SCHOLARSHIPS,

FELLOWSHIPS

AND LOANS

ISSN 1058-5699

SCHOLARSHIPS, FELLOWSHIPS AND LOANS

A GUIDE TO EDUCATION-RELATED FINANCIAL AID PROGRAMS FOR STUDENTS AND PROFESSIONALS

Volume One
Sponsors and Their Scholarships: A–H

Thirty-Eighth Edition

GALE
A Cengage Company

Scholarships, Fellowships and Loans, 38th Edition

Project Editor: Anthony Boussie

Editorial Support Services: Scott Flaugher

Composition and Electronic Prepress: Charlie Montney

Manufacturing: Cynde Lentz

© 2021 Gale, a Cengage Company

For product information and technology assistance, contact us at
Gale Customer Support, 1-800-877-4253.
For permission to use material from this text or product,
submit all requests online at **www.cengage.com/permissions.**
Further permissions questions can be emailed to
permissionrequest@cengage.com

While every effort has been made to ensure the reliability of the information presented in this publication, Gale, a part of Cengage Learning,does not guarantee the accuracy of the data contained herein. Gale accepts no payment for listing; and inclusion in the publication of any organization, agency, institution, publication, service, or individual does not imply endorsement of the editors or publisher. Errors brought to the attention of the publisher, and verified to the satisfaction of the publisher, will be corrected in future editions.

EDITORIAL DATA PRIVACY POLICY: Does this product contain information about you as an individual? If so, for more information about our editorial data privacy policies, please see our Privacy Statement at www.gale.cengage.com.

Gale
27500 Drake Rd.
Farmington Hills, MI, 48331-3535

ISBN-13: 978-0-02-867033-1 (3 vol. set)
ISBN-13: 978-0-02-867034-8 (vol. 1)
ISBN-13: 978-0-02-867035-5 (vol. 2)
ISBN-13: 978-0-02-867036-2 (vol. 3)

ISSN 1058-5699

This title is also available as an e-book.
ISBN-13: 978-0-02-867038-6
Contact your Gale sales representative for ordering information.

Printed in the United States of America
1 2 3 4 5   25 24 23 22 21

Contents

This edition of *Scholarships, Fellowships and Loans (SFL)* provides access to over 3,400 sources of education-related financial aid for students and professionals at all levels. *SFL*'s scope ranges from undergraduate and vocational/technical education through post-doctoral and professional studies. Students and others interested in education funding will find comprehensive information on a variety of programs in all educational areas, including:

- Architecture
- Area and Ethnic Studies
- Art
- Business
- Communications
- Computer Science
- Education
- Engineering
- Health Science
- Humanities
- Industrial Arts
- Language
- Law
- Literature
- Liberal Arts
- Library Science
- Life Science
- Medicine
- Mathematics
- Performing Arts
- Philosophy
- Physical Sciences
- Social Sciences
- Theology and Religion

SFL Provides Detailed Information on Awards

SFL provides all the information students need to complete their financial aid search. Entries include: administering organization name and address; purpose of award; qualifications and restrictions; selection criteria; award amount and number of awards granted; application details and deadlines; detailed contact information.

Additionally, look for the section on federal financial aid following the User's Guide for a quick summary of programs sponsored by the U.S. government, as well as information on the AmeriCorps program. There is also a section that lists higher education agencies by state.

Five Indexes Allow Quick and Easy Access to Awards

Whether you are a high school student looking for basic undergraduate financial aid, a scientist investigating research grants, or a professional attempting to finance additional career training, SFL aids your search by providing access to awards through the following indexes:

Field of Study Index categorizes awards by very specific subject fields.

Legal Resident Index targets awards restricted to applicants from specific geographic locations.

Place of Study Index provides a handy guide to awards granted for study within specific states, provinces, or countries.

Special Recipient Index lists awards that are reserved for candidates who qualify by virtue of their gender, organizational affiliation, minority or ethnic background.

Sponsor and Scholarship Index provides a complete alphabetical listing of all awards and their administering organizations.

Catchwords

SFL includes catchwords of the organization on each corresponding page, to aid the user in finding a particular entry.

As we make our way through difficult economic times, there is a growing need for a more highly-trained and educated work force. From political discussions and debates to reports from future-oriented think tanks and other groups, there is agreement that postsecondary education is a key to success. Yet how are students and their families to afford the already high (and constantly rising) cost of higher education? Searching for financial aid can be very tedious and difficult, even though hundreds of millions of dollars in aid reportedly go unclaimed every year.

Scholarships, Fellowships and Loans (SFL), the most comprehensive single directory of education-related financial aid available, can save you time, effort, and money by helping you to focus your search within the largest pool of awards and avoid pursuing aid for which you do not qualify. In most cases, the detailed descriptions contain enough information to allow you to decide if a particular scholarship is right for you to begin the application process. *SFL* lists over 8,900 major awards available to U.S. and Canadian students for study throughout the world. Included are:

- scholarships, fellowships, and grants, which do not require repayment;

- loans, which require repayment either monetarily or through service;

- scholarship loans, which are scholarships that become loans if the recipient does not comply with the award's terms;

- internships and work study programs, which provide training, work experience, and (usually) monetary compensation; and

- awards and prizes that recognize excellence in a particular field.

Also included are other forms of assistance offered by associations, corporations, religious groups, fraternal organizations, foundations, and other private organizations and companies. *SFL* includes a broad representation of government-funded awards at the national and state levels, as well as a representative sampling of lesser-known and more narrowly focused awards, such as those of a strictly local nature or programs sponsored by small organizations. Some financial aid programs administered and funded by individual colleges or universities are included in *SFL*. Both need- and merit-based awards are included. Competition-based awards and prizes are included when they offer funds that support study or research and are intended to encourage further educational or professional growth.

Students of All Types Can Benefit

Traditional students as well as those returning to school, non-degree learners, those in need of retraining, and established professionals can use the funding sources listed in *SFL* for formal and non-formal programs of study at all levels:

- high school
- vocational
- undergraduate
- graduate
- postgraduate
- doctorate
- postdoctorate
- professional development

Content and Arrangement

Scholarships, Fellowships and Loans is organized into a main section containing descriptive listings of award programs and their administering organizations, and five indexes.

The main section, Sponsors and Their Scholarships, is arranged alphabetically by name of administering organization. Entries for each organization's awards appear immediately following the entry on the organization. Each entry contains detailed contact and descriptive information, often providing users with all the information they need to make a decision about applying.

The indexes provide a variety of specific access points to the information contained within the organization and award listings, allowing users to easily identify awards of interest.

Practical Tips on How to Find Financial Aid

While there are many education-related financial aid programs for students of all types and study levels, the competition for available funds is steadily increasing. You will improve the likelihood of meeting your financial aid goals if you:

- carefully assess your particular needs and preferences;
- consider any special circumstances or conditions that might qualify you for aid; and
- carefully research available aid programs.

The following pages list some general guidelines for making your way through the search and application process.

Start Your Search Early

Any search for financial aid is likely to be more successful if you begin early. If you allow enough time to complete all of the necessary steps, you will be more likely to identify a wide variety of awards for which you qualify with plenty of time to meet their application deadlines. This can increase your chances of obtaining aid.

Some experts recommend that you start this process up to two years before you think you will need financial assistance. While you will probably be able to obtain some support if you allow less time, you might overlook some important opportunities.

Some awards are given on a first-come, first-served basis, and if you do not file your application early enough, the aid will already be distributed. In many cases, if your application is late you will not be considered, even if you have met all of the other criteria.

An early start will also allow you to identify organizations that offer scholarships to members or participants, such as student or professional associations, in time to establish membership or otherwise meet their qualifying criteria.

Assess Your Needs and Goals

The intended recipients for financial aid programs and the purposes for which awards are established can vary greatly. Some programs are open to almost anyone, while others are restricted to very specific categories of recipients. The majority of awards fall somewhere in between. Your first step in seeking financial aid is to establish your basic qualifications as a potential recipient. The following are some general questions to ask yourself to help define your educational and financial needs and goals:

- What kinds of colleges or universities interest me?
- What careers or fields of study interest me?
- Do I plan to earn a degree?
- Am I only interested in financial aid that is a gift, or will I consider a loan or work study?
- In what parts of the country am I willing to live and study?

Leave No Stone Unturned

After you have defined your goals, the next step is to identify any special factors that might make you eligible for aid programs offered only to a restricted group. Examine this area carefully, and remember that even minor or unlikely connections may be worth checking. The most common qualifications and restrictions involve:

- citizenship
- community involvement or volunteer work
- creative or professional accomplishment
- employer
- financial need
- gender
- merit or academic achievement
- military or veteran status
- organization membership (such as a union, association, or fraternal group)
- place of residence
- race or ethnic group
- religious affiliation

With many awards, you may be eligible if your spouse, parents, or guardians meet certain criteria by status or affiliations. You should be aware of your parents' affiliations even if you don't live with one (or both) of them, or if they are deceased. And given enough lead time, it may be possible for you (or your parents) to join a particular organization, or establish necessary residence, in time for you to be eligible for certain funds.

Contact Financial Aid Offices

Most colleges, universities, and other educational institutions offer their own financial aid programs. Their financial aid offices may also have information on privately sponsored awards that are specifically designated for students at those institutions. Contact their respective financial aid offices to request applications and details for all of the aid programs they sponsor and/or administer.

Use *SFL* to Identify Awards Sponsored by Private Organizations and Corporations

Scholarships, Fellowships and Loans (SFL) is the most comprehensive single source of information on major education-related financial aid programs sponsored and administered by private organizations and companies for use by students and professionals. Using *SFL* as a starting point, you can quickly compile a substantial list of financial aid programs for which you may qualify by following these simple steps:

- Compile an initial list of awards offered in your field of study.
- If you have already chosen your field of study, look in the Field of Study Index to find listings of awards grouped by more precise disciplines (such as Accounting or Journalism). If you choose this approach, your initial list is likely to be shorter but more focused. Eliminate awards that cannot be used at your chosen level of study or that do not meet your financial needs. Are you an undergraduate only interested in scholarships? Are you a graduate student willing to participate in an internship or take out a loan? Consult the User's Guide to determine which of the study level categories and award types apply to your particular situation. Both indexes clearly note the study levels at which awards may be used. The Field of Study Index also lists the type of financial aid provided.
- Eliminate awards by citizenship, residence, and other restrictions (minority status, ethnic background, gender, organizational affiliation) that make you ineligible.
- If your list is based on the Field of Study Index, you will need to look under the section for qualifications in each descriptive listing to see what requirements apply.
- Read the descriptive listings for each of the award programs left on your list. The descriptive listings should contain all the information you need to decide if you qualify and should apply for each of the awards on your list.

Expand Your List of Possibilities

If you are willing to take the initiative and do a little extra digging, you should be able to add to your list of institution-related and privately sponsored programs. In most cases, the best possibilities fall into these two areas:

Government Agencies and Programs. The Sponsors and Their Scholarships main section includes a broad representation of award programs sponsored by federal and state governments. Since these listings are not meant to be exhaustive, you should be able to identify additional programs by contacting the government agencies responsible for education-related financial aid programs listed here. On the federal level, contact the U.S. Department of Education at 400 Maryland Ave., SW, Washington, DC 20202, or on their website at https://www.ed.gov, for up-to-date information on U.S. Government award programs. For a broad overview of federal financial aid, consult the Federal Programs section. Similarly, you may contact your state department of education for details on what is offered in your particular state. Please see the State Higher Education Agencies section for state-by-state listings.

Local Sources of Awards. A surprisingly large number of financial aid programs are sponsored by small and/or lo-cal organizations. *SFL* contains a representative sampling of such programs to encourage you to seek similar programs in your own geographic area. High school guidance counselors are often aware of local programs as well, and they can usually tell you how to get in touch with the sponsoring or administering organizations. Local newspapers are also rich sources of information on financial aid programs.

Allow Enough Time for the Application Process

The amount of time needed to complete the application process for individual awards will vary, so you should pay close attention to application deadlines. Some awards carry application deadlines that require you to apply a year or more before your studies will begin. In general, allow plenty of time to:

- Write for official applications. You may not be considered for some awards unless you apply with the correct forms.
- Read all instructions carefully.
- Take note of application deadlines.
- Accurately and completely file all required supporting material, such as essays, school transcripts, and financial records. If you fail to answer certain questions, you may be disqualified even if you are a worthy candidate.
- Give references enough time to submit their recommendations. Teachers in particular get many requests for letters of recommendation and should be given as much advance notice as possible.

Make Sure You Qualify

Finally, don't needlessly submerge yourself in paperwork. If you find you don't qualify for a particular award, don't apply for it. Instead, use your time and energy to find and apply for more likely sources of aid.

Available in Electronic Format

Scholarships, Fellowships and Loans is also available online as part of Gale Directory Library and Gale eBooks. For more information, call 1-800-877-GALE.

Comments and Suggestions Welcome

We welcome reader suggestions regarding new and previously unlisted organizations and awards. Please send your suggestions to:

Scholarships, Fellowships and Loans
Gale, a Cengage Company
27500 Drake Rd.
Farmington Hills, MI 48331-3535
Phone: (248) 699-4253
Toll-free: 800-347-4253
Fax: (248) 699-8070
Email: Anthony.Boussie@cengage.com

Scholarships, Fellowships and Loans is comprised of a main section containing descriptive listings on award programs and their administering organizations, and five indexes that aid users in identifying relevant information. Each of these sections is described in detail below.

Sponsors and Their Scholarships

SFL contains two types of descriptive listings:

- brief entries on the organizations that sponsor or administer specific award programs

- descriptive entries on the award programs themselves

Entries are arranged alphabetically by administering organization; awards administered by each organization follow that organization's listings. Entries contain detailed contact and descriptive information. Users are strongly encouraged to read the descriptions carefully and pay particular attention to the various eligibility requirements before applying for awards.

The following sample organization and award entries illustrate the kind of information that is or might be included in these entries. Each item of information is preceded by a number, and is explained in the paragraph with the same number on the following pages.

Sample Entry

❙ 1 ❙ 3445
❙ 2 ❙ Microscopy Society of America
❙ 3 ❙ 4 Barlows Landing Rd., Ste. 8 Woods Hole, MA 02543
❙ 4 ❙ *Ph:* (508) 563-1155
❙ 5 ❙ *Fax:* (508) 563-1211
❙ 6 ❙ *Free:* 800-538-3672
❙ 7 ❙ *E-mail:* businessofficemsa.microscopy.com
❙ 8 ❙ *URL:* http://www.msa.microscopy.com
❙ 9 ❙ 3446
❙ 10 ❙ MSA Presidential Student Awards
❙ 11 ❙ *(Graduate, Undergraduate/*
❙ 12 ❙ *Award*

> **❙ 13 ❙** Purpose: To recognize outstanding original research by students. **❙ 14 ❙** Focus: Biological Clinical Sciences—Microscopy, Physical Sciences—Microscopy. **❙ 15 ❙** Qualif.: Candidate may be of any nationality, but must be enrolled at a recognized college or university in the United States at the time of the MSA annual meeting. **❙ 16 ❙** Criteria: Selection is done based on the applicant's

career objectives, academic record, and financial need. **❙ 17 ❙** Funds Avail.: Registration and round-trip travel to the MSA annual meeting, plus a stipend to defray lodging and other expenses. **❙ 18 ❙** Duration: Annual. **❙ 19 ❙** Number awarded: 5. **❙ 20 ❙** To Apply: Write to MSA for application form and guidelines. **❙ 21 ❙** Deadline: March 15. **❙ 22 ❙** Remarks: Established in 1979. **❙ 23 ❙** Contact: Alternate phone number: 800-538-EMSA.

Descriptions of Numbered Elements

❙ 1 ❙ Organization Entry Number. Administering organizations are listed alphabetically. Each entry is followed by an alphabetical listing of its awards. All entries (organization and award) are numbered in a single sequence. These numbers are used as references in the indexes.

❙ 2 ❙ Organization Name. The name of the organization administering the awards that follow.

❙ 3 ❙ Mailing Address. The organization's permanent mailing address is listed when known; in some cases an award address is given.

❙ 4 ❙ Telephone Number. The general telephone number for the administering organization. Phone numbers pertaining to specific awards are listed under "Contact" in the award description.

❙ 5 ❙ Fax Number. The facsimile number for the administering organization. Fax numbers pertaining to specific awards are included under "Contact" in the award description.

❙ 6 ❙ Toll-free Number. The toll-free number for the administering organization. Toll-free numbers pertaining to specific awards are included under "Contact" in the award description.

❙ 7 ❙ E-mail Address. The electronic mail address for the administering organization. Electronic mail addresses pertaining to specific awards are included under "Contact" in the award description.

❙ 8 ❙ URL and Social Media. The web address(es) for the administering organization.

❙ 9 ❙ Award Entry Number. Awards are listed alphabetically following the entry for their administering organizations. All entries (organization and award) are numbered in a single sequence. These numbers are used as references in the indexes.

❙ 10 ❙ Award Name. Names of awards are always listed. Organization titles or acronyms have been added to generic award names (for example, MSA Undergraduate Scholarships, Canadian Council Fiction Writing Grant, etc.) to avoid confusion.

▌11▐ Study Level. The level of study for which the award may be used. One or more of the following terms will be listed:

- All: not restricted to a particular level.
- High School: study at the secondary level.
- Vocational: study leading to postsecondary awards, certificates, or diplomas requiring less than two years of study.
- 2 Year: study leading to a bachelor's degree within two years
- 4 Year: study leading to a bachelor's degree within four years
- Undergraduate: study immediately beyond the secondary level, including associate, colleges and universities, junior colleges, technical institutes leading to a bachelor's degree, and vocational technical schools.
- Graduate: study leading to an M.A., M.S., LL.B., LL.M., and other intermediate degrees.
- Master's: study leading specifically to a master's degree, such as a M.A., M.S., or M.B.A.
- Postgraduate: study beyond the graduate level not specifically leading to a degree.
- Doctorate: study leading to a Ph.D., Ed.D., Sc.D., M.D., D.D.S., D.O., J.D., and other terminal degrees.
- Postdoctorate: study beyond the doctorate level; includes awards intended for professional development when candidates must hold a doctoral degree to qualify.
- Professional Development: career development not necessarily restricted by study.

▌12▐ Award Type. The type or category of award. One or more of the following terms will be listed:

- Award: generally includes aid given in recognition and support of excellence, including awards given through music and arts competitions. Non-monetary awards and awards given strictly for recognition are not included.
- Fellowship: awards granted for graduate- or postgraduate-level research or education that do not require repayment.
- Grant: includes support for research, travel, and creative, experimental, or innovative projects.
- Internship: training and work experience programs. Internships that do not include compensation of some type are not included.
- Loan: aid that must be repaid either monetarily or through service. Some loans are interest-free, others are not.
- Prize: funds awarded as the result of a competition or contest. Prizes that are not intended to be used for

study or to support professional development are not included.

- Scholarships: support for formal educational programs that does not require repayment.
- Scholarship Loan: a scholarship that becomes a loan if the recipient does not comply with the terms.
- Work Study: combined study and work program for which payment is received.
- Other: anything that does not fit the other categories, such as a travel award.

▌13▐ Purpose. The purpose for which the award is granted is listed here when known.

▌14▐ Focus. The field(s) of study that the recipient must be pursuing.

▌15▐ Qualif. Information regarding applicant eligibility. Some examples of qualification requirements include the following: academic record, citizenship, financial need, organizational affiliation, minority or ethnic background, residency, and gender.

▌16▐ Criteria Information concerning selection criteria.

▌17▐ Funds Avail. The award dollar amounts are included here along with other relevant funding information, such as the time period covered by the award, a breakdown of expenses covered (e.g., stipends, tuition and fees, travel and living allowances, equipment funds, etc.), the amount awarded to the institution, loan repayment schedules, service-in-return-for-funding agreements, and other obligations.

▌18▐ Duration. Frequency of the award.

▌19▐ Number awarded. Typical number of awards distributed.

▌20▐ To Apply. Application guidelines, requirements, and other information.

▌21▐ Deadline. Application due dates, notification dates (the date when the applicant will be notified of receipt or denial of award), disbursement dates, and other relevant dates.

▌22▐ Remarks. Any additional information concerning the award.

▌23▐ Contact. When contact information differs from that given for the administering organization, relevant addresses, telephone and fax numbers, and names of specific contact persons are listed here. When the address is that of the administering organization, the entry number for the organization is provided.

Indexes

Field of Study Index classifies awards by one or more of 450 specific subject categories, allowing users to easily target their search by specific area of study. Citations are arranged alphabetically under all appropriate subject terms. Each citation is followed by the study level and award type, which appear in parentheses and can be used to narrow the search even further.

Legal Residence Index lists awards that are restricted by the applicant's residence of legal record. Award citations are arranged alphabetically by country and subarranged by region, state or province (for U.S. and Canada). Each citation is followed by the study level and award type, which appear in parentheses and can be used to eliminate inappropriate awards.

Place of Study Index lists awards that carry restrictions on where study can take place. Award citations are arranged alphabetically under the following geographic headings:

- United States
- United States—by Region
- United States—by State
- Canada
- Canada—by Province
- International
- International—by Region
- International—by Country

Each citation is followed by the study level and award type, which appear in parentheses.

Special Recipient Index lists awards that carry restrictions or special qualifying factors relating to applicant affiliation. This index allows users to quickly identify awards relating to the following categories:

- African American
- Asian American
- Association Membership
- Disabled
- Employer Affiliation
- Ethnic Group Membership
- Fraternal Organization Membership
- Hispanic American
- Military
- Minority
- Native American
- Religious Affiliation
- Union Affiliation
- Veteran

Awards are listed under all appropriate headings. Each citation includes information on study level and award type, which appear in parentheses and can be used to further narrow the search. Users interested in awards restricted to particular minorities should also look under the general Minorities heading, which lists awards targeted for minorities but not restricted to any particular minority group.

Sponsor and Scholarship Index lists, in a single alphabetic sequence, all of the administering organizations, awards, and acronyms included in *SFL*.

Federal aid for college students is available through a variety of programs administered by the U.S. Department of Education. Most colleges and universities participate in federal programs, but there are exceptions. Contact a school's financial aid office to find out if it is a participating institution. If it participates, the student works with financial aid counselors to determine how much aid can be obtained.

Aid for students comes in three forms: grants (gifts to the student), loans (which must be repaid), and work-study jobs (a job for the student while enrolled in which his/her pay is applied to his school account). These types of aid are further explained below. More information can be found at https://www.ed.gov.

Grants

Pell Grants are intended to provide funds for any undergraduate student (who does not already have a degree) who wishes to attend college regardless of family financial background. They are available through the financial aid office at the school. The maximum Pell Grant award for the 2020-2021 award year (July 1, 2020 to June 30, 2021) is $6,345.

Federal Supplemental Educational Opportunity Grants (FSEOG) are intended for students with exceptional financial need, these grants are typically for smaller amounts (between $100 and $4,000) than Pell Grants. They are available on a limited basis.

Loans

Student loans are available a variety of ways. Loans may not be taken out for more than the cost of attendance at the school, which is determined by the financial aid administrator. Grants and other forms of aid are taken into consideration when determining the amount a student will be allowed to borrow. Loan amounts may be reduced if a student receives other forms of aid. Loans are divided into two types, subsidized and unsubsidized:

Subsidized loans: the federal government pays the interest on the loan until after schooling is complete.

Unsubsidized loans: the student incurs the interest charges while in school, but payment of the charges may be deferred until schooling is complete. The advantage of unsubsidized loans is that there are usually fewer restrictions against obtaining them. Amounts available through these programs vary depending on academic level. The total debt a student or a student's parents may accumulate for that student is $31,000 for a dependent undergraduate student, $57,500 for an independent undergraduate student (with a limit of $23,000 in subsidized loans), and $138,500 for a graduate or professional student (with a limit of $65,500 in subsidized loans) or $224,000 for health professionals.

Available Funding Programs Direct Loan Program

These low-interest loans bypass lending institutions such as banks. They are a direct arrangement between the government and the student (administered by the school). There are four repayment options for the Direct Loan program: the Income Contingent Repayment Plan, the Extended Repayment Plan, the Graduated Repayment Plan, and the Standard Repayment Plan.

Direct subsidized loans may be taken out for a maximum of $3,500 by incoming freshmen, $4,500 for sophomores, and $5,500 for juniors and seniors. The amounts for independent undergraduate students range from $9,500 to $12,500 per year for direct loans. Independent students face some restrictions on the amount of subsidized funds they can receive from the program. At least half of the funds borrowed through the Direct Loan program by independent students must come from unsubsidized loans. Graduate students may borrow up to $20,500 directly in unsubsidized loans.

Direct PLUS Loans Direct PLUS loans are federal loans that graduate or professional degree students and parents of dependent undergraduate students can use to help pay education expenses. The U.S. Department of Education makes Direct PLUS loans to eligible borrowers through schools participating in the program. The Maximum amount to be borrowed is the cost of attending the shool minus other forms of aid already obtained. For 2020-2021 the fixed rate for a Direct PLUS loan is 5.30%.

With the Direct PLUS loan, students or parents fill out a Direct PLUS Loan Application, available at the school's financial aid office. The funds are disbursed to the school. Students and parents may choose from three repayment plans: Standard, Extended, or Graduated.

Perkins Loan Program Under federal law, the authorty for schools to make new Perkins Loans ended on Sept. 30, 2017, and final disbursements were permitted through June 30, 2018. As a result, students can no longer receive Perkins Loans. A borrower who received a Perkins Loan can learn more about managing the repayment of the loan by contacting either the school that made the loan or the school's loan servicer.

Federal Work-Study Program Work-study is an arrangement that allows students to work on campus while they are enrolled to help pay their expenses. The federal government pays the majority of the student's wages, although the department where the student works also contributes. The employment must be relevant to the student's field of study and only so much time per semester may be devoted to the job. If the student earns the amount of aid prior to the end of the semester, work is terminated for the duration of the award period.

Other Considerations

Application: Applying for federal student aid is free. All federal aid is obtained by first completing a Free Application for Federal Student Aid (FAFSA). After the application is submitted, it will be processed by the Department of Education. The student then receives a Student Aid Report (SAR), which contains a figure for Expected Family Contribution. This is the amount that the student should plan on providing from non-federal sources in order to attend school.

Dependency: If a student is eligible for independent status, more money may be available in the form of loans. The interest rates and the programs for repayment, however, are the same. Independent status provides more financial aid for students who do not have the benefit of parental financial contributions.

Deadline: FAFSA deadlines are set by federal and state agencies, as well as individual schools, and vary widely. Applicants are encouraged to apply as soon as possible after January 1 of the year they plan to enroll, but no earlier.

Special Circumstances: The financial aid counselor at the school will often listen to extenuating circumstances such as unexpected medical expenses, private education expenses for other family members, or recent unemployment when evaluating requests for assistance.

Contact Information for Federal Financial Aid Programs

Call (800)433-3243 to have questions answered; (319) 337-5665 to find out if your application has been processed; (800) 730-8913 (TTY) if you are hearing impaired; (800) 647-8733 to report fraud, waste, or abuse of federal student aid funds; or visit https://www.ed.gov for application forms, guidelines, and general information.

President Clinton launched this volunteer community service program in September 1993 through the *National and Community Service Trust Act*, aimed at helping college-bound young people pay for their education while serving their communities. AmeriCorps volunteers receive minimum wage, health benefits, and a grant toward college for up to two years.

Funds for the program are distributed by the federal government in the form of grants to qualifying organizations and community groups with the goal of achieving direct results in addressing the nation's critical education, human services, public safety, and environmental needs at the community level. The program provides meaningful opportunities for Americans to serve their country in organized efforts, fostering citizen responsibility, building community, and providing educational opportunities for those who make a substantial commitment to service.

The AmeriCorps programs are run by not-for-profit organizations or partnerships, institutions of higher learning, local governments, school or police districts, states, Native American tribes, and federal agencies. Examples of participating programs include Habitat for Humanity, the American Red Cross, Boys and Girls Clubs, and local community centers and places of worship. Volunteers have nearly 1,000 different groups from which to choose. The AmeriCorps Pledge: "I will get things done for America to make our people safer, smarter, and healthier. I will bring Americans together to strengthen our communities. Faced with apathy, I will take action. Faced with conflict, I will seek a common ground. Faced with adversity, I will persevere. I will carry this commitment with me this year and beyond. I am an AmeriCorps Member and I am going to get things done."

Eligibility and Selection for Service in AmeriCorps

Citizens and legal resident aliens who are 17 years of age or older are eligible to serve in AmeriCorps before, during, or after post-secondary education. In general, participants must be high school graduates or agree to achieve their GED prior to receiving education awards. Individual programs select service participants on a nondiscriminatory and nonpolitical basis. There are national and state-wide recruiting information systems and a national pool of potential service volunteers.

Term of Service

One full-time term of service is a minimum of 1,700 hours over the course of one year or less; or a part-time term, which can range from 300 hours to 900 hours. Short-term service (such as a summer program) provides eligibility for reduced part-time status.

Compensation

You will receive a modest living allowance, health insurance, student loan deferment, and training. After you complete your term of service, you will receive an education award to help pay for your education. Serve part-time and you will receive a portion of the full amount. The amount is tied to the maximum amount of the U.S. Department of Education's Pell Grant. Since the amount of a Pell Grant can change from year to year, the amount of an education award can vary from year to year. Currently, AmeriCorps members may earn up to the value of two full-time education awards and have seven years from the date they earned each award to use it. For fiscal 2021, which began October 1, 2020, the award is $6,345 for a year of full-time service, and is pro rated for part-time service.

How Can I Use an Award?

These awards may be used to repay qualified existing or future student loans, to pay all or part of the cost of attending a qualified institute of higher education (including some vocational programs), or to pay expenses while participating in an approved school-to-work program. Awards must be used within seven years of completion of service.

Contact

Individuals interested in participating in AmeriCorps national service programs should apply directly. For basic program information, individuals can call the AmeriCorps Information Hotline at 1-800-942-2677 or visit their Web site at https://www.nationalservice.gov/programs/americorps.

The following is an alphabetic state-by-state listing of agencies located in the United States. Many of these agencies administer special federal award programs, as well as state-specific awards, such as the Tuition Incentive Program (TIP) offered by the state of Michigan for low-income students to receive free tuition at community colleges. Financial aid seekers should contact the agency in their home state for more information.

ALABAMA

Alabama Comm. on Higher Education
100 N. Union St.
P.O. Box 302000
Montgomery, AL 36104
(334)242-1998
https://ache.edu

ALASKA

Alaska Comm. on Postsecondary Education
P.O. Box 110505
Juneau, AK 99811-0505
(907)465-2962
https://acpesecure.alaska.gov

ARIZONA

Arizona Comm. for Postsecondary Education
2020 N. Central Ave.,
Ste. 650
Phoenix, AZ 85004-4503
(602)542-7230
https://highered.az.gov

ARKANSAS

Arkansas Div. of Higher Education
423 Main St., Ste. 400
Little Rock, AR 72201
(501)371-2000
https://www.adhe.edu

CALIFORNIA

California Student Aid Comm.
PO Box 419027
Rancho Cordova, CA 95741-9027
(888)224-7268
https://www.csac.ca.gov

COLORADO

Colorado Dept. of Higher Education
1600 Broadway, Ste. 2200
Denver, CO 80202
(303)862-3001
https://highered.colorado.gov

CONNECTICUT

Connecticut Office of Higher Education
450 Columbus Blvd. Ste. 707
Hartford, CT 06103-1841
(860)947-1800
www.ctohe.org

DELAWARE

Delaware Dept. of Higher Education Scholarship Incentive Program
The Townsend Building
401 Federal St., Ste. 2
Dover, DE 19901-3639
(302)735-4000
https://www.doe.k12.de.us/Page/316

DISTRICT OF COLUMBIA

District of Columbia Office of the State Superintendent of Education
1050 First Street, NE
Washington, DC 20002
(202)727-6436
https://osse.dc.gov

FLORIDA

Office of Student Financial Assistance
Dept. of Education
325 W. Gaines St.
Turlington Bldg., Ste. 1514
Tallahassee, FL 32399-0400
(800)366-3475
www.floridastudentfinancialaid.org

GEORGIA

Georgia Student Finance Comm.
2082 E. Exchange Pl.
Tucker, GA 30084
(800)505-4732
https://gsfc.georgia.gov

HAWAII

Hawaii Board of Regents
2444 Dole St.,
Bachman Hall, Rm. 209
Honolulu, HI 96822
(808)956-8213
www.hawaii.edu/offices/bor/

IDAHO

Idaho State Board of Education
PO Box 83720
Boise, ID 83720-0037
(208)334-2270
https://www.boardofed.idaho.gov

ILLINOIS

Illinois Student Assistance Comm.
1755 Lake Cook Rd.
Deerfield, IL 60015-5209
(800)899-4722
https://www.isac.org

INDIANA

Indiana Comm. for Higher Education
101 W. Ohio St., Ste. 300
Indianapolis, IN 46204-4206

(888)528-4719
https://www.in.gov/che

IOWA

Iowa College Student Aid Comm.
475 SW Fifth St., Ste. D
Des Moines, IA 50309
(877)272-4456
https://www.iowacollegeaid.gov

KANSAS

Kansas Board of Regents
1000 SW Jackson St., Ste. 520
Topeka, KS 66612-1368
(785)430-4240
https://www.kansasregents.org

KENTUCKY

Kentucky Higher Education Assistance Authority
P.O. Box 798
Frankfort, KY 40602-0798
(800)928-8926
https://www.kheaa.com/website/kheaa/home

LOUISIANA

Louisiana Office of Student Financial Assistance
602 N. Fifth St.
Baton Rouge, LA 70802
(225)219-1012
https://mylosfa.la.gov

MAINE

Finance Authority of Maine (FAME)
5 Community Dr.
P.O. Box 949
Augusta, ME 04332-0949
(207)623-3263
https://www.famemaine.com

MARYLAND

Maryland Higher Education Comm.
6 N. Liberty St.
Baltimore, MD 21201
(410)767-3300
https://mhec.state.md.us/Pages/default.aspx

MASSACHUSETTS

Massachusetts Dept. of Higher Education
One Ashburton Pl., Rm. 1401
Boston, MA 02108-1696

(617)994-6950
https://www.mass.edu/home.asp

MICHIGAN

MI Student Aid
Student Scholarships and Grants
P.O. Box 30462
Lansing, MI 48909-7962
(888)447-2687
https://www.michigan.gov/mistudentaid

MINNESOTA

Minnesota Office of Higher Education
1450 Energy Park Dr., Ste. 350
St. Paul, MN 55108-5227
(651)642-0567
www.ohe.state.mn.us/index.cfm

MISSISSIPPI

Mississippi Institutions of Higher Learning
3825 Ridgewood Rd.
Jackson, MS 39211
(601)432-6198
www.ihl.state.ms.us

MISSOURI

Missouri Dept. of Higher Education
301 W. High St.
Jefferson City, MO 65101
(573)751-2361
https://dhewd.mo.gov/

MONTANA

Montana Board of Regents
Office of Commissioner of Higher Education
Montana University System
560 N. Park, 4th Fl.
PO Box 203201
Helena, MT 59620-3201
(406)449-9124
https://www.mus.edu

NEBRASKA

Nebraska Coordinating Comm. for Postsecondary Education
P.O. Box 95005
Lincoln, NE 68509-5005
(402)471-2847
https://ccpe.nebraska.gov

NEVADA

Nevada Department of Education
700 E. Fifth St.
Carson City, NV 89701
(775)687-9115
www.doe.nv.gov

Las Vegas Office
2080 E. Flamingo Rd., Ste. 210
Las Vegas, NV 89119
(702)486-6458

NEW HAMPSHIRE

New Hampshire Dept. of Education
101 Pleasant St.
Concord, NH 03301-3494
(603)271-3494
https://www.education.nh.gov/

NEW JERSEY

Higher Education Student Assistance Authority
P.O. Box 545
Trenton, NJ 08625-0545
(800)792-8670
https://www.hesaa.org/Pages/Default.aspx

NEW MEXICO

New Mexico Higher Education Dept.
2044 Galisteo St., Ste. 4
Santa Fe, NM 87505-2100
(505)476-8400
https://hed.state.nm.us

NEW YORK

New York State Higher Education Svcs. Corp.
99 Washington Ave.
Albany, NY 12255
(888)697-4372
https://www.hesc.ny.gov

NORTH CAROLINA

North Carolina State Education Assistance Authority
PO Box 14103
Research Triangle Park, NC 27709

(919)549-8614
www.ncseaa.edu

NORTH DAKOTA

North Dakota University System
10th Fl., State Capitol
600 E. Boulevard Ave., Dept. 215
Bismarck, ND 58505-0230
(701)328-2960
https://www.ndus.edu

OHIO

Ohio Department of Higher Education
25 S. Front St.
Columbus, OH 43215
(614)466-6000
https://www.ohiohighered.org

OKLAHOMA

Oklahoma State Regents for Higher Education
655 Research Pkwy.
Suite 200
Oklahoma City, OK 73104
(405)225-9100
https://www.okhighered.org

OREGON

Oregon Student Access Comm.
1500 Valley River Dr., Ste. 100
Eugene, OR 97401
(541)687-7400
https://oregonstudentaid.gov

PENNSYLVANIA

Pennsylvania Higher Education Assistance Agency
1200 N. 7th St.
Harrisburg, PA 17102-1444
(800)692-7392
https://www.pheaa.org

RHODE ISLAND

Rhode Island Office of the Postsecondary Commissioner
560 Jefferson Blvd., Ste. 100
Warwick, RI 02886-1304

(401)736-1100
https://www.riopc.edu

SOUTH CAROLINA

South Carolina Comm. on Higher Education
1122 Lady St., Ste. 300
Columbia, SC 29201
(803)737-2260
https://www.che.sc.gov/

SOUTH DAKOTA

South Dakota Board of Regents
306 E. Capitol Ave., Ste. 200
Pierre, SD 57501
(605)773-3455
https://www.sdbor.edu/Pages/default.aspx

TENNESSEE

Tennessee Higher Education Comm.
312 Rosa Parks Ave., 9th Floor
Nashville, TN 37243
(615)741-3605
https://www.tn.gov/thec.html

TEXAS

Texas Higher Education Coordinating Board
1200 E. Anderson Ln.
Austin, TX 78752
(512)427-6101
https://www.highered.texas.gov

UTAH

Utah System of Higher Education
Two Gateway
60 South 400 West
Salt Lake City, UT 84101-1284
(800)418-8757
https://ushe.edu

VERMONT

Vermont Student Assistance Corp.
10 E. Allen St.
P.O. Box 2000

Winooski, VT 05404
(800)642--3177
https://www.vsac.org/

VIRGINIA

State Council of Higher Education for Virginia
James Monroe Bldg.
101 N. 14th St., 10th Fl.
Richmond, VA 23219
(804)225-2600
https://www.schev.edu

WASHINGTON

Washington Student Achievement Council
917 Lakeridge Way SW
Olympia, WA 98502
(360)753-7800
https://wsac.wa.gov

WEST VIRGINIA

West Virginia Higher Education Policy Comm.
1018 Kanawha Blvd., E., Ste. 700
Charleston, WV 25301
(304)558-2101
www.wvhepc.edu

WISCONSIN

Wisconsin Higher Education Aids Board
P.O. Box 7885
Madison, WI 53707-7885
(608)267-2206
heab.state.wi.us

WYOMING

Wyoming Community College Comm.
2300 Capitol Ave., 5th Fl., Ste. B
Cheyenne, WY 82002
(307)777-7763
https://communitycolleges.wy.edu

U.S. State Abbreviations

AK	Alaska
AL	Alabama
AR	Arkansas
AZ	Arizona
CA	California
CO	Colorado
CT	Connecticut
DC	District of Columbia
DE	Delaware
FL	Florida
GA	Georgia
GU	Guam
HI	Hawaii
IA	Iowa
ID	Idaho
IL	Illinois
IN	Indiana
KS	Kansas
KY	Kentucky
LA	Louisiana
MA	Massachusetts
MD	Maryland
ME	Maine
MI	Michigan
MN	Minnesota
MO	Missouri
MS	Mississippi
MT	Montana
NC	North Carolina
ND	North Dakota
NE	Nebraska
NH	New Hampshire
NJ	New Jersey
NM	New Mexico
NV	Nevada
NY	New York
OH	Ohio
OK	Oklahoma
OR	Oregon
PA	Pennsylvania
PR	Puerto Rico
RI	Rhode Island
SC	South Carolina
SD	South Dakota
TN	Tennessee
TX	Texas
UT	Utah
VA	Virginia
VI	Virgin Islands
VT	Vermont
WA	Washington
WI	Wisconsin
WV	West Virginia
WY	Wyoming

Canadian Province Abbreviations

AB	Alberta
BC	British Columbia
MB	Manitoba
NB	New Brunswick
NL	Newfoundland and Labrador
NS	Nova Scotia
NT	Northwest Territories
ON	Ontario
PE	Prince Edward Island
QC	Quebec
SK	Saskatchewan
YT	Yukon Territory

Other Abbreviations

ACT	American College Testing Program
B.A.	Bachelor of Arts
B.Arch.	Bachelor of Architecture
B.F.A.	Bachelor of Fine Arts
B.S.	Bachelor of Science
B.Sc.	Bachelor of Science
CSS	College Scholarship Service
D.D.S.	Doctor of Dental Science/Surgery
D.O.	Doctor of Osteopathy
D.Sc.	Doctor of Science
D.S.W.	Doctor of Social Work
D.V.M.	Doctor of Veterinary Medicine
D.V.M.S.	Doctor of Veterinary Medicine and Surgery
D.V.S.	Doctor of Veterinary Science
FAFSA	Free Application for Federal Student Aid
FWS	Federal Work Study
GED	General Education Development Certificate
GPA	Grade Point Average
GRE	Graduate Record Examination
J.D.	Doctor of Jurisprudence
LL.B.	Bachelor of Law
LL.M.	Master of Law
LSAT	Law School Admission Test
M.A.	Master of Arts
M.Arch.	Master of Architecture
M.B.A.	Master of Business Administration
M.D.	Doctor of Medicine
M.Div.	Master of Divinity
M.F.A.	Master of Fine Arts
MIA	Missing in Action
M.L.S.	Master of Library Science
M.N.	Master of Nursing
M.S.	Master of Science
M.S.W.	Master of Social Work
O.D.	Doctor of Optometry
Pharm.D.	Doctor of Pharmacy
Ph.D.	Doctor of Philosophy
POW	Prisoner of War
PSAT	Preliminary Scholastic Aptitude Test
ROTC	Reserve Officers Training Corps
SAR	Student Aid Report
SAT	Scholastic Aptitude Test
Sc.D.	Doctor of Science
TDD	Telephone Device for the Deaf
Th.d.	Doctor of Theology
U.N.	United Nations
U.S.	United States

1 ■ 101st Airborne Division Association

32 Screaming Eagle Blvd.
Fort Campbell, KY 42223
Ph: (931)431-0199
E-mail: membershipadmin@screamingeagle.org
URL: screamingeagle.org
Social Media: www.facebook.com/101stabndivassn

2 ■ Chappie Hall Scholarship *(Undergraduate/ Scholarship)*

Purpose: To provide financial assistance to students who have the potential to become assets to the nation. **Focus:** General studies/Field of study not specified. **Qualif.:** Applicant must maintain a "B" or better non-weighted grade average during the past school year; applicant's parents, grandparents, husband or wife is (or if deceased, was) a regular or life member (not an associate member) of the 101st Airborne Division Association; applicant shall not be attending nor accepted as a student to the United States Military Academy, the Naval Academy, the Air Force Academy, or the USCG Academy. **Criteria:** Selection and rating of applicants are eligibility, career objectives, academic record, and insight gained from the letter requesting consideration and letters of recommendation.

Funds Avail.: No specific amount. **Duration:** Annual. **To Apply:** Applicants must complete and submit the following required documents a typed personal letter; proof of membership of parent, grandparent, husband, or wife in the 101st Airborne Division Association; a transcript of school records; two letters of recommendation; small photo (head and shoulders) to be used for publication in "The screaming Eagle" if scholarship grant is awarded; letter of acceptance from a university or college and the address of the department of office at the university or college where a scholarship check could be mailed; graduating High School Students should write a essay not less than 250-words, but not exceeding 300 words on patriotism; current college/ university students - "The Importance of the U.S. Constitution." (Not less than 500 or more than 550). **Deadline:** May 22. **Contact:** Screaming Eagle Foundation, PO Box 929, Fort Campbell, KY, 42223-0929.

3 ■ 10x Digital Inc.

1001 Morehead Square Dr., Ste. 320
Charlotte, NC 28203
Free: 888-293-5649
URL: www.10xdigitalinc.com
Social Media: www.facebook.com/10xdigital
www.instagram.com/10xdigitalinc

www.linkedin.com/company/10xdigitalinc
twitter.com/10xdigitalinc

4 ■ 10x Digital Marketing Scholarship *(Undergraduate, Graduate/Scholarship)*

Purpose: To provide financial assistance to a talented student in a field related to digital marketing. **Focus:** Business; Marketing and distribution. **Qualif.:** Applicant must be a high school senior or a college undergraduate student; be majoring, or plan to major, in a field related to digital marketing; and plan to take at least 10 credits during the upcoming semester (or first semester for high school students). **Criteria:** Selection is based on the essay and narrative submitted.

Funds Avail.: $1,000. **To Apply:** Applicant must write and submit an essay on the following topic: "Digital marketing trends are changing the way we market to consumers. In your opinion, which 5 digital marketing trends are paving the way for the coming year and why. Give detailed examples of each." Applicant should also include a narrative (maximum of two paragraphs) explaining why they deserve this scholarship. **Deadline:** June 1. **Contact:** Tracy Ring; URL: www.10xdigitalinc.com/digital-marketing-scholarship/.

5 ■ 180 Medical Inc.

8516 NW Expy.
Oklahoma City, OK 73162
Fax: (888)718-0633
Free: 877-688-2729
URL: www.180medical.com
Social Media: www.facebook.com/180medical
www.instagram.com/180medical
www.linkedin.com/company/180-medical
twitter.com/180medical
www.youtube.com/channel/UCyBjhY8uL3EDL72i-7FYZ-A

6 ■ 180 Medical College Scholarship Program *(Undergraduate, Graduate, Professional development/ Scholarship)*

Purpose: To help young adults with spinal cord injuries, transverse myelitis, spina bifida, neurogenic bladder or ostomy (ileostomy, colostomy or urostomy) to pursue their goals. **Focus:** Spinal cord injuries and research. **Qualif.:** Applicants must be students attending a two-year, four-year or graduate school program and legal residents of United States; must be under a physicians' care for a spinal cord injury, transverse myelitis, spina bifida, neurogenic

Awards are arranged alphabetically below their administering organizations

bladder or ostomy (ileostomy, colostomy or urostomy). **Criteria:** Selection will be based on the committee's criteria.

Funds Avail.: $1,000. **Duration:** Annual. **Number Awarded:** 7. **To Apply:** Applicants must submit the following materials: application form; typed questions and essay that can be found at the online application form; physician's statement of diagnosis; most recent official transcript; document verifying acceptance by college or current enrollment. **Deadline:** June 1. **Contact:** Email: scholarships@180medical.com.

7 ■ 1Dental

5535 Airport Fwy.
Haltom City, TX 76117
Fax: (817)377-8826
Free: 800-372-7615
E-mail: help@1dental.com
URL: www.1dental.com

8 ■ 1Dental Scholarship *(Undergraduate, Graduate/Scholarship)*

Purpose: To help further a student's education. **Focus:** General studies/Field of study not specified. **Qualif.:** Applicant must be a resident of the U.S. and currently enrolled as a high school senior, college student or graduate student; cannot be a 1Dental.com employee or be related to any of the company's employees; 1Dental will verify enrollment. **Criteria:** Selection will be made by the scholarship committee.

Funds Avail.: $500. **Duration:** Annual. **Number Awarded:** 1. **To Apply:** Visit the scholarship page online at www.1dental.com/scholarship and complete the multiple choice and short/long-answer survey, related to dental and health opinions and issues among America's youth.**Contact:** Email: scholarships@1dental.com.

9 ■ 280 Group

142 S Santa Cruz Ave.
Los Gatos, CA 95030
Ph: (408)834-7518
E-mail: contact@280group.com
URL: 280group.com
Social Media: www.facebook.com/the280group
twitter.com/the280group
www.youtube.com/channel/UCP6-ps848wMvL9658yhRelA

10 ■ 280 Group Product Management Scholarship *(Undergraduate, Graduate/Scholarship)*

Purpose: To help students with knowledge and resume-building experience and to help them land their first product management job. **Focus:** Business; Economics. **Qualif.:** Applicant must be pursuing an undergraduate or graduate degree in business, economics, or a related field; must have a minimum 2.5 GPA. **Criteria:** Selection is based on GPA, school, and a short essay.

Funds Avail.: $500 and free online course tuition ($1,495 value). **Number Awarded:** 3. **Deadline:** November 15.

11 ■ 365 Data Science

1 Hristo Belchev St.
1000 Sofia, Bulgaria
E-mail: dataprotectionofficer@365datascience.com

URL: 365datascience.com
Social Media: facebook.com/365DataScience

12 ■ Artificial Intelligence & Ethics *(Graduate, Undergraduate/Scholarship)*

Purpose: To draw attention to the ethical debate surrounding artificial intelligence. **Focus:** General studies/Field of study not specified. **Qualif.:** Applicant must be an undergraduate or graduate student enrolled in an accredited college or university. **Criteria:** Quality of essay.

Funds Avail.: $1,000 first place; $300 second place; $200 third place. **To Apply:** Essay required.

13 ■ 4-H Alberta

c/o Diane McCann-Hiltz, Director, Government of Alberta
J.G. O'Donoghue Blvd.,7000 113 ST NW RM 108
Edmonton, AB, Canada T6H 5T6
Ph: (780)422-2249
Fax: (780)422-7755
E-mail: info@4h.ab.ca
URL: www.4h.ab.ca
Social Media: www.facebook.com/4halberta

14 ■ Grande Prairie 4-H District Scholarship *(Undergraduate/Scholarship)*

Purpose: To financially support deserving student members of the Organization who seek for continuing education. **Focus:** General studies/Field of study not specified. **Qualif.:** Applicant must be a resident of Alberta based on Student Finance Regulations, and have a minimum three year residency in Alberta immediately prior to the application date; must enrolled full time in a post secondary program recognized by Alberta advanced education, excluding first year students (students must be entering their 2nd, 3rd or 4th year of study in the Fall); must be a member of the Grande Prairie 4-H District in Alberta for a minimum of three (3) years; must have a financial need to qualify for funding (please note: students will not be eligible if they are receiving Employment Insurance, and may not be eligible if they are receiving a training allowance during their studies); must living and working in northern Alberta for a specified amount of time upon graduation; must have reasonably good prospects for employment in northern Alberta after graduation.**Criteria:** Applicants will be evaluated based on their financial need, commitment to living and working in northern Alberta for a specified amount of time upon graduation, and reasonable good prospects for employment in northern Alberta after graduation.

Funds Avail.: $1,000. **Duration:** Annual. **Number Awarded:** 2. **To Apply:** Applicants must submit complete Provincial 4-H Scholarship application and NADC scholarship application; a letter (at least 200 words) detailing their involvement with 4-H after leaving the Grande Prairie district and two (2) letters of reference. **Deadline:** May 5. **Contact:** Grande Prairie 4-H District, Scholarship Committee, Unit 90, 10001 - 101 Ave., Grande Prairie, AB T8V 0X9; Email: vandergn@xplornet.com.

15 ■ Provincial and Regional 4-H Scholarship *(Undergraduate/Scholarship)*

Purpose: To financially support deserving student members of the Organization who seek to continue their education. **Focus:** General studies/Field of study not specified. **Qualif.:** Applicants must be past or present members of Alberta 4-H Club for a minimum of 3 years and/or a full-time post-

Awards are arranged alphabetically below their administering organizations

secondary students at an officially recognized institution.

Funds Avail.: Up to $2,500. **Duration:** Annual. **Number Awarded:** Varies. **To Apply:** Applicants must register and log-in to the online application form at 4-H Alberta website; and must include an original photo along with the official transcript request for the last year's education. **Deadline:** May 15. **Contact:** 4-H Foundation of Alberta; Toll Free: 877-682-2153; Phone: 780-682-2153; E-mail: scholarship@ 4hab.com.

16 ■ Servus Credit Union 4-H Scholarship *(College, University, Undergraduate/Scholarship)*

Purpose: To provide financial assistance for Alberta 4-H members for their further education. **Focus:** General studies/Field of study not specified. **Qualif.:** Must be Alberta 4-H members who have been involved for a minimum of three years; entering their first year of study at a post-secondary institution in Alberta within one year of graduation from high school. **Criteria:** Recipients are selected based on outstanding 4-H achievement, leadership skills, community involvement, academic standing and quality of essay.

Funds Avail.: $500. **To Apply:** Completed application and essay of 750 to 1000 words on the following topic, "Using the 4-H Pledge and the 4-H Motto, write an essay on how you have fulfilled your pledge to the 4-H Program and to yourself." **Deadline:** May 5.

17 ■ 65Medicare.org

PO Box 555
Clemmons, NC 27012
Fax: (877)977-7005
Free: 877-506-3378
E-mail: help@65medicare.org
URL: 65medicare.org

18 ■ Senior Scholar Scholarship Presented by 65Medicare.org *(Two Year College, Four Year College/ Scholarship)*

Purpose: To assist an adult either returning to school or pursuing a new career trajectory to reach their educational goals. **Focus:** General studies/Field of study not specified. **Qualif.:** Applicants must be age 50 years or older; be enrolled in a two- or four-year program at an accredited collegeor university in the continental United States; U.S. citizen.

Funds Avail.: $1,000. **Duration:** Annual. **To Apply:** Preference is given to applicants who show a verifiable need/desire to further their career or start a new career as an older adult. **Deadline:** August 15. **Contact:** Email: help@ 65medicare.org.

19 ■ A-1 Auto Transport

9032 Soquel Dr., Ste. 200
Aptos, CA 95003
Fax: (888)472-6810
Free: 800-452-2880
E-mail: info@a1autotransport.com
URL: www.a1autotransport.com
Social Media: www.facebook.com/pg/a1autotransport
www.linkedin.com/company/a-1-auto-transport
twitter.com/a1autotransport
youtube.com/user/a1autotransport

20 ■ A-1 Auto Transport Scholarship *(Two Year College, Four Year College, Graduate, High School, Vocational/Occupational/Scholarship)*

Purpose: To provide educational assistance to any student. **Focus:** General studies/Field of study not specified. **Qualif.:** Applicants should be a Full-time or part-time student of an accredited institute; minimum cumulative GPA of 3.0. **Criteria:** Selection will based on A-1 Auto Transport Scholarship committee.

Funds Avail.: $1,000; $500; $250. **Duration:** Annual. **Number Awarded:** 3. **To Apply:** Applicants must write an essay/ article of at least 1000 words about a topic related to this site. **Deadline:** March 10. **Contact:** Email: scholarships@ a1autotransport.com.

21 ■ AACE International

1265 Suncrest Towne Centre Dr.
Morgantown, WV 26505-1876
Ph: (304)296-8444
Fax: (304)291-5728
E-mail: info@aacei.org
URL: web.aacei.org
Social Media: www.facebook.com/groups/2361111033
www.linkedin.com/groups/8285063/profile
twitter.com/AACE_Tweets

22 ■ AACE International Competitive Scholarships *(Undergraduate/Scholarship)*

Purpose: To advance the study of cost engineering and cost management through the integrative process of total cost management. **Focus:** Business administration; Construction; Engineering, Agricultural; Engineering, Architectural; Engineering, Chemical; Engineering, Civil; Engineering, Electrical; Engineering, Industrial; Engineering, Mechanical; Management; Manufacturing. **Qualif.:** Applicants must be full-time students pursuing a related degree in engineering and other related courses, as well as cost management; meet a minimum 3.0 or equivalent GPA. **Funds Avail.:** $2,500. **Duration:** Annual. **Deadline:** February 28.

23 ■ AAPACN Education Foundation

400 S Colorado Blvd., Ste. 600
Denver, CO 80246
Free: 800-768-1880
URL: www.aapacn.org
Social Media: www.linkedin.com/company/aapacn
twitter.com/AAPACN

24 ■ Elevating Healthcare Scholarship *(Undergraduate/Scholarship)*

Purpose: To support an RN in obtaining a BSN. **Focus:** Nursing. **Qualif.:** Applicant must be a U.S. resident and a RN working in a long-term or post-acute care facility and working towards a BSN from an accredited nursing school in the United States. **Criteria:** The foundation scholarship committee will evaluate applications and make selection.

Funds Avail.: $3,000. **Number Awarded:** 1. **To Apply:** Application must be completed at sponsor's website and submitted along with letter or reference from facility DON and administrator. **Contact:** Deborah White; E-mail: dwhite@aapacn.org.

25 ■ Lighting the Way for Nursing Scholarship *(Doctorate/Scholarship)*

Purpose: To support a LPN/LVN working to obtain a BSN or higher degree. **Focus:** Nursing. **Qualif.:** Applicant must

Awards are arranged alphabetically below their administering organizations

be a U.S. resident and a LPN/LVN working in a long-term or post-acute care facility and working towards a BSN or higher degree from an accredited nursing school in the United States. **Criteria:** The Foundation Scholarship Committee will evaluate applications and make selection.

Funds Avail.: $5,000. **Number Awarded:** 1. **Deadline:** May 6. **Contact:** Deborah White; E-mail: dwhite@aapacn.org.

26 ■ Sparking the Future in Healthcare Scholarship (Doctorate/Scholarship)

Purpose: To support a CNS working to obtain an RN, BNS, or higher degree. **Focus:** Nursing. **Qualif.:** Applicant must be a U.S. resident and a CNS working in a long-term or post-acute care facility and working towards a RN, BNS, or higher degree from an accredited nursing school in the United States. **Criteria:** The foundation scholarship committee will evaluate applications and make selection.

Funds Avail.: $4,000. **Number Awarded:** 1. **To Apply:** Application must be completed on sponsor's website and submitted along with letter of reference from facility DON and administrator. **Deadline:** May 6. **Contact:** Deborah White; E-mail: dwhite@aapacn.org.

27 ■ Cheryl M. Thomas Scholarship (Undergraduate, Graduate, Postdoctorate/Scholarship)

Purpose: To support an RN working to obtain a BSN or higher degree. **Focus:** Nursing. **Qualif.:** Applicant must be a U.S. resident and a RN working in a long-term or post-acute care facility and working to obtain a BSN or higher degree from an accredited nursing school in the United States. **Criteria:** The foundation scholarship committee will evaluate all applications and make selection.

Funds Avail.: $5,000. **Number Awarded:** 1. **To Apply:** Application must be completed at sponsor's website and submitted along with a letter of reference from facility DON and administrator. **Contact:** Deborah White; E-mail: dwhite@aapacn.org.

28 ■ AASP - The Palynological Society (AASP)
University of N Carolina at Pembroke
Geology, Old Main 213
Pembroke, NC 28372
Ph: (910)521-6478
URL: www.palynology.org
Social Media: www.facebook.com/AASP-The-Palynological
-Society-214864185270269
twitter.com/AASPTPS

29 ■ Paleontological Society Student Research Award (Graduate, Undergraduate/Grant)

Purpose: To support research in the field or any aspect related to paleontology. **Focus:** Earth sciences; Geology. **Qualif.:** Applicants must be undergraduate or graduate student members of the Paleontological Society conducting a research on any aspect of paleontology; must be a member of the Paleontological Society at the time of submission of the grant application.

Funds Avail.: $1,200. **Duration:** Annual. **Number Awarded:** Varies. **To Apply:** Online application form attached with project description, budget and references, letter of support must be submitted. **Deadline:** March 31. **Contact:** E-mail: aaspawards@gmail.com.

30 ■ Student travel awards (Graduate/Award)

Purpose: To support travel for student members **Focus:** Earth sciences; Geology. **Qualif.:** Applicants must be

member of the society. **Criteria:** Selection is based on applicant's qualifications and the quality of proposed project.

Funds Avail.: $1,500. **Duration:** Annual. **To Apply:** Applications must include one paragraph justifying the request, plus a description of the research to be presented (including the submitted abstract); a photograph; outline of the amount requested, and how the funds will be used; applicant's email and postal addresses. **Deadline:** February 15. **Contact:** Dr. Niall W. Paterson AASP – TPS Awards Committee Chair aaspawards@gmail.com.

31 ■ AAUW Legal Advocacy Fund (AAUW/LAF)
AAUW National Office
1310 L Street NW, Ste. 1000
Washington, DC 20005
Ph: (202)785-7700
URL: www.aauw.org
Social Media: www.facebook.com/AAUW.National
www.instagram.com/aauwnational
www.linkedin.com/company/aauw
twitter.com/aauw
www.youtube.com/channel/UCQRtzlArWu3kzHIL7jfRwcQ

32 ■ AAUW American Fellowships (Doctorate, Postdoctorate/Fellowship)

Purpose: To support female doctoral candidates completing dissertations or scholars seeking funds for postdoctoral research leave from accredited institutions. **Focus:** General studies/Field of study not specified. **Qualif.:** Applicant must be a women scholars who are pursuing full-time study to complete dissertations, conducting postdoctoral research full time, or preparing research for publication for eight consecutive weeks; must be U.S. citizens or permanent residents. **Criteria:** Candidates are evaluated on the basis of scholarly excellence; quality and originality of project design; and active commitment to helping women and girls through service in their communities, professions, or fields of research.

Funds Avail.: No specific amount. **Duration:** Annual. **Number Awarded:** Varies. **Deadline:** November 15. **Contact:** Email: aauw@applyists.com.

33 ■ AAUW Career Development Grants (Graduate, Advanced Professional, Professional development/Grant)

Purpose: To support women who hold a bachelor's degree and are preparing to advance their careers, change careers, or re-enter the work force. **Focus:** General studies/Field of study not specified. **Qualif.:** Applicants must be U.S. citizens or permanent residents; must hold an earned (not honorary) bachelor's degree; received their bachelor's degree on or before June 30, 2013; must not hold an earned (not honorary) graduate or professional degree; must enroll or are enrolled in courses/activities that are required for professional employment or advancement; must pass the eligibility quiz to be reviewed by the selection panel. **Criteria:** Primary consideration is given to women of color and women pursuing their first advanced degree or credentials in nontraditional fields.

Duration: Annual. **To Apply:** Applicant must submit application form along with cv/resume; narratives. **Deadline:** November 15. **Remarks:** Established in 1972. **Contact:** Email:aauw@applyists.com.

34 ■ AAUW International Fellowships (Master's, Doctorate, Postdoctorate/Fellowship)

Purpose: To award a full-time study or research in the United States to women who are not United States citizens

Awards are arranged alphabetically below their administering organizations

or permanent residents. **Focus:** General studies/Field of study not specified. **Qualif.:** Applicant must be citizenship in a country other than the U.S. or possession of a nonimmigrant visa if residing in the U.S.; must be a woment who are currently, or expect to be during the fellowship year, a U.S. citizen, U.S. permanent resident, or dual citizen with the U.S. and another country are not eligible; must hold an academic degree (earned in the U.S. or abroad) equivalent to a U.S. bachelor's degree completed by November 15, 2020; must Intend to devote herself full-time to the proposed academic plan during the fellowship year. **Criteria:** Selection is by committee.

Funds Avail.: No specific amount. **Duration:** Annual. **Number Awarded:** Up to five. **To Apply:** Applicant must submit application form along with transcripts; official letter from institution where degree was received that includes the degree completion date; proof of English proficiency; cv/resume. **Deadline:** November 15. **Remarks:** Established in 1917. **Contact:** Email:aauw@applyists.com.

35 ■ AAUW Selected Professions Fellowships
(Graduate, Master's, Doctorate/Fellowship)

Purpose: To award women who intend to pursue a full-time course of study at accredited institutions during the fellowship year. **Focus:** Architecture; Business administration; Computer and information sciences; Engineering; Law; Mathematics and mathematical sciences; Medicine; Statistics. **Qualif.:** Applicants must be U.S. citizens or permanent residents who are full-time students at an accredited U.S. institution during the fellowship year, and should be pursuing a course of study in the United States over the full academic year. **Criteria:** Selection panel of academic and practicing professionals who work in the respective selected professions fields will review and evaluate all fellowship applications for recommendation to the Program Committee of the AAUW Educational Foundation Board; final fellowship selections are approved by the Foundation Board of Directors.

Funds Avail.: $25,000. **Duration:** Annual. **Deadline:** December 1. **Remarks:** Established in 1970. **Contact:** Email: aauw@applyists.com.

36 ■ The Abramson Scholarship Foundation
PO Box 7810
Washington, DC 20044
Ph: (202)470-5425
Fax: (202)318-2482
E-mail: info@abramsonfoundation.org
URL: abramsonfoundation.org
Social Media: www.facebook.com/
  AbramsonScholarshipFoundation
www.instagram.com/abramsonscholar
www.linkedin.com/company/abramson-scholarship
  -foundation
twitter.com/AbramsonScholar
www.youtube.com/user/AbramsonFoundation

37 ■ Abramson Scholarship *(Undergraduate/Scholarship)*

Purpose: To help defer college expenses at a four-year accredited institution. **Focus:** General studies/Field of study not specified. **Criteria:** Recipients will be selected based on financial need, academic standing, and upon the decision of the foundation board of directors.

Funds Avail.: $2,000 to $5,000. **Duration:** Annual. **Number Awarded:** Varies. **To Apply:** Applicants must submit

an application form, along with the following requirements: essay; two letters of recommendation in which one is from the councilor and one is from the teacher; a copy of college financial aid application or student aid report; official transcript through midterm period of second semester of senior year including the SAT scores; budget for preferred college; letter of acceptance from college of choice; and a financial aid award letter from college of choice. **Contact:** Danielle Verbiest; Phone:202-470-5425 Email: danielle@abramsonfoundation.org.

38 ■ Academy of Art University
79 New Montgomery St.
San Francisco, CA 94105
Ph: (415)274-2222
Free: 800-544-2787
E-mail: online@academyart.edu
URL: www.academyart.edu
Social Media: www.facebook.com/AcademyofArtUniversity
www.instagram.com/academy_of_art
www.pinterest.com/academyofartuni
twitter.com/academy_of_art
www.youtube.com/user/academyofartu

39 ■ Spring Forward Scholarship *(Undergraduate/Award)*

Purpose: To assist working adults seeking a career upgrade and current college students looking to become artists and designers. **Focus:** Art. **Qualif.:** Applicant must be a new, first-time enrolled undergraduate student in the spring term; must be a U.S. citizen or eligible non-citizen; must be in a degree-seeking program at an accredited university. **Criteria:** Amount awarded is based on a short essay and artwork submission.

Funds Avail.: Up to $2,000. **To Apply:** Applicant must submit a short essay, up to three pieces of art work in digital format, and complete the application online at www.academyart.edu. **Deadline:** January 15.

40 ■ Academy of Criminal Justice Sciences (ACJS)
7339 Hanover Pky.
Greenbelt, MD 20770
Ph: (301)446-6300
Fax: (301)446-2819
Free: 800-757-2257
E-mail: info@acjs.org
URL: www.acjs.org
Social Media: www.facebook.com/Academy-of-Criminal
  -Justice-Sciences-343787695695758
twitter.com/ACJS_National

41 ■ Affirmative Action Student Scholarship Mini-Grant Travel Awards *(Undergraduate, Master's/Grant)*

Purpose: To promote the involvement of all minority groups in the academy. **Focus:** Criminal justice; Law. **Qualif.:** Applicants must be a woman or a member of a racial/ethnic group that has experienced historical discrimination, be enrolled in an undergraduate, master's, or doctoral program of criminal justice/criminology program during some part of the academic year for the Annual Meeting at which the presentation will be made, applicant must have submitted a proposal for a paper presentation for the Annual Meeting

Awards are arranged alphabetically below their administering organizations

on the ACJS website by the due date, the applicant must be willing and able to attend the Annual Meeting and present the paper described in the website submission, the paper can be self-submitted by the applicant student or submitted on the student's behalf by a faculty member, the paper submitted by the applicant may be co-authored with a faculty member; however, the student must be the first author and presenter. **Criteria:** Recipients are selected based on the AACJS Affirmative Action Committee panel's review of application materials.

Funds Avail.: Maximum of $600. **Duration:** Annual. **Number Awarded:** 2. **To Apply:** Applicants must submit a completed manuscript (not more than 30 pages in length) examining criminal justice/ criminological issue; a 10-page, double-spaced, typed proposal discussing: the nature of the research topic; why the research is important, and where relevant; the methods used; the findings of the research; the theoretical, methodological, and/or policy implications of the results. **Contact:** Denise Gosselin, Affirmative Action Committee Chair; Western New England University; Email: dgosselin@charter.net.

42 ■ Academy for Eating Disorders (AED)
11130 Sunrise Valley Dr., Ste. 350
Reston, VA 20191
Ph: (703)234-4079
Fax: (703)435-4390
E-mail: info@aedweb.org
URL: www.aedweb.org
Social Media: www.facebook.com/
 AcademyforEatingDisorders
www.instagram.com/aed_iced
www.linkedin.com/company/233404
twitter.com/aedweb
www.youtube.com/user/AEDvideoarchive

43 ■ AED Student/Early Career Investigator Travel Fellowship Program (Postgraduate/Fellowship)

Purpose: To support the students and early career investigators in attending the International Conference on Eating Disorders (ICED). **Focus:** Mental health; Psychology. **Qualif.:** Applicants must be a current student AED member; must be a full-time student in a degree program, including physicians-in-training with interest or involvement in the field of eating and related disorders, or fewer than three (3) years post training; candidates will have a demonstrated interest in research in eating and weight disorders, show promise as researchers; who have received this award more than once, or in the prior year are not eligible; individuals who have received this award once are eligible, preference will be given to applicants who have not previously received a travel fellowship. **Criteria:** Selection will be based on the committee's criteria.

Funds Avail.: $1,500. **Duration:** Annual. **Number Awarded:** up to seven. **To Apply:** Applicants should include AED common application form; current curriculum vitae; letters of recommendation; 500 words in the length and should address the importance; documentation of current training status as an undergraduate student, graduate student, postdoctoral fellow, or resident in a field of study of relevance to the understanding or treatment or prevention of eating and weight disorders; description of your academic appointment no more than three (3) years post training. **Contact:** AED Headquarters: admin@aedweb.org.

44 ■ AED Student Research Grants (Undergraduate, Graduate, Postgraduate/Grant)

Purpose: To support innovative and cutting-edge research conducted by student members of the AED. **Focus:** Mental health; Psychology. **Qualif.:** Applicants must be student members of AED by the deadline of the grants application and must be nominated by non-student members of AED; must be a full-time student in a degree program, including physicians-in-training with interest or involvement in the field of eating and related disorders; individuals who have received this award more than once, or in the prior year are not eligible. **Criteria:** Selection will be based on the committee's criteria.

Funds Avail.: $1,000 each. **Duration:** Annual. **Number Awarded:** 2. **To Apply:** Applicants should include AED common application form; current curriculum vitae; two-page, single-spaced research plan outlining the specific aims of the project, the background literature, the study procedure and methods and the timeline for completion; detailed budget that lists materials and other items and their costs; letter can be no longer than 500 words in length and should comment on your research plan, your potential as a researcher, and the potential for the successful completion of the proposed project; letter of support. **Deadline:** November 15.

45 ■ Academy of Laser Dentistry (ALD)
9900 W Sample Rd., Ste. 400
Coral Springs, FL 33065
Ph: (954)346-3776
Fax: (954)757-2598
Free: 877-527-3776
E-mail: memberservices@laserdentistry.org
URL: www.laserdentistry.org
Social Media: www.facebook.com/
 AcademyofLaserDentistry
www.linkedin.com/company/academy-of-laser-dentistry
twitter.com/aldteam

46 ■ Dr. Eugene M. Seidner Student Scholarship Program (Undergraduate, Graduate/Scholarship)

Purpose: To promote the advancement of dental laser technology education and clinical research. **Focus:** Dentistry. **Qualif.:** Applicants must be either undergraduate or graduate dental students in a general or specialty program, and they are eligible through their first year after graduation of an accredited dental program. **Criteria:** Selection will be based on the committee's criteria.

Funds Avail.: $500 (Top 1); $250 (Top 2); $100 (Top 3). **Duration:** Annual. **Number Awarded:** 3. **To Apply:** Applicants must be nominated by their dental university faculty or ALD members. must provide the following electronically through the student scholarship application: abstract for presentation and, letter of reference. Selected students are required to submit their abstract for publication in the journal of laser dentistry; scholarship application and letter of reference Form can be retrieved at the website. **Deadline:** October 31. **Remarks:** The scholarship program is named to honor the memory of Dr. Eugene M. Seidner, ALD's President 1996-97. Established in 2004. **Contact:** Applications must be sent electronically to memberservices@laserdentistry.org.

47 ■ Academy of Medical-Surgical Nurses (AMSN)
PO Box 56
Pitman, NJ 08071

Awards are arranged alphabetically below their administering organizations

Fax: (856)589-7463
Free: 866-877-2676
E-mail: amsn@ajj.com
URL: www.amsn.org
Social Media: www.facebook.com/MedSurgNurses
instagram.com/amsnmedsurg
www.linkedin.com/company/academy-of-medical-surgical
  -nurses
twitter.com/medsurgnurses
www.youtube.com/user/MedSurgNurses

48 ■ AMSN Career Mobility Scholarship
(Undergraduate, Doctorate/Scholarship)

Purpose: To provide financial assistance to AMSN members who wish to further their education. **Focus:** Medicine; Nursing; Surgery. **Qualif.:** Applicants must be members of AMSN for at least one year. **Criteria:** Applicants will be selected based on the jury's review of application materials and other supporting documents.

Funds Avail.: $2,000. **Duration:** Annual. **Number Awarded:** Up to 9. **Deadline:** March 31.

49 ■ Academy of Model Aeronautics (AMA)
5161 E Memorial Dr.
Muncie, IN 47302
Ph: (765)287-1256
Fax: (765)289-4248
Free: 800-435-9262
URL: www.modelaircraft.org
Social Media: www.facebook.com/modelaviation
www.instagram.com/amamodelaviation
twitter.com/modelaircraft
www.youtube.com/modelaircraft

50 ■ AMA/Charles H. Grant Scholarship Program
(Undergraduate/Scholarship)

Purpose: To assist students in their educational pursuits. **Focus:** Aeronautics. **Qualif.:** Applicants must be full members of AMA for 36 months prior to applying; must be high school graduates; accepted by a college/university offering a certificate or degree program. **Criteria:** Applicants will be rated based on grade average, test results, modeling activities and citizenship achievement.

Funds Avail.: Approximately $40,000. **Duration:** Annual. **To Apply:** Applicants must submit a completed application form. **Deadline:** February 1. **Contact:** The Academy of Model Aeronautics Education Department 5161 E. Memorial Dr. Muncie, IN 47302.

51 ■ Cliff and Nancy Telford Scholarship Fund
(Undergraduate/Scholarship)

Purpose: To assist students in their educational pursuits. **Focus:** Aeronautics. **Qualif.:** Applicants must be full members of AMA 36 months prior to applying; high school graduates; accepted by a college/university offering a degree program; and have participated in any of AMA and FAI activities/events. **Criteria:** Applications will be evaluated by the AMA Scholarship Committee. Selection is based on the participation in a competitive activity by AMA and FAI.

Duration: Annual. **To Apply:** Applicants must submit a Contest Classification form to list competitions that applicant participated in. **Deadline:** February 1.

52 ■ Academy of Motion Picture Arts and Sciences (AMPAS)
8949 Wilshire Blvd.
Beverly Hills, CA 90211
Ph: (310)247-3000
Fax: (310)859-9619
URL: www.oscars.org

53 ■ Academy of Motion Picture Arts and Sciences Student Academy Awards *(Undergraduate/Award)*

Purpose: To encourage and reward excellence in filmmaking at the collegiate level. **Focus:** Media arts. **Qualif.:** Filmmaker must be a full-time student in a degree-granting program at an accredited US college or university; the film must have been made in a teacher-student relationship within the curricular structure of that institution; if the filmmaker has graduated or left such a program, the film may be submitted no later than one year from the filmmaker's date of departure; for foreign filmmakers, applicants must be enrolled in CILECT-affiliated colleges and universities outside the borders of the United States and must have previous professional experience. **Criteria:** Submitted entries will be judged on four categories: Animation, Documentary, Narrative and Alternative.

Funds Avail.: No specific amount. **Duration:** Annual. **Number Awarded:** Varies. **To Apply:** All entries must be submitted electronically. The maximum running time allowed for entries in all categories is 40 minutes; domestic applicants must print a hard copy of their entry form and submit it together with their DVD to the appropriate Regional Coordinator; hard copy must contain the applicant's signature(s) and the signature of their supervising faculty advisor; foreign applicants, all entries submitted must be in English, subtitled in English or dubbed in English; entries will be accepted in the 16mm, 35mm and 70mm format or in the Digital Betacam format; film prints submitted must be composite, with optical or magnetic soundtracks. **Deadline:** June 1. **Remarks:** Established in 1972. **Contact:** Shawn Guthrie, Sr. Manager or Hector Garcia, Coordinator; Phone: 310-247-3031; Email: saa@oscars.org.

54 ■ The Academy of Neonatal Nursing
1425 N McDowell Blvd., Ste. 105
Petaluma, CA 94954
Ph: (707)568-2168
Fax: (707)569-0786
URL: www.academyonline.org

55 ■ Academy of Neonatal Nursing Conference Scholarships *(Professional development/Scholarship)*

Purpose: To support members in attending the annual National Neonatal Nurses Meeting. **Focus:** Nursing, Neonatal. **Qualif.:** Applicants must be members of the Academy in good standing for at least one year; must have a minimum of two years of neonatal practice experience; must be professionally active neonatal nurses; and have not been recipients of an ANN Conference Scholarship within the past 5 years; preference will be given to nurses who demonstrate active involvement in professional or community service activities. **Criteria:** Selection will be based on the committee's criteria; preference will be given to nurses who demonstrate active involvement in professional or community service activities.

Funds Avail.: No specific amount. **Duration:** Annual. **Number Awarded:** Up to 3. **To Apply:** Applicants must submit

---

Awards are arranged alphabetically below their administering organizations

the following completed application; a brief written explanation, no more than one paragraph, of how they intend to share information from the conference with their unit colleagues or work group; a list of contact hours obtained in the last year, including title of offering and provider; and a current curriculum vitae. **Deadline:** July 1.

56 ■ ANN Ingrid Josefin Ridky Academic Scholarships *(Undergraduate, Graduate/Scholarship)*

Purpose: To support those members who are pursuing academic advancement in neonatal nursing. **Focus:** Nursing, Neonatal. **Qualif.:** Applicants must be members of the Academy in good standing for at least one year; must have a minimum of two years of neonatal practice experience, with at least one of these years completed in the past 18 months; must be enrolled in a nursing academic degree program or a neonatal postgraduate program for one of the following: Bachelor of Nursing, Master of Nursing, Doctoral Degree in Nursing, or Post Master Certificate in a Nursing Specialty; must have successfully completed two required courses in that program; must have a GPA of 3.0 or higher; must be professionally active neonatal nurses; and have not been recipients of an ANN scholarship within the past 5 years. **Criteria:** Selection will be based on the committee's criteria.

Funds Avail.: $1,000. **To Apply:** Applicants must submit the following: completed application; a letter from their advisors or the deans of the university or other institutions of learning stating that they are enrolled in a degree program and have successfully completed two courses toward that degree; transcript of grades achieved (proof of GPA); and an essay of 200 words or less, stating why they are pursuing their education and how attainment of the degree will benefit them in their professional role as neonatal nurses. Use plain bond paper for this essay, not letterhead. **Deadline:** July 1.

57 ■ Accounting and Financial Women's Alliance (AFWA)

2365 Harrodsburg Rd., Ste. A325
Lexington, KY 40504
Ph: (859)219-3532
Free: 800-326-2163
E-mail: afwa@afwa.org
URL: www.afwa.org
Social Media: facebook.com/afwanational
instagram.com/afwanational
www.linkedin.com/company/accounting-&-financial
  -women's-alliance
www.pinterest.com/AFWAHQ/pins/
www.pinterest.com/AFWAHQ
twitter.com/afwanational

58 ■ AFWA Masters Scholarships *(Master's/Scholarship)*

Purpose: To support the costs of attending a masters program towards an accounting or finance degree. **Focus:** Accounting; Finance. **Qualif.:** Applicants must be attending an accredited College or University enrolled in a master's program, and is pursuing an accounting or finance degree. **Funds Avail.:** $750. **Duration:** Annual. **Number Awarded:** Varies. **Contact:** AFWA, 365 Harrodsburg Rd, A325, Lexington, KY, 40504; Email: foundation@afwa.org.

59 ■ AFWA Undergraduate Scholarships *(Undergraduate/Scholarship)*

Purpose: To defray the cost of attending 3rd, 4th or 5th year towards an accounting or finance degree. **Focus:** Ac-

counting; Finance. **Qualif.:** Applicants must be attending 3rd, 4th, or 5th year when pursuing an accounting or finance degree.

Funds Avail.: $500. **Duration:** Annual. **Number Awarded:** Varies. **Contact:** AFWA, 365 Harrodsburg Rd, A325, Lexington, KY, 40504; Email: foundation@afwa.org.

60 ■ Acoustical Society of America (ASA)

c/o Elaine Moran, Director of Operations
1305 Walt Whitman Rd., Ste. 300
Melville, NY 11747-4300
Ph: (516)576-2360
Fax: (631)923-2875
E-mail: asa@acousticalsociety.org
URL: acousticalsociety.org
Social Media: www.facebook.com/acousticsorg
www.instagram.com/acousticalsocietyofamerica
www.linkedin.com/company/the-acoustical-society-of
  -america
twitter.com/acousticsorg
www.youtube.com/channel/UCjCnJLVGEfqAuK5jht-FwpA

61 ■ Frederick V. Hunt Postdoctoral Research Fellowship in Acoustics *(Postdoctorate/Fellowship)*

Purpose: To further the science of and education in acoustics. **Focus:** Speech and language pathology/Audiology. **Qualif.:** Applicant must have received a doctoral degree in 2019, 2020, or shall be receiving the degree in the spring of 2021; must be a member of the Acoustical Society of America; must be conducting research on a topic in acoustics at a chosen institution. **Criteria:** Selection is based on the submitted application and materials.

Funds Avail.: No specific amount. **Duration:** Annual. **Number Awarded:** 1. **To Apply:** Applicants must submit undergraduate and graduate education record; title of doctoral thesis; three references from professional associates, supervisors or faculty; cover letter; synopsis of thesis; summary of proposed research; listing of present and recent employment, including job titles, locations, and dates; list of scientific publications; honors, awards and society affiliations; names, addresses, and relationship with those asked to provide reference letters; copy of all graduate transcripts; facilities approval form. **Deadline:** October 12. **Remarks:** Established in 1978. **Contact:** Acoustical Society of America, 1305 Walt Whitman Road, Suite 300, Melville, NY 11747-4300; Phone:516-576-2360; Email:asa@acousticalsociety.org.

62 ■ James E. West Fellowship *(Graduate/Fellowship)*

Purpose: To support minority students in their pursuit of graduate-level degrees in acoustics. **Focus:** Speech and language pathology/Audiology. **Qualif.:** Applicants must be permanent residents or citizens of the United States at the time of application; members of an ethnic minority group (Hispanic, African-American or Native American) that are underrepresented in the sciences; and accepted into, or good academic standing in, a graduate degree program. **Criteria:** Selection is based on the submitted application and materials.

Funds Avail.: No specific amount. **Duration:** Biennial. **Number Awarded:** 1. **To Apply:** Applicant must submit completed application form, official transcripts of all college and university study, graduate record exam scores, a

Awards are arranged alphabetically below their administering organizations

personal statement, and three letters of recommendation. **Deadline:** March 23. **Remarks:** Established in 1992. **Contact:** Elaine Moran, Office Manager; Acoustical Society of America; 1305 Walt Whitman Road, Suite 300, Melville, NY 11747; Phone:516-576-2360, Fax: 631-923-2875; Email: asa@acousticalsociety.org.

63 ■ Raymond H. Stetson Scholarship in Phonetics and Speech Science *(Graduate/Scholarship)*

Purpose: To facilitate the research efforts of promising graduate students. **Focus:** Speech and language pathology/Audiology. **Qualif.:** Applicants must be members of the Acoustical Society of America; evidence of good academic standing in a graduate degree program during the entire scholarship term. **Criteria:** Selection is based on the submitted application and materials.

Funds Avail.: No specific amount. **Duration:** Annual. **Number Awarded:** 2. **To Apply:** Applicant must submit completed application form, copies of transcripts of university graduate study, a personal statement, a current curriculum vitae, a research paper, and two letters of recommendation. **Deadline:** March 23. **Remarks:** Established in 1998. **Contact:** Elaine Moran, Office Manager; Acoustical Society of America; 1305 Walt Whitman Road, Suite 300, Melville, NY 11747; Phone:516-576-2360, Fax: 631-923-2875; Email: asa@acousticalsociety.org.

64 ■ Action Institute for the Study of Religion and Liberty Center for Academic Research
98 E Fulton St.
Grand Rapids, MI 49503
E-mail: info@acton.org
URL: www.acton.org
Social Media: www.facebook.com/ActonInstitute
twitter.com/actoninstitute
www.youtube.com/user/actoninstitute

65 ■ Calihan Academic Grants *(Graduate, Professional development/Fellowship, Grant)*

Purpose: To provide scholarships and research grants to future scholars and religious leaders whose academic work shows outstanding potential. **Focus:** Economics; Philosophy; Religion; Theology. **Qualif.:** Applicants must be current seminarians or graduate students in theology, philosophy, religion, history, law, politics, economics, or in related fields; must be a strong academic performance; must have a demonstrated interest in the themes of the Acton Institute; must display the potential to advance the themes of the Acton Institute. **Criteria:** Applications are reviewed and recipients selected by the research staff of the Acton Institute.

Funds Avail.: Maximum of $3,000, but typically range from $500 to $1,000. **Duration:** Semiannual. **Number Awarded:** 1. **To Apply:** Applicants must completed application and following requirements: 1-page proposal that outlines what you intend to accomplish with this award. Upload in application form; 2-page essay; recent academic paper; official transcripts; official letter of enrollment. **Deadline:** July 15 (Fall term); October 15 (Spring term). **Contact:** E-mail: Grants-Awards@acton.org.

66 ■ Calihan Travel Grants *(Other, Graduate/Grant)*

Purpose: To provide financial assistance to students who have been selected to present, at an academic conference, research relevant to themes promoted by the Acton Institute. **Focus:** Economics; Philosophy; Religion; Theology. **Qualif.:** Applicants must be a current seminarians or graduate students in theology, philosophy, religion, history, law, politics, economics, or in related fields; must be a strong academic performance; must have a demonstrated interest in the themes of the Acton Institute; must display the potential to contribute to the advancement of a free and virtuous society. **Criteria:** Selection will be based on the criteria of the research staff of the Acton Institute.

Funds Avail.: Maximum of $3,000, but typically range from $500 to $1,000. **Duration:** Annual. **To Apply:** Applicants must complete and submit the following requirements: completed application form; stated purpose of travel; abstract of paper/research (if applicable); description of how one's conference paper, research travel, or conference attendance is connected to themes promoted by the Acton Institute; disclosure of educational history; two academic references; estimated conference expenses including: travel, room and board, registration fees, and other expenses directly related to the conference/research; disclosure of additional sources of funding. **Contact:** E-mail: Grants-Awards@acton.org.

67 ■ Novak Awards *(Doctorate/Monetary, Award)*

Purpose: To support emerging scholars for outstanding new research into the interrelation of religion and economic liberty. **Focus:** Business; Economics; Philosophy; Religion; Theology. **Qualif.:** Applicants must be scholars who have received a doctorate from an accredited domestic or international program in the previous five calendar years; also current doctoral candidates in the process of completing their dissertations; must be studying theology, religion, economics, philosophy, business, or a related field; must be strong academic performance; must have a demonstrated interest in the themes of the Acton Institute and Novak Award; must also display the potential to contribute to the advancement of these ideas. **Criteria:** Selection will be based on the committee's criteria.

Funds Avail.: $15,000. **Duration:** Annual. **Number Awarded:** 1. **To Apply:** Applicant must submit an application along with: curriculum vitae; 500-word essay that describes your intellectual development, future plans, and career goals; research paper, refereed published article, or other scholarly work, such as a book, monograph, or a conference paper, on a theme relevant to religion and economic liberty; two letters of recommendation from professors or other established scholars in your field. **Deadline:** March 15. **Remarks:** The award was named after distinguished American theologian Michael Novak. **Contact:** Acton Institute Grants and Awards, 98 E Fulton St., Unit 101, Grand Rapids, MI 49503 USA; E-mail: grants-awards@acton.org.

68 ■ The Actuarial Foundation
475 N Martingale Rd., Ste. 600
Schaumburg, IL 60173-2226
Ph: (847)706-3535
E-mail: info@actfnd.org
URL: www.actuarialfoundation.org
Social Media: www.facebook.com/ActuarialFound
twitter.com/ActuarialFound

69 ■ Actuarial Diversity Scholarship *(Undergraduate/Scholarship)*

Purpose: To promote diversity within the profession through an annual scholarship program for Black/African

Awards are arranged alphabetically below their administering organizations

American, Hispanic, Native North American and Pacific Islander students. **Focus:** Actuarial science; Mathematics and mathematical sciences; Minorities. **Qualif.:** Applicants must have the intent on pursuing a career in the actuarial profession; must have at least one birth parent who is a member of one of the following minority groups Black/African American, Hispanic, Native North American, Pacific Islander; will be a full-time undergraduate student at a U.S. accredited educational institution; minimum GPA of 3.0 (on a 4.0 scale), emphasis on math or actuarial courses; and, entering college freshmen must have a minimum ACT math score of 28 or SAT math score of 600. **Criteria:** Selection exams will be an important factor in evaluating scholarship qualifications for SELECTION entering their junior year and beyond; additionally, exams passed will also be a consideration for previous award recipients applying to renew the scholarship.

Duration: Annual. **To Apply:** Applicants must visit the Foundation's website for the online application process; must complete and submit all the requirements on or before the deadline. **Deadline:** January 3.

70 ■ Caribbean Actuarial Scholarship
(Undergraduate/Scholarship)

Purpose: To support undergraduate actuarial students who demonstrate strong record of accomplishment, leadership qualities and commitment to become actuary. **Focus:** Actuarial science; Mathematics and mathematical sciences.

Remarks: Established in 2008.

71 ■ Curtis E. Huntington Memorial Scholarship
(Undergraduate/Scholarship)

Purpose: To recognize the remarkably positive impact Huntington had on the students and on the actuarial profession. **Focus:** Actuarial science; Mathematics and mathematical sciences. **Qualif.:** Applicant must be full-time college senior (seniors are undergraduate students who will receive their degree no later than August of the current year); must obtain a minimum cumulative GPA of 3.0 (on 4.0 scale); must be nominated by a professor at the affiliated school (only one nomination per school is accepted); and, have successfully completed at least one actuarial exam. **Criteria:** Selection will be based on the committee's criteria.

Funds Avail.: $2,000. **Duration:** Annual. **To Apply:** Applicants must visit the website for the online application process; must complete and submit the application on or before the deadline. **Deadline:** January 4.

72 ■ Elizabeth M. Mauro Reimbursement Awards
(Advanced Professional/Award)

Purpose: To recognize the limited resources available and to support career changers aspiring to transition into the actuarial profession. **Focus:** Actuarial science. **Qualif.:** Applicants must be 25 years or older by application deadline date; must not receive reimbursement for these exam registration fees and/or study materials from any other reimbursement program (including employee programs); must be U.S. citizens; and have passed at least one actuarial exam within the twenty-four months prior to the application due date. **Criteria:** Selection will be based on the committee's criteria.

To Apply: Applicants must meet all the eligibility requirements; must include a resume, documentation of actuarial exams passed, and one-page personal statement detailing the desire and plan to enter the actuarial profession with

the completed application; must electronically complete and submit the application. **Deadline:** August 17. **Contact:** Email: programs@actfnd.org.

73 ■ Actuary of Tomorrow - Stuart A. Robertson Memorial Scholarship *(Undergraduate/Scholarship)*

Purpose: To recognize and encourage the academic achievements of undergraduate students pursuing a career in actuarial science. **Focus:** Actuarial science; Mathematics and mathematical sciences. **Qualif.:** Applicants must be full-time students entering as a sophomore, junior or senior at a U.S accredited educational institution; must obtain a minimum cumulative GPA of 3.0 (on 4.0 scale); and, successfully completed two actuarial exams. **Criteria:** Selection will be based on the committee's criteria.

Funds Avail.: $9,000. **Duration:** Annual. **To Apply:** Applicants must visit the website for the online application process; must complete and submit all the required materials on or before the deadline. **Deadline:** January 6.

74 ■ Adelman Travel Group
6980 N Port Washington Rd.
Milwaukee, WI 53217
Ph: (414)410-8300
URL: www.adelmantravel.com
Social Media: www.facebook.com/adelmantravel
www.instagram.com/adelmantravel
www.linkedin.com/company/adelman-travel-group
twitter.com/adelmantravel
www.youtube.com/channel/UCTDIPZ_k
_LH4sCtWNYsEyyQ

75 ■ Adelman Travel Scholarship *(Undergraduate, College/Scholarship)*

Purpose: To help students pay for college. **Focus:** General studies/Field of study not specified. **Qualif.:** Applicants must be at least 18 years old, full-time students attending a U.S. college, and have a minimum 2.5 GPA.

Funds Avail.: $500. **To Apply:** Must email the following information: a 500 to 800 word essay explaining applicant's travel experience either internationally, in a different country, or a different state, that transformed them; student's name, address, phone number, and name of college attending. Essay must be in .docx format. If selected for scholarship, applicant must deliver proof of enrollment. **Deadline:** November 30. **Contact:** Sarah Paola; Email: spaola@adelmantravel.com.

76 ■ Adler Pollock & Sheehan, P.C.
One Citizens Plaza, 8th Fl.
Providence, RI 02903-1345
Ph: (401)274-7200
Fax: (401)751-0604
URL: www.apslaw.com
Social Media: www.facebook.com/AdlerPollockSheehanPc
twitter.com/AdlerPollock

77 ■ Adler Pollock & Sheehan Diversity Scholarships *(Undergraduate/Fellowship)*

Purpose: To support and encourage more diverse candidates to enter the practice of law and to diversify and enrich both the firm and profession. **Focus:** Law.

Funds Avail.: $10,000. **Duration:** Annual. **Remarks:** Established in 1960.

Awards are arranged alphabetically below their administering organizations

78 ■ Administrative Sciences Association of Canada (ASAC)

Windsor, ON, Canada N9B 3P4
E-mail: info@asac.ca
URL: www.asac.ca

79 ■ ASAC-CJAS PhD Research Grant Award
(Doctorate/Grant, Award)

Purpose: To support Canadian PhD students during their doctoral research. **Focus:** Business administration. **Qualif.:** Applicants must be full-time Canadian PhD students. **Criteria:** Applications will be assessed based on the quality and originality of the proposal, research/scholarly achievements of the applicant, and special circumstances or other factors deemed appropriate in a particular instance.

Funds Avail.: $2,500. **Duration:** Biennial.

80 ■ ADSC: The International Association of Foundation Drilling

8445 Freeport Pky., Ste. 325
Irving, TX 75063
Ph: (469)359-6000
Fax: (469)359-6007
E-mail: adsc@adsc-iafd.com
URL: www.adsc-iafd.com
Social Media: www.facebook.com/adsc.iafd
www.instagram.com/adsciafd
www.linkedin.com/in/adsc-iafd-45505b2a
twitter.com/ADSC_IAFD

81 ■ International Association of Foundation Drilling Scholarships for Civil Engineering Students
(Graduate/Scholarship)

Purpose: To support full-time civil engineering students in their continuing education. **Focus:** Engineering, Civil. **Qualif.:** Applicants must be currently full time enrolled in an ABET or CEAB accredited engineering program or be a graduate from such a program and must plan to enter or continue graduate school during the current academic yea; must be graduate students from the United States and Canada.

Funds Avail.: $3,000. **Duration:** Annual. **Number Awarded:** Minimum of 14. **Contact:** Emily Matthews, ADSC, 8445 Freeport Pkwy., Ste. 325, Irving, TX, 75063; Email: ematthews@adsc-iafd.com.

82 ■ International Association of Foundation Drilling Scholarships for Part-time Civil Engineering Graduate School Students *(Graduate/Scholarship)*

Purpose: To assist part-time civil engineering students in their continuing education. **Focus:** Engineering, Civil. **Qualif.:** Applicants must be currently part time enrolled in an ABET or CEAB accredited engineering program or be a graduate from such a program, and must plan to enter or continue graduate school during the current academic year. **Criteria:** Recipients are selected based on academic performance and financial need.

Funds Avail.: $1,500. **Duration:** Annual. **To Apply:** Applicants must submit a completed application form; current, official transcript of academic record; and two letters of reference from persons familiar with the academic or professional experience.

83 ■ Advertising Production Club of New York (APC)

Showtime Networks
1633 Broadway
New York, NY 10019
E-mail: info@apc-nyc.org
URL: www.apc-nyc.org
Social Media: www.facebook.com/apcnyc
www.instagram.com/apcny/

84 ■ APC High School Scholarship *(Graduate/ Scholarship)*

Purpose: To provide financial assistance to students studying Graphic Communications/ Arts courses. **Focus:** Communications; Graphic art and design. **Qualif.:** Applicant must be graduating high school student who has taken Graphic Communications/ Arts courses; must be a permanent United States resident from one of the five boroughs of New York City or the New York State counties of Nassau, Suffolk, Westchester or Rockland or the New Jersey State counties of Bergen, Essex, Hudson or Union with a demonstrated interest in Graphic Communications/Graphic Arts and a plan to major in a discipline leading to a career in the field.

Funds Avail.: No specific amount. **Duration:** Annual. **To Apply:** Completed application along with a scanned copy of an Official Notice of Acceptance into a two or four year college with a Graphic Communications / Design curriculum; a scanned official copy of your High School transcript showing your grades and grade average; a scanned copy of your SAT or ACT scores; three letters of support and recommendation e-mailed directly from the recommending person(s), as an attachment or in the body of the e-mail, one from a subject-related instructor; the others from principal, guidance counselor, teacher or community leader must include contact information including company/ school, e-mail address and phone number on a separate sheet of paper or e-mail; one-page double-spaced statement (300 to 500 words) discussing applicant's particular interest in Graphic Communications and why they should be considered for a Scholarship; a portfolio in your area of expertise demonstrating range and development of graphic skills, different types of work/mixed media; a minimum of five (5) pieces of your art /design work must be submitted.

85 ■ Advisory Council for Bosnia and Herzegovina (ACBH)

1510 H St. NW, Ste. 900
Washington, DC 20005
Ph: (202)347-6742
E-mail: info@acbih.org
URL: acbih.org
Social Media: www.facebook.com/ACBiH
twitter.com/acbih

86 ■ TCA-ACBH Scholarship to Turkey Program
(Undergraduate/Scholarship)

Purpose: To provide financial assistance to students who are pursuing their educational goal. **Focus:** General studies/Field of study not specified. **Qualif.:** Applicants full-time Bosnian-American undergraduates accepted to a study abroad program at a Turkish university. **Criteria:** Selection is based on merit.

Funds Avail.: $2,000. **Number Awarded:** 10. **To Apply:** Applicants must send a resume and a cover letter to ACBH

Awards are arranged alphabetically below their administering organizations

with subject title "TCA Scholarship" via email. **Contact:** E-mail: baacbh@gmail.com with subject, TCA Scholarship.

87 ■ The Advocates
737 E Winchester St.
Salt Lake City, UT 84107
Ph: (801)326-0809
E-mail: contact@utahadvocates.com
URL: www.utahadvocates.com
Social Media: www.facebook.com/TheAdvocatesUtah
twitter.com/utahadvocates

88 ■ The Utah Advocates Scholarship *(College, University/Scholarship)*

Purpose: To help students finance their higher education. **Focus:** General studies/Field of study not specified. **Qualif.:** Applicant must be enrolled in an accredited university or college, located within the United States. **Criteria:** Selection is based on the best essay submitted.

Funds Avail.: $1,000. **Duration:** Semiannual. **Number Awarded:** 1. **To Apply:** Must write a 300 to 500 word essay based on guidelines on the sponsor's website and submit with completed application. **Deadline:** January 31; June 30. **Contact:** URL: www.utahadvocates.com/the-advocates-scholarship/.

89 ■ The Advocates
611 N 31st St.
Billings, MT 59101
Ph: (406)272-6986
URL: www.montanaadvocates.com

90 ■ The Montana Advocates Scholarship *(All/ Scholarship)*

Purpose: To help students finance their higher education. **Focus:** General studies/Field of study not specified. **Qualif.:** Applicant must be enrolled in an accredited institution in the United States. **Criteria:** Selection will be based on the best essay submitted.

Funds Avail.: $1,000. **Duration:** Semiannual. **Number Awarded:** 1. **To Apply:** Applicant must submit a 300 to 500 word essay based on the guidelines provided on the sponsor's website at www.montanaadvocates.com/scholarship. **Deadline:** January 31; June 30.

91 ■ The Advocates
113 Main Ave. W Ste. 203
Twin Falls, ID 83301
Ph: (208)995-2444
URL: www.idahoadvocates.com

92 ■ The Idaho Advocates Scholarship *(University, Graduate/Scholarship)*

Purpose: To help law students finance their higher education. **Focus:** Law. **Qualif.:** Applicant must be enrolled in an accredited law school located within the United States. **Criteria:** Selection is based on the best essay submitted.

Funds Avail.: $1,000. **Duration:** Semiannual. **Number Awarded:** 1. **To Apply:** Submit a 300 to 500 word essay based on guidelines provided on sponsor's website and submit with completed application. **Deadline:** January 31; June 30. **Contact:** URL: www.idahoadvocates.com/scholarship.

93 ■ The Advocates Law
2125 Western Ave., Ste. 500
Seattle, WA 98121
Ph: (206)452-2400
URL: www.advocateslaw.com
Social Media: www.facebook.com/washingtonadovcateslaw
www.linkedin.com/company/driggs-bills-&-day-pc

94 ■ The Advocates Law Scholarship *(All/ Scholarship)*

Purpose: To help students finance their higher education. **Focus:** General studies/Field of study not specified. **Qualif.:** Applicant must be enrolled in an accredited institution in the United States. **Criteria:** Selection is based on the best essay submitted.

Funds Avail.: $1,000. **Duration:** Semiannual. **Number Awarded:** 1. **To Apply:** Applicant must write a 300 to 500 word essay should be follow a basic essay and paragraph format including an introduction with a thesis statement, body paragraphs, and a conclusion. **Deadline:** January 31; June 30.

95 ■ Advocates' Society (AS)
2700-250 Yonge St.
Toronto, ON, Canada M5B 2L7
URL: www.advocates.ca

96 ■ Catzman Award for Professionalism and Civility *(Advanced Professional, Professional development/ Award)*

Purpose: To recognize individuals who have demonstrated a high degree of professionalism and civility in the practice of law. **Focus:** Law. **Qualif.:** The recipient must be a lawyer in good standing with The Law Society of Upper Canada. **Criteria:** Selection will be based on the committee's criteria.

Funds Avail.: No specific amount. **Duration:** Annual. **To Apply:** Applicants must provide a brief statement outlining the reasons for the nomination, current curriculum vitae and two letters of support. **Deadline:** May 25. **Remarks:** Established in 2008. **Contact:** The Advocates' Society, at the above address.

97 ■ The David Stockwood Memorial Prize *(Advanced Professional, Professional development/ Prize)*

Purpose: To honor individuals who made contributions to advocacy-related fields. **Focus:** Law. **Qualif.:** Applicants must be the authors of a previously unpublished, advocacy-related article. **Criteria:** Papers will be evaluated based on their merit by a panel.

Funds Avail.: $1,000. **Duration:** Biennial; in even-numbered years. **To Apply:** Applicant should submit an article; must be a maximum of 3,500 words in length, submitted electronically in Word format. **Contact:** Robin Black, Director, Marketing and Membership, robin@advocates.ca.

98 ■ Aerospace States Association (ASA)
107 S West St., Ste. 510
Alexandria, VA 22314
Ph: (202)257-4872
Fax: (703)548-8784

Awards are arranged alphabetically below their administering organizations

E-mail: huettner@aerostates.org
URL: aerostates.org

99 ■ Edward A. O'Connor Founder's Scholarship
(Undergraduate/Scholarship)

Purpose: To help students pursue their education in an aerospace-related field. **Focus:** Aerospace sciences. **Qualif.:** Applicants must be sophomore or junior undergraduate students pursuing an aerospace-related field. **Criteria:** Selection will be based on submitted materials.

Funds Avail.: $2,000. **Duration:** Annual. **Number Awarded:** Varies. **To Apply:** Applicants must complete the application form; must submit a copy of official transcript; must submit a two-page, typed statement describing the educational career goals and interests, and how this can be related to aerospace fields; must also submit one letter of recommendation. **Deadline:** April 30.

100 ■ AFBA
909 N Washington St.
Alexandria, VA 22314
Ph: (703)549-4455
Fax: (703)706-5961
Free: 800-776-2322
E-mail: info@afba.com
URL: www.afba.com
Social Media: www.facebook.com/
  armedforcesbenefitsassociation
twitter.com/afbabenefits
www.youtube.com/user/afbaweb

101 ■ CSM Virgil R. Williams Scholarship
(Undergraduate/Scholarship)

Purpose: To support the education of EANGUS members, their spouses and their unmarried children. **Focus:** General studies/Field of study not specified. **Qualif.:** Applicants must be EANGUS Auxiliary members; must be unmarried, dependent sons and daughters of EANGUS Auxiliary members; must be spouses of EANGUS Auxiliary members. **Criteria:** Selection will be made based on the applicant's character, leadership and financial need.

Funds Avail.: $2,000. **To Apply:** Applicants must submit a transcript of high school credits and/or a transcript of college credits for applicants already in an institution of higher learning; a letter from the applicants with personal, specific facts as to why financial assistance is required; must have three letters of academic recommendation verifying the application and giving moral, personal and leadership traits. Application form and other documents must be submitted electronically via the internet to the Chairman of the Scholarship Committee except the school transcript. **Deadline:** June 1.

102 ■ AFCEA International
4400 Fair Lakes Ct.
Fairfax, VA 22033-3899
Ph: (703)631-6100
Fax: (703)631-6169
Free: 800-336-4583
E-mail: service@afcea.org
URL: www.afcea.org
Social Media: www.facebook.com/AFCEA.International
instagram.com/afcea

www.linkedin.com/company/66602
twitter.com/AFCEA
youtube.com/user/AFCEAInternational

103 ■ AFCEA Cyber Security Scholarship
(Undergraduate, Graduate/Scholarship)

Purpose: To provide scholarships, grants, and tuition assistance for aspiring engineers, technicians, programmers, military personnel, and government officials. **Focus:** Computer and information sciences; Engineering; Information science and technology; National security. **Qualif.:** Applicants must: be sophomore or junior or undergraduate students or graduate students enrolled full-time in an eligible degree-granting program; be U.S. citizens currently enrolled at the time of application in a four-year accredited college or university in the United States; obtain minimum overall GPA of 3.0 on a 4.0 scale; be majoring in a field directly related to the support of U.S. cyber security enterprises with relevance to the mission of AFCEA such as cyber security, cyber attack, computer science, digital forensics, information technology, or electronic engineering; distance-learning programs are eligible. **Criteria:** Recipients are selected based on demonstrated academic excellence, leadership, and financial need.

Funds Avail.: $5,000. **Duration:** Annual. **To Apply:** Applicants must complete and submit online application. There is one application form for all STEM Major Scholarships; applicants will be considered for all AFCEA STEM major scholarship opportunities for which they are qualified. **Deadline:** May 31. **Contact:** Email: edfoundation@afcea.org; URL: www.afcea.org/site/foundation/scholarships.

104 ■ AFCEA STEM Teacher Graduate Scholarships
(Graduate/Scholarship)

Purpose: To promote science, mathematics or information technology education at the US Secondary School, and support graduate students to become STEM teachers. **Focus:** Education; Engineering; Mathematics and mathematical sciences; Science; Technology. **Qualif.:** Applicants must be U.S. citizens who are graduate students attending an accredited U.S. college or university on-campus and majoring in secondary education for the purpose of teaching STEM (science, technology, engineering or math) subjects in a U.S. middle/intermediate and high schools; graduate-level candidates must currently be in their second semester with current overall GPA of 3.5 or higher on a 4.0 scale and taking at least two semester-equivalent classes at an accredited U.S. college or university at the time of application; current credential and licensure students must have completed a bachelor's of science degree or graduate degree in a STEM major; undergraduate students are ineligible.

Funds Avail.: $2,500. **Duration:** Annual. **Number Awarded:** 1. **To Apply:** Completed application along with current official transcript issued by the school Registrar's Office; minimum of two letters of recommendation required from faculty in the major of study; current resume and undergrad transcript - either official or unofficial (through email); one additional letter from the school principal for currently employed teacher must be submitted. **Deadline:** April 10. **Contact:** Email: edfoundation@afcea.org; URL: www.afcea.org/site/foundation/scholarships.

105 ■ AFCEA War Veterans Scholarships
(Undergraduate/Scholarship)

Purpose: To provide scholarships to war veterans. **Focus:** Communications; Engineering; Information science and

Awards are arranged alphabetically below their administering organizations

technology; Intelligence service; Mathematics and mathematical sciences; Physics. **Qualif.:** Applicants must be active-duty service personnel, honorably discharged U.S. military veterans, reservists, or National Guard personnel who served in Overseas Contingency Operations (Operation Enduring Freedom; Operation Iraqi Freedom; currently enrolled and attending classes as sophmores or juniors in an undergraduate program part time or full time in an eligible STEM major degree program at an accredited four year college or university in the U.S. (distance-learning or online programs affiliated with a major U.S. institution are eligible); have a minimum 3.0 GPA. **Criteria:** Recipients will be selected based on academic excellence, leadership and financial need.

Funds Avail.: $2,500. **Duration:** Annual. **To Apply:** Applicants may apply online at AFCEA web site; additional requirements are the following: copy of either a Certificate of Service or Discharge Form DD214; current transcript issued by the school Registrar's Office and at least two letters of recommendation from relevant faculty. **Deadline:** November 15. **Contact:** Email: edfoundation@afcea.org; URL: www.afcea.org/site/foundation/scholarships.

106 ■ Lieutenant General Douglas D. Buchholz Memorial Scholarship (Undergraduate/Scholarship)

Purpose: To provide scholarships to enlisted soldiers designated at Fort Gordon, Georgia. **Focus:** Communications; Engineering; Mathematics and mathematical sciences; Physics. **Qualif.:** Applicants must be current active duty enlisted service member assigned to Fort Gordon, Georgia; enrolled in a STEM (Science, Technology, Engineering or Mathematics) Bachelor's or Master's Degree program at an accredited university with a minimum 15 semester hours/25 quarter hours completed; have a 3.0 minimum GPA.

Funds Avail.: $2,000. **Duration:** Annual. **Number Awarded:** 1. **To Apply:** Applicants must submit: two written recommendations- for Active Duty, one from a commander or senior enlisted person in the chain of command and the other from a college professor, pastor or other respected community official; for Veterans, one from an employer (supervisor) and the other from a college professor, pastor or other respected community official; most current official transcript; a 450-650 word essay on using the degree for benefit the United States or the Department of Defense. **Deadline:** April 15. **Remarks:** Established by General Dynamics and AFCEA to honor the late LTG Douglas Buchholz and recognize the passion he shared for service members pursuing technical education. **Contact:** Horace Carney, Education Committee Chairman; Email: HRCarney@gmail.com.

107 ■ Ralph W. Shrader Diversity Scholarship (Graduate/Scholarship)

Purpose: To provide educational opportunities for talented individuals pursuing advanced STEM degrees at the master's level. **Focus:** Computer and information sciences; Engineering, Chemical; Engineering, Electrical; Mathematics and mathematical sciences; Physics. **Qualif.:** Applicants must be U.S. citizens, and women or minority students, currently enrolled full time in a master's degree program in an accredited university in the United States and currently be enrolled in their second semester and at least two (2) semester-equivalent courses per semester at a four-year accredited college or university (HBCU or non-HBCU) in the United States at the time of application; be pursuing a degree in a qualifying STEM field; have a current overall GPA of 3.5 or higher on a 4.0 scale at the time of application.

Funds Avail.: $3,000. **Duration:** Annual. **To Apply:** Applications must be submitted along with current official transcript issued by the school Registrar's Office, unofficial undergraduate transcript, resume and a minimum of two letters of recommendation required from faculty in the major of study. **Deadline:** May 31. **Contact:** Email: edfoundation@afcea.org; URL: URL: www.afcea.org/site/foundation/scholarships.

108 ■ African American Success Foundation (AASF)

7027 W Broward Blvd., Ste. 313
Fort Lauderdale, FL 33317
Ph: (954)792-1117
URL: www.blacksuccessfoundation.org

109 ■ Lydia Donaldson Tutt-Jones Memorial Research Grant (Graduate, Other, Master's/Grant)

Purpose: To provide financial support to students and professionals who conduct research study of African American success, particularly in the area of education. **Focus:** African-American studies. **Qualif.:** Applicants must be graduate students and professionals. **Criteria:** Selection will be based on the committee's criteria.

Funds Avail.: No specific amount. **Duration:** Annual. **Number Awarded:** 1.

110 ■ AFSA Chapter 155

Dover, NH 03820
Ph: (603)969-4998
Social Media: www.facebook.com/afsa155

111 ■ AFSA Chapter 155 Division 1 Scholarships - Category 1 (Undergraduate/Scholarship)

Purpose: To support students pursuing their educational goals. **Focus:** General studies/Field of study not specified. **Qualif.:** Applicants must be graduating high school seniors entering 1st year college, whose parents, grandparents and/or guardians are current members of AFSA/Auxiliary; must have a GPA of 3.0. **Criteria:** Recipients are selected based on their submitted applications.

Funds Avail.: $500. **Number Awarded:** 1. **To Apply:** Applicants must submit a completed application form (available at the website), two (2) letters of recommendation, one (1) letter from student guidance/counselor, results from SAT/ACT or equivalent, class rank or mid-term for the current year and a 5"x7" photograph. **Contact:** Clifford Wittman at wittmancm@yahoo.com.

112 ■ AFSA Chapter 155 Division 1 Scholarships - Category 2 (Undergraduate/Scholarship)

Purpose: To support students pursuing their educational goals. **Focus:** General studies/Field of study not specified. **Qualif.:** Applicants must be 2nd, 3rd and 4th year college students up to 26 years age, whose parents, grandparents and/or guardians are current members of AFSA/Auxiliary; have a GPA of 3.0. **Criteria:** Recipients are selected based on their submitted applications.

Funds Avail.: $500. **Number Awarded:** 1. **To Apply:** Applicants must submit a completed application form (available at the website), one (1) letter from student guidance/counselor, one (1) letter from senior faculty member and a 5"x7" photograph. **Contact:** Clifford Wittman at wittmancm@yahoo.com.

Awards are arranged alphabetically below their administering organizations

113 ■ AFSA Chapter 155 Division 1 Scholarships - Category 3 *(Undergraduate/Scholarship)*

Purpose: To support students pursuing their educational goals. **Focus:** General studies/Field of study not specified. **Qualif.:** Applicants must be AFSA/Auxiliary members seeking to complete advanced schooling at a credited college or trade school; must have a GPA of 3.0. **Criteria:** Recipients are selected based on their submitted applications.

Funds Avail.: $500. **Number Awarded:** 1. **To Apply:** Applicants must submit a completed application form (available at the website) and a 5"x7" photograph. **Contact:** Clifford Wittman at wittmancm@yahoo.com.

114 ■ Senior Master Sergeant William Sowers Memorial Scholarship *(Undergraduate/Grant)*

Purpose: To support students for their continuing education. **Focus:** General studies/Field of study not specified. **Qualif.:** Applicants must be members, or dependent of a parent, grandparent and/or legal guardian, who are current members of AFSA Chapter 155. **Criteria:** Recipients are selected based on their submitted applications.

Funds Avail.: $1,000. **Number Awarded:** 1. **To Apply:** Applicants must submit a handwritten essay (300 - 500 words) about your goals and what you have done toward achieving them; three (3) Letters Of Reference (not Family Members). **Deadline:** May 15. **Remarks:** Awarded in the memory of William Sowers. **Contact:** Raymond L. Drapeau, Scholarship Chairman, 1 Polk Ave., Portsmouth, NH, 03801-5729; Phone: 603-436-0880; Email: rddrapeau@comcast.net.

115 ■ After School Athlete
16810 104th Ave. SE
Renton, WA 98055
Ph: (903)600-5437
URL: www.afterschoolathlete.com

116 ■ After School Athlete Scholarship *(High School, Undergraduate/Scholarship)*

Purpose: To encourage students to self-reflect to make meaning on their journey ahead. **Focus:** General studies/Field of study not specified. **Qualif.:** High school senior or college freshman, sophomore, or junior. **Criteria:** Criteria include GPA, ACT/SAT scores, class rank, and short essays.

Funds Avail.: $250. **Duration:** Annual. **Number Awarded:** 1. **Deadline:** May 1. **Contact:** E-mail: afterschoolathlete@gmail.com.

117 ■ AfterCollege
98 Battery St., Ste. 502
San Francisco, CA 94111
Ph: (415)263-1300
Fax: (415)263-1307
Free: 877-725-7721
E-mail: info@aftercollege.com
URL: www.aftercollege.com
Social Media: www.facebook.com/AfterCollegeInc
pinterest.com/aftercollege
twitter.com/aftercollege
youtube.com/user/AfterCollegeMedia

118 ■ AfterCollege/AACN Nursing Scholarship *(Undergraduate, Master's, Doctorate/Scholarship)*

Purpose: To support students who are seeking a baccalaureate, master's or doctoral degree in nursing. **Focus:** Nursing. **Qualif.:** Applicants must already be enrolled at an AACN member institution. Special consideration will be given to students in a graduate program with the goal of becoming a nurse educator; students completing an RN-to-BSN or RN-to-MSN program; and those enrolled in an accelerated program. **Criteria:** Selection will be based on the committee's criteria.

Funds Avail.: $10,000 ($2,500 will be awarded each quarter). **Number Awarded:** Each quarter. **Deadline:** March 31; June 30; September 30; December 31. **Contact:** Email: scholarships@aftercollege.com.

119 ■ AfterCollege Business Student Scholarship *(Undergraduate, Graduate, Doctorate/Scholarship)*

Purpose: To help deserving students cover expenses during school and propel them forward into rewarding careers after college. **Focus:** Business. **Qualif.:** Applicants must be current students working toward a degree (AA, AS, BA, BS, MS, PhD) in a field of business, which can include (but is not limited to): Accounting, Advertising, Business Administration, Economics, Finance, Human Resources, International Relations, Management, Political Science, Public Relations, etc.; must have a minimum of 3.0 GPA; must be members of AfterCollege. **Criteria:** Selection will be based on the committee's criteria.

Funds Avail.: $500. **Number Awarded:** 1. **To Apply:** Interested applicants may visit the website to create a free AfterCollege account and profile and submit the online application. Finalists will be contacted by email and may be asked to submit the following: copy of unofficial transcript verifying GPA. **Deadline:** September 30. **Contact:** Email: scholarships@aftercollege.com.

120 ■ AfterCollege Engineering & Technology Student Scholarship *(Undergraduate, Graduate, Doctorate, Master's/Scholarship)*

Purpose: To support current students working toward a degree in a field of engineering and/or mathematics. **Focus:** Computer and information sciences; Engineering; Mathematics and mathematical sciences. **Qualif.:** Applicants must be current students working toward a degree (AA, AS, AAS, BA, BS, MS and PhD) in a field of engineering; and/or mathematics (may also include computer science, cybersecurity, etc.) and must have a minimum of 3.0 GPA; must be members of AfterCollege. **Criteria:** AfterCollege profiles are used as criteria to select the scholarship recipient. Primarily looking for a succinct but impactful, resume-style personal statement that describes applicant's goals and the value that they bring in an academic and/or professional context (recommend 250 words or less). May also consider GPA, honors, awards, scholarships, skills and all other information provided on the profile.

Funds Avail.: $500. **Number Awarded:** Each quarter. **To Apply:** Applicants must submit a letter of recommendation from Program Director. **Deadline:** September 30. **Contact:** Email: scholarships@aftercollege.com.

121 ■ AfterCollege Science Student Scholarship *(Undergraduate, Graduate, Doctorate/Scholarship)*

Purpose: To help deserving students cover expenses during school and propel them forward into rewarding careers after college. **Focus:** Science. **Qualif.:** Applicants must be current students working toward a degree (AA, AS, BA, BS, MS and PhD) in one of the many fields of science, including but not limited to: Astronomy, Biology, Chemistry, Geology, Meteorology, Oceanography, Physics, Zoology, etc.; must have a minimum of 3.0 GPA; must be members of Af-

Awards are arranged alphabetically below their administering organizations

terCollege. **Criteria:** Selection will be based on the committee's criteria.

Funds Avail.: $500. **Number Awarded:** 1. **To Apply:** Interested applicants must visit the website to create a free AfterCollege account and profile and submit the online application. Finalists will be contacted by email and may be asked to submit the following: copy of unofficial transcript verifying GPA; letter of recommendation from Program Director. **Deadline:** September 30. **Contact:** Email: scholarships@aftercollege.com.

122 ■ AfterCollege STEM Inclusion Scholarship
(Undergraduate, Graduate/Scholarship)

Purpose: To support students who are about to learn more on STEM education. **Focus:** Engineering; Mathematics and mathematical sciences; Science; Technology. **Qualif.:** Applicants must be currently enrolled students working toward a degree in the fields of science, technology, engineering or mathematics from a group underrepresented in their field of study; must have a minimum 3.0 GPA. **Criteria:** Selection of applicants will be based on AfterCollege profiles. GPA, honors, awards, scholarships, skills and all other information provided on the profile will also be considered.

Funds Avail.: $500. **Number Awarded:** 1. **To Apply:** Applicants must submit their succinct but impactful, resume-style personal statements (200 words or less) that describe their respective goals and values that they bring in an academic and/or professional context; they may visit the AfterCollege website to create a free AfterCollege account and profile and submit the online application. Chosen finalists will be contacted via email and will be asked to submit a copy of their unofficial transcript verifying GPA. **Deadline:** September 30. **Contact:** Email: scholarships@aftercollege.com.

123 ■ AfterCollege Succurro Scholarship
(Undergraduate, Graduate, Doctorate/Scholarship)

Purpose: To help deserving students cover expenses during school and propel them forward into rewarding careers after college. **Focus:** General studies/Field of study not specified. **Qualif.:** Applicants must be current students enrolled in an accredited program, working toward a degree (AA, AS, BA, BS, MA, MS, PhD) in any discipline; must have a minimum of 2.5 GPA; must be members of AfterCollege. **Criteria:** Selection will be based on the committee's criteria.

Funds Avail.: $500. **To Apply:** Applicants are required to visit the website to create a free AfterCollege account and profile and submit the online application. **Deadline:** September 30. **Contact:** Email: scholarships@aftercollege.com.

124 ■ Children's National Health System Pediatric Nursing Student Scholarships *(Undergraduate/Scholarship)*

Purpose: To support students who are working toward their BSN and have an interest in pediatrics. **Focus:** Nursing. **Qualif.:** Applicants must be currently enrolled students working toward their BSN and have an interest in pediatrics; must have a minimum 3.0 GPA. **Criteria:** Selection of applicants will be based on AfterCollege profiles. GPA, honors, awards, scholarships, skills and all other information provided on the profile will also be considered.

Funds Avail.: $500. **To Apply:** Applicants must submit their succinct but impactful, resume-style personal state-

ments that describe their respective goals and values that they bring in an academic and/or professional context; they may visit the AfterCollege website to create a free AfterCollege account and profile and submit the online application. **Deadline:** June 30.

125 ■ AGC Education and Research Foundation (AGCERF)
2300 Wilson Blvd., Ste. 300
Arlington, VA 22201
Ph: (703)548-3118
Fax: (703)837-5405
Free: 800-242-1767
E-mail: info@agc.org
URL: www.agc.org
Social Media: www.linkedin.com/company/agcofa
twitter.com/AGCofA
www.youtube.com/user/agcofamerica

126 ■ Saul Horowitz Jr. Memorial Graduate Award
(Graduate/Scholarship, Award)

Purpose: To provide financial support to college seniors enrolled or planning to enroll in a graduate-level construction management or construction-related engineering degree program. **Focus:** Construction; Engineering, Civil. **Qualif.:** Applicants must be undergraduate and graduate student.

Funds Avail.: Up to $7,500. **Duration:** Annual. **Contact:** Melinda Patrician, Director, AGC Education & Research Foundation, Associated General Contractors of America; Phone: 703-837-5342; Fax:703-837-5451; Email: melinda.patrician@agc.org.

127 ■ Aging Gracefully across Environments using Technology to Support Wellness, Engagement and Long Life (AGE-WELL)
12th Fl. Research
550 University Ave.
Toronto, ON, Canada M5G 2A2
Ph: (416)597-3422
Fax: (416)597-3031
E-mail: info@agewell-nce.ca
URL: agewell-nce.ca

128 ■ AGE-WELL Graduate Student and Postdoctoral Awards in Technology and Aging
(Master's, Doctorate, Postdoctorate/Award)

Purpose: To provide a unique training environment that exposes trainees to multi-disciplinary research environments and to its industry and community partners. **Focus:** Technology. **Qualif.:** Applicants must have received at least some financial support from additional sources; participate full-time in their respective program at a Canadian post-secondary institution; be engaged in academic study/research aligned with the mission and vision of AGE-WELL; applicants for doctoral awards are restricted to those entering the first or second year of their program. **Criteria:** Applications will be reviewed by a team of field experts using the following criteria: scholarly merit and quality of proposed research (40%); fit with AGE-WELL Goals and priorities (40%); quality of training environment (20%).

Funds Avail.: $10,000 for Masters students (1 year award); $15,000 for PhD students (2 year award); $20,000 for

Awards are arranged alphabetically below their administering organizations

Postdoctoral fellows (1 year award). **Duration:** Annual. **To Apply:** Applicants must complete and submit the following: online application form; two confidential letters of support (one must be from the proposed supervisor); formal evidence of enrollment in a master's or doctoral program or post-doctoral position; formal evidence of awarded funding for the current academic year; curriculum vitae. **Deadline:** May 31. **Contact:** Email: support@forum.agewell-nce.ca or training@agewell-nce.ca.

129 ■ Agricultural Institute of Canada (AIC)

70 George St., 3rd Fl.
Ottawa, ON, Canada 516589
Ph: (613)232-9459
Fax: (866)851-5689
E-mail: office@aic.ca
URL: www.aic.ca
Social Media: twitter.com/agfoodinnov

130 ■ Karl C. Ivarson Scholarship for Students in Soil Science and Related Studies *(Master's, Doctorate/Scholarship, Award)*

Purpose: To support students pursuing studies in soil science. **Focus:** Soil science. **Qualif.:** Applicants must hold Canadian citizenship; must be registered full-time in a master or doctorate program in the area of soil science (agriculture, agro-ecology, resource management, environment, geology or other related disciplines); must be enrolled in their graduate program. **Criteria:** Scholarships are awarded on the following basis but not necessarily placed in order of importance: Emphasis in research related to agricultural business/commerce/economics/trade, Academic record, Leadership and community service, Work experience and career interests, Letters of recommendation.

Funds Avail.: 2,000 Canadian dollars. **Duration:** Annual. **Number Awarded:** 1. **To Apply:** Applicants must submit a Emphasis in research related to agricultural business/commerce/economics/trade; Academic achievement; areas of stud; leadership and community service; work experience and career interests; letters of recommendation. **Deadline:** May 27. **Remarks:** The scholarship was established in memory of Karl C. Ivarson. **Contact:** E-mail: manager@cffae.ca.

131 ■ Douglas McRorie Memorial Scholarships *(Doctorate, Master's/Scholarship, Award)*

Purpose: To provide financial support to post-graduate masters or PhD students specializing in agricultural business, economics, finance or trade. **Focus:** Agribusiness; Economics; Finance. **Qualif.:** Applicants must hold Canadian citizenship or permanent resident status; must be registered full-time in a Masters or PhD program in the area of agricultural business, economics, finance or trade; must be enrolled in their graduate program; must be agricultural post-graduates majoring in agricultural business, economics, finance or trade. **Criteria:** Scholarships are awarded on the following basis but not necessarily placed in order of importance: Emphasis in research related to agricultural business/commerce/economics/trade, Academic record, Leadership and community service, Work experience and career interests, Letters of recommendation.

Funds Avail.: 3,000 Canadian dollars for Masters level (1); 5,000 Canadian dollars for PhD level (1). **Duration:** Annual. **Number Awarded:** Various. **To Apply:** Applicants must submit a Emphasis in research related to agricultural business/commerce/economics/trade; Academic achievement; areas of stud; leadership and community service; work experience and career interests; letters of recommendation. **Deadline:** February 28. **Remarks:** The scholarship was established in honor of past-president and agri-finance leader, Douglas McRorie. Established in 1990. **Contact:** E-mail: manager@cffae.ca.

132 ■ Agriculture Future of America (AFA)

11500 NW Ambassador Drive, Suite 306
Kansas City, MO 64153
Ph: (816)472-4232
Fax: (816)472-4239
Free: 888-472-4232
URL: www.agfuture.org
Social Media: www.facebook.com/
  agriculturefutureofamerica
www.instagram.com/agfutureamerica
www.linkedin.com/company/agriculture-future-of-america
twitter.com/AgFutureAmerica
www.youtube.com/user/agfuture

133 ■ Agriculture Future of America Community Scholarships *(Undergraduate/Scholarship)*

Purpose: To support local students preparing for a career in the agriculture and food industry. **Focus:** Agriculture, Economic aspects. **Qualif.:** Applicants must be 17-25 years of age, pursuing an agriculture-related bachelor's degree; must attend the entire AFA Leaders Conference; must be enrolled as a full time student. **Criteria:** Recipients will be selected on the basis of career vision and goal, leader and community involvement, and financial need.

Funds Avail.: $3,200. **To Apply:** Applicants must contact AFA to request an application form. **Contact:** Phone: 816-472-4232; E-mail: scholarship@agfuture.org.

134 ■ Agriculture Future of America Scholarships *(Undergraduate/Scholarship)*

Purpose: To encourage graduating high school seniors and current undergraduate students. **Focus:** Agriculture, Economic aspects. **Qualif.:** Applicants must be students who plan to pursue a four year degree in an agriculture-related field; must have a cumulative GPA of 3.0 or higher at the time of selection; applicants must be 17-25 years old; must attend the entire AFA Leaders Conference. **Criteria:** Recipients are selected based on an interview; an essay of 300-500 words describing the student's perception on the future of agriculture; community service; study group activities; general factors.

Funds Avail.: Amount varies. **Duration:** Annual. **To Apply:** Applicants must contact AFA to request an application form; share up-to-date school and contact information.

135 ■ Ahepa Buckeye Scholarship Foundation

c/o Tony Capranica,Chairman
601 Tall Pines Dr.
Toledo, OH 43615
Ph: (330)372-1869
URL: www.bsf.buckeyedistrict11.org

136 ■ Ahepa Buckeye Scholarship Awards *(Undergraduate/Scholarship, Award)*

Purpose: To provide financial support to students in pursuing their higher educational career. **Focus:** General studies/

Awards are arranged alphabetically below their administering organizations

Field of study not specified. **Qualif.:** Applicant must be an students entering college or in undergraduate school; must be an active member of the AHEPA, Daughters of Penelope, Sons of Pericles, Maids of Athena, or whose parent(s) have been active members of the Senior Orders for three consecutive years.**Criteria:** Recipient is selected based on scholastic achievement and financial need.

Funds Avail.: No specific amount. **To Apply:** Applicants must submit most recent high school transcript; letter of acceptance from accredited college university; IRS from 1040; for college student submit an official transcript of grades including cumulative grade point average up to the date of application and grades for the semester or term. **Deadline:** March 31. **Contact:** 601 Tall Pines Dr., Toledo, OH, 43615.

137 ■ AIA New York Chapter
536 LaGuardia Pl.
New York, NY 10012
Ph: (212)683-0023
Fax: (212)696-5022
E-mail: info@aiany.org
URL: www.aiany.org
Social Media: www.facebook.com/CenterforArchitecture
www.instagram.com/centerforarch
www.linkedin.com/company/center-for-architecture
twitter.com/CenterForArch
twitter.com/aia_newyork

138 ■ Eleanor Allwork Scholarship *(Undergraduate/ Scholarship)*

Purpose: To support architecture students seeking their first degree in architecture; and to support with demonstrated financial need. **Focus:** Architecture. **Qualif.:** Students seeking their first degree in architecture from an NAAB-accredited school in the State of New York are eligible; need not be U.S. citizens; graduate students are eligible if they have a professional undergraduate degree in a field other than architecture. **Criteria:** Selection will be based on high level of academic performance and evidence of financial need.

Funds Avail.: Up to $7,500; grant of up to $10,000. **Duration:** Annual. **To Apply:** Applicants must submit a completed application form including a portfolio and two letters of recommendation; must be submitted both electronically (PDF) and in hardcopy; cover page form; can be submitted online. **Deadline:** March 20. **Contact:** Email:scholarships@centerforarchitecture.org.

139 ■ Stewardson Keefe LeBrun Travel Grant *(Professional development/Grant, Award)*

Purpose: To further the personal and professional development of an architect in early or midcareer through travel. **Focus:** Architecture. **Qualif.:** Applicant must be a U.S. Citizen with a degree in architecture as well as a full-time practitioner, either licensed or unlicensed. **Criteria:** This award was founded to encourage student journalism on architecture, planning, or related subjects, and to foster regard for intelligent criticism among future professionals. The award is not intended as a prize for individuals, but is intended to support the ongoing publication of student-edited journals whose subject matter could include architectural design, history, or theory.

Funds Avail.: Up to $25,000. **Duration:** Annual. **Number Awarded:** Varies. **To Apply:** Applicants must submit a

completed application form; two letters of recommendation and $50 application fee; must be submitted both electronically (PDF) and in hard copy; cover page form; statement of purpose; CV; portfolios; itinerary. **Deadline:** June 15. **Contact:** Email:scholarships@centerforarchitecture.org.

140 ■ AICA Orthopedics
3166 Chestnut Dr., Ste. 100, 200
Atlanta, GA 30340
Ph: (404)855-2141
URL: www.aicaorthopedics.com

141 ■ 1-800-Pain-Free Scholarship *(Two Year College, Undergraduate, Graduate/Scholarship)*

Purpose: To help students pay for college. **Focus:** General studies/Field of study not specified. **Qualif.:** Applicants must be current or prospective students enrolled full-time at an accredited U.S. university; must be at least 18 years old. Open to all majors, but medical and law students are encouraged to apply. **Criteria:** Selection is based on the best submitted essay.

Funds Avail.: $1,000. **Number Awarded:** 1. **To Apply:** Filled out application, submit 500 - 800 word essay on distracted driving and how it has personally impacted you or someone you know, and the efforts you make to avoid driving distracted; See chiropractoratlanta.com/scholarship-program. **Deadline:** April 17. **Contact:** Jennifer Breland; Email: jbreland@aicaorthopedics.com.

142 ■ AICA Orthopedics Scholarship *(Undergraduate, Two Year College, Graduate/Scholarship)*

Purpose: To help students pay for college. **Focus:** General studies/Field of study not specified. **Qualif.:** Applicants must be current or prospective students enrolled full-time at an accredited U.S. university; must be at least 18 years old. Open to all majors, but medical and law students are encouraged to apply. **Criteria:** Selection is based on the best essay submitted.

Funds Avail.: $1,000. **Number Awarded:** 1. **To Apply:** Submit completed application, proof of enrollment and write a 500-800 word essay. Details available online. **Deadline:** April 17. **Contact:** Jennifer Breland; Email: jbreland@aicaorthopedics.com; URL: aica.com/scholarship/.

143 ■ Aiello, Harris, Marth, Tunnero, & Shiffman, P.C.
501 Watchung Ave.
Watchung, NJ 07069
Ph: (908)561-5577
URL: aielloharris.com
Social Media: facebook.com/AielloHarris
twitter.com/aielloharris

144 ■ Aiello Harris Legal Scholarships *(Undergraduate, Graduate/Scholarship)*

Purpose: To help offset the costs of education in pursuit of a program in pre-law, paralegal studies, legal assisting, or Juris Doctor. **Focus:** Law; Paralegal studies. **Qualif.:** Applicants must be currently pursuing a law-related degree or a paralegal degree, or be accepted into a legal or paralegal program; must hold or anticipate a high school diploma or GED; must have a 3.0 or higher GPA.

Funds Avail.: $1,000. **Duration:** 4 years. **Number Awarded:** 2. **To Apply:** Applicant Must Provide Unofficial

Awards are arranged alphabetically below their administering organizations

Transcript,Current Proof of Enrollment,short essay,short survey and application. **Deadline:** July 5. **Contact:** E-mail: mhepburn@aielloharris.com.

145 ■ Air Force Association (AFA)

1501 Lee Hwy.
Arlington, VA 22209
Ph: (703)247-5800
Fax: (703)247-5853
Free: 800-727-3337
E-mail: membership@afa.org
URL: www.afa.org
Social Media: www.facebook.com/AirForceAssociation
www.instagram.com/airforceassoc
www.linkedin.com/company/air-force-association
www.gr.pinterest.com/pin/331296116308752295
twitter.com/AirForceAssoc
www.youtube.com/channel/UC5V3SOz6Dp6fpHn
_wN9jSKA

146 ■ Air Force Association/Grantham Scholarships
(Undergraduate/Scholarship)

Purpose: To support and promote aerospace education, specifically the study of science, mathematics and technology. **Focus:** Aerospace sciences. **Qualif.:** Candidates must have a high school diploma or GED and must be members of AFA or their dependents. **Criteria:** Selection will be based on the committee's criteria.

To Apply: Applicants must submit a completed application form; a two-page, double-spaced essay describing the applicant's academic and career goals and explaining why they are interested in pursuing a degree via an online degree program, an explanation why this is the right time in the applicant's life and why they are committed to completing a degree; two letters of recommendation (these should be character references with descriptions of the applicant's performance and potential as a student); and proof of GED completion or high school transcripts (or college transcripts if applicable). College transcript(s) and proof of undergraduate degree are required for the graduate programs. must provide the information requested on a feedback form six months after the scholarship is awarded.

147 ■ Captain Jodi Callahan Memorial Scholarship
(Graduate, Master's/Scholarship)

Purpose: To provide scholarships for active duty of Air Force, full-time Air National Guard or full-time Air Force Reserve. **Focus:** General studies/Field of study not specified. **Qualif.:** Applicants must be active duty Air Force, full time Air National Guard or full time Air Force Reserve (officer or enlisted) pursuing a Master's Degree in a non-technical field of study; a minimum Grade Point Average of 3.0 on a scale of 4.0 is required. **Criteria:** Selection will be based on the committee's criteria.

Funds Avail.: $1,000. **Duration:** Annual. **Number Awarded:** 1. **To Apply:** Completed application must be submitted online along with one letter of recommendation from your Air Force supervisor or commander which includes a character reference, a description of your performance and an assessment of your potential as an Air Force leader and volunteer; proof of acceptance into a Master's program at an accredited college or university for those who have not begun advanced degree; a two page essay describing academic goals and degree awarded will

enhance the service to the Air Force. **Deadline:** April 30. **Remarks:** The scholarship is in memory of Captain Jodi Callahan who was an AFA Under-Forty National Director and a Trustee of the former Aerospace Education Foundation. The scholarship is made possible through contributions to the Jodi Callahan Memorial Fund by her family and friends.

148 ■ Lt Col Romeo - Josephine Bass Ferretti Scholarship *(Undergraduate/Scholarship)*

Purpose: To provide educational assistance for graduating high school students. **Focus:** Engineering; Mathematics and mathematical sciences; Science; Technology. **Qualif.:** Applicants must be minor dependents of active duty or retired Air Force, Air Force Reserve or Air National Guard enlisted airmen; they must be students pursuing an undergraduate degree in the area of science, technology, engineering or math (STEM). **Criteria:** Recipients will be selected by committee based upon high academic achievement, good character and financial need.

Funds Avail.: $5,000. **Duration:** Annual. **Number Awarded:** 1. **To Apply:** Applicants must submit a completed application form, a two-page essay describing the academic achievements and goals, one letter of recommendation, an official and original high school transcript, proof of acceptance letter must be on college/university stationery from the admissions office, registrar or financial aid office and must include a statement of the cost of tuition and fees for the first term of attendance. **Deadline:** April 30. **Remarks:** The scholarship is made possible by a bequest from the estate of Lt Col Romeo and Josephine Bass Ferretti.

149 ■ Mike and Gail Donley Spouse Scholarship
(Undergraduate, Graduate, Postgraduate/Scholarship)

Purpose: To encourage Air Force spouses worldwide to pursue associate, bachelor or graduate/postgraduate degrees. **Focus:** General studies/Field of study not specified. **Qualif.:** Applicants must be spouses of Air Force Active Duty, Air National Guard, Air Force Reserve or Department of the Air Force Civilian employees; must be in a degree program; spouses who are themselves Air Force personnel, or in ROTC, are not eligible. **Criteria:** Selection will be based on the committee's criteria and applicants' eligibility.

Funds Avail.: $2,500. **Duration:** Annual. **Number Awarded:** 2. **To Apply:** Applicants must include the following in their application: an original or copy of the most recent college/university transcript or a report card from the applicants' last semester verifying their minimum 3.5 GPA or higher; proof of acceptance into a regionally accredited community college/college/university (this may consist of a short letter on college/university stationery from either the admissions office or the registrar); a two-page double-spaced essay, describing the applicants' academic and career goals and the motivation which led them to this decision and describing how Air Force and other local community activities in which they are involved will enhance their goals; two letters of recommendation (should be character references and descriptions of performance and potential as a student, employee or volunteer); a letter of endorsement from the local AFA Chapter would be welcomed and encouraged (the two letters must be from the different sources). Letters from previous or present professors, employers and volunteer organizations referencing the work of the applicants are encouraged. **Deadline:** April 30. **Remarks:** The Air Force Association (AFA) has named its spouse scholarship program "The Mike & Gail Donley

---

Awards are arranged alphabetically below their administering organizations

Spouse Scholarship" to provide a lasting tribute to the former Secretary of the Air Force and his wife for their exemplary support of the Air Force Family.

150 ■ Pitsenbarger Award (Undergraduate, Graduate/Grant, Award)

Purpose: To provide a one-time grant to selected top USAF enlisted personnel. **Focus:** Aerospace sciences. **Qualif.:** Applicants must be top USAF enlisted personnel graduating from the Community College of the Air Force (CCAF) who plan to pursue a baccalaureate degree. **Criteria:** Selection is determined at the ESO by a committee of individuals appointed by the base education officer. The committee considers job performance, scholastic achievement, education goals and leadership qualities. Need is not a principle criterion.

Funds Avail.: $400. **Duration:** Annual. **Number Awarded:** 1. **To Apply:** Applicants must submit the following requirements: completed application form; a proof of current enrollment or intent to enroll in an accredited program leading to baccalaureate degree; citations and awards representing activities; narrative statement describing extracurricular activities and explaining their significance; and Commander's endorsement. **Deadline:** June 1. **Contact:** Air Force Association, Attn: Pitsenbarger Manager, 1501 Lee Hwy., Arlington, VA 22209-1198; Phone: 703-247-5800 ext. 4807; Fax: 703-247-5853; Email: education@afa.org.

151 ■ Michael Wilson Scholarships (Undergraduate/Scholarship)

Purpose: To support Air Force ROTC cadtes in their education. **Focus:** Aerospace sciences. **Qualif.:** Applicants must be current Air Force ROTC cadets in good standing, enrolled full-time as incoming juniors or seniors for the academic year at the Professional Air Force ROTC Officer Course program and attend both the Aerospace Studies class and Leadership Lab each semester; they must have a cumulative 2.8 GPA or better on a 4.0 scale. **Criteria:** Selection will be based on the committee's criteria.

Funds Avail.: $15,000. **Number Awarded:** 2. **To Apply:** Applicants must submit complete three essays with a uniform format prescribed by the organization; such must be submitted along with other requirements asked. **Remarks:** The scholarship program was created by the Air Force Association (AFA) in partnership with Brian Wilson. **Contact:** Staff Sergeant Darryl Andrews at 334-953-2607 or via e-mail to Darryl.Andrews@maxwell.af.mil.

152 ■ Air Force Sergeants Association (AFSA)

5211 Auth Rd.
Suitland, MD 20746
Ph: (301)899-3500
Fax: (301)899-8136
Free: 800-638-0594
E-mail: afsacomm@hqafsa.org
URL: www.hqafsa.org
Social Media: www.facebook.com/AFSAHQ
www.instagram.com/afsahq
www.linkedin.com/company/air-force-sergeants-association
twitter.com/AFSAHQ

153 ■ AFSA Scholarship Program (Undergraduate/Scholarship)

Purpose: To provide financial assistance to the studies of dependent children of the enlisted Total Air Force members.

Focus: General studies/Field of study not specified. **Qualif.:** Applicants must be AFSA members. **Criteria:** Selection will be based on applicant's academic record, character, leadership skills, writing ability, versatility and potential for success.

Funds Avail.: Amount varies. **Duration:** Annual. **Number Awarded:** 1. **To Apply:** Applicants must submit a completed application form; a copy of proof of sponsor's military status (copy of DD 214, copy of the sponsor's ID and discharge letter); official transcript of grades (high school graduates must include all grades from 9th to 12th grades, college applicants must include cumulative record of grades); a letter of recommendation written on the official school stationary with original signature (for high school graduate, letter must be written by the school principal or counselor; for college student, letter must be written by a college professor); a typed paragraph of the applicant's objectives (double-spaced) about the plans to be done after receiving the education; essay (double-spaced) about the most urgent problem facing society today and a typed, double-spaced two-page essay about a current, controversial issue; two self-addressed, stamped, blank postcards. High school graduates must include a valid record of combined SAT I or ACT scores (must be recorded on an official school transcript). **Deadline:** March 31. **Remarks:** AFSA Scholarship Program, 5211 Auth Rd., Suitland, Maryland, 20746; Phone: 800-638-0594, ext. 288. Established in 1968. **Contact:** AFSA/CMSAF/AMF Scholarship Program, 5211 Auth Rd., Suitland, MD 20746; Phone: 800-638-0594, ext. 288.

154 ■ Air Traffic Control Association (ATCA)

225 Reinekers lane, ste, 400
Alexandria, VA 22314
Ph: (703)299-2430
Fax: (703)299-2437
E-mail: info@atca.org
URL: www.atca.org
Social Media: www.facebook.com/AirTrafficControlAssociation
www.linkedin.com/feed/?trk=login_reg_redirect
twitter.com/ATCA_now
www.youtube.com/user/ATCAnow

155 ■ Air Traffic Control Association Full-time Employee Student Scholarship (Other/Scholarship)

Purpose: To provide financial assistance to full-time employees enrolled in advanced study programs that enhance employee's skills in aviation-related position. **Focus:** Aviation; Transportation. **Qualif.:** Applicants must have an attendance equal to at least half-time (6 semester hours or the equivalent) and a minimum of 30 semester or 45 hours still to be completed before graduation; must be enrolled or accepted in a two-year or greater air traffic control program at an institution approved and/or listed by the Federal Aviation Administration as directly supporting the FAA's college training initiative; must be enrolled or accepted in an accredited college or university and planning to continue the following academic year; must be enrolled in course work related to their aviation-related career and leading to a bachelor's degree or greater; must be engaged in full-time employment in an aviation-related field; must be enrolled in course work designed to enhance the applicants' skill in an air traffic control or other aviation-related discipline. **Criteria:** Recipient will be selected by the Scholarship Selection Committee based on set of criteria.

Awards are arranged alphabetically below their administering organizations

Funds Avail.: No specific amount. **Duration:** Annual. **Number Awarded:** 2. **To Apply:** Applicants must provide two letters of recommendation (from present or previous teachers, professors, instructors, supervisors, or managers) from within the last 12 months; submit certified transcript of all college coursework; if less than 30 semester or 45 quarter hours of college coursework have been completed, all high school transcripts are also required, work or experience that supports the applicant's educational and/or aviation career goals must be addressed in the application and/or essay; financial need must be addressed in the application and/or essay; submit a paper on the subject, "how do you see your career unfolding? " which should be typed, doubled spaced, 500 words maximum. **Deadline:** January 1. **Contact:** E-mail: jessica.morin@atca.org.

156 ■ Air Traffic Control Association Non-employee Student Scholarships *(Undergraduate/Scholarship)*

Purpose: To provide financial assistance to students enrolled in aviation related program of study leading to a bachelor's degree or greater. **Focus:** Aviation. **Qualif.:** Applicants must have attendance equal to at least half-time (6 semester hours or the equivalent) and a minimum of 30 semester or 45 hours still to be completed before graduation; must be enrolled or accepted in a two-year or greater air traffic control program at an institution approved and/or listed by the Federal Aviation Administration as directly supporting the FAA's college training initiative; must be enrolled or accepted in an accredited college or university and planning to continue the following academic year; must be enrolled in course work related to an aviation-related career and leading to a bachelor's degree or greater; must be engaged in full-time employment in an aviation-related field; must be enrolled in course work designed to enhance the applicant's skill in an air traffic control or other aviation-related discipline. **Criteria:** Recipient will be selected by the Scholarship Selection Committee based on set of criteria.

Funds Avail.: No specific amount. **Duration:** Annual. **To Apply:** Applicants must provide two letters of recommendation (from present or previous teachers, professors, instructors, supervisors, or managers) from within the last 12 months; submit certified transcript of all college coursework; if less than 30 semester or 45 quarter hours of college coursework have been completed, all high school transcripts are also required, work or experience that supports the applicant's educational and/or aviation career goals must be addressed in the application and/or essay; financial need must be addressed in the application and/or essay; submit a paper on the subject, "How My Education Efforts Will Enhance My Potential Contribution To Aviation." which should be typed, doubled spaced, 400 words maximum. **Deadline:** May 1. **Contact:** Air Traffic Control Association, Inc. Attn: Scholarship Fund, 1101 King St., Ste. 300 Alexandria, VA, 22314.

157 ■ Gabrial A. Hartl Scholarship *(Undergraduate/Scholarship)*

Purpose: To provide financial assistance to students enrolled in air traffic control curriculum at FAA approved institution. **Focus:** Transportation. **Qualif.:** Applicants must have an attendance equal to at least half-time (6 semester hours or the equivalent) and a minimum of 30 semester or 45 hours still to be completed before graduation; must be enrolled or accepted in a two-year or greater air traffic control program at an institution approved and/or listed by the Federal Aviation Administration as directly supporting the FAA's college training initiative; must be enrolled or ac-

cepted in an accredited college or university and planning to continue the following academic year; must be enrolled in course work related to their aviation-related career and leading to a bachelor's degree or greater; must be engaged in full-time employment in an aviation-related field; must be enrolled in course work designed to enhance the applicants' skill in an air traffic control or other aviation-related disciplines. **Criteria:** Recipient will be selected by the Scholarship Selection Committee based on set of criteria.

Funds Avail.: No specific amount. **Duration:** Annual. **Number Awarded:** 3. **To Apply:** Applicants must provide two letters of recommendation (from present or previous teachers, professors, instructors, supervisors, or managers) from within the last 12 months; submit certified transcript of all college coursework; if less than 30 semester or 45 quarter hours of college coursework have been completed, all high school transcripts are also required, work or experience that supports the applicant's educational and/or aviation career goals must be addressed in the application and/or essay; financial need must be addressed in the application and/or essay; submit a paper on the subject, "how do you see your career unfolding? " which should be typed, doubled spaced, 500 words maximum. **Deadline:** January 1. **Contact:** E-mail: jessica.morin@atca.org.

158 ■ Air & Waste Management Association (A&WMA)

Koppers Bldg.
436 Seventh Ave., Ste. 2100
Pittsburgh, PA 15219
Ph: (412)232-3444
Fax: (412)232-3450
Free: 800-270-3444
E-mail: info@awma.org
URL: www.awma.org
Social Media: www.facebook.com/
    AirandWasteManagementAssociation
www.linkedin.com/company/air-&-waste-management
    -association
twitter.com/AirandWaste

159 ■ Dave Benferado Scholarship *(Graduate/Scholarship)*

Purpose: To support the future of fields of air and waste management and to help students improve their knowledge and skills in air pollution control and waste minimization research. **Focus:** Air pollution; Waste management. **Qualif.:** Applicants must be full-time graduate students pursuing courses of study and research leading to careers in air quality, waste management, environmental management/policy/law, and/or sustainability during the academic year. **Criteria:** Selection will be based on the committee's criteria.

Funds Avail.: No specific amount. **Duration:** Annual. **To Apply:** Application materials must be submitted by online which includes: basic contact information; plan of study; statement of professional goals - two (2) page maximum; transcripts- digital copies only (un-official); letter of acceptance from Graduate School and/or Faculty Advisor; complete CV - six (6) page maximum; two reference letters. All required materials should be combined into one (1) PDF file for upload to the ShareFile site. **Deadline:** January 8.

160 ■ Milton Feldstein Memorial Scholarships *(Graduate/Scholarship)*

Purpose: To support the future of fields of air and waste management and to help students improve their knowledge and skills in air quality research. **Focus:** Air pollution; Waste management. **Qualif.:** Applicants must be full-time graduate students pursuing courses of study and research leading to careers in air quality, waste management, environmental management/policy/law, and/or sustainability during the academic year. **Criteria:** Selection will be based on the committee's criteria.

Funds Avail.: $7,500. **To Apply:** Applicants may contact the Foundation for the application process and other information. **Contact:** Robin Lebovitz, A&WMA Educational Programs Associate at rlebovitz@awma.org.

161 ■ Jacqueline Shields Memorial Scholarship
(Graduate/Scholarship)

Purpose: To support the future of fields of air and waste management and to help students improve their knowledge and skills in waste management research and study. **Focus:** Air pollution; Waste management. **Qualif.:** Applicants must be full-time graduate students pursuing courses of study and research leading to careers in air quality, waste management, environmental management/policy/law, and/or sustainability during the academic year. **Criteria:** Selection will be based on the committee's criteria.

Funds Avail.: No specific amount. **Duration:** Annual. **To Apply:** Application materials must be submitted by online which includes: basic contact information; plan of study; statement of professional goals - two (2) page maximum; transcripts- digital copies only (un-official); letter of acceptance from Graduate School and/or Faculty Advisor; complete CV - six (6) page maximum; two reference letters. All required materials should be combined into one (1) PDF file for upload to the ShareFile site. **Deadline:** January 8.

162 ■ Local A&WMA Sections and Chapter Scholarships *(Graduate/Scholarship)*

Purpose: To promote education in air quality and waste management. **Focus:** Air pollution; Environmental law; Waste management. **Qualif.:** Applicants must be a students pursuing environmental studies at universities within their geographic areas. **Criteria:** Selection is based on the application materials submitted.

Funds Avail.: No specific amount. **Duration:** Annual. **Number Awarded:** Varies. **To Apply:** Applicants are required to create a scholarship account online, and upload supporting documents.

163 ■ Richard Stessel Memorial Scholarship
(Graduate/Scholarship)

Purpose: To support the future of fields of air and waste management and to help students improve their knowledge and skills in solid and hazardous waste research. **Focus:** Air pollution; Waste management. **Qualif.:** Applicants must be full-time graduate students pursuing courses of study and research leading to careers in air quality, waste management, environmental management/policy/law, and/or sustainability during the academic year. **Criteria:** Selection will be based on the committee's criteria.

Funds Avail.: No specific amount. **Duration:** Annual. **To Apply:** Application materials must be submitted by online which includes: basic contact information; plan of study; statement of professional goals - two (2) page maximum; transcripts- digital copies only (un-official); letter of acceptance from Graduate School and/or Faculty Advisor; complete CV - six (6) page maximum; two reference letters. All required materials should be combined into one (1)

PDF file for upload to the ShareFile site. **Deadline:** January 8.

164 ■ Air and Waste Management Association Golden West Section (A&WMA-GWS)
The Petroleum Club
5060 California Ave., 12th Flr.
Bakersfield, CA 93309
E-mail: info@awma-gws.org
URL: www.awma-gws.org

165 ■ GWS Scholarship Program *(Undergraduate, Graduate/Scholarship)*

Purpose: To assist students pursuing careers in the areas of atmospheric, energy and environmental science and engineering, environmental management and sustainability, air pollution control, and waste management. **Focus:** Air pollution; Atmospheric science; Environmental science; Public health; Toxicology; Waste management; Water resources. **Qualif.:** Applicants must be accepted into full-time undergraduate and graduate programs for the academic year pursuing courses of study and/or research, leading to careers in atmospheric science, environmental science and engineering, air pollution control, public health, environmental policy, toxicology, waste management, and water resources; must be attending a college or university in the Section's Northern California geographic area (the greater Bay Area and Sacramento Valley region). **Criteria:** Selection will be based on academic record, career goals and financial need. The Student Scholarship Awards Committee will review all applications.

Funds Avail.: Up to $3,500. **Duration:** Annual. **To Apply:** Applicants must submit a completed scholarship application together with the statement of professional goals; transcripts/grade point average; a resume/work experience and letters of recommendation. Application package must be submitted in duplicate to the A&WMA-GWS Education Committee Chair.(do not staple duplicate copy). **Deadline:** March 2. **Contact:** John Koehler, Sc.D.; Education Committee; A&WMA Golden West Section; 43575 Mission Boulevard #210; Fremont CA 94539.

166 ■ Air & Waste Management Association Louisiana Section
LA
URL: la-awma.org
Social Media: www.linkedin.com/company/air-&-waste-management-association

167 ■ AWMA Louisiana Section Scholarship
(Undergraduate, Graduate/Scholarship)

Purpose: To promote education in air quality and waste management. **Focus:** Engineering; Natural sciences; Physical sciences; Public health. **Qualif.:** Applicants must: be full-time students attending a college/university located within the geographical area of the Section (Louisiana and the Sabine River Region of Eastern Texas); be at least juniors (undergraduates) and no higher than master's level graduate students; have at least two semesters (or three quarters) of schooling remaining at the time of the award; be pursuing a bachelors or master's degree with a major in engineering, physical or natural science, or public health; show through course work, projects, personal interest, etc. a desire to promote air pollution control and/or solid or hazardous waste management; and, have at least an

Awards are arranged alphabetically below their administering organizations

overall "B" average (3.00 or higher on a scale of 4.00) including all course work through the last completed semester. Must be interviewed by Louisiana Section representatives. The interview will be scheduled by the Section after the application deadline; the winning applicant should attend the Louisiana Section meeting in September to receive the scholarship award. **Criteria:** Selection will be made on the basis of academic record, plan of study, career goals, recommendations, and financial status without consideration of sex, race, national origin, age, or physical disability. The Scholarship Awards Committee reviews all applications received and its decision is final.

Funds Avail.: $5,000 (1 recipient); $3,500 (1 recipient); $2,000 (1 recipient). **Duration:** Annual. **Number Awarded:** Varies. **To Apply:** Applicants must submit a completed General Application Information Sheet together with a 1-2 page resume; 1-2 page interest and award statement; current transcripts; letter or recommendation from a major professor or department head (envelope should be signed across) and a list of current financial awards. **Deadline:** May 31. **Contact:** Louisiana Section Scholarship Award, c/o Corey Gautreaux, PPM Consultants, Inc., 7936 Office Park Blvd., Ste. A, Baton Rouge, Louisiana, 70809; Email: Corey.Gautreaux@ppmco.com.

168 ■ Air and Waste Management Association Niagara Frontier Section (AWMA-NFS)

PO Box 384
Williamsville, NY 14231
URL: awmanfs.wildapricot.org
Social Media: www.facebook.com/AWMA.nfs

169 ■ AWMA Niagara Frontier Section College Scholarship *(Graduate, Undergraduate/Scholarship)*

Purpose: To support students in their educational pursuits. **Focus:** General studies/Field of study not specified. **Qualif.:** Applicants must be full-time undergraduate or graduate students attending a recognized college/university located within the NY State counties (Allegany, Cattaraugus, Chautauqua, Erie, Niagara and Wyoming).; must be children or spouses of a current member. **Criteria:** Selection is based on applicant's environmental interests, academic record, leadership in school and the community, future academic and career potential, without consideration of sex, race, national origin, financial need, age or physical disability by Board of Directors and Education Committee.

Funds Avail.: $500-$1,000. **Duration:** One academic year. **Number Awarded:** Varies. **To Apply:** Applicants must submit a completed application form (Section I, Section II, and Section III and IV) along with grade transcripts. **Deadline:** May 15.

170 ■ Dave Sauer Memorial College Scholarship *(Undergraduate/Scholarship)*

Purpose: To support students in their educational pursuits. **Focus:** General studies/Field of study not specified. **Qualif.:** Applicants must be high school seniors in good academic standing, attending a recognized high school located within the New York State counties (Allegany, Cattaraugus, Chautauqua, Erie, Niagara or Wyoming) and will attend a recognized college/university. **Criteria:** Selection is based on applicant's environmental interests, academic record, leadership in school and the community, future academic and career potential, without consideration of sex, race, national origin, financial need, age or physical disability by Board of Directors and Education Committee.

Funds Avail.: $500-$1,000. **Duration:** Annual; One academic year. **Number Awarded:** Varies. **To Apply:** Applicants must submit a completed application form (Sections I through VI) together with a high school transcript(s). **Deadline:** May 15.

171 ■ Air and Waste Management Association - Northern and Central New Jersey Chapter (A&WMA NCNJ)

c/o Mr. Jerry Marcus, Scholarship Chair
Stonehenge Associates, LLC
304 Highland Ave.
Upper Montclair, NJ 07043
Ph: (973)746-2372
E-mail: awmamass@gmail.com
URL: www.mass-awma.net
Social Media: twitter.com/Mass_AWMA

172 ■ NCNJ-AWMA Undergraduate Scholarship *(Undergraduate/Scholarship)*

Purpose: To encourage qualified students to enter careers in environmental science. **Focus:** Environmental science; Environmental technology. **Qualif.:** Applicant must be a full-time (9 credits or more) undergraduate college student; pursuing courses of study leading to a career (or post-graduate study) in the environmental sciences/engineering or environmental management or related fields; a resident of New Jersey within the chapter area (Northern and Central New Jersey) or attending a college/university within the chapter area. **Criteria:** Selection is based on the application materials submitted for review.

Funds Avail.: $1,000 each. **Duration:** Annual. **Number Awarded:** 2. **To Apply:** Applicants must submit a completed application form or a copy of the applicant's resume, college transcript, letter of recommendation, and one-page essay on the applicant's experience and interest in environmental issues. **Deadline:** April 25. **Contact:** Mr. Jerry Z. Marcus, QEP, Stonehenge Associates, LLC, 304 Highland Avenue, Upper Montclair, NJ 07043; Phone: (973) 746-2372; E-mail: Jaziem@aol.com.

173 ■ Aircraft Electronics Association (AEA)

3570 NE Ralph Powell Rd.
Lees Summit, MO 64064
Ph: (816)347-8400
Fax: (816)347-8405
E-mail: info@aea.net
URL: www.aea.net
Social Media: www.facebook.com/
  AircraftElectronicsAssociation
www.linkedin.com/company/aircraft-electronics-association
twitter.com/aea_aero
www.youtube.com/user/AEAlive

174 ■ Aircraft Owners and Pilots Association Scholarships *(Undergraduate/Scholarship)*

Purpose: To provide financial support to students pursuing a career in avionics and/or aircraft maintenance through technical training and education at a learning institution. **Focus:** Aviation. **Qualif.:** Applicants must be high school seniors and/or college students planning to or attending an accredited school in an avionics or aircraft repair program. **Criteria:** Selection of candidates will be based on their application materials.

Awards are arranged alphabetically below their administering organizations

Funds Avail.: $2,000. To Apply: Applicants must submit complete and signed application form; recent high school or college transcript; 300-word typed-written essay.

175 ■ Chuck Peacock Memorial Scholarship
(Undergraduate/Scholarship)

Purpose: To promote and secure the future of aviation by furthering the education of students and technicians from AEA member companies. Focus: Aviation. Qualif.: Applicants must be high school seniors and/or college students who are planning to attend an accredited school in an aviation management program.

Funds Avail.: $1,000. Duration: Annual.

176 ■ David Arver Memorial Scholarship
(Undergraduate/Scholarship)

Purpose: To promote and secure the future of aviation by furthering the education of students and technicians from AEA member companies. Focus: Aviation. Qualif.: Applicants must be high school seniors and/or college students planning to or attending an accredited school in an avionics or aircraft repair program.

Funds Avail.: $1,000. Duration: Annual.

177 ■ Johnny Davis Memorial Scholarship
(Undergraduate/Scholarship)

Purpose: To provide financial support to students pursuing a career in avionics and/or aircraft maintenance through technical training and education at a learning institution. Focus: Aviation. Qualif.: Applicants must be high school seniors and/or college students planning to or attending an accredited school in an avionics or aircraft repair program.

Funds Avail.: $1,000. Duration: Annual.

178 ■ Duncan Aviation Scholarship (Undergraduate/Scholarship)

Purpose: To promote and secure the future of aviation by furthering the education of students and technicians from AEA member companies. Focus: Aviation. Qualif.: Applicants must be high school seniors and/or college students planning to or currently attending an accredited school in an avionics or aircraft repair program.

Funds Avail.: $1,000.

179 ■ Dutch and Ginger Arver Scholarship
(Undergraduate/Scholarship)

Purpose: To promote and secure the future of aviation by furthering the education of students and technicians from AEA member companies. Focus: Aviation. Qualif.: Applicants must be seniors and/or college students planning to attend an accredited school in an avionics or aircraft repair program.

Funds Avail.: $1,000. Duration: Annual.

180 ■ Field Aviation Co. Inc. Scholarship
(Undergraduate/Scholarship)

Purpose: To support individuals intending to pursue their career in aircraft electronics and aviation maintenance industry. Focus: Aviation. Qualif.: Available to a high school senior or college student who plans to attend or is attending an accredited school in an avionics or aircraft maintenance program.

Funds Avail.: $1,000. Duration: Annual.

181 ■ Lowell Gaylor Memorial Scholarships
(Undergraduate/Scholarship)

Purpose: To promote and secure the future of aviation by furthering the education of students and technicians from AEA member companies. Focus: Aviation. Qualif.: Applicants must be high school seniors and/or college students who plan to or are attending an accredited school in an avionics or aircraft repair program. Criteria: Selection of candidates will be based on their application materials.

Funds Avail.: $1,000. Duration: Annual. To Apply: Applicants are advised to contact the foundation for application forms and other required materials.

182 ■ Bud Glover Memorial Scholarships
(Undergraduate/Scholarship)

Purpose: To promote and secure the future of aviation by furthering the education of students and technicians from AEA member companies. Focus: Aviation. Qualif.: Applicants must be high school seniors and/or college students who are planning to attend an accredited school in an avionics or aircraft repair program. Criteria: Selection of candidates will be based on their application materials.

Funds Avail.: $1,500. To Apply: Applicants must submit the completed application form; official transcript of grades; one 300-word essay.

183 ■ Leon Harris/Les Nichols Memorial Scholarships to Spartan College of Aeronautics & Technology (Undergraduate/Scholarship)

Purpose: To promote and secure the future of aviation by furthering the education of students and technicians from AEA member companies. Focus: Aviation. Qualif.: Applicants must be students planning to pursue an Associate's Degree in Applied Science in Aviation Electronics (avionics) at Spartan College of Aeronautics and Technology campus in Tulsa, Oklahoma.

Funds Avail.: $35,000. Duration: Annual.

184 ■ Don C. Hawkins Memorial Scholarships
(Undergraduate/Scholarship)

Purpose: To provide financial support to students pursuing a career in aircraft electronics and aircraft maintenance through technical training and education at a learning institution. Focus: Aviation. Qualif.: Applicants must be high school seniors and/or college students planning to or attending an accredited school in an avionics or aircraft repair program. Criteria: Selection of candidates will be based on their application materials.

Funds Avail.: $1,000. To Apply: Applicants must submit complete and signed application form; recent high school or college transcript; 300-word typed-written essay.

185 ■ Honeywell Avionics Scholarships
(Undergraduate/Scholarship)

Purpose: To provide support to students pursuing a career in avionics and/or aircraft maintenance. Focus: Aviation. Qualif.: Applicants must be high school, college, or vocational/technical school students planning to or attending an accredited school in an avionics or aircraft repair program. Criteria: Selection of candidates will be based on the decision of the Scholarship Committee.

Funds Avail.: $1,000. To Apply: Applicants must submit complete and signed application form; recent high school or college transcript; 300-word typed-written essay.

186 ■ L-3 Communications Avionics Systems Scholarships (Undergraduate/Scholarship)

Purpose: To provide financial support to students pursuing a career in avionics and/or aircraft maintenance through

Awards are arranged alphabetically below their administering organizations

technical training and education at a learning institution. **Focus:** Aviation. **Qualif.:** Applicants must be high school, college, or vocational/technical school students planning to or attending an accredited school in an avionics or aircraft repair program. **Criteria:** Selection of candidates will be based on the decision of the Scholarship Committee.

Funds Avail.: $2,500. **Duration:** Annual. **To Apply:** Applicants must submit complete and signed application form; recent high school or college transcript; 300-word typed-written essay.

187 ■ Lee Tarbox Memorial Scholarship
(Undergraduate/Scholarship)

Purpose: To promote and secure the future of aviation by furthering the education of students and technicians from AEA member companies. **Focus:** Aviation. **Qualif.:** Applicants must be high school seniors and/or college students who are planning to attend an accredited school in an avionics or aircraft repair program.

Funds Avail.: $2,500. **Duration:** Annual.

188 ■ Mid-Continent Instruments and Avionics Scholarship *(Undergraduate/Scholarship)*

Purpose: To support individuals intending to pursue their career in aircraft electronics and aviation maintenance industry. **Focus:** Aviation. **Qualif.:** Applicants must be high school seniors and/or college students planning to or attending an accredited school in an avionics or aircraft repair program.

Funds Avail.: $1,000. **Duration:** Annual.

189 ■ Monte Mitchell Scholarship *(Undergraduate/Scholarship)*

Purpose: To promote and secure the future of aviation by furthering the education of students and technicians from AEA member companies. **Focus:** Aviation. **Qualif.:** Applicants must be pursuing a degree in aviation maintenance technology, avionics or aircraft repair at an accredited school; must be actively working for an AEA Member. **Criteria:** Selection of candidates will be based on their essay and employer recommendation.

Funds Avail.: $1,500. **Duration:** Annual. **To Apply:** Applicant must include Letter of recommendation from current employer; A brief essay about how he or she would benefit in their job.

190 ■ Rockwell Collins Scholarships
(Undergraduate/Scholarship)

Purpose: To promote and secure the future of aviation by furthering the education of students and technicians from AEA member companies. **Focus:** Aviation. **Qualif.:** Applicants must be high school seniors and/or college students planning to or attending an accredited school in an avionics or aircraft repair program. **Criteria:** Selection of candidates will be based on the criteria of the Scholarship Committee.

Funds Avail.: $1,000. **To Apply:** Applicants are advised to contact the foundation for application forms and other required materials.

191 ■ Thomas J. Slocum Memorial Scholarships to Redstone College *(Undergraduate/Scholarship)*

Purpose: To promote and secure the future of aviation by furthering the education of students and technicians from AEA member companies. **Focus:** Aviation. **Qualif.:** Ap-

plicants must be students who plans to attend Westwood College of Aviation Technology in Broomfield, Colorado in the avionics program. **Criteria:** Selection of candidates will be based on their application materials.

Funds Avail.: $1,000. **To Apply:** Applicants must submit the completed application form together with official transcript of grades and 300-word essay.

192 ■ Sporty's/Cincinnati Avionics Scholarships
(Undergraduate, Vocational/Occupational/Scholarship)

Purpose: To provide support to individuals intending to pursue their career in aircraft electronics and aviation maintenance industry. **Focus:** Aviation. **Qualif.:** Applicants must be high school, college, or vocational/technical school students planning to or attending an accredited school in an avionics or aircraft repair program. **Criteria:** Selection of candidates will be based on the decision of the Scholarship Committee.

Funds Avail.: No specific amount. **To Apply:** Applicants are advised to contact the foundation for application forms and other required materials. **Contact:** Mike Adamson, Executive Director; Phone: 816-347-8400; Email: mikea@ aea.net.

193 ■ Kei Takemoto Memorial Scholarships
(Undergraduate/Scholarship)

Purpose: To provide financial support to students pursuing a career in aircraft electronics and aircraft maintenance through technical training and education at a learning institution. **Focus:** Aviation. **Qualif.:** Applicants must be high school seniors and/or college students planning to or are attending an accredited school in an avionics or aircraft repair program. **Criteria:** Candidates will be selected based on the scholarship criteria.

Funds Avail.: No specific amount. **To Apply:** Applicants must submit complete and signed application form; recent high school or college transcript; 300-word typed-written essay.

194 ■ Texas State Technical College Scholarships
(Undergraduate/Scholarship)

Purpose: To promote and secure the future of aviation by furthering the education of students and technicians from AEA member companies. **Focus:** Aviation. **Qualif.:** Applicants must be students intending to pursue an associate's degree in avionics. **Criteria:** Selection of candidates will be based on the criteria of the scholarship committee.

Funds Avail.: $1,000. **To Apply:** Application form can be obtain at the website. Submit completed application form together with transcript, questions and essay to the AEA Educational Foundation.

195 ■ Tom Taylor Memorial Scholarship to Spartan College of Aeronautics & Technology
(Undergraduate/Scholarship)

Purpose: To promote and secure the future of aviation by furthering the education of students and technicians from AEA member companies. **Focus:** Aviation. **Qualif.:** Applicants must have a desire to pursue their associates degree in Applied Science or a diploma in Aviation Maintenance Technology at Spartan College of Aeronautics & Technology's campus in Tulsa, Oklahoma; must not be currently enrolled in the AMT program at Spartan.

Funds Avail.: $35,000. **Duration:** Annual.

Awards are arranged alphabetically below their administering organizations

196 ■ Airport Minority Advisory Council Educational and Scholarship Program (AMAC-ESP)

45 L Street SW
Washington, DC 20024
Ph: (703)414-2622
E-mail: info@amac-org.com
URL: www.amac-org.com
Social Media: www.facebook.com/
   AirportMinorityAdvisoryCouncil
www.instagram.com/amac_org
www.linkedin.com/company/airport-minority-advisory
   -council
twitter.com/AMAC_ORG

197 ■ AMACESP Student Scholarships
(Undergraduate/Scholarship)

Purpose: To provide financial assistance for education and outreach to full-time college students interested in pursuing aviation careers. **Focus:** Aviation. **Qualif.:** Applicant must be a U.S. citizen; must be admitted to an accredited school or university for the current school term; have a minimum GPA of 2.5; demonstrate involvement in community activities, extracurricular activities, interest and desire to pursue a career in the aviation/airport industry; and must be seeking a degree in aviation, business administration, accounting, architecture, engineering or finance. **Criteria:** Recipient will be selected by the AMACESP Scholarship Selection Committees based on a set of criteria.

Funds Avail.: $2,000. **Number Awarded:** 3. **To Apply:** Applicant must complete a current Scholarship Application; enclose transcripts to show proof of 2.5 GPA; a one-page essay (750 words or less) on overcoming barriers towards career goals; dedication to succeed in aviation and how AMAC can help; overcoming issues in the aviation industry; and two letters of recommendation from persons who are not relatives that can comment on the academic and career goals of applicant. Must also submit one 5″ x 7″ (400x600 pixels) digital color photograph, and a two-paragraph biography summarizing employment, volunteer work, awards, and academic accomplishments. **Remarks:** Established in 1998. **Contact:** Phone: 703-414-2622; Email: delianny.almonte@amac-org.com.

198 ■ Airports Council International - North America (ACI-NA)

1615 L St. NW, Ste. 300
Washington, DC 20036
Ph: (202)293-8500
Fax: (202)331-1362
E-mail: memberservices@aci-na.org
URL: www.aci-na.org
Social Media: www.facebook.com/airportscouncil
www.instagram.com/airportscouncil
www.linkedin.com/company/airports-council-international
   ---north-america
twitter.com/airportscouncil
www.youtube.com/user/ACINorthAmerica

199 ■ CAC Gerry Bruno Scholarship *(Graduate, Undergraduate/Scholarship)*

Purpose: To provide educational assistance to students at an accredited educational institution working towards a degree and a career in airport management or airport administration. **Focus:** Aviation.

Duration: Annual. **Remarks:** Established in 1993. **Contact:** University Aviation Association; Phone: 334-844-2434.

200 ■ AiryHair Inc.

4210 Creyts Rd.
Lansing, MI 48917
Free: 800-897-7708
URL: www.airyhair.com
Social Media: www.facebook.com/airyhair
www.instagram.com/airyhairextensions
twitter.com/airyhair

201 ■ AiryHair Cosmetology Scholarship
(Undergraduate, Graduate/Scholarship)

Purpose: To inspire future generations and help them achieve their goals. **Focus:** Cosmetology. **Qualif.:** Applicant must be a U.S. or Canadian citizen residing in the U.S. or Canada and studying or planning to study cosmetology. **Criteria:** Selection will be based on the most creative, well thought out essays or video submissions as judged by three AiryHair staff members.

Funds Avail.: $1,500. **Duration:** Annual. **Number Awarded:** 3. **Deadline:** July 31. **Contact:** Sam Fisher; Email: scholarships@airyhair.com; URL: www.airyhair.com/scholarship/.

202 ■ Akron Bar Association (ABA)

57 S Broadway St.
Akron, OH 44308
Ph: (303)253-5007
URL: www.akronbar.org
Social Media: www.facebook.com/AkronBarAssociation
www.linkedin.com/company/akron-bar-association
twitter.com/AkronBarAssoc

203 ■ Akron Bar Association Foundation Scholarships *(Undergraduate/Scholarship)*

Purpose: To provide scholarships to students enrolled in a law school. **Focus:** Law. **Qualif.:** Applicants must be a citizen of the United States; must have an affiliation with Summit County; will be attending a law school in Ohio; must have good academic standing with schools; must have a demonstrated history of community involvement.

Funds Avail.: No specific amount. **Duration:** Annual. **To Apply:** Applicants must complete and submit the application with the following documents: updated resume, certified transcript from the school; transcripts may be mailed directly to the foundation by your school; two letters of recommendation can be mailed; FERPA release form; copy of federal income tax return; do not submit a handwritten application. **Deadline:** March 27. **Contact:** Submit your completed application and accompanying items to: The Akron Bar Foundation, attention: Director of Foundation and Office Operations, 57 S. Broadway St., Akron, Ohio, 44308; Phone: 330-436-0103.

204 ■ Alabama Commission on Higher Education (ACHE)

100 N Union St.
Montgomery, AL 36104-3758
Ph: (334)242-1998

Awards are arranged alphabetically below their administering organizations

Fax: (334)242-0268
URL: www.ache.alabama.gov

205 ■ ACHE/American Legion Auxiliary Scholarship Program *(Undergraduate/Scholarship)*

Purpose: To support the education of Alabama students. **Focus:** General studies/Field of study not specified. **Qualif.:** Applicants must be the son, daughter, grandson, granddaughter of veterans of World War I, World War II, Korea, or Vietnam and who are residents of Alabama; and must be attending an institutions having on-campus housing. **Criteria:** Selection will be based on the committee's criteria.

Funds Avail.: No specific amount. **To Apply:** Applications are available from the American Legion Department Headquarters. **Deadline:** April 1. **Contact:** American Legion Department Headquarters, American Legion Auxiliary, 120 N Jackson St., Montgomery, AL 36104; Phone: 334-262-1176.

206 ■ ACHE Junior and Community College Athletic Scholarship Program *(Undergraduate/Scholarship)*

Purpose: To support the education of Alabama students though defraying their expenses. **Focus:** General studies/Field of study not specified. **Qualif.:** Applicants must be full-time students enrolled in public junior and community colleges in Alabama. **Criteria:** Selection is based on demonstrated athletic ability determined through try-outs.

Funds Avail.: No specific amount.

207 ■ ACHE Junior and Community College Performing Arts Scholarship Program *(Undergraduate/Scholarship)*

Purpose: To support the education of Alabama students though defraying their expenses. **Focus:** Performing arts. **Qualif.:** Applicant must be a full-time student enrolled in public junior and community colleges in Alabama. **Criteria:** Selection is based on demonstrated talent determined through competitive auditions.

Funds Avail.: No specific amount.

208 ■ ACHE Police Officer's and Firefighter's Survivors Educational Assistance Program (POFSEAP) *(Undergraduate/Scholarship)*

Purpose: To provide support to eligible spouses of Alabama police officers and firefighters killed in the line of duty. **Focus:** General studies/Field of study not specified. **Qualif.:** Applicants must be the dependent or the spouse of a police officer or firefighter killed in the line of duty; must be enrolled in an undergraduate program at a public post-secondary educational institution in Alabama. **Criteria:** Selection will be based on the submitted application.

Funds Avail.: No specific amount. **To Apply:** Applicants must submit completed application form and must include necessary documentations such as copy of natural child's birth certificate, adoption papers, marriage certificate and a death certificate or medical certification for the police officer or firefighter killed or permanently disabled as result of service in the line of duty; a letter from the employer stating the officer, firefighter or rescue squad member was killed or totally disabled in the line of duty. **Contact:** AL Communication Higher Education; PO Box 302000, Montgomery, AL, 36130-2000.

209 ■ ACHE Senior Adult Scholarship Program *(Undergraduate/Scholarship)*

Purpose: To provide support to senior citizens by giving them a free tuition program. **Focus:** General studies/Field of study not specified. **Qualif.:** Applicants must be a senior citizen (aged 60 and over) who meets the admission requirements to attend a public two-year post-secondary institution in Alabama. **Criteria:** Preference will be given to an applicant who meets the admission requirements.

Funds Avail.: No specific amount. **To Apply:** Applicants must contact the financial aid office at any public two-year post-secondary educational institutions in Alabama in order to be considered.

210 ■ ACHE Two-Year College Academic Scholarship Program *(Undergraduate/Scholarship)*

Purpose: To provide educational assistance to students who are in need. **Focus:** General studies/Field of study not specified. **Qualif.:** Applicant must be a student accepted for enrollment at public two-year post-secondary educational institutions in Alabama. **Criteria:** Selection is based on demonstrated academic merit as determined by the institutional scholarship committee. Priorities will be given to in-state residents.

Funds Avail.: No specific amount. **To Apply:** Application forms are available at the financial aid office at any public two-year post-secondary educational institution in Alabama.

211 ■ Alabama Gi Dependents' Educational Benefit Program *(Undergraduate/Scholarship)*

Purpose: To provide support to children and spouses of eligible Alabama veterans (with at least a partial disability). **Focus:** General studies/Field of study not specified. **Qualif.:** Applicants must be a dependent or spouses of eligible Alabama veterans attending a public postsecondary educational institutions in Alabama; enrolled as an undergraduate student.

Funds Avail.: No specific amount. **To Apply:** Application forms may be obtained from the Alabama State Department of Veterans Affairs or from any county veterans service officer. **Contact:** Alabama State Department of Veterans Affairs, PO Box 1509, Montgomery, AL, 36102-150; Phone: 334-242-507.

212 ■ Alabama National Guard Educational Assistance Program *(Undergraduate/Scholarship)*

Purpose: To provide educational fees and book/supplies for Alabama National Guard members. **Focus:** General studies/Field of study not specified. **Qualif.:** Applicants must be students who are active members in good standing with a federally recognized unit of the Alabama National Guard; must be residents of Alabama and at least 17 years old; must be enrolled in an accredited college, university, community college, or technical college and have completed basic training and advanced individual training; enrolled in a degree program at an accredited college or university within the State of Alabama; maintain a cumulative 2.00 GPA Undergraduate; 3.00 GPA Graduate at end of each semester; must have the Free Application for Federal Student Aid (FAFSA) on file. **Criteria:** Selection will be based on the submitted application.

To Apply: Applications are available from Alabama National Guard units. Forms must be signed by a representative of the Alabama Military Department and the financial aid officer at the college/university.

213 ■ Alabama Scholarships for Dependents of Blind Parents *(Undergraduate/Scholarship)*

Purpose: To support the education of students from families in which the head of the family is blind and whose family income is insufficient to provide educational benefits. **Focus:** General studies/Field of study not specified. **Qualif.:** Applicants must be Alabama residents; having a family in which the head of the family is blind or with family income is insufficient to provide educational benefits for attendance at an Alabama postsecondary institution. **Criteria:** Selection will be based on need.

Funds Avail.: No specific amount. **To Apply:** Applications are available in Alabama Department of Rehabilitation Services. **Contact:** Dana Barber, Statewide, Coordinator; Alabama Department of Rehabilitation Services, 2129 E S Blvd., Montgomery, AL 36116-2455; Phone: 800-441-7607; 334-613-2248; 256-362-0638.

214 ■ Alabama Student Assistance Program (ASAP)
(Undergraduate/Scholarship, Grant)

Purpose: To provide support to students in pursuing their educational goal. **Focus:** General studies/Field of study not specified. **Qualif.:** Applicants must be undergraduate students; must be Alabama residents attending an eligible Alabama institution. **Criteria:** Selection will be based on need.

Funds Avail.: $300 to $5,000. **Duration:** One academic year. **To Apply:** Applicants must submit the Free Application for Federal Student Aid available from high school guidance office or the financial aid office at the institution planning to attend. **Deadline:** October 1. **Contact:** Mrs. Cheryl Newton, Grants Coordinator; Phone:334-242-2273; Email:cheryl.newton@ache.edu.

215 ■ Alabama Student Grant Program
(Undergraduate/Grant)

Purpose: To provide educational assistance to students who are in need. **Focus:** General studies/Field of study not specified. **Qualif.:** Applicants must be part-time or full-time undergraduate students; must be Alabama resident; must not be enrolled in a course of study leading to a religious vocation; must enrolled in the following schools: Ambridge University, Birmingham Southern College, Concordia College, Faulkner University, Huntingdon College, Judson College, Miles College, Oakwood University, Samford University, South University, Spring Hill College, Stallman College, U.S. Sports Academy and University of Mobile.**Criteria:** Selection will be based on the committee's criteria.

Funds Avail.: Up to $1,200 per academic year. **To Apply:** Applications are available to the financial aid office of the institution where applicants are planning to attend. **Deadline:** September 15. **Remarks:** Established in 1978.

216 ■ Alabama Dietetic Association (ALDA)
PO Box 240757
Montgomery, AL 36124
Ph: (334)260-7970
Fax: (334)272-7128
E-mail: alda@gmsal.com
URL: www.eatrightalabama.org
Social Media: www.facebook.com/groups/37031827726/
?fref=ts
twitter.com/alda_rd
twitter.com/eatrightbama

217 ■ Birmingham District Alabama Dietetic Association Scholarships *(Graduate, Undergraduate/Scholarship)*

Purpose: To encourage and reward students majoring in the field of human nutrition, dietetics, foods, nutrition, or food systems management or admitted or enrolled in a dietetic internship who have demonstrated ability and potential in the field of dietetics and nutrition by aiding them financially. **Focus:** Nutrition. **Qualif.:** Applicants must be junior or senior undergraduate students, graduate students, or dietetic interns majoring in the field of human nutrition, dietetics, foods, nutrition, or food systems management or admitted or enrolled in a dietetic internship; must be legal residents of the following counties: Jefferson, Cullman, Walker, Bibb, Chilton, Shelby, Talladega, St. Clair and/ or an active member in the Birmingham District Dietetic Association and student members of the American Dietetic Association; must have cumulative grade point average of 3.0 or above in major courses of study. **Criteria:** Selection is based on the scholarship; potential in the field of dietetics and nutrition ascertained by, for example: leadership in activities within and outside school, professional interest, honors, activities, and work or volunteer experience; financial need; letters of recommendation; and letter of application.

Funds Avail.: $500. **To Apply:** Applicants must submit a completed application form together with the official computed cumulative GPA (all post-secondary work related to dietetics) authenticated by a faculty member; a letter of application including statements relating to financial need, immediate and future goals, leadership activities, and personal attributes such as initiation and motivation for meeting physical, emotional, and family demands as well as graduate school requirements; and resume including personal contact data, education, honors, and awards, involvement in clubs and organizations including offices held, professional and leadership activities, and work on volunteer experience.

218 ■ North Alabama Dietetic Association Scholarships *(Undergraduate, Graduate/Scholarship)*

Purpose: To encourage and reward students majoring in the field of human nutrition, dietetics, foods, nutrition, or food systems management or admitted or enrolled in a dietetic internship who have demonstrated ability and potential in the field of dietetics and nutrition by aiding them financially. **Focus:** Nutrition. **Qualif.:** Applicants must be junior or senior students majoring in the field of human nutrition dietetics, food, nutrition, or food systems management or admitted or enrolled in a dietetic internship; must be student members of the American Dietetic Association; must have cumulative grade point average of 2.5, and 3.0 or above in major sources of study; must be legal residents of North Alabama.

Funds Avail.: $500. **To Apply:** Applicants must submit a completed application form together with the official computed cumulative GPA (all post-secondary work related to dietetics) authenticated by a faculty member; a letter of application including statements relating to financial need, immediate and future goals, leadership activities, and personal attributes such as initiation and motivation for meeting physical, emotional, and family demands as well as graduate school requirements; and resume including personal contact data, education, honors, and awards, involvement in clubs and organizations including offices held, professional and leadership activities, and work on volunteer experience.

219 ■ Northeast Alabama District Dietetic Association Scholarships *(Graduate, Undergraduate/Scholarship)*

Purpose: To encourage and reward students majoring in the field of human nutrition, dietetics, foods, nutrition, or

Awards are arranged alphabetically below their administering organizations

food systems management or admitted or enrolled in a dietetic internship who have demonstrated ability and potential in the field of dietetics and nutrition by aiding them financially. **Focus:** Nutrition. **Qualif.:** Applicants must be junior or senior students majoring in the field of human nutrition dietetics, food, nutrition, or food systems management or admitted or enrolled in a dietetic internship; must have active, associate, or student membership in the Academy of Nutrition and Dietetics; must have cumulative grade point average of 2.5, and 3.0 or above in major sources of study; must be legal resident of one of the following counties: Calhoun, DeKalb, Cherokee, Cleburne, Etowah, Marshall, St. Clair or Talladega, or volunteered in a healthcare facility in one of the stated counties. **Criteria:** Selection is based on the scholarship; potential in the field of dietetics and nutrition ascertained by, for example, leadership in activities within and outside the school, professional interest, honors, activities, and work or volunteer experience; financial need; letters of recommendation; and letter of application.

Funds Avail.: $500. **To Apply:** Applicants must submit a completed application form together with the official computed cumulative GPA (all post-secondary work related to dietetics) authenticated by a faculty member; a letter of application including statements relating to financial need, immediate and future goals, leadership activities, and personal attributes such as initiation and motivation for meeting physical, emotional, and family demands as well as graduate school requirements; and resume including personal contact data, education, honors, and awards, involvement in clubs and organizations including offices held, professional and leadership activities, and work on volunteer experience.

220 ■ William E. Smith Scholarships *(Graduate/Scholarship)*

Purpose: To reward full time graduate students who have demonstrated ability and potential in the field of dietetics and nutrition by aiding them financially during graduate study. **Focus:** Nutrition. **Qualif.:** Applicants must be full-time graduate students in the field of dietetics and nutrition. **Criteria:** Selection is based on the scholarship; potential in the field of dietetics and nutrition ascertained by, for example, leadership in activities within and outside the school, professional interest, honors, activities, and work or volunteer experience; financial need; letters of recommendation; and letter of application.

Funds Avail.: $1,000. **To Apply:** Applicants must submit completed application form together with the official computed cumulative GPA (all post-secondary work related to dietetics) authenticated by a faculty member; letter of application including statements relating to financial need, immediate and future goals, leadership activities, and personal attributes such as initiation and motivation for meeting physical, emotional, and family demands as well as graduate school requirements; and resume including personal contact data, education, honors, and awards, involvement in clubs and organizations including offices held, professional and leadership activities, and work on volunteer experience.

221 ■ Southeast Alabama Dietetic Association Scholarships *(Graduate, Undergraduate/Scholarship)*

Purpose: To encourage and reward students majoring in the field of human nutrition, dietetics, foods, nutrition, or food systems management or admitted or enrolled in a dietetic internship who have demonstrated ability and potential in the field of dietetics and nutrition by aiding them

financially. **Focus:** Nutrition. **Qualif.:** Applicants must be a junior or senior majoring in the field of human nutrition, dietetics, foods, nutrition, or food systems management or admitted or enrolled in a dietetic internship; must be a legal resident of one of the following counties: Houston, Geneva, Covington, Coffee, Dale, Henry, Pike, or Barbour; or must have been employed or volunteered in a healthcare facility in one of the stated counties; or must be the child or grandchild of an active or former member of the SE Alabama Dietetic Association; and must have a cumulative GPA of 2.5 or above on a 4.0 scale, and a 3.0 or above on a 4.0 scale in major courses of study. **Criteria:** Selection is based on the scholarship; potential in the field of dietetics and nutrition ascertained by, for example, leadership in activities within and outside the school, professional interest, honors, activities, and work or volunteer experience; financial need; letters of recommendation; and letter of application.

Funds Avail.: $750. **Duration:** Annual. **To Apply:** Applicants must submit a completed application form together with the official computed cumulative GPA (all post-secondary work related to dietetics) authenticated by a faculty member; a letter of application including statements relating to financial need, immediate and future goals, leadership activities, and personal attributes such as initiation and motivation for meeting physical, emotional, and family demands as well as graduate school requirements; and resume including personal contact data, education, honors, and awards, involvement in clubs and organizations including offices held, professional and leadership activities, and work on volunteer experience.

222 ■ Wood Fruitticher Grocery Company, Inc. Scholarships *(Graduate, Undergraduate/Scholarship)*

Purpose: To encourage and reward junior level undergraduate students or full or part time graduate students in American Dietetic Association (ADA). **Focus:** Nutrition. **Qualif.:** Applicants must have been enrolled in an ACEND accredited Alabama college/university for at least one quarter or one semester. **Criteria:** Selection is based on the scholarship; potential in the field of dietetics and nutrition ascertained by, for example, leadership in activities within and outside the school, professional interest, honors, activities, and work or volunteer experience; financial need; letters of recommendation; and letter of application.

Funds Avail.: $500. **To Apply:** Applicants must submit a completed application form together with the official computed cumulative GPA (all post-secondary work related to dietetics) authenticated by a faculty member; a letter of application including statements relating to financial need, immediate and future goals, leadership activities, and personal attributes such as initiation and motivation for meeting physical, emotional, and family demands as well as graduate school requirements; and resume including personal contact data, education, honors, and awards, involvement in clubs and organizations including offices held, professional and leadership activities, and work on volunteer experience.

223 ■ Alabama Horse Council (AHC)

686 Alston Farm Rd.
Columbiana, AL 35051
URL: www.alabamahorsecouncil.org
Social Media: www.facebook.com/alhorsecouncil
www.instagram.com/alhorsecouncil
twitter.com/alhorsecouncil

Awards are arranged alphabetically below their administering organizations

224 ■ Alabama Horse Council Scholarships
(Undergraduate/Scholarship)

Purpose: To provide educational support to outstanding youth in Alabama pursuing higher education in a college or any university. **Focus:** Equine studies. **Qualif.:** Applicants or their parents/grandparents must be current members of AHC; must be majoring in a field of study for a career in the equine industry; must have demonstrated record of activity in the equine industry prior to college application. **Criteria:** Recipients are selected based on their submitted applications through mailing.

Funds Avail.: $1,000. **Duration:** Annual. **To Apply:** Applicants must submit following materials: one page-cover form; two letters of references attesting to the applicant's commitment to the equine industry, activity in the industry and character; short (500 word maximum) essay about how horses have shaped the life; list of activities and honors received (high school, college, civic, church, clubs, etc.). **Deadline:** December 30. **Contact:** Scholarship Committee, Alabama Horse Council, PO Box 553, Columbiana, AL, 35051.

225 ■ Alabama Law Foundation
415 Dexter Ave.
Montgomery, AL 36101
URL: www.alfinc.org

226 ■ Johnston Cabaniss Scholarships *(Graduate/ Scholarship)*

Purpose: To support students in furthering their law education. **Focus:** Law. **Qualif.:** Applicants must be residents of Alabama and must be law students entering second year at any accredited law school in the United States. **Criteria:** Selection will be based on the committee's criteria.

Funds Avail.: $5,000. **Duration:** Annual. **Number Awarded:** Varies. **To Apply:** Applications can be submitted online. **Deadline:** June. **Remarks:** Established in 1987.

227 ■ Justice Janie L. Shores Scholarship
(Undergraduate/Scholarship)

Purpose: To award scholarship to female Alabama residents. **Focus:** Law. **Qualif.:** Applicants must be female Alabama residents attending an Alabama law school.

Funds Avail.: No specific amount. **Duration:** Annual. **To Apply:** Applicants must visit the website for the online application process. **Deadline:** April 1.

228 ■ William Verbon Black Scholarship
(Undergraduate/Scholarship)

Purpose: To assist and support full-time students at the University of Alabama School of Law. **Focus:** Law. **Qualif.:** Applicants must be students at the University of Alabama School of Law.

Funds Avail.: No specific amount.

229 ■ Alamo Section Institute of Food Technologists (IFT)
2201 Broadway
San Antonio, TX 78215
Ph: (210)351-6341
E-mail: info@alamoift.org
URL: www.alamoift.org
Social Media: www.linkedin.com/company/alamo-ift

230 ■ Alamo IFT Scholarship *(Undergraduate/ Scholarship)*

Purpose: To provide assistance for local students pursuing their studies. **Focus:** General studies/Field of study not specified. **Qualif.:** Applicant must be an undergraduate that is currently enrolled and pursuing a degree in Food Science and Technology or the Culinary Arts.

231 ■ Alamogordo Music Theatre (AMT)
PO Box 266
Alamogordo, NM 88311
E-mail: alamogordomusictheatre.board@gmail.com
URL: alamogordomusictheatre.org
Social Media: www.facebook.com/alamogordomusictheatre
www.instagram.com/alamogordomusictheatre/?igshid
  =pp1uhyrro8bi
twitter.com/amtAlamogordo

232 ■ Don Fox Memorial Scholarship
(Undergraduate/Scholarship)

Purpose: To help students pay for their education. **Focus:** Arts. **Qualif.:** Applicants must be graduating high school seniors; must be planning to major in some aspect of fine arts. **Criteria:** Selection will be based on the committee's criteria.

Funds Avail.: No specific amount. **Duration:** Annual. **To Apply:** Applicants must complete the application form provided by Alamogordo; submit the application to AMT office and must attach a copy of high school transcript. **Deadline:** October 1. **Remarks:** The scholarship is named in memory of one of the sponsor's founding board members, Don Fox.

233 ■ Martha Julian Memorial Scholarship
(Undergraduate/Scholarship)

Purpose: To help students pay for their education. **Focus:** Arts. **Qualif.:** Applicants must be students pursuing a degree in the fine arts; must be graduating seniors or continuing college students; must have a minimum of 3.0 GPA (on a 4.0 scale). **Criteria:** Preference will be given to those majoring in some aspect of fine arts; financial need will be considered.

Funds Avail.: No specific amount. **Duration:** Annual. **To Apply:** Applicants must complete the application form provided by Alamogordo; submit the application to AMT office and must attach a copy of high school transcript. **Deadline:** October 1. **Remarks:** The scholarship is named in memory of local artist Martha Julian.

234 ■ Ted Lewis Memorial Scholarship
(Undergraduate/Scholarship)

Purpose: To provide support a graduating senior or continuing college student. **Focus:** Arts. **Qualif.:** Applicants must be graduating seniors or continuing college students; must have a minimum of 3.0 GPA on a 4.0 scale. **Criteria:** Selection will be based on the committee's criteria.

Funds Avail.: No specific amount. **Duration:** Annual. **To Apply:** Applicants must complete the application form provided by Alamogordo; submit the application to AMT office and must attach a copy of high school transcript. **Deadline:** October 1. **Remarks:** The scholarship is given in honor of founding board member Ted Lewis.

235 ■ Alaska Airmen Association (AAA)
4200 Floatplane Dr.
Anchorage, AK 99502

Awards are arranged alphabetically below their administering organizations

Ph: (907)245-1251
Fax: (888)558-1684
Free: 800-464-7030
E-mail: info@alaskaairmen.org
URL: www.alaskaairmen.org
Social Media: www.facebook.com/alaska.airmen
www.instagram.com/alaska.airmen

236 ■ John P. Culhane Professional Pilot Scholarship (Undergraduate, Vocational/Occupational/Scholarship)

Purpose: To promote development in aviation careers. **Focus:** Aviation. **Qualif.:** Applicant must be a high school senior.

Funds Avail.: $2,500. **Number Awarded:** 1. **To Apply:** Applicants must provide a letter of recommendation and acceptance letter.

237 ■ F. Atlee Dodge Maintenance Scholarship (Undergraduate/Scholarship)

Purpose: To promote development in aviation careers. **Focus:** Aviation. **Qualif.:** Applicant must be a high school senior.

Funds Avail.: $2,500. **Number Awarded:** 1. **To Apply:** Applicants must provide a letter of recommendation and acceptance letter.

238 ■ Bob Reeve Aviation Management Scholarship (Undergraduate/Scholarship)

Purpose: To promote development in aviation careers. **Focus:** Aviation. **Qualif.:** Applicant must be a high school senior.

Funds Avail.: $2,500. **To Apply:** Applicants must provide a letter of recommendation and acceptance letter.

239 ■ Alaska Broadcasters Association (ABA)
700 W 41st St., Ste. 102
Anchorage, AK 99503
Ph: (907)258-2424
Free: 888-749-8008
E-mail: akbagold@gci.net
URL: www.alaskabroadcasters.org
Social Media: www.facebook.com/Alaska-Broadcasters
  -Association-376061105799719
twitter.com/AKBroadcasters

240 ■ Linda Simmons Memorial Scholarship (Graduate/Scholarship)

Purpose: To provide encouragement and financial assistance to students who have demonstrated their interest in the communications arts. **Focus:** Broadcasting. **Qualif.:** Applicants must be pursuing a degree or certified course of study in an accredited junior/community college, college, university or professional trade school; must be pursuing radio and/or television broadcasting or broadcast engineering as a major course of study. Application from candidates pursuing major studies in journalism, public relations or advertising will be considered if there are no qualified candidates with broadcast communications or broadcast engineering majors; must be residents of the State of Alaska; student must demonstrate excellence in the following areas: academic performance; discipline/attitude; attendance. **Criteria:** Selection will be based on the submitted application materials.

Funds Avail.: $2,000. **Duration:** Annual. **To Apply:** Applicants must submit a formal application sheet; short written essay expressing applicant's personal goals; and three letters of reference that address the following criteria: academic performance, discipline/attitude and attendance. **Deadline:** April 1. **Remarks:** Established in 2001. **Contact:** ABA, Phone: 907-258-2424.

241 ■ The Alaska Community Foundation (ACF)
3201 C St., Ste. 110
Anchorage, AK 99503
Ph: (907)334-6700
Fax: (907)334-5780
Free: 855-336-6701
E-mail: info@alaskacf.org
URL: www.alaskacf.org
Social Media: www.facebook.com/AlaskaCF
www.linkedin.com/company/the-alaska-community
  -foundation
www.pinterest.com/AlaskaCF
twitter.com/akcommunity
www.youtube.com/user/AlaskaCF

242 ■ Nordic Skiing Association of Anchorage Scholarship (Graduate/Scholarship)

Purpose: To encourage scholastic performance, cross-country skiing and participation in community ski activities. **Focus:** General studies/Field of study not specified. **Criteria:** Preference will be given to students attending college in Alaska. Applicants will be selected based on their academic performance and application materials.

Funds Avail.: $1,500. **Duration:** Annual. **To Apply:** Application forms are available at the Nordic skiing association of anchorage website. applicants must have: a letter of recommendation, list of personal achievements and honors, a brief statement describing any community service, a maximum 500-word essay on the "benefits you have received from skiing", and a copy of official transcripts from all high school or university works. **Deadline:** April 9. **Contact:** The Alaska Community Foundation, Phone: 907-334-6700; Email: scholarships@alaskacf.org.

243 ■ Alaska Space Grant Program (ASGP)
University of Alaska Fairbanks
Engineering learning and innovation facility 138
1764 Tanana Loop
Fairbanks, AK 99775-5919
Ph: (907)474-6833
E-mail: ua-spacegrant-dept@alaska.edu
URL: spacegrant.alaska.edu
Social Media: www.facebook.com/Alaska-Space-Grant
  -Program-164327900265148

244 ■ ASGP Graduate Research Fellowships (Graduate/Fellowship)

Purpose: To support students in conducting research projects fostering the vision of NASA. **Focus:** Engineering; Mathematics and mathematical sciences; Science; Space and planetary sciences; Technology. **Qualif.:** Applicants must be graduate students enrolled at an Alaskan institution of higher education during the period of the award; must be U.S. citizens and in good academic standing; must be women or individuals from underrepresented groups,

Awards are arranged alphabetically below their administering organizations

specifically, Alaska Natives, Native Americans, African Americans, Hispanics, Pacific Islanders, and person with disabilities. **Criteria:** Selection is based on scholastic achievement; strength of recommendations and; proposed project merit; preference may be given to women and individuals from under-represented groups.

Funds Avail.: Up to $15,000. **To Apply:** Applicants are required to identify faculty mentors with whom they intend to work and who are available to write a letter of collaboration and must submit the following requirements: completed application form; match authorization; budget form; project description maximum of 3 pages; letter of collaboration from mentors; and academic transcript; all requirements must be submitted in one compiled PDF file. **Deadline:** December 1. **Contact:** Email: uaf-spacegrant@alaska.edu, Ph No: 907-474-6833.

245 ■ Alberta Association on Gerontology
PO Box 47022
Edmonton, AB, Canada T5J 4N1
E-mail: info@albertaaging.ca
URL: albertaaging.ca

246 ■ AAG Provincial Student Award *(Graduate/ Award)*

Purpose: To assist with the costs associated with a student's coursework, research or attendance at a workshop or conference. **Focus:** Gerontology. **Qualif.:** Applicants must be Albertans registered in a graduate degree program in an accredited post secondary institution; must not be in the last term of their program; must demonstrate interest in any aspect of aging; must agree to contribute an article for an edition of the AAGmag (e.g., a written summary of research). **Criteria:** Selection will be based on academic merit as illustrated by grades and educational attainment, relevant work/volunteer, current studies/research plans, future commitment to the field of gerontology and an indication of how this award will be used to support the applicant's interest in gerontology.

Funds Avail.: 1,000 Canadian Dollars. **Duration:** Annual. **Number Awarded:** 2. **To Apply:** Application package consists of a two-page cover letter that includes a description of the applicant's current studies or research, relevant volunteer/work experience and future plans in gerontology (academic, research, practice); a completed award application form; a copy of the applicant's curriculum vitae; a copy of post-secondary education transcripts (they do not need to be original); a letter from the student's supervisor. **Deadline:** March 10. **Contact:** Submissions must be sent to the following address: Alberta Association on Gerontology, PO Box 47022, Edmonton Ctr., Edmonton, Alberta, T5J 4N1; E-mail: info@albertaaging.ca.

247 ■ Edmonton Chapter Student Award *(Graduate/ Award)*

Purpose: To assist with the costs associated with a student's coursework, research or attendance at a workshop or conference. **Focus:** Gerontology. **Qualif.:** Applicants must be registered in a graduate degree program in an accredited post secondary institution; reside in Edmonton or surrounding communities; not be in the last term of their program; demonstrate an interest in any aspect of aging; agree to contribute an article for an edition of the AAGmag (e.g., a written summary of their research or studies). **Criteria:** Selection will be based on academic merit as illustrated by grades and educational attainment, relevant

work/volunteer, current studies/research plans, future commitment to the field of gerontology and an indication of how this award will be used to support the applicant's interest in gerontology; preference will be given to full-time students, graduate students and current AAG members.

Funds Avail.: 1,000 Canadian Dollars. **Duration:** Annual. **To Apply:** Application package consists of a two-page cover letter that includes a description of the applicant's current studies or research as well as future plans in gerontology (academic, research, practice); a completed award application form; a copy of the applicant's curriculum vitae; a copy of post-secondary education transcripts (they do not need to be original) or verification of the student's studies or research (e.g., current timetable, a letter from the student's supervisor). **Deadline:** March 10. **Contact:** Submissions must be sent to the following address: Alberta Association on Gerontology, PO Box 47022, Edmonton Ctr., Edmonton, Alberta, T5J 4N1; E-mail: info@ albertaaging.ca.

248 ■ Alberta Barley
6815 8th St. NE, No. 200
Calgary, AB, Canada T2E 7H7
Ph: (403)291-9111
Fax: (403)291-0190
Free: 800-265-9111
E-mail: barleyinfo@albertabarley.com
URL: www.albertabarley.com
Social Media: www.facebook.com/
   AlbertaBarleyCommission
twitter.com/AlbertaBarley
www.youtube.com/user/albertabarley

249 ■ Eugene Boyko Memorial Scholarship *(Undergraduate/Scholarship)*

Purpose: To recognize and encourage students studying in the field of crop production and/or crop processing technology studies. **Focus:** Agricultural sciences. **Qualif.:** Applicants must be: Canadian citizens, permanent Canadian residents or protected person living in Alberta; attending a designated post-secondary institution in Alberta; must be enrolled full-time in the second or subsequent year of undergraduate post-secondary study; must be enrolled full-time in courses with an emphasis on crop production and/or crop processing technology, and have not previously received this scholarship.**Criteria:** Selection will be based on academic achievement in their previous year of post-secondary studies.

Funds Avail.: 500 Canadian Dollars. **Duration:** Annual. **To Apply:** Applicants must submit a completed application form along with an official transcript. **Remarks:** The Scholarship is established in memory of Eugene Boyko. Established in 2002.

250 ■ Alberta Blue Cross
10009 108th St. NW
Edmonton, AB, Canada T5J 3C5
Ph: (782)498-5925
Free: 866-232-1914
URL: www.ab.bluecross.ca
Social Media: www.facebook.com/AlbertaBlueCross
www.instagram.com/albertabluecross
www.linkedin.com/company/alberta-blue-cross
twitter.com/ABBluecross

Awards are arranged alphabetically below their administering organizations

251 ■ Alberta Blue Cross Scholarships for Aboriginal Students *(Undergraduate/Scholarship)*

Purpose: To provide support for students who have demonstrated community involvement, achievement of personal goals as well as demonstrate financial need. **Focus:** General studies/Field of study not specified. **Qualif.:** Applicants must be registered Indians, Inuit or Metis; have been a resident of Alberta the during previous year of study; must be enrolling in the first year of any full-time post-secondary certificate or diploma program of two or more years duration. **Criteria:** Selection is based on scholastic achievement in diploma examinations, financial need and community involvement. personal goals.

Funds Avail.: Amount varies. **Number Awarded:** 3. **To Apply:** Applicants may also choose to submit reference letters and copies of their Alberta Education High School transcripts for evaluation. **Deadline:** September 30. **Contact:** 108 St. NW, Edmonton, Alberta, T5J 3C5, 10009; Fax: 780-498-8096.

252 ■ Alberta Child Care Association (ACCA)

No. 54 9912 - 106 St., Ste. 110
Edmonton, AB, Canada T5K 1C5
Ph: (780)421-7544
Fax: (780)428-0080
URL: www.albertachildcare.org

253 ■ Alberta Child Care Association Professional Development Grants *(Professional development/Grant)*

Purpose: To assist a Child Development Supervisor (CDS) to attend approved workshops, conferences, post-secondary credit courses and participate in professional learning communities. **Focus:** Child care. **Qualif.:** Applicants are individuals with a valid Child Development Supervisor certificate issued by the Alberta Child Care Certification office that are working as paid staff members or family child care consultants/coordinators in a licensed child care program or contracted family day home agency in Alberta, and working a minimum of 80 hours a month in a licensed child care program or family day home agency; or 40 hours each month in a licensed out-of-school care program. **Criteria:** Selection will be based on the aforesaid qualifications.

Funds Avail.: No specific amount. **Duration:** Annual. **Remarks:** Professional Development Grants are funding for three distinct approaches: workshops and conferences; postsecondary programs and courses; and professional learning communities.

254 ■ Alberta Equestrian Federation (AEF)

251 Midpark Blvd. SE, Ste. 120
Calgary, AB, Canada T2X 1S3
Ph: (403)253-4411
Fax: (403)252-5260
Free: 877-463-6233
E-mail: info@albertaequestrian.com
URL: www.albertaequestrian.com
Social Media: www.facebook.com/AlbertaEquestrian
twitter.com/ab_equestrian

255 ■ AEF Educational Scholarship *(Undergraduate/Scholarship)*

Purpose: To support active member who exemplify the objectives, vision and mission of the AEF, and are interested in pursuing an equine-related post secondary education. **Focus:** Equine studies. **Qualif.:** Applicants must be current members of AEF in good standing for 12 consecutive months at time of application; Canadian citizens over the age of 16; and enrolled or applied to an equine-related program at an accredited post-secondary college, polytechnic, or university.

Funds Avail.: 750 Canadian Dollars. **Duration:** Annual. **To Apply:** Applicant must download and complete the form on sponsor's website and submit with the following: proof of post-secondary education enrollment or acceptance; two letters of reference; current CV; photo; proof of Canadian citizenship; a 400-word essay. All submissions should be sent via email. **Deadline:** May 31. **Remarks:** Established in 1978. **Contact:** Executive Director; E-mail: execdir@albertaequestrian.com; URL: www.albertaequestrian.com/scholarships/.

256 ■ Alberta Foundation for the Arts (AFA)

10708 - 105 Ave.
Edmonton, AB, Canada T5H 0A1
Ph: (780)427-9968
E-mail: afacontact@gov.ab.ca
URL: www.affta.ab.ca
Social Media: www.facebook.com/AlbertaFoundationfortheArts
www.instagram.com/afa.1991
twitter.com/AFA1991

257 ■ AFA Film and Video Arts Project Grants *(Professional development/Grant)*

Purpose: To support the development of individual Alberta artists, arts administrators or an ensemble of artists by providing a grant for a specific film and video arts project. **Focus:** Arts; Filmmaking; Video. **Qualif.:** Applicants must be Canadian citizens; have had your primary residence in Alberta for one full year before applying; ordinarily live in Alberta for at least six months each year with the exception of attending a formal program of study. **Criteria:** Selection will be based on the committee's criteria.

Funds Avail.: 15,000 Canadian Dollars; and may include up to 3,000 Canadian Dollars per month subsistence allowance. **Duration:** Annual. **To Apply:** Applicants must provide the following in the application package: a completed application form and signed applicant agreement with original signature; ensembles must designate one member who is the contact person for all requirements of the grant; applicants must sign the applicant agreement and complete the application form; must submit the required materials if the applicants are under the age of 18 years at the time of application; an application checklist must be completed and submitted with the application; a detailed description of the project, including an outline of the objectives, planned activities, timelines and expected results and benefits; a balanced project budget detailing revenues (including the amount requested from the AFA) and expenditures in Canadian dollars; total revenues must equal total expenditures; an artistic resume of no more than four pages; students may submit a description of their dance background, including level of training, performing arts activities and other relevant dance history; applicants must also include: for all categories, film and video work, scripts or storyboards of previous productions or of the work in progress to aid the assessment process; video submissions must be a JPEG or GIF video file on VHS NTSC videocassette or one CD or DVD compatible with Microsoft

Awards are arranged alphabetically below their administering organizations

Windows operating system; for art production, a list of all principals involved in the project and their resumes; commission applicants are encouraged to submit a completed and signed contract with the commissioner and a plan for the screening, exhibition or presentation of the commissioned work; for marketing ore research, official invitations, confirmation or itineraries, as applicable; for training or career development: (I) applicants who have been accepted into a specific course must provide proof of acceptance and a detailed description, schedule and budget for the study program; applicants who have not already been accepted into a course must submit a detailed description, schedule and budget for the preferred choice. In addition, two alternate program choices should be submitted, with detailed description, schedules and budgets for each choice; applicants are encouraged to submit additional support materials that may assist in the assessment process; these may include press clippings, invitations, reference letters, reviews, catalogues, scripts published books or storyboards; applicants must submit applications in the following format to allow ease of use by juries: submit four complete, assembled application packages (one original and three copies of the application forms and all printed attachments) along with one copy of audio and/or visual support materials; assemble the parts of the packages in the same order as the checklist for this grant; clip application into four packages. Do not bind or use folders, page covers or binders; remember to make one additional copy of the complete application package and keep it for their records; audio and/or visual support materials such as CD, videocassette or DVD must be clearly labelled with the applicant's name on the media; use separate discs for different file types; all media must be compatible with Microsoft windows operating system and NTSC VHS video standards. **Deadline:** February 1; September 1.

258 ■ Music Individual Project Funding (Professional development/Grant)

Purpose: To support the development of individual Alberta artists, arts administrators or an ensemble of artists by providing a grant for a specific music project in a limited time period. **Focus:** Music. **Qualif.:** Applicants must be Canadian citizens; have had a primary residence in Alberta for one full year before applying; ordinarily, live in Alberta for at least six months each year with the exception of attending a formal program of study.

Funds Avail.: $15,000 Canadian Dollars. **Duration:** Annual. **To Apply:** Applicants must provide the following in the application package: A completed application form and signed Applicant Agreement with original signature. Ensembles must designate one member who is the contact person for all requirements of the grant. Applicants must sign the Applicant Agreement and complete the Application Form; must submit the required materials if the applicants are under the age of 18 years at the time of application; an application checklist must be completed and submitted with the application; a detailed description of the project, including an outline of the objectives, planned activities, timelines and expected results and benefits; a balanced project budget detailing revenues (including the amount requested from the AFA) and expenditures in Canadian dollars. Total revenues must equal total expenditures; an artistic resume of no more than four pages that includes past training, most recent performance highlights, compositions, discography, and ensemble experience. Applicants must also include the following: (a) for art production, include a demo recording, commercial recording, signed contract with the commissioner and a plan for the exhibition, presentation, display, publication, screening or performance of the com-

missioned work (commission applicants); for all other art production projects include one copy of audio material, including two musical selections; (b) for marketing, include: any official invitations, confirmations or itineraries; a detailed marketing plan; one copy of audio material, including two musical selection, A final copy of a commercially released recording is required for the marketing of commercial recordings or music videos; (c) for research, include: any official invitations, confirmations or itineraries; one copy of audio material, including two musical selections, if applicable; (d) for training or career development: (I) applicants who have been accepted into a specific course must submit: proof of acceptance; a detailed description; a program schedule; budget for the study program; one copy of audio material, including two musical selections. For performance programs, the two selections must be of contrasting style; (ii) applicants who have not already been accepted into a course must submit the following information for the preferred study programs including: a detailed description; a program schedule; budget for each study program; one copy of audio material, including two musical selections. For performance programs, the two selections must be of contrasting style. Applicants are encouraged to submit additional support materials that may assist in the assessment process. These may include press clippings, invitations, reference letters, reviews, catalogues, scripts, published books or storyboards. Applicants must submit applications in the following format to allow for ease of use by juries: submit four complete, assembled application packages (one original and three copies of the application form and all printed attachments) along with one copy of audio and/or visual support materials; assemble the parts of the packages in the same order as the checklist for this grant; clip applications into four packages. Do not bind or use folders, page covers or binders; remember to make one additional copy of the complete application package and keep it for their records. Audio and/or visual support materials such as CD, videocassette or DVD must be clearly labelled with the applicant's name on the media. Use separate discs for different file types. All media must be compatible with Microsoft Windows operating system and NTSC VHS video standards. The applicant is responsible for providing support materials that comply with the viewing capabilities of the AFA. **Deadline:** September 4; March 1. **Contact:** Jason Flammia, Arts Development Consultant - Music, Phone: 780-415-0297, Email: jason.flammia@gov.ab.ca.

259 ■ AFA Theatre & Performance Art Project Grants (Professional development/Grant)

Purpose: To support the development of individual Alberta artists, arts administrators or an ensemble of artist by providing a grant for a specific theatre and/or performance art project in a limited time period. **Focus:** Performing arts; Theater arts. **Qualif.:** Applicants must be Canadian citizens; have had your primary residence in Alberta for one full year before applying; ordinarily, live in Alberta for at least six months each year with the exception of attending a formal program of study.

Funds Avail.: $15,000 Canadian Dollars. **Duration:** Annual. **To Apply:** Applicants may submit only one application to the AFA each deadline across all disciplines; applicant information: Legal name and confirmation of your status (minor or Albertan); the application category (art production, marketing, research, or training or career development) and applicant status (individual, ensemble); a brief project description (20 words) and project start and end dates; applicants should submit music-related activities, which may include: past training, most recent perfor-

Awards are arranged alphabetically below their administering organizations

mances and performance highlights, compositions, discography, or ensemble experience; two musical selections such as a scratch demo from the proposed project, or high-quality demo; all video and audio files must be Windows compatible; wherever possible, support material should be uploaded as an attachment into GATE (up to 4 MB); a secondary budget outlining the applicant's ability to fund manufacturing expenses (CD pressing and artwork) (for art production projects). **Deadline:** September 4; March 1. **Contact:** Barbara Mah, Arts Development Consultant - Theatre and Performance Art, Film and Video Arts; Phone: 780-415-0306; Email: barb.mah@gov.ab.ca.

260 ■ Art Acquisition by Application (Professional development/Grant)

Purpose: To support individual artists through the purchase of art produced by Albertan artists and offers an opportunity for Albertans to experience the legacy of Alberta's visual arts community. **Focus:** Arts. **Qualif.:** Applicants must be Canadian citizens have had your primary residence in Alberta for at least one full year before applying; must be in good standing with the AFA with no open or outstanding projects or reporting.

Funds Avail.: No specific amount. **Duration:** Annual. **To Apply:** Applicants must submit legal name and confirmation of the applicant status; applicant contact Information: street and mailing address for the primary applicant or gallery; a completed applicant agreement including the e-signature of the primary applicant; an artistic resume of no more than four pages, with current mailing address which outlines any past exhibitions, achievements, teaching experience or formal education as applicable; images must be submitted a single image of a single artwork, multiple images of a single artwork; all video and audio files must be Windows compatible, MP3 and MP4 files; it may be asked for additional information to determine eligibility or any other program. **Deadline:** April 1.

261 ■ Cultural Relations Individual Project Funding (Professional development/Grant)

Purpose: To support professional artists and arts organizations in any arts discipline that will represent Alberta at a national or international level, and encourage professional artists in community residencies in partnership with an Albertan or Western Canadian community organization. **Focus:** Arts; Culture. **Qualif.:** Applicants must be Canadian citizens; have had a primary residence in Alberta for one full year before applying; ordinarily, live in Alberta for at least six months each year.

Funds Avail.: $15,000 Canadian Dollars. **Duration:** Annual. **To Apply:** Applicants must submit legal name and confirmation of the applicant status; applicant contact Information: street and mailing address for the primary applicant or gallery; a completed applicant agreement including the e-signature of the primary applicant; an artistic resume of no more than four pages, with current mailing address which outlines any past exhibitions, achievements, teaching experience or formal education as applicable; images must be submitted a single image of a single artwork, multiple images of a single artwork; all video and audio files must be Windows compatible, MP3 and MP4 files; it may be asked for additional information to determine eligibility or any other program. **Deadline:** March 31. **Contact:** Jason Flammia, Arts Development Consultant - Music, Phone: 780-415-0297, Email: jason.flammia@gov.ab.ca.

262 ■ Dance Individual Project Funding (Professional development/Grant)

Purpose: To support the development of individual Alberta artists, arts administrators or an ensemble of artists by providing a grant from a specific dance project in a limited time period. **Focus:** Arts; Dance. **Qualif.:** Applicants must be Canadian citizens; have had your primary residence in Alberta for one full year before applying; ordinarily, live in Alberta for at least six months each year with the exception of attending a formal program of study.

Funds Avail.: $15,000 Canadian Dollars. **Duration:** Annual. **To Apply:** Applicants must provide the following in the application package: a completed Application Form and signed Applicant Agreement with original signature. Ensembles must designate one member who is the contact person for all requirements of the grant. This applicant must sign the Applicant Agreement and complete the Application Form; must submit the required materials if the applicants are under the age of 18 years at the time of application; an application checklist must be completed and submitted with the application; a detailed description of the project, including an outline of the objectives, planned activities, timelines and expected results and benefits; a balanced project budget detailing revenues (including the amount requested from the AFA) and expenditures in Canadian dollars. Total revenues must equal total expenditures; an artistic resume of no more than four pages. Students may submit a description of their dance background, including level of training, performing arts activities and other relevant dance history. Applicants must also include: for art production, a list of all principals involved in the project and their resumes. To assist in the assessment process, applicants are encouraged to submit a video of previous productions of their work, or of the work-in-progress. Commission applicants are encouraged to submit a completed and signed contract with the commissioner and a plan for the exhibition, presentation, display, publication, screening or performance of the commissioned work; for marketing or research, official invitations, confirmations or itineraries, as applicable; for marketing, a detailed marketing plan; for training or career development: (I) applicants who have been accepted into a specific course must provide proof of acceptance and a detailed description, schedule and budget for the study program; (ii) applicants who have not already been accepted into a course must submit a detailed description, schedule and budget for the preferred choice. In addition, two alternate program choices should be submitted, with detailed description, schedules and budgets for each choice; (iii) for dance training programs, artists must submit two audition pieces on one VHS NTSC video cassette or DVD that is playable in a commercial DVD player. The two audition pieces together must not exceed 4 minutes in length, and must duplicate the experience of a live audition, including full body shot composition, without props or costume. One audition piece must relate to the program of study, such as classical, contemporary, jazz, modern, folk or heritage dance. The second piece must be in a contrasting style; (iv) non-performing artists must provide a resume, portfolio or videocassette/DVD of their work. Applicants are encouraged to submit additional support materials that may assist in the assessment process. These may include press clippings, invitations, reference letters, reviews, catalogues, scripts published books or storyboards. Applicants must submit applications in the following format to allow ease of use by juries: submit four complete, assembled application packages (one original and three copies of the application forms and all printed attachments) along with one copy of

Awards are arranged alphabetically below their administering organizations

audio and/or visual support materials; assemble the parts of the packages in the same order as the checklist for this grant; clip application into four packages. Do not bind or use folders, page covers or binders; remember to make one additional copy of the complete application package and keep it for their records. Audio and/or visual support materials such as CD, videocassette or DVD must be clearly labelled with the applicant's name on the media. Use separate discs for different file types. All media must be compatible with Microsoft Windows operating system and NTSC VHS video standards. **Deadline:** September 4; March 1. **Contact:** Barbara Mah, Arts Development Consultant - Theatre and Performance Art, Film and Video Arts; Phone: 780-415-0306; Email: barb.mah@gov.ab.ca.

263 ■ Indigenous Arts Individual Project Funding
(Professional development/Grant)

Purpose: To support the development of Aboriginal artists, or artists working on Aboriginal cultural themes, who seek to express and share Aboriginal culture and perspectives in a contemporary or traditional context. **Focus:** Culture; Media arts. **Qualif.:** Applicants must be Canadian citizens or landed immigrants and have their primary residence in Alberta for one full year before applying for a grant; applicants, including ensembles or collectives, must not be incorporated under either provincial or federal legislation. **Criteria:** Selection will be based on the committee's criteria.

Funds Avail.: Maximum of 15,000 Canadian Dollars. **Duration:** Annual. **To Apply:** Applicants must provide the following in the application package: a completed application form and signed Applicant Agreement with original signature; ensembles must designate one member who is the contact person for all requirements of the grant; must submit the required materials if the applicants are under the age of 18 years at the time of application; an application checklist must be completed and submitted with the application; a detailed description of the project, which demonstrates the project's connection to historical practice in a specific Aboriginal community, Protocols, and permission from the community to use traditional tribal knowledge must be addressed. Include a letter of agreement with mentor, elder or cultural resource person, and an outline of the objectives, planned activities, expected results and benefits; a balanced project budget detailing revenues and expenditures in Canadian dollars; total revenues must equal total expenditures; application category art production, marketing or research, official invitations, confirmation or itineraries, as applicable; for marketing, a detailed marketing plan; for mentorship, training or career development; applicants who have been accepted into a mentorship must provide a letter of agreement as proof of acceptance and support from the mentor, elder or cultural resource person and a detailed description, schedule and budget for the course of study; applicants are encouraged to submit additional support materials that may assist in the assessment process; clip applications into four packages; a CD, videocassette or USB must be clearly labeled with the applicant's name on the media. **Deadline:** September 4; March 1.

264 ■ Literary Individual Project Funding *(Professional development/Grant)*

Purpose: To support the development of individual Alberta artists, arts administrators or an ensemble of artists by providing a grant for a specific literary arts project in a limited time period. **Focus:** Arts; Literature. **Qualif.:** Applicants must be Canadian citizens or landed immigrants; have their primary residence in Alberta for one full year before applying for a grant. In order to be eligible from a

project grants, ensembles must be made up of members who meet the individual criteria. Applicants, including ensembles, must not be incorporated with provincial or federal corporate registries. Eligible projects must meet the criteria in one of the following categories: (a) Art production: the creation of a new literary work. Eligible projects may be a distinct phase of a new work, such as a first draft or a final draft, in one of the eligible literary genres; (b) Marketing: a program of activity for a specific period of time to disseminate a completed literary work and/or to develop audiences and markets for an artists' work. Eligible projects include, but are not limited to, promotional reading tours and book launches; on-line marketing initiatives such as book trailers; attendance at literary festivals, non-academic conference or award presentation by invitation; (c) Research: a program of activity for a specific period of time that supports or results in the development of new work in the literary arts. Eligible projects include, but are not limited to, experimentation, exploration and research of primary materials; (d) training and career development: a course or program of study to develop a writer's training in one or more of the eligible literary genres, including literary translation. Eligible projects include, but are not limited to, workshops, master classes, retreats, mentorship programs and professional courses. Except for projects in the training and career development category, eligible applicants must be professional writers who have had literary works professional published or produced. Professional literary publications or productions are literary works: (a) that have gone through an editorial process made by an independent editor/editorial board or that have gone through a dramaturgical process; (b) that have been published or produced by organizations with a majority of paid contributors who are not principals of the publishing or producing organization; (c) for which the writer has received compensation either as royalties, fees or honoraria, or as in-kind remuneration in the form of complimentary copies or a complimentary subscription; (d) of which the writer owns copyright; (e) that are available and accessible to the general public. Eligible literary arts genres are defined as the following: novels, short fiction, poetry, literary non-fiction, graphic novels, plays, young adult fiction and picture books. Professional writers of literary work are those who meet at least one of the following publication or production requirements: (a) a literary book published in print or as an e-book by a professional publishing house; (b) a minimum of two texts of short fiction, such as short stories or excerpts from a novel, published on two separate occasions in print or online literary magazines or periodicals, or in print or e-book anthologies published by professional publishing houses; (c) a minimum of five poems published on at least two separate occasions in print or online literary magazines or periodicals, or in print or e-book anthologies published by professional publishing houses; (d) a minimum of two texts of literary non-fiction published on two separate occasions in print or online literary magazines or periodicals, or in print or e-book anthologies published by professional publishing houses; (e) a play professionally produced. Applicants with a publishing or producing history established outside of Canada must provide in their artistic resumes evidence that their publications or productions are professional literary work. A statement of editorial and copyright policy of the publishes or producers may be required.

Funds Avail.: $15,000 Canadian Dollars. **Duration:** Annual. **To Apply:** Applicants must submit legal name and confirmation of the applicant status; applicant contact Information: street and mailing address for the primary applicant or gallery; a completed applicant agreement includ-

---

Awards are arranged alphabetically below their administering organizations

ing the e-signature of the primary applicant; an artistic resume of no more than four pages, with current mailing address which outlines any past exhibitions, achievements, teaching experience or formal education as applicable; images must be submitted a single image of a single artwork, multiple images of a single artwork; all video and audio files must be Windows compatible, MP3 and MP4 files; it may be asked for additional information to determine eligibility or any other program. **Deadline:** September 4; March 1. **Contact:** Brenda Hennig, Arts Development Consultant; Phone: 780-415-0285; Email: brenda.l.hennig@gov.ab.ca.

265 ■ Visual Arts and New Media Individual Project Funding *(Professional development/Grant)*

Purpose: To support the development of individual Alberta artists, arts administrators or an ensemble of artists by providing a grant for a specific literary arts project in a limited time period. **Focus:** Media arts; Visual arts. **Qualif.:** Applicants must be Canadian citizens; have had your primary residence in Alberta for one full year before applying; ordinarily, live in Alberta for at least six months each year with the exception of attending a formal program of study.

Funds Avail.: $15,000 Canadian Dollars. **Duration:** Annual. **To Apply:** Applicants may submit only one application to the AFA each deadline across all disciplines; applicant information: Legal name and confirmation of your status (minor or Albertan); the application category (art production, marketing, research, or training or career development) and applicant status (individual, ensemble); a brief project description (20 words) and project start and end dates; applicants should submit music-related activities, which may include: past training, most recent performances and performance highlights, compositions, discography, or ensemble experience; two musical selections such as a scratch demo from the proposed project, or high-quality demo; all video and audio files must be Windows compatible; wherever possible, support material should be uploaded as an attachment into GATE (up to 4 MB); a secondary budget outlining the applicant's ability to fund manufacturing expenses (CD pressing and artwork) (for art production projects). **Deadline:** September 4; March 1. **Contact:** Kari McQueen, Arts Development Consultant-Visual Arts and New Media; Phone: 780-415-0288; Email: kari.mcqueen@gov.ab.ca.

266 ■ Alberta Holstein Association

PO Box 988
Picture Butte, AB, Canada T0K 1V0
Ph: (403)335-5916
Fax: (403)732-5183
E-mail: info@albertaholstein.ca
URL: www.albertaholstein.ca
Social Media: www.facebook.com/albertaholsteinassociation

267 ■ Alberta Holstein Association Scholarships *(Undergraduate/Scholarship)*

Purpose: To encourage students to pursue their education by providing educational funds for deserving undergraduate students. **Focus:** Agriculture, Economic aspects. **Qualif.:** Applicants must have completed at least the first year of university or college; and must be returning to school within the calendar year; must be regular junior member of the Alberta Branch Holstein Canada, or a son or daughter of a

member; no individual will be eligible for a second award. **Criteria:** Recipient will be selected based on farm involvement, community participation, extracurricular activities and academic standings.

Funds Avail.: $500 each. **Duration:** Annual. **Number Awarded:** 4. **To Apply:** Applicants must submit a completed application form available from the website, a 500 to 1000-word essay explaining their farm involvement, and volunteer experience along with future employment ambitions. **Deadline:** October 31. **Contact:** Benita Hummel; Phone: 403-335-5916; Email: info@albertaholstein.ca.

268 ■ Alberta Indian Investment Corp. (AIIC)

21553 Chief Lapotac Blvd., Ste. 103
Enoch, AB, Canada T7X 3Y3
Ph: (780)470-3600
Fax: (780)470-3605
Free: 888-308-6789
E-mail: info@aiicbusiness.org
URL: www.aiicbusiness.org

269 ■ Sam Bull Memorial Scholarship *(Undergraduate/Scholarship)*

Purpose: To encourage and assist Treaty First Nations people in the pursuit of post-secondary education studies. **Focus:** Law; Political science. **Criteria:** Recipients will be evaluated by the selection committee based on academic performance, chosen area of study in relation to First Nation community development and future career aspirations.

Funds Avail.: 1,000 Canadian Dollars. **Duration:** Annual. **Number Awarded:** 2. **Deadline:** February 15. **Contact:** Alberta Indian Investment Corporation; PO Box 180 Enoch, Alberta, T7X 3Y3; Fax: 780-470-3605; Email: Info@aiicbusiness.org.

270 ■ Senator James Gladstone Memorial Scholarship *(Graduate, Undergraduate/Scholarship)*

Purpose: To encourage and assist Treaty First Nations people in the pursuit of post-secondary education studies. **Focus:** Business; Economics; Finance. **Criteria:** Recipients will be evaluated by the selection committee based on strong academic performance, chosen area of study in relation to First Nation business/economic development and future career aspirations.

Funds Avail.: 750 Canadian Dollars per year (for colleges); 1,000 Canadian Dollars per year (for universities). **Number Awarded:** 2. **To Apply:** Applicants must submit a completed application along with a 100 to 200 word statement of personal and academic objectives and certified copy of transcripts. **Deadline:** February 15. **Contact:** Alberta Indian Investment Corporation; PO Box 180 Enoch, Alberta, T7X 3Y3; Fax: 780-470-3605; Email: Info@aiicbusiness.org.

271 ■ Alberta Innovates - Health Solutions

1500, 10104 - 103 Ave.
Edmonton, AB, Canada T5J 0H8
Ph: (780)423-5727
Free: 877-423-5727
URL: www.aihealthsolutions.ca
Social Media: facebook.com/AlbertaInnovates
linkedin.com/company/alberta-innovates
twitter.com/abinnovates
www.youtube.com/user/AlbertaInnovates

Awards are arranged alphabetically below their administering organizations

272 ■ AIHS Graduate Studentships *(Master's, Doctorate/Fellowship)*

Purpose: To provide opportunities for individuals undertaking health-related research areas in pursuit of a Master's or PhD at an Alberta university. **Focus:** Health sciences; Medical research. **Qualif.:** Applicants must be currently enrolled in a graduate program at an Alberta university undertaking health-related training leading to a thesis-based graduate degree; must have completed their first year of graduate training at the time of award implementation; must be supported/sponsored by a Primary Research Supervisor. **Criteria:** Selection will be based on the following criteria: academic track record; relevant work and/or research experience; career development plans; supervisory team, the research and the mentorship environment; and research proposal; all applications will undergo a rigorous review process by a committee whose membership is both interdisciplinary and cross-sectoral.

Funds Avail.: 30,000 Canadian Dollars stipend, plus an allowance of 2,000 for research and career development. **To Apply:** Applicants must review the AIHS Training and Early Career Development Opportunity Postgraduate Fellowship program guide before applying. Application instructions are available at: albertainnovates.ca/programs/postgraduate-fellowships-in-health-innovation/. **Deadline:** April 1.

273 ■ AIHS Postgraduate Fellowships *(Postgraduate, Advanced Professional/Fellowship)*

Purpose: To support individuals who are pursuing postgraduate health-related research at an Alberta university. **Focus:** Health sciences; Medical research. **Qualif.:** Applicants must hold a PhD and/or professional health degree (e.g., MD, DDS, DVM or DPharm) without clinical accreditation in Canada, and be accepted or currently hold a postgraduate appointment at a university in Alberta. **Criteria:** Selection will be assessed on the following criteria: relevant work and/or research experience; career development plans; supervisory team and the research and mentorship environment; research proposal.

Funds Avail.: 50,000 Canadian Dollars per annum, plus 5,000 for research and career development. **Duration:** Up to 3 years. **To Apply:** Applicants must review the AIHS Training and Early Career Development Opportunity Postgraduate Fellowship program guide before applying. Application instructions are available at: albertainnovates.ca/programs/postgraduate-fellowships-in-health-innovation/.

274 ■ Alberta Innovates Technology Futures (AITF)

250 Karl Clark Rd.
Edmonton, AB, Canada T6N 1E4
Ph: (780)450-5111
Fax: (780)450-5333

275 ■ Alberta Innovates Graduate Student Scholarships *(Graduate/Scholarship)*

Purpose: To enable promising students to succeed in areas of scientific research which are strategically important to Alberta. **Focus:** Energy-related areas; Environmental technology; Health sciences; Information science and technology. **Qualif.:** Applicants must be Canadian citizens who hold a new NSERC (Natural Sciences and Engineering Research Council of Canada) or international and Canadian candidates who do not hold an NSERC award,

studying at an Alberta university to do graduate work in one of the following research areas Information and Communication Technology, Nanotechnology and Omics; in and of themselves or additionally which support the areas of Health, Bio-industries, Energy and Environment. If candidates are not yet registered at an Alberta university, their eligibility to apply for the GSS is contingent upon meeting all eligibility requirements for admission to an Alberta university; candidates should contact the university of their choice for information on those requirements. **Criteria:** Selection Alberta university will review all applications and evaluate them based on excellence and strategic alignment in areas of scientific research important to Alberta.

Funds Avail.: Amount varies. **Duration:** Annual. **Number Awarded:** Varies. **To Apply:** Application processes are specific to the applicant's university of choice.

276 ■ Alberta Innovates - Technology Futures Graduate Student Scholarships in ICT *(Doctorate, Graduate, Master's/Scholarship)*

Purpose: To help Alberta attract and retain world-class graduate students studying in an ICT related area. **Focus:** Information science and technology. **Qualif.:** Applicants must have a minimum 3.5 GPA; there are no citizenship restrictions; applying for a master's level Alberta Innovates GSS must have been admitted to their master's program; applying for a doctoral level Alberta Innovates GSS must have been admitted to their doctoral program.

Funds Avail.: Master's full value: $26,500, PhD full value: $31,500, Top-up value: $12,000. **Duration:** Four years. **To Apply:** Applicants must submit two letter of reference; copies of transcripts from all post-secondary institutions attended.

277 ■ Alberta Innovates - Technology Futures Graduate Student Scholarships in Nanotechnology *(Doctorate, Graduate/Scholarship)*

Purpose: To help Alberta attract and retain world class Master's and Doctoral students in the nanotechnology field. **Focus:** Engineering; Science. **Qualif.:** Applicants must have a minimum 3.5 GPA; there are no citizenship restrictions; applying for a master's level Alberta Innovates GSS must have been admitted to their master's program; applying for a doctoral level Alberta Innovates GSS must have been admitted to their doctoral program.

Funds Avail.: Master's full value: $26,500, PhD full value: $31,500, Top-up value: $12,000. **Duration:** Four years. **To Apply:** Applicants must submit two letter of reference; copies of transcripts from all post-secondary institutions attended.

278 ■ Alberta Innovates - Technology Futures Graduate Student Scholarships in Omics *(Doctorate, Master's, Professional development/Scholarship)*

Purpose: To enable academically superior graduate students, in a natural science or engineering discipline, to undertake full-time research training at an Alberta university, leading to a research-based Master's or Doctoral degree. **Focus:** Engineering; Science. **Qualif.:** Applicants must have a minimum 3.5 GPA; there are no citizenship restrictions; applying for a master's level Alberta Innovates GSS must have been admitted to their master's program; applying for a doctoral level Alberta Innovates GSS must have been admitted to their doctoral program.

Funds Avail.: Master's full value: $26,500, PhD full value: $31,500, Top-up value: $12,000. **Duration:** Four years. **To**

Awards are arranged alphabetically below their administering organizations

Apply: Applicants must submit two letter of reference; copies of transcripts from all post-secondary institutions attended.

279 ■ Alberta Learning Information Service - Alberta Scholarship Program

4th Fl Oxbridge Place 9820 106 Street NW
Edmonton, AB, Canada T5K 2J6
Ph: (780)427-3731
E-mail: alis.info@gov.ab.ca
URL: alis.alberta.ca

280 ■ Alberta Award for the Study of Canadian Human Rights and Multiculturalism *(Doctorate, Graduate, Master's/Award)*

Purpose: To encourage the pursuit of studies in Canadian human rights, cultural diversity and multiculturalism. **Focus:** Human rights. **Qualif.:** Applicant must be a Canadian citizen, permanent resident or protected person; enrolled or planning to enroll as a full-time graduate student (Master's or Doctoral level) at an Alberta public post-secondary institution; taking a program of study that supports the purpose of this scholarship; planning to do research that is within a Canadian context and will ultimately benefit Albertans. **Criteria:** Recipients will be selected based on information provided on application form; submitted essay; and curriculum vitae.

Funds Avail.: 10,000 Canadian Dollars - Master's level; 15,000 Canadian Dollars - Doctoral level. **Duration:** Annual. **Number Awarded:** 2. **To Apply:** Applicants must submit an application form; essay; curriculum vitae and any attachment. **Deadline:** February 1.

281 ■ Alberta Centennial Award *(Undergraduate/Scholarship)*

Purpose: To support Alberta students in their pursuit of higher education. **Focus:** General studies/Field of study not specified. **Qualif.:** Applicants must be Canadian citizens, permanent residents of Canada or protected person and must be Alberta resident and to be considered an Alberta resident one of the following conditions must apply: one parent, or legal guardian has maintained permanent residence in Canada for at least twelve (12) consecutive months immediately prior to commencing post-secondary studies and be residing in Alberta, or Alberta is the last place the student has lived for twelve (12) consecutive months immediately prior to commencing post-secondary studies, or be graduating from high school in the current academic year. **Criteria:** Selection will be based on students' involvement in volunteer activities in and outside school, leadership, citizenship and community service.

Funds Avail.: 2,005 Canadian Dollars each. **Duration:** Annual. **Number Awarded:** 25. **To Apply:** Applicants must submit a nomination form along with Two letters of reference. (References should be no longer than two pages), a reference from someone who has known the nominee for at least one year either through school or community or volunteer activities, and a reference from someone who knows the nominee well enough to support and/or elaborate on the nominee's activities and initiatives as outlined in the Record of Accomplishments Chart; a record of accomplishments chart. **Deadline:** June 1. **Remarks:** The scholarship is sponsored by the Government of Alberta to commemorate the Province of Alberta's Centennial.

282 ■ ALIS Fellowships for Full-time Studies in French *(Undergraduate/Fellowship)*

Purpose: To assist Albertans in pursuing post-secondary studies taught in French. **Focus:** Canadian studies; French studies. **Qualif.:** Applicants must be Alberta residents, Canadian citizens or permanent residents who plan to register full-time in a post-secondary program of at least one semester in length; must be enrolled in a minimum of three courses per semester in which the course content and the language of instruction are in French. **Criteria:** Selection will be based on academic achievement.

Funds Avail.: 500 Canadian Dollars-1,000 Canadian Dollars. **Duration:** Annual. **To Apply:** Applicants may obtain application form from the website or from the Students Awards Office at Alberta post-secondary institutions that offer programs taught in French and from Alberta Scholarship Programs; must include proof of Canadian citizenship: either a photocopy of Canadian birth certificate, passport or immigration papers; college applicants must include a transcript.

283 ■ ALIS Graduate Student Scholarship *(Graduate/Scholarship)*

Purpose: To recognize and reward outstanding students entering their second year of a full-time masters program in Alberta. **Focus:** General studies/Field of study not specified. **Qualif.:** Applicants must be Canadian citizens Permanent Resident or Protected Person; must be an Alberta resident, and to be considered an Alberta resident one of the following conditions must apply: one parent must currently be residing in Alberta, or Alberta is the last place the student has lived for twelve (12) consecutive months before being a full-time student, or is married to an Alberta resident before the start of the qualifying year of study; must have completed one year of a masters program and be enrolled full-time in the second year of the same program. Applicants must have been enrolled full-time in their first year and must be continuing full-time studies in the second year of the same program. Applicants are nominated by the Faculty of Graduate Studies at their school.**Criteria:** Selection is based on all marks obtained in the first year of the student's masters program.

Funds Avail.: 3,000 Canadian Dollars each.

284 ■ ALIS International Education Awards - Ukraine *(Undergraduate/Scholarship)*

Purpose: To enable Alberta post-secondary students, post-graduates, professionals and scholars to undertake career-related training, research or study in Ukraine, and Ukrainian post-secondary students, post-graduates, professionals and scholars to undertake career-related training, research or study in Alberta. **Focus:** General studies/Field of study not specified. **Qualif.:** Applicants must be Canadian citizens/permanent residents or Ukrainian residents; Canadian citizens/permanent residents must be Alberta residents, preferably attending or associated with an Alberta post-secondary institution or apprenticeship/co-op program; they must be either enrolled in a post-secondary institution at senior level, graduate students, recent post-graduates, or professionals or scholars; students applying to take a course or applying to study for one or two semesters at a post-secondary institution in Ukraine are also eligible; on the other hand, Ukrainian residents must be citizens or residents of Ukraine, preferably attending or associated with a post-secondary teaching or research institution, or apprenticeship/co-op program; they must be either enrolled in a post-secondary institution at senior level, graduate

Awards are arranged alphabetically below their administering organizations

students, recent post-graduates, or professionals or scholars; students applying to take a course or applying to study for one or two semesters at a post-secondary institution in Alberta are also eligible. **Criteria:** Recipients will be selected by a selection member representing the Alberta Ukrainian community. Selection will be based on academic merit, past accomplishments, the purpose or validity of the proposal, reference letter, and institutional support and benefit to the recipient's institution.

Funds Avail.: 5,000 Canadian Dollars each. **Duration:** Annual. **To Apply:** Applicants must submit the following: a completed and signed application form; a resume/curriculum vitae; an official transcript; an essay describing the program or research; a letter of support from the host institution, and a reference letter. **Contact:** Email: scholarships@gov.ab.ca, Toll-free: 855-606-2096.

285 ■ Arts Graduate Scholarship *(Graduate/ Scholarship)*

Purpose: To provide assistance to students who demonstrated outstanding ability in the arts pursue graduate study. **Focus:** Arts. **Qualif.:** Applicant must be a Canadian citizen, Permanent Resident or Protected Person; must be an Alberta resident, and to be considered an Alberta resident one of the following conditions must apply: Alberta is the last place the student has lived for twelve (12) consecutive months immediately prior to commencing post-secondary studies, or was married to an Alberta resident immediately prior to commencing post-secondary studies; must be enrolled full-time in a graduate program at the master level or equivalent for the fall and winter term. **Criteria:** Recipients are chosen by a Selection Committee appointed by the presidents of the universities in Alberta. Applicants are judged on previous academic accomplishments; program of study; appraiser's evaluations; answers to the essay question; and general impressions from the application form.

Funds Avail.: 15,000 Canadian Dollars each. **Duration:** Annual. **Number Awarded:** 7. **To Apply:** Applicants must submit a completed application form; official transcript; a resume that includes all universities, colleges or technical institutes attended to date, including current institution, a list of scholarships, awards, and other forms of achievement received, any publications, if any, such as the name of the journal they were published in, and any performances/exhibitions (dates, location, etc.) and a reference from the applicant's name and award name, the applicant's program of study, research (if applicable), and accomplishments. **Deadline:** January 15.

286 ■ Theodore R. Campbell Scholarship *(Undergraduate/Scholarship)*

Purpose: To reward the accomplishments of an aboriginal student from Blue Quills First Nations College. **Focus:** General studies/Field of study not specified. **Qualif.:** Applicant must be First Nations, Inuit, or Metis; must be a Canadian citizen, permanent resident, or protected person; be an Alberta resident, and to be considered an Alberta resident one of the following conditions must apply: one parent, or legal guardian has maintained permanent residence in Canada for at least twelve (12) consecutive months immediately prior to commencing post-secondary studies and be residing in Alberta, or Alberta is the last place the student has lived for twelve (12) consecutive months immediately prior to commencing post-secondary studies, or was married to an Alberta resident immediately prior to commencing post-secondary studies; have completed a minimum of 24 credits in the first year and obtained

passing marks in all courses with at least a 70% attendance record; must demonstrate financial need; must be continuing full-time in the second year of the program. **Criteria:** Selection will be based on the academic achievement during first year of study.

Funds Avail.: 1,500 Canadian Dollars. **Duration:** Annual. **To Apply:** Applicants must submit an online application form. **Remarks:** The scholarship was established by the Theodore R. Campbell family through the Alberta Heritage Scholarship Fund Endowment program.

287 ■ Robert C. Carson Memorial Bursary *(Undergraduate/Scholarship)*

Purpose: To provide financial assistance to aboriginal students who have successfully completed the first year of a program relating to criminal justice, criminology or law. **Focus:** Criminal justice; Criminology; Law. **Qualif.:** Applicants must be Canadian citizen, Permanent Resident or Protected Person; be an Alberta resident, and to be considered an Alberta resident one of the following conditions must apply: one parent, or legal guardian has maintained permanent residence in Canada for at least 12 consecutive months immediately prior to commencing post-secondary studies and be residing in Alberta, or Alberta is the last place the student has lived for twelve (12) consecutive months immediately prior to commencing post-secondary studies, or was married to an Alberta resident immediately prior to commencing post-secondary studies; must be enrolled full-time in the Law Enforcement or Criminal Justice Diploma program at Lethbridge College, Mount Royal University, or MacEwan University, or the Law program at the University of Calgary or the Law or Criminology program at the University of Alberta, and must have completed one year of the program and continuing into the second year, and be an Indigenous student.

Funds Avail.: 500 Canadian Dollars. **Duration:** Annual. **Deadline:** September 30.

288 ■ Laurence Decore Awards for Student Leadership *(Undergraduate/Scholarship)*

Purpose: To recognize those post-secondary students who have demonstrated outstanding dedication and leadership to fellow students and to their community. **Focus:** General studies/Field of study not specified. **Qualif.:** Applicant must be Canadian citizen, permanent resident or protected person; must be an Alberta resident, and to be considered an Alberta resident one of the following conditions must apply: one parent or legal guardian has maintained permanent residence in Canada for at least twelve (12) consecutive months immediately prior to commencing post-secondary studies and be residing in Alberta, or Alberta is the last place the student has lived for twelve (12) consecutive months immediately prior to commencing post-secondary studies, or was married to an Alberta resident immediately prior to commencing post-secondary studies; must be currently enrolled full-time (a minimum 60% course load) in an undergraduate program at an eligible school in Alberta; must be involved in either student government or student societies, clubs or organizations, or involved in student organizations at the provincial or national level or in non-profit community organizations; must be selected by a Selection Committee at the school. **Criteria:** Selection will be based on the committee's criteria.

Funds Avail.: 1,000 Canadian Dollars. **Duration:** Annual. **To Apply:** Applicant must provide a detailed description of their involvement and accomplishments in student government or student societies, clubs or organizations, or student

Awards are arranged alphabetically below their administering organizations

organizations at the provincial or national level or in non-profit community organizations; must submit a letter of reference. **Deadline:** February 15. **Remarks:** This scholarship honors Mr. Laurence Decore, former Edmonton mayor and leader of the Alberta Liberal Party.

289 ■ Earl and Countess of Wessex - World Championships in Athletics Scholarship
(Undergraduate/Scholarship)

Purpose: To recognize the top male and female Alberta students who have excelled in track and field. **Focus:** Athletics. **Qualif.:** Applicants must be Canadian citizens Permanent Resident or Protected Person; must be an Alberta resident, and to be considered an Alberta resident one of the following conditions must apply: one parent, or legal guardian has maintained permanent residence in Canada for at least 12 consecutive months immediately prior to commencing post-secondary studies and be residing in Alberta, or Alberta is the last place the student has lived for twelve (12) consecutive months immediately prior to commencing post-secondary studies, or the student's spouse/partner is an Alberta resident; must be enrolled full-time in post-secondary studies at the University of Alberta, the University of Calgary or the University of Lethbridge, and joined the Track and Field team at that institution as of September of the current academic year; must have completed Grade 12 requirements at a publically funded Alberta high school prior to September of the current academic year.**Criteria:** Selection will be based on students' placing in provincial and national championships, AADP standards, best performances, Mercier scores and recommendations from the applicants' coaches; academic achievement will also be a consideration.

Funds Avail.: 3,000 Canadian Dollars each. **Number Awarded:** 2. **To Apply:** Applicants must submit an online application form.

290 ■ Helen and George Kilik Scholarship
(Undergraduate/Scholarship)

Purpose: To assist students from Olds High School who are pursuing post-secondary education. **Focus:** General studies/Field of study not specified. **Qualif.:** Applicant must be a Canadian citizen, Permanent Resident or Protected Person; must be an Alberta resident, and to be considered an Alberta resident one of the following conditions must apply: one parent, or legal guardian has maintained permanent residence in Canada for at least twelve (12) consecutive months immediately prior to commencing post-secondary studies and be residing in Alberta, or Alberta is the last place the student has lived for twelve (12) consecutive months immediately prior to commencing post-secondary studies, or the student's spouse/partner is an Alberta resident; must have completed all high school grades at Olds Junior Senior High School; must be in financial need; must be involved in extra-curricular activities; must demonstrate academic achievement particularly in mathematics and science, and must be enrolled in full-time post-secondary studies. **Criteria:** Recipients will be selected by a selection member at Olds Junior Senior High School.

Funds Avail.: 1,000 Canadian Dollars. **Duration:** Annual. **Number Awarded:** 2. **To Apply:** Applicants must submit an online application form. **Deadline:** June 30. **Remarks:** This scholarship was endowment by the family of Mr. and Mrs. Kilik with the Alberta Heritage Scholarship Fund.

291 ■ Janet and Horace Allen Science Scholarship
(Undergraduate/Scholarship)

Purpose: To recognize the academic excellence of a student from Crowsnest Consolidated high School in the area of the sciences. **Focus:** Science. **Qualif.:** Applicants must be a Canadian Citizen, Permanent Resident or Protected Person; must be an Alberta resident, and to be considered an Alberta resident one of the following conditions must apply: one parent, or legal guardian has maintained permanent residence in Canada for at least twelve (12) consecutive months immediately prior to commencing post-secondary studies and be residing in Alberta, or Alberta is the last place the student has lived for twelve (12) consecutive months immediately prior to commencing post-secondary studies, or was married to an Alberta resident immediately prior to commencing post-secondary studies; be graduating from Crowsnest Consolidated High School in the current academic year; be enrolled full-time in a post-secondary program. **Criteria:** Recipient will be selected on the basis of achieving the highest average on two of the following Grade 12 courses at the 30 level biology, chemistry, physics or science.

Funds Avail.: 1,500 Canadian Dollars. **Duration:** Annual. **Number Awarded:** 1. **To Apply:** Applicants must submit an online application form. **Deadline:** August 1.

292 ■ Jason Lang Scholarship *(Undergraduate/Scholarship)*

Purpose: To reward the outstanding academic achievement of Alberta post-secondary students who are continuing full-time in an undergraduate program in Alberta. **Focus:** Dentistry; Law; Medicine; Pharmacy. **Qualif.:** Applicant must be a Canadian citizen, Permanent Resident or Protected Person; must be an Alberta resident, and to be considered an Alberta resident one of the following conditions must apply: one parent, or legal guardian has maintained permanent residence in Canada for at least 12 consecutive months immediately prior to commencing post-secondary studies and be residing in Alberta, or Alberta is the last place the student has lived for twelve (12) consecutive months immediately prior to commencing post-secondary studies, or was married to an Alberta resident immediately prior to commencing post-secondary studies; must be enrolled in an undergraduate or professional program such as Law, Medicine, Pharmacy, Dentistry, or Veterinary Medicine at a participating post-secondary educational institution in Alberta; must be enrolled in a program of study which is a minimum of two years in length or greater, i.e. a program must offer a minimum of four academic terms or 64 weeks of academic instruction, excluding work term and/or co-op, and must have completed at least 80% of a full course load and achieved a minimum Grade Point Average of 3.2 on a 4.0 scale in the previous academic year ("qualifying year") during the fall and winter semesters (excluding Spring or Summer courses); must be continuing their full-time post-secondary studies in the current academic year. **Criteria:** Applicants who meet the eligibility criteria are nominated by the Student Awards Office at the Alberta post-secondary institution where they completed their qualifying year of studies.

Funds Avail.: 1,000 Canadian Dollars. **To Apply:** Applicants must submit an online application form. **Deadline:** February 1 (Winter); October 15 (Fall). **Remarks:** This scholarship is established in the memory of Jason Lang, a 17-year-old high school student who was killed in a school shooting.

Awards are arranged alphabetically below their administering organizations

293 ■ Anna and John Kolesar Memorial Scholarship
(Undergraduate/Scholarship)

Purpose: To support those students who are academically excellent and have plan to enter in Faculty Education. **Focus:** General studies/Field of study not specified. **Qualif.:** Applicant must be a Canadian Citizen, Permanent Resident or Protected Person; must be an Alberta resident, and to be considered an Alberta resident one of the following conditions must apply: one parent, or legal guardian has maintained permanent residence in Canada for at least twelve (12) consecutive months immediately prior to commencing post-secondary studies and be residing in Alberta, or Alberta is the last place the student has lived for twelve (12) consecutive months immediately prior to commencing post-secondary studies, or was married to an Alberta resident immediately prior to commencing post-secondary studies; must be graduating from an Alberta high school in the current academic year; must be from a family where neither parent obtained a university degree, and must be enrolled or planning to enroll full-time in a program of study in an Alberta publicly funded post-secondary institution in a Faculty of Education. **Criteria:** Selection is based on the highest average obtained on three Grade 12 subjects: one of English 30, or English 30-1, 30-2, or Francais 30 30-2 and two other subjects at the 30 level; Social studies, Mathematics, Science, Biology, Chemistry, Physics and a language.

Funds Avail.: 1,500 Canadian Dollars. **Duration:** Annual. **Number Awarded:** 1. **To Apply:** Applicants must submit an online application form. **Deadline:** August 1. **Remarks:** This scholarship honors the memory of Anna and John Kolesar, the parents of Dr. Henry Kolesar, Deputy Minister of Alberta Advanced Education from 1976 to 1987.

294 ■ Language Teacher Bursary Program *(Other/Award)*

Purpose: To assist certified Alberta teachers to take a summer post-secondary program in a language other than English or language pedagogy course at an institution outside of Canada. **Focus:** Foreign languages. **Qualif.:** Applicants must be a Canadian Citizen, Permanent Resident, or Protected Person; must be an Alberta resident, and to be considered an Alberta resident one of the following conditions must apply: one parent, or legal guardian has maintained permanent residence in Canada for at least twelve (12) consecutive months immediately prior to commencing post-secondary studies and be residing in Alberta, or Alberta is the last place the student has lived for twelve (12) consecutive months immediately prior to commencing post-secondary studies, or was married to an Alberta resident immediately prior to commencing post-secondary studies; must hold a valid Alberta professional teaching certificate; must have been teaching in Alberta for a minimum of three years (FTE) by the end of the current school year; must demonstrate a background in language learning, or have recently initiated the study of this language and plan to take a summer program of at least four weeks duration in a language and/or language teaching methodology other than English outside of Canada. **Criteria:** Recipients will be selected based on statement of the program; course rigour; school authority endorsement; and potential benefit for both teacher, school authority, endorsement, and the potential benefit for both the teacher and the school authority.

Funds Avail.: 5,000 each Canadian Dollars. **Number Awarded:** Up to 10. **To Apply:** Application form can be obtained from the website; completed application form must be submitted to your local school authority for endorsement; once endorsement has been given, the school authority will mail your application to Alberta Scholarship programs; resume including education and work history; statement of Intent (one page maximum); Professional Development Summary; Course Syllabus.

295 ■ Languages In Teacher Education Scholarship
(Undergraduate/Scholarship)

Purpose: To reward Alberta students enrolled in a recognized Alberta teacher preparation program taking courses that will allow them to teach languages other than English in Alberta schools. **Focus:** Foreign languages. **Qualif.:** Applicant must be a Canadian Citizen, Permanent Resident or Protected Person; must be an Alberta resident, and to be considered an Alberta resident one of the following conditions must apply: one parent, or legal guardian has maintained permanent residence in Canada for at least twelve (12) consecutive months immediately prior to commencing post-secondary studies and be residing in Alberta, or Alberta is the last place the student has lived for twelve (12) consecutive months immediately prior to commencing post-secondary studies, or the student's spouse/partner is an Alberta resident; be enrolled full-time in the final two years of a recognized Alberta teacher preparation program offered by an Alberta Faculty of Education. **Criteria:** Selection will be based on the committee's criteria.

Funds Avail.: 2,500 Canadian Dollars. **Duration:** Annual. **Number Awarded:** 16. **To Apply:** Applicants must submit an online nomination form. **Deadline:** February 15. **Remarks:** This scholarship was created by an endowment from the Government of Alberta to the Alberta Heritage Scholarship Fund to build provincial capacity in the area of language education.

296 ■ Lois Hole Humanities and Social Sciences Scholarship *(Undergraduate/Scholarship)*

Purpose: To recognize student leadership and community service. **Focus:** Humanities; Social sciences. **Qualif.:** Applicants must be students enrolled full-time in the second or subsequent year of post-secondary study in the Faculty of Humanities, the Faculty of Social Sciences or the Faculty of Arts, at the University of Alberta, the University of Calgary, the University of Lethbridge, Athabasca University, MacEwan University or Mount Royan University; must be Canadian citizens, permanent residents. Alberta should be the last place the student has lived for twelve consecutive months before being a full-time student; must be continuing full-time in the faculty of humanities or the faculty of social sciences. **Criteria:** Selection will be based on academic merit, demonstrated leadership and community service.

Funds Avail.: 5,000 Canadian Dollars. **Duration:** Annual. **Number Awarded:** 6. **To Apply:** Applicants must submit an online nomination form. **Deadline:** November 15.

297 ■ Sir James Lougheed Award of Distinction
(Doctorate, Graduate, Master's/Award)

Purpose: To provide Alberta students in graduate programs with the opportunity for study outside of Alberta at institutions anywhere in the world. **Focus:** General studies/Field of study not specified. **Qualif.:** Applicants must be a Canadian citizen, Permanent Resident or Protected Person; must be an Alberta resident, and to be considered an Alberta resident one of the following conditions must apply: Alberta is the last place the student has lived for twelve (12) consecutive months prior to commencing post-secondary studies, or was married to an Alberta resident immediately prior to commencing post-secondary studies;

Awards are arranged alphabetically below their administering organizations

must be enrolled as a full-time student in a graduate program at an institution outside Alberta. **Criteria:** Recipients will be selected based on previous academic accomplishments, program of study, appraiser evaluations, answers to the essay question, and general impressions from the application form.

Funds Avail.: 15,000 Canadian Dollars for Masters level; 20,000 Canadian Dollars for Doctoral level. **Duration:** Annual. **Number Awarded:** Master's Level - 7; Doctoral Level - 8. **To Apply:** Applicants must submit a completed and signed application form; an official transcript; a resume that includes all universities, colleges or technical institutes attended to date, including current institution, a list of scholarships, awards, and other forms of achievement received, any publications, if any, such as the name of the journal they were published in, and any performances/exhibitions (dates, location, etc.); references, including the applicant's name and award name, and the applicant's program of study, research (if applicable), and accomplishments. **Deadline:** January 15. **Remarks:** The award honors the Calgary lawyer, parliamentarian, senator and cabinet minister who served in several federal parliaments in the late 1800s and early 1900s.

298 ■ Dr. Ernest and Minnie Mehl Scholarships
(Undergraduate/Scholarship)

Purpose: To encourage students to pursue a post-secondary education and to recognize and reward exceptional academic at the senior high school level. **Focus:** General studies/Field of study not specified. **Qualif.:** Applicants must be Canadian citizens or permanent resident of Canada; must be Alberta resident; must have completed their Grade 12 in Alberta at a school that follows the Alberta Education Curriculum; must be continuing their studies at a degree granting post-secondary institution in Canada; university transfer programs are acceptable. **Criteria:** Selection will be based on the average obtained on Diploma Examinations in one of English 30-1, 30-2 or Francais 30, 30-2 and Social Studies 30, 30-1 or 30-2 plus any three other subjects: Pure Mathematics 30, Applied Mathematics 30, Biology 30, Chemistry 30, Physics 30 or Science 30. Financial need will also be considered.

Funds Avail.: 3,500 Canadian Dollars. **Duration:** Annual. **Number Awarded:** 1. **To Apply:** No application is required; the recipient will be selected from applications received for an Alexander Rutherford Scholarship.

299 ■ Louise McKinney Post-secondary Scholarship *(Undergraduate/Scholarship)*

Purpose: To recognize exceptional academic achievement and encourage outstanding students to continue their studies at the post-secondary level. **Focus:** General studies/Field of study not specified. **Qualif.:** Applicants must be Canadian citizens, permanent resident or protected person; must be an Alberta resident, and to be considered an Alberta resident one of the following conditions must apply: one parent or legal guardian has maintained permanent residence in Canada for at least 12 consecutive months immediately prior to commencing post-secondary studies and be residing in Alberta, or Alberta is the last place the student has lived for twelve (12) consecutive months immediately prior to commencing post-secondary studies, or was married to an Alberta resident before the start of the qualifying year of study; must be nominated at the school they most recently attended, and must be continuing their full-time studies at an eligible school in Alberta in the second or subsequent year of a full-time undergraduate or professional program. **Criteria:** Selection will be based on

the academic standing and the scholarship policy of the institution.

Funds Avail.: 2,500 Canadian Dollars. **Duration:** Annual. **Number Awarded:** Up to 1,450. **To Apply:** Applicants must submit a transcript with an official signature or seal indicating that the transcript paper is issued by their school/institution; post-secondary students must contact their school to request their official transcripts. **Deadline:** September 30. **Remarks:** This scholarship established in honor of Louise McKinney.

300 ■ Charles S. Noble Scholarships for Study at Harvard *(Undergraduate/Scholarship)*

Purpose: To provide students the opportunity to pursue undergraduate studies at Harvard. **Focus:** General studies/Field of study not specified. **Qualif.:** Applicant must be a Canadian citizen, Permanent Resident or Protected Person; must be an Alberta resident, and to be considered an Alberta resident one of the following conditions must apply: one parent or legal guardian who has maintained permanent residence in Canada for at least 12 consecutive months immediately prior to commencing post-secondary studies and must be residing in Alberta, or Alberta is the last place the student has lived for twelve (12) consecutive months immediately prior to commencing post-secondary studies, or was married to an Alberta resident immediately prior to commencing post-secondary studies; intend to apply or be enrolled full-time in an undergraduate program at Harvard College. **Criteria:** Recipients are selected by the Office of Admissions at Harvard College.

Funds Avail.: $5,000 from Alberta Student Aid and up to $5,000 of financial aid. **Duration:** Annual. **Number Awarded:** 3. **To Apply:** Applicants must submit an online application form. **Deadline:** December 15. **Remarks:** The scholarship honors Sandy A. Mactaggart, the agricultural entrepreneur, innovator and farm implement manufacturer who became one of Alberta's biggest and best grain farmer.

301 ■ Northern Alberta Development Council Bursaries Program *(Undergraduate/Scholarship)*

Purpose: To increase the number of trained professionals in Northern Alberta and to encourage students from Northern Alberta to obtain a post-secondary education. **Focus:** General studies/Field of study not specified. **Qualif.:** Applicants must be residents of Alberta and planning to enroll full-time in post-secondary programs; must demonstrate financial need and be willing to live and work in northern Alberta after completion of the program; for each year of bursary funding, a student must live and work for one year in northern Alberta; students have up to six months after graduation to find a job related to their fields of study. **Criteria:** Selection will be based on the committee's following criteria: program of studies and the demand for career program in northern Alberta; knowledge of northern Alberta; academic record; answers to essay questions, and financial need.

Funds Avail.: Range of 6,000 to 12,000 Canadian Dollars. **Duration:** Annual. **To Apply:** Applicants may obtain an application form from www.benorth.ca; application forms for these bursaries are also available from Alberta Scholarship Programs, Student Awards Offices and from the Northern Alberta Development Council.

302 ■ Northern Alberta Development Council Bursary *(Undergraduate/Scholarship)*

Purpose: To assist students in pursuing a post-secondary education. **Focus:** General studies/Field of study not speci-

Awards are arranged alphabetically below their administering organizations

fied. **Qualif.:** Applicants must be residents of Alberta and planning to enroll full-time in post-secondary programs; must demonstrate financial need and be willing to live and work in northern Alberta after completion of the program; for each year of bursary funding, a student must live and work for one year in northern Alberta; students have up to six months after graduation to find a job related to their fields of study. **Criteria:** Recipients are selected by prospective employers with assistance from NADC.

Funds Avail.: 3,000 Canadian Dollars. **Duration:** Annual. **To Apply:** Applicants may obtain an application form from www.benorth.ca. Application form for these bursaries are also available from Northern Alberta Development Council. **Deadline:** April 30.

303 ■ Persons Case Scholarship *(Undergraduate, Graduate/Scholarship)*

Purpose: To assist students whose studies will ultimately contribute to the advancement of women, or who are studying in fields where members of their gender are traditionally few in number. **Focus:** General studies/Field of study not specified. **Qualif.:** Applicant must be a Canadian citizen, Permanent Resident or Protected Person; must be an Alberta resident, and to be considered an Alberta resident one of the following conditions must apply: one parent or legal guardian has maintained permanent residence in Canada for at least twelve (12) consecutive months immediately prior to commencing post-secondary studies and be residing in Alberta, or Alberta is the last place the student has lived for twelve (12) consecutive months immediately prior to commencing post-secondary studies, or the student's spouse/partner is an Alberta resident; be a full-time student in the fall and winter terms who maintains a minimum 3.0 grade point average at an approved post-secondary institution. Consideration will be given to undergraduate students studying out-of-province, however, they must identify the special nature of the out-of-province program; identify as a woman. **Criteria:** Recipients will be selected based on program of studies; academic achievement; written submission and character reference. Students pursuing graduate studies out-of-province will be given full consideration.

Funds Avail.: Range of 1,000 to 5,000 Canadian Dollars. **Duration:** Annual. **Number Awarded:** 40. **To Apply:** Applicant must submit the following with the application form: an official transcript of most current post-secondary studies; a written submission outlining how your personal, volunteer, work, or academic experience within the past two years contributes to at least one of the above criteria and to the Persons Case or the Famous Five; a curriculum vitae/resume including your volunteer experience, and a character reference letter. **Deadline:** October 31. **Remarks:** The scholarship honors the efforts of Alberta's famous five namely Emily Murphy, Louise Mckinney, Nellie McClung, Irene Parlby, and Henrietta Muir Edwards, who fought and won the right for same. Established in 1979.

304 ■ Prairie Baseball Academy Scholarship *(Undergraduate/Scholarship)*

Purpose: To reward the athletic and academic excellence of baseball players and to provide an incentive and means for these players to continue with their post-secondary education. **Focus:** General studies/Field of study not specified. **Qualif.:** Applicants must be be a Canadian citizen, Permanent Resident or Protected Person; must be an Alberta resident, and to be considered an Alberta resident one of the following conditions must apply: one parent, or legal guardian has maintained permanent residence in

Canada for at least twelve (12) consecutive months immediately prior to commencing post-secondary studies and be residing in Alberta, or Alberta is the last place the student has lived for twelve (12) consecutive months immediately prior to commencing post-secondary studies, or the student's spouse/partner is an Alberta resident; must be a participant in the Prairie Baseball Academy; must be enrolled as a full-time student at a post-secondary institution in Alberta; must have achieved a grade point average of 2.0 on a 4.0 scale in the previous term of study, and be recommended by the selection members of the Prairie Baseball Academy. **Criteria:** Selection will be based on academic achievement, community involvement and baseball achievements.

Funds Avail.: 500 Canadian Dollars - 2,500 Canadian Dollars. **Duration:** Annual. **Contact:** Tel: 855-606-2096.

305 ■ Queen Elizabeth II Graduate Scholarship *(Doctorate, Graduate, Master's/Scholarship)*

Purpose: To recognize the outstanding achievements of students pursuing graduate studies in Alberta. **Focus:** General studies/Field of study not specified. **Qualif.:** Applicants must be Canadian citizens or permanent residents of Canada and be enrolled full-time in a faculty of graduate studies at one of the following post-secondary schools in Alberta; the University of Alberta, the University of Calgary, the University of Lethbridge, Concordia University College of Alberta or Athabasca University. **Criteria:** Selection will be based on the committee's criteria.

Funds Avail.: 10,800 Canadian Dollars-Masters level; 15,000 Canadian Dollars-Doctoral level. **Duration:** Annual. **Contact:** Email: scholarships@gov.ab.ca, Toll-free: 855-606-2096.

306 ■ Registered Apprenticeship Program/CTS Scholarships (RAP) *(Undergraduate/Scholarship)*

Purpose: To provide assistance to those high school students who are taking Registered Apprenticeship Program. **Focus:** General studies/Field of study not specified. **Qualif.:** Applicants must be a Canadian citizen or Permanent Resident or Protected Person; must be an Alberta resident as defined by Alberta Student Aid; must have completed the requirements for high school diploma in June or earlier; must be registered as an Alberta apprentice in a trade while still attending high school; must have completed a minimum of 250 hours of on-the-job training and work experience in your trade; must be continuing in an approved regular apprenticeship program; have at least one period of technical training remaining, and must not be a previous RAP/CTS Scholarship award recipient. **Criteria:** Selection will be based on applicant mark.

Funds Avail.: 1,000 Canadian Dollars. **Duration:** Annual. **Deadline:** November 1.

307 ■ Alexander Rutherford High School Achievement Scholarship *(Undergraduate/Scholarship)*

Purpose: To provide assistance to those students who are pursuing post-secondary studies. **Focus:** General studies/Field of study not specified. **Qualif.:** Applicants must be Canadian citizens, permanent residents or Protected Person; must be an Alberta resident, and to be considered an Alberta resident the following conditions must apply: one parent or legal guardian must have maintained permanent residence in Canada for at least 12 consecutive months immediately prior to the applicant commencing a program of study; applicant has maintained permanent residence in Alberta at least 12-months prior to commencing a program

Awards are arranged alphabetically below their administering organizations

of study; applicant is not eligible to receive a scholarship with respect to any grade unless the applicant or the applicant's parent(s)/legal guardian were a resident in Alberta throughout the whole of that grade; must have completed high school on or after September 30, 1980; must be enrolled in, or have completed 60% of a full course load in a post-secondary or an apprenticeship program of at least one semester in length. **Criteria:** Selection will be based on student minimum combined average based on five designated courses in at least one grade: Grade 10, 11 or 12 as calculated from Alberta Residents and Completed High School Outside Alberta.

Funds Avail.: Up to 2,500 Canadian Dollars. **Duration:** Annual. **To Apply:** Applicants must provide the following: Personal Information consists of Social Insurance Number and Alberta Student Number; School Information includes Post-secondary school you are going to attend, Start date and High School attended. **Remarks:** This scholarship was named in honor of Alexander Rutherford, who had the distinction of being Alberta's first Premier and Minister of Education.

308 ■ Rutherford Scholars (Undergraduate/Scholarship)

Purpose: To provide assistance to those students who are in need. **Focus:** General studies/Field of study not specified. **Qualif.:** Applicants must be in the top ten students as determined on the first writing of diploma examination. **Criteria:** Recipients are selected on the basis of results obtained on Diploma Examinations in one of: English 30-1, 30-2 or Francais 30, 30-2, Social Studies 30 plus three other subjects; averages normally are in the 96.0 to 98.8 percent range; only the first writing of the diploma exam will be considered.

Funds Avail.: 2,500 Canadian Dollars. **Duration:** Annual. **To Apply:** Recipients are selected from applications for an Alexander Rutherford Scholarship. No separate application is required.

309 ■ Dr. Robert and Anna Shaw Scholarship (Undergraduate/Scholarship)

Purpose: To recognize and reward the academic and leadership accomplishments of three students graduating from Sexsmith Secondary School who are entering post-secondary studies. **Focus:** Agriculture, Economic aspects; Art; Art industries and trade; Engineering. **Qualif.:** Applicants must be a Canadian Citizen, Permanent Resident or Protected Person; must be an Alberta resident, and to be considered an Alberta resident one of the following conditions must apply: one parent, or legal guardian has maintained permanent residence in Canada for at least twelve (12) consecutive months immediately prior to commencing post-secondary studies and be residing in Alberta, or Alberta is the last place the student has lived for twelve (12) consecutive months immediately prior to commencing post-secondary studies, or was married to an Alberta resident immediately prior to commencing post-secondary studies; graduate from Sexsmith Secondary School in the current academic year; plan to enroll or be enrolled full-time in a post-secondary program related to agriculture, engineering, fine arts or the trades; must demonstrate a high academic standing in their Grade 12 year, and must demonstrate outstanding qualities in the areas of leadership, community spirit, involvement in extracurricular activities and a commitment to place the welfare of others above their own needs. **Criteria:** Selection will be based on the basis of demonstrated leadership; community involvement; and participation in extracurricular activities.

Funds Avail.: 500 Canadian Dollars. **Duration:** Annual. **Number Awarded:** 1. **To Apply:** Applicants must complete an application form; a summary of their leadership activities, community involvement and extracurricular activities that demonstrate community spirit and concern for others. **Deadline:** October 31. **Remarks:** The scholarship is named in honor of Dr. Robert and Anna Shaw, pioneers in the Sexsmith area.

310 ■ Dr. Robert Norman Shaw Scholarship (Undergraduate/Scholarship)

Purpose: To recognize and reward the exceptional achievement of a student graduating from Sexsmith Secondary School who is entering post-secondary studies in a health-related field. **Focus:** Health sciences. **Qualif.:** Applicants must be a Canadian Citizens, Permanent Resident, or Protected Person; must be an Alberta resident and to be considered an Alberta resident one of the following conditions must apply: one parent, or legal guardian has maintained permanent residence in Canada for at least twelve (12) consecutive months immediately prior to commencing post-secondary studies and be residing in Alberta, or Alberta is the last place the student has lived for twelve (12) consecutive months immediately prior to commencing post-secondary studies, or was married to an Alberta resident immediately prior to commencing post-secondary studies; must be graduate from Sexsmith Secondary School in the current academic year; plan to enroll or be enrolled full-time in a post-secondary program related to health, and must demonstrate a high academic standing in Grade 12. **Criteria:** Selection will be based on the highest average on five 30 level Grade 12 subjects English or French, mathematics, social studies, biology, chemistry, physics or science.

Funds Avail.: $1,500. **Duration:** Annual. **Number Awarded:** 1. **To Apply:** Applicants must submit an online application form. **Deadline:** August 1. **Remarks:** This scholarship is named in honor of Dr. Robert Norman Shaw, a pioneer in the Sexsmith area. **Contact:** Alberta Student Aid, PO Box 28000 Station Main, Edmonton, AB T5J 4R4; Toll-free: 855-606-2096.

311 ■ Alberta Teachers' Association (ATA)
11010 142 Street NW
Edmonton, AB, Canada T5N 2R1
Ph: (780)447-9400
Fax: (780)455-6481
Free: 800-232-7208
E-mail: postmaster@ata.ab.ca
URL: www.teachers.ab.ca
Social Media: www.facebook.com/ABteachers
www.instagram.com/abteachers
twitter.com/albertateachers
www.youtube.com/user/albertateachers

312 ■ Alberta Teachers Association Doctoral Fellowships in Education (Doctorate/Fellowship)

Purpose: To recognize academic excellence and to help defray the financial costs of university study. **Focus:** Education. **Qualif.:** Applicants must hold a permanent Alberta teaching certificate and have at least five years of successful teaching; must be at the highest level of membership (associate, if applicants are not qualified for active membership); must be entering or enrolled first year of full-time study in a doctoral program in education at an accredited or recognized Alberta public university; must have plan to

Awards are arranged alphabetically below their administering organizations

continue a career in Alberta; not have received a previous award; and be members in good standing. **Criteria:** Recipients will be selected based on academic standing, contribution to the association and commitment to public and excellence in teaching.

Funds Avail.: $15,000 each. **Duration:** Annual. **Number Awarded:** 2. **To Apply:** Applicant must submit all necessary documentation. The specific documentation required for each award is detailed at the end of the application form. **Deadline:** February 28. **Contact:** The Scholarship Subcommittee, The Alberta Teachers' Association, 11010 142 St. NW, Edmonton, AB, T5N 2R1, Tracey McFeeters, Administrative Officer, Scholarship Subcommittee, Phone: 780-447-9466; Toll free: 800-232-7208; E-mail: tracey.mcfeeters@ata.ab.ca.

313 ■ Alberta Teachers Association Educational Research Award (Other/Scholarship)

Purpose: To support academic research in Alberta's universities to improve teaching and learning. **Focus:** Education. **Qualif.:** Applicants must be faculty of education members or seasonal lecturers at an Alberta university who have undertaken quality research on classroom teaching and learning. **Criteria:** To qualify for an award, the research must meet the following categories: 1) be directly related to school and classroom practice; 2) be focused on school teaching and/or learning; 3) research must be current, ongoing or completed within the last two years; 4) be related to critical issues; 5) have involved classroom teachers and/or students; 6) be applicable to the Alberta context; 7) have practical benefits to teachers; and 8) have high quality in terms of purpose, methodology and originality.

Funds Avail.: $5,000. **Duration:** Annual. **To Apply:** Applicants must fill-out the application form and attach a detailed description of the research. **Deadline:** May 15. **Contact:** The Alberta Teachers' Association, 11010 142 St. NW, Edmonton, AB, T5N 2R1; E-mail: lindsay.yakimyshyn@ata.ab.ca; For Further information Dr Philip McRae; Phone: 780-447-9462; Toll Free: 800-232-7208; E-mail: philip.mcrae@ata.ab.caphilip.mcrae@ata.ab.ca.

314 ■ John Mazurek Memorial-Morgex Insurance Scholarship (Other/Scholarship)

Purpose: To help students pursue their professional development in the field of business education and/or the use of computer technology in education from a Canadian public institution. **Focus:** Computer and information sciences; Nursing. **Qualif.:** Applicants must be hold a permanent Alberta teaching certificate and have completed at least five years of successful teaching in Alberta; at the time of application, be at the highest level of membership possible (active, if the applicant is eligible for active membership, or associate, if the applicant does not qualify for active membership) and have been at the highest possible level of membership for at least five years; the area of study must focus on business education and/or the use of computer technology in education; must be an association member in good standing. **Criteria:** Selection is based upon applicability of the area of study to business education and/or the use of computer technology in education; contribution to the Association; contribution to public education, and; exemplary teaching practice in the K-12 public education system in Alberta.

Funds Avail.: $2,500. **Duration:** Annual. **To Apply:** Applicant must submit all necessary documentation. The specific documentation required for each award is detailed at the end of the application form. **Deadline:** February 28.

Remarks: The scholarship is sponsored by Morgex Insurance. **Contact:** The Scholarship Subcommittee, The Alberta Teachers' Association, 11010 142 St. NW, Edmonton, AB, T5N 2R1, Tracey McFeeters, Administrative Officer, Scholarship Subcommittee, Phone: 780-447-9466; Toll free: 800-232-7208; E-mail: tracey.mcfeeters@ata.ab.ca.

315 ■ Nadene M Thomas Graduate Research Bursary (Graduate/Scholarship)

Purpose: To financially assist graduate students of Canadian university conducting research on health issues. **Focus:** Education. **Qualif.:** Applicants must hold a permanent Alberta teaching certificate; have completed at least five years of successful teaching in Alberta; must be the highest level of membership (associate, if applicants are not qualified for active membership); must intend to continue a career in education; must be registered graduate students in an education degree program at a recognized Canadian university; must conduct research focusing on health issues affecting teacher's working conditions; must not be previous awardees; and must be members in good standing. **Criteria:** Recipients will be selected based on the following categories: 1) applicant's academic standing; 2) contributions to the association and commitment to the public; 3) excellence in teaching; and 4) applicability of the research on health issues affecting teacher's working condition.

Funds Avail.: $5,000. **Duration:** Annual. **To Apply:** Applicant must submit all necessary documentation. The specific documentation required for each award is detailed at the end of the application form. **Deadline:** February 28. **Contact:** The Scholarship Subcommittee, The Alberta Teachers' Association, 11010 142 St. NW, Edmonton, AB, T5N 2R1, Tracey McFeeters, Administrative Officer, Scholarship Subcommittee, Phone: 780-447-9466; Toll free: 800-232-7208; E-mail: tracey.mcfeeters@ata.ab.ca.

316 ■ Albuquerque Community Foundation (ACF)

624 Tijeras Ave. NW
Albuquerque, NM 87102
Ph: (505)883-6240
Fax: (505)883-3629
URL: www.albuquerquefoundation.org
Social Media: www.facebook.com/ABQFoundation
www.instagram.com/abqfoundation
www.linkedin.com/company/albuquerque-community
 -foundation
twitter.com/abqfoundation
www.youtube.com/channel/UCbL3YTXuudviJgxQkKyn7ig

317 ■ Notah Begay III Scholarship Program (Undergraduate/Scholarship)

Purpose: To provide financial assistance to Native American athletes attending college. **Focus:** General studies/Field of study not specified. **Qualif.:** Applicants must be Native American scholar athletes having a minimum GPA 3.0; and attending a community college, four-year college or university on a full time basis.

Funds Avail.: Up to $1,300. **Duration:** Annual. **Number Awarded:** One to Three. **To Apply:** Applicants must submit the following: copy of FAFSA, Student Aid Report or statement of financial aid; proof of tribal enrollment or Certificate of Indian Blood (minimum 25%); one reference from a cur-

Awards are arranged alphabetically below their administering organizations

rent academic teacher or counselor; one reference from an athletic coach. **Remarks:** Established in 1999. **Contact:** Denise Nava, Scholarship Coordinator; Email: denise@ abqcf.org; Phone: 505-883-6240.

318 ■ Bryan Cline Memorial Soccer Scholarship Program *(Undergraduate/Scholarship)*

Purpose: To support the education of graduating senior varsity soccer players. **Focus:** General studies/Field of study not specified. **Qualif.:** Applicants must be graduating senior students from Eldorado High School (EHS) who will attend a college or university full-time.

Funds Avail.: $800 each. **Duration:** Annual. **Number Awarded:** 2 (1 male; 1 female). **To Apply:** Applicants must submit a completed application form including the name of your varsity soccer team coach; two letters of reference (one from a teacher or counselor and one from a soccer coach).

319 ■ Excel Staffing Companies Scholarships for Excellence in Continuing Education *(Undergraduate/Scholarship)*

Purpose: To assist individuals who demonstrate a commitment towards reaching a career goal. **Focus:** General studies/Field of study not specified. **Qualif.:** Applicants must: be individuals who are employed full time while attending school part time; be residents of Albuquerque; have a minimum of 3.0 GPA; and, be working with a minimum of 30 hours per week. **Criteria:** Selection shall be based on the aforementioned qualifications and compliance with the application details.

Funds Avail.: $1,000 each. **Duration:** Annual. **Number Awarded:** Varies. **To Apply:** Applicants must submit a completed application form along with a resume including employment, community service, and awards or honors (maximum 4 pages); statement outlining career goals in relation to academic pursuits and financial need (grammar, spelling and punctuation do count); current/most recent transcript verifying minimum 3.0 cumulative GPA; letter from employer verifying employment of at least 30 hours per week; and letter of reference verifying community service and/or volunteer commitment (optional). Attached (sealed) or sent under separate cover: up to two letters of reference from a current or recent instructor or counselor (1-page, 1-side).

320 ■ New Mexico Manufactured Housing Association Scholarship Fund *(Undergraduate/Scholarship)*

Purpose: To provide scholarship awards to New Mexico graduating high school seniors residing in a manufactured home. **Focus:** General studies/Field of study not specified. **Qualif.:** Applicants must: live in a mobile or manufactured home; have earned a minimum GPA 3.0; and, attend a 2 or 4 year nonprofit or public educational institution or university full time.

Funds Avail.: $1,000 each. **Duration:** Annual. **Number Awarded:** One or Two. **To Apply:** Applicants must submit the following: written statement of financial need; proof of residency in a mobile or manufactured home: a copy of title or rental agreement or retail installment contract or county tax assessment; one reference from a teacher or counselor (1 page, 1 side only). **Remarks:** Established in 1996.

321 ■ Robby Baker Memorial Scholarship *(Graduate/Scholarship)*

Purpose: To provide financial support to those deserving students who are coping with dyslexia. **Focus:** General

studies/Field of study not specified. **Qualif.:** Applicants must: be La Cueva High School graduating senior students who are coping with dyslexia or other reading disability; have earned a minimum of 2.0 GPA; must be enrolled as full time students in an accredited college or university.

Funds Avail.: $850. **Duration:** Annual. **Number Awarded:** 1. **To Apply:** Applicants must submit a completed application form and two references from teachers or counselors. **Remarks:** Established in 2003.

322 ■ Barnes W. Rose, Jr. and Eva Rose Nichol Scholarship Fund *(Graduate/Scholarship)*

Purpose: To provide AHS senior pursuing a bachelor's degree in one of the STEM majors: Science, Technology, Engineering, Mathematics. **Focus:** Engineering. **Qualif.:** Applicants should demonstrate math or science interest and skill through SAT or ACF scores or strong grades in appropriate high school classes. have a minimum of 3.6 GPA; demonstrate financial need; and attend a college or university in pursuit of an engineering degree.

Funds Avail.: Upto $700. **Duration:** Annual. **Number Awarded:** 1. **To Apply:** Applicants must submit a completed application form and a minimum of one reference from an Albuquerque High School Math or Science teacher; up to two additional references programs may be submitted.

323 ■ Sussman-Miller Educational Assistance Award Program *(Undergraduate/Scholarship)*

Purpose: To provide financial assistance to students to further their education in an undergraduate program. **Focus:** General studies/Field of study not specified. **Qualif.:** Applicants must be: Attend a public or nonprofit college or university full-time. Graduating high school senior OR currently enrolled in college/university. Available statewide. MUST BE a federal financial aid recipient. Beginning Fall 2014, the Legislative Lottery Scholarship requirement includes the new minimum for number of credit hours - 15 NEW credit hours and repeating classes do not count. Preference will be given to applicants with a lower EFC (Estistamted Family Contribution).**Criteria:** Selection will be based on committee's criteria.

Funds Avail.: Between $500 and $2,000. **Duration:** Annual. **To Apply:** Applicants must fill out appropriate financial aid application and supply the required documents; signatures on application must be completed.

324 ■ Woodcock Family Education Scholarship Program *(Undergraduate/Scholarship)*

Purpose: To support students of exceptional promise in the fields of science and math. **Focus:** Mathematics and mathematical sciences; Science. **Qualif.:** Applicants must: be Albuquerque graduating high school seniors; with strong math or science credentials; attend a college or university full time; and, have a minimum GPA of 3.8 or minimum ACT composite score of 30 or minimum Math SAT of 680.

Funds Avail.: $10,000 each. **Duration:** Annual; up to 4 years. **Number Awarded:** Two to Three. **To Apply:** Applicants must attach these to their application packet: career goals in personal statement must include those in the field of math or science; one reference from a math or science teacher; one or more references from other teachers, internship or work programs, or community services. **Remarks:** Established in 1993.

325 ■ Alden Kindred of America (AKA)
105 Alden St.
Duxbury, MA 02332

Awards are arranged alphabetically below their administering organizations

Ph: (781)934-9092
E-mail: info@alden.org
URL: www.alden.org
Social Media: www.facebook.com/aldenhousehistoricsite

326 ■ Donnell B. Young Scholarships
(Undergraduate/Scholarship)

Purpose: To provide educational assistance to incoming college students. **Focus:** General studies/Field of study not specified. **Qualif.:** Applicants must be members of the Alden Kindred of America, Inc.; must be graduating high school students who are lineage members of the Alden Kindred of America, Inc. **Criteria:** Recipient will be selected based on the submitted research paper.

Funds Avail.: No specific amount. **Number Awarded:** 1. **To Apply:** Applicants must submit their high school transcripts (mailed directly by their school); a typewritten research paper of 750-1000 words is a strict requirement; the topic must be extracted from the Early American Period (1620-1750); the preface of the research paper should contain a short paragraph about the reason of the application for the scholarship; footnotes and bibliography of references should be included; volunteer work and personal information including hobbies and interests must also be provided; all application forms must have two references (one personal and one from the school). **Deadline:** March 1.

327 ■ Aleut Foundation
703 W Tudor Rd., Ste. 102
Anchorage, AK 99503-6650
Ph: (907)646-1929
Fax: (907)646-1949
Free: 800-232-4882
E-mail: taf@thealeutfoundation.org
URL: www.thealeutfoundation.org
Social Media: facebook.com/AleutFoundation

328 ■ Andrew Gronholdt Arts Scholarship
(Undergraduate, Vocational/Occupational, Graduate, Master's/Scholarship)

Purpose: To help students pursue their education in the Arts field. **Focus:** Arts. **Qualif.:** Applicants must be two-year/vocational, undergraduate, graduate or master's degree students; must have at least 3.0 GPA and must be full-time majoring in the Arts field.

Funds Avail.: No specific amount. **To Apply:** Applicants must complete the application form; must submit a letter of acceptance, two letters of recommendation, personal statement, birth certificate, class schedule and an official transcript.

329 ■ Gabe Stepetin Business Scholarship
(Undergraduate, Vocational/Occupational, Graduate, Master's/Scholarship)

Purpose: To provide financial assistance to students interested in pursuing a business field. **Focus:** Business. **Qualif.:** Applicants must be two-year/vocational, undergraduate, graduate and master's degree students; must have at least 3.0 GPA; must be enrolled full-time majoring in the business field.

Funds Avail.: No specific amount. **To Apply:** Applicants must complete an application form; must submit a letter of acceptance, two letters of recommendation, personal state-

ment, birth certificate, class schedule and an official transcript.

330 ■ Lillie Hope-McGarvey Health Scholarship
(Undergraduate, Vocational/Occupational, Graduate, Master's/Scholarship)

Purpose: To provide financial assistance to students majoring in healthcare. **Focus:** Health care services; Medicine. **Qualif.:** Applicants must be enrolled in a two-year/vocational, undergraduate, graduate or master's degree healthcare program; must maintain at least 3.0 GPA.

Funds Avail.: No specific amount. **To Apply:** Applicants must complete the application form; must submit an official transcript, letter of acceptance, two letters of recommendation, personal statement, birth certificate, class schedule and an official transcript.

331 ■ Alexander Graham Bell Association for the Deaf and Hard of Hearing (AG Bell)
3417 Volta Pl. NW
Washington, DC 20007
Ph: (202)337-5220
Fax: (202)337-8314
E-mail: info@agbell.org
URL: www.agbell.org
Social Media: www.facebook.com/AGBellAssociation
instagram.com/agbellassociation
linkedin.com/company/ag-bell-association-for-the-deaf-and
-hard-of-hearing
twitter.com/AGBellAssoc

332 ■ A.G. Bell College Scholarship Program
(Undergraduate, Graduate/Scholarship, Award)

Purpose: To support students diagnosed with a moderate to profound hearing loss prior to learning, listening and talking and who are seeking to continue their undergraduate or graduate level education in any field of study. **Focus:** Hearing and deafness. **Qualif.:** Applicants must be enrolled in or planning to attend a mainstream university and working toward a four-year undergraduate degree or a graduate degree. **Criteria:** Award will be given to applicant hearing loss must be bilateral and in the moderate to profound range; Spoken communication must be the student's primary mode of communication.

Duration: Annual. **To Apply:** Application details available on sponsor's website. **Contact:** Email: scholarships@agbell.org.

333 ■ A.G. Bell School Age Financial Aid Program
(High School/Scholarship, Monetary)

Purpose: To help students with their educational costs such as tuition, room and board, books, equipment, auditory and speech-language support services, academic tutoring, transportation, and other school-related expenses. **Focus:** General studies/Field of study not specified; Hearing and deafness. **Qualif.:** Applicants eligibility includes: bilateral hearing loss or Auditory Neuropathy (AN) must have been diagnosed before the children's fourth birthday; children's hearing loss must be in the moderate to profound range; primary mode of communication is Listening and Spoken Language; enrolled or registered as full-time students for the school year beginning in the fall of the given year between grades one and twelve in a mainstream parochial, independent or private elementary or secondary

Awards are arranged alphabetically below their administering organizations

school; and, residents of United States (including territories) or Canada. **Criteria:** Selection shall be based on the premises that the applicants are students with hearing loss who use listening and spoken language and who are in first through twelfth grades and attending a parochial, private or independent (not public) mainstream school.

Funds Avail.: $800-$1,500. **Duration:** Annual. **To Apply:** Application can be completed online as a writable pdf. **Deadline:** April 19. **Contact:** Email: financialaid@agbell.org.

334 ■ George H. Nofer Scholarship for Law and Public Policy *(Graduate/Scholarship, Monetary)*

Purpose: To support students with hearing impairments thrive in an educational setting. **Focus:** Law; Public administration. **Qualif.:** Applicants must be full-time graduate students with a pre-lingual bilateral hearing loss in the moderately-severe to profound range, use listening and spoken language as their primary method of communication, and who are attending an accredited mainstream law school or a masters or doctoral program in public policy or public administration. **Criteria:** Selection shall be based on the premises that the applicants are students with hearing loss who use listening and spoken language.

Funds Avail.: $5,000 each. **Duration:** Annual. **Number Awarded:** Up to 3. **To Apply:** Applicant Submit all pages of the application and supporting documentation on 8½" x 11" paper (or international equivalent); the application and all attachments must be in English; all pages should be single-sided; no part of the application materials should contain a staple; the application should be submitted flat, NOT folded (previously folded materials are acceptable) in a 9"x 12" or larger envelope, held together with one paper clip, and in the following order: Application, with pages in numbered order; every page of the application must be completed and the application must be signed; for applicants who use hearing aids, an unaided Audiogram performed within the last 24 months; for applicants with cochlear implants, a cochlear implant programming report performed within the last 24 months; verification of the student's application to, acceptance or enrollment in the law school or a graduate program of a mainstream and accredited university or college (a readable photocopy of a letter, tuition notice, or other correspondence confirming enrollment or acceptance is acceptable); rising graduate students—include official transcripts for all undergraduate college semesters completed. First and second year graduate students—include official transcripts of all graduate semesters completed; applicant Essay, as indicated in the application (maximum of two single-sided pages); three letters of recommendation from three different individuals; letters must be no longer than two single-sided pages, and should be provided in a sealed envelope; at least one letter must be from one of the applicant's professors in an academic or studio subject. All three letters may be from teachers/professors or two letters may be from other individuals such as a coach, extracurricular activity sponsor, hearing health professional, employer, etc. **Deadline:** April 10. **Remarks:** Established to recognize George H. Nofer's service and generosity to the Alexander Graham Bell Association for the Deaf and Hard of Hearing (A.G. Bell) and to the fields of law and deafness research and education. **Contact:** Email: scholarships@agbell.org.

335 ■ Alex's Lemonade Stand Foundation (ALSF)
Bala Pointe, 111 Presidential Blvd., Ste. 203
Bala Cynwyd, PA 19004

Ph: (610)649-3034
Fax: (610)649-3038
Free: 866-333-1213
URL: www.alexslemonade.org
Social Media: www.facebook.com/alexslemonade
www.instagram.com/alexslemonade
www.linkedin.com/company/alexs-lemonade-stand
 -foundation
www.pinterest.com/alexslemonade
twitter.com/alexslemonade
www.youtube.com/alexslemonade

336 ■ Alex's Lemonade Stand Foundation Epidemiology Grants *(Doctorate, Master's, Professional development/Grant)*

Purpose: To support research of investigators who have a specific focus on the epidemiology, early detection or the prevention of childhood cancer. **Focus:** Epidemiology; Oncology. **Qualif.:** Applicants should be at the Assistant, Associate or Full Professor level; may be M.D., M.D./Ph.D. or Ph.D; must have a history of formal training in disciplines that are relevant to the proposed research or a track record of conducting similar epidemiological or cancer research, including peer-reviewed publicationsand funding, that demonstrates the project can be accomplished by the investigator. **Criteria:** Selection will be based on the ALSF's Scientific Advisory Board.

Funds Avail.: $100,000 per year. **Duration:** Annual; two years. **To Apply:** Applicants must first complete the online form then upload the application in one PDF; scientific abstract, impact Statement, budget justification; biographical sketch; research strategy, significance, innovation, approach.

337 ■ Alex's Lemonade Stand Foundation Innovation Grants *(Other/Grant)*

Purpose: To provide critical and significant seed funding for experienced investigators with a novel and promising approach to finding causes and cures for childhood cancers. **Focus:** Oncology. **Qualif.:** Applicants must be experienced investigators with a novel and promising approach in finding causes and cures for childhood cancers. **Criteria:** Applications will be reviewed by an independent panel of experts according to the NIH recognized peer-review process and overseen by ALSF's Scientific Advisory Board.

Funds Avail.: Up to $125,000. **Duration:** Annual; two years. **To Apply:** Applicants must submit an approved letter of intent before the application will be submitted; all requests must be submitted using ALSF's online application process; can request a password or sign in by going to the guidelines and submission page; upload application as a single PDF document that is not more than 10 MB.

338 ■ Alex's Lemonade Stand Foundation Young Investigator Grants *(Doctorate, Master's, Professional development/Grant)*

Purpose: To eradicate childhood cancer through basic research, career development and helping to streamline translational clinical research. **Focus:** Oncology. **Qualif.:** Applicants should be at the early stages of their research careers as defined below; those who have their M.D., Ph.D. or dual M.D., Ph.D. but have not achieved an appointment higher than Instructor from accredited clinical fellowship programs are automatically eligible for the duration of their

Awards are arranged alphabetically below their administering organizations

training and during their first three years at the Instructor level; must be within five years from the granting of the last doctoral degree; minimum of 75% of the time during the young investigator period must be allocated as protected time for all research activities; this percentage of time includes both young investigator activities and the other research responsibilities; must not currently hold an NIH independent (R or P Award) or individual training (F or K Award) grant; institutional training grants (K12, T32) are permitted; funding from other foundations is also permitted provided there is no budgetary overlap; research mentor(s) must be identified and have a track record in pediatric oncology; if no such record exists, a co-mentor with such a record must be identified; must document mentors involvement in experimental design and execution. **Criteria:** Applications will be reviewed by an independent panel of experts using the NIH recognized peer-review process and overseen by ALSF's Scientific Advisory Board.

Funds Avail.: $50,000. **Duration:** Annual; three years. **To Apply:** Applicants must submit Application Cover Page; scientific abstract; budget or justification; biographical Sketch; mentoring plan; mentor letter of recommendation; the second and third years of funding are contingent upon a non-competitive review of annual progress reports that must demonstrate satisfactory progress toward completion of proposed research objectives and appropriate budget expenditures. **Deadline:** December 16. **Contact:** Alex's Lemonade Stand Foundation. 111 Presidential Boulevard, Suite 203, Bala Cynwyd, PA 19004. Ph. (610) 649-3034 or (866) 333-1213. Fax (610) 649-3038. E-mail: grants@ alexslemonade.com.

339 ■ AlgaeCal
300 - 22 E 5th Ave.
Vancouver, BC, Canada V6B 1C6
Ph: (510)564-7192
Fax: (855)211-7699
Free: 800-820-0184
E-mail: support@algaecal.com
URL: www.algaecal.com
Social Media: www.facebook.com/algaecal
www.instagram.com/algaecal
www.pinterest.com/algaecal
twitter.com/algaecal
www.youtube.com/user/algaecalcalcium

340 ■ AlgaeCal Health Scholarship *(Undergraduate, Graduate, Vocational/Occupational/Scholarship)*

Purpose: To financially support students in pursuit of higher education and also raise awareness for the critical issues of health and well being in our society. **Focus:** General studies/Field of study not specified. **Qualif.:** Applicants must be enrolled in a post-secondary institute for the upcoming semester in the United States or Canada; must have a minimum 3.0 GPA. **Criteria:** Selection is based on how well the applicant addresses the essay topic, strength of the idea, quality of the research, and the quality of the writing.

Funds Avail.: $1,000. **Duration:** Annual. **Number Awarded:** 1. **To Apply:** Submit an essay of up to 750 words. Topic and application available online. **Deadline:** June 30. **Contact:** Email: scholarships@algaecal.com; URL: www.algaecal.com/expert-insights/algaecal-scholarships/.

341 ■ All Smiles Dental Group
3715 Bloomington St, Ste 160
Colorado Springs, CO 80922
Ph: (719)599-0665
E-mail: allsmiles@allsmilesdentalgroup.com
URL: allsmilesdentalgroup.com
Social Media: www.facebook.com/AllSmilesDentalGroup

342 ■ All Smiles Dental Group Scholarship *(Undergraduate/Scholarship)*

Purpose: To provide an opportunity for students in the sponsor's area. **Focus:** General studies/Field of study not specified.

Funds Avail.: $2,000. **Contact:** allsmilesdentalgroup.com/winner-of-the-all-smiles-scholarship/.

343 ■ All Star Association
3121 Wall St.
Lexington, KY 40513
Free: 800-930-3644
E-mail: info@allstarpurchasing.com
URL: allstarassociation.com
Social Media: www.linkedin.com/company/all-star-association

344 ■ All Star Purchasing *(Undergraduate/Scholarship)*

Purpose: To financially support those students who are continuing their studies. **Focus:** Food science and technology. **Qualif.:** Applicants must be undergraduate degree in food science or a related field. **Criteria:** Applicants will be selected based on their academic performance, courses related to food science, apparent commitment to a career in dairy,beverage,food industry; involvement in extracurricular activities, and by the evidence of leadership ability, initiative, character and integrity.

Funds Avail.: Maximum of $15,000. **Duration:** Annual. **Number Awarded:** Up to 5. **To Apply:** Applicants must complete and print the application form; must have the official transcript from all high schools, colleges and universities attended; must submit a request letter of recommendation from a faculty member familiar with the applicant's scholastic performance; must have a recent photograph; must complete and submit the application form and other supporting documents on or before the deadline. **Deadline:** May 1. **Remarks:** The Scholarship was established in honor John D. Utterback and Henry Randolph. **Contact:** Email: susan@allstarpurchasing.com.

345 ■ Allegheny County Bar Foundation (ACBF)
400 Koppers Bldg.
Pittsburgh, PA 15219
Ph: (412)402-6641
Fax: (412)261-3622
E-mail: staff@acba.org
URL: www.acbf.org
Social Media: www.facebook.com/alleghenycountybar
twitter.com/AlleghenyCoBar

346 ■ Daniel B. Dixon Scholarship Fund *(Undergraduate/Scholarship)*

Purpose: To support a law student attending the University of Pittsburgh School of Law. **Focus:** Law. **Qualif.:** Ap-

Awards are arranged alphabetically below their administering organizations

plicants must be law students attending the University of Pittsburgh School of Law who have completed their first or second year and who have demonstrated an interest in real estate law. **Criteria:** Selection is based on academic excellence and financial need.

Funds Avail.: $1,000. **Duration:** Annual. **Number Awarded:** 1. **To Apply:** Applicants must submit a letter of recommendation from the Dean or appropriate faculty of the University of Pittsburgh School of Law; attach an essay limited to 500 words expressing your interest in real estate law. **Deadline:** June 11. **Remarks:** The Scholarship Fund was established in honor of Daniel B. Dixon who worked as an attorney in the real estate field. Established in 2007. **Contact:** Kimberly Cramer, Esq., Programs & Projects Manager; Allegheny County Bar Foundation, 400 Koppers Bldg., 436 7th Ave., Pittsburgh, PA, 15219; Phone: 412-402-6641; Fax: 412-261-3622; Email: kcramer@acba.org.

347 ■ F.C. Grote Fund *(Graduate, Undergraduate/ Scholarship)*

Purpose: To support the education of a student at the University of Pittsburgh School of Law and the University of Pennsylvania Law School. **Focus:** Law. **Qualif.:** Applicants must be students at the University of Pittsburgh School of Law or the University of Pennsylvania Law School.

Funds Avail.: $5,000. **Duration:** Annual. **To Apply:** Applicants must submit a completed application form. **Deadline:** May 15. **Contact:** Lorrie Albert; Phone: 412-402-6640; Email: lalbert@acba.org.

348 ■ Kennedy T. Friend Scholarship Fund *(Graduate, Undergraduate/Scholarship)*

Purpose: To provide support to the children of the Bar of Allegheny County in pursuing their educational goals. **Focus:** General studies/Field of study not specified. **Qualif.:** Applicants must be "member of the Bar of Allegheny County", and enrolled at Yale University in New Haven, Connecticut or at the University of Paris in France.

Funds Avail.: Varies. **Duration:** Annual. **To Apply:** Applicant should submit applications for the scholarships at the same time as the admission application is made to Yale University or the University of Paris. **Remarks:** The Scholarship Fund was established by the will of Kennedy T. Friend, a distinguished member of the Bar of Allegheny County. **Contact:** Joan S. Mastrean, Fiduciary Advisor; PNC Bank, National Association, 116 Allegheny Ctr. P8-YB35-02-Z, Pittsburgh, PA 15212; Phone: 412-762-2175.

349 ■ Honorable Carol Los Mansmann Memorial Fund *(Graduate, Undergraduate/Scholarship)*

Purpose: To support an outstanding female law student attending Duquesne University School of Law. **Focus:** Law. **Qualif.:** Applicant must be female law students attending Duquesne University School of Law who demonstrates a potential for leadership and a commitment to the advancement of women; must be enrolled in the School of Law; must have completed first year of the day division or second year of the evening or part-time day division; must be ranked in the top half of the class. **Criteria:** Selection is based on a combination of academic achievement, involvement in extracurricular and other activities, financial need and an essay.

Funds Avail.: $3,000. **Duration:** Annual. **To Apply:** Applicants must submit a completed application including transcripts and proof of class rank (most recent grade reports). **Deadline:** May 15. **Remarks:** The Scholarship

Fund was established in honor of Carol Los Mansmann by her family, friends, fellow lawyers, and the Women in the Law Committee of the Allegheny County Bar Association. **Contact:** Kimberly Cramer, Esq., Programs & Projects Manager; Allegheny County Bar Foundation, 400 Koppers Bldg., 436 7th Ave., Pittsburgh, PA, 15219; Phone: 412-402-6641; Fax: 412-261-3622; Email: kcramer@acba.org.

350 ■ The Honorable Joseph H. Ridge Memorial Scholarship Fund *(Undergraduate/Scholarship)*

Purpose: To support the education of a student at Duquesne Law School. **Focus:** Law. **Qualif.:** Applicants must be students of Duquesne Law School and must also be graduates of Central Catholic High School. **Criteria:** The Scholarship will be awarded to the highest ranking member of the graduating class at Duquesne Law School.

Funds Avail.: No specific amount. **To Apply:** Applicants must submit a letter stating interest in the scholarship; proof of graduation from Central Catholic High School; and Duquesne Law School transcript and class rank. **Remarks:** The Scholarship Fund was established in honor of Joseph H. Ridge. **Contact:** Kimberly Cramer, Esq., Programs & Projects Manager; Allegheny County Bar Foundation, 400 Koppers Bldg., 436 7th Ave., Pittsburgh, PA, 15219; Phone: 412-402-6641; Fax: 412-261-3622; Email: kcramer@ acba.org.

351 ■ James I. Smith, III Notre Dame Law School Scholarship Fund *(Graduate, Undergraduate/ Scholarship)*

Purpose: To provide scholarships to law students from Allegheny County enrolled at Notre Dame Law School. **Focus:** Law. **Qualif.:** Applicants must be Allegheny County students enrolled at Notre Dame Law School.

Funds Avail.: No specific amount. **To Apply:** Applicants must submit completed applications and include an estimated budget; must be signed by an authorized representative of the law school. **Deadline:** April 10. **Remarks:** The Scholarship Fund was established in honor of retirement of James I. Smith, and in tribute to his 38 years of devoted service to the lawyers of Allegheny County and the legal profession. Established in 2001. **Contact:** Richele Ward, Programs & Projects Manager; Allegheny County Bar Foundation, 400 Koppers Bldg., 436 7th Ave., Pittsburgh, PA, 15219; Phone: 412-402-6641; Fax: 412-261-3622; Email: rward@acba.org.

352 ■ Allen, Flatt, Balladis & Leslie Inc.
4400 MacArthur Blvd., Ste. 370
Newport Beach, CA 92660
Ph: (949)354-6882
Free: 888-329-9023
E-mail: contactus@allenflatt.com
URL: www.allenflatt.com
Social Media: www.facebook.com/allenflattballidisleslie3
www.linkedin.com/company/allen-flatt-ballidis-&-leslie
twitter.com/afbl4400
www.youtube.com/channel/UCmKSBDAe
 -dgF3cUOThBHO2g

353 ■ Rise to Shine Scholarship *(Undergraduate/ Scholarship)*

Purpose: To provide financial assistance to college students. **Focus:** General studies/Field of study not specified. **Qualif.:** Applicant must be a high school senior on

Awards are arranged alphabetically below their administering organizations

track to graduate and attend college, or a college student enrolled in an accredited four-year university or college, or a student currently enrolled in a two-year college and planning to transfer to a four-year college or university upon completion; have maintained a 3.0 or higher GPA; and be a U.S. citizen or permanent resident (DACA recipients are welcome to apply).

Funds Avail.: $1,000. **Duration:** Annual. **Number Awarded:** 1. **To Apply:** Application and essay must be submitted online. **Deadline:** May 12. **Contact:** Email: ballidisleslie@gmail.com.

354 ■ Allen Law Firm
2511 Garden Rd., Ste. A-225
Monterey, CA 93940
Ph: (831)901-3901
URL: www.sjallenlaw.com
Social Media: www.facebook.com/TheAllenLawFirm
twitter.com/sjallenlaw

355 ■ Allen Law Firm Personal Injury Scholarship
(College, Undergraduate/Scholarship)

Purpose: To help students who have suffered a personal injury or disability. **Focus:** General studies/Field of study not specified. **Qualif.:** Applicant must be enrolled in college/university or a graduating high school senior attending college in the awarding year; must be a U.S. citizen; and must be attending college or university in the United States. **Criteria:** Selection will be based on the essay and other relevant criteria.

Duration: Annual. **Number Awarded:** 1. **To Apply:** Applicant must write a 300-word essay on one of the following topics: Have you suffered a serious injury? or Do you suffer a disability? Essay details and application can be found at www.sjallenlaw.com/scholarship-contest/. **Deadline:** June 15. **Contact:** Email: scott@sjallenlaw.com.

356 ■ Alliance of the American Dental Association (AADA)
PO Box 1982
Brandon, FL 33509
Ph: (813)540-2154
Fax: (813)315-7132
E-mail: info@allianceada.org
URL: allianceada.net
Social Media: www.facebook.com/AllianceADA
twitter.com/AllianceADA

357 ■ AADA Student Spouse Scholarship *(Professional development/Scholarship)*

Purpose: To prepare the recipients for further involvement in dental health education, legislative activities and leadership positions as they continue their membership in the Alliance. **Focus:** Dentistry. **Qualif.:** Applicant must be a student spouse member of AADA; must be willing to use the skills and knowledge they acquire during Conference in continued service to the Alliance.

Funds Avail.: $700. **Duration:** Annual. **To Apply:** Applicants must submit personal statement; no more than one typed page, tell us "Why you want to attend this conference?", "How you hope to benefit from attending and how your attendance will support the Alliance?"; summary of Alliance volunteer experience at the local, state, and/or national level, including positions held; list any financial assistance received from local or state alliance. **Deadline:** February 1. **Contact:** Alliance of the ADA, PO Box 1982, Brandon, FL, 33509; Phone: 813-540-2154; Fax: 813-315-7132; E-mail: allianceoftheada@gmail.com.

358 ■ Alliance Defending Freedom (ADF)
15100 N 90th St.
Scottsdale, AZ 85260-2769
Ph: (480)444-0020
Fax: (480)444-0025
Free: 800-835-5233
URL: www.adflegal.org
Social Media: www.facebook.com/AllianceDefendingFreedom
twitter.com/alliancedefends

359 ■ Alliance Defending Freedom - Blackstone Legal Fellowships *(Undergraduate/Fellowship)*

Purpose: To prepare Christian law students for careers marked by integrity, excellence, and leadership. **Focus:** Law. **Qualif.:** Applicants must be exceptionally capable and highly motivated first year law students (second year law students are also welcome to apply). **Criteria:** Selection is based on demonstrated Christian commitment, motivation to engage in popular legal culture, leadership potential in a legal context, evidence of oral and written communication skills, and academic achievement.

Funds Avail.: No specific amount. **Duration:** Nine weeks. **To Apply:** Applicants must complete the application online. **Contact:** Alliance Defending Freedom, Blackstone Legal Fellowship, 15100 N. 90th St., Scottsdale, AZ 85260; Telephone: 480-444-0020; Facsimile: 480-444-0024; Email: Blackstone@ADFlegal.org.

360 ■ Alliance for Equality of Blind Canadians (AEBC)
RPO Town Ctr.
Kelowna, BC, Canada V1Y 9H2
Free: 800-561-4774
E-mail: info@blindcanadians.ca
URL: www.blindcanadians.ca
Social Media: www.facebook.com/blindcanadians
twitter.com/blindcanadians

361 ■ AEBC Toronto Chapter Scholarships
(Undergraduate/Scholarship)

Purpose: To support outstanding blind, deaf-blind and partially blind Canadian students in their educational pursuits. **Focus:** General studies/Field of study not specified. **Qualif.:** Applicants must: be blind, deaf-blind or partially sighted; be Canadian citizens or landed immigrants; be attending a post-secondary program (college, university or vocational) with a full-time course load or at a 40% course load if accompanied by an explanation; and Ontario residents studying in Ontario. **Criteria:** Selection is based on academic performance, community involvement and overcoming adversity.

Funds Avail.: $1,500. **To Apply:** Applicants must complete the application form online. In addition, applicants must submit a current or most recent average academic grade, calculated in percent; a personal letter; and a reference letter. **Contact:** scholarship@blindcanadians.ca.

Awards are arranged alphabetically below their administering organizations

362 ■ Business, Education and Technology Scholarships *(Graduate, Undergraduate/Scholarship)*

Purpose: To support outstanding blind, deaf-blind and partially blind Canadian students in their educational pursuits. **Focus:** General studies/Field of study not specified. **Qualif.:** Applicants must be blind, deaf-blind or partially sighted; a Canadian citizen or landed immigrant; and attending a post-secondary program (college, university or vocational) with a full-time course load or at a 40% course load if accompanied by an explanation. **Criteria:** Selection is based on academic performance, community involvement and overcoming adversity.

Funds Avail.: No specific amount. **To Apply:** Applicants must complete the application form online. In addition, Applicants must submit a current or most recent average academic grade, calculated in percent; a personal letter; and a reference letter. **Contact:** scholarship@ blindcanadians.ca.

363 ■ Alan H. Neville Memorial Scholarships *(Graduate/Scholarship)*

Purpose: To support outstanding blind, deaf-blind and partially blind Canadian students in their educational pursuits. **Focus:** General studies/Field of study not specified. **Qualif.:** Applicants must: be blind, deaf-blind or partially sighted; be Canadian citizens or landed immigrants; and attending a post-secondary program (college, university or vocational) with a full-time course load or at a 40% course load if accompanied by an explanation. **Criteria:** Selection is based on academic performance, community involvement and overcoming adversity.

Funds Avail.: $1,000. **To Apply:** Applicants must complete the application form online. In addition, applicants must submit a current or most recent average academic grade, calculated in percent; a personal letter; and a reference letter. **Contact:** scholarship@blindcanadians.ca.

364 ■ AEBC Rick Oakes Scholarships for the Arts *(Undergraduate/Scholarship)*

Purpose: To support outstanding blind, deaf-blind and partially blind Canadian students in their educational pursuits. **Focus:** General studies/Field of study not specified. **Qualif.:** Applicants must: be blind, deaf-blind or partially sighted; be Canadian citizens or landed immigrants; be attending a post-secondary program (college, university or vocational) with a full-time course load or at a 40% course load if accompanied by an explanation. **Criteria:** Selection is based on academic performance, community involvement and overcoming adversity.

Funds Avail.: $1,000. **To Apply:** Applicants must complete the application form online. In addition, applicants must submit a current or most recent average academic grade, calculated in percent; a personal letter; and a reference letter. **Contact:** scholarship@blindcanadians.ca.

365 ■ Alliance of Resident Theatres, New York (ART-NY)

520 8th Ave., Ste. 319
New York, NY 10018
Ph: (212)244-6667
E-mail: info@art-newyork.org
URL: www.art-newyork.org

366 ■ Fund for Small Theatres *(Other/Grant)*

Purpose: To support small theatre companies. **Focus:** Theater arts. **Qualif.:** Applicant must be a Full, Associate,

or Independent Producer member of A.R.T./New York in good standing; must have had annual expenses totaling under $100,000; must primarily produce in one of the five boroughs in New York City; must have participated in Organizational Planning.

Funds Avail.: $2,000 - $7,500. **To Apply:** Applicants must submit a completed application form; three page narrative statement; budget. **Deadline:** February 3. **Remarks:** Established in 1998. **Contact:** Phone: 212-244-6667 ext. 241; Email:grants@art-newyork.org.

367 ■ Alliance of Technology and Women (ATW)

909 Lake Carolyn Pkwy., Ste. 320
Irving, TX 75039
Ph: (469)378-4911
E-mail: info@dfwatw.org
URL: www.dfwatw.org
Social Media: www.facebook.com/DFWATW
www.instagram.com/dfw_atw
www.linkedin.com/company/dfw-alliance-of-technology-and
-women

368 ■ GREAT MINDS Collegiate Scholarship Program *(Undergraduate/Scholarship)*

Purpose: To help young girls become more interested in technology. **Focus:** Engineering; Mathematics and mathematical sciences; Science; Technology. **Qualif.:** Applicants must be first-time students or adult learners returning to school to pursue a new career; must be enrolled in an Associate's or Bachelor's Degree program; may have diverse levels of life experience, academic merit, age, race and religion. **Criteria:** Candidates are chosen on the basis of volunteer service, passion for technology, leadership activities, scholastic grades, letters of recommendation and previous awards. Demonstrated passion and spirit is weighted most heavily in the selection process.

Funds Avail.: No specific amount. **To Apply:** Applicants must submit a completed application form.

369 ■ Allied Van Lines Inc.

1 Parkview Plz.
Oakbrook Terrace, IL 60181
Free: 800-689-8684
URL: www.allied.com
Social Media: www.facebook.com/AlliedVanLines
www.linkedin.com/company/allied-moving
twitter.com/alliedvl

370 ■ Allied Van Lines Military Scholarship *(Undergraduate/Scholarship)*

Purpose: To support the education of military members and their relatives. **Focus:** Logistics; Transportation. **Qualif.:** Applicant must be an honorably discharged veteran or current member of the active military (including National Guard and Reserves), or a spouse or child (under the age of 21, or full-time student under the age of 23) of an honorably discharged veteran or current military member; must be a U.S. citizen or permanent resident; and must be enrolled or planning to enroll as a full-time student at an accredited college or university in the United States for completion of an undergraduate degree in logistics or an equivalent field. **Criteria:** Selection will be based on meeting the eligibility requirements as well as the committee's criteria.

Awards are arranged alphabetically below their administering organizations

Funds Avail.: $1,000. **Number Awarded:** 2. **To Apply:** Applicant must submit a 400-800 word essay detailing why they have chosen a career in logistics/supply chain management. Essay should focus on personalized tones, along with firsthand experiences and sentiments, rather than formality. Applicant must also submit a current transcript, verification of college enrollment, and a copy of the DD214 (member 4) or a signed letter from Command certifying active duty status. **Deadline:** December 15. **Contact:** URL: www.allied.com/military-scholarship.

371 ■ Allmand Law
8350 North Central Expressway,Ste 1200.
Dallas, TX 75206
Ph: (214)884-4020
E-mail: questions@allmandlaw.com
URL: www.allmandlaw.com
Social Media: www.facebook.com/allmandlawfirm
twitter.com/allmandlaw

372 ■ Allmand Law Scholarship Contest
(Undergraduate/Scholarship)

Purpose: To provide financial aid to a college student, encourage students to understand how bankruptcy relief helps small businesses, and inspire students to pursue a career in any legal field. **Focus:** Business; Finance; Law; Management. **Qualif.:** Applicant must be a high school senior or college freshman studying or planning to study business, finance, management, or law. **Criteria:** Selection is based on the best video essay.

Funds Avail.: $1,000. **Number Awarded:** 1. **To Apply:** Applicant must record a video (1 to 2 minutes, in English) explaining how bankruptcy laws help small businesses and promote economic growth. Applicant must post the video to their YouTube Channel with the title "Allmand Law Scholarship Contest" and with this link in the description: www.allmandlaw.com/scholarship-for-college-students/. Applicant must also share the video on their Facebook page and the sponsor's Facebook page. Instead of a video, applicant can submit a 1,000 to 1,500 word essay on the same subject and submit via email. **Deadline:** August 15. **Contact:** Reed Allmand; Email: AllmandScholarship@gmail.com.

373 ■ ALOA Security Professionals Association, Inc. (ALOA)
3500 Easy St.
Dallas, TX 75247
Ph: (214)819-9733
Fax: (214)819-9736
Free: 800-532-2562
E-mail: education@aloa.org
URL: www.aloa.org
Social Media: www.facebook.com/ALOA.org/

374 ■ ALOA Scholarship Foundation
(Undergraduate/Scholarship)

Purpose: To support the education of students entering the locksmithing field or already in the locksmithing field. **Focus:** Education, Vocational-technical. **Qualif.:** Applicants must be individuals desirous of entering the locksmithing field or individuals already in the field of locksmithing who wish to improve their professional skills through education. **Criteria:** Selection will be based on their financial needs,

character, aptitude for the skills necessary in locksmithing, desire for a career in locksmithing, availability to attend the event for which award is given, demonstrated commitment to the locksmith industry, letters of recommendation from locksmith industry reference, and previous scholarship awards.

Funds Avail.: No specific amount. **To Apply:** Applicants must complete the application form provided in the website of the foundation and submit it along with the three letters of recommendation at least one must be from locksmith industry; must have enclosed a 3″ x 5″ photograph; must have enclosed a copy of my most recent tax return; applications should be submitted prior to the deadline. **Remarks:** Established in 1993. **Contact:** ALOA Scholarship Foundation, Inc, 3500 Easy St., Dallas, TX 75247;-6416 Phone: 800-532-2562; Fax: 214-819-9736.

375 ■ Alpha Chi
124 W. Capitol Ave., Ste .,1630
Little Rock, AR 72201
Free: 800-477-4225
E-mail: office@alphachihonor.org
URL: www.alphachihonor.org
Social Media: www.facebook.com/alphachihonor
www.instagram.com/axalphachi
twitter.com/axalphachi

376 ■ H. Y. Benedict Fellowships *(Graduate/Fellowship)*

Purpose: To provide financial support to individuals for their first year of graduate study toward the master's, doctorate, or professional degree at any recognized institution. **Focus:** General studies/Field of study not specified. **Qualif.:** Nominees must be enrolled as graduate students with the baccalaureate degree during the school year in which application is made and must identify the graduate or professional school(s) to which they have applied for study the following fall. **Criteria:** Selection will be based on the committee's criteria.

Funds Avail.: $3,000. **Duration:** Annual. **Number Awarded:** 10. **To Apply:** Nominees must submit the official nomination form completed, signed by the sponsor and included with the entry; a letter of application from the student outlining their plans for study and detailing their extracurricular activities, maximum length of two pages, double-spaced; an academic paper or other appropriate work in the students' major field; one letter of recommendation/evaluation from a faculty member in the field represented by the paper or project addressed to the significance of the work; a self-addressed, stamped envelope. **Deadline:** February 15. **Remarks:** The scholarship is given in honor of Dr. Harry Benedict.

377 ■ Edwin W. Gaston Scholarships
(Undergraduate/Scholarship)

Purpose: To provide financial support for the education of senior undergraduate students. **Focus:** General studies/Field of study not specified. **Qualif.:** Nominee must be a senior year undergraduate student. **Criteria:** Nominee must be enrolled for the fall semester as a full-time student in undergraduate study toward the baccalaureate degree.

Funds Avail.: $3,000. **Duration:** Annual. **Number Awarded:** 2. **To Apply:** Nominee must submit the official nomination form completed, signed by the sponsor and included with the entry; a letter of application from the

Awards are arranged alphabetically below their administering organizations

student outlining plans for study and detailing extracurricular activities, maximum length of two pages, double-spaced; an academic paper or other appropriate work in the student's major field; one letter of recommendation/evaluation from a faculty member in the field represented by the paper or project addressed to the significance of the work; a self-addressed, stamped envelope. **Deadline:** February 15. **Remarks:** The scholarship is given in honor of Dr. Edwin Gaston.

378 ■ Alfred H. Nolle Scholarships (Undergraduate/Scholarship)

Purpose: To provide financial support for the education of senior undergraduate students. **Focus:** General studies/Field of study not specified. **Qualif.:** Nominees must be full-time undergraduate senior students; must be enrolled for the fall semester as full-time students in undergraduate study toward the baccalaureate degree. **Criteria:** Selection will be based on the committee's criteria.

Funds Avail.: $2,000. **Duration:** Annual. **Number Awarded:** 10. **To Apply:** Nominees must submit a completed official nomination form, signed by the sponsor and included with the entry; a letter of application from students outlining their plans for study and detailing their extracurricular activities, maximum length of two pages, double-spaced; an academic paper or other appropriate work in the students' major field; one letter of recommendation/evaluation from a faculty member in the field represented by the paper or project addressed to the significance of the work; a self-addressed, stamped envelope. **Deadline:** February 15. **Remarks:** The scholarship is given in honor of Dr. Alfred Nolle.

379 ■ Joseph E. Pryor Graduate Fellowships (Graduate/Fellowship)

Purpose: To provide financial assistance to individuals for full-time graduate or professional study (beyond the baccalaureate level). **Focus:** General studies/Field of study not specified. **Qualif.:** Applicants must be active alumni members and graduate student members at Alpha Chi institutions at the time of application. **Criteria:** Candidates will be evaluated based on criteria by the Pryor Fellowship Committee. Only complete applications will be given consideration.

Funds Avail.: $6,000 to a student who has completed at least two years of graduate or professional study and $4,000 to a first or second year student of graduate or professional study. **Duration:** Annual. **Number Awarded:** 2. **To Apply:** Applicants must submit evidence of outstanding scholarship; 300-500 word essay introducing their academic/professional goals, but not indicating financial need; two letters of recommendation from employers or professors or other persons qualified to give an evaluation; two complete official transcripts sealed by registrar; copy of official results of GRE, LSAT, MCAT or equivalent to applicant's discipline; and completed application form. **Deadline:** February 15. **Remarks:** The Fellowship is given in honor of Dr. Joseph E. Pryor.

380 ■ Robert W. Sledge Fellowships (Graduate/Fellowship)

Purpose: To provide financial support to individuals for their first year of graduate study toward the master's, doctorate or professional degree at any recognized institution. **Focus:** General studies/Field of study not specified. **Qualif.:** Nominees must be enrolled graduate students with the baccalaureate degree during the school year in which application is made and must identify the graduate or professional school(s) to which they have applied for study the following fall. **Criteria:** Selection will be based on the committee's criteria.

Funds Avail.: $4,000. **Duration:** Annual. **Number Awarded:** 2. **To Apply:** Nominees must submit the official nomination form completed, signed by the sponsor and included with the entry; a letter of application from the student outlining their plans for study and detailing their extracurricular activities, maximum length of two pages, double-spaced; an academic paper or other appropriate work in the students' major field; one letter of recommendation/evaluation from a faculty member in the field represented by the paper or project addressed to the significance of the work; a self-addressed, stamped envelope. **Deadline:** February 15. **Remarks:** The scholarship is given in honor of Dr. Robert Sledge.

381 ■ Alpha Chi Omega

5939 Castle Creek Pky.
North Dr.
Indianapolis, IN 46250
Ph: (317)579-5050
Fax: (317)579-5051
E-mail: info@alphachiomega.org
URL: www.alphachiomega.org
Social Media: www.facebook.com/alphachiomegahq
www.instagram.com/alphachiomegahq
www.linkedin.com/groups/94760/profile
www.pinterest.com/alphachiomega
twitter.com/alphachiomegahq
www.youtube.com/user/AlphaChiOmegaHQ

382 ■ Alpha Chi Omega Love and Loyalty Grants (Professional development/Grant)

Purpose: To support the educational, literary and charitable pursuits of Alpha Chi Omega, and encourage efforts that create well-rounded real, strong women. **Focus:** General studies/Field of study not specified. **Qualif.:** Applicants must be Alpha Chi Omega Fraternity, collegiate and alumnae chapters, and individual alumnae and collegiate members. **Criteria:** Selection will be based on continuous basis.

Funds Avail.: Varies. **Contact:** Amber Latta, Phone: at 317-579-5050 ext. 265, Email: alatta@alphachiomega.org.

383 ■ Alpha Chi Sigma Fraternity Inc.

6296 Rucker Rd., Ste. B
Indianapolis, IN 46220
Free: 800-252-4369
E-mail: national@alphachisigma.org
URL: www.alphachisigma.org
Social Media: www.facebook.com/AlphaChiSigma
www.linkedin.com/company/alpha-chi-sigma-fraternity
twitter.com/alphachisigma

384 ■ Alpha Chi Sigma Scholarship Awards (Graduate, Undergraduate/Scholarship)

Purpose: To encourage and recognize outstanding scholarship among Collegiate members of Alpha Chi Sigma Fraternity. **Focus:** General studies/Field of study not specified. **Qualif.:** Applicants must have been members of Alpha Chi Sigma Fraternity for at least one year, and enrolled in

Awards are arranged alphabetically below their administering organizations

an institution of higher learning at the time of nomination; and undergraduate nominees must have completed the junior year at the time of nomination; graduate nominees may be nominated based upon their undergraduate and graduate records upon the completion of their first year of graduate study; graduate students may also be nominated, based upon their graduate records alone, after admission to candidacy for the terminal degree in the field of graduate study. **Criteria:** Selection will be evaluated by the appointed award committee with established criteria.

Funds Avail.: Varies. **Duration:** Annual. **To Apply:** Application process is done through nomination. Nominee must submit the following: 1) biographical sketch; 2) two letters of recommendation by faculty of the institution from where the student is enrolled; 3) transcripts of all academic works; 4) photograph; 5) address and telephone number of a candidate including summer address if different; and 6) other information that may support the application of a nominee such as abstracts of presentations of meetings, or reprints of scientific publications. **Deadline:** February 28. **Remarks:** Established in 1913. **Contact:** Alpha Chi Sigma Scholar Award Committee at national@alphachisigma.org. If submitting hard copies, please send to 6296 Rucker Road, Suite B, Indianapolis, IN 46220.

385 ■ Alpha Delta Gamma National Fraternity

10521 Mimosa Lane.
Saint Louis, MO 63126
URL: www.alphadeltagamma.org

386 ■ Alpha Delta Gamma Educational Foundation Scholarship *(Undergraduate, Graduate/Scholarship)*

Purpose: To support and promote educational opportunities for the members of Alpha Delta Gamma National Fraternity. **Focus:** General studies/Field of study not specified. **Qualif.:** Applicants must be members of Alpha Delta Gamma National Fraternity. **Criteria:** Selection shall be based on the aforementioned applicants' qualifications and compliance with the application details.

Duration: Annual. **Number Awarded:** 2. **To Apply:** Applicants must submit a statement from the financial office of the college or university attended; one letter of recommendation from chapter moderator; one letter of recommendation from a current instructor; no larger than 5X7 photo; a letter from the ADG National Treasurer stating the membership standing; one-page biographical sketch; and one copy of transcript of records. **Deadline:** June 15.

387 ■ Alpha Kappa Alpha Educational Advancement Foundation (AKAEAF)

5656 S Stony Island Ave.
Chicago, IL 60637
Ph: (773)947-0026
Fax: (773)947-0277
Free: 800-653-6528
E-mail: akaeaf@akaeaf.net
URL: www.akaeaf.org
Social Media: facebook.com/Alpha-Kappa-Alpha
  -Educational-Advancement-Foundation-Inc
  -1696855507217868
instagram.com/akaeaf
twitter.com/akaeaf

388 ■ Alpha Kappa Alpha - Educational Advancement Foundation Undergraduate Financial Need-Based Scholarships *(Undergraduate/Scholarship)*

Purpose: To provide financial support to undergraduate and graduate students for the advancement of education. **Focus:** General studies/Field of study not specified. **Qualif.:** Applicants must be full-time undergraduate students (Sophomore or beyond) currently enrolled in an accredited degree granting institution; must have a minimum GPA of 2.5 (C average) and demonstrate community service and involvement; high school students and college freshmen are not eligible.

Funds Avail.: No specific amount. **Duration:** Annual. **To Apply:** Completed application along with personal statement; three letters of recommendation (must not be dated earlier than January of the current year); official transcript(s) from all colleges that you have attended with cumulative GPA listed; Financial Needs Analysis must be submitted. **Deadline:** April 15. **Contact:** Andrea Kerr, EAF Program Coordinator, 5656 S Stony Island Ave., Chicago, IL, 60637; Phone: 800-653-6528; Email: akerr@akaeaf.net.

389 ■ Alpha Kappa Alpha - Educational Advancement Foundation Undergraduate Merit Scholarships *(Undergraduate/Scholarship)*

Purpose: To provide financial support to undergraduate and graduate students for the advancement of education. **Focus:** General studies/Field of study not specified. **Qualif.:** Applicants must be full-time undergraduate students (Sophomore or beyond) currently enrolled in an accredited degree granting institution; must have a minimum GPA of 3.0 (B average) and demonstrate community service and involvement; high school students and college freshmen are not eligible.

Funds Avail.: No specific amount. **Duration:** Annual. **To Apply:** Completed application along with personal statement; three letters of recommendation (must not be dated earlier than January of the current year); official transcript(s) from all colleges that you have attended with cumulative GPA listed must be submitted. **Deadline:** April 15. **Contact:** Andrea Kerr, EAF Program Coordinator, 5656 S Stony Island Ave., Chicago, IL, 60637; Phone: 800-653-6528; Email: akerr@akaeaf.net.

390 ■ Youth Partners Accessing Capital (YPAC) *(Undergraduate/Scholarship)*

Purpose: To develop leadership among undergraduates in the areas of criteria development, evaluation, and fund management. **Focus:** General studies/Field of study not specified. **Qualif.:** Applicant must be an active undergraduate member of Alpha Kappa Alpha Sorority, Inc. at an accredited campus based degree granting institution and continuing a program of education in this or any other degree granting institution; must have a minimum GPA of 3.0 (at least a B average). **Criteria:** Recipients are evaluated based on demonstrated exceptional academic achievement; financial need; and leadership or volunteerism in civic or campus activities.

Funds Avail.: No specific amount. **Duration:** Annual. **To Apply:** Completed application along with two letters of recommendation: one from an instructor and the other from one who can attest to your personal character and attributes (neither should come from a relative or peer); personal goal statement stating how applicant goals support the Alpha Kappa Alpha Educational Advancement Foundation Youth P.A.C. mission, no more than two double

Awards are arranged alphabetically below their administering organizations

spaced pages with a minimum of 100 and no more than 250 words. **Deadline:** April 15. **Remarks:** Established in 1997. **Contact:** Andrea Kerr, EAF Program Coordinator, 5656 S Stony Island Ave., Chicago, IL, 60637; Phone: 800-653-6528; Email: akerr@akaeaf.net.

391 ■ Alpha Lambda Delta

6800 Pittsford-Palmyra Rd., Ste. 340
Fairport, NY 14450
Free: 800-925-7421
E-mail: ald@nationalald.org
URL: www.nationalald.org
Social Media: www.facebook.com/nationalALD
www.instagram.com/nationalald
www.linkedin.com/company/alpha-lambda-delta-honor
twitter.com/nationalald

392 ■ ALD Graduate Fellowships *(Graduate/ Fellowship)*

Purpose: To help qualified members obtain graduate or professional degrees. **Focus:** General studies/Field of study not specified. **Qualif.:** Applicants must be member of Alpha Lambda Delta who have maintained a GPA of 3.5 on a 4.0 scales or equivalent until graduation; must be enrolled or plan to be enrolled at an accredited institution within the United States. **Criteria:** Candidates will be considered on the basis of merit.

Funds Avail.: $3,000, $4,000, $5,000 and $6,500. **To Apply:** Applicants must complete application form, prepare the supplemental materials, and submit original application. **Deadline:** February 1. **Contact:** Alpha Lambda Delta National Honor Society for First-Year Success, 6800 Pittsford-Palmyra Rd., Ste. 340, Fairport, NY, 14450; Toll-free: 800-925-7421.

393 ■ Jo Anne J. Trow Undergraduate Scholarships *(Undergraduate/Scholarship)*

Purpose: To provide financial assistance to qualified members for their education. **Focus:** General studies/Field of study not specified. **Qualif.:** Applicants must be member of Alpha Lambda Delta who have maintained the cumulative grade point average of 3.5 on a 4.0 scale or equivalent. **Criteria:** Candidates will be evaluated by the chapter's scholarship selection committee.

Funds Avail.: $1,000 to $6,000. **Duration:** Annual. **Number Awarded:** 50. **To Apply:** Applicants must complete application form, prepare the supplemental materials, and submit original application. **Deadline:** April 17. **Remarks:** Established in 1988. **Contact:** Alpha Lambda Delta National Honor Society for First-Year Success, 6800 Pittsford-Palmyra Rd., Ste. 340, Fairport, NY, 14450; Toll-free: 800-925-7421.

394 ■ Alpha Mu Gamma Honor Society

855 N Vermont Ave.
Los Angeles, CA 90029
URL: www.lacitycollege.edu
Social Media: twitter.com/LACityCollege

395 ■ James Fonseca Scholarship *(Undergraduate, Graduate/Scholarship)*

Purpose: To support members to continue their foreign language studies. **Focus:** Linguistics. **Qualif.:** Applicants must be full members (undergraduates and graduates) of Alpha Mu Gamma are eligible to apply. **Criteria:** Selection will be based on demonstrate excellence in foreign language study and further study by: student's essay, participation in Chapter activities, cumulative GPA, foreign Language courses GPA; recommendations; preference is given to foreign language majors and minors.

Funds Avail.: $500. **Number Awarded:** 1. **To Apply:** Applications can be submitted online; including the personal statement (essay); three recommendations (one must be from your chapter advisor) recommenders should use the official recommendation form; official college transcript; photocopy of your AMG Full Member certificate. **Deadline:** February 1.

396 ■ Goddard, Indovina & Krakowski Scholarship *(Undergraduate, Graduate/Scholarship)*

Purpose: To support members to continue their foreign language studies. **Focus:** Linguistics. **Qualif.:** Applicants must be full members (undergraduates and graduates) of Alpha Mu Gamma are eligible to apply. **Criteria:** Selection will be based on demonstrate excellence in foreign language study and further study by: student's essay, participation in Chapter activities, cumulative GPA, foreign Language courses GPA; recommendations; preference is given to foreign language majors and minors.

Funds Avail.: $1,000. **Number Awarded:** 3. **To Apply:** Applications can be submitted online; including the personal statement (essay); three recommendations (one must be from your chapter advisor) recommenders should use the official recommendation form; official college transcript; photocopy of your AMG Full Member certificate. **Deadline:** February 1.

397 ■ Alpha Phi Sigma (APS)

3301 College Ave.
Fort Lauderdale, FL 33314
Ph: (954)262-7004
E-mail: headquarters@alphaphisigma.org
URL: www.alphaphisigma.org
Social Media: www.facebook.com/
  AlphaPhiSigmaCriminalJustice
www.linkedin.com/in/alpha-phi-sigma-the-criminal-justice
  -honor-society-1b2379189
twitter.com/alphaphisigmahq
www.youtube.com/channel/
  UCeWfUMZdZmAkwjMqioELj5A/videos

398 ■ Regina B. Shearn Scholarship *(Graduate, Undergraduate/Scholarship)*

Purpose: To assist students in their educational pursuits. **Focus:** General studies/Field of study not specified. **Qualif.:** Applicants must be National Alpha Phi Sigma members; must be enrolled in a degree program; applicants are not eligible to receive the same scholarship two years in succession. **Criteria:** Selection is based on academic performance, leadership and service, personal statement and evaluation reports and judged by panel of impartial Alpha Phi Sigma faculty members.

Funds Avail.: $2,000 each and a certificate(One undergraduate & one graduate). **To Apply:** Applicants must submit completed Scholarship Cover sheet form; current proof of enrollment in a program the semester the scholarship is awarded; must be double spaced, 12pt Times New Roman font, and 1 inch margins; evaluation reports from

Awards are arranged alphabetically below their administering organizations

three individuals who are in a position to attest to your performance, citizenship, and character; current copy of your resume with leadership, service, and honors/awards listed; Personal statement of educational perspective, purpose, and objectives, approximately 5-7 pages; must fill out one Scholarship Cover sheet for each scholarship electronically with email subject line as Regina B. Shearn SCHOLARSHIP APPLICATION to headquarters; In PDF format. **Deadline:** January 31. **Remarks:** To honor the Dr. Regina B. Shearn is the first Executive Director; The Honor Society has grown considerably and continues to grow and thrive under her leadership and tutelage. Established in 2001. **Contact:** Submit all materials and scholarship cover sheet via e-mail to headquarters@alphaphisigma.org and put Regina B. Shearn SCHOLARSHIP APPLICATION in the e-mail subject line.

399 ■ V.A. Leonard Scholarship (Graduate, Undergraduate/Scholarship)

Purpose: To assist students in their educational pursuits. **Focus:** General studies/Field of study not specified. **Qualif.:** Applicants must be National Alpha Phi Sigma members; must be enrolled in a degree program; applicants are not eligible to receive the same scholarship two years in succession. **Criteria:** Selection will be based on academic achievement, professional recommendations, and extracurricular activities and judged by a panel of impartial Alpha Phi Sigma faculty members.

Funds Avail.: $2,000 each and a certificate(One undergraduate & one graduate). **To Apply:** Applicants must submit completed Scholarship Cover sheet form; current proof of enrollment in a program the semester the scholarship is awarded; must be double spaced, 12pt Times New Roman font, and 1 inch margins; must submit a paper on applicant perception of Alpha Phi Sigma and what direction applicant would like to see the Honor Society take in the future, in approximately 5-7 pages; additional 2 pages, stating need for scholarship and how applicant intend to use the scholarship money; copy of your most recent transcript signed by your chapter advisor; submit 3 letters of recommendations, preferably from Faculty; must fill out one Scholarship Cover sheet for each scholarship electronically with email subject line as V.A Leonard SCHOLARSHIP APPLICATION to headquarters; in pdf format. **Deadline:** January 31. **Remarks:** In honor and Recognition of Dr. Leonard's leadership and hard work in the field of Criminal Justice. Established in 1982. **Contact:** Submit all materials and scholarship cover sheet via e-mail to headquarters@alphaphisigma.org and put V.A Leonard SCHOLARSHIP APPLICATION in the e-mail subject line.

400 ■ Alpha Tau Omega\Alpha Tau Omega Fraternity (ATO)

333 N Alabama St.,Ste. 220
Indianapolis, IN 46204
Ph: (317)684-1865
E-mail: info@ato.org
URL: www.ato.org
Social Media: www.facebook.com/AlphaTauOmega
www.instagram.com/atonhq
twitter.com/alphatauomega?lang=en
www.youtube.com/channel/
  UCIEgqQFJOUpoGVJFkO0w1vw

401 ■ Alpha Tau Omega Graduate Scholarship (Graduate/Scholarship)

Purpose: To provide students the highest standard of educational programs and scholarships who demonstrated leadership. **Focus:** General studies/Field of study not specified. **Qualif.:** Applicants must be students either enrolled or accepted into an accredited graduate program; must be full-time students during the academic year; must be initiated members of ATO in good standing; must have a minimum cumulative GPA of 3.5 on a 4.0 scale. **Criteria:** Selection will be based on the committee's criteria.

Funds Avail.: No specific amount. **To Apply:** Applications can be submitted online.

402 ■ Alpha Tau Omega Undergraduate Scholarships (Undergraduate/Scholarship)

Purpose: To provide students the highest standard of educational programs and scholarships who demonstrated leadership. **Focus:** General studies/Field of study not specified. **Qualif.:** Applicants must be students who have at least one undergraduate year remaining before graduation; must be an initiated member of ATO in good standing; must have a minimum cumulative grade point average of 3.5 on a 4.0 scale. **Criteria:** Selection will be based on the committee's criteria.

Funds Avail.: No specific amount. **To Apply:** Applications can be submitted online.

403 ■ William D. Krahling Excellence in Journalism Scholarship (Undergraduate/Scholarship)

Purpose: To provide students the highest standard of educational programs and scholarships who demonstrated leadership. **Focus:** Journalism. **Qualif.:** Applicants must be students majoring in journalism or a related field; must have completed one academic year of undergraduate education and have at least one undergraduate year remaining; must be initiated members of ATO in good standing; must have a minimum cumulative GPA of 3.5 on a 4.0 scale. **Criteria:** Selection will be based on the committee's criteria.

Funds Avail.: No specific amount. **To Apply:** Applications can be submitted online; must include letter of recommendation from a member of the journalism faculty. **Remarks:** The scholarship is given in honor of William D. Krahling.

404 ■ Lawrence A. Long Memorial Law Scholarship (Graduate/Scholarship)

Purpose: To provide educational programs and scholarships of the highest standards. **Focus:** General studies/ Field of study not specified. **Qualif.:** Applicants must be students who are enrolled or accepted into an accredited law school; must be full-time students during the academic year; must be an initiated member of ATO in good standing; must have a minimum cumulative grade point average of 3.5 on a 4.0 scale. **Criteria:** Selection will be based on the committee's criteria.

Funds Avail.: No specific amount. **To Apply:** Applications can be submitted online. **Remarks:** The scholarship is given in honor of Worthy Grand Chief Lawrence A. Long.

405 ■ J. Milton Richardson Theological Fellowship (Graduate/Fellowship)

Purpose: To provide students the highest standard of educational programs and scholarships who plans to attend graduate school in theology or seminary. **Focus:** Theology. **Qualif.:** Applicant must be an ATO member who plans to attend or is enrolled in an accredited graduate school in theology or the seminary, and who intends to become a member of the clergy; must have a minimum

Awards are arranged alphabetically below their administering organizations

cumulative grade point average of 3.5 on a 4.0 scale. **Criteria:** Selection will be based on the committee's criteria.

Funds Avail.: No specific amount. **To Apply:** Applications can be submitted online. **Remarks:** The Fellowship is given in honor of J. Milton Richardson. Established in 1981.

406 ■ The Alsandor Law Firm

3801 Kirby Dr., No. 720
Houston, TX 77098
Ph: (401)884-6300
Fax: (401)884-4773
URL: alsandorlaw.com
Social Media: www.facebook.com/thealsandorlawfirm
www.linkedin.com/company/the-alsandor-law-firm
twitter.com/alsandorlawfirm
www.youtube.com/channel/UC
  -zM50xEr89wgpalmWRMvqA

407 ■ The Alsandor Law Firm Scholarship Contest
(Undergraduate/Scholarship)

Purpose: To provide financial aid to college students, encourage students to understand their personal motivation for a career in the legal field, and inspire students to pursue a career in law. **Focus:** Business; Finance; Law; Management. **Qualif.:** Applicant must be financial aid to a college student, encourage students to understand their personal motivation for a career. **Criteria:** Selection is based on the best video essay.

Funds Avail.: $1,000. **Duration:** Annual. **Number Awarded:** 1. **To Apply:** Applicant must record a one- to two-minute video explaining why they want to be a lawyer; video should be in English and should be posted to the applicant's YouTube channel with the title "Fielding Law Group Scholarship Contest" and include this link in the description: www.alsandorlaw.com/scholarship-for-college-students/.Applicant should share this video on their Facebook page and the sponsor's Facebook page. Instead of a video essay, applicant can submit a 1,000 to 1,500 word essay explaining why they want to be a lawyer and post to the sponsor's page. **Deadline:** August 15.

408 ■ Alter-Cine Foundation

5369 Avenue de l'Esplanade
Montreal, QC, Canada H2T 2Z8
E-mail: altercine@videotron.ca
URL: altercine.org
Social Media: www.facebook.com/FondationAltercine

409 ■ Documentary Film Grants *(Professional development/Grant)*

Purpose: To help filmmakers in having the opportunity to assist in the production of a documentary project. **Focus:** Filmmaking. **Qualif.:** Applicants must be young video and filmmakers born and living in Africa, Asia or Latin America who want to direct a film in the language of their choice that respects the aims of the Foundation. **Criteria:** Selection will be based on the committee's criteria.

Funds Avail.: A total of 10,000 Canadian dollars; few 5,000 Canadian dollars to some filmmakers. **To Apply:** Applicants must complete the application form, available online in French, English or Spanish, including a synopsis (max. 5 pages) that describes the content, characters, situations, theme, and the treatment and style of the project; must send a Vimeo link of a previous completed documentary work; if possible the cassette should be sub-titled or versioned in French, English or Spanish; if the work does not exist in any of these three languages, please send a written transcript of the dialogue and narration in one of the three languages; Send also any visual element in support of the proposed documentary project; include a production budget for the documentary, as well as a financing plan; must include a two support letters from partners, NGOs, groups or associations supporting the project; applications must be submitted to the foundation address. **Deadline:** August 15. **Contact:** Fondation Alter-Cine, 5369 Avenue de l'Esplanade, Montreal (Quebec), H2T 2Z8, Canada; Email: altercine@videotron.ca.

410 ■ Alzheimer Society of Canada (ASC)

20 Eglinton Ave. W 16th Flr.
Toronto, ON, Canada M4R 1K8
Ph: (416)488-8772
Fax: (416)488-3778
Free: 800-616-8816
E-mail: info@alzheimer.ca
URL: alzheimer.ca
Social Media: www.facebook.com/AlzheimerCanada
www.instagram.com/alzheimercanada
twitter.com/AlzCanada
www.youtube.com/alzheimercanada

411 ■ ASC Research Grant *(University/Grant)*

Purpose: To support scientific excellence and relevance to Alzheimer's Disease. **Focus:** Medical research.

Funds Avail.: $60,000 Quality of Life; $75,000 Biomedical. **Duration:** Annual.

412 ■ Firefly Foundation/ASRP Spark Award
(Postdoctorate/Grant)

Purpose: To support unique, creative research ideas that will impact brain health and prevent, defer or effectively treat neurodegenerative disease. **Focus:** Alzheimer's disease. **Qualif.:** Applicants must be within the 18 months of completing their Ph.D. and pursue their postdoctoral fellowship in Canada. **Criteria:** Selection will be based on the research proposals of the applicants.

Funds Avail.: 100,000 Canadian Dollars per year (50,000 per annum). **Duration:** up to 2 years. **To Apply:** Applicants are required to submit proposals for studies using the Alzheimer Society of Canada (ASC) online application system for work that explicitly address the Firefly Foundation's mission to find treatment for prevention or cures to eradicate neurodegenerative disease. **Remarks:** The Spark Award is a partnership program between the Firefly Foundation and the Alzheimer Society of Canada, through its Alzheimer Society Research Program. **Contact:** Research Department, Alzheimer Society of Canada, at research@alzheimer.ca.

413 ■ NBHRF/ASRP Doctoral Training Awards
(Doctorate/Award)

Purpose: To encourage doctoral degree students to pursue research related to Alzheimer's Disease. **Focus:** Alzheimer's disease; Medical research. **Qualif.:** Applicants must be enrolled in a Canadian university-based program leading to a PhD degree; at the time of application they have been enrolled in a PhD program for 18 months or less. **Criteria:**

Awards are arranged alphabetically below their administering organizations

Selection is based on top-ranked applicants and will work with institutions in New Brunswick to administer awards.

Funds Avail.: $22,000/year; ($500/year) research allowance. **Duration:** Up to 3 years. **To Apply:** Candidates must apply to the ASRP regular research grants competition. They must also notify NBHRF of their ASRP application by email and attach to it all documents and materials submitted to the regular ASRP competition. The ASRP/NBHRF will make awards to the top-ranked applicants and will work with institutions in New Brunswick to administer awards. **Remarks:** The awards are co-sponsored by the New Brunswick Health Research Foundation and Alzheimer Society of Canada.

414 ■ Alzheimer's Association
225 N Michigan Ave., 17th Fl.
Chicago, IL 60601-7633
Ph: (312)335-8700
Free: 866-699-1246
E-mail: info@alz.org
URL: www.alz.org
Social Media: www.facebook.com/actionalz
www.instagram.com/alzassociation/
www.linkedin.com/company/alzheimer's-association
www.pinterest.com/AlzAssociation/
twitter.com/alzassociation
www.youtube.com/user/actionalz

415 ■ New Investigator Research Grant
(Postdoctorate/Grant)

Purpose: To provide newly independent investigators with funding that will allow them to develop preliminary data, to test procedures and to develop hypotheses. **Focus:** Alzheimer's disease. **Qualif.:** Applicants must be assistant professors or above at their respective institution; must be investigators who have less than ten years of research experience after receipt of their terminal degree; are faculty members who have been determined to be underrepresented faculty in biomedical and behavioral research on a national or institutional basis; in the United States will be subject to the definitions as stated by the National Institutes of Health. **Criteria:** Selection will be based on the committee's criteria.

Funds Avail.: $100,000. **Duration:** Annual; up to 2 years. **To Apply:** Applicants must submit their letter of intent; and a budget summary for the proposed research project. **Contact:** Alzheimer's Association at grantsapp@alz.org.

416 ■ Part the Cloud: Translational Research Funding *(Postgraduate/Grant)*

Purpose: To provide support for early phase studies of potential Alzheimer's therapeutics or validation of biological markers in of disease progression. **Focus:** Alzheimer's disease. **Qualif.:** Applicants must be non-profit and small for-profit agencies, or researchers with full-time staff or faculty appointments; must be international applicants. **Criteria:** Selection will be based on the committee's criteria such as significance of the question being studied & rationale of the target being pursued; applicant information; quality of the proposed trial design; quality and adequacy of available resources and budget; impact-risk.

Funds Avail.: May not exceed $500,000. **Duration:** Annual; over two years. **To Apply:** Applicants must submit the completed application form including letter of intent, annual

progress and financial reports, and budget summary for the proposed research. **Deadline:** August 20. **Contact:** Alzheimer's Association; Email: grantsapp@alz.org.

417 ■ U.S.-U.K. Young Investigator Exchange Fellowship *(Postdoctorate/Fellowship)*

Purpose: To provide new investigators with funding that will allow them to develop preliminary or pilot data. **Focus:** Alzheimer's disease. **Qualif.:** Applicants must be investigators based in the United States or United Kingdom who have less than ten years of research experience after receipt of their terminal degree. **Criteria:** Selection will be based on the committee's criteria.

Funds Avail.: $300,000 for U.S; 160,000 British Pounds for U.K. **Duration:** Annual; 3 years. **To Apply:** Applicants must complete and submit the application form and letter of intent which includes the name of principal investigator, contact information, academic rank/position title, title of the fellowship project, area of focus of the submission, brief rationale for the proposal limited to 3,000 characters, employer and identification number, a current non-profit verification for the institution, and employment verification letter.

418 ■ The Zenith Fellows Award Program (Zenith) *(Postdoctorate/Fellowship)*

Purpose: To provide major support for investigators who have: contributed significantly to the field of Alzheimer's disease research; made significant contributions to other areas of science and now focusing on problems related to Alzheimer's disease; and are likely to make substantial contributions in the future. **Focus:** Alzheimer's disease. **Qualif.:** Applicants must be successful independent investigators as evidenced by their academic appointment, external multi-year grant support on which the they are the principal investigators, independent laboratory operation, and quality of publication record. **Criteria:** Selection will be based on the committee's criteria.

Funds Avail.: $450,000. **Duration:** Annual; up to 3 years. **To Apply:** Applicants must complete and submit the application form available online; and must provide a budget summary for the proposed research project. **Deadline:** March 2; April 16. **Remarks:** Established in 1991. **Contact:** Phone: 312-335-5747 or 312-335-5862; Email: grantsapp@alz.org.

419 ■ Americal Division Veterans Association (ADVA)
PO Box 830662
Richardson, TX 75080
Ph: (830)377-8115
URL: americal.org

420 ■ Americal Legacy Foundation Scholarship *(Undergraduate/Scholarship)*

Purpose: To support high school graduate students planning to attend a college. **Focus:** General studies/Field of study not specified. **Qualif.:** Applicants must be children and grandchildren, including those by adoption, of current and deceased ADVA members, provided the deceased member held good membership standing at the time of death, or any child or adopted child of an American Division soldier who was killed or died while on active duty with the division. **Criteria:** Recipient shall be selected based on financial need.

Funds Avail.: $500 to $3,500. **Duration:** Annual. **Number Awarded:** Varies. **To Apply:** Applicant must submit a letter

Awards are arranged alphabetically below their administering organizations

from the sponsor attesting to the applicant's eligibility according to ADVA Scholarship Fund Purpose and By-Laws; a letter of admission from the applicant's college or vocational school of choice; a letter from the applicant's high school principal attesting to the applicant's character if applicant is attending or has graduated from high school (If currently attending a college, applicant may disregard this reference letter); two letters of recommendation from current teachers concerning the applicant's progress in current classes or subjects; a photocopy of the applicant's high school or college transcript; a detailed statement of the applicant's academic accomplishments, extracurricular activities, and community service involvement; an applicant must submit a 200-300 word essay on subjects pertaining to American Division history, national pride, loyalty to the nation, and patriotism. **Deadline:** May 1. **Remarks:** Established in 1994. **Contact:** Scholarship Chairman, William Bruinsma, 5425 Parmalee Rd., Middleville, Michigan 49333; Phone: 269-795-5237; Gary Noller; Phone: 830-377-8115; E-mail: gnoller@aol.com.

421 ■ American Academy of Advertising (AAA)

C/O Eric Haley, President
The University of Tennessee
1345 Circle Park Dr.
476 Communications Bldg.
Knoxville, TN 37996-0332
URL: www.aaasite.org
Social Media: www.facebook.com/
  AmericanAcademyOfAdvertising
twitter.com/adscholar

422 ■ AAA Doctoral Dissertation Grant Competition
(Doctorate/Grant)

Purpose: To support doctoral researchers with their dissertation proposals and research projects. **Focus:** Advertising. **Qualif.:** Applicants must be promote doctoral research in advertising. Recipients receive half of the award at the time of selection and half of the award when the dissertation has been defended successfully. **Criteria:** Selection based on a competitive review of dissertation proposals.
Funds Avail.: $1,000-$2,000.

423 ■ American Academy of Ambulatory Care Nursing (AAACN)

E Holly Ave.
Pitman, NJ 08071-0056
Free: 800-262-6877
E-mail: aaacn@aaacn.org
URL: www.aaacn.org
Social Media: www.facebook.com/AAACN
www.linkedin.com/company/american-academy-of
  -ambulatory-care-nursing
twitter.com/AmbCareNursing

424 ■ AAACN Conference Scholarship for Nursing Students *(Undergraduate/Scholarship)*

Purpose: To support students who are seeking initial nursing licensure. **Focus:** Nursing. **Qualif.:** Applicant must be recommended by a current member of the American Academy of Ambulatory Care Nursing; have financial need; have a willingness to give back and to write an article for the Viewpoint journal within a year of receiving the scholarship. **Criteria:** Selection will be based on the committees' criteria.

Funds Avail.: $1,000. **Duration:** Annual. **Number Awarded:** 1. **To Apply:** Applicants must be recommended by a current member of the AAACN and must submit a complete application form together with CV/resume. Application available online at www.aaacn.org/career-education/scholarships-awards/conference-scholarships. **Deadline:** November 15.

425 ■ AAACN Education Scholarship
(Undergraduate/Scholarship)

Purpose: To assist students with their tuition, books, and academic supplies to purse nursing education. **Focus:** Nursing. **Qualif.:** Applicants must be members of AAACN for a minimum of two continuous years with financial need and have the willingness to give back to the Association and publish their articles for the ViewPoint publication. **Criteria:** Selection will be based on the committees' criteria.

Funds Avail.: $1,000. **Duration:** Annual. **Number Awarded:** 1. **To Apply:** Applicants must submit the complete application form together with the applicants' CV/resume. Application available online at www.aaacn.org/career-education/scholarships-awards/education-scholarship.

426 ■ AAACN Research/Evidence Based Practice Project Awards *(Undergraduate/Grant, Scholarship)*

Purpose: To assist individuals who are conducting either nursing research or EBP project. **Focus:** Nursing. **Qualif.:** Applicants must be members of AAACN for a minimum of two continuous years with financial need and willing to contribute their knowledge to the Association and publish their articles for the ViewPoint publication, also applicants must have the eager to submit abstract for a podium or poster presentation of the nursing study or EBP project and its outcome. **Criteria:** Selection will be based on the committees' criteria.

Funds Avail.: $1,000. **Duration:** Annual. **To Apply:** Applicants must submit the complete application form together with the applicants' CV/resume. Application available online at www.aaacn.org/career-education/scholarships-awards/researchevidence-based-practice-project. **Deadline:** November 15.

427 ■ Certified in Care Coordination and Transition Management (CCCTM) Certification Grant
(Undergraduate/Scholarship)

Purpose: To provide funds to cover the exam registration fee to become CCCTM certified for members of the American Academy of Ambulatory Care Nursing. **Focus:** Nursing. **Qualif.:** Applicants must be members of American Academy of Ambulatory Care Nursing (AAACN) for a minimum of two years; currently enrolled in an accredited school of nursing or a program deemed by the committee to advance the profession of nursing; request for payment of tuition, books, academic supplies; proof of acceptance in course; must submit a research abstract and proof of acceptance of research study by academic institution or Investigational Review Board employing or sponsoring institutions; willing to present research findings at AAACN Annual Conference following receipt of award; willing to publish article in Viewpoint describing a research study and outcome. **Criteria:** Recipient will be selected by the AAACN Committee.

Funds Avail.: $255. **Duration:** Annual. **Number Awarded:** 2. **To Apply:** Applicants must complete an application form and must provide a current enrollment or proof of acceptance in an accredited school of nursing or other

Awards are arranged alphabetically below their administering organizations

academic program. Application is available online at www.aaacn.org/certified-care-coordination-and-transition-management-ccctm-certification-grant. **Deadline:** November 15.

428 ■ Candia Baker Laughlin Certification Scholarship (Undergraduate/Scholarship)

Purpose: To cover the exam fee, study materials, and other expenses related to achieving certification. **Focus:** Nursing. **Qualif.:** Applicants must be members of AAACN for a minimum of two continuous years with financial need and eligible to sit for the exam. Applicants must have the willingness to give back to the Association, contribute their knowledge, become certified in Ambulatory Care and write an article for the ViewPoint publication. **Criteria:** Selection will be based on the committees' criteria.

Funds Avail.: $1,000. **Duration:** Annual. **Number Awarded:** 1. **To Apply:** Application available online at www.aaacn.org/career-education/scholarships-awards/candia-baker-laughlin-certification-scholarship. **Remarks:** The award was established in honor of Candia Baker Laughlin for her commitment to nurses achieving certification. Established in 2013.

429 ■ American Academy of Attorney-CPAs (AAA-CPA)

PO Box 706
Warrendale, PA 15095
Ph: (703)352-8064
Fax: (703)352-8073
Free: 888-272-2889
E-mail: info@attorney-cpa.com
URL: www.attorney-cpa.com
Social Media: www.facebook.com/
  americanacademyofattorneycpas
twitter.com/attorneycpas

430 ■ Attorney-CPA Foundation Scholarships (Postgraduate/Scholarship)

Purpose: To promote the study and understanding of the fields of law and accounting and other related professions. **Focus:** Accounting; Law. **Qualif.:** Applicants must be graduating law students who have obtained CPA Certificate. **Criteria:** Selection will be based on the committee's criteria.

Funds Avail.: No specific amount. **Duration:** Annual. **To Apply:** Applicants may contact the AAA-CPA or the Attorney-CPA Foundation for more information.

431 ■ American Academy of Audiology (AAA)

11480 Commerce Park Dr., Ste. 220
Reston, VA 20191
Ph: (703)790-8466
Fax: (703)790-8631
Free: 800-222-2336
URL: www.audiology.org
Social Media: www.facebook.com/audiology
www.linkedin.com/company/american-academy-of
  -audiology
twitter.com/AcademyofAuD

432 ■ New Investigator Research Grant (Doctorate/ Grant)

Purpose: To support new investigators who have completed a doctoral degree and do not have significant sources of research funding. **Focus:** Speech and language pathology/Audiology.

Funds Avail.: Up to $10,000. **Duration:** Annual. **To Apply:** Applications will be submitted using the Academy's online grant submission system; applicants shall be required to upload several PDF documents; the body of the proposal should adhere to the following requirements: font should be a minimum of size 12 or no smaller than 6 characters per inch; should be single-spaced with no more than 6 lines per vertical inch; should be a minimum of 1 inch for all borders. **Deadline:** October 4.

433 ■ Student Investigator Research Grant - General Audiology/Hearing Science (Graduate, Doctorate/Grant)

Purpose: To support doctoral students working towards doctoral degree in audiology or hearing science who are completing a research project as part of their course of study. **Focus:** Speech and language pathology/Audiology. **Qualif.:** Applicants must be doctoral students working towards a doctoral degree in audiology or hearing science who are completing a research project as a part of their course of study; must be currently enrolled in a non-profit tax-exempt institution in the United States or Canada, public or private, as this is where grant funds will be issued; must conduct their research project under the advice and guidance of a mentor. **Criteria:** Selection will be based on rationale/purpose, methods, overall clarity, importance of work, innovation, and budget.

Funds Avail.: Up to $5,000. **Duration:** Annual. **To Apply:** Applications must be submitted using the Academy's online grant submission system; no paper copies will be accepted; applicants will be required to upload several PDF documents. The body of the proposal should adhere to the following requirements: font should be a minimum of size 12 or smaller than 6 characters per inch; single-spaced with no more than 6 lines per vertical inch; margins should be a minimum of 1 inch for all borders. **Deadline:** October 4.

434 ■ Student Investigator Research Grant - Hearing Aids, Clinical Protocols and Patient Outcomes (Graduate, Doctorate/Grant)

Purpose: To support doctoral students working towards doctoral degree in audiology or hearing science who are completing a research project as part of their course of study. **Focus:** Speech and language pathology/Audiology. **Qualif.:** Applicants must be doctoral students working towards a doctoral degree in audiology or hearing science who are completing a research project as a part of their course of study; must be currently enrolled in a non-profit tax-exempt institution in the United States or Canada, public or private, as this is where grant funds will be issued; must conduct their research project under the advice and guidance of a mentor. **Criteria:** Selection will be based on rationale/purpose, methods, overall clarity, importance of work, innovation, and budget.

Funds Avail.: Up to $5,000. **Duration:** Annual. **To Apply:** Applications must be submitted using the Academy's online grant submission system; no paper copies will be accepted; applicants will be required to upload several PDF documents. The body of the proposal should adhere to the following requirements: font should be a minimum of size 12 or smaller than 6 characters per inch; single-spaced with no more than 6 lines per vertical inch; margins should be a minimum of 1 inch for all borders. **Deadline:** October 1.

Awards are arranged alphabetically below their administering organizations

435 ■ Student Investigator Research Grant - Vestibular *(Graduate, Doctorate/Grant)*

Purpose: To support doctoral students working towards doctoral degree in audiology or hearing science who are completing a research project as part of their course of study. **Focus:** Speech and language pathology/Audiology. **Qualif.:** Applicants must be doctoral students working towards a doctoral degree in audiology or hearing science who are completing a research project as a part of their course of study; must be currently enrolled in a non-profit tax-exempt institution in the United States or Canada, public or private, as this is where grant funds will be issued; must conduct their research project under the advice and guidance of a mentor. **Criteria:** Selection will be based on rationale/purpose, methods, overall clarity, importance of work, innovation, and budget.

Funds Avail.: Up to $5,000. **Duration:** Annual. **To Apply:** Applications must be submitted using the Academy's online grant submission system; no paper copies will be accepted; required to upload several PDF documents. Body of the proposal should adhere to the following requirements: font should be a minimum of size 12 or smaller than 6 characters per inch; single-spaced with no more than 6 lines per vertical inch; margins should be a minimum of 1 inch for all borders; should include applicant's information, abstract, body of proposal, detailed budget for research proposal and budget justifications, letter of support from mentor, human and animal subjects use statement and documentation, conflict of interest statement. **Deadline:** October 4.

436 ■ Student Summer Research Fellowship *(Undergraduate, Graduate/Fellowship)*

Purpose: To support the students who will be granted for undergraduate students or doctoral students currently enrolled in a program in audiology or hearing science who wish to gain a limited, but significant, exposure to a research environment. **Focus:** Speech and language pathology/Audiology. **Qualif.:** Applicants must be one of the following: undergraduate students interested in pursuing a research doctorate in audiology or hearing science; or, graduate students who are currently enrolled in a research doctoral program in audiology or hearing science; or, graduate students who are enrolled in an AuD program with plans to pursue a research doctorate degree in audiology or hearing science; must commit to work full time in the mentor's lab for a minimum of ten weeks, uninterrupted (longer placements are certainly encouraged if they can be accommodated by both the grant recipient and the mentor). **Criteria:** Selection will be based on the committee's criteria.

Funds Avail.: $2,500. **Duration:** Annual. **To Apply:** Application process is divided for student applicants, both student applicants and mentors, and mentors; such process can be determined through the Academy's website. In general, applicants who are students must complete the online application and must secure three recommendation letters from mentors, department chairpersons, and academic advisors. **Deadline:** October 4.

437 ■ American Academy for Cerebral Palsy and Developmental Medicine (AACPDM)

555 E Wells St., Ste. 1100
Milwaukee, WI 53202
Ph: (414)918-3014
Fax: (414)276-2146
E-mail: info@aacpdm.org
URL: www.aacpdm.org

Social Media: www.instagram.com/aacpdm/
twitter.com/aacpdm

438 ■ AACPDM Student Travel Scholarship *(Professional development/Scholarship)*

Purpose: To support individuals who are conducting lessons and research regarding the health and general status of children and adults with cerebral palsy, developmental disorders and other childhood-onset disabilities. **Focus:** Child development; Disabilities; Mental health. **Qualif.:** Applicants must be student members of AACPDM who are enrolled in a full-time degree program or trainees; must be the authors of abstracts submitted to the Annual Meeting; applicants who have previously received this scholarship 3 times are disqualified from applying for again. **Criteria:** Selection will be based on the committee's criteria; preference will be given to scholarship applicants whose abstracts have been accepted.

Funds Avail.: $1,000. **To Apply:** Applicants must submit the completed application along with applications must upload a brief statement (1-2 paragraphs) outlining why they wish to have an AACPDM Scholarship; a letter of support from their Program Chief, Clinical Head or authorized official indicating that they are in a good standing with the program; curriculum vitae of no more than two pages; and a copy of their submitted abstracts. **Deadline:** April 5. **Contact:** AACPDM, 555 East Wells, Ste. 1100, Milwaukee, WI, 53202; Phone: 414-918-3014; Email: info@aacpdm.org.

439 ■ AACPDM Transformative Practice Grant Award *(Professional development/Grant)*

Purpose: To facilitate the translation of evidence-based clinical management strategies into practice. **Focus:** Clinical laboratory sciences. **Qualif.:** Applicants must be AACPDM members and have not received an AACPDM Transformative Practice Grant within the past five years; must be relevant for individuals with cerebral palsy, developmental disorders, or other childhood acquired the disability.

Funds Avail.: Up to $4,000. **To Apply:** Applicants must submit completed application form along with the following requirements: project description (max. 3 pages); engagement of the expert (max. 1 page); budget justification (max. 1 page); letter of support from the host institution must be appended to the application. **Contact:** Email: info@aacpdm.org.

440 ■ American Academy of Clinical Toxicology (AACT)

6728 Old McLean Village Dr.
McLean, VA 22101
Ph: (571)488-6000
URL: www.clintox.org
Social Media: twitter.com/aactinfo

441 ■ AACT Junior Investigator Research Grants *(Professional development/Grant)*

Purpose: To support clinical toxicology research and the development of new investigators' research skills. **Focus:** Toxicology. **Qualif.:** Applicants must be principal investigators who are new researchers within 5 years of completion of their terminal degree or postgraduate training or have professional experience greater than 5 years and no more than two externally funded research projects as principal investigators; must have senior investigators participate on

Awards are arranged alphabetically below their administering organizations

the research team as mentors/advisors; and must be members of AACT in good standing. **Criteria:** Selection will be based on the applicants' eligibility and applications.

Funds Avail.: $45,000. **Number Awarded:** 1. **To Apply:** Applications for the research grant should emphasize study objectives that focus on clinical toxicology research, sound research methods that support the study objectives, interdisciplinary collaborations, the potential for the project to be replicated, and prudent use of grant funds; the application and any appended pages should be sent as an email attachment to the AACT office, either as a Word document (.doc) or as a PDF file; in addition, the signature page (Page 5) should be sent by "fax" to the AACT office. **Deadline:** June 1.

442 ■ AACT Research Award (Professional development/Grant)

Purpose: To provide competitive funding for clinical research that encourages the development of new therapies and treatment and adds to the understanding of the principles and practice of clinical toxicology. **Focus:** Toxicology. **Qualif.:** Applicants research must focus on clinical toxicology research; The principal investigator must be a member of the American Academy of Clinical Toxicology in good standing; Multidisciplinary research teams are encouraged; The study timeline should not exceed 24 months from project initiation. **Criteria:** Selection will be based on the applicants' eligibility and applications.

Funds Avail.: Up to $5,000 plus additional $1,000 for travel. **Duration:** Annual; One year. **Deadline:** November 1.

443 ■ AACT Toxicology Trainee Research Grants (Professional development/Grant)

Purpose: To support clinical toxicology research and the development of toxicology trainees' research skills. **Focus:** Toxicology. **Qualif.:** Applicants must be principal investigators who are clinical/medical toxicology fellows-in-training within 5 years of completion of their terminal degree; must have senior investigators participate on the research team as mentors/advisors; and must be members of AACT in good standing. **Criteria:** Selection will be based on the applicants' eligibility and applications.

Funds Avail.: $4,000 ($3,000 for research study; $1,000 for travel to NACCT to present the results of the project). **Duration:** Annual. **Number Awarded:** 1. **To Apply:** Applications for the research grant should emphasize study objectives that focus on clinical toxicology research, sound research methods that support the study objectives, interdisciplinary collaborations, the potential for the project to be replicated, and prudent use of grant funds; the application and any appended pages should be sent as an email attachment to the AACT office, either as a Word document (.doc) or as a PDF file; in addition, the signature page (Page 5) should be sent by "fax" to the AACT office. **Deadline:** June 1.

444 ■ Lampe-Kunkel Memorial Award (Professional development/Grant)

Purpose: To support clinical toxicology research in natural products. **Focus:** Toxicology. **Qualif.:** An applicant must include the following: 1) Completed application form (5 pages); 2) Any attached pages required to complete Items; 3) Description of proposed project plan; 4) Four page biosketch for all investigators.

Funds Avail.: Up to $3,000 to fund one study, plus $1,000 for travel to the NACCT to present the results of the project.

Duration: Biennial. **Deadline:** December 1.

445 ■ American Academy of Cosmetic Dentistry (AACD)
402 W Wilson St.
Madison, WI 53703
Ph: (608)222-8583
Fax: (608)222-9540
Free: 800-543-9220
E-mail: info@aacd.com
URL: www.aacd.com
Social Media: www.facebook.com/theaacd25
www.instagram.com/theaacd
www.pinterest.com/theaacd
twitter.com/theaacd
www.youtube.com/user/AACD123

446 ■ AACD Dentist Fellowships (Professional development/Fellowship)

Purpose: To provide the highest level of achievement for members in accordance with the AACD's mission of education and excellence. **Focus:** Dentistry. **Qualif.:** Applicants must be members of the American Academy of Cosmetic Dentistry; must have attended three of the most recent five annual AACD scientific sessions. **Criteria:** Selection criteria will be based on the committee's criteria.

Funds Avail.: No specific amount. **Duration:** Annual. **To Apply:** Applicants may visit the website to obtain the application form; must submit 50 cases of different patients to the executive office and must pay the $550 (USD) application fee.

447 ■ American Academy of CPR & First Aid, Inc.
PO Box 251629
Plano, TX 75025-1629
URL: www.onlinecprcertification.net
Social Media: www.linkedin.com/company/ onlinecprcertification-net
twitter.com/AACPRFirstAid

448 ■ Save a Life Scholarship (College, University, Vocational/Occupational, Undergraduate, Graduate/ Scholarship)

Purpose: To further the education and career development of future doctors, nurses, technicians, professors, and teachers of all areas of specialization. **Focus:** Education; Health sciences; Medicine; Nursing; Teaching. **Qualif.:** Applicants must be currently enrolled, or applying to enroll within the next academic year, in a degree program in the fields of healthcare or education at an accredited U.S. university or college; must be at least 18 years old. Applicants who do not receive the scholarship can reapply in subsequent scholarship rounds. **Criteria:** Selection is based on the originality, expressiveness, passion, and ambition displayed by the applicant and in the essay.

Funds Avail.: $1,500. **Number Awarded:** 2. **To Apply:** Applicant must submit the following information via email: name, address, phone number, and email; scholarship essay of 750 to 1,000 words explaining applicant's career aspirations, plan to advance healthcare and/or education through their work, and what inspired applicant to commit to this field (essay should be in a Word document or Google document). **Deadline:** May 1; October 1. **Contact:** Email:

Awards are arranged alphabetically below their administering organizations

scholarship@onlinecprcertification.net;   URL: twitter.com/aafp
www.onlinecprcertification.net/scholarship.php.

449 ■ American Academy of Dermatology (AAD)

9500 W Bryn Mawr Ave., Suite 500
Rosemont, IL 60018-5216
Fax: (847)240-1859
Free: 866-503-7546
URL: www.aad.org
Social Media: www.facebook.com/AADmember
www.instagram.com/aadmember
twitter.com/AADmember

450 ■ International Society Travel Grant *(Professional development/Grant)*

Purpose: To promote and give participants the opportunity to meet foreign colleagues, and establish long-lasting professional relationship. **Focus:** Dermatology. **Qualif.:** Applicants must be dermatology residents, fellows, or young dermatologists (within five years of completing residency) from the United States and Canada willing to travel in Asia, Europe, and Latin America for dermatology meetings.

Duration: Annual. **Deadline:** June.

451 ■ American Academy of Facial Plastic and Reconstructive Surgery (AAFPRS)

310 S Henry St.
Alexandria, VA 22314
Ph: (703)299-9291
Fax: (703)299-8898
E-mail: info@aafprs.org
URL: www.aafprs.org
Social Media: www.facebook.com/AAFPRS
www.instagram.com/aafprs
www.linkedin.com/company/american-academy-of-facial
  -plastic-and-reconstructive-surgery
twitter.com/AAFPRS

452 ■ Leslie Bernstein Grant *(Professional development/Grant)*

Purpose: To encourage original research projects which will advance facial plastic and reconstructive surgery. **Focus:** Medical research; Surgery. **Qualif.:** Candidates for this grant must reside in the U.S. or Canada and be a physician (M.D.) who is an AAFPRS member in good standing.

Funds Avail.: $5,000 - $25,000. **Duration:** Annual. **Deadline:** January 15. **Contact:** Karen Sloat at ksloat@ aafprs.org.

453 ■ American Academy of Family Physicians (AAFP)

11400 Tomahawk Creek Pky.
Leawood, KS 66211-2680
Ph: (913)906-6000
Fax: (913)906-6075
Free: 800-274-2237
E-mail: aafp@aafp.org
URL: www.aafp.org/home.html
Social Media: www.facebook.com/familymed
linkedin.com/company/american-academy-of-family
  -physicians

454 ■ AAFP Minority Scholarships Program for Residents and Returning Students *(Professional development/Scholarship)*

Purpose: To provide financial assistance to students and residents for them to attend the National Conference of Family Medicine Residents and Medical Students. **Focus:** Medicine. **Qualif.:** Applicants must be family medicine residents (first-time attendees or returning) or medical students who have previously attended National Conference.

Funds Avail.: $600. **To Apply:** Applications can be submitted online; must include two text boxes to answer the following questions: Why did you choose family medicine? and Why do you want to attend National Conference? Each text box allows for 1500 characters (approximately 250 words). **Deadline:** July 1.

455 ■ AAFP Resident Community Outreach Award *(Professional development/Scholarship)*

Purpose: To recognize family medicine residents who have served in key leadership roles in community service or advocacy projects designed to meet the health care needs of special populations, and support the, in their educational pursuits. **Focus:** Medicine.

Duration: Annual. **Deadline:** May 1.

456 ■ AAFP Tomorrow's Leader Award *(Professional development/Scholarship)*

Purpose: To assist AAFP student and resident members to attend the National Conference for demonstrating leadership ability. **Focus:** Medicine.

Funds Avail.: $600 each. **Number Awarded:** Varies.

457 ■ American Academy of Neurology (AAN)

201 Chicago Ave.
Minneapolis, MN 55415
Ph: (612)928-6000
Fax: (612)454-2746
Free: 800-879-1960
E-mail: memberservices@aan.com
URL: www.aan.com
Social Media: www.facebook.com/
  AmericanAcademyofNeurology
www.instagram.com/aanbrain
twitter.com/AANMember
www.youtube.com/AANChannel

458 ■ AAN Clinical Research Training Fellowship *(Other/Scholarship)*

Purpose: To recognize the importance of good clinical research and to encourage young investigators in clinical studies. **Focus:** Neurology. **Qualif.:** Applicants must be neurologists and clinical investigators interested in academic careers in clinical research; and must be AAN members who have completed less than five years of residency. **Criteria:** Selection will be evaluated by the Clinical Research Subcommittee of the Science Committee of the AAN based on the applicants' ability and promise as clinician-scientists based on prior record of achievement and career plan, letters of reference and curriculum vitae; quality and nature of the training to be provided and the institutional, departmental and mentor-specific training

Awards are arranged alphabetically below their administering organizations

environment; quality and originality of the research plan. Priorities will be given to those applicants who are in a research career at an early stage.

Funds Avail.: $65,000 per year for two years plus; $10,000 per year for tuition fee. **Duration:** Annual. **To Apply:** Applicants must submit one complete copy of the letter of nomination from the Chair of the department of neurology, including assurance that clinical service responsibilities will be restricted to no more than 20 percent of the fellow's time; three-page research plan; copy of a current curriculum vitae; two letters of reference supporting applicants' potential for a clinical, academic research career and qualifications for the fellowship; listing of the applicants' and mentor's current and pending for support, other than the fellowship, using NIH format; letters from proposed mentor detailing the support of and commitment to the applicant and the proposed research and training plan; copy of the proposed mentor's NIH Biosketch; and document describing arrangements for formal course work including quantitative clinical epidemiology, biostatistics, study design, data analysis and ethics. **Deadline:** October 1. **Contact:** Michelle Maxwell, Program Manager, Science Committee; Activities; Phone: (612) 928-6001; Email: mmaxwell@aan.com.

459 ■ AAN International Scholarship Award *(Professional development/Scholarship, Award)*

Purpose: To provide eligible international candidates the opportunity to attend and participate in the Annual Meeting. **Focus:** Neurology. **Qualif.:** Applicants must be a resident living outside of the United States and Canada at the time of application. **Criteria:** Selection will be based on committee's criteria.

Funds Avail.: Up to $2,500. **Duration:** Annual. **Number Awarded:** Varies. **To Apply:** All nominees must provide a curriculum vitae, including a list of publications, and must submit an abstract for the Annual Meeting. **Contact:** Lynee Koester; Phone: 612-928-6127; Email: lkoester@aan.com.

460 ■ AAN Medical Student Summer Research Scholarship *(Graduate/Scholarship)*

Purpose: To stimulate students to pursue careers in neurology in either research or practice settings. **Focus:** Neurology.

Funds Avail.: $3,000. **Duration:** Annual. **Number Awarded:** Up to 20. **Deadline:** July 31. **Contact:** Genevieve Gates at ggates@aan.com.

461 ■ American Academy of Optometry (AAO)
2909 Fairgreen St.
Orlando, FL 32803
Ph: (321)319-4860
Fax: (407)893-9890
Free: 844-323-3937
E-mail: aaoptom@aaoptom.org
URL: www.aaopt.org
Social Media: www.facebook.com/AAOPT
instagram.com/aaopt
www.linkedin.com/company/aaopt
twitter.com/aaopt

462 ■ AOF/Johnson & Johnson Vision Care - Innovation in Education Grants *(Advanced Professional, Professional development/Grant)*

Purpose: To aid recently appointed faculty in advancing their teaching skills in the areas of improving delivery of information to students, new methodologies, increasing the use of new technology in all teaching settings, and the promotion of online learning tools. **Focus:** Optometry. **Qualif.:** Applicants must be faculty members at a North American optometric institution with less than 10 years experience as faculty members. **Criteria:** Selection shall be based on the aforementioned applicants' qualifications and compliance with the application details; priority will be given to innovative and creative projects of the applicants.

Funds Avail.: $18,000. **Duration:** Annual. **To Apply:** Applicants must submit a proposal electronically containing the following components: introduction; background and significance; specific aims; preliminary studies; and study design and methods. These sections should total no more than three pages. References (maximum of one page), budget and budget justification (maximum of one page), and biographical sketch(es) of principal and one co-investigator only (maximum of two pages for each investigator). Education/training; research and professional experience; honors and awards publications (refereed) for the last three years and representative earlier publications are also required. **Deadline:** July 1. **Contact:** Tracy Kitts, Foundation Coordinator: Phone: 321-710-3936; Email: AOF@aaoptom.org.

463 ■ Terrance N. Ingraham Pediatric Optometry Residency Award *(Graduate/Award)*

Purpose: To promote the practice and development of the field of Pediatric Optometry by providing incentive and support to sustain talented optometric residents who demonstrate a passion and commitment to practice, research, and education in the field of children's vision. **Focus:** Optometry. **Qualif.:** Applicants must be optometrists in an advanced practice pediatric/vision therapy residency program through a North American school or college of optometry. **Criteria:** Applicants will be evaluated primarily on the basis of their educational background and their ability and potential as teachers, researchers, and practitioners in the field of pediatric optometry; preference will be given to applicants with an interest in the utilization of soft contact lenses in pediatric populations. Proposals will be reviewed by a peer review committee established by the American Optometric Foundation with the assistance of the American Academy of Optometry Binocular Vision, Perception, and Pediatric Optometry Section chairs.

Funds Avail.: $2,750 each. **Duration:** Annual. **Number Awarded:** 2. **To Apply:** Applications and letters of recommendation must be submitted electronically (preferably as a PDF file) to the contact provided. Please include "Residency Award" and the applicant's last name in the subject line. Applications require the following: cover page that lists applicant name, any degrees, facility of residency, accredited optometric institution under which serving residency, current and permanent address information, email and daytime and evening phone contact information; applicant's education, clinical, research, and teaching experience, typically in the form of a CV; a brief description of the residency program and the names and email addresses of the three people the applicant contacted to submit letters of recommendation; one-page statement of career goals; the date/status of when AAO membership was obtained; and letters of recommendation from persons qualified to comment on educational qualifications, research abilities, and potential. One of which must be the Residency Director or Program Coordinator of the Institution. These should be emailed separately by the recommender. **Deadline:** June 1. **Contact:** Jennifer Rubin, Foundation Program Manager at Jenniferr@aaoptom.org.

Awards are arranged alphabetically below their administering organizations

464 ■ Sheldon Wechsler and George Mertz Contact Lens Residency Award (Professional development, Advanced Professional/Award)

Purpose: To promote the practice and development of the field of optometry by providing incentive and support to talented optometric residents who demonstrate a passion and commitment to practice, research, and education. **Focus:** Optometry. **Qualif.:** Applicant must be an optometrist continuing a contact lens residency program at a North-American school or college of optometry. **Criteria:** Applicants will be evaluated primarily on the basis of their educational background and their ability and potential as teachers, researchers and practitioners in the field of contact lenses.

Funds Avail.: $2,750 each. **Duration:** Annual. **Number Awarded:** 2. **To Apply:** Applicants must submit a summary of the their education, research and teaching experience; description of the residency program and plans for the next academic year; one-page statement of the applicant's career goals; and three letters of reference. **Deadline:** June 1. **Contact:** Email: aof@aaoptom.org.

465 ■ American Academy of Optometry Foundation (AOF)

2909 Fairgreen St.
Orlando, FL 32803
Ph: (321)319-4870
Fax: (407)893-9890
Free: 844-323-3937
E-mail: aaof@aaoptom.org
URL: www.aaopt.org/home/aaof
Social Media: www.facebook.com/AAOPT
www.instagram.com/aaopt/
twitter.com/aaopt

466 ■ William C. Ezell Fellowship (Graduate, Master's/Fellowship)

Purpose: To support graduate students enrolled in a full-time program of study and training in vision-related research that leads to a Master's or PhD degree. **Focus:** Optometry. **Qualif.:** Applicants must be a graduate student enrolled in a full-time program of study and training in vision-related research that leads to a Master's or PhD degree. Must be AAO members. **Criteria:** Applicants fellowship applications will be reviewed by the Research Committee of the American Academy of Optometry and recommendations will then be sent to the AOF Board which approves and funds the Ezell Fellowships through endowments and corporate sponsorship.

Funds Avail.: $8,000 plus $750 for travel grants each. **Duration:** Annual. **Number Awarded:** Varies. **To Apply:** Completed application form; three letters of recommendation from persons qualified to comment on educational qualifications of applicant, research abilities, potential and current and future teaching capabilities; one-page statement describing the applicant's educational objectives, future research and/or teaching interest and career objectives; include copies of scientific publications, copies of papers in press; applications and documents must be submitted electronically; attachments in .pdf are highly preferred, although MS Word is acceptable. **Deadline:** February 1. **Remarks:** Established in 1949. **Contact:** Jennifer Rubin, Foundation Program Manager, 2909 Fairgreen St., Orlando, FL 32803, USA; Phone: 321-319-4870; Email: AAOF@aaoptom.org.

467 ■ Antoinette M. Molinari Memorial Scholarships (Doctorate/Scholarship)

Purpose: To assist an exceptional student who has extraordinary financial needs and, as such, would have difficulty meeting the financial requirements of attending optometry school. **Focus:** Optometry. **Qualif.:** Eligible applicants must be pursuing a Doctorate of Optometry degree through a full-time course of study and maintain a grade point average of 3.5 (4 point scale) or higher for all course work taken thus far in optometry school. Students must currently hold a first to third year student status during the open application period and be a student member of the American Academy of Optometry (AAO). **Criteria:** Major criteria for selection is financial need, but academic and leadership potential are also important considerations.

Funds Avail.: $7,000. **Duration:** Annual. **Number Awarded:** 1. **To Apply:** Applicants must submit a completed application form; three letters of reference from persons who can attest the applicant's educational qualifications, leadership potential, and financial needs; one-page statement describing the educational and career objectives; and an official transcript of optometry course work. Application materials (aside from the transcript that is mailed) must be sent in an electronic format (preferably a PDF) to the contact provided. Please include the words "Molinari" and the "institution name" in the subject title. **Contact:** Tracy Kitts, Foundation Coordinator: Phone: 321-710-3936; Email: AOF@aaoptom.org.

468 ■ Vincent Salierno Memorial Scholarship (Doctorate/Award, Scholarship)

Purpose: To recognize and support a deserving optometry student. This rotating scholarship is awarded to a student chosen by the faculty. **Focus:** Optometry. **Qualif.:** Applicants must be first, second, third, and fourth year students pursuing a Doctorate of Optometry degree and be nominated by their institution for this scholarship; the students must be enrolled in a full-time course of study and must have a 3.0 average for all course work taken thus far in optometry school; the Vincent Salierno Scholarship is eligible for automatic renewal provided that the recipient maintains a 3.0 cumulative grade point average and is enrolled in a full-time course of study leading to a Doctorate of Optometry degree. **Criteria:** Selection must be based on financial need.

Funds Avail.: $2,000. **Duration:** Annual. **Number Awarded:** 2-5. **To Apply:** Applicants must submit by students. **Deadline:** September 15.

469 ■ American Academy of Otolaryngology - Head and Neck Surgery (AAO-HNS)

1650 Diagonal Rd.
Alexandria, VA 22314-2857
Ph: (703)836-4444
E-mail: memberservices@entnet.org
URL: www.entnet.org
Social Media: www.facebook.com/AAOHNS
www.instagram.com/aaohns
twitter.com/AAOHNS
www.youtube.com/user/aaohns

470 ■ AHNS/AAO-HNS Young Investigator combined Award (Other/Award)

Purpose: To support a collaborative AHNS/AAO-HNSF research project by fostering the development of contempo-

Awards are arranged alphabetically below their administering organizations

rary basic or clinical research skills focused on neoplastic disease of the head and neck among new full-time academic head and neck surgeons. **Focus:** Medical research. **Qualif.:** Applicants should be an Otolaryngologist—Head and Neck surgeon, who are active members of the AAO-HNS; Be citizens of the U.S; noncitizen nations, or have been lawfully admitted for permanent residency at the time of application; demonstrated potential for excellence in research and teaching and serious commitment to an academic research career in head and neck surgery. **Criteria:** Priority will be given to fellows or junior faculty who have completed residencies or fellowships within four years of the application

Number Awarded: 1. **To Apply:** Applications are in a similar format to the National Institutes of Health. All applications must be completed and submitted online. **Deadline:** January 1. **Contact:** Betty Mulugeta; E-mail: betty@ahns.info.

471 ■ American Academy of Periodontology (AAP)

737 N Michigan Ave., Ste. 800
Chicago, IL 60611-6660
Ph: (312)787-5518
E-mail: aap@perio.org
URL: www.perio.org
Social Media: www.facebook.com/PerioNews
twitter.com/PerioNews
www.youtube.com/user/PerioNews

472 ■ AAP Educator Scholarship *(Postdoctorate/ Scholarship)*

Purpose: To provide financial relief to students intending to pursue a career as a full-time teacher at a U.S. periodontal program upon graduation from a U.S. periodontal postdoctoral training program. **Focus:** Dentistry. **Qualif.:** Applicants must be student members of the AAP who have been accepted into or are currently enrolled in a U.S. periodontal postdoctoral training program and who intend to enter full-time teaching in a U.S. program.

Funds Avail.: $25,000. **Duration:** Annual.

473 ■ Bud and Linda Tarrson Fellowship *(Professional development/Fellowship)*

Purpose: To support professionals in their teaching and research in periodontology. **Focus:** Dentistry. **Qualif.:** Applicants must be either full-time faculty members at the instructor or assistant level or part-time faculty members; they must be affiliated for 10 years or less with a degree-granting institution, and their career goal must be teaching and research in periodontology.

Funds Avail.: Maximum of $36,000 ($12,000 per year). **Duration:** Annual; up to three years.

474 ■ American Academy of Periodontology Dr. D. Walter Cohen Teaching Fellowships *(Professional development/Fellowship)*

Purpose: To assist third-year periodontal residents in launching their careers as educators. **Focus:** Dentistry. **Qualif.:** Applicants must be in the first three years of their full-time teaching employment as defined by the institution at a U.S. periodontal program or have accepted a full-time faculty position at a U.S. periodontal program; must be students or active members of American Academy of Peri-

odontology (AAP); individuals who have not yet begun working as educators but who present a letter stating they have accepted a full-time teaching position may also apply.

Funds Avail.: $10,000. **Duration:** Annual.

475 ■ American Academy in Rome (AAR)

7 E 60th St.
New York, NY 10022-1001
Ph: (212)751-7200
Fax: (212)751-7220
URL: www.aarome.org
Social Media: www.facebook.com/aarome
www.instagram.com/amacademyrome
www.pinterest.com.au/pin/205406432978554953/?send =true
twitter.com/amacademyrome
www.youtube.com/channel/UCZqVVswAO _EfDiNKyOd12Mg

476 ■ Rome Prize *(Postdoctorate, Graduate, Undergraduate/Prize, Award)*

Purpose: To support innovative and cross-disciplinary work in the arts and humanities. **Focus:** Arts; Humanities. **Qualif.:** Applicants must be U.S. citizens at the time of application; U.S. citizens and foreign nationals who have lived in the United States for three years may apply for the National Endowment for the Humanities post-doctoral fellowships; graduate students in the humanities may apply for pre-doctoral fellowships. undergraduate students are not eligible. Applicant must not hold a full-time job during the fellowship term. **Criteria:** Selection will be based on a quality of an applicant's submission materials.

Funds Avail.: $16,000 for half term and $28,000 for full term. **Duration:** Annual. **To Apply:** Applicants must submit an application form along with project proposal and a letter of recommendation (not required for literature, musical composition, and visual arts). **Deadline:** November 1; November 15; November 30.

477 ■ American Academy of Sanitarians (AAS)

1568 LEGRAND CIRCLE
Lawrenceville, GA 30043-8191
Ph: (678)518-4028
E-mail: gnoonan@charter.net
URL: aaosi.wildapricot.org

478 ■ NEHA/AAS Scholarship *(Graduate, Undergraduate/Scholarship)*

Purpose: To encourage and support early commitment by students to a career in environmental health. **Focus:** Environmental science. **Qualif.:** Applicants pursuing a Bachelor's Degree in Environmental Health or Postgraduate Degree in Environmental Health Sciences. **Criteria:** Applicants are selected based on the committee's review of the application materials.

Funds Avail.: No specific amount. **Number Awarded:** 3. **To Apply:** Applicants must complete the online application form; provide an official academic transcript from the school in which the applicant is currently enrolled; submit one faculty letter of recommendation from the school in which the applicant is currently enrolled; incomplete applications will not be considered. **Contact:** Jonna Ashley; E-mail: jashley@neha.org.

Awards are arranged alphabetically below their administering organizations

479 ■ American Acne and Rosacea Society (AARS)

201 Claremont Ave.
Montclair, NJ 07042
Ph: (973)783-4575
Fax: (973)783-4576
Free: 888-744-3376
E-mail: info@aarsmember.org
URL: www.acneandrosacea.org
Social Media: www.facebook.com/
  AmericanAcneAndRosaceaSociety
www.linkedin.com/company/american-acne-&-rosacea
  -society
twitter.com/acneandrosacea
www.youtube.com/c/AcneandRosaceaOrgAARS

480 ■ American Acne and Rosacea Society Mentorship Grant *(Professional development/Grant)*

Purpose: To assist young dermatologists to become leaders and experts in the field of acne and rosacea by acquiring academic skills which may not be available at their training institutions. **Focus:** Dermatology. **Qualif.:** Applicants must be dermatology residents, fellows, and recent graduates (within 5 years) of U.S. dermatology residency; and the sponsor of the applicants must be a member of the AARS. **Criteria:** Selection will be based on the committee's criteria.

Funds Avail.: Not exceed to 10,000. **Duration:** Annual. **Number Awarded:** Varies.

481 ■ American Antiquarian Society (AAS)

185 Salisbury St.
Worcester, MA 01609-1634
Ph: (508)755-5221
Fax: (508)753-3311
E-mail: library@americanantiquarian.org
URL: www.americanantiquarian.org
Social Media: www.facebook.com/American.Antiquarian
instagram.com/americanantiquarian
twitter.com/AmAntiquarian
youtube.com/user/AmericanAntiquarian

482 ■ AAS-American Society for Eighteenth-Century Studies Fellowships *(Doctorate/Fellowship)*

Purpose: To enable scholars to spend an uninterrupted block of time doing research in the AAS library. **Focus:** General studies/Field of study not specified. **Qualif.:** Applicants must be enrolled in doctoral degree of accredited institutions or universities; must be holding a recognized terminal degree appropriate to the area of proposed research, such as the master's degree in library science or M.F.A. **Criteria:** Selection will be based on scholarly qualifications, the scholarly significance or importance of the project, and the appropriateness of the proposed study to the UB Library's collections.

Funds Avail.: $1,850 per month. **Duration:** Annual; one to two months during the period june 1, 2019 to may 31, 2020. **To Apply:** Applicants must fill out the online application form; must provide current CV; description of proposed research project (no longer than two double-spaced pages); one-page bibliography; two letters of recommendation. **Deadline:** January 15. **Contact:** Letters should be submitted electronically to Cheryl McRell, Program Administrator; Email: cmcrell@mwa.org.

483 ■ AAS National Endowment for the Humanities Long-Term Fellowships *(Postdoctorate/Fellowship)*

Purpose: To enable scholars to spend an uninterrupted block of time doing research in the AAS library. **Focus:** Humanities. **Qualif.:** Applicants must have completed their formal professional training; may be foreign nationals who have been residents in the United States for at least three years immediately preceding the application deadline. Applicants must have received a PhD within the last 3 years. **Criteria:** Recipients are selected based on: scholarly qualifications, significance or importance of the project; appropriateness of the proposed study to the AAS collections.

Funds Avail.: $4,200 per month. **Duration:** Annual; 4 to 12 months. **Number Awarded:** At least three. **To Apply:** Applicants must fill out the online application form including current CV; description of proposed research project (no longer than six double-spaced sides); one page bibliography; two letters of recommendation. **Deadline:** January 15. **Contact:** Letters should be submitted electronically to Cheryl McRell, Program Administrator; Email: cmcrell@mwa.org.

484 ■ American Historical Print Collectors Society Fellowship *(Doctorate/Fellowship)*

Purpose: To support research using prints. **Focus:** United States studies. **Criteria:** Recipients are selected in the spring by a committee of scholars, previous winners, and AAS curators.

Funds Avail.: $1,850 per month. **Duration:** Annual; one to two months during the period june 1, 2019 to may 31, 2020. **To Apply:** Applicants must fill out the online application form; must provide current cv; description of proposed research project (no longer than two double-spaced pages); one-page bibliography; two letters of recommendation; letters should be submitted electronically. **Deadline:** January 15. **Contact:** Nan Wolverton, Phone: 508-471-2199; Email: nwolverton@mwa.org.

485 ■ Stephen Botein Fellowships *(Doctorate/Fellowship)*

Purpose: To enable scholars to spend an uninterrupted block of time doing research in the AAS library. **Focus:** Culture; History, American. **Qualif.:** Applicants must be enrolled in doctoral degree of accredited institutions or universities; must be holding a recognized terminal degree appropriate to the area of proposed research, such as the master's degree in library science or M.F.A. **Criteria:** Selection will be based on scholarly qualifications, the scholarly significance or importance of the project, and the appropriateness of the proposed study to the society's collections.

Funds Avail.: $1,850 per month. **Duration:** Annual; one to two months during the period june 1, 2019 to may 31, 2020. **To Apply:** Applicants must fill out the online application form; must provide current CV; description of proposed research project (no longer than two double-spaced pages); one-page bibliography; two letters of recommendation. **Deadline:** January 15. **Contact:** Letters should be submitted electronically to Cheryl McRell, Program Administrator; Email: cmcrell@mwa.org.

486 ■ ACLS Frederick Burkhardt Residential Fellowships *(Other/Fellowship)*

Purpose: To support individuals for their research projects in humanities and related social sciences. **Focus:** Humanities; Social sciences. **Qualif.:** Applicants must be recently

Awards are arranged alphabetically below their administering organizations

tenured humanists; must be employed in a tenured position at a degree granting academic institution in the United States. **Criteria:** Recipients are selected based on the quality of the proposal and required qualifications.

Funds Avail.: $95,000 + funds for research costs and related scholarly activities of up to $7,500 and for relocation up to $3,000. **Duration:** one academic year. **To Apply:** Applicants must visit the website for the online fellowship application system; must submit no more than ten pages, double-spaced proposal; no more than three pages bibliography; no more than two pages publications list; three reference letters; must provide an institutional statement. **Deadline:** September 25.

487 ■ Jenny d'Héricourt Fellowship (Doctorate/ Fellowship)

Purpose: To assist individuals to do a research on any topic supported by the collections of the Society. **Focus:** Culture; History; Literature. **Qualif.:** Applicants must hold a PhD and residents of France; must be AFEA member. **Criteria:** Selection will be based on the committee's criteria.

Funds Avail.: 1,800 Euros. **Duration:** Annual; one to two months during the period june 1, 2019 to may 31, 2020. **Number Awarded:** 1. **To Apply:** Applicants must complete the application form online and must submit the following materials: current CV; description of the proposed research project (no longer than two double-spaced pages); one-page bibliography of relevant secondary literature; list of other sources of funding for the project; two letters of recommendation. **Deadline:** February 15. **Contact:** Submissions must be sent to the following address: Axel NESME, d'Hericourt Fellowship, AFEA-AAS, 10, Cours Gambetta, 69007, Lyon.

488 ■ The Drawn to Art Fellowship (Doctorate/ Fellowship)

Purpose: To enable scholars, advanced graduate students and others to spend an uninterrupted block of time doing research in the AAS library. **Focus:** Art. **Qualif.:** Applicants must be enrolled in doctoral degree of accredited institutions or universities; must be holding a recognized terminal degree appropriate to the area of proposed research, such as the master's degree in library science or M.F.A. **Criteria:** Selection will be scholarly qualifications, the scholarly significance or importance of the project, and the appropriateness of the proposed study to the society's collections.

Funds Avail.: $1,850 per month; $1,350 per month society's fellows' residence. **Duration:** Annual; one to two months during the period june 1, 2019 to may 31, 2020. **To Apply:** Applicants must fill out the online application form; must provide current CV; description of proposed research project (no longer than two double-spaced pages); one-page bibliography; two letters of recommendation. **Deadline:** January 15. **Contact:** Letters should be submitted electronically to Cheryl McRell, Program Administrator; Email: cmcrell@mwa.org.

489 ■ The Christoph Daniel Ebeling Fellowship (Postdoctorate, Doctorate/Fellowship)

Purpose: To support research at AAS by doctoral and postdoctoral candidates in American Studies at German universities. **Focus:** United States studies. **Qualif.:** Applicants must be German citizens or permanent residents at the post-graduate or postdoctoral stages of their careers. **Criteria:** Recipients are selected based on: scholarly qualifications; significance or importance of the project; ap-

propriateness of the proposed study to AAS collections.

Funds Avail.: $1,800 Euros. **Duration:** one to two months. **To Apply:** Applicants must fill out the online application form. **Deadline:** May 31.

490 ■ Fellowships for Creative and Performing Artists and Writers (Professional development/ Fellowship)

Purpose: To improve the ways in which an understanding of history is communicated to the American people. **Focus:** Culture; Filmmaking; History, American; Journalism; Performing arts; Writing. **Qualif.:** Applicants must have work for the general public which produces imaginative, non-formulaic works dealing with pre-twentieth century American history. **Criteria:** Recipients are selected based on the quality of performed task.

Funds Avail.: $1,850 stipend; (Room fees range from $700 to $500 per month.). **Duration:** Annual; four weeks during the period January 1 through December 31. **To Apply:** Applicants must fill out the online application form; should submit current resume; two letters of reference from individuals familiar with applicant's career accomplishments and goals; two to three copies of full, completed works, in addition to the 25-page work sample; references should be sent directly to AAS by email to Cheryl McRell. **Deadline:** October 5. **Contact:** Letters should be submitted electronically to Cheryl McRell, Program Administrator; Email: cmcrell@mwa.org.

491 ■ Hench Post-Dissertation Fellowship (Postdoctorate/Fellowship)

Purpose: To provide scholars with time and resources to extend research and/or to revise the dissertation for publication. **Focus:** History. **Qualif.:** Applicants must be scholars no more than three years beyond receipt of their doctorate; fellowship must be for a minimum of twelve months; intended to provide the recipient with time and resources to extend research and revise the dissertation written for publication; anything relevant to the society's library collections and programmatic scope of American history and culture through 1876 is eligible; must come from such fields as history, literature, American studies, political science, art history, music history, and others relating to America. **Criteria:** Selection will based on appropriateness of the project to the AAS collections and interests; likelihood that the revised dissertation will make a highly significant books.

Funds Avail.: $35,000. **Duration:** Annual; for twelve months. **To Apply:** Applicants must fill out the online application form. **Deadline:** October 15. **Remarks:** Established in 1998. **Contact:** Hench Fellowship: Cheryl McRell, Program Administrator, AAS; Email: cmcrell@mwa.org.

492 ■ Justin G. Schiller Fellowship (Doctorate, Postdoctorate/Fellowship)

Purpose: To support research from any disciplinary perspective on the production, distribution, literary content, or historical context of American children's books to 1876. **Focus:** Culture; History. **Qualif.:** Applicants must be doctoral or postdoctoral scholars. **Criteria:** Applicants will be selected based on the scholarly qualifications, the scholarly significance or importance of the project, and the appropriateness of the proposed study to the Society's collections.

Funds Avail.: $1,850 per month. **Duration:** Annual; one to two months during the period june 1, 2019 to may 31, 2020.

Awards are arranged alphabetically below their administering organizations

To Apply: Applicants must complete the application form online and must submit the following materials: current CV; description of the proposed research project (no longer than two double-spaced pages); one-page bibliography of relevant secondary literature; list of other sources of funding for the project; two letters of recommendation. **Deadline:** January 15. **Contact:** Cheryl McRell, Program Administrator, Email: cmcrell@mwa.org.

493 ■ Lapides Fellowships in Pre-1865 Juvenile Literature and Ephemera (Graduate, Postdoctorate/Fellowship)

Purpose: To support projects examining the creative, artistic, cultural, technological, or commercial aspects of American juvenile literature and ephemera produces between the Puritan Era and the Civil War. **Focus:** Culture; History; Literature. **Qualif.:** Applicants must be postdoctoral scholars or graduate students at work on doctoral dissertations. **Criteria:** Applicants will be selected based on the scholarly qualifications, the scholarly significance or importance of the project, and the appropriateness of the proposed study to the Society's collections.

Funds Avail.: $1,850. **Duration:** Annual; one to two months during the period june 1, 2019 to may 31, 2020. **To Apply:** Applicants must complete the application form online and must submit the following materials: current CV; description of the proposed research project (no longer than two double-spaced pages); one-page bibliography of relevant secondary literature; list of other sources of funding for the project; two letters of recommendation. **Deadline:** January 15. **Contact:** Cheryl McRell, Program Administrator, Email: cmcrell@mwa.org.

494 ■ Jay and Deborah Last Fellowships (Doctorate/Fellowship)

Purpose: To support research on American art, visual culture, or other projects that will make substantial use of graphic materials as primary sources. **Focus:** Art; Culture. **Qualif.:** Applicants must be enrolled in doctoral degree of accredited institutions or universities; must be holding a recognized terminal degree appropriate to the area of proposed research, such as the master's degree in library science or M.F.A. **Criteria:** Recipients are selected based on: scholarly qualifications; significance or importance of the project; appropriateness of the proposed study to AAS collections.

Funds Avail.: $1,850 per month. **Duration:** Annual; one to two months during the period june 1, 2019 to may 31, 2020. **To Apply:** Applicants must fill out the online application form; must provide current CV; description of proposed research project (no longer than two double-spaced pages); one-page bibliography; two letters of recommendation. **Deadline:** January 15. **Contact:** Letters should be submitted electronically to Cheryl McRell, Program Administrator; Email: cmcrell@mwa.org.

495 ■ The Legacy Fellowship (Doctorate/Fellowship)

Purpose: To enable scholars, advanced graduate students and others to spend an uninterrupted block of time doing research in the AAS library. **Focus:** History, American. **Qualif.:** Applicants must be enrolled in doctoral degree of accredited institution or universities; must be engaged in scholarly research and writing including doctoral dissertation in any field of American history and culture. **Criteria:** Selection will be based on the following: individual engaged in scholarly research and writing including doctoral dissertations in any field of American history and culture

through 1876; scholarly qualifications, the scholarly significance or importance of the project, and the appropriateness of the proposed study to the society's collections.

Funds Avail.: $1,850 per month; $1,350 per month society's fellows' residence. **Duration:** Annual; one to two months during the period june 1, 2019 to may 31, 2020. **To Apply:** Applicants must fill out the online application form; must provide current CV; description of proposed research project (no longer than two double-spaced pages); one-page bibliography; two letters of recommendation. **Deadline:** January 15. **Remarks:** Established in 1997. **Contact:** Letters should be submitted electronically to Cheryl McRell, Program Administrator; Email: cmcrell@mwa.org.

496 ■ The Barbara L. Packer Fellowship (Doctorate, Postdoctorate/Fellowship)

Purpose: To support individuals engaged in scholarly research and writing related to the Transcendentalists in general. **Focus:** Culture; History; Literature. **Qualif.:** Applicants must be doctoral or postdoctoral scholars; must be individuals engaged in scholarly research and writing related to the Transcendentalists. **Criteria:** Applicants will be selected based on the scholarly qualifications, the scholarly significance or importance of the project, and the appropriateness of the proposed study to the Society's collections.

Funds Avail.: $1,850 per month. **Duration:** Monthly; one to two months during the period june 1, 2019 to may 31, 2020. **To Apply:** Applicants must fill out the online application form; must provide current CV; description of proposed research project (no longer than two double-spaced pages); one-page bibliography; two letters of recommendation. **Deadline:** January 15. **Contact:** Cheryl McRell, Program Administrator, Email: cmcrell@mwa.org.

497 ■ Kate B. and Hall J. Peterson Fellowships (Doctorate/Fellowship)

Purpose: To enable scholars to spend an uninterrupted block of time doing research in the AAS library. **Focus:** Culture; History, American. **Qualif.:** Applicants must be enrolled in doctoral degree of accredited institution or universities; must be engaged in scholarly research and writing including doctoral dissertation in any field of American history and culture. **Criteria:** Recipients are selected based on: scholarly qualifications; significance or importance of the project; appropriateness of the proposed study to AAS collections.

Funds Avail.: $1,850 per month. **Duration:** Annual; one to two months during the period june 1, 2019 to may 31, 2020. **To Apply:** Applicants must fill out the online application form; must provide current CV; description of proposed research project (no longer than two double-spaced pages); one-page bibliography; two letters of recommendation. **Deadline:** January 15. **Contact:** Letters should be submitted electronically to Cheryl McRell, Program Administrator; Email: cmcrell@mwa.org.

498 ■ The Reese Fellowship (Doctorate/Fellowship)

Purpose: To enable scholars, advanced graduate students and others to spend an uninterrupted block of time doing research in the AAS library. **Focus:** United States studies. **Qualif.:** Applicants must be enrolled in doctoral degree of accredited institutions or universities; must be holding a recognized terminal degree appropriate to the area of proposed research, such as the master's degree in library science or M.F.A. **Criteria:** Selection will be scholarly

Awards are arranged alphabetically below their administering organizations

qualifications, the scholarly significance or importance of the project, and the appropriateness of the proposed study to the society's collections.

Funds Avail.: $1,850 per month; $1,350 per month society's fellows' residence. **Duration:** Annual; one to two months during the period june 1, 2019 to may 31, 2020. **To Apply:** Applicants must fill out the online application form; must provide current CV; description of proposed research project (no longer than two double-spaced pages); one-page bibliography; two letters of recommendation. **Deadline:** January 15. **Contact:** Letters should be submitted electronically to Cheryl McRell, Program Administrator; Email: cmcrell@mwa.org.

499 ■ The Joyce Tracy Fellowship *(Doctorate/Fellowship)*

Purpose: To enable scholars, advanced graduate students and others to spend an uninterrupted block of time doing research in the AAS library. **Focus:** History, American. **Qualif.:** Applicants must be enrolled in doctoral degree of accredited institutions or universities; must be holding a recognized terminal degree appropriate to the area of proposed research, such as the master's degree in library science or M.F.A. **Criteria:** Selection will be based on scholarly qualifications, the scholarly significance or importance of the project, and the appropriateness of the proposed study to the society's collections.

Funds Avail.: $1,850 per month; $1,350 per month society's fellows' residence. **Duration:** Annual; one to two months during the period june 1, 2019 to may 31, 2020. **To Apply:** Applicants must fill out the online application form; must provide current CV; description of proposed research project (no longer than two double-spaced pages); one-page bibliography; two letters of recommendation. **Deadline:** January 15. **Contact:** Letters should be submitted electronically to Cheryl McRell, Program Administrator; Email: cmcrell@mwa.org.

500 ■ American Art Therapy Association (AATA)

4875 Eisenhower Ave., Ste. 240
Alexandria, VA 22304
Ph: (703)548-5860
Fax: (703)783-8468
Free: 888-290-0878
E-mail: info@arttherapy.org
URL: www.arttherapy.org
Social Media: www.facebook.com/
  TheAmericanArtTherapyAssociation
www.instagram.com/arttherapyorg
twitter.com/ArtTherapyOrg

501 ■ American Art Therapy Association Anniversary Scholarship *(Graduate/Scholarship)*

Purpose: To encourage the growth of the profession by rewarding excellence and enabling access to information and resources for the members who are selected by the Scholarship Committee. **Focus:** Art therapy. **Qualif.:** Applicants must be student members with a current GPA of at least 3.25 who can demonstrate financial need and acceptance or enrollment in an American Art Therapy Association approved graduate art therapy program. **Criteria:** Selection shall be based on the aforementioned qualifications and compliance with the application details.

Funds Avail.: Up to $900. **Duration:** Annual. **Number Awarded:** 1. **To Apply:** Applicants must submit a com-

pleted application form. Other documents to be submitted are: financial form; letters of recommendation; financial information forms; and, documentation indicating acceptance or enrollment in an AATA-approved art therapy program. Please do not bind or staple documents or include extraneous information with the application. **Deadline:** May 1.

502 ■ Myra Levick Scholarship Fund *(Graduate/Scholarship)*

Purpose: To promote education in art therapy. **Focus:** Art therapy. **Qualif.:** Applicant must be an active student member of AATA; accepted or attending an AATA approved graduate art therapy program; have a GPA of 3.0; and demonstrated financial need. **Criteria:** Selection is based on the application.

Funds Avail.: Up to $900. **Duration:** Annual. **Number Awarded:** 1. **To Apply:** Applicants must submit a completed application form; one official academic transcript; two academic or work-related, signed letters of recommendation; student financial information form; one essay (maximum of two pages, double spaced, typewritten) including the biography and stating the future role as an art therapist; and documentation of acceptance or enrollment in an American Art Therapy Association approved art therapy program. **Deadline:** May 1.

503 ■ Rawley Silver Award for Excellence *(Graduate/Scholarship)*

Purpose: To promote education in art therapy. **Focus:** Art therapy. **Qualif.:** Applicant must be an active student member of AATA; accepted or attending an AATA approved graduate art therapy program; and have an excellent academic record. **Criteria:** Selection is based on the application.

Funds Avail.: Up to $900. **Duration:** Annual. **Number Awarded:** 1. **To Apply:** Applicants must submit a completed application form together with official academic transcripts; two academic/work related letters of recommendations; student financial information form; a two-page essay (biography); and proof of acceptance in an AATA approved graduate art therapy program. Submit the original and four more copies of the complete required application packets. **Deadline:** May 1.

504 ■ Rawley Silver Research Award *(Postgraduate, Postdoctorate/Award, Recognition)*

Purpose: To support an art therapy research project by a voting member of the American Art Therapy Association. **Focus:** Art therapy. **Qualif.:** Applicants must be voting members of AATA and may only submit one proposal. **Criteria:** Selection will evaluate proposals considering the following: qualifications of the researcher, quality of the proposed research, and plan for dissemination.

Funds Avail.: $1,000. **Duration:** Annual. **Deadline:** June 15. **Contact:** Email: info@arttherapy.org.

505 ■ American Association for the Advancement of Science (AAAS)

1200 New York Ave. NW
Washington, DC 20005
Ph: (202)326-6400
URL: www.aaas.org

Awards are arranged alphabetically below their administering organizations

506 ■ AAAS Mass Media Science & Engineering Fellows Program *(Undergraduate, Graduate, Postdoctorate/Fellowship)*

Purpose: To increase public understanding of science and technology. **Focus:** Engineering; Media arts; Science technologies. **Qualif.:** Applicants must be enrolled as college or university students (graduate, doctoral, or upper level undergraduates) or within one year of a completed degree in the physical, biological, geological, health, engineering, computer, or social sciences or mathematics in order to apply. The Fellowship is open to international students who are already studying in the United States and who hold visas that allow them to receive payment for work during the summer. Such is also open to US citizens studying abroad, as long as they can pay their way back into the US for the Fellowship. **Criteria:** Recipients will be selected based on telephone interview made by the AAAS staff.

Funds Avail.: $500 each. **Duration:** Annual; up to 10 weeks. **To Apply:** Applicants must fill out the online application form; they must also submit the following: applicant information; two "Recommendation Questionnaires" completed online by recommenders you identify; curriculum vitae; candidate Questions; general Writing Sample: ONE 2-3 page, double-spaced brief sample of your writing that is on any subject (science or non-science topic) and directed toward a non-scientific audience (using language appropriate for the general public); sample News Story; source Article. **Contact:** Email: mmfellowship@aaas.org.

507 ■ AAAS Science and Technology Policy Fellowships *(Professional development/Fellowship)*

Purpose: To provide professional development opportunity to individuals interested in learning about the science-policy interface while applying their scientific and technical knowledge and analytical skills to the federal policy realm. **Focus:** Engineering; Science; Science technologies. **Qualif.:** Applicants must: hold a doctoral level science degree or a master's in engineering; have solid scientific and technical credentials and three references; exhibit integrity, problem-solving ability, flexibility and leadership qualities; be U.S. citizens who are committed to serving society; have good verbal and written communication skills; and, not federal employees. AAAS seeks candidates from a broad array of backgrounds and a diversity of geographic, disciplinary, gender, and ethnic perspectives as well as disability status. Fellows represent the spectrum of career stages - from recent doctoral graduates to faculty on sabbatical and retired scientists, and sectors - from academia and industry to nonprofit organizations. **Criteria:** Selection will be based on the aforesaid qualifications and compliance with the application process.

Duration: Annual. **To Apply:** Applicants must provide a profile indicating the name and contact information; candidates' data; candidates' statement providing the qualifications for the fellowship and career goals; reasons for applying for the fellowship; they must also submit curriculum vitae; extracurricular activities; and references including three recommendation letters. **Deadline:** November 1.

508 ■ American Association of Advertising Agencies (AAAA)

1065 Avenue of the Americas, 16th Fl.
New York, NY 10018
Ph: (212)682-2500
E-mail: research@aaaa.org

URL: www.aaaa.org
Social Media: www.facebook.com/aaaaorg
www.instagram.com/4as_presents
www.linkedin.com/company/4as
www.linkedin.com/company/4as
twitter.com/4as
www.youtube.com/channel/UCrxr1ATwHXcJ6bACXusAqLw

509 ■ ANA Multicultural Excellence Scholarship Fund (MAIP) *(Graduate, Undergraduate/Internship)*

Purpose: To provide scholarships to MAIP interns upon completion of the internship program. **Focus:** Advertising.

Remarks: Established in 2003.

510 ■ Bill Bernbach Diversity Scholarships *(Undergraduate/Scholarship)*

Purpose: To provide financial assistance to creatively talented, culturally diverse students seeking an education in copywriting, art direction and design at designated colleges and portfolio schools. **Focus:** Advertising. **Qualif.:** Applicants must be African-American, American Indian/ Alaska Native, Asian-American, Native Hawaiian or other Pacific, or Hispanic students; be within 18 months of graduation; be citizens or national or legal permanent residents of the United States as of the date the application is submitted. **Criteria:** Recipients are selected by DDB Chief Creative Officers, Creative Directors, Talent Managers, and Creative Service Managers across the U.S.

Duration: Annual. **To Apply:** Applicants must contact the tuition office of the participating schools. **Deadline:** August 6. **Remarks:** Established in 1998. **Contact:** Email: bbscholarship@ny.ddb.com.

511 ■ American Association of Anatomists (AAA)

6120 Executive Boulevard, Suite 725
Rockville, MD 20852
Ph: (301)634-7910
Fax: (301)634-7965
E-mail: info@anatomy.org
URL: www.anatomy.org
Social Media: www.facebook.com/Anatomists
www.linkedin.com/company/american-association-for
 -anatomy
twitter.com/anatomyorg
www.youtube.com/user/AAAnatomists?reload=9

512 ■ AAA Education Research Scholarship *(Graduate, Postdoctorate/Scholarship)*

Purpose: To support innovative projects that hold promise as models for the resolution of important issues and problems in anatomical education and represent new and creative approaches to teaching and learning. The scholarship is supported by "Lippincott Williams & Wilkins". **Focus:** Science. **Qualif.:** Applicants must be members (graduate students in a mentored project, or postdoctoral fellows or junior faculty members (rank no higher than assistant professor) for the year in which they apply and through the completion of their scholarship project. **Criteria:** Selection is based on submission of documents.

Funds Avail.: $5,000, plus travel support (up to $1,000). **Duration:** Annual. **To Apply:** Applicants must submit an abstract of the project; letter of support from the Chairperson or Division Chief signed by the Dean or appropriate fis-

Awards are arranged alphabetically below their administering organizations

cal officer. **Deadline:** October 15. **Remarks:** Established in 2008. **Contact:** E-mail: lphares@anatomy.org.

513 ■ AAA Postdoctoral Fellowship *(Postdoctorate/ Fellowship)*

Purpose: To provide salary support to AAA members working in any aspect of biology relevant to the anatomical sciences. **Focus:** Biology. **Qualif.:** Applicants must be current AAA members and are expected to remain members for the duration of the fellowship; should be working on a research project encompassing any aspect of biology that is relevant to the anatomical sciences; approaches can include (but are not limited to) cellular, molecular, genetic or histological techniques, and/or emphasize development, evolution, morphology or human health; should have all requirements of doctoral degree completed at the time of submission of fellowship application. **Criteria:** Selection will be based on the committee's criteria.

Funds Avail.: $20,000. **Duration:** Annual. **Number Awarded:** 1. **To Apply:** Applications should be submitted electronically. Each application must include the following: curriculum vitae, NIH four-page format; four-page research proposal with the formats given by AAA; letter from the department chair stating that the candidates have completed all requirements of doctoral degrees at the time of application; evidence of an application to their institution's IACUC or IRB, as appropriate; letter describing other salary and research support available to the postdoc in the sponsor laboratory; and, three letters of recommendation, including one from the sponsor and one written by an AAA member (who may also be the sponsor). **Deadline:** October 1.

514 ■ American Association for Applied Linguistics (AAAL)

2900 Delk Rd Ste. 700,PMB 321
Marietta, GA 30067
Ph: (678)229-2892
URL: www.aaal.org
Social Media: www.facebook.com/AAALORG

515 ■ Graduate Student Award *(Doctorate, Master's, Graduate/Award)*

Purpose: To support graduate student members by helping them to attend the Association's Annual Meeting. **Focus:** Linguistics; Travel and tourism. **Qualif.:** Applicants must be student members of AAAL at the time of application and enrolled in a university Master's or Ph.D. program in applied linguistics or a related field; single authored individual submissions are eligible. **Criteria:** The primary consideration in granting the award is the academic merit of the student's proposal submitted to the conference.

Funds Avail.: No specific amount. **Number Awarded:** Varies. **To Apply:** Graduate students who are eligible to apply will be notified by the conference chair and may submit their application once they have confirmed their intention to attend the conference and arrange for their academic advisor to send a letter of recommendation. Specific information about the application submission process will be distributed to the students eligible to apply. **Remarks:** Established in 1996.

516 ■ American Association of Blacks in Energy (AABE)

1625 K St. NW, Ste. 405
Washington, DC 20006
Ph: (202)371-9530
Fax: (202)371-9218
E-mail: info@aabe.org
URL: www.aabe.org
Social Media: www.facebook.com/AABENational
twitter.com/_AABE
www.youtube.com/user/TheAABE123

517 ■ American Association of Blacks in Energy Scholarships *(Undergraduate/Scholarship)*

Purpose: To help increase the number of African Americans and other misrepresented minorities in energy-related fields. **Focus:** Energy-related areas. **Qualif.:** Applicants must have at least an overall "B" academic average and a "B" average in mathematics and science courses; must be graduating high school seniors who have applied to one or more accredited colleges/universities; must be planning to major in engineering, mathematics, or the physical sciences; must demonstrate financial need; and must be members of one of the underrepresented minority groups in the sciences and related areas of technology. **Criteria:** Applicants are evaluated based on criteria designed by the organization's National Scholarship Committee.

Duration: Annual. **To Apply:** Applicants must submit completed AABE application form; official high school transcript; complete essay that has been proofread for typing error, grammar, structure, organization, content and clarity; official proof of ACT or SAT scores; two letters of reference; completed checklist. **Deadline:** March 15.

518 ■ American Association of Blood Banks (AABB)

4550 Montgomery Avenue Suite 700, North Tower
Bethesda, MD 20814
Ph: (301)907-6977
Fax: (301)907-6895
E-mail: marketing@aabb.org
URL: www.aabb.org
Social Media: www.facebook.com/AABBupdates
twitter.com/aabb
www.youtube.com/user/aabbmedia

519 ■ AABB-Fenwal Specialist in Blood Bank Scholarship Awards *(Professional development/ Scholarship)*

Purpose: To recognize individuals who are enrolled, accepted for enrollment in, or who have recently completed training (within12 months) leading to SBB certification from an AABB-accredited institution. **Focus:** Medicine. **Qualif.:** Applicant must be any individual enrolled, accepted for enrollment in or has recently completed (within the past calendar year) a program leading to a Specialist in Blood Banking certification in an AABB accredited institution. **Criteria:** Applicants are judged upon the committee's criteria.

Funds Avail.: $1,500. **Duration:** Annual. **Remarks:** Established in 1982. **Contact:** Standards Department, AABB, 4550 Montgomery Ave., Ste. 700, North Tower, Bethesda, MD, 20814; Phone: 301-215-6493; E-mail: standards@ aabb.org.

520 ■ AABB-Fenwal Transfusion Medicine Fellows Scholarship Awards *(Doctorate/Scholarship)*

Purpose: To recognize professionals with a Doctor of Medicine or Doctor of Osteopathic Medicine degree who

Awards are arranged alphabetically below their administering organizations

are current fellows in a transfusion medicine program or training program that includes at least one continuous year in transfusion medicine training. **Focus:** Medicine. **Qualif.:** Applicant must be interested in research, development and continuing education, in the field of transfusion medicine; an MD or DO degree who is a fellow in a transfusion medicine program or training program that includes at least one continuous year in transfusion medicine training.

Funds Avail.: $1,500. **Duration:** Annual. **Remarks:** Established in 1982. **Contact:** Standards Department, AABB, 4550 Montgomery Ave., Ste. 700, North Tower, Bethesda, MD, 20814; Phone: 301-215-6493; E-mail: standards@aabb.org.

521 ■ American Association of Bovine Practitioners (AABP)

1130 East Main St., Ste. 302
Ashland, OH 44805
Ph: (419)496-0685
Fax: (419)496-0697
E-mail: aabphq@aabp.org
URL: www.aabp.org
Social Media: www.facebook.com/AABPmembers

522 ■ AABP Amstutz Scholarship (Undergraduate/Scholarship)

Purpose: To support the most superior students in the 2nd year of veterinary school that demonstrate the character, knowledge, experience, motivation, and potential to become outstanding bovine veterinarians in the United States and Canada. **Focus:** Veterinary science and medicine. **Qualif.:** Applicants must be enrolled in a college of veterinary medicine located in Canada and United States or the two Caribbean colleges of veterinary medicine accredited by the AVMA Council on Education and whose students undergo their fourth year clinical training primarily at US and Canadian schools, Ross University and St. George's University; and must be in second year of the veterinarian curriculum at the time of the application. **Criteria:** Applicants will be evaluated for the overall interest of the applicant in bovine practice, involvement in bovine medicine and bovine-related extracurricular activities, ability to express oneself in writing, and insightful answers to the essay questions.

Funds Avail.: $7,500. **Duration:** Annual. **Number Awarded:** 7. **To Apply:** Applicant must submit a current cumulative school GPA and class rank; must submit a biographical account that outlines the background of the cattle industry. Applicant must prepare a one-page or less list of factors that stimulate the interest and involvement in bovine medicine and extracurricular activities; 500 characters or less description of plans following graduation from veterinary school; 2500 characters or less answer about the experiences that stimulate in pursuing a career in food/animal/bovine medicine; 2500 characters or less answering the question "What is our role today and in the future as a veterinarian in shaping public perception of food animal welfare in United States or Canada?"; an essay about the plans for using the money acquired from the award, if considered. Must submit two letters of recommendation from either veterinarian or faculty members regarding the applicant's worthiness for the award. **Deadline:** May 29. **Contact:** AABP; 1130 East Main St. Ste. 302; Ashland, OH 44805; Phone: 1-419-496-0685; E-mail: fred@aabp.org.

523 ■ AABP Bovine Veterinary Student Recognition Award (Undergraduate/Scholarship, Award)

Purpose: To provide awards to 3rd and/or 4th year veterinary students who are interested in dairy and/or beef veterinary medicine. **Focus:** Veterinary science and medicine. **Qualif.:** Applicant must be a student member of AABP enrolled at Veterinary Colleges and Schools during the 2nd year and/or 3rd year. **Criteria:** Award committee will evaluate the student's application based on interest in bovine medicine, work experience, academic and professional experience, career goals, and recommendation letter.

Funds Avail.: $5,000. **Duration:** Annual. **Number Awarded:** 18. **To Apply:** Applicants must fill out the online application form which covers the background, work, and academic experience, primary interests in veterinary medicine, career goals, and provides an opportunity to submit the name of a faculty sponsor. **Deadline:** May 29.

524 ■ AABP Education Grants (Graduate, Postgraduate, Master's/Grant)

Purpose: To help expand the skills and knowledge base of the cattle production medicine practitioner. **Focus:** Veterinary science and medicine. **Qualif.:** Applicants must be AABP members who are incoming senior students or new graduates attending an accredited veterinary college advanced education program or another AABP approved continuing education endeavor. **Criteria:** Selection shall be based on the aforesaid qualifications and compliance with the application details.

Funds Avail.: $1,000. **Duration:** Annual. **To Apply:** Applicants must submit the following: a completed AABP Education Grant application form, including a letter of intent outlining the applicants' career goals (students) or current job description (recent graduates), prior experience with food animal production medicine, and goals for the advanced education program; brief course outline; letter of recommendation from a faculty member (who is also an AABP member) of the veterinary school the applicants graduated from or are currently enrolled in; and, a signed hold harmless agreement release form which must be emailed to the AABP office. Education Grant applications must be made online via the AABP website. Applications can be edited once submitted up to the deadline date. **Deadline:** April 15.

525 ■ AABP Student Externship Program (Undergraduate/Scholarship)

Purpose: To support veterinary students. **Focus:** Veterinary science and medicine. **Qualif.:** Applicant must be admitted to a veterinary school and completed externship of at least two weeks in bovine practice; must be a student and AABP member; must be a full-time veterinary student at an American, Canadian, or Caribbean veterinary college or be a newly admitted freshman at such college. **Criteria:** Scholarship will be given to students who have an interest in food animal practice but who may not have extensive exposure to bovine practice or cattle industry; awards will be given to underclassmen and to externships where the practice provides some tangible support for the student, such as room or board.

Funds Avail.: $1,000. **Duration:** Annual. **To Apply:** Applicants must complete the online application form including the dates of expected externship, practice where it is to take place, projected cost support to be provided by the practice and amount of aid requested, and student's career interests, prior experience with food producing animals,

Awards are arranged alphabetically below their administering organizations

and goals for the externship; must provide a letter from the practice describing what the students will be doing; a letter from a faculty member at the student's veterinary college; and must submit a completed release agreement. **Deadline:** October 1 for externships commencing between November 1; April 30 of each year; April 1 for externships commencing between May 1; October 31 of each year.

526 ■ Merial Excellence in Preventive Medicine in Beef Award *(Other/Grant)*

Purpose: To recognize ad support individual member practitioners or practices that have developed outstanding preventive medicine programs. **Focus:** Veterinary science and medicine.

Funds Avail.: $1,500. **Duration:** Annual. **Remarks:** Established in 1982.

527 ■ Merial Excellence in Preventive Medicine in Dairy Award *(Other/Grant)*

Purpose: To support individual member practitioners or practices that have developed outstanding preventive medicine programs. **Focus:** Veterinary science and medicine.

Funds Avail.: $1,500. **Duration:** Annual. **Remarks:** Established in 1982.

528 ■ American Association for Cancer Research (AACR)

615 Chestnut St., 17th Fl.
Philadelphia, PA 19106-4404
Ph: (215)440-9300
Fax: (215)440-9313
Free: 866-423-3965
E-mail: aacr@aacr.org
URL: www.aacr.org
Social Media: www.facebook.com/aacr.org
www.instagram.com/aacr_foundation
www.linkedin.com/company/american-association-for
  -cancer-research
twitter.com/aacr
www.youtube.com/channel/UCxr
  _bGdhkdyyFo5V3qDBwGg

529 ■ AACR Basic Cancer Research Fellowships
(Postdoctorate/Fellowship, Award, Recognition)

Purpose: To encourage and support mentored young investigators to conduct basic cancer research and to establish a successful career path in this field. **Focus:** Medical research; Oncology. **Qualif.:** Applicant must hold a mentored research position with the title of postdoctoral fellow, clinical research fellow, or the equivalent; have completed most recent doctoral degree within the past three years; work under the auspices of a mentor at an academic, medical, or research institution anywhere in the world; must have a doctoral degree (including PhD, MD, DO, DC, ND, DDS, DVM, ScD, DNS, PharmD, or equivalent doctoral degree) in a related field and not currently be a candidate for a further doctoral or professional degree. **Criteria:** Recipients are selected based on committee criteria.

Funds Avail.: $50,000. **Duration:** Annual. **To Apply:** Applicants to submit an application on online; applicant must have a letter of reference from a nominator accompany the online application. **Deadline:** January 22.

530 ■ AACR Minority and Minority-Serving Institution Faculty Scholar Awards *(Doctorate, Postdoctorate/Award)*

Purpose: To increase the scientific knowledge base of faculty members at Minority-Serving Institutions, and to encourage them and their students to pursue careers in cancer research. **Focus:** Oncology. **Qualif.:** Applicants must have completed doctoral studies or clinical fellowships and hold full-time faculty status at an institution designated as a Minority-Serving Institution; must have acquired doctoral degrees in fields relevant to cancer research; must be citizens or permanent residents of the United States or Canada. **Criteria:** Selection will be based on qualifications, references from mentor, abstracts, and an estimation of the potential professional benefit to the awardees.

Funds Avail.: $1,500. **Number Awarded:** 7. **To Apply:** Applicant must submit an online application form along with following: list one mentor in a supervisory capacity (i.e. dean, department head, etc.) at the candidate's institution who could certify the information in the application upon request; personal statement written by the candidate (no longer than two pages in length) describing the benefit of attending the conference and the reasons for the candidate's interest in the conference; one letter of reference from a faculty member in a supervisory role at the applicant's institution, the letter should be addressed to the MMSI faculty scholar in cancer research awards committee, and should comment on the applicant's academic and personal qualifications for this award. letter of recommendation should be on letterhead with visible signature; a copy of the abstract submitted for presentation at the meeting. candidates must indicate the temporary abstract number; curriculum vitae, including a complete bibliography (list of publications). **Contact:** AACR Minority and Minority-serving Institution Faculty Scholar in Cancer Research Awards, American Association for Cancer Research, 615 Chestnut St., 17th Fl., Philadelphia, PA 19106-4404; Phone: 215-440-9300; Fax: 215-440-9412; E-mail: micr@aacr.org.

531 ■ AACR Scholar-in-Training Awards: Other Conferences and Meetings *(Graduate, Postdoctorate/ Grant, Award)*

Purpose: To enhance the education and training of early career scientists by providing financial support for their attendance at AACR conferences and meetings. **Focus:** Medical research. **Qualif.:** Applicants must be graduate medical students, postdoctoral fellows or physicians-in-training; applicants must also be AACR members in good standing; Employees or subcontractors of private industry are not eligible. **Criteria:** Selection will be based on the qualitative rating of the abstract and the letter of recommendation. Associate members will receive priority for these awards.

Funds Avail.: No specific amount. **Duration:** Annual. **To Apply:** Applicants must submit an abstract for the conference and be listed as the presenter of the abstract; must submit a letter of recommendation from their program supervisor or department head that describes the quality of their clinical and/or experimental work. **Remarks:** Established in 1986.

532 ■ AACR-Undergraduate Scholar Awards *(Undergraduate/Award)*

Purpose: To inspire young science students to enter the field of cancer research and provide a unique educational opportunity for these students in the development of their

Awards are arranged alphabetically below their administering organizations

careers in science. **Focus:** Science. **Qualif.:** Applicants must be full-time, third-year undergraduate students majoring in science; must be AACR members at the time of application. **Criteria:** Selection will be based on the committee's criteria.

Funds Avail.: No specific amount. **Duration:** Biennial; 2 years. **Number Awarded:** Varies. **To Apply:** Applicant must provide the following: application form/online application; at least one mentor in a faculty capacity (i.e. department head, advisor, etc.) at their institution who would certify the information in the application form, upon request; a personal statement written by the candidate (no longer than one page in length) describing the benefit of attending the conference and the reasons for the candidate's interest in the conference; two letters of reference from faculty members from the applicant's institution or an institution that the applicant has attended; a copy of the abstract submitted for presentation at the meeting (if applicable); and a curriculum vitae or resume. **Remarks:** The award was established by Dr. Thomas J. Bardos, fueled by his passion for mentorship and generosity in supporting young researchers. **Contact:** AACR Membership Department; Phone: 215-440-9300; E-mail: scienceeducation@aacr.org.

533 ■ American Association for Cancer Research Minority Scholar in Cancer Research Awards (Graduate/Award)

Purpose: To provide opportunities and support for research training and career development of minorities and for involving minority institutions in cancer research, research training, education and outreach. **Focus:** Oncology. **Qualif.:** Applicants must be full-time graduate students, medical students, residents, clinical or postdoctoral fellows, or junior faculty members; must be in the minority groups that have been defined by the National Cancer Institute as being traditionally underrepresented in cancer and biomedical research; must be citizens or permanent residents of the United States or Canada. **Criteria:** Selection will be based on their qualifications, references from mentors, abstract, and an estimation of the potential professional benefit to the awardees.

Funds Avail.: $1,500. **Duration:** Annual. **Number Awarded:** 25. **To Apply:** Applicant must submit an online application form along with following; list one mentor in a faculty capacity (i.e. department head, advisor, etc.) at their institution who would certify the information in the application upon request; a personal statement written by the candidate (no longer than two pages in length) describing the benefit of attending the conference and the reasons for the candidate's interest in the conference; two letters of reference from faculty members from the applicant's institution or an institution that the applicants has attended; a copy of the abstract submitted for presentation at the meeting. candidates must indicate the temporary abstract number; and a curriculum vitae, including a complete bibliography (list of publications). **Contact:** AACR Minority Scholar in Cancer Research Awards, American Association for Cancer Research, 615 Chestnut St., 17th Fl., Philadelphia, PA 19106-4404; Phone: 215-440-9300; Fax: 215-440-9412; E-mail: micr@aacr.org.

534 ■ AACR Gertrude B. Elion Cancer Research Award (Professional development, Graduate/Award, Recognition)

Purpose: To support research in cancer etiology, diagnosis, treatment, or prevention (basic, translational, or clinical cancer research). **Focus:** Medical research; Oncology.

Qualif.: Applicants must have a doctoral degree (including PhD, MD, MD/PhD, or equivalent) in a related field and not currently be a candidate for a further doctoral degree, and medical degree must have completed their most recent doctoral degree or medical reside

Funds Avail.: $75,000. **Duration:** Annual. **Number Awarded:** 1. **To Apply:** Applicants with questions about eligibility should contact the AACR's Scientific Review and Grants Administration before submitting an application. **Deadline:** November 21. **Contact:** grants@aacr.org.

535 ■ Pancreatic Cancer Action Network-AACR Career Development Awards (Doctorate/Grant, Award)

Purpose: To encourage and support junior faculty who have completed their most recent doctoral degree or medical residency within the past 11 years at the start of the grant term to conduct pancreatic cancer research and establish successful career paths in this field. **Focus:** Medical research; Oncology. **Qualif.:** Applicant must have completed their most recent doctoral degree or medical residency within the past 11 years.

Funds Avail.: $200,000. **Duration:** 2 years. **Number Awarded:** 2. **To Apply:** Applicants to submit an application by online.

536 ■ Women in Cancer Research Scholar Awards (Graduate, Postdoctorate/Award, Monetary)

Purpose: To support Women in Cancer Research scientists-in-training and presenters of meritorious scientific papers. **Focus:** Oncology. **Qualif.:** Applicants must be members of Women in Cancer Research; must be full time scientists-in-training who are graduate students, medical students, residents, clinical fellows or equivalent, or postdoctoral fellows; may be traveling from within the United States or abroad; must be first authors on abstracts submitted for consideration for presentation at the AACR Annual Meeting. **Criteria:** Selection will be based on the committee's criteria.

Funds Avail.: $1,500 to $2,000. **Duration:** Annual. **Number Awarded:** 9. **To Apply:** Applicant must submit an online application form along with following; personal statement written by the candidate (no longer than two paragraphs in length) describing the benefit of attending the conference and the reasons for the candidate's interest in the conference; one letter of reference from a faculty member from the applicant's institution or an institution that the applicant has attended. The letters should be addressed to the Women in Cancer Scholar Awards Committee, and should comment on the applicant's academic and personal qualifications for this award. Letters of recommendation should always be on letterhead with visible signatures; a copy of the abstract submitted for presentation at the meeting. Candidates must provide the abstract control number; curriculum vitae, including a complete bibliography (list of publications). **Contact:** AACR-WICR Scholar Award Program, American Association for Cancer Research, 615 Chestnut St., 17th Fl., Philadelphia, PA 19106-4404; Phone: 215-440-9300; Fax: 215-440-9412; E-mail: micr@aacr.org.

537 ■ American Association of Candy Technologists (AACT)
711 W Water St.
Princeton, WI 54968
Ph: (920)295-6969
Fax: (920)295-6843

Awards are arranged alphabetically below their administering organizations

E-mail: aactinfo@gomc.com
URL: www.aactcandy.org

538 ■ AACT John Kitt Memorial Scholarship
(Undergraduate/Scholarship)

Purpose: To support the education of students involved in confectionery technology. **Focus:** Biology; Chemistry; Food science and technology. **Qualif.:** Applicants must be sophomores, juniors or seniors majoring in food science, chemical science, biological science, or related field at an accredited four-year college or university in north America; must also have a GPA (or equivalent on another scale) of 3.0 (out of 4.0), and be interested in confectionery technology.

Funds Avail.: $5,000 (two $2,500 installments). **Duration:** Annual. **To Apply:** Applicants must submit a completed application form together with a letter of recommendation. **Deadline:** April 3. **Contact:** Email: gretchen.bartos@warrellcorp.com.

539 ■ American Association for Clinical Chemistry (AACC)

900 7th St., NW, Ste. 400
Washington, DC 20001
Ph: (202)857-0717
Fax: (202)887-5093
Free: 800-892-1400
E-mail: custserv@aacc.org
URL: www.aacc.org
Social Media: www.facebook.com/AmerAssocforClinChem
twitter.com/_AACC
www.youtube.com/user/ClinicalChemistry

540 ■ AACC International Travel Grants *(Advanced Professional, Professional development/Grant)*

Purpose: To promote the global exchange of science and information by providing an opportunity for clinical laboratory professionals from emerging areas around the world to attend the AACC Annual Meeting. **Focus:** Chemistry; Medical research; Science. **Qualif.:** Preference will be given to AACC members and early- and mid-career scientists from underserved areas of the globe.

Funds Avail.: up to $2,500. **Duration:** Annual. **To Apply:** Application forms are available on the website and must be submitted electronically to grants@aacc.org. **Contact:** Phone: 202-835-8701; Tollfree: 800-892-1400 ext. 8701; E-mail: ITG@aacc.org.

541 ■ AACC Van Slyke Foundation Research Grants *(Professional development/Grant)*

Purpose: To encourage and support deserving clinical laboratory scientists and students throughout the world. **Focus:** Chemistry; Science.

Funds Avail.: $5,000. **Duration:** Annual. **Deadline:** March 15.

542 ■ American Association of Colleges of Nursing (AACN)

655 K St. NW, Ste. 750
Washington, DC 20001
Ph: (202)463-6930
Fax: (202)785-8320
URL: www.aacnnursing.org

Social Media: www.facebook.com/AACNursing
www.instagram.com/aacnursing
www.linkedin.com/company/american-association-of
  -colleges-of-nursing
twitter.com/AACNursing

543 ■ Johnson and Johnson/AACN Minority Nurse Faculty Scholars *(Graduate/Scholarship)*

Purpose: To provide financial support to graduate nursing students from minority backgrounds who agree to teach in a school of nursing after graduation. **Focus:** Nursing. **Qualif.:** Students must be enrolled full-time and preference is given to students in doctoral programs.

Funds Avail.: $18,000 each. **Duration:** Annual. **Number Awarded:** 5. **Deadline:** May 31. **Contact:** American Association of Colleges of Nursing, Attention: Autumn Spriggs, 655 K St. NW, Ste. 750, Washington, DC, 20001; E-mail: aspriggs@aacnnursing.org.

544 ■ American Association of Colleges of Osteopathic Medicine (AACOM)

7700 Old Georgetown Rd., Ste. 250
Bethesda, MD 20814
Ph: (301)968-4100
Fax: (301)968-4101
E-mail: aacomasinfo@liaisoncas.com
URL: www.aacom.org
Social Media: www.facebook.com/
  AmericanAssociationCollegesOsteopathicMedicine
www.instagram.com/aacom_do
www.linkedin.com/company/aacom_2
twitter.com/aacommunities
www.youtube.com/channel/
  UCdXKVgSSZmoVDlkCFLJsWsw?view_as=subscriber

545 ■ AACOM Scholar in Residence Program *(Professional development/Scholarship)*

Purpose: To provide opportunities for the college of osteopathic medicine faculty to engage in focused study and develop their competencies in medical education as a scholar-in-residence at the AACOM headquarters in Chevy Chase, Maryland. **Focus:** Medicine, Osteopathic. **Qualif.:** Applicant must be faculty and administrator candidates with responsibility for components of their college's curriculum: undergraduate, graduate or continuing medical education (CME). Applicants must be nominated by their dean and, together with the dean and department chair, develop a proposal for study that will enhance both their own college's medical education and provide leadership to the greater osteopathic medical education community.**Criteria:** Selection shall be based on the aforementioned qualifications and compliance with the application details.

Funds Avail.: No specific amount. **Contact:** Contact Mark Speicher, PhD; AACOM Senior Vice President for Medical Education and Research; 301-948-4148; meded@aacom.org.

546 ■ American Association of Colleges for Teacher Education (AACTE)

1307 New York Ave. NW, Ste. 300
Washington, DC 20005-4721
Ph: (202)293-2450
Fax: (202)457-8095

Awards are arranged alphabetically below their administering organizations

URL: aacte.org
Social Media: www.facebook.com/AACTE
twitter.com/aacte

547 ■ AACTE Outstanding Book Awards (Other/ Award, Recognition)

Purpose: To recognize as exemplary books that make a significant contribution to the knowledge base of educator preparation or of teaching and learning with implications for educator preparation. **Focus:** Teaching. **Qualif.:** Awards directly address educator preparation or teaching and learning with implications for educator preparation; must contain originality of thought in critical analyses of particular assumptions or practices, or outline proposals that reorient thinking in educator preparation. **Criteria:** Selection will be based on demonstrate high-quality scholarship in an area relevant to educator preparation; Show potential for significant impact on policy or practice in educator preparation; Demonstrate clear and effective writing.

Funds Avail.: Amount not specified. **Duration:** Annual. **To Apply:** Applicants must submit a letter of nomination addressing the criteria, brief professional biography at least 150 words and must include the contact information of the author(s) or the publisher's representative(s). **Deadline:** May 3. **Contact:** Kristin McCabe; E-mail: kmccabe@ aacte.org; Phone: 202-478-4517.

548 ■ AACTE Outstanding Dissertation Awards (Doctorate/Award)

Purpose: To recognize excellence in doctoral dissertation research that contributes to the knowledge base of teacher education or teaching and learning with implications for teacher education. **Focus:** Teaching. **Qualif.:** Applicants must be individuals receiving a doctorate in education. **Criteria:** Evaluation will be based dissertation must make a significant original contribution to the knowledge about and must address educator preparation issues, practices, or policies; dissertation must make a significant original contribution to the knowledge about or practice of educator preparation and must address educator preparation issues, practices, or policies; individual may submit only one entry each year; Authors need not be from AACTE member institutions.

Funds Avail.: $1,000. **Duration:** Annual. **To Apply:** Applicants must submit an information sheet providing the dissertation adviser's contact information; letter of support from the dissertation's adviser and explaining the importance of dissertation's question, appropriateness and completeness of the study design and significance of the analysis and interpretations; a copy of dissertation's abstract and narrative (not to exceed 10 pages, double-spaced) that answers questions stated on the online application procedures. **Deadline:** August 20. **Contact:** Kristin McCabe; E-mail: kmccabe@aacte.org; Phone: 202-478-4517.

549 ■ David G. Imig Award for Distinguished Achievement in Teacher Education (Other/Award, Recognition)

Purpose: To recognize distinguished achievements in the field of policy or research in teacher education. **Focus:** Teaching. **Qualif.:** Applicants need not be from an AACTE member institution or otherwise affiliated with AACTE, although there should be an obvious connection between the achievement recognized and AACTE's mission and work. **Criteria:** Recipients will be selected based on qualifications and submitted materials.

Funds Avail.: No specific amount. **Duration:** Annual. **To Apply:** Applicants should include letter of recommendation describing how they fulfill the selection criteria; must include their curriculum vitae; a 300-word biographical sketch of the nominee. **Remarks:** The award is named for AACTE President/CEO Emeritus David G. Imig, who led the Association from 1980 to 2005. **Contact:** Sara Hiller, Phone: 202-478-4564; E-mail: shiller@aacte.org.

550 ■ Edward C. Pomeroy Award for Outstanding Contributions to Teacher Education (Other/Award, Recognition)

Purpose: To recognize outstanding contributions to teacher education, either through distinguished service to the teacher education community through the development and promotion of outstanding practices in teacher education at the collegiate, state or national level. **Focus:** Teaching. **Qualif.:** Nominees must be individuals who have made exceptional contributions to AACTE, to a national or state organization involved in teacher education, or to persons responsible for the development of exemplary teacher education initiatives. **Criteria:** Selection criteria include evidence of outstanding contributions in one or more of the following: Distinguished service to the educator preparation community; development and promotion of outstanding practices in educator preparation at the collegiate, state, or national level; Exceptional contributions to AACTE.

Funds Avail.: No specific amount. **Duration:** Annual. **To Apply:** Applicants should include letter of recommendation describing how they fulfill the selection criteria; must include their curriculum vitae; a 300-word biographical sketch of the nominee. **Deadline:** October 10. **Remarks:** The award was established in name of Edward C. Pomeroy. **Contact:** Sara Hiller; E-mail: shiller@aacte.org; Phone: shiller@ aacte.org.

551 ■ Margaret B. Lindsey Award for Distinguished Research in Teacher Education (Other/Award, Recognition)

Purpose: To support and recognize individuals whose research over the last decade has made a major impact on the field of teacher education. **Focus:** Teaching. **Qualif.:** Candidates must be individuals or groups conducting research together, who have made exceptional contributions to research in the field of educator preparation. **Criteria:** The selection criteria include evidence of distinguished achievement in the following: research in the field of educator preparation for at least a decade; publications in peer-reviewed professional journals; presentations at AACTE professional meetings; widely cited contributions with practical applications for the field.

Duration: Annual. **To Apply:** All entries must be made through AACTE's online submissions site. Application materials must include: a 300-word biographical sketch of the nominee; one or more letters of support describing how the nominee fulfills the selection criteria; curriculum vitae. **Deadline:** October 10. **Remarks:** The award was established in memory of Margaret B. Lindsey, a longtime professor at Teachers College, Columbia University. **Contact:** Sara Hiller; Phone: 202-478-4564; E-mail: shiller@ aacte.org.

552 ■ American Association of Critical-Care Nurses (AACN)

101 Columbia
Aliso Viejo, CA 92656-4109
Ph: (949)362-2000

Awards are arranged alphabetically below their administering organizations

Fax: (949)362-2020
URL: www.aacn.org
Social Media: www.facebook.com/aacnface
www.instagram.com/exceptionalnurses
www.linkedin.com/company/aacn
twitter.com/aacnme
www.youtube.com/user/AACNTube

553 ■ AACN Continuing Professional Development Scholarships *(Advanced Professional/Scholarship)*

Purpose: To provide financial assistance to students who want to acquire knowledge and skills beyond traditional academic nursing education. **Focus:** Nursing.

Funds Avail.: Up to $3,000. **Contact:** E-mail: scholarships@aacn.org, with your last name in the subject line of your E-mail.

554 ■ American Association of Endodontists (AAE)

180 N. Stetson Ave., Suite 1500
Chicago, IL 60601
Ph: (312)266-7255
Fax: (312)266-9867
Free: 800-872-3636
E-mail: info@aae.org
URL: www.aae.org
Social Media: www.facebook.com/endodontists
www.instagram.com/savingyourteeth
www.linkedin.com/company/endodontists
twitter.com/savingyourteeth
www.youtube.com/user/rootcanalspecialists

555 ■ Competitive Research Grants *(Graduate/Grant)*

Purpose: To inspire and support research and the genesis of new knowledge in endodontics. **Focus:** Dentistry. **Qualif.:** Applicants must be submitting research that strengthens and advances the specialty of endodontics.

Funds Avail.: $500. **Duration:** Annual. **Contact:** Phone: 312-266-7255, ext. 3025.

556 ■ Endodontic Educator Fellowship Award *(Graduate, Undergraduate/Fellowship)*

Purpose: To recognize the critical role that endodontic educators play in strengthening their specialty and to address the need for more endodontic specialists to teach in dental schools. **Focus:** Dentistry. **Qualif.:** Applicants must be a citizen or hold a permanent residency card for the United States or Canada; must have been accepted for the next academic year or enrolled in the first or second year of an Advanced Specialty Education Program in Endodontics that is accredited by, or has a reciprocal agreement with, the Commission on Dental Accreditation of the American Dental Association; and has been accepted into a Master's, Doctorate or postdoctoral training program (the degree-granting institution must be an accredited U.S. university).

Funds Avail.: $50,000 per year. **Duration:** Annual; five years. **Number Awarded:** Up to 5 years. **Deadline:** April 15. **Contact:** Development Coordinator, Foundation for Endodontics, 211 E Chicago Ave., Ste. 1100, Chicago, IL 60611-2691; Fax: 866-451-9020 (North America) or 312-266-7255 (International); E-mail: ncarpenter@aae.org.

557 ■ American Association of Equine Practitioners (AAEP)

4033 Iron Works Pky.
Lexington, KY 40511
Ph: (859)233-0147
Fax: (859)233-1968
Free: 800-443-0177
E-mail: aaepoffice@aaep.org
URL: www.aaep.org
Social Media: www.facebook.com/AAEPHorseDocs
www.instagram.com/aaephorsedocs
www.linkedin.com/company/american-association-of
  -equine-practitioners-aaep-
twitter.com/AAEPHorseDocs
www.youtube.com/channel/UCRMI19tkCSAE8SKo1iJ83lg

558 ■ AAEP/ALSIC Scholarships *(Undergraduate/Scholarship)*

Purpose: To advance the health and welfare of horses by promoting the discovery and sharing of new knowledge; to enhance awareness of the need to the targeted research; to educate the public; to expand fundraising opportunities; to facilitate cooperation among funding agencies. **Focus:** Veterinary science and medicine. **Qualif.:** Applicants must be senior veterinary students who have indicated a strong desire to pursue a career in equine medicine at schools nationwide. **Criteria:** Consideration will be given to students who have demonstrated leadership qualities in any of a variety of equine-related areas including, but not limited to, involvement with the AAEP, community organizations or equined industry programs.

Funds Avail.: $2,500. **Number Awarded:** 8. **To Apply:** An applicant must fill out the online application form. Applicants must attach completed AAEP/ALSIC Scholarship Program Cover Sheet; one essay, not to exceed 1, 500 words that answers the three questions, "Why do you plan to enter equined practice and what events and/or individuals influenced your decision?", "What characteristics do you possess that uniquely qualify?"; a curriculum vitae, not to exceed two pages; a 2-page curriculum vitae. Evaluation form must be completed by a clinical instructor familiar with the applicant's performance and the other evaluation form must be completed by an equine practitioner in private practice; a self-addressed, stamped postcard by the AAEP as confirmation of receipt.

559 ■ AAEP Foundation Past Presidents' Research Fellow *(Graduate, Professional development/Scholarship)*

Purpose: To emphasize the importance of equine research, and reward a researcher for his or her contributions. **Focus:** Veterinary science and medicine. **Qualif.:** An applicant must: be a graduate of an AVMA-accredited school/college of veterinary medicine; be a current AAEP member; a graduate student or resident; and, have completed a doctorate or residency program within the past 2 years. **Criteria:** Selection will be based on Potential for proposed research to contribute to equine veterinary medicine Sincere intent for long-term career in equine veterinary research; Experience within horse industry; Experience and activity in equine veterinary medicine; Experience with equine research; Academic performance; Professional accomplishments before and after graduation.

Funds Avail.: $5,000. **Duration:** Annual. **To Apply:** An applicant must attach the complete filled out AAEP Research

Awards are arranged alphabetically below their administering organizations

Fellow Cover Sheet; must prepare a maximum one-page cover letter outlining long-term research intent, as well as how it will impact equine veterinary medicine and positively affect horse health; an applicant must include how the scholarship will help in doing the research; a maximum two-page scientific abstract and budget of the intent research project; an applicant must obtain a curriculum vitae, a completed evaluation form, a signed and sealed letter of recommendations; and an applicant must provide a self-addressed, stamped postcard to be returned as confirmation of receipt; an applicant must attend the AAEP Convention; must provide information to AAEP for AAEP Foundation Publications such as biographical sketch, benefits of fellowship, impact of research result.

560 ■ American Association of Family and Consumer Sciences (AAFCS)

107 S. W St., Ste. 816
Alexandria, VA 22314
Ph: (703)706-4600
Fax: (703)636-7648
E-mail: annualconf@aafcs.org
URL: www.aafcs.org

561 ■ American Association of Family and Consumer Sciences Undergraduate Scholarships *(Undergraduate/Scholarship)*

Purpose: To encourage undergraduate study in family and consumer sciences and its subspecialties. **Focus:** Science. **Qualif.:** Applicants must be citizens or permanent residents of the United States; must be planning to pursue or currently pursuing a degree in family and consumer sciences or its specialties at the undergraduate level on a full-time basis; must be currently enrolled in an undergraduate program that will continue into the coming academic year or have been admitted to an undergraduate program for the coming academic year; must be willing to commit themselves to meet the specific requirements of the scholarship for which they are applying. **Criteria:** Selection will be based on the ability to pursue undergraduate study; experience in relation to preparation for study in proposed field; special recognition and awards; participation in professional/community organizations and activities; evidence of professional commitment and leadership; significance of proposed area of study to families and individuals; professional goals; written communication and evaluation of applicant's recommendations.

Funds Avail.: $5,000 scholarship; $1,000 membership support. **Duration:** Annual. **Number Awarded:** 1. **To Apply:** Applicants must have maximum of three evaluators; must obtain official or unofficial copies of transcript; must mail five hard copies of labeled CDs of the completed application form. **Deadline:** January 13. **Contact:** Email: awards@aafcs.org.

562 ■ American Association of Geographers (AAG)

1710 16th St. NW
Washington, DC 20009
Ph: (202)234-1450
Fax: (202)234-2744
E-mail: gaia@aag.org
URL: www.aag.org
Social Media: www.facebook.com/geographers
twitter.com/theAAG

www.youtube.com/c/AagOrg

563 ■ AAG Dissertation Research Grants *(Doctorate/Grant)*

Purpose: To provide support for doctoral dissertation research in the field of geography. **Focus:** Geography. **Qualif.:** Applicants must be AAG members for at least one year at the time of application submission and have completed all Ph.D. **Criteria:** Selection of recipients will be based on the submitted proposals; should demonstrate high standards of scholarship.

Funds Avail.: Up to $1,000. **Duration:** Annual. **To Apply:** Application is via online; must be entered in the online application form. **Deadline:** December 31. **Remarks:** In addition to the information applicants will provide on the online application form, their dissertation supervisors must certify their eligibility by sending an email prior to the deadline. **Contact:** grantsawards@aag.org.

564 ■ Darrel Hess Community College Geography Scholarship *(Undergraduate/Scholarship)*

Purpose: To provide financial assistance to qualified individuals who want to pursue their education. **Focus:** Geography. **Qualif.:** Applicants must be students currently enrolled at a US community college, junior college, city college, or similar two-year educational institution; must have completed at least two transfer courses in geography and plan to transfer to a four-year institution as a geography major during the coming academic year. **Criteria:** Selection of applicants will be based on the overall quality of the application, scholastic excellence and academic promise. Consideration will be given to those in need of financial support.

Funds Avail.: $1,500. **Duration:** Annual. **Number Awarded:** Up to 4. **To Apply:** Applicants must complete the scholarship application available online; must submit a two-page personal statement describing the applicant's academic and personal background, as well as the applicant's academic goals and interest in pursuing geography as a major at a baccalaureate institution; must have two letters of recommendation from college instructors; must have a copy of the applicant's current unofficial transcript. **Deadline:** December 31. **Contact:** AAG Hess Scholarship, American Association of Geographers, 1710 16th St. NW, Washington, DC, 20009; E-mail: grantsawards@aag.org.

565 ■ American Association for Hand Surgery (AAHS)

500 Cummings Ctr., Ste. 4440
Beverly, MA 01915
Ph: (978)927-8330
Fax: (978)524-0498
E-mail: contact@handsurgery.org
URL: www.handsurgery.org
Social Media: www.facebook.com/handsurgery.org
www.instagram.com/handsurgeryassn
twitter.com/HandSurgeryAssn

566 ■ American Association for Hand Surgery Annual Research Awards *(Professional development/Grant)*

Purpose: To foster creativity and innovation in basic and/or clinical research in all areas pertinent to hand surgery. **Focus:** Surgery. **Qualif.:** Applicants must be therapists, Active or Affiliate AAHS member. **Criteria:** Applicants are

Awards are arranged alphabetically below their administering organizations

selected according to the potential of their research project.

Funds Avail.: $10,000. **Duration:** Annual. **Number Awarded:** Various. **To Apply:** applications include the AAHS Research Grant application form within which investigators may view requirements for and upload their project proposal. Proposals may not exceed 5 pages, not including references or senior attestation and must follow NIH formatting standards (12 point, black, Arial, Helvetica, Palatino Linotype or Georgia font, 0.5 inch margins, single spacing). Grants not in the proper format will not be reviewed and considered for funding. Proposals should include all detail listed below within a single document. Abstract: Describe the major aspects of your project (what, why, how); Aims: What are you working on?; Background and Significance: Why are you working on this?; Methods, Materials and Facilities: Why, when, where and how will you do the research? Where applicable, define patient selection and outline human investigation safety requirements, and remember that facilities must coincide with your location for 1 year following the award. Budget Justification: AAHS and the Research Committee are required by the Internal Revenue Service (IRS) to document disbursement of funds, as well as to maintain annual reports on the funded programs. Please note that this award is for support of compensation and direct costs only and cannot be used for any form of indirect costs and/or overhead assessments (personal compensation of investigators, travel, payment of hospital cost.); Collaboration: Define the role(s) of consultants, basic or clinical scientists and their percent of anticipated participation. Scientific References. **Deadline:** September 1. **Contact:** Applicants can email contact@handsurgery.org.

567 ■ American Association on Health and Disability (AAHD)

110 N Washington St., Ste. 328-J
Rockville, MD 20850
Ph: (301)545-6140
Fax: (301)545-6144
URL: www.aahd.us
Social Media: www.facebook.com/aahdus
www.linkedin.com/company/aahd?trk=hb_tab_compy_id
 _2841080
www.linkedin.com/company/aahd
twitter.com/AAHD1

568 ■ AAHD Scholarships *(Graduate, Undergraduate/ Scholarship)*

Purpose: To support students aiming a higher education in the disability and health field. **Focus:** Disabilities; Health education; Public health. **Qualif.:** Applicants must be enrolled in undergraduate or graduate school; have a documented disability and must provide documentation; be a US citizen or legal resident living in the US; and enrolled in, or accepted by, an accredited US four year university or graduate school on a full-time basis. **Criteria:** Selection will be given to students majoring in public health, disability studies, health promotion or a field related to disability and health.

Funds Avail.: $1,000. **Duration:** Annual. **To Apply:** Applicants must submit a completed application form together with a personal statement (maximum 3 pages-double spaced), including brief personal history, educational/career goals, extra-curricular activities, and reasons why they should be selected by the AAHD Scholarship Committee; two letters of recommendation (one must be from a teacher

or academic advisor); and an official copy of high school transcript as well as college transcript (if applicable); must agree to allow AAHD to use their name, picture and/or story in future scholarship materials. **Deadline:** November 15. **Contact:** Scholarship Committee, American Association on Health and Disability, 110 N. Washington St., Ste. 328-J, Rockville, MD 20850; E-mail: scholarship@aahd.us.

569 ■ American Association of Healthcare Administrative Management (AAHAM)

11240 Waples Mill Rd., Ste. 200
Fairfax, VA 22030
Ph: (703)281-4043
Fax: (703)359-7562
E-mail: info@aaham.org
URL: www.aaham.org
Social Media: www.facebook.com/AAHAMNational
instagram.com/aaham1968
twitter.com/AAHAMMember
youtube.com/user/AAHAMMembers

570 ■ National AAHAM Scholarship *(Undergraduate/ Scholarship)*

Purpose: To provide an educational scholarship to individual AAHAM members and their dependents. **Focus:** General studies/Field of study not specified. **Qualif.:** Applicants must be individuals who have been National AAHAM members for at least one year and have paid their current dues by March 31 of the year in which applications are submitted. **Criteria:** Selection will also be based on a review of the application and supporting documents, and the evidence of financial need.

Funds Avail.: $2,500 National AAHAM member ADVANCEMENT IN HEALTHCARE; $1,000 Member or Dependent of member of National AAHAM. **Duration:** Annual. **Number Awarded:** 2 for National AAHAM member ADVANCEMENT IN HEALTHCARE; 4 for Member or Dependent of member of National AAHAM. **To Apply:** Applicants must submit a written statement (no more than one page) giving evidence of financial need, including a list of other sources of financial aid such as scholarships; a letter of acceptance from the educational institution or a statement from the registrar-indicating enrollment; official transcript of grades and credits earned. **Deadline:** May 31. **Contact:** 11240 Waples Mill Rd., Ste. 200, Fairfax, VA, 22030; Fax: 703-359-7562; Email: moayad@aaham.org.

571 ■ American Association of Immunologists (AAI)

1451 Rockville Pke., Ste. 650
Rockville, MD 20852
Ph: (301)634-7178
Fax: (301)634-7887
E-mail: infoaai@aai.org
URL: www.aai.org
Social Media: www.facebook.com/ImmunologyAAI
www.linkedin.com/company/the-american-association-of
 -immunologists
twitter.com/ImmunologyAAI

572 ■ AAI Careers in Immunology Fellowship Program *(Graduate, Doctorate, Postdoctorate/ Fellowship)*

Purpose: To support the career development of immunologists by providing AAI regular members with one year of

Awards are arranged alphabetically below their administering organizations

salary support for an AAI trainee member in their labs. **Focus:** Immunology. **Qualif.:** Applicants must be AAI Regular members in good standing who have predoctoral or postdoctoral degrees. **Criteria:** Selection will be based on the Fellowship Review Committee's criteria.

Funds Avail.: Up to $250,000. **Duration:** Annual. **Number Awarded:** Varies. **To Apply:** Applicants are required to provide the PI's CV/NIH Biosketch; the trainee's curriculum vitae; documentation from your department that is signed by the student's Program or Department Chair and confirms that the trainee has passed the candidacy/qualifying exam (for predoctoral trainees only). **Deadline:** April 1. **Contact:** E-mail: fellowships@aai.org.

573 ■ AAI Public Policy Fellows Program (PPFP) (Doctorate, Postdoctorate/Fellowship)

Purpose: To help AAI members, early in their careers, better understand the role of the President and Administration, Congress, and the National Institutes of Health in determining the policies that affect biomedical research; and to teach participants how best to advocate for, and help shape, these policies that guide their careers. **Focus:** Immunology; Public health. **Qualif.:** Applicants must have received their Ph.D., M.D., or equivalent within the previous 10 years in immunology or a related field; must be members in good standing of AAI; must be committed to a career in biomedical research; must have excellent interpersonal and communication skills; and must have interest in public policy as it relates to biomedical research. **Criteria:** Selection will be based on the committee's criteria.

Duration: Annual. **Number Awarded:** Up to 10. **To Apply:** Applicants must submit the AAI PPFP application form; curriculum vitae; and two references from AAI members (regular members in good standing who do not serve on the AAI Council or AAI Committee on Public Affairs) using the PPFP recommendation form. **Deadline:** April 30.

574 ■ American Association for the Improvement of Boxing (AAIB)

PO Box 9001
Mount Vernon, NY 10552
URL: www.aaib.org
Social Media: www.facebook.com/aaiboxing
www.instagram.com/aaiboxing
twitter.com/aaiboxing
www.youtube.com/channel/
   UCEINVb63pZ8NNmCSWs7as5Q

575 ■ AAIB Scholarships (Undergraduate/Scholarship)

Purpose: To provide educational opportunities and financial assistance to young boxers who wish to obtain tertiary level education. **Focus:** General studies/Field of study not specified. **Qualif.:** Applicant must be a high school senior who has been accepted by an accredited college or university; or a current or former amateur boxer.

Remarks: Established in 1993.

576 ■ American Association on Intellectual and Developmental Disabilities (AAIDD)

8403 Colesville Rd., Ste. 900
Silver Spring, MD 20910
Ph: (202)387-1968
Fax: (202)387-2193

URL: aaidd.org
Social Media: www.facebook.com/TheAAIDD
twitter.com/_aaidd
www.youtube.com/user/aaiddvideos

577 ■ AAIDD Fellowship (Advanced Professional, Professional development/Fellowship)

Purpose: To give recognition to those active members of the Association who exhibited significant contributions to the organization. **Focus:** Disabilities; Mental retardation. **Qualif.:** Applicants must be AAIDD members who have had at least seven years of continuous, active membership in the Association; fellows shall have participated in the professional and business affairs of the Association, and shall have made a meritorious contribution to the field of intellectual disability in one or more of the following areas: contributions to program development or administration and the improvement of services for people with intellectual disability; contributions that benefit people with intellectual disability through skillful and diligent advocacy; contributions to the field of intellectual disability through academic achievements, research, publications, and presentation of professional paper.

Funds Avail.: No specific amount. **Duration:** Annual. **To Apply:** Applicants must complete the application form provided by the Association; Three letters of reference must be provided; references should be from persons who can speak to the applicant's meritorious contribution to our field; A complete list of AAIDD Fellows is on the AAIDD website.

578 ■ American Association of Japanese University Women (AAJUW)

3119 Nichols Canyon Rd
Los Angeles, CA 90046
E-mail: aajuwscholarship@gmail.com
URL: www.aajuw.org

579 ■ AAJUW Scholarship (Graduate, Undergraduate/Scholarship)

Purpose: To promote the education of women, as well as to contribute to U.S. - Japan relations, cultural exchanges, and development of leadership. **Focus:** General studies/Field of study not specified. **Qualif.:** Applicants must be female students enrolled in an accredited California college/university; have junior, senior or graduate standing by Fall; attend (at own expense) the award ceremony; demonstrate a desire and intent to fulfill a leadership role in your chosen field of study and to be a contributors to U.S.-Japan relations, cultural exchanges and the development of leadership in the area of their designated field; must not have received an AAJUW scholarship previously.

Funds Avail.: $2,000. **Duration:** Annual. **To Apply:** Applicants must submit a completed application form together with the following: a current resume; official transcript for the past two years of study (sealed and sent directly by the college/university to AAJUW); two letters of recommendation (addressed to AAJUW); and the essay explaining how you plan to use your study and knowledge for the betterment of U.S. - Japan relationship and must be specific in your essay to clarify your ideas in English or in Japanese (double-spaced, 8 1/2 x 11). **Deadline:** February 21. **Remarks:** Established in 1970. **Contact:** E-mail: aajuwscholar@gmail.com; AAJUW Scholarship Committee, 3543 W Blvd., Los Angeles, CA 90016.

580 ■ American Association for Justice (AAJ)

777 6th St. NW, Ste. 200
Washington, DC 20001

Awards are arranged alphabetically below their administering organizations

Ph: (202)965-3500
Free: 800-424-2725
URL: www.justice.org
Social Media: www.facebook.com/JusticeDotOrg
www.linkedin.com/company/american-association-for
  -justice
twitter.com/JusticeDotOrg

581 ■ AAJ Trial Advocacy Scholarship
(Undergraduate/Scholarship)

Purpose: To assist law students in furthering their studies. **Focus:** Law. **Qualif.:** Applicants must be second and third year AAJ law student members; must be enrolled in an ABA-accredited law school. **Criteria:** Selection are given to applicants who: exhibit an interest and proficiency of skills in trial advocacy; express a desire to represent victims; demonstrate a commitment and dedication to AAJ mission through involvement in an AAJ student chapter and minority caucus activities; and show financial need.

Funds Avail.: $3,000. **Duration:** Annual. **To Apply:** Applicants must submit resume; 500-word essay on how the applicants will meet the criteria; up to three recommendations from a faculty adviser, trial advocacy professor, Dean, AAJ member, or trial lawyer; and a completed form verifying applicant's student status. **Deadline:** June 1. **Contact:** AAJ Membership Dept., 777 6th St. NW, Ste. 200, Washington, DC 20001; Phone: 800-424-2727; E-mail: membership@justice.org.

582 ■ Mike Eidson Scholarship *(Graduate, Undergraduate/Scholarship)*

Purpose: To provide a support system of women lawyers to network, socialize, form professional relationships and develop female leadership for AAJ. **Focus:** Law. **Qualif.:** Applicants must be 3L (or rising 4L in a night program) female students who have demonstrated a commitment to a career as a plaintiffs lawyer or criminal defense lawyer, along with dedication to upholding and defending the principles of the Constitution, and to the concept of a fair trial, the adversary system, and a just result for the injured, the accused and those whose rights are jeopardized. **Criteria:** Selection will be based on the committee's criteria.

Funds Avail.: $5,000. **Duration:** Annual. **To Apply:** Applicants must contact the Association for the application process; resume; letter explaining your interest in a career as a trial lawyer. **Deadline:** May 1. **Remarks:** The scholarship was established in honor of AAJ Past President Mike Eidson. Established in 2008. **Contact:** AAJ Membership Department, 777 6th St. NW, Ste. 200, Washington, DC 20001; E-mail: membership@justice.org.

583 ■ Leesfield/AAJ Scholarship *(Undergraduate/ Scholarship)*

Purpose: To assist law students in furthering their studies. **Focus:** Law. **Qualif.:** Applicants must be first and second year AAJ law student members; enrolled in an ABA accredited law school. **Criteria:** Selection is based on submitted application materials.

Funds Avail.: $2,500. **Duration:** Annual. **To Apply:** Applicants must submit resume; a statement of financial need; 500-word written request substantiating the applicant's commitment to preserving the civil justice system; three recommendations from a faculty adviser, trial advocacy professor, dean AAJ member, or trial lawyer; and a completed form verifying applicant's student status. **Deadline:** June 1. **Contact:** AAJ Membership Department,777

6th St. NW, Ste. 200,Washington, DC 20001; E-mail: membership@justice.org.

584 ■ American Association of Law Libraries (AALL)
105 W Adams St., Ste. 3300
Chicago, IL 60603
Ph: (312)939-4764
Fax: (312)431-1097
URL: www.aallnet.org
Social Media: www.facebook.com/aallnet
www.linkedin.com/company/american-association-of-law
  -libraries
twitter.com/aallnet

585 ■ AALL Leadership Academy Grant *(Professional development/Grant)*

Purpose: To provide a forum for the exchange of ideas and information on academic law libraries and to represent its members interests and concerns within the Association. **Focus:** Law; Library and archival sciences. **Qualif.:** Applicants must be ALL-SIS members who are accepted into the AALL Leadership Academy and who have not received and used any ALL-SIS grants in the past. **Criteria:** Preference is given to newer members of ALL-SIS who are active participants in the ALL-SIS, AALL and/or AALL Chapters.

Funds Avail.: $1,000. **Duration:** Biennial. **To Apply:** Applicants must include the following: completed application; one letter of recommendation; brief statement (200 words maximum); copy of Leadership Academy application (no letters required) and copy of notification of acceptance into the Academy (when received). **Deadline:** November 6.

586 ■ AALL Minority Leadership Development Award *(Graduate/Award)*

Purpose: To nurture leaders for the future, and introduce minority law librarians to leadership opportunities within the Association. **Focus:** Law; Library and archival sciences. **Qualif.:** Applicants must be: members of a minority groups as defined by current US government guidelines; have a strong academic record and have earned a Master's degree in Library/Information Science; have no more than 5 years of professional (post-MLS or post-JD) library or information service work experience; be current members of AALL at the time application is submitted; have been members of AALL for at least 2 years or have 2 years of full time, professional law library work experience; demonstrate leadership potential. **Criteria:** Selection will be based on the committee's criteria.

Funds Avail.: No specific amount. **Duration:** Annual. **To Apply:** Applicants must submit the application package containing the following: completed application form; current resume or curriculum vitae; three letters of recommendation from individuals who can evaluate their law library employment experience or relevant graduate education commenting on their present and potential contributions to AALL and the field of law librarianship; a brief essay(500 to 1000 words) on how career has been influenced by belonging to a minority group and how you hope to impact the profession and the Association as you become a leader. **Deadline:** February 1. **Remarks:** Established in 2001. **Contact:** Submissions must be sent to the following committee member: Chair, Committee on Diversity & Inclusion American Association of Law Libraries, 105 W Adams St., Ste. 3300, Chicago, IL, 60603.

Awards are arranged alphabetically below their administering organizations

587 ■ AALL Research Fund *(Professional development/Grant)*

Purpose: To fund one or more projects of value to those professions that create, disseminate or use legal and law-related information. **Focus:** Law; Paralegal studies. **Qualif.:** Applicants should have experience with research projects, and an understanding of the creation, dissemination and/or use of legal and law related information; may be individuals or partnerships. **Criteria:** Preference will be given to members of AALL, working individually or in partnership with others. Selection will be based on the following: the pertinence of the research question, the appropriateness of the research and the feasibility of the work plan; the intellectual significance of the project, including its potential contribution to scholarship in librarianship, law librarianship or legal fields, and the likelihood that it will encourage research in a new direction; the qualification, expertise and level of commitment of the project director, and appropriateness of chosen staff; the promise of quality, usefulness and impact on scholarship of any resulting research product; the potential for success of the project.

Funds Avail.: $5,000 each. **Duration:** Annual. **Number Awarded:** 2. **To Apply:** Applicants must provide a resume and statement of their qualifications for carrying out the project; must submit two copies of the proposal to the Research Committee Chair; must submit their final report and project results by the scheduled date; proposal must demonstrate significance and originality in the context of existing literature and research; propose appropriate strategies for conducting the research based on the topic or issue selected, including a plan for systematic analysis that will produce objective and reliable results; show feasibility to be completed within the established time frame and budget; include a preferred means of disseminating project results. **Deadline:** April 1; December 1. **Remarks:** An endowment established by LexisNexis. Established in 2000. **Contact:** American Association of Law Libraries, AALL Research Fund: 105 W Adams St., Ste. 3300, Chicago, IL, 60603. Phone: (312) 205-8012, Fax: (312) 431-1097, Email: mmall@aall.org.

588 ■ AALL Technical Services SIS Active Member Grant *(Professional development/Grant)*

Purpose: To cover the cost of registration and travel expenses to support attendance at AALL sponsored educational events related to technical services. **Focus:** Law. **Qualif.:** Applicants must be active members of TS-SIS who have participated in TS-SIS and AALL activities, demonstrate financial need, and have not received a TS-SIS sponsored grant in past five (5) years. **Criteria:** Selection will be based on the committees' criteria.

Funds Avail.: Up to $1,000. **Duration:** Annual. **To Apply:** Applicant must submit a resume that includes current position and relevant previous positions; application form (32 KB Word version) which includes: estimate of expenses for attending the event; statement of how much financial support will be provided by the applicant's employer; brief statement (200 words maximum) explaining how attendance will help applicant achieve professional goals; and two reference letters supporting the application by individuals who are familiar with the applicant's work or the applicant's interest in professional development as a technical services law librarian. **Deadline:** March 20.

589 ■ AALL Technical Services SIS Experienced Member General Grant *(Professional development/Grant)*

Purpose: To cover the cost of registration to support attendance at AALL-sponsored educational events related to technical services. **Focus:** Law. **Qualif.:** Applicants must be members of TS-SIS for six or more years, demonstrate financial need, and have the desire for professional engagement. **Criteria:** Preference will be given to individuals who have not previously attended an AALL-sponsored educational event.

Funds Avail.: Up to $1,000. **Duration:** Annual. **To Apply:** Applicant must submit a resume that includes current position and relevant previous positions; application form (32 KB Word version) which includes: estimate of expenses for attending the event; statement of how much financial support will be provided by the applicant's employer; brief statement (200 words maximum) explaining how attendance will help applicant achieve professional goals; and two reference letters supporting the application by individuals who are familiar with the applicant's work or the applicant's interest in professional development as a technical services law librarian. **Deadline:** March 20.

590 ■ AALL Technical Services SIS Leadership Academy Grant *(Professional development/Grant)*

Purpose: To provide financial assistance to librarians who might not otherwise be able to attend an AALL-sponsored workshop due to limited financial resources. **Focus:** Law. **Qualif.:** Applicants must be members of TS-SIS. **Criteria:** Selection will be based on the committees' criteria.

Funds Avail.: Up to $1,000. **Duration:** Biennial. **To Apply:** Applicant must submit a resume that includes current position and relevant positions and application form (32 KB Word version) which includes: evidence of professional involvement; itemized estimate of transportation, lodging, meals, and/or registration expenses for attending the Academy; statement of how much financial support will be provided by the applicant's employer; brief statement (200 words maximum) connecting attendance at Academy with service to TS-SIS; indicate whether applicant will be unable to attend the Academy without funding from this grant; also submit a copy of Leadership Academy application (no letters required) and copy of notification of acceptance into the Academy and one letter of recommendation. **Deadline:** March 20.

591 ■ AALL Technical Services SIS Management Institute Grant *(Professional development/Grant)*

Purpose: To provide financial assistance to librarians who might not otherwise be able to attend an AALL-sponsored workshop due to limited financial resources. **Focus:** Law. **Qualif.:** Applicants must be members of TS-SIS. **Criteria:** Selection will be based on the committees' criteria.

Funds Avail.: Up to $1,000. **Duration:** Biennial. **To Apply:** Applicant must submit a resume that includes current position and relevant positions and application form (32 KB Word version) which includes: evidence of professional involvement; itemized estimate of transportation, lodging, meals, and/or registration expenses for attending the Institute; statement of how much financial support will be provided by the applicant's employer; statement describing their interest in the Institute and financial need; indicate whether the applicant will be unable to attend the Institute without funding from this grant; also submit a copy of registration confirmation for the institute and one letter of recommendation. **Deadline:** February 25.

Awards are arranged alphabetically below their administering organizations

592 ■ AALL Technical Services SIS New Member General Grant *(Professional development/Grant)*

Purpose: To cover the cost of registration to support attendance at AALL-sponsored educational events related to technical services. **Focus:** Law. **Qualif.:** Applicants must be members of TS-SIS for five or fewer years, demonstrate financial need, and have the desire for professional engagement; must have not received a TS-SIS sponsored educational grant previously. **Criteria:** Preference will be given to individuals who have not previously attended an AALL-sponsored educational event.

Funds Avail.: Up to $1,000. **Duration:** Annual. **To Apply:** Applicant must submit a resume that includes current position and relevant previous positions; application form (32 KB Word version) which includes: estimate of expenses for attending the event; statement of how much financial support will be provided by the applicant's employer; brief statement (200 words maximum) explaining how attendance will help applicant achieve professional goals; and two reference letters supporting the application by individuals who are familiar with the applicant's work or the applicant's interest in professional development as a technical services law librarian. **Deadline:** March 30. **Contact:** URL: www.aallnet.org/education-training/grants/sis-sponsored-grants/.

593 ■ AALL/Wolters Kluwer Law & Business Grants *(Professional development/Grant)*

Purpose: To fund one or more projects of value to those professions that create, disseminate or use legal and law-related information. **Focus:** Law; Paralegal studies. **Criteria:** Preference will be given to members of AALL, working individually or in partnership with others; will be based on the following: the pertinence of the research question, the appropriateness of the research and the feasibility of the work plan; the intellectual significance of the project, including its potential contribution to scholarship in librarianship, law librarianship or legal fields, and the likelihood that it will encourage research in a new direction; the qualification, expertise and level of commitment of the project director, and appropriateness of chosen staff; the promise of quality, usefulness and impact on scholarship of any resulting research product; the potential for success of the project.

Funds Avail.: No specific amount. **To Apply:** Applicants must provide a resume and statement of their qualifications for carrying out the project; must demonstrate significance and originality in the context of existing literature and research; propose appropriate strategies for conducting the research based on the topic or issue selected, including a plan for systematic analysis that will produce objective and reliable results; show feasibility to be completed within the established time frame and budget; include a preferred means of disseminating project results; must submit two copies of the project proposal to the Research Committee Chair. **Deadline:** December 12. **Contact:** Paula Davidson, Director of Finance and Administration, American Association of Law Libraries; Email: pdavidson@aall.org.

594 ■ Alan Holoch Memorial Grant *(Professional development/Grant)*

Purpose: To assist individuals with travel or registration expenses for the American Association of Law Libraries Annual Meeting. **Focus:** Law; Library and archival sciences. **Qualif.:** Applicants must be members of the Social Responsibilities Special Interest Section at the time of the application. **Criteria:** Preference will be given to members of the LGBTIQ community and those who have not received this grant in the past.

Funds Avail.: No specific amount. **Duration:** Annual. **To Apply:** Applicants must submit a completed application together with one letter of recommendation from either an employer or a colleague or peer; recommendations should be sought from those who are familiar with the applicants. **Deadline:** February 24.

595 ■ ALL-SIS Conference of Newer Law Librarians Grants *(Professional development/Grant)*

Purpose: To promote participation by newer academic law librarians in AALL and the ALL-SIS. **Focus:** Law; Library and archival sciences.

Funds Avail.: $500.

596 ■ FCIL Schaffer Grants for Foreign Law Librarians *(Professional development/Grant)*

Purpose: To provide financial assistance to ensure the presence and participation of a foreign librarian at the AALL Annual Meeting. **Focus:** Law; Library and archival sciences. **Qualif.:** Applicant must be a law librarian or other professional working in the legal information field, who is currently employed in a country other than the United States; must be in a position of significant responsibility for the dissemination, preservation, and/or organization of legal information; may be from any type of law library. An applicant who would not otherwise have the opportunity to attend the AALL Annual Meeting is invited and encouraged to apply; must have sufficient English proficiency to fully participate in the conference without an interpreter. **Criteria:** Applications will be evaluated on the basis of the law librarian's ability to add to the Association's knowledge of law, legal information and law librarianship from a foreign perspective; preference will be given to an applicants from an underrepresented country or region, to someone who demonstrates financial need, or to an applicant who has never attended an AALL Annual Meeting.

Funds Avail.: $2,000. **Duration:** Annual. **Number Awarded:** 1. **To Apply:** Applicant should submit a resume of their professional qualifications; documents should be in English and should be sent together either electronically or through traditional mail. **Deadline:** February 14. **Remarks:** Established in 2001. **Contact:** Mark Engsberg, Director, Hugh F. MacMillan Law Library, Emory University School of Law, 1301 Clifton Road NE, M511, Atlanta, GA 30322 USA, Email: mengsbe@emory.edu.

597 ■ Government Documents Special Interest Section - Veronica Maclay Travel Grant *(Professional development/Grant)*

Purpose: To promote and enhance the value of law libraries to the legal and public communities, to foster the profession of law librarianship, and to provide leadership in the field of legal information. **Focus:** Law; Library and archival sciences. **Qualif.:** Applicant must be a student enrolled in a library or information sciences program; must demonstrate an interest in government documents in application; must not have received a previous GD-SIS grant within three years of applying. Grant recipient will write a newsletter article for JURISDOCS; will attend the GD-SIS Breakfast/Business Meeting; will attend at least one GD-SIS-sponsored program. **Criteria:** Preference will be given to LIS students who demonstrate interest in government information and a career in law librarianship.

Funds Avail.: $1,250. **Duration:** Annual. **To Apply:** Applicants must submit a completed application and recommendation letter in electronic format. **Deadline:** April 20.

Awards are arranged alphabetically below their administering organizations

598 ■ Marcia J. Koslov Scholarship (Professional development/Scholarship)

Purpose: To provide funding for members to attend live seminars and conferences presented by the Institute for Court Management, the Center for Legal and Court Technology, the Equal Justice Conference or other programs that provide continuing education for state, court or county law librarians. **Focus:** Law; Library and archival sciences. **Qualif.:** Applicants must be current members of AALL who serve as librarians in state, court or county libraries. **Criteria:** Selection will be based on the committee's criteria; preference will be given to permanent residents of the United States and Canada.

Funds Avail.: No specific amount. **Duration:** Annual. **Number Awarded:** One or more. **To Apply:** Applicant must submit a copy of the seminar or conference information; personal statement explaining why the applicant wants to pursue continuing professional education and why the live seminar or conference they are interested in attending will meet their objectives; current resume. **Deadline:** April 1. **Contact:** Eamil:scholarships@aall.org.

599 ■ Marla Schwartz Education Grant (Professional development, Graduate/Grant)

Purpose: To enable other law librarians to attend conferences. **Focus:** Law; Library and archival sciences. **Qualif.:** Applicants must be new law librarians and graduate students in library/information studies programs. **Criteria:** Selection will be based on the financial need; individuals who have not previously attended an AALL sponsored educational event; individuals who have not previously received a TS-SIS sponsored educational grant; new or student members of TS-SIS who have demonstrated potential for professional development or scholarly activity; students in library science/information studies program who may not be a member of either AALL or TS-SIS, but who plan careers in technical services law librarianship.

Funds Avail.: No specific amount. **Duration:** Annual. **To Apply:** Applicants must submit an application which includes the current position and relevant previous positions; estimate of expenses for attending the event; statement of how much financial support will be provided by the applicant's employer; expected graduation date; maximum of 200 words brief statement explaining why the applicants is applying for the grant; two references supporting the application by individuals who are familiar with the applicant's work or the applicant's interest in professional development as a technical services law librarian. **Deadline:** March 30.

600 ■ George A. Strait Minority Scholarship (Graduate/Scholarship)

Purpose: To support the education of minority students who wish to pursue their career goals in law librarianship. **Focus:** Library and archival sciences. **Qualif.:** Applicants must be college graduates with meaningful law library experience; members of a minority group as defined by current U.S. Government guidelines; degree candidates in an ALA-accredited library school or an ABA-accredited law school; intend to have a career in law librarianship. **Criteria:** Recipients are selected based on application materials submitted and financial need.

Funds Avail.: No specific amount. **Duration:** Annual. **To Apply:** Applicants must submit a completed application form and email; A personal statement in which you include: Financial information you feel the jury could use in determining your financial need; Your interest in law librarianship and reasons for applying for this scholarship; Your career goals as a law librarian. You may also include other pertinent information such as work and family commitments that you would like the Scholarship Jury to consider when evaluating your application. Personal statements should be complete and well-written. Your personal statement should establish your financial need by thoroughly and clearly addressing your financial situation and need for a scholarship. You should also detail any leadership roles you have had in AALL or any library associations. A current resume. **Deadline:** April 1. **Contact:** Email to krundle@aall.org.

601 ■ American Association for Marriage and Family Therapy (AAMFT)

112 S Alfred St.
Alexandria, VA 22314-3061
Ph: (703)838-9808
Fax: (703)838-9805
E-mail: central@aamft.org
URL: www.aamft.org
Social Media: www.facebook.com/TheAAMFT
www.linkedin.com/company/aamft
twitter.com/theaamft
www.youtube.com/user/TheAAMFT

602 ■ AAMFT Minority Fellowship Program (MFP) (Doctorate, Graduate/Fellowship)

Purpose: To provide financial assistance to graduate students who wish to pursue their doctoral degrees in Marriage and Family therapy. **Focus:** Family/Marital therapy. **Qualif.:** Applicants must be American citizens or permanent residents with permanent resident registration card; must demonstrate a strong commitment to a career in ethnic minority mental health and substance abuse services; must be enrolled full-time in a Marriage and Family Therapy doctoral program. **Criteria:** Selection is based on the submitted application materials and financial need.

Funds Avail.: No specific amount. **Deadline:** February 14. **Contact:** Phone: 703-838-9808; Email: mfp@aamft.org.

603 ■ Dissertation Completion Fellowship (DCF) (Doctorate/Fellowship)

Purpose: To provide financial support to minority students in graduate studies in marriage and family therapy. **Focus:** Family/Marital therapy. **Qualif.:** Applicants must be U.S. citizens or have permanent U.S. residence status (I-551 or I-151); individuals on temporary or student visas are not eligible; must be AAMFT members at the time of selection and for the duration of the fellowship; must be in at least the third year of their academic program; must be enrolled in courses approved by their academic advisor that will fulfill the research requirements needed to complete their dissertation and doctoral degree; must be enrolled full-time (as defined by their academic institution) in a marriage and family therapy doctoral program for the duration of the fellowship.

Duration: Annual. **To Apply:** Applicant must provide three recommendation letters and complete all required sections in the AAMFT MFP recommendation form, including an uploaded letter and updated curriculum vita/resume; must submit undergraduate, masters and PhD program information including the dates attended and degree type for at least a full academic year within the last 10 years (must include current institution). Applicant needs to write two brief essays: essay #1 should focus on specific training interests and career goals: essay #2 should focus on choice

Awards are arranged alphabetically below their administering organizations

of university, training program, and advisor/mentor, and how choice relates to minority mental health or your specific training interests and career goals.

604 ■ American Association of Medical Assistants (AAMA)

20 N Wacker Dr., Ste. 1575
Chicago, IL 60606
Ph: (312)899-1500
Fax: (312)899-1259
Free: 800-228-2262
E-mail: info@aama-ntl.org
URL: www.aama-ntl.org
Social Media: www.facebook.com/aamaorg
www.instagram.com/aamaofficial
www.linkedin.com/company/american-association-of
  -medical-assistants
twitter.com/aamaofficial
www.youtube.com/user/AAMAchannel

605 ■ Maxine Williams Scholarship *(Undergraduate/ Scholarship)*

Purpose: To provide educational assistance to deserving medical assisting students. **Focus:** Medical assisting. **Qualif.:** Applicants must be currently enrolled in and have completed a minimum of one quarter or a semester at a post secondary medical assisting program accredited by Commission on Accreditation of Allied Health Education Programs (CAAHEP); and have a GPA of 3.0 or higher. **Criteria:** Selection is based on academic ability and financial need.

Funds Avail.: $1,000. **Duration:** Annual. **To Apply:** Applicants must be CAAHEP Program Directors to request an application from the American Association of Medical Assistants Endowment; students must contact program director for an application; applicants must request an application form electronically, including applicants name, accreditation code and program's institution name, city and state. **Deadline:** February 15. **Remarks:** The scholarship was established to honor Maxine Williams, a founder of the American Association of Medical Assistants. Established in 1959. **Contact:** AAMA Endowment, Maxine Williams Scholarship, 20 N Wacker Dr., Ste. 1575, Chicago, IL 60606.

606 ■ American Association of Neurological Surgeons (AANS)

5550 Meadowbrook Dr.
Rolling Meadows, IL 60008-3852
Ph: (847)378-0500
Fax: (847)378-0600
Free: 888-566-2267
E-mail: info@aans.org
URL: www.aans.org
Social Media: www.facebook.com/AANSNeuro
www.linkedin.com/company/aans
twitter.com/AANSneuro
www.youtube.com/aansneurosurgery

607 ■ AANS Medical Student Summer Research Fellowships (MSSRF) *(Undergraduate/Fellowship)*

Purpose: To provide support to students whose research projects are aimed at the better understanding, treatment, and prevention of neurological disorders and improved patient care. **Focus:** Neurology. **Qualif.:** Applicants must be American or Canadian medical students who wish to spend summer working in a neurosurgical laboratory, mentored by a neurosurgical investigator sponsor who is a member of the American Association of Neurological Surgeons (AANS). **Criteria:** Applicants will be judged based upon the scientific merits of the proposed project, the credentials of the applicant, letters of reference, the preceptor statement and the support provided by the sponsoring program/laboratory.

Funds Avail.: $2,500 each. **Duration:** Annual. **To Apply:** Applicants must submit applications which include the curriculum vitae and bio-sketch, a description of future plans, and a statement of why this fellowship is of interest to the applicants and why it would be beneficial to them. **Deadline:** February 1.

608 ■ William P. Van Wagenen Fellowship *(Undergraduate/Fellowship)*

Purpose: To provide financial support to a post neurosurgical resident for foreign travel for scientific enrichment, prior to beginning an academic career in neurological surgery. **Focus:** Neurology. **Qualif.:** Applicants must be senior neurosurgical residents whose country of study is different from the country of residence, in an approved neurosurgery residency programs, and whose intent is to pursue an academic career in neurological surgery. **Criteria:** Candidates will be evaluated by the Van Wagenen Selection Committee based on the originality and quality of proposal, thoroughness with which the plan for a period abroad has been designed, personal attributes, and the quality of the research environment.

Funds Avail.: $120,000 (living and travel expenses); $6,000 (family travel and living allowance); $15,000 (research support); $5,000(medical insurance.). **Duration:** One year. **To Apply:** Applicants must submit a completed application together with the letter of reference; a letter from the proposed sponsor and documentation of intent to pursue an academic career, while not required, will strengthen the application. **Deadline:** October 1. **Remarks:** The fellowship was established by the estate of Dr. Van Wagenen, one of the founders and the first President of the Harvey Cushing Society, now the AANS. Established in 1968. **Contact:** Lauren Coleman; NREF Development Coordinator; TEL 847.378.0535; EMAIL lac@nref.org.

609 ■ American Association of Neuroscience Nurses (AANN)

8735 W Higgins Rd., Ste. 300
Chicago, IL 60631
Ph: (847)375-4733
Fax: (847)375-6430
Free: 888-557-2266
E-mail: info@aann.org
URL: aann.org
Social Media: www.facebook.com/neuronurses
twitter.com/neuronursesaann

610 ■ Certified Neuroscience Registered Nurse Recertification Grant Program *(Other/Grant)*

Purpose: To provide financial assistance to those who are due to recertify their CNRN credential. **Focus:** Neuroscience; Nursing.

Funds Avail.: No specific amount. **Contact:** Email: grants@AMWF.org.

Awards are arranged alphabetically below their administering organizations

611 ■ Integra Foundation NNF Research Grant Awards (Professional development/Grant)

Purpose: To encourage qualified nurses to contribute to the advancement of neuroscience nursing through research. **Focus:** Neuroscience; Nursing. **Qualif.:** Applicant must be Principal investigator must be a registered nurse. Investigators must be ready to start the research project, or are already in the process of conducting the research, which must be congruent with NNF research priorities and must be significant to neuroscience nursing. **Criteria:** Selection will be based on the quality of the proposed research and the NNF research fund budget.

Duration: Annual. **To Apply:** Applicants must submit the following requirements: Application Form - One copy of the application form with all information included, six copies of the application form with all identifying information removed; Investigator Information Form - One copy of investigator information form (Form A) with all information included (one for each investigator), six copies of each investigator information form (Form B) for use in blind review; Budget Page - Six copies of the budget page; The Proposal - One copy of the proposal which may include names and identifying information, six additional copies of the proposal without names or identifying information; Local Institution Approval from local institutional review board indicating approval of protection of human participants (if Local institutional approval is pending, submit it when obtained). Study must have been submitted to local review committee prior to the time of application. **Deadline:** June 30.

612 ■ American Association of Occupational Health Nurses, Inc. (AAOHN)

330 N Wabash Ave., Ste. 2000
Chicago, IL 60611
Ph: (312)321-5173
Fax: (312)673-6719
E-mail: info@aaohn.org
URL: www.aaohn.org
Social Media: www.linkedin.com/groups/2972150/profile
twitter.com/AAOHN

613 ■ AAOHN Professional Development Scholarships - Academic Study (Graduate/Scholarship)

Purpose: To provide opportunities to further professional education for occupational and environmental health professionals. **Focus:** Occupational safety and health. **Qualif.:** Applicants must currently be enrolled full or part-time in either a Bachelor's Degree or Graduate Degree program. may be eligible for a scholarship to assist with the costs of furthering professional education.

Funds Avail.: $2,500 each. **Number Awarded:** 2. **Deadline:** December 1.

614 ■ AAOHN Professional Development Scholarships - Continuing Education (Professional development/Scholarship)

Purpose: To support occupational and environmental health professionals in attending and successfully completing continuing education activities that will further their professional development and continued competence. **Focus:** Occupational safety and health.

Funds Avail.: $1,500 each. **Number Awarded:** 2. **Deadline:** December 31.

615 ■ American Association for Paralegal Education (AAFPE)

222 S Westmonte Dr., Ste. 111
Altamonte Springs, FL 32714
Ph: (407)774-7880
Fax: (407)774-6440
E-mail: info@aafpe.org
URL: www.aafpe.org
Social Media: www.facebook.com/groups/
 127643713917975
www.linkedin.com/groups/2874316/profile
twitter.com/aafpe

616 ■ AAFPE LEX Scholarship (Undergraduate/Scholarship)

Purpose: To support students pursue their education in legal studies. **Focus:** Paralegal studies. **Qualif.:** Applicants must be full or part-time students who have a LEX chapter. **Criteria:** Applicants will be evaluated based on submitted materials.

Funds Avail.: $1,500 (winner); $500 (runner). **Duration:** Annual. **To Apply:** Candidates must submit a completed LEX application form with a 500 to 750 word essay; essays should be written with standard margins and type size; completed LEX Scholarship Certification form and Permission to Print form; letter indicating the applicant is a student in good standing from a faculty member, or a signed Good Standing Form. **Deadline:** January 22. **Contact:** LEX Scholarships, AAfPE; Phone: 407-774-7880; Email: info@aafpe.org.

617 ■ American Association of People with Disabilities (AAPD)

2013 H St. NW, 5th Fl.
Washington, DC 20006
Ph: (202)521-4316
Free: 800-840-8844
E-mail: communications@aapd.com
URL: www.aapd.com
Social Media: www.facebook.com/DisabilityPowered
www.linkedin.com/company/american-association-of
 -people-with-disabilities
twitter.com/AAPD
youtube.com/user/AAPDvideo

618 ■ NBCUniversal Tony Coelho Media Scholarship (Undergraduate, Graduate/Scholarship)

Purpose: To assist students with disabilities in pursuing a communications or media related degree. **Focus:** Disabilities. **Qualif.:** Applicants must be an undergraduate or graduate student; must be enrolled at a US college or university by the fall semester of the application year; self-identifies as an individual with any type of disability and is pursuing a communications or media related degree. **Criteria:** Selection will be based on the committee's criteria.

Funds Avail.: $5,625. **Number Awarded:** 8. **To Apply:** Applicants must submit the following requirements: application form in word or in PDF format; resume; unofficial transcript; one letter of recommendation from a professor, academic advisor or mentor; and two essays. Applicants must write a 300 to 350 word essay on the following topics: "what inspired you to pursue a communications or media-related degree?" and "how will you use your degree to

Awards are arranged alphabetically below their administering organizations

positively impact the disability community?". **Remarks:** The scholarship has been named in honor of Tony Coelho, a former United States Representative from California and the primary author and sponsor of the Americans with Disabilities Act (ADA). **Contact:** Email: scholarship@aapd.com; Phone: 202-521-4316.

619 ■ American Association of Physicists in Medicine (AAPM)

1631 Prince St.
Alexandria, VA 22314
Ph: (571)298-1300
Fax: (571)298-1301
E-mail: helpdesk@aapm.org
URL: www.aapm.org
Social Media: www.facebook.com/AAPM.org
instagram.com/aapmhq
www.linkedin.com/groups/2006026/profile
twitter.com/aapmHQ

620 ■ AAPM Graduate Fellowship *(Graduate/ Fellowship)*

Purpose: To support students pursuing graduate studies leading to a doctoral degree in Medical Physics. **Focus:** Physics. **Qualif.:** Applicants must be graduates of an undergraduate program in physics or equivalent majors (engineering-physics, math-physics, or nuclear engineering or applied physics) from an accredited university or college in North America; have an undergraduate GPA of greater than 3.5; and must have submitted an application for graduate study to one of the accredited programs with subsequent acceptance.

Funds Avail.: $13,000/year plus tuition support not exceeding $5,000/year. **Duration:** Two years. **To Apply:** Applicants must submit a completed application form together with all post-secondary study transcripts; graduate record exam results; two or three reference letters; and acceptance letter from the intended CAMPEP accredited Program; CV including GPAs and Publications. Application must be completed online. **Deadline:** June 8. **Contact:** Jackie Ogburn; Email: jackie@aapm.org.

621 ■ DREAM - Diversity Recruitment Recruitment through Education and Mentoring Program *(Undergraduate/Fellowship)*

Purpose: To expose minority undergraduate university students to the field of medical physics by performing research or assisting with clinical service at a U.S. institution. **Focus:** Physics. **Qualif.:** Applicants must have completed at least 2 years of undergraduate studies, but shall not have graduated; must be U.S. citizens, permanent residents, or eligible to live and work in the U.S. **Criteria:** Preference will be made to applicants who have declared a major or are eligible to declare a major in physics, engineering, or other science, which requires mathematics at least through differential equations and junior level courses in modern physics or quantum mechanics and electricity and magnetism or equivalent courses in engineering sciences.

Funds Avail.: $5,000. **Duration:** 10 weeks. **To Apply:** Applicants Combine the Application and Self Statement into one PDF and upload online; 2 signed letters of reference; send official transcripts. Application must be completed online. **Deadline:** February 3. **Contact:** Jackie Ogburn; Email: jackie@aapm.org.

622 ■ RSNA/AAPM Graduate Fellowship *(Graduate/ Fellowship)*

Purpose: To support students pursuing graduate studies leading to a doctoral degree in Medical Physics. **Focus:** Physics. **Qualif.:** Applicants must be a graduate of an undergraduate program in physics or equivalent major from an accredited university or college in North America; have an undergraduate GPA of greater than 3.5. and must have submitted an application for graduate study to accredited programs.

Funds Avail.: $13,000/year plus tuition support not exceeding $5,000/year. **Duration:** Biennial. **To Apply:** Applicants must submit a completed application form together with all post-secondary study transcripts; Graduate Record Exam results; two or three reference letters; and acceptance letter from the intended CAMPEP Accredited Program; CV including GPAs and Publications. Application must be completed online. **Deadline:** May 28. **Contact:** Jackie Ogburn; Email: jackie@aapm.org.

623 ■ Summer Undergraduate Fellowship Program *(Undergraduate/Fellowship)*

Purpose: To provide opportunities for undergraduate university students to gain experience in medical physics by performing research in a medical physics laboratory or assisting with clinical service at a clinical facility. **Focus:** Mathematics and mathematical sciences; Physics. **Qualif.:** Applicants must: have completed at least 2 years of undergraduate studies, but shall not have graduated; have declared a major or be eligible to declare a major in physics, engineering, or other science, which requires mathematics at least through differential equations and junior level courses in modern physics or quantum mechanics and electricity and magnetism or equivalent courses in engineering sciences; summer undergraduate Fellowships are restricted to U.S. citizens, Canadian citizens, and Permanent residents of the U.S.

Funds Avail.: $4,000 stipend. **Duration:** Stipend is based upon an expectation of 40-hour per week effort for 10 weeks. **To Apply:** Applicants must submit a completed application form and materials; 2 signed Letters of Reference; official transcripts. Application must be completed online. **Deadline:** February 3. **Contact:** Jackie Ogburn; Email: jackie@aapm.org.

624 ■ American Association of Physics Teachers (AAPT)

5th Floor AAPT 1 Physics Ellipse
College Park, MD 20740-3845
Ph: (301)209-3311
Fax: (301)209-0845
E-mail: marketing@aapt.org
URL: www.aapt.org

625 ■ Barbara Lotze Scholarships for Future Teachers *(Undergraduate/Scholarship)*

Purpose: To provide scholarships for future high school physics teachers. **Focus:** Physics. **Qualif.:** Applicant must be an undergraduate student enrolled in an accredited two-year college, four-year college or a university; or a high school senior accepted for such enrollment; pursuing, or planning to pursue, a course of study leading toward a career in physics teaching in the high schools; showing promise of success in their studies, and a citizen of the United States of America. **Criteria:** Recipients are selected based on merit.

Awards are arranged alphabetically below their administering organizations

Funds Avail.: $2,000. **Duration:** Annual. **To Apply:** Applicants must submit a completed application form; transcripts of all relevant academic works; a letter to the Scholarship Committee; and proof of U.S. citizenship. **Deadline:** December 1. **Contact:** American Association of Physics Teachers, 1 Physics Ellipse, College Park, MD, 20740; Phone301-209-3311 Fax: 301-209-0845; Email: eo@aapt.org.

626 ■ American Association of Plastic Surgeons (AAPS)

500 Cummings Ctr., Ste. 4400
Beverly, MA 01915
Ph: (978)927-8330
Fax: (978)524-0498
URL: www.aaps1921.org
Social Media: www.linkedin.com/groups/8592038/profile

627 ■ American Association of Plastic Surgeons Academic Scholar Program *(Professional development/Scholarship)*

Purpose: To assist surgeons in establishing a new and independent research program. **Focus:** Plastic surgery. **Qualif.:** Applicants must be plastic and reconstructive surgeons who have: completed the chief residency year within the preceding five years; and received a full-time faculty appointment in a department of surgery/plastic surgery at a medical school accredited by the Liaison Committee on Graduate Medical Education in the United States or by the Committee for Accreditation of Canadian Medical Schools in Canada. **Criteria:** Applicants who are not current recipients of major research grants are given preference.

Funds Avail.: $30,000. **Duration:** Annual. **To Apply:** Applicants must complete application online; must submit the research plan and budget; and supporting letters from the Chair of the Department/Division of Plastic Surgery. **Deadline:** July 1.

628 ■ American Association of Police Polygraphists (AAPP)

3223 Lake Ave., Unit 15c-168
Wilmette, IL 60091-1069
Ph: (847)635-3980
E-mail: nom@policepolygraph.org
URL: www.americanassociationofpolicepolygraphists.org

629 ■ William "Buddy" Sentner Scholarship Award *(Undergraduate, High School/Scholarship)*

Purpose: To provide financial support to deserving graduating high school senior or student currently attending college. **Focus:** General studies/Field of study not specified. **Qualif.:** Applicants must be graduating high school senior or student currently attending college; must be a child, grandchild, niece, nephew, or adopted or child, dependent or spouse; must have at least one parent, grandparent, uncle, aunt or legal guardian or spouse who is a full, life or honorably retired member in good standing with the AAPP. **Criteria:** Selection committee will make all decisions regarding the rules and information of the scholarship Application.

Funds Avail.: No specific amount. **Duration:** Annual. **To Apply:** Applicants must submit a completed application form; a recent official transcript of all courses and grades; and two character reference letters (from current institution's faculty and from a non-relative); completed application package must be sent to the AAPP's Office. **Deadline:** February 15. **Contact:** AAPP, 3223 Lake Ave., Unit 15c-168, Wilmette, IL, 6009-1069; Phone: 847-635-3980; Email: nom@policepolygraph.org.

630 ■ American Association of Professional Apiculturists (AAPA)

c/o Susan Cobey UCD Department of Entomology 367
Briggs Hall 318 West 12th
Davis, CA 95616
URL: aapa.cyberbee.net

631 ■ AAPA Student Research Scholarship *(Graduate, Undergraduate/Scholarship)*

Purpose: To recognize and promote outstanding research by students in the field of apiculture. **Focus:** Entomology. **Qualif.:** Applicants must be undergraduate or graduate students working in North America with completed research on apiculture; must be active AAPA members. **Criteria:** Award Committee will review proposals and rank them to the top three. Ranks will be based on scientific merit, presentation, originality and the overall value of the work within the field of apiculture.

Funds Avail.: $1,000. **To Apply:** Research proposal package must include a curriculum vitae of the nominee, one letter of recommendation, and a summary of the research problem not exceeding three pages including: objectives, significance, and methods. Nominees may also include: up to three publication reprints, submitted manuscripts or abstracts of theses or dissertations. Four copies of the proposal package should be sent to the Chair of the AAPA Student Award Committee at least one month prior to the annual meeting. **Deadline:** November 1. **Contact:** Ann W. Harman at: ahworkerb@aol.com.

632 ■ American Association of Railroad Superintendents (AARS)

PO Box 200
Lafox, IL 60147-0200
E-mail: aars@railroadsuperintendents.org
URL: supt.org
Social Media: www.linkedin.com/company/american-association-of-railroad-superintendents
www.facebook.com/AmericanAssociationOfRailroad Superintendents

633 ■ Frank J. Richter Scholarship *(Graduate, Undergraduate/Scholarship)*

Purpose: To support the education of students enrolled at an accredited college or university in the U.S. or Canada. **Focus:** Transportation. **Qualif.:** Applicant must be enrolled full-time undergraduate or graduate student at an accredited college or university; demonstrated successful completion of the previous year's study by maintaining at least a 2.75 accumulated GPA on a scale of 1 to 4 with an "A" equal to 4; have accumulated enough credits from accredited schools in time for the Fall Semester to have obtained at least a sophomore level standing at the college or university of enrollment. **Criteria:** Scholarship Commit-

Awards are arranged alphabetically below their administering organizations

tee will base its evaluation for awards on the materials submitted; points will be assigned for the narrative, recommendations, activities and honors and the applicants overall abilities.

Funds Avail.: $1,000. **Duration:** One year. **To Apply:** Applicants must submit a completed application form together with an official transcript from the schools attended; and two letters of recommendation; the application and narrative statement are to be submitted in one envelope; the two transcripts and letters of recommendation must be sent directly to AARS from the appropriate person. **Deadline:** July 1. **Contact:** Frank J. Richter; President of the AARS; email:cfoor54@msn.com.

634 ■ American Association of School Administrators (AASA)

1615 Duke St.
Alexandria, VA 22314
Ph: (703)528-0700
Fax: (703)841-1543
E-mail: info@aasa.org
URL: www.aasa.org
Social Media: www.facebook.com/AASApage
www.linkedin.com/company/american-association-of
-school-administrators
twitter.com/aasahq
www.youtube.com/user/AASAVideoCenter

635 ■ AASA Educational Administration Scholarship *(Postgraduate/Scholarship)*

Purpose: To provide incentive, honor and financial assistance for outstanding graduate students in school administration intending to make school super intendancy a career. **Focus:** Educational administration. **Qualif.:** Applicants must be recommended by the chair of the school of education in which the applicants are currently enrolled. Only one application may be submitted from each college or university campus. **Criteria:** Recipients will be selected based on academic performance.

Duration: Annual. **To Apply:** Applicants must submit completed application form available on the website; a declaration of mission consisting of no more than three separate statements (single-spaced, typewritten) addressing the following an account of how you came to be interested in school administration, what you conceive the job of a school superintendent to be, what aspects of it chiefly appeal to you, what type of contribution you would like to make in this field, the particular kind of further training and experience which you believe most essential to your best performance, and how you would apply a scholarship toward achieving your professional goals; a succinct statement of an administrative problem you have already encountered, a description of how you met it, and what, on reflection, you wish you had done about it. If you have had no administrative experience, select a problem in the field of classroom teaching or of student activities or discipline; no more than two paragraphs in which you describe specific instances in your training and experience which highlight your individual strengths and focus on your successes. These paragraphs should help the reader know you as an administrator; also submit a letter of recommendation (one original and five photocopies) from the dean of the school of education where applicants is currently enrolled; and letters of endorsement. **Deadline:** September 30. **Remarks:** Established in 1949. **Contact:** Gabriela Iturri; Phone: 703-

875-0731; Email: giturri@aasa.org.

636 ■ Stephen J. Brady Stop Hunger Scholarships *(Undergraduate/Scholarship)*

Purpose: To support the education of students who have made a significant impact in the fight against hunger. **Focus:** General studies/Field of study not specified. **Qualif.:** Applicants must be enrolled in an accredited education institution (kindergarten through college) in the United States; and must have demonstrated ongoing commitment to their community by performing volunteer services impacting hunger in the United States at least within the last 12 months. **Criteria:** Recipients will be selected based on academic performance.

Funds Avail.: $3,000. **Duration:** Annual. **Number Awarded:** 5. **To Apply:** Applicants and nominators must supply a valid e-mail address; must submit a completed application form. **Deadline:** December 5. **Remarks:** Established in 2007. **Contact:** Contact ISTS by e-mail at StopHunger@applyists.com or by phone at 615-320-3149.

637 ■ American Association of School Personnel Administrators (AASPA)

7201 W. 129th St., Ste. 220
Overland Park, KS 66213
Ph: (913)327-1222
Fax: (913)327-1223
E-mail: aaspa@aaspa.org
URL: aaspa.org

638 ■ Leon Bradley Scholarship Program *(Undergraduate/Scholarship)*

Purpose: To assist minorities seeking their initial teaching certification and/or endorsement. **Focus:** Teaching. **Qualif.:** Applicants must have an overall GPA of 3.0 or better; must be high school graduate or equivalent status; must be licensed teachers; must be residing or currently matriculating at a college or university within the following states/ provinces: Alabama, Florida, Georgia, Kentucky, North Carolina, South Carolina, Tennessee, or Virginia. **Criteria:** Selection will be based on work experience; other scholarship or financial aid support; and maintained overall GPA.

Funds Avail.: $2,500 for student's final year; $1,500 for minority paraprofessional career-charge; $1,500 for minority graduate student. **Duration:** Annual. **Number Awarded:** 2. **To Apply:** Applicants must complete an application form available on the website. **Contact:** (913) 327-1222 or tori@ aaspa.org.

639 ■ American Association of State Troopers (AAST)

1949 Raymond Diehl Rd.
Tallahassee, FL 32308
Fax: (850)385-8697
Free: 800-765-5456
URL: www.statetroopers.org
Social Media: www.facebook.com/StateTroopers

640 ■ American Association of State Troopers Scholarship Foundation First Scholarships *(Undergraduate/Scholarship)*

Purpose: To provide financial assistance for the education of students who are dependents of the members of

Awards are arranged alphabetically below their administering organizations

American Association of State Troopers, Inc. **Focus:** Law enforcement. **Qualif.:** Applicants must be high school or college students who are dependents of trooper members by natural birth, legal adoption, step child, or legal guardian. **Criteria:** Applicants will be evaluated based on academic performance and financial need.

Funds Avail.: $500. **Duration:** Annual. **To Apply:** Applicants must submit an official transcript indicating a minimum 3.0 GPA (4.0 scale) at an accredited school; for high school students: final four-year high school transcripts; for college students: a current official college transcripts indicating all grades earned through the current year which he or she is applying for; letter of acceptance from an accredited college, state university or community college for the academic year; a 500-word, typed essay entitled, "How my Education Will Advance My Career Plans"; and a small photo attached to the bottom of the application as indicated. **Deadline:** July 31. **Contact:** Joan Breeding, Phone: 800-765-5456; Email: joan@statetroopers.org.

641 ■ American Association of State Troopers Scholarship Foundation Second Scholarships
(Undergraduate/Scholarship)

Purpose: To provide financial assistance for the education of students who are dependents of the members of American Association of State Troopers, Inc. **Focus:** Law enforcement. **Qualif.:** Applicants must be high school or college students who are dependents of trooper members by natural birth, legal adoption, step child, or legal guardian. **Criteria:** Applicants will be evaluated based on academic performance and financial need.

Funds Avail.: $1,000. **Duration:** Annual. **To Apply:** Applicants must submit an original and official transcript indicating the minimum 3.5 GPA (4.0 scale) maintained during the fall through spring semesters for which the scholarship award was granted; a letter or registration notice as proof of enrollment for the academic year; and a small photo attached to the bottom of the application as indicated. **Deadline:** July 31. **Contact:** Joan Breeding, Phone: 800-765-5456; Email: joan@statetroopers.org.

642 ■ V.J. Johnson Memorial Scholarships
(Undergraduate/Scholarship)

Purpose: To provide financial assistance to a student who intend to use their education to pursue a career in law enforcement. **Focus:** Law enforcement. **Qualif.:** Applicants must be high school or college students who are dependents of trooper members by natural birth, legal adoption, step child, or legal guardian (in Florida only). **Criteria:** Recipients will be selected based on academic performance and financial need.

Funds Avail.: $1,500. **Duration:** Annual. **To Apply:** Applicants must submit an original and official transcript indicating the minimum of 3.8 GPA (4.0 scale) maintained during the fall through spring semesters for which the second scholarship award was granted; a letter or registration notice as proof of enrollment for the academic year; a 500-word, typed essay entitled, "How my Education Will Advance My Plans for a Career in Law Enforcement"; and a small photo attached to the bottom of the application as indicated. **Deadline:** July 31. **Contact:** Joan Breeding, Phone: 800-765-5456; Email: joan@statetroopers.org.

643 ■ American Association for the Study of Liver Diseases (AASLD)
1001 North Fairfax Street 4th floor
Alexandria, VA 22314

Ph: (703)299-9766
Fax: (703)299-9622
E-mail: aasld@aasld.org
URL: www.aasld.org
Social Media: www.facebook.com/AASLDNews
www.instagram.com/aasld
www.linkedin.com/company/aasld
twitter.com/AASLDtweets
www.youtube.com/user/AASLDVideo

644 ■ AASLD Advanced/Transplant Hepatology Award *(Professional development/Award)*

Purpose: To encourage the academic career of exceptional hepatology trainees. **Focus:** Health sciences; Medicine. **Qualif.:** Applicants must be members of AASLD at the time of award application and maintain active membership for the duration of the award period; must have a faculty mentor who is active in hepatology at the applicants' sponsoring institution and be members of AASLD in good standing; must have been accepted to a U.S. transplant hepatology training program. The sponsoring institution must have a United Network for Organ Sharing approved liver transplant program, which must be in good standing and must perform at least 10 liver transplantations per year. The program must have a full-time faculty member or members capable of teaching a curriculum with a broad base of knowledge in transplant medicine and hepatology; research funds portion of the award is strictly for the fellow's first year of faculty appointment at a North American (US, Canada, or Mexico) academic institution that will provide protected time to the applicant to perform mentored research. **Criteria:** Applicants will be evaluated based upon their background and their commitment to a career in adult or pediatric clinical hepatology. Specifically, candidates will be reviewed based on: professional potential of the applicants; experience, productivity, and commitment of the faculty mentor(s); clinical and/or academic environment; quality of proposed clinical program.

Funds Avail.: $30,000. **Duration:** Annual; up to 2 years. **To Apply:** To prepare an application: download the application PDF; use the forms provided in the application package as a cover pages (print or type responses); include only the required documents and provide signatures as requested; put the applicant's name (last name, first name) and the name of the award in the upper right-hand corner of each page; use half-inch margins (do not use lettering smaller than 10 point); assemble the application package in the order listed in the required documents section of this application; and, adhere to page limits and complete all sections; the completed application, letters of support or commitment, and other documents as applicable must be combined into and submitted as one PDF document; name the PDF file as follows: CTRA - last name, first name (example: CTRA - Smith, Jane); submit the application via online. **Deadline:** December 4. **Contact:** Email at awards@aasld.org.

645 ■ AASLD Autoimmune Liver Diseases Pilot Research Award *(Graduate, Doctorate, Postdoctorate, Professional development/Award, Grant)*

Purpose: To provide supplementary funding during the pilot phase of basic, translational or clinical research projects in autoimmune liver disease in preparation for future grant applications by the recipient. **Focus:** Health sciences; Medicine. **Qualif.:** Applicants must be at the predoctoral/graduate level, post-doctoral level, or junior faculty within five years of their faculty appointment date in an ac-

Awards are arranged alphabetically below their administering organizations

credited North American academic institution a the award start date; must be members of the AASLD at the time of award application and maintain active membership for the duration of the award period; and must have their respective mentors who are AASLD members in good standing for the duration of the award period. **Criteria:** Candidates will be evaluated based upon their background, their commitment to a research career, the strength of their research project and the environment in which they will conduct the project. Applications will be reviewed based on the written materials submitted. Incomplete applications and applications that fail to adhere strictly to the instructions (including the submission deadline and page limitations) will not be reviewed. All decisions are final.

Funds Avail.: $20,000. **Duration:** Annual. **To Apply:** To prepare an application: download the application PDF; use the forms provided in the application package as a cover pages (print or type responses); include only the required documents and provide signatures as requested; put the applicant's name (last name, first name) and the name of the award in the upper right-hand corner of each page; use half-inch margins (do not use lettering smaller than 10 point); assemble the application package in the order listed in the required documents section of this application; and, adhere to page limits and complete all sections; the completed application, letters of support or commitment, and other documents as applicable must be combined into and submitted as one PDF document; name the PDF file as follows: 2017 Autoimmune Pilot - last name, first name (example: 2017 Autoimmune Pilot - Smith, Jane); submit the application via online. **Deadline:** December 4. **Contact:** Email: awards@aasld.org.

646 ■ AASLD Clinical, Translational and Outcomes Research Awards *(Professional development/Grant)*

Purpose: To foster career development for individuals performing clinical or translational research in a liver-related area and who have shown commitment to excellence at an early stage of their research study. **Focus:** Health sciences; Medicine. **Qualif.:** Applicants must be either advance fellows (i.e. will have completed at least two years of fellowship training/research at the start of the award) or junior faculty members (at or below the rank of Assistant Professor) for no more than five years at the start of the award in an accredited North American (U.S., Canada, or Mexico) academic institution (at least 50% effort should be devoted to research activities); and must be members of AASLD at the time of award application and maintain active membership for the duration of the award period (they must have their respective sponsors or co-sponsors who are AASLD members in good standing). **Criteria:** Candidates will be evaluated based upon their background, their commitment to a research career, the strength of their research project and the environment in which they will conduct the project. Applications will be reviewed based on the written materials submitted. Incomplete applications and applications that fail to adhere strictly to the instructions (including the submission deadline and page limitations) will not be reviewed. All decisions are final.

Funds Avail.: $200,000 ($100,000 per year). **Duration:** Annual; up to 2 years. **To Apply:** To prepare an application: download the application PDF; use the forms provided in the application package as a cover pages (print or type responses); include only the required documents and provide signatures as requested; put the applicant's name (last name, first name) and the name of the award in the upper right-hand corner of each page; use half-inch margins (do not use lettering smaller than 10 point); assemble the

application package in the order listed in the required documents section of this application; and, adhere to page limits and complete all sections; the completed application, letters of support or commitment, and other documents as applicable must be combined into and submitted as one PDF document; name the PDF file as follows: 2017 CTRA - last name, first name (example: year CTRA - Smith, Jane); submit the application via online. **Deadline:** December 4. **Contact:** Email: awards@aasld.org.

647 ■ AASLD NP/PA Clinical Hepatology Fellowship *(Professional development/Fellowship)*

Purpose: To provide salary and benefit support for certified and licensed Nurse Practitioners or Physician Assistants pursuing a full-year of training focused on clinical care in hepatology. **Focus:** Health sciences; Medical assisting; Nursing. **Qualif.:** Applicants must be fully certified and licensed nurse practitioners, physician assistants, clinical nurse specialist or advanced practice nurses; must have no more than 18 months of experience as midlevel provider in hepatology and/or transplant hepatology (adult and/or pediatric); must be members of AASLD at the time of award application and maintain active membership for the duration of the award period (Associate or Regular Members); must be mentored during the Fellowship period by an AASLD member Clinical Hepatologists who dedicates at least 50% of their time to the care of patients with liver diseases; applicant must be a citizen or permanent resident of the US, Mexico or Canada. **Criteria:** Applicants will be evaluated based upon their professional potential of the applicant; experience, productivity, and commitment of the faculty mentor(s); clinical environment; quality of a proposed clinical program.

Funds Avail.: $78,000. **Duration:** Annual; up to 1 year. **To Apply:** Applicants must download the application form in PDF; use the forms provided in the application package as a cover pages (print or type responses); include only the required documents and provide signatures as requested; put the applicant's name (last name, first name) and the name of the award in the upper right-hand corner of each page; use half-inch margins (do not use lettering smaller than 10 point); assemble the application package in the order listed in the required documents section of this application; and adhere to page limits and complete all sections; the completed application, letters of support or commitment, and other documents as applicable must be combined into and submitted as one PDF document; name the PDF file as follows: 2017 NPPA - Last Name, First Name (example: 2017 NPPA - Smith, Jane); submit the application via online. **Deadline:** January 15. **Contact:** Email at awards@aasld.org.

648 ■ AASLD Pinnacle Research Award in Liver Disease *(Professional development/Award)*

Purpose: To develop the potential of outstanding, young scientists and encourage research in liver physiology and disease. **Focus:** Health sciences; Medicine. **Qualif.:** Applicants must commence the award within the first five years of first faculty appointment (including prior appointments in universities outside of North America); if the applicant does not have a faculty appointment at the time of application, a letter signed by the department chair confirming that the applicant will have a faculty appointment (a) no later than the Pinnacle Research Award start date and (b) for the full award cycle must be submitted; must be a member of AASLD at the time of award application and maintain active membership for the duration of the award period; must be sponsored by a research mentor (the men-

Awards are arranged alphabetically below their administering organizations

tor must be an AASLD member in good standing at the time of application and maintain active membership for the duration of the award period); and must be sponsored by a public or private non-profit institution accredited in the United States, Canada or Mexico engaged in health care and health-related research. **Criteria:** Each applicant will be evaluated based upon their background, their commitment to a research career, the scientific merit of their research project and the environment in which they will conduct the project. Applications will be reviewed based on the written materials submitted. Incomplete applications and applications that fail to adhere strictly to the instructions (including the submission deadline and page limitations) will not be reviewed. All decisions are final.

Funds Avail.: $300,000 ($100,000 per year). **Duration:** Annual; up to 3 years. **To Apply:** To prepare an application: download the application PDF; use the forms provided in the application package as a cover pages (print or type responses); include only the required documents and provide signatures as requested; put the applicant's name (last name, first name) and the name of the award in the upper right-hand corner of each page; use half-inch margins (do not use lettering smaller than 10 point); assemble the application package in the order listed in the required documents section of this application; and, adhere to page limits and complete all sections; the completed application, letters of support or commitment, and other documents as applicable must be combined into and submitted as one PDF document; Letters of Recommendation (Two letters maximum, one page each). **Deadline:** December 4. **Contact:** Email: awards@aasld.org.

649 ■ Afdhal / McHutchison LIFER Award *(Postdoctorate, Professional development/Award)*

Purpose: To develop independent and productive research careers in liver disease. **Focus:** Health sciences; Medicine. **Qualif.:** Applicants must be postdoctoral or clinical research fellows who have completed their most recent doctoral degree or medical residency within the past five years at the start of the grant term; must be either from North America, working at an academic, medical or research institution at the time of application and for the duration of the award, or outside of North America who have already been accepted into a fellowship position at a North American education institution at the time of application and for the duration of the award; and must be members of the AASLD at the time of award application and maintain active membership for the duration of the award period (they must have their respective mentors at the North American Institution who are AASLD members in good standing for the duration of the award); funded projects must be completed at the North American institution; at least 80 percent effort should be devoted to research activities related to the award. **Criteria:** Candidates will be evaluated based upon their background, their commitment to a research career, the strength of their research project and the environment in which they will conduct the project. Applications will be reviewed based on the written materials submitted. Incomplete applications and applications that fail to adhere strictly to the instructions (including the submission deadline and page limitations) will not be reviewed. All decisions are final.

Funds Avail.: $100,000 ($50,000/year). **Duration:** Annual; up to 2 years. **To Apply:** To prepare an application: download the application PDF; use the forms provided in the application package as a cover pages (print or type responses); include only the required documents and provide signatures as requested; put the applicant's name

(last name, first name) and the name of the award in the upper right-hand corner of each page; use half-inch margins (do not use lettering smaller than 10 point); assemble the application package in the order listed in the required documents section of this application; and, adhere to page limits and complete all sections; the completed application, letters of support or commitment, and other documents as applicable must be combined into and submitted as one PDF document; name the PDF file as follows: 2017 CTRA - last name, first name (example: year CTRA - Smith, Jane); submit the application via online. **Deadline:** December 4. **Contact:** Email: awards@aasld.org.

650 ■ American Association for the Surgery of Trauma (AAST)
633 N St. Clair St., Ste. 2600
Chicago, IL 60611
Fax: (312)202-5064
Free: 800-789-4006
E-mail: aast@aast.org
URL: www.aast.org
Social Media: www.facebook.com/AASTtraumasurgeons
www.instagram.com/traumadoctors
www.linkedin.com/showcase/aast-e-learning-cme
twitter.com/traumadoctors
www.youtube.com/user/AASTTrauma

651 ■ AAST/ETHICON Research Grants in Local Wound Haemostatics and Hemorrhage Control Scholarships *(Graduate, Postgraduate/Grant)*

Purpose: To support post residency research of surgeons with a major commitment in trauma surgery. **Focus:** Surgery. **Qualif.:** Program is open for individuals intending to conduct clinical research in the areas of homeostasis and resuscitation only; must have commitment to trauma surgery academic research. **Criteria:** Recipients are selected based on the Scholarship Committee's review of application materials.

Duration: Annual. **To Apply:** Applicants must submit a completed application form including curriculum vitae, bibliography and research proposals. Applicants are also required to submit one typed original copy of the application form and 4 3-hole punched photocopies. Submit completed application to Robert C. Mackersie, M.D., AAST Sec.-Treas., Trauma/Critical Care, UCSF-San Francisco Gen. Hospital, at the above address. **Remarks:** Established in 2010.

652 ■ AAST/KCI Research Grant *(Doctorate/Grant)*

Purpose: To sponsor clinical research in the area of wound care. **Focus:** Surgery. **Qualif.:** Program is open to individuals intending to conduct clinical research in the area of wound care only. **Criteria:** Recipients are selected based on the Scholarship Committee's review of application materials.

Funds Avail.: No specific amount. **Duration:** Annual. **To Apply:** Applicants must submit a completed application form including curriculum vitae, bibliography and research proposals. Applicants are also required to submit one typed original copy of the application form and four 3-hole punched photocopies. **Remarks:** Established in 2011.

653 ■ AAST Medical Student, Resident and In-Training Fellow Scholarships *(Advanced Professional/Scholarship)*

Purpose: To support those who want to attend the AAST Annual Meetings. **Focus:** Surgery. **Qualif.:** Applicants must

Awards are arranged alphabetically below their administering organizations

be medical students, residents, and in-training fellows who want to attend the AAST annual meeting. **Criteria:** Recipients will be selected based on the Scholarship Committee's review of application materials.

Duration: Annual. **To Apply:** Applicants must submit letters of recommendation, cover letter and curriculum vitae to Martin A. Croce, M.D., AAST Secretary-Treasurer. **Deadline:** June 1. **Contact:** Phone: 800-789-4006; Email: scholarships@facs.org.

654 ■ American Association of Teachers of Turkic Languages (AATT)

UCLA Center for World Languages
1333 Rolfe Hall
Los Angeles, CA 90095-1411
E-mail: aattsecretariat@gmail.com
URL: www.aatturkic.org

655 ■ ARIT Summer Fellowships for Intensive Advanced Turkish Language Study *(Graduate, Undergraduate/Fellowship)*

Purpose: To promote American and Turkish research and exchange related to Turkey. **Focus:** Foreign languages; General studies/Field of study not specified. **Qualif.:** Applicant must be a full-time students and scholars affiliated at academic institutions; must be citizen, national, or permanent resident of the United States; must currently enrolled in an undergraduate or graduate level academic program, or be faculty; must have minimum B average in current program of study; must perform at the high-intermediate level on a proficiency-based admissions examination.

Funds Avail.: No specific amount. **Duration:** Annual. **Number Awarded:** Approximately 18. **To Apply:** Applicants must submit complete application information; transcripts and three letters of reference; application fee in the amount of $25. **Deadline:** 'February. **Contact:** Dr. Sylvia Önder, Director; Division of Eastern Mediterranean Languages Department of Arabic and Islamic Studies, Georgetown University; 210 North Poulton Hall, 1437 - 37th Street N.W., Washington, D.C. 20007; Email:aritfellowship@georgetown.edu or aritoffice@gmail.com.

656 ■ American Association of Textile Chemists and Colorists (AATCC)

1 Davis Dr.
Research Triangle Park, NC 27709-2215
Ph: (919)549-8141
E-mail: allredh@aatcc.org
URL: www.aatcc.org
Social Media: www.facebook.com/AATCC.org
www.instagram.com/aatcc_
www.linkedin.com/company/american-association-of-textile
  -chemists-and-colorists
www.pinterest.com/aatcc_
twitter.com/AATCC
www.youtube.com/user/theAATCC

657 ■ Charles H. Stone-Piedmont Scholarship *(Undergraduate/Scholarship, Monetary)*

Purpose: To provide scholarships to junior and seniors, majoring in polymer or textile chemistry fields. **Focus:** Textile science. **Qualif.:** Applicants must be U.S. citizens;

juniors or senior students in an undergraduate program; must have minimum GPA of 2.85 on a 4.0 scale; must be a student at Clemson Polymer and Fiber Chemistry or North Carolina State University Polymer and Color Chemistry; must be Piedmont Section Textile employees. **Criteria:** Recipients are selected based on extracurricular activities; employment experience and financial need.

Funds Avail.: $6,000 each. **Duration:** Annual. **Number Awarded:** Up to 4. **To Apply:** Applicants must submit all the required application information. **Deadline:** February 15. **Contact:** North Carolina State University, Delisha Hinton, Student and Career Services, College of Textiles; Email: dhsmith2@ncsu.edu; Clemenson University, Professor Gary Lickfield, School of Materials Science & Engr., College of Engineering & Science; Email: lgary@clemson.edu.

658 ■ American Association for Thoracic Surgery (AATS)

800 Cummings Center, Ste. 350-V
Beverly, MA 01915
Ph: (978)252-2200
Fax: (978)522-8469
URL: www.aats.org
Social Media: www.facebook.com/AATS1917
www.linkedin.com/company/5351884
www.linkedin.com/company/american-association-for
  -thoracic-surgery-aats-
twitter.com/AATSHQ

659 ■ AATS Cardiothoracic Surgery Resident Poster Competition *(Other/Award)*

Purpose: To help offset the cost of travel and hotel accommodations at the AATS Annual Meeting. **Focus:** Health sciences; Surgery.

Funds Avail.: $500.

660 ■ AATS Perioperative/Team-Based Care Poster Competition *(Professional development/Award)*

Purpose: To provide an opportunity for professionals to participate in a scientific poster competition. **Focus:** Health sciences; Surgery. **Qualif.:** Participants must be non-MD cardiothoracic surgical team professionals (NPs, PAs, Perfusionists, and RNs). **Criteria:** Selection will be based on the submitted abstract.

Funds Avail.: $1,000. **To Apply:** Participants must submit an abstract electronically on the AATS Perioperative/Team-Based Care abstract submission website; abstracts and posters may contain material that has been previously presented; the Posters should reflect the participants' research findings and/or new and innovative ideas for successful approaches in the management of the cardiothoracic patient. **Deadline:** February 21.

661 ■ AATS Resident Critical Care Scholarships *(Professional development/Scholarship)*

Purpose: To assist individuals to attend the Cardiovascular-Thoracic (CVT) Critical Care Conference. **Focus:** Health sciences. **Qualif.:** Applicants must be residents enrolled in an ACGME-accredited cardiothoracic surgical training program in the United States or RCPSC-accredited residency program located in Canada. **Criteria:** Selection will be based on the submitted application materials.

Funds Avail.: $500. **Duration:** Annual. **Number Awarded:** Up to 35. **To Apply:** Interested applicants may visit the

Awards are arranged alphabetically below their administering organizations

website to fill out the online application. **Deadline:** July 15.

662 ■ AATS/STS Cardiothoracic Ethics Forum Scholarships (Professional development/Scholarship)

Purpose: To support CT surgeons who are interested in biomedical ethics and show promise of providing leadership for the continuing development and flourishing of ethics education for CT surgery. **Focus:** Health sciences; Surgery.

Deadline: October 30. **Remarks:** Established in 2000.

663 ■ Summer Intern Scholarships In Cardiothoracic Surgery (Undergraduate/Scholarship, Internship)

Purpose: To broaden the educational experience of medical students in cardiothoracic surgery. **Focus:** Medicine. **Qualif.:** Applicants must be first or second year medical students in a North American medical school. **Criteria:** Recipients are selected based on the committee's review of application materials.

Funds Avail.: $2,500. **Duration:** up to 8 weeks. **To Apply:** Applicants must complete an online application and include a one-page outline of what they hope to accomplish during their eight weeks internship; must also submit a letter of support from the host sponsor. **Remarks:** Established in 2007.

664 ■ American Association of University Women (AAUW)

1310 L St. NW, Ste. 1000
Washington, DC 20005
Ph: (202)785-7700
Free: 800-326-2289
E-mail: connect@aauw.org
URL: www.aauw.org
Social Media: www.instagram.com/aauwnational/
twitter.com/aauw
www.youtube.com/user/aauwinfo/

665 ■ American Association of University Women Career Development Grants (Postgraduate/Grant)

Purpose: To support women who hold bachelor's degree preparing to advance their careers, change careers, or re-enter the work force. **Focus:** General studies/Field of study not specified. **Qualif.:** Applicants must be U.S. citizens or permanent residents; must be AAUW members; hold an earned (not honorary) bachelor's degree; received their bachelor's degree on or before June 30, 2014; do not hold an earned (not honorary) graduate or professional degree. **Criteria:** Primary consideration will be given to women of color who are pursuing their first advanced degree or credentials in non-traditional fields; Reason for seeking higher education or technical training; Degree to which study plan is consistent with career objectives; Documentation of opportunities in chosen field; Quality of written proposal; Applicant is from an underrepresented racial/ ethnic background; Applicant is from an underrepresented area of the country and/or type of university other than a top-level research institution; Financial Need.

Funds Avail.: $2,000-$12,000. **To Apply:** Applicants must check online for further information about the award. **Deadline:** November 15. **Contact:** Email aauw@applyists.com.

666 ■ American Association of University Women International Fellowships (Graduate, Postgraduate, Master's/Fellowship)

Purpose: To provide fund for full-time study or research in the United States to women who are not United States

citizens or permanent residents. **Focus:** General studies/ Field of study not specified. **Qualif.:** Applicants must be a citizen in a country other than the United States, or must hold a non-immigrant visa if residing in the United States; Hold an academic degree (earned in the U.S. or abroad) equivalent to a U.S. bachelor's degree completed by November 15, 2018; Be proficient in English; Master's/first professional degree and doctoral applicants must have applied by November 15, 2018; Master's/first professional degree fellowships are intended for master's or professional degree-level programs such as J.D., M.F.A., L.L.M., M.Arch., or medical degrees such as M.D., D.D.S., etc.; Postdoctoral applicants must provide proof of their doctorate degree; hold a doctorate classified as a research degree (e.g., Ph.D., Ed.D., D.B.A., D.M.) or an M.F.A. by November 15, 2018; and indicate where they will conduct their research Doctoral fellowships are intended for doctorate degrees, such as Ph.D. or Ed.D; Postdoctoral applicants must provide proof of their doctorate degree; hold a doctorate classified as a research degree (e.g., Ph.D., Ed.D., D.B.A., D.M.) or an M.F.A. by November 15, 2018; and indicate where they will conduct their research. **Criteria:** Candidates are selected based on academic and professional qualifications, need for the specialized knowledge and skills of the country of origin, commitment to the advancement of women and girls as demonstrated by previous work and proposed study or research, documented evidence of community service in the home country concerning the improvement of the lives of women and girls.

Funds Avail.: $18,000 first professional degree; $20,000-Doctoral; $30,000-Postdoctoral. **Number Awarded:** Varies. **To Apply:** Applicants must check online for further information about the award. **Deadline:** November 15. **Remarks:** Established in 1917. **Contact:** Email aauw@applyists.com.

667 ■ American Association of University Women Master's and First Professional Awards (Professional development/Award)

Purpose: To financially support women intending to pursue a full-time course of study at accredited institutions. **Focus:** Women's studies. **Qualif.:** Applicants must be a citizen in a country other than the United States, or must hold a non-immigrant visa if residing in the United States; Hold an academic degree (earned in the U.S. or abroad) equivalent to a U.S. bachelor's degree completed by November 15, 2018; Be proficient in English; Master's/first professional degree and doctoral applicants must have applied by November 15, 2018; Master's/first professional degree fellowships are intended for master's or professional degree-level programs such as J.D., M.F.A., L.L.M., M.Arch., or medical degrees such as M.D., D.D.S., etc.; Postdoctoral applicants must provide proof of their doctorate degree; hold a doctorate classified as a research degree (e.g., Ph.D., Ed.D., D.B.A., D.M.) or an M.F.A. by November 15, 2018; and indicate where they will conduct their research Doctoral fellowships are intended for doctorate degrees, such as Ph.D. or Ed.D; Postdoctoral applicants must provide proof of their doctorate degree; hold a doctorate classified as a research degree (e.g., Ph.D., Ed.D., D.B.A., D.M.) or an M.F.A. by November 15, 2018; and indicate where they will conduct their research. **Criteria:** Candidates are selected based on academic and professional qualifications, need for the specialized knowledge and skills of the country of origin, commitment to the advancement of women and girls as demonstrated by previous work and proposed study or research, documented evidence of community service in the home country concerning the improve-

Awards are arranged alphabetically below their administering organizations

ment of the lives of women and girls.

Funds Avail.: $500 to $12,000. **To Apply:** Applicants must check online for further information about the award. **Deadline:** December 1.

668 ■ American Association of University Women Selected Professions Fellowships *(Other/Fellowship)*

Purpose: To support women in professional degree programs in fields where female participation traditionally has been low. **Focus:** Architecture; Business administration; Computer and information sciences; Engineering; Law; Medicine. **Qualif.:** Applicants must be U.S. citizens or permanent residents; Women in two categories are eligible to apply: the Science and Technology Group and the Focus Professions Group. **Criteria:** Selection of candidates based upon the following programs: Architecture (M.Arch, M.S.Arch), Computer/Information Sciences (M.S.), Engineering (M.E., M.S., Ph.D.), Engineering Dissertation Award also awarded Mathematics/Statistics (M.S.), and fellowships in the following degree programs are restricted to women of color, who have been underrepresented in these fields: Business Administration (M.B.A., E.M.B.A.), Law (J.D.), Medicine (M.D., D.O.).

Funds Avail.: $5,000-$18,000. **Duration:** Annual. **To Apply:** Applicants must check online for further information about the award. **Deadline:** December 1. **Remarks:** Established in 1970. **Contact:** Email aauw@applyists.com.

669 ■ American Dissertation Fellowships *(Doctorate, Postdoctorate/Fellowship)*

Purpose: To support female doctoral candidates and scholars completing dissertations and seeking funds for postdoctoral research leave from accredited institutions. **Focus:** General studies/Field of study not specified. **Qualif.:** Applicants must be U.S. citizens or permanent residents; Members and officers of the AAUW Board of Directors are not eligible; applicants must have completed all coursework, passed all preliminary exams, and had the dissertation research proposal or plan approved by November 1, 2020; The doctoral degree/dissertation must be completed between April 1 and June 30, 2020; Dissertation Fellows are not required to study in the U.S. **Criteria:** Candidates are evaluated on the basis of scholarly excellence, teaching experience and active commitment to help women through service in their communities, professions, or fields of research; Quality of project design; Originality of project; Qualifications of applicant; Financial Need; Applicant is from an underrepresented racial/ethnic background; Applicant is from an underrepresented area of the country and/or type of university other than a top-level research institution.

Funds Avail.: $20,000. **Duration:** Annual. **To Apply:** Applicants must check online for further information about the award. **Deadline:** November 1. **Remarks:** Established in 1888. **Contact:** Email aauw@applyists.com.

670 ■ American Association for Women in Community Colleges (AAWCC)

PO Box 3098
Gaithersburg, MD 20885
E-mail: info@aawccnatl.org
URL: www.aawccnatl.org
Social Media: twitter.com/AAWCCNatl

Awards are arranged alphabetically below their administering organizations

671 ■ American Association for Women in Community Colleges Doctoral Scholarship *(Undergraduate/Scholarship)*

Purpose: To provide support to students pursuing doctoral studies. **Focus:** General studies/Field of study not specified. **Qualif.:** Applicants must be women pursuing a doctoral degree; women who have been or are employed full-time at any community college in the United States. **Criteria:** Preference will also be given to women who document completed coursework in community colleges.

Funds Avail.: $1,500. **Duration:** Annual. **To Apply:** Applicants must submit scholarship application form along with the required supporting documents. **Deadline:** February 13. **Contact:** AAWCC, PO Box 3098, Gaithersburg, MD, 20885; E-mail: info@aawccnatl.org or members@aawccnatl.org.

672 ■ American Association for Women in Community Colleges LEADERS Institute Scholarship *(Other/Scholarship)*

Purpose: To provide leadership development opportunities for women in Community Colleges across the country. **Focus:** General studies/Field of study not specified. **Qualif.:** Applicants must be members who work in a community college. **Criteria:** Selection of recipients will be based on commitment to AAWCC, leadership plans, and the endorsement of a mentor from their home institution.

Duration: Annual. **To Apply:** Applicants must submit the online application form. **Deadline:** February 14. **Contact:** AAWCC, PO Box 3098, Gaithersburg, MD, 20885; E-mail: info@aawccnatl.org or members@aawccnatl.org.

673 ■ American Association of Women Dentists (AAWD)

7794 Grow Dr.
Pensacola, FL 32514
Fax: (850)484-8762
Free: 800-920-2293
E-mail: info@aawd.org
URL: www.aawd.org
Social Media: www.facebook.com/womendentists
www.instagram.com/womendentists
twitter.com/WomenDentists

674 ■ AAWD Colgate Research Award *(Undergraduate/Scholarship, Award, Monetary)*

Purpose: To promote an individual early career research, facilitate research related to dentistry, and to help the improvement of oral health. Innovation, creativity and forward thinking research is encouraged. **Focus:** Dentistry. **Qualif.:** Applicants must be junior and/or senior dental students, enrolled full-time, who have shown academic distinction and demonstration of excellence in dental research; the student must also be a national member of AAWD. **Criteria:** Applicants are selected based on research vision, innovation, academic performance, the potential for leadership, and overall strength of their research.

Funds Avail.: $500. **Duration:** Annual. **Number Awarded:** 10 in 2018. **To Apply:** Applicant must include a completed application, two letters of recommendation (one from a faculty member/advisor), transcripts, curriculum vitae/resume, and research proposal. **Deadline:** July 20. **Contact:** Christina C. Reeder; Email: christina.reeder@internationalamc.com.

675 ■ American Association of Zoo Keepers (AAZK)

8476 E Speedway Blvd., Ste. 204
Tucson, AZ 85710-1728
Ph: (520)298-9688
E-mail: visitor@aazk.org
URL: www.aazk.org
Social Media: www.facebook.com/AAZKinc
www.linkedin.com/company/american-association-of-zoo
  -keepers
www.pinterest.com/amdiaz1982/aazk
twitter.com/AAZKinc
www.youtube.com/user/NationalAAZK

676 ■ AAZK/AZA Advances in Animal Keeping Course Grants *(Professional development/Grant)*

Purpose: To assist members with costs associated with attending the Advances in Animal Keeping Course offered through AZA. **Focus:** Zoology. **Qualif.:** Applicants must be full-time keepers/aquarists in zoological parks and aquariums. Researchers other than zoo keepers may participate in the funded studies. The principal investigators, however, must be keepers/aquarists. **Criteria:** Selection will be based on the committee's criteria.

Funds Avail.: $1,000. **To Apply:** Application can be obtained at the members section of the AAZK website. Members are required to make an account or login at the website to access the Grant application. **Contact:** Shelly Roach, Grants Committee Chair, at the above address.

677 ■ AAZK Conservation, Preservation and Restoration Grants *(Professional development/Grant)*

Purpose: To encourage and support efforts in conservation conducted by AAZK members in zoological parks and aquariums around the world. **Focus:** Zoology. **Qualif.:** Applicants must be full-time keepers/aquarists in zoological parks and aquariums. Researchers other than zoo keepers may participate in the funded studies. The principal investigators, however, must be keepers/aquarists. **Criteria:** Selection will be based on the committee's criteria.

Funds Avail.: No specific amount. **To Apply:** Applications can be obtained at the members section of the AAZK website. Members are required to make an account or login at the website to access the Grant application. **Deadline:** May 1. **Contact:** Jessica Munson, Chair, AAZK Grants Committee, Milwaukee County Zoo, 10001 W Bluemound Rd., Milwaukee, WI, 53226-4346; or Email: Jessica.Munson@aazk.org.

678 ■ AAZK Professional Development Grants *(Professional development/Grant)*

Purpose: Jessica Biggins, Chair, AAZK Grants Committee; Email: Jessica.Munson@aazk.org. **Focus:** Zoology. **Criteria:** Selection will be based on the committee's criteria.

To Apply: Application can be obtained at the Members section of the AAZK website. Members are required to make an account or login at the website to access the Grant application. **Deadline:** March 1.

679 ■ AAZK Research Grants *(Professional development/Grant)*

Purpose: To encourage and support efforts in noninvasive research conducted by AAZK members in zoological parks and aquariums around the world. **Focus:** Zoology. **Qualif.:**

Applicants must be full-time keepers/aquarists in zoological parks and aquariums. Researchers other than zoo keepers may participate in the funded studies. The principal investigators, however, must be keepers/aquarists. **Criteria:** Selection will be based on the committee's criteria.

Funds Avail.: No specific amount. **Deadline:** May 1. **Contact:** Jessica Munson, Chair, AAZK Grants Committee, Milwaukee County Zoo, 10001 W Bluemound Rd., Milwaukee, WI, 53226-4346; or Email: Jessica.Munson@aazk.org.

680 ■ American Astronomical Society (AAS)

1667 K Street NW, Ste. 800
Washington, DC 20006
Ph: (202)328-2010
Fax: (202)234-2560
E-mail: aas@aas.org
URL: www.aas.org
Social Media: www.facebook.com/
  AmericanAstronomicalSociety
www.instagram.com/aas_office
www.linkedin.com/company/american-astronomical-society
twitter.com/AAS_Office
www.youtube.com/c/AAStronomy

681 ■ American Astronomical Society Small Research Grants *(Doctorate/Grant)*

Purpose: To promote research related to astronomy. **Focus:** Astronomy and astronomical sciences. **Qualif.:** Applicant must be a U.S. citizen or foreign astronomer with Ph.D. or equivalent and must not be connected to the institution. **Criteria:** Recipients are evaluated based on: scientific merit, student participation, budget, other funds available for the proposed project.

Funds Avail.: $500-$7,000. **To Apply:** Applicants must submit the proposal (maximum of four pages); curriculum vitae (maximum of two pages); and a cover letter; send four copies of the proposal and must mail a hardcopy of the cover page. **Deadline:** September 30. **Contact:** Melanie DeLorenzo;Email:mdl@nyct-cfi.org.

682 ■ Annie Jump Cannon Award in Astronomy *(Doctorate/Award, Recognition)*

Purpose: To honor and recognize outstanding research and promise for future research by a postdoctoral woman researcher. **Focus:** Astronomy and astronomical sciences. **Qualif.:** Applicants must be North American female astronomers within five years of receiving their PhD in the year designated for the award. **Criteria:** Selection will be based on the committee's criteria.

Funds Avail.: $1,500. **Duration:** Annual. **Number Awarded:** 1. **Deadline:** June 30. **Remarks:** Established in 1934.

683 ■ Chrétien International Research Grants *(Doctorate/Grant)*

Purpose: To promote research or projects related to astronomy. **Focus:** Astronomy and astronomical sciences. **Qualif.:** Applicants must be astronomers with PhD or equivalent. **Criteria:** Recipients are selected based on submitted proposals. Decisions will be made on the basis of quality research; importance of the proposed research to the international astronomy; ability of the applicant to carry out the research; and prudence of the budget estimates. Letters of reference will greatly affect the committee's deci-

Awards are arranged alphabetically below their administering organizations

sion; preference will be given to individuals of high promise who are otherwise unfunded.

Funds Avail.: Up to $20,000. **Duration:** Annual. **To Apply:** Applicants must submit a description of research (maximum of three pages); a statement on the applicant's ability to finish the project; a proposed budget; description of other financial resources (if applicable); curriculum vitae and bibliography of recent papers; two reference letters from astronomers who know the applicant's work; other circumstances that might help in the selection process. **Deadline:** April 1. **Contact:** Sara Asfaw, grants@aas.org.

684 ■ Rodger Doxsey Travel Prize *(Graduate, Postdoctorate/Prize)*

Purpose: To assist graduate or postdoctoral students to enable the oral presentation of their dissertation research at the AAS meeting. **Focus:** Astronomy and astronomical sciences. **Qualif.:** Applicants must be graduate students or postdocs; must be planning to present their dissertation research at a meeting of the AAS in the form of an oral dissertation talk; must be attending a North American university or have recently graduated from a North American university; must be members of AAS. **Criteria:** Selection will be based on the scientific merit of the dissertation research of the PhD.

Funds Avail.: No specific amount. **Duration:** Annual; only every winter meetings. **Number Awarded:** Varies. **To Apply:** Applicants must submit their abstract by the "on-time" abstract submission deadline; advisors of the applicants must submit a letter indicating that the applicants is within one year of receiving or receipt of the PhD. **Deadline:** October 1. **Remarks:** The prize was established through father of Rodger Doxsey, friends, family, and colleagues. Established in 2011. **Contact:** Gina Brissenden, AAS Education & Outreach Coordinator; Email:gina.brissenden@aas.org.

685 ■ American Australian Association (AAA)

50 Broadway, Ste. 2003
New York, NY 10004
Ph: (212)338-6860
Fax: (212)338-6864
E-mail: information@aaanyc.org
URL: www.americanaustralian.org
Social Media: www.facebook.com/americanaustralian
www.instagram.com/_aaausa/
www.linkedin.com/company/american-australian
 -association
twitter.com/_aaausa

686 ■ Morgan Stanley Pediatrics Fellowships
(Postgraduate, Graduate/Fellowship)

Purpose: To support Australian or American researchers who wish to conduct research in pediatrics at a top U.S. or Australian educational or research institution. **Focus:** Education, Early childhood; Medicine, Osteopathic; Medicine, Pediatric; Oncology. **Qualif.:** Applicants must be an Australian citizen or permanent resident; must be conducting graduate or post-graduate.

Funds Avail.: Up to $40,000 a year. **Duration:** Annual. **Deadline:** April 15. **Contact:** E-mail: jhelum.bagchi@aaanyc.org.

687 ■ American Bar Association Commission on Homelessness and Poverty (ABACHP)

1050 Connecticut Ave. NW, Ste. 400
Washington, DC 20036

Ph: (202)662-1693
Fax: (202)638-3844
URL: www.americanbar.org/groups/public_interest/home-
  lessness_poverty
Social Media: www.facebook.com/ABACHP
linkedin.com/company/american-bar-association
twitter.com/ABA_CHP

688 ■ John J. Curtin, Jr. Fellowships
(Undergraduate/Fellowship)

Purpose: To provide stipends to law students working to help homeless and indigent people. **Focus:** Law. **Qualif.:** Applicants must be law school students working for a bar association or legal services program designed to aid homeless or indigent clients or their advocates; must have been operational for at least one year and must have an attorney on staff or easily available to supervise the intern; must be U.S. citizens or permanent residents. **Criteria:** Selection will be based on the committee's criteria.

Funds Avail.: $3,500. **Duration:** Annual. **Number Awarded:** 3. **To Apply:** Applicants must submit a cover letter, resume, application form and a prospective program's supporting statement; must be specific about the issues on which they plan to focus and what they hope to accomplish; and both the intern and the program will be expected to submit to the ABA Commission on Homelessness and Poverty and the standing committee on Legal Aid and indigent defendants reports on the summer internship experience; the intern should assess the quality of the supervision received, describe whether the written work assigned was challenging, discuss the opportunities to work with clients, and include a summary of what the student learned from the experience; the program supervisor should describe the student's contributions to the program and provide feedback as to what skills and abilities the Curtin Justice Fund Legal Internship Program should look for in future interns. **Deadline:** March 27. **Contact:** Curtin Internship Program, American Bar Association Commission on Homelessness and Poverty; Email: homeless@americanbar.org.

689 ■ American Bar Foundation (ABF)

750 N Lake Shore Dr.
Chicago, IL 60611-4403
Ph: (312)988-6500
E-mail: info@abfn.org
URL: www.americanbarfoundation.org
Social Media: www.facebook.com/americanbarfoundation
www.instagram.com/americanbarfoundation
twitter.com/ABFResearch
www.youtube.com/user/ABFCOMM

690 ■ ABF Law and Social Science Dissertation Fellowship and Mentoring Program *(Graduate/Fellowship)*

Purpose: To promote education in Law and Social Sciences. **Focus:** Law; Social sciences. **Qualif.:** Applicants should be U.S. citizens and permanent residents who are students in a Ph.D. program in a social science department or an interdisciplinary program (third-, fourth-, and fifth-year graduate students who specialize in the field of law and social science and whose research interests include law and inequality); humanities students pursuing empirically-based social science dissertations are welcome to apply. **Criteria:** Selection is based on the application.

Awards are arranged alphabetically below their administering organizations

Funds Avail.: $30,000 stipend; $1,500 for research and travel expenses; $2,500 for relocation expenses. **Duration:** Annual. **To Apply:** Applicant should submit: a 1-2 page letter of application; a 2-3 page description of a research project or interest that relates to law and inequality (broadly defined) with a statement of how the applicant became interested in the research topic; a resume or curriculum vitae; a writing sample (a paper written for a graduate-level course or dissertation prospectus); and three letters of recommendation from faculty members (including one from the faculty member who will serve as the departmental liaison – typically the applicants' respective advisors). **Deadline:** December 1. **Contact:** Amanda Ehrhardt; Phone: 312-988-6517; Email: aehrhardt@abfn.org.

691 ■ ABF Montgomery Summer Research Diversity Fellowships in Law and Social Science
(Undergraduate/Fellowship)

Purpose: To promote undergraduate students to the rewards and demands of a research-oriented career in the field of law and/or social science. **Focus:** Law; Social sciences. **Qualif.:** Applicants must be American citizens and lawful permanent residents including, but not limited to, persons who are African American, Hispanic/Latino, Asian, Native American, or Puerto Rican, as well as other individuals who will add diversity to the field of law and social science, such as persons with disabilities and LGBTQ persons; must have a Grade Point Average of at least 3.0 (on a 4.0 scale) and be moving toward an academic major in the social sciences or humanities; must be sophomores and juniors, that is, students who have completed at least their sophomore year and who have not received a bachelor's degree by the time the fellowship begins.

Funds Avail.: $3,600 each. **Duration:** Annual; 8 weeks. **Number Awarded:** 4. **To Apply:** Candidates must submit a nomination letter, along with an official transcript to IISE. **Contact:** Breck Radulovic at bradulovic@abfn.org.

692 ■ ABF/NSF Doctoral Fellowships Program in Law & Inequality *(Doctorate/Fellowship, Award)*

Purpose: To encourage original and significant empirical and interdisciplinary research on the study of law and inequality. **Focus:** Law. **Qualif.:** candidates for Ph.D. degrees and who have completed all doctoral requirements except the dissertation by September 1, 2020. Doctoral research must be in the general area of socio-legal studies or involve social scientific approaches to the law, legal institutions, legal processes, or social justice. The research must address significant issues in the field and show promise of a major contribution to social scientific understanding of law and inequality. Students from underrepresented minority groups are especially encouraged to apply.

To Apply: Applicants must submit 1-2 page cover letter of application, including a statement of how the research project intersects with law and inequality; curriculum vitae; dissertation abstract or proposal with an outline of the substance and methods of the research; names and contact information of 3 referees that we may contact if appropriate, one of whom should be the applicant's dissertation chairperson; writing sample, reflective of a candidate's best work and appropriate to a candidate's discipline; Diversity Statement, not more than two pages, highlighting demonstrated and planned efforts to promote diversity and equity through their research, life experience, or other work.

693 ■ American Birding Association (ABA)
93 Clinton St.
Delaware City, DE 19706
Ph: (302)838-3660
Fax: (302)838-3651
Free: 800-850-2473
E-mail: info@aba.org
URL: www.aba.org
Social Media: www.facebook.com/birders
www.linkedin.com/company/american-birding-association
twitter.com/aba
www.youtube.com/user/BirdingOnline

694 ■ Richard E. Andrews Memorial Scholarship
(Undergraduate/Scholarship, Monetary)

Purpose: To provide financial assistance for young birders. **Focus:** Animal rights; Animal science and behavior. **Qualif.:** Scholarship is open to American Birding Association active members.

Funds Avail.: No specific amount. **Duration:** Annual. **To Apply:** Applicants must submit a completed application, an essay explaining why they deserve the Andrews scholarships; and a letter of recommendation from a teacher, bird club member or mentor. **Deadline:** March 1. **Remarks:** The award was established to honor Richard E. Andrews, a long-time member of the ABA, was particularly interested in studying birds, identifying them in the field, and encouraging young people in their endeavors. **Contact:** American Birding Association - Youth Scholarships, PO Box 744, Delaware City, DE, 19706; Email:scholarships@aba.org.

695 ■ Young Birder Scholarships *(Undergraduate/Scholarship, Monetary)*

Purpose: To promote the pursuit of educational and other bird-related activities. **Focus:** Animal rights; Animal science and behavior. **Qualif.:** Scholarship is open to American Birding Association active members only.

Funds Avail.: $500. **Duration:** Annual. **To Apply:** Applicants must submit a completed application form available from the ABA office and can be downloaded from the website; an essay about the importance of a bird; a letter of recommendation from a teacher, bird club member or mentor. **Deadline:** March 2. **Contact:** American Birding Association - Youth Scholarships, PO Box 744, Delaware City, DE, 19706; Email:scholarships@aba.org.

696 ■ American Board of Funeral Service Education (ABFSE)
c/o Robert C. Smith III, Executive Director
992 Mantua Pk, Ste. 108
Woodbury Heights, NJ 08097
Ph: (816)233-3747
E-mail: exdir@abfse.org
URL: www.abfse.org

697 ■ ABFSE National Scholarship Program
(Undergraduate/Scholarship)

Purpose: To provide financial awards to students enrolled in funeral service or mortuary science programs to assist them in obtaining their professional education. **Focus:** Funeral services; Mortuary science. **Qualif.:** Applicants must have at least completed one semester (or quarter) of study in a funeral service or mortuary science education accredited by the American Board of Funeral Service Educa-

Awards are arranged alphabetically below their administering organizations

tion; must have one term or semester remaining in a program which will commence after the award date in order to be considered for a full award; must be a citizen of the United States. **Criteria:** Selection of scholarship recipients is competitive; swards are made by the Scholarship Committee of ABFSE.

Funds Avail.: $500 - $2,500. **Duration:** One year. **To Apply:** Applicants must apply online; must submit the email confirmation, tax forms, letter of recommendation, enrollment verification, Federal Tax Form 1040, an essay (1-2 pages; double-spaced) addressing their decision and choice to pursue a funeral service education; and transcript of records to ABFSE Scholarship Committee. **Deadline:** March 1; September 1. **Remarks:** Established in 1960. **Contact:** Scholarship Committee, American Board of Funeral Service Education, 992 Mantua Pike, Ste. 108, Woodbury Heights, NJ 08097; E-mail: scholarships@abfse.org.

698 ■ American Brain Tumor Association (ABTA)
8550 W Bryn Mawr Ave., Ste. 550
Chicago, IL 60631
Ph: (773)577-8750
Fax: (773)577-8738
Free: 800-886-2282
E-mail: info@abta.org
URL: www.abta.org
Social Media: www.facebook.com/theABTA
www.linkedin.com/company/440727
twitter.com/theabta

699 ■ ABTA Basic Research Fellowships
(Postdoctorate/Fellowship)

Purpose: To support postdoctoral fellows conducting brain tumor research under the mentorship of an experienced investigator in the field. **Focus:** Oncology.
Funds Avail.: $100,000.00. **Duration:** Two years. **Contact:** Email: grants@abta.org.

700 ■ ABTA Discovery Grant *(Professional development/Grant)*

Purpose: To support high impact and risk projects that have the potential to change current diagnostic or treatment paradigms for brain tumors. **Focus:** Medical research. **Qualif.:** Applicants must be investigators conducting high-risk/high-impact research deemed to have the potential to change current diagnostic or treatment paradigms. **Criteria:** Selection will be based on the committees' criteria.

Funds Avail.: $50,000. **Duration:** Up to one year. **To Apply:** Applicants must submit a letter of intent and may contact the Association for the application process and other information. **Contact:** Email: grants@abta.org.

701 ■ ABTA Medical Student Summer Fellowship Program *(Undergraduate/Fellowship)*

Purpose: To motivate talented medical students to pursue a career in neuro-oncology research. **Focus:** Medical research. **Qualif.:** Applicants are not required to be U.S. citizens or residents. The institution where the research is being conducted must be in the United States or Canada.

Funds Avail.: $3,000. **Duration:** 10-12 weeks. **Deadline:** January 24. **Contact:** Email: grants@abta.org; URL: www.abta.org/research/for-researchers/.

702 ■ ABTA Translational Grant Program
(Postdoctorate/Grant)

Purpose: To support the collection of the preclinical data researchers need to apply for major funding from other

sources. **Focus:** Oncology. **Qualif.:** MDs must be within eight years of completion of their post-residency training and hold a faculty or junior faculty appointment; PhDs must be within three to ten years of having received their doctorate and hold a faculty or junior faculty appointment; if a candidate holds multiple postdoctoral degrees, the last conferred postdoctoral degree will be used to determine eligibility. **Criteria:** Selection will be based on the potential of the research, the caliber of the laboratory environment and the experience of the investigator.

Funds Avail.: $75,000. **To Apply:** Applicants must visit the website for the online application. Gathering the following information/documents in advance will expedite the completion of the online application: the year the doctorate was conferred; knowledge of previous ABTA funding history and the names of any other organizations to whom the applicants are submitting grant applications; applicants' NIH biosketch in PDF format; letter from department chair in PDF format; description of the institutional support, equipment, resources for data set analysis and other critical resources available for the proposed project. A text box is provided online; a 250 words, publishable summary of study for a non-expert reader. A text box is provided online; research proposal in PDF format, not to exceed five pages including images; the name and email address of the grant officer, within the institution, who will certify the applicants' application. All applications must be certified by a grant officer prior to submission; a note about grant officer edit and submission authority. The applicants can choose to give the grant officer the authority to edit/change the application and can choose to allow the grant officer to submit the application, once complete. These authorities can be manage once a grant officer has been entered by editing permissions in the named grant officer section; ABTA's new grant portal provides personalized user views; and grant officers see all questions and responses.

703 ■ American Burn Association (ABA)
311 S Wacker Dr., Ste. 4150
Chicago, IL 60606-6671
Ph: (312)642-9260
Fax: (312)642-9130
E-mail: info@ameriburn.org
URL: www.ameriburn.org
Social Media: www.facebook.com/
AmericanBurnAssociation
www.linkedin.com/company/16234010
twitter.com/Ameriburn

704 ■ ABA Doctoral Traveling Fellowship *(Advanced Professional, Professional development/Fellowship)*

Purpose: To support an ABA physician member or postdoctoral fellow who has given evidence of a continuing interest and productivity in the field of burn care, teaching, or research. **Focus:** Education, Medical.

705 ■ ABA President's Continuing Education Grant
(Advanced Professional, Professional development/Grant)

Purpose: To honor and recognize a non-physician member who has made significant contributions to the care of the burned patient. **Focus:** Health care services.

Funds Avail.: $500. **Duration:** Annual. **Number Awarded:** Up to 3. **Deadline:** January 1.

Awards are arranged alphabetically below their administering organizations

706 ■ American Bus Association (ABA)

111 K St. NE, 9th Fl.
Washington, DC 20002
Ph: (202)842-1645
Fax: (202)842-0850
Free: 800-283-2877
E-mail: abainfo@buses.org
URL: www.buses.org
Social Media: www.facebook.com/
AmericanBusAssociation
www.instagram.com/americanbusassn
twitter.com/AmericanBusAssn

707 ■ ABA Diversity Scholarships *(Graduate/Scholarship)*

Purpose: To mobilize greater involvement in the transportation industry. **Focus:** Transportation; Travel and tourism. **Qualif.:** Applicants must be a freshman, sophomore, junior, senior, or graduate student at an accredited University; must have a declared major or course of study relevant to the transportation, travel, and tourism industry. Transportation, travel and tourism encompass a varying range of professions from accounting to hospitality management and everything in between. **Criteria:** Recipients are selected on the basis of academic merit, character, leadership and financial need and dedication to advancing the transportation, travel and tourism industry.

Funds Avail.: $5,000. **To Apply:** Applicants are required to submit a 500-word essay discussing the role they hope to play in advancing the future of the transportation, motorcoach, travel, and tourism/hospitality industry. **Contact:** E-mail: contactus@applyists.com; Phone: 855-670-4787.

708 ■ ABA Members Scholarships *(Undergraduate, Graduate/Scholarship)*

Purpose: To financially assist deserving students who have a potential to be future leaders in the transportation, travel, and tourism industry. **Focus:** Transportation; Travel and tourism. **Qualif.:** Applicants must be an employee or a dependent children of ABA bus and tour member companies employed for at least one year; must be entering first year of college, university or professional training school by fall; must have a minimum of 3.0 GPA or on a 4.0 scale. **Criteria:** Select winners based on their academic merit, extracurricular activities, and anticipated financial need.

Funds Avail.: $5,000. **Number Awarded:** 7. **To Apply:** Applicant must submit an online application form. **Contact:** E-mail: contactus@applyists.com; Phone: 855-670-4787.

709 ■ American Bus Association Academic Merit Scholarships *(Undergraduate, Graduate/Scholarship)*

Purpose: To financially assist deserving students who have a potential to be future leaders in the transportation, travel, and tourism industry. **Focus:** Transportation; Travel and tourism. **Qualif.:** Applicants must be a freshman, sophomore, junior, senior, or graduate student at an accredited University; must have a declared major or course of study relevant to the transportation, travel, and tourism industry. Transportation, travel and tourism encompass a varying range of professions from accounting to hospitality management and everything in between. **Criteria:** Select winners based on their academic merit, extracurricular activities, and anticipated financial need.

Funds Avail.: $5,000. **Number Awarded:** 2. **To Apply:** Applicant must submit an online application form. **Contact:** E-mail: contactus@applyists.com; Phone: 855-670-4787.

710 ■ Bus & Tour Operator Scholarships *(Undergraduate, Graduate/Scholarship)*

Purpose: To financially assist deserving students who have potentials to be future leaders in the transportation, travel and tourism industry. **Focus:** Transportation; Travel and tourism. **Qualif.:** Applicants must be an employee or a dependent children of ABA bus and tour member companies employed for at least one year; must be entering first year of college, university or professional training school by fall; must have a minimum of 3.0 GPA or on a 4.0 scale. **Criteria:** Select winners based on their academic merit, extracurricular activities, and anticipated financial need.

Funds Avail.: $5,000. **Number Awarded:** 7. **To Apply:** Applicant must submit an online application form. **Contact:** E-mail: contactus@applyists.com; Phone: 855-670-4787.

711 ■ Peter L. Picknelly Honorary Scholarships *(Graduate/Scholarship)*

Purpose: To recognize the contribution of bus drivers, mechanics and maintenance personnel to the motorcoach industry. **Focus:** Transportation; Travel and tourism. **Qualif.:** Applicant must be a bus driver, mechanic, or maintenance personnel of ABA Operator Members or their dependents; must be a freshman, sophomore, junior, senior, or graduate student studying or planning to study at a technical school, trade school or in a transportation-related program; must maintain a minimum GPA of a 3.0 on a 4.0 scale. **Criteria:** Select winners based on their academic merit, extracurricular activities, and anticipated financial need.

Funds Avail.: $2,500. **To Apply:** Applicant must submit an online application form. **Contact:** E-mail: contactus@applyists.com; Phone: 855-670-4787.

712 ■ American Cancer Society (ACS)

250 Williams St. NW
Atlanta, GA 30303-1002
Free: 800-227-2345
URL: www.cancer.org
Social Media: www.facebook.com/AmericanCancerSociety
instagram.com/americancancersociety
twitter.com/americancancer

713 ■ ACS Doctoral Degree Scholarships in Cancer Nursing *(Doctorate, Graduate/Scholarship)*

Purpose: To strengthen nursing practice by providing assistance for advance preparation in the field of cancer nursing research. **Focus:** Nursing. **Qualif.:** Applicants must be currently enrolled in or applying to a doctoral degree program in nursing or a related field of research; must meet the requirements for doctoral study and must have been accepted by the institution to which they have applied at the time of funding; must have a current license to practice as registered nurses; must project a program of study that integrates cancer nursing and provides evidence of faculty support for the program of study; must take a minimum of 18 credit hours or 6 courses per year; must demonstrate a commitment to cancer nursing as evidenced by recent experience, education and/or research in the specialty area. **Criteria:** Selection will be based on the relevant professional experience in oncology; involvement in professional organizations, including leadership roles; involvement in activities of the American Cancer Society or other relevant

Awards are arranged alphabetically below their administering organizations

volunteer organizations; clear, explicit and realistic professional goals; consideration of program components, particularly oncology content, in selecting a doctoral program; conduct or plan to conduct research that is important, methodologically sound, and relevant to the health of persons affected with cancer or at risk for cancer; commitment from a faculty advisor who is experienced in the student's area of study and will provide guidance in academic and research activities; selection of a doctoral program which will support the student's professional goals and research; and dedication to cancer nursing research.

Funds Avail.: $15,000 per year. **Duration:** Annual; up to two years. **To Apply:** Applicants must visit the website for the electronic application process. **Deadline:** October 15. **Contact:** Virginia Krawiec, MPA Director, Health Professional Training in Cancer Control; Stella Jones, Program Coordinator; Phone: 404-329-5734; Email: stella.jones@cancer.org.

714 ■ ACS Graduate Scholarships in Cancer Nursing Practice *(Graduate, Master's, Doctorate/Scholarship)*

Purpose: To provide support to graduate students pursuing a master's degree in cancer nursing or doctorate of nursing practice. **Focus:** Nursing. **Qualif.:** Applicants must be currently enrolled in or applying to a master's or DNP degree graduate program with demonstrated integration of cancer content; must have a current license to practice as a registered nurse. Students in bridge programs must have passed the N-CLEX examination and updated their status with the ACS Program Office by the time the award begins; must be pursuing an advance degree and not solely a post-master's certificate. **Criteria:** Selection will be based on involvement in cancer-related professional and academic organizations; have published or contributed to scholarly publications, presentations and creative works; are the recipients of professional and academic awards and honors; have considered program content, faculty and clinical resources related to cancer in selecting a graduate program; have a focus for scholarly activity in a specific area of cancer nursing; have made a career commitment to cancer nursing; have formed explicit and realistic professional goals.

Funds Avail.: Up to $10,000. **Duration:** Up to two years. **To Apply:** Applicants must visit the website for the electronic application process. **Deadline:** November 1. **Contact:** Virginia Krawiec, MPA Director, Health Professional Training in Cancer Control; Stella Jones, Program Coordinator; Phone: 404-329-5734; Email: stella.jones@cancer.org.

715 ■ American Cancer Society - Postdoctoral Fellowships *(Doctorate/Fellowship)*

Purpose: To support the training of researchers who have received a doctoral degree to provide initial funding leading to an independent career in cancer research. **Focus:** Health care services. **Qualif.:** Applicants must have obtained their doctoral degree prior to activation of the fellowship; must be US citizens, non-citizen nationals or permanent residents of the United States. **Criteria:** Selection will be based on the committee's criteria.

Funds Avail.: $48,000; $50,000; $52,000 + ($4,000 per year fellowship allowance). **Duration:** Annual; up to three years. **To Apply:** Applicants must visit the website for the electronic grant application process and also should attach the following: a letter that includes rationale for requesting an exception to the American Cancer Society eligibility rules; a full curriculum vitae. **Deadline:** April 1; October 15. **Contact:** Email: grants@cancer.org.

716 ■ American Cancer Society - Research Scholar Grants *(Doctorate, Professional development/Grant)*

Purpose: To provide resources for investigator-initiated research in a variety of cancer-relevant areas. **Focus:** Medical research. **Qualif.:** Applicants must have an independent research or faculty position; must be independent investigators within first 6 years of independent career with no more than one current R01-like support; must be independent investigators at any stage of their career with any level of prior funding; or independent investigators at any stage of their career with any level of prior funding. **Criteria:** Selection will be based on the demonstrated intellectual independence and committed research facilities; time limit on applicant's eligibility and current grant support.

Funds Avail.: $165,000 per year. **Duration:** Up to four years. **To Apply:** Applicants must visit the website for the electronic grant application process. **Deadline:** April 1; October 15. **Contact:** Email: grants@cancer.org.

717 ■ Mentored Research Scholar Grant *(Doctorate, Professional development/Grant)*

Purpose: To support junior faculty members to become independent investigators as either clinician scientists or cancer control researchers. **Focus:** Medical research. **Qualif.:** Applicants must be within the first four years of a full-time faculty appointment or the equivalent; not be independent investigators; have four years or less postdoctoral research training/experience at the time of application; have a clinical doctoral degree; have a research doctoral degree in a clinical discipline or equivalent in nursing, nutrition, psychology, social work, etc.; or have a research doctoral degree in a cancer control discipline or equivalent in behavioral, epidemiologic, health policy, health services or psychosocial research. **Criteria:** Selection will be based on the following applicants' academic and scientific qualifications, potential to succeed as an independent investigator and commitment to research as a career; the appropriateness of the mentors' research qualifications in the proposed project area, the role of the mentors on the project, research productivity and prior success in fostering the development of cancer researchers; submitted research and training plan; documentation of the institutional commitment to the research development of the applicants.

Funds Avail.: Up to $135,000 per year including $10,000 for the mentors. **Duration:** up to five years. **To Apply:** Applicants must visit the website for the electronic grant application process. **Deadline:** October 15. **Contact:** Program Coordinator, Chanda Felton; Email: Chanda.Felton@cancer.org.

718 ■ American Center for Mongolian Studies (ACMS)

c/o Center for East Asian Studies
255 S 36th St.
642 Williams Hall
Philadelphia, PA 19104-6305
Ph: (360)356-1020
Fax: (215)573-2561
URL: mongoliacenter.org
Social Media: www.facebook.com/
   AmericanCenterForMongolianStudies
twitter.com/acmsmongolia
www.youtube.com/channel/

Awards are arranged alphabetically below their administering organizations

UCDQ5ay8BeWwSgQV2IJIFsWw

719 ■ ACMS Field Research Fellowship Program
(Postdoctorate/Fellowship)

Purpose: To support students who wish to conduct field research in Mongolia. **Focus:** General studies/Field of study not specified. **Qualif.:** Applicants must be US citizens currently enrolled full-time (students) or employed at least part-time (post-docs and faculty) at a university or college; students who have just graduated are eligible for the program; undergraduate applicants must have at least third year standing in their program, while graduate applicants can be at a masters, pre-dissertation, or doctoral candidacy level.; post-doctoral scholars and faculty must regularly teach at least one course at a US university or college to be eligible. **Criteria:** Selection process based on the selection committee.

Funds Avail.: $4,000. **Duration:** Annual. **Deadline:** February 15.

720 ■ ACMS Intensive Mongolian Language Fellowship *(Undergraduate/Fellowship)*

Purpose: To provide opportunities to intermediate-level students of the Mongolian language to enhance their communicative competence through systematic improvement of reading, writing, listening and speaking skills in an authentic environment. **Focus:** Area and ethnic studies. **Criteria:** Selection based on committee criteria.

Funds Avail.: Up to $2,000. **To Apply:** Applicants who submit their applications in March will be considered for Language Program Fellowships. **Deadline:** March 1.

721 ■ ACMS Library Fellowship *(Graduate, Professional development, Postgraduate/Fellowship)*

Purpose: To support students or faculty members in library science to conduct a short-term project and/or research in Mongolia. **Focus:** Library and archival sciences. **Qualif.:** Applicants must be advanced US graduate students, faculty members, or professionals in library and information sciences from colleges and universities. **Criteria:** Selection based on committee criteria.

Funds Avail.: Up to $4,000 (travel and living expenses). **Deadline:** February 15.

722 ■ American Center for Oriental Research
209 Commerce St.
Alexandria, VA 22314-2909
Ph: (703)789-9231
E-mail: usa.office@acorjordan.org
URL: acorjordan.org

723 ■ ACOR-CAORC Post-Doctoral Fellowships
(Postdoctorate/Fellowship)

Purpose: To support research in the natural and social sciences, humanities, and associated disciplines related to the Middle East. **Focus:** Area and ethnic studies; Humanities; Natural sciences; Social sciences. **Qualif.:** Applicants must hold a PhD degree or be scholars/professional with the equivalent terminal degree in their fields; must be pursuing research or publication projects in the natural and social sciences, humanities, and associated disciplines related to the Middle East at the time of application; must be U.S. citizens.

Funds Avail.: $32,400 for six months (which includes room and board at ACOR, transportation by a U.S. carrier, and a stipend). **Duration:** Annual; two to six months. **Number Awarded:** 2 or more. **To Apply:** Application available online at www.acorjordan.org/caorc-fellowships/. **Deadline:** February 1. **Contact:** ACOR Fellowship Committee at above address.

724 ■ ACOR-CAORC Pre-Doctoral Fellowships
(Graduate, Doctorate/Fellowship)

Purpose: To support students conducting research in Jordan. **Focus:** Area and ethnic studies. **Qualif.:** Applicants must be masters or doctoral students; must either be enrolled in a degree program, or be accepted to and planning to enroll in a degree program the next academic year at the time the award is used; must be U.S. citizens; must reside at ACOR in Jordan for the length of the fellowship (two to six months).

Funds Avail.: $23,800 for six months (which includes room and board at ACOR, transportation by a U.S. carrier, stipend, and research funds). **Duration:** Annual. **Number Awarded:** Two or more. **To Apply:** Application available online at www.acorjordan.org/caorc-fellowships/. **Deadline:** February 1. **Contact:** ACOR Fellowship Committee at address above.

725 ■ Pierre and Patricia Bikai Fellowship
(Graduate/Fellowship)

Purpose: To assist graduate students conducting archaeological research in Jordan. **Focus:** Archeology. **Qualif.:** Applicants must be enrolled graduate students of any nationality except Jordanian citizens who wish to continue study or research at ACOR after the field project has concluded and residency at the ACOR center is required.

Funds Avail.: $600 per month. **Duration:** Annual; up to 2 months. **Number Awarded:** 1 or 2. **To Apply:** Application available online at www.acorjordan.org/named-fellowships/bikai-fellowship/.

726 ■ Bert and Sally de Vries Fellowship
(Undergraduate, Graduate/Fellowship)

Purpose: To support students participating in archaeological excavations in Jordan. **Focus:** Archeology. **Qualif.:** Applicants must be undergraduate or graduate students of any nationality except Jordanian citizens for participation on an archaeological project or research in Jordan; must be enrolled students.

Funds Avail.: $1,500. **Duration:** Annual. **To Apply:** Application available online at www.acorjordan.org/named-fellowships/de-vries-fellowship/. **Remarks:** Established in 2004.

727 ■ Jennifer C. Groot Memorial Fellowship
(Undergraduate, Graduate/Fellowship)

Purpose: To assist students to participate in an archaeological excavation or survey in Jordan. **Focus:** Archeology. **Qualif.:** Applicants must be U.S. or Canadian citizens; must be undergraduate or graduate students who want to participate in an archaeological excavation or survey in Jordan.

Funds Avail.: $1,500 each. **Number Awarded:** Up to 4. **To Apply:** Application available online at www.acorjordan.org/named-fellowships/groot-memorial-fellowship/. **Deadline:** February 1. **Remarks:** Established in memory of Jennifer C. Groot, a field archaeologist who worked on many excavations in Jordan between 1974 and 1987. Established in 1989.

Awards are arranged alphabetically below their administering organizations

728 ■ Harrell Family Fellowship (Graduate/Fellowship)

Purpose: To assist in partial payment of essential expenses for graduate students to participate in an archaeological dig in Jordan. **Focus:** Archeology. **Qualif.:** Applicants must be graduate students of any nationality, except Jordanian citizens, who desire to participate on an archaeological project in Jordan; must be enrolled in graduate studies.

Funds Avail.: $2,000. **To Apply:** Application available online at www.acorjordan.org/named-fellowships/harrell-fellowship/. **Deadline:** February 1.

729 ■ Kenneth W. Russell Memorial Fellowships (Graduate/Fellowship)

Purpose: To assist students in the fields archaeology, anthropology, conservation, or related areas in Jordan. **Focus:** Anthropology; Archeology; Conservation of natural resources. **Qualif.:** Applicants must be graduate students, of any nationality except Jordanian, seeking to travel for field work or research in Jordan.

Funds Avail.: $1,800. **Duration:** Biennial. **To Apply:** Application available online at www.acorjordan.org/named-fellowships/russell-fellowship/. **Deadline:** February 1.

730 ■ Burton MacDonald and Rosemarie Sampson Fellowship (Undergraduate, Graduate/Fellowship)

Purpose: To encourage students to take part in archaeological excavations in Jordan. **Focus:** Archeology. **Qualif.:** Applicants must be Canadian citizens or Canadian landed immigrants; must be enrolled undergraduate or graduate students.

Funds Avail.: $2,000 to provide support on an archaeological project or research in Jordan; or, six weeks room and board at the ACOR center in Amman and a stipend of $400. **Duration:** Annual. **To Apply:** Application available online at www.acorjordan.org/named-fellowships/macdonald-sampson-fellowship/. **Deadline:** February 1.

731 ■ James A. Sauer Memorial Fellowships (Graduate/Fellowship)

Purpose: To support students participating in archaeological research in Jordan. **Focus:** Archeology. **Qualif.:** Applicants must be enrolled graduate students of non-Jordanian nationality.

Funds Avail.: $1,250 award without residency at ACOR, or $400 award plus one month of residency at ACOR. **Duration:** Biennial. **To Apply:** Application available online at sponsor's website. **Deadline:** February 1.

732 ■ American Ceramic Society (ACERS)

550 Polaris Pky, Ste.510
Westerville, OH 43082
Ph: (614)890-4700
Fax: (614)899-6109
Free: 866-721-3322
E-mail: customerservice@ceramics.org
URL: www.ceramics.org
Social Media: www.facebook.com/acersnews
www.linkedin.com/company/the-american-ceramic-society
twitter.com/ACerSNews
www.youtube.com/user/ceramicsociety

733 ■ Electronics Division: Lewis C. Hoffman Scholarship (Undergraduate/Scholarship)

Purpose: To encourage academic interest and excellence among undergraduate students. **Focus:** Engineering, Materials; Materials research/science. **Qualif.:** Applicant must be a junior-year student, or a student who has recently completed their junior year; must have acquired a total of 80 or more semester credits or equivalent quarter credits; must have extracurricular activities. **Criteria:** Applicants will be selected based on the application requirements.

Funds Avail.: $2,000. **Duration:** Annual. **Number Awarded:** 1. **To Apply:** Applicants must submit a recommendation letter from a faculty member in the department; write a 500 word essay on the year's topic "Tailoring Material Properties through Defect Engineering for Electronic Ceramics". **Deadline:** June 15. **Remarks:** Established in 1999. **Contact:** Edward Gorzkowski; Email: edward.gorzkowski@nrl.navy.mil; Erica Zimmerman; Email: ezimmerman@ceramics.org.

734 ■ American Chemical Society (ACS)

1155 16th St. NW
Washington, DC 20036
Ph: (202)872-4600
Free: 800-333-9511
E-mail: service@acs.org
URL: www.acs.org/content/acs/en.html
Social Media: www.facebook.com/AmericanChemicalSociety
www.linkedin.com/company/american-chemical-society
twitter.com/AmerChemSociety

735 ■ ACS Award for Research at an Undergraduate Institution (Postdoctorate/Award, Recognition, Grant, Monetary)

Purpose: To recognize the importance of research with undergraduates. **Focus:** Chemistry. **Qualif.:** Nominee must be a tenured faculty member of a predominantly undergraduate institution.

Funds Avail.: $5,000; up to $2,500 for travel expenses to attend the meeting; additional $5,000 grant. **Duration:** Annual. **Number Awarded:** 1. **To Apply:** Nominators must submit nominee's contact information, citation Including a description of the work; recommendation letter describing the nominee's work and how it is aligned with the purpose, eligibility, and/or criteria of the award, the impact on the discipline, the significance (scientific or otherwise) of this effort, and the benefits to the society; biographical sketch (2 pgs.) that focuses on the award and selection committee criteria (do not include a list of publications and patents); list of Nominee's Most Significant Publications and Patents (20 max.); support letter describing the impact of the work on the discipline, the significance of the research findings, and the way the award's purpose and criteria have been met; applicants must be completed nominations are submitted online. **Deadline:** November 1. **Remarks:** Established in 1984. **Contact:** American Chemical Society, 1155 16th St., NW Washington, D.C. 20036-4801; Phone: 202-872-4575; Fax: 202-776-8008; Email: awards@acs.org.

736 ■ Arthur C. Cope Award (Advanced Professional/Monetary, Medal, Grant, Award, Recognition)

Purpose: To honor and recognize an individual for outstanding achievement in the field of organic chemistry. **Focus:** Chemistry.

Funds Avail.: $25,000; up to $2,500 for travel expenses to the meeting; $150,000 unrestricted grant-in-aid for research in organic chemistry. **Duration:** Annual. **Number Awarded:** 1. **To Apply:** Nominators must submit nominee's contact

Awards are arranged alphabetically below their administering organizations

information, citation Including a description of the work; recommendation letter describing the nominee's work and how it is aligned with the purpose, eligibility, and/or criteria of the award, the impact on the discipline, the significance (scientific or otherwise) of this effort, and the benefits to the society; biographical sketch (2 pgs.) that focuses on the award and selection committee criteria (do not include a list of publications and patents); list of Nominee's Most Significant Publications and Patents (20 max.); support letter describing the impact of the work on the discipline, the significance of the research findings, and the way the award's purpose and criteria have been met; applicants must be completed nominations are submitted online. **Deadline:** November 1. **Remarks:** Established in 1972. **Contact:** American Chemical Society, 1155 16th St NW., Washington, D.C., 20036-4801; Phone: 202-872-4575; Fax: 202-776-8008; Email: awards@acs.org.

737 ■ American Chemical Society - Rubber Division

306 N. Cleveland Massillon Rd.
Akron, OH 44333
Ph: (330)595-5531
E-mail: lmiller@rubber.org
URL: www.rubber.org
Social Media: twitter.com/rubberdivision

738 ■ ACS Rubber Division Undergraduate Scholarship *(Undergraduate/Scholarship)*

Purpose: To support the need of chemistry-related students for financial assistance in obtaining a college degree. **Focus:** Chemistry; Engineering, Chemical; Engineering, Mechanical; Physics. **Qualif.:** Applicants must be students entering their junior or senior year for the fall-spring academic year and may have a major area study in chemistry, physics, chemical or mechanical engineering, polymer science or any other technical discipline relevant to the rubber industry. **Criteria:** Selection are given based on academic merit.

Funds Avail.: Up to $5,000 Each. **Duration:** Annual. **To Apply:** Applicants may visit the website to verify the application process and other pieces of information.

739 ■ American Choral Directors Association - Texas Chapter

7900 Ctr Pk Dr., Ste A
Austin, TX 78754
Ph: (512)474-2801
E-mail: tcda@tcda.net
URL: www.tcda.net
Social Media: www.facebook.com/texassings
www.instagram.com/texassings
twitter.com/texassings

740 ■ TCDA Carroll Barnes Student Scholarships *(Undergraduate/Scholarship)*

Purpose: To support active TCDA student members in their continuing education. **Focus:** Education, Music; Religion. **Qualif.:** Applicants must be Texas college/university undergraduate students in music education or church music majors with 60+ credit hours and must have maintained at least 3.0 GPA on a 4.0 system. **Criteria:** Selection shall be based on the aforementioned qualifications and compliance with the application details.

Funds Avail.: No specific amount. **Duration:** Annual. **To Apply:** Applicants must submit a current transcript; two sealed letters of recommendation (one from a current TCDA member); letter of application (typed or printed) detailing musical contributions and accomplishments, potential for success in the choral music profession, and professional qualifications.

741 ■ TCDA Jim and Glenda Casey Professional Scholarships *(Other/Scholarship)*

Purpose: To support active TCDA members in their professional development. **Focus:** Education, Music. **Qualif.:** Applicants must be enrolled in a Texas college/university and have three years of continuous active membership; 3.0 overall GPA average based on a 4.0 system; Completion of 60 hours by May 31 in the year of the award. **Criteria:** Selection shall be based on the aforementioned qualifications and compliance with the application details.

Funds Avail.: $1,000. **Duration:** Annual. **Number Awarded:** 1. **To Apply:** Applicants must submit a letter of application describing their qualifications, professional goals, and a description of the higher education or workshop certification sought; they must also submit their respective resume or curriculum vitae. **Contact:** Sharon Lutz; Email: sharon@tcda.net; Phone: 512-474-2801.

742 ■ TCDA Abbott IPCO Professional Scholarships *(Other/Scholarship)*

Purpose: To support active TCDA members in their professional development. **Focus:** Education, Music. **Qualif.:** Applicants must be enrolled in a Texas college/university and have three years of continuous active membership. **Criteria:** Selection shall be based on the aforementioned qualifications and compliance with the application details.

Funds Avail.: $1,000. **Duration:** Annual. **Number Awarded:** 1. **To Apply:** Applicants must submit a letter of application describing their qualifications, professional goals, and a description of the higher education or workshop certification sought; they must also submit their respective resume or curriculum vitae. **Contact:** Sharon Lutz; Email: sharon@tcda.net; Phone: 512-474-2801.

743 ■ TCDA Bill Gorham Student Scholarship *(Undergraduate/Scholarship)*

Purpose: To support active TCDA student members in their continuing education. **Focus:** Education, Music; Religion. **Qualif.:** Applicants must be Texas college/university undergraduate students in music education or church music majors with 60+ credit hours and must have maintained at least 3.0 GPA on a 4.0 system. **Criteria:** Selection shall be based on the aforementioned qualifications and compliance with the application details.

Funds Avail.: $1,000. **Duration:** Annual. **Number Awarded:** 1. **To Apply:** Applicants must submit a current transcript; two sealed letters of recommendation (one from a current TCDA member); letter of application (typed or printed) detailing musical contributions and accomplishments, potential for success in the choral music profession, and professional qualifications. **Contact:** Sharon Lutz; Email: sharon@tcda.net; Phone: 512-474-2801.

744 ■ TCDA Cloys Webb Student Scholarship *(Undergraduate/Scholarship)*

Purpose: To support active TCDA student members in their continuing education. **Focus:** Education, Music; Religion. **Qualif.:** Applicants must be Texas college/university

Awards are arranged alphabetically below their administering organizations

undergraduate students in music education or church music majors with 60+ credit hours and must have maintained at least 3.0 GPA on a 4.0 system. **Criteria:** Selection shall be based on the aforementioned qualifications and compliance with the application details.

Funds Avail.: $1,000. **Duration:** Annual. **Number Awarded:** 1. **To Apply:** Applicants must submit a current transcript; two sealed letters of recommendation (one from a current TCDA member); letter of application (typed or printed) detailing musical contributions and accomplishments, potential for success in the choral music profession, and professional qualifications. **Contact:** Sharon Lutz; Email: sharon@tcda.net; Phone: 512-474-2801.

745 ■ TCDA Gandy Ink Professional Scholarship
(Professional development/Scholarship)

Purpose: To support active TCDA members in their professional development. **Focus:** Education, Music; Religion. **Qualif.:** Applicants must be enrolled in a Texas college/ university and have three years of continuous active membership; 3.0 overall GPA average based on a 4.0 system; Completion of 60 hours by May 31 in the year of the award. **Criteria:** Selection shall be based on the aforementioned qualifications and compliance with the application details.

Funds Avail.: $1,000. **Duration:** Annual. **To Apply:** Applicants must submit a letter of application describing their qualifications, professional goals, and a description of the higher education or workshop certification sought; they must also submit their respective resume or curriculum vitae. **Contact:** Sharon Lutz; Email: sharon@tcda.net; Phone: 512-474-2801.

746 ■ TCDA General Fund Scholarships
(Undergraduate/Scholarship)

Purpose: To support active TCDA student members in their continuing education. **Focus:** Education, Music; Religion. **Qualif.:** Applicants must be Texas college/university undergraduate students in music education or church music majors with 60+ credit hours and must have maintained at least 3.0 GPA on a 4.0 system. **Criteria:** Selection shall be based on the aforementioned qualifications and compliance with the application details.

Funds Avail.: $500. **Duration:** Annual. **Number Awarded:** 1. **To Apply:** Applicants must submit a current transcript; two sealed letters of recommendation (one from a current TCDA member); letter of application (typed or printed) detailing musical contributions and accomplishments, potential for success in the choral music profession, and professional qualifications. **Deadline:** April 15. **Contact:** Sharon Lutz; Email: sharon@tcda.net; Phone: 512-474-2801.

747 ■ TCDA Past Presidents Student Scholarship
(Undergraduate/Scholarship)

Purpose: To support active TCDA student members in their continuing education. **Focus:** Education, Music; Religion. **Qualif.:** Applicants must be Texas college/university undergraduate students in music education or church music majors with 60+ credit hours and must have maintained at least 3.0 GPA on a 4.0 system. **Criteria:** Selection shall be based on the aforementioned qualifications and compliance with the application details.

Funds Avail.: $1,000. **Duration:** Annual. **Number Awarded:** 1. **To Apply:** Applicants must submit a current transcript; two sealed letters of recommendation (one from

a current TCDA member); letter of application (typed or printed) detailing musical contributions and accomplishments, potential for success in the choral music profession, and professional qualifications. **Contact:** Sharon Lutz; Email: sharon@tcda.net; Phone: 512-474-2801.

748 ■ American Civil Liberties Union of Northern California, Mid-Peninsula Chapter
39 Drumm St.
San Francisco, CA 94111
E-mail: midpen.aclu@gmail.com
URL: www.aclunc.org

749 ■ Christiane Cook Memorial Scholarship
(Undergraduate/Scholarship)

Purpose: To support students with their studies through an essay contest. **Focus:** Civil rights; Education.

Duration: Annual. **Deadline:** December 15.

750 ■ American Clan Gregor Society (ACGS)
3120 North Shannon Lakes Dr.
Tallahassee, FL 32309
E-mail: info@acgsus.org
URL: www.acgsus.org
Social Media: www.facebook.com/
  americanclangregorsocietyus
twitter.com/acgs2

751 ■ Dr. Edward May Magruder Medical Scholarships
(Undergraduate/Scholarship)

Purpose: To provide educational assistance to the students of the University of Virginia School of Medicine. **Focus:** Medicine. **Qualif.:** Applicants who are ACGHS members, children of members, or others who have lineage to the Clan Gregor are welcome to apply. Applicants must also be enrolled at least half-time or full-time for Federal Title VII programs. Those applicants who are in default on a federal loan or owe a refund on a federal grant are disqualified. Registration in Selective Service is also required for·the application. **Criteria:** Recipients will be selected based on their satisfactory academic progress and financial information.

Duration: Annual. **To Apply:** Applicants must complete both the FAFSA and the UVA School of Medicine Application (refer and download from www.healthsystem.virginia.edu). Previous year U.S Tax Returns is also required for the completion of the requirements. **Remarks:** Established in 1927. **Contact:** Ms. Nancy L. Zimmer, nlb3w@ virginia.edu.

752 ■ American Classical League (ACL)
860 NW Washington Blvd., Ste. A
Hamilton, OH 45013
Ph: (513)529-7741
Fax: (513)529-7742
Free: 800-670-8346
E-mail: info@aclclassics.org
URL: www.aclclassics.org
Social Media: www.facebook.com/ACLClassics
www.linkedin.com/company/american-classical-league
twitter.com/aclclassics

753 ■ Arthur Patch McKinlay Scholarship *(Graduate, Undergraduate/Scholarship)*

Purpose: To help our members enhance their teaching by encouraging them to travel, take courses, attend profes-

Awards are arranged alphabetically below their administering organizations

sional meetings, and engage in professional development. **Focus:** Classical studies. **Qualif.:** Applicants must be an ACL member for the preceding three years and planning to teach classics at elementary through secondary level for the current school year; ACL members at all levels of teaching are eligible to apply; ACL scholarship recipients may apply every 4 years; Undergraduate students, graduate students and new teachers with less than 3 years experience are exempt from the requirement of three consecutive years of membership.

Funds Avail.: $250-$2,000. **Duration:** Quadrennial. **To Apply:** Application form is a fillable form which you can download. After you have completed the application you may attach as an email and send to the ACL Office. **Deadline:** January 15 and March 15. **Remarks:** The scholarship was established in memory of Arthur Patch McKinlay. **Contact:** Application and signed references to info@aclclassics.org or mail to: The American Classical League Scholarship Awards; 860 NW Washington Blvd, Suite A; Hamilton, Ohio 45013.

754 ■ Glenn Knudsvig Memorial Scholarships
(Graduate, Undergraduate/Scholarship)

Purpose: To encourage teaching profession of classics by providing educational fund for deserving teacher and undergraduate or graduate member of the American Classical League. **Focus:** Classical studies. **Qualif.:** Applicants must be an ACL member for the preceding three years and planning to teach classics at elementary through secondary level for the current school year; ACL members at all levels of teaching are eligible to apply; ACL scholarship recipients may apply every 4 years.

Funds Avail.: $250-$2,000. **Duration:** Quadrennial. **To Apply:** Applicants must submit the online application form. **Deadline:** January 15 and March 15. **Remarks:** The scholarship was established in memory of Glenn Knudsvig. **Contact:** The American Classical League, Scholarship Awards, 860 NW Washington Blvd., Ste. A, Hamilton, Ohio 45013; E-mail: info@aclclassics.org.

755 ■ Ed Phinney Commemorative Scholarships
(Graduate, Undergraduate/Scholarship)

Purpose: To support teacher and student members of the American Classical League. **Focus:** Classical studies. **Qualif.:** Applicants must be an ACL member for the preceding three years and planning to teach classics at elementary through secondary level for the current school year; ACL members at all levels of teaching are eligible to apply; ACL scholarship recipients may apply every 4 years.

Funds Avail.: $250-$2,000. **Duration:** Quadrennial. **To Apply:** Applicants must submit the online application form. **Deadline:** January 15 and March 15. **Remarks:** The scholarship was established in memory of Ed Phinney. **Contact:** The American Classical League, Scholarship Awards, 860 NW Washington Blvd., Ste. A, Hamilton, Ohio 45013; E-mail: info@aclclassics.org.

756 ■ American College of Bankruptcy (ACB)
PO Box 249
Stanardsville, VA 22973
Ph: (434)939-6005
Fax: (434)939-6030
URL: www.americancollegeofbankruptcy.com
Social Media: www.facebook.com/AmColBankruptcy
www.linkedin.com/company/american-college-of
  -bankruptcy

twitter.com/AmColBankruptcy
www.youtube.com/channel/
  UCE0ulKgGlybwLWg2ChrqHWw

757 ■ ACB Foundation Grants for Pro Bono Projects *(Other/Grant)*

Purpose: To provide financial assistance to organizations whose projects are related to bankruptcy and/or debtor/creditor matters. **Focus:** Financial aid.

Funds Avail.: Up to $15,000. **Deadline:** June 1.

758 ■ American College of Chiropractic Orthopedists (ACCO)
c/o Mick McConnell, President
16730 N. Marketplace Blvd.
Nampa, ID 83687
Ph: (208)466-4600
Fax: (208)461-9236
URL: acco.wildapricot.org

759 ■ F. Maynard Lipe Scholarship Award *(Master's, Postgraduate/Scholarship)*

Purpose: To provide financial assistance to the candidate enrolled in a post-graduate orthopedic program leading to diplomate status or the masters degree program leading to a health science degree in orthopedics. **Focus:** Medicine, Chiropractic; Medicine, Orthopedic. **Qualif.:** Applicants must be enrolled in a CCE approved College of Chiropractic Post-Graduate Orthopedics course leading to Diplomate or the Masters Degree Program leading to a Health Science Degree in Orthopedics. **Criteria:** Applicants will be evaluated by the ACCO assigned Scholarship Committee.

Funds Avail.: $1,800 and $600 allowance. **Duration:** Annual. **To Apply:** Applicants should submit an article (1,000-2,500 words) on a subject current to Chiropractic Orthopedics as decided by the Scholarship Awards Committee and approved by the ACCO executive board. Articles should be doubled-spaced on white 8 1/2 x 11 inch paper. Six copies should be submitted to the Secretary of the Executive Board, with five of them being "clean" (having no identification as to the author or college), and one with full identification. Articles should include: title page; abstract and index term page; text pages or body; footnoted pages; and reference pages; A letter of authorization allowing full use of the article submitted to the ACCO; A letter of recommendation from the orthopedic course instructor/director of the program. **Deadline:** November 30; December 31. **Remarks:** The Scholarship was established in memory of Maynard F. Lipe, founding father of chiropractic orthopedics and a strong believer in the scientific principles of chiropractic, his teaching rested on a foundation of high ethical standards.

760 ■ American College of Gastroenterology (ACG)
6400 Goldsboro Rd., Ste. 200
Bethesda, MD 20817
Ph: (301)263-9000
Fax: (301)263-9025
E-mail: education@gi.org
URL: gi.org
Social Media: www.facebook.com/AmCollegeGastro
www.instagram.com/amcollegegastro
www.linkedin.com/company/american-college-of
  -gastroenterology

Awards are arranged alphabetically below their administering organizations

twitter.com/AmCollegeGastro
www.youtube.com/user/ACGastroenterology

761 ■ International GI Training Grant (Professional development/Grant)

Purpose: To provide partial financial support to physicians outside of the United States and Canada to receive clinical or clinical research training or education in Gastroenterology and Hepatology in selected medical training centers in North America. **Focus:** Gastroenterology; Medical research. **Qualif.:** Applicants must be physicians who are not citizens of, nor are currently residing in, the United States or Canada, and who are working in gastroenterology or related areas. **Criteria:** Selection will be based upon the applicant's credentials, the merit of the proposed training by the selected host training center and the potential of enhancing the field of gastroenterology in the applicant's home country.

Funds Avail.: $10,000. **Duration:** Annual. **To Apply:** Applicants must submit a completed application form, a personal statement that summarizes the reasons and objectives of additional training, a curriculum vitae, copies of all published articles and abstracts within the last five years and a completed application form from the host training center; three letters of recommendation from the training preceptor/director, from an ACG Fellow and from a person of the applicants' choosing; applicants are responsible for selecting a host training center who will voluntarily agree to participate in the program. The host training center must be able to accomplish the training goals and must complete the host training center application. **Deadline:** March 31. **Contact:** American College of Gastroenterology, 6400 Goldsboro Rd., Bethesda, MD, 20817; Phone: 301-263-9000; Maria Susano; Email: msusano@gi.org.

762 ■ American College of Healthcare Executives (ACHE)

300 S Riverside Pl., Ste. 1900
Chicago, IL 60606-3529
Ph: (312)424-2800
Fax: (312)424-0023
E-mail: contact@ache.org
URL: www.ache.org
Social Media: www.facebook.com/ACHEConnect
www.instagram.com/acheconnect
www.linkedin.com/company/american-college-of-healthcare
  -executives
twitter.com/ACHEConnect
www.youtube.com/user/ACHEhealthexecs

763 ■ Albert W. Dent Graduate Student Scholarship (Undergraduate/Scholarship)

Purpose: To help ACHE Student Associates finance their education. **Focus:** Health care services. **Qualif.:** Applicant must be a student associate in good standing in the American college of healthcare executives; must be enrolled in full-time study for the upcoming term; must demonstrate financial need; must be a U.S or Canadian citizen; must have not been a previous recipient of the scholarship. **Criteria:** Preference is given to applicants who are Student Associates of ACHE.

Funds Avail.: $5,000. **Duration:** Annual. **Number Awarded:** Up to 15. **To Apply:** Applicants must submit and complete the application form available online; must submit a current curriculum vitae or resume; an official undergradu-

ate and graduate transcript; must provide three current letters of recommendation and essay. **Deadline:** March 31.

764 ■ Foster G. McGaw Graduate Student Scholarship (Graduate/Scholarship)

Purpose: To provide financial aid to students in healthcare management graduate programs to help offset tuition costs, student loans and expenses. **Focus:** Health care services. **Qualif.:** Applicant must be a Student Associate in good standing in the American College of Healthcare Executives; enrolled in full-time study for the upcoming fall term, which is the final year of classroom work in a healthcare management graduate program; must demonstrate financial need; must be a U.S or Canadian citizen; and not a previous recipient of the scholarship. **Criteria:** Preference is given to applicants who are Student Associates of ACHE.

Funds Avail.: $5,000. **Duration:** Annual. **Number Awarded:** Up to 15. **To Apply:** Applicants must submit and complete the application form available online; must submit a current curriculum vitae or resume; an official undergraduate and graduate transcript; must provide three current letters of recommendation and essay. **Deadline:** March 31.

765 ■ American College of Medical Toxicology (ACMT)

10645 N Tatum Blvd., Ste. 200-111
Phoenix, AZ 85028
Fax: (844)226-8333
Free: 844-226-8333
E-mail: info@acmt.net
URL: www.acmt.net
Social Media: www.facebook.com/acmtmedtox
www.instagram.com/acmtmedtox
www.linkedin.com/company/acmtmedtox
twitter.com/acmt
twitter.com/acmtmedtox
www.youtube.com/c/ACMTVideos

766 ■ Michael P. Spadafora Medical Toxicology Travel Award (Professional development/Grant)

Purpose: To encourage individuals to pursue Medical Toxicology fellowship training. **Focus:** Toxicology. **Qualif.:** Applicants must be any PGY-1 or PGY-2 (or a PGY-3 in a 4 year program) members of an ACGME or AOA accredited residency program. **Criteria:** Selection will be based on the committee's criteria.

Funds Avail.: $1,500. **Duration:** Annual. **Number Awarded:** 1. **To Apply:** Applicants should provide the following information: curriculum vitae; letter documenting verification of employment; letter of support from the applicant's program director; letter of nomination from a current ACMT member (if the program director is an ACMT member, then that letter will suffice); and 1-2 page essay describing the applicants' interest and background in Medical Toxicology. **Deadline:** November 1. **Contact:** Email: info@acmt.net; American College of Medical Toxicology, 10645 N Tatum Blvd., Ste. 200-111, Phoenix, Arizona, 85028.

767 ■ American College of Nurse-Midwives Foundation (ACNM)

PO Box 380272
Cambridge, MA 02238-0272
Ph: (240)485-1850

Awards are arranged alphabetically below their administering organizations

Fax: (617)876-5822
E-mail: fdn@acnm.org
URL: www.midwife.org
Social Media: www.facebook.com/ACNMmidwives
twitter.com/ACNMmidwives
www.youtube.com/user/ACNMWEB

768 ■ A.C.N.M. Foundation, Inc. Fellowship for Graduate Education *(Doctorate, Postdoctorate/ Fellowship)*

Purpose: To encourage CNM/CMs to pursue graduate education that prepares them for leadership roles in clinical/ practice administration, education, research or policy. **Focus:** Midwifery. **Qualif.:** Applicants must be certified nurse-midwives (CNM) or certified midwives (CM); must be current members of the American College of Nurse-Midwives (ACNM); must be actively enrolled in a doctoral or post-doctoral education program; and must be graduate students in good standing as verified by the Academic Program Director. **Criteria:** Applicants are evaluated based on financial need and academic achievement.

Funds Avail.: $5,000. **Duration:** Annual. **To Apply:** Applicants must submit application form; academic/career goals and plans; academic director form; and two academic recommendations. **Deadline:** March 1. **Contact:** The A.C.N.M. Foundation, Inc., PO Box 380272, Cambridge, MA, 02238-0272; Phone: 240-485-1850; Fax: 617-876-5822; Email: foundation@acnmf.org.

769 ■ ACNM Foundation Midwives of Color-Watson Midwifery Student Scholarship *(Undergraduate/ Scholarship)*

Purpose: To increase the number of midwives of color. **Focus:** Midwifery; Nursing. **Qualif.:** Applicants must be student midwives of color. **Criteria:** Applicants will be judged based on demonstrated academic excellence and financial need.

Funds Avail.: No specific amount. **Duration:** Annual. **To Apply:** Applicants must submit application information form; statement of career goals and plans; financial assessment form; statement of financial need; program director form; and the faculty recommendation form.

770 ■ American College Personnel Association (ACPA)

1 Dupont Cir. NW, Ste. 300
Washington, DC 20036
Ph: (202)835-2272
Fax: (202)827-0601
E-mail: info@acpa.nche.edu
URL: www.myacpa.org

771 ■ ACPA Foundation Annual Fund *(Professional development/Grant)*

Purpose: To support scholarship and research activities of ACPA members. **Focus:** General studies/Field of study not specified. **Qualif.:** Applicants must be ACPA members who are conducting research that is consistent with the purposes and interests of ACPA. **Criteria:** Recipients will be selected based on the submitted project proposal.

Funds Avail.: Approximately $10,000. **Duration:** Annual. **To Apply:** Applicants must complete the online application form including the name and contact information.

772 ■ American College of Surgeons Professional Association (ACSPA)

633 N St. Clair St.
Chicago, IL 60611-3295
Ph: (312)202-5000
Fax: (312)202-5001
Free: 800-621-4111
E-mail: postmaster@facs.org
URL: www.facs.org
Social Media: www.facebook.com/AmCollSurgeons
www.linkedin.com/company/25304
www.linkedin.com/company/american-college-of-surgeons
twitter.com/amcollsurgeons
www.youtube.com/user/AmCollegeofSurgeons

773 ■ ACS Faculty Research Fellowships *(Professional development/Fellowship)*

Purpose: To assist a surgeon in the establishment of a new and independent research program. **Focus:** Surgery. **Qualif.:** Applicant must receive a full-time faculty appointment in a department of surgery or a surgical specialty at a medical school accredited by the Liaison Committee on Medical Education in the United States or by the Committee for Accreditation of Canadian Medical Schools in Canada.

Funds Avail.: $40,000 per year. **Duration:** Annual; up to two years. **To Apply:** applicant must submit a research plan up to five pages, excluding references, and budget for the two-year period of fellowship, even though renewed approval by the Scholarships Committee of the College is required for the second year. A minimum of 50 percent of the Fellow's time must be spent in the research proposed in the application. This percentage may run concurrently with the time requirements of NIH or other accepted funding. The Faculty Research Fellows are expected to attend the Clinical Congress of the American College of Surgeons in 2022 to present a report and receive a certificate at the annual meeting of the Scholarships Committee. **Deadline:** November 15.

774 ■ ACS Resident Research Scholarships *(Advanced Professional/Scholarship)*

Purpose: To encourage residents to pursue careers in academic surgery. **Focus:** Surgery. **Qualif.:** Applicants must be a Resident member of the College who has completed two postdoctoral years in an accredited surgical training program in the United States or Canada. **Criteria:** Selection will be based on the committee's criteria.

Funds Avail.: $30,000 per annum. **Duration:** Annual; up to 2 years. **To Apply:** Applicants must check the application process online. **Deadline:** September 30.

775 ■ American College of Surgeons Australia/New Zealand Traveling Fellowship *(Undergraduate/ Fellowship)*

Purpose: To encourage international exchange of information concerning surgical science, practice, and education and to establish professional and academic collaborations and friendships. **Focus:** Surgery. **Qualif.:** Applicant must hold a current full time appointment in Canada or US and should be under 50 years of age with good communication skills.

Funds Avail.: $10,000. **Duration:** Periodic. **Deadline:** November 15. **Contact:** Email: scholarships@facs.org.

Awards are arranged alphabetically below their administering organizations

776 ■ American College of Surgeons International Guest Scholarship *(Professional development/ Scholarship)*

Purpose: To provide the Scholars with an opportunity to visit clinical, teaching, and research activities in North America and to attend and participate fully in the educational opportunities and activities of the American College of Surgeons Clinical Congress. **Focus:** Surgery. **Qualif.:** Applicants must be graduates of schools of medicine who have completed their surgical training. Applicants must be at least 35 years old, but under 50, on the date that the completed application is filed. Applicants must submit their applications from the **Criteria:** Preference may be given to applicants who have not already experienced training or surgical fellowships in the U.S. or Canada.

Funds Avail.: $10,000. **Duration:** Periodic. **To Apply:** Applicants must submit a fully completed application form provided by the college on its website; must provide a list of all of their publications and must submit, in addition, three complete publications, reprints or manuscripts, of their choice from that list; must submit independently prepared letters of recommendation from three of their colleagues. **Deadline:** July 1. **Contact:** Email: kmccann@facs.org.

777 ■ George H. A. Clowes, Jr. MD, FACS, Memorial Research Career Development Award *(Professional development/Fellowship)*

Purpose: To provide support for the research of a promising young surgical investigator. **Focus:** Surgery. **Qualif.:** Applicant must have completed an accredited residency in general surgery within the preceding seven years, not including time off for maternity leave, military deployment, or medical leave; has received a full-time faculty appointment at a medical school accredited by the liaison committee on medical education in the United States or by the committee for Accreditation of Canadian medical schools in Canada. **Criteria:** Preference will be given to who have received or are working toward a K08 or K23 NIH grant.

Funds Avail.: $45,000 per year. **Duration:** Annual; up to five years. **To Apply:** Applicants must submit a cover letter of no more than 400 words describing the career objectives, how these career objectives will be achieved, and how the research protocol furthers the career development. **Remarks:** Established in 1992. **Contact:** Administrator: scholarships@facs.org or Scholarships Administrator, American College of Surgeons, 633 N. Saint Clair St., Chicago, IL 60611-3295.

778 ■ Health Policy Scholarship for General Surgeons *(Professional development/Scholarship)*

Purpose: To support general surgeons in terms of cost of tuition, travel, housing, and subsistence. **Focus:** Surgery. **Qualif.:** Applications are open to general surgeons who are members in good standing of the ACS; must be at least 30 years old up to 60 on the date that the completed application is filed. **Criteria:** Selection will be based on the committee's criteria.

Funds Avail.: $8,000. **Duration:** Annual. **Number Awarded:** 2. **To Apply:** Applications for these scholarships consist of the following items, submitted as a single PDF file one copy of the current curriculum vitae; one copy of a one-page essay, discussing why the wish to receive the scholarship; form can be downloaded at the website. **Deadline:** February 3. **Contact:** Email: scholarships@facs.org. SCHOLARSHIPS SECTION; American College of Sur-

geons; 633 N. Saint Clair St; Chicago, IL 60611-3295.

779 ■ American College of Veterinary Ophthalmologists (ACVO)
PO Box 1311
Meridian, ID 83680
Ph: (208)466-7624
Fax: (208)895-7872
E-mail: office18@acvo.org
URL: www.acvo.org
Social Media: www.facebook.com/ ACVONationalServiceAnimalEyeExam

780 ■ ACVO Best Resident Manuscript Awards *(Undergraduate/Recognition)*

Purpose: To recognize the best manuscript made by a resident. **Focus:** Optometry; Veterinary science and medicine. **Qualif.:** Applicants must be residents in an ABVO-approved residency training program or individuals who have completed their ABVO-approved residency within 18 months of the application deadline; manuscript must be published, in press, or accepted without further revisions. **Criteria:** Selection will be based on the committees' criteria.

Funds Avail.: $500. **Duration:** Annual. **Number Awarded:** 3. **To Apply:** Applicants may contact the Association for the application process and other information. **Deadline:** May 1.

781 ■ American Concrete Institute (ACI)
38800 Country Club Dr.
Farmington Hills, MI 48331-3439
Ph: (248)848-3700
Fax: (248)848-3701
E-mail: social@concrete.org
URL: www.concrete.org
Social Media: www.facebook.com/pages/American -Concrete-Institute-ACI/79308249901
www.instagram.com/concreteaci
twitter.com/concreteaci
www.youtube.com/c/aci

782 ■ ACI BASF Construction Chemicals Student Fellowship *(Graduate, Undergraduate/Fellowship)*
Purpose: To support high-potential undergraduate and graduate students whose studies relate to concrete. **Focus:** Construction; Engineering, Chemical. **Qualif.:** Applicant must attend a U.S. or Canadian university during the award year; Some of the Fellowships expect the awardee to complete a 10- to 12-week internship the summer prior to beginning the award year; must be proficient in the English language; If English is not your native language, a written statement must be attached to this application attesting this proficiency.

Duration: Annual. **To Apply:** Applicants must submit a personal and educational data; one-page resume; 500-word essay; official transcripts; application data, resume, essay, endorsements, and transcripts must be in the English language; resume must be in Microsoft Word format. **Deadline:** November 1. **Contact:** ACI Foundation, Attn: Scholarship Coordinator, 38800 Country Club Dr., Farmington Hills, MI, 48331.

783 ■ ACI Cagley Student Fellowship *(Graduate, Master's, Undergraduate/Fellowship)*
Purpose: To support high-potential undergraduate and graduate students whose studies relate to concrete. **Focus:**

Awards are arranged alphabetically below their administering organizations

Design. **Qualif.:** Applicants must have an interest in a career in design; must be undergraduates or enrolled in Master's programs; and must be serving an internship with Cagley & Associates prior to the award year; students must be nominated by an ACI-Member Faculty. **Criteria:** Selection is based on the application materials and on the interview.

To Apply: Applicants must submit a completed application form together with a resume; an essay (maximum of 500 words); two completed online reference forms; all undergraduate and graduate transcripts; and internship requirement agreement. **Deadline:** November 2.

784 ■ ACI Charles Pankow Student Fellowship
(Graduate, Undergraduate/Fellowship)

Purpose: To support high-potential undergraduate and graduate students whose studies relate to concrete. **Focus:** Construction. **Qualif.:** Applicants must be in an undergraduate or graduate class in the award year; serving an internship in a construction environment with the Charles Pankow Company prior to the award year; and must be nominated by an ACI-Member Faculty. **Criteria:** Selection is based on the application materials and on the interview.

Duration: Annual. **To Apply:** Applicants must submit a completed application form together with a resume; an essay (maximum of 500 words); two completed online reference forms; all undergraduate and graduate transcripts; and internship requirement agreement. **Deadline:** November 2.

785 ■ ACI Elmer Baker Student Fellowship
(Undergraduate/Fellowship)

Purpose: To support high-potential graduate students whose studies relate to concrete. **Focus:** Construction. **Qualif.:** Applicant must be an undergraduate student with an interest in a career in the construction industry; entering junior or senior year; studying in a civil engineering, structural engineering, or construction industry management program; serving an internship before the award period (this internship may be served with a firm other than Baker Concrete Construction) and must be nominated by an ACI-Member Faculty. **Criteria:** Selection is based on the application materials and on the interview.

To Apply: Applicants must submit a personal and educational data; one-page resume; 500-Word essay; official transcripts; application data, resume, essay, endorsements, and transcripts must be in the English language; resume must be in Microsoft word format. **Deadline:** November 2. **Contact:** ACI Foundation, Attn: Scholarship Coordinator, 38800 Country Club Dr., Farmington Hills, MI, 48331.

786 ■ ACI Foundation Scholarships *(Graduate/Scholarship)*

Purpose: To support high-potential graduate students whose studies relate to concrete. **Focus:** Architecture; Engineering; Materials research/science. **Qualif.:** Applicants must have been accepted for graduate study at an accredited college or university in an engineering, architecture, or materials science program (graduate study program shall be in the area of concrete with an emphasis on structural design, materials, construction, or any combination thereof), and must be full-time first or second-year graduate students during the entire scholarship year. **Criteria:** Selection is based on the submitted application and materials.

To Apply: Applicants must submit a completed application form along with a resume; an essay (maximum of 500

words); two completed online reference forms; and all undergraduate and graduate transcripts. **Deadline:** November 2.

787 ■ ACI President's Fellowships *(Doctorate, Master's/Fellowship)*

Purpose: To support high-potential graduate students whose studies relate to concrete. **Focus:** Construction; Design. **Qualif.:** Applicants must be Master's or Doctoral students in either construction, design, or education programs; must be nominated by an ACI-Member Faculty. **Criteria:** Selection is based on the application materials and on the interview.

To Apply: Applicants must submit a completed application form together with a resume; an essay (maximum of 500 words); two completed online reference forms; all undergraduate and graduate transcripts; and internship requirement agreement. **Deadline:** November 2. **Remarks:** Established in 2009.

788 ■ ACI Richard N. White Student Fellowship
(Graduate, Undergraduate/Fellowship)

Purpose: To support high-potential undergraduate and graduate students whose studies relate to concrete. **Focus:** Engineering, Materials. **Qualif.:** Applicant must attend a U.S. or Canadian university during the award year; Some of the Fellowships expect the awardee to complete a 10- to 12-week internship the summer prior to beginning the award year; must be proficient in the English language; If English is not your native language, a written statement must be attached to this application attesting this proficiency.

Number Awarded: 1. **To Apply:** Applicants must submit a personal and educational data; one-page resume; 500-Word essay; official transcripts; application data, resume, essay, endorsements, and transcripts must be in the English language; resume must be in Microsoft word format. **Deadline:** November 1. **Contact:** ACI Foundation, Attn: Scholarship Coordinator, 38800 Country Club Dr., Farmington Hills, MI, 48331.

789 ■ ACI W.R. Grace Scholarships *(Graduate/Scholarship)*

Purpose: To support high-potential graduate students whose studies relate to concrete. **Focus:** Architecture; Engineering; Materials research/science. **Qualif.:** Applicants must have been accepted for graduate study at an accredited college or university in an engineering, architecture, or materials science program (graduate study program shall be in the area of concrete with an emphasis on structural design, materials, construction, or any combination thereof), and must be full-time first or second-year graduate students during the entire scholarship year. **Criteria:** Selection is based on the submitted application and materials.

Funds Avail.: $3,000. **Duration:** Annual. **To Apply:** Applicants must submit a completed application form along with a resume; an essay (maximum of 500 words); two completed Online Reference Forms; and all undergraduate and graduate transcripts.

790 ■ ACI Baker Student Fellowships
(Undergraduate/Fellowship)

Purpose: To support high-potential graduate students whose studies relate to concrete. **Focus:** Construction; Engineering, Civil. **Qualif.:** Applicant must be an under-

Awards are arranged alphabetically below their administering organizations

graduate student with an interest in a career in the construction industry; entering junior or senior year; studying in a civil engineering, structural engineering, or construction industry management program; serving an internship before the award period (this internship may be served with a firm other than Baker Concrete Construction) and must be nominated by an ACI-Member Faculty. **Criteria:** Selection is based on the application materials and on the interview.

To Apply: Applicants must submit a completed application form together with a resume; an essay (maximum of 500 words); two completed online reference forms; all undergraduate and graduate transcripts; and internship requirement agreement. **Deadline:** November 2.

791 ■ Katharine & Bryant Mather Scholarship
(Graduate/Scholarship)

Purpose: To support high-potential graduate students whose studies relate to concrete. **Focus:** Architecture; Engineering; Materials research/science. **Qualif.:** Applicants Should be Finishing the graduations in the field of Concrete. **Criteria:** Selection is based on the submitted application and materials.

To Apply: Applicants must submit a completed application form along with a resume; an essay (maximum of 500 words); two completed online reference forms; and all undergraduate and graduate transcripts. **Deadline:** November 2. **Remarks:** Established in 1988.

792 ■ Kumar Mehta Scholarship *(Graduate/ Scholarship)*

Purpose: To support high-potential graduate students whose studies relate to concrete. **Focus:** Architecture; Engineering; Materials research/science. **Qualif.:** Applicants must have been accepted for graduate study at an accredited college or university in an engineering, architecture, or materials science program (graduate study program shall be in the area of concrete with an emphasis on structural design, materials, construction, or any combination thereof); must be a full-time first or second-year graduate student during the entire scholarship year; and must be pursuing a research on sustainable development of concrete. **Criteria:** Selection is based on the submitted application and materials.

Funds Avail.: No specific amount. **Number Awarded:** 1 in 2017. **To Apply:** Applicants must submit a completed application form along with a resume; an essay (maximum of 500 words); two completed online reference forms; and all undergraduate and graduate transcripts. **Deadline:** November 1. **Contact:** Julie Webb, Marketing Communications Specialist; Phone: 248-848-3148; Email: Julie.Webb@ concrete.org.

793 ■ Bertold E. Weinberg Scholarship *(Graduate/ Scholarship)*

Purpose: To support high-potential graduate students whose studies relate to concrete. **Focus:** Architecture; Engineering; Materials research/science. **Qualif.:** Applicants must have been accepted for graduate study at an accredited college or university in an engineering, architecture, or materials science program (graduate study program shall be in the area of concrete with an emphasis on structural design, materials, construction, or any combination thereof), and must be full-time first or second-year graduate students during the entire scholarship year. **Criteria:** Selection is based on the submitted application and materials.

Funds Avail.: No specific amount. **To Apply:** Applicants must submit a completed application form along with a resume; an essay (maximum of 500 words); two completed online reference forms; and all undergraduate and graduate transcripts. **Deadline:** November 2. **Remarks:** Established in 2003.

794 ■ American Conifer Society (ACS)
PO Box 1583
Maple Grove, MN 55311
Ph: (763)657-7251
E-mail: nationaloffice@conifersociety.org
URL: conifersociety.org
Social Media: www.facebook.com/conifersociety
instagram.com/americanconifersociety
www.pinterest.com/conifersociety
www.youtube.com/channel/UC0FIjX5s0dQtQ6MeuAN1FaA

795 ■ ACS Scholarship *(Undergraduate/Scholarship)*
Purpose: To provide financial assistance to ACS members to pursue their education. **Focus:** Horticulture. **Qualif.:** Applicants must be a current ACS member or sponsored by a current ACS member (including an Institutional or Corporate member); only one applicant per ACS member/sponsor is allowed per year; dependents of members may apply using their parent or guardian as sponsor; no member of ACS currently holding a National office, Regional office, or paid staff, including contracted agent, or a Reporting Person on a committee sanctioned by the Board of Directors of the ACS is eligible; applicants must have a sponsor. **Criteria:** Selection is based on grant ACS the right to use their name, a short biography, and the educational purpose, of the award in its publication CONIFERQUARTERLY and on its website as part of the scholarship announcement.

Funds Avail.: $2,500. **Duration:** Annual. **To Apply:** Corporate or Institutional sponsor or sponsoring member signature is required in the application. **Remarks:** Established in 2005. **Contact:** Dr. Lois Girton, ACS Scholarship Committee Chair; Email: scholarships@conifersociety.org.

796 ■ American Constitution Society for Law and Policy (ACS)
1899 L St., NW, Ste 200
Washington, DC 20036
Ph: (202)393-6181
Fax: (202)393-6189
E-mail: info@acslaw.org
URL: www.acslaw.org
Social Media: www.facebook.com/acslaw
www.linkedin.com/company/american-constitution-society
twitter.com/ACSLaw
www.youtube.com/c/acslaworg

797 ■ Public Interest Fellowship *(Undergraduate/ Fellowship)*
Purpose: To provide a recent law school graduate a year of legal experience and training. **Focus:** Law. **Qualif.:** Applicant must be a recent law school graduate from a U.S. law school. **Criteria:** Selection is based on the application materials.

Funds Avail.: No specific amount. **Deadline:** September 2.

798 ■ American Contact Dermatitis Society (ACDS)
555 E Wells Str., Ste. 1100
Milwaukee, WI 53202

Awards are arranged alphabetically below their administering organizations

Ph: (414)918-9805
Fax: (414)276-3349
E-mail: info@contactderm.org
URL: www.contactderm.org
Social Media: instagram.com/acds_dermatitis
twitter.com/DermatitisJrnl

799 ■ Maibach Travel Grant *(Professional development/Grant)*

Purpose: To provide travel grants to the American Contact Dermatitis Society's Annual Meeting for the presentation of work by investigators outside of the US and Canada. **Focus:** Dermatology. **Qualif.:** Applicant must be a Each of the above criteria will be rated by the committee on a scale ranging from 0-10 with the exception of Ethics which is judged on an acceptable/non-acceptable basis. The eligible abstracts with the highest total points score will

Funds Avail.: $1,000. **Duration:** Annual. **To Apply:** Application should submit via online; should Indicate their eligibility on their Abstract Submission Form; a letter stating that they would like to be considered for the Award; including a letter from your Program Director confirming your status. **Deadline:** January 3.

800 ■ American Copy Editors Society Education Fund (ACES)

7 Avenida Vista Grande, Ste. B7, No. 467
Santa Fe, NM 87508
E-mail: info@copydesk.org
URL: www.copydesk.org/blog/category/education_fund

801 ■ Aubespin Scholarships *(Undergraduate/ Scholarship)*

Purpose: To encourage young individuals to continue their career as potential professional copy editors. **Focus:** Editors and editing. **Qualif.:** Applicants must be seeking degrees as enrolled college/university juniors, seniors or graduate students during the summer and/or fall; previous scholarship winners are not eligible. **Criteria:** Selection will be based on the committee's criteria.

Funds Avail.: $2,500. **Duration:** Annual. **Number Awarded:** 5. **To Apply:** Application can send through online with entry materials. **Deadline:** November 15. **Contact:** Alex Cruden; Email: alex@copydesk.org.

802 ■ American Council of Blind Students (ACBS)

c/o American Council of the Blind
1703 N Beauregard St., Ste. 420
Alexandria, VA 22311
Ph: (202)467-5081
Fax: (202)465-5085
Free: 800-424-8666
E-mail: info@acb.org
URL: acb.org
Social Media: twitter.com/acbnational

803 ■ American Council of the Blind Scholarships *(Graduate, Undergraduate/Scholarship)*

Purpose: To support blind students in their educational pursuits. **Focus:** General studies/Field of study not specified. **Qualif.:** Applicants must be undergraduate or graduate blind students and maintain a 3.0 GPA and are involved in their school/local community. **Criteria:** Selection is based on the submitted application and materials.

Funds Avail.: $45,000. **To Apply:** All interested candidates must register for a new ACB account prior to submitting a scholarship application online. **Deadline:** February 14. **Contact:** Nancy Feela (612) 332-3242 or (800) 866-3242.

804 ■ American Council of Engineering Companies of Illinois (ACECIL)

5221 S 6th St., Ste. 120
Springfield, IL 62703
Ph: (217)529-7430
Fax: (217)529-2742
E-mail: info@acecil.org
URL: acecil.org
Social Media: www.facebook.com/ACECILLINOIS
www.linkedin.com/company/acec-il
twitter.com/ACECIllinois

805 ■ American Council of Engineering Companies of Illinois Scholarships *(Undergraduate, Postdoctorate/Scholarship)*

Purpose: To assist engineering students of Illinois in reaching their goals of higher education. **Focus:** Engineering. **Qualif.:** Applicants must be U.S. citizens, specifically, engineering students currently enrolled and pursuing a bachelor's, master's or PhD degree in an Accreditation Board for Engineering and Technology (ABET)-accredited engineering program or in an accredited land surveying program located in the state of Illinois; may be students entering their junior, senior, fifth, master's or graduate year in the fall. **Criteria:** Applicants are evaluated based on the point value indicated in the application.

Number Awarded: 9. **To Apply:** Applicants must submit the completed application form along with student's GPA; work experience; extracurricular college activities; recommendation from a professor, consulting engineering or land surveyor; and a 500-word essay. **Deadline:** March 6.

806 ■ American Council on Germany (ACG)

14 E 60th St., Ste. 1000
New York, NY 10022
Ph: (212)826-3636
Fax: (212)758-3445
URL: www.acgusa.org
Social Media: www.facebook.com/acgusa
www.linkedin.com/company/american-council-on-germany
twitter.com/acg_usa

807 ■ Dr. Guido Goldman Fellowships *(Postdoctorate/Fellowship)*

Purpose: To promote the study of German and European issues by American scholars. **Focus:** European studies; German studies. **Qualif.:** Be a U.S. citizen residing in the United States; be 40 years of age or younger at the time of the application deadline; have a minimum of five years of relevant, full-time work experience; be in the final stages of have recently completed a Ph.D.; and have a sincere commitment to furthering the transatlantic relationship. **Criteria:** Selection Committee will select applicants based on the contribution the project will make to an understanding of the economics and foreign relations of Germany, Europe and North America; the feasibility of the proposed project;

Awards are arranged alphabetically below their administering organizations

the training of the applicant; and the scholarly potential of the applicant.

Funds Avail.: $7,500 stipend, which covers transatlantic airfare and domestic travel, as well as room and board, for a minimum of 28 days. **To Apply:** A cover letter outlining your personal and professional objectives for the fellowship; a three- to five-page project proposal as described above; a current resume; and two letters of recommendation. **Remarks:** Established in 2003. **Contact:** Email: fellowships@acgusa.org.

808 ■ Dr. Richard M. Hunt Fellowships (Doctorate, Postdoctorate/Fellowship)

Purpose: To promote the study of German issues by American scholars. **Focus:** German studies. **Qualif.:** Be a U.S. citizen residing in the United States; be 40 years of age or younger at the time of the application deadline; have a minimum of five years of relevant, full-time work experience; be in the final stages of have recently completed a Ph.D.; and have a sincere commitment to furthering the transatlantic relationship.**Criteria:** The selection committee will evaluate applications based on the contribution the project will make to a better understanding of German history; the feasibility of the proposed project; the training of the applicant; and the scholarly potential of the applicant.

Funds Avail.: $7,500. **To Apply:** Applicants must submit a cover letter, outlining the applicant's professional and personal objectives for the fellowship; a 2-page project proposal; a current CV; and two letters of reference. **Remarks:** Established in 2003. **Contact:** Email: fellowships@acgusa.org.

809 ■ Anna-Maria and Stephen M. Kellen Fellowships (Professional development/Fellowship)

Purpose: To enable American and German professionals to conduct research and meet with their professional counterparts. **Focus:** Broadcasting; Journalism. **Qualif.:** Be a German citizen residing in Berlin; be 40 years of age or younger at the time of the application deadline; hold a Bachelor's Degree (or equivalent); and have a sincere commitment to furthering the transatlantic relationship. **Criteria:** Selection will be based on the committee's criteria.

Funds Avail.: $5,000. **Duration:** Annual. **To Apply:** Applicants must complete and submit the following requirements: a cover letter outlining their personal and professional objectives for the fellowship; a project proposal of at least two pages detailing the background and scope of their project, the general sources and institutions with whom they would like to consult while in the United States and the relevance of the project; a current resume; two letters of recommendation; several recent writing clips. **Contact:** Email: fellowships@acgusa.org.

810 ■ McCloy Fellowships in Agriculture (Professional development/Fellowship)

Purpose: To enable American and German professionals to conduct significant research in agriculture and meet with their professional counterparts. **Focus:** Agricultural sciences.

Funds Avail.: $5,000.

811 ■ McCloy Fellowships in Environmental Policy (Professional development/Fellowship)

Purpose: To provide German and American midcareer professionals and academics with the opportunity to travel across the Atlantic for three weeks to undertake independent research and meet with their counterparts to exchange best practices and foster professional and intellectual ties. **Focus:** Environmental law; Journalism. **Qualif.:** Applicants must be German citizens residing in Germany, between the ages of 23 and 30 at the time of the application deadline. Each applicant should demonstrate a minimum of two years of relevant, full-time work experience and hold a Bachelor's degree (or equivalent). He/she should possess a track record of outstanding academic and professional performance and have demonstrated sincere commitment to furthering the transatlantic relationship.

Funds Avail.: $5,000 stipend, which covers transatlantic airfare and domestic travel, as well as room and board, for a minimum of 21 days. **Duration:** Annual. **To Apply:** Applicants must submit the following requirements: a cover letter outlining their personal and professional objectives for the fellowship; a project proposal of at least two pages detailing the background and scope of their project, the general sources and institutions with whom they would like to consult while abroad and the relevance of the project for environmental policy and transatlantic relations; a current resume; two letters of recommendation. **Deadline:** May 31. **Contact:** Email: fellowships@acgusa.org.

812 ■ McCloy Fellowships in Journalism (Professional development/Fellowship)

Purpose: To provide print, broadcast, and new-media journalists in the relatively early stages of their career with the opportunity to travel to Europe or the United States for up to three weeks to conduct research and interviews and pursue stories of their own design. **Focus:** Journalism. **Qualif.:** Applicants must be German citizens residing in Germany, between the ages of 23 and 30 at the time of the application deadline. Each applicant should demonstrate a minimum of two years of relevant, full-time work experience and hold a Bachelor's degree (or equivalent). He/she should possess a track record of outstanding academic and professional performance and have demonstrated sincere commitment to furthering the transatlantic relationship.

Funds Avail.: $5,000. **Duration:** Annual. **Deadline:** May 31. **Contact:** Email: fellowships@acgusa.org.

813 ■ McCloy Fellowships in Urban Affairs (Professional development/Fellowship)

Purpose: To enable American and German professionals to conduct research and meet with their professional counterparts. **Focus:** Urban affairs/design/planning. **Qualif.:** Applicants must be German citizens residing in Germany, between the ages of 23 and 30 at the time of the application deadline. Each applicant should demonstrate a minimum of two years of relevant, full-time work experience and hold a Bachelor's degree (or equivalent). He/she should possess a track record of outstanding academic and professional performance and have demonstrated sincere commitment to furthering the transatlantic relationship.

Funds Avail.: $5,000. **Deadline:** May 31. **Contact:** Email: fellowships@acgusa.org.

814 ■ American Council of Independent Laboratories (ACIL)

1300 I Street, NW, Ste. 400E
Washington, DC 20005
Ph: (202)887-5872
Fax: (202)887-0021

Awards are arranged alphabetically below their administering organizations

E-mail: info@acil.org
URL: www.acil.org
Social Media: www.facebook.com/ACIL.info
www.linkedin.com/company/acil---american-council-of
  -independent-laboratories
twitter.com/acilnews

815 ■ American Council of Independent Laboratories Academic Scholarships
(Undergraduate/Scholarship, Award)

Purpose: To provide financial assistance for helping to ensure future generations of skilled employees for the laboratory testing community. **Focus:** Engineering, Civil; Physical sciences; Science. **Qualif.:** Applicants must be students attending their junior year or higher in a four-year, bachelor degree major in any of the physical sciences practiced by ACIL members physics, chemistry, engineering, geology, biology, or environmental science in granting institution or graduate program within the United States. **Criteria:** Recipient will be selected based on academic achievement, career goals, leadership, and financial need.

Funds Avail.: Up to $4,000. **Duration:** Annual. **To Apply:** Applicants must submit a completed application form, a brief resume or personal statement outlining the activities in college, including field of study and future plans; two letters of recommendation from faculty members of the university currently attending; transcript of grades; and information on any other scholarship or grant aid now being received. **Deadline:** April 6. **Contact:** American Council of Independent Laboratories, 1875 I St. NW, Ste 500, Washington, DC, 20006; Phone: 202-887-5872; Fax 202-887-0021; E-mail: bhoran@acil.org.

816 ■ American Council of Learned Societies (ACLS)
633 Third Ave.
New York, NY 10017-6706
Ph: (212)697-1505
URL: www.acls.org
Social Media: twitter.com/ACLS1919

817 ■ ACLS Collaborative Research Fellowships
(Doctorate/Fellowship)

Purpose: To offer small teams of two or more scholars the opportunity to collaborate intensively on a single, substantive project. **Focus:** Humanities; Social sciences. **Qualif.:** Applicants must have a collaborative project constitute of at least two scholars who are each seeking salary-replacement stipends for six to twelve continuous months of supported research leave to pursue full-time collaborative research during the fellowship tenure; the project coordinator must have an appointment at a US-based institution of higher education; other project members may be at institutions outside the United States or may be independent scholars; must hold a PhD degree or its equivalent in publications and professional experience at the time of application. **Criteria:** Proposals will be judged along the following criteria: Intellectual significance of the project, including its ambition and scope, and its potential contribution to scholarship in the humanities; relevance of the research questions being posed, the appropriateness of research methods, the feasibility of the work plan, the appropriateness of the field work to be undertaken, the archival or source materials to be studied and the research site; qualifications, expertise and commitment of the project

coordinator and collaborators; detail and soundness of the process and product of the collaboration, including dissemination plans; degree to which the proposed collaboration represents innovative practice in the applicants' disciplines and sub-fields; potential for success, including the likelihood that the work proposed will be completed and lead to distance results within the projected timeframe; where appropriate, the collaborators' previous record of success; and the size of the proposed budget in relation to anticipated results.

Funds Avail.: Up to $201,000. **Duration:** Annual; a total tenure period of 24 months. **To Apply:** Applications must include the following completed application forms; participant information sheet, listing all collaborators and additional project members; 10-page Proposal (double space, in Times New Roman, 11-point font); the proposal should describe the intellectual significance of the research project and explain in detail the process and product of the collaboration; two-page bibliography that places the project in intellectual context and includes relevant work in all of the disciplines involved in the project; research plan, including a timeline of the proposed research activities that specifies the location, duration and names of individuals involved in each stage; this may be in the form of a graphic timeline or narrative description; budget statement, outlining salary replacement, costs of research assistance, travel and research materials; a no more than three pages publications list for each collaborator; two reference letters that provide explicit information on the proposed collaborative project and the collaborators. **Deadline:** September 27. **Contact:** E-mail: fellowships@acls.org.

818 ■ ACLS Fellowships *(Advanced Professional, Professional development/Fellowship)*

Purpose: To help scholars devote to full-time research and writing. **Focus:** Humanities; Social sciences. **Qualif.:** Applicants must: be U.S. citizens or permanent residents as of the application deadline; have PhD degrees conferred at least two years before the application deadline; and, have a lapse of at least two years since the last supported research leave. **Criteria:** Recipients will be selected based on the following criteria: Potential of the project to advance the field of study in which it is proposed and make an original and significant contribution to knowledge; quality of the proposal with regard to its methodology, scope, theoretical framework, and grounding in the relevant scholarly literature; feasibility of the project and the likelihood that the applicant will execute the work within the proposed time frame; scholarly record and career trajectory of the applicant.

Funds Avail.: $40,000 (Assistant Professors and career equivalent); $50,000 (Associate Professors and career equivalent); $70,000 (full Professors and career equivalent). **Duration:** Annual; from 6 to 12 consecutive months. **To Apply:** Applications must be submitted online and must include: completed application form; proposal (no more than five pages, double spaced, in Times New Roman 11-point font); up to two additional pages of images, musical scores, or other similar supporting non-text materials (optional); bibliography (no more than two pages); publications list (no more than two pages); and, two reference letters. **Deadline:** December 31.

819 ■ African Humanities Program *(Postdoctorate/ Fellowship)*

Purpose: To support dissertations and projects in African studies in all disciplines of the humanities. **Focus:** African studies; Humanities. **Qualif.:** Applicants must be nationals

Awards are arranged alphabetically below their administering organizations

and residents of a country in sub-Saharan Africa, with a current affiliation at an institution in Ghana, Nigeria, South Africa, Tanzania or Uganda; should be in the final year of writing the dissertation at a university in Ghana, Nigeria, Tanzania or Uganda; Dissertation-Completion Fellowships are not available in South Africa; early career postdoctoral fellowships must be working in Ghana, Nigeria, South Africa, Tanzania or Uganda and must have completed the PhD no more than eight years ago. **Criteria:** Selection will be based on the committee's criteria.

Duration: Annual. **To Apply:** Projects must be in the humanities and must be carried out in sub-Saharan Africa; must submit a completed application by email or may be mailed to the AHP/ACLS offices in New York; invited to submit manuscripts. **Deadline:** December 4.

820 ■ American Research in the Humanities in China Fellowships *(Doctorate/Fellowship)*

Purpose: To support research that reflects an understanding of the present Chinese academic and research environment. **Focus:** Humanities; Social sciences. **Qualif.:** Applicants must be citizens or permanent residents of the United States who have lived in the United States; Program awards grants to U.S. scholars for research in China for periods of 4-12 months. **Criteria:** Selection will be based on the committee's criteria.

To Apply: Applicants must submit a carefully formulated research proposal that reflects an understanding of the present Chinese academic and research environment. The proposal should include a persuasive statement of the need to conduct the research in China. Applications must include: completed application form; proposal (no more than five pages, double spaced, in Times New Roman 11-point font); up to three additional pages of images, musical scores or other similar supporting non-text materials; copies of correspondence with Chinese contacts; bibliography (no more than two pages); curriculum vitae (no more than five pages); three reference letters.

821 ■ ACLS Frederick Burkhardt Residential Fellowships *(Other/Fellowship)*

Purpose: To support individuals for their research projects in humanities and related social sciences. **Focus:** Humanities; Social sciences. **Qualif.:** Applicants must be recently tenured humanists; must be employed in a tenured position at a degree granting academic institution in the United States. **Criteria:** Recipients are selected based on the quality of the proposal and required qualifications.

Funds Avail.: $95,000 + funds for research costs and related scholarly activities of up to $7,500 and for relocation up to $3,000. **Duration:** one academic year. **To Apply:** Applicants must visit the website for the online fellowship application system; must submit no more than ten pages, double-spaced proposal; no more than three pages bibliography; no more than two pages publications list; three reference letters; must provide an institutional statement. **Deadline:** September 25.

822 ■ Frederick Burkhardt Residential Fellowships for Recently Tenured Scholars *(Advanced Professional, Professional development/Fellowship)*

Purpose: To support long-term, unusually ambitious projects in the humanities and related social sciences. **Focus:** Humanities; Social sciences. **Qualif.:** Applicants must be a recently tenured humanists; must be employed in any tenured position at any degree-granting academic institution in the United States, remaining so for the dura-

tion of the fellowship. **Criteria:** Peer reviewers in this program are asked to evaluate all eligible proposals according to the following criteria: potential of the project to advance the field of study; the ambition and scope of the proposed project; quality of the proposal with regard to its methodology, scope, theoretical framework, and grounding in the relevant scholarly literature; feasibility of the project and the likelihood that the applicants will execute the work within the proposed timeframe; scholarly record and career trajectory of the applicant; likelihood that residence at the specified center will increase significantly the applicants' ability to carry the project forward; commitment by the scholars' institution to assist in advancing the project.

Funds Avail.: $95,000, plus funds for research costs and related scholarly activities of up to $7,500 and for relocation up to $3,000. **Duration:** Annual. **To Apply:** Applicants must submit their applications in online and must include the following: completed application form; proposal of no more than 10 pages, double spaced, in Times New Roman 11-point font; bibliography of no more than three pages; publications list of no more than two pages; three reference letters; and institutional statement; completed applications must be submitted through the ACLS Online Fellowship Application system (ofa.acls.org) no later than the fixed application deadline. **Deadline:** September 25.

823 ■ Comparative Perspectives on Chinese Culture and Society Grantees *(Doctorate/Grant)*

Purpose: To promote interchange among scholars who may not otherwise have the opportunity to work together, and to support collaborative work in China studies. **Focus:** Chinese studies. **Qualif.:** The principal organizer must be affiliated with a university or research institution and must hold a PhD. There are no restrictions as to the citizenship of participants or the location of the project. **Criteria:** Selection will be based on the committee's criteria.

Funds Avail.: Up to $25,000 for conferences; $10,000 to $15,000 for workshops and seminars; up to $6,000 for planning meetings. **To Apply:** All proposals must include the following: application information sheet (available at the website); a description of the project and its purposes. Descriptions should be no more than five double-spaced pages; a budget for the proposed event, including a statement of any other funds available; a short bibliography of relevant sources; two-page CV of principal organizer; a list of those invited with their CVs (two pages maximum). This list should clearly differentiate between those who have agreed to participate in the event and those whose participation is not confirmed. This list should also specify paper writers and discussants. Participation of scholars from academic institutions in Taiwan is expected. Participation of scholars from outside the China field is strongly encouraged; for conferences only: an appendix containing abstracts (of approximately 150-200 words) for each paper to be presented at the conference. **Deadline:** November 6. **Contact:** Email: cck@acls.org.

824 ■ Luce/ACLS Dissertation Fellowships in American Art *(Graduate, Doctorate/Fellowship)*

Purpose: To provide support for young scholars who are in the phase of completing their dissertations, as well as to advance research after being awarded the PhD. **Focus:** Art history. **Qualif.:** Applicants must be PhD candidates in a department of art history in the United States completing their dissertation which focuses on a topic in the history of the visual arts of the United States; be U.S. citizens or permanent residents; and have completed all the requirements for the PhD except the dissertation before the begin-

Awards are arranged alphabetically below their administering organizations

ning of the fellowship tenure. **Criteria:** Recipient is selected based on: The quality of the proposal with regard to its methodology, scope, theoretical framework, and grounding in the relevant scholarly literature; potential of the project to advance the field of study in art history, both generally and in the specific field(s) it engages; applicant's record of scholarly engagement and potential for scholarly achievement.

Funds Avail.: $30,000 plus up to $4,000 as a travel allowance. **Duration:** Annual. **To Apply:** Applicants must complete the application form including statement of all university and external support received during graduate study; double-spaced proposal including a timeline for the expected completion of the dissertation writing and defense (not more than five pages); up to additional three pages of supporting materials; bibliography of not more than two pages; a completed chapter of the dissertation; two reference letters, one of which must come from the applicant's dissertation advisor; List of publications, exhibitions, and/or presentations. **Deadline:** October 28. **Contact:** E-mail: fellowships@acls.org.

825 ■ Mellon/ACLS Dissertation Completion Fellowships *(Graduate, Doctorate/Fellowship)*

Purpose: To provide support for young scholars who are in the phase of completing their dissertations, as well as to advance research after being awarded the PhD. **Focus:** Humanities; Social sciences. **Qualif.:** Applicants must be PhD candidates in a humanities or social science department in the United States; have all requirements for the PhD except the dissertation completed before beginning fellowship tenure; and, be no more than six years in the degree program; must not currently hold or have previously held a dissertation completion fellowship; have not previously applied for this fellowship more than once. **Criteria:** Recipients will be selected based following four criteria: Potential of the project to advance the field of study in which it is proposed and make an original and significant contribution to knowledge; quality of the proposal with regard to its methodology, scope, theoretical framework, and grounding in the relevant scholarly literature; feasibility of the project and the likelihood that the applicant will execute the work within the proposed time frame; applicant's record of scholarly engagement and potential for scholarly achievement.

Funds Avail.: $30,000 stipend, plus funds for research costs of up to $3,000 and for university fees of up to $5,000. **Duration:** Annual; one year beginning summer. **Number Awarded:** 65. **To Apply:** Applications must be submitted online and must include: completed application form; proposal (no more than ten pages, double spaced, in Times New Roman 11-point font); one-page timeline for the expected completion of dissertation writing and defense; up to three additional pages of images, musical scores, or other similar supporting non-text materials (optional); bibliography (no more than two pages); completed chapter of the dissertation (that is neither the introduction, nor the conclusion, nor the literature review) of not more than 25 double-spaced pages, in Times New Roman 11-point font, or a representative 25-page excerpt from a longer chapter; the chapter must be in English, though citations may be in other languages (with translations provided); two reference letters; and, a statement from the applicant's institution (preferably from the applicant's department chair or dean); the provided form asks the institutional representative to (1) attest to the viability of the proposed timeline for completion; (2) stipulate that, in the event of an award, the university will not charge the student tuition or fees beyond

a limit of $5, 000 and will provide for any additional costs; and (3) pledge that if an ACLS award is made, the university will not provide the applicant with any subsequent aid. The person submitting the statement cannot be one of the reference letter writers. **Deadline:** October 28. **Contact:** E-mail: fellowships@acls.org.

826 ■ American Council for Polish Culture (ACPC)

c/o Florence Langrige, Membership Chair
78 Meadow Ln.
West Hartford, CT 06107
Ph: (860)521-4034
E-mail: flolangridge@sbcglobal.net
URL: www.polishcultureacpc.org

827 ■ Pulaski Scholarships for Advanced Studies *(Graduate, Master's/Scholarship)*

Purpose: To support qualified Polish-American graduate students in their graduate studies. **Focus:** General studies/Field of study not specified. **Qualif.:** Applicants must be a citizen of the United States and of Polish ancestry; and, a classified graduate student enrolled at an accredited university in the United States and must have completed at least one year of studies at the graduate level. **Criteria:** Selection is based on Committee members.

Funds Avail.: $5,000. **Duration:** Annual. **To Apply:** Applicants should include a resume; submit a copy of your most recent official (not downloaded) university transcript; submit a letter of recommendation from a faculty member with whom you are studying or have studied at your current postgraduate level; if the letter is sealed by the faculty member, send the sealed letter to the Committee Chairman, who will distribute copies to the other Committee Members. **Deadline:** March 16. **Contact:** Mr. Stephen Medvec, Ph.D. Chairman; 46201 Delaire Landing Rd., Philadelphia, PA, 19114-5320; Mrs. Deborah M. Majka, MS; 812 Lombard St., Ste. 12, Philadelphia, PA, 19147-1308; Mr. Peter J. Obst, MA; 67 Lower Orchard Dr., Levittown, PA, 19056-2722; Mrs. Alicia L. Dutka, 1991 Selkirk Ct, Inverness, IL, 60010; Mrs. Carolyn L. Meleski, MS; 10020 Reese Rd., Clarkston, MI, 48348-1856; E-mail: samedvec@comcast.net; Phone: 215-637-1659.

828 ■ Skalny Scholarship for Polish Studies *(Undergraduate/Scholarship)*

Purpose: To support students pursuing studies at least two years of college or university work at an accredited institution. **Focus:** General studies/Field of study not specified; Polish studies. **Qualif.:** Applicant must be a citizen of the United States who has completed two years of college or university studies at an accredited institution.

Funds Avail.: $3,000. **Duration:** Annual. **Number Awarded:** 2. **To Apply:** Applicant must submit a letter of recommendation from a faculty member who teaches Polish subjects; copy of an academic project on a Polish topic in English that was submitted as part of a course requirement, include the name, position and current address of the evaluator and the evaluation of the project; description of applicant's personal involvement in the mainstream community intended to promote Polish history and or culture or an appreciation thereof. **Deadline:** May 30.

829 ■ American Councils for International Education

1828 L St. NW, Ste. 1200
Washington, DC 20036

Awards are arranged alphabetically below their administering organizations

Ph: (202)833-7522
E-mail: info@americancouncils.org
URL: www.americancouncils.org
Social Media: www.facebook.com/AmericanCouncils
www.linkedin.com/company/american-councils-for
 -international-education
twitter.com/AC_Global

830 ■ American Councils for International Education Critical Language Scholarship Program
(Undergraduate, Graduate/Scholarship)

Purpose: To provide opportunities to a diverse range of students from across the United States at every level of language learning. **Focus:** Linguistics. **Qualif.:** Applicants must be a U.S. citizen and enrolled in an accredited U.S. degree-granting program at the undergraduate or graduate level. **Criteria:** Selection process is administered by American Councils for International Education with awards approved by the U.S. Department of State, Bureau of Educational and Cultural Affairs.

Funds Avail.: No specific amount. **To Apply:** Applicants for further application information kindly visits the society's website. **Contact:** Email: cls@americancouncils.org; URL: www.americancouncils.org/programs/critical-language-scholarship-program.

831 ■ American Counsel Association (ACA)
3770 Ridge Pike
Collegeville, PA 19426
Ph: (610)489-3300
URL: www.americancounsel.org

832 ■ American Counsel Association Scholarships
(Undergraduate/Scholarship)

Purpose: To provide scholarships to academically gifted and financially needy third-year law students. **Focus:** Law. **Qualif.:** Applicants must be enrolled in third year in a law school located within the seventh Federal Judicial District. **Criteria:** Selection will be based upon, financial need.

Funds Avail.: No specific amount. **Duration:** Annual.

833 ■ American Counseling Association (ACA)
6101 Stevenson Ave., Ste. 600
Alexandria, VA 22304
Ph: (703)823-9800
Fax: (703)823-0252
Free: 800-347-6647
E-mail: acamemberservices@counseling.org
URL: www.counseling.org
Social Media: www.facebook.com/American.Counseling
 .Association
www.instagram.com/americancounselingassociation
www.linkedin.com/company/american-counseling
 -association
twitter.com/CounselingViews

834 ■ Ross Trust Future School Counselors Essay Competition *(Undergraduate/Award, Prize)*

Purpose: To help those who endeavor to become professional counselors. **Focus:** Counseling/Guidance. **Qualif.:** Applicant must be an only ACA student members can participate in the essay competitions. **Criteria:** Selection of

applicants will be based on the following: (a) master's-level students must have an outstanding academic performance (based on a minimum of 15 graduate hours completed) and exemplary volunteer activities; (b) Doctoral-level students must have an outstanding academic performance (based on a minimum of 15 graduate hours completed), exemplary volunteer activities in schools and/or community, and scholarly research, writing and presentations.

Funds Avail.: No specific amount. **Duration:** Annual. **Number Awarded:** 17. **To Apply:** Applicants must have a statement of career goals; must provide a description of volunteer experiences in schools and/or the community for doctoral level scholarships, applicants must have statement reflecting research, writing and presentation activities. essays must be 500 words or less in length, addressing the theme given by the association. **Deadline:** December 10. **Contact:** E-mail: fburtnett@counseling.org.

835 ■ American Criminal Justice Association - Lambda Alpha Epsilon (ACJA-LAE)
PO Box 601047
Sacramento, CA 95860-1047
Ph: (916)484-6553
Fax: (916)488-2227
E-mail: acjalae@aol.com
URL: www.acjalae.org

836 ■ ACJA/LAE Student Paper Competition
(Undergraduate, Graduate/Scholarship)

Purpose: To support financially and recognize the authors of best papers among graduate and undergraduate students. **Focus:** Criminal justice; Paralegal studies. **Qualif.:** Applicants must be members of ACJA-LAE; must be enrolled in an accredited post-graduate program such as a Master's or Doctorate degree program or an accredited undergraduate degree program (upper and lower levels based on number of course hours completed). **Criteria:** Selection will be based on the submitted entries.

Funds Avail.: $200 for first place; $150 for second place; $100 for third place. **Duration:** Annual. **To Apply:** Application form can be downloaded at the website. Student's papers must be original and deal with issues and problems in the areas of criminology, law enforcement, juvenile justice, courts, corrections, prevention, planning and evaluation, career development or education in the field of criminal justice. Papers must be at least 1, 500 words with a suggested maximum of 3, 000 words (five to ten pages), typewritten, double-spaced on an 8-1/2″ x 11″ white quality paper; any standard referencing format is acceptable for the organization of papers and citations; three copies of the paper must be submitted along with the paper on CD or Flash Drive indicating what program and version was used for the word processing; must also submit three completed copies of the Student Paper Competition Application along with their papers. **Deadline:** December 31.

837 ■ ACJA/LAE Student Scholarship Program
(Undergraduate/Scholarship)

Purpose: To provide financial support to members who are upper or lower division students enrolled in a course of study in the criminal justice field. **Focus:** Criminal justice. **Qualif.:** Applicants must be upper or lower division students enrolled in a course of study in the criminal justice field; must be members of the ACJA/LAE; must be U.S. citizens or eligible non-citizens. **Criteria:** Recipients will be selected based on the following: overall GPA of 3.0 or better on a

Awards are arranged alphabetically below their administering organizations

scale of 4.0; GPA of basic courses completed in criminal justice or related field of study; and statement of career and educational goals.

Funds Avail.: $400 first place; $200 second place; $100 third place. **Duration:** Annual. **To Apply:** Applicants must fill out application form and submit with the following: official certified school transcript; certification of enrollment status; career and educational goals statement; letters of recommendation (optional). **Deadline:** December 31. **Remarks:** Established in 1979. **Contact:** Danny Hayes, Scholarship Chairman; Phone: 402-414-2520; Email: dhayes@peru.edu.

838 ■ ACJA/LAE Student Scholarship Program - Graduate Level *(Graduate, Master's, Doctorate/ Scholarship)*

Purpose: To support students enrolled in a course of study in the criminal justice field. **Focus:** Criminal justice; Law. **Qualif.:** Applicants must be U.S. citizens or eligible non-citizens; must be members of ACJA/LAE chapter or Member-at-Large in good standing (both at the time of submission and at the time of the awards); must be enrolled in an accredited post-graduate program such as a Master's or Doctorate degree program in the criminal justice field; must achieved a minimum overall GPA of a 3.0 on a scale of 4.0. **Criteria:** Recipients will be selected based on the following: overall GPA of 3.0 or better on a scale of 4.0; GPA of basic courses completed in criminal justice or related field of study; and statement of career and educational goals.

Funds Avail.: No specific amount. **To Apply:** Applicants must fill out application form and submit with the following: official certified school transcript; certification of enrollment status; career and educational goals statement; letters of recommendation (optional). **Deadline:** December 31. **Contact:** Danny Hayes, Scholarship Chairman; Phone: 402-414-2520; Email: dhayes@peru.edu.

839 ■ Richard McGrath Memorial Fund Award *(Undergraduate/Award)*

Purpose: To help the students pay the Conference Registration fee for the upcoming National Conference. **Focus:** Criminal justice; Paralegal studies. **Qualif.:** Applicants must be members of ACJA/LAE in good standing; must be currently enrolled in a degree-seeking program consistent with the criminal justice field; have been active in a chapter and regional activities; must have attended at least one regional meeting. **Criteria:** Selection will be based on the committee's criteria.

Funds Avail.: No specific amount. **Duration:** Annual. **To Apply:** Applicants can view the website for further information. **Deadline:** December 1.

840 ■ American Culinary Federation (ACF)
180 Center Place Way
Saint Augustine, FL 32095
Fax: (904)824-4468
URL: www.acfchefs.org
Social Media: www.facebook.com/ACFChefs
www.instagram.com/ACF_CHEFS
www.linkedin.com/company/american-culinary-federation
twitter.com/acfchefs

841 ■ Balestreri/Cutino Scholarship *(Undergraduate/ Scholarship)*

Purpose: To provide financial assistance to those studying culinary arts. **Focus:** Culinary arts. **Qualif.:** Applicant must

be a exemplary student and maintain a cumulative GPA of 2.75 or higher; must currently accepted to the institution with a culinary, pastry or foodservice-related major. **Criteria:** Selection will be based by points on student's overall academic progress, financial need, extracurricular activities, participation in culinary activities, competitions and answers to essay questions.

Funds Avail.: No specific amount. **Duration:** Annual. **Number Awarded:** Varies. **To Apply:** Applicants must submit a completed application form; transcript; competitor's letter or letter of participation from team coach; verification letters should include name, date and location of competition. **Deadline:** April 30; October 31. **Contact:** Toll-free: 800-624-9458, ext. 254; E-mail scholarships@acfchefs.net.

842 ■ Chaîne des Rôtisseurs Scholarships *(Undergraduate/Scholarship)*

Purpose: To provide financial assistance to those studying culinary arts. **Focus:** Culinary arts. **Qualif.:** Applicant must be a exemplary student and maintain a cumulative GPA of 2.75 or higher; must currently accepted to the institution with a culinary, pastry or foodservice-related major. **Criteria:** Selection will be based by points on student's overall academic progress, financial need, extracurricular activities, participation in culinary activities, competitions and answers to essay questions.

Funds Avail.: No specific amount. **Duration:** Annual. **To Apply:** Applicants must submit a completed application form; transcript; competitor's letter or letter of participation from team coach; verification letters should include name, date and location of competition. **Deadline:** April 30; October 31. **Contact:** Toll-free: 800-624-9458, ext. 254; E-mail scholarships@acfchefs.net.

843 ■ Linda Cullen Memorial Scholarship *(Undergraduate/Scholarship)*

Purpose: To provide financial assistance to those studying culinary arts. **Focus:** Culinary arts. **Qualif.:** Applicant must be a exemplary student and maintain a cumulative GPA of 2.75 or higher; must currently accepted to the institution with a culinary, pastry or foodservice-related major. **Criteria:** Selection will be based by points on student's overall academic progress, financial need, extracurricular activities, participation in culinary activities, competitions and answers to essay questions.

Funds Avail.: No specific amount. **Duration:** Annual. **Number Awarded:** 2. **To Apply:** Applicants must submit a completed application form; transcript; competitor's letter or letter of participation from team coach; verification letters should include name, date and location of competition. **Deadline:** April 30; October 31. **Contact:** Toll-free: 800-624-9458, ext. 254; E-mail scholarships@acfchefs.net.

844 ■ Stanley "Doc" Jensen Scholarships *(Undergraduate/Scholarship)*

Purpose: To provide financial assistance to those studying culinary arts. **Focus:** Culinary arts. **Qualif.:** Applicant must be a exemplary student and maintain a cumulative GPA of 2.75 or higher; must currently accepted to the institution with a culinary, pastry or foodservice-related major. **Criteria:** Selection will be based by points on student's overall academic progress, financial need, extracurricular activities, participation in culinary activities, competitions and answers to essay questions.

Duration: Annual. **To Apply:** Applicants must submit a completed application form; transcript; competitor's letter or

Awards are arranged alphabetically below their administering organizations

letter of participation from team coach; verification letters should include name, date and location of competition. **Deadline:** April 30; October 31. **Contact:** Toll-free: 800-624-9458, ext. 254; E-mail scholarships@acfchefs.net.

845 ■ Andrew Macrina Scholarships *(Undergraduate/Scholarship)*

Purpose: To provide financial assistance to those studying culinary arts. **Focus:** Culinary arts. **Qualif.:** Applicant must be a exemplary student and maintain a cumulative GPA of 2.75 or higher; must currently accepted to the institution with a culinary, pastry or foodservice-related major. **Criteria:** Selection will be based by points on student's overall academic progress, financial need, extracurricular activities, participation in culinary activities, competitions and answers to essay questions.

Funds Avail.: No specific amount. **Duration:** Annual. **To Apply:** Applicants must submit a completed application form; transcript; competitor's letter or letter of participation from team coach; verification letters should include name, date and location of competition. **Deadline:** April 30; October 31. **Contact:** Toll-free: 800-624-9458, ext. 254; E-mail scholarships@acfchefs.net.

846 ■ Ray and Gertrude Marshall Scholarships *(Undergraduate/Scholarship)*

Purpose: To provide financial assistance to those studying culinary arts. **Focus:** Culinary arts. **Qualif.:** Applicant must be a exemplary student and maintain a cumulative GPA of 2.75 or higher; must currently accepted to the institution with a culinary, pastry or foodservice-related major.**Criteria:** Selection will be based by points on student's overall academic progress, financial need, extracurricular activities, participation in culinary activities, competitions and answers to essay questions.

Funds Avail.: No specific amount. **Duration:** Annual. **Number Awarded:** Varies. **To Apply:** Applicants must submit a completed application form; transcript; competitor's letter or letter of participation from team coach; verification letters should include name, date and location of competition. **Deadline:** April 30; October 31. **Contact:** Toll-free: 800-624-9458, ext. 254; E-mail scholarships@acfchefs.net.

847 ■ Hermann G. Rusch Scholarship *(Other/Scholarship)*

Purpose: To support professional chefs who wished to continue education or initial certification class. **Focus:** Culinary arts. **Qualif.:** For initial certification, applicants must pass an initial ACF certification class with a "C" grade or better; for continuing education, must be certified by the American Culinary Federation as a Certified Chef d' Cuisine or higher; enrolled in a state-accredited educational institution for the purpose of enhancing culinary skills or knowledge; an active member of the American Culinary Federation in good standing for three or more years. **Criteria:** Selection shall be based on the aforementioned state-accredited qualifications and compliance with the application details.

Duration: Annual. **To Apply:** The application must be completed and signed by applicants; verification of registration to the professional development course must be submitted, along with total cost of class; will be notified by mail of any grant award or denial.

848 ■ Spice Box Grants *(Advanced Professional/Grant)*

Purpose: To support professional chefs who wish to continue their education or initial certification class. **Focus:**

Culinary arts. **Qualif.:** Applicants must meet the following requirements: be a current ACF member in good standing for a minimum of 2 years; t be a Certified Chef de Cuisine or higher. **Criteria:** Selection shall be based on a competitive basis to exemplary working culinary professionals who wish to update their skills through continuing education.

Funds Avail.: Up to $500. **Duration:** Annual. **To Apply:** Application must be completed and signed by applicants; verification of registration to the professional development course must be submitted, along with total cost of class; will be notified by mail of any grant award or denial. **Deadline:** March 31.

849 ■ Charlie Trotters's Culinary Education Foundation Scholarships *(Other, Undergraduate/Scholarship)*

Purpose: To support students in pursuing their career in culinary arts. **Focus:** Culinary arts. **Qualif.:** Applicants must be high school students, college students, professional chefs looking to further their education or become certified and student culinary teams currently competing at ACF regional and national conferences. **Criteria:** Recipients will be selected based on merit, work experience, culinary goals and skills and references.

Funds Avail.: No specific amount. **To Apply:** Applicants must submit a completed Culinary Trust Scholarship application form; a project proposal (two-page, double-spaced) illustrating their culinary goals; two letters of reference on business or personal letterhead; a current academic transcript; a non-refundable application fee of $35. **Deadline:** March 1. **Remarks:** Established in 1999.

850 ■ American Darts Organization (ADO)
PO Box 182
Stanton, CA 90680-0209
Free: 844-883-2787
E-mail: president@adodarts.com
URL: www.adodarts.com

851 ■ American Darts Organization Memorial Youth National Scholarship *(Undergraduate/Scholarship)*

Purpose: To provide financial aid for college education of young Dart players throughout the United States. **Focus:** General studies/Field of study not specified. **Qualif.:** Applicants must be U.S. citizens or must have been domiciled in the United States for a period of two years and one day; must be members in good standing of the American Darts Organization; must be Regional/National winners in the ADO Youth Playoff Program; must be under twenty-one (21) years of age as of December 1st of the year in which they plans to attend college; The student must select a program or major that leads to the earning of a degree i.e. Associate in Applied Science, Bachelor of Science etc., and must maintain a grade point average of 2.0 on a scale of 4.0.

Funds Avail.: Amount varies. **Number Awarded:** Varies. **To Apply:** Interested applicants may contact the Organization for the application process and other information.

852 ■ American Dental Association (ADA)
211 E Chicago Ave.
Chicago, IL 60611-2678
Ph: (312)440-2500
Fax: (312)440-3542
Free: 800-947-4746

Awards are arranged alphabetically below their administering organizations

URL: www.ada.org
Social Media: www.facebook.com/
   AmericanDentalAssociation
www.instagram.com/americandentalassociation
www.linkedin.com/company/19559
twitter.com/AmerDentalAssn
www.youtube.com/user/AmericanDentalAssoc

853 ■ Allied Dental Student Scholarship Program
(Undergraduate/Scholarship)

Purpose: To help dental assisting, dental hygiene, and dental laboratory technology student defray a part of their professional educational expenses. **Focus:** Dentistry.

Funds Avail.: $1,000 each (15 dental hygiene students, 10 dental assisting students and five dental laboratory technology students). **Number Awarded:** Varies.

854 ■ American Dental Association Dental Assisting Scholarship Program *(Undergraduate/Scholarship)*

Purpose: To provide financial assistance for furthering education of students in pursuing the field of dentistry. **Focus:** Dentistry. **Qualif.:** Applicants must be U.S. citizens; must be entering students at the time of application and enrolled in a dental assisting program accredited by the Commission on Dental Accreditation of the American Dental Association; enrolled as full-time students with minimum of 12 credit hours; demonstrate a minimum financial need of $1,000; have minimum accumulative grade point average of 3.5 based on a 4.0 scale; and two reference forms: one from a dentist or dental assisting representative and/or one from a school representative which must be submitted as part of the application form. **Criteria:** Applicants will be evaluated based on demonstrated financial need; academic achievement; biographical sketch questionnaire; and two completed reference forms.

Funds Avail.: $1,000. **Duration:** One year. **To Apply:** Applicants must submit an application form that is typed or printed in black ink, completed and signed by school officials; completed application form including the Academic Achievement Record Form and Financial Needs Assessment Form signed by school official; a copy of the school's letter of acceptance for those incoming first-year students; two completed reference forms, sealed and signed on the back flap of the envelope by the referrers (required forms must be used which are a part of the scholarship application form); typed, biographical sketch questionnaire (required form must be used which is a part of the scholarship application form); a self-addressed, stamped postcard which can be mailed upon receipt of the application (if the applicants wishes to have verification that the application was received).

855 ■ American Dental Association Dental Hygiene Scholarship Program *(Undergraduate/Scholarship)*

Purpose: To help students in dental assisting, dental hygiene, and dental laboratory technology students defray a part of their professional education expenses. **Focus:** Dentistry. **Qualif.:** Applicants must be U.S. citizens; entering second year students at the time of application and currently attending or enrolled at a dental school accredited by the Commission on Dental Accreditation of the American Dental Association; enrolled as full-time students with a minimum of 12 credit hours; must demonstrate a financial need of $1,000; have a minimum accumulative grade point average of 3.5 based on a 4.0 scale; and two reference forms from two dental school representatives. **Criteria:** Ap-

plicants will be evaluated based on their demonstrated financial need; academic achievement; biographical sketch questionnaire; and two completed reference forms.

Funds Avail.: $1,000. **Duration:** Annual; one year. **To Apply:** Applicant must submit an application form that is typed or printed in black ink, completed and signed by school officials; completed application form including the Academic Achievement Record Form and Financial Needs Assessment Form signed by school official; a copy of the school's letter of acceptance for those incoming first-year students; two completed reference forms, sealed and signed on the back flap of the envelope by the referrers (required forms must be used which are a part of the scholarship application form); typed, biographical sketch questionnaire (required form must be used which is a part of the scholarship application form); a self-addressed, stamped postcard which can be mailed upon receipt of the application (if the applicant wishes to have verification that the application was received).

856 ■ American Dental Association Dental Laboratory Technology Scholarship Program
(Undergraduate/Scholarship)

Purpose: To provide financial assistance for students to further their education in the field of dentistry. **Focus:** Dentistry. **Qualif.:** Applicants must be U.S. citizens (permanent resident status does not qualify); entering their final year as students at the time of application; must be currently attending a dental laboratory technology program accredited by the Commission on Dental Accreditation of the American Dental Association; must be enrolled as full-time students with minimum of 12 credit hours; must demonstrate financial need of $1,000; have a minimum accumulative grade point average of 3.5 based on a 4.0 scale; and must have two reference forms from two dental laboratory technology program representatives which must be submitted as part of the application form. **Criteria:** Applicants will be evaluated based on demonstrated financial need; academic achievement; biographical sketch questionnaire; and two completed reference forms.

Funds Avail.: $1,000. **Duration:** One year. **To Apply:** Applicant must submit an application form that is typed or printed in black ink, completed and signed by school officials; completed application form including the Academic Achievement Record Form and Financial Needs Assessment Form signed by school official; a copy of the school's letter of acceptance for those incoming first-year students; two completed reference forms, sealed and signed on the back flap of the envelope by the referrers (required forms must be used which are a part of the scholarship application form); typed, biographical sketch questionnaire (required form must be used which is a part of the scholarship application form); a self-addressed, stamped postcard which can be mailed upon receipt of the application (if the applicant wishes to have verification that the application was received). **Deadline:** March 31.

857 ■ American Dental Association Minority Dental Student Scholarships *(Undergraduate/Scholarship)*

Purpose: To help pre-doctoral dental students defray a part of their professional education expenses. **Focus:** Dentistry. **Qualif.:** Applicants must be U.S. citizens; entering second year students at the time of application and currently attending or enrolled at a dental school accredited by the Commission on Dental Accreditation of the American Dental Association; enrolled as full-time students, a minimum of 12 credit hours; demonstrate a minimum financial need of $2,500; have a minimum accumulative

Awards are arranged alphabetically below their administering organizations

grade point average of 3.0 based on a 4.0 scale; and two reference forms from two dental school representatives (i.e., professor or academic advisor) in support of the application must be submitted as part of the application form. **Criteria:** Applicants will be evaluated based on their demonstrated financial need, academic achievement, biographical sketch questionnaire and two completed reference forms.

Funds Avail.: $2,500. **Duration:** One year. **Number Awarded:** Varies. **To Apply:** Applicants must submit an application form that is typed or printed in black ink, completed and signed by school officials; completed application form, including the Academic Achievement Record Form and Financial Needs Assessment Form, which are a part of the application form, and signed by school official; a copy of the school's letter of acceptance, if entering first-year students; two completed reference forms, sealed and signed on the back flap of the envelopes by the referrers (required forms must be used which are a part of the scholarship application form); typed, biographical sketch questionnaire (required form must be used which is a part of the scholarship application form); a self-addressed, stamped postcard, which can be mailed upon receipt of the application (if the applicants wishes to have verification that the application was received).

858 ■ American Dental Hygienists' Association Institute for Oral Health (ADHA IOH)
444 N Michigan Ave., Ste. 3400
Chicago, IL 60611
Ph: (312)440-8900
E-mail: institute@adha.net
URL: www.adha.org/institute-for-oral-health
Social Media: www.facebook.com/youradha
twitter.com/YourADHA
youtube.com/ADHAdotOrg

859 ■ American Dental Hygienists' Association Institute for Oral Health Research Grants *(Master's/Grant)*

Purpose: To support professional advancement of dental hygiene educators. **Focus:** Dental hygiene. **Qualif.:** Applicants must be a licensed dental hygienists or a student pursuing a dental hygiene degree; must be a current member of ADHA or SADHA. **Criteria:** Priority will be given to proposals addressing the ADHA National Research Agenda.

Duration: Annual. **To Apply:** Applicants must contact ADHA Institute for Oral Health for application process. **Deadline:** February 28.

860 ■ Irene Woodall Graduate Scholarship *(Graduate/Scholarship)*

Purpose: To provide financial assistance to dental hygiene students and dental hygienists who demonstrate a commitment to further knowledge through academic achievement, professional excellence and desire to improve the public's overall health. **Focus:** Dental hygiene. **Qualif.:** Applicants must be pursuing a Master's degree in dental hygiene or any related fields; must have a minimum grade point average of 3.5 on a 4.0 scale. **Criteria:** Scholarship will be awarded based on how well the applicant demonstrates the goal or achievement described.

Funds Avail.: $1,000. **Duration:** Annual. **Number Awarded:** 1. **Deadline:** February 1. **Contact:** Phone: 312-

440-8944; Email: institute@adha.net.

861 ■ Sigma Phi Alpha Graduate Scholarship *(Graduate/Scholarship)*

Purpose: To provide financial assistance to dental hygiene students and dental hygienists who can demonstrate a commitment to further knowledge through academic achievement, professional excellence and desire to improve the public's overall health. **Focus:** Dental hygiene. **Qualif.:** Applicants must be Sigma Phi Alpha members pursuing a graduate degree in dental hygiene or any related fields; must have a minimum grade point average (GPA); must be a professional or student member of the American Dental Hygienists' Association (ADHA).

Funds Avail.: $1,000. **Duration:** Annual. **Number Awarded:** 1. **Deadline:** February 1.

862 ■ Wilma Motley Memorial California Merit Scholarship *(Undergraduate/Scholarship)*

Purpose: To provide financial assistance to dental hygiene students and dental hygienists who can demonstrate a commitment to further knowledge through academic achievement, professional excellence and desire to improve the public's overall health. **Focus:** Dental hygiene. **Qualif.:** Applicants must be Registered Dental Hygienists in Alternative Practice (RDHAP) or individuals pursuing associate/certificate, baccalaureate, master's or doctorate degree in dental hygiene or related field; must be residents and attending a dental hygiene program in California; must demonstrate leadership experience and have GPA of at least 3.5 on a 4.0 scale; must be active members of ADHA. **Criteria:** Applicants will be awarded based on merit.

Funds Avail.: $2,000. **Duration:** Annual. **Number Awarded:** 3. **To Apply:** Applicants must contact ADHA Institute for Oral Health office to request an application form and to ask further information. **Deadline:** February 1.

863 ■ American Diabetes Association (ADA)
2451 Crystal Dr., Ste. 900
Arlington, VA 22202
Ph: (202)331-8303
Free: 800-342-2383
E-mail: askada@diabetes.org
URL: www.diabetes.org
Social Media: www.facebook.com/AmericanDiabetesAssociation
www.instagram.com/AmDiabetesAssn
www.linkedin.com/company/american-diabetes-association
www.pinterest.com/amdiabetesassn
twitter.com/AmDiabetesAssn
www.youtube.com/user/AmericanDiabetesAssn

864 ■ ADA Junior Faculty Award *(Other/Grant, Award, Monetary)*

Purpose: To support new investigators who are establishing their independence in diabetes research. **Focus:** Medical research. **Qualif.:** Applicants must be full-time independent faculty with less than 10 years of research experience since their terminal degree who do not have previous or current NIH support (R00, R01, U01 or equivalent).

Funds Avail.: $138,000 per year for up to four years including indirect costs. **Duration:** Annual. **Number Awarded:** 12. **To Apply:** Applicants must complete the online application form. **Deadline:** July 15.

Awards are arranged alphabetically below their administering organizations

865 ■ Thomas R. Lee Career Development Award
(Professional development/Grant, Award)

Purpose: To recognize the highest scoring Career Development Award applicant. **Focus:** Medical research.

Funds Avail.: $172,500 per year. **Duration:** Annual; up to five years. **Number Awarded:** Varies.

866 ■ Mentor-Based Minority Postdoctoral Fellowship *(Postdoctorate/Fellowship, Monetary)*

Purpose: To support the training of minority scientists who are underrepresented in the field of diabetes research. **Focus:** Medical research. **Qualif.:** Applicants must be young, minority researchers who were looking to begin their career in diabetes science.

Funds Avail.: No specific amount. **Duration:** Annual. **Number Awarded:** 8. **To Apply:** Applicants must complete the online application form. **Deadline:** July 15. **Remarks:** Established in 2003.

867 ■ American Educational Research Association (AERA)
1430 K St. NW, Ste. 1200
Washington, DC 20005-2504
Ph: (202)238-3200
Fax: (202)238-3250
URL: www.aera.net
Social Media: www.facebook.com/AERAEdResearch
instagram.com/aera_edresearch
www.linkedin.com/company/79248
twitter.com/AERA_EdResearch
youtube.com/aeranews

868 ■ AERA-ETS Fellowship Program in Measurement and Education Research *(Doctorate/Fellowship)*

Purpose: To provide learning opportunities and practical experience to recent doctoral degree recipients and to early career research scientists in education research areas directed toward explaining student progress and achievement. **Focus:** Testing, educational/psychological. **Qualif.:** Applicants must be U.S citizens and permanent residents; must have completed their PhD/EdD degrees within the three years prior to application. **Criteria:** Selection of applicants will be based on the scholarship selection criteria.

Number Awarded: Up to 2. **To Apply:** Applicants must complete the application form available online; must submit a letter of recommendation; transcript of records; personal statement; dissertation abstract; dissertation/doctoral thesis summary; writing sample; and curriculum vitae. **Contact:** George Wimberly at fellowships@aera.net.

869 ■ AERA Fellows Program *(Postdoctorate/Fellowship)*

Purpose: To support early career scholars by providing intensive research and training opportunities to recent doctoral recipients in the fields and disciplines related to the scientific study of education and education processes; to increase the number of underrepresented minority professionals conducting advanced research or providing technical assistance. **Focus:** Education. **Qualif.:** Applicants must be U.S citizens and permanent residents; must have completed their PhD/EdD degrees within the three years prior to application. **Criteria:** Selection of applicants will be based on their research proposal.

Funds Avail.: $55,000-$65,000. **Duration:** Annual. **To Apply:** Applicants must complete the application form avail-

able online; must submit a letter of recommendation; transcript of records; personal statement; dissertation abstract; dissertation/doctoral thesis summary; writing sample; and curriculum vitae. **Deadline:** November 1. **Contact:** Tony Pals; Phone: 202-238-3235; E-mail: tpals@aera.net.

870 ■ AERA Minority Dissertation Fellowship in Education Research *(Doctorate/Fellowship)*

Purpose: To provide support for doctoral dissertation research to minority graduate students. **Focus:** Education. **Qualif.:** Applicants must be U.S. citizen or permanent resident; must work full-time on a dissertation and course requirements. **Criteria:** Selection will be based on the submitted application.

Funds Avail.: Up to $25,000. **To Apply:** Applicants must complete the application form available online; must submit a letter of recommendation and transcript of record. Application form and other supporting documents must be sent to AERA-AIR Fellows Program. **Deadline:** November 16.

871 ■ American Enterprise Institute
1789 Massachusetts Ave., NW
Washington, DC 20036
Ph: (202)862-5800
Fax: (202)862-7177
URL: www.aei.org
Social Media: www.facebook.com/aei
www.instagram.com/aei
www.linkedin.com/company/american-enterprise-institute
twitter.com/AEI
www.youtube.com/user/AEIVideos

872 ■ American Enterprise Institute National Research Initiative Fellowships (NRI) *(Professional development/Fellowship)*

Purpose: To help AEI collaborate with scholars who were doing important work on issues relevant to the Institute's interests and to provide the support needed for these scholars to have a greater influence on the policy debate. **Focus:** Economics; Law; Political science; Social sciences. **Qualif.:** Applicants must be university-based professors and other intellectuals to support books, monographs, working papers, edited volumes, and other types of original research on U.S. domestic public policy issues.

Funds Avail.: No specific amount. **Remarks:** Established in 2002.

873 ■ American Federation for Aging Research (AFAR)
55 W 39th St., 16th Fl.
New York, NY 10018
Ph: (212)703-9977
Fax: (212)997-0330
Free: 888-582-2327
E-mail: info@afar.org
URL: www.afar.org
Social Media: www.facebook.com/AFARorg
twitter.com/AFARorg

874 ■ AFAR Scholarships for Research in the Biology of Aging *(Graduate, Doctorate/Scholarship)*
Purpose: To give students the chance to learn more about the field of aging research, as well as increase their

Awards are arranged alphabetically below their administering organizations

understanding of the challenges involved in improving the quality of life for older people. **Focus:** Gerontology. **Qualif.:** Applicants must be MD, DO, PhD or combined degree students in good standing at a not-for-profit institution in the United States. **Criteria:** Applicants will be evaluated based on the following: qualifications and ability of the applicant, as demonstrated by academic performance, statement of purpose and letter of reference; merit and feasibility of the proposed research project and its relevance to aging; qualifications of the designated mentor, his or her endorsement of the research project, assurance of active supervision and demonstrated commitment to aging research and to the student; likelihood that the project will advance the applicant's interest and career in aging research; quality of the research environment.

Funds Avail.: $5,000. **To Apply:** Recipients will be required to submit a full report detailing their research methods and findings within 90 days of completing the research projects; mentor will be required to provide an evaluation of the student's performance and impressions of the impact of the program on the student's career. **Deadline:** December 31. **Contact:** Email: scholarship@afar.org.

875 ■ The Paul B. Beeson Emerging Leaders Career Development Award in Aging(K76) *(Professional development/Grant)*

Purpose: To sustain and promote the careers of clinically-trained faculty who are pursuing research in aging. **Focus:** Gerontology. **Qualif.:** Applicant must be clinically trained (primarily physician) early-stage investigators.

Funds Avail.: $600,000 to $800,000. **Duration:** Annual. **Remarks:** The award was established to honor Dr. Paul B. Beeson. Established in 1994.

876 ■ Glenn/AFAR Breakthroughs in Gerontology Awards *(Postgraduate/Grant)*

Purpose: To support a small number of research projects that are building on early discoveries that show translational potential for clinically-relevant strategies, treatments and therapeutics, addressing human aging and health span. **Focus:** Gerontology. **Qualif.:** To be eligible, applicants must at the time they submit their proposal be full-time faculty members at the rank of Assistant Professor or higher. **Criteria:** Applications are reviewed based on the following: qualifications and research record of the applicant; quality, promise and feasibility of the proposed research; translational potential and relevance to human aging and health span; excellence of the research environment.

Funds Avail.: Up to $100,000. **Duration:** Annual. **To Apply:** Applicants should refer to the Glenn/AFAR BIG LOI for instructions, available on the website, prior to submitting Letters of Intent. Incomplete or improperly completed LOIs cannot be considered. LOIs will be evaluated and a subset of applicants will be invited to submit a full application. **Deadline:** December 15 (Letters of Intent). **Remarks:** Established in 2005.

877 ■ Glenn Foundation for Medical Research and AFAR Grants for Junior Faculty *(Professional development/Grant)*

Purpose: To assist individuals in the development of their careers of junior investigators committed to pursuing careers in the field of aging research. **Focus:** Gerontology. **Qualif.:** Applicants must be junior investigators committed to pursuing careers in the field of aging research. **Criteria:** Applicants will be evaluated based on the following:

qualifications and research record of the applicant; quality of the proposed research in the basic biology of aging; excellence of the research environment; likelihood that the project will advance the applicant's career in aging research.

Funds Avail.: $100,000. **Duration:** Annual. **Number Awarded:** 10. **To Apply:** Applicants must submit the completed application form providing narrative and financial reports. **Contact:** Email: afarapplication@afar.org.

878 ■ American Federation of Police and Concerned Citizens (AFP&CC)
6350 Horizon Dr.
Titusville, FL 32780
Ph: (321)264-0911
E-mail: policeinfo@aphf.org
URL: www.afp-cc.org

879 ■ American Federation of Police and Concerned Citizen Educational Scholarship *(Undergraduate/Scholarship)*

Purpose: To assist family members and children of officers killed in the line of duty. **Focus:** Law enforcement. **Qualif.:** Applicants must be the surviving sons or daughters of law enforcement officers killed in the line of duty; be enrolled in a minimum of 6 credit hours; and maintain a 2.0 GPA; currently enrolled in college.

Funds Avail.: $1,000 to $4,000. **Duration:** Annual. **To Apply:** Applicants currently enrolled in college must submit a copy of their most recent school transcripts; new college students must submit a high school transcript, ACT or SAT scores, and a copy of the acceptance letter from the institution he or she plans on attending; checks will be mailed to the applicant and made payable to the school. **Contact:** AFP&CC - Police Family Survivors Fund, 6350 Horizon Dr., Titusville, FL, 32780; Phone: 321-264-0911; Fax: 321-264-0033; Email: loris@aphf.org.

880 ■ American Federation of Teachers (AFT)
555 New Jersey Ave. NW
Washington, DC 20001
Ph: (202)879-4400
Free: 800-238-1133
E-mail: servicedesk@aft.org
URL: www.aft.org
Social Media: www.facebook.com/AFTunion
twitter.com/AFTunion
www.youtube.com/user/afthq

881 ■ AFT Robert G. Porter Scholars Program *(Undergraduate/Scholarship)*

Purpose: To support graduating high school senior students who show outstanding service to their community and an understanding of the role unions can play to create a more just society. **Focus:** General studies/Field of study not specified. **Qualif.:** Applicants must be graduating high school seniors who are dependents of AFT members; must have at least one parent or legal guardian who is an AFT member; whose child or legal dependent applies for a scholarship must be a member in good standing for at least one year; children or legal dependents of AFT national, state or local union staff are not eligible for this scholarship opportunity. **Criteria:** Selection will be based on the academic achievement, commitment to community services

Awards are arranged alphabetically below their administering organizations

and school-related activities, demonstration of leadership, work experience, recommendations, special talents and skills, an essay and a commitment to advancing the interests of working people and building unions.

Funds Avail.: $8,000 scholarships, over a four- to six-year period; $1,000 one-time grants. **Duration:** Annual. **Number Awarded:** 4 (post-secondary scholarships); 10 (one-time grants). **To Apply:** Application form and details are available online at www.aft.org/member-benefits/scholarships/ robert-g-porter-scholars-program. **Deadline:** March 31. **Remarks:** The scholarship was established to honor Robert G. Porter, the secretary-treasurer of the American Federation of Teachers from 1963 to 1991. **Contact:** E-mail: PorterScholars@aft.org.

882 ■ American Federation of Teachers - Oregon (AFT)

10228 SW Capitol Hwy.
Portland, OR 97219
Ph: (971)888-5665
Fax: (503)906-3533
URL: or.aft.org
Social Media: www.facebook.com/aftoregon
twitter.com/AFTOregon

883 ■ Shirley J. Gold Scholarship *(Undergraduate, Vocational/Occupational/Scholarship)*

Purpose: To support AFT-Oregon members who are pursuing higher education at an accredited higher education institution. **Focus:** General studies/Field of study not specified. **Qualif.:** Applicants must be AFT-Oregon members planning to enroll in a college, university, or trade program. **Criteria:** Selection will be based on the committee's criteria.

Funds Avail.: $1,500. **Duration:** Annual. **Number Awarded:** 1. **To Apply:** Applicants must visit the website to obtain an application form; must also provide the following materials: a writing assignment and certification of original composition; at least two references in a stamped envelope addressed to AFT-Oregon, from a teacher or community leader who knows the applicants well and can attest to their outstanding qualities; a copy of applicant's current transcript from the college, university or trade program where they are enrolled; for college freshmen applicants, please provide a high school transcript. **Deadline:** January 31. **Contact:** AFT-Oregon Scholarship Program; E-mail: Leahl@aft-oregon.org.

884 ■ Carl J. Megel Scholarship *(Undergraduate/ Scholarship)*

Purpose: To provide assistance to dependents of AFT-Oregon members who are graduating seniors and plan to pursue higher education. **Focus:** General studies/Field of study not specified. **Qualif.:** Applicants must be children or grandchildren of AFT members; must be graduating high school students planning to enroll in an accredited institution or trade program to continue their higher education of the current year. **Criteria:** Selection will be based on the committee's criteria.

Funds Avail.: $1,500. **Duration:** Annual. **To Apply:** Applicants must visit the website to obtain an application form; must also provide the following materials: a writing assignment and certification of original composition; at least two references in a stamped envelope addressed to AFT-Oregon, from a teacher or community leader who knows the applicants well and can attest to their outstanding quali-

ties; a copy of applicant's current transcript from the college, university or trade program where they are enrolled; for college freshmen applicants, please provide a high school transcript. **Deadline:** January 31. **Remarks:** The scholarship was established in honor of Carl J. Megel was president of the American Federation of Teachers from 1952 to 1964, which was a period of tremendous growth and activity. **Contact:** AFT-Oregon Scholarship Program; E-mail: Leahl@aft-oregon.org.

885 ■ Albert F. Shanker Scholarship *(Undergraduate/ Scholarship)*

Purpose: To provide assistance to members' dependents enrolled in higher education institutions. **Focus:** General studies/Field of study not specified. **Qualif.:** Applicants must be children or grandchildren of AFT-Oregon members; must be currently attending an accredited higher education, institution or trade program and planning to continue higher education in the current academic year. **Criteria:** Selection will be based on the committee's criteria.

Funds Avail.: $1,500. **Duration:** Annual. **To Apply:** Applicants must visit the website to obtain an application form; must also provide the following materials: a writing assignment and certification of original composition; at least two references in a stamped envelope addressed to AFT-Oregon, from a teacher or community leader who knows the applicants well and can attest to their outstanding qualities; a copy of applicant's current transcript from the college, university or trade program where they are enrolled; for college freshmen applicants, please provide a high school transcript. **Deadline:** January 31. **Remarks:** The scholarship was established in honor of Albert F. Shanker who worked to build a powerful union which included not only teachers, but also paraprofessionals, public employees and health care professionals. **Contact:** AFT-Oregon Scholarship Program; E-mail: Leahl@aft-oregon.org.

886 ■ American Fisheries Society (AFS)

425 Barlow Pl.
Bethesda, MD 20814
Ph: (301)897-8616
Fax: (301)897-8096
E-mail: main@fisheries.org
URL: fisheries.org
Social Media: www.facebook.com/
  AmericanFisheriesSociety
www.instagram.com/americanfisheries
www.linkedin.com/company/1522657
twitter.com/AmFisheriesSoc

887 ■ J Frances Allen Scholarship Award *(Doctorate/Scholarship)*

Purpose: To provide funds for a female fisheries science PhD student whose research emphasis is in an area of fisheries science. **Focus:** Fisheries sciences/management; Women's studies. **Qualif.:** Applicant must be a female Ph.D. student who was an AFS member; must be conducting aquatic research in line with AFS objectives, which include "all branches of fisheries science, including but not limited to aquatic biology, engineering, fish culture, limnology, oceanography, and sociology". **Criteria:** Selection will be based on J Frances Allen Scholarship Committee of the AFS Equal opportunity section; competitive basis with an emphasis placed on research promise, scientific merit, and academic achievement.

Funds Avail.: $2,500. **Duration:** Annual. **To Apply:** Applicant should submit a resume; transcripts; three letters of

Awards are arranged alphabetically below their administering organizations

recommendation; Dissertation research proposal: do not exceed 4 single spaced pages (excluding title page, abstract, and references). **Deadline:** April 1. **Remarks:** The award was established honor Allen, who pioneered women's involvement in the AFS and in the field of fisheries. Established in 1986. **Contact:** Vivian Nguyen, Committee Chair; Email: vivian.m.n@gmail.com.

888 ■ American Fisheries Society Idaho Chapter
1905 Birch Ct.
Lewiston, ID 83501
URL: www.idahoafs.org

889 ■ ICAFS Idaho Graduate Student Scholarship
(Graduate/Scholarship)

Purpose: To provide assistance to graduate students attending any school in Idaho. **Focus:** Fisheries sciences/management. **Qualif.:** Applicants must be graduate students at any Idaho college/university during the next academic year; and must have a career goal that advances the mission and objectives of the American Fisheries Society. **Criteria:** Selection is based on professional goals; course work completed; GPA; involvement in the American Fisheries Society; and work experience with fish or aquatics.

Funds Avail.: $1,000. **Duration:** Annual; one year. **Number Awarded:** 1. **To Apply:** Applicants must submit a completed application form and resume; a statement of career goals (300 words or less); a letter of recommendation from a biology professor, faculty advisor, or administrator; and a copy of college transcript(s). **Deadline:** January 31. **Remarks:** Established in 2005. **Contact:** Lauri Monnot; Phone: 208-373-0203; Email: scholarships@idahoafs.org.

890 ■ ICAFS Idaho High School Student Scholarship *(Undergraduate/Scholarship)*

Purpose: To provide assistance to undergraduate students attending any school in Idaho pursuing higher education. **Focus:** Fisheries sciences/management. **Qualif.:** Applicants must be senior students enrolled in an Idaho high school; must have a GPA of at least 3.0; must be planning to attend a college/university located in Idaho; and have career goals that advance the mission and objectives of the American Fisheries Society. **Criteria:** Selection is based on career goals; course work; GPA; and letter of recommendation from a biology or science teacher.

Funds Avail.: $500. **Duration:** Annual. **To Apply:** Applicants must submit a application form and obtain a copy of your high school transcripts; email your completed application; e letter of recommendation must be on the letter of recommendation form which is available at scholarship website; Letters of recommendation that are emailed from the applicant. **Deadline:** January 31. **Remarks:** Established in 2005. **Contact:** Lauri Monnot; Phone: 208-373-0203; Email: scholarships@idahoafs.org.

891 ■ ICAFS Idaho Undergraduate Student Scholarship *(Undergraduate/Scholarship)*

Purpose: To provide assistance to undergraduate students attending any school in Idaho pursuing higher education. **Focus:** Fisheries sciences/management. **Qualif.:** Applicants must be undergraduate students enrolled at any Idaho college/university; and must have professional goals that support the mission of the American Fisheries Society. **Criteria:** Selection is based on professional goals, course work completed; GPA; involvement in the American Fisher-

ies Society; work experience with fish or aquatics; letter of recommendation.

Funds Avail.: $1,000. **Duration:** Annual; one year. **To Apply:** Applicants must submit a completed application form and resume; a statement of your career goals (300 words or less); a letter of recommendation from a biology professor, faculty advisor, or administrator; and a copy of college transcript(s). **Deadline:** January 31. **Remarks:** Established in 2005. **Contact:** Lauri Monnot; Phone: 208-373-0203; Email: scholarships@idahoafs.org.

892 ■ Susan B. Martin Scholarship *(Graduate/Scholarship)*

Purpose: To assist with college education costs of graduate students whose professional goals support the mission and objectives of the society. **Focus:** Fisheries sciences/management. **Qualif.:** Applicants must be graduate students at any Idaho college/university during the next academic year; and must have a career goal that advances the mission and objectives of the American Fisheries Society. **Criteria:** Selection is based on academic record; career goals; experiences that enhance the student as a professional; letter of recommendation from a biology professor, faculty advisor, or administrator; and demonstrated examples of mentoring and inspiring the growth and development of aquatic scientists.

Funds Avail.: $2,000. **Duration:** Annual. **To Apply:** Applicants must submit a completed application form and resume; a statement of career goals (300 words or less); a letter of recommendation from a biology professor, faculty advisor, or administrator; and a copy of college transcript(s). **Deadline:** January 31. **Remarks:** Established in 2008. **Contact:** Lauri Monnot; Phone: 208-373-0203; Email: scholarships@idahoafs.org.

893 ■ American Floral Endowment (AFE)
1001 N Fairfax St., Ste. 201
Alexandria, VA 22314
Ph: (703)838-5211
Fax: (703)838-5212
E-mail: afe@endowment.org
URL: endowment.org
Social Media: www.facebook.com/
  americanfloralendowment
www.instagram.com/american_floral_endowment
www.pinterest.com/floralendowment
twitter.com/floralendowment
www.youtube.com/c/EndowmentOrg

894 ■ Ball Horticultural Company Scholarship *(Undergraduate/Scholarship)*

Purpose: To support junior or senior students pursuing a career in commercial floriculture. **Focus:** Horticulture. **Qualif.:** Applicants should be junior or senior students pursuing a career in commercial floriculture. **Criteria:** Recipients are selected based on academic performance.

Funds Avail.: Varies. **Duration:** Annual. **To Apply:** Applicants must complete the online application form; must submit a letter of recommendation and endorsement by a faculty member. **Deadline:** May 1.

895 ■ Vic and Margaret Ball Student Intern Scholarships *(Undergraduate/Internship)*

Purpose: To give students the opportunity to gain practical floriculture/horticulture experience while training at a com-

Awards are arranged alphabetically below their administering organizations

mercial production greenhouse or nursery. **Focus:** Horticulture. **Qualif.:** Applicants must be full-time undergraduate students who are currently enrolled in a floriculture/environmental horticulture program at a two or four year college/university within the United States; must be U.S. citizens; must maintain "C" or better GPA with satisfactory progress in a degree or certificate program. **Criteria:** Recipients are selected based on academic performance, financial need and interest in a horticulture career.

Funds Avail.: $500 advance & $1,500 for six-month interns. **Duration:** Semiannual. **To Apply:** Applicants must submit a completed and signed application form, official transcript from all institutions attended, a statement explaining past and current involvement in floriculture activities, expectations from the program, and future career goals; pictures of the student working at the intern location must be included; must have permission to interrupt studies for the length of the training period. **Deadline:** March 1; October 1.

896 ■ Harold Bettinger Scholarship (Undergraduate, Graduate/Scholarship)

Purpose: To further the advancement of education and science in the floriculture and environmental horticulture field by funding research and studies and financing scholarships and other educational activities for individuals interested in the field. **Focus:** Horticulture. **Qualif.:** Applicants must be sophomore or graduate students pursuing a career in business and/or marketing with the intent to apply it to a horticulture-related business. **Criteria:** Recipients are selected based on academic performance.

Duration: Annual. **To Apply:** Applicants must complete the online application form; must submit a letter of recommendation and endorsement by a faculty member. **Deadline:** May 1.

897 ■ Leonard Bettinger Vocational Scholarship (Undergraduate, Vocational/Occupational/Scholarship)

Purpose: To further the advancement of education and science in the floriculture and environmental horticulture field by funding research and studies and financing scholarships and other educational activities for individuals interested in the field. **Focus:** Horticulture. **Qualif.:** Applicants must be vocational students in a one or two-year program who intend to become growers or greenhouse managers. **Criteria:** Recipients are selected based on academic performance.

Duration: Annual. **To Apply:** Applicants must complete the online application form; must submit a letter of recommendation and endorsement by a faculty member. **Deadline:** May 1.

898 ■ James Bridenbaugh Memorial Scholarship (Undergraduate/Scholarship)

Purpose: To further the advancement of education and science in the floriculture and environmental horticulture field by funding research and studies and financing scholarships and other educational activities for individuals interested in the field. **Focus:** Horticulture. **Qualif.:** Applicants must be sophomore to senior students pursuing a career in floral design and marketing fresh flowers and plants. **Criteria:** Recipients are selected based on academic performance.

Duration: Annual. **To Apply:** Applicants must complete the online application form; must submit a letter of recommendation and endorsement by a faculty member. **Deadline:** May 1.

899 ■ John Carew Memorial Scholarship (Graduate/Scholarship)

Purpose: To further the advancement of education and science in the floriculture and environmental horticulture field by funding research and studies and financing scholarships and other educational activities for individuals interested in the field. **Focus:** Horticulture. **Qualif.:** Applicants must be graduate students with an interest in greenhouse crops. **Criteria:** Recipients are selected based on academic performance.

Duration: Annual. **To Apply:** Applicants must complete the online application form; must submit a letter of recommendation and endorsement by a faculty member. **Deadline:** May 1.

900 ■ Earl Dedman Memorial Scholarship (Undergraduate/Scholarship)

Purpose: To further the advancement of education and science in the floriculture and environmental horticulture field by funding research and studies and financing scholarships and other educational activities for individuals interested in the field. **Focus:** Horticulture. **Qualif.:** Applicants must be junior or senior students maintaining a minimum 3.0 GPA who are interested in becoming greenhouse growers. **Criteria:** Recipients are selected based on academic performance.

Duration: Annual. **To Apply:** Applicants must complete the online application form; must submit two letters of recommendation and transcript of records. **Deadline:** May 1.

901 ■ Markham-Colegrave International Scholarships (Undergraduate/Scholarship)

Purpose: To further the advancement of education and science in the floriculture and environmental horticulture field by funding research and studies and financing scholarships and other educational activities for individuals interested in the field. **Focus:** Horticulture. **Qualif.:** Applicants must be sophomore or higher undergraduate or graduate students pursuing a career in horticulture marketing through international travel, either from U.S. or Europe. **Criteria:** Recipients are selected based on academic performance.

Funds Avail.: $4,500. **Duration:** Biennial; awarded in even numbered years. **To Apply:** Applicants must send a completed online application form; must submit two letters of recommendation and transcript of records; must provide relevant documentation of travel plans. **Deadline:** May 1.

902 ■ National Greenhouse Manufacturers Association (NGMA) Scholarships (Undergraduate/Scholarship)

Purpose: To further the advancement of education and science in the floriculture and environmental horticulture field by funding research and studies and financing scholarships and other educational activities for individuals interested in the field. **Focus:** Horticulture. **Qualif.:** Applicants must be junior, senior or graduate students pursuing a career in horticulture and bio-engineering or the equivalent at a four-year college. Applicants must maintain a 3.0 GPA. **Criteria:** Recipients are selected based on academic performance.

Duration: Annual. **To Apply:** Applicants must complete the online application form; must submit a letter of recommendation and endorsement by a faculty member. **Deadline:** May 1.

903 ■ Mike and Flo Novovesky Scholarship (Undergraduate/Scholarship)

Purpose: To support young married students who are working to put themselves through college. **Focus:** Horticulture.

Awards are arranged alphabetically below their administering organizations

Qualif.: Applicants must be second year to graduating married students with a GPA of 2.5 or higher. The scholarship may also go to an undergraduate with financial need and family obligations, depending on the availability of married applicants. **Criteria:** Recipients are selected based on academic performance.

Duration: Annual. **To Apply:** Applicants must complete the online application form; must submit a letter of recommendation and endorsement by a faculty member. **Deadline:** May 1.

904 ■ Lawrence "Bud" Ohlman Memorial Scholarships (Undergraduate/Scholarship)

Purpose: To further the advancement of education and science in the floriculture and environmental horticulture field by funding research and studies and financing scholarships and other educational activities for individuals interested in the field. **Focus:** Horticulture. **Qualif.:** Applicants must be in their third to final year in college, with a career goal to become a bedding plant grower for an established business. **Criteria:** Recipients are selected based on academic performance.

Duration: Annual. **To Apply:** Applicants must complete the online application form; must submit a letter of recommendation and endorsement by a faculty member. **Deadline:** May 1.

905 ■ James K. Rathmell Jr. Memorial Scholarship (Undergraduate, Graduate/Scholarship)

Purpose: To further the advancement of education and science in the floriculture and environmental horticulture field by funding research and studies and financing scholarships and other educational activities for individuals interested in the field. **Focus:** Horticulture. **Qualif.:** Applicants must be in their third to final year of undergraduate studies or be graduate students; must plan to work or study outside of the United States. **Criteria:** Recipients are selected based on academic performance.

Duration: Annual. **To Apply:** Applicants must complete the online application form; must submit a letter of recommendation and endorsement by a faculty member. **Deadline:** May 1.

906 ■ John L. Tomasovic, Sr. Scholarship (Undergraduate/Scholarship)

Purpose: To further the advancement of education and science in the floriculture and environmental horticulture field by funding research and studies and financing scholarships and other educational activities for individuals interested in the field. **Focus:** Horticulture. **Qualif.:** Applicants must be in their second to final year in college and pursuing a career in a horticulture-related field; must have 3.0-3.5 GPA. **Criteria:** Recipients are selected based on financial need and GPA.

Duration: Annual. **To Apply:** Applicants must complete the online application form; must submit a letter of recommendation and endorsement by a faculty member. **Deadline:** May 1.

907 ■ Edward Tuinier Memorial Scholarship (Undergraduate/Scholarship)

Purpose: To further the advancement of education and science in the floriculture and environmental horticulture field by funding research and studies and financing scholarships and other educational activities for individuals interested in the field. **Focus:** Horticulture. **Qualif.:** Applicants must be

in their second to final year in a floriculture program at Michigan State University. **Criteria:** Recipients are selected based on academic performance.

Duration: Annual. **To Apply:** Applicants must complete the online application form; must submit a letter of recommendation and endorsement by a faculty member. **Deadline:** May 1.

908 ■ Jacob and Rita Van Namen Marketing Scholarship (Undergraduate/Scholarship)

Purpose: To further the advancement of education and science in the floriculture and environmental horticulture field by funding research and studies and financing scholarships and other educational activities for individuals interested in the field. **Focus:** Horticulture. **Qualif.:** Applicants must be in their second to final year in college; must be interested in agribusiness marketing and distribution of floral products. **Criteria:** Recipients are selected based on academic performance.

Duration: Annual. **To Apply:** Applicants must complete the online application form; must submit a letter of recommendation and endorsement by a faculty member. **Deadline:** May 1. **Remarks:** Established in 1997. **Contact:** c/o The Jacob and Rita Van Namen Marketing Scholarship, 1601 Duke Street, Alexandria, VA 22314.

909 ■ Vocational (Bettinger, Holden & Perry) scholarship (Undergraduate, Vocational/Occupational/Scholarship)

Purpose: To further the advancement of education and science in the floriculture and environmental horticulture field by funding research and studies and financing scholarships and other educational activities for individuals interested in the field. **Focus:** Horticulture. **Qualif.:** Applicants must be vocational students in one or two-year programs with the intent of becoming growers or greenhouse managers. **Criteria:** Recipients are selected based on academic performance.

Duration: Annual. **To Apply:** Applicants must complete the online application form; must submit a letter of recommendation and endorsement by a faculty member. **Deadline:** May 1.

910 ■ Violet Wondergem Health Science Scholarship (Undergraduate, Graduate/Scholarship)

Purpose: To further the advancement of education and science in the floriculture and environmental horticulture field by funding research and studies and financing scholarships and other educational activities for individuals interested in the field. **Focus:** Horticulture. **Qualif.:** Applicants to have a career goal within the seed industry and be junior or senior level undergraduates or graduate students. **Criteria:** Recipients are selected based on academic performance.

Duration: Annual. **To Apply:** Applicants must complete the online application form; must submit a letter of recommendation and endorsement by a faculty member. **Deadline:** May 1.

911 ■ American Foreign Service Association (AFSA)

2101 E St. NW
Washington, DC 20037
Ph: (202)338-4045
Fax: (202)338-6820
E-mail: member@afsa.org

Awards are arranged alphabetically below their administering organizations

URL: www.afsa.org
Social Media: www.facebook.com/afsapage
www.linkedin.com/company/american-foreign-service
  -association
twitter.com/afsatweets
www.youtube.com/afsatube

912 ■ American Foreign Service Association Scholarship Fund Program *(Undergraduate/ Scholarship)*

Purpose: To provide financial assistance to students for their college education. **Focus:** General studies/Field of study not specified. **Qualif.:** Applicant must be a current high school senior or college freshman, sophomore or junior; Be a dependent child of a Foreign Service employee who is an American Foreign Service Association (AFSA) member. The AFSA member must be or have been an employee (active duty, retired, deceased, and/or separated) with a foreign affairs agency as defined by the Foreign Service Act of 1980 (Department of State, USAID, USIA, BBG, FCS, FAS or APHIS); Have a minimum GPA of 2.75. **Criteria:** Applicants will be evaluated on the basis of academic record and financial need.

Funds Avail.: Amount varies. **Duration:** Annual. **To Apply:** Application pieces can be sent, emailed or faxed except where noted. **Deadline:** March 15. **Contact:** Please Email: scholar2@afsa.org.

913 ■ American Foundation for the Blind (AFB)
1401 S Clark St., Ste. 730
Arlington, VA 22202
Ph: (212)502-7600
URL: www.afb.org
Social Media: www.facebook.com/
  americanfoundationfortheblind
pinterest.com/afb1921
twitter.com/afb1921
youtube.com/afb1921

914 ■ Delta Gamma Foundation Florence Margaret Harvey Memorial Scholarship *(Graduate, Undergraduate/Scholarship)*

Purpose: To provide scholarships in the field of rehabilitation and education to persons who are blind or visually impaired. **Focus:** Education; Rehabilitation, Physical/Psychological. **Qualif.:** Applicant must be blind or visually impaired; and an undergraduate or graduate student in the field of rehabilitation or education; must be U.S. citizens or naturalized citizens. **Criteria:** Selection will be based on committee's criteria.

Funds Avail.: $1,000. **Number Awarded:** 1. **To Apply:** Applicants must complete online application; includes official transcripts; two letters of recommendation; proof of legal blindness. **Deadline:** April 15. **Contact:** Aaron Preece, Scholarship Coordinator; Phone: 304-710-3034; Email: apreece@afb.net.

915 ■ Gladys C. Anderson Memorial Scholarship *(Undergraduate/Scholarship)*

Purpose: To provide scholarships in the field of music to persons who are blind or visually impaired. **Focus:** Music, Classical. **Qualif.:** Applicant should be a female undergraduate student studying music; must be U.S. citizens or naturalized citizens. **Criteria:** Selection will be based on committee's criteria.

Funds Avail.: $3,500. **Number Awarded:** 1. **To Apply:** Applicants must complete the online application; includes official transcripts; two letters of recommendation; proof of legal blindness; must submit a music performance in a digital audio format such as MP3, WAV, or OGG. **Deadline:** April 15. **Contact:** Aaron Preece, Scholarship Coordinator; Phone: 304-710-3034; Email: apreece@afb.net.

916 ■ Karen D. Carsel Memorial Scholarship *(Undergraduate/Scholarship)*

Purpose: To provide scholarships in the field of music to persons who are blind or visually impaired. **Focus:** General studies/Field of study not specified. **Qualif.:** Applicant should be a female undergraduate student studying music; must be U.S. citizens or naturalized citizens. **Criteria:** Selection will be based on committee's criteria.

Funds Avail.: $3,500. **Number Awarded:** 1. **To Apply:** Applicants must complete the online application; includes official transcripts; two letters of recommendation; proof of legal blindness; must submit a music performance in a digital audio format such as MP3, WAV, or OGG. **Deadline:** April 15. **Contact:** Aaron Preece, Scholarship Coordinator; Phone: 304-710-3034; Email: apreece@afb.net.

917 ■ Paul and Ellen Ruckes Scholarship *(Graduate, Undergraduate/Scholarship)*

Purpose: To provide scholarships in the field of engineering or in the computer, physical or life sciences to persons who are blind or visually impaired. **Focus:** Computer and information sciences; Engineering; Life sciences; Physical sciences. **Qualif.:** Applicant must be an undergraduate or graduate student in the field of engineering or in a computer, physical or life sciences; must be U.S. citizens or naturalized citizens. **Criteria:** Selection will be based on committee's criteria.

Funds Avail.: $2,000 each. **Number Awarded:** 2. **To Apply:** Applicants must complete online application; includes official transcripts; two letters of recommendation; proof of legal blindness. **Deadline:** April 15. **Contact:** Aaron Preece, Scholarship Coordinator; Phone: 304-710-3034; Email: apreece@afb.net.

918 ■ R.L. Gillette Scholarship *(Undergraduate/Scholarship)*

Purpose: To provide scholarships in the field of music to persons who are blind or visually impaired. **Focus:** Literature; Music. **Qualif.:** Applicant should be a female undergraduate student studying music; must be U.S. citizens or naturalized citizens. **Criteria:** Selection will be based on committee's criteria.

Funds Avail.: $3,500. **Number Awarded:** 1. **To Apply:** Applicants must complete the online application; includes official transcripts; two letters of recommendation; proof of legal blindness; must submit a music performance in a digital audio format such as MP3, WAV, or OGG. **Deadline:** April 15. **Contact:** Aaron Preece, Scholarship Coordinator; Phone: 304-710-3034; Email: apreece@afb.net.

919 ■ Rudolph Dillman Memorial Scholarship *(Graduate, Undergraduate/Scholarship)*

Purpose: To provide scholarships in the field of rehabilitation and education to persons who are blind or visually impaired. **Focus:** Education; Rehabilitation, Physical/Psychological. **Qualif.:** Applicant must be blind or visually impaired; and an undergraduate or graduate student in the field of rehabilitation or education; must be U.S. citizens or

---

Awards are arranged alphabetically below their administering organizations

naturalized citizens. **Criteria:** Selection will be based on committee's criteria.

Funds Avail.: $2,500 each. **Number Awarded:** 4. **To Apply:** Applicants must complete online application; includes official transcripts; two letters of recommendation; proof of legal blindness. **Deadline:** April 15. **Contact:** Aaron Preece, Scholarship Coordinator; Phone: 304-710-3034; Email: apreece@afb.net.

920 ■ Ferdinand Torres Scholarships (Graduate, Undergraduate/Scholarship)

Purpose: To financially support the education of a blind or visually impaired graduate student. **Focus:** General studies/Field of study not specified. **Qualif.:** Applicant must be a blind or visually impaired full-time undergraduate or graduate student. **Criteria:** Strong preference will be given to new immigrants to the United States, and to those residing in the New York City metropolitan area.

Number Awarded: 1. **To Apply:** Applicants must complete the online application. In addition, applicants must submit official transcripts; proof of post-secondary acceptance; two letters of recommendation; proof of U.S. citizenship; proof of legal blindness; evidence of economic need; and proof of residence in the United States (e.g. telephone bill; utility bill). Immigrants must include a description of country of origin and reason for coming to the United States. Supporting documents are to be collected and sent in one envelope to the AFB Scholarship Committee. **Contact:** AFB Information Center; Email: tannis@afb.net.

921 ■ American Foundation for Pharmaceutical Education (AFPE)

6076 Franconia Rd., Ste. C
Alexandria, VA 22310-1758
Ph: (703)875-3095
Fax: (703)875-3098
URL: afpepharm.org
Social Media: www.linkedin.com/in/afpe-foundation
-33542683
twitter.com/AFPEPharmEd

922 ■ AFPE Gateway Research Scholarships (Doctorate/Scholarship)

Purpose: To increase the number of students who undertake a faculty-mentored research program and decide to enroll in graduate programs leading to a Ph.D. in the basic, clinical, or administrative pharmaceutical sciences. **Focus:** Pharmaceutical sciences. **Qualif.:** Scholars must be selected and nominated by a faculty member; must be enrolled in a Pharm.D. program; must have completed at least two years of college; must be enrolled in at least the first year of the professional pharmacy curriculum; must be enrolled in a baccalaureate degree program; have completed at least one year of the degree program; must be enrolled for at least one full academic year after initiation of the award; and must be U.S. citizens. **Criteria:** Selection will be based on recommendation by a faculty member; demonstrated superior academic performance; submitted a proposed research topic that is relevant; provided a comprehensive mentoring plan.

Funds Avail.: $5,000. **To Apply:** Applicants should include official original transcript for current course of study; unofficial transcripts for coursework prior to the current course of study, uploaded to the application (pdf); two recommendations submitted via the online recommendation form.

Deadline: February 20. **Contact:** Sarah Devereaux-Hardimon, Development Associate, AFPE, 6076 Franconia Rd., Ste. C, Alexandria, VA 22310-1758; E-mail: hardimon@afpepharm.org.

923 ■ AFPE Pre-Doctoral Fellowships in Pharmaceutical Sciences (Doctorate/Fellowship)

Purpose: To encourage outstanding pre-doctoral students who have completed at least three semesters of graduate study and have no more than three years remaining to continue their studies and earn a Ph.D. in the pharmaceutical sciences at a U.S. school or college of pharmacy. **Focus:** Pharmaceutical sciences. **Qualif.:** Applicants must have completed at least three semesters of graduate study toward a Ph.D. and have no more than three years remaining to obtain a Ph.D. degree in a graduate program in the pharmaceutical sciences administered by, or affiliated with a U.S. school or college of pharmacy; students enrolled in joint Pharm.D./Ph.D programs are eligible to apply if they have completed the equivalent of three full semesters of graduate credit toward Ph.D., and if the Ph.D. degree will be awarded within three additional years; must be U.S. citizens or permanent residents. **Criteria:** Recipients will be selected by the Board of grant based on completed requirements.

Funds Avail.: $10,000. **To Apply:** All applications must be completed and submitted online. **Deadline:** November 28; January 9. **Contact:** Sarah Devereaux-Hardimon, Development Associate, AFPE, 6076 Franconia Rd., Ste. C, Alexandria, VA 22310-1758; E-mail: hardimon@afpepharm.org.

924 ■ AFPE Pre-Doctoral Fellowships in Pharmaceutical Sciences for Underrepresented Minorities (Doctorate, Graduate/Fellowship)

Purpose: To identify and support those students who have the potential to become leaders in the pharmaceutical profession. **Focus:** Pharmaceutical sciences. **Qualif.:** Applicants must be U.S. citizens or permanent residents; full-time students enrolled in a graduate Ph.D. program in pharmaceutical science administered by or officially affiliated with a U.S. College of Pharmacy accredited by ACPE; at least 3 semesters of study completed in the current Ph.D. program; may be students enrolled in a joint Pharm.D./Ph.D. who have completed the equivalent of 3 full semesters of graduate credit toward the Ph.D. and will be awarded the Ph.D. degree within the next 3 years. **Criteria:** Recipients are selected based on academic achievement as decided by the Board of Grant based on the completed requirements.

Contact: Sarah Devereaux-Hardimon, Development Associate, AFPE, 6076 Franconia Rd., Ste. C, Alexandria, VA 22310-1758; E-mail: hardimon@afpepharm.org.

925 ■ American Foundation for Suicide Prevention (AFSP)

199 Water St. 11th Floor
New York, NY 10038
Ph: (212)363-3500
Fax: (212)363-6237
E-mail: info@afsp.org
URL: afsp.org
Social Media: www.facebook.com/afspnational
www.instagram.com/afspnational
www.linkedin.com/company/american-foundation-for
-suicide-prevention

Awards are arranged alphabetically below their administering organizations

twitter.com/afspnational
www.youtube.com/user/afspnational

926 ■ AFSP Distinguished Investigator Grants
(Postgraduate/Grant)

Purpose: To support the work of investigators from all disciplines that contribute to the understanding of suicide and suicide prevention. **Focus:** Suicide. **Qualif.:** Applicants must be investigators from all academic disciplines, and both basic science and applied research projects will be considered, providing the study has an essential focus on suicide prevention; must be at the level of associate professor or higher with an established record of research and publication on suicide. **Criteria:** Selection will be based on the research proposals; the qualifications, experience and productivity of the applicant, innovation, the facilities available to the applicants for the purpose of the study and availability of a sufficient number of patients or subjects.

Funds Avail.: Up to $125,000. **Duration:** Two Years. **To Apply:** Applicants may apply and fill out the application form online; the application must include the following sections: cover sheet; principal investigator insurance form; abstract; certification for protection of human subjects; budget; budget justification; biographical information; project description; project timeline; references; and recommendation of mentor; completed grant applications must be submitted electronically. **Contact:** Email: grantsmanager@afsp.org.

927 ■ AFSP Pilot Innovation Grants *(Postgraduate/Grant)*

Purpose: To support the work of investigators from all disciplines that contribute to the understanding of suicide and suicide prevention. **Focus:** Suicide. **Qualif.:** Applicants at any level with research that will provide seed funding for new projects that have the potential to lead to larger investigations. **Criteria:** Selection will be based on the research proposals; the qualifications, experience and productivity of the applicant, innovation, the facilities available to the applicants for the purpose of the study and availability of a sufficient number of patients or subjects.

Funds Avail.: Up to $30,000. **Duration:** Two years. **To Apply:** Applicants may apply and fill out the application form online; the application must include the following sections: cover sheet; principal investigator insurance form; abstract; certification for protection of human subjects; budget; budget justification; biographical information; project description; project timeline; references; and recommendation of mentor; completed grant applications must be submitted electronically. **Contact:** Email: grantsmanager@afsp.org.

928 ■ AFSP Postdoctoral Research Fellowships Innovation Grants *(Postgraduate/Fellowship)*

Purpose: To support the work of investigators from all disciplines that contribute to the understanding of suicide and suicide prevention. **Focus:** Suicide. **Qualif.:** Applicants must have received a Ph.D., M.D., or other doctoral degree within the preceding six years and have had no more than three years of fellowship support. **Criteria:** Selection will be based on the research proposals; the qualifications, experience and productivity of the applicant, innovation, the facilities available to the applicants for the purpose of the study and availability of a sufficient number of patients or subjects.

Funds Avail.: Up to $112,000. **Duration:** Two years. **To Apply:** Applicants may apply and fill out the application

form online; the application must include the following sections: cover sheet; principal investigator insurance form; abstract; certification for protection of human subjects; budget; budget justification; biographical information; project description; project timeline; references; and recommendation of mentor; completed grant applications must be submitted electronically. **Contact:** Email: grantsmanager@afsp.org.

929 ■ AFSP Standard Research Innovation Grants
(Postgraduate/Grant)

Purpose: To support the work of investigators from all disciplines that contribute to the understanding of suicide and suicide prevention. **Focus:** Suicide. **Qualif.:** Applicants must be investigators from all academic disciplines, and both basic science and applied research projects will be considered, providing the study has an essential focus on suicide prevention. **Criteria:** Selection will be based on the research proposals; the qualifications, experience and productivity of the applicant, innovation, the facilities available to the applicants for the purpose of the study and availability of a sufficient number of patients or subjects.

Funds Avail.: up to $300,000. **Duration:** Two years. **To Apply:** Applicants may apply and fill out the application form online; the application must include the following sections: cover sheet; principal investigator insurance form; abstract; certification for protection of human subjects; budget; budget justification; biographical information; project description; project timeline; references; and recommendation of mentor; completed grant applications must be submitted electronically. **Contact:** Email: grantsmanager@afsp.org.

930 ■ AFSP Young Investigator Innovation Grants
(Postgraduate/Grant)

Purpose: To support the work of investigators from all disciplines that contribute to the understanding of suicide and suicide prevention. **Focus:** Suicide. **Qualif.:** Applicants must be at the level of assistant professor or lower. **Criteria:** Selection will be based on the research proposals; the qualifications, experience and productivity of the applicant, innovation, the facilities available to the applicants for the purpose of the study and availability of a sufficient number of patients or subjects.

Funds Avail.: Up to $90,000. **Duration:** Two years. **To Apply:** Applicants may apply and fill out the application form online; the application must include the following sections: cover sheet; principal investigator insurance form; abstract; certification for protection of human subjects; budget; budget justification; biographical information; project description; project timeline; references; and recommendation of mentor; completed grant applications must be submitted electronically. **Contact:** Email: grantsmanager@afsp.org.

931 ■ American Foundry Society (AFS)
1695 N Penny Ln.
Schaumburg, IL 60173
Ph: (847)824-0181
Fax: (847)824-7848
Free: 800-537-4237
E-mail: afs@afsinc.net
URL: www.afsinc.org
Social Media: www.facebook.com/americanfoundrysociety
www.instagram.com/americanfoundrysociety
www.linkedin.com/company/american-foundry-society

Awards are arranged alphabetically below their administering organizations

twitter.com/AmerFoundrySoc

932 ■ H.H. Harris Foundation Scholarship *(Professional development, Undergraduate/Scholarship, Monetary)*

Purpose: To provide educational aid to students and professionals in the metallurgical and casting of metals field. **Focus:** Metallurgy. **Qualif.:** Applicants must be students or professionals pursuing a career in the field of metallurgy or any related fields and must be U.S. citizens. **Criteria:** Recipients will be selected based on submitted application.

Funds Avail.: $1,000. **Duration:** Annual. **To Apply:** Applicants must fill out the application form and are required to submit two letters of reference and must submit a signed copy of application; applicants must be U. S. citizens; must use the current application. included in this pdf. old forms will not be accepted. **Deadline:** May 31. **Contact:** Charles L. Michod, Jr., Trustee, 333 W Wacker Dr., Ste. 2000, Chicago, IL, 60606; Email: cmichod@komdr.com.

933 ■ American Galvanizers Association (AGA)

6881 S Holy Cir., Ste. 108
Centennial, CO 80112
Ph: (720)554-0900
Fax: (720)554-0909
E-mail: aga@galvanizeit.org
URL: galvanizeit.org
Social Media: www.facebook.com/galvanizeit
www.linkedin.com/company/american-galvanizers
 -association
twitter.com/agagalvanizeit
www.youtube.com/user/AGAGalvanizeIt

934 ■ Galvanize the Future: A Richard L. Brooks Memorial Scholarship *(Undergraduate, Graduate/Scholarship)*

Purpose: To assist future specifiers with the rising cost of a college education, and teach these specifiers a little about hot-dip galvanizing. **Focus:** Architecture; Engineering, Civil; Engineering, Materials. **Qualif.:** Applicants must be full- or part-time, undergraduate or graduate students of any age enrolled at an accredited 4-year college/university only in North America during the school year; qualifying majors include architecture, civil engineering, structural engineering, construction management, material science, or other related field. **Criteria:** Selection will be based on relevance, accuracy, conciseness and ingenuity.

Funds Avail.: $2,500 (1st place); $1,500 (2nd place); $1,000 (3rd place). **Duration:** Annual. **Number Awarded:** 2. **To Apply:** Application can be submitted online; must also submit their respective essays (1000-2000 words). **Deadline:** March 31.

935 ■ American Gastroenterological Association (AGA)

4930 Del Ray Ave.
Bethesda, MD 20814
Ph: (301)654-2055
Fax: (301)654-5920
E-mail: member@gastro.org
URL: www.gastro.org
Social Media: www.facebook.com/AmerGastroAssn

www.linkedin.com/company/amergastroassn
twitter.com/AmerGastroAssn
www.youtube.com/user/AmerGastroAssn

936 ■ AGA-Elsevier Pilot Research Award *(Professional development/Award)*

Purpose: To support pilot research projects in gastroenterology or hepatology related areas. **Focus:** Medical research. **Qualif.:** Candidates must hold an MD, PhD or equivalent degree and a full-time faculty position at an accredited North American institution; research must be conducted at a North American institution; must be AGA members; women and minorities are strongly encouraged to apply. **Criteria:** Applicants will be selected based on the following criteria: significance, investigator, innovation, approach, environment, relevance to AGA's mission and evidence of institutional commitment and the overall likelihood that the project will lead to subsequent, more substantial grants.

Funds Avail.: $30,000. **Duration:** Annual. **Number Awarded:** 2. **To Apply:** Applicants must submit the following requirements: proposed research must focus on research related to gastroenterology or hepatology; allowable Costs and unallowable Costs; early career investigators are required to have a preceptor for this award; investigators who are applying for this award should state explicitly how the research being proposed is different from their previous line of research; must indicate how the investigators will use the pilot data for an extension of their work by applying to another agency; recipient must provide approval from the appropriate institution committee for use of human subjects or animals. If approval is not necessary, the recipient must provide an explanation; scientific and financial progress report must be submitted to AGA upon completion of the project and as needed upon request. **Deadline:** September 2. **Contact:** Email: awards@gastro.org.

937 ■ AGA-R. Robert & Sally Funderburg Research Award in Gastric Cancer *(Postdoctorate/Grant)*

Purpose: To support the research of an established investigator working on novel approaches to gastric cancer. **Focus:** Medical research. **Qualif.:** Candidates must hold a full-time faculty position at an accredited North American institution and must be established as an independent investigator in the field of gastric biology; candidates research must be conducted at a North American institution; women and minority investigators are strongly encouraged to apply;AGA membership is required at the time of application submission.**Criteria:** Applicants will be selected based on the following criteria: significance, investigator, innovation, approach, environment, relevance to AGA's mission and evidence of institutional commitment and relevance to AGA's mission. Preference will be given to novel approaches.

Funds Avail.: $100,000. **Duration:** Biennial. **Number Awarded:** 1. **To Apply:** Applicants must submit the following requirement: proposed research must focus on gastric cancer research, including: fields of gastric mucosal cell biology, regeneration and regulation of cell growth (not as they relate to peptic ulcer disease or repair), inflammation, genetics of gastric carcinoma, oncogenes in gastric epithelial malignancies, epidemiology of gastric cancer, etiology of gastric epithelial malignancies, clinical research in the diagnosis or treatment of gastric carcinoma; letter of recommendation should be provided by the candidate's division chief or department chair and should outline sup-

Awards are arranged alphabetically below their administering organizations

port of the candidate and their research program; allowable costs; unallowable costs; recipient must provide approval from the appropriate institution committee for use of human subjects or animals. If approval is not necessary, the recipient must provide an explanation; scientific and financial progress report must be submitted to AGA upon completion of the project and as needed upon request. **Deadline:** July 29. **Contact:** Email: awards@gastro.org.

938 ■ AGA Research Foundation Fellowship to Faculty Transition Award (Professional development/ Fellowship)

Purpose: To prepare physician scientists for independent basic science research careers in digestive diseases. **Focus:** Medicine. **Qualif.:** Candidates must hold an MD or equivalent degree (e.g. MB, ChB, MBBS, DO); have completed at least one year of research training in their current laboratory prior to the start of the award; have commitment from their home institution for a full time faculty position at the time they apply for the award; be AGA Trainee members and be sponsored by an AGA member at the time of application; and, devote at least 70 percent effort to research related to the gastrointestinal tract or liver. Women and minority investigators are strongly encouraged to apply. **Criteria:** Applicants will be select recipient will be selected based on the following criteria: significance, investigator, innovation, approach, environment, evidence of institutional commitment and relevance to AGA's mission. The applicant's potential for a future independent research career will also be considered.
Funds Avail.: $40,000 per annum. **Duration:** Annual. **Deadline:** July 29.

939 ■ AGA Research Scholar Award (AGA RSA) (Advanced Professional/Grant)

Purpose: To enable young investigators, instructors, research associates or equivalents to develop independent and productive research careers in digestive diseases by ensuring that a major proportion of their time is protected for research. **Focus:** Medical research; Medicine. **Qualif.:** Candidate must be a member of AGA; must hold an MD, PhD or equivalent degree (e.g. MB, ChB, MBBS, DO) and a full-time faculty position at a North American institution; must be an AGA member in good standing; Women, minorities and physician/scientist investigators are strongly encouraged; AGA membership must be maintained throughout the three-year duration of the award. **Criteria:** Applicants will be selected based on the following criteria: significance, investigator, innovation, approach, environment, relevance to AGA's mission and evidence of institutional commitment.
Funds Avail.: $300,000. **Duration:** Annual; up to 3 years. **Number Awarded:** 5. **To Apply:** Applicants must submit the following requirements: must allocate a minimum of 75 percent effort on the proposed project; must provide institutional approval from the appropriate committee for use of human subjects or animals; required to have a sponsor and preceptor for the award; however, one individual may serve in the capacity of both positions; must submit a progress report to AGA annually, as well as a final report 60 days after the end date of the grant period. **Deadline:** November 9. **Contact:** Email: awards@gastro.org.

940 ■ American Gastroenterological Association Research Foundation (AGAF)

c/o American Gastroenterological Association
4930 Del Ray Ave.
Bethesda, MD 20814
Ph: (301)654-2055
URL: foundation.gastro.org

941 ■ AGA Student Research Fellowship Award (Undergraduate, Graduate/Fellowship)

Purpose: To stimulate interest in research careers in digestive diseases by providing monetary support for research projects. **Focus:** Medical research.
Funds Avail.: $2,000-$3,000. **Duration:** Annual. **Number Awarded:** Up to 22.

942 ■ Moti L. & Kamla Rustgi International Travel Awards (Professional development/Grant)

Purpose: To support young investigators for their travel and related expenses to attend Digestive Disease Week (DDW). **Focus:** Medicine. **Qualif.:** Applicants must hold an MD or PhD degree or a non-US equivalent degree; must be 35 years of age or younger at the time of DDW and be fluent in English; must be AGA members; must be the first author of an abstract accepted by the AGA for presentation at DDW and provide evidence of abstract acceptance. **Criteria:** Selection is based on credentials, innovation, approach, evidence of institutional commitment.
Funds Avail.: $750. **Duration:** Annual. **Number Awarded:** 2. **To Apply:** Applications must be submitted through the AGA Grants Management System. **Deadline:** February 24.

943 ■ American Geosciences Institute (AGI)

4220 King St.
Alexandria, VA 22302-1502
Ph: (703)379-2480
Fax: (703)379-7563
E-mail: agi@americangeosciences.org
URL: www.americangeosciences.org
Social Media: www.facebook.com/americangeosciences
www.instagram.com/americangeosciences
www.linkedin.com/company/the-american-geosciences
 -institute
twitter.com/AGI_Updates
www.youtube.com/c/AmericanGeosciences

944 ■ Edward C. Roy, Jr. Award For Excellence in K-8 Earth Science Teaching (Professional development/Award)

Purpose: To recognize one teacher of grades K-8 (or the United Kingdom equivalent) each year for leadership and innovation in Earth science education. **Qualif.:** To be eligible, an applicant must be a full-time U.S. or U.K. classroom teacher who currently provides instruction in Earth science at the K-8 level. **Criteria:** Applicants will be judged on their dedication to and enthusiasm for teaching Earth science, as well as their expertise in crafting and delivering Earth science instruction for their students. Applicants will also be judged on their demonstrated commitment to improving their own Earth science understanding as lifelong learners.
Funds Avail.: $2,500 prize and an additionsl $1,000 to enable the recipient to attend the National Science Teachers Association Annual Conference. **Duration:** Annual. **To Apply:** Applications should include: current curriculum vitae or resume with complete contact information, professional development experience, and awards; letter of recommendation from the teacher's principal on school letterhead; letters of recommendation (with contact information and on

Awards are arranged alphabetically below their administering organizations

letterhead) from two other education professionals who have observed the applicant teaching Earth science; exemplary Earth system science lesson plan that emphasizes an inquiry-based approach (five pages maximum including handouts); essay (500 words maximum) describing the importance of teaching Earth science to students and how the applicant inspires students to learn Earth science concepts. **Deadline:** January 22. **Contact:** Email: awards@americangeosciences.org.

945 ■ American Geriatrics Society (AGS)
40 Fulton St., 18th Fl.
New York, NY 10038
Ph: (212)308-1414
Fax: (212)832-8646
E-mail: info.amger@americangeriatrics.org
URL: www.americangeriatrics.org
Social Media: www.facebook.com/
 AmericanGeriatricsSociety
www.instagram.com/amergeriatrics
www.linkedin.com/company/american-geriatrics-society
twitter.com/amergeriatrics

946 ■ AGS Clinical Student Research Award
(Undergraduate/Award)

Purpose: To support students with their travel expenses in attending the AGS Annual Meeting. **Focus:** Gerontology. **Qualif.:** Applicants must be undergraduate student in medicine, dentistry, nursing, social work, pharmacy, occupational therapy, or physical therapy. **Criteria:** Selection will be based on submission of a high-scoring abstract for presentation.

Funds Avail.: $500. **Duration:** Annual. **To Apply:** Applicants must submit the completed application form providing abstract of research; curriculum vitae and a letter of support from the student's advisor/research mentor. **Deadline:** December 1. **Remarks:** Established in 2007. **Contact:** Email: info.amger@americangeriatrics.org.

947 ■ American Ground Water Trust (AGWT)
50 Pleasant St., Ste. 2
Concord, NH 03301
Ph: (603)228-5444
Fax: (603)228-6557
Free: 800-423-7748
E-mail: trustinfo@agwt.org
URL: www.agwt.org
Social Media: www.facebook.com/American-Ground-Water
 -Trust-169203150484
twitter.com/Water_Education

948 ■ AGWT Baroid Scholarships *(Undergraduate/Scholarship)*

Purpose: To encourage high school students to consider careers specializing in the provision and protection of ground water resources. **Focus:** Water resources. **Qualif.:** Applicants must be high school seniors planning to attend an undergraduate academic program of study at a four-year accredited university or college located in the United States; must have a minimum 3.0 GPA; must be US citizens or legal residents of the United States. **Criteria:** Selection will be based on the submitted materials.

Funds Avail.: $2,000. **Duration:** Annual. **To Apply:** Applicants should include application form online and must submit the following materials: biographical and achievement information, countersigned by a teacher at the applicants' high school; a 500-word essay and a 300-word description of the applicants' high school ground water project and/or practical environmental work experience; two letters of recommendation; documentary evidence of scholastic achievements and references. **Deadline:** June 1.

949 ■ AGWT Thomas M. Stetson Scholarships
(Undergraduate/Scholarship)

Purpose: To encourage high school students to consider careers specializing in the provision and protection of ground water resources. **Focus:** Water resources. **Qualif.:** Applicants must be high school seniors planning to attend a college or university located west of the Mississippi River; must have a minimum 3.0 GPA; must be US citizens or legal residents of the United States. **Criteria:** Selection will be based on the submitted application materials.

Funds Avail.: $2,000. **Duration:** Annual. **To Apply:** Applicants should include application form online and must submit the following materials: biographical and achievement information, countersigned by a teacher at the applicants' high school; a 500-word essay and a 300-word description of the applicants' high school ground water project and/or practical environmental work experience; two letters of recommendation; documentary evidence of scholastic achievements and references. **Deadline:** June 1.

950 ■ Amtrol Scholarship *(High School/Scholarship)*

Purpose: To encourage high school students to consider careers specializing in the provision and protection of ground water resources. **Focus:** Water resources. **Qualif.:** Applicants must be high school seniors intending to pursue a career in a ground water related field; must have a minimum 3.0 GPA in high school; must be freshman year in a full-time academic program of study at a four-year accredited university or college located in the United States; must be U.S. citizens or legal residents of the United States. **Criteria:** Selection will be based on strength of support provided by the applicant's references; review of examination transcripts and GPA scores; written confirmation of acceptance from the college or university.

Funds Avail.: $3,000. **Duration:** Annual. **Number Awarded:** 1. **To Apply:** Applicants must include biographical and achievement information by completing the scholarship application form; a 500-word essay and a 300-word description of the applicant's high school ground water project and or practical environmental work experience must accompany the application; must be accompanied by two letters of recommendation. **Deadline:** June 1. **Remarks:** Established in 1954. **Contact:** URL: agwt.org/content/scholarship-opportunities; Email: trustinfo@agwt.org.

951 ■ American Handel Society (AHS)
c/o Marjorie Pomeroy, Secretary/Treasurer
49 Christopher Hollow Rd.
Sandwich, MA 02563-2227
Ph: (909)607-3568
E-mail: americanhandelsociety@gmail.com
URL: www.americanhandelsociety.org

952 ■ J. Merrill Knapp Research Fellowship
(Graduate/Fellowship)

Purpose: To support fellows for their scholarly projects related to Handel and his world. **Focus:** General studies/

Awards are arranged alphabetically below their administering organizations

Field of study not specified. **Qualif.:** Applicants must be graduate students. **Criteria:** Selection will be based on graduate students, scholars in the early stages of their careers, and independent scholars with no source of institutional support.

Funds Avail.: $2,000. **Duration:** Periodic. **To Apply:** Applicants must submit an outline of the project; a budget showing how and when they plans to use the funds; and a description of other grants applied for or received for the same project; must have two recommendation letters. **Remarks:** Established in 1989. **Contact:** Email; eharris@mit.edu.

953 ■ American Head and Neck Society (AHNS)

11300 W Olympic Blvd., Ste. 600
Los Angeles, CA 90064
Ph: (310)437-0559
Fax: (310)437-0585
E-mail: abstracts@ahns.info
URL: www.ahns.info
Social Media: www.facebook.com/AHNSInfo
twitter.com/AHNSinfo
www.youtube.com/user/HeadAndNeckCancer

954 ■ AHNS/AAO-HNS Young Investigator combined Award *(Other/Award)*

Purpose: To support a collaborative AHNS/AAO-HNSF research project by fostering the development of contemporary basic or clinical research skills focused on neoplastic disease of the head and neck among new full-time academic head and neck surgeons. **Focus:** Medical research. **Qualif.:** Applicants should be an Otolaryngologist—Head and Neck surgeon, who are active members of the AAO-HNS; Be citizens of the U.S; noncitizen nations, or have been lawfully admitted for permanent residency at the time of application; demonstrated potential for excellence in research and teaching and serious commitment to an academic research career in head and neck surgery. **Criteria:** Priority will be given to fellows or junior faculty who have completed residencies or fellowships within four years of the application

Number Awarded: 1. **To Apply:** Applications are in a similar format to the National Institutes of Health. All applications must be completed and submitted online. **Deadline:** January 1. **Contact:** Betty Mulugeta; E-mail: betty@ahns.info.

955 ■ AHNS Pilot Grant *(Other, Doctorate/Grant)*

Purpose: To support basic, translational or clinical researches in head and neck oncology. **Focus:** Medical research. **Qualif.:** Applicants must be medical Students, residents, Ph.D., and Junior Faculty residing in the U.S. or Canada to support basic, translational, or clinical research projects in head and neck oncology. **Criteria:** Priority will be given to projects that are also innovative with promise to develop into new long-range or expanded research programs capable of attracting funding from other sources.

Funds Avail.: $10,000. **Duration:** Annual. **Number Awarded:** 1. **To Apply:** Applications are in a similar format to the National Institutes of Health. All applications must be completed and submitted online. **Deadline:** January 1. **Remarks:** Established in 2000. **Contact:** Email: betty@ahns.info.

956 ■ Ballantyne Resident Research Grant *(Other, Graduate/Grant)*

Purpose: To support basic, translational or clinical researches in head and neck oncology. **Focus:** Medical

research. **Qualif.:** Applicants must be residents in U.S. or Canadian training programs; must be medical students, Ph.D.'s or faculty members at the rank of associate professor or below. **Criteria:** Priority will be given to projects that are also innovative with promise to develop into new long-range or expanded research programs capable of attracting funding from other sources.

Funds Avail.: maximum of $10,000. **Duration:** Annual. **Number Awarded:** 1. **To Apply:** Applications are in a similar format to the National Institutes of Health. All applications must be completed and submitted online. **Deadline:** January 1. **Remarks:** Established in 2007. **Contact:** Email: betty@ahns.info.

957 ■ American Historical Association (AHA)

400 A St. SE
Washington, DC 20003
Ph: (202)544-2422
E-mail: info@historians.org
URL: www.historians.org

958 ■ American Historical Association Fellowships in Aerospace History *(Doctorate/Fellowship)*

Purpose: To provide funding support for a research project related to aerospace history; to encourage engagement in significant and sustained advanced research in all aspects of the history of aerospace from the earliest human interest in flight to the present including cultural and intellectual history, economic history, history of law and public policy, history of science, engineering and management. **Focus:** History. **Qualif.:** Applicants must possess a doctorate degree in history or in a closely related field; may either be enrolled as students having completed all coursework in a doctoral degree-granting program; must be US citizens or permanent residents. **Criteria:** Preference will be given to scholars at early stages in their careers.

Funds Avail.: $21,250. **Duration:** Annual; from 6 to 9 months. **To Apply:** Applicants must complete the application form; applicant CV; proposal of not more than 10 pages; and at least two and not more than four letters of recommendation that address the historical competence of the applicant. **Deadline:** April 1. **Remarks:** Established in 1986. **Contact:** E-mail: awards@historians.org.

959 ■ Albert J. Beveridge Grant for Research in the History of the Western Hemisphere *(Doctorate/Grant)*

Purpose: To support research in the history of the Western hemisphere. **Focus:** History. **Qualif.:** Applicants must be members of AHA; must be doctoral students, non-tenured faculty, and unaffiliated scholars. **Criteria:** Preference will be given to those with specific research needs, such as the completion of a project or completion of a discrete segment thereof.

Funds Avail.: Up to $1,500. **Duration:** Annual. **To Apply:** Applications can be submitted online. CV (up to 5 pages), Statement (up to 750 words), Bibliography (1 page) of the most recent, relevant secondary works on the topic. **Deadline:** February 15. **Remarks:** The grant is named in honor of Albert J. Beveridge. Established in 1994. **Contact:** Prize Administrator; Email: awards@historians.org.

960 ■ J. Franklin Jameson Fellowship in American History *(Doctorate/Fellowship)*

Purpose: To support significant scholarly research in the collections of the Library Congress for one semester for

Awards are arranged alphabetically below their administering organizations

scholars who are at an early stage in their careers in history. **Focus:** History. **Qualif.:** Applicants must hold a Ph.D. degree or equivalent; must have received this degree within the past seven years; should not complete a doctoral dissertation. **Criteria:** Selection will be by a committee of the American Historical Association, in consultation with designated officers of the Library of Congress.

Funds Avail.: $5,000. **Duration:** Annual. **To Apply:** Applicants must submit an original and six copies of complete application including applicant's vita (not more than three to five pages in length); a statement concerning the proposed project and its relationship to the Library of Congress holdings; tentative schedule for residence of the fellowship; and three letters of recommendation; letters should be written by individuals qualified to judge the project and address the applicant's fitness to undertake it. **Deadline:** May 1. **Remarks:** The fellowship is named in honor of J. Franklin Jameson, a founder of the Association, longtime managing editor of the American Historical Review, formerly Chief of the Manuscript Division of the Library of Congress, and the first incumbent of the library's chair of American history. Established in 1977. **Contact:** E-mail: awards@historians.org.

961 ■ Michael Kraus Research Grants *(Doctorate/Grant)*

Purpose: To support student's travel to a library or archive; microfilming, photography, or photocopying; borrowing or access fees; and similar research expenses. **Focus:** History. **Qualif.:** Applicants must be PhD candidates and junior scholars; must be members of AHA. **Criteria:** Preference will be given to advanced doctoral students, non-tenured faculty, and unaffiliated scholars, and to those with specific research needs, such as the completion of a project or a discrete segment thereof.

Funds Avail.: Up to $800. **Duration:** Annual. **To Apply:** Applications can be submitted online. **Deadline:** February 15. **Remarks:** Established in 1994. **Contact:** Prize Administrator; E-mail: awards@historians.org.

962 ■ Littleton-Griswold Research Grant *(Doctorate/Grant)*

Purpose: To support research in U.S. legal history and in the general field of law and society. **Focus:** History. **Qualif.:** Applicants must be PhD candidates and junior scholars; must be members of AHA. **Criteria:** Preference will be given to those with specific research needs, such as the completion of a project or completion of a discrete segment thereof.

Funds Avail.: Up to $1,500. **Duration:** Annual. **To Apply:** Applications can be submitted online. **Deadline:** February 15. **Remarks:** Established in 1994. **Contact:** Prize Administrator; E-mail: awards@historians.org.

963 ■ Bernadotte E. Schmitt Grant *(Doctorate/Grant)*

Purpose: To support research in the history of Europe, Africa, and Asia. **Focus:** History. **Qualif.:** Applicants must be PhD and junior scholars; must be members of AHA. **Criteria:** Preference will be given to those with specific research needs, such as the completion of a project or completion of a discrete segment thereof.

Funds Avail.: up to $1,500. **Duration:** Annual. **To Apply:** Applications can be submitted online. **Deadline:** February 15. **Remarks:** The grant honors Bernadotte E. Schmitt, President of the Association. Established in 1996. **Contact:** Prize Administrator; E-mail: awards@historians.org.

964 ■ American Historical Print Collectors Society (AHPCS)
94 Marine St.
Farmingdale, NY 11735
URL: ahpcs.org
Social Media: www.facebook.com/
  AmericanHistoricalPrintCollectorsSociety
www.instagram.com/historicalprint
twitter.com/HistoricalPrint

965 ■ American Historical Print Collectors Society Fellowship *(Doctorate/Fellowship)*

Purpose: To support research using prints. **Focus:** United States studies. **Criteria:** Recipients are selected in the spring by a committee of scholars, previous winners, and AAS curators.

Funds Avail.: $1,850 per month. **Duration:** Annual; one to two months during the period june 1, 2019 to may 31, 2020. **To Apply:** Applicants must fill out the online application form; must provide current cv; description of proposed research project (no longer than two double-spaced pages); one-page bibliography; two letters of recommendation; letters should be submitted electronically. **Deadline:** January 15. **Contact:** Nan Wolverton, Phone: 508-471-2199; Email: nwolverton@mwa.org.

966 ■ American Horticultural Therapy Association (AHTA)
2150 N 107th St., Ste. 205
Seattle, WA 98133
Ph: (206)209-5296
E-mail: info@ahta.org
URL: www.ahta.org
Social Media: www.linkedin.com/groups/1200697
www.pinterest.com/AmHortTherapy
twitter.com/AmHortTherapy
www.youtube.com/user/AmHortTherapyAssoc/feed

967 ■ Ann Lane Mavromatis Scholarship *(Undergraduate/Scholarship)*

Purpose: To acknowledge and support a student member of AHTA in recognition of academic achievement and promoting the growth of professionalism in the field of horticultural therapy. **Focus:** Horticulture. **Qualif.:** Applicants must be a student member of AHTA in recognition of academic achievement and to promote the growth of professionalism in the field of horticultural therapy. **Criteria:** Selection will be based on the committee's criteria.

Funds Avail.: $500. **Duration:** Annual. **To Apply:** Applicants must complete all the required sections of the application. **Contact:** Complete and submit to: AHTA, 2150 N 107th St., Ste. 205, Seattle, WA, 98133; Phone: 888-294-8527; Fax: 206-367-8777; Email: info@ahta.org.

968 ■ American Hotel & Lodging Educational Foundation (AHLEF)
1250 I St. NW, Ste. 1100
Washington, DC 20005-3931
Ph: (202)289-3180
Fax: (202)289-3199
E-mail: ahleffoundation@ahla.com
URL: www.ahlafoundation.org

Awards are arranged alphabetically below their administering organizations

Social Media: www.facebook.com/AHLAfoundation
www.instagram.com/ahlafoundation
www.linkedin.com/company/american-hotel-&-lodging
  -educational-foundation
twitter.com/AHLAFoundation

969 ■ AH&LEF American Express Scholarship
(Undergraduate/Scholarship)

Purpose: To provide educational assistance to current lodging employees and their dependents. **Focus:** Hotel, institutional, and restaurant management. **Qualif.:** Applicants must be enrolled full-time or part-time; must be working a minimum of 20 hours per week at an AH & LA member hotel and with at least 12 months hotel experience.

Funds Avail.: Baccalaureate Majors - $2,000 full-time enrollment; or $1,000 part-time; Associate Majors - $1,000 full-time enrollment; or $500 part-time. **Duration:** Annual. **To Apply:** Applicants must complete all the required sections of the application. **Remarks:** Established in 1994.

970 ■ American Express Professional Development Scholarship *(Other/Scholarship)*

Purpose: To support individuals in advancing their career by growing their industry knowledge or skill set. **Focus:** Hotel, institutional, and restaurant management. **Qualif.:** Applicants must be working a minimum of 35 hours per week at an AH&LA member hotel and have at least 12 months hotel experience. **Criteria:** Applicants are selected based on professional, community and extracurricular activities; industry-related work experience; and personal attributes including career goals and their response to questions.

Funds Avail.: No specific amount. **To Apply:** Applicants must submit an application form and attach the appropriate EI distance learning enrollment form or professional certification form. **Deadline:** January 1; April 1; July 1; October 1.

971 ■ Ecolab Scholarship *(Undergraduate/ Scholarship)*

Purpose: To provide financial support to students who are enrolled in a U.S. baccalaureate or associate hospitality degree-granting program. **Focus:** Education. **Qualif.:** Applicants must be enrolled in at least 12 credit hours for both the upcoming fall and spring semesters; an undergraduate hospitality management major at a U.S. college or university. **Criteria:** Selection will be based on the committee's criteria.

Funds Avail.: $1,000 - $2,000. **Duration:** Annual. **To Apply:** Applicants must complete sections 1-8 of the AHLEF scholarship application. **Deadline:** May 1. **Remarks:** Established in 1996.

972 ■ The Hyatt Hotels Fund For Minority Lodging Management Students *(Undergraduate/Scholarship)*

Purpose: To provide educational support to minority students in a hotel management program. **Focus:** Hotel, institutional, and restaurant management. **Qualif.:** Applicants must be enrolled in at least 12 credit hours for the upcoming Fall and Spring semesters, or just the Fall semester if graduating this December; at least sophomores in a four-year program at the time of application; minority descent: African-Americans, Hispanic, American Indians, Alaskan Natives, Asian or Pacific Islanders; U.S. citizens or permanent U.S. residents.

Funds Avail.: $3,000 and a plaque. **Duration:** Annual. **To Apply:** Applicants must complete all the required sections of the application. **Deadline:** May 1. **Remarks:** Established in 1988.

973 ■ The Arthur J. Packard Memorial Scholarship
(Undergraduate/Scholarship)

Purpose: To provide educational assistance to lodging management students. **Focus:** Hotel, institutional, and restaurant management. **Qualif.:** Applicants must be enrolled full-time for the upcoming Fall and Spring semesters majoring in Hospitality Management; have a minimum GPA of 3.5 or higher; and must be U.S. residents; at least 12 credit hours for upcoming fall and spring semester, or just the fall semester if graduating this December.

Funds Avail.: First-place winner $5,000; Second-place $3,000; Third-place $2,000. **Duration:** Annual. **To Apply:** Applicants must complete all the required sections of the application. **Deadline:** May 1.

974 ■ PepsiCo Foundation Scholarships
(Undergraduate/Scholarship)

Purpose: To provide financial support to those students who are pursuing hospitality-related degree programs. **Focus:** Hotel, institutional, and restaurant management. **Qualif.:** Applicants must be an incoming freshman for the upcoming fall semester, which is defined as a student who has never been enrolled in a college or university; an undergraduate hospitality management major at a U.S. college or university; enrolled in at least 12 credit hours for the upcoming fall and spring semesters; a minimum overall GPA of 2.0; must be U.S. citizens or permanent U.S. residents. **Criteria:** Recipients are selected based on academic performance, hospitality work experience, financial need, extracurricular/professional attributes and honors, as well as personal attributes as defined in their career goal statement.

Funds Avail.: Baccalaureate Majors: $4,000; Associate Majors: $2,000. **To Apply:** Preference will be given to high school graduates of the Hospitality & Tourism Management Program (HTMP) or Lodging Management Program (LMP); applicants must complete sections 1-8 of the AHLEF Scholarship Application.

975 ■ Rama Scholarships for the American Dream
(Graduate, Undergraduate/Scholarship)

Purpose: To provide educational assistance for lodging management students. **Focus:** Hotel, institutional, and restaurant management. **Qualif.:** Applicants must be enrolled in at least nine credit hours for the upcoming Fall and Spring semesters or just the Fall semester if graduating in December; must be undergraduate or graduate hospitality management majors; must have a minimum 2.5 GPA; and must be U.S. citizens or permanent U.S. residents. **Criteria:** Applicants who are students of Asian-Indian descent and other minority groups, as well as JHM employees and their dependents will be given preference.

Funds Avail.: $1,000-$3,000. **Duration:** Annual. **To Apply:** Applicants must complete all the required sections of the application. **Deadline:** June 30. **Remarks:** Established by JHM Hotels, Inc. Established in 1998.

976 ■ Steve Hymans Extended Stay Scholarship Program *(Undergraduate/Scholarship)*

Purpose: To support students to achieve their educational goals. **Focus:** Hotel, institutional, and restaurant manage-

---

Awards are arranged alphabetically below their administering organizations

ment. **Qualif.:** Applicants must be enrolled full-time or part-time; have a minimum 3.0 GPA; be U.S. citizens or permanent U.S. residents; and have at least some experience either working or interning (paid or unpaid) at a lodging property.

Funds Avail.: $500 - $6,000 depending upon enrollment and recommended amount from school. **Duration:** Annual. **To Apply:** All Nominees must complete all sections of the AHLEF Scholarship Application. **Deadline:** May 1.

977 ■ American Indian College Fund
8333 Greenwood Blvd.
Denver, CO 80221
Ph: (303)426-8900
Fax: (303)426-1200
Free: 800-776-3863
E-mail: info@collegefund.org
URL: www.collegefund.org
Social Media: www.facebook.com/collegefund
www.instagram.com/instacollegefund
twitter.com/collegefund
www.youtube.com/playlist?list=PLLDcTqiKCHeYOpaS6V6
  -MYgz12N4q6UwP

978 ■ Citi Foundation Scholarship Program
(Undergraduate/Scholarship)

Purpose: To provide scholarship to Native students attending the following tribal colleges and universities in South Dakota. **Focus:** General studies/Field of study not specified. **Qualif.:** Applicants must be enrolled full-time at an eligible tribal college. **Criteria:** Preference will be given to those students who meet the criteria.

Funds Avail.: $50,000. **To Apply:** Applicants must complete the application process online.

979 ■ Coca-Cola First Generation Scholarships
(Undergraduate/Scholarship)

Purpose: To provide financial assistance for students who are in need. **Focus:** General studies/Field of study not specified. **Qualif.:** Applicants must have scholarship is renewable throughout students' tribal college careers if they maintain a 3.0 grade point average and are active in campus and community life. **Criteria:** Preference will be given to those students who meet the criteria.

Funds Avail.: $5,000. **To Apply:** Applicants must complete the application process online. **Contact:** Dina Horwedel, Phone: 303-430-5350, Email: dhorwedel@collegefund.org.

980 ■ Full Circle Scholarship *(Graduate, Undergraduate/Scholarship)*

Purpose: To provide a framework for undergraduate and graduate students attending accredited public and non-profit private colleges across the United States. **Focus:** Health education. **Qualif.:** Applicants must be undergraduate or graduate students attending accredited public and non-profit private colleges across the United States; US citizen or Canadian eligible to attend college in the U.S. under provisions of the Jay Treaty; must be American Indian or Alaska Native descent students attending tribal colleges and universities; must be in full-time enrollment; registered as an enrolled member of a federal or state recognized tribe, or a descendant of at least one grandparent or parent who is an enrolled tribal member. Alaska Natives may use Native Corporation membership; at least a 2.0 cumulative GPA.

To Apply: Applicants must complete the online application form and must submit the following requirements: Profile, Application, Documents; upload a digital photo that's at least 1.5 MB in size; Submit your Certificate of Indian Blood (CIB) or other proof of tribal enrollment; transcripts. **Deadline:** May 31. **Contact:** Email: scholarships@collegefund.org; Phone: 800-776-3863.

981 ■ General Mills Foundation Scholarships
(Undergraduate/Scholarship)

Purpose: To provide need-based scholarships for outstanding American Indian students. **Focus:** General studies/Field of study not specified. **Qualif.:** Applicants must be enrolled full-time at an eligible Minnesota or New Mexico tribal college. **Criteria:** Preference will be given to those who meet the criteria.

Funds Avail.: No specific amount. **To Apply:** Applicants must complete the application process online.

982 ■ Morgan Stanley Tribal Scholars Program
(Undergraduate/Scholarship)

Purpose: To provide financial support to those students who are in need. **Focus:** Business. **Qualif.:** Applicants must must be enrolled full-time at an eligible tribal college; must be American Indian with proof of enrollment; and must have demonstrated exceptional academic achievement. **Criteria:** Preference will be given to those students who meet the criteria.

To Apply: Applicants must complete the application process online.

983 ■ Nissan North America, Inc. Scholarships
(Undergraduate/Scholarship)

Purpose: To award scholarships to outstanding American Indian students who are currently enrolled in tribal colleges. **Focus:** General studies/Field of study not specified. **Qualif.:** Applicants must have at least a 2.5 grade point average; must be enrolled full-time at an eligible tribal college; and must have demonstrated exceptional academic achievement. **Criteria:** Preference will be given to students who meet the criteria.

To Apply: Applicants must complete the application process online. **Contact:** Debra Reed at 800-776-3863 or dreed@collegefund.org.

984 ■ Sovereign Nations Scholarships
(Undergraduate/Scholarship)

Purpose: To provide financial support to those students who are in need. **Focus:** General studies/Field of study not specified. **Qualif.:** Applicants must have demonstrated exceptional academic achievement by maintaining a 3.0 or higher G.P.A.; must commit to working for their tribe or an Indian organization upon completion of their degree; must be enrolled full-time at an eligible tribal college; and must be American Indian or Alaskan Native with proof of enrollment. **Criteria:** Preference will be given to those students who meet the criteria.

To Apply: Applicants must complete the application process online.

985 ■ Vine Deloria Jr. Memorial Scholarship *(Graduate, Professional development/Scholarship)*

Purpose: To provide financial support for outstanding American Indian students who are pursuing a graduate degree. **Focus:** General studies/Field of study not specified. **Qualif.:** Applicants must be pursuing graduate or

Awards are arranged alphabetically below their administering organizations

professional degree; must have a 2.0 GPA; must be U.S. citizens or Canadians eligible to attend college in the U.S. under provisions of the Jay Treaty; must be registered as an enrolled member of a federal or state recognized tribe, or a descendant of at least one grandparent or parent who is an enrolled tribal member.

Funds Avail.: $1,000. **Duration:** One year.

986 ■ Woksape Oyate: "Wisdom of the People" Distinguished Scholars Awards (Undergraduate/ Grant)

Purpose: To provide financial support to students who are in need. **Focus:** General studies/Field of study not specified. **Qualif.:** Applicants must be enrolled full-time at an eligible tribal college.

Duration: Five year.

987 ■ American Indian Education Fund (AIEF)
2401 Eglin St.
Rapid City, SD 57703
Free: 800-881-8694
E-mail: info@aiefprogram.org
URL: www.nativepartnership.org/site/PageServer?pagename=aief_home
Social Media: www.facebook.com/PWNA4hope
twitter.com/PWNA4hope

988 ■ Indian Health Service Professionals Program (Undergraduate/Scholarship)

Purpose: To provide opportunity to those Indian students who want learn and succeed in their educational career. **Focus:** Health sciences. **Qualif.:** Applicants must be enrolled members of state or federally recognized tribes; must be undergraduate or graduate students who are majoring in any health-related pre-professional program. **Criteria:** Selection will be based on the committee's criteria.

Funds Avail.: No specific amount. **Duration:** Annual. **Number Awarded:** Approximately 500. **To Apply:** Applicants must: complete AIEF Scholarship Application; provide documentation of tribal enrollment for themselves or their parents; provide transcripts with ACT and GPA scores; attach an essay that outlines the following information: introduction, academics, career plans, service to the Native American community, leadership/community service, financial needs and unique circumstances.

989 ■ International Order of the King's Daughters and Sons North American Indian Scholarship Program (Undergraduate/Scholarship)

Purpose: To provide opportunity to those Indian students who want learn and succeed in their educational career. **Focus:** General studies/Field of study not specified. **Qualif.:** Applicants must be: Native Americans who have (or whose parents have) a reservation number; undergraduates of any major. **Criteria:** Selection will be based on the committee's criteria.

Funds Avail.: $650. **Duration:** Annual. **Number Awarded:** Approximately 50. **To Apply:** Applicants must: complete AIEF Scholarship Application; provide documentation of tribal enrollment for themselves or their parents; provide transcripts with ACT and GPA scores; attach an essay that outlines the following information: introduction, academics, career plans, service to the Native American community, leadership/community service, financial needs and unique circumstances.

990 ■ Native American Education Grants (Graduate, Undergraduate/Grant)

Purpose: To provide opportunity to those Indian students who want learn and succeed in their educational career. **Focus:** General studies/Field of study not specified. **Qualif.:** Applicants must be: enrolled members of federally recognized tribes; undergraduate or graduate students of any major. **Criteria:** Selection will be based on the committee's criteria.

Funds Avail.: $3,000. **To Apply:** Applicants must: complete AIEF Scholarship Application; provide documentation of tribal enrollment for themselves or their parents; provide transcripts with ACT and GPA scores; attach an essay that outlines the following information: introduction, academics, career plans, service to the Native American community, leadership/community service, financial needs and unique circumstances.

991 ■ U.S. BIA Indian Higher Education Grants (Undergraduate/Grant)

Purpose: To provide opportunity to those Indian students who want learn and succeed in their educational career. **Focus:** General studies/Field of study not specified. **Qualif.:** Applicants must be: Native American undergraduate students of any major; enrolled in a federally recognized tribe. **Criteria:** Awards will be given based on financial need.

Funds Avail.: $300-$900. **To Apply:** Applicants must: complete AIEF Scholarship Application; provide documentation of tribal enrollment for themselves or their parents; provide transcripts with ACT and GPA scores; attach an essay that outlines the following information: introduction, academics, career plans, service to the Native American community, leadership/community service, financial needs and unique circumstances; may contact their tribe's education office for more information.

992 ■ American Indian Graduate Center (AIGC)
3701 San Mateo Blvd. NE, No. 200
Albuquerque, NM 87110
Ph: (505)881-4584
Fax: (505)884-0427
Free: 800-628-1920
URL: www.aigcs.org
Social Media: www.facebook.com/AmericanIndianGraduateCenter
instagram.com/aigc_scholarships
www.linkedin.com/company/american-indian-graduate-center
twitter.com/TeamAIGC
youtube.com/user/AIGCS/featured

993 ■ Accenture American Indian Scholarship Fund (Graduate, Undergraduate/Scholarship)

Purpose: To provide financial assistance to students who are seeking the next level of education. **Focus:** Business; Engineering; Law; Medicine; Technology. **Qualif.:** Applicants must be American Indians who are incoming freshmen with a cumulative GPA of 3.25 or greater on a 4.0 scale at the end of the seventh semester of high school or graduates/professionals who have attained a cumulative GPA of 3.25 or greater on a 4.0 scale, as measured by undergraduate transcripts; must be enrolled members of a U.S. federally-recognized American Indian tribe or Alaska Native group; must be seeking a degree and career in fields

Awards are arranged alphabetically below their administering organizations

of study including technology, engineering, medicine, law and business. **Criteria:** Applicants are evaluated on the basis of demonstrated character; personal merit evident through leadership in school, civic and extracurricular activities, academic achievement and motivation to serve and succeed; and commitment to the American Indian Community, locally and/or nationally.

Funds Avail.: No specific amount. **Duration:** Annual. **To Apply:** Applicants must submit completed application form; copy of certificate of Indian Blood (CIB); unofficial undergraduate and/or graduate academic transcripts; essay describing their character, personal merit and commitment to community and heritage. **Deadline:** June 1. **Remarks:** Established in 2006. **Contact:** AIGC: 3701 San Mateo Blvd. NE, Ste. 200, Albuquerque, NM, 87110; Fax: 505-884-0427; Email: fellowships@aigcs.org.

994 ■ AIGC Fellowships - Graduate *(Graduate/Fellowship)*

Purpose: To provide financial assistance to Native Americans and Alaska Native graduates or professional degree-seeking students in furthering their education. **Focus:** General studies/Field of study not specified. **Qualif.:** Applicants must be pursuing a post-baccalaureate graduate or professional degree as full-time students at an accredited institution in the U.S.; must be enrolled members of a federally-recognized American Indian or Alaska Native group or provide documentation of descendency; must possess one-fourth federally-recognized Indian blood. **Criteria:** Recipients are selected based on financial need.

Funds Avail.: $1,000 - $5,000. **Duration:** Annual. **To Apply:** Applicants must submit all the required application information including the Tribal Eligibility Certificate and Financial Need Form. **Deadline:** June 1. **Contact:** AIGC Fellowships - Graduate, 3701 San Mateo NE Ste. 200, Albuquerque NM 87110, Phone: 505-881-4584, Toll-free: 800-628-1920, Fax: 505-884-0427, Email: web@aigcs.org.

995 ■ Loan for Service for Graduates *(Graduate/Loan)*

Purpose: To provide financial assistance to students who are seeking graduate and professional degree. **Focus:** General studies/Field of study not specified. **Qualif.:** Applicant must be an enrolled member of a United States federally-recognized American Indian tribe or Alaska Native group or possess one-fourth federally-recognized Indian blood; must have 3.0 GPA; and must be pursuing a graduate or a professional degree as a full-time student at an accredited institution in the United States. **Criteria:** Applicants are evaluated based on financial need.

Funds Avail.: No specific amount. **To Apply:** Applicants must submit all the required application information. **Deadline:** June 1. **Contact:** AIGC: 3701 San Mateo Blvd. NE, Ste. 200, Albuquerque, NM, 87110; Fax: 505-884-0427; Email: fellowships@aigcs.org.

996 ■ Wells Fargo American Indian Scholarship Program *(Undergraduate/Scholarship)*

Purpose: To provide financial assistance to American Indian graduates in furthering their education. **Focus:** Accounting; Banking; Finance; Gaming industry; Information science and technology; Management. **Qualif.:** Applicants must be enrolled members of a United States federally-recognized American Indian tribe or Alaska Native group; must be pursuing career and degree fields relating to banking, resort management, gaming operations, management and administration, including accounting, finance, informa-

tion technology and human resources; must be full-time graduate students at a U.S. accredited college or university; and must have a cumulative average GPA of 3.0 on a 4.0 scale at the time of application. **Criteria:** Applicants are evaluated based on financial need.

Funds Avail.: No specific amount. **To Apply:** Applicants must submit all the required application information. **Deadline:** June 1. **Contact:** AIGC: 3701 San Mateo Blvd. NE, Ste. 200, Albuquerque, NM, 87110; Fax: 505-884-0427; Email: fellowships@aigcs.org.

997 ■ American Indian Library Association (AILA)

c/o Heather Devine-Hardy, Membership Coordinator
PO Box 41296
San Jose, CA 95160
E-mail: ailawebsite@gmail.com
URL: ailanet.org
Social Media: www.facebook.com/ailanet

998 ■ Virginia Mathews Memorial Scholarship *(Graduate/Scholarship)*

Purpose: To encourage the entry of qualified American Indians and Alaskan Natives into the library profession. **Focus:** Library and archival sciences. **Qualif.:** Applicants must be enrolled members of a federally recognized tribe as evidenced by the CIBC card of the applicants, or be tribal members with official documentation; able to demonstrate sustained involvement in the American Indian community and sustained commitment to American Indian concerns and initiatives; admitted to a graduate program in library and/or information sciences accredited by the American Library Association; and, enrolled for a minimum of 6 hours each semester. **Criteria:** Preference will be given to applicants who are employed in a tribal library or who are currently employed in a library serving American Indian populations. Financial need will be considered.

Funds Avail.: $4,000. **Duration:** Annual. **To Apply:** Applicants must submit a completed scholarship application together with two letters of recommendation; evidence of enrollment in a federally recognized tribe or Alaskan village or a similar official document; a personal statement (maximum of 500 words) addressing past and future sustained involvement in American Indian communities and a resume. Submit complete application package to American Indian Library Association Treasurer, Holly Tomren. **Deadline:** June 1. **Contact:** Holly Tomren-Chair, AILA Scholarship Review Board; Drexel Univ. Libraries, 3300 Market St., Philadelphia, PA 19104.

999 ■ American Indian Science and Engineering Society (AISES)

4263 Montgomery Blvd NE, Ste. 200
Albuquerque, NM 87109
Ph: (505)765-1052
Fax: (505)765-5608
E-mail: info@aises.org
URL: www.aises.org
Social Media: www.facebook.com/aises.org
www.instagram.com/aises_hq
twitter.com/AISES
www.youtube.com/user/aiseshq

1000 ■ Aises A. T. Anderson Memorial Scholarship *(Graduate, Undergraduate/Scholarship)*

Purpose: To financially assist ethnic students in furthering their education. **Focus:** Engineering; Mathematics and

Awards are arranged alphabetically below their administering organizations

mathematical sciences; Medicine; Natural resources; Science; Technology. **Qualif.:** Applicant must be a member of an American Indian tribe, an Alaska Native, or Native Hawaiian otherwise considered to be an American Indian by the tribe with which affiliation is claimed; must have a 3.0 or higher cumulative GPA; must be a full-time undergraduate or graduate student at an accredited four-year college/university; must be degree in Mathematics, Medical Sciences, Physical Science, Technology, Science, Engineering, or Natural Resources. **Criteria:** Selection will be reviewed by AISES reviewers who score each application based upon factors such as academic performance (GPA and academic record), the student's personal essay (demonstrates character, commitment, goals), strength of recommendation letters, and other activities the student has undertaken including jobs, volunteer efforts, internships, extra-curricular activities etc.

Funds Avail.: $1,000 for undergraduates; $2,000 for graduate students. **To Apply:** Applicants must complete an application form; must submit the most recent transcript and proof of tribal enrollment; two letters of recommendation; online resume. On a separate sheet, applicants must provide a personal statement with no more than 500 words. **Deadline:** March 31. **Contact:** American Indian Science and Engineering Society, at the above address.

1001 ■ AISES Intel Growing The Legacy Scholarship Program (Graduate, Undergraduate/Scholarship)

Purpose: To financially assist ethnic students in furthering their education. **Focus:** Computer and information sciences; Engineering, Chemical; Engineering, Computer; Engineering, Electrical; Engineering, Materials. **Qualif.:** Applicant must be a member of an American Indian tribe, an Alaska Native, or Native Hawaiian otherwise considered to be an American Indian by the tribe with which affiliation is claimed; must have a 3.0 or higher cumulative GPA; must be a full-time undergraduate or graduate student at an accredited four-year college/university; must be degree in Computer Science, Computer Engineering, and Electrical Engineering. Chemical Engineering and Material Science will also be considered; must be current AISES members at the time of application. **Criteria:** Selection will be reviewed by AISES reviewers who score each application based upon factors such as academic performance (GPA and academic record), the student's personal essay (demonstrates character, commitment, goals), strength of recommendation letters, and other activities the student has undertaken including jobs, volunteer efforts, internships, extra-curricular activities etc.

Funds Avail.: $5,000 for undergraduates; $10,000 for graduate students. **To Apply:** Applicants must complete an application form; must submit the most recent transcript and proof of tribal enrollment; two letters of recommendation; online resume. On a separate sheet, applicants must provide a personal statement with no more than 500 words. **Deadline:** May 15. **Contact:** AISES Scholarship Department, 6899 Winchester Circle, STE 102A, Boulder, CO 80301, Phone: 720-552-6123, Email: scholarships@aises.org.

1002 ■ AISES Oracle Academy Scholarship (Graduate, Undergraduate/Scholarship)

Purpose: To encourage and support the students pursuing degrees in Computer Science. **Focus:** Computer and information sciences; Engineering, Computer. **Qualif.:** Applicants must be currently pursuing a degree in Computer Engineering or Computer Science; must be full-time undergraduate student at an accredited college/university

or graduate student; must have a 3.5 (on a 4.0 scale) or higher cumulative GPA; must be current AISES members. **Criteria:** Selection will be based upon factors such as academic performance (GPA and academic record), the student's personal essay (demonstrates character, commitment, goals), strength of recommendation letters, and other activities the student has undertaken including jobs, volunteer efforts, internships, extra-curricular activities etc.

Funds Avail.: $2,500 (for undergraduate students); $10,000 (for graduate students). **To Apply:** Applicants must complete the OASIS general application and also include the following: resume; two letters of recommendation; essays. **Deadline:** March 31. **Contact:** Brianna Hall, Email: bhall@aises.org, Phone: 720-552-6123, Ext. 119.

1003 ■ AISES Summer Internships (Undergraduate, Graduate/Internship)

Purpose: To promote an advanced study to the graduate level and assist students in developing professional networks. **Focus:** General studies/Field of study not specified. **Qualif.:** Applicants must current AISES memberships at the time of application; must be an enrolled member or descendant of an enrolled member of a federally or state recognized American Indian Tribe, Alaska Native Village, or Native Hawai'ian or descendant of a Native Hawai'ian; must be a full-time undergraduate or graduate student at either an accredited four-year college/university, or a full-time student at a two-year college enrolled in a program leading to an academic degree. **Criteria:** Recipients will be selected based on submitted materials.

Funds Avail.: No specific amount. **Duration:** program runs in 10 weeks every year.

1004 ■ American Institute of Aeronautics and Astronautics (AIAA)
12700 Sunrise Valley Dr., Ste. 200
Reston, VA 20191-5807
Free: 800-639-2422
E-mail: custserv@aiaa.org
URL: www.aiaa.org
Social Media: www.facebook.com/AIAAfan
www.instagram.com/aiaaerospace
www.linkedin.com/company/aiaa
twitter.com/aiaa

1005 ■ AIAA Foundation Scholarship Program (Graduate, Undergraduate/Scholarship, Award, Monetary)

Purpose: To foster the professional development of those engaged in scientific and engineering activities; improves public understanding of the profession and its contributions; fosters education in engineering and science; promotes communication among engineers and scientists, as well as other professional groups; and stimulates outstanding professional accomplishments. **Focus:** Aeronautics; Astronautics. **Qualif.:** Applicant must have completed at least one academic quarter or semester of full-time college work; have a college GPA of not less than the equivalent of a 3.3 on a 4.0 scale; be enrolled in an accredited college or university; Applicant does not have to be an AIAA student member in good standing to apply, but must become one before receiving a scholarship; Applicant's scholarship plan shall be such as to provide entry into some field of science or engineering encompassed by the technical activities of AIAA; Applicant shall not have, or

Awards are arranged alphabetically below their administering organizations

subsequently receive, any other scholarship/award which, when combined with the AIAA Foundation award covers more than the cost of tuition. Applicants may be students of any nationality, not restricted by the US State Department, in full-time study at any accredited college or university within the United States. **Criteria:** Selection will be based on the committee's criteria.

Funds Avail.: No specific amount. **Duration:** Annual. **To Apply:** Applications must be received on or before the deadline. Students submitting their applications should include the essay (500-1000 words describing career goals); three references; official transcripts; and a research outline (for graduate students) of approved research topic (pdf format, 20 pages only, times new roman 10 pt. font) and also make arrangements to have their official college transcripts sent directly to AIAA. sophomore and junior students who have received one of these scholarship awards and wish to be considered for continuation of this award should arrange to have transcripts of their college academic record, and letters of recommendation from their faculty members and others supporting their continuance in the program sent to AIAA. **Deadline:** January 31.

1006 ■ American Institute of Architects Alaska
1735 New York Ave NW
Washington, DC 20006-5292
Ph: (907)276-2834
Fax: (202)626-7547
E-mail: contact@aiaalaska.org
URL: www.aia.org
Social Media: www.facebook.com/AIANational
www.instagram.com/aianational
www.linkedin.com/company/the-american-institute-of
 -architects-aia
www.pinterest.com/aianational
twitter.com/AIAnational

1007 ■ AIA Alaska College Scholarship Program
(Graduate, Undergraduate/Scholarship)

Purpose: To help Alaska resident students enroll in an accredited architectural program. **Focus:** Landscape architecture and design. **Qualif.:** Applicants must be permanent residents of the State of Alaska and have completed six or more semesters in a program leading to a Bachelor's Degree in Architecture or enrolled in a Master's Program in Architecture. **Criteria:** Selection will be based on overall ability, desire, determination and potential for successfully completing an architecture education and entering into architecture as a profession.

Funds Avail.: Up to $2,000. **Number Awarded:** 3. **To Apply:** Applicants must submit an application packet containing a personal letter stating need, qualifications and desire; in addition, a completed application form, resume and transcript, as well as a letter of recommendation from a faculty member, must be included in the package. **Contact:** AIA Alaska Scholarship Committee, PO Box 244141, Anchorage, Alaska, 99524.

1008 ■ American Institute of Architects - Northeast Illinois (AIA NEI)
1717 N Naper Blvd.
Naperville, IL 60563
Ph: (630)599-7121
E-mail: cgorniak@aianei.org

URL: www.aianei.org
Social Media: twitter.com/AIA_NEI

1009 ■ AIA Northeast Illinois Student Scholarships
(Undergraduate, Graduate/Scholarship)

Purpose: To support students enrolled in an accredited architecture program. **Focus:** Architecture. **Qualif.:** Applicants must be U.S. citizens enrolled at one of the East Central or West Central accredited Architecture schools and have a home residence of record within the AIA/NEI Chapter boundaries (Cook, DuPage, Kane, and Kendall Counties, except that the territory shall not include the area within the city limits of Chicago, nor south of Interstate 55, nor east of the Eden's Expressway).**Criteria:** Selection shall be based on the aforementioned applicants qualifications and compliance with the application details.

Funds Avail.: $3,000 each. **Number Awarded:** 2. **To Apply:** Applicants must submit a completed application form including two letters of recommendation and a self-addressed, stamped postcard. **Deadline:** April 17. **Contact:** AIA Northeast Illinois, v1717 North Naper Blvd., Ste. 102, Naperville, IL, 60563.

1010 ■ Arnold "Les" Larsen, FAIA, Memorial Scholarships *(Graduate/Scholarship)*

Purpose: To support students enrolled in an accredited architecture program. **Focus:** Architecture. **Qualif.:** Applicants must be U.S. citizens and enrolled in the Master's of Architecture program at either the University of Illinois at Chicago or at Urbana-Champaign. **Criteria:** Preference will be given to students who are participants in an AIAS chapter, demonstrated financial need and with a permanent residence within the AIA/NEI Chapter boundaries (DuPage, Kane, Kendall and suburban Cook Counties).

Funds Avail.: $1,000. **Duration:** Annual. **To Apply:** Applicants must submit a completed application form including two letters of recommendation and a self-addressed, stamped postcard. **Deadline:** April 21. **Contact:** AIA Northeast Illinois, v1717 North Naper Blvd., Ste. 102, Naperville, IL, 60563.

1011 ■ American Institute of Bangladesh Studies (AIBS)
B488 Medical Science Ctr.
1300 University Ave.
Madison, WI 53706
Ph: (608)261-1194
E-mail: aibs@southasia.wisc.edu
URL: www.aibs.net
Social Media: www.facebook.com/American-Institute-of
 -Bangladesh-Studies-AIBS-175015869231983

1012 ■ AIBS Junior Fellowships *(Doctorate/ Fellowship)*

Purpose: To support junior researchers with their travel expenses. **Focus:** General studies/Field of study not specified. **Qualif.:** Applicants must be enrolled/employed/affiliated with a US or non-US academic institution; US Citizens (unfortunately, US Permanent Residents are not eligible); must be a individual member of AIBS; must have passed the PhD exams and entered PhD candidacy before assuming the award; must be in the stage of data collection and writing. **Criteria:** Recipients are selected based on submitted applications and supporting materials.

Funds Avail.: $1,150 and allowances per month. **Duration:** Two to twelve months. **To Apply:** Application must

Awards are arranged alphabetically below their administering organizations

include: narrative proposal (10 page maximum); curriculum vitae; three letters of reference; pre-doctoral applications must also submit a transcript and a letter from their dissertation advisor (This letter can be one of the three letters of reference). **Deadline:** March 1. **Contact:** Email: sudiptaroy.aibs@gmail.com.

1013 ■ AIBS Senior Fellowships (Doctorate/Fellowship)

Purpose: To provide funding for a senior research fellowship in Bangladesh. **Focus:** General studies/Field of study not specified. **Qualif.:** Applicants must enrolled/employed/affiliated with a US or non-US academic institution (independent scholars are also welcome to apply); US Citizens (unfortunately, US permanent residents are not eligible); must be an individual member of AIBS; must have a PhD degree; must have a well-developed research agenda relevant to Bangladesh. **Criteria:** Recipients are selected based on submitted applications and supporting materials.

Funds Avail.: $1,400 and allowances per month. **Duration:** Two to twelve months. **To Apply:** Application must include: narrative proposal (10 page maximum); curriculum vitae; three letters of reference; pre-doctoral applications must also submit a transcript and a letter from their dissertation advisor (This letter can be one of the three letters of reference). **Deadline:** March 1. **Contact:** Email: sudiptaroy.aibs@gmail.com.

1014 ■ American Institute of Certified Public Accountants (AICPA)

1211 Avenue of the Americas
New York, NY 10036-8775
Ph: (212)596-6200
Fax: (212)596-6213
E-mail: service@aicpa.org
URL: www.aicpa.org
Social Media: www.facebook.com/AICPA
twitter.com/AICPA
www.youtube.com/user/AICPAMultiMedia

1015 ■ AICPA Accountemps Student Scholarship Award (Graduate/Scholarship)

Purpose: To provide financial assistance to outstanding accounting students who demonstrates potential to become leaders in the CPA profession. **Focus:** Accounting; Business. **Qualif.:** Applicant must be an outstanding accounting student; a full-time undergraduate or graduate-level accounting student; have completed at least 30 semester hours (or equivalent) of college coursework, including at least 6 semester hours (or equivalent) in accounting; have a major and overall GPA of at least 3.0. **Criteria:** Selection task force will pick recipients based on academic achievement, leadership, and future career interests in accounting.

Funds Avail.: $10,000. **Number Awarded:** 4. **To Apply:** Application should be completed at www.thiswaytocpa.com/education/aicpa-legacy-scholarships/. **Deadline:** March 1. **Contact:** scholarship@aicpa.org.

1016 ■ AICPA John L. Carey Scholarship Awards (Graduate/Scholarship)

Purpose: To encourage students to acquire professional accounting careers. **Focus:** Accounting. **Qualif.:** Applicants must be U.S. citizens or permanent residents; must be liberal arts and non-business degree holders who are pursuing both graduate studies in accounting and the CPA

licensure. **Criteria:** Recipients are selected based on academic achievement, leadership and future career interests in accounting.

Funds Avail.: $5,000. **Number Awarded:** 5. **To Apply:** Applicants must visit the website for the online application process. **Deadline:** March 1. **Contact:** Email: scholarships@aicpa.org.

1017 ■ AICPA Minority Scholarship (Undergraduate, Graduate/Scholarship)

Purpose: To assist student members in becoming CPAs. **Focus:** Accounting; Business. **Qualif.:** Applicant must be a U.S. citizen or permanent resident and an ethnic minority with plans to enroll in accounting, business, or a related field at a four-year college or university in the United States; planning to pursue CPA licensure; maintain a 3.0 GPA; enrolled as a full-time undergraduate or graduate student (exceptions may be made for an internship); be an AICPA Student Affiliate member (or have submitted a new member application); and demonstrate some financial need.

Funds Avail.: $5,000 (may vary). **To Apply:** Application should be completed at www.thiswaytocpa.com/aicpa-legacy-scholarships/scholarship-minority-accounting-students/?mm=1. **Deadline:** March 1. **Contact:** Email: scholarships@aicpa.org.

1018 ■ AICPA Two-Year Transfer Scholarship (Four Year College, Undergraduate/Scholarship)

Purpose: To aid members in gaining an accounting education and becoming CPAs. **Focus:** Accounting; Business. **Qualif.:** Applicant must be a U.S. citizen or permanent resident currently enrolled in a two-year college with plans to enroll in accounting, business, or a related field at a four-year college or university in the United States; planning to pursue CPA licensure; maintain a 3.0 GPA; enrolled as a full-time undergraduate or graduate student (exceptions may be made for an internship); be an AICPA Student Affiliate member (or have submitted a new member application); and demonstrate some financial need. **Criteria:** Recipients are selected based on academic achievement, leadership and future career interests in accounting.

Funds Avail.: $5,000. **Number Awarded:** 25. **To Apply:** Applicant should apply online at www.thiswaytocpa.com/education/aicpa-legacy-scholarships/aicpa-foundation-two-year-transfer-scholarship/. **Deadline:** March 1. **Contact:** Email: scholarships@aicpa.org.

1019 ■ American Institute of Chemical Engineers (AICHE)

120 Wall St., Fl. 23
New York, NY 10005-4020
Ph: (646)495-1371
Fax: (203)775-5177
Free: 800-242-4363
E-mail: rubing@janelia.hhmi.org
URL: www.aiche.org
Social Media: www.facebook.com/AIChE
www.instagram.com/chenected
www.linkedin.com/company/american-institute-of-chemical
 -engineers
twitter.com/ChEnected
www.youtube.com/c/AIChEChEnected

1020 ■ AIChE Minority Scholarship Awards for College Students (Undergraduate/Scholarship)

Purpose: To provide educational assistance for underrepresented chemical engineering undergraduate students.

Awards are arranged alphabetically below their administering organizations

Focus: Engineering, Chemical. **Qualif.:** Applicants shall be required to be high school graduates during the current academic year and be members of a minority group that is under-represented in chemical engineering, i.e., African-American, Hispanic, Native American, Alaskan Native, Pacific Islander. **Criteria:** Selection of winners will be based on the following criteria: I. The applicant's academic record, minimum GPA of 3.0/4.0; ii. The applicant's participation in AIChE student chapter, and professional or civic activities as outlined in the chapter advisor's, department chair's, or other faculty member's evaluation in his/her letter of nomination; iii. Applicant's career objectives and plans as outlined in his/her career essay.

Funds Avail.: $1,000 each. **Duration:** Annual. **To Apply:** Applicants must complete and submit online application. **Deadline:** August 12. **Contact:** Contact: felig@aiche.org.

1021 ■ AIChE Minority Scholarship Awards for Incoming College Freshmen *(Undergraduate/ Scholarship)*

Purpose: To provide educational assistance for chemical engineering college freshmen. **Focus:** Engineering, Chemical. **Qualif.:** Applicants shall be required to be high school graduates during the current academic year and be members of a minority group that is under-represented in chemical engineering, i.e., African-American, Hispanic, Native American, Alaskan Native, Pacific Islander; must plan to enroll during the current academic year in a four-year college or university offering a science/engineering degree; students are encouraged to choose classes leading to a degree in chemical engineering; while students admitted for science and engineering degrees are encouraged to apply for this scholarship. **Criteria:** Preference will be given to students admitted into chemical engineering degree programs.

Funds Avail.: $1,000 each. **Duration:** Annual. **Number Awarded:** 15. **To Apply:** Applicants submit the information through the online applications form. **Deadline:** August 12.

1022 ■ Donald F. & Mildred Topp Othmer Scholarship Awards *(Undergraduate/Scholarship)*

Purpose: To provide financial assistance for AIChE national student members for their undergraduate education in chemical engineering. **Focus:** Engineering, Chemical. **Qualif.:** Applicants must be AIChE national student members at the time of the nomination; must have completed approximately 50% of their degree requirement at the start of academic year (i.e. junior standing in chemical engineering in a 4-year program or equivalent for a 5-year co-op program). **Criteria:** Selection will be based on the basis of academic record, participation in AIChE Student Chapter, and other professional activities as outlined by the Student Chapter advisor in nomination letter, support of the nominee by the Student Chapter Advisor, career objectives and plans as outlined in career essay.

Funds Avail.: $1,000 each. **Duration:** Annual. **Number Awarded:** 15. **To Apply:** Applicants submit the completed application form via online along with a statement from the nominee not to exceed 300 words, outlining career plans and objectives in chemical engineering including immediate plans after graduation and long range career objectives; a letter of recommendation from the AIChE student chapter advisor containing verification of nominee's GPA and projected completion date as well as an evaluation of the student's academic performance and participation in AIChE and other professional activities. **Deadline:** June 15.

1023 ■ John J. McKetta Undergraduate Scholarship *(Undergraduate/Scholarship)*

Purpose: To provide financial assistance for chemical engineering undergraduate students planning a career in the chemical engineering process industries. **Focus:** Engineering, Chemical. **Qualif.:** Applicants must be AIChE student members at the time of the nomination; junior or senior of a 4-year program in Chemical Engineering or equivalent for a 5-year co-op program; applicant's academic record, minimum GPA of 3.0/4.0; students attending ABET accredited schools in the U.S, Canada and Mexico are eligible. **Criteria:** Preference will be given for applicant's academic record, minimum GPA of 3.0/4.0; applicant's leadership and participation in either the school's AIChE student chapter or other university-sponsored campus activity outlined in leadership activities essay; applicant's career goals in the chemical engineering process industries as outlined in career essay.

Funds Avail.: $5,000. **Duration:** Annual. **To Apply:** Applicants submit the completed application form via online along with a maximum three page (750-word) essay outlining the applicant's career goals in the Chemical Engineering process industries and minimum of two letters of recommendation (in English); one nomination letter must be from the AIChE student chapter advisor, and the other from either a department faculty or technical work supervisor (internship or REU supervisor) and official copy of student transcript sent (by the school) to AIChE. **Deadline:** June 15.

1024 ■ American Institute for Conservation of Historic & Artistic Works

727 15th St. NW, Ste. 500
Washington, DC 20005
Ph: (202)452-9545
Fax: (202)452-9328
E-mail: info@culturalheritage.org
URL: culturalheritage.org
Social Media: www.facebook.com/aiconservation
www.linkedin.com/company/american-institute-for
 -conservation
twitter.com/conservators
www.youtube.com/user/aiconservation

1025 ■ FAIC Latin American and Caribbean Scholars Program *(Other/Scholarship)*

Purpose: To provide financial support for conservation professionals from Latin America and the Caribbean to participate in the annual meeting. **Focus:** Latin American studies. **Qualif.:** Applicants must be Latin Americans. **Criteria:** Recipients will be selected based on quality of the essay, opportunities to attend international meetings, number of applicants, ability to communicate in English and availability of the financial support.

Funds Avail.: No specific amount. **To Apply:** Applicants should include resume or curriculum vitae (CV), which should include education, current employment, past employment, and conservation tasks performed for each position held; maximum three pages; either verbal (20-30 minute session) or non-verbal (poster), preferably on the topic of the conference (maximum 500 words); abstract for a presentation; commitment to attend all sessions and events in the conference and workshops; visa information; estimated cost of the round-trip economy airfare; statement on how much the applicant could personally contribute.

Awards are arranged alphabetically below their administering organizations

Deadline: September 8. **Contact:** Email: iacs@conservation-us.org.

1026 ■ Foundation of American Institute for Conservation Lecture Grants (Other/Grant)

Purpose: To provide funds for the presentation of public lectures to help advance public awareness of conservation. **Focus:** Latin American studies. **Qualif.:** Applicants should be public lectures. We will review applications and make a recommendation to the FAIC board for final approval. **Criteria:** Recipients are selected based on the ability of the project to advance public awareness of conservation; number of people reached, other project outcomes; speaker's ability to communicate the proposed topic; and feasibility of project.

Funds Avail.: Up to $500. **Duration:** Annual. **To Apply:** Applicants must complete and submit the application form via email and must attach the following materials: letter of commitment from speaker; letter of commitment from site; letter of commitment from lecture coordinator; resume of speaker; brief information about sponsor (brochure or one-page description of organization and previous activities). **Deadline:** February 15; September 15. **Contact:** Email: funding@culturalheritage.org.

1027 ■ American Institute for Economic Research (AIER)

250 Division St.
Great Barrington, MA 01230-1000
Fax: (413)528-0103
Free: 888-528-1216
E-mail: press@aier.org
URL: www.aier.org
Social Media: www.facebook.com/aierdotorg
www.linkedin.com/company/aierdotorg
www.pinterest.com/aierdotorg
twitter.com/aier
www.youtube.com/user/AIERvideo

1028 ■ American Institute for Economic Research Student Summer Fellowship (Graduate, Undergraduate/Fellowship)

Purpose: To train graduating college seniors who plan to enter doctoral programs in economics or an affiliated field, and those enrolled in such programs. **Focus:** Economics; Political science. **Qualif.:** Applicants must be graduating college seniors planning to pursue a PhD in economics or in a related field; or, current graduate students age 21 enrolled in such program for no longer than two years.

To Apply: Applicants must submit a completed application form together with a resume; personal statement; one letter of recommendation from a teacher or guidance counselor. **Remarks:** Established in 1946. **Contact:** American Institute for Economic Research, PO Box 1000, Great Barrington, MA, 01230-1000; Email: internships@aier.org.

1029 ■ American Institute of Iranian Studies (AIIRS)

118 Riverside Dr.
New York, NY 10024
E-mail: aiis@nyc.rr.com
URL: www.simorgh-aiis.org

1030 ■ AIIrS Persian Language Study in Tehran Fellowship (Graduate, Master's, Doctorate/Fellowship)

Purpose: To promote advanced language study in Tehran at the Dehkhoda Institute. **Focus:** Linguistics. **Qualif.:** Ap-

plicants must be US citizens traveling on a US passport; enrolled in a Doctoral or Masters program in the humanities or social sciences; must have an approved research topic that requires the use of Persian; have completed at least one full academic year of Persian language study.

Funds Avail.: No specific amount. **Duration:** Annual. **To Apply:** Applications must include a curriculum vitae and be made in the form of a letter, giving the following information: citizenship; research plans, level of Persian attained and what degree of proficiency is required; academic affiliation and status; names, addresses and email addresses of two referees, including the primary academic advisor. **Deadline:** April 20. **Contact:** E-mail: aiis@nyc.rr.com.

1031 ■ Short-term Senior Fellowships in Iranian Studies (Graduate, Master's, Doctorate/Fellowship)

Purpose: To enable established scholars with research interests in the field of Iranian Studies to acquaint themselves with the range of academic activities and resources in Iran today. **Focus:** Area and ethnic studies. **Qualif.:** Applicants must be US citizens traveling on a US passport. **Criteria:** Preference will be given to tenured faculty members and museum staff with some knowledge of Persian and a record of research in the humanities or the social sciences relating to Iran.

Funds Avail.: No specific amount. **Duration:** Annual; Up to four weeks. **To Apply:** Applications must include a curriculum vitae and be made in the form of a letter, giving the following information: citizenship; research plans; academic affiliation and status (stage of progress towards the doctorate); names, addresses and e-mail addresses of two referees (including the primary academic advisor). **Contact:** E-mail: aiis@nyc.rr.com.

1032 ■ American Institute for Maghrib Studies (AIMS)

Marshall Bldg., Rm. 470
845 N Park Ave.
Tucson, AZ 85721-0158
Ph: (520)626-6498
Fax: (520)621-9257
E-mail: aims@aimsnorthafrica.org
URL: aimsnorthafrica.org

1033 ■ AIMS Long-term Research Grants (Doctorate, Graduate/Grant)

Purpose: To render fund for US scholars interested in conducting research on North Africa in any Maghrib country. **Focus:** General studies/Field of study not specified. **Qualif.:** Applicants must be a U.S. citizen graduate student, independent scholar and faculty in all disciplines currently enrolled in a M.A. or Ph.D. program; and must be a member of AIMS at the time of application. **Criteria:** Recipients will be selected based on submitted application and proposal.

Funds Avail.: Maximum of $15,000. **Duration:** Annual; More than 3 months. **To Apply:** Applicants should include completed grant application cover sheet; proposal or research design of no more than 1, 500 words; proposed itinerary with approximate dates; curriculum vitae, including indication of language proficiency and institutional affiliation; one page summary of the proposed research in either French or Arabic. **Deadline:** January 31. **Contact:** Email:aimsfellowship@gmail.com.

1034 ■ AIMS Short-term Research Grants (Doctorate, Graduate/Grant)

Purpose: To render fund for US scholars interested in conducting research on North Africa in any Maghrib country.

Awards are arranged alphabetically below their administering organizations

Focus: General studies/Field of study not specified. **Qualif.:** Applicants must be a U.S. citizen graduate student, independent scholar and faculty in all disciplines currently enrolled in a M.A. or Ph.D. program; and must be a member of AIMS at the time of application. **Criteria:** Recipients will be selected based on submitted application and proposal.

Funds Avail.: Up to $6,000. **Duration:** Annual; 1-3 months. **To Apply:** Applicants should include completed grant application cover sheet; proposal or research design of no more than 1, 500 words; proposed itinerary with approximate dates; curriculum vitae, including indication of language proficiency and institutional affiliation; one page summary of the proposed research in either French or Arabic. **Deadline:** January 31. **Contact:** Email:aimsfellowship@gmail.com.

1035 ■ American Institute of Pakistan Studies (AIPS)

B488 Medical Science Ctr.
University of Wisconsin - Madison
1300 University Ave.
Madison, WI 53706
Ph: (608)265-1471
E-mail: aips@pakistanstudies-aips.org
URL: www.pakistanstudies-aips.org
Social Media: www.facebook.com/aipspage

1036 ■ AIPS Long Term Fellowships *(Doctorate, Postdoctorate/Fellowship)*

Purpose: To promote academic study of Pakistan in the US and to encourage scholarly exchange between the US and Pakistan. **Focus:** Pakistani studies. **Qualif.:** Applicants must be US citizens and enrolled/employed full-time in an institution of higher education in the USA; pre-doctoral applicants should have completed all requirements for the PhD except the dissertation. **Criteria:** Selection will be based on the Executive Committee's criteria.

Funds Avail.: $3,000 - $25,000. **To Apply:** Applicants may include a precisely stated research question, a detailed statement indicating the research methodology to be employed, including tentative timelines and list of persons to contact and/or places to visit, and expected results; should describe the intellectual merit of the project and how it relates to the goals of AIPS to promote and disseminate knowledge on Pakistan in the United States and Pakistan; also address the broader impact for your specific field and Pakistan studies as a whole; in the case of pre-doctoral fellowships, its relevance to the applicant's dissertation should be addressed, along with a timeline for the completion of the dissertation or that portion of the project for which funding is being requested from AIPS; should also include a transcripts and a letter from the dissertation advisor. **Deadline:** January 1.

1037 ■ AIPS Post-Doctoral Fellowship *(Postdoctorate/Fellowship)*

Purpose: To promote academic study of Pakistan in the U.S., and encourage scholarly exchange between the U.S. and Pakistan. **Focus:** Pakistani studies. **Qualif.:** Applicant must be an AIPS individual member; Research must be at least two months and less than nine months; If US Citizen, research can be proposed for Pakistan (limited to: Islamabad and Lahore) only, OR Countries other than Pakistan and the US; If Non-US Citizen, Research can be proposed for Pakistan, OR Countries other than Pakistan and the US.

Duration: Annual. **To Apply:** Applicants must submit a complete application package including one letter of recommendation.

1038 ■ AIPS Pre-Doctoral Fellowship *(Doctorate, Postdoctorate/Fellowship)*

Purpose: To promote academic study of Pakistan in the U.S., and encourage scholarly exchange between the U.S. and Pakistan. **Focus:** Pakistani studies. **Qualif.:** Applicants must be U.S. citizens or enrolled/employed full-time in an institution of higher education in the U.S.A. Pre-doctoral applicant should have completed all requirements for the PhD except the dissertation.

Duration: Annual. **To Apply:** Applicants must submit a complete application package which includes: two letters of recommendation (one must be from their respective dissertation advisors); letter of affiliation; and graduate transcripts.

1039 ■ AIPS Short Term Fellowships *(Doctorate, Postdoctorate/Fellowship)*

Purpose: To promote academic study of Pakistan in the US and to encourage scholarly exchange between the US and Pakistan. **Focus:** Pakistani studies. **Qualif.:** Applicants must be US citizens and enrolled/employed full-time in an institution of higher education in the USA. **Criteria:** Selection will be based on the Executive Committee's criteria.

Funds Avail.: $3,000. **To Apply:** Applicants may include a precisely stated research question, a detailed statement indicating the research methodology to be employed, including tentative timelines and list of persons to contact and/or places to visit, and expected results; should describe the intellectual merit of the project and how it relates to the goals of AIPS to promote and disseminate knowledge on Pakistan in the United States and Pakistan; also address the broader impact for your specific field and Pakistan studies as a whole; in the case of pre-doctoral fellowships, its relevance to the applicant's dissertation should be addressed, along with a timeline for the completion of the dissertation or that portion of the project for which funding is being requested from AIPS; should also include a transcripts and a letter from the dissertation advisor. **Deadline:** August 1.

1040 ■ American Institute of Physics (AIP)

1 Physics Ellipse
College Park, MD 20740
Ph: (301)209-3100
E-mail: web_management@aip.org
URL: www.aip.org

1041 ■ AIP State Department Fellowship *(Postdoctorate/Fellowship, Recognition)*

Purpose: To support at least one fellow to provide scientific and technical expertise to the U.S. State Department. **Focus:** Science; Technology. **Qualif.:** Applicant must be a U.S. citizens and eligible to receive a security clearance; membership in one or more of AIP's member societies at the time of application is required; must be a Ph.D. in a technical field of AIP's Member Societies; must interest or experience in S&T aspects of foreign policy; must have excellent scientific credentials; must have outstanding interpersonal and communications skills.

Funds Avail.: $75,000. **Duration:** Annual. **Number Awarded:** 1. **To Apply:** Applicants must submit the follow-

Awards are arranged alphabetically below their administering organizations

ing application materials: letter of intent, providing information regarding their reason for applying, scientific training and professional background, science policy interest and experience, attributes and experiences that would make applicants more effective in this position; a resume limited to two pages, with up to one additional page allowed for a list of key publications; three letters of recommendation to be submitted directly by applicant's references. letters should be from those having direct knowledge of the applicant's' character, professional competence and particular attributes or experience that would enhance the candidate's suitability for this position. applicants must visit the website for the online application and instructions on submitting the application materials. **Deadline:** October 15. **Contact:** Marissa Nielsen at scipolicyfellows@aip.org.

1042 ■ American Institute of Physics Congressional Science Fellowship (Doctorate/Fellowship)

Purpose: To help scientists broaden their experience through direct involvement with the legislative and policy processes. **Focus:** Physics. **Qualif.:** Applicants must be members in one or more of the 10 AIP Member Societies at the time of application; must be U.S. citizens; must have a PhD in physics or closely-related field prior to start of Fellowship term; must have an interest or experience in applying scientific knowledge to the solution of societal problems; must have excellent scientific credentials, outstanding interpersonal and communications skills and sound judgment and maturity in decision-making. **Criteria:** Selection will be based on the committee's criteria.

Funds Avail.: $77,500 per year. **Duration:** Annual. **Number Awarded:** 1. **To Apply:** Applicants must submit the following application materials: letter of intent, providing information regarding their reason for applying, scientific training and professional background, science policy interest and experience, attributes and experiences that would make applicants more effective in this position; a resume limited to two pages, with up to one additional page allowed for a list of key publications; three letters of recommendation to be submitted directly by applicant's references. letters should be from those having direct knowledge of the applicant's' character, professional competence and particular attributes or experience that would enhance the candidate's suitability for this position. applicants must visit the website for the online application and instructions on submitting the application materials. **Deadline:** December 15. **Contact:** Contact: Marissa Nielsen; Email: scipolicyfellows@aip.org.

1043 ■ American Institute of Physics State Department Science Fellowship (Doctorate/Fellowship)

Purpose: To contribute scientific and technical expertise to the department and raise awareness of the value of scientific input. **Focus:** Physics. **Qualif.:** Applicants must be members in one or more of the 10 AIP Member Societies at the time of application; must be U.S. citizens; must have a PhD in physics or closely-related field prior to start of Fellowship term; must be eligible for security clearance; must have an interest or experience in S&T aspects of foreign policy; must have excellent scientific credentials, outstanding interpersonal and communications skills and sound judgment and maturity in decision-making. **Criteria:** Selection will be based on the committee's criteria.

Funds Avail.: $77,500 per year. **Duration:** Annual. **Number Awarded:** 1. **To Apply:** Applicants must submit the following application materials: letter of intent, providing information regarding their reason for applying, scientific training and professional background, science policy inter-

est and experience, attributes and experiences that would make applicants more effective in this position; a resume limited to two pages, with up to one additional page allowed for a list of key publications; three letters of recommendation to be submitted directly by applicant's references. letters should be from those having direct knowledge of the applicant's' character, professional competence and particular attributes or experience that would enhance the candidate's suitability for this position. applicants must visit the website for the online application and instructions on submitting the application materials. **Contact:** Contact: Marissa Nielsen; Email: scipolicyfellows@aip.org.

1044 ■ American Institute of Polish Culture (AIPC)

1440 79th St. Causeway, Ste. 117
Miami, FL 33141
Ph: (305)864-2349
Fax: (305)865-5150
E-mail: info@ampolinstitute.org
URL: www.ampolinstitute.org

1045 ■ Harriet Irsay Scholarship (Graduate, Undergraduate/Scholarship)

Purpose: To provide financial support for American students of Polish descent who wish to continue their education after high school. **Focus:** Communications; Education; History; International affairs and relations; Journalism; Liberal arts; Media arts; Polish studies; Public relations. **Qualif.:** Applicant must be of Polish heritage; an American citizen or permanent resident; full-time graduate or undergraduate student in the field of communication, education, film, music, history, international relation, journalism, liberal arts, polish studies, public relations; or graduate student in business programs with a thesis related to Poland, or graduate student with a thesis with polish subject. **Criteria:** Recipients are selected on the basis of merits.

Funds Avail.: $1,000. **Duration:** Annual. **To Apply:** Applicants must submit a completed application form; school transcripts; resume; essay (200-400 words) about "Why should I receive the scholarship"; an article about Poland (maximum of 700 words); and three signed recommendation letters on a letterhead stationary from teachers or other person knowledgeable about the academic background. a non-refundable $10 processing fee (check or money order) must also be included. **Deadline:** July 30. **Remarks:** Established in 1992. **Contact:** Scholarship Applications: The American Institute of Polish Culture 1440 79th Street Causeway, Suite 117 Miami, FL 33141-3555.

1046 ■ American Institute for Sri Lankan Studies (AISLS)

10 Fonseka Terrace
Colombo 00500, Sri Lanka
Ph: 94 11 2583277
E-mail: vagisha.ails@gmail.com
URL: www.aisls.org
Social Media: www.facebook.com/SriLankanStudies

1047 ■ AISLS Dissertation Planning Grants (Graduate/Grant)

Purpose: To enable graduate students intending to do dissertation research in Sri Lanka to make a pre-dissertation visit to Sri Lanka to investigate the feasibility of their topic, to sharpen their research design or to make other practical arrangements for future research. **Focus:** Humanities; Social sciences. **Qualif.:** Applicants must be graduate students enrolled at a US university; must have completed most of their graduate coursework by the time of application. **Criteria:** Selection will be judged on the quality and on the potential of the dissertation research to strengthen scholarship on Sri Lanka.

Funds Avail.: $525 per week; $2,000 reimbursement for roundtrip. **Duration:** Annual. **To Apply:** Application should contain the following items: a one-page cover sheet, stating the applicant's name, mailing address, email address, home and office telephone, citizenship, major field of study, institutional affiliation, foreign languages, including proficiency, proposed dates of project, project title and a brief project description; a curriculum vitae, not to exceed two pages and may include the name and email address of the applicant's dissertation supervisor; a copy of the applicants' official or unofficial graduate transcript; a project narrative, not to exceed two single-spaced pages; a one-page project bibliography, including a selected list of publications by other scholars or primary sources that have been or will be used in the project; a confidential letter of recommendation from the applicant's dissertation supervisor. This letter should cover the applicant's academic record and be specific about the applicant's progress to date within the graduate program concerned; this letter should be sent directly to John Rogers; the project narrative should cover the following topics: a summary of the proposed dissertation project, or, if the purpose of the planning grant is to define a dissertation project, a summary of the more general questions the applicant hopes to address in their dissertation; a description of what the applicant intends to do during the grant period; the applicant's competence to carry out their proposed project, including language training; pages should have one-inch margins on all sides, 10 points or larger and should be printed on one side only; every page should be numbered and include the name of the applicant in the upper right-hand corner; five copies of the application, including the original, must be collated and fastened with staple in the following order: cover sheet, CV, project description, bibliography; a copy of the application should also be submitted in Word or PDF format by email. **Deadline:** December 1. **Contact:** For Submission: John Rogers, US Director, AISLS: rogersjohnd@aol.com.

1048 ■ AISLS Fellowships Program (Doctorate/ Fellowship)

Purpose: To strengthen ties between US and Sri Lankan scholars. **Focus:** Humanities; Social sciences. **Qualif.:** Applicants must be US citizens; must hold a PhD or equivalent academic degree or show that they will hold such a degree before taking up the fellowship; must plan to spend at least two months in Sri Lanka. **Criteria:** Selection will be based on the submitted proposal.

Funds Avail.: $3,700 per month; $2,000 for travel expenses. **Duration:** Annual. **To Apply:** Applications should contain the following items: A one-page cover sheet, stating the applicants' name, mailing address, email address, home and office telephone, citizenship, major field of study, institutional affiliation, dates of previous research in Sri Lanka, proposed dates of project, project title and a brief description; A curriculum vitae, not to exceed three pages and may include information on such matters as gender and race/ethnicity; A description of the proposed study, not to exceed three single-spaced pages; it should cover the following topics: questions to be addressed by the project,

the approach to be taken, work done to date, work to be accomplished during the fellowship period, the applicants' competence to carry out the project, how the project addresses the criteria of the competition, a statement of other support received or being sought for the project; A one-page project bibliography, including a selected list of publications by other scholars or primary sources that have been or will be used in the project; pages should have one-inch margins on all sides, 10 points or larger and should be printed on one side only; every page should be numbered and include the name of the applicants in the upper right-hand corner. Five copies of the application, including the original, must be collated and fastened with staple in the following order: cover sheet, CV, project description, bibliography; a copy of the application should also be submitted in Word or PDF format by email. **Deadline:** December 1. **Contact:** For Submission: John Rogers, US Director, AISLS: rogersjohnd@aol.com.

1049 ■ AISLS Grants for Language Instruction (Graduate/Grant)

Purpose: To provide funds that can be used to cover expenses for language instruction in Sinhala, Tamil, Pali or Arabic. **Focus:** Foreign languages. **Qualif.:** Applicants must be members of AISLS; must be US residents who hold a PhD or equivalent qualification; must be members of AISLS who are undertaking language instruction to support the needs of graduate study at a US university; must be faculty members at AISLS member institutions; must be graduate students at AISLS member institutions who are undertaking language instruction to support the needs of their program of study. **Criteria:** Selection will be based on the committee's criteria.

Funds Avail.: $400. **To Apply:** Applicants must submit a short curriculum vitae, a one-page statement that includes a description of the proposed instruction and how it supports their long-range research plans, a proposed timetable, and a budget. **Contact:** For Submission: John Rogers, US Director, AISLS: rogersjohnd@aol.com.

1050 ■ American Institute of Steel Construction (AISC)

130 E randolph, 2000 ste.
Chicago, IL 60601
Ph: (312)670-2400
E-mail: solutions@aisc.org
URL: www.aisc.org
Social Media: www.instagram.com/aisc
www.linkedin.com/company-beta/87616
twitter.com/aisc
www.youtube.com/user/AISCSteelTV

1051 ■ AISC/Great Lakes Fabricators and Erectors Association Scholarships (Graduate/Scholarship)

Purpose: To provide financial assistance to those studying civil engineering. **Focus:** Engineering, Architectural. **Qualif.:** Applicants must be U.S. citizens; must be full-time civil or architectural or construction engineering or construction management students who are currently/or will be doing masters-level work at any graduate school in Michigan.

Funds Avail.: $5,000. **Duration:** Annual. **Number Awarded:** 1. **Deadline:** May 1. **Contact:** Maria Mnookin; Phone:312-670-5418; Email: mnookin@aisc.org.

1052 ■ AISC/Ohio Structural Steel Association Scholarships (Undergraduate, Master's/Scholarship)

Purpose: To provide financial assistance to those studying civil engineering. **Focus:** Engineering, Architectural;

Awards are arranged alphabetically below their administering organizations

Engineering, Civil. **Qualif.:** Applicants must be undergraduate juniors, seniors or master's level graduate students; must be civil engineering or architectural engineering programs; must attending universities in OH full-time; must be U.S. citizen.

Funds Avail.: $2,500. **Duration:** Annual. **Number Awarded:** 1. **Deadline:** May 1. **Contact:** Maria Mnookin; Phone: 312-670-5418; E-mail: mnookin@aisc.org.

1053 ■ AISC/Rocky Mountain Steel Construction Association Scholarships *(Undergraduate, Master's/Scholarship)*

Purpose: To provide financial assistance to those studying civil engineering. **Focus:** Engineering, Architectural; Engineering, Civil. **Qualif.:** Applicants must be undergraduate, senior or master's level graduate students; must be civil engineering or architectural engineering programs; attending universities in CO or WY full-time; must be a U.S. citizen.

Funds Avail.: $3,000 each. **Number Awarded:** 2. **Deadline:** May 1. **Contact:** Maria Mnookin; Phone: 312-670-5418; E-mail: mnookin@aisc.org.

1054 ■ AISC/Southern Association of Steel Fabricators Scholarships *(Undergraduate, Master's/Scholarship)*

Purpose: To provide financial assistance to those studying civil engineering. **Focus:** Engineering, Architectural; Engineering, Civil. **Qualif.:** Applicants must be undergraduate juniors, seniors or master's level graduate students; must be civil engineering or architectural engineering programs; must attending universities in AL, FL, GA, KY, LA, MS, TN full-time; must be a U.S. citizen.

Funds Avail.: $2,500 each. **Duration:** Annual. **Number Awarded:** 2. **Deadline:** May 1. **Contact:** Maria Mnookin; Phone: 312-670-5418; E-mail: mnookin@aisc.org.

1055 ■ American Institute of Wine and Food (AIWF)
PO Box 973
Belmont, CA 94002
Ph: (415)508-6790
E-mail: info@aiwf.org
URL: www.aiwf.org

1056 ■ The AIWF Scholarship Program *(Graduate, Undergraduate/Scholarship)*

Purpose: To provide an opportunity to give back to the community, and support individuals interested in the Culinary Arts and/or Oenology. **Focus:** Culinary arts.

Remarks: Established in 1997.

1057 ■ American Jersey Cattle Association (AJCA)
6486 E Main St.
Reynoldsburg, OH 43068-2362
Ph: (614)861-3636
Fax: (614)861-8040
URL: www.usjersey.com
Social Media: www.facebook.com/usjersey

1058 ■ Cedarcrest Farms Scholarships *(Graduate, Undergraduate/Scholarship)*

Purpose: To financially support secondary students entering college freshmen through graduate school. **Focus:** General studies/Field of study not specified. **Qualif.:** Applicant must be a student (undergraduate or graduate) enrolled in a program to earn a degree in large animal veterinary practice, dairy production, dairy manufacturing, or dairy product marketing, who demonstrates through completed coursework and goal statement significant progress toward this intended degree and a clear intention for a career in agriculture. **Criteria:** Selection will be based on academic excellence, activities and accomplishments, and personal goals and commitment in the Jersey dairy business.

Funds Avail.: $1,750. **To Apply:** Applicants must submit complete scholarship application form and a copy of most recent transcript listing all completed coursework; must also provide letters of recommendation. **Deadline:** July 1.

1059 ■ Reuben R. Cowles Youth Educational Award *(Undergraduate, Graduate/Award)*

Purpose: To financially support secondary students entering as college freshmen through graduate school. **Focus:** General studies/Field of study not specified. **Qualif.:** Applicants must be young Jersey owners from Florida, Georgia, North Carolina, South Carolina, Tennessee and Virginia who are at least high school seniors but not older than 36 years of age.

Funds Avail.: No specific amount. **Duration:** Annual. **Number Awarded:** Varies. **Deadline:** July 1.

1060 ■ American Jewish Archives (AJA)
3101 Clifton Ave.
Cincinnati, OH 45220
Ph: (513)221-1875
Fax: (513)221-7812
URL: americanjewisharchives.org

1061 ■ The Loewenstein-Wiener Fellowship *(Professional development, Doctorate, Postdoctorate/Fellowship)*

Purpose: To provide fellows with an opportunity to pursue their own research, interact and exchange ideas with research peers as well as with the faculty and students of HUC-JIR. **Focus:** Jewish studies. **Qualif.:** Applicants must be conducting serious research in some area relating to the history of North American Jewry; must be post-doctoral candidates, Ph.D. candidates who are completing dissertations, and senior or independent scholars. **Criteria:** Selection will be based on the committee's criteria.

Funds Avail.: No specific amount. **To Apply:** Applicants must submit a fellowship application together with a five-page (maximum) research proposal that outlines the scope of their project and lists those collections at the American Jewish Archives that are crucial to their research; should also submit two letters of support, preferably from academic colleagues; for graduate and doctoral students, one of these two letters must be from their dissertation advisor; up-to-date curriculum vitae. **Deadline:** February 19. **Remarks:** Established in 1976. **Contact:** Assistant Director of the Fellowship Program, c/o The Jacob Rader Marcus Center of the American Jewish Archives, 3101 Clifton Ave., Cincinnati, Ohio 45220-2408; Phone: 513-487-3069; Fax: 513-487-3069; Email: dherman@huc.edu.

1062 ■ American Jewish Historical Society (AJHS)
15 W 16th St.
New York, NY 10011

Awards are arranged alphabetically below their administering organizations

Ph: (212)294-6160
Fax: (212)294-6161
E-mail: info@ajhs.org
URL: www.ajhs.org

1063 ■ Ruth B. Fein Prize *(Graduate/Prize)*

Purpose: To encourage interested students to undertake research in the field of American Jewish history. **Focus:** Area and ethnic studies. **Qualif.:** Applicants must be graduate students who will help undertake research at the American Jewish Historical Society. **Criteria:** Recipients will be selected based on qualifications.

Funds Avail.: Up to $1,000.

1064 ■ Pokross/Curhan Family Fund Prize *(Graduate, Undergraduate/Prize)*

Purpose: To assist undergraduate or graduate student pursuing an academic degree at an accredited academic institution; pokrosscurhanprize@ajhs.cjh.org. **Focus:** Area and ethnic studies. **Qualif.:** Applicants must be undergraduates and graduate students pursuing an academic degree at an accredited academic institution to help undertake research using the collections held at American Jewish Historical Society. **Criteria:** Recipients will be selected based on qualifications.

Funds Avail.: $1,000. **To Apply:** Applicants must send a two-page description of plans to produce an essay, thesis, dissertation, documentary, exhibition or other form of public program on an aspect of the American Jewish experience; and must submit a letter of support from an undergraduate or graduate mentor.

1065 ■ American Judges Association (AJA)

300 Newport Ave.
Williamsburg, VA 23185-4147
Ph: (757)259-1841
Fax: (757)259-1520
E-mail: aja@ncsc.dni.us
URL: aja.ncsc.dni.us

1066 ■ American Judges Association Law Student Essay Competition *(Undergraduate/Prize)*

Purpose: To support students who have original and unpublished work. **Focus:** Law. **Qualif.:** Applicants must be full-time law students enrolled in and attending an accredited law school in the United States or Canada. **Criteria:** Papers will be evaluated based on the following category: writing quality and clarity; interest of the topic and content to a broad segment of the judiciary; analysis and reasoning; timeliness, originality and creativity; quality and use of the research; and compliance with these rules.

Funds Avail.: $3,000 (1st Prize); $1,500 (2nd Prize); $1,000 (3rd Prize). **Duration:** Annual. **Number Awarded:** 3. **To Apply:** Applicants must submit a paper (double-spaced, 10-25 pages in length) discussing the topic given by the Committee; the cover page must be submitted in a separate document which includes the title, author's name and contact information. **Contact:** American Judges Association; Email: aja@ncsc.org.

1067 ■ American Kidney Fund (AKF)

11921 Rockville Pke., Ste. 300
Rockville, MD 20852
Free: 800-638-8299

URL: www.kidneyfund.org
Social Media: www.facebook.com/AmericanKidneyFund
www.instagram.com/americankidneyfund
twitter.com/KidneyFund
www.youtube.com/user/kidneyfund

1068 ■ AKF Clinical Scientist in Nephrology Fellowship (CSN) *(Postgraduate/Fellowship)*

Purpose: To improve the quality of care provided to kidney patients and to promote clinical research in nephrology. **Focus:** Medicine. **Qualif.:** Applicant must be a Medical Fellow/Resident Post Doctoral Fellows.

Funds Avail.: Up to $80,000 per year. **Duration:** Annual; 2 years. **Remarks:** Established in 1988. **Contact:** American Kidney Fund, Professional Education Department, 11921 Rockville Pike, Ste. 300, Rockville, MD, 20852; E-mail: education@kidneyfund.org.

1069 ■ The American Legion (AL)

700 N Pennsylvania St.
Indianapolis, IN 46206
Ph: (317)630-1200
Fax: (317)630-1223
Free: 800-433-3318
E-mail: acy@legion.org
URL: www.legion.org
Social Media: www.facebook.com/americanlegionhq
instagram.com/theamericanlegion
www.linkedin.com/company/the-american-legion
pinterest.com/talhq/pins
twitter.com/AmericanLegion
youtube.com/user/americanlegionHQ

1070 ■ The American Legion Legacy Scholarship *(Undergraduate/Scholarship)*

Purpose: To financially support the education of the dependents of active duty United States military and guard and reserve personnel. **Focus:** General studies/Field of study not specified. **Qualif.:** Applicants must be dependents of active duty United States military and guard and reserve personnel who were federalized and killed on active duty on or after September 11, 2001; must be high school seniors or high school graduates studying at an accredited institution of higher education within the United States. **Criteria:** Awards are given based on merit.

Funds Avail.: $20,000. **To Apply:** Applicants must submit a completed scholarship application with a photocopy of the deceased veteran's Certificate of Death (DD 1300).

1071 ■ Eight and Forty Lung and Respiratory Disease Nursing Scholarships *(Other/Scholarship)*

Purpose: To assist registered nurses (RN) with advanced preparation for positions in supervision, administration or teaching. **Focus:** Nursing, Pediatric. **Qualif.:** Applicants must be a registered nurse with a current state license; must have graduated at a regionally accredited school of nursing or will be graduated by the application deadline; must be a registered nurse pursuing nursing education in the field of pediatric lung and respiratory diseases on a part-time or full-time basis; must be accepted by a regionally accredited school of nursing; must be a U.S. citizen; must have leadership qualities; and must have the ability to pursue full-time employment after school. **Criteria:** Awards

Awards are arranged alphabetically below their administering organizations

are given based on personal and academic qualifications with consideration given to past experience and future employment plans as they relate to pediatric lung and respiratory disease nursing.

To Apply: Applicants must submit a completed scholarship application along with a current state Registered Nurse License or registration; three letters of recommendation; transcript of all college credit attempted; and letter of acceptance from an accredited school of nursing. **Contact:** The American Legion Americanism and Children & Youth Division, Attn: Eight and Forty Nursing Scholarship at the above address.

1072 ■ National High School Oratorical Contest Scholarship *(Undergraduate/Scholarship)*

Purpose: To provide financial support for the education of deserving high school students. **Focus:** General studies/Field of study not specified. **Qualif.:** Candidates must be high school students. **Criteria:** Students must win the oratorical contest to acquire the scholarship.

Funds Avail.: First place receives $18,000, second gets $16,000 and third takes $14,000. **Number Awarded:** 3. **Contact:** Email: oratorical@legion.org.

1073 ■ Samsung American Legion Scholarship *(Undergraduate/Scholarship)*

Purpose: To assist the education of a child, grandchild, great grandchild, etc. or a legally adopted child of a U.S. wartime veteran. **Focus:** General studies/Field of study not specified. **Qualif.:** Applicants must be high school juniors who participates in either an American Legion Boys State or American Legion Auxiliary Girls State Program and be direct descendants (children, grandchildren, great grandchildren, etc. or legally adopted children) of a U.S. wartime veteran who served on active duty during one or more of the periods of war officially designated as eligibility dates for membership in The American Legion by the United States government. **Criteria:** Awards are given based on merit.

Funds Avail.: $10,000; 10 runners-up with $5,000 for undergraduate. **Duration:** Annual. **Number Awarded:** Varies.

1074 ■ American Legion Department of Vermont
126 State St.
Montpelier, VT 05601
Ph: (802)223-7131
Fax: (802)223-0318
Free: 800-501-7131
E-mail: alvthq@myfairpoint.net
URL: vtlegion.org

1075 ■ American Legion Department of Vermont Scholarship *(Undergraduate/Scholarship)*

Purpose: To support and give educational opportunity to qualified students. **Focus:** General studies/Field of study not specified. **Qualif.:** Applicants must be seniors attending a Vermont secondary school or a similar school in an adjoining state, whose parents are legal residents of the State of Vermont, or must be seniors residing in an adjacent state whose normal high school attendance area is a Vermont secondary school; must be U.S. citizens.

Funds Avail.: $1,500. **Duration:** Annual. **To Apply:** Applicant must complete the application (available on the

sponsor's website) and submit along with high school transcripts and two letters of recommendation from members of the applicant's high school staff. **Deadline:** April 1.

1076 ■ American Library Association (ALA)
50 E Huron St.
Chicago, IL 60611-2795
Ph: (312)944-6780
Fax: (312)440-9374
Free: 800-545-2433
E-mail: ala@ala.org
URL: www.ala.org
Social Media: www.facebook.com/AmericanLibraryAssociation
twitter.com/ALALibrary
www.youtube.com/americanlibraryassociation

1077 ■ David H. Clift Scholarship *(Graduate/Scholarship, Monetary)*

Purpose: To aid individuals in pursuing an MLS in an ALA-accredited program. **Focus:** Library and archival sciences. **Qualif.:** Applicants must be American or Canadian citizens or permanent residents attending ALA accredited Master's Program and have no more than 12 semester hours towards MLS/MLIS/MIS prior to June 1 of year awarded.

Funds Avail.: $3,000. **Duration:** Annual. **Number Awarded:** 1. **To Apply:** Applicants must complete the online application. In addition, applicants must provide an official academic transcript from institutions. These can be submitted directly from the institution, or mailed in the unopened envelope as received from the degree-granting institutions along with any other materials. Only official (sealed) copies will be accepted. **Deadline:** March 1. **Remarks:** The award was named after David H. Clift, who was a former director of the American Library Association. **Contact:** ALA Library Reference Desk; Phone: 800-545-2433, ext. 2153; Fax: 312-280-3255; Email: library@ala.org.

1078 ■ Christopher Hoy/ERT Scholarship *(Graduate/Scholarship, Monetary)*

Purpose: To aid individuals in pursuing an MLS in an ALA-accredited program. **Focus:** Library and archival sciences. **Criteria:** Applicants will be evaluated based on academic excellence, leadership and evidence of commitment to a career in librarianship. A total of three references must be submitted; Transcripts from institutions where you received your bachelors degree; These can

Funds Avail.: $5,000. **Duration:** Annual. **Number Awarded:** 1. **To Apply:** Applicants are required to apply online. **Deadline:** March 1. **Remarks:** The award was established with donations from Christopher J. Hoy and the Exhibits Round Table (ERT) to honor long time ALA staff member, Christopher J. Hoy, who was director of the ALA Conference Services Office for over 20 years. **Contact:** Kimberly L. Redd, American Library Association, 50 E Huron St., Chicago, IL, 60611-2788; Phone: 312-280-4279; Fax: 312-280-3256; Email: klredd@ala.org.

1079 ■ Marshall Cavendish Scholarships *(Graduate/Scholarship, Monetary)*

Purpose: To aid those who are pursuing a master's degree in library sciences. **Focus:** Library and archival sciences.

Awards are arranged alphabetically below their administering organizations

Qualif.: Applicants must be American or Canadian citizens or permanent residents attending ALA accredited Master's Program and have no more than 12 semester hours towards MLS/MLIS/MIS prior to June 1 of year awarded. **Criteria:** Applicants will be evaluated on the basis of academic excellence, leadership and evidence of commitment to a career in librarianship.

Funds Avail.: $3,000. **Duration:** Annual. **Number Awarded:** 1. **To Apply:** Applicants are required to apply online. They may visit the program website for further application details. **Deadline:** March 1. **Contact:** Kimberly Sanders, ALA Human Resources Development and Recruitment (HRDR) Program Officer, Education and Scholarships, at the above address; Email: scholarships@ala.org.

1080 ■ American Library Association Office for Research and Statistics (ORS)
50 E Huron St.
Chicago, IL 60611-2795
Free: 800-545-2433
E-mail: ors@ala.org
URL: www.ala.org/ala/ors/researchstatistics.htm
Social Media: twitter.com/ala_ors

1081 ■ Carroll Preston Baber Research Grant
(Professional development/Grant)

Purpose: To support one or more librarians or library educators who will conduct innovative research that could lead to an improvement in services to any specified group(s) of people. **Focus:** Library and archival sciences.

Funds Avail.: $3,000. **Duration:** Annual. **Deadline:** February 10. **Remarks:** The award was established by a bequest from Hunce Voelcker. **Contact:** Kelsey Henke, Program Officer, Office of Research and Statistics, American Library Association; E-mail: khenke@ala.org.

1082 ■ American Library Association Young Adult Library Services Association (YALSA)
225 N Michigan Ave., Ste. 1300
Chicago, IL 60601
Ph: (312)280-4390
Fax: (312)280-5276
Free: 800-545-2433
E-mail: yalsa@ala.org
URL: www.ala.org/yalsa
Social Media: www.facebook.com/yalsa
twitter.com/yalsa
www.youtube.com/user/YALSA1957

1083 ■ Baker & Taylor/YALSA Collection Development Grant *(Professional development/Grant)*

Purpose: To enable librarians who work directly with young adults in public or school libraries to attend the ALA Annual Conference for the first time. **Focus:** Library and archival sciences. **Qualif.:** Candidate must be YALSA personal membership (preferably for at least two years); young adults ages 12 to 18. **Criteria:** Selection will be based on degree of need for additional materials for young adults; degree of the current collection's use and the specificity of examples used; soundness of the rationale for the selection of materials; quality of the description of the benefits this grant will bring to young adults; degree to which the applicant's approach to collection development aligns with

the principles in The Future of Library Services for and with Teens: a Call to Action.

Funds Avail.: $1,000 each. **Duration:** Annual. **Number Awarded:** 2. **To Apply:** Applicant must submit online application form; should be models of clarity and completeness. **Deadline:** December 1.

1084 ■ Frances Henne/YALSA Grant *(Undergraduate, Professional development/Grant)*

Purpose: To provide seed money for small scale projects which will encourage research that responds to the YALSA Research Agenda. **Focus:** Library and archival sciences. **Qualif.:** Applicants must be personal members of YALSA, including student members, although the research project may be undertaken by an individual, an institution, or by a group. **Criteria:** Selection will be made by the Frances Henne Jury.

Funds Avail.: $1,000. **Duration:** Annual. **Deadline:** December 1. **Contact:** Phone: 800-545-2433, ext. 4387 or Email: noconnor@ala.org.

1085 ■ American Life Fund (ALF)
3295 River Exchange Dr., No. 350
Norcross, GA 30092
Fax: (855)727-4663
Free: 877-658-1360
E-mail: info@americanlifefund.com
URL: www.americanlifefund.com
Social Media: www.facebook.com/AmericanLifeFund
twitter.com/ALifeFund

1086 ■ The American Life Fund Scholarship
(Undergraduate, Graduate/Scholarship)

Purpose: To give back to the community and support those looking to further their education. **Focus:** General studies/Field of study not specified. **Qualif.:** Applicant must be currently enrolled in an undergraduate or graduate program and have a GPA of 3.0 or higher.

Funds Avail.: $1,000. **To Apply:** Applicant must write a short essay on how they embody leadership in their everyday lives. Application form, essay, along with proof of enrollment and GPA needs to be submitted online. **Contact:** www.americanlifefund.com/scholarship/.

1087 ■ American Livebearer Association (ALA)
c/o Matt Anderson, Treasurer
2339 Country Club Dr.
Mason City, IA 50401
URL: www.livebearers.org
Social Media: www.facebook.com/AmericanLivebearerAssociation

1088 ■ Vern Parish Award *(Graduate, Postgraduate, Doctorate/Scholarship)*

Purpose: To recognize outstanding student research in the area of livebearers. **Focus:** Cooley's anemia; Fisheries sciences/management. **Qualif.:** Applicants must be agencies or college-student researchers working with live bearing fishes and not help to subsidize. Students enrolled in M.S. and Ph.D. **Criteria:** Selection will be based on the significance; approach; student background; sponsor and environment.

Funds Avail.: $1,000. **Duration:** Annual. **Number Awarded:** 1. **To Apply:** Applicants must submit the require-

Awards are arranged alphabetically below their administering organizations

ments such as project title; letter of nomination from the faculty sponsor; students' curriculum vitae; research statement. **Deadline:** March 16. **Remarks:** The award was established in memory of Vern Parish, one of ALA's early stalwart members and a great friend and benefactor to many aquarists during his lifetime. Established in 1997. **Contact:** Completed application should be submitted to: Earl Blewett, PhD, Biochemistry & Microbiology, Oklahoma State University - Center for Health Sciences; Email: earl.blewett@okstate.edu.

1089 ■ American Liver Foundation (ALF)

39 Broadway, Ste. 2700
New York, NY 10006
Ph: (212)668-1000
Fax: (212)483-8179
Free: 800-465-4837
E-mail: info@liverfoundation.org
URL: www.liverfoundation.org
Social Media: www.facebook.com/liverinfo
www.linkedin.com/company/american-liver-foundation
twitter.com/liverusa

1090 ■ ALF Postdoctoral Research Fellowship Award *(Postdoctorate, Professional development/ Fellowship)*

Purpose: To support investigational work relating to liver physiology and disease. **Focus:** Medical research. **Qualif.:** Applications are available to MD/PhD postdoctoral fellows in their first or second year; must be sponsored by an research mentor. **Criteria:** Selection will be based on the committee's criteria.

Funds Avail.: $12,500. **Duration:** Annual. **To Apply:** Applicants must submit a completed application form. **Deadline:** December 15.

1091 ■ American Liver Foundation Liver Scholar Award *(Doctorate/Award)*

Purpose: To develop the potential of outstanding, young scientists and encouraging research in liver physiology and disease. **Focus:** Medical research. **Qualif.:** Applicants must be sponsored by a public or private non-profit institution accredited in the United States, Canada or Mexico engaged in health care and health-related research; an AASLD member in good standing; and sponsored by a research mentor. **Criteria:** Awards are made to eligible institutions and are for salary support only for the awardee.

Funds Avail.: $225,000 ($75,000/year). **Duration:** Three years. **Number Awarded:** 1. **To Apply:** Applicants may download an application form online; must submit an application which contains the following sections: application information; summary and abstract; biographical sketch; research plan; research facilities; statement; letters of commitment; letters of recommendation; institution review board; signatures; original and eight copies of the completed application must be received at ALF. **Deadline:** December 15. **Contact:** Email: research@liverfoundation.org.

1092 ■ American Lung Association in the District of Columbia (ALA)

55 W Wacker Dr., Ste. 1150
Chicago, IL 60601
Free: 800-586-4872

E-mail: info@lung.org
URL: www.lung.org
Social Media: www.facebook.com/lungusa
www.instagram.com/lungassociation
www.linkedin.com/company/american-lung-association
twitter.com/LungAssociation
www.youtube.com/user/americanlung

1093 ■ ALA Allergic Respiratory Diseases Research Award *(Doctorate/Award)*

Purpose: To support research that will advance the understanding of allergic respiratory disease. **Focus:** Health sciences; Public health. **Qualif.:** Applicant must hold a doctoral degree at the time of application; have a primary faculty appointment in an allergy/immunology division/ section of an academic institution, be undertaking a project related to allergic respiratory disease, and have completed a training fellowship; must be United States citizens at the time of application or foreign nationals holding one of the following visa immigration statuses: permanent resident (Green Card), exchange visitor (J-1), temporary worker in a specialty occupation (H-1B), Canadian or Mexican citizen engaging in professional activities (TN), Australians in Specialty Occupation (E-3 visa) or temporary worker with extraordinary abilities in the sciences (O-1); at the time of application and throughout the award, an applicant must be employed by a U.S. institution. **Criteria:** Selection will be based on scientific merit, innovation, and feasibility of the research plan, and its relevance to the mission of the American Lung Association; education and experience, publications and letters of recommendation; research environment; likelihood that the applicants will continue to have a career in lung and/or other relevant research; department Chair letter clearly assuring faculty appointment with demonstrated institutional commitment before the start of an award.

Funds Avail.: $75,000. **Duration:** Annual; two years. **To Apply:** Applicants may visit the website for the application process; submit one signed original plus two copies of all application materials; must include three letters of recommendation. **Deadline:** December 10.

1094 ■ American Lung Association Biomedical Research Grants (RG) *(Doctorate/Grant)*

Purpose: To provide seed monies to junior investigators who are researching the mechanism of lung disease and general lung biology. **Focus:** General studies/Field of study not specified; Health sciences; Medical research.

Funds Avail.: $40,000. **Duration:** up to two years.

1095 ■ American Lung Association Clinical Patient Care Research Grants (CG) *(Doctorate/Grant)*

Purpose: To provide monies to investigators working on traditional clinical studies examining methods for improving patient care and treatment for lung disease. **Focus:** Health sciences; Public health.

Funds Avail.: $50,000. **Duration:** two years.

1096 ■ American Lung Association Dalsemer Research Grants (DA) *(Doctorate/Grant)*

Purpose: To provide seed monies to junior investigators who are researching the mechanism of lung disease and general lung biology. **Focus:** Health sciences; Public health. **Qualif.:** Applicants must be pursuing a career in lung health research; must be United States citizens or

Awards are arranged alphabetically below their administering organizations

foreign nationals holding one of the following visa immigration statuses permanent resident (Green Card), exchange visitor (J-1), temporary worker in a specialty occupation (H-1B), Canadian or Mexican citizen engaging in professional activities (TN), Australians in Specialty Occupation (E-3) or temporary worker with extraordinary abilities in the sciences (O-1); must be employed by a U.S. Institution. **Criteria:** Selection will be based on scientific merit, innovation, and feasibility of the research plan, and its relevance to the mission of the American Lung Association; education and experience, publications and letters of recommendation; research environment; likelihood that the applicants will continue to have a career in lung and/or other relevant research; department Chair letter clearly assuring faculty appointment with demonstrated institutional commitment before the start of an award.

Funds Avail.: $50,000. **Duration:** Annual; up to two years. **To Apply:** Applicants may visit the website for the application process; submit one signed original plus two copies of all application materials; must include three letters of recommendation. **Deadline:** December 12. **Contact:** Email: pcsupport@altum.com.

1097 ■ American Lung Association DeSousa Awards *(Postgraduate/Award)*

Purpose: To support clinical, laboratory, epidemiological, or any other kind of research that focuses on bronchiectasis, infection with a typical Mycobacteria, and infection with Nocardia species. **Focus:** Health sciences; Public health.

1098 ■ American Lung Association Senior Research Training Fellowships (RT) *(Doctorate/ Fellowship)*

Purpose: To support the training of MDs and PhDs seeking further academic training as scientific investigators with the goal of pursuing a career in pulmonary medicine and long biology research. **Focus:** Health sciences; Public health.

Funds Avail.: $32,500. **Duration:** 2 years.

1099 ■ American Lung Association Social-Behavioral Research Grants (SB) *(Doctorate/Grant)*

Purpose: To provide seed monies to junior investigators working on various disciplines of social science examining risk factors affecting lung health. **Focus:** Health sciences; Public health. **Qualif.:** Applicants must be pursuing a career in lung health research; must be United States citizens or foreign nationals holding one of the following visa immigration statuses: permanent resident (Green Card), exchange visitor (J-1), temporary worker in a specialty occupation (H-1B), Canadian or Mexican citizen engaging in professional activities (TN), Australians in Specialty Occupation (E-3) or temporary worker with extraordinary abilities in the sciences (O-1); must be employed by a U.S. Institution; must hold a doctoral degree and have a faculty appointment or equivalent with demonstrated institutional commitment (salary support, research space) in a recognized academic or other not-for-profit institution. **Criteria:** Selection will be based on scientific merit, innovation, and feasibility of the research plan, and its relevance to the mission of the American Lung Association; education and experience, publications and letters of recommendation; research environment; likelihood that the applicants will continue to have a career in lung and/or other relevant research; department Chair letter clearly assuring faculty appointment with demonstrated institutional commitment before the start of an award.

Funds Avail.: $50,000. **Duration:** Annual; two years. **To Apply:** Applicants are required to submit a letter of intent to the American Lung Association; must be an attached PDF file, no more than 3 pages, which must include: rationale for the project; planned specific aims; brief statement of the overall experimental approach; NIH Biosketch of the applicants (separate attached PDF file); submit one signed original plus two copies of all application materials. **Deadline:** December 21. **Contact:** Email: pcsupport@altum.com.

1100 ■ Lung Cancer Discovery Award (LCD) *(Doctorate/Award)*

Purpose: To support the development of novel medical treatments, advancing current treatment options and/or finding a cure for lung cancer through clinical, laboratory, epidemiological, or any other king of research. **Focus:** Health sciences; Public health. **Qualif.:** Applicants must be pursue a career in lung heath research; must be United States citizens or foreign nationals holding one of the following visa immigration statuses: permanent resident (Green Card), exchange visitor (J-1), temporary worker in a specialty occupation (H-1B), Canadian or Mexican citizen engaging in professional activities (TN), Australians in Specialty Occupation (E-3) or temporary worker with extraordinary abilities in the sciences (O-1); must be employed by a U.S. Institution; must hold a doctoral degree, have a faculty appointment at an academic institution (including research institutions not formally associated with a university), and have completed a training fellowship. **Criteria:** Selection will be based on scientific merit, innovation, and feasibility of the research plan, and its relevance to the mission of the American Lung Association; education and experience, publications and letters of recommendation; research environment; likelihood that the applicants will continue to have a career in lung and/or other relevant research; department Chair letter clearly assuring faculty appointment with demonstrated institutional commitment before the start of an award.

Funds Avail.: $100,000. **Duration:** Annual; two years. **To Apply:** Applicants are required to submit a letter of intent to the American Lung Association; must be an attached PDF file, no more than 3 pages, which must include: rationale for the project; planned specific aims; brief statement of the overall experimental approach; NIH Biosketch of the applicants (separate attached PDF file); submit one signed original plus two copies of all application materials. **Deadline:** December 10.

1101 ■ Lung Health Dissertation Grants (LH) *(Doctorate/Grant)*

Purpose: To support pre-doctoral dissertation research in the various disciplines of social science examining risk factors affecting lung health. **Focus:** Health sciences; Public health. **Qualif.:** Applicants must be pursuing a career in lung heath research; must be United States citizens or foreign nationals holding one of the following visa immigration statuses: permanent resident (Green Card), exchange visitor (J-1), temporary worker in a specialty occupation (H-1B), Canadian or Mexican citizen engaging in professional activities (TN), Australians in Specialty Occupation (E-3) or temporary worker with extraordinary abilities in the sciences (O-1); must be employed by a U.S. Institution; must be a matriculating student in good standing in a full-time academic program leading to a doctoral degree in one of the above-mentioned field. **Criteria:** Selection will be based on scientific merit, innovation, and feasibility of the research plan, and its relevance to the mission of the American Lung

Awards are arranged alphabetically below their administering organizations

Association; education and experience, publications and letters of recommendation; research environment; likelihood that the applicants will continue to have a career in lung and/or other relevant research; department Chair letter clearly assuring faculty appointment with demonstrated institutional commitment before the start of an award.

Funds Avail.: $21,000. **Duration:** Annual; two years. **To Apply:** Applicants may visit the website for the application process; submit one signed original plus two copies of all application materials; must include three letters of recommendation. **Deadline:** December 15.

1102 ■ American Marketing Association Foundation (AMAF)

130 E Randolph St., 22nd Fl.
Chicago, IL 60601
Ph: (312)542-9000
Fax: (312)542-9001
E-mail: foundation@ama.org
URL: www.ama.org/about-ama-foundation
Social Media: www.facebook.com/AmericanMarketing
twitter.com/AMA_Marketing

1103 ■ Richard A. Hammill Scholarship Fund
(Undergraduate/Scholarship)

Purpose: To support students who are enrolled in the Marketing Program. **Focus:** Marketing and distribution. **Qualif.:** Applicants must be students enrolled at Georgia State University. **Criteria:** Selection will be based on the committee's criteria.

Funds Avail.: No specific amount. **Duration:** Annual. **Remarks:** Established in 2005.

1104 ■ Robert J. Lavidge Global Marketing Research Award *(Professional development/Award)*

Purpose: To assist marketing professionals working in the nonprofit sector to further their marketing research-related education. **Focus:** Marketing and distribution. **Qualif.:** Applicants must be marketing practitioners or educators from anywhere in the world, who have demonstrated success in implementing a research procedure with practical implications, resulting in significant advancement (methodological or process based) in the marketing research field; procedures must have been implemented within the preceding five calendar years. **Criteria:** Preference will be given to advancements in closely related fields, such as marketing statistics, that also have a specific and significant impact on the marketing research field.

Funds Avail.: No specific amount. **Duration:** Annual. **Deadline:** May 15. **Remarks:** The Award was established in honor of Bob Lavidge by his friends and colleagues. Established in 1999. **Contact:** Christine Germino; Email: cgermino@ama.org.

1105 ■ Valuing Diversity PhD Scholarship
(Doctorate/Scholarship)

Purpose: To provide a scholarship to underrepresented populations in the marketing profession. **Focus:** Marketing and distribution. **Qualif.:** Applicants must be U.S. citizens or permanent U.S residents enrolled, on campus, in a full-time AACSB-accredited marketing doctoral program and have successfully completed at least one year; must have not previously received a valuing diversity scholarship; must be African American, Hispanic American, or Native Ameri-

can. **Criteria:** Selection will be based on the committee's criteria.

Funds Avail.: $1,000 each. **Duration:** Annual. **Number Awarded:** Varies. **To Apply:** Applicants must complete the online application and submit essays on how scholarship will help further the research efforts, in Microsoft Word format, within two-pages, double-spaced, in 12 pt. type (approximately 500 words); sources mentioned in essay should be credited on an additional page and do not count against the two-page maximum; must also submit two letters of recommendation(one from the applicant's advisor or Doctoral Program Coordinator, and one from another faculty member, preferably from whom the applicant has taken a course) mentioning candidate's academic work or initiatives that demonstrate a commitment to advancing diversity; essay also must address, How the dissertation research incorporates conceptual, design, or methods of issues related to diversity, any innovative theories or advanced, cutting-edge designs, methods, or approaches and contributes to advancing the field of marketing. **Deadline:** April 5. **Remarks:** Established in 2003. **Contact:** AMAF, 130 E Randolph St, 22nd Fl, Chicago, IL, 60601.

1106 ■ American Mathematical Society (AMS)

201 Charles St.
Providence, RI 02904-2213
Ph: (401)455-4000
Fax: (401)331-3842
Free: 800-321-4267
E-mail: cust-serv@ams.org
URL: www.ams.org
Social Media: www.facebook.com/amermathsoc
twitter.com/amermathsoc

1107 ■ AMS Centennial Fellowships *(Postdoctorate/ Fellowship, Monetary)*

Purpose: To promote study and research in mathematics. **Focus:** Mathematics and mathematical sciences. **Qualif.:** Applicants must have held a doctoral degree for at least three years and not more than twelve years at the inception of the award. **Criteria:** Selection will be based on the excellence of the candidate's research. Preference will be given to candidates who have not had extensive fellowship support in the past.

Funds Avail.: $93,000, plus allowance or $9,300. **Duration:** One year. **Number Awarded:** 1. **To Apply:** Applicants must submit a completed application form along with the required materials. Research description (Research Statement): please describe the research in your thesis and other work you have done (one to three pages; no more than three pages, including bibliographical references, will be accepted). **Deadline:** December 1. **Remarks:** Established in 1974.

1108 ■ American Meat Science Association (AMSA)

301 N Neil St., Ste. 400
Champaign, IL 61820-3169
Ph: (217)356-5370
Fax: (217)356-5370
Free: 800-517-2672
E-mail: information@meatscience.org
URL: www.meatscience.org
Social Media: twitter.com/meatscience

Awards are arranged alphabetically below their administering organizations

1109 ■ AMSA Graduate Student Research Poster Competition *(Graduate, Doctorate, Master's/Award)*

Purpose: To recognize individuals who have made outstanding posters relevant to any aspect of meat science. **Focus:** Science. **Qualif.:** Applicants must be graduate (MS or PhD) or undergraduate students currently members of the American Meat Association at the time of entry.

Number Awarded: 2. **To Apply:** Applicants must submit electronic poster regarding meat science. **Contact:** Deidrea Mabry, Email: dmabry@meatscience.org.

1110 ■ American Medical Association (AMA)
AMA Plz.
330 N Wabash Ave., Ste. 39300
Chicago, IL 60611-5885
Ph: (312)464-4782
Free: 800-262-3211
URL: www.ama-assn.org
Social Media: www.facebook.com/
  AmericanMedicalAssociation
www.linkedin.com/company/american-medical-association
twitter.com/AmerMedicalAssn

1111 ■ AMA Foundation Physicians of Tomorrow Scholarships *(Graduate/Scholarship)*

Purpose: To support rising fourth year medical students (third year students who are approaching their final year of medical school). **Focus:** Medicine. **Qualif.:** Applicants must be current third year medical students who are entering their fourth year of study. **Criteria:** Recipients will be selected based on academic standing and financial need.

Funds Avail.: $10,000. **Duration:** Annual. **Number Awarded:** Varies. **To Apply:** Applicants must complete the application form. Detailed requirements will be sent by the AMA Foundation to each medical school's Office of the Dean, Office of the Student Affairs, and Office of Financial Aid. **Contact:** Email: scholarships@ama-assn.org.

1112 ■ Underrepresented in Medicine award *(Graduate/Scholarship)*

Purpose: To encourage diversity in medicine and alleviates debt, and reward commitment to the elimination of healthcare disparities, outstanding academic achievements, leadership activities and community involvement. **Focus:** Medicine. **Qualif.:** Applicants must be current first or second year students and permanent residents or citizens of the U.S. They must also be African Americans, American Indians, Native Americans, Alaska Natives or Hispanics/Latinos. **Criteria:** Selection will be based on the applicant's academic standing.

Funds Avail.: No specific amount. **Duration:** Annual. **Number Awarded:** Varies. **To Apply:** Applicants must complete the application form. Detailed requirement will be sent by the AMA Foundation to each medical school's Office of the Dean, Office of the Student Affairs, and Office of Financial Aid.

1113 ■ Arthur N. Wilson, MD, Scholarships *(Undergraduate/Scholarship)*

Purpose: To support a medical student who graduated from a high school in Southeast Alaska. **Focus:** Medicine. **Funds Avail.:** $5,000.

1114 ■ American Medical Society for Sports Medicine (AMSSM)
4000 W 114th St., Ste. 100
Leawood, KS 66211

Ph: (913)327-1415
URL: www.amssm.org
Social Media: facebook.com/#!/pages/American-Medical
  -Society-for-Sports-Medicine/99144532235
www.linkedin.com/groups/4489007/profile
twitter.com/theamssm

1115 ■ AMSSM-ACSM Clinical Research Grants *(Professional development/Grant)*

Purpose: To foster original scientific investigations with a strong clinical focus among physician members of AMSSM and the ACSM. **Focus:** Medicine, Sports. **Qualif.:** Applicants must be physicians who are members of the AMSSM and the ACSM.

Funds Avail.: Maximum of $20,000 ($10,000 from AMSSM, $10,000 from ACSM). **Duration:** Annual; up to two years. **Deadline:** February 2.

1116 ■ American Men's Studies Association (AMSA)
1080 S University Ave.
Ann Arbor, MI 48109-1106
Ph: (470)333-2672
E-mail: amsamail@gmail.com
URL: mensstudies.org
Social Media: www.facebook.com/mensstudies

1117 ■ Loren Frankel Memorial Scholarship *(Undergraduate, Graduate/Scholarship)*

Purpose: To support students engaged in the critical study of men and masculinities. **Focus:** Sexuality. **Qualif.:** Applicants must be undergraduate or graduate students accepted to present a paper or poster project at the annual AMSA conference. **Criteria:** Selection will be based on content, quality, and the student's potential for making a contribution to the field of men's studies.

Funds Avail.: Up to $500. **Duration:** Annual. **To Apply:** Applicants must submit a maximum two-page document that includes brief biographical information, title and abstract of the paper and paragraph describing the importance of the project to professional and intellectual development. **Deadline:** April 1. **Remarks:** The fund is dedicated to the memory of Dr. Loren Frankel, a young professor of psychology at Shepherd University in Shepherdstown, who was known as an inspiring teacher, an accomplished scholar, and a respected colleague. Established in 2005.

1118 ■ American Meteorological Society (AMS)
45 Beacon St.
Boston, MA 02108-3693
Ph: (617)227-2425
Fax: (617)742-8718
E-mail: amsinfo@ametsoc.org
URL: www.ametsoc.org
Social Media: www.facebook.com/ametsoc
www.instagram.com/ametsoc
www.linkedin.com/company/american-meteorological
  -society
twitter.com/ametsoc
www.youtube.com/user/ametsoc

1119 ■ AMS Freshman Undergraduate Scholarship *(Undergraduate/Scholarship)*

Purpose: To encourage high school students to study in the atmospheric and related sciences. **Focus:** Meteorol-

Awards are arranged alphabetically below their administering organizations

ogy. **Qualif.:** Applicants must be a U.S. citizen or hold a permanent resident status; entering the freshman year of college as a full-time student; and plan to pursue a degree in the atmospheric or related oceanic or hydrologic sciences. **Criteria:** Selection is based on the submitted application materials.

Funds Avail.: $2,500/year. **Duration:** Annual; two years. **Number Awarded:** 1. **To Apply:** Applicants must submit a completed application form together with an official high school transcript showing grades from the past three years; a letter of recommendation from a high school teacher or guidance counselor; and a copy of scores from a SAT or similar national college entrance exam. **Deadline:** February 7. **Contact:** Donna Fernandez; Phone 617-226-3907; Email: dfernandez@ametsoc.org.

1120 ■ AMS Graduate Fellowship in the History of Science *(Graduate/Fellowship)*

Purpose: To support students who wish to complete a dissertation on the history of science. **Focus:** Science--History. **Qualif.:** Applicants must be graduate students in good standing who proposes to complete a dissertation in the history of the atmospheric or related oceanic or hydrologic sciences; must be an AMS member; student member pursuing a degree at a U.S. institution. **Criteria:** Selection is based on the submitted application materials.

Funds Avail.: $15,000. **Duration:** Annual; one year. **Number Awarded:** 1. **To Apply:** Applicants must submit a cover letter with a curriculum vitae; official transcripts from undergraduate and graduate institutions; a typewritten, detailed description of the dissertation topic and proposed research plan (10 page maximum); and three letters of recommendation (including one from dissertation advisor). **Deadline:** April 10. **Contact:** Donna Fernandez, Development and Student Program Manager; Phone: 617-227-2426 ext. 3907.

1121 ■ AMS Graduate Fellowships *(Graduate/Fellowship)*

Purpose: To encourage young scientists to prepare for careers in the meteorological, oceanic, and hydrologic fields. **Focus:** Meteorology. **Qualif.:** Applicant must be entering their first year of graduate school in the fall and provide evidence of acceptance as a full-time student at an accredited U.S. institution at the time of the award; pursuing a degree in the atmospheric or related sciences; have a minimum grade point average of 3.25 on a 4.0-point scale; must be U.S. citizens or hold permanent resident status; candidates from the fields of atmospheric sciences, chemistry, computer sciences, engineering, environmental sciences, hydrology, mathematics, oceanography, and physics. **Criteria:** Selection is based on the submitted application materials.

Funds Avail.: $25,000. **Duration:** Annual. **To Apply:** Applicants should submit three written references, relevant official transcripts, and GRE score reports. **Deadline:** January 1.

1122 ■ AMS/Industry/Government Graduate Fellowships *(Graduate/Fellowship)*

Purpose: To attract promising young scientists to prepare for careers in the atmospheric and related oceanic and hydrologic fields. **Focus:** Meteorology.

Funds Avail.: No specific amount.

1123 ■ AMS Minority Scholarships *(Undergraduate/Scholarship)*

Purpose: To help further the education of outstanding students pursuing a career in the atmospheric and related

oceanic or hydrologic sciences. **Focus:** Meteorology. **Qualif.:** Applicants must be minority students entering the freshman year of college; planning to pursue a career in the atmospheric or related oceanic and hydrologic sciences; must be U.S. citizens or hold permanent resident status; and must be pursuing a degree at a U.S. institution. **Criteria:** Selection is based on the submitted application materials.

Funds Avail.: $3,000/year. **Duration:** Annual; two years. **Number Awarded:** 1. **To Apply:** Applicants must submit a completed application form along with an official high school transcript showing grades from the past three years; a letter of recommendation from a high school teacher or guidance counselor; and a copy of scores from a SAT or similar national college entrance exam. **Deadline:** February 14. **Contact:** Donna Fernandez; Phone 617-226-3907; Email: dfernandez@ametsoc.org.

1124 ■ AMS Senior Named Scholarships *(Undergraduate/Scholarship)*

Purpose: To support students majoring in the atmospheric or related oceanic or hydrologic sciences. **Focus:** Meteorology. **Qualif.:** Applicants must be a full-time student entering the final year of undergraduate study; majoring in the atmospheric or related oceanic or hydrologic science, and/or must show clear intent to make the atmospheric or related sciences a career; enrolled full time in an accredited U.S. institution; and must have a cumulative GPA of at least a 3.25 on a scale of 4.0; must be U.S. citizens or hold permanent resident status. **Criteria:** Selection is based on the submitted application materials.

Funds Avail.: $2,000 to $10,000. **Duration:** Annual. **To Apply:** Applicants must submit a completed application form along with letters of reference and official transcripts. **Deadline:** March 13. **Contact:** Donna Fernandez; Phone 617-226-3907; Email: dfernandez@ametsoc.org.

1125 ■ The Naval Weather Service Association Scholarship *(Undergraduate/Scholarship)*

Purpose: To support students planning to pursue a career in Meteorology, Oceanography, or Space Engineering. **Focus:** Meteorology; Oceanography. **Qualif.:** Applicants must be a full-time student entering the final year of undergraduate study; majoring in the meteorology or oceanography; enrolled full time in an accredited U.S. institution; and must have a cumulative GPA of at least a 3.25 on a scale of 4.0; must be U.S. citizens or hold permanent resident status. **Criteria:** Selection is based on the submitted application materials.

Funds Avail.: $5,000. **Duration:** Annual. **Number Awarded:** 1. **To Apply:** Applicants must submit a completed application form along with letters of reference and official transcripts. **Deadline:** March 13. **Contact:** Donna Fernandez, Development and Student Program Manager; Phone: 617-227-2426 ext. 3907.

1126 ■ American MidEast Leadership Network (AMLN)
PO Box 2156
Long Island City, NY 11102
Ph: (347)924-9674
Fax: (917)591-2177
E-mail: info@amln.org
URL: amln.org

Awards are arranged alphabetically below their administering organizations

1127 ■ AMLN Scholarships for Arab American Students *(Graduate, Undergraduate/Scholarship)*

Purpose: To recognize individuals who wish to continue their higher education in the United States. **Focus:** General studies/Field of study not specified.

Funds Avail.: $1,000-$3,000. **Duration:** Annual. **Contact:** Phone: 347-924-9674; Email: fernando@amln.org.

1128 ■ American Montessori Society (AMS)
116 E 16th St.
New York, NY 10003-2163
Ph: (212)358-1250
Fax: (212)358-1256
E-mail: ams@amshq.org
URL: amshq.org
Social Media: www.facebook.com/
  AmericanMontessoriSociety
twitter.com/amshq

1129 ■ AMS Teacher Education Scholarships *(Undergraduate/Scholarship)*

Purpose: To support the growth of Montessori teachers. **Focus:** Education; Teaching. **Qualif.:** Applicants must be accepted or in the process of acceptance by an affiliated AMS teacher education program; application is considered on the basis of financial need. **Criteria:** Selection of applicants will not be based on the gender, race, creed, color or national origin or sexual orientation; applicants are considered on the basis of financial need, a compelling personal statement, three letters of recommendation and official verification of acceptance into an AMS Teacher Education Program.

Funds Avail.: $34,000. **Duration:** Annual. **Number Awarded:** Varies. **To Apply:** Applicants must submit a personal statement, three recommendation letters, financial statement and appropriate tax form and verification of TEP acceptance. **Deadline:** May 1. **Contact:** American Montessori Society 116 East 16th Street, FL 6, New York, NY 10003 E-mail:ams@amshq.org.

1130 ■ Teacher Education Scholarship *(Advanced Professional/Scholarship)*

Purpose: To support the growth of Montessori teachers of tomorrow. **Focus:** Teaching. **Qualif.:** Applicants must be individuals who have been accepted, are in the process of being accepted, or are already enrolled in an AMS-affiliated teacher education program. **Criteria:** Selection shall be based on the committee's criteria; applicants are considered on the basis of financial need, a compelling personal statement, 3 letters of recommendation, and official verification of acceptance into an AMS-affiliated program.

Funds Avail.: Varies. **Duration:** Annual. **Number Awarded:** 20. **To Apply:** Application details can be found at the program website. **Remarks:** Established in 1995.

1131 ■ American Music Therapy Association (AMTA)
8455 Colesville Rd., Ste. 1000
Silver Spring, MD 20910
Ph: (301)589-3300
Fax: (301)589-5175
E-mail: info@musictherapy.org
URL: www.musictherapy.org

Social Media: www.facebook.com/AMTAInc
instagram.com/amtainc
twitter.com/AMTAInc
youtube.com/user/AMTAmusictherapy

1132 ■ AMTA Past Presidents' Conference Scholar *(Professional development/Scholarship)*

Purpose: To support AMTA members cover the cost of attending the AMTA annual conference. **Focus:** Music therapy. **Qualif.:** Applicants must be music therapists with a current credential of MT-BC or current professional designation of ACMT, CMT or RMT; must be professional members in good standing of AMTA. **Criteria:** Selection will be based on the committee's criteria.

Funds Avail.: $500. **Duration:** Annual. **Number Awarded:** 5. **To Apply:** Applicants must submit a maximum of one page narrative application; statement of need and potential professional development should be addressed within the narrative. **Deadline:** July 31. **Contact:** Email: scholarships@musictherapy.org.

1133 ■ AMTA Student Conference Scholar *(Undergraduate, Graduate/Scholarship)*

Purpose: To support students cover the expenses of attending the AMTA National Conference. **Focus:** Music therapy. **Qualif.:** Applicants must be undergraduate, undergraduate equivalency, or graduate students enrolled in a college or university program in music therapy approved by the American Music Therapy Association. All interns in clinical training are considered eligible through their parent academic institution. Applicants must be current student members of AMTA in the year in which they apply and the year in which the award is granted. **Criteria:** Selection will be based on the committee's criteria.

Funds Avail.: $250 each. **Duration:** Annual. **Number Awarded:** 2. **To Apply:** Applicants must submit a maximum of one page narrative application. Statement of need and potential development should be addressed within the narrative. **Deadline:** July 31. **Contact:** Email: scholarships@ musictherapy.org.

1134 ■ Edwina Eustis Dick Scholarship for Music Therapy Interns *(Graduate/Scholarship)*

Purpose: To support the education of music therapy students. **Focus:** Music therapy. **Qualif.:** Applicants must be music therapy interns; must be current student members of AMTA in the year in which they apply and the year in which the award is granted. **Criteria:** Selection will be based on the committee's criteria.

Funds Avail.: $500 each. **Duration:** Annual. **Number Awarded:** 2. **To Apply:** Nomination for this award is required. Only AMTA-Approved Program Faculty may nominate students. Nominated candidates must provide the following materials: completed scholarship application form, signed and dated; personal, community, and college activities; college transcript; letter of recommendation which must be submitted by author from a music therapy professor, a professional familiar with the applicants' clinical skills or another person of the applicants' choice; participation in AMTA conferences, AMTA committees, presentations, and publications; a maximum of 800 words essay on long-term professional goals; a 400 words essay on how AMTA can impact the profession of music therapy. Any narrative must be double-spaced, 1-inch margins and in 12-point font. Narrative must be written for blind review, without specific reference to applicants' name or place of employment.

Awards are arranged alphabetically below their administering organizations

Deadline: March 15. **Contact:** Email: scholarships@musictherapy.org.

1135 ■ Arthur Flagler Fultz Research Award (Professional development/Grant)

Purpose: To encourage, promote and fund music therapy research and to explore new and innovative music therapy treatments. **Focus:** Music therapy. **Qualif.:** Applicants must be music therapists with a current credential of MT-BC or current professional designation of ACMT, CMT or RMT; must be professional members in good standing of AMTA. **Criteria:** Selection will be based on the committee's criteria.

Funds Avail.: $20,000. **Duration:** Annual. **To Apply:** Applications must be typed and submitted electronically using Fultz application form available online; download and save the application form as a new file using the member number of the principal investigators and the word "Fultz"; applicant may contact the AMTA national office get their member number; must also include all required forms and information in the order listed. **Deadline:** June 6. **Contact:** Email: fultz@musictherapy.org.

1136 ■ Anne Emery Kyllo Professional Scholarship (Professional development/Scholarship)

Purpose: To support professional music therapists in their efforts to expand their training and professional interactions through participation in continuing education opportunities. **Focus:** Music therapy. **Qualif.:** Applicants must be music therapists with a current credential of MT-BC or current professional designation of ACMT, CMT or RMT; must be professional members in good standing of AMTA. **Criteria:** Selection will be based on the committee's criteria.

Funds Avail.: $500 each for use towards CMTE credits. **Duration:** Annual. **Number Awarded:** 3. **To Apply:** Applicants must submit a maximum of two pages narrative application; statement of need, potential professional development and client impact and strength/appropriateness of continuing education goals and opportunities should be included. **Deadline:** July 31. **Contact:** Email: scholarships@musictherapy.org.

1137 ■ Theodore Meyer Scholarship (Undergraduate, Graduate/Scholarship)

Purpose: To help individuals with mental health and/or addiction issues find a path to wellness and inspiration through the joy of music. **Focus:** Music therapy. **Qualif.:** Applicants must be undergraduate, undergraduate equivalency, or graduate students enrolled in a college or university program in music therapy approved by the American Music Therapy Association. All interns in clinical training are considered eligible through their parent academic institution. Applicants must be current student members of AMTA in the year in which they apply and the year in which the award is granted. **Criteria:** Selection will be based on the committee's criteria.

Funds Avail.: $1,000. **Duration:** Annual. **Number Awarded:** 1. **To Apply:** Students must provide two short essays; the first essay should detail an interest in mental health and addiction; the second essay should describe long-term professional goals; each application narrative should be a maximum of two pages. **Deadline:** April 4.

1138 ■ Brian and Cathy Smith Memorial Fund (Graduate/Scholarship)

Purpose: To support the education of music therapy interns pursuing training in chemical dependency or in adolescent programs. **Focus:** Music therapy. **Qualif.:** Applicants must be music therapy interns pursuing training in chemical dependency or in adolescent programs; must be current student members of AMTA in the year in which they apply and the year in which the award is granted. **Criteria:** Selection will be based on the committee's criteria.

Funds Avail.: $500. **Duration:** Annual. **Number Awarded:** 1. **To Apply:** Nomination for this award is required; only AMTA-Approved Program Faculty may nominate students; nominated candidate must provide the following materials: completed scholarship application form, signed and dated; personal, community, and college activities; college transcript; letter of recommendation which must be submitted by author from a music therapy professor, a professional familiar with the applicants' clinical skills or another person of the applicants' choice; participation in AMTA conferences, AMTA committees, presentations, and publications; a maximum of 800 words essay on long-term professional goals; a 400 words essay on how AMTA can impact the profession of music therapy; any narrative must be double-spaced, 1-inch margins and in 12-point font; narrative must be written for blind review, without specific reference to applicants' name or place of employment. **Deadline:** March 15. **Remarks:** Established by the Smith family in memory of Brian Smith, a young man who valued music in his life and died in a drug-related accident. In 2006, the fund was renamed to include Brian's mother, Cathy, who passed away in 2005. **Contact:** Email: scholarships@musictherapy.org.

1139 ■ Christine K. Stevens Development Scholarship (Undergraduate, Graduate/Scholarship)

Purpose: To support music therapy students in their efforts to expand their training in the use of percussion-based strategies through continuing education opportunities with the research-based HealthRHYTHMS Group Empowerment Drumming program. **Focus:** Music therapy. **Qualif.:** Applicants must be undergraduate, undergraduate equivalency, or graduate students enrolled in a college or university program in music therapy approved by the American Music Therapy Association. All interns in clinical training are considered eligible through their parent academic institution. Applicants must be current student members of AMTA in the year in which they apply and the year in which the award is granted. **Criteria:** Selection will be based on the committee's criteria.

Funds Avail.: Full tuition for HealthRHYTHMS training (valued at $599 each). **Duration:** Annual. **Number Awarded:** 2. **To Apply:** Nomination for this award is required; only AMTA-Approved Program Faculty may nominate students; nominated candidates must submit a maximum of one page narrative; statement of need and potential professional development should be addressed within the narrative. **Deadline:** March 15. **Remarks:** Established by Remo, Inc., in Christine Stevens honor for her pioneering work. **Contact:** Email: scholarships@musictherapy.org.

1140 ■ Florence Tyson Grant to Study Music Psychotherapy (Professional development/Grant)

Purpose: To support professional music therapists in post-undergraduate training in music psychotherapy, music and psychotherapy, or psychotherapy. **Focus:** Music therapy. **Qualif.:** Applicants must be music therapists with a current credential of MT-BC or current professional designation of ACMT, CMT or RMT; must be professional members in good standing of AMTA. **Criteria:** Selection will be based on the committee's criteria.

Awards are arranged alphabetically below their administering organizations

Funds Avail.: Provides free registration to attend the upcoming Annual AMTA Conference and attend a CMTE. **Duration:** Annual. **To Apply:** Applicants must submit a maximum of two pages application narrative describing how the study of music psychotherapy, music and psychotherapy, and/or psychotherapy is important to work as music therapists; statement of need, potential professional development and client impact and strength/appropriateness of continuing education goals and opportunities should also be included. **Deadline:** July 31. **Contact:** Email: scholarships@musictherapy.org.

1141 ■ American Musicological Society (AMS)
20 Cooper Sq., 2nd Fl.
New York, NY 10003
Ph: (212)992-6340
Free: 877-679-7648
E-mail: ams@ams-net.org
URL: www.amsmusicology.org

1142 ■ M. Elizabeth C. Bartlet Fund *(Graduate, Doctorate/Grant)*

Purpose: To support doctoral students or graduates of universities in the United States and Canada who are conducting post-doctoral musicological research in France. **Focus:** Musicology. **Qualif.:** Applicants must currently attend or have graduated from a doctoral program in a north American university. If they seek to conduct research for their dissertation, they must have completed all other requirements for the Ph.D; if they seek to conduct post-doctoral research, they should have completed the Ph.D; within the past five years.

Duration: Annual. **Deadline:** April 8. **Remarks:** Established in 2005.

1143 ■ Alvin H. Johnson AMS 50 Dissertation Fellowships *(Doctorate/Fellowship)*

Purpose: To provide financial assistance for full-time studies in musicology. **Focus:** Music. **Qualif.:** Applicants are those who are registered in good standing for a doctorate at a North American university and have completed all formal degree requirements except the dissertation at the time of full application. **Criteria:** Recipients will be selected on the basis of academic merit.

Funds Avail.: $22,000. **Duration:** Annual. **Number Awarded:** Up to 3. **To Apply:** Applications should be submit a 150-word project description; current dissertation prospectus of twelve to fifteen pages (3000-4000 words);should include a detailed rationale of the project (supported by, but not limited to, an assessment of relevant secondary literature), an overview of each chapter, and a clear statement of progress to date, all written in prose; also arrange for a letter from the registrar or departmental Director of Graduate. **Deadline:** December 15. **Contact:** E-mail:ams@amsmusicology.org.

1144 ■ Jan LaRue Travel Fund *(Doctorate, Postdoctorate/Grant)*

Purpose: To encourage and assist Ph.D. candidates, postdoctorates, and junior faculty who are in all fields of musical scholarship to travel anywhere in the world to carry out the necessary work for their dissertation or other research. **Focus:** Musicology. **Qualif.:** Applicants must currently attend or have graduated from a doctoral program in a North American university; if they seek to conduct research for

their dissertation, they must have completed all other requirements for the Ph.D. (or the equivalent doctoral degree in any field of music scholarship); if they seek to conduct post-doctoral research, they should have completed the Ph.D. within the past five years. **Criteria:** Selection based on committee.

Funds Avail.: Maximum of $1,700. **Duration:** Annual. **To Apply:** The application and all materials must be submitted. **Deadline:** April 8.

1145 ■ Janet Levy Fund *(Doctorate/Grant)*

Purpose: To support professional travel and research expenses for independent scholars who are members of the American Musicological Society. **Focus:** Musicology. **Criteria:** Selection based on committee.

Funds Avail.: $500-$2,000. **Duration:** Annual. **Deadline:** May 15.

1146 ■ Howard Mayer Brown Fellowship *(Graduate/Fellowship)*

Purpose: To increase the presence of minority scholars and teachers in musicology by providing financial aid. **Focus:** Music; Musicology. **Qualif.:** Applicants must be students who have completed at least one year of graduate work, intend to pursue a Ph.D. and are in good standing at their home institution; must show evidence of academic excellence and promise of continuing achievement in music scholarship; earlier stages of the degree are particularly encouraged to apply.

Funds Avail.: $22,000. **Duration:** Annual. **To Apply:** Applications may be made directly by the student, or the student may be nominated by a faculty member of the institution at which the student is enrolled or by a member of the Society at another institution; supporting documents must include the following: a personal statement from the student (not to exceed five pages) summarizing applicants' musical and academic background and stating why they wished to pursue an advanced degree in musicology; a summary statement, not to exceed 250 words, outlining areas of research or specific topics presented in the personal statement; a curriculum vitae; samples of the applicants' work (typically not to exceed 30 pages total), such as term papers, thesis chapters, or any published material; letters of support from three faculty members, one of which may be the letter of nomination; letters should address the applicants' general intellectual and musical ability and how these might contribute to a successful career in scholarship and teaching; One letter of support must include information about the students expected funding (to the extent it can be predicted) for the given academic year; letters of recommendation should be sent as via mail. **Deadline:** December 17. **Contact:** Fax: 877-679-7648 or 212-995-4022; Email: hmb-apps@ams-net.org.

1147 ■ Harold Powers World Travel Fund *(Doctorate, Postdoctorate/Grant)*

Purpose: To encourage and assist Ph.D. candidates, postdocs, and junior faculty who are in all fields of musical scholarship who wants travel anywhere in the world to carry out the necessary work for their dissertation or other research. **Focus:** Musicology. **Qualif.:** Applicants must currently attend or have graduated from a doctoral program in a North American university; if they seek to conduct research for their dissertation, they must have completed all other requirements for the Ph.D. (or the equivalent doctoral degree in any field of music scholarship); if they seek to conduct post-doctoral research, they should have

Awards are arranged alphabetically below their administering organizations

completed the Ph.D. within the past five years. **Criteria:** Selection based on committee.

Funds Avail.: A maximum of $1,850. **Duration:** Annual. **To Apply:** The application and all materials must be submitted. **Deadline:** April 8.

1148 ■ American National Red Cross

431 18th St. NW
Washington, DC 20006
Ph: (202)303-5214
Free: 800-733-2767
URL: www.redcross.org
Social Media: www.facebook.com/redcross
www.instagram.com/americanredcross
twitter.com/redcross
www.youtube.com/user/AmRedCross

1149 ■ Jane Delano Student Nurse Scholarships
(Undergraduate, Graduate/Scholarship)

Purpose: To promote nursing as a career and the involvement of new nurses in the Red Cross. **Focus:** Nursing. **Qualif.:** Applicants must have served as Red Cross volunteers or employees within the past five (5) years; have completed the equivalent of at least one year of college/ university credits; be currently enrolled in an accredited United States nursing program; and, be currently enrolled as undergraduate or graduate students in good academic standing. **Criteria:** Selection will be based on Scholarship Selection Committee's criteria; preference will be given to student nurse volunteers.

Funds Avail.: $3,000. **Duration:** Annual. **Number Awarded:** Varies. **To Apply:** Applicants must submit the completed application form; application support documents including personal essay (attach to application), endorsement from the Red Cross Unit (attach form to application), and endorsement from Nursing School Dean (attach form to application). **Deadline:** May 10. **Contact:** Questions and application documents should be submitted via email to NationalAwards@redcross.org.

1150 ■ American Nephrology Nurses' Association (ANNA)

E Holly Ave.
Pitman, NJ 08071-0056
Ph: (856)256-2320
Fax: (856)589-7463
E-mail: anna@annanurse.org
URL: www.annanurse.org
Social Media: www.facebook.com/NephrologyNursing
www.instagram.com/annanurses
twitter.com/annanurses

1151 ■ American Nephrology Nurses' Association Evidence-Based Research Grants *(Other/Grant)*

Purpose: To encourage the discovery of new knowledge as well as the incorporation of the best scientific evidence currently available into the practice of nephrology nursing, with the ultimate goal of improving patient outcomes. **Focus:** Nephrology. **Qualif.:** Applicants must be principal or co-principal investigators must be members of ANNA within the duration of the research project; must share equal responsibility with all other co-investigators for the conceptualization and implementation of the proposed research

project; must provide an evidence of their commitment to nephrology nursing experiences and credentials; must be registered nurses who hold a master's or doctoral degree; the contributions of each of the team members must be identified and the application should describe how each investigator's role fits with their expertise and will facilitate completion of the research project. **Criteria:** Selection will be based on established research priorities and availability of funds.

Funds Avail.: $5,000 each. **Duration:** Annual. **To Apply:** Applicants must demonstrate the following; significance and applicability of the EBP project to nephrology nursing or related therapies; for EBP research proposals, sound methodology in accordance with recognized nursing research guidelines; for other EBP, sound methodology and implementation strategies depending on the type of project; for EBP research projects, approval by the appropriate institutional review board; for other EBP projects, support from the institution where the project will be implemented; feasibility and likelihood of successful completion. Applicants must submit the following items in the order specified: cover letter; ANNA Evidence-based Practice Grant Application Checklist; cover sheet; Co-investigators/consultants/collaborators sheet; detailed budget and justification; abstract; research or project plan; timeline for the research/project completion; references; appendices; copy of IRB approval for research studies or letter of support for other projects; curriculum vitae; personal research articles if available; 8 x 10 professional headshot (black and white or color); project proposals should be submitted by e-mail to the ANNA National Office. **Deadline:** November 15.

1152 ■ Nephrology Nurse Researcher Awards
(Doctorate/Award)

Purpose: To recognize outstanding nephrology nurse researchers. **Focus:** Nephrology. **Qualif.:** Applicants must be full members of ANNA, have been members for a minimum of the last two years as of the award application deadline; actively involved in nephrology nursing related health care services; active participants in ANNA at the local, regional and national level; must preferably hold a master's or doctoral degree. **Criteria:** Selection will be based on the committee's criteria.

Funds Avail.: $1,000. **Duration:** Annual. **To Apply:** Applicants packet should include documentation of the following; nominee has conducted research which contributes towards advancement of nephrology nursing; the packet should include a list of research the nominee has completed with the following information; title of the research study; list of other researchers (if applicable); date of completion of the project or projected completion of the study; the nominee has shared research findings, either through presentation at ANNA meeting or publication in appropriate journals; the nomination letter should provide the following; a list of presentations, including any co-presenters, with the title of the presentation, date, type of meeting and site of meeting; a list of publications in APA format, including other authors (if applicable), publication date, title of article, name of the journal, volume and issue and page numbers; additional comments that support the nominee as an outstanding nephrology nurse researcher. **Deadline:** October 15.

1153 ■ Barbara F. Prowant Nursing Research Grants *(Graduate/Grant)*

Purpose: To promote nursing research particularly in the area of nephrology. **Focus:** Nephrology. **Qualif.:** Applicants must be principal investigators; must be members of ANNA

Awards are arranged alphabetically below their administering organizations

within the duration of the project; must be currently certified by the Nephrology Nursing Certification Commission; must be currently enrolled in a graduate program on the masters, doctorate or post-doctorate level; must provide evidences of their experiences and credentials demonstrating the ability to complete the proposed project and commitment to nephrology nursing; must have the option of contacting a member of the ANNA Research Committee to discuss ideas and use the assistance of the committee to connect them with appropriate mentors, if needed. **Criteria:** Selection will be based on scientific merit and availability of funds.

Funds Avail.: $5,000. **Duration:** Annual. **Number Awarded:** 1. **To Apply:** Applicants must demonstrate the following; significance and applicability of the project to nursing, education or related therapies; for research proposals, sound methodology in accordance with recognized nursing research guidelines; for other proposals, sound methodology and implementation strategies depending on the type of project; approval by the appropriate institutional review board; support from institution where the project will be implemented; feasibility and likelihood of successful completion and support from faculty; must submit the following items in the order specified; cover letter; ANNA evidence-based practice grant application checklist; cover sheet; Co-investigators/consultants/collaborators sheet; detailed budget and justification; abstract; research or project plan; timeline for research/project completion; references; appendices; copy of IRB approval for research studies or letter of support for other projects; curriculum vitae; personal research articles if available; 8 x 10 professional headshot (black and white or color); project proposals should be submitted by e-mail to the ANNA national office. **Deadline:** November 15. **Remarks:** The award was established in honor and recognize Barbara F. Prowant's tremendous contributions to nephrology nursing and certification within the specialty.

1154 ■ American Neuropsychiatric Association (ANPA)

PO Box 97
Abilene, KS 67410-1707
E-mail: anpaoffice@gmail.com
URL: www.anpaonline.org
Social Media: twitter.com/anpadirect

1155 ■ ANPA Young Investigator Awards
(Postdoctorate/Grant)

Purpose: To recognize early trainees who are embarking on promising careers in the clinical neurosciences, as well as to encourage trainees who submitted abstracts for the annual meeting of the organization. **Focus:** Medicine; Neurology; Surgery. **Qualif.:** Candidate must have PGY-2 or greater resident in psychiatry or neurology, 2nd year or higher pre-doctoral candidate for PsyD or PhD, with interest in career in neuropsychiatry, behavioral neurology, or neuropsychology.

Funds Avail.: $750 each. **Duration:** Annual. **Number Awarded:** 2. **To Apply:** Applications should be accompanied by (1) a letter from the applicant's training director confirming that the work was performed during training, (2) the applicant's curriculum vitae, and (3) a statement up to 1,000 words describing the applicant's role in the submitted. **Contact:** ANPA Administrative Office, The Menninger Clinic, 12301 Main St., Houston, TX 77035; Email: anpaoffice@gmail.com.

1156 ■ American Neurotology Society (ANS)

5830 1st St. N
Saint Petersburg, FL 33703
Fax: (727)800-9428
E-mail: administrator@americanneurotologysociety.com
URL: www.americanneurotologysociety.com

1157 ■ ANS Neurotology Fellowship Award *(Other/Fellowship)*

Purpose: To subsidize travel expenses incurred while giving an oral podium presentation at the Annual Meeting of the ANS. **Focus:** Neurology. **Qualif.:** Applicants must be full-time participants in an ACGME approved Neurotology Fellowship; must be both podium presenter and first author of the paper submitted for publication. The material presented need not have been performed during the Fellowship year; i

Funds Avail.: $500. **Duration:** Annual. **Number Awarded:** Varies. **To Apply:** Completed applications can be submitted electronically, A detailed abstract describing the proposed presentation is the minimum requirement. Additional material describing the work-in-progress in greater detail may also be submitted for consideration. **Deadline:** October 15. **Remarks:** Established in 1996. **Contact:** For submission of the cover letter, electronic submission of the abstract to: Kristen Bordignon, ANS Administrator, administrator@americanneurotologysociety.com.

1158 ■ ANS Research Grant Award *(Professional development/Grant)*

Purpose: To encourage and support academic research in sciences related to the investigation of otology and neurotology. **Focus:** Hearing and deafness; Otolaryngology; Otology. **Qualif.:** Applicants must be physician investigators in the United States and Canada. **Criteria:** Selection will be on a competitive basis.

Funds Avail.: $25,000 per year. **Duration:** Annual. **Number Awarded:** 1. **To Apply:** Applicants must submit, prepare your application electronically and have everything including reference letters contained within one PDF. Please submit your final PDF application by email. Reference letters may be electronically prepared and signed as PDF documents, or may be scanned as PDF documents, in order that they may be included as part of the grant application. **Deadline:** March 1. **Remarks:** Established in 2014. **Contact:** Letters are to be submitted via email to Dr. Ronna Hertzano, Chair of the American Neurotology Society Research Committee, RHertzano@som.umaryland.edu and Kristen Bordignon, Administrator for the American Neurotology Society, administrator@americanneurotologysociety.com.

1159 ■ American Nuclear Society (ANS)

555 N Kensington Ave.
La Grange Park, IL 60526
Ph: (708)352-6611
Fax: (708)579-8314
Free: 800-323-3044
URL: www.ans.org
Social Media: www.facebook.com/www.ans.org
instagram.com/americannuclear
www.linkedin.com/groups/117546/profile
twitter.com/ans_org

Awards are arranged alphabetically below their administering organizations

1160 ■ American Nuclear Society Incoming Freshman Scholarships *(Undergraduate/Scholarship)*

Purpose: To assist students who wish to complete their post-secondary education and prepare for careers in nuclear science and technology (NS&T). **Focus:** Engineering, Nuclear. **Qualif.:** Applicants must be graduating high school seniors who have enrolled, full-time, in college courses pursuing science, technology, engineering, or mathematics (STEM) with an interest in working in nuclear science and technology. **Criteria:** Selection is evaluated based upon numerous factors, including academic preparation (GPA and test scores), awards, honors, leadership within the ANS, references, and career goals and objectives.

Funds Avail.: $1,000. **Duration:** Annual. **Number Awarded:** 4. **To Apply:** Applicants must submit all the required application information. **Deadline:** April 1.

1161 ■ American Nuclear Society Nevada Section Scholarship *(Undergraduate/Scholarship)*

Purpose: To provide financial assistance for tuition, fees and other appropriate educational expenses for CCSD Nevada seniors who plan to major in a Nuclear Engineering or a Nuclear Science related field at UNLV. **Focus:** Engineering, Nuclear; Nuclear science. **Qualif.:** Applicants must be CCSD seniors planning to major in nuclear engineering or a nuclear science related field at UNLV with a minimum 3.8 cumulative GPA. **Criteria:** Selection will be based on the application materials.

Funds Avail.: $1,000. **Duration:** Annual. **Number Awarded:** 1. **To Apply:** Applicants must submit a completed application form with an essay; two letters of recommendation; transcript; and resume of awards; a letter of recommendation from a teacher, counselor, administrator, coach or advisor. **Deadline:** January 31. **Contact:** Phone: 702-221-7422; Email: csdonnelly@ccpef.org.

1162 ■ American Nuclear Society Undergraduates Scholarships *(Undergraduate/Scholarship)*

Purpose: To help students complete their post-secondary education and prepare for careers in nuclear science and technology (NS&T). **Focus:** Engineering, Nuclear; Nuclear science. **Qualif.:** Applicants must be students who have completed at least two or more years in a course of study leading to a degree in nuclear science, nuclear engineering or a nuclear-related field. **Criteria:** Selection is evaluated based upon numerous factors, including academic preparation (GPA and test scores), awards, honors, leadership within the ANS, references, and career goals and objectives.

Funds Avail.: $2,000 - $2,500. **Duration:** Annual. **Number Awarded:** 4. **To Apply:** Applicants must submit all the required application information. **Deadline:** February 1.

1163 ■ Everitt P. Blizard Memorial Scholarship *(Graduate/Scholarship)*

Purpose: To support full-time graduate students in a program leading to an advanced degree in nuclear science, nuclear engineering, or a nuclear-related field. **Focus:** Nuclear science.

Funds Avail.: $3,000. **To Apply:** Interested applicants must visit the website to obtain an application form. Scholarship application, official transcripts, list of academic and ANS related groups in which you have participated in and any corresponding leadership positions; list of honors and awards that you received when participating in school and volunteer related groups and organizations and the level of each award; personal Statement (500 words or less) of your future plans. **Deadline:** February 1. **Remarks:** The award was established to honor Everitt Pinnell Blizard, father of reactor shielding.

1164 ■ Decommissioning, and Environmental Science Division Graduate Scholarship *(Undergraduate/Scholarship)*

Purpose: To support students who are pursuing higher education. **Focus:** Engineering; Science. **Qualif.:** Applicants must be students pursuing master's degrees in engineering or science with an emphasis on decommissioning/decontamination; management/characterization of radioactive waste; restoration of the environment; nuclear engineering. Applicants must be enrolled in a curriculum of engineering and the scholarship is limited to U.S. citizens who are enrolled in U.S. schools. **Criteria:** Selection will be based on the committee's criteria.

Funds Avail.: $2,000/each. **Duration:** Annual. **To Apply:** Applicants must submit a description of long-term and short-term professional objectives. **Deadline:** February 1.

1165 ■ Glenn T. Seaborg Congressional Science and Engineering Fellowship *(Professional development/Fellowship)*

Purpose: To promote a better understanding of public policy procedures. **Focus:** Nuclear science. **Qualif.:** Applicants must be US citizens; must be ANS members for at least two years; must fulfill a PhD in a nuclear-related discipline and at least one year of experience in a nuclear field; must fulfill a PhD in another science or engineering discipline and at least two years experience in a nuclear field; must fulfill an MS in engineering with at least three years post-degree experience in a nuclear field. **Criteria:** Selection will be based on the following criteria: competence in nuclear science and technology; demonstrated ability to participate in public policy discussions; a demonstrated ability in written and oral communications; contributions to ANS.

Funds Avail.: $60,000(Additonal travel expenses $5,000). **Duration:** Annual. **To Apply:** Applicants must submit the following information in a word, PDF, or other compatible format: applicant's name; mailing address; maximum two pages academic and professional summary; maximum two-page statement explaining the reasons for applying, what they hope to accomplish and how the fellowship will benefit them and their employer; one or two letters of reference. **Deadline:** May 1. **Contact:** Email: fellow@ans.org.

1166 ■ Allan F. Henry/Paul A. Greebler Scholarship *(Graduate/Scholarship)*

Purpose: To support full-time graduate students in a program leading to an advanced degree in nuclear science, nuclear engineering, or a nuclear-related field. **Focus:** Nuclear science.

Funds Avail.: $3,500. **Duration:** Annual. **To Apply:** Interested applicants must visit the website to obtain an application form. Scholarship application, official transcripts, list of academic and ANS related groups in which you have participated in and any corresponding leadership positions; list of honors and awards that you received when participating in school and volunteer related groups and organizations and the level of each award; personal Statement (500 words or less) of your future plans. **Deadline:** February 1. **Remarks:** The award was established to honor Dr. Paul

Awards are arranged alphabetically below their administering organizations

Greebler, who was a leader in ANS activities, an outstanding nuclear reactor physicist, and a true gentleman whose company all of his associates enjoyed.

1167 ■ Saul Levine Memorial Scholarship *(Graduate/Scholarship)*

Purpose: To support full-time graduate students in a program leading to an advanced degree in nuclear science, nuclear engineering, or a nuclear-related field. **Focus:** Nuclear science.

Funds Avail.: $3,000. **Duration:** Annual. **To Apply:** Interested applicants must visit the website to obtain an application form. Scholarship application, official transcripts, list of academic and ANS related groups in which you have participated in and any corresponding leadership positions; list of honors and awards that you received when participating in school and volunteer related groups and organizations and the level of each award; personal Statement (500 words or less) of your future plans. **Deadline:** February 1. **Remarks:** The award was established to honor Saul Levine, who was one of the pioneers in advancing the understanding of nuclear reactor safety. Established in 2001.

1168 ■ Nuclear Criticality Safety Pioneers Scholarship *(Graduate/Scholarship)*

Purpose: To support full-time graduate students in a program leading to an advanced degree in nuclear science, nuclear engineering, or a nuclear-related field. **Focus:** Nuclear science. **Criteria:** Selection will be based on the following criteria: contributions to American Nuclear Society; financial need; professional accomplishments and career objectives; academic performance.

Funds Avail.: $3,000. **Duration:** Annual. **To Apply:** Interested applicants must visit the website to obtain an application form. Scholarship application, official transcripts, list of academic and ANS related groups in which you have participated in and any corresponding leadership positions; list of honors and awards that you received when participating in school and volunteer related groups and organizations and the level of each award; personal Statement (500 words or less) of your future plans. **Deadline:** February 1.

1169 ■ James F. Schumar Scholarship *(Graduate/Scholarship)*

Purpose: To support full-time graduate students in a program leading to an advanced degree in nuclear science, nuclear engineering, or a nuclear-related field. **Focus:** Nuclear science.

Funds Avail.: $3,000. **Duration:** Annual. **To Apply:** Interested applicants must visit the website to obtain an application form. Scholarship application, official transcripts, list of academic and ANS related groups in which you have participated in and any corresponding leadership positions; list of honors and awards that you received when participating in school and volunteer related groups and organizations and the level of each award; personal Statement (500 words or less) of your future plans. **Deadline:** February 1. **Remarks:** The award was established to honor James Schumar, who was a senior scientist and the first chair of the ANS Materials Science and Technology Division.

1170 ■ American Numismatic Society (ANS)
75 Varick St., 11th Fl.
New York, NY 10013
Ph: (212)571-4470

E-mail: membership@numismatics.org
URL: www.numismatics.org
Social Media: www.facebook.com/AmericanNumismaticSociety
www.instagram.com/americannumismaticsociety
www.pinterest.com/anscoins
twitter.com/anscoins
www.youtube.com/user/ANSCoins

1171 ■ Frances M. Schwartz Fellowship *(Other/Fellowship)*

Purpose: To support the study of numismatic and museum methodology at the American Numismatic Society. **Focus:** Numismatics. **Qualif.:** Applicant must have the B.A. or the equivalent.

Funds Avail.: $5,000. **Duration:** Annual. **Remarks:** Established in 1985.

1172 ■ American Nurses Foundation (ANF)
8515 Georgia Ave., Ste. 400
Silver Spring, MD 20910-3492
Ph: (301)628-5227
Free: 800-284-2378
E-mail: givetonursing@ana.org
URL: www.nursingworld.org
Social Media: www.facebook.com/AmericanNursesAssociation
www.linkedin.com/company/american-nurses-association
twitter.com/ananursingworld
www.youtube.com/user/nursesmatter

1173 ■ ANF/ANN-FNRE Nursing Research Grants *(Professional development/Grant)*

Purpose: To support scientific research for advancing the practice of nursing, promoting health and preventing disease. **Focus:** Nursing, Neonatal. **Criteria:** Preference will be given to applicants who are members of the Academy of Neonatal Nursing; If there are no member applications, or no high-quality proposals from members, non-member applicants will be considered, with the selected grantee required to become a member of ANN in order to receive funding.

Funds Avail.: $5,000. **Remarks:** The grants are made possible by the ANF, in partnership with the Academy of Neonatal Nursing and the Foundation for Neonatal Research and Education.

1174 ■ ANF/ENRS Nursing Research Society *(Professional development/Grant)*

Purpose: To support scientific research for advancing the practice of nursing, promoting health and preventing disease. **Focus:** Nursing. **Qualif.:** Applicants must be ENRS member. **Criteria:** Selection will be based on the Foundation's criteria. Preference will be given to applicants who are members of the ENRS. If there are no member applications, or no high-quality proposal from association members, non-member applicants will be considered, with the selected grantee required to become a member of ENRS in order to receive funding.

Funds Avail.: $10,000. **Number Awarded:** 1. **Remarks:** The grants are made possible by the ANF, in partnership with the Eastern Nursing Research Society.

1175 ■ Sigma Theta Tau, International Nursing Research Grants (STTI) *(Master's, Doctorate/Grant)*

Purpose: To support scientific research for advancing the practice of nursing, promoting health and preventing

Awards are arranged alphabetically below their administering organizations

disease. **Focus:** Nursing. **Qualif.:** Applicants must be Non-US nurses and clinical nursing researchers who obtained either master's or doctorate degree, or enrolled in a doctoral program. **Criteria:** Selection will be based on the Foundation's criteria.

Funds Avail.: $7,500. **Remarks:** The grants are made possible by the ANF, in partnership with the Sigma Theta Tau International. **Contact:** For more information, contact Gisele Marshall at 301-628-5227 or email at gisele.marshall@ana.org.

1176 ■ American Occupational Therapy Foundation (AOTF)

12300 Twinbrook Pkwy., Ste. 520
Rockville, MD 20852
Ph: (240)292-1079
Fax: (240)396-6188
E-mail: aotf@aotf.org
URL: www.aotf.org
Social Media: www.facebook.com/
  americanoccupationaltherapyfoundation
linkedin.com/company/american-occupational-therapy
  -foundation
pinterest.com/aotf
twitter.com/AOTFoundation

1177 ■ Edith Weingarten Scholarship *(Postgraduate/ Scholarship)*

Purpose: To support students enrolled in a occupational therapy assistant programs. **Focus:** Occupational therapy. **Qualif.:** Applicants must Be currently enrolled as a full-time student at an AOTA accredited or developing professional level (master's or OTD) or occupational therapy assistant (OTA) program; must have completed at least one year of occupational therapy specific course work. **Criteria:** Recipients are selected based on the application and the materials submitted.

Duration: Annual. **To Apply:** Applicants must submit: applicant contact information including appropriate membership information; academic background; resume; essay question; reference/recommendation forms; program Director's statement; signature. **Deadline:** October 1. **Contact:** Phone: 240-292-1125; Email: scholarships@aotf.org.

1178 ■ Frank Oppenheimer Scholarship *(Postgraduate/Scholarship)*

Purpose: To support students enrolled in a occupational therapy assistant programs. **Focus:** Occupational therapy. **Qualif.:** Applicants must Be currently enrolled as a full-time student at an AOTA accredited or developing professional level (master's or OTD) or occupational therapy assistant (OTA) program; must have completed at least one year of occupational therapy specific course work. **Criteria:** Recipients are selected based on the application and the materials submitted.

Funds Avail.: $750. **Duration:** Annual. **To Apply:** Applicants must complete the online application, (please visit AOTF website); must prepare two personal references; curriculum Director's statement; official transcripts; financial statement; and an essay. **Deadline:** October 31. **Contact:** Phone: 240-292-1034; Email: scholarships@aotf.org.

1179 ■ Kappa Delta Phi Scholarship *(Postgraduate/ Scholarship)*

Purpose: To support students enrolled in a occupational therapy assistant programs. **Focus:** Occupational therapy.

Qualif.: Applicants must be currently enrolled as a full-time student at an AOTA accredited or developing professional level (master's or OTD) or occupational therapy assistant (OTA) program; must have completed at least one year of occupational therapy specific course work; must be a residents of AZ, CA, FL, IA, IN, KY, MO, OH. **Criteria:** Recipients are selected based on the application and the materials submitted. Priority will be given to the residents of AZ, CA, FL, IA, IN, KY, MO, OH.

Duration: Annual. **To Apply:** Applicants must submit: applicant contact information including appropriate membership information; academic background; resume; essay question; reference/recommendation forms; program Director's statement; signature. **Deadline:** October 1. **Contact:** Phone: 240-292-1125; Email: scholarships@aotf.org.

1180 ■ Mary Minglen Scholarship *(Postgraduate/ Scholarship)*

Purpose: To support students enrolled in a occupational therapy assistant programs. **Focus:** Occupational therapy. **Qualif.:** Applicants must Be currently enrolled as a full-time student at an AOTA accredited or developing professional level (master's or OTD) or occupational therapy assistant (OTA) program; must have completed at least one year of occupational therapy specific course work. **Criteria:** Recipients are selected based on the application and the materials submitted.

Funds Avail.: $1,200. **Duration:** Annual. **To Apply:** Applicants must submit: applicant contact information including appropriate membership information; academic background; resume; essay question; reference/recommendation forms; program Director's statement; signature. **Deadline:** October 1. **Contact:** Phone: 240-292-1125; Email: scholarships@aotf.org.

1181 ■ NorthCoast Medical Scholarship *(Postgraduate/Scholarship)*

Purpose: To support students enrolled in a occupational therapy assistant programs. **Focus:** Occupational therapy. **Qualif.:** Applicants must Be currently enrolled as a full-time student at an AOTA accredited or developing professional level (master's or OTD) or occupational therapy assistant (OTA) program; must have completed at least one year of occupational therapy specific course work. **Criteria:** Recipients are selected based on the application and the materials submitted.

Funds Avail.: $5,000. **Duration:** Annual. **To Apply:** Applicants must submit: applicant contact information including appropriate membership information; academic background; resume; essay question; reference/recommendation forms; program Director's statement; signature. **Deadline:** October 1. **Contact:** Phone: 240-292-1125; Email: scholarships@aotf.org.

1182 ■ Willard & Spackman Scholarship Program *(Postgraduate/Scholarship)*

Purpose: To support students enrolled in a occupational therapy assistant programs. **Focus:** Occupational therapy. **Qualif.:** Applicants must be currently enrolled as a full-time student at an AOTA accredited or developing professional level (master's or OTD) or occupational therapy assistant (OTA) program; must have completed at least one year of occupational therapy specific course work. **Criteria:** Recipients are selected based on the application and the materials submitted.

Funds Avail.: $2,000 each. **Duration:** Annual. **To Apply:** Applicants must submit: applicant contact information

---

Awards are arranged alphabetically below their administering organizations

including appropriate membership information; academic background; resume; essay question; reference/recommendation forms; program Director's statement; signature. **Deadline:** October 1. **Contact:** Phone: 240-292-1125; Email: scholarships@aotf.org.

1183 ■ American Oil Chemists' Society (AOCS)

2710 S Boulder Dr.
Urbana, IL 61802-6996
Ph: (217)359-2344
Fax: (217)351-8091
E-mail: general@aocs.org
URL: www.aocs.org
Social Media: www.facebook.com/AOCSFan
www.linkedin.com/groups/140499/profile
www.linkedin.com/company/aocs
twitter.com/AOCS
www.youtube.com/channel/UCOoXwFYZ4ZFbGKa0DF
_Y_NA

1184 ■ Ralph H. Potts Memorial Fellowship Award
(Graduate/Award, Fellowship)

Purpose: To award a graduate student doing research in fats and oils. **Focus:** Chemistry; Science. **Qualif.:** Candidate must be a scholastically outstanding graduate student from a North American university; research should involve fatty acids or their derivatives, such as long chain alcohols, amines, or other nitrogen compounds; furthermore, the research should fall within the categories of synthesis, processing utilization, or characterization.

Funds Avail.: $2,000 honorarium, and a $500 travel allowance. **Duration:** Annual. **To Apply:** Applicants must submit a completed application form; abstract tracking number and title; professor ranking form; professor letter of recommendation; submit an abstract through the AOCS Annual Meeting website, and then submit an Application through the Student Award website; the abstract number provided through the AOCS Annual Meeting abstract submission system must be included on the student application. **Deadline:** October 1. **Remarks:** The fellowship was established in recognition of Ralph H. Potts preeminence in the world of fatty acids and their derivatives, and the personal esteem in which he was held by his colleagues. Established in 1960. **Contact:** Email: awards@aocs.org.

1185 ■ American Orff-Schulwerk Association (AOSA)

147 Bell St., Ste. 300
Chagrin Falls, OH 44022
Ph: (440)600-7329
Fax: (440)600-7332
E-mail: communications@aosa.org
URL: aosa.org
Social Media: www.facebook.com/groups/146906471237
twitter.com/AOSA1968
youtube.com/user/AdminAOSA

1186 ■ AOSA Research Grant *(Professional development/Grant)*

Purpose: To promote philosophy and encourage research in varied applications of Orff Schulwerk. **Focus:** Education, Music; Music. **Qualif.:** Applicants must be AOSA members. **Criteria:** Selection will be based on committee's criteria.

Funds Avail.: $8,000. **Duration:** Annual. **To Apply:** Applicants must submit a completed application form; a resume reflecting knowledge of or expertise in Orff Schulwerk; a letter of reference and a project proposal. **Deadline:** January 15.

1187 ■ AOSA Research Partnership Grant *(Professional development/Grant)*

Purpose: To support joint research related to Orff Schulwerk by music teachers and experienced researchers. **Focus:** Music. **Qualif.:** Applicants must be groups consisting of one practicing music teacher (must be a member of the AOSA) of grades PK-12 in a school setting and one faculty member with substantial research experience at a college or university. **Criteria:** Applicants are selected based on the panel's review of the application materials.

Funds Avail.: $500-$8,000. **Duration:** Annual. **To Apply:** Applicants must submit a completed application form online; a resume reflecting knowledge of or expertise in Orff Schulwerk; a letter of reference and a project proposal. **Deadline:** January 15.

1188 ■ Barbara Potter Scholarship Fund *(Professional development/Scholarship)*

Purpose: To provide financial assistance for members of AOSA who wish to study at the Orff Institute in Salzburg, Austria. **Focus:** Music. **Qualif.:** Applicants must be a U.S. citizen or must have resided in the United States for the past five years; a current member of AOSA and must have been an AOSA member in good standing for one year; must have completed Level III Orff Schulwerk Training. **Criteria:** Applicants are selected based on the jury's review of application materials.

Funds Avail.: Amount varies. **Duration:** Biennial; in even-numbered years. **Number Awarded:** Varies. **To Apply:** Applications can be submitted online; must include basic Information; curricula vita; project Description, 1-2 pages; financial Statement; If the application is to provide instruments for school/district, the applicants must include school profile; instrument inventory and request form; reference letter; copies of the tax returns. **Deadline:** January 15. **Remarks:** The scholarship fund was established by the American Orff-Schulwerk Association to honor Barbara Potter for her passion for study at the Orff Institute in Salzburg, Austria. **Contact:** Email: info@aosa.org.

1189 ■ Shields-Gillespie Scholarship *(Other/Scholarship)*

Purpose: To support special creative projects that are associated with Orff Schulwerk and that will benefit the music education of children. **Focus:** Music. **Qualif.:** Applicants must be a U.S. citizen or must have resided in the United States for the past five years; a current member of AOSA and must have been an AOSA member in good standing for one year; must be actively involved in teaching low-income preschool or kindergarten students; must have a strong motivation to study music; and demonstrated financial need. **Criteria:** Applicants are selected based on the jury's review of application materials.

Funds Avail.: Amount varies. **Duration:** Annual. **Number Awarded:** Varies. **To Apply:** Applications can be submitted online; must include basic Information; curricula vita; project description, 1-2 pages; financial statement; copies of the tax returns. **Deadline:** January 15. **Remarks:** The scholarship honors Avon's memory and encourages the continuation of Harriette Evans Shields' philosophy of using music

Awards are arranged alphabetically below their administering organizations

as a foundation for learning in Early Childhood Education. **Contact:** Email: info@aosa.org.

1190 ■ American Oriental Society (AOS)

Hatcher Graduate Library
University of Michigan
Ann Arbor, MI 48109
URL: www.umich.edu
Social Media: twitter.com/umich

1191 ■ Louise Wallace Hackney Fellowships for the Study of Chinese Art *(Doctorate/Fellowship)*

Purpose: To permit the study of Chinese art, with special relation to painting and its reflection of Chinese culture. **Focus:** Chinese studies. **Qualif.:** Applicants must have completed three years study of the Chinese language or its equivalent and must be able to demonstrate that they have already committed themselves to the serious study of this important area of oriental art; must be post-doctoral as well as doctoral students. **Criteria:** Applicants are selected by the two committees of specialists in the field.

Funds Avail.: $8,000. **Duration:** 12 months. **To Apply:** Applicants should submit the following materials in duplicate transcript of their undergraduate and graduate course work; statement of personal finances; three or four-page summary of the proposed project to be undertaken during the year of the fellowship award, appended with a financial statement explaining the expense involved in this study; no less than three letters of recommendation. **Deadline:** March 1.

1192 ■ American Orthopaedic Foot and Ankle Society (AOFAS)

9400 W Higgins Rd., Ste. 220
Rosemont, IL 60018-4975
Ph: (847)698-4654
Fax: (847)692-3315
Free: 800-235-4855
E-mail: aofasinfo@aofas.org
URL: www.aofas.org
Social Media: www.facebook.com/aofas1
www.instagram.com/aofas1
www.linkedin.com/company/american-orthopaedic-foot-&
 -ankle-society
twitter.com/aofas
www.youtube.com/channel/UC9Jgll0MwbTIMU-3S08Z48Q

1193 ■ AOFAS Research Grants Program *(Graduate/Grant)*

Purpose: To assist members and other orthopedists in providing the highest quality foot and ankle care to the public. **Focus:** Medicine, Orthopedic. **Qualif.:** Applicants eligibility for grant funding is a benefit of membership in AOFAS, and the principle or co-principle project investigator must be an AOFAS active, candidate or international member.**Criteria:** Applications are reviewed and scored by the AOFAS Research Committee and its ad hoc reviewers on a blind basis using an NIH-style process. The committee makes recommendations to the AOFAS Board, which makes the final decision on funding.

Funds Avail.: Upto $20,000. **Duration:** One year. **To Apply:** Applications form and administrative policies and procedures are available online. **Deadline:** December 1.

Contact: Email: research@aofas.org Phone: 1-800-235-4855 or 1-847-698-4654.

1194 ■ Orthopaedic Foot and Ankle Fellowships *(Graduate, Professional development/Fellowship)*

Purpose: To assist members and other orthopedists in providing the highest quality foot and ankle care to the public. **Focus:** Medicine, Orthopedic. **Qualif.:** Applicants must be orthopedic surgeons and/or graduates from an allopathic or osteopathic medical school where fellowship is dependent upon successful completion of an approved orthopedic surgery residency program. **Criteria:** Recipients will be selected based on a consensus by foot and ankle fellowship directors.

Funds Avail.: $50,000. **Duration:** Annual; from august 1 to july 31. **Number Awarded:** Varies. **To Apply:** Applicants may download a fellowship application form online. Upon completion of the requirements, the applicants must submit their application together with program application list, curriculum vitae, personal vitae, personal statement, four letters of reference directly from the referrer, and check list of programs. **Deadline:** January 1. **Contact:** E-mail: bos@aaos.org.

1195 ■ American Osler Society (AOS)

c/o Renee Ziemer, Administrator
141 County Rd., 132 SE
Dover, MN 55929
Ph: (507)259-5125
E-mail: aosrenee@gmail.com
URL: www.americanosler.org
Social Media: www.facebook.com/American-Osler-Society
 -125835777005/timeline

1196 ■ William B. Bean Student Research Award *(Undergraduate/Grant)*

Purpose: To support research by medical students in Medical History and Medical Humanities. **Focus:** Medical research. **Qualif.:** Candidates must be current students at accredited medical schools in the U.S. or Canada.

Funds Avail.: $1,500. **Duration:** Annual. **Deadline:** March 1.

1197 ■ American Osteopathic Foundation (AOF)

142 E Ontario St., Ste. 1450
Chicago, IL 60611
Ph: (312)202-8234
Fax: (312)202-8216
E-mail: info@aof.org
URL: aof.org
Social Media: www.facebook.com/
 AmericanOsteopathicFoundation
www.linkedin.com/company/american-osteopathic
 -foundation
twitter.com/AOFDOgood
www.youtube.com/user/AOFoundation

1198 ■ William G. Anderson, DO, Minority Scholarships *(Undergraduate/Scholarship)*

Purpose: To support and recognize an outstanding minority osteopathic medical student who is committed to osteopathic principals and practice, has excelled academically, and has proven to be a leader in addressing the

Awards are arranged alphabetically below their administering organizations

educational, societal, and health needs of minorities. **Focus:** Medicine, Osteopathic. **Qualif.:** Applicants must be minority osteopathic medical students who have successfully completed their first-year of studies prior to the fall of the current year and will still be enrolled as osteopathic medical students during the same time. All applicants must be in good academic standing at an AOA accredited college of osteopathic medicine. **Criteria:** Applicants shall meet the following criteria: excellent academic achievement; demonstrated leadership efforts in addressing the educational, societal, and health needs of minorities; demonstrated leadership efforts to eliminate inequities in medical education and health care; noteworthy accomplishments, awards and honors, clerkship or special projects, and extracurricular activities in which they have shown leadership abilities. Financial need can be considered but not the determinative factor in the selection. **Funds Avail.:** $10,000. **Duration:** Annual. **Number Awarded:** 1. **Remarks:** The scholarship was established in honor of William G. Anderson. **Contact:** American Osteopathic Foundation, 142 E. Ontario St. Ste. 1450, Chicago, IL 60611; E-mail: ggottlob@aof.org.

1199 ■ Russell C. McCaughan Heritage Scholarship
(Undergraduate/Scholarship, Award)

Purpose: To provide monetary scholarship to help defer the cost of students' osteopathic medical education. **Focus:** Medicine, Osteopathic. **Qualif.:** Applicants must be osteopathic medical students who are in their last year of studies; must be committed to the science, art and philosophy of osteopathic medicine; must be enrolled in an AOA approved college/school of osteopathic medicine. **Criteria:** Selection will be based on the following criteria: demonstrated commitment to the osteopathic profession, medicine and education; promotes osteopathic ideas and unity within the osteopathic community; participation in extracurricular activities that promote osteopathic medicine to the public; demonstrates, by word and deed, the desire to advance osteopathic medicine; presents a positive image and attitude about the osteopathic profession; exhibits a unique combination of character, moral, academic and ethical behavior. **Funds Avail.:** $5,000. **Duration:** Annual. **Number Awarded:** 1. **To Apply:** Applicants must submit the following in one packet: completed application form; letters of recommendation from 3 references; letter from Dean certifying that the applicants is in good academic standing and states the applicants' class ranking; personal statement from the applicant of not more than 2 pages; official medical school academic transcript; curriculum vitae or resume. **Remarks:** Established in 1956. **Contact:** Vicki Heck, Association Dir. of Communications; vheck@aoffoundation.org or at 312-202-8232.

1200 ■ Welch Scholars Grants *(Undergraduate/Grant)*
Purpose: To provide monetary aid to students in need at each college of osteopathic medicine. **Focus:** Medicine, Osteopathic. **Qualif.:** Applicants must be osteopathic medical students who have successfully completed their first-year of studies prior to the fall of the current year and will still be enrolled as osteopathic medical students during the same time. All applicants must be in good academic standing at an AOA accredited college of osteopathic medicine. **Criteria:** Recipients are chosen because of their outstanding academic achievement, participation in extracurricular activities, strong commitment toward osteopathic medicine and financial need. **Funds Avail.:** $1,500. **Duration:** Annual. **Number Awarded:** 1. **Remarks:** Established in 2001. **Contact:**

American Osteopathic Foundation, 142 E. Ontario St. Ste. 1450, Chicago, IL 60611; E-mail: ggottlob@aof.org.

1201 ■ American Otological Society (AOS)
c/o Kristen Bordignon, Executive Administrator
5830 1st St. N
Saint Petersburg, FL 33703
Ph: (217)638-0801
Fax: (727)800-9428
E-mail: administrator@americanotologicalsociety.org
URL: www.americanotologicalsociety.org

1202 ■ AOS Research Training Fellowships
(Graduate/Fellowship)

Purpose: To further the study on otosclerosis, Meniere's disease, and related ear disorders. **Focus:** Meniere's disease; Otology; Otosclerosis.

Duration: 1-2 years. **Deadline:** January 31. **Contact:** John S. Oghalai, MD, Executive Secretary, Research Fund of the American Otological Society, Inc. E-mail: john.oghalai@med.usc.edu, Kristen Bordignon, Assistant to Dr. Oghalai; E-mail: administrator@americanotologicalsociety.org.

1203 ■ American Paint Horse Foundation (APHA)
122 East Exchange Ave. – Ste. 420
Fort Worth, TX 76164
Ph: (817)834-2742
Fax: (817)834-3152
URL: apha.com
Social Media: www.linkedin.com/company/american-paint-horse-association/about
twitter.com/APHAnews?lang=en

1204 ■ APHF Academic Scholarship *(Undergraduate/Scholarship)*

Purpose: To support and encourage hard-working young horsemen and women who are striving every day to be the best both in the horse show arena and in their academic pursuits. **Focus:** General studies/Field of study not specified. **Qualif.:** Applicants must be an APHA or AjPHA member in good standing for three years, and involved in horse activity using a Paint Horse or contributing actively to an APHA Regional Club for at least one year prior to and at the time of application; must be a high school graduate or equivalent and have never been married; must apply for the scholarship within two years from the date of high school graduation and if not awarded, can reapply during the next four years, but the award is not retroactive. **Funds Avail.:** $1,000 each. **Duration:** Annual. **Number Awarded:** 53. **To Apply:** Applicants must review application requirements on application form. APHF scholarship checklist includes the following: filled out personal and family information; completely listed all scholastic information; 500-word essay on educational plans and goals; a photograph; photograph should be approximately 3 inches by 5 inches; a transcript covering grades 1012 indicating the required cumulative 3.0 or higher GPA adjusted to a 4-point scale; official copy of SAT or ACT results if scores are not listed in transcript; listed all APHA- and horse-related activities; noted all extracurricular and community involvement; three letters of reference (each provided with a recommendation form); and, a college transcript if applicable. If they meet requirements, completely fill out application. Mail completed scholarship application to APHA at the mailing

Awards are arranged alphabetically below their administering organizations

address located on the front cover of application by the deadline. **Deadline:** March 1. **Contact:** American Paint Horse Foundation, PO Box 961023, Fort Worth, TX, 76161-0023; Phone: 817-222-6412.

1205 ■ American Parkinson Disease Association (APDA)

135 Parkinson Ave.
Staten Island, NY 10305
Ph: (718)981-8001
Fax: (718)981-4399
Free: 800-223-2732
E-mail: apda@apdaparkinson.org
URL: www.apdaparkinson.org
Social Media: www.facebook.com/APDA.INC
www.instagram.com/apdaparkinsons
www.linkedin.com/company/2880181
twitter.com/apdaparkinsons
www.youtube.com/user/APDAparkinson/videos

1206 ■ APDA Post-Doctoral Research Fellowship
(Postdoctorate/Fellowship)

Purpose: To support postdoctoral scientists whose research training holds promise into new insights of geriatric psychology, pathophysiology, etiology, and treatment of Parkinson's disease. **Focus:** Medicine, Geriatric; Parkinson's disease. **Qualif.:** Applicants must have completed their MD, DO, PhD, MD/PhD, DO/PhD or clinical residency program within two (2) years of the onset of the proposed study and must perform the research project at an academic institution within the United States whose research training focuses on new insights into the pathophysiology, etiology, and/or treatment of Parkinson's disease.

Funds Avail.: Maximum of $50,000. **Duration:** Annual; every September 1 to August 31. **To Apply:** Applicants must submit (three pages) research proposal which includes: background rationale, research plan/methods and goals; a description of where the research will be done and the resources available; a letter of reference and support from the mentor; a list of all current and pending support; and the applicant's NIH-Biosketch. **Deadline:** March 12. **Contact:** Grant Administrator, Heather Gray; Phone: 800-223-2732 ext. 117; Email: hgray@apdaparkinson.org.

1207 ■ APDA Research Grants *(Postgraduate, Professional development/Grant)*

Purpose: To provide financial support to junior investigators intending to pursue research in Parkinson's disease. **Focus:** Medical research; Parkinson's disease. **Qualif.:** Applicants must be research scientists (MD, MD/PhD, or PhD). The same investigator can reapply the following year to be considered for a second consecutive year of funding. When submitting applications for a grant on the same subject for the second consecutive year, the applicant will also submit a report of the results obtained during the prior APDA funding years. **Criteria:** Selection of recipients will be based on merit.

Funds Avail.: Maximum of $75,000. **Duration:** Annual; every September 1 to August 31. **To Apply:** Applicants must complete on-line application and submit the three pages proposal; NIH Bio-sketch and references. One (1) original of the complete application must be submitted to the attention of Heather Gray, National office. **Deadline:** March 12. **Contact:** Grant Administrator, Heather Gray; Phone: 800-223-2732 ext. 117; Email: hgray@apdaparkinson.org.

1208 ■ Dr. George C. Cotzias Memorial Fellowship
(Other, Professional development/Fellowship)

Purpose: To assist promising young neurologists in establishing careers in research, teaching, and patient service relevant to the problems, causes, prevention, diagnosis and treatment of Parkinson's disease and related neurological movement disorders. **Focus:** Neurology; Parkinson's disease. **Qualif.:** Applicant must be a physician and a U.S. citizen or a permanent resident of the U.S. who or has completed, training in a clinical discipline concerned with disorders of the nervous system (i.e. medical neurology, child neurology, neurosurgery, neuropathology); should be an instructor or assistant professor with a clear commitment for the future at sponsoring institution; must be no more than 8 years beyond receipt of their MD or OD degree and should be sponsored by a non-profit institution in the U.S. or its territories. Applicant should be no more than 6 years beyond completion of their clinical training at the time of submission and must be sponsored by a non-profit institution in the U.S. or its territories. **Criteria:** Selection will be based on the aforesaid qualifications and compliance with the application process.

Funds Avail.: $100,000 per year. **Duration:** Three consecutive years. **To Apply:** Applicants must submit the following requirements: an abstract of the proposed study; a budget for each year; resources provided or to be provided by the sponsoring institution; other sources of funding, to include sponsoring agency, amount and award period (indicate how the other sponsored research complements or supplements the present proposal); two letters of recommendation (one from the applicant's institutional sponsor and one from an academic colleague with knowledge of the applicant's professional performance). One original of the complete application must be submitted to the attention of Heather Gray, National office. **Deadline:** March 12. **Remarks:** The fellowship was established to honor the memory of the late Dr. Cotzias and to stimulate young neurologists to follow his leadership. **Contact:** Grant Administrator, Heather Gray; Phone: 800-223-2732 ext. 117; Email: hgray@apdaparkinson.org.

1209 ■ American Pediatric Surgical Nurses Association (APSNA)

5353 Wayzata Blvd., Ste. 350
Minneapolis, MN 55416
Free: 855-984-1609
E-mail: info@apsna.org
URL: www.apsna.org
Social Media: www.facebook.com/APSNAnurse
twitter.com/APSNAnurse

1210 ■ American Pediatric Surgical Nurses Association Educational Grant *(Other/Grant)*

Purpose: To assist APSNA members to further their professional education. **Focus:** Medicine, Pediatric; Nursing; Surgery. **Qualif.:** Applicants must be an APSNA member in good standing for at least one year; a registered nurse or advanced practice nurse with two years experience in pediatric surgical nursing involved in pediatric surgery patient care, education or research. **Criteria:** Selection will be made by the education committees based on potential leadership.

Funds Avail.: No specific amount. **Duration:** Annual. **To Apply:** Applicants must submit a completed application form; a documentation of program, conference or educa-

Awards are arranged alphabetically below their administering organizations

tional needs which the scholarship will be used; description of the program course; a current curriculum vitae; a letter of recommendation from co-worker; a cover letter to the Director at Large stating the applicant's credentials, experience and involvement in the pediatric surgical nursing practices and standards; and an essay about the importance of the award. **Deadline:** February 28. **Contact:** Send the following information electronically to awards@apsna.org.

1211 ■ American Philosophical Society (APS)
104 S 5th St.
Philadelphia, PA 19106-3387
Ph: (215)440-3400
Fax: (215)440-3423
E-mail: orders@dianepublishing.net
URL: amphilsoc.org

1212 ■ Daland Fellowships in Clinical Investigation
(Doctorate, Postgraduate/Fellowship)

Purpose: To provide financial support for research in the several branches of clinical medicine, including internal medicine, neurology, pediatrics, psychiatry and surgery. **Focus:** Biological and clinical sciences; Medicine, Pediatric; Neurology; Psychiatry; Surgery. **Qualif.:** Candidates must be both U.S. citizens and foreign nationals; have MD or MD/PhD degree for fewer than eight years; do not have more than two years of post-doctoral training and research; expecting to perform the research at an institution in the United States; direct contact with patients. **Criteria:** Recipients will be selected based on the jury's review of the application materials.

Funds Avail.: $40,000 for first year and $40,000 for second year. **Duration:** Annual. **To Apply:** Applicants must submit a completed application form includes all materials requested on the form; three confidential letters supporting the application. **Deadline:** September 15. **Contact:** Daland Fellowships in Clinical Investigation American Philosophical Society 104 South Fifth Street Philadelphia, PA 19106.

1213 ■ John Hope Franklin Dissertation Fellowship
(Doctorate/Fellowship)

Purpose: To support an outstanding doctoral student at an American university or an exceptional American doctoral student abroad who is completing the dissertation. **Focus:** General studies/Field of study not specified. **Qualif.:** Applicants may be U.S. citizens and residents of the United States or American citizens resident abroad; must be a doctoral student at an American university or an exceptional American doctoral student abroad who is completing the dissertation.

Duration: Annual. **To Apply:** Applicants must submit completed on-line application form and letters of support should be attached. **Remarks:** Named in honor of a distinguished member of the American Philosophical Society, John Hope Franklin. **Contact:** Linda Musumeci, Director of Grants and Fellowships; Email: lmusumeci@amphilsoc.org; Phone: 215-440-3429.

1214 ■ Franklin Research Grants *(Doctorate/Grant)*

Purpose: To support research in all areas of knowledge leading to publication. **Focus:** General studies/Field of study not specified. **Qualif.:** Applicants must have a doctorate or have published work of doctoral character and quality; can be independent scholars and faculty members at

all four-year and two-year research and non-research institutions; must be American citizens and residents of the United States. **Criteria:** Recipients will be selected based on the jury's review of the application materials.

Funds Avail.: Up to maximum of $6,000 each. **Duration:** Annual. **To Apply:** Applicants must submit a project and financial reports are due one month after completion of the funded portion of the work; Two letters of Support. **Deadline:** October 1; December 1. **Contact:** Linda Musumeci, Director of Grants and Fellowships; Email: lmusumeci@amphilsoc.org; Phone: 215-440-3429.

1215 ■ Lewis and Clark Fund for Exploration and Field Research *(Doctorate/Grant)*

Purpose: To provide funds for projects related to the astrobiological field. **Focus:** Biological and clinical sciences. **Qualif.:** Applicant must be a doctoral student and a U.S. resident performing research anywhere in the world; must be based at a U.S. institution or planning to carry out research in the United States.

Funds Avail.: Up to $5,000. **Duration:** Annual. **To Apply:** Applicants must submit brief reports on their trip for archiving in the APS Library; Letters of Support. **Deadline:** November 16. **Contact:** Linda Musumeci, Director of Grants and Fellowships; Email: lmusumeci@amphilsoc.org; Phone: 215-440-3429.

1216 ■ Short-Term Library Resident Research Fellowships *(Doctorate/Fellowship)*

Purpose: To support research in the Society's collections. **Focus:** Humanities; Science. **Qualif.:** Applicants must be US citizens or foreign nationals; may be in any relevant field of scholarship; holders of the Ph.D. or its equivalent;Ph.D. candidates who have passed their preliminary examinations and are working on their dissertation research; degreed independent scholars (without current academic affiliation). **Criteria:** Selection will be given to the candidates who live 75 or more miles from Philadelphia.

Funds Avail.: $3,000 per month. **Duration:** Annual; up to 2 months. **Number Awarded:** 25-30. **To Apply:** Applicants must visit the website for the online application process; must submit the following: cover letter; curriculum vitae; research proposal, no longer than three pages, that outlines the status of your work and what you will research at the American Philosophical Society Library; contact information for two people who will submit confidential letters of reference. **Deadline:** March 1. **Contact:** Email:libfellows@amphilsoc.org.

1217 ■ Phillips Fund for Native American Research
(Doctorate, Master's/Grant)

Purpose: To provide assistance such as travel expenses, tapes, films and consultant's fee. **Focus:** Native American studies. **Qualif.:** Applicant must be a graduate student conducting research on masters thesis or doctoral dissertation. **Criteria:** Recipients will be selected based on the jury's review of the application materials.

Funds Avail.: $3,000 to $3,500. **Duration:** Annual. **To Apply:** Applicants must submit the American Philosophical Society Library with a brief formal report and copies of any field notes; films; audio recordings; transcriptions. **Deadline:** March 1. **Contact:** Linda Musumeci, Director of Grants and Fellowships; Email: lmusumeci@amphilsoc.org; Phone: 215-440-3429.

1218 ■ American Physical Society (APS)
1 Physics Ellipse
College Park, MD 20740-3844

Awards are arranged alphabetically below their administering organizations

Ph: (301)209-3200
Fax: (301)209-0865
E-mail: social@aps.org
URL: www.aps.org
Social Media: www.facebook.com/apsphysics
twitter.com/APSphysics
www.youtube.com/user/apsphysics

1219 ■ Andreas Acrivos Dissertation Award in Fluid Dynamics *(Graduate, Doctorate/Award, Recognition, Monetary)*

Purpose: To support exceptional young scientists who have performed original doctoral thesis work of outstanding scientific quality and achievement in the area of fluid dynamics. **Focus:** Physics. **Qualif.:** Applicants must be doctoral students studying at any colleges or universities in the United States or in any education abroad program of any colleges or universities in the United States; must have been accomplished as part of the requirements for a doctoral degree; must have completed their dissertations during the previous calendar year. **Criteria:** Selection will be based on committee decision.

Funds Avail.: $1,000. **Duration:** Annual. **Number Awarded:** 1. **To Apply:** Applicants must submit a APS Prizes and Awards nomination form; copy of the nominee's Ph.D. thesis; curriculum vitae; scanned signed nomination letter from the thesis advisor; at least two letters, but not more than three, seconding the nomination; demographics form (if known/wish to specify age, gender, race, and ethnicity of the nominee). **Deadline:** May 1. **Remarks:** The award is established in the honor of Dr. Andreas Acrivos. Established in 1998. **Contact:** Email: honors@aps.org.

1220 ■ American Physical Society Minority Undergraduate Scholarships *(Undergraduate/ Scholarship)*

Purpose: To help increase the number of underrepresented minorities obtaining degrees in physics, as well as to provide funding and mentoring to minority physics students, helping them enhance their education and successfully prepare for a variety of careers. **Focus:** Physics. **Qualif.:** Applicants must be African American, Hispanic American, or Native American US citizens or permanent residents who are majoring or planning to major in physics; must be high school seniors, college freshmen or sophomores. **Criteria:** Selection is vested to the APS Committee on Minorities in Physics (COM). Recipients are selected based on financial need and academic standing.

Funds Avail.: No specific amount. **Duration:** Annual. **Number Awarded:** 1. **To Apply:** Application should include the following contains: your resume (make sure you have your contact information correct!);your essay, in the same file; your written list of STEM courses you have taken with dates and grades, still in the same file. **Deadline:** February 15. **Remarks:** Established in 1980. **Contact:** Email:apsibmin@us.ibm.com.

1221 ■ APS Scholarships for Minority Undergraduate Physics Majors *(Undergraduate/Scholarship)*

Purpose: To inspire pursuits in physics education specifically among minority undergraduates. **Focus:** Physics. **Qualif.:** Applicant should be any African-American, Hispanic American, or Native American U.S. citizen or permanent resident who is majoring or planning to major in physics; a high school senior, college freshman, or sophomore. **Criteria:** Recipient is selected based on the committee's review of their academic eligibility.

Funds Avail.: $2,000 (for new minority scholars); $3,000 (for renewal students) to be used for tuition, room & board and educational materials. **Duration:** Annual. **To Apply:** Applicants may download application materials on the website. **Remarks:** Established in 1980.

1222 ■ Award for Outstanding Doctoral Dissertation in Laser Science *(Doctorate, Postdoctorate/Award)*

Purpose: To promote doctoral research in the Laser Science area and to encourage effective written and oral presentation of research results. **Focus:** Physics. **Qualif.:** Applicants must be doctoral students at any university in the United States or abroad who have passed their dissertation defense for the Ph.D. any time during the three calendar years preceding the Laser Science Conference and who are members of DLS. **Criteria:** Applicants will be chosen by the Dissertation Award Selection Committee based on the quality of the research and the written presentation.

Funds Avail.: $1,000; $750 for travel allowance. **Duration:** Annual. **Number Awarded:** 1. **To Apply:** Applicants must submit nomination form; letter from the research advisor; letter from the department chair; two letters seconding the application; summary of the dissertation prepared by the applicant, not to exceed 1,500 words excluding figures and references; copy of or web link to the dissertation; demographics form. **Deadline:** August 17. **Remarks:** Established in 2013. **Contact:** Email: honors@aps.org.

1223 ■ Award for Outstanding Doctoral Thesis Research in Biological Physics *(Doctorate, Postdoctorate/Award, Recognition, Monetary)*

Purpose: To recognize doctoral thesis research of outstanding quality and achievement in any area of experimental, computational, engineering, or theoretical Biological Physics, broadly construed, and to encourage effective written and oral presentation of research results. **Focus:** Physics. **Qualif.:** Applicants must be doctoral students at any universities in the United States or abroad who have passed their thesis defense for the Ph.D. in any areas of experimental, computational, engineering, or theoretical Biological Physics, broadly construed. **Criteria:** Selection will be based on the committee's criteria.

Funds Avail.: $1,500 with additional $500 to $1,000 for international travel reimbursement. **Duration:** Annual. **Number Awarded:** Varies. **To Apply:** Applications package must consists of nomination form; letter from the thesis advisor; letter from the department chair or relevant program director; two letters seconding the nomination; manuscript; an abstract; curriculum vitae; demographics form. **Deadline:** June 16. **Remarks:** Established in 2009. **Contact:** Email: honors@aps.org.

1224 ■ Dissertation Award in Hadronic Physics *(Doctorate, Postdoctorate/Award, Recognition, Monetary)*

Purpose: To support outstanding young scientists who have performed original research in the area of hadronic physics. **Focus:** Physics. **Qualif.:** Applicant must have received a Ph.D. in experimental or theoretical hadronic physics. **Criteria:** Selection will be based on the committee's criteria.

Funds Avail.: $1,000 with additional $1,500 for travel reimbursement. **Duration:** Biennial. **Number Awarded:** 1. **To Apply:** Applicant must include Prizes and Awards nomination form; name and address of the candidate; a

Awards are arranged alphabetically below their administering organizations

statement of the candidate's contribution to the research; a letter of support from the candidate's Ph.D. dissertation advisor; two additional letters of support from physicists familiar with the candidate and the research; a copy of the candidate's dissertation; demographics form. **Deadline:** September 7. **Remarks:** Established in 2011. **Contact:** Email: honors@aps.org.

1225 ■ M. Hildred Blewett Fellowship *(Postdoctorate/ Fellowship, Award, Monetary)*

Purpose: To enable women to return to physics research careers after having had to interrupt those careers. **Focus:** Physics. **Qualif.:** Applicants must currently be citizens, legal residents, or resident aliens of the United States or Canada who have completed work toward a PhD. **Criteria:** Selection shall be based on the following criteria: qualifications of applicant; status of career before break; steps the applicant has taken to return to physics research; relationship of the applicant to the research community; relationship of project and award to future plans; scholarly significance of the project; quality and feasibility of the project design and timeline.

Funds Avail.: Up to $45,000. **Duration:** Annual. **Number Awarded:** Varies. **To Apply:** Application forms are available on the website. Completed application form; must provide written proof from a u. s. or Canadian institution that they will have institutional affiliation during the tenure of the grant; one to three letter(s) of recommendation, one of which may be from a designated mentor; a letter of institutional support during the tenure of the grant. **Deadline:** June 1. **Remarks:** Established in 2005. **Contact:** Email: blewett@aps.org.

1226 ■ Nicholas Metropolis Award for Outstanding Doctoral Thesis Work in Computational Physics *(Doctorate, Postdoctorate/Award, Recognition, Monetary)*

Purpose: To recognizes doctoral thesis research of outstanding quality and achievement in computational physics and encourages effective written and oral presentation of research results, **Focus:** Physics. **Qualif.:** Applicants must be doctoral students (present or past) in any country for work performed as part of the requirements for a doctoral degree; must have passed their thesis defense not more than 18 months before the nomination deadline. **Criteria:** Selection will be based on the committee's criteria.

Funds Avail.: $2,500; $1,500 travel allowance. **Duration:** Annual. **Number Awarded:** 1. **To Apply:** Applications package should include Prizes and Awards Nomination Form; recommendation letter from nominator; thesis manuscript in pdf format; thesis summary accessible to a computational scientist without specific expertise in the field of the thesis; two additional letters of support, at least one from outside the nominee's institution; nominee's cv; demographics form. **Deadline:** August 14. **Contact:** Email: honors@aps.org.

1227 ■ Cecilia Payne-Gaposchkin Doctoral Dissertation Award in Astrophysics *(Doctorate, Postdoctorate/Award, Recognition, Monetary)*

Purpose: To promote doctoral thesis in research in Astrophysics, and to encourage effective written and oral presentation of research results. **Focus:** Physics. **Qualif.:** Applicant must be doctoral students at any university in the United States or abroad who have passed their thesis defense for the Ph.D. any time during the two calendar years prior to the year of the April and who are members of the DAP are eligible. **Criteria:** Selection will be based on the committee's criteria.

Funds Avail.: $1,000; $750 for travel allowance. **Duration:** Annual. **Number Awarded:** 1. **To Apply:** Applications packet must consist of Prizes and Awards nomination form; CV, including a list of publications; letter from the thesis advisor citing the specific contributions of the nominee and the significance of those contributions; most two letters seconding a nomination; letter from the department chair certifying the date of the thesis defense; manuscript prepared by the nominee describing the thesis research; the manuscript may not exceed 1, 500 words (excluding references) and a maximum of 6 figures; abstract prepared by the nominee suitable for publication; demographics form. **Deadline:** November 29. **Remarks:** Established in 2013.

1228 ■ Richard L. Greene Dissertation Award in Experimental Condensed Matter or Materials Physics *(Doctorate, Postdoctorate/Award, Recognition, Monetary)*

Purpose: To promote doctoral thesis research of exceptional quality and importance in experimental condensed matter or experimental materials physics. **Focus:** Physics. **Qualif.:** Applicants must be doctoral students who produced doctoral dissertations about experimental condensed matter or experimental materials physics, written in English and submitted to any college or university, worldwide. **Criteria:** Selection will be based on the committee's criteria.

Funds Avail.: $2,500; $1,500 travel allowance. **Duration:** Annual. **Number Awarded:** 2. **To Apply:** Applications packet must consist: APS Prizes and Awards nomination form; copy of the Ph.D. thesis written in English; letter from the thesis advisor explaining the rationale for the nomination; two letters of support with at least one being from another institution; demographics form. **Deadline:** August 31. **Remarks:** Established in 2013. **Contact:** Email: honors@aps.org.

1229 ■ Marshall N. Rosenbluth Outstanding Doctoral Thesis Award *(Doctorate, Postdoctorate/ Award, Recognition, Monetary)*

Purpose: To provide recognition to exceptional young scientists who have performed original thesis work of outstanding scientific quality and achievement in the area of plasma physics. **Focus:** Physics. **Qualif.:** Applicants must be doctoral students at any colleges or universities in the United States or United States students abroad who have successfully passed the final thesis defense within the preceding 24 months of the current nomination deadline. **Criteria:** Selection will be based on the committee's criteria.

Funds Avail.: $2,000. **Duration:** Annual. **Number Awarded:** 1. **To Apply:** Applications package should include: APS Prizes and Awards nomination form; letter of not more than 1,000 words evaluating the nominee's qualifications for the award; at least two, but no more than four, seconding letters; nominee's thesis; demographics form. **Deadline:** May 1. **Remarks:** Established in 1985. **Contact:** Email: honors@aps.org.

1230 ■ Mitsuyoshi Tanaka Dissertation Award in Experimental Particle Physics *(Doctorate, Postdoctorate/Award, Recognition, Monetary)*

Purpose: To support exceptional young scientists who have performed original doctoral thesis work of outstanding scientific quality and achievement in the area of experimental particle physics. **Focus:** Physics. **Qualif.:** Applicants must be doctoral students studying at a college or university in North America including their study-abroad programs, for dissertation research carried out in the field of experimental

Awards are arranged alphabetically below their administering organizations

particle physics. **Criteria:** Selection will be based on the committee's criteria.

Funds Avail.: $1,500; $1,000 travel allowance. **Duration:** Annual. **Number Awarded:** 1. **To Apply:** Applicants must submit a full copy of the nominee's Ph. D. thesis, along with up to four publications and/or reports describing the work; a thesis summary of no more than two pages prepared by the nominee; a complete curriculum vitae of the nominee, including a list of publications; a nominating letter from the thesis advisor stating the date of the thesis defense and the date the final thesis document was presented to the graduate school, the role of the nominee in writing any parts of the thesis that have been published or submitted for publication (please identify these parts of the thesis), and the specific contributions of the nominee, making comparisons with others; at least two letters supporting the nomination; demographics form. **Deadline:** August 15. **Remarks:** Established in 1999. **Contact:** Email: honors@aps.org.

1231 ■ American Physical Therapy Association (APTA)
1111 N Fairfax St.
Alexandria, VA 22314-1488
Ph: (703)684-2782
Fax: (703)684-7343
Free: 800-999-2782
E-mail: memberservices@apta.org
URL: www.apta.org
Social Media: www.facebook.com/
  AmericanPhysicalTherapyAssociation
twitter.com/aptatweets
youtube.com/APTAvideo
www.youtube.com/user/APTAvideo

1232 ■ APTA Minority Scholarships - Faculty Development Scholarships *(Postdoctorate/ Scholarship, Award, Recognition)*

Purpose: To provide doctoral education support for minority faculty members, to acknowledge and reward those who demonstrate commitment to minority services and activities and show superior achievements in the profession of physical therapy. **Focus:** Physical therapy. **Qualif.:** Applicants must be U.S. citizens or legal permanent residents; must be members of one of the racial/ethnic minority groups (African-American or Black, Asian, Native Hawaiian or other Pacific Islander, American Indian/Alaska Native and Hispanic/Latino); must be physical therapists, full-time faculty members, teaching in an accredited or developing professional physical therapist education program; must possess a license to practice physical therapy in a U.S. jurisdiction or have met all the requirements for licensure in a U.S. jurisdiction; must be enrolled as students in a regionally accredited post-professional doctoral program whose content has a demonstrated relationship to physical therapy; must demonstrate continuous progress toward the completion of their post-professional doctoral program in a timely fashion; must demonstrate commitment to minority services and activities; must demonstrate a commitment to further the physical therapy profession through teaching and research; and must not have received the award in prior years. **Criteria:** Selection is based on demonstrated evidence of contributions in the area of minority affairs and services, contributions to the profession of physical therapy and scholastic achievement.
Funds Avail.: Amount varies. **Duration:** Annual. **Contact:** Email:alissapatanarut@apta.org.

1233 ■ APTA Minority Scholarships - Physical Therapist Assistant Students *(Undergraduate/ Scholarship, Award, Recognition)*

Purpose: To acknowledge and reward demonstrated participation in minority affairs and service, the potential for superior achievements as a physical therapist assistant and academic excellence. **Focus:** Physical therapy. **Qualif.:** Applicant must be a minority physical therapist assistant students by the Physical Therapy Fund. **Criteria:** Selection is based on demonstrated evidence of contributions in the area of minority affairs and services with an emphasis on contributions made while enrolled in the physical therapy education program; potential to contribute to the profession of physical therapy; and scholastic achievement.

Funds Avail.: $3,000 each. **Duration:** Annual. **Contact:** Email:alissapatanarut@apta.org.

1234 ■ APTA Minority Scholarships - Physical Therapist Students *(Undergraduate/Scholarship, Award, Recognition)*

Purpose: To acknowledge and reward demonstrated participation in minority affairs activities and services, the potential for superior achievements in the profession of physical therapy, appropriate display of professionalism as a future physical therapist and academic excellence. **Focus:** Physical therapy. **Qualif.:** Applicant must be physical therapist students by the Physical Therapy Fund. **Criteria:** Selection is based on demonstrated evidence of contributions in the area of minority affairs and services with an emphasis on contributions made while enrolled in the physical therapy education program; potential to contribute to the profession of physical therapy; and scholastic achievement.

Funds Avail.: $5,000 each. **Duration:** Annual. **Contact:** Email:alissapatanarut@apta.org.

1235 ■ American Physiological Society (APS)
6120 Executive Blvd., Ste. 600
Rockville, MD 20852-4911
Ph: (301)634-7164
Fax: (301)634-7241
URL: www.the-aps.org
Social Media: www.facebook.com/
  AmericanPhysiologicalSociety
www.linkedin.com/company/american-physiological-society
twitter.com/APSPhysiology
www.youtube.com/c/The-apsOrg

1236 ■ Lazaro J. Mandel Young Investigator Award *(Advanced Professional/Monetary, Award)*

Purpose: To recognize and support an individual demonstrating outstanding promise based on their research program in epithelial or renal physiology. **Focus:** Physiology; Science. **Qualif.:** Applicants must be a member in good standing of the APS and work within the US.

Funds Avail.: $10,000. **Duration:** Annual. **To Apply:** Applications can be submitted online. **Deadline:** November 15. **Remarks:** The award was established in 1999 in memory of Lazaro J. Mandel, professor of physiology at Duke University and long-standing APS member. Established in 1999. **Contact:** Executive Office; E-mail: awards@ the-aps.org.

Awards are arranged alphabetically below their administering organizations

1237 ■ Martin Frank Diversity Travel Award
(Undergraduate, Postdoctorate/Fellowship, Award, Monetary)

Purpose: To encourage highly qualified individuals from groups traditionally underrepresented in science to pursue professional careers in physiological/biomedical sciences. **Focus:** Physiology. **Qualif.:** Applicants must be underrepresented minority (URM) graduate students, postdoctoral fellows, and early career faculty (recently transitioned); and graduate students, postdoctoral fellows, and early career faculty (recently transitioned) with disabilities.

Funds Avail.: $1,800. **Duration:** Annual. **To Apply:** Applications can be submitted online and further details can be obtained from the website. **Deadline:** March 29;May 1. **Contact:** Brooke Bruthers, Senior Program Manager, Diversity Programs; E-mail: education@the-aps.org.

1238 ■ Porter Physiology Development Fellowship
(Doctorate/Fellowship, Award, Monetary)

Purpose: To encourage PhD students to pursue their education in physiological sciences. **Focus:** Physiology. **Qualif.:** Applicant must be underrepresented minority and diverse groups of applicants who are citizens or permanent residents of the United States or its territories and student members of the Society; applicant's advisor/PI must be a member of APS in good standin **Criteria:** Applications will be judged based on potential for success including the following: 1) academic records; 2) statement of interest; 3) previous awards and experiences; and 4) recommendation letters; applicant's proposed training environment; clarity and quality of the research.

Funds Avail.: $28,300. **Duration:** Annual; Extendable for second year. **Number Awarded:** Varies. **To Apply:** Applicant must submit an application form; documentation of educational background including transcript of records, a copy of acceptance letter to the graduate training program, current curriculum vitae, list of all undergraduate and graduate institutions have attended; must upload a biographical sketch; must provide the advisor's or program director's contact information; must complete a proposed training or research plan; and must request the uploading of two letters of recommendation from an advisor or program director. **Deadline:** January 15. **Remarks:** Established in 1967. **Contact:** Email:awardshelp@physiology.org.

1239 ■ Caroline tum Suden/Frances Hellebrandt Professional Opportunity Awards *(Postdoctorate, Graduate/Award, Monetary)*

Purpose: To encourage professionals, pre-doctoral and post-doctoral students who want to enhance their knowledge in the field of physiological sciences. **Focus:** Physiology. **Qualif.:** Applicants must be authors of an abstract submitted to American Physiological Society (APS); and must be members in good standing at the time of application.

Funds Avail.: $500 each. **Duration:** Annual. **Number Awarded:** 50. **To Apply:** Applications are only accepted via online submission. **Contact:** E-mail: members@the-aps.org.

1240 ■ Shih-Chun Wang Young Investigator Award
(Advanced Professional/Monetary, Award)

Purpose: To recognize and support an individual demonstrating outstanding promise based on their research program in the physiological sciences. **Focus:** Physiology; Science. **Qualif.:** Applicants must be a member in good standing of the APS and work within the US.

Funds Avail.: $11,000. **Duration:** Annual. **To Apply:** Applicant must provide a description of their current and pending research program; bio sketch in NIH style; full list of their current and pending grant support; copy of the abstract; letter of recommendation from their department chair or mentor; at least one additional letter of support discussing the applicant's research program. **Deadline:** November 15. **Remarks:** The award was established in the memory of Shih-Chun Wang, the Pfeiffer Professor of Pharmacology at Columbia University and a long-standing APS member. Established in 1998. **Contact:** Executive Office; E-mail: awards@the-aps.org.

1241 ■ American Planning Association (APA)
205 N Michigan Ave., Ste. 1200
Chicago, IL 60601
Ph: (312)431-9100
Fax: (312)786-6700
E-mail: customerservice@planning.org
URL: www.planning.org
Social Media: www.facebook.com/
  AmericanPlanningAssociation
instagram.com/americanplanningassociation
www.linkedin.com/groups/116818/profile
twitter.com/APA_Planning
youtube.com/user/AmericanPlanningAssn

1242 ■ American Planning Association ENRE Student Fellowship Program *(Graduate/Fellowship)*

Purpose: To provide financial support for students interested and excelling in graduate level studies in planning related to natural resources, energy or the environment. **Focus:** Energy-related areas; Natural resources; Urban affairs/design/planning. **Qualif.:** Applicants must be second-year graduate students enrolled in a PAB-accredited graduate planning program focusing on issues related to the environment, natural resources, or energy; may be full or part-time, but must be classified as a student in a Master of Planning program or related field; must have GPA above 3.0 on a 4.0 scale; focused on issues related to the environment, natural resources or energy, and pursuing a program or course of study consistent with the Division's mission. **Criteria:** Selection shall be based on the aforesaid qualifications, quality of application materials submitted, and connection of the students' course of study to Division's mission. Preference will be given to students with APA and Division memberships.

Funds Avail.: $1,500. **Duration:** Annual. **Number Awarded:** Varies. **To Apply:** Applicants must submit their respective application forms; recommendation letters from their own thesis/project faculty advisors; an 800-word description of the student's master's thesis or project, including how it relates to the division's mission; a 600-word essay describing interest in environmental planning, experience and future goals; and, curriculum vitae or resume. Completed application with the five submission requirements listed should be submitted to the contact provided. **Deadline:** June 30. **Contact:** Email: info_ENRE@planning.org.

1243 ■ Holzheimer Memorial Student Scholarship
(Graduate, Master's/Scholarship)

Purpose: To support the travel or attendance of Master's students at the national APA meeting. **Focus:** Urban affairs/

design/planning. **Qualif.:** Applicants must be Master's level students enrolled in PAB-accredited planning programs across the United States, as well as individuals who have graduated from those programs in the last year.

Funds Avail.: $2,000. **Duration:** Annual.

1244 ■ The Robert A. Catlin/David W. Long Scholarship (Graduate/Scholarship)

Purpose: To encourage the pursuit and achievement of the growing number of African American students entering the urban planning profession. **Focus:** Urban affairs/design/planning. **Qualif.:** Applicants must be African American undergraduate students who have been accepted in an urban planning program for graduate studies and graduate students, of the same affiliation, majoring in urban planning or a related field (environmental studies, geography, urban studies, urban policy etc.) Current graduate students may not be in the final semester of their programs. **Criteria:** Recipients will be selected based on the jury's review of the application materials.

Funds Avail.: $1,500. **Duration:** Annual. **To Apply:** Applicants must download and complete the fellowship application. Other requirements include personal statement, proof of enrollment in graduate planning program or letter of acceptance to graduate planning program, one recommendation letter. **Deadline:** February 9. **Contact:** Gisla Bush, PBCD Student Representative; Email: gislabush1016@gmail.com.

1245 ■ Judith McManus Price Scholarship (Undergraduate, Graduate/Scholarship)

Purpose: To provide partial funding for women and minority students. **Focus:** Urban affairs/design/planning. **Qualif.:** Applicants must be women and minority (African American, Hispanic American, or Native American) students enrolled in an approved Planning Accreditation Board (PAB) planning program who are citizens of the United States, intend to pursue careers as practicing planners in the public sector, and able to demonstrate a genuine financial need.

Funds Avail.: $2,000 and $5,000. **Duration:** Annual. **Contact:** To check on the status of application, send requests to students@planning.org.

1246 ■ American Political Science Association (APSP)

1527 New Hampshire Ave. NW
Washington, DC 20036-1206
Ph: (202)483-2512
Fax: (202)483-2657
E-mail: apsa@apsanet.org
URL: www.apsanet.org
Social Media: www.facebook.com/likeAPSA
www.linkedin.com/groups/154534/profile
twitter.com/APSAtweets

1247 ■ APSA Congressional Fellowships for Journalists (Advanced Professional, Professional development/Fellowship)

Purpose: To give early-to mid career journalists an opportunity to learn more about Congress and the legislative process through direct participation. **Focus:** Broadcasting; Journalism; Political science. **Qualif.:** Applicants must be early and mid-career print and broadcast journalists who have a professional interest in Congress; must have a bachelor's degree and two to ten years of continuous, full-

time professional experience in either print or broadcast journalism; must be U.S. citizenship or permanent residency. **Criteria:** Selection will be based on the aforesaid qualifications and compliance with the application process.

Duration: Annual; nine and a half month program. **To Apply:** Application must be submitted online and include: a detailed resume or curriculum vitae; 500-word personal statement explaining how participation in the fellowship relates to the applicants' professional goals; one writing sample (political scientists and communications scholars) or news article, broadcast script, or clip (journalists); and, the names and contact information for three professional references who have agreed to write letters of recommendation. **Contact:** APSA Congressional Fellowship Program office, Phone: 202-483-2520; Email: cfp@apsanet.org.

1248 ■ APSA Congressional Fellowships for Political Scientists (Advanced Professional, Professional development, Postdoctorate/Fellowship)

Purpose: To give early-to-mid career political scientists an opportunity to learn more about Congress and the legislative process through direct participation. **Focus:** Political science. **Qualif.:** Applicants must have completed a PhD in the last 15 years or will have defended a dissertation in political science by November of the fellowship year; can scholars in all fields of study within political science who can show a scholarly interest in Congress and the legislative process; must U.S. citizenship or permanent residency. **Criteria:** Selection will be based on the aforesaid qualifications and compliance with the application process.

Duration: Annual; nine and a half month program. **To Apply:** Application must be submitted online and include: a detailed resume or curriculum vitae; 500-word personal statement explaining how participation in the fellowship relates to the applicants' professional goals; one writing sample (political scientists and communications scholars) or news article, broadcast script, or clip (journalists); and, the names and contact information for three professional references who have agreed to write letters of recommendation. **Contact:** APSA Congressional Fellowship Program office, Phone: 202-483-2520; Email: cfp@apsanet.org.

1249 ■ APSA Fund for Latino Scholarship (Undergraduate, Graduate/Scholarship)

Purpose: To support Latino students and encourage them to enter the profession of political science. **Focus:** Political science. **Qualif.:** Applicants must be Latino or Latina graduate/undergraduate students. **Criteria:** Selection will be based on the committee's criteria.

Funds Avail.: $500-$1,000. **Duration:** Annual. **To Apply:** Applicants must submit a two-page application form available online that summarizes current research activities which are relevant to the grant; must also include certification that the host institution, department or program will provide direct financial support at least equal to the maximum amount of grant from the Fund. **Deadline:** June 15. **Contact:** E-mail: latinofund@apsanet.org; URL: www.apsanet.org/DIVERSITY/Fund-for-Latino-Scholarship.

1250 ■ APSA-MCI Communications Congressional Fellowship (Advanced Professional, Professional development, Postdoctorate/Fellowship)

Purpose: To give early-to-mid scholars and journalists an opportunity to learn more about Congress and the legisla-

Awards are arranged alphabetically below their administering organizations

tive process through direct participation. **Focus:** Communications; Journalism; Political science; Public administration. **Qualif.:** Applicants must be early and mid-career journalists and scholars in all disciplines and fields with a professional interest in public policy and telecommunications. Applicants may be scholars who have completed a PhD in the last 15 years or will have defended a dissertation by November of the fellowship year, or may be journalists who cover this topic with two to ten years of professional experience in either print or broadcast journalism (including online journalism). U.S. citizenship or permanent residency is required. **Criteria:** Preference is given to those without extensive Capitol Hill experience.

Duration: Annual; nine and a half month program. **To Apply:** Application must be submitted online and include: a detailed resume or curriculum vitae; 500-word personal statement explaining how participation in the fellowship relates to the applicants' professional goals; one writing sample (political scientists and communications scholars) or news article, broadcast script, or clip (journalists); and, the names and contact information for three professional references who have agreed to write letters of recommendation. **Contact:** APSA Congressional Fellowship Program office, Phone: 202-483-2520; Email: cfp@apsanet.org.

1251 ■ APSA Minority Fellowship Program
(Doctorate/Fellowship)

Purpose: To support minority or underrepresented students applying to enter a doctoral program in political science. **Focus:** Political science. **Qualif.:** Applicants must be members of one of the following racial/ethnic minority groups (African Americans, Asian Pacific Americans, Latinos/as, and Native Americans); must be students from underrepresented backgrounds applying to or in the early stages of doctoral programs in political science; must demonstrate interests in teaching and potential for research in political science; must be United States citizen at time of award. **Criteria:** Selection will be based on the committee's criteria.

Funds Avail.: $4,000 each. **Duration:** Annual. **Number Awarded:** 12 to 14. **To Apply:** Applicants must submit a letter of enrollment verification; an official transcript from each undergraduate and graduate institution attended; and two letters of recommendation must be submitted. **Remarks:** Established in 1969. **Contact:** Email: diversityprograms@apsanet.org; URL: www.apsanet.org/mfp.

1252 ■ APSA Small Research Grant Program
(Professional development/Grant)

Purpose: To support the research and further the careers of political scientists who are not employed at Ph.D. granting departments in the field. **Focus:** Political science. **Qualif.:** Applicants must be APSA members at the time of application; principal investigators and co-authors must be one of the following: faculty members at a college or university that does not award a PhD in political science, public administration, public policy, international relations, government or politics and whose primary appointment is in one of these departments; or political scientists not affiliated with an academic institution and are either unemployed or working in a research organization such as a think tank. **Criteria:** Selection will be based on the committee's criteria.

Funds Avail.: Up to $2,500. **Duration:** Annual. **To Apply:** Applicants must submit five single-spaced, single-sided pages proposal. Proposals should address a significant

problem in political science, should specify research design, should state how the project relates to previous research and theoretical developments, should state how the project contributes to scholarship within the field; in addition to that are the following: title page, bibliography, itemized budget, and curriculum vitae. **Deadline:** April 30. **Contact:** APSA team; Email: researchgrants@apsanet.org.

1253 ■ APSA U.S. Federal Executives Fellowships
(Advanced Professional, Professional development/Fellowship)

Purpose: To give senior-level federal executives an opportunity to learn more about Congress and the legislative process through direct participation. **Focus:** Political science. **Qualif.:** Nominees must be fellows who are employees of federal agencies and who are sponsored by their home institutions during the fellowship year; must have a minimum grade of GS-13 or equivalent at the time of nomination, at least two years of federal service in the executive branch, and long-term career goals relevant to a Congressional experience. **Criteria:** Selection will be based on the nominees' aforesaid eligibility.

Duration: Annual. **To Apply:** Application is via nomination; nominations are to be submitted to APSA by the headquarters-level training officer or coordinator for executive development; candidates, the department or agency must also submit: a detailed resume with contact information, current grade, work experience, education (degree dates and subject majors), summary of languages, special skills, and interests; a statement assessing the nominees' executive potential and need for training by the supervisor(s) or agency Executive Resources Board; and a 500-word statement by the nominees presenting a need for training, the relevance of training to career goals, and the utilization of training by the agency. **Deadline:** April 1. **Contact:** APSA Congressional Fellowship Program office, Phone: 202-483-2520; Email: cfp@apsanet.org.

1254 ■ Marguerite Ross Barnett Fund *(Graduate, Postdoctorate, Undergraduate/Grant)*

Purpose: To support research on diversity, cultural nationalism, African-American voting behavior, education policy, or urban and minority policy and politics. **Focus:** Political science; Public administration. **Qualif.:** Applicants must be APSA members, including undergraduate students, graduate students, and faculty. **Criteria:** Applications are accepted on a rolling basis.

Funds Avail.: $500 to $2,500. **Duration:** Annual. **To Apply:** Application form and details (including the categories of cost eligible for funding) are available at: connect.apsanet.org/centennialcenter/research-grants/. **Deadline:** June 30. **Contact:** Email: centennial@apsanet.org.

1255 ■ Health and Aging Policy Fellows Program
(Advanced Professional, Professional development/Fellowship)

Purpose: To make a positive contribution to the development and implementation of health policies that affect the older Americans. **Focus:** Gerontology; Health care services; Health education; Social work. **Qualif.:** Applicants must be engaged in all career stages (i.e. early, mid, and late); must be U.S. citizens or permanent residents of the U.S. territories who have career plans that anticipate continued work in the U.S. after the fellowship period; can be physicians, nurses, social workers, psychologists, dieticians, healthcare administrators, epidemiologists, economists,

Awards are arranged alphabetically below their administering organizations

and lawyers from academic and practice settings, spanning career stages from newly minted PhDs to senior professors and community leaders. **Criteria:** Recipients are selected based on the commitment to health and aging issues and improving the health and well-being of older Americans; potential for leadership in health policy; professional qualifications and achievements; impact of the fellowship experience on the applicant's career; and interpersonal and communication skills.

Duration: Annual. **Number Awarded:** Up to 15. **To Apply:** Applicants must fill out and submit the application form which can be downloaded in the website of the program; an essay stating the reasons why the applicant needs the fellowship, description of experiences or contributions in the health aging field, and plans for continued development of the health policy leadership skills after completing the fellowship; a curriculum vitae; a one-page biographical sketch; and the name and contact information of the institutional references and two professional references. **Contact:** Mica Muir, Program Coordinator; Phone: 646-774-8495; Email: hapfell@nyspi.Columbia.edu; URL: www.healthandagingpolicy.org.

1256 ■ Huang Hsing Chun-tu Hsueh Fellowship Fund *(Graduate, Postdoctorate, Undergraduate, Professional development/Grant)*

Purpose: To support international scholarship, especially in Asia. **Focus:** Asian studies; Political science. **Qualif.:** Applicants must be APSA members, including undergraduate students, graduate students, and faculty.

Funds Avail.: $500 to $2,500. **Duration:** Annual. **To Apply:** Application form and details (including the categories of cost eligible for funding) are available at: connect.apsanet.org/centennialcenter/research-grants/. **Deadline:** June 30. **Contact:** Email: centennial@apsanet.org.

1257 ■ Rita Mae Kelly Fund *(Graduate, Doctorate, Undergraduate, Professional development/Grant)*

Purpose: To support research on the intersection of gender, race, ethnicity, and political power. **Focus:** Political science; Social sciences. **Qualif.:** Applicants must be APSA members, including undergraduate students, graduate students, and faculty.

Funds Avail.: $500 to $2,500. **Duration:** Annual. **To Apply:** Application form and details (including the categories of cost eligible for funding) are available at: connect.apsanet.org/centennialcenter/research-grants/. **Deadline:** June 30. **Contact:** Email: centennial@apsanet.org.

1258 ■ Warren E. Miller Fund in Electoral Politics *(Advanced Professional, Graduate, Postdoctorate, Undergraduate/Grant)*

Purpose: To support research in national and comparative electoral politics. **Focus:** Political science. **Qualif.:** Applicants must be APSA members, including undergraduate students, graduate students, and faculty.

Funds Avail.: $500 to $2,500. **Duration:** Annual. **To Apply:** Application form and details (including the categories of cost eligible for funding) are available at: connect.apsanet.org/centennialcenter/research-grants/. **Deadline:** June 30. **Contact:** Email: centennial@apsanet.org.

1259 ■ Presidency Research Fund *(Graduate, Postdoctorate, Undergraduate, Professional development/Grant)*

Purpose: To provide supplemental support to people whose scholarly research brings them to the Washington area, to examine the relationships, institutions, and environment surrounding the President. **Focus:** History, American; Political science. **Qualif.:** Applicants must be APSA members, including undergraduate students, graduate students, and faculty.

Funds Avail.: $500 to $2,500. **Duration:** Annual. **To Apply:** Application form and details (including the categories of cost eligible for funding) are available at: connect.apsanet.org/centennialcenter/research-grants/. **Deadline:** June 30. **Contact:** Email: centennial@apsanet.org.

1260 ■ Paul A. Volcker Fund *(Undergraduate, Graduate, Doctorate, Professional development/Grant)*

Purpose: To support and promote excellence in research and theory on public administration issues affecting governance in the United States and abroad. **Focus:** Government; Public administration. **Qualif.:** Applicants must be APSA members, including undergraduate students, graduate students, and faculty.

Funds Avail.: $500 to $2,500. **Duration:** Annual. **To Apply:** Application form and details (including the categories of cost eligible for funding) are available at: connect.apsanet.org/centennialcenter/research-grants/. **Deadline:** June 30. **Contact:** Administered by the Organized Section for Public Administration; Email: volcker@apsanet.org.

1261 ■ Women & Politics Fund *(Graduate, Postdoctorate, Undergraduate, Professional development/Grant)*

Purpose: To support scholarship in the field of women and politics. **Focus:** Political science; Women's studies. **Qualif.:** Applicants must be APSA members, including undergraduate students, graduate students, and faculty.

Funds Avail.: $500 to $2,500. **Duration:** Annual. **To Apply:** Application form and details (including the categories of cost eligible for funding) are available at: connect.apsanet.org/centennialcenter/research-grants/. **Deadline:** June 30. **Contact:** Email: centennial@apsanet.org.

1262 ■ American Polygraph Association (APA)
PO Box 8037
Chattanooga, TN 37414-0037
Ph: (423)892-3992
Fax: (423)894-5435
Free: 800-272-8037
URL: www.polygraph.org
Social Media: www.facebook.com/www.polygraph.org

1263 ■ William J. Yankee Memorial Scholarship *(Undergraduate/Scholarship, Monetary, Recognition)*

Purpose: To provide financial assistance to deserving students. **Focus:** General studies/Field of study not specified. **Qualif.:** Applicants must have a 4-year degree from an accredited college or university; must select to attend an APA accredited basic polygraph examiner training course; must qualify for APA membership upon completion

Awards are arranged alphabetically below their administering organizations

of training. **Criteria:** Selection will be based on the committee's criteria.

Funds Avail.: $5,000. **Duration:** Periodic. **To Apply:** Applicants must submit an essay of up to 1000 words on detection of deception, interviewing, interrogation or related fields; must have at least two letters of recommendation. **Deadline:** June 1. **Remarks:** Established in 1999. **Contact:** American Polygraph Association; 118 Lee Pkwy, Ste. 205,Chattanooga, TN 37421; Toll-free: 800-272-8037, Fax: 423-894-5435; Email: award_nomination@ apapolygraph.org.

1264 ■ American Psychoanalytic Association (APSAA)

309 E 49th St.
New York, NY 10017
Ph: (212)752-0450
E-mail: info@apsa.org
URL: www.apsa.org
Social Media: www.linkedin.com/company/396506
twitter.com/psychoanalysis_

1265 ■ APsaA Fellowship *(Doctorate, Postdoctorate/ Fellowship)*

Purpose: To encourage interest and involvement in psychoanalysis among future leaders, researchers and educators of mental health and academia. **Focus:** Psychology. **Qualif.:** Applicants must be nominated by their Department Chairs, Program Directors, or an APsaA member; self-nominations are encouraged; must be training or working in the United States during the fellowship year. Reapplication is permitted; Psychiatry Applicants must, at the time of application, be full-time general or child psychiatry residents, PGY-2 or higher, or fellows or psychiatrists who have become board eligible within the previous three years; mustl hold at least half-time academic appointments that include training, leadership, or research responsibilities during the fellowship year; psychology applicants must be at the time of the fellowship, hold at minimum a half-time position with an academic department or clinical training program and have training, leadership, or research responsibilities; psychology graduate programs must be accredited; predoctoral, must have completed required coursework and be in or beyond the predoctoral internship; postdoctoral must have received the doctoral degree or completed a postdoctoral fellowship within the past five years; social work applicants must, at the time of the fellowship, have received an M.S.W. or doctoral degree in the last five years; must enrolled in a D.S.W. or Ph.D. program must have received their M.S.W. in the last ten years; academic and multidisciplinary applicants must be individuals from academia or non-mental health professions, such as the humanities and social sciences, neuroscience, medicine, law, theology, journalism, and the arts. **Criteria:** Selection is based on demonstrated leadership ability in their discipline; have showed special aptitude in research, teaching, artistic, writing and/or clinical endeavors; have special interest in psychodynamics, psychoanalysis, applied psychoanalysis or community outreach/development. **Funds Avail.:** No specific amount. **Duration:** Annual. **To Apply:** Applicants must submit the CV, or the fellowship nominee background summary form including the nominee's academic and employment history, professional honors, principal publications list, and other contributions to physics; up to two additional letters of support. **Remarks:** Established in 1991. **Contact:** Contact Scott Dillon MeetAdmin@apsa.org.

1266 ■ American Psychological Association (APA)

750 1st St. NE
Washington, DC 20002-4242
Ph: (202)336-5500
Free: 800-374-2721
URL: www.apa.org
Social Media: www.facebook.com/ AmericanPsychologicalAssociation
www.linkedin.com/company/american-psychological -association
twitter.com/apa
www.youtube.com/c/americanpsychologicalassociation

1267 ■ Ethel Louise Armstrong Foundation Scholarships *(Graduate, Master's/Scholarship, Monetary)*

Purpose: To provide financial assistance for female students with physical disabilities for their educational expenses. **Focus:** Disabilities. **Qualif.:** Applicant must be a woman with a physical disability; must be currently accepted to a graduate program working towards a Masters degree or above in an accredited college or university in the United States; must be active in a local, state, or national disability organization either in person or electronically which is providing services and/or advocacy for people with disabilities. **Criteria:** Selection will be based on the committee's criteria.

Funds Avail.: $1,000-$2,000. **Duration:** Annual. **To Apply:** Applicant must submit an online application form. **Deadline:** June 1. **Contact:** Deborah Lewis, Executive Director, Ethel Louise Armstrong Foundation, Inc., 2460 N Lake Ave., PO Box 128, Altadena, CA 91001; Phone: 626-398-8840; E-mail: executivedirector@ela.org.

1268 ■ American Psychological Association of Graduate Students (APAGS)

750 1st St. NE
Washington, DC 20002-4242
Ph: (202)336-5500
Free: 800-374-2721
URL: www.apa.org
Social Media: www.facebook.com/APAGradStudents
twitter.com/APAGradStudents
twitter.com/apa
www.youtube.com/theapavideo
www.youtube.com/c/americanpsychologicalassociation

1269 ■ Ellin Bloch and Pierre Ritchie Diversity Dissertation Grant *(Graduate/Grant)*

Purpose: To encourage and support graduate students in their research in the field of psychology concerning diversity issues. **Focus:** Psychology. **Qualif.:** Applicant must be a graduate student member of APAGS; must be enrolled as a student in good standing at an accredited university; must be in a doctoral program. **Criteria:** Selection will be based on the criteria.

Funds Avail.: $1,000. **Duration:** Annual. **To Apply:** Applicants must submit a cover letter that indicates the name of the nominee and the scholarship being applied for; graduate school affiliation; dissertation chair, current address, phone number and email address; a letter of recommendation supporting the application; an abbreviated dissertation proposal; and a curriculum vitae.

Awards are arranged alphabetically below their administering organizations

1270 ■ Nancy B. Forest and L. Michael Honaker Master's Grant for Research in Psychology (Graduate/Grant)

Purpose: To support dissertation research related to the field of psychology. **Focus:** Psychology. **Qualif.:** Applicant must be a graduate student member of APAGS; enrolled as a student in good standing at an accredited university; in a masters or doctoral program; undergraduates are not eligible for the scholarships. **Criteria:** Scholarship Selection Committee will review applications based on objective, qualitative and quantitative criteria.

Funds Avail.: $1,000. **Duration:** Annual. **To Apply:** Applicants must submit a cover letter that indicates the name of the scholarship; a curriculum vitae; a thesis proposal; and two letters of recommendation that supports the application. **Remarks:** Established in 1999.

1271 ■ David Pilon Scholarships for Training in Professional Psychology (Graduate/Scholarship)

Purpose: To promote supplement training and education experiences in professional practice. **Focus:** Psychology. **Qualif.:** Applicant must be a graduate student and a member of APAGS; enrolled as a student in good standing at an accredited university; in a masters or doctoral program; undergraduates are not eligible for the scholarships. **Criteria:** Scholarship Selection Committee will review applications based on objective, qualitative and quantitative criteria.

Funds Avail.: $1,000. **Duration:** Annual. **To Apply:** Applicants must submit a cover letter that indicates the name of the scholarship; a curriculum vitae; a statement (maximum 1, 000 words) addressing the applicant's short and long-term goals; a formal proposal; and two letters of recommendation that supports the application. **Remarks:** Established in 1995.

1272 ■ American Psychological Foundation (APF)

750 1st St. NE
Washington, DC 20002-4242
Ph: (202)336-5843
Fax: (202)336-5812
E-mail: foundation@apa.org
URL: www.apa.org
Social Media: twitter.com/apa
www.youtube.com/theapavideo

1273 ■ Annette Urso Rickel Foundation Dissertation Award for Public Policy (Graduate/Scholarship)

Purpose: To support of dissertation research on public policy. **Focus:** Psychology. **Qualif.:** Applicants must be Graduate student in psychology enrolled full time in good standing in a regionally accredited institution located in the U.S. or Canada. Completed doctoral candidacy, including dissertation approval by doctoral committee. Demonstrated research competence and area commitment.IRB approval must be received from host institution before funding can be awarded if human participants are involved.

Funds Avail.: $1,000. **Duration:** Annual. **Number Awarded:** 1. **To Apply:** Application must include the following in a single document (Not to exceed three pages, one-inch margins, 11-point Times New Roman/Garamond Font, single space): Goals, relevant background/literature review; Methods (must be detailed enough so that the design, assessments and procedures can be evaluated); Anticipated outcomes, significance and impact; Project timeline (not to exceed one page; typically, APF grants are for one year); Detailed budget and justification (not to exceed one page); Abbreviated CV; Letter of recommendation from your faculty advisor.

1274 ■ APA 125th Anniversary Scholarship (Doctorate, Graduate/Scholarship)

Purpose: To help graduate students further their education in psychology. **Focus:** Psychology.

Funds Avail.: $3,000. **Duration:** Annual.

1275 ■ APF High School Psychology Outreach Grants (Advanced Professional, Professional development/Grant)

Purpose: To support innovative programs that support networking, professional development and educational outreach opportunities for high school psychology teachers and students. **Focus:** Psychology; Teaching. **Qualif.:** Applicants must currently teach at least one high school psychology course and expect to teach psychology in the following academic year; high school teacher affiliates of the American Psychological Association. **Criteria:** Selection will be based on the committee's criteria.

Funds Avail.: $5,000. **Duration:** Annual. **Number Awarded:** Varies. **To Apply:** Proposals for teacher networks must include a description of the planned workshop or conference; a description of how the applicant intends to contact teachers within a region or state; should detail how many other schools and/or students will participate in the planned event, and how the applicant intends to contact the other participating schools; Conference title, date and location and proposal submission date; date. Planned session title and 300-word summary of presentation, which must focus on APA TOPSS; A budget outlining the expected costs associated with the network, workshop, conference and/or program; Resume or vitae of applicant. **Deadline:** May 15. **Contact:** Yvonne Hill, American Psychological Association, 750 First St., NE, Washington, DC, 20002-4242; Fax: 202-336-5962; Email: yhill@apa.org.

1276 ■ APF Professional Development Awards for High School Psychology Teachers (Advanced Professional, Professional development/Grant)

Purpose: To support innovative programs that support networking, professional development and educational outreach opportunities for high school psychology teachers and students. **Focus:** Psychology. **Qualif.:** Applicants must currently teach at least one high school psychology course and expect to teach psychology in the following academic year; high school teacher affiliates of the American Psychological Association. **Criteria:** Selection will be based on the committee's criteria.

Funds Avail.: Up to $500. **Duration:** Annual. **Number Awarded:** Varies. **To Apply:** Proposals for teacher networks must include a description of the planned workshop or conference; a description of how the applicant intends to contact teachers within a region or state; should detail how many other schools and/or students will participate in the planned event, and how the applicant intends to contact the other participating schools; Conference title, date and location and proposal submission date; date. Planned session title and 300-word summary of presentation, which must focus on APA TOPSS; A budget outlining the expected costs associated with the network, workshop, conference

Awards are arranged alphabetically below their administering organizations

and/or program; Resume or vitae of applicant. **Deadline:** May 15. **Contact:** Yvonne Hill, American Psychological Association, 750 First St., NE, Washington, DC, 20002-4242; Fax: 202-336-5962; Email: yhill@apa.org.

1277 ■ APF Visionary Grants *(Graduate/Grant)*

Purpose: To seed innovation through supporting research, education, and intervention projects and programs. **Focus:** Psychology. **Qualif.:** Applicants must be a graduate student or early career researcher (no more than 10 years postdoctoral); affiliated with a nonprofit charitable, educational or scientific institution, or governmental entity operating exclusively for charitable and educational purposes; demonstrated competence and capacity to execute the proposed work; Political or lobbying purposes; entertainment or fundraising expenses; conference or workshop expenses; localized direct service. **Criteria:** Applicants will be evaluated based on the following criteria: innovative and potential impact qualities; quality, viability, promise for proposed work; criticality of proposed funding for proposed work; clear and comprehensive methodology.

Funds Avail.: Up to $20,000. **Duration:** Annual. **Number Awarded:** Varies. **To Apply:** Applicants must submit a no more than seven pages, one inch margin and 11 point font proposal; relevant background, literature review, specific aims, significance; methods section (must be detailed enough so that the design, assessments and procedures can be evaluated); implications section; timeline of proposed project and detailed budget and justification (not to exceed 1 page); CV (10 page max). **Deadline:** April 1.

1278 ■ Benton-Meier Scholarships *(Graduate/Scholarship)*

Purpose: To financially support graduate students in Neuropsychology. **Focus:** Psychology. **Qualif.:** Applicants must have completed doctoral candidacy; demonstrated research competence and area commitment; IRB approval must be received from host institution before funding can be awarded, if human participants are involved.

Funds Avail.: $2,500. **Duration:** Annual. **Number Awarded:** 2. **To Apply:** Applicants must submit a proposal together with a single document (not to exceed three pages, one-inch margins, 11-point Times New Roman/Garamond Font, single space): Goals, relevant background/literature review; review. Methods (must be detailed enough so that the design assessments and procedures can be evaluated); Anticipated outcomes, significance and impact; Project timeline (not to exceed one page; typically, APF grants are for one year); Detailed budget and justification (not to exceed one page); Abbreviated CV; Letter of recommendation from faculty advisor. **Deadline:** June 1.

1279 ■ William and Dorothy Bevan Scholarship
(Graduate, Master's, Doctorate/Scholarship)

Purpose: To assist graduate students of psychology with research costs associated with the master's thesis or doctoral dissertation. **Focus:** Psychology. **Qualif.:** Applicants must be graduate students enrolled in interim master's program or doctoral program; student must intend to enroll in a PhD program. **Criteria:** Selection will be based on the following criteria: description of the context for the research; the clarity and comprehensibility of the research question; the appropriateness of the research design, the general importance of the research and the use of requested funds. Preference given for funds to actually conduct the research as opposed to tuition, travel, books and journals. Secondary criteria are related to the students'

background, including previous publications or presentations at conferences, awards won at the students' institution, the letter of recommendations from the major advisor, breadth of courses taken and grades in courses.

Funds Avail.: $5,000. **Duration:** Annual. **To Apply:** Application must completed online application form; must include the following materials, A letter of recommendation (three-page maximum) from the nominee's graduate research advisor, with original signature. On the online application form, there will be a space for you to enter your graduate advisor's email address. He or she will receive a link to upload the letter. A brief outline (three-page maximum; see review criteria below) of the nominee's thesis or dissertation research project (even if in progress) along with titles and abstracts. Outlines may be single or double-spaced, margin sizes are at the discretion of each applicant, and the outline may be followed by up to two additional pages of references. We encourage you to use your best judgment on the format and content of your application, and to get your advisor's feedback on a draft of the entire application packet before completing it. A curriculum vitae (not to exceed five pages) and a transcript (an unofficial/student copy is acceptable) of all graduate coursework completed by the nominee. **Deadline:** June 30.

1280 ■ Charles and Carol Spielberger Scholarship
(Graduate, Master's, Doctorate/Scholarship)

Purpose: To assist graduate students of psychology with research costs associated with the master's thesis or doctoral dissertation. **Focus:** Psychology. **Qualif.:** Applicants must be graduate students enrolled in interim master's program or doctoral program; student must intend to enroll in a PhD program. **Criteria:** Selection will be based on the following criteria: description of the context for the research; the clarity and comprehensibility of the research question; the appropriateness of the research design, the general importance of the research and the use of requested funds. Preference given for funds to actually conduct the research as opposed to tuition, travel, books and journals. Secondary criteria are related to the students' background, including previous publications or presentations at conferences, awards won at the students' institution, the letter of recommendations from the major advisor, breadth of courses taken and grades in courses.

Funds Avail.: $5,000. **Duration:** Annual. **To Apply:** Application must completed online application form; must include the following materials, A letter of recommendation (three-page maximum) from the nominee's graduate research advisor, with original signature. On the online application form, there will be a space for you to enter your graduate advisor's email address. He or she will receive a link to upload the letter. A brief outline (three-page maximum; see review criteria below) of the nominee's thesis or dissertation research project (even if in progress) along with titles and abstracts. Outlines may be single or double-spaced, margin sizes are at the discretion of each applicant, and the outline may be followed by up to two additional pages of references. We encourage you to use your best judgment on the format and content of your application, and to get your advisor's feedback on a draft of the entire application packet before completing it. A curriculum vitae (not to exceed five pages) and a transcript (an unofficial/student copy is acceptable) of all graduate coursework completed by the nominee. **Deadline:** June 30.

Awards are arranged alphabetically below their administering organizations

1281 ■ Elizabeth Munsterberg Koppitz Child Psychology Graduate Student Fellowship *(Graduate/Fellowship)*

Purpose: To promote the advancement of knowledge and learning in the field of child psychology. **Focus:** Psychology. **Qualif.:** Applicants must have completed doctoral candidacy; demonstrated research competence and area commitment; IRB approval must be received from host institution before funding can be awarded, if human participants are involved. **Criteria:** Applicants selection will be in conformance with stated program goals; magnitude of incremental contribution; quality of proposed work; innovation and contribution to the field; demonstrated competence and capability to execute the proposed work.

Funds Avail.: Up to $25,000. **Duration:** Annual. **Number Awarded:** Varies. **To Apply:** Applicants must apply online, include the following in a single document (Not to exceed five (5) pages, one-inch margins, 11-point Times New Roman/Garamond Font, single space): Goals, relevant background/literature review; review. Methods (must be detailed enough so that the design, assessments, and procedures can be evaluated); Anticipated outcomes, significance, and impact; Project timeline (not to exceed one (1) page; typically, APF grants are for one (1) year); Detailed budget and justification (not to exceed one (1) page); Abbreviated CV (not to exceed five (5) pages); Two letters of recommendation (one from a graduate advisor and the other from the department chair or director of graduate studies). **Deadline:** November 15.

1282 ■ Violet and Cyril Franks Scholarship *(Graduate/Scholarship)*

Purpose: To support graduate-level scholarly projects that use a psychological perspective to help understand and reduce stigma associated with mental illness. **Focus:** Psychology. **Qualif.:** Applicants must be a graduate student in good standing at an accredited university; have demonstrated commitment to stigma issues; IRB approval must be received from host institution before funding can be awarded, if human participants are involved. **Criteria:** Applicants selection will be in conformance with stated program goals; magnitude of incremental contribution; quality of proposed work; innovation and contribution to the field; demonstrated competence and capability to execute the proposed work.

Funds Avail.: $5,000. **Duration:** Annual. **Number Awarded:** 1. **To Apply:** Applicants must submit a proposal through online, together with description of proposed project to include goal, relevant background, target population, methods, and anticipated outcomes (format: 5 pages; 1-inch margins, no smaller than 11-point font, single-spaced); Detailed budget and justification; CV, 5 pages max; Letter of recommendation from faculty advisor. **Deadline:** May 15.

1283 ■ William C. Howell Scholarship *(Graduate, Master's, Doctorate/Scholarship)*

Purpose: To assist graduate students of psychology with research costs associated with the master's thesis or doctoral dissertation. **Focus:** Psychology. **Qualif.:** Applicants must be graduate students enrolled in interim master's program or doctoral program; student must intend to enroll in a PhD program. **Criteria:** Selection will be based on the following criteria: description of the context for the research; the clarity and comprehensibility of the research question; the appropriateness of the research design, the general importance of the research and the use of re-

quested funds. Preference given for funds to actually conduct the research as opposed to tuition, travel, books and journals. Secondary criteria are related to the students' background, including previous publications or presentations at conferences, awards won at the students' institution, the letter of recommendations from the major advisor, breadth of courses taken and grades in courses.

Funds Avail.: $2,500. **Duration:** Annual. **To Apply:** Application must completed online application form; must include the following materials, A letter of recommendation (three-page maximum) from the nominee's graduate research advisor, with original signature. On the online application form, there will be a space for you to enter your graduate advisor's email address. He or she will receive a link to upload the letter. A brief outline (three-page maximum; see review criteria below) of the nominee's thesis or dissertation research project (even if in progress) along with titles and abstracts. Outlines may be single or double-spaced, margin sizes are at the discretion of each applicant, and the outline may be followed by up to two additional pages of references. We encourage you to use your best judgment on the format and content of your application, and to get your advisor's feedback on a draft of the entire application packet before completing it. A curriculum vitae (not to exceed five pages) and a transcript (an unofficial/student copy is acceptable) of all graduate coursework completed by the nominee. **Deadline:** June 30.

1284 ■ Harry and Miriam Levinson Scholarship *(Graduate, Master's, Doctorate/Scholarship)*

Purpose: To assist graduate students of psychology with research costs associated with the master's thesis or doctoral dissertation. **Focus:** Psychology. **Qualif.:** Applicants must be graduate students enrolled in interim master's program or doctoral program; student must intend to enroll in a PhD program. **Criteria:** Selection will be based on the following criteria: description of the context for the research; the clarity and comprehensibility of the research question; the appropriateness of the research design, the general importance of the research and the use of requested funds. Preference given for funds to actually conduct the research as opposed to tuition, travel, books and journals. Secondary criteria are related to the students' background, including previous publications or presentations at conferences, awards won at the students' institution, the letter of recommendations from the major advisor, breadth of courses taken and grades in courses.

Funds Avail.: $5,000. **Duration:** Annual. **To Apply:** Application must completed online application form; must include the following materials, A letter of recommendation (three-page maximum) from the nominee's graduate research advisor, with original signature. On the online application form, there will be a space for you to enter your graduate advisor's email address. He or she will receive a link to upload the letter. A brief outline (three-page maximum; see review criteria below) of the nominee's thesis or dissertation research project (even if in progress) along with titles and abstracts. Outlines may be single or double-spaced, margin sizes are at the discretion of each applicant, and the outline may be followed by up to two additional pages of references. We encourage you to use your best judgment on the format and content of your application, and to get your advisor's feedback on a draft of the entire application packet before completing it. A curriculum vitae (not to exceed five pages) and a transcript (an unofficial/student copy is acceptable) of all graduate coursework completed by the nominee. **Deadline:** June 30.

Awards are arranged alphabetically below their administering organizations

1285 ■ Ruth G. and Joseph D. Matarazzo Scholarship (Graduate, Master's, Doctorate/Scholarship)

Purpose: To assist graduate students of psychology with research costs associated with the master's thesis or doctoral dissertation. **Focus:** Psychology. **Qualif.:** Applicants must be graduate students enrolled in interim master's program or doctoral program; student must intend to enroll in a PhD program. **Criteria:** Selection will be based on the following criteria: description of the context for the research; the clarity and comprehensibility of the research question; the appropriateness of the research design, the general importance of the research and the use of requested funds. Preference given for funds to actually conduct the research as opposed to tuition, travel, books and journals. Secondary criteria are related to the students' background, including previous publications or presentations at conferences, awards won at the students' institution, the letter of recommendations from the major advisor, breadth of courses taken and grades in courses.

Funds Avail.: $3,000. **Duration:** Annual. **To Apply:** Application must completed online application form; must include the following materials, A letter of recommendation (three-page maximum) from the nominee's graduate research advisor, with original signature. On the online application form, there will be a space for you to enter your graduate advisor's email address. He or she will receive a link to upload the letter. A brief outline (three-page maximum; see review criteria below) of the nominee's thesis or dissertation research project (even if in progress) along with titles and abstracts. Outlines may be single or double-spaced, margin sizes are at the discretion of each applicant, and the outline may be followed by up to two additional pages of references. We encourage you to use your best judgment on the format and content of your application, and to get your advisor's feedback on a draft of the entire application packet before completing it. A curriculum vitae (not to exceed five pages) and a transcript (an unofficial/student copy is acceptable) of all graduate coursework completed by the nominee. **Deadline:** June 30.

1286 ■ Peter and Malina James and Dr. Louis P. James Legacy Scholarship (Graduate, Master's, Doctorate/Scholarship)

Purpose: To assist graduate students of psychology with research costs associated with the master's thesis or doctoral dissertation. **Focus:** Psychology. **Qualif.:** Applicants must be graduate students enrolled in interim master's program or doctoral program; student must intend to enroll in a PhD program. **Criteria:** Selection will be based on the following criteria: description of the context for the research; the clarity and comprehensibility of the research question; the appropriateness of the research design, the general importance of the research and the use of requested funds. Preference given for funds to actually conduct the research as opposed to tuition, travel, books and journals. Secondary criteria are related to the students' background, including previous publications or presentations at conferences, awards won at the students' institution, the letter of recommendations from the major advisor, breadth of courses taken and grades in courses.

Funds Avail.: $5,000. **Duration:** Annual. **To Apply:** Application must completed online application form; must include the following materials, A letter of recommendation (three-page maximum) from the nominee's graduate research advisor, with original signature. On the online application form, there will be a space for you to enter your graduate advisor's email address. He or she will receive a

link to upload the letter. A brief outline (three-page maximum; see review criteria below) of the nominee's thesis or dissertation research project (even if in progress) along with titles and abstracts. Outlines may be single or double-spaced, margin sizes are at the discretion of each applicant, and the outline may be followed by up to two additional pages of references. We encourage you to use your best judgment on the format and content of your application, and to get your advisor's feedback on a draft of the entire application packet before completing it. A curriculum vitae (not to exceed five pages) and a transcript (an unofficial/student copy is acceptable) of all graduate coursework completed by the nominee. **Deadline:** June 30.

1287 ■ Wayne F. Placek Grants (Graduate, Doctorate/Grant)

Purpose: To support empirical research from all fields of the behavioral and social sciences on any topic related to lesbian, gay, bisexual or transgender issues. **Focus:** Behavioral sciences; Psychology. **Qualif.:** Applicants Must be either a doctoral-level researcher or graduate student affiliated with an educational institution of a 501(c)(3) nonprofit research organization. Graduate students and early career researchers are encouraged to apply. **Criteria:** Selection process will be evaluated on relevance to Place program goals, magnitude if incremental contribution, quality of proposed work; the applicants' demonstration of scholarship and research competence.

Funds Avail.: $10,000. **Duration:** Annual. **Number Awarded:** Varies. **To Apply:** Applicants must submit through online. Must include the following in single document (not to exceed five pages. one-inch margins, 11-point Times New Roman/Garamond Font, single space); Additionally, Project timeline (not to exceed one page; typically APF grants are for one year); Detailed budget and justification (not to exceed one page); Abbreviated CV (not to exceed five pages). **Deadline:** March 1.

1288 ■ Clarence J. Rosecrans Scholarship (Graduate, Master's, Doctorate/Scholarship)

Purpose: To assist graduate students of psychology with research costs associated with the master's thesis or doctoral dissertation. **Focus:** Psychology. **Qualif.:** Applicants must be graduate students enrolled in interim master's program or doctoral program; student must intend to enroll in a PhD program. **Criteria:** Selection will be based on the following criteria: description of the context for the research; the clarity and comprehensibility of the research question; the appropriateness of the research design, the general importance of the research and the use of requested funds. Preference given for funds to actually conduct the research as opposed to tuition, travel, books and journals. Secondary criteria are related to the students' background, including previous publications or presentations at conferences, awards won at the students' institution, the letter of recommendations from the major advisor, breadth of courses taken and grades in courses.

Funds Avail.: $2,000. **Duration:** Annual. **To Apply:** Application must completed online application form; must include the following materials, A letter of recommendation (three-page maximum) from the nominee's graduate research advisor, with original signature. On the online application form, there will be a space for you to enter your graduate advisor's email address. He or she will receive a link to upload the letter. A brief outline (three-page maximum; see review criteria below) of the nominee's thesis or dissertation research project (even if in progress) along with titles and abstracts. Outlines may be single or

Awards are arranged alphabetically below their administering organizations

double-spaced, margin sizes are at the discretion of each applicant, and the outline may be followed by up to two additional pages of references. We encourage you to use your best judgment on the format and content of your application, and to get your advisor's feedback on a draft of the entire application packet before completing it. A curriculum vitae (not to exceed five pages) and a transcript (an unofficial/student copy is acceptable) of all graduate coursework completed by the nominee. **Deadline:** June 30.

1289 ■ Esther Katz Rosen Fund Grants (Graduate/Grant)

Purpose: To support activities related to the psychological understanding of gifted children and youth. **Focus:** Psychology. **Qualif.:** Applicants must be affiliated with a school or education institution; must hold a doctoral degree from, or be graduate students at, an accredited university for research proposals. **Criteria:** Applicants selection will be in conformance with stated program goals; magnitude of incremental contribution; quality of proposed work; innovation and contribution to the field; demonstrated competence and capability to execute the proposed work.

Funds Avail.: Up to $50,000. **Duration:** Annual. **Number Awarded:** Varies. **To Apply:** Applicants must apply online, include proposal requirements: Detailed proposal that makes a case for the need to be addressed; describes the proposed project, methodology and the applicant's qualifications; and includes a detailed budget and justification; Appropriate use of assessment is encouraged; Current CV; Two letters of support. **Deadline:** March 1. **Remarks:** Established in 1974.

1290 ■ American Psychology-Law Society (AP-LS)

750 First St. NE
Washington, DC 20002-4242
Ph: (202)336-5500
URL: www.apadivisions.org
Social Media: www.facebook.com/APLS41
twitter.com/APLS41

1291 ■ American Psychology-Law Society Dissertation Awards (Graduate/Award)

Purpose: To supports students who complete dissertations involving basic or applied research in psychology and law. **Focus:** Law; Psychology. **Qualif.:** Applicants must be members of AP-LS and must defend their dissertation. **Criteria:** Selection will be based on the committee's criteria.

Funds Avail.: No specific amount. **Duration:** Annual. **Number Awarded:** 3. **To Apply:** Applications submitted via one email from the student, or via separate emails from the student and advisor; must attach and submit the dissertation which was submitted to the student's university; the dissertation with all author, advisor and school identifying information removed; and a signed letter of support from the dissertation advisor electronically.**Deadline:** December 31. **Contact:** Contact the chair of the Dissertation Awards Committee; Jacqueline Evans - jacevans@fiu.edu.

1292 ■ American Psychology-Law Society Student Grants-In-Aid (Graduate/Grant)

Purpose: To support empirical graduate research that addresses psycholegal issues. **Focus:** Law; Psychology. **Qualif.:** Applicants must be graduate students who are student affiliate members of AP-LS. **Criteria:** Selection will be

based on the committee's criteria.

Funds Avail.: Maximum of $750. **Duration:** Biennial. **To Apply:** Applicants must submit complete award application via email. Application includes: A short grant proposal (see proposal instructions and guidelines below).Documentation of active IRB approval status for the proposed research project from the host research institution(s).Completed appropriate tax form: W-9 tax form (PDF, 110KB) for U.S. citizens and W-8BEN tax form (PDF, 91KB) for international students. A cover sheet indicating the title of the project, name, address, phone number and email address of the investigator. An abstract of 100 words or less summarizing the project. Project background that reviews purpose, theoretical rationale and significance of the project. Project method that provides a detailed description of the project's participants, design, materials and/or procedures to be employed. Budget and justification that identifies the specific amount requested, including a detailed project budget and justification for expenses as needed. documents should be formatted according to the Publication Manual of the American Psychological Association, Sixth Edition, and submitted in an electronic format (preferably MS Word or PDF). **Deadline:** January 15; September 15. **Contact:** Email to the Grants in Aid Committee chair, Debbie Green, drdebbiegreen@gmail.com.

1293 ■ Diversity in Psychology and Law Research Award (Undergraduate, Graduate/Grant, Award)

Purpose: To support undergraduate and graduate research on issues related to psychology, law, multiculturalism and/or diversity. **Focus:** Law; Psychology. **Qualif.:** Applications are available for projects, that investigate topics related to psychology, law, diversity, and/or multiculturalism. **Criteria:** Selection will be based on a competitive basis and selected based on the quality of the proposed research, the impact of the project for promoting diversity and multiculturalism in psychology and law, and the ability for the project to be completed within one year of the project start date.

Funds Avail.: $1,000 each with an option to divide two of the awards into two $500 mini-grants. **Duration:** Annual. **Number Awarded:** Up to 5 mini-grants. **To Apply:** Application must contain a cover letter on letterhead which provides all contact information; 5-page minimum/10-page maximum description containing specific aims, background and significance, project design, budget; curriculum vitae; letter of support from the applicant's research advisor; completed W-9 (U.S. citizen) or W-8 (non-U.S. citizen) tax form; copy of the IRB approval letter for the project. **Deadline:** December 15. **Contact:** MAC Diversity Award subcommittee chair Christopher L. Bishop mailto:BishopC@trinitydc.edu & Cynthia Willis-Esqueda cwillis-esqueda1@unl.edu.

1294 ■ Grants in Aid for Early Career Professionals (Graduate/Grant)

Purpose: To support AP-LS members who are early career professionals in conducting research related to psychology and law. **Focus:** Law; Psychology. **Qualif.:** Applicants must be Early Career professionals, defined by APA as those within seven years of receiving their last degree; must submit only one award proposal per funding cycle. **Criteria:** Preference will be given to those applicants who have not ever received an AP-LS ECP Grant-In-Aid.

Funds Avail.: Up to $5,000. **Duration:** Annual. **To Apply:** Applicants must submit a cover sheet including all contact information for the primary investigator, title of the proposal, status of the human subject review for the project; an

Awards are arranged alphabetically below their administering organizations

abstract of 150-word or less describing the proposed research; a proposed budget with justifications; a curriculum vitae; a list of at least five suggested outside reviewers for the project with expertise in the area of the proposal; External reviewer suggestions must exclude those with a potential conflict of interest; a five-page maximum project description including statement of the problem and relation of the problem to the state of the field; concise overview of the relevant empirical literature, theoretical background and/or law related to the project; project method; detailed description of the methodology and analytical strategy to be employed, including an outline for expected completion of the project; anticipated contribution; statement of the significance of the project within the field of psychology and law. Project timeline, Proposed budget with budget justifications. If the applicant has secured additional funding for the proposed research from another funding source, Curriculum vitae, A list of at least five suggested reviewers for the project with expertise in the content area of the proposal. **Deadline:** October 15. **Contact:** contact the ECP Committee Chair - aplsecpgrant@gmail.com.

1295 ■ Saleem Shah Early Career Award *(Doctorate/Recognition)*

Purpose: To recognize early career excellence and contributions to the field of psychology and law. **Focus:** Law; Psychology. **Qualif.:** Applicants must have received the doctoral degree or the law degree, whichever comes later, if both have been earned within the last six years. **Criteria:** Selection will be based on the committee's criteria.

Funds Avail.: A total of $2,000. **Duration:** Annual. **Number Awarded:** 1. **To Apply:** Applicants must send a letter detailing the nominee's contributions to psychology and law, copy of the nominee's vita in PDF or Word format. Self-nominations will not be considered. **Deadline:** November 30.

1296 ■ American Public Power Association (APPA)
2451 Crystal Drive, Suite 1000
Arlington, VA 22202
Ph: (202)467-2900
URL: www.publicpower.org
Social Media: www.facebook.com/americanpublicpower
www.instagram.com/publicpowerorg
www.linkedin.com/company/american-public-power
 -association
twitter.com/publicpowerorg
www.youtube.com/c/
AmericanPublicPowerAssociationWashington

1297 ■ DEED Student Research Grant/Internships
(Undergraduate, Graduate/Grant, Internship)
Purpose: To introduce students to career opportunities in public power, support students entering technical programs and majors in short supply and high demand by the utility industry and to provide assistance to DEED members that sponsor scholarships. **Focus:** Energy-related areas. **Qualif.:** Applicants must be accepted or enrolled in a full-time vocational school or accredited college or university, this includes high school seniors through graduate students; must be studying an energy related discipline. **Criteria:** Applicants must submit a brief summary when the project is 50 percent complete. must complete a satisfactory summary abstract once their project is complete. must complete a satisfactory final report once their project is complete.

Final reports, abstracts and any other deliverable promised in the project application must be reviewed and approved by the utility before being sent to the DEED administrator. Press coverage, photos, videos, presentations and other associated materials resulting from the project are valuable. share these resources with DEED so we can promote the work that you have done. All reporting for the DEED scholarship (mid-point report, abstract, final report) must be submitted through DEED's scholarship management system, the same platform where the application was submitted.

Funds Avail.: $4,000 plus up to $1,000 in travel funds to attend applicable conference. **Duration:** Annual. **Deadline:** February 15;October 15. **Contact:** Email: DEED@PublicPower.org; Phone: 202-467-2960.

1298 ■ American Public Transportation Foundation (APFT)
1300 I St. NW, Ste. 1200 E
Washington, DC 20005
Ph: (202)496-4818
E-mail: info@aptfd.org
URL: www.aptfd.org
Social Media: www.facebook.com/
AmericanPublicTransportationAssociation

1299 ■ Dan M. Reichard, Jr. Scholarship
(Undergraduate, Graduate/Scholarship)

Purpose: To provide educational assistance to individuals in public transportation industry-related fields of study. **Focus:** Business administration; Transportation. **Qualif.:** Applicants must be enrolled in a fully accredited institution; have and maintain at least a 3.0 GPA (B) in course works that are relevant to the industry or required of a degree program; be either employed by or demonstrate a strong interest in entering the public transportation industry; and, be college sophomores (30 hours or more satisfactorily completed), juniors, seniors, or seeking advanced degree(s). **Criteria:** Selection shall be based on demonstrated interest in the public transportation industry as a career, academic achievement, essay content and quality, need for financial assistance and involvement in extracurricular citizenship and leadership activities.

Funds Avail.: No specific amount. **Duration:** Annual. **Number Awarded:** Varies. **To Apply:** Applications require the following materials: Essay (1,000 words maximum); Two (2) letters of recommendation (1 Letter for Renewing Scholars); Statement of Financial Need: explaining the financial need of the applicant, including any deficits in a financial aid package, family income and personal need (personal need may also include special circumstances, such as personal hardship or financial difficulty that contributes to the applicant's financial need). (500 words maximum); School transcript, documenting good academic standing: Enclose documentation from your school verifying you are in good academic standing and that you are maintaining the required class load. Verification of enrollment for the upcoming fall semester (letter from school or course schedule can also serve as proof of enrollment); Copy of the fee schedule from the college/university for the academic year. Signature of APTA sponsor. **Deadline:** June 15. **Remarks:** The scholarship is awarded to the applicant dedicated to a career in the business administration or management area of the transit industry.

Awards are arranged alphabetically below their administering organizations

1300 ■ Dr. George M. Smerk Scholarship
(Undergraduate, Graduate/Scholarship)

Purpose: To provide educational assistance to individuals in public transportation industry-related fields of study. **Focus:** Transportation. **Qualif.:** Applicants must be enrolled in a fully accredited institution; have and maintain at least a 3.0 GPA (B) in course works that are relevant to the industry or required of a degree program; be either employed by or demonstrate a strong interest in entering the public transportation industry; and, be college sophomores (30 hours or more satisfactorily completed), juniors, seniors, or seeking advanced degree(s). **Criteria:** Selection shall be based on demonstrated interest in the public transportation industry as a career, academic achievement, essay content and quality, need for financial assistance and involvement in extracurricular citizenship and leadership activities.

Funds Avail.: No specific amount. **Duration:** Annual. **Number Awarded:** Varies. **To Apply:** Applications require the following materials: Essay (1,000 words maximum); Two (2) letters of recommendation (1 Letter for Renewing Scholars); Statement of Financial Need: explaining the financial need of the applicant, including any deficits in a financial aid package, family income and personal need (personal need may also include special circumstances, such as personal hardship or financial difficulty that contributes to the applicant's financial need). (500 words maximum); School transcript, documenting good academic standing: Enclose documentation from your school verifying you are in good academic standing and that you are maintaining the required class load. Verification of enrollment for the upcoming fall semester (letter from school or course schedule can also serve as proof of enrollment); Copy of the fee schedule from the college/university for the academic year. Signature of APTA sponsor. **Deadline:** June 15. **Remarks:** The scholarship is awarded to the applicant dedicated to a career in public transit management.

1301 ■ Florida Public Transportation Association Scholarships (FPTA) *(Undergraduate, Graduate/Scholarship)*

Purpose: To provide educational assistance to individuals in public transportation industry-related fields of study. **Focus:** Transportation. **Qualif.:** Applicants must be enrolled in a fully accredited institution; have and maintain at least a 3.0 GPA (B) in course works that are relevant to the industry or required of a degree program; be either employed by or demonstrate a strong interest in entering the public transportation industry; and, be college sophomores (30 hours or more satisfactorily completed), juniors, seniors, or seeking advanced degree(s). **Criteria:** Selection shall be based on demonstrated interest in the public transportation industry as a career, academic achievement, essay content and quality, need for financial assistance and involvement in extracurricular citizenship and leadership activities.

Funds Avail.: No specific amount. **Duration:** Annual. **Number Awarded:** Varies. **To Apply:** Applications require the following materials: Essay (1,000 words maximum); Two (2) letters of recommendation (1 Letter for Renewing Scholars); Statement of Financial Need: explaining the financial need of the applicant, including any deficits in a financial aid package, family income and personal need (personal need may also include special circumstances, such as personal hardship or financial difficulty that contributes to the applicant's financial need). (500 words maximum); School transcript, documenting good academic standing: Enclose documentation from your school verifying you are in good academic standing and that you are

maintaining the required class load. Verification of enrollment for the upcoming fall semester (letter from school or course schedule can also serve as proof of enrollment); Copy of the fee schedule from the college/university for the academic year. Signature of APTA sponsor. **Deadline:** June 15. **Remarks:** The scholarship is awarded to an applicant from the state of Florida, and sponsored by a Florida public transit system or the FPTA.

1302 ■ Jack R. Gilstrap Scholarship *(Undergraduate, Graduate/Scholarship)*

Purpose: To provide educational assistance to individuals in public transportation industry-related fields of study. **Focus:** Transportation. **Qualif.:** Applicants must be college sophomores (30 hours or more satisfactorily completed), juniors, seniors, or those seeking advanced degrees may apply for scholarships. Enrolled in a fully accredited institution, have and maintain at least a 2.0 GPA in course work that is relevant to the industry or required of a degree program, and demonstrate a strong interest in entering the public transportation industry. All applicants must be sponsored by a member organization of the American Public Transportation Association (APTA). Any member may serve as a sponsor. **Criteria:** Selection shall be based on demonstrated interest in the public transportation industry as a career, academic achievement, essay content and quality, need for financial assistance and involvement in extracurricular citizenship and leadership activities.

Funds Avail.: No specific amount. **Duration:** Annual. **Number Awarded:** Varies. **To Apply:** Applications require the following materials: Essay (1,000 words maximum); Two (2) letters of recommendation (1 Letter for Renewing Scholars); Statement of Financial Need: explaining the financial need of the applicant, including any deficits in a financial aid package, family income and personal need (personal need may also include special circumstances, such as personal hardship or financial difficulty that contributes to the applicant's financial need). (500 words maximum); School transcript, documenting good academic standing: Enclose documentation from your school verifying you are in good academic standing and that you are maintaining the required class load. Verification of enrollment for the upcoming fall semester (letter from school or course schedule can also serve as proof of enrollment); Copy of the fee schedule from the college/university for the academic year. Signature of APTA sponsor. **Deadline:** June 15. **Remarks:** The scholarship is awarded to the applicant receiving the highest overall score.

1303 ■ Louis T. Klauder Scholarship *(Undergraduate, Graduate/Scholarship)*

Purpose: To provide educational assistance to individuals in public transportation industry-related fields of study. **Focus:** Engineering, Electrical; Engineering, Mechanical; Transportation. **Qualif.:** Applicants must be college sophomores (30 hours or more satisfactorily completed), juniors, seniors, or those seeking advanced degrees may apply for scholarships. Enrolled in a fully accredited institution, have and maintain at least a 2.0 GPA in course work that is relevant to the industry or required of a degree program, and demonstrate a strong interest in entering the public transportation industry. All applicants must be sponsored by a member organization of the American Public Transportation Association (APTA). Any member may serve as a sponsor. **Criteria:** Selection shall be based on demonstrated interest in the public transportation industry as a career, academic achievement, essay content and quality, need for financial assistance and involvement

Awards are arranged alphabetically below their administering organizations

in extracurricular citizenship and leadership activities.

Funds Avail.: No specific amount. **Duration:** Annual. **Number Awarded:** Varies. **To Apply:** Applications require the following materials: Essay (1,000 words maximum); Two (2) letters of recommendation (1 Letter for Renewing Scholars); Statement of Financial Need: explaining the financial need of the applicant, including any deficits in a financial aid package, family income and personal need (personal need may also include special circumstances, such as personal hardship or financial difficulty that contributes to the applicant's financial need). (500 words maximum); School transcript, documenting good academic standing: Enclose documentation from your school verifying you are in good academic standing and that you are maintaining the required class load. Verification of enrollment for the upcoming fall semester (letter from school or course schedule can also serve as proof of enrollment); Copy of the fee schedule from the college/university for the academic year. Signature of APTA sponsor. **Deadline:** June 15. **Remarks:** The scholarship is awarded to the applicant dedicated to a career in the rail transit industry as an electrical or mechanical engineer.

1304 ■ Parsons Brinckerhoff / Jim Lammie Scholarship *(Undergraduate, Graduate/Scholarship)*

Purpose: To provide educational assistance to individuals in public transportation industry-related fields of study. **Focus:** Transportation. **Qualif.:** Applicants must be college sophomores (30 hours or more satisfactorily completed), juniors, seniors, or those seeking advanced degrees may apply for scholarships. Enrolled in a fully accredited institution, have and maintain at least a 2.0 GPA in course work that is relevant to the industry or required of a degree program, and demonstrate a strong interest in entering the public transportation industry. All applicants must be sponsored by a member organization of the American Public Transportation Association (APTA). Any member may serve as a sponsor. **Criteria:** Selection shall be based on demonstrated interest in the public transportation industry as a career, academic achievement, essay content and quality, need for financial assistance and involvement in extracurricular citizenship and leadership activities.

Funds Avail.: No specific amount. **Duration:** Annual. **Number Awarded:** Varies. **To Apply:** Applications require the following materials: Essay (1,000 words maximum); Two (2) letters of recommendation (1 Letter for Renewing Scholars); Statement of Financial Need: explaining the financial need of the applicant, including any deficits in a financial aid package, family income and personal need (personal need may also include special circumstances, such as personal hardship or financial difficulty that contributes to the applicant's financial need). (500 words maximum); School transcript, documenting good academic standing: Enclose documentation from your school verifying you are in good academic standing and that you are maintaining the required class load. Verification of enrollment for the upcoming fall semester (letter from school or course schedule can also serve as proof of enrollment); Copy of the fee schedule from the college/university for the academic year. Signature of APTA sponsor. **Deadline:** June 15. **Remarks:** The scholarship is awarded to the applicant who is dedicated to a public transportation engineering career.

1305 ■ Reba Malone Scholarship *(Undergraduate, Graduate/Scholarship)*

Purpose: To provide educational assistance to individuals in transit or transportation marketing/ communications. **Focus:** Marketing and distribution; Transportation. **Qualif.:** Applicants must be enrolled in a fully accredited institution; have and maintain at least a 3.0 GPA (B) in course works that are relevant to the industry or required of a degree program; be either employed by or demonstrate a strong interest in entering the public transportation industry; and, be college sophomores (30 hours or more satisfactorily completed), juniors, seniors, or seeking advanced degree(s). **Criteria:** Selection shall be based on demonstrated interest in the public transportation industry as a career, academic achievement, essay content and quality, need for financial assistance and involvement in extracurricular citizenship and leadership activities.

Funds Avail.: No specific amount. **Duration:** Annual. **Number Awarded:** Varies. **To Apply:** Applications require the following materials: Essay (1,000 words maximum); Two (2) letters of recommendation (1 Letter for Renewing Scholars); Statement of Financial Need: explaining the financial need of the applicant, including any deficits in a financial aid package, family income and personal need (personal need may also include special circumstances, such as personal hardship or financial difficulty that contributes to the applicant's financial need). (500 words maximum); School transcript, documenting good academic standing: Enclose documentation from your school verifying you are in good academic standing and that you are maintaining the required class load. Verification of enrollment for the upcoming fall semester (letter from school or course schedule can also serve as proof of enrollment); Copy of the fee schedule from the college/university for the academic year. Signature of APTA sponsor. **Deadline:** June 15. **Remarks:** The scholarship is awarded to the applicant dedicated to a career in marketing/communications.

1306 ■ Richard J. Bouchard - AECOM Scholarship *(Undergraduate, Graduate/Scholarship)*

Purpose: To provide educational assistance to individuals in public transportation planning and development. **Focus:** Transportation. **Qualif.:** Applicants must be enrolled in a fully accredited institution; have and maintain at least a 3.0 GPA (B) in course works that are relevant to the industry or required of a degree program; be either employed by or demonstrate a strong interest in entering the public transportation industry; and, be college sophomores (30 hours or more satisfactorily completed), juniors, seniors, or seeking advanced degree(s). **Criteria:** Selection shall be based on demonstrated interest in the public transportation industry as a career, academic achievement, essay content and quality, need for financial assistance and involvement in extracurricular citizenship and leadership activities.

Funds Avail.: No specific amount. **Duration:** Annual. **Number Awarded:** Varies. **To Apply:** Applications require the following materials: Essay (1,000 words maximum); Two (2) letters of recommendation (1 Letter for Renewing Scholars); Statement of Financial Need: explaining the financial need of the applicant, including any deficits in a financial aid package, family income and personal need (personal need may also include special circumstances, such as personal hardship or financial difficulty that contributes to the applicant's financial need). (500 words maximum); School transcript, documenting good academic standing: Enclose documentation from your school verifying you are in good academic standing and that you are maintaining the required class load. Verification of enrollment for the upcoming fall semester (letter from school or course schedule can also serve as proof of enrollment); Copy of the fee schedule from the college/university for the academic year. Signature of APTA sponsor. **Deadline:** June

Awards are arranged alphabetically below their administering organizations

15. **Remarks:** The scholarship is awarded to the applicant dedicated to a career in public transportation planning and development.

1307 ■ American Public Works Association - Nevada Chapter (APWA)
c/o Adam Searcy, Chair
14101 Old Virginia Rd.
Reno, NV 89521
URL: nevada.apwa.net
Social Media: www.facebook.com/American-Public-Works -Association-APWA-Nevada-Chapter-175819385805858

1308 ■ Michael Koizumi APWA Internship Scholarship *(Undergraduate/Scholarship, Internship)*

Purpose: To assist students in attaining their career aspirations and building a foundation of future public works leaders. **Focus:** Public administration. **Qualif.:** Applicants must be Nevada residents or attended/graduated from a Nevada high school; must plan to enroll in a course of study leading to a career in the field of public works, public administration or a related private enterprise (e.g. business, architecture, science, engineering, etc.); and must be entering their freshman year or currently enrolled in college. **Criteria:** Awards will be given based on nominations by APWA members; financial need-income, family size; desire; achievements; grades. Preference will be given to students attending a Nevada school.

Funds Avail.: $1,500. **Duration:** Annual. **Number Awarded:** 4. **To Apply:** Applicants must submit completed application form together with copy of transcripts, reference, list of experience, a written statement on financial status, and career objectives. **Deadline:** April 15. **Contact:** Jeremy Leavitt, 333 N Rancho Dr., Las Vegas, NV 89106; Email: jeleavitt@lasvegasnevada.gov.

1309 ■ American Quarter Horse Youth Association (AQHYA)
1600 Quarter Horse Dr.
Amarillo, TX 79104
Ph: (806)376-4811
URL: www.aqha.com
Social Media: www.facebook.com/aqha1
www.instagram.com/officialaqha/
www.pinterest.com/aqha1
twitter.com/AQHA
www.youtube.com/user/aqhavideo

1310 ■ American Quarter Horse Foundation Scholarships *(Undergraduate, Graduate/Scholarship)*

Purpose: To support for youth who develop into future leaders and impact our industry. **Focus:** Education; Journalism; Nursing; Veterinary science and medicine. **Qualif.:** Applicants must be enrolled in college specializing degree programs such as education, nursing, journalism, veterinary and racing. **Criteria:** Applicants will be selected based on financial need, academic merit, equine involvement and civic activities.

Funds Avail.: No specific amount. **Duration:** Annual. **Number Awarded:** Varies. **To Apply:** Applicants must fill out the online application form and submit materials must include a completed application form with financial information, three reference letters or appraisal forms, and a high

school or college transcript. Students applying for a state or regional scholarship will also need to provide proof of membership in their state affiliate. Applicants must provide three recommendations, which may consist of a combination of uploaded reference letters or request an online recommendation. Options for submitting these items are provided when completing the online application form. **Remarks:** Established in 1976. **Contact:** For more information, contact the Foundation at 806-378-5029 or e-mail at foundation@aqha.org.

1311 ■ American Quilt Study Group (AQSG)
1610 L St.
Lincoln, NE 68508-2509
Ph: (402)477-1181
Fax: (402)477-1181
URL: www.americanquiltstudygroup.org

1312 ■ Lucy Hilty Research Grant *(Graduate/Grant)*

Purpose: To provide support for research in the industry of quilting. **Focus:** Art. **Qualif.:** Applicants can be individuals or group affiliated with quilt-related studies. **Criteria:** Selection will be according to the quality and impact of their projects; ability to complete the project; compatibility of the projects for the goal of AQSG; and how the projects will contribute to the quilting industry.

Funds Avail.: $2,000. **Duration:** Annual. **To Apply:** Applications form is available at the website; proposal should be limited to a cover letter and the application; include completed proposal description; must state the qualifications of the researcher; include letters of support from cooperating institutions or individuals; and a line-item budget for the amount of funding required; curriculum vitae; project budget. **Deadline:** February 1. **Contact:** 1610 L St., Lincoln, NE, 68508-2509; Phone/Fax: 402-477-1181; Email: AQSG2@americanquiltstudygroup.org.

1313 ■ American Radium Society (ARS)
19 Mantua Rd.
Mount Royal, NJ 08061
Ph: (310)437-0581
Fax: (856)423-3420
URL: www.americanradiumsociety.org
Social Media: www.facebook.com/AmericanRadiumSociety
www.linkedin.com/company/american-radium-society
twitter.com/radiumsociety

1314 ■ ARS Young Oncologist Travel Grants *(Professional development/Grant)*

Purpose: To recognize an individual for outstanding abstracts that are reviewed favorably for presentation at the Annual Meeting. **Focus:** Oncology; Radiology; Surgery.
Funds Avail.: $1,500. **Duration:** Annual.

1315 ■ American Railway Engineering and Maintenance-of-Way Association (AREMA)
4501 Forbes Blvd., Ste. 130
Lanham, MD 20706
Ph: (301)459-3200
E-mail: info@arema.org
URL: www.arema.org
Social Media: www.facebook.com/AREMArail

Awards are arranged alphabetically below their administering organizations

www.linkedin.com/company/american-railway-engineering
-and-maintenance-of-way-association-arema-
twitter.com/AREMArail
www.youtube.com/channel/UC-7JZpJ761kfM8IxbbBXwQw

1316 ■ AREMA Committee 12 - Rail Transit Scholarships *(Undergraduate/Scholarship)*

Purpose: To support the education of a student who is also working full-time in the railway industry. **Focus:** Engineering. **Qualif.:** Applicants must be a enrolled student who has completed at least one quarter or semester in an accredited* engineering program OR part time student working full time in the railway industry. **Criteria:** Selection will be priority given to students preference for rail transit engineering.

Funds Avail.: $2,000. **Duration:** Annual; one academic year. **Deadline:** December 8.

1317 ■ AREMA Committee 18 - Light Density and Short Line Railways Scholarships *(Undergraduate/Scholarship)*

Purpose: To support the education of an engineering student who has a potential interest in railway engineering careers. **Focus:** Engineering. **Qualif.:** Applicants must be enrolled students who have completed at least one quarter or semester in an accredited four or five year engineering or engineering technology undergraduate degree program.

Funds Avail.: $2,500. **Duration:** Annual; one academic year. **Deadline:** December 8.

1318 ■ AREMA Committee 24 - Education and Training Scholarships *(Undergraduate/Scholarship)*

Purpose: To support the education of an engineering student who has a potential interest in railway engineering careers. **Focus:** Engineering. **Qualif.:** Applicants must be current AREMA student members who have completed at least on quarter or semester in an accredited four or five year engineering or engineering technology undergraduate degree program; must have at least a 2.00 GPA (out of 4.00).

Funds Avail.: $3,000. **Duration:** Annual; one academic year. **Deadline:** December 8.

1319 ■ AREMA Committee 27 - Maintenance-of-Way Work Equipment Scholarships *(Undergraduate/Scholarship)*

Purpose: To support the education of those students whose family members work hard in the work equipment industry for railroads. **Focus:** Engineering. **Qualif.:** Applicant must be enrolled as a student in a graduate or undergraduate program leading to a degree in engineering or engineering technology; must have at least a 2.00 GPA. **Criteria:** Priority is given to a Committee 27 family member or a family member of someone in the work equipment industry for railroads.

Funds Avail.: $1,000. **Duration:** Annual; one academic year. **Number Awarded:** Varies. **Deadline:** December 8.

1320 ■ AREMA Committee 33 - Electric Energy Utilization Scholarships *(Undergraduate/Scholarship)*

Purpose: To support the education of an engineering student who has a potential interest in railway engineering careers. **Focus:** Engineering. **Qualif.:** Applicant must be demonstrating an interest in the field of rail traction electrification systems engineering.

Funds Avail.: $2,000. **Duration:** Annual; one academic year. **Deadline:** December 8.

1321 ■ AREMA Michigan Tech Alumni Scholarships *(Graduate, Undergraduate/Scholarship)*

Purpose: To support the education of engineering students at Michigan Technological University. **Focus:** Engineering. **Qualif.:** Applicant must be an undergraduate or graduate engineering student in good standing at Michigan Tech University; scholarships are also available to Railroad Engineering and Activities Club (REAC) Members and Club Officers. **Criteria:** Selection will be priority given to students who are already married or supporting a family.

Funds Avail.: $1,500. **Duration:** Annual. **Number Awarded:** 3. **To Apply:** Applicants may verify the application process through the program website. Applicants must also specify on the application if they are members of REAC. **Deadline:** December 8.

1322 ■ AREMA Presidential Spouse Scholarship *(Undergraduate/Scholarship)*

Purpose: To support the education of a female engineering student with a potential interest in railway engineering careers. **Focus:** Engineering. **Qualif.:** Applicants must be enrolled female students who have completed at least one quarter or semester in an accredited four or five-year engineering or engineering technology undergraduate degree program.

Funds Avail.: $1,000. **Duration:** Annual. **Deadline:** December 9.

1323 ■ AREMA Women's Engineering Scholarship *(Undergraduate/Scholarship)*

Purpose: To support the education of undergraduate engineering student who has potential interest in railway engineering careers. **Focus:** Engineering. **Qualif.:** All applicants include having an interest in railway engineering, maintaining a minimum GPA of 2.0 and being available for interview by the AREMA Scholarship Committee; must be enrolled female student who has completed at least one quarter or semester in an accredited* four or five-year engineering or engineering technology undergraduate degree program.

Funds Avail.: $1,500. **Duration:** varies. **Deadline:** December 8.

1324 ■ CSX Scholarships *(Undergraduate/Scholarship)*

Purpose: To support the education of an undergraduate engineering student who has potential interest in railway engineering careers. **Focus:** Engineering. **Qualif.:** All applicants include having an interest in railway engineering, maintaining a minimum GPA of 2.0 and being available for interview by the AREMA Scholarship Committee; must be enrolled female student who has completed at least one quarter or semester in an accredited* four or five-year engineering or engineering technology undergraduate degree program.

Funds Avail.: $1,000. **Duration:** Annual. **Deadline:** December 8.

1325 ■ John J. Cunningham Memorial Scholarships *(Undergraduate/Scholarship)*

Purpose: To support the education of student in a professional field that has direct applications in the passenger rail

Awards are arranged alphabetically below their administering organizations

sector. **Focus:** Engineering. **Qualif.:** Applicants must be junior or senior college students pursuing an undergraduate degree in a professional field that has direct applications in the passenger rail sector; must have at least a 2.00 GPA (out of 4.00).

Funds Avail.: $1,000. **Duration:** Annual; one academic year. **Deadline:** December 8.

1326 ■ Larry L. Etherton Scholarships (Graduate, Undergraduate/Scholarship)

Purpose: To support the continuing education of railway engineering students at the University of Illinois in the Engineering Department at Urbana-Champaign. **Focus:** Engineering. **Qualif.:** Applicants must be engineering students pursuing an undergraduate or graduate degree at the University of Illinois at Urbana-Champaign; must have at least a 2.00 GPA (out of 4.00). **Criteria:** Selection will be priority given to students who are already married or supporting a family.

Funds Avail.: $1,500. **Duration:** Annual. **To Apply:** Applicants must submit completed AREMA data form together with a cover letter (maximum of 350 words); a resume; two letters of recommendation, one from a faculty member, and another from a present employer, AREMA member, or other responsible person; and a transcript from the schools attended, and courses currently enrolled in. **Deadline:** December 9.

1327 ■ Michael W. and Jean D. Franke Family Foundation Scholarships (Graduate, Undergraduate/Scholarship)

Purpose: To support the continuing education of railway engineering students at the University of Illinois in the Engineering Department at Urbana-Champaign. **Focus:** Engineering. **Qualif.:** Applicants must be engineering students pursuing an undergraduate or graduate degree at the University of Illinois at Urbana-Champaign; must have at least a 2.00 GPA (out of 4.00).

Funds Avail.: $6,000. **Duration:** Annual. **Deadline:** December 8.

1328 ■ Michael and Gina Garcia Rail Engineering Scholarships (Undergraduate, Graduate/Scholarship)

Purpose: To support the education of an engineering student, especially to students already married or supporting a family. **Focus:** Engineering. **Qualif.:** All applicants include having an interest in railway engineering, maintaining a minimum GPA of 2.0 and being available for interview by the AREMA Scholarship Committee; must be enrolled female student who has completed at least one quarter or semester in an accredited* four or five-year engineering or engineering technology undergraduate degree program .**Criteria:** Selection will be priority given to students who are already married or supporting a family.

Funds Avail.: $3,000. **Duration:** Annual. **Deadline:** December 8.

1329 ■ Norfolk Southern Foundation Scholarships (Undergraduate/Scholarship)

Purpose: To support the education of an engineering student. **Focus:** Engineering. **Qualif.:** Applicants must be enrolled full-time in a four or five year undergraduate program in Engineering or Engineering Technology in which the institution must be located in Norfolk Southern's service area (22 states, the District of Columbia and Ontario, Canada); have completed at least one quarter or semester

in college prior to the application; and have a GPA of 2.00.

Funds Avail.: $1,000. **Duration:** Annual. **Deadline:** December 8.

1330 ■ REMSA Scholarships (Undergraduate/Scholarship)

Purpose: To support the education of an undergraduate engineering student who has potential interest in railway engineering careers. **Focus:** Engineering. **Qualif.:** All applicants include having an interest in railway engineering, maintaining a minimum GPA of 2.0 and being available for interview by the AREMA Scholarship Committee; must be enrolled female student who has completed at least one quarter or semester in an accredited* four or five-year engineering or engineering technology undergraduate degree program.

Funds Avail.: $1,000. **Duration:** Annual. **Deadline:** December 8.

1331 ■ American Rental Association Foundation (ARA)

1900 19th St.
Moline, IL 61265
Ph: (309)764-2475
Fax: (309)764-1533
Free: 800-334-2177
URL: foundation.ararental.org

1332 ■ ARA Region 10/Dorothy Wellnitz Scholarship – Canada (Undergraduate, Vocational/Occupational/Scholarship)

Purpose: To provide scholarships to promising young students looking to enter the rental industry. **Focus:** Education, Industrial. **Qualif.:** Applicants must be pursuing an education program applicable to the rental industry; must be college and technical school students from Canada; Immediate family members of the ARA Foundation board of trustees and ARA affiliated staff are not eligible. **Criteria:** Selection of applicants will be based on the scholarship application criteria.

Funds Avail.: $1,500. **Duration:** Annual. **Number Awarded:** 1. **To Apply:** Applications can be submitted online; must provide school-documented transcripts and letters of reference and essays. **Deadline:** March 2. **Remarks:** The scholarship has been named for Dorothy Wellnitz who is the former executive director of the Canadian Rental Association. Established in 2007. **Contact:** 1900 19th St., Moline, IL, 61265; Fax: 309-764-1533.

1333 ■ ARA Region Two/Ron Marshall Scholarship (Undergraduate/Scholarship)

Purpose: To financially support students within the region who is attending trade, technical or vocational school that that supports a career in the equipment and event rental industry. **Focus:** Education, Industrial. **Qualif.:** Applicants must be pursuing a trade, technical or vocational education program that supports a career in the equipment rental industry at an accredited trade or technical school, community college, college or university; applicant's business must qualify for ARA membership. **Criteria:** Applicants will be selected based on the scholarship application criteria.

Funds Avail.: $750. **Duration:** Annual. **Number Awarded:** 2. **To Apply:** Applications can be submitted online; must provide school-documented transcripts and letters of refer-

Awards are arranged alphabetically below their administering organizations

ence and essays. **Deadline:** March 2. **Contact:** 1900 19th St., Moline, IL, 61265; Fax: 309-764-1533.

1334 ■ Leonard Hawk Founders Scholarship
(Graduate, Undergraduate, Vocational/Occupational/ Scholarship)

Purpose: To provide scholarships to promising young students looking to enter the rental industry. **Focus:** Education, Industrial. **Qualif.:** Applicants must be currently employed in the equipment/event rental industry; must be an immediate family member (son, daughter or spouse) of a business owner in the equipment/event rental industry; applicant's business does not need to be an ARA member, but it must qualify for ARA membership; immediate family members of the ARA Foundation board of trustees and ARA affiliated staff are not eligible. **Criteria:** Applicants will be selected based on the scholarship application criteria.

Funds Avail.: $5,000. **Duration:** Annual. **Number Awarded:** 1. **To Apply:** Applications can be submitted online; must provide school-documented transcripts and letters of reference and essays. **Deadline:** March 1. **Remarks:** The scholarship is named after Leonard Hawk who is one of the founder and first president of the American Rental Association.

1335 ■ American Research Center in Egypt (ARCE)
909 North Washington St., Ste. 320
Alexandria, VA 22314
Ph: (703)721-3479
E-mail: info@arce.org
URL: www.arce.org
Social Media: www.facebook.com/arcenational
www.instagram.com/arcenational
twitter.com/ARCENational
www.youtube.com/user/ARCEinEgypt

1336 ■ ARCE Funded Fellowships *(Doctorate, Postdoctorate/Fellowship)*

Purpose: To provide sufficient funding to cover round-trip air transportation, living allowance, mentoring and a home base in Egypt for doctoral candidates in the all-but-dissertation stage and senior scholars conducting more advanced research. **Focus:** Anthropology; Archeology; Architecture; Art; Economics; History; Humanities; Literature; Political science; Religion. **Qualif.:** Applicants must be American pre-doctoral candidates (ABD), postdoctoral scholars, faculty and senior scholars at universities worldwide; fellowships are for a minimum stay of three months and maximum stay of 12 months; U.S. citizenship is required. **Criteria:** Selection will be based on the committee's criteria.

Funds Avail.: Amount varies. **Duration:** Annual. **Deadline:** January 18. **Contact:** Academic Programs Coordinator; Email: fellows@arce.org.

1337 ■ ARCE Research Associates Fellowship
(Doctorate, Postdoctorate, Professional development/ Fellowship)

Purpose: To supported scholars interested in conducting academic research in Egypt on a wide variety of topics. **Focus:** Anthropology; Archeology; Architecture; Art; Economics; History; Humanities; Literature; Political science; Religion. **Qualif.:** Applicants must be American pre-

doctoral candidates (ABD), postdoctoral scholars, faculty and senior scholars at universities worldwide; fellowship is for a minimum stay of three months and maximum stay of 12 months; U.S. citizenship is required. **Criteria:** Selection will be based on the committee's criteria.

Funds Avail.: No specific amount. **Duration:** Annual. **Deadline:** January 18. **Contact:** Academic Programs Coordinator; Email: fellows@arce.org.

1338 ■ The William P. McHugh Memorial Fund
(Doctorate, Graduate/Grant)

Purpose: To financially support the students enrolled in a graduate program through education, training and research initiatives. **Focus:** Anthropology; Archeology; Architecture; Art; Economics; Education, Religious; History; Literature; Political science. **Qualif.:** Applicants must be pre-doctoral ARCE Fellow in the field of Egyptian geo-archaeology and prehistory. **Criteria:** Selection of applicants will be based on the criteria given by the Scholarship Committee.

Funds Avail.: $600. **Number Awarded:** 1. **To Apply:** Applicants must submit completed applications online; must submit guiding research questions, research methodology, a clear thesis statement, and a literature review; Strong reference letters that speak directly to your research and your capacity to carry it out successfully will also support your candidacy. **Deadline:** January 15. **Contact:** Academic Programs Coordinator, Djodi Deutsch; Email: fellows@arce.org.

1339 ■ National Endowment for the Humanities Fellowship *(Graduate/Fellowship)*

Purpose: To supported scholars interested in conducting academic research in Egypt on a wide variety of topics. **Focus:** Anthropology; Archeology; Architecture; Art; Economics; Education, Religious; History; Literature; Political science. **Qualif.:** Applicants must be U.S. citizens; must be students enrolled in doctoral programs at North America universities, or postdoctoral scholars and professionals affiliated with North American universities and research institutions. **Criteria:** Selection of applicants will be based on the criteria given by the Scholarship Committee.

Funds Avail.: No specific amount. **Duration:** 4-10 months. **Number Awarded:** 1-2. **To Apply:** Applicants must submit completed applications online; must submit statement of research proposal (1, 500 words), Describes your intended research, Describes your research methodology(ies), Demonstrates the need to consult sources in Egypt, Explains the scholarly significance of your research and your qualifications to undertake the research, Assesses the feasibility of completing your research within the proposed Timeframe, Describes the final publication format (dissertation, book, chapter, etc.) of your research; Three recommendation letters for all applicants PLUS one language proficiency recommendation letter for pre-doctoral applicants; Graduate and undergraduate transcripts for pre-doctoral applicants. Please remove all password protections from transcripts prior to submission. **Deadline:** January 15. **Contact:** Academic Programs Coordinator, Djodi Deutsch; Email: fellows@arce.org.

1340 ■ The United States Department of State, Bureau of Educational & Cultural Affairs Fellowships *(Graduate/Fellowship)*

Purpose: To supported scholars interested in conducting academic research in Egypt on a wide variety of topics. **Focus:** Anthropology; Archeology; Architecture; Art; Economics; Education, Religious; History; Literature; Politi-

Awards are arranged alphabetically below their administering organizations

cal science. **Qualif.:** Applicants must be U.S. citizens; must be students enrolled in doctoral programs at North America universities, or postdoctoral scholars and professionals affiliated with North American universities and research institutions. **Criteria:** Selection of applicants will be based on the criteria given by the Scholarship Committee.

Funds Avail.: No specific amount. **Duration:** 3-12 months. **Number Awarded:** 3-6. **To Apply:** Applicants must submit completed applications online; must submit statement of research proposal (1, 500 words), Describes your intended research, Describes your research methodology(ies), Demonstrates the need to consult sources in Egypt, Explains the scholarly significance of your research and your qualifications to undertake the research, Assesses the feasibility of completing your research within the proposed Timeframe, Describes the final publication format (dissertation, book, chapter, etc.) of your research; Three recommendation letters for all applicants PLUS one language proficiency recommendation letter for pre-doctoral applicants; Graduate and undergraduate transcripts for pre-doctoral applicants. Please remove all password protections from transcripts prior to submission. **Deadline:** January 15. **Contact:** Academic Programs Coordinator, Djodi Deutsch; Email: fellows@arce.org.

1341 ■ American Research Institute in Turkey (ARIT)
3260 S St.
Philadelphia, PA 19104
Ph: (215)898-3474
URL: ccat.sas.upenn.edu

1342 ■ ARIT Fellowships in the Humanities and Social Sciences in Turkey *(Postdoctorate, Graduate/ Fellowship)*

Purpose: To help applicant's research and study facilities for researchers, as well as connections with colleagues, institutions, and authorities through its centers in Istanbul and Ankara. **Focus:** History, Ancient; Humanities; Medieval studies; Modern languages; Social sciences. **Qualif.:** Applicants must be scholars and advanced graduate students engaged in research on ancient, medieval, or modern times in turkey, in any field of the humanities and social sciences; student applicants must have fulfilled all requirements for the doctorate except the dissertation by June of the current year, and before beginning any ARIT-sponsored research; non-U.S. applicants who reside in the U.S. or Canada are expected to maintain an affiliation with an educational institution in the U.S. or Canada.

Funds Avail.: No specific amount. **Duration:** Annual. **To Apply:** Applicants must provide complete application information; three letters of recommendation; letters of reference; copy of graduate transcript; supporting documents. **Deadline:** November 1. **Contact:** University of Pennsylvania Museum, 3260 South Street, Philadelphia PA 19104-6324. For further information call (215) 898-3474, fax (215) 898-0657, or e-mail to aritoffice@gmail.com.

1343 ■ ARIT/NEH Fellowships *(Postgraduate/ Fellowship)*
Purpose: To provide longer term support for advanced research in all fields of the humanities. **Focus:** Humanities. **Qualif.:** Applicants must be scholars who have completed their formal training by the application deadline and plan to carry out research in Turkey for four months or longer; may be U.S. citizens or three-year residents of the U.S.

Funds Avail.: $4,200. **Duration:** Annual. **To Apply:** Applications can be submitted online; should submit three letters of recommendation. **Deadline:** November 1.

1344 ■ ARIT Summer Fellowships for Intensive Advanced Turkish Language Study *(Graduate, Undergraduate/Fellowship)*

Purpose: To promote American and Turkish research and exchange related to Turkey. **Focus:** Foreign languages; General studies/Field of study not specified. **Qualif.:** Applicant must be a full-time students and scholars affiliated at academic institutions; must be citizen, national, or permanent resident of the United States; must currently enrolled in an undergraduate or graduate level academic program, or be faculty; must have minimum B average in current program of study; must perform at the high-intermediate level on a proficiency-based admissions examination.

Funds Avail.: No specific amount. **Duration:** Annual. **Number Awarded:** Approximately 18. **To Apply:** Applicants must submit complete application information; transcripts and three letters of reference; application fee in the amount of $25. **Deadline:** 'February. **Contact:** Dr. Sylvia Önder, Director; Division of Eastern Mediterranean Languages Department of Arabic and Islamic Studies, Georgetown University; 210 North Poulton Hall, 1437 - 37th Street N.W., Washington, D.C. 20007; Email:aritfellowship@ georgetown.edu or aritoffice@gmail.com.

1345 ■ Critical Language Scholarships at Summer Institutes. (CLS) *(Graduate, Undergraduate/ Scholarship)*

Purpose: To expand the number of Americans studying and mastering critical need foreign languages that are critical to national security and economic prosperity. **Focus:** Business; Engineering; Humanities; Science; Social sciences. **Qualif.:** Applicants must be U.S. citizens; must be currently enrolled in a degree-granting program at the undergraduate or graduate level; enrolled in an accredited U.S. degree-granting program at the undergraduate or graduate level at the time of your application. institution must be an accredited U.S. institution. must be enrolled at this institution in the fall term of 2019. must successfully complete academic requirements for the fall term in order to remain eligible for the CLS Program. Be at least 18 years old by May 15, 2020. **Criteria:** Applicants are selected based on their commitment to language learning and plans to apply their language skills to their future academic or professional pursuits. Connection between Language and Goals; Preparation for the CLS Program; Adaptability, Sensitivity and Resilience; Contribution to the CLS Program and Program Goals.

Funds Avail.: No specific amount. **Duration:** Annual. **To Apply:** Applicants recommend online submission of all required application materials, consist of an application form, two recommendation letters, and uploaded copies of your unofficial transcripts, There are five essay questions on the application form. Your response to each essay question is strictly limited to a maximum number of words. Each applicant must obtain two recommendations. Recommendations may be provided by an academic advisor, a current or past professor or someone who knows the applicant in a professional or volunteer capacity. Each applicant must submit an unofficial transcript from the college or university they are currently attending, as well as transcripts from colleges and universities attended in the past. First-year students must submit an unofficial transcript

Awards are arranged alphabetically below their administering organizations

showing their courses in progress. High school transcripts are not necessary. **Deadline:** November 19. **Contact:** American Councils for International Education; 1828 L Street NW, Suite 1200, Washington, D.C. 20036; Telephone: 1-202-833-7522, 1-877-257-9922 (toll-free); E-mail: cls@americancouncils.org.

1346 ■ Kenan T. Erim Fellowships for Archaeological Research at Aphrodisias (Postdoctorate/Fellowship)

Purpose: To support excavation and/or research about art history and archeology at Aphrodisias in Turkey during the summer. **Focus:** Archeology; Architecture; Art history. **Qualif.:** Applicants must be advanced graduate students engaged in excavation and research at Aphrodisias. **Criteria:** Recipients are selected base on academic records and financial need.

Funds Avail.: $2,375. **To Apply:** Applicants must provide complete application information; three letters of recommendation; a 100-word abstract of the project; letters of reference; and a copy of graduate transcript. **Deadline:** November 1. **Contact:** Application form and supporting documents may sent electronically to leinwand@sas.upenn.edu.

1347 ■ Getty Research Exchange Fellowship Program for Cultural Heritage Preservation (Doctorate/Fellowship)

Purpose: To support advanced regional research and exchanges between research centers in the Mediterranean and Middle East regions. **Focus:** General studies/Field of study not specified. **Qualif.:** Applicants must be Turkish citizens who have already obtained PhD; must have professional experience in the study or preservation of cultural heritage; must be willing to undertake specific research project in overseas research centers of another country. **Criteria:** Recipients are selected based on: the significance of the proposal; value of the collaboration proposed; feasibility of the research design; and applicant's research background.

Funds Avail.: Up to $4,000. **To Apply:** Applicants must fill out the application form; submit a project abstract and project description along with a letter of recommendation and 3-page curriculum vitae. **Deadline:** December 31.

1348 ■ Ilse B. Hanfmann, George Hanfmann and Machteld J. Mellink Burslari Fellowship. (Doctorate/Fellowship)

Purpose: To enable nationals of the Republic of Turkey who are graduate students at or recent PhDs from Turkish universities in archaeology and related fields to study abroad (North America or elsewhere). **Focus:** General studies/Field of study not specified. **Qualif.:** Applicants must be candidates for M.A. or Ph.D. degrees who have finished all course work and passed all qualifying examinations for the degree before entering the tenure; archaeological fields that are eligible include Prehistory, Protohistory, Ancient Near Eastern, Anatolian, Greek and Roman, Byzantine, Seljuk and Ottoman. Those who combine archaeology with an additional concentration in Ancient History, Ancient Art History, Languages and Literatures of the Ancient Near East or of Greece and Rome, Geomorphology, or Geophysics. **Criteria:** Selection criteria are to be excellence in promise and excellence in achievement. Financial need by itself is not to be a selection criterion. Candidates also need to demonstrate proficiency in the language of the host institution. Eligible host institutions

include universities qualified in archaeology or related fields at the graduate level, institutions with important research assets (for example, research libraries, collections of antiquities, manuscripts, etc.), museums (for example, the Metropolitan Museum of Art, the British Museum, State Museums of Berlin), and archaeological schools.

Funds Avail.: $15,000 to $45,000. **Duration:** Annual. **To Apply:** Application for a Hanfmann Fellowship will consist of the following: Curriculum vitae; A one-paragraph summary of the nature and significance of the proposed project. A project proposal (no more than five pages); For graduate students: official transcripts of undergraduate and graduate course work. Demonstration of proficiency in the language or languages necessary for conducting research abroad. A minimum of three letters of recommendation from scholars familiar with the applicant's work. The letters should address the significance of the project and the capacity of the individual to complete the proposed research. The letters should be sent by the referee in single copy. **Deadline:** March 2. **Contact:** American Research Institute in Turkey, Koc University ANAMED, Istiklal Caddesi 181, 34433, Beyoglu, Istanbul; Phone: 212-393-6072; Email: aritist2@gmail.com; or American Research Institute in Turkey, Representative Sehit Ersan St. 24/9, 06680, Cankaya, Ankara; Phone: 312-427-2222; Fax: 312-427-4979.

1349 ■ National Endowment for the Humanities Advanced Fellowships for Research in Turkey (Postdoctorate/Fellowship)

Purpose: To promote American and Turkish research and exchange related to Turkey. **Focus:** Archeology; Art; History; Humanities; Linguistics; Literature; Social sciences. **Qualif.:** Applicants may be U.S. citizens or three-year residents of the U.S. (they may consult ARIT headquarters on questions of eligibility); scholars who have completed all formal training by the application deadline and plan to carry out research in Turkey for four months or longer are eligible.

Funds Avail.: $4,200. **To Apply:** Applicants must provide complete application information. Application materials and three letters of recommendation; download, save, and complete the application form appended here (.pdf); letters of reference sent directly to ARIT by mail or e-mail. Letters should support the proposed research and your capacity to carry out the project and supporting documents in paper form. **Deadline:** November 1.

1350 ■ American Respiratory Care Foundation (ARCF)
9425 N MacArthur Blvd., Ste. 100
Irving, TX 75063-4706
Ph: (972)243-2272
Fax: (972)484-2720
URL: www.arcfoundation.org
Social Media: www.linkedin.com/company/aarc
www.in.pinterest.com/pin/312155817917502676

1351 ■ Advance Degree and Clinical Research Training Grants in Alpha-1 Antitrypsin Deficiency (Master's/Grant)

Purpose: To support an RT's getting advance training in research with the subject of the deliverable research project being a meritorious project regarding alpha-1 antitrypsin deficiency. **Focus:** Respiratory therapy. **Qualif.:** Applicants must be respiratory therapists who conduct research (clinical or translational), including detection, inhalation thera-

Awards are arranged alphabetically below their administering organizations

pies, clinical care, diagnostics, and therapeutic tools in alpha-1 antitrypsin deficiency (AATD)-related lung disease. **Criteria:** The project must be deemed important and meritorious by the grant review committee and could involve any of a number of aspects regarding AATD, e.g., strategies in detection, therapy/ethical/legal/social issues, basic science, etc.

Funds Avail.: No specific amount. **To Apply:** Interested applicants may contact the Foundation for the application process and other information. **Deadline:** February 19.

1352 ■ Vyaire Fellowship for Neonatal and Pediatric Therapists *(Professional development/Fellowship)*

Purpose: To foster projects in the field of neonatal and pediatric critical care. **Focus:** Health sciences; Medical research. **Qualif.:** Candidates must be researchers having high quality abstracts accepted for presentation at the AARC Congress of the current year. **Criteria:** Selection will be based on the Trustee's criteria.

Funds Avail.: No specific amount. **Duration:** Annual. **To Apply:** No formal application is required; all fellows will be selected by ARCF trustees. **Remarks:** Funded by VIASYS Healthcare. Established in 2001.

1353 ■ Jeri Eiserman, RRT Professional Education Research Fellowship *(Professional development/Fellowship)*

Purpose: To support original university hospital research in respiratory care and airway management. **Focus:** Health sciences. **Qualif.:** Candidates must be researchers having high quality abstracts accepted for presentation at the AARC Congress of the current year.

Funds Avail.: No specific amount. **Duration:** Annual. **To Apply:** No formal application is required; all fellows will be selected by ARCF trustees. **Remarks:** Funded by the Anesthesia and Respiratory Division of Teleflex in honor of Mrs. Jeri Eiserman's dedication to advancing the respiratory care profession, and her service as an extraordinary leader, role model and educator. Established in 2015.

1354 ■ Jerome M. Sullivan Research Fund *(Professional development/Fellowship)*

Purpose: To support investigators for their clinical or basic research in respiratory care and cardiopulmonary medicine. **Focus:** Health sciences. **Qualif.:** Applicants must be respiratory care and cardiopulmonary medicine.

Funds Avail.: $10,000. **Duration:** Annual. **To Apply:** Applicants may obtain an application form online. Application must: be typewritten, using single spacing and black ribbon; be stay within the margin limitations indicated on the form and continuation pages; Continuation pages must be 8 1/2" x 11" in a good quality white bond paper. Draw all graphs, diagrams, tables, and charts with black ink. Do not include oversized documents, graphs, diagrams, tables, and chairs in the body of the application; submit them in an appendix. **Deadline:** December 31. **Remarks:** The fund was created by a grant from Jerome M. Sullivan, the 1990 President of the AARC. Established in 1990.

1355 ■ Monaghan/Trudell Fellowships for Aerosol Technique Development *(Professional development/Fellowship)*

Purpose: To support projects dealing with aerosol delivery issues. **Focus:** Health sciences; Medical research. **Qualif.:** Candidates must be researchers having high quality abstracts accepted for presentation at the AARC Congress

of the current year. **Criteria:** Selection will be based on the Trustee's criteria.

Funds Avail.: No specific amount. **Duration:** Annual. **To Apply:** No formal application is required. All fellows will be selected by ARCF Trustees. Projects may include modeling, in-vitro, or clinical studies. The focus should be on developing cost-effective approaches to aerosol delivery. **Remarks:** Funded by Trudell Medical and Monaghan Medical in the United States. Established in 1993.

1356 ■ NBRC Frederic Helmholz, Jr., MD Educational Research Fund *(Master's, Doctorate/Grant)*

Purpose: To support a research with practical value to the respiratory care profession. **Focus:** Respiratory therapy. **Qualif.:** Candidates must be Master's or PhD students. **Criteria:** Selection will be based on the Trustee's criteria.

Funds Avail.: No specific amount. **To Apply:** Applicants must submit a proposal in a format prescribed by the American Respiratory Care Foundation Board of Trustees. **Deadline:** June 1. **Contact:** ARCF Executive Office, 9425 N. MacArthur, Blvd 100, Irving, TX, 75063-4706; Phone: 972-243-2272.

1357 ■ Parker B. Francis Respiratory Research Grant *(Advanced Professional, Professional development/Grant)*

Purpose: To provide financial assistance for research programs dealing with respiratory care and related topics. **Focus:** Medical research; Respiratory therapy. **Qualif.:** Applicants must be physicians or respiratory care practitioners. **Criteria:** Selection will be based on the Trustee's criteria.

Funds Avail.: $10,000. **Duration:** Annual. **To Apply:** Applicants must use English only and avoid jargon and unusual abbreviations; type the application, using single spacing and black ribbon; stay within the margin limitations indicated on the form and continuation pages. Continuation pages must be 8 1/2" x 11", good quality, white bond paper. draw all graphs, diagrams, tables, and charts with black ink; do not include oversized documents, graphs, diagrams, tables, and chairs in the body of the application; mail or deliver the completed and signed, typewritten original and four (4) photocopies of the application. **Deadline:** December 31. **Remarks:** The grant is made possible through the provided endowment by the Parker B. Francis Foundation to the ARCF.

1358 ■ Philips Respironics Fellowships in Mechanical Ventilation *(Professional development/Fellowship)*

Purpose: To foster projects dealing with mechanical ventilation, especially outside of the intensive care unit. **Focus:** Health sciences. **Qualif.:** Candidates must be researchers having high quality abstracts accepted for presentation at the AARC Congress of the current year. **Criteria:** Selection will be based on the Trustee's criteria.

Funds Avail.: No specific amount. **Duration:** Annual. **To Apply:** No formal application is required. All fellows will be selected by ARCF Trustees. Projects can be device development, device evaluation, cost-effectiveness analysis, or education programs. **Remarks:** Funded by Respironics, Inc. Established in 1993.

1359 ■ Philips Respironics Fellowships in Non-Invasive Respiratory Care *(Professional development/Fellowship)*

Purpose: To foster projects dealing with non-invasive techniques to provide ventilator support. **Focus:** Health sci-

Awards are arranged alphabetically below their administering organizations

ences; Medical research. **Qualif.:** Candidates must be researchers having high quality abstracts accepted for presentation at the AARC Congress of the current year. **Criteria:** Selection will be based on the Trustee's criteria.

Funds Avail.: No specific amount. **Duration:** Annual. **To Apply:** No formal application is required. All fellows will be selected by ARCF Trustees. Projects can be device development, device evaluation, cost effectiveness analysis, or education programs. **Remarks:** Funded by Respironics, Inc. Established in 1993.

1360 ■ Charles W. Serby COPD Research Fellowship *(Professional development/Fellowship)*

Purpose: To promote research and education in the area of Chronic Obstructive Pulmonary Disease (COPD). **Focus:** Health sciences. **Qualif.:** Candidates must be researchers having high quality abstracts accepted for presentation at the AARC Congress of the current year. **Criteria:** Selection will be based on the Trustee's criteria.

Funds Avail.: No specific amount. **To Apply:** No formal application is required; all fellows will be selected by ARCF trustees. **Remarks:** Funded by Boehringer Ingelheim Pharmaceuticals, Inc. in honor of Dr. Charles Serby's longstanding commitment to respiratory clinical research. Established in 2002.

1361 ■ American Road & Transportation Builders Association (ARTBA)
250 E St. SW, Ste. 900
Washington, DC 20024
Ph: (202)289-4434
Fax: (202)289-4435
URL: www.artba.org
Social Media: www.facebook.com/ARTBAssociation
www.instagram.com/artbassociation
www.linkedin.com/company/artba
twitter.com/ARTBA
www.youtube.com/user/ARTBAMedia/videos

1362 ■ Lanford Family Highway Worker Memorial Scholarship Program *(High School/Scholarship)*

Purpose: To provide financial assistance to the children or legally adopted children of highway workers killed or permanently disabled in the line of duty to pursue post-high school education. **Focus:** General studies/Field of study not specified. **Qualif.:** Applicants must be the children of highway workers who have been killed or permanently disabled while working in roadway construction zones; eligible students must attend a post-secondary institution of learning that requires a high school diploma or its equivalent. this could include any public or private four-year accredited college or university; two-year accredited college; or vocational technical college or training institution. MBA candidates and master's degree students in civil engineering, construction management, and other construction-related programs will also be considered.

Funds Avail.: $5,000. **Duration:** Annual. **To Apply:** Applicants must submit completed and signed award application form. **Deadline:** April 17. **Remarks:** Established in 1999. **Contact:** Melanie Laird at mlaird@artba.org or 202.289.1029.

1363 ■ American Roentgen Ray Society (ARRS)
44211 Slatestone Ct.
Leesburg, VA 20176-5109
Ph: (703)729-3353
Fax: (703)729-4839
Free: 866-940-2777
E-mail: info@arrs.org
URL: www.arrs.org
Social Media: www.facebook.com/AmericanRoentgenRaySociety
www.instagram.com/arrs_radiology
www.linkedin.com/company/arrs
twitter.com/ARRS_Radiology
www.youtube.com/user/ARRSTube

1364 ■ ARRS/ASNR Scholarship in Neuroradiology *(Advanced Professional/Scholarship)*

Purpose: To establish the recipient as an independent investigator in the field of neuroradiology and to collect preliminary data that could lead to further funding through established mechanisms. **Focus:** Neurology; Radiology. **Qualif.:** Applicant must be a junior full-time faculty members.

Duration: Biennial.

1365 ■ American Romanian Orthodox Youth (AROY)
c/o Stephen Maxim, President
832 Indian Lake Rd.
Lake Orion, MI 48362
Ph: (586)260-3342
URL: www.roea.org/aroy.html
Social Media: www.youtube.com/user/RomanianDioceseROEA

1366 ■ A.R.F.O.R.A. Undergraduate Scholarships for Women *(Undergraduate/Scholarship)*

Purpose: To support the continuing education of student members. **Focus:** General studies/Field of study not specified. **Qualif.:** Applicant must be a female voting member of a parish of the Romanian Orthodox Episcopate of America and accepted by a duly accredited university or college. **Criteria:** Selection is based on the applicant scholastic achievement, character, worthiness, and participation in religious life.

Funds Avail.: $1,000. **Duration:** Annual. **Number Awarded:** 1. **To Apply:** Three letters of recommendation must be mailed sealed with an attached photo and must submit a formal letter projecting the plans of the applicant. **Deadline:** May 10. **Remarks:** Established in 1994. **Contact:** A.R.F.O.R.A. Scholarship Committee Corina Phillips 1122 SAFFRON TRAIL WADSWORTH OH 44281;Email: corina5dan@aol.com.

1367 ■ Pamfil and Maria Bujea Family Orthodox Christian Seminarian Scholarships *(Undergraduate/Scholarship)*

Purpose: To support the education of students seeking ordination into priesthood or wish to serve the Church in a professional manner. **Focus:** Religion. **Qualif.:** Applicants must be citizens or permanent residents of either Canada or the United States of American and show proof thereof; students must furnish written proof of enrollment in the appropriate higher education program along with a transcript of the students' grades at the designated institutions; applicant must be of good character and active in school and/or the community.**Criteria:** Award is limited to those

Awards are arranged alphabetically below their administering organizations

who either seek ordination into the priesthood or who wish to serve the Church.

Funds Avail.: $10,000. **Duration:** Annual. **Number Awarded:** 1. **To Apply:** Applicants must submit a completed application; a 300-word handwritten essay explaining their mission if they're assigned to Canada; and a posed photograph. Three letters of recommendation obtained sealed, from the authors, must be included with the application. One should be from the applicants' spiritual advisor/priest. **Deadline:** July 1. **Contact:** The Pamfil and Maria Bujea Family Orthodox Christian Seminarian Scholarship Committee, P.O. Box 309, Grass Lake Michigan 49240-0309, U.S.A.

1368 ■ A.R.F.O.R.A. Martha Gavrila Scholarships for Women *(Postgraduate/Scholarship)*

Purpose: To support the student members in post-graduate studies. **Focus:** General studies/Field of study not specified. **Qualif.:** Applicant must be a female voting member of a parish of the Romanian Orthodox Episcopate of America; a graduate of a duly accredited university/college; and accepted by a graduate school or a duly accredited university and specify her course of study. **Criteria:** Selection is based on the application materials.

Funds Avail.: $1,000. **Duration:** One year. **Number Awarded:** 1. **To Apply:** Three letters of recommendation must be mailed sealed, directly to the attention of the Scholarship Committee. A photo must be included and a formal letter projecting the plans of the applicant. **Deadline:** May 10. **Remarks:** The Award was established in memory of Mrs. Martha Gavrila, long-time president of A.R.F.O.R.A. who worked tirelessly for the Episcopate and Vatra Romaneasca. Established in 1985. **Contact:** A.R.F.O.R.A. Scholarship Committee Corina Phillips 1122 SAFFRON TRAIL WADSWORTH OH 44281;Email: corina5dan@aol.com.

1369 ■ R.O.E.A. Dumitru Golea Goldy-Gemu Scholarships *(Undergraduate, High School/Scholarship)*

Purpose: To support the continuing education of student members. **Focus:** General studies/Field of study not specified. **Qualif.:** Applicant must be of Romanian descent and a citizen or permanent resident of the United States or Canada; must be enrolled as a full-time undergraduate student in a recognized four-year educational institution. **Criteria:** Selection is based on the application.

Funds Avail.: $1,500. **Duration:** Annual. **Number Awarded:** 2. **To Apply:** Applicants must submit a completed application form; three letters of recommendation; 300 words handwritten essay explaining, "How my Romanian heritage helps make me a better American/Canadian"; and recent photo for publication. Must submit written proof of enrollment: for High School applicants, a copy of the letter of acceptance from higher education program; for current undergraduate applicants, a transcript of records at the institution; for returning undergraduate applicants, a letter of acceptance from the institution. **Deadline:** May 31. **Contact:** Goldy Scholarship Committee, PO Box 309, Grass Lake, MI, 49240-0309.

1370 ■ A.R.O.Y. Stanitz Scholarships *(Undergraduate/Scholarship)*

Purpose: To support the continuing education of student members. **Focus:** General studies/Field of study not specified. **Qualif.:** Applicants must be active AROY members; must be high school graduates; must be college students

or those who intends to enroll in a school or college or university level. **Criteria:** Selection will be based on the submitted application.

Funds Avail.: $1,000. **Duration:** Annual. **Number Awarded:** 2. **To Apply:** Applicants must submit the following application materials: a biographical history including family; an educational background and grades; list of AROY and church activities; list of extra-curricular interests or achievements; reasons why applying for the scholarship; a photograph; and a letter of recommendation from parish priest or AROY advisors regarding parish and AROY activities. **Deadline:** July 1. **Remarks:** Established in 1971. **Contact:** William R. Stanitz/AROY Scholarship, The Romanian Orthodox Episcopate of America, PO Box 309, Grass Lake, MI, 49240-0309.

1371 ■ The American-Scandinavian Foundation (ASF)
58 Park Ave.
New York, NY 10016
Ph: (212)779-3587
E-mail: info@amscan.org
URL: www.amscan.org

1372 ■ American-Scandinavian Foundation Fellowships/Grants in the United States *(Graduate, Professional development/Fellowship, Grant)*

Purpose: To promote international understanding through educational and cultural exchange between the United States and Denmark, Finland, Iceland, Norway and Sweden. **Focus:** General studies/Field of study not specified. **Qualif.:** Applicants must be citizens of Denmark, Finland, Iceland, Norway or Sweden who wish to undertake study or research programs (usually at the graduate level) in the United States. **Criteria:** Selection will be based on the standards set by the respective countries of the awardees.

Funds Avail.: Over $500,000. **Duration:** Annual. **Number Awarded:** Varies. **To Apply:** Applicants must contact the cooperating organizations of ASF.

1373 ■ American-Scandinavian Foundation Fellowships to Study in Scandinavia *(Graduate/Fellowship)*

Purpose: To support an individual to pursue research, study or creative arts projects. **Focus:** General studies/Field of study not specified. **Qualif.:** Applicants must have a well-defined research or study project that makes a stay in Scandinavia essential; must be US citizens or permanent residents; must have completed their undergraduate education by the start of their project in Scandinavia. **Criteria:** Preference will be given to candidates at the graduate level for dissertation-related study or research.

Funds Avail.: Up to $23,000. **Duration:** Annual. **Number Awarded:** Varies. **To Apply:** Applicants must complete an ASF application form; expected to devote full time to their proposed study or research, and must justify the length of time needed to complete their project; must provide evidence that you comply with research ethics and seek informed consent; three letters of recommendation are required. **Deadline:** November 1.

1374 ■ American-Scandinavian Foundation Grants to Study in Scandinavia *(Graduate/Grant)*

Purpose: To support an individual to pursue research, study or creative arts projects. **Focus:** Arts. **Qualif.:** Ap-

Awards are arranged alphabetically below their administering organizations

plicants must have a well-defined research or study project that makes a stay in Scandinavia essential; must be US citizens or permanent residents; must have completed their undergraduate education by the start of their project in Scandinavia. **Criteria:** Preference will be given to candidates at the graduate level for dissertation-related study or research.

Funds Avail.: Up to $5,000. **Duration:** Annual. **Number Awarded:** Varies. **To Apply:** Applicants must complete an ASF application form; expected to devote full time to their proposed study or research, and must justify the length of time needed to complete their project; must provide evidence that you comply with research ethics and seek informed consent; three letters of recommendation are required. **Deadline:** November 1.

1375 ■ Annika Teig Fellowship *(Postgraduate/ Internship)*

Purpose: To support Scandinavian citizens seeking experience in interior design at a leading architecture firm in New York City. **Focus:** Architecture. **Criteria:** Selection will be conducted by the review panel selected by SOM.

Funds Avail.: No specific amount. **Duration:** Annual; 3 month internship. **To Apply:** Applications must be submitted along with cover letter as to why applicant like to apply for this award; must contain work samples; portfolios should be one PDF attachment, 10-20 pages, maximum 5 MB (must be part of resume section). **Deadline:** June 1. **Remarks:** The scholarship was established to honor the memory of Annika Teig, a former Associate at SOM. **Contact:** E-mail: Judy.Betts@som.com.

1376 ■ Leif and Inger Sjöberg Award *(Advanced Professional, Professional development/Award)*

Purpose: To encourage the English translation of Scandinavian literature of the last two centuries. **Focus:** Literature; Translating. **Qualif.:** Applicants must be outstanding English translators of poetry, fiction, drama or literary prose originally written in a Nordic language. **Criteria:** Selection will be based on the committee's criteria.

Funds Avail.: $2,000. **Duration:** Annual. **Number Awarded:** Varies. **To Apply:** Applicants must consist of one copy of the translation, including a title page and a table of contents for the proposed book of which the manuscript submitted is a part and one copy of the work(s) in the original language; must also send photocopies of the following pages; a CV containing all contact information including email address for the translator; and a letter or other documents signed by the author, the author's agent or the author's estate granting permission for the translation to be entered in this competition and published in Scandinavian Review. Prose manuscripts must not be longer than 50 pages and must not be longer than 25 pages for poetry; manuscripts must be typed and double-spaced with numbered pages. **Deadline:** September 1.

1377 ■ The Nadia Christensen Prize *(All/Prize)*

Purpose: To support the most outstanding translations of poetry, fiction, drama or literary prose written by a Scandinavian author. **Focus:** General studies/Field of study not specified. **Qualif.:** Applicant must be an outstanding English translations of poetry, fiction, drama or literary prose originally written in a Nordic language. **Criteria:** Selection will be based on the committee's criteria.

Funds Avail.: $2,500. **Duration:** Annual. **Number Awarded:** 2. **To Apply:** Applicants must consist of one

copy of the translation, including a title page and a table of contents for the proposed book of which the manuscript submitted is a part and one copy of the work(s) in the original language; must also send photocopies of the following pages; a CV containing all contact information including email address for the translator; and a letter or other documents signed by the author, the author's agent or the author's estate granting permission for the translation to be entered in this competition and published in Scandinavian Review. Prose manuscripts must not be longer than 50 pages and must not be longer than 25 pages for poetry; manuscripts must be typed and double-spaced with numbered pages. **Deadline:** September 1.

1378 ■ American Schools of Oriental Research (ASOR)

PO Box 16956
Alexandria, VA 22302
Ph: (617)236-0408
E-mail: info@asor.org
URL: www.asor.org

1379 ■ Platt Excavation Fellowships *(Other, Undergraduate/Fellowship)*

Purpose: To support the participation of ASOR members as volunteers or staff on excavation projects. **Focus:** General studies/Field of study not specified. **Qualif.:** Applicants must be current members of ASOR or students enrolled at an institutional member of ASOR. **Criteria:** Preference will be given to individuals who have not received a support through the heritage programs or other funding sources.

Funds Avail.: $2,000 each. **Duration:** Annual. **To Apply:** Applicants must submit a completed application form and 250-350 words with photo (digital tiff, 300 dpi or higher); reports and photos should be sent electronically with "Platt Report" in the subject heading. **Deadline:** January 31. **Remarks:** The award was established by generous gift of the late Mrs. Katherine Barton Platt. **Contact:** Reports and photos, E-mail: asor@bu.edu; (Applications) American Schools of Oriental Research, PO Box 15729, Boston, MA, 02215.

1380 ■ American Senior Benefits Association (ASBA)

PO Box 300777
Chicago, IL 60630-0777
Free: 877-906-2722
E-mail: info@asbaonline.org
URL: www.asbaonline.org
Social Media: www.facebook.com/asbaonline
twitter.com/AmericanSenior4

1381 ■ ASBA College Scholarship Grant Program *(Professional development/Scholarship)*

Purpose: To provide and support educational financial aid to members and their grandchildren. **Focus:** General studies/Field of study not specified. **Qualif.:** Applicant must be a dependent or grandchild of an ASBA member; enrolled at least one year in college or university. **Criteria:** Awards are given based on academic merit and evaluation of the submitted essay.

Funds Avail.: Up to $1,000. **Duration:** Annual. **To Apply:** Applicants must submit an application form (please visit the website); an essay; two letters of recommendation; official

Awards are arranged alphabetically below their administering organizations

copies of high school/college transcript. **Deadline:** May 31. **Contact:** Toll-Free: 877-906-2722.

1382 ■ American Sheep Industry Association (ASI)

9785 Maroon Cir., Ste. 360
Englewood, CO 80112
Ph: (303)771-3500
E-mail: info@sheepusa.org
URL: www.sheepusa.org
Social Media: www.facebook.com/SheepUSA
twitter.com/SheepUSA
www.youtube.com/user/SheepUSA1

1383 ■ Sheep Heritage Foundation Memorial Scholarship *(Graduate, Doctorate/Scholarship)*

Purpose: To provide financial support to a graduate-level student for research toward the advancement of the sheep, lamb, and wool industry. **Focus:** Animal science and behavior. **Qualif.:** Applicants must be graduate students involved in sheep and/or wool research in such areas as animal science, agriculture economics or veterinary medicine with proof of graduate school acceptance.

Funds Avail.: $3,000. **Duration:** Annual. **To Apply:** Applicants should submit an application along with two letters of reference. **Deadline:** May 31. **Contact:** ASI, Attn: Memorial Scholarship, 9785 Maroon Cir., Ste. 360, Englewood, Colo. 80112-2692; Phone: 303-771-3500 ext. 107; Email: angela@sheepusa.org.

1384 ■ American Shotcrete Association (ASA)

38800 Country Club Dr.
Farmington Hills, MI 48331
Ph: (248)848-3780
Fax: (248)848-3740
E-mail: info@shotcrete.org
URL: www.shotcrete.org
Social Media: www.facebook.com/
  AmericanShotcreteAssociation
www.instagram.com/shotcreteasa
www.linkedin.com/company/american-shotcrete
  -association
twitter.com/shotcreteasa

1385 ■ ASA Graduate Scholarships *(Graduate/Scholarship)*

Purpose: To attract, identify and assist outstanding graduate students pursuing careers within the field of concrete with a significant interest in the shotcrete process. **Focus:** Construction. **Qualif.:** Applicant must be conducting graduate study in the area of concrete at an accredited college or university within the United States or Canada; must be a full-time first or second-year (post bachelor's degree) graduate student during the entire scholarship year. **Criteria:** Selection is based on the essay, submitted data and reference.

Funds Avail.: $3,000. **Duration:** One academic year. **Number Awarded:** 3. **To Apply:** Applicants must submit a completed, typed application form together with one-page resume; essay (1-page limit, 300 words or less, name must be on first page, include all scheduled classes for balance of academic year); two completed online reference forms; and all original undergraduate and graduate transcripts

(mailed directly to ASA in sealed envelope with a university stamp); materials must be sent together via email in one package; all materials must be in English.

1386 ■ American Society of Brewing Chemists (ASBC)

3340 Pilot Knob Rd.
Saint Paul, MN 55121
Ph: (651)454-7250
Fax: (651)454-0766
E-mail: asbc@scisoc.org
URL: www.asbcnet.org
Social Media: www.facebook.com/BrewingChemists
www.linkedin.com/groups/4662739/profile
twitter.com/BrewingChemists

1387 ■ ASBC Foundation Graduate Scholarships *(Graduate/Scholarship)*

Purpose: To provide financial support to students who are pursuing MS or Ph.D. degrees in brewing science or related areas. **Focus:** Food science and technology. **Qualif.:** Applicants must be current ASBC student members enrolled in graduate studies by the time the graduate scholarship becomes effective, or be current graduate students pursuing a course of study leading to an MS or a Ph.D. degree.

Duration: Annual. **To Apply:** Applicants must submit a completed application form; copies of transcripts; a letter of application describing career plans; and three letters of recommendation; at least two of which are from deans, department heads and/or professors who have supervised the applicant's most recent academic work; letters should present essential facts regarding scholastic record, capacity for work, extracurricular activities, career potential, ability to cooperate, character and personality and interest and capability in research. **Deadline:** April 1. **Contact:** ASBC Foundation Program Manager, Linda Schmitt; Email: lschmitt@scisoc.org.

1388 ■ ASBC Foundation Undergraduate Scholarships *(Undergraduate/Scholarship)*

Purpose: To provide financial support to students who are children of active ASBC members. **Focus:** Food science and technology; Nutrition. **Qualif.:** Applicants must be: children of active ASBC members; enrolled as undergraduate students (juniors and seniors) at a college or university; and, actively pursuing a bachelor's degree.

Funds Avail.: Up to $1,000. **Duration:** Annual. **To Apply:** Applicants must submit a completed application form; copies of transcripts; a letter of application describing career plans; and three letters of recommendation with at least two from the academic adviser and/or faculty members familiar with the applicant's academic record. The confidential letter(s) should include a general appraisal of the scholarship, extracurricular activities and abilities in particular relation to the purposes and eligibility requirements of the scholarships. **Deadline:** April 1. **Contact:** ASBC Foundation Program Manager, Linda Schmitt; Email: lschmitt@scisoc.org.

1389 ■ American Society of Business Publication Editors (ASBPE)

214 N Hale St.
Wheaton, IL 60187
Ph: (630)510-4588

Awards are arranged alphabetically below their administering organizations

Fax: (630)510-4501
E-mail: info@asbpe.org
URL: www.asbpe.org
Social Media: www.facebook.com/asbpe
www.linkedin.com/groups/81056/profile
www.linkedin.com/company/asbpe
twitter.com/asbpe
www.youtube.com/user/asbpe

1390 ■ ASBPE Young Leaders Scholarship *(Professional development/Scholarship)*

Purpose: To help young editors in their careers. **Focus:** Business. **Qualif.:** Applicant must be an editor; 30 years of age or younger; worked as an editor in a business magazine for at least two years; must be sponsored by the applicant's chief editor; pursuing a career in the business press and must not be a past winner of the ASBPE Young Leaders Scholarship.

Duration: Annual. **To Apply:** Application form is available at the website. **Deadline:** February 7.

1391 ■ American Society of Certified Engineering Technicians (ASCET)

15621 W 87th Street Pky., Ste.,205
Lenexa, KS 66219
Ph: (773)242-7238
E-mail: office@ascet.org
URL: www.ascet.org
Social Media: www.facebook.com/ASCETSocialMedia
twitter.com/ascet50

1392 ■ Joseph C. Johnson Memorial Grant
(Undergraduate/Grant)

Purpose: To diminish the cost of tuition, books, and lab fees for students. **Focus:** Engineering. **Qualif.:** Applicant must be an American citizen or a legal resident, a student, certified, regular, registered or associate member of ASCET; full or part-time student in an Engineering Technology program (students in a two year program should apply in the first year to receive the grant for their second year. Students in a four year program who apply in the third year may receive the grant for their fourth year); and be qualified for financial aid under the Federal College Work Study Program. Applicants must meet the following grade requirements: 2 points on a 3 point system, 3 points on a 4 point system, 4 points on a 5 point system, or 5 points on a 6 point system. **Criteria:** Priority will be given to applicants who have demonstrated financial need, as verified by the Dean or Registrar of Engineering Technology, or the Financial Aid Office at the institution the applicant attends.

Funds Avail.: $750. **To Apply:** Applicants must submit a fully accomplished printed or typewritten application form available online; a letter of recommendation from a faculty member of the Engineering Technology Department indicating the motivation, progress, achievements, and an evaluation of the applicant's potential in the field of Engineering Technology; letters of recommendation from two personal acquaintances, employers or former employers, outlining association, motivation and potential for success; a copy of transcript of records and be sure to pass all the requirements on time. **Deadline:** April 1. **Remarks:** The Grant was established on the honors of Joseph C. Johnson, CET, who was a long-time ASCET member and former Northeast Regional Vice President. **Contact:** ASCET Office,15621 W.

87th St Pkwy, Ste. 205,Lenexa, KS 66219; E-mail: office@ascet.org.

1393 ■ Kurt H. and Donna M. Schuler Cash Grant
(Undergraduate/Scholarship, Grant)

Purpose: To offset the cost of educational expenses as desired. **Focus:** Engineering. **Qualif.:** Applicant must either be a student, certified, regular, registered, or associate member of ASCET; a high school senior in the last five months of the academic year who will be enrolled in an Engineering Technology curriculum no later than six months following selection for award; must have passing grades in their present curriculum. **Criteria:** All applications are reviewed by the Financial Aid Committee which also selects the recipients.

Funds Avail.: $400. **Number Awarded:** Varies. **To Apply:** Applicants must provide a copy of transcript; a letter of recommendation from a personal acquaintance, faculty member, or employer outlining motivation, progress, outstanding achievements, and an evaluation of the applicant's potential in the field of Engineering Technology. **Deadline:** April 1. **Remarks:** The Grant was established on the memory of Kurt H. Schuler and Donna M. Schuler. **Contact:** ASCET Office,15621 W. 87th St Pkwy, Ste. 205,Lenexa, KS 66219; E-mail: office@ascet.org.

1394 ■ Joseph M. Parish Memorial Grants
(Undergraduate/Grant)

Purpose: To diminish the cost of tuition, books, and lab fees for students. **Focus:** Engineering. **Qualif.:** Applicants must meet the following: must have a minimum grade points average of 2 points on a 3 point system, 3 points on a 4 point system, 4 points on a 5 point system, or 5 points on a 6 point system; must be U.S. citizens or legal residents; must be student members of ASCET; must be full time students in an Engineering Technology program; must be qualified for financial aid under the Federal Work Study Program. **Criteria:** Priority will be given to applicants who have demonstrated financial need, as verified by the Dean or Registrar of Engineering Technology, or the Financial Aid Office at the institution the applicant is attending.

Funds Avail.: $500. **Duration:** Annual. **To Apply:** Applicants must submit a fully accomplished printed or typewritten application form available online; a letter of recommendation from a faculty member of the Engineering Technology Department indicating the motivation, progress, achievements, and an evaluation of the applicant's potential in the field of Engineering Technology; letters of recommendation from two personal acquaintances, employers or former employers, outlining association, motivation and potential for success; copy of transcript of records and be sure to pass all the requirements on time. **Deadline:** April 1. **Contact:** ASCET Office,15621 W. 87th St Pkwy, Ste. 205,Lenexa, KS 66219; E-mail: office@ascet.org.

1395 ■ American Society of Cinematographers (ASC)

1782 N Orange Dr.
Los Angeles, CA 90028
Ph: (323)969-4333
Free: 800-448-0145
E-mail: office@theasc.com
URL: www.theasc.com
Social Media: www.facebook.com/
  AmericanCinematographer

Awards are arranged alphabetically below their administering organizations

www.instagram.com/the_asc
twitter.com/americancine

1396 ■ William A. Fraker Student Heritage Awards
(Graduate, Undergraduate/Award)

Purpose: To recognize cinematography students who made contributions to advance the art form. **Focus:** Cinema. **Qualif.:** Applicants must be undergraduate, graduate or recently graduated (within one year) cinematography students. **Criteria:** Applicants will be judged based on artful cinematography and effective creation of the images.

Funds Avail.: No specific amount. **Number Awarded:** 2. **To Apply:** Applicants must submit a film entry.

1397 ■ American Society for Clinical Laboratory Science (ASCLS)
1861 International Dr., Ste. 200
McLean, VA 22102
Ph: (571)748-3770
E-mail: ascls@ascls.org
URL: www.ascls.org
Social Media: www.facebook.com/ASCLS
www.instagram.com/iamascls
twitter.com/ASCLS

1398 ■ Alpha Mu Tau Undergraduate Scholarships
(Undergraduate/Scholarship, Monetary)

Purpose: To provide financial assistance for professionals who are involved in advancement of clinical laboratory sciences. **Focus:** Clinical laboratory sciences. **Qualif.:** Applicants must be United States citizens or permanent residents of the United States; accepted into an NAACLS accredited program in Clinical Laboratory Science, to include Clinical Laboratory Science, Medical Technology, Clinical Laboratory Technician/Medical Laboratory Technician, Cytotechnology or Histotechnology; graduate applicants must be enrolled in the year which the award is made; undergraduate applicants must be entering in the year in which the award is made. **Criteria:** Candidates will be evaluated by the Scholarship Committee.

Funds Avail.: $1,500. **Duration:** Annual. **Number Awarded:** 6 in 2020. **To Apply:** Applicants must submit a completed application form including all required documents (letter of admission, 2 letters of recommendation and 2 performance sheets are required) to the AMTF Scholarship Coordinator. **Deadline:** April 1.

1399 ■ AMTF Graduate Scholarships *(Graduate/ Scholarship, Monetary)*

Purpose: To support student members in their graduate studies. **Focus:** Medicine. **Qualif.:** Applicants must be U.S. citizens or permanent residents and ASCLS members who are accepted into or are in an approved Masters or Doctoral program in areas related to Clinical Laboratory Science including Clinical Laboratory Education or Management Programs.

Funds Avail.: $1,000 to $3,000. **Duration:** Annual. **Number Awarded:** 3 in 2020. **To Apply:** Applicants may visit the website for the instructions regarding application process. **Deadline:** April 1.

1400 ■ Dorothy Morrison Undergraduate Scholarships *(Undergraduate/Scholarship, Monetary)*

Purpose: To provide financial assistance to professionals who are involved in advancement of clinical laboratory sci-

ences. **Focus:** Clinical laboratory sciences. **Qualif.:** Applicants must be a U.S. citizen or a permanent resident of the United States; applicants must be accepted into a NAACLS accredited program in clinical laboratory science to include Medical Laboratory Scientist or Medical Laboratory Technician programs.; applicants must be entering or in their last year of study.**Criteria:** Applicants will be evaluated by the Scholarship Committee based on the aforesaid qualifications and compliance with the application process.

Funds Avail.: Amount varies. **Duration:** Annual. **To Apply:** Applicants may verify the application process through the program website. **Deadline:** April 1.

1401 ■ American Society for Clinical Pathology (ASCP)
33 W Monroe St., Ste. 1600
Chicago, IL 60603
Ph: (312)541-4999
Fax: (312)541-4998
URL: www.ascp.org
Social Media: www.facebook.com/ASCP.Chicago
twitter.com/ASCP_Chicago

1402 ■ ASCP Foundation Garza & Becan-McBride Endowed Scholarship *(Undergraduate/Scholarship, Monetary)*

Purpose: To support phlebotomy students for their outstanding academic performance. **Focus:** Medical technology. **Qualif.:** Applicants must be ASCP members; must have completed at least 50% of training in one of the following: a NAACLS approved phlebotomy program; a phlebotomy program approved by the California Department of Public Health; or a structured program that meets the ASCP Board of Certification structured training program eligibility criteria; must have a minimum 3.0 GPA on a 4.0 scale. **Criteria:** Selection will be based on the committee's criteria.

Funds Avail.: $500. **Duration:** Annual. **To Apply:** Application is available online at www.ascp.org/content/about-ascp/ascp-foundation/providing-scholarships. **Deadline:** May 1. **Contact:** Email: scholarships@ascp.org.

1403 ■ American Society of Colon and Rectal Surgeons (ASCRS)
85 W Algonquin Rd., Ste. 550
Arlington Heights, IL 60005
Ph: (847)290-9184
Fax: (847)427-9656
E-mail: ascrs@fascrs.org
URL: www.fascrs.org
Social Media: www.facebook.com/fascrs
www.linkedin.com/company/fascrs
twitter.com/ASCRS_1

1404 ■ American Society of Colon and Rectal Surgeons International Fellowships *(Other/ Fellowship)*

Purpose: To provide research support to residents and clinical investigators from outside the U.S. or Canada to travel to the U.S. or Canada to do research. **Focus:** Surgery. **Qualif.:** ASCRS members only;ASCRS member must

Awards are arranged alphabetically below their administering organizations

be co-principal investigator or principal investigator; the applicant must be pursuing a career in colorectal surgery.

Funds Avail.: Up to $50,000. **Duration:** Annual; One year. **To Apply:** Application must complete the online; and the following items must be submitted before the ASCRS is able to process your Fellow Application: copy of an equivalent certificate of ABCRS from an appropriate national surgical board, fellowship in Royal Colleges of Surgeons, and/or certificates of higher completion of training in surgery; two (2) letters of recommendation from ASCRS Fellows; copy of your Curriculum Vitae;copy of your current medical license. **Deadline:** August 15. **Contact:** Research Foundation Administrative Office Email: rf@fascrs.org Elizabeth Wick, MD, Research Committee Chair Email: elizabeth.wick@ucsf.edu.

1405 ■ American Society of Colon and Rectal Surgeons International Travel Scholarships *(Other/ Scholarship)*

Purpose: To help colorectal surgeons further their education. **Focus:** Surgery. **Qualif.:** Applicants must have completed general surgical training and must be currently involved in colorectal surgical training; must demonstrate a commitment to practice colorectal surgery; have a guarantee of one-third funding support within their colorectal society, organization, or group; and be willing to undertake the scholarship at the next meeting.

Funds Avail.: No specific amount. **Duration:** Annual. **To Apply:** Applicants must submit a filled-out application form; two letters of recommendation (one from any official of the society where they undergo training and one from the Chairman of the Department where they are working); current activity profile; and list of publications, research work and presentations.

1406 ■ American Society of Composers, Authors and Publishers Foundation (ASCAP)

250 West 57th Street
New York, NY 10023-7142
URL: www.ascapfoundation.org
Social Media: www.facebook.com/ASCAPFoundation
www.instagram.com/ascapfoundation
twitter.com/ASCAPFoundation
www.youtube.com/channel/
  UCpJPCkzh0UGXC0BiSwhgnDg

1407 ■ Betty Rose Scholarship *(Undergraduate/ Scholarship)*

Purpose: To support students with their education. **Focus:** Filmmaking; Music. **Qualif.:** Applicant must be an ASCAP member or an unaffiliated student who is pursuing a career in television and film scoring.

Funds Avail.: No specific amount. **Duration:** Annual. **Number Awarded:** 1.

1408 ■ Charlotte V. Bergen Scholarship *(Undergraduate/Scholarship)*

Purpose: To provide scholarship to young composers, aged 18 or under, to be used for music study at an accredited college or music conservatory. **Focus:** Music.

Funds Avail.: No specific amount. **Duration:** Annual. **Number Awarded:** 1. **Remarks:** The Scholarship was established in memory of their daughter, Charlotte, a lover of classical music. Established in 2006.

1409 ■ Fran Morgenstern Davis Scholarship *(Undergraduate/Scholarship)*

Purpose: To provide educational support to students who are taking music composition. **Focus:** Music. **Qualif.:** Applicants must be full-time undergraduate music composition students at the Manhattan School of Music who demonstrate the potential to produce creative and original work and who also demonstrate financial need.

Funds Avail.: No specific amount. **Duration:** Annual. **Number Awarded:** 2. **Remarks:** The Scholarship was established in memory of Jay and Joan Morgenstern's daughter, Fran.

1410 ■ Leiber and Stoller Music Scholarship *(Undergraduate/Scholarship)*

Purpose: To provide assistance to young aspiring songwriters, musicians and vocalists. **Focus:** Music.

Funds Avail.: No specific amount. **Duration:** Annual. **Number Awarded:** 1.

1411 ■ Louis Armstrong Award Honoring W.C. Handy *(Undergraduate/Scholarship)*

Purpose: To provide assistance to Students who have abilities in music performance and composition. **Focus:** Music.

Funds Avail.: No specific amount. **Duration:** Annual. **Number Awarded:** 1. **Remarks:** Established in 2000.

1412 ■ Steve Kaplan TV & Film Studies Award *(Other/Award)*

Purpose: To provide financial assistance for an aspiring television and film composer to attend ASCAP's Film Scoring Workshop in Los Angeles. **Focus:** Filmmaking; Music. **Qualif.:** Applicants must be television and film composers.

Funds Avail.: No specific amount. **Duration:** Annual. **Number Awarded:** 1. **Remarks:** The award was established Steve Kaplan, award-winning Television and Film composer.

1413 ■ Louis Dreyfus Warner-Chappell City College Scholarship *(Undergraduate/Scholarship)*

Purpose: To award scholarships to composition students for scores written for dance, film/video or theater. **Focus:** Music. **Qualif.:** An applicant must be enrolled in either the B.A. or B.F.A. program at the City College/City University of New York, Ira Gershwin's alma mater.

Funds Avail.: No specific amount. **Duration:** Annual. **Number Awarded:** 1. **Remarks:** The Scholarship was established in honor of George and Ira Gershwin.

1414 ■ American Society for Composites (ASC)

University of Dayton
Dept. of Civil and Environmental Engineering
422 Kettering Laboratory
300 College Park Ave.
Dayton, OH 45469-0243
URL: www.asc-composites.org

1415 ■ ASC Ph.D. Research Scholarship Award *(Doctorate, Postdoctorate/Scholarship)*

Purpose: To support and recognize outstanding composite materials research by doctoral students. **Focus:** Science. **Qualif.:** Applicants must be students who are formally enrolled in a doctoral program in engineering or science, and whose dissertation research is focused on some aspect of composite materials.

Awards are arranged alphabetically below their administering organizations

Funds Avail.: $1,000 - $1,250. **Duration:** Annual. **Number Awarded:** Up to 4. **To Apply:** Applicant must complete an application form; letter of nomination; letters of recommendation; research statement; Copy of the nominee's university transcript; resume. **Deadline:** June 1.

1416 ■ American Society of Crime Laboratory Directors (ASCLD)

65 Glen Rd., Ste. 123
Garner, NC 27529
Ph: (919)773-2044
E-mail: office@ascld.org
URL: www.ascld.org
Social Media: www.linkedin.com/company/american
  -society-of-crime-lab-directors-ascld
twitter.com/ascld

1417 ■ ASCLD Scholarship Program *(Graduate, Undergraduate, Master's, Doctorate/Scholarship, Award, Monetary)*

Purpose: To provide opportunities to students intending to enter the forensic field. **Focus:** Science. **Qualif.:** Applicants must be juniors or senior students in a baccalaureate program; or graduate students (master's or doctorate) at an accredited university who is pursuing a degree in forensic science, forensic chemistry, physical or natural science. **Criteria:** Recipients will be selected based on their overall scholastic record especially in forensic science coursework, motivation or commitment to a forensic science career, personal statement and according to faculty or advisor's recommendation. At least three ASCLD members who are not affiliated with institutions from which students are applying will evaluate the pool of applicants.

Funds Avail.: $1,000. **Duration:** Annual. **To Apply:** Applicants must submit a completed application form; transcript of records; personal statement; and letter of recommendation of faculty members or a laboratory director with knowledge of the applicant. **Deadline:** April 15.

1418 ■ American Society of Criminology (ASC)

921 Chatham Ln., Ste. 108
Columbus, OH 43221
Ph: (614)826-2000
Fax: (614)826-3031
E-mail: asc@asc41.com
URL: www.asc41.com
Social Media: www.facebook.com/asc41
twitter.com/ASCRM41

1419 ■ Gene Carte Student Paper Competition Awards *(Undergraduate, Graduate/Prize)*

Purpose: To recognize students who have made outstanding scholarly works. **Focus:** Criminal justice; Criminology; Paralegal studies. **Qualif.:** Applicants must be students enrolled on a full-time basis in an academic program at either the undergraduate or graduate level. **Criteria:** Selection will be based on the committee's criteria.

Funds Avail.: $500 (First place); $300 (Second place); $200 (Third place). **Duration:** Annual. **To Apply:** Candidates may submit only one paper a year for consideration. Papers may be conceptual and/or empirical but must be directly related to criminology and must be a maximum of 7, 500 words. The criminology format for the organization

of text, citations and references should be used. Author's names and departments should appear only on the title page. The next page of the manuscript should include the title and a 100-word abstract. The authors also need to submit an electronic copy of the manuscript, as well as a letter verifying their enrollment status as full-time students, cosigned by the dean, department chair or program director, all in electronic format. **Deadline:** April 15. **Remarks:** Established in 1971.

1420 ■ Ruth D. Peterson Fellowship for Racial and Ethnic Diversity *(Doctorate/Fellowship)*

Purpose: To encourage students of color to enter the field of criminology and criminal justice. **Focus:** Criminal justice; Criminology. **Qualif.:** Applicants must be students of color, especially those from ethnic minority groups underrepresented in the field, including but not limited to, Asians, Blacks, Indigenous peoples, and Latinas/os; must be studying criminology or criminal justice issues; must be accepted into a program of doctoral studies. **Criteria:** Selection shall be based on the applicant's qualifications and compliance with the application details.

Funds Avail.: $6,000 each. **Duration:** Annual. **Number Awarded:** 3. **To Apply:** Applicants must complete and submit the following: proof of admission to a criminal justice, criminology, or related program of doctoral studies; up-to-date curriculum vitae; indication of race/ethnicity; copies of undergraduate or graduate transcripts; statement of need and prospects for financial assistance for graduate study; a letter describing career plans, salient experiences, and nature of interest in criminology and criminal justice; and, three letters of reference. **Deadline:** March 1. **Remarks:** Established in 1988. **Contact:** Kareem Jordan, Fellowship Committee Chair; Email: Jordan@American.edu.

1421 ■ American Society of Echocardiography (ASE)

2530 Meridian Parkway., Ste. 450
Durham, NC 27713
Ph: (919)861-5574
Fax: (919)882-9900
URL: www.asecho.org
Social Media: twitter.com/ase360
www.youtube.com/ase360

1422 ■ ASE Career Development Award *(Advanced Professional/Grant)*

Purpose: To support a physician/scientist who is just in the beginning of a career in academic echocardiography. **Focus:** Medicine, Cardiology.

Funds Avail.: $35,000. **Duration:** Annual. **Deadline:** March 3.

1423 ■ Alan D. Waggoner Sonographer Student Scholarship Award *(Undergraduate/Scholarship)*

Purpose: To support students enrolled in a cardiac ultrasound programs. **Focus:** Education, Medical. **Qualif.:** Applicants must be sonographer students enrolled in CAAHEP accredited educational programs who exhibit a passion for the discipline of echocardiography and demonstrate leadership abilities. **Criteria:** Selection will be based on letters of support (51% of scoring), personal accomplishments and academic record (49% of scoring); to ensure fair distribution of awards, geographic diversity will be considered when selecting the scholarship.

Awards are arranged alphabetically below their administering organizations

Funds Avail.: $1,000($500 for travel support). **Duration:** Annual. **To Apply:** Applicants must submit an application form with one letter of nomination from student's program director, plus two (2) additional letters of support; desirable to have one letter of recommendation from a Fellow of the American Society of Echocardiography (FASE); not possible to obtain a letter from a FASE, at least one letter must be an ASE member; a copy of the nominee's curriculum vitae or resume. **Deadline:** October 15. **Remarks:** The Award was named in honor of Alan D. Waggoner. Established in 2001.

1424 ■ American Society for Eighteenth-Century Studies (ASECS)

1300 Elmwood Ave, KH213
Buffalo, NY 14222
Ph: (716)878-3405
E-mail: asecsoffice@gmail.com
URL: asecs.press.jhu.edu
Social Media: www.facebook.com/asecsoffice
twitter.com/ASECSOffice

1425 ■ A.C. Elias, Jr. Irish-American Research Travel Fellowship *(Other/Fellowship)*

Purpose: To support documentary scholarship in Ireland in the period between the Treaty of Limerick (1691) and the Act of Union (1800) to enable North American-based scholars to travel in Ireland and Irish-based scholars to travel in North America for furthering their research. **Focus:** General studies/Field of study not specified. **Qualif.:** Applicants must be ASECS members who are residents of North America, or members of ASEC's Irish sister organization, Eighteenth-Century Ireland Society who are residents of the Republic of Ireland or Northern Ireland. **Criteria:** Selection will be selected based on submitted materials.

Funds Avail.: $2,500. **Duration:** Annual. **To Apply:** Applicants must submit an application form, curriculum vitae, one-page bibliography of major related books and articles, narrative description of the project and two letters of recommendation, budget. **Deadline:** November 15. **Contact:** Dr. Jason McElligott, The Keeper, Marsh's Library, St. Patrick's Close, Dublin 8, Ireland; Email: jason.mcelligott@marshlibrary.ie; Prof. James E. May, 694 Coal Hill Rd., Clearfield, PA 16830; Email: jem4@psu.edu.

1426 ■ ASECS Graduate Student Research Paper Award *(Graduate/Prize)*

Purpose: To recognize pioneering research contributions of the next generation of scholars of eighteenth-century studies. **Focus:** General studies/Field of study not specified. **Qualif.:** Applicants must be graduate scholars of eighteenth-century studies. **Criteria:** Recipients will be selected based on submitted paper.

Funds Avail.: $200. **Duration:** Annual. **To Apply:** Applicants must submit four copies of a research essay (15-30 pages) that has not been previously published; and must submit a letter of endorsement from a mentoring professor which outlines the originality and contributions in the field of eighteenth-century studies. **Deadline:** January 1.

1427 ■ ASECS Innovative Course Design Competition *(Undergraduate/Award)*

Purpose: To encourage excellence in undergraduate teaching of the eighteenth century. **Focus:** General studies/Field of study not specified. **Qualif.:** Applicants must be undergraduate student members in any ASECS constituent disciplines. **Criteria:** Selection will be evaluated based on relationship to design, readings, pedagogy and/or activities.

Funds Avail.: $500. **Duration:** Annual. **To Apply:** Applicants should submit a 750-1,500 word description of the course or unit and a draft of the syllabus. **Deadline:** October 1. **Contact:** Address: 1300 Elmwood Ave., KH213, Buffalo, NY 14222; E-mail: asecsoffice@gmail.com; Phone: 716-878-3405.

1428 ■ ASECS Women's Caucus Editing and Translation Fellowship *(Doctorate/Fellowship)*

Purpose: To support an editing or a translation work in progress of an eighteenth-century primary text on a feminist or a women's studies subject. **Focus:** Women's studies. **Qualif.:** Applicants must be ASECS members who have received a PhD degree. **Criteria:** Selection will be evaluated based on submitted proposal.

Funds Avail.: $1,000. **Duration:** Annual. **To Apply:** Applicants must submit a project translated or edited by eighteenth-century women writers or works that significantly advance the women's experience in the eighteenth century; must include curriculum vitae, three to five page proposal outlining the project, a two-page bibliography of pertinent works, two letters of recommendation and a budget explaining the candidate's plans for using the funds; winner will be asked to submit a brief written report on the progress of the project one year after receiving the award; five copies of the proposal should be submitted to the ASECS office. **Deadline:** January 15. **Contact:** ASECS office, PO Box 7867, Wake Forest University, Winston-Salem, NC 27109.

1429 ■ Aubrey L. Williams Research Travel Fellowship *(Doctorate/Fellowship)*

Purpose: To support documentary research in eighteenth-century English literature by American-based scholars. **Focus:** Literature. **Qualif.:** Applicants must be U.S.-based research doctoral student.

Funds Avail.: $1,500. **Duration:** Annual. **Contact:** ASECS, Buffalo State College, 1300 Elmwood Ave., KH213, Buffalo, NY 14222; Email: asecsoffice@gmail.com.

1430 ■ James L. Clifford Prize *(Other/Prize, Monetary)*

Purpose: To recognize authors interested in eighteenth-century studies. **Focus:** General studies/Field of study not specified. **Qualif.:** Applicants must be author(s) of an article in outstanding study of some aspect of eighteenth-century culture; must be members of the ASECS at the time of submission. **Criteria:** Recipients will be selected based on submitted article.

Funds Avail.: $500. **Duration:** Annual. **To Apply:** Applicants must submit an article of no more than 15, 000 words. Nominations must be submitted in PDF format with one hard copy. **Deadline:** January 1. **Contact:** Email: ASECSOffice@gmail.com.

1431 ■ Emilie Du Chatelet Award *(Doctorate/Award)*

Purpose: To support research in progress by independent or adjunct scholars on a feminist or women's studies subject. **Focus:** Women's studies. **Qualif.:** Applicants must be ASECS members who have received their PhD and who do not currently hold a tenured, tenure-track or job-secure position in a college or university. **Criteria:** Selection will be based on submitted project.

Funds Avail.: $500. **Duration:** Annual. **To Apply:** Applicants must include a curriculum vitae, one to three page

Awards are arranged alphabetically below their administering organizations

research proposal outlining the project and candidate's plans for using the funds; winner will be asked to submit a brief written report on the progress of the project after one year of receiving the award. **Deadline:** January 15. **Contact:** Address: 1300 Elmwood Ave., KH213, Buffalo, NY 14222; E-mail: asecsoffice@gmail.com; Phone: 716-878-3405.

1432 ■ Louis Gottschalk Prize *(Other/Prize)*

Purpose: To recognize an outstanding historical or critical study on a subject of eighteenth-century interest. Books that are primarily translations are not eligible. **Focus:** History; Literature. **Qualif.:** Applicant should be an author, who must be a member of the Society; must meet copyright date requirements. **Criteria:** Selection will be based on submitted project.

Funds Avail.: $1,000. **Duration:** Annual. **To Apply:** Applicants must submit six copies of a book. **Deadline:** November 15. **Contact:** ASECS, Buffalo State College, 1300 Elmwood Ave., KH213, Buffalo, NY 14222; Email: asecsoffice@gmail.com.

1433 ■ Gwin J. and Ruth Kolb Research Travel Fellowship *(Doctorate, Other/Fellowship)*

Purpose: To supplement costs for younger eighteenth-century scholars to travel to distant collections in North America and abroad. **Focus:** General studies/Field of study not specified.

Funds Avail.: $500. **Duration:** Annual.

1434 ■ Hemlow Prize in Burney Studies *(Graduate/Prize)*

Purpose: To recognize the best essay written by students. **Focus:** General studies/Field of study not specified. **Qualif.:** Application must be graduate students. **Criteria:** Selection will be judged based on essay's originality, coherence, use of source material, awareness of other work in the field and documentation.

Funds Avail.: $250. **Duration:** Annual. **To Apply:** Applicants must submit two copies of the essay (one appropriate for blind submission). **Deadline:** January 31. **Contact:** Dr. AnnCampbell, English Department, Boise State University, 1910 University Dr., Boise, ID, 83725-1525; Email: anncampbell@boisestate.edu.

1435 ■ Oscar Kenshur Book Prize *(Other/Prize)*

Purpose: To recognize an outstanding monograph that has value to the field of eighteenth-century studies. **Focus:** Literature. **Qualif.:** Applicants must have written a book of interest to eighteenth-century scholars. Copyright date should be for the year previous to the year the prize is awarded. **Criteria:** Selection will be based on best meet the requirements.

Funds Avail.: $1,000. **Duration:** Annual. **To Apply:** Applicants are authors or publishers must submit three copies of the book; for additional information, must contact the Director of the Center for Eighteenth-Century Studies at Indiana University. **Deadline:** February 15. **Contact:** Prof. Rebecca Spang, Director of the Center for Eighteenth-Century at Indiana University; Email: rlspang@indiana.edu.

1436 ■ Catherine Macaulay Prize *(Graduate/Prize)*

Purpose: To recognize student's paper in the field of feminist and gender studies. **Focus:** Women's studies. **Qualif.:** Applicants must be a graduate student who should submit a paper at the ASECS annual meeting. **Criteria:**

Recipients will be selected based on submitted paper.

Funds Avail.: $500. **To Apply:** Applicants must submit a paper; it should advance understanding of gender dynamics, women's experiences and/or women's contributions and offer a feminist analysis of any aspect to eighteenth-century culture and/or society. **Deadline:** September 1.

1437 ■ Paula Backscheider Archival Fellowship *(Other/Fellowship)*

Purpose: To support researchers whose projects necessitate work in archives, repositories and special collections (public and private) in foreign countries and/or in the United States. **Focus:** General studies/Field of study not specified. **Qualif.:** Applicants must be members of ASECS.

Funds Avail.: $1,000. **Duration:** Annual. **Contact:** ASECS, Buffalo State College, 1300 Elmwood Ave., KH213, Buffalo, NY 14222; Email: asecsoffice@gmail.com.

1438 ■ Robert R. Palmer Research Travel Fellowship *(Other/Fellowship)*

Purpose: To support documentary research related primarily to the history and culture of France. **Focus:** General studies/Field of study not specified. **Qualif.:** Applicants must be members of ASECS. **Criteria:** Recipients will be selected based on submitted materials.

Funds Avail.: $500. **Duration:** Annual. **To Apply:** Applicants must submit an application form, curriculum vitae, one-page bibliography of major related books and articles, narrative description of the project and two letters of recommendation, budget. **Contact:** ASECS, Buffalo State College, 1300 Elmwood Ave., KH213, Buffalo, NY 14222; Email: asecsoffice@gmail.com.

1439 ■ Theodore E.D. Braun Research Travel Fellowship *(Other/Fellowship)*

Purpose: To support researchers, regardless of rank, who are working in French literary studies. **Focus:** Area and ethnic studies. **Qualif.:** Applicants must be ASECS members.

Funds Avail.: $1,000. **Duration:** Annual. **Contact:** ASECS, Buffalo State College, 1300 Elmwood Ave., KH213, Buffalo, NY 14222; Email: asecsoffice@gmail.com.

1440 ■ Hans Turley Prize in Queer Eighteenth-Century Studies *(Graduate, Other/Prize)*

Purpose: To recognize a student's paper on a topic in Lesbian, Gay, Bisexual, Transgender or Queer studies delivered at the ASECS Annual meeting. **Focus:** General studies/Field of study not specified. **Qualif.:** Applicants must be graduate students, untenured faculty members or independent scholars. **Criteria:** Selection will be selected based on submitted paper.

Funds Avail.: No specific amount. **Duration:** Biennial. **To Apply:** Applicants must submit a paper addressing issues on Lesbian, Gay, Bisexual, Transgender or Queer studies. **Deadline:** September 1. **Contact:** Email: asecs@wfu.edu.

1441 ■ American Society for Engineering Education (ASEE)

1818 N St. NW, Ste. 600
Washington, DC 20036-2479
Ph: (202)331-3500
Fax: (202)265-8504
E-mail: board@asee.org
URL: www.asee.org

Awards are arranged alphabetically below their administering organizations

Social Media: www.facebook.com/ASEEHQ
www.instagram.com/aseehq/
www.linkedin.com/company/american-society-for
 -engineering-education
twitter.com/ASEE_DC

1442 ■ ASEE/NSF Small Business Postdoctoral Research Diversity Fellowship (SBPRDF) *(Postdoctorate/Fellowship)*

Purpose: To encourage creative and highly-trained recipients of doctoral degrees in NSF-supported science, technology, engineering and mathematical disciplines to engage in hands-on research projects in their areas of expertise at the kind of small innovative businesses that historically have fueled the nation's economic regime. **Focus:** Business; Economics. **Qualif.:** Applicants must be U.S. citizens, U.S. nationals or U.S. permanent residents, and must have received a Ph.D. degree in a NSF-supported science, technology, engineering or mathematical (STEM) discipline in the seven years prior to the application date; must not have received a prior postdoctoral fellowship in a corporate laboratory for a term of more than six months. **Criteria:** Selection will be based on the committee's criteria.

Funds Avail.: $75,000. **To Apply:** Applicants must submit online. **Deadline:** February 1;July 31. **Contact:** E-mail: nsfsbir@asee.org.

1443 ■ Naval Research Enterprise Internship Program (NREIP) *(Graduate, Undergraduate/ Internship)*

Purpose: To provide opportunities for undergraduate and graduate students to participate in research, under the guidance of an appropriate research mentor, at a participating Navy laboratory. **Focus:** Naval art and science. **Qualif.:** Applicants must be U.S. citizens (sophomore, junior, senior, or graduate students) who are enrolled at a 4-year U.S. college or university deemed accredited by the U.S. department of education. Students attending two-year colleges, who meet the major and credit requirements, may be eligible at the laboratory's discretion. Applicants should have majors relevant to the research interests of the laboratories. **Criteria:** Selection will be based upon applicant's academic achievement, personal statements, recommendation, and career & research interests.

Funds Avail.: $7,000-$11,000. **To Apply:** Application and details available at nreip.asee.org. **Deadline:** November 4. **Contact:** Email: nreip@asee.org.

1444 ■ Science and Engineering Apprenticeship Program (SEAP) *(High School/Internship)*

Purpose: To encourage participating students to pursue science and engineering careers, to further their education via mentoring by laboratory personnel and their participation in research, and to make them aware of Department of Navy research and technology efforts, which can lead to employment within the Department of Navy. **Focus:** Engineering; Science. **Qualif.:** Applicants must be high school students who have completed at least grade 9; graduating seniors are eligible to apply; must be US citizens and participation by permanent resident aliens is limited; dual citizens may be accepted at some labs.

Funds Avail.: $3,500-$4,000. **Duration:** Eight weeks. **To Apply:** Application and details available at seap.asee.org. **Deadline:** November 1. **Contact:** Email: seap@asee.org.

1445 ■ Science, Mathematics And Research for Transformation Scholarship for Service Program (SMART) *(Undergraduate, Graduate/Scholarship)*

Purpose: To increase the number of civilian scientists and engineers working at Department of Defense laboratories. **Focus:** Engineering; Mathematics and mathematical sciences; Science; Technology. **Qualif.:** Applicants must be U.S., Australia, Canada, New Zealand, or United Kingdom citizens; 18 years old and above; able to participate in summer internships at Department of Defense (DoD) facility; willing to accept post-graduate employment with the DoD; students in good standing with a minimum cumulative GPA of 3.0 on a 4.0 scale; and, pursuing undergraduate or graduate degree in one of the science, technology, engineering and mathematics (STEM) disciplines; in addition, undergraduate applicants must be enrolled in a regionally accredited U.S. college/university and have their respective high school diplomas/GED's while graduate applicants can be either currently enrolled in a regionally accredited U.S. college or university or awaiting notification of admission to such. **Criteria:** Selection shall be based on the aforementioned applicant's qualifications and compliance with the application details.

Funds Avail.: $25,000-$38,000 stipend; $1,200 for Health Insurance; $1,000 for Miscellaneous Supplies. **Duration:** Annual. **To Apply:** All applicants are required to submit applications online; applicants will need to register for a new account before they will be able to start the application; the applicant will input their name and email address and choose a password. **Deadline:** December 3. **Contact:** Phone: 202-331-3544; Fax: 202-265-8504; Email: smartparticipant@asee.org.

1446 ■ American Society for Enology and Viticulture (ASEV)

1724 Picasso Avenue, Suite E
Davis, CA 95618-0547
Ph: (530)753-3142
Fax: (530)753-3318
E-mail: info@asev.org
URL: www.asev.org
Social Media: twitter.com/ASEVtweets

1447 ■ ASEV Traditional Scholarship *(Graduate, Undergraduate/Scholarship)*

Purpose: To students pursuing a degree in enology, viticulture, or a curriculum emphasizing a science basic to the wine and grape industry. **Focus:** Viticulture. **Qualif.:** Applicants must be current ASEV Student Members prior to applying; Undergraduate and graduate students must be enrolled in or accepted into a full-time accredited four year college or university in a degree program such as for a B.S., M.S., or Ph.D.; must reside in North America during the applicable academic year; undergraduate applicants should have a minimum of junior status for the upcoming academic year (45 semester units/60 quarter units) and must have a minimum cumulative grade point average of 3.0; Graduate students must have a minimum overall grade point average of 3.2; must be accepted or enrolled in a major, or in a graduate group, emphasizing enology or viticulture, or in a curriculum emphasizing a science basic to the wine and grape industry; Student Member dues must be paid in full before deadline.**Criteria:** Undergraduate and graduate students will be rated on a separate basis.

Funds Avail.: Vary from year to year. **Duration:** Annual. **To Apply:** Applications must be submitted along with

Awards are arranged alphabetically below their administering organizations

completed and signed student questionnaire; written statement of intent; official transcripts or copies of official transcripts of all college or university courses; list of planned courses for the upcoming academic year, applicant is a graduate student who has completed the required classes for your program; letter of acceptance from the academic institution; two current letters of recommendation (at least one letter should be from an academic advisor and/or a recent instructor (within the last year of your college or university education), written specifically for the ASEV Scholarship Committee. Each letter must be signed and submitted in a sealed, return envelope with the writer's signature across the sealed envelope flap or alternatively emailed directly from the person who signed and wrote the letter. **Deadline:** March 1. **Contact:** Scholarship Committee American Society for Enology and Viticulture P.O. Box 1855 Davis, CA 95617-1855 USA; (or) Scholarship Committee American Society for Enology and Viticulture 1724 Picasso Avenue, Suite E Davis, CA 95618-0547 USA.

1448 ■ American Society for Environmental History (ASEH)

UIC Department of History - MC 198 601 S. Morgan St. Chicago, IL 60607-7109
URL: aseh.net
Social Media: www.facebook.com/pages/American-Society-for-Environmental-History/78043136293
twitter.com/ASEH_org

1449 ■ ASEH Minority Travel Grants *(Graduate, Other/Grant)*

Purpose: To support individuals present their research at ASEH's annual meetings. **Focus:** General studies/Field of study not specified. **Qualif.:** Applicants must be minority, low income scholars or graduate students. **Criteria:** Recipients will be selected based on qualifications and submitted materials. Special consideration will be given to first time applicants.

To Apply: Applicants must submit a brief vita or resume (at least two pages); one-page statement outlining their interest/objectives in attending the ASEH conference. Applicants should specify the sources of funding already received and/or applied for. Documents should be e-mailed with the subject line "Madison Travel Grant.". **Contact:** American Society for Environmental History, at the above address.

1450 ■ Rachel Carson Prize *(Other/Prize)*

Purpose: To recognize individuals who work in the field of environmental history. **Focus:** Environmental science; History. **Qualif.:** Applicants must be individuals who made the best dissertation in environmental history.

Funds Avail.: No specific amount. **Duration:** Annual. **Deadline:** November 15. **Remarks:** Established in 1993. **Contact:** E-mail: david.spatz@aseh.org.

1451 ■ Donald Worster Travel Grant *(Graduate, Other/Grant)*

Purpose: To support individuals present their research at ASEH's annual meetings. **Focus:** General studies/Field of study not specified.

Funds Avail.: up to $500. **Contact:** E-mail: david.spatz@aseh.org.

1452 ■ Ellen Swallow Richards Travel Grant *(Graduate, Other/Grant)*

Purpose: To support individuals present their research at ASEH's annual meetings. **Focus:** General studies/Field of study not specified.

Funds Avail.: up to $500. **Contact:** E-mail: david.spatz@aseh.org.

1453 ■ Alice Hamilton Prize *(Other/Prize)*

Purpose: To recognize individuals who work within the field of environmental history. **Focus:** General studies/Field of study not specified. **Qualif.:** Applicants must have published an article on outside environmental history.

Funds Avail.: No specific amount. **Duration:** Annual. **Deadline:** November 15. **Remarks:** Established in 1997. **Contact:** E-mail: david.spatz@aseh.org.

1454 ■ John D. Wirth Travel Grant *(Graduate, Other/Grant)*

Purpose: To support individuals present their research at ASEH's annual meetings. **Focus:** General studies/Field of study not specified.

Funds Avail.: up to $500. **Contact:** E-mail: david.spatz@aseh.org.

1455 ■ George Perkins Marsh Prize *(Other/Prize)*

Purpose: To recognize individuals who work in the field of environmental history. **Focus:** Environmental science; History. **Qualif.:** Applicants must be authors of a book in the field of environmental history.

Duration: Annual. **Deadline:** November 15. **Remarks:** Established in 1989. **Contact:** E-mail: david.spatz@aseh.org.

1456 ■ E.V. and Nancy Melosi Travel Grants *(Graduate, Other/Grant)*

Purpose: To support individuals present their research at ASEH's annual meetings. **Focus:** General studies/Field of study not specified. **Qualif.:** Applicants must be graduate students, low income and international scholars; must be a member of ASEH and must be presenting at our 2018 conference; presenters are eligible to apply for 2018 travel grants after they receive an acceptance notice for their session or poster proposals.

Funds Avail.: up to $500. **Duration:** Annual. **To Apply:** Applicants must submit a brief vita or resume (at least two pages) along with the title of your accepted presentation or poster.

1457 ■ Morgan and Jeanie Sherwood Travel Grant *(Graduate, Other/Grant)*

Purpose: To support individuals present their research at ASEH's annual meetings. **Focus:** General studies/Field of study not specified.

Funds Avail.: up to $500. **Contact:** E-mail: david.spatz@aseh.org.

1458 ■ Hal Rothman Dissertation Fellowship *(Doctorate, Graduate/Fellowship)*

Purpose: To recognize graduate students and to support archival research and travel. **Focus:** Environmental science; History. **Qualif.:** Applicants must be PhD students in the field of environmental history. **Criteria:** Selection will be based on qualifications and submitted materials.

Awards are arranged alphabetically below their administering organizations

Funds Avail.: $1,000. Duration: Annual. To Apply: Applicants must submit a two-page (500 words) statement explaining the project and how it is intended for the research funds, curriculum vitae and a letter of recommendation from graduate advisors. Deadline: November 15. Remarks: The award was established in honor of Hal Rothman. Contact: E-mail: david.spatz@aseh.org.

1459 ■ Samuel P. Hays Research Fellowship (Other/Fellowship)

Purpose: To advance the field of environmental history. Focus: Environmental science; History. Qualif.: Applicants must be practicing historians (either academic, public, or independent); Graduate students are ineligible. A Ph.D. is not required. Criteria: Selection will be judged based on submitted materials.

Funds Avail.: $1,000. Duration: Annual. To Apply: Applicants must submit a two-page (500 words) statement explaining the project and how it is intended for the research funds; must submit a curriculum vitae no more than three pages in length. Deadline: November 15. Contact: E-mail: david.spatz@aseh.org.

1460 ■ American Society For Legal History, Inc. (ASLH)

c/o Patricia Minter, Chair, Membership Committee
1906 College Heights Blvd., Ste. 21086
Bowling Green, KY 42101-1086
URL: aslh.net

1461 ■ Cromwell Fellowships (Graduate/Fellowship)

Purpose: To support research and writing in American legal history. Focus: History, American. Qualif.: Applicants must be graduate studies students currently enrolled in any institution, college or university. Criteria: Selection will be given to scholars at the early stage of their careers; the committee for Research Fellowships and Awards of the American Society for Legal History (ASLH) reviews the applications and makes recommendations to the foundation.

Funds Avail.: $5,000. Duration: Annual. Number Awarded: 5 to 9. To Apply: Applicants should submit a description of their proposed project,double-spaced, maximum 6 pages, with working title; a budget, a timeline, and short curriculum vitae (no longer than 3 pages); two letters of recommendation from academic referees; must be submitted electronically (preferably in one pdf file). Deadline: July 15. Contact: E-mail to:fbatlan@kentlaw.edu.

1462 ■ American Society of Genealogists (ASG)

PO Box 374
Sharon, MA 02067-0374
URL: www.fasg.org
Social Media: www.facebook.com/American-Society-of-Genealogists-231090223615835

1463 ■ The ASG Scholar Award (Professional development/Award)

Purpose: To recognize talent and build genealogical expertise by providing promising genealogists the opportunity to receive advanced academic training in genealogy and to provide financial assistance for a developing scholar to attend one of six academic programs in American genealogy. Focus: Genealogy. Qualif.: Applicants must be

genealogists, genealogical librarians, and researchers working in related fields. Criteria: Recipients are selected the ASG Scholarship Committee, chaired by the ASG vice-president.

Funds Avail.: $1,000. Duration: Annual. To Apply: Applicants must submit a published work or a manuscript of work in progress of at least 5,000 words, demonstrating an ability to conduct quality genealogical research, analyze results, and report findings in an appropriately documented fashion; a resume that emphasizes activities relating to genealogy and lists the publications in the field, if any (prior publications are not necessary); if the submission is to be returned, must be accompanied by an envelope or bagging with sufficient postage; a statement (100-150 words) which identifies the individuals' choice of program and explains why the individuals feel that attendance will enhance their growth as genealogical scholars. Deadline: August 31. Remarks: Established in 1996. Contact: David C. Dearborn, Chair ASG Scholar Award Committee PO Box 374 Sharon MA 02067 Email:dearborn@massed.net.

1464 ■ American Society of Health-System Pharmacists (ASHP)

4500 East-West Hwy., Ste. 900
Bethesda, MD 20814
Ph: (301)664-8700
Fax: (301)657-1251
Free: 866-279-0681
E-mail: custserv@ashp.org
URL: www.ashp.org
Social Media: www.facebook.com/ASHPofficial
www.instagram.com/ashpofficial/
www.linkedin.com/company/ashp
twitter.com/ASHPOfficial
www.youtube.com/user/ASHPOfficial

1465 ■ ASHP Student Research Awards (Doctorate/Award)

Purpose: To recognize pharmacy students for their published or unpublished paper that describes a completed research project related to medication use. Focus: Pharmacy. Qualif.: Applicants must be full-time students enrolled in a Doctor of Pharmacy program at an ACPE-accredited school/college of pharmacy; must be students who are authors of unpublished or published paper that describes a completed research project related to medication use. Criteria: Recipients will be selected based on originality, impact, innovation and quality of the paper.

Funds Avail.: $1,500 honorarium plus $1,000 expense allowance. Duration: Annual. To Apply: Applicants must submit an application form and published/unpublished article.

1466 ■ John W. Webb Lecture Award (Other/Award, Recognition, Monetary)

Purpose: To recognize hospital or health-system pharmacy practitioners and educators who have distinguished themselves with extraordinary dedication to foster excellence in pharmacy management. Focus: Pharmacy. Qualif.: Applicant should be pharmacy practitioners or educators who have distinguished themselves through extraordinary dedication to fostering excellence in pharmacy management or administration. Criteria: Selection will be

Awards are arranged alphabetically below their administering organizations

based on the committee's criteria.

Funds Avail.: No specific amount. **Duration:** Annual. **Number Awarded:** 1. **To Apply:** Applicants should submit the applications accompanied by a one-to-three page statement about why individuals are qualified for the award along with a copy of the nominee's curriculum vitae. **Deadline:** April 1. **Remarks:** Established in 1985. **Contact:** ASHP Section of Pharmacy Practice Leaders c/o Patricia C. Kienle, B.S.Pharm., M.P.A., FASHP Chair John W. Webb Lecture Award Selection Committee Email: awards@ashp.org.

1467 ■ American Society of Heating, Refrigerating and Air-Conditioning Engineers (ASHRAE)

1791 Tullie Cir. NE
Atlanta, GA 30329
Ph: (404)636-8400
Fax: (404)321-5478
Free: 800-527-4723
E-mail: ashrae@ashrae.org
URL: www.ashrae.org
Social Media: www.facebook.com/ASHRAEupdates
www.linkedin.com/company/ashrae
twitter.com/ashraenews
www.youtube.com/user/ASHRAEvideo

1468 ■ Alwin B. Newton Scholarship
(Undergraduate/Scholarship)

Purpose: To help reduce the financial burdens of obtaining an engineering education. **Focus:** Engineering. **Qualif.:** Applicants must be full-time undergraduate engineering students in an ABET-accredited Engineering Technology program leading to a bachelor degree, and have cumulative GPA of at least 3.0 on a scale of 4.0. **Criteria:** Recipients will be selected based on financial need; leadership ability; and character.

Funds Avail.: $5,000. **Duration:** Annual. **Number Awarded:** 1. **To Apply:** Applicants must submit: an official transcripts of college grades; a letter of recommendation; and an evaluation form from three references including a professor or faculty advisor. **Deadline:** December 1. **Remarks:** The scholarship was named for an industry pioneer, who was granted 219 patents during his lifetime. **Contact:** Lois Benedict, ASHRAE Scholarship Administrator; Phone: 678-539-1120; Email: lbenedict@ashrae.org.

1469 ■ American Society of Heating, Refrigerating, and Air-Conditioning Memorial Scholarships
(Undergraduate/Scholarship)

Purpose: To help reduce the financial burdens of obtaining an engineering education. **Focus:** Engineering. **Qualif.:** Applicants must be full-time undergraduates in an ABET-accredited Engineering Technology program leading to a Bachelor of Science or Engineering Degree and must have cumulative GPA of at least 3.0 on a 4.0 scale. **Criteria:** Recipients are selected based on the need for financial assistance; leadership ability; and character.

Funds Avail.: $5,000. **Duration:** Annual. **To Apply:** Applicants must submit an official transcript of college grades; a letter of recommendation; and an evaluation form from three references including professor or faculty advisor. **Deadline:** December 1. **Contact:** Lois Benedict, at lbenedict@ashrae.org.

1470 ■ ASHARE Undergraduate Engineering Scholarships *(Undergraduate/Scholarship)*

Purpose: To help reduce the financial burdens of obtaining an engineering education. **Focus:** Engineering. **Qualif.:** Applicants must be full-time undergraduate engineering students in an ABET-accredited Engineering Technology program leading to a bachelor degree and have cumulative GPA of at least 3.0 on a 4.0 scale. **Criteria:** Recipients will be selected based on need for financial assistance, leadership ability, and character.

Funds Avail.: $3,000 - $10,000. **Duration:** Annual. **Number Awarded:** Varies. **To Apply:** Applicants must submit: an official transcript of college grades; a letter of recommendation; and an evaluation form from three references including professor or faculty advisor. **Deadline:** December 1. **Contact:** Lois Benedict; Email: lbenedict@ashrae.org.

1471 ■ Willis H. Carrier Scholarships
(Undergraduate/Scholarship)

Purpose: To help reduce the financial burdens of obtaining an engineering education. **Focus:** Engineering. **Qualif.:** Applicants must be full-time undergraduate engineering students in an ABET-accredited Engineering Technology program leading to a bachelor degree and have cumulative GPA of at least 3.0 on a 4.0 scale. **Criteria:** Recipients will be selected based on need for financial assistance, leadership ability, and character.

Funds Avail.: $10,000. **Duration:** Annual. **Number Awarded:** 2. **To Apply:** Applicants must submit: an official transcript of college grades; a letter of recommendation; and an evaluation form from three references including professor or faculty advisor. **Deadline:** December 1. **Remarks:** The scholarship was established by The Carrier Corporation in memory of its founder, who is known widely for his numerous and significant contributions to establishing air conditioning as an industry. Carrier installed the world's first scientifically designed air conditioning system in 1902. **Contact:** Lois Benedict; Email: lbenedict@ashrae.org.

1472 ■ Frank M. Coda Scholarships *(Undergraduate/Scholarship)*

Purpose: To help reduce the financial burdens of obtaining an engineering education. **Focus:** Engineering. **Qualif.:** Applicants must be full-time undergraduate engineering students in an ABET-accredited Engineering Technology program leading to a bachelor degree and have cumulative GPA of at least 3.0 on a 4.0 scale. **Criteria:** Recipients will be selected based on need for financial assistance, leadership ability, and character.

Funds Avail.: $5,000. **Duration:** Annual. **To Apply:** Applicants must submit: an official transcript of college grades; a letter of recommendation; and an evaluation form from three references including professor or faculty advisor. **Deadline:** December 1. **Remarks:** The scholarship was established in memory of ASHRAE's former Executive Vice President, who served the Society from 1981-2004. Established in 1981. **Contact:** Lois Benedict; Email: lbenedict@ashrae.org.

1473 ■ Duane Hanson Scholarship *(Undergraduate/Scholarship)*

Purpose: To help reduce the financial burdens of obtaining an engineering education. **Focus:** Engineering. **Qualif.:** Applicants must be full-time undergraduate engineering students in an ABET-accredited Engineering Technology

Awards are arranged alphabetically below their administering organizations

program leading to a bachelor degree, and have cumulative GPA of at least 3.0 on a scale of 4.0. **Criteria:** Recipients will be selected based on financial need; leadership ability; and character.

Funds Avail.: $5,000. **Duration:** Annual. **Number Awarded:** 1. **To Apply:** Applicants must submit: an official transcript of college grades; letter of recommendation; and evaluation form from three references including professor or faculty advisor. **Deadline:** December 1. **Remarks:** The scholarship is named after the president of Gayner Engineers, a consulting mechanical/electrical engineering firm in San Francisco, California. **Contact:** Lois Benedict, ASHRAE Scholarship Administrator; Phone: 678-539-1120; Email: lbenedict@ashrae.org.

1474 ■ Henry Adams Scholarship (Undergraduate/Scholarship)

Purpose: To help reduce the financial burdens of obtaining an engineering education. **Focus:** Engineering. **Qualif.:** Applicants must be full-time undergraduate engineering students in ABET-accredited Engineering Technology program leading to bachelor degree, and have cumulative GPA of at least 3.0 on a scale where 4.0 is the highest. **Criteria:** Recipients will be selected based on financial need; leadership ability; and character.

Funds Avail.: $3,000. **Duration:** Annual. **Number Awarded:** 1. **To Apply:** Applicants must submit: an official transcript of college grades; letter of recommendation; and evaluation form from three references including professor or faculty advisor. **Deadline:** December 1. **Remarks:** The scholarship was established by Henry Adams, Inc, a consulting firm based in Baltimore, Maryland, in memory of its founder, a charter member, and sixth president of ASHRAE's predecessor society, ASHVE. **Contact:** Lois Benedict, ASHRAE Scholarship Administrator; Phone: 678-539-1120; Email: lbenedict@ashrae.org.

1475 ■ Donald E. Nichols Scholarships (Undergraduate/Scholarship)

Purpose: To help reduce the financial burdens of obtaining an engineering education. **Focus:** Engineering. **Qualif.:** Applicants must be full-time undergraduate engineering students in an ABET-accredited Engineering Technology program leading to a bachelor degree at Tennessee Technological University; they must have cumulative GPA of at least 3.0 on a 4.0 scale. **Criteria:** Recipients will be selected based on the need for financial assistance, leadership ability, and character.

Funds Avail.: $3,000. **Duration:** Annual. **To Apply:** Applicants must submit: an official transcript of college grades; a letter of recommendation; and an evaluation form from three references including professor or faculty advisor. **Deadline:** December 1. **Remarks:** The scholarship is named for a former ASHRAE vice president and graduate of Tennessee Technological University, Donald E. Nichols.

1476 ■ Reuben Trane Scholarships (Undergraduate/Scholarship)

Purpose: To help reduce the financial burdens of obtaining an engineering education. **Focus:** Engineering. **Qualif.:** Applicants must be full-time undergraduate engineering students in an ABET-accredited Engineering Technology program leading to a bachelor degree and have cumulative GPA of at least 3.0 on a 4.0 scale. **Criteria:** Recipients will be selected based on need for financial assistance, leadership ability, and character.

Funds Avail.: $10,000. **Duration:** Annual; up to 2 years. **Number Awarded:** 3. **To Apply:** Applicants must submit:

an official transcript of college grades; a letter of recommendation; and an evaluation form from three references including professor or faculty advisor. **Deadline:** December 1. **Remarks:** The scholarship was established in memory of The Trane Company founder, an engineer, inventor and business executive, whose manufacturing enterprise ranks today as one of the world's largest in the HVAC&R industry. **Contact:** Lois Benedict; Email: lbenedict@ashrae.org.

1477 ■ American Society for Horticultural Science (ASHS)
1018 Duke St.
Alexandria, VA 22314
Ph: (703)836-4606
Fax: (703)836-2024
URL: www.ashs.org
Social Media: www.facebook.com/americansocietyforhorticulturalscience
www.linkedin.com/company/american-society-for-horticultural-science
www.pinterest.com/ashs1903
twitter.com/ASHS_Hort

1478 ■ American Society for Horticultural Science Travel Grants (Graduate, Undergraduate/Grant)

Purpose: To provide financial assistance to students in the area of horticulture. **Focus:** Horticulture. **Qualif.:** Applicants must be enrolled in horticultural science as a major course of study and must have submitted an abstract title or complete abstract for presentation at the ASHS Annual Conference. **Criteria:** Grants will be awarded on the basis of merit and geographical distribution.

Funds Avail.: $500 (domestic graduate and undergraduate students); $750 (international students). **Duration:** Annual. **Number Awarded:** Varies. **To Apply:** Applicants must accomplish application and abstract. **Deadline:** April 4. **Contact:** ASHS Headquarters, 1018 Duke St., Alexandria, VA, 22314; Phone: 703-836-4606; Fax: 703-836-2024; Email: alower@ashs.org.

1479 ■ ASHS Industry Division Student Travel Grant (Graduate, Undergraduate/Grant)

Purpose: To provide financial assistance to students in the area of horticulture who are attending the ASHS Annual Conference. **Focus:** Horticulture. **Qualif.:** Applicants should be undergraduate and graduate Horticulture students. **Criteria:** Applicants will be selected based on academic achievement (30 points for 4.0 GPA), recommendation (20 points) and essay (50 points).

Funds Avail.: $1,000. **Duration:** Annual. **Number Awarded:** 4. **To Apply:** Applicants must submit transcripts, completed application; letter of recommendation from undergraduate advisor or faculty member; and a 500-word essay outlining interest in horticulture and career goals. **Deadline:** May 15. **Remarks:** Established in 2004.

1480 ■ ASHS Scholars Award (Undergraduate/Scholarship)

Purpose: To recognize and support scholastic achievement, and encourage career development in horticultural science at the undergraduate level. **Focus:** Horticulture. **Qualif.:** Applicants must be undergraduate students of any class standing at the time of the application; registered as full-time students (minimum 10 credit hours) actively pursu-

Awards are arranged alphabetically below their administering organizations

ing a degree in horticulture. **Criteria:** Recipients are chosen based on excellence in academic and scholastic performance in the major (an area of horticulture) and supporting areas of science; participation in extracurricular, leadership and research activities relating to horticulture; participation in university and community service; demonstrated commitment to the horticulture science profession and related career fields; and related horticultural experiences.

Funds Avail.: $1,500. **Duration:** Annual. **Number Awarded:** 2. **To Apply:** Applicants must be nominated by the chair or head of the department in which they are majoring; must submit completed application supported by a 250-500 essay, complete resume, three letters of reference and official university or college transcripts; incomplete applications cannot be considered. **Deadline:** February 4.

1481 ■ Miklos Faust International Travel Award (Doctorate/Grant)

Purpose: To promote international cooperation in fruit crops research and education. **Focus:** Horticulture. **Qualif.:** Applicants must be young scientists (less than 40 yrs. old) who are actively involved in fruit science research, and hold or pursuing a doctoral degree. **Criteria:** Applications are reviewed according to evidence of high originality and strong commitment to research in fruit science.

Funds Avail.: No specific amount. **Duration:** Quadrennial. **Contact:** Miklos Faust Award, c/o ASHS, 1018 Duke St., Alexandria, VA, 22314.

1482 ■ American Society of Ichthyologists and Herpetologists (ASIH)
810 E 10th St.
Lawrence, KS 66044
Ph: (785)865-9405
Free: 800-627-0326
E-mail: asih@allenpress.com
URL: www.asih.org
Social Media: www.facebook.com/groups/
   204572449594711
twitter.com/ASIHCopeia

1483 ■ Frederick and Helen Gaige Award (Professional development/Grant)

Purpose: To provide support to young herpetologists for museum or laboratory study, travel, field work, or any other activity that effectively enhances their professional careers and their contributions to the science of herpetology. **Focus:** Zoology. **Qualif.:** Applicants must be members of ASIH and should be enrolled for an advanced degree. Applicants who do not meet these basic requirements may be considered for the award under exceptional circumstances if their careers are judged to be in a developmental stage. **Criteria:** Selection will be based on merit and need.

Funds Avail.: $400 to $1,000. **Duration:** Annual. **Number Awarded:** Varies. **To Apply:** Applications for the Gaige Award and letters of recommendation should be e-mailed (not mailed) to Dr. Christopher Tracy. The application should consist of no more than two single-spaced typewritten pages (12 point font, reasonable margins) and must include the following: name, address, email address, and telephone numbers of the applicant; institutional affiliation; academic degree being sought and the year of its expected completion, or highest degree and its date of award; name of the applicant's current or most recent major professor; title of the proposed research; justification for the research;

concise description of research objectives and methods; sources of partial support for the research and pending applications for support from other funds; budget outline; short statement of the way in which the award would be used. **Deadline:** March 1.

1484 ■ Edward C. Raney Fund Award (Professional development/Grant)

Purpose: To provide support for young ichthyologists for museum or laboratory study, travel, field work, or any other activity that effectively enhances their professional careers and their contributions to the science of ichthyology. **Focus:** Zoology. **Qualif.:** Applicants must be members of ASIH and should be enrolled for an advanced degree. Applicants who do not meet these basic requirements may be considered for the award under exceptional circumstances if their careers are judged to be in a developmental stage. **Criteria:** Selection will be based on merit and need.

Funds Avail.: $400 to $1,000. **Duration:** Annual. **Number Awarded:** Varies. **To Apply:** Applications for the Raney Award and a letter of recommendation should be e-mailed (not mailed) to Dr. Raelynn Daeton Haynes. The application should consist of no more than two single-spaced pages and must include the following: name, address, email address, and telephone numbers of the applicant; institutional affiliation; academic degree being sought and the year of its expected completion, or highest degree and its date of award; name of the applicant's current or most recent major professor; title of the proposed research; justification for the research; concise description of research objectives and methods; sources of partial support for the research and pending applications for support from other funds; budget outline; short statement of the way in which the award would be used. **Deadline:** March 1.

1485 ■ American Society of Interior Designers (ASID)
1152 15th St. NW, Ste. 910
Washington, DC 20005
Ph: (202)546-3480
Fax: (202)546-3240
E-mail: membership@asid.org
URL: www.asid.org
Social Media: www.facebook.com/ASID7
www.instagram.com/asid_hq
www.linkedin.com/company/american-society-of-interior
  -designers
www.pinterest.com/asid7
twitter.com/ASID
www.youtube.com/channel/UCiDgXJ0Nav2fWIXb3m-xc5Q

1486 ■ ASID Foundation Legacy Scholarships for Graduate Students (Graduate/Scholarship)

Purpose: To encourage talented practicing interior designers to advance their professional development through graduate study and research. **Focus:** Interior design. **Qualif.:** Applicants must be enrolled in or have applied for admission to a graduate-level interior design program at a degree-granting institution; must have been practicing designers for a period of at least five years prior to graduate school. **Criteria:** Selection will be based on academic/creative accomplishment.

Funds Avail.: $4,000. **Duration:** Annual. **Number Awarded:** 1. **To Apply:** Applicants must submit the follow-

Awards are arranged alphabetically below their administering organizations

ing requirements: a maximum of 1000 words personal statement; official school transcript(s); letter of recommendation; maximum of 100 words biographical statement; headshot picture.

1487 ■ Irene Winifred Eno Grant *(Professional development/Grant)*

Purpose: To provide financial assistance to individuals or groups engaged in the creation of an educational program or an interior design research project dedicated to health, safety and welfare. **Focus:** Interior design. **Qualif.:** Applicants must be students, educators, interior design practitioners, institutions or other interior design-related groups. **Criteria:** Selection will be based on strength of the project proposal, budget, promotion plan, and expected outcome.

Funds Avail.: $5,000. **Duration:** Annual. **Number Awarded:** 1. **To Apply:** Applicant must submit Abstract; explanation of how the funds will be used; explanation of what the program will deliver and produce; promotion Plan; biographical Statement; headshot.

1488 ■ American Society of International Law (ASIL)

2223 Massachusetts Ave. NW
Washington, DC 20008
Ph: (202)939-6000
Fax: (202)797-7133
E-mail: services@asil.org
URL: www.asil.org
Social Media: www.facebook.com/
  AmericanSocietyofInternationalLaw
www.instagram.com/explore/locations/49479292/united
  -states/washington-dc/american-society-of-international
  -law
twitter.com/asilorg
www.youtube.com/asil1906

1489 ■ Arthur C. Helton Fellowship Program *(Undergraduate, Graduate/Fellowship)*

Purpose: To provide financial assistance for law students and young professionals to pursue field work and research on significant issues involving international law, human rights, humanitarian affairs, and related areas. **Focus:** Human rights; International affairs and relations; Law. **Qualif.:** Applicants must be Law students, practicing lawyers, human rights professionals, scholars, and other individuals seeking assistance in conducting international fieldwork and law-related research and in the early stages of their academic and professional careers who demonstrate the potential to make significant contributions to the use and study of international law around the world. **Criteria:** Applicants will be considered by the Helton Fellowship Selection Committee.

Funds Avail.: $2,000. **Duration:** Annual. **To Apply:** Applications must be submitted along with Project Budget; writing Sample; current CV or resume; confirmation of law student status or date of graduation from law school; Letter of support from your sponsoring organization, including details of your proposed project, impact of the project to the sponsoring organization, on the region, or in the relevant field of international law and two letters of recommendation or support. **Deadline:** January 27. **Remarks:** The fellowship was given in honor of Arthur Helton. Established in 2004. **Contact:** Email: fellowship@asil.org.

1490 ■ American Society of Landscape Architects (ASLA)

636 Eye St. NW
Washington, DC 20001-3736
Ph: (202)898-2444
Fax: (202)898-1185
Free: 888-999-2752
E-mail: info@asla.org
URL: www.asla.org
Social Media: www.facebook.com/
  AmericanSocietyofLandscapeArchitects
www.instagram.com/nationalasla
www.pinterest.com/NationalASLA
twitter.com/landarchitects

1491 ■ ASLA Council of Fellows *(Undergraduate/ Scholarship)*

Purpose: To aid outstanding students who would not otherwise have an opportunity to continue a professional degree program in the area of landscape architecture due to unmet financial need, increase the interest and participation of economically disadvantaged and underrepresented populations in the study of landscape architecture through a more diverse population, and enrich the profession of landscape architecture through a more diverse population. **Focus:** Landscape architecture and design. **Qualif.:** Applicants must be current ASLA full member or international member in good standing; have achieved at least 10 continuous years of full membership at the time of nomination; have demonstrated exceptional contributions over an extended period of time; made a significant positive impact on the public and the profession; have received recognition for those contributions from multiple sources. **Criteria:** Selection is based solely on professional excellence and outstanding accomplishments as presented in the nominations.

Duration: Annual. **To Apply:** Applicants may be nominated in up to two categories, but two separate nominations must be submitted, one for each category; Images/Powerpoints should be submitted with the Works category only; ASLA retains possession of all nomination materials and rights to their usage in conjunction with the Council of Fellows program. **Remarks:** Established in 2004. **Contact:** ASLA Council of Fellows Nominations, Attn: Curt Millay, Corporate Secretary, 636 Eye St. NW, Washington, DC, 20001; Email: cmillay@asla.org.

1492 ■ Peridian International, Inc./Rae L. Price, FASLA Scholarship *(Undergraduate/Scholarship)*

Purpose: To bring young creative individuals into the profession who may not otherwise have the financial ability to cover all the costs of their educational program. **Focus:** Landscape architecture and design. **Qualif.:** Applicants must be United States citizens who are undergraduate students in the final two years of study in Landscape Architecture at the UCLA Extension Program or Cal Poly Pomona; must demonstrate financial need and a minimum grade point average of B.

Funds Avail.: $5,000. **To Apply:** Applicants must submit all of the following: general submission form; photo; bio for the LAF website (150 word max); resume (2 page max); financial aid form; 2 Letters of recommendation; essay (2 page max). **Deadline:** February 15. **Contact:** Landscape Architecture Foundation; Email: scholarships@ lafoundation.org; Phone: 202-331-7070 x14.

Awards are arranged alphabetically below their administering organizations

1493 ■ American Society for Laser Medicine and Surgery (ASLMS)

2100 Stewart Ave., Ste. 240
Wausau, WI 54401
Ph: (715)845-9283
Fax: (715)848-2493
Free: 877-258-6028
E-mail: information@aslms.org
URL: www.aslms.org
Social Media: www.facebook.com/aslms.connect
www.instagram.com/aslmsmeeting/
www.linkedin.com/company/the-american-society-for-laser
  -medicine-and-surgery-inc-aslms-
pinterest.com/aslms/boards/
twitter.com/aslmsedu
www.youtube.com/user/AmSocLasMedSurg

1494 ■ ASLMS Educational Grants *(Undergraduate, Graduate, Professional development/Grant)*

Purpose: To help student members attend the Annual Conference. **Focus:** Medicine. **Qualif.:** Applicants must be undergraduate students, medical students, residents, interns, fellows-in-training, graduate students, and post-doctoral fellows who need financial support to attend the Annual Conference; applicants must be accepted for oral presentation of their research.

Duration: Annual. **To Apply:** Application details are available online at www.aslms.org/for-professionals/grants-awards.

1495 ■ ASLMS Research Grant *(Postdoctorate/Grant, Monetary)*

Purpose: To support research projects designed to foster the development and use of lasers and other related technologies in medical and surgical applications. **Focus:** Medicine. **Qualif.:** Applicants must presently be enrolled in or have completed postdoctoral and/or residency training; all non-ASLMS members will be required to apply for and be accepted into ALSMS membership.

Funds Avail.: Up to $70,000. **Duration:** Annual. **To Apply:** Application details are available online at www.aslms.org/for-professionals/grants-awards/research-grants/aslms-research-grant. **Deadline:** March 1.

1496 ■ Dr. Horace Furumoto Innovations Professional Development - Young Investigator Award *(Professional development/Award)*

Purpose: To recognize and encourage the development of future technology innovators and leaders. **Focus:** Medicine. **Qualif.:** Applicant must be undergoing an early stage career and/or professional development (up to 15 years in the field of lasers and related technologies in health care); non-clinical professionals, particularly those who work in industry, are especially encouraged and will receive special consideration; must display a potential for independent contribution and innovation; and have good verbal communication skills to allow for an informative and appropriate lecture.

Funds Avail.: $4,500. **Duration:** Annual. **To Apply:** Applicants must be nominated by an ASLMS member; a nomination form can be obtained at the website and must be sent electronically. **Remarks:** The Award was established in memory of Dr. Horace Furumoto. Established in 2007.

1497 ■ A. Ward Ford Memorial Research Grant *(Postdoctorate, Professional development/Grant)*

Purpose: To support direct clinical research investigating current use or potential new applications of laser or other light-based therapy. **Focus:** Medicine. **Qualif.:** Applicants must be enrolled in or have completed an MD residency or PhD postdoctoral training at the time of application and must be members or applicants for membership in ASLMS at the time of the award. **Criteria:** Priority will be given to applicants who are interested in or entering an academic teaching or research position.

Funds Avail.: Up to $65,000. **Duration:** Annual. **To Apply:** Applicants must submit the following requirements: applicant background including training, previous positions, publications, previous research; clear presentation of the clinical problem or question to be researched; presentation of the research design; a detailed budget; evidence of the institutional or other support base for the research, including collaborators; IRB approval letter for human subjects research, and approval from the institution supporting the research; have a letter of support from the training program director, and a designated mentor or research supervisor. **Deadline:** June 1. **Remarks:** Established by William B. Mark, who was an engineer by training, along with his wife, Caroline. The Marks formed the A. Ward Ford Foundation, named in honor of Caroline's grandfather, Austin Ward Ford, who was a pioneer in the early business machine industry. **Contact:** Dr. William Owen, Chair, A. Ward Ford Memorial Research Grant Committee, Community Foundation of North Central Wisconsin, 500 1st St., Ste. 2600, Wausau, WI, 54403; Phone: 715-845-9555; Email: info@cfoncw.org.

1498 ■ American Society of Mammalogists (ASM)

c/o Christy Classi, CAE
PO Box 4973
Topeka, KS 66604
Ph: (785)550-6904
E-mail: cclassi@mammalsociety.org
URL: www.mammalsociety.org
Social Media: www.facebook.com/American.Society.of
  .Mammalogists
linkedin.com/groups/American-Society-Mammalogists
  -4575484
twitter.com/mammalogists

1499 ■ Albert R. and Alma Shadle Fellowship *(Graduate/Fellowship)*

Purpose: To recognize individuals who have made significant contributions to the American Society of Mammalogists. **Focus:** Zoology.

Funds Avail.: No specific amount. **Duration:** Annual. **To Apply:** Applicants must gather the following materials: curriculum vita, 3-5 pages in length and must include peer-reviewed publications, other publications, presentations to professional meetings, research grants, memberships in professional societies, honors and awards and professional service; Arrange for three letter of recommendation to be sent via email. One letter must be from applicants' advisor. Please make sure that applicants' and other providers of letters of recommendation include their name in the subject line of the email; names and contact information for three people who the applicants have asked to provide letters in support of their applications plus name and contact information for their department head or chairperson; summary of

Awards are arranged alphabetically below their administering organizations

professional experience in mammalogy, research interests and career goals, limited to one page; abstract for thesis or dissertation research, limited to 150 words; brief statement describing how the applicants would use any support from ASM; limited to one page; description of thesis or dissertation research project organized under the following headings: title, introduction, objective, methods, present status of the Research, Significance and Literature Cited. Limited to five pages, double spaced, however, Literature Citations may be included on additional pages. **Contact:** Email to shadle@mammalsociety.org.

1500 ■ American Society of Mammalogists Grants-in-Aid of Research (Graduate, Undergraduate/Grant)

Purpose: To enhance and support graduate researchers by identifying and funding research proposals pertaining to mammals. **Focus:** Zoology. **Qualif.:** Applicants must be graduate and undergraduate students who are members of the Society at the time of application. **Criteria:** Selection will be based on the committee's criteria.

Funds Avail.: $1,500. **To Apply:** Applicants must complete the following materials; research proposal, limited to two pages, 12 pt. font, 0.5 inch margins; literature cited may be on a separate page; itemized budget for the proposed work; categorize each item as equipment, supplies or travel; indicate expected source of funds and indicate with an X if a commitment has been made for that item; give estimated total cost and amount requested from ASM; arrange for two letters of recommendation to be sent via email; one letter must be from applicant's advisor; please make sure that the advisor includes the name of the applicants in the subject line of the email; if applicants have received a Grant-in-Aid of research previously, they will have to provide the year it was awarded, title of the proposal, amount awarded, status of any resulting publications and a brief summary of progress; for the attachments, please use this name convention. **Deadline:** March 1. **Contact:** Brock McMillan; E-mail: brock_mcmillan@byu.edu.

1501 ■ American Society Of Mammalogists Fellowship In Mammalogy (Graduate/Fellowship)

Purpose: To recognize current accomplishments in mammalogy, service to ASM, and the potential for a productive, future role in professional mammalogy. **Focus:** Zoology.

Funds Avail.: $7,500. **Duration:** Annual. **To Apply:** Applicants must gather the following materials: curriculum vita, 3-5 pages in length and must include peer-reviewed publications, other publications, presentations to professional meetings, research grants, memberships in professional societies, honors and awards and professional service; Arrange for three letter of recommendation to be sent via email. One letter must be from applicants' advisor. Please make sure that applicants' and other providers of letters of recommendation include their name in the subject line of the email; names and contact information for three people who the applicants have asked to provide letters in support of their applications plus name and contact information for their department head or chairperson; summary of professional experience in mammalogy, research interests and career goals, limited to one page; abstract for thesis or dissertation research, limited to 150 words; brief statement describing how the applicants would use any support from ASM. Limited to one page; Description of thesis or dissertation research project organized under the following headings: Title, Introduction, Objective, Methods, Present Status of the Research, Significance and Literature Cited. Limited to five pages, double spaced, however, Literature Citations may be included on additional pages.

1502 ■ Graduate Student Honoraria - A. Brazier Howell Award (Master's, Doctorate/Award)

Purpose: To recognize students who have been primarily responsible for the design and/or conduct of the submitted research project. **Focus:** Zoology. **Qualif.:** Applicants must be Masters or doctoral students (or have completed their degrees during the previous Fall term) when they apply. PhD students who have completed MA/MS degrees within the previous 18 months may apply for the Alexander Award using their Master's research, but are not eligible to receive another graduate honorarium for work on a related project at the same institution; however, recipients of ASM Grant-in-Aid of Research and other student research grants (Latin American Graduate Student Field Research Award, African Graduate Student Research Fund, James L. Patton Award, Student Science Policy Award) are eligible and encouraged to apply. **Criteria:** Selection will be based on the originality, quality and presentation of research and the advisor's letter of support.

Funds Avail.: $2,000. **Duration:** Annual. **To Apply:** Applicants should submit a summary of their graduate research, not exceeding 1, 000 words, with the following clearly labeled sections: title, project significance/theoretical context, methods, results and discussion/interpretation; include key figures/tables with concise captions to support the results. A reference letter should be addressed to the committee and be written by an individual familiar with the applicant's research, ideally, the research advisor/mentor or major professor; the letter must address the following; if the students will be prepared to present the research project in the plenary session of the upcoming annual meeting; the student's role in designing and conducting the research, especially in the case of collaborative research. **Deadline:** February 15. **Contact:** Committee chair, Dr. Elizabeth Flaherty; Phone: 765-494-3567; E-mail: eflaher@purdue.edu.

1503 ■ Graduate Student Honoraria - Elmer C. Birney Award (Master's, Doctorate/Award)

Purpose: To recognize students who have been primarily responsible for the design and/or conduct of the submitted research project. **Focus:** Zoology. **Qualif.:** Applicants must be Master's or Doctoral student members of the Society. **Criteria:** Selection will be based on the originality, quality and presentation of research and the advisor's letter of support.

Funds Avail.: $2,000. **Duration:** Annual. **To Apply:** Applicants should submit a summary of their graduate research, not exceeding 1, 000 words, with the following clearly labeled sections: Title, Project Significance/ Theoretical Context, Methods, Results and Discussion/ Interpretation; include key figures/tables with concise captions to support the results. A reference letter should be addressed to the committee and be written by an individual familiar with the applicant's research, ideally, the research advisor/mentor or major professor; the letter must address the following: 1) if the students will be prepared to present the research project in the plenary session of the upcoming annual meeting; 2) the student's role in designing and conducting the research, especially in the case of collaborative research. **Deadline:** February 15. **Remarks:** Established in 1953. **Contact:** Committee Chair, Dr. Elizabeth Flaherty; E-mail: eflaher@purdue.edu.

1504 ■ Graduate Student Honoraria - Anna M. Jackson Awards (Master's, Doctorate/Award)

Purpose: To recognize excellence in pre-doctoral research. **Focus:** Zoology. **Qualif.:** Applicants must be Master's or

Awards are arranged alphabetically below their administering organizations

Doctoral student members of the Society.

Funds Avail.: No specific amount. **Duration:** Annual. **Deadline:** February 15. **Remarks:** Named in the honor of Anna M. Jackson, one of the 16 female Charter Members of ASM. Established in 1953. **Contact:** E.A. Flaherty; Email: eflaher@purdue.edu.

1505 ■ Latin American Student Field Research Award *(Graduate/Fellowship)*

Purpose: To provide support to students who are doing field projects. **Focus:** Conservation of natural resources; Zoology. **Qualif.:** Applicants must be citizens of Latin American countries (excluding Puerto Rico) and currently enrolled in a graduate program; their projects must be field-oriented investigations of natural history, conservation, ecology, systematics, wildlife biology, biogeography, or behavior. **Criteria:** Applicants are judged upon the committee's criteria.

Funds Avail.: $1,500. **Duration:** Annual. **Number Awarded:** 5. **To Apply:** Applicants must include a two-page application and two letters of recommendation from persons familiar with your scientific background and current academic program, one of which must be from your graduate advisor. **Deadline:** March 1. **Remarks:** Established in 1997.

1506 ■ Oliver P. Pearson Award *(Doctorate/ Fellowship)*

Purpose: To offer financial support to young professional mammalogists who hold academic or curatorial positions in Latin America, to help them establish or consolidate their research programs. **Focus:** Zoology. **Qualif.:** Applicant must have a Ph.D. or equivalent terminal degree conferred within the previous 5 years, an academic (post-doctoral, teaching, curatorial, or other comparable research-oriented) position in a Latin American institution; and must be a member of the American Society of Mammalogists. **Criteria:** Applicants are judged upon the committee's criteria.

Funds Avail.: $5,000 with additional $2,000 for recipient to attend the ASM meetings. **Duration:** Annual. **Number Awarded:** 1. **To Apply:** Applicants must provide a one-page statement that describes: the nature and responsibilities of their academic position; professional interests and goals for the next few years; and detailed justification documenting how and why the award would benefit the applicant's research program; a curriculum vitae; copy of one published or accepted research paper; two letters of recommendation from established professionals familiar with the applicant, based either in Latin America or abroad. **Deadline:** March 1. **Contact:** S. T. Alvarez-Castañeda; Email: sticul@yahoo.com.

1507 ■ American Society for Mass Spectrometry (ASMS)

Bldg. I-1
2019 Galisteo St.
Santa Fe, NM 87505
Ph: (505)989-4517
Fax: (505)989-1073
E-mail: office@asms.org
URL: www.asms.org
Social Media: www.facebook.com/asmsnews
www.linkedin.com/company/american-society-for-mass
  -spectrometry
twitter.com/asmsnews

1508 ■ ASMS Research Awards *(Other/Award)*

Purpose: To promote research done by young scientists in mass spectrometry. **Focus:** Science. **Qualif.:** Applicants can be academic scientists within four years of joining the tenure track faculty or equivalent in a North American university; must be members of ASMS. **Criteria:** Recipients are selected based on applications and proposals.

Funds Avail.: $35,000. **Duration:** Annual. **Number Awarded:** Varies. **To Apply:** Applicants must send seven sets of one-page fiscal proposal and justification; list of current research support; curriculum vitae; and two letters of recommendation. **Deadline:** November 30. **Contact:** ASMS Awards, 2019 Galisteo St., Bldg. 1, Santa Fe, NM 87505.

1509 ■ American Society for Microbiology (ASM)

1752 N St. NW
Washington, DC 20036
Ph: (202)737-3600
E-mail: service@asmusa.org
URL: www.asm.org
Social Media: www.facebook.com/asmfan
www.instagram.com/asmicrobiology
twitter.com/asmicrobiology

1510 ■ American Society for Microbiology International Fellowships for Africa *(Postdoctorate/ Fellowship)*

Purpose: To promote American/African collaborations in microbiological research and training. **Focus:** Microbiology.

Funds Avail.: Up to $5,000. **Duration:** Annual; from 6 weeks to 6 months.

1511 ■ American Society for Microbiology International Fellowships for Asia *(Postdoctorate/ Fellowship)*

Purpose: To promote American/Asian collaborations in microbiological research and training. **Focus:** Microbiology.

Funds Avail.: $5,000. **Duration:** Annual; from 6 weeks to 6 months.

1512 ■ American Society for Microbiology International Fellowships for Latin America and the Caribbean *(Postdoctorate/Fellowship)*

Purpose: To promote American/Latin American collaborations in microbiological research and training. **Focus:** Microbiology.

Funds Avail.: $4,000. **Duration:** Annual; from 6 weeks to 6 months.

1513 ■ American Society for Microbiology Undergraduate Research Fellowship *(Undergraduate/Fellowship, Award, Monetary)*

Purpose: To support highly competitive students who wish to pursue graduate careers in biology. **Focus:** Microbiology. **Qualif.:** Applicants must be U.S. citizens or permanent residents who are ASM members and enrolled as full-time matriculating undergraduate students during the academic year at an accredited U.S. Institution. They must be involved in a research project, have ASM members at their home institutions willing to serve as mentors, and not receive financial support for research during the Fellowship.

Funds Avail.: Up to $4,000 plus $2,000 travel support. **Duration:** Annual. **Number Awarded:** 1 in 2019. **To Ap-**

Awards are arranged alphabetically below their administering organizations

ply: Applicants must submit a complete application form; personal statement. **Deadline:** February 15. **Contact:** Shaundra Holmes; Phone: 202-942-9282; Email: fellowships@asmusa.org.

1514 ■ ASM/CDC Program in Infectious Disease and Public Health Microbiology *(Postdoctorate/Fellowship)*

Purpose: To support the development of new approaches, methodologies, and knowledge in infectious disease prevention and control in areas within the public health mission of the CDC. **Focus:** Microbiology. **Qualif.:** Applicants must have earned their doctorate degree or completed primary residency within three years from proposed start date, and may not have a faculty position or enrolled in a graduate degree program during the fellowship. **Criteria:** Recipients will be selected based on: scientific merit and training potential of the research proposal; training resources; and have significance with the Centers for Diseases public health mission.

Funds Avail.: Up to $47, 032 (annual stipend) which includes $3,000 for health benefits; $500 relocation benefits, and $2,000 for professional development. **Duration:** Annual; up to 2 years. **To Apply:** Applicants must fill out the application form. **Contact:** ASM/CDC Postdoctoral Research Fellowship Program, Education Department, American Society for Microbiology, 1752 N St. NW, Washington, DC, 20036; Phone: 202-942-9283; Email: fellowships@asmusa.org.

1515 ■ ASM Congressional Science Fellowship *(Postdoctorate/Fellowship)*

Purpose: To make practical contributions to more effective use of scientific knowledge in government, educate the scientific communities regarding public policy, and broaden the perspective of both the scientific and governmental communities regarding the value of such science-government interaction. **Focus:** Science. **Qualif.:** Applicants must: be citizens of the United States who are members of ASM for at least one year.

Funds Avail.: $65,000. **Duration:** Annual. **Contact:** ASM Congressional Science Fellowship, at hgarvey@asmusa.org.

1516 ■ ASM Research Capstone Fellowship *(Undergraduate/Fellowship, Award, Monetary)*

Purpose: To increase the number of underrepresented undergraduate students who have demonstrated the ability to pursue graduate careers in microbiology. **Focus:** Microbiology. **Qualif.:** Applicants must be ASM membership; U.S. citizenship, permanent residency, or DACA eligibility; Enrollment as a community college, undergraduate, or post-baccalaureate studentMembership of an underrepresented minority group; Conducting research in the microbiological sciencesSubmission of an abstract for presentation at ASM Microbe 2019A research mentor who is an ASM member (does not apply to the community college, undergraduate, and post-baccalaureate track).

Funds Avail.: $2,000. **Duration:** Annual. **Deadline:** March 15. **Contact:** Shaundra Holmes; Phone: 202-942-9282; Email: fellowships@asmusa.org.

1517 ■ ASM Robert D. Watkins Graduate Research Fellowship *(Postdoctorate/Fellowship, Monetary)*

Purpose: To increase the number of underrepresented groups completing doctoral degrees in the microbiological sciences. **Focus:** Microbiology. **Qualif.:** Applicants must: be formally admitted to a doctoral program in the microbiological sciences in an accredited U.S. institution; have successfully completed the first year of the graduate program; have successfully completed all graduate course work requirements for the doctoral degree by the date of activation of the fellowship; be student members of ASM; be mentored by ASM members; and, be U.S. citizens or permanent residents. **Criteria:** Recipients will be selected based on academic achievement; evidence of successful research plan developed in collaboration with research advisor/mentor; relevant career goals in the microbiological sciences; involvement in activities that serve the needs of underrepresented groups.

Funds Avail.: $63,000 ($21,000 a year for a three year period). **Duration:** Annual; up to 3 years. **Deadline:** May 1. **Contact:** ASM Robert D. Watkins Graduate Research Fellowship, Education Board, American Society for Microbiology, 1752 N St., NW, Washington, DC 20036; Phone: 202-942-9283; Email: fellowships@asmusa.org.

1518 ■ ASM Science Teaching Fellowships - Student *(Undergraduate/Fellowship)*

Purpose: To support students who are interested in a career as elementary or secondary school science teachers. **Focus:** Education. **Qualif.:** Applicants must studying, conducting research, or teaching in the microbiological and related sciences; willing to commit time and resources to participate in course activities; interested in careers that have a substantial teaching component at a non-doctoral institution.

Funds Avail.: No specific amount. **Duration:** Annual. **Contact:** Email: education@asmusa.org.

1519 ■ American Society of Military Comptrollers (ASMC)
415 N Alfred St.
Alexandria, VA 22314
Ph: (703)549-0360
Fax: (703)549-3181
Free: 800-462-5637
URL: www.asmconline.org
Social Media: www.facebook.com/ASMCNationalHQ
twitter.com/asmctweets

1520 ■ ASMC National Scholarship Program *(Graduate/Scholarship)*

Purpose: To recognize graduating high school seniors for academic achievement and provides financial assistance to seniors in order that they may accomplish their future financial management baccalaureate educational goals. **Focus:** Accounting; Business administration; Economics; Finance; Resource management. **Qualif.:** Applicant must be a graduating high school senior in the final half of the school year, or a high school graduate within six months of the application deadline. Students that have won a national scholarship in previous years may qualify for continuing assistance; must be entering a field of study directly related to financial/resource management (such as business administration, economics, accounting, finance); applications that do not fall within these fields will not be considered. **Criteria:** Recipients will be selected based on the selection panel's review of applications; the selection panel will make final recommendations to the ASMC National Executive Committee, who will approve the final award winners applicant's scholastic achievements, leadership ability,

Awards are arranged alphabetically below their administering organizations

e extracurricular activities, career/academic goals and financial need will be considered.

Funds Avail.: Amount varies. **Duration:** Annual. **Number Awarded:** 11. **To Apply:** Applicants must submit completed application form and three letters of recommendation from local ASMC chapter president, high school principal, academic dean, or guidance counselor, and a high school teacher; applications from prior winners will require document support of a GPA of 3.0 or higher and a letter from the academic institution confirming continued work in the area of financial management; endorsement letters from ASMC chapters must be submitted. **Deadline:** March 31. **Contact:** ASMC National Awards Committee, Scholarship Awards; Email: awards@asmconline.org.

1521 ■ American Society of Mining and Reclamation (ASMR)

1800 S Oak St., Ste 100
Champaign, IL 61820-6974
Ph: (217)333-9489
Fax: (217)244-3219
URL: www.asmr.us
Social Media: www.facebook.com/
AmericanSocietyMiningReclamation

1522 ■ American Society of Mining and Reclamation Memorial Scholarship Award (Undergraduate, Community College, College, University/Scholarship, Recognition)

Purpose: To support deserving students from universities, colleges, or community colleges having curricula in a scientific discipline directly related to and leading toward a profession in reclamation related work. **Focus:** Conservation of natural resources; Engineering, Mining and Mineral; Environmental science; Mining. **Qualif.:** Applicants must be full-time students who have completed at least sophomore year of curriculum in a science discipline directly relating to and leading to a profession in reclamation, and have an adequate grade point of average, carry the curriculum-required hours and participated in other curricular activities. **Criteria:** Recipients will be selected based on extracurricular activities; participation; and leadership. Preference will be given to students from schools having an ASMR student chapter.

Funds Avail.: Amount varies. **Duration:** Annual. **Number Awarded:** 3. **To Apply:** Applicants must complete the application form to be found at ASMR website; must submit: a statement outlining education and career goals; three reference letters from two academic sources, including one from advisor; college transcripts; and resume with list of awards, honors and extracurricular activities listed. **Deadline:** March 13. **Contact:** Dr. Barry Stewart; E-mail: brs40@msstate.edu.

1523 ■ American Society of Naval Engineers (ASNE)

1423 Powhatan St., Ste. 1
Alexandria, VA 22314
Ph: (703)836-6727
Fax: (703)836-7491
E-mail: asnehq@navalengineers.org
URL: www.navalengineers.org
Social Media: www.facebook.com/navalengineers
www.instagram.com/asne_navalengineers

www.linkedin.com/company/american-society-of-naval
-engineers
twitter.com/navalengineers
www.youtube.com/user/ASNE1888

1524 ■ ASNE Scholarship (Graduate, Undergraduate/ Scholarship)

Purpose: To improve the profession of naval engineering by encouraging college students to enter the field of naval engineering and by providing support to naval engineers seeking advanced education in the field. **Focus:** Engineering, Naval. **Qualif.:** Applicants must be U.S. citizens who are either: graduate candidates must be a member of ASNE to apply for a scholarship; student membership applications can be submitted with the scholarship application; undergraduate candidates do not have to be a member of ASNE to apply. **Criteria:** Selection is focused on the applicant's academic record, work history, professional promise, interest in naval engineering. Program is merit-based, however, financial need may also be considered.

Funds Avail.: $4,000 for undergraduate students; $4,000 for graduate students. **Duration:** Annual. **To Apply:** Applicants must complete and submit an application form available at the website and include three letters of reference. **Remarks:** Established in 1979. **Contact:** URL: http://www.navalengineers.org/Education/Scholarships; Phone: (703)-826-6727; Email: scholarships@navalengineers.org.

1525 ■ American Society of Nephrology (ASN)

1401 H St. NW, Ste. 900
Washington, DC 20005
Ph: (202)640-4660
Fax: (202)637-9793
E-mail: email@asn-online.org
URL: www.asn-online.org
Social Media: www.facebook.com/
AmericanSocietyofNephrology
www.instagram.com/asnkidney
www.linkedin.com/company/american-society-of
-nephrology
twitter.com/ASNKidney
www.youtube.com/user/ASNKidneyTube

1526 ■ Carl W. Gottschalk Research Scholar Grants (Professional development/Grant)

Purpose: To provide financial assistance for the development of a general nephrology investigator. **Focus:** Medical research. **Qualif.:** Applicants must: be residents of North America; be active members of ASN; hold an M.D., Ph.D., or equivalent degree; be within seven years of initial faculty appointment at the time of the award activation; have a proposed project that is independent of previous mentors; and, devote 75% of their time to research. **Criteria:** Applicants will be assessed based on their potential and the proposed project for eventual funding by a NIH R01 grant or its equivalent; qualifications with respect to prior training, productivity and independence, as well as the scientific merit of the proposed project; and commitment to the development as an independent investigator.

Funds Avail.: $100,000 a year for up to two years. **Duration:** Annual; upto two years. **Number Awarded:** Varies. **To Apply:** Applicants must submit original and three paper copies of the application (including letter from department chair or Division Director), contact information and project title; applicant's biosketch (such as a NIH Biosketch),

Awards are arranged alphabetically below their administering organizations

research project plan, letter of support from department head and three letters of reference. **Remarks:** Established in 1996. **Contact:** Phone:202-893-0008:Email:grants@asn-online.org.

1527 ■ Norman Siegel Research Scholar Grants in Pediatrics (Doctorate/Grant)

Purpose: To provide financial assistance for the development of a general nephrology investigator. **Focus:** Medicine, Pediatric. **Qualif.:** Applicants must: be residents of North America; be active members of ASN; hold an M.D., Ph.D., or equivalent degree; be within seven years of initial faculty appointment at the time of the award activation; have a proposed project that is independent of previous mentors; and, devote 75% of their time to research. **Criteria:** Applicants will be assessed based on their potential and the proposed project for eventual funding by a NIH R01 grant or its equivalent; qualifications with respect to prior training, productivity and independence, as well as the scientific merit of the proposed project; and commitment to the development as an independent investigator.

Funds Avail.: $100,000 a year for up to two years. **Duration:** Annual. **To Apply:** Applicants must submit original and three paper copies of the application (including letter from department chair or Division Director), contact information and project title; applicant's biosketch (such as a NIH Biosketch), research project plan, letter of support from department head and three letters of reference. **Remarks:** Established in 2007. **Contact:** Phone:202-893-0008:Email:grants@asn-online.org.

1528 ■ American Society of Neuroradiology (ASNR)

800 Enterprise Dr., Ste. 205
Oak Brook, IL 60523
Ph: (630)574-0220
Fax: (630)574-0661
E-mail: info@asnr.org
URL: www.asnr.org
Social Media: www.facebook.com/TheASNR
twitter.com/TheASNR

1529 ■ ARRS/ASNR Scholarship in Neuroradiology (Advanced Professional/Scholarship)

Purpose: To establish the recipient as an independent investigator in the field of neuroradiology and to collect preliminary data that could lead to further funding through established mechanisms. **Focus:** Neurology; Radiology. **Qualif.:** Applicant must be a junior full-time faculty members.

Duration: Biennial.

1530 ■ American Society for Nondestructive Testing (ASNT)

1711 Arlingate Ln.
Columbus, OH 43228-0518
Ph: (614)274-6003
Fax: (614)274-6899
Free: 800-222-2768
URL: www.asnt.org
Social Media: www.facebook.com/asntinfo
www.instagram.com/asntinfo
www.linkedin.com/company/asntinfo

twitter.com/asntinfo
www.youtube.com/user/asntinfo

1531 ■ ASNT Fellowship Award (Graduate/Fellowship, Award)

Purpose: To fund a specific research in nondestructive testing. **Focus:** Engineering; Materials research/science; Testing, educational/psychological. **Qualif.:** Applicants must be Universities or colleges with post-graduate engineering and science research programs are eligible. Specific accreditation, such as ABET accreditation, is not required. **Criteria:** Selection will be based on their experiences and the contents and quality of the submitted proposals: How novel is the research; value of potential contribution; soundness of technical approach; scope of the proposed research effort; potential for successful completion; adequacy of the proposal team; adequacy of the facilities.

Funds Avail.: Up to $20,000. **Duration:** Annual. **Number Awarded:** Up to 5. **To Apply:** Application should be in the form of a proposal for a graduate level research project from the University outlining what the program or graduate study activity will consist of and how long they will manage the fellowship; all Fellowship proposals should be formatted as follows: length; title Page; abstract; research Proposal; program of Study; research Facilities; budget. **Deadline:** October 15. **Contact:** Jessica Ames, ASNT's Program Coordinator; Email: james@asnt.org.

1532 ■ Robert B. Oliver ASNT Scholarship (Undergraduate/Scholarship)

Purpose: To assist students who have chosen a career in NDT. **Focus:** Materials research/science; Testing, educational/psychological. **Qualif.:** Applicants must be enrolled in a coursework related to nondestructive testing (NDT) leading to an undergraduate degree, an associate degree or certificate program. **Criteria:** Recipients who have the most outstanding manuscript about NDT research, investigation or development will be given preference; the manuscript is judged based on creativity, content, format and readability.

Funds Avail.: $2,500 each. **Duration:** Annual. **To Apply:** Applicants must submit completed application form (PDF) - signed by applicant & school official; original copy of the student's NDT manuscript (see manuscript criteria below); curriculum of student, showing classroom hours of NDT course work (may attach school's published curriculum if available; transcript of grades showing all of student's completed course work; letter from an instructor or school official verifying the student's enrollment; manuscript is limited to 5,000 words and a maximum of ten illustrations; Photographs should be high resolution digital images. **Deadline:** February 15. **Remarks:** The award was established in the honor of ASNT past President and Honorary Member, Robert B. Oliver. **Contact:** Jessica Ames, Awards and Honors Program, 1711 Arlingate Ln., PO Box 28518, Columbus, OH, 43228; Phone: 614-274-6003; Fax: 614-274-6899; Email: james@asnt.org.

1533 ■ American Society of Pension Professionals and Actuaries (ASPPA)

4401 N. Fairfax Dr., Ste. 600
Arlington, VA 22203
Ph: (703)516-9300
Fax: (703)516-9308
E-mail: customercare@asppa.org
URL: www.asppa.org

Awards are arranged alphabetically below their administering organizations

Social Media: twitter.com/asppa

1534 ■ Presidential Scholarship *(Master's/Scholarship)*

Purpose: To provide financial support to a junior student. **Focus:** Education. **Qualif.:** Applicants with a GPA of A on the ECTS scale or equivalent top-level grade on international grade scales who apply for and are admitted to a Master of Science programme; students enrolled in BI's Siviløkonom programme are eligible to apply in their 3rd year. **Criteria:** Applicants will be assessed according to the ECTS scale. Applicants with international bachelor's degrees will have their grades converted to the ECTS scale; other factors that may influence ranking can be other academic, GMAT/GRE/CAT scores, extracurricular achievements and special personal achievements. Certified copies of documents of these achievements and a CV must be presented; BI aims for a national and international mix in the student body. Hence, priority may be given to applicants from selected countries, selected partner schools of BI, or enrolled in priority master's programs. Preference is given to applicants seeking to earn their first master's degree.

Funds Avail.: $2,000. **Duration:** Annual. **Number Awarded:** 20 scholarships for international applicants and 10 scholarships for Norwegian applicants. **To Apply:** Applicant must write a scholarship application letter, maximum one page, outlining why applicant is deserving of this scholarship; include the application with your online admission application. **Deadline:** March 1.

1535 ■ American Society for Pharmacology and Experimental Therapeutics (ASPET)

1801 Rockville Pike, Suite 210
Rockville, MD 20852-1633
Ph: (301)634-7060
Fax: (301)634-7061
E-mail: info@aspet.org
URL: www.aspet.org
Social Media: twitter.com/aspet

1536 ■ Paul M. Vanhoutte Distinguished Lectureship in Vascular Pharmacology *(Professional development, Postgraduate/Award)*

Purpose: To recognize individuals for their outstanding contributions in Vascular Pharmacology by covering their travel expenses including registration to the Annual Spring ASPET meeting. **Focus:** Pharmacology. **Qualif.:** There are no restrictions on institutional affiliation, nationality, or age of the candidate, but the recipient must be an active member of the ASPET before receiving the award nomination. Nominations must be made by a member of the ASPET, and no member may nominate more than one candidate per year. The current division chair and secretary/treasurer and the ASPET Council president and secretary/treasurer are ineligible for division awards during their active tenure. **Criteria:** Selection will be made by Award Committee of the Division for Cardiovascular Pharmacology.

Funds Avail.: $1,000 plus $2,000 travel expenses. **Duration:** Biennial. **Number Awarded:** 1. **To Apply:** Applicant must submit a letter of nomination describing the contributions to vascular biology and pharmacology of the candidate that make him/her eligible for this Award with a listing of his/her major contributions (1000 word limit) Up to four additional letters of support describing the candidate's

contributions to vascular biology and pharmacology may also be submitted (uploaded as separate PDFs); A complete curriculum vitae; A brief biographical summary of the candidate and the importance of their work for use in award winner announcements. **Deadline:** September 15. **Remarks:** The award was established to honor Dr. Vanhoutte.

1537 ■ American Society of Plant Taxonomists (ASPT)

University of Wyoming,Department of Botany 3165, 1000 East University Ave.
Laramie, WY 82071
Ph: (307)766-2556
E-mail: aspt@uwyo.edu
URL: aspt.net
Social Media: www.facebook.com/asptsystbot
twitter.com/AmSocPlantTaxon

1538 ■ ASPT General Graduate Student Research Grant Fund *(Master's, Doctorate/Grant)*

Purpose: To support students (both master's and doctoral levels) conducting fieldwork, herbarium travel, and/or laboratory research in any area of plant systematic. **Focus:** Botany.

Duration: Annual. **Number Awarded:** 10 to 15.

1539 ■ American Society of Podiatric Medical Assistants (ASPMA)

109 First Street
Itasca, IL 60143-2114
Fax: (708)715-0071
Free: 888-882-7762
E-mail: aspmaex@aol.com
URL: www.aspma.org
Social Media: www.facebook.com/TheASPMA
twitter.com/aspma

1540 ■ Zelda Walling Vicha Memorial Scholarship *(Undergraduate/Scholarship)*

Purpose: To assist the continuing education of podiatry students. **Focus:** Podiatry. **Qualif.:** Applicants must be fourth year podiatry students throughout the United States. **Criteria:** Selection shall be based on the financial need and high scholastic achievement throughout the podiatric schooling.

Funds Avail.: $2,000 each. **Duration:** Annual. **To Apply:** Applicant must submit the application along with the required documents as follows: official Podiatry School Transcripts; two (2) Letters of Recommendations; copy of Financial Indebtedness from Podiatry School; personal Statement/Biography. **Deadline:** June 15. **Contact:** Tara Brown, PMAC-Scholarship Chair Email: tara.antoinette@gmail.com.

1541 ■ American Society for Quality (ASQ)

600 N Plankinton Ave.
Milwaukee, WI 53203
Ph: (414)272-8575
Fax: (414)272-1734
Free: 800-248-1946
E-mail: help@asq.org
URL: asq.org

Awards are arranged alphabetically below their administering organizations

Social Media: www.facebook.com/ASQ
www.linkedin.com/company/asq
twitter.com/asq
youtube.com/user/ASQhq

1542 ■ Richard A. Freund International Scholarships *(Graduate/Scholarship, Award, Monetary)*

Purpose: To support students for their graduate study of the theory and application of quality control, quality assurance, quality improvement, and total quality management. **Focus:** Quality assurance and control. **Qualif.:** Applicants must be graduate students having a 3.25 GPA or higher; concentration must be in quality control, quality assurance, quality improvement, total quality management or similar quality emphasis. **Criteria:** Selection will be based on the committee's criteria.

Funds Avail.: $5,000. **Duration:** Annual. **Number Awarded:** 1. **Deadline:** April 1. **Remarks:** The scholarship honors the memory of Richard A. Freund, a past president of ASQ.

1543 ■ Ellis R. Ott Scholarships *(Graduate, Master's/Scholarship)*

Purpose: To provide financial assistance to students who are pursuing the degree of statistics and/or quality management field. **Focus:** Quality assurance and control; Statistics. **Qualif.:** Applicants must be students who are planning to enroll or currently enrolled in a masters degree or higher level in US or Canadian program that has concentration in applied statistics and/or quality management. **Criteria:** Recipients are selected based on the following criteria: demonstrated ability; academic achievement, including honors; career objectives; faculty recommendations; involvement in campus activities, including teaching and tutoring; and industrial exposure including part-time work and internships.

Funds Avail.: $7,500. **Duration:** Annual. **To Apply:** Applicants must submit typed complete application form; resume; essay of no longer than one page, typewritten, no smaller than 10-point type, stating qualifications, career goals, reasons for seeking the scholarship; two letters of recommendation from professors in the current or intended field of study. **Deadline:** April 1. **Contact:** E-mail: lynnehare@verizon.net.

1544 ■ American Society for Radiation Oncology (ASTRO)

251 18th St. S, 8th Fl.
Arlington, VA 22202
Ph: (703)502-1550
Fax: (703)502-7852
Free: 800-962-7876
E-mail: communications@astro.org
URL: www.astro.org
Social Media: www.facebook.com/
  AmericanSocietyforRadiationOncology
www.instagram.com/astro_org
www.linkedin.com/company/american-society-for-radiation
  -oncology
twitter.com/ASTRO_org
www.youtube.com/user/ASTROTargetingCancer

1545 ■ ASTRO Junior Faculty Career Research Training Award *(Advanced Professional, Professional development/Award)*

Purpose: To stimulate interest in radiation research early in junior faculty's careers by offering them the opportunity to have focused time for research projects in radiation oncology, biology, physics or outcomes/health services. **Focus:** Oncology. **Qualif.:** Applicants must be active members of ASTRO; must be board-eligible physicians or physicists in radiation oncology or radiobiologists within the first five years of your junior faculty appointment; must provide a rich environment for career development and possesses qualified faculty in clinical, translational or basic research to serve as mentors. **Criteria:** Selection will be based on ASTRO's criteria.

Funds Avail.: $100,000 per year. **Duration:** Annual; two years. **Number Awarded:** 1. **To Apply:** Applicants must visit the website for the online application process. **Deadline:** March 31. **Contact:** Email: research@astro.org.

1546 ■ ASTRO Minority Summer Fellowship Award *(Postgraduate, Professional development/Fellowship, Award)*

Purpose: To introduce medical students from backgrounds that are underrepresented in medicine to the discipline of radiation oncology early in their medical education. **Focus:** Oncology. **Qualif.:** Applicants must be enrolled in a U.S. medical school and be in good standing at the time the application is submitted; must be able to identify a mentor with a successful record of research productivity (more information is in the application); primary mentor or co-mentor should be an ASTRO member. **Criteria:** Selection will be based on ASTRO's criteria.

Funds Avail.: $3,500 stipend for the eight-week training program and $1,000 toward the cost of travel for two students. **Duration:** Annual. **Number Awarded:** 4. **To Apply:** Applicants must visit the website for the online application process; must include head shot (photo in digital form) along application. Letters of commitment from both the mentor and the department chair at the selected institution must accompany the application. The letter of commitment from the mentor should confirm that the institution is able to fund the project. **Deadline:** February 7. **Contact:** Natalie Cain E-mail: natalie.cain@astro.org.

1547 ■ ASTRO Residents/Fellows in Radiation Oncology Research Seed Grant *(Advanced Professional, Professional development/Grant)*

Purpose: To support residents or fellows who are planning a career focusing primarily on basic science or clinical research. **Focus:** Oncology. **Qualif.:** Applicants must show a commitment to a career that focuses primarily on radiation oncology sciences; the institution has a well-established research and clinical career development program and qualified faculty in radiation oncology sciences to serve as mentors; must be an ASTRO member. **Criteria:** Selection will be based on ASTRO's criteria.

Funds Avail.: $25,000 each. **Duration:** Annual; One year. **Number Awarded:** 1. **To Apply:** Applicants must submit a letter from the proposed mentor documenting (1) the need for substitution, (2) the new mentor's qualifications for supervising the program and (3) the level of support for the applicant's career development. The letter must also document that the specific aims of the research program will remain within the scope of the original peer reviewed research program. **Deadline:** February 15.

1548 ■ ASTRO/ROI Comparative Effectiveness Research Awards *(Professional development/Award)*

Purpose: To develop comparative effectiveness research leaders within radiation oncology and to stimulate research

Awards are arranged alphabetically below their administering organizations

focused on evaluating the effectiveness, complication profile, cost and cost-effectiveness of various radiation therapy treatments, as well as the comparative effectiveness when compared to other therapies. **Focus:** Oncology. **Qualif.:** Applicants must be active members of ASTRO; must be employed by a recognized U.S. research university at the time the application is submitted; must be a board-certified or board-eligible physician or physicist in radiation oncology or a radiobiologist at the time the award commences; must show a commitment to a career that focuses primarily on academic radiation oncology; research must be conducted at a recognized U.S. research university with qualified faculty in comparative effectiveness or similar research to serve as mentors if necessary. **Criteria:** Selection will be based on ASTRO's criteria.

Funds Avail.: $50,000 per year. **Duration:** Annual; up to two years. **Number Awarded:** 1. **To Apply:** Applicants must visit the website for the online application process. **Deadline:** March 27. **Contact:** ASTRO Research Department at research@astro.org.

1549 ■ American Society of Radiologic Technologists Education and Research Foundation (ASRT)

15000 Central Ave. SE
Albuquerque, NM 87123-3909
Fax: (505)298-5063
Free: 800-444-2778
E-mail: foundation@asrt.org
URL: foundation.asrt.org
Social Media: www.facebook.com/asrtfoundation
www.linkedin.com/company/asrt-foundation

1550 ■ ASRT Research Grants (Professional development/Grant)

Purpose: To support research and analysis of issues that affect the radiologic sciences. **Focus:** Radiology. **Qualif.:** Applicants must be radiologic technologists or radiation therapists; must be ASRT members who are also registered with the American Registry of Radiologic Technologists or ASRT members who hold an unrestricted state license; proposed research projects must be for a period not to exceed two years; acceptable areas of research include radiation therapy, dosimetry, medical imaging, and radiologic science education and administration. **Criteria:** Selection will be based on significant/relevance to the profession; qualification/resources of the principal investigator and associated personnel; adequate demonstration of study protocols, assurances and agreements; appropriateness of methodology/experimental design; soundness of budget; thoroughness of literature review.

Funds Avail.: Up to $3,000 (new researcher); up to $4,000 (emerging researcher); up to $10,000-$25,000 (research). **Duration:** Annual. **To Apply:** Applicants must complete and submit the full proposal via email or mail; prior to submitting the full proposal, applicants may submit a letter of intent for preliminary review of their proposal concept; letters of intent are reviewed by the ASRT Research Department and feedback will be provided regarding the proposed research relevancy, objective and methodology. Details for specific grant levels are available at: foundation.asrt.org/what-we-do/research-grants.

1551 ■ Jerman-Cahoon Student Scholarship (Undergraduate/Scholarship)

Purpose: To provide resources for radiologic technologists intending to improve patient care and to support education

and research in the radiologic sciences. **Focus:** Radiology. **Qualif.:** Applicants must be entry-level students in radiography, sonography, magnetic resonance, or nuclear medicine who are U.S. citizens, national or permanent residents enrolled in an accredited radiologic science program; must be ASRT members and have a minimum program GPA of 3.0 on a 4.0 scale (B average).

Funds Avail.: $2,500 each. **Duration:** Annual. **Number Awarded:** 8. **To Apply:** Application details are available online at: foundation.asrt.org/what-we-do/scholarships. **Remarks:** The American Society of Radiologic Technologists established the Jerman-Cahoon Student Scholarship in honor of Edward C. Jerman, founder of the Society, and John B. Cahoon Jr., former ASRT president and one of the most highly respected educators the profession ever produced.

1552 ■ Royce Osborn Minority Scholarship (Undergraduate/Scholarship)

Purpose: To assist minority students in an entry-level radiography, sonography, magnetic resonance, radiation therapy, or nuclear medicine program. **Focus:** Radiology. **Qualif.:** Applicants must be students attending entry-level radiologic sciences program who are U.S. citizens, national or permanent residents enrolled in an accredited radiologic science program; must be ASRT members and have a minimum program GPA of 3.0 on a 4.0 scale (B average).

Funds Avail.: $4,000 each. **Duration:** Annual. **Number Awarded:** 5. **To Apply:** Application details are available online at: foundation.asrt.org/what-we-do/scholarships. **Remarks:** Created in honor of Royce Osborn and is funded through an endowment from the ASRT, as well as through contributions from individual donors.

1553 ■ Siemens Clinical Advancement Scholarship (Master's, Doctorate, Professional development/Scholarship)

Purpose: To assist medical imaging professionals seeking to enhance their clinical practice skills and provide excellent patient care. **Focus:** Radiology. **Qualif.:** Applicants must be students attending professional-level radiologic sciences program; must be ASRT members who have applied to or are currently attending an accredited degree or certificate program; must attend bachelor's, or master's degree program in radiologic sciences or certificate in a specialty discipline such as CT, MR, or sonography to enhance their clinical practice skills and provide excellent patient care.

Funds Avail.: $5,000 each. **Duration:** Annual. **Number Awarded:** 4. **To Apply:** Application details are available online at: foundation.asrt.org/what-we-do/scholarships. **Remarks:** Funded by Siemens Healthcare.

1554 ■ Varian Radiation Therapy Advancement Scholarship (Master's, Doctorate, Professional development/Scholarship)

Purpose: To ensure radiation therapists and medical dosimetrists can afford education that enhances their clinical practice skills and helps them provide excellent patient care. **Focus:** Radiology. **Qualif.:** Applicants must be students attending professional-level radiologic sciences program; must be ASRT members who have applied to or are currently be attending an accredited degree or certificate program. Those who attend certificate, bachelor's, master's or doctoral degree program to enhance their clinical practice skills and provide excellent patient care are

Awards are arranged alphabetically below their administering organizations

also eligible. Current medical imaging technologists pursuing a certificate in radiation therapy also qualify for this scholarship.

Funds Avail.: $5,000 (8 awards); $2,500 (1 award). **Duration:** Annual. **Number Awarded:** 9. **To Apply:** Application details are available online at: foundation.asrt.org/what-we-do/scholarships. **Remarks:** Funded by Varian Medical Systems because it believes in the power of education to make a difference for radiation therapists, as well as their patients.

1555 ■ American Society of Regional Anesthesia and Pain Medicine (ASRA)
3 Penn Center W, Ste. 224
Pittsburgh, PA 15276
Ph: (412)471-2718
Free: 855-795-ASRA
E-mail: asraassistant@asra.com
URL: www.asra.com
Social Media: www.facebook.com/asrameetings
www.instagram.com/asra_society
twitter.com/asra_society
www.youtube.com/channel/
  UClsMVW3YQLRJqK1iQjnV06A

1556 ■ Chronic Pain Medicine Research Grant
(Professional development/Grant)

Purpose: To promote and facilitate high quality research in pain medicine. **Focus:** Medicine. **Qualif.:** Applicants must be North American physician members of ASRA. **Criteria:** Selection will be based on the ASRA Research Committee's criteria.

Funds Avail.: Up to $200,000. **Duration:** Annual. **To Apply:** Applicants must provide letter from the chair of the department confirming the availability of time and facilities for the project; budget; applicant's and co-investigator's curriculum vitae with a listing of any past or present research support; and research plan (the components can be verified at the website); applications should be submitted in a PDF (electronic form) form. **Deadline:** May 1. **Contact:** E-mail: asraassistant@asra.com.

1557 ■ Carl Koller Memorial Research Grants
(Professional development/Grant)

Purpose: To support clinical and laboratory studies related to any aspect of regional anesthesia and analgesia and their application to surgery. **Focus:** Anesthesiology. **Qualif.:** Applicants must be North American physician members of ASRA. **Criteria:** Selection will be based on the ASRA Research Committee's criteria.

Funds Avail.: Maximum of $200,000. **Duration:** Annual. **To Apply:** Applicants must provide letter from the chair of the department confirming the availability of time and facilities for the project; budget; applicant's curriculum vitae with a listing of any past or present research support; and research plan (the components can be verified at the website); applications should be submitted in a PDF (electronic form) form. **Deadline:** August 15. **Contact:** Phone: 412-471-2718; E-mail: asraassistant@asra.com.

1558 ■ American Society of Safety Professionals
520 N Northwest Hwy.
Park Ridge, IL 60068
Ph: (847)699-2929

E-mail: customerservice@assp.org
URL: www.assp.org
Social Media: www.facebook.com/ASSESafety
www.linkedin.com/company/american-society-of-safety
  -professionals
twitter.com/ASSPSafety

1559 ■ ASSP Diversity Committee Scholarship
(Doctorate/Scholarship)

Purpose: To provide financial support to deserving students. **Focus:** Occupational safety and health. **Qualif.:** Applicants must seeking a degree in occupational safety & health or a closely related field; must have a GPA of 3.0 if applying as an undergraduate and 3.5 if applying as a graduate; enrolled in a OSH safety program. **Criteria:** Selection of applicants will be based on academic performance, leadership activity, motivation for entering the filed and letter of recommendation.

To Apply: Applicant must include APS Prizes and Awards nomination form; name and address of the candidate; a statement of the candidate's contribution to the research; a letter of support from the candidate's Ph.D. dissertation advisor; two additional letters of support from physicists familiar with the candidate and the research; a copy of the candidate's dissertation; demographics form. **Deadline:** December 1. **Contact:** Email: asspfoundation@assp.org; Phone: 847-699-2929.

1560 ■ ASSP Foundation Academic Scholarship Program *(Undergraduate, Graduate, Doctorate, Vocational/Occupational/Scholarship)*

Purpose: To support the educational efforts of students enrolled in an Occupational Safety and Health-related major. **Focus:** Occupational safety and health. **Qualif.:** Applicants must seeking a degree in occupational safety & health or a closely related field; must have a GPA of 3.0 if applying as an undergraduate and 3.5 if applying as a graduate; enrolled in a OSH safety program. **Criteria:** Selection of applicants will be based on academic performance, leadership activity, motivation for entering the field and letter of recommendation; awardees will be matched with an award based on the criteria set forth by the fund's donor.

Funds Avail.: $1,000 to $15,000. **Duration:** Annual. **Number Awarded:** Around 100 awards annually. **To Apply:** Applicants must submit one letter of recommendation with the option of including two additional letters. **Deadline:** December 1. **Contact:** URL: https://foundation.assp.org/scholarships-and-grants; Email: asspfoundation@assp.org; Phone: 847-699-2929.

1561 ■ ASSP Foundation Professional Education Grant Program *(Professional development/Grant)*

Purpose: To support the continuing education and professional development efforts of OSH professionals working in an Occupational Safety and Health-related career. **Focus:** Occupational safety and health. **Qualif.:** Applicants must be working professionals in an occupational safety & health or a closely-related field. **Criteria:** Selection of applicants is based on leadership, activity within the safety field, letters of recommendation, quality of application; awardees will be matched with an award based on the criteria set forth by the fund's donor.

Funds Avail.: $250 to $2,500. **Duration:** Annual. **Number Awarded:** Around 30 awards annually. **To Apply:** Applicant must complete application available online; provide

Awards are arranged alphabetically below their administering organizations

documentation of professional education. **Deadline:** December 1. **Contact:** URL: https://foundation.assp.org/scholarships-and-grants; Email: asspfoundation@assp.org; Phone: 847-699-2929.

1562 ■ Warren K. Brown Scholarship
(Undergraduate/Scholarship)

Purpose: To provide financial support to deserving students. **Focus:** Occupational safety and health. **Qualif.:** Applicants must seeking a degree in occupational safety & health or a closely related field; must have a GPA of 3.0 if applying as an undergraduate and 3.5 if applying as a graduate; enrolled in a OSH safety program. **Criteria:** Selection of applicants will be based on academic performance, leadership activity, motivation for entering the filed and letter of recommendation.

Deadline: December 1. **Contact:** Email: asspfoundation@assp.org; Phone: 847-699-2929.

1563 ■ Central Indiana Jim Kriner Memorial Scholarship *(Undergraduate/Scholarship)*

Purpose: To provide financial support to deserving students. **Focus:** Occupational safety and health. **Qualif.:** Applicants must seeking a degree in occupational safety & health or a closely related field; must have a GPA of 3.0 if applying as an undergraduate and 3.5 if applying as a graduate; enrolled in a OSH safety program. **Criteria:** Selection of applicants will be based on academic performance, leadership activity, motivation for entering the filed and letter of recommendation.

To Apply: Applicant must include APS Prizes and Awards nomination form; name and address of the candidate; a statement of the candidate's contribution to the research; a letter of support from the candidate's Ph.D. dissertation advisor; two additional letters of support from physicists familiar with the candidate and the research; a copy of the candidate's dissertation; demographics form. **Deadline:** December 1. **Contact:** Email: asspfoundation@assp.org; Phone: 847-699-2929.

1564 ■ Scott Dominguez - Craters of the Moon Chapter Scholarship *(Graduate, Undergraduate/Scholarship)*

Purpose: To provide financial support to deserving students. **Focus:** Occupational safety and health. **Qualif.:** Applicants must seeking a degree in occupational safety & health or a closely related field; must have a GPA of 3.0 if applying as an undergraduate and 3.5 if applying as a graduate; enrolled in a OSH safety program. **Criteria:** Selection of applicants will be based on academic performance, leadership activity, motivation for entering the filed and letter of recommendation.

To Apply: Applicant must include APS Prizes and Awards nomination form; name and address of the candidate; a statement of the candidate's contribution to the research; a letter of support from the candidate's Ph.D. dissertation advisor; two additional letters of support from physicists familiar with the candidate and the research; a copy of the candidate's dissertation; demographics form. **Deadline:** December 1. **Contact:** Email: asspfoundation@assp.org; Phone: 847-699-2929.

1565 ■ David Iden Memorial Safety Scholarships
(Undergraduate/Scholarship)

Purpose: To provide financial support to students who seek higher education. **Focus:** Occupational safety and health.

Qualif.: Applicant must be a student pursuing an undergraduate degree in occupational safety & health or a closely related field. **Criteria:** Selection of applicants will be based on the scholarship application criteria.

Funds Avail.: Varies. **Duration:** Annual. **To Apply:** Applicant must submit a transcript of records; verification by a safety faculty member; student's narrative; certification; and must attach a letter of recommendation.

1566 ■ Southwest Chapter Roy Kinslow Scholarship *(Undergraduate/Scholarship)*

Purpose: To provide financial support to deserving students. **Focus:** Occupational safety and health. **Qualif.:** Applicants must seeking a degree in occupational safety & health or a closely related field; must have a GPA of 3.0 if applying as an undergraduate and 3.5 if applying as a graduate; enrolled in a OSH safety program. **Criteria:** Selection of applicants will be based on academic performance, leadership activity, motivation for entering the filed and letter of recommendation.

To Apply: Applicant must include APS Prizes and Awards nomination form; name and address of the candidate; a statement of the candidate's contribution to the research; a letter of support from the candidate's Ph.D. dissertation advisor; two additional letters of support from physicists familiar with the candidate and the research; a copy of the candidate's dissertation; demographics form. **Deadline:** December 1. **Contact:** Email: asspfoundation@assp.org; Phone: 847-699-2929.

1567 ■ James P. Kohn Memorial Scholarship
(Doctorate/Scholarship)

Purpose: To provide financial support to deserving students. **Focus:** Occupational safety and health. **Qualif.:** Applicants must seeking a degree in occupational safety & health or a closely related field; must have a GPA of 3.0 if applying as an undergraduate and 3.5 if applying as a graduate; enrolled in a OSH safety program. **Criteria:** Selection of applicants will be based on academic performance, leadership activity, motivation for entering the filed and letter of recommendation.

To Apply: Applicant must include APS Prizes and Awards nomination form; name and address of the candidate; a statement of the candidate's contribution to the research; a letter of support from the candidate's Ph.D. dissertation advisor; two additional letters of support from physicists familiar with the candidate and the research; a copy of the candidate's dissertation; demographics form. **Deadline:** December 1. **Contact:** Email: asspfoundation@assp.org; Phone: 847-699-2929.

1568 ■ Liberty Mutual Scholarships *(Undergraduate/Scholarship)*

Purpose: To provide financial support to deserving students. **Focus:** Occupational safety and health. **Qualif.:** Applicants must seeking a degree in occupational safety & health or a closely related field; must have a GPA of 3.0 if applying as an undergraduate and 3.5 if applying as a graduate; enrolled in a OSH safety program. **Criteria:** Selection of applicants will be based on academic performance, leadership activity, motivation for entering the filed and letter of recommendation.

Funds Avail.: $10,000 each. **To Apply:** Applicant must include APS Prizes and Awards nomination form; name and address of the candidate; a statement of the candidate's contribution to the research; a letter of support from

Awards are arranged alphabetically below their administering organizations

the candidate's Ph.D. dissertation advisor; two additional letters of support from physicists familiar with the candidate and the research; a copy of the candidate's dissertation; demographics form. **Deadline:** December 1. **Contact:** Email: asspfoundation@assp.org; Phone: 847-699-2929.

1569 ■ Marsh Risk Consulting Scholarships
(Undergraduate/Scholarship)

Purpose: To provide financial support to students who seek higher education. **Focus:** Occupational safety and health. **Qualif.:** Applicant must be a student pursuing an undergraduate degree in occupational safety & health or a closely related field. **Criteria:** Selection of applicants will be based on the scholarship application criteria.

Funds Avail.: $1,500. **Number Awarded:** 1. **To Apply:** Applicant must submit a transcript of records; verification by a safety faculty member; student's narrative; certification; and must attach a letter of recommendation.

1570 ■ North Florida Chapter Safety Education Scholarships *(Undergraduate/Scholarship)*

Purpose: To provide financial support to deserving students. **Focus:** Occupational safety and health. **Qualif.:** Applicants must seeking a degree in occupational safety & health or a closely related field; must have a GPA of 3.0 if applying as an undergraduate and 3.5 if applying as a graduate; enrolled in a OSH safety program. **Criteria:** Selection of applicants will be based on academic performance, leadership activity, motivation for entering the filed and letter of recommendation.

To Apply: Applicant must include APS Prizes and Awards nomination form; name and address of the candidate; a statement of the candidate's contribution to the research; a letter of support from the candidate's Ph.D. dissertation advisor; two additional letters of support from physicists familiar with the candidate and the research; a copy of the candidate's dissertation; demographics form. **Deadline:** December 1. **Contact:** Email: asspfoundation@assp.org; Phone: 847-699-2929.

1571 ■ Harold F. Polston Scholarships *(Graduate, Undergraduate/Scholarship)*

Purpose: To provide financial support to deserving students. **Focus:** Occupational safety and health. **Qualif.:** Applicants must seeking a degree in occupational safety & health or a closely related field; must have a GPA of 3.0 if applying as an undergraduate and 3.5 if applying as a graduate; enrolled in a OSH safety program. **Criteria:** Selection of applicants will be based on academic performance, leadership activity, motivation for entering the filed and letter of recommendation.

To Apply: Applicants must complete the online application page in their website. **Deadline:** December 1. **Contact:** Email: asspfoundation@assp.org; Phone: 847-699-2929.

1572 ■ Harry Taback 9/11 Memorial Scholarships *(Undergraduate/Scholarship)*

Purpose: To provide financial support to deserving students. **Focus:** Occupational safety and health. **Qualif.:** Applicants must seeking a degree in occupational safety & health or a closely related field; must have a GPA of 3.0 if applying as an undergraduate and 3.5 if applying as a graduate; enrolled in a OSH safety program. **Criteria:** Selection of applicants will be based on academic performance, leadership activity, motivation for entering the filed and letter of recommendation.

To Apply: Applicants must complete the online application page in their website. **Deadline:** December 1. **Contact:** Email: asspfoundation@assp.org; Phone: 847-699-2929.

1573 ■ Thompson Scholarship for Women in Safety *(Doctorate/Scholarship)*

Purpose: To provide financial support to deserving students. **Focus:** Engineering; Environmental technology; Fires and fire prevention; Industrial hygiene; Medicine; Occupational safety and health; Risk management. **Qualif.:** Applicants must seeking a degree in occupational safety & health or a closely related field; must have a GPA of 3.0 if applying as an undergraduate and 3.5 if applying as a graduate; enrolled in a OSH safety program. **Criteria:** Selection of applicants will be based on academic performance, leadership activity, motivation for entering the filed and letter of recommendation.

To Apply: Applicant must include APS Prizes and Awards nomination form; name and address of the candidate; a statement of the candidate's contribution to the research; a letter of support from the candidate's Ph.D. dissertation advisor; two additional letters of support from physicists familiar with the candidate and the research; a copy of the candidate's dissertation; demographics form. **Deadline:** December 1. **Contact:** Email: asspfoundation@assp.org; Phone: 847-699-2929.

1574 ■ UPS Diversity Scholarship *(Undergraduate/Scholarship)*

Purpose: To provide financial support to deserving students. **Focus:** Occupational safety and health. **Qualif.:** Applicants must seeking a degree in occupational safety & health or a closely related field; must have a GPA of 3.0 if applying as an undergraduate and 3.5 if applying as a graduate; enrolled in a OSH safety program. **Criteria:** Selection of applicants will be based on academic performance, leadership activity, motivation for entering the filed and letter of recommendation.

Funds Avail.: $5,250 each. **To Apply:** Applicant must include APS Prizes and Awards nomination form; name and address of the candidate; a statement of the candidate's contribution to the research; a letter of support from the candidate's Ph.D. dissertation advisor; two additional letters of support from physicists familiar with the candidate and the research; a copy of the candidate's dissertation; demographics form. **Deadline:** December 1. **Contact:** Email: asspfoundation@assp.org; Phone: 847-699-2929.

1575 ■ William C. Ray, CIH, CSP Arizona Scholarship *(Doctorate/Scholarship)*

Purpose: To provide financial support to deserving students. **Focus:** Occupational safety and health. **Qualif.:** Applicants must seeking a degree in occupational safety & health or a closely related field; must have a GPA of 3.0 if applying as an undergraduate and 3.5 if applying as a graduate; enrolled in a OSH safety program. **Criteria:** Selection of applicants will be based on academic performance, leadership activity, motivation for entering the filed and letter of recommendation.

Funds Avail.: $3,000. **Number Awarded:** 1. **To Apply:** Applicant must include APS Prizes and Awards nomination form; name and address of the candidate; a statement of the candidate's contribution to the research; a letter of support from the candidate's Ph.D. dissertation advisor; two additional letters of support from physicists familiar with the candidate and the research; a copy of the candidate's dissertation; demographics form. **Deadline:** December 1. **Con-**

Awards are arranged alphabetically below their administering organizations

tact: Email: asspfoundation@assp.org; Phone: 847-699-2929.

1576 ■ American Society for Theatre Research (ASTR)

1000 Westgate Dr., Ste. 252
Saint Paul, MN 55114
Ph: (628)222-4088
E-mail: info@astr.org
URL: www.astr.org
Social Media: www.facebook.com/groups/
  1815561312006986/about

1577 ■ ASTR Research Fellowships *(Doctorate/Fellowship)*

Purpose: To underwrite some of the research expenses of scholars undertaking projects significant to the field of theatre and/or performance studies. **Focus:** Performing arts; Theater arts. **Qualif.:** Applicants must be holding a terminal degree and a member of ASTR for at least three years; rank and institutional affiliation are not considered. **Criteria:** Selection will be based on merit of the project within the field of theater/performance studies; individual scholar's academic research endeavors.

Funds Avail.: Up to $3,000. **Number Awarded:** Varies. **To Apply:** Applicants must submit a 150-word abstract of the project; a longer narrative description of the project indicating its procedures, goals and significance; a budget for the project, indicating the portion of expenses that ASTR funds will be used to underwrite, such as travel, reproductions, etc.; a two-page curriculum vitae. **Deadline:** July 16. **Contact:** Please direct questions to Committee Chair Arnab Banerji at arnab.banerji@lmu.edu.

1578 ■ Helen Krich Chinoy Dissertation Fellowship *(Doctorate/Fellowship)*

Purpose: To assist PhD candidates with the expenses of travel to national and international collections to conduct research projects connected with their dissertations. **Focus:** Theater arts. **Qualif.:** Applicants must be Ph.D. candidates who have begun working on their dissertations; the project must be part of the dissertation research. **Criteria:** Selection will be based on clarity, critical rigor, originality.

Funds Avail.: $3,000. **Duration:** Annual. **Number Awarded:** 3. **To Apply:** Applicant must submit the completed application consists of 500-word description of the proposed project, including specific information about the nature of the project, a research strategy, the current status of the project, and a rationale for the project in terms of its contribution to the discipline; a statement describing how the award will be used (i.e., a research budget and detailed summary of travel costs that will be allayed by the award) and how the research award will help the project; a curriculum vitae, including information on academic training and foreign languages relevant to the area of research; a statement of the dissertation timeline, including projected filing date; a verification statement from the dissertation chair, confirming that the applicant is in the dissertation research phase, and approving of the projected filing date indicated in the timeline; this should include the dissertation chair's signature and should be submitted by the applicant with the other application materials. **Deadline:** July 16. **Remarks:** Established in 1995.

1579 ■ Thomas Marshall Graduate Student Awards *(Postgraduate/Grant, Award)*

Purpose: To encourage students to become active members of the Society. **Focus:** General studies/Field of study not specified; Theater arts. **Qualif.:** Applicants must be an student in academic department at any level of higher education is eligible; students need not be members of ASTR at the time of application. **Criteria:** Selection will be based on the committee's criteria.

Funds Avail.: $800. **Duration:** Annual. **Number Awarded:** 3. **To Apply:** Applicants must submit a single-page essay (under 350 words, with 1.5 line spacing, 12-point type, and 1-inch margins) explaining the value of attending the next ASTR meeting to your career; a copy of curriculum vitae. **Remarks:** The Award is given in honor of the late Thomas F. Marshall.

1580 ■ American Society of Travel Agents (ASTA)

675 N Washington St., Ste. 490
Alexandria, VA 22314
Free: 800-275-2782
URL: www.asta.org
Social Media: www.facebook.com/ASTATravelAdvisors
www.instagram.com/astatraveladvisors
www.linkedin.com/company/american-society-of-travel
  -advisors
twitter.com/ASTAAdvisors
www.youtube.com/user/ASTAsVideos

1581 ■ America Express Travel Scholarships *(Undergraduate/Scholarship)*

Purpose: To encourage the pursuit of education and the growth and development of tomorrow's travel/tourism work force. **Focus:** Travel and tourism. **Qualif.:** Applicants must be travel/tourism students in either a two or four-year college/university or propriety travel school; have at least 3.0 GPA on a 4.0 scale; have relevant training in basic statistics or other social research method courses; have at least basic computer skills; and, be residents, citizens, or legal aliens of the United States or Canada. **Criteria:** Recipients will be selected based on academic standing.

Funds Avail.: $1,000. **Duration:** Annual. **Number Awarded:** 1. **To Apply:** Applicants must submit a proof of enrollment/acceptance at a travel school, community/junior college, college or university; an official school-printed description or listing of the curriculum where they enrolled; proof of enrollments in travel and tourism courses, or letter from business colleague that can attest to each of the applicant's desire to pursue a career in the travel and tourism industry; four identical collated copies of applications and required materials (one original and three photocopies); and a 500-word statement detailing the student's plans in travel and tourism as well as the student's view of the travel industry's future. **Deadline:** July 31.

1582 ■ ASTA Alaska Airlines Scholarships *(Undergraduate/Scholarship)*

Purpose: To encourage people to go into the travel and tourism business as their profession. **Focus:** Travel and tourism. **Qualif.:** Applicants must be travel/tourism students in either a four-year college/university or propriety travel school; have at least 3.0 GPA on a 4.0 scale; have relevant training in basic statistics or other social research method courses; have at least basic computer skills; and, be residents, citizens, or legal aliens of the United States or Canada. **Criteria:** Recipients will be selected based on academic standing.

Funds Avail.: $50. **Duration:** Annual. **Number Awarded:** 1. **To Apply:** Applicants must submit proof of enrollment/

Awards are arranged alphabetically below their administering organizations

acceptance at a travel school, community/junior college, college or university; an official school-printed description or listing of the curriculum where they are enrolled; proof of enrollments in travel and tourism courses, or letter from business colleague that can attest to each of the applicant's desire to pursue a career in the travel and tourism industry; four identical collated copies of applications and required materials (one original and three photocopies); and a 500-word paper on why the applicant is pursuing a career in the travel and tourism industry, which must include at least two career goals. **Deadline:** April 1. **Remarks:** Established in 2006.

1583 ■ ASTA Holland America Line Graduate Research Scholarships *(Graduate/Scholarship)*

Purpose: To provide funding support to research projects in the travel and tourism field. **Focus:** Travel and tourism. **Qualif.:** Applicants must be graduate students who are residents, citizens, or legal aliens of the United States or Canada and have a cumulative or overall minimum 3.0 grade point average. **Criteria:** Selection will be based on the aforesaid qualifications and compliance with the application process.

Funds Avail.: $4,000. **Duration:** Annual. **Number Awarded:** 1. **To Apply:** Applicants must submit the following: a proof of enrollment/acceptance at a travel school, community/junior college, or university; an official school-printed description or listing of the curriculum where applicants are enrolled; a proof of enrollment in travel and tourism courses; and a letter of recommendation from a professor, employer, or business colleague that can attest to each of the applicant's desire to pursue a career in the travel and tourism industry. **Deadline:** April 1.

1584 ■ ASTA Rigby, Healy, Simmons Scholarships *(Graduate, Undergraduate/Scholarship)*

Purpose: To encourage serious academic study in the field of travel and tourism. **Focus:** Travel and tourism. **Qualif.:** Applicants must be travel/tourism students in either a four-year college/university or propriety travel school; have at least 3.0 GPA on a 4.0 scale; have relevant training in basic statistics or other social research method courses; must have at least basic computer skills; and, be residents, citizens, or legal aliens of the United States or Canada. **Criteria:** Recipients will be selected based on academic standing.

Funds Avail.: $2,000. **Duration:** Annual. **Number Awarded:** 1. **To Apply:** Applicants must submit a proof of enrollment/acceptance at a travel school, community/junior college, college or university; an official school-printed description or listing of the curriculum where they are enrolled; proof of enrollments in travel and tourism courses, or letter from business colleague that can attest to each of the applicant's desire to pursue a career in the travel and tourism industry; four identical collated copies of applications and required materials (one original and three photocopies); and a 500-word statement suggesting improvements in the travel industry. **Deadline:** April 1.

1585 ■ Avis Budget Group Scholarships *(Graduate/Scholarship)*

Purpose: To help future travel professionals meet the need for broader business management skills, beyond those dealing solely with travel and tourism issues. **Focus:** Travel and tourism. **Qualif.:** Applicants must have a minimum of two years of full-time travel industry experience or an undergraduate degree in travel/tourism. They may be cur-

rently employed in the travel industry, or be currently enrolled in a minimum of two courses per semester in an accredited undergraduate or graduate level degree program in business or equivalent degree program. **Criteria:** Recipients will be selected based on merit.

Funds Avail.: $2,000. **Duration:** Annual. **Number Awarded:** 1. **To Apply:** Applicants must provide a proof of current employment in the travel industry; transcript from last academic term with proof of a GPA of 3.0 on a 4.0 scale, or if the applicants are returning to school after time spent in the workforce, they should submit a cover letter explaining why they are returning to school. Applicants must submit transcript showing a GPA of 3.0 on 4.0 scale; and a brief essay (500-750 words) explaining how the degree program relates to applicant's future career in the travel industry. **Deadline:** April 1.

1586 ■ David J. Hallissey Memorial Internships *(Graduate, Undergraduate/Internship)*

Purpose: To encourage academic research in the tourism field. **Focus:** Travel and tourism. **Qualif.:** Applicants must be travel/tourism students from Washington, DC metro area colleges/universities in undergraduate or graduate travel or tourism programs; have at least 3.0 GPA on a 4.0 scale; have relevant training in basic statistics or other social research method courses; have at least basic computer skills; and, be residents, citizens, or legal aliens of the United States or Canada. **Criteria:** Recipients will be selected based on academic standing.

Funds Avail.: $2,000. **Duration:** Annual. **Number Awarded:** 1. **To Apply:** Applicants must submit a proof of enrollment/acceptance at a travel school, community/junior college, college or university; an official school-printed description or listing of the curriculum where they are enrolled; proof of enrollment in travel and tourism courses, or letter from a business colleague that can attest to each of the applicant's desire to pursue a career in the travel and tourism industry. Complete application must consist of four identical collated copies of applications and required materials (one original and three photocopies). **Deadline:** April 1.

1587 ■ George Reinke Scholarships *(Other/Scholarship)*

Purpose: To support travel and tourism industry professionals who were completing their industry certification programs. **Focus:** Travel and tourism. **Qualif.:** Applicants must be travel/tourism students in either a two or four-year college/university or propriety travel school; have at least 3.0 GPA on a 4.0 scale; have a relevant training in basic statistics or other social research method courses; have at least basic computer skills; and, be residents, citizens, or legal aliens of the United States or Canada. **Criteria:** Recipients will be selected based on academic standing.

Funds Avail.: No specific amount. **Duration:** Annual. **Number Awarded:** 2. **To Apply:** Applicants must submit proof of enrollment/acceptance at a travel school, community/junior college, college or university; an official school-printed description or listing of the curriculum where they are enrolled; proof of enrollments in travel and tourism courses, or letter from business colleague that can attest to each of the applicant's desire to pursue a career in the travel and tourism industry; four identical collated copies of applications and required materials (one original and three photocopies); and a 500-word paper explaining why applicant needs the scholarship. **Deadline:** Dec 18. **Remarks:** The scholarship was established by George Reinke of

Awards are arranged alphabetically below their administering organizations

Travel Unlimited (late Trans Mark Travel). He was a long-term ASTA member from Tulsa, Oklahoma, was an area director in 1980-84 and was on the ASTA Board and Southwest Chapter President in 1974-75.

1588 ■ Allegheny Branch of Mid-America Chapter - Nancy Stewart Professional Development Scholarships *(Professional development/Scholarship)*

Purpose: To fund research projects in the travel and tourism field. **Focus:** Travel and tourism. **Qualif.:** Applicant must be a U.S permanent resident; must have a minimum of 2 years of experience in the travel industry; have successfully completed the ASTA program; must be a member of the ASTA Allegheny Branch of the Mid-America chapter (Western Pennsylvania as far east as Altoona & West Virginal).**Criteria:** Recipients are selected based on the academic standing.

Funds Avail.: $3,000. **Duration:** Annual. **To Apply:** Applicant must provide a proof of current employment in the travel industry; transcript from last academic term with proof of a GPA of 3.0 on a 4.0 scale or if the applicant is returning to school after time spent in the workforce, submit a cover letter explaining why applicant is returning to school; a letter of intent to enroll in a Travel Institute course within one year and explaining what benefits they hope to obtain from the Travel Institute program or an application to the ASTA educational program; a letter of recommendation from the official ASTA employer to confirm the employment status; and an original headshot picture. **Deadline:** November 3.

1589 ■ American Sociological Association (ASA)
1430 K St. NW, Ste. 600
Washington, DC 20005
Ph: (202)383-9005
E-mail: asa@asanet.org
URL: www.asanet.org
Social Media: www.facebook.com/
 AmericanSociologicalAssociation
twitter.com/ASANews

1590 ■ ASA Minority Fellowship Program (ASA MFP) *(Doctorate/Fellowship)*

Purpose: To support minority doctoral students who have strong interests in and commitment to a research career in sociology. **Focus:** Medicine; Psychology; Sociology. **Qualif.:** Applicants must be U.S. citizens, non-citizen nationals of the U.S., been lawfully admitted to the U.S. for permanent residence, or are eligible under DACA; members of any underrepresented racial/ethnic minority group in the U.S. (e.g. Blacks/African-Americans, Hispanics/Latinos, Asians or Pacific Islanders, or American Indians/Alaska Natives); and, enrolled in (and have completed one full academic year) in a program that grants the Ph.D. in sociology. **Criteria:** Selection will be based on their commitment to research, the focus of their research experience, academic achievement, scholarship, writing ability, research potential, financial need, and racial/ethnic minority background.

Funds Avail.: $18,000. **Duration:** Annual; every August 1 to July 31. **To Apply:** Applicants package must include: fellowship application; essays; three recommendation letters of which one should be from the mentor; official transcripts from all the undergraduate and graduate institutions that applicant has been enrolled in; curriculum vitae. **Deadline:** January 31. **Contact:** ASA Minority Fellowship Program; E-mail: diversity@asanet.org.

1591 ■ ASA Student Forum Travel Awards *(Undergraduate, Graduate/Award)*

Purpose: To assist students by defraying the expenses associated with attending the ASA Annual Meeting. **Focus:** Sociology. **Qualif.:** Applicants must be students pursuing an undergraduate or graduate sociology degree in an academic institution and current student members of ASA at the time of application; Participation in the Annual Meeting program. **Criteria:** Selection will be based on the following participation in the Annual Meeting program (e.g., paper sessions, roundtables); purpose for attending (e.g., workshop training, Honors Program participation); student financial need; availability of other forms of support, matching funds; and potential benefit to the students.

Funds Avail.: $250 each. **Duration:** Annual. **Number Awarded:** 40. **To Apply:** Applicants must complete the application form (in PDF file) and send via email or print out and mail one hard copy. **Deadline:** April 1. **Remarks:** Established in 1998. **Contact:** ASA Executive Office; Phone: 202-383-9005, ext. 322; E-mail: studentforum@ asanet.org.

1592 ■ American Sokol Organization (ASO)
9126 Ogden Ave.
Brookfield, IL 60513-1943
Ph: (708)255-5397
URL: american-sokol.org
Social Media: www.facebook.com/americansokol
twitter.com/AmericanSokol

1593 ■ American Sokol Merit Award *(Undergraduate/ Scholarship, Recognition)*

Purpose: To help incoming students pursue their studies in college. **Focus:** Education, Physical; Physical sciences. **Qualif.:** The Merit Award is designed to assist American Sokol Members in their pursuit of higher education. This is for any member of the organization planning on going full time to an accredited two-year or four –year college or university. Applicants for this award need not be limited to those who just recently graduated from high school. **Criteria:** Selection will be students who are planning a full time (at least 12 hours per semester or equivalent) course program in an accredited two-year or four-year college/university or who are already participating in such a course of study.

Funds Avail.: $1,000. **Duration:** One year. **To Apply:** Applicants must submit a recommendation and proof of the Unit or District Physical Director; a parent or guardian will be required to sign to the condition that if the candidate cannot submit the needed requirements completely they will repay the whole amount of the award. **Deadline:** June 1. **Remarks:** The award was instituted by the XIIth American Sokol Convention to be paid from the American Sokol Future Leaders Fund. **Contact:** For requesting by mail, send the completed page to: Merit Award Committee, c/o American Sokol, 9126 Ogden Ave., Brookfield, IL, 60513 or e-mail aso@american-sokol.org.

1594 ■ American Speech Language Hearing Foundation (ASHF)
2200 Research Blvd.
Rockville, MD 20850-3289
Ph: (301)296-8700
Fax: (301)296-8567

Awards are arranged alphabetically below their administering organizations

E-mail: foundation@asha.org
URL: www.ashfoundation.org
Social Media: www.facebook.com/asha.org
www.linkedin.com/company/the-american-speech
  -language-hearing-association-asha-
www.pinterest.com/ashaweb
www.youtube.com/user/ashaweb

1595 ■ American Speech Language Hearing Foundation Clinical Research Grant *(Doctorate/Grant)*

Purpose: To support investigations that will advance knowledge of the efficacy of treatment and assessment practices. **Focus:** Communications; Disabilities; Hearing and deafness; Speech and language pathology/Audiology. **Qualif.:** Applicants must have received a PhD or equivalent research doctorate within the discipline of communication sciences and disorders or related field and must demonstrate the potential and commitment to conducting independent research with a clear plan for applying for extramural research support. **Criteria:** Recipients will be selected based on the following: objectives and significance; experimental design and research method; innovation; facilities and resources; management plan and budget; investigator; mentor and mentoring plan; collaborators and collaboration plan. Priority will be given to proposals investigating promising approaches that have potential for improving the everyday functioning of individuals with, or at-risk for, communication and related impairments.

Funds Avail.: $50,000 to $75,000. **Duration:** Annual. **To Apply:** Applicants should prepare research proposals with the formats prescribed by the Foundation; such must be submitted electronically. Should a letter (addressed to the Grant Review Committee) from the administrator of your current employment setting indicating that the proposed study is endorsed and will not present a conflict of interest with your current responsibilities and commitments. **Deadline:** June 27.

1596 ■ American Speech Language Hearing Foundation Endowed Scholarships *(Graduate, Master's, Doctorate/Scholarship)*

Purpose: To support the advancement of knowledge in the area of disabilities and to improve the lives of people with speech, language, or hearing disorders. **Focus:** Communications; Disabilities; Hearing and deafness; Minorities; Speech and language pathology/Audiology. **Qualif.:** Applicants must be enrolled or accepted in a master's or doctoral in communication sciences and disorders program in the United States (in full-time study for full academic year). **Criteria:** Recipients will be selected based on the criteria set by the Foundation.

Funds Avail.: $5,000 each. **Duration:** Annual. **Number Awarded:** 6. **To Apply:** Applicants must submit the following: online student information form; letter of application and modified vitae appendix; department information form; transcripts; and confidential recommendation letters; all of those must be submitted through online application system. **Contact:** Email: foundationprograms@asha.org.

1597 ■ American Speech Language Hearing Foundation General Scholarships *(Graduate, Master's, Doctorate/Scholarship)*

Purpose: To support the advancement of knowledge in the area of disabilities and to improve the lives of people with speech, language, or hearing disorders. **Focus:** Com-

munications; Disabilities; Handicapped; Hearing and deafness; Speech and language pathology/Audiology. **Qualif.:** Applicants must be full-time master's or doctorate students who will be or who are currently enrolled in a graduate program in communication sciences and disorders. **Criteria:** Recipients will be selected based on the criteria set by the Foundation.

Funds Avail.: $5,000 each. **Duration:** Annual. **Number Awarded:** 15. **To Apply:** Applicants must submit the following: online student information form; letter of application and modified vitae appendix; department information form; transcripts; and confidential recommendation letters; all of those must be submitted through online application system. **Remarks:** Established in 1985. **Contact:** Email: foundationprograms@asha.org.

1598 ■ American Speech Language Hearing Foundation International Student Scholarship *(Graduate, Master's, Doctorate/Scholarship)*

Purpose: To support the advancement of knowledge in the area of disabilities, and improve the lives of people with speech, language, or hearing disorders. **Focus:** Communications; Hearing and deafness; Speech and language pathology/Audiology. **Qualif.:** Applicants must be full-time international graduate students studying communication sciences and disorders in the United States and demonstrating outstanding achievement. **Criteria:** Recipients will be selected based on the aforesaid qualifications and compliance with the application process.

Funds Avail.: $5,000 each. **Duration:** Annual. **Number Awarded:** 3. **To Apply:** Applicants must submit the following: online student information form; letter of application and modified vitae appendix; department information form; transcripts; and confidential recommendation letters. All of those must be submitted through online application system. **Contact:** Email: foundationprograms@asha.org.

1599 ■ American Speech Language Hearing Foundation Minority Student Scholarship *(Graduate, Master's, Doctorate/Scholarship)*

Purpose: To support the advancement of knowledge of minority students in the area of disabilities, as well as to improve the lives of people with speech, language, or hearing disorders. **Focus:** Communications; Hearing and deafness; Minorities; Speech and language pathology/Audiology. **Qualif.:** Applicants must be members of a racial or ethnic minority group and must be U.S. citizens. They must be graduate students enrolled full-time in a communication sciences and disorders program. **Criteria:** Recipients will be selected based on the aforesaid qualifications and compliance with the application process.

Funds Avail.: $5,000 each. **Duration:** Annual. **Number Awarded:** 3. **To Apply:** Applicants must submit the following: online student information form; letter of application and modified vitae appendix; department information form; transcripts; and confidential recommendation letters. All of those must be submitted through online application system. **Contact:** Email: foundationprograms@asha.org.

1600 ■ American Speech Language Hearing Foundation Scholarship for Student with A Disability *(Graduate, Master's, Doctorate/Scholarship)*

Purpose: To support the advancement of knowledge in the area of disabilities and to improve the lives of people with speech, language, or hearing disorders. **Focus:** Communications; Disabilities; Hearing and deafness; Speech

Awards are arranged alphabetically below their administering organizations

and language pathology/Audiology. **Qualif.:** Program is open to individuals who have disorders or disabilities who are enrolled in a communication sciences and disorders program. **Criteria:** Recipients are selected based on the criteria set by the Foundation.

Funds Avail.: $5,000. **Duration:** Annual. **Number Awarded:** 6. **To Apply:** Applicants must submit the following: online student information form; letter of application and modified vitae appendix; department information form; transcripts; and confidential recommendation letters; all of those must be submitted through online application system. **Contact:** Email: foundationprograms@asha.org.

1601 ■ ASHFoundation New Century Scholars Doctoral Scholarship *(Doctorate/Scholarship)*

Purpose: To support strong doctoral candidates who are committed to attaining the research doctoral degree and to working in the higher education academic community in the field of communication sciences and disorders in the United States. **Focus:** Communications; Disabilities; Speech and language pathology/Audiology. **Qualif.:** Applicants must be students who are accepted to, or currently enrolled in, a research doctoral program (PhD or equivalent) in communication sciences and disorders, and be NSSLHA or ASHA members. Students should be committed to a teacher-investigator career in communication sciences and disorders in the United States. **Criteria:** Recipients will be selected based on the following: students with either full-time status (9 hours or more per semester requirement or the university equivalent for the quarter system) or part-time statuses; and commitment of having teacher-investigator career in communication sciences and disorders in the U.S.A.

Funds Avail.: $10,000 each. **Duration:** Annual. **Number Awarded:** 15. **To Apply:** Applicants must submit the following: online student information form; letter of application and modified vitae appendix; department information form; transcripts; and confidential recommendation letters. **Contact:** Email: foundationprograms@asha.org.

1602 ■ ASHFoundation New Century Scholars Research Grant *(Doctorate/Grant)*

Purpose: To support investigations that will advance knowledge of the efficacy of treatment and assessment practices, and encourage innovative studies or unmet research. **Focus:** Communications; Disabilities; Hearing and deafness; Speech and language pathology/Audiology. **Qualif.:** Applicants must be scientists with research doctorate within the discipline of communication sciences and disorders or related field, and able to demonstrate the potential and commitment to conducting independent research with a clear plan for applying for extramural research support. **Criteria:** Recipients will be selected based on the following: objectives and significance; experimental design and research method; innovation; facilities and resources; management plan and budget; investigator; mentor and mentoring plan; collaborators and collaboration plan.

Funds Avail.: $25,000 each. **Duration:** Annual. **Number Awarded:** Up to 4. **To Apply:** Applicants should prepare research proposals with the formats prescribed by the Foundation. Such must be submitted electronically.

1603 ■ ASHFoundation New Investigators Research Grant *(Doctorate/Grant)*

Purpose: To pursue doctoral research in audiology or speech-language pathology. **Focus:** Speech and language

pathology/Audiology. **Qualif.:** Applicants must be new scientists earning their research doctorate (Ph.D.) in the discipline of communication sciences within the last 5 years. **Criteria:** Selection will be based on the committee's criteria for evaluation.

Funds Avail.: $10,000. **Duration:** Annual. **Number Awarded:** Up to 10. **To Apply:** Applicants must provide their research proposals; other documents include: investigator letter (limit 2 pages); abstract (limit 1 page); research plan (10 pages consist of specific aims, significance of research, design methods, procedures and evaluation, and facilities and resources); references (2 pages); management plan and budget (2 pages); human subjects; letter of institutional commitment; and letters of support.

1604 ■ ASHFoundation NSSLHA Scholarship *(Graduate/Scholarship)*

Purpose: To support NSSLHA student members in their graduate studies. **Focus:** Speech and language pathology/Audiology. **Qualif.:** Applicants must be undergraduate senior students with active national NSSLHA memberships and who will begin graduate study in the fall of the current year; and must be accepted for, or enrolled in, graduate study in a communication sciences and disorders program in the United States in which Master's programs in speech-language pathology or clinical doctoral programs in audiology must be accredited by the Council on Academic Accreditation in Audiology and Speech-Language Pathology (CAA). **Criteria:** Selection will be based on the committee's criteria.

Funds Avail.: $5,000 each. **Duration:** Annual. **Number Awarded:** 3. **To Apply:** Applicants must complete the online Student Information Form and upload the following required materials through the online application system: letter of application (PDF file, limit 2 pages, 12-point font, single-spaced); letter of acceptance or statement of good standing (PDF file); transcript (PDF file); essay (PDF file, limit 5 pages, 12-point font, single-spaced) responding to the question provided at the website; and confidential recommendation letters. **Contact:** Email: foundationprograms@asha.org.

1605 ■ ASHFoundation Speech Science Research Grant *(Doctorate/Grant)*

Purpose: To support investigations that will advance knowledge of the efficacy of treatment and assessment practices; to help further research activities of new investigators that have particular relevance to audiology and/or speech language pathology. **Focus:** Communications; Speech and language pathology/Audiology. **Qualif.:** Applicants must have received a doctoral degree within the past five years and wish to further research activities in the areas of speech communication. **Criteria:** Recipients will be selected based on the clearly stated project aims; significance of the research and its potential impact on the clinical needs relevant to speech-language pathology or audiology; merit of the design for answering the question, including detailed account of the methodology to be used; adequate provision for evaluating the results of the project, explicit statement of how the objectives will be measured; indication of the facilities, resources, personnel and subjects to which the applicant would have access in order to carry out the activities described in the proposal; the perceived ability of the applicant to complete the proposed research within one year period; Management plan that clearly outlines the activities and timeliness.

Funds Avail.: $10,000. **Duration:** Biennial. **To Apply:** Applicants should prepare research proposals with the formats

Awards are arranged alphabetically below their administering organizations

prescribed by the Foundation. Such must be submitted electronically. **Remarks:** The Speech Science Research Grant is supported by the Dennis Klatt Memorial Fund. The grant is designed to further research activities of new investigators and to promulgate Dr. Klatt's work. It can be used to initiate new research or supplement an existing research study. Funds may be requested for a variety of purposes; for example, equipment, subjects, research assistants, or research-related travel.

1606 ■ ASHFoundation Student Research Grant in Audiology *(Doctorate/Grant)*

Purpose: To support investigations that will advance knowledge of the efficacy of treatment and assessment practices. To help further the research activities of new investigators whose research have particular relevance to audiology and/or speech language pathology. **Focus:** Communications; Disabilities; Handicapped; Hearing and deafness; Speech and language pathology/Audiology. **Qualif.:** Applicants must be doctoral (research or clinical) degree students enrolled in, or accepted for, study in audiology or hearing science at an academic program in the United States; enrolled for full-time study for the full academic year. **Criteria:** Recipients will be selected based on the following: clearly stated project aims; the significance of the research and its potential impact on the clinical needs relevant to speech-language pathology or audiology; the merit of the design for answering the question, including detailed account of the methodology to be used; adequate provision for evaluating the results of the project, explicit statement of how the objectives will be measured; indication of the facilities, resources, personnel and subjects to which the applicant would have access in order to carry out the activities described in the proposal; the perceived ability of the applicant to complete the proposed research within a one year period; and management plan that clearly outlines the activities and timeliness.

Funds Avail.: $2,000. **Duration:** Annual. **Number Awarded:** 2. **To Apply:** Applicants should prepare research proposals with the formats prescribed by the Foundation; such must be submitted electronically. **Remarks:** The grant is supported by the Ira M. Ventry and Brad Friedrich Memorial Funds and general contributions to the annual fund. The grant competition memorializes two individuals. Ira Ventry was an audiologist whose research interests and publications focused on supra-threshold hearing, conductive hearing loss, hearing screening in the elderly and hearing handicap assessment. Brad Friedrich lectured and published widely in the field of pediatric audiology and was known for his ability to diagnose difficult-to-test children.

1607 ■ ASHFoundation Student Research Grant in Early Childhood Language Development *(Doctorate, Master's/Grant)*

Purpose: To support investigations that will advance knowledge of the efficacy of treatment and assessment practices, and help further research activities of new investigators that have particular relevance to audiology and/or speech language pathology. **Focus:** Communications; Hearing and deafness; Speech and language pathology/Audiology. **Qualif.:** Applicants must have received a master's and doctoral degree in communication sciences and disorders and aim to conduct research in early childhood language development; they must be enrolled full-time within the academic year. **Criteria:** Recipients are selected based on the following: clearly stated project aims; the significance of the research and its potential impact on the clinical needs relevant to speech-

language pathology or audiology; the merit of the design for answering the question, including detailed account of the methodology to be used; adequate provision for evaluating the results of the project, explicit statement of how the objectives will be measured; indication of the facilities, resources, personnel and subjects to which the applicant would have access in order to carry out the activities described in the proposal; the perceived ability of the applicant to complete the proposed research within one year period; and management plan that clearly outlines the activities and timeliness.

Funds Avail.: $2,000 each. **Duration:** Annual. **Number Awarded:** 2. **To Apply:** Applicants should prepare research proposals with the formats prescribed by the Foundation; such must be submitted electronically.

1608 ■ American Statistical Association (ASA)
732 N Washington St.
Alexandria, VA 22314-1943
Ph: (703)684-1221
Fax: (703)997-7299
Free: 888-231-3473
E-mail: asainfo@amstat.org
URL: www.amstat.org
Social Media: www.facebook.com/AmstatNews
www.pinterest.com/amstatnews
twitter.com/AmstatNews

1609 ■ ASA/NSF/BLS Fellowships *(Graduate/ Fellowship, Recognition, Grant)*

Purpose: To improve the collaboration between government and academic research. **Focus:** Government; Statistics. **Qualif.:** Applicants should have academically recognized research records and considerable expertise in their areas of proposed research. Moreover, applicants must be affiliated with a U.S. institution. **Criteria:** Recipients will be selected based on the proposed research project; preference will be given to those who meet the criteria.

Funds Avail.: No specific amount. **Duration:** Annual. **Number Awarded:** Varies. **To Apply:** Applicants must submit the following information via email: a curriculum vitae; names and addresses of three references; a detailed research proposal that includes background information about research topic, significance of expected results; advantages of conducting research at the bls; and detailed budget estimate (salary, relocation, travel expenses, research support). all of these must be compiled in one pdf file. **Deadline:** January 3. **Contact:** Email: joyce@amstat.org.

1610 ■ Edward C. Bryant Scholarship for an Outstanding Graduate Student in Survey Statistics *(Graduate/Scholarship)*

Purpose: To help support an outstanding graduate student in survey statistics. **Focus:** Statistics. **Qualif.:** Applicants must be full-time graduate school students. **Criteria:** Recipients will be chosen by the ASA Bryant Scholarship Award Committee. Criteria for the selection are the following: have the potential to contribute in survey statistics, experience in survey statistics; and performance in graduate studies.

Funds Avail.: $2,500. **Duration:** Annual. **Number Awarded:** 1. **To Apply:** Applicants must submit the provided application form and three letters of recommendation. **Deadline:** March 1. **Remarks:** The award was established to honor its co-founder and chair emeritus,

Awards are arranged alphabetically below their administering organizations

Edward C. Bryant. Established in 1995. **Contact:** Email: awards@amstat.org.

1611 ■ Gertrude M. Cox Scholarship *(Master's, Doctorate/Scholarship)*

Purpose: To encourage more women to enter statistically-oriented professions. **Focus:** Statistics. **Qualif.:** Applicants must be female citizens or permanent residents of the United States or Canada who are admitted to full-time study in a graduate statistical program. **Criteria:** Awards will be given based on the qualifications prescribed by the Scholarship Committee and the bestowing organization in general. **Funds Avail.:** $1,000 Each. **Duration:** Annual. **Number Awarded:** 2. **To Apply:** Applicants must submit the completed application form, academic reference letter and transcripts. These forms are available at their website. **Deadline:** February 23. **Remarks:** Established in 1989. **Contact:** Email: awards@amstat.org.

1612 ■ Samuel S. Wilks Memorial Award *(Advanced Professional/Award, Monetary)*

Purpose: To honor a distinguished individual who has made statistical contributions to the advancement of scientific or technical knowledge, ingenious application of existing knowledge, or successful activity in the fostering of cooperative scientific efforts that have been directly involved in matters of national defense or public interest. **Focus:** National security; Statistics; Technology. **Qualif.:** Nominee for the award must be a distinguished individual who has made statistical contributions to the advancement of scientific or technical knowledge, ingenious application of existing knowledge, or successful activity in the fostering of cooperative scientific efforts that have been directly involved in matters of national defense or public interest. **Criteria:** Selection will be based bestowed upon a distinguished individual who has made statistical contributions to the advancement of scientific or technical knowledge, ingenious application of existing knowledge, or successful activity in the fostering of cooperative scientific efforts that have been directly involved in matters of national defense or public interest

Funds Avail.: Total of $1,500. **Duration:** Annual. **Number Awarded:** 1. **To Apply:** Applicants are responsible for providing a current photograph and general personal information the year the award is presented. **Deadline:** February 15. **Remarks:** The award was established in memory and distinguished career of Samuel S. Wilks. Established in 1964. **Contact:** Email: awards@amstat.org.

1613 ■ American String Teachers Association - New Jersey Chapter (ASTA-NJ)

c/o Leslie Webster
8 Valley Rd.
Madison, NJ 07940
E-mail: info@astanj.com
URL: www.astanj.com

1614 ■ The Sharon Holmes ASTA/NJ Scholarship *(Undergraduate/Scholarship)*

Purpose: To help young New Jersey string students pursue a career in string teaching. **Focus:** Education, Music.

Funds Avail.: $2,000. **To Apply:** Application forms are available online. **Deadline:** April 11. **Contact:** Submissions must be sent to the following address: The Sharon Holmes ASTA/NJ Scholarship Fund, c/o Rona Landrigan, Chatham

High School, 255 Lafayette Ave, Chatham NJ 07928.

1615 ■ American Surgical Association (ASA)

500 Cummings Ctr., Ste. 4400
Beverly, MA 01915
Ph: (978)927-8330
Fax: (978)524-0498
URL: www.americansurgical.org

1616 ■ ACS/ASA Health Policy and Management Scholarships *(Professional development/Scholarship)*

Purpose: To subsidize the attendance and participation in the Executive Leadership Program in Health Policy and Management at Brandeis University. **Focus:** Health education. **Qualif.:** Applicants must be surgeons; must be members in good standing of both the ACS and ASA; planning to attend the Executive Leadership Program in Health Policy and Management at Brandeis University. **Criteria:** Selection will be based on the committee's review of the application materials.

Funds Avail.: $8,000. **Duration:** Annual. **To Apply:** Applicants must submit a completed application form; a copy of curriculum vitae; a one-page essay that discusses why the applicants need the scholarship, how the scholarship will fill a gap in applicant's training or experience, goals or plans to use the newly acquired knowledge or skills in practice. **Contact:** The application is submitted via e-mail to scholarships@facs.org.

1617 ■ American Swedish Institute (ASI)

2600 Park Ave.
Minneapolis, MN 55407
Ph: (612)871-4907
E-mail: info@asimn.org
URL: www.asimn.org

1618 ■ Lilly Lorenzen Scholarships *(Undergraduate/Scholarship)*

Purpose: To promote the study of Swedish heritage. **Focus:** Swedish studies. **Qualif.:** Applicants must be Minnesota residents must study in Sweden; should have some previous study or achievement in the field of study selected. **Criteria:** Recipients are selected based on the application materials.

Funds Avail.: $1,000. **Duration:** Annual. **To Apply:** Applicants must submit a completed application form and a transcript or a statement of professional and community achievement. **Deadline:** May 1. **Remarks:** Established in memory of Lilly Lorenzen, an instructor in Swedish University of Minnesota and the American Swedish Institute, and author of the book "Of Swedish Ways". **Contact:** Britta Walstron, ASI Programs Manager; Email:brittaw@asimn.org.

1619 ■ Malmberg Scholarships *(Undergraduate/Scholarship)*

Purpose: To provide financial assistance for individuals intending to study in Sweden. **Focus:** Swedish studies. **Qualif.:** Applicants must be U.S. citizens; enrolled in a degree-granting program in college/university or in a study or research that requires or can be enhanced by study in Sweden; and must have knowledge in the Swedish language. **Criteria:** Recipients are selected based on submitted application materials.

Awards are arranged alphabetically below their administering organizations

Funds Avail.: Up to $10,000. **Duration:** Nine months. **To Apply:** Applicants must submit a completed application form and a letter of invitation or affiliation from the Swedish institution/organization; a project summary (1000 words); transcript (optional if out of school for three years); resume; and two letters of recommendation. **Deadline:** November 15.

1620 ■ American Thoracic Society (ATS)

25 Broadway
New York, NY 10004
Ph: (212)315-8600
Fax: (212)315-6498
E-mail: atsinfo@thoracic.org
URL: www.thoracic.org
Social Media: www.facebook.com/americanthoracic
instagram.com/atscommunity
www.linkedin.com/company/248312
twitter.com/atscommunity
youtube.com/user/ThoracicTV

1621 ■ ATS Abstract Scholarships *(Undergraduate, Graduate, Doctorate/Scholarship)*

Purpose: To engage its members around the globe and to support their expenses. **Focus:** Health sciences. **Qualif.:** Applicants must be trainee members who are students, residents, fellows (holders of M.D. or Ph.D.) or equivalent; must be ATS members at the time of receiving the abstract scholarship; must be registered for and attend the ATS International Conference. **Criteria:** Selection will be based on the committee's criteria.

Funds Avail.: No specific amount. **Duration:** Annual. **Number Awarded:** Varies. **To Apply:** Applicants must submit a meritorious abstract to be presented at the ATS International Conference; must attend the ATS International Conference and must fill the questionnaire of the abstract online submission program, indicating the applicants wish that will be considered for the scholarship. **Contact:** Miriam Rodriguez, Phone: 212-315-8639; Email: mrodriguez@thoracic.org.

1622 ■ International Trainee Scholarships (ITS) *(Doctorate/Scholarship)*

Purpose: To support expenses related to attending the ATS International Conference including registration, accommodations and related daily costs such as meals and local transportation. **Focus:** Health sciences. **Qualif.:** Applicants must be trainees who are not at a U.S. or Canadian program at the time of application; must not be a U.S. or Canadian citizens; must be authors of an abstract accepted for presentation at the ATS International Conference; must not be a recipient of another travel award at the ATS International Conference; and the work in the abstract should not have been performed at a U.S. or Canadian institution. **Criteria:** Selection will be based on the committee's criteria.

Funds Avail.: No specific amount. **Duration:** Annual. **To Apply:** Applicants must submit the complete online ATS-ITS application and upload the necessary documents in PDF format within the online application; the necessary documents are abstract accepted for presentation at the ATS International Conference and curriculum Vitae limited to one page based on career aspects of work in accepted IC abstract. **Deadline:** March 22. **Contact:** Chris Hughes, Email: chughes@thoracic.org.

1623 ■ American Tinnitus Association (ATA)

522 SW 5th Ave., Ste. 825
Portland, OR 97204
Ph: (503)248-9985
Fax: (503)274-7611
Free: 800-634-8978
E-mail: tinnitus@ata.org
URL: www.ata.org
Social Media: www.facebook.com/
  AmericanTinnitusAssociation
www.instagram.com/americantinnitusassociation
linkedin.com/in/american-tinnitus-association-604354130
twitter.com/Tinnitus_USA
www.youtube.com/user/ATAJD

1624 ■ ATA Research Grants *(Professional development/Grant)*

Purpose: To assist innovative tinnitus research projects. **Focus:** Medical research.

Funds Avail.: $50,000. **Duration:** Annual. **Contact:** contact: ATA at 1-800-634-8978; Email: tinnitus@ata.org.

1625 ■ American University School of Public Affairs (AU-SPA)

4400 Massachusetts Ave. NW
Washington, DC 20016
Ph: (202)885-2940
E-mail: spa@american.edu
URL: www.american.edu
Social Media: www.facebook.com/AUSchoolofPublicAffairs
twitter.com/AU_SPA

1626 ■ Jane R. Glaser Scholarship *(Undergraduate/Scholarship)*

Purpose: To provide financial assistance to School of Public Administration students. **Focus:** Public administration. **Qualif.:** Applicant must be SPA Undergraduate studying abroad at the Hebrew University with minimum 3.2 GPA.

Funds Avail.: $10,000. **Duration:** Annual. **Number Awarded:** 1. **To Apply:** Applicants must submit personal statement detailing their proposed study abroad plans and rationale. **Remarks:** The scholarship was established by Patricia L. Glaser, BA/SPA'69 in honor of her mother, Jane R. Glaser.

1627 ■ American Veterinary Medical Association (AVMA)

1931 N Meacham Rd., Ste. 100
Schaumburg, IL 60173-4360
Fax: (847)925-1329
Free: 800-248-2862
URL: www.avma.org
Social Media: www.facebook.com/avmavets
www.instagram.com/avmavets
www.linkedin.com/company/avma
twitter.com/AVMAvets

1628 ■ AVMA Fellowship Program *(Professional development/Fellowship)*

Purpose: To support fellows in influencing key legislation affecting the veterinary profession. **Focus:** Veterinary sci-

Awards are arranged alphabetically below their administering organizations

ence and medicine. **Qualif.:** Applicants fellows must be willing to serve for one year in Washington D.C. as scientific advisors to members of Congress, and must have played vital roles in shaping and influencing key legislation affecting veterinary profession; must represent the veterinary profession in the legislative branch of government; use science-based decision making in public policy development; influence important public policy discussions; network with leaders at the top tier of federal government. **Criteria:** Selection will be based on the committee's criteria.

Funds Avail.: A stipend of $88,575; $6,000 to offset the cost of health insurance premiums. **Duration:** Annual. **To Apply:** Applicants may contact the Association for the application process and other details. **Deadline:** February 9. **Contact:** Send applications to: AVMA Fellowship Program, American Veterinary Medical Association, Government Relations Division, 1910 Sunderland Pl., NW, Washington, DC, 20036; Email: fellowship@avma.org.

1629 ■ American Water Resources Association - Colorado Section (AWRA-CO)

PO Box 9822
Denver, CO 80209
URL: www.awracolorado.org
Social Media: www.facebook.com/AWRAColorado
www.instagram.com/awra.colorado
www.linkedin.com/company/awra-colorado
twitter.com/AWRACO

1630 ■ Rich Herbert Memorial Scholarship
(Undergraduate, Master's, Doctorate/Scholarship)

Purpose: To promote interest and research in the water resources of Colorado. **Focus:** Water resources. **Qualif.:** Applicants must be enrolled as students in an undergraduate, masters, or PhD degree program at any accredited Colorado public or private college or university; must be in research or independent study pertaining to hydrology, engineering, hydrogeology, aquatic biology, water law, water-resources policy or planning, environmental science or other topics concerning water resources in Colorado. **Criteria:** Applicants are selected by a standing committee of the AWRA-Colorado section will review applications and make recommendations to the Board of Directors based on academic performance (GPA).

Funds Avail.: $500-$4,000. **Duration:** Annual. **To Apply:** Applicants must submit a completed application that includes their resume, abstract of current research and three letters of recommendation from a faculty advisor; a title page which include the applicants' full name, permanent mailing address, email address, phone number and type of scholarship; two page summary of academic interests and achievements, career goals and extracurricular interests; and transcript of records. **Deadline:** August 30. **Contact:** Laurel Stadjuhar: Phone: 303-835-9914; Email: laurel@westsagewater.com; Beorn Courtney: Phone: 720-524-6115; Email: bcourtney@elementwaterinc.com.

1631 ■ American Water Resources Association - Florida Section

c/o Roger Copp, President
1501 W. Horatio St., Unit 108
Tampa, FL 33606
Ph: (813)431-4959
E-mail: roger@wsaconsult.com
URL: awraflorida.org

Social Media: www.instagram.com/awraflorida
twitter.com/awraflorida
www.youtube.com/channel/
UCX8UuaIWR2CXve0e1d9dcnQ

1632 ■ William V. Storch Student Award
(Undergraduate, Graduate/Award)

Purpose: To support an undergraduate and a graduate student based in part on relevance of the student's curriculum to water resources and leadership in extracurricular activities related to water resources. **Focus:** Water resources. **Qualif.:** Students must be attending a Florida college/university. **Criteria:** Criteria for an undergraduate student is based on academic performance including the cumulative grade point average, relevance of the student's curriculum to water resources and leadership in extracurricular activities related to water resources. For a graduate student, selection is based on academic and/or research performance. The measures of academic performance are identical to those described for the undergraduate criteria with the addition of the quality of the student's research and its relevance to water resources.

Funds Avail.: $1,500. **Duration:** Annual. **Number Awarded:** Varies. **To Apply:** Applicants should prepare a title page and two-page summary of their academic interests and achievements, extracurricular interests and career goals as they relate to the above selection criteria. Also include a letter of reference, preferably from a professor or advisor, a transcript of all college courses and full name, permanent mailing address, email address, and phone number. **Deadline:** April 30.

1633 ■ American Water Works Association (AWWA)

6666 W Quincy Ave.
Denver, CO 80235
Ph: (303)794-7711
Fax: (303)347-0804
Free: 800-926-7337
E-mail: service@awwa.org
URL: www.awwa.org
Social Media: www.facebook.com/
  AmericanWaterWorksAssociation
www.instagram.com/americanwaterworksassociation
www.linkedin.com/company/american-water-works
  -association
twitter.com/AWWA
www.youtube.com/user/AmericanWaterWorks

1634 ■ Abel Wolman Fellowship *(Doctorate/Fellowship, Award, Monetary)*

Purpose: To support promising doctoral students in the U.S., Canada and Mexico pursuing advanced training and research in the field of water supply and treatment. **Focus:** Water resources; Water supply industry. **Qualif.:** Applicants must submit graduate and undergraduate scholarship applications. **Criteria:** Selection will be based on the committee's criteria.

Funds Avail.: No specific amount. **Duration:** Annual. **To Apply:** Applicants must submit the completed application form. **Contact:** Phone: 303-347-6201; Email: scholarships@awwa.org.

1635 ■ ARCADIS Scholarship *(Master's, Doctorate/Scholarship, Monetary)*

Purpose: To provide support to a master's or doctoral candidate student seeking a degree in the water industry.

Awards are arranged alphabetically below their administering organizations

Focus: Water resources; Water supply industry. **Qualif.:** Applicants must be students pursuing graduate degree (master's or doctoral) in water industry. **Criteria:** Selection will be based on the committee's criteria.

Funds Avail.: $5,000. **Duration:** Annual. **Number Awarded:** 1. **Contact:** Email: scholarships@awwa.org; Phone: 303-347-6201.

1636 ■ AWWA American Water Scholarship
(Master's, Doctorate/Scholarship, Monetary)

Purpose: To assist the development of professionals interested in service to the water industry. **Focus:** Water resources; Water supply industry. **Qualif.:** Applicants must be students pursuing a graduate degree (master's or doctoral). **Criteria:** Selection will be based on the committee's criteria.

Funds Avail.: $5,000. **Duration:** Annual. **To Apply:** Applicants may contact AWWA for the application process and other information. **Deadline:** December 21. **Contact:** Contact: Sr. Manager of Development Michelle Hektor; Phone: 303-734-3613; Email: mhektor@awwa.org.

1637 ■ HDR/Henry "Bud" Benjes Scholarships
(Master's/Scholarship, Monetary)

Purpose: To provide support to a student seeking a masters degree in the water industry. **Focus:** Water resources; Water supply industry. **Qualif.:** Applicants must be students pursuing master's degree in the water industry. **Criteria:** Selection will be based on the committee's criteria.

Funds Avail.: $5,000. **Duration:** Annual. **To Apply:** Applicants may contact AWWA for the application process and other information.

1638 ■ Bryant L. Bench Scholarship
(Master's/Scholarship, Monetary)

Purpose: To provide support to a master's student engaging in water-energy nexus issues for water, wastewater or water use. **Focus:** Water resources; Water supply industry. **Qualif.:** Applicants must be students pursuing master's degree. **Criteria:** Selection will be based on the committee's criteria.

Funds Avail.: $10,000. **Duration:** Annual. **To Apply:** Applicants may contact AWWA for the application process and other information. **Deadline:** December 21. **Contact:** Contact: Sr. Manager of Development Michelle Hektor; Phone: 303-734-3613; Email: mhektor@awwa.org.

1639 ■ Thomas R. Camp Scholarships
(Graduate/Scholarship, Monetary)

Purpose: To support and encourage graduate students conducting applied research in the drinking water field. **Focus:** Water resources; Water supply industry. **Qualif.:** Applicants must be in pursuit of their respective graduate degrees (either masters or doctoral). **Criteria:** Scholarship recipient will be selected based on academic record and potential to provide leadership in applied research and consulting in the drinking water field.

Funds Avail.: $5,000. **Duration:** Annual. **To Apply:** Applicants must submit the completed application form. **Contact:** Phone: 303-347-6201; Email: scholarships@awwa.org.

1640 ■ Dave Caldwell Scholarship
(Graduate/Scholarship, Monetary)

Purpose: To benefit students pursuing an engineering degree in the drinking water field. **Focus:** Engineering;

Water resources; Water supply industry. **Qualif.:** Applicants must be female and/or minority students pursuing graduate degree in the drinking water field. **Criteria:** Selection will be based on the demonstrated ability to provide leadership in applied research and consulting in the drinking water field.

Funds Avail.: $5,000. **Duration:** Annual. **To Apply:** Applicants may contact AWWA for the application process and other information. **Deadline:** December 21. **Contact:** Contact: Sr. Manager of Development Michelle Hektor; Phone: 303-734-3613; Email: mhektor@awwa.org.

1641 ■ Hazen and Sawyer Scholarship
(Master's/Scholarship, Monetary)

Purpose: To provide support to a student seeking a master's degree in the water science field. **Focus:** Water resources; Water supply industry. **Qualif.:** Applicants must be students pursuing master's degree in water science field. **Criteria:** Selection will be based on the applicant's potential to provide leadership in applied research and consulting in the drinking water field.

Funds Avail.: $5,000. **Duration:** Annual. **To Apply:** Applicants may contact AWWA for the application process and other information. **Deadline:** December 21. **Contact:** Contact: Sr. Manager of Development Michelle Hektor; Phone: 303-734-3613; Email: mhektor@awwa.org.

1642 ■ Holly A. Cornell Scholarship
(Master's/Scholarship, Monetary)

Purpose: To support and encourage outstanding female and/or minority master's students in pursuit of advanced training in the field of water supply and treatment. **Focus:** Water resources; Water supply industry. **Qualif.:** Applicants must be female and/or minority students, who are currently masters degree students anticipating completion of the requirements for a masters degree in engineering. **Criteria:** Selection will be based on the committee's criteria.

Funds Avail.: $7,500. **Duration:** Annual. **To Apply:** Applicants must submit the completed application form. **Contact:** Phone: 303-347-6201; Email: scholarships@awwa.org.

1643 ■ Larson Aquatic Research Support Scholarships (LARS)
(Graduate/Scholarship, Monetary, Recognition)

Purpose: To provide support for students interested in careers in the fields of corrosion control, treatment and distribution of domestic and industrial water supplies, aquatic chemistry, and/or environmental chemistry. **Focus:** Biochemistry; Chemistry; Water resources; Water supply industry. **Qualif.:** Applicants must be students pursuing a masters or doctoral degree in the fields of corrosion control, treatment and distribution of domestic and industrial water supplies, aquatic chemistry, and/or environmental chemistry. **Criteria:** Selection will be based on the committee's criteria.

Funds Avail.: $5,000 (Master's student); $7,000 (Doctoral student). **Duration:** Annual. **To Apply:** Applicants must submit the completed application form. **Contact:** Contact: Sr. Manager of Development Michelle Hektor at 303-734-3613 or mhektor@awwa.org.

1644 ■ Stantec Scholarship
(Master's, Doctorate/Scholarship, Monetary)

Purpose: To provide support to a master's student seeking a degree in the water industry. **Focus:** Water resources;

Awards are arranged alphabetically below their administering organizations

Water supply industry. **Qualif.:** Applicants must be students seeking master's degree in water industry. **Criteria:** Selection will be based on the committee's criteria.

Funds Avail.: $5,000. **Duration:** Annual. **To Apply:** Applicants may contact AWWA for the application process and other information. **Deadline:** December 21. **Contact:** Contact: Sr. Manager of Development Michelle Hektor; Phone: 303-734-3613; Email: mhektor@awwa.org.

1645 ■ American Water Works Association - Florida Section (FSAWWA)
1300 9th St., B-124
Saint Cloud, FL 34769
Ph: (407)957-8448
Fax: (407)957-8415
URL: www.fsawwa.org

1646 ■ Roy W. Likins Scholarship (Undergraduate, Graduate/Scholarship)

Purpose: To support students pursuing a degree related to drinking water industry. **Focus:** Water resources; Water supply industry. **Qualif.:** Applicants must be upper level undergraduate (over 65 credit hours) or graduate students enrolled in an accredited Florida Institution and currently majoring in an area related to the drinking water industry and have a minimum 3.0 grade point average based on a 4.0 system. **Criteria:** Selection will be made on the basis of academic performance, work experience, community and civic activities, honor, career goals, letters of recommendation, and evidence of leadership, motivation, character, and self-reliance.

Funds Avail.: $2,500 - $25,000. **Duration:** Annual. **To Apply:** Applicants must submit the following: completed application form (provided in Word or PDF format); official college transcripts for undergraduate and graduate courses; two recommendation letters; and a brief letter describing their interests in the FSAWWA scholarship. **Deadline:** August 1. **Remarks:** The scholarship was established in memory of Roy Likins, a life-long member of AWWA. Established in 1988. **Contact:** Likins Chair, Steve Soltau, MBA, Pinellas County Utilities, 6730 142nd Ave. N, Largo, FL, 33771; Email: ssoltau@pinellascounty.org or ssoltau@co.pinellas.fl.us; Phone: 727-453-6990.

1647 ■ American Watercolor Society (AWS)
47 5th Ave.
New York, NY 10003-4303
Ph: (212)206-8986
Fax: (212)206-1960
E-mail: info@americanwatercolorsociety.org
URL: www.americanwatercolorsociety.org

1648 ■ American Watercolor Society Scholarship Program for Art Teachers (Undergraduate, Graduate/Scholarship)

Purpose: To enhance and improve the capabilities of teachers in watercolor media. **Focus:** Art; Painting. **Qualif.:** Applicants must be art teachers currently working at a middle school, secondary school or college level institution in the United States. **Criteria:** Selection will be based on AWS I funding the cost of tuition and materials for attending an instruction period in watercolor painting of at least five days but not more than 6 months in duration.

Funds Avail.: $1,000. **Duration:** Annual. **To Apply:** Applicants must complete and submit the online application

form, at least three months in advance of the start date of the instruction; also including relevant visuals/images (max one page) evaluating workshop experience; also include the report the number of students teach per year and the number of years you have been teaching art. **Contact:** AWS Scholarship Program, 2811 Weathersfield Ctr. Rd., Perkinsville, VT, 05151.

1649 ■ American Welding Society (AWS)
8669 NW 36th St., Ste. 130
Miami, FL 33166-6672
Ph: (305)443-9353
Free: 800-443-9353
URL: www.aws.org
Social Media: facebook.com/AmericanWeldingSociety
www.instagram.com/americanweldingsociety
twitter.com/awshq
www.youtube.com/awsorg

1650 ■ Airgas - Terry Jarvis Memorial Scholarship (Undergraduate/Scholarship)

Purpose: To provide financial assistance to those individuals interested in pursuing a career in welding engineering. **Focus:** Welding. **Qualif.:** Applicants must be U.S. citizens who are full-time undergraduate students pursuing a minimum four-year degree in a welding or welding related program at an accredited university; they must be at least 18 years of age, be enrolled full-time, and have at least a 2.8 overall grade point average with a 3.0 grade point average in engineering courses; must also plan to attend an institution located within the United States or Canada. **Criteria:** Recipients are selected based on need. Priority will be given to those individuals who demonstrate an interest in pursuing a career with an industrial gas or welding equipment distributor prior to work experience, clubs, organizations, or extracurricular activities. For individuals residing or attending schools in the states of Alabama, Georgia, or Florida are also given preference.

Funds Avail.: $2,500. **Duration:** Annual. **Number Awarded:** 1. **To Apply:** Applicants must submit an application form and a high school diploma. **Contact:** AWS Foundation, Inc., 8669 NW 36 St., Ste. 130, Miami, FL, 33166-6672; Phone: 800-443-9353.

1651 ■ American Welding Society District Scholarships (Undergraduate/Scholarship)

Purpose: To provide financial assistance to students preparing for a career in the welding and related joining technologies. **Focus:** Welding. **Qualif.:** Applicants must be high school graduates or possess a GED equivalent planning to enroll in a welding course program; must attend a school located in United States or its territories. **Criteria:** Recipients are selected based on academic standing.

Funds Avail.: No specific amount. **Duration:** Annual. **Number Awarded:** Varies. **To Apply:** Application must be submitted along with statement of unmet financial need form; transcript of records; personal statement; biography and photo; when scholarship is not used during fall semester, can be used during the spring term of the same fiscal year; when entire scholarship not used during the fiscal year, the remainder will be returned to the AWS Foundation Scholarship Fund. **Deadline:** March 1. **Contact:** AWS Foundation, Inc., 8669 NW 36 St., Ste. 130, Miami, FL, 33166-6672; Phone: 800-443-9353.

Awards are arranged alphabetically below their administering organizations

1652 ■ American Welding Society Graduate Research Fellowships *(Graduate/Fellowship)*

Purpose: To advance opportunities for students preparing for a career in the welding and related joining technologies. **Focus:** Welding. **Qualif.:** Applicants must be graduate students who wish to pursue areas of research related to the welding and joining industry. **Criteria:** Selection will be based on commitee criteria.

Funds Avail.: No specific amount. **Duration:** Annual. **To Apply:** Applicants must prepare the academic credentials; plans; research history; and proposal. Technical portion of proposal should be: 25-typewritten pages; with two megabytes; 12-point font; and Times New Roman.

1653 ■ American Welding Society National Scholarships *(Undergraduate/Scholarship)*

Purpose: To support students preparing for a career in the welding and related joining technologies. **Focus:** Welding. **Qualif.:** Applicants must be students pursuing a specific degree at an accredited four-year college or university. **Criteria:** Recipients are selected based on academic standing.

Funds Avail.: $2,500 each. **Duration:** Annual. **Number Awarded:** Varies. **To Apply:** Applicants must submit a financial statement; transcript of records; personal statement; biography; and photo. **Deadline:** March 1. **Remarks:** The AWS National Scholarships are awarded in various types. **Contact:** AWS Foundation, Inc., 8669 NW 36 St., Ste. 130, Miami, FL, 33166-6672; Phone: 800-443-9353.

1654 ■ American Welding Society Past Presidents Scholarships *(Undergraduate, Graduate, Master's, Doctorate/Scholarship)*

Purpose: To provide financial assistance to individuals interested in pursuing a bachelor's degree in welding engineering, welding engineering technology, or an engineering program with an emphasis in welding. **Focus:** Welding. **Qualif.:** Applicants must be junior, senior, or graduate level (Masters or Ph.D.) students pursuing degree in Welding Engineering or Welding Engineering Technology. **Criteria:** Recipients will be selected based on financial need.

Funds Avail.: $2,500. **Duration:** Annual. **Number Awarded:** 1. **To Apply:** Applicants must complete the application form and submit it along with one or more recommendation letters from community members, local AWS officers, and/or AWS district directors attesting to the applicant's leadership capability; and (300-500 word) essay on the applicant's objectives and aspirations in the field of welding. **Contact:** AWS Foundation, Inc., 8669 NW 36 St., Ste. 130, Miami, FL, 33166-6672; Phone: 800-443-9353.

1655 ■ Arsham Amirikian Engineering Scholarship *(Undergraduate/Scholarship)*

Purpose: To provide financial assistance to an engineering student pursuing a career in the art of welding in civil and structural engineering. **Focus:** Engineering, Civil; Welding. **Qualif.:** Applicants must be U.S. citizens who are full-time undergraduate students pursuing a minimum four-year degree in civil engineering or welding related program at an accredited university; must be at least 18 years of age; must have a minimum 3.0 grade point average; must have a minimum high school diploma or equivalent; must also plan to attend an institution located within the United States. **Criteria:** Recipients are selected based on financial need.

Funds Avail.: $2,500. **Duration:** Annual; maximum time for financial aid is four years. **Number Awarded:** 1. **To Ap-**

ply: Applicants must submit an application; a high school diploma; and a financial statement. **Remarks:** The Scholarship was named in the honor of Dr. Arsham Amirikian. **Contact:** AWS Foundation, Inc., 8669 NW 36 St., Ste. 130, Miami, FL, 33166-6672; Phone: 800-443-9353.

1656 ■ Amos and Marilyn Winsand - Detroit Section Named Scholarship *(Undergraduate/Scholarship)*

Purpose: To provide financial assistance to those individuals interested in pursuing a career in welding engineering. **Focus:** Welding. **Qualif.:** Applicants must be enrolled in a Welding Engineering Program, a Welding Engineering Technology Program, a Post-Secondary Technical Program (Welding Certification targeted program), or a related field of study with a strong welding content; must be permanent residents of Michigan Attending school in the following Ontario counties Essex, Chath, am-Kent, and Sarnia-Lambton. **Criteria:** Recipients are selected based on financial need; preference will be given to students who are permanent residents of the Detroit section territory, including Ontario counties of Essex, Chatham-Kent, and Sarnia-Lambton.

Duration: Annual. **To Apply:** Application form must be submitted along with official scholastic records or grade transcripts from the high school, college or university; personal statement of 300 words or less. **Deadline:** April 1. **Remarks:** The scholarship was named in the memory of Mr. Winsand. **Contact:** E-mail: scholarship@aws.org.

1657 ■ AWS International Scholarship Program *(Undergraduate, Graduate/Scholarship)*

Purpose: To provide financial assistance to international students who wish to pursue their education in welding and related joining technologies. **Focus:** Welding. **Qualif.:** Applicants must be full time international students pursuing undergraduate or graduate studies in joining sciences; they can be matriculating in accredited joining science programs at institutions anywhere in the world; student must be in the top 20% of the institution's grading system; must be members of AWS. **Criteria:** Recipients are selected based on financial need and academic standing.

Funds Avail.: $2,500. **Duration:** Annual. **To Apply:** Applicants must submit a copy of the proposed curriculum; verification of enrollment to the institution; two letters of personal reference; two-page professional goal statement with a brief bibliography; transcript of grades or equivalent from each college; proof of country of citizenship; AWS membership number, if member; and financial information regarding tuition fees from the academic institution. **Deadline:** April 1. **Contact:** AWS Foundation, Inc., 8669 NW 36 St., Ste. 130, Miami, FL, 33166-6672; Phone: 800-443-9353.

1658 ■ Airgas - Jerry Baker Scholarship *(Undergraduate/Scholarship)*

Purpose: To provide financial assistance to those individuals interested in pursuing a career in welding engineering. **Focus:** Welding. **Qualif.:** Applicants must be U.S. or Canada citizens who are full-time undergraduate students pursuing a minimum four-year degree in a welding or welding related program at an accredited university; must be at least 18 years of age; must have at least a 2.8 overall grade point average with a 3.0 grade point average in engineering courses; must also plan to attend an institution located within the United States or Canada. **Criteria:** Recipients are selected based on need. Priority will be given to individuals who demonstrate an interest in pursuing a

Awards are arranged alphabetically below their administering organizations

career with an industrial gas or welding equipment distributor with prior to work experience, clubs, organizations, or extracurricular activities. For individuals residing or attending schools in the states of Alabama, Georgia and Florida are also given preference.

Funds Avail.: $2,500. **Duration:** Annual. **Number Awarded:** 1. **To Apply:** Applicants must submit an application form and a high school diploma. **Contact:** AWS Foundation, Inc., 8669 NW 36 St., Ste. 130, Miami, FL, 33166-6672; Phone: 800-443-9353.

1659 ■ Edward J. Brady Memorial Scholarship
(Undergraduate/Scholarship)

Purpose: To provide financial assistance to individuals interested in pursuing a career in welding engineering. **Focus:** Welding. **Qualif.:** Applicants must be undergraduate students pursuing a four-year bachelors degree in welding engineering or welding engineering technology; must be 18 years old and above; must have a minimum of 2.5 overall grade point average; must be citizens of the United States; and must plan to attend an accredited engineering school within the United States. **Criteria:** Recipient are selected based on financial need. Priority will be given to welding engineering students.

Funds Avail.: $2,500. **Duration:** Annual. **Number Awarded:** 1. **To Apply:** Applicants must complete the application form and submit it along with a high school diploma and a financial statement. **Remarks:** The scholarship was named in honor of Edward J. Brady. **Contact:** AWS Foundation, Inc., 8669 NW 36 St., Ste. 130, Miami, FL, 33166-6672; Phone: 800-443-9353.

1660 ■ Donald and Shirley Hastings Scholarship
(Undergraduate/Scholarship)

Purpose: To provide financial assistance to individuals interested in pursuing a career in welding engineering. **Focus:** Welding. **Qualif.:** Applicants must be U.S. citizens who are full-time undergraduate students pursuing a minimum four-year bachelor's degree in welding engineering (WE) or welding engineering technology (WET) at an accredited university within the United States; must be at least 18 years of age; must have a minimum 2.5 grade point average. **Criteria:** Recipients are selected based on financial need. Priority will be given to students residing or attending schools in the states of Iowa, Ohio, or California.

Duration: Annual. **To Apply:** Applicants must submit an application; a high school diploma; a copy of Free Application Financial Student Aid (FAFSA) and a financial statement. **Contact:** AWS Foundation, Inc., 8669 NW 36 St., Ste. 130, Miami, FL, 33166-6672; Phone: 800-443-9353.

1661 ■ Donald F. Hastings Scholarship
(Undergraduate/Scholarship)

Purpose: To provide financial assistance to those individuals interested in pursuing a career in welding engineering. **Focus:** Welding. **Qualif.:** Applicants must be U.S. citizens who are full-time undergraduate students pursuing a minimum four-year bachelor's degree in welding engineering (WE) or welding engineering technology (WET) at an accredited university; must be at least 18 years of age; must be enrolled full-time or part time; must have a minimum 2.5 grade point average; must plan to attend an academic institution located within the United States. **Criteria:** Recipients are selected based on financial need. Priority will be given to students residing or attending schools in the states of Ohio and California.

Funds Avail.: $2,500. **Duration:** Annual. **Number Awarded:** 1. **To Apply:** Applicants must submit an applica-

tion; a high school diploma; and a financial statement. **Contact:** AWS Foundation, Inc., 8669 NW 36 St., Ste. 130, Miami, FL, 33166-6672; Phone: 800-443-9353.

1662 ■ Howard E. and Wilma J. Adkins Memorial Scholarship
(Undergraduate/Scholarship)

Purpose: To provide financial assistance to individuals interested in pursuing a career in welding engineering. **Focus:** Welding. **Qualif.:** Applicants must be undergraduate students pursuing a four-year bachelors degree in welding engineering or welding engineering technology; be 18 years old and above; have a minimum of 2.8 overall grade point average minimum 3.20 grade point average in the engineering, scientific and technical subjects; must be citizens of the United States; and plan to attend an accredited engineering school within the United States. **Criteria:** Preference will be given to those individuals residing or attending school in the states of Wisconsin or Kentucky.

Funds Avail.: $2,500. **Duration:** Annual. **Number Awarded:** 1. **To Apply:** Applicants must complete the application form and submit it along with a high school diploma and a financial statement. **Remarks:** The fund was established in memory of Mr. Howard E. Adkins, by family and friends. Established in 1994. **Contact:** AWS Foundation, Inc., 8669 NW 36 St., Ste. 130, Miami, FL, 33166-6672; Phone: 800-443-9353.

1663 ■ Hypertherm International HyTech Leadership Scholarships
(Graduate/Scholarship)

Purpose: To provide financial assistance to those individuals interested in pursuing a graduate degree in engineering management, with a focus on becoming a technical leader within the welding and cutting industry. **Focus:** Welding. **Qualif.:** Applicants must have completed a Bachelor of Science degree or be in their final year, and have been accepted for graduate work in engineering management at an accredited graduate school (with an average GPA of 2.8); they may be citizens of any country and plan to attend an academic institution located in any country. **Criteria:** Recipients will be selected based on financial need.

Funds Avail.: $2,500. **Duration:** Annual. **Number Awarded:** 1. **To Apply:** Applicants must complete the application form and personal statement addressing a proposed advanced academic and post-academic plan. **Deadline:** February 15.

1664 ■ ITW Welding Companies Scholarships
(Undergraduate/Scholarship)

Purpose: To provide financial assistance to individuals interested in pursuing a career in welding engineering. **Focus:** Welding. **Qualif.:** Applicants must be senior, full-time undergraduate students working towards a bachelors degree in welding engineering or welding engineering technology; must be 18 years old and above; must have a minimum of 3.0 overall grade point average; must be citizens of the United States; and must plan to attend an accredited engineering school within the United States.

Contact: Vicki Pinsky at 800-443-9353, ext 212.

1665 ■ Jack R. Barckhoff Welding Management Scholarship
(Undergraduate/Scholarship)

Purpose: To provide financial assistance to individuals interested in pursuing a career in welding engineering. **Focus:** Welding. **Qualif.:** Applicants must be college juniors pursuing a four-year bachelors degree in welding engineering at the Ohio State University; must be 18 years old and

Awards are arranged alphabetically below their administering organizations

above; must have minimum of 2.5 overall grade point average; must be citizens of the United States and plan to attend an accredited engineering school within the United States; must be enrolled and must complete the two-hour credit course in Total Welding Management at the Ohio State University; Seniors entering The Ohio State University graduate school in welding engineering will be considered if there are no qualified junior welding engineering candidates. **Criteria:** Recipients will be selected based on the financial need.

Duration: Annual. **To Apply:** Applicants must complete the application form and submit it along with a high school diploma, financial statement and a transcript of records. **Remarks:** The award was established in the memory of Jack R. Barckhoff. **Contact:** AWS Foundation, Inc., 8669 NW 36 St., Ste. 130, Miami, FL, 33166-6672; Phone: 800-443-9353.

1666 ■ John C. Lincoln Memorial Scholarship
(Undergraduate/Scholarship)

Purpose: To provide financial assistance to individuals interested in pursuing a career in welding engineering. **Focus:** Welding. **Qualif.:** Applicants must be undergraduate students pursuing a four-year Bachelors Degree in a welding program at an accredited university; must have 2.5 overall grade point average; must be 18 years old and above; must be citizen of the United States and plan to attend an academic institution located within the United States. **Criteria:** Recipients are selected based on financial need. Priority will be given to those individuals residing or attending school in the States of Ohio and Arizona.

Funds Avail.: $3,500. **Duration:** Annual. **Number Awarded:** 1. **To Apply:** Applicants must complete the application form and submit it along with a high school diploma and a financial statement. **Remarks:** The scholarship is named after the founder of The Lincoln Electric Company. **Contact:** AWS Foundation, Inc., 8669 NW 36 St., Ste. 130, Miami, FL, 33166-6672; Phone: 800-443-9353.

1667 ■ Miller Electric International WorldSkills Competition Scholarship *(Undergraduate/Scholarship)*

Purpose: To provide financial assistance to individuals interested in pursuing a bachelor's degree in welding engineering, welding engineering technology, or an engineering program with an emphasis in welding. **Focus:** Welding. **Qualif.:** Applicants must compete in the National Skills USA Competition for welding and advance to the AWS Weld Trials at the AWS International Welding and Fabricating Exposition and Convention. **Criteria:** Recipients will be selected based on financial need.

Funds Avail.: $10,000 per year for a period of four consecutive years; Up to $1,000 in AWS Publications. **Duration:** Biennial. **Number Awarded:** Varies. **Contact:** E-mail: scholarship@aws.org.

1668 ■ Ronald C. and Joyce Pierce - Mobile Section Named Scholarships *(Undergraduate/Scholarship)*

Purpose: To provide financial assistance to individuals interested in pursuing a bachelor's degree in welding engineering, welding engineering technology, or an engineering program with an emphasis in welding. **Focus:** Welding. **Qualif.:** Applicants must be U.S citizen; must have a minimum 2.5 overall grade point average, and be full-time college sophomores, juniors, or seniors; must have a minimum of a high school diploma; must be attending a

four year college to pursue a degree in engineering. **Criteria:** Selection will be based on financial need; AWS members may receive greater consideration.

Duration: Annual. **To Apply:** Applicant must provide 2 letters of recommendation; must submit original official transcripts from high school, college or university; submit an essay on why applicant want to pursue a Career in Welding & Fabrication with minimum of 250 words typed and double spaced. **Deadline:** April 30. **Remarks:** The scholarship is named to honor Ronald C. Pierce, Chairman Emeritus AWS Foundation, AWS Past President, and Joyce Pierce who provide the sponsorship. **Contact:** American Welding Society, Mobile Section, PO Box 10546, Prichard, AL, 36610.

1669 ■ Praxair International Scholarship
(Undergraduate/Scholarship)

Purpose: To provide financial assistance to individuals interested in pursuing a bachelor's degree in welding engineering, welding engineering technology, or an engineering program with an emphasis in welding. **Focus:** Welding. **Qualif.:** Applicants must be undergraduate students pursuing a full time (minimum 12 credit hours) degree in Welding Engineering or Welding Engineering Technology; must be minimum 18 years old and citizens of United States or Canada planning to attend an academic institution within the United States or Canada; must maintain an overall GPA of 2.5. **Criteria:** Recipients will be selected based on financial need.

Funds Avail.: $2,500. **Duration:** Annual. **Number Awarded:** 1. **To Apply:** Applicants must complete the application form and submit it along with a high school diploma and a financial statement. **Contact:** AWS Foundation, Inc., 8669 NW 36 St., Ste. 130, Miami, FL, 33166-6672; Phone: 800-443-9353.

1670 ■ Resistance Welding Manufacturers Alliance Scholarship *(Undergraduate/Scholarship)*

Purpose: To provide financial assistance to individuals interested in the resistance of the welding process while pursuing a career in welding engineering. **Focus:** Welding. **Qualif.:** Applicant must be a student with an interest in resistance welding that has taken, or plans to take a course in resistance welding.

Duration: Annual. **To Apply:** Applicant must mark resistance welding as a Career Interest. **Deadline:** July 2. **Remarks:** Established in 2005. **Contact:** E-mail: scholarship@aws.org.

1671 ■ Robert L. Peaslee Brazing Scholarship
(Undergraduate/Scholarship)

Purpose: To provide financial assistance to individuals interested in pursuing a bachelor's degree in welding engineering, welding engineering technology, or an engineering program with an emphasis in welding. **Focus:** Welding. **Qualif.:** Applicants must be college junior or senior students pursuing a degree in Welding Engineering or Welding Engineering Technology; must have demonstrated leadership abilities; must be 18 years old and above; must be United States, Canada, or Mexico citizens and plan to attend an academic institution within the United States or Canada; must have 3.0 overall grade point average; must express an interest in the resistance welding process; must show emphasis on Brazing and Soldiering application in their coursework. **Criteria:** Recipients will be selected based on final decision of Selection Committee.

Funds Avail.: $5,000. **Duration:** Annual. **Number Awarded:** 1. **To Apply:** Applicants must complete the ap-

Awards are arranged alphabetically below their administering organizations

plication form and two letters or reference only; Personal Statement should include; Transcript; Statement of Unmet Financial Need; Verification of Enrollment. **Remarks:** The fund was established by Robert L. Peaslee and the AWS Detroit Brazing and Soldering Division of the AWS Detroit Section. Established in 2004. **Contact:** AWS Foundation, Inc., 8669 NW 36 St., Ste. 130, Miami, FL, 33166-6672; Phone: 800-443-9353.

1672 ■ James A. Turner, Jr. Memorial Scholarship
(Undergraduate/Scholarship)

Purpose: To provide financial assistance to those individuals interested in pursuing a management career in welding store operations or a welding distributorship. **Focus:** Welding. **Qualif.:** Applicants must be full-time students pursuing a four-year Bachelor of Business Degree leading to a management career in welding store operations or a welding distributorship; must be employed for at least ten hours a week at a welding distributorship; must be 18 years old and above. **Criteria:** Recipients will be selected based on financial need.

Funds Avail.: $3,500. **Duration:** Annual. **Number Awarded:** 1. **To Apply:** Applicants must complete the application form and submit it along with a high school diploma and a financial statement. **Remarks:** The scholarship is named in honor of James A. Turner, Jr. **Contact:** AWS Foundation, Inc., 8669 NW 36 St., Ste. 130, Miami, FL, 33166-6672; Phone: 800-443-9353.

1673 ■ William A. and Ann M. Brothers Scholarship
(Undergraduate/Scholarship)

Purpose: To provide financial assistance to those individuals interested in pursuing a career in welding. **Focus:** Welding. **Qualif.:** Applicants must be U.S. citizens who are full-time undergraduate students pursuing a minimum four-year degree in a welding or welding related program at an accredited university; must be at least 18 years of age and have a minimum 2.5 overall GPA. **Criteria:** Recipients are selected based on financial need; priority will be given to individuals residing or attending schools in the state of Ohio.

Funds Avail.: $6,000. **Duration:** Annual. **Number Awarded:** 1. **To Apply:** Applicants must submit an application form; high school diploma; and a financial statement. **Contact:** AWS Foundation, Inc., 8669 NW 36 St., Ste. 130, Miami, FL, 33166-6672; Phone: 800-443-9353.

1674 ■ William B. Howell Memorial Scholarship
(Undergraduate/Scholarship)

Purpose: To provide financial assistance to those individuals interested in pursuing a career in welding. **Focus:** Welding. **Qualif.:** Applicants must be U.S. citizens who are full-time undergraduate students pursuing a minimum four-year degree in a welding or welding related program at an accredited university; must be at least 18 years of age; must have a minimum 2.5 overall GPA; may be enrolled full or part time; must also plan to attend an institution located within the United States. **Criteria:** Recipients are selected based on financial need. Priority will be given to individuals residing or attending school in the states of Florida, Michigan and Ohio.

Funds Avail.: $2,500. **Duration:** Annual. **Number Awarded:** 1. **To Apply:** Applicants must submit an application form; high school diploma; and financial statement. **Deadline:** February 15. **Contact:** AWS Foundation, Inc., 8669 NW 36 St., Ste. 130, Miami, FL, 33166-6672; Phone: 800-443-9353.

1675 ■ American Wine Society Educational Foundation (AWSEF)
c/o Bonnie Huber, President
9 Summit Avenue
Butler, NJ 07405
Ph: (212)878-6277
E-mail: president@awsef.org
URL: www.awsef.org

1676 ■ American Wine Society Educational Foundation Scholarships (AWSEF) *(Graduate/Scholarship)*

Purpose: To support full-time graduate students pursuing degrees in enology, viticulture, or health aspects of wine. **Focus:** Enology; Viticulture. **Qualif.:** Applicants must be full-time graduate students who have completed at least one semester in a graduate program leading to an MS, Ph.D., or equivalent in enology, viticulture, or health aspects of wine, and who express intent to work in one of these areas upon completion of the graduate degree (Ph.D. candidates with an MS from another graduate program are eligible); must be North American (U.S., Canada, Mexico, Bahamas and West Indies Islands) citizens or permanent residents, enrolled in a degree located within North American institutions of higher learning.

Funds Avail.: $3,500 each. **Duration:** Annual. **Number Awarded:** Varies. **To Apply:** Applicants must submit a completed scholarship application form; current official transcripts of all college or university academic records; a written statement which indicates the applicant's intent to pursue a career in a wine or grape related area; a written recommendation from the applicant's academic advisor using the form supplied; three letters of recommendation including the academic advisor's written recommendation. **Deadline:** March 31. **Contact:** Kristen Lindelow, AWSEF Vice President of Scholarships; Email: vpscholarships@ awsef.org.

1677 ■ American Woman's Society of Certified Public Accountants (AWSCPA)
701 N Post Oak Rd
Houston, TX 77024
Free: 800-297-2721
E-mail: info@awscpa.org
Social Media: www.facebook.com/American-Womans
 -Society-of-CPAs-192800737440746
www.linkedin.com/groups/698867/profile
twitter.com/AWSCPANational

1678 ■ AWSCPA National Scholarships *(Graduate/ Scholarship)*

Purpose: To support students aspiring to become a Certified Public Accountant. **Focus:** Accounting. **Qualif.:** Applicant must meet the minimum education requirements to sit for the CPA exam within one year of scholarship awarding; must either be an entering Senior, 5th year student, graduate student or a graduate and eligible to take a review course within one year of scholarship awarding; must have a 3.0 GPA in accounting and a 3.0 GPA overall; and must either be a U.S. citizen or a permanent resident of the United States. **Criteria:** Selection is based on the application.

Duration: One year. **To Apply:** Applicants must submit a completed scholarship application form together with a validated transcript and an essay of no longer than 1,000

Awards are arranged alphabetically below their administering organizations

words. Applicants can also apply online. **Remarks:** Sponsored by Becker CPA Review. **Contact:** LInda Jone, CPA of Becker at 800-369-8545 or email at ljones@becker.com.

1679 ■ National Scholarships *(Graduate, Undergraduate/Award, Scholarship)*

Purpose: To provide support individuals who's aspiring to become CPAs. **Focus:** Accounting.

Duration: Annual.

1680 ■ AmericanMuscle
1 Lee Blvd., Unit 2
Malvern, PA 19355
Ph: (810)981-4720
Free: 866-727-4720
URL: www.americanmuscle.com
Social Media: www.facebook.com/AmericanMuscleFB
instagram.com/americanmusclecom
twitter.com/americanmuscle
www.youtube.com/americanmusclevideos

1681 ■ AmericanMuscle's Student Scholarship Program *(College, University/Scholarship)*

Purpose: To offer support to students and encourage solid education and motivation as the means to be successful. **Focus:** Automotive technology; Engineering, Automotive; Mechanics and repairs. **Qualif.:** Applicant must be currently enrolled full-time in a college or technical institute in the United States or be high school seniors planning to attend a college or post-secondary institution; restricted to those students pursuing an automotive degree or related field of study.

Funds Avail.: $2,000. **Duration:** Semiannual. **Number Awarded:** 2 in spring semester; 2 in fall Semester. **To Apply:** Applicant must submit an essay (750 to 1, 500 words) explaining who they are and how they plan to use their automotive education to incite positive change and innovation within the custom car industry. Essays must be submitted in Microsoft Word or PDF format. Essay should be submitted via email to scholarship@americanmuscle.com; proof of enrollment must be submitted. **Deadline:** June 15; October 15. **Contact:** Email: scholarships@ americanmuscle.com.

1682 ■ Americans United for Separation of Church and State (AUSCS)
1310 L St. NW, Ste. 200
Washington, DC 20005
Ph: (202)466-3234
E-mail: americansunited@au.org
URL: www.au.org
Social Media: www.facebook.com/americansunited
www.instagram.com/americansunited
twitter.com/americansunited

1683 ■ Student Essay Contest *(High School/Prize)*

Purpose: To encourage the separation of church and state. **Focus:** General studies/Field of study not specified. **Qualif.:** Applicant must be a high school junior or senior in the United States. Employees and board members of Americans United, and members of their families, are not eligible to participate. **Criteria:** Selection will be based on the best essay submitted. Criteria include quality of writing and

research, supported by specific examples and sources.

Funds Avail.: $1,500 (1st prize); $1,000 (2nd prize); $500 (3rd prize). **Duration:** Annual. **Number Awarded:** 3. **To Apply:** Applicant must submit a 750 to 1,000 word essay on the following topic: Why is the separation of religion and government important to you? What have you or others in your community done to oppose threats to religious freedom? What more can be done? Completed essay and application must be submitted online. **Deadline:** April 19.

1684 ■ amfAR, The Foundation for AIDS Research
120 Wall St., 13th Fl.
New York, NY 10005-3908
Ph: (212)806-1600
Fax: (212)806-1601
E-mail: info@amfar.org
URL: www.amfar.org
Social Media: www.facebook.com/
amfarthefoundationforaidsresearch
www.instagram.com/amfar
twitter.com/amfar
www.youtube.com/user/AIDSResearch

1685 ■ Mathilde Krim Fellowships in Biomedical Research *(Doctorate/Fellowship)*

Purpose: To encourage the investigators with limited experience and demonstrated interest in the field of HIV/AIDS to redirect or to embark on a career in biomedical, social or behavioral HIV/AIDS research. **Focus:** AIDS. **Qualif.:** Applicants must hold a research or clinical doctorate; must be positioned to secure an independent research position; must be mentored by an experienced investigator at the same US or international nonprofit research institution who is qualified to oversee the proposed research, has successfully supervised postdoctoral fellows and is at the associate professor level or higher; be the main author on significant publications in leading international peer-reviewed journals; have made oral and poster presentations at major scientific conferences and meetings. **Criteria:** Selections will be based on committee's criteria.

Funds Avail.: $150,000 including maximum 10% indirect costs. **To Apply:** Applicants must visit the website to obtain a letter of intent form; the LOI format for this program has been simplified; only the following will be required: eligibility details, Publications, Presentations, and Posters; fellow's biographical sketch and mentor's biographical sketch and list of fellows supervised; resources and environment form; signature form; the best-qualified eligible applicants will be invited to submit complete applications proposing original research to be conducted. **Deadline:** May 17 (Register for Portal Log-in and Instructions); May 22 (Letter of Intent Submission). **Contact:** grantapps@amfar.org.

1686 ■ AMP Global Youth
1220 L St. NW, Ste. 100-161
Washington, DC 20005
Ph: (202)709-6172
E-mail: info@aidemocracy.org
URL: www.ampglobalyouth.org
Social Media: www.facebook.com/AMPGlobalYouth
twitter.com/ampglobalyouth

1687 ■ Americans for Informed Democracy Global Scholar Program *(Undergraduate/Scholarship)*

Purpose: To support and encourage students from all different fields, backgrounds and interests who have a strong

Awards are arranged alphabetically below their administering organizations

academic records. **Focus:** International affairs and relations; Leadership, Institutional and community; Public affairs. **Qualif.:** Applicants must be high school students and visionary global leaders. **Criteria:** Applicants will be evaluated based on academic records, leadership skills; backgrounds, interests and geographic areas.

Funds Avail.: No specific amount. **To Apply:** Applicants must submit an online application form. **Remarks:** Established in 2006.

1688 ■ Amtrol Inc.
1400 Division Rd.
West Warwick, RI 02893
Ph: (401)884-6300
Fax: (401)884-4773
URL: www.amtrol.com
Social Media: twitter.com/amtroltankstour
www.youtube.com/user/AmtrolUSA

1689 ■ Amtrol Scholarship *(High School/Scholarship)*

Purpose: To encourage high school students to consider careers specializing in the provision and protection of ground water resources. **Focus:** Water resources. **Qualif.:** Applicants must be high school seniors intending to pursue a career in a ground water related field; must have a minimum 3.0 GPA in high school; must be freshman year in a full-time academic program of study at a four-year accredited university or college located in the United States; must be U.S. citizens or legal residents of the United States. **Criteria:** Selection will be based on strength of support provided by the applicant's references; review of examination transcripts and GPA scores; written confirmation of acceptance from the college or university.

Funds Avail.: $3,000. **Duration:** Annual. **Number Awarded:** 1. **To Apply:** Applicants must include biographical and achievement information by completing the scholarship application form; a 500-word essay and a 300-word description of the applicant's high school ground water project and or practical environmental work experience must accompany the application; must be accompanied by two letters of recommendation. **Deadline:** June 1. **Remarks:** Established in 1954. **Contact:** URL: agwt.org/content/scholarship-opportunities; Email: trustinfo@agwt.org.

1690 ■ Amusement & Music Operators Association (AMOA)
380 Terra Cotta Road, Ste. F
Crystal Lake, IL 60012
Ph: (847)428-7699
Fax: (847)428-7719
Free: 800-937-2662
E-mail: info@amoa.com
URL: amoa.memberclicks.net
Social Media: www.facebook.com/AMOAassociation
www.instagram.com/amoa_association/
www.linkedin.com/company/amoaassociation
twitter.com/coinop

1691 ■ Wayne E. Hesch Memorial Scholarship *(Undergraduate, Graduate/Scholarship)*

Purpose: To provide financial support to students who are, or plan or hope to be engaged in the profession. **Focus:**

General studies/Field of study not specified. **Qualif.:** Must be in a member good standing. **Criteria:** Selection will be based on the committee's criteria.

Funds Avail.: No specific amount. **Duration:** Annual. **To Apply:** Applications can be submitted online. **Deadline:** February 15. **Remarks:** The award was established in the memory of Wayne E. Hesch, a former President of AMOA. Established in 1985. **Contact:** AMOA Education Foundation, Wayne E. Hesch Memorial Scholarship Program, 380 Terra Cotta Rd, Ste F, Crystal Lake, IL, 60012.

1692 ■ AMV
c/o Lead Roster
548 Market St.
San Francisco, CA 94104
E-mail: support@leadroster.com
URL: goamv.com

1693 ■ The Lead Roster B2B Sales & Marketing Scholarship *(Undergraduate, High School/Scholarship)*

Purpose: To provide financial support to high school and college students from anywhere in the world who are interested in sales and marketing. **Focus:** Marketing and distribution. **Qualif.:** Applicants must be high school and college students interested in sales and marketing.

Funds Avail.: $1,000. **Duration:** Annual. **Number Awarded:** 1. **To Apply:** Application details are available at www.leadroster.com/scholarship-terms. **Deadline:** December 15.

1694 ■ The Publicity.ai SEO & Content Marketing Scholarship *(Undergraduate, High School/Scholarship)*

Purpose: To support high school and college students from around the world who are interested in sales and marketing. **Focus:** Marketing and distribution. **Qualif.:** Applicants must be high school and college students interested in sales and marketing.

Funds Avail.: $1,000. **Duration:** Annual. **Number Awarded:** 1. **To Apply:** Application and details are available at: publicity.ai/?scholarship. **Deadline:** December 15.

1695 ■ AMVETS
4647 Forbes Blvd.
Lanham, MD 20706-4380
Ph: (301)459-9600
Fax: (301)459-7924
Free: 877-726-8387
E-mail: amvets@amvets.org
URL: www.amvets.org
Social Media: www.facebook.com/AMVETSHQ
www.linkedin.com/company/amvets
twitter.com/AMVETSNational
twitter.com/AMVETSHQ
www.youtube.com/user/AMVETSnational

1696 ■ AMVETS National Scholarships - Entering College Freshmen *(Undergraduate/Scholarship)*

Purpose: To assist deserving children and grandchildren of veterans in attaining post-secondary education. **Focus:**

Awards are arranged alphabetically below their administering organizations

General studies/Field of study not specified. **Qualif.:** Applicant must be a graduating high school senior entering at the college freshmen level; must have a minimum high school GPA of 3.0; must be the child or grandchild of a United States veteran; must be a U.S. citizen; must have demonstrated academic promise and financial need; and must agree to authorize AMVETS to publicize the scholarship award if selected. **Criteria:** Selection is based on academic promise, financial need and merit.

Funds Avail.: $1,000 per year. **Duration:** Annual; up to 4 years. **To Apply:** Applicants must submit a copy of the veteran's honorable discharge (Form DD 214). Dependents of current military personnel must submit a letter from the base commander certifying the active duty status of the parent; an official high school transcript (must be in the 4.0 grade scale or if in a different system, translated to the 4.0 scales); SAT and/or ACT scores; a complete and signed copy of the parent(s)'/guardian(s)' 1040 tax form (applicant's name must appear on the tax form); a copy of the applicant's Free Application for Federal Student Aid (FAFSA); essay (50-100 words); acceptance letter from the accredited school to be attended; proof of college expenses; and a resume detailing extracurricular activities, volunteer activities, community services and jobs held during the past four years. **Deadline:** April 15. **Contact:** AMVETS at the above address.

1697 ■ AMVETS National Scholarships - For Veterans *(Undergraduate/Scholarship)*

Purpose: To financially assist veterans who have exhausted government aid or who might not otherwise have the financial means to further their education. **Focus:** General studies/Field of study not specified. **Qualif.:** Applicant must be a U.S. veteran; a U.S. citizen; must demonstrate financial need; must agree to authorize AMVETS to publicize the scholarship award if selected; high school diploma or GED. **Criteria:** Selection is based on academic promise, financial need and merit.

Funds Avail.: $4,000. **Duration:** Annual; up to 4 years. **To Apply:** Applicants must submit a copy of the veteran's honorable discharge or a letter certifying current service and eligibility for release from active duty prior to attending school; official college transcripts for all courses attempted and any degrees or certificates awarded (must be in the 4.0 grade scale, or if in a different system, translated to the 4.0 scales); a complete and signed copy of the applicant's 1040 tax form; a copy of the Free Application for Federal Student Aid (FAFSA); an essay (50-100 words); acceptance letter or a letter stating current student status from an accredited school; proof of college expenses; and a resume detailing military duty and awards, volunteer activities, community services and jobs held during the past four years. **Deadline:** April 30.

1698 ■ AMVETS National Scholarships - JROTC *(Undergraduate, College/Medal)*

Purpose: To support Junior ROTC cadets in pursuing study at an undergraduate college or university. **Focus:** General studies/Field of study not specified. **Qualif.:** Applicant must be an active JROTC cadet and currently a high school senior; must have a minimum high school GPA of 3.0; must be the child or grandchild of a U.S. veteran; a U.S. citizen; and agree to authorize AMVETS to publicize the scholarship award if selected. **Criteria:** Must demonstrate academic promise and financial need. Essay will be judged on theme, style, originality , and overall quality.

Funds Avail.: $1,000. **Duration:** Annual. **Number Awarded:** 1. **To Apply:** Must provide a copy of veteran's record of service demonstrating an honorable discharge (DD214) or a letter from your commanding officer certifying active duty status; official high school or college/university transcripts; Student Aid Report (SAR) from the free Application for Federal Student Aid (FAFSA); acceptance letter of letter stating student status from an accredited program; resume; essay on a topic to be determined. Children/Grandchildren must provide SAT or ACT scores.

1699 ■ Amyloidosis Foundation
7151 N Main St., Ste. 2
Clarkston, MI 48346
Ph: (248)922-9610
Fax: (248)922-9620
Free: 877-269-5643
E-mail: info@amyloidosis.org
URL: www.amyloidosis.org
Social Media: www.facebook.com/amyloidosisfdn
www.instagram.com/amyloidosisfoundation
www.linkedin.com/company/amyloidosis-foundation
twitter.com/Amyloidosisfdn

1700 ■ AF Junior Research Grant *(Professional development/Grant)*

Purpose: To support research for all types of amyloidosis being conducted by junior investigators. **Focus:** Medical research. **Qualif.:** Applicants must have completed their doctoral studies or clinical fellowship within ten years prior to application.

Duration: Annual.

1701 ■ AF Senior Research Grant *(Advanced Professional/Grant)*

Purpose: To support research for all types of amyloidosis being conducted by senior investigators. **Focus:** Medical research.

Funds Avail.: $100,000. **Duration:** Annual.

1702 ■ Anaheim Police Association
3156 E. La Palma Ave., Ste. B
Anaheim, CA 92806
Ph: (714)635-0272
URL: anaheimpa.com
Social Media: www.facebook.com/AnaheimPA

1703 ■ Anaheim Police Survivors and Scholarship Fund *(Undergraduate/Scholarship)*

Purpose: To provide financial assistance to the families of Anaheim Police Officers and other public safety personnel who are killed or severely injured in the line of duty. **Focus:** General studies/Field of study not specified.

Funds Avail.: No specific amount. **Remarks:** Established in 1979.

1704 ■ Anchor Scholarship Foundation
138 S Rosemont Rd., Ste. 206
Virginia Beach, VA 23452
Ph: (757)777-4724
URL: www.anchorscholarship.com

1705 ■ Anchor Scholarship Foundation Scholarships *(Undergraduate, Four Year College, Two Year College/Scholarship)*

Purpose: To provide scholarships to eligible dependents of active duty or retired Navy personnel. **Focus:** General

Awards are arranged alphabetically below their administering organizations

studies/Field of study not specified. **Qualif.:** Applicants must be eligible dependents (i.e. children and spouses) of active duty, retired, or honorably discharged surface U.S. Navy personnel. **Criteria:** Recipients will be selected on the basis of four equally weighted criteria; academic performance, character, extracurricular, and financial need.

Funds Avail.: $2,000 to $20,000. **Duration:** Annual. **Number Awarded:** Varies. **To Apply:** Two step process; Step one, create an account online, eligible person will receive an applicant ID number; step complete application and supply supporting documentation. **Deadline:** April 1. **Contact:** Email: scholarshipadmin@anchorscholarship.com; URL: www.anchorscholarshipapplication.com.

1706 ■ Anderson & Cummings, LLP

4200 W Vickery Blvd.
Fort Worth, TX 76107
Ph: (817)920-9000
URL: www.anderson-cummings.com
Social Media: www.facebook.com/andersoncummingsftw/
www.linkedin.com/company/andersoncummings
twitter.com/ACFortWorth

1707 ■ Anderson Cummings AC Scholarship for Higher Education *(Undergraduate/Scholarship)*

Purpose: To support and encourage exceptional leadership and achievement by Tarrant County students. **Focus:** General studies/Field of study not specified. **Qualif.:** Applicants must be Tarrant County high school seniors with a minimum GPA of 3.0; must be planning to attend an accredited two- or four-year U.S. college/university; all student applicants must plan to attend an accredited two- or four-year U.S. college or university as a full time student beginning the summer or fall immediately following high school graduation. **Criteria:** Selection will be based on the qualifications and compliance with the application process.

Funds Avail.: $500. **Duration:** Annual. **To Apply:** Applicants must visit the website to complete online application form and to upload all required documents; must also submit a minimum 500 words essay that answers the question; "How have your childhood experiences influenced your decision to continue your education at college?". **Deadline:** April 1. **Contact:** URL: www.anderson-cummings.com/scholarship.html.

1708 ■ Texas Scholarship of Academic Excellence *(Undergraduate, Graduate/Scholarship)*

Purpose: To assist full-time students currently enrolled in degree programs at a Texas university/college who have demonstrated outstanding leadership and standards on campus or in their community. **Focus:** General studies/Field of study not specified. **Qualif.:** Applicants must be currently enrolled in a full-time degree program at an accredited Texas university or college; all student applicants must be able to provide a letter of recommendation from either a university or college faculty member or someone within the community. **Criteria:** Selection will be based on the aforesaid qualifications and compliance with the application process. Preference will be given to students studying law.

Funds Avail.: $1,500. **Duration:** Annual. **To Apply:** Applicants must complete and submit the online scholarship application form with all supporting documents in required formats; applicants must also provide the following materials two recommendation letters from faculty or prominent

community members; proof of leadership via campus or community involvement; and a 500-1,500 word essay based on topic chosen by firm. **Deadline:** November 30. **Contact:** URL: www.anderson-cummings.com/collegescholarship.html.

1709 ■ The Anderson Group Summer Institute

PO Box 38334
Los Angeles, CA 90038-0334
E-mail: execsecretary@harpsociety.org
URL: www.harpsociety.org
Social Media: facebook.com/harpsociety
instagram.com/harpsociety
twitter.com/harpsociety

1710 ■ The Anderson Group Summer Institute Scholarships *(Other/Scholarship)*

Purpose: To provide opportunity to members to go in AHS National Conference by covering their expenses. **Focus:** Music. **Qualif.:** Applicants must be active members of the American Harp Society; must meet age requirements. **Criteria:** Selection is based on financial need and musical promise in the study of harp.

Funds Avail.: $1,000. **Duration:** Biennial; in odd-numbered years. **Number Awarded:** 2. **To Apply:** Applicants must submit biography including applicant's full name, legal residence, present address, telephone number, email address, proof of age, musical and academic education, personal profile, general analysis of financial need and long-range goals for harp-playing, hand-written statement, CD recording, and letter of reference.

1711 ■ Angus Foundation

3201 Frederick Ave.
Saint Joseph, MO 64506-2997
Ph: (816)383-5100
Fax: (816)233-9703
E-mail: mjenkins@angusfoundation.org
URL: www.angusfoundation.org
Social Media: www.facebook.com/AngusAssoc
www.linkedin.com/company/american-angus-association
twitter.com/AngusAssoc

1712 ■ Angus Foundation Graduate Student Degree Scholarship Program *(Graduate/Scholarship)*

Purpose: To support young men and women who are active in Angus breed pursuing an advanced degree in higher education. **Focus:** Animal science and behavior. **Qualif.:** Applicants must have been members of National Junior Angus Association and are currently junior, regular or life members of the American Angus Association. **Criteria:** Strong preference and priority will be given to applicants pursuing advanced degrees related closely to the beef industry.

Funds Avail.: $5,000 each. **Duration:** Annual. **Number Awarded:** 5. **Deadline:** May 1. **Remarks:** Established in 1998.

1713 ■ Angus Foundation Undergraduate Student Scholarships *(Undergraduate/Scholarship)*

Purpose: To support young men and women who are actively involved in the Angus breed pursuing an undergraduate degree in higher education. **Focus:** General

Awards are arranged alphabetically below their administering organizations

studies/Field of study not specified. **Qualif.:** Applicants must have been members of National Junior Angus Association and are currently junior, regular or life members of the American Angus Association.

Funds Avail.: $1,000 to $5,000. **Duration:** Annual. **Number Awarded:** 2. **Deadline:** May 1.

1714 ■ Angus/Talon Youth Educational Learning Program Endowment Fund (Graduate, Undergraduate/Scholarship)

Purpose: To support young men and women who are active in Angus breed pursuing an advanced degree in higher education. **Focus:** Animal science and behavior. **Qualif.:** Applicants must be either undergraduate or graduate students pursuing a degree related closely to the beef cattle industry. **Criteria:** Preference will be given to applicants who have successfully maintained academic progress.

Funds Avail.: Amount varies. **Duration:** Annual. **Number Awarded:** Varies. **To Apply:** Applicants must submit a signed and dated application form; must include a copy of the most recent college/university transcript, three letters of recommendation and member code.

1715 ■ Animal Behavior Society (ABS)
2111 Chestnut Ave., Ste. 145
Glenview, IL 60025
Ph: (312)893-6585
Fax: (312)896-5619
E-mail: info@animalbehaviorsociety.org
URL: www.animalbehaviorsociety.org
Social Media: www.facebook.com/animalbehaviorsociety
twitter.com/animbehsociety

1716 ■ ABS Student Research Grant (Graduate/Grant)

Purpose: To encourage graduate students of animal behavior to participate in meaningful conservation-related research. **Focus:** Animal science and behavior; Conservation of natural resources. **Qualif.:** Applicants must be Animal Behavior Society student members; must be enrolled in a graduate program.

Funds Avail.: $500-$2,000. **To Apply:** Application must be uploaded as a single, eight-page pdf file including sections such as Research Proposal (Pages 1-4), Budget and Justification (Pages 5), Curriculum Vitae (Pages 6-7), Animal Care Questionnaire (Page 8); Must be single-spaced, Arial 11 pt. font, 1″ (2.5 cm) margins on the top, bottom and two sides, pages numbered successively from 1-8 at the bottom center. **Deadline:** December 15.

1717 ■ ABS Amy R. Samuels Cetacean Behavior and Conservation Award (Graduate/Grant)

Purpose: To provide financial support for graduate students studying cetacean behavior and/or cetacean conservation in natural environments. **Focus:** Animal science and behavior; Environmental conservation. **Qualif.:** Candidates must be Animal Behavior Society student members; must be enrolled in a graduate program.

Funds Avail.: $500-$2,000. **Duration:** Annual. **Number Awarded:** 2. **To Apply:** Application must be uploaded as a single, eight-page pdf file including sections such as Research Proposal (Pages 1-4), Budget and Justification (Pages 5), Curriculum Vitae (Pages 6-7), Animal Care Questionnaire (Page 8); Must be single-spaced, Arial 11 pt

font, 1″ (2.5 cm) margins on the top, bottom and two sides, pages numbered successively from 1-8 at the bottom center. **Deadline:** December 15.

1718 ■ Annapolis Rotary Club
PO Box 3175
Annapolis, MD 21403
URL: www.annapolisrotary.org

1719 ■ Rotary Club of Annapolis Scholarship (Graduate/Scholarship)

Purpose: To support graduating high school students defray their college expenses. **Focus:** General studies/Field of study not specified. **Qualif.:** Applicants must meet the following qualifications: must be a graduating senior; must be a resident of Anne Arundel County; must attend a high school in the Annapolis Area (including home schooled students); Children and grandchildren of Rotarians are not eligible; members of a Rotary "Interact" high school organization can apply; plan to attend an accredited community college, college or university; must have a minimum GPA of 3.0; must have demonstrated involvement in school activities; must have demonstrated significant involvement in community service activities. **Criteria:** Preference will be given to those who have demonstrated significant involvement in school and in the community.

Funds Avail.: $1,500. **Number Awarded:** 4. **To Apply:** Applicants must complete and submit the application form with required information available in the website. **Deadline:** April 1. **Contact:** Scholarship Committee, Rotary Club of Annapolis, PO Box 3175, Annapolis, MD, 21403; Email: cf1729@yahoo.com.

1720 ■ Annmarie Skin Care
821 Bancroft Way
Berkeley, CA 94710
Ph: (510)679-1794
Free: 866-729-9434
URL: www.annmariegianni.com/home
Social Media: www.facebook.com/annmarieskincare
www.instagram.com/annmarieskincare
www.linkedin.com/company/annmarie-organic-skin-care
www.pinterest.com/annmariegianni
twitter.com/AnnmarieBeauty

1721 ■ Honest. Wild. Beautiful. Scholarship Program (Undergraduate, Graduate/Scholarship)

Purpose: To recognize and award a student who chose an ongoing commitment to make the planet more beautiful through their studies, work, or volunteer efforts. **Focus:** General studies/Field of study not specified. **Qualif.:** Applicants must be currently enrolled in an undergraduate or graduate program at an accredited college or university OR be a senior in high school who has already been accepted to an undergraduate program; be enrolled full-time; maintain a GPA of 3.0 or higher; demonstrate a strong interest and commitment to issues and initiatives relating to making our planet a better place for all. **Criteria:** Content and creativity of video submission.

Funds Avail.: $1,000. **Duration:** Annual. **Number Awarded:** 1. **To Apply:** Create a short (2-3 minutes) video describing what you've done, what you're going to do, and what your vision is for a more honest, wild, and beautiful planet. Submit at www.annmariegianni.com/

Awards are arranged alphabetically below their administering organizations

scholarship.html. **Deadline:** September 30.

1722 ■ Annual Young, Marr & Associates

3554 Hulmeville Rd., No. 102
Bensalem, PA 19020
Ph: (215)515-6389
URL: www.youngmarrlaw.com
Social Media: www.facebook.com/youngmarrlaw
www.linkedin.com/company/young-marr-law
twitter.com/youngmarrlaw

1723 ■ Annual Young, Marr & Associates Scholarship *(Undergraduate/Scholarship)*

Purpose: To support those pursuing legal careers. **Focus:** Law. **Qualif.:** Applicant must be a U.S. citizen; have a minimum 3.0 GPA; have proof of admission to law school. **Criteria:** Selection is based on merit and the quality of the application materials.

Funds Avail.: $1,000. **Duration:** Annual. **Number Awarded:** 1. **To Apply:** Applicant must fill out application, write essay, and send transcript. **Deadline:** August 1. **Contact:** Email: scholarships@youngmarrlaw.com; URL: www.youngmarrlaw.com/scholarship/.

1724 ■ antibodies-online Inc.

PO Box 5201
Limerick, PA 19468
Fax: (888)205-9894
Free: 877-302-8632
E-mail: info@antibodies-online.com
URL: www.antibodies-online.com

1725 ■ antibodies-online Annual University Scholarship *(Undergraduate, Graduate/Scholarship)*

Purpose: To help young scientists and prospective scientists in the life sciences to help cover the costs of their education. **Focus:** Life sciences. **Qualif.:** Applicant must be enrolled as a freshman, undergraduate, or graduate student at an accredited college or university for the upcoming fall or spring term with a major in life sciences or related fields. **Criteria:** Selection is based on the written responses supplied by the applicant.

Funds Avail.: $1,000. **Duration:** Annual. **Number Awarded:** 2. **To Apply:** Application should be completed online along with a 250-word abstract on why the applicant has decided to enter the field of life science and how they plan to use their degree to further advance this field, and a 150-word abstract on what their favorite discovery is and why. **Deadline:** January 20; July 20. **Contact:** Email: scholarship@antibodies-online.com; URL: www.antibodies-online.com/scholarship/.

1726 ■ Antioch University New England - Center for Tropical Ecology and Conservation (CTEC)

40 Avon St.
Keene, NH 03431-3516
Free: 800-553-8920
E-mail: ctec.ane@antioch.edu
URL: www.antioch.edu/new-england/resources/centers
-institutes/center-tropical-ecology-conservation
Social Media: www.facebook.com/The-Center-for-Tropical
-Ecology-and-Conservation-71367975972

1727 ■ CTEC Internships *(Undergraduate/Internship)*

Purpose: To support individuals who wish to conduct studies related to tropical ecology and conservation. **Focus:** Ecology; Environmental conservation. **Qualif.:** Applicants must be students who are interested to further their study relevant to tropical ecology and conservation. **Criteria:** Selection will be based on the committees' criteria.

Funds Avail.: No specific amount. **To Apply:** Applicants may contact the Center for application process and other information.

1728 ■ CTEC Scholarships *(Graduate/Scholarship)*

Purpose: To provide financial support to students studying tropical ecology and conservation at Antioch University New England. **Focus:** Ecology. **Qualif.:** Applicants must be AUNE graduate students who are members of CTEC and are conducting research or projects pertaining to ecology, sustainable development, natural resource management, or conservation.

1729 ■ APA Division 16: School Psychology

c/o American Psychological Association
750 1st St. NE
Washington, DC 20002-4242
Fax: (202)336-6040
URL: apadivision16.org
Social Media: www.facebook.com/apadivision16
twitter.com/apadivision16

1730 ■ Paul E. Henkin School Psychology Travel Grant *(Doctorate/Grant)*

Purpose: To support travel expenses for students members of the APA Division 16 to attend the annual APA convention. **Focus:** Psychology. **Qualif.:** Applicant must have a student membership in APA Div. 16; Demonstrated commitment to pursuit of a school psychology career; Those receiving any APA travel reimbursement for convention attendance are ineligible.

Funds Avail.: $1,500. **Duration:** Annual. **To Apply:** Applicants must complete interested may find all application instructions and necessary materials on APF's website. **Deadline:** April 15.

1731 ■ APA Division 35: Society for the Psychology of Women

750 First St. NE
Washington, DC 20002-4242
Ph: (202)336-5500
URL: www.apadivisions.org

1732 ■ Janet Hyde Graduate Student Research Grant *(Doctorate, Graduate/Grant)*

Purpose: To support psychology students who are supporting feminist research. **Focus:** Psychology; Women's studies. **Qualif.:** Applicants must be currently enrolled in doctoral programs in psychology. **Criteria:** Selection will be based on the committee's criteria.

Funds Avail.: $500. **To Apply:** Application requirements are the following: cover page with project title, investigator's name, address, phone, fax and email address; a 100-word abstract; a proposal (five-page maximum, double-spaced) addressing the project's purpose, theoretical rationale and procedures, including how the method and data analysis

Awards are arranged alphabetically below their administering organizations

stem from the proposed theory and purpose (references are not included in this five-page limit); a one-page statement articulating the study's relevance to feminist goals and importance to feminist research. The expected timeline for progress and completion of the project (including the date of the research proposal committee meeting if applicable) and the project timeline should not exceed two years; a faculty sponsor's recommendation, which includes why the research cannot be funded, or funded in full, by other sources (the letter should be attached to the email with the application materials, and please do not send such separately); status of IRB review process, including expected date of IRB submission and approval (preference will be given to proposals that have received approval); an itemized budget (if additional funds are needed to ensure completion of the project, please specify sources, and funds cannot be used for tuition, living expenses or travel to present research at a conference); applicant's curriculum vitae; all sections of the proposal should be typed and prepared according to APA style (e.g., please use 12-point font). Applicants should submit no more than two files (i.e., one with the letter of recommendation and one with all the other required materials). **Deadline:** March 15; September 15. **Contact:** Hyde Award co-chairs, Stephanie Parisien, PhD, and Alexandra Zelin, PhD;.

1733 ■ APA Division 39: Psychoanalysis
750 First St. NE
Washington, DC 20002-4242
Ph: (202)336-5500
URL: www.apadivisions.org
Social Media: www.facebook.com/APADiv39
twitter.com/APADiv39

1734 ■ APA Division 39 Scholars Program
(Graduate/Scholarship)

Purpose: To promote learning about psychoanalysis and to facilitate open dialogue and exchange of ideas about the future of psychoanalytic thinking, research and practice in the field of psychology and the role of psychologists in the future of psychoanalysis. **Focus:** Psychology. **Qualif.:** Applicant may be any US-based, non-profit organizations or associations with a tax designation and nonprofit associations; those outside of the United States may also eligible as long as the content of the entry is in English; both members and non-members of ASAE may submit entries; must be inscribed with the name of the organization or association the communication was produced for, not the name of the individual employed by said organization or association who created the communication.

Funds Avail.: $1,000. **To Apply:** Applications can be submitted online and further details can be obtained from the website. **Deadline:** September 15.

1735 ■ APA Division 44: Society for the Psychology of Sexual Orientation and Gender Diversity
750 First St. NE
Washington, DC 20002-4242
Ph: (202)336-5500
URL: www.apadivisions.org

1736 ■ Bisexual Foundation Scholarships
(Graduate/Scholarship, Award)

Purpose: To support emerging scholars who are researching about the growing bisexuality to the field of LGBT is-

sues in psychology. **Focus:** Psychology. **Qualif.:** Applicants must be currently enrolled full-time in a psychology or therapy/counseling graduate program; applications from students in allied disciplines, such as gender studies, social work and sociology, cannot be considered at this time. **Criteria:** Selection will based on the application materials submitted.

Funds Avail.: Up to $1,000. **Duration:** Annual. **To Apply:** Applicants must submit an application consisting of one cover sheet; curriculum vitae; one copy of the project description; and a letter from the supervisor addressing their qualifications and quality/feasibility of the project. **Deadline:** March 30.

1737 ■ Malyon Smith Scholarship Research Award
(Graduate/Scholarship)

Purpose: To support the advancement of research about psychology of sexual orientation and gender identity. **Focus:** Psychology. **Qualif.:** Applicants must be full-time graduate students in a department of Psychology. **Criteria:** Selection will be based on the proposal.

Funds Avail.: Up to $1,000. **Duration:** Annual. **To Apply:** Applicants must submit an application consisting of one cover sheet; curriculum vitae; one copy of the project description; and a letter from the supervisor addressing their qualifications and quality/feasibility of the project. **Deadline:** March 30. **Remarks:** Established in 1994. **Contact:** Email:malyon.smith.award@gmail.com.

1738 ■ APA Division 54: Society of Pediatric Psychology (SPP)
PO Box 3968
Lawrence, KS 66046
Ph: (785)856-0713
Fax: (785)748-2034
E-mail: apadiv54@gmail.com
URL: www.societyofpediatricpsychology.org

1739 ■ Lizette Peterson Homer Injury Prevention Grant *(Other, Undergraduate, Graduate/Grant)*

Purpose: To support research related to the prevention of injuries in children and adolescents. **Focus:** Medicine, Pediatric. **Qualif.:** Applicants must be students and/or faculty members at an accredited university with demonstrated research competence and area commitment. **Criteria:** Selection will be based on the committee's criteria.

Funds Avail.: $5,000. **Number Awarded:** 1. **To Apply:** Applicants must submit the following: research proposal, which should be no more than four single spaced pages including (1) 100-word abstract, (2) description of the project with introduction, methods and procedures, (3) detailed budget, and (4) references (all in one MS Word document); a current curriculum vitae; supporting faculty supervisor letter (if the applicants are student); and proof of IRB approval or statement that IRB approval is pending. **Deadline:** October 1.

1740 ■ Marion and Donald Routh Student Research Grant *(Graduate/Grant)*

Purpose: To provide assistance to research related to the field of pediatric psychology. **Focus:** Medicine, Pediatric. **Qualif.:** Applicants must be student members of SPP in full-time psychology graduate programs. Postdoctoral fellows are not eligible for this award. **Criteria:** Recipients are selected based on committee's review of proposal.

Awards are arranged alphabetically below their administering organizations

Funds Avail.: $1,000. **Number Awarded:** 2. **To Apply:** Applicants must submit a summary of proposed research (maximum of 100 words); project objectives (maximum of 4 pages); Project objectives, aims and hypotheses; Relevant literature review; Design, method and procedures; Data analytic plan; References. **Deadline:** October 15. **Contact:** SPP Executive Committee, contact Idia Thurston.

1741 ■ APhA Foundation

2215 Constitution Ave. NW
Washington, DC 20037
Ph: (202)429-7565
Fax: (202)638-3793
E-mail: info@aphafoundation.org
URL: www.pharmacist.com
Social Media: www.facebook.com/APhAFoundation
twitter.com/pharmacists
www.youtube.com/user/aphafoundation

1742 ■ Mary Louise Andersen Scholarship
(Undergraduate/Scholarship)

Purpose: To support students who choose to invest their time in their school's APhA - ASP chapter to help shape the future of the profession while managing the demands of a full-time pharmacy curriculum. **Focus:** Pharmacy. **Qualif.:** Applicants must: complete at least one academic year in the professional sequence of courses; earn cumulative grade point average of at least 2.75 on a 4.0 scale (or equivalent grading system) in professional coursework during pharmacy school; be active members in the APhA Academy of Student Pharmacists (APhA-ASP) in the United States or Puerto Rico. **Criteria:** Applications will be scored according to the following points system: academic performance, 10 points; pharmacy related activities, 25 points; non-pharmacy community activities/work, 25 points; essay, 20 points; letters of recommendation, 20 points.

Funds Avail.: $1,000. **Duration:** Annual. **Number Awarded:** 1. **To Apply:** Application and details are available online at www.aphafoundation.org/student-scholarship-program. **Deadline:** December 1. **Contact:** John Little, Executive Fellow; Email: jlittle@aphanet.org.

1743 ■ APhA Foundation Scholarship
(Undergraduate/Scholarship)

Purpose: To support students who choose to invest their time in their school's APhA - ASP chapter to help shape the future of the profession while managing the demands of a full-time pharmacy curriculum. **Focus:** Pharmacy. **Qualif.:** Applicants must complete at least one academic year in the professional sequence of courses; earn cumulative grade point average of at least 2.75 on a 4.0 scale (or equivalent grading system) in professional coursework during pharmacy school; active members in the APhA Academy of Student Pharmacists (APhA-ASP) in the United States or Puerto Rico. **Criteria:** Applications will be scored according to the following points system: academic performance, 10 points; pharmacy related activities, 25 points; non-pharmacy community activities/work, 25 points; essay, 20 points; letters of recommendation, 20 points.

Funds Avail.: $1,000. **Duration:** Annual. **Number Awarded:** 1. **To Apply:** Application and details are available online at www.aphafoundation.org/student-scholarship-program. **Deadline:** December 1. **Contact:** John Little, Executive Fellow; Email: jlittle@aphanet.org.

1744 ■ George F. Archambault Scholarship
(Undergraduate/Scholarship)

Purpose: To support students who choose to invest their time in their school's APhA - ASP chapter to help shape the future of the profession while managing the demands of a full-time pharmacy curriculum. **Focus:** Pharmacy. **Qualif.:** Applicants must: complete at least one academic year in the professional sequence of courses; earn cumulative grade point average of at least 2.75 on a 4.0 scale (or equivalent grading system) in professional coursework during pharmacy school; be active members in the APhA Academy of Student Pharmacists (APhA-ASP). **Criteria:** Applications will be scored according to the following points system: academic performance, 10 points; pharmacy related activities, 25 points; non-pharmacy community activities/work, 25 points; essay, 20 points; letters of recommendation, 20 points. Preference given to those indicating further USPHS service, including a USPHS residency program, and completion of a COSTEP program or equivalent clerkship experience at a USPHS facility, or child of a USPHS pharmacist.

Funds Avail.: $1,500. **Duration:** Annual. **Number Awarded:** 1. **To Apply:** Application and details are available online at www.aphafoundation.org/student-scholarship-program. **Deadline:** December 1. **Remarks:** Established by the Archambault Foundation to honor the late George F. Archambault, PhG, PhC, JD, for his long career of dedicated service to the pharmacy profession and the Public Health Service. Established in 2011. **Contact:** John Little, Executive Fellow; Email: jlittle@aphanet.org.

1745 ■ Boyle Family Scholarship *(Undergraduate/Scholarship)*

Purpose: To support student pharmacists who will provide much needed pharmaceutical care. **Focus:** Pharmacy. **Qualif.:** Applicants must complete at least one academic year in the professional sequence of courses; earn cumulative grade point average of at least 2.75 on a 4.0 scale (or equivalent grading system) in professional coursework during pharmacy school; be active members in the APhA Academy of Student Pharmacists (APhA-ASP) in the United States or Puerto Rico. **Criteria:** Applications will be scored according to the following points system: academic performance, 10 points; pharmacy related activities, 25 points; non-pharmacy community activities/work, 25 points; essay, 20 points; letters of recommendation, 20 points.

Funds Avail.: $1,000. **Duration:** Annual. **Number Awarded:** 1. **To Apply:** Application and details are available online at www.aphafoundation.org/student-scholarship-program. **Deadline:** December 1. **Contact:** John Little, Executive Fellow; Email: jlittle@aphanet.org.

1746 ■ Marvin and Joanell Dyrstad Scholarship
(Undergraduate/Scholarship)

Purpose: To support students who choose to invest their time in their school's APhA - ASP chapter to help shape the future of the profession while managing the demands of a full-time pharmacy curriculum. **Focus:** Pharmacy. **Qualif.:** Applicants must: complete at least one academic year in the professional sequence of courses; earn cumulative grade point average of at least 2.75 on a 4.0 scale (or equivalent grading system) in professional coursework during pharmacy school; be active members in the APhA Academy of Student Pharmacists (APhA-ASP) in the United States or Puerto Rico. **Criteria:** Applications will be scored according to the following points system: academic performance, 10 points; pharmacy related activities, 25

Awards are arranged alphabetically below their administering organizations

points; non-pharmacy community activities/work, 25 points; essay, 20 points; letters of recommendation, 20 points.

Funds Avail.: $1,000. **Duration:** Annual. **Number Awarded:** 1. **To Apply:** Application and details are available online at www.aphafoundation.org/student-scholarship-program. **Deadline:** December 1. **Contact:** John Little, Executive Fellow; Email: jlittle@aphanet.org.

1747 ■ Gloria Francke Scholarship *(Undergraduate/ Scholarship)*

Purpose: To support students who choose to invest their time in their school's APhA - ASP chapter to help shape the future of the profession while managing the demands of a full-time pharmacy curriculum. **Focus:** Pharmacy. **Qualif.:** Applicants must complete at least one academic year in the professional sequence of courses; must earn cumulative grade point average of at least 2.75 on a 4.0 scale (or equivalent grading system) in professional coursework during pharmacy school; must be active members in the APhA Academy of Student Pharmacists (APhA-ASP). **Criteria:** Applications will be scored according to the following points system: academic performance, 10 points; pharmacy related activities, 25 points; non-pharmacy community activities/work, 25 points; essay, 20 points; letters of recommendation, 20 points.

Funds Avail.: $1,000. **Duration:** Annual. **Number Awarded:** 1. **To Apply:** Application and details are available online at www.aphafoundation.org/student-scholarship-program. **Deadline:** December 1. **Contact:** John Little, Executive Fellow; Email: jlittle@aphanet.org.

1748 ■ John A. Gans Scholarship *(Undergraduate/ Scholarship)*

Purpose: To support students who choose to invest their time in their school's APhA - ASP chapter to help shape the future of the profession while managing the demands of a full-time pharmacy curriculum. **Focus:** Pharmacy. **Qualif.:** Applicants must: complete at least one academic year in the professional sequence of courses; earn cumulative grade point average of at least 2.75 on a 4.0 scale (or equivalent grading system) in professional coursework during pharmacy school; be active members in the APhA Academy of Student Pharmacists (APhA-ASP) in the United States or Puerto Rico. **Criteria:** Applications will be scored according to the following points system: academic performance, 10 points; pharmacy related activities, 25 points; non-pharmacy community activities/work, 25 points; essay, 20 points; letters of recommendation, 20 points.

Funds Avail.: $1,000. **Duration:** Annual. **Number Awarded:** 1. **To Apply:** Application and details are available online at www.aphafoundation.org/student-scholarship-program. **Deadline:** December 1. **Contact:** John Little, Executive Fellow; Email: jlittle@aphanet.org.

1749 ■ Robert D. Gibson Scholarship *(Undergraduate/Scholarship)*

Purpose: To support students who choose to invest their time in their school's APhA - ASP chapter to help shape the future of the profession while managing the demands of a full-time pharmacy curriculum. **Focus:** Pharmacy. **Qualif.:** Applicants must: complete at least one academic year in the professional sequence of courses; earn cumulative grade point average of at least 2.75 on a 4.0 scale (or equivalent grading system) in professional coursework during pharmacy school; active members in the APhA Academy of Student Pharmacists (APhA-ASP) in the United States and Puerto Rico. **Criteria:** Applications will be scored ac-

cording to the following points system: academic performance, 10 points; pharmacy related activities, 25 points; non-pharmacy community activities/work, 25 points; essay, 20 points; letters of recommendation, 20 points.

Funds Avail.: $1,000. **Duration:** Annual. **Number Awarded:** 1. **To Apply:** Application and details are available online at www.aphafoundation.org/student-scholarship-program. **Deadline:** December 1. **Contact:** John Little, Executive Fellow; Email: jlittle@aphanet.org.

1750 ■ Sam Kalman Scholarship *(Undergraduate/ Scholarship)*

Purpose: To support students who choose to invest their time in their school's APhA - ASP chapter to help shape the future of the profession while managing the demands of a full-time pharmacy curriculum. **Focus:** Pharmacy. **Qualif.:** Applicants must complete at least one academic year in the professional sequence of courses; earn cumulative grade point average of at least 2.75 on a 4.0 scale (or equivalent grading system) in professional coursework during pharmacy school; active members in the APhA Academy of Student Pharmacists (APhA-ASP). **Criteria:** Applications will be scored according to the following points system: academic performance, 10 points; pharmacy related activities, 25 points; non-pharmacy community activities/work, 25 points; essay, 20 points; letters of recommendation, 20 points.

Funds Avail.: $1,000. **Duration:** Annual. **Number Awarded:** 1. **To Apply:** Application and details are available online at www.aphanet.org/student-scholarship-progam.**Deadline:** December 1. **Remarks:** Established by a lead gift from Elizabeth Keyes and supported by gifts from current and former APhA staff members to honor Samuel H. Kalman. **Contact:** John Little, Executive Fellow; Email: jlittle@aphanet.org.

1751 ■ Juan and Esperanza Luna Scholarship *(Undergraduate/Scholarship)*

Purpose: To support students who choose to invest their time in their school's APhA - ASP chapter to help shape the future of the profession while managing the demands of a full-time pharmacy curriculum. **Focus:** Pharmacy. **Qualif.:** Applicants must complete at least one academic year in the professional sequence of courses; earn cumulative grade point average of at least 2.75 on a 4.0 scale (or equivalent grading system) in professional coursework during pharmacy school; active members in the APhA Academy of Student Pharmacists (APhA-ASP) in the United States or Puerto Rico. **Criteria:** Applications will be scored according to the following points system: academic performance, 10 points; pharmacy related activities, 25 points; non-pharmacy community activities/work, 25 points; essay, 20 points; letters of recommendation, 20 points.

Funds Avail.: $1,000. **Duration:** Annual. **Number Awarded:** 1. **To Apply:** Application and details are available online at www.aphafoundation.org/student-scholarship-program. **Deadline:** December 1. **Remarks:** Established by Nancy A. Alvarez and named in honor of her parents. Established in 2013. **Contact:** John Little, Executive Fellow; Email: jlittle@aphanet.org.

1752 ■ Paul Pumpian Scholarship *(Undergraduate/ Scholarship)*

Purpose: To support students who choose to invest their time in their school's APhA - ASP chapter to help shape the future of the profession while managing the demands of a full-time pharmacy curriculum. **Focus:** Pharmacy. **Qualif.:**

Awards are arranged alphabetically below their administering organizations

Applicants must complete at least one academic year in the professional sequence of courses; earn cumulative grade point average of at least 2.75 on a 4.0 scale (or equivalent grading system) in professional coursework during pharmacy school; active members in the APhA Academy of Student Pharmacists (APhA-ASP) in the United States and Puerto Rico. **Criteria:** Applications will be scored according to the following points system: academic performance, 10 points; pharmacy related activities, 25 points; non-pharmacy community activities/work, 25 points; essay, 20 points; letters of recommendation, 20 points.

Funds Avail.: $1,000. **Duration:** Annual. **Number Awarded:** 1. **To Apply:** Application and details are available online at www.aphafoundation.org/student-scholarship-program. **Deadline:** December 1. **Contact:** John Little, Executive Fellow; Email: jlittle@aphanet.org.

1753 ■ Colonel Jerry W. Ross Scholarship
(Undergraduate/Scholarship)

Purpose: To support students who choose to invest their time in their school's APhA - ASP chapter to help shape the future of the profession while managing the demands of a full-time pharmacy curriculum. **Focus:** Pharmacy. **Qualif.:** Applicants must complete at least one academic year in the professional sequence of courses; earn cumulative grade point average of at least 2.75 on a 4.0 scale (or equivalent grading system) in professional coursework during pharmacy school; active members in the APhA Academy of Student Pharmacists (APhA-ASP); be an Air Force pharmacy technician pursuing a degree in pharmacy, or family member of an Air Force pharmacist or technician enrolled in an accredited college of pharmacy; demonstrate the Air Force core values of excellence, selflessness, integrity, leadership and academics. **Criteria:** Applications will be scored according to the following points system: academic performance, 10 points; pharmacy related activities, 25 points; non-pharmacy community activities/work, 25 points; essay, 20 points; letters of recommendation, 20 points. Preference given to those indicating further Air Force Service.

Funds Avail.: $1,000. **Duration:** Annual. **Number Awarded:** 1. **To Apply:** Application and details are available online at www.aphafoundation.org/student-scholarship-program. **Deadline:** December 1. **Contact:** John Little, Executive Fellow; Email: jlittle@aphanet.org.

1754 ■ Charles C. Thomas Scholarship
(Undergraduate/Scholarship)

Purpose: To support students who choose to invest their time in their school's APhA - ASP chapter to help shape the future of the profession while managing the demands of a full-time pharmacy curriculum. **Focus:** Pharmacy. **Qualif.:** Applicants must complete at least one academic year in the professional sequence of courses; earn cumulative grade point average of at least 2.75 on a 4.0 scale (or equivalent grading system) in professional coursework during pharmacy school; active members in the APhA Academy of Student Pharmacists (APhA-ASP) in the United States or Puerto Rico; members of Phi Lambda Sigma (PLS). **Criteria:** Applications will be scored according to the following points system: academic performance, 10 points; pharmacy related activities, 25 points; non-pharmacy community activities/work, 25 points; essay, 20 points; letters of recommendation, 20 points.

Funds Avail.: $1,000. **Duration:** Annual. **Number Awarded:** 1. **To Apply:** Application and details available online at www.aphafoundation.org/student-scholarship-program. **Deadline:** December 1. **Contact:** John Little, Executive Fellow; Email: jlittle@aphanet.org.

1755 ■ Appalachian School of Law (ASL)
1169 Edgewater Dr.
Grundy, VA 24614
Ph: (276)935-4349
Fax: (276)935-8496
Free: 800-895-7411
E-mail: admissions@asl.edu
URL: www.asl.edu
Social Media: www.facebook.com/
  theAppalachianSchoolofLaw
www.instagram.com/appalachian_law/
twitter.com/Appalachian_Law
www.youtube.com/user/AppalachianLaw

1756 ■ Appalachian School of Law Merit Scholarship Program *(Undergraduate/Scholarship)*

Purpose: To support students financially in the form of credit against tuition charged. **Focus:** Law. **Qualif.:** Applicants must be at least incoming first year law students. **Criteria:** Recipients will be selected based on the Law School Admission Test (LSAT) and Undergraduate Grade Point Average (UGPA); eligibility for retention of an award during the students' first three years in law school will be based on their academic performance; scholarship will be awarded on a first come, first serve basis.

Funds Avail.: $5,000 to $35,000 for three years as a credit against tuition. **To Apply:** Application details available at www.asl.edu/scholarships/. **Contact:** Financial Aid Office; Phone: 800-895-7411 ext. 1211; Email: financialaid@asl.edu.

1757 ■ Appel Law Firm L.L.P.
100 Pringle Ave., Ste. 730
Walnut Creek, CA 94596
Ph: (925)938-2000
Free: 855-262-7735
URL: www.appellawyer.com
Social Media: www.linkedin.com/company/2240137
www.linkedin.com/company/appel-law-firm-llp
twitter.com/AppelLawyer

1758 ■ Auto Accident Law Firm Survivor Scholarships *(Graduate/Scholarship)*

Purpose: To assist students with their educational expenses. **Focus:** General studies/Field of study not specified. **Qualif.:** Applicants must be U.S. citizens or permanent residents; have sustained injuries from a car or truck accident or been affected by someone else's accident; enrolled in an accredited college or university within the United States; and have a cumulative GPA of 3.00 or higher. Graduate and Law school students are encouraged to apply. **Criteria:** Selection will be based on the committee's criteria.

Funds Avail.: $1,000. **Duration:** Annual. **To Apply:** Applicants must submit the following requirements: completed application; official copy of a current academic transcript; copy of a police report or other proof of the applicants' accident; and personal essay of not more than three pages describing the car accident, how it affected the applicants and what are the changes since the accident. **Deadline:** August 1.

Awards are arranged alphabetically below their administering organizations

1759 ■ Applied Behavior Analysis EDU

1200 Broad St.
Bellingham, WA 98229
Ph: (760)385-3643
URL: www.appliedbehavioranalysis.org

1760 ■ Applied Behavior Analysis EDU $1,000 Excellence in Practice Scholarship *(Graduate/Scholarship)*

Purpose: To help a student pay for their masters degree in applied behavioral analysis. **Focus:** Behavioral sciences; Psychology. **Qualif.:** Applicant must be a graduate student or starting a graduate program in applied behavioral analysis with a minimum GPA of 3.5. **Criteria:** Selection is based on the strength of the written essay.

Funds Avail.: $1,000. **Duration:** Annual. **Number Awarded:** 1. **To Apply:** Applicant must write and submit an essay in 2,500 words or less that tells their story, focusing on what inspired them to start thinking about a career in applied behavioral analysis. Applicant must complete the application form and submit along with the written essay and proof of GPA (transcript or other verifiable document). **Deadline:** May 1. **Remarks:** Established in 2019.

1761 ■ Applied Motion Products Inc.

404 Westridge Dr.
Watsonville, CA 95076
Ph: (831)761-6555
Fax: (831)761-6544
Free: 800-525-1609
E-mail: djoyce@applied-motion.com
URL: www.applied-motion.com
Social Media: www.facebook.com/AppliedMotionProducts
www.linkedin.com/company/applied-motion-products
twitter.com/ampmotion

1762 ■ The Make It Move Scholarships *(Undergraduate/Scholarship)*

Purpose: To assist those who want to turn their brilliant ideas into moving, working realities. **Focus:** General studies/Field of study not specified. **Qualif.:** Applicants must be U.S. citizens and international students enrolled in high school or an undergraduate/graduate program at an accredited U.S. institution. **Criteria:** Selection will be reviewed by a selection committee compose of managing staff members of Applied Motion; will be based on which students creation best exemplified the originality, ingenuity, and mechanical skill to drive the advancement of today's technological society.

Funds Avail.: $1,000. **Number Awarded:** 1. **To Apply:** Applicants need to film your final creation in action using instagram; include a short description about your creation; upload it to Instagram including the hashtag #ampmakeitmove. **Deadline:** October 16.

1763 ■ Appraisal Institute Education and Relief Foundation (AI)

200 W Madison St., Ste. 1500
Chicago, IL 60606
Ph: (312)335-4133
Fax: (312)335-4134
E-mail: aierf@appraisalinstitute.org
URL: www.aierf.org
Social Media: www.facebook.com/AppraisalInstitute
www.linkedin.com/company/appraisal-institute
twitter.com/AI_National

1764 ■ AIERF Undergraduate Scholarship *(Undergraduate/Scholarship)*

Purpose: To help finance the education endeavors of individuals concentrating in real estate appraisal, land economics, real estate or allied fields. **Focus:** Land management; Real estate. **Qualif.:** Applicants must be students majoring in real estate appraisal, land economics, real estate or allied fields; must be sophomore, junior or senior students seeking an associate or bachelor's degree; must be full- or part-time students in any U.S. degree granting college or university; must have a strong academic record. **Criteria:** Selection will be based on the applicants' academic excellence.

Funds Avail.: $1,000. **Duration:** Annual. **To Apply:** Applicants must submit a completed application together with two-hundred (200) word personal statement discussing academic achievements, financial need, career aspirations, involvement in real estate field; and any qualifications considered relevant by the applicants; current resume; official copies of all college transcripts; two (2) letters of recommendation attesting to applicants' work ethic, character and pursuit of career in real estate appraisal, land economics, real estate or allied fields. Letters of recommendation should be sent directly to the Appraisal Institute Education Trust. **Deadline:** April 15. **Contact:** Appraisal Institute Education Trust at educationtrust@appraisalinstitute.org.

1765 ■ Arab American Institute (AAI)

1600 K St. NW, Ste. 601
Washington, DC 20006
Ph: (202)429-9210
Fax: (202)429-9214
E-mail: communications@aaiusa.org
URL: www.aaiusa.org
Social Media: www.facebook.com/ArabAmericanInstitute
twitter.com/aaiusa

1766 ■ Al Muammar Scholarships for Journalism *(Undergraduate/Scholarship)*

Purpose: To provide scholarship opportunities to American students who are of Arab descent. **Focus:** Journalism. **Qualif.:** Applicants must be Arab American college students who are majoring in journalism, as well as college seniors who have been accepted to a graduate journalism school; be a UC citizen or permanent resident of Arab descent; be a full-time student at an accredited college or university in the United States; have current GPA of 3.3 or higher. **Criteria:** Selection will be based on the committee's criteria.

Funds Avail.: $5,000. **Number Awarded:** 4. **To Apply:** Applicants may download an application from the foundation's website; must also include an official transcript and letter of recommendation (one letter must be from the professor in the applicant's journalism program and second would be ideally be from a leader in an Arab American community organization with which the applicant has had a relationship). Must send five copies of the following items, collated into five complete packets, each with one copy of completed application form: unofficial transcript; resume; short essay; work samples. **Remarks:** Established in 2005.

Awards are arranged alphabetically below their administering organizations

1767 ■ Barakat Trust and Barakat Foundation Scholarships (Graduate, Postdoctorate/Scholarship)

Purpose: To provide financial support for students and scholars of Islamic culture. **Focus:** General studies/Field of study not specified. **Qualif.:** Applicants must have completed at least a B.A. degree and have been accepted for graduate study or an apprenticeship at an accredited university or institution. **Criteria:** Selection will be based on the committee's criteria.

Funds Avail.: Amount varies. **Duration:** Annual. **To Apply:** Applicants may contact the Barakat Trust and Barakat Foundation for the application requirements. **Deadline:** February 15. **Contact:** Barakat Trust and Barakat Foundation, 2665 Kimball Pomona, CA 91767; rc101@earthlink.net.

1768 ■ Ameen Rihani Scholarship Program (Undergraduate/Scholarship)

Purpose: To promote academic excellence and provide an opportunity for outstanding student to reach their fullest potential. **Focus:** Literature; Philosophy; Political science. **Qualif.:** Applicants should be individuals who are of Lebanese or other Arab descent; are citizens/legal permanent residents of the United States; have attained a cumulative GPA of at least 3.25 on a 4.0 scale; will enter a college or university as full-time, degree-seeking freshmen in the fall of the year; and, have demonstrated leadership abilities through participation in the community service, extracurricular or other activities. **Criteria:** Selection shall be based on the aforementioned qualifications and compliance with the application details.

Funds Avail.: $1,500. **Duration:** Annual. **Number Awarded:** 1. **To Apply:** Application is via nomination by teachers, counselors, and principals are invited to nominate students with outstanding academic qualifications, particularly those who would promote success in the fields of literature, philosophy, or political science. **Deadline:** March 15. **Contact:** Ameen Rihani Scholarship Program, The Ameen Rihani Organization, 7979 Old Georgetown Rd., Ste. 700 Bethesda, MD 20814.

1769 ■ Arab American Medical Association Houston Chapter (AAMA)
John P. McGovern Bldg.
1515 Hermann Dr.
Houston, TX 77004-7126
Ph: (713)524-4267
Fax: (713)526-1434
URL: www.aama-houston.org

1770 ■ AAMA Houston Chapter Health Training Scholarships (Other/Scholarship)

Purpose: To support Arab students in their educational pursuit. **Focus:** Education, Medical; Medicine. **Qualif.:** Applicants must be of Arab heritage; enrolled full-time in an internationally recognized health care related school; accepted to spend greater than 3 months at one of Houston's medical institutions or any affiliated hospitals; willing to provide a written report describing their experience during the elective training; willing to attend AAMA meetings during the training months in Houston; and, become members of NAAMA/AAMA-Houston Chapter. **Criteria:** Selection shall be based on the aforementioned applicants' qualifications and compliance with the application details.

Funds Avail.: $750-$3,000. **Duration:** Annual. **To Apply:** Applicants must submit a completed scholarship applica-

tion form along with an updated CV; a letter verifying enrollment in a medical/health institution/school; a letter of acceptance for elective training at any of the medical institutions in Houston and two letters or recommendation from current instructors.

1771 ■ Archaeological Institute of America (AIA)
44 Beacon St.
Boston, MA 02108
Ph: (617)353-9361
Fax: (617)353-6550
URL: www.archaeological.org
Social Media: www.facebook.com/Archaeological.Institute
www.instagram.com/archaeology_aia
twitter.com/archaeology_aia
www.youtube.com/archaeologytv

1772 ■ AIA Graduate Student Travel Awards (Graduate/Grant, Award)

Purpose: To assist graduate students who are presenting papers at the AIA Annual Meeting with their travel expenses. **Focus:** Archeology. **Qualif.:** Applicants must be graduate students and must be AIA members in good standing. **Criteria:** Selection will be based on the committee's criteria.

Funds Avail.: No specific amount. **Duration:** Annual. **To Apply:** Applicant must submit online application form; become available in the fall, attach your cv and a scanned copy of your student id or fax. **Deadline:** November 15. **Contact:** Christine Dziuba; Phone: 857-305-9361; E-mail: cdziuba@archaeological.org.

1773 ■ Archaeological Institute of America Fellowships for Study in the US (Postdoctorate/Fellowship)

Purpose: To provide support to scholars who are pursuing highest quality on various aspects of archeology. **Focus:** Archeology. **Qualif.:** Applicants who are archaeologists must have a PhD degree; architects must have their diploma; must demonstrate professional competence in archaeology in their applications; preference will be given to applicants who are at an early stage of their professional careers. **Criteria:** Selection will be on the basis of scholarly promise as indicated by the applicant's academic record, prior publications and the merits of the proposed research projects.

Funds Avail.: No specific amount. **Duration:** Annual. **Number Awarded:** 1. **To Apply:** Applicants must submit a completed online application form; curriculum vitae, including a list of publications; two references; in case of project collaborator, must submit brief description of DAI project they are involved in, and the nature of their participation And letter of recommendation from a DAI project supervisor. **Deadline:** November 1. **Contact:** Laurel Nilsen Sparks, Fellowship Coordinator; E-mail: fellowships@archaeological.org; Phone: 857-305-9360; E-mail: fellowships@archaeological.org.

1774 ■ Archaeology of Portugal Fellowship (Professional development, Graduate/Fellowship)

Purpose: To support projects pertaining to the archaeology of Portugal. **Focus:** Archeology. **Qualif.:** Applicants must be Portuguese, American or other scholars; must be members of the AIA at the time of application and until the end of the fellowship term. **Criteria:** Selection will be based on the committee's criteria.

Funds Avail.: range of $2,000 to $8,000 ($7,500 is the current maximum). **Duration:** Annual. **Number Awarded:**

Awards are arranged alphabetically below their administering organizations

Varies. **To Apply:** Applicant must submit an online application form including references and transcripts. **Deadline:** November 1. **Contact:** AIA Fellowship Coordinator; E-mail: fellowships@archaeological.org.

1775 ■ Anna C. and Oliver C. Colburn Fellowships
(Doctorate/Fellowship)

Purpose: To support studies undertaken at the American School of Classical Studies at Athens, Greece for no more than a year. **Focus:** Archeology. **Qualif.:** Applicants must be citizens or permanent residents of the United States or Canada; must be members of the AIA at the time of application and until the end of the fellowship term; must be at the pre-doctoral stage or have received a PhD within five years of application. **Criteria:** Selection will be based on the committee's criteria.

Funds Avail.: $5,500 each. **Duration:** Annual; even years. **Number Awarded:** 2. **To Apply:** Applicants must submit all materials including references and transcripts. **Deadline:** January 15. **Contact:** AIA Fellowship Coordinator; E-mail: fellowships@archaeological.org.

1776 ■ DAI Fellowship for Study in Berlin
(Postdoctorate/Fellowship)

Purpose: To provide two post-doctoral research fellowships to AIA members based in North America who wish to use the library facilities of the DAI in Berlin. **Focus:** Archeology. **Qualif.:** Applicants must be members of the Archaeological Institute of America and must be residents of a North American country. **Criteria:** Selection will be on the basis of scholarly promise as indicated by the applicant's academic record, prior publications and the merits of the proposed research projects.

Funds Avail.: No specific amount. **Duration:** Annual; Duration of two months. **Number Awarded:** 2. **To Apply:** Applications, including a research proposal, a curriculum vitae, and a publication list online. **Deadline:** November 30. **Contact:** Dr. Barbara Sielhorst, Fellowship Coordinator; E-mail: Barbara.Sielhorst@dainst.de; Application E-mail: generalsekretaer@dainst.de; Application address: Dr. Philipp von Rummel, Podbielskiallee 69-71, 14195, Berlin.

1777 ■ Jane C. Waldbaum Archaeological Field School Scholarship *(Undergraduate, Graduate/ Scholarship, Award)*

Purpose: To help students who are planning to participate in archaeological field work for the first time. **Focus:** Archeology. **Qualif.:** Applicants must be juniors and senior undergraduate students who have not yet completed their first year of graduate school and currently enrolled at a college or university in United States or Canada; must be at least 18 years old and have not previously participated in an archaeological excavation. **Criteria:** Applicants will be judged based on academic achievements and financial need.

Funds Avail.: $1,000 each. **Duration:** Annual. **Number Awarded:** Varies. **To Apply:** Applicants must complete the online application form; a brief cover letter (300 words or less) in the applicant's own words; an outline of anticipated expenses associated with participation on the project and a statement from the applicant indicating any other financial resources available to help cover expenses and two references for letters of recommendation from professors or academic advisors at the applicant's college or university. **Deadline:** March 1. **Remarks:** The scholarship was established in honor of AIA Honorary President Jane Waldbaum. **Contact:** Laurel Sparks, Lecture & Fellowship

Coordinator,857-305-9360,lsparks@archaeological.org.

1778 ■ Samuel H. Kress Grants for Research and Publication in Classical Art and Architecture
(Professional development, Graduate/Grant, Award)

Purpose: To provide financial support to individuals who have publication activities critical to both current and future archaeological research. **Focus:** Archeology; Architecture; Art. **Qualif.:** Applicants must still be in the research stage and must have a publication contract in place with either a non-profit or commercial publisher; must be members of AIA; in good standing for two consecutive years (or one year for graduate students). **Criteria:** Selection will be based on the committee's criteria.

Funds Avail.: $3,000. **Duration:** Annual. **To Apply:** Applicants must include a timetable for completion of the manuscript, specific plans for publication including budget information and a description of how the grant will be utilized. **Deadline:** November 1; March 1. **Remarks:** Established in 1929. **Contact:** AIA Fellowship Coordinator; Phone: 857-305-9360; E-mail: fellowships@ archaeological.org.

1779 ■ Olivia James Traveling Fellowship *(Professional development/Fellowship)*

Purpose: To support fellows to travel and study in Greece, Cyprus, the Aegean Islands, Sicily, Southern Italy, Asia Minor (Turkey) or Mesopotamia. **Focus:** Archeology. **Qualif.:** Applicants must be US citizens; must have been AIA members in good standing for at least two consecutive years (or one year for graduate students) by the application deadline. **Criteria:** Preference will be given to individuals engaged in dissertation research or to those who received their PhD within five years of the application deadline.

Funds Avail.: $25,000. **Duration:** Annual. **Number Awarded:** 1. **To Apply:** Applicants must have been AIA members in good standing for at least two consecutive years (or one year for graduate students) by the application deadline. **Deadline:** November 1. **Contact:** AIA Fellowship Coordinator; E-mail: fellowships@aia.bu.edu.

1780 ■ Harriet and Leon Pomerance Fellowships
(Graduate/Fellowship)

Purpose: To support an individual project of a scholarly nature, related to Aegean Bronze Age Archaeology. **Focus:** Archeology. **Qualif.:** Applicants must be citizens or permanent residents of the United States or Canada, or be actively pursuing an advance degree at a North American College or University; must must have been AIA members in good standing for at least two consecutive years (or one year for graduate students) by the application deadline. **Criteria:** Preference will be given to candidates whose project requires travel to the Mediterranean for the purpose of the fellowship.

Funds Avail.: $5,000. **Duration:** Annual. **Number Awarded:** 1. **To Apply:** Applicants must be citizens; applicants must good standing for at least two consecutive years (or one year for graduate students) by the application deadline and (including references and transcripts). **Deadline:** November 1. **Contact:** AIA Fellowship Coordinator, E-mail: fellowships@archaeological.org.

1781 ■ Helen M. Woodruff Fellowships
(Postdoctorate/Fellowship)

Purpose: To support pre- or post-doctoral fellowship for study of archaeology and classical studies. **Focus:** Archeol-

Awards are arranged alphabetically below their administering organizations

ogy. **Qualif.:** Applicants must be citizens or permanent residents of the United States. **Criteria:** Selection will be based on the committee's criteria.

Funds Avail.: $10,000. **Duration:** Biennial; Odd years. **Number Awarded:** 1. **To Apply:** Applicant must be a citizen or permanent resident of the United States; American Academy in Rome receives all applications; conclusion of the fellowship tenure, recipients must submit a report to the chair and the president of the American academy in Rome. **Deadline:** November 1. **Contact:** American Academy in Rome, 7 E 60th St., New York, NY, 10022; Fellowship Coordinator; Phone: 857-305-9360 (AIA) or 212-751-7200 (AAR); E-mail: fellowships@archaeological.org.

1782 ■ Architectural Engineering Institute of ASCE (AEI)

c/o American Society of Civil Engineers
1801 Alexander Bell Dr.
Reston, VA 20191
Ph: (703)295-6300
Free: 800-548-2723
E-mail: aei@asce.org
URL: www.asce.org
Social Media: www.facebook.com/ASCE.org
www.instagram.com/asce_hq
twitter.com/ascetweets
www.youtube.com/user/AmerSocCivilEng

1783 ■ ASCE Freeman Fellowship *(Graduate/ Fellowship, Award)*

Purpose: To recognize an individual for their contribution in hydraulic science and art. **Focus:** Engineering, Civil. **Qualif.:** Applicants must be a member of the Society in any grade and in good standing at the time of application and award; the fellowship may be awarded only to those students who will continue their formal graduate education at a recognized educational institution; and previous recipients of the fellowship are eligible to apply. **Criteria:** Selection is based on the quality of the application which shall be submitted to the ASCE Honors and Awards Program office by February 10 of the year of award; society awards committee or its designee for recommendation to the executive committee for final approval; the committee reserves the right to recommend that no award be made in a particular year if no meritorious applications are received.

Funds Avail.: $2,000-$5,000. **Duration:** Annual. **To Apply:** Applicants should submit completed application form; personal essay on why they should receive this fellowship; an essay (of no more than 500 words) highlighting why they chose to become a civil engineer, specific involvement, any special financial needs, and long term goals and plans; detailed financial statement stating the amount of and purposes for which the funds will be used and how they will assist the applicant; description of the proposed research and its objectives; a statement from the institution at which the research is to be conducted indicating that the and proposed research are acceptable to the institution must be included; minimum of two sealed letters of recommendation, one of which must be from a faculty member; sealed official transcript; one- to two-page resume; and include honors, activities, organizations, activities (including any offices held), and any work experience. **Deadline:** February 10. **Remarks:** Established in 1924. **Contact:** Submit the completed application to: American Society of Civil Engineers, Attn: Honors and Awards Program, 1801

Alexander Bell Dr., Reston, Virginia, 20191-4400.

1784 ■ Architectural League of New York (AL)

594 Broadway, Ste. 607
New York, NY 10012
Ph: (212)753-1722
E-mail: info@archleague.org
URL: www.archleague.org
Social Media: www.facebook.com/archleague
www.instagram.com/archleague
twitter.com/archleague
www.youtube.com/user/archleague

1785 ■ The Deborah J. Norden Fund *(Graduate/ Grant)*

Purpose: To assist students and recent graduates in the fields of architecture, architectural history, and urban studies. **Focus:** Architecture.

Funds Avail.: $5,000. **Duration:** Annual. **Number Awarded:** Varies.

1786 ■ Architectural Precast Association (APA)

325 John Knox Rd., Ste. L103
Tallahassee, FL 32303
Ph: (850)205-5637
Fax: (850)222-3019
E-mail: info@archprecast.org
URL: www.archprecast.org
Social Media: www.facebook.com/APAMembers
twitter.com/ArchPrecast

1787 ■ Tom Cory Scholarships *(Undergraduate, Graduate/Scholarship)*

Purpose: To provide financial assistance for architecture students. **Focus:** Architecture. **Qualif.:** Applicants must have a cumulative GPA of 3.0 or higher; must have at least two semesters of school left to complete from date of award; must be involved in activities related to the architectural field. **Criteria:** Recipients are selected based on academic merit and committee's review of the application.

Funds Avail.: $2,000. **Duration:** Annual. **To Apply:** Applicants must send a completed application form; transcript of two years college through the last grading period to the date of application; letter of recommendation from a faculty member of the college or university; a typed description of your career plans after graduation; a typed essay (essay 1) explaining why you chose this career; a typed essay (essay 2) of 300 – 500 words on a topic of your choice related to the precast concrete industry.

1788 ■ Arctic Institute of North America (AINA)

University of Calgary
2500 University Dr. NW , ES-1040
Calgary, AB, Canada T2N 1N4
Ph: (403)220-7515
Fax: (403)282-4609
E-mail: arctic@ucalgary.ca
URL: arctic.ucalgary.ca
Social Media: www.facebook.com/
  arcticinstituteofnorthamerica
www.instagram.com/aina_arcticsynthesis

Awards are arranged alphabetically below their administering organizations

twitter.com/ArcticSynthesis

1789 ■ Lorraine Allison Scholarship *(Graduate/ Scholarship)*

Purpose: To support academic excellence, a demonstrated commitment to northern research, and a desire for research results to be beneficial to northerners, especially Native northerners. **Focus:** Natural sciences; Social sciences. **Qualif.:** Applicants must be students enrolled at a Canadian university in a program of graduate study related to northern issues; candidates in biological science fields will be preferred, but social science topics will also be considered; scholars from Yukon, the Northwest Territories and Nunavut are encouraged to apply. **Criteria:** Candidates will be selected based on selection committee's review of the application materials.

Funds Avail.: 3,000 Canadian Dollars. **Duration:** Annual. **Number Awarded:** 1. **To Apply:** Applicants must provide a two-page description of the northern studies program and relevant project(s) being undertaken; must submit three letters of reference from the applicant's current or past professors; complete curriculum vitae with academic transcript and list of the current source and amounts of research funding, including scholarships, grants and bursaries. **Deadline:** January 10. **Remarks:** The scholarship honor the memory of Lorraine Allison, a remarkable woman who was a biologist, environmental advocate and Arctic scholar. **Contact:** University of Calgary, 2500 University Dr., N.W., ES-1040, Calgary, Alberta, Canada, T2N 1N4; Phone: 403-220-7515; Fax: 403-282-4609; E-mail: arctic@ucalgary.ca.

1790 ■ Jim Bourque Scholarship *(Undergraduate/ Scholarship)*

Purpose: To support a Canadian Aboriginal student who intends to take, or is enrolled in, post-secondary training in education, environmental studies, traditional knowledge or telecommunications. **Focus:** Environmental technology; Telecommunications systems. **Qualif.:** Applicants must be Canadian Aboriginal students currently, or intending to enroll in education, environmental studies, traditional knowledge, or telecommunication. **Criteria:** Scholarships will be given based on financial need, relevance of study, achievements, return on investment and overall presentation of the application.

Funds Avail.: 1,000 Canadian Dollars. **Duration:** Annual. **Number Awarded:** 1. **To Apply:** Applicants must submit a description of their intended program of study and the reason for their choice of program (500 words); a copy of the recent high school or college/university transcript; letter of recommendation from a community leader; a statement of financial need; proof of enrollment to post-secondary institution; and must also provide a proof of Canadian Aboriginal descent. **Deadline:** July 12. **Remarks:** The scholarship honor the legacy of the late Hon. James W. Bourque, PC. **Contact:** University of Calgary, 2500 University Dr., N.W., ES-1040, Calgary, Alberta, Canada, T2N 1N4; Phone: 403-220-7515; Fax: 403-282-4609; E-mail: arctic@ucalgary.ca.

1791 ■ Northern Scientific Training Program *(Graduate/Scholarship)*

Purpose: To support projects on northern topics from all disciplines and in multi-disciplinary fields. **Focus:** Biology; Science. **Qualif.:** Applicants must be enrolled in a degree program at a Canadian university; Summer and winter projects are eligible; Students supported by training funds must be Canadian citizens or permanent residents. **Crite-**

ria: Candidates will be selected based on selection committee's review of the application materials.

Funds Avail.: Up to 5,000 Canadian Dollars. **Duration:** Annual. **Number Awarded:** Varies. **To Apply:** Completed application form including; student contact information; detailed budget showing any other funding and its source being provided to the project; Official academic transcripts; independent letter of support. **Deadline:** November 8. **Contact:** Northern Studies Committee, NSTP, University of Calgary, 2500 University Dr., N.W., ES-1040; E-mail:arctic@ucalgary.ca.

1792 ■ Jennifer Robinson Memorial Scholarship *(Graduate/Scholarship)*

Purpose: To support a graduate student in northern biology. **Focus:** Biology. **Qualif.:** Applicants must be graduate students enrolled at a Canadian university, and studying Northern biology ("northern" is defined as locations that lie north of the southern limit of the discontinuous permafrost zone). **Criteria:** Applicants are judged upon the committee's criteria.

Funds Avail.: 5,000 Canadian Dollars. **Duration:** Annual. **Number Awarded:** 1. **To Apply:** Applicants must include one page cover letter; brief description of the proposed research (maximum 3 pages including references), including a clear hypothesis, relevance, title and statement of the purpose of the research, the area and type of study, the methodology and plan for evaluation of findings; three reference letters; complete curriculum vitae; official transcripts; a list of current sources and amounts of research funding, including scholarships, grants and bursaries. **Deadline:** January 10. **Remarks:** The scholarship honor the memory of Jennifer J. Robinson, a dedicated field worker. Established in 1987. **Contact:** University of Calgary, 2500 University Dr., N.W., ES-1040, Calgary, Alberta, Canada, T2N 1N4; Phone: 403-220-7515; Fax: 403-282-4609; E-mail: arctic@ucalgary.ca.

1793 ■ Arctic Physical Therapy Fairbanks
308 Old Steese Hwy.
Fairbanks, AK 99701
Ph: (907)374-3000
Fax: (907)451-7244
URL: www.physicaltherapyfairbanks.com
Social Media: www.facebook.com/
    ArcticPhysicalTherapyAndRehabilitation

1794 ■ Arctic Physical Therapy Scholarship *(Undergraduate/Scholarship)*

Purpose: To support college and university students enrolled in college or university. **Focus:** General studies/ Field of study not specified. **Qualif.:** Applicants must be attending college or university no later than January; attending college or university on a full-time or part-time basis by January; must have achieved a GPA of 3.0 or greater during their last academic year; must be attending a school in the U.S. or Canada; must be U.S. or Canadian residents.

Funds Avail.: $500. **To Apply:** Applications can be submitted online at: physicaltherapyfairbanks.com/physical_therapy_fairbanks.php. **Deadline:** August 31.

1795 ■ Arent Fox L.L.P.
1301 Ave. Americas, 42nd Fl.
New York, NY 10019-5820
Ph: (212)484-3900

Awards are arranged alphabetically below their administering organizations

Fax: (212)484-3990
E-mail: andrew.silfen@arentfox.com
URL: www.arentfox.com
Social Media: www.linkedin.com/company/arent-fox
twitter.com/arentfox
www.youtube.com/user/arentfox

1796 ■ Diversity Scholarship *(Graduate/Scholarship, Award)*

Purpose: To provide financial assistance to qualified individuals intending to pursue their law career. **Focus:** Law. **Qualif.:** Candidates must be in good standing at an ABA-accredited law school in the US; students who are members of a population that historically has been underrepresented in the legal profession are encouraged to apply. **Criteria:** Selection will be based on excellent college and law school academic performance;excellent oral and written communication skills.

Funds Avail.: $20,000. **Duration:** Annual. **Number Awarded:** 1. **To Apply:** Applicants must submit a completed electronic application; personal statement; resume; undergraduate transcript; law school transcript; legal writing sample; contact information of three professional and academic references. **Deadline:** August 15. **Contact:** Email: attorneyrecruit@arentfox.com.

1797 ■ Arizona Airports Association (AZAA)
107 S Southgate Dr.
Chandler, AZ 85226
Ph: (480)403-4618
Fax: (480)893-7775
E-mail: info@azairports.org
URL: azairports.site-ym.com

1798 ■ Marty Rosness Student Scholarship *(Other/ Scholarship)*

Purpose: To enhance careers in the aviation industry. **Focus:** Aviation. **Qualif.:** Applicants must be enrolled in an aviation related degree or program in the state of Arizona. **Criteria:** Recipients are selected based on academic performance.

Funds Avail.: $2,500. **Duration:** Annual. **Number Awarded:** One or multiple. **To Apply:** Applicants must submit a completed application form; current copy of college academic transcript of records; resume; and must attach a sheet that includes a reference to the questions or sections from which the applicant is responding to. **Deadline:** March 13. **Contact:** Email: info@azairports.org.

1799 ■ Arizona Artist Blacksmith Association (AABA)
7070 E Dogwood Tr.
Cornville, AZ 86325-5154
URL: azblacksmiths.org

1800 ■ Read Carlock Memorial Scholarship Fund *(Other/Scholarship)*

Purpose: To provide financial assistance to interested blacksmiths and/or immediate family members of AABA members for skills and abilities development. **Focus:** General studies/Field of study not specified. **Qualif.:** Applicants must be members of the Arizona Artist Blacksmith Association. **Criteria:** Selection is based on evidence of applicant's

strong desire for continued and serious investigation of the craft and for a novice blacksmith, must demonstrate a history of commitment and a legitimate interest in the blacksmith craft; desire to promote the craft of blacksmithing.

Funds Avail.: $1,000. **Duration:** Annual. **Number Awarded:** Varies. **To Apply:** Applicants must submit all the required application information to the scholarship committee.

1801 ■ Arizona Christian School Tuition Organization (ACSTO)
PO Box 6580
Chandler, AZ 85246
Ph: (480)820-0403
Fax: (480)820-2027
E-mail: social@acsto.org
URL: www.acsto.org
Social Media: www.facebook.com/acstoconnect

1802 ■ Original Tax Credit Scholarship *(Master's, Doctorate/Scholarship)*

Purpose: To provide educational support to students who are in need. **Focus:** General studies/Field of study not specified. **Qualif.:** Applicants must be students planning to attend K-12 in a Christian private school. **Criteria:** Awards are given based on the submitted application.

Duration: Annual. **To Apply:** Applicants must complete the application form available online. **Remarks:** Established in 1998.

1803 ■ Overflow Scholarships *(Undergraduate/ Scholarship)*

Purpose: To give private schools additional help with their students' cost of tuition while still ensuring that the end result is budget positive for the state. **Focus:** Education. **Qualif.:** Applicants must be transferring from a District or Charter Public School; must be a Kindergarten Student; must be Pre-K Student with Disabilities; must be US Armed Forces Dependent; must be Previously Received Corporate or Overflow/PLUS Scholarship.

Funds Avail.: No specific amount.

1804 ■ Arizona City/County Management Association (ACMA)
1820 W Washington St.
Phoenix, AZ 85007
Ph: (602)258-5786
Fax: (602)253-3874
E-mail: info@azmanagement.org
URL: azmanagement.org
Social Media: www.facebook.com/pg/AZCMA
twitter.com/azmanagers

1805 ■ Marvin A. Andrews Scholarships/Internships *(Graduate, Undergraduate/Internship, Scholarship)*

Purpose: To financially assist Arizona graduate students in public administration who aspire to a career in local government management. **Focus:** Public administration. **Qualif.:** Applicants must be full-time students attending either Arizona State University, Northern Arizona University or the University of Arizona who have exhibited strong academic achievement. **Criteria:** Recipients are selected based on

Awards are arranged alphabetically below their administering organizations

interest in local government administration, career plans, academic achievement, school and/or community honors and activities and financial need.

Funds Avail.: $6,000. **To Apply:** Applicants must submit: completed application form; resume; two letters of recommendation; an official graduate-level transcript; a letter addressed to Robert Flatley, ACMA President addressing their interest in local government management, career goals, and financial need or plans for using the scholarship. **Deadline:** November 25. **Remarks:** The scholarship was established in honor of Marvin Andrews, former City Manager of Phoenix, to local government in Arizona. Established in 1990. **Contact:** URL: azmanagement.org/membership/scholarships/.

1806 ■ Charles A. Esser Memorial Scholarships (Graduate/Scholarship)

Purpose: To honor and financially assist Arizona graduate students in public administration who aspire to a career in local government management. **Focus:** Public administration. **Qualif.:** Applicant must be a part-time MPA student attending Arizona State University, Grand Canyon University, Northern Arizona University or the University of Arizona who is currently working in local government and who has exhibited strong academic achievement. **Criteria:** Recipients are selected based on interest in local government administration, career plans, academic achievement, school and/or community honors and activities and financial need.

Duration: Annual. **To Apply:** Applicants must submit the following: completed application form; resume; two letters of recommendation; an official graduate-level transcript; a letter addressed to Robert Flatley, ACMA President addressing their interest in local government management, career goals, and financial needs or plans for using the scholarship. **Deadline:** November 25. **Remarks:** The scholarship was established in honor and memory of Charles A. Esser, former City Manager of Phoenix. Established in 1973. **Contact:** URL: azmanagement.org/membership/scholarships/.

1807 ■ Arizona Hydrological Society (AHS)
PO Box 65062
Tucson, AZ 85728
E-mail: info@azhydrosoc.org
URL: azhydrosoc.org
Social Media: www.facebook.com/azhydrosoc
www.linkedin.com/company/arizona-hydrological-society

1808 ■ Arizona Hydrological Society Academic Scholarships (Graduate, Undergraduate/Scholarship)

Purpose: To encourage full-time students to excel in the field of hydrology, hydrogeology or any water-resource related fields. **Focus:** Hydrology. **Qualif.:** Applicants must be junior, senior or graduate students at any university or college in Arizona. **Criteria:** Selection will be based on GPA; strength of recommendation letter; application letter describing the interest and goals in hydrology and water resources; and degree of need.

Funds Avail.: $2,000. **Duration:** Annual. **Number Awarded:** Up to 3. **To Apply:** Applicants must submit an application form; official transcripts; and at least one letter of recommendation; application letter, including description of financial need. **Deadline:** April 30. **Contact:** Dennis Hall, Email: dhall@elmontgomery.com.

1809 ■ Arizona Library Association (AZLA)
2532 N 4th St Ste. 271
Flagstaff, AZ 86001

Ph: (928)288-2011
URL: www.azla.org
Social Media: www.facebook.com/arizonalibraryassociation
twitter.com/azlalib

1810 ■ Friends of the Oro Valley Public Library Support Staff Scholarship Award (Undergraduate/ Scholarship, Monetary, Award)

Purpose: To provide continuing education via community college, university, or national conference, to any non-M.L.S. degreed library staff member employed by any library within the State of Arizona. **Focus:** Library and archival sciences. **Qualif.:** Applicant must be enrolled in a college or university program with a grade point average of 3.0 or above; must be actively pursuing an A.A.S degree in Library Technology, a B.A. or B.S. degree in any major with the goal of pursuing, upon graduation, a Master's Degree in Library Science; member in AzLA.

Funds Avail.: $500. **Duration:** Annual. **To Apply:** Applicants must submit a 500 word essay that includes the following: name of school for which scholarship will be used; currently working in a library setting, any accomplishments made; what goals you have after you graduate and how the scholarship will help in achieving those goals; how you plan to use your education in promoting library services and AzLA; must have a minimum of two (2) additional letters of support. **Deadline:** September 12. **Contact:** C/OMargie Farmer, Joel Valdez Main Library, 101 N Stone Ave., Tucson, AZ, 85701; Phone: 520-594-5530; Email: ginamacaluso@email.arizona.edu.

1811 ■ Arizona Nursery Association (ANA)
1430 W Broadway Rd., Ste. 110
Tempe, AZ 85282
Ph: (480)966-1610
Fax: (480)966-0923
E-mail: info@azna.org
URL: azna.org

1812 ■ Arizona Nursery Association Scholarships (Undergraduate, Graduate, College, University/ Scholarship)

Purpose: To financially assist students in the horticultural related curriculum. **Focus:** Horticulture. **Qualif.:** Applicants must be residents of Arizona currently or planning to be enrolled in a horticultural-related curriculum at a university, community college or continuing education program; must be currently employed in or have an interest in the nursery industry as a career; must have above-average scholastic achievement or at least two years work experience in the industry; must display involvement in extracurricular activities related to industry. **Criteria:** Selection will be based on academic performance.

Funds Avail.: $500-$3,000. **Duration:** Annual. **To Apply:** Applicants must complete the online application form. **Deadline:** April 15. **Contact:** Arizona Nursery Association, 1430 W. Broadway, Ste. 110, Tempe, AZ 85282; Phone: 480-966-1610; Fax: 480-966-0923; E-mail: scholarship@azna.org.

1813 ■ Arizona Nurses Association (AZNA)
1850 E Southern Ave., Ste. 1
Tempe, AZ 85282
Ph: (480)831-0404

Awards are arranged alphabetically below their administering organizations

Fax: (480)839-4780
E-mail: info@aznurse.org
URL: www.aznurse.org
Social Media: www.facebook.com/
  arizonanursesassociation
twitter.com/ArizonaNurses

1814 ■ Arizona Nurses Foundation Scholarships
(Graduate/Scholarship)

Purpose: To enhance the development of Arizona nurses and further the nursing profession in Arizona. **Focus:** Nursing. **Qualif.:** Applicants may be enrolled part-time or full-time. **Criteria:** Selection is potential for leadership in nursing; commitment to professional nursing in Arizona.

Funds Avail.: A.D.N. applicants: $500; BSN, RN-BSN, Masters: $1,000; doctoral applicants: $2,500. **Duration:** Annual. **Deadline:** March 1; October 1. **Remarks:** Established in 1998.

1815 ■ Arizona Society of Certified Public Accountants (ASCPA)
4801 E Washington St., Ste. 180
Phoenix, AZ 85034
Ph: (602)252-4144
Fax: (602)252-1511
Free: 888-237-0700
URL: www.ascpa.com
Social Media: www.facebook.com/ASCPA
twitter.com/ASCPA

1816 ■ ASCPA High School Scholarships *(Graduate/Scholarship, Monetary)*

Purpose: To support students pursuing an accounting degree. **Focus:** Accounting. **Qualif.:** Applicants must be high school seniors enrolling in an Arizona university/community college as full time students majoring in accounting, and be legal U.S. residents and current residents of Arizona. **Criteria:** Selection is based on academic achievement (as documented through GPA, class ranking and standardized test scores) and community involvement and leadership potential (as demonstrated by the student's personal statement and letters of recommendation).

Funds Avail.: $500. **Number Awarded:** Up to 2. **To Apply:** Applicants must submit a completed application form along with a certified high school transcript (contains student's class rank, GPA and test scores); a personal statement on community involvement, career goals and desire to contribute to the community (maximum of 2 pages); and a one-page letter of recommendation from a teacher or a school official.

1817 ■ ASCPA Private University Scholarships
(Master's, Graduate/Scholarship)

Purpose: To support students pursuing an accounting degree. **Focus:** Accounting. **Qualif.:** Applicants must be accounting major; be legal U.S. and Arizona residents; be full-time students (12 or more credits per semester or 24 credits per year); have earned at least 12 college/university credits at the time of application; have completed at least one accounting course at a college/university; and have a GPA of 3.0 or better. **Criteria:** Selection is based on academic achievement (as documented through GPA and success in accounting or accounting-related courses), likelihood of becoming a CPA and remaining in Arizona, and

community involvement and leadership potential (as demonstrated by the student's personal statement and letter of recommendation).

Funds Avail.: $1,000. **Number Awarded:** Up to 3. **To Apply:** Applicants must submit a completed application form along with the college/university transcripts for all schools attended; resume (includes work experience and information such as extra-curricular activities, public service activities, awards and honors); a one-page essay on future career interests and professional goals (include 2-year and 5-year goals); letter of recommendation from an instructor or employer.

1818 ■ Sam Gallant Memorial Scholarships *(Graduate, Undergraduate/Scholarship)*

Purpose: To support students pursuing an accounting degree. **Focus:** Accounting. **Qualif.:** Applicant must be an accounting major; have a 3.5 minimum GPA; be studying in an Arizona State University Main; an African American; and a legal U.S. resident. **Criteria:** Selection is based on the submitted application materials.

Funds Avail.: $1,000. **Number Awarded:** 1. **To Apply:** Applicants must complete a detailed scholarship application form together with a statement of career goals and a formal resume. Students may contact Arizona State University Main Campus for more information on the scholarship.

1819 ■ Public University Senior and Master's Program Scholarships *(Graduate/Scholarship)*

Purpose: To support students pursuing an accounting degree. **Focus:** Accounting. **Qualif.:** Applicants must: be accounting major who will begin their senior year or master's program; have a 3.5 minimum GPA; be studying in an Arizona public university (Arizona State University Main, University of Arizona and Northern Arizona University) and legal U.S. residents. **Criteria:** Selection is based on the submitted application materials.

Funds Avail.: $2,000. **Number Awarded:** Up to 3. **To Apply:** Applicants must complete a detailed scholarship application form together with a statement of career goals and a formal resume. Students may contact the individual university for applications and to learn more about the process.

1820 ■ Arkansas Association of Family and Consumer Sciences (ARAFCS)
201 Donaghey Ave.
McAlister Hall 100
Conway, AR 72032
E-mail: arkafcs@gmail.com
URL: www.aafcs.org
Social Media: www.facebook.com/AAFCSheadquarters
www.instagram.com/aafcs_hq
www.pinterest.com/aafcs
twitter.com/aafcs

1821 ■ ARAFCS Doctoral Scholarship *(Doctorate, Graduate/Scholarship)*

Purpose: To encourage family and consumer sciences professionals by providing financial assistance for graduate education. **Focus:** General studies/Field of study not specified. **Qualif.:** Applicant must be a legal resident of Arkansas; must be a family and consumer sciences major at an Arkansas university. **Criteria:** Applicants will be selected by the scholarship committee.

Awards are arranged alphabetically below their administering organizations

Funds Avail.: No specific amount. **Duration:** Annual. **To Apply:** Applicants must complete the application form available on the website; must submit an official transcript of record. **Deadline:** March 9. **Contact:** Dr. Renee Ryburn, 201 Donaghey Ave., McAlister Hall 100, Conway, AR 72035.

1822 ■ ARAFCS Masters Scholarship (Graduate, Master's/Scholarship)

Purpose: To encourage family and consumer sciences professionals by providing financial assistance for graduate education. **Focus:** General studies/Field of study not specified. **Qualif.:** Applicant must be a legal resident of Arkansas; must be a family and consumer sciences major at an Arkansas university. **Criteria:** Applicants will be selected by the scholarship committee.

Funds Avail.: No specific amount. **Duration:** Annual. **To Apply:** Applicants must complete the application form available on the website; must submit an official transcript of record. **Deadline:** March 9. **Contact:** Dr. Renee Ryburn, 201 Donaghey Ave., McAlister Hall 100, Conway, AR 72035.

1823 ■ Arkansas Environmental Federation (AEF)

415 North McKinley, Ste. 835
Little Rock, AR 72205
Ph: (501)374-0263
Fax: (501)374-8752
E-mail: aroberts@environmentark.org
URL: environmentark.org
Social Media: www.facebook.com/
ArkEnvironmentalFederation
twitter.com/arkenvfed

1824 ■ Randall Mathis Scholarship for Environmental Studies Fund (Undergraduate/Scholarship)

Purpose: To provide financial assistance for selected students from Arkansas universities. **Focus:** Environmental science; Health education; Natural resources. **Qualif.:** Applicants must be U.S. citizens residing in Arkansas and must be undergraduates or graduate students with at least 2.8 cumulative GPA based on 4.0 system.

Duration: Annual. **Number Awarded:** 1. **To Apply:** Applicants must submit a completed application form; transcript of records; letter of nomination from a faculty member; and two additional letters of recommendation that address candidate's scholastic and personal attributes. **Deadline:** July 24. **Remarks:** The award was established in honor of Randall Mathis of Arkadelphia, the former longtime director of the Arkansas Department of Environmental Quality.

1825 ■ Arkansas Green Industry Association (AGIA)

9 Shackleford Plz., Ste. 1
Little Rock, AR 72221-1715
Ph: (501)225-0029
Fax: (501)224-0988
E-mail: office@argia.org
URL: www.argia.org
Social Media: www.facebook.com/pages/Arkansas-Green
-Industry-Association/105497262821260
twitter.com/ArkansasAGIA

1826 ■ Arkansas Green Industry Association Professional Grants (Professional development/Grant)

Purpose: To encourage young or new business owners and students to become involved in the AGIA by encouraging participation in AGIA events. **Focus:** Business; Horticulture. **Qualif.:** Applicants must be young or business owners for less than 3 years, or students or recent graduates in horticulture. **Criteria:** Selection will be based on the committee's criteria.

Funds Avail.: No specific amount. **Duration:** Periodic. **To Apply:** Applicant must submit an online application form.

1827 ■ Arkansas Green Industry Association Student Scholarships (Undergraduate/Scholarship)

Purpose: To provide financial assistance to Arkansas students pursuing study in botany and related field. **Focus:** Botany; Horticulture. **Qualif.:** Applicants must be Arkansas students pursuing degrees in horticulture-related fields. **Criteria:** Selection will be based on the committee's criteria.

Funds Avail.: No specific amount. **Duration:** Annual. **To Apply:** Application form and details available on sponsor's website.

1828 ■ Arkansas Library Association (ARLA)

3416 Primm Ln.
Birmingham, AL 35216
Free: 800-241-4590
E-mail: arlib2@sbcglobal.net
URL: www.arlib.org
Social Media: www.facebook.com/arlibassoc
twitter.com/ArLALibrary

1829 ■ ArLA Scholarship (Graduate/Scholarship)

Purpose: To encourage a higher standard of professional training in Arkansas libraries. **Focus:** Library and archival sciences. **Qualif.:** Applicant must hold or be completing work toward a bachelor's degree from an accredited college or university and must not currently hold a master's degree in library science; applicant must be currently accepted and enrolled in a program leading to a master's degree in library science; applicant may be currently employed in a library in Arkansas provided all other conditions are met. **Criteria:** Selection shall be based on applicant's interest in librarianship as a profession, academic record and compliance with application requirements.

Duration: Annual. **Number Awarded:** 1. **To Apply:** Applicants must submit a completed application form together with an official graduate transcript or proof of enrollment; letter of application; resume; and three letters of reference from individuals qualified to address the academic and professional potential of the applicant. **Deadline:** July 1; September 1. **Remarks:** The scholarships are classified into two: the Arkansas Library Association Annual Scholarship, and the Arkansas Library Association School Library Media Specialist (SLMS) Scholarship. Both are awarded at the annual conference. **Contact:** Arkansas Library Association, PO Box 3821, Little Rock, AR, 72203; Email: info@arlib.org.

1830 ■ Arkansas Nurses Association (ARNA)

1123 S University, Ste. 1015
Little Rock, AR 72204
Ph: (501)244-2363
E-mail: arna@arna.org

Awards are arranged alphabetically below their administering organizations

Social Media: www.facebook.com/arknurses
www.instagram.com/arknurses

1831 ■ Arkansas Nursing Foundation - Dorothea Fund Scholarships *(Other/Scholarship)*

Purpose: To provide financial assistance to nurses throughout the state of Arkansas. **Focus:** Nursing. **Qualif.:** Applicants must be registered nurses who can give a statement of commitment to community health nursing, seeking a degree into result in an advanced practice nurse, and demonstrate a need. **Criteria:** Selection will be based on the committee's criteria.

Funds Avail.: No specific amount. **Duration:** Annual. **To Apply:** Applicants must complete the application packet and must include the following completed application form; cover letter stating desire for the scholarship and intended use of funds (including a statement regarding other financial assistance); statement regarding institutional financial assistance toward the planned degree (tuition waivers or reductions); current resume (one page including education, work experience, achievements and honors, if applicable); two letters of recommendation (with one being from current supervisor or faculty) including information concerning leadership and academic ability of the applicant; official undergraduate and graduate transcript(s) from all nursing programs attended (in sealed envelope with Registrar's signature or stamp on flap); letter of acceptance into degree program accredited by NLNAC or CCNE; and extracurricular activities (achievements, organization memberships, volunteer work). **Deadline:** June 1.

1832 ■ Arkansas Nursing Foundation - Mary Gray Scholarships *(Other/Scholarship)*

Purpose: To provide financial assistance to nurses throughout the state of Arkansas. **Focus:** Nursing. **Qualif.:** Applicants must be registered nurses seeking an advanced degree in nursing, interested or involved in advanced practice nursing (Advance Nurse Practitioner, Clinical Nurse Specialist, Certified Nurse Midwife, and Certified Nurse Anesthetist). **Criteria:** Selection will be based on the committee's criteria.

Funds Avail.: No specific amount. **Duration:** Annual. **To Apply:** Applicants must complete the application packet and must include the following completed application form; cover letter stating desire for the scholarship and intended use of funds (including a statement regarding other financial assistance); statement regarding institutional financial assistance toward the planned degree (tuition waivers or reductions); current resume (one page including education, work experience, achievements, and honors, if applicable); two letters of recommendation (with one being from current supervisor or faculty) including information concerning leadership and academic ability of the applicant; official undergraduate and graduate transcript(s) from all nursing programs attended (in sealed envelope with Registrar's signature or stamp on flap); letter of acceptance into degree program accredited by NLNAC or CCNE; and extracurricular activities (achievements, organization memberships, volunteer work). **Deadline:** June 1.

1833 ■ Arkansas Public Health Association (APHA)

PO Box 250327
Little Rock, AR 72225
Ph: (501)661-2794
URL: www.arkpublichealth.org

Social Media: www.facebook.com/
ArkansasPublicHealthAssociation
www.linkedin.com/company/american-public-health
-association
www.pinterest.com/americanpha
twitter.com/PublicHealth
youtube.com/user/aphadc

1834 ■ APHA Student Scholarship *(Undergraduate, Graduate/Scholarship)*

Purpose: To provide support for their attainment of a public health degree Students. **Focus:** Public health. **Qualif.:** Applicants must be Arkansas residents; be enrolled, or plan to enroll in the field of public health; must have cumulative GPA of 3.0 or higher and be in good standing; must be a student member; High school senior, undergraduate or graduate student. **Criteria:** Selection will be based on the GPA, goals in public health, honors, organizations, volunteering with health-related organizations, letter from major professor, personal reference letter, present or past public health experience, full-time student, part-time student, financial need.

Funds Avail.: $1,000. **Duration:** Annual. **To Apply:** Applicants must submit two letters of support be provided from individuals familiar with the student's work and professional activities; transcripts. **Deadline:** April 15. **Contact:** Brandi Roberts; E-mail: brandi.roberts@arkansas.gov.

1835 ■ Arkansas Single Parent Scholarship Fund (ASPSF)

614 E Emma Ave., Ste. 119
Springdale, AR 72764
URL: www.aspsf.org
Social Media: www.facebook.com/aspsf
www.instagram.com/aspsf1990/

1836 ■ Arkansas Single Parent Scholarship *(Undergraduate, Graduate/Scholarship)*

Purpose: To provide supplemental financial assistance to those single parents living in Arkansas who are pursuing a course of instruction that will improve their income-earning potential. **Focus:** General studies/Field of study not specified. **Qualif.:** Applicants eligibilities are single parents living in Arkansas who are considered economically disadvantaged and who have custodial care of one or more children under the age of eighteen; and, those who have not previously earned a diploma or degree from a four-year institution of higher learning; have at least a 2.0 cumulative GPA; legal resident of the United States (or a resident with DACA status. **Criteria:** Selection will be based on committee's criteria.

Funds Avail.: Amount varies. **Duration:** Annual. **To Apply:** Applicants are encouraged to contact the Single Parent Scholarship Fund in their county; proof of enrollment; proof of income; Pell Grant (FAFSA); current transcript; proof of marital status; three letters of recommendation; statement of goals. **Deadline:** July 15; September 15. **Remarks:** Established in 1990.

1837 ■ Arkansas State University (ASU)

1600 S College St.
Mountain Home, AR 72653
Ph: (870)508-6100
Fax: (870)508-6287

Awards are arranged alphabetically below their administering organizations

URL: asumh.edu
Social Media: www.facebook.com/ASUMH
www.instagram.com/asumountainhome
www.pinterest.com/asumh
twitter.com/asumountainhome
www.youtube.com/user/ASUMountainHome

1838 ■ Benbrook Scholarship *(Graduate/Scholarship)*

Purpose: To provide financial support to the students enrolled in ASUMH. **Focus:** General studies/Field of study not specified. **Qualif.:** Applicants must be students graduated or will graduate from norfork high school, in norfork, Arkansas, or students who live in the geographical area of the norfork school district; must be admitted to a college, university, vocational-technical school or other school described in section 170(b)(1)(A)(ii) of the Internal revenue code as a candidate for a certificate or an undergraduate or graduate degree, on a full-time basis.

Funds Avail.: Varies. **To Apply:** Applicants must submit complete application form available online; should include current official high school transcript and ACT/SAT scores or current official college transcript, and proof of attendance at Norfork High School; signed letter from applicant providing information about themselves and their need for this Scholarship; two signed character reference letters from persons other than family members. **Deadline:** April 5. **Remarks:** Established in 2007.

1839 ■ Armed Forces Communications and Electronics Association San Diego Chapter

PO Box 80666
San Diego, CA 92138-0666
URL: sandiego.afceachapters.org
Social Media: www.facebook.com/AFCEASanDiego
twitter.com/afceasd

1840 ■ Buck Bragunier Leadership Scholarship *(Four Year College, University/Scholarship)*

Purpose: To provide scholarship for the students of San Diego military community. **Focus:** Computer and information sciences; Engineering; Mathematics and mathematical sciences; Natural sciences; Science. **Qualif.:** Applicants must be U.S. citizens and residents of San Diego county; high school seniors with a record of leadership and volunteering activities during high school, church, and community; must have GPA of at least 3.7; and eventual attendance at an accredited four year college or University anywhere within United States in a 4-year degree granting full-time curriculum; must major in science, technology, engineering or math curriculums. **Criteria:** Selection will be based on records of leadership and volunteering activities within the high school, church, community which are the focuses of the program.

Funds Avail.: $2,000. **Duration:** Annual. **Number Awarded:** 1. **To Apply:** Applicants must submit a copy of your college/university acceptance letter; copy of your SAT/ACT scores; your most recent grade transcript; two letters of recommendation. **Deadline:** June 1. **Remarks:** The Scholarship was established to honor Buck's memory and unique contributions to the San Diego Chapter of AFCEA. **Contact:** Gloria McKearney, Scholarship Chair, Email: Gloria9391@aol.com.

1841 ■ Armenian American Medical Society (AAMS)

PO Box 32
Glendale, CA 91209

URL: aamsc.org
Social Media: www.facebook.com/
ArmenianAmericanMedicalSociety

1842 ■ Armenian American Medical Association Scholarship Program *(Undergraduate, Graduate/Scholarship)*

Purpose: To provide financial assistance to medical students of Armenian descent. **Focus:** Medicine. **Qualif.:** Applicants must be students of Armenian descent and enrolled in an accredited medical, pharmacy, dental, physician assistant, nursing, or other professional healthcare schools in the United States. **Criteria:** Awards granted on the basis of need, merit, special interest in Armenian medical causes, and Armenian medical/health community service.

Number Awarded: Varies. **To Apply:** Applicants must check the sponsor's website for the required materials. **Deadline:** October 20.

1843 ■ Armenian American Pharmacists' Association (AAPA)

PO Box 550046
Waltham, MA 02451
Ph: (617)600-8661
URL: www.aapha.org

1844 ■ Armenian American Pharmacists' Association Scholarship *(Graduate/Scholarship)*

Purpose: To provide financial support to Armenian American students who are pursuing pharmacy degrees. **Focus:** Pharmacy. **Qualif.:** Applicants must be students of Armenian descent, and a full-time Doctor of Pharmacy student residing in New England. **Criteria:** Awards will be based on academic excellence and financial need.

Funds Avail.: No specific amount. **Duration:** Annual. **To Apply:** Application is available on sponsor's website. **Deadline:** February 1.

1845 ■ Armenian Bar Association

PO Box 29111
Los Angeles, CA 90029
E-mail: info@armenianbar.org
URL: armenianbar.org
Social Media: www.facebook.com/
ArmenianBarAssociation/

1846 ■ Armenian Bar Association Scholarships *(Graduate/Scholarship)*

Purpose: To provide support students of Armenian descent attending, or accepted for admission to, an approved law school in the United States, Armenia or elsewhere. **Focus:** Law. **Qualif.:** Applicants must be enrolled in or admitted to, if in the United States, an American Bar Association-accredited or state-accredited law school, or if in Armenia or another country, a law school approved by the Armenia Bar Association; have a strong academic potential as demonstrated by academic performance; must have strong academic potential as demonstrated by your academic performance (i.e., grades). **Criteria:** Selection will be based on the committee's criteria.

Funds Avail.: No specific amount. **Duration:** Annual. **To Apply:** Applicants must submit a completed application

Awards are arranged alphabetically below their administering organizations

form; cover letter; resume; personal essay (maximum: 3, 000 words); two letters of recommendation (from professors, school administrators, Armenian community leaders or others in official capacities who have knowledge of the applicant's academic performance and potential and/or commitment to the Armenian community); official grade transcripts from undergraduate college and law school; and proof of entrance or acceptance into, or continuation in, an approved law school. **Deadline:** June 1. **Contact:** The Armenian Bar Association Grants & Scholarship Committee; Email: scholarship@armenianbar.org.

1847 ■ Armenian Educational Foundation (AEF)

600 W Broadway, Ste. 130
Glendale, CA 91204
Ph: (818)242-4154
Fax: (818)242-4913
E-mail: aef@aefweb.org
URL: aefweb.org
Social Media: www.facebook.com/
  ArmenianEducationalFoundation
twitter.com/AEFweb

1848 ■ Richard R. Tufenkian Scholarships
(Undergraduate/Scholarship)

Purpose: To provide financial support to qualified students of Armenian parentage. **Focus:** General studies/Field of study not specified. **Qualif.:** Applicants must be outstanding college and university students in California; must have minimum 3.0 GPA; must have undergraduate status in fall 2018; Father and/or mother and/or grandparent of Armenian origin. **Criteria:** Selection will be based on superior academic records.

Funds Avail.: $3,000 each. **Duration:** Annual. **Number Awarded:** 3. **To Apply:** Applicants should include: proof of acceptance to an accredited U.S. university/college; first 2 pages of income tax returns for previous year; first 2 pages of parent's tax returns for previous year; sealed official transcripts; current academic reference letter; and a one page double spaced essay. **Deadline:** July 31. **Remarks:** Established in 1990. **Contact:** For further information, applicants may e-mail: aef@aefweb.org.

1849 ■ Armenian General Benevolent Union (AGBU)

55 E 59th St.
New York, NY 10022-1112
Ph: (212)319-6383
E-mail: agbuny@agbu.org
URL: agbu.org
Social Media: www.facebook.com/agbu.org
twitter.com/agbu
www.youtube.com/user/AGBUvideo

1850 ■ AGBU Heritage Scholar Grant
(Undergraduate/Scholarship, Grant)

Purpose: To support the higher education of students graduated from AGBU high schools. **Focus:** General studies/Field of study not specified. **Qualif.:** Applicants must be college-bound high school seniors graduating from each of the three AGBU high schools in the United States with a GPA of 3.5 (out of 4.0) and above at any of the following: AGBU Manoogian-Demirdjian School in Canoga Park, CA; AGBU Alex and Marie Manoogian School in

Southfield, MI; AGBU Vatche & Tamar Manoukian High School in Pasadena, CA; must be admitted to a selective university and must be nominated for the grant by the principal and faculty of their respective high school. **Criteria:** Applicants will be approved for the grant based on the following criteria: academic excellence; financial need; involvement in community service, with particular attention to their involvement in the Armenian community.

Funds Avail.: Up to $2,000. **Duration:** Annual. **Number Awarded:** Up to 2. **To Apply:** Application form and details are available at www.agbu-scholarship.org. **Deadline:** April 15. **Contact:** AGBU Scholarship Program; E-mail: scholarship@agbu.org.

1851 ■ Armenian Professional Society (APS)

PO Box 10134
Glendale, CA 91209
URL: www.armenianprofessionalsociety.org
Social Media: www.facebook.com/
  ArmenianProfessionalSocietyLosAngeles
www.linkedin.com/groups/4333408/profile
twitter.com/aps_losangeles

1852 ■ Armenian Professional Society Graduate Student Scholarship *(Graduate/Scholarship)*

Purpose: To provide scholarships to Graduate students of Armenian decent who are or will be attending a university in the United States. **Focus:** General studies/Field of study not specified. **Qualif.:** Applicants must be Armenian descent and enrolled in a graduate degree program in the current year fall. **Criteria:** Selection will be based on financial need, scholastic achievements, faculty recommendations and involvement in the Armenian community.

Funds Avail.: No specific amount. **Duration:** Annual. **To Apply:** Applicants must submit completed application form along with current resume; official transcript for the last degree you received; if current graduate student, include a transcript documenting your time in graduate school thus far; up to two letters of recommendation, at least one of which must be from a current or former employer (an internship supervisor suffices) and an essay explaining applicant's strong work ethic, academic excellence and passionate about Armenian community service must be submitted. **Deadline:** July 31. **Contact:** Email: scholarships@armenianprofessionalsociety.org.

1853 ■ Armenian Relief Society of Eastern U.S.A. (ARSER)

80 Bigelow Ave., Ste. 200
Watertown, MA 02472
Ph: (617)926-3801
Fax: (617)924-7238
E-mail: arseastus@gmail.com
URL: www.arseastusa.org
Social Media: www.facebook.com/ARSEasternUSA
www.instagram.com/arseastus

1854 ■ ARS Lazarian Graduate Scholarship *(Graduate, Master's, Doctorate/Scholarship)*

Purpose: To encourage educational pursuits among graduate students of Armenian descent. **Focus:** Business; Business administration; Economics; Government; History; International affairs and relations; Journalism; Law; Medicine; Political science; Public service. **Qualif.:** Ap-

Awards are arranged alphabetically below their administering organizations

plicants must be of Armenian descent pursuing their studies at the graduate level (Master's Degree or Doctorate) in the fields of law, history, political science, international relations, journalism, government, economics, business administration, medicine and public service or similar field; must have graduated from an accredited four year college or university in the U.S; must be in need of financial assistance. **Criteria:** Selection is made on the basis of financial need, merit and involvement in the Armenian community.

Funds Avail.: No specific amount. **Duration:** Annual; up to 1 year only. **Deadline:** April 1. **Contact:** Phone: 617-926-3801; Fax: 617-924-7238; URL: arseastusa.org/our-programs/youth-education/.

1855 ■ ARS Undergraduate Scholarship
(Undergraduate/Scholarship)

Purpose: To support Armenian students who plan to attend or are attending an accredited four-year college or university in the U.S. **Focus:** General studies/Field of study not specified. **Qualif.:** Applicants must be of Armenian descent who are undergraduate students and have completed at least one semester at an accredited four-year college or university in the United States, or must be enrolled in a two-year college and are transferring to a four-year college or university as full-time students in the Fall. **Criteria:** Selection is made on the basis of financial need, merit and involvement in the Armenian community.

Funds Avail.: No specific amount. **Duration:** Annual; up to 1 year only. **To Apply:** Must provide income tax returns, official transcript, two letters of recommendation, completed application. **Deadline:** April 1. **Contact:** URL: arseastusa.org/our-programs/youth-education/.

1856 ■ Armenian Students' Association of America (ASA)
333 Atlantic Ave.
Warwick, RI 02888
Ph: (401)461-6114
E-mail: asa@asainc.org
URL: www.asainc.org/index.php

1857 ■ Harry E. Adrian Memorial Grant
(Undergraduate/Scholarship)

Purpose: To help students of Armenian descent pay for college. **Focus:** General studies/Field of study not specified; Political science. **Qualif.:** Applicants must be American-born and of Armenian descent; must be students enrolled full-time and have completed one full year of academics at a four-year accredited U.S. college or university, or must be enrolled in a two-year college or university and transferring to a four-year college or university as a full-time student; must be U.S. citizens or possess the appropriate visa status in order to study in the U.S. **Criteria:** Preference given to those specializing in political science.

Duration: Annual. **To Apply:** Forms and details available online at www.asainc.org/national/scholarships.shtml; application, essay, transcripts, three letters of reference, and profile form must be mailed. **Deadline:** March 15.

1858 ■ Samuel Agabian Memorial Grant
(Undergraduate/Scholarship)

Purpose: To help students of Armenian descent pay for college. **Focus:** General studies/Field of study not speci-

fied. **Qualif.:** Applicants must be of Armenian descent; must be students enrolled full-time and have completed one full year of academics at a four-year accredited U.S. college or university, or must be enrolled in a two-year college or university and transferring to a four-year college or university as a full-time student; must be U.S. citizens or possess the appropriate visa status in order to study in the U.S.

Duration: Annual. **To Apply:** Forms and details available online at www.asainc.org/national/scholarships.shtml; application, essay, transcripts, three letters of reference, and profile form must be mailed. **Deadline:** March 15.

1859 ■ Melkon and Negdar Aijian Memorial Grant
(Undergraduate/Scholarship)

Purpose: To help students of Armenian descent pay for college. **Focus:** General studies/Field of study not specified. **Qualif.:** Applicants must be of Armenian descent; must be students enrolled full-time and have completed one full year of academics at a four-year accredited U.S. college or university, or must be enrolled in a two-year college or university and transferring to a four-year college or university as a full-time student; must be U.S. citizens or possess the appropriate visa status in order to study in the U.S.

Duration: Annual. **To Apply:** Forms and details available online at www.asainc.org/national/scholarships.shtml; application, essay, transcripts, three letters of reference, and profile form must be mailed. **Deadline:** March 15.

1860 ■ T. Thomas Amirian Memorial Grant
(Undergraduate/Scholarship)

Purpose: To help students of Armenian descent pay for college. **Focus:** General studies/Field of study not specified. **Qualif.:** Applicants must be of Armenian descent; must be students enrolled full-time and have completed one full year of academics at a four-year accredited U.S. college or university, or must be enrolled in a two-year college or university and transferring to a four-year college or university as a full-time student; must be U.S. citizens or possess the appropriate visa status in order to study in the U.S.

Duration: Annual. **To Apply:** Forms and details available online at www.asainc.org/national/scholarships.shtml; application, essay, transcripts, three letters of reference, and profile form must be mailed. **Deadline:** March 15.

1861 ■ Ararat Association Scholarship Grant
(Undergraduate/Scholarship)

Purpose: To help students of Armenian descent pay for college. **Focus:** General studies/Field of study not specified. **Qualif.:** Applicants must be of Armenian descent; must be students enrolled full-time and have completed one full year of academics at a four-year accredited U.S. college or university, or must be enrolled in a two-year college or university and transferring to a four-year college or university as a full-time student; must be U.S. citizens or possess the appropriate visa status in order to study in the U.S.

Duration: Annual. **To Apply:** Forms and details available online at www.asainc.org/national/scholarships.shtml; application, essay, transcripts, three letters of reference, and profile form must be mailed. **Deadline:** March 15.

1862 ■ Armenian American Veterans' Association of Worcester Scholarship *(Undergraduate/Scholarship)*

Purpose: To help students of Armenian descent pay for college. **Focus:** General studies/Field of study not speci-

Awards are arranged alphabetically below their administering organizations

fied. **Qualif.:** Applicants must be of Armenian descent; must be students enrolled full-time and have completed one full year of academics at a four-year accredited U.S. college or university, or must be enrolled in a two-year college or university and transferring to a four-year college or university as a full-time student; must be U.S. citizens or possess the appropriate visa status in order to study in the U.S.

Duration: Annual. **To Apply:** Forms and details available online at www.asainc.org/national/scholarships.shtml; application, essay, transcripts, three letters of reference, and profile form must be mailed. **Deadline:** March 15.

1863 ■ Ardemis, Armenoohy, and Arpi Arsenian Memorial Grant *(Undergraduate/Scholarship)*

Purpose: To help students of Armenian descent pay for college. **Focus:** General studies/Field of study not specified. **Qualif.:** Applicants must be of Armenian descent; must be students enrolled full-time and have completed one full year of academics at a four-year accredited U.S. college or university, or must be enrolled in a two-year college or university and transferring to a four-year college or university as a full-time student; must be U.S. citizens or possess the appropriate visa status in order to study in the U.S.

Duration: Annual. **To Apply:** Forms and details available online at www.asainc.org/national/scholarships.shtml; application, essay, transcripts, three letters of reference, and profile form must be mailed. **Deadline:** March 15.

1864 ■ ASA Inc. Journalism Internship Program *(Undergraduate/Internship)*

Purpose: To help journalism students of Armenian descent gain experience by interning with two English-language Armenian newspapers in the United States and Canada: The Armenian Weekly and The Armenian Mirror-Spectator. **Focus:** Journalism. **Qualif.:** Applicants must be journalism students of Armenian descent; open to high school seniors, undergraduates, and enrolled graduate students

Funds Avail.: $1,000 stipend. **Duration:** Annual. **To Apply:** Application and transcripts should be sent directly to the publication; form and details available online at www.asainc.org/ASA_JIP/journalism.shtml. **Deadline:** May 29.

1865 ■ Marguerite Chapootian Atamian Memorial Grant *(Undergraduate/Scholarship)*

Purpose: To help students of Armenian descent pay for college. **Focus:** General studies/Field of study not specified. **Qualif.:** Applicants must be of Armenian descent; must be students enrolled full-time and have completed one full year of academics at a four-year accredited U.S. college or university, or must be enrolled in a two-year college or university and transferring to a four-year college or university as a full-time student; must be U.S. citizens or possess the appropriate visa status in order to study in the U.S.

Duration: Annual. **To Apply:** Forms and details available online at www.asainc.org/national/scholarships.shtml; application, essay, transcripts, three letters of reference, and profile form must be mailed. **Deadline:** March 15.

1866 ■ Sarkis Bogosian Memorial Grant *(Undergraduate/Scholarship)*

Purpose: To help students of Armenian descent pay for college. **Focus:** General studies/Field of study not speci-

fied. **Qualif.:** Applicants must be of Armenian descent; must be students enrolled full-time and have completed one full year of academics at a four-year accredited U.S. college or university, or must be enrolled in a two-year college or university and transferring to a four-year college or university as a full-time student; must be U.S. citizens or possess the appropriate visa status in order to study in the U.S.

Duration: Annual. **To Apply:** Forms and details available online at www.asainc.org/national/scholarships.shtml; application, essay, transcripts, three letters of reference, and profile form must be mailed. **Deadline:** March 15.

1867 ■ Ara S. Boyan Scholarship Grant *(Undergraduate/Scholarship)*

Purpose: To help students of Armenian descent pursuing a degrees in humanities. **Focus:** Humanities. **Qualif.:** Applicants must be of Armenian descent; must be students enrolled full-time and have completed one full year of academics at a four-year accredited U.S. college or university, or must be enrolled in a two-year college or university and transferring to a four-year college or university as a full-time student; must be U.S. citizens or possess the appropriate visa status in order to study in the U.S. **Criteria:** Must be studying in the field of humanities.

Duration: Annual. **To Apply:** Forms and details available online at www.asainc.org/national/scholarships.shtml; application, essay, transcripts, three letters of reference, and profile form must be mailed.

1868 ■ Hermine Buchakian Scholarship Grant *(Undergraduate/Scholarship)*

Purpose: To help students of Armenian descent pay for college. **Focus:** General studies/Field of study not specified. **Qualif.:** Applicants must be of Armenian descent; must be students enrolled full-time and have completed one full year of academics at a four-year accredited U.S. college or university, or must be enrolled in a two-year college or university and transferring to a four-year college or university as a full-time student; must be U.S. citizens or possess the appropriate visa status in order to study in the U.S.

Duration: Annual. **To Apply:** Forms and details available online at www.asainc.org/national/scholarships.shtml; application, essay, transcripts, three letters of reference, and profile form must be mailed. **Deadline:** March 15.

1869 ■ Charlotte Calfian Scholarship Grant *(Undergraduate/Scholarship)*

Purpose: To help students of Armenian descent pay for college. **Focus:** General studies/Field of study not specified. **Qualif.:** Applicants must be of Armenian descent; must be students enrolled full-time and have completed one full year of academics at a four-year accredited U.S. college or university, or must be enrolled in a two-year college or university and transferring to a four-year college or university as a full-time student; must be U.S. citizens or possess the appropriate visa status in order to study in the U.S.

Duration: Annual. **To Apply:** Forms and details available online at www.asainc.org/national/scholarships.shtml; application, essay, transcripts, three letters of reference, and profile form must be mailed. **Deadline:** March 15.

1870 ■ Arthur H. Dadian Scholarship Grants *(Undergraduate/Scholarship)*

Purpose: To help students of Armenian descent pay for college. **Focus:** Armenian studies; General studies/Field of

Awards are arranged alphabetically below their administering organizations

study not specified. **Qualif.:** Applicants must be of Armenian descent; must be students enrolled full-time and have completed one full year of academics at a four-year accredited U.S. college or university, or must be enrolled in a two-year college or university and transferring to a four-year college or university as a full-time student; must be U.S. citizens or possess the appropriate visa status in order to study in the U.S. **Criteria:** Preference given to those pursuing Armenian studies.

Duration: Annual. **To Apply:** Forms and details available online at www.asainc.org/national/scholarships.shtml; application, essay, transcripts, three letters of reference, and profile form must be mailed. **Deadline:** March 15.

1871 ■ Thomas Richard Dadourian Memorial Grant
(Undergraduate/Scholarship)

Purpose: To help students of Armenian descent pay for college. **Focus:** General studies/Field of study not specified. **Qualif.:** Applicants must be of Armenian descent; must be students enrolled full-time and have completed one full year of academics at a four-year accredited U.S. college or university, or must be enrolled in a two-year college or university and transferring to a four-year college or university as a full-time student; must be U.S. citizens or possess the appropriate visa status in order to study in the U.S.

Duration: Annual. **To Apply:** Forms and details available online at www.asainc.org/national/scholarships.shtml; application, essay, transcripts, three letters of reference, and profile form must be mailed. **Deadline:** March 15.

1872 ■ Alexander A. Dadourian Scholarship
(Undergraduate/Scholarship)

Purpose: To help students of Armenian descent pay for college. **Focus:** General studies/Field of study not specified. **Qualif.:** Applicants must be of Armenian descent; must be students enrolled full-time and have completed one full year of academics at a four-year accredited U.S. college or university, or must be enrolled in a two-year college or university and transferring to a four-year college or university as a full-time student; must be U.S. citizens or possess the appropriate visa status in order to study in the U.S.

Duration: Annual. **To Apply:** Forms and details available online at www.asainc.org/national/scholarships.shtml; application, essay, transcripts, three letters of reference, and profile form must be mailed. **Deadline:** March 15.

1873 ■ Dadour Dadourian Scholarship Fund
(Undergraduate/Scholarship)

Purpose: To help students of Armenian descent pay for college. **Focus:** General studies/Field of study not specified. **Qualif.:** Applicants must be of Armenian descent; must be students enrolled full-time and have completed one full year of academics at a four-year accredited U.S. college or university, or must be enrolled in a two-year college or university and transferring to a four-year college or university as a full-time student; must be U.S. citizens or possess the appropriate visa status in order to study in the U.S.

Duration: Annual. **To Apply:** Forms and details available online at www.asainc.org/national/scholarships.shtml; application, essay, transcripts, three letters of reference, and profile form must be mailed. **Deadline:** March 15.

1874 ■ Garabed and Almast Der Megrditchian Scholarship Grants *(Undergraduate/Scholarship)*

Purpose: To help students of Armenian descent pay for college. **Focus:** General studies/Field of study not speci-

fied. **Qualif.:** Applicants must be of Armenian descent; must be students enrolled full-time and have completed one full year of academics at a four-year accredited U.S. college or university, or must be enrolled in a two-year college or university and transferring to a four-year college or university as a full-time student; must be U.S. citizens or possess the appropriate visa status in order to study in the U.S.

Duration: Annual. **To Apply:** Forms and details available online at www.asainc.org/national/scholarships.shtml; application, essay, transcripts, three letters of reference, and profile form must be mailed. **Deadline:** March 15.

1875 ■ Enkababian Family and Sarian Family Memorial Grant *(Undergraduate/Scholarship)*

Purpose: To help students of Armenian descent pursue college degrees in history or political science. **Focus:** History; Political science. **Qualif.:** Applicants must be of Armenian descent; must be students enrolled full-time and have completed one full year of academics at a four-year accredited U.S. college or university, or must be enrolled in a two-year college or university and transferring to a four-year college or university as a full-time student; must be U.S. citizens or possess the appropriate visa status in order to study in the U.S. **Criteria:** Must be a history or political science major attending a private college.

Duration: Annual. **To Apply:** Forms and details available online at www.asainc.org/national/scholarships.shtml; application, essay, transcripts, three letters of reference, and profile form must be mailed. **Deadline:** March 15.

1876 ■ Parsegh and Thora Essefian Memorial Grant
(Undergraduate/Scholarship)

Purpose: To help students of Armenian descent pursue a degree in Armenian studies. **Focus:** Armenian studies. **Qualif.:** Applicants must be of Armenian descent; must be students enrolled full-time and have completed one full year of academics at a four-year accredited U.S. college or university, or must be enrolled in a two-year college or university and transferring to a four-year college or university as a full-time student; must be U.S. citizens or possess the appropriate visa status in order to study in the U.S. **Criteria:** Must be pursuing Armenian studies.

Duration: Annual. **To Apply:** Forms and details available online at www.asainc.org/national/scholarships.shtml; application, essay, transcripts, three letters of reference, and profile form must be mailed. **Deadline:** March 15.

1877 ■ Lionel Galstaun Memorial Grant
(Undergraduate/Scholarship)

Purpose: To help students of Armenian descent pay for college. **Focus:** General studies/Field of study not specified. **Qualif.:** Applicants must be of Armenian descent; must be students enrolled full-time and have completed one full year of academics at a four-year accredited U.S. college or university, or must be enrolled in a two-year college or university and transferring to a four-year college or university as a full-time student; must be U.S. citizens or possess the appropriate visa status in order to study in the U.S.

Duration: Annual. **To Apply:** Forms and details available online at www.asainc.org/national/scholarships.shtml; application, essay, transcripts, three letters of reference, and profile form must be mailed. **Deadline:** March 15.

1878 ■ Maro Ajemian Galstaun Memorial Grant
(Undergraduate/Scholarship)

Purpose: To help students of Armenian descent pursue degrees in humanities, especially music. **Focus:** Humani-

Awards are arranged alphabetically below their administering organizations

ties; Music. **Qualif.:** Applicants must be of Armenian descent; must be students enrolled full-time and have completed one full year of academics at a four-year accredited U.S. college or university, or must be enrolled in a two-year college or university and transferring to a four-year college or university as a full-time student; must be U.S. citizens or possess the appropriate visa status in order to study in the U.S. **Criteria:** Must be studying humanities. Preference given to music majors.

Duration: Annual. **To Apply:** Forms and details available onlIne at www.asainc.org/national/scholarships.shtml; application, essay, transcripts, three letters of reference, and profile form must be mailed. **Deadline:** March 15.

1879 ■ George Gurdjian Memorial Grant
(Undergraduate/Scholarship)

Purpose: To help students of Armenian descent pay for college. **Focus:** General studies/Field of study not specified. **Qualif.:** Applicants must be of Armenian descent; must be students enrolled full-time and have completed one full year of academics at a four-year accredited U.S. college or university, or must be enrolled in a two-year college or university and transferring to a four-year college or university as a full-time student; must be U.S. citizens or possess the appropriate visa status in order to study in the U.S.

Duration: Annual. **To Apply:** Forms and details available online at www.asainc.org/national/scholarships.shtml; application, essay, transcripts, three letters of reference, and profile form must be mailed. **Deadline:** March 15.

1880 ■ Antranik and Alice Gurdjian Scholarship Grant *(Undergraduate/Scholarship)*

Purpose: To help students of Armenian descent pay for college. **Focus:** General studies/Field of study not specified. **Qualif.:** Applicants must be of Armenian descent; must be students enrolled full-time and have completed one full year of academics at a four-year accredited U.S. college or university, or must be enrolled in a two-year college or university and transferring to a four-year college or university as a full-time student; must be U.S. citizens or possess the appropriate visa status in order to study in the U.S.

Duration: Annual. **To Apply:** Forms and details available online at www.asainc.org/national/scholarships.shtml; application, essay, transcripts, three letters of reference, and profile form must be mailed. **Deadline:** March 15.

1881 ■ Garabed, Zabel and Vahe Hachikian Scholarship Grant *(Undergraduate/Scholarship)*

Purpose: To help students of Armenian descent pay for a degree in business of chemistry. **Focus:** Business; Chemistry; General studies/Field of study not specified. **Qualif.:** Applicants must be of Armenian descent; must be students enrolled full-time and have completed one full year of academics at a four-year accredited U.S. college or university, or must be enrolled in a two-year college or university and transferring to a four-year college or university as a full-time student; must be U.S. citizens or possess the appropriate visa status in order to study in the U.S. **Criteria:** Preference given to students pursuing degrees in chemistry or business.

Duration: Annual. **To Apply:** Forms and details available online at www.asainc.org/national/scholarships.shtml; application, essay, transcripts, three letters of reference, and profile form must be mailed. **Deadline:** March 15.

1882 ■ Jack Hajinian Memorial Grant
(Undergraduate/Scholarship)

Purpose: To help students of Armenian descent pursue degrees in the medical field. **Focus:** Medicine. **Qualif.:** Applicants must be of Armenian descent; must be students enrolled full-time and have completed one full year of academics at a four-year accredited U.S. college or university, or must be enrolled in a two-year college or university and transferring to a four-year college or university as a full-time student; must be U.S. citizens or possess the appropriate visa status in order to study in the U.S. **Criteria:** Must be pursuing a degree in the medical field.

Duration: Annual. **To Apply:** Forms and details available online at www.asainc.org/national/scholarships.shtml; application, essay, transcripts, three letters of reference, and profile form must be mailed. **Deadline:** March 15.

1883 ■ Margaret Shumavonian Harnischfeger Scholarship *(Undergraduate/Scholarship)*

Purpose: To help students of Armenian descent pay for college. **Focus:** General studies/Field of study not specified. **Qualif.:** Applicants must be of Armenian descent; must be students enrolled full-time and have completed one full year of academics at a four-year accredited U.S. college or university, or must be enrolled in a two-year college or university and transferring to a four-year college or university as a full-time student; must be U.S. citizens or possess the appropriate visa status in order to study in the U.S.

Duration: Annual. **To Apply:** Forms and details available online at www.asainc.org/national/scholarships.shtml; application, essay, transcripts, three letters of reference, and profile form must be mailed. **Deadline:** March 15.

1884 ■ Hekemian Family Scholarship Grants
(Undergraduate/Scholarship)

Purpose: To help students of Armenian descent pursue business degrees in college. **Focus:** Business. **Qualif.:** Must be of Armenian descent; enrolled full-time and have completed one full year of academics at a four-year accredited U.S. college or university, or must be enrolled in a two-year college or university and transferring to a four-year college or university as a full-time student; must be U.S. citizens or possess the appropriate visa status in order to study in the U.S; must be studying in the field of business.

Duration: Annual. **To Apply:** Forms and details available online at www.asainc.org/national/scholarships.shtml; application, essay, transcripts, three letters of reference, and profile form must be mailed. **Deadline:** March 15.

1885 ■ George Holopigian Memorial Grants
(Undergraduate/Scholarship)

Purpose: To help students of Armenian descent attend college. **Focus:** General studies/Field of study not specified. **Qualif.:** Applicants must be of Armenian descent; must be students enrolled full-time and have completed one full year of academics at a four-year accredited U.S. college or university, or must be enrolled in a two-year college or university and transferring to a four-year college or university as a full-time student; must be U.S. citizens or possess the appropriate visa status in order to study in the U.S.

Duration: Annual. **To Apply:** Forms and details available online at www.asainc.org/national/scholarships.shtml; ap-

Awards are arranged alphabetically below their administering organizations

plication, essay, transcripts, three letters of reference, and profile form must be mailed. **Deadline:** March 15.

1886 ■ The Husenig Foundation Scholarship Grant
(Undergraduate/Scholarship)

Purpose: To help students of Armenian descent attend college. **Focus:** General studies/Field of study not specified. **Qualif.:** Applicants must be of Armenian descent; must be students enrolled full-time and have completed one full year of academics at a four-year accredited U.S. college or university, or must be enrolled in a two-year college or university and transferring to a four-year college or university as a full-time student; must be U.S. citizens or possess the appropriate visa status in order to study in the U.S.

Duration: Annual. **To Apply:** Forms and details available online at www.asainc.org/national/scholarships.shtml; application, essay, transcripts, three letters of reference, and profile form must be mailed. **Deadline:** March 15.

1887 ■ Armenag and Armenhooi Kalustian Memorial Grant *(Undergraduate/Scholarship)*

Purpose: To help students of Armenian descent attend college. **Focus:** Education; General studies/Field of study not specified. **Qualif.:** Applicants must be of Armenian descent; must be students enrolled full-time and have completed one full year of academics at a four-year accredited U.S. college or university, or must be enrolled in a two-year college or university and transferring to a four-year college or university as a full-time student; must be U.S. citizens or possess the appropriate visa status in order to study in the U.S. **Criteria:** Preference will be given to students studying education.

Duration: Annual. **To Apply:** Forms and details available online at www.asainc.org/national/scholarships.shtml; application, essay, transcripts, three letters of reference, and profile form must be mailed. **Deadline:** March 15.

1888 ■ Aram and Adrine Kamparosyan Memorial Grant *(Undergraduate/Scholarship)*

Purpose: To help students of Armenian descent attend college. **Focus:** General studies/Field of study not specified. **Qualif.:** Applicants must be of Armenian descent; must be students enrolled full-time and have completed one full year of academics at a four-year accredited U.S. college or university, or must be enrolled in a two-year college or university and transferring to a four-year college or university as a full-time student; must be U.S. citizens or possess the appropriate visa status in order to study in the U.S.

Duration: Annual. **To Apply:** Forms and details available online at www.asainc.org/national/scholarships.shtml; application, essay, transcripts, three letters of reference, and profile form must be mailed. **Deadline:** March 15.

1889 ■ Koren and Alice Odian Kasparian Memorial Grant *(Undergraduate/Scholarship)*

Purpose: To help Armenian students studying international law, foreign languages, and diplomatic studies attend college. **Focus:** International affairs and relations; Law; Linguistics. **Qualif.:** Applicants must be of Armenian descent; must be students enrolled full-time and have completed one full year of academics at a four-year accredited U.S. college or university, or must be enrolled in a two-year college or university and transferring to a four-year college or university as a full-time student; must be

U.S. citizens or possess the appropriate visa status in order to study in the U.S.; must be studying in the fields of international law, foreign language, or diplomatic studies.

Duration: Annual. **To Apply:** Forms and details available online at www.asainc.org/national/scholarships.shtml; application, essay, transcripts, three letters of reference, and profile form must be mailed. **Deadline:** March 15.

1890 ■ Araxy Kechejian Memorial Grant
(Undergraduate/Scholarship)

Purpose: To help students of Armenian descent pursue degrees in the field of medicine. **Focus:** Medicine. **Qualif.:** Applicants must be of Armenian descent; must be students enrolled full-time and have completed one full year of academics at a four-year accredited U.S. college or university, or must be enrolled in a two-year college or university and transferring to a four-year college or university as a full-time student; must be U.S. citizens or possess the appropriate visa status in order to study in the U.S.; must be studying in the field of medicine.

Duration: Annual. **To Apply:** Forms and details available online at www.asainc.org/national/scholarships.shtml; application, essay, transcripts, three letters of reference, and profile form must be mailed. **Deadline:** March 15.

1891 ■ George Keverian Public Service Scholarship
(Undergraduate/Scholarship)

Purpose: To help students of Armenian descent study public service or principles of democracy. **Focus:** Political science; Public service. **Qualif.:** Applicants must be of Armenian descent; must be students enrolled full-time and have completed one full year of academics at a four-year accredited U.S. college or university, or must be enrolled in a two-year college or university and transferring to a four-year college or university as a full-time student; must be U.S. citizens or possess the appropriate visa status in order to study in the U.S.; must be studying in the fields of public service or principles of democracy.

Duration: Annual. **To Apply:** Forms and details available online at www.asainc.org/national/scholarships.shtml; application, essay, transcripts, three letters of reference, and profile form must be mailed. **Deadline:** March 15.

1892 ■ Haig Koumjian Memorial Grant
(Undergraduate/Scholarship)

Purpose: To help students of Armenian descent attend college. **Focus:** General studies/Field of study not specified. **Qualif.:** Applicants must be of Armenian descent; must be students enrolled full-time and have completed one full year of academics at a four-year accredited U.S. college or university, or must be enrolled in a two-year college or university and transferring to a four-year college or university as a full-time student; must be U.S. citizens or possess the appropriate visa status in order to study in the U.S. **Criteria:** Preference given to New Jersey residents.

Duration: Annual. **To Apply:** Forms and details available online at www.asainc.org/national/scholarships.shtml; application, essay, transcripts, three letters of reference, and profile form must be mailed. **Deadline:** March 15.

1893 ■ Harry A. Kuljian Memorial Grant
(Undergraduate/Scholarship)

Purpose: To help Armenian students studying theology attend college. **Focus:** Theology. **Qualif.:** Applicants must be of Armenian descent; must be students enrolled full-time and have completed one full year of academics at a four-

Awards are arranged alphabetically below their administering organizations

year accredited U.S. college or university, or must be enrolled in a two-year college or university and transferring to a four-year college or university as a full-time student; must be U.S. citizens or possess the appropriate visa status in order to study in the U.S.; must be studying in the field of theology.

Duration: Annual. **To Apply:** Forms and details available online at www.asainc.org/national/scholarships.shtml; application, essay, transcripts, three letters of reference, and profile form must be mailed. **Deadline:** March 15.

1894 ■ Manasel Manasselian Memorial Grant
(Undergraduate/Scholarship)

Purpose: To help students of Armenian descent attend college. **Focus:** General studies/Field of study not specified. **Qualif.:** Applicants must be of Armenian descent; must be students enrolled full-time and have completed one full year of academics at a four-year accredited U.S. college or university, or must be enrolled in a two-year college or university and transferring to a four-year college or university as a full-time student; must be U.S. citizens or possess the appropriate visa status in order to study in the U.S.

Duration: Annual. **To Apply:** Forms and details available online at www.asainc.org/national/scholarships.shtml; application, essay, transcripts, three letters of reference, and profile form must be mailed. **Deadline:** March 15.

1895 ■ K. Cyrus Melikian Memorial Grant
(Undergraduate/Scholarship)

Purpose: To help students of Armenian descent attend college. **Focus:** General studies/Field of study not specified. **Qualif.:** Applicants must be of Armenian descent; must be students enrolled full-time and have completed one full year of academics at a four-year accredited U.S. college or university, or must be enrolled in a two-year college or university and transferring to a four-year college or university as a full-time student; must be U.S. citizens or possess the appropriate visa status in order to study in the U.S.

Duration: Annual. **To Apply:** Forms and details available online at www.asainc.org/national/scholarships.shtml; application, essay, transcripts, three letters of reference, and profile form must be mailed. **Deadline:** March 15.

1896 ■ Dikran Missirlian Scholarship Grant
(Undergraduate/Scholarship)

Purpose: To help students of Armenian descent pay for college. **Focus:** General studies/Field of study not specified. **Qualif.:** Applicants must be of Armenian descent; must be students enrolled full-time and have completed one full year of academics at a four-year accredited U.S. college or university, or must be enrolled in a two-year college or university and transferring to a four-year college or university as a full-time student; must be U.S. citizens or possess the appropriate visa status in order to study in the U.S.

Duration: Annual. **To Apply:** Forms and details available online at www.asainc.org/national/scholarships.shtml; application, essay, transcripts, three letters of reference, and profile form must be mailed. **Deadline:** Marcrh 15.

1897 ■ Satenik & Adom Ourian Education Foundation Scholarship *(Undergraduate/Scholarship)*

Purpose: To help students of Armenian descent pay for college. **Focus:** General studies/Field of study not speci-

fied. **Qualif.:** Applicants must be of Armenian descent; must be students enrolled full-time and have completed one full year of academics at a four-year accredited U.S. college or university, or must be enrolled in a two-year college or university and transferring to a four-year college or university as a full-time student; must be U.S. citizens or possess the appropriate visa status in order to study in the U.S.

Duration: Annual. **To Apply:** Forms and details available online at www.asainc.org/national/scholarships.shtml; application, essay, transcripts, three letters of reference, and profile form must be mailed. **Deadline:** March 15.

1898 ■ Larry A. Peters Endowment Fund Scholarship *(Undergraduate/Scholarship)*

Purpose: To help students of Armenian descent pay for college. **Focus:** General studies/Field of study not specified. **Qualif.:** Applicants must be of Armenian descent; must be students enrolled full-time and have completed one full year of academics at a four-year accredited U.S. college or university, or must be enrolled in a two-year college or university and transferring to a four-year college or university as a full-time student; must be U.S. citizens or possess the appropriate visa status in order to study in the U.S.

Duration: Annual. **To Apply:** Forms and details available online at www.asainc.org/national/scholarships.shtml; application, essay, transcripts, three letters of reference, and profile form must be mailed. **Deadline:** March 15.

1899 ■ Francis Poloshian Memorial Grant
(Undergraduate/Scholarship)

Purpose: To help students of Armenian descent pay for college. **Focus:** General studies/Field of study not specified. **Qualif.:** Applicants must be of Armenian descent; must be students enrolled full-time and have completed one full year of academics at a four-year accredited U.S. college or university, or must be enrolled in a two-year college or university and transferring to a four-year college or university as a full-time student; must be U.S. citizens or possess the appropriate visa status in order to study in the U.S.

Duration: Annual. **To Apply:** Forms and details available online at www.asainc.org/national/scholarships.shtml; application, essay, transcripts, three letters of reference, and profile form must be mailed. **Deadline:** March 15.

1900 ■ James Poloshian Memorial Grant
(Undergraduate/Scholarship)

Purpose: To help students of Armenian descent pay for college. **Focus:** General studies/Field of study not specified. **Qualif.:** Applicants must be of Armenian descent; must be students enrolled full-time and have completed one full year of academics at a four-year accredited U.S. college or university, or must be enrolled in a two-year college or university and transferring to a four-year college or university as a full-time student; must be U.S. citizens or possess the appropriate visa status in order to study in the U.S.

Duration: Annual. **To Apply:** Forms and details available online at www.asainc.org/national/scholarships.shtml; application, essay, transcripts, three letters of reference, and profile form must be mailed. **Deadline:** March 15.

1901 ■ Dr. Henry Seneca Charitable Trust Scholarship *(Undergraduate/Scholarship)*

Purpose: To help students of Armenian descent pursue degrees in medicine. **Focus:** Medicine. **Qualif.:** Applicants

Awards are arranged alphabetically below their administering organizations

must be of Armenian descent; must be students enrolled full-time and have completed one full year of academics at a four-year accredited U.S. college or university, or must be enrolled in a two-year college or university and transferring to a four-year college or university as a full-time student; must be U.S. citizens or possess the appropriate visa status in order to study in the U.S.; must be studying medicine.

Duration: Annual. **To Apply:** Forms and details available online at www.asainc.org/national/scholarships.shtml; application, essay, transcripts, three letters of reference, and profile form must be mailed. **Deadline:** March 15.

1902 ■ Archak and Meroum Senekjian Memorial Grant *(Undergraduate/Scholarship)*

Purpose: To help students of Armenian descent pay for college. **Focus:** General studies/Field of study not specified. **Qualif.:** Applicants must be of Armenian descent; must be students enrolled full-time and have completed one full year of academics at a four-year accredited U.S. college or university, or must be enrolled in a two-year college or university and transferring to a four-year college or university as a full-time student; must be U.S. citizens or possess the appropriate visa status in order to study in the U.S.

Duration: Annual. **To Apply:** Forms and details available online at www.asainc.org/national/scholarships.shtml; application, essay, transcripts, three letters of reference, and profile form must be mailed. **Deadline:** March 15.

1903 ■ Julia Shahan and Shahan Siran Nevshehir Memorial Grant *(Undergraduate/Scholarship)*

Purpose: To help students of Armenian descent pay for college. **Focus:** Arts. **Qualif.:** Applicants must be of Armenian descent; must be students enrolled full-time and have completed one full year of academics at a four-year accredited U.S. college or university, or must be enrolled in a two-year college or university and transferring to a four-year college or university as a full-time student; must be U.S. citizens or possess the appropriate visa status in order to study in the U.S.; must be studying in the fields of arts.

Duration: Annual. **To Apply:** Forms and details available online at www.asainc.org/national/scholarships.shtml; application, essay, transcripts, three letters of reference, and profile form must be mailed. **Deadline:** March 15.

1904 ■ Arthur A. Thovmasian, Jr. Memorial Grant *(Undergraduate/Scholarship)*

Purpose: To help students of Armenian descent pay for college. **Focus:** General studies/Field of study not specified. **Qualif.:** Applicants must be of Armenian descent; must be students enrolled full-time and have completed one full year of academics at a four-year accredited U.S. college or university, or must be enrolled in a two-year college or university and transferring to a four-year college or university as a full-time student; must be U.S. citizens or possess the appropriate visa status in order to study in the U.S. **Criteria:** Preference given to students who are Rhode Island residents.

Duration: Annual. **To Apply:** Forms and details available online at www.asainc.org/national/scholarships.shtml; application, essay, transcripts, three letters of reference, and profile form must be mailed. **Deadline:** March 15.

1905 ■ Dr. Harry Jeffrey Tourigian Memorial Grant *(Undergraduate/Scholarship)*

Purpose: To help students of Armenian descent pay for college. **Focus:** General studies/Field of study not speci-

fied; Medicine. **Qualif.:** Applicants must be of Armenian descent; must be students enrolled full-time and have completed one full year of academics at a four-year accredited U.S. college or university, or must be enrolled in a two-year college or university and transferring to a four-year college or university as a full-time student; must be U.S. citizens or possess the appropriate visa status in order to study in the U.S. **Criteria:** Preference will be given to those studying medicine.

Duration: Annual. **To Apply:** Forms and details available online at www.asainc.org/national/scholarships.shtml; application, essay, transcripts, three letters of reference, and profile form must be mailed. **Deadline:** March 15.

1906 ■ Aram Zakian Memorial Fund Scholarship *(Undergraduate/Scholarship)*

Purpose: To help students of Armenian descent pay for college. **Focus:** General studies/Field of study not specified. **Qualif.:** Applicants must be of Armenian descent; must be students enrolled full-time and have completed one full year of academics at a four-year accredited U.S. college or university, or must be enrolled in a two-year college or university and transferring to a four-year college or university as a full-time student; must be U.S. citizens or possess the appropriate visa status in order to study in the U.S.

Duration: Annual. **To Apply:** Forms and details available online at www.asainc.org/national/scholarships.shtml; application, essay, transcripts, three letters of reference, and profile form must be mailed. **Deadline:** March 15.

1907 ■ Araxie Zakian Memorial Grant *(Undergraduate/Scholarship)*

Purpose: To help students of Armenian descent pay for college. **Focus:** General studies/Field of study not specified. **Qualif.:** Applicants must be of Armenian descent; must be students enrolled full-time and have completed one full year of academics at a four-year accredited U.S. college or university, or must be enrolled in a two-year college or university and transferring to a four-year college or university as a full-time student; must be U.S. citizens or possess the appropriate visa status in order to study in the U.S.

Duration: Annual. **To Apply:** Forms and details available online at www.asainc.org/national/scholarships.shtml; application, essay, transcripts, three letters of reference, and profile form must be mailed. **Deadline:** March 15.

1908 ■ Charles Zarigian, Esq. Memorial Award *(Undergraduate/Scholarship)*

Purpose: To help students of Armenian descent pay for college. **Focus:** General studies/Field of study not specified; Law; Religion; Teaching. **Qualif.:** Applicants must be of Armenian descent; must be students enrolled full-time and have completed one full year of academics at a four-year accredited U.S. college or university, or must be enrolled in a two-year college or university and transferring to a four-year college or university as a full-time student; must be U.S. citizens or possess the appropriate visa status in order to study in the U.S. **Criteria:** Preference given to those studying law, teaching, or Christian ministry.

Duration: Annual. **To Apply:** Forms and details available online at www.asainc.org/national/scholarships.shtml; application, essay, transcripts, three letters of reference, and profile form must be mailed. **Deadline:** March 15.

Awards are arranged alphabetically below their administering organizations

1909 ■ George Zartarian Memorial Grant
(Undergraduate/Scholarship)

Purpose: To help Armenian students pay for college. **Focus:** General studies/Field of study not specified. **Qualif.:** Applicants must be of Armenian descent; must be students enrolled full-time and have completed one full year of academics at a four-year accredited U.S. college or university, or must be enrolled in a two-year college or university and transferring to a four-year college or university as a full-time student; must be U.S. citizens or possess the appropriate visa status in order to study in the U.S. **Criteria:** Preference given to students who are Rhode Island residents.

Duration: Annual. **To Apply:** Forms and details available online at www.asainc.org/national/scholarships.shtml; application, essay, transcripts, three letters of reference, and profile form must be mailed. **Deadline:** March 15.

1910 ■ Army Aviation Association of America (AAAA)
593 Main St.
Monroe, CT 06468-2830
Ph: (203)268-2450
Fax: (203)268-5870
E-mail: aaaa@quad-a.org
URL: www.quad-a.org
Social Media: www.facebook.com/ArmyAviationAssociation
www.instagram.com/armyaviationassociation
twitter.com/army_aviation

1911 ■ AAAA Scholarship Program *(Undergraduate, Graduate/Scholarship)*

Purpose: To provide grants and loans to members who seek further education as well as the member's family who sought college-entry financial aid. **Focus:** General studies/Field of study not specified. **Qualif.:** Applicant must be a current member of the Army Aviation Association of America; or spouse of a current AAAA member or deceased member; or son or daughter of a current member or deceased member; or grandchild of a current member or deceased member; or unmarried sibling of a current member or deceased member.

Duration: Annual. **To Apply:** Applicants must submit the completed application including current transcript of grades; proof of admission to an accredited college or university; photograph; essay: maximum 300-word essay; reference: to be completed by an individual who is aware of the applicant's abilities and potential (teacher, employer, coach, etc.). Do not include relatives; academic reporting form. **Deadline:** May 1. **Remarks:** Established in 1963. **Contact:** Sue Stokes; Phone: 203-268-2450; Email: scholarship@quad-a.org.

1912 ■ Army, Navy & Air Force Veterans in Canada (ANAVETS)
6 Beechwood Ave., Ste. 2
Ottawa, ON, Canada K1L 8B4
URL: anavets.ca

1913 ■ Judge Daniel F. Foley Memorial Scholarship
(Undergraduate/Scholarship)

Purpose: To support a goodwill partnership between veterans of the United States and Canada. **Focus:** General studies/Field of study not specified. **Qualif.:** Applicants should be direct descendants (children, grandchildren, great grandchildren) of members of The Army, Navy & Air Force Veterans in Canada attending any year of university or college courses leading to a degree or diploma. **Criteria:** Selection will be based on National Executive Committeeman and on the Advisory Committee.

Funds Avail.: $1,000. **Duration:** Annual. **Number Awarded:** 1. **Deadline:** August 1.

1914 ■ Army Nurse Corps Association (ANCA)
8000 IH-10 W, Ste. 600
San Antonio, TX 78230-3887
Ph: (210)650-3534
Fax: (210)650-3534
Free: 888-742-9910
E-mail: membership@e-anca.org
URL: e-anca.org
Social Media: www.facebook.com/ArmyNurseCorpsAssociation

1915 ■ ANCA Scholarships *(Undergraduate/Scholarship)*

Purpose: To provide financial assistance to nursing students. **Focus:** Nursing. **Qualif.:** Applicant must be currently enrolled in an accredited baccalaureate or advanced degree nursing or nurse anesthesia program who: serving or have previously served in any branch, at any rank, of a component of the US Army (active army, army national guard, or army reserve); are not currently receiving funding by a component of the US Army (e.g., ROTC scholarship students and students receiving full GI Bill benefits are not eligible); and as applicable, have received an honorable discharge; must be nursing or anesthesia students whose parent(s), spouse, or child(ren) have current or previous service in a component of the US Army. **Criteria:** Applicants who are students planning to enter the Army Nurse Corps, Army Reserve or National Guard; previously served in the United States Army, Army Reserve or National Guard; Army Nurse Corps officers enrolled in undergraduate or graduate nursing programs not funded by United States Army, Army Reserve or National Guard; members of Army Medical Department pursuing baccalaureate degree in nursing not funded by United States Army, Army Reserve or National Guard will be given preference.

Funds Avail.: No specific amount. **Duration:** Annual. **Number Awarded:** 17. **To Apply:** Applicants must submit application template consist of school and location; agency accreditation; internal revenue status; scholarship program; support of army nurse corps recruitment activities; award criteria; application for specific student; and agreement to Education Committee.

1916 ■ Army Scholarship Foundation
11700 Preston Rd., Ste. 660-301
Dallas, TX 75230
E-mail: contactus@armyscholarshipfoundation.org
URL: www.armyscholarshipfoundation.org
Social Media: www.facebook.com/ArmyScholarshipFoundation

1917 ■ The First Lieutenant Scott McClean Love Memorial Scholarship - Children of Soldiers
(Undergraduate, Vocational/Occupational/Scholarship)

Purpose: To financially support deserving children of current or former United States Army personnel in their pursuit

Awards are arranged alphabetically below their administering organizations

of higher education. **Focus:** General studies/Field of study not specified. **Qualif.:** Applicants must be sons or daughters of regular duty, active duty Reserve or active duty National Guard U.S. Army members in good standing; or must be sons or daughters of former U.S. Army who received an honorable discharge or medical discharge or who were killed while serving in the U.S. Army; must be high school seniors, high school graduates or registered as undergraduate students at an accredited college or vocational/technical institution; must be U.S. citizens not reaching 24th birthday by application deadline.

Duration: Annual. **To Apply:** Applicants must submit a completed scholarship application form along with a Free Application for Federal Student Aid (FAFSA); a signed copy of the appropriate income tax return for the previous year; a certificate of good service or the parent's/spouse's DD 214; a high school transcript and transcripts from all post high school educational institutions (if applicable); an essay; and a photograph. **Deadline:** April 15. **Remarks:** The Scholarship was established in memory of Scott McClean Love. **Contact:** Army Scholarship Foundation, 11700 Preston Rd., Ste. 660-301, Dallas, Texas, 75230; E-mail: ContactUs@armyscholarshipfoundation.org.

1918 ■ The First Lieutenant Scott McClean Love Memorial Scholarship - Spouses of Soldiers
(Undergraduate, Vocational/Occupational/Scholarship)

Purpose: To financially assist deserving spouses of current or former United States Army personnel in their pursuit of higher education. **Focus:** General studies/Field of study not specified. **Qualif.:** Applicants must be spouses of a serving enlisted regular active duty, active duty Reserve or active duty National Guard U.S. Army member in good standing; or must be spouses of former U.S. Army who received an honorable discharge or medical discharge or who were killed while serving in the U.S. Army; must be high school seniors, high school graduates or registered as undergraduate students at an accredited college or vocational/technical institution; must be U.S. citizens not reaching 24th birthday by application deadline.

Duration: Annual. **To Apply:** Applicants must submit a completed scholarship application form along with a Free Application for Federal Student Aid (FAFSA); a signed copy of the appropriate income tax return for the previous year; a certificate of good service or the parent's/spouse's DD 214; a high school transcript and transcripts from all post high school educational institutions (if applicable); an essay; and a photograph. **Deadline:** April 15. **Remarks:** The Scholarship was established in memory of Scott McClean Love. **Contact:** Army Scholarship Foundation, 11700 Preston Rd., Ste. 660-301, Dallas, Texas, 75230; E-mail: ContactUs@armyscholarshipfoundation.org.

1919 ■ The Captain Jennifer Shafer Odom Memorial Scholarship - Children of Soldiers *(Undergraduate, Vocational/Occupational/Scholarship)*

Purpose: To financially support deserving children of current or former United States Army personnel in their pursuit of higher education. **Focus:** General studies/Field of study not specified. **Qualif.:** Applicants must be sons or daughters of regular duty, active duty Reserve or active duty National Guard U.S. Army members in good standing; or must be sons or daughters of former U.S. Army who received an honorable discharge or medical discharge or who were killed while serving in the U.S. Army; must be high school seniors, high school graduates or registered as undergraduate students at an accredited college or vocational/technical

institution; must be U.S. citizens not reaching 24th birthday by application deadline.

Duration: Annual. **To Apply:** Applicants must submit a completed scholarship application form along with a Free Application for Federal Student Aid (FAFSA); a signed copy of the appropriate income tax return for the previous year; a certificate of good service or the parent's/spouse's DD 214; a high school transcript and transcripts from all post high school educational institutions (if applicable); an essay; and a photograph. **Deadline:** April 15. **Remarks:** The Scholarship was established in memory of Jennifer Shafer Odom. **Contact:** Army Scholarship Foundation, 11700 Preston Rd., Ste. 660-301, Dallas, Texas, 75230; E-mail: ContactUs@armyscholarshipfoundation.org.

1920 ■ The Captain Jennifer Shafer Odom Memorial Scholarship - Spouses of Soldiers *(Undergraduate, Vocational/Occupational/Scholarship)*

Purpose: To financially assist deserving spouses of current or former United States Army personnel in their pursuit of higher education. **Focus:** General studies/Field of study not specified. **Qualif.:** Applicants must be spouses of a serving enlisted regular active duty, active duty Reserve or active duty National Guard U.S. Army member in good standing; or must be spouses of former U.S. Army who received an honorable discharge or medical discharge or who were killed while serving in the U.S. Army; must be high school seniors, high school graduates or registered as undergraduate students at an accredited college or vocational/technical institution; must be U.S. citizens not reaching 24th birthday by application deadline.

Duration: Annual. **To Apply:** Applicants must submit a completed scholarship application form along with a Free Application for Federal Student Aid (FAFSA); a signed copy of the appropriate income tax return for the previous year; a certificate of good service or the parent's/spouse's DD 214; a high school transcript and transcripts from all post high school educational institutions (if applicable); an essay; and a photograph. **Deadline:** April 15. **Remarks:** The Scholarship was established in memory of Jennifer Shafer Odom. **Contact:** Army Scholarship Foundation, 11700 Preston Rd., Ste. 660-301, Dallas, Texas, 75230; E-mail: ContactUs@armyscholarshipfoundation.org.

1921 ■ Aaron Arnoldsen Memorial
1325 Airmotive Way, Ste. 220
Reno, NV 89502
E-mail: info@aamemorial.com
URL: aamemorial.com

1922 ■ Aaron Edward Arnoldsen Memorial Scholarship *(Undergraduate/Scholarship)*

Purpose: To provide financial support to aid students' educational endeavors. **Focus:** General studies/Field of study not specified. **Qualif.:** Applicant may be either male or female; applicants must be junior or senior students; must graduate of Nevada high school; 3.0 Grade Point Average (G.P.A.) or below; must be full time student at the University of Nevada, Reno; must continued employment through forthcoming school-year. **Criteria:** Selection based on meeting the set criteria.

Funds Avail.: Over $200,000. **Duration:** Annual. **Number Awarded:** Varies. **To Apply:** Applicants must submit completed application form and the other requirements needed. **Remarks:** Established in 1993. **Contact:** Phone: 775-784-4666.

Awards are arranged alphabetically below their administering organizations

1923 ■ ARRL Foundation (ARRLF)
225 Main St.
Newington, CT 06111-1494
Ph: (860)594-0200
Fax: (860)594-0259
Free: 888-277-5289
E-mail: hq@arrl.org
URL: www.arrl.org

1924 ■ American Radio Relay League Louisiana Memorial Scholarships (Undergraduate/Scholarship)

Purpose: To provide financial assistance to students who have the license for higher education. **Focus:** Radio and television. **Qualif.:** Applicants must hold an FCC amateur radio license, and be Louisiana residents or attending a four-year college/university in Louisiana; must have a 3.0 GPA. **Criteria:** Award is given based on the submitted materials.

Funds Avail.: $750. **To Apply:** Applicants must submit a completed scholarship application form along with a recent high school (or equivalent) or college transcript.

1925 ■ Earl I. Anderson Scholarships (Undergraduate/Scholarship)

Purpose: To provide financial assistance to students who have the license for post-secondary education. **Focus:** Radio and television. **Qualif.:** Applicant must hold an FCC amateur radio license; be a resident of, or attending classes in Illinois, Indiana, Michigan, or Florida; and must be an ARRL member. **Criteria:** Award is given based on the submitted materials. The ARRL Foundation Scholarship Committee will review all applicants for eligibility and award decisions. Preference will be given to applicants studying in Electronic Engineering or related technical field.

Duration: Annual. **To Apply:** Applicant must submit a completed scholarship application form online along with a pdf format of recent high school (or equivalent) or college transcript.

1926 ■ The ARRL General Fund Scholarship (Undergraduate/Scholarship)

Purpose: To provide financial assistance to students who have the license for post-secondary education. **Focus:** Radio and television. **Qualif.:** Applicants must hold an FCC amateur radio license. **Criteria:** Award is given based on the submitted materials. The ARRL Foundation Scholarship Committee will review all applicants for eligibility and award decisions.

Funds Avail.: $2,000. **Duration:** Annual. **Number Awarded:** Varies. **To Apply:** Applicants must submit a completed scholarship application form along with a recent high school (or equivalent) or college transcript. **Deadline:** December 31.

1927 ■ The Ernest L. Baulch, W2TX, and Marcia E. Baulch, WA2AKJ, Scholarship (Undergraduate/Scholarship)

Purpose: To provide financial support to students who are holding a license for post-secondary education. **Focus:** Radio and television. **Qualif.:** Applicants must hold an FCC amateur radio license; and be attending a four-year college/university. **Criteria:** Award is given based on the submitted materials.

Funds Avail.: $3,500. **Duration:** Annual. **Number Awarded:** 1. **To Apply:** Applicants must submit a com-pleted scholarship application form along with a recent high school (or equivalent) or college transcript. **Deadline:** December 31.

1928 ■ The Richard W. Bendicksen, N7ZL, Memorial Scholarship (Undergraduate/Scholarship)

Purpose: To provide financial assistance to students who have the license for higher education. **Focus:** Radio and television. **Qualif.:** Applicants must hold an FCC amateur radio license and be attending a four-year college/university. **Criteria:** Award is given based on the submitted materials.

Funds Avail.: $1,000. **Duration:** Annual. **Number Awarded:** 1. **To Apply:** Applicants must submit a completed scholarship application form along with a recent high school (or equivalent) or college transcript. **Deadline:** December 31.

1929 ■ The William Bennett, W7PHO, Memorial Scholarship (Undergraduate/Scholarship)

Purpose: To support the education of students holding a valid FCC-granted Amateur Radio license for post-secondary education. **Focus:** Radio and television. **Qualif.:** Applicants must hold an FCC amateur radio license; be a Northwest, Pacific or Southwest division resident; be enrolled in a four-year college/university; and have a GPA of 3.0 or better for an ongoing course of study. **Criteria:** Award is given based on submitted materials.

Funds Avail.: $500. **Duration:** Annual. **Number Awarded:** 1. **To Apply:** Applicants must submit a completed scholarship application form along with a recent high school (or equivalent) or college transcript. **Deadline:** December 31.

1930 ■ The Henry Broughton, K2AE, Memorial Scholarship (Undergraduate/Scholarship)

Purpose: To provide financial support to students who are holding a license for post-secondary education. **Focus:** Engineering; Radio and television; Science. **Qualif.:** Applicants must hold an FCC amateur radio license; reside within 70 miles of Schenectady NY; studying in baccalaureate or higher courses of study in engineering, sciences or a similar field in an accredited four-year college/university. **Criteria:** Award is given based on the submitted materials.

Funds Avail.: $1,000. **Duration:** Annual. **Number Awarded:** 1. **To Apply:** Applicants must submit a completed scholarship application form along with a recent high school (or equivalent) or college transcript. **Deadline:** December 31.

1931 ■ The Mary Lou Brown Scholarship (Undergraduate/Scholarship)

Purpose: To support the education of students holding a valid FCC-granted Amateur Radio license for post-secondary education. **Focus:** Radio and television. **Qualif.:** Applicants must hold an FCC amateur radio license; be a resident of ARRL Northwest Division (AK, ID, MT, OR, WA); studying baccalaureate or higher courses; and have a GPA of 3.0 or higher. **Criteria:** Awards are given based on the submitted materials; preference will be given to those applicants who have demonstrated an interest in promoting Amateur Radio Service.

Funds Avail.: $2,500. **Duration:** Annual. **Number Awarded:** Varies. **To Apply:** Applicants must submit a completed scholarship application form along with a recent high school (or equivalent) or college transcript. **Deadline:** December 31.

Awards are arranged alphabetically below their administering organizations

1932 ■ The Central Arizona DX Association Scholarship (Undergraduate/Scholarship)

Purpose: To provide financial support to students who are holding a license for post-secondary education. **Focus:** Radio and television. **Qualif.:** Applicants must hold an FCC amateur radio license; be a resident of Arizona; and have a GPA of 3.2 or above. **Criteria:** Graduating high school students will be considered before current college students.

Funds Avail.: $1,000. **Duration:** Annual. **Number Awarded:** 1. **To Apply:** Applicants must submit a completed scholarship application form along with a recent high school (or equivalent) or college transcript. **Deadline:** December 31.

1933 ■ The Challenge Met Scholarship (Undergraduate/Scholarship)

Purpose: To provide financial support to students who are holding a license for post-secondary education. **Focus:** Radio and television. **Qualif.:** Applicants must hold an FCC amateur radio license; and be attending an accredited two or four-year college technical school or university. **Criteria:** Preference is given to application with documented learning disability (by physician or school) and indications that the applicant is putting forth substantial effort regardless of resulting academic grades.

Funds Avail.: $500. **Duration:** Annual. **Number Awarded:** Varies. **To Apply:** Applicants must submit a completed scholarship application form along with a recent high school (or equivalent) or college transcript. **Deadline:** December 31.

1934 ■ The Chicago FM Club Scholarship (Undergraduate/Scholarship)

Purpose: To provide financial assistance to students who are pursuing post-secondary education. **Focus:** Radio and television. **Qualif.:** Applicants must be a U.S. citizen or within three months of citizenship; residency in FCC Ninth Call district (IN, IL, WI). **Criteria:** Awards are given based on the submitted materials, eligibility and award decisions by the ARRL Foundation Scholarship Committee.

Funds Avail.: $500. **Duration:** Annual. **Number Awarded:** Varies. **To Apply:** Applicants must submit a completed scholarship application form online along with a pdf format of recent high school (or equivalent) or college transcript. **Deadline:** December 31.

1935 ■ The Tom and Judith Comstock Scholarship (Undergraduate/Scholarship)

Purpose: To support students with their education who have the license for post-secondary education. **Focus:** Radio and television. **Qualif.:** Applicants must be a U.S. citizen or within three months of citizenship; Residence in TX or OK. **Criteria:** Award is given based on the submitted materials. The ARRL Foundation Scholarship Committee will review all applicants for eligibility and award decisions.

Funds Avail.: $2,000. **Duration:** Annual. **Number Awarded:** 1. **To Apply:** Applicants must submit a completed scholarship application form along with a recent high school (or equivalent) or college transcript. **Deadline:** December 31.

1936 ■ The Irving W. Cook WA0CGS Scholarship (Undergraduate/Scholarship)

Purpose: To provide financial support to students who have the license for post-secondary education. **Focus:** Communications; Electronics; Radio and television. **Qualif.:** Ap-

plicants must be a U.S. citizen or within three months of citizenship; Resident of KS. **Criteria:** Award is given based on the submitted materials.

Funds Avail.: $1,000. **Duration:** Annual. **Number Awarded:** 1. **To Apply:** Applicants must submit a completed scholarship application form online along with a pdf format of recent high school (or equivalent) or college transcript. **Deadline:** December 31.

1937 ■ The Charles Clarke Cordle Memorial Scholarship (Undergraduate/Scholarship)

Purpose: To provide financial assistance to students who have the license for post-secondary education. **Focus:** Communications; Electronics; Radio and television. **Qualif.:** Applicants must be a U.S. citizen or within three months of citizenship; Resident of GA or AL. **Criteria:** Award is given based on the submitted materials.

Funds Avail.: $1,000. **Duration:** Annual. **Number Awarded:** 1. **To Apply:** Applicants must submit a completed scholarship application form along with a recent high school (or equivalent) or college transcript. **Deadline:** December 31.

1938 ■ The Dayton Amateur Radio Association Scholarship (Undergraduate/Scholarship)

Purpose: To provide financial assistance to students who have the license for post-secondary education. **Focus:** Radio and television. **Qualif.:** Applicants must be a U.S. citizen or within three months of citizenship; Resident of Any. **Criteria:** Award is given based on the submitted materials. The ARRL Foundation Scholarship Committee will review all applicants for eligibility and award decisions.

Funds Avail.: $1,000. **Duration:** Annual. **Number Awarded:** 4. **To Apply:** Applicants must submit a completed scholarship application form online along with a pdf format of recent high school (or equivalent) or college transcript. **Deadline:** December 31.

1939 ■ The Charles N. Fisher Memorial Scholarship (Undergraduate/Scholarship)

Purpose: To provide financial assistance to students who have the license for post-secondary education. **Focus:** Communications; Electronics; Radio and television. **Qualif.:** Applicants must hold an FCC amateur radio license; must be a resident of ARRL Southwestern Division (AZ, Los Angeles, Orange, San Diego, and Santa Barbara); studying in electronics, communications or related fields of a regionally accredited institution. **Criteria:** Award is given based on the submitted materials.

Duration: Annual. **Number Awarded:** 1. **To Apply:** Applicants must submit a completed scholarship application form online along with a pdf format of recent high school (or equivalent) or college transcript. **Deadline:** December 31.

1940 ■ William R. Goldfarb Memorial Scholarships (Undergraduate/Scholarship)

Purpose: To provide financial assistance to students who have the license for post-secondary education. **Focus:** Business; Computer and information sciences; Engineering; Medicine; Nursing; Radio and television; Science. **Qualif.:** Applicant must hold an FCC amateur radio license; must be studying baccalaureate courses in business-related, computers, medical, nursing, engineering or sciences; be a high school senior; and must demonstrate financial need. **Criteria:** Award is given based on the

Awards are arranged alphabetically below their administering organizations

submitted materials. The ARRL Foundation Scholarship Committee will review all applicants for eligibility and award decisions.

To Apply: Applicant must submit a completed scholarship application form along with a recent high school (or equivalent) or college transcript and the Free Application for Federal Student Aid (FAFSA) or Student Aid Report (SAR).

1941 ■ The Paul and Helen L. Grauer Scholarships
(Undergraduate/Scholarship)

Purpose: To provide financial assistance to students who have the license for post-secondary education. **Focus:** Communications; Electronics; Radio and television. **Qualif.:** Applicants must be a U.S. citizen or within three months of citizenship; Resident of ARRL Midwest Division (IA, KS, MO, NE). **Criteria:** Award is given based on the submitted materials.

Funds Avail.: $1,000. **Duration:** Annual. **Number Awarded:** 1. **To Apply:** Applicants must submit a completed scholarship application form online along with a pdf format of recent high school (or equivalent) or college transcript. **Deadline:** December 31.

1942 ■ The K2TEO Martin J. Green, Sr. Memorial Scholarship *(Undergraduate/Scholarship)*

Purpose: To provide financial assistance to students who have the license for post-secondary education. **Focus:** Radio and television. **Qualif.:** Applicants must be a U.S. citizen or within three months of citizenship; Resident of any. **Criteria:** Preference is given to a student from a "ham family".

Funds Avail.: $1,000. **Duration:** Annual. **Number Awarded:** 1. **To Apply:** Applicants must submit a completed scholarship application form along with a recent high school (or equivalent) or college transcript. **Deadline:** December 31.

1943 ■ Perry F. Hadlock Memorial Scholarships
(Undergraduate/Scholarship)

Purpose: To provide financial assistance to students who have the license for post-secondary education. **Focus:** Engineering, Electrical; Radio and television; Technology. **Qualif.:** Applicant must hold an FCC amateur radio license; must be studying in baccalaureate or higher courses in a technology-related field; preference to electrical and electronics engineering. **Criteria:** Preference is given to applicant studying at Clarkson University, Potsdam NY, or any Atlantic or Hudson Division.

To Apply: Applicant must submit a completed scholarship application form along with a recent high school (or equivalent) or college transcript.

1944 ■ The Albert H. Hix, W8AH, Memorial Scholarship *(Undergraduate/Scholarship)*

Purpose: To provide financial assistance to students who have the license for higher education. **Focus:** Radio and television. **Qualif.:** Applicants must be a U.S. citizen or within three months of citizenship; Resident of any; and have a GPA of 3.0 or higher. **Criteria:** Award is given based on the submitted materials.

Funds Avail.: $500. **Duration:** Annual. **Number Awarded:** 1. **To Apply:** Applicants must submit a completed scholarship application form along with a recent high school (or equivalent) or college transcript. **Deadline:** December 31.

1945 ■ Seth Horen, K1LOM Memorial Scholarships
(Undergraduate/Scholarship)

Purpose: To provide financial assistance to students who have the license for higher education. **Focus:** Radio and television. **Qualif.:** Applicant must hold an FCC amateur radio license and be attending a four-year college/university. **Criteria:** Award is given based on the submitted materials.

Funds Avail.: $500. **To Apply:** Applicant must submit a completed scholarship application form along with a recent high school (or equivalent) or college transcript.

1946 ■ IRARC Memorial, Joseph P. Rubino, WA4MMD, Scholarship *(Undergraduate/Scholarship)*

Purpose: To provide financial assistance to students who have the license for higher education. **Focus:** Electronics; Radio and television. **Qualif.:** Applicants must hold an FCC amateur radio license; have a minimum 2.5 GPA on a 4.0 scale; and be enrolled in an undergraduate degree or electronic technician certification program at an accredited institution. **Criteria:** Preference is given to the residents of Florida (Brevard County).

Funds Avail.: $750. **Duration:** Annual. **Number Awarded:** Varies. **To Apply:** Applicants must submit a completed scholarship application form along with a recent high school (or equivalent) or college transcript. **Deadline:** December 31.

1947 ■ The Dr. James L. Lawson Memorial Scholarship *(Undergraduate/Scholarship)*

Purpose: To provide financial assistance to students who have the license for higher education. **Focus:** Communications; Electronics; Radio and television. **Qualif.:** Applicants must hold an FCC amateur radio license; be a resident of one of the New England states (ME, NH, VT, CT, RI, MA) or New York State; and be studying in baccalaureate or higher courses in electronics, communications or related fields. **Criteria:** Award is given based on the submitted materials.

Funds Avail.: $500. **Duration:** Annual. **Number Awarded:** 1. **To Apply:** Applicants must submit a completed scholarship application form along with a recent high school (or equivalent) or college transcript. **Deadline:** December 31.

1948 ■ The Fred R. McDaniel Memorial Scholarship
(Undergraduate/Scholarship)

Purpose: To provide financial assistance to students who have the license for higher education. **Focus:** Communications; Electronics; Radio and television. **Qualif.:** Applicants must hold an FCC amateur radio license; be a resident of the FCC 5th call district (TX, OK, AR, LA, MS, NM); be studying in baccalaureate or higher courses of study in electronics, communications or related fields. **Criteria:** Preference is given to students with GPA of 3.0 or higher.

Funds Avail.: $500. **Duration:** Annual. **Number Awarded:** 1. **To Apply:** Applicants must submit a completed scholarship application form along with a recent high school (or equivalent) or college transcript. **Deadline:** December 31.

1949 ■ The Edmond A. Metzger Scholarship
(Undergraduate/Scholarship)

Purpose: To provide financial assistance to students who have the license for higher education. **Focus:** Engineering, Electrical; Radio and television. **Qualif.:** Applicants must hold an FCC amateur radio license; be residents of ARRL Central Division (IL, IN, WI); be studying in baccalaureate or higher courses of study in electrical engineering; be

Awards are arranged alphabetically below their administering organizations

ARRL members; and attending school in the Central Division. **Criteria:** Award is given based on the submitted materials.

Funds Avail.: $500. **Duration:** Annual. **Number Awarded:** 1. **To Apply:** Applicants must submit a completed scholarship application form along with a recent high school (or equivalent) or college transcript. **Deadline:** December 31.

1950 ■ The Mississippi Scholarship *(Undergraduate/ Scholarship)*

Purpose: To provide financial assistance to students who have the license for higher education. **Focus:** Communications; Electronics; Radio and television. **Qualif.:** Applicants must hold an FCC amateur radio license; be a Mississippi resident; be studying in baccalaureate or higher courses of study in electronics, communications or related fields; and be under 30 years of age. **Criteria:** Selection will be Bachelor's degree or higher in electronics, communications, or related fields

Funds Avail.: $500. **Duration:** Annual. **Number Awarded:** 1. **To Apply:** Applicants must submit a completed scholarship application form along with a recent high school (or equivalent) or college transcript. **Deadline:** December 31.

1951 ■ The New England FEMARA Scholarship *(Undergraduate/Scholarship)*

Purpose: To provide financial assistance to students who have the license for post-secondary education. **Focus:** Radio and television. **Qualif.:** Applicants must be a U.S. citizen or within three months of citizenship; Resident of Resident of New England states (ME, NH, VT, CT, RI, MA). **Criteria:** Award is given based on the submitted materials. The ARRL Foundation Scholarship Committee will review all applicants for eligibility and award decisions.

Funds Avail.: $1,000. **Duration:** Annual. **Number Awarded:** Varies. **To Apply:** Applicants must submit a completed scholarship application form along with a recent high school (or equivalent) or college transcript. **Deadline:** December 31.

1952 ■ Northern California DX Foundation Scholarships *(Undergraduate/Scholarship)*

Purpose: To provide financial assistance to students who have the license for higher education. **Focus:** Radio and television. **Qualif.:** Applicant must hold an FCC amateur radio license; be attending a junior college, four-year college/university or trade school in the U.S.; and must demonstrate activity and interest in DXing. **Criteria:** Awards are given based on the submitted materials.

To Apply: Applicant must submit a completed scholarship application form along with a recent high school (or equivalent) or college transcript.

1953 ■ The Peoria Area Amateur Radio Club Scholarship *(Undergraduate/Scholarship)*

Purpose: To provide financial assistance to students who have the license for higher education. **Focus:** Radio and television. **Qualif.:** Applicants must hold an FCC amateur radio license; be a resident of Central Illinois in one of these counties: Peoria, Tazewell, Woodford, Knox, McLean, Fulton, Logan, Marshall or Stark; and attending an accredited two or four-year college/university. **Criteria:** Award is given based on the submitted materials.

Funds Avail.: $500. **Duration:** Annual. **Number Awarded:** 1. **To Apply:** Applicants must submit a completed scholarship application form along with a recent high school (or

equivalent) or college transcript. **Deadline:** December 31.

1954 ■ The PHD Scholarship *(Undergraduate/ Scholarship)*

Purpose: To provide financial assistance to students who have the license for higher education. **Focus:** Computer and information sciences; Electronics; Journalism; Radio and television. **Qualif.:** Applicants must hold an FCC amateur radio license; be a resident of ARRL Midwest Division (IA, KS, MO, NE); with a course of study in journalism, computer science or electronic engineering; and be the child of a deceased radio amateur. **Criteria:** Award is given based on the submitted materials.

Funds Avail.: $1,000. **Duration:** Annual. **Number Awarded:** 1. **To Apply:** Applicants must submit a completed scholarship application form along with a recent high school (or equivalent) or college transcript. **Deadline:** December 31.

1955 ■ The Thomas W. Porter, W8KYZ, Scholarship Honoring Michael Daugherty, W8LSE *(Undergraduate/Scholarship)*

Purpose: To provide financial support to students who are in need. **Focus:** Radio and television. **Qualif.:** Applicants must be a U.S. citizen or within three months of citizenship; Resident of Ohio or West Virginia; Accredited 2 or 4-year college, university, or technical school. **Criteria:** Preference is given to the resident of Ohio or West Virginia.

Funds Avail.: $1,000. **Duration:** Annual. **Number Awarded:** 1. **To Apply:** Applicants must submit a completed scholarship application form along with a recent high school (or equivalent) or college transcript. **Deadline:** December 31.

1956 ■ The Ray, NØRP, & Katie, WØKTE, Pautz Scholarship *(Undergraduate/Scholarship)*

Purpose: To provide financial assistance to students who have the license for higher education. **Focus:** Computer and information sciences; Electronics; Radio and television. **Qualif.:** Applicants must hold an FCC amateur radio license; be a resident of the ARRL Midwest Division (IA, KS, MO, NE); be enrolled in electronics, computer science or related field at an accredited 4-year college/university; and be an ARRL member. **Criteria:** Award is given based on the submitted materials.

Funds Avail.: $500-$1,000. **Duration:** Annual. **Number Awarded:** 1. **To Apply:** Applicants must submit a completed scholarship application form along with a recent high school (or equivalent) or college transcript. **Deadline:** December 31.

1957 ■ The Don Riebhoff Memorial Scholarship *(Undergraduate/Scholarship)*

Purpose: To provide financial support to students who are in need. **Focus:** Radio and television. **Qualif.:** Applicants must hold an FCC amateur radio license; be studying in baccalaureate or higher courses of study in international studies at an accredited post-secondary school; and be an ARRL member. **Criteria:** Award is given based on the submitted materials.

Funds Avail.: $1,000. **Duration:** Annual. **Number Awarded:** 1. **To Apply:** Applicants must submit a completed scholarship application form along with a recent high school (or equivalent) or college transcript. **Deadline:** December 31.

Awards are arranged alphabetically below their administering organizations

1958 ■ The Bill, W2ONV, and Ann Salerno Memorial Scholarship *(Undergraduate/Scholarship)*

Purpose: To provide financial support to students who are in need. **Focus:** Radio and television. **Qualif.:** Applicants must hold an FCC amateur radio license; have a high school GPA of 3.7 or higher; Aggregate income of family household no greater than $100,000 per year; Recipient may receive this scholarship only once; accredited 4-year college or university. **Criteria:** Award is given based on the submitted materials.

Funds Avail.: $1,000. **Duration:** Annual. **Number Awarded:** 2. **To Apply:** Applicants must submit a completed scholarship application form along with a recent high school (or equivalent) or college transcript. **Deadline:** December 31.

1959 ■ The Eugene "Gene" Sallee, W4YFR, Memorial Scholarship *(Undergraduate, Graduate/ Scholarship)*

Purpose: To provide financial support to students who are in need. **Focus:** Radio and television. **Criteria:** Award is given based on the submitted materials.

To Apply: Applicant must submit a completed scholarship application form along with a recent high school (or equivalent) or college transcript. **Deadline:** January 31.

1960 ■ The Scholarship of the Morris Radio Club of New Jersey *(Undergraduate/Scholarship)*

Purpose: To provide financial assistance to students who have the license for higher education. **Focus:** Radio and television. **Qualif.:** Applicants must be a U.S. citizen or within three months of citizenship; Institution: 4-year college or university; Resident of Any. **Criteria:** Award is given based on the submitted materials.

Funds Avail.: $1,000. **Duration:** Annual. **Number Awarded:** 1. **To Apply:** Applicants must submit a completed scholarship application form along with a recent high school (or equivalent) or college transcript. **Deadline:** December 31.

1961 ■ The Six Meter Club of Chicago Scholarship *(Undergraduate/Scholarship)*

Purpose: To provide financial support to students who are in need. **Focus:** Radio and television. **Qualif.:** Applicants must hold an FCC amateur radio license; be a resident of Illinois ARRL Central Division (Indiana, Wisconsin); and Part-time or full-time post-secondary student at a regionally accredited technical school, community college, college or university leading to an undergraduate degree; Preference to applicants with GPA of 2.5 or better and in good academic standing.**Criteria:** Award is given based on the submitted materials.

Funds Avail.: $500. **Duration:** Annual. **Number Awarded:** 1. **To Apply:** Applicants must submit a completed scholarship application form along with a recent high school (or equivalent) or college transcript. **Deadline:** December 31.

1962 ■ The Zachary Taylor Stevens Scholarship *(Undergraduate/Scholarship)*

Purpose: To provide financial support to students who have the license for post-secondary education. **Focus:** Radio and television. **Qualif.:** Applicants must hold an FCC amateur radio license and be enrolled in an accredited two or four-year college/university or technical school; be residence in the "8" call area (MI, OH WV). **Criteria:** Prefer-

ence is given to the residents of Amateur radio call areas in MI, OH and WV.

Funds Avail.: $750. **Duration:** Annual. **Number Awarded:** 1. **To Apply:** Applicants must submit a completed scholarship application form along with a recent high school (or equivalent) or college transcript. **Deadline:** December 31.

1963 ■ The Carole J. Streeter, KB9JBR, Scholarship *(Undergraduate/Scholarship)*

Purpose: To provide financial support to students who have the license for post-secondary education. **Focus:** Radio and television. **Qualif.:** Applicants must be a U.S. citizen and be enrolled in an accredited college/university studying healing arts; Any class of active Amateur Radio license with preference for basic Morse code capability. **Criteria:** Preference is given to applicants with basic morse code proficiency, healing arts study or courses at teaching hospitals or local colleges.

Funds Avail.: $1,000. **Duration:** Annual. **Number Awarded:** 1. **To Apply:** Applicants must submit a completed scholarship application form along with a recent high school (or equivalent) or college transcript. **Deadline:** December 31.

1964 ■ The Norman E. Strohmeier, W2VRS, Memorial Scholarship *(Undergraduate/Scholarship)*

Purpose: To provide financial support to students who have the license for post-secondary education. **Focus:** Radio and television. **Qualif.:** Applicants must hold an FCC amateur radio license; be a resident of Western New York; and have a cumulative GPA of 3.2 or better on a 4.0 scale; documentation of Amateur Radio activities and achievements and any honor from community service. **Criteria:** Preference is given to graduating high school seniors.

Funds Avail.: $500. **Duration:** Annual. **Number Awarded:** 1. **To Apply:** Applicants must submit a completed scholarship application form along with a recent high school (or equivalent) or college transcript. **Deadline:** December 31.

1965 ■ The Gary Wagner, K3OMI, Scholarship *(Undergraduate/Scholarship)*

Purpose: To provide financial support to students who have the license for post-secondary education. **Focus:** Engineering; Radio and television. **Qualif.:** Applicants must hold an FCC amateur radio license; be a resident of NC, VA, WV, MD or TN; enrolled in an accredited four-year college/ university (NC, VA, WV, MD, or TN) working towards a Bachelor's of Science in any field of engineering; and have financial need. **Criteria:** Selection will be based in financial need of the applicants.

Funds Avail.: $1,000. **Duration:** Annual. **Number Awarded:** 1. **To Apply:** Applicants must submit a completed scholarship application form along with a recent high school (or equivalent) or college transcript. **Deadline:** December 31.

1966 ■ The L. Phil and Alice J. Wicker Scholarship *(Undergraduate/Scholarship)*

Purpose: To provide financial support to students who have the license for post-secondary education. **Focus:** Communications; Electronics; Radio and television. **Qualif.:** Applicants must hold an FCC amateur radio license; be a resident of, and attending in ARRL Roanoke Division (NC, SC, VA, WV); enrolled in a baccalaureate or higher course in electronics, communications and related fields. **Criteria:** Award is given based on the submitted materials.

Awards are arranged alphabetically below their administering organizations

Funds Avail.: $500. **Duration:** Annual. **Number Awarded:** 1. **To Apply:** Applicants must submit a completed scholarship application form along with a recent high school (or equivalent) or college transcript. **Deadline:** December 31.

1967 ■ Yankee Clipper Contest Club Youth Scholarship *(Undergraduate/Scholarship)*

Purpose: To provide financial support to students who have the license for post-secondary education. **Focus:** Radio and television. **Qualif.:** Applicants must hold an FCC amateur radio license; residency or college/university attendance within 175 miles of YCCC Center in Erving MA, including MA, RI, CT, Long Island NY, some of VT, NH, ME, PA, and NJ; and be enrolled in a two or four-year degree program at an accredited college/university. **Criteria:** Award is given based on the submitted materials.

Funds Avail.: $1,200. **Duration:** Annual. **Number Awarded:** 1. **To Apply:** Applicants must submit a completed scholarship application form along with a recent high school (or equivalent) or college transcript. **Deadline:** December 31.

1968 ■ The YASME Foundation Scholarship *(Undergraduate/Scholarship)*

Purpose: To provide financial support to students who have the license for post-secondary education. **Focus:** Engineering; Radio and television; Science. **Qualif.:** Applicants must have been licensed for at least two years and currently hold a General Class or higher Amateur Radio license. **Criteria:** Preference is given to high school applicants ranked in top 5%-10%, or to college students in the top 10%; participation in local Amateur Radio club and community service is important to selection.

Funds Avail.: $3,000. **Duration:** Annual. **To Apply:** Applicants must submit a completed scholarship application form along with a recent high school (or equivalent) or college transcript. **Deadline:** December 31.

1969 ■ Arthritis Foundation (AF)
1355 Peachtree St. NE, Ste. 600
Atlanta, GA 30309
Ph: (404)872-7100
Free: 800-283-7800
URL: www.arthritis.org
Social Media: www.facebook.com/Arthritis.org •
instagram.com/arthritisfoundation
www.linkedin.com/company/arthritis-foundation
twitter.com/ArthritisFdn

1970 ■ Arthritis Champions Scholarship *(Undergraduate, Graduate/Scholarship, Monetary)*

Purpose: To provide financial assistance to students with rheumatic diseases. **Focus:** General studies/Field of study not specified. **Qualif.:** Applicants must be doctor-diagnosed with arthritis or related rheumatic disease; must be U.S. citizens or legal permanent residents; must be accepted or enrolled full-time in an accredited undergraduate, graduate, or medical program in the United States; must have and maintain a minimum 2.5 GPA; must be engaged Arthritis Foundation advocates, fundraisers, participants, volunteers, or supporters.

Funds Avail.: Up to $7,500 per academic year for up to four years. **Duration:** Annual. **To Apply:** Application details are available online at www.arthritis.org/juvenile-arthritis/arthritis-champion-scholarship. **Deadline:** March 31. **Re-**

marks: Generously funded by Dr. & Mrs. Walter J. Winterhoff and Dr. Smriti Bardhan. **Contact:** Email: scholarship@arthritis.org.

1971 ■ Arthritis Foundation Investigator Awards *(Doctorate/Award)*

Purpose: To support outstanding established investigator with innovative, creative ideas that have the potential to move arthritis research toward better treatments and a cure. **Focus:** Arthritis. **Qualif.:** Applicants must hold an MD, PhD, DO, DVM, or equivalent degree and a university faculty position at the associate professor level or above; must hold or have held in the past 12 months an NIH R01 or equivalent award (such as VA Merit, DOD, etc.); must be US citizens or have permanent residence at the time of application. **Criteria:** Selection will be based on the committee's criteria.

Funds Avail.: $100,000. **Duration:** 5 years. **To Apply:** Applications can be submitted online. **Deadline:** August 30.

1972 ■ Arts Council of Princeton (ACP)
Paul Robeson Center for the Arts
102 Witherspoon St.
Princeton, NJ 08542
Ph: (609)924-8777
Fax: (609)921-0008
E-mail: info@artscouncilofprinceton.org
URL: www.artscouncilofprinceton.org
Social Media: www.facebook.com/ArtsCouncilofPrinceton
twitter.com/ArtsPrinceton

1973 ■ George Dale Scholarship Fund *(Undergraduate/Scholarship)*

Purpose: To make art experiences meaningful, instructive, fun and accessible for people of all ages, backgrounds and skill levels. **Focus:** General studies/Field of study not specified. **Qualif.:** Applicants must be children living in the John-Witherspoon neighborhood. **Criteria:** Selection will be based on the committee's criteria.

Funds Avail.: No specific amount. **Duration:** Annual. **To Apply:** Applicants must fill out the scholarship application available online and must return it to the Paul Robeson Center or may contact the Scholarship Awards Committee for the application process and other information; must attach a copy of most recently filed income tax form; must be mailed, delivered, or faxed. **Deadline:** March 24 for Spring Classes; May 1 for Summer Camp.

1974 ■ Arts Foundation of Cape Cod
396 Main St., Ste. 10
Hyannis, MA 02601
Ph: (508)362-0066
E-mail: info@artsfoundation.org
URL: artsfoundation.org
Social Media: www.facebook.com/artsfoundation
www.instagram.com/artsfoundationofcc
www.pinterest.com/artsfoundation
twitter.com/artsfoundofcc

1975 ■ Arts Foundation of Cape Cod Scholarships *(Undergraduate, Vocational/Occupational/Scholarship)*

Purpose: To support Cape Cod students interested in pursuing higher education in creative arts fields such as

Awards are arranged alphabetically below their administering organizations

music, dance, drama, visual arts, fashion design, and creative writing. **Focus:** Arts; Creative writing; Dance; Fashion design; Music; Visual arts. **Qualif.:** Applicant must live on Cape Cod and be a current high school senior in a registered public, charter, private, or home education program; must have been accepted into an accredited college, university, or arts-specific trade school. **Criteria:** Selection is based upon completed application and portfolio.

Duration: Annual. **To Apply:** Apply online at artsfoundation.org/programs/scholarships/. **Deadline:** June 30. **Contact:** Arts Foundation of Cape Cod, Julie Wake, Executive Director; Phone: 508-362-0066, ext. 111; Email: jwake@artsfoundation.org.

1976 ■ ASAE: The Center for Association Leadership

1575 I St. NW
Washington, DC 20005
Ph: (202)371-0940
Fax: (202)371-8315
Free: 888-950-2723
E-mail: asaeservice@asaecenter.org
URL: www.asaecenter.org
Social Media: www.facebook.com/ASAEfan
instagram.com/asaecenter/
www.instagram.com/asaecenter
www.linkedin.com/company/162539
www.linkedin.com/company/asae-the-center-for
  -association-leadership
twitter.com/ASAEcenter
www.youtube.com/user/asaecenter

1977 ■ Diversity Executive Leadership Program Scholarship (DELP) *(Other/Scholarship)*

Purpose: To provide support, education, access and service opportunities to individuals from identity groups who are under-represented in the association community. **Focus:** Leadership, Institutional and community; Management. **Qualif.:** Applicant must be member of a racial or ethnic minority group, be GLBT, or have a disability; must be currently employed as a mid-to-senior level association employee with minimum of three years experience in association management or as an association CEO for a minimum of one year; must have professional, volunteer, civic or community leadership experience. **Criteria:** Applicants must be ASAE members; recipients are selected on the basis of commitment to participate in a variety of ASAE activities and to pursue CAE certification.

Funds Avail.: No specific amount. **Duration:** Biennial. **Number Awarded:** Varies. **Deadline:** March 19. **Contact:** Marilu Morada, Manager, DELP; Phone:202-326-9527; Email: mmorada@asaecenter.org.

1978 ■ Ascend, Inc.

60 Broadway, E Bulng., 6th Fl.
New York, NY 10038
Ph: (212)248-4888
E-mail: info@ascendleadership.org
URL: www.ascendleadership.org
Social Media: www.facebook.com/ascendleadership
www.instagram.com/ascendleader
twitter.com/ascendleader
www.youtube.com/user/ascendleadership

1979 ■ Ernst and Young Scholarships
(Undergraduate/Scholarship)

Purpose: To support and honor students who have made excellent scholastic performance and contribution to the community. **Focus:** Accounting; Finance. **Qualif.:** Applicants must have a 3.3 GPA or higher(on a 4.0 scale); must be major in Accounting. **Criteria:** Selection will be based on the demonstrated leadership skills.

Funds Avail.: $5,000. **Number Awarded:** 5. **To Apply:** Applicants must complete and submit the application form together with the following materials: unofficial transcript, resume and 500-word minimum personal essay.

1980 ■ ASET - The Neurodiagnostic Society

402 E Bannister Rd., Ste. A
Kansas City, MO 64131-3019
Ph: (816)931-1120
Fax: (816)931-1145
E-mail: info@aset.org
URL: www.aset.org
Social Media: www.facebook.com/ASETsociety
www.linkedin.com/company/aset-society
twitter.com/asetsociety?lang=en
www.youtube.com/user/ASETLIVE1959

1981 ■ American Society of Electroneurodiagnostic Technologists Student Education Grants
(Undergraduate/Grant)

Purpose: To assist and encourage students to further their education in neurodiagnostic and for working professionals to continue their interests, enhance their knowledge and improve their skills in the field. **Focus:** Health sciences. **Qualif.:** Applicant must be a student enrolled full-time in a CAAHEP accredited END school; or an employee of ASET member companies or individuals; relatives of the Foundation Selection Committee and the Foundation Board of Directors are not qualified for grants. **Criteria:** Selection Committees will review all submitted applications based on applicant's interest in pursuing a career; scholastic achievement including GPA; interest in pursuing a degree; upon references and recommendations by instructors, employers and other pertinent individuals.

Funds Avail.: Up to $1,500. **To Apply:** Applicants must submit an application; copies of transcript; recommendations and reference letters; an outline of the proposed program of study. **Contact:** Arlen Reimnitz, Executive Director; Email: arlene@aset.org.

1982 ■ ASET Scholarships *(Other/Scholarship)*

Purpose: To provide conference, seminars, and other educational opportunities to ASET members. **Focus:** Neuroscience. **Qualif.:** Applicant must be a member of ASET in good standing, candidates must have been a member of ASET for at least one year prior to the year of making the application. **Criteria:** Selection is based on financial need and educational needs.

Funds Avail.: No specific amount. **Duration:** Annual. **Number Awarded:** Varies. **To Apply:** Applicants should include typed, signed statement of general activities and interests, career and professional goals, responsibilities of current position and how attending the annual conference or education seminar, or enrolling in an ASET online course, would better help applicant in the course of their day-to-day job, long-term career, and/or professional goals; letter of recom-

Awards are arranged alphabetically below their administering organizations

mendation from the applicant's supervisor or administration approving or noting their support for applicant's participation in the event or course enrollment. **Deadline:** May 15.

1983 ■ Ashburn Institute (AI)
198 Okatie Village Dr., Ste. 103
Bluffton, SC 29909
Ph: (703)728-6482
Fax: (843)705-7643
URL: www.ashburninstitute.org

1984 ■ Mayme and Herb Frank Scholarship Program *(Graduate/Scholarship)*

Purpose: To support the study of international integration and federalism at the graduate level. **Focus:** International affairs and relations. **Qualif.:** Applicants must be graduate students. **Criteria:** Selection is based on best papers which meet the goals of the conference, as outlined in the "Call"; priority for the half of funds will be given to U.S. citizens.

Duration: Annual. **To Apply:** Applicants must submit a Call For Papers to be eligible. **Remarks:** Funding is provided by the gracious endowment left by Mayme and Herb Frank. Established in 1991.

1985 ■ Asian Pacific American Advocates (OCA)
1322 18th St. NW
Washington, DC 20036-1803
Ph: (202)223-5500
Fax: (202)296-0540
E-mail: oca@ocanational.org
URL: www.ocanational.org
Social Media: www.facebook.com/ocanational
www.instagram.com/ocanational
twitter.com/OCANational

1986 ■ Organization of Chinese Americans Scholarships *(Undergraduate/Scholarship)*

Purpose: To provide financial assistance to high school seniors in pursuing their educational career. **Focus:** General studies/Field of study not specified. **Qualif.:** Applicants must be current APA high school seniors entering their first year of college in the upcoming fall semester/quarter; must demonstrate financial need; must be permanent residents or U.S. citizens; and have a cumulative grade point average (GPA) of 3.0 or above (on a 4.0 scale). **Criteria:** Candidates will be selected based on achievements and financial needs.

Funds Avail.: No amount mentioned. **To Apply:** Applicants must submit resume; one-page essay; high school transcript(s); letter of acceptance from college or university; printed student aid Report (SAR); and financial Aid award notification (FAN) from college or university. **Deadline:** April 1.

1987 ■ Asian Pacific American Bar Association of Silicon Valley (APABASV)
PO Box 60988
Palo Alto, CA 94306
E-mail: apabasv@gmail.com
URL: www.apabasv.com
Social Media: www.facebook.com/groups/131858536851

1988 ■ APABA Silicon Valley Achievement Scholarship *(Advanced Professional/Scholarship)*

Purpose: To support law students in the Bay Area. **Focus:** Law. **Qualif.:** Applicants must be law students in the bay area who have overcome personal hardship or challenges, shown excellence and achievement in law school or demonstrated leadership and service to the Asian pacific American community. **Criteria:** Preference will be given to law students who have demonstrated a commitment to immigration issues, language access issues and human trafficking issues.

Funds Avail.: $10,000 each. **Duration:** Annual. **Number Awarded:** 2 or 4. **To Apply:** Applicants must submit a resume (with GPA) and an essay (maximum of 2 pages, double-spaced). **Deadline:** June 19. **Contact:** E-mail: scholarship@apabasv.com.

1989 ■ Asian Pacific American Librarians Association (APALA)
c/o Lessa Pelayo-Lozada
Executive Director
PO Box 1598
San Pedro, CA 90733
URL: www.apalaweb.org
Social Media: www.facebook.com/apalaweb
twitter.com/ala_apala

1990 ■ APALA Scholarship *(Doctorate, Master's/Scholarship)*

Purpose: To provide financial assistance to a student of Asian or Pacific background who is enrolled in, or has been accepted into, a master's or doctoral degree program in library and/or information science at a school accredited by the American Library Associati **Focus:** Information science and technology; Library and archival sciences. **Qualif.:** Applicant must be attending or admitted into a master's degree or doctoral program in library and/or information science at a school accredited by ALA. Students pursuing archives and other information studies concentrations are also eligible to apply. Applicant may be either a full-time or part-time student. Applicant must be in library school by Fall 2020. Applicant must be of Asian/Pacific Islander heritage. Applicant must be an APALA member in good standing by application deadline. Recipient may not receive more than one APALA scholarship award. Recipient will serve on the Scholarship Committee the following year. **Criteria:** Recipients are selected based on the Scholarship Committee's review of the application materials.

Funds Avail.: $1,000. **Duration:** Annual. **Number Awarded:** 1. **To Apply:** Completed application along with a resume; letter of acceptance to an ALA accredited library school; library graduate school transcript or undergraduate transcript; first letter of recommendation: letters should highlight the applicant's academic and personal abilities and their potential to make positive contributions to the library profession; second letter of recommendation: letters should highlight the applicant's academic and personal abilities and their potential to make positive contributions to the library profession. **Deadline:** April 1. **Contact:** please contact the APALA Scholarships & Awards Committee: scholarships@apalaweb.org.

1991 ■ Asian/Pacific Bar Association of Sacramento (ABAS)
Metro Station
Sacramento, CA 95812-2215
E-mail: abassacramento@gmail.com
URL: www.abassacramento.com
Social Media: www.facebook.com/groups/129940792852

Awards are arranged alphabetically below their administering organizations

www.instagram.com/abassacramento
twitter.com/abassacramento

1992 ■ The Abas Law Foundation Scholarship
(Graduate, Postgraduate/Scholarship)

Purpose: To support law students and recent law school graduates who possess extraordinary skills, desire and potential to serve and lead the greater Sacramento Asian-Pacific Islander community. **Focus:** Law. **Qualif.:** Applicants must: be either currently enrolled and in good standing at a Sacramento area (including U.C. Davis) law school or currently residing in the Sacramento area and must graduate from law school. **Criteria:** Recipients will be selected based on potential for community service; leadership in the Asian Pacific Islander community; academic achievement; and financial need.

Funds Avail.: $1,000 to $10,000. **Duration:** Annual. **To Apply:** Applicants must submit evidence of scholarship eligibility (a copy of current law school registration or law school diploma will suffice); a personal statement; a current resume; current law school transcripts; financial information; and two references. **Deadline:** April 9. **Remarks:** Established in 1997. **Contact:** Katie Konz and Jeannie Lee Jones; Email: scholarships@abaslawfoundation.org.

1993 ■ Asian and Pacific Islander American Scholarship Fund
1850 M St. NW Ste. 245
Washington, DC 20036
Ph: (202)986-6892
Free: 877-808-7032
E-mail: info@apiascholars.org
URL: www.apiasf.org
Social Media: www.facebook.com/apiascholar
www.instagram.com/apiascholars
www.linkedin.com/company/apia-scholars
twitter.com/APIA_Scholars
www.youtube.com/channel/UCRfN4lat5oX4H9BtYKZ-Y2g

1994 ■ APIASF Scholarships *(Undergraduate/Scholarship)*

Purpose: To support and encourage all Asian and Pacific Islander American students to pursue higher education by developing future leaders who will contribute back to their communities. **Focus:** General studies/Field of study not specified. **Qualif.:** Applicants must be: of Asian and/or Pacific Islander ethnicity as defined by the U.S. census; U.S. citizens, U.S. Nationals, legal permanent residents or citizens of the Federated States of Micronesia, Republic of the Marshall Islands or the Republic of Palau; and, first-time, incoming college students enrolled full-time in a two or four-year program at a U.S. accredited college or university in the U.S., Guam, American Samoa, or the Commonwealth of the Northern Mariana Islands for the coming school year. (In the Freely Associated States, this includes the Community Colleges of the Federated States of Micronesia, the Republic of Marshall Islands and the Republic of Palau.) Applicants must have cumulative, unweighted grade point average (GPA) of 2.7 or higher on a 4.0 scale. **Criteria:** Recipient will be selected based on academic record and future plans; community service and leadership; and financial need.

Funds Avail.: $2,500 to $20,000. **Duration:** Annual. **To Apply:** Applicants must complete the application form online, available at the website of APIASF. Other instruc-

tions for the application. **Deadline:** January 22. **Contact:** Email:applicant@apiascholars.org.

1995 ■ ASIS International (ASIS)
1625 Prince St.
Alexandria, VA 22314-2882
Ph: (703)519-6200
E-mail: asis@asisonline.org
URL: www.asisonline.org
Social Media: www.facebook.com/SecMgmtMag
www.linkedin.com/company/asis-international
twitter.com/SecMgmtMag
www.youtube.com/user/ASISInternational

1996 ■ ASIS Foundation Chapter Matching Scholarship *(Undergraduate/Scholarship)*

Purpose: To provide educational assistance to chapter members, student members or student nonmembers pursuing a security career. **Focus:** General studies/Field of study not specified. **Qualif.:** Applicants must be part- or full-time students who have completed one year of study at an accredited college, university or community college towards a career in security profession; must be undergraduate students (their chapter will set the grade point average required, for them to be qualified for the scholarship) or graduate students who earned at least a 3.0 GPA on a 4.0 scale. **Criteria:** Selection will be based on the committee's criteria.

Funds Avail.: $500-$1,000. **Duration:** Annual. **To Apply:** Applicant must submit the application, a copy of official school transcripts including a cumulative GPA, a letter of recommendation from a faculty member or colleague, and a 250-word narrative that describes your plan for a career in the security profession, including degrees and/or professional development courses, applicable memberships, and specific areas of interest. **Deadline:** February 28. **Contact:** Phone Number:602-331-7000 or Email:sheri@andersonsecurity.com.

1997 ■ ASME International
2 Park Ave.
New York, NY 10016-5990
URL: www.asme.org
Social Media: www.facebook.com/ASME.org
www.instagram.com/asmedotorg
www.linkedin.com/company/asme
twitter.com/asmedotorg

1998 ■ Auxiliary Undergraduate Scholarships *(Undergraduate/Scholarship)*

Purpose: To provide scholarships and new developments in Mechanical Engineering; to honor students who demonstrate outstanding personal and academic characteristics. **Focus:** Engineering, Mechanical. **Qualif.:** Applicant must be U.S. citizen; must be enrolled in U.S. school in an ABET accredited Mechanical Engineering Department. **Criteria:** Recipients will be selected based on submitted application, needs, character, and ASME participation.

Funds Avail.: No specific amount. **Duration:** Annual. **To Apply:** Applicants must submit online. **Deadline:** March 1.

1999 ■ Elisabeth M. and Winchell M. Parsons Scholarship *(Doctorate/Scholarship)*

Purpose: To assist students in pursuing educational program in mechanical engineering or mechanical engineer-

Awards are arranged alphabetically below their administering organizations

ing technology. **Focus:** Engineering, Mechanical. **Qualif.:** Applicant must be a US Citizen and be enrolled in a mechanical engineering program; scholarship is to be used for a Doctoral Degree in Engineering. **Criteria:** Selection is based on strong ASME leadership role and participation with ASME extra-curricular activities such as holding office in the ASME student section or on an ASME committee; leadership within the engineering academic context specified above, and a strong potential for contribution to the mechanical engineering profession identified in a recommendation letter; high level of financial need.

Funds Avail.: $3,000. **Duration:** Annual. **Number Awarded:** Up to 2. **To Apply:** Applicant must submit US Citizen and be enrolled in a mechanical engineering program. This scholarship is to be used for a Doctoral Degree in Engineering. **Deadline:** March 1.

2000 ■ Lucy and Charles W.E. Clarke Scholarship
(Undergraduate/Scholarship, Award)

Purpose: To assist students in pursuing educational program in mechanical engineering or mechanical engineering technology. **Focus:** Engineering, Mechanical. **Qualif.:** Applicants must be graduating high school seniors active on a FIRST FTC or FRC team; planning to enroll full-time in an ABET-accredited or substantially equivalent mechanical engineering or mechanical engineering technology program, no later than the fall after their senior year in high school. **Criteria:** Selection is based on strong ASME leadership role and participation with ASME extra-curricular activities such as holding office in the ASME student section or on an ASME committee; leadership within the engineering academic context specified above, and a strong potential for contribution to the mechanical engineering profession identified in a recommendation letter; high level of financial need.

Funds Avail.: $5,000. **Duration:** Annual. **Number Awarded:** Varies. **To Apply:** Applicants must submit an online Form; should include a resume with GPA information and a list of school and extracurricular activities; transcript with first semester GPA or grade percentage; school grading profile; letter shall not be written by your nominator, parent and/or relative; letter shall attest to the student's technical, creative and leadership contributions to the first team. **Deadline:** March 15. **Contact:** RuthAnn Bigley; Phone: 212-591-7650; Email: bigleyr@asme.org.

2001 ■ Rice-Cullimore Scholarship *(Graduate/Scholarship)*

Purpose: To assist students in pursuing educational program in mechanical engineering or mechanical engineering technology. **Focus:** Engineering, Mechanical. **Qualif.:** Applicant must be a foreign student intending to do graduate work for a Master's or Doctoral Degree in mechanical engineering in the United States; applications for that Program must be obtained from and filed with the local Institute of International Education (IIE) Office.

Funds Avail.: $2,000. **Duration:** Annual. **Number Awarded:** 1. **Deadline:** March 1.

2002 ■ Marjorie Roy Rothermel Scholarship
(Master's/Scholarship)

Purpose: To support students in pursuing their educational goal. **Focus:** Engineering, Mechanical. **Qualif.:** Applicants must be U.S. citizens and must be currently enrolled in a mechanical engineering program; scholarship is to be used for a Master's Degree in Engineering. **Criteria:** Selection is based on strong ASME leadership role and participation

with ASME extra-curricular activities such as holding office in the ASME student section or on an ASME committee; leadership within the engineering academic context specified above, and a strong potential for contribution to the mechanical engineering profession identified in a recommendation letter; high level of financial need.

Funds Avail.: $2,000. **Duration:** Annual. **Number Awarded:** Up to 2. **To Apply:** Applicant must submit US citizen and be enrolled in a mechanical engineering program. This scholarship is to be used for a master's degree in engineering. **Deadline:** March 1.

2003 ■ ASPRS, The Imaging and Geospatial Information Society

425 Barlow Place, Suite 210,
Bethesda, MD 20814-2160
Ph: (301)493-0290
Fax: (301)493-0208
E-mail: office@asprs.org
URL: www.asprs.org
Social Media: www.facebook.com/ASPRS.org
twitter.com/ASPRSorg

2004 ■ Robert E. Altenhofen Memorial Scholarships
(Graduate, Undergraduate/Scholarship)

Purpose: To encourage and commend college students who display exceptional interest and ability in the theoretical aspects of photogrammetry. **Focus:** Photogrammetry. **Qualif.:** Applicants must be undergraduate or graduate student members of ASPRS. **Criteria:** Recipients are selected based on the highest overall ranking.

Funds Avail.: $2,000; certificate. **To Apply:** Applicants must submit an application form; a statement (2 pages) regarding plans for continuing studies in theoretical photogrammetry; evidence of capabilities of the applicants in these fields; and academic transcripts.

2005 ■ ERDAS Internship *(Graduate/Internship)*

Purpose: To provide individuals an opportunity to carry out a small research project of their own choice, or to work on an existing ERDAS project as part of a team. **Focus:** Photogrammetry; Remote sensing. **Qualif.:** Applicant must be a graduate student of photogrammetric and remote sensing and a student member of ASPRS. **Criteria:** Applicants are selected based on submitted applications.

Funds Avail.: $2,500. **Duration:** Eight weeks. **To Apply:** Applicants must submit an application form; two letters of recommendation; official transcripts from each college and university attended; a proposal (maximum of 1, 000 words) stating the significance of the research, the proposed methodology, the expected results and a schedule. Research topics should be in the general area of digital photogrammetry and remote sensing. **Remarks:** Funded by ERDAS Inc. **Contact:** ASPRS Scholarship Administrator at scholarships@asprs.org.

2006 ■ Francis H. Moffitt Scholarship *(Graduate, Undergraduate/Scholarship)*

Purpose: To encourage upper-division undergraduate and graduate-level college students to pursue a course of study in surveying and photogrammetry leading to a career in the geospatial mapping profession. **Focus:** Photogrammetry; Remote sensing. **Qualif.:** Applicants must be students currently enrolled or intending to enroll in a college or

Awards are arranged alphabetically below their administering organizations

university in the United States or Canada, who are pursuing a program of study in surveying or photogrammetry leading to a career in the geospatial mapping profession. **Criteria:** Applicants are selected based on the submitted applications.

Funds Avail.: $5,500. **Duration:** Annual. **To Apply:** Applicants must submit an application form; a listing of courses taken and/or those to be taken in surveying and photogrammetry and other related geospatial information technologies; a transcript of all college/university level courses completed; a listing of internships, special projects or work experience; two letters of recommendation or reference form; a statement (maximum of two pages) detailing the applicant's educational and research goals.

2007 ■ Kenneth J. Osborn Scholarship
(Undergraduate/Scholarship)

Purpose: To encourage and commend college students who display exceptional interest, desire, ability and aptitude to enter the profession of surveying, mapping, photogrammetry, or geospatial information and technology. **Focus:** Photogrammetry. **Qualif.:** Applicant must be an undergraduate student enrolled or planning to enroll in a college/university in the United States, who is pursuing a program of study in preparation for entering the profession in the general area of surveying, mapping, photogrammetry, or geospatial information and technology. **Criteria:** Scholarship will be given to an applicant who has the highest overall ranking.

Funds Avail.: $2,000. **Duration:** Annual. **To Apply:** Applicants must submit an application form; a listing of courses taken in surveying, mapping, photogrammetry and geospatial information and technology and the academic grades received; a transcript of all college or university level courses completed; two letters of recommendation from faculty members or professionals; evidence materials of the applicant's capabilities in this field; a statement of work experience and a personal statement (maximum of 2 pages).

2008 ■ Leica Scholarship *(Graduate/Scholarship)*

Purpose: To support graduate-level studies addressing new and innovative uses of signal processing, image processing techniques and the application of photogrammetry to real-world techniques. **Focus:** Photogrammetry. **Qualif.:** Applicant must be a member of ASPRS; planning to enroll in graduate studies in a college/university in the United States or elsewhere. **Criteria:** Scholarship will be given to an applicant who has the highest overall ranking.

Funds Avail.: $2,000. **Duration:** Annual. **To Apply:** Applicants must submit an application form; a statement (2 pages) detailing educational and career plans for continuing studies in photogrammetric applications; two reference forms/letters from faculty members who have knowledge of the applicant's capabilities; and evidence materials of the applicant's capabilities in this field.

2009 ■ Robert N. Colwell Fellowship *(Doctorate/ Fellowship)*

Purpose: To encourage and commend college/university graduate students at the PhD level who display exceptional interest, desire, ability and aptitude in the field of remote sensing or other related geospatial information technologies, and who have a special interest in developing practical uses of these technologies. **Focus:** Remote sensing. **Qualif.:** Applicant must be a graduate student (Ph.D. level); enrolled or planning to enroll in a college/university

in the United States or Canada; or recently graduated post-doctoral researcher pursuing a study in remote sensing or related geospatial information technologies. **Criteria:** Recipients are selected based on the application materials submitted; based on highest overall ranking.

Funds Avail.: $6,500. **Duration:** Annual. **To Apply:** Applicants must submit completed application form; a listing of courses taken; transcript of all college/university level courses completed; a listing of internships, special projects or work experience; two letters of recommendation and a statement (maximum of two pages) detailing the applicant's educational or research goals.

2010 ■ Ta Liang Award *(Graduate/Award)*

Purpose: To support research-related travel in remote sensing. **Focus:** Remote sensing. **Qualif.:** Applicant must be a graduate student member of ASPRS. **Criteria:** Applicants are selected based on scholastic record, research travel plan, letters of recommendation and community service activities.

Funds Avail.: $2,000. **Duration:** Annual. **To Apply:** Applicants must submit an application form; a letter of recommendation; a statement (2 pages) detailing the plan for research-related travel; a transcript of all college-level courses completed and grades received; class rank; a description of extracurricular activities (particularly relating to community service).

2011 ■ William A. Fischer Scholarship *(Graduate/ Scholarship)*

Purpose: To facilitate studies and career goals directed towards new and innovative uses of remote sensing data/techniques. **Focus:** Remote sensing. **Qualif.:** Applicants must be current or prospective graduate student members of ASPRS. **Criteria:** Applicants are selected based on the highest overall ranking.

Funds Avail.: $2,000. **Duration:** One year. **To Apply:** Applicants must submit an application form; two letters of recommendation; a statement (2 pages) detailing educational and career plans for continuing studies in remote sensing applications; transcript of grades. **Remarks:** The award is presented by ASPRS with funding provided by a grant from the ASPRS Foundation, on behalf of individual and corporate contributions to the Foundation in memory of William A. Fischer, a pioneer in the use of remote sensing from space for the study of the planet Earth.

2012 ■ Paul R. Wolf Memorial Scholarships
(Graduate/Scholarship)

Purpose: To encourage and commend college students who displays exceptional interest, desire, ability, and aptitude to enter the profession of teaching Surveying, Mapping or Photography. **Focus:** Education; Photogrammetry. **Qualif.:** Applicant must be a graduate student member of ASPRS; enrolled or planning to enroll in a college/university in the United States; pursuing a program of study in preparation for entering the teaching profession in the general area of Surveying, Mapping or Photogrammetric. **Criteria:** The committee evaluates each application and will select the applicants who best meets the criteria.

Funds Avail.: $3,000; certificate. **To Apply:** Applicants must submit an application form; a listing of courses taken in Surveying, Mapping and Photogrammetry and the academic grades received; a transcript of all college or university level courses; two letters of recommendation from faculty members having knowledge of the applicant's

Awards are arranged alphabetically below their administering organizations

capabilities as an educator in this field; evidence materials of the applicant's capabilities in this field; and a statement of teaching experience.

2013 ■ Associated Colleges of the Midwest (ACM)

180 N. Michigan Avenue, Suite 2020
Chicago, IL 60601
Ph: (312)263-5000
Fax: (312)263-5879
E-mail: acm@acm.edu
URL: www.acm.edu
Social Media: www.facebook.com/ACMedu
www.instagram.com/acmedu
twitter.com/ACMedu
www.youtube.com/user/ACMoffcampus

2014 ■ Newberry Library ACM/GLCA Faculty Fellowships *(Other/Fellowship)*

Purpose: To provide assistance to researchers who wish to use the Newberry Library's collections. **Focus:** General studies/Field of study not specified.

Funds Avail.: $4,200 per month. **Duration:** Annual.

2015 ■ Associated General Contractors of America (AGC)

2300 Wilson Blvd., Ste. 300
Arlington, VA 22201
Ph: (703)548-3118
Fax: (240)396-2470
Free: 800-242-1767
E-mail: info@agc.org
URL: www.agc.org
Social Media: www.facebook.com/AGCofA
www.linkedin.com/company/67031
twitter.com/AGCofA
www.youtube.com/user/agcofamerica

2016 ■ AGC Foundation Outstanding Educator Awards *(Other/Award, Monetary)*

Purpose: To recognize an educator who makes a significant mark in the field of construction education, and support the education of the students of the winning educator. **Focus:** Construction. **Qualif.:** Applicant must be a full-time teaching faculty member of a university construction program or a construction-related engineering program or with an institution-approved construction option, with at least four years full-time teaching experience. **Criteria:** Recipients shall be chosen based on the teaching responsibilities and activities with AGC and/or other construction industry organizations.

Funds Avail.: $10,000 ($5,000 for the educator); $2,500 scholarships for the two students chosen by the winning educator. **Duration:** Annual. **Number Awarded:** 1. **To Apply:** Applicants must submit two copies of nomination form and attachments; the joint letter of nomination; the nomination checklist; a maximum of three letters of reference; submitted by email as an application package (one pdf). **Deadline:** November 15. **Remarks:** Established in 1985. **Contact:** Melinda Patrician, AGC Education and Research Foundation, 2300 Wilson Blvd, Ste. 300, Arlington, VA 22201; Phone: 703-837-5342; Email: patricianm@agc.org.

2017 ■ Associated General Contractors of New York State

10 Airline Dr., Ste. 203
Albany, NY 12205
Ph: (518)456-1134
Fax: (518)456-1198
URL: agcnys.org
Social Media: www.facebook.com/AGCNYS
twitter.com/agc_nys
www.youtube.com/user/agcnys

2018 ■ AGC NYS Scholarship Program *(Undergraduate, Graduate/Scholarship)*

Purpose: To provide financial assistance to students pursuing a degree in Civil engineering, Construction Technology and Construction Management at colleges or universities. **Focus:** Engineering, Civil. **Qualif.:** Applicants must be entering the 2nd, 3rd or 4th year of a two or four-year college; must seriously intend upon a career in the highway construction industry. Applicants must have 2.50 GPA. **Criteria:** Applicants will be evaluated by the Selection Committee of the New York State Chapter Inc., Associated General Contractors.

Funds Avail.: $2,500-$5,000. **Duration:** Annual; one year. **Deadline:** May 1. **Remarks:** Established in 1988. **Contact:** AGC NYS, LLC, 10 Airline Dr. Ste. 203, Albany, NY, 12205; Phone: 518-456-1134; Fax: 518-456-1198.

2019 ■ Associated Medical Services (AMS)

162 Cumberland St., Ste. 228
Toronto, ON, Canada M5R 3N5
URL: www.ams-inc.on.ca

2020 ■ Hannah Post-doctoral Fellowship *(Postdoctorate/Fellowship)*

Purpose: To support scholarship of exceptional promise at the post-doctoral level. **Focus:** Medical research. **Qualif.:** Candidates must be a Canadian citizen in order to qualify for Fellowship; a period of full time post-PhD degree studies.

Funds Avail.: $45,000. **Duration:** Annual.

2021 ■ Associated Press Television and Radio Association (APTRA)

1850 N Central Ave., Ste. 640
Phoenix, AZ 85004
URL: www.aptra.com

2022 ■ APTRA-Clete Roberts/Kathryn Dettman Memorial Journalism Scholarship *(Undergraduate/Scholarship)*

Purpose: To help students pursue a broadcast journalism course. **Focus:** Broadcasting. **Qualif.:** Applicants must be college students enrolled at a college or university in one of the 13 APTRA states; must be pursuing a career in Broadcast Journalism. (Incoming freshmen and high school seniors are not eligible). **Criteria:** Judges will evaluate based on academic achievement, financial need and broadcast career goals.

Funds Avail.: $1,500. **Duration:** Annual. **Number Awarded:** 1. **To Apply:** Applicants must complete the application form and must attach tapes or writing samples of

Awards are arranged alphabetically below their administering organizations

broadcast-related work. **Deadline:** February 27.

2023 ■ Associates of the American Foreign Service Worldwide (AAFSW)

4001 N 9th St., Ste. 214
Arlington, VA 22203
Ph: (703)820-5420
Fax: (703)820-5421
E-mail: office@aafsw.org
URL: www.aafsw.org
Social Media: www.facebook.com/aafsw
twitter.com/aafsw

2024 ■ AAFSW "Twice Exceptional" Merit Scholarship for High School Seniors, Gap Year, and College Students *(Undergraduate/Scholarship)*

Purpose: To support outstanding high school seniors or gap year students in their education. **Focus:** General studies/Field of study not specified. **Qualif.:** Applicants must be high school seniors with an IEP or equivalent, gap year students entering college in the fall with an IEP or equivalent, or college freshmen or sophomores with an IEP or equivalent from their junior or senior year of high school, whose families are part of the foreign affairs agency community. An immediate family member must be a current member of AAFSW at the time of application.

Funds Avail.: $2,500 each. **Duration:** Annual. **Number Awarded:** 2. **To Apply:** Application form and details are available on the sponsor's website. **Deadline:** April 15. **Remarks:** Established in 2018.

2025 ■ AAFSW Merit Scholarship for College Students *(College, Undergraduate/Scholarship)*

Purpose: To recognize an outstanding student currently enrolled in college. **Focus:** General studies/Field of study not specified. **Qualif.:** Applicants must be current college freshmen, sophomores, or juniors enrolled in a 4-year college or university, whose families are part of the foreign affairs agency community. An immediate family member must be a current member of AAFSW at the time of application.

Funds Avail.: $2,500 each. **Duration:** Annual. **Number Awarded:** 2. **To Apply:** Application form is available on the sponsor's website and must be submitted with the following: original 500-word essay; college transcript; two letters of recommendation. **Deadline:** April 15.

2026 ■ The Judy Felt Memorial Volunteerism Scholarship *(College, Undergraduate/Scholarship)*

Purpose: To recognize student with an exceptional record of community service. **Focus:** General studies/Field of study not specified. **Qualif.:** Applicants must be high school seniors, gap year students, or college students enrolled in a 4-year college or university, whose families are part of the foreign affairs agency community. An immediate family member must be a current member of AAFSW at the time of application.

Funds Avail.: $1,500. **Number Awarded:** 1. **To Apply:** Application and details are available on the sponsor's website. **Deadline:** April 15.

2027 ■ Association for Academic Surgery (AAS)

11300 W Olympic Blvd., Ste. 600
Los Angeles, CA 90064
Ph: (310)437-1606

Fax: (310)437-0585
URL: www.aasurg.org

2028 ■ AAS/AAS Trainee Research Fellowship Awards *(Professional development/Fellowship)*

Purpose: To provide an eligible resident or fellow who has completed at least two years of postgraduate training in a surgical discipline the opportunity to spend one year in a full-time basic research position with an AAS member. **Focus:** Medical research; Surgery. **Qualif.:** Applicants must be residents or fellows who are currently enrolled in an accredited training program and have completed at least two years of postgraduate training in a surgical discipline; must be also candidate members or active members of the AAS; must be at least one mentor who is an active or senior member of the AAS. **Criteria:** Selection will be based on the proposals of the applicants; selection will be Academic Surgical Congress.

Funds Avail.: $20,000. **Duration:** Annual. **Number Awarded:** 2. **To Apply:** Applicants submit the materials such as a Cover Letter outlining their academic development plan for their one-year research period, their short and long-term career goals, and any other relevant information that they wish the committee to consider with their application; curriculum vitae or NIH-Style Biosketch, maximum of 4 pages; Lay Summary of the project, 200-300 words only; Comprehensive Research Plan, no more than five single-spaced, Arial 11pt, 1″ margin, pages inclusive of the following items, abstract for research proposal, significance of research, background information, preliminary observations, experimental plan methods, materials, potential limitations and pitfalls and references; evidence of institutional approval, IRB, IND, University Animal Use Committee; letter of support from sponsoring AAS mentor; letter of support of protected time from the chair of their department; and NIH-style Bio-sketch from their AAS mentor maximum of 4 pages. **Deadline:** August 5. **Remarks:** Established in 1988.

2029 ■ Association for the Advancement of Baltic Studies (AABS)

PO Box 353420
Seattle, WA 98195-3420
E-mail: aabs@uw.edu
URL: www.aabs-balticstudies.org

2030 ■ Association for the Advancement of Baltic Studies Dissertation Grants for Graduate Students *(Doctorate/Grant)*

Purpose: To support doctoral dissertation research and write-up in any field of Baltic Studies. **Focus:** General studies/Field of study not specified. **Qualif.:** Applicants must currently be enrolled in a PhD program and have completed all requirements for a PhD except the dissertation; must be current AABS members at the time of application. **Criteria:** Proposals will be evaluated according to the scholarly potential of the applicant, and the quality and scholarly importance of the proposed work, especially to the development of Baltic Studies

Funds Avail.: Up to $2,000. **Duration:** Annual. **Number Awarded:** 1. **To Apply:** Applicants must submit: online application form; 500-word proposal (in English); one-page budget specifying expenses (in English); curriculum Vitae (in English); evidence of current enrollment in a PhD program; writing sample of no more than 25 pages (in English). **Contact:** Dr. Ineta Dabašinskien, Vice President

Awards are arranged alphabetically below their administering organizations

of Professional Development; Email: aabs@uw.edu.

2031 ■ Association for the Advancement of Scandinavian Studies in Canada

University of Victoria
3800 Finnerty Rd.
Victoria, BC, Canada V8P 5C2
URL: aassc.com

2032 ■ The AASSC Gurli Aagaard Woods Undergraduate Publication Award *(Undergraduate/Award)*

Purpose: To develop skills and knowledge of undergraduate students about Scandinavian cultures and studies. **Focus:** General studies/Field of study not specified. **Qualif.:** Applicants must be undergraduate students who have an interest in Scandinavian-Canadian Studies.

Funds Avail.: No specific amount. **To Apply:** Applicants must submit a 2,000 to 4,000 words essay (excluding footnotes and bibliography) in Chicago style and must attach a title sheet with the following information: the student's name and contact information; the instructor's name; institutional affiliation; contact information; and the title and dates of the course in which the work was produced. **Deadline:** January 15.

2033 ■ The AASSC Marna Feldt Graduate Publication Award *(Graduate/Award)*

Purpose: To develop skills and knowledge of the students about Scandinavian cultures and studies. **Focus:** General studies/Field of study not specified. **Qualif.:** Applicants must be graduate students who have interest in Scandinavian-Canadian Studies.

Funds Avail.: No specific amount. **To Apply:** Applicants must submit a 5,000 to 7,000 words essay (excluding footnotes and bibliography) in Chicago style and must attach a title sheet with the following information: the student's name and contact information; the instructor's name; institutional affiliation; contact information; and the title and dates of the course in which the work was produced. **Deadline:** January 15.

2034 ■ AASSC Norwegian Travel Grant *(Undergraduate, College, University/Grant)*

Purpose: To help students attend and present papers at the Congress of the Canadian Federation for the Humanities and Social Sciences (CFHSS). **Focus:** General studies/Field of study not specified. **Qualif.:** Applicants must be student members of AASSC/AAESC presenting a papers at the Congress.

Funds Avail.: No specific amount. **Duration:** Annual. **To Apply:** Applicants must submit Confirmation of valid AASSC membership; Proof of affiliation with an educational institution in Canada and Resume or CV. **Deadline:** April 1.

2035 ■ Association on American Indian Affairs (AAIA)

966 Hungerford Dr., Ste. 30-A
Rockville, MD 20850
Ph: (240)314-7155
E-mail: general.aaia@indian-affairs.org
URL: indian-affairs.org
Social Media: www.facebook.com/
    AssociationAmericanIndianAffairs
www.linkedin.com/company/association-on-american
    -indian-affairs
twitter.com/IndianAffairs
www.youtube.com/channel/UCttH2SWzzBFt
    -h266Gd9MDg/videos

2036 ■ AAIA Allogan Slagle Memorial Scholarship *(Undergraduate, Graduate/Scholarship)*

Purpose: To provide financial assistance to non-federally recognize tribe members who are aiming higher education. **Focus:** Native American studies. **Qualif.:** Applicants must be full-time students from the Continental US or Alaska; must be graduate or undergraduate students pursuing a degree in public health or science. **Criteria:** Selection will be based on the above mentioned qualifications and compliance with the application details.

Funds Avail.: No specific amount. **Duration:** Annual. **To Apply:** Applicants must submit one application package only for the scholarship; Other details about application can be verified at the program website; Applicants must submit a current class schedule and transcript. **Deadline:** July 16. **Remarks:** Established in 2004.

2037 ■ Adolf Van Pelt Scholarship *(Undergraduate/Scholarship)*

Purpose: To provide financial assistance to federally recognize tribe members who are aiming higher education. **Focus:** Native American studies. **Qualif.:** Applicants must be students who are enrolled in federally recognized tribes and who are seeking a degree in any curriculum. **Criteria:** Selection will be based on the above mentioned qualifications and compliance with the application details.

Funds Avail.: No specific amount. **Duration:** Annual. **To Apply:** Applicants must submit one application package only for the scholarship; Other details about application can be verified at the program website; Applicants must submit a current class schedule and transcript. **Deadline:** July 16. **Remarks:** Established in 1987.

2038 ■ Elizabeth and Sherman Asche Memorial Scholarship *(Graduate, Undergraduate/Scholarship)*

Purpose: To provide financial assistance to Native American people aiming for higher education. **Focus:** Public health. **Qualif.:** Applicants must be full-time students from the Continental US or Alaska; must be graduate or undergraduate students pursuing a degree in public health or science; applicants have a minimum 2.5 out of 4.0 GPA. **Criteria:** Applicants will be selected based on the submitted materials.

Duration: Annual. **Number Awarded:** Varies. **To Apply:** Applicants must submit one application package only for the scholarship; Other details about application can be verified at the program website; Applicants must submit a current class schedule and transcript. **Deadline:** May 31. **Remarks:** Established with a bequest from the late Elizabeth Hill Asche.

2039 ■ Florence Young Memorial Scholarships *(Master's/Scholarship)*

Purpose: To provide financial assistance to students for their educational expenses. **Focus:** Law.

To Apply: Applicants submit a copy of Tribal enrollment (there is no minimum blood quantum requirement for eligibility). This can be a copy of the student's Tribal I.D. card or a copy of an official letter from the Tribe; Applicant

Awards are arranged alphabetically below their administering organizations

must submit a current class schedule and transcript. **Deadline:** June 1.

2040 ■ Sequoyah Graduate Scholarship *(Master's/Scholarship)*

Purpose: To provide financial assistance to students for their educational expenses. **Focus:** General studies/Field of study not specified.

To Apply: Applicants submit a copy of Tribal enrollment (there is no minimum blood quantum requirement for eligibility). This can be a copy of the student's Tribal I.D. card or a copy of an official letter from the Tribe; Applicant must submit a current class schedule and transcript. **Deadline:** June 1.

2041 ■ Association of American Indian Physicians (AAIP)

1225 Sovereign Row, Ste. 103
Oklahoma City, OK 73108
Ph: (405)946-7072
Fax: (405)946-7651
URL: aaip.org
Social Media: www.facebook.com/The-Association-of
   -American-Indian-Physicians-156976135945
twitter.com/associationofa4
www.youtube.com/channel/
   UCwCrT22n5B484jRZESdpiWQ

2042 ■ Full Circle Scholarship *(Graduate, Undergraduate/Scholarship)*

Purpose: To provide a framework for undergraduate and graduate students attending accredited public and non-profit private colleges across the United States. **Focus:** Health education. **Qualif.:** Applicants must be undergraduate or graduate students attending accredited public and non-profit private colleges across the United States; US citizen or Canadian eligible to attend college in the U.S. under provisions of the Jay Treaty; must be American Indian or Alaska Native descent students attending tribal colleges and universities; must be in full-time enrollment; registered as an enrolled member of a federal or state recognized tribe, or a descendant of at least one grandparent or parent who is an enrolled tribal member. Alaska Natives may use Native Corporation membership; at least a 2.0 cumulative GPA.

To Apply: Applicants must complete the online application form and must submit the following requirements: Profile, Application, Documents; upload a digital photo that's at least 1.5 MB in size; Submit your Certificate of Indian Blood (CIB) or other proof of tribal enrollment; transcripts. **Deadline:** May 31. **Contact:** Email: scholarships@collegefund.org; Phone: 800-776-3863.

2043 ■ Association of American Medical Colleges (AAMC)

655 K St. NW, Ste. 100
Washington, DC 20001-2399
Ph: (202)828-0400
E-mail: amcas@aamc.org
URL: www.aamc.org
Social Media: www.facebook.com/aamctoday
www.instagram.com/aamctoday
www.linkedin.com/company/aamc

twitter.com/aamctoday
www.youtube.com/user/AAMCvideo

2044 ■ Herbert W. Nickens Medical Student Scholarships *(Advanced Professional/Scholarship)*

Purpose: To support outstanding students who have shown leadership in efforts to eliminate inequities in medical education and health care and have demonstrated leadership efforts in addressing educational, societal, and health care needs of racial and ethnic minorities in the United States. **Focus:** Education, Medical. **Qualif.:** Applicants must be U.S. citizen, permanent resident, or an individual granted deferred action for childhood arrivals (DACA) status; Entering the third year of study in a LCME-accredited U.S. medical school; Students enrolled in combined degree programs (such as MD/PhD) are eligible when they are entering their third year of medical school-.Criteria: Recipients will be selected based on academic standing.

Funds Avail.: $5,000. **Duration:** Annual. **Number Awarded:** 5. **To Apply:** Applicants must include nomination letter from the medical school's dean or dean's designee (not to exceed four double-spaced pages) stating verbatim that the candidate has maintained good academic standing throughout the first two years; A letter of recommendation from the institutional GSA diversity affairs officer (not to exceed four double-spaced pages). Should the institution not have a GSA diversity affairs officer, the nominator must be noted in the cover sheet as the replacement. A letter of recommendation from a faculty member (not to exceed four double-spaced pages). A personal statement by the nominee assessing their leadership efforts in eliminating inequities in medical education and health care for racial and ethnic minorities (not to exceed two double-spaced pages). A curriculum vitae (CV) for the nominee, which clearly highlights awards and scholarships. **Deadline:** April 24.

2045 ■ Association of Applied Paleontological Sciences (AAPS)

96 E 700 S
Logan, UT 84321-5555
Ph: (435)752-7145
URL: www.aaps.net

2046 ■ Dan Rigel Memorial Educational Grant *(Professional development, Advanced Professional/Grant)*

Purpose: To promote the education of their students in geology and paleontology. **Focus:** Geology; Paleontology. **Qualif.:** Applicants must be high school teachers or high school educators. **Criteria:** Awardees will be selected based upon need and the proposed use of funds.

Funds Avail.: $250 to $1,000. **Duration:** Annual. **To Apply:** Applicants must submit application form along with a letter stating how they propose to use the grant. **Deadline:** December 1. **Remarks:** The grant established in the memory of Dan Rigel who ran Caveman Lapidary along with his wife. Established in 2011. **Contact:** Neal Larson, Scholarship and Grant Chairperson; C/O Larson Paleontology, PO Box 1313, Hill City, SD, 57745, USA; Email: ammoniteguy@gmail.com.

2047 ■ A. Allen Graffham Research Grant *(Advanced Professional, Professional development/Grant)*

Purpose: To support researchers that will publish on specimens collected by, or in collaboration with, AAPS

Awards are arranged alphabetically below their administering organizations

members. **Focus:** Geology; Paleontology. **Qualif.:** Applicants must be scientists, researchers or students in paleontology. **Criteria:** Selection will be based on the Board of Directors criteria.

Funds Avail.: $1,000. **Duration:** Annual. **Number Awarded:** 1 in 2006. **To Apply:** Applicants must submit a letter of application explaining the focus of their research, which AAPS member they collected with or acquired the fossils from, and what they plan on using the money for; must also submit a copy of their resume, publication, and a copy of their paper. **Deadline:** December 1. **Remarks:** The grant established in the memory of Allen Graffham. **Contact:** Neal Larson, Scholarship and Grant Chairperson; C/O Larson Paleontology, PO Box 1313, Hill City, SD, 57745, USA; Email: ammoniteguy@gmail.com.

2048 ■ Charles Sternberg Scholarship (Graduate/Scholarship)

Purpose: To support graduate level students in paleontology who are conducting various studies about macro vertebrate fossils. **Focus:** Paleontology. **Qualif.:** Applicants must be graduate level students in paleontology attending universities worldwide; must be active in field research and collecting. **Criteria:** Applicants are selected based on the criteria set by the Association and if they meet the approval of the board of directors and the membership.

Funds Avail.: $1,000. **Duration:** Annual. **Number Awarded:** Up To 2. **To Apply:** Applicants must submit the following requirements: application letter explaining the focus of the study and thesis subject; recommendation letter from one or more professors; curriculum vitae or college transcript. **Deadline:** December 1. **Remarks:** Established in 2001. **Contact:** Neal Larson, Scholarship and Grant Chairperson; C/O Larson Paleontology, PO Box 1313, Hill City, SD, 57745, USA; Email: ammoniteguy@gmail.com.

2049 ■ René M. Vandervelde Research Grants (Professional development/Grant)

Purpose: To qualified researchers working on the marine paleontology, geology, or stratigraphy of the Late Cretaceous Pierre and Bearpaw Shales of North America. **Focus:** Geology; Paleontology. **Qualif.:** Applicants must be students and researchers working in the marine paleontology, geology or stratigraphy of the Late Cretaceous Pierre and Bearpaw Shales of North America. **Criteria:** Recipients will be selected by the AAPS Board of Directors.

Funds Avail.: $1,000. **Duration:** Annual. **To Apply:** Applicants must submit a letter of request, a brief synopsis of planned research goals (no more than two pages), resume (including publications and abstracts), and a letter of support from either a professor and/or associates. **Deadline:** December 1. **Remarks:** Established in 2007. **Contact:** Neal Larson, Scholarship and Grant Chairperson; C/O Larson Paleontology, PO Box 1313, Hill City, SD, 57745, USA; Email: ammoniteguy@gmail.com.

2050 ■ James R. Welch Scholarship (Graduate/Scholarship)

Purpose: To support graduate level students in paleontology who are conducting various studies about macro invertebrate fossils. **Focus:** Paleontology. **Qualif.:** Applicants must be graduate level students in paleontology attending universities worldwide; must be active in field research and collecting. **Criteria:** Applicants are selected based on the criteria set by the Association and if they meet the approval of the board of directors and the membership.

Funds Avail.: $1,000. **Duration:** Annual. **Number Awarded:** Up To 3. **To Apply:** Applicants must submit the following requirements: application letter explaining the focus of the study and thesis subject; recommendation letter from one or more professors; curriculum vitae or college transcript. **Deadline:** December 1. **Contact:** Neal Larson, Scholarship and Grant Chairperson; C/O Larson Paleontology, PO Box 1313, Hill City, SD, 57745, USA; Email: ammoniteguy@gmail.com.

2051 ■ Association for Applied and Therapeutic Humor (AATH)
220 E State St., Fl. G
Rockford, IL 61104
Ph: (815)708-6587
E-mail: info@aath.org
URL: www.aath.org
Social Media: www.facebook.com/groups/6605272722
www.linkedin.com/groups/134293
twitter.com/AATH_Assoc
www.youtube.com/user/GOAATH

2052 ■ Ed Dunkelblau Scholarship (All/Scholarship)

Purpose: To honor the work, dedication, commitment and contribution to AATH and the field of therapeutic humor. **Focus:** Recreational therapy. **Qualif.:** Applicants must be practitioners of color or researchers interested in the cultural applications of therapeutic humor. **Criteria:** Selection will be based on the applicant's awareness of AATH mission.

Funds Avail.: No specific amount. **Duration:** Annual. **To Apply:** Applicants must submit an essay (up to 250 words) demonstrating their interest in therapeutic humor, documenting their work in the field of therapeutic humor, and expressing their awareness of the mission of AATH. **Deadline:** November 15. **Remarks:** Established in honor of Ed Dunkelblau, AATH past conference chair. Established in 2005.

2053 ■ The Margie Klein "Paper Plate" Scholarships (All/Scholarship)

Purpose: To honor the work, dedication, commitment and contribution to AATH and in the field of therapeutic humor. **Focus:** Recreational therapy. **Qualif.:** Applicants must show interest in therapeutic humor. **Criteria:** Selection will be based on clarity; innovation/originality/creativity; and impact.

Funds Avail.: Conference registration. **Duration:** Annual. **Number Awarded:** 1. **To Apply:** Applicants must submit an essay describing how humor helped them in work-related situations. Examples can come from the corporate world, the nonprofit arena, or the self-employed. If possible, please provide at least three examples. Essays should range from approximately 250 to 500 words. They must also indicate their AATH membership status. **Remarks:** In memory of Margie Klein, the mother of Allen Klein, 2005/2006 president of AATH. Throughout the 95-plus-years of her life, Allen's mother continually used her sense of humor and was inspirational in Allen's teaching others about the power of humor.

2054 ■ Lenny Ravich "Shalom" Scholarships (Advanced Professional/Scholarship)

Purpose: To help cultivate the next generation of AATH members. **Focus:** Recreational therapy. **Qualif.:** Applicants

Awards are arranged alphabetically below their administering organizations

must be individuals whose works in humor and laughter clearly and tangibly demonstrate commitment to world peace. **Criteria:** Selection will be based on the impact of the applicant's essay.

Funds Avail.: $100 and conference registration. **Number Awarded:** 1. **To Apply:** Applicants must submit three essays (up to 250 words each) answering these questions: How do you presently apply (or plan to apply) your knowledge and experience in humor and laughter to advance world peace?; How has your mission and purpose in life brought you to this moment?; Why do you feel that you are deserving of this scholarship. **Remarks:** The scholarship was established by Lenny Ravich, Director of the Gestalt Institute of Tel Aviv.

2055 ■ Patty Wooten Scholarships *(Professional development/Scholarship, Award, Recognition)*

Purpose: To support nurses who are currently involved in creating humor interventions that are being used in a therapeutic manner for patients, family, and/or staff. **Focus:** Recreational therapy. **Qualif.:** Applicants must be nurses (R.N., L.P.N., L.V.N. or C.N.A) who are currently involved in creating humor interventions that are being used in a therapeutic manner for patients, family, and/or staff. **Criteria:** Selection will be based on the AATH's criteria.

Funds Avail.: Conference registration. **Duration:** Annual. **Number Awarded:** 1. **To Apply:** Applicants are required to write an essay describing how they perceive humor to be therapeutic and how their work, program, or intervention efforts have benefited patients, family, or staff. They must also indicate their AATH membership status. **Remarks:** Established in loving memory of Patty Wooten, AATH past conference chair.

2056 ■ Association of Art Museum Curators (AAMC)

174 E 80th St.
New York, NY 10075
Ph: (646)405-8057
Fax: (212)537-5571
E-mail: aamc@artcurators.org
URL: www.artcurators.org
Social Media: www.facebook.com/ArtCuratorsAssoc
www.instagram.com/art_curators
twitter.com/Art_Curators

2057 ■ AAMC Foundation Engagement Program for International Curators Grants *(Advanced Professional, Professional development/Grant)*

Purpose: To provide opportunities for professional development and exchange, as well as to expand and strengthen the international curatorial community and give primacy to the curatorial voice in the international dialogue between museum professionals. **Focus:** Museum science. **Qualif.:** Application is open to non-U.S. based curators and U.S. liaisons working on or having worked within exhibitions and projects that explore historic American Art (c. 1500-1980), including painting; sculpture; works on paper, including prints, drawing and photography; decorative arts; and excluding architecture; design; and performance. U.S. liaisons must be AAMC members in good standing. Non-U.S. based curators must be proficient in oral and written English. **Criteria:** Selection will be based on the AAMC Foundation's criteria.

Funds Avail.: Amount varies. **Duration:** Annual; up to 2 years. **Number Awarded:** 4. **To Apply:** Applicants must

contact the AAMC Foundation for more information regarding the separate application process for the U.S. liaisons and non U.S. based curators. **Deadline:** October 24.

2058 ■ Kress/AAR Fellowships *(Professional development/Fellowship)*

Purpose: To provide essential funding for curators to develop projects that require research in Italy. **Focus:** Museum science. **Qualif.:** Applicants must be art curators at non-profit organizations, with direct responsibility for works of art. In addition, curators and others that work a minimum of 50% of the time for/with non-profit organizations will be considered. **Criteria:** Selection will be based on the research proposal of the applicants; priority will be given to those without fund to support travel research.

Funds Avail.: No specific amount. **Duration:** Annual. **Number Awarded:** 1. **To Apply:** Applicants must provide a letter of support from institution director, project director and/or host of project; they are required to list preferred period of residency, indicating a first and second choice; research can be exhibition related or for written scholarly work, but should not be in conjunction with completing a dissertation. **Deadline:** January 31.

2059 ■ Association for Asian Studies (AAS)

825 Victors Way, Ste. 310
Ann Arbor, MI 48108
Ph: (734)665-2490
Fax: (734)665-3801
E-mail: ads@asianstudies.org
URL: www.asian-studies.org
Social Media: www.facebook.com/AASAsianStudies
www.instagram.com/associationforasianstudies
twitter.com/AASAsianStudies

2060 ■ AAS CIAC Small Grants *(Graduate/Grant)*

Purpose: To support funding requests for indirect costs of research. **Focus:** General studies/Field of study not specified. **Qualif.:** Applicants must be AAS members, junior and independent scholars, adjunct faculties, and dissertation-level graduate students. **Criteria:** Preference will be given to applicants who show sincere interest in research, particularly in Chinese or Inner Asia studies.

Funds Avail.: Up to $2,000. **Duration:** Annual. **To Apply:** Applicants must submit a completed application form along with 200-word abstract of the project; a detailed budget of anticipated expenses, including other sources of funding; a two-page (maximum) curriculum vitae; in the case of graduate students, a letter of support from their dissertation advisor, without which the application will not be considered. **Deadline:** November 1. **Contact:** Peter Carroll, CIAC Vice Chair; Email: p-carroll@northwestern.edu.

2061 ■ AAS Korean Studies Scholarship Program *(Graduate/Scholarship)*

Purpose: To provide scholarship for graduate students majoring in Korean studies in North America for their coursework and/or research. **Focus:** General studies/Field of study not specified. **Qualif.:** Applicants must be M.A. or Ph.D. students majoring in Korean studies in any university in North America. Applicants must exhibit sufficient ability to use Korean-language sources in their research and study. **Criteria:** Selection will be based on the submitted applications.

Awards are arranged alphabetically below their administering organizations

Funds Avail.: range of $10,000–$20,000. **Duration:** Annual. **To Apply:** Applicants must complete a Foundation Application Form, a three-page proposal outlining research interests and academic progress of the student, with a separate one-page bibliography; grade transcripts of coursework; and three letters of recommendation, one of which must be from someone able to attest to the applicant's language ability. **Deadline:** January.

2062 ■ Association for Behavior Analysis International (ABAI)

550 W Centre Ave., Ste. 1
Portage, MI 49024
Ph: (269)492-9310
Fax: (269)492-9316
E-mail: mail@abainternational.org
URL: www.abainternational.org
Social Media: www.facebook.com/ABAInternational.org
twitter.com/abaievents

2063 ■ Marian Breland Bailey Award *(Graduate, Undergraduate/Award)*

Purpose: To promote research and scholarly activity by students in the applied analysis of animal behavior. **Focus:** Animal science and behavior.

Contact: SIG president, Dr. Terri Bright, E-mail: terribright@comcast.net.

2064 ■ Student Researcher Award, From the Behavioral Gerontology SIG *(Undergraduate, Graduate/Award)*

Purpose: To support research and scholarly activity by students in behavioral gerontology. **Focus:** Behavioral sciences; Gerontology. **Qualif.:** Any graduate or undergraduate student who is first author on a behavioral gerontology related talk or poster is invited to submit a presentation for consideration. **Criteria:** Selection will be based on the committee's criteria and the application materials submitted.

Funds Avail.: $50. **Duration:** Annual. **Number Awarded:** 1. **To Apply:** There is no formal submission process; any presentation that addresses issues relevant to behavioral gerontology is eligible.

2065 ■ Association of Black Cardiologists (ABC)

122 E 42nd St., 18th Fl.
New York, NY 10168-1898
Fax: (888)281-3574
Free: 800-753-9222
URL: www.abcardio.org
Social Media: www.facebook.com/abcardio
www.instagram.com/abcardio1/
www.linkedin.com/company/213425
www.linkedin.com/company/association-of-black
  -cardiologists
twitter.com/abcardio1
www.youtube.com/theabcardio

2066 ■ The Dr. Richard Allen Williams and Genita Evangelista Johnson Scholarship,AMA Foundation Scholarship *(Undergraduate/Scholarship)*

Purpose: To promote diversity in medicine, encourage commitment to eliminating health care disparities and sup-

port future Cardiologists, while helping to alleviate medical student debt. **Focus:** Medicine, Cardiology. **Qualif.:** Applicant must be an African American and other minority 1st, 2nd, 3rd, and 4th year medical students. **Criteria:** Selection based on committee criteria.

Funds Avail.: $5,000. **Duration:** Annual. **Number Awarded:** Varies. **To Apply:** Applicants should submit the following documents via the online form below: A one-page statement of interest Official medical school transcript Recent curriculum vitae; Two letters of recommendation from a professor at current medical school. **Deadline:** August 28.

2067 ■ Association of Black Women Lawyers of New Jersey

PO Box 22524
Trenton, NJ 08607
Ph: (609)285-3512
E-mail: law860@verizon.net
URL: abwl-nj.org
Social Media: www.facebook.com/ABWLNJ
twitter.com/ABWL_NJ

2068 ■ Bernadine Johnson-Marshall and Martha Bell Williams Scholarships *(Undergraduate/ Scholarship)*

Purpose: To encourage greater participation of African-American women in the field of law. **Focus:** Law. **Qualif.:** Applicants must be either enrolled at an accredited law school in New Jersey or New Jersey permanent residents enrolled at an accredited law school outside of New Jersey; female of African descent; student must be a 1L, 2L or part time 3L. **Criteria:** Scholarships will be awarded on the basis of demonstrated community service/civic involvement, personal financial need, academic achievement and a brief writing sample or essay.

Funds Avail.: $10,000. **Number Awarded:** 1. **To Apply:** Applicants must visit the website to obtain an application. Completed applications can be sent via electronic mail or via US Postal Service mail. **Deadline:** March 1.

2069 ■ Association of Black Women Physicians (ABWP)

4712 Admiralty Way, Ste. No. 175
Marina del Rey, CA 90292
Ph: (213)277-7022
E-mail: abwpcorrespondence@gmail.com
URL: www.blackwomenphysicians.org
Social Media: www.facebook.com/Blackfemaledoctors
www.instagram.com/blackwomenphysicians
www.linkedin.com/company/association-of-black-women
  -physicians/about
twitter.com/ABWP_Drs

2070 ■ Rebecca Lee Crumpler, M.D. Scholarship *(Advanced Professional/Scholarship)*

Purpose: To financially support the Southern California female medical students and for the improvement of public health and welfare through the advancement of knowledge concerning women and community health. **Focus:** Medicine. **Qualif.:** Applicants must be female medical students who are permanent residents of Southern California at any medical school, or students at a Southern California medi-

---

Awards are arranged alphabetically below their administering organizations

cal school, who are in good academic standing. **Criteria:** Selection is based on financial need and academic merit.

Funds Avail.: No specific amount. **Duration:** Annual. **To Apply:** Applicants must submit academic transcripts; financial aid award letter/verification; medical school acceptance letter or medical school deans letter of good standing; three letters of recommendation; curriculum vitae; short bio (250 words or less); high quality photo (.jpeg preferred format); and a typed personal statement. **Deadline:** September 1. **Contact:** Association of Black Women Physicians ATTN: Rebecca Lee Crumpler, MD - Scholarship Committee; 4712 Admiralty Way, #175 Marina del Rey, CA 90292 abwpcorrespondence@gmail.com or Call (213) 277-7022.

2071 ■ Association of Business Information & Media Companies (ABM)

675 3rd Ave., 7th Fl.
New York, NY 10017-5704
Ph: (212)661-6360
URL: www.abmassociation.com
Social Media: www.facebook.com/abmassociation

2072 ■ McAllister Fellowship *(Professional development/Fellowship)*

Purpose: To promote the study of business media. **Focus:** Business Communications. **Qualif.:** Applicants must be editors or executives. **Criteria:** Selection is based on judging panel and screening board.

Funds Avail.: No specific amount. **Duration:** Annual. **Number Awarded:** 1. **To Apply:** Applicants may contact the ABM for the application process and other related information.

2073 ■ Association of California Nurse Leaders Kern County Chapter

1810 Eye St.
Bakersfield, CA 93301
URL: www.kcacnl.com

2074 ■ AKCNL Nightingale Scholarship *(Graduate, Undergraduate/Scholarship)*

Purpose: To financially support undergraduate and graduate nurses in Kern County. **Focus:** Nursing. **Qualif.:** Applicants must be enrolled in an accredited entry level or graduate RN Program; plan on staying in Kern County after graduation; undergraduate student must maintain at least a 3.0 GPA; graduate student must maintain at least a 3.5 GPA. **Criteria:** Selection is based on the student's qualifications, application materials, and on the research.

Funds Avail.: $1,000. **Number Awarded:** 10. **To Apply:** Applicants must submit a completed application form along with a written recommendation from your immediate supervisor or instructor; transcript of program courses to date including GPA; essay (no longer than 500 words). **Deadline:** March 16. **Contact:** Email: Kim Jenkins, Kimberley.A.Jenkins@kp.org.

2075 ■ Association of California Water Agencies (ACWA)

980 9th St., Ste. 1000
Sacramento, CA 95814
Ph: (916)441-4545

Free: 888-666-2292
E-mail: acwabox@acwa.com
URL: www.acwa.com
Social Media: www.facebook.com/acwawater
www.linkedin.com/company/association-of-california-water
-agencies
twitter.com/ACWAWater

2076 ■ Association of California Water Agencies Scholarship *(Undergraduate/Scholarship)*

Purpose: To promote study focusing on water resources. **Focus:** Water resources. **Qualif.:** Applicants must be residents of California attending one of the selected California schools full-time as juniors or seniors during the current academic year. **Criteria:** Applicant will be selected based on: Scholastic achievement; Demonstrated motivation to the vocation of water resources-related management; The quality of the student's essay; and Commitment to full-time enrollment for the entire academic year.

Funds Avail.: $3,500. **Duration:** Annual. **Number Awarded:** 2. **To Apply:** Applicants must submit at least two current letters of recommendation (but no more than three), with at least one of the letters originating from a college professor or employer on business letterhead; all letters of recommendation must include contact information for the letter writer. official transcripts for each college they have attended; acceptable formats include photocopied or scanned official transcripts, or unofficial transcripts issued by the school; however, printed class schedules will not be accepted. submit an essay responding to specific prompt (no more than 1,000 words). **Deadline:** March 1. **Contact:** Phone: 916-441-4545; Email: scholarships@acwa.com.

2077 ■ Clair A. Hill Scholarship *(Undergraduate/ Scholarship)*

Purpose: To support students pursuing degrees in water resources-related fields. **Focus:** Water resources. **Qualif.:** Applicants must be residents of California attending one of the selected California schools full-time as sophomores, juniors or seniors during the current academic year. **Criteria:** Applicant will be selected based on: Scholastic achievement; Demonstrated motivation to the vocation of water resources-related management; The quality of the student's essay; and Commitment to full-time enrollment for the entire academic year.

Funds Avail.: $5,000. **Duration:** Annual. **Number Awarded:** 1. **To Apply:** Applicant must submit at least two current letters of recommendation (but no more than three), with at least one of the letters originating from a college professor or employer on business letterhead; all letters of recommendation must include contact information for the writer. official transcripts for each college they have attended; acceptable formats include photocopied or scanned official transcripts, or unofficial transcripts issued by the school; however, printed class schedules will not be accepted. an essay responding to specific prompt (no more than 1,000 words). **Deadline:** March 1. **Contact:** Phone: 916-441-4545; Email: scholarships@acwa.com.

2078 ■ Stephen K. Hall ACWA Water Law and Policy Scholarship *(Graduate/Scholarship)*

Purpose: To encourage talented and innovative students to join the effort to ensure California's water quality and to implement sound water management policies. **Focus:** Water resources. **Qualif.:** Applicant must be attending an accredited, public or private U.S. college at the start of the

Awards are arranged alphabetically below their administering organizations

academic year. must be pursuing a graduate degree (Master's, PhD, or Law School) in water law, water policy or public administration with a demonstrated concentration in the field of water resources. **Criteria:** Applicant will be selected based on: Scholastic achievement; Demonstrated motivation to the vocation of water resources-related management; The quality of the student's essay; and Commitment to full-time enrollment for the entire academic year.

Funds Avail.: $7,000. **Duration:** Annual. **Number Awarded:** 1. **To Apply:** Applicant must submit at least three current letters of recommendation, with at least one of the letters originating from a college professor or employer; and submit official transcripts for each college they have attended; printed class schedules will not be accepted. an essay responding to specific prompt (no more than 1,000 words). **Deadline:** March 1. **Remarks:** Established in 2007. **Contact:** Email scholarships@acwa.com or call (916) 441-4545.

2079 ■ Association for Canadian Studies in the United States (ACSUS)

University at Buffalo - The State University of New York
732 Clemens Hall
Buffalo, NY 14260
E-mail: info@acsus.org
URL: www.acsus.org

2080 ■ ACSUS Distinguished Dissertation Award
(Doctorate/Award)

Purpose: To honor outstanding doctoral research on Canada at American institutions. **Focus:** General studies/Field of study not specified. **Qualif.:** Applicants must be nominated by a faculty member serving on dissertation committees at universities in the United States; must be members of ACSUS; who have completed the Ph.D. degree. **Criteria:** Successful nominees should represent an original work that makes a contribution to the nominee's discipline; must contain at least 50% content on Canada; and the topic must be comparative in nature; the dissertation will be judged on substantive and methodological quality, originality of thought and clarity.

Funds Avail.: $500. **Duration:** Biennial. **To Apply:** Applications must be accompanied by a letter of support from the student's dissertation advisor and one from an additional reference who is not a member of ACSUS; each nomination must be accompanied by a copy of the dissertation (not to exceed 500 words), typed and double-spaced; a one page resume of the nominee; and materials should be submitted electronically. **Deadline:** August 1. **Contact:** E-mail: info@acsus.org.

2081 ■ Enders Student Fellowship *(Graduate/Fellowship)*

Purpose: To encourage advanced scholarship on Canada-U.S. relations by funding fellowship for US scholars conducting research in Canada. **Focus:** General studies/Field of study not specified. **Qualif.:** Applicants can be in any discipline or professional school who are in the process of preparing a graduate thesis or doctoral dissertation related in substantial part to the study of Canada, Canada-U.S. relations or comparative policies in North America; must be U.S. citizens or permanent residents; must be enrolled in full-time masters or doctoral programs at any institution in the United States; and must have obtained, in writing, the support of a faculty member or research scientist at a Canadian university, or the head of an organization or business who agrees to act as the student's academic sponsor during the tenure of their award. **Criteria:** Applicants will be selected according to the following criteria: clarity of the proposal and its methodology; proposal's potential contribution to the enhancement of the Canada-U.S. relationship or to comparative policymaking in North America; likelihood of the project's being accomplished during the period of the award; demonstrated need for the research to be carried out in Canada; strength of the letters of support; part academic awards/achievement demonstrated by transcripts, awards, and distinctions.

Funds Avail.: $3,500. **To Apply:** Applicants must submit a curriculum vitae; one-page proposal outlining the thesis/dissertation project that states why research at the selected university is essential to the project and how such a visit will enhance the quality of the student's research; schedule of the activities; one letter of support from the student's thesis/dissertation chair and another one from the departmental chair or dean of the school; and a letter of invitation from the faculty member or organization head where student will be conducting research. **Deadline:** March 31. **Contact:** Dr. Andrew Holman, Chair, Selection Committee, a2holman@bridgew.edu.

2082 ■ Association Canadienne des Chefs de Police (ACCP)

300 Terry Fox Dr., Unit 100
Kanata, ON, Canada K2K 0E3
URL: cacp.ca

2083 ■ Jack Ackroyd Scholarships *(Other/Scholarship)*

Purpose: To support members of police forces across Canada to further their education with a view of promoting professionalism and excellence throughout the policing community. **Focus:** Law enforcement. **Qualif.:** Applicants must be uniform and civilian members of police forces who have completed a degree or certificate program in police studies, criminology, law, or other programs related to law enforcement in an accredited Canadian university or community college. **Criteria:** Selection is based on demonstrated academic excellence in police related studies will be given preference.

Funds Avail.: 100 Canadian Dollars each. **Duration:** Annual. **Number Awarded:** 5. **To Apply:** Applicants must submit documents pertaining to their personal information, police service of employment, date of graduation, official transcripts of courses and grades, and any other information which may be considered relevant including any letter of support from the police service of which they are members. **Contact:** Further information or inquiries may be made to Trevor McCagherty, Executive Support, CACP Research Foundation, at 905-242-2146.

2084 ■ L'Association Canadienne Des Géographes (CAG)

60 University Private, Simard Hall, Rm. 031
Ottawa, ON, Canada K1N 6N5
Ph: (613)562-5208
E-mail: info@cag-acg.ca
URL: www.cag-acg.ca
Social Media: www.facebook.com/canadiangeographers
twitter.com/cangeographers

Awards are arranged alphabetically below their administering organizations

2085 ■ CAG Health and Health Care Study Group Awards (Graduate/Award)

Purpose: To facilitate the exchange of ideas and information among researchers interested in health geography issues. **Focus:** General studies/Field of study not specified. **Qualif.:** Applicants must be members of the Canadian Association of Geographers; must be graduate students or supervisors who are members of the HHCSG at the time of the CAG meeting. **Criteria:** Selection will be given based on applicants who conducted the best research.

Funds Avail.: No specific amount. **To Apply:** Applicants must submit an application form. **Contact:** Jennifer Dean, at jennifer.dean@uwaterloo.ca.

2086 ■ Canadian Historical Geography Award (Master's, Graduate, Undergraduate/Prize)

Purpose: To promote collegiality and scholarly exchange among historical geographers, and to advance the interdisciplinary interests of historical geography within the academic community and beyond. **Focus:** Geography. **Qualif.:** Applicants must be full-time or part-time undergraduates or Master's students attending a credited Canadian college or university or to anyone who has graduated from an undergraduate or Masters program at a credited Canadian college or university within the 12-month period preceding competition; Doctoral students are not eligible. **Criteria:** Selection will be based on originality, research quality, and style of the submitted essay.

Funds Avail.: $100. **Duration:** Annual. **To Apply:** Applicants must submit an essay; must be a research paper discussing Canadian historical geography and have been written anytime after January 2017; essay must be submitted in French or English not exceeding 6,000 words including references, footnotes or endnotes. In addition, must also submit the following information; name and contact details; an abstract no longer than 250 words; name of the institution attended at the time of writing the essay; course by which the essay was written; and name of the course instructor. **Deadline:** May 15. **Contact:** Essays must be submitted by electronic mail to Matt Dyce at m.dyce@uwinnipeg.ca.

2087 ■ Robin P. Armstrong Memorial Prize for Excellence in Indigenous Studies (Graduate/Award, Monetary)

Purpose: To promote excellence in applied research related to First Nation/Aboriginal/Indigenous peoples in Canada. **Focus:** Geography. **Qualif.:** Applicant must completed a Master's or PhD thesis in First Nations/Indigenous Studies or Geography on research related to First Nations/Aboriginal/Indigenous peoples in·Canada. **Criteria:** Selection will be ranked based on the following categories; significance of the problem; conceptualization, design and execution of the study; quality of the results; potential for improving theory; and clarity, insight and originality of the work.

Funds Avail.: $500. **Duration:** Annual. **Number Awarded:** 1. **To Apply:** Applicants must submit a cover letter; curriculum vitae; and 1,000-1,500 words abstract outlining the problem or question studied, review of related literature, design and methodology, statistical results and conclusions, and statement of significance. **Deadline:** January 31. **Contact:** Applications should be sent by e-mail to gail.fondahl@unbc.ca.

2088 ■ Association Canadienne d'Études Cinématographiques (ACEC)

c/o Edward Jurkowski, Dean
Faculty of Fine Arts, University of Lethbridge
4401 University Dr.
Lethbridge, AB, Canada T1K 3M4
Ph: (403)329-2126
URL: www.filmstudies.ca
Social Media: www.facebook.com/FSAC.ACEC
twitter.com/_filmstudies

2089 ■ Gerald Pratley Award (Doctorate, Graduate/Scholarship)

Purpose: To help graduate students (masters or doctorates) with an excellent academic record and whose research will improve knowledge of Canadian / Quebec cinema in Canada or abroad. **Focus:** Cinema. **Qualif.:** Applicants must be students entering or completing a graduate program in Film Studies (or any related discipline) at any recognized post-secondary institution in or outside Canada; applicants need not be Canadian citizens. **Criteria:** Selection is based on the student's previous academic performance, intentions for a specific paper or body of research on Canadian/Quebec cinema.

Funds Avail.: 1,000 Canadian Dollars. **Duration:** Annual. **To Apply:** Applicants must prepare a brief research proposal (500 words) including bibliography; two letters of recommendation; one sample of previous work (3000 to 5000 words); and official university transcripts or unofficial grade reports. **Deadline:** August 31. **Remarks:** The award was established to tribute Gerald Pratley's (1923-2011) contribution to the advancement of Canadian film studies. Established in 1991. **Contact:** Email: president@filmstudies.ca.

2090 ■ Association Canadienne du Diabete

1300-522 University Ave.
Toronto, ON, Canada M5G 2R5
E-mail: info@diabetes.ca
URL: www.diabetes.ca
Social Media: www.instagram.com/DiabetesCanada/
www.linkedin.com/company/diabetescanada
twitter.com/DiabetesCanada

2091 ■ Eli Lilly Graduate Scholarship (Graduate, Postgraduate/Scholarship)

Purpose: To encourage members to pursue their graduate or post-secondary graduate studies in a diabetes field. **Focus:** Diabetes. **Qualif.:** Applicants must be active DES members for a minimum of two years; must be Canadian citizens or landed immigrants; must not have received another DES or Canadian Diabetes Association scholarships or bursary for the same academic year; will be given to those who are studying at a Canadian university. **Criteria:** Selection is based on the deliberations of the DES Awards Selection Committee.

Funds Avail.: $5,000. **Duration:** Annual; 5 years only. **To Apply:** Applicant must submit one current copy of the applicant's curriculum vitae; three letters of reference in total – one must be from academic supervisor or advisor; and a head shot (high resolution jpgs (300 dpi) and 4 x 6 size). **Deadline:** May 1.

2092 ■ Association Canadienne des Infirmieres et Infirmiers en Sciences Neurologiques (ACIISN)

PO Box 47143 Creekside
Calgary, AB, Canada T3P 0A0

Awards are arranged alphabetically below their administering organizations

URL: www.cann.ca

2093 ■ Lynn Ann Baldwin Scholarships *(Master's/ Scholarship)*

Purpose: To provide financial assistance to qualified nurses to pursue master's level education with neuroscience nursing as a focus. **Focus:** Neuroscience. **Qualif.:** Applicants must be registered nurses who have worked in neurosciences and are members of Canadian Association of Neuroscience Nursing in good standing for at least two years; must be in the master's program of study. **Criteria:** Selection will be based on the committee's criteria.

To Apply: Applicants must submit a completed application form; proof of acceptance into the master's program for which the scholarship is being sought, or proof of registration to write the certification exam; evidence of amount of registration fees; proof of current registration with provincial nursing association; one letter of reference from a person who has had the opportunity to assess their work. **Remarks:** Established in 2007.

2094 ■ Jessie Young Certification Bursary *(Other/ Award)*

Purpose: To provide financial support to qualified nurses to pursue additional training in neuroscience nursing. **Focus:** Neuroscience. **Qualif.:** Applicants must be registered nurses who have worked in neurosciences and are members of the Canadian Association of Neuroscience Nurses in good standing. The program or course of study for the Jessie Young Bursary must have a clear Neuroscience focus or component. **Criteria:** Selection will be based on the committee's criteria.

Funds Avail.: No specific amount. **To Apply:** Applicants must submit a completed application form; proof of acceptance into the educational program or course of study which the bursary is being sought, or proof of registration to write the certification exam; evidence of amount of registration fees; proof of current registration with provincial nursing association; one letter of reference from a person who has had the opportunity to assess their work. **Deadline:** May 31. **Remarks:** Established in 1983.

2095 ■ Neuroscience Certification Bursary Awards *(Other/Award)*

Purpose: To provide financial assistance to qualified nurses to pursue additional training in neuroscience nursing. **Focus:** Neuroscience. **Qualif.:** Applicants must be registered nurses who have worked in neurosciences and are members of the Canadian Association of Neuroscience Nurses in good standing. The program or course of study for the Jessie Young Bursary must have a clear Neuroscience focus or component. **Criteria:** Selection will be based on the committee's criteria.

Funds Avail.: No specific amount. **To Apply:** Applicants must submit a completed application form; proof of acceptance into the educational program or course of study which the bursary is being sought, or proof of registration to write the certification exam; evidence of amount of registration fees; proof of current registration with provincial nursing association; and one letter of reference from a person who has had the opportunity to assess the applicant's work.

2096 ■ Association Canadienne des Parajuristes
c/o Mrs. Cara Subirana
2606 Adhemar-Raynault Ave.

Montreal, QC, Canada J5W 0E1
URL: www.caplegal.ca

2097 ■ Lise M. Duchesneau Scholarship *(Undergraduate/Scholarship)*

Purpose: To encourage and support students who stood out during their paralegal studies. **Focus:** Paralegal studies. **Qualif.:** Applicants must be graduating students from participating institutions. **Criteria:** Selection shall be based on the criteria of the teachers of the Paralegal Program at participating institutions.

Funds Avail.: 500 Canadian Dollars. **Duration:** Annual. **To Apply:** Applicants may contact the Association for the application process and other information.

2098 ■ Association Canadienne des Professeurs de Langues Secondes (ACPLS)
2490 Don Reid Dr.
Ottawa, ON, Canada K1H 1E1
URL: www.caslt.org
Social Media: www.facebook.com/CASLT.ACPLS
www.instagram.com/caslt_acpls
twitter.com/CASLT_ACPLS

2099 ■ Robert Roy Award *(Advanced Professional/ Award, Recognition)*

Purpose: To recognize outstanding contributions by educators and researchers to the second language education field. **Focus:** Education, Bilingual and cross-cultural; Linguistics. **Qualif.:** Applicants must have been active members of the CASLT for at least two years; must have distinguished themselves in teaching, research, or writing to the improvement of second language teaching and learning in Canada. **Criteria:** Applicants will be selected based on submitted nomination.

Funds Avail.: No specific amount. **Duration:** Annual. **To Apply:** Applicants must submit the background information of the colleague they want to nominate to the contact provided; submit a brief text (no longer than 400 words). **Deadline:** March 31. **Remarks:** Established with a bequest from the late Robert Roy, a distinguished Canadian second language educator and founding president of CASLT. Established in 1983. **Contact:** Submit to: Email: admin@ caslt.org.

2100 ■ H.H. Stern Award *(Advanced Professional/ Award)*

Purpose: To support innovative classroom practices in second language learning. **Focus:** Education, Bilingual and cross-cultural. **Qualif.:** Applicants must be CASLT members. **Criteria:** Candidates will be chosen based on the submitted proposal which must: be innovative through the application of new techniques, strategies and/or approaches to learning; identify the impact of the project in the classroom, school or community; demonstrate the related improvement of student language learning; have the potential for duplication in other classrooms, schools, and communities; and include a brief plan for evaluating the innovation.

Funds Avail.: $300. **Duration:** Annual. **To Apply:** Applications should include a completed application form clearly identifying the teaching level and target second language, short Applicants biography and a current electronic photograph; completed project description answering the

Awards are arranged alphabetically below their administering organizations

five focus questions provided above; and, endorsement by a colleague or supervisor related to the impact of the project. **Deadline:** March 31. **Remarks:** The award was established in honor of Dr. H. H. Stern, was a highly respected educator and the visionary initiator of the National Core French Study. **Contact:** Send your applications to CASLT's National Office via email to admin@ caslt.org.

2101 ■ Association Canadienne de Radio-Oncologie (ACRO)

20 Crown Steel Dr., Unit 6
Markham, ON, Canada L3R 9X9
Ph: (905)415-3917
Fax: (905)415-0071
Free: 855-415-3917
E-mail: caro-acro@secretariatcentral.com
URL: www.caro-acro.ca
Social Media: www.facebook.com/caroacrocommunication
www.fr-ca.facebook.com/caroacrocommunication
twitter.com/caro_acro_ca

2102 ■ CARO-ELEKTA Research Fellowship Program *(Professional development/Fellowship)*

Purpose: To foster the development of highly qualified clinicians, researchers and future Radiation Oncology leaders. **Focus:** Oncology.

Funds Avail.: No specific amount. **Duration:** Annual; One year.

2103 ■ Association Canadienne de la Recherche Théâtrale (ACRT)

c/o Dr. Barry Freeman, Theatre and Performance Studies
University of Toronto Scarborough
1265 Military Trail
Toronto, ON, Canada M1C 1A4
E-mail: catr.membership@gmail.com
URL: catracrt.ca
Social Media: www.facebook.com/CATRACRT
twitter.com/catr_acrt

2104 ■ Heather McCallum Scholarship *(Professional development/Scholarship, Award)*

Purpose: To allow researchers to enrich their projects in ways otherwise unaffordable, through travel, access to archives or events, or the purchase of materials. **Focus:** Interdisciplinary studies. **Qualif.:** Applicants must be graduate students and emerging scholars (within five years upon completion of a PhD) in the fields of theatre, drama and performance studies, with a preference given to topics with a Canadian focus. **Criteria:** Recipients will be chosen based on the following criteria: 1) excellence of the project and its contribution to the discipline; 2) a project which can be completed in a reasonable time; 3) academic records and potential of the applicants; 4) if the request indicates a purchase of anything at an archival value that can be deposited subsequently in the public domain. Preference will be given to those applicants who have not fully established their careers and are not eligible for funds for the particular project applied for from federal, provincial and municipal arts councils or institutions.

Funds Avail.: $1,000. **Duration:** Annual. **To Apply:** Applicants must submit letter (1 to 2 pages) describing the

project for which assistance is required; his paper presents the results of the research and development of the project in the context of the project association; the letter should indicate which of the scholarships the candidate would like to be considered for; are welcome to apply for both scholarships and the same application for both; current curriculum vitae; One reference letter, sent directly to the Secretary of the Committee by the deadline; these papers should comment on the project and on the candidate's scholarly achievements, and research potential. **Deadline:** May 1. **Remarks:** Established in 1987. **Contact:** Heather Davis-Fisch; Email: heather.davisfisch@ufv.ca.

2105 ■ Robert G. Lawrence Prize *(Doctorate, Graduate/Prize, Award)*

Purpose: To recognize research of scholars who have presented an outstanding paper during the CATR annual conference. **Focus:** Theater arts. **Qualif.:** Applicants must be graduate students and scholars who recently completed their PhD (less than five years) and who make a presentation at the annual conference. **Criteria:** Recipients will be selected by the committee based on the depth and details of the submitted paper and quality of the presentation.

Funds Avail.: $200. **Duration:** Annual. **Deadline:** May 24. **Remarks:** Established in 1995.

2106 ■ Association Canadienne des Ressources Hydriques (ACRH)

176 Gloucester St., Ste. 320
Ottawa, ON, Canada K2P 0A6
Ph: (613)237-9363
Fax: (613)594-5190
E-mail: services@aic.ca
URL: www.cwra.org/en
Social Media: www.facebook.com/CWRA2015
www.linkedin.com/company/cwra
twitter.com/CWRA_Flows

2107 ■ Canadian Water Resources Association Harker/Cameron Women in Water Scholarship *(Graduate/Scholarship)*

Purpose: To raise awareness of the value of water; to promote responsible and effective water resource management in Canada. **Focus:** Water resources. **Qualif.:** Applicants must be women and either Canadian citizens or Permanent Residents attending a Canadian University or college; must be graduate students whose programs of study focus on applied, natural, or social science aspects of water resources. **Criteria:** Awarded to the highest ranked female applicant whom has not already been awarded a higher scholarship.

Funds Avail.: 2,000 Canadian dollars. **Duration:** Annual. **To Apply:** Application is available at cwra.org/en/scholarships/. **Deadline:** January 31. **Remarks:** Presented to recognize the ongoing legacy of Jennifer Harker and Valerie Cameron. **Contact:** Email: scholarships@cwra.org.

2108 ■ Dillon Consulting Scholarship *(Graduate/Scholarship)*

Purpose: To recognize graduate students whose programs of study focus on applied, natural, or social science aspects of water resources. **Focus:** Water resources. **Qualif.:** Applicant must be the second-highest ranked graduate student whose program of study focuses upon applied, natural or social science aspects of water resources; must

Awards are arranged alphabetically below their administering organizations

be a Canadian citizen or landed immigrant attending a Canadian University or college; must be enrolled in full-time graduate studies in any discipline. **Criteria:** Recipients are selected based on academic excellence and project relevance to water management and development.

Funds Avail.: 5,000 Canadian Dollars. **Duration:** Annual. **To Apply:** Applicants must provide a statement from the chairman/director of the department which verifies that the application is reflective of the project; a 500-word statement which outlines the applicant's research project and its relevance to sustainable water resources; official transcript of records; two references to be sent directly to the Scholarship Committee by the referees or appropriate official of the university or college; a statement from the program chairman or director endorsing the application from that program, including confirmation of the applicant's full-time registration; and completed application form. **Deadline:** January 31. **Contact:** Email: scholarships@cwra.org; URL: cwra.org/en/scholarships/.

2109 ■ Ken Thomson Scholarship (Graduate/Scholarship)

Purpose: To raise awareness of the value of water; to promote responsible and effective water resource management in Canada. **Focus:** Water resources. **Qualif.:** Applicant must be a graduate student whose program of study focuses upon applied, natural or social science aspects of water resources; must be a Canadian citizen or landed immigrant attending a Canadian University or college; must be enrolled in full-time graduate studies in any discipline. **Criteria:** Recipients are selected based on academic excellence and project relevance to water management and development.

Funds Avail.: 2,000 Canadian Dollars. **Duration:** Annual. **Number Awarded:** 1. **To Apply:** Applicants must provide a statement from the chairman/director of the department which verifies that the application is reflective of the project; a 500-word statement which outlines the applicant's research project and its relevance to sustainable water resources; official transcript of records; two references to be sent directly to the Scholarship Committee by the referees or appropriate official of the university or college; a statement from the program chairman or director endorsing the application from that program, including confirmation of the applicant's full-time registration; and completed application form. **Deadline:** January 31. **Remarks:** This scholarship is presented to honor the legacy of the late Ken Thomson. **Contact:** Email: scholarships@cwra.org; URL: cwra.org/en/scholarships/.

2110 ■ Association Canadienne de Science Politique (ACSP)
260 Dalhousie St., Ste. 204
Ottawa, ON, Canada K1N 7E4
URL: www.cpsa-acsp.ca

2111 ■ Donald Smiley Prize (Advanced Professional/Prize, Award, Recognition)

Purpose: To encourage the ideals of scholarship represented by the great Canadian scientists. **Focus:** Political science. **Qualif.:** Applicants books must be single-authored or multi-authored; textbooks, edited books, collections of essays, translations and memoirs are not eligible. **Criteria:** Preference will be given to the best book published in French or English in the field related to the study of government and politics in Canada.

Funds Avail.: No specific amount. **Duration:** Annual. **To Apply:** Applicants must submit a book published in France or Canada. **Deadline:** December 11. **Remarks:** The prize was established to honor the life and work of Donald V. Smiley (1921-1990). **Contact:** Nomination to be sent to CPSA Secretariat at cpsa-acsp@cpsa-acsp.ca. Also the packages or e-mails must be clearly marked Donald Smiley Prize Entry and sent to the following members: Donald Smiley Prize Jury (paper copy), Canadian Political Science Association, 260 Dalhousie St., Ste. 204, Ottawa, Ontario, K1N 7E4, Canada; Phone: 613-562-1202; Andre Blais (paper copy), Department de science politique University de Montreal, 3150 rue Jean-Brillant, local C-4012, Montreal, QC, H3C 3J7, Canada; Phone: 514-343-6111, Ext. 40564; Bruce Smardon (paper copy), Department of Political Science, McLaughlin College 228, York University, 4700 Keele St., Toronto, ON, M3J 1P3, Canada; Phone: 416-736-2100, ext. 30080; Jennifer Wallner (paper copy), School of Political Studies, Faculty of Social Sciences, University of Ottawa, 120 University, Ottawa, ON, K1N 6N5, Canada; Phone: 613-562-754.

2112 ■ Jill Vickers Prize (Other/Award)

Purpose: To support the authors of papers in the fields of Political Science and related studies. **Focus:** Political science. **Qualif.:** Applicants must be the authors of papers related to the topic of gender and politics presented in English or French. **Criteria:** Recipients will be selected based on the quality of their submissions.

Funds Avail.: No specific amount. **Duration:** Annual. **To Apply:** Applicants must submit their electronic copy of the paper to be e-mailed directly to each member of the Prize jury. **Deadline:** June 15. **Remarks:** The prize was established in honor of Professor Jill Vickers, an activist and a leader in Canadian feminist scholarship, and the author of numerous books and articles in the fields of feminist political science, epistemology and interdisciplinary methodology, feminist theory and movements for change. **Contact:** Emails must clearly be marked Jill Vickers Prize Entry and send to each of the following: Canadian Political Science Association, cpsa-acsp@cpsa-acsp.ca; Alana Cattapan (University of Saskatchewan), alana.cattapan@usask.ca; Maya Eichler (Mount Saint Vincent University), maya.eichler@msvu.ca; Shannon Sampert (University of Winnipeg), s.sampert@uwinnipeg.ca.

2113 ■ Association Canadienne de Securite Incendie
2800 - 14th Ave., Ste. 210
Markham, ON, Canada L3R 0E4
Ph: (416)492-9417
Fax: (416)491-1670
E-mail: cfsa@taylorenterprises.com
URL: canadianfiresafety.com

2114 ■ CFSA Randal Brown & Associates Awards (Undergraduate/Award)

Purpose: To inspire pursuits on fire safety awareness by providing financial support for students attending an approved Fire Safety Technology Course in a post-secondary school in Canada. **Focus:** Fires and fire prevention. **Qualif.:** Applicants must be 2nd year students in a three-year full time Fire Protection Technology course at a Canadian college or university; must have exceptional overall skills in Codes/Standard Technology; have an academic proficiency of 3.3/4.00; and must be students entering the second and

Awards are arranged alphabetically below their administering organizations

subsequent years of an approved course. **Criteria:** Selection will be based on the committees' criteria.

Funds Avail.: 1,000 Canadian Dollars. **Duration:** Annual. **Number Awarded:** 2. **To Apply:** Applicant must submit a written response of up to 300 words in paragraph form, providing a brief description of: the applicant's interest in fire safety and knowledge of CFSA and the donor organization; the course the applicant's are enrolled in and how they would like to utilize their education; any experience of the applicant in fire safety, either work related, through attendance at conferences and CFSA functions, etc.; and a statement of the applicant's extracurricular involvement. Must also submit a letter of reference from faculty about applicant. **Deadline:** March 18.

2115 ■ CFSA Aon Fire Protection Engineering Award *(Undergraduate/Scholarship)*

Purpose: To support and provide financial assistance to qualified persons who desire to make their careers in the field of fire safety. **Focus:** Fires and fire prevention. **Qualif.:** Applicants must be students enrolled in a Technician or Technology Program at a Canadian college or university with a primary focus on Sprinkler Technology - Code and Design and an academic proficiency or 3.3 GPA. **Criteria:** Selection will be based on the committees' criteria.

Funds Avail.: $1,000. **Duration:** Annual. **Number Awarded:** 1 to 2. **To Apply:** Applicants must submit a written response of up to 300 words in paragraph form, providing a brief description of: the applicants' interest in fire safety and knowledge of CFSA and the donor organization; the course of the applicants' they are enrolled in and how they would like to utilize their education; any experience of the applicants in the fire safety either work related, attendance of conferences, CFSA functions etc. and a statement of the applicants' extracurricular involvement and; letter of reference from faculty about individual. **Deadline:** March 18.

2116 ■ CFSA City of Markham, Buildings Standards Department Award *(Undergraduate/Scholarship)*

Purpose: To support and provide financial assistance to qualified persons who desire to make their careers in the field of fire safety. **Focus:** Fires and fire prevention. **Qualif.:** Applicants must be students enrolled in Fire Protection Engineering or related Fire and Life Safety Diploma Program and an academic proficiency = 3.3 GPA. **Criteria:** Selection will be based on the committee's criteria.

Funds Avail.: $500. **Duration:** Annual. **Number Awarded:** 1. **To Apply:** Applicants must submit a written response of up to 300 words in paragraph form, providing a brief description of: the applicant's interest in fire safety and knowledge of CFSA and the donor organization; the course of the applicant's they are enrolled in and how they would like to utilize their education; any experience of the applicants in the fire safety either work related, attendance of conferences, CFSA functions etc. and a statement of the applicant's extracurricular involvement and; letter of reference from faculty about individual. **Deadline:** March 20. **Contact:** Attention: Scholarship Form, Canadian Fire Safety Association, 2800 14th Ave., Ste. 210, Markham, ON, L3R 0E4.

2117 ■ CFSA Fire Safety Awards *(Postgraduate/ Scholarship)*

Purpose: To expand fire safety awareness by providing financial assistance for individuals attending an approved Fire Safety Technology Course in a post-secondary school

in Canada. **Focus:** Fires and fire prevention. **Qualif.:** Applicants must be enrolled in a Fire Protection Technology course at a Canadian college or university; must have excelled with outstanding leadership, motivation and technical skills and an overall academic proficiency = 3.3 GPA; must be students entering the second and subsequent years of an approved course. **Criteria:** Selection will be based on the committee's criteria.

Funds Avail.: 1,000 Canadian Dollars. **Duration:** Annual. **Number Awarded:** 1. **To Apply:** Applicant must submit a written response of up to 300 words in paragraph form, providing a brief description of: the applicant's interest in fire safety and knowledge of CFSA and the donor organization; the course the applicant's are enrolled in and how they would like to utilize their education; any experience of the applicant in fire safety, either work related, through attendance at conferences and CFSA functions, etc.; a statement of the applicant's extracurricular involvement and a letter of reference from faculty about applicant. **Deadline:** March 20. **Remarks:** The award was established in memory of Rich Morris. **Contact:** Canadian Fire Safety Association, 2800 14th Ave., Ste. 210, Markham, ON, L3R 0E4.

2118 ■ CFSA Founders Award for Leadership & Excellence *(Graduate, Postgraduate/Scholarship)*

Purpose: To engage in, assist and contribute to promote the development, diffusion and application of knowledge to the advancement of all forms of fire safety in Canada. **Focus:** Fires and fire prevention. **Qualif.:** Applicant must be enrolled 3-year full-time Fire Protection Technology or University degree. **Criteria:** Selection will be based on academic excellence, outstanding leadership, motivation and community service.

Funds Avail.: 1,000 Canadian Dollars. **Duration:** Annual. **To Apply:** Applicants must submit a written response of up to 300 words in paragraph form, providing a brief description of; your interest in fire safety and knowledge of CFSA and the donor organization; any experience you have in fire safety either work related, attendance at conferences, CFSA functions etc; and a statement on your extracurricular involvement (i.e. student clubs, mentoring, tutoring, athletics & community volunteering); letter of reference from faculty about individual. **Deadline:** March 20. **Contact:** Canadian Fire Safety Association, 2800 14th Ave., Ste. 210, Markham, ON, L3R 0E4.

2119 ■ CFSA Leber Rubes Inc. Awards *(Postgraduate/Award, Monetary)*

Purpose: To inspire pursuits on fire safety awareness by providing financial support for students attending an approved Fire Safety Technology Course in a post-secondary school in Canada. **Focus:** Fires and fire prevention. **Qualif.:** Applicants must be 2nd year students in a three-year full-time Fire Protection Technology course at a Canadian college or university; must have exceptional overall skills in Fire Alarm System Technology; have an academic proficiency of 3.3/4.00; and must be students entering the second and subsequent years of an approved course. **Criteria:** Applicants will be evaluated based on academic achievement and letter of application as required by the association.

Funds Avail.: 850 Canadian Dollars. **To Apply:** Applicants must submit their academic grades together with completed application form.

Awards are arranged alphabetically below their administering organizations

2120 ■ CFSA LRI Engineering Award
(Undergraduate/Scholarship)

Purpose: To support and provide financial assistance to qualified persons who desire to make their careers in the field of fire safety. **Focus:** Fires and fire prevention. **Qualif.:** Applicants must be students enrolled in a Fire Protection Technology Course at a Canadian college or university with exceptional overall skills in Fire Alarm System Technology and an academic proficiency = 3.3 GPA. **Criteria:** Selection will be based on the committee's criteria.

Funds Avail.: $1,000. **Duration:** Annual. **Number Awarded:** 2. **To Apply:** Applicants must submit a written response of up to 300 words in paragraph form, providing a brief description of: the applicant's interest in fire safety and knowledge of CFSA and the donor organization; the course of the applicant's they are enrolled in and how they would like to utilize their education; any experience of the applicants in the fire safety either work related, attendance of conferences, CFSA functions etc. and a statement of the applicant's extracurricular involvement and; letter of reference from faculty about individual. **Deadline:** March 20. **Contact:** Attention: Scholarship Form, Canadian Fire Safety Association, 2800 14th Ave., Ste. 210, Markham, ON, L3R 0E4.

2121 ■ CFSA Nadine International Awards
(Undergraduate/Scholarship)

Purpose: To expand pursuits on fire safety awareness by providing financial assistance for students enrolled in an approved Fire Safety Technology Course in a post-secondary school in Canada. **Focus:** Fires and fire prevention. **Qualif.:** Applicants must be 2nd year students in a three-year full-time Fire Protection Technology course at a Canadian college or university; must have exceptional overall skills in Fire Suppression Technology; must have an academic proficiency = 3.3 GPA; must be students entering the second and subsequent years of an approved course. **Criteria:** Selection will be based on the committee's criteria.

Funds Avail.: 1,000 Canadian Dollars. **Duration:** Annual. **Number Awarded:** 2. **To Apply:** Applicant must submit a written response of up to 300 words in paragraph form, providing a brief description of: the applicant's interest in fire safety and knowledge of CFSA and the donor organization; the course the applicant's are enrolled in and how they would like to utilize their education; any experience of the applicant in fire safety, either work related, through attendance at conferences and CFSA functions, etc.; and a statement of the applicant's extracurricular involvement. Must also submit a letter of reference from faculty about applicant. **Deadline:** March 20. **Contact:** Canadian Fire Safety Association, 2800 14th Ave., Ste. 210, Markham, ON, L3R 0E4.

2122 ■ CFSA Siemens Canada Award
(Undergraduate/Scholarship)

Purpose: To support and provide financial assistance to qualified persons who desire to make their careers in the field of fire safety. **Focus:** Fires and fire prevention. **Qualif.:** Applicants must be students enrolled in a Technician or Technology Program at a Canadian college or university with a primary focus on Fire Alarm - Code and Design and an academic proficiency = 3.3 GPA. **Criteria:** Selection will be based on the committee's criteria.

Funds Avail.: $1,000. **Duration:** Annual. **Number Awarded:** 1 to 2. **To Apply:** Applicants must submit a written response of up to 300 words in paragraph form, providing a brief description of: the applicant's interest in fire safety and knowledge of CFSA and the donor organization; the course of the applicant's they are enrolled in and how they would like to utilize their education; any experience of the applicants in the fire safety either work related, attendance of conferences, CFSA functions etc. and a statement of the applicant's extracurricular involvement and; letter of reference from faculty about individual. **Deadline:** March 20. **Contact:** Attention: Scholarship Form, Canadian Fire Safety Association, 2800 14th Ave., Ste. 210, Markham, ON, L3R 0E4.

2123 ■ CFSA Underwriters' Laboratories of Canada Awards *(Undergraduate/Scholarship)*

Purpose: To inspire pursuits on fire safety awareness by providing financial assistance for students attending an approved Fire Safety Technology Course in a post-secondary school in Canada. **Focus:** Fires and fire prevention. **Qualif.:** Applicants must be top 1st and 2nd year students in a three-year full-time Fire Protection Technology course at a Canadian college or university; must have exceptional academic skills in Codes and Standards; must have an overall proficiency = 3.3 GPA. **Criteria:** Selection will be based on the committee's criteria.

Funds Avail.: 500 Canadian Dollars. **Duration:** Annual. **Number Awarded:** 1. **To Apply:** Applicant must submit a written response of up to 300 words in paragraph form, providing a brief description of: the applicant's interest in fire safety and knowledge of CFSA and the donor organization; the course the applicant's are enrolled in and how they would like to utilize their education; any experience of the applicant in fire safety, either work related, through attendance at conferences and CFSA functions, etc.; and a statement of the applicant's extracurricular involvement. Must also submit a letter of reference from faculty about applicant. **Deadline:** March 20. **Contact:** Canadian Fire Safety Association, 2800 14th Ave., Ste. 210, Markham, ON, L3R 0E4.

2124 ■ Association Canadienne du Stationnement (ACS)
350-2255 St. Laurent Blvd.
Ottawa, ON, Canada K1G 4K3
Ph: (613)727-0700
Fax: (613)727-3183
E-mail: info@canadianparking.ca
URL: canadianparking.ca
Social Media: www.facebook.com/Canadian-Parking-Association-173429676044219
www.linkedin.com/groups/4401936/profile
twitter.com/canadianparking
www.youtube.com/channel/UCCA2ol1lij4X1rw0Da9Wr4A

2125 ■ The Canadian Parking Association Scholarship (CPA) *(Undergraduate/Scholarship)*

Purpose: To provide financial assistance to students in their pursuit of academic excellence and to encourage post-secondary study that enhances the parking industry in Canada. **Focus:** General studies/Field of study not specified. **Qualif.:** Applicants must be a registered CPA members, their spouses and dependents, and members' employees whose job function is 50% related to parking; must have a minimum cumulative average of 70% (or equivalent) in the last three semesters of available marks; non-academic courses such as career or personal development-related courses will not be considered; must be entering or already enrolled in full time studies in a first

Awards are arranged alphabetically below their administering organizations

bachelor degree program or first diploma program. **Criteria:** Selection will be evaluated based on academic performance; extracurricular activities or volunteer/community involvement, excluding those which are included in the high school curriculum; and quality of reference letters (one from a teacher and one from a person familiar with extracurricular activities or community involvement, excluding family members).

Funds Avail.: 2,000 Canadian Dollars each. **Duration:** Annual. **Number Awarded:** Up to 9. **To Apply:** Applicants must submit the completed application form along with official transcript of the last three semesters; description of extracurricular activities or volunteer/community involvement; two signed letters of reference; and the parental consent form. **Deadline:** April 30. **Remarks:** Established in 2004. **Contact:** Scholarship Partners Canada, Ref: The Canadian Parking Association Scholarship, 1710-350 Albert St., Ottawa, ON, K1R 1B1; Phone: 613-563-1236; Toll-free: 844-567-1237; Fax: 613-563-9745; Email: awards@univcan.ca.

2126 ■ Association Canadienne des Thérapeutes du Sport (CATA)

400 5th Ave. SW, Ste. 300
Calgary, AB, Canada T2P 0L6
URL: www.athletictherapy.org

2127 ■ Larry Ashley Memorial Scholarship Award
(Other/Award, Scholarship)

Purpose: To recognize an outstanding athletic trainer in professional hockey. **Focus:** Medicine, Sports; Physical therapy. **Qualif.:** Applicants must demonstrate a commitment to developing practical and academic athletic therapy skills in the field of professional hockey.

Duration: Annual.

2128 ■ Association Canadienne des Troubles d'apprentissage (ACTA)

2420 Bank St., Ste. 20
Ottawa, ON, Canada K1V 8S1
Ph: (613)238-5721
E-mail: info@ldac-acta.ca
URL: www.ldac-acta.ca
Social Media: www.facebook.com/ldacacta
twitter.com/ldacacta

2129 ■ Joanna Townsend Applied Arts Scholarship
(All/Scholarship)

Purpose: To encourage students with learning disabilities to pursue an education and/or career in any of the various applied arts programs. **Focus:** Art; Art, Caricatures and cartoons; Dance; Graphic art and design; Illustrators and illustrations; Music; Performing arts. **Qualif.:** Applicant must be a Canadian citizen or a permanent resident who has lived in Canada for at least two years; and is diagnosed with a documented learning disability which is the primary disability. **Funds Avail.:** $1,000. **Duration:** One academic year. **Number Awarded:** 1. **To Apply:** Applicant must submit a completed application form along with a letter from a doctor, teacher, principal or service provider confirming the diagnosis with information about the learning disability; two additional letters of reference (one of which is from a teacher outlining the student's talents in the art area); and

a 200-word outline on description of their learning disability, how creative art has been influenced by their learning disability, involvement as a volunteer and/or employment experience in the art world, and career goals as it pertains to an art program. **Deadline:** May 15. **Contact:** Learning Disabilities Association of Canada, The JoAnna Townsend Applied Arts Scholarship, 323 Chapel St., Ste. 200, Ottawa, Ontario, K1N 7Z2; Phone: 613-238-5721; Fax: 613-235-5391; Email: information@ldac-taac.ca.

2130 ■ Doreen Kronick Scholarships *(Graduate/Scholarship)*

Purpose: To encourage graduate students whose programs of study will lead them to a field that will assist persons with learning disabilities. **Focus:** General studies/Field of study not specified. **Qualif.:** Applicants must be graduate study in a university that will assist learning disabled students and must be a Canadian citizen or landed immigrant. **Criteria:** Selection is based on the submitted application materials.

Funds Avail.: $500. **Duration:** One academic year. **Deadline:** May 15.

2131 ■ Association of Certified Fraud Examiners (ACFE)

The Gregor Bldg.
716 West Ave.
Austin, TX 78701-2727
Ph: (512)478-9000
Fax: (512)478-9297
Free: 800-245-3321
E-mail: memberservices@acfe.com
URL: www.acfe.com
Social Media: www.facebook.com/
 AssociationofCertifiedFraudExaminers
www.instagram.com/theacfe
twitter.com/theacfe

2132 ■ Ritchie-Jennings Memorial Scholarship Program *(Undergraduate, Graduate/Scholarship)*

Purpose: To support the education of students who have an interest in pursuing a career in fraud examination. **Focus:** Accounting; Business administration; Criminal justice; Finance. **Qualif.:** Applicants must currently be enrolled full-time and similarly enrolled during the given academic year at an accredited, four-year college or university. They must have a declared major or minor in accounting, business administration, finance or criminal justice and demonstrate a desire to pursue a career in fraud examination or similar anti-fraud profession. **Criteria:** Scholarships are awarded on the basis of: completed application form; fraud-related interests, activities, goals, and desired career paths; overall academic achievement demonstrated by transcripts; and letters of recommendations.

Funds Avail.: $1,000-$10,000. **Duration:** Annual. **Number Awarded:** Varies. **To Apply:** Applicants must submit a completed Ritchie-Jennings Memorial Scholarship Application together with official transcript(s) showing all completed college or university courses; and three letters of recommendation (which must be submitted on behalf of the applicants). **Deadline:** February 1. **Remarks:** The scholarship was named after two members of the ACFE, Larry Jennings, CFE, CPA, 49; and Tracy Ritchie, CFE, CPA, 41; both of Houston, Texas. **Contact:** Scholarship Program Coordinator, Global Headquarters - The Gregor Bldg., 716

Awards are arranged alphabetically below their administering organizations

W Ave., Austin, TX 78701 USA; Phone: 800-245-3321 (U.S. & Canada only) & 512-478-9000; Fax: 512-276-8127; E-mail: scholarships@ACFE.com.

2133 ■ Association of Certified Fraud Examiners - Georgia Area Chapter (ACFE)

PO Box 79498
Atlanta, GA 30357-7498
URL: www.gacfe.org

2134 ■ GACFE Scholarship Program *(Graduate, Undergraduate/Scholarship)*

Purpose: To provide continuing education in fraud detection, deterrence and prevention. **Focus:** Accounting. **Qualif.:** Applicants must be currently employed full time in the fraud examination and investigative fields (private or government sectors). Candidates must have two (2) or more years of experience in fraud investigations and or examination, as well as either be a current or new member of our Chapter. **Criteria:** Scholarships will be awarded on the basis of (a) overall academic achievement demonstrated by notarized transcripts; (b) two letters of faculty recommendation, at least one of which must be from an instructor in the students' accounting, criminal justice, risk management or law degree program; and (c) an interest in fraud detection, deterrence, and prevention, demonstrated through courses of study or career goals.

Funds Avail.: $500 to $2,000. **Duration:** Annual. **To Apply:** Applicant must fill out the application via the link below and email your entire packet, application, and scanned documents (scanned documents are to comprise one PDF doc); attaching the following enclosures: Proof of GA State Residency; Proof that you are currently employed in the public or private sector for at least two years and that your job duties relate to fraud examination and investigations; Two letters of recommendation from your employer, one being from a supervisor or manager; Proof of military service; if applicable (DD-214 or other official document); Copy of College or University Degree Diploma; Resume or Curriculum Vitae; Complete a 300-500 word essay via the GACFE scholarship application explaining why you deserve the scholarship to enroll in the CFE Exam prep course and how becoming a CFE would enhance your career and your organization's fraud deterrence goals. **Deadline:** October 15. **Contact:** careeraffairs@gacfe.org.

2135 ■ Association of College and Research Libraries - Delaware Valley Chapter

c/o Eleanor Goldberg, Treasurer
901 Media Line Rd.
Media, PA 19063
Ph: (610)325-2742
URL: acrldvc.org

2136 ■ ACRL/DVC Student Stipend *(Undergraduate/Scholarship)*

Purpose: To foster and support future academic librarians. **Focus:** Library and archival sciences. **Qualif.:** Applicants must be library school students living or working in the chapter's service area (eastern Pennsylvania and Delaware) and who are currently enrolled in an ALA-accredited program, including distance education programs.

Funds Avail.: $1,000. **Duration:** Annual.

2137 ■ Association of College Unions International (ACUI)

1 City Centre Ste. 200
120 W 7th St.
Bloomington, IN 47404-3925
Ph: (812)245-2284
E-mail: acui@acui.org
URL: www.acui.org
Social Media: www.facebook.com/acui.org
instagram.com/acui_gallery
www.linkedin.com/company/acui
twitter.com/ACUITweets
youtube.com/user/ACUItv

2138 ■ ACUI Research and Education Grant *(Undergraduate, Graduate, Professional development/Grant)*

Purpose: To fund research-based projects that increase the knowledge base of the student activities, college unions, ACUI, and the profession in general. **Focus:** General studies/Field of study not specified. **Qualif.:** Applicants must be Individuals with ACUI membership. **Criteria:** Selection will be based on the credentials and research of the qualified applicants.

Funds Avail.: Up to $1,500. **Duration:** Annual. **To Apply:** Applicants must submit: Name, institution, and contact information for all contributors; One compiled packet--that is no more than 10 double-spaced typed page, and that contains no identifying information to ensure a blind review--which addresses: Research rationale and brief literature review, Description of the methodology, Justification as to how the project supports the published ACUI research agenda and makes a significant contribution to the profession, Detailed budget showing how the awarded funds will be utilized, Anticipated project timeline. An acknowledgement by the applicant that, if selected.

2139 ■ Gretchen Laatsch Scholarships *(Graduate/Scholarship)*

Purpose: To encourage graduate students to submit professional quality articles in the field of college unions and students activities. **Focus:** General studies/Field of study not specified. **Qualif.:** Applicants must be recognized by an institution as students in pursuit of graduate degrees in any academic area. **Criteria:** Consideration will be given to students either currently in the field of college union and student activities or those intending to enter the profession.

Funds Avail.: $1,000. **Duration:** Annual. **To Apply:** Applicants must submit an article containing a minimum of 500 words; must have a letter of recommendation from a college union or student activities professional. **Contact:** ACUI at jrudisil@acui.org.

2140 ■ Association for Compensatory Educators of Texas (ACET)

PO Box 220
Floresville, TX 78114
Ph: (832)644-5020
Fax: (832)644-8520
URL: acetx.org
Social Media: www.facebook.com/ACETXorg

2141 ■ Association for Compensatory Educators of Texas Paraprofessionals Scholarships *(Other/Scholarship)*

Purpose: To support paraprofessionals who wish to return to school to pursue a degree and teacher certification.

Awards are arranged alphabetically below their administering organizations

Focus: General studies/Field of study not specified. **Qualif.:** Applicants must be paraprofessionals who wish to return to school to pursue a degree and teacher certification; must be currently working with a school district in a compensatory program.

Funds Avail.: $1,000. **Duration:** Annual. **Number Awarded:** 4. **To Apply:** Applicants must submit proof of a high school diploma or GED and currently be working with a school district in a compensatory program. **Deadline:** February 14. **Contact:** Catherine Eubanks, Humble I.S.D. Scholarship Chairperson; 4810, Magnolia Cove Dr. Kingwood, Texas, 77345, Ph. No:281-641-8389; E-mail: catherine.eubanks@humbleisd.net.

2142 ■ Association for Compensatory Educators of Texas Students (Graduate/Scholarship)

Purpose: To provide remedial assistance and support for students who have failed STAAR or are at-risk of dropping out of school. include programs for migrant, Title I, Bilingual/ESL, and pregnant or parenting students. **Focus:** General studies/Field of study not specified. **Qualif.:** Applicants must be graduating high school students. student applicants must provide documented proof of participation in a compensatory education program sometime during their school career.

Funds Avail.: $1,000. **Duration:** Annual. **Number Awarded:** 20. **To Apply:** Applicants must submit a completed application form. **Deadline:** February 14. **Contact:** Catherine Eubanks, Humble I.S.D. Scholarship Chairperson; 4810, Magnolia Cove Dr. Kingwood, Texas, 77345, Ph. No:281-641-8389; E-mail: catherine.eubanks@humbleisd.net.

2143 ■ Association of Desk and Derrick Clubs (ADDC)

5014 Fm 1500
Paris, TX 75460
Ph: (405)543-3464
E-mail: ado@addc.org
URL: www.addc.org
Social Media: twitter.com/ADDCeducation

2144 ■ Frances C. Hidell Scholarship
(Undergraduate/Scholarship)

Purpose: To provide financial assistance for college students planning a career in the petroleum energy or allied industries. **Focus:** Energy-related areas; Engineering, Mechanical; Engineering, Nuclear; Engineering, Petroleum; Geology; Geophysics. **Qualif.:** Applicants must have completed at least two years or be currently enrolled in the second year of undergraduate study at an accredited college or university; be a U.S. or Canadian citizen; maintain a GPA of 3.2 or above on a 4.0 scale (United States) or 80% and above (Canada); be pursuing a career in the field of petroleum, energy or allied industry. **Criteria:** Preference will be given to applicants with financial need.

Duration: Annual. **To Apply:** Applicants must submit the online application form along with transcript and letters of recommendation. **Deadline:** April 1. **Remarks:** The scholarship was established in honor of Frances C. Hidell. **Contact:** Desk and Derrick Educational Trust, C/o Shirley Bridwell, Burk Royalty Co., Ltd., PO Box 94903, Wichita Falls, TX, 76308, USA.

2145 ■ Association universitaire canadienne d'études nordique (ACUNS)

32 Colonnade Rd., Ste. 200
Ottawa, ON, Canada K2E 7J6
Ph: (613)820-8300
E-mail: awards@acuns.ca
URL: acuns.ca
Social Media: www.facebook.com/ACUNSAUCEN
www.instagram.com/acunsaucen
twitter.com/ACUNSAUCEN

2146 ■ CNST Scholarship (Doctorate, Graduate/Scholarship)

Purpose: To support Canadian students enrolled in a doctoral program at a Canadian university. **Focus:** General studies/Field of study not specified. **Qualif.:** Applicants must be citizens or permanent residents of Canada presently enrolled in a doctoral program at a Canadian university. **Criteria:** Selection will based on academic record, the quality of the application, potential benefit of the research, originality, letters of reference and the applicants' interest in, and commitment to, the north and northern scholarship.

Funds Avail.: $10,000. **Duration:** Annual. **Number Awarded:** 1. **To Apply:** Applicants must submit a completed application form together with two letters of reference; all transcript of grades; and copy of the research license. **Deadline:** January 31. **Remarks:** Established in 1982. **Contact:** Canadian Northern Studies Trust Program, c/o Association of Canadian Universities for Northern Studies, 32 Colonnade Rd., Ste. 200, Ottawa, Ontario K2E 7J6.

2147 ■ POLAR Northern Resident Scholarship (Doctorate, Master's/Scholarship)

Purpose: To support Canadian students who are long-term residents of Nunavut, Northwest Territories, Yukon or the Provincial North. **Focus:** General studies/Field of study not specified. **Qualif.:** Applicants must be Canadian citizens or permanent residents of Canada identified as long-term residents of Nunavut, Northwest Territories, Yukon or the Provincial North and currently enrolled in a masters or doctoral level program at a Canadian university. **Criteria:** Selection will based on academic record, the quality of the application, potential benefit of the research, originality, letters of reference and the applicants' interest in, and commitment to, the north and northern scholarship.

Funds Avail.: $10,000. **Duration:** Annual. **Number Awarded:** 4. **To Apply:** Applicants must submit a completed application form together with two letters of reference; all official transcript of grades; and a copy of the research license. **Deadline:** January 31. **Contact:** Canadian Northern Studies Trust Program, c/o Association of Canadian Universities for Northern Studies, 32 Colonnade Rd., Ste. 200, Ottawa, Ontario K2E 7J6.

2148 ■ Polar Scholarship (Doctorate, Graduate/Scholarship)

Purpose: To support Canadian students enrolled in a doctoral program at a Canadian university. **Focus:** General studies/Field of study not specified. **Qualif.:** Applicants must be Canadian citizens or permanent residents of Canada presently enrolled in a doctoral program at a Canadian university. **Criteria:** Selection will based on academic record, the quality of the application, potential benefit of the research, originality, letters of reference and the applicants' interest in, and commitment to, the north and northern scholarship.

Awards are arranged alphabetically below their administering organizations

Funds Avail.: $10,000. **Duration:** Annual. **Number Awarded:** 1. **To Apply:** Applicants must submit a completed application form together with two letters of reference; all transcript of grades; and a copy of the research license. **Deadline:** January 31. **Contact:** Canadian Northern Studies Trust Program, c/o Association of Canadian Universities for Northern Studies, 32 Colonnade Rd., Ste. 200, Ottawa, Ontario K2E 7J6.

2149 ■ Association of Donor Recruitment Professionals (ADRP)

1717 K St., NW, Ste. 900
Washington, DC 20006
Ph: (202)393-5725
Fax: (202)393-1282
E-mail: info@adrp.org
URL: www.adrp.org
Social Media: www.facebook.com/adrp.org
www.instagram.com/adrpgiveblood

2150 ■ Association of Donor Recruitment Professionals Hughes Scholarships (Other/Scholarship)

Purpose: To help individuals enhance their professional development. **Focus:** General studies/Field of study not specified. **Qualif.:** Applicant must be a current member of ADRP; have been involved in donor recruitment/community relations for less than two years. ADRP board members are not eligible to apply. **Criteria:** Recipients will be selected based on submitted application.

Funds Avail.: No specific Amount. **Duration:** Annual. **To Apply:** Must submit a typewritten 500 words essay describing a creative recruitment idea that applicant has developed or wants to implement; and a typewritten letter of endorsement from an immediate supervisor. **Remarks:** Established in 1999.

2151 ■ Association of Donor Recruitment Professionals Presidential Scholarships (Other/Scholarship)

Purpose: To provide financial assistance to members who wish to acquire education and networking opportunities. **Focus:** General studies/Field of study not specified. **Qualif.:** Applicant must be a member of ADRP; have been a donor recruiter for two or more years. ADRP board members are not eligible to apply. **Criteria:** Judging will be based on submitted application.

Funds Avail.: No specific amount. **Duration:** Annual. **To Apply:** Applicant must submit a 500 word essay stating why this scholarship would enhance their professional development; a letter of endorsement from an immediate supervisor; and a letter of endorsement from a blood drive coordinator. Materials must be submitted in a typewritten format. **Remarks:** Established in 1995.

2152 ■ Nancy J. Chapman Scholarships (Other/Scholarship)

Purpose: To help individuals enhance their professional development. **Focus:** General studies/Field of study not specified. **Qualif.:** Applicant must be a current member of ADRP; must be in a management position in donor recruitment. ADRP board members are not eligible to apply. **Criteria:** Recipients will be selected based on submitted application.

Funds Avail.: No specific amount. **Duration:** Annual. **To Apply:** Applicant must submit a typewritten 500-word es-

say stating why this scholarship would enhance their professional development and typewritten letter of endorsement from applicant's immediate supervisor. **Deadline:** December 6. **Remarks:** Established in 1991. **Contact:** Shirley Nimsky, Executive Director, Association of Donor Recruitment Professionals (ADRP), at the above address.

2153 ■ Charles Drew Scholarships (Other/Scholarship)

Purpose: To help individuals enhance their professional development. **Focus:** General studies/Field of study not specified. **Qualif.:** Applicants must be current members of ADRP. Board members are not eligible to apply. **Criteria:** Recipients will be selected based on submitted applications.

Funds Avail.: No specific amount. **Duration:** Annual. **To Apply:** Applicants must submit a 500-word essay describing a successful technique they have developed which resulted in an increase in minority donations; and a typewritten letter of endorsement from their immediate supervisor. **Remarks:** Established in 2002.

2154 ■ Association for Educational Communications and Technology (AECT)

320 W 8th St., Ste. 101
Bloomington, IN 47404-3745
Ph: (812)335-7675
Free: 877-677-2328
E-mail: aect@aect.org
URL: www.aect.org
Social Media: www.facebook.com/AECT1
www.linkedin.com/company/aect1
twitter.com/aect

2155 ■ AECT Foundation Mentor Endowment Scholarship (Doctorate, Graduate/Scholarship)

Purpose: To support graduate study at the doctoral level in the field of educational communications and technology. **Focus:** Education. **Qualif.:** Applicants must be graduate students in educational communications and technology pursuing a graduate study during an academic year or a summer session in any accredited college/university in the United States or Canada; must be members of AECT and must be accepted in or enrolled in a doctoral level program. **Criteria:** Selection is based on: scholarship; leadership potential; experience in the field of educational communications and technology (such as employment, field experience, course work, assistantships, presentations, and publications); and letters of recommendation.

Funds Avail.: $2,000. **Duration:** One academic year or one summer session. **Number Awarded:** 1. **To Apply:** Applicants must submit a completed application form along with three letters of recommendation. **Deadline:** August 15. **Contact:** Denise Tolbert, ECT Foundation Awards Chair; E-mail: dtolbert@nu.edu.

2156 ■ AECT Legacy Graduate Scholarship (Master's, Graduate, Professional development/Scholarship)

Purpose: To improve the teaching/learning process in the library and classroom and to supplement the recipient's training by extending the use of educational communications and technology. **Focus:** Education, Bilingual and cross-cultural; Education, Elementary; Education, Special; Library and archival sciences. **Qualif.:** Applicants must be

Awards are arranged alphabetically below their administering organizations

practicing K-12 school teachers or school library/media specialists pursuing a Master's degree or professional certificate in the field; must be enrolled or planning to attend an accredited college. **Criteria:** Selection is based on: scholarship; experience in the field of educational media, information literacy, research skills and involvement in innovative programs; service and leadership in the profession; applicant's statement; and letters of recommendation.

Funds Avail.: $500. **Number Awarded:** 1. **To Apply:** Applicants must complete and submit the application form and three letters of recommendation. Application and references may be emailed by the deadline, but letters of recommendation must be received from the writer no later than a week after the deadline. **Deadline:** August 15. **Contact:** Denise Tolbert; Email: dtolbert@nu.edu.

2157 ■ AECT McJulien Graduate Student Scholarship Award *(Graduate, Doctorate/Scholarship)*

Purpose: To support a minority graduate student pursuing educational communications and technology. **Focus:** Education. **Qualif.:** Applicant must be enrolled in a degree-granting program in educational technology at the Master's, (MS), Specialist (EdS) or Doctoral (Ph.D./EdD) level; must provide evidence of an average of "B" or better; and must be a member of AECT. **Criteria:** Selection is based on AECT's Culture, Learning and Technology Division awards committee which manages the scholarship.

Funds Avail.: $500. **Duration:** Annual. **Number Awarded:** 1. **To Apply:** Applicants must submit a completed nomination form; Include any additional electronic materials as directed or contact AECT for alternative submission procedures; must be received from at least one and preferably three references. **Deadline:** July 15. **Contact:** Holly Marshburn, CLT Vice President Finance, and Awards; Email: marshburn.holly@gmail.com.

2158 ■ Association of Energy Engineers (AEE)

3168 Mercer University Dr.
Atlanta, GA 30341
Ph: (770)447-5083
URL: www.aeecenter.org
Social Media: www.facebook.com/
  AssociationofEnergyEngineers
twitter.com/AEE

2159 ■ Association of Energy Engineers Foundation Scholarship Program *(Graduate, Undergraduate/Scholarship)*

Purpose: To encourage qualified practitioners in energy engineering and energy management by awarding scholarships to further education in the field. **Focus:** Energy-related areas. **Qualif.:** Applicants must be undergraduates and graduate degree candidates who are enrolled in engineering or management programs at accredited colleges or universities; and must be nominated by AEE Chapters. **Criteria:** Applicants are evaluated based on the criteria designed by the Scholarship Selection Committee.

Funds Avail.: No specific amount. **Duration:** Annual. **To Apply:** Applicants should include student application; personal recommendation from a faculty member; student's current transcript; statement of 50-100 words from student "Why I wish to study energy engineering and/or energy management". **Deadline:** May 1. **Contact:** Email: privere@aeefoundation.org.

2160 ■ Association of Environmental & Engineering Geologists

3053 Nationwide Pky.
Brunswick, OH 44212
Ph: (330)578-4900
Fax: (216)803-9900
Free: 844-331-7867
E-mail: contact@aegweb.org
URL: www.aegweb.org
Social Media: www.facebook.com/AEGweb
www.instagram.com/aegweb
twitter.com/AEGweb

2161 ■ Marliave Scholarship Fund *(Graduate/Scholarship)*

Purpose: To support academic activity and reward outstanding scholarship in Engineering Geology and Geological Engineering. **Focus:** Engineering, Geological. **Qualif.:** Applicants must be senior or graduate students presently enrolled full-time; in a college or university degree program that is directly applicable to engineering geology or geological engineering, and student members of AEG.

Funds Avail.: $3,000. **Duration:** Annual. **Number Awarded:** 1. **To Apply:** Applications are accepted online only; with all supporting materials, including transcripts, letters of recommendation, etc. **Deadline:** February 1. **Remarks:** The scholarship fund honors the memory, work, and professional contributions of Elmer C. Marliave (1910-1967), a founding member of the Association of Environmental & Engineering Geologists, Burton H. Marliave (1917-1991), a president of the Association, and their father, Chester E. Marliave (1885-1958), a pioneer engineering geologist. Established in 1968.

2162 ■ Martin L. Stout Scholarships *(Graduate, Undergraduate/Scholarship)*

Purpose: To supports environmental and engineering geologic studies by students at the undergraduate and graduate levels. **Focus:** Engineering, Geological. **Qualif.:** Applicants must be maintain student membership in the Association. **Criteria:** Selection will be made based on demonstrated ability, scholarship, potential for contributions to the profession, character, and activities in student/professional societies.

Funds Avail.: $1,000 Undergraduate; $1,500 Masters; $2,000 Doctoral. **Duration:** Annual. **Number Awarded:** 2. **To Apply:** Applicants must submitted with the scholarship application.

2163 ■ Association of Environmental Engineering and Science Professors Foundation (AEESP)

1211 Connecticut Ave NW, Suite 650
Washington, DC 20036
Ph: (202)640-6591
E-mail: bschorr@aeesp.org
URL: www.aeespfoundation.org

2164 ■ CH2M/AEESP Outstanding Doctoral Dissertation Award *(Doctorate/Award)*

Purpose: To recognize outstanding doctoral dissertation that contributes to the advancement of environmental science and engineering. **Focus:** Engineering; Environmental science. **Qualif.:** Candidates must be doctoral students. **Criteria:** Submitted dissertations will be evaluated on the

Awards are arranged alphabetically below their administering organizations

basis of: the scientific and technical merit of the research; originality of the research; contribution to the advancement of environmental engineering and science; clarity of presentation.

Funds Avail.: $1,500 for the student; $500 for the faculty advisor; $750 for travel support. **Duration:** Annual. **Number Awarded:** 1. **To Apply:** Applications must submit nominations letter containing their email and mailing address and telephone numbers for the students and advisors; an indication as to when the dissertations was completed; a one paragraph description of the importance of the student's work and its relevance to environmental engineering and science; a concise statement defining the student's intellectual contribution to the work; the statement regarding intellectual contribution is necessary for all entries, but it is especially important if multiple authors contributed to the work under consideration; Dissertation abstract, written by the student, not to exceed 1, 000 words. **Contact:** John E. Tobiason, Ph.D., P.E., BCEE, Department of Civil and Environmental Engineering, University of Massachusetts at Amherst; Phone: 413-545-5397; Email: tobiason@umass.edu.

2165 ■ Paul V. Roberts/AEESP Outstanding Doctoral Dissertation Award *(Doctorate/Prize, Monetary)*

Purpose: To recognize a rigorous and innovative doctoral thesis that advances the science and practice of water quality engineering for either engineered or natural systems. **Focus:** Engineering. **Qualif.:** Applicants must be doctoral students. **Criteria:** Submitted dissertations will be evaluated on the basis of: the scientific and technical merit of the research; originality of the research; contribution to the advancement of environmental engineering and science; clarity of presentation.

Funds Avail.: $1,500 for the student; $500 for the faculty advisor; $750 travel allotment. **Duration:** Annual. **To Apply:** Faculty advisors are encouraged to nominate dissertations completed under their supervision but must limit themselves to a single entry; nominations letter must contain the following information: the email and mailing address and telephone numbers for the students and advisors; an indication as to when the dissertations was completed; a one paragraph description of the importance of the student's work and its relevance to environmental engineering and science; concise statement defining the students' intellectual contribution to the work; the statement regarding intellectual contribution is necessary for all entries, but it is especially important if multiple authors contributed to the work under consideration; Dissertation abstract, written by the student, not to exceed 1,000 words. **Contact:** John E. Tobiason, Ph.D., P.E., BCEE, Department of Civil and Environmental Engineering, University of Massachusetts at Amherst; Phone: 413-545-5397; Email: tobiason@umass.edu.

2166 ■ William Brewster Snow Award *(Master's/Award, Monetary)*

Purpose: To recognize an environmental engineering graduate student who has made significant accomplishments in an employment or academic engineering project. **Focus:** Engineering; Environmental science. **Qualif.:** Applicants for this award must be enrolled part- or full-time in an environmental engineering graduate program pursuing or have completed a master's degree in environmental engineering or a closely related program. **Criteria:** Eligible applicants will be judged based on academic program and performance (45%), professional or community service

(15%), engineering project accomplishment (25%), purpose and goals (10%), and any other evidence provided (5%).

Funds Avail.: $250. **Duration:** Annual. **Number Awarded:** 1. **To Apply:** Electronic nomination packages should include: nomination form; transcript verifying that the student has achieved a minimum GPA of 3.3 (on a 4.0 scale) in Master's degree program coursework; documented successful completion of the Fundamentals of Engineering Exam; two academic letters of recommendation; evidence of active participation in a student or regular chapter of an engineering related professional society; statement of purpose in pursuing a Master's degree and goals for first 5 years of professional practice; any other evidence of merit, papers, honors, recognition. **Contact:** John E. Tobiason, Ph.D., P.E., BCEE, Department of Civil and Environmental Engineering, University of Massachusetts at Amherst; Phone: 413-545-5397; Email: tobiason@umass.edu.

2167 ■ Virginia Tech Student Travel Award *(Undergraduate, Graduate/Award)*

Purpose: To support the recipients' travel to attend the biennial AEESP Education and Research Conference. **Focus:** Engineering; Environmental science. **Qualif.:** Applicants must be undergraduate or graduate students of Virginia Tech. **Criteria:** Selection will be based on merit.

Funds Avail.: Up to $750. **Duration:** Biennial; in odd-numbered years. **To Apply:** Interested applicants may contact the Foundation or Virginia Tech for the application process and other information. **Remarks:** Established in 2007.

2168 ■ W. Wesley Eckenfelder Graduate Research Award *(Master's, Doctorate/Award)*

Purpose: To recognize an environmental engineering or environmental science graduate student whose research contributes to the knowledge pool of wastewater management. **Focus:** Engineering; Environmental science. **Qualif.:** Applicants must either be a Master's or Ph.D. student. **Criteria:** Award selection will be based on academic program performance (45%), professional or community service (15%), project significance (25%), purpose and goals,(10%), and any other evidence provided (5%).

Funds Avail.: $1,500; $500 travel allotment. **Duration:** Annual. **To Apply:** Electronic nomination packages should include: letter from the faculty advisor of the applicant indicating completed substantive requirements for the graduate degree sought, and earned a minimum GPA of 3.3/4 in the current program; two academic letters of recommendation; 25-page copy of a publication (or manuscript submitted for publication) derived from the subject research for which the applicant is the first author; professional resume of the student applicant, listing all professional affiliations, publications, honors, service, and relevant experience; and applicant-prepared statement of professional purpose in pursuing the graduate degree and goals for the first five years of professional practice limited to 500 words. **Contact:** John E. Tobiason, Ph.D., P.E., BCEE, Department of Civil and Environmental Engineering, University of Massachusetts at Amherst; Phone: 413-545-5397; Email: tobiason@umass.edu.

2169 ■ Association des Etudiantes Infirmiereres du Canada
50 Driveway
Ottawa, ON, Canada K2P 1E2
Ph: (613)237-2133

Awards are arranged alphabetically below their administering organizations

Fax: (613)237-3520
Free: 800-361-8404
URL: cna-aiic.ca
Social Media: www.facebook.com/CNA.AIIC
twitter.com/canadanurses
www.youtube.com/user/CNAVideos

2170 ■ Saint Elizabeth Health Care Scholarship for Community Health Nursing (Undergraduate/Scholarship)

Purpose: To support a nursing student who shows a significant interest in community health nursing. **Focus:** Nursing. **Qualif.:** Applicants must be students registered in a nursing school with current membership in the CNSA; must be students in their graduating year at the time of application with an intention to enter the field of community health nursing; must have successfully completed the academic year in which the application is made; must be current members of the CNSA Board of Directors are not eligible for the award in their year of office. **Criteria:** Applicants are judged upon the committee's criteria.

Funds Avail.: $2,000. **Duration:** Annual. **Number Awarded:** 1. **To Apply:** Applicants must provide two letters of reference, one should be from a professor and or clinical instructor who can validate the information provided in the application; must submit an official transcript of his or her marks to date with the application. **Deadline:** December 12. **Contact:** Completed application form and supporting documents must be sent to: Canadian Nursing Students' Association, C/o Awards Committee, Fifth Ave. Crt., 99 Fifth Ave., Ste. 15, Ottawa, ON, K1S 5K4.

2171 ■ Association des Facultes de Pharmacie du Canada (AFPC)

PO Box 59025
Ottawa, ON, Canada K1G 5T7
URL: www.afpc.info

2172 ■ Merck Frosst Canada Inc. Postgraduate Pharmacy Fellowship Award (Postgraduate, Graduate, Doctorate/Fellowship)

Purpose: To support the best student entering or continuing postgraduate studies in pharmacy at a Canadian university. **Focus:** Pharmacology. **Qualif.:** Applicants are final year students in a pharmacy or pharmaceutical sciences degree program (B.Sc. or entry level Pharm D) or pharmacy practitioners (including hospital pharmacy residents) who are entering postgraduate (M.Sc. or Ph.D.) studies in a Faculty, College or School of Pharmacy in Canada. First-year graduate students who have a pharmacy or pharmaceutical sciences degree (but no advanced degrees) and are enrolled in an M.Sc. or Ph.D. program in a Faculty, College or School of Pharmacy in Canada are also eligible. This program is designed primarily for applicants who are Canadian citizens or permanent residents of Canada. Awards may also be made to exceptional candidates who are neither Canadian citizens nor permanent residents at the time of application. **Criteria:** Selection of applicants will be based on academic performance, publication activity, and fields of research in need of support.

Funds Avail.: 15,000 Canadian Dollars. **Duration:** Annual. **Number Awarded:** 1. **To Apply:** Applications can be submitted online and further details can be obtained from the website. **Deadline:** December 15.

2173 ■ Merck Frosst Canada Ltd. Postgraduate Pharmacy Fellowships (Graduate, Postgraduate, Doctorate/Fellowship)

Purpose: To encourage students to pursue their postgraduate studies in Pharmacy at a Canadian University. **Focus:** Pharmacy. **Qualif.:** Applicants must be in the final year in a pharmacy or pharmaceutical sciences degree program or pharmacy practitioners who are entering postgraduate studies in a faculty, College or School of Pharmacy in Canada or first year graduate students who have a pharmacy or pharmaceutical sciences degree and are enrolled in an M.Sc. or PhD degree in Faculty, College or School of Pharmacy in Canada; must be Canadian citizens or permanent residents of Canada. **Criteria:** Selection of applicants will be based on academic performance, publication activity, and fields of research in need of support.

Funds Avail.: $15,000. **Duration:** Annual. **Number Awarded:** 1. **To Apply:** Applicants must submit the complete application form together with their official transcript of academic records. **Deadline:** December 15.

2174 ■ Association for Federal Information Resources Management (AFFIRM)

2800 Eisenhower Ave., Ste. 210
Alexandria, VA 22314
Ph: (703)778-4646
Fax: (703)683-5480
E-mail: info@affirm.org
URL: www.affirm.org
Social Media: www.facebook.com/AFFIRM.org
twitter.com/affirmtweets

2175 ■ Affirm Scholarship Program (Undergraduate/Scholarship)

Purpose: To support greater educational opportunities for students attending DC, MD & VA area STEM educational institutions. **Focus:** Information science and technology; Technology. **Qualif.:** Applicants must be full-time students (12 credits or more); must be junior or above; must have a minimum of 3.0 cumulative GPA; and must be majoring in some aspect of information technology or related field; must be U.S. Citizen; must demonstrate financial need. **Criteria:** Preference will be given to U.S. Citizens.

Funds Avail.: No specific amount. **Contact:** Help Center; Phone: 800-888-8682.

2176 ■ Association of Field Ornithologists (AFO)

c/o CLA
700 Pleasant St., 3rd Fl.
New Bedford, MA 02740
URL: www.afonet.org
Social Media: www.facebook.com/field.ornithology
www.linkedin.com/groups/8228183/profile
twitter.com/FieldOrnith
www.youtube.com/channel/
  UCHJz4GgHIBYkbARZ1qMd2KQ

2177 ■ The E. Alexander Bergstrom Memorial Research Award (Undergraduate, Master's/Award)

Purpose: To promote field studies of birds by supporting a specific research or analysis project. **Focus:** Ornithology. **Qualif.:** Applicant and/or their primary research supervisor must be a member of the Association of Field Ornithologists prior to the application deadline.

Funds Avail.: $1,500 each(U.S./Canada/Latin America). **Duration:** Annual. **Number Awarded:** Varies. **To Apply:** Applicant must complete the application form along with A curriculum vitae no longer than two pages; A research proposal, not exceeding three single-spaced pages, which describes the purpose of the study and its scientific or conservation significance, contains a brief description of the methods to be used and the facilities available for the study, and includes any critical, supporting citations; budget itemizing total costs for the proposed project and indicating the amount you are requesting in the form of a Bergstrom award; A description of other funding for the study that has been awarded/received or has been (or will be) requested in the near future. **Deadline:** January 15 (U.S./Canada); July 15 (Latin America). **Remarks:** The award honors E. Alexander Bergstrom (1919-1973) memory and dedication to bird research. **Contact:** Valentina Ferretti, Chair of the Bergstrom Awards Committee; Email: ferrettivale@gmail.com.

2178 ■ Association of Flight Attendants - CWA (AFA-CWA)

501 3rd St. NW
Washington, DC 20001
Ph: (202)434-1300
Free: 800-424-2401
URL: www.afanet.org
Social Media: www.facebook.com/afacwa
twitter.com/afa_cwa
www.youtube.com/user/myafacwa

2179 ■ Association of Flight Attendants Scholarship Fund *(Undergraduate/Scholarship)*

Purpose: To further the education of promising young men and women who are dependents of AFA members in good standing who otherwise would not have the opportunity for higher education. **Focus:** Aviation. **Qualif.:** Applicants must be dependents of AFA members in good standing seeking to further education at an accredited college or university. **Criteria:** Selection will be based on students' rank on their high school class; SAT or ACT scores; demonstrated financial need.

Funds Avail.: Up to $5,000. **Duration:** Annual. **To Apply:** Applicants must submit a completed application form (available on the website), 300-word essay, three references; transcripts, grades and SAT scores. **Deadline:** April 30. **Contact:** Association of Flight Attendants Scholarship Fund, PO Box 56, Hartwood, VA, 22471-0056.

2180 ■ Association of Food and Drug Officials (AFDO)

155 W. Market St. 3rd Floor
York, PA 17401
Ph: (717)757-2888
Fax: (717)650-3650
E-mail: afdo@afdo.org
URL: www.afdo.org
Social Media: www.facebook.com/Association-of-Food-and -Drug-Officials-368401966580523
www.twitter.com/afdonews
www.linkedin.com/company/association-of-food-and-drug -officials
youtube.com/user/afdo1896

2181 ■ George M. Burditt Scholarships *(Undergraduate/Scholarship)*

Purpose: To provide financial assistance for students to further their education. **Focus:** General studies/Field of study not specified. **Qualif.:** Applicants should have demonstrated a desire to serve in a career of research, regulatory work, quality control, or teaching in an area related to some aspect of foods, drugs or consumer product safety; should have demonstrated leadership capabilities; and must have at least a 3.0 grade average during the first two years of undergraduate study on a scale of 4.0. **Criteria:** Selection will be based on the aforesaid qualifications.

Funds Avail.: $1,500. **Duration:** Annual. **To Apply:** Completing an application, an official and complete college transcript must be submitted along with letters of recommendation from two faculty members. recipients should have demonstrated a desire to serve in a career of research, regulatory work, quality control, or teaching in an area related to some aspect of foods, drugs or consumer product safety; should have demonstrated leadership capabilities. **Deadline:** March 1. **Remarks:** Established in 1981. **Contact:** Dr. Joanne M. Brown, Chair, AFDO Awards Committee; Association of Food and Drug Officials, 155 West Market Street, 3rd Floor, York, PA 17401; Phone: 717-757-2888; FAX: 717-650-3650; E-Mail: afdo@afdo.org.

2182 ■ Betsy B. Woodward Scholarships *(Undergraduate/Scholarship)*

Purpose: To provide financial assistance for students to further their education. **Focus:** General studies/Field of study not specified. **Qualif.:** Applicants should have demonstrated a desire to serve in a career of research, regulatory work, quality control, or teaching in an area related to some aspect of foods, drugs or consumer product safety; should have demonstrated leadership capabilities; and must have at least a 3.0 grade average during the first two years of undergraduate study on a scale of 4.0. **Criteria:** Selection will be based on the aforesaid qualifications.

Funds Avail.: $1,500. **Duration:** Annual. **To Apply:** Completing an application, an official and complete college transcript must be submitted along with letters of recommendation from two faculty members. recipients should have demonstrated a desire to serve in a career of research, regulatory work, quality control, or teaching in an area related to some aspect of foods, drugs or consumer product safety; should have demonstrated leadership capabilities. **Deadline:** March 1. **Remarks:** Established in 1981. **Contact:** Dr. Joanne M. Brown, Chair, AFDO Awards Committee; Association of Food and Drug Officials, 155 West Market Street, 3rd Floor, York, PA 17401; Phone: 717-757-2888; FAX: 717-650-3650; E-Mail: afdo@afdo.org.

2183 ■ Association of Former Intelligence Officers (AFIO)

7700 Leesburg Pke., Ste. 324
Falls Church, VA 22043
Ph: (703)790-0320
Fax: (703)991-1278
E-mail: afio@afio.com
URL: www.afio.com

2184 ■ David L. Boren Undergraduate Scholarships *(Graduate, Undergraduate/Scholarship)*

Purpose: To provide funding for graduate and undergraduate study in a number of targeted countries and fields.

Awards are arranged alphabetically below their administering organizations

Focus: General studies/Field of study not specified. **Qualif.:** Applicants must be students currently enrolled in undergraduate study or graduates planning to attend graduate school. Students applying for this scholarship must desire to study a foreign language in addition to any major-related study. **Criteria:** Preference is given to students interested in studying critical languages or fields related to security interest as well as to those interested in study in selected areas.

Funds Avail.: $10,000 per semester or $20,000 per academic year. **Duration:** Annual. **To Apply:** Applicants for Scholarships may choose to complete an official hardcopy application form, which can be obtained from the Loyola College faculty representative, or may submit their application forms online. In addition, 3 letters of recommendation and 4 semesters' worth of transcripts are required. For those who have attended college for less than 4 semesters, high school records indicating achievements during the last 2 years must be included. **Deadline:** February 10. **Remarks:** Established in 1991. **Contact:** Boren Scholarships and Fellowships, Institute of International Education, 1400 K St. NW, 7th Fl., Washington, DC, 20005-2403; Telephone: 800-618-NSEP (6737); E-mail: boren@iie.org.

2185 ■ CIA Undergraduate Scholarships
(Undergraduate/Scholarship)

Purpose: To assist minority, disabled and non-disabled deserving students to increase knowledge and academic skills. **Focus:** General studies/Field of study not specified. **Qualif.:** Applicants must be entering their junior or senior year of college by the fall of 2020; applications must be submitted no earlier than your senior undergraduate year of college and no later than your second year of graduate school studies. **Criteria:** Selection is based on merit, character, serious academic commitment, and relevance of your studies to national security interests and career ambitions.

Funds Avail.: $18,000. **Duration:** Annual. **To Apply:** Applicants must provide - via the online form is best - the following SEVEN items. Any of these formats for your attachments are acceptable: PDF, DOC, DOCX, TXT, JPG, TIF, RTF, ODT, including common archive files - e.g., ZIP, ZIPX. Do not send dat or htm files. Verify your attachments open to be certain they are valid files and not empty shortcut files. Keep attachments per email under 15 MB. Cover Letter: explaining your need for scholarship, your career goals, your views of U.S. world standing and role U.S. intelligence community should play; Resume; A copy of your academic transcript - need not be original or "official"; One recommendation (have person send to us by email; Recent photograph - can be sent as a high resolution digital image file via email attachment, or printed and mailed. Image should show full face sitting, standing, or portrait only. JPG, TIF, GIF, PDF, other major graphic image formats acceptable; Indicate for WHICH scholarships you wish to be considered. No need to send multiple copies of your materials, however, since we will consider you for all scholarships we offer; College or University you will be attending in 2020-2021 and your intended course of study (your declared 'major' or 'area of concentration'). **Deadline:** June 1. **Contact:** AFIO Scholarships, 7700 Leesburg Pike Ste 324, Falls Church, VA 22043; scholarships@afio.com.

2186 ■ Association of Government Accountants (AGA)
2208 Mt. Vernon Ave.
Alexandria, VA 22301-1314

Awards are arranged alphabetically below their administering organizations

Ph: (703)684-6931
Fax: (703)519-0039
Free: 800-242-7211
URL: www.agacgfm.org
Social Media: www.facebook.com/AGACGFM
twitter.com/agacgfm

2187 ■ Association of Government Accountants Graduate Scholarships for Community Service
(Graduate/Scholarship)

Purpose: To provide financial assistance to qualified professionals who exemplify and promote excellence in federal, state or local government financial management. **Focus:** Accounting; Economics; Public administration. **Qualif.:** Applicants must be AGA members or family members; must be applied toward full time graduate study in a financial management academic discipline, such as accounting, economics, finance, information systems/technology and public administration; must have a minimum GPA of 3.0 on a 4.0 scale; must be actively involved in community service projects. **Criteria:** Applicants will be selected based on community service involvement and accomplishments.

Funds Avail.: $1,500. **Duration:** Annual. **Number Awarded:** Up to 2. **To Apply:** Applicants must submit the application form along with a reference letter from an AGA member; a reference letter from a community service organization addressing the applicant's community service involvement, written on professional letterhead; must submit an essay (cannot be more than two double-spaced pages) on How applicant made a difference in the lives of others through community service, in Microsoft Word format with full name on the document and specify what scholarship applying for. **Deadline:** April 16. **Contact:** Email: awards@agacgfm.org.

2188 ■ Association of Government Accountants Graduate Scholarships for Full-time study
(Graduate/Scholarship)

Purpose: To provide financial assistance to qualified professionals who exemplify and promote excellence in federal state or local government financial management. **Focus:** Accounting; Economics; Public administration. **Qualif.:** Applicants must be AGA members or family members; must be applied toward full time graduate study in a financial management academic discipline, such as accounting, economics, finance, information systems/technology and public administration; must have a minimum GPA of 3.0 on a 4.0 scale; graduate-level full-time is defined as 9 credit hours per semester. **Criteria:** Applicants will be selected based on candidate's potential for making a meaningful contribution to public financial management.

Funds Avail.: $3,000. **Duration:** Annual. **Number Awarded:** Up to 2. **To Apply:** Applicants must submit the application form along with a reference letter from an AGA member; a reference letter from another professional such as a professor, guidance counselor, employer; a recommendation letter written on professional letterhead; must submit an essay (cannot be more than two double-spaced pages) on what should a government do to be more accountable and transparent to its constituents, in Microsoft Word format with full name on the document and specify what scholarship applying for. **Deadline:** April 16. **Contact:** Email: awards@agacgfm.org.

2189 ■ Association of Government Accountants Graduate Scholarships for Part-time study (Graduate/Scholarship)

Purpose: To provide financial assistance to qualified professionals who exemplify and promote excellence in federal, state or local government financial management. **Focus:** Accounting; Economics; Public administration. **Qualif.:** Applicants must be AGA members or family members; must be applied toward part time graduate study in a financial management academic disciplines, such as accounting, economics, finance, information systems/technology and public administration; must have a minimum GPA of 3.0 on a 4.0 scale. **Criteria:** Applicants will be selected based on candidate's potential for making a meaningful contribution to public financial management.

Funds Avail.: $1,500. **Duration:** Annual. **Number Awarded:** Up to 1. **To Apply:** Applicants must submit the application form along with a reference letter from an AGA member; a reference letter from another professional such as a professor, guidance counselor, employer; a recommendation letter written on professional letterhead; must submit an essay (cannot be more than two double-spaced pages) on what should a government do to be more accountable and transparent to its constituents, in Microsoft Word format with full name on the document and specify what scholarship applying for. **Deadline:** April 16. **Contact:** Email: awards@agacgfm.org.

2190 ■ Association of Independent Colleges and Universities of Pennsylvania (AICUP)

101 N Front St.
Harrisburg, PA 17101-1405
Ph: (717)232-8649
Fax: (717)233-8574
E-mail: info@aicup.org
URL: www.aicup.org
Social Media: www.facebook.com/AICUP1
www.instagram.com/paprivatecolleges
twitter.com/aicup

2191 ■ Air Products and Chemicals, Inc. Scholarships (Undergraduate/Scholarship)

Purpose: To promote the engineering and information technology profession to individuals from groups historically underrepresented in engineering. **Focus:** Computer and information sciences; Engineering, Chemical; Engineering, Mechanical. **Qualif.:** Applicants must be full-time undergraduate students majoring only in chemical engineering, Mechanical engineering, Information technology (computer science, management information systems, IST); be enrolled as a junior in fall; have a minimum GPA of 3.0; be women and/or members of the following minority groups: American Indian or Alaska Native, Asian, Black or African American, Hispanic or Latino, Native Hawaiian or other Pacific Islander. Student must be accepted at, or currently attending, one of 84 member colleges and universities of the Association of Independent Colleges and Universities of Pennsylvania. **Criteria:** Selection will be based on the committee's criteria.

Funds Avail.: $7,500. **Duration:** Annual. **Number Awarded:** 1. **To Apply:** Application forms are available at the Financial Aid office; applicant must submit complete application materials to Mary Maronic, Foundation Associate, Association of Independent Colleges and Universities of Pennsylvania. A complete application consists of a completed, signed application form, a copy of the student's transcript, a resume and an essay; the candidate may submit a letter of recommendation.

2192 ■ Michael Baker Corp. Scholarship for Diversity in Engineering (Undergraduate/Scholarship)

Purpose: To promote the engineering and information technology profession to individuals from groups historically underrepresented in engineering. **Focus:** Engineering, Architectural; Engineering, Civil. **Qualif.:** Applicants must be full-time undergraduate students majoring in Civil, Environmental, or Architectural Engineering only;. **Criteria:** Selection will be based on the committee's criteria.

To Apply: Applicants must visit the website for the online application process.

2193 ■ Commonwealth "Good Citizen" Scholarships (Undergraduate/Scholarship)

Purpose: To provide scholarship to the students who have shown an extraordinary commitment to community service and who have demonstrated creativity in shaping their volunteer activities. **Focus:** General studies/Field of study not specified. **Qualif.:** Applicant must be an AICUP student.

Funds Avail.: No specific amount.

2194 ■ The McLean Scholarship for Nursing and Physician Assistant Majors (Undergraduate/Scholarship)

Purpose: To help full-time undergraduate students who are enrolled in a Nursing or Physician's Assistant program. **Focus:** Nursing. **Qualif.:** Applicants must be graduated in an AICUP institution that offers a nursing or physician assistant program.

Funds Avail.: No specific amount.

2195 ■ Association for Institutional Research (AIR)

1983 Centre Pointe Blvd., No. 101
Tallahassee, FL 32308
Ph: (850)385-4155
Fax: (850)385-5180
E-mail: air@airweb.org
URL: www.airweb.org
Social Media: www.facebook.com/air4data
www.instagram.com/air4data
www.linkedin.com/company/association-for-institutional
 -research
twitter.com/air4data

2196 ■ AIR Dissertation Grants (Doctorate/Grant)

Purpose: To support dissertation research and writing under the guidance of a faculty dissertation advisor. **Focus:** General studies/Field of study not specified. **Qualif.:** Applicants must be support year-long research projects for recipients affiliated with a non-profit U.S. postsecondary institution or relevant higher education organization. **Criteria:** Selection will be based on the panel of national experts' criteria.

Funds Avail.: Up to $25,000.

2197 ■ AIR Research Grants (Professional development/Grant)

Purpose: To support research available to faculty, practitioners, and scholars. **Focus:** General studies/Field of study

Awards are arranged alphabetically below their administering organizations

not specified. **Qualif.:** Applicants must be support year-long research projects for recipients affiliated with a non-profit U.S. postsecondary institution or relevant higher education organization. **Criteria:** Selection will be based on the panel of national experts' criteria.

Funds Avail.: Up to $40,000. **Remarks:** Established in 1995.

2198 ■ Edward Delaney Scholarship *(Professional development/Scholarship)*

Purpose: To facilitate the professional growth and development of early career institutional research professionals by providing travel assistance to AIR's annual Forum. **Focus:** General studies/Field of study not specified. **Qualif.:** Applicants must meet the following criteria: hold current year AIR membership; be currently employed in the institutional research (IR) field; have worked for 3 years in a campus-based IR/assessment office for full- or part-time; and, have never attended the AIR Forum. **Criteria:** Selection will be based on the committee's criteria.

Funds Avail.: $1,000. **Duration:** Annual. **Number Awarded:** 1. **To Apply:** Applicants must submit an essay, maximum 750 words, addressing the impact of this award and briefly describe the applicant's current work in IR and provide a summary review of their current skills and accomplishments in the field; a letter of support from the applicant's supervisor approving their participation in the professional development activity must also be submitted. **Remarks:** Named in honor of Edward Delaney, who served as AIR President from 1992-93.

2199 ■ Julia M. Duckwall Scholarship *(Professional development/Scholarship)*

Purpose: To facilitate the professional growth and development of early career institutional research professionals. **Focus:** General studies/Field of study not specified. **Qualif.:** Applicants must meet the following criteria: hold current year AIR membership; be currently employed in the institutional research (IR) field; have worked for 3-5 years in a campus-based IR/assessment office for full- or part-time; have never attended the AIR Forum. **Criteria:** Selection will be based on the committee's criteria.

Funds Avail.: No specific amount. **Number Awarded:** 3. **To Apply:** Applicants must submit an essay, maximum 750 words, addressing the impact this award and briefly describe the applicant's current work in IR and provide a summary review of their current skills and accomplishments in the field; a letter of support from the applicant's supervisor approving their participation in the professional development activity must also be submitted. **Remarks:** Named in honor of the late Julia M. Duckwall, a prominent member of AIR.

2200 ■ Association of International Education Administrators (AIEA)
811 9th St., Ste. 215
Durham, NC 27705
Ph: (919)893-4980
E-mail: info@aieaworld.org
URL: www.aieaworld.org
Social Media: www.facebook.com/AIEAWorld
www.linkedin.com/groups/4060235
twitter.com/AIEAWorld

2201 ■ AIEA Presidential Fellows Program
(Undergraduate/Fellowship)

Purpose: To give mentorship to new Senior International Officers (SIO). **Focus:** Education. **Qualif.:** Applicants must

be current AIEA members. **Criteria:** Selections will be based on the following criteria: need and perceived benefit; promise/potential of applicants; quality of statement and application materials.

Funds Avail.: $2,000. **Duration:** Annual. **Number Awarded:** 1. **To Apply:** Applicants should submit their CV, Statement of Purpose, and a list of 3 references. **Deadline:** May 1.

2202 ■ Association of International Petroleum Negotiators (AIPN)
11767 Katy Freeway, Ste. 412
Houston, TX 77079
Ph: (281)558-7715
Fax: (281)558-7073
E-mail: membership@aipn.org
URL: www.aipn.org
Social Media: www.facebook.com/AIPN.HQ
www.linkedin.com/company/
   associationofinternationalpetroleumnegotiators
twitter.com/aipnHQ

2203 ■ AIPN Student Scholarships *(Graduate, Undergraduate/Scholarship)*

Purpose: To supports students in financial need who possess the potential to make a significant contribution to the field of international oil and gas negotiations. **Focus:** Energy-related areas. **Qualif.:** Applicants may be working towards an energy, commercial or law degree, but must be attending a university that supports the AIPN by having professor on AIPN's Education Advisory Board. **Criteria:** Selection will be based on the following criteria: potential to make a significant contribution to the field of international oil and gas negotiations; academic ability; leadership and negotiation ability; year in school; financial need.

Funds Avail.: A total of $5,000; $2,500 for each semester. **Duration:** Annual. **To Apply:** Applicants must submit two (2) letters of recommendation and the "AIPN Reference Letter" forms, from individuals who can speak from personal knowledge concerning the applicant's character, ability, and potential to make a significant contribution to the field of international oil and gas negotiations. **Deadline:** April 27. **Remarks:** Established in 2009. **Contact:** education@aipn.org.

2204 ■ Association for Iron and Steel Technology (AIST)
186 Thorn Hill Rd.
Warrendale, PA 15086-7528
Ph: (724)814-3000
Fax: (724)814-3001
E-mail: memberservices@aist.org
URL: www.aist.org/home.aspx
Social Media: www.facebook.com/
   AssociationForIronAndSteelTechnology
www.instagram.com/aist_aistech
www.linkedin.com/company/aist---association-for-iron-&
   -steel-technology
twitter.com/AISTech
www.youtube.com/user/AIST186

2205 ■ AIST Foundation Engineering Scholarship
(Undergraduate/Scholarship)

Purpose: To support talented and dedicated students to encourage them to pursue careers within iron-and steel-

Awards are arranged alphabetically below their administering organizations

related industries. **Focus:** Metallurgy. **Qualif.:** Applicant must be student in the following engineering/engineering technology majors may apply: metallurgy, materials science, electrical, mechanical, chemical, industrial, environmental, computer science and safety; will be accepted from university freshmen, sophomore and junior applicants and for seniors planning to attend graduate school; must be enrolled full-time in a four-year undergraduate or graduate program at an accredited North American university; should have a minimum cumulative GPA of 2.5 on a 4.0 scale; must be a citizen of a NAFTA country (USA, Canada, Mexico). **Criteria:** Recipients are selected based on the application materials submitted.

Funds Avail.: $3,000 for one year. **Duration:** Annual. **Number Awarded:** Up to 3. **To Apply:** Applicants must submit following documents along with application form: a resume; three letters of recommendation which address the applicant's character, academic status, leadership potential and career commitment from a college academic advisor, professor and previous employer; transcripts; and an essay (maximum of 2 pages) about the applicant's professional goals, interest in a career in the iron and steel industry, and how the applicant's skills could be applied to enhance the industry. **Deadline:** October 30. **Contact:** E-mail: lwharrey@aist.org.

2206 ■ AIST Globe-Trotters Member Chapter Scholarship *(Undergraduate, Postgraduate/Scholarship)*

Purpose: To support students in pursuing the career within the iron and steel industry. **Focus:** General studies/Field of study not specified. **Qualif.:** Applicant must be the child or grandchild of an active Globe-Trotters chapter member in good standing; must be currently enrolled in an accredited college or university; postgraduate students are also eligible. **Criteria:** Selection will be based on submitted essay, academic achievement, and extracurricular activities.

Funds Avail.: $3,000 each for one year. **Duration:** Annual. **Number Awarded:** Up to 5. **To Apply:** Applicants must submit following documents along with application form: a resume; an essay of 300 words or less, explaining the reason the candidate has selected a particular field of study; copy of SAT/ACT scores and a copy of current high school or college transcripts. **Deadline:** April 30. **Contact:** AIST Globe-Trotters Member Chapter Scholarship, c/o Noah Hanners, 439 S Sleight St., Naperville, IL 60540.

2207 ■ AIST Midwest Member Chapter – Tom Cipich Non-Engineering Scholarship *(Undergraduate/Scholarship)*

Purpose: To support students in pursuing the career within the iron and steel industry. **Focus:** General studies/Field of study not specified. **Qualif.:** Applicant must be a graduating senior in high school who will be enrolling in college for the fall semester, or a first, second or third year student currently enrolled in a full accredited college or university; must be a full time student in good academic standing; must be members of the AIST Midwest chapter or the dependent of a member of the AIST Midwest chapter. **Criteria:** Selection will be based on impartial Scholarship Committee criteria.

Funds Avail.: $3,000 for one year. **Duration:** Annual. **Number Awarded:** 1. **To Apply:** Applicants must submit a following documents along with application form: a resume; two recommendations or evaluations; a brief essay (1 to 2 pages) describing the Student's objectives for College and career; copy of SAT/ACT scores; copy of current high

school or college transcripts. **Deadline:** January 31. **Contact:** Rich Trzcinski, Chapter Scholarship Chair; Email: richtrzcinski@gmail.com.

2208 ■ AIST Midwest Member Chapter - Betty McKern Scholarship *(Undergraduate/Scholarship)*

Purpose: To support female students in pursuing careers within the iron and steel industry. **Focus:** Engineering; Metallurgy. **Qualif.:** Applicant must be a graduating female senior in high school who will be enrolling in college for the fall semester, or a first, second or third year student currently enrolled in a full accredited college or university; must be a full time student in good academic standing; must be a member of the AIST Midwest chapter or the dependent of a member of the AIST Midwest chapter. **Criteria:** Selection will be based on impartial Scholarship Committee criteria.

Funds Avail.: $3,000 for one year. **Duration:** Annual. **Number Awarded:** 1. **To Apply:** Applicants must submit following documents along with application form: a resume; two recommendations or evaluations; a brief essay (1 to 2 pages) describing the Student's objectives for College and career; copy of SAT/ACT scores; copy of current high school or college transcripts. **Deadline:** January 31. **Contact:** Rich Trzcinski, Chapter Scholarship Chair; Email: richtrzcinski@gmail.com.

2209 ■ AIST Midwest Member Chapter - Don Nelson Scholarship *(Undergraduate/Scholarship)*

Purpose: To provide educational assistance to engineering students. **Focus:** Engineering; Metallurgy. **Qualif.:** Applicant must be a graduating senior in high school who will be enrolling in college for the fall semester, or a first, second or third year student currently enrolled in a full accredited college or university; must be a full time student in good academic standing; must be members of the AIST Midwest chapter or the dependent of a member of the AIST Midwest chapter. **Criteria:** Selection will be based on impartial Scholarship Committee criteria.

Funds Avail.: $3,000 for one year. **Duration:** Annual. **Number Awarded:** 1. **To Apply:** Applicants must submit following documents along with application form: a resume; two recommendations or evaluations; a brief essay (1 to 2 pages) describing the Student's objectives for College and career; copy of SAT/ACT scores; copy of current high school or college transcripts. **Deadline:** January 31. **Contact:** Rich Trzcinski, Chapter Scholarship Chair; Email: richtrzcinski@gmail.com.

2210 ■ AIST Midwest Member Chapter - Engineering Scholarships *(Undergraduate/Scholarship)*

Purpose: To provide educational assistance for engineering students. **Focus:** Engineering; Metallurgy. **Qualif.:** Applicant must be a graduating senior in high school who will be enrolling in college for the fall semester, or a first, second or third year student currently enrolled in a full accredited college or university; must be a full time student in good academic standing; must be members of the AIST Midwest chapter or the dependent of a member of the AIST Midwest chapter. **Criteria:** Selection will be based on impartial Scholarship Committee criteria.

Funds Avail.: $3,000 for four years. **Duration:** Annual. **Number Awarded:** 2. **To Apply:** Applicants must submit following documents along with application form: a resume; two recommendations or evaluations; a brief essay (1 to 2 pages) describing the Student's objectives for College and career; copy of SAT/ACT scores; copy of current high

Awards are arranged alphabetically below their administering organizations

school or college transcripts. **Deadline:** January 31. **Contact:** Rich Trzcinski, Chapter Scholarship Chair; Email: richtrzcinski@gmail.com.

2211 ■ AIST Midwest Member Chapter - Jack Gill Scholarship *(Undergraduate/Scholarship)*

Purpose: To provide educational assistance for engineering students. **Focus:** Engineering; Metallurgy. **Qualif.:** Applicant must be a graduating senior in high school who will be enrolling in college for the fall semester, or a first, second or third year student currently enrolled in a full accredited college or university; must be a full time student in good academic standing; must be members of the AIST Midwest chapter or the dependent of a member of the AIST Midwest chapter. **Criteria:** Selection will be based on impartial Scholarship Committee criteria.

Funds Avail.: $3,000 for one year. **Duration:** Annual. **Number Awarded:** 1. **To Apply:** Applicants must submit following documents along with application form: a resume; two recommendations or evaluations; a brief essay (1 to 2 pages) describing the Student's objectives for College and career; copy of SAT/ACT scores; copy of current high school or college transcripts. **Deadline:** January 31. **Contact:** Rich Trzcinski, Chapter Scholarship Chair; Email: richtrzcinski@gmail.com.

2212 ■ AIST Midwest Member Chapter - Mel Nickel Scholarship *(Undergraduate/Scholarship)*

Purpose: To provide educational assistance for engineering students. **Focus:** Engineering; Metallurgy. **Qualif.:** Applicant must be a graduating senior in high school who will be enrolling in college for the fall semester, or a first, second or third year student currently enrolled in a full accredited college or university; must be a full time student in good academic standing; must be members of the AIST Midwest chapter or the dependent of a member of the AIST Midwest chapter. **Criteria:** Selection will be based on impartial Scholarship Committee criteria.

Funds Avail.: $3,000 for one year. **Duration:** Annual. **Number Awarded:** 1. **To Apply:** Applicants must submit following documents along with application form: a resume; two recommendations or evaluations; a brief essay (1 to 2 pages) describing the Student's objectives for College and career; copy of SAT/ACT scores; copy of current high school or college transcripts. **Deadline:** January 31. **Contact:** Rich Trzcinski, Chapter Scholarship Chair; Email: richtrzcinski@gmail.com.

2213 ■ AIST Midwest Member Chapter - Western States Award *(Undergraduate/Scholarship)*

Purpose: To provide educational assistance for engineering students. **Focus:** Engineering; Metallurgy. **Qualif.:** Applicant must be a graduating senior in high school who will be enrolling in college for the fall semester, or a first, second or third year student currently enrolled in a full accredited college or university; must be a full time student in good academic standing; must be members of the AIST Midwest chapter or the dependent of a member of the AIST Midwest chapter. **Criteria:** Selection will be based on impartial Scholarship Committee criteria.

Funds Avail.: $3,000 for one year. **Duration:** Annual. **Number Awarded:** 1. **To Apply:** Applicants must submit following documents along with application form: a resume; two recommendations or evaluations; a brief essay (1 to 2 pages) describing the Student's objectives for College and career; copy of SAT/ACT scores; copy of current high school or college transcripts. **Deadline:** January 31. **Con-**

tact: Rich Trzcinski, Chapter Scholarship Chair; Email: richtrzcinski@gmail.com.

2214 ■ AIST Northeastern Ohio Member Chapter - Alfred B. Glossbrenner Scholarship *(Undergraduate/Scholarship)*

Purpose: To provide educational assistance for students who wish to pursue their education and career in engineering and metallurgy. **Focus:** Engineering; Metallurgy. **Qualif.:** Applicant must be the children (natural, step-children, adopted or ward) of a United States citizen or landed immigrant who is a member, in good standing and paid for the past two years, of the Association for Iron & Steel Technology; must also be accepted in an eligible full-time course at an accredited North American university or college studying engineering or metallurgy; students must maintain and document a GPA of 2.5 or greater in a technical major to remain eligible for the scholarship program. **Criteria:** Selection will be based on academic achievements with respect to high school GPA, Rank in class ACT / SAT scores, extra-curricular activities, and planned major course of study; Consideration will also be given to a required essay from the student.

Funds Avail.: $2,000 per year for up to four years. **Duration:** Annual. **Number Awarded:** 1. **To Apply:** Applicants must submit following documents along with application form: a resume; a brief essay (1 to 2 pages); a recommendation or evaluation from a Counselor, Teacher or Professor; copy of SAT/ACT scores; copy of current high school or college transcripts. **Deadline:** April 30. **Remarks:** The award was established to honor the founding chairman of the AISE Canton District Section. Established in 1988. **Contact:** AIST Northeastern Ohio Member Chapter Scholarships, C/o Jaime Hart, AIST Northeastern Ohio Chapter Scholarship Chair, Rudolph Libbe Group, 5505 Valley Belt Rd., Ste. F, Independence, Ohio, 44131; Phone: 216-217-2499; E-mail: Jaime.Hart@RLGbuilds.com.

2215 ■ AIST Northeastern Ohio Member Chapter - John Klusch Scholarships *(Undergraduate/Scholarship)*

Purpose: To encourage talented and dedicated students to pursue careers within iron and steel-related industries. **Focus:** Engineering; Metallurgy. **Qualif.:** Applicant must be the children (natural, step-children, adopted or ward) of a United States citizen or landed immigrant who is a member, in good standing and paid for the past two years, of the Association for Iron & Steel Technology; must also be accepted in an eligible full-time course at an accredited North American university or college studying engineering or metallurgy; students must maintain and document a GPA of 2.5 or greater in a technical major to remain eligible for the scholarship program. **Criteria:** Selection will be based on academic achievements with respect to High School GPA, Rank in class ACT / SAT Scores, extra-curricular activities, and planned major course of study; Consideration will also be given to a required essay from the student.

Funds Avail.: $2,000 per year for up to four years. **Duration:** Annual. **Number Awarded:** 1. **To Apply:** Applicants must submit following documents along with application form: a resume; a brief essay (1 to 2 pages); a recommendation or evaluation from a Counselor, Teacher or Professor; copy of SAT/ACT scores; copy of current high school or college transcripts. **Deadline:** April 30. **Remarks:** The scholarship was given in honor of John Klusch for working more than 35 years as Canton Section Secretary. **Contact:** Jaime Hart, AIST Northeastern Ohio Chapter

Awards are arranged alphabetically below their administering organizations

Scholarship Chair, Rudolph Libbe Group, Address: 5505 Valley Belt Rd., Ste. F, Independence, Ohio 44131; Phone: 216.217.2499; E-mail: Jaime.Hart@RLGbuilds.com.

2216 ■ AIST Northern Pacific Member Chapter Scholarships *(Undergraduate/Scholarship)*

Purpose: To provide educational assistance for students who wish to pursue their education. **Focus:** General studies/Field of study not specified. **Qualif.:** Applicant must be child, grandchild (natural, adopted or ward), spouse, niece/nephew of an AIST Northern Pacific Chapter Member in good standing; members of the Material Advantage program are also eligible; must be enrolled full-time at an accredited North American college or university for the fall semester of the year of the application. **Criteria:** Selection will be based on committee's criteria.

Funds Avail.: $3,000 (1); $1,500 (up to 2). **Duration:** Annual. **Number Awarded:** Up to 3. **To Apply:** Applicants must submit following documents along with application form: a resume; current copy of high school or college transcripts; a recommendation letter from a non-family member familiar with the student's character, such as a Counselor, Teacher or Professor; a brief essay (no more than 1 page). **Deadline:** June 1. **Contact:** Adrian Deneys, Praxair Inc.; Phone: 925-866-6838.

2217 ■ AIST Ohio Valley Member Chapter Scholarships *(Undergraduate/Scholarship)*

Purpose: To support students who are pursuing an education in engineering, metallurgy, physical science, computer technology or an engineering technology field. **Focus:** Biology; Chemistry; Computer and information sciences; Engineering, Electrical; Engineering, Mechanical; Engineering, Metallurgical; Microbiology; Physical sciences. **Qualif.:** Applicant must be the child (including step-children, adopted children or wards) of a member in good standing of the Ohio Valley Chapter of the AIST or a Student member in good standing; must be accepted into, planning to attend, or currently enrolled in an eligible, full-time curriculum at an accredited university or college. **Criteria:** Selection will be based on overall academic performance especially achievement in mathematics and science; extra-curricular activities and the applicant's essay.

Funds Avail.: $1,000 per year. **Duration:** Annual. **Number Awarded:** 1-2. **To Apply:** Applicants must submit an online application form together with the following materials: a resume; a recommendation/evaluation from a counselor and teacher or professor; copy of SAT/ACT scores; copy of transcripts; an essay (maximum of 2 pages) with either one of the topics: purpose in going to college; beneficial experience during the last two summers; most significant experiences and effect on future plans; accomplishments providing the greatest satisfaction; reasons why they should be chosen as the recipient of the award. **Deadline:** March 31. **Contact:** Mark E. Shircliff; E-mail: mshircliff@amroll.com; Phone: 412-952-2007.

2218 ■ AIST Southeast Member Chapter - Gene Suave Scholarship *(Undergraduate/Scholarship)*

Purpose: To provide financial support for students who are pursuing a career in engineering, science, or other steel-related fields. **Focus:** Engineering; Metallurgy; Science. **Qualif.:** Applicant must be a Southeast Chapter student; planning to take up courses in engineering, sciences or other majors related to iron and steel production; must be accepted in an eligible full or part time course of study at an accredited university or college; students members of

the Material Advantage program are also eligible. **Criteria:** Recipient will be selected based on the SAT or ACT scores for college applicants and on the applicant's GPA from an accredited college or institution (non-first year student). Extra-curricular activities and student's written essays are also considered.

Funds Avail.: $3,500. **Duration:** Annual. **Number Awarded:** 1. **To Apply:** Applicants must submit following documents along with application form: a resume; a brief essay (250 words or less); recommendation or evaluation from a Counselor, Teacher or Professor; copy of SAT/ACT scores; copy of current high school or college transcripts. **Deadline:** April 30. **Contact:** Mike Kinney; Address: CMC Steel-South Carolina, 310 New State Rd., Cayce, SC, 28033; E-mail: mike.kinney@cmc.com.

2219 ■ AIST Southern California Member Chapter Scholarship *(Undergraduate/Scholarship)*

Purpose: To support students who are pursuing education. **Focus:** General studies/Field of study not specified. **Qualif.:** Applicant must be the child (including step-children, adopted children or wards), grandchild, niece, nephew or the spouse of an active AIST Southern California Chapter member in good standing; must be accepted into, planning to attend, or currently enrolled in an eligible, full-time curriculum at an accredited university or college. **Criteria:** Selection will be based on the committee's criteria.

Funds Avail.: $1,500 each. **Duration:** Annual. **Number Awarded:** Up to 2. **To Apply:** Applicants must submit following documents along with application form: a resume; three letters of recommendation which address the applicant's character, academic status, leadership potential and career commitment from a college academic advisor, professor and previous employer; transcripts; and an essay (not more than 250). **Deadline:** April 30. **Contact:** Moses Ramirez, California Steel Industries, 14000 San Bernardino Ave., Fontana, CA 92335; Phone: 909-350-5925; Email: moses.ramirez@californiasteel.com.

2220 ■ AIST Benjamin F. Fairless Scholarship *(Undergraduate/Scholarship)*

Purpose: To provide educational assistance for students who wish to pursue their education. **Focus:** Engineering; Metallurgy. **Qualif.:** Applicant must be student in the following engineering/engineering technology majors may apply: metallurgy, materials science, electrical, mechanical, chemical, industrial, environmental, computer science and safety; will be accepted from university freshmen, sophomore and junior applicants and for seniors planning to attend graduate school; must be enrolled full-time in a four-year undergraduate or graduate program at an accredited North American university; should have a minimum cumulative GPA of 2.5 on a 4.0 scale; must be a citizen of a NAFTA country (USA, Canada, Mexico). **Criteria:** Recipients are selected based on the application materials submitted.

Funds Avail.: $3,000. **Duration:** Annual. **Number Awarded:** 2. **To Apply:** Applicants must submit following documents along with application form: a resume; three letters of recommendation which address the applicant's character, academic status, leadership potential and career commitment from a college academic advisor, professor and previous employer; transcripts; and an essay (maximum of 2 pages) about the applicant's professional goals, interest in a career in the iron and steel industry, and how the applicant's skills could be applied to enhance the industry. **Deadline:** October 30. **Remarks:** The scholarship was established in memory of Benjamin F. Fairless,

Awards are arranged alphabetically below their administering organizations

longtime Chairman of the Board. Established in 1954. **Contact:** E-mail: lwharrey@aist.org.

2221 ■ AIST Willy Korf Memorial Fund (Undergraduate, Graduate/Scholarship)

Purpose: To support students in pursuing a career within iron- and steel-related industries. **Focus:** Engineering; Metallurgy. **Qualif.:** Applicant must be student in the following engineering/engineering technology majors may apply: metallurgy, materials science, electrical, mechanical, chemical, industrial, environmental, computer science and safety; will be accepted from university freshmen, sophomore and junior applicants and for seniors planning to attend graduate school; must be enrolled full-time in a four-year undergraduate or graduate program at an accredited North American university; should have a minimum cumulative GPA of 2.5 on a 4.0 scale; must be a citizen of a NAFTA country (USA, Canada, Mexico). **Criteria:** Recipients are selected based on the application materials submitted.

Funds Avail.: $3,000 for one year. **Duration:** Annual. **Number Awarded:** 4. **To Apply:** Applicants must submit following documents along with application form: a resume; three letters of recommendation which address the applicant's character, academic status, leadership potential and career commitment from a college academic advisor, professor and previous employer; transcripts; and an essay (maximum of 2 pages) about the applicant's professional goals, interest in a career in the iron and steel industry, and how the applicant's skills could be applied to enhance the industry. **Deadline:** October 30. **Remarks:** The scholarship was established to honor the late Willy Korf, founder of the Korf Group. **Contact:** E-mail: lwharrey@aist.org.

2222 ■ AIST Ronald E. Lincoln Memorial Scholarship (Undergraduate/Scholarship)

Purpose: To support students who are pursuing education in iron- and steel-related industries. **Focus:** Engineering; Metallurgy. **Qualif.:** Applicant must be student in the following engineering/engineering technology majors may apply: metallurgy, materials science, electrical, mechanical, chemical, industrial, environmental, computer science and safety; will be accepted from university freshmen, sophomore and junior applicants and for seniors planning to attend graduate school; must be enrolled full-time in a four-year undergraduate or graduate program at an accredited North American university; should have a minimum cumulative GPA of 2.5 on a 4.0 scale; must be a citizen of a NAFTA country (USA, Canada, Mexico). **Criteria:** Recipients are selected based on the application materials submitted. Awarded to individuals who best exemplify the qualities of leadership and innovation.

Funds Avail.: $3,000 for one year. **Duration:** Annual. **Number Awarded:** 3. **To Apply:** Applicants must submit following documents along with application form: a resume; three letters of recommendation which address the applicant's character, academic status, leadership potential and career commitment from a college academic advisor, professor and previous employer; transcripts; and an essay (maximum of 2 pages) about the applicant's professional goals, interest in a career in the iron and steel industry, and how the applicant's skills could be applied to enhance the industry. **Deadline:** October 30. **Remarks:** The scholarship was established in memory of Ronald Lincoln. **Contact:** E-mail: lwharrey@aist.org.

2223 ■ AIST Judith A. Quinn Detroit Member Chapter Scholarship (Undergraduate/Scholarship)

Purpose: To provide financial support for students who are pursuing a career in engineering. **Focus:** Engineering;

Metallurgy. **Qualif.:** Applicant must be a child or grandchild of an AIST Detroit Member Chapter member in good standing for two or more consecutive years; must be an undergraduate student enrolled full-time and majoring in the field of engineering, metallurgy or materials science program at an accredited North American University; should have a minimum cumulative GPA of 3.0 on a 4.0 scale, with a demonstrated interest in a career, or plans to pursue a career, in the iron and steel industry. **Criteria:** Selection will be based on the committee's criteria.

Funds Avail.: Two at $2,500 and two at $5,000. **Duration:** Annual. **Number Awarded:** 4. **To Apply:** Applicants must submit an application form available along with a resume; an essay, not to exceed two pages in length; three letters of recommendation which address character, academic status, leadership potential and career commitment; copy of SAT/ACT scores; copy of current high school or college transcripts. **Deadline:** April 30. **Remarks:** Named in honor and memory of Judith A. Quinn, who was a pioneer for women in the Detroit area steel industry. She passionately served as Detroit Member Chapter Secretary-Treasurer for the AISE Detroit District Section in both 1985 and 1998 and served as the AIST Detroit Member Chapter secretary 2004-2013.

2224 ■ AIST David H. Samson Canadian Scholarship (Undergraduate/Scholarship)

Purpose: To provide financial support for students who are pursuing a career in engineering. **Focus:** Engineering. **Qualif.:** Applicant must be student in the following engineering/engineering technology majors may apply: metallurgy, materials science, electrical, mechanical, chemical, industrial, environmental, computer science and safety; will be accepted from university freshmen, sophomore and junior applicants and for seniors planning to attend graduate school; must be enrolled full-time in a four-year undergraduate or graduate program at an accredited North American university; should have a minimum cumulative GPA of 2.5 on a 4.0 scale; must be a citizen of a NAFTA country (USA, Canada, Mexico). **Criteria:** Recipients are selected based on the application materials submitted. Selected by the AIST Northern Member Chapter.

Funds Avail.: $3,000 for one year. **Duration:** Annual. **Number Awarded:** 1. **To Apply:** Applicants must submit following documents along with application form: a resume; three letters of recommendation which address the applicant's character, academic status, leadership potential and career commitment from a college academic advisor, professor and previous employer; transcripts; and an essay (maximum of 2 pages) about the applicant's professional goals, interest in a career in the iron and steel industry, and how the applicant's skills could be applied to enhance the industry. **Deadline:** October 30. **Remarks:** The scholarship was established to honor David H. Samson, past vice president engineering at Dofasco and past president of the AISE. **Contact:** E-mail: lwharrey@aist.org.

2225 ■ AIST William E. Schwabe Memorial Scholarship (Undergraduate/Scholarship)

Purpose: To support students who are pursuing education in iron- and steel-related industries. **Focus:** Engineering; Metallurgy. **Qualif.:** Applicant must be student in the following engineering/engineering technology majors may apply: metallurgy, materials science, electrical, mechanical, chemical, industrial, environmental, computer science and safety; will be accepted from university freshmen, sophomore and junior applicants and for seniors planning to attend graduate school; must be enrolled full-time in a four-year

Awards are arranged alphabetically below their administering organizations

undergraduate or graduate program at an accredited North American university; should have a minimum cumulative GPA of 2.5 on a 4.0 scale; must be a citizen of a NAFTA country (USA, Canada, Mexico). **Criteria:** Recipients are selected based on the application materials submitted.

Funds Avail.: $3,000 for one year. **Duration:** Annual. **Number Awarded:** 1. **To Apply:** Applicants must submit following documents along with application form: a resume; three letters of recommendation which address the applicant's character, academic status, leadership potential and career commitment from a college academic advisor, professor and previous employer; transcripts; and an essay (maximum of 2 pages) about the applicant's professional goals, interest in a career in the iron and steel industry, and how the applicant's skills could be applied to enhance the industry. **Deadline:** October 30. **Remarks:** The scholarship was established in memory of William E. Schwabe. Established in 2005. **Contact:** E-mail: lwharrey@aist.org.

2226 ■ Association of Jewish Libraries
PO Box 1118
Teaneck, NJ 07666
Ph: (201)371-3255
E-mail: info@jewishlibraries.org
URL: jewishlibraries.org
Social Media: www.facebook.com/jewishlibraries
www.pinterest.com/AssociationofJewishLibraries
twitter.com/JewishLibraries

2227 ■ AJL Conference Stipends (Graduate/Award)

Purpose: To assist members with the expense of attending AJL's annual conference. **Focus:** General studies/Field of study not specified.

Funds Avail.: Up to $ 20,000. **Deadline:** March 29.

2228 ■ AJL Scholarship Fund (Graduate/Scholarship)

Purpose: To encourage students to train for, and enter, the field of Judaica librarianship. **Focus:** Library and archival sciences. **Qualif.:** Applicants must be attending or planning to attend an ALA-accredited graduate library school or equivalent; should have an interest in, and demonstrate a potential for, pursuing a career in Judaica librarianship; ALA accredited library school in the United States or Canada; accredited library school in either the United Kingdom, Australia, or New Zealand; graduate library school programs at the David Yellin College and at Bar Ilan University. **Criteria:** Selection is based on the application.

Funds Avail.: $1,000. **To Apply:** Applicants must complete and submit the application form available online; a documentation of acceptance or enrollment; documentation of Jewish studies completed at an academic or less formal level or of experience working in Judaic libraries; and Personal statement as a Word or rtf format. **Deadline:** April 15. **Contact:** Sarah Barnard, 5646 Hunters Lake, Cincinnati, OH 45249,Phone: 513-405-2057.

2229 ■ AJL Scholarship for Library School Students (Graduate/Scholarship)

Purpose: To encourage students to train for and enter the field of Judaica librarianship. Candidates must be attending or planning to attend a graduate school of library and information science. **Focus:** Jewish studies; Library and archival sciences. **Qualif.:** Applicant must be a student enrolled or accepted in a graduate school of library and information science and a conference subvention award for attending the Association of Jewish Libraries' annual conference. **Criteria:** Selection will be merit-based rather than need-based.

Funds Avail.: $1,000. **Duration:** Annual. **Number Awarded:** up to two. **To Apply:** Applicants must submit proof of acceptance for the next academic year or proof of current enrollment; Transcripts and/or letters on official letterhead should be submitted. **Deadline:** April 15. **Remarks:** Established in 1989. **Contact:** E-mail:scholarship@jewishlibraries.org.

2230 ■ Association of Latino Professionals For America (ALPFA)
801 S Grand Ave., Ste. 400
Los Angeles, CA 90017
Free: 855-266-7883
E-mail: info@national.alpfa.org
URL: www.alpfa.org
Social Media: www.facebook.com/ALPFA
instagram.com/ALPFA
www.linkedin.com/company/alpfa
twitter.com/ALPFA
www.youtube.com/alpfa

2231 ■ ALPFA Scholarship (Graduate, Undergraduate, Master's/Scholarship)

Purpose: To financially support Hispanic students pursuing studies in accounting, finance, IT or related field. **Focus:** Accounting; Business; Finance. **Qualif.:** Applicant must be Hispanic origin or DACA status; Must be a degree seeking student enrolled at a two-year college, four-year university, or graduate program. Majors: Business, Accounting, Finance or STEM. Classifications: rising Sophomores, rising Juniors, rising Seniors, Graduate students; Cumulative Grade Point Average: 3.0 or higher (out of 4.0). **Criteria:** Essays will be judged on grammar, spelling, punctuation, and clarity of composition. Consideration is also given for financial need, first- or second-generation student.

Duration: Annual. **Deadline:** May 15.

2232 ■ Association of Leadership Educators, Inc. (ALE)
c/o Jill Arensdorf, Chair and Associate Professor, Department of Leadership Studies
Fort Hays State University, 600 Park St., Rarick Hall 235
Hays, KS 67601
Ph: (785)628-4303
URL: www.leadershipeducators.org
Social Media: www.facebook.com/American.Counseling
.Association
www.linkedin.com/groups/4090399/profile
twitter.com/ALE_Leadership

2233 ■ Founding Mothers Student Scholarships - Graduate (Graduate/Scholarship)

Purpose: To provide funds for outstanding students who show promise in the field and present at the conference. **Focus:** Leadership, Institutional and community. **Qualif.:** Applicants must be graduate students in good academic standing and may not have already received the award; recipients for this award are required to present or co-present at the ALE Conference. **Criteria:** Selection will be based on the committee's criteria.

Awards are arranged alphabetically below their administering organizations

Funds Avail.: No specific amount. **Duration:** Annual. **Number Awarded:** Up to 4. **To Apply:** Applicants must submit the following requirements in PDF format and upload to the application website: personal info - name, address, phone number, e-mail, college/university, major, year in school and expected graduation date; current GPA; career goal(s) in 50 words or less; titles and categories of proposals submitted to the ALE conference and; name of person who will provide a letter of reference - name, position, address and e-mail; applicants must also submit a response to the following questions (maximum of 50 words per question): What are your particular interests/concerns/goals in studying leadership?; How would you benefit from attending the ALE conference?; How would you share what you learned at the ALE with others?; What experiences drew you to leadership education? and; What role do you see leadership education playing in our world's future?. **Deadline:** April 2. **Contact:** Gina Matkin ALE Director of Awards & Recognition Associate Professor Agricultural Leadership, Education, & Communication University of Nebraska – Lincoln 402. 472. 4454 gmatkin1@unl.edu.

2234 ■ Association for Library Collections & Technical Services (ALCTS)

50 E Huron St.
Chicago, IL 60611-2795
Ph: (312)280-5037
Fax: (312)280-5033
Free: 800-545-2433
E-mail: alcts@ala.org
URL: www.ala.org
Social Media: twitter.com/alcts

2235 ■ First Step Award - Wiley Professional Development Grant *(Professional development/Grant, Award)*

Purpose: To provide librarians new to the continuing resources field with the opportunity to broaden their perspective and to encourage professional development in ALA Conference and participation in Continuing Resources Section activities. **Focus:** Library and archival sciences. **Qualif.:** Applicant must be a ALCTS member with five or fewer years of professional experience in the continuing resources field. **Criteria:** Selection will be based on commitment to professional development in the serials field as evidenced by participation in continuing education activities, workshops, previous participation in professional activities. Commitment to and interest in continuing-resources related work; personal and professional development; financial need.

Funds Avail.: $1,500. **Duration:** Annual. **Number Awarded:** 1. **To Apply:** Applicant must include current resume or vita; candidate's written justification; two letters of reference. **Deadline:** December 1. **Contact:** Shirleanne Ackerman Gahan, Chair; Email: gahan@up.edu.

2236 ■ Association for Library Service to Children (ALSC)

225 N Michigan Ave., Ste. 1300
Chicago, IL 60601
Free: 800-545-2433
E-mail: alsc@ala.org
URL: www.ala.org
Social Media: twitter.com/wearealsc

2237 ■ ALSC Bound to Stay Bound Books Scholarship *(Graduate/Scholarship)*

Purpose: To provide financial assistance for individuals pursuing a master's or advanced degree in children's librarianship. **Focus:** Library and archival sciences. **Qualif.:** Applicants must be U.S. or Canadian citizens pursuing a master or advanced degree in children's librarianship; should be men and women who intend to pursue an MLS degree and who plan to work in children's librarianship; should be serving children up to and including the age of 14 in any type of library. **Criteria:** Selection will be selected on the basis of academic excellence, leadership qualities and the desire to work with children in any type of library.

Funds Avail.: $8,000. **Duration:** Annual. **Number Awarded:** 4. **To Apply:** Applicants must submit a completed application form; a personal statement describing career interests and goals; a commitment to library service to children; and three references (must be completed online); academic transcripts. **Deadline:** March 1. **Contact:** Elizabeth Serrano (Staff Liaison, October 21, 2019, to June 30, 2022) -; eserrano@ala.org; Work Phone: (312) 280-2164; American Library Association; 225 N Michigan Ave Ste 1300; Chicago, IL 60601-7616.

2238 ■ ALSC Summer Reading Program Grant *(Other/Grant)*

Purpose: To recognize outstanding summer reading programs by providing financial assistance, while recognizing ALSC members for outstanding program development. **Focus:** Library and archival sciences. **Qualif.:** Applicants must be personal members of ALSC as well as ALA. **Criteria:** Application will be judged on the following: plan and outline submitted for a theme-based summer reading program in a public library; committee encourages innovative proposals involving children with physical or mental disabilities.

Funds Avail.: $3,000. **Duration:** Annual. **Number Awarded:** 1. **To Apply:** Applications can be submitted online. **Deadline:** December 1. **Contact:** Allison Cline, Deputy Executive Director; Email:acline@ala.org.

2239 ■ Louise Seaman Bechtel Fellowship *(Professional development/Fellowship)*

Purpose: To provide librarians the opportunity to read and study at the Baldwin Library of the George Smathers Libraries, University of Florida. **Focus:** Library and archival sciences. **Qualif.:** Applicants must have personal membership in the Association for Library Service to Children (ALSC); have at least 8 years professional experience in direct service to children; have a graduate degree from an ALA-accredited program; and, demonstrate ongoing commitment to motivating children to read; must be prepared to spend a minimum of four weeks in Gainesville; the time spent does not have to be successive weeks. **Criteria:** Selection will be based on the description of the topic of study for the fellowship period; the applicant's demonstration of ongoing commitment to motivating children to read.

Funds Avail.: $4,000. **Duration:** Annual. **Number Awarded:** 1. **To Apply:** Application must be submitted online. **Deadline:** October 1. **Contact:** Allison Cline, Deputy Executive Director; Email:acline@ala.org.

2240 ■ Frederic G. Melcher Scholarships *(Graduate/Scholarship)*

Purpose: To provide financial assistance for individuals pursuing a master's or advanced degree in children's li-

---

Awards are arranged alphabetically below their administering organizations

brarianship. **Focus:** Library and archival sciences. **Qualif.:** Applicants must be citizens of the U.S. or Canada. Each scholarship will be granted to four/two candidates whose educational and personal qualifications indicate fitness for professional preparation at the graduate level in the field of library work with children. Factors considered are academic excellence, leadership qualities and a desire to work with children in any type of library. A Personal Statement describing career interests and goals, and a commitment to library service to children must be included with the application. The applicant may not have earned more than 12 semester hours toward an MLS/MLIS prior to June 1 of the year awarded. The recipients will be expected to accept positions after graduation in the field of library service to children for at least one year. These positions shall be in the United States or Canada, or in a library provided for dependents of military personnel of the United States or Canada. Within a year of graduation, each recipient is expected to submit to the Association for Library Service to Children a letter from an institution's director or personnel department verifying appointment as a children's librarian. If the recipient does not complete this requirement, for any reason within the recipient's control, the scholarship money must be refunded. Failure to fulfill requirements will result in forfeiture, or repayment of scholarship monies. The recipients are expected to become members of the American Library Association and the Association for Library Service to Children. For the Melcher scholarship, money will be paid in two equal amounts at the beginning of the first two semesters or quarters in which the recipient is enrolled.**Criteria:** Selection will be selected on the basis of academic excellence, leadership qualities and the desire to work with children in any type of library.

Duration: One year. **Number Awarded:** 2. **To Apply:** Applicants must submit a completed application form; a personal statement describing career interests and goals; a commitment to library service to children; and three references (must be completed online). **Deadline:** March 1. **Remarks:** The scholarship was established as a tribute to Frederic G. Melcher, a great leader in promoting better books for children. **Contact:** Elizabeth Serrano (Staff Liaison, October 21, 2019, to June 30, 2022) -; eserrano@ ala.org; Work Phone: (312) 280-2164; American Library Association; 225 N Michigan Ave Ste 1300; Chicago, IL 60601-7616.

2241 ■ Penguin Random House Young Readers Group Award (Professional development/Grant, Award)

Purpose: To provide funds for children's librarians in school or public libraries with ten or fewer years of experience. **Focus:** Library and archival sciences. **Qualif.:** Applicants must be personal members of ALSC as well as ALA; must work directly with children in elementary, middle schools or public libraries; must have less than ten years, but more than one year, of experience as a children's librarian by the opening of the Annual Conference. **Criteria:** Applicant will be judged on the following: involvement in ALSC, as well as any other professional or educational association of which the applicant was a member, officer, chairman, etc.; new programs or innovations started by the applicants at the library in which they work; library experience.

Funds Avail.: $600. **Duration:** Annual. **Number Awarded:** 4. **Deadline:** October 1. **Contact:** ALA Scholarship Clearinghouse; 225 N. Michigan Ave., Ste., 1300, Chicago, IL 60601; Toll Free: 800-545-2433 ext. 4279; Email: scholarships@ala.org.

2242 ■ Association Minéralogique du Canada
490, rue de la Couronne
Quebec City, QC, Canada G1K 9A9
URL: www.mineralogicalassociation.ca

2243 ■ MAC Foundation Scholarship (Graduate, Postdoctorate/Scholarship)

Purpose: To honor a graduate student involved in MSC or PhD thesis program in the fields of mineralogy, crystallography, petrology, geochemistry or mineral deposits. **Focus:** Mineralogy. **Qualif.:** Applicants must be a students, one to a student enrolled in an MSc program and one to a student in a PhD program.

Funds Avail.: 5,000 Canadian Dollar. **Duration:** Annual. **Number Awarded:** 2. **Remarks:** Established in 1999.

2244 ■ Mineralogical Association of Canada Scholarships (Doctorate, Graduate/Scholarship)

Purpose: To support graduate students engaged in research in any field currently supported by MAC. **Focus:** Mineralogy. **Qualif.:** Applicants must be students entering their second year of an M.Sc. program or the second or third year of a Ph.D. program at any Canadian university or students who are Canadian citizens attending a university located outside of Canada.

Funds Avail.: 5,000 Canadian Dollars. **Duration:** Annual. **Number Awarded:** 2. **To Apply:** Applications must be accompanied by an official academic transcript (undergraduate and graduate). Applicants must provide an outline of their thesis project using two pages of single text. Five copies of the application form and thesis project should be provided. **Deadline:** May 1.

2245 ■ Association of Moving Image Archivists (AMIA)
1313 N Vine St.
Hollywood, CA 90028
Ph: (323)463-1500
Fax: (323)463-1506
URL: www.amianet.org
Social Media: www.facebook.com/amiarchivists
www.instagram.com/AMIArchivists
twitter.com/AMIAnet

2246 ■ Rick Chace Foundation Scholarships (Graduate/Scholarship)

Purpose: To provide financial assistance to deserving students who want to pursue a career in the field of moving image archiving. **Focus:** Library and archival sciences; Museum science. **Qualif.:** Applicants must be enrolled full-time in a graduate-level or other advanced program in moving image studies or production, library or information services, archival administration, museum studies or a related discipline; must have a GPA of at least 3.0. **Criteria:** Selection will be based on their commitment in pursuing a career in the field of moving image archiving, academic records and strength of a student's program of study.

Funds Avail.: $4,000. **Duration:** Annual. **To Apply:** Applicants must complete the application form available online; must have the official transcript from the applicant's most recent academic program; must provide an essay of no more than 1, 000 words describing applicant's major field of study, interest in moving image archiving, relevant experience and/or education and career goals; must submit

Awards are arranged alphabetically below their administering organizations

two letters of recommendation. **Deadline:** June 1. **Remarks:** The award was established in honor of Rick Chace. Established in 2002. **Contact:** Kristina Kersels, E-mail kkersels@amianet.org.

2247 ■ Kodak Fellowships in Film Preservation
(Graduate/Fellowship)

Purpose: To provide financial assistance to deserving students who want to pursue a career in the field of moving image archiving. **Focus:** Library and archival sciences; Museum science. **Qualif.:** Applicants must be enrolled full-time in a graduate-level or other advanced program in moving image studies or production, library or information services, archival administration, museum studies or a related discipline; must be accepted into such a program for the next academic year; must have a GPA of at least 3.0; must have strong organizational and interpersonal skills and demonstrate an interest in pursuing a career in the moving image archival field; must be at least 21 years of age and must possess a valid driver's license; must be a US citizen or have a US work visa. **Criteria:** Recipients will be selected based on the following criteria; commitment to pursuing a career in moving image archiving; academic record; program of study as it applies to moving image archiving.

To Apply: Applicants must complete the application form available online; must have the official transcript from the applicant's most recent academic program; must provide an essay of no more than 1, 000 words describing applicant's major field of study, interest in moving image archiving, relevant experience and/or education and career goals; must submit two letters of recommendation.

2248 ■ Mary Pickford Scholarships *(Graduate/Scholarship)*

Purpose: To provide financial assistance to deserving students who want to pursue a career in the field of moving image archiving. **Focus:** Library and archival sciences; Museum science. **Qualif.:** Applicants must be enrolled full-time in a graduate-level or other advanced program in moving image studies or production, library or information services, archival administration, museum studies or a related discipline; must have a GPA of at least 3.0. **Criteria:** Recipient will be selected based on the scholarship application criteria.

To Apply: Applicants must complete the application form available online; must have the official transcript from the applicant's most recent academic program; must provide an essay of no more than 1, 000 words describing applicant's major field of study, interest in moving image archiving, relevant experience and/or education and career goals; must submit two letters of recommendation. **Remarks:** Established in 1997.

2249 ■ Sony Pictures Scholarship *(Graduate/Scholarship)*

Purpose: To provide financial assistance to deserving students who want to pursue a career in the field of moving image archiving. **Focus:** Library and archival sciences; Museum science. **Qualif.:** Applicants must be enrolled full-time in a graduate-level or other advanced program in moving image studies or production, library or information services, archival administration, museum studies or a related discipline; must have a GPA of at least 3.0. **Criteria:** Selection will be based on their commitment in pursuing a career in the field of moving image archiving, academic records and strength of a student's program of study.

Funds Avail.: $4,000. **Duration:** Annual. **To Apply:** Applicants must complete the application form available online; must have the official transcript from the applicant's most recent academic program; must provide an essay of no more than 1, 000 words describing applicant's major field of study, interest in moving image archiving, relevant experience and/or education and career goals; must submit two letters of recommendation. **Deadline:** June 1. **Remarks:** Established in 1998. **Contact:** Kristina Kersels, E-mail kkersels@amianet.org.

2250 ■ Universal Studios Preservation Scholarships
(Graduate/Scholarship)

Purpose: To provide financial assistance to deserving students who want to pursue their career in the field of moving image archiving. **Focus:** Library and archival sciences; Museum science. **Qualif.:** Applicants must be enrolled full-time in a graduate-level or other advanced program in moving image studies or production, library or information services, archival administration, museum studies or a related discipline; must have a GPA of at least 3.0. **Criteria:** Selection will be based on their commitment in pursuing a career in the field of moving image archiving, academic records and strength of a student's program of study.

Funds Avail.: $4,000. **Duration:** Annual. **To Apply:** Applicants must complete the application form available online; must have the official transcript from the applicant's most recent academic program; must provide an essay of no more than 1, 000 words describing applicant's major field of study, interest in moving image archiving, relevant experience and/or education and career goals; must submit two letters of recommendation. **Deadline:** June 1. **Remarks:** Established in 2003. **Contact:** Kristina Kersels, E-mail kkersels@amianet.org.

2251 ■ Association for Nonprofit and Social Economy Research
c/o Institute for Nonprofit Studies
Mount Royal University
4825 Mount Royal Gate SW
Calgary, AB, Canada T3E 6K6
E-mail: anser.ares@gmail.com
URL: www.anser-ares.ca
Social Media: twitter.com/anserares

2252 ■ ANSER Graduate Student Awards for Research on Nonprofits and the Social Economy
(Graduate/Award)

Purpose: To encourage and foster graduate research excellence and innovation in the field of nonprofits and the social economy in Canada. **Focus:** Economics; Nonprofit sector. **Qualif.:** Applicants must be landed immigrants or Canadian graduate students who are focusing on non-profit and social economy research. **Criteria:** Selection will be based on: research scholarship; quality of research; relevance to nonprofits and the social economy; contribution to policy, governance, or sustainability of nonprofits and the social economy; and innovation in methodology, theory or area of focus.

Funds Avail.: 1,500 Canadian Dollars. **Duration:** Annual. **Number Awarded:** 2. **To Apply:** Applicants must submit the following by the deadline date: a two page outline of the research question/methodology/research partners/ expected contribution/relationship to nonprofits and the social economy/research timetable; curriculum vitae (4

Awards are arranged alphabetically below their administering organizations

pages maximum) to include stage of study/expected completion date/bursaries or funding/publications/research experience; and a letter of support from supervisor or other to comment on quality of research scholarship and relevance to nonprofit and social economy. **Deadline:** December 20. **Contact:** ANSER-ARES Awards Committee Chair at luct@unb.ca.

2253 ■ Association of Occupational Health Professionals in Healthcare (AOHP)
125 Warrendale Bayne Rd., Ste. 375
Warrendale, PA 15086
Fax: (724)935-1560
Free: 800-362-4347
E-mail: info@aohp.org
URL: www.aohp.org
Social Media: www.facebook.com/AOHP-Association-of
  -Occupational-Health-Professional-in-Healthcare
  -128269079138
twitter.com/AOHP_Org

2254 ■ Sandra Bobbitt Continuing Education Scholarship *(Undergraduate/Scholarship)*
Purpose: To provide annual continuing education scholarships to subsidize the educational efforts of members. **Focus:** General studies/Field of study not specified. **Qualif.:** Applicants must be AOHP active members in good standing. **Criteria:** Applicants will be evaluated based on the information required on the application.

Duration: Annual. **Number Awarded:** 1. **To Apply:** Applicants may verify the application process through the program website. **Deadline:** July 1.

2255 ■ Julie Schmid Research Scholarship
(Advanced Professional/Scholarship)
Purpose: To encourage, promote and strengthen the knowledge base and expertise of the occupational health professional in healthcare. **Focus:** Occupational safety and health. **Qualif.:** Applicants must have proposals for an original research project on current and/or anticipated issues in healthcare-related occupational health. **Criteria:** Applicants will be selected based on merit in accordance with the evaluation tool.

Funds Avail.: $2,000. **To Apply:** Applicants must submit a formal title for the project; state the one category from the following list that best describes the area the research project will address: employment examinations, medical surveillance, immunizations, infectious diseases, employee health records, work injuries, administration, marketing occupational health services or other healthcare-related topics; briefly describe the impact/significance of the research project to the occupational health professional in a healthcare setting; list the objectives and goals of the research project; describe the activities that will be implemented to achieve the goals of the project, e.g., questionnaire. As appropriate, describe the target population, e.g., clinical (nursing, etc.) nonclinical employees. **Deadline:** July 1. **Contact:** AOHP Research Committee Chair: info@aohp.org.

2256 ■ Association of PeriOperative Registered Nurses (AORN)
2170 South Parker Rd., Ste. 400
Denver, CO 80231

Ph: (303)755-6300
Fax: (800)847-0045
Free: 800-755-2676
E-mail: custsvc@aorn.org
URL: www.aorn.org
Social Media: www.facebook.com/AORN
www.instagram.com/aornpics
www.linkedin.com/company/aorn
www.pinterest.ph/aorn
twitter.com/aorn
www.youtube.com/user/aornvideos

2257 ■ AORN Academic Scholarships *(Undergraduate, Master's, Doctorate/Scholarship, Monetary)*
Purpose: To support students who are pursuing a career in perioperative nursing; and to support registered nurses who are continuing their education in perioperative nursing by pursuing a bachelor's, master's or doctoral degree. **Focus:** Nursing. **Qualif.:** Applicants must be students who are pursuing a career in perioperative nursing and registered nurses who are continuing their education in perioperative nursing by pursuing a bachelor's, master's, or doctoral degree.

Deadline: June 14. **Contact:** E-mail: foundation@aorn.org.

2258 ■ AORN Foundation Scholarship Program
(Undergraduate, Doctorate, Master's/Scholarship, Monetary)
Purpose: To provide financial assistance to students enrolled in nursing schools and to perioperative nurses pursuing bachelors, masters, or doctoral degrees. **Focus:** Nursing. **Qualif.:** The AORN Foundation supports your professional goals and helps you maintain evidence-based knowledge and competencies. We have awarded scholarships to more than 3,000 nurses working to earn a degree, achieve advanced certification, and complete continuing nurse education. **Criteria:** The Foundation offers professional development grants to help nurses maintain competency and to ensure safe and high-quality care.

Deadline: June 14. **Contact:** AORN Foundation: Phone: 800-755-2676; E-mail: foundation@aorn.org.

2259 ■ Association of Postgraduate PA Programs (APPAP)
PO Box 60005
Pittsburgh, PA 15211
Ph: (703)778-5570
Fax: (703)548-5539
URL: www.appap.org
Social Media: instagram.com/therealAPPAP
linkedin.com/company/the-association-of-postgraduate-pa
  -programs/about
twitter.com/therealappap

2260 ■ Linda Brandt Research Award *(Postgraduate/Award)*
Purpose: To support research regarding physician assistant postgraduate training programs, PA residents, fellows, graduates. **Focus:** Medicine. **Qualif.:** Applicants must be Physician Assistant Post-Graduate Residents; must be Physician Assistant students who have a research focus on PA Post-Graduate training, impact or outcomes; must be professionals who have a research interest in PA Post-Graduate education, impact or outcomes. **Criteria:** Selec-

Awards are arranged alphabetically below their administering organizations

tion will be based on the committee's criteria.

Funds Avail.: $2,000. **Number Awarded:** One. **To Apply:** Applicants must submit a typed, double-spaced proposal that includes the following sections: title page; title; applicants' name, postal and email address, phone and fax numbers; abstract, not more than 500 words; research description, not more than four pages, which includes the background and rationale, methods, identification and qualifications of key personnel, and expected timeline for completion of the project; CV of applicants; CV of mentors; mentor statement of support; statement of institutional support. This may be a letter from an appropriate individual or representative who can affirm that the applicant has access to facilities and personnel to aid in the successful completion of the project. It may be included in the mentor statement if appropriate; students and residents should identify a mentor or mentor team. Up to 3 persons may be included. Mentor identification is optional for graduates and other professionals. However, mentor identification is encouraged for those with limited experience in research; importance to PA post-graduate education; feasibility and likelihood of completion (timeline, mentor, facility, etc.); considerations: writing organization, detail and style. **Deadline:** March 30. **Remarks:** The award is given in honor of Linda Brandt, was one of the founding members the AP-PAP and served as its first president. **Contact:** APPAP Linda Brandt Research Award, Amber Brooks-Gumbert, PA-C, Mayo Clinic, Division of Hospital Internal Medicine, 5777 E. Mayo Blvd., Phoenix, AZ 85054; Email: brooksgumbert.amber@mayo.edu.

2261 ■ Association for Preservation Technology International (APT)

3085 Stevenson Dr., Ste. 200
Springfield, IL 62703
Ph: (217)529-9039
Fax: (888)723-4242
E-mail: info@apti.org
URL: www.apti.org
Social Media: www.facebook.com/aptpreservation
www.instagram.com/aptpreservation/
www.pinterest.com/aptint/apt-bulletin/
twitter.com/APT_Intl_Conf

2262 ■ Association for Preservation Technology International Student Scholarships *(Graduate, Undergraduate/Scholarship)*

Purpose: To promote research or projects on preservation technology. **Focus:** Historic preservation. **Qualif.:** Applicants must be enrolled in a trade, undergraduate or graduate program which is affiliated with a trade school, college or university. **Criteria:** Selection will be based on the quality of a submitted abstract and a personal statement.

Funds Avail.: No specific amount. **Duration:** Annual. **Number Awarded:** Varies. **To Apply:** Applicants are required to submit their personal as well as their professor's contact information. **Contact:** Jeff Greene, Committee Co-Chair; Email: jgreene@evergreene.com.

2263 ■ Association of Professional Schools of International Affairs (APSIA)

1615 L St., NW 8th Fl.
Washington, DC 20036

Ph: (202)559-5831
URL: www.apsia.org

2264 ■ Harold W. Rosenthal Fellowship in International Relations *(Professional development/ Fellowship)*

Purpose: To support students who pursuing a career in international relations. **Focus:** International affairs and relations. **Qualif.:** Applicants must be a graduate student in international relations; must be planning to continue education after the summer internship.

Remarks: The fellowship was established in honor of Harold Rosenthal, a Senate staff member. Established in 1977.

2265 ■ Association for Psychological Science (APS)

1800 Massachusetts Ave. NW, Ste. 402
Washington, DC 20036
Ph: (202)293-9300
Fax: (202)293-9350
URL: www.psychologicalscience.org
Social Media: www.facebook.com/PsychologicalScience
twitter.com/PsychScience
www.youtube.com/user/PsychologicalScience

2266 ■ APS Student Research Award (APS) *(Undergraduate, Graduate/Award)*

Purpose: To promote and acknowledge outstanding research conducted by student members. **Focus:** Psychology. **Qualif.:** Applicants must be either graduate or undergraduate APS student members. **Criteria:** Award will be given on a competitive basis.

Funds Avail.: $300. **Duration:** Annual. **Number Awarded:** 5. **To Apply:** Students affiliated must submit the following information: project title and an abstract; project summary. The project should detail the purpose, methodology and results of the research and include introduction/background, methods, results and discussion/theoretical implications. **Contact:** Email: studentresearch@psychologicalscience.org.

2267 ■ Association for Psychological Science Student Grants (APS) *(Graduate, Undergraduate/ Grant)*

Purpose: To encourage student research in psychological science. **Focus:** Psychology. **Qualif.:** Applicant must be an APS undergraduate or graduate student. **Criteria:** Committees will evaluate each research proposal based on its clarity, ability to explain some psychological phenomenon and ability to advance research in a specified area.

Funds Avail.: $500. **Duration:** Annual. **Number Awarded:** Up to 8. **To Apply:** Applicants must submit a cover letter; project summary; and review board approval. All materials must be submitted through e-mail with a subject, APSSC Student Grant Submission, except the cover letter, and Project Summary which should be submitted in separate Microsoft Word or Open Format documents. **Contact:** Email: apssc.graduate@psychologicalscience.org.

2268 ■ Association of Public Health Laboratories (APHL)

8515 Georgia Ave., Ste. 700
Silver Spring, MD 20910

Awards are arranged alphabetically below their administering organizations

Ph: (240)485-2745
Fax: (240)485-2700
E-mail: info@aphl.org
URL: www.aphl.org
Social Media: www.facebook.com/PublicHealthLabs
www.instagram.com/aphl/
www.linkedin.com/company/association-of-public-health
  -laboratories-aphl
twitter.com/APHL

2269 ■ APHL-CDC Infectious Diseases Laboratory Fellowship *(Doctorate/Fellowship)*

Purpose: To train and prepare scientists for careers in public health laboratories and support public health initiatives related to infectious disease research and to provide a high quality training experience for the fellow while providing workforce capacity to the public health laboratory community. **Focus:** Public health. **Qualif.:** Applicants must be US citizens or permanent residents; must have completed a master's degree in a science-related discipline by the program start date; must be able to participate in the orientation session and start their appointment at the host laboratory following the program; must hold (or expect to complete by July 2017) a recent master's-level degree (for example, MS, MPH, or MSPH) in biology, microbiology, virology, chemistry, public health or a related discipline; degree must have been received within the last 5 years. **Criteria:** Selection will be based on the committee's criteria.

Funds Avail.: No specific amount. **To Apply:** Applicants must includes a narrative statement; resume; 3 letters of recommendation; official transcripts from all degree-granting institutions; proof of US citizenship or permanent residency. **Contact:** Email: fellowships@aphl.org.

2270 ■ Association of Public Treasurers of the United States and Canada (APT US & C)

PO Box 591
Tawas City, MI 48764
Ph: (989)820-5205
E-mail: info@aptusc.org
URL: www.aptusc.org
Social Media: www.facebook.com/aptusc.org

2271 ■ APT US&C Scholarships *(Advanced Professional/Scholarship)*

Purpose: To give assistance to any active member who needs financial assistance to attend an APT US & C conference or to attend an affiliated APT US & C institute. **Focus:** General studies/Field of study not specified. **Qualif.:** Applicants must be active members in good standing. **Criteria:** Selection is based on financial need.

Funds Avail.: Up to $500 to attend a national APT US & C conference; $250 to attend an affiliated APT US & C institute. **Duration:** Annual. **To Apply:** Applicants must submit a completed APT US & C Scholarship application form together with a letter from the applicant's city, town, county (councilor, selectman, city manager, etc. confirming the necessity). **Contact:** association of Public Treasurers of the United States and Canada P.O. Box 591, Tawas City, Michigan 48764 info@aptusc.org 989.820.5205.

2272 ■ Association of Rehabilitation Nurses (ARN)

8735 W Higgins Rd., Ste. 300
Chicago, IL 60631-2738

Free: 800-229-7530
E-mail: info@rehabnurse.org
URL: www.rehabnurse.org
Social Media: www.instagram.com/associrehabnurse/
twitter.com/associrehabnurse
www.youtube.com/channel/UC-JoUwW2EZQGTywY1Ts
  _TaA

2273 ■ Mary Ann Mikulic Scholarship *(Other/ Scholarship)*

Purpose: To provide financial assistance covering full tuition of the Professional Rehabilitation Nursing course. **Focus:** Nursing. **Qualif.:** Applicants must be registered nurses with current license practicing in the specialty of rehabilitation nursing and able to meet all the financial responsibilities incurred by participating in the course; must be a first-time attendee to ARN conference.

Funds Avail.: one full tuition. **Duration:** Annual. **Deadline:** July 1.

2274 ■ Association for Research on Nonprofit Organizations and Voluntary Action (ARNOVA)

441 W Michigan St.
Indianapolis, IN 46202
Ph: (317)684-2120
Fax: (317)684-2128
URL: www.arnova.org
Social Media: www.facebook.com/arnovacommunity
www.instagram.com/arnovacommunity
www.linkedin.com/company/arnovacommunity
twitter.com/ARNOVA
www.youtube.com/channel/UCjMY
  -_6IPFRU5TmW0awTZlw

2275 ■ Emerging Scholars Award *(Graduate/Award)*

Purpose: To help and support students and scholars spread their research into practice, and enhance their knowledge. **Focus:** Nonprofit sector. **Qualif.:** Applicant must be an ARNOVA member with an active membership at the time of application; must have a paper accepted for the current year ARNOVA Conference. **Criteria:** Selection will be based on strength of the applicant's nomination letter; priority is given to applicants who will present at the ARNOVA conference.

Funds Avail.: No specific amount. **Duration:** Annual. **Number Awarded:** 10. **To Apply:** Applicants must submit the following requirements; (1) cover letter; (2) copy of ARNOVA conference proposal; (3) letter of acceptance from the Conference Committee Chairs; (4) letter of recommendation from a faculty member or a letter of recommendation from someone who knows the research or work; (5) resume, containing a mailing address, email address, and telephone number; (6) official transcript of record. **Deadline:** August 3. **Contact:** Email:awards@arnova.org.

2276 ■ Association of School Business Officials of Maryland and the District of Columbia (ASBO-MD&DC)

1200-C Agora Dr., Ste 241
Bel Air, MD 21014
E-mail: jlaporta@asbo.org
URL: www.asbo.org

Awards are arranged alphabetically below their administering organizations

2277 ■ Dwight P. Jacobus Scholarships
(Undergraduate/Scholarship)

Purpose: To assist those individuals who require financial assistance to secure a college education. **Focus:** Business; Education. **Qualif.:** Applicants must have been residents of Maryland or District of Columbia for at least one year preceding the date of the award; and, accepted for admission as full-time students; they must demonstrate financial need, and have a minimum 2.0 overall GPA. **Criteria:** Selection scholarships are made by the Association of School Business Officials of Maryland and the District of Columbia based upon: scholastic achievement; financial need; Scholastic Assessment Test (SAT) scores or American College Test (ACT) scores; and quality of extracurricular achievements.

Funds Avail.: $1,000 each. **Duration:** Annual. **Number Awarded:** 10. **To Apply:** Applicants must file an application and supporting documents with the Chair of the Scholarship Committee for ASBO of Maryland and the District of Columbia. Applications are available from guidance or financial aid offices, or may be requested in writing from the Chair of the Scholarship Committee. **Deadline:** March 1. **Remarks:** The scholarship was established to honor Dwight P. Jacobus, the first Executive Director of ASBO. **Contact:** Margaret Ellen Kalmanowicz margaretellen.kalmanowicz@qacps.org ASBO MD&DC Scholarship Committee Chair Queen Anne's County Public Schools 202 Chesterfield Road Centreville, MD 21617.

2278 ■ Association of Schools and Programs of Public Health (ASPPH)
1615 L St. NW, Ste. 510
Washington, DC 20036
Ph: (202)296-1099
Fax: (202)296-1252
E-mail: info@aspph.org
URL: www.aspph.org
Social Media: www.facebook.com/ASPPH
www.linkedin.com/company/1274952
twitter.com/ASPPHtweets

2279 ■ ASPPH/CDC Public Health Fellowship Program *(Doctorate, Graduate/Fellowship)*

Purpose: To address emerging needs of public health, and to provide leadership and professional opportunities at the Centers for Disease Control and Prevention (CDC) for students and graduate students of ASPH member graduate schools of public health. **Focus:** Public health. **Qualif.:** Applicants must have received an MPH or Doctorate degree prior to the beginning of the fellowship; or be an early career professional with MPH or Doctorate degrees (within 5 years of graduation); have received degree(s) from an ASPH-member, CEPH-accredited, graduate school of public health; and be a U.S. citizen or hold a visa permitting permanent residence in the U.S. **Criteria:** All applications to the program undergo a two-phase review process.

To Apply: Applicants must complete the application online. In addition, applicants must submit a hard copy documents of two generic recommendation letters; graduate transcripts (of all ASPH member school(s) of public health attended); and the signature page (available after submitting the online application). **Deadline:** February 2. **Remarks:** Established in 1995. **Contact:** ASPPH Graduate Training Programs; Email: trainingprograms@aspph.org.

2280 ■ ASPPH/EPA Environmental Health Fellowship Program *(Doctorate, Postdoctorate/Fellowship)*

Purpose: To provide professional training and opportunities for early career public health professionals by enabling them to work in EPA on current and emerging environmental public health needs. **Focus:** Public health. **Qualif.:** Applicants must have received an MPH or Doctorate degree prior to the beginning of the fellowship (no later than August of the application year); or be an early career professional with MPH or Doctorate degree (within 5 years of graduation); must have received degree(s) from an ASPH-member, CEPH-accredited, graduate school of public health; and must be a U.S. citizen or hold a visa permitting permanent residence in the U.S. **Criteria:** All applications to the program undergo a two-phase review process.

Funds Avail.: Varies. **Duration:** One year. **To Apply:** Applicants must complete the application online. In addition, applicants must submit a hard copy documents of two generic recommendation letters; graduate transcripts (of all ASPH member school(s) of public health attended); and the signature page (available after submitting the online application).

2281 ■ ASPPH/NHTSA Public Health Fellowship Program *(Doctorate, Master's/Fellowship)*

Purpose: To provide training opportunities to graduates of accredited schools of public health. **Focus:** Public health. **Qualif.:** Applicants must have received an MPH or Doctorate degree prior to the beginning of the fellowship; or be a career professional with MPH or Doctorate degree (within 5 years of graduation); must have received their degree(s) from an ASPH-member, CEPH-accredited, graduate school of public health; and be a U.S. citizen or hold a visa permitting permanent residence in the U.S. **Criteria:** Selection will based on the quality of essay, strength of credentials, previous professional experience; and letters of recommendation.

Funds Avail.: Varies. **Duration:** One year. **To Apply:** Applicants must complete the application online. In addition, applicants must submit a hard copy documents of two generic recommendation letters; graduate transcripts (of all ASPH member school(s) of public health attended); and the signature page (available after submitting the online application). **Deadline:** February 9. **Contact:** ASPPH Graduate Training Programs; Email: trainingprograms@aspph.org.

2282 ■ ASPPH Public Health Fellowship Program *(Doctorate, Postdoctorate/Fellowship)*

Purpose: To provide leadership and professional opportunities at the Centers for Disease Control and Prevention (CDC) for students and graduate students of ASPPH member graduate schools and programs of public health. **Focus:** Public health.

Deadline: February 2. **Contact:** ASPPH Graduate Training Programs; Email: trainingprograms@aspph.org.

2283 ■ ASPPH Public Health Preparedness Fellowship Program *(Postdoctorate/Fellowship)*

Purpose: To provide opportunities for a motivated and experienced individual to play a role in helping to shape United States health policy. **Focus:** Public health. **Qualif.:** Applicants must have received an MPH or Doctorate degree prior to the beginning of the fellowship; or be an early career professional with MPH or Doctorate degrees (within 5 years of graduation); have received degree(s)

Awards are arranged alphabetically below their administering organizations

from an ASPH-member, CEPH-accredited, graduate school of public health; and a U.S. citizen or hold a visa permitting permanent residence in the U.S. **Criteria:** All applications to the program undergo a two-phase review process.

Funds Avail.: No specific amount. **Duration:** Annual. **To Apply:** Applicants must submit a hard copy documents of two generic recommendation letters; graduate transcripts (of all ASPH member school(s) of public health attended); and the signature page (available after submitting the online application). **Deadline:** September 30.

2284 ■ ASPPH/CDC Allan Rosenfield Global Health Fellowship Program *(Postdoctorate, Postgraduate/Fellowship)*

Purpose: To enhance the training of graduates of schools of public health with an interest in global health. **Focus:** Public health. **Qualif.:** Applicants must have received their Master's or Doctorate degree prior to the beginning of the fellowship or within the last five years (graduate degrees must come from an ASPH member graduate school of public health accredited by the Council on Education for Public Health); and must be a U.S. citizen or hold a visa permitting permanent residence in the U.S. **Criteria:** Selection will based on the quality of essay, strength of credentials, previous professional experience; and letters of recommendation.

Funds Avail.: No specific amount. **To Apply:** Applicants must complete the application online. In addition, applicants must submit a hard copy documents of two generic recommendation letters; graduate transcripts (of all ASPH member school(s) of public health attended); and the signature page (available after submitting the online application).

2285 ■ Association of Science-Technology Centers (ASTC)
818 Connecticut Ave. NW, 7th Fl.
Washington, DC 20006-2734
Ph: (202)783-7200
Fax: (202)783-7207
E-mail: info@astc.org
URL: www.astc.org

2286 ■ Lee Kimche McGrath Worldwide Fellowship *(Other/Fellowship)*

Purpose: To support individuals from a science center or museum who wishes to participate in the ASTC Annual Conference. **Focus:** Museum science. **Criteria:** Applications are reviewed by the ASTC International Advisory Board. Preference will be given to institutions that cannot afford to send a representative to an ASTC conference; whose participation will benefit other science centers in addition to their own; and who have limited opportunities to meet professionally with science center colleagues.

Funds Avail.: No specific amount. **Duration:** Annual. **Remarks:** Established in 2004. **Contact:** Email:conference@astc.org.

2287 ■ Association of Seventh-Day Adventist Librarians (ASDAL)
E-mail: asdal@asdal.org
URL: www.asdal.org
Social Media: www.facebook.com/Association-of-Seventh-day-Adventist-Librarians-ASDAL-106412606200541

2288 ■ D. Glenn Hilts Scholarship *(Graduate, Undergraduate/Scholarship)*

Purpose: To recognize excellence in scholarship and to encourage individuals with leadership potential to seek employment in a Seventh-day Adventist library. **Focus:** General studies/Field of study not specified; Library and archival sciences. **Qualif.:** Applicant must be a Seventh-day Adventist in good standing; Applicant must be accepted to a graduate library and information science program in an American Library Association (ALA) accredited program, OR, if attending outside the United States or Canada, the program must be recognized by the International Federation of Library Associations.

To Apply: Applicants must submit an online application form including GPA and GRE scores, if available; official college transcripts. Include library school transcripts, if currently enrolled; copy of the official letter of acceptance from an accredited library school; personal statement in an essay of 600 words; curriculum vitae; three letters of reference (one should be a character reference from your Seventh-day Adventist pastor). **Deadline:** May 4. **Remarks:** Established in 1985. **Contact:** Melissa Hortemiller; Chair, ASDAL Scholarship and Awards Committee; Library Director; Union College Library; 3800 South 48th Street; Lincoln, NE 68506; 402.486.2600 x2154; melissa.hortemiller@ucollege.edu.

2289 ■ Association for the Sociology of Religion (ASR)
Ball State University
Department of Sociology
2000 W University Ave., N Quad 222
Muncie, IN 47306
E-mail: asreo@bsu.edu
URL: www.sociologyofreligion.com

2290 ■ Joseph H. Fichter Research Grant *(Postdoctorate/Grant)*

Purpose: To financially assist scholars involved in promising research in the area of women and religion. **Focus:** Religion; Women's studies. **Qualif.:** Applicants must be ASR members at least during the year prior the submission of their application; who are pursuing or currently have a Ph.D. in a range of disciplines, the proposed research must be sociological in nature. **Criteria:** Recipients will be selected based on submitted materials.

Funds Avail.: $12,000. **Duration:** Annual. **To Apply:** Applicants must submit a proposal of not more than five double-spaced pages (1,250 words); detailed, one-page budget; updated curriculum vitae; statement of his/her qualifications to carry out the proposed research, and a current email address at which he/she can be contacted during the summer months. **Deadline:** May 1. **Contact:** E-mail: dawne.moon@marquette.edu.

2291 ■ Robert J. McNamara Student Paper Award *(Graduate/Award, Monetary)*

Purpose: To recognize outstanding student papers in the sociology of religion. **Focus:** Religion. **Qualif.:** Applicants must be currently enrolled graduate students who have not defended their doctoral dissertation at the time their paper is submitted; membership in the Association for the Sociology of Religion is required either at the time of application or pr **Criteria:** Applicants will be judged based on submitted paper.

Awards are arranged alphabetically below their administering organizations

Funds Avail.: $500. **Duration:** Annual. **To Apply:** Applicants must submit an abstract from the ASR Program Chair following the guidelines of all standard paper submissions. It should be in the form of articles with a maximum length of 40 double-spaced, single-sided pages inclusive of all materials: text, title, notes, table, figures, etc. The title page should include an abstract of no more than 200 words. Texts should not exceed 12, 000 words, approximately 36 double-spaced pages of 12 point font. Applicants should attach their paper as a file, formatted in Microsoft Word. **Deadline:** June 8. **Contact:** E-mail: stuart.wright@lamar.edu.

2292 ■ Association of Specialized and Cooperative Library Agencies (ASCLA)
225 N Michigan Ave., Ste. 1300
Chicago, IL 60601
Fax: (312)440-9374
Free: 800-545-2433
E-mail: ala@ala.org
URL: www.ala.org
Social Media: twitter.com/ala_ascla

2293 ■ ALA Century Scholarship *(Master's, Doctorate/Scholarship)*
Purpose: To fund services or accommodations that are either not provided by law or otherwise by the university that will enable the student or students to successfully complete the course of study for a Master's in Library Science and become a library or information studies professional. **Focus:** Library and archival sciences. **Qualif.:** Applicants must be citizens of the United States or Canada and must have a disability. **Criteria:** Proof of disability and need for financial assistance.

Funds Avail.: $2,500. **Duration:** Annual. **To Apply:** Applicants must be citizens of the United States or Canada; submit medical documentation of their disability or disabilities, accommodations and or services the applicant would need for their studies; documentation should identify the applicant's disability and how it affects their ability to complete a course of study. **Remarks:** Established in 2000. **Contact:** Kimberly L. Redd, klredd@ala.org Work Phone: (312) 280-4279 Fax: (312) 280-3256 American Library Association 225 N Michigan Ave Ste 1300 Chicago, IL 60601-7616.

2294 ■ Association of State Dam Safety Officials (ASDSO)
239 S Limestone
Lexington, KY 40508-2501
Ph: (859)550-2788
Fax: (202)550-2795
E-mail: info@damsafety.org
URL: www.damsafety.org
Social Media: www.facebook.com/DamSafety.org
www.instagram.com/dam_safety
www.linkedin.com/company/association-of-state-dam
-safety-officials-asdso-
twitter.com/Dam_Safety
www.youtube.com/channel/
UCnpC7rQGbNAhkyhDdGw00NA

2295 ■ ASDSO Undergraduate Scholarship *(Undergraduate/Scholarship)*
Purpose: To reward excellence in the study of civil engineering and related fields, and to make students more aware of dam safety as a career opportunity. **Focus:** Engineering, Civil.

Funds Avail.: $5,000-$10,000. **Duration:** Annual. **Remarks:** Established in 1992.

2296 ■ Association of State Dam Safety Officials memorial Undergraduate Scholarship *(Undergraduate/Scholarship)*
Purpose: To promote the study of civil engineering and related fields as a career. **Focus:** Engineering, Civil. **Qualif.:** Applicants must be a U.S. citizen; enrolled in a civil engineering program and in their senior year; pursuing a career in hydraulics, hydrology or geotechnical disciplines or related to design, construction and operation of dams; have 2.5 GPA for the first three years in college and recommended by advisor. **Criteria:** Selection will be based on academic scholarship, financial need, work experience or activities and essay.

Funds Avail.: $5,000-$10,000. **Duration:** Annual. **Number Awarded:** 2. **To Apply:** Applicants must send an application form; transcript; three letters of recommendation; and (500-word) essay describing the proposed study and its importance. **Remarks:** Established in 1992.

2297 ■ Association of Surgical Technologists (AST)
6 W Dry Creek Cir., Ste. 200
Littleton, CO 80120
Ph: (303)694-9130
Fax: (303)694-9169
Free: 800-637-7433
URL: www.ast.org
Social Media: www.facebook.com/
AssociationofSurgicalTechnologists
www.instagram.com/astsurgtech
www.linkedin.com/company/association-of-surgical-tech-
nologists?trk=company_name
www.pinterest.com/assnsurgtechs
twitter.com/AST_SurgTech
www.youtube.com/user/AssnSurgTech

2298 ■ Foundation for Surgical Technology Scholarships *(Graduate/Scholarship)*
Purpose: To encourage and reward educational excellence as well as to respond to the financial need demonstrated by the surgical technology student and offer assistance to those who seek a career in surgical technology. **Focus:** Surgery. **Qualif.:** Applicants must be currently enrolled in an accredited surgical technology program and eligible to sit for the NBSTSA national surgical technologist certifying examination; must demonstrate superior academic ability; and must have a need for financial assistance. **Criteria:** Selection will be based on academic excellence and financial need.

Funds Avail.: No specific amount. **Duration:** Annual. **To Apply:** Applicants should include instructor's email address; contact information, including mailing address and email address; name and mailing address of applicant's surgical technology program. **Deadline:** March 1.

2299 ■ Association of Texas Professional Educators Foundation (ATPE)
305 E Huntland Dr., Ste. 300
Austin, TX 78752

Awards are arranged alphabetically below their administering organizations

Fax: (512)467-2203
Free: 800-777-2873
E-mail: info@atpe.org
URL: www.atpe.org
Social Media: www.facebook.com/OfficialATPE
www.instagram.com/officialatpe
www.linkedin.com/company/atpe
www.pinterest.com/atpe
twitter.com/OfficialATPE
www.youtube.com/user/OfficialATPE

2300 ■ Barbara Jordan Memorial Scholarships
(Undergraduate, Graduate/Scholarship)

Purpose: To support outstanding students currently enrolled in educator preparation programs. **Focus:** Education. **Qualif.:** Applicants must be juniors, seniors or graduate students enrolled in an accredited college/university educator preparation program. **Criteria:** Selection shall be based on the aforementioned applicants' qualifications and compliance with the application details.

Funds Avail.: No specific amount. **Duration:** Annual. **Number Awarded:** Varies. **To Apply:** Applicants must submit a completed application form along with college transcripts with official university imprint (do not fax); a detailed description of participation in any academic, honorary, civic or extracurricular activities in college; an essay (maximum of 2 typed, double-spaced 8 1/2x11 pages) including the applicant's personal educational philosophy, why the applicant wants to become an educator, who influenced the applicant the most in making career decision and why the applicant is applying for the award; and at least two (no more than three) letters of recommendation. **Deadline:** June 2. **Contact:** ATPE Foundation, at the above address.

2301 ■ Fred Wiesner Educational Excellence Scholarships *(Undergraduate, Graduate/Scholarship)*

Purpose: To support outstanding students currently enrolled in educator preparation programs. **Focus:** Education. **Qualif.:** Applicant must be college students enrolled in an accredited college/university educator preparation program. **Criteria:** Selection shall be based on the aforementioned applicants' qualifications and compliance with the application details.

Funds Avail.: No specific amount. **Duration:** Annual. **Number Awarded:** Varies. **To Apply:** Applicants must submit a completed application form along with college transcripts with official university imprint (do not fax); a detailed description of participation in any academic, honorary, civic or extracurricular activities in college; an essay (maximum of 2 typed, double-spaced 8 1/2x11 pages) including the applicant's personal educational philosophy, why the applicant wants to become an educator, who influenced the applicant the most in making career decision and why the applicant is applying for the award; and at least two (no more than three) letters of recommendation. **Deadline:** June 2. **Contact:** ATPE Foundation, at the above address.

2302 ■ Association of the United States Navy (AUSN)
5904 Richmond Hwy Ste 530
Alexandria, VA 22303
Ph: (703)548-5800
Fax: (703)683-3647
Free: 877-628-9411
E-mail: info@ausn.org

URL: www.ausn.org
Social Media: www.facebook.com/AUSN1
twitter.com/AUSNTweets

2303 ■ Association of the United States Navy Scholarships *(Undergraduate/Scholarship)*

Purpose: To provide educational assistance for the sons and daughters of members of the Association of the United States Navy. **Focus:** General studies/Field of study not specified. **Qualif.:** Applicants must be undergraduate students who are accepted or enrolled in college or accredited technical institution; may apply during their senior year of high school and up to their senior year in college; must remain a full time student defined as maintaining an average course load of 15 credit hours, with a minimum of 12 credit hours in any semester or quarter throughout the year at an accredited college or technical institution in the U.S; must maintain a grade point average (GPA) of 2.5 or above; scholarships are school-year specific and must be applied for annually; no more than two will be awarded to any scholarship recipients. **Criteria:** Selection will be based on financial need, scholastic and leadership ability, potential, character and personal qualities.

Funds Avail.: $1,000 to $2,000. **Duration:** Annual. **To Apply:** Applicants must submit the completed application along with photograph; copy of your most recent grades from high school, college or technical institution; Letter of Reference from someone with whom you have a non-social relationship; Autobiography. **Deadline:** June 1. **Contact:** Association of the United States Navy, Kathryn Moats, Scholarship Program, 3601 Eisenhower Ave, Ste 110, Alexandria, VA, 22304; Email: kathryn.moats@ausn.org.

2304 ■ Association of University Programs in Health Administration (AUPHA)
1730 M St. NW, Ste. 407
Washington, DC 20036
Ph: (202)763-7283
E-mail: aupha@aupha.org
URL: www.aupha.org/home
Social Media: facebook.com/aupha
linkedin.com/company/association-of-university-programs
  -in-health-administration
twitter.com/aupha

2305 ■ Corris Boyd Scholarship *(Graduate/Scholarship)*

Purpose: To support the education of students of color entering a graduate degree program. **Focus:** Health care services. **Qualif.:** Applicants must have applied and been accepted to a Master's AUPHA full-member program (but not yet enrolled); must be full-time student; must be student of color (African American, American Indian/Alaska Native, Asian American, Hawaiian/Pacific Islander, Latino/Hispanic, Multiracial); must have a minimum 3.0 GPA (out of 4.0) in undergraduate coursework; and must be U.S. citizens. **Criteria:** Selection is based on the applicant's leadership qualities; academic achievements; community involvement; commitment to healthcare; and financial need (may be considered when all other factors are equal).

Funds Avail.: $40,000. **Duration:** Annual. **To Apply:** Applicants must complete the application form online. In addition, applicants must submit GRE or GMAT score and score report (uploaded in PDF format or sent by mail or fax); program information (list of the AUPHA Full-Member,

Awards are arranged alphabetically below their administering organizations

CAHME accredited programs applied); cumulative GPA (submit via online application); current resume (uploaded in Word or PDF format); a personal statement (maximum of 1,000 words, uploaded in Word or PDF format); three signed letters of recommendation, one must be from a faculty member, one from an employer/supervisor (uploaded in PDF format or sent by mail or fax); and official transcripts (from all higher education institutions attended). **Deadline:** April 17. **Remarks:** The program was established in honor of Corris Boyd, a healthcare leader who dedicated his life to diversity and excellence in leadership – especially among people of color. Established in 2006. **Contact:** E-mail: csanyer@aupha.org.

2306 ■ Foster G. McGaw Scholarship *(Undergraduate, Graduate/Scholarship)*

Purpose: To provide financial support to students enrolled in health administration programs. **Focus:** Health services administration. **Qualif.:** Applicants must be undergraduate or graduate students in healthcare administration; enrolled in their final year (fall/spring) of full-time study in a healthcare management graduate program; with demonstrates financial need.

Duration: Annual. **To Apply:** Applicants must submit current resume or curriculum vitae; official undergraduate and graduate transcripts; three current letters of recommendation (one must be from graduate program director); application essay including information on applicant's reason for pursuing a career in healthcare management and their career aspirations and goals. Information on financial need, community/civic engagement, and volunteerism should also be provided. **Remarks:** Established in 1975. **Contact:** E-mail: mcgaw@aupha.org.

2307 ■ David A. Winston Health Policy Scholarship *(Graduate/Scholarship)*

Purpose: To increase the number and quality of individuals trained in healthcare policy at the state and federal level. **Focus:** Health care services. **Qualif.:** Applicants must be current first year graduate students in their second full-time equivalent semester or third full-time equivalent quarter for those in two-year programs or for those in longer programs, their next to final year, studying at any AUPHA or ASPPH member graduate program; must be scheduled to complete the didactic portion of their degree not later than December of the year following the awarding of the scholarship; must be U.S. citizens; applicants from health policy, public policy, health administration, business, economics, and law graduate programs (e.g. MPH, MPP, MHA, MBA, MA, JD) as well as joint degree programs (e.g. JD/MPH) are strongly encouraged to apply; students of all political ideological perspectives are encouraged to apply. **Criteria:** Selection is based on the applicant's expressed and demonstrated commitment to improvement of the U.S. health care system, leadership, academic achievement, community involvement and long term career interest.

Funds Avail.: $10,000. **Duration:** Annual. **Number Awarded:** 10. **To Apply:** Applicants must complete the application form online. In addition, applicants must submit a resume detailing both professional and extracurricular activities; a personal statement detailing the applicant's interest in and commitment to health policy and how they intend to pursue policy within their career, this statement should be roughly one and one half single spaced pages in length and should provide detail on what experiences in your life have directed you towards a career in health policy and what your future career aspirations are, the statement should outline how your academic preparation has and will

continue to prepare you for a career in health policy; Undergraduate and graduate registrar-issued transcripts (at least one full-time equivalent semester of graduate work in health management or health policy must appear on graduate transcript); two letters of nomination, one letter must be from a faculty member in your degree program, the second letter must be from a preceptor or employer, both letters should be on letterhead, signed, and speak specifically to your qualifications for this scholarship. **Deadline:** April 1. **Contact:** Lydia Middleton, Winston Fellowship Executive Director; Phone: 703-894-0940 ext. 131; E-mail: info@winstonfellowship.org.

2308 ■ Association for Women in Architecture and Design (AWA+D)
1315 Storm Pky.
Torrance, CA 90501
Ph: (310)534-8466
Fax: (877)257-9666
URL: awaplusd.org
Social Media: www.facebook.com/AWAplusD
www.instagram.com/AWAplusD
www.linkedin.com/groups/3863498/profile
www.linkedin.com/company/awaplusd
twitter.com/AWAplusD

2309 ■ Association for Women in Architecture Scholarships *(Undergraduate/Scholarship)*

Purpose: To advance and support the positions of women in architecture and allied fields. **Focus:** Architecture. **Qualif.:** Applicants must be residents of California or attending a California school, and must be enrolled in one of the qualifying majors for the current school term; must have completed a minimum of 18 units in their major by the application due date. **Criteria:** Selection will based on merit as evidenced by grades, personal statement, letter of recommendation and quality of student work.

Funds Avail.: $2,500. **Duration:** Annual. **Number Awarded:** Varies. **To Apply:** Applicants must complete the application form; must submit an official transcript of records from each college and university attended, two sealed letters of recommendation with signature over the seal from an instructor who has taught in their major; must submit a typewritten personal statement stating the reasons for studying the chosen field and career objectives; must submit a portfolio in "11x17" format showing one-to-three projects from their school work and self-addressed stamped envelope, standard business size. **Deadline:** March 27. **Contact:** Jana Wehby, Scholarship Chair; Phone: 310-534-8466; Email: scholarships@awaplusd-foundation.org.

2310 ■ Association for Women in Computing - Houston Chapter
PO Box 421316
Houston, TX 77242-1316
Ph: (713)222-0955
E-mail: info@awchouston.org
URL: awchouston.org

2311 ■ Kathi Bowles Scholarships for Women in Technology *(Undergraduate, Graduate/Scholarship)*

Purpose: To support and assist women who are pursuing technology degrees and have contributed leadership and service to their school, university, or community. **Focus:**

Awards are arranged alphabetically below their administering organizations

Computer and information sciences; Information science and technology; Technology.

2312 ■ Association for Women Geoscientists (AWG)

1333 West 120th Ave, Ste 211
Westminster, CO 80234
Ph: (303)412-6219
Fax: (303)253-9220
E-mail: office@awg.org
URL: www.awg.org
Social Media: www.facebook.com/AWGeoscientists
www.instagram.com/awg_org
twitter.com/AWG_org

2313 ■ AWG Minority Scholarship *(Undergraduate/ Scholarship)*

Purpose: To encourage young minority women to pursue an education and later a career in the geosciences. **Focus:** Geosciences. **Qualif.:** Applicants must be women who are African-American, Hispanic, or Native American and are full-time students pursuing undergraduate degree in geosciences at an accredited college or university. **Criteria:** Selection shall be based on the premises that the applicants may contribute to the larger world community through their academic and personal strengths.

Funds Avail.: Up to $6,000. **Duration:** Annual. **Number Awarded:** Varies. **To Apply:** Applicants must download the provided application form; the application calls for a statement of academic and career goals, two letters of recommendation, high school and college transcripts, and SAT or ACT scores. **Deadline:** June 30. **Contact:** Association for Women Geoscientists, Attn. Minority Scholarship, 1333 W 120th Ave., Ste. 211, Westminster, Colorado, 80234; For Queries, Christina Tapia; E-mail: minorityscholarship@awg.org.

2314 ■ Chrysalis Scholarship *(Graduate/Scholarship)*

Purpose: To support a geoscience graduate student with their thesis/ dissertation. **Focus:** Geosciences. **Qualif.:** Applicant must be a female geoscience graduate student who has had an interruption in academic progress due to life circumstances; who has contributed to and will continue to contribute to, both the geosciences and the larger world community through academic and personal strengths. **Criteria:** Selection is based on the application materials by Chrysalis Scholarship Committee.

Funds Avail.: $2,000. **Duration:** One year. **To Apply:** Applicants must submit a letter describing background, career goals and objectives, how the scholarship will be used, and the nature and length of the interruption of education; applicants must also submit two reference letters.

2315 ■ AWG Maria Luisa Crawford Field Camp Scholarships *(Undergraduate/Scholarship)*

Purpose: To encourage promising young women to pursue geoscience careers through attendance at field camp. **Focus:** Geosciences. **Qualif.:** Applicants must be full-time students who are pursuing an undergraduate degree in the geosciences at an accredited college or university, and have a GPA of 3.0 or higher. **Criteria:** Selection will be based on the committee's criteria.

Funds Avail.: $750 each. **Duration:** Annual. **Number Awarded:** 2. **To Apply:** Applicant must download and

complete the provided application form. Also, applicants must provide the following: a 250-word essay explaining how the field-camp experience fits into their long-term academic and career goals; a transcript of all of their college work (an unofficial transcript is acceptable); names and contact information for two instructors who are acquainted with the applicant's work and are willing to write letters of recommendation for the applicant (noting the ethnic origin, if applicable). The organization will contact them directly and ask them to submit their recommendations. **Deadline:** February 14. **Remarks:** Named for Louisa (Weecha) Crawford for whom the combination of science, outdoor adventure, the chance to travel, and the joy of working with others made a career of teaching geology a perfect choice. **Contact:** Crawford committee; E-mail: crawford@awg.org.

2316 ■ Janet Cullen Tanaka Geosciences Undergraduate Scholarship *(Undergraduate/ Scholarship)*

Purpose: To encourage the participation of women in the study of geosciences. **Focus:** Geosciences. **Qualif.:** Applicants should be undergraduate women (sophomore, junior, or senior women enrolled in a university or two-year college in Oregon or Washington State) committed to completing a Bachelor's Degree and pursuing a career or graduate work in the geosciences, including geology, environmental/engineering geology, geochemistry, geophysics, hydrogeology or hydrology. They must have a minimum of 3.2 GPA (or equivalent academic achievement). **Criteria:** Applicants will be judged based on their potential for professional success, academic achievement and financial need.

Funds Avail.: $1,200. **To Apply:** Applicant must submit their name, address, phone number, and email (if available); one paragraph each describing financial needs, current resources, and academic achievements; one-page essay summarizing applicant's commitment to a career in the geosciences; copies of all college transcripts (photocopies accepted); three letters of reference; provide names, affiliations, phone numbers of references. **Deadline:** December 1. **Contact:** AWG-PNW Scholarship Committee (Attn.: Sarah Dewey) 529-B 11th Ave E Seattle WA 98102 Email:awg.pnw.scholarships@gmail.com.

2317 ■ Association for Women in Mathematics (AWM)

11240 Waples Mill Rd., Ste. 200
Fairfax, VA 22030
Ph: (703)934-0163
Fax: (703)359-7562
E-mail: awm@awm-math.org
URL: awm-math.org
Social Media: www.facebook.com/awmmath
www.instagram.com/awmmath
twitter.com/AWMmath

2318 ■ AWM Mathematics Travel Grants *(Doctorate/ Grant)*

Purpose: To promote women mathematicians to attend conferences in their fields provides them a valuable opportunity to advance their research activities and their visibility in the research community. **Focus:** Mathematics and mathematical sciences. **Qualif.:** Applicant must be a woman holding a doctorate degree and with a work address in the USA.; applicant's research must be in an area

Awards are arranged alphabetically below their administering organizations

supported by DMS. **Criteria:** Recipients will be determined on a competitive basis by a selection panel consisting of distinguished mathematicians appointed by the AWM.

Duration: Annual. **Number Awarded:** 3. **To Apply:** Application materials include: a research proposal (two to three pages in length, references are not included in page limit); a curriculum vitae; a proposed budget which must be a separate page in your application in addition to fill out the amounts in the required fields online; current or pending funding available to the applicant. **Deadline:** February 1; May 30; October 1. **Contact:** AWM Administrative Specialist; Phone: 401-455-4042; Email: awm@awm-math.org.

2319 ■ Mathematics Mentoring Travel Grants
(Doctorate/Grant)

Purpose: To help young women to develop a long-term working and mentoring relationship with senior mathematicians. **Focus:** Mathematics and mathematical sciences. **Qualif.:** Applicants must be women holding a doctorate degree or equivalent with a work address in the United States; must be in a field supported by the Division of the Mathematical Sciences of the National Science Foundation. **Criteria:** Awards will be determined on a competitive basis by a selection panel consisting of distinguished mathematicians appointed by the AWM.

Funds Avail.: $5,000. **Duration:** Annual. **Number Awarded:** 7. **To Apply:** Applicants must have a curriculum vitae; must provide a research proposal which specifies why the proposed travel would be particularly beneficial; must submit a supporting letter from the proposed mentor with the curriculum vitae of the proposed mentor; must have a proposed budget and information about other sources of funding available. **Deadline:** February 1. **Contact:** AWM Administrative Specialist; Phone: 401-455-4042; Email: awm@awm-math.org.

2320 ■ Association for Women in Sports Media (AWSM)
21317 Estero Preserve Run
Estero, FL 33928
E-mail: awsmboard@gmail.com
URL: www.awsmonline.org
Social Media: www.facebook.com/awsmonline
www.instagram.com/awsm_sportsmedia
twitter.com/awsm_sportmedia

2321 ■ Association for Women in Sports Media Internship Program *(Undergraduate/Scholarship, Internship)*

Purpose: To assist female college students interested in sports media careers through paid internships with employers. **Focus:** Media arts; Sports writing. **Qualif.:** Applicants must be full-time female students interested in sports media careers. **Criteria:** Applications will be evaluated by the AWSM board members and appropriate media professionals.

Funds Avail.: $1,000. **Duration:** Annual. **Number Awarded:** Varies. **To Apply:** Applicants may contact the AWSM for more information. **Deadline:** October 31. **Remarks:** Established in 1990. **Contact:** Email: awsminternships@gmail.com.

2322 ■ AWSM Broadcasting Scholarship
(Undergraduate/Scholarship)

Purpose: To provide scholarship to female college students interested in sports media careers. **Focus:** Broadcasting.

Qualif.: Applicants must be full-time female students interested in sports media careers.

Funds Avail.: $1,000. **Duration:** Annual.

2323 ■ AWSM Public Relations Scholarship/ Internships *(Scholarship, Internship)*

Purpose: To provide scholarship and paid internship to female college students interested in sports media careers. **Focus:** Public relations.

Funds Avail.: $1,000. **Duration:** Annual.

2324 ■ Association of Zoo Veterinary Technicians (AZVT)
c/o Dianna Lydick, RVT, Executive Director
650 S RL Thornton Fwy.
Dallas, TX 75203
URL: www.azvt.org
Social Media: www.facebook.com/
AssociationOfZooVeterinaryTechniciansazvt

2325 ■ AZVT Laurie Page-Peck Scholarship
(Graduate/Scholarship)

Purpose: To provide educational assistance for veterinary or medical technology students. **Focus:** Veterinary science and medicine. **Qualif.:** Applicant must be a veterinary or medical technology student interested in zoo veterinary technology.

Funds Avail.: Up to $1,500. **To Apply:** Applicants must submit a paper about zoo veterinary technology. **Deadline:** May 15. **Contact:** Kim Aubuchon, RVT Saint Louis Zoo; E-mail:kaubuchon@stlzoo.org.

2326 ■ Association of Zoos and Aquariums (AZA)
8403 Colesville Rd., Ste. 710
Silver Spring, MD 20910-3314
Ph: (301)562-0777
Fax: (301)562-0888
E-mail: membership@aza.org
URL: www.aza.org
Social Media: www.facebook.com/zoosaquariums
www.instagram.com/zoos_aquariums
www.pinterest.com/AZAanimals
twitter.com/zoos_aquariums
www.youtube.com/user/zooaquariumnetwork

2327 ■ Margaret A. Dankworth Management Scholarship *(Professional development/Scholarship)*

Purpose: To support and assist AZA members with their chosen course that led them to demonstrate leadership ability or leadership potential and a commitment to professional growth. **Focus:** Leadership, Institutional and community; Zoology. **Qualif.:** Applicants must be AZA individual members employed in an AZA zoo, aquarium or related facility; members of international AZA institutions are welcome to apply. **Criteria:** Selection will be based on merit; recipients are chosen by the AZA Professional Development Committee.

Duration: Annual. **To Apply:** Narratives include Program Analysis, Program Design, Program Development, Program Implementation Significance, value and innovation(maximum of six (6) pages) and evaluation maximum of two (2)

Awards are arranged alphabetically below their administering organizations

pages. Letter of Reference; Resume. **Deadline:** July 31. **Contact:** E-mail: scholarships@aza.org.

2328 ■ Robert O. Wagner Professional Development Scholarship *(Professional development/Scholarship)*

Purpose: To support professionals that demonstrates involvement in AZA programs or conservation activities, leadership ability or leadership potential and a commitment to professional growth. **Focus:** Zoology. **Qualif.:** Applicant must be an AZA individual member employed in an AZA zoo, aquarium or related facility. **Criteria:** Selection will be based on merit alone and not on need.

Duration: Annual. **To Apply:** Applications can be submitted online and further details can be obtained from the website; At least one letter of support must be from a supervisor must be submitted. **Deadline:** July 31. **Contact:** E-mail: scholarships@aza.org.

2329 ■ ASTM International
100 Barr Harbor Dr.
West Conshohocken, PA 19428-2959
Ph: (610)832-9500
Fax: (610)832-9555
E-mail: service@astm.org
URL: www.astm.org

2330 ■ Mary R. Norton Memorial Scholarship Award for Women *(Graduate/Award, Scholarship, Monetary, Recognition)*

Purpose: To encourage women college seniors or first-year graduate students to pursue the study of Physical Metallurgy or Materials Science, with emphasis on relationship of microstructure and properties. **Focus:** Mining. **Qualif.:** Applicants must be registered full-time and must expect to be classified as a senior for first-year graduate student during the academic year. **Criteria:** Selection will be based on interest or potential interest in a career in Physical Metallurgy or Materials Science as evidenced by the application statement and faculty recommendation.

Funds Avail.: $500. **Duration:** Annual. **Remarks:** Established in 1975. **Contact:** Travis Murdock; Phone: 610-832-9826; E-mail: tmurdock@astm.org.

2331 ■ Astronaut Scholarship Foundation (ASF)
651 Danville Drive, Suite 101
Orlando, FL 32825
Ph: (407)362-7900
E-mail: info@astronautscholarship.org
URL: www.astronautscholarship.org
Social Media: www.facebook.com/AstronautScholarship
www.instagram.com/astroscholarfdn
www.linkedin.com/company/astronaut-scholarship
  -foundation
twitter.com/astroscholarfdn
www.youtube.com/user/AstronautScholars/feed

2332 ■ Astronaut Scholarship Foundation Scholarship *(Undergraduate/Scholarship)*

Purpose: To ensure that the United States would maintain its leadership in science and technology by supporting some of the very best science, technology, engineering and math college students. **Focus:** Engineering; Mathematics and mathematical sciences; Science. **Qualif.:** Applicants

must be nominated by faculty members; must be U.S citizens; must be at least a sophomore applying for junior; must be enrolled in one of the participating universities; must be enrolled for both semesters as a full-time student for the ASF-supported academic year; must be seeking a STEM degree with intentions to pursue research or advance their field upon completion of their final degrees; intending to perform biomedical research are eligible. **Criteria:** Recipients will be selected by the ASF Scholarship Committee.

Funds Avail.: $10,000. **Duration:** Annual. **Number Awarded:** 50. **To Apply:** Applicants must submit the completed application form including two letters of recommendation, personal statement, a copy of academic transcripts, a copy of birth certificate, naturalization form, or U.S. passport to authenticate and confirm, C.V. or resume. **Deadline:** March 30. **Remarks:** Established in 1986. **Contact:** Phone: 407-362-7900; Email: info@ astronautscholarship.org.

2333 ■ Athenaeum of Philadelphia (PAT)
219 S 6th St.
Philadelphia, PA 19106-3794
Ph: (215)925-2688
Fax: (215)925-3755
URL: www.philaathenaeum.org
Social Media: www.facebook.com/philaathenaeum
www.instagram.com/philaathenaeum
www.linkedin.com/company/athenaeum-of-philadelphia
www.pinterest.com/PhilaAthenaeum
twitter.com/PhilaAthenaeum
www.youtube.com/user/PhilaAthenaeum

2334 ■ Charles E. Peterson Fellowships *(Other/ Fellowship)*

Purpose: To support professionals in the study, recording, and preservation of early American architecture and building technology (pre-1860) and the teaching of conservation skills in American schools of architecture. **Focus:** General studies/Field of study not specified. **Qualif.:** Applicants must be persons who hold a terminal degree and possess a distinguished record of accomplishment. **Criteria:** Applications are reviewed by a Committee of Architects, Architectural Historians and Educators appointed by the Athenaeum Board of Directors; preference will be given to those applicants who have research on Delaware Valley topics.

Funds Avail.: Maximum of $15,000. **Duration:** Annual. **To Apply:** Applicants should submit the application in the form of a single-page letter setting forth a brief statement of the project, with attached budget, schedule for completion, professional resume, and two letters of reference. **Deadline:** March 1. **Contact:** Peterson Fellowship Committee, The Athenaeum of Philadelphia, 219 S. 6th St., Philadelphia, PA 19106-3794.

2335 ■ Athletic Equipment Managers Association (AEMA)
c/o Sam Trusner
207 E. Bodman
Bement, IL 61813
Ph: (217)678-1004
Fax: (217)678-1005
E-mail: aema@frontiernet.net

Awards are arranged alphabetically below their administering organizations

URL: www.equipmentmanagers.org
Social Media: www.facebook.com/
AthleticEquipmentManagersAssociation
twitter.com/aema_74

2336 ■ Russell Athletics Scholarship
(Undergraduate/Scholarship)

Purpose: To assist students in furthering their professional abilities to athletic equipment management. **Focus:** General studies/Field of study not specified. **Qualif.:** Applicants must be full-tlme college students with one year collegiate athletic equipment management experience who display an interest in the field of athletic equipment management. **Criteria:** Selection will be based on academic achievement, community involvement, displayed interest in athletic equipment management, completion of an essay and letters of recommendation.

Funds Avail.: $500 each. **Duration:** Annual. **Number Awarded:** 3. **To Apply:** Applicants must provide three character references with letters of recommendation; one of these references must come from the Supervising Equipment Manager. They must also submit an original essay of no more than 200 words on the topic of "What Athletic Equipment Management Means to Me"; must submit the said documents along with the completed application form provided by AEMA. **Contact:** AEMA Office, c/o Sam Trusner, 207 E. Bodman, Bement, IL 61813.

2337 ■ Atkinson Charitable Foundation
1 Yonge St., Ste. 702
Toronto, ON, Canada M5E 1E5
Ph: (416)368-5152
Fax: (416)865-3619
E-mail: info@atkinsonfoundation.ca
URL: atkinsonfoundation.ca
Social Media: www.facebook.com/AtkinsonFoundation
www.ca.linkedin.com/company/atkinson-foundation
twitter.com/AtkinsonCF

2338 ■ Atkinson Fellowships in Public Policy
(Professional development/Fellowship)

Purpose: To financially assist professionals with undertaking a research project on a topical public policy issue. **Focus:** Broadcasting; Journalism; Public affairs. **Qualif.:** Applicants must be Canadian citizens or landed immigrants who are full-time journalists in print or broadcast media. **Criteria:** Selection will be given to issues that are at the forefront of public policy debate and have significant implications for Canadian society.

Funds Avail.: 75,000 Canadian Dollars stipend; 25,000 Canadian Dollars for research expenses. **Duration:** Annual. **Number Awarded:** 1. **To Apply:** Applicants must provide curriculum vitae; story that contains the importance to Canadian society; and related articles in a three-page letter of intent; in the letter, they should demonstrate considerable familiarity with their chosen topic; they should also articulate the specific policy questions they want to pursue; letters may be submitted in either English or French. **Remarks:** Established in 1988.

2339 ■ Atlanta Association of Legal Administrators (AALA)
c/o Brennan Fulton
1201 W Peachtree St.

One Atlantic Ctr.
Atlanta, GA 30309
E-mail: info@myaala.com
URL: www.myaala.com
Social Media: www.facebook.com/AtlantaALA
www.linkedin.com/company/atlanta-association-of-legal
-administrators
twitter.com/AtlantaALA
www.youtube.com/channel/UCQqCd5XLsuODC3iF_woM-
xlg

2340 ■ Gene Henson Scholarship *(Undergraduate/Scholarship)*

Purpose: To recognize and support outstanding graduating high school students in metro Atlanta. **Focus:** General studies/Field of study not specified. **Qualif.:** Applicants must be outstanding seniors attending high school in metro Atlanta; must be enrolling in a Georgia college or university and must have an acceptance letter from school of choice.

Funds Avail.: $10,000. **Duration:** Annual. **Number Awarded:** 1. **To Apply:** Application can be completed online at www.myaala.com/page/HensonScholarship. **Deadline:** April 30. **Remarks:** Established in 2004.

2341 ■ Atlantic County Bar Association
1201 Bacharach Boulevard
Atlantic City, NJ 08401
Ph: (609)345-3444
URL: www.atcobar.org
Social Media: www.facebook.com/Atcobara
twitter.com/ATCOBAR

2342 ■ The Vincent S. Haneman - Joseph B. Perskie Scholarship *(Graduate, Undergraduate/Fellowship)*

Purpose: To support law students with their educational pursuit. **Focus:** Law. **Qualif.:** Applicants must be admitted to an American bar association accredited law school; must be residents of Atlantic county for one year prior to application; and be law students in any year including the first year. **Criteria:** Selection is based on academic ability, financial need, leadership potential and character.

Funds Avail.: No specific amount. **Duration:** Annual. **To Apply:** Applicants must submit a completed application form. **Deadline:** January 1; May 1. **Contact:** Haneman-Perskie Scholarship Foundation, c/o Atlantic County Bar Association, 1201 Bacharach Blvd., Atlantic City, NJ, 08401.

2343 ■ Atlantic Provinces Library Association (APLA)
Kenneth C. Rowe Management Bldg., Dalhousie University
6100 University Ave., Ste. 4010
Halifax, NS, Canada B3H 4R2
E-mail: president@apla.ca
URL: www.apla.ca
Social Media: twitter.com/APLAcontact

2344 ■ APLA Merit Award *(Professional development/Scholarship)*

Purpose: To provide financial assistance to individuals to undertake or complete the academic requirement leading to a degree in Library and Information Science. **Focus:**

Awards are arranged alphabetically below their administering organizations

General studies/Field of study not specified; Library and archival sciences. **Criteria:** Selection is based on leadership in library associations, contributions to the development, application and utilization of library services and library systems, significant contribution to library literature.

Funds Avail.: No specific amount. **To Apply:** Applicants must submit application including nominee's achievements and letters of support. **Deadline:** April 30. **Contact:** Suzanne van den Hoogen, APLA Past President, Public Services Librarian, St. Francis Xavier University, Antigonish, NS B2G 2W5; Phone: 902-867-4535; Fax: 902-867-5153; Email: svandenh@stfx.ca.

2345 ■ Carin Alma E. Somers Scholarship (Undergraduate/Scholarship)

Purpose: To provide financial assistance to individuals to undertake or complete the academic requirement leading to a degree in Library and Information Science. **Focus:** Library and archival sciences. **Qualif.:** Applicants must be Canadian citizens; must be residents of Atlantic Provinces; and must have demonstrated financial need. **Criteria:** Selection of recipients will be recommended by a committee of the four Provincial Vice Presidents and the President-Elect to the Executive Committee.

Funds Avail.: $1,000. **Duration:** Annual. **To Apply:** Applicants must submit a completed application form. **Deadline:** March 31. **Contact:** VP, President Elect Patricia Doucette Holland College, 140 Weymouth St. Charlottetown, PE C1A 8Z3; Phone: 902-566-9350; Email: pmdoucette@hollandcollege.com.

2346 ■ Atlantic Salmon Federation (ASF)
15 Rankine Mill Rd.
Chamcook, NB, Canada E5B 3A9
E-mail: savesalmon@asf.ca
URL: www.asf.ca
Social Media: twitter.com/SalmonNews
www.youtube.com/user/ASFatlanticsalmon

2347 ■ Atlantic Salmon Federation Olin Fellowships (Graduate/Fellowship)

Purpose: To improve knowledge or skills in advanced fields while looking for solutions to current problems in Atlantic salmon biology, management and conservation. **Focus:** Biology, Marine. **Qualif.:** Applicants must be legal residents of the United States or Canada. At any accredited university, research laboratory or active management program. **Criteria:** Recipients are selected based on the committee's review of all applications.

Funds Avail.: $1,000-$3,000. **Duration:** Annual. **To Apply:** Applicants can collect the application forms from the Atlantic Salmon Federation Office in Canada or in USA; must attach a statement of qualifications; transcript of grades, if applicable; description of the program or project; and supporting documentation, if required. **Deadline:** March 15. **Contact:** Email:emansfield@asf.ca, phone (506) 529-1062.

2348 ■ Audio Engineering Society, Inc. (AES)
551 Fifth Ave., Ste. 1225
New York, NY 10176
Ph: (212)661-8528
URL: www.aes.org
Social Media: www.facebook.com/AES.org

www.instagram.com/aes_org
twitter.com/AESorg
www.youtube.com/user/AESorg

2349 ■ AES Graduate Studies Grants (Graduate/Grant, Award)

Purpose: To encourage the entry of talented students into the profession of audio engineering and related fields. **Focus:** Engineering. **Qualif.:** Applicants must have successfully completed an undergraduate degree program (typically four years) at a recognized college or university; demonstrated commitment to audio engineering (or a related field) as a career choice; acceptance or a pending application for graduate studies leading to a masters or higher degree, or an internationally recognized equivalent; and, be members in good standing of the Audio Engineering Society (any membership grade qualifies). **Criteria:** Selection will be based on the committee's criteria.

Funds Avail.: No specific amount. **Duration:** Annual. **To Apply:** Applicants must submit three letters of recommendation, which attest to the applicant's satisfactory progress toward the degree. **Deadline:** July 1. **Remarks:** Established in 1984.

2350 ■ Auto Care Association
7101 Wisconsin Ave., Ste. 1300
Bethesda, MD 20814-3415
Ph: (301)654-6664
Fax: (301)654-3299
E-mail: info@autocare.org
URL: www.autocare.org
Social Media: www.facebook.com/autocareorg
www.linkedin.com/groups/4869479/profile
twitter.com/autocareorg
www.youtube.com/user/AAIAssociation

2351 ■ Tom Babcox Memorial Scholarships (Professional development/Scholarship)

Purpose: To support continuing education tailored specifically for the business needs of the automotive service industry. **Focus:** Automotive technology. **Qualif.:** Applicants must work in mechanical repair industry; must demonstrate an interest in self-improvement through management education; must own or work for a business that as an ASA Collision division member in good standing. If an applicant is not a business owner, he/she must be recommended by a business owner.**Criteria:** Recipients are selected based on academic performance and demonstrated interest in automotive industry.

Funds Avail.: No specific amount. **Duration:** Annual. **To Apply:** Applicants must submit a completed application form. **Deadline:** August 17.

2352 ■ Florida Automotive Industry Scholarships (Undergraduate/Scholarship)

Purpose: To provide and promote practical business management service. Focus: Automotive technology. **Focus:** Automotive technology. **Qualif.:** Applicants must be high school seniors, or high school graduates, or persons possessing a GED. **Criteria:** Recipients are selected based on the academic achievement, merit, and need.

Funds Avail.: No specific amount. **To Apply:** Applicants must submit a complete application form. **Contact:** Phone: 813-962-4445.

Awards are arranged alphabetically below their administering organizations

2353 ■ Sloan Northwood University Heavy-Duty Scholarships *(Undergraduate/Scholarship)*

Purpose: To provide and promote practical business management service. **Focus:** Automotive technology. **Qualif.:** Applicants must be enrolled in the university's Automotive Aftermarket Management curriculum, Heavy Duty Management program or the Heavy Duty Vehicle Technology program; must be U.S. citizens and maintain a 2.5 cumulative grade point average. **Criteria:** Recipients are selected based on financial need and demonstrated career interest.

Funds Avail.: No specific amount. **To Apply:** Applicants must submit a complete application form. **Contact:** Phone: 616-395-5620.

2354 ■ Auto-Pets

2900 Auburn St.
Auburn Hills, MI 48326
Fax: (248)254-1797
Free: 877-250-7729
URL: www.litter-robot.com
Social Media: www.facebook.com/LitterRobot
instagram.com/thelitterrobot
www.linkedin.com/company/automated-pet-care-products
 -inc.
pinterest.com/litterrobot
twitter.com/litter_robot
youtube.com/user/TheLitterRobot

2355 ■ Auto-Pets "Out-of-the-Box Thinking" Scholarships *(All/Scholarship)*

Purpose: To get young people thinking about innovation. **Focus:** Business; Engineering; Marketing and distribution. **Qualif.:** Applicants must be U.S. Students; must be current students at an accredited university, community college, certificate program, graduate school, or equivalent institute within the United States. **Criteria:** Selection will be made for the person those who are unique and innovative pet product that makes pet care more enjoyable and completely fulfills the essay requirements.

Funds Avail.: $500 to $1,500. **Deadline:** July 18.

2356 ■ Automotive Industries Association of Canada (AIAC)

180 Elgin St., Ste. 1400
Ottawa, ON, Canada K2P 2K3
Ph: (613)728-5821
Fax: (613)728-6021
Free: 800-808-2920
E-mail: info@aiacanada.com
URL: www.aiacanada.com
Social Media: www.facebook.com/AIAofCanada
www.linkedin.com/company/aia-canada
twitter.com/AIAOFCANADA

2357 ■ AIA and the Global Automotive Aftermarket Symposium Scholarships *(Undergraduate/Scholarship)*

Purpose: To support deserving secondary students, college and university students who want to pursue a career in the automotive aftermarket. **Focus:** Automotive technology. **Qualif.:** Applicants must be graduating high school seniors or have graduated from high school within the past two years; must be enrolled in a college-level program, university or an accredited automotive technical program through either a CAMPE college or a CARS-approved institute; must be attending a full-time program in Canada or the United States. **Criteria:** Applicants will be selected based on their academic merit.

Funds Avail.: 1,000 Canadian Dollars. **Duration:** Annual. **To Apply:** Applicant must submit application along with essay; high school transcript; if applicant attending a post-secondary program, a copy of your current school transcript with official school seal; letter of recommendation (from a non family member, preferably an employer, teacher or someone other than a family friend). **Deadline:** June 15. **Contact:** Peter Kornafel; Phone: 816-584-0511; Email: pete@petekornafel.com.

2358 ■ Hans McCorriston Grant *(Undergraduate/Grant)*

Purpose: To support students pursuing careers as motive power machinists. **Focus:** Automotive technology. **Qualif.:** Applicants must be enrolled in the AIA Motive Power Machinist Training Program or a college-level machinist training program within Canada.

Funds Avail.: 1,000 Canadian Dollars. **Duration:** Annual. **Number Awarded:** 5. **To Apply:** Applicants must complete and submit online application. **Contact:** Didina Kyenge; Email: didina.kyenge@aiacanada.com; Phone: 800-808-2920 ext. 231.

2359 ■ Arthur Paulin Automotive Aftermarket Scholarship Awards *(Postgraduate, Undergraduate/Scholarship)*

Purpose: To provide monetary assistance to deserving students in the automotive field. **Focus:** Automotive technology. **Qualif.:** Applicants must be enrolled in an automotive aftermarket industry-related program or curriculum at a Canadian college or university. This includes students pursuing their studies as an automotive apprentice. It also includes studies in any of the following automotive sectors: auto body, hard parts, heavy duty or motive power (machinists). **Criteria:** Recipients are selected based on Scholarship Committee's review of applications and other supporting documents.

Funds Avail.: 700 Canadian Dollars. **Duration:** Annual. **Number Awarded:** Varies. **To Apply:** Application form; letter from the applicant stating his/her long-term automotive goals; letter from the applicant's primary automotive instructor stating why the instructor feels the scholarship applicant is worthy of receiving the scholarship; letter from the applicant's primary automotive instructor stating why the instructor feels the scholarship applicant is worthy of receiving the scholarship; letter from the applicant's primary automotive instructor stating why the instructor feels the scholarship applicant is worthy of receiving the scholarship; letter from the applicant's primary automotive instructor stating why the instructor feels the scholarship applicant is worthy of receiving the scholarship. **Deadline:** November 30. **Remarks:** Award was named after long time AIA volunteer Arthur Paulin, who served as President of H. Paulin and Company Limited for over 35 years and he became Chairman of the Board in 1990. **Contact:** Emial:info@aiacanada.com; Phone:613-728-6021.

2360 ■ Marion Roberts Memorial Scholarships *(Undergraduate/Scholarship)*

Purpose: To provide financial assistance and encouragement enabling students to further their education at the

---

Awards are arranged alphabetically below their administering organizations

post-secondary school level. **Focus:** General studies/Field of study not specified. **Qualif.:** Applicant must be a dependent child or spouse of a full-time employee in an active AIA member company; confirmation of the parent's/spouse employment must be provided by the member company. Applicant must be enrolled in a full-time post-secondary program leading to a degree, certificate or diploma at an accredited university, college, technical school or C.E.G.E.P. **Criteria:** Recipients are selected based on Scholarship Committee's review of applications.

To Apply: Applicants must fill out the application form available at the website; must prepare a letter that demonstrates leadership ability in school, social or other activities; must have a transcript indicating academic achievement, with an official seal or photocopy of the seal of the school; recent passport-sized photo.

2361 ■ Automotive Parts and Service Association of Illinois
5330 Wall St.
Madison, WI 53718-7929
Ph: (217)786-2850
Fax: (608)240-2069
Free: 800-236-6332
E-mail: info@apsail.com
URL: apsail.com

2362 ■ Ralph Silverman Memorial Scholarship
(Undergraduate/Scholarship)

Purpose: To further promote quality and high standards through education within the automotive aftermarket industry. **Focus:** Automotive technology. **Qualif.:** Applicants must be students who intend to pursue a career in the automotive aftermarket industry. Applicants must be residents of Illinois and members of APSA Illinois. **Criteria:** Recipients are selected based on academic performance and demonstrated an interest in the automotive industry.

Duration: Annual. **To Apply:** Applications can be submitted online. **Deadline:** Mary 31.

2363 ■ Automotive Recyclers Association (ARA)
9113 Church St.
Manassas, VA 20110
Ph: (571)208-0428
URL: www.a-r-a.org
Social Media: www.instagram.com/astatraveladvisors

2364 ■ ARA Scholarship Awards *(Undergraduate/Scholarship)*
Purpose: To assist outstanding students to pursue their educational goal. **Focus:** Business; Education, Vocational-technical. **Qualif.:** Applicant must be parent employed at least 1 year, whose business organization (Owner) is a member of the ARA in good standing. Owners, or children of owners, and those owning over $100,000 of stock in the employing firm are not eligible. Be enrolled in a post-high school program at a college, university, or accredited school providing trade, business or technical programs, taking a minimum of 12 credit hours or equivalent of a full-time student. College/University applicants - have achieved at least a 3.0 grade point average, or the equivalent, in their previous educational program. Accredited Trade, Business or Technical School/Program applicants - have achieved at least a 2.0 grade point average, or the equivalent, in their

previous educational program. Previous recipients may reapply annually for a maximum of 3 awards. A renewal application is required.**Criteria:** Applicants will be selected based on their academic achievement.

Funds Avail.: No specific amount. **Duration:** Annual. **Number Awarded:** Over 40. **To Apply:** Applicants must submit a completed application form and profile sheet; transcript; A letter of verification from the ARA member company that the applicant or the parent of the applicant is currently employed and in good standing with their employer; parent completed certification form if not an employee. **Deadline:** March 15. **Remarks:** Established in 1963. **Contact:** ARA Director of Member Services, Kelly Badillo at (571) 208-0428 or via email at kelly@a-r-a.org.

2365 ■ Automotive Women's Alliance Foundation (AWAF)
PO Box 4305
Troy, MI 48099
Fax: (248)239-0291
Free: 877-393-2923
E-mail: admin@awafoundation.org
Social Media: www.facebook.com/groups/67060378726
www.linkedin.com/groups/1919546/profile
twitter.com/AutomotiveWomen

2366 ■ Automotive Women's Alliance Foundation Scholarships *(Undergraduate/Scholarship)*

Purpose: To support the advancement of automotive professionals and motivate current and future students studying an automotive related field. **Focus:** Automotive technology. **Qualif.:** Applicants must be Must be an undergraduate student, a graduate student or a postgraduate student. Must attend a university, a four-year college or two-year college. Minimum 3.0 GPA. Restricted to female students. Both full-time and part-time students. Restricted to residents of Mississippi. Restricted to students studying Applied Sciences, Accounting, Business/Consumer Services, Chemical Engineering, Communications, Computer Science/Data Processing, Civil Engineering, Economics, Electrical Engineering/Electronics, Energy and Power Engineering, Engineering-Related Technologies, Engineering/Technology, Environmental Science, Finance, Graphics/Graphic Arts/Printing, Human Resources, Industrial Design, International Studies, Law/Legal Services, Meteorology/Atmospheric Science, Mechanical Engineering, Mathematics, Marketing, Materials Science, Engineering, and Metallurgy, Advertising/Public Relations, Statistics, Science, Technology, and Society, Transportation.**Criteria:** Scholarships are given based on academic merit.

Funds Avail.: No specific amount. **Contact:** RoseAnn Nicolai, Administrator, admin@AWAFoundation.org, Tel: 877-393-2923.

2367 ■ AVAC: Global Advocacy for HIV Prevention
423 W 127th St., 4th Fl.
New York, NY 10027
Ph: (212)796-6423
Fax: (646)365-3452
E-mail: avac@avac.org
URL: www.avac.org
Social Media: www.facebook.com/HIVpxresearch
twitter.com/hivpxresearch

Awards are arranged alphabetically below their administering organizations

www.youtube.com/user/HIVPxResearch

2368 ■ HIV Prevention Research Advocacy Fellowships *(Professional development/Fellowship)*

Purpose: To provide support to emerging and mid-career advocates to design and implement advocacy projects focused on biomedical HIV prevention research and implementation activities in their countries and communities. **Focus:** AIDS. **Qualif.:** Applicants must be emerging or mid-career community leaders and advocates involved or interested in advocacy around HIV prevention research and implementation; must be individuals with some experience or education in the areas of HIV and AIDS, public health, medicine, international development, women's rights, communications or advocacy with key populations, such as sex workers, LGBT people and drug users; must be based in low and middle-income countries where biomedical HIV prevention clinical research is planned or ongoing and/or where there is current work on implementation of voluntary medical male circumcision, pre-exposure prophylaxis, treatment as prevention and combination prevention packages that link biomedical strategies. Advocates can also develop proposals that seek to catalyze plans and policies in the country where little activity on these issues has happened to date; must be able to collaborate with English-speaking mentors; must demonstrate strategic analysis of how Fellowship-related activities will relate to this work. **Criteria:** Selection will be based on the committee's criteria.

Funds Avail.: No specific amount. **To Apply:** Applications form can be downloaded at the website. Applicants must submit the individual and host organization information forms, the essay/short answer questions, the host organization letter of support and applicants' CV/resume. **Deadline:** September 20. **Contact:** Email: fellows@avac.org.

2369 ■ AvaCare Medical
1665 Corporate Rd. W
Lakewood, NJ 08701
Free: 877-813-7799
E-mail: info@avacaremedical.com
URL: avacaremedical.com
Social Media: www.facebook.com/avacaremedical
www.pinterest.com/avacaremedical
twitter.com/AvaCareMedical

2370 ■ AvaCare Medical Scholarship
(Undergraduate/Scholarship)

Purpose: To support students by providing them a scholarship toward college tuition. **Focus:** Dentistry; Medicine; Nursing; Nutrition. **Qualif.:** Applicants must be citizens of the united states or in a possession of an alien registration card; must be a high school senior or enrolled in an accredited U.S. college or university; must have a minimum cumulative GPA of 3.0; must be pursuing a degree in the medical field such as therapy, nursing, medicine, nutrition, laboratory science, dentistry, etc. **Criteria:** Selection will be judged on content, creativity and quality of work; must be own unique work and cannot be published anywhere else online.

Funds Avail.: $1,000. **Duration:** Annual. **Number Awarded:** 1. **To Apply:** Applicants must send a project about an act of kindness that inspired them along with their transcript, name, email address, phone number, and the field they are pursuing via mail or email; may choose to

complete any one of the following projects Blog post (up to 800 words), relevant pictures may be included; video, up to 1.5 minutes; Image, up to 8.5" x 11", along with a short description. **Deadline:** December 15. **Contact:** AvaCare Medical, Scholarship Department, 1665 Corporate Rd W, Lakewood, NJ, 08701; Email: scholarships@avacaremedical.com.

2371 ■ Aviation Distributors and Manufacturers Association (ADMA)
PO Box 3948
Parker, CO 80134
Ph: (720)249-0999
URL: www.adma.org

2372 ■ ADMA International Scholarship
(Undergraduate/Scholarship)

Purpose: To provide assistance for students pursuing careers in the aviation field. **Focus:** Aviation. **Qualif.:** Applicants must be third year students enrolled in a four year program at an accredited post secondary institution majoring in Aviation Management or a Professional Pilot program; a first year student in an A&P program at a two-year accredited program.

Funds Avail.: No specific amount. **Duration:** Annual. **Deadline:** April 2.

2373 ■ AVS Science and Technology Society (AVS)
125 Maiden Ln., 15th Fl.
New York, NY 10038
Ph: (212)248-0200
Fax: (212)248-0245
E-mail: yvonne@avs.org
URL: www.avs.org
Social Media: www.facebook.com/AmericanVacuumSociety
www.linkedin.com/groups/1309457/profile
twitter.com/AVS_Members

2374 ■ AVS Applied Surface Science Division
(Graduate/Award)

Purpose: To provide a forum for research and education in the preparation, characterization, modification, and utilization of surfaces and interfaces in practical applications. **Focus:** Science technologies. **Qualif.:** Applicants must be graduate students that will need to present a poster or talk during any Applied Surface Science Division sessions, plus an additional capsule (3-slide, 5-minute) presentation to the judges. **Criteria:** Selection will be based on the scientific merit and originality of students' work.

Funds Avail.: $1,000. **Duration:** Annual. **To Apply:** Applicants wishing to participate in the competition should contact the ASSD Student Award Chair when submitting an abstract. **Deadline:** May 2. **Contact:** All documents including the nomination form and the supporting letters should be sent to the ASSD Awards committee at ASSDAwards@avs.org.

2375 ■ AVS Biomaterial Interfaces Division - Early Career Researchers Awards (BID-ECR) *(Graduate/Monetary)*

Purpose: To recognize and encourage excellence in continuing graduate studies in the sciences and technolo-

Awards are arranged alphabetically below their administering organizations

gies of interest to American Vacuum Society. **Focus:** Science technologies. **Qualif.:** Applicants must have a Ph.D. or equivalent degree which was earned less than 10 years prior to January 1 of the award year. **Criteria:** Selection will be based on the committee's criteria.

Funds Avail.: $250. **Duration:** Annual. **To Apply:** Applicants must submit: a letter and two supporting letters; a biography and CV of the nominee; and a copy of the abstract. **Deadline:** May 1. **Contact:** Application materials should be sent by email to: Prof Axel Rosenhahn at axel.rosenhahn@rub.de.

2376 ■ AVS Electronic Materials and Photonic Division Postdoctoral Award (Postdoctorate/Award)

Purpose: To recognize postdoctoral fellows who will be presenting EMPD papers at the International Symposium. **Focus:** Science technologies. **Qualif.:** Applicants must be postdoctoral fellows who have an accepted abstract.

Funds Avail.: $500. **To Apply:** Applicants must submit a copy of the accepted abstract with program number; a recommendation letter from their advisor; their curriculum vitae; and a cover letter of request. **Deadline:** September 7.

2377 ■ AVS Manufacturing Science and Technology Group (Graduate/Award)

Purpose: To encourage participation of students in the MSTG program and to acknowledge the valuable contributions they make in advancing state-of-the-art in manufacturing science and technology. **Focus:** Science technologies. **Qualif.:** Applicants must be full-time university graduate students with primary appointments at universities. **Criteria:** Selection process will give preference to applicants who give oral presentations of their papers.

Funds Avail.: No specific amount. **Duration:** Annual. **Number Awarded:** Up to 2. **To Apply:** Applicants must submit the following: a 1-page letter of application describing the students research; letter of endorsement by the student's research advisor; copy of submitted abstract; completed application. **Deadline:** May 2.

2378 ■ AVS MEMS and NEMS Technical Group Best Paper Award (Undergraduate, Graduate/Monetary)

Purpose: To promote outstanding scientific research and technological innovation. **Focus:** Science technologies. **Qualif.:** Applicants must be undergraduate or graduate students. **Criteria:** Applicants will be judged on the quality, originality of their research and their skill in presentation (oral/poster).

Funds Avail.: $500. **Duration:** Annual. **To Apply:** Applicants should submit a cover letter describing their intent to compete along with a copy of their AVS abstract, current resume. **Deadline:** May 2.

2379 ■ AVS Nanometer-Scale Science and Technology Division Graduate Award (Graduate/Monetary)

Purpose: To give recognition to outstanding research by graduate students giving oral presentations in NSTD sessions at AVS international symposia. **Focus:** Science technologies. **Qualif.:** Applicants must be graduate students. **Criteria:** Selection will based on the quality of the talk, the responses to questions, and the level of the research.

Funds Avail.: $500. **Duration:** Annual. **To Apply:** Applicants must submit a completed application, a copy of the abstract, an extended abstract written by the student of no

more than three pages, and a recommendation letter from the students' research advisor, who must be a member of AVS. **Deadline:** May 2.

2380 ■ AVS Spectroscopic Ellipsometry Focus Topic Graduate Student Awards (Graduate/Award)

Purpose: To recognize graduate students and young postdoc researchers in a Focus Topic on SE session at the Annual Symposium. **Focus:** Science technologies. **Qualif.:** Interested applicants must be competitive graduate students and young post-doctoral researchers. **Criteria:** Selection will be based on the submitted application materials.

Funds Avail.: $500. **Duration:** Annual. **To Apply:** Interested applicants must submit the following: curriculum vitae; a copy of their submitted AVS abstract; and a letter of recommendation from their research advisor.

2381 ■ AVS Thin Film Division James Harper Awards (Graduate/Monetary)

Purpose: To recognize the best oral presentation by a graduate student in a Thin Film Division session at the Annual Symposium. **Focus:** Science technologies. **Qualif.:** Applicants must be currently registered graduate students. **Criteria:** Selection will be based on the committee's criteria.

Funds Avail.: $800; two $500 for the runner-ups. **Duration:** Annual. **To Apply:** Applicants must submit the curriculum vitae; a copy of their submitted AVS abstract; and a letter of recommendation from their research advisor. **Deadline:** May 2.

2382 ■ John Coburn and Harold Winters Student Award in Plasma Science and Technology (Graduate/Award)

Purpose: To promote outstanding scientific research and technological innovation. **Focus:** Science technologies. **Qualif.:** Applicants must be students. **Criteria:** Selection will be based on the oral presentation, the quality of research, the clarity of the presentation and the potential for the research to advance the field of plasma science.

Funds Avail.: $500. **Duration:** Annual. **To Apply:** Applicants must submit a curriculum vitae of the nominee; a one-page letter of endorsement from the student's research advisor/mentor; a copy of the nominee's submitted abstract for the AVS International Symposium. **Deadline:** May 2. **Remarks:** Established in 1994.

2383 ■ Dorothy M. and Earl S. Hoffman Award (Graduate/Award)

Purpose: To recognize and encourage excellence in continuing graduate studies in the sciences and technologies of interest to American Vacuum Society. **Focus:** Science technologies. **Qualif.:** Applicant must be a registered graduate student in an accredited academic institution at the time when the applications are due; expected not to graduate before the award selection. **Criteria:** Selection will be based on the excellence in research and academic record.

Remarks: Established in 2002.

2384 ■ Magnetic Interfaces & Nanostructures Division - Leo M. Falicov Student Award (Graduate/Grant)

Purpose: To recognize outstanding research performed by a graduate student in areas of interest to the MIND. **Focus:** Science technologies. **Qualif.:** Applicants must be gradu-

Awards are arranged alphabetically below their administering organizations

ate students. **Criteria:** Selection will be based on the oral presentation, considering quality of research and clarity of presentation.

Funds Avail.: No specific amount. **Duration:** Annual. **To Apply:** Selection will be based on the oral presentation, considering quality of research and clarity of presentation. **Deadline:** May 2.

2385 ■ Morton M. Traum Surface Science Student Award *(Graduate, Doctorate/Prize)*

Purpose: To recognize and support the best student presenter at the AVS International Symposium. **Focus:** Science technologies. **Qualif.:** Applicants must be either current graduate students or have received the Ph.D. degree in the year of the Symposium. **Criteria:** Selection will be based on the scientific content and presentation skill.

Funds Avail.: $1,000. **Duration:** Annual. **To Apply:** Candidates must submit the following: a copy of the abstract that includes the abstract submission number; an extended abstract that does not exceed two pages (including tables, figures and references); and expected graduation date. **Deadline:** May 2. **Remarks:** Established in 1981.

2386 ■ Russell & Sigurd Varian Award *(Graduate/Recognition)*

Purpose: To recognize and encourage excellence in continuing graduate studies in the sciences and technologies of interest to AVS. **Focus:** Science technologies. **Qualif.:** Applicants must be registered graduate students in an accredited academic institution at the time when the applications are due; expected not to graduate before the award selection. **Criteria:** Selection will be based on the excellence in research and academic record.

Funds Avail.: No specific amount. **Duration:** Annual. **Remarks:** The award was established to commemorate the pioneering work of Russell and Sigurd Varian in the field of vacuum science and technology. Established in 1982.

2387 ■ Nellie Yeoh Whetten Award *(Graduate/Recognition)*

Purpose: To recognize and encourage excellence by women in graduate studies in the sciences and technologies of interest to AVS. **Focus:** Science technologies. **Qualif.:** Applicants must be registered female graduate students in an accredited academic institution at the time when the applications are due; applicants are normally expected not to graduate before the award selection. **Criteria:** Selection will be based on the excellence in research and academic record.

Funds Avail.: No specific amount. **Duration:** Annual. **To Apply:** Applicants must submit a completed application form, the Report on Candidate Form, abstract to the AVS International Symposium. **Remarks:** Established to honor Nellie Yeoh Whetten. Established in 1989.

2388 ■ AWeber Communications
1100 Manor Dr.
Chalfont, PA 18914
Free: 877-293-2371
E-mail: abuse@aweber.com
URL: www.aweber.com

2389 ■ The Aweber Developing Futures Scholarship *(Undergraduate/Scholarship)*

Purpose: To invest in the young individuals who will be the entrepreneurs, business owners, and hard-working professionals of the future. **Focus:** Advertising; Business; Communications; Marketing and distribution. **Qualif.:** Applicants must be undergraduate students studying in the business/marketing/communications fields.

Funds Avail.: $2,500. **Duration:** Annual. **Deadline:** May 31.

2390 ■ AX Control Inc.
55 rue Murray St., Ste. 330
Ottawa, ON, Canada K1N 5M3
URL: www.raic.org

2391 ■ AX Control, Inc. Academic Scholarship *(College/Scholarship)*

Purpose: To support the educational pursuits of a student who has an interest in the impact a small business can have on the American economy. **Focus:** General studies/Field of study not specified. **Qualif.:** Applicant must be at least 18 years old by the selection date and be enrolled full- or part-time in an undergraduate program. **Criteria:** Selection is based on the essay that best exemplifies a passion for small business in the United States.

Funds Avail.: $1,000. **Number Awarded:** 1. **To Apply:** Applicant must submit an 800-1,200 word essay based on a personal account of how a small business impacted the applicant, or an ambition applicant may have to start a small business of their own. Applicant must also provide their student ID number and proof of age if asked. Submission form is located on the sponsor's website at www.axcontrol.com/scholarship. **Deadline:** June 1.

2392 ■ AXA Equitable Life Insurance Co.
1290 Avenue of the Americas
New York, NY 10104
URL: www.axa-equitable.com
Social Media: www.facebook.com/AXAUS
www.linkedin.com/company/axa-us
twitter.com/axa_us

2393 ■ AXA Achievement Scholarship *(Undergraduate/Scholarship)*

Purpose: To provide scholarships to high school seniors and college students who demonstrated outstanding achievement. **Focus:** General studies/Field of study not specified. **Qualif.:** Applicants must be US citizens or legal residents; be current high school seniors who plan to enroll full-time in an accredited two-year or four-year college or university in the US; demonstrate ambition and self-drive as evidence by outstanding achievement in an activity in school, the community or the workplace.

Funds Avail.: $2,500 - $25,000 each. **Duration:** Annual.

2394 ■ Ayn Rand Institute (ARI)
6 Hutton Centre Drive, Suite 600
Santa Ana, CA 92707
Ph: (949)222-6550
Fax: (949)222-6558
E-mail: mail@aynrand.org
URL: www.aynrand.org
Social Media: www.facebook.com/AynRandOrg
www.instagram.com/aynrandorg
www.pinterest.com/aynrandorg

Awards are arranged alphabetically below their administering organizations

twitter.com/aynrandorg
www.youtube.com/user/AynRandInstitute

2395 ■ Atlas Shrugged Essay Contest *(Graduate, Undergraduate, High School/Prize)*

Purpose: To encourage students to use and practice their writing skills through essay contests. **Focus:** General studies/Field of study not specified. **Qualif.:** Applicant must be a 12th grader, college undergraduate or graduate student for any part of the school year in which the contest is held. ARI reserves the right to make exceptions to this rule, on a case-by-case basis, for international students or for students with nonstandard school years. **Criteria:** Essays will be judged on whether the student is able to argue for and justify their view--not on whether the Institute agrees with the view the student expresses. Judges will look for writing that is clear, articulate and logically organized. Winning essays must demonstrate an outstanding grasp of the philosophic meaning of Atlas Shrugged.

Funds Avail.: $25,000 - 1st prize; $2,500 - 2nd prize; $500 - 3rd prize; $100 - finalists. **Number Awarded:** 1 - 1st prize; 3 -2nd place; 5 - 3rd place; 50 - finalists. **To Apply:** Applicants must read Atlas Shrugged and write an 800 to 1,600-word essay on one of three assigned topics available on aynrand.org/contests; applicants may submit the essay online or by mail. **Deadline:** September 21. **Contact:** Email: essays@aynrand.org.

2396 ■ Ayn Rand Institute Anthem Essay Contest *(High School, Undergraduate/Prize)*

Purpose: To support high school and college students for the best essay on Ayn Rand's fiction. **Focus:** General studies/Field of study not specified. **Qualif.:** Applicant must be in the 8th, 9th, 10th, 11th or 12th grade at the time of the current contest deadline. ARI reserves the right to make exceptions to this rule, on a case-by-case basis, for international students or for students with nonstandard school years. **Criteria:** Essays will be judged on whether the student is able to argue for and justify their view - not on whether the Institute agrees with the view the student expresses. Judges will look for writing that is clear, articulate and logically organized. Winning essays must demonstrate an outstanding grasp of the philosophic meaning of Anthem.

Funds Avail.: $2,000 - 1st prize; $250 - 2nd prize; $100 - 3rd prize; $25 - finalists. **Number Awarded:** 1 - 1st place; 3 - 2nd place; 5 - 3rd place; 50 -finalists. **To Apply:** Applicants must read Anthem and write a 600 to 1, 200-word essay on one of three assigned topics available on aynrand.org/contests. **Deadline:** May 28. **Contact:** Email: essays@aynrand.org.

2397 ■ Ayn Rand Institute Fountainhead Essay Contest *(High School, Undergraduate/Prize)*

Purpose: To support and help high school students for the best essay on Ayn Rand's fiction. **Focus:** General studies/ Field of study not specified. **Qualif.:** Applicant must be in the 11th or 12th grade for any part of the school year in which the contest is held. ARI reserves the right to make exceptions to this rule, on a case-by-case basis, for international students or for students with nonstandard school years. **Criteria:** Essays will be judged on whether the student is able to argue for and justify their view--not on whether the Institute agrees with the view the student expresses. Judges will look for writing that is clear, articulate and logically organized. Winning essays must demonstrate an outstanding grasp of the philosophic meaning of The Fountainhead.

Funds Avail.: $10,000 - 1st prize; $2,500 - 2nd prize; $500 - 3rd prize; $50 - finalists. **Number Awarded:** 1 - 1st place; 3 - 2nd place; 5 - 3rd place; 50 -finalists. **To Apply:** Applicants must read The Fountainhead and write an 800-1, 600 word essay on one of three assigned topics available on aynrand.org/contests. **Deadline:** May 28. **Contact:** Email: essays@aynrand.org.

2398 ■ The Azarian Group LLC

6 Prospect St.ste. 2A
Midland Park, NJ 07432
Ph: (201)444-7111
E-mail: info@azariangroup.com
URL: www.azariangroup.com

2399 ■ John M. Azarian Memorial Armenian Youth Scholarship Fund *(Undergraduate/Scholarship)*

Purpose: To provide financial assistance to students of Armenian descent. **Focus:** General studies/Field of study not specified. **Qualif.:** Applicants must be undergraduate students of Armenian descent attending a college or university in the United States.

To Apply: Application form and details available at www.azariangroup.com/scholarship-program/how-to-apply/. **Deadline:** May 31. **Remarks:** Established in 1976. **Contact:** Email: Jcifuentes@azariangroup.com.

2400 ■ BadCredit.org

15 SE 1st Ave., Ste. B
Gainesville, FL 32601
Free: 888-217-5962
URL: www.badcredit.org
Social Media: www.facebook.com/BadCredit.org
twitter.com/BadCreditorg

2401 ■ BadCredit.orgs Wealth Wise Scholarship *(Undergraduate, Graduate/Scholarship)*

Purpose: To provide support to future professionals of the finance industry. **Focus:** Accounting; Business; Finance; Mathematics and mathematical sciences. **Qualif.:** Applicant must be majoring in the finance industry (finance, business, accounting, mathematics, management, communications, and related majors); must be a U.S. resident; must be a current or future college student (high school senior) with a minimum 3.5 GPA. **Criteria:** Selection will be based on the essay: writing quality; knowledge of essay topic; and thought leadership.500-900 words. The essay should be written in 12-point font, Times New Roman, double-spaced, 1-inch margins.

Funds Avail.: $1,000. **Duration:** Annual. **Number Awarded:** 1. **To Apply:** Applicant must submit an essay and official transcript. Application details available online at www.badcredit.org/scholarship. **Deadline:** December 31. **Contact:** Email: jena@badcredit.org.

2402 ■ The Bailey Family Foundation (BFF)

912 W Platt St.
Tampa, FL 33606
Ph: (813)549-6140
Fax: (813)549-6141
E-mail: contact@bailey-family.org
URL: www.bailey-family.org
Social Media: www.facebook.com/BFFTampa

Awards are arranged alphabetically below their administering organizations

www.linkedin.com/company/8696861
www.linkedin.com/company/the-bailey-family-foundation

2403 ■ The Bailey Family Foundation College Scholarship Program (Undergraduate/Scholarship)

Purpose: To financially assist students in continuing their education. **Focus:** General studies/Field of study not specified. **Qualif.:** Applicant must be a U.S. residents and college student pursuing an undergraduate degree; and must possess a minimum cumulative GPA of 2.5 and demonstrate financial need. **Criteria:** Applicants will be evaluated based on academic achievement and financial need.

Funds Avail.: $5,000. **Duration:** Annual. **To Apply:** Applicants must submit a completed scholarship application form including an essay of no more than 300 words describing any community service or other activities that have influenced them or telling the reviewers about the their goals. **Deadline:** February 29.

2404 ■ The Bailey Family Foundation High School Scholarships Program (Undergraduate/Scholarship)

Purpose: To provide financial assistance for high school seniors intending to continue their post-secondary education. **Focus:** General studies/Field of study not specified. **Qualif.:** Applicants must be U.S. residents and be graduating seniors who possess a minimum cumulative GPA of 2.5 and demonstrate financial need; must be from a participating high school and pursuing an undergraduate degree. **Criteria:** Applicants will be evaluated based on academic achievement and financial need.

Funds Avail.: $5,000. **Duration:** Annual; renewable up to 4 years. **To Apply:** Applicants must submit a completed scholarship application form including an essay of no more than 300 words describing any community service or other activities that have influenced them or telling the reviewers about the their goals. **Deadline:** February 29.

2405 ■ Baker, Donelson, Bearman, Caldwell and Berkowitz, P.C.

165 Madison Ave., Ste. 2000
Memphis, TN 38103
Ph: (901)526-2000
Fax: (901)577-2303
E-mail: contact@bakerdonelson.com
URL: www.bakerdonelson.com
Social Media: www.facebook.com/BakerDonelson
www.linkedin.com/company/baker-donelson
twitter.com/Baker_Donelson

2406 ■ Baker Donelson Diversity Scholarship (Undergraduate/Scholarship)

Purpose: To help law students defray the cost of law school tuition and related expenses. **Focus:** Law. **Qualif.:** Applicants must be diverse law students. **Criteria:** Selection will be based on the committee's criteria.

Funds Avail.: $10,000 each. **Duration:** Annual. **Number Awarded:** 3. **To Apply:** Applicants must visit the website for the online application tool. **Deadline:** June 15.

2407 ■ Baker and Hostetler LLP

191 N Wacker Dr., Ste. 3100
Chicago, IL 60606-1901
Ph: (312)416-6200

Fax: (312)416-6201
E-mail: rokada@bakerlaw.com
URL: www.bakerlaw.com
Social Media: www.facebook.com/BakerHostetler/
www.instagram.com/bakerhostetler/
www.linkedin.com/company/bakerhostetler/
twitter.com/BakerHostetler
www.youtube.com/user/BakerHostetlerLaw

2408 ■ BakerHostetler Diversity Fellowship Program (Undergraduate/Fellowship)

Purpose: To recruit candidates with diverse backgrounds and perspectives to foster an inclusive workplace. **Focus:** Law. **Qualif.:** Applicants must be enrolled full-time in an ABA-accredited law school and in good standing as a second-year law student at the time of application; member of one of the under-represented racial/ethnic groups set forth by the Equal Employment Opportunity Commission or a member of the LGBT community; not a recipient of a similar diversity award from another law firm for the same time period; must spend at least eight weeks with the firm; splitting time between two offices may be permitted based upon approval of the two offices' Hiring Partners; a US citizens or otherwise authorized to work in the United States. **Criteria:** Selection will be based on the demonstrated superior academic performance during college and law school, significant personal achievements and strong community involvement; law school students will need to possess strong oral and written communication skills, demonstrated leadership achievements and a sincere interest and commitment to join BakerHostetler.

Funds Avail.: $25,000. **To Apply:** Applicants must provide the completed application form; current resume; unofficial or official undergraduate and law school transcripts; personal statement; two professional or academic references. **Deadline:** November 1. **Contact:** Dee Driscole, Attorney Recruitment and Development Manager, BakerHostetler; Email: ddriscole@bakerlaw.com.

2409 ■ Paul D. White Scholarship Program (Undergraduate/Scholarship)

Purpose: To provide minority law students with valuable experience early in their careers. **Focus:** Law. **Qualif.:** Applicants must be law students of Black or African American, Hispanic or Latino, Native Hawaiian or Pacific Islander, Asian, American Indian or Alaska Native descent.

Funds Avail.: $7,500 and a paid summer clerkship. **Duration:** Annual. **Number Awarded:** 3. **To Apply:** Applications for sponsor offices in Cincinnati, Cleveland, and Columbus are available online at: www.bakerlaw.com/diversity/firmdiversityscholarship.

2410 ■ Baker McKenzie

300 E Randolph St., Ste. 5000
Chicago, IL 60601
Ph: (312)861-8000
Fax: (312)861-2899
URL: www.bakermckenzie.com
Social Media: www.facebook.com/officialbakermckenzie
twitter.com/bakermckenzie
www.youtube.com/BakerMcKenzieGlobal

2411 ■ Baker McKenzie Diversity Fellowship (Postgraduate, Professional development/Fellowship)

Purpose: To encourage and support upcoming law students who are contributing essentially to the diversity of

Awards are arranged alphabetically below their administering organizations

legal community. **Focus:** Law; Minorities. **Qualif.:** Applicants must be qualified rising second-year law students who show promise of contributing meaningfully to the diversity of the legal community; must meet the academic and hiring criteria of Baker and McKenzie's summer associate program; must receive an offer of summer employment for their second-year summer; and must be members of a population that historically has been underrepresented in the legal profession. **Criteria:** Selection will be based on the applicant's eligibility and compliance with the application process.

Funds Avail.: $10,000. **Duration:** Annual. **To Apply:** Applicants must complete the application and submit the following: current resume; a copy of undergraduate transcript; a copy of law school transcript; a personal statement, not to exceed 500 words, which describes their talents, qualities, and experiences and how they would contribute to Baker and McKenzie's diversity and inclusion efforts. Send the application and the supporting documents to the Diversity Fellowship mailbox. **Deadline:** September 15. **Contact:** E-mail: diversityfellowship@bakermckenzie.com.

2412 ■ Baker McKenzie Graduate Legal Studies Scholarships *(Graduate, Professional development/ Scholarship)*

Purpose: To support Firm associates in their full-time graduate legal study outside their home jurisdictions. **Focus:** Law. **Qualif.:** Applicants must be Baker and McKenzie associates who have been with the Firm for at least two years and are interested in studying for a graduate law degree (Ll.M., M.C.L., or similar).

Funds Avail.: No specific amount.

2413 ■ Baltimore City Community College (BCCC)

2901 Liberty Heights Ave.
Baltimore, MD 21215-7807
Ph: (410)462-8300
Free: 800-735-2258
E-mail: online@bccc.edu
URL: www.bccc.edu
Social Media: www.facebook.com/MyBCCC
www.instagram.com/my_bccc
twitter.com/my_bccc

2414 ■ BCCC Foundation General Scholarship Fund *(Undergraduate/Scholarship)*

Purpose: To provide financial assistance to individuals who have the desire and commitment to pursue their educational goals. **Focus:** General studies/Field of study not specified. **Qualif.:** Applicants must demonstrate financial need and be a Maryland resident.

Funds Avail.: Amount varies. **Duration:** Annual. **Contact:** Phone: 410-462-8498.

2415 ■ BCCC Workforce Creation Scholarship *(Undergraduate/Scholarship)*

Purpose: To provide financial assistance to those who have the desire and commitment to pursue their educational goals. **Focus:** General studies/Field of study not specified. **Qualif.:** Applicants must be Baltimore City residents only, who are US Citizens, or eligible non-citizens, in the biotechnology program either as a full-time or part-time student taking more than 6 credits; new BCCC student

may apply with supplemental supporting documents; must complete a FASFA and write a letter of interest, expressing the student's personal commitment to this area of study and future career goals.

Funds Avail.: No specific amount. **Duration:** Annual.

2416 ■ Banff Centre for Arts and Creativity

107 Tunnel Mountain Dr.
Banff, AB, Canada T1L 1H5
Ph: (403)762-6100
E-mail: leadership@banffcentre.ca
URL: banffcentre.ca
Social Media: www.facebook.com/BanffCentre
www.instagram.com/banffcentre
www.linkedin.com/school/banff-centre
twitter.com/banffcentre
www.youtube.com/user/TheBanffCentre

2417 ■ Alliance Pipeline Scholarships *(Other/ Scholarship)*

Purpose: To support non-profit leaders of Canadian charities in improving their leadership skills. **Focus:** Leadership, Institutional and community. **Qualif.:** Applicants must be employees of a registered Canadian charity under the Income Tax Act (Canada). **Criteria:** Priority will be given to individuals with organizations operating in a location where Alliance Pipelines has a business interest or association.

Funds Avail.: No specific amount. **Duration:** Annual. **To Apply:** Applicants must submit a completed application form along with a brief outline (on letterhead) of the applicants' organization's history, mission and activities and the role, responsibilities and length of service with the organization; reasons why assistance is required; anticipated benefits from participating in the program; a description of how the applicants will share the learning from the program with the team, organization and throughout the sector; the name of Supervisor or Board Chair; and the registered charity number with the Canada Revenue Agency (CRA).

2418 ■ Fraser Milner Casgrain Scholarships *(Other/ Scholarship)*

Purpose: To support non-profit leaders of Canadian charities in improving their leadership skills. **Focus:** Leadership, Institutional and community. **Qualif.:** Applicant must be an employee, officer, director or designated agent of a registered Canadian charity under the Income Tax Act (Canada). **Criteria:** Selection is based on the submitted application materials

Funds Avail.: No specific amount. **Duration:** Annual. **To Apply:** Applicants must submit a completed application form together with a brief outline (on letterhead, one page) of the applicant's financial contribution to the program and the organization; the names of other agencies applied for funding and the amounts requested; reasons why assistance is required; the anticipated benefits from participating in the program; name of Supervisor of Board Chair; and the registered charity number with the Canada Revenue Agency (CRA).

2419 ■ Investors Group Scholarship *(Other/ Scholarship)*

Purpose: To support non-profit leaders of Canadian charities in improving their leadership skills. **Focus:** Leadership,

---

Awards are arranged alphabetically below their administering organizations

Institutional and community. **Qualif.:** Applicants must be employees of a registered Canadian charity under the Income Tax Act (Canada) and the organization must be located in Manitoba. **Criteria:** Priority will be given to individuals with organizations in the city of Winnipeg.

Funds Avail.: $4,583 each. **Duration:** Annual. **To Apply:** Applicants must submit a completed application form along with a brief outline (on letterhead) of the applicants' organization's history, mission, activities and the role, responsibilities and length of service with the organization; reasons why assistance is required; anticipated benefits from participating in the program; a description of how the applicants will sharing the learning from the program with the team, organization and throughout the sector; the name of Supervisor or Board Chair; and the registered charity number with the Canada Revenue Agency (CRA).

2420 ■ Lafarge Community Leaders Scholarships (Other/Scholarship)

Purpose: To support non-profit leaders of Canadian charities in improving their leadership skills. **Focus:** Leadership, Institutional and community. **Qualif.:** Applicants must be an employee of a Canadian non-profit organization. **Criteria:** Selection is based on the submitted application materials.

Funds Avail.: $4,000 each. **Duration:** Annual; 3 years. **Number Awarded:** 3. **To Apply:** Applicants must submit a completed application form along with a brief outline (on letterhead) of the applicant's organization's history, mission, activities and the role, responsibilities and length of service with the organization; reasons why assistance is required; anticipated benefits from participating in the program; a description of how the applicant will share the learnings from the program with the team, organization and throughout the sector; and the name of Supervisor or Board Chair. **Remarks:** Established in 2009.

2421 ■ Youth or the Environment Scholarships (Other/Scholarship)

Purpose: To support non-profit leaders of Canadian charities in improving their leadership skills. **Focus:** Leadership, Institutional and community. **Qualif.:** Applicant must be an employee, officer, director or designated agent of a Canadian registered charity under the Income Tax Act (Canada). The organization must have a substantial focus on either youth or the environment and be at a mid- or upper-level management position. The annual revenue of the organization must be under $3,000,000. **Criteria:** Selection is based on the submitted application materials.

Funds Avail.: No specific amount. **To Apply:** Applicants must submit a completed application form along with a brief outline (on letterhead) of the applicant's organization's history, mission, activities and role within the areas of focus; the applicant's role and responsibilities and length of service with the organization; the name of Supervisor or Board Chair; a resume; organization's most recent audited financial statements; and registered charity number with CRA.

2422 ■ Bank of Canada
234 Wellington St.
Ottawa, ON, Canada K1A 0G9
Ph: (613)782-8111
Fax: (613)782-7713
Free: 800-303-1282
E-mail: info@bankofcanada.ca
URL: www.bankofcanada.ca

Social Media: www.linkedin.com/company/bank-of-canada
twitter.com/bankofcanada
www.youtube.com/user/bankofcanadaofficial

2423 ■ Bank of Canada Fellowship Award (Doctorate, Other/Fellowship)

Purpose: To provide financial support to students who have been recognized for their expertise and excellence in bank-related issues. **Focus:** Banking; Economics; Finance; Marketing and distribution. **Qualif.:** Applicants must be Canadian citizens, permanent residents or legally permitted to work in Canada; must have obtained a Ph.D. degree; and be employed by a Canadian university during the tenure of the fellowship.

Funds Avail.: $50,000 for research grant; $40,000 for research expense allowance; $5,000university for administration of the award funds. **Duration:** Annual; up to five years. **Number Awarded:** Varies. **To Apply:** Applicants must submit letter of nomination from the university; must need reference letter. **Deadline:** November 30.

2424 ■ Bank of Canada Governor's Awards (Doctorate, Other/Award)

Purpose: To provide funds to exceptional assistant and associate professors working at Canadian universities who have made contributions in their fields. **Focus:** Business; Economics; Finance.

Funds Avail.: $25,000. **Duration:** Annual; up to two years. **To Apply:** Applicants must submit letter of nomination from the university; must need reference letter.

2425 ■ Bank of Nova Scotia - Barbados
Broad St, Bridgetown
Saint Michael, Barbados
Ph: (246)227-4455
Free: 800-744-2672
URL: www.scotiabank.com

2426 ■ Scotiabank Scholarship (Undergraduate/Scholarship)

Purpose: To provide support for Black Canadian students who want to pursue education in the field of business studies. **Focus:** Business. **Qualif.:** Applicants must be Canadian citizens or permanent residents who are members of the Canadian Black community (i.e. Black persons of discernible African ancestry and self identity); maximum 30 years of age and enrolled in a full-time student in the academic year at an accredited post-secondary institution (as determined by the NSF) in the field of business studies. **Criteria:** Selection will be based on strong academics, demonstrated financial need, leadership skills, and commitment to helping in their community.

Funds Avail.: 5,000 Canadian Dollars each. **Duration:** Annual. **Number Awarded:** 2. **To Apply:** Applicants must complete the online application form and attach the following: Letter of Recommendation from teacher, guidance counsellor, principal or vice-principal who knows applicant well and can write about academic accomplishments and other outstanding attributes written on official letterhead; letter of Recommendation from a member of applicant community, high-school transcript (attachments in PDF format); hardcopy original of high school transcript must be sent to NSF Office within 14 days of application online deadline. **Remarks:** Sponsored by the Bank of Nova Scotia.

2427 ■ Banner & Witcoff Ltd.
71 South Wacker Drive Ste. 3600
Chicago, IL 60606

Awards are arranged alphabetically below their administering organizations

Ph: (312)463-5000
Fax: (312)463-5001
E-mail: info@bannerwitcoff.com
URL: www.bannerwitcoff.com
Social Media: www.linkedin.com/company/bannerwitcoff
twitter.com/BannerWitcoff

2428 ■ Donald W. Banner Diversity Fellowship for Law Students *(Graduate/Fellowship)*

Purpose: To foster the development of intellectual property lawyers from diverse backgrounds. **Focus:** Law. **Qualif.:** Applicants must be either 1L or 2L students who have entered into a JD program at an ABA-accredited law school in the United States. **Criteria:** Selection will be based on the committee's criteria; Priority will be given to those students who are members of a historically underrepresented minority group in IP law.

Funds Avail.: $5,000 each. **Duration:** Annual. **Number Awarded:** Minimum 1. **To Apply:** Applicants must complete the Donald W. Banner Diversity Scholarship application form, available online; must submit a resume, academic transcripts (law, undergraduate/graduate school), a writing sample (5-10 pages), three references including contact information, and a one-page statement describing how diversity has impacted the candidate. **Remarks:** The scholarship was established in memory of Donald W. Banner. **Contact:** Donald W. Banner Diversity Scholarship, c/o Christopher Hummel, Banner & Witcoff, Ltd., 1100 13th St., NW, Ste. 1200, Washington, DC, 20005.

2429 ■ Baptist Communicators Association (BCA)

c/o Margaret Dempsey-Colson
4519 Lashley Ct. NE
Marietta, GA 30068
Ph: (678)641-4457
URL: www.baptistcommunicators.org
Social Media: www.facebook.com/BaptistComm
www.instagram.com/BaptistCommunicators
www.linkedin.com/company/baptist-communicators-assn
twitter.com/BaptistComm

2430 ■ Al Shackleford and Dan Martin Professional Scholarship *(Professional development/Scholarship)*

Purpose: To provide financial assistance for attending BCA events. **Focus:** General studies/Field of study not specified. **Qualif.:** Applicants must be full-time BCA members. **Criteria:** Selection of scholarship recipients will be made by the executive committee.

Funds Avail.: Not to exceed $1,000. **Duration:** Annual. **To Apply:** Application materials must include: a) name, address, and phone number of applicant; b) Current position/title, department and agency; c) Number of years worked in public relations/communications and number of years at the applicant's institution; d) Highest level of formal education attained and name of other professional development conferences or workshops attended in the past; e) copy of applicant's job description and resume; f) title and name of person to whom the applicant reports; g) statement of why financial assistance is needed and how much money is required. **Deadline:** March 1. **Contact:** Baptist Communicators Association, Scholarship Committee, 4519 Lashley Court, Marietta, GA, 30068; Phone: 678-641-4457; E-mail: margaretcolson@bellsouth.net.

2431 ■ Alan Compton and Bob Stanley Professional Scholarship *(Professional development/Scholarship)*

Purpose: To provide financial assistance to qualified or prospective members for attendance at a BCA-related workshop. **Focus:** General studies/Field of study not specified. **Qualif.:** Applicants must be minority-ethnic and international BCA members or prospective members. **Criteria:** Selection of scholarship recipients will be made by the executive committee.

Funds Avail.: Not to exceed $500. **Duration:** Annual. **To Apply:** Application materials must include: a) name, address, and phone number of applicant; b) Current position/title, department and agency; c) race or country of origin d) Number of years worked in public relations/communications and number of years at the applicant's institution; e) Highest level of formal education attained and name of other professional development conferences or workshops attended in the past; f) copy of applicant's job description and resume; g) title and name of person to whom the applicant reports; h) statement of why financial assistance is needed and how much money is required. **Deadline:** March 1. **Contact:** Baptist Communicators Association, Scholarship Committee, 4519 Lashley Court, Marietta, GA, 30068; Phone: 678-641-4457; E-mail: margaretcolson@bellsouth.net.

2432 ■ Bar Association of San Francisco (BASF)

301 Battery St., 3rd Fl.
San Francisco, CA 94111
Ph: (415)982-1600
Fax: (415)477-2388
URL: www.sfbar.org
Social Media: www.facebook.com/sfbar
www.instagram.com/sfbarassn
www.linkedin.com/company/the-bar-association-of-san
  -francisco
www.pinterest.com/sfbar
twitter.com/sfbar
www.youtube.com/user/sfbarassociation

2433 ■ Bay Area Minority Law Student Scholarship *(Graduate, Undergraduate/Scholarship)*

Purpose: To provide financial assistance to qualified students from minority groups underrepresented in the law schools. **Focus:** Law. **Qualif.:** Applicants must be students from minority groups who are underrepresented in bay area law schools and have received a "letter of admission" from one of the eight Northern California law schools. **Criteria:** Selection will be based on the submitted application materials.

Funds Avail.: $10,000. **Duration:** Annual; up to three years. **To Apply:** Applicants must submit the following; a completed application with official undergraduate or graduate transcript; 500-word personal statement; copies of current IRS tax forms; statement of economic need (optional); and, copies of "letters of admissions" from any ABA accredited law school in northern California. **Deadline:** April 17. **Remarks:** Established in 1998. **Contact:** sakwei@sfbar.org.

2434 ■ Bariatric Surgery Source, LLC

151 NC Hwy. 9, No. B105
Black Mountain, NC 28711
Free: 888-847-9158

Awards are arranged alphabetically below their administering organizations

URL: www.bariatric-surgery-source.com
Social Media: www.facebook.com/BariatricSurgerySource

2435 ■ The Future of Bariatric Surgery Scholarship
(Undergraduate, Graduate, Vocational/Occupational/ Scholarship)

Purpose: To encourage bright, motivated students to enter and influence the direction of the bariatric field, and to increase awareness of the life-changing and potentially society-changing benefits of weight loss surgery. **Focus:** Medicine. **Qualif.:** Applicants must be currently majoring in any medically-related degree or attending any medically-related certification program; attending (or accepted by) school full-time at an accredited two-year or four-year college or university, or vocational-technical school located in the U.S. **Criteria:** Essay with the most insightful and well-supported predictions about the future of bariatric surgery will be selected as the winner.

Funds Avail.: $1,000. **Duration:** Semiannual. **Number Awarded:** 1-2. **To Apply:** Applicant must submit essay (minimum 2,000 words) describing how the field of bariatric surgery will evolve over the next 5 years. Include two letters of recommendation and a current, complete official transcript of grades. **Deadline:** January 1; July 1. **Contact:** Bariatric Surgery Source, 4495-304 Roosevelt Blvd. Ste. 198, Jacksonville, FL, 32210.

2436 ■ Baron and Budd P.C.
3102 Oak Lawn Ave., Ste. 1100
Dallas, TX 75219-4283
Free: 866-723-1890
E-mail: info@baronbudd.com
URL: baronandbudd.com
Social Media: www.facebook.com/Baron.and.Budd
www.linkedin.com/company/baron-&-budd-p-c-
twitter.com/baronandbudd
www.youtube.com/user/baronbudd

2437 ■ Baron and Budd Attorneys Mesothelioma Cancer Victims Memorial Scholarships (College, University/Scholarship)

Purpose: To honor the legacy of mesothelioma victims and their loved ones but offering scholarships in their honor. **Focus:** General studies/Field of study not specified. **Qualif.:** Applicant must be entering a US-based two- or four-year college or university as a first year student.

Funds Avail.: $2,500. **Number Awarded:** 2. **To Apply:** Applicant must submit a written essay (800 to 1, 250 words) or video essay (2 to 3 minute YouTube video) along with two letters of recommendation. Application and details are available online at www.baronandbudd.com/mesothelioma-lawyers/scholarships/. **Deadline:** July 16.

2438 ■ Barrientos Scholarship Foundation (BSF)
PO Box 7173
Omaha, NE 68107
E-mail: info@barrientosscholarship.org
URL: www.barrientosscholarship.org
Social Media: www.facebook.com/ BarrientosScholarshipFoundation
twitter.com/BSF_Omaha

2439 ■ BSF General Scholarship Awards (College, University/Scholarship)

Purpose: To provide financial assistance to qualified students who want to pursue their studies. **Focus:** Interdis-ciplinary studies. **Qualif.:** Applicants must not be receiving major financial assistance from other outside sources, such as Pell Grant, Goodrich Scholarship, Susan Thompson Buffett award, or NU Regents Scholarship. **Criteria:** Selection of applicants will be based on the criteria of the Scholarship Selection Committee.

Funds Avail.: Varies. **Deadline:** April 24.

2440 ■ Barth Syndrome Foundation (BSF)
2005 Palmer Ave., Ste. 1033
Larchmont, NY 10538
Ph: (914)303-6323
Fax: (518)213-4061
URL: www.barthsyndrome.org
Social Media: www.facebook.com/ barthsyndromefoundation
twitter.com/BarthSyndrome
www.youtube.com/user/shelleybow1

2441 ■ BSF Research Grants (Professional development/Grant)

Purpose: To advance the state of knowledge about Barth Syndrome so that progress can be made in finding a specific treatment or cure for this unusual mitochondrial disease. **Focus:** Disabilities; Genetics.

Funds Avail.: Idea Grant (US $50,000 maximum for 1-2 years); for a Development Grant (US $100,000 maximum over 2-3 years). **Deadline:** October 31.

2442 ■ Barton Springs/Edwards Aquifer Conservation District (BSEACD)
1124 Regal Row
Austin, TX 78748
Ph: (512)282-8441
Fax: (512)282-7016
E-mail: bseacd@bseacd.org
URL: www.bseacd.org
Social Media: www.facebook.com/pg/BSEACD
twitter.com/bseacd
www.youtube.com/channel/UCLwV7V9j-cx-XokRcHR-cUQ

2443 ■ Kent S. Butler Memorial Groundwater Stewardship Scholarship Essay Contest
(Undergraduate/Scholarship, Award)

Purpose: To award high school juniors, seniors, and immediate graduates for best essay. **Focus:** Conservation of natural resources. **Qualif.:** Applicant must be high school juniors, seniors, and immediate graduates. Must attend (or have attended) a public, private, or other accredited school located within the boundaries of these school districts: Austin, Del Valle, Dripping Springs, Eanes, Hays Consolidated, Lockhart, San Marcos Consolidated, and Wimberley. **Criteria:** Applicant will be judged on the basis of originality (30%), quality and style of writing (20%), grammar and spelling (20%), the accuracy of information (20%), and bibliography and proper citation of information used in the essay (10%).

Funds Avail.: $2,500. **Duration:** Annual. **Number Awarded:** Varies. **To Apply:** Applicants must submit completed application form that contains contestant's name and contact information; essays should be titled, but the

Awards are arranged alphabetically below their administering organizations

contestant's name should not appear anywhere on the pages of the essay so that they may remain anonymous during the judging; applications and essays may be stapled together and need not be put in a folder or slick report cover. **Deadline:** March 25. **Contact:** BSEACD, 1124 Regal Row, Austin, TX, 78748.

2444 ■ Bat and Ball Game

8345 NW 66th St., No. C7592
Miami, FL 33166-7896
Ph: (844)873-2875
URL: batandballgame.com

2445 ■ Bat and Ball Game Womens Sports Scholarship *(Undergraduate/Scholarship)*

Purpose: To ease the financial burden faced by students and their families. **Focus:** Sports studies. **Qualif.:** Applicant must be a female student studying for any sports-related degree, including: sports science, sports physiotherapy, sports management, physical and sport education, sport psychology, sports nutrition, and sports rehabilitation. **Criteria:** Selection will be based on essay and other applicant information. Essays will be judged on thoughtfulness, creativity, and demonstrated knowledge of sport.

Funds Avail.: $1,000. **Duration:** Annual. **Number Awarded:** Varies. **To Apply:** Applicant must write an original essay (400 to 600 words, in English) on one of the following topics: 1. Are there women in sports today that you see as role models? Who and why?; 2. Why is baseball important to the sporting world in general?; 3. Where will the sport of baseball be 10 years from now?; 4. In your perspective, how has sport changed in the last tow decades? Essays and personal details should be submitted via email to: scholarship@batandballgame.com. **Deadline:** May 30.

2446 ■ Bat Conservation International (BCI)

500 N Capital of Texas Hwy., Bldg. 1
Austin, TX 78746
Ph: (512)327-9721
Free: 800-538-2287
URL: www.batcon.org
Social Media: www.facebook.com/BatCon
www.instagram.com/batconservationinternational
www.linkedin.com/company/bat-conservation-international
twitter.com/BatConIntl
www.youtube.com/user/batconservation

2447 ■ Bat Conservation International Granting Programs *(Graduate, Undergraduate/Scholarship)*

Purpose: To support students in research initiatives that is essential in conserving bats and ecosystems. **Focus:** Wildlife conservation, management, and science.

Funds Avail.: Varies. **Duration:** Annual. **Remarks:** Established in 1982. **Contact:** Email:rpatterson@batcon.org.

2448 ■ Baurkot & Baurkot: The Immigration Law Group

205 S 7th St.
Easton, PA 18042
Ph: (484)544-0022
Fax: (201)604-6791

URL: www.baurkotlaw.com

2449 ■ Attorney Raymond Lahoud Scholar Program *(Undergraduate, Graduate/Scholarship)*

Purpose: To provide quality academic opportunities to the upcoming generation of attorneys. **Focus:** Law. **Qualif.:** Applicants must be either enrolled in a 4-year college or university program as a sophomore, junior, or senior, or be accepted to/enrolled in an ABA-accredited law school in their first, second, or third year; minimum GPA of 3.0. **Criteria:** Academic performance, activities in and outside of college, and the depth of the essay written.

Funds Avail.: $10,000. **Number Awarded:** 5. **To Apply:** Submit application, resume, unofficial transcripts, and an essay (minimum 3,000 words) discussing why you wish to pursue a career in the legal profession. **Deadline:** March 1. **Contact:** nationalimmigrationlawyers.com/legalscholars; Yenny Bautista, legalscholars@baurkotlaw.com.

2450 ■ John Bayliss Broadcast Foundation

PO Box 51126
Pacific Grove, CA 93950
Ph: (831)655-5229
E-mail: khfranke@baylissfoundation.org
Social Media: twitter.com/BEAWebTweets

2451 ■ John Bayliss Broadcast Foundation Internship Programs *(Undergraduate/Internship)*

Purpose: To enhance students' education at Bayliss Schools across the nation. To provide practical skills that will prepare them for a rewarding future. **Focus:** Broadcasting. **Criteria:** Recipients are selected based on financial need and academic record.

Funds Avail.: No specific amount. **To Apply:** Applicants must submit a resume and complete the application form. **Contact:** PO Box 51126, Pacific Grove, CA, 93950; Ph: 831-655-5229; Fax: 831-655-5228; E-mail: cbutrum@ baylissfoundation.org.

2452 ■ John Bayliss Broadcast Foundation Radio Scholarships *(Undergraduate/Scholarship)*

Purpose: To provide financial assistance to outstanding broadcast students. **Focus:** Broadcasting. **Qualif.:** Juniors and seniors majoring in Broadcast Communications who have maintained a 3.0 GPA. **Criteria:** Selection based on financial need; preference is given to students of merit with an extensive history of radio-related activities.

Funds Avail.: $5,000. **Duration:** Annual. **Number Awarded:** Multiple. **To Apply:** Applicants must provide an official transcript, a resume, three letters of recommendation evaluating their scholastic and personal strengths, and a descriptive essay outlining future broadcasting goals. **Remarks:** Established in 2010.

2453 ■ B.C. Road Builders and Heavy Construction Association (BCRB & HCA)

8678 Greenall Ave., Ste. 307
Burnaby, BC, Canada V5J 3M6
Ph: (604)436-0220
Fax: (604)436-2627
E-mail: info@roadbuilders.bc.ca
URL: www.roadbuilders.bc.ca
Social Media: www.instagram.com/bcroadbuilders
www.linkedin.com/company/bc-roadbuilders-and-heavy
-construction-association

Awards are arranged alphabetically below their administering organizations

twitter.com/BCRoadBuilders

2454 ■ Betty Spalton Scholarships (Undergraduate/Scholarship)

Purpose: To provide financial support to individuals obtaining an education in fields associated with the road building and heavy construction industry. **Focus:** Construction. **Qualif.:** Applicants must be students entering or continuing studies leading to a career in road building, road maintenance or heavy construction; must be Canadian citizens; must be either full or part-time at any BC college, university, technical or trades Institute; must be Canadian citizens.**Criteria:** Preference will be given to students who are female and/or members of minority groups.

Funds Avail.: 1,500 Canadian Dollars. **Duration:** Annual. **To Apply:** Complete applications must include the following: a brief 250-500 words essay explaining the interest in obtaining an education in the field and career goals; transcripts from any secondary and post-secondary institutions attended; a resume. **Deadline:** May 31. **Remarks:** The scholarship was established after Betty Spalton, who served as District Highways Manager in McBride and went on to become President and General Manager of the Okanagan South (Penticton) Division of Argo Road Maintenance and was an acknowledged expert in maintenance policy, standards, business management and construction in general. Established in 1999. **Contact:** Betty Spalton Trust Fund, B.C. Road Builders and Heavy Construction Association, Ste. 307, 8678 Greenall Ave., Burnaby, BC, V5J 3M6.

2455 ■ BDPA Education and Technology Foundation (BETF)
4423 Lehigh Rd., No. 277
College Park, MD 20740
Free: 800-343-5015
E-mail: ExecDirector@betf.org
URL: www.betf.org
Social Media: www.facebook.com/pg/BDPAFoundation
twitter.com/BDPA

2456 ■ Eli Lilly And Company/BDPA Scholarship (Undergraduate, Graduate, Master's/Scholarship)

Purpose: To provide outstanding minority students financial assistance in pursuing an information technology-related degree. **Focus:** Information science and technology. **Qualif.:** Applicant must be a citizen or permanent resident of the United States; must be a graduating high school senior or current college student in good standing at the time of their application and graduating high school seniors at the time of their application; must be an active member of BDPA; must demonstrate academic achievement with a cumulative GPA of 3.0 or higher; must be pursuing a bachelors or masters degree in information systems, computer science, computer engineering, or an information technology related discipline. **Criteria:** Selection is evaluated based on academic excellence; exceptional leadership potential and impact through service to their communities.

Funds Avail.: $2,500. **Duration:** Annual. **To Apply:** Completed application along with passport-sized photo in a professional style and context; current and sealed official school transcript (for high school applicants, official transcript must include senior year grades); two letters of recommendation from individuals of no familial relation (at least one letter must be from a faculty member and at least one letter should reflect applicant interest in information systems, computer science, computer engineering, or an information technology related discipline); typed 500 word essay describing the importance of Information Technology and how it has changed our day to day lives. **Deadline:** July 16. **Contact:** Eli Lilly and Company, Cherise Poole, Lilly Corporate Ctr., Drop Code 6220, Indianapolis, IN, 46285; Email: c_poole@lilly.com.

2457 ■ The Beatitudes Society
2345 Channing Way
Berkeley, CA 94704

2458 ■ Beatitudes Fellowships (Professional development/Fellowship)

Purpose: To assist young entrepreneurial faith leaders with the resources and relationships that empower them to create new models for church and the pursuit of social justice. **Focus:** Christian education. **Qualif.:** Applicants are emerging faith leaders who are: under the age of 40; within seven years of divinity school graduation; based in a community of faith; actively working to engage faith with social justice using a unique approach. **Criteria:** Selection will be based on a proven track record of leadership; a commitment to faith and to social justice; a willingness to take risks; a desire to collaborate with others; a specific project that matches up their deep gladness with the world's great need.

Duration: Annual. **To Apply:** Applicants are nominated and then complete an application process that includes an online application and description of their project due, as well as a personal interview.

2459 ■ BECA Foundation
PO Box 936
Escondido, CA 92033
Ph: (858)779-4157
URL: www.becafoundation.org

2460 ■ Alice Newell Joslyn Medical Scholarship (Undergraduate, Doctorate, Master's/Scholarship)

Purpose: To seek promising students and provide them with the necessary financial assistance, moral support and guidance to complete their education, thereby promoting higher educational and leadership standards within the Hispanic community. **Focus:** Education, Medical. **Qualif.:** Applicants must be entering medical/health care professions (dental/medical assistant, nursing, physical therapist, or seeking their Bachelor of Science, Master's or Doctorate in the health field); must be living or attending a high school or college in San Diego County at the time of application. **Criteria:** Recipients are selected based on financial need, scholastic determination, community and cultural awareness.

Funds Avail.: $500 - $2,000. **Duration:** Annual. **To Apply:** Applicants must complete the application form online and must submit all required materials including an essay, two letters of recommendation in PDF or Word format and official transcripts. **Deadline:** March 30. **Contact:** BECA Foundation, PO Box 936, Escondido, CA, 92033; Email: scholarship@becafoundation.org.

2461 ■ BECA General Scholarship (Undergraduate/Scholarship)

Purpose: To seek promising students and provide them with the necessary financial assistance, moral support and guidance to complete their education, thereby promoting higher educational and leadership standards within the Hispanic community. **Focus:** General studies/Field of study not specified. **Qualif.:** Applicants must be a San Diego County High School graduate who is entering college. **Criteria:** Recipients are selected based on financial need and merit; GPA; and community involvement.

Funds Avail.: $500 - $1,000. **To Apply:** Applicants must complete the application form online and must submit all required materials including an essay, two letters of recommendation in PDF or Word format and official transcripts. **Deadline:** March 30. **Contact:** BECA Foundation, PO Box 936, Escondido, CA, 92033; Email: scholarship@ becafoundation.org.

2462 ■ LAFS - Cal State University San Marcos General Scholarships *(Undergraduate/Scholarship)*

Purpose: To seek promising students and provide them with the necessary financial assistance, moral support and guidance to complete their education, thereby promoting higher educational and leadership standards within the Hispanic community. **Focus:** General studies/Field of study not specified. **Qualif.:** Applicants must be Latino students enrolled at CSU San Marcos. **Criteria:** Recipients are selected based on financial need, scholastic determination and community and cultural awareness.

Funds Avail.: No specific amount. **Duration:** Annual. **Number Awarded:** Varies. **To Apply:** Applicants must complete the application form and must submit all required materials and official transcripts. **Deadline:** March 30.

2463 ■ Beinecke Rare Book & Manuscript Library
8 Dock ,344 Winchester Ave.
New Haven, CT 06511
Ph: (203)432-2977
Fax: (203)432-4047
E-mail: beinecke.library@yale.edu
URL: beinecke.library.yale.edu

2464 ■ Beinecke Rare Book and Manuscript Library Visiting Postdoctoral Scholar Fellowships *(Postdoctorate/Fellowship)*

Purpose: To support visiting scholars, and provide access to the library for scholars who live outside the greater New Haven area. **Focus:** Library and archival sciences.

Funds Avail.: $4,000 per month.

2465 ■ Research Fellowships for Yale Graduate & Professional School Students *(Graduate, Professional development/Fellowship)*

Purpose: To support students who wish to use Beinecke collections as a primary resource for their dissertations or culminating projects. **Focus:** Library and archival sciences. **Criteria:** Selection will be based on a competitive basis.

Funds Avail.: Range from $3,000 to $13,650. **Duration:** Annual. **To Apply:** Applicants must submit the following materials to the Director of the Beinecke Library; an application form; curriculum vitae; a maximum of 1,200 words proposal explaining in detail the specific relationship between the Beinecke Collection and the applicant's research; a detailed list of specific research materials to be consulted at Beinecke during the fellowship; two confidential letters of recommendation sent to the Beinecke Director, one of which must come from the principal director of the

applicant's dissertation or culminating project; for graduate students, approved or pending prospectus; for professional school students, a statement explaining how their project fulfills the culminating requirement in their school. **Deadline:** March 1; November 1.

2466 ■ Bel Canto Vocal Scholarship Foundation
55 Tremont St.
Cranston, RI 02920
URL: www.belcantoscholarship.com

2467 ■ Bel Canto Vocal Scholarship Foundation *(Graduate/Scholarship)*

Purpose: To support the education of young, talented opera singers. **Focus:** Opera. **Qualif.:** Applicants must be U.S. citizens with proof of citizenship and must be 21 to 36 years old. **Criteria:** Selection will be based on overall quality of the submissions.

Funds Avail.: No specific amount. **Duration:** Annual. **Number Awarded:** 4. **To Apply:** Applicants must submit a resume, along with a cover letter; must provide a DVD (no CDs, please), with three operatic arias, two of which must be in Italian, and the third in the language of choice; 3 letters of recommendation, two of which must be from reputable voice teachers, and the third from a respected professional in the field of opera; proof of United States citizenship via a copy of either your passport or your birth certificate. **Remarks:** Established in 1988.

2468 ■ Max Bell Foundation
105 12 Ave., SE Ste. 970
Calgary, AB, Canada T2G 1A1
Ph: (403)215-7310
E-mail: amccarry@maxbell.org
URL: maxbell.org

2469 ■ Max Bell Senior Fellow Grants *(Advanced Professional/Grant)*

Purpose: To add value to debates over critical public policy issues in health and wellness, education and environment. **Focus:** Environmental science; Health education; Public health.

Funds Avail.: Amount varies. **Duration:** Annual. **Number Awarded:** 1. **To Apply:** Applicants must follow the application process described on the.

2470 ■ Belmont University
1900 Belmont Blvd.
Nashville, TN 37212
Ph: (615)460-6000
URL: belmont.edu
Social Media: www.facebook.com/BelmontUniversity
www.instagram.com/belmontu
twitter.com/BelmontUniv
www.youtube.com/user/belmontu

2471 ■ Belmont University Commercial Music Showcase Scholarship Fund *(Undergraduate/ Scholarship)*

Purpose: To provide financial assistance to students attending Belmont University who are majoring in a commercial music degree. **Focus:** Music. **Qualif.:** Applicants

Awards are arranged alphabetically below their administering organizations

must attend Belmont University majoring in a commercial music degree.

Funds Avail.: No specific amount. **Deadline:** March 15. **Remarks:** Established in 1998.

2472 ■ Benign Essential Blepharospasm Research Foundation (BEBRF)

PO Box 12468
Beaumont, TX 77726-2468
Ph: (409)832-0788
Fax: (409)832-0890
E-mail: bebrf@blepharospasm.org
URL: www.blepharospasm.org

2473 ■ Benign Essential Blepharospasm Research Foundation Research Grants *(Doctorate/Grant)*

Purpose: To support research directly related to blepharospasm or Meige's Syndrome, both forms of cranial dystonia. **Focus:** Medicine. **Qualif.:** Applicants must be principal investigators hold M.D. or Ph.D. and intend to conduct researches that relate specifically to benign essential blepharospasm and Meige covering new treatments, pathophysiology and genetics, photophobia and dry eye; non-US citizens working at institutions abroad are eligible to apply. **Criteria:** Selection will based on committee's review of the proposal.

Funds Avail.: $100,000. **Duration:** Annual. **To Apply:** Applicants must send curriculum vitae and eight copies of proposals with consent form and necessary signatures. Specific grant guidelines and forms are available on the website. **Deadline:** September 30.

2474 ■ Benson & Bingham

11441 Allerton Park Dr., No. 100
Las Vegas, NV 89135
Ph: (702)684-6900
Fax: (702)382-9798
E-mail: info@bensonbingham.com
URL: www.bensonbingham.com
Social Media: www.facebook.com/bensonbingham
twitter.com/bensonbingham

2475 ■ Benson & Bingham First Annual Scholarship *(Graduate/Scholarship)*

Purpose: To help alleviate the financial strain of attending law school. **Focus:** Law. **Qualif.:** Applicant must be a U.S. citizen or permanent resident; currently enrolled in or recently accepted to an accredited law school; have a cumulative GPA of 3.0 or higher. **Criteria:** Essays are judged on: originality of thought or provocativeness; attention to current law as well as statistical knowledge of the area of investigation.

Funds Avail.: $2,000 for the winner; $250 for runners up (2). **Duration:** Annual. **Number Awarded:** 1. **To Apply:** Along with an essay, applications must include an unofficial college transcript and proof of law school acceptance or attendance. Submit a minimum 600-word essay on one of the following topics: 1) Premises security; 2) Consumer product safety. Submissions must be 100% original and never published or disseminated at a previous time. Candidates may site case law or historical record with appropriate citations to the source. **Deadline:** August 31. **Remarks:** Established in 2017. **Contact:** Justin Simpson;

Email: scholarship@bensonbingham.com.

2476 ■ Benson Law Firm

The Hanna Bldg.
1422 Euclid Ave., Ste. 970
Cleveland, OH 44115
Ph: (216)230-3787
URL: bensonbankruptcyattorney.com

2477 ■ Benson Law Firm Scholarship Contest *(Undergraduate/Scholarship)*

Purpose: To provide financial aid to college students, encourage students to understand how bankruptcy relief helps small businesses, and inspire students to pursue a career in any legal field. **Focus:** Business; Finance; Law; Management. **Qualif.:** Applicant must be a high school senior or college freshman in the U.S. studying, or planning to study, business, finance, management, or law. **Criteria:** Selection is based on the best video essay or essay submitted.

Funds Avail.: $1,000. **Duration:** Annual. **Number Awarded:** 1. **To Apply:** Applicant must record a video (1 to 2 minutes, in English) explaining how bankruptcy laws help small businesses and promote economic growth. Applicant must post the video to their YouTube Channel with the title "Benson Law Firm Scholarship" and with this link in the description: www.bensonbankruptcyattorney.com/scholarship-for-college-students/. Applicant must also share the video on their Facebook page and the sponsor's Facebook page. Instead of a video, applicant can submit a 1,000 to 1,500 word essay on the same subject and submit via email. **Deadline:** August 15. **Contact:** David Benson; Email: BensonScholarship@gmail.com.

2478 ■ Benton Community Foundation (BCF)

660 NW Harrison Blvd.
Corvallis, OR 97330
Ph: (541)753-1603
URL: www.bcfgives.org
Social Media: www.facebook.com/
  BentonCommunityFoundation
twitter.com/BCFgives

2479 ■ David W. Schacht Native American Student Scholarship *(Undergraduate/Scholarship)*

Purpose: To provide scholarship to the students of Oregon State University. **Focus:** General studies/Field of study not specified. **Qualif.:** Applicants must: be students of Native American descent, defined as self-identified individuals with tribal affiliation; have demonstrated ability and scholarship during high school or during previous college years; must qualify for financial assistance as defined by the Financial Aid Office of OSU. **Criteria:** Selection will be based on the committee's criteria.

Funds Avail.: No specific amount. **Duration:** Annual. **To Apply:** Applicants may contact the Foundation for application form and other requirements.

2480 ■ William Harrison Gill Education Fund *(Undergraduate/Scholarship)*

Purpose: To provide scholarship to the students of Oregon State University. **Focus:** General studies/Field of study not specified. **Qualif.:** Applicants must: be of Native American descent; be an American citizen with a permanent or guardian residence in one of the following states: Arizona, California, Colorado, Idaho, Montana, Nevada, New Mexico, Oregon, Utah, Washington or Wyoming; and must be students enrolled at Oregon State University. **Criteria:** Selection will be based on the committee's criteria.

Funds Avail.: $3,000. **Duration:** Annual. **To Apply:** Applicants may contact the Foundation for application process and other requirements.

2481 ■ Helen J. & Harold Gilman Smith Scholarship *(Graduate, Undergraduate/Scholarship)*

Purpose: To provide scholarship to the students pursuing their first baccalaureate or graduate degree in any field of study. **Focus:** General studies/Field of study not specified. **Qualif.:** Applicants must: be a Native American student; have a minimum GPA of 2.75 for their undergraduate freshman year; graduate students must maintain the minimum GPA level required by their college graduate degree program. Preference is given to students graduating from an American Indian high school; Applicants must qualify for financial assistance as defined by the Financial Aid Office of OSU. **Criteria:** Selection will be based on the committee's criteria.

Funds Avail.: $13,000. **Duration:** Annual. **To Apply:** Applicants may contact the Foundation for application form and other requirements.

2482 ■ Hugh & Helen Wood Nepalese Scholarship *(Undergraduate/Scholarship)*

Purpose: To provide scholarship to the students who are current citizens of Nepal. **Focus:** General studies/Field of study not specified. **Qualif.:** Applicants must be current students who are citizens of Nepal; primary preference in awarding the scholarship shall be given to those candidates who agree to become a public servant in Nepal for at least five years following graduation. Other requirements include: a 3.5 GPA; a minimum TOEFL score of 550 or other language competency score satisfactory to the university: and all preparatory work completed in Nepal. Secondary consideration will be given to African American students if no Nepalese students meet the requirements. **Criteria:** Selection will be based on the committee's criteria.

Funds Avail.: No specific amount. **Duration:** Annual. **To Apply:** Applicants may contact the Foundation for application form and other requirements. **Remarks:** Established in 1988.

2483 ■ Joel R. Friend Scholarship *(Undergraduate/Scholarship)*

Purpose: To provide scholarship opportunity to the students from OSU. **Focus:** General studies/Field of study not specified. **Qualif.:** Applicants must be foreign students from Thailand, Taiwan (Republic of China) in attendance at OSU in any field of study; must qualify for financial assistance as defined by the Financial Aid Office of OSU. **Criteria:** Selection will be based on the committee's criteria.

Funds Avail.: $7,000. **Duration:** Annual. **To Apply:** Applicants may contact the Foundation for application form and other requirements.

2484 ■ Kilbuck Family Native American Scholarship *(Undergraduate/Scholarship)*

Purpose: To provide scholarship opportunity to the students enrolled at Oregon State University. **Focus:** General studies/Field of study not specified. **Qualif.:** Applicants must have a cumulative GPA of 3.0 or above; have at least

1/16 enrolled or documented tribal affiliation; must be a graduate of Oregon or Alaska high schools; scholarship is renewable for up to 12 terms if a 3.0 cumulative GPA is maintained. **Criteria:** Selection will be based on the committee's criteria.

Funds Avail.: No specific amount. **Duration:** Annual. **To Apply:** Applicants may contact the Foundation for application process and other requirements.

2485 ■ Lucy Hsu Ho Scholarship *(Undergraduate/Scholarship)*

Purpose: To award scholarship to the foreign students of ethnic Chinese descent. **Focus:** General studies/Field of study not specified. **Qualif.:** Applicants must be foreign students of ethnic Chinese descent; primary preference in awarding the scholarship shall be given to those candidates who have demonstrated leadership in student and/or community activities and organizations, as well as the desire to serve others in the candidate's future chosen field of work; secondary preference shall be determined by level of financial need; must re-apply for this scholarship each year; must qualify for financial assistance as defined by the Financial Aid Office of OSU. **Criteria:** Selection will be based on the committee's criteria.

Funds Avail.: No specific amount. **Duration:** Annual. **To Apply:** Applicants may contact the Foundation for the application process and other required materials.

2486 ■ Margaret Dowell-Gravatt, M.D. Scholarship *(Undergraduate/Scholarship)*

Purpose: To encourage and support ethnic minority undergraduate women enrolled in the College of Science. **Focus:** Medical technology; Medicine; Microbiology; Nursing; Occupational therapy; Physical therapy; Zoology. **Qualif.:** Applicants must be pursuing a degree in Zoology or Microbiology or one of the following pre-health programs: Medical Technology, Medicine, Nursing, Physical and/or Occupational therapy. Applicants must be enrolled full-time at the sophomore, junior or senior level; have a GPA of 2.5 overall and 3.0 in science courses required in their major field or pre-health curriculum; and qualify for financial assistance as defined by the Financial Aid Office of OSU. **Criteria:** Selection will be based on the committee's criteria.

Funds Avail.: No specific amount. **Duration:** Annual. **To Apply:** Applicants may contact the Foundation for application form and other requirements.

2487 ■ Berks County Community Foundation
237 Court St.
Reading, PA 19601
Ph: (610)685-2223
Fax: (610)685-2240
E-mail: info@bccf.org
URL: www.bccf.org
Social Media: www.facebook.com/
  berkscountycommunityfoundation
www.instagram.com/berksfoundation
www.linkedin.com/company/berks-county-community
  -foundation
twitter.com/BerksFoundation
www.youtube.com/channel/UCx4IJuMK9nCXYpzQHi3sVEg

2488 ■ Howard Fox Memorial Law Scholarship Fund *(Graduate/Scholarship)*

Purpose: To provide scholarships to graduates of Berks County, PA, high schools who are entering their second year at an accredited law school, who demonstrate financial need, without discrimination to color, race, national origin or religion. **Focus:** Law. **Qualif.:** Applicants must be Berks County residents entering their second year at an accredited law school who demonstrate financial need, without discrimination to color, race, national origin or religion. **Criteria:** Recipients will be selected based on financial need; preference will be given to students entering their second year of law school.

Funds Avail.: $3,000. **Duration:** Annual. **Number Awarded:** 1. **To Apply:** Applicants must submit the following: completed application form with two letters of reference from people who are not related to them; a copy of law school transcript; and a written recommendation from a professor at the law school they are attending. **Deadline:** April 1. **Remarks:** The fund is in memory of Howard Fox who was a member of the Berks County Bar Association and an attorney in the Public Defenders Office at the time of his accidental death.

2489 ■ The Bert Saperstein Communications Scholarship Fund

PO Box 42
Robert Merrill Sta.
New Rochelle, NY 10804
Ph: (914)636-1281
E-mail: info@bsc-scholarshipfund.org
URL: www.bsc-scholarshipfund.org

2490 ■ The Bert Saperstein Communication Scholarship Fund *(Undergraduate/Scholarship)*

Purpose: To provide the financial help for tuition. **Focus:** Communications. **Qualif.:** Applicant must be a full time college and university students, pursuing degrees in the communication arts. **Criteria:** Selection will be based on the criteria set by the Board of Trustees.

Funds Avail.: No specific amount. **Remarks:** Established in 1983.

2491 ■ The Best Hoverboard

228 Park Ave. S
New York, NY 10003
URL: thebesthoverboard.com

2492 ■ The Best Hoverboard Scholarship Era *(College, University/Scholarship)*

Purpose: To help students pay for their college educations. **Focus:** General studies/Field of study not specified. **Qualif.:** Applicant must be attending a college or university during the academic year. **Criteria:** Selection is based attending a college or university during the semester/year academic year. • Must be in good academic standing with your current educational institution.

Funds Avail.: $1,000. **Number Awarded:** 1. **To Apply:** Applicant must write an essay (1,000 word) and submit essay online along with name, email, contact details, and name of the college or university attending, and a profile picture (optional). **Deadline:** February 25. **Contact:** www.iefa.org/scholarships/3281/ The_Best_Hoverboard_Scholarship_Era.

2493 ■ Beta Beta Beta

University of North Alabama
Math Bldg. M1 - A

1 Harrison Plz.
Florence, AL 35632
Ph: (256)765-6220
E-mail: tribeta@una.edu
URL: www.tribeta.org

2494 ■ TriBeta Research Grant Awards *(Undergraduate/Grant)*

Purpose: To support selected research activities by undergraduates who are regular members of Tri-Beta. **Focus:** Science.

Duration: Annual. **Remarks:** Established in 2008.

2495 ■ Beta Phi Mu

PO Box 42139
Philadelphia, PA 19101
Ph: (267)361-5018
E-mail: headquarters@betaphimu.org
URL: www.betaphimu.org
Social Media: twitter.com/betaphimu

2496 ■ Blanche E. Woolls Scholarship *(Graduate/ Scholarship)*

Purpose: To provide support for a student beginning Library and Information Studies at an ALA-accredited school with the intention of pursuing a career in school library media service. **Focus:** Library and archival sciences. **Qualif.:** Applicants must be admitted to graduate programs in library and information studies accredited by the American Library Association and have not completed more than 12 hours by the Fall semester following the application deadline; must have the clear intention of pursuing a career in school library and media service. **Criteria:** Selection will be judged on several factors but the autobiographical note is the prime importance.

Funds Avail.: $2,250. **Duration:** Annual. **Number Awarded:** 1. **To Apply:** Applicants must submit the completed application form together with typed one-page autobiography; current transcripts from all institutions of higher learning; and five letters of recommendation from academic instructors, employers or supervisors of paid volunteer work experience; all applications and documents must be scanned and sent via e-mail. **Deadline:** March 15. **Contact:** headquarters@betaphimu.org.

2497 ■ Eugene Garfield Doctoral Dissertation Fellowship *(Doctorate/Fellowship)*

Purpose: To support doctoral students who are working on their dissertations in Library and Information Science, Information Studies, Informatics, or a related field. **Focus:** Information science and technology; Library and archival sciences. **Qualif.:** Applicants must be enrolled in a doctoral-level research program at an institution with ALA, CILIP, or other Beta Phi Mu Executive Board approved accreditation.

Funds Avail.: $3,000 each. **Duration:** Annual. **Number Awarded:** Up to 6. **To Apply:** Applicants must submitted curriculum vitae; meeting your program's requirements for advancement to candidacy; abstract of dissertation (300 word limit); letter from Dean or Director indicating dissertation topic has been approved; proof that applicant's candidacy has been advanced and that all requirements for degree except writing and defense of dissertation have been completed; three letters of recommendation; and personal statement not to exceed 500 words relating to

Awards are arranged alphabetically below their administering organizations

post-dissertation plans. **Deadline:** March 15. **Contact:** headquarters@betaphimu.org.

2498 ■ Harold Lancour Scholarship for Foreign Study *(Professional development/Scholarship)*

Purpose: Provided to Librarians for research or a special course of study to survey foreign libraries or programs outside North America. **Focus:** Library and archival sciences. **Qualif.:** Applicants must be degreed professionals working in a library, archives, or other approved information setting. LIS faculty are not eligible, nor are students currently enrolled in LIS doctoral or master's degree programs.

Funds Avail.: $1,750. **Duration:** Annual.

2499 ■ Frank B. Sessa Scholarship *(Professional development/Scholarship)*

Purpose: For a Beta Phi Mu member to increase professional skills through additional study or attendance at a formal program or workshop. **Focus:** General studies/Field of study not specified. **Qualif.:** Applicants must be a Beta Phi Mu member.

Funds Avail.: $150 each. **Duration:** Annual. **To Apply:** Applicants must submit curriculum vitae; name of Beta Phi Mu chapter and year of induction; and one or two page description of applicant's plan for study and its relevance to the present job and plans for the future. **Deadline:** March 15.

2500 ■ Beta Pi Sigma Sorority, Inc. (BPSSI)

PO Box 11108
Carson, CA 90749
Ph: (702)533-3068
E-mail: betapisigsor@gmail.com
URL: betapisigmasorority.org
Social Media: www.linkedin.com/company/beta-pi-sigma
-sorority-inc

2501 ■ Beta Pi Sigma Sorority Local Chapter Scholarship (BPSSS) *(Undergraduate/Scholarship)*

Purpose: To provide educational assistance to graduating high school seniors. **Focus:** General studies/Field of study not specified. **Qualif.:** Applicants must be graduating high school seniors who will enroll in an undergraduate course of study during the current school year at an accredited two- or four-year college or university; must have at least a 3.0 cumulative GPA. **Criteria:** Selection is determined by scholastic achievement, leadership ability, and financial need.

Funds Avail.: Varies. **Duration:** Annual. **Number Awarded:** 1. **To Apply:** Applicants must submit completed application; an essay describing any special family circumstances or needs; one original and one photocopy of official high school transcript in the registrars sealed envelope; and three letters of recommendation. **Contact:** URL: betapisigmasorority.org/scholarship-high-school-app/.

2502 ■ Beta Theta Pi

5134 Bonham Rd.
Oxford, OH 45056
Fax: (513)523-2381
Free: 800-800-2382
E-mail: beta@beta.org
URL: beta.org
Social Media: www.facebook.com/betathetapi

www.instagram.com/betathetapi
www.linkedin.com/groups/46380
twitter.com/BetaThetaPi

2503 ■ W. H. (Bert) Bates Oxford Cup Scholarship *(Undergraduate, Graduate/Scholarship)*

Purpose: To financially assist Betas in completing undergraduate or graduate degrees. **Focus:** General studies/ Field of study not specified. **Qualif.:** Applicants must be undergraduate or graduate students and initiated members of Beta Theta Pi who will be enrolled as full-time students in the upcoming school year. **Criteria:** Selection based on final scores from a three-judge panel.

Funds Avail.: $1,425. **Duration:** Annual. **Number Awarded:** 1. **To Apply:** Application must be completed online at: beta.org/foundation/merit-scholarships/. **Deadline:** April 15. **Contact:** Laura Lednik, Director of Development; Email: laura.lednik@beta.org.

2504 ■ Stephen D. Bechtel, Jr. Oxford Cup Scholarship *(Undergraduate, Graduate/Scholarship)*

Purpose: To financially support Betas in pursuing undergraduate and graduate degrees. **Focus:** General studies/ Field of study not specified. **Qualif.:** Applicants must be undergraduate and graduate students and initiated members of Beta Theta Pi who will be enrolled as full-time students in the upcoming school year. **Criteria:** Selection is based on final scores from a three-judge panel.

Funds Avail.: $700. **Duration:** Annual. **Number Awarded:** 1. **To Apply:** Application must be completed online at: beta.org/foundation/merit-scholarships/. **Deadline:** April 15. **Contact:** Laura Lednik, Director of Development; Email: laura.lednik@beta.org.

2505 ■ Bertram W. Bennett Memorial Scholarship *(Undergraduate, Graduate/Scholarship)*

Purpose: To financially assist Betas in pursuing undergraduate and graduate degrees. **Focus:** General studies/ Field of study not specified. **Qualif.:** Applicants must be undergraduate and graduate students and initiated members of Beta Theta Pi who will be enrolled as full-time students in the upcoming school year. **Criteria:** Selection is based on final scores from a three-judge panel.

Funds Avail.: $1,025 each. **Duration:** Annual. **Number Awarded:** 2. **To Apply:** Application must be completed online at: beta.org/foundation/merit-scholarships/. **Deadline:** April 15. **Contact:** Laura Lednik, Director of Development; Email: laura.lednik@beta.org.

2506 ■ Beta Foundation Merit Scholarships *(Graduate, Undergraduate/Scholarship)*

Purpose: To support full-time students who are members of Beta Theta Pi as they pursue higher education. **Focus:** General studies/Field of study not specified. **Qualif.:** Applicants must be undergraduate and graduate student initiated members of Beta Theta Pi who will be enrolled as full-time students in the current academic year. **Criteria:** Recipients will be evaluated by a panel of independent judges.

Funds Avail.: $250-$2,250. **Duration:** Annual. **To Apply:** Application available online at beta.org/foundation/merit-scholarships/. **Deadline:** April 15. **Contact:** Laura Lednik, Beta's Director of Development; Email: laura.lednik@ beta.org.

2507 ■ Kyle R. Blanco Memorial Scholarship *(Undergraduate, Graduate/Scholarship)*

Purpose: To financially assist Betas in pursuing undergraduate and graduate degrees. **Focus:** General studies/

Awards are arranged alphabetically below their administering organizations

Field of study not specified. **Qualif.:** Applicants must be undergraduate and graduate students and initiated members of Beta Theta Pi who will be enrolled as full-time students in the upcoming school year. **Criteria:** Selection is based on final scores by a three-judge panel.

Funds Avail.: $250. **Duration:** Annual. **Number Awarded:** 1. **To Apply:** Application must be completed online at: beta.org/foundation/merit-scholarships/. **Deadline:** April 15. **Contact:** Laura Lednik, Director of Development; Email: laura.lednik@beta.org.

2508 ■ Seth R. and Corinne H. Brooks Memorial Scholarships (Undergraduate/Scholarship)

Purpose: To financially assist students in their pursuit of academic achievement. **Focus:** General studies/Field of study not specified. **Qualif.:** Applicants must be students who will be attending college (including post-graduate students), and are also sons or daughters of a Beta alumnus.

Funds Avail.: $1,325 each. **Duration:** Annual. **Number Awarded:** 2. **To Apply:** Application available online at beta.org/foundation/merit-scholarships/. **Deadline:** April 15.

2509 ■ Fred and Mary Jane Brower Scholarship (Undergraduate, Graduate/Scholarship)

Purpose: To financially assist Betas in pursuing undergraduate and graduate degrees. **Focus:** General studies/Field of study not specified. **Qualif.:** Applicants must be undergraduate and graduate students and initiated members of Beta Theta Pi who will be enrolled as full-time students in the upcoming school year. **Criteria:** Selection is based on final scores by a three-judge panel.

Funds Avail.: $600. **Duration:** Annual. **Number Awarded:** 1. **To Apply:** Application must be completed online at: beta.org/foundation/merit-scholarships/. **Deadline:** April 15. **Contact:** Laura Lednik, Director of Development; Email: laura.lednik@beta.org.

2510 ■ Edward M. Brown Oxford Cup Scholarship (Undergraduate, Graduate/Scholarship)

Purpose: To financially assist Betas completing undergraduate and graduate degrees. **Focus:** General studies/Field of study not specified. **Qualif.:** Applicants must be undergraduate or graduate students and initiated members of Beta Theta Pi who will be enrolled as full-time students in the upcoming school year. **Criteria:** Selection based on final scores from a three-judge panel. Preference given to applicants from the Miami (Ohio) chapter.

Funds Avail.: $1,275 each. **Duration:** Annual. **Number Awarded:** 2. **To Apply:** Application must be completed online at: beta.org/foundation/merit-scholarships/. **Deadline:** April 15. **Contact:** Laura Lednik, Director of Development; Email: laura.lednik@beta.org.

2511 ■ Frederick S. Bucholz Scholarship (Undergraduate, Graduate/Scholarship)

Purpose: To financially assist Betas in pursuing post-secondary education. **Focus:** General studies/Field of study not specified. **Qualif.:** Applicants must be undergraduate or graduate students and initiated members of Beta Theta Pi in the Iowa State chapter who will be enrolled as full-time students in the upcoming school year. **Criteria:** Selection is based on final scores from a three-judge panel.

Funds Avail.: $1,150 each. **Duration:** Annual. **Number Awarded:** 2. **To Apply:** Application must be completed online at: beta.org/foundation/merit-scholarships/. **Dead-line:** April 15. **Contact:** Laura Lednik, Director of Development; Email: laura.lednik@beta.org.

2512 ■ Adam S. Burford Memorial Scholarship (Undergraduate, Graduate/Scholarship)

Purpose: To financially assist Betas in pursuing undergraduate and graduate degrees. **Focus:** General studies/Field of study not specified. **Qualif.:** Applicants must be undergraduate and graduate students and initiated members of Beta Theta Pi who will be enrolled as full-time students in the upcoming school year. **Criteria:** Selection is based on final scores by a three-judge panel. Preference will be given to applicants from the West Virginia chapter.

Funds Avail.: $400. **Duration:** Annual. **Number Awarded:** 1. **To Apply:** Application must be completed online at: beta.org/foundation/merit-scholarships/. **Deadline:** April 15. **Contact:** Laura Lednik, Director of Development; Email: laura.lednik@beta.org.

2513 ■ Thad Byrne Memorial Scholarship (Undergraduate, Graduate/Scholarship)

Purpose: To financially assist Betas in completing undergraduate and graduate degrees. **Focus:** General studies/Field of study not specified. **Qualif.:** Applicants must be undergraduate or graduate students and initiated members of Beta Theta Pi who will be enrolled as full-time students in the upcoming school year. **Criteria:** Selection based on final scores from a three-judge panel.

Funds Avail.: $1,425. **Duration:** Annual. **Number Awarded:** 1. **To Apply:** Application must be completed online at: beta.org/foundation/merit-scholarships/. **Deadline:** April 15. **Contact:** Laura Lednik, Director of Development; Email: laura.lednik@beta.org.

2514 ■ John L. Calvert Memorial Scholarship (Undergraduate, Graduate/Scholarship)

Purpose: To financially assist Betas in pursing undergraduate and graduate degrees. **Focus:** General studies/Field of study not specified. **Qualif.:** Applicants must be undergraduate or graduate students and initiated members of Beta Theta Pi who will be enrolled as full-time students in the upcoming school year. **Criteria:** Selection is based on final scores by a three-judge panel. Preference will be given to applicants from Georgia Tech chapter.

Funds Avail.: $1,150 each. **Duration:** Annual. **Number Awarded:** 2. **To Apply:** Application must be completed online at: beta.org/foundation/merit-scholarships/. **Deadline:** April 15. **Contact:** Laura Lednik, Director of Development; Email: laura.lednik@beta.org.

2515 ■ Thomas D. and Karen H. Cassady Scholarship (Undergraduate, Graduate/Scholarship)

Purpose: To financially assist Betas in pursuing undergraduate and graduate degrees. **Focus:** General studies/Field of study not specified. **Qualif.:** Applicants must be undergraduate and graduate students and initiated members of Beta Theta Pi who will be enrolled as full-time students in the upcoming school year. **Criteria:** Selection is based on final scores from a three-judge panel. Preference will be given to applicants from the Cincinnati chapter.

Funds Avail.: $975. **Duration:** Annual. **Number Awarded:** 1. **To Apply:** Application must be completed online at: beta.org/foundation/merit-scholarships/. **Deadline:** April 15. **Contact:** Laura Lednik, Director of Development; Email: laura.lednik@beta.org.

Awards are arranged alphabetically below their administering organizations

2516 ■ Oscar Chapman Memorial Scholarship
(Undergraduate, Graduate/Scholarship)

Purpose: To financially assist Betas in pursuing undergraduate and graduate degrees. **Focus:** General studies/Field of study not specified. **Qualif.:** Applicants must be undergraduate or graduate students and initiated members of Beta Theta Pi in the DePauw chapter who will be enrolled as full-time students in the upcoming school year. **Criteria:** Selection is based on final scores from a three-judge panel.

Funds Avail.: $1,125 each. **Duration:** Annual. **Number Awarded:** 3. **To Apply:** Application must be completed online at: beta.org/foundation/merit-scholarships/. **Deadline:** April 15. **Contact:** Laura Lednik, Director of Development; Email: laura.lednik@beta.org.

2517 ■ Cleveland Alumni Association Scholarship
(Undergraduate, Graduate/Scholarship)

Purpose: To financially assist Betas in pursuing undergraduate and graduate degrees. **Focus:** General studies/Field of study not specified. **Qualif.:** Applicants must be undergraduate or graduate students and initiated members of Beta Theta Pi who will be enrolled as full-time students in the upcoming school year. **Criteria:** Selection is based on final scores by a three-judge panel. Preference will be given to applicants from chapters in Ohio and residents of Ohio.

Funds Avail.: $1,050 each. **Duration:** Annual. **Number Awarded:** 4. **To Apply:** Application must be completed online at: beta.org/foundation/merit-scholarships/. **Deadline:** April 15. **Contact:** Laura Lednik, Director of Development; Email: laura.lednik@beta.org.

2518 ■ L. Robert Clough Memorial Scholarship
(Undergraduate, Graduate/Scholarship)

Purpose: To financially assist Betas in pursuing undergraduate and graduate degrees. **Focus:** General studies/Field of study not specified. **Qualif.:** Applicants must be undergraduate and graduate students and initiated members of Beta Theta Pi in the South Dakota chapter who will be enrolled as full-time students in the upcoming school year. **Criteria:** Selection is based on final scores from a three-judge panel.

Funds Avail.: $1,000. **Duration:** Annual. **Number Awarded:** 1. **To Apply:** Application must be completed online at: beta.org/foundation/merit-scholarships/. **Deadline:** April 15. **Contact:** Laura Lednik, Director of Development; Email: laura.lednik@beta.org.

2519 ■ William W. Dawson Memorial Scholarship
(Undergraduate, Graduate/Scholarship)

Purpose: To financially assist Betas in pursuing their college degrees. **Focus:** General studies/Field of study not specified. **Qualif.:** Applicants must be undergraduate or graduate students and initiated members of Beta Theta Pi who will be enrolled as full-time students in the upcoming school year. **Criteria:** Selection based on final scores by three-judge panel.

Funds Avail.: $1,100 each. **Duration:** Annual. **Number Awarded:** 2. **To Apply:** Application must be completed online at: beta.org/foundation/merit-scholarships/. **Deadline:** April 15. **Contact:** Laura Lednik, Director of Development; Email: laura.lednik@beta.org.

2520 ■ Delta Tau Scholarship *(Undergraduate, Graduate/Scholarship)*

Purpose: To financially assist Betas in pursuing undergraduate and graduate degrees. **Focus:** General studies/Field of study not specified. **Qualif.:** Applicants must be undergraduate and graduate students and initiated members of Beta Theta Pi who will be enrolled as full-time students in the upcoming school year. **Criteria:** Selection is based on final scores from a three-judge panel.

Funds Avail.: $700. **Duration:** Annual. **Number Awarded:** 1. **To Apply:** Application must be completed online at: beta.org/foundation/merit-scholarships/. **Deadline:** April 15. **Contact:** Laura Lednik, Director of Development; Email: laura.lednik@beta.org.

2521 ■ John Holt Duncan Memorial Scholarship
(Undergraduate, Graduate/Scholarship)

Purpose: To financially assist Betas in pursuing undergraduate and graduate degrees. **Focus:** General studies/Field of study not specified. **Qualif.:** Applicants must be undergraduate and graduate students and initiated members of Beta Theta Pi who will be enrolled as full-time students in the upcoming school year. **Criteria:** Selection based on final scores from a three-judge panel.

Funds Avail.: $2,300. **Duration:** Annual. **Number Awarded:** 1. **To Apply:** Application must be completed online at: beta.org/foundation/merit-scholarships/. **Deadline:** April 15. **Contact:** Laura Lednik, Director of Development; Email: laura.lednik@beta.org.

2522 ■ East Carolina Scholarship *(Undergraduate, Graduate/Scholarship)*

Purpose: To financially assist Betas in pursuing undergraduate and graduate degrees. **Focus:** General studies/Field of study not specified. **Qualif.:** Applicants must be undergraduate and graduate students and initiated members of Beta Theta Pi in the East Carolina chapter who will be enrolled as full-time students in the upcoming school year. **Criteria:** Selection is based on final scores from a three-judge panel.

Funds Avail.: $750. **Duration:** Annual. **Number Awarded:** 1. **To Apply:** Application must be completed online at: beta.org/foundation/merit-scholarships/. **Deadline:** April 15. **Contact:** Laura Lednik, Director of Development; Email: laura.lednik@beta.org.

2523 ■ W. Todd Elias Memorial Scholarship
(Undergraduate, Graduate/Scholarship)

Purpose: To financially assist Beta students in completing undergraduate and graduate degrees. **Focus:** General studies/Field of study not specified. **Qualif.:** Applicants must be undergraduate or graduate students and initiated members of Beta Theta Pi who will be enrolled as full-time students in the upcoming school year. **Criteria:** Selection will be based on final scores from a three-judge panel. Preference will be given to applicants from the Nebraska chapter.

Funds Avail.: $1,550. **Duration:** Annual. **Number Awarded:** 1. **To Apply:** Application must be completed online at: beta.org/foundation/merit-scholarships/. **Deadline:** April 15. **Contact:** Laura Lednik, Director of Development; Email: laura.lednik@beta.org.

2524 ■ James L. Gavin Memorial Scholarship
(Undergraduate, Graduate/Scholarship)

Purpose: To financially assist Betas in pursuing undergraduate and graduate degrees. **Focus:** General studies/Field of study not specified. **Qualif.:** Applicants must be undergraduate or graduate students and initiated members of Beta Theta Pi who will be enrolled as full-time students

Awards are arranged alphabetically below their administering organizations

in the upcoming school year. **Criteria:** Selection based on final scores by a three-judge panel.

Funds Avail.: $1,100 each. **Duration:** Annual. **Number Awarded:** 3. **To Apply:** Application must be completed online at: beta.org/foundation/merit-scholarships/. **Deadline:** April 15. **Contact:** Laura Lednik, Director of Development; Email: laura.lednik@beta.org.

2525 ■ Burton L. Gerber Scholarship
(Undergraduate/Scholarship)

Purpose: To help Betas pursue undergraduate and graduate degrees. **Focus:** International affairs and relations; Military science and education. **Qualif.:** Applicants must be senior undergraduate students and initiated members of Beta Theta Pi who will be enrolled as full-time students in the upcoming school year; must be pursuing a career in military or international affairs. **Criteria:** Selection is based on final scores from a three-judge panel.

Funds Avail.: $1,600. **Duration:** Annual. **Number Awarded:** 1. **To Apply:** Application must be completed online at: beta.org/foundation/merit-scholarships/. **Deadline:** April 15. **Contact:** Laura Lednik, Director of Development; Email: laura.lednik@beta.org.

2526 ■ Thomas Boston Gordon Memorial Scholarship *(Undergraduate, Graduate/Scholarship)*

Purpose: To financially assist Betas in pursuing undergraduate and graduate degrees. **Focus:** General studies/Field of study not specified. **Qualif.:** Applicants must be undergraduate and graduate students and initiated members of Beta Theta Pi who will be enrolled as full-time students in the upcoming school year. **Criteria:** Selection based on final scores from a three-judge panel.

Funds Avail.: $2,300. **Duration:** Annual. **Number Awarded:** 1. **To Apply:** Application must be completed online at: beta.org/foundation/merit-scholarships/. **Deadline:** April 15. **Contact:** Laura Lednik, Director of Development; Email: laura.lednik@beta.org.

2527 ■ Charles Henry Hardin Memorial Scholarship *(Undergraduate, Graduate/Scholarship)*

Purpose: To financially assist Betas in pursuing undergraduate and graduate degrees. **Focus:** General studies/Field of study not specified. **Qualif.:** Applicants must be undergraduate and graduate students and initiated members of Beta Theta Pi who will be enrolled as full-time students in the upcoming school year. **Criteria:** Selection is based on final scores from a three-judge panel.

Funds Avail.: $2,300. **Duration:** Annual. **Number Awarded:** 1. **To Apply:** Application must be completed online at: beta.org/foundation/merit-scholarships/. **Deadline:** April 15. **Contact:** Laura Lednik, Director of Development; Email: laura.lednik@beta.org.

2528 ■ Ronald, Randall and Roger Helman Scholarship *(Undergraduate, Graduate/Scholarship)*

Purpose: To financially assist undergraduate and graduate Betas complete their degrees. **Focus:** General studies/Field of study not specified. **Qualif.:** Applicants must be undergraduate or graduate students and initiated members of Beta Theta Pi who will be enrolled as full-time students in the upcoming school year; must be members of the Miami, Central Michigan, or Michigan Beta chapters (alternating between the three, when possible). **Criteria:** Selection is based on final scores from a three-judge panel.

Funds Avail.: $1,550. **Duration:** Annual. **Number Awarded:** 1. **To Apply:** Application must be completed

online at: beta.org/foundation/merit-scholarships/. **Deadline:** April 15. **Contact:** Laura Lednik, Director of Development; Email: laura.lednik@beta.org.

2529 ■ George L. and June L. Herpel Memorial Scholarship *(Graduate/Scholarship)*

Purpose: To financially assist Betas in pursuing graduate degrees, especially in medicine and theology. **Focus:** General studies/Field of study not specified; Medicine; Theology. **Qualif.:** Applicants must be graduate students and initiated members of Beta Theta Pi who will be enrolled as full-time students in the upcoming school year; preference is for medical or theology majors (no political science or sociology majors). **Criteria:** Selection based on final scores by a three-judge panel. In the case of a tie, preference is for applicants from Vanderbilt or Villanova.

Funds Avail.: $1,075 each. **Duration:** Annual. **Number Awarded:** 5. **To Apply:** Application must be completed online at: beta.org/foundation/merit-scholarships/. **Deadline:** April 15. **Contact:** Laura Lednik, Director of Development; Email: laura.lednik@beta.org.

2530 ■ Douglas W. Hill, Jr. Scholarship *(Undergraduate, Graduate/Scholarship)*

Purpose: To financially assist Betas in pursuing undergraduate and graduate degrees. **Focus:** General studies/Field of study not specified. **Qualif.:** Applicants must be undergraduate or graduate students and initiated members of Beta Theta Pi who will be enrolled as full-time students in the upcoming school year. **Criteria:** Selection is based on final scores by a three-judge panel. Preference will be given to applicants from the Michigan State chapter.

Funds Avail.: $1,100 each. **Duration:** Annual. **Number Awarded:** 3. **To Apply:** Application must be completed online at: beta.org/foundation/merit-scholarships/. **Deadline:** April 15. **Contact:** Laura Lednik, Director of Development; Email: laura.lednik@beta.org.

2531 ■ John A. Hill Memorial Scholarship *(Undergraduate, Graduate/Scholarship)*

Purpose: To financially assist Betas in completing undergraduate and graduate degrees. **Focus:** General studies/Field of study not specified. **Qualif.:** Applicants must be undergraduate or graduate students and initiated members of Beta Theta Pi from the Denver chapter who will be enrolled as full-time students in the upcoming school year. **Criteria:** Selection is based on final scores from a three-judge panel.

Funds Avail.: $1,325. **Duration:** Annual. **Number Awarded:** 1. **To Apply:** Application must be completed online at: beta.org/foundation/merit-scholarships/. **Deadline:** April 15. **Contact:** Laura Lednik, Director of Development; Email: laura.lednik@beta.org.

2532 ■ Dr. Marshall E. Hollis Scholarship *(Undergraduate, Graduate/Scholarship)*

Purpose: To financially assist Betas in pursuing undergraduate and graduate degrees. **Focus:** General studies/Field of study not specified. **Qualif.:** Applicants must be undergraduate and graduate students and initiated members of Beta Theta Pi in the Mississippi chapter who will be enrolled as full-time students in the upcoming school year. **Criteria:** Selection is based on final scores by a three-judge panel.

Funds Avail.: $450. **Duration:** Annual. **Number Awarded:** 1. **To Apply:** Application must be completed online at:

Awards are arranged alphabetically below their administering organizations

beta.org/foundation/merit-scholarships/. **Deadline:** April 15. **Contact:** Laura Lednik, Director of Development; Email: laura.lednik@beta.org.

2533 ■ James P. Kirkgasser Memorial Scholarship
(Undergraduate, Graduate/Scholarship)

Purpose: To financially assist Betas in pursuing undergraduate and graduate degrees. **Focus:** General studies/Field of study not specified. **Qualif.:** Applicants must be undergraduate and graduate students and initiated members of Beta Theta Pi who will be enrolled as full-time students in the upcoming school year; restricted to Betas from District IV schools, with preference for Syracuse (Colgate, Cornell, St. Lawrence). **Criteria:** Selection is based on final scores from a three-judge panel.

Funds Avail.: $1,825. **Duration:** Annual. **Number Awarded:** 1. **To Apply:** Application must be completed online at: beta.org/foundation/merit-scholarships. **Deadline:** April 15. **Contact:** Laura Lednik, Director of Development; Email: laura.lednik@beta.org.

2534 ■ John G. F. Knight Memorial Scholarship
(Undergraduate, Graduate/Scholarship)

Purpose: To financially assist Betas in pursuing undergraduate and graduate degrees. **Focus:** General studies/Field of study not specified. **Qualif.:** Applicants must be undergraduate and graduate students and initiated members of Beta Theta Pi in Florida who will be enrolled as full-time students in the upcoming school year. **Criteria:** Selection is based on final scores from a three-judge panel.

Funds Avail.: $1,025. **Duration:** Annual. **Number Awarded:** 1. **To Apply:** Application must be completed online at: beta.org/foundation/merit-scholarships/. **Deadline:** April 15. **Contact:** Laura Lednik, Director of Development; Email: laura.lednik@beta.org.

2535 ■ Carl A. Kroch Oxford Cup Memorial Scholarship *(Undergraduate, Graduate/Scholarship)*

Purpose: To financially assist Betas in pursuing college degrees. **Focus:** General studies/Field of study not specified. **Qualif.:** Applicants must be undergraduate or graduate students and initiated members of Beta Theta Pi who will be enrolled as full-time students in the upcoming school year. **Criteria:** Selection is based on final scores by a three-judge panel.

Funds Avail.: $1,150. **Duration:** Annual. **Number Awarded:** 1. **To Apply:** Application must be completed online at: beta.org/foundation/merit-scholarships/. **Deadline:** April 15. **Contact:** Laura Lednik, Director of Development; Email: laura.lednik@beta.org.

2536 ■ Otho E. Lane Memorial Scholarship
(Undergraduate, Graduate/Scholarship)

Purpose: To financially assist Betas in completing undergraduate and graduate degrees. **Focus:** General studies/Field of study not specified. **Qualif.:** Applicants must be undergraduate or graduate students and initiated members of Beta Theta Pi who will be enrolled as full-time students in the upcoming school year. **Criteria:** Selection will be based on final score from a three-judge panel. Preference will be given to applicants from the Miami (Ohio) chapter.

Funds Avail.: $1,350. **Duration:** Annual. **Number Awarded:** 1. **To Apply:** Application must be completed online at: beta.org/foundation/merit-scholarships/. **Deadline:** April 15. **Contact:** Laura Lednik, Director of Development; Email: laura.lednik@beta.org.

2537 ■ David Linton Memorial Scholarship
(Undergraduate, Graduate/Scholarship)

Purpose: To help Betas pursue undergraduate and graduate degrees. **Focus:** General studies/Field of study not specified. **Qualif.:** Applicants must be undergraduate and graduate students and initiated members of Beta Theta Pi who will be enrolled as full-time students in the upcoming school year. **Criteria:** Selection is based on final scores from a three-judge panel.

Funds Avail.: $2,300. **Duration:** Annual. **Number Awarded:** 1. **To Apply:** Application must be completed online at: beta.org/foundation/merit-scholarships/. **Deadline:** April 15. **Contact:** Laura Lednik, Director of Development; Email: laura.lednik@beta.org.

2538 ■ Horace G. Lozier Memorial Scholarship
(Undergraduate, Graduate/Scholarship)

Purpose: To financially assist Betas in pursuing undergraduate and graduate degrees. **Focus:** General studies/Field of study not specified. **Qualif.:** Applicants must be undergraduate and graduate students and initiated members of Beta Theta Pi who will be enrolled as full-time students in the upcoming school year. **Criteria:** Selection is based on final scores from a three-judge panel.

Funds Avail.: $1,850. **Duration:** Annual. **Number Awarded:** 1. **To Apply:** Applications must be completed online at: beta.org/foundations/merit-scholarships/. **Deadline:** April 15. **Contact:** Laura Lednik, Director of Development; Email: laura.lednik@beta.org.

2539 ■ Samuel Taylor Marshall Scholarship *(Graduate, Undergraduate/Scholarship)*

Purpose: To help Betas pursue undergraduate and graduate degrees. **Focus:** General studies/Field of study not specified. **Qualif.:** Applicants must be undergraduate and graduate students and initiated members of Beta Theta Pi who will be enrolled as full-time students in the upcoming school year. **Criteria:** Selection is based on final scores from a three-judge panel.

Funds Avail.: $2,300. **Duration:** Annual. **Number Awarded:** 1. **To Apply:** Application must be completed online at: beta.org/foundation/merit-scholarships/. **Deadline:** April 15. **Contact:** Laura Lednik, Director of Development; Email: laura.lednik@beta.org.

2540 ■ Men of Principle Scholarship *(Undergraduate, Graduate/Scholarship)*

Purpose: To help individual Beta chapters and colonies of the Fraternity recognize unaffiliated (non-Greek) male students on college campuses. **Focus:** General studies/Field of study not specified. **Qualif.:** Applicants must be male students enrolled in post-secondary education. **Criteria:** Selection will be based on devotion to the values the Fraternity holds dear: mutual assistance, intellectual growth, trust, integrity, and responsible conduct. Selection is done by the individual chapters.

Duration: Annual. **To Apply:** Application must be completed online at: beta.org/scholarship/. Application will be forwarded to the respective chapter or colony president on applicant's campus.

2541 ■ John K. Merrell Scholarship *(Undergraduate, Graduate/Scholarship)*

Purpose: To financially assist Betas in pursuing undergraduate and graduate degrees. **Focus:** General studies/Field of study not specified. **Qualif.:** Applicants must be

Awards are arranged alphabetically below their administering organizations

undergraduate and graduate students and initiated members of Beta Theta Pi in the Purdue chapter who will be enrolled as full-time students in the upcoming school year. **Criteria:** Selection is based on final scores from a three-judge panel.

Funds Avail.: $1,050 each. **Duration:** Annual. **Number Awarded:** 7. **To Apply:** Application must be completed online at: beta.org/foundation/merit-scholarships/. **Deadline:** April 15. **Contact:** Laura Lednik, Director of Development; Email: laura.lednik@beta.org.

2542 ■ Steven Craig Merrill Memorial Scholarship
(Undergraduate, Graduate/Scholarship)

Purpose: To financially assist Betas in pursuing college degrees. **Focus:** General studies/Field of study not specified. **Qualif.:** Applicants must be undergraduate or graduate students and initiated members of Beta Theta Pi in the Virginia chapter who will be enrolled as full-time students in the upcoming school year. **Criteria:** Selection based on final scores by a three-judge panel.

Funds Avail.: $1,225 each. **Duration:** Annual. **Number Awarded:** 2. **To Apply:** Application must be completed online at: beta.org/foundation/merit-scholarships/. **Deadline:** April 15. **Contact:** Laura Lednik, Director of Development; Email: laura.lednik@beta.org.

2543 ■ Shelby L. Molter Music Education Scholarship *(Undergraduate, Graduate/Scholarship)*

Purpose: To financially support Betas pursuing music degrees. **Focus:** Music. **Qualif.:** Applicants must be undergraduate and graduate students and initiated members of Beta Theta Pi who will be enrolled as full-time students in the upcoming school year; must be music majors. **Criteria:** Selection is based on final scores by a three-judge panel.

Funds Avail.: $475. **Duration:** Annual. **Number Awarded:** 1. **To Apply:** Application must be complete online at: beta.org/foundation/merit-scholarships/. **Deadline:** April 15. **Contact:** Laura Lednik, Director of Development; Email: laura.lednik@beta.org.

2544 ■ M. Steve Moore Memorial Scholarship
(Undergraduate, Graduate/Award)

Purpose: To financially assist Betas in completing their college degrees. **Focus:** General studies/Field of study not specified. **Qualif.:** Applicants must be undergraduate or graduate students and initiated members of Beta Theta Pi who will be enrolled as full-time students in the upcoming school year. **Criteria:** Selection based on final scores by a three-judge panel. Preference given to applicants from the Clemson chapter.

Funds Avail.: $1,225. **Duration:** Annual. **Number Awarded:** 1. **To Apply:** Application must be completed online at: beta.org/foundation/merit-scholarships/. **Deadline:** April 15. **Contact:** Laura Lednik, Director of Development; Email: laura.lednik@beta.org.

2545 ■ Edith Cantor Morrison Memorial Scholarship
(Undergraduate, Graduate/Scholarship)

Purpose: To financially assist Betas who are pursuing teaching careers. **Focus:** Teaching. **Qualif.:** Applicants must be undergraduate and graduate students and initiated members of Beta Theta Pi who will be enrolled as full-time students in the upcoming school year; must be majoring in education (teaching, specifically). **Criteria:** Selection is based on final scores from a three-judge panel.

Funds Avail.: $850. **Duration:** Annual. **Number Awarded:** 1. **To Apply:** Application must be completed online at: beta.org/foundation/merit-scholarships/. **Deadline:** April 15. **Contact:** Laura Lednik, Director of Development; Email: laura.lednik@beta.org.

2546 ■ Douglas J. Neeley Memorial Scholarship
(Undergraduate, Graduate/Scholarship)

Purpose: To financially assist Betas in completing their undergraduate and graduate degrees. **Focus:** General studies/Field of study not specified. **Qualif.:** Applicants must be undergraduate or graduate students and initiated members of Beta Theta Pi in the Kenyon chapter who will be enrolled as full-time students in the upcoming school year. **Criteria:** Selection is based on final scores by a three-judge panel.

Funds Avail.: $1,250. **Duration:** Annual. **Number Awarded:** 2. **To Apply:** Application must be completed online at: beta.org/foundation/merit-scholarships/. **Deadline:** April 15. **Contact:** Laura Lednik, Director of Development; Email: laura.lednik@beta.org.

2547 ■ E. William Palmer Memorial Scholarship
(Undergraduate, Graduate/Scholarship)

Purpose: To financially assist Betas in completing undergraduate and graduate degrees. **Focus:** General studies/Field of study not specified. **Qualif.:** Applicants must be undergraduate or graduate students and initiated members of Beta Theta Pi who will be enrolled as full-time students in the upcoming school year. **Criteria:** Selection based on final scores from a three-judge panel. Preference given to applicants from the Lehigh chapter.

Funds Avail.: $1,275. **Duration:** Annual. **Number Awarded:** 1. **To Apply:** Application must be completed online at: beta.org/foundation/merit-scholarships/. **Deadline:** April 15. **Contact:** Laura Lednik, Director of Development; Email: laura.lednik@beta.org.

2548 ■ Caroline Previdi of Sandy Hook Elementary Memorial Scholarship *(Undergraduate, Graduate/Scholarship)*

Purpose: To support sons or daughters of Betas who are pursuing education degrees. **Focus:** Education. **Qualif.:** Applicants must be education majors who are sons or daughters of Betas. **Criteria:** Selection based on final scores from a three-judge panel.

Funds Avail.: $1,200 each. **Duration:** Annual. **Number Awarded:** 2. **To Apply:** Application must be completed online at: beta.org/foundation/merit-scholarships/. **Deadline:** April 15. **Contact:** Laura Lednik, Director of Development; Email: laura.lednik@beta.org.

2549 ■ John J. and Elizabeth Rhodes Scholarship
(Undergraduate, Graduate/Scholarship)

Purpose: To financially assist Betas in completing undergraduate and graduate degrees. **Focus:** General studies/Field of study not specified. **Qualif.:** Applicants must be undergraduate or graduate students and initiated members of Beta Theta Pi who will be enrolled as full-time students in the upcoming school year. **Criteria:** Selection based on final scores from a three-judge panel. Preference given to applicants from the Arizona, Arizona State, and Kansas State chapters.

Funds Avail.: $1,425 each. **Duration:** Annual. **Number Awarded:** 2. **To Apply:** Application must be completed online at: beta.org/foundation/merit-scholarships/. **Dead-

Awards are arranged alphabetically below their administering organizations

line: April 15. **Contact:** Laura Lednik, Director of Development; Email: laura.lednik@beta.org.

2550 ■ Ben C. Rich Memorial Scholarship
(Undergraduate, Graduate/Scholarship)

Purpose: To financially assist Betas in pursuing undergraduate and graduate degrees. **Focus:** General studies/ Field of study not specified. **Qualif.:** Applicants must be undergraduate and graduate students and initiated members of Beta Theta Pi who will be enrolled as full-time students in the upcoming school year. **Criteria:** Selection based on final scores from a three-judge panel.

Funds Avail.: $1,825. **Duration:** Annual. **Number Awarded:** 1. **To Apply:** Applications must be completed online at: beta.org/foundation/merit-scholarships/. **Deadline:** April 15. **Contact:** Laura Lednik, Director of Development; Email: laura.lednik@beta.org.

2551 ■ Michael Clarkson Ryan Memorial Scholarship *(Undergraduate, Graduate/Scholarship)*

Purpose: To financially assist Betas in pursuing undergraduate and graduate degrees. **Focus:** General studies/ Field of study not specified. **Qualif.:** Applicants must be undergraduate and graduate students and initiated members of Beta Theta Pi who will be enrolled as full-time students in the upcoming school year. **Criteria:** Selection is based on final scores from a three-judge panel.

Funds Avail.: $2,300. **Duration:** Annual. **Number Awarded:** 1. **To Apply:** Application must be completed online at: beta.org/foundation/merit-scholarships/. **Deadline:** April 15. **Contact:** Laura Lednik, Director of Development; Email: laura.lednik@beta.org.

2552 ■ Fred A. Seaton Memorial Scholarship
(Undergraduate, Graduate/Scholarship)

Purpose: To financially assist Betas in completing undergraduate and graduate degrees. **Focus:** General studies/ Field of study not specified. **Qualif.:** Applicants must be undergraduate or graduate students and initiated members of Beta Theta Pi who will be enrolled as full-time students in the upcoming school year. **Criteria:** Selection is based on final scores from a three-judge panel. Preference given to applicants from the Kansas State chapter.

Funds Avail.: $1,475. **Duration:** Annual. **Number Awarded:** 2. **To Apply:** Application must be completed online at: beta.org/foundation/merit-scholarships/. **Deadline:** April 15. **Contact:** Laura Lednik, Director of Development; Email: laura.lednik@beta.org.

2553 ■ William C. Scheetz Memorial Scholarship
(Undergraduate, Graduate/Scholarship)

Purpose: To financially support Betas completing undergraduate and graduate degrees. **Focus:** General studies/ Field of study not specified. **Qualif.:** Applicants must be undergraduate or graduate students and initiated members of Beta Theta Pi who will be enrolled as full-time students in the upcoming school year. **Criteria:** Selection is based on final scores by a three-judge panel. Preference will be given to applicants from the Pennsylvania chapter.

Funds Avail.: $1,250 each. **Duration:** Annual. **Number Awarded:** 2. **To Apply:** Application must be completed online at: beta.org/foundation/merit-scholarships/. **Deadline:** April 15. **Contact:** Laura Lednik, Director of Development; Email: laura.lednik@beta.org.

2554 ■ Col. Richard R. (Misty) and Sally Shoop Scholarship *(Undergraduate, Graduate/Scholarship)*

Purpose: To financially assist Betas in pursuing undergraduate and graduate degrees. **Focus:** General studies/

Field of study not specified. **Qualif.:** Applicants must be undergraduate and graduate students and initiated members of Beta Theta Pi who will be enrolled as full-time students in the upcoming school year. **Criteria:** Selection is based on final scores by a three-judge panel.

Funds Avail.: $825. **Duration:** Annual. **Number Awarded:** 1. **To Apply:** Application must be completed online at: beta.org/foundation/merit-scholarships/. **Deadline:** April 15. **Contact:** Laura Lednik, Director of Development; Email: laura.lednik@beta.org.

2555 ■ Col. John R. Simpson Memorial Scholarship
(Undergraduate, Graduate/Scholarship)

Purpose: To financially assist Betas in pursuing undergraduate and graduate degrees. **Focus:** General studies/ Field of study not specified. **Qualif.:** Applicants must be undergraduate and graduate students and initiated members of Beta Theta Pi who will be enrolled as full-time students in the upcoming school year. **Criteria:** Selection is based on final scores from a three-judge panel. Preference will be given to applicants from the Miami (Ohio) chapter.

Funds Avail.: $1,000 each. **Duration:** Annual. **Number Awarded:** 8. **To Apply:** Application must be completed online at: beta.org/foundation/merit-scholarships/. **Deadline:** April 15. **Contact:** Laura Lednik, Director of Development; Email: laura.lednik@beta.org.

2556 ■ James George Smith Memorial Scholarship
(Undergraduate, Graduate/Scholarship)

Purpose: To provide financial assistance to Betas pursuing undergraduate and graduate degrees. **Focus:** General studies/Field of study not specified. **Qualif.:** Applicants must be undergraduate and graduate students and initiated members of Beta Theta Pi who will be enrolled as full-time students in the upcoming school year. **Criteria:** Selection is based on final scores from a three-judge panel.

Funds Avail.: $2,300. **Duration:** Annual. **Number Awarded:** 1. **To Apply:** Application must be completed online at: beta.org/foundation/merit-scholarships/. **Deadline:** April 15. **Contact:** Laura Lednik, Director of Development; Email: laura.lednik@beta.org.

2557 ■ H. H. Stephenson, Jr. Oxford Cup Scholarship *(Undergraduate, Graduate/Scholarship)*

Purpose: To financially assist Betas in pursuing undergraduate and graduate degrees. **Focus:** General studies/ Field of study not specified. **Qualif.:** Applicants must be undergraduate and graduate students and initiated members of Beta Theta Pi who will be enrolled as full-time students in the upcoming school year. **Criteria:** Selection is based on final scores from a three-judge panel.

Funds Avail.: $575. **Duration:** Annual. **Number Awarded:** 1. **To Apply:** Applications must be completed online at: beta.org/foundation/merit-scholarships/. **Deadline:** April 15. **Contact:** Laura Lednik, Director of Development; Email: laura.lednik@beta.org.

2558 ■ Hugh E. Stephenson, Jr. Oxford Cup Scholarship *(Undergraduate, Graduate/Scholarship)*

Purpose: To financially assist Betas in pursuing undergraduate and graduate degrees. **Focus:** General studies/ Field of study not specified. **Qualif.:** Applicants must be undergraduate and graduate students and initiated members of Beta Theta Pi who will be enrolled as full-time students in the upcoming school year. **Criteria:** Selection is based on final scores from a three-judge panel.

Awards are arranged alphabetically below their administering organizations

Funds Avail.: $725. **Duration:** Annual. **Number Awarded:** 1. **To Apply:** Application must be completed online at: beta.org/foundation/merit-scholarships/. **Deadline:** April 15. **Contact:** Laura Lednik, Director of Development; Email: laura.lednik@beta.org.

2559 ■ Michael W. Toennis Scholarship
(Undergraduate, Graduate/Scholarship)

Purpose: To financially assist Betas in pursuing college degrees. **Focus:** General studies/Field of study not specified. **Qualif.:** Applicants must be undergraduate and graduate students and initiated members of Beta Theta Pi who will be enrolled as full-time students in the upcoming school year. **Criteria:** Selection is based on final scores by a three-judge panel. Preference will be given to applicants from the Houston chapter.

Funds Avail.: $850. **Duration:** Annual. **Number Awarded:** 1. **To Apply:** Application must be completed online at: beta.org/foundation/merit-scholarships/. **Deadline:** April 15. **Contact:** Laura Lednik, Director of Development; Email: laura.lednik@beta.org.

2560 ■ Gupton A. Vogt Oxford Cup Memorial Scholarship *(Undergraduate, Graduate/Scholarship)*

Purpose: To financially assist Betas in pursuing college degrees. **Focus:** General studies/Field of study not specified. **Qualif.:** Applicants must be undergraduate and graduate students and initiated members of Beta Theta Pi who will be enrolled as full-time students in the upcoming school year. **Criteria:** Selection is based on final scores from a three-judge panel.

Funds Avail.: $850. **Duration:** Annual. **Number Awarded:** 1. **To Apply:** Application must be completed online at: beta.org/foundation/merit-scholarships/. **Deadline:** April 15. **Contact:** Laura Lednik, Director of Development; Email: laura.lednik@beta.org.

2561 ■ Bethesda Lutheran Communities
600 Hoffmann Dr.
Watertown, WI 53094
Ph: (920)261-3050
Fax: (920)261-8441
Free: 800-369-4636
URL: bethesdalc.org
Social Media: www.facebook.com/BethesdaLutheran Communities
www.instagram.com/bethesdalc
www.pinterest.com/bethesdalc
twitter.com/BethesdaLC
www.youtube.com/user/BethesdaVideos

2562 ■ Lutheran Student Scholastic and Service Scholarships - College and University Students
(Undergraduate/Scholarship)

Purpose: To financially support Lutheran students pursuing degrees in any area of service to people with developmental disabilities. **Focus:** Mental health. **Qualif.:** Applicants must be active communicant members of a Lutheran church; have achieved sophomore status or higher at a college or university; have a 3.0 overall GPA; and have an interest in a career in the field of developmental disabilities. **Criteria:** Selection of recipients will be in a competitive basis. Criteria include are the said qualifications and compliance with the application process.

Funds Avail.: $3,000. **Duration:** Annual. **Number Awarded:** 5. **To Apply:** Application must documentation

of100 hours of service to people with intellectual and/or developmental disabilities, volunteer or paid. Service must be completed within the past two years; a 250-300-word essay on how the intended academic course of study will support their career in the field of intellectual and/ or developmental disabilities; four letters of recommendation (pastor, professor/teacher and two unrelated others);an official college/university transcript(s);submit pictures of applicant volunteering/interacting with people with intellectual and/or developmental disabilities. **Deadline:** May 15. **Contact:** Bethesda Lutheran Communities, Attn: Barb Schultz, 600 Hoffmann Dr., Watertown, WI 53094; Phone: 920-206-4427; 800-369-4636, ext. 4427; Email: barb.schultz@mailblc.org.

2563 ■ Bethune-Cookman University (B-CU)
640 Dr. Mary McLeod Bethune Blvd.
Daytona Beach, FL 32114
URL: www.cookman.edu
Social Media: www.facebook.com/bethunecookmanuniv
www.instagram.com/bethunecookman
twitter.com/bethunecookman
www.youtube.com/channel/UCtxafoO19WK_ihP97cVi51w

2564 ■ Bethune-Cookman University Excelsior Level 1 Scholarship *(Undergraduate/Scholarship)*

Purpose: To provide financial assistance for students intending to pursue their education. **Focus:** General studies/Field of study not specified. **Qualif.:** Applicants must be students who complete high school in May or June prior to enrolling into B-CU in the subsequent Fall semester; they must have a cumulative GPA of 3.5 (must earn and maintain 3.3 cumulative GPA to renew the award) and have test scores of SAT 1130 or ACT composite 23. **Criteria:** Selection will be based on merit.

Funds Avail.: No specific amount. **Duration:** Annual. **To Apply:** Applicant must complete and submit your FAFSA; must submit pay the required $300 (non-refundable) enrollment fee by February 20, 2017, by contacting the cashier's office and copy of Social Security Card. **Deadline:** December 1.

2565 ■ Bethune-Cookman University Presidential Scholarship *(Undergraduate/Scholarship)*

Purpose: To provide financial assistance to students intending to pursue their education. **Focus:** General studies/Field of study not specified. **Qualif.:** Applicants must be students who complete high school in May or June prior to enrolling into B-CU in the subsequent Fall semester; they must have a cumulative GPA of 3.75 (must earn and maintain 3.5 cumulative GPA to renew the award) and have test scores of SAT 1820 or ACT composite 26. **Criteria:** Selection will be based on merit.

Funds Avail.: No specific amount. **Duration:** Annual; up to 3 years. **To Apply:** Applicant must complete and submit your FAFSA; must submit pay the required $300 (non-refundable) enrollment fee by February 1, 2019, by contacting the cashier's office and copy of Social Security Card. **Deadline:** February 1.

2566 ■ Bibliographical Society of America (BSA)
PO Box 1537
New York, NY 10021
Ph: (212)452-2710
URL: www.bibsocamer.org

Awards are arranged alphabetically below their administering organizations

2567 ■ The Katharine Pantzer Fellowship in the British Book Trades *(Other/Fellowship)*

Purpose: To support sustained research in topics relating to book production history in Britain and other related aspects. **Focus:** Library and archival sciences; Printing--History. **Qualif.:** Applicants must be conducting research on topics relating to book production and distribution in Britain during the hand-press period as well as studies of authorship, reading and collecting based on the examination of British books published in that period. **Criteria:** Selection are given based on merit.

Funds Avail.: $6,000. **Duration:** Annual.

2568 ■ Bibliographical Society of Canada (BSC)
360 Bloor St. W
Toronto, ON, Canada M5S 3C9
URL: www.bsc-sbc.ca

2569 ■ Bernard Amtmann Fellowship *(Postgraduate, Other/Fellowship)*

Purpose: To support the work of a scholar engaged in some area of bibliographical research, including textual studies and publishing history and with a particular emphasis on Canada. **Focus:** General studies/Field of study not specified. **Qualif.:** Applicants must be members of the Bibliographical Society of Canada. **Criteria:** Selection will be based on scholastic ability; preference is given to applicants who display great interest in research work.

Funds Avail.: $2,000. **Duration:** Every three years. **To Apply:** Application must submit the online application form. **Deadline:** December 13. **Remarks:** The Fellowship was established in memory of Bernard Amtmann (1907-1979), the noted bookseller and specialist in Canadian. Established in 1992. **Contact:** Ruth Panofsky, Chair, Awards Committee, Bibliographical Society of Canada, 350 Victoria St., Toronto, ON, M5B 2K3, Canada, Email: panofsky@ryerson.ca.

2570 ■ Marie Tremaine Fellowship *(Postgraduate, Other/Fellowship)*

Purpose: To support the work of a scholar engaged in some area of bibliographical research, including textual studies and publishing history, with a particular emphasis on Canada. **Focus:** General studies/Field of study not specified. **Qualif.:** Applicants must be members of the Bibliographical Society of Canada. **Criteria:** Scholarship recipient will be selected based on scholastic ability; preference is given to applicants who display great interest in research work.

Funds Avail.: $2,000. **Duration:** One year. **Number Awarded:** 1. **To Apply:** Application must complete the online application form, should includes the summary and description of the project, budget and must provide references. **Deadline:** December 13. **Remarks:** The Fellowship was established in memory of and through the generosity of Marie Tremaine, the doyenne of Canadian bibliographers. Established in 1987. **Contact:** Ruth Panofsky, Chair, Awards Committee, Bibliographical Society of Canada, 350 Victoria St., Toronto, ON, M5B 2K3, Canada.

2571 ■ Big Sandy Community and Technical College (BSCTC)
1 Bert T. Combs Dr.
Prestonsburg, KY 41653
Ph: (606)886-3863

Free: 855-462-7282
URL: www.bigsandy.kctcs.edu
Social Media: www.facebook.com/BigSandyCTC
twitter.com/BSCTC05
www.youtube.com/user/BigSandyCTC1

2572 ■ Kentucky Educational Excellence Scholarship *(Undergraduate/Scholarship)*

Purpose: To provide financial support for deserving Kentucky high school students and GED recipients who are intending to pursue their education. **Focus:** General studies/Field of study not specified. **Qualif.:** Applicants must: be high school students; be U.S. citizens, nationals or permanent residents; be residents of Kentucky; have earned at least a 2.5 GPA in any year of high school while meeting the KEES curriculum requirements; attend and graduate from a certified Kentucky high school or other approved high school; and, not be convicted felons. High school graduates applying for a KEES bonus award must have at least an ACT composite score of 15 or a score of 810 or higher on the SAT and must have earned at least a 2.5 GPA in any year of high school while meeting the KEES curriculum requirements. Homeschool graduates applying for a KEES bonus award must have an ACT composite score of 15 or better on a national exam; GED graduate applicants must have an ACT composite score of 15 or better on a national exam; must have earned a GED in Kentucky within five years of turning 18 years old. **Criteria:** Selection will be based on merit.

Funds Avail.: No specific amount. **Duration:** Annual.

2573 ■ KHEAA Teacher Scholarship *(Undergraduate/Scholarship)*

Purpose: To provide financial aid for highly qualified Kentucky students intending to pursue initial teacher certification at participating Kentucky institutions. **Focus:** Teaching. **Qualif.:** Applicants must: be residents of Kentucky who are enrolled full-time in a teacher certification program; demonstrate financial need; and, meet school's satisfactory academic progress requirements. **Criteria:** Priority will be given to financially incapable applicants.

Funds Avail.: Up to $2,500. **Duration:** Annual. **Deadline:** May 1.

2574 ■ BioCommunications Association (BCA)
389 Newport Ave.
Attleboro, MA 02703-5617
E-mail: office@bca.org
URL: www.bca.org
Social Media: www.facebook.com/BioCommunicationsAssociation
twitter.com/BCA_update
www.youtube.com/channel/UCxlMxMTmhdl3EH4hEtAlBxQ

2575 ■ Endowment Fund for Education Grants *(Undergraduate/Grant)*

Purpose: To provide funds for projects which assist in the education of persons actively pursuing careers in biological imaging. **Focus:** Biological and clinical sciences. **Qualif.:** Applicants must be students, trainees, biocommunicators, or institutional programs that can demonstrate a need for project funding; members of the Selection Committee, or their relatives, are ineligible. **Criteria:** Selection of applicants will be based on merit and availability of funds.

Awards are arranged alphabetically below their administering organizations

Funds Avail.: Maximum of $500. **Duration:** Annual. **To Apply:** Applicants must submit the following documentation: (1) Current curriculum vitae; (2) A full and complete statement of what the applicant/ applicants intend(s) to accomplish within the field of biological photography; (3) Time frame for the project; (4) Details of how the project will benefit biomedical communications and biocommunicators as a whole, and of how this will be measured; (5) An agreement to provide the EFFE Committee with a final report describing the results of the project and its impact on biocommunication; (6) Description of plan to share the resulting educational benefits with the BCA membership; (7) An agreement that the BioCommunications Association, Inc., shall have the right of first publication on any results from project funded wholly or partially from the Endowment Fund for Education. **Deadline:** February 1.

2576 ■ Endowment Fund for Education Scholarships (EFFE) (Undergraduate/Grant, Scholarship)

Purpose: To provide funds for projects which assist in the education of persons actively pursuing careers in biological imaging. **Focus:** Biological and clinical sciences. **Qualif.:** Applicants must be enrolled in accredited college or technical school program as 2nd, 3rd or 4th year student. **Criteria:** Selection committees will evaluate all the submitted applications; will be based on merit and availability of funds.

Funds Avail.: $500. **Duration:** Annual. **Number Awarded:** 2. **To Apply:** Applicant must submit resume; Portfolio; Reference Contact Information; Transcripts; Proof of Enrollment; Include a short essay, no more than one page in length, explaining what inspired you to pursue a course of study in scientific/biomedical visual communications and share any related future goals or aspirations you may have in this field. **Deadline:** February 1. **Contact:** Endowment Funds for Education Chair, BioCommunications Association, 389 Newport Ave., Attleboro, MA 02703-5617; E-mail: office@bca.org.

2577 ■ Biomedical Engineering Society (BMES)

8201 Corporate Dr., Ste. 1125
Landover, MD 20785-2224
Ph: (301)459-1999
Fax: (301)459-2444
Free: 877-871-2637
E-mail: membership@bmes.org
URL: www.bmes.org
Social Media: www.facebook.com/BMESociety
www.instagram.com/bmesociety
www.linkedin.com/company/biomedical-engineering
-society
twitter.com/BMESociety
www.youtube.com/user/BMESociety

2578 ■ BMES Graduate and Undergraduate Student Awards (Graduate, Undergraduate/Award)

Purpose: To promote the future of the biomedical engineering profession. **Focus:** Biomedical sciences; Engineering, Biomedical. **Qualif.:** Applicants must be graduates or undergraduate students and must be BMES members in good standing. **Criteria:** Selection will be based on committee's criteria.

Funds Avail.: $500 for graduate; $400 for undergraduate. **Duration:** Annual. **To Apply:** Applicants must submit an abstract at the time of the official abstract-submission deadline for the annual meeting and pay the abstract-submission fee; for the undergraduate submission submit two-to-three pages, single spaced, (10-12 font type size) and one inch margins in all sides; a letter of support from the scientific advisor or department chair certifying the originality of the student effort must be uploaded at the time of submission; for the graduate submission submit three-to-four pages single spaced, (10-12 font type size) and one inch margins in all sides; a letter of support from the scientific advisor or department chair certifying the originality of the student effort must be uploaded at the time of submission. **Contact:** Biomedical Engineering Society, at the above address.

2579 ■ Birmingham Public School

31301 Evergreen Rd.
Beverly Hills, MI 48025
Ph: (248)203-3000
Fax: (248)203-3144
E-mail: info@birmingham.k12.mi.us
URL: www.birmingham.k12.mi.us
Social Media: www.facebook.com/
  BirminghamPublicSchools
www.linkedin.com/company/birmingham-public-schools
twitter.com/BirminghamPS
www.youtube.com/user/BirminghamPS

2580 ■ Birmingham Student Scholarships (Undergraduate/Scholarship)

Purpose: To provide college financial assistance for students who reside within the boundaries of the Birmingham School District upon high school graduation. **Focus:** General studies/Field of study not specified. **Qualif.:** Applicants must be high school and/or college students living in the Birmingham Public School District at the time of their high school graduation. **Criteria:** Selection will be based on the committee's criteria.

Funds Avail.: Amount varies. **Duration:** Annual. **Number Awarded:** Varies. **To Apply:** Applicants must submit completed application to the student's high school counselor prior to the filing date set by the Scholar Board each year; the application must be signed by both the student and one parent certifying the truth of the application; the application requires student's and parents' current income tax information, as well as information regarding family housing, unless there is independent written verification of an established pattern of non-support by a parent; scholarship grants will be reduced by 50 percent if information is not received from both parents; the application and instructions can be printed from the webpage.

2581 ■ Bisnar Chase, Personal Injury Attorneys LLP

1301 Dove St., No. 120
Newport Beach, CA 92660
Ph: (949)203-3814
Fax: (949)752-2777
Free: 800-561-2777
E-mail: marketing@bestattorney.com
URL: www.bestattorney.com

2582 ■ The Branch Out Scholarship (Undergraduate, College, University/Scholarship)

Purpose: To help U.S. students pay for college. **Focus:** General studies/Field of study not specified. **Qualif.:** Applicants must be high school seniors or college students committed to expanding their education and using their education to improve their communities. **Criteria:** Selection will be based on the best submitted essay.

Funds Avail.: $1,000 award, plus $500 for a charity chosen by the scholarship recipient. **Duration:** Semiannual. **Number Awarded:** 2 per year. **To Apply:** Application details and form available at www.bestattorney.com/giving-back/branch-out-scholarship/. **Deadline:** June 15; December 15. **Contact:** K. Feathers at email and phone number above.

2583 ■ Mary E. Bivins Foundation
2311 W 16th Ave.
Amarillo, TX 79102-2303
Ph: (806)379-9400
Fax: (806)379-9404
E-mail: info@bivinsfoundation.org
URL: www.bivinsfoundations.org

2584 ■ The Mary E. Bivins Ministry Scholarship Program *(Graduate, Undergraduate/Scholarship)*

Purpose: To educate ministers to preach the Christian religion. **Focus:** Education, Religious. **Criteria:** Priority will be given to students intending to serve as pulpit pastors upon graduation.

Funds Avail.: $2,500 for juniors or seniors; $3,500 for graduate students. **Duration:** Annual. **To Apply:** Applicants must submit the completed application form. **Contact:** Jessica Tudyk, Program Officer, Mary E. Bivins Foundation, PO Box 1727, Amarillo, TX, 79105; Phone: 806-379-9400; Email: Jessica@bivinsfoundation.org.

2585 ■ Black Business and Professional Association (BBPA)
180 Elm St.
Toronto, ON, Canada M5T 3M4
Ph: (416)504-4097
E-mail: info@bbpa.org
URL: www.bbpa.org
Social Media: www.facebook.com/thebbpa
twitter.com/thebbpa

2586 ■ Hon. Lincoln Alexander Scholarship *(Undergraduate, Graduate/Scholarship)*

Purpose: To provide support for Black Canadian students who want to pursue education. **Focus:** General studies/Field of study not specified. **Qualif.:** Applicants must be Canadian citizens or permanent residents who are members of the Canadian Black community (i.e. Black persons of discernible African ancestry and self identity); maximum 30 years of age and enrolled in a full-time student in the academic year at an accredited post-secondary institution (as determined by the NSF). **Criteria:** Selection will be based on academic achievement, financial need, recognized contribution to the Black community and some donor prescribed criteria.

Funds Avail.: 1,000 to 2,000 Canadian Dollars. **Duration:** Annual. **Number Awarded:** 1. **To Apply:** Applicants must complete the online application form and attach the following: Letter of Recommendation from teacher, guidance counsellor, principal or vice-principal who knows applicant well and can write about academic accomplishments and other outstanding attributes written on official letterhead;

letter of Recommendation from a member of applicant community, high-school transcript (attachments in PDF format); hardcopy original of high school transcript must be sent to NSF Office within 14 days of application online deadline. **Remarks:** The scholarship is in honor of the widely respected first Black Lieutenant Governor of Ontario, who continues to emphasize the need for fairness and equity for all citizens.

2587 ■ BBPA First Generation Scholarships *(College, University, Undergraduate/Scholarship)*

Purpose: To support students whose parents have not participated in post-secondary education studies. **Focus:** General studies/Field of study not specified. **Qualif.:** Applicants must be must be residents of Ontario or permanent residents who are members of the Canadian Black community (i.e. Black persons of discernible African ancestry and self identity); maximum 30 years of age and enrolled in a full-time student in the academic year at an accredited post-secondary institution (as determined by the NSF); and the first in their family to attend university. **Criteria:** Selection will be based on academic achievement, financial need, recognized contribution to the Black community and some donor prescribed criteria.

Funds Avail.: 1,000 to 2,000 Canadian Dollars. **Duration:** Annual. **To Apply:** Applicants must complete the online application form and attach the following: Letter of Recommendation from teacher, guidance counsellor, principal or vice-principal who knows applicant well and can write about academic accomplishments and other outstanding attributes written on official letterhead; letter of Recommendation from a member of applicant community, high-school transcript (attachments in PDF format); hardcopy original of high school transcript must be sent to NSF Office within 14 days of application online deadline. **Remarks:** Established in 1986. **Contact:** E-mail: scholarships@BBPA.org.

2588 ■ Beverley Mascoll Scholarship *(Undergraduate/Scholarship)*

Purpose: To provide support for Black Canadian students. **Focus:** General studies/Field of study not specified. **Qualif.:** Applicants must be Canadian citizens or permanent residents who are members of the Canadian Black community (i.e. Black persons of discernible African ancestry and self identity); maximum 30 years of age and enrolled in a full-time student in the academic year at an accredited post-secondary institution (as determined by the NSF). **Criteria:** Selection will be based on academic achievement, financial need, recognized contribution to the Black community and some donor prescribed criteria.

Funds Avail.: 1,000 to 2,000 Canadian dollars. **Duration:** Annual. **To Apply:** Applicants must complete the online application form and attach the following: Letter of Recommendation from teacher, guidance counsellor, principal or vice-principal who knows applicant well and can write about academic accomplishments and other outstanding attributes written on official letterhead; letter of Recommendation from a member of applicant community, high-school transcript (attachments in PDF format); hardcopy original of high school transcript must be sent to NSF Office within 14 days of application online deadline. **Remarks:** The scholarship honors the memory of Mrs. Mascoll, a well known and respected entrepreneur who often helped out less fortunate members of our community.

2589 ■ Robert K. Brown Scholarships *(Undergraduate, Master's/Scholarship)*

Purpose: To support a student pursuing a career in the field of Social Services at the bachelor's or master's degree

Awards are arranged alphabetically below their administering organizations

level. **Focus:** Social work. **Qualif.:** Applicants must be: enrolled in a course of study in the field of social services; Canadian citizens or permanent residents; maximum of 30 years of age; and, enrolled in a full-time bachelor's or master's degree level at a Canadian college or university for the academic year. **Criteria:** Selection will be based on academic achievement, financial need, and recognized contribution to the Black community. Special consideration for Black males.

Funds Avail.: 1,500 Canadian Dollars. **Duration:** Annual. **Number Awarded:** 1. **To Apply:** Applicants must complete the application form and submit along with a letter describing the reasons why they would be worthy recipients of a BBPA National Scholarship; a completed financial information schedule stating their budget for the coming year including information on their expected sources of funding, family income and related information; a letter of reference from the two individuals named in their application (must be a teacher from their high school, college or university, and an individual who is familiar with their community service); and two passport size photos - head shot. Application form and requirements must be sent to The Board of Trustees, BBPA National Scholarship Fund. **Remarks:** The scholarship is sponsored by Tropicana Community Services (Robert K. Brown was a founding father) which is a not-for-profit organization providing culturally appropriate social services to youth in east Toronto.

2590 ■ Herb Carnegie Scholarship *(Undergraduate/ Scholarship)*

Purpose: To provide support to under-privileged Black Canadian students. **Focus:** General studies/Field of study not specified. **Qualif.:** Applicants must be Canadian citizens or permanent residents who are members of the Canadian Black community (i.e. Black persons of discernible African ancestry and self identity); maximum 30 years of age and enrolled in a full-time student in the academic year at an accredited post-secondary institution (as determined by the NSF). **Criteria:** Selection will be based on academic achievement, financial need, recognized contribution to the Black community and some donor prescribed criteria.

Funds Avail.: 1,000 to 2,000 Canadian Dollars. **Duration:** Annual. **Number Awarded:** 1. **To Apply:** Applicants must complete the online application form and attach the following: Letter of Recommendation from teacher, guidance counsellor, principal or vice-principal who knows applicant well and can write about academic accomplishments and other outstanding attributes written on official letterhead; letter of Recommendation from a member of applicant community, high-school transcript (attachments in PDF format); hardcopy original of high school transcript must be sent to NSF Office within 14 days of application online deadline. **Remarks:** The scholarship is in honor of the late Mr. Herb Carnegie, an outstanding athlete who fought against systemic obstacles to be acknowledged as a first rate hockey player. He was awarded the Order of Canada, to recognize his contributions helping many youth overcome obstacles to their success. Established in 1986.

2591 ■ C.I.B.C Scholarship *(Undergraduate, Graduate/Scholarship)*

Purpose: To provide support for Black Canadian students who demonstrated social responsibility through work in the community. **Focus:** General studies/Field of study not specified. **Qualif.:** Applicants must be Canadian citizens or permanent residents who are members of the Canadian Black community (i.e. Black persons of discernible African ancestry and self identity); maximum 30 years of age and

enrolled in a full-time student in the academic year at an accredited post-secondary institution (as determined by the NSF). **Criteria:** Selection will be based on demonstrated social responsibility through work in the community.

Funds Avail.: 5,000 Canadian Dollars. **Duration:** Annual. **Number Awarded:** 1. **To Apply:** Applicants must complete the online application form and attach the following: Letter of Recommendation from teacher, guidance counsellor, principal or vice-principal who knows applicant well and can write about academic accomplishments and other outstanding attributes written on official letterhead; letter of Recommendation from a member of applicant community, high-school transcript (attachments in PDF format); hardcopy original of high school transcript must be sent to NSF Office within 14 days of application online deadline.

2592 ■ Harry Gairey Scholarship *(Undergraduate/ Scholarship)*

Purpose: To provide support for Black Canadian students who want to pursue education. **Focus:** General studies/ Field of study not specified. **Qualif.:** Applicants must be Canadian citizens or permanent residents who are members of the Canadian Black community (i.e. Black persons of discernible African ancestry and self identity); maximum 30 years of age and enrolled in a full-time student in the academic year at an accredited post-secondary institution (as determined by the NSF). **Criteria:** Selection will be based on academic achievement, financial need, recognized contribution to the Black community and some donor prescribed criteria.

Funds Avail.: 2,000 Canadian Dollars. **Duration:** Annual. **Number Awarded:** 1. **To Apply:** Applicants must complete the online application form and attach the following: Letter of Recommendation from teacher, guidance counsellor, principal or vice-principal who knows applicant well and can write about academic accomplishments and other outstanding attributes written on official letterhead; letter of Recommendation from a member of applicant community, high-school transcript (attachments in PDF format); hardcopy original of high school transcript must be sent to NSF Office within 14 days of application online deadline. **Remarks:** The scholarship is sponsored by the BBPA, in honor of Mr. Gairey's important role as a community activist and his many valuable contributions to the Black community over the years.

2593 ■ Lucille May Gopie Scholarships *(Undergraduate, Graduate/Scholarship)*

Purpose: To support a young person who has been encouraged by a single parent to pursue higher education as a means of self-fulfillment. **Focus:** General studies/Field of study not specified. **Qualif.:** Applicants must be: persons who have been encouraged by a single parent to pursue higher education; Canadian citizens or permanent residents; maximum of 30 years old; and, enrolled in a full-time degree bachelor's degree at a Canadian college or university for the academic year. **Criteria:** Selection will be based on academic achievement, financial need, and recognized contribution to the Black community.

Funds Avail.: 2,000 Canadian Dollars. **Duration:** Annual. **Number Awarded:** 1. **To Apply:** Applicants must complete the application form and submit along with a letter describing the reasons why they would be worthy recipients of a BBPA National Scholarship; a completed financial information schedule stating their budget for the coming year including information on their expected sources of funding, family income and related information; a letter of reference

Awards are arranged alphabetically below their administering organizations

from the two individuals named in their application (must be a teacher from their high school, college or university, and an individual who is familiar with their community service); and two passport size photos - head shot. Application form and requirements must be sent to The Board of Trustees, BBPA National Scholarship Fund. **Remarks:** The scholarship is sponsored by Kamala Jean Gopie. Such is named for her mother, who came from humble beginnings and encouraged her children to dream and to achieve through education.

2594 ■ Guntley-Lorimer Science and Arts Scholarships *(Undergraduate/Scholarship)*

Purpose: To provide support to Black Canadian students enrolled in Science and Arts programs at the university and college levels. **Focus:** Arts; Science. **Qualif.:** Applicants must be Canadian citizens or permanent residents enrolled in Science and Arts programs at a Canadian college or university levels. **Criteria:** Selection will be based on academic achievement, financial need, and recognized contribution to the Black community.

Funds Avail.: 2,000 Canadian Dollars (for student in Arts); 3,000 Canadian Dollars (for student in Science). **Duration:** Annual. **Number Awarded:** 4. **To Apply:** Applicants must complete the application form and submit along with a letter describing the reasons why they would be worthy recipients of a BBPA National Scholarship; a completed financial information schedule stating their budget for the coming year including information on their expected sources of funding, family income and related information; a letter of reference from the two individuals named in their application (must be a teacher from their high school, college or university, and an individual who is familiar with their community service); and two passport size photos - head shot. Application form and requirements must be sent to The Board of Trustees, BBPA National Scholarship Fund. **Remarks:** The scholarship is sponsored by Dr. Edith Guntley-Lorimer and Professor Michael Lorimer.

2595 ■ Al Hamilton Scholarship *(Undergraduate/Scholarship)*

Purpose: To provide support to under-privileged Black Canadian students. **Focus:** General studies/Field of study not specified. **Qualif.:** Applicants must be Canadian citizens or permanent residents who are members of the Canadian Black community (i.e. Black persons of discernible African ancestry and self identity); maximum 30 years of age and enrolled in a full-time student in the academic year at an accredited post-secondary institution (as determined by the NSF). **Criteria:** Selection will be based on academic achievement, financial need, recognized contribution to the Black community and some donor prescribed criteria.

Funds Avail.: 1,000 to 2,000 Canadian Dollars. **Duration:** Annual. **Number Awarded:** 1. **To Apply:** Applicants must complete the online application form and attach the following: Letter of Recommendation from teacher, guidance counsellor, principal or vice-principal who knows applicant well and can write about academic accomplishments and other outstanding attributes written on official letterhead; letter of Recommendation from a member of applicant community, high-school transcript (attachments in PDF format); hardcopy original of high school transcript must be sent to NSF Office within 14 days of application online deadline. **Deadline:** June 16; June 30. **Remarks:** The scholarship honors the late Al Hamilton, journalist, founder of an ethnocultural newspaper for the Black community, and a respected community activist.

2596 ■ Hon. Michaelle Jean Scholarship *(Undergraduate/Scholarship)*

Purpose: To provide support for Black Canadian students who want to pursue education. **Focus:** General studies/Field of study not specified. **Qualif.:** Applicants must be Canadian citizens or permanent residents who are members of the Canadian Black community (i.e. Black persons of discernible African ancestry and self identity); maximum 30 years of age and enrolled in a full-time student in the academic year at an accredited post-secondary institution (as determined by the NSF). **Criteria:** Selection will be based on academic achievement, financial need, recognized contribution to the Black community and some donor prescribed criteria.

Funds Avail.: 1,000 to 2,000 Canadian Dollars. **Duration:** Annual. **Number Awarded:** 1. **To Apply:** Applicants must complete the online application form and attach the following: Letter of Recommendation from teacher, guidance counsellor, principal or vice-principal who knows applicant well and can write about academic accomplishments and other outstanding attributes written on official letterhead; letter of Recommendation from a member of applicant community, high-school transcript (attachments in PDF format); hardcopy original of high school transcript must be sent to NSF Office within 14 days of application online deadline. **Remarks:** The scholarship honors the first Afro-Canadian Governor General. After the expiration of her appointment in September 2010, she continues to contribute significantly to humanitarian issues. She was named UNESCO Special Envoy for Haiti, immediately after her term.

2597 ■ Harry Jerome Legacy Scholarship *(Undergraduate, Graduate/Scholarship)*

Purpose: To provide support for Black Canadian students who have demonstrated superior achievement in academics, athletics and their involvement in helping those who need, assistance or support in the Black community. **Focus:** General studies/Field of study not specified. **Qualif.:** Applicants must be Canadian citizens or permanent residents who are members of the Canadian Black community (i.e. Black persons of discernible African ancestry and self identity); maximum 30 years of age and enrolled in a full-time student in the academic year at an accredited post-secondary institution (as determined by the NSF). **Criteria:** Selection will be based on academic achievement, financial need, recognized contribution to the Black community and some donor prescribed criteria.

Funds Avail.: 2,000 Canadian Dollars. **Duration:** Annual. **Number Awarded:** 1. **To Apply:** Applicants must complete the online application form and attach the following: Letter of Recommendation from teacher, guidance counsellor, principal or vice-principal who knows applicant well and can write about academic accomplishments and other outstanding attributes written on official letterhead; letter of Recommendation from a member of applicant community, high-school transcript (attachments in PDF format); hardcopy original of high school transcript must be sent to NSF Office within 14 days of application online deadline. **Remarks:** The scholarship is sponsored by the BBPA to honor Harry Jerome, an outstanding Black Canadian who was an Olympian, Officer of the Order of Canada, and world renowned for his sports achievements. Established in 1996.

2598 ■ Minerva Scholarships *(Undergraduate/Scholarship)*

Purpose: To provide support for Black Canadian students who want to pursue education. **Focus:** General studies/

Awards are arranged alphabetically below their administering organizations

Field of study not specified. **Qualif.:** Applicants must be Canadian citizens or permanent residents who are members of the Canadian Black community (i.e. Black persons of discernible African ancestry and self identity); maximum 30 years of age and enrolled in a full-time student in the academic year at an accredited post-secondary institution (as determined by the NSF). **Criteria:** Selection will be based on academic achievement, financial need, recognized contribution to the Black community and some donor prescribed criteria.

Funds Avail.: 2,000 Canadian Dollars each. **Duration:** Annual. **Number Awarded:** 4. **To Apply:** Applicants must complete the online application form and attach the following: Letter of Recommendation from teacher, guidance counsellor, principal or vice-principal who knows applicant well and can write about academic accomplishments and other outstanding attributes written on official letterhead; letter of Recommendation from a member of applicant community, high-school transcript (attachments in PDF format); hardcopy original of high school transcript must be sent to NSF Office within 14 days of application online deadline.

2599 ■ Robert Sutherland/Harry Jerome Entrance Award *(Undergraduate/Scholarship)*

Purpose: To support students pursuing an undergraduate degree at Queen's University. **Focus:** General studies/ Field of study not specified. **Qualif.:** Applicant must be a black student entering the first year of any direct-entry undergraduate degree program at Queen's University. **Criteria:** Selection is base on demonstrated financial need, academic achievement and contribution to the community or other volunteer activities, reviewed by a committee of the Student Awards Office at Queen's Univ.

Funds Avail.: $5,000 Canadian Dollars. **Duration:** 3 Year. **To Apply:** Applicants must complete the online application form and attach the following: Letter of Recommendation from teacher, guidance counsellor, principal or vice-principal who knows applicant well and can write about academic accomplishments and other outstanding attributes written on official letterhead; letter of Recommendation from a member of applicant community, high-school transcript (attachments in PDF format); hardcopy original of high school transcript must be sent to NSF Office within 14 days of application online deadline. **Deadline:** March 1. **Remarks:** The scholarship honors Robert Sutherland (BA, 1852), the first student of African heritage to graduate from Queen's University, Ontario, Canada. Established in 2008.

2600 ■ Royal Bank Scholarships *(Undergraduate, Master's, Graduate/Scholarship)*

Purpose: To provide support for Black Canadian students who want to pursue education in a business-related field. **Focus:** Business administration; Economics; Finance. **Qualif.:** Applicants must be Canadian citizens or permanent residents who are members of the Canadian Black community (i.e. Black persons of discernible African ancestry and self identity); maximum 30 years of age and enrolled in a full-time student in the academic year at an accredited post-secondary institution (as determined by the NSF) in business administration or a related field. **Criteria:** Selection will be based on academic achievement, financial need, recognized contribution to the Black community and some donor prescribed criteria.

Funds Avail.: 4,000 Canadian Dollars each. **Duration:** Annual. **Number Awarded:** 2. **To Apply:** Applicants must complete the online application form and attach the following: Letter of Recommendation from teacher, guidance

counsellor, principal or vice-principal who knows applicant well and can write about academic accomplishments and other outstanding attributes written on official letterhead; letter of Recommendation from a member of applicant community, high-school transcript (attachments in PDF format); hardcopy original of high school transcript must be sent to NSF Office within 14 days of application online deadline. **Remarks:** Sponsored by the Royal Bank of Canada.

2601 ■ Scotiabank Scholarship *(Undergraduate/ Scholarship)*

Purpose: To provide support for Black Canadian students who want to pursue education in the field of business studies. **Focus:** Business. **Qualif.:** Applicants must be Canadian citizens or permanent residents who are members of the Canadian Black community (i.e. Black persons of discernible African ancestry and self identity); maximum 30 years of age and enrolled in a full-time student in the academic year at an accredited post-secondary institution (as determined by the NSF) in the field of business studies. **Criteria:** Selection will be based on strong academics, demonstrated financial need, leadership skills, and commitment to helping in their community.

Funds Avail.: 5,000 Canadian Dollars each. **Duration:** Annual. **Number Awarded:** 2. **To Apply:** Applicants must complete the online application form and attach the following: Letter of Recommendation from teacher, guidance counsellor, principal or vice-principal who knows applicant well and can write about academic accomplishments and other outstanding attributes written on official letterhead; letter of Recommendation from a member of applicant community, high-school transcript (attachments in PDF format); hardcopy original of high school transcript must be sent to NSF Office within 14 days of application online deadline. **Remarks:** Sponsored by the Bank of Nova Scotia.

2602 ■ Portia White Scholarship *(Undergraduate/ Scholarship)*

Purpose: To provide support for Black Canadian students who want to pursue education. **Focus:** Music. **Qualif.:** Applicants must be Canadian citizens or permanent residents who are members of the Canadian Black community (i.e. Black persons of discernible African ancestry and self identity); maximum 30 years of age and enrolled in a full-time student in the academic year at an accredited post-secondary institution (as determined by the NSF) in the field of musical arts. **Criteria:** Selection will be based on academic achievement, financial need, recognized contribution to the Black community and some donor prescribed criteria.

Funds Avail.: 1,000 to 2,000 Canadian Dollars. **Duration:** Annual. **Number Awarded:** 1. **To Apply:** Applicants must complete the online application form and attach the following: Letter of Recommendation from teacher, guidance counsellor, principal or vice-principal who knows applicant well and can write about academic accomplishments and other outstanding attributes written on official letterhead; letter of Recommendation from a member of applicant community, high-school transcript (attachments in PDF format); hardcopy original of high school transcript must be sent to NSF Office within 14 days of application online deadline. **Remarks:** The scholarship is in honor of the late Ms. Portia White, a renowned opera singer in past decades, who overcame personal obstacles to establish an out-standing musical career.

2603 ■ Black Canadian Scholarship Fund
PO Box 8002
Ottawa, ON, Canada K1G 5H6

Awards are arranged alphabetically below their administering organizations

URL: www.bcsf.ca

2604 ■ BCSF Scholarships *(Undergraduate/ Scholarship)*

Purpose: To encourage academic excellence among black students in their chosen fields of study. **Focus:** General studies/Field of study not specified. **Qualif.:** Applicants must be Black Canadian students graduating from a high school in the city of Ottawa; must be admissible to a recognized Canadian university; demonstrate a need of financial assistance; be Canadian citizens; demonstrate leadership in community involvement; and, have an interim or final average of at least 75% in 6 grade 12 courses. **Criteria:** Selection will be based on the criteria set by the bestowing organization.

Funds Avail.: $6,000. **Duration:** Annual. **To Apply:** Applicants must submit a two-page essay explaining why the scholarship is important to them and how they will satisfy the eligibility criteria. They must also: provide a photocopy of the applicant's latest official transcript of 6 Grade 12 courses with above 75% average; have a letter of recommendation from a teacher/guidance counselor in current academic year; have proof of community service; have proof of Canadian citizenship; and, have a detailed statement indicating the amount of money expected from various sources. **Deadline:** May 31. **Remarks:** Established in 1996. **Contact:** Janet Adams, Senior Associate, Development and Donor Services at the Ottawa Community Foundation; Phone: 613-236-1616; ext. 231.

2605 ■ Black Caucus of the American Library Association (BCALA)

PO Box 174
New York, NY 10159-0174
Ph: (917)856-8923
E-mail: info@bcala.org
URL: www.bcala.org
Social Media: www.facebook.com/blackcaucusala/
twitter.com/BC_ALA

2606 ■ E.J. Josey Scholarship *(Graduate/ Scholarship)*

Purpose: To support African American students in library and information science. **Focus:** Library and archival sciences. **Qualif.:** Applicants must be an African American Citizen of the U.S. or Canada, and enrolled or accepted by ALA-accredited graduate program leading to a degree in library and information science at the time of application. **Criteria:** Selection is based on the essay's argument development and critical analysis, clear language, conciseness and creativity.

Funds Avail.: $2,000. **Duration:** One year. **Number Awarded:** 2. **To Apply:** Applicants must write an essay on a given theme. Essays (typed, double-spaced, and in Microsoft word or Corel) must include a cover letter providing the applicant's name, address, phone numbers, graduate program, and name of school and anticipated date of graduation; use the MLA style and include a minimum of six bibliographical references; essays submitted electronically will only be considered and include E.J. Josey in the subject line of your electronic submission.

2607 ■ Black Note Inc.

1340 Reynolds 116 Ave.
Irvine, CA 92614

Free: 800-949-3095
URL: www.blacknote.com
Social Media: facebook.com/blacknotevape
instagram.com/blacknotevape
pinterest.com/blacknotevape
twitter.com/blacknotevape
youtube.com/channel/UCGMRyNv4BmVNWn29clk4oPw

2608 ■ Get A Boost $2,000 Scholarship *(All/ Scholarship)*

Purpose: To provide scholarships for students. **Focus:** General studies/Field of study not specified. **Qualif.:** Applicant must be at least 18 years old.

Funds Avail.: $2,000. **Duration:** Annual. **Number Awarded:** 2. **To Apply:** Applicant must meet the lineup of requirements, complete an online application, and submit an essay discussing their smoke-free world ideas. Application available at www.blacknote.com/scholarship/. **Deadline:** July 31.

2609 ■ Black Nurses Association of Greater Washington D.C. Area (BNA-GWDCA)

PO Box 55285
Washington, DC 20040
Ph: (202)291-8866
E-mail: contactus@bnaofgwdca.org
URL: www.bnaofgwdca.org
Social Media: www.facebook.com/bnaofgwdca

2610 ■ Dr. Johnella Banks Memorial Scholarships *(Undergraduate/Scholarship)*

Purpose: To provide financial assistance to students who are in need. **Focus:** Nursing. **Qualif.:** Applicants must be African American with permanent residency in the District of Columbia or one of the adjacent counties of the State of Maryland (Anne Arundel, Calvert, Charles, Howard and Montgomery, Prince Georges); must be sophomore, junior or first-semester senior nursing students in a registered nursing or practical nursing program; must be currently enrolled in a National League for Nursing accredited program and be in good academic standing with a cumulative grade point average of at least 2.8; and must be U.S. citizens. **Criteria:** Recipients are selected based on financial need.

Funds Avail.: No specific amount. **Duration:** Annual. **To Apply:** Applicants must submit a current official transcript from their nursing program, two letters of recommendation from which one must come from current faculty member and one must come from the Nursing Faculty Advisor or Designee; must submit a written essay that describes the applicant's objectives and need-based reasons for scholarship application; documented evidence to add support for the applicant's desirability that includes participation in student and nursing activities, community service in the Greater Washington area, awards, letters and certificates; must provide a proof of United States citizenship and evidence of financial need. **Deadline:** January 31.

2611 ■ Margaret Pemberton Scholarships *(Undergraduate/Scholarship)*

Purpose: To provide financial assistance to students who are in need. **Focus:** Nursing. **Qualif.:** Applicants must be African American with permanent residency in the District of Columbia or one of the adjacent counties of the State of

Awards are arranged alphabetically below their administering organizations

Maryland (Anne Arundel, Calvert, Charles, Howard and Montgomery, Prince Georges); must be graduating senior, currently enrolled in a high school in the District of Columbia or one of the adjacent counties of the State of Maryland; must be in good academic standing with a cumulative grade point average of at least 2.8 (on a scale of 4.0). **Criteria:** Recipients are selected based on financial need.

Funds Avail.: Up to $2,000. **Duration:** Annual. **To Apply:** Applicants must submit at least one-page long written essay describing personal and educational goals, contributions to the community and reasons why they should be selected; must submit a documented evidence for support, including participation in activities and organizations, awards, certificates, and/or letters of commendation; must submit an official high school transcript, copy of letter of acceptance to a Baccalaureate Nursing Program in a college or university in the United States of America; must submit two letters of recommendation, from which one must come from a high school counselor or designee and the other one must come from non-related adult who has knowledge of the applicant's potential for success. **Deadline:** April 15.

2612 ■ Black Rock Arts Foundation (BRAF)
660 Alabama St.
San Francisco, CA 94110
Ph: (415)626-1248
E-mail: info@blackrockarts.org
URL: www.blackrockarts.org
Social Media: www.facebook.com/
BlackRockArtsFoundation
twitter.com/braf
www.youtube.com/user/blackrockarts

2613 ■ Global Art Grant *(Graduate/Grant)*
Purpose: To support artists and organizations in promoting interactive arts in the community. **Focus:** Art. **Qualif.:** Grant is open to all individual artists, artist collectives or organizations regardless of their geographic location; the grant is applied towards creation of interactive artworks or towards the development of community programs that support interactive artworks; funded projects must be art that is accessible to the public; cost of the materials necessary to fulfill the project's vision. **Criteria:** Selection will be projects that are highly interactive, community-driven, and collaborative works of art that are accessible to the public and civic scope are given priority; taking risks and providing seed funding that stimulates new explorations and fosters new artists; validation and support for artists; created by the community for benefit of that community.

Funds Avail.: $500-$10,000. **Duration:** Annual. **To Apply:** Applicants must first submit their letter of inquiry; if selected by the committee, they will be invited to submit a full proposal; It is mandatory that applicant must submit the LOI through online process; In order to access the online form, applicant will need to create a burner profile; complete proposal includes: completion of the online proposal, timeline, budget, supplemental images and materials. **Deadline:** Letter of Intent (LOI)-December 18; Full proposal form February 12. **Contact:** Laura Dane, Burning Man Grant Program Manager; Email: artgrants@burningman.org.

2614 ■ Black Theatre Network (BTN)
c/o Renee Charlow Business Manager
8306 Bluebird Way
Lorton, VA 22079

E-mail: president@blacktheatrenetwork.org
URL: www.blacktheatrenetwork.org

2615 ■ S. Randolph Edmonds Young Scholars Competition *(Graduate, Undergraduate/Scholarship)*
Purpose: To encourage research and scholarship in black theatre and to expose the beauty and complexity of the inherited theatre work of our African American ancestors, as well as, preserve and develop Black Theatre's unique art form. **Focus:** Theater arts. **Qualif.:** Applicants must be college/university undergraduates or graduates working on a paper concerned with an aspect of the Black Theatre in either the United States or throughout the world. **Criteria:** Selection will be based on the criteria of the panel of judges.

Funds Avail.: 1st Place-$250; 2nd Place-$100. **Duration:** Annual. **To Apply:** Applicants must submit their own work; papers must be typed, double-spaced and in MLA format with a works cited page; if applicable, also include endnotes that demonstrate awareness of formal methods of documentation; papers should be approximately 10 pages in length, not including endnotes. **Deadline:** April 1. **Remarks:** Established in 1988. **Contact:** phone (610-350-7527); Email: ksaine@shepherd.edu.

2616 ■ Black Wynn PLLC
40 N Central Ave., Ste. 1400
Phoenix, AZ 85004
Ph: (480)665-7324
URL: www.bwphoenixpersonalinjurylawyers.com
Social Media: www.facebook.com/blackwynnlaw

2617 ■ Autism Scholarship *(High School, Two Year College, Four Year College, Graduate, Vocational/ Occupational, Professional development/Scholarship)*
Purpose: To defray the cost of tuition. **Focus:** General studies/Field of study not specified. **Qualif.:** U.S. citizen who has been diagnosed with autism spectrum disorder (ASD). **Criteria:** Short statement and optional essay.

Funds Avail.: $1,000. **To Apply:** Complete online application form; upload statement of not more than 100 words describing your educational goals. Optional: upload essay up to 650 words telling us how autism has impacted your education. **Deadline:** February 15. **Contact:** Black Wynn Personal Injury Lawyers, 40 N Central Ave., Ste. 1850 Phoenix, Arizona, 85004; Phone: 480-665-7324; Email: michael@bwphoenixpersonalinjurylawyers.com.

2618 ■ Law School Scholarship *(Graduate/ Scholarship)*
Purpose: To provide a degree of assistance in tuition payments. **Focus:** Law. **Qualif.:** U.S. citizen who is or will be attending a U.S. law school accredited by the ABA.

Funds Avail.: $1,000. **To Apply:** Complete online application form; upload a short statement of up to 100 words explaining why you want to obtain a law degree. Optional: upload essay of 700 words or less discussing how you intend to use your law degree to make a difference in your community. **Deadline:** February 23. **Contact:** Black Wynn Personal Injury Lawyer. 40 North, Central Avenue, Ste., 1850, Phoenix, Arizona, 85004; Phone: 480-665-7324; Email: michael@bwphoenixpersonalinjurylawyers.com.

2619 ■ Blair Chiropractic Society
550 E Carson Plaza Dr., Ste. 122
Carson, CA 90746

Awards are arranged alphabetically below their administering organizations

URL: www.blairchiropractic.com

2620 ■ Beatrice K. Blair Scholarships
(Undergraduate/Scholarship)

Purpose: To enhance the educational opportunities of chiropractic students with an interest in specific upper cervical Blair technique by providing financial assistance to eligible students attending chiropractic schools. **Focus:** Medicine, Chiropractic. **Qualif.:** Applicant must be a student in good standing at an accredited chiropractic college; be a member of a student Blair club (if available at their school); have a GPA of at least 2.5 out of 4.0 (C+); have completed at least one Primary Blair seminar.

Funds Avail.: No specific amount. **Duration:** Annual. **To Apply:** Applicants must submit a copy of their chiropractic college transcript (grades); two letters of reference from Blair instructors, chiropractic college teachers or DC's;a list of Blair seminars they have attended; a short essay (1-2 pages) on why they want to practice the Blair technique.

2621 ■ Blakemore Foundation
801 Second Ave., Ste. 800
Seattle, WA 98104
Ph: (206)427-4838
E-mail: contactus@blakemorefoundation.org
URL: www.blakemorefoundation.org
Social Media: www.facebook.com/blakemorefoundation
www.instagram.com/blakemorefoundation/

2622 ■ Blakemore Freeman Fellowships
(Undergraduate, Advanced Professional/Fellowship)

Purpose: To award fellowship to students for one academic year of advanced level language study in East or Southeast Asia in approved language programs. **Focus:** Foreign languages. **Qualif.:** Applicants must be pursuing a professional, business, technical or academic career that involves the regular use of a modern East or Southeast Asian language; must have a college undergraduate degree; must be at or near an advanced level in the language as defined in the grant guidelines; minimum requirement is three years of study of the language at college level or equivalent fluency; must be able to devote oneself exclusively to full-time intensive language study during the term of the grant; must be US citizens or permanent residents of the United States. **Criteria:** Selection will be based on the following criteria: a focused, well-defined career objective involving Asia in which regular use of the language is an important aspect; the potential to make a significant contribution to a field of study or area of professional or business activity in an Asian country; prior experience in the Asian country or involvement or participation in activities related to the country; good academic, professional or business background, appropriate to the career program.

Funds Avail.: No specific amount. **Duration:** Annual. **To Apply:** Applicant must submit a list of all classes/training they have taken in their chosen language of study; a list of any academic and professional honors they have been awarded; a copy in PDF format of their curriculum vitae or resume; a personal essay, three to four pages in length, double-spaced, in PDF format detailing applicant's career path and goals, which discusses their academic, professional or business background, prior study of the language and involvement with the Asian country, and how the language will be used to achieve their career objectives; two professional contacts to submit letters of recommendation on applicant's behalf; official transcripts from all college-level institutions from which applicant received a degree or is currently attending. Official electronic transcripts, sent by the issuing institution's electronic transcript; if a college or university does not issue official electronic transcripts, official paper transcripts will be accepted. **Deadline:** December 30.

2623 ■ Blinded Veterans Association (BVA)
400 New Jersey Ave NW
Washington, DC 20001
Ph: (202)371-8880
Fax: (202)371-8258
Free: 800-669-7079
E-mail: bva@bva.org
URL: bva.org
Social Media: www.facebook.com/blindedveteransassociation
twitter.com/blindedveterans
www.youtube.com/user/BlindedVeterans

2624 ■ Kathern F. Gruber Scholarship Program
(Undergraduate, Graduate/Scholarship)

Purpose: To financially assist the spouses and dependent children of blinded veterans. **Focus:** General studies/Field of study not specified. **Qualif.:** Applicants must be spouses and dependent children of blinded veterans. **Criteria:** Recipients will be selected based on merit.

Funds Avail.: No specific amount. **Duration:** Annual. **Number Awarded:** 6. **To Apply:** Applicants must submit a completed application form along with three letters of reference; must include transcripts. **Deadline:** April 17. **Contact:** Mail your application and required material to: Blinded Veterans Association, Attn: Scholarship Program, 125 N. West St., 3rd Fl., Alexandria, VA 22314.

2625 ■ Blood Assurance Foundation
705 E 4th St.
Chattanooga, TN 37403-1916
Free: 800-962-0628
URL: www.bloodassurance.org
Social Media: www.facebook.com/bloodassurance
www.instagram.com/bloodassurance
twitter.com/bloodassurance

2626 ■ Crystal Green Memorial Scholarship
(Graduate/Scholarship)

Purpose: To encourage educational pursuits by providing financial assistance. **Focus:** General studies/Field of study not specified. **Qualif.:** Applicants must be high school senior students planning to enter an accredited two or four-year college or university, It must be a public, or private, not-for-profit institution from which you can receive an associate or bachelor's degree. You must have a 3.0 GPA and score at least a 20 on the ACT or 950 on the SAT (cumulative). and have at least "B" average Financial need is a consideration. Applicants who have all educational expenses and/or grants are ineligible.**Criteria:** Selection will be based on the written application, high school transcript, school and community service, letters of recommendation and a marketing plan for a blood drive.

Funds Avail.: $1,500 each. **Number Awarded:** 12. **To Apply:** Applicants must submit a detailed marketing plan for a new drive promotion; must secure two letters of recom-

Awards are arranged alphabetically below their administering organizations

mendation and obtain an official high school transcript which includes the first semester senior grades and ACT/ SAT test scores. **Deadline:** March 1. **Remarks:** The scholarship fund is dedicated to Crystal Green who was a valiant and loving young woman that set forth the example of kindness and care to all that she met. Established in 1999. **Contact:** Caitlyn Mantooth, Marketing Coordinator Email: caitlynmantooth@bloodassurance.org; Phone: 423-756-0966.

2627 ■ Bloom Legal LLC

839 St. Charles Ave., No. 310
New Orleans, LA 70130
URL: www.bloomlegal.com
Social Media: www.facebook.com/bloomlegalNOLA
www.linkedin.com/company/bloom-legal-llc
twitter.com/sethbloomnola

2628 ■ Annual Bloom Legal Scholarship for Students Affected by Cerebral Palsy *(Community College, Undergraduate/Scholarship)*

Purpose: To provide a scholarship for those affected by cerebral palsy. **Focus:** General studies/Field of study not specified. **Qualif.:** Applicant must have cerebral palsy and be a high school senior or current college student enrolling or currently enrolled in an undergraduate program for the upcoming fall semester at a four-year university or community college in the United States.

Funds Avail.: $1,000. **Duration:** Annual. **Number Awarded:** 1. **To Apply:** Applicant must submit either a 300 to 500 word essay or a 1 to 3 minute video addressing the following: Tell us about yourself! How have you overcome adversity in your life? What are your educational aspirations? What do you want to study in college and what experiences do you hope to have? Where do you see yourself in ten years? Applicant should send this to the contact via email with the subject line: Bloom Legal Scholarship followed by the applicant's name. General application form must filled out at the sponsor's website. **Deadline:** June 15. **Contact:** Garret Travis; Email: tgarrettravis@bloomlegal.com; URL: www.bloomlegal.com/about/scholarship/.

2629 ■ BluePay Processing L.L.C.

184 Shuman Blvd., Ste. 350
Naperville, IL 60563-8433
Free: 866-495-0423
E-mail: merchantservices@bluepay.com
URL: www.bluepay.com
Social Media: www.facebook.com/BluePayProcessing
www.linkedin.com/company/bluepay-inc
twitter.com/BluePay

2630 ■ Bluepay Stem Scholarship *(Graduate, Undergraduate/Scholarship)*

Purpose: To support students pursuing degrees in STEM fields. **Focus:** Engineering; Mathematics and mathematical sciences; Science; Technology. **Qualif.:** Applicant must be an undergraduate or graduate student majoring in a STEM (science, technology, engineering, and math) field. **Criteria:** Selection will be based on essay.

Funds Avail.: $1,000. **Number Awarded:** 3 (one first prize, two runner up prizes). **To Apply:** Applicant must submit an essay of 500 to 1,000 words answering one of the following

question: 1. What recent innovation has meant the most to your daily life?; 2. What do your imagine or have you experienced to be the single greatest challenge that arises when you start your own business?; 3. What do you think is the biggest threat to the security of your personal information? Applicant can fill out the form and submit the essay. **Deadline:** August 16. **Contact:** Email: info@bluepay.com.

2631 ■ Blues Heaven Foundation (BHF)

2120 S Michigan Ave.
Chicago, IL 60616
Ph: (312)808-1286
E-mail: info@bluesheaven.com
URL: www.bluesheaven.com

2632 ■ Muddy Waters Scholarships *(Undergraduate, Graduate/Scholarship)*

Purpose: To provide financial assistance for students in Chicago. **Focus:** African-American studies; Education, Music; Folklore; Journalism; Music; Performing arts; Radio and television. **Qualif.:** Applicants must have full-time enrollment status in an Illinois area college or university; must be in at least their first year of undergraduate studies or graduate program; be pursuing a degree in one of the following areas or related fields; music, music education, African-American studies, folklore, performing arts, arts management, journalism, radio/TV/film music composers/songwriters, artist's legal rights, studio recording engineers; be based on projected expenses, student and family income; special consideration will be given to demonstrating need for financial assistance. **Criteria:** Selection will be based on academic achievement, concentration of studies and financial need.

Funds Avail.: $2,000. **To Apply:** Application form is available from the website. **Deadline:** April 30. **Contact:** Blues Heaven Foundation, Attn: Scholarship Committee, 2120 S Michigan Ave., Chicago, IL, 60616.

2633 ■ BMI Foundation

7 World Trade Ctr.
250 Greenwich St.
New York, NY 10007-0030
Ph: (212)220-3103
E-mail: info@bmifoundation.org
URL: bmifoundation.org
Social Media: www.facebook.com/BMIFoundation
instagram.com/bmifoundation
twitter.com/bmifoundation

2634 ■ Pete Carpenter Fellowship *(Professional development/Fellowship)*

Purpose: To give aspiring TV and film composers the opportunity to work with the composer Mike Post at his studio in Los Angeles. **Focus:** Music composition. **Qualif.:** Applicants must be an aspiring composer under the age of 35.

Funds Avail.: $2,000. **Duration:** Annual. **Deadline:** April 1. **Remarks:** Established in 1989.

2635 ■ John Lennon Scholarships *(Undergraduate/Scholarship)*

Purpose: To support songwriters and composers who are current students. **Focus:** Music composition. **Qualif.:** Applicants must be current students or alumnus or alumna of a U.S. college or university and be between the ages of 17 and 24. **Criteria:** Selection is based on the submitted original song in any genre.

Funds Avail.: $20,000. **Duration:** Annual. **Number Awarded:** 3. **Deadline:** April 1. **Remarks:** Established in 1997.

2636 ■ Peermusic Latin Scholarship *(Undergraduate/ Scholarship)*

Purpose: To support songwriters and composers who are current students. **Focus:** Music composition. **Qualif.:** Applicants must be students enrolled at a college or university located in the U.S. or Puerto Rico; between the ages of 17 and 24 as of time of submission; must have never had any musical work commercially recorded or distributed; not a prior peermusic Latin Scholarship winner (excluding Honorable Mentions). **Criteria:** Selection is based on the submitted original song or instrumental work in a Latin genre.

Funds Avail.: $5,000. **Duration:** Annual. **Deadline:** April 1. **Remarks:** Established in 2003.

2637 ■ Woody Guthrie Fellowship *(Professional development/Fellowship)*

Purpose: To support students pursuing research topics or themes related to Woody Guthrie which explore his creative work and contribution to American music and culture. **Focus:** History, American; Humanities; Musicology; Social sciences. **Qualif.:** Applicants must be pursuing research topics or themes related to Woody Guthrie.

Funds Avail.: Up to $5,000. **Duration:** Annual. **Deadline:** April 1. **Remarks:** Established in 2005. **Contact:** Email: archives@woodyguthriecenter.org.

2638 ■ B.O.G. Pest Control

645 Central Ave. E, Number 200
Edgewater, MD 21037
Ph: (410)867-1002
E-mail: office@bladesofgreen.com
URL: www.bogpestcontrol.com
Social Media: facebook.com/BOGPestControl
linkedin.com/company/blades-of-green-and-b-o-g-pest
-control

2639 ■ The B.O.G. Pest Control Scholarship Funds *(Undergraduate, Graduate/Scholarship)*

Purpose: To support students who demonstrate academic excellence, as well as a passion for the pursuit of further study in environmental education at an accredited college or university. **Focus:** Biology; Chemistry; Engineering, Chemical; Environmental science. **Qualif.:** Applicants must be seeking undergraduate or graduate level education in chemistry, chemical engineering, biology, environmental studies or related fields. **Criteria:** Selection will be based on the submitted application materials.

Funds Avail.: $1,000. **Duration:** Annual. **To Apply:** Applicants must prepare a 350 - 500 words essay describing the career path they plan to seek after graduation, passion for their intended field, and what inspired them to pursue their intended career path; submit completed application form together with essay, letter of intent, and a high school transcript to Angela Osborne. **Deadline:** March 15. **Remarks:** Established in 1989. **Contact:** Submission: Angela Osborne, B.O.G. Pest Control, 645 Central Ave. E 200,

Edgewater, MD, 21037; questions: Email: aosborne@ bladesofgreen.com.

2640 ■ Bogliasco Foundation - Liguria Study Center for the Arts and Humanities

1 E 53rd St.
New York, NY 10022
Ph: (212)713-7628
E-mail: info@bfny.org
URL: www.bfge.org

2641 ■ Aaron Copland Bogliasco Fellowships in Music *(Professional development/Fellowship)*

Purpose: To provide funds to assist fellows who otherwise might not be able to afford the cost of travel to and from Genoa. **Focus:** Arts; Music. **Qualif.:** Applicants must be American composers.

Funds Avail.: No specific amount. **Duration:** Annual.

2642 ■ Leo Biaggi de Blasys Bogliasco Fellowships *(Undergraduate/Scholarship)*

Purpose: To provide funds to assist fellows who otherwise might not be able to afford the cost of travel to and from Genoa. **Focus:** Arts; Humanities. **Qualif.:** Applicants must be living in those parts of the world where the cost of travel to Genoa may be prohibitive. **Criteria:** Preference will be given to person whose applications suggest that they would be comfortable working in an intimate, international, multilingual community of scholars and artists.

Funds Avail.: No specific amount. **Duration:** Annual. **To Apply:** Applications should include completed application form; three letters of reference; a short-form curriculum vitae, three pages in length; a one-page description of the project that the applicants would pursue during their stay at the Liguria Study Center; a sample of the applicants' work that has been published, performed, exhibited or otherwise publicly presented during the last five years. **Deadline:** Varies.

2643 ■ Bogliasco Fellowships *(Professional development/Fellowship)*

Purpose: To award qualified persons working in the various disciplines of the Arts and Humanities without regard to nationality, age, race or gender. **Focus:** Arts; Humanities. **Qualif.:** Applicants must be working in all disciplines of the Arts and Humanities without regard to nationality, age, race, religion or gender. **Criteria:** Preference will be given to person whose applications suggest that they would be comfortable working in an intimate, international, multilingual community of scholars and artists.

Funds Avail.: No specific amount. **To Apply:** Applications should include completed application form; three letters of reference; a short-form curriculum vitae, three pages in length; a one-page description of the project that the applicants would pursue during their stay at the Liguria Study Center; a sample of the applicants' work that has been published, performed, exhibited or otherwise publicly presented during the last five years. **Deadline:** January 15; April 15.

2644 ■ John Burroughs Bogliasco Fellowships *(Professional development/Fellowship)*

Purpose: To provide funds honor of the American naturalist and essayist who was active in the evolution of the U.S.

Awards are arranged alphabetically below their administering organizations

conservation movement. **Focus:** Arts; Literature.

Funds Avail.: No specific amount.

2645 ■ Jerome Robbins Bogliasco Fellowships in Dance *(Professional development/Fellowship)*

Purpose: To provide funds to assist fellows who otherwise might not be able to afford the cost of travel to and from Genoa. **Focus:** Arts; Choreography. **Qualif.:** Applicants must be American choreographers. **Criteria:** Preference will be given to person whose applications suggest that they would be comfortable working in an intimate, international, multilingual community of scholars and artists.

Funds Avail.: No specific amount. **To Apply:** Applications should include completed application form; three letters of reference; a short-form curriculum vitae, three pages in length; a one-page description of the project that the applicants would pursue during their stay at the Liguria Study Center; a sample of the applicants' work that has been published, performed, exhibited or otherwise publicly presented during the last five years. **Deadline:** Varies.

2646 ■ New Museum Bogliasco Fellowship in Visual Art *(Professional development/Fellowship)*

Purpose: To provide funds to assist fellows who otherwise might not be able to afford the cost of travel to and from Genoa. **Focus:** Visual arts.

Funds Avail.: No specific amount.

2647 ■ Roger Sessions Memorial Bogliasco Fellowships in Music *(Professional development/Fellowship)*

Purpose: To provide funds to assist fellows who otherwise might not be able to afford the cost of travel to and from Genoa. **Focus:** Arts; Music. **Qualif.:** Applicants must be American composers. **Criteria:** Preference will be given to person whose applications suggest that they would be comfortable working in an intimate, international, multilingual community of scholars and artists.

Funds Avail.: No specific amount. **To Apply:** Applications should include completed application form; three letters of reference; a short-form curriculum vitae, three pages in length; a one-page description of the project that the applicants would pursue during their stay at the Liguria Study Center; a sample of the applicants' work that has been published, performed, exhibited or otherwise publicly presented during the last five years. **Deadline:** Varies.

2648 ■ Bohemian Lawyers' Association of Chicago (BLAC)

c/o Joseph E. Kolar (President) 321 N. Clark Street, Suite 900
Chicago, IL 60654
URL: www.bohemianlawyers.org

2649 ■ Bohemian Lawyers Association of Chicago Scholarships *(Graduate/Scholarship)*

Purpose: To financially assist the qualified individuals who wish to pursue their law careers in Chicago. **Focus:** Law. **Qualif.:** Applicants must be ancestry enrolled in an accredited law school in the greater Chicagoland area are eligible. **Criteria:** Selection will be based on the application materials given.

Funds Avail.: $2,500 - $5,000. **Duration:** Annual. **To Apply:** Applicants must complete the application form; attach an essay (limit 750 words) discussing; attach a current

copy of your law school transcript and resume. **Deadline:** March 26. **Contact:** Email: scholarships@bohemianlawyers.org.

2650 ■ Fondation J. Armand Bombardier

1155 Rue Metcalfe, Ste. 2100
Montreal, QC, Canada H3B 2V6
Ph: (514)876-4555
E-mail: fondation@fjab.qc.ca
URL: www.fondationbombardier.ca
Social Media: www.facebook.com/FondationBombardier
www.linkedin.com/company/fondation-j-armand-bombardier
twitter.com/FondationJAB

2651 ■ Yvonne L. Bombardier Visual Arts Scholarship Program *(Master's, Doctorate/Scholarship)*

Purpose: To support the Quebec's next generation of artists. **Focus:** Drawing; Painting; Photography; Sculpture. **Qualif.:** Applicants must be enrolled in a Masters art program in a Quebec university who practices one or more of the following disciplines: Drawing Engraving/stamping Painting Photography Sculpture;and enrolled in the program full-time; must be Canadian citizens or have the status of permanent resident. **Criteria:** Selection will be based on the committee's criteria.

Funds Avail.: $10,000. **Duration:** Annual. **To Apply:** Applicants must submit a completed application form; a presentation letter describing the students' artistic and creative approach as well as their future projects and the developments of their approach (maximum 1,000 words); two letters of recommendation signed by a professor, a teacher, or a lecturer; a portfolio consisting of a DVD (maximum 5 minutes) or a CD (maximum 15 images) presenting original works produces by students over the last two year; a curriculum vitae (maximum 3 pages); an academic file containing all statement of grades for the current program of studies; if students are in the first year of their program, statement of grades for the last year in the previous program of studies must be submitted.Applications must be sent in electronic version via the WeTransfer or mailed. **Deadline:** Fall 2019 (the date will be published at the end of summer). **Contact:** J. Armand Bombardier Foundation, 1155, Metcalfe St., Ste. 2100, Montreal, Quebec, H3B 2V6; Phone: 514-876-4555; Email: fondation@fjab.qc.ca;.

2652 ■ Booksrun LLC

620 E Erie Ave.
Philadelphia, PA 19134
Free: 866-249-9769
URL: booksrun.com
Social Media: www.facebook.com/booksrun
www.instagram.com/tom_booksrun
www.pinterest.com/booksrun
twitter.com/booksrun

2653 ■ Booksrun Scholarship Financial Aid *(Undergraduate, Graduate/Scholarship)*

Purpose: To help gifted, diligent, and hard working students reduce the enormous costs for a chance of obtaining a higher education. **Focus:** General studies/Field of study not specified. **Qualif.:** Applicant must be a high school graduate, current undergraduate, or graduate student at a college or university in the United States; must have a

Awards are arranged alphabetically below their administering organizations

minimum 2.75 GPA and be at least 17 years old; must be a Books run follower on Instagram, Facebook, or Twitter.

Funds Avail.: $1,000. **Number Awarded:** 1. **To Apply:** Applicant must Fill out the application form; Write an essay "Life after death: my college textbooks" pointing out the following topics: What do I generally do with your used textbooks? Where and how is it convenient to sell my used textbooks? ideas on how to make bookselling more attractive for students. Online bookstores that I have found trustworthy and why? Which % of my textbooks are e-Books? Which websites are interesting for students? Which websites do I surf during the week?. **Deadline:** September 30. **Contact:** https://booksrun.com/scholarship.

2654 ■ Boomer Benefits
2601 Meacham Blvd., Ste. 500
Fort Worth, TX 76137
Ph: (817)249-8600
Free: 855-732-9055
URL: boomerbenefits.com
Social Media: www.facebook.com/BoomerBenefits
instagram.com/boomerbenefits
www.linkedin.com/company/boomer-benefits
pinterest.com/boomerbenefits
twitter.com/boomerbenefits

2655 ■ Boomer Benefits Scholarship *(Undergraduate, Graduate/Scholarship)*

Purpose: To recognize and empower students who have returned to school later in life to better themselves, advance their current career path, or pursue a new career. **Focus:** General studies/Field of study not specified. **Qualif.:** Applicant must be U.S. citizen age 50 or older who are currently enrolled in a four-year or undergraduate or graduate program at an accredited public or private school including community colleges and universities; must have a minimum 3.0 GPA. **Criteria:** Selection will be based on the applicants' GPA, amount and nature of community service, and the strength of letters of recommendation submitted. Priority will be given to applicants who demonstrate a passion for service to others - particularly an older American, and a seriousness of purpose and sound character.

Funds Avail.: $1,000. **Duration:** Annual. **Number Awarded:** 1. **To Apply:** Applicants must download the provided scholarship application form from the website and submit per instructions given in the same packet; additional documents include: recommendation letter from a professor in the last 2 years, or facilitator of a verifiable community service organization; transcript; and a letter describing current goals and how this education will help to achieve those goals, and community service history. **Deadline:** August 15. **Contact:** Attn: Scholarship Review Board; Email: scholarship@boomerbenefits.com; URL: boomerbenefits.com/scholarship-requirements/.

2656 ■ Boot Camp Digital
1847 WALKER St.
Cincinnati, OH 45204
Social Media: www.facebook.com/bootcampdigital
www.instagram.com/bootcampdigital
www.linkedin.com/company/boot-camp-digital
www.pinterest.com/bootcampdigital

2657 ■ Future Digital Marketers Scholarship *(College, University/Scholarship)*

Purpose: To help students in digital marketing fields of study to show their talents in social media, share their

insights about the future of digital marketing, and pay for higher education. **Focus:** Computer and information sciences; Marketing and distribution. **Qualif.:** Applicant must be a U.S. resident enrolled in a college or university in a digital marketing field of study. **Criteria:** Selection will be based on the social media post submitted.

Funds Avail.: $1,000. **Number Awarded:** 1. **To Apply:** Applicant must complete the application on the sponsor's website and create a social media post answering the question: What is the future of digital marketing? Social media post entries must be publicly posted and tagged with the hashtags and mentions as described on the scholarship page. **Deadline:** December 31. **Contact:** Allison Chaney; E-mail: Allison@bootcampdigital.com; URL: bootcampdigital.com/scholarship.

2658 ■ Aaron J. Boria, PLLC
352 N Main St., Ste. 4
Plymouth, MI 48170
Ph: (734)453-7878
Fax: (734)468-1515
E-mail: borialaw@gmail.com
URL: thelawyermichigan.com

2659 ■ Aaron J. Boria, PLLC, Scholarship *(Undergraduate, Graduate/Scholarship)*

Purpose: To assist students who are interested in the legal field. **Focus:** Law. **Qualif.:** Undergraduate students who are attending an accredited university in the U.S. with an interest in law school who have a minimum 3.0 GPA; or current law school students who are attending an American Bar Association accredited law school with a minimum 2.5 GPA.

Funds Avail.: $500. **Duration:** Semiannual. **Number Awarded:** 1. **To Apply:** Write an essay in 1,000 words or fewer that describe why you are interested in the law; your favorite community involvement and why it is your favorite; and how higher education can help reduce crime in our communities. **Deadline:** March 30; November 30. **Contact:** Aaron Boria.

2660 ■ Bottlinger Law LLC
4909 S 135th St., Ste. 206
Omaha, NE 68137
Ph: (402)810-8573
URL: www.bottlingerlaw.com
Social Media: www.facebook.com/bottlingerlaw
www.instagram.com/bottlingerlawllc
twitter.com/bottlingerlaw

2661 ■ Bowties and Books Scholarship *(Undergraduate, College, University/Scholarship)*

Purpose: To help deserving students pay for college. **Focus:** General studies/Field of study not specified. **Qualif.:** Applicant must be a high school senior on track to graduate or a college student enrolled in an accredited four-year university or college, or currently enrolled in a two-year college and planning to transfer to a four-year university upon completion; have a minimum 3.0 GPA; and be a U.S. citizen or permanent resident (DACA recipients are welcome to apply).

Funds Avail.: $1,000. **Number Awarded:** Varies. **To Apply:** Application and essay must be submitted online. **Dead-**

Awards are arranged alphabetically below their administering organizations

line: April 15. **Contact:** Scholarship Manager; Email: jbottlinger@bottlingerlaw.com; URL: www.bottlingerlaw .com/ scholarship/.

2662 ■ Bourse de Montreal Inc.

1800 - 1190 Ave. des Canadiens-de-Montréal
Montreal, QC, Canada H3B 0G7
Ph: (514)871-2424
Fax: (514)871-3514
Free: 800-361-5353
URL: www.m-x.ca
Social Media: www.fr-ca.facebook.com/montrealexchange
www.linkedin.com/company/montreal-exchange
twitter.com/MtlExchange
www.youtube.com/channel/
UCMkvCi8jMdCAqNoNvJsCaJg

2663 ■ Canadian Derivatives Scholarship
(Postgraduate/Scholarship)

Purpose: To support the education of the students interested in Canadian derivative markets. **Focus:** Finance. **Qualif.:** Applicants must be in full-time postgraduate programs in a Canadian university and must conduct a research project on stock derivatives or a subject related to the activities of the Montreal Exchange. **Criteria:** Selection will be based on how the applicants demonstrate the following criteria: innovative aspect of the research project; interest in research and show enthusiasm toward chosen topic; leadership and initiative in academic and professional activities; outstanding academic performance.

Funds Avail.: $25,000. **To Apply:** Applicants must submit the following required documents; duly completed form; plan for the research project (maximum of two pages); one page letter of motivation; curriculum vitae; official transcript of all previous university studies; two letters of recommendation, One of the two recommendations must be signed by your supervisor and the second may be from a professor or an employer. **Deadline:** June 5.

2664 ■ Bowen

250 Fulton Ave., Ste. G
Garden City Park, NY 11040
Ph: (516)308-3539
E-mail: hello@bowenmedia.com
URL: www.bowenmedia.com

2665 ■ Web Design Scholarship *(Undergraduate/ Scholarship)*

Purpose: To help young designers alleviate the stress of paying for college during their academic pursuit. **Focus:** Computer and information sciences; Graphic art and design. **Qualif.:** Applicant must be a student at an accredited school or accepted and to begin at an accredited school within six months of application; must be attending a school in the United States. Applicants can win the award up to twice. **Criteria:** Selection committee will look for web designs that are visually appealing, have high-quality user experience, navigation, and good content structure throughout.

Funds Avail.: $1,500 each. **Duration:** Semiannual. **Number Awarded:** 2 per year. **To Apply:** Complete application and submit an example of web design at www.bowenmedia.com/web-design-scholarship. **Deadline:**

July 15; December 15. **Contact:** Natalie Bowen; Email: natalie@bowenmedia.com.

2666 ■ Mila Boyd Law Offices

2412 Main St.
Vancouver, WA 98660
Ph: (360)869-0857
URL: www.uptowninjurylaw.com
Social Media: www.facebook.com/MilaBoydLaw
www.linkedin.com/in/mila-boyd-440150140

2667 ■ Mila Boyd Law Offices Scholarship Contest
(Undergraduate/Scholarship)

Purpose: To provide financial aid to college students, encourage students to understand their personal motivation for a career in the legal field, and inspire students to pursue a career in law. **Focus:** Law. **Qualif.:** Applicant must be a high school senior or college freshman in the United States who is studying, or planning to study, law. **Criteria:** Selection is based on the best video essay or essay submitted.

Funds Avail.: $1,000. **Duration:** Annual. **Number Awarded:** 1. **To Apply:** Applicant must record a video (1 to 2 minutes, in English) explaining why they want to be a lawyer. Applicant must post the video to their YouTube Channel with the title "Mila Boyd Law Offices Scholarship Contest" and with this link in the description: www.milaboydlaw.com/scholarship-for-college-students/. Applicant must also share the video on their Facebook page and the sponsor's Facebook page. Instead of a video, applicant can write a 1,000 to 1,500 word essay on the same subject and submit via email. **Deadline:** August 15. **Contact:** Mila Boyd; Email: milaboydscholarship@ gmail.com.

2668 ■ Boys and Girls Club of Ottawa

2825 Dumaurier Ave.
Ottawa, ON, Canada K2B 7W3
Ph: (613)232-0925
Fax: (613)230-0891
URL: ottawa.bgccan.com
Social Media: www.facebook.com/BGCOttawa
www.instagram.com/bgcottawa
www.linkedin.com/company/boys-and-girls-club-of-ottawa
twitter.com/bgcottawa
www.youtube.com/user/BGCOChannel

2669 ■ Brian Smith Memorial Scholarships
(Undergraduate/Scholarship)

Purpose: To promote, encourage and sponsor promising individuals who would otherwise experience extreme hardships in pursuing a post-secondary education. **Focus:** General studies/Field of study not specified. **Qualif.:** Applicants must be graduating students from a high school in the Ottawa area planning to attend any university or college in the city of Ottawa. **Criteria:** Recipients will be selected based on financial need and demonstrated participation as a community volunteer.

Funds Avail.: $5,000. **Duration:** Annual. **Number Awarded:** 2. **To Apply:** Applicants must submit: a completed application form; completed expenses and income form; up-to-date resume; two letters of recommendation; copy of most recent school transcript; proof of citizenship status; copy of letter of acceptance to an accredited post-

Awards are arranged alphabetically below their administering organizations

secondary school; professional quality color photo; and a 300-1,000-word essay discussing their community involvement, financial need, accomplishment and academics. **Deadline:** May 13. **Remarks:** Established in 1996. **Contact:** Ashley Tripp at 613-232-0925, x263 or atripp@ bgcottawa.org.

2670 ■ Brain Canada Foundation

1200 McGill College Ave., Ste. 1600
Montreal, QC, Canada H3B 4G7
Ph: (514)989-2989
E-mail: info@braincanada.ca
URL: www.braincanada.ca
Social Media: www.facebook.com/brain.canada
www.linkedin.com/company/brain-canada
twitter.com/intent/follow?source=followbutton&variant=1
.0&screen_name=BrainCanada
www.youtube.com/channel/
UCLuWPIyAVRu7ZmwfJmtZVxA

2671 ■ Azrieli Neurodevelopmental Research Program *(Advanced Professional/Grant)*

Purpose: To support translational research in the area of neurodevelopmental disorders. **Focus:** Mental health; Neuroscience. **Qualif.:** Applicant must be an excellent systems or translational research in the area of neurodevelopmental disorders, with a special focus on Autism spectrum disorder and Fragile X syndrome. **Criteria:** Selection will be based on the letter of intent and full application stages. Specific criteria include innovation and originality; collaboration; feasibility; and impact.

To Apply: Applicants must submit a letter of intent (LOI) since the application for funding is competitive. LOI application components are: project summary; project team details; budget; attachments (figures and references); optional information such as names and contact information for up to three individuals who are not in conflict and would be competent to review the LOI and the subsequent full application, if invited; and signatures and certification. Submitted letters of intent will be subjected for review. Only those invited by Brain Canada following the LOI review will be able to submit full applications. All LOIs must be submitted using Brain Canada's electronic grant management system. **Remarks:** The research program is made possible through the joint venture of Brain Canada Foundation and The Azrieli Foundation.

2672 ■ Brain Canada-ALS Canada Career Transition Awards *(Postdoctorate, Advanced Professional, Professional development/Grant)*

Purpose: To identify and engage a rising star pursuing innovative research in laboratories and academic institutions in Canada. **Focus:** Amyotrophic lateral sclerosis; Neurology. **Qualif.:** Applicants must be either senior postdoctoral trainees or recently hired junior faculty members wanting to secure or maintain a faculty job in Canada. **Criteria:** Selection will be based on the committee's criteria.

Funds Avail.: $315,000. **Duration:** Annual. **To Apply:** Applicants must submit a letter of intent describing the project to the partners; letters of intent are considered highly promising and those aligned with the program objectives will be invited to submit a full project proposal. **Remarks:** The Career Transition Award is part of the joint funding program of the Brain Canada Foundation and the ALS Canada.

2673 ■ Brain Canada-ALS Canada Discovery Grants *(Advanced Professional, Professional development/ Grant)*

Purpose: To encourage new basic research focused on identifying causes of, or treatments for ALS and related neurological disorders. **Focus:** Amyotrophic lateral sclerosis; Mental health; Neurology; Neuroscience. **Qualif.:** Applicants must be A minimum of 2 investigators are required, from different institutions (or distinct departments within the same institution). A lead investigator must be named who will assume the administrative and financial responsibilities for the team grant. The lead investigator's institution will be deemed the host institution for the grant and will receive the funding disbursements from Brain Canada. For options I and ii above, each co-investigator must be an independent researcher who has a PhD or equivalent, or a health professional degree (MD). Clinical researchers should have completed residency training which includes research experience, or the individual should have previous research experience. The PI must hold an academic position at a qualifying Canadian institution; For option iii above, the principal investigator must be a clinician with an MD or a non-physician professional with experience treating or working with people living with ALS. The PI must hold an academic position at a qualifying Canadian institution. **Criteria:** Selection will be based on the research proposals of the applicants and other criteria of the committee.

Funds Avail.: 100,000 Canadian Dollars. **Duration:** Annual. **To Apply:** Complete applications should be submitted via email; 1) Cover page 2) Abstract (scientific) (limit page) 3) Research Plan (limit 6 pages) 4) Figures and Tables (limit 3 pages) 5) Bibliography 6) Budget Page(s) 7) Curriculum Vitae (see below for format) (limit 5 pages per CV) 8) Supporting Documents 9) Other funding currently held or applied. **Deadline:** September 25. **Remarks:** The grant is part of the joint funding program of the Brain Canada Foundation and the ALS Canada.

2674 ■ Brain Canada-ALS Canada Hudson Translational Team Grants *(Advanced Professional, Professional development/Grant)*

Purpose: To support series of research that are relevant to ALS and related neurological disorders. **Focus:** Amyotrophic lateral sclerosis; Mental health; Neurology; Neuroscience. **Qualif.:** Applicants must be teams of independent investigators from multiple independent Canadian institutions proposing such a translational research approach with a sound and feasible rationale, supported by preliminary data. **Criteria:** Selection will be based on the research proposals of the applicants and other criteria of the committee.

Funds Avail.: Upto a maximum of $50,000. **To Apply:** Applicants may contact the Foundation for the application process and other required materials. **Deadline:** April 26 (letter of intent submission); June 30 (full proposal submission). **Remarks:** The Hudson Translational Team Grant is part of the joint funding program of the Brain Canada Foundation and the ALS Canada.

2675 ■ Brain Canada/CQDM *(Advanced Professional/ Grant)*

Purpose: To identify, fund and support the development of breakthrough technologies that enhance biopharmaceutical research and development productivity and accelerate the development of new, safe and effective drugs for disorders of the brain and nervous system. **Focus:** Mental health; Neuroscience. **Qualif.:** Applicants must be from a team of

Awards are arranged alphabetically below their administering organizations

two or more eligible investigators from at least two Canadian provinces; investigators are those appointed by and working at a University, hospital, affiliated research institution or employed by SMEs in the field of life sciences, biotechnologies, biopharmaceuticals, medical devices, diagnostics, engineering, imaging, or contract research organizations ("CRO"). **Criteria:** Selection will be based on the submitted letter of intent and full proposals.

Funds Avail.: Up to 1,500,000 Canadian Dollars over three years. **Duration:** Annual; Three years. **Number Awarded:** Approximately 3-4. **To Apply:** Applicants must submit a letter of intent describing the project to the partners; letters of intent are considered highly promising and those aligned with the program objectives will be invited to submit a full project proposal. **Deadline:** Varies. **Remarks:** The "Focus on Brain" is a joint program of Brain Canada Foundation and Quebec Consortium for Drug Discovery (CQDM).

2676 ■ Brain Canada/NeuroDevNet Developmental Neurosciences Research Training Awards (Postdoctorate, Advanced Professional, Professional development/Grant)

Purpose: To enhance the training of talented young scientists conducting research focused on the key aspects of developmental neurosciences under the direction of leading Canadian researchers. **Focus:** Mental health; Neuroscience. **Qualif.:** Applicants can be from any nation; however, training must be undertaken at a participating institution located within Canada. **Criteria:** Selection will be based on the committee's criteria.

Funds Avail.: 30,000 Canadian Dollars per year; 50,000 Canadian Dollars per year for postdoctoral fellowships; 5,000 Canadian Dollars per year for career development. **To Apply:** Applicants may verify the website for further instructions regarding the application process. **Remarks:** The award is made possible by the joint cooperation of Brain Canada Foundation and NeuroDevNet. **Contact:** programs@braincanada.ca.

2677 ■ Brain Canada/RBC Research Partnership in Mental Health Services for Children and Youth Funds (Advanced Professional/Grant)

Purpose: To support multi-investigator research projects focused on improved delivery of mental health services through the identification and validation of innovative interventions and practices that are cost-effective, and delivered at the right place and time to support both affected individuals and their families. **Focus:** Mental health. **Qualif.:** Applicants must be two or more investigators in any scientific discipline who are eligible to apply for research grants from the Canadian federal granting agencies (CIHR, NSERC, and SSHRC). **Criteria:** Selection will be based on the research proposals and compliance with the application details. To be recommended for funding, proposals will demonstrate: innovation and originality; multidisciplinarity and teamwork; and potential for impact.

Number Awarded: 1 team. **To Apply:** Applicants must submit a letter of intent (LOI) since the application for funding is competitive. LOI application components are: project summary; project team details; budget; attachments (figures and references); optional information such as names and contact information for up to three individuals who are not in conflict and would be competent to review the LOI and the subsequent full application, if invited; and signatures and certification. Submitted letters of intent will be subjected for review. Only those invited by Brain Canada following the LOI review will be able to submit full applica-

tions. All LOIs must be submitted using Brain Canada's electronic grant management system. **Remarks:** The research partnership is made possible by the Brain Canada Foundation and the Royal Bank of Canada. **Contact:** programs@braincanada.ca.

2678 ■ Platform Support Grants (Advanced Professional/Grant)

Purpose: To support major research platforms, local, regional or national, that provide enhanced technical and research capability to multiple investigators working in the brain sciences. **Focus:** Mental health; Neuroscience. **Qualif.:** Applicants must be User Groups of investigators working in the brain sciences; User Groups are composed of investigators based in Canada whose research depends on use of the platform for which support is requested, or who are involved in the development of the platform; members of the User Group must be eligible to receive funding from the federal granting agencies; the User Group may be based in one or several research institutions. **Criteria:** Selection will be based on the following attributes of the excellence and impact of the research that is conducted using the platform; distinctiveness of the platform; management of the platforms; the added value of Brain Canada and Partner(s) support; sustainable commitment to platform support; and data sharing and standardization.

Funds Avail.: Maximum of 2,000,000 Canadian Dollars (over a period of three years). **Duration:** Three years. **To Apply:** Applicants must submit a letter of intent (LOI) since the application for funding is competitive; LOI application components are platform summary; user group details; budget; impact; attachments (figures and references); optional information such as names and contact information for up to three individuals who are not in conflict and would be competent to review the LOI and the subsequent full application, if invited; and signatures and certification; submitted letters of intent will be subjected for review; only those invited by Brain Canada following the LOI review will be able to submit full applications; all LOIs must be submitted using Brain Canada's electronic grant management system. **Deadline:** February 4. **Contact:** Brain Canada - platformgrant@braincanada.ca.

2679 ■ Brandeis University - Hadassah-Brandeis Institute (HBI)
515 S St., MS 079
Waltham, MA 02454-9110
Ph: (781)736-2064
Fax: (781)736-2078
E-mail: hbi@brandeis.edu
URL: www.brandeis.edu/hbi
Social Media: facebook.com/brandeisuniversity
instagram.com/brandeisuniversity
twitter.com/BrandeisU
youtube.com/brandeis

2680 ■ HBI Gilda Slifka Internship Program (Graduate, Undergraduate/Internship)

Purpose: To provide undergraduate and graduate students with a variety of opportunities to learn about the work of Jewish women's studies scholars and centers, and try their hand at research in the field. **Focus:** Jewish studies; Women's studies. **Qualif.:** Applicants must be undergraduate or graduate students with a demonstrated interest in women's studies, Jewish women's studies, or topics related to Jewish women/Jewish gender issues around the world.

Awards are arranged alphabetically below their administering organizations

Funds Avail.: Weekly stipend. **Number Awarded:** 8 (6 undergraduate students; 2 graduate students). **To Apply:** Application form and details available at www.brandeis.edu/hbi/programs/internship/index.html. **Deadline:** April 15. **Contact:** Debby Olins, Assistant Director for Administration; Email: dolins@brandeis.edu.

2681 ■ HBI Scholar-in-Residence Program
(Undergraduate, Graduate, Postgraduate/Scholarship)

Purpose: To give outstanding scholars, writers, and artists the opportunity to be in residence at HBI at different points during the year. **Focus:** Jewish studies; Women's studies. **Qualif.:** Applicants must be scholars working on any aspect of Jewish women's and gender studies. Applicants living outside the U.S. and those whose work has an international dimension are especially encouraged to apply **Criteria:** Selection will be based on the committee's criteria.

Funds Avail.: $5,000 monthly stipend. **To Apply:** Application form and details are available online at www.brandeis.edu/hbi/programs/residencies/index.html. **Contact:** Debby Olins, Assistant Director for Administration; Email: dolins@brandeis.edu.

2682 ■ Brandner Law Firm
3621 Veterans Memorial Blvd.
Metairie, LA 70002
Ph: (504)345-1111
URL: www.brandnerlawfirm.com
Social Media: www.facebook.com/BrandnerLawFirm
www.linkedin.com/company/mike-brandner-injury-attorneys
twitter.com/MikeBrandner

2683 ■ Scholarships for a Higher Education in Law
(Graduate/Scholarship)

Purpose: To support college-bound students wishing to pursue a legal degree. **Focus:** Law. **Qualif.:** Applicants must be currently enrolled in a Louisiana college or university and must have a minimum GPA of 3.0. **Criteria:** Selection are determined solely by selection committee as appointed by Brandner Law Firm.

Funds Avail.: $1,500. **Duration:** Annual; non-renewable. **Number Awarded:** 1. **To Apply:** Applicants must submit the following application materials official copy of high school transcript; essay of 500 to 1,400 words in PDF format, with the file name as lastname_firstname_blf.pdf; filled-out application form. **Deadline:** November 30.

2684 ■ Breast Cancer Car Donations
11601 Wilshire Blvd., Ste. 101
Los Angeles, CA 90025
Free: 866-540-5069
URL: www.cardonations4cancer.org

2685 ■ Breast Cancer Car Donations Annual College Scholarship *(Undergraduate/Scholarship)*

Purpose: To help students pay for STEM educations and thus pave the way for tomorrows leaders. **Focus:** Engineering; Mathematics and mathematical sciences; Science. **Qualif.:** Applicants must be undergraduate students majoring in a STEM field of study at an accredited college or university in the United States. **Criteria:** Selection is based on the best essay submitted.

Funds Avail.: $1,000 (1); $250 (2). **Duration:** Annual. **Number Awarded:** 3. **To Apply:** Complete the application, write essay, and upload transcripts online. **Deadline:** August 15. **Contact:** Email: scholarship@cardonations4cancer.org; URL: www.cardonations4cancer.org/about-us/breast-cancer-car-donations-annual-college-scholarship/.

2686 ■ Hilda E. Bretzlaff Foundation (HEBF)
1550 N Milford Rd., Ste. 101
Milford, MI 48381
Ph: (248)684-3408
Fax: (248)684-2648
URL: www.hebf.org
Social Media: www.linkedin.com/company/hilda-e.-bretzlaff-foundation

2687 ■ Hilda E. Bretzlaff Foundation Scholarships
(Undergraduate/Scholarship, Grant)

Purpose: To assist individuals in attending educational institutions in the United States of America and/or England. **Focus:** General studies/Field of study not specified. **Qualif.:** Applicants must maintain a minimum 2.0 grade point average; demonstrate financial need; be moral, conservative, ambitious, and proven to be a credit to America. **Criteria:** Selection will be based on the aforesaid qualifications.

Funds Avail.: No specific amount. **To Apply:** Applicants must obtain an application by contacting a school or institution who is currently working within a proposal with HEBF; must submit all qualifying completed applications to HEBF for review by the June due date; if applicant did not get application from the financial aid department of their school, they will need to complete a "financial aid Form" and submit it to their financial aid department, who will then forward it on to HEBF.

2688 ■ Breyer Law Offices PC
3840 E Ray Rd.
Phoenix, AZ 85044
URL: www.breyerlaw.com
Social Media: www.facebook.com/husbandandwifelawteam
twitter.com/arizonalawteam

2689 ■ The Husband and Wife Law Team Scholarship *(Undergraduate/Scholarship)*

Purpose: To give back to exceptional students, and to stress the importance of higher education and students being able to follow their dream career path after high school. **Focus:** General studies/Field of study not specified. **Criteria:** One recipient will be from Arizona, and one from anywhere else in the United States.

Funds Avail.: $1,000. **Number Awarded:** 2. **To Apply:** Application and essay must be submitted online. **Deadline:** MAY 5. **Contact:** www.breyerlaw.com/scholarship/.

2690 ■ BrightFocus Foundation
22512 Gateway Center Dr.
Clarksburg, MD 20871
Fax: (301)258-9454
Free: 800-437-2423
E-mail: info@brightfocus.org
URL: www.brightfocus.org
Social Media: www.facebook.com/BrightFocusFoundation
www.instagram.com/brightfocus

Awards are arranged alphabetically below their administering organizations

www.linkedin.com/company/brightfocus-foundation
www.pinterest.com/BrightFocusFdn
twitter.com/_BrightFocus
www.youtube.com/c/BrightfocusOrg

2691 ■ ADR Postdoctoral Fellowship Awards
(Advanced Professional, Professional development/ Fellowship)

Purpose: To support young researchers in their final stages of mentored training. **Focus:** Medical research.

Funds Avail.: $200,000. **Duration:** for two years.

2692 ■ Alzheimer's Disease Research Standard Award *(Doctorate/Award)*

Purpose: To provide significant funding for researchers pursuing pioneering research leading to greater understanding, prevention, and treatment of Alzheimer's disease. **Focus:** Medical research. **Qualif.:** Fellowships are limited to researchers within 5 years of doctoral degree conferral (or end of residency). All other applicants are encouraged to apply for a standard award.

Funds Avail.: $400,000. **Duration:** up to three years. **Deadline:** November 4.

2693 ■ Macular Degeneration Research Program Grant *(Doctorate/Grant)*

Purpose: To support research on the cause or treatment of macular degeneration. **Focus:** Medical research.

Funds Avail.: $300,000. **Duration:** Annual; up to two years. **Deadline:** December 3.

2694 ■ National Glaucoma Research Program Grant *(Professional development/Grant)*

Purpose: To support pioneering research leading to greater understanding, prevention, and treatment of glaucoma. **Focus:** Medical research.

Funds Avail.: $200,000. **Duration:** up to two years. **To Apply:** Applicants must Proposal Central application portal using Microsoft Internet Explorer, then switch to another web browser, such as Mozilla Firefox or Google Chrome. Attachments are required and must be submitted; Upon doing so, a system-defined password will be emailed.

2695 ■ British American Foundation of Texas (BAFTX)
PO Box 421234
Houston, TX 77242
Ph: (281)310-0321
E-mail: info@baftx.org
URL: baftx.org
Social Media: www.facebook.com/BAFTX
www.linkedin.com/in/baftx-british-american-foundation-of
 -texas-069485123
twitter.com/baftx

2696 ■ BAFTX Early Starters Award *(Undergraduate/ Award)*

Purpose: To provide assistance to students on the right track. Further education is a costly business and requires significant financial resources and planning. **Focus:** General studies/Field of study not specified. **Qualif.:** Applicants must be permanent residents of Texas; enrolled in full-time education at the Middle School level; must maintain an average A grade and hold an excellent school attendance record. **Criteria:** Applicants are evaluated based on financial need.

Funds Avail.: $1,000. **To Apply:** Applicants must submit the completed application form; essay a British person (past or present) whom they admire; current transcript signed by a member of their teaching staff; letter of recommendation which must come from a teacher in whose class they were enrolled within the past year, or from a guidance counselor at their school (letter must be on school letterhead paper); and a recent photograph. **Deadline:** January 31. **Contact:** Email: info@baftx.org.

2697 ■ BAFTX Graduate Award *(Graduate/Award)*

Purpose: To provide financial assistance to aspiring individuals from Great Britain or Texas, USA that are intent on furthering their education in their chosen field. **Focus:** General studies/Field of study not specified. **Qualif.:** Applicants must be permanent residents of Texas; must be enrolled in full time education; between 21 and above; must hold an undergraduate degree with a GPA of 3.5 or above for U.S. applicants and 2.1 (65+) for U.K. applicants. **Criteria:** Applicants are evaluated based on academic achievement and financial need.

Funds Avail.: No specific amount. **To Apply:** Applicants must submit an essay, 450 and 450 words. on one of the topics given in the application form found at the website of BAFTX; a letter of recommendation which must come from a teacher in whose class they were enrolled within the past year or from a guidance counselor at their university (letter must be on university letterhead paper); current transcript of their academic performance signed by a member of the teaching staff; financial statement declaring their eligibility for the program; budget outline stating the sum being requested for tuition fees and other costs associated with their education for one semester; and a recent photograph. **Deadline:** March 31. **Contact:** Email: info@baftx.org.

2698 ■ BAFTX Junior Achievers Award *(Undergraduate/Award)*

Purpose: To provide a summer study program and cultural exchange for academically adept students from low income families in the Houston area. **Focus:** General studies/Field of study not specified. **Qualif.:** Applicants must be permanent residents of Texas; enrolled in full-time education; must be a high school junior; and must maintain a competitive GPA and excellent school attendance record. **Criteria:** Applicants are evaluated based on financial need.

Funds Avail.: No specific amount. **To Apply:** Applicants must submit completed application form; an essay regarding a British person (past or present) whom they admire; current transcript of academic performance signed by a member of the teaching staff; letter of recommendation which must come from a teacher in whose class they were enrolled within the past year or from a guidance counselor at their school (letter must be on school letterhead); and a recent photograph. **Deadline:** January 31. **Contact:** Email: info@baftx.org.

2699 ■ BAFTX Undergraduate Award *(Undergraduate/Award)*

Purpose: To alleviate the financial burden of funding the college fees. **Focus:** General studies/Field of study not specified. **Qualif.:** Applicants must be permanent residents of Texas; must be enrolled in full time education; must be between 18 and above; and must maintain a GPA of 3.25. **Criteria:** Applicants are evaluated based on merit and financial need.

Awards are arranged alphabetically below their administering organizations

Funds Avail.: No specific amount. **To Apply:** Applicants must submit an essay, 450 and 450 words. on one of the topics given in the application form found at the website of BAFTX; a letter of recommendation which must come from a teacher in whose class they were enrolled within the past year or from a guidance counselor at their university (letter must be on university letterhead paper); current transcript of their academic performance signed by a member of the teaching staff; financial statement declaring their eligibility for the program; budget outline stating the sum being requested for tuition fees and other costs associated with their education for one semester; and a recent photograph. **Deadline:** March 31. **Contact:** Email: info@baftx.org.

2700 ■ British Columbia Historical Federation (BCHF)

PO Box 448
Fort Langley, BC, Canada V1M 2R7
URL: www.bchistory.ca

2701 ■ W. Kaye Lamb Award for the Best Student works *(Undergraduate/Scholarship)*

Purpose: To support student essays relating to the history of British Columbia. **Focus:** Canadian studies; Writing. **Qualif.:** Applicant must be a student registered in university or college in British Columbia.

Funds Avail.: $750 - 1st or 2nd year students; $1,000 3rd or 4th year students. **Duration:** Annual. **Number Awarded:** 2. **To Apply:** Applicants must submit their application for this scholarship and include a covering letter of application; letter of recommendation from the instructor for whose course the essay was written; an essay of 1500-3000 words for 1st or 2nd year or 1500-5000 words for 3rd or 4th-year students on a topic relating to the history of British Columbia; website or podcast; artwork; performance either created or directed; video, film, documentary, or multimedia installation created by the student. **Deadline:** March 15. **Contact:** Submissions must be sent to the following Committee Member: Shannon Bettles W. Kaye Lamb Essay Scholarship BC Historical Federation, PO Box 448, Fort Langley, BC, Canada, V1M 2R7.

2702 ■ Broadcast Education Association (BEA)

1 M St. SE
Washington, DC 20003
Ph: (202)602-0584
Fax: (202)609-9940
E-mail: help@beaweb.org
URL: www.beaweb.org/wp
Social Media: www.facebook.com/groups/34744282858
twitter.com/BEAWebTweets

2703 ■ Abe Voron Award *(Graduate/Scholarship)*

Purpose: To provide a broad range of services to academic and professional members to keep them abreast with the latest electronic media developments in radio, television, news technologies, management, sales, news reporting, production, research, communication, law, policy and international systems. **Focus:** Broadcasting. **Qualif.:** Applicants must be professors, industry professionals and students involved in teaching and research related to radio, television and electronic media; must be juniors, seniors and graduate students at BEA Member institutions; must be studying toward a career in radio. **Criteria:** Recipients are selected based on academic performance and potential as professionals.

Funds Avail.: $3,000. **Number Awarded:** 1. **To Apply:** Applicants must submit official application form from the campus faculty; must submit transcript of records, broadcast and other experiences; written statement of goals and supportive statement from three references. **Deadline:** October 12.

2704 ■ Walter S. Patterson Scholarships *(Graduate/Scholarship)*

Purpose: To provide a broad range of services to academic and professional members to keep them abreast with the latest electronic media developments in radio, television, news technologies, management, sales, news reporting, production, research, communication, law, policy and international systems. **Focus:** Broadcasting. **Qualif.:** Applicants must be professors, industry professionals and students involved in teaching and research related to radio, television and electronic media; must be juniors, seniors and graduate students at BEA Member institutions. **Criteria:** Recipients are selected based on academic performance and potential as professionals.

Funds Avail.: $1,750 each. **Duration:** Annual. **Number Awarded:** 2. **To Apply:** Applicants must submit official application form from the campus faculty; must submit transcript of records, broadcast and other experiences; written statement of goals and supportive statement from three references. **Deadline:** October 12.

2705 ■ Helen J. Sioussat/Fay Wells Scholarships *(Graduate/Scholarship)*

Purpose: To provide a broad range of services to its academic and professional members to keep them abreast with the latest electronic media developments in radio, television, news technologies, management, sales, news reporting, production, research, communication, law, policy and international systems. **Focus:** Broadcasting. **Qualif.:** Applicants must be professors, industry professionals and students involved in teaching and research related to radio, television and electronic media; must be juniors, seniors and graduate students at BEA Member institutions. **Criteria:** Recipients are selected based on academic performance and potential as professionals.

Funds Avail.: $1,250 each. **Number Awarded:** 2. **To Apply:** Applicants must submit an official application form from the campus faculty; must submit transcript of records, broadcast and other experiences; written statement of goals and supportive statement from three references.

2706 ■ Alexander M. Tanger Scholarships *(Graduate/Scholarship)*

Purpose: To provide a broad range of services to academic and professional members to keep them abreast with the latest electronic media developments in radio, television, news technologies, management, sales, news reporting, production, research, communication, law, policy and international systems. **Focus:** Broadcasting. **Qualif.:** Applicants must be professors, industry professionals and students involved in teaching and research related to radio, television and electronic media; must be juniors, seniors and graduate students at BEA Member institutions. **Criteria:** Recipients are selected based on academic performance and potential as professionals.

Funds Avail.: $5,000. **Number Awarded:** 1. **To Apply:** Applicants must submit official application form from the campus faculty; must submit transcript of records, broadcast and other experiences; written statement of goals and supportive statement from three references. **Deadline:** October 12.

Awards are arranged alphabetically below their administering organizations

2707 ■ Two Year/Community Broadcast Education Association Scholarship Awards (Other/Scholarship)

Purpose: To provide a broad range of services to academic and professional members to keep them abreast with the latest electronic media developments in radio, television, news technologies, management, sales, news reporting, production, research, communication, law, policy and international systems. **Focus:** Broadcasting.

2708 ■ Vincent T. Wasilewski Award (Graduate/ Scholarship)

Purpose: To provide a broad range of services to academic and professional members to keep them abreast with the latest electronic media developments in radio, television, news technologies, management, sales, news reporting, production, research, communication, law, policy and international systems. **Focus:** Broadcasting. **Qualif.:** Applicants must be professors, industry professionals and students involved in teaching and research related to radio, television and electronic media; must be juniors, seniors and graduate students at BEA Member institutions. **Criteria:** Recipients are selected based on academic performance and potential as professionals.

Funds Avail.: $4,000. **Number Awarded:** 1. **To Apply:** Applicants must submit official application forms from the campus faculty; must submit transcript of records, broadcast and other experiences; written statement of goals and supportive statement from two references. **Deadline:** October 12. **Contact:** Dr. Peter B. Orlik, BEA Scholarship Committee Chair, 613 Kane St., Mt. Pleasant, MI, 48858; Email: orlik1pb@cmich.edu.

2709 ■ Bronx County Bar Association (BCBA)
851 Grand Concourse, Rm. 124
Bronx, NY 10451
Ph: (718)293-2227
URL: www.bronxbar.com
Social Media: www.facebook.com/bronxbarassociation
www.linkedin.com/company/bronx-county-bar-association/ about

2710 ■ Craig Lensch Memorial Scholarship
(Undergraduate/Scholarship)

Purpose: To provide financial Aid Officers at local law schools students who are domiciled in Bronx County. **Focus:** Law. **Qualif.:** Applicants must be first, second, or third year law students who are graduating in May or June; enrolled at an A.B.A. accredited school; first year students must have completed one semester of study; Applicant's Domicile must be Bronx county. **Criteria:** Applicants will be evaluated based on academics, financial need, writing sample, personal interview, law school transcript and personal statement.

Funds Avail.: $5,000. **Duration:** Annual. **Number Awarded:** 1. **To Apply:** Application along with official college and law school transcripts and writing sample must be mailed with subject line 'scholarship'.

2711 ■ Hon. Peggy Bernheim Memorial Scholarship
(Undergraduate/Scholarship)

Purpose: To provide financial assistance for the education of law school students who are domiciled in Bronx County. **Focus:** Law. **Qualif.:** Applicants must be first, second, or third year law students who are graduating in May or June; enrolled at an A.B.A. accredited school; first year students

must have completed one semester of study; Applicant's Domicile must be Bronx county. **Criteria:** Applicants will be evaluated based on academics, financial need, writing sample, personal interview, law school transcript and personal statement.

Funds Avail.: $5,000. **Duration:** Annual. **Number Awarded:** 1. **To Apply:** Application along with official college and law school transcripts and writing sample must be mailed with subject line 'scholarship'. Applicants interested in applying for this scholarship should pay particular attention to the question regarding athletic experiences, skills and accomplishments.

2712 ■ The Brookdale Foundation
300 Frank W Burr Blvd., Ste. 13
Teaneck, NJ 07666
Ph: (201)836-4602
Fax: (201)836-4342
URL: www.brookdalefoundation.org

2713 ■ The Brookdale Leadership in Aging Fellowship Program (Other/Fellowship)

Purpose: To foster the development of a new generation of leaders in the field of aging by supporting investigators in the developmental stages of their careers. **Focus:** Gerontology. **Qualif.:** Applicants must demonstrate leadership potential; must provide evidence of an ongoing commitment to a career in aging.

Funds Avail.: No specific amount. **Duration:** Annual. **Remarks:** Established in 1985.

2714 ■ Brookings Doha Center (BDC)
1775 Massachusetts Ave. NW
Washington, DC 20036
URL: www.brookings.edu

2715 ■ BDC Visiting Fellowship (Advanced Professional, Professional development/Fellowship)

Purpose: To Leading academics and practitioners from mid-to-senior ranks publish research. **Focus:** General studies/Field of study not specified.

Funds Avail.: No specific amount.

2716 ■ Angela Faye Brown & Associates
3800 N Lamar Blvd., Ste 200
Austin, TX 78756
Ph: (512)814-5711
E-mail: client@afbfamilylaw.com
URL: www.afbfamilylaw.com
Social Media: www.facebook.com/brownfamilylaw

2717 ■ Angela Faye Brown Video Essay Contest
(Graduate/Scholarship)

Purpose: To help ease the stress of paying for college. **Focus:** Law. **Qualif.:** Applicant must be a senior at Texas college or university planning to attend law school or a current law student at a Texas college or university; have a minimum 2.8 GPA; and identify as African-American, Hispanic, or LatinX. **Criteria:** Selection will be based on the creativity, originality, and feasibility of the video essay.

Funds Avail.: $2,000. **Number Awarded:** 1. **To Apply:** Applicant must submit a video essay on the following topic:

Awards are arranged alphabetically below their administering organizations

There are some people who believe a paternity test should be required prior to a father's name being listed on the birth certificate, and there are others who are strongly opposed to this idea? Do you think paternity tests should be mandatory at the moment a child is born? Why or why not? Application and video essay should be submitted via email. **Deadline:** August 31. **Contact:** Angela Brown; Email: scholarship@afbfamilylaw.com; URL: www.afbfamilylaw.com/scholarships-for-texas-law-students/.

2718 ■ John Carter Brown Library

94 George St.
Providence, RI 02906
Ph: (401)863-2725
Fax: (401)863-3477
URL: www.brown.edu
Social Media: www.facebook.com/BrownUniversity
www.facebook.com/jcblibrary
instagram.com/brownu
www.instagram.com/johncarterbrownlibrary
www.linkedin.com/school/brown-university
www.linkedin.com/company/john-carter-brown-library
www.pinterest.com/pin/205476801718829652
twitter.com/jcblibrary
www.youtube.com/brownuniversity

2719 ■ Long-term Fellowship *(Graduate, Doctorate/Fellowship)*

Purpose: To give scholars from the U.S. and abroad an opportunity to pursue their work in proximity to a distinguished collection of primary sources. **Focus:** General studies/Field of study not specified. **Qualif.:** Applicant must be a citizens of the United States or to those applicants residing in the U.S. for the three years preceding application. **Criteria:** Recipients will be selected based on academic standing and financial need.

Funds Avail.: $4,200 per month. **Duration:** Annual; from 5 to 10 months. **To Apply:** Applicants must complete the application form; must send three letters of recommendation; a narrative description, in English, of the proposed project, including an explanation of its historiographical significance, progress to date on the project, identification of specific materials to be consulted at the JCB, and plan for work to be completed while in residence; must current curriculum vitae. **Deadline:** December 1. **Remarks:** The fellowships are funded by the National Endowment for the Humanities (NEH).

2720 ■ John Carter Brown Library Short-Term Fellowships *(Doctorate, Postdoctorate/Fellowship)*

Purpose: To support and assist scholars in any area of research related to the Library's holdings. **Focus:** General studies/Field of study not specified. **Qualif.:** Applicants must be citizens of the United States and foreign nationals who are engaged in pre- or post-doctoral, or independent, research; graduate students must have passed their preliminary or general examinations at the time of application. **Criteria:** Recipients will be selected based on the academic standing and financial need.

Funds Avail.: $2,100 per month. **Duration:** Annual; from 2 to 4 months. **To Apply:** Applicants must complete the application form; must send two letters of recommendation; must current curriculum vitae. **Deadline:** December 1.

2721 ■ Ron Brown Scholar Program

1160 Pepsi Pl., Ste. 206
Charlottesville, VA 22901
Ph: (434)964-1588
Fax: (434)964-1589
E-mail: info@ronbrown.org
URL: www.ronbrown.org
Social Media: www.facebook.com/ronbrownscholarprogram
www.linkedin.com/company/ron-brown-scholar-program
twitter.com/ronbrownscholar

2722 ■ Ron Brown Scholarship *(Undergraduate/Scholarship)*

Purpose: To advance higher education and improve the lives of public service-minded and intellectually gifted African Americans and to accelerate their progress into impactful leadership roles and opportunities. **Focus:** General studies/Field of study not specified. **Criteria:** Selection will be made by members of the Ron Brown Selection Committee.

Funds Avail.: $40,000 ($10,000 per year for four years). **Duration:** Annual; for 4 years. **Number Awarded:** Varies. **To Apply:** Applicants must mail the application materials in one packet; transcripts and letters of recommendation should not be sent under separate cover; must provide SAT/ACT scores; incomplete, e-mailed or faxed applications will not be considered. **Deadline:** January 9. **Remarks:** Established by CAP Charitable Foundation, the Ron Brown Scholar Program (RBSP) honors the legacy of Ronald H. Brown, the late Secretary of Commerce, through a selective, multilevel scholarship and leadership program which focuses on academic achievement, community service and career immersion for African American college bound high school seniors. Established in 1996. **Contact:** Ron Brown Scholar Program, 485 Hillsdale Dr., Ste. 206, Charlottesville, VA, 22901; Phone: 434-964-1588; Fax: 434-964-1589; Email: info@ronbrown.org.

2723 ■ Brown University - Pembroke Center for Teaching and Research on Women

172 Meeting St.
Providence, RI 02912
Ph: (401)863-2643
Fax: (401)863-1298
E-mail: pembroke_center@brown.edu
URL: www.brown.edu
Social Media: www.facebook.com/PembrokeCenter
www.instagram.com/pembrokecenter_brown
twitter.com/PembrokeCenter
www.youtube.com/playlist?list=PLTiEffrOcz_41We8G8P
-5vXxOqBZC00T5

2724 ■ Pembroke Center's Faculty Research Fellowships *(Professional development/Fellowship)*

Purpose: To support the participation of Brown faculty members in the Pembroke Seminar, an interdisciplinary research seminar that meets weekly throughout the academic year. **Focus:** General studies/Field of study not specified. **Qualif.:** Applicant must be a campus-based full-time regular tenure and tenure line faculty member. **Criteria:** Selection will be based on the committee criteria.

Funds Avail.: No specific amount. **Duration:** Annual. **Number Awarded:** Varies. **To Apply:** Applicants must submit

Awards are arranged alphabetically below their administering organizations

an application package which includes a current curriculum vitae and a 1,000 words project proposal that describes their research. Faculty participants should have an active interest in the seminar's topic, but the research project may be in any related field and need not directly address the topic. **Deadline:** February 14. **Contact:** Materials should be submitted, Pembroke Center, Box 1958, 172 Meeting St., Rm. 111, Phone: 401-863-2643; Email: Pembroke_Center@Brown.edu, For questions, Bonnie Honig; Phone: 401-863-3466; Email: Bonnie_Honig@Brown.edu.

2725 ■ Pembroke Center Graduate Student Fellowships *(Graduate, Postdoctorate/Fellowship)*

Purpose: To provide students an enhanced context that gives the opportunity for presentation of work and benefits or critique from an exciting group of Pembroke Center Faculty. **Focus:** General studies/Field of study not specified. **Qualif.:** Applicants must be graduate students enrolled and currently studying at Brown University.

Funds Avail.: $1,000. **Duration:** Annual. **To Apply:** Applicants must submit a cover sheet indicating their name, current year, department and dissertation director; a three-page description of their research project, including a brief representative bibliography; a brief letter of support from a faculty member who knows their work. **Deadline:** March 12. **Contact:** Box 1958, 172 Meeting St., Room 111; Phone: 863-2643, Email: Pembroke_Center@Brown.edu.

2726 ■ Pembroke Center Seed Grants *(Professional development/Grant)*

Purpose: To support the formation of focused interdisciplinary groups working across fields and academic divisions to creatively explore social issues of representation. **Focus:** Arts; Health sciences; Humanities; Science technologies; Social sciences. **Qualif.:** Applicants must be from the humanities, social sciences, creative arts, health sciences and science and technology studies. **Criteria:** Preference will be given to projects that involve faculty across academic divisions.

Funds Avail.: $10,000. **Duration:** Annual. **Number Awarded:** 1. **To Apply:** Applicants must complete the following requirements: one faculty project director, plus a minimum of one additional faculty member from a different field; one-page bios of research group participants, including their disciplines, research interest as they relate to the seed grant application and their other interdisciplinary projects; title of research project and a two- to three-page description that details the central research questions, common themes and project goals; plan to involve other faculty researchers, visiting scholars, postdoctoral fellows, and students; dissemination plan for research findings. **Deadline:** April 1. **Contact:** Send applications electronically, Email: Pembroke_Center@brown.edu or deliver hard copy to, The Pembroke Center - Box 1958, Pembroke Hall, Rm. 111, 172 Meeting St., Brown University, Providence, RI, 02912.

2727 ■ Pembroke Center for Teaching and Research on Women Postdoctoral Research Associateships *(Postdoctorate/Fellowship)*

Purpose: To support the educational development of scholars from any field whose research relates to the theme of "Fatigue". **Focus:** General studies/Field of study not specified. **Qualif.:** Applicants must have a Ph.D. and may not hold a tenured position. **Criteria:** Selection will be based on the basis of their scholarly potential and the

relevance of their work to the research theme.

Funds Avail.: $50,000 plus $1,500 for research expenses. **Duration:** Annual. **To Apply:** Applicants must complete and submit the following completed application form; cover letter; one page document including title and 250-word abstract of proposed research project; project statement of five typed pages (double-spaced); brief representative bibliography for research proposal; curriculum vitae; course syllabus with a course description and schedule of assigned readings; three confidential recommendation letters. **Deadline:** December 5. **Contact:** Phone: 401-863-2643; Email: donna_goodnow@brown.edu.

2728 ■ Peggy Browning Fund (PBF)
100 S Broad St., Ste. 1208
Philadelphia, PA 19110
Ph: (267)273-7990
Fax: (267)273-7688
URL: www.peggybrowningfund.org
Social Media: www.facebook.com/peggybrowningfund

2729 ■ Peggy Browning Fund - Chicago School-Year Fellowships *(Graduate, Undergraduate/Fellowship)*

Purpose: To provide assistance for the education of law students about the human rights and needs of workers. **Focus:** Law. **Qualif.:** Applicants must be students in good standing at a participating law school in proximity to the fellowship location and must have completed at least one year of law school. **Criteria:** Selection is based on submitted application materials.

Funds Avail.: $6,000. **Duration:** Annual; ten-weeks. **To Apply:** Applicants must submit a cover letter, a completed application form and resume. **Deadline:** January 17.

2730 ■ Bryant Surety Bonds Inc.
73 Old Dublin Pke., Ste. 10, No. 306
Doylestown, PA 18901
Fax: (866)450-3414
Free: 866-450-3412
URL: www.bryantsuretybonds.com
Social Media: www.facebook.com/BryantSuretyBonds
www.linkedin.com/company/bryant-surety-bonds-inc-
pinterest.com/bryantsurety
twitter.com/bryantsurety
youtube.com/channel/UCh_q58hRS5cTikJyEChBS7w

2731 ■ Bryant Essay Scholarships *(Undergraduate, Graduate/Scholarship)*

Purpose: To help individuals start a new business that they have dreamed of by bonding their start up. **Focus:** General studies/Field of study not specified. **Qualif.:** Applicants must be currently enrolled in graduate or undergraduate degree program in an accredited U.S. college, university, or trade school. **Criteria:** Selection will be based on the committee's criteria.

Funds Avail.: $1,000. **Number Awarded:** 1. **To Apply:** Applicants must submit an essay of 500-2,000 words and an email regarding scholarships along with the following information: first and last name, school name, and expected date of graduation. **Deadline:** June 15. **Contact:** scholarships@bryantsuretybonds.com.

2732 ■ Bryant Visual Content Scholarships *(Undergraduate, Graduate/Scholarship)*

Purpose: To help individuals start a new business that they have dreamed of by bonding their start up. **Focus:**

Awards are arranged alphabetically below their administering organizations

General studies/Field of study not specified. **Qualif.:** Applicants must be currently enrolled in a graduate or undergraduate degree program in an accredited U.S. college, university, or trade school. **Criteria:** Selection will be based on the committee's criteria.

Funds Avail.: $1,000. **Number Awarded:** 1. **To Apply:** Applicants must provide the following images and infographics with high resolution in png, jpeg, jpg, or gif format; 1-3 minutes long video; slides deck with 5-20 slides; email regarding scholarships along with the following information first and last name, school name and expected date of graduation. **Deadline:** June 15. **Contact:** scholarships@ bryantsuretybonds.com.

2733 ■ Brylak Law
15900 La Cantera Pkwy., ste. 19245
San Antonio, TX 78256
Ph: (210)733-5533
Fax: (210)558-4804
Free: 866-883-5533
URL: www.brylaklaw.com
Social Media: www.linkedin.com/company/brylak-&
-associates-l.l.c.

2734 ■ Brylak Law Safety Scholarship Contest
(Undergraduate/Scholarship)

Purpose: To provide financial aid to college students; encourage students to explore the role personal injury lawyers play in minimizing hazards, helping those injured, and encouraging people everywhere to think about consumer safety; and inspire students to pursue a career in any legal field. **Focus:** Business; Finance; Law; Management. **Qualif.:** Applicant must be a high school senior or college freshman in the United States who is studying, or plans to study, business, management, finance, or law. **Criteria:** Selection is based on the best video or written essay submitted.

Funds Avail.: $1,000. **Duration:** Annual. **Number Awarded:** 1. **To Apply:** Applicant must record a video (one to two minutes long, in English) explaining how lawyers make the world a safer place. Video must be uploaded to applicant's YouTube channel with the title "Brylak Law Safety Scholarship Contest" and the following link in the description: www.brylaklaw.com/safety-scholarship-for-law-students/. Applicant must also share the video on their Facebook page and the sponsor's Facebook page. Instead of a video essay, applicant may submit a 1,000 to 1,500 word essay on the same subject via email. **Deadline:** August 15. **Contact:** Wallace Brylak; Email: brylakscholarship@gmail.com.

2735 ■ Buckfire & Buckfire, P.C.
29000 Inkster Rd, Ste., 150
Southfield, MI 48034
Ph: (248)595-7544
Free: 888-797-8787
URL: www.buckfirelaw.com
Social Media: www.facebook.com/buckfirelaw
www.linkedin.com/company/buckfire-
twitter.com/BuckfireLaw
www.youtube.com/c/buckfirelaw

2736 ■ Buckfire & Buckfire, P.C. Law School Diversity Scholarships *(Graduate/Scholarship)*

Purpose: To help law students who are in need of financial assistance achieve their academic and professional dreams. **Focus:** Law. **Qualif.:** Applicants must be U.S. citizens currently attending or have completed at least one semester of classes at an accredited law school within the United States; must have a minimum 3.0 GPA; must be members of ethnic or racial minority or any individuals who demonstrates a defined commitment to issues of diversity within their academic career. **Criteria:** Selection will be based on the committee's criteria.

Funds Avail.: $2,000. **Number Awarded:** 1. **To Apply:** Applicants must submit a completed scholarship application form; a one page typed essay describing how the applicants utilized their time promoting ethnic diversity within their community - alternatively, applicants may write about how they will use their law degree to promote ethnic diversity in the future; and a certified official copy of law school transcript. **Deadline:** April 1. **Remarks:** Established in 2013. **Contact:** Law School Diversity Scholarship, 29000 Inkster Rd., Ste. 150, Southfield, MI, 48034; Email: info@ buckfirelaw.com.

2737 ■ Buckfire & Buckfire, P.C. Medical Diversity Scholarships *(Advanced Professional/Scholarship)*

Purpose: To recognize medical school students who do outstanding work to promote ethnic diversity in their community. **Focus:** Medical assisting. **Qualif.:** Applicants must be U.S. citizens currently attending or have completed at least one semester of classes at an accredited medical school within the United States; must have a minimum 3.0 GPA; must be members of ethnic or racial minority or any individuals who demonstrates a defined commitment to issues of diversity within their academic career. **Criteria:** Selection will be based on the committee's criteria.

Funds Avail.: $2,000. **Duration:** Annual. **Number Awarded:** 1. **To Apply:** Applicants must submit a completed scholarship application form; a one page typed essay describing how the applicants utilized their time promoting ethnic diversity within their community - alternatively, applicants may write about how they will use their law degree to promote ethnic diversity in the future; and a certified official copy of law school transcript. **Deadline:** April 1. **Remarks:** Established in 2014. **Contact:** Medical Diversity Scholarship, 29000 Inkster Rd., Ste. 150, Southfield, MI, 48034; Email: info@buckfirelaw.com.

2738 ■ Susan Thompson Buffett Foundation
222 Kiewit Plz.
Omaha, NE 68131
Ph: (402)943-1383
E-mail: scholarships@stbfoundation.org
URL: www.buffettscholarships.org

2739 ■ Susan Thompson Buffett Foundation Scholarship *(Undergraduate, Two Year College/ Scholarship)*

Purpose: To provide financial assistance to qualified individuals. **Focus:** General studies/Field of study not specified. **Criteria:** Selection will be based on financial need; academic merit; personal essay; a strength of recommendations.

Duration: Annual. **To Apply:** Applicants must submit the information via online application form and attach two recommendations; Student Aid Report; high school transcript; essay (1000 to 1500 words); consent form. **Deadline:** February 1. **Contact:** Phone: 402-943-1383; Email: scholarships@stbfoundation.org.

Awards are arranged alphabetically below their administering organizations

2740 ■ Building Owners and Managers Association of Greater New York (BOMANY)

1 Penn Plz., 22nd Fl., Ste. 2205
New York, NY 10119
Ph: (212)239-3662
URL: www.bomany.org
Social Media: www.facebook.com/pg/BOMANewYork/
  about
twitter.com/boma_ny?lang=en
www.youtube.com/channel/UCdtMfrEi1
  _pOGCaP7QFRPPA

2741 ■ BOMA/NY Scholarship *(Undergraduate/ Scholarship)*

Purpose: To financially assist students to further their professional education. **Focus:** General studies/Field of study not specified. **Qualif.:** Applicants must be a BOMA New York member; must have completed, and passed, at least one BOMI course in any designation. **Criteria:** Scholarship committee determines each award based on the points addressed in the required essay, completed application form, and the in-person interview; must attend an in-person interview with the scholarship committee at the BOMA/NY office.

Funds Avail.: No specific amount. **Duration:** Annual. **To Apply:** Applicants must submit completed application form along with a one page essay and letter of recommendation from current employer. **Deadline:** July 30. **Remarks:** Established in 1988. **Contact:** BOMA New York Office: One Penn Plaza, Ste 2205, 22nd Fl, New York, NY 10119.

2742 ■ Bulletin of the Atomic Scientists

1307 E 60th St
Chicago, IL 60637-3283
Ph: (773)834-3779
URL: thebulletin.org

2743 ■ Rieser Fellowships *(Undergraduate/ Fellowship)*

Purpose: To provide financial support for undergraduate students pursuing a project relating to interaction of science, global security, and public policy. **Focus:** National security; Peace studies. **Qualif.:** Applicant must be an undergraduate student at a U.S. college/university. **Criteria:** Selection is based on academic interests, extracurricular activities and career aspiration.

Funds Avail.: $4,000. **Duration:** One year. **Number Awarded:** 2. **To Apply:** Applicants must send an application form (available at the website); resume; proposal (800-1000 words); official letters confirming internships, acceptance to conference; an essay (one-page, single-spaced) explaining how the fellowship would be benefit the applicant; project budget; and two letters of recommendation. **Deadline:** March 15.

2744 ■ Bunker Family Association (BFA)

c/o Gil Bunker, President
9 Sommerset Rd.
Turnersville, NJ 08012-2122
Ph: (856)589-6140
E-mail: membership@bunkerfamilyassn.org
URL: www.bunkerfamilyassn.org

2745 ■ Annabelle Moore Scholarship *(Undergraduate/Scholarship)*

Purpose: To support the continuing education of the relative of an Association member. **Focus:** General studies/ Field of study not specified. **Qualif.:** Applicants must be a child or grandchild of a Bunker Family Association member in good standing, and must be a high school graduating senior or college freshman. **Criteria:** Selection will be based on the following; scholarship attainment, goals and worthiness, financial need, and activities and awards.

Funds Avail.: $500. **Duration:** Annual. **Number Awarded:** 1. **To Apply:** Applicants shall complete the following application process; the current application form; provide a genealogy chart showing Bunker lineage; and, forward a complete high school transcript (with official HS seal) containing marks for the most recent term or semester. **Deadline:** July 30. **Contact:** LiAnn Pennington, 2632, 52nd Ave., Greeley, CO 80634-4005; Email: lianngrannyp@gmail.com.

2746 ■ Burger King McLamore Foundation

5505 Blue Lagoon Dr.
Miami, FL 33126
Ph: (305)378-3186
E-mail: bk_mclamorefoundation@whopper.com
URL: bkmclamorefoundation.org
Social Media: www.youtube.com/channel/
  UC3SPrA1aXFWHgzeof70gTOA

2747 ■ Burger King Employee Scholars Program *(Undergraduate/Scholarship)*

Purpose: To provide scholarship awards to assist students who excel academically while also working part-time and being actively involved in their community. **Focus:** General studies/Field of study not specified. **Qualif.:** Applicants must be high school seniors who are salaried or hourly team members of a Burger King restaurant; active on BK payroll for at least 12 months of the current year's application deadline; maintain at least a 2.0 GPA throughout high school or college; enrolled at an accredited college/vocational school in the fall of the scholarship year; participate in extracurricular activities or community service; receive written recommendation from their employer. **Criteria:** Selection will be based on financial need, community involvement, employment at a participating restaurant location, academic achievements and records.

Funds Avail.: $1,000 to $50,000. **To Apply:** Applicants must log on to www.applyists.net to get an application and must follow the onscreen instructions. **Deadline:** Dec. 15. **Remarks:** Established in 2000. **Contact:** For additional information, applicants must contact the International Scholarship and Tuition Services, Inc.; Phone: 615-320-3149; Fax: 615-320-3151. Application form and supporting documents can be faxed at 615-627-9685 or 615-627-9673 or can be emailed at bkscholars@applyists.com.

2748 ■ Burger King Scholars Program *(Undergraduate/Scholarship)*

Purpose: To provide support to employees, employees' spouses or domestic partners, employees' children, and high school seniors in the United States. **Focus:** General studies/Field of study not specified. **Qualif.:** Applicants must be high school seniors who: maintain a cumulative GPA of 2.5 or higher on a 4.0 scale or the equivalent; demonstrate participation in community service activities; demonstrate financial need; plan to enroll in an accredited two-year or four-year college, university or vocational/technical school; graduating high school seniors or graduating from home school education; must be U.S. or Canada residents. **Criteria:** Selection will be based on the submitted application.

Awards are arranged alphabetically below their administering organizations

Funds Avail.: $1,000 to $50,000. **Duration:** Annual. **To Apply:** Applications will be accepted via online submission process at: burgerking.scholarsapply.org. **Deadline:** December 18. **Remarks:** Administered by Scholarship America. Established in 2000. **Contact:** Scholarship Management Services; Phone: 507-931-8340; Email: burgerkingscholars@scholarshipamerica.org.

2749 ■ Burroughs Wellcome Fund

21 T.W. Alexander Dr.
Research Triangle Park, NC 27709
Ph: (919)991-5100
URL: bwfund.org
Social Media: www.facebook.com/BWFundRTP
www.instagram.com/bwfund
www.linkedin.com/company/burroughs-wellcome-fund
twitter.com/BWFUND
www.youtube.com/user/BWFUND55

2750 ■ Burroughs Wellcome Fund Collaborative Research Travel Grants (CRTG) *(Doctorate, Postdoctorate/Grant)*

Purpose: To support researchers from degree-granting institutions with travel either domestically or internationally to acquire new research techniques, to promote collaborations and to attend courses. **Focus:** Biology; Chemistry; Computer and information sciences; Engineering; Mathematics and mathematical sciences; Physics; Statistics. **Qualif.:** Applicants must hold a Ph.D. in mathematics, physics, chemistry, computer science, statistics, or engineering at the time of application and interested in investigating research opportunities in the biological sciences are eligible; biologists holding a doctorate degree at the time of application who are interested in working with physical scientists, mathematicians, engineers, chemists, statisticians, or computer scientists to incorporate their ideas and approaches to answering biological questions are eligible to apply; only proposals addressing questions in the biomedical sciences will be accepted; all proposals must be cross-disciplinary; grants must be made to U.S. or Canadian degree-granting institutions only. **Criteria:** Selection will be made on the basis of the proposal's scientific quality of the proposed activities and the career development potential and impact of the collaboration/visit. BWF does not provide critiques or written comments of unfunded proposals.

Funds Avail.: $15,000. **Duration:** Annual. **Number Awarded:** Varies. **To Apply:** Applicants must read all information provided in the program website to ensure successful application; prepare, in advance, the documents required in the proposal elements; combine and order the supporting materials into one (1) PDF file (prescribed formats are provided in the program website); upload the combined file of supporting documents as one attachment on the "Attachments" page of the submission website. Other procedures must confer to the program and submission websites. **Deadline:** February 12. **Contact:** Email: travel.progress@bwfund.org.

2751 ■ Career Awards for Medical Scientists (CAMS) *(Postdoctorate/Grant)*

Purpose: To support research and other scientific and educational activities of career medical scientists. **Focus:** Biomedical sciences; Medical research. **Qualif.:** Applicants must hold an M.D., D.D.S., D.V.M., or D.O. degree; must not be more than 13 years past their clinical doctorate degree; to meet this requirement, applicants must have received their clinical doctorate degree on or after January 1, 2005; may hold a junior faculty appointment (Lecturer, Instructor, Assistant Professor-non-tenure track, etc.); however, candidates with tenure track appointments are not eligible; must have non-tenure track faculty appointments with institutional start-up funds or hold an NIH R01 are not eligible; must submit proposals through accredited, degree-granting institutions in the U.S. or Canada; must obtain approval and signature by an authorized official at the degreegranting university in the U.S. or Canada; authorized official at the degree-granting institution must verify candidate's immigration status as part of the application; primary mentor or faculty sponsor of a candidate must hold an appointment at the same accredited, degree-granting institution in the U.S. or Canada as the applicant; citizens and non-citizen permanent and temporary residents of the U.S. and Canada who are legally qualified to work in the U.S. or Canada are eligible; candidates who are temporary U.S. residents must hold a valid U.S. visa (J-1, H1B, F-1 or O-1 visas); temporary Canadian residents must hold a valid Canadian visa (Study Permit, C-43, C-44, C-10, or C-20 work permits/visas); as a candidate, your visa status must allow you to remain in the U.S. or Canada during the award period of the CAMS grant; If a grant is awarded and your visa does not allow for such a stay, BWF may terminate the grant. BWF will not intercede on behalf of non-citizens whose stay in the U.S. or Canada falls out of visa compliance; proposals must be in the area of basic biomedical, disease-oriented, or translational research; proposals in health services research or involving large-scale clinical trials will not be considered; candidates with a clinical degree not awarded in the U.S. or Canada must be fully licensed to practice in the U.S. or Canada or have completed a residency in the U.S. or Canada; candidates must be committed to a full-time career in research as an independent investigator at a North American degree-granting institution; recipients are required to devote at least 75% of their time to research-related activities. **Criteria:** Selection will be based on CAMS Advisory Committee review applications, interview finalists, and make recommendations for approval to BWF's Board of Directors.

Funds Avail.: $700,000. **Duration:** Annual; over five years. **Number Awarded:** Varies. **To Apply:** Applicants will be required to complete a web-based questionnaire assessing their eligibility to apply; proposal consists of data entry fields submitted through the online Internet Grant Application Module (IGAM) plus a single PDF attachment and four (4) confidential letters of support; proposal elements (required except where noted): cover page (template provided); scientific and lay abstract (templates provided); nih biosketch (5-page limit); research plan (6-page limit); submitted manuscripts (optional; 3 maximum); bibliography (optional); personal statement (template provided); confidential faculty sponsor or mentor letter; three additional confidential letters of support; signature page form (template provided); institutional certification form (template provided). **Deadline:** October 1. **Contact:** Rolly L. Simpson, Jr., Senior Program Officer, Eligibility and Competitiveness Discussion; Email: rsimpson@bwfund.org; Phone: 919-991-5110 or Debra J. Holmes, Senior Program Associate; Email: dholmes@bwfund.org; Phone: 919-991-5134 or Kendra Tucker, Senior Programs Assistant; Email: ktucker@bwfund.org; Phone: 919-991-5115.

2752 ■ Career Awards for Science and Mathematics Teachers *(Other/Award)*

Purpose: To recognize teachers who have demonstrated solid knowledge of science and/or mathematics content

---

Awards are arranged alphabetically below their administering organizations

and have outstanding performance records in educating children. **Focus:** Mathematics and mathematical sciences; Science. **Qualif.:** Applicants must be currently licensed North Carolina public school science and/or mathematics teachers who teach in grades K-12 in North Carolina public schools and have completed at least five-years of teaching experience at the time of application, with at least 70 percent of their time devoted to teaching science and/or mathematics courses; must be in elementary schools, who also can be science and/or mathematics specialists, must have completed at least five-years of teaching at the time of application; with at least 30 percent of the candidate's time spent teaching science and/or mathematics; at least 20 percent of their time should be spent working with other teachers. If they are specialists; must have superior knowledge of science and/or mathematics, excellent teaching skills, demonstrated leadership and a commitment to continue teaching in the North Carolina Public School system and must be citizens of the United States. **Criteria:** Selection will be based primarily on the following; candidate's qualifications and potential to conduct high-quality science and/or mathematics teaching; significant contributions to enhancing students' knowledge of science and/or mathematics; knowledge of subject content and effectiveness of communications skills; abilities in the classroom that should demonstrate learner-centered, knowledge-centered, assessment-centered and community-centered learning styles; support from the principal and superintendent.

Funds Avail.: $175,000. **Duration:** Annual; five years. **To Apply:** Applications will require signatures and letters of support from the principal of the candidate's school and the superintendent of the school district; more than one candidate from a school or school district is eligible to apply; in support of, the principal and superintendent must demonstrate that the necessary environment for successful science and/or mathematics teaching exists at the school and that there are opportunities for the teacher to be mentored and to mentor other teachers; the principal and superintendent must clearly outline in letters of support how the teaching professional will be supported and developed as a teacher leader in the districts. **Deadline:** September 30. **Contact:** Alfred Mays Senior Program Officer Email: amays@bwfund.org, 919-991-5103;Tiffanie Traylor Senior Program Associate Email: ttaylor@bwfund.org, 919-991-5116.

2753 ■ Career Awards at the Scientific Interface (CASI) *(Undergraduate, Postdoctorate, Graduate/ Grant)*

Purpose: To advance post-doctoral training and to foster the early career development of researchers whose works are dedicated to pursuing a career in academic research. **Focus:** Biochemistry; Biology; Biophysics; Chemistry; Computer and information sciences; Engineering; Mathematics and mathematical sciences; Medicine; Physics; Statistics. **Qualif.:** Applicants must hold a Ph.D. degree in one of the fields of mathematics, physics, chemistry, computer science, statistics, or engineering. Ph.D. is in biochemistry/biophysics/biology/cell biology/chemistry or who have an engineering degree, M.D. are also eligible, provided, they meet other eligibility criteria or any other qualifications set by the BWF for this program. **Criteria:** The Interfaces in Science Advisory Committee will review all prepoposals, select candidates to invite for submission of full applications, interview finalists, and make recommendations for awards to the BWF Board of Directors; selection will be based on depth and rigor of training in a

scientific discipline other than biology; importance of biological questions identified in the proposal, and innovation in the approaches chosen to answer them; interdisciplinary nature of research plan, the degree to which non-biological methods are integrated, and the degree to which the proposed work will open new fields of inquiry; potential of candidate to establish a successful independent research career, evidenced by productivity during the postdoctoral period prior to application; and, quality of proposed collaborations.

Funds Avail.: $500,000. **Duration:** Five years. **Number Awarded:** Varies. **To Apply:** Applicants must read all information provided in the program website to ensure successful application; prepare, in advance, the documents required in the proposal elements; combine and order the supporting materials into one (1) PDF file (prescribed formats are provided in the program website); upload the combined file of supporting documents as one attachment on the "Attachments" page of the submission website; other procedures must confer to the program and submission websites. **Deadline:** September 1; January 8. **Contact:** Program Officer Dr. Kelly Rose.

2754 ■ Investigators in the Pathogenesis of Infectious Disease *(Doctorate, Postdoctorate/Grant)*

Purpose: To support accomplished investigators at the assistant professor level to study pathogenesis, with a focus on the interplay between human and microbial biology, shedding light on how human and microbial systems are affected by their encounters; and to provide opportunities for accomplished investigators still early in their careers to study what happens at the points where human and microbial systems connect. **Focus:** Biology; Infectious diseases; Pathology; Veterinary science and medicine. **Qualif.:** Applicants must have an established record of independent research; citizens and non-citizen permanent and temporary residents of the U.S. and Canada who are legally qualified to work in the U.S. or Canada are eligible; citizens and non-citizen permanent and temporary residents of the U.S. and Canada who are legally qualified to work in the U.S. or Canada are eligible; candidates who are temporary U.S. residents must hold a valid U.S. visa (J-1, H1B, F-1 or O-1 visas). Temporary Canadian residents must hold a valid Canadian visa (Study Permit, C-43, C44, C-10, or C-20 work permits/visas); candidates who will be promoted to Associate Professor by November 15, 2018, are not eligible to apply; candidates who have completed a Burroughs Wellcome Fund career development award (CAMS or CASI) are encouraged to apply but must contact BWF before writing the pre-proposal. Having had BWF travel, career guidance for trainees, preterm birth, regulatory science, or PDEP grants does not impact PATH support. **Criteria:** Selection will be based on PATH Advisory Committee will review pre-proposals and full proposals, interview finalists, and make recommendations to BWF's Board of Directors for funding.

Funds Avail.: $500,000. **Duration:** Annual. **To Apply:** Applicants must read all information provided in the program website to ensure successful application; prepare, in advance, the documents required in the proposal elements; combine and order the supporting materials into one (1) PDF file (prescribed formats are provided in the program website); upload the combined file of supporting documents as one attachment on the "Attachments" page of the submission website; other procedures must be confer to the program and submission websites. **Deadline:** November 13. **Contact:** Email: vmcgovern@bwfund.org.

Awards are arranged alphabetically below their administering organizations

2755 ■ Bush Foundation

101 5th St. E, Ste. 2400
Saint Paul, MN 55101
Ph: (651)227-0891
Fax: (651)297-6485
E-mail: info@bushfoundation.org
URL: bushfoundation.org
Social Media: www.facebook.com/bushfoundation
twitter.com/bushfoundation
www.youtube.com/channel/UCecHEN-aevpu3VqTICenr_Q

2756 ■ Bush Fellowship *(Professional development/ Fellowship)*

Purpose: To support and develop more leaders who are better equipped and better networked to effectively lead change. **Focus:** Arts. **Qualif.:** Applicants must be at least 24-years old at the time of the application deadline; must be a resident who lives in Minnesota, North Dakota, South Dakota or one of the 23 Native nations that shares the same geography, for one continuous year immediately prior to the application deadline. **Criteria:** Selection will be based on a record of success; outstanding character; active Learner.

Funds Avail.: $100,000. **Duration:** 12 to 24 month. **To Apply:** Applications will be accepted via online submission process. **Deadline:** September 17. **Remarks:** Established in 1976.

2757 ■ Bush Fellowship Program *(Professional development/Fellowship)*

Purpose: To motivate individuals who are eager to prepare themselves for greater leadership opportunities and to create positive change in their communities. **Focus:** Leadership, Institutional and community. **Qualif.:** Applicants must be a U.S. citizen or permanent resident; be 24 years or older at the application deadline date; have lived or worked for at least one continuous year immediately prior to the application deadline in Minnesota, North Dakota or South Dakota; and not a former Bush Leadership Fellows. **Criteria:** Selection committees review applicants' records with attention to leadership, learning and impact.

Funds Avail.: Up to $100,000. **Duration:** Annual. **To Apply:** Applications will be accepted via online submission process. **Deadline:** September 17. **Remarks:** Established in 1965.

2758 ■ Business Broker Network

375 Northridge Rd.
Atlanta, GA 30350
Fax: (770)391-5061
URL: www.businessbroker.net

2759 ■ $2,000 College Scholarship for the Business Leaders of Tomorrow *(Undergraduate/Scholarship)*

Purpose: To help students' with college expenses and encourage entrepreneurial activity. **Focus:** General studies/ Field of study not specified. **Qualif.:** Applicant must be a current college freshmen, sophomore, or senior enrolled in a college or university in the United States or U.S. territories; must be between the ages of 17-24. **Criteria:** Selection based on the strength of the applicant's essay.

Funds Avail.: $2,000. **Number Awarded:** 1. **To Apply:** Applicant must submit an 800-word or less essay on the following prompt "Choose an entrepreneur or business

leader that you admire and answer the following questions": What entrepreneurial qualities do you believe have allowed them to achieve their success? How has this person positively impacted society? What have you learned from your person's journey? As a future business leader, what do you hope to accomplish that will positively affect society? Essay should be submitted via email. File name should be applicant's full name and date of birth; subject line should have year and name of scholarship. **Deadline:** October 30.

2760 ■ Business and Professional Women's Foundation (BPW)

1030 15th Street, N.W. Suite B1 Ste. 148
Washington, DC 20005
Ph: (202)293-1100
E-mail: foundation@bpwfoundation.org
URL: bpwfoundation.org
Social Media: www.facebook.com/BPWFoundation
www.linkedin.com/company/business-and-professional
 -women's-foundation
twitter.com/BPW_CEO

2761 ■ BPW Foundation Career Advancement Scholarships *(Undergraduate/Scholarship)*

Purpose: To provide financial assistance to disadvantaged women seeking to further their education. **Focus:** General studies/Field of study not specified. **Qualif.:** Applicants must be female; must be U.S. citizens 25 years of age or older who are within two years of completing their bachelors degree; and pursuing a bachelor's degree from an accredited institution in the fields of science, technology, engineering, or mathematics (STEM)-or a related field. **Criteria:** Applications will be reviewed by the scholarship committee.

Funds Avail.: No specific amount. **To Apply:** Applications and supporting documents must be sent to BPW foundation. **Remarks:** Established in 1969.

2762 ■ Business Professionals of America (BPA)

700 Morse Rd., Ste. 201
Columbus, OH 43214
Ph: (614)895-7277
Fax: (614)895-1165
Free: 800-334-2007
E-mail: bpamembership@bpa.org
URL: www.bpa.org
Social Media: www.facebook.com/
 businessprofessionalsofamerica
instagram.com/bpanational
twitter.com/National_BPA

2763 ■ National Technical Honor Society Scholarships *(Professional development/Scholarship)*

Purpose: To assist outstanding seniors of Business Professionals of America in the Secondary Division. **Focus:** Business. **Qualif.:** Applicants must be outstanding Business Professionals of America members in either the secondary or post-secondary divisions. **Criteria:** Selection will be based on academic success, involvement within BPA, and membership in the NTHS.

Funds Avail.: $1,000. **Duration:** Annual. **Number Awarded:** 3. **To Apply:** Applicants must submit completed application form along with the school grade transcript or

Awards are arranged alphabetically below their administering organizations

letter from school principal verifying GPA; a one-page, typed resume of activities involving both Business Professionals of America and other school and community activities; three signed recommendation letters on official letterhead from local advisor and two individuals of their choice; a one-page, double-spaced, typed essay on topic, "What ideals have you taken from BPA and implemented into both your professional and personal lives?" and "How do you interpret the phrase 'Uncover Your Magic' and give an example of how you have been embodied the phrase in your life?". **Deadline:** April 1. **Contact:** Directed to Brigette Bethea Email: bbethea@bpa.org.

2764 ■ BusinessStudent.com

2033 San Elijio Ave.,
Cardiff, CA 92007
URL: www.businessstudent.com
Social Media: www.facebook.com/BusinessStudent
-586984355048513
twitter.com/bizstudentcom

2765 ■ BusinessStudent.com Business Leaders Scholarship *(College, University, Undergraduate, Graduate, Doctorate/Scholarship)*

Purpose: To help students pay for their college expenses, either on campus or online. **Focus:** Business. **Qualif.:** Applicant must be a current student at an accredited U.S. university or college (online programs included) and have a minimum 3.2 GPA on a 4.0 scale. **Criteria:** Selection is based on the quality of the essay and the applicant's GPA.

Funds Avail.: $1,500. **Number Awarded:** 2. **To Apply:** Applicant must submit completed application and essay. **Deadline:** May 1; October 1. **Contact:** URL: www.businessstudent.com/scholarsh.

2766 ■ The Bussey Law Firm PC

12 E Boulder St.
Colorado Springs, CO 80903
Ph: (719)419-8493
Fax: (719)475-0046
URL: thebusseylawfirm.com
Social Media: www.facebook.com/BusseyLawFirm
www.instagram.com/busseylawfirm
twitter.com/CODefenseLawyer
www.youtube.com/user/busseylawfirm

2767 ■ New Heights Scholarship *(Undergraduate/ Scholarship)*

Purpose: To help a deserving student pay for college. **Focus:** General studies/Field of study not specified. **Qualif.:** Applicant must have earned, or will earn this year, their high school diploma; have maintained a minimum 3.0 GPA; and be a U.S. citizen or permanent resident.

Funds Avail.: $500. **Number Awarded:** 1. **To Apply:** Application and essay must be submitted online. **Deadline:** April 21. **Contact:** Scholarship Manager; Email: sarah@timothybussey.com; URL: www.thebusseylawfirm.com/scholarship/.

2768 ■ Buzzell, Welsh & Hill

200 Third St.
Macon, GA 31202
Ph: (478)217-2072

Fax: (352)392-4873
E-mail: info@bwhlegal.com
URL: www.bwhlegal.com
Social Media: www.facebook.com/bwhlegal
www.linkedin.com/company/buzzell-welsh-hill-llp
twitter.com/bwhlegal

2769 ■ Buzzell, Welsh & Hill College Scholarship Program *(Graduate/Scholarship)*

Purpose: To help the next generation of college and technical students bring their academic and professional goals to life. **Focus:** General studies/Field of study not specified. **Qualif.:** Applicant must be a U.S. citizen enrolled at an accredited college or university in the United States. **Criteria:** Selection will be based on the best essay submitted.

Funds Avail.: $2,500. **Duration:** Annual. **Number Awarded:** 1. **To Apply:** Applicant must submit an essay on the topic for that scholarship year. Details on the essay subject and submission format can be found on the scholarship webpage. **Deadline:** April 30.

2770 ■ BWI Scholarship Fund

108 Ninth St.
Wilmette, IL 60091
Ph: (847)736-4142
E-mail: info@bwi.org
URL: www.bwi.org/scholarship-fund

2771 ■ BWI Scholarship *(Undergraduate, Community College, University/Scholarship)*

Purpose: To honor an undergraduate college student who has demonstrated a passion for the field of boating media and has a clear career goal in the areas of writing, photography, video, broadcasting, film, or art. **Focus:** General studies/Field of study not specified. **Qualif.:** Applicant must be enrolled in an undergraduate college or university program. **Criteria:** Ideal candidates will be talented communicators with boating interests who can demonstrate a record of accomplishment in, and commitment to, the field. Judges will look for applicants with talent, promise, and firsthand knowledge of the boating life. Applications will be judged on clarity, organization, and originality.

Funds Avail.: $2,000. **Number Awarded:** 1. **To Apply:** The application must be properly completed and include a recommendation from a faculty advisor, professor or school administrator; most recent transcript; examples of boating media work; one-page statement by the nominee that details career goals; optional letters of recommendation. **Deadline:** January 15. **Contact:** E-mail: info@bwi.org.

2772 ■ Cactus and Succulent Society of America (CSSA)

PO Box 1000
Claremont, CA 91711-1000
Ph: (626)405-3504
URL: www.cssainc.org
Social Media: www.facebook.com/
CactusAndSucculentSocietyOfAmerica
twitter.com/CactiSucculents

2773 ■ CSSA Research Grants Program *(Undergraduate, Graduate, Advanced Professional, Other/Grant)*

Purpose: To support research on succulent plants. **Focus:** Botany. **Qualif.:** Eligibility is open to all without respect to

Awards are arranged alphabetically below their administering organizations

gender, age, nationality, or affiliation. **Criteria:** Selection will be based on the grant applications being reviewed on the basis of merit of the proposal and the competence of the investigator(s) to conduct the proposed research.

Funds Avail.: $1,200 to $3,000. **Duration:** Semiannual. **To Apply:** Applicants must submit their respective research proposals on or before the deadline; details of the proposal and application are enumerated on the sponsor's website. **Contact:** Phuc Huynh, CSSA Research Committee Chair; Email: huynhphu7@gmail.com.

2774 ■ The Calgary Foundation
1180 - 105 12 Ave., SE
Calgary, AB, Canada T2G 1A1
Ph: (403)802-7700
Fax: (403)802-7701
E-mail: info@calgaryfoundation.org
URL: calgaryfoundation.org
Social Media: www.facebook.com/calgaryfoundation
www.instagram.com/calgfoundation
twitter.com/CalgFoundation
www.youtube.com/user/calfound

2775 ■ Kathryn Huget Leadership Award *(Master's, Doctorate/Award)*

Purpose: To improve the role of leadership in business and specifically the advancement of women in leadership roles. **Focus:** Leadership, Institutional and community.

Funds Avail.: Minimum of $1,000. **Duration:** Annual. **To Apply:** Applications can be submitted online and brief summary (one-page) of their involvement in business and views of leadership; two letters from business references. **Deadline:** June 30.

2776 ■ Calhoun Community College
6250 Hwy. 31 N
Tanner, AL 35671
Ph: (256)306-2500
Fax: (256)890-4700
Free: 800-626-3628
URL: www.calhoun.edu
Social Media: www.facebook.com/CalhounCollege
www.instagram.com/calhoun_college
twitter.com/CalhounCollege
www.youtube.com/user/CETV2

2777 ■ Calhoun Valedictorian, Salutatorian/Top 5% Scholarships *(Other/Scholarship)*

Purpose: To provide educational assistance to Calhoun students. **Focus:** General studies/Field of study not specified.

Funds Avail.: $1,000 ($500 per semester). **Duration:** Annual. **Number Awarded:** Varies. **Deadline:** February 1.

2778 ■ California Association for the Education of Young Children
950 Glenn Dr., Ste. 150
Folsom, CA 95630
Ph: (916)486-7750
Fax: (916)486-7765
URL: caeyc.org

Social Media: www.facebook.com/CAEYC
www.instagram.com/caaeyc
twitter.com/caeyc

2779 ■ CAEYC Presidents Education Award *(Graduate/Award, Scholarship)*

Purpose: To encourage pursuit of advanced educational degrees and leadership in the profession. **Focus:** Education. **Qualif.:** Applicant must be a current CAEYC member in good standing with a demonstrated financial need; current enrollment in an accredited academic degree program in Early Childhood Education or Child Development is required; must also have a record of service or contribution to AEYC at the Local Affiliate or State Affiliate level. **Criteria:** Selection will be based on the committee's criteria.

Funds Avail.: $1,000. **Duration:** Annual. **Number Awarded:** 1. **To Apply:** Applications can be submitted online; proof of current enrollment from the academic institution; copy of current membership card from NAEYC; two letters of recommendation. **Deadline:** February 20. **Remarks:** The award was established in honor of Docia Zavitkovsky, a president of Play Matters by CAEYC. **Contact:** CAEYC at (916) 486-7750, or email info@caeyc.org.

2780 ■ California Association for Health, Physical Education, Recreation, and Dance (CAHPERD)
1501 El Camino Ave., Ste. 3
Sacramento, CA 95815
Ph: (916)922-3596
Fax: (916)922-0133
E-mail: reception@cahperd.org
URL: www.cahperd.org
Social Media: www.facebook.com/CAHPERD
instagram.com/cahperd
twitter.com/cahperd

2781 ■ James Echols Scholarship Award *(Undergraduate/Recognition, Award, Scholarship)*

Purpose: To support the highest ranked minority applicants in their continuing education. **Focus:** Dance; Education, Physical; Health sciences. **Qualif.:** Applicants must be Asian, African American, Latino, or Native American students majoring in Health, Physical Education, Recreation or Dance; have completed (or be enrolled in) a minimum of 60 semester/90 quarter units of college work; be residents of California and attend a two- or four-year college/university within California; have a minimum 3.0 overall GPA; and be CAHPERD members for a minimum of 30 days prior to application. **Criteria:** Criteria for selection includes the following: scholastic proficiency; leadership ability; and, personal qualities.

Funds Avail.: $1,000. **Duration:** Annual. **To Apply:** Applicants must submit a completed application form, three letters of recommendation, and scholastic verification by the university registrar's office or transcripts of all college work. **Deadline:** November 1.

2782 ■ John F. Kennedy Scholarship Award *(Undergraduate/Recognition, Award, Scholarship)*

Purpose: To support the highest ranked undergraduate applicants in their continuing education. **Focus:** Dance; Education, Physical; Health sciences. **Qualif.:** Applicants must be undergraduate students majoring in Health, Physi-

Awards are arranged alphabetically below their administering organizations

cal Education, Recreation or Dance; have completed (or be enrolled in) a minimum of 60 semester/90 quarter units of college work; be residents of California and attend a two- or four-year college/university within California; have a minimum 3.0 overall GPA; and be CAHPERD members for a minimum of 30 days prior to application. **Criteria:** Criteria for selection includes the following: scholastic proficiency; leadership ability; and, personal qualities.

Funds Avail.: $1,000. **Duration:** Annual. **To Apply:** Applicants must submit a completed application form, three letters of recommendation, and scholastic verification by the university registrar's office or transcripts of all college work. **Deadline:** November 1.

2783 ■ Winifred Van Hagen/Rosalind Cassidy Scholarship Award *(Undergraduate, Graduate/ Recognition, Award)*

Purpose: To support the highest ranked applicants in their continuing education. **Focus:** Dance; Education, Physical; Health sciences. **Qualif.:** Applicants must be students majoring in Health, Physical Education, Recreation or Dance; have completed (or be enrolled in) a minimum of 60 semester/90 quarter units of college work; be residents of California and attend a two- or four-year college/ university within California; have a minimum 3.0 overall GPA; and be CAHPERD members for a minimum of 30 days prior to application. **Criteria:** Criteria for selection includes the following: scholastic proficiency; leadership ability; and, personal qualities.

Funds Avail.: $1,000. **Duration:** Annual. **To Apply:** Applicants must submit a completed application form, three letters of recommendation, and scholastic verification by the university registrar's office or transcripts of all college work. **Deadline:** November 1.

2784 ■ California Association of Pest Control Advisers (CAPCA)

2600 River Plaza Dr., Ste. 250
Sacramento, CA 95833
Ph: (916)928-1625
Fax: (916)928-0705
URL: capca.com
Social Media: www.facebook.com/CAPestControlAdvisers
www.instagram.com/capca_plant_health
twitter.com/CAPCA3
www.youtube.com/channel/UCR2re585N5DnlZH7xMltiXA

2785 ■ Stanley W. Strew Scholarship *(Undergraduate/Scholarship)*

Purpose: To support and promote agricultural pest control advisers or professional production consultants who serve California agricultural and horticultural producers. **Focus:** Agricultural sciences. **Qualif.:** Applicants must currently attend college in an agricultural or horticultural related field; master's degree or doctorate students are not eligible; students attending junior or community college are eligible; students who hold a DPR license (QAC, QAL, PCA, etc.). **Criteria:** Selection will be based on the committee's criteria.

Funds Avail.: $3,000. **Duration:** Annual. **To Apply:** Applicants must submit a completed application form; must include a current official transcript of records; must submit required letters of recommendation. **Deadline:** May 1. **Contact:** C/O CAPCA, 2600 River Plaza Drive, Suite 250, Sacramento, California 95833.

2786 ■ California Association of Private Postsecondary Schools (CAPPS)

2520 Venture Oaks., Ste. 170
Sacramento, CA 95833
E-mail: info@cappsonline.org
URL: www.cappsonline.org
Social Media: www.facebook.com/CAPPSonline
www.linkedin.com/company/california-association-private
  -postsecondary-schools?trk=biz-companies-cym
twitter.com/CAPPSonline

2787 ■ Sue Fleming Memorial Scholarship for Allied Health *(Undergraduate/Scholarship)*

Purpose: To helping students achieve their dreams and assist students to achieve their vocational objectives. **Focus:** Cosmetology; Health sciences; Nursing. **Qualif.:** Applicants must be enrolled in an allied health program at a CAPP's member School.

Remarks: The schlorship is established in memory of Sue Fleming. **Contact:** 2520 Venture Oaks, Stee 170, Sacramento, CA, 95833; E-mail: info@cappsonline.org; Phone: 916-447-5500.

2788 ■ California Change Lawyers

180 Howard St.,Ste.1220
San Francisco, CA 94105
URL: www.calbarfoundation.org
Social Media: facebook.com/CaliforniaBarFoundation
www.facebook.com/ChangeLawyers
twitter.com/ChangeLawyers
www.youtube.com/channel/
  UC04peLQXbn5j2SxwFVy1eQQ

2789 ■ California Bar Foundation 3L Diversity Scholarship *(Undergraduate/Scholarship)*

Purpose: To help offset high cost of law school education. **Focus:** Law. **Qualif.:** Candidate must be diverse 3L who intends to take the California bar exam, has a commitment to social justice/public interest, and can demonstrate their California-oriented career goals. **Criteria:** Selection will be based on the committee's criteria.

Funds Avail.: No specific amount. **Duration:** Annual. **Deadline:** February 15. **Contact:** Email: scholarships@ calbarfoundation.org.

2790 ■ California ChangeLawyers 1L scholarship *(Graduate/Scholarship)*

Purpose: To defray the cost of the students' 1L year. **Focus:** Law.

Funds Avail.: $7,500. **Duration:** Annual.

2791 ■ California Consumer Attorneys, P.C.

10900 Wilshire Blvd., Ste. 300
Los Angeles, CA 90024
Ph: (310)872-2600
Fax: (310)730-7377
E-mail: info@thelemonfirm.com
URL: www.thelemonfirm.com

2792 ■ California Consumer Attorney P.C.s Annual Consumer Advocacy Scholarship *(Undergraduate, Graduate/Scholarship)*

Purpose: To help law students with a passion for advocacy pay for college. **Focus:** Law. **Qualif.:** Applicant must be at

Awards are arranged alphabetically below their administering organizations

least 18 years old; enrolled in an accredited California university, college, or law school or intending to attend law school. **Criteria:** Writing that is creative, informative, clear, and logically organized.

Funds Avail.: $1,000. **Duration:** Annual. **Number Awarded:** 1. **To Apply:** Complete application and submit 400-600 word essay. Topic available online. **Deadline:** October 1. **Contact:** Sepehr Daghighian, Esq.; Email: scholarship@thelemonfirm.com; URL: thelemonfirm.com/scholarship/.

2793 ■ California Council of the Blind (CCB)
2143 Hurley Way, Ste. 250
Sacramento, CA 95825
Ph: (916)441-2100
Fax: (916)441-2188
Free: 800-221-6359
E-mail: ccotb@ccbnet.org
URL: ccbnet.org
Social Media: www.facebook.com/ccbnet.org
twitter.com/ccb_org

2794 ■ California Council of the Blind Scholarships
(Undergraduate, Graduate, Vocational/Occupational/Scholarship)

Purpose: To provide financial assistance to legally blind students in California for their educational expenses. **Focus:** General studies/Field of study not specified. **Qualif.:** Applicants must be legally blind and attending, or will be attending, a college, university, or vocational school; must be full-time undergraduate or graduate students; must be permanent California residents.

Funds Avail.: No specific amount. **Duration:** Annual. **To Apply:** Applicants must have doctor's statement or a statement from a qualified professional. Application details are available on the sponsor's website February 1st of each year. **Deadline:** May 15. **Remarks:** Established in 1934.

2795 ■ California Grocers Association (CGA)
1215 K St., Ste. 700
Sacramento, CA 95814-3946
Ph: (916)448-3545
Fax: (916)448-2793
URL: www.cagrocers.com
Social Media: www.facebook.com/CAGrocers
www.linkedin.com/company/california-grocers-association
twitter.com/CalGrocers

2796 ■ Al Plamann Legacy Scholarship
(Undergraduate/Scholarship)

Purpose: To provide proactive leadership, education, advocacy and information. **Focus:** General studies/Field of study not specified. **Qualif.:** Applicants must be high school seniors, college freshmen, sophomores and juniors who are dependents of employees or are themselves, employees of a CGA member company; must be planning to enroll as full-time college students at an accredited, non-profit college or university in the United States. **Criteria:** Recipients are selected based on academic merit, evidence of outstanding character and leadership potential.

Funds Avail.: $1,000. **To Apply:** Applicants must submit a completed application form.

2797 ■ Classic Wines of California Scholarships
(Undergraduate/Scholarship)

Purpose: To provide proactive leadership, education, advocacy and information. **Focus:** General studies/Field of study not specified. **Qualif.:** Applicants must be high school seniors, college freshmen, sophomores and juniors who are dependents of employees or are themselves employees of a CGA member company; must be planning to enroll as full-time college students at an accredited, non-profit college or university in the United States. **Criteria:** Recipients are selected based on academic merit, evidence of outstanding character and leadership potential.

To Apply: Applicants must submit a completed application form. **Contact:** CGA Educational Foundation; Email: foundation@cagrocers.com.

2798 ■ Don C. Beaver Memorial Scholarship
(Undergraduate/Scholarship)

Purpose: To provide financial aid to student who pursuing a career in grocery industry. **Focus:** General studies/Field of study not specified. **Qualif.:** Applicants must be a full-time college students who are also CGA member company employees and/or their dependent sons and daughters. **Criteria:** Recipients are selected based on academic merit, evidence of outstanding character and leadership potential.

Funds Avail.: $2,000. **To Apply:** Applicants must submit application via online.

2799 ■ Hall of Achievement Scholarship
(Undergraduate/Scholarship)

Purpose: To provide proactive leadership, education, advocacy and information. **Focus:** General studies/Field of study not specified. **Qualif.:** Applicants must be a full-time college students who are also CGA member company employees and/or their dependent sons and daughters; be an undergraduate or graduate student. **Criteria:** Recipients are selected based on academic merit, evidence of outstanding character and leadership potential.

Funds Avail.: $2,000. **Duration:** Annual. **Number Awarded:** Varies. **To Apply:** Applicants must submit application via online. **Deadline:** April 1. **Contact:** Email: donotreply@applyISTS.com and ContactUs@applyISTS.com.

2800 ■ Paul A. Hughes Memorial Scholarships
(Undergraduate/Scholarship)

Purpose: To provide proactive leadership, education, advocacy and information. **Focus:** General studies/Field of study not specified. **Qualif.:** Applicants must be high school seniors, college freshmen, sophomores and juniors who are dependents of employees or are themselves employees of a CGA member company; must be planning to enroll as full-time college students at an accredited, non-profit college or university in the United States. **Criteria:** Recipients are selected based on academic merit, evidence of outstanding character and leadership potential.

Funds Avail.: $1,000. **To Apply:** Applicants must submit a completed application form. **Deadline:** April 1.

2801 ■ Illuminator Educational Foundation Scholarships
(Undergraduate, Graduate/Scholarship)

Purpose: To provide proactive leadership, education, advocacy and information. **Focus:** General studies/Field of study not specified. **Qualif.:** Applicants must be a full-time college students who are also CGA member company employees and/or their dependent sons and daughters. **Criteria:** Recipients are selected based on academic merit, evidence of outstanding character and leadership potential.

Funds Avail.: $1,000. **Duration:** Annual. **Number Awarded:** varies. **To Apply:** Applicants must submit ap-

Awards are arranged alphabetically below their administering organizations

plication via online. **Deadline:** April 1. **Contact:** Email: donotreply@applyISTS.com and ContactUs@ applyISTS.com.

2802 ■ Jack H. Brown Future Leaders Scholarships
(Undergraduate/Scholarship)

Purpose: To provide proactive leadership, education, advocacy and information. **Focus:** General studies/Field of study not specified. **Qualif.:** Applicants must be a full-time college students who are also CGA member company employees and/or their dependent sons and daughters. **Criteria:** Recipients are selected based on academic merit, evidence of outstanding character and leadership potential.

Funds Avail.: $1,000. **To Apply:** Applicants must submit application via online. **Deadline:** April 1. **Contact:** Email: donotreply@applyISTS.com and ContactUs@ applyISTS.com.

2803 ■ Don Kaplan Legacy Scholarships
(Undergraduate/Scholarship)

Purpose: To provide proactive leadership, education, advocacy and information. **Focus:** General studies/Field of study not specified. **Qualif.:** Applicants must be high school seniors, college freshmen, sophomores and juniors who are dependents of employees or are themselves employees of a CGA member company; must be planning to enroll as full-time college students at an accredited, non-profit college or university in the United States.

To Apply: Applicants must submit a completed application form.

2804 ■ Lou & Dorie Amen Legacy Scholarship
(Undergraduate/Scholarship)

Purpose: To provide proactive leadership, education, advocacy and information. **Focus:** General studies/Field of study not specified.

Funds Avail.: $1,000. **Duration:** Annual. **Number Awarded:** Varies. **To Apply:** Applicants must submit a completed application form. **Deadline:** April 1. **Contact:** Email: donotreply@applyISTS.com and ContactUs@ applyISTS.com.

2805 ■ Bill MacAloney Legacy Scholarships
(Undergraduate/Scholarship)

Purpose: To provide proactive leadership, education, advocacy and information. **Focus:** General studies/Field of study not specified. **Qualif.:** Applicants must be high school seniors, college freshmen, sophomores and juniors who are dependents of employees or are themselves employees of a CGA member company; must be planning to enroll as full-time college students at an accredited, non-profit college or university in the United States. **Criteria:** Recipients are selected based on academic merit, evidence of outstanding character and leadership potential.

Funds Avail.: $1,000. **To Apply:** Applicants must submit a completed application form. **Deadline:** April 1.

2806 ■ Peter and Jody Larkin Legacy Scholarship
(Undergraduate/Scholarship)

Purpose: To provide proactive leadership, education, advocacy and information. **Focus:** General studies/Field of study not specified. **Qualif.:** Applicants must be high school seniors, college freshmen, sophomores and juniors who are dependents of employees or are themselves, employees of a CGA member company; must be planning to enroll as full-time college students at an accredited, non-profit

college or university in the United States. **Criteria:** Recipients are selected based on academic merit, evidence of outstanding character and leadership potential.

Funds Avail.: $1,000. **To Apply:** Applicants must submit a completed application form.

2807 ■ Roger K. Hughes Legacy Scholarship
(Undergraduate/Scholarship)

Purpose: To provide proactive leadership, education, advocacy and information. **Focus:** General studies/Field of study not specified. **Qualif.:** Applicants must be high school seniors, college freshmen, sophomores and juniors who are dependents of employees or are themselves, employees of a CGA member company; must be planning to enroll as full-time college students at an accredited, non-profit college or university in the United States. **Criteria:** Recipients are selected based on academic merit, evidence of outstanding character and leadership potential.

Funds Avail.: $1,000. **To Apply:** Applicants must submit a completed application form.

2808 ■ Save Mart Legacy Scholarships
(Undergraduate/Scholarship)

Purpose: To provide proactive leadership, education, advocacy and information. **Focus:** General studies/Field of study not specified. **Qualif.:** Applicants must be high school seniors, college freshmen, sophomores and juniors who are dependents of employees or are themselves employees of a CGA member company; must be planning to enroll as full-time college students at an accredited, non-profit college or university in the United States. **Criteria:** Recipients are selected based on academic merit, evidence of outstanding character and leadership potential.

Duration: Annual. **Number Awarded:** Varies. **To Apply:** Applicants must submit a completed application form. **Deadline:** April 1. **Contact:** Email: donotreply@applyISTS.com and ContactUs@applyISTS.com.

2809 ■ Trelut Family Legacy Scholarship
(Undergraduate/Scholarship)

Purpose: To provide proactive leadership, education, advocacy and information. **Focus:** General studies/Field of study not specified. **Qualif.:** Applicants must be high school seniors, college freshmen, sophomores and juniors who are dependents of employees or are themselves, employees of a CGA member company; must be planning to enroll as full-time college students at an accredited, non-profit college or university in the United States. **Criteria:** Recipients are selected based on academic merit, evidence of outstanding character and leadership potential.

Funds Avail.: $1,000. **To Apply:** Applicants must submit a completed application form.

2810 ■ Bob Wilson Legacy Scholarships
(Undergraduate/Scholarship)

Purpose: To provide proactive leadership, education, advocacy and information. **Focus:** General studies/Field of study not specified. **Qualif.:** Applicants must be high school seniors, college freshmen, sophomores and juniors who are dependents of employees or are themselves employees of a CGA member company; must be planning to enroll as full-time college students at an accredited, non-profit college or university in the United States. **Criteria:** Recipients are selected based on academic merit, evidence of outstanding character and leadership potential.

To Apply: Applicants must submit a completed application form. **Deadline:** April 1.

Awards are arranged alphabetically below their administering organizations

2811 ■ California Groundwater Association (CGA)

700 R St., Ste. 200
Sacramento, CA 95811
Ph: (916)231-2134
E-mail: info@groundh2o.org
URL: www.groundh2o.org

2812 ■ CGA Scholarships *(Undergraduate/ Scholarship)*

Purpose: To provide financial assistance to those students who are in need. **Focus:** General studies/Field of study not specified. **Qualif.:** Applicants must be California residents; must be pursuing a major course of study in groundwater; must have a family affiliation with a member of the California groundwater association; must show proof of current admission or entry acceptance at an educational institution within 6 months of scholarship award; grade point average to enter and retain eligibility shall be that grade point average required by the educational institution in its scholarship program; provide a 500 word essay demonstrating their interest in ground water technology. **Criteria:** Preference will be given to those who meet the criteria; Letters of recommendation from professor, teacher, employer, etc. are highly valued.

Funds Avail.: $2,000-$4,000. **Duration:** Annual. **Number Awarded:** Varies. **To Apply:** Applicants must obtain a CGA sponsor; submit transcript and letter of recommendation; and provide a 500 word essay about their interest in the groundwater field or their chosen field of study; must check the available website for the additional requirements. **Deadline:** March 15. **Remarks:** Established in 1989. **Contact:** California Groundwater Association, 1017 L Street, PMB #312, Sacramento, CA, 95814; Phone: 916-231-2134; Fax: 614-898-7791; E-mail: ecardwell@groundh2o.org.

2813 ■ California-Hawaii Elks Association (CHEA)

5450 E Lamona Ave.
Fresno, CA 93727
Ph: (559)255-4531
Fax: (559)456-2659
E-mail: chea@chea-elks.org
URL: www.chea-elks.org
Social Media: www.facebook.com/CaliforniaHawaiiElks
twitter.com/CalHawaiiElks

2814 ■ CHEA Undergraduate Scholarship Program for Students with Disabilities *(Undergraduate/ Scholarship)*

Purpose: To provide financial assistance to students with disabilities wishing to further their education. **Focus:** General studies/Field of study not specified. **Qualif.:** Applicants must be U.S. citizens and be residents of California or Hawaii; must have a physical impairment, neurological impairment, visual, hearing or speech-language disorder; must be current or graduating high school students; must have passed the General Educational Development (GED) Examination or the California High School Proficiency Examination (CHSPE). **Criteria:** Recipients will be selected based on academic achievement and financial need.

Funds Avail.: $1,000 to $2,000 each. **Duration:** Annual. **Number Awarded:** 20 to 30. **To Apply:** Application details area available online at: chea-elks.org/youth-activities/

scholarships/. **Deadline:** March 15. **Remarks:** Established in 1981. **Contact:** Jack Geiger, Chairman, CHEA Scholarship; Email: jackbgeiger@gmail.com.

2815 ■ CHEA Vocational Grants *(Vocational/ Occupational, Two Year College/Grant)*

Purpose: To assist students who are planning to pursue eligible vocational or technical courses. **Focus:** General studies/Field of study not specified. **Qualif.:** Applicants must be high school students; must be residents of California or Hawaii who are U.S. citizens; and must have plans to pursue vocational or technical courses. **Criteria:** Applicants will be judged based on motivation, need, skills, grades, completeness, and neatness of the given directions.

Funds Avail.: Up to $2,000 per year for up to two years. **Duration:** Annual. **To Apply:** Applicants must complete the application form; must fill-out the date of application issued; must submit a BPO Elks Lodge endorsement, transcript of grades or work records; must provide a budget for school year projected, financial information and exhibit. **Contact:** Jack Geiger, Chairman, CHEA Scholarship; Email: jackbgeiger@gmail.com.

2816 ■ Elks National Foundation Most Valuable Student Scholarship Contest *(Undergraduate/ Scholarship)*

Purpose: To support students with the highest-rated applicants in the competition each year. **Focus:** General studies/Field of study not specified. **Qualif.:** Applicants must be high school senior students who are citizens of the United States. **Criteria:** Selection will be based on scholarship, leadership, and financial need. Male and female applicants compete separately.

Funds Avail.: $200 to $700 (District Awards); $800 to $3,500 (State Awards); $4,000 to $50,000 (National Awards). **Duration:** Annual. **Number Awarded:** 114 (District); 286 (State); 500 (National). **To Apply:** Applications are available online at www.elks.org/enf/scholars/mvs.cfm. **Deadline:** November 15.

2817 ■ California Landscape Contractors Association (CLCA)

1491 River Park Dr., Ste. 100
Sacramento, CA 95815
Ph: (916)830-2780
Fax: (916)830-2788
E-mail: info@clca.org
URL: www.clca.org
Social Media: twitter.com/clcainside

2818 ■ CLCA Landscape Educational Advancement Foundation Scholarship *(Undergraduate/Scholarship)*

Purpose: To provide financial assistance to landscape programs for special needs. **Focus:** Landscape architecture and design. **Qualif.:** Applicants must be students attending an accredited California community college or state university, majoring in ornamental horticulture and taking a minimum of six units. **Criteria:** Selection must includes career goals, extracurricular activity, work experience, financial need and letters. of recommendation

Funds Avail.: No specific amount. **To Apply:** Applicants must fill-up completely the provided application form available online. **Deadline:** June 1. **Remarks:** Established in 1988. **Contact:** LEAF Foundation 1491 River Park Drive,

Awards are arranged alphabetically below their administering organizations

Suite 100 Sacramento, CA 95815 Email:leaf@clca.org.

2819 ■ California Narcotics Officers' Association (CNOA)

28245 Avenue Crocker, Ste. 230
Santa Clarita, CA 91355-1201
Ph: (661)775-6960
Fax: (661)775-1648
Free: 877-775-6272
E-mail: info@cnoa.org
URL: www.cnoa.org
Social Media: www.facebook.com/cnoainfo
twitter.com/cnoanews

2820 ■ CPYC/CNOA Youth Leadership Scholarship
(Undergraduate/Scholarship)

Purpose: To support twelfth grade students who have engaged in meaningful leadership and citizenship volunteer activities during the past year. **Focus:** General studies/ Field of study not specified. **Qualif.:** Applicants must be high school seniors who wish to pursue their studies in college; must be a biological or adopted child of an active or retired law enforcement officer within the State of California; must be California citizens. **Criteria:** Recipients are selected based on their essay they have received.

Funds Avail.: $500-$1,000. **Number Awarded:** Varies. **To Apply:** Applicants must submit a completed application form and essay.

2821 ■ California Police Youth Charities (CPYC)

1129 Firehouse Alley
Sacramento, CA 95814
Ph: (916)787-4201
URL: www.calpyc.com

2822 ■ CPYC/CNOA Youth Leadership Scholarship
(Undergraduate/Scholarship)

Purpose: To support twelfth grade students who have engaged in meaningful leadership and citizenship volunteer activities during the past year. **Focus:** General studies/ Field of study not specified. **Qualif.:** Applicants must be high school seniors who wish to pursue their studies in college; must be a biological or adopted child of an active or retired law enforcement officer within the State of California; must be California citizens. **Criteria:** Recipients are selected based on their essay they have received.

Funds Avail.: $500-$1,000. **Number Awarded:** Varies. **To Apply:** Applicants must submit a completed application form and essay.

2823 ■ California Psychological Association (CPA)

1231 I St., Ste. 204
Sacramento, CA 95814-2933
Ph: (916)286-7979
Fax: (916)286-7971
E-mail: cpa@cpapsych.org
URL: www.cpapsych.org
Social Media: www.facebook.com/pages/California
  -Psychological-Association/289165669667
twitter.com/jlccpa
twitter.com/CPA_psych

2824 ■ CPA-F Scholarship *(Graduate/Scholarship)*

Purpose: To strengthen the field of psychology by increasing the number of psychologists from California's ethnically diverse communities. **Focus:** Psychology. **Qualif.:** Applicants must be members of one or more established ethnic minority groups; be graduated from a regionally accredited undergraduate institution; have been accepted into a doctoral program in psychology at a regionally accredited or approved institution in the State of California; and, enrolled as full-time graduate students. **Criteria:** Selection will be judged on their potential for pursuing doctoral level work in psychology.

Funds Avail.: $2,000. **Number Awarded:** 3. **To Apply:** Applicants must submit a completed application form which includes an essay along with three letters of recommendation (Applicant Evaluation Form); official copy of most recent transcript (mailed directly from the academic institution to the Foundation); a letter of acceptance directly from the respective graduate program; and financial information. **Deadline:** November 3.

2825 ■ California School Library Association (CSLA)

6444 E Spring St., Ste. 237
Long Beach, CA 90815-1553
Fax: (888)655-8480
Free: 888-655-8480
E-mail: info@csla.net
URL: www.csla.net
Social Media: www.facebook.com/4CSLA
twitter.com/cslainfo

2826 ■ Above and Beyond Scholarship *(Graduate/ Scholarship)*

Purpose: To encourage practicing Teacher Librarians to pursue either a Master's or Doctorate degree in librarianship or in a related field. **Focus:** Library and archival sciences. **Qualif.:** Applicants must be professional members of the California School Library Association who are enrolled in advanced degree programs.

Funds Avail.: $1,000. **Duration:** Annual. **Number Awarded:** 1. **Deadline:** October 15.

2827 ■ Jewell Gardiner Scholarship *(Undergraduate/ Scholarship)*

Purpose: To support members with their teacher librarian credential program. **Focus:** Library and archival sciences. **Qualif.:** Applicants must be professional members of the California School Library Association who are enrolled in advanced degree programs.

Funds Avail.: $1,000. **Deadline:** October 15.

2828 ■ Leadership for Diversity Paraprofessional Scholarship *(Advanced Professional/Scholarship)*

Purpose: To assist school library paraprofessionals who reflect the diversity of California's multicultural, multilingual population. **Focus:** Library and archival sciences. **Qualif.:** Applicants must be a current CSLA member; be from a traditionally underrepresented group; be working in a classified position in the library field; be enrolled in a community college program for school library technical service certification. **Criteria:** Selection of applicants will be based on the criteria of the selection committee.

Funds Avail.: $1,500. **Duration:** Annual. **To Apply:** Applicants must provide two letters of recommendation and a

Awards are arranged alphabetically below their administering organizations

college transcript or other enrollment verification must be submitted; Candidates for letters of recommendations include current supervisor, course instructor, classroom teacher or principal. **Deadline:** October 15. **Contact:** Email the materials to info@csla.net, or fax them to 888-655-8480.

2829 ■ Leadership for Diversity TL Scholarship
(Master's/Scholarship)

Purpose: To assist teacher librarians who reflect the diversity of California's multicultural, multilingual population. **Focus:** Library and archival sciences. **Qualif.:** Applicants must be current CSLA member; be from a traditionally underrepresented group; be working, or intend to work, as a teacher librarian in California; be enrolled in a California Commission on Teacher Credentialing accredited teacher librarian credential program. **Criteria:** Selection of applicants will be based on the criteria of the selection committee.

Funds Avail.: $1,500. **Duration:** Annual. **To Apply:** Applicants must provide two letters of recommendation and a college transcript or other enrollment verification must be submitted; Candidates for letters of recommendations include current supervisor, course instructor, classroom teacher or principal. **Deadline:** October 15. **Contact:** Email the materials to info@csla.net, or fax them to 888-655-8480.

2830 ■ California Scottish Rite Foundation (CSRF)
2100 N Broadway, Ste. 350
Santa Ana, CA 92706
Ph: (714)547-7325
Fax: (714)541-7602
E-mail: info@casrf.org
URL: www.casr-foundation.org
Social Media: www.facebook.com/
  californiascottishritefoundation
www.instagram.com/ca_scottish_rite_foundation
www.youtube.com/channel/
  UCLZmEOvJjm1Fp8lwuF7ZAgw

2831 ■ Ruppert Scholarship *(Undergraduate/Scholarship)*

Purpose: To provide financial assistance to young men and women who want to pursue their education at the university and graduate level. **Focus:** General studies/Field of study not specified. **Qualif.:** Applicants must be undergraduate students who are residents of California state aged between 17 to 25 years old; must have a grade point average of 3.0 or better; study must be in medicine, engineering, forestry, and public School Administration only. **Criteria:** Applicants are evaluated based on demonstrated high ideals and ability; high grades in school; financial need and part-time employment.

Funds Avail.: $3,000 per year. **Duration:** One year. **To Apply:** Applicants must submit completed application form along with a certified transcript of grades for the previous semester, planned courses in the coming quarter/semester and current mailing address. **Deadline:** February 21. **Contact:** California Scottish Rite Foundation, 2100 N Broadway Ste. 350, Santa Ana, CA, 92706.

2832 ■ California Sea Grant
University of California
9500 Gilman Dr., Dept. 0232
La Jolla, CA 92093-0232

Ph: (858)534-4440
Fax: (858)534-2231
E-mail: jeckman@ucsd.edu
URL: www-csgc.ucsd.edu
Social Media: www.facebook.com/CASeaGrant
twitter.com/CASeaGrant

2833 ■ California Sea Grant State Fellowship
(Graduate/Fellowship)

Purpose: To provide a unique educational opportunity for graduate students who are interested both in marine resources and in the policy decisions affecting those resources. **Focus:** Water resources. **Qualif.:** Applications may be submitted by a graduate student close to completing degree (Masters, Ph.D., or J.D) in a field related to conservation, management, protection, stewardship, public policy, or law of marine and/or coastal environments, or areas that impact marine and coastal environments, at a California university. **Criteria:** Recipients will be evaluated based on submitted application and supporting documents; host selection will depend on the following categories: quality of the fellowship opportunity; level of educational benefit for the fellow; the host office's previous experience working with interns, fellows or other mentoring/educational programs; and level of financial commitment.

Funds Avail.: $46,860, health insurance reimbursement $3,120 and travel $2,400. **To Apply:** Applicants must submit personal and academic curriculum vitae (not to exceed two pages using 12 point font); a personal education and career goal statement that emphasizes the applicant's abilities and interests, and the applicant's expectations of the career development experience (1,000 words or less); two letters of professional recommendation, including one from the student's major professor. If no major professor exists, the faculty member who is most familiar with the applicant academically may be substituted; copies of all undergraduate and graduate student transcripts; unofficial copies will be accepted. **Deadline:** July 27. **Contact:** Email: sgproposal@ucsd.edu.

2834 ■ California Society of Radiologic Technologists (CSRT)
4747 N. First Street, Ste. 140
Fresno, CA 93726
Ph: (415)278-0441
E-mail: info@csrt.org
URL: www.csrt.org
Social Media: www.facebook.com/groups/298778630785
twitter.com/CSRTorg

2835 ■ Anna B. Ames Clinical Excellence Student Grant *(Undergraduate/Grant)*

Purpose: To provide financial assistance to radiologic science students enrolled in JRCERT-approved California schools. **Focus:** Radiology. **Criteria:** Selection will be based on the committee's criteria including Clinical Excellence and Sense of Leadership.

Funds Avail.: $500. **Duration:** Annual. **To Apply:** Applicants must submit a completed application form obtained from the CSRT office or website; must submit other required materials listed in the application for the Grant. **Deadline:** September 13. **Remarks:** The award was established in the memory of Anna B. Ames who lived a life of service to others as a radiographer, a founding leader of CSRT, and as a responsible and active citizen of her community.

Awards are arranged alphabetically below their administering organizations

Contact: California Society of Radiologic Technologists, ATTN: Scholarship Committee, 4747 N. First St., No.140 Fresno, CA, 93726; Phone: 415-278-0441; Email: info@csrt.org.

2836 ■ Ruth McMillan Academic Excellence Student Scholarship *(Undergraduate, Four Year College, Two Year College/Grant)*

Purpose: To provide financial assistance to radiologic science students enrolled in approved California schools. **Focus:** Radiology. **Qualif.:** Applicants must be CSRT members enrolled full-time in a California Department of Health Services Joint Review Committee for Education in Radiologic Technology (JRCERT) accredited education program of Radiologic Sciences; at least 6 months enrolled in the program at the time of receipt of the award; considered to possess exceptional skills in the clinical environment; considered ineligible if a holder of certification in another allied health profession that provides advanced standing in the said educational program. **Criteria:** Selection will be based on the committee's criteria including Academic Excellence and Leadership Attributes.

Funds Avail.: $500. **Duration:** Annual. **Number Awarded:** 1. **To Apply:** Applicants must submit a completed application form obtained from the CSRT office or website; must submit other required materials listed in the application for the Grant. **Deadline:** October 1. **Remarks:** The award was established in the memory of Ruth McMillan who lived a life of service to others as a radiographer, as an educator, and as a responsible and active citizen of her community. **Contact:** Email: info@csrt.org; URL: www.csrt.org/education/student-corner/scholarships-awards.

2837 ■ Superior District Legislative Mentoring Student Grants *(Undergraduate/Grant)*

Purpose: To provide an opportunity to radiologic science students enrolled in approved California schools, through financial assistance, in order for them to participate in the legislative process. **Focus:** Radiology.

Funds Avail.: No specific amount. **Remarks:** Established in 1944.

2838 ■ Superior District Legislative Mentoring Student Grants RT to DC *(Undergraduate/Grant)*

Purpose: To provide an opportunity to radiologic science students enrolled in approved California schools, through financial assistance, in order for them to participate in the legislative process. **Focus:** Radiology.

2839 ■ California State University San Marcos Alumni Association

333 S. Twin Oaks Valley Rd.
San Marcos, CA 92096
Ph: (760)750-4406
E-mail: alumni@csusm.edu
URL: www.csusm.edu
Social Media: www.facebook.com/CSUSMAlumniAssociation

2840 ■ Alumni Endowed Scholarship *(Undergraduate/Scholarship)*

Purpose: To support fellow and future alumni in furthering their education. **Focus:** General studies/Field of study not specified. **Qualif.:** Applicants must be alumni returning to school or current undergraduates.

Funds Avail.: No specific amount. **Duration:** Annual. **Number Awarded:** 5.

2841 ■ California Waterfowl Association (CWA)

1346 Blue Oaks Blvd.
Roseville, CA 95678
Ph: (916)648-1406
Fax: (916)648-1665
E-mail: cwa@calwaterfowl.org
URL: www.calwaterfowl.org
Social Media: www.facebook.com/CaliforniaWaterfowl
www.instagram.com/calwaterfowl
twitter.com/CalWaterfowl
www.youtube.com/user/CaliforniaWaterfowl

2842 ■ California Waterfowl Association College Scholarships *(Undergraduate/Scholarship)*

Purpose: To support student(s) with a desire to pursue a career in waterfowl or wetlands ecology. **Focus:** Botany; Ecology; Wildlife conservation, management, and science; Zoology. **Qualif.:** Applicants must be students with a desire to pursue a career in waterfowl or wetlands ecology. **Criteria:** Recipients are selected based on candidates resolve, high academic achievement and project merit.

Funds Avail.: $2,000 (Fist place); $1,000 (Second place). **Duration:** Annual. **Number Awarded:** 2. **To Apply:** Applicants must submit a. **Deadline:** October 31. **Contact:** California Waterfowl Association, Nicole Chavez, 1346 Blue Oaks Blvd., Roseville, CA, 95678; Email: nchavez@calwaterfowl.org.

2843 ■ Calvin Alumni Association (CAA)

3201 Burton Street, S.E.
Grand Rapids, MI 49546-4301
Ph: (616)526-6000
Fax: (616)526-8551
Free: 800-688-0122
E-mail: info@calvin.edu
URL: www.calvin.edu
Social Media: www.facebook.com/calvinuniversity
www.instagram.com/calvinuniversity
www.linkedin.com/school/calvin-college
twitter.com/Calvin_Uni
www.youtube.com/calvinuniversity

2844 ■ Calvin Alumni Association-Washington, D.C. Scholarships *(Undergraduate/Scholarship)*

Purpose: To support students who display evidence of faith commitment in the areas of leadership, volunteerism and service to the community. **Focus:** General studies/Field of study not specified. **Qualif.:** Applicant must be a current Calvin student accepted into the semester in Washington D.C.; must have cumulative GPA of 3.20 or higher; must demonstrate personal and intellectual maturity, seriousness of purpose as demonstrated in academic work, and interest in civic engagement.**Criteria:** Recipients are selected based on Christian commitment, scholastic achievement, personal character and professional promise.

Funds Avail.: $500. **Number Awarded:** Up to 2. **To Apply:** Applicants must submit the attached application with the required essay of up to 750 words, a resume and an unofficial transcript (available on portal). **Deadline:** October

Awards are arranged alphabetically below their administering organizations

11. **Contact:** Kevin den Dulk, Henry Institute Director; Phone:616-526-6234; Email:krd33@calvin.edu; or Ellen Hekman; Phone: 616-526-6565; Email: elh4@calvin.edu.

2845 ■ Camden County Bar Association (CCBA)

1040 N Kings Highway, Ste. 201
Cherry Hill, NJ 08034
Ph: (856)482-0620
E-mail: info@camdencountybar.org
URL: www.camdencountybar.org
Social Media: www.facebook.com/
  CamdenCountyBarAssociation
www.linkedin.com/in/camdencountybarassociation
twitter.com/camdencountybar

2846 ■ Benjamin Asbell Memorial Awards (Graduate, Undergraduate/Scholarship)

Purpose: To help law students defray the cost of law school tuition. **Focus:** Law; Law enforcement. **Qualif.:** Applicants for the first award must be day or evening students at the Rutgers-Camden School of Law, who are residents of South Jersey and must not be first-year students; must also demonstrate genuine financial need, scholastic ability and a history or desire to work in the areas of law enforcement and/or the administration of justice; for the second award, applicants must be students at any of the following law schools: Rutgers-Camden, Rutgers-Newark, Penn, Seton Hall, Temple, Villanova, or Widener.

Funds Avail.: $1,000 each. **Number Awarded:** 2. **To Apply:** Application form available on sponsor's website. **Deadline:** February 28. **Contact:** Executive Director-Law School Awards.

2847 ■ Eivind H. Barth, Jr. Memorial Award (Undergraduate, Graduate/Scholarship)

Purpose: To help law students defray the cost of law school tuition. **Focus:** Law. **Qualif.:** Applicants must be law students attending either the Rutgers-Camden School of Law or the Temple Law School; must demonstrate genuine financial need and show a bona fide intention to practice law in Camden County.

Funds Avail.: $1,000. **To Apply:** Application form available on sponsor's website. **Deadline:** February 28. **Contact:** Executive Director-Law School Awards.

2848 ■ Hon. Joseph W. Cowgill Memorial Award (Undergraduate, Graduate/Scholarship)

Purpose: To help law students defray the cost of law school tuition. **Focus:** Law. **Qualif.:** Applicants must be Rutgers-Camden School of Law students who are in the upper half of their class; must demonstrate genuine financial need as well as be a resident of Camden County.

Funds Avail.: $1,000. **To Apply:** Application form available on sponsor's website. **Deadline:** February 28. **Contact:** Executive Director-Law School Awards.

2849 ■ Hon. Ralph W.E. Donges Memorial Award (Undergraduate, Graduate/Scholarship)

Purpose: To help law students defray the cost of law school tuition. **Focus:** Law. **Qualif.:** Applicants must be part-time, evening law students attending one of the following law schools: Rutgers-Camden, Rutgers-Newark, Penn, Seton Hall, Temple, Villanova, or Widener. Applicants must show a bonafide intention to practice law in Camden County and

demonstrate genuine financial need as well as scholastic achievement.

Funds Avail.: $1,000. **To Apply:** Application form available on sponsor's website. **Deadline:** February 28. **Contact:** Executive Director-Law School Awards.

2850 ■ DuBois Brothers Award (Undergraduate, Graduate/Scholarship)

Purpose: To help law students defray the cost of law school tuition. **Focus:** Law. **Qualif.:** Applicants must be students of any Delaware Valley law school; must show a bonafide intention to practice law in South Jersey as well as exhibit professionalism and high character in their personal and academic lives; and must also demonstrate genuine financial need.

Funds Avail.: $1,000. **To Apply:** Application form available on sponsor's website. **Deadline:** February 28. **Contact:** Executive Director-Law School Awards.

2851 ■ George F. Kugler, Jr. Award (Undergraduate, Graduate/Scholarship)

Purpose: To help law students defray the cost of law school tuition. **Focus:** Law. **Qualif.:** Applicants must be second or third-year students attending any New Jersey law school; must demonstrate genuine financial need as well as a history of and/or desire to work in public service law.

Funds Avail.: $1,000. **To Apply:** Application form available on sponsor's website. **Deadline:** February 28. **Contact:** Executive Director-Law School Awards.

2852 ■ Harold and Harriet Plum Memorial Award (Undergraduate, Graduate/Scholarship)

Purpose: To help law students defray the cost of law school tuition. **Focus:** Law. **Qualif.:** Applicants must be students of any accredited law school; must demonstrate scholastic achievement as well as genuine financial need.

Funds Avail.: $1,000. **To Apply:** Application form available on sponsor's website. **Deadline:** February 28. **Contact:** Executive Director-Law School Awards.

2853 ■ Louis C. Portella Memorial Award (Undergraduate, Graduate/Scholarship)

Purpose: To help law students defray the cost of law school tuition. **Focus:** Law. **Qualif.:** Applicants must be second or third year full-time students at either Rutgers-Camden or Temple law schools who reside in and intend to practice law in Camden County; must be in good academic standing and active in both extracurricular and community activities.

Funds Avail.: $1,000. **To Apply:** Application form available on sponsor's website. **Deadline:** February 28. **Contact:** Executive Director-Law School Awards.

2854 ■ Hon. Rudolph J. Rossetti Memorial Award (Undergraduate, Graduate/Scholarship)

Purpose: To help law students defray the cost of law school tuition. **Focus:** Law. **Qualif.:** Applicants must be students attending any Delaware Valley law school. Applicants must demonstrate scholastic achievement and a genuine financial need.

Funds Avail.: $1,000. **To Apply:** Application form available on sponsor's website. **Deadline:** February 28. **Contact:** Executive Director-Law School Awards.

2855 ■ Jay A. Strassberg Memorial Scholarship (Undergraduate/Scholarship)

Purpose: To support law students pursuing degrees in Journalism, Public Relations, Advertising, Communications,

Awards are arranged alphabetically below their administering organizations

or Theater Arts. **Focus:** Advertising; Journalism; Law; Public relations. **Qualif.:** Applicants must be any Rutgers-Camden School of Law student or Temple University undergraduate students majoring in Journalism, Public Relations and Advertising Department of the School of Communications and Theater Arts who demonstrates both financial need and academic achievement. **Criteria:** Preference will be given to candidates from Camden County or the South Jersey area.

Duration: Annual. **To Apply:** Applicants must submit the application form along with following: a brief letter from the applicants detailing their personal and educational background, work history, course of study and plans after graduation; current transcript of undergraduate courses including GPA; letter of recommendation submitted by a member of the Journalism, Public Relations and Advertising Department at Temple University; a disclosure of financial information revealing all sources of funding being received or being offered to the applicants. **Deadline:** May 18. **Remarks:** The scholarship was established to honor Jay A. Strassberg, a 1961 Communications graduate of Temple University, who served as the Executive Director of the Camden County Bar Association from 1974 to 1998. **Contact:** Laurence Pelletier, Executive Director, Camden County Bar Foundation, 1040 N. Kings Hwy., Ste. 201, Cherry Hill, NJ, 08034; Phone: 856-482-0620; Fax: 856-482-0637; E-mail: lbp@camdencountybar.org.

2856 ■ Daniel B. Toll Memorial Award (Undergraduate, Graduate/Scholarship)

Purpose: To help law students defray the cost of law school tuition. **Focus:** Law. **Qualif.:** Applicants must be law students who are not in their final year of study; must be residents of South Jersey, preferably Camden County; must have demonstrated a commitment to the area in charitable, humanitarian, and community service activities.

Funds Avail.: $1,000. **To Apply:** Application form available on sponsor's website. **Deadline:** February 28. **Contact:** Executive Director-Law School Awards.

2857 ■ William Tomar Memorial Award (Undergraduate, Graduate/Scholarship)

Purpose: To help law students defray the cost of law school tuition. **Focus:** Law. **Qualif.:** Applicants must be incoming, full or part-time law students at Rutgers School of Law – Camden; should demonstrate genuine financial need and scholastic achievement from previous educational experiences.

Funds Avail.: $1,000. **To Apply:** An official acceptance letter from Rutgers must be submitted with the application form which is available on sponsor's website. **Deadline:** February 28. **Contact:** Executive Director-Law School Awards.

2858 ■ Bruce A. Wallace Memorial Award (Undergraduate, Graduate/Scholarship)

Purpose: To help law students defray the cost of law school tuition. **Focus:** Law. **Qualif.:** Applicants must be third-year students at Rutgers-Camden School of Law; must be from the South Jersey area; must be in the upper half of their class; must demonstrate genuine financial need.

Funds Avail.: $1,000. **To Apply:** Application form available on sponsor's website. **Deadline:** February 28. **Contact:** Executive Director-Law School Awards.

2859 ■ Camden County College Camden City Campus (CCC)

200 N Broadway
Camden, NJ 08102
Ph: (856)338-1817
URL: www.camdencc.edu
Social Media: www.facebook.com/camdencc
www.instagram.com/camdencc
twitter.com/camdencc
www.youtube.com/camdencc

2860 ■ Camden County College Foundation Scholarships (Undergraduate/Scholarship, Award)

Purpose: To provide support to the outstanding individuals who want to pursue higher education and career goals at CCC. **Focus:** General studies/Field of study not specified. **Criteria:** Selection is based on demonstrate a financial need, but others are awarded to students possessing academic merit.

Funds Avail.: No specific amount. **Duration:** Annual. **To Apply:** Students have to apply through the online application form. **Contact:** Melissa Daly at mdaly@camdencc.edu. Phone: 856-227-7200, ext. 4946.

2861 ■ Cameco Corp.

2121-11th St. W
Saskatoon, SK, Canada S7M 1J3
Ph: (306)956-6200
Fax: (306)956-6201
URL: www.cameco.com
Social Media: www.facebook.com/Cameco.Careers
instagram.com/camecocommunity
www.linkedin.com/company/cameco-corporation
twitter.com/cameconews
youtube.com/user/CamecoCorporation

2862 ■ Bernard Michel Scholarship (Undergraduate/Scholarship)

Purpose: To provide support for a Saskatchewan aboriginal student entering their second or third year of study. **Focus:** Engineering; Liberal arts. **Qualif.:** Applicants must be Saskatchewan aboriginal students entering their first or second year of study within the Colleges of Engineering, Commerce or Arts and Science at the University of Saskatchewan. **Criteria:** Applicants will be selected based on scholarship application form and requirements.

Funds Avail.: $5,000. **Number Awarded:** 2. **To Apply:** Applicants must complete the application form available online and must be sent to University of Saskatchewan. **Deadline:** June 1. **Contact:** Phone: 306-966-1212; Email: awards@usask.ca.

2863 ■ Cameco Corporation Scholarships in the Geological Sciences - Continuing Students (Undergraduate/Scholarship)

Purpose: To support students who want to pursue their career in geological sciences. **Focus:** Geology. **Qualif.:** Applicants must be full-time students who are Canadian citizens entering their second year of university study and pursuing Bachelor of Science degrees; must have declared majors in the geological sciences; must be registered in 200 level courses related to their majors; must have a sessional weighted average of at least 70% for all credit units

Awards are arranged alphabetically below their administering organizations

attempted in the last regular session. **Criteria:** Applicants will be selected based on scholarship application form and requirements.

Funds Avail.: $5,000. **Duration:** Annual. **Number Awarded:** 2. **To Apply:** Applications form can be obtained from the Continuing Students, Student Central, University of Saskatchewan. **Deadline:** June 1. **Contact:** Continuing Students, Student Central, University of Saskatchewan, 105 Administration Place, Saskatoon, SK S7N 5A2; Phone: 306-966-1212; Email:askus@usask.ca.

2864 ■ Cameco Corporation Scholarships in the Geological Sciences - Entering Students
(Undergraduate/Scholarship)

Purpose: To support students who want to pursue their career in geological sciences. **Focus:** Geology. **Qualif.:** Applicants must be full-time students who are Canadian citizens pursuing Bachelor of Science degrees and are entering their first year of university study and are registered in specified courses as outlined in guidelines. **Criteria:** Applicants will be selected based on scholarship application form and requirements.

Funds Avail.: $5,000. **Duration:** Annual. **Number Awarded:** 2. **To Apply:** Applications form can be obtained from the Recruitment and Admissions, University of Saskatchewan. **Deadline:** June 1. **Contact:** Phone: 306-966-5788; Email: admissions@usask.ca.

2865 ■ Camp Network
1033 Demonbreun St., Ste. 300
Nashville, TN 37203
URL: www.campnetwork.com
Social Media: www.facebook.com/campnetwork
twitter.com/campnetwork

2866 ■ Camp Network Counselor Appreciation Scholarships (Undergraduate/Scholarship)

Purpose: To reward and support the education of select few counselors. **Focus:** General studies/Field of study not specified. **Qualif.:** Applicants must be U.S. citizens who are currently high school seniors attending a school in the United States; must be anticipating completion of high school diploma at time of application; and must currently have a minimum of 3.0 GPA. **Criteria:** Selection will be based on the applicants' exhibited humility, passion, unity, servanthood, and thankfulness.

Funds Avail.: $1,000. **To Apply:** Applicants must create a short, exciting video (3-5 minutes max) that explains their experiences as camp counselors, how they exhibit the five qualities above, and how they intend to use the college degree. Upload the video to DropBox.com, YouTube, Vimeo, or another reputable file sharing service (make sure the visibility is set to public). To submit your application send an email to the contact provided. **Deadline:** November 1. **Contact:** Send e-mail to Andrew Downing at scholarships@campnetwork.com.

2867 ■ Campus Compact
45 Temple Pl.
Boston, MA 02111
Ph: (617)357-1881
Fax: (617)357-1889
E-mail: campus@compact.org
URL: www.compact.org
Social Media: www.facebook.com/CampusCompact
www.linkedin.com/company/campus-compact
twitter.com/campus_compact

2868 ■ Newman Civic Fellowship (Undergraduate/Fellowship)

Purpose: To honor inspiring college student leaders who have demonstrated an investment in finding solutions for challenges facing communities throughout the country. **Focus:** General studies/Field of study not specified. **Qualif.:** Applicants must be undergraduate students at Campus Compact member colleges and universities.

Funds Avail.: No specific amount. **Duration:** Annual. **Number Awarded:** Varies. **To Apply:** Applicants may contact the Campus Compact for the application process and other information. **Contact:** Molly Leiper, Communications Manager; Email:mleiper@compact.org.

2869 ■ Campus Pride
1433 Emerywood Dr.
Charlotte, NC 28210
Ph: (704)277-6710
E-mail: info@campuspride.org
URL: www.campuspride.org
Social Media: www.facebook.com/LeadwithPRIDE
www.instagram.com/campuspride
www.linkedin.com/company/campus-pride
twitter.com/campuspride
www.youtube.com/campuspride

2870 ■ Campus Pride Summer Fellows (Undergraduate, Graduate, Postgraduate/Fellowship)

Purpose: For LGBTQ+ college students and allies with a desire to learn more about campus organizing and social justice. **Focus:** Leadership, Institutional and community; Nonprofit sector. **Qualif.:** Requires strong writing, editing, and communication skills, as well as adaptability, self-motivation, and knowledge of the various Campus Pride programs; must work 40 hours per week from the office in Charlotte, NC.

Funds Avail.: $650 monthly stipend plus host housing. **Number Awarded:** Varies. **To Apply:** Submit application online with cover letter detailing your interest and qualifications, professional resume, and two letters of recommendations from faculty/staff/mentors. **Deadline:** April 8. **Remarks:** Due to COVID, in person Summer Fellows applications may not be accepted. Non-paid remote opportunities are still an available. **Contact:** Email: ally@campuspride.org; URL: www.campuspride.org/connect/fellowships/.

2871 ■ Canada Council for the Arts
150 Elgin St.
Ottawa, ON, Canada K1P 5V8
Ph: (613)566-4414
Fax: (613)566-4390
Free: 800-263-5588
E-mail: info@canadacouncil.ca
URL: canadacouncil.ca
Social Media: www.facebook.com/canadacouncil
www.linkedin.com/company/canada-council-for-the-arts
twitter.com/canadacouncil

2872 ■ Peter Dwyer Scholarships (Undergraduate/Scholarship)

Purpose: To support the most promising students at the National Ballet School and the National Theatre School.

Awards are arranged alphabetically below their administering organizations

Focus: Dance; Theater arts. **Qualif.:** Applicants must be most promising students at both the National Ballet School and the National Theatre School of Canada.

Funds Avail.: Up to 10,000 Canadian Dollars. **Duration:** Annual. **Contact:** Sarah Brown, Program Officer, Prizes, Canada Council for the Arts, 150 Elgin St., PO Box 1047, Ottawa, ON, K1P 5V8; Phone: 613-566-4414, ext. 6004; Toll free: 800-263-5588, ext. 6004; TTY: 866-585-5559; Email: sarah.brown@canadacouncil.ca.

2873 ■ J. B. C. Watkins Award *(Professional development/Fellowship)*

Purpose: To support professional Canadian artists in any field who are graduates of any Canadian university, postsecondary art institution, or training school and who choose to carry out their postgraduate studies any country other than Canada. **Focus:** Art. **Qualif.:** Applicant must be Canadian professional architect wishing to pursue post-graduate studies outside Canada, ideally in Denmark, Norway, Sweden or Iceland; Canada council for the Arts, you must be a Canadian citizen or have permanent resident status; must also be an architecture graduate of a Canadian university, postsecondary art institution or training school. **Criteria:** Preference will be given to those wishing to carry out their studies in Denmark, Norway, Sweden or Iceland.

Funds Avail.: 5,000 Canadian Dollars. **Duration:** Annual. **Number Awarded:** Varies. **To Apply:** Nominator is responsible for providing all the information and support material requested; Canada council will make eligibility decisions based on the information provided in the nomination; printed on one side only; separate sheets of white paper (letter format, 81/2 x 11 inches). **Deadline:** 'October 1. **Contact:** Sarah Brown, Program Officer, Prizes, Canada Council for the Arts, 150 Elgin St., PO Box 1047, Ottawa, ON, K1P 5V8; Phone: 613-566-4414, ext. 6004; Toll free: 800-263-5588, ext. 6004; TTY: 866-585-5559; Email: sarah.brown@canadacouncil.ca.

2874 ■ Canadian Aeronautics and Space Institute (CASI)
350 Terry Fox Dr., Ste. 104
Kanata, ON, Canada K2K 2W5
Ph: (613)591-8787
Fax: (613)591-7291
E-mail: casi@casi.ca
URL: www.casi.ca
Social Media: www.facebook.com/Canadian-Aeronautics
   -and-Space-Institute-428049723903708
www.linkedin.com/company/canadian-aeronautics-and
   -space-institute/
twitter.com/CASInstitute
www.youtube.com/channel/
   UCsOK2VxIhQV0ERvKSSNN1oQ

2875 ■ Charles Luttman Scholarship
(Undergraduate/Scholarship)

Purpose: To support students who demonstrated qualities of leadership and involvement in any area of student affairs and excellence in communication and organizational skills. **Focus:** General studies/Field of study not specified. **Qualif.:** Applicants must be Canadian citizens and student members in good standing of CASI. **Criteria:** Selection will be based on the committee's criteria.

Funds Avail.: $3,000. **Duration:** Annual. **To Apply:** Applicants should provide a short outline of their activities and

accomplishments in each of three areas: technical achievement; leadership and involvement in student affairs; communication and organizational skills; a statement about the goals the students have set for themselves should be included. **Deadline:** March 16.

2876 ■ Canadian Anesthesiologists Society (CAS)
1 Eglinton Ave. E, Ste. 208
Toronto, ON, Canada M4P 3A1
URL: www.cas.ca
Social Media: twitter.com/CASUpdate

2877 ■ Baxter Corporation Canadian Research Awards in Anesthesia *(Other/Award, Monetary)*

Purpose: To support anesthesia-related research in Canada. **Focus:** Anesthesiology. **Qualif.:** Applicants must be associate/active members of CAS who propose to carry out an original project and are eligible for the New Investigator Awards. **Criteria:** Award winner is chosen based on the scientific merit, importance, and feasibility of the project.

Duration: Annual. **To Apply:** Application forms are available online. Applicants must submit documentation of institutional approval of human and/or animal experimentation.

2878 ■ CAS/GE Healthcare Canada Inc. Research Awards *(Other/Award)*

Purpose: To provide support for infrastructure costs related to a specific research project or program. **Focus:** Medical research. **Qualif.:** Applicants must be associate or active members of the society who are eligible for an award in the field of perioperative imaging related to anesthesia and/or critical care. **Criteria:** Selection is chosen based on scientific merit, importance, and feasibility of the project.

Funds Avail.: No specific amount. **Duration:** Annual. **To Apply:** Application forms are available online; must submit documentation of institutional approval of human and or animal experimentation. **Contact:** For further information, applicants may send an e-mail at research@cas.ca.

2879 ■ CAS Research Award in Neuroanesthesia *(Other/Award)*

Purpose: To support anesthesia-related research in Canada. **Focus:** Anesthesiology.
Funds Avail.: Up to $10,000. **Duration:** Annual.

2880 ■ CAS/Vitaid-LMA Residents' Research Grant Competition *(Other/Award)*

Purpose: To promote and support anesthesia-related research performed by a resident in Canada. **Focus:** Anesthesiology. **Qualif.:** Nominees must be resident physicians who are in good standing at a Canadian university department of anesthesia. Nominees must be members of the CAS and must propose to carry out an original project within Canada. **Criteria:** Award winner is chosen based on scientific merit, importance, and feasibility of the project.

To Apply: Application forms are available online. Applicants must submit a curriculum vitae; letter from the supervisor that specifies the extent to which the applicant will contribute towards the research project; letter from the residency program director.

2881 ■ David S. Sheridan Canadian Research Awards *(Other/Award)*

Purpose: To support anesthesia-related research in Canada. **Focus:** Anesthesiology. **Qualif.:** Applicants must

Awards are arranged alphabetically below their administering organizations

be associate/active members of CAS who propose to carry out an original project and are eligible for the New Investigator Awards. **Criteria:** Award winner is chosen based on the scientific merit, importance, and feasibility of the project.

Funds Avail.: 10,000 Canadian Dollars. **Duration:** Annual. **To Apply:** Applicants must fill out the application forms available online. Applicants must submit documentation of institutional approval of human and/or animal experimentation.

2882 ■ Canadian Association of Black Lawyers (CABL)

20 Toronto St.
Toronto, ON, Canada M5C 2B8
E-mail: info@cabl.ca
URL: www.cabl.ca
Social Media: www.facebook.com/Canadian-Association-of
-Black-Lawyers-150574661678680
www.instagram.com/cablnational
twitter.com/cablnational

2883 ■ Lucie and Thornton Blackburn Scholarship (CABL) *(Graduate, Juris Doctorate/Scholarship)*

Purpose: To financially assist minority students pursuing an education at a Canadian law school. **Focus:** Law. **Qualif.:** Applicants must be minority students entering their second year of study in an LLB or JD program at a Canadian law school. **Criteria:** Selection will be based on financial need; determination of the scholarship recipient will be made by the scholarship awards committee.

Funds Avail.: $5,000. **Duration:** Annual. **To Apply:** Applicants must submit an application form along with an essay, in the context of a globalized economy and local laws, discuss the pros and cons of the policy rational behind the Supreme Court of Canada's findings in Google Inc. v. Equustek Solutions Inc. Do you agree or disagree with the decision, and why? (approximately 750-1250 words). **Contact:** Lucie and Thornton Blackburn Scholarship Awards Committee, c/o Canadian Association of Black Lawyers, 20 Toronto St., Ste. 300, Toronto, Ontario, M5C 2B8; E-mail: info@cabl.ca. Please name your PDF file as follows: LAST-NAME_BlackburnScholarship.pdf, substituting your own last name in the title.

2884 ■ Canadian Association for Business Economics (CABE)

31 Adelaide St. E
Toronto, ON, Canada M5C 2J1
Free: 855-222-3321
E-mail: info@cabe.ca
URL: www.cabe.ca
Social Media: www.facebook.com/CABEconomics
www.linkedin.com/company/canadian-association-for
-business-economics/
twitter.com/CABE_Economics

2885 ■ Doug Purvis Prize *(Other/Prize)*

Purpose: To recognize authors who made contributions to Canadian economic policy. **Focus:** Economics. **Qualif.:** Applicants must have written book(s) in relevance to Canadian economic policy; must have had a series of articles in newspapers or magazines, journals, or govern-

ment studies including monographs done for Royal Commissions, other official documents and think-tank reports; materials must be primarily, but not exclusively in the public domain.

Funds Avail.: 15,000 Canadian Dollars. **Duration:** Annual. **To Apply:** Electronic submissions must be in PDF format including the full details of the nominees, name and address of the nominator and affiliation. **Deadline:** March 15. **Remarks:** The award was established in honour and memory of noted Canadian economist Doug Purvis. Established in 1994. **Contact:** Vivian Tran; Email: cea.execdir@gmail.com.

2886 ■ Canadian Association of Cardiovascular Prevention and Rehabilitation (CACPR)

20 Crown Steel Dr. Unit 6
Markham, ON, Canada L3R 9X9
URL: www.cacpr.ca

2887 ■ Canadian Association of Cardiac Rehabilitation Graduate Scholarship Awards *(Graduate/Scholarship)*

Purpose: To recognize the research of graduate students in the area of cardiac rehabilitation and to reflect CACR's support of their educational endeavors in this area. **Focus:** Medicine, Cardiology. **Qualif.:** Applicants must be a member of the CACR. **Criteria:** Selection will be based on strength of research methodology; feasibility of successfully completing the study; importance and relevance to the field of cardiac rehabilitation; strength of the letter of support; and potential for continuing to make a valuable contribution to the field of cardiac rehabilitation.

Funds Avail.: $3,000. **Duration:** Annual. **Number Awarded:** 4. **To Apply:** Applicants must submit the auto-fill abstract form in English in word format together with one letter of reference from a current supervisor; and letter of application: a letter outlining the student's current research in the area of cardiac rehabilitation and future directions in this field; the letter should be maximum of two pages in length and must specifically address the rating criteria related to methodology, feasibility, importance and relevance. **Deadline:** May 2. **Contact:** Marilyn Thomas, 204-488-5857; email: mthomas@cacr.ca.

2888 ■ Canadian Association of Critical Care Nurses (CACCN)

PO Box 25322
London, ON, Canada N6B 6B1
Ph: (519)649-5284
Fax: (519)649-1458
Free: 866-477-9077
E-mail: caccn@caccn.ca
URL: www.caccn.ca
Social Media: www.facebook.com/CanACCN
www.youtube.com/channel/UCSLRIj-j606rWo_gQmndECg
twitter.com/CACCN1

2889 ■ CACCN/Baxter Corporation Guardian Scholarship *(Professional development/Scholarship)*

Purpose: To support an individual or an interdisciplinary team who propose to make significant contributions toward patient and/or caregiver safety in the critical care environment. **Focus:** Nursing. **Qualif.:** Applicant must be a member of CACCN in good standing for a minimum of one

Awards are arranged alphabetically below their administering organizations

year; be licensed to practice nursing in Canada; CNA certification preferred. **Criteria:** Selections will be reviewed for their contribution to patient safety, evidence of transferability of the project, innovation, sustainability, and leadership withiin critical care practice areas.

Funds Avail.: $2,500 each. **Duration:** Annual. **Number Awarded:** Up to 2. **Deadline:** June 1.

2890 ■ CACCN Educational Awards *(Professional development/Grant)*

Purpose: To provide funds to assist critical care nurses to attend continuing education programs at the baccalaureate, masters, and doctorate of nursing levels. **Focus:** Nursing. **Qualif.:** Applicants must be an critical care nurses in Canada; active member of CACCN in good standing for a minimum of one (1) year; accepted to an accredited school of nursing or recognized critical care program. **Criteria:** Recipients will be selected based on the quality of their submissions.

Funds Avail.: 1,000 Canadian dollars. **Duration:** Annual. **Number Awarded:** 2. **To Apply:** Applicants must submit a letter of reference from current employer; Oral and Poster Presentations will be considered; Presentations considered for merit points; incomplete applications will not be considered. **Deadline:** January 31 and September 1. **Contact:** Send applications to CACCN National Office; Email: caccn@caccn.ca or Fax: 519-649-1458 or Mail to: CACCN, PO Box 25322, London, ON, N6C 6B1.

2891 ■ CACCN Research Grant *(Professional development/Grant)*

Purpose: To support the research activities of a CACCN member that is relevant to the practice of critical care nursing. **Focus:** Nursing. **Qualif.:** Applicants must be a member of CACCN in good standing for a minimum of one year; licensed to practice nursing in Canada; Conduct the research in Canada; members enrolled in a graduate nursing program. **Criteria:** Selection will be based on the committee's criteria.

Funds Avail.: 2,500 Canadian Dollars. **Duration:** Annual. **To Apply:** Applicants must completed application form; Proof of CACCN active membership and Canadian citizenship; grant proposal not in excess of five single spaced pages; letter of support from the sponsoring agency; brief Curriculum Vitae for the principal investigator and co-investigator. **Deadline:** June 1. **Contact:** Send applications to CACCN National Office; Email: caccn@caccn.ca or Fax: 519-649-1458 or Mail to: CACCN, PO Box 25322, London, ON, N6C 6B1.

2892 ■ Canadian Association of Gerontology (CAG)

c/o Department of Occupational Science & Occupational Therapy
University of Toronto
Toronto, ON, Canada M5G 1V7
Ph: (855)224-2240
URL: cagacg.ca
Social Media: www.facebook.com/CdnAssocGero
www.linkedin.com/company/canadian-association-on
  -gerontology
twitter.com/cagacg

2893 ■ Margery Boyce Bursary Award *(Graduate/ Award, Scholarship)*

Purpose: To support post-baccalaureate students who have made a significant contribution to their community through volunteer activities. **Focus:** Gerontology. **Qualif.:** Applicant must be a CAG member; must be registered, or formally accepted as a full-time student in a post-baccalaureate program at a recognized Canadian university at the time the application is submitted; must be a Canadian citizen or have permanent resident status; must have made a significant contribution to their community through volunteer activities with or on behalf of seniors and who are registered in a program of study focused on aging or the aged. **Criteria:** Recipient will be recommended by the awards committee; preference will be given to persons returning to university after an absence from formal study.

Funds Avail.: $500. **Duration:** Annual. **To Apply:** Applicants must submit an application form with transcripts; proof of registration or acceptance in a university program; letter of support from the faculty supervisor or program Chair which addresses the criteria for the bursary and the letter of support from any community organization that can address the amount and quality of the applicant's volunteer activities as related to the criteria. Applicants must submit a photo and a short biographical profile for the CAG Newsletter. **Deadline:** July 3. **Contact:** URL: cagacg.ca/awards/boyce/.

2894 ■ Donald Menzies Bursary Award *(Postgraduate/Scholarship, Award)*

Purpose: To support post-baccalaureate students registered in a program of study focused on aging or the aged. **Focus:** Gerontology. **Qualif.:** Applicant must be a CAG member; must be registered, or formally accepted as a full-time student in a post-baccalaureate program at a recognized Canadian university at the time the application is submitted; must be a Canadian citizen or have permanent resident status. **Criteria:** Recipient will be selected by the Awards Committee based on academic merit among students demonstrating financial need.

Funds Avail.: $1,500. **Duration:** Annual. **To Apply:** Applicants must submit the application form with the university transcript; proof of registration, or acceptance in university program; a letter of support from the faculty supervisor; and an approved thesis/research project proposal (if applicable). Applicants must submit a photo and a short biographical profile for the CAG Newsletter. **Deadline:** July 3. **Contact:** URL: cagacg.ca/awards/menzies/.

2895 ■ Schlegel-UW RIA Scholarship *(Doctorate/ Scholarship)*

Purpose: To support students completing their first year of a doctoral program with a program of study related to gerontology. **Focus:** Gerontology. **Qualif.:** Applicant must be a Canadian citizen or have a permanent resident status; must be CAG members; must be completing their first year of a doctoral program, with a program of study relevant to the field of gerontology; must have a minimum of 80% academic average in the program of study preceding the doctoral program; and must have at least two years of practice and/or volunteer service with older adults. **Criteria:** Selection will be based on the committee's criteria.

Funds Avail.: $1,000. **Duration:** Annual. **To Apply:** Applicants must submit one original version of each of the following documents together with the online application form; all university transcripts; proof of acceptance in the first year of a doctoral program; a letter of support from the previous or current faculty supervisor or program chair which addresses program of study and its relevance to the field of gerontology; at least 1 letter of support from any community organizations (on letterhead) who can address

Awards are arranged alphabetically below their administering organizations

the amount, quality and duration of the volunteer activities as related to the criteria; must submit a photo and a short biographical profile for the CAG Newsletter. **Deadline:** July 3. **Contact:** URL: cagacg.ca/awards/schlegel-ria/.

2896 ■ Canadian Association of Insolvency and Restructuring Professionals (CAIRP)
277 Wellington St. W
Toronto, ON, Canada M5V 3H2
URL: www.cairp.ca

2897 ■ Lloyd Houlden Fellowship *(Advanced Professional, Professional development/Fellowship)*

Purpose: To support an original analysis of innovative ways to improve the insolvency system. **Focus:** Banking; Economics; Law. **Qualif.:** Applicants must be the authors from any part of the insolvency community – practicing Licensed Insolvency Trustees and lawyers, as well as academics and students.

Funds Avail.: $20,000. **Duration:** Annual. **Contact:** The Fellowship is named after the late Justice of the Court of Appeal of Ontario, Lloyd Houlden who had a long and distinguished career both as a practicing jurist and author specializing in insolvency.

2898 ■ Canadian Association of Law Libraries (CALL)
1 Eglinton Avenue East, Suite 705
Toronto, ON, Canada M4P 1E8
URL: www.callacbd.ca

2899 ■ CALL/ACBD Education Reserve Fund Grant *(Professional development/Grant)*

Purpose: To provide funding support for members of CALL/ACBD intending to further their education in pursuits that do not fit the guidelines of the association's already established scholarships. **Focus:** Law. **Qualif.:** Applicants must be members of the Canadian Association of Law Libraries/Association canadienne des bibliotheques de droit who have been in good standing for a minimum of 12 months; pursuits must be relevant to their career in law libraries or law librarianship. **Criteria:** Selection will be based on merit.

Funds Avail.: No specific amount. **Duration:** Annual. **Number Awarded:** Varies. **To Apply:** Application form is available online; must submit completed application form along with a resume and a letter of support from your employer. **Deadline:** April 1. **Contact:** National Office: 1 Eglinton Avenue East, Suite 705; Toronto ON M4P 3A1; Tel: 647.346.8723; Email: office@callacbd.ca.; Completed applications to: Dolores Noga, Chair, CALL/ACBD Scholarships and Awards Committee; Email: dnoga@mross.com.

2900 ■ CALL/ACBD Research Grants *(Graduate/Grant)*

Purpose: To provide members with financial assistance to carry out research in areas of interest to members and to the association. **Focus:** Law. **Qualif.:** Applicants must be members of CALL/ACBD who are intending to do research projects that promote an understanding of legal information sources or law librarianship. **Criteria:** Selection will be based on the recommendation of the committee to promote proposed research.

Funds Avail.: $3,000. **Duration:** Annual. **Number Awarded:** 1. **To Apply:** Applicants may apply individually

or in partnership with another member of CALL/ACBD. They must submit completed application available in the website outlining the proposed project, the amount of money requested and a brief budget setting out how funds will be spent. They should be prepared to demonstrate that they have completed a preliminary investigation as to the feasibility of their proposed project. **Deadline:** March 15. **Remarks:** Established in 1996. **Contact:** National Office: 1 Eglinton Avenue East, Suite 705; Toronto ON M4P 3A1; Tel: 647.346.8723; Email: office@callacbd.ca.; Michelle LaPorte, Co-Chair, CALL/ACBD Committee to Promote Research; e-mail: mlaporte@lerners.ca Or to Elizabeth Brutonm, Co-Chair, CALL.

2901 ■ Diana M. Priestly Memorial Scholarship *(Undergraduate/Scholarship)*

Purpose: To encourage and support professional development in the area of law librarianship. **Focus:** Law. **Qualif.:** Applicants must be Canadian citizens and have previous law library experience and will be enrolled in an accredited Canadian Library School during the next academic term or year; have a degree from or are currently enrolled in an accredited Canadian Library School and will be enrolled in an approved Canadian Law School during the next academic term or year, or who have a degree from or are currently enrolled in an approved Canadian law School and will be enrolled in an accredited Canadian Library school during the next academic term/year, or who will be concurrently enrolled in an approved Canadian Law School and an accredited Canadian Library School during the next academic term/year. **Criteria:** Recipients will be chosen based on applicant's work experience, letter of application and letters of reference; preference will be given to members of the Canadian Association of Law Libraries/Association canadienne des bibliotheques de droit.

Funds Avail.: $2,500. **Duration:** Annual. **Number Awarded:** 1. **To Apply:** Applicants must submit the completed application form available on the website along with resume; written statement from applicant; transcripts; and references. **Deadline:** February 1. **Remarks:** Established with a bequest from the late Diana M. Priestly, a distinguished Canadian law librarian. **Contact:** National Office: 1 Eglinton Avenue East, Suite 705; Toronto ON M4P 3A1; Tel: 647.346.8723; Email: office@callacbd.ca.; Completed applications to: Dolores Noga, Chair, CALL/ACBD Scholarships and Awards Committee; Email: dnoga@mross.com.

2902 ■ James D. Lang Memorial Scholarship *(Graduate/Scholarship)*

Purpose: To support attendance at a continuing education program, be it a workshop, certificate program or other similar activity deemed appropriate by the CALL/ACBD Scholarships and Awards Committee. **Focus:** Law. **Qualif.:** Applicants must be members of CALL/ACBD who have been in good standing for a minimum of 12 months. **Criteria:** Scholarship will be given based on merit.

Funds Avail.: No specific amount. **Duration:** Annual. **Number Awarded:** Varies. **To Apply:** Application form is available online; must submit the completed application form along with resume and a letter of support from their employer. **Deadline:** February 1; August 1. **Remarks:** The award was established in honor of James D. Lang, a long time employee of Carswell and member of CALL/ACBD. **Contact:** National Office: 1 Eglinton Avenue East, Suite 705; Toronto ON M4P 3A1; Tel: 647.346.8723; Email: office@callacbd.ca.; Completed applications to: Dolores Noga, Chair, CALL/ACBD Scholarships and Awards Com-

Awards are arranged alphabetically below their administering organizations

mittee; Email: dnoga@mross.com.

2903 ■ Canadian Association of Law Teachers (CALT)
Western University
London, ON, Canada
URL: www.acpd-calt.org
Social Media: www.facebook.com/Calt-Acpd
  -1494599754141388
twitter.com/CALT_ACPD

2904 ■ CALT Prize for Academic Excellence *(Other/Prize)*
Purpose: To honor exceptional contribution to research and law teaching by a Canadian law teacher in mid-career. **Focus:** Law. **Qualif.:** Applicants must be Canadian law teachers in mid-career; and must be nominated by one or more colleagues. **Criteria:** Candidates will be evaluated based on the following criteria: quality and innovation in teaching and learning; quality and impact of legal scholarship and are considered by a selection committee composed of three people (either law teachers or members of the judiciary) appointed by the president of CALT.

Funds Avail.: No specific amount. **Duration:** Annual. **To Apply:** Nominees must submit a complete curriculum vitae; three letters of reference; and representative student's evaluations. **Deadline:** January 21. **Contact:** Professor Angela Cameron; Email: a.cameron@uottawa.ca.

2905 ■ Canadian Association of Oilwell Drilling Contractors (CAODC)
717 7th Ave. SW, Ste. 2050
Calgary, AB, Canada T2P 0Z3
Ph: (403)264-4311
Fax: (403)263-3796
E-mail: info@caodc.ca
URL: www.caodc.ca
Social Media: www.facebook.com/thecaodc
www.instagram.com/thecaodc/
www.linkedin.com/company/5607531?
twitter.com/thecaodc
www.youtube.com/user/TheCAODC

2906 ■ Tim Downing Memorial Scholarship Program *(Professional development/Scholarship)*
Purpose: To help employees of CAODC achieve a higher education. **Focus:** General studies/Field of study not specified. **Qualif.:** Applicants must be CAODC drilling or service rig member employees with minimum of 12 months on-the-job experience and who are currently employed in one of the following: 1) as motorhands, derrickhands or drillers on a drilling rig; 2) as derrickhands or operators on a service rig; and 3) in a safety related position within the drilling or service rig member company.

Funds Avail.: 7,260 Canadian Dollars. **Duration:** Annual. **Number Awarded:** 1. **To Apply:** Application details available at: caodc.ca/ohs_scholarship.

2907 ■ Canadian Association for the Practical Study of Law in Education (CAPSLE)
c/o Lori Pollock, Secretariat
37 Moultrey Cres.

Georgetown, ON, Canada L7G 4N4
Ph: (905)702-1710
E-mail: info@capsle.ca
URL: capsle.ca
Social Media: twitter.com/_CAPSLE

2908 ■ CAPSLE Bursary. *(Graduate/Fellowship)*
Purpose: To provide students an open forum who are studying legal issues affecting education. **Focus:** Law. **Qualif.:** Applicant must have been accepted to a Canadian university program in a recognized Faculty of Education and/or Faculty of Law. **Criteria:** Recipients will be selected based on submitted proposal and is by CAPSLE Board's decision.

Funds Avail.: $1,000. **Duration:** Annual. **Number Awarded:** 1. **To Apply:** Applications can be submitted online; must submit documentary proof; short essay, up to 500 words; resume. **Deadline:** June 30. **Contact:** Email: info@capsle.ca.

2909 ■ Canadian Association of Principals (CAP)
300 Earl Grey Dr., Ste. 220
Kanata, ON, Canada K2T 1C1
E-mail: info@cdnprincipals.com
URL: cdnprincipals.com

2910 ■ CAP Student Leadership Award *(Undergraduate/Scholarship)*
Purpose: To afford principals the opportunity to recognize one of their student leaders and to enter that student as a nominee for a national scholarship. **Focus:** General studies/Field of study not specified. **Qualif.:** Applicant should be in the top 20% of their class. **Criteria:** Selection will be based on Leadership in school activities; leadership in the community; academic achievement; essay; recognition, awards, honors and scholarships.

Funds Avail.: $250 each. **Duration:** Annual. **Number Awarded:** 12. **To Apply:** Applicants must complete the questionnaire following these instructions; advisors should aid students in filling out the questionnaire and in furnishing and verifying entries that are part of the student's official school records. **Deadline:** March 1.

2911 ■ Canadian Association for Studies in Co-operation (CASC)
c/o Centre for the Study of Co-operatives
University of Saskatchewan
101 Diefenbaker Pl.
Saskatoon, SK, Canada S7N 5B8
E-mail: casc.acec@usask.ca
URL: www.coopresearch.coop
Social Media: www.facebook.com/CCRNRCRC
twitter.com/CCRNRCRC

2912 ■ Amy and Tim Dauphinee Scholarship *(Graduate/Scholarship)*
Purpose: To support research on co-operative studies. **Focus:** Banking; Finance. **Qualif.:** Applicants must either undertake studies at Canadian universities or university-equivalent colleges (regardless of citizenship) or are Canadian citizens or landed immigrants studying at such institutions outside Canada. **Criteria:** Selection will be based on the applicant's respective academic records, as

Awards are arranged alphabetically below their administering organizations

well as on the importance of the proposed research activities to the development of the co-op movement in Canada or abroad.

Funds Avail.: 3,000 Canadian Dollars. **To Apply:** Applicants must submit a completed application form along with background information; previous degree(s) or official transcripts; academic awards/distinctions/scholarships; two letters of reference (one must be academic); statement of interest in co-operatives; experience with co-operatives (either as volunteer or employee); and a description of the project (3-5 pages). **Deadline:** March 30. **Remarks:** Established in recognition of the outstanding contribution these two leaders made to the development of the credit union movement and the Ontario Credit Union Charitable Foundation. **Contact:** Paul Cabaj, Attn: CASC Scholarships, Co-operatives and Mutuals Canada, 275 Bank St., 4th fl., Ottawa, Ontario, Canada, K2P 2L6; Email: pcabaj@canada.coop.

2913 ■ Alexander Fraser Laidlaw Fellowship
(Graduate/Fellowship)

Purpose: To support research on co-operative studies. **Focus:** Banking; Finance. **Qualif.:** Applicants must either undertake studies at Canadian universities or university-equivalent colleges (regardless of citizenship) or are Canadian citizens or landed immigrants studying at such institutions outside Canada. **Criteria:** Selection will be based on the applicant's respective academic records, as well as on the importance of the proposed research activities to the development of the co-op movement in Canada or abroad.

Funds Avail.: 1,000 Canadian Dollars. **Duration:** Annual. **To Apply:** Applicants must submit a completed application form along with background information; previous degree(s) or official transcripts; academic awards/distinctions/ scholarships; two letters of reference (one must be academic); statement of interest in co-operatives; experience with co-operatives (either as volunteer or employee); and a description of the project (3-5 pages). **Deadline:** March 30. **Remarks:** Established to honor Dr. Alexander Fraser Laidlaw, the father of the non-profit co-operative housing movement in Canada. **Contact:** Paul Cabaj, Attn: CASC Scholarships, Co-operatives and Mutuals Canada, 275 Bank St., 4th Fl., Ottawa, ON K2P 2L6; Email: pcabaj@canada.coop.

2914 ■ Lemaire Co-operative Studies Award
(Undergraduate, Graduate/Scholarship)

Purpose: To encourage students to undertake studies and research which will help them contribute to the development of co-operative in Canada or elsewhere. **Focus:** Banking; Finance. **Qualif.:** Applicants must be undergraduate or graduate students either undertaking studies at Canadian universities or university-equivalent colleges (regardless of citizenship) or are Canadian citizens or landed immigrants studying at such institutions outside Canada. Full-time or part-time students, taking full- or partial-credit courses at any university or university equivalent college are eligible to apply. Eligible candidates must take a minimum of one course about co-operatives. **Criteria:** Selection will be proportional to the significance and contribution of the studies to the advancement of co-operatives.

Funds Avail.: 1,000 to 3,000 Canadian Dollars. **To Apply:** Applicants must submit a completed application form along with background information; previous degree(s) or official transcripts; academic awards/distinctions/scholarships; two

letters of reference (one must be academic); statement of interest in co-operatives; experience with co-operatives (either as volunteer or employee); and a description of the project (3-5 pages for graduate students, 1 page for undergraduates). **Deadline:** March 30. **Remarks:** The award was named in the honor of Louis Lemaire, a cooperative pioneer. **Contact:** Paul Cabaj, Attn: CASC Scholarships, Co-operatives and Mutuals Canada, 275 Bank St., 4th Fl., Ottawa, Ontario, Canada, K2P 2L6; Email: pcabaj@canada.coop.

2915 ■ Canadian Authors Association-National Capital Region
192 Spadina Ave., Ste. 107
Toronto, ON, Canada M5T 2C2
Ph: (416)975-1756
Fax: (705)955-0716
E-mail: NCRadmin@canadianauthors.org
URL: canadianauthors.org/nationalcapitalregion
Social Media: www.facebook.com/groups/CanadianAuthor-sNCR/?fref=ts
twitter.com/caa_ncr

2916 ■ CAA National Capital Region Writing Contest *(All/Award, Prize, Monetary)*

Purpose: To recognize outstanding short stories or poetry. **Focus:** Literature; Writing. **Criteria:** Winners will be selected based on submitted essays.

Funds Avail.: $300 First Place; $200 Second Place; $100 Third Place. **Duration:** Annual. **Number Awarded:** 3. **To Apply:** Applicants must submit an essay or poem to be considered as entry for the contest. Formats are provided and can be found at the program website. **Deadline:** February 3.

2917 ■ The Canadian Bar Association (CBA)
66 Slater St., Ste. 1200
Ottawa, ON, Canada K1P 5H1
Ph: (613)237-2925
Fax: (613)237-0185
Free: 800-267-8860
E-mail: info@cba.org
URL: www.cba.org
Social Media: www.facebook.com/CanadianBarAssociation
twitter.com/CBA_News

2918 ■ Viscount Bennett Fellowship *(Graduate/ Fellowship)*

Purpose: To encourage a high standard of legal education, training and ethics. **Focus:** Law. **Qualif.:** Applicants must be Canadian citizens who have graduated from an approved law school in Canada, and be members of Canadian Bar Association in good standing. **Criteria:** The CBA Awards Committee is responsible for selecting the successful candidates. Recipients will be selected based on the result of the conducted interview.

Funds Avail.: $25,000. **Duration:** Annual. **Number Awarded:** Varies. **To Apply:** Applicants must fill out completely the provided application form and such must be submitted together with the following: photocopy of birth or citizenship certificate, one certified copy of law transcripts, academic distinctions, curriculum vitae, one-page synopsis of the extra-curricular interests as well as activities during

Awards are arranged alphabetically below their administering organizations

the post-secondary studies, one-page statement outlining the course of study to be pursued, and two letters of reference. **Deadline:** November 15. **Remarks:** The Viscount Bennett Fellowship is made possible by a donation from the Right Honorable Viscount Bennett, a CBA Past President from 1929-30 who established a trust fund to provide income to be used to encourage a high standard of legal education, training and ethics. **Contact:** Completed application must be submitted to: Viscount Bennett Fellowship, c/o: Senior Director of Communications and Marketing, The Canadian Bar Association, 865 Carling Ave., Ste. 500, Ottawa, ON K1S 5S8; E-mail: viscount-vicomte@cba.org.

2919 ■ Canadian Blood Services

1800 Alta Vista Dr.
Ottawa, ON, Canada K1G 4J5
Ph: (613)739-2300
Fax: (613)731-1411
Free: 888-236-6283
E-mail: feedback@blood.ca
URL: www.blood.ca/en
Social Media: www.facebook.com/itsinyoutogive
www.linkedin.com/company/canadian-blood-services
twitter.com/@itsinyoutogive

2920 ■ Canadian Blood Services Graduate Fellowship Program (Graduate/Fellowship)

Purpose: To attract and support young investigators to initiate or continue training in the field of blood transfusion science. **Focus:** Blood banking. **Qualif.:** Applicants must be engaged in full-time training in research in a Canadian graduate school leading to a PhD or combined health professional Ph.D. program; must demonstrate acceptance into a PhD program to receive continued support; in a training program which includes actual involvement in research and not only courses in research methods; and must not hold another award at the same time. **Criteria:** Selection is based on the applicant's academic qualifications, research experience and ability; relevance of the proposed project; and merit of the proposed project and research environment. **Funds Avail.:** $25,000. **Duration:** Annual. **To Apply:** Applicants must submit a completed application form including all attachments with four complete, collated copies and official, original transcript(s).

2921 ■ Canadian Blood Services Postdoctoral Fellowship Program (Postdoctorate/Fellowship)

Purpose: To foster careers related to transfusion science in Canada. **Focus:** Blood banking. **Qualif.:** Applicants must hold a relevant prerequisite degree (PhD, MD, DDS, or DVM) from a recognized academic institution; must be within five years of completing the degree; must not be holding another award. **Criteria:** Selection is based on the applicants' academic qualifications, research experience and ability; relevance of the proposed project; and merit of the proposed project and research environment. **Funds Avail.:** $10,000. **Duration:** 1-3 years. **To Apply:** Applicants must submit a completed application form including all attachments with four complete, collated copies and official, original transcript(s).

2922 ■ Canadian Breast Cancer Foundation - BC/Yukon

300 - 1090 W Pender St.
Vancouver, BC, Canada V6E 2N7

Ph: (604)683-2873
Free: 800-561-6111
E-mail: cbcfbc@cbcf.org
URL: www.cbcf.org/bc/Pages/default.aspx
Social Media: www.facebook.com/canadianbreastcancerccs

2923 ■ Annual Research Doctoral and Postgraduate Fellowship Grant Program (Doctorate, Postdoctorate, Postgraduate, Advanced Professional/Fellowship, Grant)

Purpose: To support the most qualified breast cancer research projects in BC. **Focus:** Medical research; Medicine; Oncology. **Qualif.:** Applicants for the program are the following PhD students, health care professionals, MD graduates, or recent PhD graduates. **Criteria:** Selection will be based on the committee's criteria. **Funds Avail.:** No specific amount. **Duration:** Annual. **To Apply:** Applicants must follow these guidelines when applying: confirm the program criteria and eligibility to apply by reviewing the Grants Fellowship Program Guidebook and Criteria; follow the registration instructions within the Fellowship Webgrants User Manual to register to use the WebGrants system; ensure familiarity with the user guide before completing application online; access WebGrants to complete application. **Contact:** bcgrants@cbcf.org.

2924 ■ CBCF - BC/Yukon Region Breast Cancer Research Grants Competition (Advanced Professional/Grant)

Purpose: To initiate new projects in breast cancer in British Columbia. **Focus:** Oncology. **Qualif.:** Applicants must be investigators from all research disciplines in British Columbia and Yukon Territory. **Criteria:** Recipients are selected based on the premise that projects must demonstrate direct impact on the issue of breast cancer, including strategies for knowledge translation so that the work being done in the laboratory transfers as quickly as possible to the clinic and to the people affected by breast cancer. **Funds Avail.:** Up to 250,000 Canadian Dollars. **Duration:** Two years. **To Apply:** Applicants may verify the website for further information on the application process. **Contact:** Grants Allocation Manager at bcgrants@cbcf.org.

2925 ■ CBCF - BC/Yukon Region Breast Cancer Survivor Dragon Boat Grants (Professional development/Grant)

Purpose: To support breast cancer survivor dragon boat teams across the province. **Focus:** Oncology. **Qualif.:** Applicants must be members of breast cancer survivor dragon boat teams across British Columbia and Yukon Region. **Criteria:** Selection will be based on the committee's criteria. **Funds Avail.:** No specific amount. **Number Awarded:** Over 20. **To Apply:** Applicants must visit the website for the online application process. **Remarks:** Established in 1996. **Contact:** Grants Allocation Manager at bcgrants@cbcf.org.

2926 ■ CBCF - BC/Yukon Region Community Health Grants (Professional development/Grant)

Purpose: To provide locally tailored breast cancer programs throughout British Columbia and the Yukon, which allow sustainable and accountable community based initiatives in the areas of prevention, early detection, treatment and cure for breast cancer. **Focus:** Oncology. **Qualif.:** Applicants must be community organizations throughout British

Awards are arranged alphabetically below their administering organizations

Columbia and the Yukon Territory that delve on breast cancer issues across the provinces. **Criteria:** Selection will be based on the committee's criteria.

Funds Avail.: No specific amount. **To Apply:** Applicants must visit the website for the online application process and other required materials. **Contact:** Grants Allocation Manager at bcgrants@cbcf.org.

2927 ■ CBCF - BC/Yukon Region Small Initiative Funds *(Professional development/Grant)*

Purpose: To provide funding for small scale community initiatives in breast cancer and breast health education and awareness. **Focus:** Oncology. **Qualif.:** Applicants must be small scale community organizations throughout British Columbia and Yukon Territory. **Criteria:** Selection will be based on the committee's criteria.

To Apply: Applicants must visit the website for the online application process and other required materials. **Contact:** Grants Allocation Manager at bcgrants@cbcf.org.

2928 ■ Canadian Breast Cancer Foundation - Ontario
55 St. Clair Ave., W Ste. 500
Toronto, ON, Canada M4V 2Y7
Ph: (416)815-1313
Free: 866-373-6313
URL: www.cbcf.org/ontario
Social Media: www.facebook.com/
  CanadianBreastCancerCCS
twitter.com/breastcancerccs

2929 ■ CBCF - Ontario Nurse and Allied Health Professional Fellowships *(Advanced Professional, Professional development/Fellowship)*

Purpose: To support nurses and allied health professionals with a strong emphasis on women's health to focus on pursuing formal or informal advanced study or training focused on gaining expertise in clinical disciplines involving the prevention, screening, diagnosis and/or treatment of breast cancer; survivorship; quality of life; conducting basic, translational, participatory or community-based research relevant to breast cancer, or a combination thereof. **Focus:** Nursing, Oncological; Oncology. **Qualif.:** Applicants must be Canadian residents or permanent residents and nurses or allied health professionals who are registered and licensed by their respective professional college. **Criteria:** Selection will be based on the following (in order of importance) relevance to breast cancer; applicants' supervision/training environment/training and career development plan; detailed project proposal; applicants academic performance; applicants publications/abstracts; knowledge translation plan; and anticipated impact; preference will be given to candidates who demonstrate interest in and commitment to breast health/breast cancer issues, and intent to continue their careers in Ontario.

To Apply: Applicants may apply via the WebGrants system and must provide all required application materials. **Deadline:** September 17 (intent to apply); October 15 (for both application and submission of letters of reference).

2930 ■ CBCF - Ontario Physician Fellowships
(Doctorate, Professional development/Fellowship)

Purpose: To encourage medical doctors to focus on gaining expertise in research and/or clinical disciplines involv-

ing the prevention, screening, diagnosis and/or treatment of breast cancer; survivorship; quality of life; conducting basic, translational, participatory or community-based research relevant to breast cancer, or a combination thereof. **Focus:** Oncology. **Qualif.:** Applicants must be medical doctors who are registered in or have completed a Royal College of Physicians and Surgeons of Canada certified program or a College of Family Physicians certified program. **Criteria:** Selection will be based on the following (in order of importance): relevance to breast cancer; applicants' supervision/training environment/training and career development plan; applicants' mentor and mentorship plan; detailed project proposal; applicant academic performance; applicant publications/abstracts; knowledge translation plan; and anticipated impact. Preference will be given to candidates who demonstrate interest in and commitment to breast health/breast cancer issues, and intent to continue their careers in Ontario.

To Apply: Interested applicants may apply via the WebGrants system and must provide all required application materials. **Deadline:** September 17 (intent to apply); October 15 (for both application and submission of letters of reference).

2931 ■ CBCF - Ontario Research Fellowships
(Doctorate, Postdoctorate, Professional development/ Fellowship)

Purpose: To develop the expertise and capacity of doctoral and postdoctoral researchers in the fields of breast cancer and breast health research. **Focus:** Oncology. **Qualif.:** Applicants must be Canadian citizens or permanent residents; must be university baccalaureate graduates; and must be enrolled for studies in a graduate program in Ontario, Canada at the doctoral level or accepted for postdoctoral studies in Ontario, Canada. **Criteria:** Selection will be based on the following (in order of importance): relevance to breast cancer; applicants' publications/abstracts; applicants' academic performance; applicants' supervision/ training environment/training plan; detailed project proposal; knowledge translation plan; and anticipated impact. Preference will be given to candidates who demonstrate interest in and commitment to breast health/breast cancer issues, and intent to continue their careers in Ontario.

Funds Avail.: 35,000 Canadian Dollars per 12 months of full-time training (doctoral); 45,000 Canadian Dollars per 12 months of full-time training (postdoctoral). **Duration:** Annual. **To Apply:** Applicants may apply via WebGrants system and must provide all required application materials.

2932 ■ CBCF - Ontario Research Project Grants
(Advanced Professional, Professional development/ Grant)

Purpose: To support individuals in their research on breast cancer. **Focus:** Oncology. **Qualif.:** Applicants must be individuals who are conducting research with direct impact and relevance to breast cancer. **Criteria:** Selection will be on a competitive basis.

Funds Avail.: Up to 450,000 Canadian Dollars. **Duration:** Five years. **To Apply:** Applicants must submit their respective research proposals. They may propose studies ranging from laboratory, pre-clinical and clinical investigations to psychosocial, survivorship, and health services research. All proposals must include a knowledge translation strategy. **Deadline:** October 31.

Awards are arranged alphabetically below their administering organizations

2933 ■ Canadian Breast Cancer Foundation - Prairies/NWT Region

First Edmonton Pl.
Edmonton, AB, Canada T5J 3S9
Ph: (780)452-1166
Free: 866-302-2223
URL: www.cbcf.org/prairies

2934 ■ CBCF - Prairies/NWT Grants in Basic Biomedical Research *(Advanced Professional, Professional development/Grant)*

Purpose: To support high-quality research in all areas including biology of breast cancer, prevention, screening, early detection, diagnosis, prognosis, treatment, cancer control, psychosocial, health care delivery and outcomes. **Focus:** Oncology.

Funds Avail.: Funding for each project may not exceed $125,000 per year and $375,000 in total. **Duration:** Annual; three years.

2935 ■ CBCF - Prairies/NWT Grants in Clinical Research *(Advanced Professional, Professional development/Grant)*

Purpose: To support high-quality research in all areas including biology of breast cancer, prevention, screening, early detection, diagnosis, prognosis, treatment, cancer control, psychosocial, health care delivery and outcomes. **Focus:** Oncology. **Criteria:** Selection will be on a competitive basis.

Funds Avail.: Funding for each project may not exceed $125,000 per year and $375,000 in total. **Duration:** Annual; three years. **To Apply:** Applicants must provide their respective clinical projects and epidemiological studies addressing etiology, prevention, early detection, diagnosis, prognosis, treatment (clinical applications), evaluation of delivery methods and interventions. **Deadline:** March 9.

2936 ■ CBCF - Prairies/NWT Grants in Health Services and Policy Research *(Advanced Professional, Professional development/Grant)*

Purpose: To support high-quality research in all areas including biology of breast cancer, prevention, screening, early detection, diagnosis, prognosis, treatment, cancer control, psychosocial, health care delivery and outcomes. **Focus:** Oncology. **Qualif.:** Applicants must be researchers in Manitoba, Saskatchewan, Alberta, Northwest Territories and Nunavut. **Criteria:** Selection will be on a competitive basis.

Funds Avail.: Up to 125,000 Canadian Dollars per year. **To Apply:** Applicants must provide their respective research proposals on financial and health-care delivery issues such as quality of care, access to care (including timeliness and equity) and factors associated with variations in quality and access.

2937 ■ CBCF - Prairies/NWT Postdoctoral Fellowships *(Postdoctorate, Professional development/ Fellowship)*

Purpose: To provide assistance in launching a career in social, clinical or basic science breast cancer research. **Focus:** Oncology. **Qualif.:** Applicants must be recent Ph.D. graduates across Alberta, Saskatchewan, Manitoba, Northwest Territories and Nunavut. Research project must be relevant to the study of breast cancer. **Criteria:** Selection will be based on the submitted research proposals.

To Apply: Applicants must submit one original signed hard copy of their completed application and one electronic copy, either through e-mail or USB to the CBCF-Prairies/NWT Region's Edmonton Office.

2938 ■ CBCF - Prairies/NWT Research Grants in Psychosocial, Cultural and Environmental Determinants of Health *(Advanced Professional, Professional development/Grant)*

Purpose: To support high-quality research in all areas including biology of breast cancer, prevention, screening, early detection, diagnosis, prognosis, treatment, cancer control, psychosocial, health care delivery and outcomes. **Focus:** Oncology. **Qualif.:** Applicants must be researchers in Manitoba, Saskatchewan, Alberta, Northwest Territories and Nunavut. **Criteria:** Selection will be on a competitive basis.

Funds Avail.: Up to 125,000 Canadian Dollars per year. **To Apply:** Applicants must provide their respective research proposals addressing psychosocial issues, supportive care, survivorship and outcomes, quality of life issues and interventions, behavioural research, cancer control, education, communication.

2939 ■ Canadian Bureau for International Education (CBIE)

220 Laurier Ave. W, Ste. 1550
Ottawa, ON, Canada K1P 5Z9
Ph: (613)237-4820
Fax: (613)237-1073
E-mail: communication@cbie.ca
URL: www.cbie.ca
Social Media: www.facebook.com/cbie.ca
www.linkedin.com/company/the-canadian-bureau-for
  -international-education-cbie-
twitter.com/CBIE_BCEI
www.youtube.com/user/cbiebcei

2940 ■ EDC International Business Scholarships *(Undergraduate/Scholarship)*

Purpose: To support Canadian students interested in pursuing studies in international business. **Focus:** Business. **Qualif.:** Applicants must be Canadian citizens or permanent residents enrolled in a full-time accredited bachelor's degree at a Canadian university or college; must be studying business (international business, commerce, finance, economics, accounting, etc.) or business combined with environmental or sustainability courses and returning to full-time studies for the upcoming academic year; and must be in excellent academic standing. **Criteria:** Scholarships are awarded by a selection committee who evaluates applications based on the following: demonstrated interest in pursuing a career in international business; academic achievement (as reflected in the transcripts and/or honors); experience in Canada and abroad (work, internships, volunteering, study exchanges) during the current program, or concrete plans for obtaining international experience during the academic year; leadership potential (as reflected in extracurricular activities); strength of letters of reference; and language skills.

To Apply: Applicants may visit the program website for further information regarding the application process and other requirements needed to submit. **Remarks:** The EDC International Business Scholarship is administered on behalf of Export Development Canada by the Canadian

---

Awards are arranged alphabetically below their administering organizations

Bureau for International Education.

2941 ■ Canadian Cancer Society Research Institute (CCSRI)
55 Saint Clair Ave. W, Ste. 300
Toronto, ON, Canada M4V 2Y7
Ph: (416)961-7223
E-mail: research@cancer.ca
URL: www.cancer.ca/research
Social Media: twitter.com/cancersociety

2942 ■ Canadian Cancer Society Travel Awards
(Doctorate, Master's, Postdoctorate/Award)

Purpose: To defray the travel costs associated with making a scientific presentation as a first author or presenter at a conference, symposium or other appropriate professional meeting. **Focus:** Health sciences. **Qualif.:** Applicants must be one of the following: registered students in Ph.D. or M.D. program; post-doctoral fellows within 5 years of attaining a Ph.D.; or medical residents/clinical fellows within 5 years of attaining an M.D. **Criteria:** Selection will be based on a competitive basis.

Funds Avail.: Maximum of $2,000. **Duration:** Annual. **Number Awarded:** 30. **To Apply:** Applicants must submit the following requirements: details of the conference; Curriculum Vitae; project summary including the relevance to cancer; budget along with information regarding the applicant's supervisor; and letter of support. **Deadline:** January 15; May 15; September 15. **Contact:** Email: egrams@cancer.ca.

2943 ■ Canadian Cartographic Association (CCA)
c/o Byron Moldofsky, Treasurer
177 Brookdale Ave.
Toronto, ON, Canada M5M 1P4
URL: www.cca-acc.org

2944 ■ Deed of Award *(Undergraduate/Scholarship, Award)*

Purpose: To recognize and encourage exceptional student achievement and ability in any aspect of cartography. **Focus:** Cartography/Surveying. **Qualif.:** Applicant must be a full-time student in a recognized college or university program; must be a Canadian citizen or landed immigrant and the student will be in one of the following situations; must be entering the final year of a community college or CEGEP program in cartography; must be entering the final year of an undergraduate honors program with a concentration in cartography; must be a student accepted into or enrolled in a graduate program with a concentration in cartography; any student awarded this scholarship is not eligible in any subsequent year; the award is tenable only in the year in which it is granted. **Criteria:** Applicants are selected based on committee's review of the application materials.

Funds Avail.: $500. **Duration:** Annual. **To Apply:** Applicants must submit an official transcript of all college or university courses complete with grades received; letters of recommendation from two faculty members who are familiar with the student's works and capabilities; one-page statement from the student regarding plans for continuing education in cartography. **Deadline:** March 15. **Remarks:** The scholarship was established in memory of Dr. Nicholson who was a well known and respected educator and member

of the Canadian Cartographic Association. He had a long and distinguished career in government and academe, where his interests lay in the history of cartography and Canadian government mapping, in particular the National Atlas of Canada. **Contact:** Claire Gosson; E-mail: secretary@cca-acc.org.

2945 ■ Canadian Centre for Occupational Health and Safety (CCOHS)
135 Hunter St. E
Hamilton, ON, Canada L8N 1M5
URL: www.ccohs.ca

2946 ■ Dick Martin Scholarships *(Postgraduate/Scholarship, Award)*

Purpose: To support financially those students who wants to continue their career in occupational health and safety. **Focus:** Occupational safety and health. **Qualif.:** Applicants must be students, who are enrolled, either full-time or part-time, in an occupational health and safety related course or program. **Criteria:** Recipients will be selected based on Essay and Cover letter they submitted.

Funds Avail.: 500 Canadian dollars-3,000 Canadian dollars. **Duration:** Annual. **Number Awarded:** 2. **To Apply:** Applicants must submit complete online application form; one page cover letter and 1,000 to 1,200 word essay either of the two: Prevention Essay or Technical Essay. **Deadline:** January 31. **Remarks:** Established in 2002.

2947 ■ Canadian Civil Liberties Association
90 Eglinton Ave. E, Ste. 900
Toronto, ON, Canada M4P 1A6
Ph: (416)363-0321
Fax: (416)861-1291
E-mail: mail@ccla.org
URL: ccla.org
Social Media: www.facebook.com/cancivlib
www.instagram.com/cancivlib
twitter.com/cancivlib
www.youtube.com/user/CanCivLib

2948 ■ CCLA Summer Legal Volunteer Opportunities for Law Students and Law Graduates *(Graduate, Undergraduate/Internship)*

Purpose: To help students engage in legal work relating to CCLA's ongoing advocacy efforts in civil liberties and human rights. **Focus:** Civil rights; Law. **Qualif.:** Applicants opportunities are open to law students and law graduates. Applicants should be reliable, well-organized and self-motivated, with a demonstrated interest in civil liberties, human rights, and public policy. Strong writing skills are essential. Personal or professional experience working with non-governmental organizations is highly desirable. Bilingualism and the ability to read and write professionally in French is a strong plus. CCLA is an equal opportunity organization, and is committed to diversity and inclusiveness in its practices.

Funds Avail.: No specific amount. **Duration:** Annual. **To Apply:** Applicants must submit a resume, cover letter, and law school transcripts. **Deadline:** February 10. **Contact:** Email: volunteer@ccla.org.

2949 ■ Bernard Chernos Essay Contest *(High School/Prize)*

Purpose: To commemorate the work of Bernard Chernos. **Focus:** Civil rights. **Qualif.:** Applicants must be high school

Awards are arranged alphabetically below their administering organizations

students. **Criteria:** Applicants will be selected based on submitted essay.

Funds Avail.: $500 plus book (first place); $150 plus book (second place); $100 plus book (third place). **Duration:** Annual. **Number Awarded:** 1. **To Apply:** Applicants can locate current year's question, find instructions, and submit entry online at: ccla.org/education/student-contests/.

2950 ■ Canadian Co-operative Association (CCA)

275 Bank St., Ste. 400
Ottawa, ON, Canada K2P 2L6
URL: cdfcanada.coop
Social Media: www.facebook.com/CDFCanada
www.linkedin.com/company/canadian-co-operative
 -association
twitter.com/CDFCanada

2951 ■ Canadian Association for Studies in Co-operation Scholarships - Alexander Fraser Laidlaw Fellowship *(Graduate/Fellowship)*

Purpose: To support studies about co-operative businesses and organizations. **Focus:** Business. **Qualif.:** Applicants must be graduate students either undertaking studies at a Canadian university or a university-equivalent college (regardless of citizenship) or be Canadian citizens or landed immigrant studying at such institutions outside Canada. **Criteria:** Selection is based on the applicant's academic record as well as on the importance of the proposed research activities to the development of the co-op movement in Canada or abroad.

Funds Avail.: 1,000 Canadian Dollars. **To Apply:** Applicants must submit a completed application form along with background information; previous degree(s) or official transcripts; academic awards/distinctions/scholarships; two letters of reference (one must be academic); statement of interest in co-operatives; experience with co-operatives (either as volunteer or employee); and a description of the project (maximum 4 pages for graduate students, 1 page for undergraduates). **Deadline:** April 30. **Contact:** Paul Cabaj, Attn: CASC Scholarships, Co-operatives and Mutuals Canada, 275 Bank St., 4th fl., Ottawa, ON K2P 2L6; Email: pcabaj@canada.coop.

2952 ■ Canadian Association for Studies in Co-operation Scholarships - Amy and Tim Dauphinee Scholarship *(Graduate/Scholarship)*

Purpose: To support studies about co-operative businesses and organizations. **Focus:** Business. **Qualif.:** Applicants must be graduate students. **Criteria:** Selection will be based on the committee's criteria.

Funds Avail.: 3,000 Canadian Dollars. **To Apply:** Applicants must submit a completed application form along with background information; previous degree(s) or official transcripts; academic awards/distinctions/scholarships; two letters of reference (one must be academic); statement of interest in co-operatives; experience with co-operatives (either as volunteer or employee); and a description of the project (3-5 pages for graduate students, 1 page for undergraduates). **Contact:** Paul Cabaj, Attn: CASC Scholarships, Co-operatives and Mutuals Canada, 275 Bank St., 4th fl., Ottawa, ON K2P 2L6; Email: pcabaj@canada.coop.

2953 ■ Canadian Association for Studies in Co-operation Scholarships Lemaire Co-operative Studies Award *(Graduate, Undergraduate/Scholarship)*

Purpose: To encourage students to undertake studies which will help them contribute to the development of co-operatives in Canada or elsewhere. **Focus:** Business. **Qualif.:** Applicants must be undergraduate or graduate students taking full or partial credit courses at any university or university-equivalent college, and must take a minimum of one course about co-operatives. **Criteria:** Selection is based on the submitted application materials.

Funds Avail.: 1,000 to 3,000 Canadian Dollars. **Duration:** Annual. **To Apply:** Applicants must submit a completed application form along with background information; previous degree(s) or official transcripts; academic awards/distinctions/scholarships; two letters of reference (one must be academic); statement of interest in co-operatives; experience with co-operatives (either as volunteer or employee); and a description of the project) Please attach an outline of your research project. (Maximum of 4 pages for graduate students; 1 page for undergraduates. **Deadline:** March 30. **Contact:** Paul Cabaj, Attn: CASC Scholarships, Co-operatives and Mutuals Canada, 275 Bank St., 4th fl., Ottawa, ON K2P 2L6; Email: pcabaj@canada.coop.

2954 ■ Canadian Communication Association (CCA)

c/o Tanner Mirrlees, Pres., Ontario Tech University
Oshawa, ON, Canada L1G 0C5
URL: www.acc-cca.ca
Social Media: twitter.com/CCA_ACdC

2955 ■ Beaverbrook Media at McGill Student Paper Prize *(Undergraduate/Prize)*

Purpose: To recognize the promising scholars in Canadian Communication Studies. **Focus:** Communications. **Qualif.:** Applicants must be students currently enrolled in a graduate program in Communications at a Canadian university; must be fully paid members of the CCA at the time they submit their paper for consideration.

Funds Avail.: 1,000 Canadian Dollars. **Duration:** Annual. **Number Awarded:** 1. **To Apply:** Applicants must submit a single-authored essay. Paper must be between 6000-8000 words in Word, RTF, or PDF format. **Deadline:** April 3.

2956 ■ Gertrude J. Robinson Book Prize *(Professional development/Prize, Award)*

Purpose: To recognize Canadian scholars and promote scholarly excellence in Communication fields. **Focus:** Communications. **Qualif.:** Applicants for the prize must have published a monograph in the previous calendar year, and be members of the Canadian Communication Association.

Funds Avail.: No specific amount. **Duration:** Annual. **Deadline:** March 8. **Contact:** Email: acc.cca.ca@gmail.com.

2957 ■ Canadian Consumer Specialty Products Association (CCSPA)

130 Albert St., Ste. 800
Ottawa, ON, Canada K1P 5G4
Ph: (613)232-6616
Fax: (613)233-6350
E-mail: assoc@ccspa.org
URL: www.ccspa.org
Social Media: twitter.com/CCSPA_ACPCS

2958 ■ Chevalier Award Scholarship *(Undergraduate/Scholarship)*

Purpose: To support those students who demonstrated outstanding extracurricular contributions and accomplishments. **Focus:** General studies/Field of study not specified. **Qualif.:** Applicants must be sons or daughters of employees of a member company of the Canadian Consumer Specialty Products Association. **Criteria:** Selection will be based on good citizenship, humanitarian service, interest in communal affairs and leadership skills.

Funds Avail.: 2,500 Canadian Dollars. **Duration:** Annual. **To Apply:** Applicants may download an application form online.

2959 ■ Canadian Council of Muslim Women (CCMW)
21-59 King St E
Gananoque, ON, Canada K7G 1E8
Ph: (416)999-6059
E-mail: info@ccmw.com
URL: www.ccmw.com
Social Media: www.facebook.com/CCMWNational
www.instagram.com/ccmwnational
www.linkedin.com/company/ccmw
twitter.com/ccmwcanada
www.youtube.com/channel/UCOF
 -BIKxWy8jjPOL12GGY0A

2960 ■ Lila Fahlman Scholarship *(Undergraduate, Graduate/Scholarship)*

Purpose: To assist Canadian Muslim women students in their education. **Focus:** Education; Women's studies. **Qualif.:** Applicant must be a Canadian Muslim woman enrolled in a full-time undergraduate or graduate degree or certificate programs at a Canadian college or university; committed to completing the full academic year; candidates not completing the year, must return the funds; must be making a recognized positive contribution to society through civic engagement and/or volunteering experience; must be a Canadian citizen or a permanent resident of Canada. **Criteria:** Preference may be given to those who have supported CCMW through their volunteer work.

Funds Avail.: No specific amount. **Duration:** Annual. **To Apply:** Applicant must submit an essay describing the reasons why they would be a worthy recipient of this scholarship include=ing their contribution to civic engagement at the community level, other volunteer activities, academic achievements, most important accomplishments and future goals. (No more than 500 words); a brief outline of the budget for the coming year including information on expected sources of funding (e.g. employment contribution, parents contribution, and other scholarship and loans) housing, travel, food, books, student loans; two letters of reference, which may be a teacher from their high school, college or university; and someone who is familiar with their community service and provide the name of the institution they are enrolled in, name of the department scholarship has to be sent to, address of the department and student number; transcripts and resume. **Deadline:** July 2. **Remarks:** Chair of the scholarship selection committee: Dr. Nafeesa Sheikh at nafeesa.ccmw@gmail.com. **Contact:** Dr. Nafeesa Sheikh, Email: nafeesa.ccmw@gmail.com.

2961 ■ Canadian Energy Law Foundation (CELF)
15th Flr., Dentons
850 - 2 St., SW
Calgary, AB, Canada T2P 0R8
URL: www.energylawfoundation.ca

2962 ■ Canadian Energy Law Foundation Graduate Scholarship in Law *(Advanced Professional/Scholarship)*

Purpose: To contribute to the advancement of energy law by means of supporting law students in their education. **Focus:** Law. **Qualif.:** Applicants must be Canadian and foreign students enrolled in a Canadian University LLM or PHD program who are confirmed as the designated candidate by the Law School; only one designated candidate per law school is eligible. **Criteria:** Selection will be made by CELF's Scholarship Subcommittee based on thesis topic(s) that are of interest to Canadian energy lawyers; recipient(s) intending to make a significant contribution to the Canadian energy legal practice.

Funds Avail.: Up to 20,000 Canadian Dollars. **Duration:** Annual. **Number Awarded:** 1. **To Apply:** Applicants must submit a statement describing their thesis topic and why it would be of interest to Canadian energy lawyers and/or a description of the activities undertaken by the applicants that are intended to make a significant contribution to the Canadian energy legal practice; must be accompanied by a letter from the Law School confirming that the applicants are the designated candidates for the Law School for the Scholarship Program.

2963 ■ Canadian Engineering Memorial Foundation (CEMF)
2- 555 Hall Ave E
Renfrew, ON, Canada K7V 4M7
Fax: (613)432-6840
Free: 866-883-2363
E-mail: info@cemf.ca
URL: www.cemf.ca
Social Media: www.facebook.com/
 CanadianEngineeringMemorialFoundation
twitter.com/CEMF

2964 ■ CEMF Engineering Ambassador Awards *(Undergraduate/Award)*

Purpose: To support a woman enrolled full-time in an engineering undergraduate program at a Canadian university. **Focus:** Engineering. **Qualif.:** Applicant must be a Canadian citizen or a Landed Immigrant with a Permanent Residence Card; self-identify as female and be currently enrolled full-time in a chemical engineering program at a Canadian university.

Funds Avail.: $5,000. **Duration:** Annual. **Number Awarded:** 6. **Contact:** Phone: 866-883-2363; Email: info@cemf.ca; URL: www.cemf.ca/en/undergraduate-ambassador-awards.

2965 ■ CEMF Rona Hatt Chemical Engineering Ambassador Award *(Graduate, Undergraduate/Award)*

Purpose: To encourage women to pursue their career path in engineering while inspiring others to follow in their footprints. **Focus:** Engineering. **Qualif.:** Applicant must be a Canadian citizen or a Landed Immigrant with a Permanent Residence Card; self-identify as female and be enrolled full-time in an accredited engineering program at a Canadian university but cannot be in the final year of their undergraduate program.

Funds Avail.: $5,000. **Duration:** Annual. **Number Awarded:** 1. **Remarks:** The Foundation named this award after the first known woman in Canada who became a chemical engineer.

Awards are arranged alphabetically below their administering organizations

2966 ■ Claudette Mackay Lassonde Ambassador Award *(Doctorate, Undergraduate/Award)*

Purpose: To recognize and support a woman studying engineering full-time at the PhD level. **Focus:** Engineering. **Qualif.:** Applicants must be Canadian citizens or a Landed Immigrant with a Permanent Residence Card; must be a graduate of an accredited engineering program from a Canadian university or have a P. Eng. designation or be a recognized E.I.T. in their providence of residence and currently enrolled as a full-time graduate student in an engineering program at a Canadian university; self-identify as female. **Criteria:** Recipients are selected based on the following: quality of presentation, extent and scope of involvement, assessment of passion for engineering, leadership potential, communication and interpersonal skills, perseverance and creativity.

Funds Avail.: $15,000. **Duration:** Annual. **Number Awarded:** 1. **To Apply:** Applicants must submit the following: an application form; applicant declaration; proof of citizenship; informational letter; extracurricular and community activities; summary of community, extracurricular and sports activities; resume or CV; references; letter of support; voice sound clip(2 minutes maximum); presentation; video clip of demonstration of an engineering principle. **Remarks:** The award was established in the memory of the late Claudette MacKay-Lassonde, P.Eng., who a pioneer for women and a leader in the engineering community. **Contact:** Questions: info@cemf.ca; Toll-Free: 866-883-2363.

2967 ■ Vale Master's Engineering Ambassador Award *(Master's/Award)*

Purpose: To support a woman enrolled full-time in an engineering master's program at a Canadian university. **Focus:** Engineering. **Qualif.:** Applicants must be women in Canada who are pursuing their studies in mining and metallurgical engineering or a related discipline.

Funds Avail.: 10,000 Canadian Dollars. **Number Awarded:** 1.

2968 ■ Canadian Federation of University Women

331 Cooper St., Ste. 502
Ottawa, ON, Canada K2P 0G5
Ph: (613)234-8252
Fax: (613)234-8221
Free: 888-220-9606
URL: cfuw.org
Social Media: www.facebook.com/cfuw.fcfdu
twitter.com/cfuwfcfdu
www.youtube.com/channel/UC1t_06P1lINjxkExDamY46w

2969 ■ Canadian Home Economics Association Fellowship (CHEA) *(Postgraduate/Fellowship)*

Purpose: To support individuals in studying one or more aspects in the field of Human Ecology/Home Economics/Family and Consumer Sciences, at the masters or doctoral level. **Focus:** Home Economics. **Qualif.:** Candidates must be studying one or more aspects of Human Ecology/Home Economics/Family and Consumer Sciences at the masters or doctoral level; must be accepted or enrolled in a postgraduate program in Canada at the time of application. **Criteria:** Selection will be based on the committee's criteria.

Funds Avail.: 6,000 Canadian Dollars. **Duration:** Annual. **Number Awarded:** 1. **To Apply:** Applicants must complete

and submit the completed application form with completed filing fee payment form or a copy of the electronic receipt of the approved transaction for the online credit card payment of filing fee; completed personal information consent; statement of intent; curriculum vitae; completed referee assessment; confirmation of enrollment in a graduate program from the host Institution; letter of acceptance into the program of proposed study from the host institution, if not enrolled at the time of application; ethics application/approval or approximate date of projected application, if applicable. **Deadline:** January 14. **Contact:** Program Manager, CFUW Fellowships Committee, Canadian Federation of University Women, 331 Cooper St., Ste. 502, Ottawa, Ontario, K2P 0G5.

2970 ■ CFUW Aboriginal Women's Award *(Postgraduate/Fellowship)*

Purpose: To honor a student enrolled in a full-time course of studies at any level of a second master's or doctoral program. **Focus:** Women's studies. **Qualif.:** Applicants must be post-graduate students and applicant must be a woman.

Funds Avail.: 11,500 Canadian Dollars. **Duration:** Annual. **Number Awarded:** 1. **Deadline:** January 14. **Contact:** Program Manager, 331 Cooper St., Ste. 502, Ottawa, Ontario, K2P 0G5, Toll-free in Canada & the US: 1-888-220-9606; Phone: 613-234-8252 ext. 104, Email: fellowships@cfuw.org; cfuwfls@rogers.com.

2971 ■ CFUW Memorial Fellowship *(Master's/Fellowship)*

Purpose: To honor and recognize those for whom the CFUW Charitable Trust receives memorial donations. **Focus:** Engineering, Civil; Science; Women's studies. **Qualif.:** Candidate must be enrolled in masters studies in science; mathematics; or engineering. **Criteria:** Selection will be based on the committee's criteria.

Funds Avail.: 8,000 Canadian Dollars each. **Duration:** Annual. **Number Awarded:** 1. **To Apply:** Applicant must include copies of the electronic receipt; must include two section statement of Intent; and curriculum vitae; there must be three referee's assessments completed and signed by each referee. **Deadline:** January 14. **Contact:** Program Manager, 331 Cooper St., Ste. 502, Ottawa, Ontario, K2P 0G5, Toll-free in Canada & the US: 1-888-220-9606; Phone: 613-234-8252 ext. 104, Email: fellowships@cfuw.org; cfuwfls@rogers.com.

2972 ■ École Polytechnique Commemorative Awards *(Master's, Doctorate, Graduate/Fellowship)*

Purpose: To promote the status of women. **Focus:** General studies/Field of study not specified. **Qualif.:** Applicants must be students at the masters or doctoral level of study. **Criteria:** Selection will be based on the committee's criteria.

Funds Avail.: $7,000 for doctoral each; $5,000 for masters for each. **Duration:** Annual. **Number Awarded:** 2. **To Apply:** Applicants must complete and submit the completed application form with completed filing fee payment form or a copy of the electronic receipt of the approved transaction for the online credit card payment of filing fee; completed personal information consent; statement of intent; curriculum vitae; completed referee assessment; confirmation of enrollment in a graduate program from the host institution; letter of acceptance into the program of proposed study from the host institution, if not enrolled at the time of application; ethics application/approval or approximate date of projected application, if applicable. **Deadline:** January

---

Awards are arranged alphabetically below their administering organizations

14. **Contact:** Program Manager, 331 Cooper St., Ste. 502, Ottawa, Ontario, K2P 0G5, Toll-free in Canada & the US: 1-888-220-9606; Phone: 613-234-8252 ext. 104, Email: fellowships@cfuw.org; cfuwfls@rogers.com.

2973 ■ Bourse Georgette LeMoyne *(Graduate/Fellowship)*

Purpose: To honor and recognize graduates at a Canadian university where one of the languages of administration and instruction is French. **Focus:** Women's studies. **Qualif.:** Applicant must be studying in French and write the Statement of Intent (Section I) of the application in French; must be Canadian citizen or permanent resident status in Canada; must be a woman; at least a bachelor degree or equivalent from a recognized university. **Criteria:** Selection will be based on the committee's criteria.

Funds Avail.: 5,000 Canadian Dollars each. **Duration:** Annual. **Number Awarded:** 2. **To Apply:** Applicant must include copies of the electronic receipt; must include two section statement of Intent; and curriculum vitae; there must be three referee's assessments completed and signed by each referee. **Deadline:** January 14. **Contact:** Program Manager, 331 Cooper St., Ste. 502, Ottawa, Ontario, K2P 0G5, Toll-free in Canada & the US: 1-888-220-9606; Phone: 613-234-8252 ext. 104, Email: fellowships@cfuw.org; cfuwfls@rogers.com.

2974 ■ Elizabeth Massey Award *(Postgraduate/Award)*

Purpose: To support post-graduate students who are studying visual arts, such as painting or sculpture; or in music. **Focus:** Visual arts. **Qualif.:** Applicants must be post-graduate students in the visual arts. **Criteria:** Selection will be based on the committee's criteria.

Funds Avail.: 5,000 Canadian Dollars. **Duration:** Annual. **Number Awarded:** 1. **To Apply:** Applicants must complete and submit the completed application form with completed filing fee payment form or a copy of the electronic receipt of the approved transaction for the online credit card payment of filing fee; completed personal information consent; statement of intent; curriculum vitae; completed referee assessment; confirmation of enrollment in a graduate program from the host institution; letter of acceptance into the program of proposed study from the host institution, if not enrolled at the time of application; ethics application/approval or approximate date of projected application, if applicable. **Deadline:** January 14. **Remarks:** The award was established in memory of Elizabeth Massey, a young lawyer and member of CFUW whose life was greatly enriched by her love of the creative arts. Established in 2006. **Contact:** Program Manager, CFUW Fellowships Committee, Canadian Federation of University Women, 331 Cooper St., Ste. 502, Ottawa, Ontario, K2P 0G5.

2975 ■ Dr. Margaret McWilliams Pre-Doctoral Fellowship *(Doctorate/Fellowship)*

Purpose: To recognize a woman who dedicated her life to furthering the status of women through improved access to higher education and the active involvement of woman in public life. **Focus:** Women's studies. **Qualif.:** Applicants must be woman who has completed at least one calendar year in a full-time doctoral program and is enrolled in full-time studies in Canada or abroad. **Criteria:** Selection will be based on the committee's criteria.

Funds Avail.: 11,000 Canadian Dollars each. **Duration:** Annual. **Number Awarded:** 1. **To Apply:** Applicant must include copies of the electronic receipt; must include two

section statement of Intent; and curriculum vitae; there must be three referee's assessments completed and signed by each referee. **Deadline:** January 14. **Remarks:** Established in 1952. **Contact:** Program Manager, 331 Cooper St., Ste. 502, Ottawa, Ontario, K2P 0G5, Toll-free in Canada & the US: 1-888-220-9606; Phone: 613-234-8252 ext. 104, Email: fellowships@cfuw.org; cfuwfls@rogers.com.

2976 ■ Dr. Alice E. Wilson Awards *(Master's, Doctorate/Fellowship)*

Purpose: To promote the status of women. **Focus:** General studies/Field of study not specified. **Qualif.:** Applicants must be masters or doctoral students. **Criteria:** Selection will be based on the committee's criteria.

Funds Avail.: 5,000 Canadian Dollars each. **Duration:** Annual. **Number Awarded:** 4. **To Apply:** Applicants must complete and submit the completed application form with completed filing fee payment form or a copy of the electronic receipt of the approved transaction for the online credit card payment of filing fee; completed personal information consent; statement of intent; curriculum vitae; completed referee assessment; confirmation of enrollment in a graduate program from the host institution; letter of acceptance into the program of proposed study from the host institution, if not enrolled at the time of application; ethics application/approval or approximate date of projected application, if applicable. **Deadline:** January 14. **Contact:** Program Manager, 331 Cooper St., Ste. 502, Ottawa, Ontario, K2P 0G5, Toll-free in Canada & the US: 1-888-220-9606; Phone: 613-234-8252 ext. 104, Email: fellowships@cfuw.org; cfuwfls@rogers.com.

2977 ■ Canadian Federation of University Women, Edmonton Branch

c/o Amy Macleod, Membership Chair
7504-156 St. NW
Edmonton, AB, Canada T5R 1X5
E-mail: cfuwedmonton@cfuwedmonton.org
URL: www.cfuwedmonton.org
Social Media: www.facebook.com/groups/
  CFUWEdmonton/1281987935168654
twitter.com/cfuwedmonton

2978 ■ Margaret Brine Graduate Scholarships For Women *(Graduate, Master's, Doctorate/Scholarship)*

Purpose: To support women in their education. **Focus:** General studies/Field of study not specified. **Qualif.:** Applicants must be full-time female graduate students with a current minimum GPA of 3.8; must be registered in a research-based degree program. Master's students must have completed at least one term of their Master's program at the University of Alberta and have received grades for courses taken at the graduate level. Doctoral students must have completed at least one year of their Doctoral program at the University of Alberta. **Criteria:** Selection will be based on the applicants' demonstrated academic excellence and embodying the values of CFUW.

Funds Avail.: 3,000 Canadian Dollars. **Duration:** Annual. **Number Awarded:** 4 (2 Master's, 2 Doctoral). **To Apply:** Applicants must include official, sealed transcripts; letter of intent; two or three original reference letters; and resume. **Deadline:** February 14. **Remarks:** Established in 1985. **Contact:** Margaret Brine Graduate Scholarships for Women, CFUW Edmonton Academic Awards, The Office of the Dean of Students, SUB 5-02, University of Alberta,

Awards are arranged alphabetically below their administering organizations

Edmonton, AB, Canada, T6G 2J7. Email: scholarship@cfuwedmonton.org.

2979 ■ Canadian Fertility and Andrology Society (CFAS)

301 - 1719 rue Grand Trunk
Montreal, QC, Canada H3K 1M1
E-mail: info@cfas.ca
URL: cfas.ca
Social Media: twitter.com/cdnfertility

2980 ■ Dr. Biljan Memorial Awards *(Advanced Professional/Award, Grant)*

Purpose: To recognize a reproductive endocrinologist or fertility specialist who made a contribution to clinical research. **Focus:** Biological and clinical sciences; Endocrinology. **Qualif.:** Applicants must be CFAS members; must be clinicians working in the field of reproductive endocrinology and infertility. **Criteria:** Preference will be given to abstracts that address novel approaches to ovulation induction/IVF or that address innovations in patient-focused strategies that improve administrative or clinical care.

Funds Avail.: 5,000 Canadian Dollars. **Duration:** Biennial. **To Apply:** Applicants must submit abstracts of their own; abstracts must adhere to the CFAS and/or BFS requirements for submission as appropriate. **Contact:** CFAS, at the above address.

2981 ■ Canadian Frailty Network (CFN)

Kidd House
100 Stuart St.
Kingston, ON, Canada K7L 3N6
Ph: (613)549-6666
E-mail: info@cfn-nce.ca
URL: www.cfn-nce.ca
Social Media: www.facebook.com/canadianfrailtynetwork
www.linkedin.com/company/tvn-technology-evaluation-in
  -the-elderly-network-
twitter.com/cfn_nce

2982 ■ CFN Interdisciplinary Fellowships Program *(Graduate, Postdoctorate, Advanced Professional/Fellowship)*

Purpose: To provide a unique learning experience to trainees and adapt an experiential learning approach to allow fellows to: develop expertise on frailty and late life issues; understand interdisciplinary perspectives and collaborative practice; and, develop skills to be successful in professional settings. **Focus:** Gerontology.

Funds Avail.: 25,000 Canadian Dollars (Master's level); 35,000 Canadian Dollars (doctorate level); 50,000 Canadian Dollars (postdoctorate/health professionals). **To Apply:** Applicant must submit a pre-application intent to apply for the fellowship competition, to be eligible to submit a full application package; applications will not be considered unless a pre-application intent to apply has been submitted on-line; applicant should read the Application Instructions before registering at the Intent to apply. A complete Application Package is comprised of: application form; applicants' respective CV; transcripts for all post-secondary and clinical/medical school studies; applicants' and supervisors' Capacity Disclosure Form; application signatures form; supervisor endorsement; two professional references

form; partner letters of support. **Deadline:** November 8.

2983 ■ Canadian Friends of the Hebrew University of Jerusalem (CFHU)

Madison Ctr.
4950 Yonge St., Ste. 1202
Toronto, ON, Canada M2N 6K1
Ph: (416)485-8000
Fax: (416)485-8565
Free: 888-432-7398
E-mail: info@cfhu.org
URL: www.cfhu.org
Social Media: www.facebook.com/CdnFriendsHU
twitter.com/CdnFriendsHU

2984 ■ Canadian Zionist Federation - Dr. Leon Aryeh Kronitz Scholarship *(Undergraduate, Graduate/Scholarship)*

Purpose: To support outstanding students looking to study abroad. **Focus:** Teaching. **Qualif.:** Applicants must be Canadian citizens; must be recent high school graduates, university students or graduate students pursuing teacher training or general studies in Israel; must be accepted for at least one year at an accredited postsecondary program; must demonstrate financial need. **Criteria:** Selection will be based on the committee's criteria.

Funds Avail.: No specific amount. **Number Awarded:** Varies. **To Apply:** Applicants must submit three letters of recommendation required, one of which must be by a high school principal or university studies director and may contact the Association for other application information needed. **Deadline:** May 31. **Contact:** Florence Simon, Canadian Zionist Federation; 5151 Cote St. Catherine, Ste. 206, Montreal H3W 1M6; Phone: 514-739-7300 ext. 3100; czf.national@federationcja.org.

2985 ■ Hushy Lipton Memorial Scholarship Fund *(Undergraduate, Graduate, Postgraduate/Scholarship)*

Purpose: To support outstanding students looking to study abroad. **Focus:** General studies/Field of study not specified. **Qualif.:** Applicants must be Canadian in need of financial aid; must be undergraduate, graduate or postgraduate students who are residing in Canada and planning to study for a full academic year; must have Ontario Secondary Diploma (OSSD) or its equivalent; and must be eligible for full-time attendance at associated recognized institutions of higher learning in Israel. **Criteria:** Selection will be based on the committee's criteria.

Funds Avail.: No specific amount. **To Apply:** Applicants may visit the UJA website for updated application form and other relevant information. **Deadline:** May. **Contact:** Miriam Daniels; 416-635-2883 ext. 5116; mdaniels@ujafed.org; jewishtoronto.com/scholarships.

2986 ■ Morris M. Pulver Scholarship Fund *(Undergraduate, Graduate, Postgraduate/Scholarship)*

Purpose: To support outstanding students looking to study abroad. **Focus:** General studies/Field of study not specified. **Qualif.:** Applicants must be Canadian in need of financial aid; must be undergraduate, graduate or postgraduate students who are residing in Canada and planning to study for a full academic year; must have Ontario Secondary Diploma (OSSD) or its equivalent; and must be eligible for full-time attendance at associated recognized

Awards are arranged alphabetically below their administering organizations

institutions of higher learning in Israel. **Criteria:** Selection will be based on the committee's criteria.

Funds Avail.: No specific amount. **To Apply:** Applicants may visit the UJA website for updated application form and other relevant information. **Deadline:** May. **Contact:** Miriam Daniels; 416-635-2883 ext. 5116; mdaniels@ujafed.org; jewishtoronto.com/scholarships.

2987 ■ Rothberg International School Graduate Merit Scholarship (Graduate, Master's/Scholarship)

Purpose: To support outstanding students looking to study abroad. **Focus:** General studies/Field of study not specified. **Qualif.:** Candidates must have completed their undergraduate degree and have a minimum GPA of 3.8 or equivalent. Any candidate for an M.A. program may apply and those selected will be eligible for a two-year fellowship, conditional on maintenance of academic performance. Candidates for any other graduate program are not eligible to apply for the Graduate Merit Scholarship. **Criteria:** Selection will be based on the committee's criteria.

Funds Avail.: No specific amount. **To Apply:** Applicants may visit the website for online application and other information. **Contact:** Email: overseas.huji.ac.il/scholarships; gradmiss@savion.huji.ac.il.

2988 ■ Canadian Gerontological Nursing Association (CGNA)
1202-71 Charles St. E
Toronto, ON, Canada M4Y 2T3
Ph: (416)927-8654
E-mail: cgna.office@gmail.com
URL: www.cgna.net

2989 ■ Ann C. Beckingham Scholarship (Graduate, Other/Scholarship)

Purpose: To support outstanding registered nurses undertaking further education in a graduate degree program. **Focus:** Gerontology; Nursing. **Qualif.:** Applicant must be outstanding Registered Nurses undertaking further education in a graduate degree program relevant to career development. **Criteria:** Selection will be based on the committee's criteria.

Funds Avail.: No specific amount. **Duration:** Annual. **To Apply:** Applicants must enclose a copy of their certificate to practice nursing in a Canadian province/territory; copy of current national/provincial/territorial gerontological nursing association membership card (or copy of completed CGNA/provincial/territorial association application form); evidence from an academic institution of part-time or full-time student status; academic transcript of most recently completed nursing degree program (please indicate as well those courses with gerontological content); curriculum vitae; and letter of support/recommendation from a current CGNA member; must complete the application by answering the following questions (in no more than one page for each): Describe your past contributions to gerontological nursing in Canada; Describe why you are interested in furthering your education in gerontological nursing and indicate how this additional education will assist your career plans. **Deadline:** February 14. **Contact:** Email: lori.schindelmartin@ryerson.ca.

2990 ■ CGNA Memorial Scholarship (Graduate, Other/Scholarship)

Purpose: To help students further their education in a graduate degree program. **Focus:** Gerontology; Nursing.

Qualif.: Applicants must be in a post-basic undergraduate nursing degree program with a gerontological nursing focus. **Criteria:** Selection will be based on the committee's criteria.

Funds Avail.: No specific amount. **Duration:** Annual. **To Apply:** Applicants must enclose a copy of their certificate to practice nursing in a Canadian province/territory; copy of current national/provincial/territorial gerontological nursing association membership card (or copy of completed CGNA/provincial/territorial association application form); evidence from an academic institution of part-time or full-time student status; academic transcript of most recently completed nursing degree program which should indicate as well those courses with gerontological content; curriculum vitae; and letter of support/recommendation from a current CGNA member; must complete the application by answering the following questions (in no more than one page for each): Describe your past contributions to gerontological nursing in Canada; Describe why you are interested in furthering your education in gerontological nursing and indicate how this additional education will assist your career plans. **Deadline:** February 14.

2991 ■ Canadian Golf Superintendents Association (CGSA)
2605 Summerville Ct., Unit A2082
Mississauga, ON, Canada L4X 0A2
Ph: (416)626-8873
Fax: (416)626-1958
Free: 800-387-1056
E-mail: cgsa@golfsupers.com
URL: golfsupers.com
Social Media: www.facebook.com/Canadian-Golf-Superintendents-Association-151227228150
twitter.com/GolfSupers

2992 ■ CGSA Student Scholarship Awards (Undergraduate/Award, Scholarship)

Purpose: To support student members attending educational programs as a means of enhancing their knowledge and skills for the turfgrass profession as well as becoming better qualified for their current or future employment. **Focus:** General studies/Field of study not specified. **Qualif.:** Applicants must be a Canadian Citizen and have a minimum of one season as an employee on a Golf Course; CGSA student members who are currently enrolled in at least the second year of a recognized; two (2) years duration (or longer) or are enrolled in a one year mechanic course are eligible to apply. **Criteria:** Selection will be based on the committee criteria.

Funds Avail.: $1,500; $1,000; $500. **Duration:** Annual. **Number Awarded:** 1. **To Apply:** Applicant must submit all of the necessary information to the CGSA scholar's fund; 500- 1, 000 Word essay from student included in proper font size and double spaced; report from your instructor included. **Deadline:** November 30.

2993 ■ Canadian Group Psychotherapy Association (CGPA)
c/o First Stage Enterprises
1 Concorde Gate Ste. 109
Toronto, ON, Canada M3C 3N6
Ph: (416)426-7229
Fax: (416)426-7280

Awards are arranged alphabetically below their administering organizations

Free: 866-433-9695
E-mail: admin@cgpa.ca
URL: cgpa.ca

2994 ■ CGPF Endowments Conference Scholarships *(Undergraduate/Scholarship)*

Purpose: To financially assist trainees who wish to acquire professional development and to defray the cost of attending the CGPA Annual conference. **Focus:** General studies/Field of study not specified. **Qualif.:** Applicants must be trainees in group psychotherapy in a GCPA-accredited training program or academic degree program. **Criteria:** Recipients will be evaluated based on training background, work experience, perspective on development of group therapy practice and being associated with the individual's life experience.

Duration: Annual. **Number Awarded:** 4. **To Apply:** Applicants must submit a letter of intent, curriculum vitae and letter of support from a mentor. **Deadline:** August 31 or December 31. **Contact:** Email: info@cgpf.ca.

2995 ■ Martin Fischer Training Award *(Undergraduate/Award)*

Purpose: To recognize and support outstanding Canadian trainees or students who are receiving training in group therapy from an established program. **Focus:** General studies/Field of study not specified. **Qualif.:** Applicants must be students nominated by a training faculty member. **Criteria:** Applicants will be evaluated based on submitted paper, clinical and research achievements.

Funds Avail.: 500-1,500 Canadian Dollars. **Duration:** Annual. **Number Awarded:** Varies. **To Apply:** Applicants must submit three copies of paper accompanying the letter of support and documentation of clinical and research achievements. **Deadline:** August 31 or December 31. **Contact:** Email: info@cgpf.ca.

2996 ■ Canadian Hard of Hearing Association (CHHA)

75 Albert Str.Ste 901
Ottawa, ON, Canada K1V 7P2
URL: www.chha.ca

2997 ■ Canadian Hard of Hearing Association Scholarship Program *(Undergraduate/Scholarship)*

Purpose: To offer financial assistance to hard of hearing and deafened students. **Focus:** General studies/Field of study not specified. **Qualif.:** Applicants must be students registered in a full-time program at a recognized Canadian college or university; must be either hard-of-hearing, deaf or orally deaf; must be a Canadian citizen, permanent resident/landed immigrant, convention refugee or a protected person living in Canada, as defined in the Immigration and Refugee Protection Act; mature students are also eligible. **Criteria:** Selection of applicants will be judged by a number of criteria including academic achievement, determination to cope with hearing loss and community involvement.

Funds Avail.: No specific amount. **Duration:** Annual. **To Apply:** Interested applicants must visit the website for the online application process. **Deadline:** June 1. **Remarks:** Established in 2002. **Contact:** CHHA National Office, 2415 Holly Ln., Ste 205, Ottawa, Ontario, K1V 7P2; Phone: 613-526-1584, Fax: 613-526-4718, Toll free: 800-263-8068, Email: scholarship@chha.ca.

2998 ■ Canadian Hard of Hearing Association - Newfoundland and Labrador (CHHA-NL)

1081 Topsail Rd.
Mount Pearl, NL, Canada A1N 5G1
Ph: (709)753-3224
Fax: (709)753-5640
Free: 888-753-3224
E-mail: info@chha-nl.ca
URL: chha-nl.ca
Social Media: www.facebook.com/betterhearingNL
www.linkedin.com/company/canadian-hard-of-hearing
  -association---newfoundland-and-labrador
twitter.com/betterhearingNL

2999 ■ Glenna Stone Memorial Scholarship *(Undergraduate/Scholarship)*

Purpose: To offer financial assistance and recognition to hard of hearing, late-deafened and oral deaf students registered in a full time program at a recognized Canadian college or university, in any area of study, with the ultimate goal of obtaining a diploma, certificate or degree. **Focus:** General studies/Field of study not specified. **Criteria:** Applications will be judged by a number of criteria including academic achievement, determination to cope with hearing loss and community involvement.

Funds Avail.: 2,000 Canadian Dollars. **Duration:** Annual. **Number Awarded:** 1. **To Apply:** Applicants must submit completed application form with a signed audiogram; a copy of your most recent school transcript; two reference letters in accordance with reference guidelines. **Deadline:** June 30. **Remarks:** Established in memory of Glenna Stone, a former President of the Association who was a strong advocate for the rights of persons with hearing loss and persons with disabilities. **Contact:** CHHA-NL, 1081 Topsail Rd., Mount Pearl, NL, A1N5G1; TollFree: 1-888-753-3224; Text: 709-725-3224; Fax: 709-753-5640; Email: info@chha-nl.ca.

3000 ■ Canadian Hemophilia Society (CHS)

301-666 Sherbrooke St. W
Montreal, QC, Canada H3A 1E7
Ph: (514)848-0503
Fax: (514)848-9661
Free: 800-668-2686
E-mail: chs@hemophilia.ca
URL: www.hemophilia.ca
Social Media: www.facebook.com/
  CanadianHemophiliaSociety
www.instagram.com/chs_national/
twitter.com/CHShemophilia
www.youtube.com/user/CanadianHemophilia

3001 ■ CHS - Bursary Program Scholarships *(Undergraduate/Scholarship)*

Purpose: To bring young volunteers into the CHS while recognizing the importance of education. **Focus:** General studies/Field of study not specified. **Qualif.:** Applicants must possess academic standards sufficient to allow admission into the post-secondary educational institution and program to which the bursary would be applied. **Criteria:** Priority is given to those who have financial needs.

Funds Avail.: 5,000 Canadian dollars. **Duration:** Annual. **To Apply:** Applicant must provide three letters of reference

Awards are arranged alphabetically below their administering organizations

with the application stating the abilities and suitability of the candidate; must provide a letter from a physician or any medical authority confirming medical status; must submit an original essay (500 words) to emphasize the logical thinking and adequate writing skills of the applicant; and must submit the original transcript of grades for the last year in secondary school. Application forms are available from the website. **Deadline:** April 30.

3002 ■ CHS - Mature Student Bursary Program Scholarships *(Undergraduate/Scholarship)*

Purpose: To support students returning to or beginning a course of studies at any post-secondary institution. **Focus:** General studies/Field of study not specified. **Qualif.:** Applicants must be at least 30 years of age. **Criteria:** Recipients are selected based on application materials and financial need as reviewed by a committee of academics and lay persons.

Funds Avail.: 5,000 Canadian dollars. **Duration:** Annual. **To Apply:** Applicants must submit a detailed budget showing their source of income and their projected expenses for a year of study at the institution of their choice; must submit an essay of intent describing past employment and assessment of new career; must provide three letters of reference with their application, none of which may be from a relative (such letters should attest to the abilities and suitability of the candidate for the program being applied for as well as act as a character reference for the candidate); must provide a separate letter from their physician or some medical authority confirming their medical status regarding eligibility to this program. **Deadline:** April 30.

3003 ■ CHS James Kreppner Memorial Scholarship and Bursary Program *(Undergraduate/Scholarship)*

Purpose: To bring young volunteers into the CHS while recognizing the importance of education. **Focus:** General studies/Field of study not specified. **Qualif.:** Applicants must possess academic proficiency of 3.0 GPA on a 4.0 scale; must have an experience in community service at a volunteer level and must possess leadership qualities; have hemophilia (factor VIII or IX) or another inherited bleeding disorder, carriers, and those who contracted HIV through a blood transfusion; their spouses and children may also apply. **Criteria:** Priority will be given to those who might not be able to succeed in a vocational course requiring strenuous physical labor.

Funds Avail.: 5,000 Canadian dollars. **Duration:** Annual. **Number Awarded:** 2. **To Apply:** Applicant must provide three letters of reference with the application stating the abilities and suitability of the candidate; must provide a letter from a physician or any medical authority confirming their medical status; must submit an original 500-word essay to emphasize the logical thinking and adequate writing skills of the applicant; and must submit the original transcript of grades of the last year in secondary school; application forms are available on the website. **Deadline:** April 30. **Remarks:** The schlorship established to honour James Kreppner's dedication, intelligence, and commitment to the CHS and community service.

3004 ■ Canadian Hospitality Foundation (CHF)
1155 Queen Street West
Toronto, ON, Canada M6J 1J4
Ph: (416)649-4239
E-mail: info@thechf.ca
URL: www.thechf.ca
Social Media: www.facebook.com/Canadian-Hospitality
-Foundation-681832381955389
www.linkedin.com/company/canadian-hospitality
-foundation
twitter.com/CanadianHospFdn

3005 ■ Culinary Scholarship (2-year Program) *(Undergraduate/Scholarship)*

Purpose: To provide scholarship to the students enrolled in a two-years culinary program. **Focus:** Culinary arts. **Criteria:** Selection will be based on work experience; leadership and ability; extra curricular activities; educational record; professional promise.

Funds Avail.: Varies. **Duration:** Annual. **To Apply:** Applicants should include completed and signed application form (pen or typewritten only); resume or curriculum vitae; an official transcript of records; letter(s) of recommendation from a current faculty member and/or school administrator; letter(s) of recommendation from past or present employer(s) (reference letters for volunteer activities will also be considered); include photo that must be a color 5 by 7 inch head and shoulders portrait, with a resolution of 300 dpi or higher.

3006 ■ John A. Rothschild Bachelor Degree in Hospitality Scholarship *(Undergraduate, Community College/Scholarship)*

Purpose: To provide scholarship to the students enrolled in Hospitality, Hotel & Food, Tourism & Hospitality degree programs. **Focus:** Hotel, institutional, and restaurant management; Travel and tourism. **Criteria:** Selection will be based on work experience; leadership and ability; extra curricular activities; educational record; professional promise and Essay.

Funds Avail.: $2,500. **Duration:** Annual. **To Apply:** Applicants should include completed and signed application form (pen or typewritten only); resume or curriculum vitae; an official transcript of records; letter(s) of recommendation from a current faculty member and/or school administrator; a photo must be color 5 by 7 inch head and shoulders portrait, with a resolution of 300 dpi or higher; 300 word essay on one of the topics listed on the application form. **Deadline:** July 20. **Contact:** Canadian Hospitality Foundation, Attn: Scholarship Committee, 300 Adelaide St., E Rm.339, Toronto, ON, M5A 1N1.

3007 ■ Canadian Hydrographic Association
4900 Yonge St., Ste 1205
Toronto, ON, Canada M2N 6A6
URL: hydrography.ca

3008 ■ Canadian Hydrographic Association Student Award *(Undergraduate/Award)*

Purpose: To advance the knowledge of hydrography, cartography and associated disciplines. **Focus:** Engineering, Ocean; Hydrology; Oceanography. **Qualif.:** Applicants must be full time students in an accredited post-secondary program in the field of Geomatics in a university or technological college anywhere in Canada. **Criteria:** Selection will be based on the following criteria: demonstrated bonafide financial need, coupled with an above average academic performance.

Funds Avail.: Deserving Student $2,000. **Duration:** Annual. **Number Awarded:** 1. **To Apply:** Applicants will be required to write a short paragraph explaining their financial need in a clear, concise manner on the application form or,

Awards are arranged alphabetically below their administering organizations

if necessary, attached piece of paper. the importance of this aspect of the application is emphasized. applicants must submit one letter of reference from an official of the university or college where the applicant spent the previous year. letter of reference must include the address and phone number of this official. **Deadline:** June 30. **Remarks:** Established in 1992. **Contact:** Kirsten Greenfield, Canadian Hydrographic Association, 4900 Yonge St., Ste. 1205, Toronto, Ontario, M2N 6A6; Email: kirsten.greenfield@pwgsc.gc.ca.

3009 ■ Canadian Identification Society (CIS)

Ontario Police College
10717 Haceinda Rd.
Aylmer, ON, Canada N5H 2R3
Ph: (416)808-6899
Fax: (416)808-6852
E-mail: michelle.pflug@ontario.ca
URL: cis-sci.ca

3010 ■ Canadian Identification Society Essay/ Scholarship Awards *(Advanced Professional, Professional development/Award)*

Purpose: To help CIS members conduct their research. **Focus:** Criminology; Law enforcement; Science. **Qualif.:** Applicants must be CIS members or immediate family members employed in law enforcement. **Criteria:** Essays will be evaluated based on originality of the technique, merit as a method of collecting/processing forensic evidence and the quality of writing.

Duration: Annual. **Number Awarded:** 3. **To Apply:** Applicants must submit an essay (minimum of 3000 words in either French or English) on forensic identification evidence that describes a successful method of locating, processing or presenting such evidence. **Contact:** Canadian Identification Society, at the above address.

3011 ■ The William Donald Dixon Research Grant *(Graduate, Undergraduate, Advanced Professional/ Grant)*

Purpose: To provide opportunities to individuals engaged in forensic research. **Focus:** Chemistry; Law enforcement; Science. **Qualif.:** Applicants must be members of CIS who have submitted a relevant research paper in the field of forensic science; must have a bachelor's degree in any discipline but should not be employed in law enforcement; graduates of three-year programs are required to be employed in law enforcement. **Criteria:** Recipients will be selected based on submitted research proposals. Priority may be given to graduates in science or chemistry.

Funds Avail.: 500 Canadian Dollars each. **Duration:** Annual. **Number Awarded:** 2. **To Apply:** Applicants must submit a research proposal, or outline on a topic related to forensic identification. The summary and/or research must be submitted for publishing in the Identification Canada Journal. Letters of recommendation should be obtained from a senior official of their police department, law enforcement official(s), or academic head and employer.

3012 ■ Edward Foster Award *(Advanced Professional/ Award)*

Purpose: To recognize the contribution of the recipient to the Forensic Identification field throughout his/her career. **Focus:** Criminology; Science. **Qualif.:** Applicants must be nominated by the two CIS members. **Criteria:** Awards will

be given to applicants based on Photographic quality, Evidential value, Ingenuity/utilization of techniques and equipment. Judge decision is final.

Duration: Annual. **To Apply:** Applicants must submit an outline of their contributions to the field of forensic identification. **Remarks:** The award is named after Edward Foster, the founder of the fingerprint system in Canada.

3013 ■ Canadian Imperial Bank Of Commerce (CIBC)

Commerce Ct., 199 Bay St.
Toronto, ON, Canada M5L 1A2
Ph: (416)980-2211
Fax: (416)980-7012
E-mail: corpcommmailbox@cibc.com
URL: www.cibc.com
Social Media: www.facebook.com/CIBC
www.linkedin.com/company/cibc
twitter.com/cibc
youtube.com/user/CIBCVideos

3014 ■ C.I.B.C Scholarship *(Undergraduate, Graduate/Scholarship)*

Purpose: To provide support for Black Canadian students who demonstrated social responsibility through work in the community. **Focus:** General studies/Field of study not specified. **Qualif.:** Applicants must be Canadian citizens or permanent residents who are members of the Canadian Black community (i.e. Black persons of discernible African ancestry and self identity); maximum 30 years of age and enrolled in a full-time student in the academic year at an accredited post-secondary institution (as determined by the NSF). **Criteria:** Selection will be based on demonstrated social responsibility through work in the community.

Funds Avail.: 5,000 Canadian Dollars. **Duration:** Annual. **Number Awarded:** 1. **To Apply:** Applicants must complete the online application form and attach the following: Letter of Recommendation from teacher, guidance counsellor, principal or vice-principal who knows applicant well and can write about academic accomplishments and other outstanding attributes written on official letterhead; letter of Recommendation from a member of applicant community, high-school transcript (attachments in PDF format); hardcopy original of high school transcript must be sent to NSF Office within 14 days of application online deadline.

3015 ■ Canadian Indigenous Nurses Association (CINA)

50 The Driveway
Ottawa, ON, Canada K2P 1E2
URL: www.indigenousnurses.ca
Social Media: www.facebook.com/
CanadianIndigenousNursesAssociation
twitter.com/cinanurses

3016 ■ Jean Goodwill Scholarship *(Graduate/ Scholarship)*

Purpose: To encourage and help nurses of Aboriginal ancestry to obtain the specialized knowledge they require. **Focus:** Nursing. **Qualif.:** Applicants must be students who are graduating from a registered nurse course and are accepted into one of the following specialized training programs: community health nursing, outpost nursing,

Awards are arranged alphabetically below their administering organizations

midwifery; must be or will be enrolled in a bachelor level nursing program; can be graduate nurses already serving in isolated communities and who are accepted into community health nursing, outpost nursing or midwifery program; those who are or will be enrolled in a Bachelor level nursing program. **Criteria:** Selection is based on the selection board's review of the application materials; preference will be given to applicants of aboriginal ancestry who intend to serve in the North.

Funds Avail.: 2,500 Canadian dollars. **Duration:** Annual. **To Apply:** Applicants must submit a complete application and it must be received by the President of the Aboriginal Nurses Association of Canada. **Deadline:** May 31. **Contact:** Canadian Indigenous Nurses Association, 50 Driveway, Ottawa, ON, K2P 1E2; T: 613-724-4677; Toll Free: 1-866-724-3049; Fax: 613-724-4718; Email: info@indigenousnurses.ca.

3017 ■ Canadian Institute for the Administration of Justice (CIAJ)
5950 Chemin de la Côte-des-Neiges Office 450
Montreal, QC, Canada H3S 1Z6
Ph: (514)731-2855
Fax: (514)731-3247
E-mail: ciaj@ciaj-icaj.ca
URL: ciaj-icaj.ca
Social Media: www.facebook.com/ciaj.icaj
twitter.com/ciaj_icaj

3018 ■ Charles D. Gonthier Research Fellowship
(Graduate, Advanced Professional/Fellowship)

Purpose: To support and recognize an academic selected by the jury who will best research the topic of CIAJ's annual conference. **Focus:** Social sciences. **Qualif.:** Applicants must be faculty members and graduate students at Canadian universities. **Criteria:** Selection will be based on the CIAJ's criteria.

Funds Avail.: $7,500. **Duration:** Annual. **Number Awarded:** 1. **To Apply:** Completed application form along with a completed research report and complete account of expenditures must be submitted. **Deadline:** March 31. **Remarks:** The fellowship is named in honor of the late Mr. Justice Charles D. Gonthier of the Supreme Court of Canada, a former President of CIAJ. Established in 2009. **Contact:** Email: ciaj@ciaj-icaj.ca.

3019 ■ Canadian Institute for Advanced Research (CIFAR)
MaRS Ctr, W Twr., 661 University Ave., Ste. 505
Toronto, ON, Canada M5G 1M1
Ph: (416)971-4251
Fax: (416)971-6169
Free: 888-738-1113
E-mail: info@cifar.ca
URL: www.cifar.ca
Social Media: www.facebook.com/CIFAR
www.linkedin.com/company/canadian-institute-for
  -advanced-research
www.linkedin.com/company/cifar
twitter.com/cifar_news
www.youtube.com/channel/UCZj1nnTIiutUjEg-22e8UTA

3020 ■ CIFAR Azrieli Global Scholars program
(Professional development/Scholarship)

Purpose: To identify some of the world's most promising early-career researchers to become members of a CIFAR

research program. **Focus:** General studies/Field of study not specified. **Qualif.:** Applicants must be individuals within the first five years of having completed their PhD; and must have demonstrated outstanding scholarship and research potential.

Funds Avail.: $100,000. **Duration:** over two years. **Number Awarded:** Varies. **To Apply:** Applicant must submit a brief description of significant paper or research achievement (150 words maximum); a summary of how research complements and contributes to the themes andgoals of the CIFAR research program you would like to join (150 words maximum); a summary of most important leadership experience to date (150 wordsMaximum); a summary of your engagement to date with non-academic communities to extend the impact of your research (150 words maximum); Applicant must submit two recommendation letters. **Contact:** E-mail: globalscholars@cifar.ca.

3021 ■ Canadian Institute of Geomatics (CIG)
900 rue Dynes Rd., Ste. 100 D
Ottawa, ON, Canada K2C 3L6
URL: www.cig-acsg.ca

3022 ■ Hans Klinkenberg Memorial Scholarship
(Undergraduate/Scholarship)

Purpose: To provide scholarship to students in the Geomatics sciences at technical institutes and community colleges in Canada. **Focus:** Geography. **Qualif.:** Applicants must be students in the geomatics sciences at technical institutes and community colleges in Canada. **Criteria:** Selection will be based on scholastic achievement and various required documents.

Funds Avail.: 500 to 2,000 Canadian Dollars. **Duration:** Annual. **Number Awarded:** Up to 2. **Deadline:** February 15. **Remarks:** The award was named after Hans Klinkenberg who was a well-known and respected field surveyor, mathematician, foreign advisor, and professor. **Contact:** Completed application must be set to: Chair, Board of Trustees, Hans Klinkenberg Memorial Scholarship, c/o Canadian Institute of Geomatics, 900 Dynes Rd., Ste. 100 D, Ottawa, ON, K2C 3L6.

3023 ■ Canadian Institute of Planners (CIP)
141 Laurier Ave. W, Ste. 1112
Ottawa, ON, Canada K1P 5J3
Ph: (613)237-7526
Fax: (613)237-7045
Free: 800-207-2138
E-mail: communications@cip-icu.ca
URL: www.cip-icu.ca
Social Media: www.facebook.com/cdnplanners
www.instagram.com/cdnplanners
www.linkedin.com/company/canadian-institute-of-planners
twitter.com/CIP_ICU
www.youtube.com/channel/UCX91bjgH9xo_VHV
  -LRMdM3Q

3024 ■ College of Fellows Travel Scholarship
(Undergraduate/Scholarship)

Purpose: To provide opportunity for the student to travel, observe, and study, innovative, leading-edge planning projects first hand, thus contributing to their education, anticipation and excitement for the profession they are about to enter. **Focus:** General studies/Field of study not

---

Awards are arranged alphabetically below their administering organizations

specified. **Qualif.:** Applicant must be a student member who is in the final year of an undergraduate planning program recognized by the Canadian Institute of Planners. **Criteria:** Recipients will be selected based on demonstrated leadership and commitment to their chosen profession and professional association; academic achievement; and a proposal to travel and explore a leading-edge, innovative or new planning initiative or project that will contribute to the depth and breadth of the student's educational experience as reviewed by a jury consisting of three members of the College of Fellows and the Vice President of the Student Scholarship Trust Fund.

Funds Avail.: 4,000 Canadian Dollars. **Duration:** Annual. **To Apply:** Applicant must provide their contact information, university and program enrollment information, official transcript, a recommendation letter from the department head and from someone who is familiar with the applicant's commitment to community service, a list of accomplishments, and a travel proposal (not more than 4-5 pages in length). Applicants is required to submit six originals and one copy on CD of the submission materials. **Deadline:** February 17. **Contact:** CIP; Phone: 800-207-2138 or 613-237-7526; Email: cip-icu.ca.

3025 ■ Canadian Institute of Ukrainian Studies (CIUS)

4-30 Pembina Hall
University of Alberta
Edmonton, AB, Canada T6G 2H8
Ph: (780)492-2972
E-mail: cius@ualberta.ca
URL: www.ualberta.ca/~cius
Social Media: www.facebook.com/canadian.institute.of
  .ukrainian.studies
instagram.com/ualberta
twitter.com/UAlberta
www.youtube.com/channel/UCjHj-JpnElzXCZ8SbliMs2Q

3026 ■ Helen Darcovich Memorial Doctoral Fellowship (Doctorate/Fellowship)

Purpose: To support a student writing a dissertation on a Ukrainian or Ukrainian-Canadian topic in one of areas of education, history, law, humanities, arts, social sciences, women's studies, and library sciences. **Focus:** Ukrainian studies. **Qualif.:** Applicant must be doctoral student writing a dissertation on a Ukrainian or Ukrainian-Canadian topic in library sciences, education, history, law, humanities, arts, social sciences, or women's studies.

Funds Avail.: Up to 13,000 Canadian Dollars. **Duration:** Annual. **To Apply:** Completed applications can be submitted electronically, date of submission and further information can be obtained from the website. **Deadline:** March 1.

3027 ■ Marusia and Michael Dorosh Fellowship (Master's, Graduate/Fellowship)

Purpose: To support a student writing a master's thesis on a Ukrainian or Ukrainian-Canadian topic in one of areas of education, history, law, humanities, arts, social sciences, women's studies, and library sciences. **Focus:** Education; History; Law; Library and archival sciences; Social sciences; Women's studies. **Qualif.:** Applicant must be a student in a graduate degree program undertaking a thesis on a Ukrainian or Ukrainian-Canadian topic in library sciences, education, history, law, humanities, arts, social sciences, or women's studies.

Funds Avail.: Up to 10,000 Canadian Dollars. **Duration:** Annual. **Number Awarded:** 1. **To Apply:** Completed applications can be submitted electronically, date of submission and further information can be obtained from the website. **Deadline:** March 1. **Contact:** Canadian Institute of Ukrainian Studies, 430 Pembina Hall, University of Alberta, Edmonton, Alberta T6G 2H8; Phone: 780-492-2972; Email: cius@ualberta.ca.

3028 ■ Ivan Franko School of Ukrainian Studies Ukraine Travel Award (Undergraduate/Grant)

Purpose: To support students seeking additional exposure to Ukrainian history, literature, geography, culture and language. **Focus:** Geography; History; Linguistics; Literature. **Qualif.:** Applicants must be students who have completed at least one year of study at the post-secondary level and who have also completed Ukrainian 30 or equivalent. They are required to enroll in a Ukrainian studies course/program to be offered in Ukraine by an accredited post-secondary institution, or to take courses for one semester or more at a post-secondary institution in Ukraine. **Criteria:** Selection will be based on overall academic achievement, performance in Ukrainian courses, and submitted essay.

Funds Avail.: $2,000 Canadian Dollars. **Duration:** Annual. **Deadline:** March 1.

3029 ■ Steven Kobrynsky Memorial Scholarship (Undergraduate/Scholarship)

Purpose: To assist an undergraduate student enrolled at the University of Alberta who demonstrates outstanding achievement or proficiency in the Ukrainian language. **Focus:** General studies/Field of study not specified. **Qualif.:** Applicant must be enrolled at the University of Alberta and demonstrate outstanding achievement or proficiency in the Ukrainian language.

Funds Avail.: 1,000 Canadian Dollars. **Duration:** Biennial. **Deadline:** March 1. **Remarks:** Established in 1986.

3030 ■ Leo J. Krysa Family Undergraduate Scholarships (Undergraduate/Scholarship)

Purpose: To help students pursue their final year of study in the faculty of Arts or Education. **Focus:** Ukrainian studies. **Qualif.:** Applicants must be Canadian citizens or permanent residents of Canada at the time of application; must be students in the faculty of Arts and Education about to enter their final year of study in pursuit of an undergraduate degree; have a program which emphasizes Ukrainian and/or Ukrainian-Canadian studies based on the following areas: Education, History, Humanities and Social Sciences; must have a record of above average grades in their Ukrainian-content courses. **Criteria:** Recipients will be judged on a point system that emphasizes academic achievement, performance in Ukrainian-content course, writing sample (paper or essay), and community involvement.

Funds Avail.: Up to $3,500. **Duration:** Annual. **To Apply:** Application form can be obtained at University of Alberta, Canadian Institute of Ukrainian Studies; applicants must complete and submit the application form together with their official transcript of records. **Deadline:** March 1.

3031 ■ The Remeza Family Research and Publications Grant (Professional development/Grant)

Purpose: To support research and publications pertaining to the work and legacy of Bohdan Lepky and the general

---

Awards are arranged alphabetically below their administering organizations

areas of his intellectual and creative interests. **Focus:** Literature.

Duration: Annual. **Deadline:** March 1.

3032 ■ Stasiuk Master's Research Fellowship
(Master's/Fellowship)

Purpose: To support a student writing a thesis on a Ukrainian or Ukrainian-Canadian topic in any of the following areas: education, history, law, humanities, social sciences, arts, women's studies, library sciences. **Focus:** Ukrainian studies; Writing. **Qualif.:** Applicant must be enrolled in a thesis-based Master's program in one of the following areas education, history, law, humanities, arts, social sciences, women's studies, library sciences, women's studies, library sciences; applications in other areas will be considered on an individual basis; the thesis itself must be on a Ukrainian or Ukrainian Canadian topic. **Criteria:** Selection will be based on the submitted applications; will be judged on a points system based on the thesis proposal, academic grades, letters of reference, and writing sample.

Funds Avail.: $10,000 Canadian Dollars. **Duration:** Annual. **Deadline:** March 1.

3033 ■ Ukrainian Canadian Professional and Business Club Scholarships in Education
(Undergraduate/Scholarship)

Purpose: To support students who wish to pursue their final year of study in the faculty of Education. **Focus:** Ukrainian studies. **Qualif.:** Applicant must be a full-time undergraduate student completing the third or fourth year in the faculty of Education at the University of Alberta; must have taken one course in language acquisition or teaching and one senior course in Ukrainian language or literature; must have both academic standing and demonstrated involvement in the Ukrainian community; and have an overall GPA of no less than 7.0. **Criteria:** Recipients will be judged on a points system that emphasizes academic achievement, performance in Ukrainian-content course, writing sample (paper or essay), and community involvement.

Funds Avail.: $800. **Duration:** Annual. **Number Awarded:** 1. **To Apply:** Application form can be obtained at University of Alberta, Canadian Institute of Ukrainian Studies; applicants must complete and submit the application form together with their official transcript of records. **Deadline:** March 1.

3034 ■ Canadian Iranian Foundation (CIF)
PO Box 91231
West Vancouver, BC, Canada V7V 3N6
Ph: (604)800-1977
Fax: (604)922-8584
E-mail: info@cif-bc.com
URL: cif-bc.com
Social Media: www.facebook.com/
CanadianIranianFoundation
www.instagram.com/canadian_iranian_foundation
twitter.com/CIFBC
www.youtube.com/user/canadianiranianfound

3035 ■ Canadian Iranian Foundation Scholarship
(Undergraduate/Scholarship)

Purpose: To assist immigrant students who wish to pursue their academic goals. **Focus:** General studies/Field of study not specified. **Qualif.:** Applicants must have legal im-

migrant's status (canadian citizen or permanent resident of canada) and reside in canada; have shown a great effort in trying to integrate into canadian society by volunteering at least 100 hours of community service; have active interest in iranian and canadian culture and heritage; must be accepted into a canadian post-secondary institute in a full degree program by the end of academic year; must be a member of C.I.F. for at least past 2 years and volunteers. **Criteria:** Selection will be based on the committee's criteria.

Funds Avail.: No specific amount. **Duration:** Annual. **To Apply:** Applicants must provide one letter of reference supporting extra-curricular and volunteering activities in a sealed envelope; one letter of reference supporting academics in a sealed envelope; sealed official transcript of applicant's most recent academic year; 300 words essay about "what sets you apart from other applicants?". **Deadline:** April 28. **Contact:** PO Box 91231, West Vancouver, BC, Canada, V7V 3N6.

3036 ■ Canadian Library Association (CLA)
1150 Morrison Dr., Ste. 400
Ottawa, ON, Canada K2H 8S9
Ph: (613)232-9625
Fax: (613)563-9895
E-mail: info@cla.ca
URL: cla.ca
Social Media: www.facebook.com/
CanadianLibraryAssociation
twitter.com/cla_web

3037 ■ Dafoe Scholarship *(Undergraduate, Master's/Scholarship)*

Purpose: To recognize and support a student entering an accredited Masters degree in library and information studies. **Focus:** Library and archival sciences. **Qualif.:** Applicant must be Canadian citizenship or a permanent resident; must be commencing studies for their first professional library/information science degree at an institution offering an ALA accredited masters degree in library and information studies. **Criteria:** Preference will be given to academic achievement, leadership potential and demonstrated interest in the profession.

Funds Avail.: $5,000. **Duration:** Annual. **Deadline:** May 1. **Remarks:** Established in 1982.

3038 ■ World Book Graduate Scholarships in Library and Information Science *(Graduate/Scholarship)*

Purpose: To support individuals who wish to pursue a PhD degree in library and information studies. **Focus:** Library and archival sciences. **Qualif.:** Applicant must be an individual who holds a MLS/MLIS degree and is pursuing a PhD degree in library and information studies in either Canada or the United States; must be a Canadian citizen or landed immigrant. **Criteria:** Recipients are selected based on the application and other supporting documents.

Funds Avail.: No specific amount. **Duration:** Annual. **To Apply:** Application form is available at the website.

3039 ■ Canadian Meteorological and Oceanographic Society (CMOS)
10N196 - 200 Kent St.
Ottawa, ON, Canada K1A 0E6
Ph: (613)990-0300

Awards are arranged alphabetically below their administering organizations

E-mail: cmos@cmos.ca
URL: www.cmos.ca
Social Media: www.facebook.com/cmos.scmo.canada
www.linkedin.com/groups/8421835/profile

3040 ■ Andrew Thomson Prize in Applied Meteorology *(Professional development/Award, Prize)*

Purpose: To recognize a member or members of the Society for an outstanding contribution to the application of meteorology in Canada. **Focus:** Meteorology; Oceanography. **Qualif.:** Applicants must be members of the Society with outstanding contribution to the application of meteorology in Canada. **Criteria:** Selection will be based on the committee's criteria.

Funds Avail.: No specific amount. **Duration:** Annual. **Number Awarded:** Varies. **To Apply:** Application letters should include the current title, full address and phone number of the nominee; an up-to-date CV and a summary of the candidate's work must be included; the nomination should be accompanied by, at least one and at most four, additional letters of support indicating the extent of influence of the candidate's work. Electronic format is preferred; however, hard-copy material will be accepted. **Deadline:** February 15. **Remarks:** The award is named after Andrew Thomson, founder of the Canadian Branch of the Royal Meteorological Society in 1939. Established in 1966. **Contact:** Canadian Meteorological and Oceanographic Society, PO Box 3211, Sta. D, Ottawa, ON, K1P 6H7, Canada; Email: cmos@cmos.ca.

3041 ■ CMOS-SCMO President's Prize *(Professional development/Prize)*

Purpose: To recognize members for a recent paper or book of special merit in the fields of meteorology or oceanography. **Focus:** Meteorology; Oceanography. **Qualif.:** Applicants must be members of the Society with a recent paper or book of special merit in the fields of meteorology or oceanography; the paper must have been accepted for publication in Atmosphere-Ocean or another refereed journal. **Criteria:** Selection will be based on the committee's criteria.

Funds Avail.: No specific amount. **Duration:** Annual. **To Apply:** Application letters should include the current title, full address and phone number of the nominee; an up-to-date CV and a summary of the candidate's work must be included; the nomination should be accompanied by, at least one and at most four, additional letters of support indicating the extent of influence of the candidate's work. Electronic format is preferred; however, hard-copy material will be accepted. **Deadline:** February 15. **Remarks:** Established in 1967. **Contact:** Email at awards-coord@cmos.ca.

3042 ■ CMOS Undergraduate Scholarships *(Undergraduate/Scholarship)*

Purpose: To support students planning a career in atmospheric, hydrological, oceanographic or limnological sciences. **Focus:** Meteorology. **Qualif.:** Applicants must be Canadian citizens or have landed immigrant status and be in their penultimate undergraduate year; students should be taking four or more half courses in one or more of the following areas in their final year: meteorology, physical or chemical oceanography or limnology, hydrology or climatology. **Criteria:** Selection will be based on the committee's criteria.

Funds Avail.: $500. **Duration:** Annual. **Number Awarded:** 1. **To Apply:** Applicants must submit a cover letter; this let-

ter should include a current civic address, phone numbers and e-mail address of the applicant; will be changing address during the year, it is suggested that a more permanent address and a home telephone number, be included as well; a transcript of academic studies; a statement of interest and intent to pursue a career in the relevant sciences; any details of relevant work experience; two letters of recommendations in confidence, from university professors who are directly acquainted with and knowledgeable about the work of the student; the professors can send these directly to the awards coordinator; electronic format, pdf is preferred; however, hard-copy material will be accepted; receipt of submissions will not be acknowledged unless requested; acknowledgement, when requested, will be by e-mail. **Deadline:** March 15. **Remarks:** Established in 2001.

3043 ■ Roger Daley Postdoctoral Publication Awards *(Postdoctorate/Monetary, Award)*

Purpose: To recognize excellence of a publication in the fields of meteorology or oceanography that has appeared, or is in press, at the time of nomination. **Focus:** Meteorology; Oceanography. **Qualif.:** Applicants must be working in Canada in a non-permanent position as a postdoctoral fellows or research associates and must have received their doctoral degree within five years. **Criteria:** Selection will based on the excellence of a publication in the fields of meteorology or oceanography that has appeared or is in press at the time of nomination.

Funds Avail.: 2,000 Canadian Dollars. **Duration:** Annual. **To Apply:** Application letters should include the current title, full address and phone number of the nominee; an up-to-date CV and a summary of the candidate's work must be included; the nomination should be accompanied by, at least one and at most four, additional letters of support indicating the extent of influence of the candidate's work. Electronic format is preferred; however, hard-copy material will be accepted. **Deadline:** February 15. **Remarks:** The award is named after Roger Willis Daley, UCAR Distinguished Scientific Visitor at the Naval Research Lab in Monterey. Established in 2005. **Contact:** Awards Coordinator at e-mail: awards-coord@cmos.ca.

3044 ■ Tertia M.C. Hughes Memorial Graduate Student Prize *(Graduate/Award, Prize)*

Purpose: To recognize contributions of special merit by graduate students registered at a Canadian university or Canadian graduate students registered at a foreign university. **Focus:** Meteorology; Oceanography. **Qualif.:** Applicants must be graduate students registered at a Canadian university or by Canadian graduate students registered at a foreign university. **Criteria:** Selection will be based on the committee's criteria.

Funds Avail.: $500. **Duration:** Annual. **Number Awarded:** Varies. **To Apply:** Application letters should include the current title, full address and phone number of the nominee. An up-to-date CV and a summary of the candidate's work must be included; the nomination should be accompanied by, at least one and at most four, additional letters of support indicating the extent of influence of the candidate's work. Electronic format is preferred; however, hard-copy material will be accepted. **Deadline:** February 15. **Remarks:** The award was made at the 2000 CMOS congress in Victoria, B.C to honor Tertia M.C. Hughes by CMOS. Established in 1967. **Contact:** Canadian Meteorological and Oceanographic Society, PO Box 3211, Sta. D, Ottawa, ON, K1P 6H7, Canada; Email: cmos@cmos.ca.

Awards are arranged alphabetically below their administering organizations

3045 ■ François J. Saucier Prize in Applied Oceanography *(Professional development/Award, Prize)*

Purpose: To recognize an individual for an outstanding contribution to the application of oceanography in Canada. **Focus:** Meteorology; Oceanography. **Qualif.:** Applicants must be members of the Society with outstanding contribution to the application of meteorology in Canada. **Criteria:** Selection will be based on the committee's criteria.

Funds Avail.: No specific amount. **Duration:** Annual. **To Apply:** Applicants must submit the nomination letters which includes the current title, full address and phone number of the nominee, an up-to-date CV and a summary of the candidate's work. Electronic format (e.g., pdf) is preferred; however, hard-copy material will be accepted. Receipt of submissions will not be acknowledged unless requested. Acknowledgement when requested will be by e-mail. **Deadline:** February 15. **Remarks:** The award is given in remembrance of Francois J. Saucier, an oceanographer with the Department of Fisheries and Oceans Canada (DFO), researcher in physical oceanography at the Institute Maurice-Lamontagne (IML), located in Mont-Joli, Quebec. Established in 1982. **Contact:** Canadian Meteorological and Oceanographic Society, PO Box 3211, Sta. D, Ottawa, ON, K1P 6H7, Canada; Email: cmos@cmos.ca; Awards Coordinator at e-mail: awards-coord@cmos.ca.

3046 ■ Canadian National Institute for the Blind (CNIB)

1929 Bayview Ave.
Toronto, ON, Canada M4G 3E8
Ph: (416)486-2500
Free: 800-563-2642
E-mail: info@cnib.ca
URL: www.cnib.ca
Social Media: www.linkedin.com/company/cnib
www.facebook.com/myCNIB
www.instagram.com/cnibfoundation
twitter.com/CNIB
www.youtube.com/user/cnibnatcomm

3047 ■ CNIB Master's Scholarships *(Master's/Scholarship)*

Purpose: To encourage and support people who are blind or partially sighted to undertake studies at the post-graduate level. **Focus:** General studies/Field of study not specified. **Qualif.:** Applicant must be blind or partially sighted (less than 20/70 corrected vision); must be a Canadian citizen or have held landed immigrant status for one year prior to the date of application; must be a university graduate who is entering a post-graduate education program; plan to study at a Canadian university, or a foreign university where a commitment to return to Canada is expressed; must be a high academic standing with demonstrated superior intellectual ability and judgment. **Criteria:** Selection will be based on a high academic standing with demonstrated superior intellectual ability and judgment; will be given to students planning to undertake theoretical and practical research at a Canadian university.

Funds Avail.: $12,500. **Duration:** Annual. **Number Awarded:** 2. **To Apply:** Applicants must download the Application Form (either English or French application) and submit to Shampa Bose, Executive Assistant and Research Coordinator of CNIB. **Deadline:** June 15. **Contact:** April Assenza, Executive Business Partner and Lead, Opera-

tions and Special Events, at April.Assenza@cnib.ca.

3048 ■ Nalini Perera Little Lotus Bud Master's Scholarships *(Master's/Scholarship)*

Purpose: To encourage and support people who are blind or partially sighted to undertake studies at the post-graduate level. **Focus:** General studies/Field of study not specified. **Qualif.:** Applicants must be blind or partially sighted (less than 20/70 corrected); must be university school graduates entering a post-graduate education program; and must be Canadian citizens (or landed immigrants, permanent residents, protected refugees for at least one year prior to the date of application). **Criteria:** Selection will be based on the applicant's academic standing and must have demonstrated superior intellectual ability and judgment; preference will be given to those who will undertake theoretical and practical research at a Canadian university.

Funds Avail.: $5,000. **Duration:** Annual. **To Apply:** Applicants must download the Application Form (either English or French application) and submit to Shampa Bose, Executive Assistant and Research Coordinator of CNIB. **Contact:** April Assenza, Executive Business Partner and Lead, Operations and Special Events, at April.Assenza@cnib.ca.

3049 ■ Ross C. Purse Doctoral Fellowship *(Graduate/Award, Fellowship)*

Purpose: To support and encourage research in the social sciences, engineering, or other fields of study that are immediately relevant to the field of vision loss. **Focus:** Medical research; Visual impairment. **Qualif.:** Applicants must be studying at a Canadian university or college, or at a foreign university where a commitment to work in the field of vision loss in Canada for at least two years can be demonstrated; must have achieved a high academic standing and must have demonstrated superior intellectual ability and judgment. **Criteria:** Selection will be given to people doing research at a Canadian university or college.

Funds Avail.: 12,500 Canadian Dollars. **Duration:** Annual. **Number Awarded:** 1. **To Apply:** Applications can be submitted online. **Deadline:** June 30. **Remarks:** Established in 1996. **Contact:** Cheryl-Ann Ali; Phone: 416-486-2500 ext.7637; E-mail: cheryl-ann.ali@cnib.ca.

3050 ■ Scholarship Award of the Bell Aliant Pioneer Volunteers *(Graduate/Scholarship)*

Purpose: To provide financial assistance to a person with vision lost while attending a post-secondary educational program. **Focus:** General studies/Field of study not specified. **Qualif.:** Candidates must be aged 25 years or under, have visual acuity of 20/70 or less with correction and be Canadian Citizen residing in Nova Scotia or Prince Edward Island. They must also be graduating from Grade 12 during the application year (or be a high school graduate) and registered in a post-secondary educational program. **Criteria:** Candidates will be selected based on the review of the application materials; priority is given to candidates with financial need.

Funds Avail.: No specific amount. **Duration:** Annual. **To Apply:** Candidates must submit a completed application form (available on the website); must submit two letters of reference: (1) educational letter of recommendation, and (2) personal or community letter of recommendation including contact information (address, telephone, fax and e-mail); letter of acceptance from post-secondary education institution; must provide a documentation about the

Awards are arranged alphabetically below their administering organizations

candidate's visual acuity. **Contact:** Selection Committee, Scholarship Award of the Bell Aliant Pioneer Volunteers, c/o Wendy Constable; Email: wendy.constable@cnib.ca.

3051 ■ Canadian National Railway Co.

935 de la Gauchetiere St. W
Montreal, QC, Canada H3B 2M9
Free: 888-888-5909
E-mail: contact@cn.ca
URL: www.cn.ca
Social Media: www.facebook.com/CNrail
www.linkedin.com/company/cn
twitter.com/cnrailway

3052 ■ CN Scholarships for Women *(Undergraduate/ Scholarship)*

Purpose: To encourage women to pursue non-traditional careers in areas such as trade, technology and operations; to promote employment equity in Canada. **Focus:** Technology. **Qualif.:** Applicants must be Canadian students who demonstrate desire in the field of trade, technology and operation, and have been accepted in one of those programs at an accredited educational institutions. **Criteria:** Applicants will be evaluated on the basis of their demonstrated interests in a non-traditional career. Scholarships are awarded regardless of whatever other financial assistance applicants may have obtained and may be used to ease financial constraints while studying.

Funds Avail.: 3,000 Canadian Dollars. **Duration:** Annual. **Number Awarded:** Varies. **To Apply:** Applicants must submit letter of recommendation written by one of their educators, employers, or someone who can assess their personality; and must include a (one-page) essay describing their interest with the chosen program. Aspiring applicants may also go to the website of the Canadian National Railways for other details regarding the application process. **Deadline:** May 13.

3053 ■ Canadian Nurses Foundation (CNF)

50 Driveway
Ottawa, ON, Canada K2P 1E2
URL: www.cnf-fiic.ca

3054 ■ Aplastic Anemia and Myelodysplasia Association of Canada Scholarships *(Graduate, Master's/Scholarship)*

Purpose: To support students who want to pursue their education. **Focus:** Hematology; Oncology. **Qualif.:** Applicants must be nurses who will be focusing their research in the field of hematology or oncology; must be willing to increase awareness of Aplastic, Anemia and Myelodysplasia issues by presenting to colleagues or sitting on the Board of the Association; must have at least three semesters remaining in their program after June 30; must be Canadian citizens or permanent resident status; must be studying in Canada; must be RNs enrolled in a Masters program in a health related field; must be non-nurses who hold a degree in a health-related field or a nursing-related program, which will qualify them as RNs at the Master's level. **Criteria:** Selection will be given to CANO members.

Funds Avail.: $5,000. **Duration:** Annual. **To Apply:** Applicants must include the confirmation of registration in the next semester of their program; recent transcripts or web-based grades; and two references (from academic supervi-

sors where possible). **Contact:** Email: info@cnf-fiic.ca.

3055 ■ AstraZeneca Award *(Doctorate/Award)*

Purpose: To support students who want to pursue their education. **Focus:** Nursing. **Qualif.:** Applicants must be students at the doctoral level desiring to enhance their knowledge and improve their expertise in diabetic nursing; must be a Canadian citizen or permanent resident status; must be studying in Canada; must have at least three semesters remaining in their program after June 30. **Criteria:** Selection of applicants will be based on the Scholarship application criteria.

Funds Avail.: 9,000 Canadian Dollars. **Duration:** Annual. **To Apply:** Applicants must include the confirmation of registration in the next semester of their program; recent transcripts or web-based grades; and two references (from academic supervisors where possible). **Contact:** Email: info@cnf-fiic.ca.

3056 ■ Dr. Ann C. Beckingham Scholarships *(Doctorate/Scholarship)*

Purpose: To support students who want to pursue their education. **Focus:** Nursing. **Qualif.:** Applicants must specialize in gerontology; must be Canadian citizens or with a permanent resident status; must be studying in Canada; must have at least three semesters remaining in their program after June 30. **Criteria:** Selection of applicants will be based on the Scholarship application criteria.

Funds Avail.: $5,000. **Duration:** Annual. **To Apply:** Applicants must include the confirmation of registration in the next semester of their program; recent transcripts or web-based grades; and two references (from academic supervisors where possible). **Contact:** Email: info@cnf-fiic.ca.

3057 ■ Canadian Nurses Foundation Northern Award *(Undergraduate/Scholarship)*

Purpose: To support students who want to pursue their education. **Focus:** Nursing. **Qualif.:** Applicant must be a student intending to work in Canada's North; must be a Canadian citizen or have permanent resident status; must be studying in Canada; must have at least three semesters remaining in their program after June 30. **Criteria:** Selection will based on nurses of Aboriginal origin, or who have worked in the north for at least 2 years.

Funds Avail.: $3,000. **Duration:** Annual. **To Apply:** Applicants must include the confirmation of registration in the next semester of their program; recent transcripts or web-based grades; and two references (from academic supervisors where possible). **Contact:** Email: info@cnf-fiic.ca.

3058 ■ Canadian Nurses Foundation Scholarships *(Undergraduate, Master's, Doctorate/Scholarship)*

Purpose: To support students in all areas of nursing practice. **Focus:** Nursing. **Qualif.:** Applicants must be Canadian citizens or permanent resident status; must be studying in Canada; must be entering at least year 2 as full-time students of a baccalaureate-nursing program. **Criteria:** Selection of applicants will be based on the Scholarship application criteria.

Funds Avail.: Varies. **Duration:** Annual. **To Apply:** Applicants must complete and print the application form available online. For further information, applicants are advice to contact, Jacqueline Solis, Foundation Coordinator at 613-237-2159. **Contact:** Email: info@cnf-fiic.ca.

Awards are arranged alphabetically below their administering organizations

3059 ■ Extendicare Scholarships in Gerontology
(Master's/Scholarship)

Purpose: To support students who want to pursue their education. **Focus:** Gerontology. **Qualif.:** Applicants must be nurses who intend to practice, teach or do research in gerontology/long term care; must be Canadian citizens or have permanent resident status; must be studying in Canada; must be a student at the Master's level; must have at least three semesters remaining in their program after June 30. **Criteria:** Selection of applicants will be based on the scholarship application criteria.

Funds Avail.: $5,000. **Duration:** Annual. **To Apply:** Applicants must include the confirmation of registration in the next semester of their program; recent transcripts or web-based grades; and two references (from academic supervisors where possible). **Contact:** Email: info@cnf-fiic.ca.

3060 ■ Dr. Helen Preston Glass Fellowships
(Master's/Fellowship)

Purpose: To support students who want to pursue their education. **Focus:** Nursing. **Qualif.:** Applicant must be Canadian citizen or have permanent resident status; must be studying in Canada; must be a student at the Master's level; must have at least three semesters remaining in their program after June 30. **Criteria:** Selection will be given to those focused on Primary Health Care.

Funds Avail.: $5,000. **Duration:** Annual. **To Apply:** Applicants must include the confirmation of registration in the next semester of their program; recent transcripts or web-based grades; and two references (from academic supervisors where possible). **Contact:** Email: info@cnf-fiic.ca.

3061 ■ Judy Hill Memorial Scholarships
(Undergraduate/Scholarship)

Purpose: To support students who want to pursue their education. **Focus:** Nursing. **Qualif.:** Applicants must be students currently working in Canada's North, or who have worked there and want to upgrade their skills/knowledge to be of better service to continue working there; must provide details of their plans to work there for at least 12 months; must be Canadian citizens or have permanent resident status; must be studying in Canada; must have at least three semesters remaining in their program after June 30. **Criteria:** Selection of applicants will be based on the Scholarship application criteria.

Funds Avail.: $3,000. **Duration:** Annual. **To Apply:** Applicants must include the confirmation of registration in the next semester of their program; recent transcripts or web-based grades; and two references (from academic supervisors where possible). **Contact:** Email: info@cnf-fiic.ca.

3062 ■ Johnson & Johnson Scholarships
(Undergraduate/Scholarship)

Purpose: To support students who want to pursue their education. **Focus:** Nursing. **Qualif.:** Applicant must be a student who plans to practice nursing in an operating room or a critical care area; must be a Canadian citizen or have permanent resident status; must be studying in Canada; must have at least three semesters remaining in their program after June 30. **Criteria:** Selection of applicants will be based on the Scholarship application criteria.

Funds Avail.: $3,000. **Duration:** Annual. **To Apply:** Applicants must include the confirmation of registration in the next semester of their program; recent transcripts or web-based grades; and two references (from academic supervisors where possible). **Contact:** Email: info@cnf-fiic.ca.

3063 ■ Dr. Dorothy J. Kergin Fellowships *(Doctorate, Master's/Fellowship)*

Purpose: To support students who want to pursue their education. **Focus:** Nursing. **Qualif.:** Applicant must be a Canadian citizen or have permanent resident status; must be studying in Canada; must have at least three semesters remaining in their program after June 30; must be a student at the doctoral or Master's level. **Criteria:** Selection of applicants will be based on the Scholarship application criteria.

Funds Avail.: $5,000. **Duration:** Annual. **To Apply:** Applicants must include the confirmation of registration in the next semester of their program; recent transcripts or web-based grades; and two references (from academic supervisors where possible). **Contact:** Email: info@cnf-fiic.ca.

3064 ■ Tecla Lin & Nelia Laroza Memorial Scholarships *(Undergraduate/Scholarship)*

Purpose: To support students who want to pursue their education. **Focus:** Nursing. **Qualif.:** Applicant must be a foreign educated nurse working towards baccalaureate degree; must be a Canadian citizen or have permanent resident status; must be studying in Canada; must have at least three semesters remaining in their program after June 30. **Criteria:** Applicants will be based on the Scholarship application criteria.

Funds Avail.: $3,000. **Duration:** Annual. **To Apply:** Applicants must include the confirmation of registration in the next semester of their program; recent transcripts or web-based grades; and two references (from academic supervisors where possible). **Contact:** Email: info@cnf-fiic.ca.

3065 ■ Eleanor Jean Martin Award *(Master's/ Scholarship)*

Purpose: To support students who want to pursue their education. **Focus:** Nursing. **Qualif.:** Applicants must be students interested in studying either neurosurgical or cancer nursing fields; must be Canadian citizens or have permanent resident status; must be studying in Canada; must be students at the Master's level; must have at least three semesters remaining in their program after June 30. **Criteria:** Selection of applicants will be based on the Scholarship application criteria.

Funds Avail.: $5,000. **Duration:** Annual. **To Apply:** Applicants must include the confirmation of registration in the next semester of their program; recent transcripts or web-based grades; and two references (from academic supervisors where possible). **Contact:** Email: info@cnf-fiic.ca.

3066 ■ Military Nurses Association Scholarships
(Master's/Scholarship)

Purpose: To support students who want to pursue their education. **Focus:** Nursing. **Qualif.:** Applicants must be Canadian citizens or have permanent residents status; must be studying in Canada; must be students at the Master's level; must have at least three semesters remaining in their program after June 30. **Criteria:** Preference will be given to military nurses, or former military.

Funds Avail.: $5,000. **Duration:** Annual. **To Apply:** Applicants must include the confirmation of registration in the next semester of their program; recent transcripts or web-based grades; and two references (from academic supervisors where possible). **Contact:** Email: info@cnf-fiic.ca.

3067 ■ Margaret Munro Award *(Undergraduate/ Scholarship)*

Purpose: To support students who want to pursue their education. **Focus:** Nursing. **Qualif.:** Applicant must be a

Awards are arranged alphabetically below their administering organizations

student from Prince Edward Island; must be a Canadian citizen or have permanent resident status; must be studying in Canada; must have at least three semesters remaining in their program after June 30. **Criteria:** Selection will be given to students from PEI or those studying at UPEI.

Funds Avail.: $3,000. **Duration:** Annual. **To Apply:** Applicants must include the confirmation of registration in the next semester of their program; recent transcripts or web-based grades; and two references (from academic supervisors where possible). **Contact:** Email: info@cnf-fiic.ca.

3068 ■ Dr. Helen K. Mussallem Fellowships
(Master's/Fellowship)

Purpose: To support students who want to pursue their education. **Focus:** Nursing. **Qualif.:** Applicants must be students at Master's level; must be Canadian citizens or have permanent residents status; must be studying in Canada; must have at least three semesters remaining in their program after June 30. **Criteria:** Recipients will be evaluated based on academic aptitude, personal strengths and leadership potential. Final decision will be made based on merit, strategic directions of CNF, financial and resources considerations.

Funds Avail.: $5,000. **Duration:** Annual. **To Apply:** Applicants must include the confirmation of registration in the next semester of their program; recent transcripts or web-based grades; and two references (from academic supervisors where possible).

3069 ■ New Brunswick Nurses Association Scholarships *(Master's/Scholarship)*

Purpose: To support students who want to pursue their education. **Focus:** Nursing. **Qualif.:** Applicants must be students from New Brunswick; must be Canadian citizens or have permanent resident status; must be studying in Canada; must be students at the Master's level; must have at least three semesters remaining in their program after June 30. **Criteria:** Selection of applicants will be based on the Scholarship application criteria.

Funds Avail.: $5,000. **Duration:** Annual. **To Apply:** Applicants must include the confirmation of registration in the next semester of their program; recent transcripts or web-based grades; and two references (from academic supervisors where possible). **Contact:** Email: info@cnf-fiic.ca.

3070 ■ Sharon Nield Memorial Scholarships
(Undergraduate/Scholarship)

Purpose: To support students who want to pursue their education. **Focus:** Nursing. **Qualif.:** Applicants must be registered diploma nurses returning to school; must be Canadian citizens or have permanent resident status; must be studying in Canada; must have at least three semesters remaining in their program after June 30. **Criteria:** Selection of applicants will be based on the Scholarship application criteria.

Funds Avail.: $3,000. **Duration:** Annual. **To Apply:** Applicants must include the confirmation of registration in the next semester of their program; recent transcripts or web-based grades; and two references (from academic supervisors where possible). **Contact:** Email: info@cnf-fiic.ca.

3071 ■ Senator Norman Paterson Fellowships (TBC)
(Doctorate/Scholarship)

Purpose: To support students who want to pursue their education. **Focus:** Nursing. **Qualif.:** Applicant must be a Canadian citizen or have permanent resident status; must

be studying in Canada; must be a student at the doctoral level; must have at least three semesters remaining in their program after June 30. **Criteria:** Selection of applicants will be based on the Scholarship application criteria.

Funds Avail.: 3,000 Canadian Dollars. **Duration:** Annual. **To Apply:** Applicants must include the confirmation of registration in the next semester of their program; recent transcripts or web-based grades; and two references (from academic supervisors where possible). **Contact:** Email: info@cnf-fiic.ca.

3072 ■ Sanofi Pasteur Scholarships *(Master's/Scholarship)*

Purpose: To support students who want to pursue their education. **Focus:** Nursing. **Qualif.:** Applicants must be Canadian citizens or have permanent residents status; must be studying in Canada; must be enrolled in a Master's program in a health related field; must have at least three semesters remaining in their program after June 30. **Criteria:** Selection of applicants will be based on the Scholarship application criteria.

Funds Avail.: $5,000. **Duration:** Annual. **To Apply:** Applicants must include the confirmation of registration in the next semester of their program; recent transcripts or web-based grades; and two references (from academic supervisors where possible). **Remarks:** Established in 1990. **Contact:** Email: info@cnf-fiic.ca.

3073 ■ Sigma Theta Tau International Scholarships
(Doctorate/Scholarship)

Purpose: To support students who want to pursue their education. **Focus:** Nursing. **Qualif.:** Applicants must be nurses who are working on their PhD dissertation; must be Canadian citizens or permanent resident status; must be studying in Canada; must have at least three semesters remaining in their program after June 30. **Criteria:** Selection of applicants will be based on the Scholarship application criteria.

Funds Avail.: $1,800. **Duration:** Annual. **To Apply:** Applicants must include the confirmation of registration in the next semester of their program; recent transcripts or web-based grades; and two references (from academic supervisors where possible). **Contact:** Email: info@cnf-fiic.ca.

3074 ■ TD Meloche Monnex Centennial Doctoral Scholarship *(Doctorate/Scholarship)*

Purpose: To support students who want to pursue their education. **Focus:** Nursing. **Qualif.:** Applicant must be a Canadian citizen or have permanent resident status; must be studying in Canada; must have at least three semesters remaining in their program after June 30; must be a student at the doctoral level. **Criteria:** Selection will be Canada's leading provider of insurance and added-value financial services, known for its exceptional quality of customer service.

Funds Avail.: $10,000. **Duration:** Annual. **To Apply:** Applicants must include the confirmation of registration in the next semester of their program; recent transcripts or web-based grades; and two references (from academic supervisors where possible). **Contact:** Email: info@cnf-fiic.ca.

3075 ■ John Vanderlee Award *(Undergraduate/Scholarship)*

Purpose: To support students who want to pursue their education. **Focus:** Nursing. **Qualif.:** Applicant must be a Canadian citizen or have permanent resident status; must

Awards are arranged alphabetically below their administering organizations

be studying in Canada; must have at least three semesters remaining in their program after June 30. **Criteria:** Selection of applicants will be based on the Scholarship application criteria.

Funds Avail.: $3,000. **Duration:** Annual. **To Apply:** Applicants must include the confirmation of registration in the next semester of their program; recent transcripts or web-based grades; and two references (from academic supervisors where possible). **Contact:** Email: info@cnf-fiic.ca.

3076 ■ Canadian Occupational Therapy Foundation (COTF)

2420 Bank St., Ste. 64
Ottawa, ON, Canada K1V 8S1
URL: www.cotfcanada.org

3077 ■ COTF Graduate Scholarships *(Doctorate, Master's/Scholarship)*

Purpose: To support an individual pursuing graduate studies and as such may be used at the recipient's discretion to offset the costs of fees, books, supplies, and so on. **Focus:** Occupational therapy. **Qualif.:** Applicants must be life or student members of CAOT enrolled full-time or part-time in a master's or doctoral program related to occupational therapy research.

Funds Avail.: $3,000 doctoral; $1,500 master's. **Duration:** Annual. **Number Awarded:** 1. **Deadline:** October 1. **Contact:** Email: skamble@cotfcanada.org or amcdonald@cotfcanada.org.

3078 ■ COTF/Invacare Master's Scholarship *(Master's/Scholarship)*

Purpose: To support an individual pursuing graduate studies and as such may be used at the recipient's discretion to offset the costs of fees, books, supplies, and so on. **Focus:** Occupational therapy. **Qualif.:** Applicants must be individual, life or student members of CAOT enrolled full-time or part-time in a master's program related to occupational therapy.

Funds Avail.: $2,000. **Duration:** Annual. **Number Awarded:** 1. **Deadline:** October 1. **Remarks:** Established in 2006. **Contact:** Email: skamble@cotfcanada.org or amcdonald@cotfcanada.org.

3079 ■ COTF Mental Health Research Grant *(Undergraduate/Award, Grant)*

Purpose: To individual, life or student members of CAOT who have been sponsored by an employer or educational institution to pursue research directly applicable to the practice of client-centered occupational therapy. **Focus:** Medicine.

Funds Avail.: $10,000. **Duration:** Annual. **Deadline:** February 28. **Remarks:** Established in 2018. **Contact:** Email: skamble@cotfcanada.org or amcdonald@cotfcanada.org.

3080 ■ Goldwin Howland Scholarship *(Master's, Doctorate/Scholarship)*

Purpose: To support an individual pursuing graduate studies and as such may be used at the recipient's discretion to offset the costs of fees, books, supplies, and so on. **Focus:** Occupational therapy. **Qualif.:** Applicants must be enrolled in graduate studies related to occupational therapy in Canada; must be CAOT individual, life or student members in good standing; those enrolled in a university program

outside Canada should indicate their intention to return to practice and/or to take up an academic appointment in Canada. **Criteria:** Selection of applicants will be based on scholarship reviewer criteria.

Funds Avail.: $2,000. **Duration:** Annual. **Number Awarded:** 1. **Deadline:** October 1. **Remarks:** The scholarship was founded in appreciation of Dr. Howland's leadership and vision, and is awarded to an individual who has demonstrated these qualities within the profession of occupational therapy and is enrolled in full-time studies. Established in 1945.

3081 ■ Isobel Robinson Historical Research Grant *(Professional development/Grant)*

Purpose: To support individual, life or student members of CAOT undertaking historical research on some aspect of occupational therapy. **Focus:** Occupational safety and health. **Qualif.:** Applicants must be life or student undertaking historical research on some aspect of occupational therapy.

Funds Avail.: 2,000 Canadian Dollars. **Duration:** Biennial. **Deadline:** February 28. **Remarks:** Established in 2004. **Contact:** Email: skamble@cotfcanada.org or amcdonald@cotfcanada.org.

3082 ■ Thelma Cardwell Scholarship *(Master's, Doctorate/Scholarship)*

Purpose: To support an individual pursuing graduate studies and as such may be used at the recipient's discretion to offset the costs of fees, books, supplies, and so on. **Focus:** Occupational therapy. **Qualif.:** Applicants must be individual, life or student members of CAOT enrolled full-time in a master's or doctoral level program who have demonstrated an outstanding contribution to occupational therapy. **Criteria:** Selection of applicants will be based on scholarship panel's criteria.

Funds Avail.: $2,000. **Duration:** Annual. **Number Awarded:** 1. **Deadline:** October 1. **Remarks:** The scholarship is established to acknowledge Dr. Cardwell's outstanding contribution to occupational therapy, and is awarded to an individual enrolled in full-time studies who has demonstrated significant involvement and leadership in such field. Established in 1985. **Contact:** Email: skamble@cotfcanada.org.

3083 ■ Canadian Office Products Association (COPA)

101-1335 Morningside Ave.
Scarborough
Toronto, ON, Canada M1B 5M4
Ph: (905)624-9462
Fax: (905)624-0830
E-mail: info@copa.ca
URL: www.copa.ca
Social Media: www.facebook.com/
  canadianofficeproductsassociation
www.linkedin.com/company/canadian-office-products
  -association
twitter.com/COPA_network

3084 ■ COPA Scholarship Fund *(Undergraduate/ Scholarship)*

Purpose: To assist undergraduate students in their post-secondary education. **Focus:** General studies/Field of study not specified. **Qualif.:** Applicants must be students

---

Awards are arranged alphabetically below their administering organizations

entering their first or second post-secondary studies; must be former or current employees, or with parents, guardians, or grandparents who are currently employed by a COPA member company; must be citizens or permanent residents of Canada; must have received a high school diploma within the last five years; must have completed the final two years of high school in not more than two years (this should not be consecutive); must have achieved an overall average of at least 80% in the final two years of high school prior to graduation or a GPA of at least 75% in the first year of college or university; be enrolling the first or second year of study at a university or college recognized by the Association of Universities and Colleges of Canada. **Criteria:** Applicants with GPA averages of 90 per cent and above will receive three ballots; applicants with averages of 85-89 per cent will receive two ballots; all other qualifying averages will receive one ballot.

Funds Avail.: Varies. **Duration:** Annual. **Number Awarded:** Varies. **To Apply:** Completed application consisting of the application questionnaire; a letter of employment from employer or parent/grandparent/guardians employer verifying candidate connection to a COPA member company; proof of Canadian citizenship or Permanent Resident status, copy of your official transcript for the past academic year; a copy of your preliminary acceptance letter from college or university (first year students) and a copy of your tuition invoice(second year students) must be submitted. **Deadline:** July 31. **Contact:** Phone: 905-624-9462, ext. 223 or E-mail: scholarship@copa.ca.

3085 ■ Canadian Pain Society (CPS)
250 Consumers Rd., Ste. 301
Toronto, ON, Canada M2J 4V6
URL: canadianpainsociety.site-ym.com

3086 ■ Canadian Pain Society Post-Doctoral Fellowship Awards *(Postdoctorate/Fellowship)*

Purpose: To financially assist PhD students to engage in pain research in and outside Canada. **Focus:** Education, Medical. **Qualif.:** Applicants must have completed their PhD in a pain-related field; must be Canadian citizens or landed immigrants with permanent Canadian residence. **Criteria:** Award will be given to applicants who best meet the requirements.

Funds Avail.: No specific amount. **To Apply:** Applicants must submit a cover letter; two-page summary of the proposed research; curriculum vitae; two letters of reference, one of which must come from a PhD supervisor; and a letter of support from the proposed supervisor.

3087 ■ CPS Clinical Pain Management Fellowship Awards *(Postgraduate/Fellowship)*

Purpose: To support graduates of Canadian post-graduate medical education programs who wish to further study in pain management at any institution in and outside Canada. **Focus:** Education, Medical. **Qualif.:** Applicants must have completed an MD; have completed a residency program accredited by the Royal College of Physicians and Surgeons of Canada or the College of Family Physicians of Canada; must be Canadian citizens or landed immigrants with permanent Canadian residence. **Criteria:** Award will be given to applicants who best meet the requirements.

Funds Avail.: No specific amount. **Duration:** Annual. **To Apply:** Applicants must submit a cover letter; curriculum vitae; two letters of reference, one of which must be from the Director of the residency program. If applicants have

already completed specialty training, then a copy of the Royal College of Physicians and Surgeons of Canada or College of Family Physicians of Canada certificate should be submitted along with two letters of reference. A letter of support from the Director of the program the candidate proposes for their fellowship year is also required.

3088 ■ CPS Excellence in Interprofessional Pain Education Awards *(Other/Award)*

Purpose: To support CPS members who have made significant contributions in interprofessional pain education. **Focus:** Education, Medical. **Qualif.:** Applicants must be CPS members who have demonstrated excellence in interprofessional pain education in an accredited setting with various community healthcare professionals. **Criteria:** Submitted documents will be evaluated based on demonstration of innovation, scholarship, relevance to pain education, and contribution and impact of the work to the field.

Funds Avail.: No specific amount. **Duration:** Annual. **To Apply:** Each nomination should include a two-page letter submitted to the CPS that documents the nominee's area of educational focus. It should be accompanied by a supporting letter from another CPS member external to the nominee's institution but familiar with the nominee's achievements in IPE; and must submit a curriculum vitae.

3089 ■ CPS Interprofessional Nursing Project Awards *(Other/Award)*

Purpose: To support CPS members who have made significant contributions in interprofessional pain education. **Focus:** Education, Medical. **Qualif.:** Applicants must be registered nurses who have been members of the Canadian Pain Society (CPS) for at least one year and not been recipients of this award for three years. **Criteria:** This award will be given to applicants who best demonstrate excellence as principal investigators of an interprofessional project on changing pain management practices and improving patient outcomes. All submissions will be ranked according to innovation, feasibility, methodology, ethical considerations and relevance to current practice issues.

Funds Avail.: No specific amount. **Duration:** Annual. **To Apply:** Applicants must submit a brief proposal to the CPS that describes the project including the purpose, objectives, method, evaluation and budget. Proposal should be a maximum of two pages and the project must be completed within one year. Recipients must submit results in an abstract form to be considered for poster presentation at the subsequent scientific meeting; must present five minutes summary of the project at the CPS Special Interest Group-Nursing Issues Luncheon meeting and be present for the award presentation; and must submit receipts for all the travel costs.

3090 ■ CPS Knowledge Translation Research Awards *(Other/Grant)*

Purpose: To assist a pain-related knowledge translation research project. **Focus:** Education, Medical. **Qualif.:** Applicants must be registered nurses who have been members of the Canadian Pain Society (CPS) for at least one year and not been recipients of this grant for three years. **Criteria:** Submissions will be ranked according to feasibility, methodology, ethical considerations and relevance to current practice issues.

Funds Avail.: No specific amount. **Duration:** Annual. **To Apply:** Applicants must submit a two-page written proposal for the use of the money, purpose, objectives, method, evaluation and budget along with a reference letter from a

Awards are arranged alphabetically below their administering organizations

CPS member; must submit a project which aims to improve patient outcomes using knowledge translation strategies and should be completed within one year; applicants must submit the results in an abstract form to be considered for the presentation at the subsequent CPS Scientific meeting.

3091 ■ CPS Nursing Excellence in Pain Management Awards *(Professional development/Award)*

Purpose: To assist and support nurses who consistently exemplify leadership in an area of nursing practice, education, or research in pain management. **Focus:** Education, Medical. **Qualif.:** Applicants must be CPS member in good standing.

Duration: Annual.

3092 ■ CPS Nursing Research and Education Awards *(Other/Grant)*

Purpose: To provide support a pain-related research project. **Focus:** Education, Medical. **Qualif.:** Applicants must be registered nurses who have been members of the Canadian Pain Society (CPS) for at least one year and not been recipients of this award for three years. **Criteria:** Submissions will be ranked according to feasibility, methodology, ethical considerations and relevance to current practice issues.

Funds Avail.: No specific amount. **Duration:** Annual. **To Apply:** Applicants must submit a two-page written proposal for the use of money, purpose, objectives, method, evaluation and budget along with a reference letter from a CPS member; must submit the results in an abstract form to be considered for poster presentation at the subsequent CPS Scientific meeting.

3093 ■ CPS Outstanding Pain Mentorship Award *(Other/Award)*

Purpose: To support and assist a researcher and/or clinician who consistently exemplifies outstanding mentorship in the training of future pain researchers and/or clinicians. **Focus:** Education, Medical. **Qualif.:** Applicants must be CPS members for at least two years and not been recipients of this award; and must be nominated by at least one colleague. **Criteria:** Award will be given to applicants who best meet the requirements.

Funds Avail.: $1,000. **Duration:** Annual. **To Apply:** Nominations must be made in writing; must include the nominee's curriculum vitae, narrative endorsement (maximum of 750 words) describing the mentorship qualities of the candidate. Endorsements must be signed by the nominee(s) before submission. **Deadline:** September 24. **Contact:** Canadian Pain Society office, Phone: 416-642-6379; Email: awards@canadianpainsociety.ca.

3094 ■ CPS Trainee Research Awards *(Doctorate/Grant, Award)*

Purpose: To support trainees who are working in any field of pain research projects. **Focus:** Education, Medical. **Qualif.:** Applicants must be trainees who are in the first three years of a PhD program; must be members of the Canadian Pain Society (CPS); must not hold other sources of external operating funds used to support research. **Criteria:** Judges will evaluate applications according to the trainee's qualifications/research background, academic excellence and merit of the proposed project.

Funds Avail.: $2,000. **Duration:** Annual. **Number Awarded:** 2. **To Apply:** Applicants must submit curriculum vitae; official (sealed) transcripts from all previous post-secondary institutions; one-page research summary outlining the research and indication of its related category; one-page budget with detailed justification of how funds will be used; and two letters of recommendation that address the trainee's academic and research abilities. Each letter must be sealed and signed across the seal by the writer. **Contact:** Canadian Pain Society office, Phone: 416-642-6379; Email: awards@canadianpainsociety.ca.

3095 ■ Canadian Physiotherapy Association - Physiotherapy Foundation of Canada
567 Queen St. W
Toronto, ON, Canada M5V 2B6
Ph: (647)565-9823
E-mail: info@physiotherapyfoundation.ca
URL: www.physiotherapyfoundation.ca

3096 ■ Physiotherapy Foundation of Canada Research Grant *(Other/Grant)*

Purpose: To fund a physiotherapy research in Canada that aims to improve the mobility, health and well-being of society. **Focus:** Physiology. **Qualif.:** Applicants must be Canadian citizens, landed immigrants, or people who reside in Canada (for the duration of the grant) with a valid work or student visa. **Criteria:** Application will be considered from the standpoint of its scientific merit and budget within the framework of the aforementioned regulations.

Funds Avail.: $4,000. **Number Awarded:** 1. **To Apply:** Applicants must submit an electronic copy of the completed application and all attachments as a single PDF file; submissions in other formats will not be considered; applications and attachments should be typed single spaced and minimum font size 11; illustrations should be drawn with clean black lines. **Deadline:** January 29. **Contact:** Email: foundation@physiotherapy.ca.

3097 ■ B.E. Schnurr Memorial Fund Research Grants *(Other/Grant)*

Purpose: To provide grants for students involved in physiotherapy research programs. **Focus:** Physiology. **Qualif.:** Applicants must be Canadian citizens, landed immigrants, or people who reside in Canada (for the duration of the grant) with a valid work or student visa. Special consideration will be given to blind individuals. **Criteria:** Recipients will be selected based on scientific merit, budget within framework of the aforementioned regulations. Priority will be given to research projects that are perceived to be of maximum benefit to the practice of physiotherapy and society as a whole.

Funds Avail.: Up to $7,200. **To Apply:** Applicants must submit an electronic copy of the completed application and all attachments as a single PDF file; submissions in other formats will not be considered; applications and attachments should be typed single spaced and minimum font size 11; illustrations should be drawn with clean black lines. **Deadline:** January 29. **Remarks:** The B.E. Schnurr Memorial Fund was established by the family, friends and colleagues of Bodil Elizabeth Schnurr in commemoration of her dedication to research in physiotherapy. **Contact:** Email: foundation@physiotherapy.ca.

3098 ■ Ann Collins Whitmore Memorial Scholarship (ACWMS) *(Graduate/Scholarship)*

Purpose: To provide scholarship for students involved in a research project that is part of the academic requirements

Awards are arranged alphabetically below their administering organizations

for completion of their program. **Focus:** Physiology. **Qualif.:** Applicants must have completed a professional physiotherapy program and are enrolled full-time in a PhD or post-professional masters program; must be Canadian citizens, landed immigrants, or people who reside in Canada (for the duration of the grant) with a valid work or student visa. **Criteria:** Special consideration will be given to visually impaired applicants.

Funds Avail.: Up to $4,000. **Number Awarded:** 1. **To Apply:** Applicants must submit one hard copy and one soft copy of the completed application and all appendices; appendices should be typed single spaced, minimum font size 11 and should include the applicant's and supervisor's curriculum vitae; must also submit a letter of appraisal from their supervisor, or advisor that also outlines the proposed research programme; two additional letters of appraisal; and a letter from the Head of the Department at the university confirming acceptance into one of the programmes described in the regulations for The Dominion of Canada General Insurance Scholarship. If the applicant is not enrolled at the time of the application, any scholarship will be conditional upon the receipt of written confirmation of enrollment in the programme in question; and certified transcripts of all university-level courses (graduate and undergraduate). **Deadline:** January 29. **Remarks:** The Scholarship was named in the honor of Ann Collins Whitmore, a dedicated physiotherapist. **Contact:** Grants Program Manager; Email: rkelly@physiotherapy.ca.

3099 ■ Canadian Picture Pioneers (CPP)

225 The E Mall, Ste. 1762
Toronto, ON, Canada M9B 0A9
Ph: (416)368-1139
Fax: (416)368-1139
E-mail: cdnpicturepioneers@rogers.com
URL: canadianpicturepioneers.ca
Social Media: www.facebook.com/groups/
116714111684364
www.instagram.com/canadianpicturepioneers/

3100 ■ Canadian Picture Pioneers Scholarship
(Undergraduate/Scholarship)

Purpose: To assist students who are in need of financial assistance, and who are enrolled in full time studies. **Focus:** Filmmaking; Media arts. **Qualif.:** Applicants must be legal residents of Canada (including residents of Quebec); be 30 years of age and under; currently enrolled in full time studies at a post-secondary institution; and currently work or have worked in the film industry within the past 6 months, or children/grandchildren of individuals who currently work or who have worked in the film industry in the past 6 months (or has retired from a career in the film industry and was employed for at least five (5) years prior to retirement). **Criteria:** Essays will be judged on the following criteria: inclusion of all of the information requested; clarity of thought and communication of content; essay structure; creativity / originality; grammar and spelling.

Funds Avail.: Two $5,000 Canadian Dollars; Ten $4,000 Canadian Dollars; Thirteen $2,000 Canadian Dollars. **Duration:** Annual. **Number Awarded:** 25. **To Apply:** Applicants must submit to write a 500 word essay telling the judging Trustees about themselves and explain how the scholarship money would benefit them, and how their life and education will benefit society, must also include information on any volunteer service with dates of volunteer activities; Financial information including current year school costs

and any accumulated school debts. **Deadline:** August 31. **Remarks:** Established in 2003.

3101 ■ Canadian Poultry Research Council (CPRC)

225 Metcalfe St., Ste. 314
Ottawa, ON, Canada K2P 1P9
URL: www.cp-rc.ca

3102 ■ The Canadian Poultry Research Council Postgraduate Scholarship *(Postgraduate/Scholarship)*

Purpose: To encourage and support graduate students to carry out research in an aspect of poultry science. **Focus:** Poultry science.

Funds Avail.: $5,000. **Duration:** Annual. **Number Awarded:** 1. **To Apply:** Applicants must complete and submit the following; a completed CPRC Postgraduate scholarship application form (available at the website); updated academic transcripts; a two-page resume describing the goals and academic and extracurricular activities that support their interests in poultry research; a statement of endorsement from research supervisor describing why they are particularly suitable for this award; outline of proposed research; contributions and statements.

3103 ■ Canadian Public Relations Society (CPRS)

411 Richmond St. E, Ste 200
Toronto, ON, Canada M5A 3S5
Ph: (416)239-7034
Fax: (416)929-5256
URL: www.cprs.ca
Social Media: www.facebook.com/CPRSNational
www.instagram.com/CPRSNational
www.linkedin.com/company/canadian-public-relations
-society-inc.
twitter.com/CPRSNational

3104 ■ Torchia Scholarship in Public Relations
(Undergraduate/Scholarship)

Purpose: To provide support to students who chose to study public relations/communications. **Focus:** Public relations. **Qualif.:** Applicant must be enrolled in an undergraduate public relations/communications degree program at a Canadian university or multi-year diploma or certificate program at a community college; completed the first year satisfactorily and entering the second year; studying in one of Canada's two official languages that is not the first language or mother tongue of applicant; able to demonstrate overall comprehension of public relations/communications, its theoretical and practical elements, values and principles and high ethical standards; commitment to a career in public relations/communications.

Funds Avail.: $1,500 Canadian Dollars. **Duration:** Annual. **To Apply:** Applicants should submit a copy of your curriculum vitae; attach a letter from their university or college that attests to their status and how they meet the scholarship criteria; attach a two-page submission in their language of study addressing the Scholarship criteria and their understanding of why culture and language will be important to their career planning. **Deadline:** June 15. **Contact:** CPRS Foundation; c/o 507 Millwood Road, Toronto, Ontario, M4S 1K6; Phone: 416 570 8031; Email: info@cprsfoundation.ca.

Awards are arranged alphabetically below their administering organizations

3105 ■ Canadian Simmental Association (CSA)
4101 19th St. NE, No. 13
Calgary, AB, Canada T2E 7C4
URL: www.simmental.com

3106 ■ Dr. Allan A. Dixon Memorial Scholarships
(Postgraduate/Scholarship)

Purpose: To support members of the Canadian Simmental Association and their children. **Focus:** General studies/ Field of study not specified. **Qualif.:** Application is used for the Friends of Canadian Simmental Foundation Scholarship, Dr. Allan A. Dixon Memorial Scholarship and Trevor Vance Memorial Scholarship. Open to all youth involved in the beef cattle industry who are attending a post-secondary institution in the application year. Available to students pursuing post-secondary education and recognized scholastic achievement. Applicants must be Canadian citizens. You may only apply for scholarships not previously awarded from the Foundation and a maximum of 2 FCSF scholarships in your lifetime.

Funds Avail.: $2,000 each. **Duration:** One year. **Number Awarded:** 2. **Deadline:** September 30. **Remarks:** The scholarship is in the memory of Dr. Allan A. Dixon. **Contact:** Friends of Canadian Simmental Foundation, 4101 - 19th St. NE, Ste. 13, Canada, T2E 7C4; Toll-free: 866-860-6051; Fax: 403-250-5121; Email: fcsf@simmental.com.

3107 ■ Canadian Society of Agronomy (CSA)
PO Box 637
Pinawa, MB, Canada R0E 1L0
URL: www.agronomycanada.com

3108 ■ Graduate Student Pest Management Award
(Graduate/Grant, Award)

Purpose: To support qualified graduate students enrolled in any aspect of pest management at Canadian universities. **Focus:** Agricultural sciences. **Qualif.:** Applicant must be a member of CSA; must be enrolled at a Canadian University with research programs relevant to pest management. **Criteria:** Selection will be based on scholarship panel's criteria.

Funds Avail.: 500 Canadian Dollars, accompanied by a travel grant of up to 1,000 Canadian Dollars. **Duration:** Annual. **To Apply:** Application must submit online. **Deadline:** April 15.

3109 ■ Canadian Society of Biblical Studies (CSBS)
c/o Jonathan Vroom
University of Toronto Dept. of Near and Middle Eastern Civilizations
4 Bancroft Ave 2nd flr.
Toronto, ON, Canada M5S1C1
URL: csbs-sceb.ca

3110 ■ CSBS Annual Student Prize Competition
(Graduate/Prize)

Purpose: To help students demonstrate their research related to Biblical studies. **Focus:** Religion.
Duration: Annual.

3111 ■ Canadian Society for Civil Engineering (CSCE)
521-300 rue St-Sacrement
Montreal, QC, Canada H2y 1X4

Ph: (514)933-2634
Fax: (514)933-3504
E-mail: info@csce.ca
URL: csce.ca
Social Media: www.facebook.com/
  Canadiansocietyforcivilengineering
www.linkedin.com/groups/1812786
twitter.com/csce2

3112 ■ Donald Jamieson Fellowship *(Graduate/ Fellowship)*

Purpose: To support individuals who are pursuing full-time graduate studies in structural engineering at a Canadian University. **Focus:** Engineering, Civil. **Qualif.:** Applicants must be full-time graduate students in Canadian universities.

Funds Avail.: 5,000 - 7,000 Canadian Dollars. **Duration:** Annual. **Remarks:** The award was established in honor of Donald Jamieson, a prominent civil engineer in British Columbia. Established in 1987. **Contact:** 521-300 rue St-Sacrement Montreal, QC, H2Y 1X4; Phone: 514-933-2634.

3113 ■ Canadian Society of Club Managers (CSCM)
703 Evans Ave. Suite 202A
Etobicoke, ON, Canada M9C 5E9
URL: www.cscm.org

3114 ■ Val Mason Scholarship *(Graduate, Professional development/Scholarship, Award)*

Purpose: To provide financial assistance to individuals pursuing a career in club management. **Focus:** Management. **Qualif.:** The applicant must be nominated by a member of CSCM and a covering letter of recommendation must accompany the application package. The applicant must be employed, or have been recently employed, at a member Club of the CSCM. The applicant must have shown a keen interest in pursuing a career in our industry.**Criteria:** Selection will be based on the committee's criteria.

Funds Avail.: 2,000 Canadian dollars. **Duration:** Annual. **Number Awarded:** 1. **To Apply:** Applicant must submit 500-word essay written by the Nominee explaining their interest in the club management profession; An explanation by the Nominee describing how their education is presently funded. If they are the recipient of other scholarships or bursaries, the value of each award is indicated; A copy of an official transcript from their college/ university. **Deadline:** July 13. **Contact:** Email:events@cscm.org.

3115 ■ Canadian Society of Exploration Geophysicists (CSEG)
Roslyn Bldg., Ste.570
400 5th Ave. SW
Calgary, AB, Canada T2P 0L6
URL: www.cseg.ca

3116 ■ CSEG Scholarship Trust Fund *(Graduate, Undergraduate/Scholarship)*

Purpose: To provide financial support for promising graduate students pursuing careers in the field of exploration geophysics. **Focus:** Geophysics. **Qualif.:** An applicant may

Awards are arranged alphabetically below their administering organizations

be either a high school student, an undergraduate student with above average grades or a graduate student. A student must be pursuing a course of studies directed toward a career in exploration geophysics or a dependent of a CSEG member who will be entering university. Certain scholarships administered by the Trust Fund impose additional qualifications. Completion of the questionnaire will aid in determining whether an applicant meets these qualifications. Applicants must be a CSEG student member or have a parent who is a CSEG member. Scholarships are awarded on the basis of academic performance, financial need, interest in geophysics and extra-curricular activities. **Criteria:** Applicants are selected based on academic performance, financial need, interest in geophysics and extra-curricular activities.

Funds Avail.: No specific amount. **Duration:** Annual. **Number Awarded:** Varies. **To Apply:** Applicants must provide a transcript of post-secondary education accompanied by a list of courses currently in progress and recommendation letters from two faculty members or a past or current employer mailed directly to the Committee by the author. **Deadline:** November 1. **Remarks:** Established in 1970. **Contact:** Canadian Society of Exploration Geophysicists; c/o Scholarship Committee; Suite 570, 400 – 5th Avenue SW; Calgary, Alberta T2P 0L6.

3117 ■ Canadian Society for Medical Laboratory Science (CSMLS)

33 Wellington St. N
Hamilton, ON, Canada L8R 1M7
URL: www.csmls.org

3118 ■ CSMLS Student Scholarship *(Postgraduate/ Scholarship, Monetary, Award)*

Purpose: To help and support students in their final year of a Canadian training program. **Focus:** Medical laboratory technology. **Qualif.:** Applicant must be enrolled with the CSMLS as a student member. Be enrolled in the final year of education in a Canadian accredited program, or a program which has sought but not yet, achieved accreditation, in medical laboratory technology, cytotechnology, clinical genetics or medical laboratory assistant program in Canada. Be a Canadian citizen OR a permanent resident of Canada.

Funds Avail.: $500 each. **Number Awarded:** 2. **To Apply:** Applicants must submit the application forms together with the official transcript of records; two letters of recommendation, one should be from a faculty member or college official and one should be from a community leader or other person. **Deadline:** November 1. **Contact:** Grants, Scholarships & Awards Committee, 33 Wellington Street North, Hamilton, Ontario L8R 1M7; Email:awards@csmls.org.

3119 ■ Canadian Society of Otolaryngology - Head and Neck Surgery (CSOHNS)

68 Gilkison Rd.
Elora, ON, Canada N0B 1S0
URL: www.entcanada.org

3120 ■ Educational Excellence Award *(Graduate/ Award)*

Purpose: To help students pursue advanced training in Canada. **Focus:** General studies/Field of study not specified. **Qualif.:** Applicant must be a Society member is eligible to make a nomination. **Criteria:** Selection will be based on the committee's criteria.

Funds Avail.: No specific amount. **Duration:** Annual. **Number Awarded:** 1 in 2019. **To Apply:** Application forms must be signed by the nominator and seconder; letter shall not exceed 250 words; three letters of support from the nominee's peers; current abbreviated CV of the nominee (maximum 4 pages); list of graduate trainees mentored by the nominee. **Deadline:** FEBRUARY 28.

3121 ■ Canadian Society of Petroleum Geologists (CSPG)

150, 540 - 5th Ave. SW
Calgary, AB, Canada T2P 0M2
URL: www.cspg.org

3122 ■ Glen Ruby Memorial Scholarships *(Undergraduate/Scholarship)*

Purpose: To promote excellence in petroleum geology and geophysics by assisting in the development of future geoscientists. **Focus:** Geosciences. **Qualif.:** Applicants must be students in their second, third or fourth year of studies in areas related to petroleum geology and geophysics. **Criteria:** Selection will be based on merit.

Funds Avail.: $2,000 (2nd year students); $3,000 (3rd year students); $5,000 (4th year students). **Duration:** Annual. **Number Awarded:** Varies. **To Apply:** Applicants must submit the completed application form together with copy of transcripts; application forms are available online.

3123 ■ Canadian Society for the Study of Higher Education (CSSHE)

260 Dalhousie St., Ste. 204
Ottawa, ON, Canada K1N 7E4
Ph: (613)241-0018
Fax: (613)241-0019
E-mail: csshe-scees@csse.ca
URL: csshe-scees.ca

3124 ■ CSSHE Masters Thesis/Project Awards *(Master's/Award)*

Purpose: To support outstanding Master's thesis or project in Canadian universities in the area of higher education. **Focus:** Education; Educational administration. **Qualif.:** Candidates must have completed the requirements for a Masters degree at a Canadian university during the calendar year prior to the award. They must have passed the final examination and the supervisory committee must have accepted the thesis or project by 31 December of the year prior to the award. **Criteria:** Selection is based on the scholarly excellence, but not limited to: readability, clarity and contribution to increased understanding of the dynamics of higher education.

Funds Avail.: No specific amount. **Duration:** Annual. **To Apply:** Faculty members must submit two nominations; each submission must include five copies of an expanded abstract (1000-1500 words); it should contain the problem statement, significance of the study, methodology, major findings and recommendations; separate file with the full text of the thesis or project should also be submitted. **Deadline:** January 31. **Contact:** Mr. Tim Howard, CSSHE Secretariat, Email: csshe-scees@csse.ca.

3125 ■ CSSHE Research and Scholarship Award *(Professional development/Award)*

Purpose: To honor scholars in mid-career for publishing outstanding research on any aspect of Canadian post-

Awards are arranged alphabetically below their administering organizations

secondary education. **Focus:** Education; Educational administration. **Qualif.:** Applicants must be scholars with demonstrated contributions in research focusing on Canadian post-secondary education. **Criteria:** Award will be made on the basis of published research with particular emphasis given to work published in the last five years. **Funds Avail.:** No specific amount. **Duration:** Annual. **To Apply:** Applicants must submit a letter of nomination describing the candidate and stating the reason(s) why they have been chosen for a research award; must also submit a curriculum vitae or example(s) of the published scholarship. **Deadline:** January 31. **Contact:** Email: csshescees@csse.ca.

3126 ■ Canadian Student Leadership Association (CSLA)

Three Oaks Senior High School
Summerside, PE, Canada C1N 4V9
Ph: (519)222-6718
E-mail: info@studentleadership.ca
URL: studentleadership.ca
Social Media: www.facebook.com/studentleadersedge
twitter.com/CSLA_Leaders

3127 ■ CSLA Leaders of Distinction Award *(Professional development/Recognition)*

Purpose: To recognize and support professionals for their outstanding leadership at the advisor level. **Focus:** General studies/Field of study not specified. **Qualif.:** Application must be nominated for consideration by CSLA's provincial representatives. May be individuals; informal groups of faculty or students, or both; local faculty associations; local student councils; departments; or alumni. **Criteria:** Recipients will be selected based on demonstrated leadership. **Funds Avail.:** No specific amount. **To Apply:** Application must be submitted for consideration by CSLA's provincial representatives. **Deadline:** June 1. **Contact:** Nomination should be mailed to Bill Conconi, CSLA Executive Director; E-mail: bconconi@studentleadership.ca.

3128 ■ CSLA Leadership Scholarship
(Undergraduate/Scholarship)

Purpose: To support eligible students who have made significant contribution to student leadership initiatives in their home community. **Focus:** General studies/Field of study not specified. **Qualif.:** Applicants must be enrolled in their senior year in a Canadian high school; must be currently members of CSLA; must have minimum average of 70% in their graduating year; must have plan to attend an accredited Canadian post-secondary institution; must have superior contribution through membership; and must have made a significant contribution to student leadership initiatives in their community. **Criteria:** Applicants will be selected based on merit. **Funds Avail.:** $1,000. **Duration:** Annual. **To Apply:** Applicants must submit a completed application form, resume, list of leadership activities completed during high school years, transcript of records and letter of reference from the chairperson or leadership advisor. Applicants must also submit an essay on how they would engage student leaders to make a positive and democratic difference in their school and community.

3129 ■ Canadian Technical Asphalt Association (CTAA)

174 2417 Main St.
West Kelowna, BC, Canada V4T 2H8

Ph: (250)768-9187
URL: www.ctaa.ca

3130 ■ Canadian Technical Asphalt Association Scholarships *(Undergraduate/Scholarship)*

Purpose: To support students preparing for careers as scientists, technologists or engineers in the general area of asphalt paving technology. **Focus:** Engineering, Chemical; Engineering, Civil. **Criteria:** Recipients will be chosen based on their submitted application form and supporting documents. **Funds Avail.:** $2,000. **Duration:** Annual. **To Apply:** Applicants must submit a completed application form; resume; current academic transcripts; maximum of 500 words statement explaining why they deserve to receive the scholarship; and three letters of reference (one from advisor and two from individuals knowledgeable in technical or academic qualifications of the applicant). **Deadline:** July 1. **Contact:** Canadian Technical Asphalt Association 174-2417 Main Street West Kelowna, BC, Canada V4T 2H8; Phone / Fax: 250-768-9187; Email: admin@ctaa.ca.

3131 ■ Canadian Technology Law Association

PO Box 918
Thornhill, ON, Canada L4J 8G7
Ph: (905)889-0640
URL: www.cantechlaw.ca
Social Media: ca.linkedin.com/company/can-tech-law
twitter.com/cantechlaw

3132 ■ Canadian IT Law Association Student Writing Contest *(Undergraduate/Prize)*

Purpose: To support law students who are encouraged to have an interest in information technology law. **Focus:** Law. **Qualif.:** Applicants must be students in any Canadian University. **Criteria:** Selection will be reviewed based on quality, originality and creativity of argument, quality of writing, sophistication and depth of the research. **Funds Avail.:** No specific amount. **Duration:** Annual. **To Apply:** Applications should be between approximately 25 to 50 typed pages, should contain endnotes and not footnotes, should be written in word format, 12-point font and double-spaced; submissions may be in English or French; subject line for the entries should be "IT Can Student Writing Competition."

3133 ■ Canadian Transportation Research Forum (CTRF)

PO Box 23033
Woodstock, ON, Canada N4T 1R9
Ph: (519)421-9701
URL: www.ctrf.ca
Social Media: twitter.com/ForCTRF

3134 ■ CTRF Scholarships for Graduate Study in Transportation *(Graduate/Scholarship)*

Purpose: To encourage graduate students to specialize in the transportation field. **Focus:** Business administration; Economics; Geography; Law; Religion. **Qualif.:** Applicants must be canadian citizen or full-time student at a canadian university. **Criteria:** Selection will be based on committee's criteria. **Funds Avail.:** $4,000-$6,000. **Duration:** Annual. **Number Awarded:** Varies. **To Apply:** Applicants must submit a

Awards are arranged alphabetically below their administering organizations

covering letter (including name, address, telephone, fax number, and e-mail address); official transcripts; a 300-word summary outlining graduate research project or field of study; and two letters of reference. **Deadline:** January 31. **Contact:** Email: cawoudsma@ctrf.ca.

3135 ■ Canadian Water and Wastewater Association (CWWA)
1010 Polytek St., Unit 11
Ottawa, ON, Canada K1J 9H9
Ph: (613)747-0524
Fax: (613)747-0523
URL: www.cwwa.ca
Social Media: www.facebook.com/
CanadianWaterAndWastewaterAssociation

3136 ■ Steve Bonk Scholarship (Undergraduate, Graduate/Scholarship)
Purpose: To provide educational assistance to those embarking on careers associated with municipal water supply or wastewater. **Focus:** Water resources. **Qualif.:** Applicants shall be Canadian citizens or permanent residents of Canada and have completed successfully at least one year of post secondary education. **Criteria:** Selection is based on academic achievement, statement/essay, and work experience/extra-curricular activities.

Funds Avail.: $500. **Duration:** Annual. **To Apply:** Submit a copy of the post-secondary course transcripts completed to date; a description or list of planned further studies; and a 500-word statement or essay of the applicant's interest, knowledge and future goals in the water or wastewater industry together with applicable work experience or extracurricular activities. **Deadline:** June 1. **Remarks:** The scholarship was established in recognition of Steve Bonk's guidance and development of CWWA and his roles as leader and ambassador of the water and wastewater sectors. Established in 1995. **Contact:** URL: www.acwwa.ca/committees/scholarship/stevebonk.

3137 ■ Cancer for College (CFC)
981 Park Center Dr.
Vista, CA 92081
Ph: (760)599-5096
E-mail: info@cancerforcollege.org
URL: www.cancerforcollege.org
Social Media: www.facebook.com/cancerforcollege
www.instagram.com/cancerforcollege
twitter.com/CFCcharity

3138 ■ Cancer for College Scholarship (Graduate, Undergraduate/Scholarship)
Purpose: To support current and former cancer patients in their educational pursuits. **Focus:** General studies/Field of study not specified. **Qualif.:** Applicants must be U.S. residents enrolled in an accredited university, community college or trade school; and must be cancer patients, cancer survivors and/or amputees.

Funds Avail.: $1,000-$5,000. **Duration:** Annual. **Number Awarded:** 1. **To Apply:** Applications can be submitted online. **Deadline:** January 31. **Contact:** Phone: 760-599-5096; Email: applications@cancerforcollege.org.

3139 ■ Cancer Research Institute (CRI)
4 Fl,29 Broadway.
New York, NY 10006
Ph: (212)688-7515
Fax: (212)832-9376
Free: 800-992-2623
E-mail: jtormey@cancerresearch.org
URL: www.cancerresearch.org
Social Media: www.facebook.com/
CancerResearchInstituteInc
www.instagram.com/cancerresearchinstitute
www.linkedin.com/company/the-cancer-research-institute
twitter.com/CancerResearch
www.youtube.com/user/cancerresearchinst

3140 ■ Clinic & Laboratory Integration Program (CLIP) (Professional development/Grant)
Purpose: To support scientists who are working to explore clinically relevant questions aimed at improving the effectiveness of cancer immunotherapies. **Focus:** Immunology. **Qualif.:** Applicants must hold a faculty appointment as a tenure-track assistant professor at the time of award activation.

Funds Avail.: $100,000. **Duration:** Two years. **To Apply:** Applicants must submit a letter of intent and invited application. Letters of intent must be submitted electronically; must visit the website to access the online application and attach the supporting document about brief description of current research; curriculum vitae and bibliography; abstract of research in nontechnical English explaining the importance of the proposed research and its clinical relevance. Not to exceed 250 words; an initial research concept (succinct description of the proposed research, description of the relevance of the proposed research to cancer immunology, description of how your proposed project bridges laboratory and clinical discovery), not to exceed 3 pages. **Deadline:** February 1.

3141 ■ CRI Irvington Postdoctoral Fellowships (Postdoctorate/Fellowship)
Purpose: To support qualified young scientists at leading universities and research centers around the world who wish to receive training in cancer immunology. **Focus:** Immunology. **Criteria:** Selection will be based on the committee's criteria.

Funds Avail.: Up to $175,500. **Duration:** Annual; three years. **Number Awarded:** 3. **To Apply:** Applicants must submit an entire PDF application form, beginning with the cover sheet; a brief description of the applicant's background and research accomplishments; list of other funding sources to which application has been or will be submitted, with due dates; applicant's curriculum vitae and bibliography; brief summary of the project, including a description of how the proposed research is relevant to understanding the role of the immune system in cancer and/or the treatment of cancer through immunological means; an abstract of research in nontechnical English explaining the importance of the proposed research and its potential clinical relevance; concise research proposal not to exceed 6 pages inclusive of tables and figures, exclusive of references; a letter from the sponsor introducing the applicants and describing the sponsor's qualifications to direct the proposed research; must contain two letters of recommendation; one letter must be from the applicant's thesis advisor. **Deadline:** April 1, October 1. **Remarks:** Established in 1971.

3142 ■ Student Training and Research in Tumor Immunology Grants (Graduate/Grant)
Purpose: To attract students to promising careers as cancer immunologists. **Focus:** Immunology. **Qualif.:** Ap-

Awards are arranged alphabetically below their administering organizations

plicants must be graduate students conducting thesis research in the area of tumor immunology. **Criteria:** Selection will be based on the committee's criteria.

Funds Avail.: Up to $30,000. **To Apply:** Applicants may contact the Institute for the application process and other information.

3143 ■ Cancer Research Society (CRS)
625 President-Kennedy Ave., Ste. 402
Montreal, QC, Canada H3A 3S5
Ph: (514)861-9227
Fax: (514)861-9220
URL: www.societederecherchesurlecancer.ca
Social Media: www.facebook.com/recherchecancer
www.instagram.com/recherchecancer
twitter.com/SRC_CRS
www.youtube.com/user/CRScommunications/featured

3144 ■ Scholarships for the Next Generation of Scientists *(Postdoctorate/Scholarship)*

Purpose: To support the transition of postdoctoral researchers, who become members of team of researchers in universities, and those who want to continue their work as independent researchers in a Canadian university. **Focus:** Medical research.

Funds Avail.: 160,000 Canadian Dollars. **Duration:** Annual. **To Apply:** Applicants must submit official transcripts for all university degrees; three reference letters; a proof of Canadian citizenship or permanent resident document (certificate of Canadian citizenship or birth certificate / copy of an act issued by the proper provincial government authority or valid passport or permanent resident card) along with completed application. **Deadline:** May 22. **Contact:** Lucille Beaudet, Ph.D., MBA; Phone: 514-861-9227, ext. 234; Toll-free: 866-343-2262, ext. 234; E-mail: grants@src-crs.ca.

3145 ■ Cancer Survivors' Fund
PO Box 792
Missouri City, TX 77459-0792
Ph: (281)437-7142
Fax: (281)596-7244
E-mail: csf@cancersurvivorsfund.org
URL: www.cancersurvivorsfund.org

3146 ■ Cancer Survivors' Fund Scholarship *(Undergraduate/Scholarship)*

Purpose: To augment the expenses associated with the college education of young cancer survivors. **Focus:** General studies/Field of study not specified. **Qualif.:** Applicants must be cancer survivors or currently diagnosed with cancer does not have to be receiving treatment; must be enrolled in or accepted for enrollment in an undergraduate school. **Criteria:** Selection is based on applicants' personal hardship and financial need.

Funds Avail.: No specific amount. **Duration:** Annual. **To Apply:** Applicants must submit online application form including two letters of recommendation from two different academic teachers addressing why they should receive the scholarship; a letter from an attending physician verifying their medical history and current medical situation; must agree to do volunteer work to use their cancer experience to help other young cancer patients and survivors coping

with a life threatening or life-altering event; must submit an essay discussing the following question: How has my experience with cancer impacted my life values and career goals?, minimum of 500 words and a maximum of 1200 words; copy of an acceptance letter from the college/university; applicants and their parents if they are minors, must sign a release, that they agree to have their name and photo published in the news media or any CSF publication as a recipient of Cancer Survivors' Fund scholarship.

3147 ■ Cape Coral Community Foundation (CCCF)
1405 SE 47th St., Unit 2
Cape Coral, FL 33904
Ph: (239)542-5594
E-mail: cccf@capecoralcf.org
URL: www.capecoralcf.org
Social Media: www.facebook.com/CapeCoralCF
twitter.com/Capecoralcf

3148 ■ The Helen and Edward Brancati Teacher Development Scholarship *(Professional development, Postgraduate/Scholarship)*

Purpose: To assist teachers employed by an accredited school in the United States who wish to continue their education. **Focus:** General studies/Field of study not specified. **Qualif.:** Applicants must be teachers employed by an accredited school in the United States who are seeking to continue their education; must be a U.S. Citizen. **Criteria:** Selection will be based on the basis of the applicant demonstrating the ability to create an atmosphere of learning for students across the broad spectrum of a mainstream classroom.

Duration: Annual. **To Apply:** Applicants must show proof of employment; must provide a copy of teaching certificate, written evaluations from their school principal; must outline a plan for how these funds will be used to increase their professional development or enhance their classroom; must provide a 500-word original essay discussing their reasons for becoming a teacher and how this scholarship will be beneficial; must submit a proof of enrollment or most recent transcript. **Deadline:** October 31. **Contact:** Beth Rivera, Operations Manager; 1405 SE 47th St., Unit 2, Cape Coral, FL, 33904; Phone: 239-542-5594; Email: brivera@capecoralcf.org.

3149 ■ The Rotary Club of Cape Coral Goldcoast Scholarship *(Undergraduate/Scholarship)*

Purpose: To assist eligible high school seniors to further their education by attending college. **Focus:** General studies/Field of study not specified. **Criteria:** Applicants are selected based on academic standing, academic history, school and community involvement, career and academic goals and three letters of recommendation.

Funds Avail.: $4,000 ($1,000/year). **Duration:** Up to 4 years. **To Apply:** Applicants must submit a completed application form. **Deadline:** April 1.

3150 ■ Cape Fear Community College Foundation (CFCC)
411 N. Front Street
Wilmington, NC 28401
Ph: (910)362-7000
Free: 877-799-2322

Awards are arranged alphabetically below their administering organizations

E-mail: admissions@cfcc.edu
URL: cfcc.edu
Social Media: www.facebook.com/capefearcc
www.instagram.com/capefearcc
twitter.com/cfcc
www.youtube.com/user/cfccnc

3151 ■ CFCC Foundation Merit Scholarship
(Undergraduate/Scholarship)

Purpose: To assist the local high school students throughout the course of their studies who exhibit academic excellence. **Focus:** General studies/Field of study not specified. **Criteria:** Selection is based on academic achievement; consideration will be given to non-school activities, work record, community service.

Funds Avail.: $2,600 for first year at CFCC: $1,300 in the fall semester, and another $1,300 in the spring semester (if the student continues to be qualified as a Merit Scholar). **Duration:** Annual. **To Apply:** Applicants must submit all required application information including the letter of recommendation from high school principal, guidance counselor or high school teacher; official, sealed high-school transcript, containing both weighted and non-weighted GPAs and class rank; a typed essay (maximum of 500 words) stating the applicants career and personal goals; writing sample will be consider for determining applicants; resume or bulleted list of work, community and/or school involvement. **Deadline:** April 30. **Contact:** CFCC Foundation, Merit Scholarships, 411 North Front St., Wilmington, NC, 28401.

3152 ■ Capital City AIDS Fund (CCAF)
1912 F St., Ste. 105
Sacramento, CA 95811
Ph: (916)448-1110
E-mail: capcityaidsfund@yahoo.com
URL: www.capcityaidsfund.org
Social Media: twitter.com/capcityaidsfund

3153 ■ Helen Veress-Mitchell Scholarship Fund
(Undergraduate/Scholarship)

Purpose: To help and support people living with HIV/AIDS attend college and pursue a two-year, four-year, or graduate degree. **Focus:** General studies/Field of study not specified.

Funds Avail.: No specific amount. **Duration:** Annual. **Remarks:** Established in 2002.

3154 ■ CarBrain LLC
7900 NW 154th, Ste. 200
Miami Lakes, FL 33016
Free: 877-877-7911
E-mail: info@carbrain.com
URL: carbrain.com
Social Media: www.facebook.com/thecarbrain
www.instagram.com/thecarbrain
twitter.com/theCarBrain
www.youtube.com/channel/UCPqxXA__Ws46
-udCD4VR9Rg

3155 ■ The CarBrain.com Scholarship *(Two Year College, Undergraduate, Graduate, High School/ Scholarship)*

Purpose: To provide scholarships to students with an interest in the automotive industry. **Focus:** General studies/

Field of study not specified. **Qualif.:** Must be a current high school senior in the United States OR be enrolled in a college or university in the United States as a freshman, sophomore or junior. **Criteria:** Selection is merit-based and focuses on the submitted essay.

Funds Avail.: $1,000. **Duration:** Annual. **Number Awarded:** 1. **To Apply:** Submit an answer to one of two essay questions available on the website. **Deadline:** April 1. **Contact:** Email: scholarship@carbrain.com; URL: carbrain.com/scholarship.

3156 ■ The DamagedCars.com Summer Scholarship
(Two Year College, Undergraduate, Graduate, High School/Scholarship)

Purpose: To provide scholarships to students with an interest in the automotive industry. **Focus:** General studies/ Field of study not specified. **Qualif.:** Must be a current high school senior in the United States or be enrolled in a college or university in the United States as a freshman, sophomore or junior. **Criteria:** Selection is merit-based and focused on the submitted essay.

Funds Avail.: $1,000. **Duration:** Annual. **Number Awarded:** 1. **To Apply:** Submit an answer to one of the two essay questions, email application and essay details. **Deadline:** April 1. **Contact:** Email: scholarship@ damagedcars.com; URL: www.damagedcars.com/ scholarship.

3157 ■ Cardiac Health Foundation of Canada
901 Lawrence Ave. W. Suite 201
Toronto, ON, Canada M6A 1C3
URL: cardiachealth.ca

3158 ■ Cardiac Health Foundation of Canada Scholarship *(Graduate/Scholarship)*

Purpose: To support educational endeavors of graduate students in the area of cardiac rehabilitation. **Focus:** Health care services. **Qualif.:** Applicants must be graduate student members of Canadian Association of cardiovascular prevention and rehabilitation (CACPR) and; must submit a scientific abstract and it must be accepted for presentation at the CACPR Annual Symposium.

Funds Avail.: $1,500- $2,000. **Duration:** Annual. **To Apply:** Applications can be submitted online. **Deadline:** May 7.

3159 ■ The Dr. Terry Kavanagh Fellowship
(Graduate/Fellowship)

Purpose: To support educational endeavors of graduate students. **Focus:** Health care services. **Qualif.:** Applicants must be graduate students of University of Toronto.

Funds Avail.: $6,000-$7,000. **Duration:** Annual. **Number Awarded:** 2.

3160 ■ CardRates.com
c/o Digital Brands Inc.
15 SE 1st Ave., Ste. B
Gainesville, FL 32601
URL: www.cardrates.com
Social Media: www.facebook.com/CardRatesCom
twitter.com/CardRates

3161 ■ CardRates.com Financial Futures Scholarship *(Community College/Scholarship)*

Purpose: To support student education and the future of the financial industry. **Focus:** General studies/Field of study

Awards are arranged alphabetically below their administering organizations

not specified. **Qualif.:** Must be a current or future college student (high school senior) and a U.S. resident; must have a minimum 3.5 GPA; must have an interest and goal to pursue a career in the financial industry. **Criteria:** Selection will be based on academic achievement and the submitted essay.

Funds Avail.: $1,000. **Duration:** Annual. **Number Awarded:** 1. **To Apply:** Applicant must submit an official transcript and original essay to the address above. **Deadline:** July 31.

3162 ■ Career Transition For Dancers (CTFD)
5757 Wilshire Blvd., Ste. 400
Los Angeles, CA 90036
Ph: (212)221-7300
E-mail: info@actorsfund.org
URL: www.actorsfund.org
Social Media: www.facebook.com/theactorsfund
www.instagram.com/theactorsfund
twitter.com/theactorsfund
www.youtube.com/actorsfundorg

3163 ■ Caroline H. Newhouse Scholarship Fund
(Professional development/Scholarship, Grant)

Purpose: To support current and former professional dancers who can demonstrate earning their livelihood from performing as a dancer. **Focus:** Dance. **Qualif.:** Applicants must be dancers who have performing dance careers of 7 or more years; performing years need not be consecutive or current; must have 100 weeks or more of paid dance employment in the United States within a career-span of 7 or more years; must have total gross earnings of minimum of $56,000 arrived at by combining the annual gross income of the 7 highest earning years of performing dance careers. **Criteria:** Selection shall be based on the applicants' respective work history as professional dancers.

Remarks: Established in 1985. **Contact:** Ann Barry, Grants Administrator; Phone: 212-764-0172 ext. 224.

3164 ■ CareerFitter.com
502 Long Shoals Road
Arden, NC 28704
URL: www.careerfitter.com
Social Media: www.facebook.com/careerfitter
www.youtube.com/user/careerfitter

3165 ■ CareerFitter Online Scholarship *(Undergraduate, Graduate/Scholarship)*

Purpose: To support students in their educational pursuits. **Focus:** General studies/Field of study not specified. **Criteria:** Selection will be based on the committee's criteria.

Funds Avail.: $1,000. **Duration:** Annual. **Number Awarded:** Varies. **To Apply:** Applicants may visit the scholarship section of the bestowing organization's website for further information regarding the application details. **Deadline:** January 31. **Contact:** Email: scholarship@careerfitter.com.

3166 ■ Caribbean Hotel and Tourism Association (CHTA)
2655 Le Jeune Rd., Ste. 800
Coral Gables, FL 33134

Ph: (305)443-3040
E-mail: events@caribbeanhotelandtourism.com
URL: www.caribbeanhotelandtourism.com
Social Media: www.facebook.com/
CaribbeanHotelAndTourismAssociation
www.instagram.com/chtafeeds/
www.linkedin.com/company/caribbean-hotel-and-tourism
-association
twitter.com/chTAfeeds

3167 ■ Caribbean Hotel and Tourism Association Scholarship *(Graduate, Undergraduate/Scholarship)*

Purpose: To support the education of Caribbean tourism industry personnel and students pursuing tourism & hospitality careers. **Focus:** Hotel, institutional, and restaurant management. **Qualif.:** Applicants have minimum GPA of 3.0 or equivalent. **Criteria:** Applicants are selected based by Selection Committee; based on the merit of the application.

Funds Avail.: $500 - $5,000. **Duration:** Annual. **Number Awarded:** Varies. **To Apply:** Applicants must complete the application form; endorsement letter; 3 letters of reference or recommendation; transcripts; recent photo of the applicant in jpeg or similar format; 400-words or less statement. **Deadline:** April 15. **Contact:** E-mail: Foundation@CaribbeanHotelandTourism.com.

3168 ■ Carnegie Corporation of New York
437 Madison Ave.
New York, NY 10022
Ph: (212)371-3200
URL: www.carnegie.org
Social Media: www.facebook.com/CarnegieCorporation
www.linkedin.com/company/carnegie-corporation-of-new
-york
twitter.com/carnegiecorp
www.youtube.com/user/carnegiecorpofny

3169 ■ Next Generation Social Sciences in Africa: Doctoral Dissertation Completion Fellowship *(Doctorate/Fellowship)*

Purpose: To support the advancement of social science faculty toward completion of doctoral degrees and to promote next-generation social science research in Ghana, Nigeria, South Africa, Tanzania, and Uganda. **Focus:** Social sciences. **Criteria:** Selection will be based on the committee's criteria.

Funds Avail.: $15,000. **Duration:** Annual. **Number Awarded:** 1. **To Apply:** Applications must be submitted using the online application portal; strong proposals will offer clear and concise descriptions of the project and its significance; proposals should display thorough knowledge of the relevant social science literature that will engage and the methodologies relevant to the project; in addition, must demonstrate that all proposed activities are feasible and can be completed in a timely manner; fellows must be willing to attend two workshops sponsored by the SSRC each year that are intended to help early-career faculty produce scholarly publications. **Deadline:** January 10. **Contact:** Email: nextgenafrica@ssrc.org.

3170 ■ Next Generation Social Sciences in Africa: Doctoral Dissertation Proposal Fellowship *(Doctorate/Fellowship)*

Purpose: To support short-term research costs to develop a doctoral dissertation proposal. **Focus:** Social sciences.

Awards are arranged alphabetically below their administering organizations

|

Qualif.: Applicants must be citizens of and reside in a sub-Saharan African country while holding a current faculty position at an accredited college or university in Ghana, Nigeria, South Africa, Tanzania or Uganda; must have a master's degree and be working toward completion of a doctoral degree; must be admitted to a graduate program but have yet to undertake dissertation research. **Criteria:** Selection will be based on the committee's criteria.

Funds Avail.: $3,000. **Duration:** Annual. **To Apply:** Applications must be submitted using the online application portal; strong proposals will offer clear and concise descriptions of the project and its significance; proposals should display thorough knowledge of the relevant social science literature that will engage and the methodologies relevant to the project; in addition, must demonstrate that all proposed activities are feasible and can be completed in a timely manner; fellows must be willing to attend two workshops sponsored by the SSRC each year that are intended to help early-career faculty produce scholarly publications. **Deadline:** November 17. **Contact:** Email: nextgenafrica@ssrc.org.

3171 ■ Next Generation Social Sciences in Africa: Doctoral Dissertation Research Fellowship
(Doctorate/Fellowship)

Purpose: To support the advancement of social science faculty toward completion of doctoral degrees and to promote next-generation social science research in Ghana, Nigeria, South Africa, Tanzania, and Uganda. **Focus:** Social sciences. **Criteria:** Selection will be based on the committee's criteria.

Funds Avail.: $15,000. **Duration:** Annual; 6-12 months. **To Apply:** Applicants must be submitted online. **Deadline:** January 10. **Contact:** Email: nextgenafrica@ssrc.org.

3172 ■ Carnegie Institution for Science
1530 P St. NW
Washington, DC 20005
Ph: (202)387-6400
Fax: (202)387-8092
URL: carnegiescience.edu
Social Media: www.facebook.com/carnegiescience
www.instagram.com/carnegiescience
twitter.com/carnegiescience
www.youtube.com/user/CarnegieInstitution/videos

3173 ■ Carnegie Observatories Graduate Research Fellowships *(Graduate, Doctorate/Fellowship)*

Purpose: To support graduate students interested in carrying out all or part of their thesis research under the supervision of a Carnegie Staff member. **Focus:** General studies/Field of study not specified. **Qualif.:** Applicants must have completed all requisite coursework and examinations at their home institution, and be ready to conduct full-time research toward their PhD dissertation, at the start of the appointment; since a PhD degree will be awarded by the home institution, must obtain written approval from the department chair or head granting permission for the applicants to participate in the program. **Criteria:** Selection will be based on the committee's criteria.

Funds Avail.: No specific amount. **To Apply:** Applicants must submit a brief cover letter summarizing the application and its contents; department head/chair approval letter; a list of potential advisors and projects; title of research project to be conducted with the Carnegie advisor; letters

of recommendation sent by the three individuals familiar with the academic qualifications and scientific potential of the applicant; if English is not the native language, letters should assess their English proficiency; letters should be submitted by email; an official transcript of the courses and grades to be mailed by the university registrar; curriculum vitae and publication record; a four page maximum statement of previous and current research; a four page maximum summary of the research project; materials, except for the transcript of grades should be submitted online; documents should be uploaded in PDF format. **Deadline:** April 19. **Contact:** Carnegie Observatories, at the above address; Email: gradfellowships@obs.carnegiescience.edu.

3174 ■ Carpenters' Company of the City and County of Philadelphia
320 Chestnut St., Carpenters Hall
Philadelphia, PA 19106
Ph: (215)925-0167
E-mail: carphall@carpentershall.com
URL: www.carpentershall.org
Social Media: instagram.com/carpentershall
twitter.com/CarpentersHall

3175 ■ Carpenters' Company Scholarship Program
(Undergraduate/Scholarship)

Purpose: To aid young adults pursuing a career in Architecture, Structural Engineering, or Construction Management/Engineering. **Focus:** Architecture; Construction; Engineering, Architectural. **Criteria:** Selection shall be based on the aforementioned applicant's qualifications and compliance with the application details.

Funds Avail.: $5,000. **Duration:** Annual; up to 4 years. **To Apply:** Applicants must submit a completed scholarship application form.

3176 ■ CartVela
Peshawar, Khyber Pakhtunkhwa 25000, Pakistan
Ph: 92 345 9896627
E-mail: cartvela@gmail.com
URL: www.cartvela.com

3177 ■ Digital Marketing Scholarship Program
(Undergraduate/Scholarship)

Purpose: To help needy students in fulfilling their aims for future so that they can be the best of themselves. **Focus:** General studies/Field of study not specified. **Qualif.:** Applicant must be a college or university student; must be at least 15 years old.

Funds Avail.: $1,500. **Number Awarded:** September 15. **To Apply:** Application details available at cartvela.com/scholarship/. **Contact:** Email: scholarship@cartvela.com.

3178 ■ Cascade Blues Association (CBA)
PO Box 6566
Portland, OR 97228-6566
URL: cascadebluesassociation.org
Social Media: www.facebook.com/groups/cascadebluesassociation
www.instagram.com/cascadebluesassociation
twitter.com/BluesCascade

Awards are arranged alphabetically below their administering organizations

3179 ■ Christopher Mesi Memorial Music Scholarships *(Undergraduate/Scholarship)*

Purpose: To encourage anyone to pursue an undergraduate degree at a local college. **Focus:** Music. **Qualif.:** Applicants must be high school seniors or college music students; must have GPA of 2.75 or better. **Criteria:** Recipients are selected based on demonstrated achievement through their involvement in school or community activities.

Funds Avail.: $500. **To Apply:** Applicants must submit their transcript of records; two letters of recommendation from which one must come from a music teacher and one must come from a counselor, employer or teacher; and a proof of college enrollment. **Deadline:** July 1. **Remarks:** CBA Scholarship Committee P.O. Box 14493, P.O. Box 14493 Portland, OR 97293-0493, Portland, OR 97293-0493. Established in 1997.

3180 ■ Cascara Vacation Rentals

57100 Beaver Dr., Bldg. 6, Ste. 160
Sunriver, OR 97707
Ph: (541)593-3225
Fax: (541)593-6652
E-mail: cascara@cascaravacations.com
URL: www.cascaravacations.com
Social Media: www.facebook.com/CascaraVacations
instagram.com/cascaravacations
twitter.com/cascarasunriver

3181 ■ Cascara Vacation Rentals Hospitality Matters Scholarships *(Undergraduate, Graduate/ Scholarship)*

Purpose: To offer scholarships to students to use at the college of choice. **Focus:** General studies/Field of study not specified. **Qualif.:** Applicants must be students currently enrolled in a graduate or undergraduate degree program at an accredited U.S. college, university or trade school. **Criteria:** Submitted essay will be evaluated based on the thoroughness of thought; creative approach; correct spelling and grammar; a representation of hospitality service true to the values of personal contact; supporting evidence behind claims.

Funds Avail.: $500. **Duration:** Annual. **Number Awarded:** 1. **To Apply:** Applicants must prepare a 750-word essay describing what personal service is and ways it can be implemented in a modern accommodation businesses. **Contact:** evan@cascaravacations.com.

3182 ■ Casualty Actuarial Society (CAS)

4350 N Fairfax Dr., Ste. 250
Arlington, VA 22203
Ph: (703)276-3100
Fax: (703)276-3108
E-mail: office@casact.org
URL: www.casact.org
Social Media: www.facebook.com/
  CasualtyActuarialSociety
www.instagram.com/cas.act
www.linkedin.com/company/casualty-actuarial-society
twitter.com/casact
www.youtube.com/user/CASwebmaster

3183 ■ CAS Trust Scholarship Program *(Undergraduate/Scholarship, Monetary, Award)*

Purpose: To support student's interest in the property/ casualty actuarial profession. **Focus:** Actuarial science.

Qualif.: Applicants must be U.S. or Canadian citizens or permanent residents; must be continuing or currently attending a U.S. or Canadian college or university as full-time students in the current academic year; You must be a member of Student Central. **Criteria:** Selection preference will be given to applicants who have not yet won the CAS Trust Scholarship.

Funds Avail.: $10,000 for the first place; $5,000 each for the second and third place. **Duration:** Annual. **Number Awarded:** 3. **To Apply:** Applicants must submit a CAS Trust Scholarship application and attached essay; two recommendation letters, preferably completed by internship supervisors, instructors and/or advisors at the applicant's educational institution who know them well and a current official transcript. **Deadline:** January 31. **Remarks:** Established in 2002. **Contact:** CAS Trust Scholarship Coordinator, Casualty Actuarial Society, 4350 N Fairfax Dr., Ste. 250, Arlington, VA 22203; Phone: 703-276-3100.

3184 ■ Harold W. Schloss Memorial Scholarship Fund *(Undergraduate/Scholarship, Monetary)*

Purpose: To support and give benefit to deserving and academically outstanding students in the actuarial program of the Department of Statistics and Actuarial Science at the University of Iowa. **Focus:** Actuarial science. **Qualif.:** Applicants must be members of CAS society. **Criteria:** Selection preference will be given to applicants who have not yet won the CAS Trust Scholarship.

Funds Avail.: $500. **Duration:** Annual. **Number Awarded:** 1. **To Apply:** Applicants may contact the CAS society for the application details. **Remarks:** Established in 1984.

3185 ■ Catholic Biblical Association of America (CBA)

Catholic University of America
433 Caldwell Hall
Washington, DC 20064
Ph: (202)319-5519
E-mail: cba-office@cua.edu
URL: catholicbiblical.org
Social Media: www.linkedin.com/company/catholic-biblical
  -association-of-america/

3186 ■ Roland E. Murphy, O.Carm., Scholarship *(Undergraduate/Scholarship)*

Purpose: To provide support to students who want to pursue their biblical studies. **Focus:** Bible studies. **Qualif.:** Applicant must be a full-time student in doctoral programs on biblical studies at four institutions; Catholic University of America; Graduate Theological Union at Berkeley; University of Notre Dame; Fordham University; will be nominated by the institution and will be granted the scholarship by the CBA; must be a graduate student with the potential to become a scholar who would be a credit to the CBA and the university by exemplifying the best traditions of Catholic biblical scholarship. **Criteria:** Selection will be based on the following criteria; Doctoral programs in both Old Testament and New Testament, which include a theological component; Quality programs, as judge on faculty and on course requirements, including biblical language requirements resembling those of the Pontifical Biblical Institute for the S.S.L., including both Hebrew and Greek.

Funds Avail.: Full tuition fee and a stipend of $15,500. **Duration:** Annual. **To Apply:** For further information, applicants are advised to contact the Association at Catholic University of America.

Awards are arranged alphabetically below their administering organizations

3187 ■ Catholic Relief Services (CRS)

228 W Lexington St.
Baltimore, MD 21201-3443
Free: 888-277-7575
E-mail: info@crs.org
URL: www.crs.org
Social Media: www.facebook.com/CatholicReliefServices
www.instagram.com/catholicreliefservices
twitter.com/catholicrelief

3188 ■ Catholic Relief Services Summer Internship
(Undergraduate, Graduate/Internship)

Purpose: To provide interns the professional experience, knowledge and skills that could help them enter the world of international non-government organizations. **Focus:** General studies/Field of study not specified. **Qualif.:** Applicants must be currently enrolled undergraduate or graduate college students or have graduated within the last year; must be authorized to work in the United States at the time of application. **Criteria:** Selection of interns will based on who possess strong organizational skills and the ability to collaborate in a team environment. Proactive individuals with strong interpersonal skills and oral/written communications and the commitment and ability to produce high quality, accurate work in an efficient and timely manner are the most successful. Proficiency in MS Outlook, Word, Excel, and PowerPoint is highly desirable.

Funds Avail.: No specific amount. **Duration:** Annual; period of 10 to 12 weeks or longer in some cases. **To Apply:** Applicants must submit a cover letter and resume to available internships related to their field of study and academic requirement. **Deadline:** May 1.

3189 ■ Catholic United Financial

3499 Lexington Ave. N
Saint Paul, MN 55126
Ph: (651)490-0170
Free: 800-568-6670
E-mail: info@catholicunited.org
URL: www.catholicunitedfinancial.org
Social Media: www.facebook.com/catholicunited
www.instagram.com/catholic.united.financial
www.linkedin.com/company/catholicunitedfinancial
twitter.com/catholicuf
www.youtube.com/c/CatholicUnitedFinancialSaintPaul

3190 ■ Post-High School Tuition Scholarship Program *(Undergraduate/Scholarship)*

Purpose: To provide financial assistance to students to pursue their education. **Focus:** General studies/Field of study not specified. **Criteria:** Applicants will be selected based on submitted application.

Funds Avail.: $500 for students attending a Catholic college or university; $300 for those attending a non-Catholic college, university or institution. **Duration:** Annual. **Number Awarded:** 1. **To Apply:** Applicants can submit applications through the online Member Portal system. **Deadline:** April 30. **Remarks:** Established in 1955. **Contact:** E-mail: info@catholicunited.org; engage@catholicunited.org; Phone: 800-568-6670; 651-490-0170.

3191 ■ Cave Conservancy Foundation

c/o Ms. Kate Britton, Program Director
13131 Overhill Lake Ln.
Glen Allen, VA 23059

Ph: (804)798-3432
Fax: (804)798-4894
E-mail: cavecv@aol.com
URL: www.caveconservancyfoundation.org

3192 ■ CCF Academic Fellowships in Karst Studies - Graduate *(Master's, Doctorate/Fellowship)*

Purpose: To promote the study of caves and conservation. **Focus:** Cave studies; Environmental conservation. **Qualif.:** Applicants must be students who are currently enrolled in either a master's or doctorate degree level at any accredited U.S. university or college, and interested in the study of caves and karst.

Funds Avail.: $7,000 for Master's degree; $20,000 for Doctorate degree. **To Apply:** Applicants for the fellowship must include a letter of intent, a curriculum vita, a thesis proposal, graduate transcripts, and two letters of recommendation, one being from the thesis advisor. **Deadline:** May 1. **Remarks:** Established in 1997. **Contact:** Dr. Annette S. Engel; Email: aengel1@utk.edu; cavecv@aol.com.

3193 ■ CCF Academic Fellowships in Karst Studies - Undergraduate *(Undergraduate/Fellowship)*

Purpose: To assist undergraduate students in their further education in cave studies. **Focus:** Cave studies; Conservation of natural resources. **Qualif.:** Applicants must be students who are currently enrolled in an undergraduate degree level at any accredited U.S. university or college, and interested in the study of caves and karst.

Funds Avail.: $6,000. **To Apply:** Applicants for the fellowship must include a letter of intent, a research proposal not exceeding 5,000 words, a letter of support from the undergraduate advisor, and undergraduate transcripts. **Deadline:** May 1. **Contact:** Dr. Daniel W. Fong; Email: dfong@american.edu.; cavecv@aol.com.

3194 ■ Cave Conservancy of the Virginias (CCV)

13131 Overhill Lake Ln.
Glen Allen, VA 23059
Ph: (804)798-4893
URL: www.caveconservancyofvirginia.org
Social Media: www.facebook.com/
caveconservancyofthevirginias

3195 ■ Graduate and Undergraduate Fellowship Awards *(Doctorate, Graduate, Undergraduate/Fellowship, Award)*

Purpose: To promote study and research on caves and karst in any field. **Focus:** Archeology; Biology; Cave studies; Engineering, Geological; Geography; Geology; Social sciences. **Qualif.:** Applicant must involve caves and karst areas anywhere in the world, but applicants must be full-time students at a U.S. college or university. **Criteria:** Selection will be based on the committee's criteria.

Funds Avail.: $6,000 (undergraduate); $7,000 (graduate students); $20,000 (PhD Students). **Duration:** Annual. **Number Awarded:** Varies. **To Apply:** Applicants must submit a letter of intent, a proposal of the research (maximum of 5000 words), a letter of support and undergraduate transcripts. Graduate applicants (MS and PhD) must submit a letter of intent, a curriculum vitae, a thesis proposal, graduate transcript and two letters of recommendation (one from the thesis advisor). **Deadline:** May 1. **Contact:** Dr. Annette S. Engel; Email: aengel1@utk.edu.

3196 ■ CCNMA: Latino Journalists of California

ASU Walter Cronkite School of Journalism and Mass Communication

Awards are arranged alphabetically below their administering organizations

---

725 Arizona Ave., Ste. 404
Santa Monica, CA 90401-1734
Ph: (424)229-9482
Fax: (424)238-0271
E-mail: ccnmainfo@ccnma.org
URL: ccnma.org
Social Media: www.facebook.com/ccnma.latinojournalists/
www.instagram.com/latinojournos/
twitter.com/ccnma

3197 ■ Frank del Olmo Memorial Scholarships
(Undergraduate/Scholarship)

Purpose: To support qualified Latino students who are planning to pursue a career in journalism. **Focus:** Journalism. **Qualif.:** Applicants must be Latino college students or graduating high school seniors attending a college or university in California (California residents may attend a college or university outside of California) and majoring in journalism. **Criteria:** Selection will be based on commitment to the field of journalism, scholastic achievement, community awareness, and financial need.

Funds Avail.: $500-$1,000 per student. **Duration:** Annual. **To Apply:** Applicants must submit a completed application form together with an autobiographical essay (300-500 words); two reference letters, including at least one from a faculty member (no family members); current official transcripts; and work samples (which include newspaper articles, TV or radio audition tapes, or photographs produced by student applicants). **Remarks:** Established in memory of Frank del Olmo, a founding member of the CCNMA who also served on its Board of Directors.

3198 ■ Joel Garcia Memorial Scholarship
(Undergraduate/Scholarship)

Purpose: To provide support to qualified Latino students who are planning to pursue a career in journalism. **Focus:** Journalism. **Qualif.:** Applicant must be a Latino college student or graduating high school senior attending a college or university in California (residents of California may attend school elsewhere) and must major in journalism.

Funds Avail.: $500-$1,000 per student. **Duration:** Annual. **To Apply:** Application details are available on the sponsor's website. **Remarks:** Established in honor of Joel Garcia, a Los Angeles journalist who first proposed founding a professional association for Chicano journalists in 1972. That group would eventually become CCNMA: Latino Journalists of California.

3199 ■ CDA Foundation

1201 K St., 14th Fl.
Sacramento, CA 95814
Free: 800-232-7645
URL: www.cdafoundation.org
Social Media: www.facebook.com/cdacares
www.instagram.com/cdadentists/
www.linkedin.com/company/california-dental-association
twitter.com/CDA_Dentists
www.youtube.com/user/CDADentists

3200 ■ Webb Family Grant *(Postdoctorate/ Scholarship)*

Purpose: To provide support to those pursuing dental degrees. **Focus:** Dentistry. **Criteria:** Selection is based on the submitted application and materials.

Funds Avail.: Up to $5,000 for educational expenses. **Number Awarded:** 1. **To Apply:** Applicants should contact the sponsoring organization for application details.

3201 ■ CDC Foundation

600 Peachtree St. NE, Ste. 1000
Atlanta, GA 30308
Ph: (404)653-0790
Fax: (404)653-0330
E-mail: info@cdcfoundation.org
URL: www.cdcfoundation.org
Social Media: www.facebook.com/CDCFoundation
www.instagram.com/cdcfound
www.linkedin.com/company/cdc-foundation?trk=fc_b
www.br.pinterest.com/cdcfoundation
twitter.com/CDCFound
www.youtube.com/user/CDCFoundation

3202 ■ Pappaioanou Veterinary Public Health and Applied Epidemiology Fellowships *(Undergraduate/ Fellowship)*

Purpose: To provide an opportunity for third and fourth-year medical and veterinary students to gain public health experience in an international setting. **Focus:** Medicine; Veterinary science and medicine. **Qualif.:** Applicants must be third or fourth year students in the veterinary medicine. **Criteria:** Applicants will be selected on a highly competitive basis.

Funds Avail.: No specific amount. **Duration:** Annual; up to one full year. **To Apply:** Applicants are required to submit one to two page research proposal (not to exceed two single-spaced pages with an 11-font size) that contains the following information: name of the applicants and their respective contact information; date of submission; brief description of career objectives, focus/pursuits/plans; title/ name of proposed fellowship opportunity; public health purpose/objective of the proposed opportunity; learning objective of proposed opportunity (how will the experience assist achieving career pursuits); CDC program that would be hosting the experience; name of CDC mentor that would supervise/oversee learning experience; proposed start date and time period to be spent at CDC for learning opportunity; and, amount of funding being sought and what funding would be used to support. **Contact:** Helene Erenberg E-mail:herenberg@cdcfoundation.org.

3203 ■ CEDAM International

2 Fox Rd.
Croton on Hudson, NY 10520
Ph: (914)271-5365
URL: cedaminternational.org

3204 ■ Lloyd Bridges Scholarship *(Graduate/ Scholarship)*

Purpose: To inspire individuals to help protect one of the world's most fragile ecosystems and to have educators experience the wonders of the underwater world and share it to their students. **Focus:** Aquaculture. **Qualif.:** Applicants must be a certified scuba diver, a teacher (elementary or secondary level), or actively engaged in an education program at an institution or environmental organization, such as an aquarium, science center or relevant non-profit organization. **Criteria:** Selection is based on the applicant's merit and financial need.

Awards are arranged alphabetically below their administering organizations

---

Funds Avail.: up to $1,200. **Duration:** Annual. **To Apply:** Applicants must complete the application form; must submit a 500-word essay; a resume and one letter of recommendation. **Deadline:** April 1. **Contact:** Susan Sammon & Jan Rosenfeld; Email: susansammon@gmail.com or janrosenfeld@gmail.com.

3205 ■ Celler Legal, P.A.

10368 W State Rd. 84, Ste. 103
Davie, FL 33324
Ph: (954)903-7475
E-mail: richard@floridaovertimelawyer.com
URL: www.floridaovertimelawyer.com
Social Media: www.facebook.com/richardcellerlegalpa/
twitter.com/CellerLegalPA
www.youtube.com/user/cellerlegalpa

3206 ■ Celler Legal P.A. Employment Skills Scholarship Program *(Undergraduate/Scholarship)*

Purpose: To support exceptional young students looking to advance their work and career skills with the intent of using their education in service of their community. **Focus:** General studies/Field of study not specified. **Qualif.:** Applicants must be entering or attending first year in a Florida college or university; must have maintained a high school GPA of 3.0 of higher; must be U.S. citizens or have permanent residency. **Criteria:** Applicants will be reviewed by members of Celler Legal P.A. and evaluated based on factors including financial need, the personal story share, and the accomplishment of the students.

Funds Avail.: $1,000. **Duration:** Annual. **To Apply:** Application form and details are available online at www.floridaovertimelawyer.com/scholarship/. **Deadline:** November 12. **Remarks:** Established in 2016.

3207 ■ Center for Advanced Study in the Behavioral Sciences (CASBS)

75 Alta Rd.
Stanford, CA 94305
Ph: (650)736-0100
E-mail: casbs-info@stanford.edu
URL: casbs.stanford.edu
Social Media: twitter.com/casbsstanford
www.youtube.com/user/casbsbehavsci

3208 ■ CASBS Fellowships *(Doctorate, Other/Fellowship)*

Purpose: To extend knowledge of the principles governing human behavior to help solve the critical problems of contemporary society. **Focus:** Behavioral sciences. **Qualif.:** Applications from scholars who are three to four years past the doctorate. **Criteria:** Selection process is based on an online application system.

Duration: Annual. **To Apply:** Applications can be submitted online; full curriculum vitae; two reference letters; If applicable, a statement of your project's fit with one of our partner fellowship programs (150-250 words). **Remarks:** Established in 1954. **Contact:** Ting Liu or Sally Schroeder; Email: casbs-fellowships@stanford.edu.

3209 ■ Center for Book Arts (CBA)

28 W 27th St., 3rd Fl.
New York, NY 10001

Ph: (212)481-0295
E-mail: info@centerforbookarts.org
URL: centerforbookarts.org

3210 ■ Artist-in-Residence Workspace Grant *(Professional development/Grant)*

Purpose: To promote experimentation in making book art. **Focus:** Art. **Qualif.:** Applicants must be artists, live/work in New York State and must reside in the greater NYC metropolitan area at the time of application and during the residency. **Criteria:** Selection will be based on the committees' criteria.

Funds Avail.: $750-$1,500. **Duration:** Annual. **Number Awarded:** Up to 5. **To Apply:** Applicants may contact the Association for application process and other information. **Deadline:** October 13.

3211 ■ Center for Craft, Creativity and Design (CCCD)

67 Broadway St.
Asheville, NC 28801
Ph: (828)785-1357
E-mail: info@centerforcraft.org
URL: www.craftcreativitydesign.org
Social Media: www.facebook.com/centerforcraft
www.instagram.com/centerforcraft
www.linkedin.com/company/the-center-for-craft-creativity-and-design

3212 ■ Craft Research Fund Grants *(Other/Grant)*

Purpose: To encourage, expand and support scholarly craft research in the United States. **Focus:** Crafts. **Qualif.:** Applicants must be researchers, scholars or museum curators and graduate students.

Funds Avail.: Up to $15,000. **Duration:** Annual. **Number Awarded:** 1. **To Apply:** Applicants must submit five copies of the proposal in the following order by page; cover sheet; one-page summary of the proposal; three other scholars/colleagues who have written the three most significant works of the chosen topic; timeline and schedule for completing the project; budget page; curriculum vitae; no more than five pages project description; letter of support from a field scholar and from an institution, publication, organization, participant or anyone who is affiliated with the project; image(s) that would compliment or may add to the clarity of the proposal (optional). **Deadline:** October 1. **Contact:** E-mail: grants@craftcreativitydesign.org.

3213 ■ Center For Religious Humanism

3307 3rd Ave. W
Seattle, WA 98119
Ph: (206)281-2988
Fax: (206)281-2979
Free: 866-481-0688
E-mail: image@imagejournal.org
URL: imagejournal.org
Social Media: www.facebook.com/imagejournal
instagram.com/image_journal
twitter.com/image_journal

3214 ■ Milton Postgraduate Fellowship *(Postgraduate/Fellowship)*

Purpose: To support writers of poetry, fiction and creative nonfiction who seek to animate the Christian imagination,

Awards are arranged alphabetically below their administering organizations

promote intellectual integrity, and explore the human condition with honesty and compassion. **Focus:** Creative writing. **Qualif.:** Applicants must be U.S. citizens, or be able to show proof of permanent residency, unexpired temporary residency, or a current valid visa, and possess at least an M.A. in English Literature, Creative Writing, or the humanities, or an MFA in Creative Writing. **Criteria:** Selection will be based on clearly formulated proposal, a high quality of writing, and a demonstrated ability to complete the project.

Duration: Annual. **To Apply:** Applicants must submit a book proposal, including synopsis and description of its audience (limit 2000 words); an autobiographical essay about the applicant's development as a writer and a person of faith (limit 2000 words); 30 to 50 double-spaced pages of prose or 8 to 12 poems; a brief explanation of what the Applicants aim to accomplish next year at the Center; and a $25 application fee (make check payable to Image).

3215 ■ Luci Shaw Fellowship *(Undergraduate/Fellowship)*

Purpose: To expose a promising undergraduate student. **Focus:** Literature. **Qualif.:** Applicants must be currently enrolled undergraduate institution. **Criteria:** Selection is based on the application.

Funds Avail.: No specific amount. **Duration:** Annual. **To Apply:** Applicants must submit a completed application form along with a letter of introduction; a resume; a writing sample of 10-15 pages (this could be a term paper, a personal essay, or creative writing. It can include poetry, but it shouldn't be all poetry); and two letters of recommendation from teachers, work or volunteer supervisors, or other mentors who know you well. **Contact:** Phone: 206-281-2988; Email: image@imagejournal.org.

3216 ■ Center for Global Initiatives
FedEx Global Education Ctr.
CB 5145
301 Pittsboro St., Ste. 3000
Chapel Hill, NC 27599-5145
Ph: (919)962-3094
Fax: (919)962-5375
E-mail: cgi@unc.edu
URL: cgi.unc.edu
Social Media: www.facebook.com/unccgi
www.instagram.com/unccgi/
twitter.com/unccgi

3217 ■ UNC-CGI C.V. Starr Scholarship *(Undergraduate, Graduate/Scholarship)*

Purpose: To support University of North Carolina students who demonstrate financial need to undertake an independent internationally-oriented experience. **Focus:** General studies/Field of study not specified. **Qualif.:** Applicants must be undergraduate and graduate students. Undergraduate applicants should be "Pell-eligible" based on demonstrated financial need; must have at least 2.8 GPA; graduate must not be U.S. citizens or permanent residents (green card holders); must have plan of returning to UNC for at least one semester upon completing their internationally-oriented experience. **Criteria:** Applications will be evaluated based on feasibility and planning, need, impact and budget.

Funds Avail.: $1,500 - $6,000 each. **Duration:** Annual. **Number Awarded:** Varies. **To Apply:** Applicants must complete an online application form and must include the

following basic biography; project title and summary; short answer questions; letter of affiliation; list of three references; detailed budget; list of additional funding sources; unofficial transcript; and international student need analysis worksheet. **Remarks:** Established in 2004. **Contact:** Brandy Arellano, Program Manager, Center for Global Initiatives; Phone: 919-962-6857; Email: brandy_arellano@unc.edu.

3218 ■ Center for International Environmental Law (CIEL)
1101 15th St. NW, 11th Fl.
Washington, DC 20005
Ph: (202)785-8700
Fax: (202)785-8701
E-mail: info@ciel.org
URL: www.ciel.org
Social Media: www.linkedin.com/company/the-center-for -international-environmental-law-ciel-/
twitter.com/ciel_tweets

3219 ■ Louis B. Sohn Fellowships in Human Rights and Environment *(Graduate/Fellowship)*

Purpose: To offer fellowship positions to recent law school graduates and members of the bar who wish to develop or increase their knowledge of the practice of public interest, international environmental law. **Focus:** Law. **Qualif.:** Applicants must be public interest lawyers that have had significant on the ground experience working on human rights issues. **Criteria:** Selection is based on the submitted application materials.

Funds Avail.: No specific amount. **Duration:** Annual. **To Apply:** Applicants must submit a letter, resume, writing sample, and an additional essay that describes applicants' interest and background in human rights and the environment and how these legal instruments can or should be used to protect human rights and the environment (maximum of 500 words); must indicate in the cover letter that they would like to be considered for the fellowship.

3220 ■ Center for Jewish History (CJH)
15 W 16th St.
New York, NY 10011
Ph: (212)294-8301
E-mail: inquiries@cjh.org
URL: www.cjh.org
Social Media: www.facebook.com/centerforjewishhistory
instagram.com/centerforjewishhistory
twitter.com/cjewishhistory

3221 ■ CJH Graduate Research Fellowships *(Doctorate/Fellowship)*

Purpose: To support original research at the Center for Jewish History in the field of Jewish Studies. **Focus:** Jewish studies. **Qualif.:** Applicants must be qualified doctoral candidates in accredited institutions. They must have the appropriate visa for acceptance of the stipend and for the required duration of the award. **Criteria:** Preference will be given to those candidates who draw on the library and archival resources of more than one partner.

Funds Avail.: $22,500. **Duration:** Annual; Up to one year. **To Apply:** Applicants must complete the following requirements: cover letter stating area of interest, knowledge of

Awards are arranged alphabetically below their administering organizations

relevant languages, and how the project relates to the mission of the Center for Jewish History; curriculum vitae, including contact information, education, publications, scholarly and/or museum activities, teaching experience and any other relevant work experience; specific research proposal of no more than five pages, including specific reference to the collections at the Center and clearly stated goals for research during the period of the fellowship; official graduate school transcript; three letters of recommendation, including from the students' academic advisors, which address the significance of the candidate's work for the field as well as the candidate's ability to fulfill the proposed work. **Deadline:** February 2. **Contact:** Judah Bernstein, Ph.D., Academic Programs Coordinator, Center for Jewish History, 15 W 16th St., New York, NY 10011, United States of America, Email: fellowships@cjh.org.

3222 ■ CJH-NEH Fellowships for Senior Scholars
(Doctorate/Fellowship)

Purpose: To support college and university faculty as they worked to complete their dissertations using the partner collections. **Focus:** European studies; German studies; Humanities; Jewish studies; Russian studies. **Qualif.:** Applicants must: be college and university faculty members who received a PhD more than six years prior to the start of the fellowship; be U.S. citizens as well as foreigners who have lived in the United States for at least three years prior to the application deadline; and, have the appropriate visa for acceptance of the stipend for the duration of the award. **Criteria:** Selection will be based on the committee's criteria.

Funds Avail.: A stipend of up to $50,400. **Duration:** Annual. **To Apply:** Applicants must complete the following requirements: cover letter stating area of interest, knowledge of relevant languages, and how the project relates to the mission of the Center for Jewish History; curriculum vitae, including contact information, education, publications, scholarly and/or museum activities, teaching experience and any other relevant work experience; specific research proposal of no more than five pages, including specific reference to the collections at the Center and clearly stated goals for research during the period of the fellowship; three letters of recommendation, which address the significance of the candidates' work for their field as well as the candidates' ability to fulfill the proposed work. **Deadline:** January 3. **Contact:** Christopher Barthel, Ph.D., Director of Academic Programs, Center for Jewish History; Email: fellowships@cjh.org.

3223 ■ CJH-Prins Foundation Fellowships for Senior Scholars *(Doctorate/Fellowship)*

Purpose: To support international senior scholars as they worked to complete their dissertations using the partner collections. **Focus:** European studies; German studies; Humanities; Jewish studies; Russian studies. **Qualif.:** Applicants must be foreign senior scholars in any field who have completed a PhD more than six years prior to the start of the fellowship and whose research will benefit substantially from consultation of materials housed at the Center. **Criteria:** Selection will be based on the committee's criteria; preference will be given to candidates from Eastern Europe and the former Soviet Union.

Funds Avail.: A stipend of $75,000 as well as a relocation stipend of up to $15,000. **To Apply:** Applicants must complete the following requirements: curriculum vitae, including information, education, publications, scholarly and/or museum activities, teaching experience and any other relevant work experience; detailed research proposal consisting of four to five pages, including specific reference

to the collections at the Center and clearly stated goals for research during the period of the fellowship; three letters of recommendation that address the significance of the candidate's work for their field as well as the candidate's ability to fulfill the proposed research project; two recent publications consisting of either an article published in a scholarly journal, a chapter in an edited collection, or the introduction and a subsequent chapter from a recently published book; 1- to 2-page essay articulating why they wish to emigrate and what they hope to accomplish after concluding the fellowship. Send all application materials together electronically as one PDF continuous document. Applicants are responsible for ensuring that letters of recommendation are submitted electronically by recommenders by the deadline. **Contact:** Christopher Barthel, PhD, Senior Manager for Academic and Public Programs Center for Jewish History; Email: fellowships@cjh.org.

3224 ■ CJH-Prins Foundation Post-Doctoral and Early Career Fellowship for Emigrating Scholars
(Professional development, Postdoctorate/Fellowship)

Purpose: To support international scholars as they worked to complete their dissertations using the partner collections. **Focus:** European studies; German studies; Humanities; Jewish studies; Russian studies. **Qualif.:** Applicants must be scholars from outside the United States who seek permanent teaching and research positions who are at the beginning of their career. They must have the appropriate visa for acceptance of the stipend for the duration of the award. **Criteria:** Selection will be based on the committee's criteria; preference will be given to candidates from Eastern Europe and the former Soviet Union.

Funds Avail.: $35,000. **Duration:** Annual. **To Apply:** Applicants must complete the following requirements: cover letter stating area of interest, knowledge of relevant languages, and how the project relates to the mission of the Center for Jewish History; curriculum vitae, including contact information, education, publications, scholarly and/or museum activities, teaching experience and any other relevant work experience; specific research proposal of no more than five pages, including specific reference to the collections at the Center and clearly stated goals for research during the period of the fellowship; three letters of recommendation, which address the significance of the candidates' work for their field as well as the candidates' ability to fulfill the proposed work. **Deadline:** January 16. **Contact:** Christopher Barthel, Ph.D., Director of Academic Programs, Center for Jewish History; Email: fellowships@cjh.org.

3225 ■ CJH Visiting Scholars Program *(Doctorate/Fellowship)*

Purpose: To support visiting scholars as they worked to complete their dissertations using the partner collections. **Focus:** Jewish studies. **Qualif.:** Applicants must be scholars who: have their PhD or equivalent terminal degree; and, working on projects that make use of the Center partner collections. **Criteria:** Selection will be based on the committee's criteria.

Funds Avail.: No specific amount. **Duration:** Up to three months. **To Apply:** Applicants must complete the following requirements: a complete curriculum vitae; a description of the proposed research, maximum of three pages in length, including an explanation of which of the Center partners' collections will be used; the names and contact information of two references. Send all application materials together electronically as one continuous PDF document. **Contact:** Judah Bernstein, Ph.D., Academic Programs Coordinator,

Awards are arranged alphabetically below their administering organizations

Center for Jewish History, 15 W 16th St., New York, NY 10011, United States of America, Email: fellowships@cjh.org.

3226 ■ Joseph S. Steinberg Emerging Jewish Filmmaker Fellowship (Undergraduate, Graduate/Fellowship)

Purpose: To help further existing projects, or to start new projects, whose subject matter is in line with the collections housed at the Center. **Focus:** Jewish studies. **Qualif.:** Applicants must be undergraduate and graduate emerging filmmakers working on their own original projects on topics related to modern Jewish history. **Criteria:** Students will be selected for one academic year of research through a rigorous and competitive process.

Funds Avail.: Up to $5,000. **Duration:** Annual. **To Apply:** Applicants must complete the application; submit CV; at least one, preferably two, letter(s) of recommendation/support.

3227 ■ The Center for Justice & Accountability
1 Hallidie Plz., Ste. 406
San Francisco, CA 94102
Ph: (415)544-0444
Fax: (415)544-0456
E-mail: center4justice@cja.org
URL: www.cja.org
Social Media: www.facebook.com/CenterForJusticeAndAccountability
www.linkedin.com/company/113494
twitter.com/cja_news

3228 ■ Legal Internships (Professional development/Internship)

Purpose: To encourage and train law students in preparation for their chosen profession. **Focus:** Law. **Qualif.:** Applicants must be second and third year law students who want to undergo training at CJA's office in San Francisco. Exceptional first year law students may be considered for the summer term. **Criteria:** Selection will be based on need; the center are particularly interested in students have familiarity with human rights law, international criminal and humanitarian law, and evidence.

Funds Avail.: No specific amount. **To Apply:** Applicants must send an email which contains the following: cover letter, resume, and transcript. They must state their names and the term for which they are applying in the subject line. Cover letter of the applicants should consist of the following: the term which they are applying; any relevant coursework (especially evidence, advanced civil procedure, federal courts, trial advocacy, international criminal law, international humanitarian law, human rights law, public international or comparative law, and immigration law), and your professor(s) for any human rights law, humanitarian law, or related international law courses; any language abilities, especially Spanish, French, Somali, Khmai, Arabic, Farsi, Haitian, Creole, Swahili or any Southeast Asian languages; and any deadlines the applicants need to secure funding for their internship. **Deadline:** December 15. **Contact:** One Hallidie Plaza, Ste. 406, San Francisco, CA, 94102; Phone: 415-544-0444; Fax: 415-544-0456; Email: info@cja.org.

3229 ■ Center for Justice and International Law
1630 Connecticut Ave. NW, Ste. 401
Washington, DC 20009-1053

Ph: (202)319-3000
Fax: (202)319-3019
E-mail: brasil@cejil.org
URL: cejil.org
Social Media: www.facebook.com/CEJIL
www.linkedin.com/company/center-for-justice-and-international-law---cejil
twitter.com/cejil
youtube.com/user/cejilddhh/videos

3230 ■ CEJIL Communications Internships (Professional development, Graduate/Internship)

Purpose: To encourage students and graduates who wish to have more practical experience in the field of human rights to complement their academic and professional training. **Focus:** Communications; Human rights. **Qualif.:** Applicants must be students or graduates with concentrations in communications or journalism that are interested in promoting and protecting human rights, with a particular emphasis in Latin America; students or graduates with a career orientation towards human rights work are also considered. **Criteria:** Selection will be based on the applications of the aspiring interns.

Funds Avail.: No specific amount. **Duration:** Periodic. **To Apply:** Applications can be submitted online. **Deadline:** October 15; February 15; June 15.

3231 ■ CEJIL Legal Internships (Graduate, Professional development/Internship)

Purpose: To encourage students and graduates who wish to have more practical experience in the field of human rights to complement their academic and professional training. **Focus:** Human rights; Law. **Qualif.:** Applicants must be law students or law graduates interested in a career in international human rights law, with a particular interest in Latin America; students or graduates with careers oriented towards human rights work will also be considered; furthermore, must have solid command of the Spanish language; have excellent writing skills; have willingness and ability to handle a wide variety of tasks; and have experience in working in non-government organizations; knowledge of Portuguese and/or English language is valuable, depending also upon the office where the internship is held. **Criteria:** Selection will be based on the applications of the aspiring interns.

Funds Avail.: No specific amount. **Duration:** Periodic. **To Apply:** Applications for the internship (in Washington D.C.) will be accepted on a rolling basis. Interested applicants should fill out the online application form for the office in which they hope to carry out the internship. After filling out all of the necessary information on the application, they will also have the option of attaching a copy of their resume. **Deadline:** October 15; February 15; June 15.

3232 ■ Center for LGBTQ Studies (CLAGS)
365 5th Ave., Rm. 7115
New York, NY 10016
Ph: (212)817-1955
Fax: (212)817-1567
E-mail: info@clags.org
URL: www.clags.org
Social Media: www.facebook.com/clags.org
twitter.com/CLAGSNY
www.youtube.com/user/clagsny

Awards are arranged alphabetically below their administering organizations

3233 ■ CLAGS Fellowship Award *(Graduate, Advanced Professional/Award, Fellowship)*

Purpose: To give scholars the most help possible in furthering their respective works on LGBTQ studies. **Focus:** Sexuality. **Qualif.:** Applicant may be a graduate student, an academic, or an independent scholar who is contributing to the field of LGBTQ studies.

Funds Avail.: $2,000. **Duration:** Annual. **Number Awarded:** 1. **To Apply:** Application along with cover letter stating your name, address, contact information, school/campus affiliation and project description; submit the most complete version of your dissertation and one copy of the abstract, in case of first or second book manuscript, submit at least three chapters from your proposed project and one copy of your prospectus should be send electronically; Files saved on CD are also accepted but no printed copies. **Deadline:** June 1. **Contact:** E-mail: clagsfellowships@gmail.com.

3234 ■ The Duberman-Zal Fellowship *(Graduate/Scholarship)*

Purpose: To award a senior scholar from any country doing scholarly research on the lesbian, gay, bisexual, transgender, and queer experience. **Focus:** Homosexuality. **Qualif.:** Applicants must be a graduate student, senior scholar (tenured university professor or advanced independent scholar) from any country doing scholarly research on the lesbian/gay/bisexual/transgender/queer (LGBTQ) experience.

Funds Avail.: $7,500. **Duration:** Annual. **To Apply:** Applicants must submit a completed application form; a cover letter with contact information; a proposal of 7-10 pages; curriculum vitae; an evidence of contribution to the field of LGTBQ studies; and two letters of recommendation. **Remarks:** The fellowship was named for CLAGS founder and first executive director, Martin Duberman, and partner, Eli Zal. **Contact:** E-mail: clagsfellowships@gmail.com.

3235 ■ The Robert Giard Fellowship *(Graduate/Fellowship)*

Purpose: To provide fund to support research, travel or writing. **Focus:** Homosexuality. **Qualif.:** Applicants must be graduate students, academic or independent scholars who work on dissertation. **Criteria:** Applicants will be selected by the fellowships committee of the Center for Lesbian and Gay Studies based on the review of the application materials.

Funds Avail.: $7,500. **Duration:** Annual. **To Apply:** Applicant must submit completed application with CV, cover letter, description of proposed project. **Remarks:** The fellowship was named for Robert Giard, a portrait, landscape, and figure photographer whose work often focused on LGBTQ lives and issues. **Contact:** E-mail: clagsfellowships@gmail.com.

3236 ■ Joan Heller-Diane Bernard Fellowships *(Graduate, Undergraduate/Fellowship)*

Purpose: To supports research into the impact of lesbians and/or gay men on U.S. society and culture. **Focus:** Homosexuality. **Qualif.:** Applicants must be junior scholars, graduate students, untenured professors, independent researchers, or senior scholars; those conducting research on lesbian issues are encouraged to apply.

Contact: For further information, applicants may contact the Fellowship Coordinator by phone: 212-817-1958 or by e-mail: clagsfellowships@gmail.com.

3237 ■ Center for Plant Conservation (CPC)

15600 San Pasqual Valley Rd.
Escondido, CA 92027-7000
Ph: (760)796-5686
E-mail: info@saveplants.org
URL: www.saveplants.org
Social Media: www.facebook.com/
  CenterForPlantConservation
www.instagram.com/centerforplantconservation
twitter.com/cpcplants

3238 ■ Catherine H. Beattie Fellowships *(Graduate/Fellowship)*

Purpose: To promote conservation of rare and endangered flora in the United States through the programs of the Center for Plant Conservation in partnership with the Garden Club of America. **Focus:** Biology; Horticulture. **Qualif.:** Applicants must be graduate students in biology or horticulture. **Criteria:** Preference will be given to students focusing on endangered flora of the Carolina or the southeastern united states.

Funds Avail.: up to $4,500. **Duration:** Annual. **To Apply:** Applications should be submitted to the center for plant conservation and must include the following: one page cover letter; two page (maximum) project narrative; one page project budget and timeline; curriculum vitae; letter of recommendation from major advisor or equivalent. **Deadline:** January 31.

3239 ■ Central Farm Service

233 W Ciro St.
Truman, MN 56088
Ph: (507)776-2831
Fax: (507)776-2871
Free: 800-657-3282
URL: www.cfscoop.com
Social Media: www.facebook.com/WFS.COOP
twitter.com/cfscoop

3240 ■ Working for Farmers' Success Scholarships *(Undergraduate/Scholarship)*

Purpose: To encourage young people to pursue an agricultural career. **Focus:** Agriculture, Economic aspects. **Qualif.:** Applicants must be senior students who are graduating from the WFS trade territory. **Criteria:** Recipients will be selected based on academic performance, qualities of leadership, integrity and good community citizenship. Financial need is also given consideration.

Funds Avail.: $500 each. **Number Awarded:** Up to 20. **To Apply:** Applicants must submit a completed application form.

3241 ■ Central Florida Jazz Society (CFJS)

3208 W Lake Mary Blvd., Ste. 1720
Lake Mary, FL 32746-3476
Ph: (407)539-2357
E-mail: jazz@centralfloridajazzsociety.com
URL: centralfloridajazzsociety.com
Social Media: www.facebook.com/centralfloridajazzsociety
www.instagram.com/centralfloridajazzsociety/?hl=bn
twitter.com/CFjazz

3242 ■ Central Florida Jazz Society Scholarships *(Undergraduate/Scholarship)*

Purpose: To support amateur jazz musicians in furthering their education. **Focus:** Music, Jazz. **Criteria:** Selection

Awards are arranged alphabetically below their administering organizations

will based on: technique; expression; style (interpretation); performance presence (showmanship) and overall performance.

Funds Avail.: $1,000 to $ 2,500. **Duration:** Annual. **Number Awarded:** 4. **To Apply:** Initial screening of all applicants will require an audition cassette tape, CD or DVD containing 1 or 2 improvised choruses of two selections of different tempos (labeled with the student's name on the recording); in addition to the musical recording, a letter of recommendation, from an individual familiar with the applicant's musicianship, character and commitment to jazz study, must be submitted. **Deadline:** April 2. **Contact:** Send audio or video files as attachments in an e-mail to greg_glennmillerproductions@yahoo.com.

3243 ■ Central Intelligence Agency (CIA)

Office of Public Affairs
Washington, DC 20505
Ph: (703)482-0623
URL: www.cia.gov
Social Media: www.facebook.com/Central.Intelligence
.Agency
twitter.com/CIA
www.youtube.com/user/ciagov

3244 ■ CIA Undergraduate Scholarships
(Undergraduate/Scholarship)

Purpose: To assist minority, disabled and non-disabled deserving students to increase knowledge and academic skills. **Focus:** General studies/Field of study not specified. **Qualif.:** Applicants must be entering their junior or senior year of college by the fall of 2020; applications must be submitted no earlier than your senior undergraduate year of college and no later than your second year of graduate school studies. **Criteria:** Selection is based on merit, character, serious academic commitment, and relevance of your studies to national security interests and career ambitions.

Funds Avail.: $18,000. **Duration:** Annual. **To Apply:** Applicants must provide - via the online form is best - the following SEVEN items. Any of these formats for your attachments are acceptable: PDF, DOC, DOCX, TXT, JPG, TIF, RTF, ODT, including common archive files - e.g., ZIP, ZIPX. Do not send dat or htm files. Verify your attachments open to be certain they are valid files and not empty shortcut files. Keep attachments per email under 15 MB. Cover Letter: explaining your need for scholarship, your career goals, your views of U.S. world standing and role U.S. intelligence community should play; Resume; A copy of your academic transcript - need not be original or "official"; One recommendation (have person send to us by email; Recent photograph - can be sent as a high resolution digital image file via email attachment, or printed and mailed. Image should show full face sitting, standing, or portrait only. JPG, TIF, GIF, PDF, other major graphic image formats acceptable; Indicate for WHICH scholarships you wish to be considered. No need to send multiple copies of your materials, however, since we will consider you for all scholarships we offer; College or University you will be attending in 2020-2021 and your intended course of study (your declared 'major' or 'area of concentration'). **Deadline:** June 1. **Contact:** AFIO Scholarships, 7700 Leesburg Pike Ste 324, Falls Church, VA 22043; scholarships@afio.com.

3245 ■ Central Texas Bluegrass Association (CTBA)

PO Box 9816
Austin, TX 78766-9816
E-mail: ctba@centraltexasbluegrass.org
URL: www.centraltexasbluegrass.org
Social Media: www.facebook.com/
CentralTexasBluegrassAssociation
www.instagram.com/centraltexasbluegrass

3246 ■ Willa Beach-Porter CTBA Music Scholarship Fund *(Undergraduate/Scholarship)*

Purpose: To support students who have demonstrated a serious interest and performance talent in bluegrass music, and who show a need for financial assistance to support their musical studies. **Focus:** Music. **Qualif.:** Applicants must be between the ages of 12 and 21; must be Texas residents. **Criteria:** Recipients are selected based on financial need.

Funds Avail.: No specific amount. **Duration:** Annual. **Number Awarded:** Varies. **To Apply:** Applicants must complete an application form and two recommendation letters (mailed separately). **Deadline:** May 15. **Remarks:** The scholarship is named after Willa Beach-Porter, a long-time supporter of bluegrass music and of the Central Texas Bluegrass Association. **Contact:** Central Texas Bluegrass Association, PO Box 9816, Austin, TX 78766-9816; Phone: 512-261-9440; E-mail: ctba@centraltexasbluegrass.org.

3247 ■ CentraState Healthcare Foundation

225 Willow Brook Rd, Ste. 5
Freehold, NJ 07728
Ph: (732)294-7030
E-mail: foundation@centrastate.com
URL: www.centrastatefoundation.org
Social Media: www.facebook.com/centrastatefoundation
www.instagram.com/centrastatefoundation
twitter.com/centrastatefndn
www.youtube.com/user/CentraStateFndn

3248 ■ CentraState Associated Auxiliaries Scholarship *(Undergraduate/Scholarship)*

Purpose: To provide scholarship assistance to deserving students who want to pursue the healthcare field. **Focus:** Health care services. **Qualif.:** Applicants must be students or adult who live and volunteer in the CentraState service area; must be graduating high school seniors or an adult returning to college to pursue a career in the healthcare field.

Funds Avail.: $500 each. **Duration:** Annual. **Number Awarded:** 3. **To Apply:** Applicants must submit the application form along with transcripts (for the high school seniors), two letters of recommendation (one must be from the person or organization for whom you volunteer), and the completed essay requirement. **Deadline:** May 22. **Contact:** Mrs. Valerie Mac Phee, PO Box 32, Perrineville, NJ, 08535.

3249 ■ CentraState Band Aid Open Committee Scholarship *(Undergraduate/Scholarship)*

Purpose: To support students who are planning to pursue a career in the health professions. **Focus:** Health sciences. **Funds Avail.:** $2,000. **Duration:** Annual. **Number Awarded:** 2. **To Apply:** Applicants must submit the ap-

Awards are arranged alphabetically below their administering organizations

plication form along with a current transcript, two letters of recommendation, and the completed essay requirement. **Contact:** Olive Taylor, CentraState Healthcare Foundation, 225 Willow Brook Rd., Ste. 5, Freehold, NJ, 07728; Phone: 732-294-7030; Email: otaylor@centrastate.com.

3250 ■ CentraState Healthcare Foundation Health Professions Scholarships *(Undergraduate/ Scholarship)*

Purpose: To provide scholarship assistance to deserving students who want to pursue the healthcare field. **Focus:** Health care services. **Qualif.:** Applicants must be high school seniors who live and/or attend school within the CentraState Healthcare System service area and have chosen to pursue a career in the health professions. **Criteria:** Selection will be based on the aforesaid qualifications and compliance with the application process.

Funds Avail.: $500 each. **Duration:** Annual. **Number Awarded:** 3. **To Apply:** Applicants must submit a current transcript, letters of recommendation from two teachers and/or counselors and the completed essay requirement; the application form may be obtained from the CentraState Healthcare Foundation office. **Deadline:** April 21.

3251 ■ DCH Freehold Toyota Scholarship *(Undergraduate/Scholarship)*

Purpose: To support students who are planning to pursue a career in the health professions. **Focus:** Health sciences. **Qualif.:** Applicants must be graduating high school seniors attending the Freehold Regional High School District's medical sciences program; must be planning to pursue a career in the health professions.

Funds Avail.: $1,000. **Duration:** Annual. **Number Awarded:** 1. **To Apply:** Applicants must submit the application form along with a current transcript, two letters of recommendation, and the completed essay requirement. **Contact:** Olive Taylor, CentraState Healthcare Foundation, 225 Willow Brook Rd., Ste. 5, Freehold, NJ, 07728; Phone: 732-294-7030; Email: otaylor@centrastate.com.

3252 ■ Centre for Interdisciplinary Research in Music Media and Technology (CIRMMT)
527 W Sherbrooke St.
Montreal, QC, Canada H3A 1E3
URL: www.cirmmt.org

3253 ■ CIRMMT Student Awards *(Graduate, Master's, Doctorate/Award)*

Purpose: To support students who are pursuing interdisciplinary research projects within the Center's mandate. **Focus:** Music; Technology. **Qualif.:** Applicants must be new and returning graduate student members; Master's and Doctoral students may submit single or group applications; to be eligible, students must be enrolled during the full period of the award funding. **Criteria:** Selection will be based on disciplinarity of the proposal.

Funds Avail.: $3,000 to $5,000. **Duration:** Annual. **Number Awarded:** Varies. **To Apply:** Applicants must submit one complete electronic copy, in a single PDF document, of the form and all additional documents; applicants must submit CV's. **Deadline:** February 1. **Contact:** Email: reception@cirmmt.mcgill.ca.

3254 ■ Centre International de Criminologie Comparée (CICC)
University of Montreal
Pavillon Lionel-Groulx

3150, rue Jean-Brillant
Ste. C-4086
Montreal, QC, Canada H3T 1N8
Ph: (514)343-7065
Fax: (514)343-2269
E-mail: cicc@umontreal.ca
URL: www.cicc.umontreal.ca
Social Media: www.facebook.com/CICCUdeM
twitter.com/CICCTweet
www.youtube.com/user/CICCTV

3255 ■ CICC Postdoctoral Fellowship *(Postdoctorate/ Fellowship)*

Purpose: To conduct advanced research on the processes by which criminal behaviour is regulated and the control mechanisms put in place by public, private and community institutions. **Focus:** Criminology. **Qualif.:** Applicant must be a postdoctoral student. **Criteria:** Priority will be given to candidates from other universities.

Funds Avail.: 32,825 Canadian Dollars. **Duration:** Annual. **To Apply:** Application can be written in English; the research project (three pages maximum) should detail the following: issue, objectives, methodology, schedule, references, the statement of motivations to carry out the project at CICC; a curriculum vitae outlining applicant's main achievements; a schedule of goals for the duration of the fellowship; a reference letter from the research director. Must submit the original signed letter by postal mail along with a transcript of marks. **Deadline:** July 15. **Remarks:** Established in 2004.

3256 ■ Centre for International Sustainable Development Law (CISDL)
Chancellor Day Hall
3644 Peel St.
Montreal, QC, Canada H3A 1W9
Ph: (818)685-9931
Fax: (514)398-4659
E-mail: secretariat@cisdl.org
URL: www.cisdl.org
Social Media: www.facebook.com/intsustainlaw
twitter.com/intsustainlaw

3257 ■ CISDL Global Research Fellowship - Associate Fellows *(Graduate/Fellowship)*

Purpose: To promote sustainable societies and the protection of ecosystems by advancing understanding, development and implementation of international sustainable development law. **Focus:** Law. **Qualif.:** Applicant may be a law or legal graduate student from a developing country or from one of the leading international law programs of university law faculties around the world.

Funds Avail.: No specific amount. **Duration:** Annual. **To Apply:** Applicants must submit a completed application form along with a cover letter and current CV. **Deadline:** October 1.

3258 ■ CISDL Global Research Fellowship - Legal Research Fellows *(Graduate/Fellowship)*

Purpose: To promote sustainable societies and the protection of ecosystems by advancing understanding, development and implementation of international sustainable development law. **Focus:** Law. **Criteria:** Selection is based

Awards are arranged alphabetically below their administering organizations

on academic and professional qualifications. Preference is given to applications from research fellows presently based in Montreal or in the country of a CISDL Lead Counsel.

Funds Avail.: No specific amount. **Duration:** Annual. **To Apply:** Applicants must submit a completed application form together with a curriculum vitae and a cover letter.

3259 ■ CISDL Global Research Fellowships - Senior Research Fellows (Other/Fellowship)

Purpose: To promote sustainable societies and the protection of ecosystems by advancing understanding, development and implementation of international sustainable development law. **Focus:** Law. **Criteria:** Preference is given to CISDL fellows from developing countries, and those who are based in universities or international law institutions affiliated with CISDL.

Funds Avail.: No specific amount. **Duration:** Annual. **To Apply:** Applicants must submit a completed application form together with a current resume. **Deadline:** October 1.

3260 ■ Centre pour l'Innovation dans la Gouvernance Internationale (CIGI)

67 Erb St. W
Waterloo, ON, Canada N2L 6C2
URL: www.cigionline.org

3261 ■ International Law Research Program's Graduate Scholarship Competition (CIGI ILRP)
(Advanced Professional, Professional development/Scholarship)

Purpose: To encourage leading scholars, senior practitioners and legal experts in the government or private sector to take part in research on international law. **Focus:** Law. **Qualif.:** Applicants must be Canadian and foreign students currently enrolled in masters or doctoral level studies at a Canadian university. **Criteria:** Selection will be based on the applicant's high quality academic qualifications, professional experience, established networks, a proven track record of publications in prominent journals, and participation in public discourse and debate; are subjected to a two stage ranking and review process by a Selection Committee consisting of CIGI senior management and external members; proposals should align with the three core streams of the ILRP and programmatic streams of CIGI.

Funds Avail.: Up to $16,000. **Duration:** Annual. **To Apply:** Applicants should provide Statement of Interest, indicating a clearly specified explanation of why you wish to spend a period of residency at CIGI's ILRP; Research Proposal (not more than 1,500-words); curriculum vitae; One letter of support; Three references, at least two of which are academic references; Transcripts from all post-secondary institutions; Letter of recommendation from the student's doctoral supervisor; Student's letter requesting renewal. **Deadline:** April 15. **Contact:** E-mail at lawcareers@cigionline.org.

3262 ■ Centre de Recherches pour le Développement International (CRDI)

PO Box 8500
Ottawa, ON, Canada K1G 3H9
URL: www.idrc.ca

3263 ■ The Bentley Cropping Systems Fellowship
(Graduate/Fellowship)

Purpose: To provide funding for field research aimed at increasing the yield of food crops, improving farmers' livelihoods, and improving soil fertility. **Focus:** Agricultural sciences; Food science and technology.

Funds Avail.: No specific amount. **Duration:** Biennial. **Remarks:** Established with a bequest from the late Dr. Bentley and his wife, Helen S. Bentley, was a member of the founding Board of IDRC. Established in 1999.

3264 ■ IDRC Research Awards (Master's, Doctorate/Award)

Purpose: To aid the research of Canadian citizens or permanent residents, and citizens of developing countries who are pursuing master's or doctoral studies at a recognized university or having completed a master's or doctoral program at a recognized university. **Focus:** General studies/Field of study not specified. **Qualif.:** Applicant must be a Canadians, permanent residents of Canada, and citizens of developing countries pursuing a master's or a doctoral degree at a recognized university OR who have completed a master's or a doctoral degree at a recognized university. **Criteria:** The following criteria will be used to evaluate applications: relevance of the proposal to IDRC's mission; relevance of the proposal to the chosen development outcome area; clarity and quality of the proposal; clarity and appropriateness in addressing the ethical considerations and gender dimensions of the proposed research; applicant's capacity to conduct the proposed program of research, including academic training, local language capacity, and related experience.

Funds Avail.: 15,000 Canadian Dollars. **Duration:** Annual. **Number Awarded:** 12. **Deadline:** September 16.

3265 ■ Cereals & Grains Association

3340 Pilot Knob Rd.
Saint Paul, MN 55121
Ph: (651)454-7250
Fax: (651)454-0766
E-mail: info@cerealsgrains.org
URL: www.cerealsgrains.org
Social Media: www.facebook.com/cerealsgrains
www.linkedin.com/groups/4163868/profile
www.linkedin.com/company/cerealsgrains
twitter.com/aaccintl
twitter.com/cerealsgrains

3266 ■ American Association of Cereal Chemists Graduate Fellowship Program (Graduate/Fellowship)

Purpose: To encourage graduate research in grain-based food science and technology. **Focus:** Food science and technology. **Qualif.:** Applicants must be a current Cereals & Grains Association Student Member; must be enrolled in graduate studies by the time the fellowship becomes effective, or be a current graduate student pursuing a course of study leading to an MS or a Ph.D. degree; must be conducting fundamental investigations for the advancement of cereal science and technology, including oilseeds; must be enrolled in an academic schedule that meets the minimum requirements of the university involved, for full-time graduate study. **Criteria:** Selection based on age, sex, race, financial need, or previous receipt or non-receipt.

Funds Avail.: Up to $3,000. **Duration:** Annual. **Number Awarded:** Up to 2. **To Apply:** Applicants must submit completed application along with letter of application, copies of transcripts of all college or university undergraduate work you have completed to date, two (2) letters of recommendation with at least one from (and signed by) academic

Awards are arranged alphabetically below their administering organizations

adviser and/or faculty member familiar with your academic record. **Deadline:** May 29. **Contact:** Email:hq@cerealsgrains.org.

3267 ■ Raymond J. Tarleton Graduate Fellowships
(Graduate/Fellowship)

Purpose: To support a Fellowship Program that encourages graduate research in grain-based food science and technology. **Focus:** Food science and technology.

Funds Avail.: $2,500. **Duration:** Annual. **Number Awarded:** 1. **Remarks:** Established in 2003.

3268 ■ CGTrader
Antakalnio St. 17
LT-10312 Vilnius, Lithuania
E-mail: info@cgtrader.com
URL: www.cgtrader.com
Social Media: www.facebook.com/cgtrader
www.linkedin.com/company/cgtrader
twitter.com/CG_Trader

3269 ■ Annual CGTrader Scholarship *(High School, Undergraduate, Graduate/Scholarship)*

Purpose: To spread scholarship opportunity among students in any field of study. **Focus:** General studies/Field of study not specified. **Qualif.:** Applicant must be high school senior, undergraduate, or graduate student enrolled full-time in an academic institution; minimum 2.5 GPA.

Funds Avail.: $2,000 for first place; $500 each for second and third place. **Duration:** Annual. **Number Awarded:** 3. **To Apply:** Application form should be completed and submitted along with essay online at www.cgtrader.com/scholarships. **Deadline:** December 2. **Contact:** Email: scholarship@cgtrader.com.

3270 ■ CH2M HILL Companies, Ltd.
9191 S Jamaica St.
Englewood, CO 80112-5946

3271 ■ CH2M/AEESP Outstanding Doctoral Dissertation Award *(Doctorate/Award)*

Purpose: To recognize outstanding doctoral dissertation that contributes to the advancement of environmental science and engineering. **Focus:** Engineering; Environmental science. **Qualif.:** Candidates must be doctoral students. **Criteria:** Submitted dissertations will be evaluated on the basis of: the scientific and technical merit of the research; originality of the research; contribution to the advancement of environmental engineering and science; clarity of presentation.

Funds Avail.: $1,500 for the student; $500 for the faculty advisor; $750 for travel support. **Duration:** Annual. **Number Awarded:** 1. **To Apply:** Applications must submit nominations letter containing their email and mailing address and telephone numbers for the students and advisors; an indication as to when the dissertations was completed; a one paragraph description of the importance of the student's work and its relevance to environmental engineering and science; a concise statement defining the student's intellectual contribution to the work; the statement regarding intellectual contribution is necessary for all entries, but it is especially important if multiple authors contributed to the work under consideration; Dissertation abstract, written by the student, not to exceed 1, 000 words. **Contact:** John E.

Tobiason, Ph.D., P.E., BCEE, Department of Civil and Environmental Engineering, University of Massachusetts at Amherst; Phone: 413-545-5397; Email: tobiason@umass.edu.

3272 ■ Holly A. Cornell Scholarship *(Master's/Scholarship, Monetary)*

Purpose: To support and encourage outstanding female and/or minority master's students in pursuit of advanced training in the field of water supply and treatment. **Focus:** Water resources; Water supply industry. **Qualif.:** Applicants must be female and/or minority students, who are currently masters degree students anticipating completion of the requirements for a masters degree in engineering. **Criteria:** Selection will be based on the committee's criteria.

Funds Avail.: $7,500. **Duration:** Annual. **To Apply:** Applicants must submit the completed application form. **Contact:** Phone: 303-347-6201; Email: scholarships@awwa.org.

3273 ■ ChairScholars Foundation
16101 Carencia Lane
Odessa, FL 33556-3278
Ph: (813)926-0544
URL: chairscholars.org

3274 ■ ChairScholars Florida Scholarship Program *(Undergraduate/Scholarship)*

Purpose: To provide tuition for college or vocational school with Florida Prepaid Tuition Scholarships. **Focus:** Disabilities. **Qualif.:** Applicants must: have serious physical disability; be eligible for their school's "Free or Reduced Lunch Program"; have at least a B average; be' enrolled in any Florida public school. **Criteria:** Selection will be based on the committee's criteria.

Funds Avail.: No specific amount. **Duration:** Annual. **To Apply:** Interested applicants may contact the Foundation for the application process and other information.

3275 ■ ChairScholars National Scholarship Program *(Undergraduate/Scholarship)*

Purpose: To support low-income students with severe physical disabilities - giving them the opportunity to pursue their dreams because "no physical impairment should deter a motivated mind". **Focus:** General studies/Field of study not specified. **Qualif.:** Applicants must: have serious physical challenge and may or may not use a wheelchair for mobility (no minor disability will be considered); have verifiable unmet financial need; have at least a B average; be a high school senior or college undergraduate; and, show some form of significant community service or social contribution in the past. **Criteria:** Selection will be based on the committee's criteria.

Duration: Annual. **To Apply:** Applicants must submit: good quality recent photograph, full body shot as opposed to head shot; 300 to 500 word essay that outlines how became physically challenged, how the situation has affected the family, and goals and aspirations for the future; three letters of recommendation; Parent's or Guardian's Federal income tax return from last year (if parents are divorced, please send both tax returns); High School transcripts, including SAT and ACT scores and any honors or achievements earned; Physician's documentation of your disability; and if obtained any other scholarships already, inform the bestowing organization of that fact.

Awards are arranged alphabetically below their administering organizations

3276 ■ Charlotte-Mecklenburg Schools Curriculum Research Center
PO Box 30035
Charlotte, NC 28202
URL: www.cms.k12.nc.us

3277 ■ Charlotte-Mecklenburg Schools Scholarship Incentive Fund *(Undergraduate/Scholarship)*

Purpose: To graduates of Charlotte-Mecklenburg public high schools with financial need. **Focus:** General studies/Field of study not specified. **Qualif.:** Applicants must be graduating seniors at a Charlotte-Mecklenburg public high school; must be participants in the Communities in Schools Think College Program or the Charlotte-Mecklenburg Schools AVID Program; must be legal residents of Mecklenburg County, NC; and must have 2.5 minimum cumulative grade point average on a 4.0 scale.

Funds Avail.: No specific amount. **Deadline:** January 3. **Contact:** Qiana Austin; Phone: 704-973-4535; Email: qaustin@fftc.org.

3278 ■ Charlotte Pride
PO Box 32362
Charlotte, NC 28232
Ph: (704)910-8824
URL: charlottepride.org
Social Media: www.facebook.com/cltpride
www.instagram.com/cltpride
twitter.com/cltpride

3279 ■ Charlotte Pride Scholarship *(Community College, Two Year College, Undergraduate, Four Year College/Scholarship)*

Purpose: To improve economic mobility for LGBTQ and Straight Ally college students from the Charlotte metro area. **Focus:** General studies/Field of study not specified. **Qualif.:** Applicant must be LGBTQ or a Straight Ally student who has demonstrated service to the LGBTQ community or a desire to serve the LGBTQ community; must have taken the ACT or SAT; must have a significant unmet financial need; must be enrolled or intending to enroll in a two- or four-year college in North or South Carolina; must be from one of the following counties: Mecklenburg, York, Union, Gaston, Cabarrus, Iredell, Rowan, Cleveland, Lancaster, Lincoln, Stanly, Chester, Catawba, Chesterfield, Alexander, or Anson. **Criteria:** Applicants will be selected based on academic performance and essay/art work quality. Preference will be given to full-time students and to part-time students in their junior or senior year; other part-time students who demonstrate passion, willingness, and ability to complete their degrees will be considered.

Funds Avail.: Up to $2,500. **To Apply:** Applicants should apply online. **Deadline:** July 13. **Contact:** Email: scholarships@charlottepride.org; URL: charlottepride.org/scholarship/.

3280 ■ Chartway Federal Credit Union
5700 Cleveland St.
Virginia Beach, VA 23462
Free: 800-678-8765
URL: www.chartway.com
Social Media: www.facebook.com/chartwayfcu
www.instagram.com/chartwayfcu
twitter.com/chartwayfcu

3281 ■ Chartway Federal Credit Union Director's Memorial Scholarship *(Undergraduate, Graduate/Scholarship)*

Purpose: To help a member pay for college. **Focus:** General studies/Field of study not specified. **Qualif.:** Applicant must be a Chartway Federal Credit Union member, with an account in good standing, who is pursuing an undergraduate or graduate degree. **Criteria:** Selection is based on need, academic performance, essays, and reference letter.

Funds Avail.: $3,000. **Duration:** Annual. **Number Awarded:** 7. **To Apply:** Application must be completed online. **Contact:** URL: app.smarterselect.com/programs/64323-Chartway-Federal-Credit-Union.

3282 ■ Cherokee Nation
17675 S. Muskogee Ave.
Tahlequah, OK 74464
Ph: (918)453-5000
Free: 800-256-0671
E-mail: communications@cherokee.org
URL: www.cherokee.org
Social Media: www.facebook.com/TheCherokeeNation
instagram.com/thecherokeenation
twitter.com/CherokeeNation
youtube.com/user/CherokeeTV

3283 ■ Cherokee Nation Graduate Scholarship *(Graduate/Scholarship)*

Purpose: To support Cherokee Nation Tribal Citizens pursuing degrees at a college or university. **Focus:** General studies/Field of study not specified. **Qualif.:** Applicants must be pursuing a Graduate Degree (Masters or Doctoral) at an accredited College/University, residing within the 14-county jurisdictional or contiguous counties; must maintain a 2.0 GPA and fulfill community service requirements. **Criteria:** Selection is based on the following preferences: 1. Continuing students; 2. Classification order of new applicants (Senior, Junior, Sophomore, Freshman); 3. Academic performance.

Funds Avail.: $2,000. **To Apply:** Applicants must submit Student Aid Report; most recent transcript. **Deadline:** June 15.

3284 ■ Cherokee Nation Pell Scholarships *(Undergraduate/Scholarship)*

Purpose: To support Cherokee Nation Tribal Citizens pursuing degrees at a college or university. **Focus:** General studies/Field of study not specified. **Qualif.:** Applicants must be a Cherokee Nation tribal citizen who qualified for Federal Pell Grant funding regardless of permanent residence. **Criteria:** Selection is based on the following preferences: 1. Continuing students; 2. Classification order of new applicants (Senior, Junior, Sophomore, Freshman); 3. Academic performance.

Funds Avail.: No specific amount. **Duration:** Annual. **To Apply:** Applicants must submit a completed application form together with Student Aid Report (all pages); copy of Social Security card; copy of Tribal Citizenship card (blue); official high school transcript (7 semester) or GED scores (Freshmen only); copy of ACT/SAT or College Placement Test Scores (Freshmen only); and official Undergraduate Transcript with most recent semester grades (if applicable). **Deadline:** June 15.

Awards are arranged alphabetically below their administering organizations

3285 ■ Undergraduate Scholarship *(Undergraduate/ Scholarship)*

Purpose: To support Cherokee Nation Tribal Citizens pursuing degrees at a college or university. **Focus:** General studies/Field of study not specified. **Qualif.:** Applicants must be students pursuing a first Associate or Bachelor's degree, not includingAssociate of Applied Science; residing outside the 14-county jurisdictional or contiguous counties-must be eligible for the federal Pell grant to receive the Undergraduate scholarship.

Funds Avail.: $2,000. **Deadline:** June 15.

3286 ■ Chicago Railroad Mechanical Association (CRMA)

c/o Joe Malacina, Secretary-Treasurer
14007 S Bell Rd., Ste. 243
Homer Glen, IL 60491
E-mail: crma@thecrma.org
URL: www.thecrma.org

3287 ■ CRMA Scholarship *(Graduate, Undergraduate/ Scholarship)*

Purpose: To provide financial assistance to eligible college or university students. **Focus:** General studies/Field of study not specified. **Criteria:** Selection will be based on the evaluation of narrative; transcript; recommendations; activities; honors and overall abilities.

Funds Avail.: Up to $2,000. **Duration:** Annual. **Number Awarded:** 2. **To Apply:** Applicants must submit a completed application form including the narrative requested in Section E of the application; official transcript from learning institute's Bursar office including work completed; two recommendation letters; the application, narrative statement, transcript and recommendation letters must be submitted in one envelope. **Deadline:** September 15. **Contact:** CRMA, Joe Malacina, Secretary/Treasurer, 14007 S. Bell Rd., Ste. 243, Homer Glen, IL 60491.

3288 ■ Chicana/Latina Foundation (CLF)

1419 Burlingame Ave., Ste. W2
Burlingame, CA 94010
Ph: (650)548-1040
Fax: (650)477-2605
E-mail: clfinfo@chicanalatina.org
URL: www.chicanalatina.org
Social Media: www.facebook.com/ ChicanaLatinaFoundation
www.instagram.com/chicanalatinafoundation
www.pinterest.com.mx/pin/503629170799033233
twitter.com/CLF_says

3289 ■ Chicana / Latina Foundation Scholarship Program *(Graduate, Undergraduate/Scholarship)*

Purpose: To assist Latina students in completing their undergraduate and graduate college education. **Focus:** General studies/Field of study not specified. **Criteria:** Selection will be based on the committee's criteria.

Funds Avail.: $1,500. **Duration:** Annual. **Number Awarded:** 35. **To Apply:** The application process is online. **Deadline:** March 31.

3290 ■ Childhood Cancer Canada

20 Queen St. W. Unit 702
Toronto, ON, Canada M5H 3R3
Ph: (416)489-6440
Fax: (416)489-9812
Free: 800-363-1062
E-mail: info@childhoodcancer.ca
URL: www.childhoodcancer.ca
Social Media: www.facebook.com/ ChildhoodCancerCanada
www.instagram.com/childhoodcancercanada
twitter.com/chldhdcancercan

3291 ■ Childhood Cancer Survivor Scholarship *(Undergraduate, College, University, Vocational/ Occupational/Scholarship)*

Purpose: To support young adult cancer survivors and assist them financially with their post-secondary school education. **Focus:** General studies/Field of study not specified. **Qualif.:** Applicant must have been treated (or are currently being treated) for childhood cancer (diagnosis must have occurred before their 18th birthday); be a legal resident of, and currently living in, Canada; be a student in any full-time university, college, or vocational training program, in any year of their studies provided that they are enrolled in school for the fall term that the scholarship covers.

Funds Avail.: 1,500 Canadian Dollars. **Duration:** Annual. **To Apply:** Application can be completed online at www.childhoodcancer.ca/scholarship. **Deadline:** May 29.

3292 ■ TEVA Canada Survivor Scholarship *(Undergraduate, University/Scholarship)*

Purpose: To provide scholarships to young Canadians who are in treatment for or who have survived childhood cancer. **Focus:** Health sciences; Medicine; Pharmacy. **Qualif.:** Applicant must have been treated (or are currently being treated) for childhood cancer (diagnosis must have occurred before their 18th birthday); be a legal resident of, and currently living in, Canada; and be enrolled in a Canadian university in the fields of pharmacy, medicine, or health sciences (students may be in any year of their studies provided that they are enrolled in school for the fall term in which the scholarships are awarded).

Funds Avail.: 5,000 Canadian dollars. **Duration:** Annual. **Number Awarded:** Up to 10. **To Apply:** Application can be completed online at www.childhoodcancer.ca/scholarship. **Deadline:** May 29.

3293 ■ Children of Fallen Patriots Foundation (CFPF)

44900 Prentice Dr.
Dulles, VA 20166
Fax: (703)956-3009
Free: 866-917-2373
URL: www.fallenpatriots.org
Social Media: www.facebook.com/FallenPatriots
instagram.com/fallenpatriots
linkedin.com/company/children-of-fallen-patriots-foundation
pinterest.com/fallenpatriots
twitter.com/fallenpatriots
youtube.com/user/FallenPatriotsFound

3294 ■ Children of Fallen Patriots Scholarships *(Community College, Undergraduate, Graduate, Vocational/Occupational/Scholarship)*

Purpose: To provide college funding to military children who have lost a parent in the line of duty or due to service

Awards are arranged alphabetically below their administering organizations

connection, seeking to bridge the gap in funding between the Veteran's Administration resources and the total cost of undergraduate college education. **Focus:** General studies/ Field of study not specified. **Qualif.:** Applicant must have a military parent who has fallen in peacetime or in combat, whether they were listed as active, reserve, or guard at the time of their passing.

Funds Avail.: $6,250. **To Apply:** Apply online at www.fallenpatriots.org/enroll-a-student. **Remarks:** Enrollments are accepted at any time; scholarships are processed on a semester-by-semester basis. Eligible students will receive up to $6, 250 in scholarship funding per academic year. **Contact:** E-mail: enrollments@fallenpatriots.org.

3295 ■ Children's Literature Association (CHLA)
3525 Piedmont Rd., Ste. 300, Bldg. 5
Atlanta, GA 30305
Ph: (630)571-4520
Fax: (708)876-5598
E-mail: info@childlitassn.org
URL: chla.memberclicks.net

3296 ■ Hannah Beiter Graduate Student Research Grants *(Master's, Graduate/Grant, Recognition)*

Purpose: To encourage young individuals to pursue their research that may be related to the dissertation or Master's thesis. **Focus:** Literature, Children's. **Qualif.:** Applicant must be a graduate degree (e.g., applied to tuition), but as support for research that may be related to the dissertation or master's thesis. **Criteria:** Selection is based on proposals which are read and judged by the ChLA Grants Committee.

Funds Avail.: $500-$1,500 individual awards. **Duration:** Annual. **To Apply:** Applicants must provide a cover letter including the name, telephone number, mailing address and email address, academic institution and status; must submit curriculum vitae and two reference letter; detailed description of the research proposal (not to exceed three single-spaced pages), indicating the nature and significance of the project, where it will be carried out, rough budget, and the expected date of completion. **Deadline:** February 1. **Remarks:** The Grant was established on the memory of Dr. Hannah Beiter, a long-time supporter of student participation in the Children's Literature Association.

3297 ■ ChLA Faculty Research Grants *(Professional development/Grant)*

Purpose: To fund proposals dealing with criticism or original scholarship with the expectation that the undertaking will lead to publication and make a significant contribution to the field of children's literature in the area of scholarship or criticism. **Focus:** Literature, Children's. **Qualif.:** Applicants should not be members of the ChLA Executive Board or ChLA Grants Committee. **Criteria:** Applications will be evaluated based upon the quality of the proposal and the potential of the project to enhance or advance Children's Literature studies.

Funds Avail.: $500 to $1,500. **Duration:** Annual. **Number Awarded:** 1. **To Apply:** applications should include: cover page with name, telephone number, mailing address and e-mail address. academic institution and status/rank (professor, librarian, etc.); or institution applicant is affiliated with (library, publisher, etc.); detailed description of the research proposal (not to exceed three single-spaced pages), indicating the nature and significance of the project,

where it will be carried out, rough budget, and the expected date of completion; and vita that includes a bibliography of major publications and scholarly achievements. **Deadline:** February 1;December 15.

3298 ■ The Children's Tumor Foundation (CTF)
370 Lexington Avenue, Suite 2100
New York, NY 10017
Ph: (212)344-6633
Fax: (212)747-0004
Free: 800-323-7938
E-mail: info@ctf.org
URL: www.ctf.org
Social Media: www.facebook.com/childrenstumor
www.instagram.com/childrenstumor
www.linkedin.com/company/children's-tumor-foundation
twitter.com/childrenstumor
www.youtube.com/childrenstumor

3299 ■ CTF Young Investigator Award (YIA) *(Graduate, Postdoctorate, Doctorate/Award)*

Purpose: To accelerate progress toward finding effective NF therapies. **Focus:** Neuroscience.

Funds Avail.: Varies. **Duration:** Annual. **Deadline:** January 1. **Contact:** Email: grants@ctf.org.

3300 ■ A Child's Hope Int'l, Inc.
2430 E Kemper Rd.
Cincinnati, OH 45241
Ph: (513)771-2244
Fax: (513)828-6852
E-mail: office@achildshopeintl.org
URL: thechildrenarewaiting.org
Social Media: www.facebook.com/AChildsHopeIntl

3301 ■ Linsley Scholarship Fund *(Undergraduate, Vocational/Occupational/Scholarship)*

Purpose: To support young adults pursuing post-secondary education. **Focus:** General studies/Field of study not specified. **Qualif.:** Applicant must be an active follower of Jesus Christ; must be a regular attendee of a bible believing church; must been in public or private foster care for the 12 consecutive months prior to their 18th birthday, or have been adopted or placed into legal guardianship from foster care, or have been orphaned for at least one year at the time of their 18th birthday; must have been accepted into or expect to be accepted into an accredited Pell-eligible college, post-secondary school or vocational program; must be under the age of 25 on March 31 of the year in which they first apply; must have been in foster care or orphaned while living in the United States; and must have U.S. citizenship. **Criteria:** Selection will be based on the combination of merits and needs of the applicants.

Funds Avail.: $1,000 to $3,000. **Duration:** Annual. **Number Awarded:** Varies. **To Apply:** Applicant must download an application form at thechildrenarewaiting.org/fostercare/fund/ and submit completed form with supporting documentation to the address above. **Remarks:** The scholarship was established in recognition of Paul and Deanna Linsley's selfless lives.

3302 ■ Jane Coffin Childs Memorial Fund for Medical Research
333 Cedar St.
New Haven, CT 06520-8000

Awards are arranged alphabetically below their administering organizations

Ph: (203)785-4612
URL: jccfund.org
Social Media: www.facebook.com/JaneCoffinChildsFund

3303 ■ Jane Coffin Childs Memorial Fund - Medical Research Postdoctoral Fellowship *(Postdoctorate, Doctorate/Fellowship)*

Purpose: To award fellowships to suitably qualified individuals for full-time postdoctoral studies in the medical and related sciences bearing on cancer. **Focus:** Oncology.

Funds Avail.: Basic stipend is $52,000 for the first year, $52,500 for the second year, and $53,000 the third year, with an additional $1,000 for each dependent child. **Duration:** Annual. **To Apply:** Applicant must submit evidence as to pre and postdoctoral training must supply (a) the names and addresses of three individuals personally acquainted both with the applicant and with the applicant's professional work, one of whom should be the principal pre-doctoral advisor, (b) a suitably documented outline of the research problem proposed, and (c) the written consent of the chief of laboratory and a responsible fiscal officer of the host institution indicating their willingness to accept and provide necessary facilities for the Fellow. **Deadline:** February 1.

3304 ■ ChinaSona Foundation

401 N Garfield Ave., Ste. 1
Alhambra, CA 91801
Ph: (626)282-9186
Fax: (626)282-9252
E-mail: chinasonaorg@gmail.com
URL: www.chinasona.org

3305 ■ "A Better World" Spirituality and Technology Advancement Scholarship *(Undergraduate, Graduate/Scholarship)*

Purpose: To promote a better world through spiritual and technological advancements. **Focus:** General studies/Field of study not specified. **Qualif.:** Applicant must be a high school or college student. **Criteria:** Selection based on the quality of the essay or invention.

Funds Avail.: $1,000. **Duration:** Annual. **To Apply:** Applicant must write about how they would like to promote a better world. (Mandatory reading: "Abduction to the 9th Planet" also known as "Thiaoouba Prophecy." Other suggested readings: "Conversations with God", or books of a similar kind. Sample topics to consider: What can we do to increase people's spiritual awareness and development? How can we use technology to assist the spiritual development of a person?); Describe and send one thing that you invented to assist in the spiritual development of a person; Application details available at www.chinasona.org/scholarship.html. **Deadline:** July 19.

3306 ■ Chinese American Medical Society (CAMS)

11 East Broadway, Suite 4C
New York, NY 10038
Ph: (212)334-4760
Fax: (646)304-6373
URL: camsociety.org

3307 ■ CAMS Summer Research Fellowship *(Undergraduate/Fellowship)*

Purpose: To promote and support clinical and basic science research among Chinese American medical and dental students. **Focus:** Dental laboratory technology; Medical technology. **Qualif.:** Applicants must be first, second, or third year medical or dental students who are in good standing at an accredited US medical or dental school in the USA at the time of application. **Criteria:** Special consideration will be given to projects involving Chinese American health issues.

Funds Avail.: $400 per week. **Duration:** 8 to 10 weeks. **To Apply:** Applicants must submit completed CAMS Summer Research Fellowship Application; project description; personal statement; curriculum vitae; a two letters from a supervising investigator supporting the research project and from the Dean verifying good standing. **Deadline:** March 31. **Contact:** Scholarship Committee, 265 Canal St., Ste. 515, New York, NY, 10013.

3308 ■ Esther Lim Memorial Scholarships *(Undergraduate/Scholarship)*

Purpose: To provide educational assistance to medical, dental students, and scientists. **Focus:** Dental laboratory technology; Medical technology. **Qualif.:** Applicant must be a medical or dental student or scientist matriculated in a medical or dental school. **Criteria:** Selection is based on merit.

Funds Avail.: No specific amount. **Duration:** Annual. **To Apply:** Application form is available at the website. Applicants must submit completed application form along with a letter from the Dean of Students verifying good standing; two letters of recommendation; a personal statement; and a current vitae. **Deadline:** March 31. **Remarks:** Established in 1989.

3309 ■ Ruth Liu Memorial Scholarship *(Undergraduate/Scholarship)*

Purpose: To provide scholarships to outstanding medical students in need of financial assistance. **Focus:** Dental laboratory technology; Medical technology. **Qualif.:** Applicant must be a medical or dental student or scientist matriculated in a medical or dental school. **Criteria:** Selection is based on merit.

Funds Avail.: $1,000 each. **Duration:** Annual. **Number Awarded:** 3-5. **To Apply:** Applicants must submit completed application form along with a letter from the Dean of Students verifying good standing; two letters of recommendation; a personal statement; and a current curriculum vitae. **Deadline:** March 31. **Contact:** CAMS, Scholarship Committee, 265 Canal St., Ste. 515, New York, NY, 10013.

3310 ■ Chinese Professionals Association of Canada (CPAC)

4150 Finch Ave. E
Toronto, ON, Canada M1S 3T9
Ph: (416)298-7885
Fax: (416)298-0068
E-mail: office@cpac-canada.ca
URL: cpac-canada.ca

3311 ■ Chinese Professionals Association of Canada Professional Achievement Awards (PAA) *(Professional development/Award)*

Purpose: To recognize and celebrate the achievements of professional immigrants. **Focus:** General studies/Field of study not specified. **Qualif.:** Applicants must have achieved an outstanding stature in their profession in Canada; must have used CPAC's services (including bridging program)

Awards are arranged alphabetically below their administering organizations

for them to land new jobs; and must have achieved a successful accomplishment on a different profession other than the training they had before; recognizing their community or professional accomplishments locally or abroad by an outstanding individual aged 29 and below.

Remarks: Established in 2009.

3312 ■ ChiroHealth USA
250 Katherine Dr.
Flowood, MS 39232
Free: 888-719-9990
E-mail: info@chirohealthusa.com
URL: www.chirohealthusa.com
Social Media: facebook.com/ChiroHealthUSA
twitter.com/1CHUSA
www.youtube.com/channel/
UC7ujuFBqFmNtC54VTL0CXGQ

3313 ■ ChiroHealthUSA Foxworth Family Scholarship *(Doctorate/Scholarship)*

Purpose: To recognize students' ability to lead and serve and their commitment to making a lasting impact on their communities and the chiropractic profession. **Focus:** Medicine, Chiropractic. **Qualif.:** Applicant must be a full-time student enrolled in a Doctorate of Chiropractic program at an accredited college or university in the United States; must have a minimum 2.7 GPA; must agree to keep award confidential until announced at the FCA National Convention. **Criteria:** Selection is achievement-based.

Funds Avail.: $15,000. **Duration:** Annual. **Number Awarded:** 1.

3314 ■ Chopin Foundation of the United States
1440 79th Street Cswy., Ste. 117
Miami, FL 33141
Ph: (305)868-0624
Fax: (305)865-5150
E-mail: info@chopin.org
URL: www.chopin.org
Social Media: www.facebook.com/chopinus
www.instagram.com/ChopinMiami
twitter.com/ChopinMiami
www.youtube.com/user/Chopinfoundationusa

3315 ■ Chopin Foundation Scholarship *(Other/Scholarship)*

Purpose: To support and encourage young, talented American pianists through up to four years of preparation for the national chopin piano competition of the united states. **Focus:** Music, Piano. **Qualif.:** Applicants must be American pianists (citizens or legal residents); not younger than 14 and not older than 17 years; studying in the field of music, majoring in piano. **Criteria:** Applicants are selected based on merit.

Funds Avail.: $1,000. **Duration:** Annual. **To Apply:** Applicants must submit a statement of career goals; minimum of two references from piano teachers or performers; a video tape of Chopin's works, registration fee of $25 and proof of enrollment; proof of current school enrollment or statement of being home schooled; optionally, upload additional page(s) to list significant repertoire studied. **Deadline:** June 15. **Contact:** The Chopin Foundation of the United States, Inc., Scholarship Committee, 1440 79th

Street Causeway, Ste. 117, Miami, FL, 33141;Phone: 305-868-0624; Fax: 305-865-5150; E-mail: info@chopin.org.

3316 ■ Choristers Guild (CG)
12404 Park Central Dr., Ste. 100
Dallas, TX 75251-1802
Ph: (469)398-3606
Free: 800-246-7478
URL: www.choristersguild.org
Social Media: www.facebook.com/ChoristersGuild
twitter.com/ChoristersGuild
www.youtube.com/channel/UC55kqa2D
_OlosQ1Wr6mCClw

3317 ■ Ruth K. Jacobs Memorial Scholarship *(Graduate/Scholarship)*

Purpose: To provide financial aid to full-time students preparing for church music ministry. **Focus:** Music. **Qualif.:** Applicant must be a music major with choral church music as a primary interest; must be registered as a junior, senior, or graduate student in an accredited university; must be registered as a full-time student; must demonstrate talent and leadership ability and promise of future in church music. **Criteria:** Selection will be based on academic merit; passion for leading children and youth in music; intention to serve in church music ministry.

Funds Avail.: Up to $1,500. **Duration:** Annual. **To Apply:** Applicants must submit an application form; transcript of records; and four references who are acquainted with the applicants' qualifications. **Deadline:** February 1.

3318 ■ Christian Missionary Scholarship Foundation (CMSF)
1899 Orchard Lake Rd., Ste. 203
Sylvan Lake, MI 48320
Ph: (616)526-7731
Fax: (616)526-6777
E-mail: cmsf01@gmail.com
URL: www.christianmissionaryscholarship.org
Social Media: www.facebook.com/
christianmissionaryscholarshipfoundation

3319 ■ CMSF Scholarship *(Graduate/Scholarship)*

Purpose: To provide financial support for the education of the children of missionaries who have made significant financial sacrifices to serve the Lord. **Focus:** General studies/Field of study not specified.

Funds Avail.: Amount varies. **Duration:** Annual. **Number Awarded:** Varies. **To Apply:** Applications can be submitted online. **Deadline:** February 1.

3320 ■ Christian Pharmacists Fellowship International (CPFI)
531 Old Jonesboro Rd.
Bristol, TN 37621-1154
Ph: (423)844-1043
Fax: (423)844-1005
Free: 888-253-6885
E-mail: info@cpfi.org
URL: www.cpfi.org
Social Media: twitter.com/CPFI_students

Awards are arranged alphabetically below their administering organizations

3321 ■ Christian Pharmacists Fellowship International (CPFI) (Advanced Professional/ Scholarship)

Purpose: To assist Christian students in pursuing a career on pharmacy. **Focus:** Pharmacy. **Qualif.:** Applicants must be a national CPFI member; enrolled in an accredited pharmacy college/university or training program. **Criteria:** Preference will be given to students who have been a member over a sustained period of time and/or a member of a college chapter of CPFI.

Funds Avail.: Upto $250 per year. **Duration:** Annual. **To Apply:** Applicants must send completed application form; description of the plan or project; an email support from the Dean and from an instructor/mentor; and a resume. **Deadline:** October 1; March 1; June 1.

3322 ■ Christian Record Services for the Blind (CRSB)

5900 S 58th St., Ste. M
Lincoln, NE 68516
Ph: (402)488-0981
Fax: (402)488-7582
Free: 888-213-0003
E-mail: info@christianrecord.org
URL: www.christianrecord.org
Social Media: www.facebook.com/christianrecord
www.instagram.com/crsbfriends
www.linkedin.com/company/crsbfriends
twitter.com/CRSBfriends
www.youtube.com/user/ChRecord

3323 ■ Anne Lowe Scholarship (Undergraduate/ Scholarship, Award)

Purpose: To assist blind young people who wish to pursue their college education. **Focus:** General studies/Field of study not specified. **Qualif.:** Applicants must be college students. **Criteria:** Scholarship recipients will be selected based on academic achievement, the citizenship which is supported through reference letters, and verification of blindness.

Duration: Annual. **Remarks:** Tom Lowe established the scholarship in the memory of his wife, Anne, who loved education and the mission of Christian Record. Established in 1989. **Contact:** Christian Record Services, Inc., 5900 S 58th St., Ste. M, Lincoln, NE, 68516.

3324 ■ Christian Scholarship Foundation, Inc. (CSF)

409 Prospect St.
New Haven, CT 06511
URL: www.christianscholars.org

3325 ■ CSF Graduate Fellowship (Graduate/ Fellowship)

Purpose: To provide financial assistance to ministers enrolled in doctoral programs in religion and related fields. **Focus:** Bible studies; Religion; Theology.

Funds Avail.: $2,000-$10,000. **Duration:** Annual. **Number Awarded:** 3-5. **To Apply:** Applicants should include summary statement of plans for the academic year for which application is made, including signature of approval by the applicant's faculty advisor or major professor; estimated budget which includes income and expenditures for the academic year for which application is made; official transcripts of all previous academic work, undergraduate and graduate; four (4) letters of recommendation regarding personal, religious and intellectual development; a research paper or other example of the applicant's most scholarly written work (not more than 50 pp. in length). **Deadline:** January 15. **Contact:** Christian Scholarship Foundation, c/o Dr. Gregory E. Sterling, Yale Divinity School, 409 Prospect St., New Haven, CT, 06511; Email: gregory.sterling@yale.edu.

3326 ■ Church Hill Classics Ltd.

594 Pepper St.
Monroe, CT 06468
Fax: (203)268-2468
Free: 800-477-9005
E-mail: info@diplomaframe.com
URL: www.diplomaframe.com
Social Media: www.facebook.com/ChurchHillClassics
www.instagram.com/diplomaframe
www.linkedin.com/company/church-hill-classics
www.pinterest.com/diplomaframe
twitter.com/diplomaframe
www.youtube.com/user/churchhillclassics

3327 ■ Frame My Future Scholarship Contest (Undergraduate, Graduate/Scholarship, Prize)

Purpose: To provide students the funds they need for their educational expenses. **Focus:** General studies/Field of study not specified. **Qualif.:** Applicants must be legal U.S. residents and full-time students at a college or university in the United States for the current academic year. **Criteria:** Judges will select finalist based on creativity of the full entry, including the image and accompanying description.

Funds Avail.: $5,000 (grand prize); $1,000 (1st runner up); $500 (2nd runner up). **Duration:** Annual. **Number Awarded:** 3. **To Apply:** Applicant must submit an original creation conveying the theme for that year. Application details are available online at www.diplomaframe.com/ contests/frame-my-future-scholarship.aspx. **Deadline:** April 1.

3328 ■ Church, Langdon, Lopp, Banet Law

318 Pearl St., Ste. 200
New Albany, IN 47150
Ph: (812)370-8934
Fax: (812)813-4020
URL: www.cllblegal.com
Social Media: www.facebook.com/CLLBLEGAL

3329 ■ The Church, Langdon, Lopp, Banet Law Scholarships (Undergraduate, Four Year College/ Scholarship)

Purpose: To encourage and reward individuals who are deeply involved in the community that surrounds them. **Focus:** General studies/Field of study not specified. **Qualif.:** Applicants must be high school seniors, who have been accepted to a 4-year college institution or a student currently enrolled in a 4-year college institution; college students must reside in one of these counties when they are not in school Jefferson County, Kentucky and Clark, Floyd, Harrison, Washington, Scott, and Jefferson County,

Awards are arranged alphabetically below their administering organizations

Indiana; be a US citizen or authorized to work in the U.S.**Criteria:** Published articles will be judged on creativity, originality, and ability to convey a complex message.

Funds Avail.: $500. **Duration:** Annual. **Number Awarded:** 1. **To Apply:** Applicants must provide all current contact information including: full name, mailing address, email address, and phone number; color photograph; proof of attendance or acceptance at an accredited school as outlined in the requirements; copy of the applicant's official transcript for their most recently completed semester of school; write a 500 to 1,000 word essay. **Deadline:** June 1. **Contact:** URL: www.cllblegal.com/community-involvement-scholarship/.

3330 ■ Winston Churchill Foundation of the United States

600 Madison Ave., Ste. 1601
New York, NY 10022-1737
Ph: (212)752-3200
Fax: (212)246-8330
E-mail: info@churchillscholarship.org
URL: www.churchillscholarship.org

3331 ■ The Churchill Scholarships *(Postgraduate/Scholarship)*

Purpose: To provide finance to American students seeking doctorate degree opportunities in United Kingdom. **Focus:** Engineering; Mathematics and mathematical sciences.

Funds Avail.: No specific amount. **Duration:** Annual. **To Apply:** Applicants must complete the application form; four letters of reference; proposed program of the study; personal statement. **Deadline:** November 2. **Contact:** Email: info@churchillscholarship.org; Phone: 212-752-3200.

3332 ■ CIMON Inc.

2435 W Horizon Ridge Pkwy.,NO.100
Henderson, NV 89052
Free: 800-300-9916
URL: www.cimon.com
Social Media: www.facebook.com/cimoninc
www.linkedin.com/company/cimonautomation
twitter.com/CIMONsns

3333 ■ CIMON Inc Scholarship *(College, University/Scholarship)*

Purpose: To help students in the process of pursuing college degrees in STEM fields. **Focus:** Engineering; Mathematics and mathematical sciences; Science. **Qualif.:** Applicant must be a U.S. citizen accepted to or currently attending a college or university in the United States and obtaining a degree in a STEM field.

Funds Avail.: $1,000. **Number Awarded:** 1. **To Apply:** Application can be filled out at www.cimon.com/scholarship. **Deadline:** December 1.

3334 ■ Cincinnati Scholarship Foundation (CSF)

324 East 4th St. 2nd Floor
Cincinnati, OH 45202
Ph: (513)345-6701
Fax: (513)345-6705
E-mail: info@cincinnatischolarshipfoundation.org

URL: www.cincinnatischolarshipfoundation.org
Social Media: www.facebook.com/
CincinnatiScholarshipFoundation
www.instagram.com/cincinnati_sf
twitter.com/CincinnatiSF

3335 ■ Ach Family Scholarship Fund *(Undergraduate/Scholarship)*

Purpose: To support high school graduates who reside in Greater Cincinnati and are beginning college in the fall of their graduation. **Focus:** General studies/Field of study not specified. **Qualif.:** Applicants must be high school graduates; must reside in Greater Cincinnati; must beginning college in the fall of their graduation; must have proven financial need. **Criteria:** Selection is based on proven financial need; priority given to students attending Dater Junior or Senior High School.

Funds Avail.: No specific amount. **Duration:** Annual. **To Apply:** Applicant must submit a completed scholarship application form through online; along with a transcript up to the first semester of the current academic year; resume; Student Aid Report (SAR) in its entirety; financial Aid Award Notification from the college applicant plan to attend. **Deadline:** May 15. **Contact:** Cincinnati Scholarship Foundation, 324 E 4th St. 2nd Fl., Cincinnati, OH, 45202; Phone: 513-345-6701; Fax: 513-345-6705; E-mail: info@cincinnatischolarshipfoundation.org.

3336 ■ Annie Wagner Memorial Scholarship Fund *(Undergraduate/Scholarship)*

Purpose: To encourage students to achieve their highest academic potential. **Focus:** General studies/Field of study not specified. **Qualif.:** Applicants must reside in the Greater Cincinnati area; must be a students attending Xavier University, Northern Kentucky University or the College Conservatory of Music at the University of Cincinnati and majoring in a music-related field. **Criteria:** Selection are based on need.

Funds Avail.: No specific amount. **Duration:** Annual. **To Apply:** Applicant must submit a completed scholarship application form through online; along with a transcript up to the first semester of the current academic year; resume; Student Aid Report (SAR) in its entirety; financial Aid Award Notification from the college applicant plan to attend. **Deadline:** May 15. **Contact:** Cincinnati Scholarship Foundation, 324 E 4th St. 2nd Fl., Cincinnati, OH, 45202; Phone: 513-345-6701; Fax: 513-345-6705; E-mail: info@cincinnatischolarshipfoundation.org.

3337 ■ Barr Foundation Scholarship *(Undergraduate/Scholarship)*

Purpose: To help students from Greater Cincinnati area to achieve the dream of a college education. **Focus:** General studies/Field of study not specified. **Qualif.:** Applicants must be high school graduates who reside in Greater Cincinnati and are beginning college in the fall of their graduation; must have proven financial need. **Criteria:** Selection is based on proven financial need.

Funds Avail.: No specific amount. **Duration:** Annual. **To Apply:** Applicant must submit a completed scholarship application form through online; along with a transcript up to the first semester of the current academic year; resume; Student Aid Report (SAR) in its entirety; financial Aid Award Notification from the college applicant plan to attend. **Deadline:** May 15. **Contact:** Cincinnati Scholarship Foundation, 324 E 4th St. 2nd Fl., Cincinnati, OH, 45202; Phone: 513-

Awards are arranged alphabetically below their administering organizations

345-6701; Fax: 513-345-6705; E-mail: info@cincinnatischolarshipfoundation.org.

3338 ■ Barrett Family Scholarship Fund
(Undergraduate/Scholarship)

Purpose: To help students from Greater Cincinnati area to achieve the dream of a college education. **Focus:** General studies/Field of study not specified. **Qualif.:** Applicants must be high school graduates who reside in Greater Cincinnati and are beginning college in the fall of their graduation; must have proven financial need. **Criteria:** Selection is based on proven financial need.

Funds Avail.: No specific amount. **Duration:** Annual. **To Apply:** Applicant must submit a completed scholarship application form through online; along with a transcript up to the first semester of the current academic year; resume; Student Aid Report (SAR) in its entirety; financial Aid Award Notification from the college applicant plan to attend. **Deadline:** May 15. **Contact:** Cincinnati Scholarship Foundation, 324 E 4th St. 2nd Fl., Cincinnati, OH, 45202; Phone: 513-345-6701; Fax: 513-345-6705; E-mail: info@cincinnatischolarshipfoundation.org.

3339 ■ Bob and Linda Kohlhepp Scholarship Fund
(Undergraduate/Scholarship)

Purpose: To support high school graduates who reside in Greater Cincinnati and are beginning college in the fall of their graduation. **Focus:** General studies/Field of study not specified. **Qualif.:** Applicants must be high school graduates who reside in Greater Cincinnati and are beginning college in the fall of their graduation; must have proven financial need. **Criteria:** Selection is based on proven financial need.

Funds Avail.: No specific amount. **Duration:** Annual. **To Apply:** Applicant must submit a completed scholarship application form through online; along with a transcript up to the first semester of the current academic year; resume; Student Aid Report (SAR) in its entirety; financial Aid Award Notification from the college applicant plan to attend. **Deadline:** May 15. **Contact:** Cincinnati Scholarship Foundation, 324 E 4th St. 2nd Fl., Cincinnati, OH, 45202; Phone: 513-345-6701; Fax: 513-345-6705; E-mail: info@cincinnatischolarshipfoundation.org.

3340 ■ Borden Inc. Scholarship Fund
(Undergraduate/Scholarship)

Purpose: Cincinnati Scholarship Foundation, 324 E 4th St. 2nd Fl., Cincinnati, OH, 45202; Phone: 513-345-6701; Fax: 513-345-6705; E-mail: info@cincinnatischolarshipfoundation.org. **Focus:** General studies/Field of study not specified. **Qualif.:** Applicants must be high school graduates who reside in Greater Cincinnati and are beginning college in the fall of their graduation. **Criteria:** Awards are given based on need.

Funds Avail.: No specific amount. **Duration:** Annual. **To Apply:** Applicant must submit a completed scholarship application form through online; along with a transcript up to the first semester of the current academic year; resume; Student Aid Report (SAR) in its entirety; financial Aid Award Notification from the college applicant plan to attend. **Deadline:** May 15. **Contact:** Phone: 513-345-6701; Fax: 513-345-6705; E-mail: info@cincinnatischolarshipfoundation.org.

3341 ■ Carl H. Lindner Family Fund *(Undergraduate/Scholarship)*

Purpose: To support students from Greater Cincinnati area to pursue a college education. **Focus:** General studies/

Field of study not specified. **Qualif.:** Applicants must be high school graduates who reside in Greater Cincinnati and are beginning college in the fall of their graduation. **Criteria:** Awards are given based on need.

Funds Avail.: No specific amount. **Duration:** Annual. **To Apply:** Applicant must submit a completed scholarship application form through online; along with a transcript up to the first semester of the current academic year; resume; Student Aid Report (SAR) in its entirety; financial Aid Award Notification from the college applicant plan to attend. **Deadline:** May 15. **Contact:** Cincinnati Scholarship Foundation, 324 E 4th St. 2nd Fl., Cincinnati, OH, 45202; Phone: 513-345-6701; Fax: 513-345-6705; E-mail: info@cincinnatischolarshipfoundation.org.

3342 ■ Castellini Foundation Scholarship
(Undergraduate/Scholarship)

Purpose: To help students from Greater Cincinnati area to achieve the dream of a college education. **Focus:** General studies/Field of study not specified. **Qualif.:** Applicants must be high school graduates who reside in Greater Cincinnati and are beginning college in the fall of their graduation. **Criteria:** Awards are given based on need.

Funds Avail.: No specific amount. **Duration:** Annual. **To Apply:** Applicant must submit a completed scholarship application form through online; along with a transcript up to the first semester of the current academic year; resume; Student Aid Report (SAR) in its entirety; financial Aid Award Notification from the college applicant plan to attend. **Deadline:** May 15. **Contact:** Cincinnati Scholarship Foundation, 324 E 4th St. 2nd Fl., Cincinnati, OH, 45202; Phone: 513-345-6701; Fax: 513-345-6705; E-mail: info@cincinnatischolarshipfoundation.org.

3343 ■ CFT/ACPSOP Scholarship Fund
(Undergraduate/Scholarship)

Purpose: To help students from Greater Cincinnati area to achieve their dream of a college education. **Focus:** General studies/Field of study not specified. **Qualif.:** Applicant must be a senior in High School or an undergraduate attending an accredited, non-proprietary college or university; must be a resident of the Greater Cincinnati area; must be a member or child of a member of CFT/ACPSOP. **Criteria:** Selection are based on need; Priority is given to minorities pursuing a degree in education.

Funds Avail.: No specific amount. **Duration:** Annual. **To Apply:** Applicant must submit a completed scholarship application form through online; along with a transcript up to the first semester of the current academic year; resume; Student Aid Report (SAR) in its entirety; financial Aid Award Notification from the college applicant plan to attend. **Deadline:** May 15. **Contact:** Cincinnati Scholarship Foundation, 324 E 4th St. 2nd Fl., Cincinnati, OH, 45202; Phone: 513-345-6701; Fax: 513-345-6705; E-mail: info@cincinnatischolarshipfoundation.org.

3344 ■ Charles and Claire Phillips Scholarship Fund *(Undergraduate/Scholarship)*

Purpose: To help students from Greater Cincinnati area to achieve their dream of a college education. **Focus:** General studies/Field of study not specified. **Qualif.:** Applicant must be a senior in High School or an undergraduate attending an accredited, non-proprietary college or university; must be a resident of the Greater Cincinnati area. **Criteria:** Selection is based on proven academic ability and financial need.

Funds Avail.: No specific amount. **Duration:** Annual. **To Apply:** Applicant must submit a completed scholarship ap-

Awards are arranged alphabetically below their administering organizations

plication form through online; along with a transcript up to the first semester of the current academic year; resume; Student Aid Report (SAR) in its entirety; financial Aid Award Notification from the college applicant plan to attend. **Deadline:** May 15. **Contact:** Cincinnati Scholarship Foundation, 324 E 4th St. 2nd Fl., Cincinnati, OH, 45202; Phone: 513-345-6701; Fax: 513-345-6705; E-mail: info@cincinnatischolarshipfoundation.org.

3345 ■ Charlotte R. SchmidLapp Scholarship Fund
(Undergraduate/Scholarship)

Purpose: To support high school graduates who reside in Greater Cincinnati and are beginning college in the fall of their graduation. **Focus:** General studies/Field of study not specified. **Qualif.:** Applicants must be high school graduates; must reside in Greater Cincinnati; must beginning college in the fall of their graduation; must have proven financial need. **Criteria:** Selection is based on proven financial need.

Funds Avail.: No specific amount. **Duration:** Annual. **To Apply:** Applicant must submit a completed scholarship application form through online; along with a transcript up to the first semester of the current academic year; resume; Student Aid Report (SAR) in its entirety; financial Aid Award Notification from the college applicant plan to attend. **Deadline:** May 15. **Contact:** Cincinnati Scholarship Foundation, 324 E 4th St. 2nd Fl., Cincinnati, OH, 45202; Phone: 513-345-6701; Fax: 513-345-6705; E-mail: info@cincinnatischolarshipfoundation.org.

3346 ■ Christopher Todd Grant Memorial Fund
(Undergraduate/Scholarship)

Purpose: To support students from Greater Cincinnati area to pursue a college education. **Focus:** General studies/Field of study not specified. **Qualif.:** Applicant must be a graduating senior of a Northern Kentucky high school in Kenton, Boone, and Campbell counties and has played soccer in grade or high school and has proven financial need; must reside in Greater Cincinnati. **Criteria:** Selection is based on proven financial need.

Funds Avail.: No specific amount. **Duration:** Annual. **To Apply:** Applicant must submit a completed scholarship application form through online; along with a transcript up to the first semester of the current academic year; resume; Student Aid Report (SAR) in its entirety; financial Aid Award Notification from the college applicant plan to attend. **Deadline:** May 15. **Contact:** Cincinnati Scholarship Foundation, 324 E 4th St. 2nd Fl., Cincinnati, OH, 45202; Phone: 513-345-6701; Fax: 513-345-6705; E-mail: info@cincinnatischolarshipfoundation.org.

3347 ■ Cincinnati Bell Foundation Scholarship
(Undergraduate/Scholarship)

Purpose: To support students from Greater Cincinnati area to pursue a college education. **Focus:** General studies/Field of study not specified. **Qualif.:** Applicants must be high school graduates; must reside in Greater Cincinnati; must beginning college in the fall of their graduation; must have proven financial need. **Criteria:** Selection is based on proven financial need.

Funds Avail.: No specific amount. **Duration:** Annual. **To Apply:** Applicant must submit a completed scholarship application form through online; along with a transcript up to the first semester of the current academic year; resume; Student Aid Report (SAR) in its entirety; financial Aid Award Notification from the college applicant plan to attend. **Deadline:** May 15. **Contact:** Cincinnati Scholarship Foundation,

324 E 4th St. 2nd Fl., Cincinnati, OH, 45202; Phone: 513-345-6701; Fax: 513-345-6705; E-mail: info@cincinnatischolarshipfoundation.org.

3348 ■ Cincinnati Financial Corporation Fund
(Undergraduate/Scholarship)

Purpose: To support high school graduates who reside in Greater Cincinnati and are beginning college in the fall of their graduation. **Focus:** General studies/Field of study not specified. **Qualif.:** Applicants must be high school graduates; must reside in Greater Cincinnati; must beginning college in the fall of their graduation; must have proven financial need. **Criteria:** Selection is based on proven financial need.

Funds Avail.: No specific amount. **Duration:** Annual. **To Apply:** Applicant must submit a completed scholarship application form through online; along with a transcript up to the first semester of the current academic year; resume; Student Aid Report (SAR) in its entirety; financial Aid Award Notification from the college applicant plan to attend. **Deadline:** May 15. **Contact:** Cincinnati Scholarship Foundation, 324 E 4th St. 2nd Fl., Cincinnati, OH, 45202; Phone: 513-345-6701; Fax: 513-345-6705; E-mail: info@cincinnatischolarshipfoundation.org.

3349 ■ Corinne and Fred Capuder Memorial Scholarship (Undergraduate/Scholarship)

Purpose: To support students from Greater Cincinnati area to pursue a college education. **Focus:** General studies/Field of study not specified. **Qualif.:** Applicants must be a non-traditional student (over the age of 25) who is beginning or continuing pursuit of a post-secondary degree; must be a resident of the Greater Cincinnati area and Ripley County in Indiana. **Criteria:** Selection are based on need.

Funds Avail.: No specific amount. **Duration:** Annual. **To Apply:** Applicant must submit a completed scholarship application form through online; along with a transcript up to the first semester of the current academic year; resume; Student Aid Report (SAR) in its entirety; financial Aid Award Notification from the college applicant plan to attend. **Deadline:** May 15. **Remarks:** Established in 1989. **Contact:** Cincinnati Scholarship Foundation, 324 E 4th St. 2nd Fl., Cincinnati, OH, 45202; Phone: 513-345-6701; Fax: 513-345-6705; E-mail: info@cincinnatischolarshipfoundation.org.

3350 ■ Corwin Nixon Scholarship Fund
(Undergraduate/Scholarship)

Purpose: To assist student residing in the 84th Ohio Congressional District pursuing a degree in the medical field. **Focus:** General studies/Field of study not specified. **Qualif.:** Applicant must be a student residing in the 84th Ohio Congressional District pursuing a degree in the medical field and with a proven financial need. **Criteria:** Selection is based on proven financial need.

Funds Avail.: No specific amount. **Duration:** Annual. **To Apply:** Applicant must submit a completed scholarship application form through online; along with a transcript up to the first semester of the current academic year; resume; Student Aid Report (SAR) in its entirety; financial Aid Award Notification from the college applicant plan to attend. **Deadline:** May 15. **Contact:** Cincinnati Scholarship Foundation, 324 E 4th St. 2nd Fl., Cincinnati, OH, 45202; Phone: 513-345-6701; Fax: 513-345-6705; E-mail: info@cincinnatischolarshipfoundation.org.

Awards are arranged alphabetically below their administering organizations

3351 ■ Crosset Family Foundation Scholarship
(Undergraduate/Scholarship)

Purpose: To support high school graduates who reside in Greater Cincinnati and are beginning college in the fall of their graduation. **Focus:** General studies/Field of study not specified. **Qualif.:** Applicants must be high school graduates; must reside in Greater Cincinnati; must beginning college in the fall of their graduation; must have proven financial need. **Criteria:** Selection is based on proven financial need.

Funds Avail.: No specific amount. **Duration:** Annual. **To Apply:** Applicant must submit a completed scholarship application form through online; along with a transcript up to the first semester of the current academic year; resume; Student Aid Report (SAR) in its entirety; financial Aid Award Notification from the college applicant plan to attend. **Deadline:** May 15. **Contact:** Cincinnati Scholarship Foundation, 324 E 4th St. 2nd Fl., Cincinnati, OH, 45202; Phone: 513-345-6701; Fax: 513-345-6705; E-mail: info@cincinnatischolarshipfoundation.org.

3352 ■ Dater Foundation Scholarship
(Undergraduate/Scholarship)

Purpose: To support students attending Dater Junior or Senior High School who are in financial need. **Focus:** General studies/Field of study not specified. **Qualif.:** Applicants must be students coming from Hamilton, Clermont, Butler and Warren counties attending college in Ohio, Indiana or Kentucky; must have proven financial need; must reside in the Greater Cincinnati area. **Criteria:** Priority given to students attending Dater Junior or Senior High School

Funds Avail.: No specific amount. **Duration:** Annual. **To Apply:** Applicant must submit a completed scholarship application form through online; along with a transcript up to the first semester of the current academic year; resume; Student Aid Report (SAR) in its entirety; financial Aid Award Notification from the college applicant plan to attend. **Deadline:** May 15. **Contact:** Cincinnati Scholarship Foundation, 324 E 4th St. 2nd Fl., Cincinnati, OH, 45202; Phone: 513-345-6701; Fax: 513-345-6705; E-mail: info@cincinnatischolarshipfoundation.org.

3353 ■ David J. Joseph Company Scholarship Fund
(Undergraduate/Scholarship)

Purpose: To support students from Greater Cincinnati area to pursue a college education. **Focus:** General studies/Field of study not specified. **Qualif.:** Applicant must be a senior in High School or an undergraduate attending an accredited, non-proprietary college or university; must be a resident of the Greater Cincinnati area; must be dependent children of employees of the David J. Joseph Company. **Criteria:** Awards are given based on need.

Funds Avail.: No specific amount. **Duration:** Annual. **To Apply:** Applicant must submit a completed scholarship application form through online; along with a transcript up to the first semester of the current academic year; resume; Student Aid Report (SAR) in its entirety; financial Aid Award Notification from the college applicant plan to attend. **Deadline:** May 15. **Contact:** Cincinnati Scholarship Foundation, 324 E 4th St. 2nd Fl., Cincinnati, OH, 45202; Phone: 513-345-6701; Fax: 513-345-6705; E-mail: info@cincinnatischolarshipfoundation.org.

3354 ■ Dee Wacksman Scholarship Fund
(Undergraduate/Scholarship)

Purpose: To assist students majoring in the performing arts who are chosen by the Association of Community

Theaters. **Focus:** General studies/Field of study not specified. **Qualif.:** Applicant must be a students majoring in the performing arts who are chosen by the Association of Community Theaters; must reside in the Greater Cincinnati area. **Criteria:** Selection are based on need.

Funds Avail.: No specific amount. **Duration:** Annual. **To Apply:** Applicant must submit a completed scholarship application form through online; along with a transcript up to the first semester of the current academic year; resume; Student Aid Report (SAR) in its entirety; financial Aid Award Notification from the college applicant plan to attend. **Deadline:** May 15. **Contact:** Cincinnati Scholarship Foundation, 324 E 4th St. 2nd Fl., Cincinnati, OH, 45202; Phone: 513-345-6701; Fax: 513-345-6705; E-mail: info@cincinnatischolarshipfoundation.org.

3355 ■ Dwight Hibbard Scholarship Fund
(Undergraduate/Scholarship)

Purpose: To support high school graduates who reside in Greater Cincinnati and are beginning college in the fall of their graduation. **Focus:** General studies/Field of study not specified. **Qualif.:** Applicants must be high school graduates; must reside in Greater Cincinnati; must beginning college in the fall of their graduation; must have proven financial need. **Criteria:** Selection is based on proven financial need.

Funds Avail.: No specific amount. **Duration:** Annual. **To Apply:** Applicant must submit a completed scholarship application form through online; along with a transcript up to the first semester of the current academic year; resume; Student Aid Report (SAR) in its entirety; financial Aid Award Notification from the college applicant plan to attend. **Deadline:** May 15. **Contact:** Cincinnati Scholarship Foundation, 324 E 4th St. 2nd Fl., Cincinnati, OH, 45202; Phone: 513-345-6701; Fax: 513-345-6705; E-mail: info@cincinnatischolarshipfoundation.org.

3356 ■ Ella Wilson Johnson Scholarship Fund
(Undergraduate/Scholarship)

Purpose: To help students from Greater Cincinnati area to achieve the dream of a college education. **Focus:** General studies/Field of study not specified. **Qualif.:** Applicant must be a graduate of Cincinnati Public Schools attending the University of Cincinnati; must reside in the Greater Cincinnati area. **Criteria:** Awards are given based on need.

Funds Avail.: No specific amount. **Duration:** Annual. **To Apply:** Applicant must submit a completed scholarship application form through online; along with a transcript up to the first semester of the current academic year; resume; Student Aid Report (SAR) in its entirety; financial Aid Award Notification from the college applicant plan to attend. **Deadline:** May 15. **Contact:** Cincinnati Scholarship Foundation, 324 E 4th St. 2nd Fl., Cincinnati, OH, 45202; Phone: 513-345-6701; Fax: 513-345-6705; E-mail: info@cincinnatischolarshipfoundation.org.

3357 ■ E.W. Scripps Foundation Scholarship
(Undergraduate/Scholarship)

Purpose: To help students from Greater Cincinnati area to achieve the dream of a college education. **Focus:** General studies/Field of study not specified. **Qualif.:** Applicants must be high school graduates who reside in Greater Cincinnati and are beginning college in the fall of their graduation; must have proven financial need. **Criteria:** Selection will be based on applicants proven financial need.

Funds Avail.: No specific amount. **Duration:** Annual. **To Apply:** Applicant must submit a completed scholarship ap-

Awards are arranged alphabetically below their administering organizations

plication form through online; along with a transcript up to the first semester of the current academic year; resume; Student Aid Report (SAR) in its entirety; financial Aid Award Notification from the college applicant plan to attend. **Deadline:** May 15. **Contact:** Cincinnati Scholarship Foundation, 324 E 4th St. 2nd Fl., Cincinnati, OH, 45202; Phone: 513-345-6701; Fax: 513-345-6705; E-mail: info@cincinnatischolarshipfoundation.org.

3358 ■ Farmer Family Scholarship Fund
(Undergraduate/Scholarship)

Purpose: To help students from Greater Cincinnati area to achieve the dream of a college education. **Focus:** General studies/Field of study not specified. **Qualif.:** Applicants must be high school graduates who reside in Greater Cincinnati and are beginning college in the fall of their graduation; must have proven financial need. **Criteria:** Selection is based on proven financial need.

Funds Avail.: No specific amount. **Duration:** Annual. **To Apply:** Applicant must submit a completed scholarship application form through online; along with a transcript up to the first semester of the current academic year; resume; Student Aid Report (SAR) in its entirety; financial Aid Award Notification from the college applicant plan to attend. **Deadline:** May 15. **Contact:** Cincinnati Scholarship Foundation, 324 E 4th St. 2nd Fl., Cincinnati, OH, 45202; Phone: 513-345-6701; Fax: 513-345-6705; E-mail: info@cincinnatischolarshipfoundation.org.

3359 ■ Fifth Third Bank Scholarship Fund
(Undergraduate/Scholarship)

Purpose: To help students from Greater Cincinnati area to achieve the dream of a college education. **Focus:** General studies/Field of study not specified. **Qualif.:** Applicants must be high school graduates who reside in Greater Cincinnati and are beginning college in the fall of their graduation; must have proven financial need. **Criteria:** Selection is based on proven financial need.

Duration: Annual. **To Apply:** Applicant must submit a completed scholarship application form through online; along with a transcript up to the first semester of the current academic year; resume; Student Aid Report (SAR) in its entirety; financial Aid Award Notification from the college applicant plan to attend. **Deadline:** May 15. **Contact:** Cincinnati Scholarship Foundation, 324 E 4th St. 2nd Fl., Cincinnati, OH, 45202; Phone: 513-345-6701; Fax: 513-345-6705; E-mail: info@cincinnatischolarshipfoundation.org.

3360 ■ Fletemeyer Family Scholarship Fund
(Undergraduate/Scholarship)

Purpose: To help students from Greater Cincinnati area to achieve the dream of a college education. **Focus:** General studies/Field of study not specified. **Qualif.:** Applicant must be a senior in High School or an undergraduate attending an accredited, non-proprietary college or university with preference to those attending Purdue University; must be a resident of the Greater Cincinnati area. **Criteria:** Selection are based on need; preference to those attending Purdue University.

Funds Avail.: No specific amount. **Duration:** Annual. **To Apply:** Applicant must submit a completed scholarship application form through online; along with a transcript up to the first semester of the current academic year; resume; Student Aid Report (SAR) in its entirety; financial Aid Award Notification from the college applicant plan to attend. **Deadline:** May 15. **Contact:** Cincinnati Scholarship Foundation,

324 E 4th St. 2nd Fl., Cincinnati, OH, 45202; Phone: 513-345-6701; Fax: 513-345-6705; E-mail: info@cincinnatischolarshipfoundation.org.

3361 ■ Florette B. Hoffheimer Scholarship Fund
(Undergraduate/Scholarship)

Purpose: To help students from Greater Cincinnati area to achieve the dream of a college education. **Focus:** General studies/Field of study not specified. **Qualif.:** Applicants must be high school graduates who reside in Greater Cincinnati and are beginning college in the fall of their graduation; must have proven financial need. **Criteria:** Selection is based on proven financial need.

Duration: Annual. **To Apply:** Applicant must submit a completed scholarship application form through online; along with a transcript up to the first semester of the current academic year; resume; Student Aid Report (SAR) in its entirety; financial Aid Award Notification from the college applicant plan to attend. **Deadline:** May 15. **Contact:** Cincinnati Scholarship Foundation, 324 E 4th St. 2nd Fl., Cincinnati, OH, 45202; Phone: 513-345-6701; Fax: 513-345-6705; E-mail: info@cincinnatischolarshipfoundation.org.

3362 ■ Frank Foster Skillman Fund *(Undergraduate/ Scholarship)*

Purpose: To help students from Greater Cincinnati area to achieve the dream of a college education. **Focus:** General studies/Field of study not specified. **Qualif.:** Applicants must be students residing in the city of Cincinnati attending the college of their choice. **Criteria:** Awards are given based on need.

Funds Avail.: No specific amount. **Duration:** Annual. **To Apply:** Applicant must submit a completed scholarship application form through online; along with a transcript up to the first semester of the current academic year; resume; Student Aid Report (SAR) in its entirety; financial Aid Award Notification from the college applicant plan to attend. **Deadline:** May 15. **Contact:** Cincinnati Scholarship Foundation, 324 E 4th St. 2nd Fl., Cincinnati, OH, 45202; Phone: 513-345-6701; Fax: 513-345-6705; E-mail: info@cincinnatischolarshipfoundation.org.

3363 ■ Gardner Foundation Scholarship
(Undergraduate/Scholarship)

Purpose: To help students from Greater Cincinnati area to achieve the dream of a college education. **Focus:** General studies/Field of study not specified. **Qualif.:** Applicants must be graduating seniors; must have demonstrated need; must reside in the Greater Cincinnati area. **Criteria:** Selection are based on need; priority is given to students from Middletown, Ohio.

Funds Avail.: No specific amount. **Duration:** Annual. **To Apply:** Applicant must submit a completed scholarship application form through online; along with a transcript up to the first semester of the current academic year; resume; Student Aid Report (SAR) in its entirety; financial Aid Award Notification from the college applicant plan to attend. **Deadline:** May 15. **Contact:** Cincinnati Scholarship Foundation, 324 E 4th St. 2nd Fl., Cincinnati, OH, 45202; Phone: 513-345-6701; Fax: 513-345-6705; E-mail: info@cincinnatischolarshipfoundation.org.

3364 ■ GE Aviation Scholarship Fund
(Undergraduate/Scholarship)

Purpose: To help students from Greater Cincinnati area to achieve the dream of a college education. **Focus:** General

---

Awards are arranged alphabetically below their administering organizations

studies/Field of study not specified. **Qualif.:** Applicants must be high school graduates who reside in Greater Cincinnati and are beginning college in the fall of their graduation; must have proven financial need. **Criteria:** Selection will be based on financial need.

Funds Avail.: No specific amount. **Duration:** Annual. **To Apply:** Applicant must submit a completed scholarship application form through online; along with a transcript up to the first semester of the current academic year; resume; Student Aid Report (SAR) in its entirety; financial Aid Award Notification from the college applicant plan to attend. **Deadline:** May 15. **Contact:** Cincinnati Scholarship Foundation, 324 E 4th St. 2nd Fl., Cincinnati, OH, 45202; Phone: 513-345-6701; Fax: 513-345-6705; E-mail: info@cincinnatischolarshipfoundation.org.

3365 ■ Goldman, Sachs and Company Fund
(Undergraduate/Scholarship)

Purpose: To help students from Greater Cincinnati area to achieve the dream of a college education. **Focus:** General studies/Field of study not specified. **Qualif.:** Applicants must be high school graduates who reside in Greater Cincinnati and are beginning college in the fall of their graduation; must have proven financial need. **Criteria:** Selection is based on proven financial need.

Funds Avail.: No specific amount. **Duration:** Annual. **To Apply:** Applicant must submit a completed scholarship application form through online; along with a transcript up to the first semester of the current academic year; resume; Student Aid Report (SAR) in its entirety; financial Aid Award Notification from the college applicant plan to attend. **Deadline:** May 15. **Contact:** Cincinnati Scholarship Foundation, 324 E 4th St. 2nd Fl., Cincinnati, OH, 45202; Phone: 513-345-6701; Fax: 513-345-6705; E-mail: info@cincinnatischolarshipfoundation.org.

3366 ■ H.C. Schott Foundation Scholarship
(Undergraduate/Scholarship)

Purpose: To help students from Greater Cincinnati area to achieve the dream of a college education. **Focus:** General studies/Field of study not specified. **Qualif.:** Applicants must be high school graduates who reside in Greater Cincinnati and are beginning college in the fall of their graduation; must have proven financial need. **Criteria:** Selection will be based on financial need.

Funds Avail.: No specific amount. **Duration:** Annual. **To Apply:** Applicant must submit a completed scholarship application form through online; along with a transcript up to the first semester of the current academic year; resume; Student Aid Report (SAR) in its entirety; financial Aid Award Notification from the college applicant plan to attend. **Deadline:** May 15. **Contact:** Cincinnati Scholarship Foundation, 324 E 4th St. 2nd Fl., Cincinnati, OH, 45202; Phone: 513-345-6701; Fax: 513-345-6705; E-mail: info@cincinnatischolarshipfoundation.org.

3367 ■ HCRTA/Glen O. & Wyllabeth Scholarship
Fund *(Undergraduate/Scholarship)*

Purpose: To help students from Greater Cincinnati area to achieve the dream of a college education. **Focus:** General studies/Field of study not specified. **Qualif.:** Applicants must be graduating senior in Hamilton county; must have strong academic record, majoring in education, and has proven financial need; must reside in the Greater Cincinnati area. **Criteria:** Awards are given based on strong academic record, majoring in education, and has proven financial need.

Funds Avail.: No specific amount. **Duration:** Annual. **To Apply:** Applicant must submit a completed scholarship application form through online; along with a transcript up to the first semester of the current academic year; resume; Student Aid Report (SAR) in its entirety; financial Aid Award Notification from the college applicant plan to attend. **Deadline:** May 15. **Contact:** Cincinnati Scholarship Foundation, 324 E 4th St. 2nd Fl., Cincinnati, OH, 45202; Phone: 513-345-6701; Fax: 513-345-6705; E-mail: info@cincinnatischolarshipfoundation.org.

3368 ■ Heidelberg Distributing Scholarship Fund
(Undergraduate/Scholarship)

Purpose: To help students from Greater Cincinnati area to achieve the dream of a college education. **Focus:** General studies/Field of study not specified. **Qualif.:** Applicants must be high school graduates who reside in Greater Cincinnati and are beginning college in the fall of their graduation; must have proven financial need. **Criteria:** Selection is based on proven financial need.

Funds Avail.: No specific amount. **Duration:** Annual. **To Apply:** Applicant must submit a completed scholarship application form through online; along with a transcript up to the first semester of the current academic year; resume; Student Aid Report (SAR) in its entirety; financial Aid Award Notification from the college applicant plan to attend. **Deadline:** May 15. **Contact:** Cincinnati Scholarship Foundation, 324 E 4th St. 2nd Fl., Cincinnati, OH, 45202; Phone: 513-345-6701; Fax: 513-345-6705; E-mail: info@cincinnatischolarshipfoundation.org.

3369 ■ Heinz Pet Products Scholarship Fund
(Undergraduate/Scholarship)

Purpose: To help students from Greater Cincinnati area to achieve the dream of a college education. **Focus:** General studies/Field of study not specified. **Qualif.:** Applicants must be high school graduates who reside in Greater Cincinnati and are beginning college in the fall of their graduation; must have proven financial need. **Criteria:** Selection is based on proven financial need.

Funds Avail.: No specific amount. **Duration:** Annual. **To Apply:** Applicant must submit a completed scholarship application form through online; along with a transcript up to the first semester of the current academic year; resume; Student Aid Report (SAR) in its entirety; financial Aid Award Notification from the college applicant plan to attend. **Deadline:** May 15. **Contact:** Cincinnati Scholarship Foundation, 324 E 4th St. 2nd Fl.; Cincinnati, OH, 45202; Phone: 513-345-6701; Fax: 513-345-6705; E-mail: info@cincinnatischolarshipfoundation.org.

3370 ■ Helen Steiner Rice Scholarship Fund
(Undergraduate/Scholarship)

Purpose: To help students from Greater Cincinnati area to achieve the dream of a college education. **Focus:** General studies/Field of study not specified. **Qualif.:** Applicants must be high school graduates who reside in Greater Cincinnati and are beginning college in the fall of their graduation; must have proven financial need. **Criteria:** Selection is based on proven financial need.

Duration: Annual. **To Apply:** Applicant must submit a completed scholarship application form through online; along with a transcript up to the first semester of the current academic year; resume; Student Aid Report (SAR) in its entirety; financial Aid Award Notification from the college applicant plan to attend. **Deadline:** May 15. **Contact:** Cincinnati Scholarship Foundation, 324 E 4th St. 2nd Fl.,

Awards are arranged alphabetically below their administering organizations

Cincinnati, OH, 45202; Phone: 513-345-6701; Fax: 513-345-6705; E-mail: info@cincinnatischolarshipfoundation.org.

3371 ■ Johnny Bench Scholarship Fund
(Undergraduate/Scholarship)

Purpose: To help students from Greater Cincinnati area to achieve the dream of a college education. **Focus:** General studies/Field of study not specified. **Qualif.:** Applicants must be students residing within the I-275 boundary and attending the University of Cincinnati, Miami University, Mt. St. Joseph University, Northern Kentucky University, Thomas More College and Cincinnati State; also for students residing in Binger OK attending college in Oklahoma; must have participated in athletics.**Criteria:** Awards are given based on need.

Funds Avail.: No specific amount. **Duration:** Annual. **To Apply:** Applicant must submit a completed scholarship application form through online; along with a transcript up to the first semester of the current academic year; resume; Student Aid Report (SAR) in its entirety; financial Aid Award Notification from the college applicant plan to attend. **Deadline:** May 15. **Remarks:** Established in 1983. **Contact:** Cincinnati Scholarship Foundation, 324 E 4th St. 2nd Fl., Cincinnati, OH, 45202; Phone: 513-345-6701; Fax: 513-345-6705; E-mail: info@cincinnatischolarshipfoundation.org.

3372 ■ Joseph S. Stern Scholarship Fund
(Undergraduate/Scholarship)

Purpose: To support high school graduates who reside in Greater Cincinnati and are beginning college in the fall of their graduation. **Focus:** General studies/Field of study not specified. **Qualif.:** Applicants must be high school graduates who reside in Greater Cincinnati and are beginning college in the fall of their graduation; must have proven financial need. **Criteria:** Selection is based on proven financial need.

Funds Avail.: No specific amount. **Duration:** Annual. **To Apply:** Applicant must submit a completed scholarship application form through online; along with a transcript up to the first semester of the current academic year; resume; Student Aid Report (SAR) in its entirety; financial Aid Award Notification from the college applicant plan to attend. **Deadline:** May 15. **Contact:** Cincinnati Scholarship Foundation, 324 E 4th St. 2nd Fl., Cincinnati, OH, 45202; Phone: 513-345-6701; Fax: 513-345-6705; E-mail: info@cincinnatischolarshipfoundation.org.

3373 ■ Judge Benjamin Schwartz Memorial Fund
(Undergraduate/Scholarship)

Purpose: To help students from Greater Cincinnati area to achieve the dream of a college education. **Focus:** General studies/Field of study not specified. **Qualif.:** Applicants must be former residents of Hillcrest School; must have a proven financial need; must reside in the Greater Cincinnati area. **Criteria:** Selection is based on proven financial need.

Funds Avail.: No specific amount. **Duration:** Annual. **To Apply:** Applicant must submit a completed scholarship application form through online; along with a transcript up to the first semester of the current academic year; resume; Student Aid Report (SAR) in its entirety; financial Aid Award Notification from the college applicant plan to attend. **Deadline:** May 15. **Contact:** Cincinnati Scholarship Foundation, 324 E 4th St. 2nd Fl., Cincinnati, OH, 45202; Phone: 513-345-6701; Fax: 513-345-6705; E-mail: info@cincinnatischolarshipfoundation.org.

3374 ■ Juilfs Foundation Scholarship
(Undergraduate/Scholarship)

Purpose: To support high school graduates who reside in Greater Cincinnati and are beginning college in the fall of their graduation. **Focus:** General studies/Field of study not specified. **Qualif.:** Applicants must be high school graduates who reside in Greater Cincinnati and are beginning college in the fall of their graduation; must have proven financial need. **Criteria:** Selection is based on proven financial need.

Funds Avail.: No specific amount. **Duration:** Annual. **To Apply:** Applicant must submit a completed scholarship application form through online; along with a transcript up to the first semester of the current academic year; resume; Student Aid Report (SAR) in its entirety; financial Aid Award Notification from the college applicant plan to attend. **Deadline:** May 15. **Contact:** Cincinnati Scholarship Foundation, 324 E 4th St. 2nd Fl., Cincinnati, OH, 45202; Phone: 513-345-6701; Fax: 513-345-6705; E-mail: info@cincinnatischolarshipfoundation.org.

3375 ■ Kroger Cincinnati/Dayton Scholarship Fund
(Undergraduate/Scholarship)

Purpose: To support high school graduates who reside in Greater Cincinnati and are beginning college in the fall of their graduation. **Focus:** General studies/Field of study not specified. **Qualif.:** Applicants must be high school graduates who reside in Greater Cincinnati and are beginning college in the fall of their graduation; must have proven financial need. **Criteria:** Selection is based on proven financial need.

Funds Avail.: No specific amount. **Duration:** Annual. **To Apply:** Applicant must submit a completed scholarship application form through online; along with a transcript up to the first semester of the current academic year; resume; Student Aid Report (SAR) in its entirety; financial Aid Award Notification from the college applicant plan to attend.**Deadline:** May 15. **Contact:** Cincinnati Scholarship Foundation, 324 E 4th St. 2nd Fl., Cincinnati, OH, 45202; Phone: 513-345-6701; Fax: 513-345-6705; E-mail: info@cincinnatischolarshipfoundation.org.

3376 ■ L. & T. Woolfolk Memorial Scholarship Fund
(Undergraduate/Scholarship)

Purpose: To support an African-American student who are in financial need. **Focus:** General studies/Field of study not specified. **Qualif.:** Applicant must be an African-American student with proven financial need; must reside in the Greater Cincinnati area. **Criteria:** Selection is based on proven financial need.

Funds Avail.: No specific amount. **Duration:** Annual. **To Apply:** Applicant must submit a completed scholarship application form through online; along with a transcript up to the first semester of the current academic year; resume; Student Aid Report (SAR) in its entirety; financial Aid Award Notification from the college applicant plan to attend. **Deadline:** May 15. **Contact:** Cincinnati Scholarship Foundation, 324 E 4th St. 2nd Fl., Cincinnati, OH, 45202; Phone: 513-345-6705; Fax: 513-345-6705; E-mail: info@cincinnatischolarshipfoundation.org.

3377 ■ Louis B. Zapoleon Memorial Fund
(Undergraduate/Scholarship)

Purpose: To support students who are in financial need who are resident of the Greater Cincinnati area. **Focus:** General studies/Field of study not specified. **Qualif.:** Ap-

Awards are arranged alphabetically below their administering organizations

plicant must be a student with proven financial need; a senior in high school or an undergraduate attending an accredited, non-proprietary college or university; must be a resident of the Greater Cincinnati area. **Criteria:** Selection will be based on financial need.

Funds Avail.: No specific amount. **Duration:** Annual. **To Apply:** Applicant must submit a completed scholarship application form through online; along with a transcript up to the first semester of the current academic year; resume; Student Aid Report (SAR) in its entirety; financial Aid Award Notification from the college applicant plan to attend. **Deadline:** May 15. **Contact:** Cincinnati Scholarship Foundation, 324 E 4th St. 2nd Fl., Cincinnati, OH, 45202; Phone: 513-345-6701; Fax: 513-345-6705; E-mail: info@cincinnatischolarshipfoundation.org.

3378 ■ Lowe Simpson Scholarship Fund
(Undergraduate/Scholarship)

Purpose: To support high school graduates who reside in Greater Cincinnati and are beginning college in the fall of their graduation. **Focus:** General studies/Field of study not specified. **Qualif.:** Applicants must be high school graduates who reside in Greater Cincinnati and are beginning college in the fall of their graduation; must have proven financial need. **Criteria:** Selection is based on proven financial need.

Funds Avail.: No specific amount. **Duration:** Annual. **To Apply:** Applicant must submit a completed scholarship application form through online; along with a transcript up to the first semester of the current academic year; resume; Student Aid Report (SAR) in its entirety; financial Aid Award Notification from the college applicant plan to attend. **Deadline:** May 15. **Contact:** Cincinnati Scholarship Foundation, 324 E 4th St. 2nd Fl., Cincinnati, OH, 45202; Phone: 513-345-6701; Fax: 513-345-6705; E-mail: info@cincinnatischolarshipfoundation.org.

3379 ■ Lyle Everingham Scholarship Fund
(Undergraduate/Scholarship)

Purpose: To support high school graduates who reside in Greater Cincinnati and are beginning college in the fall of their graduation. **Focus:** General studies/Field of study not specified. **Qualif.:** Applicants must be high school graduates who reside in Greater Cincinnati and are beginning college in the fall of their graduation; must have proven financial need. **Criteria:** Selection is based on proven financial need.

Funds Avail.: No specific amount. **Duration:** Annual. **To Apply:** Applicant must submit a completed scholarship application form through online; along with a transcript up to the first semester of the current academic year; resume; Student Aid Report (SAR) in its entirety; financial Aid Award Notification from the college applicant plan to attend. **Deadline:** May 15. **Contact:** Cincinnati Scholarship Foundation, 324 E 4th St. 2nd Fl., Cincinnati, OH, 45202; Phone: 513-345-6701; Fax: 513-345-6705; E-mail: info@cincinnatischolarshipfoundation.org.

3380 ■ Lyle and Rlene Everingham Family Fund
(Undergraduate/Scholarship)

Purpose: To support high school graduates who reside in Greater Cincinnati and are beginning college in the fall of their graduation. **Focus:** General studies/Field of study not specified. **Qualif.:** Applicants must be high school graduates who reside in Greater Cincinnati and are beginning college in the fall of their graduation; must have proven financial need. **Criteria:** Selection is based on proven financial need.

Funds Avail.: No specific amount. **Duration:** Annual. **To Apply:** Applicant must submit a completed scholarship application form through online; along with a transcript up to the first semester of the current academic year; resume; Student Aid Report (SAR) in its entirety; financial Aid Award Notification from the college applicant plan to attend. **Deadline:** May 15. **Contact:** Cincinnati Scholarship Foundation, 324 E 4th St. 2nd Fl., Cincinnati, OH, 45202; Phone: 513-345-6701; Fax: 513-345-6705; E-mail: info@cincinnatischolarshipfoundation.org.

3381 ■ Martha W. Tanner Memorial Fund
(Undergraduate/Scholarship)

Purpose: To support a student of Appalachian descent. **Focus:** General studies/Field of study not specified. **Qualif.:** Applicant must be a student of Appalachian descent; must be a senior in High School or an undergraduate attending an accredited, non-proprietary college or university and a resident of the Greater Cincinnati area. **Criteria:** Selection are based on need.

Duration: Annual. **To Apply:** Applicant must submit a completed scholarship application form through online; along with a transcript up to the first-semester of the current academic year; resume; Student Aid Report (SAR) in its entirety; financial Aid Award Notification from the college applicant plan to attend. **Deadline:** May 15. **Contact:** Cincinnati Scholarship Foundation, 324 E 4th St. 2nd Fl., Cincinnati, OH, 45202; Phone: 513-345-6701; Fax: 513-345-6705; E-mail: info@cincinnatischolarshipfoundation.org.

3382 ■ Marvin Rammelsberg Scholarship Fund
(Undergraduate/Scholarship)

Purpose: To assist a graduate of Cincinnati Public Schools attending Morehead State University. **Focus:** General studies/Field of study not specified. **Qualif.:** Applicant must be a graduate of Cincinnati Public Schools attending Morehead State University. **Criteria:** Selection are based on need.

Funds Avail.: No specific amount. **Duration:** Annual. **To Apply:** Applicant must submit a completed scholarship application form through online; along with a transcript up to the first semester of the current academic year; resume; Student Aid Report (SAR) in its entirety; financial Aid Award Notification from the college applicant plan to attend. **Deadline:** May 15. **Contact:** Cincinnati Scholarship Foundation, 324 E 4th St. 2nd Fl., Cincinnati, OH, 45202; Phone: 513-345-6701; Fax: 513-345-6705; E-mail: info@cincinnatischolarshipfoundation.org.

3383 ■ Mary Roberts Scholarship Fund
(Undergraduate/Scholarship)

Purpose: To support a student majoring in Nursing; especially to graduates of Jewish Hospital School of Nursing returning to school for a bachelors degree. **Focus:** General studies/Field of study not specified. **Qualif.:** Applicant must be a resident of Greater Cincinnati; must be a student majoring in Nursing. **Criteria:** Priority given to graduates of Jewish Hospital School of Nursing returning to school for a bachelors degree.

Funds Avail.: No specific amount. **Duration:** Annual. **To Apply:** Applicant must submit a completed scholarship application form through online; along with a transcript up to the first semester of the current academic year; resume; Student Aid Report (SAR) in its entirety; financial Aid Award Notification from the college applicant plan to attend. **Deadline:** May 15. **Contact:** Cincinnati Scholarship Foundation,

Awards are arranged alphabetically below their administering organizations

324 E 4th St. 2nd Fl., Cincinnati, OH, 45202; Phone: 513-345-6701; Fax: 513-345-6705; E-mail: info@cincinnatischolarshipfoundation.org.

3384 ■ McCall Educational Fund (Undergraduate/ Scholarship)

Purpose: To support African-American students attending a college in Hamilton County or Miami University. **Focus:** General studies/Field of study not specified. **Qualif.:** Applicant must be a resident of Greater Cincinnati; must be African-American students attending a college in Hamilton County or Miami University. **Criteria:** Awards are given based on need.

Funds Avail.: No specific amount. **Duration:** Annual. **To Apply:** Applicant must submit a completed scholarship application form through online; along with a transcript up to the first semester of the current academic year; resume; Student Aid Report (SAR) in its entirety; financial Aid Award Notification from the college applicant plan to attend. **Deadline:** May 15. **Contact:** Cincinnati Scholarship Foundation, 324 E 4th St. 2nd Fl., Cincinnati, OH, 45202; Phone: 513-345-6701; Fax: 513-345-6705; E-mail: info@cincinnatischolarshipfoundation.org.

3385 ■ Michael Bany Memorial Scholarship Fund (Undergraduate/Scholarship)

Purpose: To assist a student with a proven musical ability and financial need pursing a degree in a field of music. **Focus:** General studies/Field of study not specified. **Qualif.:** Applicant must be a resident of Greater Cincinnati; a student with a proven musical ability and financial need pursuing a degree in a field of music. **Criteria:** Selection is based on proven financial need.

Funds Avail.: No specific amount. **Duration:** Annual. **To Apply:** Applicant must submit a completed scholarship application form through online; along with a transcript up to the first semester of the current academic year; resume; Student Aid Report (SAR) in its entirety; financial Aid Award Notification from the college applicant plan to attend. **Deadline:** May 15. **Contact:** Cincinnati Scholarship Foundation, 324 E 4th St. 2nd Fl., Cincinnati, OH, 45202; Phone: 513-345-6701; Fax: 513-345-6705; E-mail: info@cincinnatischolarshipfoundation.org.

3386 ■ Midland Company Scholarship Fund (Undergraduate/Scholarship)

Purpose: To support high school graduates who reside in Greater Cincinnati and are beginning college in the fall of their graduation. **Focus:** General studies/Field of study not specified. **Qualif.:** Applicants must be high school graduates who reside in Greater Cincinnati and are beginning college in the fall of their graduation; must have proven financial need. **Criteria:** Selection is based on proven financial need.

Funds Avail.: No specific amount. **Duration:** Annual. **To Apply:** Applicant must submit a completed scholarship application form through online; along with a transcript up to the first semester of the current academic year; resume; Student Aid Report (SAR) in its entirety; financial Aid Award Notification from the college applicant plan to attend. **Deadline:** May 15. **Contact:** Cincinnati Scholarship Foundation, 324 E 4th St. 2nd Fl., Cincinnati, OH, 45202; Phone: 513-345-6701; Fax: 513-345-6705; E-mail: info@cincinnatischolarshipfoundation.org.

3387 ■ Milacron Geier Scholarship Fund (Undergraduate/Scholarship)

Purpose: To support high school graduates who reside in Greater Cincinnati and are beginning college in the fall of their graduation. **Focus:** General studies/Field of study not specified. **Qualif.:** Applicants must be high school graduates; must reside in Greater Cincinnati; must beginning college in the fall of their graduation; must have proven financial need. **Criteria:** Selection is based on proven financial need.

Funds Avail.: No specific amount. **Duration:** Annual. **To Apply:** Applicant must submit a completed scholarship application form through online; along with a transcript up to the first semester of the current academic year; resume; Student Aid Report (SAR) in its entirety; financial Aid Award Notification from the college applicant plan to attend. **Deadline:** May 15. **Contact:** Cincinnati Scholarship Foundation, 324 E 4th St. 2nd Fl., Cincinnati, OH, 45202; Phone: 513-345-6701; Fax: 513-345-6705; E-mail: info@cincinnatischolarshipfoundation.org.

3388 ■ Milton and Edith Brown Memorial Scholarship Fund (Undergraduate/Scholarship)

Purpose: To support residents of Ohio studying for the ministry or have relatives in the ministry. **Focus:** General studies/Field of study not specified. **Qualif.:** Applicants must be residents of Ohio studying for the ministry or have relatives in the ministry. **Criteria:** Awards are given based on need.

Funds Avail.: No specific amount. **Duration:** Annual. **To Apply:** Applicant must submit a completed scholarship application form through online; along with a transcript up to the first semester of the current academic year; resume; Student Aid Report (SAR) in its entirety; financial Aid Award Notification from the college applicant plan to attend. **Deadline:** May 15. **Contact:** Cincinnati Scholarship Foundation, 324 E 4th St. 2nd Fl., Cincinnati, OH, 45202; Phone: 513-345-6701; Fax: 513-345-6705; E-mail: info@cincinnatischolarshipfoundation.org.

3389 ■ Nelson Schwab Jr. Scholarship Fund (Undergraduate/Scholarship)

Purpose: To support high school graduates who reside in Greater Cincinnati and are beginning college in the fall of their graduation. **Focus:** General studies/Field of study not specified. **Qualif.:** Applicants must be high school graduates who reside in Greater Cincinnati and are beginning college in the fall of their graduation; must have proven financial need. **Criteria:** Selection is based on proven financial need.

Funds Avail.: No specific amount. **Duration:** Annual. **To Apply:** Applicant must submit a completed scholarship application form through online; along with a transcript up to the first semester of the current academic year; resume; Student Aid Report (SAR) in its entirety; financial Aid Award Notification from the college applicant plan to attend. **Deadline:** May 15. **Contact:** Cincinnati Scholarship Foundation, 324 E 4th St. 2nd Fl., Cincinnati, OH, 45202; Phone: 513-345-6701; Fax: 513-345-6705; E-mail: info@cincinnatischolarshipfoundation.org.

3390 ■ Nethercott Family Scholarship Fund (Undergraduate/Scholarship)

Purpose: To support high school graduates who reside in Greater Cincinnati and are beginning college in the fall of their graduation. **Focus:** General studies/Field of study not specified. **Qualif.:** Applicants must be high school graduates who reside in Greater Cincinnati and are beginning college in the fall of their graduation; must have proven financial need. **Criteria:** Selection is based on proven financial need.

Awards are arranged alphabetically below their administering organizations

Funds Avail.: No specific amount. **Duration:** Annual. **To Apply:** Applicant must submit a completed scholarship application form through online; along with a transcript up to the first semester of the current academic year; resume; Student Aid Report (SAR) in its entirety; financial Aid Award Notification from the college applicant plan to attend. **Deadline:** May 15. **Contact:** Cincinnati Scholarship Foundation, 324 E 4th St. 2nd Fl., Cincinnati, OH, 45202; Phone: 513-345-6701; Fax: 513-345-6705; E-mail: info@cincinnatischolarshipfoundation.org.

3391 ■ Ohio National Foundation Scholarship
(Undergraduate/Scholarship)

Purpose: To support high school graduates who reside in Greater Cincinnati and are beginning college in the fall of their graduation. **Focus:** General studies/Field of study not specified. **Qualif.:** Applicants must be high school graduates who reside in Greater Cincinnati and are beginning college in the fall of their graduation; must have proven financial need. **Criteria:** Selection is based on proven financial need.

Funds Avail.: No specific amount. **Duration:** Annual. **To Apply:** Applicant must submit a completed scholarship application form through online; along with a transcript up to the first semester of the current academic year; resume; Student Aid Report (SAR) in its entirety; financial Aid Award Notification from the college applicant plan to attend. **Deadline:** May 15. **Contact:** Cincinnati Scholarship Foundation, 324 E 4th St. 2nd Fl., Cincinnati, OH, 45202; Phone: 513-345-6701; Fax: 513-345-6705; E-mail: info@cincinnatischolarshipfoundation.org.

3392 ■ Pepper Family Scholarship Fund
(Undergraduate/Scholarship)

Purpose: To support high school graduates who reside in Greater Cincinnati and are beginning college in the fall of their graduation. **Focus:** General studies/Field of study not specified. **Qualif.:** Applicants must be high school graduates who reside in Greater Cincinnati and are beginning college in the fall of their graduation; must have proven financial need. **Criteria:** Selection is based on proven financial need.

Funds Avail.: No specific amount. **Duration:** Annual. **To Apply:** Applicant must submit a completed scholarship application form through online; along with a transcript up to the first semester of the current academic year; resume; Student Aid Report (SAR) in its entirety; financial Aid Award Notification from the college applicant plan to attend. **Deadline:** May 15. **Contact:** Cincinnati Scholarship Foundation, 324 E 4th St. 2nd Fl., Cincinnati, OH, 45202; Phone: 513-345-6701; Fax: 513-345-6705; E-mail: info@cincinnatischolarshipfoundation.org.

3393 ■ Pichler Family Scholarship Fund
(Undergraduate/Scholarship)

Purpose: To support high school graduates who reside in Greater Cincinnati and are beginning college in the fall of their graduation. **Focus:** General studies/Field of study not specified. **Qualif.:** Applicants must be high school graduates who reside in Greater Cincinnati and are beginning college in the fall of their graduation; must have proven financial need. **Criteria:** Selection is based on proven financial need.

Funds Avail.: No specific amount. **Duration:** Annual. **To Apply:** Applicant must submit a completed scholarship application form through online; along with a transcript up to the first semester of the current academic year; resume;

Student Aid Report (SAR) in its entirety; financial Aid Award Notification from the college applicant plan to attend. **Deadline:** May 15. **Contact:** Cincinnati Scholarship Foundation, 324 E 4th St. 2nd Fl., Cincinnati, OH, 45202; Phone: 513-345-6701; Fax: 513-345-6705; E-mail: info@cincinnatischolarshipfoundation.org.

3394 ■ PNC Scholarship Fund
(Undergraduate/Scholarship)

Purpose: To support high school graduates who reside in Greater Cincinnati and are beginning college in the fall of their graduation. **Focus:** General studies/Field of study not specified. **Qualif.:** Applicants must be high school graduates who reside in Greater Cincinnati and are beginning college in the fall of their graduation; must have proven financial need. **Criteria:** Selection is based on proven financial need.

Funds Avail.: No specific amount. **Duration:** Annual. **To Apply:** Applicant must submit a completed scholarship application form through online; along with a transcript up to the first semester of the current academic year; resume; Student Aid Report (SAR) in its entirety; financial Aid Award Notification from the college applicant plan to attend. **Deadline:** May 15. **Contact:** Cincinnati Scholarship Foundation, 324 E 4th St. 2nd Fl., Cincinnati, OH, 45202; Phone: 513-345-6701; Fax: 513-345-6705; E-mail: info@cincinnatischolarshipfoundation.org.

3395 ■ Priscilla Gamble Scholarship Fund
(Undergraduate/Scholarship)

Purpose: To support high school graduates who reside in Greater Cincinnati and are beginning college in the fall of their graduation. **Focus:** General studies/Field of study not specified. **Qualif.:** Applicants must be high school graduates who reside in Greater Cincinnati and are beginning college in the fall of their graduation; must have proven financial need. **Criteria:** Selection is based on proven financial need.

Funds Avail.: No specific amount. **Duration:** Annual. **To Apply:** Applicant must submit a completed scholarship application form through online; along with a transcript up to the first semester of the current academic year; resume; Student Aid Report (SAR) in its entirety; financial Aid Award Notification from the college applicant plan to attend. **Deadline:** May 15. **Contact:** Cincinnati Scholarship Foundation, 324 E 4th St. 2nd Fl., Cincinnati, OH, 45202; Phone: 513-345-6701; Fax: 513-345-6705; E-mail: info@cincinnatischolarshipfoundation.org.

3396 ■ Procter and Gamble Foundation Scholarship
(Undergraduate/Scholarship)

Purpose: To support high school graduates who reside in Greater Cincinnati and are beginning college in the fall of their graduation. **Focus:** General studies/Field of study not specified. **Qualif.:** Applicants must be high school graduates who reside in Greater Cincinnati and are beginning college in the fall of their graduation; must have proven financial need. **Criteria:** Selection is based on proven financial need.

Funds Avail.: No specific amount. **Duration:** Annual. **To Apply:** Applicant must submit a completed scholarship application form through online; along with a transcript up to the first semester of the current academic year; resume; Student Aid Report (SAR) in its entirety; financial Aid Award Notification from the college applicant plan to attend. **Deadline:** May 15. **Contact:** Cincinnati Scholarship Foundation, 324 E 4th St. 2nd Fl., Cincinnati, OH, 45202; Phone: 513-

Awards are arranged alphabetically below their administering organizations

345-6701; Fax: 513-345-6705; E-mail: info@cincinnatischolarshipfoundation.org.

3397 ■ Raymond and Augusta Klink Scholarship Fund (Undergraduate/Scholarship)

Purpose: To support high school graduates who reside in Greater Cincinnati and are beginning college in the fall of their graduation. **Focus:** General studies/Field of study not specified. **Qualif.:** Applicants must be high school graduates who reside in Greater Cincinnati and are beginning college in the fall of their graduation; must have proven financial need. **Criteria:** Selection is based on proven financial need.

Funds Avail.: No specific amount. **Duration:** Annual. **To Apply:** Applicant must submit a completed scholarship application form through online; along with a transcript up to the first semester of the current academic year; resume; Student Aid Report (SAR) in its entirety; financial Aid Award Notification from the college applicant plan to attend. **Deadline:** May 15. **Contact:** Cincinnati Scholarship Foundation, 324 E 4th St. 2nd Fl., Cincinnati, OH, 45202; Phone: 513-345-6701; Fax: 513-345-6705; E-mail: info@cincinnatischolarshipfoundation.org.

3398 ■ Richard Heekin Scholarship Fund (Undergraduate/Scholarship)

Purpose: To help students from Greater Cincinnati area to achieve the dream of a college education. **Focus:** General studies/Field of study not specified. **Qualif.:** Applicants must be high school graduates who reside in Greater Cincinnati and are beginning college in the fall of their graduation. **Criteria:** Awards are given based on need.

Funds Avail.: No specific amount. **Duration:** Annual. **To Apply:** Applicant must submit a completed scholarship application form through online; along with a transcript up to the first semester of the current academic year; resume; Student Aid Report (SAR) in its entirety; financial Aid Award Notification from the college applicant plan to attend. **Deadline:** May 15. **Contact:** Cincinnati Scholarship Foundation, 324 E 4th St. 2nd Fl., Cincinnati, OH, 45202; Phone: 513-345-6701; Fax: 513-345-6705; E-mail: info@cincinnatischolarshipfoundation.org.

3399 ■ Robert H. Reakirt Scholarship Fund (Undergraduate/Scholarship)

Purpose: To help students from Greater Cincinnati area to achieve the dream of a college education. **Focus:** General studies/Field of study not specified. **Qualif.:** Applicants must be high school graduates who reside in Greater Cincinnati and are beginning college in the fall of their graduation. **Criteria:** Selection are based on need.

Funds Avail.: No specific amount. **Duration:** Annual. **To Apply:** Applicant must submit a completed scholarship application form through online; along with a transcript up to the first semester of the current academic year; resume; Student Aid Report (SAR) in its entirety; financial Aid Award Notification from the college applicant plan to attend. **Deadline:** May 15. **Contact:** Cincinnati Scholarship Foundation, 324 E 4th St. 2nd Fl., Cincinnati, OH, 45202; Phone: 513-345-6701; Fax: 513-345-6705; E-mail: info@cincinnatischolarshipfoundation.org.

3400 ■ Roger and Joyce Howe Scholarship Fund (Undergraduate/Scholarship)

Purpose: To help students from Greater Cincinnati area to achieve the dream of a college education. **Focus:** General

studies/Field of study not specified. **Qualif.:** Applicants must be high school graduates who reside in Greater Cincinnati and are beginning college in the fall of their graduation. **Criteria:** Awards are given based on need.

Funds Avail.: No specific amount. **Duration:** Annual. **To Apply:** Applicant must submit a completed scholarship application form through online; along with a transcript up to the first semester of the current academic year; resume; Student Aid Report (SAR) in its entirety; financial Aid Award Notification from the college applicant plan to attend. **Deadline:** May 15. **Contact:** Cincinnati Scholarship Foundation, 324 E 4th St. 2nd Fl., Cincinnati, OH, 45202; Phone: 513-345-6701; Fax: 513-345-6705; E-mail: info@cincinnatischolarshipfoundation.org.

3401 ■ S. David Shor Scholarship Fund (Undergraduate/Scholarship)

Purpose: To help students from Greater Cincinnati area to achieve the dream of a college education. **Focus:** General studies/Field of study not specified. **Qualif.:** Applicants must be high school graduates who reside in Greater Cincinnati and are beginning college in the fall of their graduation. **Criteria:** Awards are given based on need.

Funds Avail.: No specific amount. **Duration:** Annual. **To Apply:** Applicant must submit a completed scholarship application form through online; along with a transcript up to the first semester of the current academic year; resume; Student Aid Report (SAR) in its entirety; financial Aid Award Notification from the college applicant plan to attend. **Deadline:** May 15. **Contact:** Cincinnati Scholarship Foundation, 324 E 4th St. 2nd Fl., Cincinnati, OH, 45202; Phone: 513-345-6701; Fax: 513-345-6705; E-mail: info@cincinnatischolarshipfoundation.org.

3402 ■ S.C. Johnson, A Family Company Scholarship Fund (Undergraduate/Scholarship)

Purpose: To help students from Greater Cincinnati area to achieve the dream of a college education. **Focus:** General studies/Field of study not specified. **Qualif.:** Applicants must be high school graduates who reside in Greater Cincinnati and are beginning college in the fall of their graduation. **Criteria:** Awards are given based on need.

Duration: Annual. **To Apply:** Applicant must submit a completed scholarship application form through online; along with a transcript up to the first semester of the current academic year; resume; Student Aid Report (SAR) in its entirety; financial Aid Award Notification from the college applicant plan to attend. **Deadline:** May 15. **Contact:** Cincinnati Scholarship Foundation, 324 E 4th St. 2nd Fl., Cincinnati, OH, 45202; Phone: 513-345-6701; Fax: 513-345-6705; E-mail: info@cincinnatischolarshipfoundation.org.

3403 ■ Semple Foundation Scholarship (Undergraduate/Scholarship)

Purpose: To support students from Greater Cincinnati area to pursue a college education. **Focus:** General studies/Field of study not specified. **Qualif.:** Applicants must be high school graduates who reside in Greater Cincinnati and are beginning college in the fall of their graduation. **Criteria:** Awards are given based on need.

Funds Avail.: No specific amount. **Duration:** Annual. **To Apply:** Applicant must submit a completed scholarship application form through online; along with a transcript up to the first semester of the current academic year; resume; Student Aid Report (SAR) in its entirety; financial Aid Award

Awards are arranged alphabetically below their administering organizations

Notification from the college applicant plan to attend. **Deadline:** May 15. **Contact:** Cincinnati Scholarship Foundation, 324 E 4th St. 2nd Fl., Cincinnati, OH, 45202; Phone: 513-345-6701; Fax: 513-345-6705; E-mail: info@cincinnatischolarshipfoundation.org.

3404 ■ Thomas J. Emery Memorial Fund Scholarship (Undergraduate/Scholarship)

Purpose: To support students from Greater Cincinnati area to pursue a college education. **Focus:** General studies/Field of study not specified. **Qualif.:** Applicants must be high school graduates who reside in Greater Cincinnati and are beginning college in the fall of their graduation. **Criteria:** Awards are given based on need.

Funds Avail.: No specific amount. **Duration:** Annual. **To Apply:** Applicant must submit a completed scholarship application form through online; along with a transcript up to the first semester of the current academic year; resume; Student Aid Report (SAR) in its entirety; financial Aid Award Notification from the college applicant plan to attend. **Deadline:** May 15. **Contact:** Cincinnati Scholarship Foundation, 324 E 4th St. 2nd Fl., Cincinnati, OH, 45202; Phone: 513-345-6701; Fax: 513-345-6705; E-mail: info@cincinnatischolarshipfoundation.org.

3405 ■ T.L. Conlan Scholarship Fund (Undergraduate/Scholarship)

Purpose: To support students from Greater Cincinnati area to pursue a college education. **Focus:** General studies/Field of study not specified. **Qualif.:** Applicants must be high school graduates who reside in Greater Cincinnati and are beginning college in the fall of their graduation. **Criteria:** Awards are given based on need.

Funds Avail.: No specific amount. **Duration:** Annual. **To Apply:** Applicant must submit a completed scholarship application form through online; along with a transcript up to the first semester of the current academic year; resume; Student Aid Report (SAR) in its entirety; financial Aid Award Notification from the college applicant plan to attend. **Deadline:** May 15. **Contact:** Cincinnati Scholarship Foundation, 324 E 4th St. 2nd Fl., Cincinnati, OH, 45202; Phone: 513-345-6701; Fax: 513-345-6705; E-mail: info@cincinnatischolarshipfoundation.org.

3406 ■ US Bank NA Scholarship Fund (Undergraduate/Scholarship)

Purpose: To support students from Greater Cincinnati area to pursue a college education. **Focus:** General studies/Field of study not specified. **Qualif.:** Applicants must be high school graduates who reside in Greater Cincinnati and are beginning college in the fall of their graduation. **Criteria:** Awards are given based on need.

Funds Avail.: No specific amount. **Duration:** Annual. **To Apply:** Applicant must submit a completed scholarship application form through online; along with a transcript up to the first semester of the current academic year; resume; Student Aid Report (SAR) in its entirety; financial Aid Award Notification from the college applicant plan to attend. **Deadline:** May 15. **Contact:** Cincinnati Scholarship Foundation, 324 E 4th St. 2nd Fl., Cincinnati, OH, 45202; Phone: 513-345-6701; Fax: 513-345-6705; E-mail: info@cincinnatischolarshipfoundation.org.

3407 ■ Walter and Marilyn Bartlett Scholarship Fund (Undergraduate/Scholarship)

Purpose: To support students from Greater Cincinnati area to pursue a college education. **Focus:** General studies/

Field of study not specified. **Qualif.:** Applicants must be high school graduates who reside in Greater Cincinnati and are beginning college in the fall of their graduation. **Criteria:** Awards are given based on need.

Funds Avail.: No specific amount. **Duration:** Annual. **To Apply:** Applicant must submit a completed scholarship application form through online; along with a transcript up to the first semester of the current academic year; resume; Student Aid Report (SAR) in its entirety; financial Aid Award Notification from the college applicant plan to attend. **Deadline:** May 15. **Contact:** Cincinnati Scholarship Foundation, 324 E 4th St. 2nd Fl., Cincinnati, OH, 45202; Phone: 513-345-6701; Fax: 513-345-6705; E-mail: info@cincinnatischolarshipfoundation.org.

3408 ■ Western-Southern Foundation Scholarship (Undergraduate/Scholarship)

Purpose: To help students from Greater Cincinnati area to achieve the dream of a college education. **Focus:** General studies/Field of study not specified. **Qualif.:** Applicants must be high school graduates who reside in Greater Cincinnati and are beginning college in the fall of their graduation. **Criteria:** Awards are given based on need.

Funds Avail.: No specific amount. **Duration:** Annual. **To Apply:** Applicant must submit a completed scholarship application form through online; along with a transcript up to the first semester of the current academic year; resume; Student Aid Report (SAR) in its entirety; financial Aid Award Notification from the college applicant plan to attend. **Deadline:** May 15. **Contact:** Cincinnati Scholarship Foundation, 324 E 4th St. 2nd Fl., Cincinnati, OH, 45202; Phone: 513-345-6701; Fax: 513-345-6705; E-mail: info@cincinnatischolarshipfoundation.org.

3409 ■ William A. Friedlander Scholarship Fund (Undergraduate/Scholarship)

Purpose: To help students from Greater Cincinnati area to achieve the dream of a college education. **Focus:** General studies/Field of study not specified. **Qualif.:** Applicants must be high school graduates who reside in Greater Cincinnati and are beginning college in the fall of their graduation. **Criteria:** Selection are based on need.

Funds Avail.: No specific amount. **Duration:** Annual. **To Apply:** Applicant must submit a completed scholarship application form through online; along with a transcript up to the first semester of the current academic year; resume; Student Aid Report (SAR) in its entirety; financial Aid Award Notification from the college applicant plan to attend. **Deadline:** May 15. **Contact:** Cincinnati Scholarship Foundation, 324 E 4th St. 2nd Fl., Cincinnati, OH, 45202; Phone: 513-345-6701; Fax: 513-345-6705; E-mail: info@cincinnatischolarshipfoundation.org.

3410 ■ William J. Rielly/MCURC Scholarship Fund (Undergraduate/Scholarship)

Purpose: To help students from Greater Cincinnati area to achieve the dream of a college education. **Focus:** General studies/Field of study not specified. **Qualif.:** Applicants must be students residing in Madisonville and attending the college of their choice. **Criteria:** Selection are based on need.

Funds Avail.: No specific amount. **Duration:** Annual. **To Apply:** Applicant must submit a completed scholarship application form through online; along with a transcript up to the first semester of the current academic year; resume; Student Aid Report (SAR) in its entirety; financial Aid Award

Awards are arranged alphabetically below their administering organizations

Notification from the college applicant plan to attend. **Deadline:** May 15. **Contact:** Cincinnati Scholarship Foundation, 324 E 4th St. 2nd Fl., Cincinnati, OH, 45202; Phone: 513-345-6701; Fax: 513-345-6705; E-mail: info@cincinnatischolarshipfoundation.org.

3411 ■ Woodward Trustees Foundation Scholarship
(Undergraduate/Scholarship)

Purpose: To help students from Greater Cincinnati area to achieve the dream of a college education. **Focus:** General studies/Field of study not specified. **Qualif.:** Applicants must be graduates of Cincinnati Public Schools attending the University of Cincinnati. **Criteria:** Selection are based on need.

Funds Avail.: No specific amount. **Duration:** Annual. **To Apply:** Applicant must submit a completed scholarship application form along with a copy of recent transcript; expected Family Contribution (EFC) from Student Aid Report (SAR), which comes as a result of filing the FAFSA; copy of Financial Aid Award Letter from the chosen college to be attended and resume. **Deadline:** April 30. **Contact:** Phone: 513-345-6701; Fax: 513-345-6705; E-mail: info@cincinnatischolarshipfoundation.org.

3412 ■ Wynne Family Memorial Fund
(Undergraduate/Scholarship)

Purpose: To help students from Greater Cincinnati area to achieve the dream of a college education. **Focus:** General studies/Field of study not specified. **Qualif.:** Applicants must be students attending the University of Cincinnati majoring in liberal arts. **Criteria:** Selection are based on need.

Funds Avail.: No specific amount. **Duration:** Annual. **To Apply:** Applicant must submit a completed scholarship application form through online; along with a transcript up to the first semester of the current academic year; resume; Student Aid Report (SAR) in its entirety; financial Aid Award Notification from the college applicant plan to attend. **Deadline:** May 15. **Contact:** Cincinnati Scholarship Foundation, 324 E 4th St. 2nd Fl., Cincinnati, OH, 45202; Phone: 513-345-6701; Fax: 513-345-6705; E-mail: info@cincinnatischolarshipfoundation.org.

3413 ■ Cinestory Foundation
PO Box 661962
Los Angeles, CA 90066
E-mail: info@cinestory.org
URL: www.cinestory.org
Social Media: www.facebook.com/CineStoryorg
www.instagram.com/cinestoryfoundation
twitter.com/CineStory
www.youtube.com/channel/UCpn2PExhJgCkvxxtR-qx4zQ

3414 ■ CineStory Feature Fellowship *(Professional development/Fellowship)*

Purpose: To help the Fellow advance their craft and career. **Focus:** Screenwriting. **Criteria:** CineStory notifies winners only. Entrants are advised to check Cines Tory's website and e-newsletter for judging announcements; selection is based on the committee's criteria.

Funds Avail.: $20,000 in cash and prizes($10,000 cash award). **To Apply:** Applicants may check with the Cines Tory Foundation website for the application process and other details; there are submission fees for the deadlines. **Deadline:** Early Deadline – January 19; Regular Deadline

– February 9; Late Deadline – March 15; Extended Late Deadline – April 19.

3415 ■ Cintas Foundation
8724 Sunset Drive, PMB 528
Miami, FL 33173
E-mail: info@cintasfoundation.org
URL: www.cintasfoundation.org
Social Media: www.facebook.com/CintasFoundation
www.instagram.com/cintasfoundation
twitter.com/cintasfoundatio

3416 ■ Brandon Fradd Fellowship in Music Composition *(Professional development/Fellowship)*

Purpose: To encourage the development of artists in music composition. **Focus:** Music. **Qualif.:** Applicants must be creative artists of Cuban citizenship or direct lineage (having a Cuban parent or grandparent).

Funds Avail.: $20,000. **Duration:** Annual. **To Apply:** Applicants must submit an original application (completed either in English or Spanish); must submit two narrative statements, two letters of recommendation and work samples (three to five recordings); samples should be on DVDs or CDs in MP3 format. **Deadline:** June 1. **Contact:** Laurie Escobar, CINTAS Administrator, MDC Museum of Art + Design, Freedom Tower at Miami Dade College; 600 Biscayne Blvd., Miami, Florida, 33132; Phone: 305-237-7901, Email: info@cintasfoundation.org.

3417 ■ CINTAS Foundation Fellowship in Architecture & Design *(Professional development/ Fellowship)*

Purpose: To encourage the development of artists in architecture. **Focus:** Architecture. **Qualif.:** Applicants must be artists living outside of Cuba; must be Cuban citizens or with direct lineage (having a Cuban parent or grandparent); applicants engaged in research, students, or performing artists are not eligible. **Criteria:** Selection will be based on the committee's criteria.

Funds Avail.: $20,000. **Duration:** Annual. **To Apply:** Applicants must submit a completed, original application (completed either in English or Spanish); must prepare two narrative statements, two letters of recommendation and work samples; acceptable formats are DVDs and CDs accompanied by a corresponding image list; materials must be accompanied by the work sample form; limit submission to ten samples. **Deadline:** June 1. **Contact:** Laurie Escobar, CINTAS Administrator, MDC Museum of Art + Design, Freedom Tower at Miami Dade College; 600 Biscayne Blvd., Miami, Florida, 33132; Phone: 305-237-7901, Email: info@cintasfoundation.org.

3418 ■ CINTAS-Knight Fellowship intheVisual Arts
(Professional development/Fellowship)

Purpose: To encourage the development of artists in visual arts. **Focus:** Visual arts.

Funds Avail.: No specific amount. **Duration:** Annual. **To Apply:** Applicants must submit an original application (completed either in English or Spanish); must prepare two narrative statements, two letters of recommendation and work samples; Applicants may submit maximum of 10 digital images; acceptable formats are DVDs and CDs accompanied by a corresponding image list. **Deadline:** June 1.

Awards are arranged alphabetically below their administering organizations

3419 ■ Civic Music Association of Milwaukee
2625 S Greeley St., Ste. 3A
Milwaukee, WI 53207
Ph: (414)483-3223
E-mail: info@civicmusicmilwaukee.org
URL: www.civicmusicmilwaukee.org
Social Media: www.facebook.com/civicmusicmilwaukee
twitter.com/CivicMusicMke
www.youtube.com/channel/
  UCpm5fHDUCkjPOZQ3JDbgHXg

3420 ■ CMA Private Lesson Program: Instrumental Scholarships for Elementary and Middle School Students *(Undergraduate/Scholarship)*
Purpose: To encourage one or more students who have demonstrated exceptional musical potential but are not presently taking private lessons. **Focus:** Music. **Qualif.:** Applicants must be 4th to a 9th-grade band and orchestra students who have not yet had the opportunity for private study; must be a resident of Milwaukee, Waukesha, Washington, Ozaukee or Racine County. **Criteria:** Selection will be based on the committee's criteria.

Funds Avail.: No specific amount. **To Apply:** Applicants must undergo an audition and prepare an essay about their experiences in school music activities. **Deadline:** February 28.

3421 ■ Civil Air Patrol (CAP)
105 S Hansell St., Bldg. 714
Maxwell AFB, AL 36112-6332
Free: 877-227-9142
URL: www.gocivilairpatrol.com
Social Media: www.facebook.com/capnhq
www.instagram.com/civil__air__patrol
www.linkedin.com/company/civil-air-patrol
twitter.com/civilairpatrol
www.youtube.com/user/CAPMember

3422 ■ Col Mary Feik Cadet Flight Scholarship *(Undergraduate/Scholarship)*
Purpose: To provide academic and flight scholarships to deserving cadets and seniors. **Focus:** Aeronautics; Aviation.

Funds Avail.: No specific amount. **Duration:** Annual. **To Apply:** Applicants must submit a questionnaire (word doc), (pdf version) rather than a submitting a resume; letter of recommendation from a CAP senior member that has first-hand knowledge of your academic abilities, leadership and character; a statement describing how applicant will spend the scholarship, including flight training plan, place of fly, start and end of training period, place of fly, how often will be flying etc. **Deadline:** December 31. **Contact:** CAP National Headquarters, CadetInvest, 105 S Hansell St., Maxwell AFB, 36112; Email: CadetInvest@capnhq.gov.

3423 ■ Civitan International (CI)
PO Box 130744
Birmingham, AL 35213-0744
Ph: (205)591-8910
Free: 800-248-4826
E-mail: civitan@civitan.org
URL: civitan.org
Social Media: twitter.com/civitan

3424 ■ Civitan Shropshire Scholarship *(Undergraduate, Vocational/Occupational/Scholarship)*
Purpose: To provide financial assistance to students enrolled in undergraduate or graduate studies. **Focus:** General studies/Field of study not specified. **Criteria:** Recipients are selected based on academic record; professional objectives; civitan involvement; community-service activities; and financial need.

Funds Avail.: $1,000. **Duration:** Annual. **To Apply:** Applicants must submit all required application materials. must submit a letter of endorsement coming from an advisor or school principal. **Deadline:** January 31.

3425 ■ Clan Ross America
1015 Archer St.
San Diego, CA 92109
E-mail: info@clanross.org
URL: clanross.org

3426 ■ Clan Ross Foundation Scholarships *(Undergraduate/Scholarship)*
Purpose: To enhance the knowledge of the youth about Scottish culture. **Focus:** Scottish studies. **Qualif.:** Applicants must be current members of Clan Ross Association of the United States, Inc. for at least a year. Applicants who are also related with the current members of the Association are also welcome to apply. Families or members of the Clan Ross Scholarship Committee are disqualified for the scholarships. **Criteria:** Recipients will be selected based on their objectives, commitment, demonstrated proficiency, development and future goals.

Duration: One year. **To Apply:** Applicants must write or call the Clan Ross Association for complete information and application form. **Contact:** Virgil Bumann, 1867 Via Acorde, Camarillo, CA 93010.

3427 ■ Claremont McKenna College - Henry Kravis Leadership Institute
850 Columbia Ave.
Claremont McKenna College
Claremont, CA 91711-6420
Ph: (909)621-8743
Fax: (909)607-5252
E-mail: kli@cmc.edu
URL: kravisleadershipinstitute.org
Social Media: www.facebook.com/
  KravisLeadershipInstitute
twitter.com/kravisinstitute

3428 ■ CMC-KLI Leadership Research Fellowship *(Undergraduate/Fellowship)*
Purpose: To encourage and support students research on projects related to all areas of leadership. **Focus:** Leadership, Institutional and community. **Qualif.:** Applicants must be a Claremont McKenna College students and be in good standing with the college. Final research paper must be completed, approved by faculty sponsor. **Criteria:** Selections will be based on the following criteria: proposed research must be interesting and relevant to the study of leadership; significant learning will be as a result of the proposed research; proposed research are well-planned and can reasonably be completed in an academic year; methodology are appropriate and well considered.

Awards are arranged alphabetically below their administering organizations

Funds Avail.: $1,500 (up to $500 on travel stipend). **Duration:** Annual. **To Apply:** Applicants must submit the following requirements: online application form; resume; CMC transcript; research proposal; faculty sponsor confirmation. **Deadline:** October 2. **Contact:** Dr. Sherylle J. Tan, Director of Internships and KLI Research, Kravis Leadership Institute, Kravis Center 446, Phone: 909-607-8136; Email: Stan@cmc.edu.

3429 ■ CMC-KLI Leadership Thesis Fellowship
(Undergraduate/Fellowship)

Purpose: To encourage and support students research on projects related to social entrepreneurship and the social sector. **Focus:** Leadership, Institutional and community. **Qualif.:** Applicants must be a Claremont McKenna College students and be in good standing with the college. Final research paper must be completed, approved by faculty sponsor. **Criteria:** Selections will be based on the following criteria: proposed research must be interesting and relevant to the study of leadership; significant learning will be as a result of the proposed research; proposed research are well-planned and can reasonably be completed in an academic year; methodology are appropriate and well considered.

Funds Avail.: $1,500 (up to $500 on travel stipend). **Duration:** Annual. **To Apply:** Applicants must submit the following requirements: online application form; resume; CMC transcript; research proposal; faculty sponsor confirmation. **Deadline:** October 2. **Contact:** Dr. Sherylle J. Tan, Director of Internships and KLI Research, Kravis Leadership Institute, Kravis Center 446, Phone: 909-607-8136; Email: Stan@cmc.edu.

3430 ■ CMC-KLI Social Sector Internship Program
(Undergraduate/Internship)

Purpose: To allow student involvement in the management of the organization. **Focus:** Leadership, Institutional and community. **Qualif.:** Applicants must be Claremont McKenna College students and be in good standing with the college. **Criteria:** Selection will be based on the committee's criteria.

Duration: Annual. **To Apply:** Applicants may contact the CMC Career Services Center for the application process and other information.

3431 ■ Willis W. and Ethel M. Clark Foundation
PO Box 89
Pebble Beach, CA 93953-0089
Ph: (831)625-1175
Fax: (831)625-1175
E-mail: clarkfoundation@redshift.com
URL: www.theclarkfoundation.org

3432 ■ Willis W. and Ethel M. Clark Foundation Investment in Community Fellowship *(Graduate/Fellowship)*

Purpose: To provide financial assistance to deserving students who are attending graduate school or who have been accepted to a graduate school. **Focus:** Public service. **Qualif.:** Applicants must have been born, raised and/or have lived in one of the coastal communities of the Monterey Peninsula; must be enrolled in an advanced program of study in a field of significant public interest and benefit; must have above average academic achievement; have potential to make a significant contribution to society

in general and, in particular, the coastal communities of the Monterey Peninsula; must have proven commitment to volunteerism and public service; must have demonstrated passion for community betterment and must be able to document a continuing philosophy toward community service for the area; and have responsible career goals for advancement in the chosen field. **Criteria:** Selection will be based on above average academic achievement; potential to make a significant contribution to society in general and, in particular, the coastal communities of the Monterey Peninsula; proven commitment to volunteerism and public service; demonstrated passion for community betterment and able to document a continuing philosophy toward community service for the area; responsible career goals.

Funds Avail.: Up to $10,000. **Duration:** Annual; one academic year. **To Apply:** Applicants must submit a completed, typed original plus one copy of the application form together with a resume/curriculum vitae (original plus one copy); a narrative autobiography (original plus one copy, maximum of two pages, double-spaced); statement of community service (original plus one copy, maximum of two pages, double-spaced); career goals (original plus one copy, maximum of one page, double-spaced); official transcripts (original plus one copy); proof of enrollment; and two letters of recommendation. **Deadline:** January 31. **Remarks:** Established in 2002.

3433 ■ Cleveland Leadership Center (CLC)
1 Cleveland Ctr., 1375 E 9th St., Ste.1100
Cleveland, OH 44114
Ph: (216)592-2400
Fax: (216)621-7733
E-mail: info@cleveleads.org
URL: www.cleveleads.org
Social Media: www.facebook.com/cleveleads
www.linkedin.com/company/cleveland-leadership-center
twitter.com/cleveleads

3434 ■ Cleveland Executive Fellowships (CEF)
(Other/Fellowship)

Purpose: To accelerate the professional development of civic leaders for Greater Cleveland. **Focus:** Public affairs. **Qualif.:** Applicants must have significant professional achievements and substantial organizational responsibilities; must have an average of 5-10 years of experience; have a minimum of five years of experience and/or a master's degree. **Criteria:** Selection is based on submitted applications.

Funds Avail.: $40,000. **Duration:** Annual. **Number Awarded:** Varies. **To Apply:** Applicantss must submit a completed application electronically; application requires: two copies of completed application form, including written essays; two copies of a professional-quality resume (maximum of 2 pages); three letters of recommendation; and official academic transcripts for all higher education institutions attended. **Contact:** hbelsito@cleveleads.org.

3435 ■ Clinic for the Rehabilitation of Wildlife (CROW)
3883 Sanibel Captiva Rd.
Sanibel, FL 33957
Ph: (239)472-3644
E-mail: info@crowclinic.org
URL: crowclinic.org

Awards are arranged alphabetically below their administering organizations

Social Media: www.facebook.com/CROWClinic
www.pinterest.com/crowclinic
twitter.com/crowclinic

3436 ■ Wildlife and Conservation Medicine Internship *(All/Fellowship)*

Purpose: To provide individuals with a thorough understanding of the rehabilitation process for injured and orphaned wildlife on the Gulf Coast of Southwest Florida. **Focus:** Wildlife conservation, management, and science. **Qualif.:** Applicants must be over 18 years of age; must agree to and sign rules and regulations in regard to commitment, housing, dress code, code of conduct, photo policies. **Criteria:** Selection will be based on the committee's criteria.

Funds Avail.: $150 bi-monthly. **Duration:** Semiannual. **To Apply:** Applicants must provide proof of current tetanus immunizations and proof of pre-exposure rabies series. **Contact:** PO Box 150, Sanibel, FL, 33957; Phone: 239-472-3644, ext. 231; Email: students@crowclinic.org.

3437 ■ Clinical Nurse Specialist Foundation
801 E Park Dr., Ste. 100
Harrisburg, PA 17111
Ph: (717)703-0033
Fax: (717)234-6798
URL: www.cns-foundation.org

3438 ■ Jan Bingle Scholarships *(Master's, Doctorate/Scholarship)*

Purpose: To increase the number of CNSs who are educated and prepared and thus, address the shortage of CNSs in the United States. **Focus:** Nursing. **Qualif.:** Applicants must be students who are pursuing a master's degree in an accredited CNS program or Clinical Nurse Specialists pursuing a research or practice doctorate. **Criteria:** Scholarship is competitive and is based on academic performance, clinical excellence, and demonstrated leadership.

Funds Avail.: $1,000. **To Apply:** Applicants must complete and submit their application and must attach the following documents: documentation of admission as a student in a CNS master's or DNP program, or a CNS DNP or PhD program; documentation of current active student status by registrar, faculty member or dean; a current official transcript provided by a Registrar or by an academic advisor that confirms their current minimum cumulative GPA of 3.0 or higher; evidence of outstanding achievement in CNS course work in their specialty by recommendation of two program faculty; evidence of past or present (five years preceding entry into the academic program) leadership activity related to nursing; evidence of experiences resulting in improvement or positive change with other cultures, minority groups and/or vulnerable populations; evidence of professional citizenship as exemplified in local, state, national initiative to improve nursing or health care.

3439 ■ Christine Filipovich Scholarships *(Master's, Doctorate/Scholarship)*

Purpose: To increase the number of CNSs who are educated and prepared and thus, address the shortage of CNSs in the United States. **Focus:** Nursing. **Qualif.:** Applicants must be students who are pursuing a master's degree in an accredited CNS program or Clinical Nurse Specialists pursuing a research or practice doctorate. **Crite-**

ria: Scholarship is competitive and is based on academic performance, clinical excellence, and demonstrated leadership.

Funds Avail.: $500 each. **Number Awarded:** 2. **To Apply:** Applicants must complete and submit their application and must attach the following documents: documentation of admission as a student in a CNS master's or DNP program, or a CNS DNP or PhD program; documentation of current active student status by registrar, faculty member or dean; a current official transcript provided by a Registrar or by an academic advisor that confirms their current minimum cumulative GPA of 3.0 or higher; current curriculum vitae and description of their background/expertise related to the project; letter from the current employer. Applicants applying for funds to support research related to CNS outcomes must attach the following: overview of the project, abstract and timeline; letters of support; proposed budget; plans for dissemination of findings; IRB review documentation or anticipated date of IRB review. Applicants applying to support health policy activities must attach a description of intended use of funds and a description of expected outcome or how they will use the project.

3440 ■ Lippincott Williams and Wilkins Scholarships (LWW Scholarship) *(Master's, Doctorate/Scholarship)*

Purpose: To increase the number of CNSs who are educated and prepared and thus, address the shortage of CNSs in the United States. **Focus:** Nursing. **Qualif.:** Applicants must be students who are pursuing a master's degree in an accredited CNS program or Clinical Nurse Specialists pursuing a research or practice doctorate. **Criteria:** Scholarship is competitive and is based on academic performance, clinical excellence, and demonstrated leadership.

To Apply: Applicants must complete and submit their application and must attach the following documents: documentation of admission as a student in a CNS master's or DNP program, or a CNS DNP or PhD program; documentation of current active student status by registrar, faculty member or dean; a current official transcript provided by a Registrar or by an academic advisor that confirms their current minimum cumulative GPA of 3.0 or higher; evidence of outstanding achievement in CNS course work in their specialty by recommendation of two program faculty; evidence of past or present (five years preceding entry into the academic program) leadership activity related to nursing; evidence of experiences resulting in improvement or positive change with other cultures, minority groups and/or vulnerable populations; evidence of professional citizenship as exemplified in local, state, national initiative to improve nursing or health care.

3441 ■ Club Managers Association of America (CMAA)
1733 King St.
Alexandria, VA 22314
Ph: (703)739-9500
Fax: (703)739-0124
E-mail: crc@cmaa.org
URL: www.cmaa.org
Social Media: www.facebook.com/MyCMAA
www.linkedin.com/company/club-managers-assn-of
 -america-cmaa
twitter.com/CMAA
www.youtube.com/user/MyCMAA

Awards are arranged alphabetically below their administering organizations

Sponsors and Their Scholarships

3442 ■ CMAA Student Conference Travel Grants
(Undergraduate/Grant, Award)

Purpose: To help student chapters offset the costs associated with attending the CMAA World Conference on Club Management. **Focus:** Management. **Qualif.:** Applicants must be student chapters of CMAA.

Funds Avail.: No specific amount. **Duration:** Annual. **Deadline:** May 1. **Remarks:** Established in 1988. **Contact:** The Club Foundation, Attn: Carrie Wosicki, 1733 King St., Alexandria, VA, 22314-2720; Phone: 703- 739-9500; Fax: 703-739-0124.

3443 ■ Joe Perdue Scholarship *(Undergraduate/ Scholarship, Award)*

Purpose: To support and enhance the life cycle of club managers professional development, beginning at the university level and building throughout their career. **Focus:** Management. **Qualif.:** Candidates must be pursuing managerial careers in the private club industry; must have completed their freshman year of college and be enrolled for the full academic year in an accredited four-year institution and must have achieved and maintained a grade point average of at least 2.5 on a 4.0 scale, or 4.5 on a 6.0 scale. **Criteria:** Applicants who are CMAA student chapter members are given additional points.

Funds Avail.: No specific amount. **Duration:** Annual. **Number Awarded:** Varies. **To Apply:** Applicants must submit the online application form along with contact information; CMAA member ID# (if applicable); education information: current University/College name and address; major and minor (if applicable); cumulative GPA; any other colleges/ universities and/or vocational/technical schools attended; kits of Extra-curricular activities; employment information; list of all positions held in the hospitality industry to date (to be filled in the online application); essay(500-1,000 words); electronic copy of college transcript; 2 recommendations; current resume. **Deadline:** July 1.

3444 ■ Willmoore H. Kendall Scholarships *(Professional development/Scholarship)*

Purpose: To provide tuition support to assist club managers interested in pursuing the Certified Club Manager (CCM) designation. **Focus:** Management. **Qualif.:** Applicants must be member of CMAA; must be an assistant manager; must committed to a career in the club industry; must actively pursuing the CCM designation; have at least one BMI course remaining to complete; nominated for the scholarship by their CMAA chapter.**Criteria:** Recipients are selected based on management experience; CMAA Chapter and community activities; quality of essay; General Manager letter of recommendation; overall quality.

Funds Avail.: No specific amount. **Duration:** Annual. **Number Awarded:** Varies. **To Apply:** Applicants must submit online application form along with letter of support must be provided by chapter; letter of recommendation from the general manager; letter of recommendation from a club member; current resume; CMAA credit history; essay (between 500-1000 words). **Deadline:** October 1;November 1. **Remarks:** The Award is given in Honor of Willmoore H. Kendall. **Contact:** Carrie Wosicki; Email: carrie.wosicki@ cmaa.org; Phone: 703-299-4283.

3445 ■ Clubs of America
484 Wegner Rd.
Lakemoor, IL 60051

Ph: (815)363-4000
Fax: (815)363-4677
E-mail: Info@GreatClubs.com
URL: www.greatclubs.com
Social Media: www.facebook.com/ClubsOfAmerica
www.instagram.com/clubsofamerica/
pinterest.com/clubsofamerica/
twitter.com/clubsofamerica

3446 ■ Clubs of America Scholarship Program
(Undergraduate/Scholarship)

Purpose: To help students pursue career dreams and aspirations. **Focus:** General studies/Field of study not specified. **Qualif.:** Applicants must be current college students enrolled in any accredited U.S. college or university with a cumulative GPA of at least 3.0.

Funds Avail.: $1,000. **Duration:** Annual. **Number Awarded:** 1. **To Apply:** Applicants must submit an essay of no fewer than 600 words about their career aspirations and how their current studies will help them achieve success in their careers; where do the applicants see themselves 10 years from now?; essay must be submitted as a doc or pdf attachment via email; YouTube submissions are optional, video should be no longer than 5 minutes. **Deadline:** August 31. **Contact:** Email:scholarship@ greatclubs.com; URL: www.greatclubs.com/scholarship/.

3447 ■ Coaching Association of Canada (CAC)
1155 Lola St., Ste. 201
Ottawa, ON, Canada K1K 4C1
Ph: (613)235-5000
Fax: (613)235-9500
E-mail: coach@coach.ca
URL: www.coach.ca
Social Media: www.facebook.com/coach.ca
twitter.com/CAC_ACE

3448 ■ Women in Coaching National Coaching Institute Scholarships *(Undergraduate/Scholarship)*

Purpose: To financially assist women attending one of the seven National Coaching Institutes in Canada. **Focus:** General studies/Field of study not specified. **Qualif.:** Applicants must be Canadian citizens or landed immigrants currently coaching Canadian athletes; must be certified NCCP level 3; and must be on the program at one of the seven National Coaching Institutes across Canada. **Criteria:** Recipients will be selected based on submitted application form and supporting documents.

Funds Avail.: Amount varies. **Duration:** Annual. **To Apply:** Applicants must contact Ms. Sheilagh Croxon for application form and needed materials.

3449 ■ Coalition of Higher Education Assistance Organizations (COHEAO)
777 6th St. NW, Ste. 510
Washington, DC 20001
Ph: (202)349-2303
E-mail: hwadsworth@bosepublicaffairs.com
URL: www.coheao.com
Social Media: twitter.com/COHEAO

3450 ■ COHEAO Scholarship *(Undergraduate/ Scholarship)*

Purpose: To provide financial assistance to those students who are in need. **Focus:** General studies/Field of study not

Awards are arranged alphabetically below their administering organizations

specified. **Qualif.:** Applicants must be U.S citizens; must attend a COHEAO member school; only undergraduate students who are entering their sophomore, junior or senior year are eligible to apply; freshmen and graduate students are not eligible. **Criteria:** Preference will be given to those students who meet the criteria.

Funds Avail.: $1,000. **Duration:** Annual. **Number Awarded:** 4. **To Apply:** Applicants must submit the following completed application form; essay/testimonial response(s); academic recommendation letter; sealed official copy of transcript. **Deadline:** April 12. **Contact:** COHEAO, C/O Bose Washington Partners, 777 6th St., NW, Ste., 510, Washington, DC, 2000; Email: gmarak@ bosewashingtonpartners.com.

3451 ■ Coalition for Networked Information (CNI)

21 Dupont Cir., Ste. 800
Washington, DC 20036
Ph: (202)296-5098
Fax: (202)872-0884
URL: www.cni.org
Social Media: www.facebook.com/cni.org
twitter.com/cni_org
www.youtube.com/user/cnivideo

3452 ■ Paul Evan Peters Fellowship *(Master's, Doctorate, Graduate/Fellowship)*

Purpose: To support and assist students pursuing graduate studies in the information sciences, librarianship, or closely related field, that advance the frontiers of digital information and technology. **Focus:** Information science and technology; Library and archival sciences. **Criteria:** Selection will be judged on how well they meet the academic and personal standards for the award, not on financial need.

Funds Avail.: $5,000 for doctoral; $2,500 for master's. **Duration:** Biennial. **Number Awarded:** 2. **To Apply:** Applications process will be posted to the CNI-ANNOUNCE Lister and CNI News feed; must complete applications include the following; a completed form, which includes space for a 300-500-word essay explaining the qualification, intellectual interests, and academic and career objectives; essay include a discussion of how will advance scholarship in digital information and technology and apply their knowledge to problems of scholarship, intellectual productivity, or public life; a curriculum vitae or resume that includes the complete contact information (address, phone number and email); two letters of recommendation from faculty members, work supervisors or others who can comment on the academic and personal qualifications for the fellowship; these letters must be sent by email directly from the recommenders' email accounts; a copy of student's letter of acceptance into a university graduate program in information science or librarianship, or closely related field; proof of US citizenship or permanent residency; official transcript may also be requested, if have already completed courses toward the graduate degree.

3453 ■ Coast Guard Foundation (CGF)

394 Taugwonk Road
Stonington, CT 06378
Ph: (860)535-0786
Fax: (860)535-0944
E-mail: info@cgfdn.org
URL: www.coastguardfoundation.org

Social Media: www.facebook.com/coastguardfoundation
www.instagram.com/coastguardfoundation
twitter.com/CoastGuardFound
www.youtube.com/user/CoastGuardFoundation

3454 ■ Commander Ronald J. Cantin Scholarships *(Undergraduate/Scholarship)*

Purpose: To support Coast Guard enlisted personnel and their dependents. **Focus:** General studies/Field of study not specified. **Criteria:** Selection will be based on scholastic promise, motivation, moral character, leadership qualities and good citizenship.

Funds Avail.: $2,500. **Duration:** Annual. **Remarks:** The Scholarship honors the career of CDR Ronald J. Cantin. **Contact:** Family Resource Specialist (FRS) at Health, Safety and Work-Life (HSWL) Regional Practice (RP); Phone: 800-872-4957 or 252-335-6214.

3455 ■ Commander Daniel J. Christovich Scholarship *(Undergraduate/Scholarship)*

Purpose: To provide support to Coast Guard personnel and to their family in aiming higher education. **Focus:** General studies/Field of study not specified. **Criteria:** Selection will be based on scholastic promise, motivation, moral character, leadership qualities and good citizenship.

Funds Avail.: $2,500. **Duration:** Annual. **Remarks:** The Scholarship honors the career of CDR Daniel J. Christovich.

3456 ■ Clay Maitland CGF Scholarship *(Undergraduate/Scholarship)*

Purpose: To provide support to Coast Guard personnel and to their family in aiming higher education. **Focus:** General studies/Field of study not specified. **Qualif.:** Applicants must be dependent children of enlisted men and women of the US Coast Guard on active duty, retired or deceased and dependent children of enlisted personnel in the Coast Guard Reserve currently on extended active duty 180 days or more. **Criteria:** Selection will be based on scholastic promise, motivation, moral character, leadership qualities and good citizenship.

Funds Avail.: $5,000. **Duration:** Annual; renewable for up to four consecutive years. **To Apply:** Applicants must submit an application package which includes: completed foundation scholarship application form; student's college entrance scores; letter of recommendation from a school official where the student is currently attending high school, or college transcript signed by school official; letter to the president of the selection committee; letter of acceptance from the college or vocational school the student plans to attend; and completed Foundation financial statement. Application packages should include originals plus five copies of all original materials, with the exception of official transcripts which are to remain sealed. **Contact:** Commandant (G-1112), 2100 2nd St., SW, STOP 7902 Washington, DC 20593-7902.

3457 ■ Coast Guard Foundation Enlisted Education Scholarship *(Advanced Professional/Scholarship)*

Purpose: To support for education is a cornerstone of our commitment to the men and women of the U.S. Coast guard and their families. **Focus:** General studies/Field of study not specified. **Qualif.:** Applicants must be Unmarried dependent children of enlisted men and women of the U.S. Coast Guard that are: active duty, retired, or deceased; coast Guard Reserve currently on extended active duty 180 days or more; must be a college bound high school

Awards are arranged alphabetically below their administering organizations

senior entering an accredited college or technical school for the fall semester of this year or a full-time undergraduate student already enrolled in an accredited four-year undergraduate program or technical school for the fall semester of this year. **Criteria:** Selection will be based on scholastic promise, motivation, moral character, leadership qualities and good citizenship.

Funds Avail.: $1,000 to $5,000. **Duration:** Annual. **Deadline:** March 29. **Contact:** Sage Williams; Email: swilliams@cgfdn.org.

3458 ■ The Fallen Heroes Scholarship
(Undergraduate/Scholarship)

Purpose: To provide support to Coast Guard personnel and to their family in aiming higher education. **Focus:** General studies/Field of study not specified. **Criteria:** Selection will be based on scholastic promise, motivation, moral character, leadership qualities and good citizenship.

Funds Avail.: No specific amount. **Duration:** Annual. **Remarks:** The Scholarship was established by John and Delinda Statts in memory of Mr. Statts' parents, Captain Frederick Statts and his wife Sara. **Contact:** Email Sage Williams at swilliams@cgfdn.org.

3459 ■ Captain Ernest W. Fox Perpetual Scholarship *(Advanced Professional/Scholarship)*

Purpose: To provide support to Coast Guard personnel and to their family in aiming higher education. **Focus:** General studies/Field of study not specified. **Qualif.:** Applicants must be qualified active duty Coast Guard, civil service employee personnel or their dependents at the Coast Guard Aviation Logistic Center. **Criteria:** Selection will be based on scholastic promise, motivation, moral character, leadership qualities and good citizenship.

Duration: Annual. **Deadline:** March 15. **Remarks:** The Scholarship was established to honor the memory of late son/brother Captain Ernest W. Fox. **Contact:** Email Sage Williams at swilliams@cgfdn.org.

3460 ■ Roy Vander Putten *(Advanced Professional/Scholarship)*

Purpose: To assist active duty and reserve Coast Guard personnel with their educational expenses. **Focus:** General studies/Field of study not specified. **Qualif.:** Applicants must be active enlisted personnel in pay grades E-3 to E-9 with two or more years of Coast Guard service. **Criteria:** Selection will be based on scholastic promise, motivation, moral character, leadership qualities and good citizenship.

Funds Avail.: Up to $500. **To Apply:** Applicants should complete the application form 1560/10a, available through the Coast Guard Institute.

3461 ■ Coastal Bend Community Foundation (CBCF)
555 N Carancahua St., Ste. 900
Corpus Christi, TX 78401
Ph: (361)882-9745
Fax: (361)882-2865
URL: www.cbcfoundation.org
Social Media: www.facebook.com/
CoastalBendCommunityFoundation

3462 ■ Alejandro "Alex" Abecia Reaching High Scholarships *(Undergraduate/Scholarship)*

Purpose: To provide resources for educational opportunities including vocational schools, two and four-year universities. **Focus:** General studies/Field of study not specified. **Qualif.:** Applicants must be a graduating senior from Mary Carroll High School; must be an active member of the Mary Carroll High School Band or a member of the Mary Carroll Varsity Soccer Team; must currently be on the A or the A/B Honor Roll; must be enrolled in honors classes in high school; must have the respect of peers, coaches and band leaders for showing dedication and commitment; must enroll as a full time college student the fall following high school graduation at an accredited college or university (at least 12 semester credits).**Criteria:** Applicants may focus on achievement, community service or financial need.

Funds Avail.: Varies. **Duration:** Annual. **Number Awarded:** 4. **To Apply:** Applicant must submit current official transcript; ACT/SAT Score reports; FAFSA Student Aid Report(all pages); one letter of recommendation; two essays. **Deadline:** March 1. **Remarks:** Established in memory of Alejandro (Alex), who died in a tragic automobile accident on July 29, 2003. **Contact:** Nicole Ross, Program Director; Phone: 361-882-9745; Email: nross@cbcfoundation.org.

3463 ■ Barriger - Zachary Barriger Memorial Scholarship Fund *(Undergraduate/Scholarship)*

Purpose: To provide financial assistance to high school seniors who are planning to pursue a career in computer or electrical engineering. **Focus:** Engineering, Computer; Engineering, Electrical. **Qualif.:** Applicants must be a graduating senior at Tuloso-Midway high school planning to pursue a degree in the fields of engineering or medicine; must be enrolled full time at a publicly supported two or four-year accredited college or university in Texas; must maintain a GPA of 2.75 on a 4.0 scale.**Criteria:** Applicants are evaluated based on merit. Preference will be given to jazz musicians.

Funds Avail.: Varies. **Duration:** Annual. **To Apply:** Applicant must submit current official transcript; ACT/SAT Score reports; FAFSA Student Aid Report(all pages); one letter of recommendation; two essays (essay titled "Keeping These United States Free & at Peace with the World"). **Deadline:** March 1. **Remarks:** The scholarship was established in memory of Zachary Barriger who was a senior at Tuloso-Midway High School. **Contact:** Nicole Ross, Program Director; Phone: 361-882-9745; Email: nross@cbcfoundation.org.

3464 ■ Beck – O.J. Beck, Jr. Memorial Scholarship *(Undergraduate/Scholarship)*

Purpose: To provide educational assistance to students who are seeking a bachelor's degree in building construction. **Focus:** Construction. **Qualif.:** Applicants must be a graduating high school senior or current college student planning to or currently pursuing a bachelor of science degree in building construction; must have permanent residence in the area served by the South Texas Chapter of Associated General Contractors (22 counties); must attend any accredited four year college or university.**Criteria:** Recipients will be selected based on financial need.

Funds Avail.: Varies. **Duration:** Annual. **To Apply:** Applicant must submit current official transcript; ACT/SAT Score reports; FAFSA Student Aid Report(all pages); one letter of recommendation; two essays (essay titled "Keeping These United States Free & at Peace with the World"). **Deadline:** March 1. **Remarks:** The scholarship was established in memory of O.J. (Junior) Beck, Jr., a respected general contractor and builder in the Coastal Bend with a reputation for attention to his projects and

Awards are arranged alphabetically below their administering organizations

friendly relations with owners. **Contact:** South Texas Associated General Contractors; Phone: 361-289-0996.

3465 ■ Bennett – Reverend E.F. Bennett Scholarship *(Undergraduate/Scholarship)*

Purpose: To provide financial support to graduating seniors from a Coastal Bend high school. **Focus:** General studies/Field of study not specified. **Qualif.:** Applicants must be a graduating senior from high schools in CBCF seven-county area; must be in top 10% of graduating class; must enroll full-time at Del Mar College, TAMUCC or TAMUK; must establish financial need based on the Median Family Income of their county.**Criteria:** Applicants will be evaluated based on financial need.

Funds Avail.: Varies. **Duration:** Annual. **To Apply:** Applicant must submit current official transcript; ACT/SAT Score reports; FAFSA Student Aid Report(all pages); one letter of recommendation; two essays (essay titled "Keeping These United States Free & at Peace with the World"). **Deadline:** March 1. **Remarks:** The scholarship was established by a group of business leaders in Corpus Christi, Texas to honor Reverend Bennett's outstanding record of community service. **Contact:** Nicole Ross, Program Director; Phone: 361-882-9745; Email: nross@cbcfoundation.org.

3466 ■ Brem - Marion Luna Brem/Pat McNeil Health and Education Endowment *(Undergraduate/Scholarship)*

Purpose: To provide financial assistance to teenage parents in Coastal Bend to pursue a college education while raising and supporting their children. **Focus:** General studies/Field of study not specified. **Qualif.:** Applicants must have attended (GED recipient) or be a graduated from a high school in CBCF seven-county area; graduate with a GPA of 2.5 on a 4.0 scale; must attend Coastal Bend College, Del Mar College, TAMUCC or TAMUK (Kingsville campus only); must maintain a GPA of 2.0 on a 4.0 scale; must complete at least 9.0 credit hours each semester.**Criteria:** Applicants are evaluated based on academic achievement and financial need.

Funds Avail.: Varies. **Duration:** Annual. **To Apply:** Applicant must submit current official transcript; ACT/SAT Score reports; FAFSA Student Aid Report(all pages); one letter of recommendation; two essays (essay titled "Keeping These United States Free & at Peace with the World"). **Deadline:** March 1. **Contact:** Nicole Ross, Program Director; Phone: 361-882-9745; Email: nross@cbcfoundation.org.

3467 ■ D.C. and Virginia Brown Scholarship *(Undergraduate/Scholarship)*

Purpose: To provide financial assistance to students in need. **Focus:** General studies/Field of study not specified. **Qualif.:** Applicants must be graduates of Mathis High School or Mathis High School students who have earned their GED certificate and who have good potential and character; must maintain a course-load of 12 semester hours; must maintain a 2.5 GPA on a 4.0 scale. **Criteria:** Applicants will be evaluated based on academic merit and personal attributes.

Funds Avail.: $4,000 for four-year college student; $2,200 for two-year and trade school student; $1,000 for handicapped student. **Duration:** Annual. **Number Awarded:** 4. **To Apply:** Applicant must submit current official transcript; ACT/SAT Score reports; FAFSA Student Aid Report(all pages); one letter of recommendation; two essays (essay

titled "Keeping These United States Free & at Peace with the World"). **Deadline:** March 1. **Contact:** Nicole Ross, Program Director; Phone: 361-882-9745; Email: nross@cbcfoundation.org.

3468 ■ Burney – Cecil E. Burney Scholarship *(Undergraduate/Scholarship)*

Purpose: To provide financial assistance to high school seniors or graduates of a Coastal Bend high school in furthering their college education. **Focus:** Education; History; Liberal arts; Music; Political science. **Qualif.:** Applicants must be a graduating senior or current college student who graduated from a high school in the CBCF seven-county area; must maintain a GPA of 3.0 on a 4.0 scale; must attend an accredited college or university in the United States of America and be enrolled full-time.**Criteria:** Applicants are evaluated based on academic performance.

Funds Avail.: Varies. **Duration:** Annual. **To Apply:** Applicant must submit current official transcript; ACT/SAT Score reports; FAFSA Student Aid Report(all pages); one letter of recommendation; two essays (essay titled "Keeping These United States Free & at Peace with the World"). **Deadline:** March 1. **Remarks:** The scholarship was established in memory of Cecil E. Burney, founder and president of the Coastal Bend Community Foundation from 1981 to 1989. He was a prominent attorney, banker, community leader and historian. **Contact:** Nicole Ross, Program Director; Phone: 361-882-9745; Email: nross@cbcfoundation.org.

3469 ■ C.C.H.R.M.A. Scholarships *(Undergraduate/Scholarship)*

Purpose: To assist students majoring in business with an interest in human resources. **Focus:** Business; Personnel administration/human resources. **Qualif.:** Applicants must be residents and college students enrolled full-time in the Coastal Bend seven-county service area universities, including University of the Incarnate Word online courses; must maintain a 3.0 GPA on a 4.0 scale. **Criteria:** Applicants will be evaluated based on academic achievement and financial need.

Funds Avail.: $700. **To Apply:** Applicants must submit a complete application form, including a one page essay on "Why I am interested in Human Management?" and college transcript.

3470 ■ Justin Forrest Cox "Beat the Odds" Memorial Scholarships *(Undergraduate/Scholarship)*

Purpose: To provide educational support to students who are in need. **Focus:** General studies/Field of study not specified. **Qualif.:** Applicants must be graduate from a Victoria ISD high school; must have a "C" average or better; must be studying for a four-year baccalaureate degree; must complete at least 12 credit hours per semester; must overcome a significant difficulty in graduating from high school; must maintain a 2.5 GPA to receive carried-over funds.**Criteria:** Applicants will be evaluated based on academic achievement and financial need.

Funds Avail.: Varies. **Duration:** Annual. **To Apply:** Applicant must submit current official transcript; ACT/SAT Score reports; FAFSA Student Aid Report(all pages); one letter of recommendation; two essays (essay titled "Keeping These United States Free & at Peace with the World"). **Deadline:** April 1. **Contact:** Nicole Ross, Program Director; Phone: 361-882-9745; Email: nross@cbcfoundation.org.

Awards are arranged alphabetically below their administering organizations

3471 ■ Dean – Derek Lee Dean Soccer Scholarships
(Undergraduate/Scholarship)

Purpose: To assist outstanding high school students of W.B. Ray High School who have a passion for soccer. **Focus:** General studies/Field of study not specified. **Qualif.:** Applicants must be a graduating senior at W. B. Ray High School; must be in the top 25% of the class; must be a member of the soccer team who exhibits a love of soccer, teamwork and sportsmanship. **Criteria:** Applicants are evaluated based on academic achievement and personal involvement in the sport.

Funds Avail.: Varies. **Duration:** Annual. **To Apply:** Applicant must submit current official transcript; ACT/SAT Score reports; FAFSA Student Aid Report(all pages); one letter of recommendation; two essays (essay titled "Keeping These United States Free & at Peace with the World"). **Deadline:** March 1. **Remarks:** The scholarship was established in honor of Derek Lee Dean, who was killed in a tragic accident in 1998. **Contact:** NIcole Ross, Program Director; Phone: 361-882-9745; Email: nross@cbcfoundation.org.

3472 ■ Doraine "Pursuit of Educational Excellence" Scholarship *(Undergraduate/Scholarship)*

Purpose: To promote educational excellence in Coastal Bend. **Focus:** General studies/Field of study not specified. **Qualif.:** Applicants must be graduating senior from any high school in the CBCF seven-county area; must be ranked in top ten percent (10%) of their graduating class; must enrolled full time at any accredited college or university and maintain a GPA of 3.0 on a 4.0 scale. **Criteria:** Applicants are evaluated based on academic performance and merit.

Funds Avail.: Varies. **Duration:** Annual. **To Apply:** Applicant must submit current official transcript; ACT/SAT Score reports; FAFSA Student Aid Report(all pages); one letter of recommendation; two essays (essay titled "Keeping These United States Free & at Peace with the World"). **Deadline:** March 1. **Contact:** NIcole Ross, Program Director; Phone: 361-882-9745; Email: nross@cbcfoundation.org.

3473 ■ Downes - Jay and Rheba Downes Memorial Scholarship *(Undergraduate/Scholarship)*

Purpose: To provide financial assistance to students who are pursuing college. **Focus:** General studies/Field of study not specified. **Qualif.:** Applicants must be a graduating Alice High School senior; must letter in the UIL-sanctioned sport of golf at least two years; must have an overall high school GPA of "B" or better; must have participated in extracurricular activities other than athletics; must exemplify the high ideals and spirit of good conduct and sportsmanship benefiting a "Fighting Alice Coyote;" must attend a four-year college or university; must register for at least 12 hours of classes; must maintain a minimum college GPA of 2.5 on a 4.0 scale. **Criteria:** A scholarship committee will select the recipients.

Funds Avail.: Varies. **Duration:** Annual. **To Apply:** Applicant must submit current official transcript; ACT/SAT Score reports; FAFSA Student Aid Report(all pages); one letter of recommendation; two essays (essay titled "Keeping These United States Free & at Peace with the World"). **Deadline:** March 1. **Remarks:** The scholarship was established in memory of James Ed (Jay) Downes, an Alice businessman and civic leader, and his wife, Rheba. Mr. Downes founded and served as chief executive of Energy Dynamics, an oilfield equipment and service provider in the domestic and international markets. **Contact:** NIcole Ross, Program Director; Phone: 361-882-9745; Email: nross@cbcfoundation.org.

3474 ■ Eidson - John R. Eidson Jr.,'38 Scholarship *(Undergraduate/Scholarship)*

Purpose: To assist Engineering Students attending Texas A & M University - College Station. **Focus:** Engineering. **Qualif.:** Applicants must be students (sophomore year or more) attending Texas A & M University - College Station; graduate of high school in one of seven counties served by CBCF; majoring in Engineering; must have participated in professional and social societies; and maintained full-time status and a GPA of 3.0 higher. **Criteria:** Preference given to students of Asian or Eastern Indian heritage.

Funds Avail.: Varies. **Duration:** Annual. **To Apply:** Applicant must submit current official transcript; ACT/SAT Score reports; FAFSA Student Aid Report(all pages); one letter of recommendation; two essays (essay titled "Keeping These United States Free & at Peace with the World"). **Deadline:** March 1. **Contact:** NIcole Ross, Program Director; Phone: 361-882-9745; Email: nross@cbcfoundation.org.

3475 ■ Flynn - Barney Flynn Memorial Scholarship *(Undergraduate/Scholarship)*

Purpose: To provide financial assistance to graduating seniors of Corpus Christi, Flour Bluff or Tuloso-Midway ISD high schools in furthering their education. **Focus:** General studies/Field of study not specified. **Qualif.:** Applicants must be graduating seniors from any high school in CCISD, Tuloso-Midway or Flour Bluff; must be currently active, with a high performance level and achievement level in band; and must be enrolled full-time at any accredited college or university. **Criteria:** Applicants will be evaluated based on merit.

Funds Avail.: Varies. **Duration:** Annual. **To Apply:** Applicant must submit current official transcript; ACT/SAT Score reports; FAFSA Student Aid Report(all pages); one letter of recommendation; two essays (essay titled "Keeping These United States Free & at Peace with the World"). **Deadline:** March 1. **Remarks:** The scholarship was established to memorialize Barney Flynn, who died on June 11, 1991. Barney was a freshman at Richard King High School in Corpus Christi when he and his father, Captain Dan Flynn, were killed in a tragic automobile accident. **Contact:** Nicole Ross, Program Director; Phone: 361-882-9745; Email: nross@cbcfoundation.org.

3476 ■ Guerra - Melissa Ann (Missy) Guerra Scholarship *(Undergraduate/Scholarship)*

Purpose: To provide educational assistance to senior students of Mary Caroll High School. **Focus:** General studies/Field of study not specified. **Qualif.:** Applicants must be a graduating senior from Mary Carroll High School; must demonstrate financial need; must be enrolled full time in a state-funded college in Texas; must maintain a 3.0 GPA on a 4.0 scale. **Criteria:** Preference will be given to students who are Tigerette Drill team members and/or members of the National Honor Society, those who plan to study pre-law, education or nursing, and those attending Del Mar College or TAMUCC.

Funds Avail.: Varies. **Duration:** Annual. **To Apply:** Applicant must submit current official transcript; ACT/SAT score reports; FAFSA Student Aid Report(all pages); one letter of recommendation; two essays. **Deadline:** March 1. **Remarks:** The scholarship was established in memory of

Awards are arranged alphabetically below their administering organizations

Melissa Ann (Missy) Guerra, who lost her life in a tragic automobile accident the night she graduated from Mary Carroll High School. **Contact:** Nicole Ross, Program Director; Phone: 361-882-9745; Email: nross@cbcfoundation.org.

3477 ■ Hernandez – Manuel Hernandez, Jr. Memoral Scholarship *(Undergraduate/Scholarship)*

Purpose: To provide students the financial assistance they need. **Focus:** General studies/Field of study not specified. **Qualif.:** Applicants must be a graduating seniors from Roy Miller High School, who will be entering college in the fall semester immediately following graduation; must have minimum GPA of 80% on a 100% scale; must demonstrate financial need; must be enrolled at any accredited college or university in the United States of America.**Criteria:** Applicants will be evaluated based on financial need.

Funds Avail.: Varies. **Duration:** Annual. **To Apply:** Applicant must submit current official transcript; ACT/SAT Score reports; FAFSA Student Aid Report(all pages); one letter of recommendation; two essays (essay titled "Keeping These United States Free & at Peace with the World"). **Deadline:** March 1. **Remarks:** Established in memory of Corporal Manuel Hernandez, Jr., who honorably served his country in the Republic of South Vietnam in 1969. **Contact:** Nicole Ross, Program Director; Phone: 361-882-9745; Email: nross@cbcfoundation.org.

3478 ■ A. Joseph Huerta "Puedo" Scholarships *(Undergraduate/Scholarship)*

Purpose: To provide financial assistance to students who pursue education in college. **Focus:** General studies/Field of study not specified. **Qualif.:** Applicants must be a graduating seniors from Carroll, Collegiate, King, Moody, Miller, Veteran's Memorial or WB Ray high schools or Harold T. Branch in Corpus Christi, Texas; must have a minimum GPA of 90% on a 100% scale; must be enrolled full-time at an accredited college or university; must maintain a GPA of at least 3.0 on a 4.0 scale to receive second semester check (only $2,500 and $5,000 awards).**Criteria:** Applicants are evaluated based on academic achievement and financial need.

Funds Avail.: Varies. **Duration:** Annual. **To Apply:** Applicant must submit current official transcript; ACT/SAT Score reports; FAFSA Student Aid Report(all pages); one letter of recommendation; two essays (essay titled "Keeping These United States Free & at Peace with the World"). **Deadline:** March 1. **Remarks:** The scholarship was established by Joseph Huerta to provide that opportunity. **Contact:** Nicole Ross, Program Director; Phone: 361-882-9745; Email: nross@cbcfoundation.org.

3479 ■ Laine - Casey Laine Armed Services Scholarship *(Undergraduate/Scholarship)*

Purpose: To assist students who are seeking financial resources to further their college education. **Focus:** General studies/Field of study not specified. **Qualif.:** Applicants must be a graduating senior from any high school in the CBCF seven-county service area who has participated in JROTC in high school or intends to join ROTC in college, or current college student participating in college ROTC program or reservist (Army, Air Force, Navy, or Marines) or member of Texas National Guard, or a member of the U.S. Armed Forces (Army, Air Force, Navy, or Marines) who has served at least three years active duty, OR an honorably discharged veteran of the U.S. Armed Forces, or the dependent of someone currently on active duty in the U.S.

Armed Forces who has served at least three years, OR an honorably discharged veteran of the U.S. Armed Forces, or high school applicants should be in top one-half of class; must be enrolled full-time at an accredited college or university; must maintain a minimum 2.5 GPA on a 4.0 scale, and complete at least 12 credit hours per semester to be eligible for renewal.**Criteria:** Applicants are evaluated based on academic performance; preference will be given to an applicant residing in a single parent home, where parent is not remarried, and female if all other criteria are met (ROTC/veteran and single parent).

Funds Avail.: Varies. **Duration:** Annual. **To Apply:** Applicant must submit current official transcript; ACT/SAT Score reports; FAFSA Student Aid Report(all pages); one letter of recommendation; two essays. **Deadline:** March 1. **Remarks:** Established in honor of Lieutenant Casey Laine Swakon, to honor her success in college and in the ROTC program. **Contact:** Nicole Ross, Program Director; Phone: 361-882-9745; Email: nross@cbcfoundation.org.

3480 ■ Lay – Sue Kay Lay Memorial Scholarship *(Undergraduate/Scholarship)*

Purpose: To assist high school seniors seeking financial resources to further their education. **Focus:** General studies/Field of study not specified. **Qualif.:** Applicants must be graduating seniors from any high school in the CBCF seven-county service area; must be a permanent resident of the CBCF seven-county service area; must be enrolled full-time at any accredited college or university in the United States; must maintain a minimum GPA of 3.0 on a 4.0 scale to receive subsequent 3 years.**Criteria:** Applicants are evaluated based on financial need.

Funds Avail.: Varies. **Duration:** Annual. **To Apply:** Applicant must submit current official transcript; ACT/SAT Score reports; FAFSA Student Aid Report(all pages); one letter of recommendation; two essays. **Deadline:** March 1. **Remarks:** Established in memory of Sue Kay Lay, a Baker Junior High School student killed in an automobile accident on June 23, 1970, while visiting the family ranch in Brackettville, Texas. She was 13 years old at the time. **Contact:** Nicole Ross, Program Director; Phone: 361-882-9745; Email: nross@cbcfoundation.org.

3481 ■ Martin " Marty" Allen Scholarship *(Undergraduate/Scholarship)*

Purpose: To provide financial assistance to students who are majoring in Music. **Focus:** Music. **Qualif.:** Applicants must be a graduating senior or current college student with a permanent residence in the CBCF seven-county area; must be a music major (preference given to jazz musician); must enrolled full time at an accredited college or university; must maintain a GPA of 2.5 on a 4.0 scale.**Criteria:** Applicants who are jazz musicians will be given preference.

Funds Avail.: Varies. **Duration:** Annual. **To Apply:** Applicant must submit current official transcript; ACT/SAT Score reports; FAFSA Student Aid Report(all pages); one letter of recommendation; two essays (essay titled "Keeping These United States Free & at Peace with the World"). **Deadline:** March 1. **Remarks:** Established in memory of Marty Allen, a professional jazz musician who died suddenly in February 2003. **Contact:** Nicole Ross, Program Director; Phone: 361-882-9745; Email: nross@cbcfoundation.org.

3482 ■ Miller – Brian and Colleen Miller Math and Science Scholarship *(Undergraduate/Scholarship)*

Purpose: To provide financial assistance to students who needs college education. **Focus:** General studies/Field of

Awards are arranged alphabetically below their administering organizations

study not specified. **Qualif.:** Applicants must be a graduating seniors from any high school in the CBCF seven-county service area, and residents of the CBCF service area; must be enrolled full time in any accredited college or university in the United States. **Criteria:** Preference given to students taking AP Math and Science courses and involved in extracurricular math and science competitions, groups and events.

Funds Avail.: Varies. **Duration:** Annual. **To Apply:** Applicant must submit current official transcript; ACT/SAT Score reports; FAFSA Student Aid Report(all pages); one letter of recommendation; two essays. **Deadline:** March 1. **Remarks:** Established by Brian and Colleen Miller of Corpus Christi, Texas to honor and show appreciation to the many donors and organizations that assisted them with their college educations through scholarships. **Contact:** Nicole Ross, Program Director; Phone: 361-882-9745; Email: nross@cbcfoundation.org.

3483 ■ Rains - J.J. Rains Memorial Scholarship (Undergraduate/Scholarship)

Purpose: To provide financial assistance to senior students for their college education. **Focus:** General studies/Field of study not specified. **Qualif.:** Applicants must be graduating CCISD high school seniors, with a minimum GPA of 75% on a 100% scale (2.5 on a 4.0 scale); must be enrolled full time at any accredited college or university; must minimum GPA of 2.5 on a 4.0 scale. **Criteria:** Preference will be given to students with demonstrated financial need and those who participated in HS speech and/or debate classes or activities.

Funds Avail.: Varies. **Duration:** Annual. **To Apply:** Applicant must submit current official transcript; ACT/SAT Score reports; FAFSA Student Aid Report(all pages); one letter of recommendation; two essays (essay titled "Keeping These United States Free & at Peace with the World"). **Deadline:** March 1. **Remarks:** Established in memory of J.J. Rains, a speech and debate teacher at Mary Carroll High School for over 25 years. **Contact:** Nicole Ross, Program Director; Phone: 361-882-9745; Email: nross@cbcfoundation.org.

3484 ■ W.B. Ray High School Class of '56 Averill Johnson Scholarship (Undergraduate/Scholarship)

Purpose: To provide financial assistance to graduating seniors of W.B. Ray High School. **Focus:** General studies/Field of study not specified. **Qualif.:** Applicants must be a graduating high school senior from WB Ray High School; must have minimum GPA of 90% on a 100% scale; must enrolled in college in the fall of their graduating year; must attend any accredited college or university in the United States.**Criteria:** Recipients are selected based on academic achievement and financial need.

Funds Avail.: Varies. **Duration:** Annual. **To Apply:** Applicant must submit current official transcript; ACT/SAT Score reports; FAFSA Student Aid Report(all pages); one letter of recommendation; two essays (essay titled "Keeping These United States Free & at Peace with the World"). **Deadline:** March 1. **Remarks:** The scholarship was established in honor Averill Johnson Walters to thank her for organizing reunion festivities. Established in 1956. **Contact:** Nicole Ross, Program Director; Phone: 361-882-9745; Email: nross@cbcfoundation.org.

3485 ■ Rotary Club of Corpus Christi Scholarship (Undergraduate/Scholarship)

Purpose: To support the advancement of higher education in the immediate Corpus Christi area. **Focus:** General studies/Field of study not specified. **Qualif.:** Applicant must be a graduating high school seniors from any high school within the city limits of Corpus Christi, Texas; must enrolled full time at Del Mar College or Texas A&M – Corpus Christi; must maintain a minimum GPA of 2.0 on a 4.0 scale for renewal of scholarship.**Criteria:** Applicants are evaluated based on financial need.

Funds Avail.: Varies. **Duration:** Annual. **To Apply:** Applicant must submit current official transcript; ACT/SAT Score reports; FAFSA Student Aid Report(all pages); one letter of recommendation; two essays (essay titled "Keeping These United States Free & at Peace with the World"). **Deadline:** March 1. **Remarks:** Established by the Rotary Club of Corpus Christi to benefit students with their post-secondary education. **Contact:** Nicole Ross, Program Director; Phone: 361-882-9745; Email: nross@cbcfoundation.org.

3486 ■ Saunders – Kevin Saunders Wheelchair Success Scholarship (Undergraduate/Scholarship)

Purpose: To provide an opportunity for people permanently confined to a wheelchair to attend college or technical school. **Focus:** General studies/Field of study not specified. **Qualif.:** Applicants must be graduating seniors or current college students who are permanent residents of the CBCF seven-county service area; must be a wheelchair-bound individual or have a family member who is confined to a wheelchair, and be involved in sports competition and activities necessary for success in competition.**Criteria:** Applicants will be evaluated based on scholastic performance and financial need.

Funds Avail.: Varies. **Duration:** Annual. **To Apply:** Applicant must submit current official transcript; ACT/SAT Score reports; FAFSA Student Aid Report(all pages); one letter of recommendation; two essays (essay titled "Keeping These United States Free & at Peace with the World"). **Deadline:** March 1. **Remarks:** The scholarship was established by Kevin Saunders to help provide an opportunity for people permanently confined to a wheelchair to attend college or technical school. **Contact:** Nicole Ross, Program Director; Phone: 361-882-9745; Email: nross@cbcfoundation.org.

3487 ■ Seaman Family Scholarship (Undergraduate/Scholarship)

Purpose: To provide financial assistance for Coastal Bend students who are home-schooled and need financial aid. **Focus:** General studies/Field of study not specified. **Qualif.:** Applicants must be a graduating home-schooled seniors or returning recipients from the CBCF seven-county service area or Calhoun County, Texas; must members in the Home Schoolers Association; must be enrolled full-time at an accredited college or university. **Criteria:** Preference will be given to first time applicants.

Funds Avail.: Varies. **Duration:** Annual. **To Apply:** Applicant must submit current official transcript; ACT/SAT Score reports; FAFSA Student Aid Report(all pages); one letter of recommendation; two essays (essay titled "Keeping These United States Free & at Peace with the World"). **Deadline:** March 1. **Remarks:** Established by former State Representative Gene Seaman and his wife, Ellen. **Contact:** Nicole Ross, Program Director; Phone: 361-882-9745; Email: nross@cbcfoundation.org.

3488 ■ Shamsie – Judge Terry Shamsie Scholarship (Undergraduate/Scholarship)

Purpose: To provide financial support to students with their post-secondary school education. **Focus:** General studies/

Awards are arranged alphabetically below their administering organizations

Field of study not specified. **Qualif.:** Applicants must be a graduating high school senior from Banquete High School with a minimum HS GPA of 3.0 on a 4.0 scale (80% on a 100% scale); must be a graduating high school senior from Robstown High School with a minimum HS GPA of 3.0 on a 4.0 scale (80% on a 100% scale); must be a graduating high school senior from Nueces or Kleberg counties, attending Texas A&M Corpus Christi or Texas A&M Kingsville with a minimum HS GPA of 3.0 on a 4.0 scale (80% on a 100% scale); must be a graduating high school senior from any high school in the CBCF seven-county service area majoring in economics or agriculture, attending any accredited college or university in the United States, with a minimum HS GPA of 3.5 on a 4.0 scale (85% on a 100% scale); must be enrolled full-time and have permanent residence in the CBCF seven-county service area.**Criteria:** Applicants will be evaluated based on academic achievement and financial need.

Funds Avail.: Varies. **Duration:** Annual. **To Apply:** Applicant must submit current official transcript; ACT/SAT Score reports; FAFSA Student Aid Report(all pages); one letter of recommendation; two essays (essay titled "Keeping These United States Free & at Peace with the World"). **Deadline:** March 1. **Remarks:** Established in honor of Judge Terry Shamsie to assist studens with their post-secondary school education. **Contact:** Nicole Ross, Program Director; Phone: 361-882-9745; Email: nross@cbcfoundation.org.

3489 ■ Springer - Jim Springer Memorial Scholarship *(Undergraduate/Scholarship)*

Purpose: To provide financial assistance to further the education of deserving students in Coastal Bend. **Focus:** Advertising; Marketing and distribution; Public relations. **Qualif.:** Applicants must be a current college students who have reached sophomore level or above; must be a majoring in Public Relations, Marketing Advertising or Communications; must be a permanent resident of the CBCF seven-county service area; must maintain a minimum GPA of 2.5 on a 4.0 scale to receive the second half of the scholarship.**Criteria:** Applicants are evaluated based on academic performance and financial need.

Funds Avail.: Varies. **Duration:** Annual. **To Apply:** Applicant must submit current official transcript; ACT/SAT Score reports; FAFSA Student Aid Report(all pages); one letter of recommendation; two essays (essay titled "Keeping These United States Free & at Peace with the World"). **Deadline:** March 1. **Remarks:** Established in memory of Jim Springer, a well-known master of ceremonies of Chamber of Commerce breakfasts and many other events in Corpus Christi. **Contact:** Nicole Ross, Program Director; Phone: 361-882-9745; Email: nross@cbcfoundation.org.

3490 ■ Talbert Family Memorial Scholarship *(Undergraduate/Scholarship)*

Purpose: To provide financial support to deserving students who are studying accounting. **Focus:** Accounting. **Qualif.:** Applicants must be a graduating high school senior, or current college student wo is a permanent resident of the CBCF seven-county service area; must major in accounting or financial management; must enrolled full-time at any accredited college or university in the state of Texas; must maintain a college GPA of 3.0 on a 4.0 scale and submit transcripts and a personal note regarding college experience to date and intended major for renewal.**Criteria:** Applicants must submit all the required application information.

Funds Avail.: Varies. **Duration:** Annual. **To Apply:** Applicant must submit current official transcript; ACT/SAT

Score reports; FAFSA Student Aid Report(all pages); one letter of recommendation; two essays (essay titled "Keeping These United States Free & at Peace with the World"). **Deadline:** March 1. **Remarks:** Established by Dr. William L. Talbert to honor his parents and to encourage worthy students to pursue higher education. The scholarship honors his parents, Mr. and Mrs. William O. Talbert, and grandparents, Mr. Laurel Talbert and Mrs. Rena Talbert. the Talbert family farmed in the Robstown area from 1913 into the 1960s. **Contact:** Nicole Ross, Program Director; Phone: 361-882-9745; Email: nross@cbcfoundation.org.

3491 ■ Webb – Faye and Rendell C Webb JR Scholarship *(Undergraduate/Scholarship)*

Purpose: To provide financial assistance to students who are in need. **Focus:** Education. **Qualif.:** Applicants must be graduates of Miller or Moody high schools in Corpus Christi, Texas with a minimum GPA of 85% on a 100% scale; must be enrolled full time in a college or university in the state of Texas (preference given to students attending TAMUCC, TAMUK or Del Mar College); must be enrolled full-time at any accredited college or university in the United States. **Criteria:** Preference will be given to students who attended Los Encinos, Lamar or Lozano Elementary Schools for at least one year and those majoring in Elementary Education or Engineering.

Funds Avail.: Varies. **Duration:** Annual. **To Apply:** Applicant must submit current official transcript; ACT/SAT Score reports; FAFSA Student Aid Report(all pages); one letter of recommendation; two essays (essay titled "Keeping These United States Free & at Peace with the World"). **Deadline:** March 1. **Remarks:** Established in honor of Faye Webb to assist students with their post-secondary school education. **Contact:** Nicole Ross, Program Director; Phone: 361-882-9745; Email: nross@cbcfoundation.org.

3492 ■ Williams – Dr. Dana Williams Scholarship *(Undergraduate/Scholarship)*

Purpose: To provide educational assistance to students planning to become teachers or public school administrators. **Focus:** Education. **Qualif.:** Applicant must be a graduating senior from any high school in the CCISD; must enrolled full-time at any accredited college or university in the United States; must maintain a minimum GPA of 3.0 on a 4.0 scale and submit a transcript and personal note regarding college experience to date and intended major to CBCF for continued receipt of award. **Criteria:** Preference will be given to students who major in education pursuing a teaching certificate and to students who are permanent residents of Nueces County.

Funds Avail.: Varies. **Duration:** Annual. **To Apply:** Applicant must submit current official transcript; ACT/SAT Score reports; FAFSA Student Aid Report(all pages); one letter of recommendation; two essays (essay titled "Keeping These United States Free & at Peace with the World"). **Deadline:** March 1. **Remarks:** The scholarship was established by the Coastal Bend Community Foundation to honor Dr. Dana Williams, superintendent of the Corpus Christi Independent School District from 1962 to 1981 and founding Executive Director of the Coastal Bend Community Foundation from 1981 to 1998. **Contact:** Nicole Ross, Program Director; Phone: 361-882-9745; Email: nross@cbcfoundation.org.

3493 ■ Coca-Cola Scholars Foundation (CCSF)

PO Box 442
Atlanta, GA 30301

Awards are arranged alphabetically below their administering organizations

Free: 800-306-2653
URL: www.coca-colascholars.org
Social Media: www.facebook.com/cokescholars
www.instagram.com/cokescholars
www.linkedin.com/company/cokescholars/about
twitter.com/cokescholars
www.youtube.com/user/CocaColaScholars

3494 ■ Coca-Cola Scholars Program Scholarship
(Undergraduate/Scholarship)

Purpose: To provide scholarships to high school seniors for them to pursue higher education. **Focus:** General studies/Field of study not specified. **Criteria:** Selection will be based on the committee's criteria.

Funds Avail.: $20,000. **Duration:** Annual. **Number Awarded:** 200. **To Apply:** Applicants may apply online and must complete all parts of the application process.

3495 ■ Code Play Learn
132 N Ridgeland
Oak Park, IL 60302
Ph: (708)374-8286
E-mail: contact@codeplaylearn.com
URL: www.codeplaylearn.com

3496 ■ Code Play LEARN Scholarship *(Two Year College, Undergraduate, Graduate/Scholarship)*

Purpose: To provide financial aid to students to pursue education. **Focus:** General studies/Field of study not specified. **Qualif.:** Applicants must be U.S. citizens accepted to or currently attending a college or university in the United States.

Funds Avail.: $1,000. **Duration:** Annual. **Number Awarded:** 1. **To Apply:** Application is available at the sponsor's website. **Deadline:** November 30.

3497 ■ Coit Cleaning and Restoration Services
865 Hinckley Rd.
Burlingame, CA 94010
Ph: (650)697-6190
Free: 800-367-2648
URL: www.coit.com
Social Media: www.facebook.com/COITClean
instagram.com/coitclean
linkedin.com/company/coit-services
twitter.com/coitclean

3498 ■ The COIT Clean GIF Scholarship Contest
(Undergraduate, Graduate/Scholarship)

Purpose: To provide financial support to undergraduate and graduate students. **Focus:** General studies/Field of study not specified. **Qualif.:** Applicants must be enrolled in an undergraduate or graduate program at an accredited college or university in the U.S. or Canada. COIT employees and family members are ineligible from competing in the scholarship.**Criteria:** Quality of graphic design and humor/cleverness of submission.

Funds Avail.: $2,000. **Number Awarded:** 1. **To Apply:** Create a lightly animated GIF that shows us a fast way to get your space cleaned. Your GIF should be designed for posting on social media and can be as many frames as you like, just keep it short. Post your design on your personal Facebook and Twitter accounts, using the hashtag #CoitScholarship on both. Email it in GIF format, with the subject line COIT Scholarship, to coit.scholarship.2017@gmail.com. Include: full name; personal Facebook URL; personal Twitter username; mailing address; phone number; qualifying school name; proof of enrollment (attach a copy/scan of a valid class schedule or other similar document from the school); date of birth (mm/dd/yyyy); name of parent or legal guardian (if under 18). **Deadline:** August 31. **Contact:** Email: coit.scholarship.2017@gmail.com.

3499 ■ COLAGE
509 10th Ave. E.
Seattle, WA 98102
Ph: (828)782-1938
E-mail: colage@colage.org
URL: www.colage.org
Social Media: www.facebook.com/colage
www.instagram.com/colagenational
twitter.com/colagenational

3500 ■ Lee Dubin Memorial Scholarship
(Undergraduate/Scholarship)

Purpose: To recognize students who have one or more LGBTQ parent/guardian and have demonstrated ability and commitment to effecting change in the LGBTQ community. **Focus:** Social sciences.

Funds Avail.: $1,000. **Duration:** Annual. **Number Awarded:** 4.

3501 ■ The Coleopterists Society (CS)
c/o Anthony I. Cognato, PhD
Dept. of Entomology, Michigan State University
288 Farm Ln.
243 Natural Science Bldg.
East Lansing, MI 48824
E-mail: coleopsoctreas@gmail.com
URL: www.coleopsoc.org
Social Media: www.facebook.com/coleopterists.society
twitter.com/coleopsoc

3502 ■ Coleopterists Society - Youth Incentive Award *(High School/Award, Grant)*

Purpose: To provide encouragement and assistance to young beetle enthusiasts (grades 7-12). **Focus:** Entomology. **Qualif.:** Applicants must be students in grades 7-12 who are beetle enthusiasts. **Criteria:** The Youth Incentive Award Committee from the Coleopterists Society will evaluate the applications and will select up to two winners annually; one each in junior (grades 7-9) and senior (grades 10-12)

Funds Avail.: $400 (senior); $200 (junior). **Duration:** Annual. **Number Awarded:** 2. **To Apply:** Applicant must submit an online application form. **Deadline:** November 1. **Remarks:** Established in 1989. **Contact:** Dr. David G. Furth, Entomology, NHB, MRC 165, PO Box 37012, Smithsonian Institution, Washington, D. C. 20013-7012; Phone: 202-633-0990; Fax: 202-786-2894; E-mail: furthd@si.edu.

3503 ■ College Art Association (CAA)
50 Broadway, 21st Fl.
New York, NY 10004

Awards are arranged alphabetically below their administering organizations

Ph: (212)691-1051
Fax: (212)627-2381
E-mail: nyoffice@collegeart.org
URL: www.collegeart.org
Social Media: www.facebook.com/caavisual
www.instagram.com/caavisual
www.pinterest.cl/pin/227854062368990563/?send=true
twitter.com/caavisual
www.youtube.com/c/CAAvisual

3504 ■ Wyeth Foundation For American Art Publication Grant *(Other/Grant)*

Purpose: To support book-length, scholarly manuscripts in the history of American art. **Focus:** History, American; Publishing; Visual arts. **Qualif.:** Applicants must be publishers of book-length scholarly manuscripts in the history of American art, visual studies, and related subjects that have been accepted by the publishers on their merits but cannot be published in the most desirable form without a subsidy.

Funds Avail.: No specific amount. **Duration:** Annual. **Number Awarded:** Varies. **To Apply:** Applicants must submit a curriculum vitae, narrative description, authors' response to peer reviews, publishers' cover letter, partial manuscript and two or more peer reviews of the manuscript that have been submitted to the publishers. **Deadline:** September 15. **Remarks:** Established in 2005. **Contact:** Aakash Suchak; Phone: 212-392-4435; Email: asuchak@collegeart.org.

3505 ■ College of Healthcare Information Management Executives (CHIME)

710 Avis Dr., Ste. 200
Ann Arbor, MI 48108
Ph: (734)665-0000
Fax: (734)665-4922
E-mail: staff@chimecentral.org
URL: chimecentral.org
Social Media: www.facebook.com/CIOCHIME
www.instagram.com/chime.transforminghealthcare
www.linkedin.com/company/chime
twitter.com/CIOCHIME

3506 ■ John Glaser Scholarships *(Undergraduate/Scholarship)*

Purpose: To acknowledge IT staff members who show potential for advancement to a CIO and who are dedicated to professional development. **Focus:** Health care services. **Qualif.:** Candidates must be employed and nominated by a current CHIME member. **Criteria:** Recipients are selected based on Committee's review of the CIO potential and dedication to professional development.

Funds Avail.: $3,000. **Duration:** One year. **Number Awarded:** 2. **To Apply:** Applicants must provide resume; and (500 to 1,000-word) essay describing: visions and goals; handling their responsibilities; financial challenges that prohibit them to participate in leadership development activities; and benefits they can get to the program they choose to attend. Applicant's direct supervisor is required to complete the questions on the application. **Deadline:** September 6.

3507 ■ The College Monk

2035 Sunset Lake Rd., Ste. B-2
Newark, DE 19702

URL: thecollegemonk.com
Social Media: www.facebook.com/thecollegemonkcom
www.instagram.com/thecollegemonk
www.linkedin.com/company/thecollegemonk
www.pinterest.com/thecollegemonk
twitter.com/thecollegemonk

3508 ■ $1500 College Monk Short Essay Scholarship *(Undergraduate, Graduate/Scholarship)*

Purpose: To provide financial assistance to high school graduating students or college students who are going to attend an accredited institution in the United States. **Focus:** General studies/Field of study not specified. **Qualif.:** Applicant must be pursuing or looking to pursue an undergraduate or graduate education in the United States during the next 12 months; must be a citizen of the U.S. or an international student with a valid student visa. **Criteria:** Selection will be based on the essay submitted and done by a qualified panel of judges. Criteria for the essay will be writing ability, creativity, originality, and overall excellence.

Funds Avail.: $1,500. **Number Awarded:** 1. **To Apply:** Applicant must submit an original essay and addresses the following: Please tell us about yourself and why you are applying for this scholarship; how this scholarship will help you achieve your personal and professional goals; and any past achievements at the state, national, or international level. Application should be submitted through the sponsor's website at www.thecollegemonk.com/scholarships. **Deadline:** January 31. **Contact:** Email: info@thecollegemonk.com.

3509 ■ College Raptor

3578 Perch Dr. SE
Iowa City, IA 52240
Ph: (319)849-7101
URL: www.collegeraptor.com

3510 ■ $2,500 College Raptor Scholarship *(College, University, Undergraduate, Graduate, Community College/Scholarship)*

Purpose: To help students with college expenses. **Focus:** General studies/Field of study not specified. **Qualif.:** Applicant must be a legal resident of the United States, District of Columbia, or a U.S. territory; must be at least 16 years old and enrolled, or planning to enroll in fall of the scholarship year, in an accredited post-secondary institution (high school juniors and seniors and current college students). **Criteria:** Selection based on strength of the application and the essay submitted.

Funds Avail.: $2,500. **Number Awarded:** 1. **To Apply:** Application available at www.collegeraptor.com/2500scholarship/. **Deadline:** September 30.

3511 ■ College Reading and Learning Association (CRLA)

7044 S. 13th St.
Oak Creek, WI 53154
Ph: (414)908-4961
E-mail: customercare@crla.net
URL: www.crla.net

3512 ■ Cengage Travel Award for Teachers of Reading at a Community College *(Professional development/Monetary)*

Purpose: To support a member who seeks professional development. **Focus:** Education; Reading. **Qualif.:** Ap-

Awards are arranged alphabetically below their administering organizations

plicant must be a CRLA member teaching reading at a community college who seeks professional development through participation in the annual CRLA conference; at least three years of experience in teaching basic and/or college reading at a community college.

To Apply: Applicants must submit a 500-700-word essay describing how the Cengage travel award would be used to foster their professional development and/or research and scholarship. Applicants should be as specific as possible about how they will select strands and sessions to facilitate the growth they are seeking. **Deadline:** August 1. **Contact:** Email: wbb001@shsu.edu.

3513 ■ College Success Foundation (CSF)
Eastgate Bldg.
15500 SE 30th Pl., Ste. 200
Bellevue, WA 98007
Ph: (425)416-2000
Fax: (425)416-2001
Free: 877-655-4097
E-mail: info@collegesuccessfoundation.org
URL: www.collegesuccessfoundation.org
Social Media: www.facebook.com/CollegeSuccessFndn
www.instagram.com/collegesuccessfdn/
www.linkedin.com/company/college-success-foundation
twitter.com/College_Success
www.youtube.com/user/collegesuccessfndn

3514 ■ College Success Foundation Chateau Ste. Michelle Scholarship Fund *(Undergraduate/Scholarship)*

Purpose: To provide financial support for underserved students who would like to obtain four-year college degree. **Focus:** General studies/Field of study not specified. **Qualif.:** Applicants must have plan to attend, or currently attending an eligible four-year college or university in Washington State; must be residents of Washington; must have plan to file or have already filed a FAFSA, if eligible; must have 2.75 cumulative GPA; and be enrolled full-time (12 credits per quarter or equivalent for semester) as college students.

Funds Avail.: No specific amount. **Duration:** Four years. **Number Awarded:** Varies. **To Apply:** Applicants must submit the online application and then mail transcript and a letter of recommendation to College Success Foundation. **Deadline:** February 28. **Remarks:** Established in 2001. **Contact:** Email: ScholarshipServices@collegesuccessfoundation.org.

3515 ■ College Success Foundation Leadership 1000 Scholarship *(Undergraduate/Scholarship)*

Purpose: To provide college scholarships to deserving students who need assistance attending an eligible four-year college or university in Washington State. **Focus:** General studies/Field of study not specified. **Qualif.:** Applicants must have plan to attend, or currently attending an eligible four-year college or university in Washington State; must be enrolled in a full-time basis; must be Washington State residents; must have plan to file or have already filed a FAFSA, if eligible; must have 2.50 cumulative GPA.

Funds Avail.: Up to $5,000 per academic year. **Duration:** Annual. **To Apply:** Application and details are available on the Sponsor's website. **Deadline:** February 5. **Contact:** Email: ScholarshipServices@

collegesuccessfoundation.org; URL: www.collegesuccessfoundation.org/wa/scholarships/l1000/eligibility.

3516 ■ College Success Foundation Washington State Governors' Scholarship for Foster Youth *(Undergraduate/Scholarship)*

Purpose: To help young men and women who are currently in an open dependency court order in Washington State, or an open dependency tribal court order, continue their education and earn a college degree. **Focus:** General studies/Field of study not specified. **Qualif.:** Applicants must be Washington State High School seniors and on track to graduate from high school; must have cumulative GPA of 2.0 or higher; must have plan to enroll in a college on a full-time basis; must have resided in Washington State for at least three academic years prior to high school graduation. Applicants must meet one of the following criteria: placed by Washington State in foster care, guardianship, or dependency guardianship; placed in federally recognized care classified as an unaccompanied minor and rendered a legal permanent residency in the United States; placed under a dependency tribal court order outside of their home. Renewable for up to 5 years or completion of undergraduate degree.

Funds Avail.: $2,000-$4,000 per year. **Number Awarded:** 40-50. **To Apply:** Application and details are available on the sponsor's website. **Deadline:** February 5. **Contact:** Email: ScholarshipServices@collegesuccessfoundation.org.

3517 ■ College and University Public Relations and Associated Professionals (CUPRAP)
237 S Fraser St.
State College, PA 16805-0034
URL: www.cuprap.org

3518 ■ CUPRAP Communications Internship Award for Students of Color *(Undergraduate/Award)*

Purpose: To grant scholarship to make it financially easier for students of color to obtain valuable internship experience in a communications field. **Focus:** Communications. **Qualif.:** Applicants must be members of racial minority groups such as African-American, Asian/Pacific Islander, Hispanic/Latino, Native American; must be enrolled as a full-time undergraduate student at an accredited college or university having individual membership representation in CUPRAP. **Criteria:** Selection will be based on applicant's academic ability, communication skills and creativity as demonstrated through work samples and financial needs.

Funds Avail.: $2,000. **Duration:** Annual. **To Apply:** Applications can be submitted online; include a cover letter; resume of your academic or work experience; an official grade transcript from your school; faculty recommendation. **Deadline:** January 5. **Contact:** Dan Hanson, 105 Taylor Dr., Wallingford, PA, 19086; Email: danwhanson@yahoo.com.

3519 ■ Colonial Ghosts, LLC
4900 Trailview
Williamsburg, VA 23188
Ph: (757)598-1805
URL: colonialghosts.com
Social Media: www.facebook.com/ColonialGhosts
instagram.com/colonialghosts

Awards are arranged alphabetically below their administering organizations

pinterest.com/colonialghosts
twitter.com/colonialghosts

3520 ■ Colonial Ghosts Scholarships for History & Marketing Students (Undergraduate/Scholarship)

Purpose: To support students majoring in Marketing. **Focus:** Marketing and distribution. **Qualif.:** Applicants must be students currently enrolled in an accredited college with a declared major in Marketing.

To Apply: Interested applicants must fill out the online form and submit the essay via the scholarship link. They must include an essay (1,000 word minimum) explaining their education goals and plans after graduating college. Explain why they deserve to win and what the scholarship means to them. **Deadline:** December 15. **Contact:** Email: scholarships@colonialghosts.com.

3521 ■ Colorado Association of Law Libraries (CoALL)

2080 S High St.
Denver, CO 80210
E-mail: coall@coallnet.org
URL: www.coallnet.org
Social Media: www.facebook.com/CoLawLib
twitter.com/coallnet

3522 ■ Martha W. Keister Memorial Travel Grant (Professional development/Grant)

Purpose: To fund members attending library related educational programs or help defray the cost of library school education. **Focus:** Law; Library and archival sciences.

Funds Avail.: $400. **Duration:** Annual. **Remarks:** The award was established to honor the contributions and legacy of Martha Keister, a well-respected former member of the Colorado law library community. **Contact:** Grants and Scholarships Chair, Kathryn Michaels, Phone: 720.625.5106; Email: kathryn.michaels@judicial.state.co.us.

3523 ■ Colorado Association of Stormwater and Floodplain Managers - Metro Denver Region (CASFM)

c/o Drew Beck, PE, CFM, Representative
1601 Blake St., Ste. 200
Denver, CO 80202
Ph: (303)572-0200
URL: www.casfm.org
Social Media: www.facebook.com/groups/casfm
twitter.com/CASFMOrg

3524 ■ CASFM-Ben Urbonas Scholarship (Graduate/Scholarship)

Purpose: To promote interest among students and the engineering community in CASFM and to promote the goals of the organization. **Focus:** Atmospheric science; Hydrology; Meteorology. **Criteria:** Selection will be based on the evaluation of applications and specific criteria.

Funds Avail.: $2,500. **Duration:** Annual. **To Apply:** Applicants must submit a completed application form; a short essay (up to 500 words) describing personal and career goals. **Deadline:** October 30. **Remarks:** Established in

2002. **Contact:** CASFM Scholarship Committee, c /o Town of Parker, Jacob James, 20120 E Main St., Parker, CO, 80138; Email: jjames@parkeronline.org.

3525 ■ Colorado Broadcasters Association (CBA)

333 W Hampden Ave., Ste. 400
Englewood, CO 80110
Ph: (720)536-5427
Fax: (720)536-5259
E-mail: cba@coloradobroadcasters.org
URL: www.coloradobroadcasters.org
Social Media: twitter.com/JustinSasso

3526 ■ Broadcast Education and Development Program (Other/Scholarship)

Purpose: To foster continual development of Colorado's radio and television workforce. **Focus:** Broadcasting. **Qualif.:** Applicant must be program is for regular, full-time broadcast employees who are seeking to improve their education while continuing to work. **Criteria:** Preference will be forprojects leading to degrees or certificates.

Duration: Annual. **To Apply:** Applications should be submitted to the Colorado Broadcasters Association. **Contact:** Colorado Broadcasters Association, at the above address or Email: CBA@ColoradoBroadcasters.org. Fax: (720) 536-5259, United States Postal Service: Colorado Broadcasters Association, 333 W. Hampden Avenue; ste., 400, Englewood, CO 80110.,.

3527 ■ Colorado Christian University Alumni Association (CCU)

8787 W Alameda Ave.
Lakewood, CO 80226
Ph: (303)963-3000
Free: 800-443-2484
URL: www.ccu.edu
Social Media: www.facebook.com/myCCU
www.instagram.com/myccu
www.linkedin.com/school/colorado-christian-university
www.pinterest.com/ccucags
twitter.com/my_ccu

3528 ■ CCU Endowed Scholarships (Undergraduate/Scholarship)

Purpose: To assist students with the cost of post-secondary education. **Focus:** General studies/Field of study not specified.

Funds Avail.: No specific amount.

3529 ■ Colorado Hotel and Lodging Association (CH&LA)

1701 California St., Ste. L-1061
Denver, CO 80202
Ph: (303)297-8335
E-mail: info@chla.com
URL: chla.com
Social Media: www.facebook.com/coloradohotelandlodging
www.instagram.com/chla_colorado
twitter.com/coloradolodging

3530 ■ Karl Mehlmann Scholarship (Undergraduate/Scholarship)

Purpose: To support students pursuing degrees in the hospitality and tourism industry. **Focus:** Culinary arts. **Cri-**

Awards are arranged alphabetically below their administering organizations

teria: Recipients are selected based on the grammar and spelling of the essay.

Funds Avail.: $16,000. **To Apply:** Applicants must submit one official transcript from current school or most recent if not currently attending school; must submit a brief autobiography; a one-page, typewritten essay answering why you've selected the hospitality industry for your career and what definition of hospitality is; must submit a type, signed and on letterhead recommendation letter from College or University; signature from Director/Dean. **Deadline:** April 24. **Contact:** CHLA office, Phone: 303-297-8335 or Email: info@chla.com.

3531 ■ Colorado Nurses Foundation (CNF)
PO Box 3406
Englewood, CO 80155
Ph: (720)457-1004
Fax: (303)200-7099
E-mail: info@coloradonursesfoundation.com
URL: www.coloradonursesfoundation.com

3532 ■ Colorado Nurses Association: Virginia Paulson Memorial Scholarship *(Graduate, Undergraduate/Scholarship)*

Purpose: To provide scholarships for qualified nursing students from both rural and urban settings. **Focus:** Nursing. **Qualif.:** Applicants must be Colorado residents committed to practicing nursing in Colorado; must be students in an approved Colorado Nursing Program; must have a minimum of 3.25 GPA (for undergraduate applicants) or 3.5 GPA (for graduate applicants); must have one of the following student statuses: (1) Junior or senior level BSN undergraduate students; (2) RN enrolled in a baccalaureate or higher degree nursing program in a school of nursing; (3) Students in second year of nursing studies in an associate degree in nursing program; (4) RN with master's degree in nursing, currently practicing in Colorado and enrolled in a doctoral program; (5) Students in second or third year of a Doctorate Nursing Practice (DNP) program. **Criteria:** Selection will be based on professional philosophy and goals; dedication to the improvement of patient care in Colorado; demonstrated commitment to nursing, critical thinking skills and potential for leadership; involvement in community and professional organizations; GPA-minimum of 3.25 undergraduate, 3.5 graduate; financial need; recommendation of one faculty member; and employer/supervisor recommendation.

Funds Avail.: $1,200. **Duration:** Annual. **Number Awarded:** 1. **To Apply:** Applicant must submit a copy of transcript from earned (must be completed) baccalaureate or higher degree in a field other than nursing; financial need statement and narrative explanation; recommendation of one faculty member; recommendation from employer/supervisor. **Deadline:** October 31. **Contact:** Email: support@civicamanagement.zendesk.com; Phone: 720-457-1004.

3533 ■ Colorado Nurses Foundation Nightingale Named Scholarship *(Graduate, Undergraduate/Scholarship)*

Purpose: To provide scholarships for qualified nursing students from both rural and urban settings. **Focus:** Nursing. **Qualif.:** Applicants must be Colorado residents committed to practicing nursing in Colorado; must be students in an approved Colorado Nursing Program; must have a minimum of 3.25 GPA (for undergraduate applicants) or 3.5

GPA (for graduate applicants); and must have one of the following student statuses: (1) Junior or senior level BSN undergraduate students; (2) RN enrolled in a baccalaureate or higher degree nursing program in a school of nursing; (3) Students in second year of nursing studies in an associate degree in nursing program; (4) RN with master's degree in nursing, currently practicing in Colorado and enrolled in a doctoral program; (5) Students in second or third year of a Doctorate Nursing Practice (DNP) program. **Criteria:** Selection will be based on professional philosophy and goals; dedication to the improvement of patient care in Colorado; demonstrated commitment to nursing, critical thinking skills and potential for leadership; involvement in community and professional organizations; GPA-minimum of 3.25 undergraduate, 3.5 graduate; financial need; recommendation of one faculty member; and employer/supervisor recommendation.

Funds Avail.: No specific amount. **Duration:** Annual. **Number Awarded:** Varies. **Deadline:** September 1. **Contact:** Email: support@civicamanagement.zendesk.com; Phone: 720-457-1004.

3534 ■ Lola Fehr: Nightingale Scholarships *(Graduate, Undergraduate/Scholarship)*

Purpose: To provide scholarships for qualified nursing students from both rural and urban settings. **Focus:** Nursing. **Qualif.:** Applicants must be Colorado residents committed to practicing nursing in Colorado; must be students in an approved Colorado Nursing Program; must have a minimum of 3.25 GPA (for undergraduate applicants) or 3.5 GPA (for graduate applicants); and must have one of the following student statuses: (1) Junior or senior level BSN undergraduate students; (2) RN enrolled in a baccalaureate or higher degree nursing program in a school of nursing; (3) Students in second year of nursing studies in an associate degree in nursing program; (4) RN with master's degree in nursing, currently practicing in Colorado and enrolled in a doctoral program; (5) Students in second or third year of a Doctorate Nursing Practice (DNP) program. **Criteria:** Scholarship application will be rated based on the following: (1) Professional philosophy and goals; (2) Dedication to the improvement of patient care in Colorado; (3) Demonstrated commitment to nursing, critical thinking skills and potential for leadership; (4) Involvement in community and professional organizations; (5) GPA-minimum of 3.25 undergraduate, 3.5 graduate; (6) Financial need; (7) Recommendation of one faculty member; and (8) Employer/Supervisor recommendation.

To Apply: Applicants must submit a cover sheet, financial need statement, resume, recommendation form from Faculty and Employer in a separated sealed envelope, copy of transcript including the last semester grades. Student essay must be no more than three pages, double-spaced in a 12pt. font with 1″ each margin. **Contact:** Vicki Carroll; Phone: 970-416-6811; Fax: 970-416-6820; Email: CNFScholarships@aol.com.

3535 ■ H.M. Muffly Memorial Scholarship *(Graduate, Undergraduate/Scholarship)*

Purpose: To provide scholarships for qualified nursing students from both rural and urban settings. **Focus:** Nursing.

Funds Avail.: $1,500. **Duration:** Annual. **Number Awarded:** 3. **To Apply:** Applicant must submit a copy of transcript from earned (must be completed) baccalaureate or higher degree in a field other than nursing; financial need statement and narrative explanation; recommenda-

Awards are arranged alphabetically below their administering organizations

tion of one faculty member; recommendation from employer/supervisor. **Deadline:** October 31. **Contact:** Email: support@civicamanagement.zendesk.com; Phone: 720-457-1004.

3536 ■ Roy Anderson Memorial Scholarship (Graduate, Undergraduate/Scholarship)

Purpose: To provide scholarships for qualified nursing students from both rural and urban settings. **Focus:** Nursing. **Qualif.:** Applicants must be Colorado residents committed to practicing nursing in Colorado; must be students in an approved Colorado Nursing Program; must have a minimum of 3.25 GPA (for undergraduate applicants) or 3.5 GPA (for graduate applicants); must have one of the following student statuses: (1) Junior or senior level BSN undergraduate students; (2) RN enrolled in a baccalaureate or higher degree nursing program in a school of nursing; (3) Students in second year of nursing studies in an associate degree in nursing program; (4) RN with master's degree in nursing, currently practicing in Colorado and enrolled in a doctoral program; (5) Students in second or third year of a Doctorate Nursing Practice (DNP) program. **Criteria:** Selection will be based on professional philosophy and goals; dedication to the improvement of patient care in Colorado; demonstrated commitment to nursing, critical thinking skills and potential for leadership; involvement in community and professional organizations; GPA-minimum of 3.25 undergraduate, 3.5 graduate; financial need; recommendation of one faculty member; and employer/supervisor recommendation.

Funds Avail.: $1,500. **Duration:** Annual. **Number Awarded:** 3. **To Apply:** Applicant must submit a copy of transcript from earned (must be completed) baccalaureate or higher degree in a field other than nursing; financial need statement and narrative explanation; recommendation of one faculty member; recommendation from employer/supervisor. **Deadline:** October 31. **Contact:** Email: support@civicamanagement.zendesk.com; Phone: 720-457-1004.

3537 ■ Patty Walter Memorial Scholarships (Graduate, Undergraduate/Scholarship)

Purpose: To provide Colorado Nurses Foundation is dedicated to improving health care and nursing practice in Colorado. The foundation began Oct. 3, 1987, as the Nursing Institute of Colorado. Although the name has changed, the mission of the organization has remained essentially the same: to advance nursing in Colorado through education, advocacy, and recognition. **Focus:** Nursing. **Qualif.:** Applicants must be Colorado residents committed to practicing nursing in Colorado; must be students in an approved Colorado Nursing Program; must have a minimum of 3.25 GPA (for undergraduate applicants) or 3.5 GPA (for graduate applicants); and must have one of the following student statuses: (1) Junior or senior level BSN undergraduate students; (2) RN enrolled in a baccalaureate or higher degree nursing program in a school of nursing; (3) Students in second year of nursing studies in an associate degree in nursing program; (4) RN with master's degree in nursing, currently practicing in Colorado and enrolled in a doctoral program; (5) Students in second or third year of a Doctorate Nursing Practice (DNP) program. **Criteria:** Selection will be based on professional philosophy and goals; dedication to the improvement of patient care in Colorado; demonstrated commitment to nursing, critical thinking skills and potential for leadership; involvement in community and professional organizations; GPA-minimum of 3.25 undergraduate, 3.5 graduate; financial need; recommendation of

one faculty member; and employer/supervisor recommendation.

Funds Avail.: No specific amount. **To Apply:** Applications can be submitted through online. **Deadline:** October 31. **Contact:** Phone: 720-457-1004.

3538 ■ Colorado Society of Certified Public Accountants (COCPA)
7887 E Belleview Ave., Ste. 200
Englewood, CO 80111-6076
Ph: (303)773-2877
Free: 800-523-9082
E-mail: info@cocpa.org
URL: www.cocpa.org
Social Media: www.facebook.com/cocpa
www.instagram.com/co_cpas
www.linkedin.com/company/colorado-society-of-certified
 -public-accountants
twitter.com/COCPAs
www.youtube.com/user/CSCPA

3539 ■ CSCPA College Scholarships (Graduate, Undergraduate/Scholarship)

Purpose: To support undergraduate and graduate accounting students. **Focus:** Accounting. **Qualif.:** Applicant must be an accounting major who has completed at least eight semester hours of accounting courses including one upper division accounting course; attend a Colorado college/university with an accredited accounting program; enrolled in courses equal to six semester/quarter hours or more for the semester/quarter for which the student is applying; have a college/university cumulative GPA of 3.0 or better on a 4.0 scale; and a U.S. citizen, or non-U.S. citizen legally living and studying in Colorado with a valid visa. **Criteria:** Selection is based on the application materials submitted.

Funds Avail.: $2,500. **To Apply:** Applicants must submit a completed application form together with an official or unofficial transcript from the current school that includes cumulative overall GPA.

3540 ■ CSCPA High School Scholarships (Undergraduate, Graduate/Scholarship)

Purpose: To support high school seniors who plan to major in accounting at Colorado community colleges and Colorado colleges/universities. **Focus:** Accounting. **Qualif.:** Applicants must be a Colorado high school senior who will major in accounting at a Colorado community college or Colorado college or university with an accredited accounting program. **Criteria:** Selection is based on the application materials submitted.

Funds Avail.: $2,500. **Duration:** Biennial. **To Apply:** Applicants must submit a completed application form together with an official high school transcript that includes the applicant's cumulative GPA, class ranking and SAT/ACT test scores. **Deadline:** June 1.

3541 ■ CSCPA Sophomore Scholarships (Undergraduate/Scholarship)

Purpose: To financially support outstanding sophomore accounting students. **Focus:** Accounting. **Qualif.:** Applicant must be a sophomore who has maintained a 3.0 or better GPA on a 4.0 scale during the prior year and plans to major in accounting; enrolled in a Principles of Accounting class with a 3.0 GPA, and enroll in courses equal to six semester/

Awards are arranged alphabetically below their administering organizations

quarter hours or more for the term for which the student is applying; and be a U.S. citizen, or non-U.S. citizen legally living and studying in Colorado with a valid visa. **Criteria:** Selection is based on the application materials submitted.

To Apply: Applicants must submit a completed application form along with an official or unofficial transcript that includes the previous year's cumulative overall GPA.

3542 ■ Columbus Citizens Foundation (CCF)

8 E 69th St.
New York, NY 10021
Ph: (212)249-9923
Fax: (212)737-4413
E-mail: ccf@columbuscitizens.org
URL: www.columbuscitizensfd.org
Social Media: www.facebook.com/
  columbuscitizensfoundation
www.instagram.com/ccfdn
www.linkedin.com/organization-guest/company/columbus
  -citizens-foundation
twitter.com/ccfdn
www.youtube.com/user/ColumbusCitizensFdn

3543 ■ Columbus Citizens Foundation College Scholarships *(Undergraduate/Scholarship)*

Purpose: To provide financial assistance to underwrite the cost of Italian descent students' college tuition. **Focus:** General studies/Field of study not specified. **Qualif.:** Applicants must be students of Italian descent; with GPA of 3.0 or higher; and must come from households where the total gross income does not exceed $20, 000 per capita; only 8th graders who will enter high school as freshman are eligible. **Criteria:** Applicants are evaluated based on existence of Italian-American ancestry; financial need; academic excellence; and service to school and community.

Funds Avail.: No specific amount. **Duration:** for 4 years. **To Apply:** Applicants must submit letters of recommendation; an essay; academic performance verification form and attachments; financials. **Remarks:** Established in 1984.

3544 ■ Columbus Citizens Foundation High School Scholarships *(Undergraduate/Scholarship)*

Purpose: To provide educational assistance for students of Italian descent. **Focus:** General studies/Field of study not specified. **Qualif.:** Applicants must be students of Italian descent; with GPA of 3.0 or higher; and must come from households where the total gross income does not exceed $20, 000 per capita. **Criteria:** Applicants are evaluated based on existence of Italian-American ancestry; academic achievement and school/community service; and financial need.

Funds Avail.: No specific amount. **Duration:** for 4 years. **To Apply:** Applicants must submit letters of recommendation; an essay; academic performance verification form and attachments; financials. **Remarks:** Established in 1994.

3545 ■ Colvin Law Offices

205 S High St.
Winchester, TN 37398
Ph: (931)962-1044
Fax: (931)962-1094
Free: 877-380-3017
URL: www.colvin-law.com

3546 ■ John Colvin Law Award *(Graduate/ Scholarship)*

Purpose: To help students finance their first semester of law school and give them a strong foothold for continuing their law degree. **Focus:** Law. **Qualif.:** Applicants must be U.S. citizens or authorized to work/go to school in the United States; must have a published article in print or digital; must be commencing law school (1L) in August of the current year. **Criteria:** Selection will be based on creativity, originality, and ability to clearly convey a complex message of the submitted article.

Funds Avail.: $1,000. **Duration:** Annual. **Number Awarded:** 1. **To Apply:** Applicants must submit the following; a completed online scholarship application form; a copy of law school acceptance letter; copy of previously published article or link to its online location. **Contact:** jrclaw309@gmail.com.

3547 ■ Colwell Law Group

200 Great Oaks Blvd., Ste. 224
Albany, NY 12203
Ph: (518)213-4204
E-mail: mcolwell@colwell-law.com
URL: colwell-law.org
Social Media: www.facebook.com/finnegan
www.linkedin.com/company/finnegan-henderson-farabow
  -garrett-&-dunner-llp

3548 ■ Colwell Law Group Single Parent Scholarship *(Community College, University, Undergraduate/ Scholarship)*

Purpose: To help children of single parents, or single parents, afford college. **Focus:** General studies/Field of study not specified. **Qualif.:** Applicant must be the child of a single parent or a single parent themselves; be attending an accredited four-year college or university or two-year community college in the fall semester; have a minimum 3.0 GPA; and be a U.S. citizen or permanent resident. **Criteria:** Selection is based on the best essay submitted.

Funds Avail.: $2,000. **Duration:** Annual. **Number Awarded:** 1. **To Apply:** Applicant must submit a current transcript and a 500-word essay explaining how living in a single-parent household has affected their life. **Deadline:** May 31. **Contact:** Kevin Colwell; Email: kcolwell@colwell-law.com; URL: www.colwell-law.org/scholarship/.

3549 ■ Committee of 200 (C200)

980 N Michigan Ave., Ste. 1575
Chicago, IL 60611
Ph: (312)255-0296
Fax: (312)255-0789
E-mail: info@c200.org
URL: www.c200.org
Social Media: www.instagram.com/c200advancingwomen
www.linkedin.com/company/the-committee-of-200
twitter.com/committeeof200

3550 ■ C200 Scholar Awards *(Graduate/Scholarship)*

Purpose: To support outstanding MBA women students for their extraordinary leadership potential, entrepreneurial spirit, and a commitment to giving back and supporting other women. **Focus:** Business. **Qualif.:** Applicants must be women MBA students enrolled in business school host-

Awards are arranged alphabetically below their administering organizations

ing a C200 outreach seminar. **Criteria:** Selections will be based on work experience, GPA, recommendations and essays.

Funds Avail.: Up to $10,000. **Duration:** Annual. **Number Awarded:** Varies. **To Apply:** Applicant must submit a recommendation and essay. **Contact:** Meghan McRae at mmcrae@c200.org.

3551 ■ The Commonwealth Fund
1 E 75th St.
New York, NY 10021
Ph: (212)606-3800
Fax: (212)606-3500
E-mail: info@cmwf.org
URL: www.commonwealthfund.org
Social Media: www.facebook.com/commonwealthfund
www.linkedin.com/company/the-commonwealth-fund
twitter.com/commonwealthfnd

3552 ■ AHCJ Reporting Fellowships on Health Care Performance *(Other/Fellowship)*

Purpose: To pursue a significant reporting project examining health care systems. **Focus:** Health care services. **Qualif.:** Applicants must be health care journalists. **Criteria:** Selection will be based on the committee's criteria.

Duration: Annual. **To Apply:** Applicants must complete application form and other required attachments. **Remarks:** Established in 2010. **Contact:** Barry Scholl, Senior Vice President for Communications and Publishing, The Commonwealth Fund; Email: bas@cmwf.org.

3553 ■ Australian-American Health Policy Fellowships *(Doctorate, Graduate/Fellowship)*

Purpose: To offer a unique opportunity for outstanding, mid-career U.S. health policy researchers and practitioners to spend up to 10 months in Australia. **Focus:** Health care services.

Duration: Annual. **To Apply:** Applicants must complete a formal application including an applicant summary sheet, statement of professional objectives, preliminary research proposal for a policy-oriented research project that fits within the program's priority areas, curriculum vitae, institutional letter of reference from the director of the applicant's institution or organization; two other professional references from senior health policymakers, managers or researchers who can comment on the applicant's past work and potential contributions of their proposed project and samples of up to three published articles or reports. **Remarks:** Established in 2004. **Contact:** Robin Osborn, Vice President and Director, International Health Policy and Practice Innovations, The Commonwealth Fund; Tel: 212-606-3809; Fax: 212-606-3875; Email: ro@cmwf.org.

3554 ■ The Commonwealth Fund Mongan Fellowship in Minority Health Policy *(Other/Fellowship)*

Purpose: To promote a high performing health care system that achieves better access, improved quality, and greater efficiency. **Focus:** General studies/Field of study not specified. **Qualif.:** Applicants must be physicians who have completed residency, either BE/BC in the United States; must have additional experience beyond residency, such as chief residency is preferred; have experience or interest in addressing and improving the health needs of minorities, disadvantaged and vulnerable populations; have strong

evidence of leadership experience or potential, especially as related to community efforts, quality improvements and/or health policy; have an intention to pursue a career in policy, public health practice or academia; and must be U.S. citizens. **Criteria:** Selection will be reviewed for academic and training qualifications; commitment to a multicultural perspective in program planning, program implementation and policy analysis; experience in projects devoted to increasing quality care and access and improving the capacity of the health care system to address health needs of minority, disadvantaged and vulnerable populations; and evidence of leadership potential.

Funds Avail.: No specific amount. **Duration:** Annual. **To Apply:** Applicants must complete the application form, both the Commonwealth Fund/Harvard University Fellowship in Minority Health Policy and the Master of Public Health Program of the Harvard School of Public Health, including application for financial aid at HSPH; for those who already have an MPH degree, applications to both the Commonwealth Fund/Harvard University Fellowship (CFHUF) in Minority Health Policy and the Master of Public Administration Program of the Harvard Kennedy School will be required, including application for financial aid at HKS; once applicants have filled out and submitted all of the required information in the Request for Application Form, they should download the appropriate CFHUF application documents online. **Deadline:** December 2. **Remarks:** Established in 1996. **Contact:** Joan Y. Reede, MD, MPH, MS, MBAJoan Y. Reede, MD, MPH, MS, MBA; Director 164 Longwood Avenue, 2nd floor Boston, MA 02115-5818; Tel: 617-432-2922 Fax: 617-432-3834 E-mail: mfdp_cff@hms.harvard.edu.

3555 ■ Harkness Fellowships in Health Care Policy and Practice *(Doctorate, Graduate/Fellowship)*

Purpose: To provide opportunities for mid-career health services researchers and practitioners from Australia, Canada, Germany, The Netherlands, New Zealand, Norway, Sweden, Switzerland and the United Kingdom. **Focus:** Economics; Health care services; Political science.

Funds Avail.: Up to $130,000. **To Apply:** Applicants must complete a formal application, including: statement of professional objectives, curriculum vitae, five page preliminary proposal for a policy-oriented research project that fits within the fund's national program areas; letter of reference from the department chair or from the director of their institution; three professional references from senior health policy researchers, policymakers or senior level managers who can comment on the applicants' past work and the potential contribution of their proposed project. **Remarks:** Established in 1998. **Contact:** Email: mf@cmwf.org.

3556 ■ Communal Studies Association (CSA)
PO Box 122
Amana, IA 52203
Ph: (319)622-6446
E-mail: info@communalstudies.org
URL: www.communalstudies.org
Social Media: www.facebook.com/Communal-Studies-Association-109993645753235

3557 ■ Communal Studies Association Research Fellowships *(Graduate/Fellowship)*

Purpose: To support research on historic or contemporary intentional communities. **Focus:** General studies/Field of study not specified. **Qualif.:** Applicants must be CSA

Awards are arranged alphabetically below their administering organizations

members in good standing at the time of application and at presentation of the research. **Criteria:** Fellowships will be given to those who meet the qualifications.

Funds Avail.: $1,600. **Duration:** Annual. **To Apply:** Applicants should provide: a curriculum vitae or resume and letters from two relevant references; a two-page description of the overall project, plan, goals, timeline, and how research will be presented at the CSA conference (paper, panel, A/V presentation, performance, exhibition, etc.); a bibliography of intended resources to be consulted during the grant project and a statement that these resources are open to the applicants; and a detailed budget, specifying if funds other than this grant are to be used and their sources. **Deadline:** March 1. **Contact:** CSA at info@communalstudies.org.

3558 ■ Communications Workers of America Canada (CWA)

301-2200 Prince of Wales Dr.
Ottawa, ON, Canada K2E 6Z9
URL: www.cwa-scacanada.ca

3559 ■ Morton Bahr Scholarship *(Undergraduate/Scholarship)*

Purpose: To assist union members and other workers by furthering their educational goals and enhancing educational access through distance learning. **Focus:** General studies/Field of study not specified. **Qualif.:** Applicants must be Union workers, family members and/or domestic partners interested in registering for degree studies with Empire State College; must be individuals pursuing a degree at Empire State College. **Criteria:** Preference will be given to members of the Communications Workers of America. Criteria include an ability to succeed in college studies, a program match with educational and career goals, leadership qualities, financial need and diversity.

Funds Avail.: No specific amount. **Duration:** Annual. **To Apply:** Applicants may download an application form online and must submit all required materials. **Deadline:** May 31. **Contact:** Email: scholarships@esc.edu.

3560 ■ Communities Adolescent Nutrition and Fitness Program (CANFIT)

2140 Shattuck Ave., Ste. 1110
Berkeley, CA 94704
Ph: (510)644-1533
Fax: (510)843-9705
E-mail: info@canfit.org
URL: www.canfit.org
Social Media: www.facebook.com/canfit
twitter.com/canfit
youtube.com/user/CANFitVideo

3561 ■ CANFIT Nutrition, Physical Education and Culinary Arts Scholarships *(Graduate, Undergraduate/Scholarship)*

Purpose: To encourage students to consider careers that will improve adolescent nutrition and fitness. **Focus:** Culinary arts; Education, Physical; Nutrition; Public health. **Criteria:** Selection will be based on the committee's criteria.

Funds Avail.: No specific amount. **Duration:** Annual. **To Apply:** Applicants must submit a completed statement of financial status; two recommendation letters from two

individuals; letter describing academic goals and involvement in community nutrition; a 500-1, 000-word essay; photograph (billfold size or larger); one copy of an official transcript of graduate course work to 12-15 units (for graduate applicants) or official transcripts of all college work to accrue 50 units (for undergraduate applicants). **Deadline:** March 31. **Contact:** CANFIT Scholarships, PO Box 3989, Berkeley, CA, 94703; Phone: 510-644-1533, ext 112; Email: info@canfit.org.

3562 ■ Community Foundation of the Eastern Shore, Inc. (CFES)

1324 Belmont Ave., Ste. 401
Salisbury, MD 21804
Ph: (410)742-9911
Fax: (410)742-6638
E-mail: htrader@cfes.org
URL: cfes.org
Social Media: www.facebook.com/CFEasternShore
www.instagram.com/communityfoundationES
twitter.com/cfesnonprofit

3563 ■ Drew Smith Memorial Scholarship *(Undergraduate/Scholarship)*

Purpose: To assist a turfgrass management student who has a passion for the golf industry, demonstrates drive, determination, and financial need. **Focus:** Turfgrass management. **Qualif.:** Applicants must be adults or graduating public or private high school seniors who are pursuing a degree in golf turf management from an accredited college or university and must be domiciled residents of the Eastern Shore Counties of Maryland and Virginia or the State of Delaware; must also be enrolled in college for a minimum of six credit hours per scholastic year. **Criteria:** Recipients are selected based on academic record, financial need, extracurricular activities or community service.

Funds Avail.: $1,000. **Duration:** Annual. **To Apply:** Applicants must submit a completed application form, Career Goal Information, and two letters of recommendation. **Deadline:** July 14. **Contact:** Drew Smith Memorial Scholarship, PO Box 1607, Ocean Pines, MD, 21811.

3564 ■ Duane V. Puerde Memorial Scholarship Fund *(Undergraduate/Scholarship)*

Purpose: To aid graduating students from Parkside High School in their pursuit of higher education. **Focus:** General studies/Field of study not specified. **Qualif.:** Applicants must be past graduates or current 12th-grade students of Parkside High school who are residents of rural Eastern Wicomico County, Maryland including but not exclusive to the communities of Parsonburg, Pittsville, Powellville, Williards or Melson who have been accepted for admission as full-time college students or vocational school. **Criteria:** Recipients are selected based on academic performance and participation in extracurricular activities.

Funds Avail.: $500. **Duration:** Annual. **To Apply:** Applicants must submit a completed application form, an official high school transcript of grades and two letters of recommendation from non-family members. **Deadline:** April 1. **Contact:** Elaine W. Purdue, Chair, Duane V. Perdue Memorial Scholarship, PO Box 5, Willards, MD, 26874.

3565 ■ Elizabeth Brittingham Pusey Scholarship *(Graduate/Scholarship)*

Purpose: To support those graduating in the public school systems of Wicomico County. **Focus:** General studies/Field

Awards are arranged alphabetically below their administering organizations

of study not specified. **Qualif.:** Applicants must be graduating seniors at any Wicomico County high school who have selected their college and have been accepted for admission as full-time students and are in the top 10% of their class. **Criteria:** Recipients shall be selected based on financial need.

Funds Avail.: $1,500 each. **Duration:** Annual. **Number Awarded:** 3. **To Apply:** Applicants must submit a completed application form, an official transcript of grades ad letter of acceptance from college or university. **Deadline:** April 1. **Contact:** Community Foundation of the Eastern Shore, 1324 Belmont Ave., Ste. 401, Salisbury, MD, 21804; Fax: 410-742-6638; Direct questions, B.J. Summers; Phone: 410-742-9911; Email: summers@cfes.org.

3566 ■ Esther M. Smith Scholarship Fund
(Undergraduate/Scholarship)

Purpose: To support selected students with disabilities from Maryland in their continuing education. **Focus:** General studies/Field of study not specified. **Qualif.:** Applicants must: be graduating seniors with a disability as accepted defined by the Americans with Disabilities Act (ADA) who attended in Wicomico County; be nominated by their school principal, guidance counselor or teacher; have a minimum GPA of 2.0; and, have been accepted for admission as full-time students at an accredited four-year college or university or a two-year education or career training institution.

Funds Avail.: $2,000 for one academic year ($1,000 per semester). **Duration:** Annual. **To Apply:** Applicants must submit completed application form; an official high school transcript of grades; essay; letter of recommendation from non-family members. **Deadline:** April 1. **Contact:** Community Foundation of the Eastern Shore, 1324 Belmont Ave., Ste. 401, Salisbury, MD, 21804.

3567 ■ Federalsburg Rotary Club Scholarship
(Undergraduate/Scholarship)

Purpose: To aid graduates of Colonel Richardson High School for their pursuit of higher education in their respective colleges or universities. **Focus:** General studies/Field of study not specified. **Qualif.:** Applicants must be graduating seniors of Colonel Richardson High School who have selected their college and have been accepted for admission as full-time students; must have 2.5 GPA. **Criteria:** Recipients are selected based on financial need.

Funds Avail.: Minimum of $500. **Duration:** Annual. **To Apply:** Applicants must submit a completed application form; an official high school transcript of grades and letter of acceptance from college or university. **Deadline:** April 1. **Contact:** Community Foundation of the Eastern Shore, 1324 Belmont Ave., Ste. 401, Salisbury, MD, 21804; Fax: 410-742-6638; Direct questions, B.J. Summers; Phone: 410-742-9911; Email: summers@cfes.org.

3568 ■ Green Hill Yacht and Country Club Scholarship *(Undergraduate, High School/Scholarship)*

Purpose: To empower donors to make a profound difference in the quality of life in Maryland's Lower Eastern Shore; to provide community leadership through grants, non-profit support programs, charitable partnerships and local initiatives in Somerset, Wicomico, and Worcester counties. **Focus:** General studies/Field of study not specified.

Funds Avail.: $1,000. **Duration:** Annual. **Number Awarded:** 1. **To Apply:** Applicants must submit a completed application form, an official high school transcript of grades and two letters of recommendation from non-family

member. **Deadline:** April 15. **Contact:** Green Hill Yacht and Country Club, 5471 Whitehaven Rd., Quantico, MD, 21856-2134.

3569 ■ Gruwell Scholarship *(Undergraduate/ Scholarship)*

Purpose: To help students in their pursuance of higher education. **Focus:** General studies/Field of study not specified. **Qualif.:** Applicants must be residents of Lake Forest School District, Kent County, Delaware who have selected their college and have been accepted for admission as full-time students. **Criteria:** Recipients are selected based on financial need, community involvement, academic achievement and extracurricular activities.

Funds Avail.: $500. **Duration:** Annual. **To Apply:** Applicants must submit a completed application form, an official high school transcript of grades and letter of acceptance from college or university; a copy of parent or guardian and student's most recent income tax return; two letters of recommendation from non-family members. **Deadline:** April 1. **Contact:** Community Foundation of the Eastern Shore, 1324 Belmont Ave., Ste. 401, Salisbury, MD, 21804; Fax: 410-742-6638; Direct questions, B.J. Summers; Phone: 410-742-9911; Email: summers@cfes.org.

3570 ■ Hancock Family Snow Hill High School Scholarship *(Graduate/Scholarship)*

Purpose: To support graduating high school seniors from Snow Hill High School in their continuing education. **Focus:** General studies/Field of study not specified. **Qualif.:** Applicants must: be graduating seniors at Snow Hill High School who have been accepted by an Accredited academic college program; have 2.5 GPA in appropriate course work indicating the students are able to be successful at the college level; have three or more year residents of Snow Hill area; be active in school activity, church, community and youth clubs; must have a good moral character. **Criteria:** Recipients are selected based on academic performance, financial need and participation in extracurricular activities.

Funds Avail.: $2,000. **Duration:** Annual. **To Apply:** Applicants must submit a completed application form; an official high school transcript of grades; letter of acceptance from college or university; a copy of parent or guardian and student's most recent income tax return and two letters of recommendation from non-family members. **Deadline:** April 21.

3571 ■ Herb And Ann Fincher Scholarship Fund
(Undergraduate/Scholarship)

Purpose: To support Maryland students who are about to pursue Mathematics or Engineering courses. **Focus:** Engineering; Mathematics and mathematical sciences. **Qualif.:** Applicants must be graduates of the four public high schools in Wicomico County, Maryland (James M. Bennett High, Wicomico High, Parkside High, and Mardela High) who have been accepted into a course of study for either math or engineering. **Criteria:** Recipients shall be selected based on demonstrated maturity and commitment to succeed in college level courses of study.

Funds Avail.: $1,500 per annum. **Duration:** Annual. **To Apply:** Applicants must submit a completed application form, an official high school transcript of grades, letter of acceptance from college or university; two letters of recommendation from non-family members. **Deadline:** April 1. **Contact:** Community Foundation of the Eastern Shore, 1324 Belmont Ave., Ste. 401, Salisbury, MD, 21804; Fax:

Awards are arranged alphabetically below their administering organizations

410-742-6638; Direct questions, B.J. Summers; Phone: 410-742-9911; Email: summers@cfes.org.

3572 ■ Martin S. Kane Memorial Community Service Award Scholarships (Undergraduate/Scholarship)

Purpose: To aid the continuing education of high school seniors from Wicomico High School. **Focus:** General studies/Field of study not specified. **Qualif.:** Applicants must be graduating high school seniors from Wicomico High School. **Criteria:** Recipients are selected based on financial need.

Funds Avail.: $600. **To Apply:** Application can be obtain from Wicomico High School Guidance Office. **Contact:** Community Foundation of the Eastern Shore, at the above address.

3573 ■ M. William and Frances J. Tilghman Scholarship (Undergraduate/Scholarship)

Purpose: To assist the graduates of Wicomico High School or Somerset County Public High School in their pursuance of higher education. **Focus:** General studies/Field of study not specified. **Qualif.:** Applicants must be graduating high school senior students from Wicomico or Somerset County public high school. **Criteria:** Selection shall be based on academic achievement, extracurricular activities and financial need.

Funds Avail.: Minimum of $1,000. **Duration:** Annual. **To Apply:** Applicants must submit a completed application form; an official high school transcript of grades; letter of acceptance from a college or university and two letters of recommendation from non-family members. **Deadline:** April 1. **Contact:** Community Foundation of the Eastern Shore, 1324 Belmont Ave., Ste. 401, Salisbury, MD, 21804; Fax: 410-742-6638; Direct questions, B.J. Summers; Phone: 410-742-9911; Email: summers@cfes.org.

3574 ■ Maryland Building Industry Association, Eastern Shore Chapter Scholarship Fund (Undergraduate, High School/Scholarship)

Purpose: To encourage and support those students who are pursuing a career in architecture, engineering, or a construction related study. **Focus:** Architecture; Construction; Engineering. **Qualif.:** Applicants must be current 12th-grade students of high schools in Eastern Shore of Maryland counties of Kent, Queen Anne's, Caroline, Talbot, Dorchester, Somerset and Worcester who have been accepted for admission as full-time students. They must have a minimum of 2.5 GPA on a 4.0 scale and participated in some extracurricular activities. **Criteria:** Recipients are selected based on academic performance, financial need and extracurricular activities.

Funds Avail.: $500. **Duration:** Annual. **To Apply:** Applicants must submit a completed application form; an official high school transcript of grades; letter of acceptance from college or university; an essay describing the reasons of choosing the career path and two letters of recommendation from non-family members. **Deadline:** April 1. **Contact:** Home Builders Association of Maryland, Eastern Shore Chapter Scholarship, 11825 W. Market Place, Fulton, MD, 20759.

3575 ■ Minority Scholarship Award (Undergraduate/Scholarship)

Purpose: To assist past or current graduating high school senior from Parkside High School in their pursuance of higher education. **Focus:** General studies/Field of study

not specified. **Qualif.:** Applicants must be past graduates or current 12th-grade students of Parkside High School, Wicomico County, Maryland who have been accepted for admission as full-time college students; and have successfully completed a minimum of three advanced placement social studies during the enrollment at Parkside High School. **Criteria:** Selection will be based on committee's criteria.

Funds Avail.: $5,000. **Duration:** Annual. **To Apply:** Applicants must submit a completed application form; official high school transcript of grades; letter of acceptance from college or university; and an essay describing the personal character; three letters of recommendation two from teachers, and one from a non-family member resume. **Deadline:** April 1. **Contact:** Community Foundation of the Eastern Shore, 1324 Belmont Ave., Ste. 401, Salisbury, MD, 21804; Fax: 410-742-6638; Direct questions, B.J. Summers; Phone: 410-742-9911; Email: summers@cfes.org.

3576 ■ Progress Lane Scholarship Fund (Undergraduate/Scholarship)

Purpose: To support the continuing education of high school graduating seniors from Washington High School. **Focus:** General studies/Field of study not specified. **Criteria:** Recipients are selected based on academic performance and financial need.

Funds Avail.: $500. **Duration:** Annual. **To Apply:** Applicants must submit a completed application form; an official high school transcript of grades; a letter of acceptance from college; university or training institute and 250-word essay describing the reasons of wanting to attend college. **Contact:** Community Foundation of the Eastern Shore, 1324 Belmont Ave., Ste. 401, Salisbury, MD, 21804; Fax: 410-742-6638; Direct questions, B.J. Summers; Phone: 410-742-9911; Email: summers@cfes.org.

3577 ■ Richard and Patricia Hazel Minority Scholarship Award (Undergraduate/Scholarship)

Purpose: To support the education of minority students who are about to commit to teaching for two years within the public education systems of Somerset, Wicomico, or Worcester Counties. **Focus:** Education. **Criteria:** Recipients are selected based on financial need, community involvement, academic achievement and extracurricular activities.

Funds Avail.: Up to $2,000. **Duration:** Annual. **To Apply:** Applicants must submit a completed application form; "one-page" describing the reasons of wanting to teach; an official high school transcript of grades; letter of acceptance from college or university and summary of financial assistance from college/university financial aid and office; must also submit a copy of parent/guardian and student's most recent income tax return and two letters of recommendation from non-family members. **Deadline:** May 1. **Contact:** Community Foundation of the Eastern Shore, at the above address.

3578 ■ Lana K. Rinehart Scholarships (Undergraduate/Scholarship)

Purpose: To support the students from Parkside High School who are pursuing higher education. **Focus:** General studies/Field of study not specified. **Qualif.:** Applicants must be graduating senior students at Parkside High School. **Criteria:** Recipients are selected based on academic performance and financial need.

Funds Avail.: $1,000. **To Apply:** Applicants must submit a completed application form. Applications are available from

Awards are arranged alphabetically below their administering organizations

Parkside High School Guidance Office. **Deadline:** May 1. **Contact:** Community Foundation of the Eastern Shore, at the above address.

3579 ■ TFC Edward A. Plank, Jr. Memorial Scholarship *(Undergraduate/Scholarship)*

Purpose: To support those graduating in the public school systems of Maryland in Somerset County. **Focus:** General studies/Field of study not specified. **Qualif.:** Applicants must be graduating seniors from any Somerset County School, and have 3.0 overall GPA.

Funds Avail.: $2,000. **Duration:** Annual. **To Apply:** Applicants must submit a completed application form, a 500-word essay on how crimes or drug abuse have been affected today's society; personal letters of recommendation from two responsible adults other than relatives. **Deadline:** March 31. **Contact:** Community Foundation of the Eastern Shore, 1324 Belmont Ave., Ste. 401, Salisbury, MD, 21804; Fax: 410-742-6638; Direct questions, B.J. Summers; Phone: 410-742-9911; Email: summers@cfes.org.

3580 ■ Wicomico High School Class of '55 Schloarship *(Undergraduate/Scholarship)*

Purpose: To assist the graduates of Wicomico High School in their pursuance of higher education. **Focus:** General studies/Field of study not specified. **Qualif.:** Applicants must: be graduating senior students of Wicomico High School who have spent at least their junior and senior years in that school's program; have selected their college and have been accepted for admission as full-time students; and, have 3.0 cumulative GPA. **Criteria:** Recipients are selected based on community involvement, academic achievement and extracurricular activities.

Funds Avail.: $1,000. **Duration:** Annual. **To Apply:** Applicants must submit a completed application form; an official high school transcript of grades; letter of acceptance from college or university; three letters of recommendation from non-family members; 250 word essay on how they can make a difference. **Contact:** Community Foundation of the Eastern Shore, 1324 Belmont Ave., Ste. 401, Salisbury, MD, 21804; Fax: 410-742-6638; Direct questions, B.J. Summers; Phone: 410-742-9911; Email: summers@cfes.org.

3581 ■ William R. Bowen Scholarship *(Undergraduate/Scholarship)*

Purpose: To assist high school graduating students in their pursuit of continuing education. **Focus:** General studies/Field of study not specified. **Qualif.:** Applicants must be graduating seniors of Snow Hill High School. **Criteria:** Recipients are selected based on academic performance and financial need.

Funds Avail.: $500. **To Apply:** Applicants must submit a completed application form; an official high school transcript of grades; letter of acceptance from college or university; a copy of parent or guardian and student's most recent income tax return and two letters of recommendation from non-family members. **Deadline:** April 1. **Contact:** Community Foundation of the Eastern Shore, 1324 Belmont Ave., Ste. 401, Salisbury, MD, 21804; Fax: 410-742-6638; Direct questions, B.J. Summers; Phone: 410-742-9911; Email: summers@cfes.org.

3582 ■ William T. Burbage Family Memorial Scholarship *(Undergraduate/Scholarship)*

Purpose: To assist high school graduating students in their pursuit of continuing education. **Focus:** General studies/

Field of study not specified. **Qualif.:** Applicants must be graduating seniors of Stephen Decatur High School who have selected their college and have been accepted for admission as full-time students and have 3.0 GPA. **Criteria:** Selection will be based on work experience as a substitute for extracurricular activities.

Funds Avail.: $1,000. **Duration:** Annual. **To Apply:** Applicants must submit a completed application form; an official high school transcript of grades; letter of acceptance from college or university; two letters of recommendation from non-family members; a detailed listing by high school year of activities and an essay explaining how growing up on the Eastern Shore has contributed the individual leadership style. **Contact:** scholarship applications should be directed to: Heather Trader: Htrader@cfes.org or 410-742-9911.

3583 ■ Community Foundation of the Fox River Valley
111 W Downer Pl., Ste. 312
Aurora, IL 60506-6106
Ph: (630)896-7800
Fax: (630)896-7811
E-mail: info@cffrv.org
URL: www.communityfoundationfrv.org
Social Media: www.facebook.com/cffrv
www.linkedin.com/company/community-foundation-of-the
-fox-river-valley
twitter.com/CFFRVfoundation
www.youtube.com/user/CFFRV

3584 ■ Community Foundation of the Fox River Valley Scholarship *(Undergraduate, Graduate, High School/Scholarship)*

Purpose: To enhance and support local students with their continued education. **Focus:** General studies/Field of study not specified. **Qualif.:** Applicants must be students who will attend an accredited institution of higher education within the United States of America on a full-time basis in the current year. **Criteria:** Recipients are selected based on academic ability and financial need.

Funds Avail.: No specific amount. **Duration:** Annual. **Number Awarded:** 1. **To Apply:** Applicants must submit a completed application form. **Remarks:** Established in 1948. **Contact:** Rhonda, Director of Scholarships; Phone: 630-896-7800 x1008 or 331-208-9421; Email: scholarship@cffrv.org.

3585 ■ Community Foundation for Greater Atlanta
191 Peachtree St. NE, Ste. 1000, 10th Fl.
Atlanta, GA 30303
Ph: (404)688-5525
Fax: (404)688-3060
URL: www.cfgreateratlanta.org
Social Media: www.facebook.com/cfgreateratlanta
www.linkedin.com/company/the-community-foundation-for
-greater-atlanta
twitter.com/philanthropyATL
www.youtube.com/user/cfgreateratlanta

3586 ■ George and Pearl Strickland Scholarship Fund *(Graduate, Undergraduate/Scholarship)*

Purpose: To provide financial assistance to undergraduate and graduate students pursuing a degree at Atlanta

Awards are arranged alphabetically below their administering organizations

University Center colleges. **Focus:** General studies/Field of study not specified. **Qualif.:** Applicants must be legal residents of Georgia; must be enrolled or accepted at Clark Atlanta University, Morehouse College, Morehouse School of Medicine or Spelman College; and have a minimum GPA of 2.0. **Criteria:** Recipients will be selected based on demonstrated commitment to community service, potential for success in chosen field and financial need.

Funds Avail.: $1,000 to $2,000. **Duration:** Annual. **Number Awarded:** UP to 30. **Deadline:** February 14. **Contact:** Email: scholarships@cfgreateratlanta.org.

3587 ■ Steve Dearduff Scholarship Fund (Graduate, Undergraduate/Scholarship)

Purpose: To provide financial assistance to undergraduate and graduate students pursuing degrees in medicine and social work. **Focus:** Medicine; Social work. **Criteria:** Recipients will be selected based on submitted documents and financial need.

Funds Avail.: UP to $2,500. **Duration:** Annual. **Number Awarded:** 3. **Deadline:** February 15.

3588 ■ Community Foundation for Greater New Haven

70 Audubon St.
New Haven, CT 06510-9755
Ph: (203)777-2386
Fax: (203)787-6584
E-mail: contactus@cfgnh.org
URL: www.cfgnh.org
Social Media: www.facebook.com/cfgnh
www.linkedin.com/company/community-foundation-for
 -greater-new-haven
twitter.com/cfgnh

3589 ■ Bambi Bailey Scholarship Fund (Undergraduate/Scholarship)

Purpose: To create positive and sustainable change in Greater New Haven by increasing the amount of and enhancing the impact of community philanthropy and to provide college scholarships based on financial need. **Focus:** General studies/Field of study not specified. **Qualif.:** Applicants must be students from New Haven. **Criteria:** Recipients are selected based on financial need.

Remarks: Established in 2001. **Contact:** 70 Audubon StreetNew Haven, CT 06510; Phone: 203-777-2386; E-mail: ContactUs@cfgnh.org.

3590 ■ George J. Bysiewicz Scholarship Fund (Other/Scholarship)

Purpose: To create changes in Greater New Haven by enhancing the impact of community philanthropy. **Focus:** General studies/Field of study not specified. **Qualif.:** Applicants must be students from New Haven, Catholic School planning to attend Sacred Heart Academy and Notre Dame High School. **Criteria:** Recipients are selected based on financial need.

Remarks: Established in 2000. **Contact:** 70 Audubon StreetNew Haven, CT 06510; Phone: 203-777-2386; E-mail: ContactUs@cfgnh.org.

3591 ■ John S. Martinez and Family Scholarship Fund (Undergraduate/Scholarship)

Purpose: To create changes in Greater New Haven by enhancing the impact of community philanthropy. **Focus:**

General studies/Field of study not specified. **Qualif.:** Applicants must be students in an institution or university. **Criteria:** Recipients are selected based on financial need.

Remarks: Established in 2003. **Contact:** 70 Audubon StreetNew Haven, CT 06510; Phone: 203-777-2386; E-mail: ContactUs@cfgnh.org.

3592 ■ Murtha Cullina LLP Scholarship Fund (Undergraduate/Scholarship)

Purpose: To create changes in Greater New Haven by enhancing the impact of community philanthropy. **Focus:** General studies/Field of study not specified. **Qualif.:** Applicants must be students from the greater New Haven area planning to attend a Metropolitan Business Academy. **Criteria:** Recipients are selected based on financial need.

Remarks: Established in 1999. **Contact:** 70 Audubon StreetNew Haven, CT 06510; Phone: 203-777-2386; E-mail: ContactUs@cfgnh.org.

3593 ■ Ruth and Sherman Zudekoff Scholarship Fund (Undergraduate/Scholarship)

Purpose: To create positive and sustainable change in Greater New Haven by increasing the amount of and enhancing the impact of community philanthropy. **Focus:** General studies/Field of study not specified. **Qualif.:** Applicants must be students from Hyde Leadership School. **Criteria:** Recipients are selected based on financial need.

Funds Avail.: No specific amount. **Duration:** Annual. **Remarks:** Established in 2000. **Contact:** 70 Audubon Street-New Haven, CT 06510; Phone: 203-777-2386; E-mail: ContactUs@cfgnh.org.

3594 ■ Curtis M. Saulsbury Scholarship Fund (Undergraduate/Scholarship)

Purpose: To provide young people the opportunity to obtain an education in music. **Focus:** Music. **Qualif.:** Applicants must be graduating from secondary school (James Hillhouse High School) in the region serviced by the community foundation. **Criteria:** Recipients are selected based on financial need.

Number Awarded: 1. **To Apply:** The application process is online. **Remarks:** Established in 2001. **Contact:** 70 Audubon StreetNew Haven, CT 06510; Phone: 203-777-2386; E-mail: ContactUs@cfgnh.org.

3595 ■ Community Foundation of Greene County (CFGC)

108 E High St.,
Waynesburg, PA 15370
Ph: (724)627-2010
Fax: (724)627-2011
E-mail: cfgcpa@gmail.com
URL: www.cfgcpa.org
Social Media: www.facebook.com/cfgcpa

3596 ■ The Thelma S. Hoge Memorial Scholarship (Graduate/Scholarship)

Purpose: To support students of West Greene School District who are pursuing a college education. **Focus:** General studies/Field of study not specified. **Qualif.:** Applicants must be graduating seniors from West Greene school district. Be accepted at a post-secondary, four-year college or university. **Criteria:** Possess a cumulative GPA of at least 3.0.

Awards are arranged alphabetically below their administering organizations

Funds Avail.: $2,000. **Duration:** Annual. **Number Awarded:** 2. **To Apply:** Applications must be submitted to the West Greene High School Guidance office. **Deadline:** April 1.

3597 ■ Renardo A. Matteucci Family Scholarship
(Undergraduate/Scholarship)

Purpose: To provide an annual need-based scholarship to the Jefferson-Morgan High School students. **Focus:** General studies/Field of study not specified. **Qualif.:** Applicants must be graduating students from Jefferson-Morgan High School; must be planning to pursue a Bachelor Degree, an Associate Degree or a Diploma from a trade school; must have a minimum GPA of 2.75. **Criteria:** Applicants are selected based on financial need.

Funds Avail.: $1,000. **Duration:** Annual. **Number Awarded:** 2. **To Apply:** Applicants should submit a copy of their FAFSA, Student Aid Report (including the EFC), verification of their GPA from a guidance counselor, a copy of an official attendance record and copy of any post-secondary acceptance and scholarship award letter(s) along with completed application form. **Deadline:** April 2. **Contact:** The Community Foundation of Greene County, ATTN: Grant Making Committee, PO Box 768, Waynesburg, PA, 15370.

3598 ■ Walter Samek III Memorial Scholarship
(Graduate/Scholarship)

Purpose: To assist graduating senior class members of Carmichaels High School to continue post-secondary education. **Focus:** General studies/Field of study not specified. **Qualif.:** Applicants must be Carmichaels area senior boys or girls who are enrolled in an approved post-secondary college/university; must have a 3.5 GPA or higher. **Criteria:** Recipients are selected based on financial need and community service.

Funds Avail.: No specific amount. **Duration:** Annual. **Number Awarded:** 1. **To Apply:** Applicants must submit online; a copy of the official school transcript. **Deadline:** April 1. **Contact:** Phone: 724-627-2010; Email: cfgcpa@gmail.com.

3599 ■ William H. Davis, Jr. Scholarship
(Undergraduate/Scholarship)

Purpose: To support students attending the Westmoreland County Community College. **Focus:** General studies/Field of study not specified. **Qualif.:** Applicants must be residents of Green County; must be graduating students or previous graduates of any Greene County high school; have made application and be accepted at Westmoreland County Community College. **Criteria:** Recipients are selected based on financial need.

Funds Avail.: Up to $1,000. **Duration:** Annual. **Number Awarded:** 3. **To Apply:** Applicants must these applications must be submitted to the school guidance counselors' office. **Deadline:** April 2, June 1, August 1, or November 1. **Contact:** The Community Foundation of Greene County; Bettie Stammerjohn; phone: 724-627-2010; Email: cfgc@gmail.com.

3600 ■ Community Foundation of Middle Tennessee (CFMT)
3833 Cleghorn Ave., Ste. 400
Nashville, TN 37215-2519
Ph: (615)321-4939
Fax: (615)327-2746
Free: 888-540-5200
E-mail: givingback@cfmt.org
URL: www.cfmt.org
Social Media: www.instagram.com/communityfoundationmidtn
www.linkedin.com/company/the-community-foundation-of-middle-tennessee
twitter.com/CFMT
www.youtube.com/user/CommFoundMidTn

3601 ■ Archie Hartwell Nash Memorial Scholarship Fund *(Graduate, Undergraduate/Scholarship)*

Purpose: To benefit Middle Tennessee State University students who embody his work ethic and commitment to education. **Focus:** General studies/Field of study not specified. **Qualif.:** Applicants must be Middle Tennessee State University sophomores. **Criteria:** Recipients are selected based on academic records, test scores, extracurricular activities, work experience, community involvement, recommendations about leadership and character, merit, financial need.

Funds Avail.: No specific amount. **Number Awarded:** 1. **To Apply:** Applications can be submitted online including two recommendations, one academic and one personal/employment; transcripts and financial information. **Deadline:** March 15. **Remarks:** The scholarship was created by his wife in memory of Archie Nash. Established in 1997. **Contact:** Pat Cole, Scholarship Coordinator; Phone: 615-321-4939, Ext. X116; Email: pcole@cfmt.org.

3602 ■ B. J. Runnels Dean Scholarship Fund
(Undergraduate/Scholarship)

Purpose: To provide financial assistance to students pursuing a specific field of study and who are most in need. **Focus:** General studies/Field of study not specified. **Qualif.:** Applicants must be female and entering the field of ministry. **Criteria:** Recipients are selected based on academic records, test scores, extracurricular activities, work experience, community involvement, recommendations about leadership and character, merit, financial need.

Funds Avail.: No specific amount. **To Apply:** Applications can be submitted online including two recommendations, one academic and one personal/employment; transcripts and financial information. **Deadline:** March 15. **Remarks:** The scholarship was established by Myrte Veach and the many friends of B.J. Dean in memory of B.J. Runnels Dean. Established in 1995. **Contact:** Pat Cole, Scholarship Coordinator; Phone: 615-321-4939, Ext. X116; Email: pcole@cfmt.org.

3603 ■ Barbara Hagan Richards Scholarship Fund
(Undergraduate/Scholarship)

Purpose: To encourage young people to pursue an education, just as she encouraged her own children. **Focus:** General studies/Field of study not specified. **Qualif.:** Applicants must be graduating seniors, undergraduates, and/or graduate students currently enrolled in a college/university and/or alumni of any high school located and serving Giles County, Tennessee; must have GPA of 3.0. **Criteria:** Recipients are selected based on academic records, test scores, extracurricular activities, work experience, community involvement, recommendations about leadership and character, merit, financial need.

Funds Avail.: No specific amount. **Number Awarded:** 2. **To Apply:** Applications can be submitted online including two recommendations, one academic and one personal/employment; transcripts and financial information. **Dead-**

Awards are arranged alphabetically below their administering organizations

line: March 15. **Remarks:** This award established memory of Barbara Hagan Richards. Established in 2001. **Contact:** Pat Cole, Scholarship Coordinator; Phone: 615-321-4939, Ext. X116; Email: pcole@cfmt.org.

3604 ■ Belmont University Commercial Music Showcase Scholarship Fund *(Undergraduate/ Scholarship)*

Purpose: To provide financial assistance to students attending Belmont University who are majoring in a commercial music degree. **Focus:** Music. **Qualif.:** Applicants must attend Belmont University majoring in a commercial music degree.

Funds Avail.: No specific amount. **Deadline:** March 15. **Remarks:** Established in 1998.

3605 ■ Buster Pool Memorial Scholarship Fund *(Undergraduate/Scholarship)*

Purpose: To provide financial assistance to students pursuing a specific field of study and who are most in need. **Focus:** General studies/Field of study not specified. **Qualif.:** Applicants must be graduating seniors of Meridian High School in Meridian, Mississippi. **Criteria:** Recipients are selected based on academic records, test scores, extracurricular activities, work experience, community involvement, recommendations about leadership and character, merit, financial need.

Funds Avail.: No specific amount. **Number Awarded:** 1. **To Apply:** Applications can be submitted online including two recommendations, one academic and one personal/ employment; transcripts and financial information. **Deadline:** March 15. **Remarks:** The scholarship was established in memory of Buster Pool. Established in 2002. **Contact:** Pat Cole, Scholarship Coordinator; Phone: 615-321-4939, Ext. X116; Email: pcole@cfmt.org.

3606 ■ Leigh Carter Scholarship Fund *(Undergraduate/Scholarship)*

Purpose: To provide financial assistance to students pursuing a specific field of study and who are most in need. **Focus:** Health care services. **Qualif.:** Applicants must be full-time students attending one of the nation's accredited chiropractic colleges or universities. **Criteria:** Recipients are selected based on financial need, interest in health care delivery, extracurricular and civic participation; preference will be given to students from Tennessee.

Funds Avail.: No specific amount. **Number Awarded:** 1. **To Apply:** Applications can be submitted online including two recommendations, one academic and one personal/ employment; transcripts and financial information. **Deadline:** March 15. **Remarks:** The scholarship honors Leigh Carter and her passion for learning. Established in 2001. **Contact:** Pat Cole, Scholarship Coordinator; Phone: 615-321-4939, Ext. X116; Email: pcole@cfmt.org.

3607 ■ The Cheatham County Scholarship Fund *(Undergraduate/Scholarship)*

Purpose: To provide financial assistance to students pursuing a specific field of study and who are most in need. **Focus:** General studies/Field of study not specified. **Qualif.:** Applicants must be Cheatham County, Tennessee residents for a minimum period of one year; must have a high school diploma or GED with a GPA of 2.0 or better; must attend an accredited college, university, or technical school and maintain a grade point average of 2.0 or better. **Criteria:** Recipients are selected based on academic

records, test scores, extracurricular activities, work experience, community involvement, recommendations about leadership and character, merit, financial need.

Funds Avail.: No specific amount. **To Apply:** Applications can be submitted online including two recommendations, one academic and one personal/employment; transcripts and financial information. **Deadline:** March 15. **Remarks:** Established in 2002. **Contact:** Pat Cole, Scholarship Coordinator; Phone: 615-321-4939, Ext. X116; Email: pcole@cfmt.org.

3608 ■ Choose Your Future Scholarship Fund *(Undergraduate/Scholarship)*

Purpose: To provide financial assistance to students pursuing a specific field of study and who are most in need. **Focus:** General studies/Field of study not specified. **Qualif.:** Applicants must be graduates of the Metropolitan Nashville Public School of Davidson County with a minimum GPA of 2.5 and a score of 21 on the ACT; must be attending a college or university in the United States. **Criteria:** Recipients are selected based on financial need; preference will be given to students who are the first in their families to attend college.

Funds Avail.: No specific amount. **Number Awarded:** 1. **To Apply:** Applications can be submitted online including two recommendations, one academic and one personal/ employment; transcripts and financial information. **Deadline:** March 15. **Remarks:** Established in 2007. **Contact:** Pat Cole, Scholarship Coordinator; Phone: 615-321-4939, Ext. X116; Email: pcole@cfmt.org.

3609 ■ Cynthia and Alan Baran Fine Arts and Music Scholarship Fund *(Undergraduate/Scholarship)*

Purpose: To provide an opportunity for young people to pursue their passion early in life in the areas of visual arts and music. **Focus:** Art; Music. **Qualif.:** Applicants must be rising sophomores, juniors, seniors in college and graduate students at an accredited college, university, or institute full-time or part-time (six or more credits); and must maintain at least 3.0 GPA or better. **Criteria:** Recipients are selected based on academic records, test scores, extracurricular activities, work experience, community involvement, recommendations about leadership and character, merit, financial need.

Funds Avail.: No specific amount. **To Apply:** Applications can be submitted online including two recommendations, one academic and one personal/employment; transcripts and financial information. **Deadline:** March 15. **Remarks:** Established in 2004. **Contact:** Pat Cole, Scholarship Coordinator; Phone: 615-321-4939, Ext. X116; Email: pcole@cfmt.org.

3610 ■ Colonel Richard M. Dawson Highway Patrol Scholarship Fund *(Undergraduate/Scholarship)*

Purpose: To provide financial assistance to students pursuing a specific field of study and who are most in need. **Focus:** Criminal justice. **Qualif.:** Applicants must be children of employees of the Tennessee Highway Patrol who serve in uniform, undercover, or plainclothes; must be rising sophomores, juniors, or seniors in college who demonstrate a commitment to a career in criminal justice through their course of study. **Criteria:** Recipients are selected based on academic records, test scores, extracurricular activities, work experience, community involvement, recommendations about leadership and character, merit, financial need.

Funds Avail.: No specific amount. **Number Awarded:** 2. **To Apply:** Applications can be submitted online including

Awards are arranged alphabetically below their administering organizations

two recommendations, one academic and one personal/employment; transcripts and financial information. **Deadline:** March 15. **Remarks:** The Scholarship was established by friends and co-workers to honor Colonel Richard Dawson dedication to family, friends and the Tennessee Highway Patrol. Established in 2004. **Contact:** Pat Cole, Scholarship Coordinator; Phone: 615-321-4939, Ext. X116; Email: pcole@cfmt.org.

3611 ■ DBI Scholarship Fund (Undergraduate/Scholarship)

Purpose: To provide financial assistance to students pursuing a specific field of study and who are most in need. **Focus:** General studies/Field of study not specified. **Qualif.:** Applicants must be the children of current employees of Ingram Entertainment Inc. or DBI Beverage Inc. with at least two years of service; must be graduating high school seniors, undergraduates and graduates enrolling or enrolled at an accredited college/university, junior college or technical/vocational school on a full-time basis maintaining a B average or better. **Criteria:** Recipients are selected based on academic records, test scores, extracurricular activities, work experience, community involvement, recommendations about leadership and character, merit, financial need.

Number Awarded: '15. **To Apply:** Applications can be submitted online including two recommendations, one academic and one personal/employment; transcripts and financial information. **Deadline:** March 15. **Remarks:** Established in 2003. **Contact:** Pat Cole, Scholarship Coordinator; Phone: 615-321-4939, Ext. X116; Email: pcole@cfmt.org.

3612 ■ Dr. Mac Scholarship Fund (Undergraduate/Scholarship)

Purpose: To provide financial assistance to students pursuing a specific field of study and who are most in need. **Focus:** Dentistry. **Qualif.:** Applicants must be enrolled at the University of Tennessee at Memphis School of Dentistry and entering their third year of school with a minimum of 2.7 GPA. **Criteria:** Recipients are selected based on academic records, test scores, extracurricular activities, work experience, community involvement, recommendations about leadership and character, merit, financial need.

Funds Avail.: No specific amount. **To Apply:** Applications can be submitted online including two recommendations, one academic and one personal/employment; transcripts and financial information. **Deadline:** March 15. **Remarks:** The scholarship was established to honor Dr. James W. McPherson. Established in 2004. **Contact:** Pat Cole, Scholarship Coordinator; Phone: 615-321-4939, Ext. X116; Email: pcole@cfmt.org.

3613 ■ Dody Boyd Scholarship Fund (Undergraduate/Scholarship)

Purpose: To provide financial assistance to students pursuing a specific field of study and who are most in need. **Focus:** General studies/Field of study not specified. **Qualif.:** Applicants must be seniors graduating from Cheatham County Central High School and wishing to attend a two-year community college/technical school or four-year university; must have GPA of at least 2.5 or better and an ACT score of 20 or better. **Criteria:** Recipients are selected based on academic records, test scores, extracurricular activities, work experience, community involvement, recommendations about leadership and character, merit, financial need.

Funds Avail.: No specific amount. **Number Awarded:** 1. **To Apply:** Applications can be submitted online including two recommendations, one academic and one personal/employment; transcripts and financial information. **Deadline:** March 15. **Remarks:** Established in 2006. **Contact:** Pat Cole, Scholarship Coordinator; Phone: 615-321-4939, Ext. X116; Email: pcole@cfmt.org.

3614 ■ Drue Smith / Society of Professional Journalists' Scholarship Fund (Undergraduate/Scholarship)

Purpose: To provide financial assistance to students pursuing a specific field of study and who are most in need. **Focus:** Journalism. **Qualif.:** Applicants must be college juniors, seniors or graduate students who have graduated from high school in Middle Tennessee and have chosen journalism or broadcast news for a career, or mid-career working journalists who seek training to develop professionally or further their careers. **Criteria:** Recipients are selected based on academic records, test scores, extracurricular activities, work experience, community involvement, recommendations about leadership and character, merit, financial need.

Funds Avail.: No specific amount. **To Apply:** Applications can be submitted online including two recommendations, one academic and one personal/employment; transcripts and financial information. **Deadline:** March 15. **Remarks:** This Fund was established in memory of Drue upon her death in 2001. Established in 2004. **Contact:** Pat Cole, Scholarship Coordinator; Phone: 615-321-4939, Ext. X116; Email: pcole@cfmt.org.

3615 ■ Educational Loan Program for Gay and Lesbian Students (Undergraduate/Loan)

Purpose: To provide financial assistance to students pursuing a specific field of study and who are most in need. **Focus:** General studies/Field of study not specified. **Qualif.:** Applicants must be young men or women whose parents have discontinued financial support for their education because they are gay or lesbian. **Criteria:** Recipients are selected based on academic records, test scores, extracurricular activities, work experience, community involvement, recommendations about leadership and character, merit, financial need.

Funds Avail.: No specific amount. **To Apply:** Applications can be submitted online including two recommendations, one academic and one personal/employment; transcripts and financial information. **Deadline:** March 15. **Remarks:** Established in 1997. **Contact:** Pat Cole, Scholarship Coordinator; Phone: 615-321-4939, Ext. X116; Email: pcole@cfmt.org.

3616 ■ Eloise Pitts O'More Scholarship Fund (Undergraduate/Scholarship)

Purpose: To support the students in interior design, fashion design and merchandising, and graphic design and advertising. **Focus:** Interior design. **Qualif.:** Applicants must attend O'Mara College of Design. **Criteria:** Recipients are selected based on academic records, test scores, extracurricular activities, work experience, community involvement, recommendations about leadership and character, merit, financial need.

Funds Avail.: No specific amount. **To Apply:** Applications can be submitted online including two recommendations, one academic and one personal/employment; transcripts and financial information. **Deadline:** March 15. **Remarks:** The scholarship was established in memory of Eloise

Awards are arranged alphabetically below their administering organizations

O'More. Established in 2001. **Contact:** Pat Cole, Scholarship Coordinator; Phone: 615-321-4939, Ext. X116; Email: pcole@cfmt.org.

3617 ■ Emmett H. Turner Scholarship Fund
(Undergraduate/Scholarship)

Purpose: To provide financial assistance to students pursuing a specific field of study and who are most in need. **Focus:** Criminal justice. **Qualif.:** Applicants must be students enrolling or currently enrolled at Tennessee University in the Criminal Justice program. **Criteria:** Recipients are selected based on academic records, test scores, extracurricular activities, work experience, community involvement, recommendations about leadership and character, merit, financial need.

Funds Avail.: No specific amount. **Number Awarded:** 1. **To Apply:** Applications can be submitted online including two recommendations, one academic and one personal/employment; transcripts and financial information. **Deadline:** March 15. **Remarks:** Established in 2003. **Contact:** Pat Cole, Scholarship Coordinator; Phone: 615-321-4939, Ext. X116; Email: pcole@cfmt.org.

3618 ■ Frank and Charlene Harris Scholarship Fund
(Undergraduate/Scholarship)

Purpose: To provide financial assistance to students pursuing a specific field of study and who are most in need. **Focus:** General studies/Field of study not specified. **Qualif.:** Applicants must be graduating seniors of Cumberland Gap High School in Claiborne County, TN; must have GPA of 3.0 or higher at the time of the application. **Criteria:** Recipients are selected based on academic records, test scores, extracurricular activities, work experience, community involvement, recommendations about leadership and character, merit, financial need.

Funds Avail.: No specific amount. **Number Awarded:** 1. **To Apply:** Applications can be submitted online including two recommendations, one academic and one personal/employment; transcripts and financial information. **Deadline:** March 15. **Remarks:** The scholarship was established by Beth and Greg Cashion, in their loving memory, of Charlene Harris and Frank. Established in 2005. **Contact:** Pat Cole, Scholarship Coordinator; Phone: 615-321-4939, Ext. X116; Email: pcole@cfmt.org.

3619 ■ George Oliver Benton Memorial Scholarship Fund *(Undergraduate/Scholarship)*

Purpose: To provide financial assistance to students pursuing a specific field of study and who are most in need. **Focus:** Government. **Qualif.:** Applicants must be Tennessee's Legislative Interns. **Criteria:** Recipients are selected based on academic records, test scores, extracurricular activities, work experience, community involvement, recommendations about leadership and character, merit, financial need.

Funds Avail.: No specific amount. **To Apply:** Applications can be submitted online including two recommendations, one academic and one personal/employment; transcripts and financial information. **Deadline:** March 15. **Remarks:** This Scholarship is a memorial of George Oliver Benton. Established in 2001. **Contact:** Pat Cole, Scholarship Coordinator; Phone: 615-321-4939, Ext. X116; Email: pcole@cfmt.org.

3620 ■ Diane G. Lowe and John Gomez, IV Scholarship Fund *(Undergraduate/Scholarship)*

Purpose: To financial assistance for students to take qualifying entrance exams to institutions of higher learning, such as the SAT and ACT exams, and to attend academic programs that offer special challenges or accelerated content. **Focus:** General studies/Field of study not specified. **Qualif.:** Applicants must be students with financial need in Grades 6-12 who reside in Rutherford, Cannon, DeKalb, or Wilson Counties; students taking qualifying entrance exams to institutions of higher learning, such as the SAT and ACT exams, and will attend academic programs that offer special challenges or accelerated content.**Criteria:** Recipients are selected based on academic records, test scores, extracurricular activities, work experience, community involvement, recommendations about leadership and character, merit, financial need.

Funds Avail.: No specific amount. **To Apply:** Applications can be submitted online including two recommendations, one academic and one personal/employment; transcripts and financial information. **Deadline:** March 15. **Remarks:** Established to honor Diane G. Lowe and in memory of John Gomez IV. Established in 2006. **Contact:** Pat Cole, Scholarship Coordinator; Phone: 615-321-4939, Ext. X116; Email: pcole@cfmt.org.

3621 ■ Heloise Werthan Kuhn Scholarship Fund
(Undergraduate/Scholarship)

Purpose: To help teen parents develop self-esteem through education or technical training in order to qualify for better jobs. **Focus:** General studies/Field of study not specified. **Qualif.:** Applicants must be pregnant or parenting teens living in the State of Tennessee; must be enrolled or planning to enroll in post-secondary education at an accredited college, university, junior college, technical school, or job training program as a way to increase their job skills and become more employable. **Criteria:** Recipients are selected based on academic records, test scores, extracurricular activities, work experience, community involvement, recommendations about leadership and character, merit, financial need.

Funds Avail.: No specific amount. **To Apply:** Applications can be submitted online including two recommendations, one academic and one personal/employment; transcripts and financial information. **Deadline:** March 15. **Remarks:** Established in 2001. **Contact:** Pat Cole, Scholarship Coordinator; Phone: 615-321-4939, Ext. X116; Email: pcole@cfmt.org.

3622 ■ Howard A. Clark Horticulture Scholarship Fund *(Undergraduate/Scholarship)*

Purpose: To provide financial assistance to students pursuing a specific field of study and who are most in need. **Focus:** Horticulture. **Qualif.:** Applicants must be graduating seniors from Avery County High School, North Carolina attending a two or four-year college to study horticulture or agriculture; and must have at least a 2.5 GPA in high school. **Criteria:** Recipients are selected based on academic records, test scores, extracurricular activities, work experience, community involvement, recommendations about leadership and character, merit, financial need.

Funds Avail.: No specific amount. **Number Awarded:** 1. **To Apply:** Applications can be submitted online including two recommendations, one academic and one personal/employment; transcripts and financial information. **Deadline:** March 15. **Remarks:** The scholarship was created by Howard's family as a testament to Howard A. Clark who spent almost five decades cultivating the earth, learning the lay of it, and growing shrubs and trees of remarkable quality. Established in 2008. **Contact:** Pat Cole, Scholarship Coordinator; Phone: 615-321-4939, Ext. X116; Email: pcole@cfmt.org.

Awards are arranged alphabetically below their administering organizations

3623 ■ Jennifer Ingrum Scholarship Fund
(Undergraduate/Scholarship)

Purpose: To provide financial assistance to students pursuing a specific field of study and who are most in need. **Focus:** General studies/Field of study not specified. **Qualif.:** Applicants must be students of Gallatin High School and Station Camp High School area who qualify academically for college but need financial assistance. **Criteria:** Recipients are selected based on academic records, test scores, extracurricular activities, work experience, community involvement, recommendations about leadership and character, merit, financial need.

Funds Avail.: $2,000. **Duration:** Annual. **Number Awarded:** At least 2. **To Apply:** Applications can be submitted online including two recommendations, one academic and one personal/employment; transcripts and financial information. **Deadline:** March 15. **Remarks:** The scholarship was established to honor a born educator, Jennifer Ingrum. Established in 2005. **Contact:** Pat Cole, Scholarship Coordinator; Phone: 615-321-4939, Ext. X116; Email: pcole@cfmt.org.

3624 ■ Jerry Newson Scholarship Fund
(Undergraduate/Scholarship)

Purpose: To provide financial assistance to students pursuing a specific field of study and who are most in need. **Focus:** General studies/Field of study not specified. **Qualif.:** Applicants must currently reside in Davidson County, Tennessee; must attend a four-year accredited institution of higher education which may be out-of-state; must be pursuing a degree in the social sciences or areas where they will be helping and giving back to their community. **Criteria:** Recipients are selected based on academic records, test scores, extracurricular activities, work experience, community involvement, recommendations about leadership and character, merit, financial need.

Funds Avail.: No specific amount. **Number Awarded:** 2. **To Apply:** Applications can be submitted online including two recommendations, one academic and one personal/employment; transcripts and financial information. **Deadline:** March 15. **Remarks:** The scholarship was established in memory of Jerry Newson Jr. Established in 1997. **Contact:** Pat Cole, Scholarship Coordinator; Phone: 615-321-4939, Ext. X116; Email: pcole@cfmt.org.

3625 ■ Jimmy Edwards Scholarship Fund
(Undergraduate/Scholarship)

Purpose: To provide financial assistance to students pursuing a specific field of study and who are most in need. **Focus:** General studies/Field of study not specified. **Qualif.:** Applicants must be past students or graduates of Donelson High School, Donelson, Tennessee, and any descendants of alumni of Donelson High School. **Criteria:** Recipients are selected based on academic records, test scores, extracurricular activities, work experience, community involvement, recommendations about leadership and character, merit, financial need.

Funds Avail.: No specific amount. **Number Awarded:** 1. **To Apply:** Applications can be submitted online including two recommendations, one academic and one personal/employment; transcripts and financial information. **Deadline:** March 15. **Remarks:** Established in 2001. **Contact:** Pat Cole, Scholarship Coordinator; Phone: 615-321-4939, Ext. X116; Email: pcole@cfmt.org.

3626 ■ John E. Mayfield ABLE Scholarship Fund
(Graduate/Scholarship)

Purpose: To provide financial assistance to students pursuing a specific field of study and who are most in need.

Focus: General studies/Field of study not specified. **Qualif.:** Applicants must be graduating seniors and be participants of the ABLE program; must attend an accredited college, university, junior college, technical school or job training program; individuals who have previously received scholarship assistance are welcome to re-apply. **Criteria:** Recipients are selected based on academic records, test scores, extracurricular activities, work experience, community involvement, recommendations about leadership and character, merit, financial need.

Funds Avail.: No specific amount. **To Apply:** Applications can be submitted online including two recommendations, one academic and one personal/employment; transcripts and financial information. **Deadline:** March 15. **Remarks:** Established in 2002. **Contact:** Pat Cole, Scholarship Coordinator; Phone: 615-321-4939, Ext. X116; Email: pcole@cfmt.org.

3627 ■ Juliann and Joe Maxwell Scholarship Fund for Employees of Tractor Supply *(Undergraduate/Scholarship)*

Purpose: To provide financial assistance to students pursuing a specific field of study and who are most in need. **Focus:** General studies/Field of study not specified. **Qualif.:** Applicants must be high school seniors, college freshmen, sophomores and juniors who are dependent children, including adopted and stepchildren of full or part-time employees of the Tractor Supply Company; employees must have minimum of one year of service with Tractor Supply Company with at least one year of employment.**Criteria:** Recipients are selected based on academic records, test scores, extracurricular activities, work experience, community involvement, recommendations about leadership and character, merit, financial need.

Funds Avail.: No specific amount. **Number Awarded:** 7. **To Apply:** Applications can be submitted online including two recommendations, one academic and one personal/employment; transcripts and financial information. **Deadline:** March 15. **Remarks:** Established in 2006. **Contact:** Pat Cole, Scholarship Coordinator; Phone: 615-321-4939, Ext. X116; Email: pcole@cfmt.org.

3628 ■ Juliann King Maxwell Scholarship Fund for Riverview High School *(Undergraduate, Vocational/Occupational/Scholarship)*

Purpose: To provide financial assistance to students pursuing a specific field of study and who are most in need. **Focus:** General studies/Field of study not specified. **Qualif.:** Applicants must be graduating seniors from Riverview High School in Searcy, Arkansas, or prior recipients of the scholarship, who want to pursue vocational training as well as those pursuing a college degree. **Criteria:** Recipients are selected based on academic records, test scores, extracurricular activities, work experience, community involvement, recommendations about leadership and character, merit, financial need.

Funds Avail.: No specific amount. **Number Awarded:** 12. **To Apply:** Applications can be submitted online including two recommendations, one academic and one personal/employment; transcripts and financial information. **Deadline:** March 15. **Remarks:** Established in 2006. **Contact:** Pat Cole, Scholarship Coordinator; Phone: 615-321-4939, Ext. X116; Email: pcole@cfmt.org.

3629 ■ Kathy D. and Stephen J. Anderson Scholarship Fund *(Undergraduate/Scholarship)*

Purpose: To provide financial assistance to students pursuing a specific field of study and who are most in need.

Awards are arranged alphabetically below their administering organizations

Focus: General studies/Field of study not specified. **Qualif.:** Applicants must be graduate students from a public high school in Williamson County after attending for a minimum of three years; must be good standing as a citizen in the school and community; must have a 3.2 or better GPA, minimum ACT score of 22 or SAT of 1100; must be involved in at least one outside extra-curricular activity (which could include working part-time).**Criteria:** Recipients are selected based on academic records, test scores, extracurricular activities, work experience, community involvement, recommendations about leadership and character, merit, financial need.

Funds Avail.: Up to $10,000 per student. **Duration:** Up to 4 years. **Number Awarded:** 4. **To Apply:** Applications can be submitted online including two recommendations, one academic and one personal/employment; transcripts and financial information. **Deadline:** March 15. **Remarks:** The scholarship was established by Stephen J. Anderson. Established in 2005. **Contact:** Pat Cole, Scholarship Coordinator; Phone: 615-321-4939, Ext. X116; Email: pcole@cfmt.org.

3630 ■ Knox Hume Scholarship Fund
(Undergraduate/Scholarship)

Purpose: To provide financial assistance to students pursuing a specific field of study and who are most in need. **Focus:** General studies/Field of study not specified. **Qualif.:** Applicants must be graduates of Hume-Fogg High School. **Criteria:** Recipients are selected based on academic records, test scores, extracurricular activities, work experience, community involvement, recommendations about leadership and character, merit, financial need.

Funds Avail.: No specific amount. **Number Awarded:** 22. **To Apply:** Applications can be submitted online including two recommendations, one academic and one personal/ employment; transcripts and financial information. **Deadline:** March 15. **Remarks:** Established in 2007. **Contact:** Pat Cole, Scholarship Coordinator; Phone: 615-321-4939, Ext. X116; Email: pcole@cfmt.org.

3631 ■ Mike and Mary Jean Kruse Scholarship Fund *(Graduate, Undergraduate/Scholarship)*

Purpose: To provide financial assistance to students pursuing a specific field of study and who are most in need. **Focus:** Accounting. **Qualif.:** Applicants must be rising juniors, seniors and graduate students majoring in accounting with goals in becoming a Certified Public Accountant; must be residents of Tennessee and attend an accredited college/university in the State of Tennessee; must maintain a minimum GPA of 3.2 or better. **Criteria:** Extra consideration will be given to married students.

Funds Avail.: No specific amount. **Number Awarded:** 2. **To Apply:** Applications can be submitted online including two recommendations, one academic and one personal/ employment; transcripts and financial information. **Deadline:** March 15. **Remarks:** The scholarship was created by friends and colleagues to honor the company founder, Mike Kruse. Established in 2003. **Contact:** Pat Cole, Scholarship Coordinator; Phone: 615-321-4939, Ext. X116; Email: pcole@cfmt.org.

3632 ■ Lt. Holly Adams Memorial Scholarship Fund
(Undergraduate/Scholarship)

Purpose: To provide financial assistance to students pursuing a specific field of study and who are most in need. **Focus:** General studies/Field of study not specified. **Qualif.:** Applicants must be students from the Page High School area in Williamson County who not only achieve, but also possess the integrity, courage and caring spirit to help others achieve. **Criteria:** Recipients are selected based on academic records, test scores, extracurricular activities, work experience, community involvement, recommendations about leadership and character, merit, financial need.

Funds Avail.: No specific amount. **Duration:** Annual. **Number Awarded:** 1. **To Apply:** Applications can be submitted online including two recommendations, one academic and one personal/employment; transcripts and financial information. **Deadline:** March 15. **Remarks:** The scholarship was established in memory of Lt. Holly Adams. Established in 2006. **Contact:** Pat Cole, Scholarship Coordinator; Phone: 615-321-4939, Ext. X116; Email: pcole@cfmt.org.

3633 ■ Edna L. Martin Scholarship Fund
(Undergraduate/Scholarship)

Purpose: To provide financial assistance to students pursuing a specific field of study and who are most in need. **Focus:** Education. **Qualif.:** Applicants must be graduating high school seniors, or individuals who previously graduated from the Davidson County-Metropolitan Nashville Public School System; must have a desire to pursue a career in teaching in elementary, middle or high school. **Criteria:** Recipients are selected based on academic records, test scores, extracurricular activities, work experience, community involvement, recommendations about leadership and character, merit, financial need.

Funds Avail.: No specific amount. **Number Awarded:** 6. **To Apply:** Applications can be submitted online including two recommendations, one academic and one personal/ employment; transcripts and financial information. **Deadline:** March 15. **Remarks:** The scholarship was established to honor Edna Martin. Established in 2004. **Contact:** Pat Cole, Scholarship Coordinator; Phone: 615-321-4939, Ext. X116; Email: pcole@cfmt.org.

3634 ■ Maude Keisling / Cumberland County Extension Homemakers Scholarship Fund
(Undergraduate/Scholarship)

Purpose: To assist students majoring in home economics who pursue degrees in fields of study that will prepare them to work directly with families and children. **Focus:** Ecology; Education; Social work. **Qualif.:** Applicants must be Cumberland County students pursuing degrees in fields of study that will prepare them to work directly with families and children. **Criteria:** Recipients are selected based on academic records, test scores, extracurricular activities, work experience, community involvement, recommendations about leadership and character, merit, financial need.

Funds Avail.: No specific amount. **Number Awarded:** 1. **To Apply:** Applications can be submitted online including two recommendations, one academic and one personal/ employment; transcripts and financial information. **Deadline:** March 15. **Remarks:** This scholarship was established in memory of Maude E. Keisling, former University of Tennessee Extension agent in Cumberland County. Established in 2000. **Contact:** Pat Cole, Scholarship Coordinator; Phone: 615-321-4939, Ext. X116; Email: pcole@cfmt.org.

3635 ■ John E. Mayfield Scholarship Fund for Cheatham County Central High School
(Undergraduate/Scholarship)

Purpose: To provide financial assistance to students pursuing a specific field of study and who are most in need. **Focus:** General studies/Field of study not specified. **Qua-**

Awards are arranged alphabetically below their administering organizations

lif.: Applicants must be alumni and/or graduating seniors of Cheatham County Central High School in Cheatham County, Tennessee; must be residents of Cheatham County and have grade point average of 2.0 or better. **Criteria:** Recipients are selected based on academic records, test scores, extracurricular activities, work experience, community involvement, recommendations about leadership and character, merit, financial need.

Funds Avail.: No specific amount. **Number Awarded:** 1. **To Apply:** Applications can be submitted online including two recommendations, one academic and one personal/employment; transcripts and financial information. **Deadline:** March 15. **Remarks:** Established in 2000. **Contact:** Pat Cole, Scholarship Coordinator; Phone: 615-321-4939, Ext. X116; Email: pcole@cfmt.org.

3636 ■ John E. Mayfield Scholarship Fund for Harpeth High School (Undergraduate/Scholarship)

Purpose: To provide financial assistance to students pursuing a specific field of study and who are most in need. **Focus:** General studies/Field of study not specified. **Qualif.:** Applicants must be alumni and/or graduating seniors of Harpeth High School in Cheatham County, Tennessee; must be residents of Cheatham County and have GPA of 2.0 or better. **Criteria:** Recipients are selected based on academic records, test scores, extracurricular activities, work experience, community involvement, recommendations about leadership and character, merit, financial need.

Funds Avail.: No specific amount. **Number Awarded:** 1. **To Apply:** Applications can be submitted online including two recommendations, one academic and one personal/employment; transcripts and financial information. **Deadline:** March 15. **Remarks:** Established in 2000. **Contact:** Pat Cole, Scholarship Coordinator; Phone: 615-321-4939, Ext. X116; Email: pcole@cfmt.org.

3637 ■ John E. Mayfield Scholarship Fund for Pleasant View Christian High School (Undergraduate/Scholarship)

Purpose: To provide financial assistance to students pursuing a specific field of study and who are most in need. **Focus:** General studies/Field of study not specified. **Qualif.:** Applicants must be alumni and/or graduating seniors of Pleasant View Christian School in Cheatham County, Tennessee; must be residents of Cheatham County and have GPA of 2.0 or better. **Criteria:** Recipients are selected based on academic records, test scores, extracurricular activities, work experience, community involvement, recommendations about leadership and character, merit, financial need.

Funds Avail.: No specific amount. **Number Awarded:** 1. **To Apply:** Applications can be submitted online including two recommendations, one academic and one personal/employment; transcripts and financial information. **Deadline:** March 15. **Remarks:** Established in 2001. **Contact:** Pat Cole, Scholarship Coordinator; Phone: 615-321-4939, Ext. X116; Email: pcole@cfmt.org.

3638 ■ John E. Mayfield Scholarship Fund for Sycamore High School (Undergraduate/Scholarship)

Purpose: To provide financial assistance to students pursuing a specific field of study and who are most in need. **Focus:** General studies/Field of study not specified. **Qualif.:** Applicants must be alumni and/or graduating seniors of Sycamore High School in Cheatham County, Tennessee; must be residents of Cheatham County and have GPA of 2.0 or better. **Criteria:** Recipients are selected based on

academic records, test scores, extracurricular activities, work experience, community involvement, recommendations about leadership and character, merit, financial need.

Funds Avail.: No specific amount. **Number Awarded:** 1. **To Apply:** Applications can be submitted online including two recommendations, one academic and one personal/employment; transcripts and financial information. **Deadline:** March 15. **Remarks:** Established in 2000. **Contact:** Pat Cole, Scholarship Coordinator; Phone: 615-321-4939, Ext. X116; Email: pcole@cfmt.org.

3639 ■ Meyer D. and Dorothy C. Silverman Scholarship Fund (Undergraduate/Scholarship)

Purpose: To provide financial assistance to students pursuing a specific field of study and who are most in need. **Focus:** General studies/Field of study not specified. **Qualif.:** Applicants must be students in Grade 7 to 12 in Oak Ridge Public Schools who are committed in developing their talents as string instrument players but who, otherwise, would be financially unable to take private string instruction. **Criteria:** Recipients are selected based on academic records, test scores, extracurricular activities, work experience, community involvement, recommendations about leadership and character, merit, financial need.

Funds Avail.: No specific amount. **To Apply:** Applications can be submitted online including two recommendations, one academic and one personal/employment; transcripts and financial information. **Deadline:** March 15. **Remarks:** Established in 2007. **Contact:** Pat Cole, Scholarship Coordinator; Phone: 615-321-4939, Ext. X116; Email: pcole@cfmt.org.

3640 ■ JoAhn Brown Nash Memorial Scholarship Fund (Undergraduate/Scholarship)

Purpose: To provide financial assistance to students pursuing a specific field of study and who are most in need. **Focus:** General studies/Field of study not specified. **Qualif.:** Applicants must be female students at Fisk University, entering their junior year, who exemplify outstanding leadership skills, with a GPA of 3.2 or above. **Criteria:** Recipients are selected based on academic records, test scores, extracurricular activities, work experience, community involvement, recommendations about leadership and character, merit, financial need.

Funds Avail.: No specific amount. **Number Awarded:** 1. **To Apply:** Applications can be submitted online including two recommendations, one academic and one personal/employment; transcripts and financial information. **Deadline:** March 15. **Remarks:** The Scholarship was established in honor of JoAhn Brown-Nash. Established in 2002. **Contact:** Pat Cole, Scholarship Coordinator; Phone: 615-321-4939, Ext. X116; Email: pcole@cfmt.org.

3641 ■ Pauline LaFon Gore Scholarship Fund (Undergraduate/Scholarship)

Purpose: To provide financial assistance to students pursuing a specific field of study and who are most in need. **Focus:** General studies/Field of study not specified. **Qualif.:** Applicants must be high school seniors and current college underclassmen who are from Smith County, Tennessee and have lived there for the majority of their pre-college schooling. **Criteria:** Recipients are selected based on academic records, test scores, extracurricular activities, work experience, community involvement, recommendations about leadership and character, merit, financial need.

Funds Avail.: No specific amount. **Number Awarded:** 2. **To Apply:** Applications can be submitted online including

Awards are arranged alphabetically below their administering organizations

two recommendations, one academic and one personal/employment; transcripts and financial information. **Deadline:** March 15. **Remarks:** The scholarship was established in memory of Pauline LaFon Gore. Established in 1998. **Contact:** Pat Cole, Scholarship Coordinator; Phone: 615-321-4939, Ext. X116; Email: pcole@cfmt.org.

3642 ■ Regina Higdon Scholarship *(Undergraduate/Scholarship)*

Purpose: To provide financial assistance to students pursuing a specific field of study and who are most in need. **Focus:** Art. **Qualif.:** Applicants must be graduating eighth graders of Christ the King School and/or former graduates of Christ the King School attending Father Ryan High School or St. Cecilia Academy; must have at least a 2.5 GPA or equivalent; must exhibit a love for the arts. **Criteria:** Recipients are selected based on academic records, test scores, extracurricular activities, work experience, community involvement, recommendations about leadership and character, merit, financial need.

Funds Avail.: No specific amount. **To Apply:** Applications can be submitted online including two recommendations, one academic and one personal/employment; transcripts and financialinformation. **Deadline:** March 15. **Remarks:** The scholarship was created by friends and family in memory of Regina Higdon. Established in 2003. **Contact:** Pat Cole, Scholarship Coordinator; Phone: 615-321-4939, Ext. X116; Email: pcole@cfmt.org.

3643 ■ James Edward "Bill" Richards Scholarships *(Undergraduate/Scholarship)*

Purpose: To provide financial assistance to students pursuing a specific field of study and who are most in need. **Focus:** General studies/Field of study not specified. **Qualif.:** Applicants must be high school seniors, undergraduates or graduate students who have graduated from East High School in Nashville, Tennessee; and must have GPA of at least 3.0. **Criteria:** Recipients are selected based on academic records, test scores, extracurricular activities, work experience, community involvement, recommendations about leadership and character, merit, financial need.

Funds Avail.: No specific amount. **Number Awarded:** 1. **To Apply:** Applications can be submitted online including two recommendations, one academic and one personal/employment; transcripts and financial information. **Deadline:** March 15. **Remarks:** The Scholarship was established in honor of James Richards. Established in 2001. **Contact:** Pat Cole, Scholarship Coordinator; Phone: 615-321-4939, Ext. X116; Email: pcole@cfmt.org.

3644 ■ Senator Carl O. Koella, Jr. Memorial Scholarship Fund *(Undergraduate/Scholarship)*

Purpose: To provide financial assistance to students pursuing a specific field of study and who are most in need. **Focus:** Law. **Qualif.:** Applicants must be from East Tennessee and seeking an internship in the Tennessee State Legislature. **Criteria:** Recipients are selected based on financial need, extracurricular and civic participation; consideration will be given to extracurricular activities in the areas of government and politics.

Funds Avail.: No specific amount. **Number Awarded:** 1. **To Apply:** Applications can be submitted online including two recommendations, one academic and one personal/employment; transcripts and financial information. **Deadline:** March 15. **Remarks:** The scholarship was established in memory of Senator Carl O. Koella. Established in 1999. **Contact:** Pat Cole, Scholarship Coordinator; Phone: 615-

321-4939, Ext. X116; Email: pcole@cfmt.org.

3645 ■ Richie Stevenson Scholarship Fund *(Undergraduate/Scholarship)*

Purpose: To provide financial assistance to students pursuing a specific field of study and who are most in need. **Focus:** General studies/Field of study not specified. **Qualif.:** Applicants must be a graduating senior of Benton Hall School. **Criteria:** Recipients are selected based on academic records, test scores, extracurricular activities, work experience, community involvement, recommendations about leadership and character, merit, financial need.

Funds Avail.: No specific amount. **To Apply:** Applications can be submitted online including two recommendations, one academic and one personal/employment; transcripts and financial information. **Deadline:** March 15. **Remarks:** The Scholarship was established in honor of Richie Stevenson. Established in 2000. **Contact:** Pat Cole, Scholarship Coordinator; Phone: 615-321-4939, Ext. X116; Email: pcole@cfmt.org.

3646 ■ Teddy Wilburn Scholarship Fund *(Undergraduate/Scholarship)*

Purpose: To provide financial assistance to students pursuing a specific field of study and who are most in need. **Focus:** General studies/Field of study not specified. **Qualif.:** Applicants must be students enrolling or currently enrolled at Tennessee State University or Vanderbilt University; must have at least "B" overall GPA during the last two years of high school; must have attended high school within the 40 counties of Middle Tennessee for the majority of high school. **Criteria:** Recipients are selected based on academic records, test scores, extracurricular activities, work experience, community involvement, recommendations about leadership and character, merit, financial need.

Funds Avail.: No specific amount. **Number Awarded:** 15. **To Apply:** Applications can be submitted online including two recommendations, one academic and one personal/employment; transcripts and financial information. **Deadline:** March 15. **Remarks:** Established in 2005. **Contact:** Pat Cole, Scholarship Coordinator; Phone: 615-321-4939, Ext. X116; Email: pcole@cfmt.org.

3647 ■ Tennessee Trucking Foundation Scholarship Fund *(Undergraduate/Scholarship)*

Purpose: To provide financial assistance to students pursuing a specific field of study and who are most in need. **Focus:** General studies/Field of study not specified. **Qualif.:** Applicants must be Tennessee residents who are dependent children, spouses or employees who are members in good standing of the Tennessee Trucking Association; must be entering their junior or senior years at accredited colleges or universities located in the State of Tennessee. **Criteria:** Recipients are selected based on academic records, test scores, extracurricular activities, work experience, community involvement, recommendations about leadership and character, merit, financial need.

Funds Avail.: No specific amount. **Number Awarded:** 8. **To Apply:** Applications can be submitted online including two recommendations, one academic and one personal/employment; transcripts and financial information. **Deadline:** March 15. **Remarks:** Established in 2003. **Contact:** Pat Cole, Scholarship Coordinator; Phone: 615-321-4939, Ext. X116; Email: pcole@cfmt.org.

Awards are arranged alphabetically below their administering organizations

3648 ■ William and Clara Bryan Scholarship Fund
(Undergraduate/Scholarship)

Purpose: To provide financial assistance to students pursuing a specific field of study and who are most in need. **Focus:** General studies/Field of study not specified. **Qualif.:** Applicants must be high school seniors and/or college underclassmen from Giles County. **Criteria:** Recipients are selected based on academic records, test scores, extracurricular activities, work experience, community involvement, recommendations about leadership and character, merit, financial need.

Funds Avail.: No specific amount. **Number Awarded:** 4. **To Apply:** Applications can be submitted online including two recommendations, one academic and one personal/employment; transcripts and financial information. **Deadline:** March 15. **Remarks:** The Scholarship was established in memory of William and Clara Bryan. Established in 1994. **Contact:** Pat Cole, Scholarship Coordinator; Phone: 615-321-4939, Ext. X116; Email: pcole@cfmt.org.

3649 ■ Woman's Club of Nashville Scholarship Endowment Fund *(Undergraduate/Scholarship)*

Purpose: To provide financial assistance to students pursuing a specific field of study and who are most in need. **Focus:** General studies/Field of study not specified. **Qualif.:** Applicants must be women residing in Davidson County, Tennessee; must be graduating high school seniors or high school graduates with a GPA of 3.0 or higher. **Criteria:** Recipients are selected based on leadership, achievement, community involvement, poise, personality, and a sense of personal goals.

Funds Avail.: No specific amount. **Duration:** Annual. **Number Awarded:** 3. **To Apply:** Applications can be submitted online including two recommendations, one academic and one personal/employment; transcripts and financial information. **Deadline:** March 15. **Remarks:** Established in 2001. **Contact:** Pat Cole, Scholarship Coordinator; Phone: 615-321-4939, Ext. X116; Email: pcole@cfmt.org.

3650 ■ John W. Work III Memorial Foundation Scholarship Fund *(Undergraduate/Scholarship)*

Purpose: To provide financial assistance to students pursuing a specific field of study and who are most in need. **Focus:** Music. **Qualif.:** Applicants must be undergraduate juniors, seniors or graduate students pursuing a degree in music at an accredited university, college or institute; must have "B" average and demonstrate potential for excellence in music. **Criteria:** Recipients are selected based on academic records, test scores, extracurricular activities, work experience, community involvement, recommendations about leadership and character, merit, financial need; preference will be given to African Americans.

Funds Avail.: No specific amount. **Number Awarded:** 1. **To Apply:** Applications can be submitted online including two recommendations, one academic and one personal/employment; transcripts and financial information. **Deadline:** March 15. **Remarks:** The Scholarship was established in honor of John W. Work III. Established in 2002. **Contact:** Pat Cole, Scholarship Coordinator; Phone: 615-321-4939, Ext. X116; Email: pcole@cfmt.org.

3651 ■ Community Foundation of Northeast Alabama (CFNEA)
Quintard Towers
1130 Quintard Ave., Ste. 100
Anniston, AL 36201

Ph: (256)231-5160
URL: www.yourcommunityfirst.org
Social Media: www.facebook.com/CFNEA
twitter.com/CFNEA

3652 ■ Cleve Holloway Memorial Scholarship
(Undergraduate/Scholarship)

Purpose: To provide full or supplemental funding for full-time enrolled students at an accredited state college or university within Alabama. **Focus:** General studies/Field of study not specified. **Criteria:** Recipients are selected based on priority will be given to seniors with documented economic need, strong moral character, and promising academic ability.

Duration: Annual. **To Apply:** Applicants must submit a completed application form, transcript of records and an essay describing their personal aspirations, educational or career goals and how this scholarship will help in achieving their career goals. **Deadline:** March 1. **Remarks:** The Scholarship was established in memory of Cleve Holloway by Mrs. Maudine Holloway.

3653 ■ Farley Moody Galbraith Scholarship
(Graduate/Scholarship)

Purpose: To graduating seniors from any accredited public or private high school, including home school. **Focus:** General studies/Field of study not specified. **Criteria:** Priority will be given to seniors with: (1) a minimum grade point average of no less than 3.0; (2) demonstrated financial need; and, (3) good character in both school and society attested by the letters of recommendation.

Duration: Annual. **To Apply:** Applicants must submit a completed application form and an essay describing their personal aspirations, educational or career goals and how this scholarship will help in achieving their career goals. **Deadline:** March 1. **Remarks:** The Scholarship was established in honor of Farley Moody Galbraith.

3654 ■ Whitney Laine Gallahar Memorial Scholarship Fund *(Undergraduate/Scholarship)*

Purpose: To provide supplemental funding for full- or part-time enrolled students at an accredited state college or university within Alabama. **Focus:** General studies/Field of study not specified. **Qualif.:** Applicants must be graduating seniors of Ohatchee High school; must have 2.5 GPA; must be enrolled as a part- or full-time; members of Gallahar family, and all donors and relatives of those donors, who contribute more than two percent of the Fund's assets, are ineligible. **Criteria:** Recipients are selected based on financial need, academic ability, recommendations sighting attributes, team spirit in the classroom, on an athletic field or other extracurricular association, strong character and personal initiative.

To Apply: Applicants must submit a completed application form and an essay describing their personal aspirations, educational or career goals and how this scholarship will help in achieving their career goals. **Deadline:** March 1. **Remarks:** The Scholarship was established in memory of Whitney Laine Gallahar by Whitney's parents, Ricky and Donna; Whitney's brother, Blake; and, grandparents, Travis and Gayle Reaves.

3655 ■ Guin-Stanford Scholarship *(Advanced Professional/Scholarship)*

Purpose: To enhance the quality of life in Calhoun County, Alabama. **Focus:** General studies/Field of study not speci-

Awards are arranged alphabetically below their administering organizations

fied. **Qualif.:** Applicants must have earned a bachelor's degree from an accredited college or university, and must be accepted into the University of Alabama School or Law or College of Education; Applicants applying under the pool of Alabama teachers pursuing masters or doctorate degrees must have a valid Alabama Teaching certificate; Members of the Guin and Stanford families, and all donors and relatives of those donors, who contribute more than two percent of the Fund's assets, are ineligible. **Criteria:** Recipients are selected based on financial need, exhibit civic or community service, illustrate academic ability and strong moral character.

Funds Avail.: No specific amount. **Duration:** Annual. **To Apply:** Applicants must submit a completed application form, letter of enrollment from their religious leader attesting to the applicant's participation in any Christian church or denomination, essay describing applicant's career goals and how their Biblically-founded beliefs and values make them a suitable candidate, concluding the statement with the main reason why the committee should award him or her, the scholarship and two letters of recommendation. **Deadline:** March 1. **Remarks:** The Scholarship was established in honor of Dorace Guin, and Hon. J. Foy Guin, Jr. By the University Church of Christ.

3656 ■ Joseph and Amelia Saks Scholarship
(Undergraduate/Scholarship)

Purpose: To foster educational opportunities for graduates of Saks High School; to provide full or supplemental funding for full-time enrolled students over a four-year period at an accredited college or university within the United States. **Focus:** General studies/Field of study not specified. **Qualif.:** Applicants must be graduating senior students of Saks High School or its successor institution; must have maintained high personal standards and moral character; must be full-time students completing academics aligned with their specific major or degree; members of the Saks family, and all donors and relatives of those donors, who contribute more than two percent of the Fund's assets, are ineligible. **Criteria:** Selection priority will be given to seniors with strong moral character, discernable academic ability, aptitude in mathematics or English, recognized school and community service, and financial need.

Funds Avail.: No specific amount. **Duration:** Annual. **To Apply:** Applicants must submit a completed application form; an essay describing their personal aspirations, educational or career goals and how this scholarship will help in achieving their career goals; a signed letter of acceptance; certified proof of enrollment from an institution and confirmation that the recipient is enrolled; and an official college or university transcript at the end of academic term. **Remarks:** The Scholarship was established in memory of Amelia and Joseph Saks by his parents.

3657 ■ Leslie and Mary Ella Scales Scholarship
(Undergraduate/Scholarship)

Purpose: To recognize the value of higher education and provide support for graduates of Anniston High School. **Focus:** General studies/Field of study not specified. **Criteria:** Recipients are selected based on financial need, may be a full-time or part-time enrolled student.

Duration: Annual. **Remarks:** The Scholarship was established in memory of Mr. and Mrs. Leslie Scales by Dr. and Mrs. James S. Daniel.

3658 ■ E.C. Lloyd and J.C.U. Johnson Scholarship Fund *(Undergraduate/Scholarship)*

Purpose: To provide supplemental funding for full or part-time enrolled students at any accredited two-or-four-year college or university within the United States. **Focus:** General studies/Field of study not specified. **Qualif.:** Applicants must be graduating seniors from any public or private high school including home schools within the Community Foundation of Northeast Alabama service region; Members of the Lloyd and Johnson families, and all donors and relatives of those donors, who contribute more than two percent of the Fund's assets, are ineligible. **Criteria:** Priority will be given to seniors with financial need, discernable academic ability and good character. Preference will be given to applicants who are the first in their family to attend college.

Duration: Annual; for four years. **To Apply:** Applicants must submit a completed application form and an essay describing their personal aspirations, educational or career goals and how this scholarship will help in achieving the career goal. **Deadline:** March 1. **Remarks:** The Scholarship was established in honor of Mrs. Mary Elizabeth Johnson, a retired school teacher.

3659 ■ Gertie S. Lowe Nursing Scholarship Awards
(Undergraduate/Scholarship)

Purpose: To promote and celebrate the nursing profession. **Focus:** Nursing. **Qualif.:** Applicants must be full- or part-time students in the LPN or RN program at Gadsten State Community College. **Criteria:** Recipients are selected based on character, academic ability, school/community service and financial need.

Funds Avail.: No specific amount. **To Apply:** Applicants must submit a completed application form and an essay describing their personal aspirations and contributions to nursing profession.

3660 ■ Melanie and Todd Edmondson Memorial Scholarship *(Undergraduate/Scholarship)*

Purpose: To encourage young people to follow their dreams and to help lessen some of life's challenges. **Focus:** General studies/Field of study not specified. **Qualif.:** Applicants must be graduates of Oxford High School or its successor; must have 3.0 or "B" average; must be actively involved in their community, school and religious activities; must be full or part-time enrolled students at an accredited institution of higher learning in the United States; may be pursuing any field of academic study or technical training; members of the Edmondson family and all relatives of donors who contribute more than two percent of the Fund's assets, are ineligible. **Criteria:** Recipients are selected based on financial need and academic performance.

Duration: Annual. **To Apply:** Applicants must submit a completed application form, transcript of records, an essay describing their personal aspirations, educational or career goals and how this scholarship will help in achieving their career goals. **Remarks:** The Scholarship was established in memory of Melanie and Todd Edmondson by Bobby and Elaine Edmondson.

3661 ■ Reverend John S. Nettles Scholarships
(Undergraduate/Scholarship)

Purpose: To foster hope, self-confidence and ambition in the graduates of Anniston High School. **Focus:** General studies/Field of study not specified. **Qualif.:** Applicants must be graduating seniors from Anniston high School; must have 2.5 GPA or above on a 4.0 scale. **Criteria:** Recipients are selected based on character, academic ability, school, church and community service and financial need.

Funds Avail.: $1,000. **To Apply:** Applicants must submit a completed application form and an essay describing the

Awards are arranged alphabetically below their administering organizations

personal aspirations, educational and career goals. **Deadline:** February 1.

3662 ■ Jean L. Phillips Auburn Scholarship Fund
(Undergraduate/Scholarship)

Purpose: To provide financial resources enabling local students to pursue higher education at Auburn University. **Focus:** General studies/Field of study not specified. **Qualif.:** Applicants must be graduates of an accredited public or private high school within Calhoun County; must be ranked within the top 25% of high school graduating class; members of the Phillips Family, and all donors and relatives of those donors, who contribute more than two percent of the Fund's assets, are ineligible. **Criteria:** Recipients are selected based on financial need, proven academic ability, strong moral character. be recognized for school and community service, show financial need.

Duration: Annual. **To Apply:** Applicants must submit a completed application form and an essay describing their personal aspirations, educational and career goals. **Deadline:** March 1. **Remarks:** The Scholarship was established in honor of Jean L. Phillips, an Auburn University alumni, and resident of Calhoun County has donated assets to establish this scholarship fund due to her gratitude to Auburn University.

3663 ■ Gerald Powell Scholarships *(Undergraduate/Scholarship)*

Purpose: To support tuition assistance for students attending Sacred Heart of Jesus Catholic School in Anniston, Alabama. **Focus:** General studies/Field of study not specified.

Funds Avail.: No specific amount.

3664 ■ Nathan Sparks Memorial Scholarship
(Undergraduate/Scholarship)

Purpose: To provide supplemental funding for full or part-time enrolled students at an accredited college, university or technical institution within the united states. **Focus:** General studies/Field of study not specified. **Qualif.:** Applicants must be graduating seniors of saks high school. **Criteria:** Recipients are selected based on financial need; priority will be given to seniors recommended as a positive role model, mentor, advocate or leader; recognized for character and promoting the betterment of saks high school; noted for having a team spirit in the nathan jackson sparks classroom, on an athletic field or other extracurricular association; and, motivated academically to succeed at an institution of higher learning.

Duration: Annual. **To Apply:** Applicants must submit a completed application form, an essay describing their personal character and two letters of recommendation. **Remarks:** The Scholarship was established in honor of Nathan Jackson Sparks.

3665 ■ Mary Katherine "Kathy" Williamson Scholarship Fund *(Undergraduate/Scholarship)*

Purpose: To provide financial aid to deserving individuals pursuing an associate or bachelor degree in medical field. **Focus:** General studies/Field of study not specified. **Qualif.:** Applicants must be individuals who have a diploma from an any accredited public or private high school or who have earned the General Education Development (GED) certificate; must be residents of Calhoun County; must have a 2.5 overall GPA or better on a 4.0 scale. **Criteria:** Recipients are selected based on financial need, passion

to serve the needs of others, demonstrated academic ability, and community service.

Duration: Annual. **To Apply:** Applicants must submit a completed application form, transcript of records, and an essay describing their aspirations, educational or career goals and how this scholarship will help in achieving their career goals; applications are available to the guidance counselors at schools in Calhoun County or directly from the Community Foundation office or website (www.yourcommunityfirst.org).

3666 ■ Community Foundation of Northern Illinois (CFNIL)
946 N 2nd St.
Rockford, IL 61107
Ph: (815)962-2110
Fax: (815)962-2116
E-mail: info@cfnil.org
URL: www.cfnil.org
Social Media: www.facebook.com/cfnil
www.instagram.com/the_cfnil
twitter.com/The_CFNIL

3667 ■ Ashley E. Ketcher Memorial Scholarship
(Undergraduate/Scholarship)

Purpose: To provide educational funds to support an Auburn High School CAPA student planning to attend an accredited college or university. **Focus:** General studies/Field of study not specified. **Qualif.:** Applicants must be graduating Auburn High School seniors in the CAPA program who have an interest in and prior experience in the performing arts; must have a cumulative GPA of at least 2.5/4.0. **Criteria:** Recipients are selected based on financial need.

Funds Avail.: Varies. **Duration:** Annual. **To Apply:** Applicants must submit a completed application form along with one recommendation from a CAPA teacher and an essay discussing applicant's interest in the performing arts and how applicant overcame adversity in life. **Deadline:** February 1. **Contact:** Sarah Lambert; Phone: 779-210-8207; Email: slambert@cfnil.org.

3668 ■ Richard L. Bernardi Memorial Scholarship
(Undergraduate/Scholarship)

Purpose: To provide educational resources for students pursuing higher education, especially at the community college level. **Focus:** General studies/Field of study not specified. **Qualif.:** Applicants must be attending Rock Valley College in the upcoming year; must have an at least 2.0 GPA; must have a history of involvement in sports, but do not have to necessarily have participated at the high school level. **Criteria:** Recipients are selected based on demonstrated enthusiasm and leadership; preference may be given to applicants who play or have played tennis.

Funds Avail.: Varies. **Duration:** Annual. **To Apply:** Applicants must submit a completed application form along with an essay demonstrating applicant's enthusiasm and leadership, and the role sports have played in their life. **Deadline:** February 1. **Remarks:** The scholarship was established to honor Richard L. Bernardi. **Contact:** ciara stahly Phone: 779-210-8207; Email: csthly@cfnil.org.

3669 ■ Bonnie Sorenson Scudder Memorial Scholarship *(Undergraduate/Scholarship)*

Purpose: To serve the four county area (Boone, Ogle, Stephenson and Winnebago) through philanthropy; to

Awards are arranged alphabetically below their administering organizations

provide leadership in meeting charitable needs and to be a responsible steward to the Foundation's donors and of the Foundation's endowment. **Focus:** Education, Physical. **Qualif.:** Applicant must be a female senior attending Harvard High School; must have exhibited an interest in women's physical education and plan to pursue a degree in women's physical education.

Funds Avail.: Varies. **Duration:** Annual. **To Apply:** The scholarship does not have an online application. **Deadline:** February 1. **Remarks:** The scholarship is in memory of Bonnie Sorenson Scudder. **Contact:** Marcia Miller, Harvard High School, 1103 N Jefferson, Harvard, IL 60033; Questions: Ciara Stahly; Phone: 779-210-8209; Email: cstahly@cfnil.org.

3670 ■ Buster Lindsay Memorial Scholarship
(Undergraduate, High School/Scholarship)

Purpose: To provide educational resources to student athletes from Jefferson High School to assist them in college. **Focus:** General studies/Field of study not specified. **Qualif.:** Applicant must be a graduating senior from Jefferson High Schoo;have participated in high school sports for a minimum of three years (including senior year);have a minimum GPA of 2.5/4.0; and plan to attend a two- or a four-year college or university. **Criteria:** Selection will be based on the committee's criteria.

Funds Avail.: Varies. **Duration:** Annual. **Number Awarded:** 1. **To Apply:** Applicants must submit a completed application form along with an essay demonstrating applicant's past academic or personal achievements, leadership skills, community and school involvement or obstacles overcame in the past. **Deadline:** February 1. **Contact:** Phone: +1 779 210-8209; Email: cstahly@cfnil.org.

3671 ■ Carolyn Wones Recruitment Grant
(Undergraduate/Grant)

Purpose: To provide educational resources for women, and to promote the professional and personal growth of women educators and excellence in education. **Focus:** General studies/Field of study not specified. **Qualif.:** Applicants must be females graduating from a high school within Boone or Winnebago county; must have plans to pursue a degree in secondary teaching; must exhibit academic potential and have participated in a number of high school activities.

Funds Avail.: Varies. **Duration:** Annual. **To Apply:** Applicants must submit a completed application form along with an essay describing applicant's academic potential and high school activities. **Deadline:** February 1. **Contact:** Sarah Lambert; Phone: 779-210-8207; Email: slambert@cfnil.org.

3672 ■ CFNIL Senior Memorial Scholarship
(Undergraduate/Scholarship)

Purpose: To provide educational resources to a high school graduating senior from the Rockford Public School District 205. **Focus:** General studies/Field of study not specified. **Qualif.:** Applicants must be a graduating senior from a Rockford district no. 205 high school and plan to attend a college, university or other post-secondary institution; nominated by your Rockford public high school principal. **Criteria:** Recipients are selected based on academic potential and financial need.

Funds Avail.: Varies. **Duration:** Annual. **To Apply:** Applicants must submit a completed application form along

with an essay demonstrating applicant's past academic or personal achievements, leadership skills, community and school involvement or obstacles overcame in the past. **Deadline:** February 1. **Contact:** Ciara Stahly; Phone: 779-210-8209; Email: cstahly@cfnil.org.

3673 ■ Harry H. and Floy B. Chapin Scholarships
(Undergraduate/Scholarship)

Purpose: To provide scholarships to selected graduating seniors from high schools who do their trading and business regularly in the Durand area. **Focus:** General studies/ Field of study not specified. **Qualif.:** Applicants must be graduating senior students from Durand, Dakota or Pecatonica High school; must rank in top 15% of graduating class; must plan to attend a recognized college or university; must have frequent businesses in Durand.

Funds Avail.: Varies. **Duration:** Annual. **To Apply:** Applicants must submit a completed application form along with an essay demonstrating applicant's frequent businesses in Durand. **Deadline:** February 1. **Remarks:** Established in 1977. **Contact:** Sarah Lambert; Phone: 779-210-8207; Email: slambert@cfnil.org.

3674 ■ Charles Lee Anderson Memorial Scholarship
(Undergraduate/Scholarship)

Purpose: To provide college scholarships to graduates of Rock Valley College and Sycamore High School who plan to pursue a degree in education. **Focus:** Education. **Qualif.:** Applicant must be a graduating Rock Valley College student or graduating senior from Sycamore High School; must be entering college or university to pursue a degree in education; must be demonstrate optimism, determination and love of neighbor as exemplified by Dr. Anderson's life. **Criteria:** Recipients are selected based on demonstrated optimism, determination and love of neighbor.

Funds Avail.: Varies. **Duration:** Annual. **To Apply:** Applicants must submit a completed application form along with contact information for high school academic verifier; cumulative unweighted GPA from second semester of junior year; class rank; list of senior year courses. **Deadline:** February 1. **Contact:** Ciara Stahly, Program Officer; Phone: 779-210-8209; Email: cstahly@cfnil.org.

3675 ■ Community Foundation of Northern Illinois Scholarship *(Undergraduate/Scholarship)*

Purpose: To serve the four county area (Boone, Ogle, Stephenson and Winnebago) through philanthropy; to provide leadership in meeting charitable needs and to be a responsible steward to the Foundation's donors and of the Foundation's endowment. **Focus:** General studies/Field of study not specified. **Qualif.:** Applicant must be a graduating senior from Winnebago County; must have a minimum GPA of 2.75/4.0; and have an EFC of less than 100. **Criteria:** Recipients are selected based on financial need.

Funds Avail.: Varies. **Duration:** Annual. **To Apply:** Applicants must submit a completed application form along with an essay discussing an obstacle that made it especially difficult for the applicant to complete your high school education and how will the experience help to be successful in college and beyond. **Deadline:** February 1. **Contact:** Sarah Lambert; Phone: 779-210-8207; Email: slambert@cfnil.org.

3676 ■ Deborah Jean Rydberg Memorial Scholarship *(Undergraduate/Scholarship)*

Purpose: To provide educational resources for Guilford High School students to pursue their dreams through higher

Awards are arranged alphabetically below their administering organizations

education. **Focus:** General studies/Field of study not specified. **Qualif.:** Applicants must be graduating female senior athletes from Guilford High school who have a minimum GPA of 2.3/4.0 planning to attend college with strong work ethic. **Criteria:** Selection will be past academic or personal achievements, leadership skills, community and school involvement, or obstacles you've overcome.

Funds Avail.: Varies. **Duration:** Annual. **To Apply:** Applicants must submit a completed application form along with an essay demonstrating applicant's past academic or personal achievements, leadership skills, community and school involvement or obstacles overcame in the past. **Deadline:** February 1. **Remarks:** The scholarship was established to honor Deborah Jean Rydberg. **Contact:** Ciara Stahly; Phone: 779-210-8209; Email: cstahly@cfnil.org.

3677 ■ Ernest and Charlene Stachowiak Memorial Scholarship *(Undergraduate/Scholarship)*

Purpose: To provide educational resources for residents in Boone and Winnebago Counties. **Focus:** General studies/Field of study not specified. **Qualif.:** Applicant must be a high school senior in Winnebago and Boone Counties who has been nominated by their high school principal (current college students and non-traditional students may apply without nomination); must have a permanent address in Winnebago or Boone County and GPA of at least 2.5/4.0; must exhibit sincerity, high character, and the ability to overcome obstacles. **Criteria:** Recipients are selected based on financial need.

Funds Avail.: Varies. **Duration:** Annual. **To Apply:** Applicants must submit a completed application form along with an essay demonstrating applicant's financial need, sincerity, high character, and ability to overcome obstacles. **Deadline:** February 1. **Contact:** Ciara Stahly; Phone: (779) 210-8209; Email: cstahly@cfnil.org.

3678 ■ Susan Kay Munson Gilmore Memorial Scholarship *(Undergraduate, Vocational/Occupational, Graduate/Scholarship)*

Purpose: To provide financial support to those students who are pursuing their educational goal. **Focus:** General studies/Field of study not specified. **Qualif.:** Applicants must be a graduating senior from or graduate of Guilford High School or a Mendota Township High School; must have GPA of at least 2.0/4.0; must have financial need; must be pursuing a vocational career. **Criteria:** Recipients are selected based on financial need.

Funds Avail.: Varies. **Duration:** Annual. **Number Awarded:** 2. **To Apply:** Applicants must submit a completed application form along with contact information for high school academic verifier; cumulative unweighted GPA from second semester of junior year; class rank; list of senior year courses. **Deadline:** February 1. **Remarks:** The scholarship was established to honor Susan Munson Gilmore. **Contact:** Ciara Stahly, Program Officer; Phone: 779-210-8209; Email: cstahly@cfnil.org.

3679 ■ Helen R. (Finley) Loescher and Stephen B. Loescher Scholarship *(High School/Scholarship)*

Purpose: To provide educational resources to Freeport High School students who wish to pursue further education in the fine arts. **Focus:** Arts. **Qualif.:** Applicants must be Freeport High School students demonstrating academic achievement, self-motivation and an interest in the arts; must have exhibited artistic talent through participation in the high school arts curriculum; must have plans to pursue

an education in fine arts. **Criteria:** Selection will be based on the committee criteria.

Funds Avail.: Varies. **Duration:** Annual. **To Apply:** The scholarship does not have an online application. **Deadline:** February 1. **Contact:** Ciara Stahly, Call +1 (779) 210-8209, Email:cstahly@cfnil.org.

3680 ■ Amber Huber Memorial Scholarship *(Undergraduate/Scholarship)*

Purpose: To provide educational resources in recognition of a graduating senior at Byron High School who has made a positive contribution to the high school track and/or cheerleading program. **Focus:** General studies/Field of study not specified. **Qualif.:** Applicants must be graduating senior females from Byron High School who have participated in the Byron High School girls track program or Byron High School Cheerleading program for at least three seasons including their senior year; must have a minimum GPA of 2.0/4.0. **Criteria:** Recipients are selected based on past academic or personal achievements, leadership skills, community and school involvement.

Funds Avail.: Varies. **Duration:** Annual; renewable for four years. **Number Awarded:** 1. **To Apply:** Applicants must submit a completed application form along with an essay demonstrating applicant's past academic or personal achievements, leadership skills, community and school involvement or obstacles overcame in the past. **Deadline:** February 1. **Remarks:** The scholarship was established to honor Amber Humer. **Contact:** Ciara Stahly; Phone: 779-210-8209; Email: cstahly@cfnil.org.

3681 ■ International Management Council Scholarship (IMC) *(Undergraduate/Scholarship)*

Purpose: To provide educational resources to Winnebago County high school graduating seniors to pursue a degree in business. **Focus:** Business. **Qualif.:** Applicants must be graduating seniors residing in Winnebago County who are pursuing a degree in business; must have a GPA of at least 3.0 on a 4.0 scale and have been active in community service.

Funds Avail.: Varies. **Duration:** Annual. **Number Awarded:** 1. **To Apply:** Applicants must submit a completed application form along with an essay discussing applicant's involvement in community service. **Deadline:** February 1. **Remarks:** Established in 1970. **Contact:** Ciara Stahly; Phone: 779-210-8209; Email:cstahly@cfnil.org.

3682 ■ John Flynn Memorial Scholarship *(Undergraduate/Scholarship)*

Purpose: To provide educational resources to Pecatonica High School Senior students who are pursuing higher education. **Focus:** General studies/Field of study not specified. **Qualif.:** Applicants must be graduating Pecatonica High School senior students pursuing higher education; must have at least a 2.0 GPA on a 4.0 scale and have been involved in community service.

Funds Avail.: Varies. **Duration:** Annual. **To Apply:** Applicants must submit a completed application form along with an essay demonstrating the applicant's involvement in community service and agricultural background. **Deadline:** February 1. **Remarks:** The scholarship was established in loving memory of John Flynn. **Contact:** Sarah Lambert; Phone: 779-210-8207; Email: slambert@cfnil.org.

3683 ■ Keith Maffioli Scholarship *(Undergraduate/Scholarship)*

Purpose: To provide financial support to those students who are pursuing their educational goal. **Focus:** General

Awards are arranged alphabetically below their administering organizations

studies/Field of study not specified. **Criteria:** Recipients are selected based on financial need.

Funds Avail.: Varies. **Duration:** Annual. **Number Awarded:** 1. **To Apply:** Applicants must submit a completed application form along with an essay demonstrating applicant's past academic or personal achievements, leadership skills, community and school involvement or obstacles overcame in the past. **Deadline:** February 1. **Remarks:** The scholarship was established through a bequest from Flora June Fredine in memory of Keith Maffioli. **Contact:** Ciara Stahly; Phone: (779) 210-8209; Email: cstahly@cfnil.org.

3684 ■ La Voz Latina Scholarship *(Undergraduate/ Scholarship)*

Purpose: To serve the four county area (Boone, Ogle, Stephenson and Winnebago) through philanthropy; to provide leadership in meeting charitable needs and to be a responsible steward to the Foundation's donors and of the Foundation's endowment. **Focus:** Education, Secondary. **Qualif.:** Applicants must be of Hispanic descent and resident of Winnebago, Boone, Stephenson or Jo Daviess Counties; must be classified as a graduating senior by the time award is granted and be enrolled at an accredited college or university in order to receive funds; must maintain a 2.5 scholastic average or equivalent. **Criteria:** Recipients are selected based on academic achievements which indicate a high potential for success in post-secondary education; a level of involvement in school and community activities.

Funds Avail.: Varies. **Duration:** Annual. **To Apply:** Applicants must submit a completed application form along with a description of projected financial needs; at least two letters of recommendation. (3-4 are encouraged). At least one of the letters must be written by a teacher, school counselor or administrator. **Deadline:** January 18. **Contact:** Ciara Stahly; Phone: (779) 210-8209; Email: cstahly@cfnil.org.

3685 ■ Leopold Education Project Scholarship *(Undergraduate/Scholarship)*

Purpose: To provide students the financial assistance they need in pursuing their chosen degree of education. **Focus:** General studies/Field of study not specified. **Qualif.:** Applicants must be graduating high school seniors or high school graduates who are enrolled or planning to enroll in a full-time course of study at an accredited four-year college or university in a natural resources field; must have a GPA of at least 3.0 on a 4.0 scale and have their permanent address in Boone, Cook, Dekalb, DuPage, Kane, Lake, Mchenry, Will or Winnebago counties.

Funds Avail.: Varies. **Duration:** Annual. **To Apply:** The scholarship does not have an online application. **Deadline:** February 15. **Contact:** Jennifer Becker; Phone: 815-544-2677 ext.3.

3686 ■ Margaret T. Craig Community Service Scholarship *(Undergraduate/Scholarship)*

Purpose: To reward, promote and encourage youth to be involved in their community. **Focus:** General studies/Field of study not specified. **Qualif.:** Applicants must be an undergraduate college student of at least freshman status; have a permanent address in Winnebago County; must have completed at least 50 hours of community service while in college; must have a minimum GPA of 2.75/4.0. **Criteria:** Recipients are selected based on financial need, community involvement and a strong commitment to

improving the quality of life for people in their school, community and country.

Funds Avail.: Varies. **Duration:** Annual. **Number Awarded:** 1. **To Apply:** Applicants must submit a completed application form along with an essay discussing community service experience and its impact. **Deadline:** February 1. **Contact:** Ciara Stahly, Call +1 (779) 210-8209, Email:cstahly@cfnil.org.

3687 ■ Mark A. Reid Memorial Scholarship *(Undergraduate/Scholarship)*

Purpose: To provide students the financial assistance they need in pursuing their chosen degree of education. **Focus:** Music. **Qualif.:** Applicants must be a graduating senior at Oregon High School; demonstrate enthusiasm and optimism; have actively participated in music or drama; exhibit leadership in the school and encourage other students; must be actively involved in extracurricular activities.

Funds Avail.: Varies. **Duration:** Annual. **To Apply:** The scholarship does not have an online application. **Deadline:** February 1. **Contact:** Ciara Stahly; Phone:779-210-8209; Email:csahly@cfnil.org.

3688 ■ May-Cassioppi Scholarship *(Undergraduate/ Scholarship)*

Purpose: To provide financial support to those students who are pursuing their educational goal. **Focus:** General studies/Field of study not specified. **Qualif.:** Applicants must be graduating senior swimmers or divers of Guilford High school planning to attend a college, university, junior college, or trade school; must have been on the team for three or more years including their senior year; must exhibit character traits of strength, discipline, leadership, teamwork and loyalty. **Criteria:** Recipients are selected based on financial need.

Funds Avail.: Varies. **Duration:** Annual. **Number Awarded:** 1. **To Apply:** Applicants must submit a completed application form along with an essay demonstrating applicant's past academic or personal achievements, leadership skills, community and school involvement or obstacles overcame in the past. **Deadline:** February 1. **Remarks:** The scholarship was established to honor the coaching careers of Don May and Gene Cassioppi. **Contact:** Sarah Lambert; Phone: 779-210-8207; Email: slambert@cfnil.org.

3689 ■ Paul and Ruth Neidhold Business Scholarship *(Undergraduate/Scholarship)*

Purpose: To provide financial support to those students who are pursuing their educational goal. **Focus:** Business. **Qualif.:** Applicants must be Harvard High School seniors with a minimum GPA of 2.0; must have plans to pursue an education or training in a business field. **Criteria:** Recipients are selected based on financial need.

Funds Avail.: Varies. **Duration:** Annual. **Number Awarded:** 1. **To Apply:** Applicants must submit a completed application form along with an essay demonstrating applicant's past academic or personal achievements, leadership skills, community and school involvement or obstacles overcame in the past. **Deadline:** February 1. **Remarks:** The scholarship was established to honor Paul and Ruth Neidhold. **Contact:** Sarah Lambert; Phone: 779-210-8207; Email: slambert@cfnil.org.

3690 ■ Nettie and Jesse Gorov Scholarship *(Undergraduate/Scholarship)*

Purpose: To provide educational resources to current college students or non-traditional students planning to attend

Awards are arranged alphabetically below their administering organizations

a college or university to pursue a degree. **Focus:** General studies/Field of study not specified. **Qualif.:** Applicants must be a current college student or non-traditional student with a permanent address within Boone, Ogle, Stephenson, or Winnebago County; attend or plans to attend an accredited two or four year school; have an EFC of less than 5, 000. **Criteria:** Recipients are selected based on financial need, character and scholastic achievement.

Funds Avail.: Varies. **Duration:** Annual. **Number Awarded:** 1. **To Apply:** Applicants must submit a completed application form along with an essay demonstrating applicant's character, scholastic achievement, and financial need. **Deadline:** February 1. **Contact:** Ciara Stahly, Program Officer; Phone: 779-210-8209; Email: cstahly@cfnil.org.

3691 ■ Northwest Community Center Scholarship
(Undergraduate/Scholarship)

Purpose: To provide educational resources for program participants and volunteers at the Northwest Community Center in Rockford. **Focus:** General studies/Field of study not specified. **Qualif.:** Applicants must be graduating senior students or graduates from a Rockford high school who have a GPA of at least 2.0; must have plans to attend a college, university or trade school; must have a history of involvement at the Northwest Community Center as either a volunteer or participant; past recipients may reapply. **Criteria:** Recipients are selected based on financial need.

Funds Avail.: Varies. **Duration:** Annual. **To Apply:** Applicants must submit a completed application form along with an essay demonstrating applicant's involvement with the Northwest Community Center. **Deadline:** February 1. **Contact:** Ciara Stahly, Call +1 (779) 210-8209, Email:cstahly@cfnil.org.

3692 ■ Richard J. Schnell Memorial Scholarship
(Postdoctorate/Scholarship)

Purpose: To provide financial support to those students who are pursuing their educational goal. **Focus:** General studies/Field of study not specified. **Qualif.:** Applicants must be enrolled in an American Dental Association accredited dental or dental hygiene program, or a graduate post-doctoral program, for the upcoming school year; must be attending a two- or four-year college or university in the state of Illinois, or the Indiana University School of Dentistry; must show evidence of financial need. **Criteria:** Recipients are selected based on financial need.

Funds Avail.: Varies. **Duration:** Annual. **Deadline:** July 3. **Contact:** Sarah Lambert; Phone: 779-210-8207; Email: slambert@cfnil.org.

3693 ■ Rockford Area Habitat for Humanity College Scholarship *(Undergraduate/Scholarship)*

Purpose: To provide educational resources for the owners and their dependents of homes built by Rockford Area Habitat for Humanity, Inc. **Focus:** General studies/Field of study not specified. **Criteria:** Selection will be based and recipients may re-apply. Vocational training programs are not eligible for the scholarship.

Funds Avail.: Varies. **Duration:** Annual. **Number Awarded:** 1. **To Apply:** Applicants must submit a completed application form along with an essay demonstrating applicant's past academic or personal achievements, leadership skills, community and school involvement or obstacles overcame in the past. **Deadline:** February 1. **Remarks:** Established in 2005. **Contact:** Sarah Lambert;

Phone: 779-210-8207; Email: slambert@cfnil.org.

3694 ■ William Pigott Memorial Scholarship
(Undergraduate/Scholarship)

Purpose: To provide educational resources to individuals pursuing higher education. **Focus:** Engineering. **Qualif.:** Applicants must be graduating senior students from McHenry, Boone or Winnebago county and plan to major in Engineering in post-secondary studies; must have a minimum GPA of 3.2 on4.0 scale.

Funds Avail.: Varies. **Duration:** Annual. **To Apply:** Applicants must submit a completed application form along with an essay demonstrating why the applicant wants to study engineering. **Deadline:** February 1. **Contact:** Sarah Lambert; Phone: 779-210-8207; Email: slambert@cfnil.org.

3695 ■ William R. Durham Drama and Theater Scholarship *(Undergraduate/Scholarship)*

Purpose: To encourage teaching or working professional theater in either acting or the technical aspects of theater. **Focus:** Theater arts. **Qualif.:** Applicants must be high school graduates or graduating seniors having a permanent address within Winnebago or Boone County with a GPA of at least 3.0 on a 4.0 scale; must plan to attend an accredited four-year college or university to obtain an M.A. or B.A.; must intend to teach theater or work professionally as a performer or technician in theater. **Criteria:** Selection will be based on the committee's criteria.

Funds Avail.: Varies. **Duration:** Annual. **To Apply:** Applicants must submit a completed application form along with an essay addressing the applicant's intention as a theater teacher, professional performer, or technician. **Deadline:** February 1. **Contact:** Ciara stahly; Phone: 779-210-8207; Email: cstahly@cfnil.org.

3696 ■ Gary S. Wilmer/RAMI Music Scholarship
(Undergraduate/Scholarship)

Purpose: To provide financial support to those students who are pursuing an education in music. **Focus:** Music. **Criteria:** Committees make recommendations for scholarship awards based on the purpose and specific criteria of each scholarship as established by its donors.

Funds Avail.: Varies. **Duration:** Annual. **To Apply:** Completed application along with two recommendations of which one must be from a music teacher; an essay demonstrating applicant's commitment to continued active involvement in school or community music groups; a recording of a performance identifying the name of the piece and the composer of each recording, especially if the recording was written or improvised by the applicant, indicating which voice or voices in the recording are theirs; going beyond the five minute time period will not be penalized. **Deadline:** February 1. **Remarks:** The scholarship was established to honor the memory and continue the legacy of Gary Wilmer. **Contact:** Sarah Lambert; Phone: 779-210-8207; Email: slambert@cfnil.org.

3697 ■ Women of Today's Manufacturing Scholarship *(Undergraduate/Scholarship)*

Purpose: To provide educational resources to promote the study and development of the many areas of manufacturing technology through scholarships. **Focus:** Manufacturing. **Qualif.:** Applicants must be male or female residents of Ogle, Winnebago, Boone, Stephenson or Rock County who plan to attend a college, university or trade/technical school; must demonstrate how their coursework will impact

Awards are arranged alphabetically below their administering organizations

manufacturing technology in the region; additional funding may be available for students attending Western Illinois University.

Funds Avail.: Varies. **Duration:** Annual. **To Apply:** Applicants must submit a completed application form along with an essay describing how the coursework will impact manufacturing technology in the Northern Illinois region. **Deadline:** February 1. **Contact:** Sarah Lambert; Phone: 779-210-8207; Email: slambert@cfnil.org.

3698 ■ Margaret Wyeth Scholarships
(Undergraduate/Scholarship)

Purpose: To provide financial support to those students who are pursuing their educational goal. **Focus:** General studies/Field of study not specified. **Qualif.:** Applicants must be graduating public high school senior students and residing in Boone, Ogle or Winnebago County; must plan to attend a college or university. **Criteria:** Recipients are selected based on financial need and demonstrated active involvement in social studies organizations, clubs and classes such as student government, political campaigns, social service and community service.

Funds Avail.: No specific amount. **Duration:** Annual. **To Apply:** Applicants must submit a completed application form, verification form, an official transcript in a sealed envelope, two letters of recommendation and a copy of their FAFSA. **Contact:** Laura Schweitzer at 815-926-2110 x17 or lschweitzer@cfnil.org.

3699 ■ Zeta Chapter Memorial Award
(Undergraduate/Award)

Purpose: To provide educational resources for women, and to promote the professional and personal growth of women educators and excellence in education. **Focus:** General studies/Field of study not specified. **Qualif.:** Applicants must be females who are graduating from a public high school within Boone or Winnebago county; must have plans to teach at any level; must exhibit academic potential and have participated in a number of high school activities.

Funds Avail.: Varies. **Duration:** Annual. **Number Awarded:** 1 or 2. **To Apply:** Applicants must submit a completed application form along with an essay describing applicant's potential and high school activities. **Deadline:** February 1. **Contact:** Sarah Lambert; Phone: 779-210-8207; Email: slambert@cfnil.org.

3700 ■ Community Foundation of Prince Edward Island (CFPEI)
119 Queen St., Ste. 102
Charlottetown, PE, Canada C1A 4B3
Ph: (902)892-3440
Fax: (902)892-0880
Free: 800-566-7307
E-mail: info@cfpei.ca
URL: www.cfpei.ca

3701 ■ Architects Association of PEI Scholarship
(Master's, Doctorate, Graduate/Scholarship)

Purpose: To provide financial assistance to qualified individuals who want to pursue their education. **Focus:** Architecture. **Criteria:** Selection will made by external award selection committee.

Funds Avail.: $2,300. **To Apply:** Applicants must complete the application form available online. **Deadline:** May 1.

Remarks: Established in 2004.

3702 ■ Joan Auld Scholarship *(Undergraduate/ Scholarship)*

Purpose: To provide financial assistance to qualified individuals who want to pursue their education. **Focus:** Art; Crafts; Design. **Criteria:** Recipient will be selected based on the scholarship application criteria.

Funds Avail.: $870. **To Apply:** Applicants must complete the application form available online; must provide an outline of the proposed course of study and the name of the institution where they will attend the class; must submit an essay about their background, interest, aims and ambitions; must submit a letter of reference and portfolio demonstrating previous work, samples of craft-related work, sketches, video or pictures; must include written verification of acceptance. **Deadline:** May 1. **Remarks:** The award is established by the Prince Edward Island Crafts Council in honor of Joan Auld. Joan's was as a Craft Development Officer with the PEI Department of Business Development. Established in 2000. **Contact:** 119, Queen st. Charlottetown, PE, C1A 4B3, Phone: 902-892-3440; Fax: 902-892-0880; Email: info@cfpei.ca.

3703 ■ Orin Carver Scholarship *(Undergraduate/ Scholarship)*

Purpose: To provide financial assistance to qualified individuals who want to pursue their education. **Focus:** General studies/Field of study not specified. **Qualif.:** Applicant must be a graduate of a PEI High School with a Grade 12 overall average of 75%; a student entering Holland College or UPEI; demonstrates a high level of excellence and leadership in either athletics, arts, community service or any combination. **Criteria:** Selection will be made by CFPEI Granting Committee.

Funds Avail.: 1,120 Canadian Dollars. **Duration:** Annual. **Number Awarded:** Varies. **To Apply:** Completed application along with personal statement; transcript of marks; two reference letters; confirmation of Acceptance from a Canadian Post-Secondary Institution; certification and authorization must be submitted. **Deadline:** May 1. **Remarks:** The award was established in honor of Orin Carver who served as President of the games. Mr. Carver passed in 2001. Established in 1991. **Contact:** Community Foundation of Prince Edward Island, 119 Queen St., Charlottetown, PE CIA 4B3.

3704 ■ Lorne and Ruby Bonnell Scholarship
(Master's, Graduate/Scholarship)

Purpose: To provide scholarship assistance to qualified individuals who want to pursue their studies. **Focus:** General studies/Field of study not specified. **Qualif.:** Applicants must be a graduating student from UPEI; accepted into a Canadian university for graduate studies in the masters of science field (Chemistry, Physics, Biology). **Criteria:** Recipient will be selected by the selection committee following the guidelines of conditions of eligibility.

Funds Avail.: $1,050. **To Apply:** Applicants must complete the application form available online. **Remarks:** The Scholarship was established by the late Dr. Lorne and Ruby Bonnell for a student pursuing a Master's degree of Science. Established in 2000. **Contact:** 119, Queen st. Charlottetown, PE, C1A 4B3, Phone: 902-892-3440; Fax: 902-892-0880; Email: info@cfpei.ca.

3705 ■ Lowell Phillips Scholarship *(Undergraduate/ Scholarship)*

Purpose: To provide financial assistance to qualified individuals who want to pursue their education. **Focus:**

Awards are arranged alphabetically below their administering organizations

General studies/Field of study not specified. **Qualif.:** Applicants must be a student with a defined physical disability; a resident of PEI; enrolled in a post-secondary school. **Criteria:** Selection will made by CFPEI Granting Committee based on effort and dedication to academic studies; financial need.

Funds Avail.: $800. **To Apply:** Applicant must complete the application form available online; must submit a copy of their final grades; must have a brief description of their physical disability and what they hope to gain from their studies; must have a letter of acceptance for the next year's study. **Deadline:** May 1. **Remarks:** The Scholarship was created by friends and associates of Lowell Phillips to honor and celebrate how Mr. Phillips faced adversity. Established in 1989.

3706 ■ Summerside-Natick International Friendship Hockey Fund *(Undergraduate/Scholarship)*

Purpose: To provide financial assistance to qualified individuals who want to pursue their education. **Focus:** General studies/Field of study not specified. **Criteria:** Selection will made by CFPEI Granting Committee; preference will be given to the individuals who have played with the Summerside Area Minor Hockey Association; demonstrate a financial need.

Funds Avail.: $520. **Duration:** Annual. **Number Awarded:** 2. **To Apply:** Applicants must complete the application form available online. **Deadline:** May 1. **Remarks:** Established in 2001.

3707 ■ Community Foundation of Sarasota County

2635 Fruitville Rd.
Sarasota, FL 34237
Ph: (941)955-3000
Fax: (941)952-1951
E-mail: info@cfsarasota.org
URL: www.cfsarasota.org
Social Media: www.facebook.com/
   CommunityFoundationSarasotaCounty
www.instagram.com/cfsarasota
www.linkedin.com/company/community-foundation-of
   -sarasota-county
twitter.com/CFSarasota

3708 ■ Emily and Roland Abraham Educational Fund *(Undergraduate/Scholarship)*

Purpose: To help students pursue a college degree or vocational training. **Focus:** General studies/Field of study not specified. **Qualif.:** Applicants must be seniors graduating from public high school in Charlotte, Manatee or Sarasota Counties; must have a 3.2 GPA or higher. **Criteria:** Selection will be based on financial need, leadership potential, academic performance, work experience, and commitment to school and community through volunteerism.

Funds Avail.: No specific amount. **To Apply:** Applicants must complete the application form and must submit all required documents including essay, supporting documents and copy of student aid report. **Remarks:** The scholarship was established by Roland Abraham to honor the memory of his late wife, Emily. **Contact:** Earl Young, Manager, Scholarships and Special Initiatives; 2635 Fruitville Rd., Sarasota, FL, 34237; Phone: 941-955-3000; Fax: 941-952-1951.

3709 ■ The ABWA Sunrise Chapter Scholarship Fund *(Undergraduate, Vocational/Occupational/Scholarship)*

Purpose: To provide financial assistance to needy individuals to attend an accredited college or university. **Focus:** Business. **Qualif.:** Applicants must be female students with 3.0 unweighted high school GPA and must be of good character and have a career goal related to their college or university studies; must be residents of Manatee or Sarasota Counties. **Criteria:** Recipients are selected based on financial need.

Funds Avail.: No specific amount. **To Apply:** Applicants must complete the application form and must submit all required documents including essay, supporting documents and copy of student aid report. **Remarks:** Established in 2003.

3710 ■ The byourself Scholarship Fund *(Undergraduate, Vocational/Occupational/Scholarship)*

Purpose: To provide financial assistance to students who are pursuing their educational goal. **Focus:** Nursing. **Qualif.:** Applicants must be adult learners, men or women in Sarasota County pursuing RN, LPN, or CNA; must be accepted into the nursing programs at Manatee Community College or Sarasota County Technical Institute; and must maintain a 2.8 GPA. **Criteria:** Recipients are selected based on financial need.

Funds Avail.: No specific amount. **To Apply:** Applicants must complete the application form and must submit all required documents including official college transcript; copy of resume; student aid report; one letter of reference; copy of student's financial aid package or financial aid rejection letter. **Remarks:** Established in 2002.

3711 ■ The Davis Educational Fund *(Undergraduate, Vocational/Occupational/Scholarship)*

Purpose: To help students obtain a college degree or vocational training to pursue a career in nursing or the medical field. **Focus:** Education, Medical. **Qualif.:** Applicants must be adult learners, men and women, who are residents of Sarasota County. **Criteria:** Recipients are selected based on financial need and on their educational objectives that will lead to a career in the health care field.

Funds Avail.: No specific amount. **To Apply:** Applicants must complete the application form and must submit all required documents including official college transcript; copy of resume; student aid report; one letter of reference; copy of student's financial aid package or financial aid rejection letter.

3712 ■ The Father Connie Dougherty Scholarship Fund *(Undergraduate, Vocational/Occupational/Scholarship)*

Purpose: To support students to attend a college, university, or institution of higher learning including education in advanced vocational training. **Focus:** General studies/Field of study not specified. **Qualif.:** Applicants must be high school seniors and recent graduates of Sarasota County; must be under the age of 24. **Criteria:** Recipients are selected based on financial need.

Funds Avail.: No specific amount. **To Apply:** Applicants must complete the application form and must submit all required documents including essay, supporting documents and copy of student aid report.

Awards are arranged alphabetically below their administering organizations

3713 ■ James Franklin and Dorothy J. Warnell Scholarship Fund *(Undergraduate, Vocational/Occupational/Scholarship)*

Purpose: To provide financial assistance to students who are pursuing their educational goal. **Focus:** General studies/Field of study not specified. **Qualif.:** Applicants must be residents of Sarasota County for post high school education. **Criteria:** Recipients are selected based on financial need and on their educational objectives.

Funds Avail.: No specific amount. **To Apply:** Applicants must complete the application form and must submit all required documents including official college transcript; copy of resume; student aid report; one letter of reference; copy of student's financial aid package or financial aid rejection letter. **Remarks:** Established in 2003.

3714 ■ The George W. and Ethel B. Hoefler Fund *(Undergraduate/Scholarship)*

Purpose: To provide educational assistance to students who wish to study again. **Focus:** General studies/Field of study not specified. **Qualif.:** Applicants must be adult learners who are Sarasota County residents. **Criteria:** Recipients will be selected on the basis of financial need and demonstrated aptitude and seriousness of purpose.

Funds Avail.: No specific amount. **To Apply:** Applicants must complete the application form and must submit all required documents including official college transcript; copy of resume; student aid report; one letter of reference; copy of student's financial aid package or financial aid rejection letter. **Remarks:** Established in 2009. **Contact:** 2635 Fruitville Rd., Sarasota, FL, 34237; Phone: 941-955-3000; Fax: 941-952-1951; E-mail: info@cfsarasota.org.

3715 ■ Helen F. "Jerri" Rand Memorial Scholarships *(Undergraduate, Vocational/Occupational/Scholarship)*

Purpose: To provide financial assistance to students who are pursuing their educational goal. **Focus:** Cosmetology. **Qualif.:** Applicants must be adult learners who are accepted to any accredited beauty school in Sarasota County pursuing a professional certificate in hairdressing. **Criteria:** Recipients are selected based on financial need.

Funds Avail.: No specific amount. **To Apply:** Applicants must complete the application form and must submit all required documents including official college transcript; copy of resume; student aid report; one letter of reference; copy of student's financial aid package or financial aid rejection letter. **Remarks:** The scholarship was honor the memory of The Helen F. "Jerri" Rand. Established in 2006.

3716 ■ Community Foundation for Southeast Michigan

333 W Fort St., Ste. 2010
Detroit, MI 48226-3134
Ph: (313)961-6675
Fax: (313)961-2886
URL: www.cfsem.org
Social Media: www.facebook.com/cfsem
www.linkedin.com/company/cfsoutheastmi/?originalSubdomain=in
www.pinterest.com/cfsem
twitter.com/cfsem
www.youtube.com/channel/
   UCrhCRFjcPJUdnAm4ZXzSHxg

3717 ■ Chris M. Kurzweil Scholarship *(Undergraduate/Scholarship)*

Purpose: To assist the legal dependents of employees of Intertape Polymer Group in pursuing a program of undergraduate education. **Focus:** General studies/Field of study not specified. **Qualif.:** Applicants must be the son or daughter of a current employee of Intertape Polymer Group (Marysville, Michigan) who is in good standing and has been employed for at least three years. **Criteria:** Recipients will be selected based on their: strong scholastic performance; leadership qualities in school, extracurricular activities and community involvement; and, class rank.

Funds Avail.: $1,000 each. **Duration:** Annual. **Number Awarded:** 2. **To Apply:** Applicants must submit the completed online application form. **Remarks:** The scholarship was established by Mr. Chris M. Kurzweil, former Chief Executive Officer of American Tape. **Contact:** Phone: 313-961-6675 Email: scholarships@cfsem.org.

3718 ■ Dick Depaolis Memorial Scholarship *(Undergraduate/Scholarship)*

Purpose: To provide educational scholarship support to scholar-athletes who are graduates of North Farmington High School. **Focus:** General studies/Field of study not specified. **Criteria:** Recipients will be evaluated based on their academic records, recommendations, statement of goals and financial need.

Funds Avail.: No specific amount. **Duration:** Annual. **To Apply:** Applicants must submit the completed online application form. **Deadline:** March 24. **Remarks:** The scholarship was established in Honor of Dick DePaolis by his family. Established in 2004. **Contact:** Phone: 313-961-6675 Email: scholarships@cfsem.org.

3719 ■ Detroit Economic Club Scholarship *(Undergraduate/Scholarship)*

Purpose: To assist students from Detroit and Macomb, Oakland, and Wayne counties in pursuing a program of undergraduate education. **Focus:** General studies/Field of study not specified. **Qualif.:** Applicants must be graduates of any high school located in the City of Detroit, or Wayne, Oakland, or Macomb counties and entering their first year of college in the fall. **Criteria:** Recipients will be selected based on their demonstrate financial need, extra-curricular activities, service in the school and the community, volunteer involvement and paid work experience.

Funds Avail.: $2,000 each. **Duration:** Annual. **Number Awarded:** 2. **To Apply:** Applicants must complete and submit online application. **Deadline:** March 15. **Contact:** Phone: 313-961-6675 Email: scholarships@cfsem.org.

3720 ■ Robert Holmes Scholarship *(Undergraduate/Scholarship)*

Purpose: To assist the legal dependents of Michigan Teamsters in pursuing a program of undergraduate education. **Focus:** General studies/Field of study not specified. **Qualif.:** Applicants must be entering their first year of college in the fall and be legal dependents of members of Michigan locals of the International Brotherhood of Teamsters; members must be active or have been placed on a seniority list. **Criteria:** Recipients will be selected based on their: strong scholastic performance while in high school; class rank; and demonstrated qualities of leadership in school, extracurricular activities and community involvement.

Funds Avail.: $1,000 each. **Duration:** Annual. **Number Awarded:** 6. **To Apply:** Applicants must submit the

Awards are arranged alphabetically below their administering organizations

completed online application form. **Deadline:** March15. **Contact:** Phone: 313-961-6675 Email: scholarships@cfsem.org.

3721 ■ Detroit Tigers Willie Horton Scholarship
(Undergraduate/Scholarship)

Purpose: To provide educational scholarship support to the graduates of Detroit Collegiate Preparatory High School at Northwestern. **Focus:** General studies/Field of study not specified. **Qualif.:** Applicants must be graduating seniors at Northwestern High School in Detroit; have applied or have been accepted as full-time students in an accredited educational institution in the United States. **Criteria:** Applicants will be evaluated based on their demonstrate exemplary desire, ability and good grades; demonstrate leadership and character through extracurricular activities, volunteer involvement and work experience in school and the community.

Funds Avail.: No specific amount. **Duration:** Annual. **Number Awarded:** 1. **To Apply:** Applicants must submit a complete application form including the following: official academic transcript at the end of their year of award. **Deadline:** March 15. **Remarks:** The Detroit Tigers established the Detroit Tigers Willie Horton Scholarship to honor the on field and civic contributions of hometown hero, Willie Horton. Established in 2000. **Contact:** Phone: 313-961-6675 Email: scholarships@cfsem.org.

3722 ■ Imelda *(Graduate, High School/Scholarship)*

Purpose: To provide educational scholarship support to scholar-athletes who graduate of Fowlerville High School. **Focus:** Chemistry; Engineering, Electrical; Engineering, Mechanical; Physics. **Qualif.:** Applicants must be Employees of the Foundation, members of the Board of Trustees of the Foundation as well as dependents of employees of Fowlerville High School, dependents of the Fowlerville School District and dependents of the scholarship selection committee are ineligible for scholarship consideration. **Criteria:** Applicants will be evaluated based on their leadership and character through extracurricular activities, volunteer involvement and work experience in school and in the community.

Funds Avail.: No specific amount. **Duration:** Annual. **To Apply:** Applicants must Get the Scholarship Application Form from the Counseling Office at Fowlerville High School. Complete the Scholarship Application Form and submit it to the Counseling Office at Fowlerville High School. Your signed personal statement about those who have influenced you and your educational and career goals is crucial. Remember to include it with your application with your printed name and signature. release of your official copy of your high school transcript to the scholarship committee. Request that one of your teachers complete the Recommendation Form. **Deadline:** March 15. **Remarks:** The scholarship was established by Imelda and Ralph LeMar to support student who graduate from Fowlerville public schools. Established in 2000. **Contact:** Community Foundation for Southeast Michigan at (313) 961-6675 or scholarships@cfsem.org.

3723 ■ Jean and Tom Rosenthal Scholarship Program *(Undergraduate/Scholarship)*

Purpose: To provide educational scholarship support to graduates of Pontiac High School. **Focus:** General studies/Field of study not specified. **Qualif.:** Applicants must be members of the graduating class at Pontiac Northern High School or Pontiac Central High School; must enroll full-time at a non-profit or state supported two- or four-year college or university in the United States. recipient withdraws from the educational institution, the award will be cancelled and the unspent portion will be returned to the Community Foundation. **Criteria:** Applicants will be evaluated based on their desire, ability, and good grades; demonstrate leadership and character through dedicated community service; financial need; participation and leadership in school activities and extracurricular involvement.

Funds Avail.: No specific amount. **Duration:** Annual. **To Apply:** Applicants must submit the completed online application form. **Deadline:** March 15. **Contact:** Phone: 313-961-6675 Email: scholarships@cfsem.org.

3724 ■ Jeptha Wade Schureman Scholarship Program *(Undergraduate/Scholarship)*

Purpose: To provide financial assistance to students of Southeast Michigan region for their education. **Focus:** Dentistry; Law; Medicine; Nursing. **Qualif.:** Applicants must be residents of Wayne, Oakland, Macomb, Lenawee, Monroe, Livingston, Washtenaw, or St. Clair counties at the time of high school graduation; must demonstrate strong scholastic performance while in high school or college with an equivalent of a 3.0 grade point average; must be pursuing, or plan to pursue, a degree in the fields of law, nursing, medicine or dentistry. **Criteria:** Applicants will be evaluated based on demonstrate leadership and character through extracurricular activities, service in school and community, volunteer involvement and paid work experience; candidates between the ages of 17-27 at the time of application and to those pursuing full-time education; must demonstrate financial need.

Funds Avail.: $7,500 each. **Duration:** Annual. **Number Awarded:** Up to 10. **To Apply:** Applicants must submit the completed application form; write a personal statement that describes their educational plans, career goals, motivating factors, and important experiences which have helped to shape their personal philosophy and future goals. **Deadline:** March 15. **Contact:** Phone: 313-961-6675; E-mail: scholarships@cfsem.org.

3725 ■ Virgil K. Lobring Scholarship Program *(Undergraduate/Scholarship)*

Purpose: To provide educational scholarship support to graduates of Western International High School. **Focus:** General studies/Field of study not specified. **Qualif.:** Applicants must be members of the graduating class at western International High School; have applied or been accepted as full-time students in an accredited educational institution in the United States; must enroll full-time at a non-profit or state supported four year college or university in the United States. **Criteria:** Applicants will be evaluated based on their desire, ability, and good grades; demonstrate leadership and character through dedicated community service; financial need.

Funds Avail.: No specific amount. **Duration:** Annual. **To Apply:** Applicants must submit the completed online application form. **Deadline:** March 15. **Contact:** Phone: 313-961-6675 Email: scholarships@cfsem.org.

3726 ■ Community Foundation of Western Massachusetts (CFWM)
333 Bridge St.
Springfield, MA 01103
Ph: (413)732-2858
Fax: (413)733-8565

Awards are arranged alphabetically below their administering organizations

E-mail: wmass@communityfoundation.org
URL: www.communityfoundation.org
Social Media: www.facebook.com/
  CommunityFoundationWMass
twitter.com/CFWM413
www.youtube.com/user/cfwm413

3727 ■ African American Achievement Scholarship Fund *(Undergraduate/Scholarship)*

Purpose: To help bring higher education within reach of residents in Massachusetts who might not otherwise be able to afford it. **Focus:** General studies/Field of study not specified. **Qualif.:** Applicants must be residents of Franklin, Hampden or Hampshire Counties who attend four-year colleges and have participated in extracurricular activities.

To Apply: Applicants must submit completed online application; applicant's most recent academic transcript; completed copy of the applicant's student aid report. **Deadline:** March 31. **Contact:** Phone:413-732-2858; Email:scholar@communityfoundation.org.

3728 ■ Community Legal Services of Philadelphia (CLS)

1424 Chestnut St.
Philadelphia, PA 19102-2505
Ph: (215)981-3700
E-mail: dfreedman@clsphila.org
URL: clsphila.org
Social Media: www.facebook.com/clsphila
www.linkedin.com/company/community-legal-services
twitter.com/CLSphila

3729 ■ Community Legal Services of Philadelphia Fellowships *(Postgraduate, Graduate/Fellowship)*

Purpose: To deliver high quality legal services to a diverse client population. **Focus:** Law; Paralegal studies. **Qualif.:** Candidates must be graduates or judicial law clerks interested in a public interest law career. Candidates with diverse cultural backgrounds and/or oral proficiency in languages other than English, people of color, gay men and lesbians, and members of under-served or disadvantage communities are also encouraged to apply. **Criteria:** Selection will be based on demonstrated passion for, interest in and commitment to public interest and poverty law; a demonstrated ability to providing the highest quality legal services to individual clients; excellent legal analysis and research, writing and oral advocacy skills; an interest in policy and advocacy work; strong networking, relationship building and communications skills; sound professional and legal judgment; a high level of commitment to racial justice and serving low-income communities and clients.

Funds Avail.: No specific amount. **Duration:** Annual. **Number Awarded:** Varies. **To Apply:** Applicants must submit the following requirements: resume; cover letter addressing their interest and experience in public interest and poverty law and describing any ideas for a fellowship proposal; two brief legal writing samples; law school transcript; list of three references. **Contact:** Brenda Marrero; Email: bmarrero@clsphila.org; Jennifer Burdick; Email: jburdick@clsphila.org.

3730 ■ Concordia University Faculty of Arts and Science (SDBI) - Simone de Beauvoir Institute

1455 de Maisonneuve Blvd. W
Montreal, QC, Canada H3G 1M8

URL: www.concordia.ca

3731 ■ Provost Entrance Scholarship *(Undergraduate/Scholarship)*

Purpose: To support students who are in the Major in Women's Studies and have completed or are currently registered in WSDB 290, 291 and 292. **Focus:** Women's studies. **Qualif.:** Applicants must be full-time students; can be Canadians, permanent residents or international students; must be in their first-year; cumulative GPA or "cote R" at entrance (calculated by Concordia University). **Criteria:** Selection will be based on Cumulative GPA or "cote R" at the entrance.

Duration: Annual. **To Apply:** Applicant must submit application form along with statement of contribution; curriculum vitae. **Deadline:** February 28.

3732 ■ Mair Verthuy Scholarship *(Undergraduate/Scholarship)*

Purpose: To support students who are in the Major in Women's Studies and have completed or are currently registered in WSDB 290, 291 and 292. **Focus:** Women's studies. **Qualif.:** Applicant must be a full-time student; must be a Canadian or permanent resident; with 60 credits completed at least 30 credits in WSDB; must have a minimum of 3.5 GPA. **Criteria:** Selection will be based on, cumulative GPA; if two students end up having the same cumulative GPA, need to split the scholarship in two.

Duration: Annual. **Deadline:** February 28.

3733 ■ Conference on Asian Pacific American Leadership (CAPAL)

1875 Connecticut Ave NW, 12th Fl., No.12181
Washington, DC 20009
Ph: (202)643-0190
E-mail: info@capal.org
URL: www.capal.org
Social Media: www.facebook.com/capaldc
twitter.com/capalDC

3734 ■ CAPAL Public Service Scholarships *(Graduate, Undergraduate/Scholarship)*

Purpose: To provide financial assistance to students with leadership potential to pursue public service internships in Washington, DC. **Focus:** Public service.

To Apply: Applicants must submit a completed online application form; resume and academic transcripts; one to three letters of recommendation; a statement of purpose that answers two out of three questions found on the online application. **Deadline:** February 13. **Contact:** E-mail: applications@capal.org.

3735 ■ Conference of State Bank Supervisors (CSBS)

1129 20th St. NW, 9th Fl.
Washington, DC 20036
Ph: (202)296-2840
Fax: (202)296-1928
URL: www.csbs.org

3736 ■ Conference of State Bank Supervisors Graduate Schools of Banking and Trust Scholarships *(Graduate/Scholarship)*

Purpose: To award scholarships to three state banking department personnel to attend the graduate school of

Awards are arranged alphabetically below their administering organizations

banking or graduate trust school of their choice. **Focus:** Banking. **Qualif.:** Applicants must be outstanding and deserving examiners who demonstrate excellence in their work by supporting their attendance at the graduate banking or graduate trust school of their choice; continue to be employed by a state banking department. **Criteria:** Selection will be made by panel of judges.

Funds Avail.: Up to $3,000 plus $1,250 from the Graduate School of Banking at Colorado. **Duration:** Annual. **Number Awarded:** 3. **To Apply:** Applicants must submit completed application form; complete program description, containing contact information, qualifications, and program procedures. **Remarks:** Established in 1972. **Contact:** C. Thomas McVey, Director of Learning Services, CSBS Education Foundation, 1129 20th St. NW, 9th Fl., Washington, DC, 20036-4306; E-mail: tmcvey@csbs.org.

3737 ■ Congressional Black Caucus Foundation, Inc. (CBCF)
1720 Massachusetts Ave. NW
Washington, DC 20036
Ph: (202)263-2800
E-mail: info@cbcfinc.org
URL: www.cbcfinc.org
Social Media: www.facebook.com/CBCFInc
www.instagram.com/cbcfinc
www.linkedin.com/company/congressional-black-caucus
 -foundation
twitter.com/CBCFInc
www.youtube.com/user/CBCFINC

3738 ■ CBC Spouses Education Scholarship
(Graduate, Undergraduate/Scholarship)

Purpose: To provide support to students in pursuing their educational goals. **Focus:** General studies/Field of study not specified. **Criteria:** Selection is based on submitted application and materials.

Funds Avail.: $500-$8,200. **Duration:** Annual. **To Apply:** Applicants must submit a completed CBC Spouses scholarship application; a sealed official high school or college transcript; a personal statement essay from the student (500-1, 000 words) that addresses all four (4) of the topics listed on the application in one essay; two letters of recommendation (one should come from a community or public service leader-church leader, community leader, etc.); if a first year student, an acceptance letter from the college/university where the student will enroll; and a recent photograph suitable for publication. **Deadline:** April 30. **Contact:** Phone: 202-263-2800; Email: scholarships@cbcfinc.org.

3739 ■ CBC Spouses Performing Arts Scholarship
(Undergraduate/Scholarship)

Purpose: To support students pursuing a career in the field of performing arts. **Focus:** Performing arts. **Criteria:** Selection is based on submitted application and materials.

Funds Avail.: Up to $3,000. **Duration:** Annual. **Number Awarded:** 10. **To Apply:** Applicants must submit resume; recent photograph suitable for publication; two electronically submitted letters of recommendation; Official transcript; electronic copy of detailed Federal Student Aid Report; 2 minute visual recording sample. **Deadline:** April 22. **Contact:** Phone: 202-263-2800; Email: scholarships@cbcfinc.org.

3740 ■ CBC Spouses Visual Arts Scholarship
(Undergraduate/Scholarship)

Purpose: To support students pursuing a career in the visual arts to achieve their goals. **Focus:** Visual arts. **Criteria:** Selection is based on submitted application and materials.

Funds Avail.: $3,000. **Duration:** Annual. **Number Awarded:** 2. **To Apply:** Applicants must submit resume; recent photograph suitable for publication; two electronically submitted letters of recommendation; Official transcript; electronic copy of detailed Federal Student Aid Report; 2 minute visual recording sample. **Deadline:** April 30. **Contact:** Phone: 202-263-2800; Email: scholarships@cbcfinc.org.

3741 ■ Congressional Fellowship *(Other/Fellowship)*

Purpose: To increase the number of African Americans working as professional staff in the U.S. Congress. **Focus:** General studies/Field of study not specified.

Funds Avail.: No specific amount. **Duration:** Annual. **To Apply:** Applicants must submit a completed application form along with a resume; three letters of recommendation; three transcripts (at least one must be an official transcript); and three essays (each essay no more than two pages in length); submit three copies of the complete application under one cover. **Contact:** CBCF Congressional Fellowship Programs, Congressional Black Caucus Foundation, Inc, 1720 Massachusetts Ave, N.W., Washington, DC, 20036; Phone: 202-263-2800; Email: fellowships@cbcfinc.org.

3742 ■ Louis Stokes Health Scholars Program
(Undergraduate/Scholarship)

Purpose: To provide support to students in pursuing their educational goals. **Focus:** Health care services; Health education; Health sciences; Health services administration; Occupational safety and health; Public health. **Criteria:** Preference will be given to students who demonstrate an interest to work in underserved communities.

Funds Avail.: $8,000. **Duration:** Annual. **Number Awarded:** 4. **To Apply:** Applicants must submit resume; recent photograph suitable for publication; two electronically submitted letters of recommendation; Official transcript; electronic copy of detailed Federal Student Aid Report; 2 minute visual recording sample. **Deadline:** April 30. **Contact:** Phone: 202-263-2800; Email: scholarships@cbcfinc.org.

3743 ■ Louis Stokes Urban Health Policy Fellows Program *(Other/Fellowship)*

Purpose: To bring together individuals with diverse interests in policy areas in order to complement and enrich the experiences of all program participants. **Focus:** Behavioral sciences; Biological and clinical sciences; Health sciences; Social sciences. **Qualif.:** Applicants must be U.S. citizens or permitted to work in the United States; must be graduate or have professional degree in a health-related field (behavioral science, social sciences, biological sciences and health professions) from an accredited institution completed prior to the fellowship start date; must familiar with the federal legislative process, Congress and the Congressional Black Caucus (CBC); and must have demonstrated interest in public policy, and commitment to creating and implementing policy to improve the living conditions for underserved and underrepresented individuals. **Criteria:** Selection is based on a combination of the

Awards are arranged alphabetically below their administering organizations

following criteria: a record of academic and professional achievement; evidence of leadership skills and the potential for further growth; study of how health policies affect African Americans and minorities; demonstrated interest in public health policy; and quality of paper application and interview performance.

Funds Avail.: No specific amount. **Duration:** Annual. **To Apply:** Applicants must submit a completed application form along with a resume; three letters of recommendation; three transcripts (at least one must be an official transcript); and three essays (each essay no more than two pages in length); submit three copies of the complete application under one cover; bind application with paperclips (do not use staples).

3744 ■ Congressional Hispanic Caucus Institute

1128 16th St., NW
Washington, DC 20036
Ph: (202)543-1771
Fax: (202)548-8799
URL: www.chci.org
Social Media: www.facebook.com/CHCIDC
instagram.com/chcidc
www.linkedin.com/company/congressional-hispanic-caucus
  -institute
twitter.com/chci
youtube.com/user/chcicommunications

3745 ■ CHCI Congressional Internship Program
(Undergraduate/Internship)

Purpose: To allow promising Latino undergraduate students to experience it's like to work in a congressional office, while participating in weekly professional and leadership development and civic engagement through community service. **Focus:** Political science. **Qualif.:** Applicants must be U.S. citizens, lawful permanent residents, asylees, or individuals who are lawfully authorized to work full-time without restriction for any U.S. employer and who, at the time of application, possess lawful evidence of employment authorization; must be Latino undergraduate students; must have minimum 3.0 GPA; must have demonstrated financial need; consistent, active participation in public and/or community service activities; have strong writing skills. **Criteria:** Selection will be on competitive basis.

Funds Avail.: $3,750 (Fall/Spring), $3,125 (Summer). **Duration:** Triennial. **To Apply:** Application form and details are available online at chci.org/programs/congressional-internship-program/. **Deadline:** October 1 (Spring); December 1 (Summer); February 15 (Fall).

3746 ■ CHCI Graduate Fellowship Program *(Graduate, Professional development/Fellowship)*

Purpose: To enhance individuals' leadership abilities, strengthen professional skills and ultimately produce more competent and competitive Latino professionals in public policy areas. **Focus:** Education; Engineering; Health care services; Housing; Law; Mathematics and mathematical sciences; Public administration; Public service; Science; Technology. **Qualif.:** Applicants must be emerging Latino leaders who are U.S. citizens, lawful permanent residents, asylees, or individuals who are lawfully authorized to work full-time without restriction for any U.S. employer and who, at the time of application, possess lawful evidence of employment authorization; must have earned a Bachelor's degree within two years of the program start date; have

high academic achievement (preference of 3.0 GPA or higher); have evidence of leadership skills and potential for leadership growth; have demonstrated commitment to public service-oriented activities; and have superior analytical skills and outstanding oral and written communication skills. **Criteria:** Selection will be on competitive basis; applications are reviewed by a selection committee composed of program alumni, members of the CHCI Board of Directors and Advisory Council, and CHCI staff.

Funds Avail.: $29,700 over nine months, plus benefits. **Duration:** Annual. **To Apply:** Application form and details are available online at chci.org/programs/graduate-fellowship-program/. **Deadline:** January 15.

3747 ■ CHCI Public Policy Fellowships *(Professional development/Fellowship)*

Purpose: To enhance individuals' leadership abilities, strengthen professional skills and ultimately produce more competent and competitive Latino professionals in public policy areas. **Focus:** Public administration; Public service. **Qualif.:** Applicants must be U.S. citizens, lawful permanent residents, asylees, or individuals who are lawfully authorized to work full-time without restriction for any U.S. employer and who, at the time of application, possess lawful evidence of employment authorization; must have earned a Bachelor's degree within two years of the program start date; have high academic achievement (preference of 3.0 GPA or higher); have evidence of leadership skills and potential for leadership growth; have demonstrated commitment to public service-oriented activities; and have superior analytical skills and outstanding oral and written communication skills. **Criteria:** Selection will be on competitive basis; applications are reviewed by a selection committee composed of program alumni, members of the CHCI Board of Directors and Advisory Council, and CHCI staff.

Funds Avail.: $26,100 over nine months, plus other benefits. **Duration:** Annual. **To Apply:** Application form and details are available online at chci.org/programs/public-policy-fellowship-program/. **Deadline:** January 15.

3748 ■ Connecticut Association of Assessing Officers (CAAO)

PO Box 427
Windsor, CT 06095-0427
URL: www.caao.com

3749 ■ Alexander Standish Memorial Scholarship
(Professional development/Scholarship)

Purpose: To support member of CAAO in career development. **Focus:** General studies/Field of study not specified. **Qualif.:** Applicants must be members of CAAO member. **Criteria:** Selection will be based on the committee's criteria.

Funds Avail.: $500. **Duration:** Annual. **Number Awarded:** 1. **Deadline:** June.

3750 ■ Connecticut Association of Land Surveyors (CALS)

78 Beaver Road, Suite 2-J
Wethersfield, CT 06109
Ph: (860)563-1990
URL: ctsurveyors.org
Social Media: www.facebook.com/pg/Connecticut-Association-of-Land-Surveyors-108774842572976/about/¿ref
  =page_internal

Awards are arranged alphabetically below their administering organizations

3751 ■ CALS Memorial Scholarship *(Undergraduate/ Scholarship)*

Purpose: To provide students the financial assistance they need in surveying. **Focus:** Cartography/Surveying. **Criteria:** Selection will be based on the committee's criteria.

Funds Avail.: No specific amount. **Duration:** Annual. **Number Awarded:** 4. **To Apply:** Applicants must submit a statement outlining qualifications, transcript, resume and other pertinent information. **Deadline:** June 1. **Remarks:** Established in honor of CALS members Harry E. Cole (1909-1984), Oliver H. Paquette (1931-1992), William G. Berglund (1918-1989) and William W. Seymour (1947-1998). **Contact:** CALS Scholarship committee, C/O Jay Doody, 49 Arlington St., West Haven, CT 06516.

3752 ■ Connecticut Association of Latinos in Higher Education (CALAHE)

Central Connecticut State University
1615 Stanley St.,Willard-DiLoreto, Ste. D311
New Britain, CT 06050
URL: calahe.org
Social Media: www.facebook.com/CALAHE
twitter.com/CALAHE1978

3753 ■ Thomas M. Blake Memorial Scholarships *(Undergraduate/Scholarship)*

Purpose: To promote different areas of postsecondary education participated by Latinos. **Focus:** Education. **Qualif.:** Applicants must be accepted for admission to an accredited institution of higher education; have a "B" average (3.0 GPA) for all completed enrollment periods at the time of application; be U.S. citizens or permanent residents; have been Connecticut residents during the preceding 12 months; be Latino students from Connecticut; and must demonstrate financial need. **Criteria:** Selection is based on the application materials.

Funds Avail.: $1,000. **To Apply:** Applicants must submit a completed scholarship application together with an official copy of educational transcripts; copy of Student Aid Report (SAR) sent by the U.S. Department of Education; and an essay on. **Contact:** Dr. Wilson Luna, Gateway Community College, at the above address.

3754 ■ Connecticut Association of Latinos in Higher Education Scholarships *(Undergraduate/ Scholarship)*

Purpose: To award a scholarship to the students entering or enrolled as undergraduates in an accredited college or university. **Focus:** General studies/Field of study not specified. **Qualif.:** Applicants must be a high school senior/ged equivalent or undergraduate college student; must be latinx student from Connecticut; must demonstrated financial need; must accepted to or attending an accredited institution of higher education; must cumulative gpa of 2.75 or greater for all completed course work at the time of application; must attend full time and be seeking their first undergraduate degree; must demonstrated community service within the latinx community. **Criteria:** Selection are based on scholarship chair.

Funds Avail.: $1,000. **Duration:** Annual. **Number Awarded:** Varies. **To Apply:** Applicants must submit completed application; letter of acceptance from college or university (for high school seniors or GED Students); two letters of recommendation – one must be from a teacher; official high school or college transcript; Copy of either:

Federal Student Aid Report or undocumented/DACA students must submit the State of Connecticut Student Aid Report; essay. **Deadline:** June 30. **Contact:** Dr. Wilson Luna, Scholarship Chair, Gateway Community College, 20 Church St., New Haven, CT, 06510; Email:70harvest@ gmail.com.

3755 ■ Rosa Quezada Memorial Education Scholarships *(Undergraduate/Scholarship)*

Purpose: To promote different areas of postsecondary education participated by Latinos. **Focus:** Education.

Funds Avail.: $1,000. **To Apply:** Applicants must submit a completed scholarship application together with an official copy of educational transcripts; copy of Student Aid Report (SAR) sent by the U.S. Department of Education; and an essay on "How do you feel education is going to impact your ability to continue assisting others to pursue an education?" (Maximum of 2 pages typewritten, double spaced statement). **Contact:** Dr. Wilson Luna, Gateway Community College, at the above address.

3756 ■ John Soto Scholarships *(Undergraduate/ Scholarship)*

Purpose: To promote different areas of postsecondary education participated by Latinos. **Focus:** Education. **Qualif.:** Applicants must be accepted for admission to an accredited institution of higher education; have a "B" average (3.0 GPA) for all completed enrollment periods at the time of application; a U.S. citizen or permanent resident; have been a Connecticut resident during the preceding 12 months; a Latino student from Connecticut; and must demonstrate financial need. **Criteria:** Selection is based on the application materials.

Funds Avail.: $1,000. **Duration:** Annual. **Number Awarded:** 1. **To Apply:** Applicants must submit a completed scholarship application together with an official copy of educational transcripts; copy of Student Aid Report (SAR) sent by the U.S. Department of Education; and an essay on. **Deadline:** June 30. **Contact:** Dr. Wilson Luna, Gateway Community College, at the above address.

3757 ■ Marta Vallin Memorial Scholarships *(Undergraduate/Scholarship)*

Purpose: To promote the participation of Latinos in different areas of postsecondary education in Connecticut. **Focus:** Education. **Qualif.:** Applicants must be attending Gateway Community College; have a "B" average (3.0 GPA) for all completed enrollment periods at the time of application; a U.S. citizen or permanent resident; have been a Connecticut resident during the preceding 12 months; a Latino student from Connecticut; and must demonstrate financial need. **Criteria:** Selection is based on the application materials.

Funds Avail.: $1,000. **To Apply:** Applicants must submit a completed scholarship application together with an official copy of educational transcripts; copy of Student Aid Report (SAR) sent by the U.S. Department of Education; and an essay on "How do you feel education is going to impact your ability to continue assisting others to pursue an education?" (Maximum of 2 pages typewritten, double spaced statement).

3758 ■ Connecticut Construction Industries Association

912 Silas Deane Hwy.
Wethersfield, CT 06109-3433

Awards are arranged alphabetically below their administering organizations

Ph: (860)529-6855
Fax: (860)563-0616
E-mail: ccia-info@ctconstruction.org
URL: ctconstruction.org
Social Media: www.facebook.com/
  connecticutconstructionindustriesassociation
twitter.com/CCIA_info

3759 ■ Associated General Contractors of Connecticut Scholarships (AGC/CT Scholarship)
(Undergraduate/Scholarship)

Purpose: To support students enrolled in a construction management or construction related engineering programs. **Focus:** Construction; Engineering, Civil. **Qualif.:** Applicants must be Connecticut residents enrolled in, or graduating high school seniors applying for and planning to enter, a four-year building and construction technology or civil engineering program, or entering a two-year technical school with a construction course of study, with the intent of entering a four-year accredited college upon completion of the technical school. Applicants must desire a career in construction.

Funds Avail.: $5,000 ($2,500 per year for two years). **Duration:** Annual. **To Apply:** Applicants must complete the "four-page" signed application; must submit one faculty evaluation form completed by high school faculty member with scholastic achievement and school history, two personal evaluation forms and official transcript of records. **Deadline:** February 28. **Contact:** John W. Butts, Phone: 860-529-6855; Email: jbutts@ctconstruction.org.

3760 ■ Connecticut Space Grant Consortium
University of Hartford, Dana 203, 200 Bloomfield Ave.
West Hartford, CT 06117
Ph: (860)768-4813
E-mail: ctspgrant@hartford.edu
URL: ctspacegrant.org
Social Media: www.facebook.com/ConnecticutSpaceGrant
twitter.com/CTSpaceGrant

3761 ■ Connecticut Space Grant College Consortium Undergraduate Research Fellowships
(Undergraduate/Fellowship)

Purpose: To support outstanding students' education and research who exemplify interest in STEM field. **Focus:** Space and planetary sciences. **Qualif.:** Applicants must be undergraduate full-time students with a minimum GPA of 3.0 or higher; must provide a proof of U.S. Citizenship through the Grant Verification Form. **Criteria:** Selection will be based on the committee's criteria.

To Apply: Applicants must submit complete requirements via email. The email must include two attachments, the Contact/Demographic Info form and a single PDF containing the appropriate cover sheet, abstract, proposal narrative, letters of support, resume/CV, transcript and the Grant Verification Form. **Contact:** Email: csgcinfo@hartford.edu.

3762 ■ Connecticut Women's Hall of Fame
320 Fitch St.
New Haven, CT 06515
Ph: (203)392-9008
Fax: (203)392-9012
E-mail: info@cwhf.org

URL: www.cwhf.org
Social Media: www.facebook.com/ctwomen
twitter.com/ctwomen

3763 ■ Eileen Kraus Scholarship *(Two Year College, Four Year College/Scholarship)*
Purpose: To recognize an outstanding young Connecticut student embarking on their first year of college or university. **Focus:** General studies/Field of study not specified. **Qualif.:** Female resident of Connecticut who is a high school senior or recent graduate intending to enroll in an accredited two or four-year university.

Funds Avail.: $5,000. **Duration:** $5,000. **Number Awarded:** 1. **Remarks:** The Scholarship was established in memory of Eileen Kraus was the first woman to head a major regional financial institution, and was the founding Chairman of the Connecticut Women's Hall of Fame Board of Trustees. Established in 2016. **Contact:** The Eileen Kraus Scholarship, c/o The Connecticut Women's Hall of Fame, 320 Fitch St., Schwartz Hall B-3, New Haven, CT, 06515; Phone: 203-392-9007.

3764 ■ The Connor Group Kids & Community Partners
10510 Springboro Pike
Miamisburg, OH 45342
URL: connorgroup.com

3765 ■ The Connor Group Kids & Community Partners Scholarship *(Two Year College, Undergraduate, Graduate/Scholarship)*
Purpose: To provide disadvantaged high school seniors or college students with financial assistance to purse higher education. **Focus:** General studies/Field of study not specified. **Qualif.:** Applicant must be high school seniors or college students attending or planning to attend an accredited U.S. college or university; must have a combined family income of $75,000 or less. **Criteria:** Selection will be based on demonstrating alignment with the sponsor's core values. Preference will be given to students who reside in one of the markets in which the sponsor operates: Atlanta, Austin, Charlotte, Chicago, Cincinnati, Columbus, Dallas, Dayton, Denver, Louisville, Minneapolis, Nashville, Raleigh-Durham, and Tampa.

Funds Avail.: $2,500 each. **Number Awarded:** 6. **To Apply:** Submit application, basic demographic information, evidence of school and community involvement, volunteer work and other activities. **Deadline:** January 15. **Contact:** Email: rojohnson@connorgroup.com; URL: connorgroup.com/kids-and-community/scholarship/.

3766 ■ Conquer Cancer
2318 Mill Rd. Ste. 800
Alexandria, VA 22314
E-mail: info@conquer.org
URL: conquer.org
Social Media: www.facebook.com/
  ConquerCancerFoundation
www.instagram.com/conquercancerfoundation
twitter.com/ConquerCancerFd
www.youtube.com/user/ConquerCancerFdtn

3767 ■ ASCO/CCF Young Investigator Awards
(Professional development, Advanced Professional/Grant)
Purpose: To fund physicians during the transition from a fellowship program to a faculty appointment. **Focus:** Oncol-

Awards are arranged alphabetically below their administering organizations

ogy. **Qualif.:** Applicants must: be physicians working with MD, DO, or international equivalent working in any country; be on their last two years in a clinical department at an academic medical institution at the time of grant submission; have a valid and active medical license at the time of application; must be members of ASCO; and, have a mentor from the sponsoring institution who must provide a letter of support. **Criteria:** Preference will be given to those with proposals that are hypothesis-driven with a clinical research focus on generating the rationale for future clinical studies; strength of the mentor in supporting the applicants' proposal and in facilitating the applicants' career development; potential to pursue an academic clinical oncology career; availability of institutional resources to support the proposed project.

Funds Avail.: $50,000. **Duration:** Annual. **Number Awarded:** 1. **To Apply:** Applicants must accomplish their online application process at Grants Website and should be submitted in accordance to the requirements and instructions of the Request for Proposals (RFP); all application materials must be in English and must include the following components: contact information; project information (includes Abstract, IRB and Animal Use Assurances); specific aims; personal statements; applicants' biosketch; research strategy; cited references; project timeline; budget and justification; mentor's biosketch; mentor's letter of support; institutional letter of support from Department Chair or Dean; institutional approval face sheet signed by the Institutional Approver. **Deadline:** October 29.

3768 ■ Bradley Stuart Beller Special Merit Award (Doctorate, Postdoctorate/Award)

Purpose: To support fellows who have the highest ranking abstract overall in the Merit Award category as determined by the Scientific Program Committee. **Focus:** Medical research; Oncology.

Funds Avail.: $2,000. **Duration:** Annual. **Deadline:** February 11.

3769 ■ CCF Career Development Award (Professional development/Grant)

Purpose: To provide funding to clinical investigators who have received their initial faculty appointment to establish an independent clinical cancer research program. **Focus:** Oncology. **Qualif.:** Applicants must be physicians working in any country and in the first to third year of a full-time, primary faculty appointment in a clinical department at an academic medical institution; must have a valid and active medical license at the time of application; must have completed productive postdoctoral research; must be ASCO members; should not have any current career development award and have not been a Principal Investigator on any large project grants; and must have a mentor from the sponsoring institution who must provide a letter of support. **Criteria:** The Conquer Cancer Foundation Grants selection committee will select the recipient based on the following criteria: potential for the applicants to pursue an academic clinical oncology career; strength of the hypothesis-driven proposal with a clinical research focus; strength of the mentor in supporting the applicants' proposal and in facilitating the applicants' career development; and availability of institutional resources to support the proposed project.

Funds Avail.: $200,000. **Duration:** Annual; paid in three annual increments. **To Apply:** Applicants must accomplish their online application process and must be submitted in accordance to the requirements and instructions of the

Request for Proposals (RFP); all application materials must be in English. **Deadline:** September 24. **Remarks:** Established in 1992.

3770 ■ CCF Improving Cancer Care Grants (Professional development, Doctorate/Grant)

Purpose: To encourage multi-disciplinary research that will have a major impact in breast cancer care. **Focus:** Oncology. **Qualif.:** Eligible research teams must be focused on implementing and/or evaluating new solutions to existing problems in quality of, access to, and delivery of care with general applicability to breast cancer; must be led by a single Principal Investigator, who must be an active ASCO member (or have submitted a membership application) with an MD, DO, PhD or equivalent degree; must have a multidisciplinary team of investigators that may include clinicians, nurses, pharmacists, statisticians, epidemiologists, information technologists and other research experts. **Criteria:** Selection will be based on the committee's criteria.

To Apply: Interested applicants must visit the Easygrants website to create an account and to access the online application system. Applicants must provide a letter of intent to be submitted online **Contact:** ASCO Cancer Foundation at grants@asco.org.

3771 ■ CCF Merit Award (Professional development, Doctorate/Award)

Purpose: To support fellows and residents whose research is addressed in high-quality abstracts and recognized for its scientific merit. **Focus:** Oncology. **Qualif.:** Applicants must be authors of an abstract; must hold a doctoral degree or be doctoral degree candidates at the time of abstract submission; must be enrolled in an oncology fellowship training program or equivalent; must work in an oncology laboratory or clinical research setting. **Criteria:** Selection will be based on the committee's criteria.

Funds Avail.: $1,000. **Duration:** Annual. **To Apply:** Consideration for the award is available on the abstract submitter for the appropriate meeting; must present the abstract at the annual meeting and must provide a letter of support from their training program director and two-page curriculum vitae.

3772 ■ Comparative Effectiveness Research Professorship (CERP) (Professional development, Doctorate/Grant)

Purpose: To assist consumers, clinicians, purchasers, and policy makers to make informed decisions that will improve health care at both the individual and population levels. **Focus:** Oncology. **Qualif.:** Applicants must have an MD, PhD or equivalent degree; must have the rank of full professors; must have full-time faculty appointment at an academic medical center; must have a full-time faculty appointment at an academic medical center; must have made significant contributions that have changed the direction of breast cancer research; must be serving as a research mentor to one or more researcher(s) in training; must lead a research team in conducting research on comparative effectiveness in breast cancer; must be active members of ASCO; must commit to spend 75% of time during the award period dedicated to research including leading a team of researchers and mentoring physician-scientists. **Criteria:** Selection will be based on the following criteria: qualifications, experience and productivity of the applicants; commitment to mentoring the next generation of researchers in comparative effectiveness research; scientific impact, merit and originality of the applicants' ongoing research, and the

Awards are arranged alphabetically below their administering organizations

ongoing research that the applicants are mentoring; documented effective research team leadership; facilities and resources available to the applicants to continue their research career and attain their career goals.

Funds Avail.: A total of $500,000. **Duration:** Annual; paid in 5 annual increments. **To Apply:** Domestic and international applications must be submitted in accordance with the requirements and instructions of request for proposal (RFP); must provide a letter of intent; all application materials must be in English and must be submitted online.

3773 ■ Drug Development Research Professorship (*Professional development/Internship*)

Purpose: To provide flexible funding to outstanding researchers who have made, and are continuing to make significant contributions that may change the direction of cancer research. **Focus:** Medical research.

Funds Avail.: $100,000 per year. **Duration:** Annual; up to 5 years. **To Apply:** Applications must be submitted in accordance to the requirements and instructions of the Research Professorship Request for Proposals (RFP); all materials must be in English and must be submitted through the Grants Portal; paper applications or applications sent by e-mail or fax will not be accepted. **Contact:** Conquer Cancer Foundation, at the above address.

3774 ■ International Development and Education Award in Palliative Care (*Professional development/ Award*)

Purpose: To provide medical education in palliative care, assist with career development and helps establish strong relationships with leading ASCO members in the field of palliative care who serves as scientific Mentors to each recipient. **Focus:** Oncology. **Qualif.:** Applicants must have a current passport that does not expire before December of the current year; must be current residents of a country classified by the World Bank as Low-Income, Lower-Middle-Income, or Upper-Middle-Income, and have limited resources to attend the ASCO Annual Meeting; must be full members, members in training or international corresponding members of ASCO or willing to submit an application for ASCO membership; must have a demonstrated interest in integrating palliative and supportive care into their institution; must be less than ten years past their oncology program training; must be fluent in English. **Criteria:** Selection will be based on the submitted applications.

Funds Avail.: No specific amount. **Duration:** Annual. **To Apply:** All applications must be submitted in accordance to the requirements and instructions of the Request for Applications; must include the following mandatory components: contact information; personal statement; applicant information; biographical sketch; senior oncologist or palliative care specialist letter of recommendation; institutional approval. **Deadline:** October 1.

3775 ■ International Development and Education Awards (*Professional development, Doctorate/Grant*)

Purpose: To support early-career oncologists in developing countries and facilitates the sharing of knowledge between these oncologists and ASCO members. **Focus:** Oncology. **Qualif.:** Applicants must have a current passport; must be current residents of a country classified by the World Bank as low-income, lower-middle-income or upper-middle-income and have limited resources to attend the ASCO annual meeting; not have completed more than one year of "formal training"; must be member of ASCO (full, member-in-training, or international corresponding); must be less

than ten years past their oncology program; must be fluent in English (writing and speaking); must have demonstrated interest in integrating palliative and supportive care into his/ her institution. **Criteria:** Selection will be based on the committee's criteria.

Funds Avail.: Amount not specified. **Duration:** Annual. **Number Awarded:** Varies. **To Apply:** Applicants must visit the website for the online application process; all application materials must be in English. **Deadline:** October 31,2019.

3776 ■ International Innovation Grants (*Professional development/Grant*)

Purpose: To provide research funding in support of novel and innovative project that can have a significant impact on cancer control in low- and middle-income countries. **Focus:** Oncology. **Criteria:** Selection will be based on the committee's criteria.

Funds Avail.: Up to $20,000. **Duration:** Annual. **To Apply:** applications sent by e-mail or fax will not be accepted. All application materials must be in English and must be submitted through the Application Portal. **Deadline:** July 31.

3777 ■ Brigid Leventhal Special Merit Award (*Postdoctorate, Professional development/Award*)

Purpose: To support fellows who submitted the top abstract in Pediatric Oncology. **Focus:** Oncology. **Qualif.:** Special Merit Awards are presented each year to trainees and junior faculty who have the top-ranking abstracts for the ASCO Annual Meeting. In addition to the stipend, recipients receive a plaque and are recognized at the ASCO Annual Meeting. Hold a doctoral degree (including but not limited to MD, DO, PharmD, or PhD) Be enrolled in an oncology fellowship training program, a radiation oncology residency program, or an equivalent oncology training program at the time of abstract submission Work in an oncology laboratory or clinical research setting. **Criteria:** Selection will be based on the committee's criteria.

Funds Avail.: $1,000. **Duration:** Annual. **To Apply:** This award is given to the fellow who submitted the top abstract in Pediatric Oncology as determined by the Scientific Program Committee.

3778 ■ Long-term International Fellowships (*Professional development/Fellowship*)

Purpose: To provide early-career oncologists in low- to middle-income countries the support and resources needed to advance their training. **Focus:** Oncology. **Qualif.:** Applicants must be full member or international corresponding member of ASCO; must be physicians who have completed a subspecialty training program or the equivalent; must have less than 10 years of experience; must commit to returning to their home country within one year following the completion of the fellowship; must have a pre-existing relationship with a mentor of ASCO and are employed in U.S. or Canada. **Criteria:** Selection will be based on the committee's criteria.

Funds Avail.: A total of $115,000. **Duration:** Annual. **To Apply:** Applicants must accomplish their online application process submitted through the Application Portal. and submitted in accordance to the requirements and instructions of the Request for Proposals (RFP). All application materials must be in English and must include the following components: contact Information; project information; personal statement questions; biographical sketch; letter of

Awards are arranged alphabetically below their administering organizations

recommendation from home institution; publications; budget; mentor information; the following must be completed by the mentor: fellowship description from US or Canadian mentor; mentor NIH biographical sketch; mentor letter of support; institutional approval facesheet, signed by host institution. **Deadline:** January 14.

3779 ■ Medical Student Rotation for Underrepresented Populations *(Graduate, Master's/Grant)*

Purpose: To facilitate the recruitment and retention of individuals from populations underrepresented in medicine to cancer careers and increase access to quality care for underserved communities. **Focus:** Oncology. **Qualif.:** Applicants must meet the following criteria to qualify for the Medical Student Rotation: must be enrolled in a DO or MD program at a U.S. medical school; must be a U.S. citizen, U.S. national, or permanent resident; must be an ASCO member; must have a record of good academic standing; and must be of an underrepresented population in medicine. **Criteria:** Selection will be based on the committee's criteria.

Funds Avail.: $5,000 stipend for the rotation; $1,500 for future travel to the ASCO Annual Meeting; additional $2,000 to students mentor. **Duration:** Annual. **Number Awarded:** Varies. **To Apply:** Interested applicants may visit the website to obtain an application form. **Deadline:** November 12.

3780 ■ James B. Nachman Endowed ASCO Junior Faculty Award in Pediatric Oncology *(Doctorate, Professional development/Grant, Monetary)*

Purpose: To support faculty members who submits the highest ranking abstract in pediatric oncology for the ASCO Annual Meeting. **Focus:** Oncology. **Qualif.:** -Hold a medical or doctoral degree (MD, PhD, DO, or DNP)-Be within 7 years of their first faculty appointment at the time of abstract submission-Conduct laboratory, population-based, or clinical research focused on childhood cancer-Agree to present the abstract at the ASCO Annual Meeting-In addition, the abstract must be selected for presentation in an Oral Abstract Session

Funds Avail.: $3,000. **Duration:** Annual. **To Apply:** Consideration for a Merit Award is available on the abstract submitter for the ASCO Annual Meeting and other ASCO thematic meetings. **Deadline:** February 11.

3781 ■ Pain and Symptom Management Special Merit Award *(Postdoctorate, Professional development/Award)*

Purpose: To support fellow who submitted the top abstract in Pain and Symptom Management Research. **Focus:** Oncology. **Qualif.:** Applicant must be the First Author on the abstract submission and agree to present the abstract if selected for presentation at the Meeting; hold a doctoral degree (including but not limited to MD, DO, PharmD, or PhD); must be enrolled in an oncology fellowship training program, a radiation oncology residency program, or an equivalent oncology training program at the time of abstract submission; Work in an oncology laboratory or clinical research setting; provide a letter of support from their training program director, indicating eligibility for the award; provide a curriculum vitae. **Criteria:** Selection will be based on the committee criteria.

Funds Avail.: $1,000. **Duration:** Annual. **Number Awarded:** Varies. **To Apply:** This award is given to the fellow who submitted the top abstract in Pain and Symptom Management Research as determined by the Scientific

Program Committee. **Deadline:** February 1 1.

3782 ■ Patient Advocate Scholarship Program *(Professional development/Scholarship)*

Purpose: To support the awardees to be able to attend the Annual Meeting of The American Society of Clinical Oncology (ASCO) and ASCO Symposia. **Focus:** Medical research; Oncology. **Criteria:** Based primarily on financial need, advocacy experience, current advocacy activities and involvement.

Contact: Email: patientadvocates@asco.org; Phone: 571-483-1426.

3783 ■ Resident Travel Award for Underrepresented Populations *(Professional development/Award)*

Purpose: To support financially the residents from underrepresented populations to attend the ASCO Annual Meeting. **Focus:** Oncology.

Funds Avail.: $1,500. **Duration:** Annual. **To Apply:** Applicants must visit the website for the online application process. **Deadline:** November 12.

3784 ■ Translational Research Professorship *(Professional development/Internship)*

Purpose: To provides funding to full professors who have made significant contributions to cancer research and are dedicated to mentoring the next generation of researchers. **Focus:** Medical research. **Qualif.:** Be a physician (MD, DO, or international equivalent with explanation) working in any country with a full-time faculty appointment in a clinical department at an academic medical center; full member of the American Society of Clinical Oncology (ASCO) in good standing or submit a membership application with grant application. Currently hold the rank of full professor or equivalent at an academic medical center. **Criteria:** Significant contributions in the area of breast cancer disparities research.

Funds Avail.: $500,000. **Duration:** 5 years. **To Apply:** Applications must be submitted in accordance to the requirements and instructions of the Research Professorship Request for Proposals (RFP); all materials must be in English and must be submitted through the Grants Portal. Paper applications or applications sent by e-mail or fax will not be accepted. **Deadline:** May 27.

3785 ■ Conseil des Arts de l'Ontario (OAC)
121 Bloor St. W, 7th Fl.
Toronto, ON, Canada M4W 3M5
Ph: (416)961-1660
Fax: (416)961-7796
Free: 800-387-0058
E-mail: info@arts.on.ca
URL: www.arts.on.ca
Social Media: www.facebook.com/OntarioArts
twitter.com/ONArtsCouncil
www.youtube.com/user/OntarioArts

3786 ■ Orford String Quartet Scholarship *(Professional development/Scholarship)*

Purpose: To assist a Canadian string musician with studies, commissions, or performances related to work in chamber music. **Focus:** Music. **Qualif.:** Applicants must be musicians. **Criteria:** Applicants are judged upon the committees criteria.

Funds Avail.: $3,000. **Duration:** Biennial. **To Apply:** Applicants can view the website for further details. **Remarks:** Established in 1993.

Awards are arranged alphabetically below their administering organizations

3787 ■ Conseil Canadien pour le Commerce Autochtone (CCAB)
2 Berkeley St., Ste. 310
Toronto, ON, Canada M5A 4J5
URL: www.ccab.com
Social Media: www.facebook.com/
 CanadianCouncilforAboriginalBusiness
www.linkedin.com/company/canadian-council-for-aboriginal
 -business
twitter.com/ccab_national

3788 ■ Foundation for the Advancement of Aboriginal Youth Bursary Program *(Undergraduate/ Scholarship)*

Purpose: To provide scholarship assistance to qualified individuals who want to pursue their post-secondary education. **Focus:** General studies/Field of study not specified. **Qualif.:** Applicant must be a Canadian resident, of First Nation, Metis or Inuit heritage and attending either a high school or a post-secondary institute full-time within Canada. **Criteria:** Recipient will be selected based on financial need, academic and career commitment, contribution to family and community and leadership and role model qualities.

Funds Avail.: No specific amount. **To Apply:** Applicant must complete the application form available online; must provide a proof of First Nations, Inuit or Metis ancestry; must have two signed, original letters of support; must provide a copy of the most recent official school transcripts and report card; must include a letter of acceptance; must provide a recent color photo. **Contact:** 1-866-566-3229.

3789 ■ Foundation for the Advancement of Aboriginal Youth Scholarships *(Undergraduate/ Scholarship)*

Purpose: To provide scholarship assistance to qualified individuals who want to pursue their post-secondary education. **Focus:** General studies/Field of study not specified. **Qualif.:** Applicant must be a Canadian resident, of First Nation, Metis or Inuit heritage and attending either high school or a post-secondary institute full-time within Canada. **Criteria:** Recipient will be selected based on financial need, academic and career commitment, contribution to family and community, and leadership and role model qualities.

Funds Avail.: No specific amount. **To Apply:** Applicant must complete the application form available online; must provide proof of First Nation, Inuit or Metis ancestry; must have two signed, original letters of support; must provide a copy of the most recent official school transcripts and report card; must include a letter of acceptance; must provide a recent color photo. Application form and other supporting documents must be sent to Foundation for the Advancement of Aboriginal Youth, c/o Canadian Council for Aboriginal Business, 250 The Esplanade, Ste. 204, Toronto, ON M5A 1J2. **Contact:** 1-866-566-3229.

3790 ■ Conseil Canadien des Infirmieres et Infirmiers en Soins Cardiovasculaires (CCCN)
202-300 March Rd.
Ottawa, ON, Canada K2K 2E2
Ph: (613)406-3548
Fax: (613)595-1155
E-mail: info@cccn.ca
URL: www.cccn.ca
Social Media: www.facebook.com/CCCnurses/¿ref=aymt
 _homepage_panel

www.linkedin.com/company/cccn
twitter.com/CCCnurses

3791 ■ CCCN Research Grant Program *(Professional development/Grant)*

Purpose: To provide funds to CCCN members for research pertaining to cardiovascular or cerebrovascular nursing in Canada. **Focus:** Medicine, Cardiology; Nursing. **Qualif.:** Applicants must be Canadian citizens or permanent residents; current members of the CCCN. **Criteria:** Preference will be given to the applicant who has not received funding from CCCN in the past five years; has contributed the most to CCCN endeavors.

Funds Avail.: 2,500 Canadian Dollars. **Duration:** Biennial. **Deadline:** March 31.

3792 ■ Conseil Canadien des Techniciens et Technologues (CCTT)
2197 Riverside Dr., Ste. 301
Ottawa, ON, Canada K1H 7X3
Ph: (613)238-8123
Fax: (613)238-8822
E-mail: cctt@cctt.ca
URL: www.cctt.ca

3793 ■ Manulife Financial Scholarship *(Undergraduate/Scholarship)*

Purpose: To assist the child of a certified member with expenses incurred undertaking a course of studies leading to a technician or technology diploma in a recognized program of studies in Engineering or Applied Science Technology. **Focus:** Engineering; Science technologies. **Qualif.:** Applicant must be a son or daughter of an individual member of a Constituent member (CM) of CCTT. **Criteria:** Selection shall be based on the aforementioned qualifications and compliance with the application details.

Funds Avail.: 1,000 Canadian Dollars. **Duration:** Annual. **Number Awarded:** 2. **To Apply:** Applicant must secure a letter from a Provincial Association of the council, attesting to the fact that their parents are members in good standing or with better standing; proof of enrollment as full-time student in an Engineering or Applied Science Technology Program in Canada. **Deadline:** December 15. **Contact:** CCTT Awards, 2197 Riverside Dr., Ste. 405, Ottawa, ON, K1H7X3; Email: cctt@cctt.ca.

3794 ■ Conseil Consultatif Canadien de la Radio (CCCR)
811-116 Albert St.
Ottawa, ON, Canada K1P 5G3
URL: www.rabc-cccr.ca

3795 ■ William Taylor in Radiocommunications Scholarships *(Undergraduate/Scholarship)*

Purpose: To encourage careers in telecommunications especially among engineering students. **Focus:** Telecommunications systems. **Qualif.:** Applicants must be enrolled in an accredited Canadian university and must have completed at least the second year in an engineering programme. **Criteria:** Selection of applicants will be based on their academic excellence; recognized involvement with the industry; continuing contribution to the community at large.

Awards are arranged alphabetically below their administering organizations

Funds Avail.: $3,500. **Duration:** Annual. **To Apply:** Scholarship applications may be obtained by contacting RABC or log on to www.electrofed.com; completed applications must be submitted to RABC. **Deadline:** May 31. **Remarks:** Administered by the Electro-Federation Canada.

3796 ■ Conseil de recherches en sciences humaines (SSHRC)
350 Albert St.
Ottawa, ON, Canada K1P 6G4
URL: www.sshrc-crsh.gc.ca

3797 ■ SSHRC Doctoral Fellowship Program
(Doctorate/Fellowship, Scholarship)

Purpose: To develop research skills and assist in the training of highly-qualified academic personnel by supporting students who demonstrate a high standard of scholarly achievement in undergraduate and graduate studies in the social sciences and humanities. **Focus:** Humanities; Social sciences. **Criteria:** Selection will be based on academic merit.

Funds Avail.: $20,000 per year. **Duration:** 12 to 48 months. **To Apply:** Applicants must ensure that they meet the requirements; complete and submit only one application form together with the CV and the required attachments; will find the application instructions when they begin to create it online; must determine their current registration status and submit their complete application to the appropriate institution. **Deadline:** October 17. **Contact:** Phone: 613-943-7777; Email: fellowships@sshrc-crsh.gc.ca.

3798 ■ SSHRC Postdoctoral Fellowships
(Postdoctorate/Fellowship)

Purpose: To support the most promising Canadian new scholars in the social sciences and humanities and assist them in establishing a research base at an important time in their research careers. **Focus:** Social sciences. **Criteria:** selection committees review an entire cohort of applications and make recommendations about funding that are subject to SSHRC approval. The scores assigned to each application indicate the relative standing of an application within a given committee.

Funds Avail.: $40,500 per year. **Duration:** Annual; 1 to 2 years. **Deadline:** September 16. **Contact:** Phone: 613-943-7777; Email: fellowships@sshrc-crsh.gc.ca.

3799 ■ Conseil International d'Études Canadiennes (CIEC)
Holland Cross RO
1620 Scott St., Unit 8
Ottawa, ON, Canada K1Y 4V1
URL: www.iccs-ciec.ca
Social Media: www.facebook.com/pages/International
  -Council-for-Canadian-Studies/193445340684256
twitter.com/ICCS_CIEC
www.youtube.com/channel/UCV3vOSP
  -nHS2DEawqfdtP0w

3800 ■ Canadian Studies Postdoctoral Fellowships
(Postdoctorate/Fellowship)

Purpose: To enable young Canadian and foreign academics to visit a Canadian or foreign university with a Canadian Studies program for a teaching or research fellowship. **Focus:** Canadian studies. **Qualif.:** Applicants must be in post-doctoral level that have completed a doctoral thesis on a topic primarily related to Canada and are not employed as a full-time; must obtain a formal commitment from such universities concerning the services and teaching and/or research opportunities which would be available to them. **Criteria:** Selection will be based on the committee's criteria.

Funds Avail.: 2,500 canadian dollers per month plus the cost of a return airline ticket for a maximum of CDN$10,000. **Duration:** Annual; minimum of one month and maximum of three months. **To Apply:** Applicants must submit the following materials: up-to-date curriculum vitae; copy of the doctoral thesis; full description of the project proposed during fellowship; an official letter from the host university indicating its support of the young researcher (availability of research tools, library, archives, computer, office, accommodation, teaching load and other responsibilities); two letters of reference from university professors knowledgeable with the candidates' studies; and letter from the senior researcher's host outlining the research project and the work to be assigned to the young researcher during the fellowship. For applicants applying for a research fellowship, they must include a budget detailing travel expenses, material, photocopies, etc. and for applicants applying for a teaching fellowship, they must also include a course outline maximum of two pages. Application files must be submitted to the ICCS with a recommendation from the national Canadian Studies Association. **Deadline:** November 24. **Contact:** Postdoctoral Fellowships in Canadian Studies International Council for Canadian Studies Holland Cross RO, 1620 Scott Street, Unit 8, PO Box 64016 Ottawa ON K1Y 4V1; Email: jkoustas@brocku.ca.

3801 ■ International Council for Canadian Studies Graduate Student Scholarships *(Graduate/ Scholarship)*

Purpose: To support the works of young scholars, by enabling successful candidates for their research related to their thesis or dissertation in the field of Canadian Studies. **Focus:** Canadian studies. **Qualif.:** Applicants must be students in the social sciences or humanities who are in the process of preparing a graduate thesis or doctoral dissertation in Canada; must be at the thesis or dissertation stage; and must obtain, in writing, the support of a faculty member at a Canadian University who has agreed to act as the students' academic sponsor during the tenure of their award. **Criteria:** Applicants will be evaluated based on clarity of the proposal and its methodology; the proposal's potential contribution; must demonstrate the need for the research to be carried out in Canada and by the strength of the letter of support. Nominations will be evaluated and ranked by the adjudication committee appointed by the International Council for Canadian Studies.

Funds Avail.: Up to 4,000 Canadian Dollars. **Duration:** Annual. **Number Awarded:** 6. **To Apply:** Applicants completed application form available in PDF format, which will be signed by the candidate and the president of the national association. Applicants must submit a two-page proposal outlining the thesis/dissertation project; an official university transcript; copy of a letter from the faculty member in a Canadian University indicating their willingness to act as the student's academic sponsor; and a letter of support from the student's thesis/dissertation supervisor; a copy of the letter from the faculty member in a Canadian university indicating willingness to act as the student's academic sponsor. **Deadline:** November 24. **Contact:** Graduate Student Scholarships; International Council for Canadian Studies; Holland Cross RO, 1620 Scott Street,

Awards are arranged alphabetically below their administering organizations

Unit8, PO Box 64016; Ottawa ON K1Y 4V1; CANADA;
E-mail: jkoustas@brocku.ca.

3802 ■ Conseil de Recherches en Sciences Naturelles et en Génie du Canada
350 Albert St.
Ottawa, ON, Canada K1A 1H5
Ph: (855)275-2861
URL: www.nserc-crsng.gc.ca
Social Media: www.facebook.com/nserccanada
www.linkedin.com/company/natural-sciences-and
  -engineering-research-council-of-canada
twitter.com/nserc_crsng
www.youtube.com/user/NSERCTube

3803 ■ Alexander Graham Bell Canada Graduate Scholarships-Doctoral Program *(Doctorate, Master's/Scholarship)*

Purpose: To provide financial support to high calibre scholars who are engaged in a doctoral program in the natural sciences or engineering. **Focus:** Natural sciences; Pre-Columbian studies. **Qualif.:** Applicants must be Canadian citizens or permanent residents of Canada; must intend to pursue, in the following year, full-time graduate studies and research at the master's or doctoral level in an eligible program in one of the areas of the natural sciences and engineering supported by NSERC; and must have obtained a first-class average (a grade of "A-") in each of the last two completed years of study. **Criteria:** Selection of recipients is based on academic excellence, research ability or potential and communication, interpersonal, and leadership abilities.

Funds Avail.: 35,000 Canadian Dollars. **Duration:** Up to three years. **Number Awarded:** 1. **To Apply:** Applicants must complete the online Form 201 (available on-line) and submit with other supporting materials. **Deadline:** October 17. **Contact:** Email: schol@nserc-crsng.gc.ca.

3804 ■ Banting Postdoctoral Fellowships Program *(Postdoctorate/Fellowship)*

Purpose: To provides funding to the very best postdoctoral applicants, both nationally and internationally, who will positively contribute to the country's economic, social and research-based growth. **Focus:** General studies/Field of study not specified. **Qualif.:** Applicant must be a Canadian citizens; permanent residents of Canada; foreign citizens. **Criteria:** Selection will be based on the committee's criteria.

Funds Avail.: $70,000. **Duration:** Biennial; non-renewable. **Deadline:** October 1.

3805 ■ Industrial R&D Fellowships *(Postdoctorate/Fellowship)*

Purpose: To provide financial support and to enable recent doctoral graduates to engage in research and development in the private sector. **Focus:** Engineering. **Qualif.:** Applicant must have completed a doctoral degree within the last five years; must not have been employed for more than six months in an R&D position in the Canadian private sector after receipt of a doctoral degree; and must not have received an offer of employment from the nominating company except an offer of this fellowship; postdoctoral fellows who have already held a Mitacs Elevate award are not eligible to apply again to Elevate or to apply afterwards to Accelerate but who have held a Mitacs Accelerate award as a Masters, or PhD student are eligible to apply. **Criteria:**

Selection is based on Peer assessment criteria which are grouped into the technical merit of the proposed research project and the excellence of the proposed fellow.

Funds Avail.: $55,000 minimum annual stipend and training curriculum valued at $7,500 per year. **Duration:** Annual; upto 2 years. **To Apply:** Completed application form along with memorandum; applicant's CV; proposed academic supervisor's CV; One letter of support from the proposed academic supervisor, One letter of support from a former supervisor or person familiar with the fellow's research expertise, One letter of support from an eligible partner organization on partner organization letterhead that confirms the amount of the financial commitment must be submitted as separate documents. **Deadline:** July 11. **Contact:** Phone: 613-996-1900.

3806 ■ NSERC Postgraduate Scholarships-Doctoral Program *(Doctorate/Scholarship)*

Purpose: To provide financial support to high-calibre students who are engaged in doctoral programs in the natural sciences or engineering. **Focus:** Natural sciences; Pre-Columbian studies. **Criteria:** Selection of recipients is based on academic excellence, research ability or potential and communication, interpersonal, and leadership abilities.

Funds Avail.: 21,000 Canadian Dollars. **Duration:** Up to three years. **To Apply:** Applicants must complete the online Form 201 (available on-line) and submit with other supporting materials. **Deadline:** October 17.

3807 ■ NSERC's E.W.R Steacie Memorial Fellowships *(Professional development/Fellowship)*

Purpose: To enhance the career development of outstanding and highly promising university faculty who are earning a strong international reputation for original research. **Focus:** Science. **Qualif.:** Applicants recognize early-stage academic researchers in the natural sciences and engineering and support them to enhance their research capacity, so that they can become leaders in their field and inspire others.

Funds Avail.: $250,000 over two years. **Duration:** Annual; up to two years. **Number Awarded:** Up to 6. **To Apply:** Applicants must complete a NSERC Personal Data Form (Form 100). When completing this form: contributions do not need to be limited to those in the last six years; there is no page limit; page one of an Application for a Grant (Form 101); only the top part, including the Certification/Requirements box, needs to be completed; no signatures are required on this form; a completed Environmental Information Form (Appendix A), if required; a two-page summary of the research that would be pursued during tenure; copies of the nominee's three most significant research contributions; the names and addresses (mail and email) of five to seven Canadian and/or international researchers who, in the opinion of the nominators, could be approached by NSERC to conduct an impartial review of the nomination; external reviewers should not be members of the nominee's university, former professors or supervisors, or present or former collaborators or colleagues; applicants must not contact suggested external reviewers in advance; NSERC reserves the right to select all or none of the suggested reviewers; a Terms and Conditions Form for Nominees signed by the nominee; a Terms and Conditions Form for Nominators signed by the nominator. **Deadline:** June 7. **Remarks:** The award was established to honor the memory of Dr. Edgar William Richard Steacie, an outstanding chemist and research leader who made major contributions to the development of science in Canada during, and

Awards are arranged alphabetically below their administering organizations

immediately following, World War II. **Contact:** Steacie Fellowships, NSERC, 350 Albert St., Ottawa, Ontario K1A 1H5; Phone: 613-943-7653; Email: inquiries.steacie@nserc-crsng.gc.ca.

3808 ■ Vanier Canada Graduate Scholarships Program *(Graduate/Scholarship)*

Purpose: To support students who demonstrate a high standard of scholarly achievement in graduate studies in the social sciences and humanities, natural sciences and engineering, and health and to those who demonstrate leadership skills. **Focus:** Health sciences; Humanities; Natural sciences; Social sciences. **Qualif.:** Applicant must be Canadian and international students; who demonstrate both leadership skills and a high standard of scholarly achievement in graduate studies in the natural sciences and engineering, social sciences and humanities, or health sciences. **Criteria:** Selection will be based on the committee's criteria.

Funds Avail.: 50,000 Canadian Dollars per year. **Duration:** Annual. **To Apply:** Applicants must visit the Vanier CGS website for further instructions and application procedures. **Deadline:** November 3. **Contact:** Email: vanier@cihr-irsc.gc.ca.

3809 ■ Constangy, Brooks, Smith & Prophete L.L.P.

230 Peachtree St. NW, Ste. 2400
Atlanta, GA 30303-1557
Ph: (404)525-8622
URL: www.constangy.com
Social Media: www.facebook.com/Constangy
twitter.com/ConstangyLaw
www.youtube.com/channel/
  UC5uLdysVswASipoUBZIYUFw

3810 ■ Diversity Scholars Awards *(Undergraduate/Award, Recognition)*

Purpose: To honor and recognize the achievements of law students who have demonstrated academic achievement, a commitment to diversity in their community, school or work environment, and personal achievements in overcoming challenges to reach goals. **Focus:** Law. **Criteria:** Selection will be based on accomplishments in academics, a commitment to diversity in the community, school or work environment, and personal achievement in overcoming challenges to reach goals.

Funds Avail.: $5,000. **Duration:** Annual. **Number Awarded:** 1. **To Apply:** Applicants must apply in online application process. **Contact:** Kian Cheng; Constangy, Brooks, Smith & Prophete, LLP, 230 Peachtree St. NW, Ste. 2400, Atlanta, GA, 30303.

3811 ■ Consumer Attorneys of California (CAOC)

770 L St., Ste. 1200
Sacramento, CA 95814
Ph: (916)442-6902
Fax: (916)442-7734
E-mail: info@caoc.org
URL: www.caoc.org
Social Media: www.facebook.com/ConsumerAttorneys
www.instagram.com/consumer_attorneys_ca
twitter.com/ConsumerAttysCA
www.youtube.com/user/consumerattorneysca

3812 ■ California Bar Foundation 3L Diversity Scholarship *(Undergraduate/Scholarship)*

Purpose: To help offset high cost of law school education. **Focus:** Law. **Qualif.:** Candidate must be diverse 3L who intends to take the California bar exam, has a commitment to social justice/public interest, and can demonstrate their California-oriented career goals. **Criteria:** Selection will be based on the committee's criteria.

Funds Avail.: No specific amount. **Duration:** Annual. **Deadline:** February 15. **Contact:** Email: scholarships@calbarfoundation.org.

3813 ■ Consumers Credit Union

1075 Tri-State Pky., Ste. 850
Gurnee, IL 60031
Free: 877-275-2228
E-mail: ccu_info@myconsumers.org
URL: www.myconsumers.org
Social Media: www.facebook.com/consumerscreditunion
www.linkedin.com/company/consumers-credit-union-illinois
www.youtube.com/user/ConsumersCreditUnion

3814 ■ Consumers Credit Union Scholarship *(Undergraduate, College, Vocational/Occupational, Two Year College, University/Scholarship)*

Purpose: To provide high school seniors in the Lower Peninsula of Michigan with an opportunity to help pay for their higher education. **Focus:** General studies/Field of study not specified. **Qualif.:** Applicants must be high school seniors in the Lower Peninsula of Michigan with a minimum 2.5 GPA. **Criteria:** Selection is based on academic qualifications and contest of essay question response.

Funds Avail.: $20,000 (1); $1,000 (10). **Number Awarded:** 11. **To Apply:** Complete application; provide high school transcript, letter of acceptance from an accredited college, university or trade school; letter of recommendation; documentation of school activities, community service and/or volunteer work; essay, minimum 300 words, topic can be found online. **Deadline:** March 1. **Contact:** Email: scholarships@consumerscu.org; URL: www.consumerscu.org/about/scholarships.

3815 ■ Contra Costa County Bar Association (CCCBA)

2300 Clayton Rd., Ste. 520
Concord, CA 94520
Ph: (925)686-6900
Fax: (925)686-9867
E-mail: feedback@cccba.org
URL: www.cccba.org
Social Media: www.facebook.com/CCCBA/
twitter.com/CCCBAR

3816 ■ Richard E. Arnason Court Scholarship Program *(Undergraduate/Scholarship)*

Purpose: To help adults or juveniles gain the education they need to get ahead. **Focus:** Criminal justice. **Qualif.:** Applicants must be adults or juveniles currently residing in Contra Costa County who have been through the criminal justice system resulting in a conviction; must be out of custody as of March 31st of the current year and not in a residential treatment program or on electronic home detention.

Awards are arranged alphabetically below their administering organizations

Funds Avail.: Up to $2,500. **Duration:** Annual. **To Apply:** Applicants must submit a completed application form; if selected for consideration, applicants must provide references and documentation to support their request, including school transcripts. **Deadline:** April 1. **Contact:** Contra Costa County Bar Association, Richard E. Arnason Court Scholarship Committee; Email: awolf@cccba.org.

3817 ■ Jack Kent Cooke Foundation (JKCF)

44325 Woodridge Pky.
Lansdowne, VA 20176
Ph: (571)799-8000
Fax: (703)723-8030
E-mail: scholarships@jkcf.org
URL: www.jkcf.org
Social Media: www.facebook.com/
  JackKentCookeFoundation
instagram.com/thejkcf
www.linkedin.com/company/the-jack-kent-cooke-foundation
twitter.com/TheJKCF

3818 ■ Jack Kent Cooke Dissertation Fellowship Award *(Doctorate/Fellowship)*

Purpose: To support advanced doctoral students completing dissertations that further the understanding of the educational pathways and experiences of high-achieving, low-income students. **Focus:** General studies/Field of study not specified. **Qualif.:** Applicants may be U.S. citizens, U.S. permanent residents, or non-U.S. citizens; must be currently studying in an accredited U.S. institution; must be advanced doctoral students who have completed all pre-dissertation requirements; must have successfully defended their dissertation proposal before the application deadline; must not have previously received a scholarship or other funding from the foundation. **Criteria:** The Foundation will select fellows based on the their superior academic ability and achievement; dissertation's significant contribution to exploring; the quality of the proposal with regard to its methodology, scope, theoretical framework, and grounding in the relevant scholarly literature; and the feasibility of the project and the likelihood that the applicant will execute the work within the proposed timeframe.

Funds Avail.: $100,000. **Duration:** Annual. **Number Awarded:** 4. **To Apply:** Interested applicants must provide and submit the following via the electronic site or mail: online application form; cover letter describing the relevance of proposed research with the mission of the Foundation; summary of the proposal, limited to six pages; work plan or timeline for completing dissertation; one letter of support; an official graduate transcript; and curriculum vitae.

3819 ■ Jack Kent Cooke Graduate Arts Awards *(Graduate/Award)*

Purpose: To recognize and rewards America's promising up-and-coming artists from lower-income backgrounds with the nation's leading graduate scholarship in the visual arts, performing arts, and creative writing. **Focus:** Creative writing; Performing arts; Visual arts. **Qualif.:** Candidates must have senior standing or have graduated from an accredited four-year US college or university within the past five years; must have a cumulative undergraduate GPA of 3.20 or better on a scale of 4.0; must demonstrate unmet financial need; must have a bachelor's degree by the start of the fall of the current semester; must have plans to begin their first graduate degree program in the performing arts, visual arts

or creative writing at an accredited college or university in the fall of the current year. **Criteria:** Criteria will be based on the applicants academic achievement, artistic or creative merit, financial need, and resilience.

Funds Avail.: $50,000. **Duration:** Annual. **Number Awarded:** 20. **To Apply:** Interested applicants may visit the website for the online application process and other information.

3820 ■ Jack Kent Cooke Foundation College Scholarship Program *(Undergraduate/Scholarship)*

Purpose: To support deserving students with their educational expenses. **Focus:** Education. **Qualif.:** Applicants must be high school senior students; must have a cumulative unweighted GPA of 3.5 or above; must have an SAT combined score of 1200 or above (CR and M) and/or ACT composite score of 26 or above; and must have demonstrated unmet financial need and intend to enroll full-time in an accredited college. **Criteria:** Selection will be based on exceptional academic ability and achievement, financial need, persistence, a desire to help others, and leadership.

Funds Avail.: Up to $40,000. **Duration:** Annual. **To Apply:** Applicants must visit the Foundation's website for the online application system. The College Scholarship Program application requires information from several different people. Each person must have a unique email address in order to receive the required forms via email from the online application system. **Deadline:** September 6. **Contact:** Email: scholarships@jkcf.org.

3821 ■ Jack Kent Cooke Foundation Undergraduate Transfer Scholarship *(Undergraduate/Scholarship)*

Purpose: To support community college students to transfer and complete their bachelor's degrees at the top four-year colleges/universities. **Focus:** General studies/ Field of study not specified. **Qualif.:** Applicants must be current students at an accredited U.S. community college or two-year institution with sophomore status, or recent graduates; plan to enroll full-time in a baccalaureate program at an accredited college/university; have a cumulative undergraduate GPA of 3.5 or better on a scale of 4.0 (or the equivalent). **Criteria:** Selection will be based on achievement and academic ability; financial need; persistence; leadership; service to others.

Funds Avail.: Up to $40,000. **Duration:** Annual. **To Apply:** Applicants must complete the application form and also include: information of teacher recommenders and personal recommender. **Deadline:** April 10. **Contact:** Email: scholarships@jkcf.org.

3822 ■ Jack Kent Cooke Foundation Young Scholars Program *(Undergraduate/Scholarship)*

Purpose: To support students in their educational pursuits. **Focus:** General studies/Field of study not specified. **Qualif.:** Applicants must be in the 7th grade entering 8th grade; have mostly 'A' grades and no 'Cs' or below in the past two years; have a family with unmet financial need; and planning to attend high school in the U.S.; must reside in the U.S. or a U.S. territory. **Criteria:** Selection is based on academic ability and high achievement and intelligence, unmet financial need, will to succeed, leadership and public service, critical-thinking ability and appreciation for, or participation in, the arts and humanities, music, art, literature or similar fields.

Funds Avail.: No specific amount. **Duration:** Annual. **Number Awarded:** Varies. **To Apply:** Applicants must submit a

Awards are arranged alphabetically below their administering organizations

completed application (application checklist: student application, parent/guardian form, custodial parent(s)/ guardian(s) financial form and tax forms; noncustodial parent(s)/guardian(s) financial form and tax forms (if applicable); school report; teacher recommendation; personal recommendation; survey form). **Deadline:** April 26. **Contact:** Phone: 800-941-3300; Email: scholarships@jkcf.org.

3823 ■ Cool Club
16 Panteli Katelari St., Office 303
Nicosia 1097, Cyprus
URL: cool.club
Social Media: www.facebook.com/writerscoolclub
twitter.com/WritersCoolClub

3824 ■ $1,500 Video Contest Scholarship for Students Who Enjoy Writing *(High School, College, University/Scholarship)*

Purpose: To assist aspiring writers with educational costs. **Focus:** General studies/Field of study not specified. **Qualif.:** Applicant must be a high school, college, or university student from any country. **Criteria:** Selection is based on the video submitted which will be evaluated by an editorial team for creativity, usefulness, and production quality.

Funds Avail.: $1,000 (1); $500 (1). **Number Awarded:** 2. **To Apply:** Applicant must record an original video; criteria available on sponsor's website. Applicant must like and share the contest video description on Facebook or Twitter and subscribe to the Cool. Club YouTube channel. The following should be sent to the sponsor via email: a link to the uploaded video, a screenshot proving the applicant's subscription to the Cool. Club YouTube channel, and the answer to the question "Where did you find out about the Cool. Club Contest? **Deadline:** October 7. **Contact:** Email: scholarship@cool.club; URL: cool.club/blog/scholarship/.

3825 ■ Cooley L.L.P.
3175 Hanover St.
Palo Alto, CA 94304-1130
Ph: (650)843-5000
Fax: (650)849-7400
URL: www.cooley.com
Social Media: www.facebook.com/CooleyLLP
www.linkedin.com/company/cooleyllp
twitter.com/CooleyLLP

3826 ■ Cooley Diversity Fellowship *(Graduate, Undergraduate/Fellowship)*

Purpose: To financially assist law students. **Focus:** Law. **Criteria:** Selection is based on commitment to promoting diversity and inclusion; undergraduate and law school academic achievement; personal achievement; demonstrated leadership ability; community service.

Funds Avail.: Up to $30,000. **Duration:** Annual. **To Apply:** Applicants must submit a completed application form online along with a brief personal statement; a current resume; law school transcript; and undergraduate transcript; also submit up to two letters of recommendation; up to three references; and a legal writing sample. **Deadline:** January 10. **Contact:** Amie Santos, Cooley's Diversity and Inclusion Manager; Email: diversityfellowship@cooley.com.

3827 ■ Coordinating Council for Women in History (CCWH)
608 N. 5th Ave.
Phoenix, AZ 85003

URL: theccwh.org
Social Media: www.facebook.com/theccwh
twitter.com/TheCCWH

3828 ■ CCWH / Berks Graduate Student Fellowship *(Graduate/Fellowship)*

Purpose: To support the completion of a dissertation in a history department either in the crucial stage of research or in the final year of writing. **Focus:** History. **Qualif.:** The applicant must be a graduate student historian in a history department in a U.S. institution; must have passed to A.B.D. status by the time of application; may specialize in any field of history; may hold this award and others simultaneously; and need not attend the award ceremony to receive the award. **Criteria:** Selection will be based on the committee's criteria.

Funds Avail.: $1,000. **Duration:** Annual. **Number Awarded:** 1. **To Apply:** Applicants must submit a current curriculum vitae; summary of the dissertation project, including an explanation of how the dissertation project will advance understanding of the issue(s) under study, a survey of the major primary sources, a discussion of the historiography, a summary of research already accomplished, and an indication of plans for completion of the dissertation in no more than 1200 words, double-spaced; two letters of recommendation from members of the dissertation committee in a separate e-mails with name of applicants and CCWH/Berks Award in the subject line; if a signature is not obtained, at least one of the letters should state that applicant has advanced to A.B.D. status. **Deadline:** June 15. **Remarks:** Established in 1991. **Contact:** ccwhberksaward@theccwh.org.

3829 ■ CCWH Nupur Chaudhuri Article Prize *(Professional development/Prize)*

Purpose: To support the best first article published in the field of history. **Focus:** History. **Qualif.:** Applicants must be current CCWH members; need not attend the award ceremony to receive the award; have published an article with full scholarly apparatus in a refereed journal. **Criteria:** Selection will be based on the committee's criteria.

Funds Avail.: $1,000. **Duration:** Annual. **Number Awarded:** Varies. **To Apply:** Applicants must submit the following information in an email and attachments: name; mailing address; home phone; email; institutional affiliation if any; bibliographical Information; article title; journal, volume and date of publication and page numbers; current CV; article. **Deadline:** June 15. **Remarks:** Named to honor long-time CCWH board member and former executive director and co-president from 1995-1998 Nupur Chaudhuri. **Contact:** E-mail: ChaudhuriAward@theccwh.org.

3830 ■ Catherine Prelinger Award *(Postdoctorate/ Scholarship)*

Purpose: To provide support to scholars whose career has not followed a traditional path through secondary and higher education, and whose work has contributed to women in the historical profession. **Focus:** General studies/Field of study not specified; History; Women's studies. **Qualif.:** Applicants must be members of CCWH and must hold either A.B.D. status or the Ph.D.; shall be actively engaged in scholarship that is historical in nature, although the degree may be in related fields.

Funds Avail.: $20,000. **Duration:** Annual. **Number Awarded:** 1. **To Apply:** Applicants must submit a curriculum vitae (limited to 4 pages); a personal statement of

Awards are arranged alphabetically below their administering organizations

the applicant's non-traditional career path, challenges faced, contributions to women in the profession, and activism on behalf of women (limited to one single-spaced page, 11-point font, 1-inch margins); the project statement (limited to three single-spaced pages, 11-point font, 1-inch margins); confidential letters of recommendation. **Deadline:** June 15. **Remarks:** The award is named in the memory of Catherine Prelinger, a former CCWH president and nontraditional scholar. Established in 1998. **Contact:** Committee chair, Stephanie Moore; E-mail: PrelingerAward@theccwh.org.

3831 ■ Ida B. Wells Graduate Student Fellowship
(Graduate/Fellowship)

Purpose: To support graduate students working in historical dissertation that interrogates race and gender, not necessarily in a history department. **Focus:** General studies/Field of study not specified; History; Women's studies. **Qualif.:** Applicant must be a CCWH member; must be a graduate student in any department of a U.S. institution; must have passed to A.B.D. status by the time of application; may hold this award and others simultaneously; need not attend the award ceremony to receive the award. **Criteria:** Applicants are judged upon the committee's criteria.

Funds Avail.: $1,000. **Duration:** Annual. **Number Awarded:** 2. **To Apply:** Applicants must include current curriculum vitae; a summary of the dissertation project, an explanation of how the dissertation project will advance our understanding of the issue(s) under study, a survey of the major primary sources, a discussion of the historiography, a summary of research already accomplished, and an indication of plans for completion of the dissertation in no more than 1200 words, double-spaced; two letters of recommendation from members of the dissertation committee in a separate e-mails. **Deadline:** June 15. **Remarks:** Established in 1999. **Contact:** Committee, E-mail: WellsAward@ccwh.org.

3832 ■ Copper and Brass Servicenter Association (CBSA)
6734 W 121st St.
Overland Park, KS 66209
Ph: (913)396-0697
Fax: (913)345-1006
E-mail: cbsahq@copper-brass.org
URL: www.copper-brass.org
Social Media: www.facebook.com/CBSAHQ
www.linkedin.com/company/copper-and-brass-servicenter -association
twitter.com/CBSAHQ
www.youtube.com/CBSATV

3833 ■ Copper and Brass Servicenter Association Scholarship Program *(Undergraduate/Scholarship)*

Purpose: To provide financial educational assistance to a child of CBSA employees or any associate member companies. **Focus:** General studies/Field of study not specified. **Qualif.:** Applicant must be employed by a CBSA member company; Be a child of an employee of a CBSA member company; Be enrolled in an undergraduate industrial distribution degree program; Be pursuing an undergraduate degree at an accredited four-year college or university; Be taking at least six credit hours in the upcoming school year Have a grade point average (GPA) of at least 3.0 (on a 4.0 scale). **Criteria:** Recipients are selected based on academic achievement, extracurricular activities and financial of

Funds Avail.: No specific amount. **Duration:** Annual. **To Apply:** Applicant must submit current unofficial transcript. If you are a college freshman, please send both high school and college transcripts; A letter of recommendation from a principal or dean, department head or instructor from your school; A 500-word (one-page) essay; The signature addendum page of the application, signed by both the student and a parent or guardian. **Deadline:** June 7. **Contact:** Jean McClure; Phone: 913-396-0697.

3834 ■ Cores & Associates
200 Daniels Way, Ste., 200
Freehold, NJ 07728
Ph: (732)414-6669
E-mail: info@amysaracores.com
URL: amysaracores.com
Social Media: www.facebook.com/CoresAssociates
twitter.com/coresassociates

3835 ■ Cores & Associates Scholarship Contest
(Undergraduate/Scholarship)

Purpose: To provide financial aid to college students, encourage students to understand how lawyers help family law proceedings, and inspire students to pursue a career in the legal field. **Focus:** Law. **Qualif.:** Applicant must be high school senior or college freshman in the United States who is studying, or planning to study, law. **Criteria:** Selection is based on the best video essay or written essay submitted.

Funds Avail.: $1,000. **Duration:** Annual. **Number Awarded:** 1. **To Apply:** Applicant must record a video essay (one to two minutes long, in English) than answer the essay topic. Video must be uploaded to the applicant's YouTube channel with the title "Cores & Associates Scholarship Contest" and with the following link in the description: amysaracores.com/scholarship-for-college-students/. Applicant must also share the video on their Facebook page and the sponsor's Facebook page. Instead of a video essay, applicant may submit a 1,000 to 1,500 word essay on the same subject via email. **Deadline:** August 15. **Contact:** Amy Cores; Emai: info@coresandassociates.com.

3836 ■ Corporate Counsel Women of Color (CCWC)
Radio City Sta.
New York, NY 10101-2095
Ph: (646)483-8041
E-mail: info@ccwomenofcolor.org
URL: ccwomenofcolor.org
Social Media: www.instagram.com/ccwomenofcolor
twitter.com/ccwomenofcolor

3837 ■ My Life As A Lawyer Scholarship *(Graduate/Scholarship)*

Purpose: To support law students with their educational pursuit. **Focus:** Law. **Qualif.:** Applicants must be first or second year students enrolled in an accredited law school in any state of the United States of America. **Criteria:** Selection is based on the submitted application materials.

Funds Avail.: No specific amount. **Duration:** Annual. **To Apply:** Applicants must submit (through first-class mail only) a completed application form together with a list of any publications, academic awards, honors, scholarships, memberships, and/or extracurricular activities; an essay of

Awards are arranged alphabetically below their administering organizations

no more than 350 words; and a copy of law school transcript. **Deadline:** June 30. **Contact:** Corporate Counsel Women of Color, Attention: My Life As a Lawyer 2019 Scholarship; Radio City Station, PO Box 2095, New York, New York, 10101-2095; Email: info@ccwomenofcolor.org.

3838 ■ Corporation des Associations de Detaillants d'Automobiles (CADA)

123 Commerce Valley Dr. E Ste. 303
Thornhill, ON, Canada L3T 7W8
Ph: (905)940-4959
Free: 800-463-5289
URL: www.cada.ca

3839 ■ Richard C. Gauthier CADA Scholarship
(Undergraduate/Scholarship)

Purpose: To support a student, in any year, in taking Bachelor of Applied Business in Automotive Management program. **Focus:** Automotive technology; Business. **Criteria:** Selection will be made by the ECAC Fellowships Selection Committee.

Funds Avail.: 2,500 Canadian Dollars. **Duration:** Annual. **Number Awarded:** 1. **To Apply:** Applicants need to forward a cover letter explaining how they meet the criteria, a resume, an academic transcript (copy acceptable) and a copy of their successful co-op placement evaluation completed in a new car or truck dealership; letter of recommendation from their immediate superior to this concession is also required. **Remarks:** The Award was established in honor of Richard C. Gauthier, who was the President and CEO of the CADA from 1996 to 2016. **Contact:** ABSC Georgian College Awards Officer; Phone: 705-728-1968, ext. 1211.

3840 ■ Correctional Education Association (CEA)

PO Box 3430
Laurel, MD 20709
Ph: (443)459-3080
Fax: (443)459-3088
E-mail: office@ceanational.org
URL: ceanational.org
Social Media: www.facebook.com/CEANatl
www.instagram.com/ceanational
twitter.com/ceanatl

3841 ■ Correctional Education Association Scholarships *(Graduate, Undergraduate/Scholarship)*

Purpose: To encourage students to continue a course of study in correctional education. **Focus:** Criminal justice. **Qualif.:** Applicant must be a graduate or undergraduate student in correctional education; must be a voting member of the Correctional Education Association and have been a member for a minimum of two years prior to application. **Criteria:** Application materials (quality of the application will be taken into consideration) will be evaluated by the Scholarship Committee; priority will be given to first time applicants.

Funds Avail.: Up to $500. **Duration:** Annual. **To Apply:** Applicants forms are available in the website (application format must be completed in full in order to be considered by the Committee); application materials must be sent to Correctional Educational Association, Scholarship Committee. **Contact:** Correctional Education Association, Attn:

Awards Committee, PO Box 3430, Laurel, MD, 20709; Phone: 443-459-3984; Fax: 443-459-3088; E-mail: kwilson@ceanational.org; CEA National Secretary (Awards Committee Chair), Susan Nell, OSU/CETE 1900 Kenny Rd., Columbus, OH, 43210; E-mail: nell.5@osu.edu.

3842 ■ Costume Society of America (CSA)

PO Box 852
Columbus, GA 31902-0852
Free: 800-272-9447
E-mail: national.office@costumesocietyamerica.com
URL: costumesocietyamerica.com

3843 ■ Stella Blum Research Grant *(Graduate, Undergraduate/Grant)*

Purpose: To provide financial assistance to a student member working in the field of North American costume. **Focus:** Design. **Criteria:** Applicants will be evaluated based on the following: significance, creativity, and innovation of the proposed research topic; impact of the research on the broad field of costume (beyond simply increasing the student's own knowledge and experience) and applicant's awareness of the interdisciplinary nature of the field of costume; feasibility of time frame, work plan, and budget of the proposed project; time frame/work plan/time table; methodology of the research plan and appropriateness of research sources and bibliography; applicant's qualifications, including familiarity with the subject and previous experience; recommendation letters.

Funds Avail.: $3,000. **Duration:** Annual. **To Apply:** Applicants must Send six (6) copies of the following: application form; budget form; project proposal (double spaced and no more than 1, 000 words), including: introduction to research project, its background and significance; purposes and goals of the research, specific objectives of work to be accomplished, and what questions will be answered; qualifications of researcher, familiarity with subject, course work completed and related courses to be taken during the project, previous research experience, and how the project will benefit the student at this point in their academic career and in the long run; methodology, structure of research design, name of research supervisor, and project schedule; application/scholarly presentation of results, and the value of this information to the field of costume research; select bibliography and related resources (not included in word limit); Send one (1) copy of the following: proof of current student enrollment; official transcripts from all relevant academic work sent via US mail under seal or directly from the institution using a secure electronic transfer process; letters of permission from any research site, museum, or library that the applicant intends to visit for research. To be sent separately, two (2) recommendations (on form that can be downloaded here), one from the research project supervisor and another from someone familiar with the applicant's academic record, preferably a faculty member. **Deadline:** May 1. **Remarks:** The grant was named in honor of Stella Blum (1916-1985), a costume curator, educator, writer, scholar, and founding member and Fellow of the Costume Society of America. Established in 1987. **Contact:** Ann Wass, 903 60th aver, Riverdale, MD, 20737; E-mail: annbwass@aol.com.

3844 ■ CSA College and University Collection Care Grant *(Other/Grant)*

Purpose: To assist the costume and textiles collection of a college or university that receives little or no financial support from its institution. **Focus:** Design. **Qualif.:** Applying institutions must meet the following requirements: have a degree program in apparel, textiles, or theatre; have a collection consisting of dress, textiles, and related objects that is intended for preservation; legally own the collection (a private collection housed in a college/university is not eligible); provide institutional support for the collection; provide institutional endorsement of the collection by some expression of commitment for the care and management of the collection; must be or become an Institutional Member of the Costume Society of America or have an active staff member who is an Individual CSA member; an institution is not eligible to receive a grant more than once in three years. **Criteria:** Evaluations will be based upon: high impact of the project on collection's well-being and mission; feasibility of the project in terms of budget, timeline, and personnel to carry it out; significance of the collection to the academic unit.

Funds Avail.: $1,500. **Duration:** Annual. **To Apply:** Applications are available on the web site and should be submitted online. **Deadline:** October 15. **Remarks:** Established in 2006. **Contact:** Committee Chair, Kelly Richardson, Email: ksrichar@indiana.edu.

3845 ■ CSA Travel Research Grants (Advanced Professional/Grant)

Purpose: To provide financial assistance and to enable an individual (non-student) member to travel to a library, archive, museum, or other collection or site to further an on-going research project. **Focus:** Design. **Qualif.:** Applicants must have been members of the CSA for at least the preceding two years; provide proof that work on the project is already underway; have confirmed that the collection they propose to visit will grant them a research appointment and that the material to be consulted will be available. **Criteria:** Applications will be evaluated based on the following: feasibility of time frame, work plan and budget of the proposed project; methodology of the research plan and appropriateness of research sources and bibliography; evidence of work accomplished to date; applicant's qualification's, including familiarity with subject and previous experience; impact of the research on the broad field of costume.

Funds Avail.: $2,100. **Duration:** Annual. **To Apply:** Applicants should submit the following: a letter of application, including a description of the project under way, evidence of work accomplished to date, name of the collection to be visited, reasons for visiting the designated collection, project dates for visiting the collection and completion date for project, audience that will benefit from the project; current resume or CV (no more than two pages); letter from the collection they proposed to visit granting a research appointment at the time required and confirming that the material to be consulted will be available; summary of projected budget (one page maximum). **Deadline:** October 15. **Remarks:** Established in 1996. **Contact:** Catherine Amoroso Leslie, Committee Chair; E-mail: cleslie1@kent.edu.

3846 ■ Adele Filene Student Presenter Grant (Graduate, Undergraduate/Grant)

Purpose: To provide financial assistance to students who have been selected to present papers at the CSA national symposium. **Focus:** Design. **Qualif.:** Applicants must be full-time undergraduate or graduate university students; must be current members of the Costume Society America; must have received notice that their proposal for an oral research paper or research exhibit has been accepted for that yea's National Symposium; must reside outside a 200

mile radius of that symposium site; recipients will be expected to attend the symposium, present their research, and receive their check at the awards ceremony. **Criteria:** Applicants will be evaluated based on the following: significance of the research to be presented; quality of student's scholarship and future professional promise; applicant's interest in the broad field of costume; evidence of applicant's interest in continuing involvement with CSA; and recommendation letter.

Funds Avail.: $600. **Duration:** Annual. **Number Awarded:** 2. **To Apply:** Applicants must complete and submit the following: name, email, mailing address, name of college or university, major, and date of graduation; a 1, 000-1, 500 words essay on their involvement with dress and fashion, their career goals, and what they hope to gain from attending the CSA National Symposium; a letter of recommendation from an academic advisor or professor, which may be sent separately or emailed. **Deadline:** January 15. **Remarks:** The grants are named in honor of Adele Filene (1909-2010), designer of couture, sportswear, and handbags as well as a teacher and costume restoration specialist. Established in 1996. **Contact:** Michelle Finamore, Committee Chair; E-mail: Mfinamore@mfa.org.

3847 ■ Council for the Advancement of Science Writing (CASW)

PO Box 17337
Seattle, WA 98127
Ph: (206)880-0177
E-mail: sylviakantor@casw.org
URL: www.casw.org
Social Media: www.facebook.com/SciWriting
twitter.com/ScienceWriting

3848 ■ Taylor/Blakeslee University Fellowships (Graduate/Award)

Purpose: To provide financial support to students who want to pursue a career in science writing. **Focus:** Journalism. **Qualif.:** Applicants must be working journalists and students of outstanding ability who have been accepted for enrollment in graduate-level programs in science writing; with at least two years of mass media experience are particularly invited to apply; must have an undergraduate degree and must convince the CASW selection committee; must be accepted by at least one institution prior to the fellowship application deadline; must be U.S. citizens or permanent residents. **Criteria:** Applications will be evaluated by CASW Selection Committee based on criteria; journalists with at least two years of mass media experience will receive preferential treatment in the selection process.

Funds Avail.: $5,000. **Duration:** Annual. **To Apply:** Applicants must complete the application form; must submit resume; samples of writing; description of science-writing program and list of courses to be pursued; and statement (not to exceed 500 words). **Deadline:** January 1. **Contact:** Rennie Taylor at P.O Box 910 Hedgesville, WV 25427.

3849 ■ Council of American Overseas Research Centers (CAORC)

PO Box 37012
Washington, DC 20013
Ph: (202)633-1599
Fax: (202)633-3141
E-mail: info@caorc.org

Awards are arranged alphabetically below their administering organizations

URL: www.caorc.org
Social Media: www.facebook.com/caorc
www.instagram.com/caorc_council
www.linkedin.com/company/council-of-american-overseas
  -research-centers
twitter.com/caorc
www.youtube.com/channel/
  UCAC7nz6zzzWWa4RFBjP6HDg

3850 ■ ARIT Fellowships in the Humanities and Social Sciences in Turkey *(Postdoctorate, Graduate/Fellowship)*

Purpose: To help applicant's research and study facilities for researchers, as well as connections with colleagues, institutions, and authorities through its centers in Istanbul and Ankara. **Focus:** History, Ancient; Humanities; Medieval studies; Modern languages; Social sciences. **Qualif.:** Applicants must be scholars and advanced graduate students engaged in research on ancient, medieval, or modern times in turkey, in any field of the humanities and social sciences; student applicants must have fulfilled all requirements for the doctorate except the dissertation by June of the current year, and before beginning any ARIT-sponsored research; non-U.S. applicants who reside in the U.S. or Canada are expected to maintain an affiliation with an educational institution in the U.S. or Canada.

Funds Avail.: No specific amount. **Duration:** Annual. **To Apply:** Applicants must provide complete application information; three letters of recommendation; letters of reference; copy of graduate transcript; supporting documents. **Deadline:** November 1. **Contact:** University of Pennsylvania Museum, 3260 South Street, Philadelphia PA 19104-6324. For further information call (215) 898-3474, fax (215) 898-0657, or e-mail to aritoffice@gmail.com.

3851 ■ Multi-Country Research Fellowship *(Doctorate, Postdoctorate/Fellowship)*

Purpose: To support advanced regional or trans-regional research in the humanities, social sciences or allied natural sciences for US doctoral candidates and scholars who have already earned their PhD. **Focus:** Humanities; Natural sciences; Social sciences. **Criteria:** Preference will be given to candidates examining comparative and/or cross-regional research.

Funds Avail.: Up to $11,000 each. **Duration:** Annual. **Number Awarded:** Approximately 8. **To Apply:** Applications must consist of a project description (maximum of 1500 words); project bibliography/literature review (one page); two separate letters of recommendation; a maximum three pages curriculum vitae; graduate transcript; project bibliography/literature review and curriculum vitae, in MS Word format, via email. **Remarks:** Established in 1993. **Contact:** Email: fellowships@caorc.org.

3852 ■ Council for Children with Behavior Disorders (CCBD)

Council for Exceptional Children
2900 Crystal Dr., Ste. 1000
Arlington, VA 22202-3557
Ph: (703)620-3660
Free: 888-232-7733
E-mail: service@cec.sped.org
URL: www.ccbd.net
Social Media: www.facebook.com/cechq
www.linkedin.com/company/council-for-exceptional
  -children-cec-

twitter.com/cecmembership

3853 ■ Eleanor Guetzloe Undergraduate Scholarship *(Undergraduate/Scholarship)*

Purpose: To support an outstanding undergraduate students who are pursuing teaching certification in the area of behavioral needs. **Focus:** Behavioral sciences. **Qualif.:** Applicants must be current members of the Council for Exceptional Children (CEC), and registered to attend either graduate or undergraduate studies directly related to working with students with behavioral needs at an accredited institution of higher education.

Duration: Annual.

3854 ■ Council for European Studies (CES)

Columbia University
420 W 118 St., MC 3307
New York, NY 10027
Ph: (212)854-4172
Fax: (212)854-8808
E-mail: info@ces-europe.org
URL: councilforeuropeanstudies.org
Social Media: www.facebook.com/CESEurope
www.linkedin.com/company/2696778
twitter.com/ces_europe

3855 ■ Alliance-CES Pre-Dissertation Research Fellowship *(Graduate/Fellowship)*

Purpose: To facilitate the transition from coursework to fieldwork, and to enable students to make rapid progress in refining their initial ideas into a feasible, interesting and fundable doctoral project. **Focus:** European studies. **Qualif.:** Applicants must be enrolled in a doctoral program at a university that is a member of Alliance. **Criteria:** Selection will be based on the committee's criteria.

Funds Avail.: $4,500. **Duration:** Annual. **To Apply:** Applicants must submit the CES Pre-Dissertation Fellowship Application Form and return three completed Faculty Recommendation Forms; must submit a Language Competency Form for every language in which they will require functional knowledge to complete their proposed research. **Deadline:** February 1. **Remarks:** Established in 2002. **Contact:** Email to awards@ces-europe.org.

3856 ■ CES Conference Travel Grants *(Graduate, Professional development/Grant)*

Purpose: To provide support trans-Atlantic travel for junior faculty and graduate students already scheduled to present at the Council's International Conference of Europeanists. **Focus:** European studies. **Qualif.:** Applicants must be junior faculty and graduate students already scheduled to present at CES' International Conference of Europeanists. **Criteria:** Selection will be based on submission of form.

Funds Avail.: $500. **Duration:** Annual. **To Apply:** Interested applicants must visit the website for the online application process; must include CV; cover letter. **Deadline:** January 9.

3857 ■ European Studies First Article Prize *(Professional development/Prize)*

Purpose: To honor the writers of the best first articles in European studies published within a two-year period. **Focus:** European studies; Humanities; Social sciences. **Criteria:** Selection will be based on submission of form.

Awards are arranged alphabetically below their administering organizations

Funds Avail.: $250. **Duration:** in odd years. **Number Awarded:** 2. **To Apply:** Nominations must be submitted by the publisher, editor, author or admiring colleagues, and must be accompanied by a nomination form and digital copy of the nominated article. **Deadline:** October 1. **Contact:** Email to awards@ces-europe.org.

3858 ■ Mellon-CES Dissertation Completion Fellowships in European Studies. *(Graduate/Fellowship)*

Purpose: To facilitate the timely completion of the doctoral degree by late-stage graduate students on topics that focus on European Studies. **Focus:** European studies. **Qualif.:** Applicants must be US citizen or green card holder; ABD (year 5 and above); must be enrolled at a higher education institution in US; must be graduate students; applicant must also have exhausted the dissertation completion funding normally provided by current academic department or university for the coming academic year (applicants who still have a potential to receive funding from their institution for the fellowship year are not eligible to apply). The applicant must be working on a topic within or substantially overlapping European Studies. **Criteria:** Selection will be based on the committee's criteria.

Funds Avail.: $27,500. **Duration:** Semiannual. **To Apply:** Applicants must submit completed application form; three faculty recommendations. **Deadline:** January 15. **Contact:** Email to awards@ces-europe.org.

3859 ■ Council on Foreign Relations (CFR)
The Harold Pratt House
58 E 68th St.
New York, NY 10065
Ph: (212)434-9400
Fax: (212)434-9800
E-mail: corporate@cfr.org
URL: www.cfr.org
Social Media: www.facebook.com/
  councilonforeignrelations
instagram.com/cfr_org
www.linkedin.com/company/council-on-foreign-relations
twitter.com/CFR_org
youtube.com/user/cfr/featured

3860 ■ CFR Military Fellowships *(Professional development/Fellowship)*

Purpose: To enable selected military officers to broaden their understanding of international relations. **Focus:** International affairs and relations. **Qualif.:** Applicants must be military officers nominated by the Chiefs of Staff of the Army and the Air Force, the Chief of Naval Operations, and the Commandants of the Coast Guard and the Marine Corps. **Criteria:** Selection will be based on the CFR's criteria.

Duration: Annual. **To Apply:** Applicants from the U.S. Army, U.S. Air Force, U.S. Coast Guard, U.S. Marine Corps, and U.S. Navy should contact their human resources officer to learn more about the fellowship application process. **Contact:** Email: fellowships@cfr.org; URL: www.cfr.org/fellowships/military-fellowship.

3861 ■ CFR National Intelligence Fellowships
(Professional development/Fellowship)

Purpose: To provide the opportunity to senior intelligence officers to participate in and contribute to the Council on Foreign Relations activities and events. **Focus:** Intelligence

service; International affairs and relations. **Qualif.:** Applicants must be senior intelligence officers; must be nominated by the Office of the Director of National Intelligence and interviewed by CFR. **Criteria:** Selection will be based on the CFR's criteria.

Duration: Annual. **To Apply:** Applicants should contact their human resources officer to learn more about the application process. **Remarks:** Established in 1999. **Contact:** Phone: 212.434.9740; Email: fellowships@cfr.org; URL: www.cfr.org/fellowships/national-intelligence-fellowship.

3862 ■ CFR Stanton Nuclear Security Fellowship
(Doctorate, Postdoctorate, Advanced Professional/Fellowship)

Purpose: To encourage younger scholars studying nuclear security issues and stimulate the development of the next generation of thought leaders in nuclear security. **Focus:** International affairs and relations; National security. **Qualif.:** Applicants must be U.S. citizens and permanent residents who are eligible to work in the United States; and must be junior (non-tenured) faculty, postdoctoral fellows, or predoctoral candidates from any discipline, including law, who are working on a nuclear security related issue. **Criteria:** Selection will be based on the following criteria: scholarly qualifications; professional accomplishments; merits of an application proposal that focuses on nuclear security issues.

Funds Avail.: $110,000 (junior, non-tenured); $80,000 (postdoctoral). **Duration:** Annual. **Number Awarded:** 2. **To Apply:** Applicants who meet the program's eligibility requirements can apply online. **Deadline:** December 15. **Remarks:** The fellowship is sponsored by the Stanton Foundation. **Contact:** Phone: 212.434.9740; Email: fellowships@cfr.org; URL: www.cfr.org/fellowships/stanton-nuclear-security-fellowship.

3863 ■ CFR Volunteer Internships *(Undergraduate, Graduate/Internship)*

Purpose: To offer outstanding volunteer opportunities for college students and graduate students focusing on international relations and who are pursuing a career in foreign policy or a related field. **Focus:** International affairs and relations. **Qualif.:** Applicants must be U.S. citizens or permanent residents; must be undergraduate and graduate students with majors in international relations, political science, economics, or related fields; regional specialization and language skills may also be required for some internships; in addition to meeting the intellectual requirements, applicants should have excellent skills in administration, writing, research, and computers, as well as previous office experience; must also be willing to commit to fourteen to eighteen hours per week. **Criteria:** Selection will be on highly competitive basis.

Funds Avail.: Interns will be paid a competitive hourly wage. **Duration:** Annual. **To Apply:** Application details and information on specific internships is available online at www.cfr.org/career-opportunities/internships. **Contact:** Email: humanresources@cfr.org.

3864 ■ International Affairs Fellowships in Japan (IAF) *(Professional development/Fellowship)*

Purpose: To provide the opportunity to mid-career U.S. citizens to expand their professional horizons by spending a period of research or other professional activity in Japan. **Focus:** International affairs and relations. **Qualif.:** Applicants must be U.S. Citizens; must be mid-career professionals; must have a strong record of professional achieve-

Awards are arranged alphabetically below their administering organizations

ment; must have an interest in U.S.-Japan relations; must hold at least a bachelor's degree. **Criteria:** Selection will be based on scholarly qualifications; professional experience; firm grounding in foreign policy; merits and feasibility of a project proposal that relates to U.S.-Japan relations; character and personal qualities conducive to promoting cross-cultural communication and cooperation.

Funds Avail.: No specific amount. **Duration:** Annual. **To Apply:** Applications can be submitted online. **Deadline:** October 31. **Remarks:** The fellowship is sponsored by Hitachi, Ltd. Established in 1977. **Contact:** Phone: 212.434.9740; Email: fellowships@cfr.org; URL: www.cfr.org/fellowships/international-affairs-fellowship-japan.

3865 ■ International Affairs Fellowships in Nuclear Security (IAF-NS) (Professional development/ Fellowship)

Purpose: To offer university-based scholars valuable hands-on experience in the nuclear security policymaking field. **Focus:** International affairs and relations. **Qualif.:** Applicants must be U.S. citizens or permanent residents who are eligible to work in the United States and be between the ages of twenty-nine and fifty. **Criteria:** Selection will be based on a combination of the following criteria: scholarly qualifications, achievements and promise, depth and breadth of professional experience, firm grounding in foreign policy and international relations, and the contribution the fellowship will make to the applicants' career development.

Funds Avail.: $125,000. **Duration:** Annual. **Number Awarded:** 2. **To Apply:** Applicants those who meet the program's eligibility requirements can apply online. **Remarks:** The fellowship is sponsored by the Stanton Foundation. **Contact:** Phone: 212.434.9740; Email: fellowships@cfr.org.; URL: www.cfr.org/international-affairs-fellowship-nuclear-security.

3866 ■ Edward R. Murrow Press Fellowships (Professional development/Fellowship)

Purpose: To promote the quality of responsible and discerning journalism **Focus:** Journalism. **Qualif.:** Applicants must be those who have distinguished credentials in the field of journalism and who have covered international news as a working journalist for print, broadcast, or online media widely available in the United States; limited to those individuals who are authorized to work in the United States and who will continue to be authorized for the duration of the fellowship. **Criteria:** Selection will be highly competitive and will be based on the following criteria: professional experience as a foreign correspondent or editor; firm grounding in foreign policy; and clear, creative, and original application statement

Funds Avail.: $75,000 along with a modest travel grant. **Duration:** Annual; Ten months. **To Apply:** Applicants who meet the program's eligibility requirements can apply online. **Deadline:** March 1. **Remarks:** Established in 1949. **Contact:** Phone: 212.434.9740; Email: fellowships@cfr.org.

3867 ■ Council of Graduate Schools (CGS)

1 Dupont Cir. NW, Ste. 230
Washington, DC 20036
Ph: (202)223-3791
Fax: (202)331-7157
URL: www.cgsnet.org
Social Media: www.facebook.com/
CouncilOfGraduateSchools

www.linkedin.com/company/council-of-graduate-schools
twitter.com/CGSGradEd

3868 ■ ETS/CGS Award for Innovation in Promoting Success in Graduate Education (Graduate/Award)

Purpose: To support institutional changes that result in enhancing student success through completion of programs at the master's or doctoral level. **Focus:** Educational administration. **Qualif.:** Applicants must be member institutions of CGS. **Criteria:** Selection will be based on the degree of innovation in the institution's approach; the extent of institutional collaboration and commitment; the source of the institution's match; the sustainability plan; the project's potential for replicability.

Funds Avail.: $20,000. **Duration:** Annual. **To Apply:** Applicant must include Letter of Application (1 page); Project Description including budget (maximum 4 pages); Letter of endorsement from Chief Academic Officer or President (1 page). **Deadline:** September 10. **Contact:** Anna Naranjo; Email: anaranjo@cgs.nche.edu.

3869 ■ Council on Library and Information Resources (CLIR)

1707 NW L St., Ste. 650
Washington, DC 20036
E-mail: chenry@clir.org
URL: www.clir.org
Social Media: www.facebook.com/CLIRNews
twitter.com/clirnews
youtube.com/user/DLFCLIR

3870 ■ Mellon Fellowships for Dissertation Research in Original Sources (Doctorate/Fellowship)

Purpose: To help junior scholars in the humanities and related social science fields gain skills and creativity in developing knowledge from original sources. **Focus:** Humanities; Social sciences. **Qualif.:** Applicant must be currently enrolled in a doctoral program in a graduate school in the United States; have a plan to do dissertation research, primarily in original source material in the holdings of archives, libraries, historical societies, museums, related repositories, or a combination; and write their dissertation and receive the Ph.D. degree in a field of the humanities or in a related element of the social sciences. **Criteria:** Selection committee will assess quality with reference to the following criteria: originality and creativity of the research proposal; importance of the proposed dissertation to the Applicant's field; appropriateness of the primary-source collections and institutions in which the Applicants proposes to do research; competence of the Applicants for proposed research as indicated by references, transcripts, language skills, research experience and other academic achievements; prospects for completing specified research within the time projected and funds awarded.

Funds Avail.: up to $25,000 per year. **Duration:** Annual; 9-12 months. **Number Awarded:** 15. **To Apply:** Applicants must submit an online application form; must provide transcripts covering all graduate study and three letters of reference; all reference letters must be submitted by reference providers through the online application system. **Deadline:** December 8. **Contact:** E-mail: mellon@clir.org.

3871 ■ Rovelstad Scholarship (Undergraduate, Graduate/Scholarship)

Purpose: To provide financial support to students of library and information science who wish to attend the World

Library and Information Congress of the International Federation of Library Associations and Institutions (IFLA). **Focus:** Humanities; Library and archival sciences. **Qualif.:** Applicants must be enrolled in an accredited school of library and information science at the time of the current IFLA annual meeting; must be citizens or permanent residents of the United States, and should have an interest in cooperative endeavors with international libraries, international standards or other international library and information issues. **Criteria:** Selection will be based on the committee's criteria.

Funds Avail.: No specific amount. **Duration:** Annual. **To Apply:** Applicants must complete and submit the application form available online together with official transcripts of undergraduate and graduate school records and two letters of reference submitted by reference providers through the online application system. **Deadline:** January 26. **Contact:** E-mail: rovelstad@clir.org.

3872 ■ Council on Social Work Education (CSWE)
1701 Duke St., Ste. 200
Alexandria, VA 22314
Ph: (703)683-8080
Fax: (703)683-8099
E-mail: info@cswe.org
URL: www.cswe.org
Social Media: www.facebook.com/CSocialWorkEd
www.linkedin.com/company/740571
twitter.com/CSocialWorkEd
www.youtube.com/user/CSWEvideo

3873 ■ Carl A. Scott Book Scholarship
(Undergraduate/Scholarship)

Purpose: To promote equity and social justice in social work. **Focus:** Social work. **Qualif.:** Applicants must be in the last year of study for a social work degree in a baccalaureate or master's degree program accredited by the Council on Social Work Education; must be African American, American Indian, Asian American, Mexican American or Puerto Rican; must have a cumulative GPA of at least 3.0 on a 4.0 scale and must be enrolled in 12 credit hours. **Criteria:** Recipients are selected based on the demonstrated commitment in promoting equity and social justice.

Funds Avail.: $500. **Duration:** Annual. **Number Awarded:** 2. **To Apply:** Applicants must submit a two-three page, double-spaced, typewritten statement that include professional interests, and experiences; two letters of recommendation preferably from a professor, a field instructor, or a community-based leader; an official letter from the school's registrar verifying that the applicants are enrolled and in good standing with the university or college and an official academic transcript from university/college. **Contact:** Email: cas@cswe.org.

3874 ■ Council on Social Work Education Minority Fellowship Program for Doctoral Students
(Postdoctorate/Fellowship)

Purpose: To provide leadership in practice, research, teaching, and policy promulgation in government or private organizations serving underrepresented and underserved persons with or at risk for mental health and/or substance abuse disorders. **Focus:** Mental health; Social work. **Qualif.:** Applicants must be currently enrolled in a doctoral

program in a school of social work; must be an American citizen, non citizen national, or have permanent residence status; must have a master's degree in social work from a CSWE-accredited program. **Criteria:** Recipients will be selected based on the potential for assuming a leadership role providing mental health and substance abuse services to ethnic/racial minority individuals and communities and potential for success in doctoral studies; evidence of strong fit with and commitment to behavioral health services for underserved racial/ethnic populations; life experiences relevant to and/or volunteer or work experience with racial/ethnic populations.

Funds Avail.: No specific amount. **Duration:** Annual. **To Apply:** Applicants must submit an application instruction sheet. All permanent residents must provide the following: photocopy of Permanent Resident Card signed by the notary public; official transcript of records; GRE and MAT scores; letter of admission; resume; financial list of information including the resources applied for, personal financial costs and anticipated income.

3875 ■ Council on Social Work Education Scholars Program *(Doctorate/Scholarship)*

Purpose: To promote research projects and initiatives of interest to the scholar as well as to CSWE. **Focus:** Social work. **Qualif.:** Applicants must be senior scholars, faculty member and junior scholars such as doctoral students or individuals recently completing their doctoral dissertation. **Criteria:** Selection will be based on proposed research.

Funds Avail.: No specific amount. **Duration:** Annual. **To Apply:** Applicants must submit completed application together with project proposal; budget; task list; and curriculum vitae.

3876 ■ Counseil Canadien de droit International (CCIL)
275 Bay St.
Ottawa, ON, Canada K1R 5Z5
Ph: (613)238-4870
Fax: (613)236-2727
E-mail: ccil-ccdi@intertaskconferences.com
URL: www.ccil-ccdi.ca
Social Media: www.facebook.com/Canadian-Council-on
-International-Law-CCIL-240331419338849
www.linkedin.com/company/canadian-council-on
-international-law
twitter.com/ccil_ccdi

3877 ■ John Peters Humphrey Student Fellowships
(Graduate/Fellowship)

Purpose: To inspire educational achievement by providing support for outstanding students pursuing graduate studies at leading graduate institutions in Canada or worldwide. **Focus:** Law; Political science. **Qualif.:** Applicants must be students of Canadian law and political science (or their equivalent) faculties. **Criteria:** Selection committee appointed by the President of the CCIL will review the applications and base its determination on the Applicant's academic accomplishments, proposed program of study, letter of reference, and other information contained in the application.

Funds Avail.: 20,000 Canadian Dollars. **Duration:** Annual. **Number Awarded:** Up to 3. **To Apply:** Applicants must submit the official transcript from each post-secondary academic institution, three letters of reference which speak

Awards are arranged alphabetically below their administering organizations

both of the candidate's academic strengths and weaknesses and the likelihood of success in a programme of graduate studies. **Remarks:** The Fellowship was established in memory of John Peters Humphrey, a renowned Canadian international lawyer and scholar. Established in 1974.

3878 ■ Leslie C. Green Veterans Scholarship *(Juris Doctorate, Advanced Professional/Scholarship)*

Purpose: To provide tuition support to Canadian Armed Forces veterans entering or pursuing legal studies in a Canadian law school. **Focus:** Law. **Qualif.:** Applicants must be Canadian Armed Forces veterans who are entering or pursuing legal studies; intending to follow a career dedicated to international humanitarian law. **Criteria:** Selection will be based on the committee's criteria.

Funds Avail.: 2,000 Canadian Dollars. **Duration:** Annual. **Number Awarded:** 1. 2015. **Deadline:** September 30. **Remarks:** Established in 2013.

3879 ■ CouponBirds

2443 Fillmore St., No. 380-3240
San Francisco, CA 94115
URL: www.couponbirds.com
Social Media: www.facebook.com/couponbirdscom
www.instagram.com/couponbirds
www.pinterest.com/couponbirds
twitter.com/couponbirdscom
www.youtube.com/c/couponbirds

3880 ■ "Help to Save" Scholarship *(College, University/Scholarship)*

Purpose: To assist students in reducing their tuition fee burden and collect their smart ways of saving money. **Focus:** General studies/Field of study not specified. **Qualif.:** Applicant must be at least sixteen years old, enrolled at an accredited university or college in US or Canada, must have a legitimate acceptance letter from an accredited university or college. Employees of CouponBirds.com, their parent or affiliate companies are ineligible to apply, immediate family members of employees are also ineligible. **Criteria:** Completing the submission accounts for 30 percent, quality of submission accounts for 30 percent, the uniqueness and helpfulness of ideas presented in the video account for 40 percent.

Funds Avail.: $1,000. **Number Awarded:** 1. **To Apply:** Applicant should complete the form online at www.couponbirds.com/scholarship, take a short survey on your daily online and in-store shopping habits, upload a video to YouTube with the title "CouponBirds Scholarship", follow CouponBirds YouTube channel and add a link to CouponBirds Scholarship Page in the video description, after each of these steps are complete, submit your application with one click at the bottom of the application page. **Deadline:** October 10. **Contact:** Email: scholarship@couponbirds.com.

3881 ■ Coupons for Save

72A Royal City
Hanoi, Vietnam
URL: www.couponsforsave.com

3882 ■ Coupons for Save Scholarship *(All/Scholarship)*

Purpose: To help a student pay for her/his education. **Focus:** General studies/Field of study not specified. **Qua-**

lif.: Applicant must be a student from anywhere in the world.

Funds Avail.: $3,000. **Number Awarded:** 1. **To Apply:** Application is available online at www.couponsforsave.com. **Deadline:** December 31. **Contact:** Email: jeniferalien.couponsforsave@gmail.com.

3883 ■ Courage To Grow Scholarship

PO Box 2507
Chelan, WA 98816
Ph: (509)731-3056
E-mail: support@couragetogrowscholarship.com
URL: couragetogrowscholarship.com

3884 ■ Courage to Grow Scholarships *(Undergraduate/Scholarship)*

Purpose: To help and support students achieve their higher education goals. **Focus:** General studies/Field of study not specified. **Qualif.:** Applicants must be U.S. citizens who are juniors or high school seniors or college students with a minimum GPA of 2.5.

Funds Avail.: $500. **Duration:** Monthly; 1 month. **To Apply:** Applicants must explain a GPA and maximum of 250 words. **Deadline:** August 31.

3885 ■ Course Hero Inc.

2000 Seaport Blvd.
Redwood City, CA 94063
Free: 888-634-9397
URL: www.coursehero.com
Social Media: www.facebook.com/coursehero
www.instagram.com/coursehero
www.linkedin.com/company/coursehero
www.pinterest.com/coursehero
twitter.com/coursehero
www.youtube.com/channel/UCt_TSquDx7B-2RX6y3dx3_g

3886 ■ Academic Hero Scholarship *(College, University/Scholarship)*

Purpose: To award a student for their academic performance, personal growth, and desire to continue their success as a college student. **Focus:** General studies/Field of study not specified. **Qualif.:** Applicant must be at least 16 years old and enrolled in a U.S. high school or college; must be a U.S citizen; must have a minimum 3.0 GPA. **Criteria:** Selection will be made by a panel of judges that reads the applicants' essays. Essays will be judged on the following criteria: sincerity, creativity, thoughtfulness, and factual credibility.

Funds Avail.: $10,000. **Duration:** Semiannual. **Number Awarded:** 1. **To Apply:** Applicant must fill out the scholarship form on the website at www.coursehero.com/. Applicant must create a free account, fill out an application, complete the essay, and submit their application on the portal. **Deadline:** October 31.

3887 ■ CourseHorse, Inc.

220 E 23rd St., Ste. 500
New York, NY 10010
Ph: (914)227-2800
URL: coursehorse.com
Social Media: www.facebook.com/CourseHorse

Awards are arranged alphabetically below their administering organizations

twitter.com/coursehorse

3888 ■ Tennessee Learner's Scholarship *(College, High School/Scholarship)*

Purpose: To strengthen our commitment to learning locally. **Focus:** General studies/Field of study not specified. **Qualif.:** High school seniors planning to attend college in Tennessee, or anyone enrolled in part- or full-time college classes in Tennessee. **Criteria:** Quality and originality of written or video submission.

Funds Avail.: $1,000. **Number Awarded:** 1. **To Apply:** Submit a short video (up to 2 minutes) or short essay (up to 1,000 words) explaining your personal goals and how taking classes will help achieve them. Email learn@coursehorse.com with a link to your video or your essay text in the body of the email. Include "Tennessee 2017 Learner's Scholarship" in the subject line. **Deadline:** March 15. **Contact:** coursehorse.com/nashville-tn#scholarship; E-mail: learn@coursehorse.com.

3889 ■ The Cover Guy

2315 Whirlpool St., Ste. 968
Niagara Falls, NY 14305
Fax: (866)607-7639
Free: 866-652-6837
E-mail: info@thecoverguy.com
URL: www.thecoverguy.com
Social Media: www.facebook.com/thecoverguy
instagram.com/thecoverguy
twitter.com/thecoverguy

3890 ■ The Cover Guy Annual Scholarship *(Undergraduate, Graduate/Scholarship)*

Purpose: To help students with their higher education and to give back to the communities we serve. **Focus:** General studies/Field of study not specified. **Qualif.:** Applicants must be students enrolled in an undergraduate or graduate program at a university, college or trade school in the United States or Canada. **Criteria:** Selection will be made by dedication to education and volunteer work in their community.

Funds Avail.: $500. **Duration:** Annual. **To Apply:** Applicants must visit the website for the online application process and other information; must submit an article consisting of 500-1000 words, covering the applicants experience with hot tubs, backyard experiences, how hot tubs improve life, etc.; must include name, phone number, address, school name, program; provide an explanation of why you should be considered for the award (grades, volunteer work, etc.), and student ID number. **Deadline:** July 1.

3891 ■ CoverWallet

100 Avenue of the Americas, 3rd. Fl.
New York, NY 10013
Ph: (646)844-9933
E-mail: info@coverwallet.com
URL: www.coverwallet.com
Social Media: www.facebook.com/coverwallet
twitter.com/coverwallet

3892 ■ CoverWallet Small Business Scholarship *(Two Year College, Four Year College, Graduate/Scholarship)*

Purpose: To help students take on an entrepreneurial mindset and view small businesses through a more holistic

perspective. **Focus:** General studies/Field of study not specified. **Criteria:** Readability and thoughtfulness of the submitted essay.

Funds Avail.: $500. **To Apply:** Submit a short essay highlighting their favorite local business and risks they face.

3893 ■ George W. Crawford Black Bar Association

PO Box 2715
Hartford, CT 06146-2715
Ph: (860)578-4764
URL: www.georgecrawfordblackbar.org
Social Media: www.facebook.com/gwcblackbarct
www.linkedin.com/company/george-w-crawford-black-bar
  -association
twitter.com/gwcblackbarct

3894 ■ Priscilla Green Scholarships *(Undergraduate/Scholarship)*

Purpose: To support minority students who are practicing law in the State of Connecticut. **Focus:** Law. **Qualif.:** Applicants must be minority law students at accredited law schools who demonstrate a commitment to both practicing law in the state of Connecticut and furthering Crawford's mission. **Criteria:** Selection will be based on academic and extracurricular achievement and submitted application.

Funds Avail.: $2,000. **Duration:** Annual. **Contact:** Thamar Esperance at TEsperance@ghla.org; or Stephanie Johnson at StephanieA.Johnson@TheHartford.com.

3895 ■ Creative Diagnostics

45-1 Ramsey Rd.
Shirley, NY 11967
Fax: (631)614-7828
E-mail: info@creative-diagnostics.com
URL: www.creative-diagnostics.com
Social Media: www.facebook.com/CreativeDiagnostics
www.linkedin.com/company/creative-diagnostics
twitter.com/winsletkerry

3896 ■ Creative Diagnostics Fall Scholarship Program *(Undergraduate, Graduate/Scholarship)*

Purpose: To help science students achieve their goals in a college education. **Focus:** Science. **Qualif.:** Applicants must be actively pursuing a degree related to science; be enrolled as an undergraduate, postgraduate, PhD, or postdoctoral student at an accredited college or university; have a cumulative GPA of 3.0.

Funds Avail.: $1,000. **To Apply:** Complete online scholarship application form, send copy of transcript, and submit essay of at least 600 words on one of the following topics: adaptive immunity, autoimmunity, cytokines, immunological disorders, infectious diseases, inflammation, innate immunity, plant immunology, signal transduction, or tumor immunology and vaccines. **Deadline:** June 16. **Contact:** Email: contact@creative-diagnostics.com.

3897 ■ Creative Glass Center of America (CGCA)

1501 Glasstown Rd.
Millville, NJ 08332-1566
Ph: (856)825-6800
Fax: (856)825-2410

Awards are arranged alphabetically below their administering organizations

Free: 800-998-4552
E-mail: cgca@wheatonarts.org
URL: www.wheatonarts.org/artists-2/creative-glass-center-of-america

3898 ■ Creative Glass Fellowship Program
(Advanced Professional/Fellowship)

Purpose: To offer direct support to emerging and mid-career artists who work with glass. **Focus:** General studies/Field of study not specified.

Funds Avail.: No specific amount. **Duration:** Annual; Three-Month. **Number Awarded:** 4. **To Apply:** Applicants must submit two reference letters; ten images of the applicants work; special note about video; image information sheet (include Title of Piece, Medium, Description/Technique, Dimensions, Date of Completion); One paragraph biography; statement of intent; Current Resume/C.V.; Language Proficiency Documentation. **Contact:** Pamela Weichmann; Creative Glass Fellowship Program at WheatonArts; 1501 Glasstown Rd., Millville, NJ 08332-1566; E-mail: pweichmann@wheatonarts.org.

3899 ■ Creative Soul Music School
5633 Wauauga Rd.
Watauga, TX 76148
Ph: (817)485-7464
URL: www.creativesoulmusic.com
Social Media: www.facebook.com/creativesoulmusic
twitter.com/CSmusicschool

3900 ■ Creative Soul Music School Scholarship
(Graduate/Scholarship)

Purpose: To encourage and contribute to music education. **Focus:** Music. **Qualif.:** Applicant must be High School Seniors - Graduate Students, Music Majors, GPA of 3.0 or higher, United States residents. **Criteria:** All applicants who complete the online application with honest, appropriate answers and who meet the eligibility requirements, will be entered into a drawing for the scholarship.

Funds Avail.: $500. **Number Awarded:** 1. **To Apply:** Application must be filled out in full at www.creativesoulmusic.com/music-scholarship. **Deadline:** April 14. **Contact:** E-mail: scholarships@creativesoulmusic.com.

3901 ■ Credible
22 4th St. Fl. 8
San Francisco, CA 94103
E-mail: support@credible.com
URL: www.credible.com
Social Media: www.facebook.com/crediblelabs
twitter.com/credible

3902 ■ Credible $2,500 Scholarship *(Graduate/Scholarship)*

Purpose: To help fund part of a student's education. **Focus:** General studies/Field of study not specified. **Qualif.:** Applicant must be a undergraduate or graduate student actively enrolled in a college or university in the United States: must be a U.S. resident. **Criteria:** Selection will be via a random drawing.

Funds Avail.: $2,500. **To Apply:** Applicant should complete the entry form online at www.credible.com/blog/

mycrediblefuture/2500/. Once applicant enters, they can share it with their friends and receive bonus entries when friends enter through their link. **Contact:** Email: scholarship@credible.com.

3903 ■ Crescent Electric Supply Co.
7750 Dunleith Dr.
East Dubuque, IL 61025
Ph: (815)747-3145
E-mail: onlinesupport@cesco.com
URL: www.cesco.com
Social Media: www.facebook.com/crescentelectricsupply
www.linkedin.com/company/crescent-electric-supply
pinterest.com/crescentelec
twitter.com/CrescentElectrc
youtube.com/user/Cescovideo

3904 ■ Crescent Electric Sustainability Scholarship
(Undergraduate/Scholarship)

Purpose: To provide scholarship opportunity for a student who practices sustainable lifestyle choices. **Focus:** General studies/Field of study not specified. **Qualif.:** Applicant must be a graduating senior in high school or a freshman, sophomore, or junior in college; between the ages of 16 and 22.

Funds Avail.: $1,000. **Number Awarded:** 1. **Deadline:** August 8.

3905 ■ Crisis Intervention and Suicide Prevention Centre of British Columbia
763 E Broadway
Vancouver, BC, Canada V5T 1X8
Ph: (604)872-1811
Fax: (604)879-6216
Free: 800-784-2433
E-mail: info@crisiscentre.bc.ca
URL: crisiscentre.bc.ca

3906 ■ Steve Cowan Memorial Scholarships
(Undergraduate/Scholarship)

Purpose: To support individuals who have made a positive contribution to their school and/or local or global community. **Focus:** General studies/Field of study not specified. **Qualif.:** Applicants must be currently enrolled in grade 12 at a Lower Mainland/Sea-to-Sky Corridor high school; must possess the academic skills to successfully enter and complete a post-secondary education. **Criteria:** Selection will be based on applicant's dedication to the humanitarian ideals and community service ideals of the Crisis Centre, their volunteer experience, community leadership and their participation in community service.

Funds Avail.: $500-$1,000. **To Apply:** Applicants must submit an application form, two reference letters and an official transcript of the past two years of schooling.

3907 ■ Crohn's and Colitis Canada
600-60 St. Clair Ave. E
Toronto, ON, Canada M4T 1N5
URL: crohnsandcolitis.ca

3908 ■ The Crohn's and Colitis Canada Grants-in-Aid of Research program *(Advanced Professional, Professional development/Grant)*

Purpose: To advance prevention, treatments, health policy, and ultimately find cures on inflammatory bowel disease

Awards are arranged alphabetically below their administering organizations

(IBD). **Focus:** Gastroenterology. **Criteria:** Selection will be based on committee.

Duration: Annual. **To Apply:** Applicants must complete the online applications. **Deadline:** January 17.

3909 ■ Crohn's and Colitis Canada Innovations in IBD Research *(Advanced Professional, Professional development/Grant)*

Purpose: To stimulate and support research which may not be encompassed within the boundaries of traditional medical research. **Focus:** Gastroenterology; Medical research.

Funds Avail.: Maximum of 50,000 Canadian Dollars. **Number Awarded:** 1. **To Apply:** Applications must be submitted through the online application form available on the Crohn's and Colitis Canada website. **Deadline:** January 18. **Contact:** Crohn's and Colitis Canada, 600-60 St., Clair Ave., East Toronto, Ontario, M4T 1N5; Attn: Research Grants & Evaluation Specialist; Phone: 416-920-5035 x252; Email: research@crohnsandcolitis.ca.

3910 ■ Crohn's & Colitis Foundation (CCFA)
733 3rd Ave., Ste. 510
New York, NY 10017
Free: 800-932-2423
E-mail: info@ccfa.org
URL: www.crohnscolitisfoundation.org
Social Media: www.facebook.com/ccfafb
www.instagram.com/crohnscolitisfoundation
www.linkedin.com/company/crohn's-&-colitis-foundation-of
  -america

3911 ■ CCFA Career Development Awards
(Doctorate/Grant, Award)

Purpose: To support a research that will help prepare for a career of independent basic or clinical investigation in the area of inflammatory bowel disease. **Focus:** Medicine. **Qualif.:** Individuals who are already well established in the field of IBD research are not considered eligible for this award. Applicants should identify a senior investigator to act as a mentor to facilitate the transition to independence. At the time of application, applicants must be employed by an institution (public non-profit, private non-profit, or government) engaged in health care and/or health related research within the United States. Research is not restricted by citizenship; however, proof of legal work status is required. Applicants must hold an MD and/or PhD (or equivalent degree). Candidates holding MD degrees must have five years of experience after receiving their terminal degree—two years of which must be documented research experience relevant to IBD. Applicants holding PhDs must have at least two years of documented post-doctoral research relevant to IBD. Generally, candidates should not be in excess of ten years beyond the attainment of their doctoral degree.

Funds Avail.: Total of $90,000. **Duration:** Annual; one to three years. **To Apply:** Each applicant must submit a letter of intent (LOI) prior to submitting a full proposal for consideration. The LOI is reviewed seriously by the review committee who determines whether or not the applicant is invited to submit a full proposal. Each section of the LOI should be completed fully to be eligible for funding consideration. **Deadline:** June 1st-15th; June 22nd -July 6th. **Contact:** Orlando Green at ogreen@ crohnscolitisfoundation.org.

3912 ■ CCFA Research Fellowship Awards *(Doctorate, Graduate/Fellowship, Award)*

Purpose: To support a research that will help prepare for a career of independent basic or clinical investigation in the area of Crohn's disease and ulcerative colitis. **Focus:** Medicine. **Qualif.:** Applicants must be employed in an institution; engaged in health care or health related research within the United States; have MD, PhD or equivalent. Applicants with MD degrees must have at least two years of post doctoral experience. Candidates with PhD degrees must have at least one year of post-doctoral research experience related to IBD; proposals must be relevant to inflammatory bowel disease (Crohn's Disease or ulcerative colitis); already well established in individuals the field of IBD research are not considered eligible.

Funds Avail.: Up to $45,000. **Duration:** Annual; one to three years. **To Apply:** Each applicant must submit a letter of intent (LOI) prior to submitting a full proposal for consideration. The LOI is reviewed seriously by the review committee who determines whether or not the applicant is invited to submit a full proposal. Each section of the LOI should be completed fully to be eligible for funding consideration. **Deadline:** January 14; July 1. **Remarks:** Established in 1967. **Contact:** E-mail: mmbesch@ crohnscolitisfoundation.org; Phone: 646) 943-7501.

3913 ■ CCFA Student Research Fellowship Awards *(Graduate, Undergraduate/Grant, Fellowship, Award)*

Purpose: To fund a research on topics relevant to inflammatory bowel disease. **Focus:** Medicine. **Qualif.:** Applicants must be undergraduate, medical, or graduate students at an accredited institution in the United States.

Funds Avail.: Up to $2,500. **Number Awarded:** Up to 16. **To Apply:** Each applicant must submit a letter of intent (LOI) prior to submitting a full proposal for consideration. The LOI is reviewed seriously by the review committee who determines whether or not the applicant is invited to submit a full proposal. Each section of the LOI should be completed fully to be eligible for funding consideration. **Deadline:** March 15. **Contact:** E-mail: mmbesch@ crohnscolitisfoundation.org; Phone: 646) 943-7501.

3914 ■ Crohn's and Colitis Foundation of America Senior Research Awards *(Doctorate, Graduate/Grant, Award)*

Purpose: To provide established researchers with funds to generate sufficient preliminary data to become competitive for funds from other sources such as the National Institutes of Health (NIH). **Focus:** Medicine. **Qualif.:** Applicant must hold an MD and/or PhD (or equivalent degree) and must be employed by an institution (public non-profit, private non-profit, or government) that is engaged in health care and/or health-related research. He/she must have attained independence from his/her mentor. Eligibility is not restricted by citizenship or geography.

Funds Avail.: Up to $115,830. **Duration:** One to three years. **To Apply:** Each applicant must submit a letter of intent (LOI) prior to submitting a full proposal for consideration. The LOI is reviewed seriously by the review committee who determines whether or not the applicant is invited to submit a full proposal. Each section of the LOI should be completed fully to be eligible for funding consideration. **Contact:** Orlando Green at ogreen@ crohnscolitisfoundation.org.

3915 ■ Crop Science Society of America (CSSA)
5585 Guilford Rd.
Madison, WI 53711-5801

Awards are arranged alphabetically below their administering organizations

Ph: (608)273-8080
URL: www.crops.org
Social Media: www.facebook.com/CSSA.crops
www.linkedin.com/company/crop-science-society-of
 -america
twitter.com/ASA_CSSA_SSSA

3916 ■ Gerald O. Mott Award *(Graduate/Award)*

Purpose: To support a meritorious graduate student in crop science. **Focus:** Agricultural sciences.

Duration: Annual. **To Apply:** Applications can be submitted online and further details can be obtained from the website. **Deadline:** February 27. **Remarks:** The award was established in Honor of CSSA President Gerald O. Mott, who trained 75 graduate students during his 45 year career at Purdue University and the University of Florida.

3917 ■ Crosley Law Firm

3303 Oakwell Ct., Ste. 200
San Antonio, TX 78218
Ph: (210)529-3000
Fax: (210)444-1561
E-mail: info@crosleylaw.com
URL: www.crosleylaw.com
Social Media: www.facebook.com/CrosleyLaw
instagram.com/CrosleyLaw
twitter.com/crosleylaw
www.youtube.com/user/crosleylaw

3918 ■ Crosley Law Firm Distracted Driving Scholarship *(Four Year College/Scholarship)*

Purpose: To help a student pay for college while publicizing the dangers of distracted driving. **Focus:** General studies/Field of study not specified. **Qualif.:** Applicant must be a high school senior enrolling in a community college or 2- or 4-year college/university; must reside in San Antonio, Texas, and have a minimum 3.0 GPA. **Criteria:** Selection will be Confirmation of enrollment at a community college or 4-year institution

Funds Avail.: $1,000. **Duration:** Annual. **Number Awarded:** 1. **To Apply:** Applicant must write an essay of 750 to 2,000 words on how distracted driving has impacted their life. Application form is available online at crosleylaw.com/scholarship. **Deadline:** June 30.

3919 ■ Cross & Smith, LLC

907 17th Ave.
Tuscaloosa, AL 35401
Ph: (205)391-0618
URL: www.crossandsmith.com
Social Media: www.facebook.com/crossandsmith
www.linkedin.com/company/cross-&-smith-llc
twitter.com/ALInjuryLawPros
www.youtube.com/user/crossandsmith

3920 ■ Cross & Smith Annual $1,000 College Scholarship *(Two Year College, Undergraduate, Graduate/Scholarship)*

Purpose: To help students pay for their college education in legal studies. **Focus:** Law. **Qualif.:** Applicant must be a high school senior or already in college and intending to pursue a degree in law. **Criteria:** Selection will be based on a combination of writing skills, academic qualifications, and extracurricular activities.

Funds Avail.: $1,000. **Duration:** Annual. **Number Awarded:** 1. **To Apply:** Applicant must write a 500 to 1,000 word essay that explains their motivation for pursuing a law degree, including any obstacles they think they may encounter and how they plan to address them. An email must be sent to the contacts with the essay and the following information: full name, phone number, address, current school, current GPA, intended college and major, and any extracurricular or volunteer activities. **Deadline:** November 2. **Contact:** Email: dell.cross@crossandsmith.com, justin.smith@crossandsmith.com; URL: www.crossandsmith.com/firm-news/cross-smith-offering-annual-1000-college-scholarship/.

3921 ■ CrossLites

c/o Samuel Certo, Faculty Advisor
1000 Holt Ave.
Winter Park, FL 32789
E-mail: crosslites@gmail.com
URL: www.crosslites.org
Social Media: www.facebook.com/Crosslites

3922 ■ CrossLites Scholarship *(Undergraduate, Graduate/Scholarship)*

Purpose: To provide financial aid to students who wish to pursue their education. **Focus:** General studies/Field of study not specified. **Qualif.:** Applicants must be high school, college or graduate school students; there are no minimum GPA or test score requirements in order to qualify for the scholarship contest. **Criteria:** Selection shall be based on the submitted essay's originality, reflection, punctuation/grammar, and content.

Funds Avail.: 1st Place: $4,000|2nd Place: $2,500|3rd Place: $1,500|4th Place: $1,000|5th Place: $750|6th Place: $500|3 Lottery Winners win $150 each. **Duration:** Annual. **Number Awarded:** Varies. **To Apply:** Applicants must submit their name; email address; name of the institution that the applicants is attending or planning to attend; a 400-600 word reflective essay (based on Dr. Parker's quotes or messages); Official transcripts. **Deadline:** December 31. **Contact:** C/O Samuel Certo, 1000 Holt Ave., Winter Park, FL 32789; Email: Crosslites@gmail.com.

3923 ■ CRUSH the CPA Exam

888 Prospect St.
La Jolla, CA 92037
Ph: (858)888-9063
E-mail: crushthecpaexam@gmail.com
URL: crushthecpaexam.com
Social Media: www.facebook.com/CRUSHtheCPAExam
twitter.com/CRUSHTheCPAExam

3924 ■ Crush The CPA Exam Scholarship *(Undergraduate, Professional development/ Scholarship)*

Purpose: To help pay for test fees and test prep review courses for the Certified Public Accountant (CPA) exam. **Focus:** Accounting. **Qualif.:** Applicants must be college students in their last year of obtaining an accounting degree or a recent graduate; cumulative GPA of 3.0 or higher; planning to take the CPA Exam. **Criteria:** Selection based on academic achievement, leadership, and future career interests.

Awards are arranged alphabetically below their administering organizations

Funds Avail.: $1,000. **Duration:** Annual. **To Apply:** Complete application form at crushthecpaexam.com/crush-the-cpa-exam-scholarship-program.**Deadline:** November 30. **Contact:** Email: bryce@crushthecpaexam.com.

3925 ■ Crush Empire
10505 Roselle St.
San Diego, CA 92121
Ph: (858)263-4188
E-mail: crush@crushempire.com
URL: crushempire.com

3926 ■ Crush the GMAT Scholarship Program
(Undergraduate, Graduate/Scholarship)

Purpose: To help professionals pay for test fees and test prep review courses for the Graduate Management Admission Test (GMAT). **Focus:** Business; Business administration. **Qualif.:** Applicants must be actively pursuing a business school degree; cumulative GPA of 3.0 or higher.

Funds Avail.: $649. **Number Awarded:** 1. **To Apply:** Submit an essay of 500-1000 words that answer: "What made you decide to go to business school? What career path or industry do you plan on pursuing? Why?" **Deadline:** May 31.

3927 ■ Crush the GRE Scholarship Program
(Undergraduate, Graduate/Scholarship)

Purpose: To help pay for test fees and test prep review courses for the Graduate Record Examinations (GRE). **Focus:** General studies/Field of study not specified. **Qualif.:** Applicants should be enrolled in the last year of collegiate education, or be recent graduates of college or university; minimum cumulative GPA of 3.0.

Funds Avail.: $559. **Number Awarded:** 1. **To Apply:** Submit a short essay of 500-1000 words that answers: "What made you decide to pursue an advanced degree? What career path or industry do you plan on pursuing? Why?" **Deadline:** May 31.

3928 ■ Crush the LSAT Scholarship Program
(Undergraduate, Graduate/Scholarship)

Purpose: To help professionals pay for test fees and test prep review courses for the Law School Admission Test (LSAT). **Focus:** Law. **Qualif.:** Applicants should be in the last year of collegiate education or be a recent graduate of a college or university; minimum GPA of 3.0. **Criteria:** Applicants my benefit from being on a law school track, but it's not required.

Funds Avail.: $574. **Number Awarded:** 1. **To Apply:** Submit a short of 500-1,000 words that answers, "What made you decide to go to law school? What career path or legal industry do you plan on pursuing? Why?" **Deadline:** May 31.

3929 ■ Crush the NCLEX Scholarship Program
(Four Year College, Graduate/Scholarship)

Purpose: To help professionals pay for test fees and test prep review courses for the National Council Licensure Examination (NCLEX). **Focus:** Nursing.

Funds Avail.: $589. **Number Awarded:** 1. **Deadline:** May 31.

3930 ■ Crush the PMP Scholarship Program
(Undergraduate, Graduate/Scholarship)

Purpose: To help pay for test fees and test prep review courses for the Project Management Professional (PMP)

exam. **Focus:** Business; Management. **Qualif.:** Applicants should be in the last semester of collegiate education, a recent graduate of a college or university, or employed within the project management industry; minimum GPA of 3.0.

Funds Avail.: $1,154. **Number Awarded:** 1. **To Apply:** Submit an essay of 200-400 words that answers, "What made you decide you are ready for the PMP? Tell us about how you decided to become a PMP? Why do you want to be a PMP?" **Deadline:** May 31.

3931 ■ Crush the USMLE Scholarship Program
(Undergraduate, Graduate/Scholarship)

Purpose: To help pay for test fees and test prep review courses for the United States Medical Licensing Examination (USMLE). **Focus:** Medicine. **Qualif.:** Applicants should be actively pursuing the first step of medical certification toward a license to practice medicine. **Criteria:** College GPA, work experience, and medical school performance.

Funds Avail.: $894. **Number Awarded:** 1. **To Apply:** Submit an essay of 500-1,000 words that answers, "What made you decide to go to medical school? What career path or medical industry do you plan on pursuing? Why?"**Deadline:** May 31.

3932 ■ CSA Fraternal Life
2050 Finley Rd., Ste. 70
Lombard, IL 60148
Ph: (630)472-0500
Fax: (630)472-1100
Free: 800-543-3272
URL: csalife.com
Social Media: www.facebook.com/CSAFraternalLife

3933 ■ CSA Fraternal Life Scholarships
(Undergraduate/Scholarship)

Purpose: To help students on their financial needs for studying in college. **Focus:** General studies/Field of study not specified. **Qualif.:** Applicant must be a member in good standing of CSA Fraternal Life for a minimum of two (2) continuous years at the time of application; applicant must have at least $5,000 face value in permanent life insurance or $1,000 cash value in an Annuity; must have cumulative 3.0 or higher GPA (based on a 4.0 scale) upon graduation from high school; attending college must have a 3.0 GPA (based on a 4.0 scale); must not yet completed a full year of undergraduate studies; ACT or SAT score sheets must be included. **Criteria:** Selection will be made based on class rank, grade point average, college placement test scores, extracurricular activities including CSA activities, and essay made.

Funds Avail.: No specific amount. **Duration:** Annual. **To Apply:** Applicants must submit a completed application form to the Fraternal Department; a complete official transcript to be sent to CSA; photo for publication in the Journal. Please do not staple photo to your application; typed or legibly written essay of 400-500 words on a subject of applicants' interests. **Deadline:** March 23. **Contact:** CSA Fraternal Department, 2050 Finley Rd., Ste. 70, Lombard, IL, 60148; Amanda Lovell; Email: alovell@csalife.com; Toll-free: 800-543-3272; Fax: 630-472-1100.

3934 ■ Cuban American Bar Association (CABA)
Holland & Knight
701 Brickell Ave., Ste. 3300
Miami, FL 33131

Awards are arranged alphabetically below their administering organizations

Ph: (305)857-7229
E-mail: info@cabaonline.com
URL: cabaonline.com
Social Media: www.facebook.com/cabamiami
www.instagram.com/cabamiami
www.linkedin.com/groups/2097510
twitter.com/cabamiami

3935 ■ Cuban American Bar Association Scholarships *(Professional development/Scholarship)*

Purpose: To provide financial assistance to Cuban-American law students and law students interested in activities of importance to the Cuban-American community. **Focus:** Law. **Qualif.:** Applicants must be a Cuban-American law student, distinguished academically and/or in service-oriented activities; any law student who has distinguished them self in research, writing, community services, and/or other activities of importance to the Cuban-American community; must be a currently enrolled student in good academic standing at an accredited law school; must be a citizen or legal permanent resident of the United States. **Criteria:** Selection will be based on academic accomplishments, community service,References, personal essay and financial need.

Duration: Annual. **To Apply:** Applicants must submit a typed Scholarship application; competitive essay (no more than 1,000 words) focusing on, and describing in detail, the activities and achievements that qualify them for the award, as well as a statement of financial need; updated resume; copy of transcripts. **Deadline:** April 30. **Remarks:** To providescholarships for deserving law students in accredited law schools and honored the memory of distinguished lawyers and judges by awarding scholarships in their memory. **Contact:** Daniel Espinosa, Director of Operations; Email: despinosa@cabaonline.com.

3936 ■ Cultural Vistas

233 Broadway, Ste. 2120
New York, NY 10279
Ph: (212)497-3500
E-mail: info@culturalvistas.org
URL: culturalvistas.org
Social Media: www.facebook.com/CulturalVistas
instagram.com/culturalvistas
www.linkedin.com/company/cultural-vistas/
twitter.com/culturalvistas
www.youtube.com/user/culturalvistas

3937 ■ IAESTE United States Internships *(Undergraduate/Internship)*

Purpose: To allow students and recent graduates experience the cultural exchange and mutual understanding between the United States and other countries. **Focus:** Cross-cultural studies. **Qualif.:** Applicants must be Non U.S. citizen; minimum 18 years old; proficiency in English; Currently enrolled full-time and actively pursuing studies at a ministerially-recognized degree or certificate-granting post-secondary academic institution outside the United States or have graduated from such an institution no more than 12 months prior to desired internship start date; must not intend to change status while in the United States; must intend to enter the United States solely for the purpose of internship or training; not to abandon non-immigrant status.

Funds Avail.: No specific amount. **Duration:** Annual; Minimum of 3 weeks up to maximum of 12 months. **Number**

Awarded: Varies. **To Apply:** Applicants may verify the application process through the program website. **Remarks:** Established in 1950.

3938 ■ Jessica King Scholarships *(Other/Scholarship)*

Purpose: To enable talented, driven, and adventurous young Americans to have a life-changing international experience and succeed in the international hospitality field. **Focus:** Management; Public relations. **Qualif.:** Applicants must be at least 18 years old but not older than 35 having an offer of training/work contract from an employer in the hospitality industry for a position outside the US; be participants in an AIPT program; have an educational degree (Associate or Bachelor degree or ACF certification) from a hospitality/culinary school or program; have had at least 2 years of employment in the hospitality industry; and, be US citizens. **Criteria:** Selection shall be based on the merit, and not on the financial need.

Funds Avail.: $2,500. **Duration:** Annual. **To Apply:** Applicants must complete and submit a filled-out application form and must include two letters of reference, two copies of resume and a copy of school transcripts. They must also submit an essay of at least 500 words but not exceeding 1000 words, describing the applicant's motivation for participating in a practical work experience abroad; describing the skills that they expect to learn from their international work experience. Applicants must also include how they will apply the experience to their future endeavors upon return to the US. **Remarks:** Established in 2002.

3939 ■ The Cure Starts Now Foundation

10280 Chester Rd.
Cincinnati, OH 45215
URL: www.thecurestartsnow.org
Social Media: www.facebook.com/TheCureStartsNow

3940 ■ The Cure Starts Now Foundation Grants *(Graduate, Doctorate/Grant)*

Purpose: To support institutions and medical professionals whose research focuses on cancers that present the greatest opportunities for a homerun cancer cure. **Focus:** Medicine; Oncology. **Criteria:** Selection will be based on scientific merit, disease impact, innovation, feasibility, and expertise of investigators.

Funds Avail.: $100,000-$200,000. **Duration:** Annual. **To Apply:** Applicants must submit a completed application form; applications must be submitted as a researcher account within the snapgrant.com system; grants must be assigned the "The Cure Starts Now" affiliation when posting within snapgrant.com; must be In English and single spaced; progress report must be submitted by the investigator(s) on annual intervals. **Contact:** Keith Desserich; Email: keith@thecurestartsnow.org;.

3941 ■ Cushman Foundation for Foraminiferal Research (CFFR)

PO Box 7065
Lawrence, KS 66044-7065
Ph: (785)865-9405
Fax: (785)843-6153
E-mail: cushmanfoundation@allenpress.com
URL: www.cushmanfoundation.org
Social Media: www.facebook.com/groups/

Awards are arranged alphabetically below their administering organizations

CushmanFoundationForamResearch
twitter.com/cushmanfdn?lang=en

3942 ■ Loeblich and Tappan Student Research Award *(Graduate, Undergraduate/Grant)*

Purpose: To support undergraduate and graduate students' research on any aspect of living or fossil foraminifera or other protists, such as diatoms, coccolithophorids, dinoflagellates, acritarchs, or radiolaria. **Focus:** Paleontology. **Qualif.:** Applicants must be current students with developed research projects; must be Cushman Foundation members at the time of application. **Criteria:** Selection will be based on the committee's criteria; scientific merit and financial need.

Funds Avail.: $2,000. **Duration:** Annual. **Number Awarded:** Varies. **To Apply:** Applicants must complete the application form providing one- to three-page description of the proposed research; a detailed budget with justification; curriculum vitae; letter of support from the student's faculty advisor; should be sent to the Cushman Foundation by email; preferred format for electronic submission is pdf, ideally with all required items in one file, although the advisor's letter may be sent separately; other acceptable formats are MSWord, rtf, and Wordperfect. **Deadline:** March 1. **Remarks:** The award was established in memory of Alfred R. Loeblich, Jr. and Helen Tappan. Established in 2004. **Contact:** Email to cushmanfoundation@gmail.com.

3943 ■ Custom Creatives

30141 Agoura Rd., Ste. 210
Agoura Hills, CA 91301
Ph: (818)865-1267
Fax: (818)865-8363
Free: 877-865-1267
E-mail: info@customcreatives.com
URL: customcreatives.com
Social Media: www.facebook.com/customcreatives
www.linkedin.com/company-beta/2390257
twitter.com/customcreatives
youtube.com/user/customcreatives

3944 ■ Custom Creatives Digital Marketing Scholarship Program *(Community College, Four Year College/Scholarship)*

Purpose: To support the next generation of students interested in various aspects of the ever-changing, fast-growing digital marketing industry. **Focus:** Marketing and distribution. **Qualif.:** Applicant must be a U.S. residents or permanent residents currently attending a college or junior college, who will still be enrolled by the Custom Creatives Digital Marketing Scholarship December 1st notification date.

Funds Avail.: $1,000. **Number Awarded:** 2. **To Apply:** Complete online form and submit a 400-500 word essay on one of the following topics: 1) Describe what you plan on doing after you graduate from college as it relates to digital marketing, and why; 2) What are some clever or innovative ways to foster customer-business relationships online?; 3) How can social media help business students?. **Deadline:** May 31. **Contact:** Email: scholarships@customcreatives.com; Email: info@customcreatives.com.

3945 ■ CustomerServ

19901 Southwest Fwy., Ste. 163
Sugar Land, TX 77479

Free: 855-997-7281
URL: www.customerserv.com
Social Media: www.facebook.com/customerservltd
www.linkedin.com/company/customerserv-ltd
twitter.com/CustomerServLTD
www.youtube.com/user/CustomerServLTD

3946 ■ CustomerServ Scholarship *(University/Scholarship)*

Purpose: To help current or prospective business students relieve some financial stress in the upcoming school year. **Focus:** Business. **Qualif.:** Applicant must be enrolled or accepted at an accredited university and have a minimum 3.0 GPA.

Funds Avail.: $7,500. **Duration:** Annual. **Number Awarded:** 1. **To Apply:** Applicant must write a 500-word essay on the following topic: Who/what inspired you to enter the business industry? Application and complete instructions are available on the sponsor's website. **Deadline:** June 1. **Contact:** Email: admin@customerserv.com; URL: www.customerserv.com/customerserv-scholarship/.

3947 ■ Cystic Fibrosis Foundation

4550 Montgomery Ave., Ste. 1100 N
Bethesda, MD 20814
Ph: (301)351-4422
Free: 800-344-4823
E-mail: info@cff.org
URL: www.cff.org
Social Media: www.facebook.com/cysticfibrosisfoundation
instagram.com/cf_foundation
twitter.com/CF_Foundation
www.youtube.com/user/CysticFibrosisUSA

3948 ■ CFF Grants *(Other/Grant)*

Purpose: To encourage the development of new information that contributes to the understanding of the basic etiology and pathogenesis of Cystic Fibrosis. **Focus:** Medical research. **Qualif.:** Applicants study may be carried out at the subcellular, cellular, animal or patient levels; to be considered, proposals must be hypothesis-driven and provide sufficient preliminary data to justify Cystic Fibrosis Foundation support. **Criteria:** Scholarships are awarded based on a combination of financial need, academic achievement and leadership.

Funds Avail.: $100,000. **Duration:** Annual; 2 years. **To Apply:** Applicants can view information and form is available online. **Deadline:** April 19; September 6.

3949 ■ CFF/NIH-Unfunded Award *(Professional development/Grant)*

Purpose: To support excellent CF-related research projects that have been submitted to and approved by the National Institutes of Health but cannot be supported by available NIH funds. **Focus:** Medical research. **Qualif.:** Applications must have been reviewed by an NIH study section and presented to an institute council within 12 months of applying for CFF support; application must fall within the upper 40th percentile.

Funds Avail.: $125,000 per year. **Duration:** Annual; up to two years. **To Apply:** Applications can be submitted online. **Deadline:** October 31. **Contact:** Grants and Contracts Office, Cystic Fibrosis Foundation, 4550 Montgomery Ave.,

Awards are arranged alphabetically below their administering organizations

Ste. 1100 N, Bethesda, MD 20814; Tollfree: 800-FIGHT-CF; Phone: 301-841-2614; Email: grants@cff.org.

3950 ■ CFF Pilot and Feasibility Awards (Professional development/Grant)

Purpose: To support basic science research studies promising new investigators, focused on developing and testing new hypotheses in areas relevant to cystic fibrosis. **Focus:** Medical research. **Qualif.:** Applicant may be U.S. residents and from outside the U.S. are welcome to apply; International applicants and institutions are required to submit additional information in accordance with U.S. anti-terrorist restrictions. **Criteria:** Funding priority will be placed on those projects proposing to better understand the mechanisms behind disease pathophysiology and to develop strategies to prevent or treat it.

Funds Avail.: Up to $50,000 per year. **Duration:** Annual; up to a two years. **To Apply:** Applications must be submitted online. **Deadline:** May 7. **Contact:** Grants and Contracts Office, Cystic Fibrosis Foundation, 4550 Montgomery Ave., Ste. 1100 N, Bethesda, MD 20814; Tollfree: 800-FIGHT-CF; Phone: 301-841-2614; Email: grants@cff.org.

3951 ■ Summer Scholarships in Epidemiology (Undergraduate/Scholarship)

Purpose: To provide financial support for M.D.s currently working in cystic fibrosis to increase skills in epidemiology. **Focus:** General studies/Field of study not specified. **Qualif.:** Applicants may either be individuals entering college or vocational school or those who have already completed two semesters of college or vocational school. **Criteria:** Scholarships are awarded based on a combination of financial need, academic achievement, and leadership.

Funds Avail.: $2,000. **Duration:** Annual. **To Apply:** Applicant must completed the applications and submit online. **Deadline:** 01/04/01. **Contact:** Grants and Contracts Office, Cystic Fibrosis Foundation, 4550 Montgomery Ave., Ste. 1100 N, Bethesda, MD 20814; Tollfree: 800-FIGHT-CF; Phone: 301-841-2614; Email: grants@cff.org.

3952 ■ Daedalian Foundation (DF)
PO Box 249
Universal City, TX 78148
Ph: (210)945-2111
E-mail: info@daedalians.org
URL: www.daedalians.org

3953 ■ Daedalian Foundation Matching Scholarships (Undergraduate/Scholarship)

Purpose: To support high school students who wants to be a military pilot. **Focus:** Aerospace sciences. **Qualif.:** Applicants must be college/university students pursuing a career as military aviators.

To Apply: Applicants must submit a completed application form together with a 3″ x 5″ photograph to the Chairman. **Contact:** Scholarship program manager; Email: info@daedalians.org.

3954 ■ Descendants Scholarships (Undergraduate/Scholarship)

Purpose: To recognize objectives of the Daedalians insofar as assisting in the education of deserving young persons. **Focus:** Aerospace sciences. **Qualif.:** Applicants must be a direct descendant (natural or adopted) of a founder, named, or hereditary member in good standing (living or deceased)

of the Order of Daedalians; a citizen of the United States of America; accepted by or attending an accredited college/university and enrolled in an academic program which leads to a baccalaureate or higher degree; physically and mentally qualified with demonstrated aptitude for commissioned US military service; in good scholastic standing; and not a recipient of another Daedalian scholarship in the same year. **Criteria:** Applicants will be evaluated by the selection boards based on the requirements especially financial need.

Funds Avail.: $2,000. **Duration:** Annual. **Number Awarded:** 3. **Deadline:** August 1. **Contact:** Applicant must send copies of this application to both the sponsoring Daedalian Flight and to the Daedalian Foundation, PO Box 249, JBSA-Randolph, Texas, 78148.

3955 ■ John and Alice Egan Multi-Year Mentioning Scholarship Program (Undergraduate/Scholarship)

Purpose: To support high school students who wants to be a military pilot. **Focus:** Aerospace sciences. **Qualif.:** Applicants must be college/university students pursuing a career as military aviators; Must be in ROTC; Must have and maintain a cumulative 3.00 or better GPA (on a 4-point scale); Must be medically qualified for flight training. Copy of ROTC Physical examination required; Must plan to apply for and must be awarded a military aviator training allocation at the appropriate juncture in the student's chosen ROTC program; Must stay in contact with sponsoring flight (attend a minimum of one flight meeting annually) and arrange for official grade reports and ROTC progress details to be provided by the university to the flight each semester to qualify for successive year's funding; Freshmen are not eligible. **Criteria:** Selection is based on the application.

Funds Avail.: $500-$2,000. **Duration:** Annual. **To Apply:** Applicants must submit a completed application form together with a 3″ x 5″ photograph; complete transcripts (sent directly by the educational institution); a copy of FAA medical certificate and annotated copy of the Flight Physical Standards Questionnaire. **Deadline:** August 1. **Contact:** Applicant must send copies of this application to both the sponsoring Daedalian Flight and to the Daedalian Foundation, PO Box 249, JBSA-Randolph, Texas, 78148.

3956 ■ Navy, Army or Air Force ROTC Program (Graduate/Scholarship)

Purpose: To support high school students who wants to be a military pilot. **Focus:** Aerospace sciences. **Qualif.:** Applicants must be college/university students pursuing a career in military and must be nominated by local commander. **Criteria:** Selection is made by various ROTC headquarters.

Duration: Annual. **Contact:** Applicant must send copies of this application to both the sponsoring Daedalian Flight and to the Daedalian Foundation, PO Box 249, JBSA-Randolph, Texas, 78148.

3957 ■ Dairy Farmers of America Inc. (DFA)
1405 N. 98th St.
Kansas City, KS 66111
Ph: (816)801-6455
Free: 888-337-2407
URL: www.dfamilk.com
Social Media: www.facebook.com/dfamilk
www.instagram.com/dfamilk
www.linkedin.com/company/dairy-farmers-of-america
twitter.com/dfamilk

Awards are arranged alphabetically below their administering organizations

3958 ■ DFA Cares Foundation Scholarship Program
(Undergraduate/Scholarship)

Purpose: To support outstanding students pursuing careers in the dairy industry. **Focus:** Dairy science. **Qualif.:** Applicants must be pursuing a career in the dairy industry and enrolled in or applying for an accredited degree program. **Criteria:** Selection is based on applicant's commitment and passion to have a career in the dairy industry, and responses to essay questions; extracurricular activities, awards, recognition and work experience; academic achievement.

Funds Avail.: No specific amount. **Duration:** Annual. **To Apply:** Applicants must submit a completed application form along with a recent transcript and two letters of recommendation. **Deadline:** January 15.

3959 ■ The Dalai Lama Trust (DLT)
18579 Burke Ave.
Shoreline, WA 98133
Ph: (202)643-7085
URL: www.dalailamatrust.org

3960 ■ DLF Graduate Scholarship Program
(Graduate/Scholarship)

Purpose: To further human capital development of the Tibetan people by supporting the pursuit of excellence among Tibetan students in the graduate field of their choice. **Focus:** General studies/Field of study not specified.

Funds Avail.: Up to $10,000. **Duration:** Annual. **To Apply:** Applicants must submit a complete application form; photograph of applicant; curriculum vitae; two essay responses; official undergraduate transcript record; copy of acceptance letter or enrollment form for intended graduateInstitution; three signed written letters of recommendation. **Remarks:** Established in 2009. **Contact:** Scholarship Committee, The Dalai Lama Foundation, 18579 Burke Ave. N, Shoreline, WA, 98133, USA; Email: scholarship@dalailamatrust.org.

3961 ■ Dalcroze Society of America (DSA)
c/o Anne Farber
161 W 86th St., No. 7A
New York, NY 10024-3411
Ph: (212)724-5009
E-mail: president@dalcrozeusa.org
URL: www.dalcrozeusa.org

3962 ■ Dalcroze Society of America Memorial Scholarships *(Graduate/Scholarship)*

Purpose: To provide financial aid to students attending institutions offering Dalcroze certification or graduate credits devoted to the Dalcroze approach. **Focus:** Education, Music. **Qualif.:** Applicants must be attending an institution offering Dalcroze graduate credits and must not have been previously awarded a DSA scholarship. **Criteria:** Committees will award scholarships based on merit, financial need, intention to work towards Dalcroze certification within United States, residency and previous experience.

Funds Avail.: No specific amount. **Duration:** 3 weeks to one semester. **To Apply:** Applicants must submit a resume, proof of acceptance at a Dalcroze Training Center, three letters of recommendation, statement of financial need such as recent tax return or other documents, and a personal statement describing teaching and Dalcroze experiences or reasons for pursuing the training. **Deadline:** April 30. **Contact:** Jessica Schaeffer, Secretary at secretary@dalcrozeusa.org.

3963 ■ Dallas Area Paralegal Association (DAPA)
PO Box 12533
Dallas, TX 75225-0533
E-mail: info@dallasparalegals.org
URL: dallasparalegals.org
Social Media: www.facebook.com/pages/Dallas-Area -Paralegal-Association/119148899846
www.linkedin.com/groups/2031005/profile
twitter.com/DAPA_Paralegals

3964 ■ DAPA Student Member Scholarships
(Undergraduate, Postgraduate/Scholarship)

Purpose: To promote the professional development of the paralegal profession and individual paralegals. **Focus:** Paralegal studies. **Qualif.:** Applicants must be enrolled and actively participating in a minimum of six hours of study in a Baccalaureate, Post-baccalaureate, or Associate Degree paralegal education program at a college and/or paralegal school which has attained American Bar Association approval or in institutionally accredited and in substantial compliance with the ABA Guidelines within Dallas/Fort Worth and the contiguous counties; demonstrate financial need; have not been convicted of a felony; have and maintain a minimum 3.0 GPA on a 4.0 scale average at the institution they are currently attending. **Criteria:** Scholarships will be awarded without regard to race, color, creed, sex or age.

Funds Avail.: Up to $1,500. **Duration:** Annual. **Number Awarded:** 1. **To Apply:** Applicants must complete and submit fully completed on-line application, which is appointed by Communities Foundation of Texas, Inc.; an essay, to be submitted on-line, which shall be 750 words or less on a topic to be chosen by the Selection Committee; two letters of recommendation; one should be from an instructor or counselor who can attest to the applicant's working ethic and general character; copy of current transcript. Students who maintain a minimum of 3.0 GPA may apply and/or reapply for additional scholarship funds on an annual basis; the institutions will be asked to submit an unlimited number of applications on behalf of applicants meeting all scholarship recipient requirements to the selection committee; each institution and the programs presented shall be licensed and accredited. **Deadline:** January 4.

3965 ■ Dance Films Association (DFA)
252 Java St., Ste. 333
Brooklyn, NY 11222
Ph: (347)505-8649
E-mail: info@dancefilms.org
URL: www.dancefilms.org
Social Media: www.facebook.com/dancefilms
www.instagram.com/dancefilms/
twitter.com/DanceFilms

3966 ■ DFA Production Grant *(Professional development/Grant)*

Purpose: To support dance film productions. **Focus:** Dance. **Qualif.:** Applicants must be DFA members and available to attend the festival at the Film Society of Lincoln Center.

Awards are arranged alphabetically below their administering organizations

Funds Avail.: one award for $2,500; two $500 awards. **Duration:** Annual. **Number Awarded:** 3. **To Apply:** Applicants should include: project description; team description; timeline and schedule; budget and budget notes; script, storyboard and/or outline; current needs to complete film; and visual support.

3967 ■ Danish America Heritage Society (DAHS)

1717 Grant St.
Blair, NE 68008
URL: www.danishheritage.org
Social Media: www.facebook.com/danishheritage

3968 ■ Edith and Arnold N. Bodtker Grants
(Undergraduate, Graduate/Grant, Internship)

Purpose: To provide stipends for students interested in studying and performing research in the area of Danish immigration to North America. **Focus:** Cross-cultural studies. **Qualif.:** Applicants must be currently enrolled at or graduated from a university level institution; must have a designed research or internship project that makes a stay in the USA or Canada (for Danish or North American students) or in Denmark (for North American students) necessary for their research.

Funds Avail.: Up to $5,000. **Duration:** Annual. **To Apply:** Applicants must submit proposals including name, contact information, project description, tentative timeline, estimated budget, curriculum vitae or resume and least two letter of reference. **Deadline:** April 15; September 15. **Remarks:** The DAHS created the Grants for Research and Internship to allow Bodtker funds to be used to support historical research in areas of interest. Established in 1998.

3969 ■ Dante Society of America (DSA)

PO Box 600616
Newtonville, MA 02460
Ph: (617)876-5160
E-mail: dantesociety@gmail.com
URL: www.dantesociety.org

3970 ■ Dante Prize *(Undergraduate/Prize, Monetary)*

Purpose: To support best student essay in competition on a subject related to the life or works of Dante. **Focus:** Renaissance studies. **Qualif.:** Applicants must be undergraduates in any American or Canadian college or university, or by anyone not enrolled as graduate students who have received the degree of A.B., or its equivalent, within the past year. **Criteria:** Selection will be based on the best student essay on a subject related to the life or works of Dante Alighieri. The committee may, at its discretion, split the award between two contestants (each to receive one half of the prize), or it may make no award.

Funds Avail.: $500. **Duration:** Annual. **To Apply:** Applications must be sent as an e-mail attachment to the Dante Society; undergraduate essays should be no longer than 7,500 words, graduate essays should be no longer than 10,000 words including bibliographies and any other material; the writer's name should not appear on the essay title page or on any other page of the essay since the essays are submitted anonymously to the readers; and Quotations from Dante's works should be cited in the original language and the format of an essay should conform to either the Chicago or MLA Style Sheet guidelines. **Deadline:** June 30. **Remarks:** Established in 1887. **Contact:** URL: www.dantesociety.org/prizes-and-awards#Dante_Prize_Grandgent_Award.

3971 ■ Charles Hall Grandgent Award *(Graduate/Award, Monetary)*

Purpose: To support the student with the best essay on a subject related to the life or works of Dante. **Focus:** Renaissance studies. **Qualif.:** Applicants must be American or Canadian students enrolled in any graduate program. **Criteria:** Selection will be based on the best student essay on a subject related to the life or works of Dante Alighieri. The committee may, at its discretion, split the award between two contestants (each to receive one half of the prize), or it may make no award.

Funds Avail.: $750. **Duration:** Annual. **To Apply:** Applications must be sent as an e-mail attachment to the Dante Society; undergraduate essays should be no longer than 7,500 words, graduate essays should be no longer than 10,000 words including bibliographies and any other material; the writer's name should not appear on the essay title page or on any other page of the essay since the essays are submitted anonymously to the readers; and Quotations from Dante's works should be cited in the original language and the format of an essay should conform to either the Chicago or MLA Style Sheet guidelines. **Deadline:** June 30. **Remarks:** The award is named for Charles Hall Grandgent, professor of Italian and Romance linguistics at Harvard University who served as president of the Dante Society from 1915-1932. Established in 1961. **Contact:** URL: www.dantesociety.org/prizes-and-awards#Dante_Prize_Grandgent_Award.

3972 ■ David Library of the American Revolution (DLAR)

1201 River Rd.
Washington Crossing, PA 18977
Ph: (215)493-6776
Fax: (215)493-5492
URL: www.dlar.org
Social Media: www.facebook.com/The-David-Library-of-the-American-Revolution-102378867681
twitter.com/davidlibrary

3973 ■ David Library Fellowships *(Doctorate, Postdoctorate/Fellowship)*

Purpose: To support the education of doctoral and postdoctoral students and encourage the scholarly use of the Library's Resources. **Focus:** General studies/Field of study not specified.

Funds Avail.: Range from $1,000-$1,600. **Duration:** One month. **To Apply:** Applicants should submit seven sets of the following: proposal, curriculum vitae and writing sample; two letters of recommendation. **Deadline:** March 6. **Remarks:** Established in 1985. **Contact:** Academic Advisory Council, David Library of the American Revolution, PO Box 748, Washington Crossing, PA, 18977;.

3974 ■ Davis Levin Livingston '

400 Davis Levin Livingston Pl., 851 Fort St.,Ste. 400
Honolulu, HI 96813
Ph: (808)740-0633
E-mail: mdavis@davislevin.com
URL: www.davislevin.com
Social Media: www.facebook.com/DavisLevinLivingston

Awards are arranged alphabetically below their administering organizations

www.instagram.com/davislevinlivingston

3975 ■ Davis Levin Livingston Public Interest Law Scholarships (Postgraduate/Scholarship)

Purpose: To support law students intending to pursue public interest law. **Focus:** Law. **Criteria:** Selection will be based on the applicants' eligibility and compliance with the application process.

Funds Avail.: $3,000. **Duration:** Annual. **To Apply:** Applicants must complete the application form and submit the following: one to three page typed essay; a stated intention of pursuing a legal career in public interest law; an official and complete copy of undergraduate college transcripts; an acceptance letter from an accredited law school within the United States; and proof of legal residency in the U.S. (i.e., birth certificate, passport, permanent resident card, etc.). **Contact:** Application materials should be mailed (or e-mailed in PDF format) to Lynne Agbalog at lynne@ davislevin.com.

3976 ■ Davis Memorial Foundation

356 Digital Dr.
Morgan Hill, CA 95037
Ph: (650)938-5441
Fax: (650)938-5407
URL: www.davisfoundation.org

3977 ■ Davis Memorial Foundation Scholarship (Graduate, Undergraduate/Scholarship)

Purpose: To develop qualified professionals through education and to award those who have the desire to continue to improve their quality of life. **Focus:** General studies/Field of study not specified. **Criteria:** Applicants will be evaluated based on both academic and personal performance. judgment of the selection committee, candidates are otherwise ranked equally.

Funds Avail.: $5,000 each. **Duration:** Annual. **Number Awarded:** Varies. **To Apply:** Applicants must submit six copies of each official application form; official transcript of all high school and college records; letter from college, university or technical trade school where the undergraduate or graduate work will be undertaken, indicating provisional acceptance of the proposed course of study; and current picture. **Deadline:** April 9. **Contact:** Phone: 650-938-5441.

3978 ■ Davis Wright Tremaine L.L.P. (DWT)

188 W Northern Lights Blvd., Ste. 1100
Anchorage, AK 99503-3985
Ph: (907)257-5300
Fax: (907)257-5399
E-mail: info@dwt.com
URL: www.dwt.com
Social Media: www.facebook.com/dwtlaw
www.instagram.com/dwtlaw
www.linkedin.com/company/davis-wright-tremaine-llp
twitter.com/dwtlaw

3979 ■ Davis Wright Tremaine 1L Diversity Scholarship (Undergraduate/Scholarship)

Purpose: To provide financial assistance to qualified students intending to pursue their law degree. **Focus:** Law. **Criteria:** Applicants will be selected based on their academic performance and commitment to a successful career in law.

Duration: Annual. **Number Awarded:** Varies. **To Apply:** Applicants must submit a current resume; a complete undergraduate transcript; a grade from the first semester of law school; a short, personal essay indicating the applicant's eligibility for and interest in the scholarship, and a legal writing sample; and two or three references (one of whom should be a person qualified to comment on the applicant's law school work). **Deadline:** January 5.

3980 ■ DealRoom

205 W Wacker Dr.,
Chicago, IL 60606
Ph: (312)344-3442
E-mail: sales@dealroom.net
URL: dealroom.net
Social Media: www.facebook.com/dealroom.net
www.linkedin.com/company/dealroom
twitter.com/dealroominc
www.youtube.com/channel/
   UClpm6DNXKbZqS0cLyKraQUg

3981 ■ Scholarship Contest from Dealroom (College, University/Scholarship)

Purpose: To find creative students ready to move forward and look for innovative solutions in business, m&a, and virtual data room industry. **Focus:** General studies/Field of study not specified. **Qualif.:** Applicant must be a full-time student for the upcoming school year and must show some level of interest in m&a or the virtual data room industry. **Criteria:** Essay will be judged on writing skills, style, and innovative business solutions.

Funds Avail.: $500. **Number Awarded:** 1. **To Apply:** Applicant must write an essay (roughly 800 words) on one of the topics suggested on the sponsor's site. Application and essay should be submitted online. **Deadline:** July 30. **Contact:** Email: scholarship@dealroom.net; URL: dealroom.net/ dealroom-scholarship.

3982 ■ Dealsshutter

SCO -113, 2nd Fl., Darbara Complex, B - Block, Ranjit Ave.
Amritsar 143 001, Punjab, India
Ph: 91 980 3749711
E-mail: info@dealsshutter.com
URL: www.dealsshutter.com
Social Media: www.facebook.com/Dealsshutter
www.instagram.com/dealsshutterofficial
www.linkedin.com/company/deals-shutter
www.pinterest.com/dealsshutter
twitter.com/Dealsshutter
www.youtube.com/channel/UCe-liD4lAaAMs5CM3F8pZLg

3983 ■ Dealsshutter.com Scholarship (College, University/Scholarship)

Purpose: To allow students anywhere in the world to pursue and education. **Focus:** General studies/Field of study not specified. **Qualif.:** Applicant must be attending a college or university anywhere in the world. **Criteria:** Entries will be judged by the Dealsshutter editorial team.

Funds Avail.: $500. **Duration:** Semiannual. **Number Awarded:** 1. **To Apply:** Applicants should submit full name,

Awards are arranged alphabetically below their administering organizations

---

photo, email, address, contact number, name and address of university attending, and an essay at www.dealsshutter.com/scholarship. PC users should submit entries in Microsoft Word, Mac users should submit entries in Text Edit. **Deadline:** January 30. **Contact:** Email: scholarship@dealsshutter.com.

3984 ■ Death Valley '49ers Inc.
24601 Glen Ivy Rd., No. 39
Corona, CA 92883
URL: www.deathvalley49ers.org
Social Media: www.facebook.com/pages/Death-Valley
 -49ers-Inc/179046718816309
twitter.com/DeathValley49er

3985 ■ Death Valley '49ers Scholarships
(Undergraduate/Scholarship)

Purpose: To assist high school graduates living in the Death Valley Unified School District. **Focus:** Historic preservation. **Qualif.:** Applicants must be residents of the death valley unified school district and/or death valley national park for a minimum of two years and/or parent(s) are employed within the boundaries of death valley national park and/or attended death valley elementary school for a minimum of two years; must have completed all the required subjects for high school graduation in their junior and senior academic years at Beatty, Pahrump, or Shoshone high schools; must maintain 24 to 30 required units per academic year; freshmen must have 2.5 GPA, sophomores must have 2.75, juniors and seniors must have 3.0 GPA. **Criteria:** Selection is based on a four-year program and will be renewed each year based on the academic progress of the student; the scholarship committee will review academic progress at the end of each semester.

Funds Avail.: $4,000. **Duration:** Annual. **Number Awarded:** 1. **To Apply:** Applicants must submit a Death Valley '49ers Scholarship Application to the Scholarship Committee by the application deadline in the senior year of high school. **Remarks:** Established in 1976. **Contact:** Virginia E. Stockman, Chairman, Death Valley '49ers Scholarship Committee, PO Box 365, 243 N Clay St., Independence, California 93526; Phone: 760-878-2337; E-mail: rvstockman@aol.com.

3986 ■ Debt.com
5701 W Sunrise Blvd., Ste. 100
Plantation, FL 33313
Free: 800-810-0989
URL: www.debt.com
Social Media: www.facebook.com/debtcom
instagram.com/debtcom
linkedin.com/company/debt-com
pinterest.com/debtcom
twitter.com/debtcom
youtube.com/c/DebtDotCom

3987 ■ Debt.com Scholarship *(All/Scholarship)*

Purpose: To offer scholarships to students pursuing higher education. **Focus:** General studies/Field of study not specified. **Qualif.:** Applicants must be students in the United States. **Criteria:** Selection will be based on the committee's criteria and the quality of the essay.

Funds Avail.: $500. **Number Awarded:** 1. **To Apply:** Applicants Write a short letter telling us about yourself and

Why do you need our $500 cash? What are your plans in life? How did you feel applying for all those other scholarships? Did you learn anything from that? Did you win any?. **Deadline:** September 1. **Contact:** Debt.com, Daniel Rosenstein; Phone: 954-377-9154; Email: editor@debt.com.

3988 ■ The Decorative Arts Trust
20 S Olive St., Ste. 204
Media, PA 19063
Ph: (610)627-4970
Fax: (610)627-4971
E-mail: thetrust@decorativeartstrust.org
URL: www.decorativeartstrust.org
Social Media: www.facebook.com/TheDecorativeArtsTrust
www.instagram.com/decorativeartstrust
www.linkedin.com/company/decorativeartstrust
twitter.com/DecArtsTrust
www.youtube.com/channel/UCktIYxqlMkDgEuyoExdUq1w

3989 ■ Dewey Lee Curtis Symposium Scholarships
(Advanced Professional/Scholarship)

Purpose: To support individuals actively working in the field of American decorative arts with their education. **Focus:** Art. **Qualif.:** Applicants must be individuals who are actively working in the field of American decorative arts. **Criteria:** Candidates will be selected based on the application.

Funds Avail.: No specific amount. **Duration:** Semiannual. **Number Awarded:** 2. **To Apply:** Applicant must submit an online application form along with recommendation letter. **Remarks:** The award was named in memory of the late Dewey Lee Curtis, a decorative arts historian and founding father of the Trust. **Contact:** The Dewey Lee Curtis Scholarship, The Decorative Arts Trust, 20 S Olive St., Ste. 204, Media, PA, 19063.

3990 ■ Deedal Studio Inc.
4470 W Sunset Blvd., No. 90149
Los Angeles, CA 90027
E-mail: info@driversedhub.com
URL: driversedhub.com
Social Media: www.facebook.com/usdrivertest
twitter.com/deedalstudio?lang=en

3991 ■ CitizenshipTests.org Engineering and Science Scholarship *(Undergraduate/Scholarship)*

Purpose: To provide financial assistance to engineering and science students with good academic standing and involvement in the community. **Focus:** Engineering; Science. **Qualif.:** Applicant must be an undergraduate university student (or the equivalent) who is currently attending a college or university in the United States or Canada in the fields of engineering or science and are at their third of final year of study; must also be a legal resident of the United States or Canada. **Criteria:** Selection will be based on the following equally weighted criteria: community or campus involvement, academic references, and grade point average (GPA).

Funds Avail.: $1,000. **Number Awarded:** 1. **To Apply:** Applicant must review and accept the Official Rules of the Scholarship and submit a cover letter explaining how they've contributed to their campus or community through

Awards are arranged alphabetically below their administering organizations

extracurricular activities or volunteer work, an unofficial transcript with the application, an two written academic references. **Deadline:** April 30. **Contact:** URL: citizenshiptests.org/scholarship/.

3992 ■ DriversEdHub.com Scholarship
(Undergraduate/Scholarship)

Purpose: To provide financial assistance to students with good academic standing and involvement in the community. **Focus:** General studies/Field of study not specified. **Qualif.:** Applicant must be an undergraduate students who is currently attending an accredited college or university in the United States or Canada and must be a legal resident of Canada or the United States. **Criteria:** Selection will be based on the following equally weighted criteria: community or campus involvement, academic references, and grade point average (GPA).

Funds Avail.: $2,000. **Number Awarded:** 1. **To Apply:** Applicant must review and accept the Official Rules of the Scholarship and submit a cover letter explaining how they have contributed to their campus or community through extracurricular activities or volunteer work, an unofficial transcript with application, and two written academic references. **Deadline:** April 30. **Contact:** www.driversedhub.com/scholarship/.

3993 ■ DefensiveDriving.com
11 Greenway Plz., Ste. 3150
Houston, TX 77046
Ph: (713)488-4000
E-mail: help@defensivedriving.com
URL: www.defensivedriving.com
Social Media: www.facebook.com/defensivedrivingonline
www.youtube.com/user/defensivedriving1

3994 ■ Defensive Driving scholarship
(Undergraduate/Scholarship)

Purpose: To supply college students with funds to pay for their school. **Focus:** General studies/Field of study not specified. **Qualif.:** Applicants must be high school seniors or college students who are legal residents of the United States and enrolled in semester beginning no later than fall of the current year; home-schooled students may apply as long as their course of study is equivalent to a high school senior. **Criteria:** Selection committee's decision is final; selection is not based on financial need; applicants may not be relatives of employees, officers, or owners of defensive driving.

Funds Avail.: $1,000. **Duration:** Annual. **Number Awarded:** 1. **To Apply:** Applications can be submitted online; applicants must Respond to the following prompt: My Future Major - tell what they are going to major in, and why they are choosing it using #MyFutureMajor on Facebook, Instagram or Twitter must tag defense driving in the post to be eligible. **Deadline:** June1. **Contact:** Email: marketing@defensivedriving.com.

3995 ■ Delaware Community Foundation (DCF)
100 W 10th St., Ste. 115
Wilmington, DE 19899-1636
Ph: (302)571-8004
Fax: (302)571-1553
E-mail: info@delcf.org
URL: delcf.org

Social Media: www.facebook.com/DelawareCF
www.linkedin.com/company/delaware-community
-foundation
twitter.com/DelCommunity

3996 ■ Chrysler Technical Scholarship Fund
(Undergraduate/Scholarship)

Purpose: To support students pursuing their respective careers in design, engineering, manufacturing or repair of automotive products. **Focus:** General studies/Field of study not specified. **Qualif.:** Applicants must be residents of Delaware and not older than 23 years of age at the time of application; have a minimum 2.75 GPA and plan to obtain a degree or certificate from a community college, trade school or university in a technical field related to the design, engineering, manufacturing or repair of automotive products, including but not limited to, automotive repair, skilled trades and engineering. **Criteria:** Applicants will be selected based on demonstrated academic ability, leadership traits and financial need.

Funds Avail.: Up to $10,000 per year. **Duration:** Annual. **To Apply:** Applicants must download and fill out the application form at the Delaware Community Foundation website. **Deadline:** March 15. **Contact:** Joyce Darling at jdarling@delcf.org or call 302-571-8004.

3997 ■ Delta Delta Delta
14951 N Dallas Pky. Ste. 500
Dallas, TX 75254
Ph: (817)633-8001
Fax: (817)471-1801
E-mail: info@trideltaeo.org
URL: www.tridelta.org
Social Media: www.facebook.com/TriDeltaEO
www.instagram.com/explore/tags/tridelta
www.linkedin.com/company/delta-delta-delta
www.pinterest.com/deltadeltadelta
twitter.com/TriDelta
www.youtube.com/user/TriDeltaEO

3998 ■ Nancy Ashley Adams/Ashley Adams Koetje Scholarships *(Undergraduate/Scholarship)*

Purpose: To provide financial assistance to qualified undergraduate students. **Focus:** General studies/Field of study not specified. **Qualif.:** Applicants must be Alpha Eta chapter members in Florida State University.

Funds Avail.: No specific amount.

3999 ■ Atlanta Alumnae Chapter Achievement Scholarship *(Undergraduate/Scholarship)*

Purpose: To provide financial assistance to qualified undergraduate students. **Focus:** General studies/Field of study not specified. **Qualif.:** Applicant must be graduated from a Georgia high school in one of the following four counties: Fulton, Dekalb, Cobb or Gwinnett.

Funds Avail.: No specific amount.

4000 ■ Beta Gamma Memorial Scholarship
(Undergraduate/Scholarship)

Purpose: To provide financial assistance to qualified undergraduate students. **Focus:** General studies/Field of study not specified. **Qualif.:** Applicants must be Beta Gamma chapter members at Jacksonville University.

Awards are arranged alphabetically below their administering organizations

Funds Avail.: No specific amount.

4001 ■ Durning Sisters Scholarships (Graduate/Scholarship)

Purpose: To provide financial assistance to graduate students. **Focus:** General studies/Field of study not specified. **Qualif.:** Applicants must be Tri Delta members who have completed 12 hours of graduate study and are unmarried.

Funds Avail.: No specific amount.

4002 ■ Harriet Erich Graduate Fellowship (Graduate/Fellowship)

Purpose: To provide financial assistance to graduate students. **Focus:** General studies/Field of study not specified. **Qualif.:** Applicants must be Tri Delta members enrolled in an accredited graduate program at the University of Alabama.

Funds Avail.: No specific amount.

4003 ■ Hazel D. Isbell Foundation Fellowships (Graduate/Fellowship)

Purpose: To provide financial assistance to graduate students. **Focus:** General studies/Field of study not specified.

Funds Avail.: No specific amount.

4004 ■ Houston Alumnae Chapter Graduate Fellowship (Graduate/Fellowship)

Purpose: To provide financial assistance to graduate students. **Focus:** General studies/Field of study not specified. **Qualif.:** Applicants must accredited graduate program full-time whose permanent residence is in Houston, Texas.

Funds Avail.: No specific amount.

4005 ■ Louise Bales Gallagher Scholarship (Undergraduate/Scholarship)

Purpose: To provide financial assistance to qualified undergraduate students. **Focus:** General studies/Field of study not specified. **Qualif.:** Applicants must be Delta Epsilon chapter members at Milliken University.

Funds Avail.: No specific amount.

4006 ■ Margaret McFarlane Alkek Undergraduate Scholarship (Undergraduate/Scholarship)

Purpose: To provide financial assistance to qualified undergraduate students. **Focus:** Education; Music; Theater arts.

Funds Avail.: No specific amount.

4007 ■ Martin Sisters Scholarship (Undergraduate/Scholarship)

Purpose: To provide financial assistance to qualified undergraduate students. **Focus:** General studies/Field of study not specified.

Funds Avail.: No specific amount.

4008 ■ McKinney Sisters Scholarship (Undergraduate/Scholarship)

Purpose: To provide financial assistance to qualified undergraduate students. **Focus:** General studies/Field of study not specified. **Qualif.:** Applicants must be graduates from high school in San Antonio, TX or have permanent residence in San Antonio.

4009 ■ Northern Virginia Alumnae Chapter Scholarship (Undergraduate/Scholarship)

Purpose: To provide financial assistance to qualified undergraduate students. **Focus:** General studies/Field of study not specified.

Funds Avail.: No specific amount.

4010 ■ Cissy McDaniel Parker Scholarships (Undergraduate/Scholarship)

Purpose: To provide financial assistance to qualified undergraduate students. **Focus:** General studies/Field of study not specified. **Qualif.:** Applicants must be Theta Zeta chapter members at the University of Texas. **Criteria:** Applicants will be judged based on academic achievement, campus and community involvement, and financial need.

Funds Avail.: No specific amount. **Duration:** one academic year.

4011 ■ Peg Hart Harrison Memorial Scholarship (Undergraduate/Scholarship)

Purpose: To provide financial assistance to qualified undergraduate students. **Focus:** General studies/Field of study not specified. **Qualif.:** Applicants must be Beta Lambda chapter members at the University of Central Florida.

Funds Avail.: No specific amount.

4012 ■ Cheryl White Pryor Memorial Scholarship (Undergraduate/Scholarship)

Purpose: To provide financial assistance to qualified undergraduate students. **Focus:** General studies/Field of study not specified. **Qualif.:** Applicants must be members of Delta Sigma chapter member at Tennessee, and be initiated sophomore or junior members.

Funds Avail.: No specific amount.

4013 ■ Sarah Shinn Marshall Scholarship (Undergraduate, Graduate/Scholarship)

Purpose: To provide financial assistance to qualified undergraduate students. **Focus:** General studies/Field of study not specified.

Funds Avail.: No specific amount.

4014 ■ Tri Delta Alpha Eta Scholarships (Undergraduate/Scholarship)

Purpose: To provide financial assistance to qualified undergraduate students. **Focus:** General studies/Field of study not specified. **Qualif.:** Applicants must be Alpha Eta chapter members in Florida State University.

Funds Avail.: No Specific amount.

4015 ■ Tri Delta Alpha Rho Leadership Scholarships (Undergraduate/Scholarship)

Purpose: To provide financial assistance to qualified undergraduate students. **Focus:** General studies/Field of study not specified. **Qualif.:** Applicants must be Alpha Rho chapter members at the University of Georgia and be initiated sophomore or junior members.

Funds Avail.: No specific amount.

4016 ■ Delta Epsilon Sigma
c/o Dr. Claudia Marie Kovach
Aston, PA 19014-1298

Awards are arranged alphabetically below their administering organizations

Ph: (610)558-5573
E-mail: info@deltaepsilonsigma.org
URL: www.deltaepsilonsigma.org

4017 ■ Delta Epsilon Sigma Graduate Fellowship
(Graduate/Fellowship)

Purpose: To provide financial support for the education of member students. **Focus:** General studies/Field of study not specified. **Qualif.:** Applicants must be members who are in the senior years of study; Fellowships are awarded for full-time study in graduate or professional school. **Criteria:** Applicants will be judged by the Scholarship Committee based on scholastic achievement, leadership and service activities.

Duration: Annual. **Deadline:** March 15. **Contact:** Scanned document should be emailed to: Contact@DeltaEpsilonSigma.org.

4018 ■ Delta Epsilon Sigma Undergraduate Scholarships *(Undergraduate/Scholarship)*

Purpose: To provide financial support for the education of member students. **Focus:** General studies/Field of study not specified. **Qualif.:** Applicants must be members and full-time students who are in their senior year of study.

Duration: Annual. **Contact:** Return Application and Supporting Information to: Delta Epsilon Sigma, University of St. Thomas, Mail 4073, 2115 Summit Ave., Saint Paul, MN, 55105.

4019 ■ Delta Gamma
3250 Riverside Dr.
Columbus, OH 43221
Ph: (614)481-8169
E-mail: dgfoundation@deltagamma.org
URL: www.deltagamma.org
Social Media: www.facebook.com/deltagamma
www.instagram.com/deltagamma_eo
www.linkedin.com/company/delta-gamma
www.pinterest.com/deltagamma
twitter.com/deltagamma

4020 ■ Delta Gamma Undergraduate Merit-Based Scholarships *(Undergraduate/Scholarship)*

Purpose: To encourage the Delta Gammas to pursue a career in science. **Focus:** Science. **Qualif.:** Applicant must have a 3.0 or higher GPA; must be a full-time undergraduate student in the current and next academic year; must be an initiated member of Delta Gamma by December end of current year.

Funds Avail.: No specific amount. **Duration:** Annual. **To Apply:** Completed application along with a resume; transcripts (official or unofficial) from all the universities attended; recommendation letter from Advisory Team Chairman must be submitted. **Deadline:** March 1.

4021 ■ The Delta Kappa Gamma Society International (DKP)
416 W 12th St.
Austin, TX 78701-1817
Fax: (512)478-3961
URL: www.dkg.org
Social Media: www.facebook.com/dkgorg
www.instagram.com/dkgsi

www.pinterest.com/dkgsi
twitter.com/dkg_si
www.youtube.com/user/dkgaustin

4022 ■ Delta Kappa Gamma Society International World Fellowship *(Graduate/Fellowship)*

Purpose: To enable international female students to pursue advanced study in the United States and/or Canada. **Focus:** General studies/Field of study not specified. **Qualif.:** Applicants must be female graduate students from various countries other than the United States or Canada.

Funds Avail.: Amount varies. **Duration:** Annual. **Number Awarded:** Varies. **To Apply:** Applicants who wish to study in the United States may ask the Cultural Affairs Office of the United States Embassy in their home country to obtain further information on the application process; must submit the application forms and other documents required to the international World Fellowship committee for evaluation and ranking. **Remarks:** The World Fellowship Program began as a project to aid women in war-torn countries. Established in 1946.

4023 ■ Delta Phi Epsilon Sorority (DPHIE)
251 S Camac St.
Philadelphia, PA 19107
Ph: (215)732-5901
Fax: (215)732-5906
E-mail: info@dphie.org
URL: www.dphie.org
Social Media: www.facebook.com/DeltaPhiEpsilonSorority
www.instagram.com/dphieihq
twitter.com/dphieihq
www.youtube.com/channel/
  UCRZbAS4lo2xQoGVGyBmnB8w

4024 ■ Delta Phi Epsilon Educational Foundation Scholarships *(Graduate/Scholarship)*

Purpose: To develop social conscience and a willingness to think in terms of the common good in order to assure for its members continuous development and achievement in the collegiate and fraternity world. **Focus:** General studies/Field of study not specified.

Duration: Annual; one academic year.

4025 ■ Delta Tau Lambda Sorority, Inc.
PO Box 7714
Ann Arbor, MI 48107

4026 ■ Lydia Cruz and Sandra Maria Ramos Scholarships *(Graduate/Scholarship)*

Purpose: To assist young Latinas in reaching their goals through education. **Focus:** General studies/Field of study not specified. **Qualif.:** Applicants must be current Latina high school seniors who are entering their first year of college at a two or four year higher learning institution. **Criteria:** Selection of applicants will be based on academic excellence and community service.

Funds Avail.: No specific amount. **Duration:** Annual. **To Apply:** Applicants must complete the application form, available on the website, including the essays; must provide the official high school transcript and a copy of University/College Acceptance Letter. **Remarks:** The scholarship was named after Darilis Garcia-McMillian's grandmother and

Awards are arranged alphabetically below their administering organizations

Maria Victoria Ramos' sister. The two women chosen greatly influenced the lives of the Founding Mothers. Established in 1995. **Contact:** E-mail: DTL-VicePresident@gmail.com.

4027 ■ Delta Zeta (DZ)
202 E Church St.
Oxford, OH 45056
Ph: (513)523-7597
E-mail: dzs@dzshq.com
URL: www.deltazeta.org
Social Media: www.facebook.com/
 DeltaZetaSororityNational
www.instagram.com/deltazetanatl
www.pinterest.com/deltazeta
twitter.com/DeltaZetaNatl
www.youtube.com/user/DZSorority

4028 ■ Betsy B. and Garold A. Leach Scholarship
(Undergraduate/Scholarship)

Purpose: To provide financial assistance to all qualified undergraduate students. **Focus:** Museum science. **Qualif.:** Applicants must be an undergraduate student.

Duration: Annual. **Deadline:** February 15.

4029 ■ Charline Chilson Scholarships
(Undergraduate/Scholarship)

Purpose: To provide financial assistance to all qualified undergraduate students. **Focus:** Science. **Qualif.:** Applicants must be an undergraduate student.

Funds Avail.: No specific amount. **Duration:** Annual. **Deadline:** February 15.

4030 ■ Arlene Davis Scholarships *(Undergraduate/Scholarship)*

Purpose: To provide financial assistance to all qualified undergraduate students. **Focus:** Aviation. **Qualif.:** Applicants must be initiated, active, continuing members entering their sophomore or junior year, who are enrolled in courses showing an interest in aviation; must have a 3.0 grade average. **Criteria:** Candidate will be selected based on academic standing and financial need.

Funds Avail.: No specific amount. **Duration:** Annual. **To Apply:** Scholarship applications are available on the website and must be completed properly. Applicant must have the FAFSA reply form. **Deadline:** February 15. **Contact:** Application must be submitted at dzfoundation@dzshq.com.

4031 ■ Gail Patrick Undergraduate Scholarships
(Undergraduate/Scholarship)

Purpose: To provide financial assistance to all qualified undergraduate students. **Focus:** General studies/Field of study not specified. **Qualif.:** Applicants must be an undergraduate student.

Duration: Annual. **Deadline:** February 15.

4032 ■ Edith Head Undergraduate Scholarships
(Undergraduate/Scholarship)

Purpose: To provide financial assistance to all qualified undergraduate students. **Focus:** Fashion design. **Qualif.:** Applicants must be an undergraduate student.

Duration: Annual. **Deadline:** February 15.

4033 ■ Elizabeth M. Gruber Scholarship *(Graduate/Scholarship)*

Purpose: To provide financial assistance to all qualified graduate students. **Focus:** Liberal arts. **Qualif.:** Applicants must be an Graduate student.

Duration: Annual. **Deadline:** February 15.

4034 ■ Elsa Ludeke Scholarship *(Graduate/Scholarship)*

Purpose: To provide financial assistance to all qualified graduate students. **Focus:** General studies/Field of study not specified. **Qualif.:** Applicants must be an Graduate student.

Duration: Annual. **Deadline:** February 15.

4035 ■ Heghinian Scholarships *(Undergraduate/Scholarship)*

Purpose: To provide financial assistance to all qualified undergraduate students. **Focus:** General studies/Field of study not specified. **Qualif.:** Applicants must be an undergraduate student.

Duration: Annual. **Deadline:** February 15.

4036 ■ Houston/Nancy Holliman Scholarship
(Undergraduate/Scholarship)

Purpose: To provide financial assistance to all qualified undergraduate students. **Focus:** Health sciences; Hearing and deafness; Speech and language pathology/Audiology. **Qualif.:** Applicants must be an undergraduate student.

Duration: Annual. **Deadline:** February 15.

4037 ■ Sarah Jane Houston Scholarships
(Undergraduate/Scholarship)

Purpose: To provide financial assistance to all qualified undergraduate students. **Focus:** Education, English as a second language. **Qualif.:** Applicants must be an undergraduate student.

Duration: Annual. **Deadline:** February 15.

4038 ■ Huenefeld/Denton Scholarships
(Undergraduate/Scholarship)

Purpose: To provide financial assistance to all qualified undergraduate students. **Focus:** Child development; Education; Library and archival sciences. **Qualif.:** Applicants must be junior or senior initiated, active continuing members in need of financial help, seeking an undergraduate degree in child development/primary education or library science. **Criteria:** Applicants will be evaluated based on their academic achievements, campus activities, and service to Delta Zeta.

Funds Avail.: No specific amount. **Duration:** Annual. **To Apply:** Scholarship applications are available on the website and must be completed properly. Applicants must have the FAFSA reply form. **Deadline:** February 15. **Contact:** Application must be submitted at dzfoundation@dzshq.com.

4039 ■ John L. and Eleanore I. Mckinley Scholarships *(Undergraduate/Scholarship)*

Purpose: To provide financial assistance to all qualified undergraduate students. **Focus:** General studies/Field of study not specified. **Qualif.:** Applicants must be an undergraduate student.

Duration: Annual. **Deadline:** February 15.

Awards are arranged alphabetically below their administering organizations

4040 ■ Helen Woodruff Nolop Scholarships in Audiology and Allied Fields *(Graduate/Scholarship)*

Purpose: To provide financial assistance to all qualified graduate students. **Focus:** Health sciences; Speech and language pathology/Audiology. **Qualif.:** Applicants must be an Graduate student. **Criteria:** Selection of applicant will be based on academic achievement and financial need.

Funds Avail.: No specific amount. **Duration:** Annual. **To Apply:** Applicant must provide a transcript of record; must submit a statement indicating special service to Delta Zeta, activities and/or community involvement, academic honors and/or honor societies, and personal statement about need and desire to get the award; must have a list of employment records and at least two recommendation letters from a Delta Zeta (Alumnae Chapter President, College Chapter Director, and/or Regional Collegiate Coordinator), and one from Academic Graduate Advisor and/or Employer. **Deadline:** February 15.

4041 ■ Gail Patrick Charitable Trust Scholarships *(Graduate/Scholarship)*

Purpose: To provide financial assistance for qualified graduate students. **Focus:** General studies/Field of study not specified. **Qualif.:** Applicants must be an Graduate student. **Criteria:** Applicants will be evaluated based on academic achievements and campus activities.

Funds Avail.: $2,500. **Duration:** Annual. **To Apply:** Scholarship applications are available on the website and must be completed properly. Applicants must have the FAFSA reply form. **Deadline:** February 15.

4042 ■ Dorothy Worden Ronken Scholarships *(Graduate/Scholarship)*

Purpose: To provide financial assistance to all qualified graduate students. **Focus:** Business; Education. **Qualif.:** Applicants must be Delta Zeta graduate students working on a degree in education or business; must be initiated continuing members in good standing in a collegiate chapter with 3.0 cumulative grade average. **Criteria:** Preference will be given to applicants from the Alpha Alpha chapter of Northwestern University.

Funds Avail.: No specific amount. **Duration:** Annual. **To Apply:** Applicants must provide a transcript of record; must submit a statement indicating their special service to Delta Zeta, activities and/or community involvement, academic honors and/or honor societies, and personal statement about need and desire to get the award; must have a list of employment records and at least two recommendation letters from a Delta Zeta (Alumnae Chapter President, College Chapter Director, and/or Regional Collegiate Coordinator), and one from Academic Graduate Advisor and/or employer. **Deadline:** February 15. **Contact:** dzfoundation@dzshq.com.

4043 ■ Sandra Sebrell Bailey Scholarship *(Undergraduate/Scholarship)*

Purpose: To provide financial assistance to all qualified undergraduate students. **Focus:** General studies/Field of study not specified. **Qualif.:** Applicants must be an undergraduate student.

Duration: Annual. **Deadline:** February 15.

4044 ■ Elizabeth Coulter Stephenson Scholarships *(Undergraduate/Scholarship)*

Purpose: To provide financial assistance to all qualified undergraduate students. **Focus:** General studies/Field of

study not specified. **Qualif.:** Applicants must be outstanding in campus and chapter activities; must have held, or must currently hold, an executive board position; must have at least 3.0 GPA; must have been adversely affected, or parents have been adversely affected, by a disaster. **Criteria:** Preference will be given to initiated, active, continuing members of Delta Zeta in their junior or senior year who need financial assistance.

Duration: Annual. **To Apply:** Application forms are available on the website. Applicants must provide the official transcript; must have statement about special service to Delta Zeta, campus activities and/or community involvement, and academic honors; must have the list of employment record; must submit a recommendation letter from the college chapter director (CCD) and if chapter has no CCD, a letter from RCC will suffice. **Contact:** Application materials must be sent at dzfoundation@dzshq.com.

4045 ■ Thornberg/Havens Scholarship *(Undergraduate/Scholarship)*

Purpose: To provide financial assistance to all qualified undergraduate students. **Focus:** General studies/Field of study not specified. **Qualif.:** Applicants must be an undergraduate student.

Duration: Annual. **Deadline:** February 15.

4046 ■ Democrats for Life of America (DFLA)
10521 Judicial Dr., Unit 200
Fairfax, VA 22030
Ph: (703)424-6663
E-mail: info@democratsforlife.org
URL: www.democratsforlife.org

4047 ■ Democrats for Life of America Scholarship Essay *(College, Community College, High School, Undergraduate, Graduate, Vocational/Occupational/ Scholarship)*

Purpose: To increase awareness of the Democrats for Life of America (DFLA), to foster and reward respectful dialogue, and to promote and reward original and creative thinking. **Focus:** General studies/Field of study not specified. **Qualif.:** Applicant must be between the ages of 17-26, a U.S. citizen, and a full-time student. **Criteria:** Essays will be judged on originality, creativity, and feasibility of thoughts and ideas, along with acknowledgement of alternative perspectives.

Funds Avail.: $2,500 (first place); $1,000 (second place); $500 (third place). **Number Awarded:** 3. **To Apply:** Applicant should submit a 500 to 800 word essay and contact information online. **Deadline:** June 7.

4048 ■ DeMolay International
10200 NW Ambassador Dr.
Kansas City, MO 64153
Ph: (816)891-8333
Fax: (816)891-9062
Free: 800-336-6529
E-mail: demolay@demolay.org
URL: www.demolay.org
Social Media: www.facebook.com/DeMolay.International

4049 ■ Frank S. Land Scholarship *(Undergraduate/ Scholarship)*

Purpose: To provide financial assistance for eligible members of DeMolay. **Focus:** General studies/Field of

Awards are arranged alphabetically below their administering organizations

study not specified. **Qualif.:** Applicants must be active members of DeMolay with a high school diploma.

Funds Avail.: No specific amount. **Duration:** Annual. **Number Awarded:** 1. **To Apply:** Applicants must submit application and letters of reference from appropriate professors; current copy high school or college transcript; include documentation of your SAR score obtained from your most recent FAFSA application; signed and dated copy of this scholarship application. **Deadline:** April 1.

4050 ■ Dentistry by John Barras DDS

1330 Post Oak Blvd., Ste. 1300
Houston, TX 77056
Ph: (713)993-9814
URL: www.johnbarrasdds.com
Social Media: www.facebook.com/dentistrybyjohnbarras
twitter.com/johnbarrasdds
youtube.com/dentistrybyjohnbarrasddshouston

4051 ■ Autism Scholarship *(High School, Two Year College, Four Year College, Graduate, Vocational/ Occupational, Professional development/Scholarship)*

Purpose: To encourage individuals diagnosed with autism to continue their education, and thereby to achieve their career goals, at the same time lessening the financial burden associated with attendance at an educational institution. **Focus:** General studies/Field of study not specified. **Qualif.:** U.S. citizen who has been diagnosed with autism spectrum disorder (ASD). **Criteria:** Short statement and optional essay.

Funds Avail.: $1,000. **To Apply:** Complete online application form; upload statement (135 words or less) describing your educational goals. Optional: upload essay (850 words or less) explaining how ASD or autism has impacted your education. **Deadline:** February 19. **Contact:** John Barras, DDS, 1330 Post Oak Blvd. #1300, Houston, TX, 77056; Phone: 713-993-9814.

4052 ■ Denver Scholarship Foundation (DSF)

789 Sherman Street, Suite 610
Denver, CO 80203
Ph: (303)951-4140
Fax: (303)951-4143
E-mail: info@denverscholarship.org
URL: denverscholarship.org
Social Media: www.facebook.com/
  DenverScholarshipFoundation
www.linkedin.com/company/denver-scholarship-foundation
twitter.com/DenvScholarFdtn

4053 ■ Denver Scholarship Foundation General Scholarship Fund *(Graduate/Scholarship)*

Purpose: To inspire and empower Denver Public School (DPS) students to achieve their post-secondary goals. **Focus:** General studies/Field of study not specified. **Qualif.:** Applicants must be a DPS graduate; must have at least a 2.0 GPA.

Funds Avail.: No specific amount. **Duration:** Annual. **To Apply:** Applicants must submit application form. **Deadline:** July 15.

4054 ■ Deutsche Gesellschaft fur Amerikastudien (DGFA)

Universitat Mannheim
Historisches Institut

Lehrstuhl fur Zeitgeschichte
D-68131 Mannheim, Germany
Ph: 49 931 3180293
E-mail: executive_director@dgfa.de
URL: dgfa.de

4055 ■ The Christoph Daniel Ebeling Fellowship *(Postdoctorate, Doctorate/Fellowship)*

Purpose: To support research at AAS by doctoral and postdoctoral candidates in American Studies at German universities. **Focus:** United States studies. **Qualif.:** Applicants must be German citizens or permanent residents at the post-graduate or postdoctoral stages of their careers. **Criteria:** Recipients are selected based on: scholarly qualifications; significance or importance of the project; appropriateness of the proposed study to AAS collections.

Funds Avail.: $1,800 Euros. **Duration:** one to two months. **To Apply:** Applicants must fill out the online application form. **Deadline:** May 31.

4056 ■ Deutscher Akademischer Austausch Dienst (DAAD)

871 United Nations Plz.
New York, NY 10017
Ph: (212)758-3223
Fax: (212)755-5780
E-mail: daadny@daad.org
URL: www.daad.org
Social Media: www.facebook.com/daad.usa
twitter.com/daadnewyork
www.youtube.com/user/daadny

4057 ■ Leo Baeck Institute - DAAD Fellowships *(Doctorate/Fellowship)*

Purpose: To provide financial assistance to the students doing dissertation research work and to academics writing a scholarly essay or book. **Focus:** German studies. **Qualif.:** Applicants must be US citizens and Ph.D. candidates or recent Ph.D.'s (degree awarded within the last two years). **Criteria:** Selection shall be based on the aforementioned qualifications and compliance with the application details.

Funds Avail.: $2,000. **Number Awarded:** 2. **To Apply:** Applicants must submit the following: completed application form; curriculum vitae; a full description of the research project; for doctoral students, send official transcripts for graduate and undergraduate work, evidence of enrollment in a PhD program, one letter of recommendation by their doctoral advisor and one by another scholar familiar with their work; for PhDs, evidence of their degree (transcripts not required); and two letters of recommendation from two colleagues familiar with their research. **Deadline:** November 1; May 31. **Contact:** Michael Thomanek; Email: thomanek@daad.org.

4058 ■ DAAD Learn German in Germany Grants *(Doctorate/Grant)*

Purpose: To encourage faculty members who are not in German Studies, German Language and Literature, and German Translation and Interpretation to attend intensive language courses at Goethe-Institutes in Germany. **Focus:** German studies. **Qualif.:** Applicants must be citizens or permanent residents of the United States or Canada and they are scholars who hold a Ph.D. (or equivalent) and

Awards are arranged alphabetically below their administering organizations

have been working in research or teaching full-time at a university or research institution in the United States or Canada for at least two years after receipt of the doctorate; must be in mid-career and are under 46 years of age; must have a basic knowledge of German; must not have previously studied in a German-speaking country for more than two months and/or received a grant to attend a German language course from DAAD or any other organization within the last three years. **Criteria:** Preference will be given to applicants in the social sciences, the natural sciences, engineering and professional schools.

Funds Avail.: 1,800 Euros. **Number Awarded:** 2. **To Apply:** Applicants must submit a completed DAAD application form; curriculum vitae not to exceed five pages; a detailed statement explaining why the applicant wants to attend a Goethe Institute language course in Germany; accomplish the language evaluation (self-test form enclosed with application); must have the list of publications and a list of courses taught during the previous academic year. **Deadline:** January 31. **Contact:** Ms. Uta Gaedeke; Email: gaedeke@daad.org.

4059 ■ DAAD Study Scholarship Awards (Graduate, Undergraduate/Scholarship)

Purpose: To provide the opportunity to study in Germany, or complete a Master's degree course and obtain a degree from a German higher education institution. **Focus:** Dentistry; Medicine; Pharmacy; Veterinary science and medicine. **Qualif.:** Applicants must be graduating seniors (fourth or final year of undergraduate studies) or those with undergraduate degree in all academic fields; must be enrolled full-time at any North American University; citizens of US or Canada, but open to foreigners who have studied at any accredited US or Canadian university for two years; must have a study project that makes a stay in Germany essential. **Criteria:** Preference will be given to applicants who have been invited by a faculty member at a German university to study at a particular university department.

Funds Avail.: No specific amount. **Duration:** Annual. **To Apply:** Applicants must submit the application form with the supplemental form (for music, fine arts, dance only), CV/Resume, study proposal, two letters of recommendation, evidence of contact with German Institution, DAAD Language evaluation form and transcript of records. **Contact:** Study Scholarship, 871 United Nations Plaza, New York, NY 10017; Email: gradscholar@daad.org.

4060 ■ DAAD Undergraduate Scholarship Program (Undergraduate/Scholarship)

Purpose: To support undergraduate US and Canadian students interested in studying, doing research or completing an internship in Germany. **Focus:** General studies/Field of study not specified. **Qualif.:** Applicants must be currently second or third year students and will be in their third and fourth year during their stay in Germany; must be U.S., Canadian citizens or permanent residents; has interest in contemporary German and European affairs; and full-time students in an undergraduate degree-granting program at an accredited North American college or university. Students with outstanding academic records and personal integrity as evinced by both their grades and letters of recommendation are eligible to apply. **Criteria:** Preference will be given to students whose projects or programs are based at an organized by a German university.

Funds Avail.: 650 Euros. **Duration:** One semester. **To Apply:** Applicants must submit the original printout of the application with their signature and three copies of the follow-

ing supplemental documents: resume; an approximately three pages of project proposal; two recommendation letters from major professors; acceptance into Study Abroad Program, Exchange Program, letter by mentor or invitation from a German university; transcripts; and language evaluation certificate.

4061 ■ Faculty Research Visit Grants (Doctorate/ Grant)

Purpose: To pursue research at universities, libraries, archives, institutes or laboratories in Germany. **Focus:** General studies/Field of study not specified. **Qualif.:** Applicants must be citizens or permanent residents of the United States or Canada. German nationals must have been affiliated with a US or Canadian institution in full-time employment for at least ten consecutive years; should possess adequate knowledge of the German language to carry out the proposed research; may not hold a DAAD grant and a grant from another German or German-American organization concurrently for the same project; former recipients of DAAD research grants who wish to apply again may do so after a lapse of at least three years; a change of dates for recipients of the Research Grant for University Academics and Scientists is a rare exception granted only in special circumstances. **Criteria:** Scholarship decisions are made by an independent academic selection committee based on an outstanding academic record and potential; validity and feasibility of the proposed project; and the necessity to carry it out in Germany.

Funds Avail.: 2,000 Euros; 2,150 Euros; 2,300 Euros. **Duration:** One to three months program. **To Apply:** Application requires the following: curriculum vitae; list of academic publications; comprehensive statement about research/ working project; time schedule and itinerary of the planned research stay; letter from host which refers to the applicant's proposal and guarantees that a workplace will be provided. The invitation letter should be a PDF document that can be uploaded to the portal by the applicant. **Deadline:** October 15.

4062 ■ German Studies Research Grants (Undergraduate/Grant)

Purpose: To encourage research and promote the study of cultural, political, historical, economic, and social aspects of modern and contemporary German affairs from an inter and multidisciplinary perspective. **Focus:** German studies. **Qualif.:** Applicants must be undergraduate students with at least junior standing pursuing German Studies nominated by their department and/or program chair; must be U.S. citizens who are enrolled full time at the university that nominates them; have completed at least two years of college degree in German; and with a minimum of three courses in German Studies. **Criteria:** Selection of applicants will be based on the application and other supporting documents.

Funds Avail.: $2,000-$3,000. **To Apply:** Applicants must submit a completed DAAD application form; curriculum vitae; detailed description of the research project or the pre-dissertation proposal; budget statement; list of German language and German Studies courses taken; two letters of recommendation wherein, one must come from professor supervising the German Studies curriculum or the research project; DAAD language evaluation form signed by a German Department faculty member; and an official transcript of records. **Deadline:** November 1; May 1. **Contact:** DAAD (German Academic Exchange Service), German Studies Research Grant, 871 United Nations Plz., New York, NY, 10017. Email:grandel@daad.org.

Awards are arranged alphabetically below their administering organizations

4063 ■ Hochschulsommerkurse *(Undergraduate/ Award)*

Purpose: To attend a broad range of summer courses at German universities which focus mainly on literary, cultural, political and economic aspects of modern and contemporary Germany. **Focus:** German studies. **Qualif.:** Applicants can be students from bachelor's and master's degrees in all disciplines; bachelor students must have completed at least two academic years at the beginning of the scholarship; graduates with a master's degree and doctoral students are excluded from the application. **Criteria:** Applicants will be assessed on the basis of their academic and professional future.

Funds Avail.: 850 Euros. **To Apply:** Applicants must submit a completed DAAD application form; autobiographical essay in German; a detailed, English statement of approximately 500 words explaining why the applicants wants to attend a university summer course; recommendation letter written by a professor in the applicant's major field of study but the recommendation should be different from professor who evaluates the language proficiency; complete, official transcripts of all post-secondary studies; DAAD language evaluation form (Sprachzeugnis) signed by any member of German Department at the applicant's institution or by an official of a Goethe Institute. **Contact:** Branch Office New York, German Academic Exchange Service, 871 United Nations Plaza, New York, NY 10017 USA; Phone: 212-758-3223; Fax: 212-755-5780; Email: daadny@daad.org.

4064 ■ Intensive Language Course Grant *(Graduate, Undergraduate/Grant)*

Purpose: To enhance language proficiency in Germany. **Focus:** German studies. **Qualif.:** Applicants must be full-time students currently enrolled in a graduate program in all fields of study except German, or any other modern language or literature; German language skills should be equivalent to at least level A1 and no higher than B1 of the Common European Framework of Reference for Languages. **Criteria:** Applicants will be assessed based on academic record and statements of project and professional future.

Duration: Eight weeks. **Deadline:** December 1.

4065 ■ Research Internships in Science and Engineering (RISE) *(Undergraduate/Internship)*

Purpose: To provide internship opportunities in Germany for U.S. and Canadian undergraduate students in the fields of biology, chemistry, physics, earth sciences, and engineering. **Focus:** Biology; Chemistry; Earth sciences; Engineering; Physics. **Qualif.:** Applicants must be undergraduate students from the United States, Canada, or the UK, studying in the fields of biology, chemistry, physics, earth sciences, or engineering. **Duration:** Annual. **Contact:** Email: rise-germany@daad.de.

4066 ■ Study Scholarship for Artists or Musicians *(Graduate, Postdoctorate/Scholarship)*

Purpose: To provide the opportunity to study in Germany, or complete a postgraduate degree course and obtain a degree from a German higher education institution. **Focus:** Architecture; Art; Dance; Music. **Qualif.:** Applicants should be in the fields of Fine Arts, Architecture, Music and Dance. Graduating seniors must be full-time at an accredited university for two years. Open to U.S. or Canadian citizens. **Criteria:** Preference will be given to applicants who have

been invited by a faculty member at a German university to study at a particular university department.

Funds Avail.: 750 Euros. **Duration:** Annual. **To Apply:** Applicant must complete the online application form available in the website and must have the following: Supplemental materials, CV/Resume, Study proposal, two letters of recommendation, evidence of contact with German Institution and transcript of records. **Contact:** Applications must be submitted to our head office: DAAD - German Academic Exchange Service, Section ST23 - North America, Kennedyallee 50, 53175 Bonn, Germany.

4067 ■ Development Fund for Black Students in Science and Technology (DFBSST)
2705 Bladensburg Rd. NE
Washington, DC 20018
Ph: (202)635-3604
URL: www.dfbsstscholarship.org

4068 ■ Development Fund for Black Students in Science and Technology Scholarship *(Undergraduate/Scholarship)*

Purpose: To provide scholarships to African American undergraduate students enroll in scientific or technical fields of study at Historically Black Colleges and Universities. **Focus:** Science; Technology. **Qualif.:** Applicants must meet the following criteria: African-American heritage; undergraduate students majoring (or intending to major) in a technical field of study (i.e., engineering, math, science, etc.); enrollment at one of the predominantly Black colleges or universities; U.S. citizenship or permanent residency. **Criteria:** Selection is based on academic achievement, personal essay describing career goals, current and past relevant extracurricular activities, recommendations from teachers and guidance counselors and financial need.

Funds Avail.: $3,000. **Duration:** Annual; up to 4 years. **Number Awarded:** 1. **To Apply:** Applicants must submit a completed application form. **Deadline:** June 15.

4069 ■ DeVries & Associates
75-5591 Palani Rd., Ste. 2001
Kailua Kona, HI 96740
Ph: (808)339-3200
URL: www.devriespc.com
Social Media: www.facebook.com/devrieslaw
twitter.com/devries_aal

4070 ■ DeVries Law School Scholarship *(Undergraduate/Scholarship)*

Purpose: To provide financial aid to college students, encourage students to understand how lawyers help businesses thrive, and inspire students to pursue a career in any legal field. **Focus:** Business; Finance; Law; Management. **Qualif.:** Applicant must be a high school senior or college freshman in the U.S. who is studying, or plans to study, business, finance, management, or law. **Criteria:** Selection is based on the quality of the video essay or written essay submitted.

Funds Avail.: $1,000. **Duration:** Annual. **Number Awarded:** 1. **To Apply:** Applicant must record a video (one to two minutes long, in English) explaining how lawyers help businesses thrive. Video must be published on the applicant's YouTube page with the title "DeVries Law Scholarship Contest" and this link in the description: devriespc.com/

Awards are arranged alphabetically below their administering organizations

scholarship-for-college-students. Applicant must also share the video on their Facebook page and the sponsor's Facebook page. Instead of a video essay, applicant may submit a 1,000 to 1,500 word essay on the same subject via email. **Deadline:** August 15. **Contact:** Porter DeVries; Email: DeVriesScholarship@gmail.com.

4071 ■ Diabetes Hope Foundation (DHF)
6150 Dixie Rd., Unit 1
Mississauga, ON, Canada L5T 2E2
Ph: (905)670-0557
E-mail: info@diabeteshopefoundation.com
URL: www.diabeteshopefoundation.com
Social Media: www.facebook.com/diabeteshopefoundation
www.linkedin.com/company/diabetes-hope-foundation
twitter.com/DiabetesHopeFDN
www.youtube.com/channel/
UCWnZWK8zJ1bJBd0AXRp4aRg

4072 ■ Diabetes Hope Scholarship Program
(Undergraduate/Scholarship)

Purpose: To provide educational assistance to students with diabetes in continuing their studies. **Focus:** General studies/Field of study not specified. **Qualif.:** Applicant must be young adults who are residents of Ontario, Canada; must be final year of high school and entering an accredited post-secondary institution in the fall of 2020. **Criteria:** Selection will ne nased on student Background/Leadership/Community Development;student Transcrip;about Diabetes Hope Foundation;diabetes Care;mentor's Comments;essay Question.

Funds Avail.: $2,000 each. **Duration:** Annual; one year. **Number Awarded:** Varies. **To Apply:** All application submissions must be completed online. **Deadline:** March 9. **Contact:** Anita Nardella, Program Coordinator, Diabetes Hope Foundation, 6150 Dixie Rd., Unit 1, Mississauga, ON, L5T 2E2; Email: anita@diabeteshopefoundation.com.

4073 ■ Diabetes Scholars Foundation (DSF)
310 Busse Hwy., Ste. 256
Park Ridge, IL 60068
Ph: (312)215-9861
Fax: (847)991-8739
E-mail: scholars@beyondtype1.org
URL: www.diabetesscholars.org

4074 ■ The Lilly Diabetes Tomorrow's Leaders Scholarship *(Undergraduate/Scholarship)*

Purpose: To financially support incoming college students with Type 1 diabetes who are seeking a higher education at an accredited four year university, college, technical or trade school. **Focus:** General studies/Field of study not specified. **Qualif.:** Applicants must be high school seniors and incoming freshmen with Type 1 diabetes; should be seeking a higher education at an accredited four year university, college, technical or trade school; must be U.S. citizens or permanent residents. **Criteria:** Selection is based on activities, grades, volunteering, advocacy, leadership, essays and recommendations from both a treating physician/CDE and from a high school teacher/counselor; not based on financial need.

Funds Avail.: $5,000. **Duration:** Annual. **To Apply:** Submission of application and recommendations must be

completed online at diabetesscholars.org/college-scholarship/. **Deadline:** April 15. **Contact:** Email: scholars@beyondtype1.org.

4075 ■ Diagnosis Delayed
525 State Hwy. 73, Ste. 117
Marlton, NJ 08053
Ph: (856)778-5500
Fax: (856)778-1918
E-mail: info@diagnosisdelayed.com
URL: www.diagnosisdelayed.com

4076 ■ Diagnosis Delayed Scholarship *(Graduate/Scholarship)*

Purpose: To help offset the costs of obtaining a medical or legal degree. **Focus:** Law; Medicine.

Funds Avail.: $500. **Number Awarded:** 1. **Contact:** Email: info@diagnosisdelayed.com.

4077 ■ DiBella Law Offices PC
45 Osgood St., Ste. 302
Methuen, MA 01844
Ph: (978)965-8057
URL: www.dibellalawoffice.com
Social Media: www.facebook.com/DiBellaLawOfficesPC
twitter.com/DIBellaLaw

4078 ■ Writing the Future *(Undergraduate, College, University/Scholarship)*

Purpose: To help a diligent and deserving student pay for college. **Focus:** General studies/Field of study not specified. **Qualif.:** Applicant must be a high school senior on track to graduate or a college student enrolled in an accredited four-year university or college, or currently enrolled in a two-year college and planning to transfer to a four-year university upon completion; have a minimum 3.0 GPA; and be a U.S. citizen or permanent resident (DACA recipients are welcome to apply).

Funds Avail.: $500. **Number Awarded:** 1. **To Apply:** Application and essay must be submitted online. **Deadline:** April 14. **Contact:** Scholarship Manager; Email: chris.dibella@dibellalawoffice.com; URL: www.dibellalawoffice.com/scholarship/.

4079 ■ Dickey Rural Networks (DRN)
9628 Hwy. 281
Ellendale, ND 58436
Ph: (701)344-5000
Free: 877-559-4692
URL: www.drtel.net

4080 ■ Dickey Rural Networks Scholarship
(Undergraduate, Vocational/Occupational/Scholarship)

Purpose: To provide financial assistance to those students who want to further their college education. **Focus:** Telecommunications systems. **Criteria:** Selection will be based on the based on the committee's criteria.

Funds Avail.: Twenty-two $500; Thirty $2,000; additional $500. **Duration:** Annual. **Number Awarded:** 1. **To Apply:** Applicants must complete an application form and submit an transcript (3 copies); a 300-word essay (2 copies); es-

Awards are arranged alphabetically below their administering organizations

say portion of the application is worth 35% of your total score; educator's statement (2 copies); one letter of recommendation from a local community leader other than an educator. **Deadline:** February 28. **Contact:** Janell Hauck, Customer Care Manager; DRN, PO Box 69, Ellendale, ND, 58436-0069; Phone: 701-344-5000; Email: foundation@frs.org.

4081 ■ Bill Dickey Scholarship Association (BDSA)

1241 E Washington St.
Phoenix, AZ 85034
Ph: (602)258-7851
Fax: (602)258-3412
E-mail: info@billdickey.org
URL: billdickey.org
Social Media: www.facebook.com/
  billdickeyscholarshipassociation
twitter.com/billdickey_org
www.youtube.com/channel/UCgEjM9VtFcpn8plWSWrxtaw

4082 ■ Bill Dickey Scholarship Association Scholarship *(Undergraduate, High School/Scholarship)*

Purpose: To provide financial support to deserving undergraduate students. **Focus:** General studies/Field of study not specified. **Qualif.:** Applicants must be school and college students; must pursue an undergraduate degree at a college or university of their choice; must be accepted to a college or university within the U.S; must be a U.S. citizen; must be a full time student, maintain a 2.5 GPA on a term and cumulative basis. **Criteria:** Selection will be based on academic achievement, leadership, financial need, evidence of community service and golfing ability.

Funds Avail.: Up to $14,000. **Duration:** Annual; up to 4 years. **To Apply:** Applications can be submitted online; must provide official transcript; essay must be a minimum of 500 words and it must be typed and double-spaced, no exceptions; additional pages to application; two personal reference forms should be completed by your high school principal, guidance counselor or other professional(s) who are knowledgeable of your: (a) academic record, (b) potential for successful college level academic immersion, (c) history of active participation in golf and (d) financial need. **Deadline:** May 24. **Contact:** Scholarship Committee, 1241 East Washington St., Ste. 101, Phoenix, AZ, 85034.

4083 ■ Dietetics in Health Care Communities (DHCC)

PO Box 4489
Carol Stream, IL 60197-4489
Free: 800-877-1600
URL: www.dhccdpg.org
Social Media: www.facebook.com/
  dieteticsinhealthcarecommunities15

4084 ■ Gaynold Jensen Education Stipends *(Post-doctorate, Other/Scholarship)*

Purpose: To provide learning programs to improve the contributions of consultant dietitians to health care. **Focus:** Health care services. **Qualif.:** Applicants must be American Dietetic Association members; must be at least a two-year member in Consultant Dietitians in Health Care Facilities; a registered dietitian; currently practicing as a consultant dietitian; planning to expand knowledge in the consultant

role. **Criteria:** Candidates are chosen on the basis of volunteer service, passion for technology, leadership activities, scholastic grades, letters of recommendation and previous awards. Demonstrated passion and spirit is weighted most heavily in the selection process.

Funds Avail.: No specific amount. **Duration:** Annual. **To Apply:** Applicants must send the application forms (available at the website).

4085 ■ Digital Entertainment Group

10635 Santa Monica Blvd.
Los Angeles, CA 90027
Ph: (424)248-3809
Fax: (424)248-3816
URL: degonline.org

4086 ■ Hedy Lamarr Achievement Award for Emerging Leaders in Entertainment Technology *(Undergraduate/Award)*

Purpose: To recognize a female college junior whose studies in the fields of entertainment and technology have shown exceptional promise. **Focus:** Filmmaking; Media arts; Music; Theater arts. **Qualif.:** Applicant must be a female student in good standing, in junior year at an accredited U.S-based academic institution; must be a citizen of the U.S.; must have a minimum 3.0 GPA. **Criteria:** Selection will be made by a judging panel based on innovation, leadership, excellence.

Funds Avail.: $10,000. **Duration:** Annual. **To Apply:** Applications can be submitted online; must provide resume or curriculum vitae; essay; letter of recommendation from professor or dean; short summary of any additional factors. **Deadline:** February 15.

4087 ■ Digital Health Canada

1100 – 151 Yonge Street
Toronto, ON, Canada M5C 2W7
URL: digitalhealthcanada.com

4088 ■ Steven Huesing Scholarships *(Graduate, Undergraduate/Scholarship)*

Purpose: To encourage health education by providing financial assistance for post-secondary education. **Focus:** Health education. **Qualif.:** Scholarship applications are accepted from any student currently enrolled in a Health Informatics or related program at an accredited post-secondary institution. The applicant should be of sound academic standing, demonstrate active involvement and achievement in HI, and show how his/her educational work has made a recognized contribution to advancing the thinking in HI. **Criteria:** Selection will be based on academic standing and potential contribution to advance health informatics.

Funds Avail.: $1,000. **Duration:** One year. **To Apply:** Applicant must submit transcript of marks; assessment by an academic advisor; proof of enrolment in and current attendance at a recognized Canadian post-secondary institution in a HI or related program; and description of the applicant's involvement and achievements in health informatics (written submission of 500 words). **Deadline:** March 22. **Remarks:** Established in recognition of Founding President Steven Huesing's contribution to COACH. Established in 1999. **Contact:** contact Shannon Bott, Executive Director, Operations, Digital Health Canada at

Awards are arranged alphabetically below their administering organizations

sbott@digitalhealthcanada.com; or 647.775.8555.

4089 ■ Digital Responsibility
3561 Homestead, Ste. 113
Santa Clara, CA 95051-5161
E-mail: info@digitalresponsibility.org
URL: www.digitalresponsibility.org

4090 ■ E-Waste Scholarship *(High School, Undergraduate, Graduate/Scholarship)*

Purpose: To help students understand the impact of e-waste and what can be done to reduce e-waste. **Focus:** General studies/Field of study not specified. **Qualif.:** High school freshmen, sophomores, juniors; or seniors; current or entering college or graduate school students of any level; U.S. citizen or legal resident. Home schooled students are also eligible. **Criteria:** Content and creativity of essay.

Funds Avail.: $1,000. **Duration:** Annual. **To Apply:** Complete online application form including a 140-character statement about e-waste. Ten finalists will then write an essay between 500 and 1,000 words on the topic. **Deadline:** April 30. **Contact:** Email: scholarship@digitalresponsibility.org; URL: http://www.digitalresponsibility.org/ewaste-scholarship.

4091 ■ Diplomatic and Consular Officers, Retired, Inc. (DACOR)
1801 F St. NW
Washington, DC 20006
Ph: (202)682-0500
URL: www.dacorbacon.org
Social Media: www.facebook.com/DACOR-and-DACOR
  -Bacon-House-Foundation-135980179779310
twitter.com/DACORtweets

4092 ■ Gantenbein Medical Fund Fellowship *(Graduate/Fellowship)*

Purpose: To provide financial assistance, in education aspect, to American students pursuing medical degree/studies. **Focus:** Medicine. **Qualif.:** Applicants must be first-year American students enrolled in accredited U.S. medical schools with a program in Global Health that is integrated into the regular medical school program. **Criteria:** Selection will be based on the committee's criteria.

Funds Avail.: $30,000. **Duration:** Annual. **To Apply:** Applicants may contact the Organization for the application process and other details. **Remarks:** The Gantenbein Medical Fund was established through the bequest of Mary F. Gantenbein in memory of her husband, FSO James W. Gantenbein.

4093 ■ Graduate Fellowships for Study of International Affairs *(Graduate, Master's/Fellowship)*

Purpose: To support students pursuing Master's degree in international affairs. **Focus:** International affairs and relations. **Qualif.:** Applicant must be U.S. citizens pursuing Master's degree in international affairs; must be planning to study at any accredited graduate school in the United States. **Criteria:** Selection will be based on the Education Committee's criteria.

Funds Avail.: $10,000 each. **Duration:** Annual. **To Apply:** Applicants may contact the Organization for the application process and other details.

4094 ■ Direct Energy L.P.
12 Greenway Plz., Ste. 250
Houston, TX 77046
Ph: (713)877-3500
Fax: (800)346-2233
URL: www.directenergy.com
Social Media: www.facebook.com/directenergy
www.instagram.com/directenergy
twitter.com/directenergy
www.youtube.com/user/TheDirectEnergy

4095 ■ The Direct Energy Live Brighter Scholarship *(Undergraduate/Scholarship)*

Purpose: To support and recognize the people making a positive impact in their communities. **Focus:** General studies/Field of study not specified. **Qualif.:** Applicant must be a registered college student for the upcoming school year and be at least 18 years old; have a minimum 3.0 on a 4.0 scale; and be a resident of any of the states where Direct Energy offers energy services: Connecticut, Delaware, Illinois, Indiana, Maryland, Massachusetts, Michigan, New Jersey, New York, Ohio, Pennsylvania, Texas, New Hampshire, Rhode Island, and the District of Columbia. **Criteria:** Selection is based on the following criteria equally: academic performance of the applicant based on submitted transcript, creativity and innovation of the video or essay, understanding the mission of the applicant and how it makes a positive difference in people's lives, and how application aligns with the sponsor's brand of qualities (being innovative, thoughtful, and inspiring).

Funds Avail.: $2,500. **Number Awarded:** 1. **To Apply:** Application must be completed and essay submitted online. **Deadline:** December 31. **Contact:** Email: DEscholarship@directenergy.com; URL: https://www.directenergy.com/scholarship/official-rules.

4096 ■ Direct Textbooks
1525 Chemeketa St. NE
Salem, OR 97301
E-mail: service@directtextbook.com
URL: directtextbook.com

4097 ■ DirectTextbook.com Scholarship Essay Contest *(College, Undergraduate, University/Scholarship)*

Purpose: To help students pay for their education. **Focus:** General studies/Field of study not specified. **Qualif.:** Applicant must be a U.S. citizen currently enrolled in an accredited two- or four-year college or university for the upcoming fall semester; and must have a recent GPA of 2.0 or higher.

Funds Avail.: $3,000 (1st place); $2,000 (2nd place); $1,000 (3rd place). **To Apply:** Applicant must write an essay (500 words or less) in response to the following question: What is independence? What is the importance of independence in your life? Application and complete instructions are available on the website. **Contact:** URL: www.directtextbooks.com/scholarship.php.

4098 ■ Directed Energy Professional Society (DEPS)
7770 Jefferson St. NE, Ste. 440
Albuquerque, NM 87109
Ph: (505)998-4910

Awards are arranged alphabetically below their administering organizations

Fax: (505)998-4917
E-mail: office@deps.org
URL: www.deps.org

4099 ■ DEPS Graduate Scholarship *(Graduate/ Scholarship)*

Purpose: To provide support of research and development of DE technology. **Focus:** Chemistry; Engineering, Aerospace/Aeronautical/Astronautical; Engineering, Chemical; Engineering, Electrical; Engineering, Optical; Materials research/science; Physics. **Qualif.:** Applicants must be U.S. citizens or individuals who have demonstrated interest in American citizenship; must be full-time graduate students at a U.S. school; must be pursuing or currently studying DE technology areas of HEL or HPM with scopes similar to those researches published in the Journal of Directed Energy. **Criteria:** Selection is based on the reviews conducted by the DEPS Board of Scientific and Engineering Advisors' (BSEA).

Funds Avail.: Up to $10,000. **Duration:** Annual. **Number Awarded:** Varies. **To Apply:** Applicants must submit completed application form available at the website; official transcripts of undergraduate and graduate studies sent directly from the school; letter of interest in DE technology and statement of proposed research; and a reference letter from a potential or current research advisor including an assessment of the applicant's potential and description of facilities to be employed for the research; and letter of intent to become U.S. citizen. **Deadline:** April 30. **Contact:** Mark Neice, DEPS Executive Director, Email: mark@deps.org.

4100 ■ Dirksen Congressional Center

2815 Broadway
Pekin, IL 61554-4219
Ph: (309)347-7113
E-mail: twhite@dirksencenter.org
URL: dirksencenter.org

4101 ■ Congressional Research Grants *(Graduate/ Grant)*

Purpose: To fund research on congressional leadership and related studies about the U.S. Congress. **Focus:** Government. **Criteria:** Selection is based on the project design; plan of work; dissemination; applicant's qualifications; a relationship of the project to the Centers Program goals and to current work in the field; and appropriateness of the budget request for the requirements.

Funds Avail.: Few hundred dollars to $3,500. **Duration:** Annual. **To Apply:** Applicants must submit the general information along with congressional research grant project description; budget; curriculum vitae and reference letter. **Remarks:** Established in 1978. **Contact:** Frank H. Mackaman, The Dirksen Congressional Center, 2815 Broadway, Pekin, IL, 61554-4219 USA; Phone; 309-347-7113; Email: fmackaman@dirksencenter.org.

4102 ■ Ray and Kathy LaHood Scholarships for the Study of American Government *(Undergraduate/ Scholarship)*

Purpose: To provide financial support for Bradley University juniors who are majoring in a discipline related to The Dirksen Center's purpose and interest or in subjects related to the study of Federal Government. **Focus:** Government. **Qualif.:** Must attend Bradley University, be a junior in good standing who will enter their senior year of study in a field related to the study of the U.S. government, maintain a grad point of at least 3.0 overall and 3.5 in their major. **Criteria:** Selection is based on scholastic records.

Funds Avail.: No specific amount. **Duration:** Annual. **Number Awarded:** Varies. **To Apply:** Applicants must fill out the required scholarship form; must agree to write a 250-word evaluation of the impact of their scholarship before the end of their senior year. **Contact:** Brad McMillan, Executive Director, Institute for Principled Leadership, bmcmillan@bradley.edu.

4103 ■ The Disability Care Center

2875 S Orange Ave., Ste. 500
Orlando, FL 32806
Free: 888-504-0035
URL: www.disabilitycarecenter.org
Social Media: www.facebook.com/disabilitycarecenter
twitter.com/disability_care

4104 ■ Disability Care Center Disabled Student Scholarships *(Undergraduate/Scholarship)*

Purpose: To assist students who are suffering from a debilitating condition(s) while continuing their education at a college institution. **Focus:** General studies/Field of study not specified. **Qualif.:** Applicants must be enrolled in a U.S. college institution with at least 12 credit hours of classes for the upcoming fall semester; must be legal residents of the United States; must have a GPA of 2.5 from their most recent transcript (high school or college); and must have a medically diagnosed impairment. **Criteria:** Selection will be based on the aforementioned qualifications and the submitted essays.

Funds Avail.: $500. **To Apply:** Applicants will be required to write a short essay between 500 and 1,500 words about the essay topic given; additional requirement is their most recent transcript. **Deadline:** August 1. **Contact:** Email: scholarship@disabilitycarecenter.org.

4105 ■ Disability Care Center Special Education Scholarships *(Undergraduate/Scholarship)*

Purpose: To support students who are pursuing a degree in special education. **Focus:** Education; Education, Special. **Qualif.:** Applicants must be enrolled in a U.S. college institution with at least 12 credit hours of classes for the upcoming fall semester; must be legal residents of the United States; must have a GPA of 2.5 from their most recent transcript (high school or college); and must be currently majoring in special education.**Criteria:** Selection will be based on the aforementioned qualifications and the submitted essays.

Funds Avail.: $500. **To Apply:** Applicants will be required to write a short essay between 500 and 1,500 words about the essay topic given here; must explain why they are pursuing a degree in special education and how they plan to make a difference in the lives of the disabled; additional requirement is a letter of recommendation from a creditable source. **Deadline:** August 1.

4106 ■ Disabled American Veterans (DAV)

PO Box 14301
Cincinnati, OH 45250-0301
Free: 877-426-2838
E-mail: service@dav.org
URL: www.dav.org

Awards are arranged alphabetically below their administering organizations

Social Media: www.facebook.com/DAV
www.instagram.com/daveterans
www.linkedin.com/company/disabled-american-veterans
www.pinterest.com/daveterans
twitter.com/davhq
www.youtube.com/c/disabledamericanveterans

4107 ■ Jesse Brown Memorial Youth Scholarship Program *(Advanced Professional/Scholarship)*

Purpose: To provide financial assistance to young volunteers who play active roles in the Department of Veterans Affairs Voluntary Service programs to continue their education. **Focus:** General studies/Field of study not specified. **Qualif.:** Applicants must be any volunteers who are at the age of 21 or younger and have volunteered for a minimum of 100 hours at a VA medical center during the previous year; immediate family members of the DAV national organization are also eligible. **Criteria:** Applicants will be evaluated based on criteria designed by the Scholarship Selection Committee.

Funds Avail.: Varies. **Duration:** Annual. **Number Awarded:** 8. **To Apply:** Nominations must be submitted by the Voluntary Service Program Manager at the VA medical center, DAV Department Commander. Students must submit a self-nomination form which is available online, including an essay and any supporting documentation. **Deadline:** February 28. **Contact:** DAV National Headquarters, ATTN: Jesse Brown Scholarship Submissions, 3725 Alexandria Pike, Cold Spring, KY, 41076, Email: JBMYS@ dav.org.

4108 ■ Discover Financial Services (DFS)

2500 Lake Cook Rd.
Riverwoods, IL 60015-3851
Free: 800-347-2683
E-mail: emailwatch@discover.com
URL: www.discover.com
Social Media: www.facebook.com/discover
www.instagram.com/discover/
www.linkedin.com/company/discover-financial-services
twitter.com/discover

4109 ■ Discover Bar Exam Loans *(Graduate/Loan, Scholarship)*

Purpose: To help cover the bar exam prep classes and living expenses. **Focus:** Law. **Qualif.:** Applicants must have graduated from law school within the past 6 months or be enrolled in a final year of study in a graduate law degree program; must be US citizens; permanent residents or international students. International students require a Social Security number and a cosigner; must be 16 years or older at the time of application; must pass a credit check.

Funds Avail.: No specific amount. **Duration:** Annual. **To Apply:** Applicants must complete the online submission. **Contact:** Repayment Assistance Department at 800-STUDENT.

4110 ■ Discover Graduate Loans *(Graduate, Master's, Doctorate/Loan, Scholarship)*

Purpose: To address the needs of students enrolled in a master's or doctoral degree programs. **Focus:** General studies/Field of study not specified. **Qualif.:** Applicants must have graduated from law school within the past 6 months or be enrolled in a final year of study in a graduate

law degree program; must be US citizens; permanent residents or international students. International students require a Social Security number and a cosigner; must be 16 years or older at the time of application; must pass a credit check.

Funds Avail.: No specific amount. **Duration:** Annual. **To Apply:** Applicants must complete the online submission. **Contact:** Repayment Assistance Department at 800-STUDENT.

4111 ■ Discover Health Professions Loans *(Graduate/Loan, Scholarship)*

Purpose: To address the needs of students enrolled in a health professions graduate program. **Focus:** Dentistry; Medical assisting; Medicine, Osteopathic; Nursing; Occupational therapy; Optometry; Pharmacy; Physical therapy; Podiatry; Veterinary science and medicine. **Qualif.:** Applicants must be students enrolled at least half-time in a graduate program at an eligible law school; must be seeking a degree; must be making satisfactory academic progress as defined by their school; must be US citizens, permanent residents or international students. International students require a Social Security number and a cosigner; must be 16 years or older at the time of application; must pass a credit check.

Funds Avail.: No specific amount. **Duration:** Annual. **To Apply:** Applicants must complete the online submission. **Contact:** Repayment Assistance Department at 800-STUDENT.

4112 ■ Discover Law Loans *(Graduate/Loan, Scholarship)*

Purpose: To address the needs of students enrolled in a graduate program at an eligible law school. **Focus:** Law. **Qualif.:** Applicants must be students enrolled at least half-time in a graduate program at an eligible law school; must be seeking a degree; must be making satisfactory academic progress as defined by their school; must be US citizens, permanent residents or international students. International students require a Social Security number and a cosigner; must be 16 years or older at the time of application; must pass a credit check.

Funds Avail.: No specific amount. **Duration:** Annual. **To Apply:** Applicants must complete the online submission. **Contact:** Repayment Assistance Department at 800-STUDENT.

4113 ■ Discover MBA Loans *(Graduate/Loan, Scholarship)*

Purpose: To address the needs of students enrolled in a graduate program at an eligible business school. **Focus:** Business. **Qualif.:** Applicants must be enrolled at least half-time in a graduate program at an eligible business school; must be seeking a degree; must be making satisfactory academic progress as defined by their school; must be US citizens, permanent residents or international students. International students require a Social Security number and a cosigner; must be 16 years or older at the time of application; must pass a credit check.

Funds Avail.: No specific amount. **Duration:** Annual. **To Apply:** Applicants must complete the online submission. **Contact:** Repayment Assistance Department at 800-STUDENT.

4114 ■ Discover Residency Loans *(Graduate/Loan, Scholarship)*

Purpose: To cover the cost of residency, internship, relocation and board exam review. **Focus:** Dentistry; Medical as-

---

Awards are arranged alphabetically below their administering organizations

sisting; Medicine, Osteopathic; Nursing; Occupational therapy; Optometry; Pharmacy; Physical sciences; Podiatry; Veterinary science and medicine. **Qualif.:** Applicants must have graduated within the past 12 months or be enrolled at least half-time and making satisfactory academic progress in their final year of study in a graduate health professions program; must be US citizens, permanent residents or international students. International students require a Social Security number and a cosigner; must be 16 years or older at the time of application; must pass a credit check. **Funds Avail.:** No specific amount. **Duration:** Annual. **To Apply:** Applicants must complete the online submission. **Contact:** Repayment Assistance Department at 800-STUDENT.

4115 ■ The Distinguished Flying Cross Society (DFCS)

PO Box 502408
San Diego, CA 92150
Free: 866-332-6332
URL: www.dfcsociety.org
Social Media: www.facebook.com/
   DistinguishedFlyingCross
www.instagram.com/dfcsociety
twitter.com/dfcsociety

4116 ■ Distinguished Flying Cross Society Scholarship *(Undergraduate/Scholarship)*

Purpose: To support dependents of DFC Society members in the pursuit of continuing higher education. **Focus:** Aviation. **Qualif.:** Applicants must be descendants or legally adopted children of a DFC Society member. **Criteria:** Selection will be selected based on academic achievement.

To Apply: Applicants must provide a 500-word essay on why they deserve a DFCS Scholarship; SAT/SCAT/ACT scores; official high school transcript; and a letter from DFCS member attesting that they are a descendant of a DFCS member. **Deadline:** June 30.

4117 ■ Distinguished Young Women

751 Government St.
Mobile, AL 36602
Ph: (251)438-3621
Fax: (251)431-0063
Free: 800-256-5435
E-mail: kendra@distinguishedyw.org
URL: distinguishedyw.org
Social Media: www.facebook.com/DistinguishedYW
www.instagram.com/distinguishedyw
twitter.com/distinguishedyw
www.youtube.com/user/distinguishedyw

4118 ■ Distinguished Young Women - Cash Scholarships *(High School/Scholarship)*

Purpose: To give every young woman the opportunity to further their education and prepare for a successful future. **Focus:** General studies/Field of study not specified. **Qualif.:** Applicants must be females in their junior or senior years of high school; must be willing to participate in the DYW program. **Criteria:** Selection will be based on interview (25%), talent (20%), scholastics (25%), fitness (15%) and self-expression (15%).
Funds Avail.: No specific amount. **Duration:** Annual. **To Apply:** Applications can be submitted online at

distinguishedyw.org/apply-now/.

4119 ■ District of Columbia Library Association (DCLA)

50 Massachusetts Ave. NE
Washington, DC 20002
URL: www.dcla.org
Social Media: www.facebook.com/groups/24861967157
www.instagram.com/dclalibrarians
twitter.com/DCLALibrarians

4120 ■ Ruth Fine Memorial Student Loans *(Undergraduate/Grant, Loan)*

Purpose: To assist student members who are pursuing a professional career in the library/information science field. **Focus:** Library and archival sciences. **Qualif.:** Applicant must be attending a university in an American Library Association-accredited graduate program. **Criteria:** Applicants will be selected by the committee criteria.

Funds Avail.: $6,000 each. **Duration:** Annual. **Number Awarded:** 1. **Deadline:** May 15. **Remarks:** Established in 2002.

4121 ■ DO Supply Inc.

6305 Lake Wheeler Rd.
Raleigh, NC 27603
Ph: (919)205-4392
E-mail: sales@dosupply.com
URL: www.dosupply.com
Social Media: www.facebook.com/DoSupplyCompany
www.linkedin.com/company/do-supply-company
twitter.com/dosupplycompany

4122 ■ DO Supply Academic Scholarship *(Undergraduate/Scholarship)*

Purpose: To help students fund their college education. **Focus:** General studies/Field of study not specified. **Qualif.:** Applicant must be at least 18 years old and enrolled full- or part-time in a college or university in an undergraduate program. **Criteria:** Scholarship will be given to the applicant who best demonstrates their passion for small business in the United States by creating a well-researched and personal account of a small business that impacted their life, or of a dream they have to establish their own small business.

Funds Avail.: $1,000. **Number Awarded:** 1. **To Apply:** Application and essay must be submit. **Deadline:** June 1. **Contact:** Isaac Wittenberg; Email Iwittenb@dosupply.com; URL: www.dosupply.com/scholarship.php.

4123 ■ Jim Dodson Law

310 Wildwood Way
Clearwater, FL 33756
Ph: (727)446-0840
Free: 888-815-6398
URL: www.jimdodsonlaw.com
Social Media: www.facebook.com/jimdodsonlaw
www.instagram.com/jimdodsonlaw
www.linkedin.com/company/2362295
twitter.com/jimdodsonlaw
www.youtube.com/user/jimdodsonlawflorida

Awards are arranged alphabetically below their administering organizations

4124 ■ Jim Dodson Law Scholarship for Brain Injury Victims & Their Caregivers *(Undergraduate/Scholarship)*

Purpose: To further the education of victims of traumatic brain injuries. Open to both students who have suffered such injuries, or students' of family members who have had a TBI. **Focus:** General studies/Field of study not specified. **Qualif.:** Applicants must be either a graduating senior in high school or currently enrolled part time or full time in college. must have a 2.75 GPA; and must demonstrate a capacity for success in their chosen field.

Funds Avail.: $1,000. **Duration:** Annual. **To Apply:** Applicants should apply online and also include a 500 word essay on this topic: Tell us how having a brain injury has changed your life. If you are a caregiver or a family member of someone who has a brain injury, please write your essay on how it has impacted you and/or your family's life. Your essay should not exceed 500 words and should briefly relate your personal experience with a traumatic brain injury or the traumatic brain injury of a loved one. **Deadline:** June 20. **Remarks:** Jim has seen the life-changing toll TBIs take on their victims and their caregivers. Jim's personal experience representing brain injury victims and his strong belief in the value of a college education lead him to create a scholarship offered specifically to injury victims and their loved ones. **Contact:** Kati; Email: kati@jimdodsonlaw.com.

4125 ■ Dollar-A-Day Scholarship Fund, Inc
PO Box 811882
Boca Raton, FL 33481-1882
Free: 888-728-2521
E-mail: info@muslimscholarship.org
URL: www.muslimscholarship.org

4126 ■ Dollar-A-Day Academic Scholarships *(Graduate, Undergraduate/Scholarship)*

Purpose: To provide educational assistance to Muslim university students in their chosen field of study. **Focus:** General studies/Field of study not specified. **Qualif.:** Applicants must be permanent residents or citizens of the United States; college or graduate students; must be Muslims; must demonstrate financial need; and have filed the FAFSA for the applicable year. **Criteria:** Selection will be based on evaluation of submitted documents and specific criteria; preference will be given to students enrolled in an advanced degree program, but undergraduate students are still encouraged to apply.

Funds Avail.: $1,000. **Duration:** Annual. **To Apply:** Applicants must submit a completed application form; university enrollment form; most recent transcripts; two recommendation letters; student aid report; and updated resume. **Deadline:** May 1. **Contact:** Dollar-A-Day Scholarship Fund, at the above address.

4127 ■ Dolphin Scholarship Foundation (DSF)
4966 Euclid Rd., Ste. 109
Virginia Beach, VA 23462
Ph: (757)671-3200
Fax: (757)671-3330
E-mail: info@dolphinscholarship.org
URL: www.dolphinscholarship.org
Social Media: www.facebook.com/
  DolphinScholarshipFoundation
twitter.com/DolphinScholars

4128 ■ DOLPHIN SCHOLARSHIPS *(Undergraduate/Scholarship)*

Purpose: To support the education of children/stepchildren of members or former members of the Submarine Force or who have served in the Submarine Force. **Focus:** General studies/Field of study not specified. **Criteria:** Selection of Student Dolphin Scholars is determined by evaluating the following criteria:academic proficiency;extracurricular activities;community service;two references;student essay.

Funds Avail.: $2,000 or $3,400. **Duration:** Annual. **Number Awarded:** 25-30. **To Apply:** Applicant must completing the Online Application. **Deadline:** March 15.

4129 ■ Dominican Bar Association (DBA)
PO Box 203
New York, NY 10013
E-mail: dominicanbarassoc@gmail.com
URL: www.dominicanbarassociation.org
Social Media: www.facebook.com/dominicanbarassociation/?fref=ts
www.instagram.com/dominicanbarassoc/
www.linkedin.com/groups/4120959/profile
twitter.com/dominicanbar

4130 ■ DBA Scholarships *(Undergraduate/Scholarship)*

Purpose: To help undergraduate students pursue their education in a law school. **Focus:** Law. **Qualif.:** Applicants must be first, second, or third, fourth- year, undergraduate students in the field of law; must be enrolled full-time or part-time.

Funds Avail.: $3,000. **Duration:** Annual. **To Apply:** Applicants must submit a completed and signed the DBA scholarship application form, current resume, cover letter, an official undergraduate transcript or a photocopy and letter from the law school's financial aid office indicating the amount of aid awarded. **Deadline:** June 22. **Contact:** Email: DBAScholarship@gmail.com.

4131 ■ DontPayFull
Zece Mese St., No. 9
24062 Bucharest, Romania
URL: www.dontpayfull.com
Social Media: facebook.com/DontPayFull
instagram.com/dontpayfull
linkedin.com/company/dontpayfull-ltd
pinterest.com/dontpayfull
twitter.com/DontPayFull

4132 ■ DontPayFull $500 Annual Student Scholarship *(High School, College, University, Undergraduate/Scholarship)*

Purpose: To invest in students who need financial help. **Focus:** General studies/Field of study not specified. **Qualif.:** Applicant must be living in the United States and currently a high school, college, or university student. **Criteria:** Selection will be decided by a panel of expert judges and based on answers to the three essay questions included in the application.

Funds Avail.: $500. **Duration:** Annual. **Number Awarded:** 1. **To Apply:** Application is available at www.dontpayfull.com/page/scholarships-apply/. **Deadline:**

Awards are arranged alphabetically below their administering organizations

October 31. **Contact:** Email: irinav@dontpayfull.com.

4133 ■ Dotcom-Monitor, Inc.
2500 Shadywood Rd., Ste. 820
Excelsior, MN 55331
Free: 888-479-0741
URL: www.dotcom-monitor.com
Social Media: www.facebook.com/dotcommonitor
www.linkedin.com/company/dotcom-monitor
twitter.com/dotcom_monitor
www.youtube.com/user/dotcommonitor

4134 ■ Dotcom-Monitor Women in Computing Scholarship *(Undergraduate/Scholarship)*
Purpose: To encourage and support female undergraduate students who are pursuing careers in computing by assisting them with the rising cost of higher education. **Focus:** Computer and information sciences. **Qualif.:** Applicants must be female students; enrolled as full-time undergraduate students at an accredited college or university in the U.S. or Canada; have either already declared their major or have completed at least one academic year in computer science, computer engineering, or closely related technical field.

Funds Avail.: $1,000. **Duration:** Annual. **To Apply:** Applicant must compose essay answers (up to 500 words each) answering three questions. Essay questions and application must be completed online at www.loadview-testing.com/scholarship/. **Deadline:** April 1. **Remarks:** Established in 2016.

4135 ■ Douglas-Coldwell Foundation (DCF)
300-279 Laurier Ave., W
Jack Layton Bldg.
Ottawa, ON, Canada K1P 5J9
Ph: (613)232-1918
Fax: (613)230-9950
E-mail: info@dcf.ca
URL: www.dcf.ca
Social Media: twitter.com/officialtommyd
www.youtube.com/channel/UCHX-L8RlehYAbYov_zN2r0w

4136 ■ Beverlee Bell Scholarships in Human Rights and Democracy *(Graduate/Scholarship)*
Purpose: To provide support to qualified students who want to pursue their education. **Focus:** Human rights. **Qualif.:** Applicants must be graduate students making a significant contribution to human rights and democracy in developing countries; must be faculty of arts and social sciences, faculty of public affairs and management. **Criteria:** Selection will be made by Dean, Faculty of Graduate Studies and Research.

Funds Avail.: 1,000 Canadian Dollars. **Duration:** Annual. **To Apply:** Applicants are advised to contact the Carleton University for further information about the scholarship application form and requirements. **Deadline:** January. **Remarks:** Established in 2002. **Contact:** Carleton University, Academic Department, 1125 Colonel By Dr., Ottawa, ON; Phone: 613-520-2525; Fax: 613-520-4049.

4137 ■ Douglas-Coldwell Foundation Scholarships in Social Affairs *(Graduate/Scholarship)*
Purpose: To support deserving student who wants to pursue their study. **Focus:** Education, English as a second language; History; Political science; Social work; Sociology. **Qualif.:** Applicants must be fully-qualified graduate students preparing a thesis on a topic involving some aspect of Canadian social theory or history.

Funds Avail.: 3,000 Canadian Dollars. **To Apply:** Applicants must be faculty of graduate studies using a titled scholarship application form and research proposal.**Deadline:** October 31. **Contact:** Carleton University, Academic Department, 1125 Colonel By Dr., Ottawa, ON; Phone: 613-520-2525; Fax: 613-520-4049.

4138 ■ Kalmen Kaplansky Scholarships in Economic and Social Rights *(Graduate/Scholarship)*
Purpose: To provide support to qualified students who want to pursue their education. **Focus:** Civil rights; Economics. **Qualif.:** Applicants must be graduate students researching economic and social rights in a School or Department in the Faculty of Public Affairs and Management at Carleton University. **Criteria:** Selection will be based on research projects involving economic and social rights.

Funds Avail.: 1,000 Canadian Dollars. **Duration:** Annual. **To Apply:** Applicants are advised to contact the Carleton University for further information about the scholarship application form and requirements. **Deadline:** February 1. **Remarks:** Established in 1998. **Contact:** Carleton University, Academic Department, 1125 Colonel By Dr., Ottawa, ON; Phone: 613-520-2525; Fax: 613-520-4049.

4139 ■ Douglas Psychotherapy Service
136 Madison Ave.
New York, NY 10016
Ph: (212)828-7473
URL: www.douglasgrppractice.com
Social Media: www.facebook.com/Douglas-Psychotherapy
 -Services-PC-100811531565178
www.instagram.com/epagov
www.linkedin.com/company/douglas-psychotherapy
 -services
twitter.com/epa
www.youtube.com/user/USEPAgov

4140 ■ The Douglas Psychotherapy Do Good General Education Scholarship *(Undergraduate, Graduate/Scholarship)*
Purpose: To provide financial aid to students to pursue education. **Focus:** General studies/Field of study not specified. **Qualif.:** Applicants must be U.S. citizens accepted to or currently attending a college or university within the United States. **Criteria:** Selection will be based on clarity of thought, passion, and proper grammar/syntax provided by the applicant in the question answer.

Funds Avail.: $1,000. **Duration:** Annual. **Number Awarded:** 5. **To Apply:** Complete application and 200 word essay online. **Deadline:** November 30. **Contact:** URL: www.douglasgrppractice.com/scholarship.

4141 ■ Downeast Energy and Building Supply
18 Spring St.
Brunswick, ME 04011
Free: 800-339-9921
URL: www.downeastenergy.com
Social Media: www.facebook.com/downeastenergy

4142 ■ Downeast Energy Scholarships *(Undergraduate/Scholarship)*
Purpose: To provide support to students in pursuing their educational goal. **Focus:** General studies/Field of study not

Awards are arranged alphabetically below their administering organizations

specified. **Qualif.:** Applicants must be students who are high school seniors or graduates planning to enroll, or students already enrolled in a full-time course of study leading to a bachelor's degree at an accredited post-secondary college or university, an associate's degree at a junior or community post secondary school, or a certificate at an approved vocational technical institute. **Criteria:** Selection award will be based on a combination of selection factors including but not limited to scholastic merit and participation in extracurricular activities.

Duration: One academic year. **Number Awarded:** Varies. **To Apply:** Applicants must submit completed application; high school transcripts; two or more non-family character references; and a word processed cover letter describing applicant's intended course of study and anything else that might help with the decision.

4143 ■ Downtown Apartment Company (DAC)

730 N Wells St.
Chicago, IL 60654
Ph: (312)772-3929
URL: www.downtownapartmentcompany.com
Social Media: www.facebook.com/
  DowntownApartmentCompany
www.instagram.com/downtownapartmentcompany
www.linkedin.com/company/downtown-apartment-company
www.pinterest.com/chicagoloopapt
twitter.com/CityLifeChicago

4144 ■ Downtown Apartment Companys Scholarship Program *(Undergraduate/Scholarship)*

Purpose: To help a student pursuing a career in real estate pay for their education. **Focus:** Real estate. **Qualif.:** Undergraduate students considering a career in real estate and attending an accredited college or university in the United States. **Criteria:** Selection is based on the best essay submitted.

Funds Avail.: $500. **Duration:** Annual. **Number Awarded:** 1. **To Apply:** Complete application; submit essay explaining who you are and why you feel drawn to the real estate field; provide current transcript or proof of acceptance. **Deadline:** December 1. **Contact:** URL: www.downtownapartmentcompany.com/scholarship-program/.

4145 ■ Drake University Law School

2507 University Avenue
Des Moines, IA 50311-4505
Ph: (515)271-2824
Free: 800-443-7253
URL: www.drake.edu
Social Media: www.facebook.com/drakelawschool
instagram.com/drakeuniversity
www.instagram.com/drakelawschool
www.linkedin.com/school/drake-university-law-school
twitter.com/DrakeLawSchool
youtube.com/GoDrakeBulldogs
www.youtube.com/user/DrakeLawSchool

4146 ■ William Stone Ayres Scholarship *(Graduate/Scholarship)*

Purpose: To support the education of law students at the Drake University Law School. **Focus:** Law. **Qualif.:** Ap-

plicants must be students of Drake University Law School. **Criteria:** Recipients will be selected based on merit and academic achievement.

Funds Avail.: No specific amount. **Duration:** Annual. **To Apply:** Applicants must file FAFSA and application form. **Deadline:** April 1. **Remarks:** The scholarship was established by a bequest from Gladys L. Ayres in memory of her husband, an 1894 Law School graduate. **Contact:** Phone: 515-271-2782 Email: law-admit@drake.edu.

4147 ■ Beverly Estate Scholarship *(Undergraduate/Scholarship)*

Purpose: To support the education of law students at the Drake University Law School. **Focus:** Law. **Qualif.:** Applicants must be students of Drake University Law School. **Criteria:** Recipients will be selected based on merit and academic achievement.

Funds Avail.: No specific amount. **Duration:** Annual. **To Apply:** Applicants must file FAFSA and application form. **Remarks:** The scholarships are made possible by bequests from Francis Cecile Beverly, LW'15, and Adda Brown Beverly, ED'14. **Contact:** Phone: 515-271-2782; E-mail: law-admit@drake.edu.

4148 ■ George and Mary Brammer Scholarship *(Undergraduate/Scholarship)*

Purpose: To support the education of law students at the Drake University Law School. **Focus:** Law. **Qualif.:** Applicants must be students of Drake University Law School. **Criteria:** Recipients will be selected based on merit and academic achievement.

Funds Avail.: No specific amount. **Duration:** Annual. **To Apply:** Applicants must file FAFSA and application form. **Remarks:** The scholarship was established by Mary and John Harper as a memorial to Mary's parents, 1908 and 1907 graduates of the Law School. **Contact:** Phone: 515-271-2782 Email: law-admit@drake.edu.

4149 ■ Raymond DiPaglia Endowment Scholarship *(Undergraduate/Scholarship)*

Purpose: To support the education of law students at the Drake University Law School. **Focus:** Law. **Qualif.:** Applicants must be returning law students who are in good standing at the Drake University Law School. **Criteria:** Recipients will be selected based on merit and academic achievement.

Funds Avail.: No specific amount. **Duration:** Annual. **To Apply:** Applicants must file FAFSA and application form. **Remarks:** The endowed scholarship was established by Mr. Raymond DiPaglia, LW'91. **Contact:** Phone: 515-271-2782 Email: law-admit@drake.edu.

4150 ■ Grace O. Doane Scholarship *(Undergraduate/Scholarship)*

Purpose: To provide a scholarship for a second-year Iowa resident who ranks in the top one-half of their class. **Focus:** Law. **Qualif.:** Applicants must be second year Iowa residents who rank in the top one-half of their class. **Criteria:** Recipients will be selected based on merit and academic achievement.

Funds Avail.: No specific amount. **Duration:** Annual. **To Apply:** Applicants must file FAFSA and an application form. **Contact:** Phone: 515-271-2782 Email: law-admit@drake.edu.

4151 ■ Joseph M. Dorgan Scholarship *(Undergraduate/Scholarship)*

Purpose: To support the education of law students at the Drake University Law School. **Focus:** Law. **Qualif.:** Ap-

Awards are arranged alphabetically below their administering organizations

plicants must be African-American law students. **Criteria:** Recipients will be selected based on merit and academic achievement, as well as financial need.

Funds Avail.: No specific amount. **Duration:** Annual. **To Apply:** Applicants must file FAFSA and application form. **Contact:** Phone: 515-271-2782 Email: law-admit@ drake.edu.

4152 ■ Drake University Law School Law Opportunity Scholarship - Disadvantage
(Undergraduate/Scholarship)

Purpose: To provide financial assistance to entering students who are from educationally, economically, or socially disadvantaged backgrounds, or who demonstrate that their enrollment will significantly contribute to the diversity of the student body. **Focus:** Law. **Qualif.:** Applicants must have been admitted to the Law School and able to demonstrate financial need as determined by the Free Application for Federal Student Aid. **Criteria:** Recipients will be selected based on the following factors: (1) applicants' showing of diversity, disadvantage or both; (2) academic record; (3) personal achievements and leadership; and (4) financial need; preference will be given to students whose enrollment will significantly contribute to the diversity of the Drake Law School student body, or to those who have overcome economic, educational or other significant disadvantages.

Funds Avail.: No specific amount. **Duration:** Annual. **To Apply:** Applicants must have the FAFSA form completed between January 1 and March 1, and must submit the completed scholarship application form. **Deadline:** March 1. **Contact:** Drake Law School, Office of Admission and Financial Aid, 2507 University Ave, Des Moines, IA 50311-4505; Phone: 515-271-2782.

4153 ■ Drake University Law School Law Opportunity Scholarship - Diversity *(Undergraduate/Scholarship)*

Purpose: To provide financial assistance to entering students who are from educationally, economically, or socially disadvantaged backgrounds, or who demonstrate that their enrollment will significantly contribute to the diversity of the student body. **Focus:** Law. **Qualif.:** Applicants must have been admitted to the law school and able to demonstrate financial need as determined by the Free Application for Federal Student Aid. **Criteria:** Recipients will be selected based on the following factors: (1) applicants' showing of diversity, disadvantage or both; (2) academic record; (3) personal achievements and leadership; and (4) financial need; preference will be given to students whose enrollment will significantly contribute to the diversity of the Drake University law school student body, or to those who have overcome economic, educational or other significant disadvantages.

Funds Avail.: No specific amount. **Duration:** Annual. **To Apply:** Applicants must have the FAFSA form completed between January 1 and March 1, and must submit the completed scholarship application form. **Deadline:** March 1. **Contact:** Drake Law School, Office of Admission and Financial Aid, 2507 University Ave., Des Moines, IA 50311-4505.

4154 ■ Drake University Law School Public Service Scholarships *(Undergraduate/Scholarship)*

Purpose: To encourage them to explore the wide variety of public service career opportunities. **Focus:** Law. **Qualif.:**

Applicants must be entering students who exhibit an extraordinary history of public service work and plan to continue that commitment during and after law school. **Criteria:** Recipients will be selected based merit, academic achievement, and financial need.

Funds Avail.: No specific amount. **Duration:** Annual. **To Apply:** Applicants must submit completed application form along with essay, a short description of past work experiences/activities, letters of recommendation, relevant academic curriculum and statement of reasons for award. **Deadline:** March 15. **Remarks:** Established in 2004. **Contact:** Drake Law School, Office of Admission and Financial Aid, 2507 University Ave, Des Moines, IA, 50311-4505; E-mail: lawadmit@drake.edu; Fax: 515-271-1990.

4155 ■ Robert E. Early Memorial Scholarship
(Undergraduate/Scholarship)

Purpose: To support the education of law students at the Drake University Law School. **Focus:** Law. **Qualif.:** Applicants must be second or third year full time students who are in need of financial assistance. **Criteria:** Recipients will be selected based on merit, academic achievement, and financial need.

Funds Avail.: No specific amount. **Duration:** Annual. **To Apply:** Applicants must file FAFSA and application form. **Remarks:** The scholarship was established by Margaret M. Early in memory of her husband, LW'41. **Contact:** Phone: 515-271-2782 Email: law-admit@drake.edu.

4156 ■ Herman E. Elgar Memorial Scholarship
(Undergraduate/Scholarship)

Purpose: To provide financial assistance to full-time students enrolled in the J.D. program. **Focus:** Law. **Qualif.:** Applicants must be third year law students at Drake University. **Criteria:** Recipients will be selected based on merit, academic achievement, and financial need.

Funds Avail.: No specific amount. **Duration:** Annual. **To Apply:** Applicants must file FAFSA and application form. **Remarks:** The scholarship was established in memory of Mr. Elgar, LW'11, by his wife Clara Elgar and children, John Elgar, LW'50, Alanson Elgar, LW'51 and Elizabeth Elgar Anderson, ED'41. **Contact:** Office of Admission and Financial Aid - Phone: 515-271-2782; E-mail: law-admit@drake.edu.

4157 ■ D.J. Fairgrave Education Trust
(Undergraduate/Scholarship)

Purpose: To provide financial assistance to full-time students enrolled in the J.D. program. **Focus:** Law. **Qualif.:** Applicants must be students of Drake University Law School. **Criteria:** Recipients will be selected based on: financial need; character; academic record; personal achievements; future goals and anticipated contributions to the profession.

Funds Avail.: No specific amount. **Duration:** Annual. **To Apply:** Applicants must file FAFSA and application form. **Remarks:** The scholarship trust was established by Denio John Fairgrave. **Contact:** Office of Admission and Financial Aid - Phone: 515-271-2782; E-mail: law-admit@drake.edu.

4158 ■ Leland Stanford Forrest Scholarship
(Undergraduate/Scholarship)

Purpose: To support the education of law students at the Drake University Law School. **Focus:** Law. **Qualif.:** Applicants must be students who are graduates of Iowa high schools or colleges. **Criteria:** Recipients will be selected

Awards are arranged alphabetically below their administering organizations

from among entering students who are graduates of Iowa high schools or colleges.

Funds Avail.: No specific amount. **Duration:** Annual. **To Apply:** Applicants must file FAFSA and application form. **Remarks:** The scholarship was established through the bequest of Leland Stanford Forrest, former dean of the law school. **Contact:** Phone: 515-271-2782 Email: law-admit@drake.edu.

4159 ■ Lex and Scott Hawkins Endowed Scholarship *(Undergraduate/Scholarship)*

Purpose: To provide financial assistance to full-time students enrolled in the J.D. program. **Focus:** Law. **Qualif.:** Applicants must be the president of the Law School's Moot Court Board.

Funds Avail.: No specific amount. **Duration:** Annual. **Remarks:** The scholarship was established by Lex Hawkins, LW'51, and Scott Hawkins, LW'81. **Contact:** Office of Admission and Financial Aid - Phone: 515-271-2782; E-mail: law-admit@drake.edu.

4160 ■ Edward and Cora Hayes Scholarship *(Undergraduate/Scholarship)*

Purpose: To provide financial assistance to full-time students enrolled in the J.D. program. **Focus:** Law. **Qualif.:** Applicants must be accepted as first year students at Drake University Law School and not graduates of Iowa high schools or colleges. **Criteria:** Recipients will be selected based on merit.

Funds Avail.: No specific amount. **Duration:** Annual. **To Apply:** Applicants must file FAFSA and application form. **Remarks:** The scholarship was established by the former associate dean (Edward) and his wife (Cora). **Contact:** Office of Admission and Financial Aid - Phone: 515-271-2782; E-mail: law-admit@drake.edu.

4161 ■ Annamae Heaps Law Scholarship *(Undergraduate/Scholarship)*

Purpose: To provide financial assistance to full-time students enrolled in the J.D. program. **Focus:** Law. **Qualif.:** Applicants must be second year students who demonstrate financial need. **Criteria:** Recipients will be selected based on merit and academic achievement.

Funds Avail.: No specific amount. **Duration:** Annual. **To Apply:** Applicants must file FAFSA and application form. **Contact:** Office of Admission and Financial Aid - Phone: 515-271-2782; E-mail: law-admit@drake.edu.

4162 ■ John M. Helmick Law Scholarship *(Undergraduate/Scholarship)*

Purpose: To provide financial assistance to full-time students enrolled in the J.D. program. **Focus:** Law. **Qualif.:** Applicants must be students of Iowa backgrounds planning to enter the legal or educational professions in Iowa. **Criteria:** Recipients will be selected based on merit and academic achievement.

Funds Avail.: No specific amount. **Duration:** Annual. **To Apply:** Applicants must file FAFSA and application form. **Remarks:** The scholarship was established by Robert H. Helmick, LW'60, in memory of his grandfather, John Miller Helmick. **Contact:** Office of Admission and Financial Aid - Phone: 515-271-2782; E-mail: law-admit@drake.edu.

4163 ■ Iowa Association of Electric Cooperatives - Electric Cooperative Pioneer Trust Fund Scholarship *(Undergraduate/Scholarship)*

Purpose: To support the education of law students at the Drake University Law School. **Focus:** Law. **Qualif.:** Ap-

plicants must be second or third year law students interested in agricultural law.

Funds Avail.: No specific amount. **Duration:** Annual. **Contact:** Phone: 515-271-2782; E-mail: law-admit@drake.edu.

4164 ■ James P. Irish Scholarship *(Undergraduate/Scholarship)*

Purpose: To support the education of law students at the Drake University Law School. **Focus:** Law. **Qualif.:** Applicants must be students graduated from Southeast Polk High School or members of the Law Review Board of Editor. **Criteria:** Selection will be based on the committee's criteria.

Funds Avail.: No specific amount. **Duration:** Annual. **To Apply:** The application process is online. **Remarks:** The scholarship was established by Edwin Skinner and Donald Beattie in honor of their associate and law partner, James P. Irish, LW'31. **Contact:** Office of Admission and Financial Aid at 515-271-2782; law-admit@drake.edu.

4165 ■ Martin Luther King Law Scholarship *(Undergraduate/Scholarship)*

Purpose: To provide financial assistance to full-time students enrolled in the J.D. program. **Focus:** Law. **Qualif.:** Applicants must be female African-American law students who embody the spirit and values of Martin Luther King and who have demonstrated financial need. **Criteria:** Recipients will be selected based on merit and academic achievement.

Funds Avail.: No specific amount. **Duration:** Annual. **To Apply:** Applicants must file FAFSA and application form. **Remarks:** The scholarship was established by Naomi Mercer, LW'68. **Contact:** Office of Admission and Financial Aid - Phone: 515-271-2782; E-mail: law-admit@drake.edu.

4166 ■ Forest A. King Scholarship *(Undergraduate/Scholarship)*

Purpose: To provide financial assistance to full-time students enrolled in the J.D. program. **Focus:** Law. **Qualif.:** Applicants must be students of Drake University Law School. **Criteria:** Recipients will be selected based on merit and academic achievement.

Funds Avail.: No specific amount. **Duration:** Annual. **To Apply:** Applicants must file FAFSA and application form. **Remarks:** The scholarship was established in memory of Mr. King, LW'25, by his wife, Nonnie. **Contact:** Office of Admission and Financial Aid - Phone: 515-271-2782; E-mail: law-admit@drake.edu.

4167 ■ Verne Lawyer Scholarship *(Undergraduate/Scholarship)*

Purpose: To provide financial assistance to full-time students enrolled in the J.D. program. **Focus:** Law. **Qualif.:** Applicants must be students of Drake University Law School. **Criteria:** Recipients will be selected based on merit and academic achievement.

Funds Avail.: No specific amount. **Duration:** Annual. **To Apply:** Applicants must file FAFSA and application form. **Remarks:** The scholarship was established by an anonymous donor to honor D. Verne Lawyer, a 1949 graduate of the Law School. Established in 1992. **Contact:** Office of Admission and Financial Aid - Phone: 515-271-2782; E-mail: law-admit@drake.edu.

4168 ■ Frederick D. Lewis Jr. Scholarships *(Undergraduate/Scholarship)*

Purpose: To provide financial assistance to full-time students enrolled in the J.D. program. **Focus:** Law. **Qualif.:**

Awards are arranged alphabetically below their administering organizations

Applicants must be students of Drake University Law School. **Criteria:** Recipients will be selected based on merit and academic achievement.

Funds Avail.: No specific amount. **Duration:** Annual. **To Apply:** Applicants must file FAFSA and application form. **Remarks:** The scholarship fund was established by Patrick D. Kelly, LW'53, in memory of Frederick D. Lewis Jr., a professor at Drake Law School from 1949 to 1959. **Contact:** Office of Admission and Financial Aid - Phone: 515-271-2782; E-mail: law-admit@drake.edu.

4169 ■ Gordon and Delores Madson Scholarship
(Undergraduate/Scholarship)

Purpose: To provide financial assistance to full-time students enrolled in the J.D. program. **Focus:** Law. **Qualif.:** Applicants must be students of Drake University Law School. **Criteria:** Recipients will be selected based on merit and academic achievement.

Funds Avail.: No specific amount. **Duration:** Annual. **To Apply:** Applicants must file FAFSA and application form. **Remarks:** The scholarship was established by Gordon Madson, LW'57, and his wife, Delores. **Contact:** Office of Admission and Financial Aid - Phone: 515-271-2782; E-mail: law-admit@drake.edu.

4170 ■ Jake S. More Scholarship *(Undergraduate/Scholarship)*

Purpose: To provide financial assistance to full-time students enrolled in the J.D. program. **Focus:** Law. **Qualif.:** Applicants must be students of Drake University Law School. **Criteria:** Recipients will be selected based on merit and academic achievement.

Funds Avail.: No specific amount. **Duration:** Annual. **To Apply:** Applicants must file FAFSA and scholarship application form. **Remarks:** The scholarship was established by Jake S. More, LW'28. **Contact:** Office of Admission and Financial Aid - Phone: 515-271-2782; E-mail: law-admit@drake.edu.

4171 ■ Dwight D. Opperman Scholarships
(Undergraduate/Scholarship)

Purpose: To support the education of law students at the Drake University Law School. **Focus:** Law. **Qualif.:** Applicants must be accepted as first-year students at Drake Law School. **Criteria:** Selection will be based on evidence of superior academic record and potential; demonstrate significant community and extracurricular experiences; must achieve noteworthy law entrance exam scores.

Funds Avail.: $10,000 each. **Duration:** Annual. **Number Awarded:** 3. **To Apply:** Applicants must complete the application packet (application for admission and the general scholarship information sheet). **Contact:** Phone: 515-271-2782; E-mail: law-admit@drake.edu.

4172 ■ Janet Reynoldson Memorial Scholarship
(Other/Scholarship)

Purpose: To provide financial assistance to full-time students enrolled in the J.D. program. **Focus:** Law. **Qualif.:** Applicants must be students of Drake University Law School. **Criteria:** Recipients will be selected based on students' contributions to community and family, academic achievement, need and significant change in career.

Funds Avail.: No specific amount. **Duration:** Annual. **To Apply:** Applicants must file FAFSA and application form. **Remarks:** The scholarship was established by the family of Janet Reynoldson, LW'65. **Contact:** Office of Admission

and Financial Aid - Phone: 515-271-2782; E-mail: law-admit@drake.edu.

4173 ■ Walter and Rita Selvy Scholarship
(Undergraduate/Scholarship)

Purpose: To provide financial assistance to full-time students enrolled in the J.D. program. **Focus:** Law. **Qualif.:** Applicants must be students of Drake University Law School. **Criteria:** Recipients will be selected based on merit and academic achievement.

Funds Avail.: No specific amount. **Duration:** Annual. **To Apply:** Applicants must file FAFSA and application form. **Remarks:** The scholarship was established by Walter, LW'28, and his late wife, Rita Selvy, Awarded under the direction of the president of Drake University. **Contact:** Office of Admission and Financial Aid - Phone: 515-271-2782; E-mail: law-admit@drake.edu.

4174 ■ Charles "Buck" and Dora Taylor Scholarship
(Undergraduate/Scholarship)

Purpose: To provide financial assistance to full-time students enrolled in the J.D. program. **Focus:** Law. **Qualif.:** Applicants must be students with financial need and have demonstrated a history of academic success while participating in sports at the undergraduate school level. **Criteria:** Recipients will be selected based on merit, academic achievement, and financial need.

Funds Avail.: No specific amount. **Duration:** Annual. **To Apply:** Applicants must submit the General Information Form for Scholarships along with the application for admission. **Remarks:** The scholarship was established in honor of Charles Taylor, LW'33. **Contact:** Office of Admission and Financial Aid - Phone: 515-271-2782; E-mail: law-admit@drake.edu.

4175 ■ Haemer Wheatcraft Scholarship
(Undergraduate/Scholarship)

Purpose: To provide financial assistance to full-time students enrolled in the J.D. program. **Focus:** Law. **Qualif.:** Applicants must be students of Drake University Law School. **Criteria:** Recipients are selected based on merit and academic achievement.

Funds Avail.: No specific amount. **Duration:** Annual. **To Apply:** Applicants must file the FAFSA and the scholarship application. **Remarks:** The scholarship was established by friends and associates in honor of Haemer Wheatcraft, LW'33. **Contact:** Office of Admission and Financial Aid - Phone: 515-271-2782; E-mail: law-admit@drake.edu.

4176 ■ Zarley, McKee, Thomte, Voorhees, Sease Law Scholarship *(Undergraduate/Scholarship)*

Purpose: To provide financial assistance to full-time students enrolled in the J.D. program. **Focus:** Law. **Qualif.:** Applicants must be students interested in intellectual property law. **Criteria:** Recipients will be selected based on merit and academic achievement.

Funds Avail.: No specific amount. **Duration:** Annual. **To Apply:** Applicants must file FAFSA and application form. **Remarks:** The scholarship was established by Donald H. Zarley, LW'54; Bruce W. McKee; Dennis L. Thomte; Michael G. Voorhees, LW'68; Edmund J. Sease, LW'67; and John Beehner. **Contact:** Office of Admission and Financial Aid - Phone: 515-271-2782; E-mail: law-admit@drake.edu.

4177 ■ The Drama Therapy Fund
1626 Leavenworth St.
Manhattan, KS 66502

Awards are arranged alphabetically below their administering organizations

E-mail: info@dramatherapyfund.org
URL: www.dramatherapyfund.org

4178 ■ Wilder Dimension Scholarships for Advanced Study in Theatre Arts *(Graduate/Scholarship)*

Purpose: To provide drama therapist the assistance they need. **Focus:** Theater arts. **Qualif.:** Applicants must be registered drama therapists working on continuing education and graduate students preparing for careers as drama therapists either through an approved NADT university program or through NADT alternative learning program. **Criteria:** Selection will be based on evaluation of submitted documents and specific criteria; applications will be reviewed by a team of three registered drama therapists.

Funds Avail.: Up to $400. **To Apply:** Applicants must submit a contact information page along with a letter of intent which includes contact information, name of proposed course, where the course will be offered, and dates of the course, rational for wanting to study theater history or literature and contribution to practice as drama therapist. Send via online or send via mail (applicants must send four hard copies for mail applications). **Contact:** Sally Bailey, Treasurer, at the above address; or Email: dtfund@ dramatherapyfund.org.

4179 ■ Camille and Henry Dreyfus Foundation, Inc.

555 Madison Ave., 20th Fl.
New York, NY 10022-3301
Ph: (212)753-1760
Fax: (212)593-2256
URL: www.dreyfus.org
Social Media: www.facebook.com/dreyfusfoundation
twitter.com/dreyfusfndn
www.youtube.com/user/CandHDreyfusFdn

4180 ■ Camille and Henry Dreyfus Foundation - Senior Scientist Mentor Program *(Professional development/Grant)*

Purpose: To support emeritus faculty who maintain active research programs with undergraduates in the chemical sciences. **Focus:** Science. **Qualif.:** Open to all academic institutions in the States, Districts, and Territories of the United States of America that grant a bachelor's degree or higher in the chemical sciences, including biochemistry, materials chemistry, and chemical engineering; faculty with emeritus status on or before October of the current year, and who maintain active research programs in the chemical sciences, may apply. **Criteria:** Selection will be based on the assessment of the research proposed and the plans for undergraduate participation in the research.

Funds Avail.: $20,000. **Duration:** Annual; two years. **To Apply:** Applicants may visit the website to obtain an application form; the original application should be formatted on 8 1/2 x 11-inch paper, using 12-point font size, and assembled as: the online application form; a no more than four pages describing the specific projects or project types in which the undergraduates will participate, ongoing research with undergraduates, and how they will interact with and mentor the undergraduates; a maximum of five pages CV that includes a list of up to 15 relevant publications in which contributions by undergraduate co-authors are clearly identified; a letter from an institutional representative highlighting the applicants' achievements with undergraduates and confirming that the institutional facilities required for the proposed research are available; letter of support must be sent directly to the Foundation from a colleague, preferably from outside the institution, which is familiar with the applicants' research, teaching and experience in mentoring and advising undergraduates; generate all the materials as a single PDF document and should be sent through email. **Deadline:** May 18.

4181 ■ Camille Dreyfus Teacher-Scholar Awards *(Professional development/Grant)*

Purpose: To support and assist young faculties who have research and teaching careers in chemical sciences. **Focus:** Chemistry. **Qualif.:** Applicant must be bachelor's or master's degree in the chemical sciences, including biochemistry, materials chemistry, and chemical engineering; must hold a full-time tenure-track academic appointment, be after the fourth and not after the twelfth years of their independent academic careers, and be engaged in research and teaching primarily with undergraduates. **Criteria:** Selection are based upon research achievements and assessed by a panel of distinguished faculty in the chemical sciences.

Funds Avail.: $75,000. **Duration:** Annual. **Number Awarded:** Varies. **To Apply:** Applicants must send the online nomination form (available mid December) and a letter of nomination from an institutional representative highlighting the nominee's achievements, and the basis for selection (limited to three pages); CV; budget. **Deadline:** February 4. **Contact:** Email: programs@dreyfus.org.

4182 ■ Drone Pilot Ground School

404 GLEN WEST DR
Nashville, TN 37215-2966
URL: tnbear.tn.gov

4183 ■ Drone Technology College Scholarshi p *(High School, Undergraduate/Scholarship)*

Purpose: To support students who demonstrate an interest in pushing the drone industry forward. **Focus:** General studies/Field of study not specified. **Qualif.:** Applicant must be a current or rising college students who demonstrate an interest in pushing the drone industry forward. High school seniors are eligible to apply. **Criteria:** Selection will be based on the committee's criteria.

Funds Avail.: $1,000 each. **Duration:** Annual. **Number Awarded:** 2. **To Apply:** Applicant must submit an essay of 750 to 1, 000 words on one of the following topics: How drones can be used for good; how drones will change our world over the next ten years; how drones can be used for STEM education. Applicant should also include a paragraph about themselves, including where they are from, their education, field of study, career plans, interest in drones, and any other relevant information. A letter of support from an educator in their school is also required. Application form is available online at www.dronepilotgroundschool.com/scholarship/#college. **Deadline:** May 15.

4184 ■ Drones Globe

2545 Rinehart Rd.
Miami, FL 33128
Ph: (850)515-7630
E-mail: scholarship@drones-globe.com
URL: www.drones-globe.com

Awards are arranged alphabetically below their administering organizations

Social Media: www.facebook.com/dronesglobe1
www.pinterest.com/mydronesglobe
twitter.com/mydronesglobe

4185 ■ Science Environment Scholarship by Drones Globe *(Undergraduate, Graduate, Postgraduate/ Scholarship)*

Purpose: To provide financial assistance to college students with a passion for writing. **Focus:** General studies/Field of study not specified. **Qualif.:** Applicants must be undergraduate or graduate students. **Criteria:** Criteria of essay submission, including: creativity and imagination power, ability of expression, writing skills, organizing skills, consistency and strong logic ability, and article topic.

Funds Avail.: $1,000. **To Apply:** Submit essay (in PDF or DOC format) between 1,000 and 1,500 words on a drone-related topic provided at www.drones-globe.com/scholarship. Include your personal details, school/college name, area of study, and proof of student identity. **Contact:** Email: scholarship@drones-globe.com.

4186 ■ DrugRehab.org

483 Mandalay Ave.
Clearwater, FL 33767
Ph: (231)640-0169
URL: www.drugrehab.org
Social Media: facebook.com/DrugRehab.org
pinterest.com/drugrehaborg
twitter.com/DrugRehab_org

4187 ■ Substance Abuse and Mental Health Awareness in Veterans Scholarship *(Undergraduate, Graduate/Scholarship)*

Purpose: To increase awareness of the effects of drugs and alcohol on veterans and their families. **Focus:** General studies/Field of study not specified. **Qualif.:** Applicant must be a veteran or an active member of the United States Armed Forces, or a family member of a veteran or active member of the United States Armed Forces; must be enrolled or soon to be enrolled as an undergraduate or graduate student at a post-secondary institution in the United States; must be at least 18 years old at time of scholarship entry. **Criteria:** Selection will be based on the essay, with consideration given to originality, good structure, logical arguments, and a passion for spreading awareness about the effects of drugs and alcohol addiction on veterans and their families.

Funds Avail.: $5,000. **Number Awarded:** 1. **To Apply:** Applicant must submit an essay (not to exceed 2,000 words) on the specific topic for that year's scholarship. Applications available online at www.drugrehab.org/veterans-scholarship/. **Deadline:** May 1. **Contact:** Joe Belfry; Email: joe@drugrehab.com.

4188 ■ Drummond Law Firm

810 S Casino Center Blvd., No. 101
Las Vegas, NV 89183
Ph: (702)935-2983
Fax: (702)508-9440
URL: www.drummondfirm.com

4189 ■ Drummond Law Firm Scholarship *(Graduate, College/Scholarship)*

Purpose: To help ROTC students and military veterans gain an education. **Focus:** General studies/Field of study

not specified. **Qualif.:** Applicant must be a high school student currently in a JROTC or Boy Scout Explorer program that has been accepted to and will be attending a post-secondary education institution in the United States, a student currently enrolled in college and a member of their college's ROTC program, or a U.S. military veteran that is currently enrolled in a post-secondary education institution or graduate school. **Criteria:** Selection will be based on the applicant's essay response and extracurricular activities.

Funds Avail.: $1,000. **Duration:** Annual. **Number Awarded:** 1. **To Apply:** Applicant should submit the following: a 500+ word essay about why they want to or have served our country or how our service members who serve our country affect the applicant's daily living; a letter of recommendation from their JROTC, ROTC, or former military supervisor; documentation of being enrolled in a post-secondary education institution. any other documentation the applicant would like considered. Application can be completed online at www.drummondfirm.com/news-resources/scholarship/. **Deadline:** August 15. **Contact:** Email: office@drummondfirm.com.

4190 ■ Dublin San Ramon Services District

7051 Dublin Blvd.
Dublin, CA 94568-3018
Ph: (925)828-0515
Fax: (925)829-1180
E-mail: contact@dsrsd.com
URL: www.dsrsd.com
Social Media: www.facebook.com/freerecycledwater
twitter.com/DSRSDnews

4191 ■ DSRSD James B. Kohnen Scholarships *(Undergraduate, High School/Scholarship)*

Purpose: To promote a career in water resources. **Focus:** Water resources.

Funds Avail.: $1,000. **Duration:** Annual. **Remarks:** To honor Mr. Kohnen's public service in the water resources field and inspire young people to follow in his footsteps.

4192 ■ Doris Duke Charitable Foundation (DDCF)

650 5th Ave., 19th Fl.
New York, NY 10019
Ph: (212)974-7000
Fax: (212)974-7590
URL: www.ddcf.org
Social Media: twitter.com/DorisDukeFdn

4193 ■ International Clinical Research Fellowship *(Graduate/Fellowship)*

Purpose: To encourage medical students who are pursuing careers in clinical research. **Focus:** Biological and clinical sciences. **Qualif.:** Applicants must be students matriculated at any US medical school who are in good academic standing and have completed two or more years of medical school prior to the start of the fellowship. **Criteria:** Selection will be based on the committee's criteria.

Funds Avail.: $30,000.

4194 ■ Duke University and University of North Carolina Rotary Peace Center

Sanford School of Public Policy
Duke Center for International Development

Awards are arranged alphabetically below their administering organizations

Rubenstein Hall, Rm. 286
Durham, NC 27708-0237
Ph: (919)613-9222
Fax: (919)962-5375
URL: rotarypeacecenternc.org
Social Media: www.facebook.com/DukeUncRotaryCenter
www.instagram.com/dukeuncrotarycenter
twitter.com/DukeUNCRotary

4195 ■ Rotary Peace Fellowship Program *(Graduate, Master's/Fellowship)*

Purpose: To empower, educate, and increase the capacity of peace builders through rigorous academic training, practice, and global networking opportunities. **Focus:** Peace studies. **Criteria:** Selection will be based on consists of three levels club, district, and world.

Funds Avail.: No specific amount. **Duration:** Annual. **Number Awarded:** 50. **To Apply:** Applicants must submit completely the necessary requirements which include curriculum vitae, personal statement, complete transcripts, two to three copies of recommendations and test scores; must contact their local Rotary club to begin the process of endorsement and pass the interview, either in person or via phone, by the Rotary district; those who want to study at Duke or UNC should rank the Duke-UNC Rotary Center as number one. **Deadline:** July 1.

4196 ■ Duluth Superior Area Community Foundation (DSACF)

324 West Superior Street, Ste. 700
Duluth, MN 55802
Ph: (218)726-0232
E-mail: info@dsacommunityfoundation.com
URL: www.dsacommunityfoundation.com
Social Media: www.facebook.com/
dsacommunityfoundation

4197 ■ Amelia and Emanuel Nessell Family Scholarship Fund *(Undergraduate/Scholarship)*

Purpose: To provide educational opportunities for students who are in financial need, especially those Jewish applicants. **Focus:** General studies/Field of study not specified. **Criteria:** Applicants are evaluated based on academic record, financial need, written recommendations (one of which must come from a clergy), involvement in community and extra-curricular activities; priority consideration will be given to Jewish applicants.

Funds Avail.: $1,000 each. **Duration:** Annual. **Number Awarded:** Varies. **To Apply:** Applicants must include an academic transcript (including standardized test scores);recommendations (from at least one educator and one clergy) and financial need documentation. **Deadline:** January 15. **Remarks:** The scholarship was established as a memorial to Amelia and Emanuel Nessell. The Nessells moved to Duluth in 1920 and Emanuel served as a manager for the First Street Department Store. Established in 1997. **Contact:** Duluth-Superior Area Community Foundation, 222 E Superior St., Ste. 302, Duluth, MN, 55802; Phone: 218-726-0232.

4198 ■ Anderson Niskanen Scholarship Fund *(Graduate/Scholarship)*

Purpose: To provide financial assistance to Duluth public high schools graduating students who are in financial need for post-secondary education at the University of Minnesota Duluth or the University of Minnesota-Twin Cities. **Focus:** General studies/Field of study not specified. **Qualif.:** Applicants must be graduating seniors from Duluth public high schools who will attend either the University of Minnesota-Duluth or the University of Minnesota-Twin Cities; and must be in the top 25% of their class. **Criteria:** Applicants are evaluated based on financial need; academic achievement; recommendations.

Funds Avail.: $2,000 each. **Duration:** Annual. **Number Awarded:** Varies. **To Apply:** Applicants must submit a completed application form; academic transcript (including standardized test scores); two letters of recommendation; and financial documentation. **Deadline:** January 15. **Remarks:** The scholarship was established by Suama Niskanen Anderson as a memorial to Anderson Niskanen. Established in 1998. **Contact:** Duluth-Superior Area Community Foundation, 222 E Superior St., Ste. 302, Duluth, MN, 55802; Phone: 218-726-0232.

4199 ■ Darrell and Palchie Asselin Scholarship Fund *(Undergraduate/Scholarship)*

Purpose: To provide financial assistance to the non-traditional, older students in financial resources for their education. **Focus:** General studies/Field of study not specified. **Qualif.:** Applicants must be students over the age of 22 who are the primary care givers to one or more children; must have a grade point average of 2.5 or higher. **Criteria:** Applicants are evaluated based on financial need; academic achievement; recommendations.

Funds Avail.: $2,000 each. **Duration:** Annual. **Number Awarded:** 1. **To Apply:** Applicants must complete the application form; academic transcript; letters of recommendation; and financial need documentation. **Deadline:** January 15. **Remarks:** The scholarship was established as a memorial to Darrell and Palchie Asselin. Mr. Asselin, originally from Crookston, established and built Northern Photo Company in Duluth. Established in 1993. **Contact:** Duluth-Superior Area Community Foundation, 222 E Superior St., Ste. 302, Duluth, MN, 55802; Phone: 218-726-0232.

4200 ■ William E. Barto Scholarship Fund *(Undergraduate/Scholarship)*

Purpose: To provide financial assistance for art students. **Focus:** Arts; Visual arts. **Criteria:** Applicants are evaluated based on financial need, academic record, written recommendations, and seriousness of purpose.

Funds Avail.: $2,000. **Duration:** Annual. **Number Awarded:** 1. **To Apply:** Applicants must submit a completed application form; academic transcript; letters of recommendation; and financial need documentation. **Remarks:** The scholarship was established in memory of William E. Barto. Established in 1995. **Contact:** Duluth-Superior Area Community Foundation, 222 E Superior St., Ste. 302, Duluth, MN, 55802; Phone: 218-726-0232.

4201 ■ Bernard B. and Mary L. Brusin Scholarship Fund *(Undergraduate/Scholarship)*

Purpose: To provide assistance to Jewish and Roman Catholic students who are in need financial of aid for their college education. **Focus:** General studies/Field of study not specified. **Qualif.:** Applicants must be either Jewish or Roman Catholic graduating seniors from St. Louis County public or private high schools who are in the top 25% of their high school. **Criteria:** Applicants are evaluated based on financial need, academic record, written recommendations, and seriousness of purpose.

Awards are arranged alphabetically below their administering organizations

Funds Avail.: About $5,000. **Duration:** Annual. **Number Awarded:** Varies. **To Apply:** Applicants should complete and submit an application form; academic transcript (including standardized test scores); recommendations from one educator and one to the clergy; and financial need documentation. **Remarks:** The scholarship was established as a memorial to Bernard B. and Mary Reilly Brusin. Both Mr. and Mrs. Brusin were longtime residents of Duluth and pursued separate business careers during their lifetimes. Established in 1987. **Contact:** Duluth-Superior Area Community Foundation, 222 E Superior St., Ste. 302, Duluth, MN, 55802; Phone: 218-726-0232.

4202 ■ Dr. Mark Rathke Family Scholarship Fund (Graduate/Scholarship)

Purpose: To help future generations of Marshall School students to pursue their educational goals. **Focus:** General studies/Field of study not specified. **Qualif.:** Applicants must be graduating seniors of the Marshall School who will be attending a college or university as full-time students; and, have demonstrated school or community involvement, leadership qualities and hardworking behavior; can be used at any accredited college or university. **Criteria:** Applicants are evaluated based on academic record; hard-working behavior; good citizenship; leadership qualities; serious commitment to college education; written recommendations; and involvement in community and extra-curricular activities. Preference will be given to those students who are not in the top ten percent of their graduating class.

Funds Avail.: $1,000 each. **Duration:** Annual. **Number Awarded:** 1. **To Apply:** Applicants must submit a completed application form; academic transcript (including standardized test scores); and two letter of recommendation. **Remarks:** The scholarship was established as a memorial to Dr. Mark Rathke. Established in 1999. **Contact:** Duluth-Superior Area Community Foundation, 222 E Superior St., Ste. 302, Duluth, MN, 55802; Phone: 218-726-0232.

4203 ■ DSACF Modern Woodmen of America Scholarship Fund (Undergraduate/Scholarship)

Purpose: To provide financial assistance to the non-traditional students who are in financial need. **Focus:** General studies/Field of study not specified. **Qualif.:** Applicants must be single parents who are the primary caregivers to one or more children. **Criteria:** Applicants are evaluated based on academic record, written recommendations, and involvement in community and church activities.

Funds Avail.: $1,000. **Duration:** Annual. **Number Awarded:** 1. **To Apply:** Applicants must submit a completed application form together with academic transcript (including standardized test scores), two recommendations, and financial need documentation. **Deadline:** January 15. **Contact:** Duluth-Superior Area Community Foundation, 222 E Superior St., Ste. 302, Duluth, MN, 55802; Phone: 218-726-0232.

4204 ■ Duluth Building and Construction Trades Council Scholarship Fund (Graduate/Scholarship)

Purpose: To provide financial assistance to children of members of unions affiliated with the Duluth Building Trades Council. **Focus:** Health care services. **Qualif.:** Applicants must be graduating high school seniors, whose parent or guardian is a member of one of the 17 unions affiliated with the Duluth Building Trades Council; and, have grade point average of 2.75, based on 4.0 scale, or higher. **Criteria:** Preference will be given to students entering the health care field.

Funds Avail.: $2,500. **Duration:** Annual. **Number Awarded:** 2. **To Apply:** Applicants must submit a completed application form; academic transcript (including standardized test scores); two letters of recommendation; and financial need documentation; essay. **Deadline:** January 15. **Remarks:** Established in 1980. **Contact:** Duluth-Superior Area Community Foundation, 222 E Superior St., Ste. 302, Duluth, MN, 55802; Phone: 218-726-0232.

4205 ■ Duluth Central High School Alumni Scholarship Fund (Graduate/Scholarship)

Purpose: To assist students who ever attended Central High School to help them achieve their educational goals. **Focus:** General studies/Field of study not specified. **Qualif.:** Applicants must be graduating seniors from Duluth Central High School who will attend the College of St. Scholastic, University of Minnesota-Duluth, University of Wisconsin-Superior, Lake Superior College, or Wisconsin Indianhead Technical College. **Criteria:** Applicants are evaluated based on academic record, financial need, written recommendations, and seriousness of purpose.

Funds Avail.: $1,000. **Duration:** Annual. **Number Awarded:** Varies. **To Apply:** A complete application will also include an academic transcript (including standardized test scores), two recommendations and financial need documentation. **Remarks:** The scholarship was established in honor of Mr. Beck, principal of Duluth Central High School from 1939 until his retirement in 1965. Established in 1944. **Contact:** Duluth-Superior Area Community Foundation, 222 E Superior St., Ste. 302, Duluth, MN, 55802; Phone: 218-726-0232.

4206 ■ Peter M. Gargano Scholarship Fund (Undergraduate/Scholarship)

Purpose: To provide financial assistance for post-secondary education to the children of employees of Ulland Brothers. **Focus:** General studies/Field of study not specified. **Criteria:** Applicants are evaluated based on academic record (including GPA, class rank, and test scores when relevant), financial need, written recommendations, and seriousness of purpose.

Funds Avail.: $2,000. **Duration:** Annual. **Number Awarded:** 1. **To Apply:** Applicants must submit a completed application form and recently completed Student Aid Report (SAR) from the Free Application for Federal Student Aid (FAFSA); a completed application must also include an academic transcript (including standardized test scores), one recommendation and financial need documentation. **Deadline:** January 15. **Remarks:** Established in 1992. **Contact:** Duluth-Superior Area Community Foundation, 222 E Superior St., Ste. 302, Duluth, MN, 55802; Phone: 218-726-0232.

4207 ■ Patricia S. Gustafson '56 Memorial Scholarship Fund (Graduate/Scholarship)

Purpose: To provide financial assistance to graduating female seniors from Denfeld High School or the Marshall School who exemplifies the characteristics and life exhibited by Patricia Gustafson. **Focus:** General studies/Field of study not specified. **Qualif.:** Applicants must be those with a 3.4 or higher GPA and who intend to attend UMD, CSS, or LSC should contact their guidance counselors. **Criteria:** Recipients are selected based on ability to live a full life following the example of Patricia Gustafson; contributions to their schools; high academic achievement; potential and intention to make contributions in the field of education; high level of moral character; and, level of financial need.

Awards are arranged alphabetically below their administering organizations

Funds Avail.: $800 each. **Duration:** Annual. **Number Awarded:** 1. **Remarks:** Established in 2007. **Contact:** Duluth-Superior Area Community Foundation, 222 E Superior St., Ste. 302, Duluth, MN, 55802; Phone: 218-726-0232.

4208 ■ Jeanne H. Hemmingway Scholarship Fund
(Undergraduate/Scholarship)

Purpose: To assist students with financial need from the three counties of Minnesota's Arrowhead region to attend the area's largest school, the University of Minnesota Duluth. **Focus:** General studies/Field of study not specified. **Qualif.:** Eligible applicants must be a resident of the DSACF service area (Aitkin, Carlton, Cook, Itasca, Koochiching, Lake or St. Louis in Minnesota or Ashland, Bayfield or Douglas in Wisconsin); must enroll in the University of Minnesota Duluth the following fall; must have significant financial need; must meet ONE or more of the following "Adversity" criteria: is a survivor of physical or sexual abuse; has experienced homelessness in the past five years; has participated in an alternative education program or completed a GED; speaks English as a second language; has been assessed as chemically dependent; has ever missed a significant amount of school for medical or care-giving reasons. **Criteria:** Applicants are evaluated based on financial need, academic record, written recommendations, and seriousness of purpose.

Funds Avail.: $2,500. **Duration:** Annual. **Number Awarded:** Varies. **To Apply:** Applicants must submit a completed application form and a recently completed Student Aid Report (SAR) from the Free Application for Federal Student Aid (FAFSA). **Deadline:** January 15. **Remarks:** The scholarship was established in honor of Jeanne H. Hemmingway; former resident of Duluth and Tower and greatly enjoyed the Minnesota lake country. Established in 1990. **Contact:** Duluth-Superior Area Community Foundation, 222 E Superior St., Ste. 302, Duluth, MN, 55802; Phone: 218-726-0232.

4209 ■ Gus and Henrietta Hill Scholarship Fund
(Graduate/Scholarship)

Purpose: To provide financial assistance to graduates of Duluth East High School pursuing post-secondary education. **Focus:** General studies/Field of study not specified. **Qualif.:** Applicants must be graduating seniors from Duluth East High School who are active in the sport of pole vaulting and/or music activities can be nominated by a member of the Duluth East faculty. **Criteria:** Applicants will be evaluated based on participation in pole vaulting or music activities, financial need, academic record, written recommendations, and seriousness of purpose.

Funds Avail.: About $5,000 per year. **Duration:** Annual. **Number Awarded:** 1. **To Apply:** Applicants must submit a completed application form; academic transcript (including standardized test scores); two letters of recommendation; and financial documentation. **Remarks:** The scholarship was established in honor of Roger C. Hill; long time resident of Duluth and recognized the importance of higher education; he participated in sports, specifically pole vaulting. Established in 2000. **Contact:** Duluth-Superior Area Community Foundation, 222 E Superior St., Ste. 302, Duluth, MN, 55802; Phone: 218-726-0232.

4210 ■ Max and Julia Houghton Duluth Central Scholarships *(Undergraduate/Scholarship)*

Purpose: To provide financial assistance to graduating Central seniors for post-secondary education. **Focus:** Gen-

eral studies/Field of study not specified. **Qualif.:** Applicants must be graduating seniors from Duluth Central High School who are in the top 25% of their high school class. **Criteria:** Applicants are evaluated based on financial need, academic performance, and involvement in community and/or school activities.

Funds Avail.: Amount varies. **Number Awarded:** Varies. **To Apply:** Applicants must submit all the required application information. **Contact:** Duluth-Superior Area Community Foundation, at the above address.

4211 ■ Greg Irons Award Fund *(Undergraduate/Award)*

Purpose: To recognize and reward the efforts of students in Duluth Public Schools and teachers who help students succeed. **Focus:** General studies/Field of study not specified. **Qualif.:** Applicants must be 12th-grade students who have been able to attain their personal goals through self motivation, perseverance and through guidance of a mentor who characterizes Greg Irons; have positive influences through their enthusiastic participation in school activities; and, be students with academic, physical, or emotional needs. **Criteria:** Recipients will be selected based on academic record and other factors described on the application; preference will be given to students who have desire to enter the teaching profession or other helping professions.

Funds Avail.: $1,000. **Duration:** Annual. **Number Awarded:** 2. **To Apply:** Applicants must submit a completed application form including transcript of records. **Contact:** Duluth-Superior Area Community Foundation, 222 E Superior St., Ste. 302, Duluth, MN, 55802; Phone: 218-726-0232.

4212 ■ Jackson Club Scholarship Fund
(Undergraduate/Scholarship)

Purpose: To provide financial awards for post secondary education, including college and vocational training to graduating seniors from Hermantown High School. **Focus:** General studies/Field of study not specified. **Qualif.:** Applicants must be residents of Hermantown and graduates of Hermantown High School planning to attend any accredited post-secondary institution on a full-time basis, and have a 2.75 or higher. **Criteria:** Applicants are evaluated based on academic record, written recommendation, and involvement in community activities.

Funds Avail.: $500. **Duration:** Annual. **Number Awarded:** Varies. **To Apply:** Applicants must submit a completed application form; transcript of records (including standardized test scores); one letter of recommendation; and an essay stating the meaning of growing up in Hermantown. **Remarks:** Established in 1910. **Contact:** Duluth-Superior Area Community Foundation, 222 E Superior St., Ste. 302, Duluth, MN, 55802; Phone: 218-726-0232.

4213 ■ Cory Jam Memorial Award *(Undergraduate/Scholarship)*

Purpose: To provide financial assistance to Duluth East High School graduates. **Focus:** General studies/Field of study not specified. **Criteria:** Applicants are evaluated based on academic records, written recommendations, and involvement in community and church activities.

Funds Avail.: $1,000. **Duration:** Annual. **Number Awarded:** 1. **To Apply:** Applicants must submit a completed application form; academic transcript (including standardized test scores); and two letters of recommendation. **Deadline:** January 15. **Remarks:** The scholarship was established in honor of Cory Jam memorial award with memorial gifts from family members and friends. Established in 1988. **Contact:** Duluth-Superior Area Community Foundation, 222 E Superior St., Ste. 302, Duluth, MN, 55802; Phone: 218-726-0232.

4214 ■ Lawrence E. and Mabel Jackson Rudberg Scholarship Fund *(Undergraduate/Scholarship)*

Purpose: To provide financial assistance to students pursuing a college degree. **Focus:** General studies/Field of study not specified. **Qualif.:** Applicants must be graduating seniors from Duluth public and Two Harbors Senior High intending to pursue a post-secondary education at an accredited four-year public or private college or university. **Funds Avail.:** $5,000 each. **Duration:** Annual. **Number Awarded:** 2. **To Apply:** Applicants must submit a completed DSACF Common Scholarship application form; academic transcript (including standardized test scores); two letters of recommendation; and financial need documentation. **Deadline:** January 15. **Remarks:** The scholarship was established as a memorial to Lawrence and Mabel Rudberg. From Duluth and Two Harbors respectively, Dr. and Mrs. Rudberg both spent their professional lives teaching. Established in 1999. **Contact:** Duluth-Superior Area Community Foundation, 222 E Superior St., Ste. 302, Duluth, MN, 55802; Phone: 218-726-0232.

4215 ■ Minnesota Power Community Involvement Scholarship Fund *(Undergraduate/Scholarship)*

Purpose: To provide financial assistance for graduating high school seniors within Minnesota Power's service area who are active volunteers in their communities. **Focus:** General studies/Field of study not specified. **Qualif.:** Applicants must be full-time high school seniors residing within Minnesota Power's service territory who have a 3.0 GPA or above. **Criteria:** Applicants are evaluated based on community involvement.

Funds Avail.: $2,500 each per year. **Duration:** Annual. **Number Awarded:** 10. **To Apply:** Applicants must submit an application form; supporting documentation from community leaders; and a high school transcript. **Deadline:** January 15. **Remarks:** Established in 1998. **Contact:** Duluth-Superior Area Community Foundation, 222 E Superior St., Ste. 302, Duluth, MN, 55802; Phone: 218-726-0232.

4216 ■ Hubert A. Nelson Scholarship Fund *(Graduate/Scholarship)*

Purpose: To provide financial assistance for students studying business and accounting. **Focus:** Accounting; Business. **Qualif.:** Applicants must be graduating seniors of public or private high schools in Duluth and Superior; planning to major in business or accounting at the University of Minnesota-Duluth or the University of Wisconsin-Superior; and, in the top 25% of their high school. **Criteria:** Applicants are evaluated based on academic record, financial need, written recommendations, involvement in community; and extra-curricular activities.

Funds Avail.: $1,000. **Duration:** Annual; Up to 4 years. **Number Awarded:** Varies. **To Apply:** Applicants must submit a completed application form; academic transcript (including standardized test scores); one letter of recommendation; and financial need documentation. **Remarks:** The scholarship was established to honor his memory and to provide financial assistance to students studying business and accounting. Established in 1995. **Contact:** Duluth-

Superior Area Community Foundation, 222 E Superior St., Ste. 302, Duluth, MN, 55802; Phone: 218-726-0232.

4217 ■ Phil Shykes Memorial Scholarship Fund *(Graduate/Scholarship)*

Purpose: To provide financial assistance to graduating seniors from Hermantown High School for post-secondary education at vocational school, college or university. **Focus:** General studies/Field of study not specified. **Qualif.:** Applicants must be graduating seniors from Hermantown High School who are intending to pursue post-secondary education; have achieved a 2.5 or higher cumulative GPA in high school. **Criteria:** Recipients will be selected based on the following criteria; financial need; family profile; involvement in community service; major field of interest; determination to pursue a higher education or vocation; and employment.

Funds Avail.: $1,000. **Duration:** Annual. **Number Awarded:** 1. **To Apply:** Applicants must submit a completed DSACF Common Scholarship Application form; academic transcript (including standardized test scores); one letter of recommendation; and financial need documentation. **Deadline:** January 15. **Remarks:** The scholarship was established as a memorial to Phil Shykes, a long time resident of Duluth. Mr. Shykes was a well-respected businessman and established and built Miller Mall Auto Parts Inc. Established in 1999. **Contact:** Duluth-Superior Area Community Foundation, 222 E Superior St., Ste. 302, Duluth, MN, 55802; Phone: 218-726-0232.

4218 ■ Robert B. and Sophia Whiteside Scholarship Fund *(Graduate/Scholarship)*

Purpose: To provide financial assistance to students of Duluth high schools who are going to attend college. **Focus:** General studies/Field of study not specified. **Qualif.:** Applicants must be high school seniors graduating from schools, including home schools, in Duluth and seek admission to any fully-accredited, degree granting college or university; and must be in top 10% of their class. **Criteria:** Applicants are evaluated based on academic achievement.

Funds Avail.: $5,000 each. **Duration:** Annual. **Number Awarded:** Varies. **To Apply:** Applicants must submit a completed application form; academic transcript (including standardized test scores); and two letters of recommendation. **Deadline:** January 15. **Remarks:** The scholarship was established in memory of Robert and Sophia Whiteside by the will of their daughter Marion Whiteside Meining. Established in 1976. **Contact:** Duluth-Superior Area Community Foundation, 222 E Superior St., Ste. 302, Duluth, MN, 55802; Phone: 218-726-0232.

4219 ■ Dale and Betty George Sola Scholarships *(Undergraduate/Scholarship)*

Purpose: To provide financial assistance for graduating seniors who reside in the central area of Duluth, who attend the Marshall School or several alternative schools in Duluth. **Focus:** General studies/Field of study not specified. **Qualif.:** Applicants must be students of Duluth Central High School, the Marshall School, Lakeview Christian Academy and alternative schools (including Unity School and the Harbor City International School) in the central areas of Duluth; or, graduates residing within the Central Hillside or Park Point areas who have a grade point average of 2.75 (on a 4.0 scale) or higher. **Criteria:** Recipients will be selected based on the following criteria: (1) demonstrated leadership; (2) hard-working behavior; (3) financial need; (4) good work ethic; (5) involvement in community and school activities; and (6) academic performance.

Awards are arranged alphabetically below their administering organizations

Preference will be given to students who are not in the top ten percent of the graduating class.

To Apply: Applicants must complete the DSACF Common Scholarship Application available from the Guidance Offices; academic transcript (including standardized test scores); two letters of recommendation; and financial need documentation. **Remarks:** Established in 2003. **Contact:** Duluth-Superior Area Community Foundation, at the above address.

4220 ■ John A. and Jean Quinn Sullivan Scholarship Funds (Undergraduate/Scholarship)

Purpose: To provide financial assistance for students majoring in education who are in financial need. **Focus:** Education. **Qualif.:** Applicants must be graduates of Senior High in Superior, Wisconsin who will attend their junior and senior years at the University of Wisconsin-Superior majoring in education.

Funds Avail.: Around $1,000 per year. **Duration:** Annual. **Number Awarded:** Varies. **Remarks:** Established in 1996. **Contact:** Duluth-Superior Area Community Foundation, 222 E Superior St., Ste. 302, Duluth, MN, 55802; Phone: 218-726-0232.

4221 ■ Dumbarton Oaks Research Library and Collection

1703 32nd St. NW
Washington, DC 20007
Ph: (202)339-6401
Fax: (202)625-0279
E-mail: museum@doaks.org
URL: www.doaks.org
Social Media: www.facebook.com/doaksDC
twitter.com/DumbartonOaks

4222 ■ Dumbarton Oaks Fellowship (Doctorate, Graduate/Fellowship)

Purpose: To promote research in Byzantine studies, Pre-Columbian studies and Garden and Landscape Studies. Awarded in various categories. **Focus:** Byzantine studies; Pre-Columbian studies. **Qualif.:** Applicants must be graduate students who expects to have a PhD prior to taking up residence at Dumbarton Oaks. **Criteria:** Selection is based on the submitted application materials.

Funds Avail.: $35,000. **Duration:** One academic year. **To Apply:** Applicants are required to complete the application online; must submit three letters of recommendation. **Deadline:** November 1. **Contact:** Email: FellowshipPrograms@doaks.org.

4223 ■ Dumbarton Oaks Junior Fellowship (Graduate/Fellowship)

Purpose: To promote research in Byzantine studies, Pre-Columbian studies and Garden and Landscape Studies. **Focus:** Byzantine studies; Pre-Columbian studies. **Qualif.:** Applicants must be graduate students who expects to have a PhD prior to taking up residence at Dumbarton Oaks. **Criteria:** Selection is based on the submitted application materials.

Funds Avail.: $21,000. **Duration:** one academic year. **To Apply:** Applicants are required to complete the application online. In addition, applicants must submit three letters of recommendation and a transcript of graduate record (sent by university registrar). **Deadline:** November 1. **Contact:**

Manager of Academic Programs, Dumbarton Oaks, 1703 32nd St. NW, Washington, DC, 20007.

4224 ■ Dumbarton Oaks Research Library and Collection Bliss Symposium Award (Undergraduate, Graduate/Award)

Purpose: To provide travel expenses for Harvard students wishing to attend the annual symposia in Byzantine, Pre-Columbian, or Garden and Landscape studies at Dumbarton Oaks. **Focus:** Byzantine studies. **Qualif.:** Applicants must be Harvard students wishing to attend Dumbarton Oaks' annual symposia in Byzantine, Pre-Columbian, or Garden and Landscape Studies. **Criteria:** Selection will be based on the committee's criteria.

Funds Avail.: $500. **To Apply:** Applicants should prepare an application consisting of a brief cover letter stating why the conference is of interest, curriculum vitae, and one letter of recommendation, which should be from the applicant's advisor or department chair; must be received at least four weeks prior to the symposium, and should be marked "Bliss Awards" and directed to the appropriate study program. **Contact:** Email: Byzantine@doaks.org or Landscape@doaks.org or Pre-Columbian@doaks.org.

4225 ■ Dumbarton Oaks Research Library and Collection Graduate Research Workshops (Undergraduate, Graduate/Fellowship)

Purpose: To support student groups in their research workshops that intersect with the Institute's particular fields of study and resources. **Focus:** Byzantine studies. **Qualif.:** Applicants must be groups of students about 4-8 members, graduate or undergraduate, and have already formed or planning to form a research workshop at Harvard University. **Criteria:** Selection will be based on the committee's criteria.

Funds Avail.: No specific amount. **Duration:** No less than two days and no longer than a week. **To Apply:** Applicants must submit a 250-word proposal outlining the nature and purpose of the workshop, the names and resumes of student participants and the principal student coordinator. The proposal should include at least three possible bands of time when the visits to Dumbarton Oaks could take place. **Contact:** Proposals should be sent to Professor Jan Ziolkowski, Director; Dumbarton Oaks Research Library and Collection; 1703 32nd St., NW, Washington DC 20007-2934.

4226 ■ Dumbarton Oaks Research Library and Collection One-Month Research Stipends (Doctorate/Monetary)

Purpose: To engage students in advance research in one of Dumbarton Oaks subject specialties. **Focus:** Byzantine studies. **Qualif.:** Applicants must be scholars holding PhD or other relevant terminal degree and working on research projects in Byzantine studies, Pre-Columbian studies, or Garden and Landscapes studies. **Criteria:** Selection will be given to applicants who live 75 or more miles from Washington, D.C.

Funds Avail.: $3,000. **To Apply:** Applicants must submit an online application prior to the deadline of the applicants proposed research visit and must notify the department to which they are applying via email; must include a project proposal of no more than 1, 000 words and two letters of reference; must contain an overview of the project, its significance in the applicant's discipline and ways in which research will complement; and the challenge in studying their field; must provide a copy of an original Social Security

Awards are arranged alphabetically below their administering organizations

card and a U.S. Social Security number or an International Taxpayer Identification Number (ITIN) for the non-U.S. citizens for stipend disbursement. **Deadline:** October 1. **Contact:** Manager of Academic Programs; Email: FellowshipPrograms@doaks.org.

4227 ■ Dumbarton Oaks Research Library and Collection Post-Baccalaureate Media Fellowships
(Professional development/Fellowship)

Purpose: To develop and apply their research skills while gaining experience in related professional fields and contributing to the institutional mission of Dumbarton Oaks. **Focus:** Byzantine studies. **Qualif.:** Applicants must be Harvard college graduates.

Deadline: November 1.

4228 ■ Dumbarton Oaks Research Library and Collection Project Grants *(Doctorate/Grant)*

Purpose: To assist scholars in conducting research about Byzantine, Pre-Columbian, or Garden and Landscape Studies. **Focus:** Byzantine studies. **Qualif.:** Applicants must be individuals who have earned a doctorate or equivalent degree. **Criteria:** Selection are based upon ability and preparation of the principal project personnel (including knowledge of the requisite languages); interest and value of the project to the specific field of study.

Funds Avail.: $3,000-$10,000. **To Apply:** Applicant must complete an online application form; which includes three letters of reference posted directly by the recommenders to the online application system. **Deadline:** November 1. **Contact:** Email: Byzantine@doaks.org or Landscape@doaks.org or Pre-Columbian@doaks.org.

4229 ■ Dumbarton Oaks Research Library and Collection Short-Term Predoctoral Residencies Grants
(Undergraduate/Grant)

Purpose: To support scholars in doing their research in the field of Byzantine, Pre-Columbian, or Garden and Landscape studies. **Focus:** Byzantine studies. **Qualif.:** Applicants must be advanced graduate students who are preparing for their PhD general exams, writing their doctoral dissertations, or expecting relevant final degrees in the field of Byzantine, Pre-Columbian, or Garden and Landscape studies. **Criteria:** Selection will be based on the committee's criteria.

Funds Avail.: No specific amount. **To Apply:** Applicants must send the following to the appropriate Director of Studies and subject librarian, at least 60 days before the preferred residency dates letter of request specifically the desired period of stay and the purpose of the visit; and brief curriculum vitae with address and telephone number, U.S. Social Security number, education, awards and honors, present and past positions (if applicable), publication, papers read, field research, etc. and a statement about language competences; applicants must have their academic adviser send a letter of recommendation directly to the appropriate Director of Studies at Dumbarton Oaks. **Contact:** Director of Byzantine, Pre-Columbian, Garden and Landscape Studies, Dumbarton Oaks Research Library and Collection, 1703 32nd St. NW, Washington, DC, 20007; Email: Byzantine@doaks.org or Landscape@doaks.org or Pre-Columbian@doaks.org.

4230 ■ Dumbarton Oaks Research Library and Collection Summer Fellowship *(Graduate/Fellowship)*

Purpose: To support students who are interested in learning and conducting research in Byzantine, Garden and Landscape, and Pre-Columbian studies. **Focus:** Byzantine studies. **Qualif.:** Applicants must be Byzantine, Pre-Columbian, or Garden and Landscape Scholars on any level of advancement beyond the first year of graduate (post-baccalaureate) study. **Criteria:** Selection will be based on the committee's criteria.

Funds Avail.: $250. **Duration:** period of seven weeks. **To Apply:** Applicants are required to complete the application online. In addition, applicants must submit three letters of recommendation and a transcript of graduate record (sent by university registrar).

4231 ■ Dumbarton Oaks Research Library and Collection Summer Internships for Harvard Students
(Undergraduate, Graduate/Internship)

Purpose: To support educational expenses of the students in studying Byzantine, Pre-Columbian, or Garden and Landscape Studies. **Focus:** Byzantine studies. **Qualif.:** Applicants must be undergraduate or graduate students of Harvard. **Criteria:** Selection will be based on the committee's criteria.

Funds Avail.: No specific amount. **Contact:** Email: Internships@doaks.org.

4232 ■ Dumbarton Oaks Research Library and Collection Post-Doctoral Teaching Fellowships
(Postdoctorate/Fellowship)

Purpose: To promote research in Byzantine studies, Pre-Columbian studies, and Garden and Landscape Studies. **Focus:** Byzantine studies; Pre-Columbian studies. **Qualif.:** Applicants must have completed all requirements for the doctoral degree; a citizen of the U.S. or Canada or a graduate of a North American university; and must have an excellent command of spoken and written English. **Criteria:** Selection is based on demonstrated scholarly accomplishment and overall academic excellence and promise; potential future impact on the field of Byzantine studies through teaching and writing; significance and quality of the research project(s) to be carried out at Dumbarton Oaks; knowledge of the relevant ancient and modern languages; and ability to contribute to the academic community at Dumbarton Oaks and local area universities.

Funds Avail.: No specific amount. **Duration:** three years. **To Apply:** Applicants must submit six copies of an application consisting of a cover letter that includes a statement of teaching experience and proposed courses; a curriculum vitae; a writing sample of not more than forty pages; a 1000-word description of the research project(s) to be carried out during the term of the fellowship; and three letters of recommendation.

4233 ■ Mellon Fellowships in Urban Landscape Studies *(Graduate, Master's, Doctorate/Fellowship)*

Purpose: To support devoted students to pursue research about garden and landscape studies. **Focus:** Landscape architecture and design. **Qualif.:** Applicants must be currently-enrolled graduate students or undergraduate juniors or seniors at Harvard University; preference will be given to students in concentrations relevant to the programs of study at Dumbarton Oaks. **Criteria:** Selection is based on the suitability and clarity of the research objectives, the relevance to the fellowship project, the feasibility of the budget and schedule, and the potential contribution to the field of urban landscape studies.

Funds Avail.: No specific amount. **To Apply:** Applicants must submit three letters of recommendation. **Deadline:**

Awards are arranged alphabetically below their administering organizations

February 1. **Contact:** mellon@doaks.org.

4234 ■ William R. Tyler Fellowships *(Graduate/ Fellowship)*

Purpose: To provide funds to graduate students with genuine intellectual interests on Pre-Columbian/early Colonial or Mediterranean/Byzantine worlds or in Garden and Landscape history. **Focus:** Byzantine studies. **Qualif.:** Applicants must be Harvard graduate students in art history, archaeology, history and literature of the Pre-Columbian/early Colonial or Mediterranean/Byzantine worlds or in Garden and Landscape history; must have completed all departmental requirements, (including course work, residence, general and preliminary examinations, and approval of the prospectus); full-time residence during the entire term or academic year of their contribution to an institutional project. **Criteria:** Applications will be judged on the originality and solidity of their contribution to their fields.

Funds Avail.: $29,500. **To Apply:** Applicants must provide three letters of recommendation, two of which should be from professors in their department at Harvard Universities and one of which should be from their dissertation supervisor. **Contact:** Manager of Academic Programs, Dumbarton Oaks, 1703 32nd St. NW, Washington, DC, 20007; Email: FellowshipPrograms@doaks.org.

4235 ■ Gabriel Dumont Institute of Native Studies and Applied Research (GDI)

917 - 22nd St. W
Saskatoon, SK, Canada S7M 0R9
Ph: (306)242-6070
Fax: (306)242-0002
Free: 877-488-6888
E-mail: apprenticeships@gdins.org
URL: www.gdins.org
Social Media: www.facebook.com/gabrieldumontinstitute
twitter.com/gdins_org

4236 ■ Gabriel Dumont College Graduate Student Bursary *(Postgraduate, Master's, Doctorate/ Scholarship)*

Purpose: To provide financial assistance and encourage Saskatchewan Metis to pursue full time graduate studies and conduct research in fields related to Metis people. **Focus:** Culture. **Qualif.:** Applicants must be Metis students who are pursuing full-time academics at the postgraduate level, masters or doctorate at a recognized university in Canada or abroad.

Duration: Annual. **Number Awarded:** Varies. **To Apply:** Applicants must submit the most recent two years of the official transcript of post-secondary education. **Deadline:** October 1. **Contact:** Secretary, Selection Committee - GDC Graduate Student Bursary Program c/o Gabriel Dumont Institute of Native Studies and Applied Research, 917- 22nd St W, Saskatoon, SK, S7M 0R9; Phone: 306-242-6070; Fax: 306-242-0002.

4237 ■ Duncan Aviation Inc.

3701 Aviation Rd.
Lincoln, NE 68524
Ph: (402)475-2611
Fax: (402)475-5541
Free: 800-228-4277
URL: www.duncanaviation.com

4238 ■ Duncan Aviation Scholarship *(Undergraduate/ Scholarship)*

Purpose: To promote and secure the future of aviation by furthering the education of students and technicians from AEA member companies. **Focus:** Aviation. **Qualif.:** Applicants must be high school seniors and/or college students planning to or currently attending an accredited school in an avionics or aircraft repair program.

Funds Avail.: $1,000.

4239 ■ Dutchess County Bar Association (DCBA)

PO Box 1837
Poughkeepsie, NY 12601
Ph: (845)473-2488
URL: www.dutchesscountybar.org

4240 ■ Joseph H. Gellert Scholarship *(Graduate/ Scholarship)*

Purpose: To provide financial assistance for the residents of Dutchess County attending an accredited law school. **Focus:** Law.

Funds Avail.: $1,000. **Duration:** Annual. **Contact:** URL: communityfoundationshv.org/Scholarships/Gellert-Dutchess-Bar-Scholarship.

4241 ■ DW Simpson Global Actuarial Recruitment

1801 W Warner Ave., Ste. 203
Chicago, IL 60613
Ph: (312)867-2300
E-mail: actuaries@dwsimpson.com
URL: www.dwsimpson.com
Social Media: www.facebook.com/dwsimpson
www.linkedin.com/company/dwsimpson
twitter.com/dwsimpson
www.youtube.com/channel/
   UCOZ0WL41rfquAVMdstWvX4g

4242 ■ DW Simpson Actuarial Science Scholarship *(Undergraduate/Scholarship)*

Purpose: To provide financial support to deserving students who are pursuing study in actuarial science. **Focus:** Actuarial science. **Criteria:** Applicants will be evaluated on the basis of academic performance.

Funds Avail.: $1,000 each. **Duration:** Annual. **Number Awarded:** 2. **To Apply:** Applicants must fill out the online application form electronically. **Deadline:** April 30 for the Fall scholarship; October 31 for the Spring scholarship.

4243 ■ Dystonia Medical Research Foundation (DMRF)

1 E Wacker Dr., Ste. 1730
Chicago, IL 60601-1980
Ph: (312)755-0198
Fax: (312)803-0138
Free: 800-377-3978
E-mail: dystonia@dystonia-foundation.org
URL: www.dystonia-foundation.org
Social Media: www.facebook.com/dystonia.foundation
www.instagram.com/dystoniamrf

Awards are arranged alphabetically below their administering organizations

twitter.com/dmrf
www.youtube.com/user/FacesofDystonia

4244 ■ Dystonia Medical Research Foundation Clinical Fellowships (Postdoctorate/Fellowship)

Purpose: To assist post-doctoral fellows in establishing careers in research relevant to dystonia. **Focus:** Muscular dystrophy. **Criteria:** Selection To become eligible, an institution must provide information on the training environment, program curriculum, available resources and the expected amount of exposure to patients with dystonia.

To Apply: Applicants must submit a proposal in addition, applicants should include the following attachments application Cover Sheet (use form provided); Budget (use form provided); biographical sketch of principal investigator and all key personnel (Use standard NIH form); Research Funding Terms and Conditions, signed by applicants and applicant's institutional official; letters of support (one letter from a mentor); and relevant articles, video clips, or other items, if applicable. **Deadline:** January 3.

4245 ■ Eagle Touch Technologies Co. Ltd.
10 Jones St.
New York, NY 10014
Ph: (833)288-5965
URL: www.eagle-touch.com

4246 ■ Technology - Students Scholarship Program (College, University/Scholarship)

Purpose: To give back to society and help students in need pursue their dreams. **Focus:** General studies/Field of study not specified. **Qualif.:** Applicant must be currently enrolled in high school, university, or college as a full-time student. **Criteria:** Essays will be evaluated based on the following criteria: writing quality, originality of ideas, logic and clarity of organization, and evidence of understanding of the topic.

Funds Avail.: $3,000. **Number Awarded:** 2. **To Apply:** Applicant must write an essay (2,000 words) on the subject: How does touch display technology change your life? What do you expect for the future of touch technology? And why are you interested in winning this scholarship? **Deadline:** December 14. **Contact:** www.eagle-touch.com/scholarship/.

4247 ■ Early American Industries Association (EAIA)
PO Box 524
Hebron, MD 21830-0524
URL: www.earlyamericanindustries.org

4248 ■ EAIA Research Grants (Other/Grant)

Purpose: To preserve and present historic trades, crafts and tools that will reflect their impact on our lives. **Focus:** Crafts; Industry and trade. **Qualif.:** Applicants must be individuals with a research related to trades, crafts and tools. **Criteria:** Recipients will be evaluated based on submitted research.

Funds Avail.: Up to $3,000. **Duration:** Annual. **Number Awarded:** Varies. **To Apply:** Applicants must submit a research; project must be related to the purpose of the EAIA; the total length including the form may not exceed ten pages; successful applicants will be required to file a report on the project attached on a form; one copy of the final form of the completed project must be deposited to the Research Grants Committee, whether or not the final

form is published; applicants are asked to give the names and addresses of their local newspapers, so the Research Grants Committee can announce new grant recipients; Official acknowledgment of the support of EAIA must be listed in any published material connected with the project; An abstract of the grantees research must be furnished with a report within 60 days of the scheduled completion of the funded work. **Deadline:** March 15. **Contact:** John H. Verrill, Executive Director, PO Box 524, Hebron, MD, 21830-0524.

4249 ■ Earthquake Engineering Research Institute (EERI)
499 14th St., Ste. 320
Oakland, CA 94612-1934
Ph: (510)451-0905
Fax: (510)451-5411
E-mail: eeri@eeri.org
URL: www.eeri.org
Social Media: instagram.com/eerigrams
www.linkedin.com/groups/1082697/profile
twitter.com/eeri_tweets
youtube.com/user/EERIvideos

4250 ■ EERI/FEMA NEHRP Graduate Fellowship in Earthquake Hazard Reduction (Graduate/Fellowship)

Purpose: To support study and research that may contribute to the science and practice of earthquake hazard mitigation. **Focus:** Earth sciences. **Qualif.:** Applicants must be enrolled in a graduate degree program at an accredited U.S. college/university and must hold U.S. citizenship or permanent resident status. **Criteria:** Selection is based All application materials must be submitted electronically to EERI, including a letter of nomination from a faculty sponsor at the student's institution and two additional reference letters.

Funds Avail.: $12,000. **Duration:** Annual. **Number Awarded:** 2. **To Apply:** Applicants must include an academic transcript; a statement of educational and career goals that also describes involvement in EERI; letter of nomination from a faculty sponsor at the student's institution and two additional reference letters.

4251 ■ Eason & Tambornini, A Law Corporation
1234 H St.
Sacramento, CA 95814
Ph: (916)438-1819
Fax: (916)438-1820
E-mail: info@capcitylaw.com
URL: www.capcitylaw.com
Social Media: www.facebook.com/sacramentolawyers

4252 ■ Injury to Opportunity Scholarship (Vocational/Occupational/Scholarship)

Purpose: To provide a benefit to the children of persons who have been permanently injured or killed in a Personal Injury Accident or work related injury (Workers Compensation). **Focus:** General studies/Field of study not specified. **Qualif.:** Applicant must be under 21 and have had a parent who suffered an injury resulting in permanent disability or wrongful death; must have a high school diploma/GED, or be a high school student in good standing. **Criteria:** Academic achievement, aptitude, extracurricular activities, and

Awards are arranged alphabetically below their administering organizations

community service will be considered in selection. Answers to the personal questions and living situation will also be considered.

Funds Avail.: $2,000. **To Apply:** Applicants must include directions on how to submit scholarship to their school, including: tuition acceptance deadline, best person to contact about scholarship for applicant's program; how the check should be written; and address to send check to. **Contact:** Email:matthew@capcitylaw.com.

4253 ■ East Tennessee Foundation (ETF)
520 W. SUMMIT HILL DRIVE, SUITE 1101
Knoxville, TN 37902
Ph: (865)524-1223
Fax: (865)637-6039
Free: 877-524-1223
E-mail: etf@etf.org
URL: www.easttennesseefoundation.org
Social Media: www.youtube.com/user/easttennfoundation

4254 ■ B&W Y-12 Scholarship Fund *(Undergraduate/Scholarship)*

Purpose: To benefit graduating high school seniors wishing to pursue careers in science, math or pre-engineering related fields. **Focus:** Engineering; Mathematics and mathematical sciences; Science.

Funds Avail.: $1,400. **Duration:** Annual; Up to 1 year. **Number Awarded:** 1. **To Apply:** Applicants must check the application process online; must include a Letter of Recommendation. **Remarks:** Established in 2004.

4255 ■ Ruby A. Brown Memorial Scholarships *(Undergraduate/Scholarship)*

Purpose: To benefit health nurses seeking to continue their nursing education. **Focus:** Nursing.

Funds Avail.: $3,300. **Duration:** Up to 1 year. **To Apply:** Applicants must check the application process online; must include a Letter of Recommendation. **Remarks:** Established in 2003.

4256 ■ Gordon W. and Agnes P. Cobb Scholarship *(Undergraduate/Scholarship)*

Purpose: To benefit graduates of high schools in Blount, Loudon, and Knox counties in Tennessee who wish to pursue or who are pursuing college education in a health care or medical-related field. **Focus:** Health sciences.

Funds Avail.: $10,000 per year. **Duration:** Up to 4 years. **To Apply:** Applicants must check the application process online; must include a Letter of Recommendation. **Remarks:** Established in 1996.

4257 ■ Michael D. Curtin Renaissance Student Memorial Scholarship *(Graduate/Scholarship)*

Purpose: To recognize and benefit students who demonstrate leadership or achievement in a balanced array of activities, including the arts, athletics, citizenship, community/religious service and academics. **Focus:** General studies/Field of study not specified. **Qualif.:** Applicants must be enrolled as full time students in an accredited public or private not-for-profit university; must be a Graduating seniors of Anderson County High School.

Funds Avail.: $1,250. **Duration:** Up to 4 years. **To Apply:** Applicants must check the application process online; must

include a Letter of Recommendation. **Deadline:** June 1. **Remarks:** Established in 2000.

4258 ■ R.G. and Ruth Crossno Scholarship *(Undergraduate/Scholarship)*

Purpose: To benefit graduating seniors of Anderson County High School who wish to pursue an advanced degree. **Focus:** General studies/Field of study not specified.

Funds Avail.: $1,500. **Duration:** Annual; Up to 4 years. **To Apply:** Applicants must check the application process online; must include a Letter of Recommendation. **Deadline:** June 1. **Remarks:** Mr. R.G. Crossno, past mayor of Norris, Tennessee and 21-year member of the Anderson County School Board dedicated his life to promoting better education throughout the state of Tennessee. Established in 1990.

4259 ■ Steven L. Coffey Memorial Scholarship *(Undergraduate/Scholarship)*

Purpose: To assist students who possess the potential for excellence but may require some additional support in achieving their educational goals. **Focus:** General studies/Field of study not specified. **Criteria:** Selection will be based on the committee's criteria.

Funds Avail.: $1,500-$2,500. **Duration:** Up to 4 years. **To Apply:** Applicants must check the application process online; must include a Letter of Recommendation. **Remarks:** Established in 1988.

4260 ■ East-West Center (EWC)
1601 E West Rd.
Honolulu, HI 96848-1601
Ph: (808)944-7111
Fax: (808)944-7212
E-mail: ewccontact@eastwestcenter.org
URL: www.eastwestcenter.org
Social Media: www.facebook.com/EastWestCenter.org
www.youtube.com/user/EastWestCenter

4261 ■ Asian Development Bank - Japan Scholarship Program *(Graduate, Master's/Scholarship)*

Purpose: To provides support for Master's degree study in ADB-JSP approved fields of study at the University of Hawai'i at M?noa (UHM), and for participation in the educational, residential, and leadership development programs at the East-West Center (EWC). **Focus:** General studies/Field of study not specified. **Criteria:** Selection will be based on the committee's criteria.

Funds Avail.: No specific amount. **Duration:** Annual. **To Apply:** Applicants must complete the following materials ADB Scholarship Application Form; University of Hawai'i Graduate Admissions Application; curriculum vitae; completed essays 1-3; writing sample; application fee; two official transcripts from each institution attended; one official degree certificate for every degree earned; three letters of reference; official TOEFL or IELTS test score report received directly by East-West Center from the Testing Center; official GRE; official GMAT test scores; application form, letter of reference form and letter of reference-community service can be downloaded at the website. **Contact:** East-West Center, Award Services Office, John A. Burns Hall, Room 2066, 1601 East-West Road, Honolulu, HI 96848-1601 USA; Phone: 808-944-7738; Fax: 808-944-7730; E-mail: adbjsp@eastwestcenter.org.

Awards are arranged alphabetically below their administering organizations

4262 ■ East-West Center Graduate Degree Fellowship (Master's, Doctorate, Graduate/Fellowship)

Purpose: To support students to participate in educational and research programs at the East-West Center while pursuing graduate study at the University of Hawai'i. **Focus:** General studies/Field of study not specified. **Qualif.:** Applicants must be citizens or permanent residents of the United States and citizens of countries in the Pacific and Asia, including Russia. **Criteria:** Selection will be based on the committee's criteria.

Funds Avail.: No specific amount. **Duration:** Annual. **To Apply:** Applicants may contact the Center for the application process and other information. **Deadline:** December 1. **Contact:** East-West Center, Award Services Office; Phone: 808-944-7735; Fax: 808-944-7730; Email: scholarships@eastwestcenter.org.

4263 ■ Indonesian Directorate General of Higher Education Scholarships (DIKTI) (Graduate/Scholarship)

Purpose: To support students to participate in educational and research program at the East-West Center while pursuing graduate study at the University of Hawaii. **Focus:** General studies/Field of study not specified. **Qualif.:** Applicants must be citizens of Indonesia pursuing graduate study at the University of Hawaii. **Criteria:** Selection will be based on the committee's criteria.

Funds Avail.: No specific amount. **To Apply:** Applicant must submit official transcripts be received from each college or university where credits and grades have been earned; An official graduation and/or degree certificate must accompany transcripts that do not include the date of graduation and type of degree awarded; All transcripts and certificates must bear the actual (not copied) signature of the registrar and actual embossed seal or official stamp of the issuing institution; All transcripts and certificates, to be considered official, must be received by the East-West Center in sealed official envelopes of the issuing institution; Non-English transcripts or certificates must be issued in the original language and be accompanied by English translations. **Deadline:** November 1. **Contact:** Award Services Office/DIKTI, East-West Center, 1601 East-West Rd., Honolulu, HI 96848-1601 USA.

4264 ■ Obuchi Student Scholarship (Graduate/Scholarship)

Purpose: To support students to participate in educational, cultural, residential and leadership programs at the East-West Center while pursuing a Master's degree at the University of Hawaii or for study in the Asia Pacific Leadership Program. **Focus:** General studies/Field of study not specified. **Qualif.:** Applicants must be residents of Okinawa, Japan, who have the intention of returning to Okinawa on completion of study, to contribute to the development needs of Okinawa; must be enrolled or planning to enroll in an MA program at the University of Hawaii at Manoa. **Criteria:** Selection will be based on the committee's criteria.

Funds Avail.: No specific amount. **Duration:** Annual. **To Apply:** Applicants must submit Copy of passport biodata page; Photocopy of permanent domicile in Okinawa or certificate of residence for Okinawa; Confidential Financial Statement Form; Two (2) official transcripts from each institution attended. **Deadline:** December 1. **Contact:** To learn more about the program, Junko Itokazu, Obuchi Program Okinawa PR Desk, NPO Okinawa Language Center; Email: itokazu@okilc.org; For specific questions regarding the application forms or process, mail to scholarships@eastwestcenter.org with Obuchi Student Scholarship as subject line.

4265 ■ Seameo-Vietnam Scholarship Program (Graduate/Scholarship)

Purpose: To support students to participate in educational and research program at the East-West Center while pursuing graduate study at the University of Hawaii. **Focus:** General studies/Field of study not specified. **Qualif.:** Applicants must be a master's and doctoral programs in approved fields of study at the University of Hawai'i at Minoa; must be citizens of Vietnam. **Criteria:** Selection will be based on the committee's criteria.

Funds Avail.: No specific amount. **To Apply:** Interested applicants may contact the Center for the application process and other information. **Contact:** Overseas Study Department OSD, Phone: 84-8-3824 5618, ext. 118-119; Manager; Email: ptnmai@vnseameo.org.

4266 ■ Easter Seals Ontario
1 Concorde Gate, St. 700
Toronto, ON, Canada M3C 3N6
Ph: (416)421-8377
Fax: (416)696-1035
Free: 800-668-6252
E-mail: info@easterseals.org
URL: www.easterseals.org
Social Media: www.facebook.com/EasterSealsON
instagram.com/eastersealson
www.linkedin.com/company/easter-seals-ontario
twitter.com/eastersealson
youtube.com/user/Eastersealsont

4267 ■ The Leaders of Tomorrow Award (Award)

Purpose: To assist Easter Seals youth who displays commendable leadership skills, dedication and commitment to Easter Seals through their volunteer role and is an advocate for individuals with physical disabilities. **Focus:** Education, Vocational-technical.

4268 ■ Beatrice Drinnan Spence Scholarship (Undergraduate, Vocational/Occupational/Scholarship)

Purpose: To assist young adults with physical disabilities with the cost of post-secondary education or vocational training. **Focus:** Education, Vocational-technical. **Qualif.:** Applicants must be resident students of Ontario with physical disabilities who are registered for post-secondary education entering their second to final year of study; must have achieved a minimum grade point average of 75% or equivalent in their previous year of study at a postsecondary educational facility; served as a model and inspiration to fellow students; must have applied for alternate financial assistance and still require assistance; must demonstrate consistent level of scholastic achievement throughout their secondary school and post-secondary curriculum. **Criteria:** Applicants are evaluated based on personal attributes and financial need.

Funds Avail.: $5,000. **Duration:** Annual. **Number Awarded:** 1. **To Apply:** Applicants must submit the completed application form along with a one-page letter outlining qualifications for the award including scholastic achievement, motivation, initiative and extra-curricular activities; copy of secondary and, if applicable, post-

Awards are arranged alphabetically below their administering organizations

secondary transcripts; any interim marks that are available before the deadline; proof of application to applicable alternate sources of financial assistance; a current letter from a medical physician outlining your physical disability, if not a registered client or previously registered client of Easter Seals Ontario; an academic reference from your secondary school principal or a current postsecondary institution professor; a personal reference from an individual who is familiar with your current extracurricular activities and outstanding characteristics and cannot be written by a family member; all reference letters must be signed, dated within the last 12 months, and where appropriate provided on official letterhead. **Deadline:** May 4. **Remarks:** Established in memory of Beatrice Drinnan Spence, mother of Judy McIntosh. Established in 2004. **Contact:** Scholarship Selection Committee, c/o Alison Morse, Provincial Coordinator – Special Education, Easter Seals Ontario, One Concorde Gate Ste. 700 Toronto, ON, M3C 3N6; Phone: 416-421-8778 Ext. 335; Toll-free: 800-668-6252; Email: scholarships@easterseals.org.

4269 ■ Eastern Communication Association (ECA)

University of Scranton 800 Linden St. STT 4106
Scranton, PA 18510
Ph: (614)392-1558
E-mail: info@ecacomm.org
URL: www.ecasite.org
Social Media: www.facebook.com/ECACOMM
twitter.com/ECAComm
www.youtube.com/channel/UC60rwfoPsailZ5cK7LmvOFg

4270 ■ Applied Urban Communication Research Grants *(Professional development/Grant)*

Purpose: To foster and promote significant inter-disciplinary communication research contributions that extend the boundaries of. **Focus:** Communications. **Qualif.:** Applicants must be members of the Eastern Communication Association. **Criteria:** Applicants will be evaluated based on the potential impact of their work as well as the quality and rigor of their contributions.

Funds Avail.: $2,500. **Duration:** Annual. **To Apply:** Applicants must include a cover letter explaining why the applicant deserves the award; a 500-word essay describing, outlining the anticipated outcomes, intended mode of dissemination of the research; anticipated budget and timetable for completion of the project; copy of the curriculum vitae; and at least one supporting letter from someone well-acquainted with the nominee. **Deadline:** February 1. **Contact:** ECA Past President, Jason Wrench, Email: wrenchj@newpaltz.edu.

4271 ■ ECA Centennial Scholarships *(Master's, Doctorate/Scholarship)*

Purpose: To assist deserving PhD and M.A. students in their education. **Focus:** Communications. **Qualif.:** Applicants must be Ph.D., M.A., M.S. students in Communication who are current ECA members. **Criteria:** Recipients will be selected based on submitted materials.

Funds Avail.: No specific amount. **Duration:** Annual. **Number Awarded:** 2. **To Apply:** Applications must include a letter of nomination from the thesis or dissertation advisor attesting the nominees' student status; must submit a four-page, 1500-word project summary. **Deadline:** March 1. **Contact:** ECA Past President, Jason Wrench, Email: wrenchj@newpaltz.edu.

4272 ■ Eastman Community Music School (ECMS)

26 Gibbs St.
Rochester, NY 14604
Ph: (585)274-1400
Fax: (585)274-1005
E-mail: community@esm.rochester.edu
URL: www.esm.rochester.edu
Social Media: www.facebook.com/eastmancommunitymusicschool
www.instagram.com/eastmancommunityschool
www.youtube.com/user/eastmancms

4273 ■ Need-based and Merit Scholarships *(Undergraduate/Scholarship)*

Purpose: To assist ECMS students in their continuing education. **Focus:** Music. **Qualif.:** Applicants must be ECMS students enrolled in a diploma program. **Criteria:** Selection shall be based on merit and financial need.

Funds Avail.: No specific amount. **Duration:** Annual. **To Apply:** Applicants must submit a completed application form along with Financial Assistance Application Form; teacher recommendation; and copy of the first page of the applicant's federal tax form. **Deadline:** August 1.

4274 ■ Echoing Green

494 8th Ave., 2nd Fl.
New York, NY 10165
Ph: (212)689-1165
Fax: (212)689-9010
E-mail: info@echoinggreen.org
URL: www.echoinggreen.org
Social Media: facebook.com/echoinggreen
instagram.com/echoinggreen
linkedin.com/company/echoing-green
twitter.com/echoinggreen
youtube.com/user/echoinggreen1

4275 ■ Echoing Green Black Male Achievement Fellowships *(Professional development/Fellowship)*

Purpose: To encourage individuals who are dedicated to improving the life outcomes of black men and boys in the United States. **Focus:** Social work. **Qualif.:** Applicants must be social entrepreneurs who are starting up new and innovative organizations in the field of black male achievement. **Criteria:** Selection will be based on the committee's criteria.

Funds Avail.: $80,000 for individuals; $90,000 for two-person partnerships. **To Apply:** Applicants may apply as individuals or as partners. They may contact Echoing Green for the application process.

4276 ■ Echoing Green Climate Fellowships *(Professional development/Fellowship)*

Purpose: To encourage individuals who are committed to working on innovations in mitigation and adaptation to climate change. **Focus:** Social work. **Qualif.:** Applicants must be next-generation social entrepreneurs committed to working on innovations in mitigation and adaptation to climate change. **Criteria:** Selection will be based on the committee's criteria.

Funds Avail.: $80,000 for individuals; $90,000 for two-person partnerships. **To Apply:** Applicants may apply as

Awards are arranged alphabetically below their administering organizations

individuals or as partners. They may contact Echoing Green for the application process.

4277 ■ Echoing Green Global Fellowships *(Professional development/Fellowship)*

Purpose: To support emerging leaders working to bring about positive social change. **Focus:** Leadership, Institutional and community. **Qualif.:** Applicants must be emerging social entrepreneurs from any part of the world working to disrupt the status quo. **Criteria:** Selection will be based on the committee's criteria.

Funds Avail.: $80,000 for individuals; $90,000 for two-person partnerships. **To Apply:** Applicants may apply as individuals or as partners. They may contact Echoing Green for the application process.

4278 ■ Ecological Society of America (ESA)

1990 M St. NW, Ste. 700
Washington, DC 20036
Ph: (202)833-8773
Fax: (202)833-8775
E-mail: esahq@esa.org
URL: www.esa.org
Social Media: www.facebook.com/esa.org
www.instagram.com/ecologicalsociety
twitter.com/esa_org
www.youtube.com/user/ESAVideos

4279 ■ The Jasper Ridge Restoration Fellowship *(Graduate, Undergraduate/Fellowship)*

Purpose: To provide financial support to deserving students. **Focus:** General studies/Field of study not specified. **Qualif.:** Applicants must be post-doctoral students up to senior faculty. **Criteria:** Applications will be assessed based on an individual's past accomplishments and on potential to take full advantage of the ecosystems and past research at Jasper Ridge, as well as the intellectual community at Stanford.

Funds Avail.: $80,000. **To Apply:** Applicants must submit a CV, a 3-page description of their proposed program, and contact information for 3 references. **Deadline:** May 1. **Contact:** Dr. Philippe Cohen, Administrative Director, Jasper Ridge Biological Preserve, 4001 Sand Hill Rd., Woodside, CA 94062; E-mail: philippe.cohen@stanford.edu.

4280 ■ Economic History Association (EHA)

McClelland Hall, 401GG
Dept. of Economics
University of Arizona
Tucson, AZ 85721-0108
Ph: (520)621-6224
Fax: (520)621-8450
URL: eh.net

4281 ■ Arthur H. Cole Grants in Aid *(Doctorate/Grant)*

Purpose: To support research in economic history, regardless of time period or geographic area. **Focus:** History, Economic. **Qualif.:** Applicants must be members of the Association and must hold the Ph.D. degree. **Criteria:** Preference is given to recent Ph.D. recipients.

Funds Avail.: Up to $5,000. **Deadline:** March 1. **Contact:** Professor Tracy Dennison, Committee on Research in

Economic History; E-mail: tkd@hss.caltech.edu.

4282 ■ EHA Exploratory Travel and Data Grants *(Doctorate/Grant)*

Purpose: To provide students the financial assistance they need in research. **Focus:** History, Economic. **Qualif.:** Applicants must be doctoral students and current association members. **Criteria:** Recipients will be selected based on Committee's review of the application materials submitted.

Funds Avail.: Up to $2,500. **To Apply:** Applicants must submit 3 pages of project description; should upload a reference letter. **Deadline:** January 18. **Contact:** Professor Tracy Dennison, chair, Committee on Research in Economic History; E-mail: tkd@hss.caltech.edu.

4283 ■ EHA Graduate Dissertation Fellowships *(Graduate/Fellowship)*

Purpose: To support students whose thesis topics have been approved and who have made some progress towards writing their dissertation. **Focus:** History, Economic. **Qualif.:** Applicants must be current association members. Applicant at early stages of dissertation development are not eligible for fellowship support. **Criteria:** Recipients will be selected based on the committee's review of the application materials submitted.

Funds Avail.: $10,000. **Deadline:** January 18. **Contact:** Professor Tracy Dennison, chair, Committee on Research in Economic History; E-mail: tkd@hss.caltech.edu.

4284 ■ EDiS Company

110 S Poplar St., Ste. 400
Wilmington, DE 19801-5053
Free: 800-995-3347
E-mail: info@ediscompany.com
URL: www.ediscompany.com
Social Media: www.facebook.com/ediscompany
www.linkedin.com/company/edis-company
twitter.com/EDiSCompany

4285 ■ Generation III Scholarship *(Undergraduate/Scholarship)*

Purpose: To support students who are planning to pursue an associate or bachelor's degree. **Focus:** Architecture; Business; Engineering. **Criteria:** Awards are given based on academic achievement, financial aid and field of study.

Funds Avail.: $1,000. **Duration:** Annual; up to four years. **Number Awarded:** 1. **Deadline:** March 15. **Remarks:** Established in 1998. **Contact:** Delaware Community Foundation Scholarships, C/o ETS Scholarship & Recognition Programs, PO Box 6730, Princeton, NJ, 08541; Mr. Adam DiSabatino, Scholarship Administrator; Phone: 302-421-5700.

4286 ■ EditMyPaper.ca

Toronto, ON, Canada M2h1J8
E-mail: info@editmypaper.ca
URL: editmypaper.ca
Social Media: www.facebook.com/EditMyPaper
twitter.com/editmypaper

4287 ■ The Edit My Paper Proofreading Scholarships *(Undergraduate/Scholarship)*

Purpose: To reward great writers and allow them to showcase their rhetoric skills. **Focus:** Writing. **Qualif.:** Ap-

Awards are arranged alphabetically below their administering organizations

plicants must be enrolled in high school, college or university (North America/Europe). **Criteria:** Selection will be based on the following criteria: depth of thought; creativity; spelling and grammar.

Funds Avail.: $250-$1,000. **Duration:** Annual. **Number Awarded:** 3. **To Apply:** Applicants must write a 500 to 1000 word essay on the prompt located on the scholarship info page and submit it along with some basic information; may contact the Foundation for application process and other information. **Deadline:** December 30.

4288 ■ Editors Association of Canada (EAC)
1507-180 Dundas St. W
Toronto, ON, Canada M5B 1L2
URL: www.editors.ca

4289 ■ Claudette Upton Scholarships
(Undergraduate/Scholarship)

Purpose: To support continuing professional development in editing. **Focus:** Editors and editing. **Qualif.:** Applicants must be student members of EAC. **Criteria:** Scholarship will be given to a student who demonstrates an aptitude for editing, commitment to pursuing a career as an editor, and other qualifications reminiscent of honorary life member Claudette Upton.

Funds Avail.: $1,000. **Duration:** Annual. **To Apply:** Applicants must submit a reference letter from an instructor; maximum two-page resume; 300-word statement in response to the question "At the end of a long career as an editor, what would be the one thing you hope to be the most proud of?". **Remarks:** Established in 2009. **Contact:** Claudette Upton Scholarship Coordinator; 1507-180 Dundas St., West, Toronto, ON, M5G 1Z8.

4290 ■ Edmonton Community Foundation
9910 103 St. NW
Edmonton, AB, Canada T5K 2K7
Ph: (780)426-0015
Fax: (780)425-0121
Free: 866-626-0015
E-mail: info@ecfoundation.org
URL: www.ecfoundation.org
Social Media: facebook.com/pages/Edmonton-Community -Foundation/172806652795178

4291 ■ Don and Norine Lowry Awards for Women of Excellence *(Undergraduate, Graduate, Advanced Professional/Scholarship)*

Purpose: To provide assistance to women of all ages in pursuit of their goals in the fields of water, power, finance, energy, accounting, healthcare, safety or community relations. **Focus:** General studies/Field of study not specified. **Qualif.:** Applicants must be female residents in the City of Edmonton who are able to demonstrate permanent residence or citizenship of Canada; must be pursuing a program of study in the fields of water, power, finance, energy, accounting, healthcare, safety and/or community relations leading to a recognized certificate, diploma, undergraduate or graduate degree, or professional designation at a school operating in Edmonton; and must clearly demonstrate how the proposed course of study will help the applicants reach their career aspirations. **Criteria:** Consideration and priority will be given to those with commitment to an ongoing career in their field of study in

Edmonton, community involvement or leadership, participation in sports and recreation, educational goals related to establishing their excellence as a leader in their chosen field, and financial need.

Funds Avail.: $1,000-$5,000. **Number Awarded:** Varies. **To Apply:** Applicants must submit the completed application form and must provide two reference letters which recommend the student and the course of study. Reference letters must be from a third party individual (e.g. employer, volunteer contact, teacher); should clearly address how the applicants meet the criteria and priorities described above; should be signed, dated and current, and with contact information for the writer; should have summary which outlines the applicants' employment and educational history; and should have statement of marks for most recent studies. Official transcripts are not required, a photocopy or print out from a school website is acceptable. Before an award is confirmed, recipients must provide proof of enrollment in the program of choice. **Deadline:** May 31. **Contact:** Email: studentawards@ecfoundation.org.

4292 ■ Al Maurer Awards *(Undergraduate, Graduate, Advanced Professional/Scholarship)*

Purpose: To assist public service employees with furthering their education in areas that will promote public service excellence. **Focus:** Public service. **Qualif.:** Applicants must be permanent public sector employees; must demonstrate permanent public service employment within Edmonton city limits; must have residence in the greater Edmonton area and permanent residence or citizenship in Canada; and must be pursuing a program of study leading to a recognized certificate, diploma, undergraduate or graduate degree or professional designation at a school operating in Edmonton. **Criteria:** Priority will be given to applicants who demonstrate commitment to an ongoing career in the public service, educational goals related to refining the employees' ability to promote public service excellence, and financial need to cover educational costs beyond those provided by the employer.

Funds Avail.: $500-$2,500. **Duration:** Annual. **Number Awarded:** Varies. **To Apply:** Applicants must submit the completed application form; must provide a reference letter from their managers or supervisors which recommends the students and the course of study (reference letters should clearly address how the applicant meets the criteria and priorities); must provide a personal reference from someone (not a relative) who can address how the applicants meet the criteria; must provide a resume which outlines the applicants' employment and educational (including training provided by the employer) history. Before an award is confirmed, recipients must provide proof of enrollment in the program of choice. **Deadline:** August 31. **Contact:** Email: studentawards@ecfoundation.org.

4293 ■ Edmonton Epilepsy Association (EEA)
11215 Groat Rd. NW
Edmonton, AB, Canada T5M 3K2
Ph: (780)488-9600
Fax: (780)447-5486
Free: 866-374-5377
E-mail: info@edmontonepilepsy.org
URL: www.edmontonepilepsy.org
Social Media: www.facebook.com/edmonton.epilepsy twitter.com/EEdmonton

Awards are arranged alphabetically below their administering organizations

4294 ■ Edmonton Epilepsy Association Scholarship
(Undergraduate/Scholarship)

Purpose: To assist students who are currently under a Canadian physician's care for epilepsy to advance to or continue with college or university studies. **Focus:** General studies/Field of study not specified. **Qualif.:** Applicants must be Greater- Edmonton students who are Canadian citizens or who have permanent resident status (please include a copy of your immigration papers) and who are currently under a Canadian physician's care for epilepsy. **Funds Avail.:** 1,000 Canadian Dollars. **Duration:** Annual. **Number Awarded:** 2. **To Apply:** Applicants must submit application form along with a short essay (no fewer than 600 and no more than 1, 200 words in length). The essay must be typewritten and double-spaced. **Deadline:** March 1.

4295 ■ Edmonton Epilepsy Continuing Education Scholarships *(Undergraduate/Scholarship)*

Purpose: To open doors for incoming or continuing Canadian college students who are under epilepsy care. **Focus:** General studies/Field of study not specified. **Qualif.:** Applicants must be Canadian citizens entering or continuing in college or University studies who have landed immigrant status and currently be under a Canadian physician's care for epilepsy. **Criteria:** Recipients will be selected based on Committee's review of all applications and supporting documents. **Funds Avail.:** $1,000. **Duration:** Annual. **Number Awarded:** 2. **To Apply:** Applicants must submit three letter of recommendation of which one must come from someone from academia; a copy of immigration papers (if landed immigrant); an unofficial copy of the current academic transcript; and a copy of university, college, or graduate school application(s)/acceptance letter, or confirmation of enrollment. **Deadline:** March 1.

4296 ■ Edon Farmers Cooperative Association Inc.
205 S Michigan St.
Edon, OH 43518
Ph: (419)272-2121
Fax: (419)272-2304
Free: 800-878-4093
URL: www.edonfarmerscoop.com
Social Media: www.facebook.com/edon-farmers-co-op-162000213885568

4297 ■ Edon Farmers Cooperative Scholarships
(Undergraduate/Scholarship)

Purpose: To provide financial assistance for high school seniors to further their education as full-time students in any post high school institution. **Focus:** Agricultural sciences. **Qualif.:** Applicants must be dependents of a stockholder going into any field of study or any students going into an agricultural field; and must be high school seniors in any post high school institutions. **Funds Avail.:** $1,000. **Duration:** Annual. **To Apply:** Applicants must submit all the required application information. **Contact:** Edon farmers association Po Box 308, Edon, OH, 43518.

4298 ■ Educational Audiology Association (EAA)
700 McKnight Park Dr., Ste. 708
Pittsburgh, PA 15237

Fax: (888)729-3489
Free: 800-460-7322
E-mail: admin@edaud.org
URL: edaud.org
Social Media: www.facebook.com/educationalaudiology
www.linkedin.com/groups/4300870/profile
twitter.com/EduAud

4299 ■ Fred Berg Awards *(Undergraduate/Award)*

Purpose: To promote educational audiology. **Focus:** Speech and language pathology/Audiology. **Qualif.:** Applicants may be members or nonmembers of EAA. **Criteria:** Awards will be given based on the committee's criteria. The Nominations and Awards Committee reviews the nominations and makes recommendations to the EAA Executive Committee for approval. **Funds Avail.:** No specific amount. **Duration:** Irregular. **Number Awarded:** Varies. **To Apply:** Applicants must submit a letter stating the applicant's specific qualifications for the award; two additional letters of support; and the applicant's vitae.

4300 ■ Educational Audiology Association Doctoral Scholarship *(Doctorate/Scholarship)*

Purpose: To provide financial assistance to a member of EAA, practicing as an educational audiologist who are pursuing doctoral degree. **Focus:** Speech and language pathology/Audiology. **Qualif.:** Applicant must be a member of EAA; practicing as an educational audiologist; be matriculated in an official doctoral program. **Criteria:** Selection is based on committee's review of all applications. **Funds Avail.:** $500-$1,000. **Duration:** Annually. **Number Awarded:** 3. **To Apply:** Applicants must submit all supporting documentation. **Deadline:** Rolling submissions will be accepted all year. **Contact:** EAA headquarters, 700 McKnight Park Dr., Ste. 708, Pittsburgh, PA, 15237; Email: admin@edaud.org.

4301 ■ Noel D. Matkin Awards *(Undergraduate/Award)*

Purpose: To promote educational audiology. **Focus:** Speech and language pathology/Audiology. **Qualif.:** Applicants must be a member of EAA. **Criteria:** Award will be given to practitioners and students who are EAA members. **Funds Avail.:** No specific amount. **Duration:** Annual. **To Apply:** Applicants are encouraged to submit proposals for these awards; proposals should be typed, double-spaced, and should include the requested information on the pdf rule; proposals should include section headings and number pages; must submit a letter of support from their academic advisor, research mentor or program director. **Deadline:** February 1. **Contact:** EAA Headquarters, 3030 W 81st Ave., Westminster, Colorado 80031.

4302 ■ The Educational Foundation for Women in Accounting (EFWA)
136 S Keowee St.
Dayton, OH 45402
Ph: (937)424-3391
Fax: (937)222-5794
E-mail: info@efwa.org
URL: www.efwa.org

4303 ■ EFWA Moss Adams Foundation Scholarships *(Undergraduate/Scholarship)*

Purpose: To provide financial assistance to female reentry students who wish to pursue a degree in accounting. **Fo-**

Awards are arranged alphabetically below their administering organizations

cus: Accounting. **Qualif.:** Applicants must be women returning to school with undergraduate status; incoming, current, or reentry junior or seniors; must be minority women; or pursuing their fifth year requirement through either general studies or within a graduate program. **Criteria:** Selection will be based on commitment to the goal of pursuing a degree in accounting, including evidence of continued commitment after receiving the award; aptitude for accounting and business; clear evidence that the candidate has established goals and a plan for achieving those goals, both personal and professional; financial need. **Funds Avail.:** $1,000. **Duration:** Annual. **To Apply:** Applications must be submitted online. **Deadline:** April 30. **Contact:** Phone: 937-424-3391; Email: info@efwa.org.

4304 ■ Michele L. McDonald Scholarships
(Undergraduate/Scholarship)

Purpose: To provide financial assistance to female reentry students who wish to pursue a degree in accounting. **Focus:** Accounting. **Qualif.:** Applicants must be women returning to college from the work force or after raising children. **Criteria:** Selection will be based on commitment to the goal of pursuing a degree in accounting, including evidence of continued commitment after receiving the award; aptitude for accounting and business; clear evidence that the candidate has established goals and a plan for achieving those goals, both personal and professional; financial need. **Funds Avail.:** $1,000. **Duration:** Annual. **To Apply:** Applications must be submitted online. **Deadline:** April 30. **Contact:** Phone: 937-424-3391; Email: info@efwa.org.

4305 ■ Rhonda J.B. O'Leary Memorial Scholarship
(Undergraduate, Graduate/Scholarship)

Purpose: To support students who are pursuing a degree in accounting. **Focus:** Accounting. **Qualif.:** Applicants must be undergraduate or graduate student. **Criteria:** Selection will be based on commitment to the goal of pursuing a degree in accounting, including evidence of continued commitment after receiving the award; aptitude for accounting and business; clear evidence that the candidate has established goals and a plan for achieving those goals, both personal and professional; financial need. **Funds Avail.:** Up to $2,000. **To Apply:** Applications must be submitted online. **Deadline:** April 30. **Contact:** Phone: 937-424-3391; Email: info@efwa.org.

4306 ■ Women In Need Scholarships
(Undergraduate/Scholarship)

Purpose: To provide financial assistance to female reentry students who wish to pursue a degree in accounting. **Focus:** Accounting. **Qualif.:** Applicants should be incoming, current, or reentry juniors or seniors. **Criteria:** Selection will be based on commitment to the goal of pursuing a degree in accounting, including evidence of continued commitment after receiving the award; aptitude for accounting and business; clear evidence that the candidate has established goals and a plan for achieving those goals, both personal and professional; financial need. **Funds Avail.:** $2,000. **Duration:** Two years. **Number Awarded:** 1. **To Apply:** Applications must be submitted online. **Deadline:** April 30.

4307 ■ Women In Transition Scholarships
(Undergraduate/Scholarship)

Purpose: To provide financial assistance to female reentry students who wish to pursue a degree in accounting. **Fo-**

cus: Accounting. **Qualif.:** Applicants should be incoming or current freshmen and women returning to school with a freshman status. **Criteria:** Selection will be based on commitment to the goal of pursuing a degree in accounting, including evidence of continued commitment after receiving the award; aptitude for accounting and business; clear evidence that the candidate has established goals and a plan for achieving those goals, both personal and professional; financial need.

Funds Avail.: Up to $16,000. **Duration:** Four years. **Number Awarded:** 1. **To Apply:** Applications must be submitted online. **Deadline:** April 30. **Contact:** Phone: 937-424-3391; Email: info@efwa.org.

4308 ■ Educational Research Center of America (ERCA)
2 Dubon Ct.
Farmingdale, NY 11735
Ph: (561)586-1003
E-mail: info@studentresearch.org
URL: www.studentresearch.org

4309 ■ Student Research Foundation Personal Achievement Scholarship *(Undergraduate/ Scholarship)*

Purpose: To help high school students further their education and professional development. **Focus:** General studies/Field of study not specified. **Qualif.:** Applicants must be high school students and legal residents of the United States. **Criteria:** Selection shall be based on (1) describe a personal achievement story, (2) determine and explain instances of struggle or adversity, (3) and display how they overcame adversity to reach their goals.

Funds Avail.: $25,000 (One (1) First Place Award of $15,000; One (1) Second Place Awards of $5,000; Two (2) Third Place Awards of $2,500 each). **Duration:** Annual. **Number Awarded:** 4. **To Apply:** Applicants must be completed and submitted online; personal information including Parent/Guardian's full name and permanent address, city, state, zip; phone number, and email address; applicant's full name and permanent address, city, state, ZIP code; phone number; e-mail address; name of applicant's high school; high school graduation year; high school address (including city, state, and zip); description of up to 1,000 words of the personal achievement. **Deadline:** July 26. **Contact:** Student Research Foundation, PO Box 311, Midtown Station, New York, NY, 10018.

4310 ■ Educational Testing Service (ETS)
660 Rosedale Rd.
Princeton, NJ 08541
Ph: (609)921-9000
E-mail: etsinfo@ets.org
URL: www.ets.org
Social Media: www.linkedin.com/company/educational
  -testing-service-ets
twitter.com/etsinsights

4311 ■ ETS Postdoctoral Fellowships *(Postdoctorate/ Fellowship)*

Purpose: To provide research opportunities to individuals who have recently earned their doctoral degrees. **Focus:** Linguistics; Psychology; Speech and language pathology/ Audiology; Statistics; Teaching. **Qualif.:** Applicants must be

Awards are arranged alphabetically below their administering organizations

doctorate in a relevant discipline within the past three years and have evidence of prior research. **Criteria:** Selection will be based on the applicants scholarship and the technical strength of the proposed research topic.

Funds Avail.: No specific amount. **Duration:** Annual. **To Apply:** Applicants must send a one-page abstract about the research and a letter of intent. If the submitted abstract is approved, applicants must submit a detailed proposal (approximately 5 double-spaced pages) describing the research that will be carried out at ETS and how it relates to current ETS research; a current curriculum vita; official graduate academic transcripts; and names and e-mail addresses of three individuals familiar with the applicant's work and willing to complete a recommendation form. Submit all application materials via e-mail (provided at the contact) as PDF attachments, except for the transcripts which must be sent via regular mail. **Deadline:** January 1 (Preliminary application materials) March 1 (Final application materials). **Contact:** Email: internfellowships@ets.org; Phone: 609-734-5543.

4312 ■ Harold Gulliksen Psychometric Research Fellowship *(Doctorate, Graduate/Fellowship)*

Purpose: To increase the number of well-trained scientists in educational assessment, psychometrics and statistics. **Focus:** Linguistics; Psychology; Speech and language pathology/Audiology; Statistics; Teaching. **Qualif.:** Applicants must be enrolled in a doctoral program; have completed all the coursework toward the PhD; be at the dissertation stage of the program (dissertation topics in the areas of psychometrics, statistics, educational or psychological measurement or quantitative methods will be given priority). **Criteria:** Selection will be based on the strength of the applicant's academic credentials and the suitability and technical strength of the proposed research project.

Funds Avail.: No specific amount. **Duration:** Annual. **To Apply:** Applicants must submit a letter of interest (approximately five double-spaced pages) describing the research that would be undertaken during the award year and how the research fits with ETS research efforts; a nomination letter (either as an e-mail or as an e-mail with a PDF attachment) from an academic advisor; and a current curriculum vitae. For final application, applicants must submit a detailed project description (approximately 15 double-spaced pages) of the research the applicant will carry out at the host university, including the purpose, goals and methods of the research; official graduate academic transcripts; and evidence of scholarship (presentations, manuscripts, etc.). Submit all application materials via e-mail (provided at the contact) as PDF attachments. **Deadline:** December 29 (preliminary application); February 16 (final application). **Contact:** Email: internfellowships@ets.org.

4313 ■ Sylvia Taylor Johnson Minority Fellowships in Educational Measurement *(Doctorate/Fellowship)*

Purpose: To encourage original and significant research for early-career scholars. **Focus:** Linguistics; Psychology; Speech and language pathology/Audiology; Statistics; Teaching. **Qualif.:** Applicants must be U.S citizens.

Funds Avail.: No specific amount. **Duration:** Annual. **Contact:** Caldwell Hall, Cornell University, Ithaca, NY, 14853-2602; Phone: 607-255-5820; Fax: 607-255-1816.

4314 ■ EducationDynamics L.L.C.
111 River St., 10th Fl.
Hoboken, NJ 07030

Ph: (201)377-3000
Free: 888-567-2008
URL: www.educationdynamics.com
Social Media: www.facebook.com/EducationDynamics
www.linkedin.com/company/educationdynamics
twitter.com/EdDynamics

4315 ■ Cyber Security Scholarship *(College, University, Undergraduate, Vocational/Occupational/ Scholarship)*

Purpose: To help students fund their educations. **Focus:** Computer and information sciences; Security. **Qualif.:** Applicant must be a U.S. resident enrolled or enrolling in college in the field of cyber security. **Criteria:** Best essay submitted will be awarded scholarship.

Funds Avail.: $1,000. **Number Awarded:** 1. **To Apply:** Applicant must submit 250 word essay and fill out application at website: cyber-security.degree/1k-scholarship. **Deadline:** July 15. **Contact:** E-mail: scholarships@ educationdynamics.com.

4316 ■ GradSchools.com Minority Graduate Nursing Scholarship *(Graduate/Scholarship)*

Purpose: To help minority students pursuing a graduate degree in nursing. **Focus:** Nursing. **Qualif.:** Applicant must be a minority (African American, Hispanic, Native American, Pacific Islander); must be enrolled in a full-time graduate nursing program; must be a legal resident of the United States and at least 18 years old.

Funds Avail.: $2,000. **Number Awarded:** 1. **To Apply:** Applicant must submit a 250-word essay. Applications available online at www.gradschools.com/programs/nursing/ minority-nursing-scholarships. **Deadline:** July 15. **Contact:** Email: jholland@educationdynamics.com.

4317 ■ Edvisors Network Inc.
10000 W Charleston Blvd., Ste. 200
Las Vegas, NV 89135
URL: www.edvisors.com

4318 ■ Federal Student Loans for Graduate Students *(Graduate/Loan)*

Purpose: To address the needs of graduate students enrolled in a college or university. **Focus:** General studies/ Field of study not specified. **Qualif.:** Applicants must be attending graduate school or professional school. **Criteria:** Selection will be based on submitted application.

Funds Avail.: Varies. **To Apply:** Applicants must file the free application for Federal Student Aid; once the application is complete, the school's financial aid office will send an award letter, detailing the amount of aid available.

4319 ■ The Edwards Law Firm
8282 S Memorial Dr., Ste. 304
Tulsa, OK 74133
Ph: (918)221-0516
Free: 800-304-9246
E-mail: medwards@edwardslawok.com
URL: www.edwardslawok.com

4320 ■ The Edwards Annual College Scholarships *(Undergraduate/Scholarship)*

Purpose: To provide scholarships to deserving students towards their tuition costs. **Focus:** General studies/Field of

Awards are arranged alphabetically below their administering organizations

study not specified. **Qualif.:** Applicants must be currently enrolled in an Oklahoma college or university, and must have a minimum GPA of 2.5. **Criteria:** Selection will be based on the committee's criteria.

Funds Avail.: $1,500. **Duration:** Annual. **To Apply:** Applicants must visit the website to complete the application process and must provide the official copy of high school transcript and a minimum 500-word essay using the specified prompt; prepare an essay in a.PDF format, with the file name: lastname_firstname_blf.pdf. **Deadline:** December 1.

4321 ■ EGIA Foundation
3800 Watt Ave., Ste. 105
Sacramento, CA 95821
Ph: (507)931-1682
Free: 866-562-9060
URL: egiafoundation.org

4322 ■ EGIA Foundation Scholarship Program
(Vocational/Occupational, Two Year College/ Scholarship)

Purpose: To assist students passionately committed to a career in the HVACR industry. **Focus:** Heating, air conditioning, and refrigeration. **Qualif.:** Applicants must be committed to a career in the HVACR industry; planning to enroll or enrolled at a two-year vocational school, technical school, or approved technical institute; have a minimum GPA of 2.0; be U.S. citizens, nationals, or permanent residents. **Criteria:** Selection is based on eligibility requirements, academic merit, financial need, and interest of pursuing a career in residential HVAC or home performance contracting.

Funds Avail.: $2,500 each. **Duration:** Annual. **Number Awarded:** Up to 20. **To Apply:** Application form and details are available at: egiafoundation.org/what-we-do/scholarship. **Deadline:** March 31.

4323 ■ The Eichholz Law Firm
530 Stephenson Ave., No. 500
Savannah, GA 31405
Free: 855-551-1019
E-mail: info@thejusticelawyer.com
URL: www.thejusticelawyer.com
Social Media: www.facebook.com/TheEichholzLawFirm
www.instagram.com/theeichholzlawfirm
www.linkedin.com/company/the-eichholz-law-firm
twitter.com/Eichholz_Law
www.youtube.com/user/TheEichholzLawFirm

4324 ■ Annual Eichholz Scholarship *(Graduate/ Scholarship)*

Purpose: To further students' education in Law. **Focus:** Law. **Qualif.:** Applicants must be enrolled or accepted in an accredited community college or university in Georgia; must have a minimum GPA of3.25 unweighted. **Criteria:** Selection will be based on committee's criteria.

Funds Avail.: $1,500. **Duration:** Annual. **Number Awarded:** 1. **To Apply:** Applicants must include an original essay of at least 500 words on the provided topic; application forms must be filled out completely. **Deadline:** June 15.

4325 ■ Eisbrouch Marsh L.L.C.
50 Main St.
Hackensack, NJ 07601

Ph: (201)342-5545
E-mail: david@emlawoffices.com
URL: emlawoffices.com
Social Media: www.facebook.com/EisbrouchMarshLLC
twitter.com/deisbrouch
youtube.com/channel/UCnGyQFvZb8Z1QtlbPRKtbag

4326 ■ Eisbrouch & Marsh Scholarship Awards
(Undergraduate, Graduate/Scholarship)

Purpose: To assist single mothers who are equally committed to completing their degree and raising their families. **Focus:** General studies/Field of study not specified. **Qualif.:** Applicants must be accepted/enrolled in a junior college with plans to attend a 4-year college or university program, or accepted/enrolled in a 4-year college or university program, or accepted/enrolled in a graduate program, or enrolled in high school with plans to attend a 4-year college or university program; must be single mothers; and must have maintained a minimum 3.0 GPA at their current educational institution according to their most recent transcript. **Criteria:** Selection will be based on the committee's criteria.

Funds Avail.: $500. **To Apply:** Applicants are required to write about their dual roles as both mothers and students. Essays should be a minimum of 1,000 words and should address the following: "describe some of the challenges motherhood has imposed on your academic goals", "how your role as a mother prepared you for the challenges you face as a student?" and "what will earning your degree mean to you?". The following additional requirements are necessary for all applicants: application attachments must be in word or PDF formats only (kindly complete and sign the attached PDF application form and submit with other required materials); applications must be sent via email (only emailed applications will be considered); applicants must include their most current contact information including full name, mailing address, email address and phone number; proof of attendance or acceptance at one of the learning institutions; copy of the applicants' official transcript for their most recently completed semester of school that reflects the minimum 3.0 GPA requirement.

4327 ■ El Dorado County Mineral and Gem Society
PO Box 950
Placerville, CA 95667
Ph: (530)676-2472
E-mail: info@eldoradomineralandgem.org
URL: www.eldoradomineralandgem.org

4328 ■ El Dorado County Mineral and Gem Society Scholarship *(Graduate/Scholarship)*

Purpose: To provide support to students who are pursuing a degree and/or career in earth sciences, lapidary arts and other related fields at an accredited college or university. **Focus:** Earth sciences. **Qualif.:** Applicants must be a graduate of an El Dorado County high school, who may now be attending a college or graduate school outside of the County. **Criteria:** Selection is based on the application.

Funds Avail.: $500 - $1,000. **Duration:** Annual. **Number Awarded:** 1. **To Apply:** Applicants must submit a completed application form along with a current transcript; a personal essay of 300-500 words; and two letters of reference, one of which is from a faculty member and the other from someone who is not a member of the applicant's fam-

Awards are arranged alphabetically below their administering organizations

ily. **Contact:** Scholarship Committee, El Dorado County Mineral and Gem Society, PO Box 950, Placerville, CA, 95667; Phone: 530-676-2472.

4329 ■ El Pomar Foundation

10 Lake Cir.
Colorado Springs, CO 80906
Ph: (719)633-7733
Fax: (719)577-5702
Free: 800-554-7711
E-mail: grants@elpomar.org
URL: www.elpomar.org
Social Media: www.facebook.com/elpomarfoundation
www.instagram.com/el_pomar

4330 ■ El Pomar Fellowship *(Graduate/Fellowship)*

Purpose: To provide students the passion for leadership, dedication to self-improvement and a desire to invest in the communities of Colorado. **Focus:** General studies/Field of study not specified. **Criteria:** Selection is based on submitted application materials.

Funds Avail.: No specific amount. **Duration:** Annual. **Number Awarded:** Varies. **To Apply:** Applicants must submit letter of intent (not to exceed two pages): describe your interest in the fellowship and in serving the communities of Colorado. In addition, please cite a specific example from your resume highlighting a lesson you have learned about leadership; resume; college transcripts; two recommendations from supervisors, professors, or community leaders who can speak to your leadership skills, work ethic, and ability to work as a member of a team; 150 words or fewer each: 1. Please describe the candidate's leadership skills, capabilities, and experience; 2. Please comment on the candidate's receptiveness to critical feedback and ability to be coached; 3. Please describe an area for improvement for the candidate. **Contact:** Email: recruiting@elpomar.org.

4331 ■ eLearners.com

5 Marine View Plz.
Hoboken, NJ 07030
Ph: (201)377-3000
URL: www.elearners.com
Social Media: www.facebook.com/eLearners
twitter.com/eLearners

4332 ■ eLearners Online College Scholarship *(Undergraduate/Scholarship)*

Purpose: To ease the financial burden of attending an online educational program. **Focus:** General studies/Field of study not specified. **Qualif.:** Applicants must be enrolled or enrolling in an online college and/or an online for-credit degree program at an accredited post-secondary institution of higher learning; be a legal U.S. resident of the 50 United States and the District of Columbia; be 18 years of age or older at the time of application. **Criteria:** Application completeness, timeliness, eligibility criteria, originality, and creativity.

Funds Avail.: $1,000. **To Apply:** Submit application and short essay no more than 250 words answering the question, "How has choosing an online college enabled you to finish your education?". **Deadline:** February 28.

4333 ■ The eLearners Scholarship for Military Personnel, Veterans, and Spouses *(College, Vocational/Occupational/Scholarship)*

Purpose: To ease the financial burden of attending an online educational program for active military, veterans, and spouses. **Focus:** General studies/Field of study not specified. **Qualif.:** Applicants must be military active duty, honorably discharged, veteran, or a spouse from any branch of the military; be currently enrolled or expect to enroll in an accredited post-secondary institution of higher learning (college, university, or trade school); be legal residents of the 50 United States and the District of Columbia; and be 18 years of age or older at the time of application.

Funds Avail.: $1,000. **To Apply:** Complete online application and submit 250-word essay answering a given prompt. **Deadline:** February 28.

4334 ■ eLearning.net

12345 Lakecity Way, Ste 150
Seattle, WA 98125
Free: 866-771-4449
E-mail: help@elearning.net
URL: elearning.net
Social Media: www.facebook.com/elearningnetwork
www.linkedin.com/company/the-elearning-network
twitter.com/elearningnetwrk

4335 ■ Instructional Design & Learning Technologies Scholarships *(Undergraduate, Graduate/Scholarship)*

Purpose: To help learning and development professionals pursue their own continuing education and apply the latest in instructional design theory and educational technologies to their work to build better training programs. **Focus:** General studies/Field of study not specified. **Qualif.:** Applicants must possess a minimum of 5 years of post-high school work experience; must have applied for and been accepted to an eligible program of study. **Criteria:** Essays will be reviewed for items including: essay completeness, detail, and thoughtfulness; alignment of the program of study to the applicants' stated goals; grammatical correctness.

Funds Avail.: $750-$1,500. **Duration:** Annual. **Number Awarded:** 4. **To Apply:** Applicant must submit a typewritten (PDF document) personal essay that includes, at a minimum: first and last name, name of current employer or most recent employer if currently between jobs, describe experiences in developing online training programs either individually or as part of a team, and a link to personal LinkedIn profile (if applicant has one) or other online professional biography; and answer the following questions: Why are you pursuing an education in instructional design, eLearning development, learning technologies, or related field?; How do you intend to apply what you learn to the work you will do in the future?; What educational institution did you select and how did you go about selecting that institution as the one best suited to your learning needs?; What program of study did you select and how did you go about selecting that program as the one best suited to your learning needs; List any other information you feel will help the scholarship judges evaluate your application. Applicants must provide two scholarship recommendation letters from professional associates. Letters should include: first and last name of referral source; relationship of referral source to applicants (e.g. direct supervisor, co-worker, former manager, etc.); a description of why the referral source believes the applicant would benefit from the chosen program of study. **Deadline:** August 12. **Contact:** learningscholarships@gmail.com.

Awards are arranged alphabetically below their administering organizations

4336 ■ Electro-Federation Canada (EFC)

180 Attwell Dr., Ste. 300
Toronto, ON, Canada M9W 6A9
Ph: (905)602-8877
Fax: (416)679-9234
Free: 866-602-8877
URL: www.electrofed.com
Social Media: www.linkedin.com/company/electro
 -federation-canada/
twitter.com/EFC_Tweets

4337 ■ Affiliated Distributors Electrical Industry Scholarship Awards *(Undergraduate/Scholarship)*

Purpose: To help students across Canada reach their education and career objectives. **Focus:** Engineering, Electrical. **Qualif.:** Applicants must be students in any post-secondary institution across Canada who have successfully completed at least the first year of any degree, diploma or electrical apprenticeship program. **Criteria:** Priority will be given to students who have an electrical or electronics concentration; successful students will have above-average marks in their current program and will have shown leadership in their school and community.

Funds Avail.: 3,500 Canadian Dollars. **Duration:** Annual. **To Apply:** Applicants may visit the website for them to create an account to apply for the scholarship, as well as for the other application materials required. **Deadline:** May 31. **Remarks:** The scholarship is co-sponsored by the Affiliated Distributors.

4338 ■ Burndy Canada Inc. Academic Achievement Awards *(Undergraduate/Scholarship)*

Purpose: To help students across Canada reach their education and career objectives. **Focus:** Engineering, Electrical. **Qualif.:** Applicants must be college or university students who have completed at least one year of study in any area related to the electrical industry; and must either be current employees of Burndy Canada Inc. or related to someone currently employed with the Company or employed or related to a current employee of any electrical distributor or manufacturer in the Canadian Electrical Industry. **Criteria:** Selection will be based on the committee's criteria.

Funds Avail.: 3,500 Canadian Dollars. **Duration:** Annual. **To Apply:** Applicants may visit the website to create an account to apply for the scholarship and for other application requirements. **Deadline:** May 31. **Remarks:** The scholarship is co-sponsored by Burndy Canada, Inc.

4339 ■ Convectair Sustainable Development Scholarship Awards *(Undergraduate/Scholarship)*

Purpose: To help students across Canada reach their education and career objectives. **Focus:** Electronics; Engineering, Electrical; Engineering, Mechanical; Environmental science. **Qualif.:** Applicants must be college or university students across Canada in sustainable development, engineering (electrical and mechanical), electronics and environmental studies; and must have completed at least one year of academic studies with an above-average mark; also open to employees or relatives of full-time employees of any Electro-Federation Canada members. **Criteria:** Selection will be based on the applicants' eligibility and other criteria of the committee.

Funds Avail.: 3,500 Canadian Dollars. **Duration:** Annual. **To Apply:** Applicants may visit the website to create an ac-count to apply for the scholarship and for the other application requirements. **Deadline:** May 31. **Remarks:** The scholarship is co-sponsored by the Convectair.

4340 ■ Bob Dyer/OEL Apprenticeship Scholarships *(Undergraduate/Scholarship)*

Purpose: To help students across Canada reach their education and career objectives. **Focus:** Electronics; Engineering, Electrical. **Qualif.:** Applicants must be apprentices who have, within the last 12 months, completed any of the levels of schooling at an approved Ontario College Electrical Apprenticeship program; must have at least a 75% average; and must be OEL member company employees or immediate relatives of an OEL member company employee. **Criteria:** Selection will be based on the applicants' eligibility and other criteria of the committee.

Funds Avail.: 500 Canadian Dollars each. **Duration:** Annual. **To Apply:** Applicants may visit the website for them to create an account to apply for the scholarship, as well as for the other application materials required. **Deadline:** May 31. **Remarks:** The scholarship is co-sponsored by the Ontario Electrical League.

4341 ■ Eaton Awards of Academic Achievement *(Undergraduate/Scholarship)*

Purpose: To help students across Canada reach their education and career objectives. **Focus:** Electronics; Engineering, Electrical. **Qualif.:** Applicants must be university or college students who have completed at least one year of academic studies with a minimum 80% average (2.5 GPA) whose parent/legal guardian is a full-time employee of an Electro-Federation Canada member in good standing. **Criteria:** Selection will be based on the applicants' eligibility and other criteria of the committee.

Funds Avail.: 3,500 Canadian Dollars each. **Duration:** Annual. **To Apply:** Applicants may visit the website for them to create an account to apply for the scholarship, as well as for the other application materials required. **Deadline:** May 31. **Remarks:** The scholarship is co-sponsored by Eaton.

4342 ■ EFC Atlantic Region Scholarships *(Undergraduate/Scholarship)*

Purpose: To help students across Canada reach their education and career objectives. **Focus:** Electronics; Engineering, Electrical. **Qualif.:** Applicants must be students enrolled full-time in a two-year electrical/electronics program at either Nova Scotia Community College, New Brunswick Community College or PEI Holland College and successfully completed their first year of study with a minimum 75% average. **Criteria:** Selection will be based on the applicants' eligibility and other criteria of the committee.

Funds Avail.: $1,000 Each. **Number Awarded:** 5. **To Apply:** Applicants may visit the website for them to create an account to apply for the scholarship, as well as for the other application materials required. **Deadline:** May 31. **Remarks:** The scholarship is co-sponsored by the EFC Atlantic Region.

4343 ■ EFC University and College Scholarships *(Undergraduate/Scholarship)*

Purpose: To help students across Canada reach their education and career objectives. **Focus:** Electronics; Engineering, Electrical. **Qualif.:** Applicants must be students who have completed at least their first year of study in electrical engineering, electrical technology, or

Awards are arranged alphabetically below their administering organizations

business administration, and maintained a minimum cumulative average of 75%. **Criteria:** Selection will be based on the applicants' eligibility and other criteria of the committee.

Funds Avail.: 1,000 Canadian Dollars each. **Duration:** Annual. **To Apply:** Applicants may visit the website for them to create an account to apply for the scholarship, as well as for the other application materials required. **Deadline:** May 31.

4344 ■ Franklin Empire Scholarship Awards
(Undergraduate/Scholarship)

Purpose: To help students across Canada reach their education and career objectives. **Focus:** Engineering, Electrical. **Qualif.:** Applicants must be university, college, or trade school students, in Quebec or Ontario; must have completed two years of study in the field of electrical apprenticeship, electrical technician, engineering/technology (electrical, mechanical, industrial), or a discipline related to the electrical industry; and must have maintained an average of 80%. **Criteria:** Selection will be based on the applicants' eligibility and other criteria of the committee.

Funds Avail.: 3,500 Canadian Dollars. **Duration:** Annual. **To Apply:** Applicants may visit the website to create an account to apply for the scholarship and for the other application requirements. **Deadline:** May 31. **Remarks:** The scholarship is co-sponsored by the Franklin Empire.

4345 ■ G.E. Lighting Canada Community Leadership Awards *(Undergraduate/Award)*

Purpose: To help students across Canada reach their education and career objectives. **Focus:** Business; Engineering, Electrical. **Qualif.:** Applicants must be undergraduate university students in either an Engineering or Business program who have completed at least their first year of study with a minimum cumulative average of 80% and have also established a commitment to community service through volunteerism. **Criteria:** Selection will be based on the applicants' eligibility and other criteria of the committee.

Funds Avail.: 3,500 Canadian Dollars. **Duration:** Annual. **To Apply:** Applicants may visit the website for them to create an account to apply for the scholarship, as well as for the other application materials required. **Deadline:** May 31. **Remarks:** The scholarship is co-sponsored by the G.E. Lighting Canada.

4346 ■ Gerrie Electric Memorial Scholarship Awards *(Undergraduate/Scholarship)*

Purpose: To help students across Canada reach their education and career objectives. **Focus:** Engineering, Electrical. **Qualif.:** Applicants must be Canadian citizens; must be students entering second year at Ontario college or university in the field of electrical apprenticeship, electrical engineering technology, or electrical technician; must have demonstrated community service through volunteerism; and must have achieved a cumulative average of 75%. **Criteria:** Preference will be given to relatives of Gerrie Electric, its customers and its vendor partners.

Funds Avail.: 3,500 Canadian Dollars. **Duration:** Annual. **To Apply:** Applicants may visit the website to create an account to apply for the scholarship and for the other application requirements. **Deadline:** May 31. **Remarks:** The scholarship is co-sponsored by the Gerrie Electric.

4347 ■ Graybar Canada Award of Excellence Scholarships *(Undergraduate/Scholarship)*

Purpose: To help students across Canada reach their education and career objectives. **Focus:** Arts; Business;

Electronics; Engineering, Electrical; Information science and technology. **Qualif.:** Applicants must be students who have completed their first year of post-secondary education in either a business program, general arts, IT or a discipline related to the electrical industry; and must have maintained a minimum cumulative average of at least 80%. **Criteria:** Selection will be based on the applicants' eligibility and other criteria of the committee.

Funds Avail.: 3,500 Canadian Dollars. **Duration:** Annual. **To Apply:** Applicants may visit the website for them to create an account to apply for the scholarship, as well as for the other application materials required. **Deadline:** May 31. **Remarks:** The scholarship is co-sponsored by the Graybar Canada.

4348 ■ Hammond Power Solutions Inc. Outstanding Electrical Scholar Awards (HPS) *(Undergraduate/Award)*

Purpose: To help students across Canada reach their education and career objectives. **Focus:** Electronics; Engineering, Electrical. **Qualif.:** Applicants must be Ontario or Quebec university/college students currently enrolled in an approved post-secondary electrical program; must have completed at least their second year of study in Electrical Engineering, Electrical Technology, Electrical Technician, Electrical Technologist, Industrial Electrician, or working towards completing an electrical apprenticeship; and must have a minimum cumulative average of 75%. **Criteria:** Selection will be based on the applicants' eligibility; preference will be given to students who commit to their industry through active membership with OACETT and/or PEO, or to those who demonstrate active leadership in their school or community.

Funds Avail.: 3,500 Canadian Dollars. **Duration:** Annual. **To Apply:** Applicants may visit the website to create an account to apply for the scholarship and for the other application requirements. **Deadline:** May 31. **Remarks:** The scholarship is co-sponsored by the Hammond Power Solutions Inc.

4349 ■ E.B. Horsman & Son Scholarships *(Undergraduate/Scholarship)*

Purpose: To help students across Canada reach their education and career objectives. **Focus:** Engineering, Electrical. **Qualif.:** Applicants must be students attending any post-secondary institution in a region where EBH is located; must have completed at least their first year of study in electrical apprenticeship, electrical technician, engineering/technology electrical, or a discipline related to the electrical industry. **Criteria:** Preference will be given to relatives of EBH, its customers and its supplier partners.

Funds Avail.: $1,750; $1,250; $750. **Duration:** Annual. **To Apply:** Applicants may visit the website to create an account to apply for the scholarship and for the other application requirements. **Deadline:** May 31. **Remarks:** The scholarship is co-sponsored by the E.B. Horsman & Son.

4350 ■ Hubbell Canada LP "Electrical Industry Leadership" Scholarship Awards *(Undergraduate/Scholarship)*

Purpose: To support students who have demonstrated interests in a career path that will drive innovation and leadership in the electrical industry in Canada. **Focus:** Electronics; Engineering, Electrical. **Qualif.:** Applicants must be students enrolled in a Canadian university who have completed at least their first year of study in Busi-

Awards are arranged alphabetically below their administering organizations

ness, Engineering or Science with a minimum cumulative average of 80%. **Criteria:** Selection will be based on the applicants' eligibility and other criteria of the committee.

Funds Avail.: 3,500 Canadian Dollars. **Duration:** Annual. **To Apply:** Applicants may visit the website for them to create an account to apply for the scholarship, as well as for the other application materials required. **Deadline:** May 31. **Remarks:** The scholarship is co-sponsored by the Hubbell, Inc.

4351 ■ Kerrwil's J.W. Kerr Continuing Education Scholarship Awards *(Undergraduate/Scholarship)*

Purpose: To help students across Canada reach their education and career objectives. **Focus:** Business; Electronics; Engineering, Electrical; Marketing and distribution. **Qualif.:** Applicants must be university or college graduates in a Canadian school; must have completed at least their second year in an engineering or business program with a minimum cumulative average of 75% and with a desire to drive forward in a marketing or product management in the electrical industry; and must also be either current employees or relatives of someone currently employed within the Canadian Electrical industry, including electrical wholesale, electrical equipment manufacturing representatives or electrical manufacturing. **Criteria:** Selection will be based on the applicants' eligibility and other criteria of the committee.

Funds Avail.: 3,500 Canadian Dollars. **Duration:** Annual. **To Apply:** Applicants may visit the website for them to create an account to apply for the scholarship, as well as for the other application materials required. **Deadline:** May 31. **Remarks:** The scholarship is co-sponsored by the Kerrwil.

4352 ■ Osram Sylvania Scholastic Achievement Awards *(Undergraduate/Scholarship)*

Purpose: To help students across Canada reach their education and career objectives. **Focus:** Business administration; Engineering, Electrical; Engineering, Mechanical. **Qualif.:** Applicants must be university students who have completed at least the second year of study with a minimum cumulative average of 85%; eligible fields of study include electrical and mechanical engineering and business administration. **Criteria:** Selection will be based on the applicants' eligibility and other criteria of the committee.

Funds Avail.: 3,500 Canadian Dollars. **Duration:** Annual. **To Apply:** Applicants may visit the website for them to create an account to apply for the scholarship, as well as for the other application materials required. **Deadline:** May 31. **Remarks:** The scholarship is co-sponsored by the Osram Sylvania.

4353 ■ Philips Lighting Continuing Education Awards *(Undergraduate/Scholarship)*

Purpose: To help students across Canada reach their education and career objectives. **Focus:** Business administration; Engineering, Electrical; Engineering, Mechanical. **Qualif.:** Applicants must be either a current employee or relative of someone currently employed within the Canadian Electrical Industry including electrical distributors, electrical engineers, lighting specifiers and electrical contractors. **Criteria:** Selection will be based on the applicants' eligibility and other criteria of the committee.

Funds Avail.: 3,500 Canadian Dollars. **Duration:** Annual. **To Apply:** Applicants may visit the website for them to create an account to apply for the scholarship, as well as for the other application materials required. **Deadline:** May 31.

Remarks: The scholarship is co-sponsored by the Philips Lighting Canada.

4354 ■ RAB Design Lighting Award of Excellence *(Undergraduate/Scholarship)*

Purpose: To help students across Canada reach their education and career objectives. **Focus:** Electronics; Engineering, Electrical; Engineering, Mechanical. **Qualif.:** Applicants must be Canadian university or college students who have completed at least their first year of study in an Electrical, Electronics or Mechanical Engineering program; must demonstrate a minimum overall average of at least 75%. **Criteria:** Selection will be based on the applicants' eligibility and other criteria of the committee.

Funds Avail.: 3,500 Canadian Dollars. **Duration:** Annual. **To Apply:** Applicants may visit the website for them to create an account to apply for the scholarship, as well as for the other application materials required. **Deadline:** May 31. **Remarks:** The scholarship is co-sponsored by the RAB Design Lighting Inc.

4355 ■ Schneider Electric Student Merit Awards *(Undergraduate/Scholarship)*

Purpose: To help students across Canada reach their education and career objectives. **Focus:** Business administration; Engineering, Electrical. **Qualif.:** Applicants must be university, college or apprenticeship students who have completed at least their first year of study in Engineering, Business Administration or an Electrical Apprenticeship program; and maintained a minimum cumulative average of 85%. **Criteria:** Selection will be based on the applicants' eligibility and other criteria of the committee.

Funds Avail.: 5,000 Canadian Dollars. **Duration:** Annual. **To Apply:** Applicants may visit the website to create an account to apply for the scholarship, as well as for the other application materials required. **Deadline:** May 31. **Remarks:** The scholarship is co-sponsored by the Schneider Electric.

4356 ■ Siemens Canada Academic Awards *(Undergraduate/Scholarship)*

Purpose: To help students across Canada reach their education and career objectives. **Focus:** Engineering, Electrical; Engineering, Mechanical. **Qualif.:** Applicants must be university or college students who have completed at least their second year of study in an electrical, mechanical engineering/technology program with a minimum 80% average. **Criteria:** Selection will be based on the applicants' eligibility and other criteria of the committee.

Funds Avail.: 3,500 Canadian Dollars each. **Duration:** Annual. **To Apply:** Applicants may visit the website for them to create an account to apply for the scholarship, as well as for the other application materials required. **Deadline:** May 31. **Remarks:** The scholarship is co-sponsored by the Siemens Canada.

4357 ■ Sonepar Canada Scholarship Awards *(Undergraduate/Scholarship)*

Purpose: To help students across Canada reach their education and career objectives. **Focus:** Electronics; Engineering, Electrical. **Qualif.:** Applicants must be university or college students in a Canadian school who have completed at least their second year in an Engineering or Business program with a minimum cumulative average of 80%. **Criteria:** Selection will be based on the applicants' eligibility and other criteria of the committee.

Awards are arranged alphabetically below their administering organizations

Funds Avail.: 3,500 Canadian Dollars. **To Apply:** Applicants may visit the website for them to create an account to apply for the scholarship, as well as for the other application materials required. **Remarks:** The scholarship is co-sponsored by the Sonepar Canada.

4358 ■ The Standard Recognition of Excellence Awards (Undergraduate/Scholarship)

Purpose: To assist Canadian university or college students who demonstrate academic excellence. **Focus:** Electronics; Engineering, Electrical. **Qualif.:** Applicants must be Canadian university or college students who have completed two years of study in business administration/commerce and must have maintained a minimum cumulative average of 80%. **Criteria:** Selection will be based on the applicants' eligibility and other criteria of the committee.

Funds Avail.: 3,500 Canadian Dollars. **Duration:** Annual. **To Apply:** Applicants may visit the website for them to create an account to apply for the scholarship, as well as for the other application materials required. **Deadline:** May 31. **Remarks:** The scholarship is co-sponsored by the Standard Products, Inc.

4359 ■ Stelpro Scholarship 360: Energizing Potential (Undergraduate/Scholarship)

Purpose: To support native Quebec students in their continuing education. **Focus:** Electronics; Engineering, Electrical. **Qualif.:** Applicants must be native Quebec residents, studying within the province, whose academic and/or professional path have led them to pursue a career in the electrical industry; must be enrolled in either a vocational training program, college or university degree program. **Criteria:** Selection will be based on the applicants' eligibility and other criteria of the committee.

Funds Avail.: 3,500 Canadian Dollars. **Duration:** Annual. **To Apply:** Applicants may visit the website to create an account to apply for the scholarship, as well as for the other application materials required. **Deadline:** May 31. **Remarks:** The scholarship is co-sponsored by the Stelpro.

4360 ■ RABC William Taylor Scholarships (Undergraduate/Scholarship)

Purpose: To help students across Canada reach their education and career objectives. **Focus:** Telecommunications systems. **Qualif.:** Applicants must be engineering students who have completed at least their second year in an accredited Canadian University and plan on pursuing a career in telecommunications. **Criteria:** Selection will be based on the applicants' eligibility and other criteria of the committee.

Funds Avail.: 3,500 Canadian Dollars. **Duration:** Annual. **To Apply:** Applicants may visit the website to create an account to apply for the scholarship, as well as for the other application materials required. **Deadline:** May 31. **Remarks:** The scholarship is co-sponsored by the Radio Advisory Board of Canada.

4361 ■ The WESCO Student Achievement Award (Undergraduate/Scholarship)

Purpose: To help students across Canada reach their education and career objectives. **Focus:** Business administration; Electronics; Engineering, Electrical. **Qualif.:** Applicants must be university or college students who have completed at least their first year of study in electrical engineering, electrical technology, or business administration, and maintained a minimum cumulative average of

80%. **Criteria:** Selection will be based on the applicants' eligibility and other criteria of the committee.

Funds Avail.: 3,500 Canadian Dollars. **Duration:** Annual. **To Apply:** Applicants may visit the website for them to create an account to apply for the scholarship, as well as for the other application materials required. **Deadline:** May 31. **Remarks:** The scholarship is co-sponsored by the WESCO Distribution Canada.

4362 ■ Electrochemical Society (ECS)

Bldg. D
65 S Main St.
Pennington, NJ 08534-2839
Ph: (609)737-1902
Fax: (609)737-2743
E-mail: ecs@electrochem.org
URL: www.electrochem.org
Social Media: www.facebook.com/
  TheElectrochemicalSociety
www.linkedin.com/company/ecs---the-electrochemical
  -society/
twitter.com/ECSorg
www.youtube.com/user/ECS1902

4363 ■ Oronzio de Nora Industrial Electrochemistry Fellowships (Postdoctorate/Fellowship)

Purpose: To support students who are conducting research about industrial electrochemistry. **Focus:** Electrochemistry. **Qualif.:** Applicant must be a postdoctoral scientist or engineer continuing research in industrial electrochemistry. **Criteria:** Selection is based on the proposed research topics in the areas of electrochemistry.

Funds Avail.: $25,000. **Duration:** Annual. **To Apply:** Applicants must submit an essay (1, 000 words or less) addressing personal interests/career goals related to the fellowship position, and talents brought to the fellowship, along with a curriculum vitae; three letters of recommendation (should include letter of support from the group receiving the fellow); and transcripts. **Remarks:** Established in 2003. **Contact:** ECS; E-mail: awards@electrochem.org.

4364 ■ Elements Behavioral Health

103 Powell Court Ste 100
Brentwood, TN 37027
Free: 844-875-5609
URL: www.elementsbehavioralhealth.com
Social Media: www.facebook.com/
  PromisesBehavioralHealth
www.linkedin.com/company/promises-behavioral-health
twitter.com/PromisesBHealth
www.youtube.com/user/elementsbhealth

4365 ■ Elements Behavioral Health Scholarship (College, University, Undergraduate/Scholarship)

Purpose: To further the message of addiction recovery. **Focus:** General studies/Field of study not specified. **Qualif.:** Applicant must be currently enrolled or accepted for enrollment at a college or university in the United States. **Criteria:** Essays will be judged based on relevance to topic, originality, creativity, and/or emotional impact.

Funds Avail.: $10,000 total. **Number Awarded:** 3. **To Apply:** Applicant must submit an essay. Details are available

Awards are arranged alphabetically below their administering organizations

online at www.elementsbehavioralhealth.com/scholarship. **Deadline:** December 31.

4366 ■ Elevate Pest Control
60 W 1000 N
Logan, UT 84321
Ph: (435)753-3825
URL: elevatepestcontrol.com

4367 ■ Utah ROLF Scholarship *(Community College/ Award)*

Purpose: To give back to the community by providing a scholarship. **Focus:** General studies/Field of study not specified. **Qualif.:** Applicant must be a high school senior or college freshman from the state of Utah; achievements include earning a 4.0 GPA; being a member of the Snow College soccer team. **Criteria:** Selection will be based on athletics and academics.

Funds Avail.: $500. **Number Awarded:** 1. **To Apply:** Applicant must submit a application in online. **Deadline:** May 30.

4368 ■ Elite Entrepreneurs
1260 S Spectrum Blvd.
Chandler, AZ 85286
Ph: (480)499-6693
E-mail: info@growwithelite.com
URL: growwithelite.com
Social Media: www.facebook.com/growwithelite
www.linkedin.com/company/elite-entrepreneurs
twitter.com/eliteentrepren5

4369 ■ Elite Entrepreneurs Scholarship Contest
(Undergraduate, Graduate, High School/Scholarship)

Purpose: To provide financial aid to college students, encourage students who have ideas and want to become entrepreneurs, and inspire students to grow their business ideas. **Focus:** Business; Finance; Law; Management. **Qualif.:** Applicant must be a high school senior or college freshman in the U.S. who is studying, or plans to study, in the fields of business, finance, management, or law. **Criteria:** Selection is based on the best video essay or written essay submitted.

Funds Avail.: $1,000. **Number Awarded:** 1. **To Apply:** Applicant must record a video (one to two minutes long, in plain English) explaining the greatest challenges for entrepreneurs and their plans for overcoming these challenges. Video must be published on the applicant's YouTube channel with the title "Elite Entrepreneurs Scholarship Contest" and this link in the description: growwithelite.com/college-scholarship-for-entrepreneurs. Applicant must also share the video on their Facebook page and the sponsor's Facebook page. Instead of a video, applicant may submit a 1,000 to 1,500 word essay on the same subject via email. **Deadline:** August 15. **Contact:** Stephanie Hitchins; Email: eliteentrepreneursscholarship@gmail.com.

4370 ■ Elks National Foundation (ENF)
2750 N Lakeview Ave.
Chicago, IL 60614-1889
Ph: (773)755-4700
Fax: (773)755-4790
URL: www.elks.org

4371 ■ Elks National Foundation Most Valuable Student Scholarship Contest *(Undergraduate/ Scholarship)*

Purpose: To support students with the highest-rated applicants in the competition each year. **Focus:** General studies/Field of study not specified. **Qualif.:** Applicants must be high school senior students who are citizens of the United States. **Criteria:** Selection will be based on scholarship, leadership, and financial need. Male and female applicants compete separately.

Funds Avail.: $200 to $700 (District Awards); $800 to $3,500 (State Awards); $4,000 to $50,000 (National Awards). **Duration:** Annual. **Number Awarded:** 114 (District); 286 (State); 500 (National). **To Apply:** Applications are available online at www.elks.org/enf/scholars/mvs.cfm. **Deadline:** November 15.

4372 ■ Most Valuable Student scholarships
(Undergraduate/Scholarship)

Purpose: To provide educational support to outstanding students for their college or university expenses. **Focus:** General studies/Field of study not specified. **Qualif.:** Applicant must be a current high school seniors, or the equivalent, who are citizens of the United States are eligible to apply. **Criteria:** Recipients are selected based on leadership, financial need and scholastic standing.

Funds Avail.: $4,000 to $50,000. **Duration:** Annual. **Number Awarded:** 500. **To Apply:** Applicants can obtain the application at the Foundation's website; completed application must be submitted to the Elks Lodge nearest to the applicant's home. **Deadline:** November 15.

4373 ■ Emerald Creek Capital
575 Lexington Ave., 31 Fl.
New York, NY 10022
Free: 800-313-2616
E-mail: info@emeraldcreekcapital.com
URL: www.emeraldcreekcapital.com
Social Media: www.linkedin.com/company/emerald-creek -capital
twitter.com/EmeraldCreekNY

4374 ■ Emerald Creek Capital Scholarship
(Undergraduate/Scholarship)

Purpose: To help deserving students in the New York City area pay for their education. **Focus:** General studies/Field of study not specified. **Qualif.:** Applicant must be assistance to young outstanding students; and must be from the NYC area. **Criteria:** Selection will be based on merit, financial need, and the essay submitted.

Funds Avail.: $10,000. **Number Awarded:** 1. **To Apply:** Application must be completed on the sponsor's website. **Deadline:** June 15. **Contact:** Email: rjurbala@ emeraldcreekcapital.com;   URL: www.emeraldcreekcapital.com/scholarship.

4375 ■ Emergency Nurses Association (ENA)
915 Lee St.
Des Plaines, IL 60016-6569
Ph: (847)460-4123
Free: 800-900-9659
E-mail: education@ena.org
URL: www.ena.org

Awards are arranged alphabetically below their administering organizations

Social Media: www.facebook.com/ENAorg
instagram.com/enaorg
twitter.com/ENAorg
www.youtube.com/c/enaorg

4376 ■ Board of Certification for Emergency Nursing (BCEN) Undergraduate Scholarship
(Undergraduate/Scholarship)

Purpose: To provide support to individuals and emergency nurses who are seeking a higher level of education. **Focus:** Nursing. **Qualif.:** Applicants must be nurses with a current BCEN credential (CEN, CPEN, CFRN or CTRN) who are pursuing a baccalaureate degree in nursing; must be ENA members for at least one year and with a minimum GPA of 3.0.

Funds Avail.: $2,000 each. **Duration:** Annual. **To Apply:** Applicants must submit two letters of recommendation; one of which must be from a current ENA member in good standing. **Contact:** Phone:847-460-4100; Email:ena.foundation@ena.org.

4377 ■ ENA Foundation Annual Conference Scholarships (Professional development, Advanced Professional/Scholarship)

Purpose: To support members to attend the Annual Conference. **Focus:** Nursing. **Qualif.:** Applicants must be members of ENA. **Criteria:** Selection will be based on the committee's criteria.

Duration: Annual. **Number Awarded:** 43. **To Apply:** Applicants must complete the application form provided by ENA Foundation, then submit such, together with other documents asked by the organization. **Remarks:** Established in 1991. **Contact:** Phone: 847-460-4100; Email: ena.foundation@ena.org.

4378 ■ ENA Foundation Seed Grants (Master's, Advanced Professional/Grant)

Purpose: To provide funding for research that will advance the specialized practice of emergency nursing. **Focus:** Nursing. **Criteria:** Selection will be based on the committee's criteria.

Funds Avail.: $500 each. **Duration:** Annual. **Number Awarded:** 5. **To Apply:** Applicants must complete the entire application form available at the website and submit the completed application together with the signed research agreement electronically or via mail. **Deadline:** September 30 or January 31. **Contact:** Email: ena.foundation@ena.org; Phone: 847-460-4100.

4379 ■ ENA Foundation Undergraduate State Challenge Scholarship (Undergraduate/Scholarship)

Purpose: To provide support to individuals and emergency nurses who are seeking a higher level of education. **Focus:** Nursing. **Qualif.:** Applicants must be nurses pursuing a baccalaureate degree in nursing (RN to BSN); must be a current ENA member in good standing; must be attending an ACEN or CCNE accredited institution and must provide verification of the institution's current accreditation; must be a minimum of a 3.0 Grade Point Average (GPA).

Funds Avail.: $3,000. **Duration:** Annual. **To Apply:** Applicants must submit two letters of recommendation; one of which must be from a current ENA member in good standing. **Contact:** Phone:847-460-4100; Email:ena.foundation@ena.org.

4380 ■ Employment Boost
755 W Big Beaver Rd., Ste. 2100
Troy, MI 48084

Free: 888-468-6495
URL: employmentboost.com
Social Media: www.facebook.com/ResumeBOOST

4381 ■ Employment Boost College Scholarship
(College, University/Scholarship)

Purpose: To help students obtain meaningful work and grow their careers. **Focus:** General studies/Field of study not specified. **Qualif.:** Applicant must be enrolled in a U.S.-based high school or college (high school students must plan to attend college during the fall semester of the year applying for the scholarship); must attend or plan to attend a 2- or 4-year college/university; must have a minimum 3.6 GPA.

Funds Avail.: $1,000. **Duration:** Quarterly. **Number Awarded:** 2 per quarter; 8 per year. **To Apply:** Applicant must submit an essay (500 to 1,000 words). Essay requirements depend on the applicant's major. Essay details and scholarship form are available online at employmentboost.com/scholarship. **Deadline:** January 1; April 1; July 1; October 1. **Contact:** Email: ebteam@employmentboost.com.

4382 ■ Endocrine Society
2055 L St. NW, Ste. 600
Washington, DC 20036
Ph: (202)971-3636
Fax: (202)736-9705
Free: 888-363-6274
E-mail: hormone@endocrine.org
URL: www.endocrine.org
Social Media: www.facebook.com/EndocrineSociety
www.instagram.com/theendocrinesociety
www.linkedin.com/company/the-endocrine-society
twitter.com/TheEndoSociety

4383 ■ Endocrine Society Summer Research Fellowships (Graduate, Undergraduate/Fellowship)

Purpose: To encourage promising undergraduate students, medical students and first year graduate school students to pursue careers in endocrinology. **Focus:** Endocrinology. **Qualif.:** Applicants must be currently enrolled full-time in school and may not be employed as research assistants. Student's academic levels must fall into one of the three categories at the time they apply: undergraduate students who are currently in their Four year of schooling or beyond; first year graduate students; medical students who are beyond their first year of schooling; mentors must be active members of the Endocrine Society and projects must be under the direction of the mentor; only one application per mentor may be submitted. Mentors who won a fellowship in 2019 are ineligible to sponsor an application. **Criteria:** Selection will be based on the committee's criteria.

Funds Avail.: No specific amount. **Duration:** Annual; 8-12 weeks. **Number Awarded:** Varies. **To Apply:** Applicant should complete online application form and submit: summary of research project, jointly prepared by Mentor and Student (1 page); mentor statement which includes mentor's role in the research project including plans for training, student's role in the research project, student's qualifications; student statement explaining why they chose Mentor's lab and project; mentor's biosketch (NIH Style; 5 page maximum); transcripts from all advanced academic institutions in which student has been enrolled (transcripts do not need to be official, but must be submitted in English);

Awards are arranged alphabetically below their administering organizations

curriculum vitae or resume; disclosure of funding statements. **Contact:** E-mail: awards@endocrine.org.

4384 ■ Endourological Society
4100 Duff Pl., Lower Level
Seaford, NY 11783
Ph: (516)520-1224
Fax: (516)520-1225
URL: www.endourology.org
Social Media: www.facebook.com/EndourologySociety/
  timeline
twitter.com/EndourolSoc

4385 ■ Western University - Endourology Fellowship *(Professional development/Fellowship)*

Purpose: To facilitate the development of academic and clinical excellence in endourology and minimally Invasive Surgery. **Focus:** Urology.

Funds Avail.: No specific amount. **Duration:** Annual; two years.

4386 ■ Energy and Mineral Law Foundation (EMLF)
340 S Broadway, Ste. 101
Lexington, KY 40508
Ph: (859)231-0271
E-mail: emagee@jacksonkelly.com
URL: www.emlf.org
Social Media: www.facebook.com/EnMinLaw
www.instagram.com/EnMinLaw
www.linkedin.com/company/energy-and-mineral-law
  -foundation
twitter.com/enminlaw

4387 ■ EMLF Law Student Scholarships *(Undergraduate/Scholarship)*

Purpose: To support law students studying energy, environmental, natural resource, and mineral law at schools holding membership in the energy & mineral law foundation. **Focus:** Energy-related areas; Environmental law; Environmental science; Mineralogy; Natural resources. **Qualif.:** Applicants must be law school students for the current academic year and must demonstrate an interest in the study of natural resources, energy or mineral law. **Criteria:** Recipient will be selected based on potential to make a significant contribution in the field of energy, mineral and natural resources law; academic ability; leadership ability; financial need.

Funds Avail.: $1,000-$5,000. **Duration:** Annual. **To Apply:** Applicants must submit a complete application form; transcript of records; and two letters of recommendation from school dean, faculty member, or member of the legal profession. **Deadline:** March 15. **Contact:** EMLF Scholarship Application, 340 S Bwy., Ste. 101, Lexington, KY 40508, Fax: 859-226-0485; E-mail: carolyn@emlf.org.

4388 ■ Enlisted Association of National Guard of the United States (EANGUS)
1 Massachusetts Ave. NW, Ste. 880
Washington, DC 20001
Fax: (703)519-3849
Free: 800-234-3264

E-mail: eangus@eangus.org
URL: eangus.org
Social Media: twitter.com/EANGUS72

4389 ■ CSM Virgil R. Williams Scholarship *(Undergraduate/Scholarship)*

Purpose: To support the education of EANGUS members, their spouses and their unmarried children. **Focus:** General studies/Field of study not specified. **Qualif.:** Applicants must be EANGUS Auxiliary members; must be unmarried, dependent sons and daughters of EANGUS Auxiliary members; must be spouses of EANGUS Auxiliary members. **Criteria:** Selection will be made based on the applicant's character, leadership and financial need.

Funds Avail.: $2,000. **To Apply:** Applicants must submit a transcript of high school credits and/or a transcript of college credits for applicants already in an institution of higher learning; a letter from the applicants with personal, specific facts as to why financial assistance is required; must have three letters of academic recommendation verifying the application and giving moral, personal and leadership traits. Application form and other documents must be submitted electronically via the internet to the Chairman of the Scholarship Committee except the school transcript. **Deadline:** June 1.

4390 ■ Ennis Arts Association (EAA)
122 Old Virginia City Hwy.
Ennis, MT 59729
URL: www.ennisartsassociation.org

4391 ■ EAA Members Memorial Scholarship *(Undergraduate/Scholarship)*

Purpose: To help students pursue their education in an arts related curriculum. **Focus:** Arts. **Qualif.:** Scholarships are available to individual residents of Madison County who are current or past graduates of Madison County high schools (Ennis, Harrison, Sheridan or Twin Bridges) or to those who have graduated from high school (or its equivalent) in these districts. **Criteria:** Recipients will be evaluated based on submitted materials.

Funds Avail.: $1,000. **Duration:** Annual. **To Apply:** Applicants must contact the Guidance Counselor at their prospective school. **Deadline:** April 15.

4392 ■ EAA Workshop Scholarships *(Undergraduate/Scholarship)*

Purpose: To support the total cost of an art related single activity, workshop, adult education class or camp. **Focus:** Arts. **Qualif.:** Applicants must be individuals living in Madison County (Ennis, Harrison, Sheridan or Twin Bridges) school district boundaries. **Criteria:** Selection will be based on the committee's criteria.

Funds Avail.: $100 to $200. **Duration:** Annual. **To Apply:** Applicants must contact the Guidance Counselor at their prospective school.

4393 ■ Entertainment Software Association (ESA)
601 Massachusetts Ave. NW, Ste. 300
Washington, DC 20001
E-mail: esafinfo@theesa.com
URL: www.theesa.com
Social Media: www.facebook.com/

Awards are arranged alphabetically below their administering organizations

---

TheEntertainmentSoftwareAssociation
www.linkedin.com/company/entertainment-software
 -association/
twitter.com/theESA

4394 ■ ESA Foundation Scholarship *(Undergraduate/ Scholarship)*

Purpose: To assist women and minority students who plan to continue their education in fields supporting Video Game Development. **Focus:** Computer and information sciences; Graphic art and design. **Criteria:** Selection will be based on academic performance; academic honors; career plans and goals; extracurricular activities and leadership; prior work experience; special circumstances (i.e., military service).

Funds Avail.: $3,000 each. **Duration:** Annual. **Number Awarded:** 30 (15 graduating high school seniors and 15 current college students). **To Apply:** Applications can be submitted online. **Deadline:** March 2. **Remarks:** Established in 2007.

4395 ■ The Entomological Foundation
3 Pk. Pl., Ste. 307
Annapolis, MD 21401
URL: www.entfdn.org

4396 ■ Kenneth and Barbara Starks Plant Resistance to Insects Graduate Student Award *(Graduate/Award)*

Purpose: To support graduate students with their studies in entomology or plant breeding/genetics for innovative research that contributes significantly to knowledge of plant resistance to insect. **Focus:** Entomology. **Qualif.:** Applicants must be graduate students in entomology or plant breeding/genetics for innovative research that contributes significantly to knowledge of plant resistance to insects; must be a candidate for a Master's or doctoral degree at an accredited university; must be an ESA and P-IE Section member. **Criteria:** Selection will be based on points of applicants and proposed research.

Funds Avail.: $500. **Duration:** Annual. **To Apply:** Applicants must include a letter of nomination from the student's advisor (maximum 2 pages); statement from the nominee that includes the title of the research, duration, and background information concerning the significance of the research to the field of plant resistance to insects (maximum 2 pages); curriculum vitae or resume; one letter of support from a person familiar with the nominee's qualifications (maximum 2 pages). **Deadline:** June 1.

4397 ■ Jeffery P. LaFage Graduate Student Research Award *(Master's, Doctorate/Grant)*

Purpose: To recognize graduate students who proposes innovative research that advances or contributes significantly to the knowledge of the biology or control of pests in the urban environment, especially termites or other wood-destroying organisms. **Focus:** Biology; Entomology. **Qualif.:** Applicants must be candidates for a Masters or doctoral degree at an accredited university; priority will be given to proposals demonstrating a creative and realistic approach to the fields of interest.

Funds Avail.: No specific amount. **Duration:** Annual. **To Apply:** All nomination packages must be submitted electronically. The entire nomination package must not exceed 20 pages total. This includes letters of nomination

or recommendation and publication lists. Letters of nomination and recommendation must be included in the electronic package. Only the following file formats will be accepted: PDF, RTF, TIF or JPG graphic files. Files created on either PC or MAC platforms will be accepted; font size for text may not be smaller than 10 point; contain no more than six separate files and the size of each file must not exceed 3 MB. Complete packages may be submitted either by Nomination Submission Website or by email as attached files to the awards administrator. **Deadline:** July 1.

4398 ■ Lillian and Alex Feir Graduate Student Travel Award in Insect Physiology, Biochemistry, or Molecular Biology *(Master's, Doctorate/Award)*

Purpose: To encourage graduate students working with insects or other arthropods in the broad areas of physiology, biochemistry and molecular biology to affiliate with ESA's Integrative Physiological and Molecular Insect Systems Section and to attend the ESA Annual Meeting or an International Congress of Entomology. **Focus:** Entomology. **Qualif.:** Applicants must be students who are using arthropods to study any aspect of basic or applied physiology, biochemistry or molecular biology in the broadest sense for their Master's or doctoral research; must be ESA student members; students from all science departments are encouraged to apply. **Criteria:** Selection will be based on enthusiasm and interest in attending the meeting; academic credentials; reasonable budget to attend meeting; topic or areas of thesis research; recommendations from colleagues, peer groups, etc.

Funds Avail.: No specific amount. **Duration:** Annual. **Number Awarded:** 1. **To Apply:** Applications must be submitted electronically; letters of nomination must be included in the electronic package, letter of recommendation may be included in the package or submitted via e-mail; printed letters will not be accepted; letters of recommendation cannot exceed two pages each; file formats must be PDF, RTF, TIF graphic files, or JPG graphic files; font size for text may not be smaller than 10 point; must provide a curriculum vitae; two letters of endorsement from professional colleagues and clientele. **Deadline:** June 1. **Contact:** Email: awards@entsoc.org.

4399 ■ Shripat Kamble Urban Entomology Graduate Student Award for Innovative Research *(Doctorate/ Award)*

Purpose: To support and recognize a doctoral student who is currently conducting research which demonstrates innovative and realistic approaches to urban entomology. **Focus:** Entomology. **Qualif.:** Candidates must be students for a doctoral degree at an accredited university in the U.S.; must be ESA members with a genuine interest in urban entomology excluding turf and ornamental pests.

Funds Avail.: $500. **Duration:** Annual. **Number Awarded:** 1. **To Apply:** Applicants must submit a nomination letter to the MUVE president; curriculum vitae; two additional letters of reference; university transcripts; all documents should be merged into one PDF file for ease of review by the panel; the entire nomination package must not exceed 20 pages. **Deadline:** June 1. **Contact:** For questions, MUVE VP-Elect, Dr. Dana Nayduch; Email: dana.nayduch@ ars.usda.gov.

4400 ■ Entomological Society of America (ESA)
3 Park Pl., Ste. 307
Annapolis, MD 21401-3722
Ph: (301)731-4535

Awards are arranged alphabetically below their administering organizations

Fax: (301)731-4538
URL: www.entsoc.org
Social Media: www.facebook.com/entsoc
twitter.com/EntsocAmerica
www.youtube.com/user/entsoc

4401 ■ Henry and Sylvia Richardson Research Grant *(Postdoctorate/Grant)*

Purpose: To provide research funds to postdoctoral members of the Entomological Society of America. **Focus:** Entomology. **Qualif.:** A nominee must be an ESA member and postdoctoral scholar, working in insect control by attractants, repellents, biological controls, thermocontrols, or chemical controls; grade point average of 3.0 on a 4.0 scale is also required. **Criteria:** Priority will be given to those candidates working in insect control of medical or veterinary importance.

Funds Avail.: No specific amount. **Duration:** Annual. **Number Awarded:** 1. **To Apply:** Nominee must be submitted electronically; letters of nomination must be included in the electronic package, letter of recommendation may be included in the package or submitted via e-mail; letters of recommendation cannot exceed two pages each; file formats must be PDF, RTF, TIF graphic files, or JPG graphic files; font size for text may not be smaller than 10 point; must provide a CV which includes Background Information, Research, Teaching, Extension or Outreach and Service; letter of nomination; letter of application describing eligibility; two letters of recommendation, one from a major professor and one from a previous instructor. **Deadline:** June 1. **Contact:** Email: awards@entsoc.org.

4402 ■ Entomological Society of Canada (ESC)

500-386 Broadway
Winnipeg, MB, Canada R3C 3R6
Ph: (204)282-9823
Free: 888-821-8387
E-mail: info@esc-sec.ca
URL: www.esc-sec.ca
Social Media: twitter.com/CanEntomologist

4403 ■ Ed Becker Conference Travel Awards *(Undergraduate, Graduate/Award)*

Purpose: To provide financial assistance to students to attend a Joint Annual Meeting and present a paper or poster. **Focus:** Entomology. **Qualif.:** Applicants must be students in graduate or undergraduate program at a Canadian university and an active member in the ESC; students must present a paper or a poster at the Joint Annual Meetings of ESC on their own original research; no student may receive more than one ESC Ed Becker Conference Travel Award while registered for the same degree. **Criteria:** Applications will be reviewed by a committee of the Society.

Funds Avail.: $500 each. **Duration:** Annual. **Number Awarded:** Varies. **To Apply:** Applicant must submit the application in a single PDF file with the following documents: cover page including award being applied for, name and email address of the applicant's and email addresses of those providing letters of support; curriculum vitae containing name and address, phone number, email address, date, education (degrees and dates), work and volunteer experience, awards and scholarships, list of scientific contributions like refereed and non-refereed publications, talks and posters at meetings, other communications and other interests or achievements; scanned set of transcripts, either

of originals, or copies certified as such by a graduate secretary/administrator or graduate supervisor, showing undergraduate and post graduate (if applicable) grades; an abstract of the paper or poster (250 word maximum); letter from the applicant's supervisor of research stating that the applicant is engaged in a graduate or undergraduate program; recommendation letter from a faculty member who is familiar to the applicant's research. **Deadline:** March 1. **Contact:** ESC Association Coordinator via email.

4404 ■ Biological Survey of Canada Scholarship *(Postgraduate/Scholarship)*

Purpose: To assist a student studying insect or terrestrial arthropod biodiversity in Canada. **Focus:** Entomology. **Qualif.:** Applicants must be post-graduate students studying at a Canadian university and carrying out a project on insect (or terrestrial arthropod) faunistics in a Canadian habitat. **Criteria:** Applications will be reviewed by a committee of the Society. Selection will be based on the basis of high scholastic achievement and excellence in faunistics.

Funds Avail.: $2,000. **Duration:** Biennial; in even numbered years. **Number Awarded:** 1. **To Apply:** Applicants must submit the application in a single PDF file with the following documents: cover page including award being applied for, name and email address of the applicants and email addresses of those providing letters of support; Curriculum Vitae containing name and address, phone number, email address, date, education (degrees and dates), work and volunteer experience, awards and scholarships, list of scientific contributions like refereed and non-refereed publications, talks and posters at meetings, other communications and other interests or achievements; scanned set of transcripts, either of originals, or copies certified as such by a graduate secretary/administrator or graduate supervisor, showing undergraduate and post graduate (if applicable) grades; a one page statement answering to the question "why you are studying entomology?" and a summary of the applicant's thesis research and; reference letters from applicant's supervisor and one other person which clearly indicate the applicant's academic abilities, communication skills, progress as a graduate student and the novelty and scholastic contribution of the applicant's research to the field of entomology. Letter of the applicants should indicate the contribution of their work. **Deadline:** March 1. **Contact:** ESC Association Coordinator via email.

4405 ■ John H. Borden Scholarship *(Postgraduate/Scholarship)*

Purpose: To assist students in postgraduate programs who are studying Integrated Pest Management (IPM) with an entomological emphasis. **Focus:** Entomology. **Qualif.:** Applicants must be full time postgraduate students studying Integrated Pest Management (IPM) at a degree granting institution in Canada. **Criteria:** Applications will be reviewed by a committee of the Society.

Funds Avail.: $1,000. **Duration:** Annual. **Number Awarded:** 1. **To Apply:** Applicants must submit the application in a single PDF file with the following documents: cover page including award being applied for, name and email address of the applicants and email addresses of those providing letters of support; curriculum vitae containing name and address, phone number, email address, date, education (degrees and dates), work and volunteer experience, awards and scholarships, list of scientific contributions like refereed and non-refereed publications, talks and posters at meetings, other communications and other interests or achievements; scanned set of transcripts, either of originals, or copies certified as such by a graduate secretary/administrator or graduate supervisor, showing undergraduate and post graduate (if applicable) grades; a one page statement answering to the question "why you are studying entomology?"; a summary of the applicant's thesis research; and reference letters from applicant's supervisor and one other person which clearly indicate the applicant's academic abilities, communication skills, progress as a graduate student and the novelty and scholastic contribution of the applicant's research to the field of entomology. Letter of the applicants should indicate the contribution of their work. **Deadline:** March 1. **Remarks:** In honor of Dr. John H. Borden, and his prestigious contributions in the field of forest pest ecology. **Contact:** ESC Association Coordinator via email.

4406 ■ Dr. Lloyd M. Dosdall Memorial Scholarships
(Postgraduate/Scholarship)

Purpose: To assist students conducting research in the area of arthropod community ecology. **Focus:** Entomology. **Qualif.:** Applicants must be full-time postgraduate students in the field of arthropod community ecology and studying at a degree granting institution in Canada. **Criteria:** Preference will be given to those applicants with a focus on aquatic or agro-ecosystems.

Funds Avail.: $1,000 each. **Duration:** Annual. **Number Awarded:** 2. **To Apply:** Applicants must submit the application in a single PDF file with the following documents: cover page including award being applied for, name and email address of the applicants and email addresses of those providing letters of support; curriculum vitae containing name, address, phone number, email address, date, education, work and volunteer experience, awards and scholarships, list of scientific contributions like refereed and non-refereed publications, talks and posters at meetings, other communications and other interests or achievements; scanned set of transcripts, either of originals, or copies certified as such by a graduate secretary/administrator or graduate supervisor, showing undergraduate and post graduate (if applicable) grades; one page statement answering to the question "why you are studying entomology?" and summary of the applicant's thesis research; reference letters from applicant's supervisor and one other person which clearly indicate the applicant's academic abilities, communication skills, progress as a graduate student and the novelty and scholastic contribution of the applicant's research to the field of entomology. **Deadline:** March 1. **Remarks:** The scholarship was endowed by Teresa Height-Dosdall to honor the memory of Dr. Lloyd M. Dosdall and commemorate his many contributions to crop protection, insect ecology, and aquatic entomology in Canada. **Contact:** ESC Association Coordinator via email.

4407 ■ Entomological Society of Canada Danks Scholarship *(Postgraduate/Scholarship)*

Purpose: To assists students in studies and researches leading to a postgraduate degree in entomology. **Focus:** Entomology. **Qualif.:** Applicants must be full time postgraduate students at a degree granting institution in Canada involved in studies that aim to increase knowledge of the taxonomy, life history or environmental relationships of part of the native Canadian arthropod fauna, but without any focus or bias towards species of direct economic importance. **Criteria:** Applications will be reviewed by a committee of the Society.

Funds Avail.: $1,500 each. **Duration:** Annual. **Number Awarded:** 2. **To Apply:** Applicants must submit the application in a single PDF file with the following documents: cover page including award being applied for, name and

email address of the applicants and email addresses of those providing letters of support; Curriculum Vitae containing name and address, phone number, email address, date, education (degrees and dates), work and volunteer experience, awards and scholarships, list of scientific contributions like refereed and non-refereed publications, talks and posters at meetings, other communications and other interests or achievements; scanned set of transcripts, either of originals, or copies certified as such by a graduate secretary/administrator or graduate supervisor, showing undergraduate and post graduate (if applicable) grades; a one page statement answering to the question "why you are studying entomology?"; a summary of the applicant's thesis research; and reference letters from applicant's supervisor and one other person which clearly indicate the applicant's academic abilities, communication skills, progress as a graduate student and the novelty and scholastic contribution of the applicant's research to the field of entomology. **Deadline:** March 1. **Remarks:** Established in memory of David Danks (1974-2008), reflecting the interests of David and of his father Hugh in environmental science and entomology. **Contact:** ESC Association Coordinator via email.

4408 ■ Graduate Research Travel Scholarships
(Graduate/Scholarship)

Purpose: To foster graduate education in entomology and to help students increase the scope of the graduate training. **Focus:** Entomology. **Qualif.:** Applicants must be enrolled as a full-time graduate student; be studying at a Canadian University; be pursuing scientific studies on insects or other related terrestrial arthropods. **Criteria:** Applications will be judged on scientific merit and normally one will be given to a Ph.D. student and one to an M.Sc. Student.

Funds Avail.: $500 to $2,000. **Duration:** Annual. **Number Awarded:** 2. **To Apply:** Applicants must submit the application in a single PDF file with the following documents: cover page including award being applied for, name and email address of the applicants and email addresses of those providing letters of support; curriculum vitae containing name and address, phone number, email address, date, education (degrees and dates), work and volunteer experience, awards and scholarships, list of scientific contributions like refereed and non-refereed publications, talks and posters at meetings, other communications and other interests or achievements; scanned set of transcripts, either of originals, or copies certified as such by a graduate secretary/administrator or graduate supervisor, showing undergraduate and post graduate (if applicable) grades; and approximately four pages of proposal. Proposal will be in the format of a grant proposal and the applicants will provide the following information: the subject of the thesis; a pertinent review of the literature in the field; a concise presentation of the status of the ongoing thesis research; a description of the research or course work to be undertaken, clearly indicating the relevance to the overall goal of the thesis, an explanation of why such work cannot be carried out at the student's own university and the justification of the site where the research/course work will be carried out; a budget for the proposed project; and anticipated dates of travel and date on which scholarship money is needed. **Deadline:** March 1. **Contact:** ESC Association Coordinator via email.

4409 ■ Keith Kevan Scholarship *(Postgraduate/Scholarship)*

Purpose: To assist students in postgraduate programs who are studying systematic in entomology. **Focus:** Ento-

Awards are arranged alphabetically below their administering organizations

mology. **Qualif.:** Applicants must be post-graduate students studying at Canadian university or Canadian citizens studying abroad. **Criteria:** Applications will be reviewed by a committee of the Society.

Funds Avail.: $2,000. **Duration:** Biennial; in odd numbered years. **To Apply:** Applicants must submit the application in a single PDF file with the following documents: cover page including award being applied for, and name and email addresses including the email addresses of those providing letters of support; curriculum vitae containing name and address, phone number, email address, date, education (degrees and dates), work and volunteer experience, awards and scholarships, list of scientific contributions like refereed and non-refereed publications, talks and posters at meetings, other communications and other interests or achievements; scanned set of transcripts, either of originals, or copies certified as such by a graduate secretary/administrator or graduate supervisor, showing undergraduate and post graduate (if applicable) grades; one page statement answering to the question "why you are studying entomology?"; summary of the thesis research; and reference letters from the supervisor and one other person which clearly indicate the applicant's academic abilities, communication skills, progress as a graduate student and the novelty and scholastic contribution of the applicant's research to the field of entomology. Letters of the applicants should indicate the contribution of their work to biosystematics. **Deadline:** March 1. **Remarks:** The scholarship was established in memory of In memory of Dr. D. Keith McE. Kevan. **Contact:** ESC Association Coordinator via email.

4410 ■ Entomological Society of Saskatchewan
c/o Iain Phillips, Secretary
Saskatoon, SK, Canada S7N 3R3
Ph: (306)933-7474
E-mail: iain.phillips@wsask.ca
URL: www.entsocsask.ca

4411 ■ Brooks Scholarship *(Graduate/Scholarship)*
Purpose: To support students in studies related to entomology and to provide them the opportunity to gain research experience in the field of entomology. **Focus:** Entomology. **Qualif.:** Applicants must be registered for at least one academic year as full-time students in the field of entomology in the College of Graduate Studies and Research at the Universities of Saskatchewan or Regina; must have an academic average equivalent to a "B" standing or above; and must have demonstrated the ability to make an outstanding contribution to entomology in Saskatchewan.

Funds Avail.: $500. **Duration:** Annual. **To Apply:** Applicants must send their academic records, a list of publications, and a statement of interests, activities and accomplishments related to entomology. **Deadline:** October 1. **Contact:** Tyler Wist, Treasurer; Email: tyler.wist@agr.gc.ca; Iain Phillips, Secretary; Email: iain.phillips@swask.ca.

4412 ■ Entomological Society of Saskatchewan Student Presentation Award *(Undergraduate/Award)*
Purpose: To support students giving a scientific presentation at the Entomological Society of Saskatchewan ESS Annual Meeting. **Focus:** Entomology. **Qualif.:** Applicants must be students studying entomology at any level including those from universities outside Saskatchewan. **Criteria:** Selection will be based on on merit, regardless of the number of students entered according to presentation and

preparation of the material; knowledge of the subject; scope of the work, experimental design.

Funds Avail.: $100. **Duration:** Annual. **Number Awarded:** Varies. **To Apply:** Applicants may contact the Society for the application process and other required materials. **Contact:** Tyler Wist, Treasurer, Entomological Society of Saskatchewan, 107 Science Pl., Saskatoon SK, S7N 0X2; Phone: 306-956-7667; Email: tyler.wist@agr.gc.ca.

4413 ■ Entomological Society of Saskatchewan Travel Awards *(Professional development/Award)*
Purpose: To support members of ESS by helping them attend an entomological conference or conduct entomological research or activities. **Focus:** Entomology. **Qualif.:** Applicants must be members of the Entomological Society of Saskatchewan in good standing. **Criteria:** Selection will be based on the committee's criteria.

Funds Avail.: $500 (Maximum). **Duration:** Annual; fiscal year. **Number Awarded:** Varies. **To Apply:** Applicants must submit a statement indicating why it is important for the ESS to lend its support and budget; budget should include a breakdown of the expected costs, the anticipated sources of funding for the conference, project or event and where the ESS support will be applied.

4414 ■ Environmental Law Institute (ELI)
1730 M St. NW, Ste. 700
Washington, DC 20036
Ph: (202)939-3800
Fax: (202)939-3868
URL: www.eli.org
Social Media: www.facebook.com/pg/
   EnvironmentalLawInstitute
www.linkedin.com/company/environmental-law-institute
twitter.com/ELIORG

4415 ■ Public Interest Environmental Law Fellowships *(Graduate/Fellowship)*
Purpose: To provide a recent law school graduate a year of legal experience and training. **Focus:** Law. **Qualif.:** Applicants must be a law school graduate or a candidate, who has graduated recently, and have a top academic record and possess superior legal research and writing skills. **Criteria:** Selection is based on the application materials.

Duration: Annual. **To Apply:** Applicants must submit a complete application package which must include: cover letter; current resume; completed.

4416 ■ Environmental Research and Education Foundation (EREF)
3301 Benson Dr., Ste. 101
Raleigh, NC 27609
Ph: (919)861-6876
Fax: (919)861-6878
E-mail: foundation@erefdn.org
URL: www.erefdn.org
Social Media: www.facebook.com/erefdn
www.linkedin.com/groups/4240923/profile
twitter.com/erefnews
www.youtube.com/user/EREFDN

4417 ■ EREF Doctoral Scholarship *(Doctorate/Scholarship)*
Purpose: To promote the waste management research and education. **Focus:** Waste management. **Qualif.:** Ap-

Awards are arranged alphabetically below their administering organizations

plicant must be a doctoral student; have a clearly demonstrated interest in solid waste management research. EREF defines solid waste management to pertain to municipal solid waste, construction & demolition waste, industrial waste. **Criteria:** Selection will be based on academic performance; professional experience; relevance of one's work to the advancement of solid waste management science; the potential for success.

Funds Avail.: Up to $14,400 per year (up to 3 years). **Duration:** Annual. **To Apply:** Applicant must complete an application form; must submit an official college transcript; admission test scores; three recommendations; an essay of not more than 500 words that includes an autobiographical statement and discussion of research topic. Essay should be typewritten, double-spaced, unbound and unstapled.

4418 ■ Epilepsy Foundation
8301 Professional Pl. W, Ste. 230
Landover, MD 20785
Ph: (301)459-3700
Fax: (301)577-2684
Free: 800-332-1000
URL: www.epilepsyfoundation.org
Social Media: www.facebook.com/
  EpilepsyFoundationofAmerica
www.instagram.com/epilepsyfdn
twitter.com/epilepsyfdn

4419 ■ Epilepsy Foundation Behavioral Sciences Post-Doctoral Fellowships (Postdoctorate/Fellowship)
Purpose: To provide financial assistance for post-doctoral training of behavioral scientists committed to epilepsy research. **Focus:** Behavioral sciences; Epilepsy; Social sciences. **Qualif.:** Applicants must receive their doctoral degrees in the field of social sciences by the time the fellowship commences; have an acceptable research plan; and have an access to institutional resources in conducting the project. **Criteria:** Applications are evaluated based on the quality of the proposed project; applicant's and preceptor's qualifications; and adequacy of the facility.

Funds Avail.: No specific amount. **To Apply:** Applicants must complete an application form with letters of recommendation included.

4420 ■ Epilepsy Foundation Behavioral Sciences Student Fellowships (Graduate, Undergraduate/ Fellowship)
Purpose: To encourage individuals to pursue careers in epilepsy in either the research or practice setting. **Focus:** Behavioral sciences; Epilepsy. **Qualif.:** Applicants must be undergraduates or graduate students who are studying a field related to epilepsy research or clinical care; have (three months) free period to conduct the research; have qualified mentor; and have access to institutional resources including clinics and laboratories to conduct the project. **Criteria:** Applications are evaluated based on the quality of the proposed project; interest in the field; applicant's and mentor's qualifications; adequacy of facilities and quality of the training environment.

Funds Avail.: No specific amount. **To Apply:** Applicants must complete an application form with letters of recommendation included.

4421 ■ Epilepsy Foundation Health Sciences Student Fellowships (Doctorate, Graduate/Fellowship)
Purpose: To stimulate individuals to pursue careers in epilepsy in either research or practice settings. **Focus:**

Epilepsy; Health sciences. **Qualif.:** Applicants must be pre-doctoral training students in Health Sciences; be enrolled or accepted for enrollment in medical school, in doctoral program or other graduate program; have an epilepsy-related study or research plan; have three months free period; have a qualified mentor; have an access to institutional resources including clinics or laboratories in conducting the project. **Criteria:** Applications are evaluated based on the quality of the proposed project; relevance of the proposed work to epilepsy; interest in the field of epilepsy; applicants' qualifications; adequacy of facility and quality of the training environment.

Funds Avail.: $2,000. **To Apply:** Applicants must complete an application form with letters of recommendation included. **Contact:** Epilepsy Foundation at the above address.

4422 ■ Epilepsy Foundation Post-doctoral Research and Training Fellowships (Postdoctorate/Fellowship)
Purpose: To support the post-doctoral training of academic physicians and scientists committed to epilepsy research. **Focus:** Epilepsy; Neuroscience. **Qualif.:** Applicants must be physicians or PhD neuroscientists. **Criteria:** Applications are evaluated based on the quality of the proposed project. Applications are considered from individuals interested in acquiring experience either in basic laboratory research or in the conduct of human clinical studies.

Funds Avail.: No specific amount. **To Apply:** Applicants may visit the website or contact Epilepsy Foundation for more details. **Contact:** Epilepsy Foundation at the above address.

4423 ■ Epilepsy Foundation Pre-doctoral Research Training Fellowships (Graduate/Fellowship)
Purpose: To support pre-doctoral students with dissertation research related to epilepsy. **Focus:** Biochemistry; Epilepsy; Genetics; Neuroscience; Nursing, Cardiovascular and cerebrovascular; Pharmacology; Pharmacy; Physiology; Psychology. **Qualif.:** Applicants must be graduate students enrolled in a full-time doctoral (PhD) program with academic focus on Neuroscience, Physiology, Pharmacology, Psychology, Biochemistry, Genetics, Nursing, or Pharmacy; must have a defined dissertation research project; must have a qualified preceptor with expertise to supervise and provide guidance on the aspects of the research related to epilepsy; must have access to institutional resources to conduct the proposed research project. **Criteria:** Applications are evaluated based on academic record and potential and commitment to develop as an independent and productive epilepsy.

Funds Avail.: $19,000 for stipend and $1,000 to support travel. **Duration:** Annual. **To Apply:** Applicants must complete an application form with letters of recommendation included. **Deadline:** August 22.

4424 ■ Epilepsy Foundation Research Grants (Doctorate/Grant)
Purpose: To support clinical investigators or basic scientists by providing funds for biological or behavioral research that will advance the understanding, treatment, and prevention of epilepsy. **Focus:** Behavioral sciences; Epilepsy. **Qualif.:** Applicants must be conducting a biological or behavioral research that may advance the treatment, understanding and prevention of epilepsy. **Criteria:** Applications are evaluated based on the quality of the proposed project.

Funds Avail.: No specific amount. **Duration:** Annual. **To Apply:** Applicants may visit the website or contact Epilepsy Foundation for more details.

Awards are arranged alphabetically below their administering organizations

4425 ■ Epilepsy Foundation Research and Training Fellowships for Clinicians *(Doctorate, Other/Grant)*

Purpose: To provide support for study and research by clinically trained professionals. **Focus:** Epilepsy; Medicine, Internal; Neurology; Psychiatry. **Qualif.:** Applicant must hold an MD, PhD, ScD, PharmD, RN, or equivalent degree in a relevant clinical discipline; must be a clinical fellow, postdoctoral fellow, or newly appointed clinical faculty member (within two years of first full-time appointment) at an appropriate institution by the beginning of the project term (Researchers with appointments at the level of Adjunct Professor or Associate Professor are not eligible, nor are research assistants, graduate or medical students, medical residents, permanent government employees, or employees of private industry); must have a defined research plan and access to institutional resources to conduct the proposed project and be able to devote at least 50% of their time to the Research and Training Fellowship; must have a qualified mentor with expertise to supervise and provide guidance on epilepsy-related research. **Criteria:** Applications are evaluated based on academic record and potential and commitment to develop as an independent and productive epilepsy.

Funds Avail.: $49,000 for stipend and $1,000 to support travel. **Duration:** Annual. **To Apply:** Applications can be submitted through online. **Deadline:** January 31.

4426 ■ Partnership for Pediatric Epilepsy Research *(Doctorate/Grant)*

Purpose: To support innovative investigator-initiated studies on epilepsies that begin in infancy and childhood. **Focus:** Epilepsy. **Qualif.:** Applicants must hold a relevant advanced degree (MD or PhD); must have completed all research training; and must be based at corporations and academic/university settings. **Criteria:** Applications are evaluated based on the quality of the proposed project. Grants will be awarded to applicants based on need and timetable for the proposed work.

Duration: 1-3 years. **To Apply:** Applicants may visit the website or contact Epilepsy Foundation for more details.

4427 ■ Targeted Research Initiative for Health Outcomes *(Doctorate/Grant)*

Purpose: To support research that generates initial data leading to more extensive projects that will generate knowledge and will ultimately improve the healthcare of persons with epilepsy. **Focus:** Behavioral sciences; Epilepsy. **Qualif.:** Applicants must hold a relevant advanced degree; have completed all research training; and must be based at corporations as well as academic/university settings. **Criteria:** Applications are evaluated based on proposal's scientific validity; relevance to the program's goals and feasibility; applicant's qualifications and adequacy of the research. Grants will be awarded to applicants who have provided a clear justification based on need and timetable of the work proposed.

Funds Avail.: No specific amount. **To Apply:** Applicants may visit the website or contact Epilepsy Foundation for more details. **Contact:** Epilepsy Foundation at the above address.

4428 ■ Epilepsy Newfoundland and Labrador (ENL)

351 Kenmount Rd.
Saint John's, NL, Canada A1B 3P9
Ph: (709)722-0502

Free: 866-374-5377
E-mail: info@epilepsynl.com
URL: www.epilepsynl.com

4429 ■ Jim Hierlihy Memorial Scholarship *(Undergraduate/Scholarship)*

Purpose: To support a mature student with epilepsy who has taken the initiative to return to studies to advance in their present job or train for a new career. **Focus:** General studies/Field of study not specified. **Qualif.:** Applicants must: have a family member diagnosed with epilepsy, be a member in good standing of Epilepsy NL at the time of application. Becoming a member is easy - applications are available at www.epilepsynl.com. - submit a copy of their most recent transcript or marks with their application. **Criteria:** Evaluations will be based on a combination of the applicant's grades, extracurricular activities, and financial need.

Funds Avail.: $1,000. **Duration:** Annual. **Number Awarded:** 1. **To Apply:** Award holders must be prepared to enter or be currently enrolled in a post-secondary training institution in the academic year of application. The award holder must submit to Epilepsy Newfoundland and Labrador confirmation of admission or enrollment to the training institution as soon as possible after the selection, but no later than January 15 of the academic year. **Deadline:** November 1. **Remarks:** The scholarship honor Jim Hierlihy, who was on the Executive of the ENL support group in Gander and a great supporter of all those living with seizures. **Contact:** Epilepsy Newfoundland and Labrador, 351 Kenmount Rd, St. John's, NL, A1B 3P9, Phone: 709-722-0502; Fax: 709-722-0999; Tollfree: 866-EPILEPSY; E-mail: info@epilepsynl.com.

4430 ■ Mature Student Scholarship *(Undergraduate/Scholarship)*

Purpose: To widen horizons of ENL student members by providing financial support as they pursue college or university studies. **Focus:** General studies/Field of study not specified. **Qualif.:** Applicants must be 21 years or older; must be diagnosed with epilepsy; and be members in good standing of Epilepsy Newfoundland and Labrador at the time of the scholarship application. Scholarship is not open to current ENL board and staff members. Former board or staff members and/or their family members can apply for scholarships if they have been out of the service of Epilepsy Newfoundland and Labrador for two years. **Criteria:** Selection is based on the review of application records.

Funds Avail.: $1,000. **Duration:** Annual. **Number Awarded:** 1. **To Apply:** Applicants must submit a personal statement on how their research will contribute or be of value to Newfoundland and Labrador; an official transcript of marks from Memorial University of Newfoundland and from any other university attended; a letter of recommendation from the dean of the faculty or school in which the applicants was registered as an undergraduate at Memorial University of Newfoundland; a letter of recommendation from the head of the department in which applicants majored as an undergraduate at Memorial University of Newfoundland; a letter of recommendation from the applicant's present master's level supervisor. **Deadline:** January 15. **Contact:** 261 Kenmount Road, St. John's, NL A1B 3P9; Telephone: 709-722-0502; Toll Free: 1-866-epilepsy; Fax: 709-722-0999; Email: info@epilepsynl.com.

4431 ■ Epsilon Sigma Alpha (ESA)

363 W Drake Rd.
Fort Collins, CO 80526

Awards are arranged alphabetically below their administering organizations

Ph: (970)223-2824
Fax: (970)223-4456
E-mail: esainfo@epsilonsigmaalpha.org
URL: www.epsilonsigmaalpha.org/Homepage
Social Media: facebook.com/collegiateESA
linkedin.com/groups/Epsilon-Sigma-Alpha-ESA-69177
pinterest.com/esapins
twitter.com/ESAtweets
youtube.com/user/CollegiateESA

4432 ■ Career Enhancement Grant *(Professional development/Grant)*

Purpose: To assist persons who seek further study/training, workshops, seminars, intern training, etc. for the development of their skills and job advancement. **Focus:** General studies/Field of study not specified. **Qualif.:** Applicants must be professionals looking to attend workshops and seminars that help them increase their job ability or knowledge in their current field of employment or assist them in starting a new job.

Funds Avail.: $2,000. **To Apply:** Application and details available online at www.epsilonsigmaalpha.org/scholarships-and-grants/grants/life-grant. **Contact:** ESA Grants Chairman.

4433 ■ Equal Justice Initiative (EJI)

122 Commerce St.
Montgomery, AL 36104
Ph: (334)269-1803
Fax: (334)269-1806
E-mail: contact_us@eji.org
URL: www.eji.org
Social Media: www.facebook.com/equaljusticeinitiative
www.instagram.com/eji_org
twitter.com/eji_org
www.youtube.com/user/ejiorg

4434 ■ EJI Justice Fellowship *(Graduate, Postgraduate, Professional development/Fellowship)*

Purpose: To provide opportunity to those talented and ambitious recent college graduates, post graduates and young professionals to work for two years as a full-time, paid staff member at EJI. **Focus:** Nonprofit sector; Social work. **Qualif.:** Applicants must be recent college graduates, post graduates, or young professionals; an opportunity to work for two years as a full-time, paid staff member at EJI.

Duration: Annual. **To Apply:** Applicants must send a letter of interest and resume. **Deadline:** December 13. **Contact:** Rachel Judge; Email: rjudge@eji.org.

4435 ■ Equal Justice Works

1730 M St. NW, Ste. 800
Washington, DC 20036-4511
Ph: (202)466-3686
URL: www.equaljusticeworks.org
Social Media: www.facebook.com/EqualJusticeWorks
www.linkedin.com/company/equal-justice-works
twitter.com/EJW_org
www.youtube.com/equaljusticeworks

4436 ■ Equal Justice Works Fellowships *(Graduate, Undergraduate/Fellowship)*

Purpose: To support qualified and passionate lawyers in developing new and innovative legal projects that can impact lives and serve communities in desperate need of legal assistance. **Focus:** Law. **Qualif.:** Applicants must be third year law students, a recent law school graduate who has not held a full-time, permanent public interest attorney position, or an experienced private attorney from an EJW member law school who are committed to public interest; applicant who has had a previous postgraduate legal fellowship through equal justice works or any other major fellowship program (e.g. Skadden, Soros, Echoing Green). However, equal justice works AmeriCorps legal fellows are eligible to apply, as well as those candidates who have previously received a law school fellowship such as a clinical fellow position or a judicial clerkship. **Criteria:** Applications will be judged based on quality of the proposed project; the individual fellowship candidate, and the host organization, taking into consideration other factors such as issue area, geographic diversity and sponsor preferences; must sit for the bar exam before beginning their Fellowship.

Funds Avail.: No specific amount. **To Apply:** Identify an issue; identify a host organization; design the project; complete the application. **Deadline:** September 17. **Contact:** Email: Fellowships@equaljusticeworks.org.

4437 ■ Boomer Esiason Foundation (BEF)

483 10th Ave., Ste. 300
New York, NY 10018
Ph: (646)292-7930
Fax: (646)292-7945
E-mail: info@esiason.org
URL: esiason.org
Social Media: www.facebook.com/
  BoomerEsiasonFoundation
instagram.com/boomeresiasonfoundation
twitter.com/cysticfibrosis
www.youtube.com/channel/UCQ6aIx6sTZYqH8VDFg13l_g

4438 ■ BEF General Academic Scholarships *(Undergraduate, Graduate/Scholarship)*

Purpose: To help people living with cystic fibrosis and those students who are the children of parents with cystic fibrosis (living or deceased) who are pursuing undergraduate and graduate degrees. **Focus:** General studies/Field of study not specified. **Qualif.:** Applicants must be undergraduate and graduate students proven to have been diagnosed with cystic fibrosis. **Criteria:** Grantees will be selected based on scholastic ability, character, leadership potential, service to the community and financial need.

Funds Avail.: Up to $5,000. **To Apply:** Applicants must submit a completed application form available at the website; recent photo; letter from physician confirming CF diagnosis and therapy routine; recent W2 form; one-page essay stating goals; detailed breakdown of tuition costs; and transcript of records. **Contact:** Email: scholarships@esiason.org.

4439 ■ BEF Sacks For CF Scholarship *(Graduate, Undergraduate/Scholarship)*

Purpose: To provide educational assistance for students with cystic fibrosis. **Focus:** General studies/Field of study not specified. **Qualif.:** Applicants must be proven to have been diagnosed with cystic fibrosis. **Criteria:** Grantees will be selected based on their academic achievements and adherence to daily CF therapy.

Funds Avail.: $3,000 to $10,000. **Duration:** Annual. **Number Awarded:** 30. **To Apply:** Applicants must submit an

Awards are arranged alphabetically below their administering organizations

application form (downloaded from the website); recent photo; essay; an official/unofficial high school/college transcript; tuition breakdown; and W2 form for verification for both parents; letter from physician (on letterhead) confirming CF diagnosis and therapy routine. **Deadline:** January 10. **Contact:** Email: scholarships@esiason.org.

4440 ■ BEF Scholarship of the Arts *(Graduate, Undergraduate/Scholarship)*

Purpose: To provide educational assistance for students with cystic fibrosis who are engaged in arts. **Focus:** Art. **Qualif.:** Applicants must be artists with cystic fibrosis (CF). **Criteria:** Grantees will be selected according to credits.

Funds Avail.: $500-$1,000. **Duration:** Annual. **To Apply:** Applicants must submit an application form (available at the website); a recent photo; letter from the doctor confirming diagnosis of cystic fibrosis and list of daily medication routine; 2-part essay; an official/unofficial high school/college transcript; tuition breakdown; W2 form for verification for both parents and picture of the art entry; one or more photos of art entry. **Deadline:** May 15. **Contact:** Email: scholarships@esiason.org.

4441 ■ Exercise For Life Athletic Scholarship *(Undergraduate/Scholarship)*

Purpose: To provide educational assistance for student athletes with cystic fibrosis. **Focus:** General studies/Field of study not specified. **Qualif.:** Applicants must be a high school senior or undergraduate student who has cystic fibrosis. **Criteria:** Grantees will be selected according to financial need, academic accomplishment and athletic ability.

Funds Avail.: $10,000. **Duration:** Annual. **Number Awarded:** 4. **To Apply:** Applicants must submit an application form (available at the website); EFL training log (print from website); an essay (one-page, single-spaced) on the importance of exercise and compliance; recent photo; letter from physician (on letterhead) confirming CF diagnosis and therapy routine; recent W2 form verification for both parents; high school transcript; letter of acceptance from a college institution; and signed waiver. **Deadline:** June 5. **Contact:** Email: scholarships@esiason.org.

4442 ■ Rosemary Quigley Memorial Scholarship *(Undergraduate, Graduate/Scholarship)*

Purpose: To enable and inspire young adults with cystic fibrosis to engage in academic studies that will lead them to lives and careers of personal and professional fulfillment. **Focus:** General studies/Field of study not specified. **Qualif.:** Applicants must be students with cystic fibrosis who are pursuing undergraduate or graduate degrees with a clear sense of life goals and whose commitment to living life to the fullest despite having CF is exemplary. **Criteria:** Selection will be chosen based on a majority vote based on ALL parts of the application.

Funds Avail.: $500-$2,000. **To Apply:** Applicants must submit all of the following requirements in order to be considered: application; essay discussing the applicants' post-graduation goals and importance of compliance to CF therapies and daily practices to stay healthy; recent photo; letter from physician (on letterhead) confirming CF diagnosis and therapy routine; transcript (high school, college and/or graduate school); letter of acceptance from academic institution; detailed breakdown of tuition costs from academic institution; and W2 form for both parents. **Deadline:** June 5. **Contact:** Email: scholarships@esiason.org.

4443 ■ Rimington Trophy Scholarship *(Undergraduate, Graduate/Scholarship)*

Purpose: To recognize and support individuals who are living, breathing and succeeding with cystic fibrosis. **Focus:** General studies/Field of study not specified. **Qualif.:** Applicants must be proven to have been diagnosed with cystic fibrosis. **Criteria:** Selection will be based on the applicant's demonstrated scholastic ability, character, leadership potential, service to the community and need for financial assistance.

Funds Avail.: $1,000-$2,000. **To Apply:** Applicants must submit all the following documents in order to be considered: application; essay discussing the applicants' post-graduation goals and importance of compliance to CF therapies and daily practices to stay healthy; recent photo; letter from physician (on letterhead) confirming CF diagnosis and therapy routine; transcript (high school, college and/or graduate school); letter of acceptance from academic institution; detailed breakdown of tuition costs from academic institution; and W2 form for both parents OR tax return if self-employed. **Deadline:** May 8. **Remarks:** Established in association with Rimington Trophy, the college football award named in honor of BEF President and former University of Nebraska center Dave Rimington. Established in 2012. **Contact:** Email: scholarships@esiason.org.

4444 ■ Essay Service
8 The Green, Ste. 4982
Dover, DE 19901
URL: www.essayservice.com
Social Media: www.facebook.com/essayservicecom
www.instagram.com/essayservicecom/
twitter.com/essayservicecom
www.youtube.com/channel/UCUWg2GHTZE
_97Di6KERzEng/featured

4445 ■ Essay Service Writer's Encouragement Scholarship *(Undergraduate/Scholarship)*

Purpose: To support and encourage members of EssayService.com. **Focus:** General studies/Field of study not specified. **Qualif.:** Applicants must be able to demonstrate evidence that they are enrolled in high school or a tertiary institution; must be members of Essay Service.

Funds Avail.: $500 for Gold; $250 for Silver; $250 for Bronze. **Duration:** Semiannual. **Number Awarded:** 3. **To Apply:** Applicant must complete the form online and submit with an essay of 600 to 1,200 words on a given topic. **Deadline:** January 14; August 14. **Contact:** Email: support@essayservice.com.

4446 ■ EssayPro
332 Hawthorne Ln.
Charlotte, NC 28204
Ph: (424)218-9577
URL: essaypro.com
Social Media: www.facebook.com/essayprocom
twitter.com/EssayPro_

4447 ■ Essay Writing Contest *(Undergraduate, Graduate/Scholarship)*

Purpose: To assist students enrolled in an accredited college or university. **Focus:** General studies/Field of study not specified. **Qualif.:** Applicants must be enrolled in an

Awards are arranged alphabetically below their administering organizations

accredited college or university.

Funds Avail.: $500 for first place; $250 for second and third place. **Duration:** Quarterly. **Number Awarded:** 3. **To Apply:** Applicant must submit 600-800-word scholarship essay on a given topic, in Microsoft Word format; Include your contact information in the document. **Deadline:** May 20; September 20; December 20. **Contact:** E-mail: team@ essaypro.com.

4448 ■ Etruscan Foundation (EF)
PO Box 26
Fremont, MI 49412-0026
Ph: (231)519-0675
Fax: (231)924-0777
E-mail: office@etruscanfoundation.org
URL: www.etruscanfoundation.org
Social Media: www.facebook.com/Etruscanfoundation

4449 ■ Fieldwork Fellowship *(Undergraduate, Graduate/Award, Fellowship)*

Purpose: To support participation in field schools or archaeological fieldwork at Etruscan and indigenous sites of non-Greek Italy from the Neolithic through the 1st Century BCE. **Focus:** Archeology; Culture. **Qualif.:** All applicants must be members of The Etruscan Foundation. **Criteria:** Applicants will be evaluated by The Etruscan Foundation Fellowship Review Committee; the recommendations of the Committee will be forwarded to the Board of Directors for final approval.

Funds Avail.: $2,000. **Duration:** Annual. **To Apply:** Applicants must submit completed Cover Form and Curriculum Vitae; one signed letter of recommendation from a professor other than the director of the field school to which the student is applying; Include a narrative defining your interests in the field school you plan to attend; include a narrative (minimum 300 words) defining how the field school experience will further your graduate studies with focus upon specific research activities and anticipated outcomes. **Deadline:** February 14. **Contact:** Richard String, Executive Director, Etruscan Foundation, PO Box 26, Fremont, MI, 49412.

4450 ■ Études d'Oiseaux Canada
115 Front St.
Port Rowan, ON, Canada N0E 1M0
Free: 888-448-2473
E-mail: hello@birdscanada.org
URL: www.bsc-eoc.org
Social Media: www.facebook.com/birdscanada
www.instagram.com/birds.canada
twitter.com/BirdStudiesCan
twitter.com/BirdsCanada
www.youtube.com/user/BirdStudiesCanada

4451 ■ James L. Baillie Memorial Fund - Student Award for Field Research *(Graduate/Grant)*

Purpose: To support a graduate student conducting field studies on Canadian birds in their natural environment. **Focus:** Ornithology. **Qualif.:** Applicant must be a graduate student who conducting field studies on Canadian birds in their natural environment.

Funds Avail.: $2,000. **Duration:** Annual. **Deadline:** February 15. **Remarks:** Established in 1978. **Contact:** Baillie

Fund, Secretary; email at acoughlan@birdscanada.org or phone 1-866-518-0212.

4452 ■ Evans Warncke Robinson LLC
191 Peachtree St., Ste. 3980
Atlanta, GA 30303
Ph: (404)236-6835
URL: disabilityinsurancelawfirm.com

4453 ■ Evans Warncke Robinson, LLC Scholarship Contest *(Undergraduate/Scholarship)*

Purpose: To provide financial aid to college students, encourage students to understand their personal motivation for a career in the legal field, and inspire students to pursue a career in law. **Focus:** Business; Finance; Law; Management. **Qualif.:** Applicant must be U.S. college student. **Criteria:** Selection is based on the video essay submitted.

Funds Avail.: $1,000. **Duration:** Annual. **Number Awarded:** 1. **Deadline:** August 15.

4454 ■ Everglades Foundation
18001 Old Cutler Rd., Ste. 625
Miami, FL 33157
Ph: (305)251-0001
E-mail: info@evergladesfoundation.org
URL: evergladesfoundation.org
Social Media: www.facebook.com/evergladesfoundation
www.instagram.com/evergladesfoundation
www.linkedin.com/company/evergladesfoundation
twitter.com/evergfoundation
www.youtube.com/channel/UCSOxA
  -CPaTmxtXwfyEB4-ew

4455 ■ FIU ForEverglades Scholarship *(Graduate, Doctorate, Master's/Scholarship)*

Purpose: To support graduate research students in pursuing the development of innovative scientific methods in advancing the understanding of Everglades physical, chemical, or biological processes, or research in economic impacts of environmental changes. **Focus:** Biological and clinical sciences; Earth sciences; Economics; Engineering; Geography; Resource management. **Qualif.:** Applicants must be full-time graduate research students pursuing degrees in sciences, engineering and economics; only graduate students from FIU are welcome to apply for the FIU ForEverglades Scholarship.

Funds Avail.: $10,000-$20,000. **Duration:** Annual. **Number Awarded:** 2. **To Apply:** Application entries should contain the following: a cover letter; a proposal describing the research that the award would support (no more than 5, 000 words); proposed budget; a personal essay of no more than 2 pages on the candidate's career goals and how scholarship will support those goals; a curriculum vitae including transcripts; at least one and up to three academic or professional letter(s) of reference; and other relevant or supporting work products or documentation. Electronic submission is preferred, and the package and letters of reference should be emailed. **Deadline:** July 31. **Contact:** Everglades Foundation Fellowship Program, Everglades Foundation, 18001 Old Cutler Rd., Ste. 625, Palmetto Bay, FL, 33157.

4456 ■ ForEverglades Scholarship *(Graduate, Master's, Doctorate/Scholarship)*

Purpose: To support graduate research students in pursuing the development of innovative scientific methods in

Awards are arranged alphabetically below their administering organizations

advancing the understanding of Everglades physical, chemical, or biological processes, or research in economic impacts of environmental changes. **Focus:** Biological and clinical sciences; Earth sciences; Economics; Engineering; Geography; Resource management. **Qualif.:** Applicants must be full-time graduate research students pursuing degrees in earth sciences, biological sciences, engineering, geography, planning and resource management and economics.

Funds Avail.: $10,000 - $20,000. **Duration:** Annual. **Number Awarded:** Varies. **To Apply:** Application entries should contain the following: a cover letter; a proposal describing the research that the award would support (no more than 5, 000 words); proposed budget; a personal essay of no more than 2 pages on the candidate's career goals and how scholarship will support those goals; a curriculum vitae including transcripts; at least one and up to three academic or professional letter(s) of reference; and other relevant or supporting work products or documentation. Electronic submission is preferred, and the package and letters of reference should be emailed. **Deadline:** July 31.

4457 ■ John Marshall Everglades Internship Program *(Undergraduate/Internship)*

Purpose: To support graduate research students in pursuing the development of innovative scientific methods in advancing the understanding of Everglades physical, chemical, or biological processes, or research in economic impacts of environmental changes. **Focus:** Biological and clinical sciences; Earth sciences; Economics; Engineering; Geography; Resource management. **Qualif.:** Applicants must have an interest in a range of topics related to Everglades restoration; must be an undergraduate student. **Criteria:** Selection criteria will be based on the submitted application.

Funds Avail.: Not to exceed $2,000. **Duration:** Annual. **To Apply:** Applicants must submit the following as one PDF document: A detailed cover letter explaining how the John Marshall Everglades Internship will benefit your career. A two-page double spaced essay answering the following question: "How do policy and science work together in conservation?". Unofficial copy of transcripts.

4458 ■ Evoke Strategy LLC
3902 henderson blvd., ste. 208
Tampa, FL 33609
URL: www.evokestrategy.com

4459 ■ Evoke Strategy Writing Scholarship *(Undergraduate/Scholarship)*

Purpose: To help usher in the next generation of professional writers. **Focus:** English language and literature; Marketing and distribution; Public relations; Writing. **Qualif.:** Applicant must be currently attending a U.S. college or university with a focus on English, writing, public relations, or marketing; must have a cumulative minimum 3.25 GPA. **Criteria:** Selection will be based on quality of the writing.

Funds Avail.: $500. **Duration:** Annual. **Number Awarded:** 1. **To Apply:** Applicant must submit a writing-related piece of undergraduate work from the previous year and an official transcript; submissions must include applicant's full name and university (.edu) email address. **Deadline:** December 31. **Contact:** Email: scholarship@evokestrategy.com.

4460 ■ Exabeam Inc.
1051 E Hillsdale Blvd., 4th Fl.
Foster City, CA 94404

Free: 844-392-2326
E-mail: info@exabeam.com
URL: www.exabeam.com
Social Media: www.facebook.com/exabeam
instagram.com/exabeam
www.linkedin.com/company/exabeam
twitter.com/exabeam
youtube.com/channel/UC8Ur9wIfXAtFNB-cMCPNY2g

4461 ■ Exabeam Cyber Security Scholarship *(Undergraduate, Graduate/Scholarship)*

Purpose: To support the next generation of cyber security leaders by identifying students who show passion for driving innovative solutions in the fight against the next wave of online threats. **Focus:** General studies/Field of study not specified. **Qualif.:** Applicants must be legal residents of the United States and the District of Columbia who are sixteen years of age or older at the time of application and who are currently enrolled (or have been accepted to enroll) in an accredited post-secondary institution of higher learning (college or university) with a minimum 3.0 GPA. **Criteria:** Selection will be based on the criteria of originality and creativity (80%) and grade point average (GPA) (20%).

Funds Avail.: $1,000. **To Apply:** Applicant must submit name and contact information, academic transcripts, and either a 600- to 1,000-word essay or a link to a 5-minute video that answers the question prompt at www.exabeam.com/scholarship/. **Deadline:** June 30. **Contact:** Email: scholarship@exabeam.com.

4462 ■ Executive Women International (EWI)
1288 Summit Ave. Ste.107 PMB 124
Oconomowoc, WI 53066
Ph: (262)269-5625
E-mail: ewi@ewiconnect.com
URL: www.ewiconnect.com
Social Media: www.instagram.com/ewicorporate
twitter.com/ewicorporate

4463 ■ ASIST Scholarship (ASIST) *(Professional development/Scholarship)*

Purpose: To financially support students for their continuous education. **Focus:** General studies/Field of study not specified. **Qualif.:** Applicants must be adults facing economic, social, or physical challenges, who are looking to improve their situation through educational opportunities. **Criteria:** Recipients are selected based on financial need; socially, physically and economically challenged adults; responsibility for small children.

Funds Avail.: $2,000-$10,000. **Duration:** Annual. **To Apply:** Applicants must submit the application form along with unofficial transcript of grades from educational provider; two letters of Recommendation; copy of the financial package letter from the school you are attending; for United States students, include a copy of your Student Aid Report which is the report you received when you completed the Free Application for Federal Student Aid; for Canadian students, include a copy of the Assessment Calculator Information which you can print from your online Student Loan Application for your Federal and Provincial funding; application must be typed in black ink in a font size no smaller than 11 point.

4464 ■ Executive Women International Scholarship Program (EWISP) *(Undergraduate/Scholarship)*

Purpose: To financially help qualified applicants achieve their academic goals. **Focus:** General studies/Field of study

Awards are arranged alphabetically below their administering organizations

not specified. **Qualif.:** Applicants must be high school seniors. **Criteria:** Selection will be based on their scholastic achievement, leadership qualities, good citizenship and extra-curricular activities.

Duration: Annual. **To Apply:** Applicants must submit a completed application form available on the website; two letters of recommendation (use the Personal Recommendation Form) and official transcript of grades. Applications should be submitted to the EWI Chapter near the applicant's residency.

4465 ■ ExeptionalNurse.com
13019 Coastal Cir.
Palm Beach Gardens, FL 33410
E-mail: exceptionalnurse@aol.com
URL: www.exceptionalnurse.com
Social Media: www.facebook.com/ExceptionalNurse

4466 ■ ExeptionalNurse.com Scholarships
(Undergraduate/Scholarship)

Purpose: To support students with disabilities who wish to continue their education in a nursing education program. **Focus:** Nursing. **Qualif.:** Applicants must be students with a documented disability who have applied to, or already been admitted to, a college or university program on a full-time basis.

Funds Avail.: No specific amount. **Duration:** Annual. **Number Awarded:** Varies. **To Apply:** Applicants must submit a completed and signed application form along with three letters of recommendation attesting to the applicant's academic abilities and personal character (may not be relatives); a 1-2 page essay; official transcripts of high school or college courses completed; and Medical Verification of Disability Form. **Contact:** Scholarship Committee, ExceptionalNurse.com, 13019 Coastal Circle Palm Beach, Gardens, Fl, 33410.

4467 ■ The Expert Institute
48 Wall St, 32nd Flr
New York, NY 10005
Free: 888-858-9511
E-mail: info@expertinstitute.com
URL: www.theexpertinstitute.com
Social Media: www.facebook.com/TheExpertInstitute
www.linkedin.com/company/the-expert-institute
twitter.com/ExpertInst

4468 ■ The Expert Institute Legal Blog Post Writing Contest *(Graduate/Scholarship)*

Purpose: To help law students ease some of their financial burden. **Focus:** Law. **Qualif.:** Applicants must be current law school students. **Criteria:** Selection will be based on committee's criteria.

Funds Avail.: $2,000. **Duration:** Annual. **Number Awarded:** 3. **To Apply:** Applicants must submit a 1,500-2,500 words essay written in a blog post format; full name of author (First, Middle, and Last); contact information for author, including e-mail address and phone number; school name and mailing address.

4469 ■ The Explorers Club
46 E 70th St.
New York, NY 10021

Ph: (212)628-8383
Fax: (212)288-4449
E-mail: president@explorers.org
URL: www.explorers.org
Social Media: www.facebook.com/TheExplorersClubNYC
www.instagram.com/the_explorers_club
twitter.com/explorersclub

4470 ■ The Scott Pearlman Field Awards *(Professional development/Award)*

Purpose: To provide grants to artists, writers, filmmakers, still and video photographers, and journalists recommended by a member of The Explorers Club who is also leading the expedition. **Focus:** Filmmaking; Journalism; Photography. **Qualif.:** Applicants must be professional artists, writers, photographers, filmmakers and journalists. **Criteria:** Selection will be based on the committee's criteria.

Funds Avail.: No specific amount. **Duration:** Annual. **Number Awarded:** 1. **To Apply:** The application process is online.

4471 ■ Express Medical Supply
218 Seebold Spur
Fenton, MO 63026
Free: 800-633-2139
E-mail: sales@exmed.net
URL: www.exmed.net
Social Media: www.facebook.com/ExMed.net
twitter.com/Express_Medical

4472 ■ Express Medical Supply Scholarship Program *(Undergraduate/Scholarship)*

Purpose: To contribute to higher education and learning by offering the winning student financial assistance to help cover the expenses of tuition and books. **Focus:** General studies/Field of study not specified. **Qualif.:** Applicants must be students enrolled part-time or full-time at any two- or four-year college or university in the United States; must be a legal resident of the United States or hold a valid student visa. **Criteria:** Selection will be based on the applicants' photo, which will be deemed as displayed to be most creative in their Twitter account.

Funds Avail.: $500. **Duration:** Biennial. **Number Awarded:** 2. **To Apply:** Application details are available online at www.exmed.net/t-scholarships.aspx. **Deadline:** June 1; December 30. **Contact:** Email: scholarships@exmed.net.

4473 ■ EZstorit.com
270 Cobb Pkwy. SE, Ste. 140-256
Marietta, GA 30060
Fax: (888)390-8740
Free: 888-686-2849
E-mail: info@ezstorit.com
URL: ezstorit.com
Social Media: www.facebook.com/ezstorit
www.instagram.com/ezstorit/
twitter.com/ezstorit

4474 ■ Get Ahead Scholarship *(Undergraduate, Graduate/Scholarship)*

Purpose: To assist students financially. **Focus:** General studies/Field of study not specified. **Qualif.:** Applicants

Awards are arranged alphabetically below their administering organizations

must be enrolled as a full-time undergraduate or graduate student at an accredited college or university in the United States, Canada, or Puerto Rico; must have a minimum 2.75 accumulated GPA. **Criteria:** Selection will be made by the sponsor for the well-written and clearly and creatively address the topic.

Funds Avail.: $500. **Duration:** Annual. **Number Awarded:** 1. **To Apply:** Applicant must submit completed application, proof of enrollment (class schedule, housing contract, etc.), proof of GPA (unofficial transcripts are acceptable), and 300-750 word essay. Application must be completed and submitted online at ezstorit.com/ezstorit-get-ahead-scholarship. **Deadline:** July 25.

4475 ■ Facebook, Inc.
1601 Willow Rd.
Menlo Park, CA 94025
Ph: (650)543-4800
URL: www.facebook.com
Social Media: facebook.com/security/hsts-pixel.gif

4476 ■ Facebook Fellowship Program (Doctorate/Fellowship)

Purpose: To encourage and support promising doctoral students who are engaged in innovative and relevant research in areas related to computer science and engineering. **Focus:** Computer and information sciences; Engineering. **Qualif.:** Applicants must be full-time PhD students who are currently involved in on-going research and enrolled in an accredited university in any country. Students work must be related to one or more of the following disciplines: Applied Statistics; AR/VR Photonics and Optics; CommAI; Computational Social Science; Computer Vision; Computer Storage and Efficiency; Distributed Systems; Economics and Computation; Hardware and Software Infrastructure for Machine Learning; Machine Learning; Natural Language Processing; Networking and Connectivity; Programming Languages; Security/Privacy; Spoken Language Processing and Audio Classification; UX/Instagram Well-being. **Criteria:** Applications will be evaluated based on the strength of the student's research statement, publication record, and recommendation letters.

Funds Avail.: A stipend of $37,000 each year, and up to $5,000 in conference travel support. **Duration:** Annual; Up to two years. **To Apply:** Applicants must submit a 1-2 page research summary which clearly identifies the area of focus, importance to the field, and applicability to Facebook of the anticipated research during the award; a current resume or CV with email, phone and mailing address, including applicable coursework; 2 letters of recommendation (one must be from an academic advisor). **Deadline:** October 4. **Contact:** E-mail: facebookfellowship@fb.com.

4477 ■ Fadel Educational Foundation, Inc. (FEF)
PO Box 212135
Augusta, GA 30917-2135
URL: fadelfoundation.wordpress.com
Social Media: www.facebook.com/FadelFoundation
twitter.com/fadelfoundation

4478 ■ FEF Scholarship (Undergraduate/Scholarship)

Purpose: To encourage American Muslims to pursue post-secondary education. **Focus:** General studies/Field of study not specified. **Qualif.:** Applicants must be a recent

history of movement for agricultural employment - priority will be given to currently interstate migrant youth; scholastic potential; enrolled in or accepted at an accredited public or private college, technical or vocational school, or a dropout or a potential dropout from high school who shows promise of ability to continue schooling.

Duration: Annual. **Contact:** Fadel Educational Foundation, Inc., PO Box 212135, Augusta, GA, 30917-2135.

4479 ■ Faegre Baker Daniels L.L.P.
2200 Wells Fargo Ctr. 90 S Seventh St.
Minneapolis, MN 55402-3903
Ph: (612)766-7000
Fax: (612)766-1600
URL: www.faegre.com
Social Media: www.facebook.com/FaegreBD
www.linkedin.com/company/faegre-baker-daniels-llp
www.youtube.com/FaegreBD

4480 ■ Faegre Baker Daniels Diversity & Inclusion Fellowships (Graduate/Fellowship)

Purpose: To promote diversity in the legal profession. **Focus:** Law. **Qualif.:** Applicants must be enrolled in a J.D. program at any accredited law school in the United States; must be interested in a summer associate position in one of FaegreBD's U.S. offices. **Criteria:** Selection will be based on the submitted application materials.

Funds Avail.: $10,000. **Duration:** Annual. **To Apply:** Candidates must complete the online application, including a cover letter indicating office preference, a resume, a law school transcript, and a two-page personal statement describing how or why they will contribute meaningfully to diversity and inclusion at Faegre Baker Daniels and/or in the legal profession.

4481 ■ Families of Freedom Scholarship Fund
Scholarship America
Saint Peter, MN 56082
Free: 877-862-0136
E-mail: info@familiesoffreedom.org
URL: www.familiesoffreedom.org

4482 ■ Families of Freedom Scholarship Fund - Scholarship America (Undergraduate, Vocational/Occupational/Scholarship)

Purpose: To provide education assistance for post-secondary study to dependents - children and spouses of those killed or permanently disabled as a result of terrorist attacks on September 11, 2001 and during the rescue activities to those attacks. **Focus:** General studies/Field of study not specified.

Funds Avail.: No specific amount. **To Apply:** Applicant must register, download and print the registration form and complete, and mail with requested documentation. **Remarks:** Managed by Scholarship America. **Contact:** Families of Freedom Scholarship Fund, Scholarship America, One Scholarship Way, Saint Peter, MN, 56082; Toll-free: 877-862-0136; Email: info@familiesoffreedom.org.

4483 ■ Families USA
1225 New York Ave. NW, Ste. 800
Washington, DC 20005
Ph: (202)628-3030

Awards are arranged alphabetically below their administering organizations

Fax: (202)347-2417
E-mail: info@familiesusa.org
URL: www.familiesusa.org
Social Media: www.facebook.com/FamiliesUSA
www.instagram.com/familiesusa
www.linkedin.com/company/families-usa
twitter.com/familiesusa

4484 ■ Wellstone Fellowships for Social Justice
(Graduate/Fellowship)

Purpose: To foster the advancement of social justice through participation in health care advocacy work that focuses on the unique challenges facing many communities of color. **Focus:** Social work. **Qualif.:** Applicants must be authorized to work in the United States and have a college degree or plan to receive a degree. **Criteria:** Selection will be based on the applicants' demonstrable passion for social justice.

Duration: Annual. **To Apply:** Applicants must submit a completed application form along with a personal essay and a resume; in addition, Families USA must receive an official copy of most recent college or graduate school transcript sent directly from the school registrar's office, three letters of recommendation from academic and/or professional references who can attest the applicant's community involvement. **Deadline:** February 12. **Contact:** Send application materials to: wellstonefellowship@familiesusa.org.

4485 ■ Family, Career and Community Leaders of America (FCCLA)
1910 Association Dr.
Reston, VA 20191-1584
Ph: (703)476-4900
Fax: (703)439-2662
E-mail: national@fcclainc.org
URL: www.fcclainc.org
Social Media: www.facebook.com/nationalfccla
www.instagram.com/nationalfccla
www.pinterest.com/nationalfccla
www.youtube.com/user/NationalFCCLA1945

4486 ■ Beth Middleton Memorial Scholarships
(Undergraduate/Scholarship)

Purpose: To support leadership potential and develop skills for life planning, goal setting, problem solving, decision making and interpersonal communications. **Focus:** General studies/Field of study not specified. **Qualif.:** Applicant must be a member for a minimum of 2 years; must be a current or former FCCLA state or national officer; must currently be a senior (grade 12) in high school; must have minimum 3.5 cumulative GPA (based on a non-weighted 4.0 scale); must maintain 3.0 GPA in their post-secondary courses; must be affiliated with National FCCLA. **Criteria:** Applicants will be judged solely on information contained on the online form and letters of recommendation.

Funds Avail.: $400 for tuition, room and/or board. **Number Awarded:** 1. **To Apply:** Applicant must fill out the online application form; must attach the most recent official high school transcript of record including the first semester of the senior year along with standardized college entrance exam scores (ACT and/or SAT); must provide a copy of the chapter affiliation verifying national dues have been paid. Applicant must include recommendations from a local

adviser, state adviser, and one other person knowledgeable of student's non-FCCLA activities. **Deadline:** March 1. **Remarks:** The Scholarship was named in the memory of Beth Middleton.

4487 ■ National Technical Honor Society Scholarships (NTHS) *(Undergraduate/Scholarship)*

Purpose: To support qualified FCCLA members that have applied to a degree granting institution leading to an associate's or bachelor's degree in any field of study. **Focus:** General studies/Field of study not specified. **Qualif.:** Applicants must be a member of the National Technical Honor Society; must be a senior and must have taken the ACT or SAT examination; must have applied to a degree granting institution leading to an associate's or bachelor's degree in any field of study. **Criteria:** Recipient will be selected based on outstanding leadership, academic excellence and significant volunteer experience; also, judges will base the evaluation to the style and expression as well as content.

Funds Avail.: $1,000. **Duration:** Annual. **Number Awarded:** 2. **To Apply:** Applicant must fill out the online application form; must attach the most recent official high school transcript of record including the first semester of the senior year along with standardized college entrance exam scores (ACT and/or SAT); must provide a copy of the chapter affiliation verifying national dues have been paid. Applicant must include recommendations from a local adviser, state adviser, and one other person knowledgeable of student's non-FCCLA activities. **Deadline:** April 1. **Contact:** Phone: 703-476-4900.

4488 ■ Family Life Today
27 Cherokee Rd.
Arlington, MA 02474
Ph: (617)686-3087
URL: familylivingtoday.com

4489 ■ Child Welfare and Development (CWD) Scholarship *(Undergraduate/Scholarship)*

Purpose: To aid students who plan to pursue a career in the field of child welfare, and to help build a world where every child can grow up healthy, protected from harm or trauma, and educated so they can reach their full potential. **Focus:** Psychology; Social work; Sociology. **Qualif.:** Applicant must be currently enrolled in good standing in an accredited sociology, psychology, or social sciences undergraduate program in the United States; must have a current overall GPA of 3.0 or higher; must have a demonstrated history of working with or on behalf of children who have experienced neglect or abuse (through advocacy, community involvement, volunteerism, or research efforts); must have demonstrated financial need. **Criteria:** Selection will be on review by the CWD Scholarship Award committee, which will score each submission and essay on a scale of 1 to 20 based on merit and need factors.

Funds Avail.: $1,000. **Duration:** Annual. **Number Awarded:** 1. **To Apply:** Applicant must submit an 1 to 2 page essay on that explains the following: 1. Why you've chosen to pursue a career in social work and child welfare; 2. What your specific extracurricular experience is working with or on behalf of at-risk or traumatized children; 3. How you intend to use this award. Applicant must also provide first and last name, email address, phone number, current college or university, current GPA, expected graduation date, and current course of study. All materials should be submitted to cwdscholarship@familylivingtoday.com. **Dead-**

Awards are arranged alphabetically below their administering organizations

line: January 31. **Contact:** URL: familylivingtoday.com/cwd-social-work-scholarship/.

4490 ■ Fanconi Anemia Research Fund (FARF)

1801 Willamette St., Ste. 200
Eugene, OR 97401
Ph: (541)687-4658
Free: 888-326-2664
E-mail: info@fanconi.org
URL: www.fanconi.org
Social Media: www.facebook.com/
  fanconianemiaresearchfund
www.instagram.com/fanconianemiaresearchfund
www.linkedin.com/company/fanconi-anemia-research-fund/
twitter.com/FAresearchfund
www.youtube.com/channel/UCV4Bfk33arbdYF_5HsIYM9Q

4491 ■ Fanconi Anemia Research Grants *(Postdoctorate, Doctorate/Grant)*

Purpose: To help researchers advance the science relating to Fanconi anemia. **Focus:** Health sciences. **Qualif.:** Applicant should hold doctorate or equivalent degree from US and non-US. **Criteria:** Selection will be based on the committee's criteria.

Funds Avail.: Varies. **Remarks:** Established in 1989. **Contact:** Email: research@fanconi.org.

4492 ■ The Fantasy Sports Daily

2540 S Ocean Blvd.
Highland Beach, FL 33487
Ph: (561)274-6504
Fax: (561)274-6507
URL: www.fantasysportsdaily.com

4493 ■ The Fantasy Sports Daily Scholarship Program - General Scholarship for Advanced Education *(Undergraduate, Graduate, Master's/Scholarship)*

Purpose: To support and motivate students to value and make the most of their education, and to give scholarship awards to deserving students to achieve higher quality education, and actively promote education to encourage students to improve their knowledge and strive for excellence. **Focus:** General studies/Field of study not specified. **Qualif.:** Applicants must be legal residents of the United States and must be students who are at least 16 years of age enrolled in an accredited post-secondary academic institution in the United States in a two year, four year or a graduate program. **Criteria:** Students are selected based on their responses, as judged by the executive management team.

Duration: Annual; each fall and spring semester. **To Apply:** Applicants must submit one complete contest application via sponsor's website in English language before the deadline and must answer four personal, open-ended, and thought-provoking questions to be considered as finalist. **Deadline:** October 15.

4494 ■ Farella Braun + Martel L.L.P.

235 Montgomery St.
Russ Bldg., 17th Fl.
San Francisco, CA 94104

Ph: (415)954-4400
Fax: (415)954-4480
URL: www.fbm.com
Social Media: www.facebook.com/FarellaBraunMartel/
www.instagram.com/farellabraunmartel/
www.linkedin.com/company/farella-braun---martel-llp
twitter.com/FarellaBraun

4495 ■ Farella Braun + Martel LLP 1L Diversity Scholarship Program *(Undergraduate/Scholarship)*

Purpose: To assist diverse Bay Area law students who are pursuing their legal careers. **Focus:** Law. **Qualif.:** Applicants must be current first-year students with full- or part-time class loads attending one of the following law schools: University of California, Berkeley, School of Law; University of California Davis School of Law; University of California, Hastings College of the Law; Santa Clara University School of Law; Stanford Law School; or University of San Francisco School of Law; the program is open to law students of underrepresented groups whose background or personal experience would otherwise contribute to the diversity of the legal profession. **Criteria:** Recipients will be selected based on a combination of merit and financial need; preference will be given to applicants who demonstrate a commitment to working and living in the Bay Area.

Funds Avail.: $30,000. **Duration:** Annual. **Number Awarded:** 3. **To Apply:** Applicants must submit the completed application form together with the other requirements asked by the bestowing organization. **Contact:** Maggie Owyang; Email: DiversityScholarship@fbm.com; URL: www.fbm.com/diversity-equality-inclusion-committee/diversity-scholarship/.

4496 ■ Farm Equipment Manufacturers Association (FEMA)

1000 Executive Pky., Ste. 100
Saint Louis, MO 63141-6369
Ph: (314)878-2304
Fax: (314)732-1480
E-mail: info@farmequip.org
URL: www.farmequip.org
Social Media: twitter.com/Shortliner

4497 ■ Harold B. Halter Memorial Scholarship *(Undergraduate/Scholarship)*

Purpose: To provide scholarships to outstanding students to apply at any two-year or four-year college of their choice. **Focus:** General studies/Field of study not specified. **Qualif.:** Applicants must be students who have been enrolled in the Pope County Community High School for at least two previous years; must have a GPA of 2.5 based upon a 4 point system; must have been accepted for enrollment as full-time students in a junior or four-year accredited college or university. **Criteria:** Selection will be based on the following criteria: excellence in scholarship; contribution to the favorable image of Pope County Community High School, including improvement in academic work; demonstrated leadership ability; outstanding character and personal development; desire to grow academically and socially; and has shown a level of financial self-support.

Funds Avail.: $1,000. **Duration:** Annual. **Remarks:** The award was established in memory of Harold Halter who was Executive Vice President of this association for 29-years.

Awards are arranged alphabetically below their administering organizations

4498 ■ Federal Alliance For Safe Homes (FLASH)

1427 E Piedmont Dr., Ste. 2
Tallahassee, FL 32308
Fax: (850)201-1067
Free: 877-221-7233
E-mail: flash@flash.org
URL: www.flash.org
Social Media: twitter.com/FederalAlliance

4499 ■ FLASH Social Science Scholarships
(Graduate/Scholarship)

Purpose: To support graduate students seeking academic degrees that underpin disaster safety and mitigation, including construction, engineering, financial services, risk communication, social sciences and other related fields. **Focus:** Engineering; Risk management; Social sciences. **Qualif.:** Applicants must be master or doctorate degree students performing research on behavior change, societal effects, or other social aspects as they relate to natural disaster mitigation. **Criteria:** Selection will be based on the committee's criteria.

Funds Avail.: $1,500. **Duration:** Annual. **To Apply:** Applicants must submit the following: a fully-completed application form; unofficial transcripts of undergraduate and graduate records; a statement of appraisal and agreement to direct the applicants' graduate research program from the proposed faculty advisor; must respond to all questions on the application form in typewritten and no additional sheet should be attached. **Deadline:** May 15.

4500 ■ Huber Engineered Woods Product Evaluation Scholarships *(Graduate/Scholarship)*

Purpose: To support graduate students seeking academic degrees that underpin disaster safety and mitigation, including construction, engineering, financial services, risk communication, social sciences and other related fields. **Focus:** Architecture; Construction; Engineering; Materials research/ science. **Qualif.:** Applicants must be master or doctorate degree students performing research on new structural product testing/evaluation and new structural product testing/evaluation procedures. **Criteria:** Selection will be based on the committee's criteria.

Funds Avail.: $1,500. **Duration:** Annual. **To Apply:** Applicants must submit the following: a fully-completed application form; unofficial transcripts of undergraduate and graduate records; a statement of appraisal and agreement to direct the applicants graduate research program from the proposed faculty advisor. Applicants must respond to all questions on the application form in typewritten and no additional sheet should be attached.

4501 ■ International Code Council Scholarship
(Graduate/Scholarship)

Purpose: To support graduate students seeking academic degrees that underpin disaster safety and mitigation, including construction, engineering, financial services, risk communication, social sciences and other related fields. **Focus:** Construction; Engineering. **Criteria:** Applicants will be selected based on the merits of the application.

Funds Avail.: $1,500. **Duration:** Annual. **Number Awarded:** 1. **To Apply:** Applicants must submit the following: a fully-completed application form; unofficial transcripts of undergraduate and graduate records; a statement of appraisal and agreement to direct the applicants' graduate research program from the proposed faculty advisor; must respond to all questions on the application form in typewritten and no additional sheet should be attached. **Deadline:** May 15.

4502 ■ John Jeffries Meteorology Scholarship
(Graduate/Scholarship)

Purpose: To support graduate students seeking academic degrees that underpin disaster safety and mitigation, including construction, engineering, financial services, risk communication, social sciences and other related fields. **Focus:** Meteorology. **Qualif.:** Applicants must be master or doctorate degree students performing research on meteorology or meteorological risk modeling as it relates to natural disasters. **Criteria:** Selection will be based on the committee's criteria.

Funds Avail.: $1,500. **Duration:** Annual. **To Apply:** Applicants must submit the following a fully-completed application form; unofficial transcripts of undergraduate and graduate records; a statement of appraisal and agreement to direct the applicants' graduate research program from the proposed faculty advisor; must respond to all questions on the application form in typewritten and no additional sheet should be attached. **Deadline:** May 15. **Contact:** Tim Smail, Phone: 850-728-0348; Email: tim@flash.org.

4503 ■ Portland Cement Association Scholarship
(Graduate/Scholarship)

Purpose: To support graduate students seeking academic degrees that underpin disaster safety and mitigation, including construction, engineering, financial services, risk communication, social sciences and other related fields. **Focus:** Construction. **Qualif.:** Applicants must be master or doctorate degree students or fourth or fifth year architectural students performing research on the following topics: innovative use of concrete systems to improve the resilience of new production homes; quantification of the impacts significant loss of housing stock has on post disaster community recovery and continuity; life cycle cost analysis examining short and long term financial and social impacts of more resilient concrete home construction; innovative use of concrete to improve the resilience of homes that are rebuilt after being damaged or destroyed in a natural disaster. **Criteria:** Selection will be based on the committee's criteria.

Funds Avail.: $1,500. **Duration:** Annual. **Number Awarded:** 1. **To Apply:** Applicants must submit the following: a fully-completed application form; unofficial transcripts of undergraduate and graduate records; a statement of appraisal and agreement to direct the applicants' graduate research program from the proposed faculty advisor; must respond to all questions on the application form in typewritten and no additional sheet should be attached. **Deadline:** May 15. **Contact:** Tim Smail, Phone: 850-728-0348; Email: tim@flash.org.

4504 ■ Resilience Action Fund Scholarship
(Graduate/Scholarship)

Purpose: To support graduate students seeking academic degrees that underpin disaster safety and mitigation, including construction, engineering, financial services, risk communication, social sciences and other related fields. **Focus:** Architecture; Business; Construction; Economics; Urban affairs/design/planning. **Qualif.:** Applicants must be master and doctorate degree students performing research on policy cost-benefit analysis, risk assessment and construction economics, or correlation between housing prices/ affordability and construction costs related to mitigation.

Awards are arranged alphabetically below their administering organizations

Criteria: Selection will be based on the committee's criteria.

Funds Avail.: $1,500. **Duration:** Annual. **To Apply:** Applicants must submit the following: a fully-completed application form; unofficial transcripts of undergraduate and graduate records; a statement of appraisal and agreement to direct the applicants' graduate research program from the proposed faculty advisor; must respond to all questions on the application form in typewritten and no additional sheet should be attached. **Deadline:** May 15. **Contact:** Tim Smail, Phone: 850-728-0348; Email: tim@flash.org.

4505 ■ Federal Circuit Bar Association (FCBA)

1620 I St. NW, Ste. 801
Washington, DC 20006-4033
Ph: (202)466-3923
Fax: (202)833-1061
E-mail: brookshire1@fedcirbar.org
URL: www.fedcirbar.org

4506 ■ William S. Bullinger Scholarships *(Doctorate/ Scholarship)*

Purpose: To support individuals who have an interest in the subject matter of the Federal Circuit's legal community. **Focus:** Law. **Qualif.:** Applicants must be pursuing a juris doctor degree; must be enrolling for the upcoming academic year in any law school accredited by the American Bar Association; must demonstrate financial need and interest in one of the many topics that lie within the procedure, substance or scope of the jurisdiction of the United States Court of Appeal for the Federal Circuit. **Criteria:** Selection is based primarily on economic need, although other criteria including academic promise and an interest in the subject matter of the Federal Circuit's legal community are considered.

Funds Avail.: $5,000. **Duration:** Annual. **Number Awarded:** 1. **To Apply:** Applicants must include curriculum vitae; undergraduate and, if applicable, graduate law school transcripts; an original, typed essay written by the Applicants alone; essay is limited to no more than 450 words on one page and should address the Applicant's financial need, any interests in particular areas of the law, and any qualifications for a particular scholarship considered relevant by the Applicants; must include unofficial transcripts, and need not include a letter of recommendation. **Deadline:** May 31. **Remarks:** The scholarship is given in memory of William S. Bullinger, a respected practitioner who tirelessly advanced the Association's encouragement of professionalism, civility in practice, and dialogue between the Bench and Bar.

4507 ■ Howard T. Markey Memorial Scholarship *(Undergraduate/Scholarship)*

Purpose: To provide financial support for qualified individuals intending to pursue their studies. **Focus:** Law. **Qualif.:** Applicants must be law students showing financial need, demonstrated academic promise, and service, either in undergraduate or in law school. **Criteria:** Selection will be given based on a written submission of no more than one page setting out the applicant's financial need, any interests in particular areas of the law, and any qualifications for the awards considered relevant by the applicant; application materials will be considered, and prior academic performance will not be the primary criteria for selection.

Funds Avail.: $10,000. **Duration:** Annual; one year. **Number Awarded:** 1. **To Apply:** Applicants must submit a col-

lege and law school transcript and a one-page curriculum vitae. **Deadline:** May 31.

4508 ■ Need-Based Scholarships *(Doctorate/ Scholarship)*

Purpose: To provide scholarship to law students in need of financial help. **Focus:** Law. **Qualif.:** Applicants must be pursuing a juris doctor degree; must be enrolling for the upcoming academic year in any law school accredited by the American Bar Association; must demonstrate financial need and interest in one of the many topics that lie within the procedure, substance or scope of the jurisdiction of the United States Court of Appeal for the Federal Circuit. **Criteria:** Selection will be based on the committee's criteria.

Funds Avail.: $5,000. **Duration:** Annual. **To Apply:** Applicants must include curriculum vitae; undergraduate and, if applicable, graduate law school transcripts; an original, typed essay written by the Applicants alone; essay is limited to no more than 450 words on one page and should address the Applicant's financial need, any interests in particular areas of the law, and any qualifications for a particular scholarship considered relevant by the Applicants; must include unofficial transcripts, and need not include a letter of recommendation. **Deadline:** May 31.

4509 ■ Helen W. Nies Memorial Scholarship *(Postgraduate/Scholarship)*

Purpose: To provide financial support for qualified individuals intending to pursue their studies. **Focus:** Law. **Qualif.:** Applicants must be women law students showing financial need, demonstrated academic promise and service, either in undergraduate or in law school. **Criteria:** Selection will be based on financial need.

Funds Avail.: $10,000. **Duration:** Annual. **To Apply:** Applicants must include curriculum vitae; undergraduate and, if applicable, graduate law school transcripts; an original, typed essay written by the Applicants alone; essay is limited to no more than 450 words on one page and should address the Applicant's financial need, any interests in particular areas of the law, and any qualifications for a particular scholarship considered relevant by the Applicants; must include unofficial transcripts, and need not include a letter of recommendation. **Deadline:** May 31. **Remarks:** The award was established in the memory of Helen W. Nies, former Chief Judge of the United States Court of Appeals for the Federal Circuit. **Contact:** Scholarship Coordinator, Jonathan Bean; E-mail: j.bean@arizona.edu.

4510 ■ Federal Communications Bar Association (FCBA)

1020 19th St. NW, Ste. 325
Washington, DC 20036
Ph: (202)293-4000
Fax: (202)293-4317
E-mail: fcba@fcba.org
URL: www.fcba.org
Social Media: www.facebook.com/CommunicationsBar
www.facebook.com/communicationsbar

4511 ■ FCBA Foundation College Scholarship Program *(Undergraduate/Scholarship)*

Purpose: To provide financial assistance for local high school students intending to pursue college studies. **Focus:** General studies/Field of study not specified. **Criteria:** Selec-

Awards are arranged alphabetically below their administering organizations

tion will review applications from high school students of diverse backgrounds with an interest in communications-related fields, including media, journalism, technology, engineering or law.

Funds Avail.: Up to $28,000. **Number Awarded:** Varies. **To Apply:** Application is via online; may visit the website for further information on the application process. **Deadline:** February 23.

4512 ■ FCBA Foundation Law School Scholarship Programs (Postgraduate/Scholarship)

Purpose: To support the education of law students across the country. **Focus:** Law. **Qualif.:** Applicants must be second or third year students currently enrolled in accredited law schools in the United States who have a demonstrated interest in pursuing a career in communications law. **Criteria:** Selection will be based on need and merit.

Funds Avail.: $2,000-$5,000. **Deadline:** April 9.

4513 ■ FCBA Foundation Law School Summer Internship Stipend Program (Professional development/Internship)

Purpose: To support law students in their job trainings with a connection to their field of study. **Focus:** Law. **Qualif.:** Applicants must be U.S. law students attending an accredited college or university. **Criteria:** Selection will be based on the committee's criteria.

Funds Avail.: Amount varies. **Duration:** Annual. **Number Awarded:** Varies. **Deadline:** March 31.

4514 ■ Federal Employee Education and Assistance Fund (FEEA)

1641 Prince St.
Alexandria, VA 22314
Ph: (202)554-0007
Fax: (202)559-1298
E-mail: fedshelpingfeds@feea.org
URL: www.feea.org
Social Media: www.facebook.com/FedsHelpingFeds
www.linkedin.com/company/feea
twitter.com/FedsHelpingFeds

4515 ■ FEEA-NTEU Scholarships (Graduate, Postgraduate, Undergraduate/Scholarship)

Purpose: To provide financial assistance to civilian employees of the US Federal Government. **Focus:** General studies/Field of study not specified. **Qualif.:** Applicants must be current civilian federal employees and their dependent family members (spouse/child); adult children and other relatives are eligible if claimed on the sponsoring employee's tax return; active duty military members and their dependents are eligible only through a sponsoring civilian employee spouse; military retirees and dependents are eligible if the retiree (or retiree's spouse) is a current civilian federal employee; must have at least three (3) years of civilian federal service; must have at least a 3.0 cumulative grade point average (CGPA) unweighted on a 4.0 scale; must be current high school seniors or college students working toward an accredited degree and enrolled in a two or four year undergraduate, graduate or postgraduate program; dependents must be full-time students; and federal employees may be part-time students. **Criteria:** Selection will be judged by Scholarship Committee.

Funds Avail.: $5,000. **Duration:** Annual. **To Apply:** Applicants must submit FEEA Scholarship Application Form;

essay; written recommendation/character reference; transcript; a list and brief description of awards, extracurricular and community service activities; copy of ACT, SAT or other examination scores; copy of most recent standard form 50 "notice of personnel action", and two self-addressed, stamped, No. 10 business-size envelopes with first class postage properly affixed. **Remarks:** Established in 1986.

4516 ■ FMA-FEEA Scholarship Program (Graduate/Scholarship)

Purpose: To provide financial assistance for the educational pursuits of current civilian employees and retirees who are FMA members and their dependent family members. **Focus:** General studies/Field of study not specified. **Criteria:** Selection will be based on academic and personal achievement; community service and engagement; recommendation of the academic or professional contact; substance and quality of writing throughout the application.

Funds Avail.: $1,000-$5,000. **Duration:** Annual. **Number Awarded:** Varies. **To Apply:** Applicants must submit complete application package containing the FMA-FEEA Scholarship Application Form; essay; written recommendation/character reference; transcript of scholastic record; brief description of awards, extracurricular and community service activities; copy of ACT, SAT or other examination scores; copy of most recent standard Form 50, Notice of Personnel Action (Federal employee applicants); and two self-addressed, stamped, No. 10 business-size envelopes with first class postage properly affixed. **Remarks:** Established in 1994.

4517 ■ NARFE-FEEA Scholarship Awards Program (Undergraduate/Scholarship)

Purpose: To provide financial assistance for the education of children and grandchildren of federal employees. **Focus:** General studies/Field of study not specified.

Duration: Annual. **Remarks:** Established in 1987. **Contact:** NARFE-FEEA Fund, c/o FEEA, 1641 Prince St., Alexandria, VA, 22314; Email: scholarship@narfe.org.

4518 ■ Federal Law Enforcement Officers Association (FLEOA)

7945 MacArthur Blvd., Ste. 201
Cabin John, MD 20818
Ph: (202)870-5503
Free: 866-553-5362
E-mail: fleoa@fleoa.org
URL: www.fleoa.org

4519 ■ The FLEOA Foundation Scholastic Program (Undergraduate/Scholarship)

Purpose: To provide educational assistance for the children of current, retired or deceased Federal Law Enforcement Officers. **Focus:** General studies/Field of study not specified. **Qualif.:** Applicants must be high school graduates, who are the children of current, retired or deceased members of the federal law enforcement officers association. **Criteria:** Selection will be based on the committee's criteria; grants will be awarded in the order of the highest cumulative ranking; special consideration will be given to those applicants who are the children of federal law enforcement officers who were killed or disabled in the line of duty.

Funds Avail.: $500 or $1,000. **Duration:** Annual. **To Apply:** Applications must be submitted along with high school

Awards are arranged alphabetically below their administering organizations

final transcripts, with class ranking, SAT or other aptitude test scores; letters that support community service activity; acceptance from a college or university. **Deadline:** July 1. **Contact:** FLEOA Foundation; 7945 MacArthur Blvd, Suite 201; Cabin John, MD 20818; efebus@fleoa.org.

4520 ■ Federal Managers Association (FMA)

1641 Prince St.
Alexandria, VA 22314-2818
Ph: (703)683-8700
Fax: (703)683-8707
E-mail: info@fedmanagers.org
URL: www.fedmanagers.org
Social Media: www.facebook.com/fedmanagers
twitter.com/FedManagers

4521 ■ FMA-FEEA Scholarship Program *(Graduate/Scholarship)*

Purpose: To provide financial assistance for the educational pursuits of current civilian employees and retirees who are FMA members and their dependent family members. **Focus:** General studies/Field of study not specified. **Criteria:** Selection will be based on academic and personal achievement; community service and engagement; recommendation of the academic or professional contact; substance and quality of writing throughout the application.

Funds Avail.: $1,000-$5,000. **Duration:** Annual. **Number Awarded:** Varies. **To Apply:** Applicants must submit complete application package containing the FMA-FEEA Scholarship Application Form; essay; written recommendation/character reference; transcript of scholastic record; brief description of awards, extracurricular and community service activities; copy of ACT, SAT or other examination scores; copy of most recent standard Form 50, Notice of Personnel Action (Federal employee applicants); and two self-addressed, stamped, No. 10 business-size envelopes with first class postage properly affixed. **Remarks:** Established in 1994.

4522 ■ The Federalist Society

1776 I St. NW, Ste. 300
Washington, DC 20006
Ph: (202)822-8138
Fax: (202)296-8061
E-mail: info@fedsoc.org
URL: fedsoc.org
Social Media: www.facebook.com/Federalist.Society
www.linkedin.com/company/the-federalist-society
twitter.com/FedSoc
www.youtube.com/user/TheFederalistSociety

4523 ■ Olin-Searle-Smith-Darling Fellows in Law *(Other/Fellowship)*

Purpose: To provide young legal thinkers the opportunity to spend one or two years working full time on writing and developing their scholarship with the goal of entering the legal academy. **Focus:** Law. **Qualif.:** Applicants must be J.D. and have extremely strong academic qualifications; committed to the rule of law and intellectual diversity and legal academia; and have the promise of a distinguished career as a legal scholar and teacher. **Criteria:** Selection is based upon a distinguished group of academics selecting the Fellows based on qualifications and the submitted application materials.

Funds Avail.: $60,000 plus benefits. **Duration:** Annual. **To Apply:** Applicants must submit a resume and law school transcript; academic writing sample(s) (50 page limit); a brief discussion of the applicants' areas of intellectual interest (approximately 2 pages); a statement of commitment to teaching law; and at least two, and generally no more than three, letters of support. **Deadline:** March 13. **Contact:** Olin-Searle-Smith-Darling Fellows in Law Program, ATTN: Jim Pennell, c/o The Federalist Society, 1776 I St., NW, Ste. 300; Washington, D.C. 20006.

4524 ■ Federated Women's Institutes of Ontario

7382 Wellington Rd. 30, RR5
Guelph, ON, Canada N1H 6J2
Ph: (519)836-3078
Fax: (519)836-9456
E-mail: fwio@fwio.on.ca
URL: fwio.on.ca
Social Media: www.facebook.com/FWIOntario
twitter.com/fwiontario

4525 ■ Ontario Women's Institute Scholarships *(Undergraduate/Scholarship)*

Purpose: To assist students studying at the university of guelph, college of social and applied human sciences. **Focus:** Hotel, institutional, and restaurant management; Management. **Qualif.:** Applicants must be female students from Ontario with a minimum of 70% cumulative average; have completed 4.00 credits in the BASc Program and who have involvement in extracurricular activities.

Funds Avail.: $1,000. **Duration:** Annual. **Deadline:** May 15. **Remarks:** Established in 1947.

4526 ■ Federation of American Consumers and Travelers (FACT)

318 Hillsboro Ave.
Edwardsville, IL 62025
Fax: (618)656-5369
Free: 800-872-3228
E-mail: cservice@usafact.org
URL: usafact.org
Social Media: www.facebook.com/usafactmembers
www.linkedin.com/company/usafact
www.pinterest.com/FACTAdvantage

4527 ■ FACT "Second Chance" Scholarship Program *(Undergraduate/Scholarship)*

Purpose: To support the education of FACT members and their families. **Focus:** General studies/Field of study not specified. **Qualif.:** Applicants must be FACT members and their immediate families; must be graduating from an accredited public, private or parochial high school and maintain a "C" grade point average to remain in the funds (if considered); students currently enrolled in two- or four-year education in accredited colleges or universities. **Criteria:** Applicants will be evaluated by the Scholarship Committee based on academic records and quality of the essay submitted.

Funds Avail.: $2,500 to $10,000. **Duration:** Annual. **Number Awarded:** 4. **To Apply:** Applicants must submit completed application form; Release Authorization and Membership Verification Form; Certification Form; Official Copy of High School Transcript signed by the applicant's

Awards are arranged alphabetically below their administering organizations

high school principal or academic advisor; and a two-page, double-spaced essay. **Deadline:** September 30.

4528 ■ Federation of Asian Canadian Lawyers
20 Toronto St., Ste. 300
Toronto, ON, Canada M5C 2B8
URL: facl.ca
Social Media: www.facebook.com/on.facl.ca
www.instagram.com/faclontario
www.linkedin.com/company/federation-of-asian-canadian
  -lawyers
twitter.com/faclontario

4529 ■ Omatsu FACL Scholarships *(Juris Doctorate, Advanced Professional/Scholarship)*

Purpose: To support FACL student members in their legal education. **Focus:** Law. **Criteria:** Selection will be based on leadership and community involvement, law student vision, academics, financial need, and personal statement.

Funds Avail.: 1,000 Canadian Dollars each. **To Apply:** Applicants must complete the provided Application Form and submit via email, along with their curriculum vitae, university and law school transcripts. **Contact:** Email: awardss@facl.ca.

4530 ■ Fédération Canadienne des Épiciers Indépendants (FCEI)
105 Gordon Baker Rd., Ste. 401
North York, ON, Canada M2H 3P8
URL: www.cfig.ca

4531 ■ Canadian Federation of Independent Grocers National Scholarship *(Undergraduate/ Scholarship)*

Purpose: To provide financial assistance to Canadian students for their further educational enrichment. **Focus:** General studies/Field of study not specified. **Criteria:** Applicants are evaluated based on the essay they have written, respectively.

Funds Avail.: 6,000 Canadian dollars. **Duration:** Annual. **Number Awarded:** 1. **To Apply:** Applicants must submit application form with all pertinent information properly filled in. **Deadline:** August 4.

4532 ■ Federation of Diocesan Liturgical Commissions (FDLC)
415 Michigan Ave. NE
Washington, DC 20017
Ph: (202)635-6990
Fax: (202)529-2452
E-mail: nationaloffice@fdlc.org
URL: www.fdlc.org

4533 ■ Tabat Scholarship Award *(Graduate/ Scholarship)*

Purpose: To support graduate students in liturgical studies by providing assistance with the payment of tuition, the purchase of books, or the continuation of research. **Focus:** Religion; Theology. **Qualif.:** Applicants must be pursuing a graduate degree in a program of liturgical studies to prepare for service in the Church of the United States in an academic, diocesan, or parish setting. **Criteria:** Selection

will be evaluated by the Scholarship Committee.

Funds Avail.: $1,000. **Duration:** Annual. **To Apply:** Applicants must submit curriculum vitae; a short description of how the grant will be used; and two letters of recommendation, in a sealed envelope, from professors or from someone knowledgeable about the person's work. **Deadline:** June 1. **Remarks:** Established in 2001.

4534 ■ Jonathan M. Feigenbaum, Esquire
184 High St., No. 503
Boston, MA 02110
Ph: (617)934-7488
URL: www.erisaattorneys.com
Social Media: www.facebook.com/jonathan-m-feigenbaum
  -esquire-1433084030300422
linkedin.com/company/jonathan-m.-feigenbaum
www.youtube.com/channel/UCEu7P6lfLuGhY-KSQMktZ8A

4535 ■ City of Boston Disability Scholarship Contest *(Undergraduate/Scholarship)*

Purpose: To help needy college students who have family members suffering from a disability and encourage students to explore what they have learned about a disability that can have a positive impact on family and community. **Focus:** General studies/Field of study not specified. **Qualif.:** Applicant must be a current college student attending a part-time or full-time degree granting program; have a family member that has an occupationally impairing disability; and work in public sector or have a family member who works in the public sector. **Criteria:** Selection is based on the best video essay submitted.

Funds Avail.: $1,000. **Duration:** Annual. **Number Awarded:** 3. **To Apply:** Applicant must record a video (one to two minutes long) explaining what they have learned from a family member or loved one who has a disability. Video should be published on the applicant's YouTube channel with the title "City of Boston Disability Contest" and this link in the description: www.erisaattorneys.com/city-boston-disability-scholarship-college-students-family-member-suffering-disability/. Applicant must also share the video to their Facebook page. **Deadline:** August 15. **Contact:** Nancy Rand; Email: Nancy@nrand.com.

4536 ■ The Feldman Law Firm, PLLC
1 E Washington St., #2240
Phoenix, AZ 85004
Ph: (602)540-7887
E-mail: attorney@afphoenixcriminalattorney.com
URL: www.afphoenixcriminalattorney.com
Social Media: www.facebook.com/TheFeldmanLawFirmPllc
www.linkedin.com/company/the-feldman-law-firm-llp
twitter.com/phxattorney
www.youtube.com/channel/UCQyCx1I
  -JgW131EoT1EHYLQ

4537 ■ Autism Scholarship *(Community College, Four Year College, Vocational/Occupational/Scholarship)*

Purpose: To provide tuition assistance to encourage those with autism spectrum disorder (ASD) to continue their education. **Focus:** General studies/Field of study not specified. **Qualif.:** Applicant must be diagnosed with autism/ASD and intending to further their schooling at a college or vocational/trade school. **Criteria:** Selection will be based

Awards are arranged alphabetically below their administering organizations

on Short statement and optional essay.

Funds Avail.: $1,000. **To Apply:** Applicants must complete online application on sponsor's website. Applicant must also upload a statement (up to 100 words in length) explaining educational goals, or prepare and upload an essay (up to 700 words or less in length) discussing how ASD has affected applicant's education. **Deadline:** February 21. **Contact:** Email: mike@afphoenixcriminalattorney.com.

4538 ■ Disabled Veterans Scholarship *(Community College, College, Vocational/Occupational/Scholarship)*

Purpose: To provide scholarships for disabled veterans who want to continue their educations. **Focus:** General studies/Field of study not specified. **Qualif.:** Applicants must be disable veterans of the United States Armed Forces with a disability rating of at least 30 percent or higher, who plan to attend a trade or vocational school, or a college or junior college.

Funds Avail.: $1,000. **To Apply:** Applicant must complete the online application form on the scholarship website, including agreeing to the terms and conditions of the scholarship program and upload the following materials: a short statement of 125 words or less explaining their educational goals; and an essay of not more than 850 words that discusses how their life has been affected by their military service and/or disability. **Deadline:** February 5.

4539 ■ Law Student Scholarship *(Graduate/Scholarship)*

Purpose: To defray a portion of the cost of tuition at an ABA-accredited U.S. law school. **Focus:** Law. **Qualif.:** Applicant must be a U.S. citizen attending or planning to attend an ABA-accredited school. **Criteria:** Selection will be based on the short statement and optional essay.

Funds Avail.: $1,000. **To Apply:** Applicant must complete online application and upload a statement up to 125 words or less explaining why they want to obtain a law degree, or upload an essay up to 900 words discussing how a law degree will enable the applicant to make a difference in the world.

4540 ■ FHE Health
505 S Federal Hwy., No. 2
Deerfield Beach, FL 33441
Free: 877-650-0726
URL: www.fherehab.com
Social Media: www.facebook.com/fhehealth
www.youtube.com/user/fherehab

4541 ■ Hope for Healing Scholarship *(Undergraduate, Graduate, Doctorate, Master's/Scholarship)*

Purpose: To encourage more of America's best and brightest to pursue a vocation in the field of addiction and mental health. **Focus:** Behavioral sciences; Mental health; Nursing. **Qualif.:** Applicants must be undergraduate or graduate students. Undergraduate applicants must be currently enrolled in a four-year degree program or show evidence of acceptance to such a program; have a GPA of 3.0 or higher in the last completed academic year at a four-year institution, in the most recent quarter or semester, or if no college has been completed a minimum 3.5 or high school GPA; and an academic focus in the area of mental and behavioral health or psychiatric nursing as demonstrated by major or minor course of study. Graduate applicants

must be currently enrolled in a graduate degree program or show proof of acceptance to an institution that offers Masters and Doctorate degrees; have graduated from an accredited four-year institution with a 3.0 or higher GPA; and have an academic focus in an area of study related to mental and behavioral health, nursing, or addiction medicine. **Criteria:** All applicants are required to complete a form on the website page. From those applicants, finalists will be selected. Applicants will be judged on: academic performance; quality of essay; and potential for positive impact on the field of mental and behavioral health (as demonstrated by the essay and level of current volunteer activities or employment in the field).

Funds Avail.: $5,000 (one undergraduate, one graduate). **Duration:** Annual. **Number Awarded:** 2. **To Apply:** Applicants must submit the following: high school or college transcripts; proof of current college enrollment or acceptance; documentation of course of study; a typed essay that describes why applicant is pursuing study in mental health, nursing or addiction medicine, and what they want to contribute to the field; and a completed application form. **Deadline:** January 15.

4542 ■ Fibrose Kystique Canada (CF)
2323 Yonge St., Ste. 800
Toronto, ON, Canada M4P 2C9
Free: 800-378-2233
E-mail: info@cysticfibrosis.ca
URL: www.cysticfibrosis.ca
Social Media: www.facebook.com/CysticFibrosisCanada
twitter.com/CFCanada

4543 ■ CCFF Clinical Fellowships *(Doctorate, Graduate/Fellowship)*

Purpose: To train physicians to become CF specialists so that they can provide ongoing clinical care to individuals with CF in Canada. **Focus:** Cystic fibrosis. **Qualif.:** Applicants must be a Canadian citizen or permanent resident; have an MD degree; have recently completed the clinical training, exam and have obtained medical licensure in Canada. **Criteria:** Selection is based on the applicant's merit and potential.

Funds Avail.: No specific amount. **Duration:** One year. **To Apply:** Applicants must submit three letters of recommendation (one from the recent supervisor); description of the proposed clinical training program; one- to two-page letters should indicate the period of time and in what capacity the supervisor has known the Applicants, and should elaborate on academic and clinical capabilities and competence; including a clinical research component if applicable, and official transcripts of the applicant's complete academic record. **Deadline:** October 3.

4544 ■ CCFF Fellowships *(Doctorate, Graduate/Fellowship)*

Purpose: To support basic or clinical research training in the areas of biomedical or behavioral sciences pertinent to cystic fibrosis. **Focus:** Cystic fibrosis. **Qualif.:** Applicants must hold an MD or PhD degree or must be graduates who have already completed basic residency training and are eligible for Canadian licensure. **Criteria:** Selection is based on the applicant's merit and potential.

Funds Avail.: Varies. **Duration:** 2 years. **To Apply:** Applicants must submit three letters of recommendation (one from a current supervisor); a description of the proposed

Awards are arranged alphabetically below their administering organizations

research and training program; and official transcripts. Twelve copies of the application are required (1 with original signatures and 11 double-sided photocopies, with each copy stapled in the upper left hand corner). **Deadline:** October 1. **Contact:** amackesy@cysticfibrosis.ca.

4545 ■ CCFF Scholarships (Doctorate, Graduate/ Scholarship)

Purpose: To attract investigators to cystic fibrosis research. **Focus:** Cystic fibrosis. **Qualif.:** Applicant must hold an MD or PhD degree; must be sponsored by the chairman of the appropriate department and by the dean of the faculty; and has recently completed the training and wish to devote the majority of the time to cystic fibrosis research. **Criteria:** Selection is based on the caliber of the applicant's research and the potential of the applicant to make an outstanding contribution to cystic fibrosis research.

Funds Avail.: No specific amount. **To Apply:** Applicants must submit a completed application form together with the required materials.

4546 ■ Field Museum of Natural History
1400 S Lake Shore Dr.
Chicago, IL 60605-2496
Ph: (312)922-9410
URL: www.fieldmuseum.org
Social Media: www.facebook.com/fieldmuseum
www.instagram.com/fieldmuseum/
twitter.com/fieldmuseum
www.youtube.com/user/thefieldmuseum

4547 ■ Graduate Student Fellowships (Graduate/ Fellowship)

Purpose: To support graduate students engaged in dissertation research associated with the field museum. **Focus:** General studies/Field of study not specified. **Qualif.:** Applicants must be graduate students residing in the Chicago area; graduate students must have completed the preliminary examination. **Criteria:** Selection will be based on evaluation of submitted research including relevance of the field museum's collections to the project, collaboration(s) with Field Museum curators (if any), procedures and methods used in the project.

Funds Avail.: $32,000. **Duration:** Annual. **Number Awarded:** 2. **To Apply:** Applicants must submit full curriculum vitae with names and contact information of two references in addition to sponsor; a copy of thesis proposal uploaded as supplemental material with the application; requires an endorsement letter from a Field Museum scientific sponsor. **Deadline:** February 3.

4548 ■ Fielding Law Group
16400 Southcenter Pkwy., No. 210
Tukwila, WA 98188
Ph: (206)686-5454
E-mail: spencer@fieldinglawgroup.com
URL: www.fieldinglawgroup.com
Social Media: www.facebook.com/fieldinglawgroup

4549 ■ Fielding Law Group Scholarship Contest (Undergraduate/Scholarship)

Purpose: To provide financial aid to college students, encourage students to understand their personal motivation

for a career in the legal field, and inspire students to pursue a career in law. **Focus:** Law. **Qualif.:** Applicant must be a high school senior or college freshman in the U.S. who is studying, or plans to study, in the field of law. **Criteria:** Selection is based on the best video essay submitted.

Funds Avail.: $1,000. **To Apply:** Applicant must record a video (one to two minutes long, in plain English) explaining why the want to be a lawyer. Video must be published on the applicant's YouTube channel with the title "Fielding Law Group Scholarship Contest" and this link in the description: www.fieldinglawgroup.com/scholarship-for-college-students.html. Applicant must also share the video on their Facebook page and the sponsor's Facebook page. Instead of a video, applicant may submit a 1,000 to 1,500 word essay on the same subject via email. **Deadline:** August 15. **Contact:** Spencer Fielding; Email: scholarship@fieldinglawgroup.com.

4550 ■ Fields Institute
222 College St.
Toronto, ON, Canada R3B 2E9
Ph: (416)348-9710
Fax: (416)348-9714
E-mail: inquiries@fields.utoronto.ca
URL: www.fields.utoronto.ca
Social Media: www.facebook.com/fieldsinstitute
www.instagram.com/fieldsinstitute
www.linkedin.com/company/the-fields-institute-for-research
  -in-mathematical-sciences
twitter.com/FieldsInstitute
www.youtube.com/channel/UCSzx
  -qTK2639JBWgrb6mTmw

4551 ■ Fields Research Fellowship (Postdoctorate/ Fellowship)

Purpose: To support individuals with high potential to re-enter an active research career after an interruption due to family responsibilities. **Focus:** Mathematics and mathematical sciences. **Qualif.:** Applicants must be faculty member at our Principal Sponsoring Universities are invited to apply or to nominate a mathematical scientist for the purpose of collaborative research. **Criteria:** Selection will be made by the directors of the Institute, in consultation with the Scientific Advisory Panel.

Funds Avail.: Upto $3,500. **Duration:** Triennial; 1 to 3 months. **Number Awarded:** Varies. **To Apply:** Applicants must submit a cover sheet indicating interest; a curriculum vitae; a research proposal which includes the name(s) of faculty who may be appropriate as supervisors/research advisors; other applicants must submit letter of nomination and recommendation from a faculty member at one of our principal sponsoring Universities. **Deadline:** September 15, January 15, and May 15.

4552 ■ Fields Postdoctoral Fellowships (FPDF) (Postdoctorate/Fellowship)

Purpose: To support postdoctoral fellows in the field of mathematical sciences. **Focus:** Mathematics and mathematical sciences. **Qualif.:** Applicants must be major in thematic programs.

Funds Avail.: $30,000. **Duration:** 6 months. **To Apply:** Applicants must include cover sheet of their application, and include the names of faculty members at Affiliate or Principal Sponsoring Universities who may be appropriate supervisors.

Awards are arranged alphabetically below their administering organizations

4553 ■ Filipino Bar Association of Northern California (FBANC)

268 Bush St., No. 2928
San Francisco, CA 94104
E-mail: info@fbanc.org
URL: fbanc.org
Social Media: www.facebook.com/groups/23799184288/
  ?mc_cid=79ffcddd43&mc_eid=UNIQID
twitter.com/fbancorg
www.youtube.com/channel/UCKoSVB4R-50C6FyRd
  -euSpg/featured

4554 ■ FBANC Foundation NAPABA Convention Scholarship *(Advanced Professional/Scholarship)*

Purpose: To support law students in their educational pursuit. **Focus:** Law. **Qualif.:** Applicant must be a current law student in good academic standing and admitted to a law school.

Funds Avail.: No specific amount. **Duration:** Annual. **To Apply:** Applicants must submit a current law school transcript or admittance letter from a law school; a resume; and not longer than two page essay (double-spaced). **Remarks:** Established in 1998. **Contact:** Lorna Garcia de Guzman; Email: LGarcia779@yahoo.com.

4555 ■ Film Independent

5670 Wilshire Blvd., 9th Fl.
Los Angeles, CA 90036
Ph: (323)556-9300
Fax: (323)556-9303
E-mail: spiritawards@filmindependent.org
URL: www.filmindependent.org
Social Media: www.facebook.com/filmindependent
www.instagram.com/filmindependent
twitter.com/filmindependent
www.youtube.com/user/filmindependent

4556 ■ Truer Than Fiction Award *(Professional development/Award)*

Purpose: To support an emerging director of non-fiction features who has not yet received significant attention. **Focus:** Filmmaking. **Qualif.:** Applicant must an emerging director of non-fiction features who has not yet received significant attention.

Funds Avail.: $25,000. **Duration:** Annual. **Number Awarded:** 1.

4557 ■ Filson Historical Society

1310 S 3rd St.
Louisville, KY 40208
Ph: (502)635-5083
Fax: (502)635-5086
E-mail: info@filsonhistorical.org
URL: filsonhistorical.org
Social Media: www.facebook.com/TheFilsonHS
www.instagram.com/filsonhistorical
www.youtube.com/user/FilsonHistoricalKY

4558 ■ Ballard Breaux Visiting Fellowships *(Postdoctorate/Fellowship)*

Purpose: To assist and support a post doctoral student living outside of Kentucky for a one-month residence at Fil-

son Historical Society research collections. **Focus:** History, American. **Qualif.:** Applicant must have a Ph.D. or equivalent terminal degree.

Funds Avail.: $2,000. **Duration:** Periodic. **To Apply:** Cover sheet with name, mailing address, telephone and fax numbers, e-mail address, present rank and institution name, name of fellowship or internship you applying for, title of project, history of financial aid received during the last five years; A description of your research project; A resume of no more than three pages; Three letters of recommendation from colleagues familiar with your work. **Deadline:** October 15; February 15. **Contact:** The Filson Historical Society, 1310 S Third St., Louisville, Kentucky 40208; For questions; Email: fellowships@ filsonhistorical.org; The Filson's collections and holdings; Email:research@filsonhistorical.org.

4559 ■ Filson Fellowships *(Postdoctorate, Doctorate/Fellowship)*

Purpose: To support doctoral candidates at the dissertation stage in the use of the Filson Historical Society research collections for period of one week. **Focus:** History, American. **Qualif.:** Applicants must have practical experience in collections management and research for graduate students.

Funds Avail.: $500. **Duration:** Semiannual; one week. **To Apply:** Cover sheet with name, mailing address, telephone and fax numbers, e-mail address, present rank and institution name, name of fellowship or internship you applying for, title of project, history of financial aid received during the last five years; A description of your research project; A resume of no more than three pages; Three letters of recommendation from colleagues familiar with your work. **Deadline:** October 15; February 15. **Contact:** The Filson Historical Society, 1310 S Third St., Louisville, Kentucky 40208; Email: fellowships@filsonhistorical.org.

4560 ■ Filson Historical Society Master's Thesis Fellowship *(Master's/Fellowship)*

Purpose: To support Master's students who are developing and researching thesis topics on the history of Kentucky and the regions of the Ohio Valley and the Upper South. **Focus:** History, American. **Qualif.:** Applicant must be an M.A. candidate at the thesis stage.

Funds Avail.: $500. **Duration:** Semiannual; one week. **To Apply:** Cover sheet with name, mailing address, telephone and fax numbers, e-mail address, present rank and institution name, name of fellowship or internship you applying for, title of project, history of financial aid received during the last five years; a description of your research project; a resume of no more than three pages; three letters of recommendation from colleagues familiar with your work. **Contact:** The Filson Historical Society, 1310 S Third St., Louisville, Kentucky 40208; For questions, LeeAnn Whites; Email: whites@filsonhistorical.org.

4561 ■ Financial CAD Corp.

13450 102nd Ave., Ste. 1750 Central City
Surrey, BC, Canada V3T 5X3
URL: www.fincad.com

4562 ■ FINCAD Women in Finance Scholarships *(Graduate/Scholarship)*

Purpose: To encourage and support outstanding women in the field of finance. **Focus:** Finance. **Qualif.:** Applicants must be women of any age who are studying Finance in an

Awards are arranged alphabetically below their administering organizations

accredited graduate-level program. **Criteria:** Selection will be based on the committee's criteria.

Funds Avail.: $10,000. **Duration:** Annual. **To Apply:** Applicants may contact the Company for the application process and other information. **Deadline:** June 30.

4563 ■ Fine Arts Association (FAA)

38660 Mentor Ave.
Willoughby, OH 44094
Ph: (440)951-7500
Fax: (440)975-4592
URL: www.fineartsassociation.org
Social Media: www.facebook.com/TheFineArtsAssociation
www.instagram.com/fineartsassoc
twitter.com/TheFineArtsAssn
www.youtube.com/channel/
  UCVWbEY1Uq9JqrorupWl8DYg

4564 ■ Fine Arts Association Minority Scholarship
(Undergraduate/Scholarship)

Purpose: To ensure that the opportunity for art education is available to all who deserve it and to create customized educational arts experiences in music, dance, drama, visual arts and music therapy. **Focus:** Art. **Qualif.:** Applicants must be students residing in Lake County; family income should be based on the HSS Poverty Guidelines. **Criteria:** Scholarships are awarded based on financial need.

To Apply: Applicants must complete the application form with parents/guardians if they are dependents. Forms are available at the FAA Customer Service Center and are also available for download at the website. First time applicants must include a copy of the first page of their most recent IRS 1040 form. **Contact:** Phone: 440-951-7500.

4565 ■ Fine Arts Association United Way Scholarship *(Undergraduate/Scholarship)*

Purpose: To ensure that the opportunity for art education is available to all who deserve it and to create customized educational arts experiences in music, dance, drama, visual arts and music therapy. **Focus:** Art. **Qualif.:** Applicants must be students residing in Lake County; family income should be based on the HSS Poverty Guidelines. **Criteria:** Scholarships are awarded based on merit.

Funds Avail.: No specific amount. **To Apply:** Applicants must complete the application form with parents/guardians if they are dependents. Forms are available at the FAA Customer Service Center and are also available for download at the website. First time applicants must include a copy of the first page of their most recent IRS 1040 form. **Deadline:** July 17,April 1. **Contact:** Phone: 440-951-7500.

4566 ■ Gwen Yarnell Theatre Scholarship
(Undergraduate/Scholarship)

Purpose: To ensure that the opportunity for art education is available to all who deserve it and to create customized educational arts experiences in music, dance, drama, visual arts and music therapy. **Focus:** Art; Theater arts. **Qualif.:** Applicants must have enrolled in classes or lessons at The Fine Arts Association within the past year. preference will be given to currently enrolled students. applicants must have achievements in art, dance, music or theater; scholarships are not transferable; unused scholarships are not carried forward to subsequent sessions. **Criteria:** Scholarships are awarded based on merit.

To Apply: Applicants must complete and submit the achievement scholarship application to the Customer Service Center; must complete an Instructor recommendation Form for Achievement Scholarship and return it to the Customer Service Center; scholarship Application forms must be completed by the parents/guardians of students who are dependents; director of Education will review all applications and make recommendations to the CEO and Scholarship. **Contact:** Customer Service Center at 440-951-7500.

4567 ■ Finnegan, Henderson, Farabow, Garrett and Dunner, LLP

901 New York Ave. NW
Washington, DC 20001-4413
Ph: (202)408-4000
URL: www.finnegan.com
Social Media: www.facebook.com/finnegan
www.linkedin.com/company/finnegan-henderson-farabow
  -garrett-&-dunner-llp
twitter.com/FinneganIPLaw

4568 ■ Finnegan Diversity Scholarship *(Juris Doctorate/Scholarship)*

Purpose: To develop diversity in the workplace and in the field of intellectual property law. **Focus:** Law.

Funds Avail.: $15,000. **Duration:** Annual. **Deadline:** February 1. **Remarks:** Established in 2003. **Contact:** Finnegan Diversity Scholarship, c/o Laurie Taylor, Recruitment Manager Personal Statement; Finnegan, Henderson, Farabow, Garrett & Dunner, L.L.P; Email: diversityscholarship@finnegan.com.

4569 ■ Firefly Foundation

87 Avenue Rd.
Toronto, ON, Canada M5R 3R9
E-mail: contact@fireflyfoundation.org
URL: www.fireflyfoundation.org
Social Media: www.instagram.com/firefly_foundation
twitter.com/mizzfirefly

4570 ■ Firefly Foundation/ASRP Spark Award
(Postdoctorate/Grant)

Purpose: To support unique, creative research ideas that will impact brain health and prevent, defer or effectively treat neurodegenerative disease. **Focus:** Alzheimer's disease. **Qualif.:** Applicants must be within the 18 months of completing their Ph.D. and pursue their postdoctoral fellowship in Canada. **Criteria:** Selection will be based on the research proposals of the applicants.

Funds Avail.: 100,000 Canadian Dollars per year (50,000 per annum). **Duration:** up to 2 years. **To Apply:** Applicants are required to submit proposals for studies using the Alzheimer Society of Canada (ASC) online application system for work that explicitly address the Firefly Foundation's mission to find treatment for prevention or cures to eradicate neurodegenerative disease. **Remarks:** The Spark Award is a partnership program between the Firefly Foundation and the Alzheimer Society of Canada, through its Alzheimer Society Research Program. **Contact:** Research Department, Alzheimer Society of Canada, at research@alzheimer.ca.

4571 ■ Firland Foundation

1700 NE 150th St.
Shoreline, WA 98155

Awards are arranged alphabetically below their administering organizations

Ph: (206)363-4349
Fax: (206)365-4751
E-mail: president@firland.org
URL: www.firland.org
Social Media: www.facebook.com/pages/Firland-Sheltered
-Workshop-Foundation/850329921754689
www.linkedin.com/company/firland-sheltered-workshop

4572 ■ Graduate Pulmonary Nursing Fellowship
(Professional development/Fellowship, Scholarship)

Purpose: To recruit and retain high caliber graduate nursing students who are committed to nursing practice, education, or research in tuberculosis (TB) or other pulmonary diseases. **Focus:** Tuberculosis. **Qualif.:** Applicant must be a graduate nursing student in the MS, MN, DNP or PhD programs at the UW SoN; previous clinical experience caring for patients with TB or other pulmonary diseases; commitment to the study of nursing care for TB or other pulmonary diseases and to full-time enrollment (minimum 10 credits/quarter) in all quarters of funding; agree to present at a Firland Board meeting, progress and accomplishments at the end of each funding year. **Criteria:** Preference will be given to students who are focused on nursing care of individuals with TB and plan to practice in the Pacific Northwest after graduation.

Funds Avail.: $30,000 per year. **Duration:** Annual; Two years. **Number Awarded:** 1. **To Apply:** Applicants may contact the Foundation for the application process and other required materials. **Deadline:** March 31. **Remarks:** Established in 2009.

4573 ■ Northrop-Park Fellowship *(Professional development/Fellowship)*

Purpose: To provide opportunity to develop independent faculty-level tuberculosis research funding. **Focus:** Tuberculosis. **Qualif.:** Applicants must be investigators interested in tuberculosis research. **Criteria:** Selection will be based on the committee's criteria.

Funds Avail.: No specific amount. **Duration:** Annual; three years. **Number Awarded:** 1. **To Apply:** Applicants must submit a letter of intent via online application; if approved, within a few days a unique link to the application proper will be received. **Deadline:** March 31. **Contact:** For Questions can be sent to Bijan Ghassemieh, Email: bijang@uw.edu.

4574 ■ First Catholic Slovak Ladies Association (FCSLA)

24950 Chagrin Blvd.
Beachwood, OH 44122-5634
Ph: (216)464-8015
Fax: (216)464-9260
Free: 800-464-4642
E-mail: info@fcsla.com
URL: www.fcsla.org
Social Media: www.facebook.com/First-Catholic-Slovak
-Ladies-Association-National-Headquarters
-829643137092360

4575 ■ FCSLA Graduate Scholarships *(Graduate/Scholarship)*

Purpose: To assist young members of the association in their educational pursuits. **Focus:** General studies/Field of study not specified. **Qualif.:** Applicants must be members in good standing with the Association for at least three years prior to applying and hold one of the following policies in their name: $1,000 minimum permanent life insurance certificate; $5,000 minimum term certificate; an annuity certificate. Applicants must be full-time graduate students. **Criteria:** Selection is done by a committee of impartial judges based on the following criteria: academic standing, 40%; church/community service value, 30%; school involvement/essay, 30%.

Funds Avail.: $1,750 each. **Duration:** Annual. **Number Awarded:** 19. **To Apply:** Submit official transcripts; an autobiographical statement of approximately 500 words of the applicant's goals and objectives; include a wallet-sized photo; completed application. **Deadline:** February 25. **Contact:** Email: Scholarship@fcsla.com; URL: www.fcsla.org/scholarship.shtml.

4576 ■ FCSLA High School Scholarships *(High School, College, Graduate/Scholarship)*

Purpose: To assist young members of the association with their educational pursuits. **Focus:** General studies/Field of study not specified. **Qualif.:** Applicants must be members in good standing with the Association for at least three years prior to applying and hold one of the following policies in their name: $1,000 minimum permanent life insurance certificate; $5,000 minimum term certificate; an annuity certificate. Applicants must be high school students. **Criteria:** Selection is done by a committee of impartial judges based on the following criteria: academic standing, 40%; church/community service value, 30%; school involvement/essay, 30%.

Funds Avail.: $1,000 each. **Duration:** Annual. **Number Awarded:** 9 freshmen; 9 sophomore; 9 junior; 9 senior. **To Apply:** Application form and details are available on the Association's website. **Deadline:** February 28. **Contact:** Email: Scholarship@fcsla.com.

4577 ■ FCSLA Seminary or Diaconate or Religious Life Scholarships *(Graduate/Scholarship)*

Purpose: To help members pursue graduate degrees in the Catholic priesthood, diaconate, or religious life. **Focus:** Christian education; Religion. **Qualif.:** Applicants must be members in good standing with the Association for at least three years prior to applying and hold one of the following policies in their name: $1,000 minimum permanent life insurance certificate; $5,000 minimum term certificate; an annuity certificate. Applicants must be preparing for the Catholic priesthood (seminarians) or preparing for the Catholic diaconate or religious life.

Duration: Annual. **To Apply:** Submit official transcripts; an autobiographical statement of approximately 500 words of the applicant's goals and objectives; include a wallet-sized photo; completed application. **Deadline:** February 25. **Contact:** Email: Scholarship@fcsla.com; URL: www.fcsla.org/scholarship.shtml.

4578 ■ FCSLA Undergraduate College Scholarships *(Undergraduate, Two Year College, Four Year College/Scholarship)*

Purpose: To support the educational pursuits of young members of the Association. **Focus:** General studies/Field of study not specified. **Qualif.:** Applicants must be members in good standing with the Association for at least three years prior to applying and hold one of the following policies in their name: $1,000 minimum permanent life insurance certificate; $5,000 minimum term certificate; an annuity certificate. Applicants must be undergraduate students. **Criteria:** Selection is done by a committee of judges based

Awards are arranged alphabetically below their administering organizations

on the following criteria: academic standing, 40%; church/community service value, 30%; school involvement/essay, 30%.

Funds Avail.: $1,250 each. **Duration:** Annual. **Number Awarded:** 60 freshmen; 31 sophomore; 18 junior; 18 senior. **To Apply:** Submit official transcripts; an autobiographical statement of approximately 500 words of the applicant's goals and objectives; include a wallet-sized photo; completed application. **Deadline:** February 25. **Contact:** Email: Scholarship@fscla.com; URL: www.fcsla.org/scholarship.shtml.

4579 ■ FCSLA Vocational/Technical/Trade Scholarships *(Vocational/Occupational/Scholarship)*

Purpose: To assist young members of the association with their educational pursuits. **Focus:** General studies/Field of study not specified. **Qualif.:** Applicants must be members in good standing with the Association for at least three years prior to applying and hold one of the following policies in their name: $1,000 minimum permanent life insurance certificate; $5,000 minimum term certificate; an annuity certificate. Applicants must be vocational, technical, or trade students. **Criteria:** Selection is done by a committee of impartial judges based on the following criteria: academic standing, 40%; church/community service value, 30%; school involvement/essay, 30%.

Funds Avail.: $1,250 each. **Duration:** Annual. **Number Awarded:** 5. **To Apply:** Submit official transcripts; a letter of recommendation; an autobiographical statement of approximately 500 words of the applicant's goals and objectives; include a wallet-sized photo; completed application. **Deadline:** February 25. **Contact:** Email: Scholarship@fcsla.com.

4580 ■ First Community Foundation Partnership of Pennsylvania (FCFP)

201 West Fourth Street
Williamsport, PA 17701
Ph: (570)321-1500
Fax: (570)321-6434
URL: www.wlfoundation.org
Social Media: www.facebook.com/FCFPGIVES

4581 ■ Ruth D. Adams Fund *(Undergraduate/Scholarship)*

Purpose: To provide financial assistance for Montoursville Area High School seniors who are seeking higher education beyond graduation from high school (full-time) and who represent the top 10% GPA of graduating seniors. **Focus:** General studies/Field of study not specified. **Qualif.:** Applicants shall be approved for full-time admission to any accredited two or four-year college or university of their choice and be enrolled in a course of study of their choice which leads to a degree. **Criteria:** Selection may be based on the essay.

Funds Avail.: No specific amount. **Number Awarded:** 5. **To Apply:** Applicants should include essay; resume; letter of recommendation; transcripts; acceptance letter from institutions from which you've applied; Student Aid Report (SAR) from your FAFSA. **Contact:** Betty Gilmour, Director of Grantmaking; Phone: 570-321-1500; Email:bettyg@fcfpartnership.org.

4582 ■ Albert and Alice Nacinovich Music Scholarship Fund *(Undergraduate/Scholarship)*

Purpose: To provide financial assistance for Lycoming County high school seniors graduating from public or private schools with a demonstrated interest in music, planning to attend a qualified institution of higher education in a music-related field of study. **Focus:** Music. **Qualif.:** Applicants must be graduating high school seniors from any Lycoming County high school, public or private (secular or Christian), or as part of a qualified home-schooling arrangement within Lycoming County; must have been accepted to a qualified institution of higher education with the intention of pursuing further education or a career in music in a degree-granting program in music education or a music-related field of study; and must have a demonstrated interest in music, which may include participation in band, chorus, music theory and composition, and performance service at school, church, or community; must have maintained a GPA of 80 or higher.

Funds Avail.: No specific amount. **To Apply:** Applicants must include list of school and/or community involvement; most recent transcripts; recommendation letter; and paragraph of how they have shared their music talents with their school, church, and/or community. **Deadline:** April 15. **Contact:** Betty Gilmour, Director of Grantmaking; Phone: 570-321-1500; Email:bettyg@fcfpartnership.org.

4583 ■ Anne L. "Annie" Alexander and Blaise Robert "B R" Alexander *(Undergraduate/Scholarship)*

Purpose: To provide scholarship for graduating seniors from Mount Carmel Area High School and Montoursville Area High School. **Focus:** General studies/Field of study not specified. **Qualif.:** Applicants must attend an accredited four-year college or university and be enrolled in a business or technical program; must exhibit good citizenship and community involvement.

Funds Avail.: No specific amount. **Number Awarded:** 2. **To Apply:** Applicants should include essay; resume; letter of recommendation; transcripts; acceptance letter from institutions from which you've applied; Student Aid Report (SAR) from your FAFSA. **Deadline:** March 19. **Contact:** Betty Gilmour, Director of Grantmaking; Phone: 570-321-1500; Email:bettyg@fcfpartnership.org.

4584 ■ B-Brave McMahon/Stratton Scholarship Fund *(Undergraduate/Scholarship)*

Purpose: To provide financial assistance for graduates who have been in the foster care system or have legal adopted status and who have shown remarkable achievement despite the obstacles in their life. **Focus:** General studies/Field of study not specified. **Qualif.:** Applicant must be a graduating senior from a Lycoming County High School or Clinton County high school; must have been accepted into a full-time continuing education program, preferably in Pennsylvania; must have exhibited good citizenship and have no known drug or alcohol record or juvenile offenses; and must show evidence that they have a current minimum GPA of 2.8.

Funds Avail.: No specific amount. **To Apply:** Applicants must include list of school and/or community involvement; most recent transcripts; recommendation letter; Essay; Student Aid Report (SAR) from your FAFSA form. **Contact:** Betty Gilmour, Director of Grantmaking, the First Community Foundation Partnership of PA; Phone: 570-321-1500; Email: BettyG@fcfpartnership.org.

4585 ■ Gina L. Barnhart Memorial Scholarship Fund *(Undergraduate/Scholarship)*

Purpose: To provide financial assistance for Milton Area High school seniors planning to pursue a major in elementary education. **Focus:** Education, Elementary. **Qualif.:** Ap-

Awards are arranged alphabetically below their administering organizations

plicants must attend an accredited institution of higher education and plan to major in elementary education. **Criteria:** Preference for applicants in good standing on the cheerleading squad.

Funds Avail.: No specific amount. **To Apply:** Applicants must include a resume; essay; transcripts; Letter of recommendation; Student Aid Report (SAR) from your FAFSA; Acceptance letter from institutions from which you've applied. **Contact:** Betty Gilmour, Director of Grantmaking; Phone: 570-321-1500; Email:bettyg@fcfpartnership.org.

4586 ■ Joseph R. Calder, Jr., MD Scholarship Fund
(Undergraduate/Scholarship)

Purpose: To support the education of current and/or aspiring Lycoming County medical professionals who plan to dedicate their lives to helping others. **Focus:** Health sciences; Medicine; Nursing; Pharmacy. **Qualif.:** Applicant must be students returning to school to pursue a career in a part-time or full-time medical related program; must resident in Lycoming County. **Criteria:** Selection will be based on merit.

Funds Avail.: No specific amount. **Duration:** Annual. **To Apply:** Applicants must submit a completed application form together with a proof of acceptance into an accredited two or four year college or university in a medical related program; must submit an essay not to exceed one page outlining why they are pursuing a career in the medical field and summarizing their ultimate career objectives; and at least one letter of reference or testimonial; resume including job experience, volunteer experience and community or school involvement. **Deadline:** July 15. **Contact:** Betty Gilmour, Director of Grantmaking; Phone: 570-321-1500; Email:bettyg@fcfpartnership.org.

4587 ■ Carl & Lucille Jarrett Scholarship Fund
(Undergraduate/Scholarship)

Purpose: To provide scholarship for Montgomery Area High School seniors and/or graduated alumni who have been accepted and will attend an accredited 2 or 4-year college or university, full-time or part-time. **Focus:** General studies/Field of study not specified. **Qualif.:** Applicants should be accepted, part-time or full-time, at an accredited 2- or 4-year institution of higher education; must exhibit good citizenship; must be honest; must have integrity; must have shown through job or volunteer history their ability to succeed; must be self-motivated; and must have strong ethics.

Number Awarded: 5. **To Apply:** Applicants should include essay; resume; letter of recommendation; transcripts; acceptance letter from institutions from which you've applied; Student Aid Report (SAR) from your FAFSA. **Contact:** Betty Gilmour, Director of Grantmaking; Phone: 570-321-1500; Email:bettyg@fcfpartnership.org.

4588 ■ The Warren E. "Whitey" Cole A.S.H.E. Scholarship Fund *(Undergraduate/Scholarship)*

Purpose: To provide scholarship awards for students enrolled in a Civil Engineering curriculum. **Focus:** Engineering, Civil. **Qualif.:** Applicants must be enrolled in civil engineering, civil engineering technology or civil technology curriculum; must be a current student of Penn State University, Bucknell University or Pennsylvania College of Technology OR resident of Bradford, Columbia, Lycoming, Montour, Northumberland, Snyder, Sullivan, Tioga or Union counties and attend another college; must have completed at least sophomore year of a 4-year curriculum or the freshman year of 2-year curriculum.

Funds Avail.: No specific amount. **To Apply:** Applicants should include essay; resume; letter of recommendation;

transcripts; acceptance letter from institutions from which you've applied; Student Aid Report (SAR) from your FAFSA. **Contact:** Betty Gilmour, Director of Grantmaking; Phone: 570-321-1500; Email:bettyg@fcfpartnership.org.

4589 ■ Marion Jones Donaldson Scholarship Fund
(Undergraduate/Scholarship)

Purpose: To provide financial assistance for Canton Area High School seniors who are pursuing a course of study in elementary or secondary education. **Focus:** Education, Elementary; Education, Secondary. **Qualif.:** Applicants must be attending an accredited institution of higher education, pursuing a major in the area of elementary or secondary education; must have a four-year overall minimum grade average of 85%. **Criteria:** Selection will be based on involvement in community service, extra-curricular activities, and financial need.

Funds Avail.: No specific amount. **To Apply:** Applicants should include essay; resume; letter of recommendation; transcripts; acceptance letter from institutions from which you've applied; Student Aid Report (SAR) from your FAFSA. **Deadline:** April 2. **Contact:** Betty Gilmour, Director of Grantmaking; Phone: 570-321-1500; Email:bettyg@fcfpartnership.org.

4590 ■ Nolan W. Feeser Scholarship Fund
(Undergraduate/Scholarship)

Purpose: To provide financial assistance for South Williamsport Area High School seniors who are pursuing a higher education degree at an accredited college or university. **Focus:** General studies/Field of study not specified. **Qualif.:** Applicant must be one male student and one female student; must demonstrated academic achievement. **Criteria:** Preference of attendees of Lycoming College, Gettysburg College or Pennsylvania College of Technology.

Funds Avail.: No specific amount. **Number Awarded:** 2. **To Apply:** Applicants should include essay; resume; letter of recommendation; transcripts; acceptance letter from institutions from which you've applied; Student Aid Report (SAR) from your FAFSA. **Contact:** Betty Gilmour, Director of Grantmaking; Phone: 570-321-1500; Email:bettyg@fcfpartnership.org.

4591 ■ Benjamin Franklin Trust Fund *(Undergraduate, Vocational/Occupational/Scholarship)*

Purpose: To provide academic support for students who are attending Pennsylvania College and have graduated from Bradford County, Clinton County, Lycoming County, Potter County, Sullivan County or Tioga County. **Focus:** General studies/Field of study not specified. **Qualif.:** Applicants must be enrolled at the Pennsylvania College of Technology; must be enrolled in an approved Tech prep high school program and subsequently enroll in a Certificate, Associate or Bachelor's Degree program at the Pennsylvania College of Technology. In schools without approved Tech Prep programs, students must enroll in a high school vocational-technical program and subsequently enroll in a Certificate, Associate, or Bachelor's Degree program at the Pennsylvanian College of Technology. Applicants must have a GPA of "B" or higher and must be enrolled full-time. Preference will be given to continuing students in subsequent years if a cumulative GPA of 2.80 is maintained in the program.

Funds Avail.: No specific amount. **Duration:** Annual. **To Apply:** Applicants must submit a writing sample as defined by the Penn College Outreach for K-12 office. **Contact:** Betty Gilmour, Director of Grantmaking; Phone: 570-321-

Awards are arranged alphabetically below their administering organizations

1500; Email:bettyg@fcfpartnership.org.

4592 ■ Daniel G. and Helen I. Fultz Scholarship Fund *(Undergraduate/Scholarship)*

Purpose: To assist students graduating senior from Mifflin County High School. **Focus:** General studies/Field of study not specified. **Qualif.:** Applicants must attend full-time an undergraduate program at Lycoming College, Williamsport, PA; have exhibited good citizenship and community involvement, be a leader with a sense of humor, be grounded, show tolerance of others, is honest, has integrity, and makes a difference in the school community.

Funds Avail.: No specific amount. **Duration:** Annual. **Number Awarded:** 1. **Contact:** Betty Gilmour, Director of Grantmaking; Phone: 570-321-1500; Email:bettyg@fcfpartnership.org.

4593 ■ Morton and Beatrice Harrison Scholarship Fund *(Undergraduate/Scholarship)*

Purpose: To provide financial assistance for Lycoming County young adults who demonstrate the potential to succeed in pursuing higher education goals. **Focus:** General studies/Field of study not specified. **Qualif.:** Applicants must be young adults who, as a result of legal offenses as juveniles or young adults, that have come to the attention of the Lycoming County's Probation Department OR the Lycoming County Children & Youth Services Agency OR the Nurse Family Partnership; must graduating from a Lycoming County High School who have been identified with at-risk behavior in their school district throughout their secondary education (grades 6 through 12) may be considered; must attend or currently enrolled in a two- or four-year college/university, technical college, or trade school.**Criteria:** Selection will be based on the committee's criteria.

Funds Avail.: No specific amount. **Duration:** Annual. **Number Awarded:** 1. **To Apply:** Applicants must include completed application; proof of acceptance to a qualified institution of higher education, including but not limited to a 2- or 4-year college or university, a technical college, trade school or other approved education or training program; one letter of reference; essay outlining why they have decided to pursue higher education. **Deadline:** April 20. **Contact:** Betty Gilmour, Director of Grantmaking; Phone: 570-321-1500; Email:bettyg@fcfpartnership.org.

4594 ■ ISCALC International Scholarship Fund *(Undergraduate/Scholarship)*

Purpose: To provide financial assistance for Lycoming County high school seniors who have demonstrated an interest in furthering their education in international studies. **Focus:** Foreign languages; International affairs and relations. **Qualif.:** Applicants must attend an accredited institution of higher learning who plans to pursue major coursework in the area of international studies, including but not limited to international affairs, foreign languages, overseas exchange programs, multicultural studies, or related areas.

Funds Avail.: No specific amount. **To Apply:** Applicants should include essay; resume; letter of recommendation; transcripts; acceptance letter from institutions from which you've applied; Student Aid Report (SAR) from your FAFSA. **Deadline:** April 15. **Contact:** Betty Gilmour, Director of Grantmaking; Phone: 570-321-1500; Email:bettyg@fcfpartnership.org.

4595 ■ Lindsay M. Entz Memorial Scholarship Fund *(Undergraduate/Scholarship)*

Purpose: To provide financial assistance for the Jersey Shore High School seniors intending to pursue a course of study in elementary education, preferably with an emphasis on education of special-needs children. **Focus:** Education, Elementary. **Qualif.:** Applicants must attend a full-time continuing education program, preferably in Pennsylvania; exhibit good citizenship, be a leader with a sense of humor, be grounded, show tolerance of others, is honest and has integrity; pursuing a course of study in education. **Criteria:** Preference of education for children with special needs.

Funds Avail.: No specific amount. **Duration:** Annual. **To Apply:** Applicants should include essay; resume; letter of recommendation; transcripts; acceptance letter from institutions from which you've applied; Student Aid Report (SAR) from your FAFSA. **Deadline:** April 1. **Contact:** Betty Gilmour, Director of Grantmaking; Phone: 570-321-1500; Email:bettyg@fcfpartnership.org.

4596 ■ Margaret E. Waldron Memorial Fund *(Undergraduate/Scholarship)*

Purpose: To provide financial assistance for Muncy High School seniors who are pursuing higher education. **Focus:** General studies/Field of study not specified. **Qualif.:** Applicant must be one male student and one female student; must have completed grades 10,11,12 at Muncy Jr./Sr. High School; must rank in upper 1/5 of the class for Junior and Senior years.

Funds Avail.: $14,000 paid over four years ($3,000 for the freshman and sophomore years; $4,000 for the junior and senior years). **Duration:** Annual. **Number Awarded:** 2. **To Apply:** Applicants must include transcript through the 3rd (latest) marking period of senior year; recommendation letter; financial aid and award package; copy of parents' current U.S. individual income tax return. **Deadline:** April 13. **Contact:** Betty Gilmour, Director of Grantmaking; Phone: 570-321-1500; Email:bettyg@fcfpartnership.org.

4597 ■ Joseph and Catherine Missigman Memorial Nursing Scholarships *(Undergraduate/Scholarship)*

Purpose: To provide financial assistance for Bloomsburg University students who are pursuing a career in nursing. **Focus:** Nursing. **Qualif.:** Applicants must be Bloomsburg University students who have identified nursing as their major; must be completing their second or third year's curricula in the University's nursing education program; have a GPA of 2.5 or greater for all nursing coursework; and have a demonstrated financial need as determined by Bloomsburg University's methods and practices for assessing its student's financial capacities. **Criteria:** Selection will be based on the committee's criteria.

To Apply: Applicants must have completed and filed an application for the scholarship and must include a one-page cover letter describing reason for applying for the scholarship and interest in the nursing field. **Contact:** Dr. Margie Eckroth-Bucher; Phone: 570-389-4607; Email: meckroth@bloomu.edu.

4598 ■ Missigman Scholarship Fund *(Undergraduate/Scholarship)*

Purpose: To provide financial assistance for Sullivan County High School seniors who have been accepted into a full-time undergraduate program at an accredited institution of higher education, preferably in Pennsylvania. **Focus:** General studies/Field of study not specified. **Qualif.:** Candidate must be a graduating senior at Sullivan County High School and must demonstrate a strong potential to succeed in pursuing their higher education objectives. **Criteria:** Selection will be based on the committee's criteria.

Funds Avail.: No specific amount. **To Apply:** Applicants may request an application from the Sullivan County High

Awards are arranged alphabetically below their administering organizations

School or from the First Community Foundation of Pennsylvania. **Contact:** Jill Sysock, Guidance Office, Sullivan County High School, Beech and South St., Laporte, PA 18626, 570-947-7001, sysojill@sulcosd.k12.pa.us.

4599 ■ Robert E. and Judy More Scholarship Fund
(Undergraduate/Scholarship)

Purpose: To provide financial assistance for Montgomery Area High School students intending to pursue higher education in finance, engineering, business or science. **Focus:** Business; Engineering; Finance; Science. **Qualif.:** Applicants must be accepted, full-time, at an accredited institution of higher education, preferably in Pennsylvania; must exhibit leadership qualities, academic excellence and a cooperative spirit. **Criteria:** Preference will be given to students pursuing higher education in the areas of finance, engineering, business or science.

Funds Avail.: No specific amount. **To Apply:** Applicants should include essay; resume; letter of recommendation; transcripts; acceptance letter from institutions from which you've applied; Student Aid Report (SAR) from your FAFSA. **Contact:** FCFP Philanthropy Center, 201 W Fourth St., Williamsport, PA, 17701.

4600 ■ Muncy Rotary Club Scholarship Fund
(Undergraduate/Scholarship)

Purpose: To provide financial assistance for Muncy High School seniors who have been accepted into a full-time continuing education program. **Focus:** General studies/Field of study not specified. **Qualif.:** Applicants must attend, full-time, an accredited institution of higher learning; exhibit community involvement.

Funds Avail.: No specific amount. **Duration:** Annual. **To Apply:** Applicants must include recommendation letter from a member of the community that has not recommended another student for this scholarship; brief paragraph expressing applicants' need for the scholarship. **Contact:** Betty Gilmour, Director of Grantmaking; Phone: 570-321-1500; Email:bettyg@fcfpartnership.org.

4601 ■ Muncy Scholars Awards Fund
(Undergraduate/Scholarship)

Purpose: To assist students graduating senior from Graduating senior from Muncy Jr/Sr High School, Lycoming County. **Focus:** General studies/Field of study not specified. **Qualif.:** Applicants must attend Muncy high school from freshman year through senior year; attend full-time, a four-year college or university; must also exhibit continued growth in citizenship; possess qualities of leadership, honesty and integrity, and determination to succeed.

Funds Avail.: No specific amount. **To Apply:** Applicants should include essay; resume; letter of recommendation; transcripts; acceptance letter from institutions from which you've applied; Student Aid Report (SAR) from your FAFSA. **Deadline:** April 13. **Contact:** Betty Gilmour, Director of Grantmaking; Phone: 570-321-1500; Email:bettyg@fcfpartnership.org.

4602 ■ Ralph and Josephine Smith Fund
(Undergraduate/Scholarship)

Purpose: To defray all or a portion of the costs of attending college or other undergraduate institutions of higher learning beyond the secondary level for Warrior Run High School seniors. **Focus:** General studies/Field of study not specified. **Qualif.:** Applicants must be attending college or other undergraduate institution of higher learning beyond the

secondary level; must maintain a 2.5 grade average.

Funds Avail.: No specific amount. **To Apply:** Applicants should include essay; resume; letter of recommendation; transcripts; acceptance letter from institutions from which you've applied; Student Aid Report (SAR) from your FAFSA. **Contact:** Betty Gilmour, Director of Grantmaking; Phone: 570-321-1500; Email:bettyg@fcfpartnership.org.

4603 ■ Kimberly Marie Rogers Memorial Scholarship Fund *(Undergraduate, Vocational/Occupational/Scholarship)*

Purpose: To provide financial assistance for Montoursville Area High School seniors who are seeking higher education beyond graduation from high school (full-time) and who represent the top 10% GPA of graduating seniors. **Focus:** General studies/Field of study not specified. **Qualif.:** Applicants must attend a vocational or technical college; strong scholastic achievement.

Funds Avail.: No specific amount. **To Apply:** Applicants should include essay; resume; letter of recommendation; transcripts; acceptance letter from institutions from which you've applied; Student Aid Report (SAR) from your FAFSA. **Contact:** Betty Gilmour, Director of Grantmaking; Phone: 570-321-1500; Email:bettyg@fcfpartnership.org.

4604 ■ Dr. Wayne F. Rose Scholarship Fund
(Undergraduate/Scholarship)

Purpose: To provide financial assistance for Loyalsock High School seniors intending to attend a qualified institution of higher education in pursuit of a career in education who have a demonstrated interest in working with children and who exhibit an appreciation of the arts. **Focus:** General studies/Field of study not specified. **Qualif.:** Applicants must be attending a qualified institution of higher education; pursuing a career in education; and demonstrates interest in working with children; must demonstrate family financial need; must demonstrate active involvement working or volunteering with children outside of their own school and typical class responsibilities; must demonstrate participation in the arts while in school and/or through extracurricular activities; and must be in good academic standing with potential for success.

Funds Avail.: No specific amount. **To Apply:** Applicants should include essay; resume; letter of recommendation; transcripts; acceptance letter from institutions from which you've applied; Student Aid Report (SAR) from your FAFSA. **Deadline:** April 3. **Contact:** Betty Gilmour, Director of Grantmaking; Phone: 570-321-1500; Email:bettyg@fcfpartnership.org.

4605 ■ John A. Savoy Scholarship Fund
(Undergraduate/Scholarship)

Purpose: To provide financial assistance for South Williamsport Area High School seniors who have been accepted into a full-time undergraduate program at an accredited institution of higher education, preferably in Pennsylvania. **Focus:** General studies/Field of study not specified. **Qualif.:** Applicants must attend, full-time, an undergraduate program at an accredited institution of higher education, preferably in Pennsylvania; must have exhibited good citizenship and community involvement.

Funds Avail.: $2,000. **Duration:** Annual. **To Apply:** Applicants should include essay; resume; letter of recommendation; transcripts; acceptance letter from institutions from which you've applied; Student Aid Report (SAR) from your FAFSA. **Contact:** Betty Gilmour, Director of Grant-

Awards are arranged alphabetically below their administering organizations

making; Phone: 570-321-1500; Email:bettyg@fcfpartnership.org.

4606 ■ Monica M. Weaver Memorial Fund
(Undergraduate/Scholarship)

Purpose: To provide scholarship for Montoursville Area High School seniors of high scholastic standing who are enrolled at a college or other educational institution. **Focus:** Physical therapy. **Qualif.:** Applicants must be female students with high scholastic standing; attending an accredited four-year college or university or other educational institution, majoring in physical therapy; majors in occupational therapy, nursing or other related health care profession can also apply, but preference to majors in physical therapy; must have resided in Montoursville area school district for a minimum of three (3) years prior to graduation. **Criteria:** Selection will be based on the committee's criteria. Preference will be given to a student who has not received other scholarships and demonstrates financial need.

Funds Avail.: No specific amount. **Contact:** Betty Gilmour, Director of Grantmaking; Phone: 570-321-1500; Email:bettyg@fcfpartnership.org.

4607 ■ Eleanor M. Wolfson Memorial Scholarship Fund *(Undergraduate/Scholarship)*

Purpose: To provide scholarship for Montoursville Area High School seniors who will be attending Yale College. **Focus:** Creative writing. **Qualif.:** Applicants must attend Yale College; must be attending an accredited four year college or university with an outstanding academic record and a demonstrated talent in creative writing.

Funds Avail.: No specific amount. **To Apply:** Applicants should include essay; resume; letter of recommendation; transcripts; acceptance letter from institutions from which you've applied; Student Aid Report (SAR) from your FAFSA. **Contact:** Betty Gilmour, Director of Grantmaking; Phone: 570-321-1500; Email:bettyg@fcfpartnership.org.

4608 ■ Wendy Y. Wolfson Memorial Scholarship Fund *(Undergraduate/Scholarship)*

Purpose: To provide scholarship for Montoursville Area High School seniors who will be attending Yale College. **Focus:** Criticism (Art, Drama, Literary); Music. **Qualif.:** Applicants must attend Yale College; must have outstanding academic record and a demonstrated talent in music or drama (secondary preference) and attend any other accredited institution of higher education/.

Funds Avail.: No specific amount. **To Apply:** Applicants should include essay; resume; letter of recommendation; transcripts; acceptance letter from institutions from which you've applied; Student Aid Report (SAR) from your FAFSA. **Contact:** Betty Gilmour, Director of Grantmaking; Phone: 570-321-1500; Email:bettyg@fcfpartnership.org.

4609 ■ Fish Finder Guides
193 Long St.
Jacksonville, FL 32216
Ph: (708)877-6751

4610 ■ Fish Finder Guides Scholarship *(Undergraduate, Graduate/Scholarship)*

Purpose: To support students who have excellent writing skills and can write about the fishing industry. **Focus:** General studies/Field of study not specified. **Qualif.:** Ap-

plicant must be an undergraduate or graduate student. **Criteria:** Selection will be based on the quality of the content.

Funds Avail.: $1,000. **Duration:** Annual. **Number Awarded:** 1. **To Apply:** Application including name, email address, college name & ID proof along with the content. **Deadline:** February 2. **Contact:** Email: scholarship@fishfinderguides.com.

4611 ■ Fish & Richardson
One Marina Park Dr.
Boston, MA 02210-1878
Ph: (617)542-5070
Fax: (617)542-8906
E-mail: info@fr.com
URL: www.fr.com
Social Media: www.facebook.com/fishrichardson
www.instagram.com/fishrichardson
www.linkedin.com/company/fish-&-richardson-p-c-
twitter.com/fishrichardson
www.youtube.com/user/fishandrichardson

4612 ■ Fish & Richardson 1L Diversity Fellowship Program *(Undergraduate/Fellowship)*

Purpose: To promote diversity in the legal profession. **Focus:** Law. **Qualif.:** Applicants must be in good standing as a first-year law student at an ABA accredited law school; must demonstrate a record of academic and professional achievement; contribute meaningfully to the diversity of the firm and legal community. **Criteria:** Selection is based on the submitted application and materials.

Funds Avail.: $5,000. **Duration:** Annual. **Number Awarded:** Varies. **To Apply:** Applicants must submit a completed application form. **Deadline:** January 3. **Remarks:** Established in 2005. **Contact:** Email: diversity@fr.com.

4613 ■ Flamenco de la Isla Society
2568 Vancouver St.
Victoria, BC, Canada V8T 4A7
E-mail: info@flamencodelaisla.org
URL: www.flamencodelaisla.org

4614 ■ Flamenco Student Scholarship *(Undergraduate, Professional development/Scholarship)*

Purpose: To support students defray the cost of obtaining an education. **Focus:** Dance. **Qualif.:** Applicants must be members of the Flamenco de la Isla Society; must be willing to, or have in the past, volunteered for the society's events. **Criteria:** Selection will be given to those students who meet the criteria; demonstrated commitment to volunteering for the Flamenco de la Isla Society; further develop flamenco skills and knowledge, and financial need.

Funds Avail.: Up to $500. **Duration:** Annual. **To Apply:** Applicants must submit a completed application form. **Deadline:** September 1. **Contact:** Flamenco de la Isla Society Attention: Scholarship Application, 2568 Vancouver St., Victoria, BC, V8T 4A7.

4615 ■ Flexible Packaging Association (FPA)
185 Admiral Cochrane Dr., Ste. 105
Annapolis, MD 21401

Awards are arranged alphabetically below their administering organizations

Ph: (410)694-0800
E-mail: fpa@flexpack.org
URL: www.flexpack.org
Social Media: www.linkedin.com/company/flexible
-packaging-association
twitter.com/FlexPackOrg
www.youtube.com/channel/
UC4UYar4TQBDtNk2eP2I1AEQ

4616 ■ FPA Summer Internships Program
(Undergraduate/Internship)

Purpose: To support students financially regarding their internship. **Focus:** Education, Industrial; Industrial design. **Qualif.:** Applicants must be enrolled in an AA, BA, BS or MS degree program; have a 2.7 GPA; have 24 credit hours, nine credits of which are in packaging, printing or other areas in the converting industry.

Funds Avail.: $3,000. **Duration:** Annual. **To Apply:** Applicants are advised to visit the website for the online application system; prepare a recommendation letter (academic or professional); and an essay (maximum of 500 words). **Deadline:** February 13. **Remarks:** Established in 2005. **Contact:** Flexible Packaging Association, Attn: Debbie Lillard, 185 Admiral Cochrane Dr., Ste. 105, Annapolis, MD, 21401; E-mail: dlillard@flexpack.org.

4617 ■ Flexographic Technical Association (FTA)
3920 Veterans Memorial Hwy., Ste. 9
Bohemia, NY 11716-1074
Ph: (631)737-6020
Fax: (631)737-6813
URL: www.flexography.org
Social Media: www.facebook.com/flextechassn
www.instagram.com/flextechassn
www.linkedin.com/company/flextechassn
twitter.com/FlexTechAssn

4618 ■ FIRST Operator Certification Awards *(Professional development/Internship)*

Purpose: To assist individuals who desire to improve their skills in the pursuit of certification training. **Focus:** Printing trades and industries. **Criteria:** Selection will be based on submitted applications.

Funds Avail.: No specific amount. **Duration:** Annual. **To Apply:** Applicants must submit an electronic format of a completed application form together with supporting documents such as work history, letters of recommendation and must attach a school transcript. **Contact:** Flexographic Technical Association, at the above address; or Email: memberinfo@flexography.org.

4619 ■ Florida A&M University - School of the Environment (SOE)
FSH Science Research Ctr.
Tallahassee, FL 32307
Ph: (850)599-3550
Fax: (850)599-8183
E-mail: famuesi@famu.edu
URL: www.famu.edu/index
.cfm?environmentalscience&About
Social Media: facebook.com/FAMU1887
instagram.com/famu_1887
twitter.com/FAMU_1887

youtube.com/user/FAMUTube1887

4620 ■ FAMU Presidential Scholarship - Florida Community College Scholarships *(Undergraduate/ Scholarship)*

Purpose: To assist high achieving Florida community/junior college graduates. **Focus:** Environmental science. **Qualif.:** Applicants must be Florida community/junior college graduates; must be AA/AS degree transfer student who has a minimum cumulative 2.50 GPA and is not enrolled as a FAMU student. **Criteria:** Selection will be based on the committee's criteria.

Duration: Annual. **To Apply:** Applicants may contact the Center for application process and other information. **Deadline:** November 1.

4621 ■ FAMU Presidential Scholarship - George W. Gore Assistantship Scholarship *(Undergraduate/ Scholarship)*

Purpose: To assist incoming freshmen students in meeting the cost of college education. **Focus:** Education. **Qualif.:** Applicants must be incoming freshmen who have at least 1200 on the SAT or 27 on the ACT and a minimum unweighted 3.5 high school GPA. **Criteria:** Selection will be based on the committee's criteria.

To Apply: Applicants may contact the University for the application process and other information. **Deadline:** November 1.

4622 ■ Florida Association of Directors of Nursing Administration (FADONA)
400 Executive Center Dr., No. 208
West Palm Beach, FL 33401
Ph: (561)683-0037
Fax: (561)689-6324
E-mail: fadona@fadona.org
URL: www.fadona.org
Social Media: www.instagram.com/fadonaltc

4623 ■ The Imogene Ward Nursing Scholarship
(Undergraduate/Scholarship)

Purpose: To provide financial assistance to individuals who wants to pursue their education in the LTC setting. **Focus:** Nursing. **Criteria:** Selection will be based on demonstrated determination to overcome personal and/or professional obstacles to pursue nursing education, track record of excellence and the potential for future leadership in long-term care.

Funds Avail.: $500. **Duration:** Annual. **To Apply:** Applicants must submit a completed application form including name and full contact information; Must submit a 300-word or less narrative essay which outlines what it takes to be an exceptional nurse and also expresses reasons they should be considered for the Imogene Ward Nursing Scholarship Award; Letter of recommendation. **Remarks:** The Scholarship is honored in the memory of a true long-term care leader, Imogene Ward. Established in 2008.

4624 ■ Florida Association for Media in Education (FAME)
PO Box 941169
Maitland, FL 32794-1169
Ph: (863)585-6802
E-mail: fame@floridamediaed.org

Awards are arranged alphabetically below their administering organizations

URL: www.floridamedia.org
Social Media: www.facebook.com/floridamedia
www.instagram.com/floridamediaed
www.pinterest.com/FloridaMediaEd
twitter.com/FloridaMediaEd
www.youtube.com/channel/UCabpbwNViKfop4j4ZeN9ajQ

4625 ■ Sandy Ulm Scholarships *(Undergraduate, Master's/Scholarship)*

Purpose: To help students in Florida be involved in and have open access to a quality school library media program, administered by a highly competent, certified library media specialist. **Focus:** Media arts. **Criteria:** Selection will be based on academic performance.

Funds Avail.: No specific amount. **Duration:** Annual. **To Apply:** Applicants must submit a completed application form and a copy of the transcript of all college credits for the graduate program in which they are currently enrolled, two letters of recommendation (one must come from a professor) and a notarized statement (found in application). **Remarks:** Established in 2001.

4626 ■ Florida Department of Business and Professional Regulation (DBPR)
2601 Blair Stone Rd.
Tallahassee, FL 32399-1027
Ph: (850)487-1395
Free: 866-532-1440
E-mail: ula@myfloridalicense.com
URL: www.myfloridalicense.com
Social Media: www.facebook.com/FloridaDBPR
www.instagram.com/florida.dbpr
www.linkedin.com/company/department-of-business-and
-professional-regulation
twitter.com/FloridaDBPR
www.youtube.com/user/FloridaDBPR

4627 ■ Clay Ford Florida Board of Accountancy Minority Scholarships *(Undergraduate/Scholarship)*

Purpose: To encourage students to remain in school for the fifth year required to sit for the CPA exam. **Focus:** Accounting. **Qualif.:** Applicants must be individuals with ethnicity, gender or racial minority status pursuant to section 288.703(3) F.S.; and be Florida residents who are in the fifth year of an accounting program at an accredited Florida institution. **Criteria:** Selection shall be based on financial need, on the aforementioned applicants' qualifications, and compliance with the application details.

Funds Avail.: $3,000 to $6,000 per semester. **Duration:** Annual. **Number Awarded:** Up to 2. **To Apply:** Applicants must submit a completed application form along with a copy of current transcripts; a copy of most recent FAFSA; and a financial release form completed by the financial aid office. **Deadline:** June 1. **Contact:** Florida Board of Accountancy Clay Ford Scholarship Application, 240 NW 76th Drive, Suite A, Gainesville, Florida 32607.

4628 ■ Florida Education Fund, Inc (FEF)
201 E Kennedy Blvd., Ste. 1525
Tampa, FL 33602
Ph: (813)272-2772
Fax: (813)272-2784
E-mail: office@fefonline.org

URL: www.fefonline.org

4629 ■ Florida Education Fund McKnight Doctoral Fellowship *(Graduate/Fellowship)*

Purpose: To address the under-representation of african american and hispanic faculty at colleges and universities in the state of florida by increasing the pool of citizens qualified with phd degrees to teach at the college and university levels. **Focus:** Arts; Business; Engineering; Health sciences; Nursing; Performing arts; Science; Visual arts.

Funds Avail.: $17,000 in tuition, fees and stipend. **Duration:** Annual. **Number Awarded:** Up to 50. **To Apply:** Applicants must submit application materials; three (3) individuals who can speak to your academic potential complete the McKnight doctoral fellowship program confidential recommendation form; submit a letter of recommendation; submit a copy of your resume or vita to the fef office; submit original sets of transcripts and standardized test scores to the fef office. **Deadline:** January 15. **Remarks:** Established in 1984. **Contact:** Charles Jackson, Program Manager, Phone: 813-272-2772.

4630 ■ Florida Engineering Society (FES)
PO Box 750
Tallahassee, FL 32302-0750
Ph: (850)224-7121
E-mail: fes@fleng.org
URL: www.fleng.org
Social Media: www.facebook.com/
FloridaEngineeringSociety
www.instagram.com/floridaengineeringsociety
www.linkedin.com/company/florida-engineering-society
twitter.com/FICE_ACECFL

4631 ■ Raymond W. Miller, PE Scholarships *(Undergraduate/Scholarship)*

Purpose: To encourage and assist students in pursuing engineering careers; to educate the public about engineering and to promote and enhance engineering education in Florida in order to position the state as a technological leader in a global economy. **Focus:** Engineering. **Qualif.:** Applicants must be enrolled in an ABET-accredited Florida engineering school and must plan to attend the University of Florida. **Criteria:** Preference will be given to students desiring to attend the University of Florida.

Funds Avail.: $2,500. **To Apply:** Applicants must submit completed application form; an official transcript; and letter of recommendation from any appropriate source.

4632 ■ Eric Primavera Memorial Scholarships *(Undergraduate/Scholarship)*

Purpose: To encourage and assist students in pursuing engineering careers; to educate the public about engineering and to promote and enhance engineering education in Florida in order to position the state as a technological leader in a global economy. **Focus:** Engineering. **Qualif.:** Applicants must be enrolled in an ABET-accredited Florida engineering school and plan to attend the Florida Institute of Technology. **Criteria:** Preference will be given to students desiring to attend Florida Institute of Technology.

Funds Avail.: $1,000. **To Apply:** Applicants must submit completed application form; an official transcript; and letter of recommendation from any appropriate source.

Awards are arranged alphabetically below their administering organizations

4633 ■ Florida Fertilizer & Agrichemical Association (FFAA)

605 E Main St
Bartow, FL 33830
Ph: (863)686-4827
Fax: (863)682-8626
E-mail: mhartney@ffaa.org
URL: www.ffaa.org
Social Media: www.facebook.com/Florida-Fertilizer
 -Agrichemical-Association-115164458792
twitter.com/FFAAtweets

4634 ■ Florida Fertilizer and Agrichemical Association Scholarships *(Undergraduate/Scholarship)*

Purpose: To promote the study of agriculture in higher education and to encourage students pursuing agriculture studies. **Focus:** Agricultural sciences. **Qualif.:** Applicants must be agriculture junior, senior or graduate students at the University of Florida A&M or Florida Southern; must plan to enroll for the semester immediately following the fall semester; must have a minimum GPA of 3.0 on a 4.0 scale. **Criteria:** Recipients are selected based on academic performance and financial need.

Funds Avail.: No specific amount. **Duration:** Annual. **To Apply:** Applicants must submit a completed application form; copy or screenshot of transcripts. **Contact:** Phone:863-686-4827,E-mail:mhartney@ffaa.org.

4635 ■ Florida Institute of Certified Public Accountants (FICPA)

3800 Esplanade Way, Ste. 210
Tallahassee, FL 32311
Ph: (850)224-2727
Fax: (850)222-8190
Free: 800-342-3197
E-mail: msc@ficpa.org
URL: www.ficpa.org
Social Media: www.facebook.com/FloridaInstituteofCPAs
www.instagram.com/ficpa
www.linkedin.com/company/florida-institute-of-cpas-ficpa
twitter.com/FICPA

4636 ■ FICPA Educational Foundation 1040K Race Scholarships *(Undergraduate/Scholarship, Award)*

Purpose: To offset the educational costs for accounting students at Florida's colleges and universities. **Focus:** Accounting. **Qualif.:** Applicants must be an African American; a permanent resident of Miami-Dade, Broward, Palm Beach, or Monroe Counties; and must be a full-time, 4th or 5th year accounting major at: Barry University, Florida Atlantic University, Florida International University, Florida Memorial College, Nova Southeastern University, St. Thomas University, and University of Miami. **Criteria:** Selection will be given based on the application materials submitted.

Funds Avail.: $3,000 each. **Duration:** Annual. **Number Awarded:** Varies. **To Apply:** Students must submit a completed application along with official transcripts to the Accounting Scholarship Chairman by the school's deadline for review by the accounting faculty; if the application is selected. **Deadline:** February 15.

4637 ■ Florida Nursery, Growers and Landscape Association (FNGLA)

1533 Park Center Dr.
Orlando, FL 32835

Free: 800-375-3642
E-mail: info@fngla.org
URL: www.fngla.org
Social Media: www.facebook.com/FNGLA
www.instagram.com/fngla_florida
twitter.com/fngla

4638 ■ The James H. Davis Memorial Scholarship *(Undergraduate, Postgraduate/Scholarship)*

Purpose: To encourage students to pursue careers in Florida's horticulture industry and related pursuits by providing financial assistance for undergraduate, post-graduate, or other advanced education programs in Florida. **Focus:** Horticulture. **Criteria:** Selection will be based on financial need and students' ability to maintain a 2.0 grade point average.

Funds Avail.: No specific amount. **Duration:** Annual. **To Apply:** Applicants must complete the application form; must submit a high school or college transcript; an essay and two letters of recommendation. **Remarks:** The award was established in honor of James H. Davis, a respected tree farm owner and member of the Florida Nursery, Growers and Landscape Association (FNGLA). **Contact:** Completed application and attachments to: James H. Davis Memorial Scholarship, National Horticulture Foundation, 1533 Park Center Dr., Orlando, FL, 32835.

4639 ■ Florida Nurses Association (FNA)

1235 E Concord St.
Orlando, FL 32803
Ph: (407)896-3261
Fax: (407)896-9042
E-mail: info@floridanurse.org
URL: www.floridanurse.org
Social Media: www.facebook.com/
 FloridaNursesAssociation
www.linkedin.com/company/florida-nurses-association
twitter.com/FLNurses

4640 ■ Florida Nurses Foundation Scholarships *(Undergraduate, Master's, Doctorate/Scholarship)*

Purpose: To serve and support all registered nurses through professional development, advocacy and the promotion of excellence at every level of professional nursing practice. **Focus:** Nursing. **Qualif.:** Applicants must be enrolled in a nationally accredited nursing program; applicants must be resides within the Northeast Florida area (Nassau, Duval, Baker, Clay, & Bradford Counties).

Funds Avail.: No specific amount. **Duration:** Annual. **Deadline:** June 1.

4641 ■ The Florida Ornithological Society (FOS)

4806 West Beach Drive
Tampa, FL 33609
URL: www.fosbirds.org
Social Media: www.facebook.com/groups/42478406968

4642 ■ Helen G. and Allan D. Cruickshank Education Award *(Undergraduate, Doctorate, Postdoctorate/Grant)*

Purpose: To support projects dealing with wild birds in Florida. **Focus:** Ornithology.

Funds Avail.: $2,000-$2,500. **Duration:** Annual. **Number Awarded:** 1. **To Apply:** Applicant should provide a two-

Awards are arranged alphabetically below their administering organizations

page written description of the proposed use of the award; should send three copies of their proposal and a curriculum vitae. **Deadline:** September 1. **Remarks:** Established in 1999. **Contact:** Adam Kent; 222 SE 12th St., Gainesville, FL, 32641.

4643 ■ Florida Outdoor Writers Association, Inc. (FOWA)
235 Apollo Beach Blvd., Unit 271
Apollo Beach, FL 33572
Ph: (813)579-0990
E-mail: info@fowa.org
URL: www.fowa.org
Social Media: www.facebook.com/FOWAOrg
twitter.com/FOWAORG

4644 ■ Florida Outdoor Writers Association Scholarships (FOWA) *(Undergraduate/Scholarship)*

Purpose: To motivate and encourage young people to enter outdoor communications career fields. **Focus:** Communications; Journalism. **Qualif.:** Applicants must be students at Florida Colleges and Universities, or must be students whose applications are endorsed by a FOWA member or a faculty advisor.

Funds Avail.: $1,000. **Duration:** Annual. **To Apply:** Applicants must submit a completed application form; must submit an essay, 500-1, 000-words, that expresses their appreciation for the outdoor experience; an up-to-date resume; a letter of endorsement from a FOWA member or faculty advisor. **Deadline:** June 11.

4645 ■ Florida Police Chiefs Association (FPCA)
2636 Mitcham Dr.
Tallahassee, FL 32308
Ph: (850)219-3631
E-mail: info@fpca.com
URL: www.fpca.com
Social Media: www.facebook.com/TheFPCA
twitter.com/FloridaChiefs

4646 ■ The Judge Ralph Fisch Police Explorer Scholarship Program *(Undergraduate/Scholarship)*

Purpose: To support number of programs including youth career development. **Focus:** Government. **Criteria:** Selection will be based on the committee's criteria.

Funds Avail.: $1,000. **Duration:** Annual. **To Apply:** Applicants must submit a completed application form along with major field of academic interest, currently active school and community organizations, leadership positions, important awards and recognitions with name of the organizations presented them, written statement of up to 1, 000 words stating reasons for seeking this scholarship; three letters of recommendation should come from (1) school officials, (2) post or organizational leaders, and (3) community or church leaders. **Contact:** Florida Police Chiefs Education and Research Foundation: 2636 Mitcham Dr. Tallahassee, Florida, 32308; Phone: 850-219-3631.

4647 ■ Florida Public Health Association (FPHA)
1605 Pebble Beach Blvd.
Green Cove Springs, FL 32043-8077
Ph: (904)657-2009
Fax: (904)657-2235

E-mail: floridapha@bellsouth.net
URL: www.fpha.org
Social Media: www.facebook.com/FLPublicHealth

4648 ■ Florida Public Health Association Public Health Graduate Scholarships *(Graduate, Undergraduate/Scholarship)*

Purpose: To support the studies of students who are studying public health. **Focus:** Public health. **Qualif.:** Applicants must be a FPHA member; must be in a Master's Degree or Doctoral Degree program in the field of public health; must intend to remain in Florida and contribute to Florida's Public Health System following graduation.

Funds Avail.: $150. **Duration:** Annual. **Number Awarded:** 1. **To Apply:** Applicants must submit the complete application form together with a narrative (1-2 pages) that explains professional goals and reasons for seeking Master's or Doctoral degree, curriculum vitae, two original letters of recommendation from two non-family references, and copy of current transcript showing GPA. **Deadline:** May 14. **Contact:** Email: fpha@srahec.org.

4649 ■ Florida Public Health Association Public Health Undergraduate Scholarships *(Undergraduate/Scholarship)*

Purpose: To support the students displaying financial need who are majoring in public health or nutrition science. **Focus:** Public health. **Qualif.:** Applicants must be working on degrees in health-related or public health programs; must be nominated by an FPHA active member.

Funds Avail.: $100. **Duration:** Annual. **To Apply:** Applicants must submit the completed application form together with a narrative (1-2 pages) that explains professional goals and reasons for interest in health or public health, curriculum vitae, two original letters of recommendation from two non-family references, and a copy of current transcript showing GPA.

4650 ■ Florida Retired Educators Association (FREA)
10051 5th St. N, Ste. 108
Saint Petersburg, FL 33702
Ph: (727)577-6400
E-mail: info@frea.org
URL: www.frea.org
Social Media: www.facebook.com/
FloridaRetiredEducatorsAssociation

4651 ■ FREA Scholarship *(Undergraduate/Scholarship)*

Purpose: To provide an opportunity to high school seniors who wish to teach in the State of Florida. **Focus:** Education. **Qualif.:** Applicants must be graduating high school seniors. **Criteria:** Selection will be based on the committee's criteria.

Funds Avail.: Amount varies. **Duration:** Annual. **To Apply:** Applicants must completed Application; Single page typed Essay; Recommendation Letters; Official high school transcript with ACT or SAT scores circled. In the event the ACT/SAT scores are not printed on the transcript, a student applying for this scholarship must send an official copy of these scores along with this application in order for consideration; Mail your application by your local unit deadline. **Deadline:** December; January. **Remarks:** Estab-

Awards are arranged alphabetically below their administering organizations

lished in 1980. **Contact:** Phone: 727-577-6400; Email: info@frea.org.

4652 ■ Flow Feet Orthopedic Shoes
17503 La Cantera Pkwy., Ste. 104188
San Antonio, TX 78257
Free: 877-926-0133
E-mail: customerservice@flowfeet.com
URL: flowfeet.com
Social Media: www.facebook.com/FlowFeetShoes
www.instagram.com/flowfeetshoes
twitter.com/flowfeetshoes

4653 ■ Flow Feet Foot the Bill Scholarship *(Two Year College, University/Award)*

Purpose: To help students "foot the bill" for their education. **Focus:** General studies/Field of study not specified. **Qualif.:** Applicant must be a current, full-time student enrolled in an accredited U.S. university or college and have a cumulative GPA of at least 3.0. **Criteria:** Selection will be based on the creativity and writing skills displayed in the submitted essay.

Funds Avail.: $500. **Number Awarded:** 1. **To Apply:** Applicant must submit a 500 word essay about why people should help others and how helping others is important for future success. Applicant must also provide an example of how they have helped someone or something in the past and how their good deed impacted the recipient. Applicant may submit a video essay (up to four minutes) instead of a written essay. Applicant must submit the essay via email and include: scanned application of student ID verifying student status and a current transcript. **Deadline:** September 30. **Contact:** E-mail: scholarships@flowfeet.com.

4654 ■ Fondation des Prix Michener
Ottawa, ON, Canada
E-mail: information@michenerawards.ca
URL: www.michenerawards.ca

4655 ■ The Michener-Deacon Fellowship for Investigative Journalism *(Professional development/ Fellowship)*

Purpose: To encourage excellence in investigative print, broadcast, and online journalism that serves the public interest. **Focus:** Journalism. **Qualif.:** Applicants must be Canadian citizens who are active in Canadian journalism, and mature journalists with at least five years of experience for four month's leave. **Criteria:** Applications will be judged by an independent panel to be selected.

Funds Avail.: $30,000 and accountable expenses of up to $5,000. **Duration:** Annual. **To Apply:** Applicants are expected to submit a written outline for a proposed project. the application must include a letter of reference attesting to the capacity of the candidates to deliver the proposed project and, where applicable, employer support for the candidates. additional documentation such as undertakings of access or cooperation from third parties will be welcome. the judges will take into consideration the quality of the candidates' presentation. applications must include an expression by an employer or a news organization of intent or, preferably, a commitment to publish or broadcast the completed project. the publication or broadcast must indicate that the project was supported and funded by the Michener Awards Foundation. in addition, the project or a

summary must be made available for posting on the website of the Michener Awards Foundation.

4656 ■ The Michener-Deacon Fellowship for Journalism Education *(Professional development/ Fellowship)*

Purpose: To strengthen the education of both of the successful applicant and the regular student in the journalism program. **Focus:** Journalism. **Criteria:** Judges will award the fellowship on the merits of the applicant's proposal for a course of study over one semester.

Funds Avail.: $30,000 and accountable expenses of up to $5,000. **Duration:** Annual. **To Apply:** Applicants must submit the following requirements: written outline for a course of study in PDF format; resume that includes detailed work history; written authorization for leave from an employer and; letter from the host department providing approval from the application and describing how it will support the candidate. The letter should confirm that the school will organize one public lecture for the journalist-in-residence and facilitate arrangements for other lectures or mentoring during the semester. **Deadline:** February 28.

4657 ■ Fondation Savoy
230 Foch St.
Saint-Jean-sur-Richelieu, QC, Canada J3B 2B2
Ph: (450)358-9779
Fax: (450)346-1045
E-mail: info@savoy-foundation.ca
URL: www.savoy-foundation.ca
Social Media: www.facebook.com/SavoyFoundation
twitter.com/SavoyFoundation

4658 ■ Savoy Foundation Postdoctoral and Clinical Research Fellowships *(Postdoctorate/Fellowship)*

Purpose: To support study and research in the field of epilepsy. **Focus:** Epilepsy. **Qualif.:** Applicant must be a Canadian researchers for research conducted in Canada or abroad and to foreign nationals for projects conducted in Canada. **Criteria:** Selection will be based on the committee's criteria.

Funds Avail.: $30,000. **Duration:** Annual; 1 year. **Number Awarded:** 1. **To Apply:** The application process is online.

4659 ■ Fonds de la Société canadienne d' évaluation pour l'éducation
1485 Laperriere Ave.
Ottawa, ON, Canada K1Z 7S8
Ph: (613)725-2526
Fax: (613)729-6206
E-mail: secretariat@evaluation-education.org
URL: cesef.memberlodge.org

4660 ■ CESEF Postgraduate Scholarship Program *(Postdoctorate/Scholarship)*

Purpose: To provide scholarship for graduate students wishing to further their knowledge within the field of program evaluation. **Focus:** General studies/Field of study not specified. **Qualif.:** Applicants who are pursuing studies for the purpose of improving the theory and practice of program evaluation; they must be in master's or doctoral level. **Criteria:** Selection will be based on merit and contribution to the field.

Awards are arranged alphabetically below their administering organizations

Funds Avail.: $5,000. **Duration:** Annual. **To Apply:** Applicants may contact the society for information about the submission process and deadlines. **Deadline:** December 9. **Contact:** Email: secretariat@evaluation-education.org.

4661 ■ Food Distribution Research Society (FDRS)

c/o Jonathan Baros
600 Laureate Way
Kannapolis, NC 28081
Ph: (704)250-5458
URL: www.fdrsinc.org
Social Media: twitter.com/FDRSInc

4662 ■ Richardson-Applebaum Award *(Doctorate, Master's, Graduate/Scholarship)*

Purpose: To recognize an outstanding graduate student with an interest in a career in the food industry. **Focus:** Food service careers. **Qualif.:** Applicants must be graduate students with scholarly interest and career aspirations in the food distribution system who have completed the degree. **Criteria:** Selection is based on the submitted application materials.

Funds Avail.: $1,250 (Ph.D. degree level competition); $750 (M.S. degree level); $750 (Masters level, non-thesis paper). **Duration:** Annual. **To Apply:** Applicants must complete the entire application form and submit cover letter; a copy of the dissertation/thesis/case study; a letter of recommendation from the academic advisor; a brief synopsis of: academic training, any food industry experience and/or research experience, and career interests, goals, and objectives; applicant's contact information (name, mailing address, phone number, and e-mail). **Deadline:** February 1. **Remarks:** The award was named in the memory of William Applebaum. Established in 1978. **Contact:** Kathy Kelley, Vice President of Education, Penn State University, 6 Tyson Bldg., University Park, PA, 16802; E-mail: KathyKelley@psu.edu.

4663 ■ Food and Drug Law Institute (FDLI)

1155 15th St. NW, Ste. 910
Washington, DC 20005
Ph: (202)371-1420
Fax: (202)371-0649
Free: 800-956-6293
E-mail: info@fdli.org
URL: www.fdli.org
Social Media: www.facebook.com/foodanddruglaw
twitter.com/foodanddruglaw

4664 ■ H. Thomas Austern Memorial Writing Competition *(Doctorate/Award, Prize)*

Purpose: To encourage students interested in the areas of law that affect food, drugs, animal drugs, biologics, cosmetics, diagnostics, dietary supplements, medical devices and tobacco. **Focus:** Law. **Qualif.:** Applicants must be currently enrolled in a J.D. program at any of the nations' "ABA accredited" law schools.

Funds Avail.: $750 for first place, $500 for second, and $250 for third. **Duration:** Annual. **Number Awarded:** 2. **To Apply:** Submissions must be typewritten, double-spaced on 8.5 x 11 inch paper; electronic submissions in word documents are acceptable; students joining the short paper

competition; candidates submitting in a long paper category cannot exceed 100 pages including footnotes; text and footnote shall be type-written, 12 pt.; Times New Roman format; papers must have one-inch margin in all sides; must also include a cover sheet with entrant's full name and contact information, law school, year of study, and date of submission. **Deadline:** June 19.

4665 ■ Food Processing Suppliers Association (FPSA)

1451 Dolley Madison Blvd., Ste. 101
McLean, VA 22101-3850
Ph: (703)663-1200
Fax: (703)761-4334
URL: www.fpsa.org
Social Media: www.facebook.com/FPSAorg
www.linkedin.com/company/food-processing-suppliers
 -association
twitter.com/fpsaorg

4666 ■ Career Development Scholarships *(Postgraduate/Scholarship)*

Purpose: To attract and retain qualified personnel for the food processing industry. **Focus:** Food science and technology; Food service careers. **Qualif.:** Applicants must be a full-time employee, spouse of a full-time employee, or a child of a full-time employee of firms which are members in good standing of the Food Processing Suppliers Association; the employee must have been employed by a member firm for at least one year as of January 1 of the year in which the scholarships are awarded and must still be employed by a member firm when the scholarships are awarded; must be high school seniors, college students, or graduate students. **Criteria:** Selection will be based on academic achievements and records; and ACT/SAT Test Scores (if applicable); essay content; extracurricular activities; community involvement.

Funds Avail.: $5,000. **Duration:** One year. **Number Awarded:** Up to 15. **To Apply:** Applicants must complete the online application. **Deadline:** May 15.

4667 ■ Foot Locker Foundation, Inc.

112 W 34th St.
New York, NY 10120
URL: www.footlockerscholarathletes.com

4668 ■ Foot Locker Scholar Athletes *(Undergraduate/Scholarship)*

Purpose: To support U.S. students who are currently involved in high school sports, intramural sports, or community-based sports. **Focus:** General studies/Field of study not specified. **Qualif.:** Applicant must be a current high school senior entering a four-year, accredited U.S. college or university in the Fall; a member (in good standing) of a high school sports team or be involved in after-school sports (e.g. intramurals, martial arts, etc.); maintained an unweighted GPA of 3.0 or higher from ninth grade to first semester of 12th grade; be a U.S. citizen or U.S. permanent legal resident. Foot Locker employees and their immediate family members are ineligible. **Criteria:** Selection will be evaluated based on the following embody good sportsmanship and strong moral character; are passionate and committed to empowering the community in which they live; are confident and enthusiastic leaders; display academic excel-

Awards are arranged alphabetically below their administering organizations

lence; or have come from diverse backgrounds.

Funds Avail.: $20,000 each. **Number Awarded:** 20. **To Apply:** Applications can be submitted online. **Deadline:** December 15.

4669 ■ For the Love of Chocolate Scholarship Foundation

4533 W North Ave.
Melrose Park, IL 60160
Ph: (773)972-1927
E-mail: franco@ftloc.org
URL: www.fortheloveofchocolatefoundation.org
Social Media: www.facebook.com/ftloc
www.instagram.com/forloveofchocolate
www.linkedin.com/company/for-the-love-of-chocolate
  -scholarship-foundation
twitter.com/FLoveChocolate
www.youtube.com/channel/UCh1XVR75ryytlRTxBbLxk2w

4670 ■ For the Love of Chocolate Foundation Scholarships *(Undergraduate, Graduate, Professional development/Scholarship)*

Purpose: To encourage and assist aspiring students, career changers and culinary career professionals to advance their knowledge of the pastry arts. **Focus:** Culinary arts. **Qualif.:** Applicants must demonstrate a desire to develop their pastry art skills; must agree to work or volunteer a minimum of 40 hours in a food service establishment prior to or during the semester, and their work must be documented by a direct supervisor; must be U.S. citizens or foreign nationals who currently hold a federally issued Permanent Resident ("green") Card. **Criteria:** Selection will be based on committee's criteria.

Funds Avail.: No specific amount. **To Apply:** Applicants must submit a completed scholarship application form along with a personal essay, two letters of recommendation and a copy of previous year's tax return; must submit the essay questions and budget. **Deadline:** May 1; June 1; October 1. **Contact:** Email: franco@ftloc.org.

4671 ■ Ford Foundation

320 E 43rd St.
New York, NY 10017
Ph: (212)573-5000
Fax: (212)351-3677
URL: www.fordfoundation.org
Social Media: www.facebook.com/FordFound
www.linkedin.com/company/ford-foundation
twitter.com/FordFoundation
www.youtube.com/user/fordfoundationTV

4672 ■ Ford Foundation Dissertation Fellowship *(Postdoctorate/Fellowship)*

Purpose: To provide support for individuals working to complete a dissertation leading to a Doctor of Philosophy or Doctor of Science degree. **Focus:** Area and ethnic studies; Interdisciplinary studies; Peace studies.

Funds Avail.: $25,000. **Duration:** Annual. **Number Awarded:** 36. **To Apply:** Applicants must complete the online application form including personal and contact information; personal statement describing the applicant's background and experience and commitment to the goals

of the Ford Foundation Fellowship Programs; statement of previous research and scholarly productivity including a list of publications and presentations; proposed plan of graduate study and research and the applicant's long-range career goals; names and contact information of a minimum of three individuals who will upload a letter of recommendation on the applicant's behalf (four letters are highly recommended; five letters maximum); and also must include supplementary materials: baccalaureate degree transcript; graduate transcript; letters of recommendation (maximum 4 MB); fewer than three letters of recommendation; prepare essays in advance and save each in a separate pdf file (maximum 4 MB) so that you are ready to upload these documents. **Deadline:** December 17 for online application; January 7 for supplementary materials. **Contact:** Email: fordapplications@nas.edu.

4673 ■ Ford Foundation Postdoctoral Fellowship *(Postdoctorate/Fellowship)*

Purpose: To provide support for individuals engaged in postdoctoral study after the attainment of the Doctor of Philosophy or Doctor of Science degree. **Focus:** Area and ethnic studies; Interdisciplinary studies; Peace studies.

Funds Avail.: $45,000. **Duration:** Annual. **Number Awarded:** 24. **To Apply:** Applicants must complete the online application form including personal and contact information; personal statement describing the applicant's background and experience and commitment to the goals of the Ford Foundation Fellowship Programs; statement of previous research and scholarly productivity including a list of publications and presentations; proposed plan of graduate study and research and the applicant's long-range career goals; names and contact information of a minimum of three individuals who will upload a letter of recommendation on the applicant's behalf (four letters are highly recommended; five letters maximum); and also must include supplementary materials: baccalaureate degree transcript; graduate transcript; letters of recommendation (maximum 4 MB); fewer than three letters of recommendation; prepare essays in advance and save each in a separate pdf file (maximum 4 MB) so that you are ready to upload these documents. **Deadline:** December 17 for online application; January 7 for supplementary materials.

4674 ■ Ford Foundation Predoctoral Fellowship *(Graduate, Doctorate/Fellowship)*

Purpose: To provide support for individuals engaged in graduate study leading to a Doctor of Philosophy or Doctor of Science degree. **Focus:** Area and ethnic studies; Interdisciplinary studies; Peace studies.

Funds Avail.: $24,000. **Duration:** Annual; up to 3 years. **To Apply:** Applicants must complete the online application form including personal and contact information; personal statement describing the applicant's background and experience and commitment to the goals of the Ford Foundation Fellowship Programs; statement of previous research and scholarly productivity including a list of publications and presentations; proposed plan of graduate study and research and the applicant's long-range career goals; names and contact information of a minimum of three individuals who will upload a letter of recommendation on the applicant's behalf (four letters are highly recommended; five letters maximum); and also must include supplementary materials: baccalaureate degree transcript; graduate transcript; letters of recommendation (maximum 4 MB); fewer than three letters of recommendation; prepare essays in advance and save each in a separate pdf file (maximum 4 MB) so that you are ready to upload these

Awards are arranged alphabetically below their administering organizations

documents. **Deadline:** December 17 for online application; January 8 for supplementary materials.

4675 ■ The Forensic Sciences Foundation, Inc (FSF)

410 N 21st St.
Colorado Springs, CO 80904
Ph: (719)636-1100
Fax: (719)636-1993
URL: fsf.aafs.org

4676 ■ Jan S. Bashinski Criminalistics Graduate Thesis Assistance Grant *(Graduate/Grant)*

Purpose: To support graduate students in completing their thesis or independent research project required for a graduate degree in criminalistics forensic sciences. **Focus:** Law enforcement; Psychology. **Qualif.:** Applicant must be a full or part-time student completing graduate degree requirements by conducting a research project at an educational institution accredited in the U.S. by a recognized academic body; should have made a significant scientific contribution to their field. **Criteria:** Selection is based on submission of documents.

Funds Avail.: $1,700 cash and $1,300 for travel expenses. **Duration:** Annual. **Number Awarded:** Varies. **To Apply:** Applicants must complete the application and submit with the required attachments. **Deadline:** July 31.

4677 ■ FSF Field Grant *(Professional development/Grant)*

Purpose: To help the investigator/researcher initiate original problem oriented research. **Focus:** Science. **Qualif.:** Must be a member or an affiliate of the American Academy of Forensic Sciences. **Criteria:** Selection is based on submission of documents.

Funds Avail.: Up to $1,500. **Duration:** Annual. **To Apply:** Research proposals must include: an abstract not to exceed three pages containing a well-developed title and research question; a brief literature review of not more than ten references pertinent to the subject of the research; a detailed budget and timetable; disclose of current or previous FSF research grants awarded; and curriculum vitae. All materials may be submitted electronically or by mail. **Deadline:** June 15. **Contact:** Kimberly Wrasse; Email: kwrasse@aafs.org.

4678 ■ FSF Student Travel Grant *(Undergraduate, Graduate/Grant)*

Purpose: To assist students by helping them attend the American Academy of Forensic Sciences (AAFS) Annual Meeting. **Focus:** Criminology. **Qualif.:** Applicants must be AAFS members/affiliates or AAFS applicants applying for membership; must be 4th year undergraduate or graduate students at an accredited four-year college, university or professional school whose accreditation is acceptable to the FSF Board of Trustees. **Criteria:** Selection is based on submission of documents.

Funds Avail.: Up to $1,500 per student. **Duration:** Annual. **To Apply:** Applicants must submit an abstract either as presenters or co-authors for the annual meeting they will be attending; must have a letter of recommendation from their advisor or professor; must submit a 400-600 word essay explaining how attendance at an AAFS meeting will impact their career decision; must submit a curriculum vitae to include specific regarding their involvement in forensic

science and their current GPA. **Deadline:** June 15. **Contact:** Kimberly Wrasse, FSF, 410 N. 21st St., Colorado Springs, CO 80904; Email: kwrasse@aafs.org.

4679 ■ Lucas Grant *(Professional development/Grant)*

Purpose: To help the investigator/researcher in original in-depth problem oriented research. **Focus:** Science. **Qualif.:** Must be a member or an affiliate of the American Academy of Forensic Sciences. **Criteria:** Selection is based on submission of documents.

Funds Avail.: $1,501-$6,000. **Duration:** Annual. **To Apply:** Research proposals must include: an abstract not to exceed three pages containing a well-developed title and research question; a brief literature review of not more than ten references pertinent to the subject of the research; a detailed budget and timetable; disclose of current or previous FSF research grants awarded; and curriculum vitae. All materials may be submitted electronically or by mail. **Deadline:** June 15. **Contact:** Kimberly Wrasse; Email: kwrasse@aafs.org.

4680 ■ Forest History Society (FHS)

2925 Academy Rd.
Durham, NC 27705-9311
Ph: (919)682-9319
Fax: (919)682-2349
URL: www.foresthistory.org
Social Media: www.facebook.com/foresthistory
www.linkedin.com/company/forest-history-society
twitter.com/foresthistory
www.youtube.com/user/foresthistor

4681 ■ Alfred D. Bell, Jr. Travel Grants *(Graduate/Grant)*

Purpose: To provide financial assistance for researchers conducting in-depth studies using resources in the society's archive and library. **Focus:** General studies/Field of study not specified. **Qualif.:** Applicants must be persons whose research topics are covered in the FHS library and archives. **Criteria:** Preference is given to applicant's whose research topics are well-covered in the FHS library and archives; preference is also given to young scholars, per the wishes of the Bell family.

Funds Avail.: $950. **Duration:** Annual. **Number Awarded:** Varies. **To Apply:** Applicants must submit a completed hard copy of the application form and resume at the FHS office. **Remarks:** The scholarship was established in honor of the memory of wholesale lumberman, forest industry editor, and former FHS vice president Alfred D. Bell Jr. **Contact:** Eben Lehman; Bell Travel Grants, Forest History Society, 2925 Academy Rd., Durham, NC 27705; E-mail: eben.lehman@foresthistory.org.

4682 ■ Frederick K. Weyerhaeuser Forest History Fellowship *(Graduate/Fellowship)*

Purpose: To support the research of a Duke University graduate student whose research examines in some way forest and conservation history. **Focus:** Environmental conservation; Forestry; History. **Qualif.:** Applicants must be Duke University graduate students pursuing research in the fields of forest, conservation or environmental history. **Criteria:** Selection will be a basis of merit; proposals are judged in terms of overall significance and quality of presentation.

Funds Avail.: $11,000. **Duration:** Annual. **To Apply:** Applicants must submit a narrative description of research (up

Awards are arranged alphabetically below their administering organizations

to eight pages), including significance of topic, research approach, author's background, research and writing schedule, and budget; attachments are not necessary but may include previous publications, written chapters and basic bibliography; curriculum vitae and 2-3 letters of recommendation from persons knowledgeable of the applicant's research; letters of recommendation should address the author's qualifications and may describe the significance of the topic to forest and conservation history; five hard copies of the proposal and an electronic copy of the proposal without supporting documents; must provide a cover letter that states the title of the proposed research, a one-paragraph summary of the significance of the project and a description of the historical nature of the project. **Deadline:** January 31. **Remarks:** Established to honor the memory of Frederick K. Weyerhaeuser. Established in 1986. **Contact:** Forest History Society, 2925 Academy Road, Durham, NC, 27705; Email: andrea.anderson@foresthistory.org.

4683 ■ Forestry Suppliers Inc.
401 S Wright Rd.
Janesville, WI 53546
Fax: (800)628-2068
Free: 800-241-6401
URL: www.benmeadows.com
Social Media: www.facebook.com/benmeadowsco
linkedin.com/company/forestry-suppliers-inc-
pinterest.com/forestrysup
twitter.com/ForestrySup
youtube.com/user/ForestrySuppliers1

4684 ■ Ben Meadows Natural Resource Scholarships - Academic Achievement Scholarships (Undergraduate/Scholarship)
Purpose: To provide fund for students enrolled in a natural resource program. **Focus:** Environmental science; Fisheries sciences/management; Forestry; Natural resources; Wildlife conservation, management, and science. **Qualif.:** Applicant must be a junior or senior student enrolled in a natural resource program working toward a bachelor of arts or science degree, which includes, but is not limited to, agro forestry, urban forestry, environmental studies, natural resource management, natural resource recreation, wildlife management, wood science and fisheries management. **Criteria:** Selection based on the application.
Funds Avail.: $2,500. **Duration:** Annual.

4685 ■ Ben Meadows Natural Resource Scholarships - Leadership Scholarships (Undergraduate/Scholarship)
Purpose: To provide fund for students enrolled in a natural resource program. **Focus:** Environmental science; Fisheries sciences/management; Forestry; Natural resources; Wildlife conservation, management, and science. **Qualif.:** Applicant must be a junior or senior student enrolled in a natural resource program working toward a bachelor of arts or science degree, which includes, but is not limited to, agro forestry, urban forestry, environmental studies, natural resource management, natural resource recreation, wildlife management, wood science and fisheries management. **Criteria:** Selection based on the application.
Funds Avail.: $2,500. **Duration:** Annual.

4686 ■ Formsbirds.com
South Ashland Ave.
Chicago, IL 60608

URL: www.formsbirds.com

4687 ■ FormsBirds Scholarship (Undergraduate/Scholarship)
Purpose: To help outstanding students to complete their college education. **Focus:** General studies/Field of study not specified. **Qualif.:** Applicants must be either currently enrolled or planning to enroll at an accredited college or university; must have a minimum 3.0 GPA; must be at least 16 years old at the time of application; current employees, officers, directors and agents of Formsbirds and its related companies and members of their immediate families (defined as spouse, parents, siblings and children) and persons residing at the same address are not eligible. Applicants must agree to Formsbirds official scholarship rules and follow all application instructions. **Criteria:** Selection will be based on the scoring criteria (material organization, vocabulary and style, creativity and originality, grammar, punctuation, and spelling and neatness.
Funds Avail.: $500. **Duration:** Annual. **Number Awarded:** 1. **To Apply:** Applicants must compose a 600-1,000 word essay in Word; must complete an application form; an academic transcript and a photo. **Deadline:** September 15. **Contact:** Email: scholarship@formbirds.com.

4688 ■ Forté Foundation
9600 Escarpment, Ste. 745
Austin, TX 78749
Ph: (512)535-5157
URL: www.fortefoundation.org
Social Media: facebook.com/fortefoundation
instagram.com/fortefoundation
linkedin.com/company/forte-foundation
twitter.com/fortefoundation
youtube.com/user/fortefoundation

4689 ■ Forté Fellowships (Master's/Fellowship)
Purpose: To increase the number of women applying to and enrolling in MBA programs by offering fellowships. **Focus:** Business.
Funds Avail.: No specific amount. **Duration:** Annual. **Number Awarded:** 1. **To Apply:** Applicants must first submit an MBA application to a participating school; schools are encourage to nominate fellows who represent diverse educational and work backgrounds, career goals, ethnicities and citizenship. **Deadline:** July 12.

4690 ■ Foss Maritime Co.
450 Alaskan Way S., Ste. 706
Seattle, WA 98104
Ph: (206)281-3800
Free: 800-426-2885
E-mail: info@foss.com
URL: www.foss.com
Social Media: www.facebook.com/FossMaritime
www.instagram.com/fossmaritime
www.linkedin.com/company/foss-maritime-company
twitter.com/FossMaritime
www.youtube.com/channel/
 UCV81oQRIKeHA88nrqYn0m9w

4691 ■ Norm Manly YMTA Maritime Education Scholarship (Undergraduate/Scholarship)
Purpose: To support students pursuing maritime training and education in community colleges, technical and

Awards are arranged alphabetically below their administering organizations

vocational programs, colleges, universities, maritime academies or other educational institutions. **Focus:** Maritime studies. **Qualif.:** Applicants must currently be enrolled as seniors in a high school or affiliated high school program (including GED program) in the State of Washington; plan to pursue post-secondary training or educational program leading to a maritime or marine-related career; and, have a grade point average of at least 2.5; relatives of the PSM Board of Governors, the YMTA Committee, the executive management team, or the owners of businesses or organizations sponsoring YMTA scholarships are not eligible. **Criteria:** Selection will be based on YMTA Committee's criteria; Essays will be judged for content, organization, grammar, spelling and neatness.

Funds Avail.: $1,000 to $5,000. **Duration:** Annual. **To Apply:** Applicants must submit completed application form along with current unofficial high school transcript; essay stating course of study planned to pursue and how this scholarship will assist candidate to secure a marine-related career; letters of support from a teacher (if GPA is less than 2.5, a second letter from a teacher is required), and from a member of the maritime community (optional). **Deadline:** February 24. **Contact:** URL: http://ymta.net/ymta-scholarships; Alicia Barnes, E-mail: ymta@pugetmaritime.org; Phone: 206-812-5464.

4692 ■ Foster Care to Success (FC2S)
23811 Chagrin Blvd., Ste. 210
Cleveland, OH 44122
Ph: (571)203-0270
Free: 855-773-8299
E-mail: info@fc2success.org
URL: www.fc2success.org
Social Media: www.facebook.com/FosterCare2Success
twitter.com/fc2success
www.youtube.com/fc2success

4693 ■ Casey Family Services Alumni Scholarship
(Undergraduate, Master's, Vocational/Occupational/Scholarship)

Purpose: To provide funds for students to cover their tuition and/or other expenses directly related to educational pursuits. **Focus:** Health care services. **Criteria:** Recipients are selected based on financial needs and scholastic standing.

Funds Avail.: Up to $10,000. **Duration:** Annual. **To Apply:** Applicants are suggested to visit the website to create an account and for the online application process.

4694 ■ Dr. Nancy Foster Scholarship Program
NOAA Office of National Marine Sanctuaries
1305 East-West Hwy., 11th Fl., Rm. 11423
Silver Spring, MD 20910
E-mail: fosterscholars@noaa.gov
URL: fosterscholars.noaa.gov

4695 ■ Dr. Nancy Foster Scholarships *(Graduate/Scholarship)*

Purpose: To provide support for independent graduate-level studies in oceanography, marine biology, or maritime archaeology (including all science, engineering, social science and resource management of ocean and coastal areas), particularly by women and members of minority groups. **Focus:** Biology, Marine; Maritime studies; Oceanography.

Duration: Annual. **Number Awarded:** Varies. **To Apply:** Applicants must submit a completed application form along with general information sheet; statement of intent; transcripts; enrollment verification or list of graduate schools applied; research proposal; two letters of recommendation; statement of financial need. **Deadline:** December 6. **Contact:** Dr. Nancy Foster Scholarship Program, NOAA Office of National Marine Sanctuaries, 1305 East-West Highway, 11th Fl., Rm. 11622, Silver Spring, MD, 20910.

4696 ■ Foundation for Advancement of Diversity In IP Law
1400 Crystal Dr., Ste. 600
Arlington, VA 22202
Ph: (703)412-1313
E-mail: admin@diversityinIPlaw.org
URL: www.diversityiniplaw.org
Social Media: www.facebook.com/diversityinIPLaw
twitter.com/diversityIPL

4697 ■ Jan Jancin Award *(Undergraduate/Award)*

Purpose: To promote the study of intellectual property law. **Focus:** Law. **Qualif.:** Applicants must be law students nominated by their schools who have excelled in the study of intellectual property law; best grades in IP courses overall; outstanding achievement in specified IP courses; best IP paper written by a student; determination by a faculty consensus; or membership and activity in student IP organizations. **Criteria:** Selection will be based on the committee's criteria.

Funds Avail.: $5,000. **To Apply:** Applicants must include the following in the nomination package: letter of recommendation on Law School letterhead; Jan Jancin Application Summary completed by the student candidate; a one-page essay by the student candidate discussing their personal achievements in the field of IP law. **Deadline:** May 24. **Contact:** American Intellectual Property Law Education Foundation, 1400 Crystal Dr., Ste., 600 Arlington, VA, 22202; Phone: 703-415-0780; Fax: 703-415-0786; Email: admin@aiplef.org.

4698 ■ Sidney B. Williams, Jr. Scholarships
(Undergraduate/Scholarship)

Purpose: To increase the number of underrepresented minority groups serving as intellectual property law practitioners in law firms and departments of corporations. **Focus:** Law. **Qualif.:** Applicants must be students entering or attending law school in Fall 2018 or 2019. **Criteria:** Recipients are selected based on demonstrated commitment to developing a career in intellectual property law; academic performance during the undergraduate, graduate and law school levels; financial need; leadership skills; and community activities or special accomplishments.

Funds Avail.: $10,000. **Duration:** Annual. **To Apply:** Applicants must submit completed scholarship application form; FAFSA form (or similar form) and other supporting documentation required; they must also submit: undergraduate transcript and graduate law transcript (if applicable); two letters of recommendation from, but not limited to former teachers, college administrators, community leaders, or other similar persons concerning the academic ability, character, reputation or professional aptitude of the applicant; evidence of being US citizens; personal or telephonic interview; and recent resume. **Dead-**

Awards are arranged alphabetically below their administering organizations

line: March 15. **Remarks:** Established in 2001. **Contact:** Deshuandra Walker, Manager, Student Support Programs, Thurgood Marshall College Fund; 1770 St. James Place, Ste. 414, Houston, TX 77056; Phone: 713-955-1073; Fax: 202-448-1017; E-mail: deshuandra.walker@tmcfund.org.

4699 ■ Foundation of the American Institute for Conservation of Historic and Artistic Works

727 15th St. NW, Ste. 320
Washington, DC 20005
Ph: (202)452-9545
Fax: (202)452-9328
E-mail: info@conservation-us.org
Social Media: www.facebook.com/aiconservation

4700 ■ FAIC Individual Professional Development Scholarships *(Professional development/Scholarship)*

Purpose: To help defray professional development costs for individual members of AIC who are Professional Associates or Fellows. **Focus:** Art conservation. **Qualif.:** Applicants must be AIC members seeking professional development. **Criteria:** Preference may be given to applicants who have not received FAIC funding within the past three years; and to applicants who will publish/lecture on the proposed project (thereby disseminating knowledge/skills gained).

Funds Avail.: Up to $1,000. **Duration:** Annual. **To Apply:** Applicants must complete and submit five copies of application and supporting materials to FAIC. Applicants may also submit application electronically only if all of materials (with the exception of letters of support) can be submitted electronically. Send the application form and all supporting materials in PDF, RTF or Microsoft Word format via email attachments. Name the files to include last name ("Lastname.doc" or "Lastname.pdf"). **Deadline:** February 15 or September 15. **Contact:** FAIC-Logo-web, Sarah Saetren, Education Coordinator; Phone: 202- 661-8071; Email: faicgrants@conservation-us.org.

4701 ■ Foundation for Anesthesia Education and Research (FAER)

200 First Street SW, WF6-674
Rochester, MN 55905
Ph: (507)284-9700
E-mail: faer@faer.org
URL: www.faer.org
Social Media: facebook.com/FAERinfo
twitter.com/FAERanesthesia

4702 ■ FAER Mentored Research Training Grants *(Professional development/Grant)*

Purpose: To help anesthesiologists develop the skills, preliminary data for subsequent grant applications and research publications needed to become independent investigators. **Focus:** Anesthesiology. **Criteria:** Selection will be based on the committee's criteria.

Funds Avail.: $175,000 ($75,000 for the 1st year; $100,000 for the 2nd year). **Duration:** Two years. **To Apply:** Applicants must be able to provide research projects in basic science, clinical or translational, or health service research; applicants and mentors must submit their biographical sketches (applicants must use the latest FAER version of the current NIH biosketch template while mentors must use

the standard NIH biosketch template); other documents required are abstracts; resubmission statement (if the applicants have previously submitted any research proposal to FAER); research plan; budget; letters of commitment and recommendation; and human use or animal review (with IRB or IACUC approval); applicants must also remember that the mentorship and career development sections are major elements of FAER research grant applications and are weighted heavily in the scoring. **Deadline:** February 28.

4703 ■ FAER Research in Education Grants *(Advanced Professional/Grant)*

Purpose: To advance the careers and knowledge of anesthesiologists interested in improving the concepts, methods and techniques of education in anesthesiology. **Focus:** Anesthesiology. **Qualif.:** Applicants must: be U.S. citizens, permanent residents, or holders of H-1 or O-1 visa with minimum of three years remaining; be graduate physicians with an unexpired, permanent, unconditional and unrestricted license to practice medicine or osteopathy in at least one state or jurisdiction of the United States; be certified by the American Board of Anesthesiology or in the examination system; be active members of the American Society of Anesthesiologists; and, have no more than ten years from completion of initial core anesthesiology residency training, whether or not from an ACGME-accredited program. **Criteria:** Selection will be based on the committee's criteria.

Funds Avail.: $100,000 ($50,000 per annum). **Duration:** up to two years. **To Apply:** Applicants and mentors must submit their biographical sketches (applicants must use the latest FAER version of the current NIH biosketch template while mentors must use the standard NIH biosketch template). Other documents required are abstracts; resubmission statement (if the applicants have previously submitted any research proposal to FAER); research plan; budget; letters of commitment and recommendation; and human use or animal review (with IRB or IACUC approval). Applicants must also remember that the mentorship and career development sections are major elements of FAER research grant applications and are weighted heavily in the scoring. **Deadline:** August 15 (summer/fall); February 15 (winter/spring). **Contact:** FAER office; Phone: 630-912-2554; Email: FAER@faer.org.

4704 ■ FAER Research Fellowship Grants *(Postdoctorate, Postgraduate, Graduate/Grant)*

Purpose: To provide anesthesiology residents and fellows the opportunity to obtain significant training in research techniques and scientific methods. **Focus:** Anesthesiology. **Qualif.:** Applicants must be U.S. citizens, permanent U.S. residents, Anesthesiology trainees after CA-1 year. **Criteria:** Selection will be based on the committee's criteria.

Funds Avail.: $75,000. **Duration:** Annual. **To Apply:** Applicants should contact FAER for the application process and other related information. **Deadline:** August 15 fall; February 15 spring. **Contact:** FAER office; Phone: 630-912-2554; Email: FAER@faer.org.

4705 ■ Foundation for Appalachian Ohio (FAO)

35 Public Sq.
Nelsonville, OH 45764
Ph: (740)753-1111
Fax: (740)753-3333
E-mail: info@ffao.org
URL: www.appalachianohio.org

Awards are arranged alphabetically below their administering organizations

Social Media: www.facebook.com/
foundationforappalachianohio

4706 ■ Ora E. Anderson Scholarship *(Undergraduate, High School/Scholarship)*

Purpose: To provide financial support to the most outstanding eligible scholars who are committed to environmental protection and conservation. **Focus:** Natural sciences. **Criteria:** Applicants will be selected based on academic performance and demonstrated commitment to environmental protection and conservation will be considered; ethical character, extracurricular activities, volunteerism and financial need will also be evaluated.

Funds Avail.: No specific amount. **Duration:** Annual. **Number Awarded:** Varies. **Deadline:** March 15. **Remarks:** The scholarship was established to honor Ora Eaton Anderson, in memory of his lifelong contributions toward the conservation and protection of Appalachian Ohio's natural environment. **Contact:** To learn more about the application process, Phone: 740-753-1111; 35 Public Square, Nelsonville, Ohio 45764; Email: scholarships@ffao.org.

4707 ■ Susan K. Ipacs Nursing Legacy Scholarship *(Undergraduate, High School/Scholarship)*

Purpose: To provide financial assistance to nursing students. **Focus:** Nursing. **Qualif.:** Applicants must be second year Hocking College students pursuing a degree in a nursing program; must have at least 3.0 GPA on a 4.00 scale. **Criteria:** Selection of applicants will be based on financial need and character as evidenced by personal conduct, values, attitude and behavior applicable to the nursing field, and submitted statement and nomination forms.

Funds Avail.: No specific amount. **Duration:** Annual. **Number Awarded:** Varies. **Remarks:** The Susan K. Ipacs Nursing Legacy Scholarship Fund was established at the Foundation for Appalachian Ohio to honor the work and life of Susan Ipacs - nurse, instructor, mother, wife and friend. **Contact:** To learn more about the application process, Phone: 740-753-1111.

4708 ■ Bob Evans And Wayne White Scholarship *(Graduate, High School/Scholarship)*

Purpose: To financially assist senior high school students in Appalachian Ohio. **Focus:** General studies/Field of study not specified. **Criteria:** Preference will be given to those with financial need, who demonstrate the desire to succeed and overcome obstacles.

Duration: Annual. **Number Awarded:** 2. **Deadline:** March 15. **Remarks:** The Bob Evans and Wayne F. White Legacy Scholarship was established by family and friends of the two, including Bob's wife, Jewell Evans to honor the legacy and commitment these two friends had to the Appalachian Ohio region. **Contact:** Foundation for Appalachian Ohio P.O. Box 456.

4709 ■ Zelma Gray Medical School Scholarship *(Graduate, Doctorate/Scholarship)*

Purpose: To provide scholarship assistance to promising medical provider from Guernsey County High School in order to improve the medical access and healthcare in Ohio. **Focus:** Education, Medical. **Qualif.:** Applicants must be residents and high school graduates of Guernsey County who are pursuing a Doctor of Medicine or Doctor of Osteopathic Medicine degree; must be enrolled full-time in an accredited medical school within united states. **Criteria:**

Applicants will be selected based on MCAT scores and college transcripts on a non-discriminatory basis without regard to race, creed, national origin, religion, or sex and the amount is at the discretion of the Fund Trustee.

Funds Avail.: No specific amount. **Duration:** Annual. **Deadline:** June 1. **Remarks:** The scholarship was established by Zelma Gray Before her death. **Contact:** Zelma Gray Scholarship Fund c/o Foundation for Appalachian Ohio 35 Public Square Nelsonville, Ohio 45764. Phone: 740-753-1111.

4710 ■ Foundation Asie Pacifique du Canada

900-675 W Hastings St.
Vancouver, BC, Canada V6B 1N2
Ph: (604)684-5986
Fax: (604)681-1370
E-mail: info@asiapacific.ca
URL: www.asiapacific.ca
Social Media: www.facebook.com/
   asiapacificfoundationofcanada
www.linkedin.com/company/asia-pacific-foundation-of
   -canada
twitter.com/AsiaPacificFdn

4711 ■ Asia Pacific Foundation of Canada Junior Research Fellowships *(Undergraduate, Master's/Fellowship)*

Purpose: To support undergraduates and master's level program graduates with their work and research in Vancouver. **Focus:** General studies/Field of study not specified. **Qualif.:** Applicants must be Canadian citizens or permanent residents (international students with an off-campus work permit will be considered in some cases); must be available to work at the Foundation's Vancouver or Toronto offices; and must be enrolled in an undergraduate or master's-level program. **Criteria:** Selection will be based on the committee's criteria.

Funds Avail.: $1,000-$4,000. **Duration:** Annual. **To Apply:** Applicants must submit the following documents: resume detailing the applicants' academic background, skills and professional experiences; a short writing sample (published or unpublished); copy of the applicants' university transcript (scanned or electronic copies will suffice); a 1-2 page cover letter detailing the applicants' career interests and goals, how they hope to benefit from the fellowship and why are they interested in working in the thematic area specified in the call for applications; name, title and contact information (email and phone number) for two references. Applications are accepted in English and French. **Contact:** Serena Ko, Post-Graduate Research Fellow, Email: serena.ko@asiapacific.ca.

4712 ■ Asia Pacific Foundation of Canada Media Fellowships *(Professional development/Fellowship)*

Purpose: To help Canadian journalists provide more insightful reportage and analysis on Asia and the Canada-Asia relationship while connecting journalists working on this dynamic part of the world. **Focus:** Journalism. **Qualif.:** Applicants must be journalists who are citizens or permanent residents of Canada; must be employed by a Canadian magazine, newspaper, news service, business publication, radio, television station, new media or multimedia outlet as reporters, feature writers, columnists or as freelancers; must have at least three years of experience in their field and have an established history of publication in Canadian

Awards are arranged alphabetically below their administering organizations

news media. **Criteria:** Selection of applicants will be based on the jury formed by APF Canada; the key criteria are significance of the topic, project feasibility, potential impact and personal qualifications.

Funds Avail.: Upto-$10,000. **Duration:** Annual. **Number Awarded:** 3. **To Apply:** Applicants must submit curriculum vitae; two examples of written or broadcast work, if possible, provide links to the examples of previous work or include copies as a PDF format or as digital media files; budget proposal of up to $7,000 including materials and other basic expenses but excluding trans-Pacific travel; letter from their prospective editor/producer, stating a willingness, in principle, to run stories resulting from this trip, subject to normal editorial judgment; and 750 words research proposal. **Deadline:** April 16. **Contact:** Communications Manager, Asia Pacific Foundation of Canada, 900-675 West Hastings St., Vancouver, B.C., V6B 1N2; Email: communications@asiapacific.ca.

4713 ■ Asia Pacific Foundation of Canada Post-Graduate Research Fellowships *(Master's, Doctorate/Fellowship)*

Purpose: To support Masters or PhD graduates in their work and conducting research. **Focus:** General studies/Field of study not specified. **Qualif.:** Applicants must be Canadian citizens and permanent residents who have graduated from a Master's or doctoral program within 18 months of the application as defined by the date of the graduation ceremony. **Criteria:** Selection will be based on the committee's criteria.

Funds Avail.: $40,000-$42,000. **Duration:** Annual; nonrenewable. **Number Awarded:** 3. **To Apply:** Applicants must submit the following documents: resume detailing the applicants' academic background; writing sample (published or unpublished); 500-750 words description of the project that would be undertaken at the Foundation; and two letters of recommendation from individuals who know the applicant. If sending hard copies, referees should mail them directly to the Foundation at the address; if sending by email, the letter should be in the form of a signed PDF document, sent from the referee's institutional email address. **Deadline:** June 29. **Contact:** Serena Ko, Post-Graduate Research Fellow, Email: serena.ko@asiapacific.ca.

4714 ■ Foundation for the Carolinas (FFTC)

220 N Tryon Street
Charlotte, NC 28202
Ph: (704)973-4500
E-mail: reception@fftc.org
URL: www.fftc.org
Social Media: www.facebook.com/foundationforthecarolinas
www.instagram.com/fftcarolinas
www.linkedin.com/company/foundation-for-the-carolinas
twitter.com/FFTC_RCCL

4715 ■ African American Network - Carolinas Scholarship Fund *(Undergraduate/Scholarship)*

Purpose: To provide scholarships for college-bound students from North and South Carolina who are pursuing a major in engineering, math, science, computer science, accounting, finance or business administration. **Focus:** Accounting; Business administration; Computer and information sciences; Engineering; Finance; Mathematics and mathematical sciences; Science. **Qualif.:** Applicants must

be graduating seniors at a North or South Carolina high school; must have a 3.0 minimum GPA; must attend a four-year college or university located in North or South Carolina; must plan to major in engineering, computer science, the sciences, accounting, finance or business administration. **Criteria:** Committees made up of various community individuals make recommendations for awarding based upon the specific purpose and criteria established by its donor.

Funds Avail.: No specific amount. **Duration:** Annual. **Number Awarded:** 2. **Deadline:** March 6. **Contact:** Qiana Austin, Vice President & Scholarships Program Officer; Phone: 704-973-4535; Email: scholars@fftc.org.

4716 ■ The William Tasse Alexander Scholarship *(Undergraduate/Scholarship)*

Purpose: To provide financial assistance to undergraduate students from Mecklenburg County, North Carolina; primarily in the field of education. **Focus:** Education. **Qualif.:** Applicants must be legal residents of Mecklenburg County, NC who are matriculating full-time juniors or seniors in college; must have a minimum cumulative grade point average of 3.0 on a 4.0 scale; and must be majoring in the field of education or taking courses leading to a career in teaching.

Funds Avail.: No specific amount. **Deadline:** March 12. **Remarks:** The Scholarship was established by the will of Margery Alexander. Established in 1982. **Contact:** Qiana Austin; Email: qaustin@fftc.org.

4717 ■ Andersen Nontraditional Scholarships for Women's Education and Retraining (ANSWER) *(Undergraduate/Scholarship)*

Purpose: To provide financial support and encouragement for adult women. **Focus:** General studies/Field of study not specified. **Qualif.:** Applicants must be nontraditional female students age 25 or older at the time of the application deadline; legal residents of Mecklenburg County, NC or contiguous county in North Carolina or South Carolina; enrolled or planning to enroll as full-time, degree-seeking students at an accredited institution in North Carolina or South Carolina; and must be primary caregivers to at least one school-age child (enrolled in K-12). This includes natural born or legally adopted children for whom legal guardianship has been granted. **Criteria:** Applicants who are single parents are given preference, with the following basis criteria: financial need as determined by the costs of college attendance compared with an applicants' household income and other financial factors; demonstrated potential for academic success.

Funds Avail.: No specific amount. **To Apply:** Applicants must submit a completed application form; copy of the Student Aid Report from FAFSA; official transcripts of grades for the applicant's most recently completed coursework; three recommendation forms from non-related adults such as instructors or other campus administrators, employers, mentors, etc.; updated, typed resume; one to two-page typed personal statement expressing why the applicant is applying for the scholarship and the applicant's educational and career goals; and copy of the applicant's federal tax return for the preceding year showing dependents and adjusted gross income. **Deadline:** January 16. **Contact:** Qiana Austin at qaustin@fftc.org.

4718 ■ Annabel Lambeth Jones Brevard College Merit Scholarship Fund *(Undergraduate/Scholarship)*

Purpose: To provide financial assistance to students at Queens University and Brevard College. **Focus:** General

Awards are arranged alphabetically below their administering organizations

studies/Field of study not specified. **Qualif.:** Applicants must be incoming freshmen at Queens University of Charlotte in Charlotte, NC or Brevard College in Brevard, NC; must have high academic merit; and must have demonstrated leadership potential.

Funds Avail.: No specific amount. **Contact:** Financial Aid Offices, Brevard College; For Question: Qiana Austin, Email: qaustin@fftc.org.

4719 ■ Bank of America Junior Achievement Scholarship in honor of Donna Champion Fund
(Undergraduate/Scholarship)

Purpose: To provide financial support for undergraduate students who have expressed an interest in business through their service to Junior Achievement in Atlanta, GA. **Focus:** Business; Technology. **Qualif.:** Applicants must be graduating high school seniors with a minimum cumulative GPA of 3.0 on a 4.0 scale and who have actively participated in Junior Achievement of Georgia; and must be planning to major in business or computer technology.

Funds Avail.: No specific amount. **Contact:** Junior Achievement, Phone: 404-257-1932; For questions: Qiana Austin, Email: qaustin@fftc.org.

4720 ■ Ben Robinette Scholarship Fund
(Undergraduate/Scholarship)

Purpose: To assist graduates of high schools in Charlotte-Mecklenburg (public or private schools) to attend the University of North Carolina at Chapel Hill. **Focus:** General studies/Field of study not specified. **Qualif.:** Applicants must be graduating seniors at public or private high school in Charlotte-Mecklenburg with minimum of 3.0 grade point average on 4.0 scale.

Funds Avail.: No specific amount. **Contact:** Qiana Austin; Email: qaustin@fftc.org.

4721 ■ Pete and Ellen Bensley Memorial Scholarship Fund *(Undergraduate/Scholarship)*

Purpose: To assist graduating seniors from East Mecklenburg High School who demonstrates an interest in foreign languages or journalism. **Focus:** Foreign languages; Journalism. **Qualif.:** Applicants must be legal residents of Mecklenburg County and graduating seniors at East Mecklenburg high school who are planning to major in foreign languages and/or journalism.

Funds Avail.: No specific amount. **Contact:** Scholarship Coordinator at East Mecklenburg High School, Phone: 980-343-6430; Questions: Qiana Austin, Email: qaustin@fftc.org.

4722 ■ Cadmus Communications Corporation Graphics Scholarship Endowment Fund
(Undergraduate/Scholarship)

Purpose: To assist students who are enrolled in the associate degree in Graphic Arts Management Program at Central Piedmont Community College. **Focus:** Graphic art and design. **Qualif.:** Applicants must have completed at least two semesters of the CPCC Graphic Arts and Imaging Technology Program with 3.0 minimum cumulative grade point average on 4.0 scale.

Funds Avail.: No specific amount. **Duration:** Annual. **Remarks:** Established in 1989. **Contact:** Qiana Austin; Email: qaustin@fftc.org.

4723 ■ Kasie Ford Capling Memorial Scholarship Endowment Fund *(Undergraduate/Scholarship)*

Purpose: To provide financial assistance to high school seniors graduating from Charlotte-Mecklenburg high schools (public or private) who have experienced the death of one or both parents. **Focus:** General studies/Field of study not specified. **Qualif.:** Applicants must be graduating high school seniors from a high school located in Mecklenburg County, NC (public or private) planning to enter a four-year degree program at an accredited institution; must be a legal resident of Mecklenburg County, NC; must have experienced the death of one or both parents.

Funds Avail.: No specific amount. **Duration:** Annual. **Deadline:** May 1. **Contact:** Edwenda Avery; Email: eavery@fftc.org.

4724 ■ The Carolina Panthers Players Sam Mills Memorial Scholarship *(Undergraduate/Scholarship)*

Purpose: To assist athletes from Mecklenburg County, NC and Spartanburg County, SC who wish to pursue a four-year undergraduate degree. **Focus:** General studies/Field of study not specified. **Qualif.:** Applicants must be graduating senior athletes at high schools (public or private) located in Mecklenburg County, NC or Spartanburg County, SC; have earned a varsity letter in high school; with 3.0 minimum cumulative unweighted grade point average on a 4.0 scale; demonstrated outstanding leadership and citizenship; and must attend an accredited four-year college or university as full-time students.

Funds Avail.: No specific amount. **Duration:** Annual. **Deadline:** March 6. **Contact:** Qiana Austin; Email: qaustin@fftc.org.

4725 ■ Carolinas-Virginias Hardware Scholarship
(Undergraduate/Scholarship)

Purpose: To support the children of employees of member firms of the Carolinas-Virginias Region of the National Retail Hardware Association. **Focus:** General studies/Field of study not specified. **Qualif.:** Applicant must be the child of an employee of member firms of the National Retail Hardware Association; must have a minimum cumulative grade point average of 2.5 (on a 4.0 scale). **Criteria:** Committees made up of various community individuals make recommendations for awarding based upon the specific purpose and criteria established by its donor.

Funds Avail.: No specific amount. **Deadline:** March 6. **Contact:** Qiana Austin, Vice President & Scholarships Program Officer; Phone: 704-973-4535; Email: scholars@fftc.org.

4726 ■ Charlotte Housing Authority Scholarship Fund (CHASF) *(Undergraduate/Scholarship)*

Purpose: To provide scholarships for college, technical or vocation school to residents of housing owned or managed by the Charlotte Housing Authority. **Focus:** General studies/Field of study not specified. **Qualif.:** Applicants must be residents of public housing owned or managed by the Charlotte Housing Authority. Applicants attending a college, vocational or technical school for the first time must not be over 21 years of age as of September 1 of the school year for which the scholarship award is to be made; those who have previously attended a college, vocational or technical school must not be over 24 years of age as of September 1 of the school year for which the scholarship award is to be made. **Criteria:** Applicants are evaluated based on financial need; academic performance; personal achievements; school and community involvement; and commitment to and demonstrated potential for success in college, technical or vocational school.

Funds Avail.: No specific amount. **To Apply:** Applicants must submit a completed application form; official transcript(s) of coursework; one to two pages typed personal statement expressing the applicant's educational and career goals and financial need for scholarship assistance; and a copy of the applicant's FAFSA or student aid report; copy of the "Cost of Attendance" for the college(s) you are applying. **Contact:** Qiana Austin, Vice President & Scholarships Program Officer; Phone: 704-973-4535; Email: scholars@fftc.org.

4727 ■ Charlotte-Mecklenburg Schools Scholarship Incentive Fund *(Undergraduate/Scholarship)*

Purpose: To graduates of Charlotte-Mecklenburg public high schools with financial need. **Focus:** General studies/Field of study not specified. **Qualif.:** Applicants must be graduating seniors at a Charlotte-Mecklenburg public high school; must be participants in the Communities in Schools Think College Program or the Charlotte-Mecklenburg Schools AVID Program; must be legal residents of Mecklenburg County, NC; and must have 2.5 minimum cumulative grade point average on a 4.0 scale.

Funds Avail.: No specific amount. **Deadline:** January 3. **Contact:** Qiana Austin; Phone: 704-973-4535; Email: qaustin@fftc.org.

4728 ■ Childrens Scholarship Fund-Charlotte *(Undergraduate/Scholarship)*

Purpose: To provide scholarship assistance to students who are in grades K-8. **Focus:** General studies/Field of study not specified. **Qualif.:** Applicants must be legal residents of Mecklenburg County, NC in grades K-8 attending or planning to attend a tuition-based school in the Charlotte-Mecklenburg region.

Funds Avail.: $100 to $10,000+. **Contact:** Phone- 704-973-4529; Email: donorrelations@fftc.org.

4729 ■ The Communities in Schools Jack Tate ThinkCollege Scholarship *(Undergraduate/Scholarship)*

Purpose: To provide educational assistance to participants who attend Central Piedmont Community College. **Focus:** General studies/Field of study not specified. **Qualif.:** Applicants must achieve 90% of the benchmark goal for attendance set for their high school during their senior year (Charlotte-Mecklenburg School System sets individual school goals each year for attendance, academics and behavior, copies are available in the school offices); must have earned a minimum 2.5 cumulative grade point average (on a 4.0 scale) at the end of the first semester of senior year; must be graduating seniors at Communities In Schools site; and must have at least one full academic year of enrollment and participation in the ThinkCOLLEGE Program (upon graduation).

Funds Avail.: No specific amount. **Deadline:** January 3. **Contact:** Qiana Austin; Email: qaustin@fftc.org.

4730 ■ Judy Crocker Memorial Scholarship Fund *(Undergraduate/Scholarship)*

Purpose: To provide financial assistance to students with an interest in Education, Human Services, and related majors. **Focus:** Education. **Qualif.:** Applicants must be rising junior or senior at Winthrop University, located in Rock Hill, SC; must be majoring in education, human services or a related field; must have 2.9 minimum cumulative grade point average (on a 4.0 scale); must legal resident of York County, SC; must demonstrate financial need.

Funds Avail.: No specific amount. **Contact:** Edwenda Avery; Email: eavery@fftc.org.

4731 ■ Crowder Scholarship *(Undergraduate/Scholarship)*

Purpose: To provide children of employees of general contracting companies headquartered in Mecklenburg County, NC. **Focus:** General studies/Field of study not specified. **Qualif.:** Applicants parents must work for general contracting companies who are members of ACG and headquartered in Mecklenburg County, N.C. **Criteria:** Committees made up of various community individuals make recommendations for awarding based upon the specific purpose and criteria established by its donor.

Funds Avail.: $500 to $6,000. **To Apply:** Applicants must submit a completed application form; necessary transcript;. **Deadline:** January 31. **Contact:** Qiana Austin, Vice President & Scholarships Program Officer; Phone: 704-973-4535; Email: scholars@fftc.org.

4732 ■ E.R. and Lillian B. Dimmette Scholarship *(Undergraduate/Scholarship)*

Purpose: To provide financial assistance to students who deserve it. **Focus:** General studies/Field of study not specified.

Funds Avail.: No specific amount. **Deadline:** January 31. **Contact:** Qiana Austin, Vice President & Scholarships Program Officer; Phone: 704-973-4535; Email: scholars@fftc.org.

4733 ■ Foundation for the Carolinas Rotary Scholarship Fund *(Undergraduate/Scholarship)*

Purpose: To provide scholarships to children of Mecklenburg County police officers and firefighters **Focus:** General studies/Field of study not specified.

Funds Avail.: No specific amount. **Duration:** Annual.

4734 ■ Henry S. and Carolyn Adams Scholarship *(Undergraduate/Scholarship)*

Purpose: To provide financial assistance to deserving undergraduate students of Union County, North Carolina who have been nominated by their principal. **Focus:** General studies/Field of study not specified. **Qualif.:** Applicants must be legal residents of Union County, North Carolina; must nominated by the principal of their high school; must have minimum cumulative grade point average of 3.0 (on a 4.0 grading scale); must demonstrate a substantial need for financial assistance.

Funds Avail.: No specific amount. **Deadline:** March 6. **Contact:** Qiana Austin, Vice President & Scholarships Program Officer; Phone: 704-973-4535; Email: scholars@fftc.org.

4735 ■ Herb Adrian Memorial Scholarship Endowment *(Undergraduate/Scholarship)*

Purpose: To provide financial assistance to college juniors and seniors of Virginia Tech who has a great interest in the multi-housing industry, including but not limited to finance, construction, and management. **Focus:** Construction; Finance; Management. **Qualif.:** Applicant must be a rising Virginia Tech junior or senior; must have interest in the multi-housing industry, including but not limited to finance, construction and management; and must demonstrate financial need.

Funds Avail.: No specific amount. **To Apply:** Applicants must contact the Virginia Tech Residential Property Management School. **Contact:** Qiana Austin, Vice President & Scholarships Program Officer; Phone: 704-973-

Awards are arranged alphabetically below their administering organizations

4535; Email: scholars@fftc.org.

4736 ■ Howard B. Higgins South Carolina Dental Scholarships (Undergraduate/Scholarship)

Purpose: To provide financial assistance to students who are attending College at the Medical University of South Carolina. **Focus:** Dentistry. **Qualif.:** Applicants must be students at the College of Dental Medicine at the Medical University of South Carolina; must have at least 3.0 cumulative grade point average (on a 4.0 scale); and must be legal residents of South Carolina. **Criteria:** Applicants are evaluated based on the criteria designed by the Scholarship Selection Committee.

Funds Avail.: No specific amount. **To Apply:** Applicants must submit all the required application information. **Contact:** Qiana Austin at qaustin@fftc.org.

4737 ■ James V. Johnson Scholarship Endowment Fund (Undergraduate/Scholarship)

Purpose: To provide students at Pfeiffer University in Misenheimer, NC and Mitchell Community College in Statesville, NC. **Focus:** General studies/Field of study not specified. **Qualif.:** Applicants must be legal residents of Iredell or Alexander County in North Carolina; must be incoming freshmen at Pfeiffer University in Misenheimer, NC or first-year students at Mitchell Community College in Statesville, NC.

Funds Avail.: No specific amount. **Contact:** Qiana Austin, Vice President & Scholarships Program Officer; Phone: 704-973-4535; Email: scholars@fftc.org.

4738 ■ Julian E. Carnes Scholarship Endowment Fund (Undergraduate/Scholarship)

Purpose: To provide students of Clemson University and the University of North Carolina at Charlotte who is preparing for a career in a technological field appropriate to meet the requirements of the U.S. Patent Office as a patent agent or attorney. **Focus:** Biology; Chemistry; Computer and information sciences; Engineering; Physics. **Qualif.:** Applicants must be rising junior or senior at Clemson University or UNC Charlotte; must legal resident of North or South Carolina; academic major appropriate to meet the requirements of the U.S. Patent Office for admission as a patent agent or attorney (Including but not limited to engineering, chemistry, physics, biology and computer science); must have 3.0 minimum cumulative grade point average (on a 4.0 scale).

Funds Avail.: No specific amount. **Contact:** Clemson University Office of Student Financial Aid, Phone: 864-656-2280 or UNC Charlotte Student Financial Aid Office, Phone: 704-687-2461; For Question, Qiana Austin, Email: qaustin@fftc.org.

4739 ■ The Mary and Millard Kiker Scholarship (Undergraduate/Scholarship)

Purpose: To provide financial assistance to undergraduate students who are a legal resident of Anson or Union County, NC and have been nominated by the Superintendent of Schools in their county. **Focus:** General studies/Field of study not specified. **Qualif.:** Applicants must be legal residents of Anson or Union County, NC who are nominated by the Superintendent of Schools in their county with a minimum cumulative grade point average of 2.5.

Funds Avail.: No specific amount. **Deadline:** April 3. **Contact:** Qiana Austin; Email: qaustin@fftc.org.

4740 ■ Laura M. Fleming Scholarship (Undergraduate, Vocational/Occupational/Scholarship) -

Purpose: To provide financial assistance to children of Founders Federal Credit Union members to attend an accredited college, vocational or technical school of their choice. **Focus:** Education, Vocational-technical. **Qualif.:** Applicants must be children of founders Federal Credit Union members shall be defined to include natural born or legally adopted children and stepchildren and wards of employees; must be high school seniors scheduled to graduate in the spring of the current school year; must have a minimum 3.5 cumulative grade point average (on a 4.0 scale); parents or legally appointed guardians of applicants must be Founders Federal Credit Union members in good standing for a minimum two years (24 months) prior to the application deadline; must required to perform 40 hours of community service per year to be eligible for renewal for the following year. **Criteria:** Scholarship Committee will consider the following when selecting recipients: financial need as determined by the costs of college attendance compared with an applicant's household income and other financial factors; record of good citizenship, as evidenced by school and community involvement beyond required school activities and customary faith-based (church) involvement; prior academic achievement, including cumulative grade point average; preference is given to applicants who demonstrate a positive influence in their school and community and exemplify sound morals and character.

Funds Avail.: No specific amount. **Deadline:** March 6. **Remarks:** Established in 2004. **Contact:** Qiana Austin; Email: qaustin@fftc.org.

4741 ■ Law Enforcement Memorial Scholarship Endowment Fund (Undergraduate/Scholarship)

Purpose: To provide educational support to outstanding undergraduate students of Central Piedmont Community College or the University of North Carolina at Charlotte who is pursuing a degree in a law enforcement field. **Focus:** Law enforcement. **Qualif.:** Applicants must be students at Central Piedmont Community Collegeor the University of North Carolina at Charlotte; must be majoring in a law enforcement field; must have 2.5 minimum cumulative grade point average (on a 4.0 scale).

Funds Avail.: No specific amount. **Contact:** CPCC Financial Aid Office, Phone: 704-330-6942 or the UNC Charlotte Student Financial Aid Office, Phone: 704-687-5900; For Question: Qiana Austin, Email: qaustin@fftc.org.

4742 ■ George T. Lewis, Jr. Academic Scholarship Fund (Undergraduate/Scholarship)

Purpose: To provide motivation and encouragement to George T. Lewis, Jr. Academic Center graduates intending to pursue post-secondary education or training. **Focus:** General studies/Field of study not specified. **Qualif.:** Applicants must meet or exceed the benchmark goals for attendance set for the George T. Lewis, Jr. Academic Center during their senior year; must have earned a minimum 2.0 cumulative grade point average (on a 4.0 scale) at the end of the first semester of senior year; and must be graduating seniors at the George T. Lewis, Jr. Academic Center and must have at least one full academic year of enrollment and participation in the ThinkCOLLEGE Program (upon graduation). **Criteria:** Applicants are evaluated based on academic achievement; school involvement and personal achievements and financial need.

Funds Avail.: No specific amount. **To Apply:** Applicants must submit completed application form; copy of the SAR

Awards are arranged alphabetically below their administering organizations

from FAFSA; official copy of high school transcript(s), including SAT/ACT scores; two recommendation forms (one from a teacher, counselor or other school administrator and one from employer, community leader or other non-related adult); a one to two-paged typed personal statement on one of the following topics: (1) Discuss who or what has been the biggest influence on your decisions to attend college and why or (2) Present and explain the 'personal mission' or 'personal vision' you have adopted for yourself and discuss why you think these goals are important; and a copy of the applicant's completed FAFSA. **Contact:** Qiana Austin at qaustin@fftc.org.

4743 ■ Lula Faye Clegg Memorial Scholarship Endowment Fund *(Undergraduate/Scholarship)*

Purpose: To provide financial assistance to students who are majoring in education at the University of North Carolina at Charlotte. **Focus:** Education. **Qualif.:** Applicants must be graduates of a high school in the Charlotte-Mecklenburg public school system; must rank in the top 10% of graduating high school class; and must have strong interest and commitment to a career in teaching.

Funds Avail.: $5,000. **Contact:** Brad Smith; Phone: 704-687-8815; scholarships@uncc.edu.

4744 ■ Mary and Elliot Wood Foundation Graduate Scholarship *(Graduate/Scholarship)*

Purpose: To further the knowledge of the scholars for their careers that will contribute to the Goals of the Foundation. **Focus:** Ecology; Economics; Education; Environmental science; Government; Humanities; Nutrition; Peace studies. **Qualif.:** To be eligible to apply for a MEWF graduate scholarship, a college graduate must have been chosen as a recipient or a finalist for a MEWF undergraduate scholarship. The applicant must have been an undergraduate recipient, finalist or super finalist who has graduated within the previous five years. The applicant must commit to a course of graduate study and eventual career that will contribute to the Goals of the Foundation. The applicant must specify in the application the graduate school and the degree to be earned. Each graduate scholarship is school-specific and degree-specific; it is not transferable to another school or another degree. The recipient must maintain full-time enrollment (9 semester hours) for each semester for which the scholarship is paid. The graduate scholarship is eligible for annual renewal for a maximum of 4 years for a full-time student, provided the recipient makes satisfactory progress toward the specified degree.

Funds Avail.: No specific amount. **Duration:** Annual. **Deadline:** May 8.

4745 ■ The Mary and Elliott Wood Foundation Undergraduate Scholarship *(Undergraduate/Scholarship)*

Purpose: To provide financial support for the most gifted future leaders who have the capability, desire, energy, enthusiasm, and determination to improve our civilization and to enhance the quality of all life cultural, civic, and ecological. **Focus:** General studies/Field of study not specified. **Qualif.:** Applicants must be students graduating from high schools in the districts of Guilford County, Davidson County, Randolph County, or Moore County; must have a GPA of at least 4.0 and 1800 on SAT total scores.

Funds Avail.: No specific amount. **Duration:** Annual. **Deadline:** February 2. **Contact:** Qiana Austin; Email: qaustin@fftc.org.

4746 ■ Albert and Eloise Midyette Memorial Scholarship Fund *(Undergraduate/Scholarship)*

Purpose: To provide educational support to students who are pursuing degrees in the fields of religious and ministry studies, nursing, and other medical academic fields. **Focus:** Education, Medical; Nursing. **Qualif.:** Applicants must be a full-time student at Limestone College; must be majoring in the fields of religious and ministry studies, nursing or other medical academic fields; must cumulative unweighted grade point average of at least 2.5 (on a 4.0 scale); must be a U.S. citizen.

Funds Avail.: No specific amount. **Duration:** Annual. **Contact:** Edwenda Avery; Email: eavery@fftc.org.

4747 ■ Carolina Panthers Players Sam Mills Memorial Scholarships *(Undergraduate/Scholarship)*

Purpose: To assist athletes from North and South Carolina who wish to pursue their next level of education. **Focus:** General studies/Field of study not specified. **Qualif.:** Applicants must be graduating senior athletes at high schools (public or private) located in Mecklenburg County, NC or Spartanburg County, SC; have earned a varsity letter in high school; with 3.0 minimum cumulative unweighted grade point average on a 4.0 scale; demonstrated outstanding leadership and citizenship; and must attend an accredited four-year college or university as full-time students.

Funds Avail.: No specific amount. **Duration:** Annual. **Deadline:** March 6. **Remarks:** Established in 2001. **Contact:** Qiana Austin, Vice President and Scholarships Program Officer; Phone: 704-973-4535; Email: qaustin@fftc.org.

4748 ■ The North Carolina League For Nursing Academic Scholarship *(Graduate, Master's/Scholarship)*

Purpose: To provide financial assistance for graduate students pursuing either a master's degree in nursing or a doctoral degree in nursing or a related discipline. **Focus:** Nursing. **Qualif.:** Applicants must be legal residents of North Carolina; must have completed a minimum of six semester hours of course work in their graduate program of study by the application deadline; and must be granted unconditional admission to a master's degree program in nursing or doctoral degree program in nursing or a related discipline and be classified as a graduate degree student by the college or university.

Funds Avail.: $500 to $2,000. **Deadline:** March 6. **Contact:** please contact Scholarships Department at scholars@fftc.org.

4749 ■ North Mecklenburg Teachers' Memorial Scholarship Fund *(Undergraduate/Scholarship)*

Purpose: To provide financial support to students who intend to pursue a degree in education. **Focus:** Education. **Qualif.:** Applicant must be a a North Mecklenburg High School student who intends to pursue a degree in education.

Funds Avail.: No specific amount. **Remarks:** The Award was established as a memory of two very special teachers, Mrs. Jean Holtzclaw and Mr. Jerry Taylor. Established in 2007. **Contact:** North Mecklenburg High School Guidance Office, Phone: 980-343-3840; For questions: Qiana Austin, Email: qaustin@fftc.org.

4750 ■ The Henry Dewitt Plyler Scholarship *(Undergraduate/Scholarship)*

Purpose: To provide financial support to students who are attending Winthrop University. **Focus:** General studies/

Awards are arranged alphabetically below their administering organizations

Field of study not specified. **Qualif.:** Applicants must be graduating seniors or graduates of Lancaster County public high schools; must have 3.0 minimum cumulative grade point average (on a 4.0 scale); and must be legal residents of Lancaster County, SC.

Funds Avail.: No specific amount. **Deadline:** January 3. **Contact:** Qiana Austin; Email: qaustin@fftc.org.

4751 ■ Richard Goolsby Scholarship - Created by William and Martha Debrule *(Graduate, Undergraduate/Scholarship)*

Purpose: To provide financial assistance to graduate undergraduate students who have shown a career interest or demonstrate practical experiences in the plastics industry. **Focus:** General studies/Field of study not specified. **Qualif.:** Applicants must be full-time rising college sophomore, junior or senior students at a four-year college or two-year technical school, who are in good academic standing and majoring in or taking courses that would be suited to a career in the plastics industry (includes but not limited to chemistry, physics, chemical engineering, mechanical engineering, industrial engineering and business administration); or must be graduate students seeking to obtain a post-secondary graduate degree.

Funds Avail.: No specific amount. **Deadline:** March 6. **Contact:** Qiana Austin; Email: qaustin@fftc.org.

4752 ■ The Rotary Club of Charlotte Public Safety Scholarship Fund *(Undergraduate/Scholarship)*

Purpose: To provide financial assistance to the children of Mecklenburg County first responders. **Focus:** Public service. **Qualif.:** Applicants must be high school seniors intending to enter a two-year or four-year degree program with a minimum of 2.5 cumulative grade point average (on a 4.0 scale), whose mother or father are full time employees of the Charlotte Fire Department, Charlotte-Mecklenburg Police Department, Mecklenburg County Sheriff's Office or MEDIC with minimum of one year of service.

Funds Avail.: $1,500. **Deadline:** March 1. **Contact:** Qiana Austin; Email: qaustin@fftc.org.

4753 ■ The Sally Cole Visual Arts Scholarship Program *(Undergraduate/Scholarship)*

Purpose: To provide financial assistance to Richmond County, NC students with demonstrated talent and career interests in the visual arts. **Focus:** Visual arts. **Qualif.:** Applicants must be planning to attend an accredited two-year or four-year post-secondary institution with a degree program in visual arts; must be high school seniors in good academic standing scheduled to graduate in the spring of the current school year; must have an expressed and demonstrated interest in the visual and/or studio arts which primarily includes, but are not limited to, painting, drawing, sculpture, illustration and ceramics; must be legal residents of Richmond County, NC.

Funds Avail.: No specific amount. **Deadline:** January 3. **Contact:** Qiana Austin; Email: qaustin@fftc.org.

4754 ■ The Spirit Square Center for Arts and Education Scholarship Fund *(Undergraduate/ Scholarship)*

Purpose: To provide financial assistance for undergraduate students who can demonstrate aptitude and career potential in arts. **Focus:** General studies/Field of study not specified. **Qualif.:** Applicants must be college juniors or senior students in good academic standing who have demonstrated talent and with a declared major that indicates potential for a significant career contribution to arts. **Criteria:** Recipients are selected based on academic performance; school and community involvement and personal achievements; and commitment to and demonstrated potential for a career in arts. Preference will be given to students who are legal residents of Mecklenburg or contiguous counties in North or South Carolina and those who attend colleges and universities in North Carolina.

Funds Avail.: No specific amount. **To Apply:** Applicants must submit a completed application form; official transcript(s) of academic coursework and grades for at least the last two years; three recommendation forms, two of which must come from individuals who are able to evaluate the applicants' aptitude and career potential in arts; one to two pages typed statement expressing 1) reasons for applying for the scholarship, 2) interest in arts, 3) educational and career goals in arts; and 4) a copy of the estimated expense budget for tuition, room and board, books, etc. **Deadline:** March 6. **Contact:** Qiana Austin at qaustin@fftc.org.

4755 ■ Mary Stewart and William T. Covington, Jr. Scholarship Fund *(Undergraduate/Scholarship)*

Purpose: To provide financial support to students who graduated from a public high school. **Focus:** General studies/Field of study not specified. **Qualif.:** Applicants must be legal residents of Hoke County, NC; must have 2.75 minimum cumulative grade point average (on a 4.0 scale); and must attend a four-year college or university.

Funds Avail.: No specific amount. **Deadline:** March 6. **Contact:** Scholarship Coordinator, Hoke County High School, Phone: 910-875-2156; For questions: Qiana Austin, Email: qaustin@fftc.org.

4756 ■ T. Frank Booth Memorial Scholarship Endowment Fund *(Undergraduate/Scholarship)*

Purpose: To provide financial assistance to accounting students at East Carolina University. **Focus:** Accounting. **Qualif.:** Applicants must be legal residents of North Carolina who are juniors or seniors with a 3.0 minimum cumulative grade point average (on 4.0 scale) who have declared major in accounting.

Funds Avail.: No specific amount. **Contact:** East Carolina University's Accounting Department, Phone: 252-328-6623; Questions: Qiana Austin, Email: qaustin@fftc.org.

4757 ■ Tacy Anna Smith Memorial Scholarship Endowment Fund *(Undergraduate/Scholarship)*

Purpose: To provide financial support to graduating seniors who are studying at Providence High School in Charlotte, NC. **Focus:** General studies/Field of study not specified. **Qualif.:** Applicants must be graduating seniors at Providence high school with a 2.5 minimum cumulative grade point average (on a 4.0 scale), planning to attend a four-year college or university. **Criteria:** Applicants are evaluated based on criteria designed by the Scholarship Committee.

Funds Avail.: No specific amount. **Contact:** Providence High School's guidance office, Phone: 980-343-5390; For questions: Qiana Austin, Email: qaustin@fftc.org.

4758 ■ The Donald H. Bernstein and John B. Talbert Jr. Scholarship *(Undergraduate/Scholarship)*

Purpose: To assist natural-born or legally-adopted dependent children, stepchildren, and wards of employees. **Fo-**

Awards are arranged alphabetically below their administering organizations

cus: General studies/Field of study not specified. **Qualif.:** Applicants must be graduating high school seniors who have a minimum cumulative grade point average of 3.0 (on a 4.0 scale); parents or legal guardians of applicants must be employees who have completed at least two years (24 months) of full-time service with Hanes Companies, Inc. USA prior to the application deadline; must be defined to include natural-born or legally-adopted dependent children, stepchildren, and wards of employees.

Funds Avail.: No specific amount. **Deadline:** February 15. **Contact:** Qiana Austin; Email: qaustin@fftc.org.

4759 ■ Ted Ousley Scholarship Endowment Fund
(Undergraduate/Scholarship)

Purpose: To provide undergraduate scholarships for graduating seniors at North Mecklenburg High School in Huntersville, NC. **Focus:** General studies/Field of study not specified. **Qualif.:** Applicants must be graduating seniors at North Mecklenburg high school, Hopewell High School, William Amos Hough High School; must have a minimum cumulative grade point average of 2.5 (on a 4.0 scale); and must be planning to attend a post-secondary institution in North Carolina.

Funds Avail.: No specific amount. **Contact:** Qiana Austin at qaustin@fftc.org.

4760 ■ Turner Family Scholarships *(Undergraduate, Vocational/Occupational/Scholarship)*

Purpose: To provide financial assistance for graduating high school seniors in Mecklenburg County intending to attend an accredited college or vocational school in Mecklenburg County. **Focus:** Education, Vocational-technical. **Qualif.:** Applicants must be graduating high school seniors who have a minimum cumulative grade point average of 2.5 (on a 4.0 scale); residing in Mecklenburg County, NC; must attend an accredited college or vocational school in Mecklenburg County, North Carolina. **Criteria:** Applicants are evaluated based on academic achievement including grade point average and performance on tests designed to measure preparation and ability for postsecondary study; involvement in extracurricular activities and leadership roles held; and record of community service and other personal achievements. Preference will be given to applicants who are children of National Welders Suppliers employees.

Funds Avail.: No specific amount. **Deadline:** April 22. **Contact:** please contact the Scholarship Department at 704.973.4500 or scholars@fftc.org.

4761 ■ The Sybil Jennings Vorheis Memorial Undergraduate Scholarships *(Undergraduate/Scholarship)*

Purpose: To assist North Iredell High School graduates in obtaining a degree in physical therapy, medicine or nursing from a post-secondary accredited institution. **Focus:** Medicine; Nursing; Physical therapy. **Qualif.:** Applicants must be graduating or have graduated from North Iredell high school with a minimum cumulative grade point average of 3.0 (on 4.0 scale). **Criteria:** Recipients are selected on the basis of academic achievement; school and community involvement; and personal achievements.

Funds Avail.: No specific amount. **To Apply:** Applicants must submit completed application form; verification of acceptance into the accredited graduate program; official copy of college transcript; two recommendation forms and letters of recommendation; and a typewritten application statement of eligibility expressing applicant's educational and

career goals, reasons for applying for the scholarship, and why the applicant feels they are a good candidate for the scholarship. **Contact:** Qiana Austin at qaustin@fftc.org.

4762 ■ Laramie Walden Memorial Fund
(Undergraduate/Scholarship)

Purpose: To provide financial assistance to children of Charlotte, NC firefighters. **Focus:** General studies/Field of study not specified. **Qualif.:** Applicants must be seniors scheduled to graduate in the spring of the academic year; must have 3.5 minimum cumulative weighted grade point average (on a 4.0 scale) whose parent(s) are full-time employees of the Charlotte Fire Department with at least one year of service; and must participate in state-sanctioned school sport. **Criteria:** Applicants are evaluated based on academic merit and extracurricular involvement.

Funds Avail.: No specific amount. **To Apply:** Applicants must submit completed application form; official transcript(s) of academic coursework and grades for at least the last two years; three recommendation forms (two from instructor or other school administrator and one from a non-related adult in the Charlotte-Mecklenburg area such as an employer, coach, scout leader, etc.); and a one-paged typed statement expressing the reason for applying for the scholarship, qualifications, educational and career goals. **Contact:** Qiana Austin at qaustin@fftc.org.

4763 ■ The Fred C. Wikoff Jr. Scholarship
(Undergraduate, Vocational/Occupational/Scholarship)

Purpose: To provide students who are children of employees of Wikoff Color Corporation. **Focus:** General studies/Field of study not specified. **Qualif.:** Applicants must be children of employees (defined to include natural-born or legally-adopted dependent children and stepchildren and wards of employees). Parents or legally-appointed guardians of applicants must be full-time employees who have worked for Wikoff Color Corporation for at least two years prior to the application deadline. Applicants enrolled in high school at the time of application must have a minimum cumulative grade point average 2.5 (on a 4.0 scale). Applicants enrolled in college at the time of application must have a minimum cumulative grade point average of 2.0 (on a 4.0 scale). Applicant's age must not be over 25 as of the application deadline but a student over the age of 25 will be considered on a case to case basis if the student is permanently disabled or has some other special circumstance that requires them to be financially dependent upon their parents.

Funds Avail.: No specific amount. **Deadline:** March 8. **Contact:** Qiana Austin; Email: qaustin@fftc.org.

4764 ■ The Wilbert L. and Zora F. Holmes Scholarship *(Undergraduate/Scholarship)*

Purpose: To provide financial assistance for graduating seniors from South Carolina's York School District One intending to attend an accredited college or technical school of their choice. **Focus:** Education, Vocational-technical. **Qualif.:** Applicants must be graduating seniors at York Comprehensive high school (currently the only high school in the York School District One) and must have been students at York Comprehensive high school for a minimum of two years as of the application deadline; must be legal residents of York County, South Carolina; and must have a minimum of 3.0 cumulative grade point average (on 4.0 scale) at the end of the first semester of senior year.

Funds Avail.: $500. **Deadline:** May 1. **Contact:** York Comprehensive High School, Phone: 803-684-2336; For

Awards are arranged alphabetically below their administering organizations

Questions: Qiana Austin, Email: qaustin@fftc.org.

4765 ■ The Harriet Glen Wilmore Scholarship
(Undergraduate, Vocational/Occupational/Scholarship)

Purpose: To provide financial assistance to residents who wish to attend college technical or vocational school. **Focus:** Education, Vocational-technical. **Qualif.:** Applicants must be residents of the Wilmore Neighborhood which is defined by Summit Avenue on the north, Interstate 77 on the west, South Tryon Street on the east and Wilmore Drive on the south; must have lived in Wilmore Neighborhood for at least one year (12 months) prior to the application deadline; and must have a minimum cumulative grade point average of 2.0 (on a 4.0 scale) for the last completed years of education.

Funds Avail.: No specific amount. **Deadline:** June 15. **Contact:** Qiana Austin; Email: qaustin@fftc.org.

4766 ■ Foundation for Community Association Research
6402 Arlington Blvd., Ste. 500
Falls Church, VA 22042
Ph: (703)970-9220
Fax: (703)970-9558
Free: 888-224-4321
E-mail: foundation@caionline.org
URL: foundation.caionline.org
Social Media: www.facebook.com/CAIsocial
www.instagram.com/caisocial
twitter.com/caisocial
www.youtube.com/user/fcaronline

4767 ■ Byron Hanke Fellowships *(Doctorate, Graduate, Undergraduate/Fellowship)*

Purpose: To promote positive charge for all stakeholders who live in homeowner associations by discovering future trends and opportunities; to support and conduct research; to facilitate and promote cooperation among industry partners and provide resources that help educate the public. **Focus:** General studies/Field of study not specified. **Qualif.:** Applicants must be enrolled in an accredited master's, doctoral or law program in United States of America or Canada; in all discipline are welcome to apply provided their research projects or studies are related to community associations. **Criteria:** Recipients are selected based on academic achievements; faculty recommendations; research and writing ability; and the nature of the proposed topic and its benefit to the study and understanding of community associations.

Funds Avail.: $3,000-$5,000. **Duration:** Annual. **To Apply:** Applicants must submit a completed application form and research proposal. **Deadline:** May 1.

4768 ■ Foundation for Contemporary Arts (FCA)
820 Greenwich St.
New York, NY 10014
Ph: (212)807-7077
E-mail: info@contemporary-arts.org
URL: www.foundationforcontemporaryarts.org
Social Media: www.facebook.com/
foundationforcontemporaryarts
www.instagram.com/foundationforcontemporaryarts

4769 ■ Grants to Artists *(Advanced Professional/Grant)*

Purpose: To provide recipients with the financial means to engage in whatever artistic endeavors they wish to pursue, to research and develop ideas, embark on projects, and complete projects already under way. **Focus:** Dance; Music; Performing arts; Poetry; Visual arts. **Qualif.:** Applicants must be artists working in any of the following areas dance, music/sound, theater/performance art, poetry and the visual arts. **Criteria:** Administered by a confidential nomination and selection process.

Funds Avail.: $40,000. **Duration:** Annual. **To Apply:** The FCA invites distinguished artists and arts professionals to serve as nominators and propose one exceptional individual, collective or performing group whom they feel deserves and will benefit from an award. **Remarks:** Established in 1992.

4770 ■ Foundation for Educational Exchange between Canada and the United States of America
350 Albert St., Ste. 2015
Ottawa, ON, Canada K1R 1A4
URL: www.fulbright.ca

4771 ■ Killam Fellowships *(Undergraduate/Fellowship)*

Purpose: To provide an opportunity for exceptional undergraduate students from universities in the United States to spend either one semester or a full academic year as an exchange student in Canada. **Focus:** General studies/Field of study not specified.

Funds Avail.: $10,000. **Duration:** Annual. **To Apply:** Applications can be submitted online.

4772 ■ Foundation for Enhancing Communities (TFEC)
200 N. 3rd Street 8th Floor
Harrisburg, PA 17101
Ph: (717)236-5040
Fax: (717)231-4463
E-mail: info@tfec.org
URL: www.tfec.org
Social Media: www.facebook.com/tfec.hbg
www.instagram.com/tfec.pa
www.linkedin.com/company/the-foundation-for-enhancing
-communities
twitter.com/tfechbg

4773 ■ Adrienne Zoe Fedok Art and Music Scholarship *(Undergraduate/Scholarship)*

Purpose: To provide financial support to students of either Central Dauphin High School or Central Dauphin East High School. **Focus:** Art; Music. **Qualif.:** Applicants must be graduating high school senior from Central Dauphin High School or Central Dauphin East High School, Interest in art and/or music education, Academic achievement, Leadership and community service, Financial need.

Funds Avail.: $1,000. **Number Awarded:** 1. **To Apply:** Application and the required attachments must be completed on online application download the fill-in Word document that you should complete, save, and attach to your application. Student Resume, Completed Supplemental Form, FAFSA Student Aid Report, Personal Essay: Describe your educational and career goals. 300 words maximum, typewritten, 12 pt. font, double spaced. Also Official Transcript. School Counselor Form. **Deadline:** April 6.

Awards are arranged alphabetically below their administering organizations

Contact: Faith Elmes; Scholarship Associate; 200 N 3rd St., 8th fl., PO Box 678 Harrisburg, PA, 17108-0678; Email: felmes@tfec.org.

4774 ■ Anil and Neema Thakrar Family Fund #1
(Undergraduate/Scholarship)

Purpose: To assist graduating seniors from any high school in Cumberland, Dauphin, or Perry County. **Focus:** Engineering; Mathematics and mathematical sciences; Science. **Qualif.:** Applicants must be graduating seniors from any high school in Cumberland, Dauphin, or Perry county OR current college students with permanent residences in Cumberland, Dauphin, or Perry county; plans to attend college for the study of math, science, or engineering; academic performance, including a GPA between a 2.0 and 3.0; Financial need. **Criteria:** Selection will be based on the committee's criteria.

Funds Avail.: Amount varies. **To Apply:** Applicants must complete and submit the application and other required attachments on or before the deadline; applicants must provide the following attachments: official transcript of complete high school/college records including GPA; must attach a 300-word essay stating the biggest life challenge and the lesson acquired from the experience; and two personal reference letters from a high school teacher; letters from family members will not be accepted; reference should be sealed in an envelope. **Deadline:** March 15. **Contact:** Faith Elmes; Scholarship Associate; 200 N 3rd St., 8th fl., PO Box 678 Harrisburg, PA, 17108-0678; Email: felmes@tfec.org.

4775 ■ Carrie and George Lyter Scholarship
(Undergraduate/Scholarship)

Purpose: To provide educational assistance for students attending Greenwood High School, Newport High School, Susquenita High School and West Perry High School. **Focus:** Education, Elementary; Mathematics and mathematical sciences; Science. **Criteria:** Selection will be based on extracurricular activities;demonstrated talent for leadership;high moral character (attend and be involved in church activities).

Funds Avail.: Amount varies. **Number Awarded:** 1. **To Apply:** The application process is online. **Deadline:** April 1. **Remarks:** Established in 2002. **Contact:** Faith Elmes; Scholarship Associate; 200 N 3rd St., 8th fl., PO Box 678 Harrisburg, PA, 17108-0678; Email: felmes@tfec.org.

4776 ■ Erin L. Jenkins Memorial Scholarship
(Undergraduate/Scholarship)

Purpose: To provide educational support to deserving students attending Cumberland Valley High School. **Focus:** General studies/Field of study not specified. **Qualif.:** Applicants must reside in Cumberland Valley School District, or its successor; must demonstrate academic achievement, community service and financial need.

Funds Avail.: $1,500. **Number Awarded:** 1. **To Apply:** Applicants must complete and return the application and attachments to the Foundation. Students must also submit the following: official school transcript; two recommendations; FAFSA Student Aid Report Form; and (300-word) personal essay. **Deadline:** April 1. **Contact:** Faith Elmes; Scholarship Associate; 200 N 3rd St., 8th fl., PO Box 678 Harrisburg, PA, 17108-0678; Email: felmes@tfec.org.

4777 ■ Norma Gotwalt Scholarship Fund
(Undergraduate/Scholarship)

Purpose: To provide financial assistance to students for their college tuition expenses. **Focus:** Education, Elementary. **Qualif.:** Applicants must be female junior or senior students studying Elementary Education at the Penn State Capital College and who have maintained a minimum of 3.25 cumulative GPA while at Capital College. **Criteria:** Recipients will be selected based on financial need; community service; submitted essay; and career goals.

Funds Avail.: $3,000. **Number Awarded:** 1. **To Apply:** Applicants must complete the application form; must submit an official transcript of post-secondary academic records; FAFSA Student Aid Report Form; (300-word) personal essay; and a written recommendation from a professor who can assess the potential ability as an elementary school teacher. **Deadline:** March 15. **Contact:** Faith Elmes, Scholarship Associate; Phone: 717-236-5040; Email: felmes@tfec.org.

4778 ■ Carol Hoy Scholarship Fund *(Undergraduate/Scholarship)*

Purpose: To provide educational support to students who are pursuing a career in early childhood education. **Focus:** Education, Early childhood; Education, Elementary. **Qualif.:** Applicants must be graduating senior of Mechanicsburg Area high school who desire to pursue a career in elementary education or early childhood education; show academic achievement, leadership, and community service; and demonstrate financial need.

Funds Avail.: No specific amount. **Number Awarded:** 1. **To Apply:** Application and the required attachments must be completed and postmarked on or before the deadline; the required attachments include: completed student background sheet; high school transcript; FAFSA student aid report form (financial aid form); completed student essay; resume including leadership and community service; and two personal reference letters; one letter should be from a teacher and the other letter should be from an individual who can speak to applicant's ability to successfully complete studies, such as a teacher, employer, or mentor; application form can be obtained online. **Deadline:** April 7. **Remarks:** Established in 2006. **Contact:** Faith Elmes; Scholarship Associate; 200 N 3rd St., 8th fl., PO Box 678 Harrisburg, PA, 17108-0678; Email: felmes@tfec.org.

4779 ■ J. Ward Sleichter and Frances F. Sleichter Memorial Fund *(Undergraduate/Scholarship)*

Purpose: To provide aid for needy and deserving students who otherwise would not have the financial means to obtain a four-year college education. **Focus:** General studies/Field of study not specified. **Qualif.:** Applicants must be full-time students who maintain a "B" or 2.5 grade point average or equivalent; must reside in the area defined by the Shippensburg Area School District, or its successor; and must have plan to attend a four-year college or university.

Funds Avail.: Up to $5,000. **Duration:** Up to 4 years. **Number Awarded:** 1. **To Apply:** Applicants must complete the following required attachments: application; official school transcript; two recommendations (one from the student's guidance counselor and one from a teacher who can discuss the student's personal characteristics such as motivation, character, ability and potential); and FAFSA Student Aid Report (make sure to include the cover letter of the report, which will indicate the student's Estimated Family contribution). **Deadline:** April 1. **Contact:** Faith Elmes; Scholarship Associate; 200 N 3rd St., 8th fl., PO Box 678 Harrisburg, PA, 17108-0678; Email: felmes@tfec.org.

Awards are arranged alphabetically below their administering organizations

4780 ■ Jan DiMartino Delany Memorial Scholarship
(Undergraduate/Scholarship)

Purpose: To assist students with their college tuition expenses. **Focus:** General studies/Field of study not specified. **Qualif.:** Applicants must be a graduating senior of Cumberland Valley high school who will attend a two or four-year institution of higher learning.

Funds Avail.: $3,000. **Number Awarded:** 1. **To Apply:** Applicant must complete and submit the application to the Cumberland Valley High School Guidance Office; include an official transcript; completed personal essay explaining how they have overcome personal challenges; FAFSA Student Aid Report; Two Personal Reference Letters, One letter must be from a high school teacher on school letterhead; the other letter must be from an employer, supervisor, or community advisor on letterhead. **Deadline:** April 1. **Contact:** Faith Elmes; Scholarship Associate; 200 N 3rd St., 8th fl., PO Box 678 Harrisburg, PA, 17108-0678; Email: felmes@tfec.org.

4781 ■ Oliver Rosenberg Educational Trust
(Undergraduate/Scholarship)

Purpose: To assist students with business, technical or trade school tuition expenses. **Focus:** General studies/Field of study not specified. **Qualif.:** Graduating seniors from Harrisburg High School, Sci-Tech High, Bishop McDevitt, or Dauphin County Technical School; must attend a college or university in Pennsylvania **Criteria:** Financial need.

Funds Avail.: Amount varies. **Number Awarded:** Varies. **To Apply:** Required documents include the application; official transcript of complete high school records, including GPA, through first half of final year, on which the raised school seal is imprinted; a 300-word essay explaining how applicant has overcome challenges in life and how they will apply these lessons to a vocation; must list their most significant extracurricular or non-academic activities, emphasizing work experience and community volunteer service. Scholarships require a copy of SAR to be included in application; applications missing the SAR will not be considered. **Deadline:** April 1. **Contact:** Faith Elmes; Scholarship Coordinator; 200 N 3rd St., 8th fl., PO Box 678 Harrisburg, PA, 17108-0678; Email: scholarshipapplications@tfec.org; URL: www.tfec.org/scholarships/oliver-rosenberg-educational-trust/.

4782 ■ The Ruth Cook Pfautz Memorial Scholarship Fund
(Undergraduate/Scholarship)

Purpose: To assist Susquenita High School students with their college expenses in the field of Elementary Education. **Focus:** Education, Elementary. **Qualif.:** Applicants must be graduating senior students of Susquenita high school who have a GPA of 2.5 on a 4.0 point scale; plans to study early elementary education.

Funds Avail.: Amount varies. **Number Awarded:** 1. **To Apply:** Application form can be obtained online; must complete the attached form and requested supporting documents and send to the Foundation; the supporting documents include: official transcript of the complete high school record; list of extracurricular or non-academic activities; reference letter; and a 300-word student essay explaining why they have chosen Elementary Education as a career path and describing their educational plans to achieve their career goal. **Deadline:** April 1. **Contact:** Faith Elmes; Scholarship Associate; 200 N 3rd St., 8th fl., PO Box 678 Harrisburg, PA, 17108-0678; Email: felmes@tfec.org.

4783 ■ Soroptimist International of Chambersburg Fund
(Undergraduate/Scholarship)

Purpose: To provide assistance for female seniors of Chambersburg Area Senior High School. **Focus:** General studies/Field of study not specified. **Qualif.:** Applicants must be female graduating seniors of Chambersburg Area high school; must be accepted at an accredited college or university.

Funds Avail.: Amount varies. **Number Awarded:** 1. **To Apply:** Applicant must complete the required attachments, which include: application; two letters of recommendation (one from applicant's guidance counselor, and the other from one of the applicant's teachers containing a general character assessment of the applicant as a person and a student); FAFSA Student Aid Report; a paragraph of approximately 150 words answering the question "Why I Have Chosen to Continue My Education". **Deadline:** April 1. **Contact:** THOMAS BRADLEY; Scholarship Associate; 200 N 3rd St., 8th fl., PO Box 678 Harrisburg, PA, 17108-0678; Email: tbradley@tfec.org.

4784 ■ Sue & Ken Dyer Foundation Travel Scholarship
(Other/Scholarship)

Purpose: To assist students with travel expenses for educational or service trips. **Focus:** Travel and tourism. **Qualif.:** Applicants must be junior or senior students enrolled at one of the following schools: Cedar Cliff, Camp Hill, Mechanicsburg, Trinity or the Harrisburg Academy.

Funds Avail.: $2,000. **Duration:** Annual. **Number Awarded:** Varies. **To Apply:** Applicant must complete and return the application and required attachments to the Foundation; required attachments include: scholastic record and extracurricular activities; an essay on the topic: "The purpose of my proposed trip and what I expect to gain from this experience"; essay should be titled, typewritten, double-spaced and maximum of 300 words; two reference letters from individuals who can speak to the quality of applicant's character, academic prowess, and/or their likelihood of utilizing the proposed travel experience as a tool for personal growth; also include financial information. **Deadline:** March 15. **Contact:** Faith Elmes; Scholarship Associate; 200 N 3rd St., 8th fl., PO Box 678 Harrisburg, PA, 17108-0678; Email: felmes@tfec.org.

4785 ■ Foundation of the Federal Bar Association (FFBA)
1220 N Fillmore St., Ste. 444
Arlington, VA 22201
Ph: (571)481-9100
Fax: (571)481-9090
E-mail: fba@fedbar.org
URL: www.fedbar.org/about-us/affiliated-organizations/foundation-of-the-federal-bar-association
Social Media: www.facebook.com/FederalBar
www.linkedin.com/company/federal-bar-association
twitter.com/federalbar

4786 ■ Foundation Public Service Scholarship Award
(Undergraduate/Scholarship)

Purpose: To provide financial assistance to high school students for their continuing higher education. **Focus:** General studies/Field of study not specified. **Qualif.:** Applicants must be graduating high school seniors planning to attend a four-year college or university; and, students currently enrolled full-time at a four-year college or university or

Awards are arranged alphabetically below their administering organizations

graduate students enrolled full-time in a graduate or professional degree program; at least one of the parents or guardians must be current federal government attorneys or federal judges and members of the Federal Bar Association. **Criteria:** Selection will be evaluated based on academic record, leadership recognition, school and community activities and service, and compelling essay response - exhibiting both substance and written communication skills.

Funds Avail.: $5,000. **Duration:** Annual. **To Apply:** Applicants must submit the completed application along with most recent transcripts (official copy); letter of acceptance from their college, university or graduate/professional school for new enrolls; and an essay. **Deadline:** May 15. **Contact:** Phone: 571-481-9100; Email: foundation@fedbar.org.

4787 ■ Foundation Fighting Blindness (FFB)
890 Yonge St., 12th Fl.
Toronto, ON, Canada M4W 3P4
Ph: (416)360-4200
Fax: (416)360-0060
Free: 800-461-3331
E-mail: info@fightingblindness.ca
Social Media: www.facebook.com/
  FightingBlindnessCanada
twitter.com/ffbcanada
youtube.com/user/FFBCanada/featured

4788 ■ FFB-C Postdoctoral Fellowships
(Postdoctorate/Fellowship)

Purpose: To increase the number of Canadian scientists being trained to investigate the causes, means of detection, prevention and cure of retinitis pigmentosa (RP), macular degeneration and related diseases of the retina. **Focus:** Optometry. **Qualif.:** Applicants must hold an MD, PhD, DDS, DVM, PharmD, or equivalent degree in a field appropriate to retinal degenerative disease research (molecular genetics, molecular biology, physiology, biochemistry, cell biology, or immunology). **Criteria:** Selection is based on the submitted application and materials.

Funds Avail.: No specific amount. **To Apply:** Applicants must complete the application online.

4789 ■ Foundation of the National Student Nurses Association (FNSNA)
45 Main Street, Suite 606
Brooklyn, NY 11201
Ph: (718)210-0705
Fax: (718)797-1186
E-mail: fnsna@forevernursing.org
URL: www.forevernursing.org
Social Media: www.facebook.com/ForeverNursing
www.instagram.com/nsnainc
twitter.com/ForeverNursing

4790 ■ Breakthrough to Nursing Scholarships
(Undergraduate/Scholarship)

Purpose: To provide financial support to qualified nursing students. **Focus:** Nursing. **Qualif.:** Applicant must be a student committed to providing quality health care services to underserved population; must possess the necessary leadership skills to influence the delivery of quality care;

must be a U.S citizen or Alien with U.S permanent resident status/Alien Registration Number; must establish academic achievement; must have an involvement in student nursing organizations and community health activities; must be attending classes and taking no less than six credits per semester. **Criteria:** Selection of applicants will be based on academic achievement, financial need and involvement in student nursing organizations and community health activities. Selection committee of faculty and students from various nursing programs is appointed to select recipients.

Funds Avail.: No specific amount. **Duration:** Annual. **To Apply:** Applicants must submit and complete the application form available online; must submit an official transcript of records. Application form and other supporting documents must be sent to Foundation of the National Nurses' Association.

4791 ■ Career Mobility Scholarships *(Graduate, Undergraduate, Vocational/Occupational/Scholarship)*

Purpose: To provide financial support to qualified nursing students. **Focus:** Nursing. **Criteria:** Selection will be based on academic achievement, financial need and involvement in student nursing organizations and community health activities.

Funds Avail.: $1,000-$7,500. **Duration:** Annual. **To Apply:** Applicants should submit official transcript of records; application form and other supporting documents must be sent to Foundation of the National Nurses' Association. **Deadline:** January.

4792 ■ Specialty Nursing Scholarships
(Undergraduate/Scholarship)

Purpose: To provide financial support to qualified nursing students. **Focus:** Nursing.

Funds Avail.: No specific amount. **Duration:** Annual. **To Apply:** Applicants must submit and complete the application form available online; must submit an official transcript of records. Application form and other supporting documents must be sent to Foundation of the National Nurses' Association. **Deadline:** January.

4793 ■ Foundation for Neonatal Research and Education (FNRE)
200 E Holly Ave.
Sewell, NJ 08080
Ph: (856)256-2343
Fax: (856)589-7463
E-mail: contact@fnre.com
URL: ajj.com/fnre
Social Media: www.facebook.com/NeonatalResearchand
  Education
twitter.com/ajjinc

4794 ■ Foundation for Neonatal Research and Education Scholarship *(Doctorate, Graduate, Postgraduate, Undergraduate/Scholarship)*

Purpose: To support students and professionals pursue a higher education. **Focus:** Nursing, Neonatal. **Qualif.:** Applicants must be neonatal nurses admitted to a college or school of higher education on one of the following areas: Bachelor of Science in Nursing (current RN); Master in Science in Nursing for Advanced Practice in Neonatal Nursing; Doctoral degree in Nursing; and Master's or Post-Master degree in Nursing Administration or Business Management; must be actively engaged in a service, research, or

Awards are arranged alphabetically below their administering organizations

educational role; active members of a professional association and must demonstrate an ongoing professional education in neonatal nursing; must have not received a FNRE scholarship or grant in the past five years; if awarded both an FNRE scholarship and grant concurrently, then only one can be kept: members of the FNRE Board and the FNRE Scholarship Review Committee are ineligible to apply during their term.

Funds Avail.: No specific amount. **To Apply:** Applicants must submit a completed application form, current resume or curriculum vitae, an official transcript from each college or school of higher education, a letter of verification of enrollment and acceptance to a college or school, three evaluations, transcripts. **Contact:** Foundation for Neonatal Research and Education (FNRE), Anthony J. Jannetti, Inc., East Holly Ave., Box 56, Pitman, New Jersey, 08071-0056; Phone: 856-256-2343; Fax: 856-589-7463.

4795 ■ Foundation of the Pennsylvania Medical Society
777 E Park Dr.
Harrisburg, PA 17105-8820
Ph: (717)558-7750
Fax: (717)558-7818
Free: 800-228-7823
E-mail: foundation@pamedsoc.org
URL: www.foundationpamedsoc.org
Social Media: www.facebook.com/FoundationPAMED
www.linkedin.com/company/the-foundation-of-the
 -pennsylvania-medical-society
twitter.com/foundationpamed
www.youtube.com/channel/UCym5YvcZnqMCrTrltnEWH7A

4796 ■ Allegheny County Medical Society Medical Student Scholarship *(Advanced Professional/Scholarship)*

Purpose: To assist local students with the cost of attending a Pennsylvania medical school. **Focus:** Medicine. **Criteria:** Applicants are evaluated based on financial need.

Funds Avail.: $4,000. **Duration:** Annual. **To Apply:** Applicants must submit completed scholarship application form; two reference letters from persons other than family members, documenting integrity, interpersonal skills and potential as a future physician (one must come from either a medical school professor or a physician); a letter, on school letterhead, from the applicants' medical school verifying that they are enrolled full time as a third or fourth-year medical student at that institution; and a typed, one-page essay addressing the following where do you see yourself in 10 years? How do you plan to give back to the community?. **Deadline:** September 30.

4797 ■ Alliance Medical Education Scholarship (AMES) *(Undergraduate, Graduate/Scholarship)*

Purpose: To financially assist a deserving medical student enrolled in a Pennsylvania medical school. **Focus:** Medicine. **Criteria:** Selection will be evaluated based on financial need.

Funds Avail.: $2,500 each. **Duration:** Annual. **Number Awarded:** Varies. **To Apply:** Applicants must submit a completed application form; two reference letters (personal and academic from persons other than family members documenting the integrity, interpersonal skills, and potential as a future physician); a letter on school letterhead, from

the medical school verifying full time enrollment as a second-year or third-year medical student; a typed essay, one page, must be submitted describing the vision for the future of Pennsylvania medicine; a completed Pennsylvania Medical Society membership application (if not a current member). **Deadline:** February 29. **Remarks:** Established in 2000. **Contact:** Deborah K. Monko Director, Student Financial Services Phone: (717) 558-7854 studentservices-foundation@pamedsoc.org,.

4798 ■ Scott A. Gunder, MD, DCMS Presidential Scholarship *(Undergraduate, Graduate/Scholarship)*

Purpose: To financially assist deserving second-year medical students at Penn State College of Medicine. **Focus:** Medicine. **Criteria:** Selection will be evaluated based on financial need.

Funds Avail.: $1,500. **Duration:** Annual. **To Apply:** Applicant must submit: completed application form; two reference letters, from persons other than family members, documenting the integrity, interpersonal skills and potential as future physicians; letter, on school letterhead, from Penn State College of Medicine verifying that they are enrolled full-time and second-year medical students; one-page essay (12-pt. type, double spaced) describing the person or event that most influenced them to become a physician and how they see themselves leading others into medicine; and completed Pennsylvania Medical Society membership applications if students are not current members. **Remarks:** The Scholarship Established in memory of the 39-year-old Harrisburg gastroenterologist will continue. Established in 2000.

4799 ■ Lycoming County Medical Society Scholarship *(Undergraduate, Graduate/Scholarship)*

Purpose: To provide financial assistance for medical students who are residents of Lycoming County. **Focus:** Medicine. **Criteria:** Selection will be evaluated based on financial need.

Funds Avail.: $3,000 each. **Duration:** Annual. **Number Awarded:** 3. **To Apply:** Applicants must submit completed application form; two reference letters, from persons other than family members, documenting the applicants' integrity, interpersonal skills, and potential as future physicians; a letter, on school letterhead, from medical school verifying that they are enrolled full-time as medical students at their respective institutions; and, one-page, typed essay specifically describing why they chose to become physicians and what contributions they expect to make to the health profession. **Deadline:** September 30. **Remarks:** The Scholarship established by county's medical society the scholarship within the Foundation.

4800 ■ Montgomery County Medical Society – William W. Lander, MD, Medical Student Scholarship *(Undergraduate/Scholarship)*

Purpose: To provide financial assistance for medical students who are residents of Montgomery County. **Focus:** Medicine. **Criteria:** Selection will be evaluated based on financial need.

Funds Avail.: $2,000 each. **Duration:** Annual. **Number Awarded:** 2. **To Apply:** Applicants must submit a completed application form; two reference letters, from persons other than family members, documenting the integrity, interpersonal skills and potential as physicians; a letter, on school letterhead, from their medical schools verifying that they are enrolled full time as first-year medical students at that institution; one-page, typed essay addressing the

Awards are arranged alphabetically below their administering organizations

reasons for pursuing medical career, personal goals and plans for future within the profession. **Deadline:** September 30. **Remarks:** The Scholarship established by contributions from Montgomery County Medical Society and physicians.

4801 ■ Myrtle Siegfried, MD, and Michael Vigilante, MD Scholarship *(Undergraduate/Scholarship)*

Purpose: To provide financial assistance to qualified first-year medical students residing in Berks, Lehigh, or Northampton County. **Focus:** Medicine. **Criteria:** Selection will be evaluated based on financial need.

Funds Avail.: $1,000. **Duration:** Annual. **To Apply:** Applicants must submit a completed application form; two reference letters documenting the applicants' integrity, interpersonal skills and potential as future physicians (letters must come from persons who know the applicants well but are not family members); a letter, on school letterhead, from their medical school verifying that they are enrolled full-time at that institution and first-year medical students; one-page, typed essay specifically describing why they chose to become physicians and what contributions they expect to make to the health profession; materials will be accepted beginning July 1 of the current year, and must be postmarked on or before September 30 of the current year; and will be notified of the committee's decision by December 1 of the current year. **Deadline:** September 30. **Remarks:** The Scholarship established by memorial contribution from Mrs. Elena Pascal, Foundation trustee, and her sister, Mrs. Carla Vigilante, in honor of their parents, Drs. Siegfried and Vigilante, who practiced medicine in Allentown for more than 50 years. Established in 1999.

4802 ■ Foundation for the Preservation of Honey Bees, Inc.
c/o Molly Sausaman, Executive Director
3525 Piedmont Road, Building Five, Suite 300
Atlanta, GA 30305
Ph: (404)760-2875
URL: preservationofhoneybees.org

4803 ■ Foundation for the Preservation of Honey Bees Scholarship *(Graduate/Scholarship)*

Purpose: To allow the recipients to attend the annual North American Beekeeping Conference, where they will have an opportunity to meet other researchers and beekeepers and to present their research to the industry. **Focus:** Life sciences. **Qualif.:** Applicants must be a graduate student in apiculture.

Funds Avail.: $3,000. **Duration:** Annual. **Number Awarded:** 4. **To Apply:** Applicants must submit a cover letter from the advisor outlining the applicant's progress toward graduate degree, tentative graduation date, and any other information about the applicants and the research that would help the committee "get to know" the applicant; a curriculum vitae, or resume, not to exceed 2 pages; and the research proposal (not to exceed 3 pages); applications must be submitted as one PDF document electronically, including name, address, e-mail address and phone number. **Deadline:** September 28. **Remarks:** Established in 2005. **Contact:** Molly Sausaman, Executive director; Phone: 404-760-2875; msausaman@abfnet.org.

4804 ■ Foundation for Seacoast Health (FFSH)
100 Campus Dr., Ste. 1
Portsmouth, NH 03801

Ph: (603)422-8200
URL: www.ffsh.org
Social Media: www.facebook.com/Foundation-for-Seacoast-Health-431317490236981

4805 ■ Edwina Foye Award for Outstanding Graduate Student *(Undergraduate, Graduate/Scholarship)*

Purpose: To honor the memory of Edwina Foye, RN, a nurse who dedicated twenty-five years of service to Portsmouth Hospital. **Focus:** Health care services; Health education. **Criteria:** Selection will be based on scholastic aptitude and performance, personal achievements, leadership, and community involvement.

Funds Avail.: Up to $5,000. **Duration:** Annual. **To Apply:** Applicants must submit a completed Scholarship Application form along with three Student Assessment Forms (in sealed envelopes); official school transcripts; test scores; essay and current resume. **Deadline:** May 1. **Remarks:** Established in 1985.

4806 ■ FPDA Motion and Control Network
180 Admiral Cochrane Dr., Ste. 370
Annapolis, MD 21401
Ph: (410)940-6347
Fax: (410)263-1659
E-mail: info@fpda.org
URL: www.fpda.org
Social Media: www.facebook.com/theFPDA
www.linkedin.com/company/fpda
twitter.com/TheFPDA

4807 ■ Tom D. Ralls Memorial Scholarship *(Professional development/Scholarship)*

Purpose: To support young executives for their full tuition to the University of Innovative Distribution. **Focus:** Industrial design. **Qualif.:** Applicant must be an employee in good standing of a FPDA Regular (Distributor) Member organization; must be a qualified member of the FPDA Young Executives (YES).

Duration: Annual. **To Apply:** Applicants must provide a letter of recommendation from a company principal; must provide an essay detailing their desire to attend the University of Innovative Distribution program. **Deadline:** November 14. **Contact:** Patricia A. Lilly, FPDA Executive Director, Phone: 410-904-6362, Email: plilly@fpda.org.

4808 ■ Fragile X Research Foundation of Canada (FXRFC)
167 Queen St. W
Brampton, ON, Canada L6Y 1M5
Ph: (905)453-9366
E-mail: info@fragilexcanada.ca
URL: fragilexcanada.ca

4809 ■ Postdoctoral Fellowships *(Postdoctorate/Fellowship)*

Purpose: To promote research aimed at finding a specific treatment for Fragile X syndrome. **Focus:** Medical research. **Qualif.:** Applicants must be postdoctoral fellows who want to pursue research in Fragile X. **Criteria:** Selection is based on submitted application materials.

Funds Avail.: $45,000 (includes salary plus research travel allowance). **Duration:** Annual. **To Apply:** Application pack-

Awards are arranged alphabetically below their administering organizations

age must include a brief letter of inquiry describing the proposed project; a 6-12 page description of the proposed project (background, objectives, approach, methodological detail, significance, originality, and key references); curriculum vitae for the principal investigator; curriculum vitae for the postdoctoral fellow to be supported under the grant; three references; financial accounting of how the funds will be spent; a full accounting of any other current and submitted sources of support for the project; and requested start date of the project. **Deadline:** February 1. **Contact:** Dr. Carlo Paribello, Fragile X Research Foundation of Canada; Phone: 905-453-9366; Fax: 905-453-0095; Email: medical@fragilexcanada.ca.

4810 ■ Joe Francis Haircare Scholarship Foundation
PO Box 50625
Minneapolis, MN 55405
Ph: (651)769-1757
E-mail: contact@joefrancis.com
URL: www.joefrancis.com

4811 ■ Joe Francis Haircare Scholarship
(Undergraduate/Scholarship)

Purpose: To provide support to deserving students who want to pursue their professional training in hairstyling. **Focus:** Cosmetology. **Qualif.:** Applicants must be actively enrolled in cosmetology school or planning to enroll in cosmetology/barber school. **Criteria:** Recipient will be selected by the independent committee composed of individuals drawn from the professional beauty industry; selection is based on their potential, financial need, and commitment to a long-term career in cosmetology.

Funds Avail.: $1,200. **Duration:** Annual. **To Apply:** Applicants must complete the application form available online; must have a letter of recommendation from an employer, instructor, counselor, or someone qualified to offer testimony of character. **Contact:** Kim Larson, Phone: 651-769-1757; Email: contact@joefrancis.com.

4812 ■ Anne Frank Center for Mutual Respect
1325 Ave. of the Americas, 28th Fl.
New York, NY 10019
Ph: (212)431-7993
E-mail: info@annefrank.com
URL: www.annefrank.com
Social Media: www.facebook.com/
   AnneFrankCenterforMutualRespect
instagram.com/annefrankcenter
twitter.com/AnneFrankCenter
youtube.com/user/AnneFrankCenterUSA

4813 ■ Spirit of Anne Frank Scholarship Award
(Undergraduate/Scholarship)

Purpose: To support students who have proven themselves exceptional leaders in combating intolerance, prejudice and injustice in their communities. **Focus:** Human rights; Social sciences. **Qualif.:** Applicants must be high school seniors in the United States who will be attending a four-year college in the fall; must exhibit extraordinary leadership in combating intolerance and prejudice in their communities. **Criteria:** Selection is based on their level of activism in their community in combating issues of prejudice, intolerance and inequality; this activism is detailed in the ap-

plicant's personal essay and in two supporting letters of recommendation.

Funds Avail.: $5,000. **Duration:** Annual. **To Apply:** Applicants must complete the online application form, which includes a 1, 000-word personal essay and two supporting letters of recommendation that detail their commitment to social justice and their fight for equality in their community.

4814 ■ Franklin District Medical Society
85 Post Office Pk., Ste. 8518
Wilbraham, MA 01095
Ph: (413)596-9231
Fax: (413)596-9901
Free: 800-522-3112
E-mail: franklin@massmed.org
URL: www.massmed.org
Social Media: www.facebook.com/massmed
twitter.com/massmedical
www.youtube.com/user/MassMedicalSociety

4815 ■ Percy W. Wadman, M.D. Scholarship
(Postgraduate/Scholarship)

Purpose: To support medical students based on merit and financial need. **Focus:** Medicine. **Qualif.:** Applicants' one or both parents or guardians must live in Franklin County.

Funds Avail.: $1,000-$2,000. **Duration:** Annual. **To Apply:** Application letter of matriculation must be submitted from applicants' medical school; a copy of the letter of recommendation from the applicants' undergraduate school to the medical school must be submitted; and a copy of parent's or guardian's 1040 Federal Tax Form for the last tax year. **Deadline:** April 30.

4816 ■ Fraser Stryker
500 Energy Plz., 409 S 17th St.
Omaha, NE 68102-2663
Ph: (402)341-6000
Fax: (402)341-8290
URL: www.fraserstryker.com
Social Media: www.facebook.com/FraserStrykerPCLLO
www.linkedin.com/company/fraser-stryker-pc-llo
twitter.com/FraserStryker

4817 ■ Fraser Stryker Diversity Scholarship Program *(Undergraduate/Scholarship)*

Purpose: To provide financial aid for college-bound students from low-income families in the Omaha metro area who are interested in pursuing a career in law. **Focus:** Law.

Funds Avail.: $2,500 per academic year. **Duration:** Annual. **Number Awarded:** 1. **To Apply:** Applicants must submit application and all related documents; resume, including list of leadership positions, honors and awards, extra-curricular activities and community service; essay (1000-1500 words) discussing career goals; official transcript of high school courses; Two (2) letters of recommendation from teachers and/or guidance counselor; copies of applications for financial aid if applicant checked "YES" under the financial information section. **Deadline:** March 6. **Contact:** Stephen M. Bruckner, 500 Energy Plaza, 409 S 17th St., Omaha, NE 68102-2663; Phone: 402-341-6000; Fax: 402-341-8290; Email: sbruckner@fraserstryker.com. Kathryn A. Dittrick; Email: kdittrick@fraserstryker.com.

Awards are arranged alphabetically below their administering organizations

4818 ■ FRAXA Research Foundation

10 Prince Pl., Ste. 203
Newburyport, MA 01950
Ph: (978)462-1866
E-mail: info@fraxa.org
URL: www.fraxa.org
Social Media: www.facebook.com/fraxaresearch
www.instagram.com/fraxaresearch
www.linkedin.com/company/fraxa-research-foundation
twitter.com/fraxaresearch
www.youtube.com/c/FraxaOrg

4819 ■ FRAXA Fellowships *(Postdoctorate, Master's/ Fellowship, Recognition, Monetary)*

Purpose: To encourage research aimed at finding a specific treatment for fragile X syndrome. **Focus:** General studies/Field of study not specified.

Funds Avail.: $45,000 per year. **Duration:** Annual; Two years. **To Apply:** Applicants must provide the following information with their application description of the proposed project (8-15 pages recommended); curriculum vitae for the principal investigator; curriculum vitae for the postdoctoral fellow to be supported under the grant; names of three references who are willing to be contacted to provide recommendations for candidate postdoctoral fellow; financial accounting of how the funds will be spent, with dollar distribution into major component items; a full accounting of any other current and submitted sources of support for this project and other lab research; requested start date of the project; the earliest possible state date is three months after receipt of the application; completed application must be submitted via email; application must be in a PDF format of less than 15 MB. **Deadline:** Feb 1. **Contact:** Dr. Michael Tranfaglia, CSO of FRAXA; E-mail: mtranfaglia@fraxa.org; Email: kclapp@fraxa.org.

4820 ■ Freedom Alliance

22570 Markey Ct., Ste. 240
Dulles, VA 20166
Ph: (703)444-7940
Fax: (703)444-9893
Free: 800-475-6620
URL: freedomalliance.org
Social Media: www.facebook.com/FreedomAlliance
www.linkedin.com/company/freedom-alliance
twitter.com/FreedomAlliance
www.youtube.com/thefreedomalliance

4821 ■ Freedom Alliance Scholarship Fund *(Undergraduate/Scholarship)*

Purpose: To support the children of military personnel who have been killed or permanently disabled. **Focus:** General studies/Field of study not specified. **Qualif.:** Must be a dependent child of an active military service member killed or disabled as the result of an operational mission/training accident; a senior high school, high school graduate or enrolled in an institution of higher learning; and must under the age of 26 years old. **Criteria:** Applicants are selected based on the committee's review of the application materials.

Funds Avail.: No specific amount. **Duration:** Annual. **To Apply:** Copy of your government issued photo identification; proof of dependency: birth certificate, tax form which lists dependents, or military child ID card; certificate of death (DD 1300) or rating letter (DD Form 214) from the Veterans Administration stating disability; official high school or college transcripts; provide a high resolution photo of applicant and qualifying parent; and write a 500 Word Essay or Personal Statement: What does your parent's service mean to you? **Remarks:** Freedom of Alliance will mail scholarship check to the school. **Contact:** Wanda Cruz, Email: wanda.cruz@freedomalliance.org.

4822 ■ Freedom From Religion Foundation

PO Box 750
Madison, WI 53701
Ph: (608)256-8900
Fax: (608)204-0422
E-mail: info@ffrf.org
URL: ffrf.org
Social Media: www.facebook.com/4ffrf
twitter.com/FFRF
youtube.com/user/FFRForg

4823 ■ Brian Bolton Graduate/Mature Student Essay Awards *(Graduate/Award)*

Purpose: To promote the constitutional principle of separation of state and church. **Focus:** General studies/Field of study not specified. **Qualif.:** Applicants must be currently enrolled graduate students of any age or any currently enrolled undergraduate ages 25 to 30 who attend a North American college or university. **Criteria:** Selection will be based on the submitted essay.

Funds Avail.: $200-$3,500. **Duration:** Annual. **To Apply:** Applicants must submit an essay with 750-950 words covering the topic noted online; must be typed, stapled and double-spaced with standard margins. Include word count. Place name and essay title on each page; choose own title and include one-paragraph biography on separate page at end of essay; include name, age and birth date, hometown, university or college, year in school, intended major and interests, previous degrees and anticipated graduation date. Application can be completed online at ffrf.org/outreach/ffrf-student-scholarship-essay-contests. **Deadline:** August 1.

4824 ■ Michael Hakeem Memorial Essay Contest for Ongoing College Students *(Undergraduate/ Scholarship)*

Purpose: To reward students for critical thinking. **Focus:** General studies/Field of study not specified. **Qualif.:** Applicants must be college students.

Funds Avail.: $200 to $3,500. **Duration:** Annual. **Number Awarded:** Varies. **To Apply:** Application available online at ffrf.org/outreach/ffrf-student-scholarship-essay-contests.

4825 ■ David Hudak Memorial Essay Contest for Freethinking Students of Color *(Undergraduate/ Scholarship)*

Purpose: To provide support and acknowledgement for freethinking students of color, as a minority within a minority. **Focus:** General studies/Field of study not specified. **Qualif.:** Applicants must be freethinking students of color between the ages of 17-21, who are either graduating high school seniors who will be attending a North American college or university in the fall, or students who are currently enrolled in the same. People of color includes all racial groups that are not white.

Awards are arranged alphabetically below their administering organizations

Funds Avail.: $200 to $3,500. **Duration:** Annual. **Number Awarded:** 1. **To Apply:** Applicant must fill out the online application and submit along with their essay. Essay must be double-spaced, standard margins, font size of 11 to 14 points; applicant's name and the name of the essay must be on each page and pages must be numbered; applicants are encouraged to use inclusive language (don't presume male, for example, use "humanity" or "humankind" instead of "mankind"). Essay prompt is available on the sponsor's website. **Deadline:** July 15. **Contact:** URL: ffrf.org/outreach/ffrf-student-scholarship-essay-contests.

4826 ■ Fried, Frank, Harris, Shriver and Jacobson L.L.P.
One New York Plz.
New York, NY 10004
Ph: (212)859-4000
Fax: (212)859-8000
URL: www.friedfrank.com

4827 ■ 1L Diversity Fellowships *(Graduate/Fellowship)*

Purpose: To support recent law school graduates. **Focus:** Law. **Qualif.:** Applicant must be a full-time first-year law student enrolled in an ABA-accredited law school. **Criteria:** Selection will be based on the committee's criteria.

Funds Avail.: $10,000 each. **Duration:** Annual. **To Apply:** Applicants must complete the online application, submit a resume, undergraduate transcript and copy of current law school transcript. **Contact:** Email: fellowships@goodwinlaw.com.

4828 ■ Friends of Canadian Broadcasting (FCB)
200/238 - 131 Bloor St. W
Toronto, ON, Canada M5S 1R8
Free: 866-833-1282
E-mail: friends@friends.ca
URL: www.friends.ca
Social Media: www.facebook.com/friendscb
twitter.com/friendscb

4829 ■ Dalton Camp Awards *(Professional development/Award, Monetary)*

Purpose: To support individuals who write essays on the link between democracy and the media in Canada. **Focus:** Media arts. **Qualif.:** Applicants must be Canadian citizens or permanent residents of Canada.

Funds Avail.: 10,000 Canadian Dollars for the first award; 2,500 Canadian Dollars for the second award. **Duration:** Annual. **To Apply:** Applicants must submit an essay that is written in English and does not exceed 2,000 words; each entry shall be accompanied by the author's full name and contact information, including postal address, email address and a telephone number. Each entry should also include: a biographical sketch not exceeding 50 words; the word count of the essay; written confirmation that the entry complies with the Rules of The Dalton Camp Award; essays submitted by email attachment should include, on the first page of the essay, a title followed by the full name of the author; subsequent pages should be numbered and contain no information identifying the author; essays submitted using the online submission form should contain no information identifying the author in the body of the essay. **Deadline:** March 20. **Remarks:** Established in 2002.

Contact: E-mail: submissions@daltoncampaward.ca.

4830 ■ Friends of Project 10 Inc.
115 W California Blvd., Ste. 116
Pasadena, CA 91105
Ph: (626)399-1118
E-mail: project10@hotmail.com
URL: www.friendsofproject10.org
Social Media: www.facebook.com/Friendsofproject10

4831 ■ Friends of Project 10 Models of Excellence Scholarship *(Undergraduate/Scholarship)*

Purpose: To support students who have advanced the civil rights of the lesbian, gay, bisexual, and transgender communities. **Focus:** Sexuality. **Qualif.:** Applicants are limited to graduating senior high school students residing in these Southern California counties Imperial, Kern, Los Angeles, Orange, Riverside, Santa Barbara, San Bernardino, San Diego, San Luis Obispo, Ventura; they must be from public, private and parochial schools who have advanced the civil rights of the lesbian, gay, bisexual, and transgender (LGBT) population.

Funds Avail.: $1,000-$3,000. **Duration:** Annual. **Number Awarded:** Varies. **Deadline:** May 5. **Remarks:** Established in 1994.

4832 ■ Full Stack Talent
1646 W Snow Ave., Ste. 10
Tampa, FL 33605
Ph: (813)517-8488
URL: www.fullstacktalent.com
Social Media: www.facebook.com/FullStackTalent
www.instagram.com/fullstacktalent
www.linkedin.com/company/fullstacktalent
twitter.com/FullStackTalent

4833 ■ Full Stack Student Scholarship *(Graduate/Scholarship)*

Purpose: To assist with financial relief for a technology student. **Focus:** Technology. **Qualif.:** Applicant must be enrolled in a U.S. based college or university and majoring in a technology related field. **Criteria:** Selection will be based on the submitted essay.

Funds Avail.: $500. **Duration:** Annual. **Number Awarded:** 1. **To Apply:** Applicant must submit a 300-500 word essay.

4834 ■ The Fuller Foundation, Inc.
c/o GMA Foundations 2 Liberty Square, Suite 500
Boston, MA 02109
Ph: (617)391-3094
URL: www.fullerfoundation.org

4835 ■ The Dr. George T. Bottomley Scholarship *(Undergraduate/Scholarship)*

Purpose: To support outstanding young men and women employed at New Hampshire golf courses in pursuing higher education. **Focus:** General studies/Field of study not specified. **Qualif.:** Applicants must be a graduate of an accredited high school or enrolled in a bachelor or associate degree college program, a minimum academic GPA of 2.5 on a 4.0 scale; must have a minimum of two summers of successful work at a NH golf course as a caddie, in the

Awards are arranged alphabetically below their administering organizations

Pro Shop, on the grounds crew, or in the clubhouse; must be of proven character, integrity, and citizenship; must be a qualified Abenaqui scholar or to a young man or woman from the Seacoast area.

Duration: Annual. **To Apply:** Completed application along with an official copy of your transcript (through Fall of previous year); copy of Free Application for Student Aid (FAFSA) report (the 5 page report, not the application); letter from the club or course where you have completed the employment requirement, certifying you have worked at least 2 seasons (for new applicant); copy of the acceptance letter from the school, college or university, applicant going to attend and confidential school report completed by high school principal or guidance counselor (for high school senior) must be submitted. **Deadline:** May 15. **Remarks:** The Scholarship established in memory by The Fuller Foundation, and his family in recognition of his lifelong support of golf at Abenaqui Country Club and in New Hampshire. **Contact:** McDonough Scholarship Foundation; c/o Kerri Coughlin; 61 N St., Manchester, NH, 03104; Email: mcDonoughapplication@comcast.net.

4836 ■ Fund for American Studies (TFAS)

1706 New Hampshire Ave. NW
Washington, DC 20009
Ph: (202)986-0384
Fax: (202)986-0390
E-mail: info@tfas.org
URL: tfas.org
Social Media: www.facebook.com/TFASorg
instagram.com/tfasorg
twitter.com/TFASorg
youtube.com/c/tfasorg

4837 ■ Congressional and Business Leadership Awards *(Undergraduate/Scholarship)*

Purpose: To provide financial support for students who wish to attend the Institute on Business and Government Affairs (IBGA) at Georgetown University. **Focus:** Business; Local government.

Funds Avail.: No specific amount. **Duration:** Annual. **Number Awarded:** 1. **Remarks:** Established in 1990. **Contact:** Mr. Ed Turner; Phone: 202-986-0384; Email: eturner@TFAS.org.

4838 ■ Eben Tisdale Fellowship *(Undergraduate/Fellowship, Monetary)*

Purpose: To support outstanding students who are interested technology and public policy. **Focus:** Technology. **Qualif.:** Applicants must be junior or senior students interested in public policy and the high-tech industry, or in a graduate program. **Criteria:** The Advisory Committee will evaluate submitted materials.

Funds Avail.: Full scholarship of $8,695; $1,000 Stipends. **Duration:** Annual. **To Apply:** Applicants must submit a completed application form; professional resume; official academic transcripts; evaluation forms from two academic references (in a sealed envelope, author's signature must be across the seal); a 500-word statement on reasons of wanting to be a Tisdale fellow. **Remarks:** Established after the death of Eben Tisdale, general manager of government affairs for the Hewlett-Packard Company.

4839 ■ Fundación Educativa Carlos M. Castañeda (FECMC)

1925 Brickell Ave. D-1108
Miami, FL 33129

Ph: (305)283-4963
E-mail: fecmc@me.com
URL: www.fecmc.org

4840 ■ Carlos M. Castaneda Journalism Scholarship *(Graduate/Scholarship)*

Purpose: To support the education and development of Spanish speaking journalists. **Focus:** Journalism.

Funds Avail.: $7,000 each. **Duration:** Annual. **Number Awarded:** Varies. **To Apply:** Applicants must submit a completed application form together with all transcript(s) of academic work (in sealed envelopes with official school seal or a signature across the flap); proof of acceptance into a graduate journalism program; applicant's (or applicant's parents') most recent 1040 tax form or equivalent tax documents (if from a foreign country); Curriculum Vitae listing educational background, work history, awards, internships, language proficiency and any work done for school or community newspaper; three reference letters in separate sealed envelopes (professors, advisors, employers, etc.); a portfolio with three of the best stories published by professional or school publications in Spanish; and a 2000-word essay. **Remarks:** Established in 2006.

4841 ■ Funeral Service Foundation, Inc. (FSF)

13625 Bishops Dr.
Brookfield, WI 53005
Free: 877-402-5900
URL: www.funeralservicefoundation.org
Social Media: twitter.com/fsf1945

4842 ■ Brenda Renee Horn and Steve Mack Memorial Scholarships *(Undergraduate/Scholarship)*

Purpose: To provide financial assistance for top-scoring mortuary science students via the Key Memories scholarship essay contest. **Focus:** Mortuary science. **Qualif.:** Applicants must be open to full-time or part-time students in good standing who are enrolled in ABFSE- or Canadian-accredited institutions/programs, must be attending class of degree in mortuary science. **Criteria:** Applicants must be Submit on online only.

Deadline: November 1.

4843 ■ Joseph E. Hagan Memorial Scholarship *(Graduate/Scholarship)*

Purpose: To provide financial assistance for mortuary science school students. **Focus:** Mortuary science. **Qualif.:** Applicant must be full-time or part-time students in good standing who are enrolled in ABFSE- or Canadian-accredited institutions/programs; must be attending classes and actively pursuing a degree in mortuary science at the time of application.

Funds Avail.: $2,500. **Duration:** Annual. **To Apply:** Applicant must be submit application along with: essay & video; recent transcripts; letter of good standing from an instructor or program director; headshot; signature. **Deadline:** November 1. **Remarks:** Established in 2000.

4844 ■ NFDA Professional Women's Conference Scholarship *(Undergraduate/Scholarship)*

Purpose: To provide financial assistance for tuition and travel stipend for selected individuals who attended the National Funeral Directors Association Professional Women's Conference. **Focus:** Funeral services; Mortuary science.

Awards are arranged alphabetically below their administering organizations

Funds Avail.: $1,000. **Duration:** Annual. **To Apply:** Applicants must submit 750 to 1, 000-word essay and a brief five-minute (maximum) video.

4845 ■ Fur Takers of America (FTA)
PO Box 3
Buckley, IL 60918
Ph: (217)394-2577
URL: www.furtakersofamerica.com

4846 ■ Charles Dobbins FTA Scholarships
(Undergraduate, Vocational/Occupational/Scholarship)

Purpose: To promote interest in the accumulation and dissemination of knowledge concerning the trapping of fur bearing animals among persons interested therein. **Focus:** Agricultural sciences; Biology; Wildlife conservation, management, and science. **Qualif.:** Applicants must be members of FTA or their immediate relatives; must be majoring in agriculture, biology, wildlife management or related courses in an accredited two-year or four-year college, university, or vocational/technical school. **Criteria:** Recipients are selected based on academic records and quality of the essay submitted.

Funds Avail.: $500. **Duration:** Annual. **To Apply:** Applicants must provide a proof of high school graduation or pending graduation; official documents indicating that they have been accepted in an institution as first year students, or registration of classes if applicants are already in school; must also submit an essay that discusses career goals and how the scholarship would help to achieve these goals. **Deadline:** June 1. **Contact:** Jerry Schilling; Address: 21 Schilling Lane, New Harmony, IN 47631; Phone: 812-783-1097.

4847 ■ Gallery Collection
65 Challenger Rd.
Ridgefield Park, NJ 07660
Ph: (201)641-0070
Fax: (800)772-1144
Free: 800-950-7064
E-mail: service@gallerycollection.com
URL: www.gallerycollection.com

4848 ■ The Gallery Collection's Create-A-Greeting-Card Scholarship *(Undergraduate/Scholarship)*

Purpose: To encourage students to use their talents and pursue their education. **Focus:** Art; Graphic art and design; Photography. **Qualif.:** Applicants must be currently enrolled in high school, college or university; must have a talent in fine arts, graphic design or photography; and must be U.S. citizens; must be 14 years of age or older at the time of entry, unless prohibited by law.

Funds Avail.: $10,000 for the winner; $1,000 for the selected school. **Duration:** Annual. **To Apply:** Applicants must submit an original photograph a piece of artwork or graphics file for the front cover. **Contact:** Scholarship Administrator, The Gallery Collection, Prudent Publishing Company, Inc.; Email: scholarshipadmin@gallerycollection.com.

4849 ■ Gallery Karin Carton
305 N Coast Hwy.
Laguna Beach, CA 92651

E-mail: info@gallerycartonfineart.com
URL: www.gallerycartonfineart.com

4850 ■ Karin Carton Scholarship *(Graduate/Scholarship)*

Purpose: To help students pay for qualified college expenses, including tuition, books, and on-campus room and board. **Focus:** Art; Business; General studies/Field of study not specified. **Qualif.:** Applicant must be currently enrolled in a two- or four-year program at an accredited college or university. **Criteria:** Selection is based on relevance and originality.

Funds Avail.: $300. **Duration:** Annual. **Number Awarded:** 1. **To Apply:** Applicant must write an essay answering these questions: What is the future of art? What does this mean for artists and galleries? **Deadline:** February 15. **Remarks:** Established in 2019.

4851 ■ Gamewardens Association, Vietnam to Present
PO Box 354
Murrieta, CA 92564-0354
Free: 866-220-7477
URL: www.tf116.org
Social Media: www.facebook.com/Gamewardens

4852 ■ Gamewardens Scholarship Program *(High School/Scholarship)*

Purpose: To discuss military history, military news and other topics of concern or interest about Vietnam. **Focus:** Vietnamese studies. **Qualif.:** Applicants must be in need of the assistance; must be the son, daughter or grandchild of a member of Game wardens. **Criteria:** Committee will consider the application based on the need of the applicant.

Funds Avail.: $1,500. **Duration:** Annual. **To Apply:** Applicants must fill out the application form and send to Game warden of Vietnam Association Office. **Deadline:** July 15. **Contact:** Gamewardens Scholarship Program, Attn. Glen Slay, 1074 Buena Vista Dr. La Selva Beach, CA; E-mail: scholarship@tf116.org.

4853 ■ The Gamma Mu Foundation
PO Box 23520
Fort Lauderdale, FL 33307-3520
Ph: (866)463-6007
E-mail: info@gammamufoundation.org
URL: gammamufoundation.org

4854 ■ The Gamma Mu Scholarships Program
(Vocational/Occupational, Professional development, Undergraduate, Graduate, Postgraduate/Scholarship)

Purpose: To support gay men who want to further their education at a college, university, vocational, or professional training program. Resources are targeted to rural and/or underserved areas. **Focus:** General studies/Field of study not specified. **Qualif.:** Must be a citizen of the United States, a gay male, under 35 years of age at time of application, have completed high school or the GED by June of the application year, admitted to an accredited college, university, or vocational institution for fall of the current year or spring of the following year. **Criteria:** Financial need, community and extracurricular involvement, experience overcoming discrimination and/or marginalization, work/academic achievement, educational and career goals,

Awards are arranged alphabetically below their administering organizations

involvement in the LGBTQ community, leadership in promoting diversity and tolerance.

Funds Avail.: $1,000 to $2,500. **Duration:** Annual. **Number Awarded:** Varies. **To Apply:** Submit a completed application online, complete transcripts, school enrollment, or other relevant information when requested. **Deadline:** March 31. **Contact:** Email: scholarships@gammamufoundation.org; URL: gammamufoundation.org/scholarship-guidelines/.

4855 ■ Gamma Sigma Alpha (GSA)

PO Box 3948
Parker, CO 80134
Free: 844-705-3291
E-mail: director@gammasigmaalpha.org
URL: gammasigmaalpha.org
Social Media: www.facebook.com/gammasigmaalpha
www.instagram.com/gammasigmasigma
twitter.com/gammasigmaalpha

4856 ■ Gamma Sigma Alpha Graduate Scholarship *(Graduate/Scholarship)*

Purpose: To assist qualified members pursuing graduate studies at an accredited institution. **Focus:** General studies/Field of study not specified. **Qualif.:** Applicants must be members of Gamma Sigma Alpha with a cumulative GPA of 3.5 or better (applicants must have been initiated prior to their application submission). **Criteria:** Selection will be based upon academic record, recommendations submitted, the applicant's statement, and scholarly, campus and community activities.

Funds Avail.: $2,000 each. **Duration:** Annual. **Number Awarded:** 2. **To Apply:** Applications can submitted through online. Applicants must submit a completed application form together with a two letters of recommendation; resume; one page essay; and official transcript(s) of all academic work. **Deadline:** May 31. **Remarks:** Established in 2005. **Contact:** Phone: (844) 705-3291, Email: director@gammasigmaalpha.org.

4857 ■ Garden Club of America (GCA)

14 E 60th St., 3rd Fl.
New York, NY 10022
Ph: (212)753-8287
E-mail: gca@gcamerica.org
URL: www.gcamerica.org
Social Media: www.facebook.com/thegardenclubofamerica
www.instagram.com/thegardenclubofamerica
www.linkedin.com/company/gcamerica
twitter.com/GCAScholarships

4858 ■ Catherine H. Beattie Fellowships *(Graduate/Fellowship)*

Purpose: To promote conservation of rare and endangered flora in the United States through the programs of the Center for Plant Conservation in partnership with the Garden Club of America. **Focus:** Biology; Horticulture. **Qualif.:** Applicants must be graduate students in biology or horticulture. **Criteria:** Preference will be given to students focusing on endangered flora of the Carolina or the southeastern united states.

Funds Avail.: up to $4,500. **Duration:** Annual. **To Apply:** Applications should be submitted to the center for plant

conservation and must include the following: one page cover letter; two page (maximum) project narrative; one page project budget and timeline; curriculum vitae; letter of recommendation from major advisor or equivalent. **Deadline:** January 31.

4859 ■ Garden Club of America Awards in Tropical Botany (GCA) *(Doctorate/Award)*

Purpose: To promote the preservation of tropical forests by enlarging the body of botanists with field experience. **Focus:** Botany. **Qualif.:** Applicants must be PhD enrolled in United States university; open to U.S. Citizens and permanent residents who are enrolled in a U.S. based institution. **Criteria:** Selection will be based on the committee's criteria.

Funds Avail.: $5,500. **Duration:** Annual. **Number Awarded:** 2. **To Apply:** Applicants must submit a curriculum vitae; (two-page) statement of proposed research; personal letter describing plans for the future and commitment to tropical conservation; letter of recommendation from student's graduate advisor including an evaluation of the student's progress. **Deadline:** January 15. **Remarks:** Established in 1983. **Contact:** Andrea Santy, Director, Education for Nature Program, World Wildlife Fund, 1250 24th St. NW, Washington, DC, 20037. Phone: 202-495-4447; e-mail: andrea.santy@wwfus.org.

4860 ■ Katherine M. Grosscup Scholarships in Horticulture *(Undergraduate, Graduate/Scholarship)*

Purpose: To encourage the study of horticulture and related fields. **Focus:** Horticulture. **Qualif.:** Applicants must be current college sophomores, juniors, seniors or graduate students from Ohio, Pennsylvania, West Virginia, Michigan, Indiana and Kentucky, and have "B" GPA or better. **Criteria:** Selection will be based on the committee's criteria.

Funds Avail.: $3,500. **Duration:** Annual. **To Apply:** Applicants must submit a completed application form; two letter of recommendation one should be from your advisor or professor of the department of your major; the other should be from current and/or former employer; Also include how your proposed course of study will support you in your endeavor; transcript of college records; and personal statement explaining the career goals and how the chosen area of study will help achieve the objectives. **Deadline:** January 15. **Remarks:** The scholarship is given in in memory of her friend Katharine MacConnell Grosscup. Established in 1981. **Contact:** The Garden Club of America, Attn: Scholarship Applications, 14 E 60th St., New York, NY, 10022-1006; Phone: 212-753-8287; Fax: 212-753-0134; Email: grosscupscholarship@gmail.com; and scholarshipapplications@gcamerica.org.

4861 ■ Garden State Association of Christian Schools

c/o Donald A. Netz, President
151 Golf Club Rd.
Sewell, NJ 08080
Ph: (856)589-1665
E-mail: mdavis@gccs.co
URL: gsacsnj.com

4862 ■ Rev. Alfred E. Monson Scholarship *(Other/Fellowship)*

Purpose: To assist a teacher in GSACS who plans further study or attend a summer institute. **Focus:** Teaching. **Qua-**

Awards are arranged alphabetically below their administering organizations

lif.: Applicant must be a teacher in GSACS who plans further study.

Funds Avail.: $300. **Duration:** Annual. **Number Awarded:** 1. **Deadline:** May 1. **Remarks:** The Award Is Established In Memory Rev. Alfred E. Monson, Founder And President Of The Garden State Association Of Christian Schools.

4863 ■ The Gardeners of America
PO Box 40545
Bay Village, OH 44140-0545
URL: www.gardenersofamerica.club/scholarships

4864 ■ Gardeners of America/Men's Garden Clubs of America Scholarship *(Undergraduate/Scholarship)*

Purpose: To promote the study of horticulture and floriculture. **Focus:** Horticulture. **Qualif.:** Applicants must be students enrolled in an accredited community college, university, or college offering a major in horticulture or floriculture as the major subject leading toward a degree in horticulture, floriculture or other field of study. **Criteria:** Selection are based upon committee criteria.

Funds Avail.: $1,000. **Duration:** Annual. **Number Awarded:** 1. **To Apply:** Applicants must include copy of transcripts; three letters of recommendation one from their major professor, and two from other professors or instructors or employer; essay or autobiography identifying specific needs and goals and accomplishments in student affairs and societies.

4865 ■ Gatti, Keltner, Bienvenu & Montesi PLC
219 Adams Ave.
Memphis, TN 38103
Ph: (901)526-2126
Fax: (901)577-5424
URL: www.gkbm.com
Social Media: www.facebook.com/
gattikeltnerbienvenumontesi
www.linkedin.com/company/gkbm
www.youtube.com/channel/UCi1QpBmXOjTQK-nkUT9Ot-A

4866 ■ Montesi Scholarship *(Undergraduate/Scholarship)*

Purpose: To provide a student with the opportunity to pursue a higher education. **Focus:** General studies/Field of study not specified. **Qualif.:** Applicant must show proof of acceptance or active enrollment in undergrad school. **Criteria:** Selection will take into account the quality of writing, as well as the applicant's ability to follow the instructions.

Funds Avail.: $2,500. **To Apply:** Applicant must submit an essay; essays should be written in English and typed in 12-point, legible font; all submissions should be 500 words or LESS; applications can be filled out and submitted online at www.gkbm.com/montesi-scholarship/. **Deadline:** May 30. **Contact:** Email:scholarship@gkbm.com.

4867 ■ Gay and Lesbian Armenian Society (GALAS)
8721 Santa Monica Blvd., Box 654
West Hollywood, CA 90069-4511
Ph: (310)203-1587
URL: www.galasla.org
Social Media: www.facebook.com/GALASLosAngeles

www.instagram.com/galas_la/
twitter.com/galasLA

4868 ■ GALAS Scholarship *(Undergraduate, Graduate/Scholarship)*

Purpose: To help students of Armenian descent who are active in LGBTQ activism to pay for college. **Focus:** General studies/Field of study not specified. **Qualif.:** Applicants must be undergraduate or graduate students of Armenian descent who have demonstrated LGBTQ activism, such as involvement with an LGBTQ nonprofit or LGBTQ campus initiative, club or organization, or collective; must be attending a college or university in the United States.

Funds Avail.: $1,000 each. **Number Awarded:** 3. **To Apply:** Applicant must complete the application form and submit with current transcripts, two letters of recommendation (in PDF format), and a letter of interest (minimum 500 words in PDF format) demonstrating applicant's connection/experience with the LGBTQ community and why applicant is the ideal recipient of the scholarship. **Deadline:** November 14.

4869 ■ Gay and Lesbian Business Association of Santa Barbara (GLBA)
PO Box 90907
Santa Barbara, CA 93190
Ph: (805)684-4442
URL: glbasb.org

4870 ■ Carl Joseph Adelhardt Memorial Scholarship *(Undergraduate/Scholarship)*

Purpose: To provide financial assistance to those students who are in need. **Focus:** General studies/Field of study not specified. **Qualif.:** Applicants must be students enrolled or planning to enroll at a post-secondary institution in Santa Barbara County. **Criteria:** Applicants are awarded based upon the potential for lasting contribution to the Santa Barbara gay and lesbian community, career goals, and financial need.

Funds Avail.: No specific amount. **Duration:** Annual. **To Apply:** Applicants must submit the following: completed application including statements of community involvement and financial need; an autobiography/personal statement; a copy of current college and/or high school transcript of records; two letters of recommendation from a community member and the other one must come from a teacher or faculty member of their institution. **Deadline:** July 30. **Remarks:** Established in memory of Carl Joseph Adelhardt, a resident of Santa Barbara for over three decades, an entrepreneur, noted decorator, and generous supporter of local causes. Established in 2005. **Contact:** GLBA Scholarship, PO Box 90907, Santa Barbara, CA 93190-0907.

4871 ■ The Robert L. Johns Vocational Scholarship *(Vocational/Occupational/Scholarship)*

Purpose: To ensure that LGBT vocational students have the opportunity to fulfill their professional goals. **Focus:** General studies/Field of study not specified. **Qualif.:** Applicants must be students enrolled or planning to enroll at a post-secondary institution in Santa Barbara County. **Criteria:** Applicants are awarded based upon the potential for lasting contribution to the Santa Barbara gay and lesbian community, career goals, and financial need.

Funds Avail.: No specific amount. **Duration:** Annual. **To Apply:** Applicants must submit the following: completed

Awards are arranged alphabetically below their administering organizations

application including statements of community involvement and financial need; an autobiography/personal statement; a copy of current college and/or high school transcript of records; two letters of recommendation from a community member and the other one must come from a teacher or faculty member of their institution. **Deadline:** July 30. **Remarks:** Named after Robert Johns, a prominent Santa Barbara cosmetologist and businessman. Established in 2003. **Contact:** GLBA Scholarship, PO Box 90907, Santa Barbara, CA 93190-0907.

4872 ■ Stephen Logan Memorial Scholarship
(Undergraduate/Scholarship)

Purpose: To provide financial assistance to students who are in need. **Focus:** General studies/Field of study not specified. **Qualif.:** Applicants must attendance at a post-secondary institution in Santa Barbara County; must demonstrate academic excellence, leadership skills, community involvement, and financial need; enrolled in undergraduate or graduate programs. **Criteria:** Applicants will be selected based upon the potential contribution to the Santa Barbara gay and lesbian community; career goals; and financial need.

Funds Avail.: No specific amount. **Duration:** Annual. **Number Awarded:** 1. **To Apply:** Applicants must submit the following: completed application including statements of community involvement and financial need; an autobiography/personal statement; a copy of current college and/or high school transcript of records; two letters of recommendation from a community member and the other one must come from a teacher or a faculty member of their institution. **Deadline:** July 30. **Remarks:** The scholarship is named for the well-known Santa Barbara contractor whose generous bequest upon his death in 2000 ensured grants would be available to help gay and lesbian youth in the future. Established in 2000. **Contact:** GLBA Scholarship, PO Box 90907, Santa Barbara, CA 93190-0907.

4873 ■ The Raffin-Gathercole Scholarship
(Undergraduate/Scholarship)

Purpose: To help LGBT youth succeed and achieve academically. **Focus:** General studies/Field of study not specified. **Qualif.:** Applicants must be enrolled or planning to enroll at a post-secondary institution in Santa Barbara County. **Criteria:** Applicants are awarded based upon the potential for lasting contribution to the Santa Barbara gay and lesbian community, career goals, and financial need.

Funds Avail.: No specific amount. **Duration:** Annual. **To Apply:** Applicants must submit the following: completed application including statements of community involvement and financial need; an autobiography/personal statement; a copy of current college and/or high school transcript of records; two letters of recommendation from a community member and the other one must come from a teacher or faculty member of their institution. **Remarks:** Established in honor of Claude Raffin and Jon Gathercole they provided exceptional and ongoing support for GLBA. Established in 2003. **Contact:** GLBA Scholarship, PO Box 90907, Santa Barbara, CA 93190-0907.

4874 ■ Gemological Institute of America (GIA)
The Robert Mouawad Campus
5345 Armada Dr.
Carlsbad, CA 92008
Ph: (760)603-4000
Fax: (760)603-4080
Free: 800-421-7250

URL: www.gia.edu
Social Media: www.facebook.com/GIAEducation
instagram.com/giagrams
www.linkedin.com/company/gia
pinterest.com/giapins
twitter.com/GIAnews
youtube.com/user/officialGIAchannel

4875 ■ Color Masters Scholarship *(Undergraduate/Scholarship)*

Purpose: To provide financial support to applicants employed by a jewelry store that carries ColorMasters products. **Focus:** Gemology. **Qualif.:** Applicants must be U.S. citizens and permanent residents.

Funds Avail.: $10,000. **To Apply:** Applicants must complete the GIA Scholarship application (available on the website), with a letter of recommendation from a person in the jewelry industry; passport/driver's license/national identify card. **Deadline:** March 31 and September 30. **Contact:** Phone: 760-603-4131; Toll-free: 800-421-7250 ext. 4131.

4876 ■ Eunice Miles Scholarship *(Graduate/Scholarship)*

Purpose: To provide educational assistance for students. **Focus:** General studies/Field of study not specified. **Qualif.:** Applicants must be U.S. citizens and permanent residents.

Funds Avail.: No specific amount. **Duration:** Annual. **Number Awarded:** 2. **To Apply:** Applicants must complete the GIA Scholarship application (available on the website), with a letter of recommendation from a person in the jewelry industry; passport/driver's license/national identify card. **Deadline:** March 31 and September 30. **Contact:** Phone: 760-603-4131; Toll-free: 800-421-7250 ext. 4131.

4877 ■ George W. Juno Scholarship *(Graduate/Scholarship)*

Purpose: To promote the study of gemology. **Focus:** Gemology. **Qualif.:** Applicants must be U.S. citizens and permanent residents.

Funds Avail.: $1,500. **To Apply:** Applicants must complete the GIA Scholarship application (available on the website), with a letter of recommendation from a person in the jewelry industry; passport/driver's license/national identify card. **Deadline:** March 31 and September 30. **Contact:** Phone: 760-603-4131; Toll-free: 800-421-7250 ext. 4131; Email: scholarship@gia.edu.

4878 ■ GIA Scholarship - Distance Education eLearning *(Graduate/Scholarship)*

Purpose: To promote the study of gemology. **Focus:** Gemology. **Qualif.:** Applicants must be U.S. citizens and permanent residents.

Funds Avail.: Varies. **To Apply:** Applicants must complete the GIA Scholarship application (available on the website), with a letter of recommendation from a person in the jewelry industry; passport/driver's license/national identify card. **Deadline:** March 31 and September 30. **Contact:** Phone: 760-603-4131; Toll-free: 800-421-7250 ext. 4131.

4879 ■ Lone Star GIA Associate and Alumni Scholarships *(Undergraduate/Scholarship)*

Purpose: To support individuals who are pursuing a gemology program. **Focus:** General studies/Field of study not

Awards are arranged alphabetically below their administering organizations

specified. **Qualif.:** Applicants must: be U.S. citizens and permanent residents. **Criteria:** Applications will be reviewed by the GIA Scholarship committee; preference will be given to applicants residing in Texas, Oklahoma, Louisiana, New Mexico and Arkansas.

Funds Avail.: $500. **Number Awarded:** 1. **To Apply:** Applicants must complete the GIA Scholarship application (available at the website), with a letter of recommendation from a person in the jewelry industry. **Deadline:** March 31 and September 30.

4880 ■ Mikimoto Scholarship (Graduate/Scholarship)

Purpose: To support individuals who are pursuing a gemology program. **Focus:** Gemology. **Qualif.:** Applicants must be U.S. citizens and permanent residents.

Funds Avail.: $950. **Duration:** Annual. **To Apply:** Applicants must complete the GIA Scholarship application (available on the website), with a letter of recommendation from a person in the jewelry industry; passport/driver's license/national identify card. **Deadline:** March 31 and September 30. **Contact:** Phone: 760-603-4131; Toll-free: 800-421-7250 ext. 4131.

4881 ■ North Texas GIA Alumni Association Scholarship (Undergraduate/Scholarship)

Purpose: To provide educational assistance for students. **Focus:** General studies/Field of study not specified. **Qualif.:** Applicants must be U.S. citizens and permanent Texas residents.

Funds Avail.: $1,500. **To Apply:** Applicants must complete the GIA Scholarship application (available on the website), with a letter of recommendation from a person in the jewelry industry; passport/driver's license/national identify card. **Deadline:** March 31 and September 30. **Contact:** Phone: 760-603-4131; Toll-free: 800-421-7250 ext. 4131.

4882 ■ Richard T. Liddicoat Scholarship (Graduate/Scholarship)

Purpose: To support individuals who are pursuing a gemology program. **Focus:** Gemology. **Qualif.:** Applicants must be U.S. citizens and permanent residents.

Funds Avail.: $23,233. **To Apply:** Applicants must complete the GIA Scholarship application (available on the website), with a letter of recommendation from a person in the jewelry industry; passport/driver's license/national identify card. **Deadline:** March 31 and September 30. **Contact:** Email: scholarship@gia.edu; Phone: 760-603-4131; Toll-free: 800-421-7250 ext. 4131.

4883 ■ William Goldberg Scholarship (Undergraduate/Scholarship)

Purpose: To support individuals who are pursuing a gemology program for Carlsbad campus. **Focus:** Gemology. **Qualif.:** Applicants must be U.S. citizens and permanent residents.

Funds Avail.: $15,000. **Number Awarded:** 1. **To Apply:** Applicants must complete the GIA Scholarship application (available at the website), with a letter of recommendation; Letter must be signed and dated within past 12 months, and must include all contact information. **Deadline:** March 31 and September 30. **Contact:** Phone: 760-603-4131; Toll-free: 800-421-7250 ext. 4131.

4884 ■ General Aviation Manufacturers Association (GAMA)

1400 K St. NW, Ste. 801
Washington, DC 20005-2485

Ph: (202)393-1500
Fax: (202)842-4063
E-mail: info@gama.aero
URL: www.gama.aero
Social Media: www.facebook.com/General.Aviation
  .Manufacturers.Association
www.instagram.com/gamanufacturers
www.linkedin.com/company/general-aviation
  -manufacturers-association
twitter.com/GAManufacturers
www.youtube.com/channel/UCojAj8YPWAN
  -vtNy5SSDSnw

4885 ■ ICAS Foundation / GAMA Scholarship (College, Undergraduate, University/Scholarship)

Purpose: To provide assistance to students seeking an aviation related degree. **Focus:** Aviation. **Qualif.:** Student must be enrolled in an aviation-related degree program; completed at least two semesters with an aviation-related declared major. **Criteria:** Applicant must distinguish themselves from their peers.

Funds Avail.: $2,000. **Duration:** Annual. **Number Awarded:** 1. **To Apply:** Complete application including essay, biographical, and demographic information; provide GPA, record of extracurricular and community participation; winners will be asked to provide a photograph. **Contact:** Email: scholarships@icasfoundation.org; URL: icasfoundation.org/scholarships/gama-scholarship/.

4886 ■ Edward W. Stimpson Aviation Excellence Award Scholarship (Undergraduate, College, University/Scholarship)

Purpose: To provide assistance to students seeking an aviation related degree. **Focus:** Aviation. **Qualif.:** Must be a current student at a U.S. high school accepted to and enrolling in an institution for an aviation-related degree program (flight training, aviation management, aerospace engineering, aviation maintenance); have a 3.0 or better grade point average **Criteria:** Academic achievements, involvement in extra-curricular activities, and essay question responses.

Funds Avail.: $2,000. **Duration:** Annual. **Number Awarded:** 1. **To Apply:** Must submit completed application, essay, high school transcript, two letters of recommendation. **Deadline:** April 15. **Contact:** Phone: 202-393-1500; Email: lhaertlein@gama.aero; URL: gama.aero/opportunities-in-ga/scholarships/.

4887 ■ General Board of Higher Education and Ministry (GBHEM)

1001 19th Ave. S
Nashville, TN 37212
Ph: (615)340-7400
E-mail: communications@gbhem.org
URL: www.gbhem.org
Social Media: www.facebook.com/gbhem
www.linkedin.com/company/gbhem
twitter.com/gbhem
youtube.com/user/gbhem

4888 ■ Baker Scholarship (Doctorate, Professional development/Scholarship)

Purpose: To assist campus ministers in pursuing further education. **Focus:** General studies/Field of study not speci-

Awards are arranged alphabetically below their administering organizations

fied. **Qualif.:** Applicants must have an M.Div. degree or its equivalent; must be current campus ministers who have been in campus ministry for at least three years; must be committed to remaining in campus ministry; must be pursuing advanced training (such as doctorate degree, certification, independent study) and must have a minimum 3.0 GPA.

To Apply: Application available online at www.gbhem.org/loans-scholarships/scholarships/list-of-scholarships/.

4889 ■ Rosalie Bentzinger Scholarships *(Doctorate/Scholarship)*

Purpose: To assist deacons furthering their studies in Christian education. **Focus:** Religion. **Qualif.:** Applicants must be ordained deacons pursuing a Ph.D. in Christian Education, enrolled in a University Senate approved Seminary; must have a 3-year membership in the UMC; must have a GPA of 3.0+.

Funds Avail.: $5,000. **Duration:** Annual. **To Apply:** Application available online at www.gbhem.org/loans-scholarships/scholarships/list-of-scholarships/. **Contact:** For eligibility questions, Email: umscholar@gbhem.org; For technical questions, Email: GBHEM@applyists.com.

4890 ■ Esther Edwards Graduate Scholarships *(Doctorate, Professional development/Scholarship)*

Purpose: To assist female administrators and faculty members pursuing doctorates in leadership. **Focus:** General studies/Field of study not specified. **Qualif.:** Applicant must be a female administrator or faculty member pursuing a Ph.D. in leadership working for a United Methodist-related institution.

Funds Avail.: $5,000. **Duration:** Annual. **To Apply:** Application available online at www.gbhem.org/loans-scholarships/scholarships/list-of-scholarships/. **Contact:** For eligibility questions, Email: umscholar@gbhem.org; For technical questions, Email: GBHEM@applyists.com.

4891 ■ HANA Scholars *(Undergraduate, Graduate, Doctorate/Scholarship)*

Purpose: To assist students from various backgrounds working towards various higher education degrees. **Focus:** General studies/Field of study not specified. **Qualif.:** Applicants must be of Hispanic, Asian, and/or Native American ethnicity; must be in junior year or higher of undergraduate study (up through doctorate); minimum 3-year membership in the UMC; minimum 2.85 GPA.

Funds Avail.: $1,000-$3,000. **To Apply:** Application available online at www.gbhem.org/loans-scholarships/scholarships/list-of-scholarships/.

4892 ■ Miriam Hoffman Scholarship *(Undergraduate, Graduate/Scholarship)*

Purpose: To assist students from various backgrounds working towards various higher education degrees. **Focus:** Music. **Qualif.:** Applicants must be undergraduate or graduate students; must be pursuing a vocational career in music education or music ministry; must have minimum 2.5 GPA.

Funds Avail.: $500-$1,000. **To Apply:** Application available online at www.gbhem.org/loans-scholarships/scholarships/list-of-scholarships/.

4893 ■ Journey Toward Ordained Ministry Scholarships *(Undergraduate, Graduate/Scholarship)*

Purpose: To assist students from various backgrounds working towards various higher education degrees. **Focus:**

Religion. **Qualif.:** Applicants must be an undergraduate or graduate level racial-ethnic minority student pursuing ordained ministry (deacon or elder); age 30 or under; minimum 2-year membership in the UMC; enrolled at a UM-related institution; minimum 2.85 GPA for undergrad, minimum 3.0 GPA for graduate level.

Funds Avail.: $5,000. **Duration:** Annual. **To Apply:** Application available online at www.gbhem.org/loans-scholarships/scholarships/list-of-scholarships/. **Contact:** For eligibility questions, Email: umscholar@gbhem.org; For technical questions, Email: GBHEM@applyists.com.

4894 ■ Elvina Jane Owen Scholarship *(Graduate, Undergraduate/Scholarship)*

Purpose: To assist students from various backgrounds working towards various higher education degrees. **Focus:** General studies/Field of study not specified. **Qualif.:** Applicants must be undergraduate or graduate students with a minimum 2.85 GPA and at least one year of membership in the UMC. **Criteria:** First preference is given to students in theJohnstown District of the Western Pennsylvania Annual Conferenceenrolled at Allegheny College. Second preference goes to graduate students fromthe Western Pennsylvania Annual Conferencemajoring in education.

Funds Avail.: $500-$1,000. **Duration:** Annual. **To Apply:** Application available online at www.gbhem.org/loans-scholarships/scholarships/list-of-scholarships/. **Contact:** For eligibility questions, Email: umscholar@gbhem.org; For technical questions, Email: GBHEM@applyists.com.

4895 ■ United Methodist General Scholarships *(Undergraduate, Graduate/Scholarship)*

Purpose: To provide financial support to those students who are pursuing their educational goals. **Focus:** General studies/Field of study not specified. **Qualif.:** Applicants must be undergraduate or graduate level students, with a minimum 1-year active membership in the UMC, and a minimum 2.5 GPA.

Funds Avail.: $500-$1,000 for undergraduate; 500-$2,000 for graduate students. **To Apply:** Application available online at www.gbhem.org/loans-scholarships/scholarships/list-of-scholarships/.

4896 ■ General Federation of Women's Clubs of Massachusetts (GFWC)

PO Box 679
Sudbury, MA 01776-0679
Ph: (978)443-1617
E-mail: gfwcma@aol.com
URL: www.gfwcma.org

4897 ■ Boston City Federation "Return to School" Scholarships *(Undergraduate, Graduate/Scholarship)*

Purpose: To support a woman returning to college after an absence of at least four years. **Focus:** General studies/Field of study not specified. **Qualif.:** Applicants must be women maintaining legal residence in Massachusetts and returning to college after an absence of at least four years.

Funds Avail.: $500. **Duration:** Annual. **Deadline:** February 1. **Contact:** All other inquiries may be directed to GFWC of Massachusetts 978-443-4569.

4898 ■ Catherine E. Philbin Scholarship *(Undergraduate, Graduate/Scholarship)*

Purpose: To support graduate or undergraduate students residing in Massachusetts and majoring in Public Health.

Awards are arranged alphabetically below their administering organizations

Focus: Public health. **Qualif.:** Applicants must be undergraduate or graduate students maintaining legal residence in Massachusetts and pursuing study in Public Health.

Funds Avail.: $500. **Duration:** Annual. **To Apply:** Applicants must submit a completed application together with a personal statement (maximum of 500 words) addressing professional goals and financial need; a letter of reference from the department chair (original on school letterhead); and official transcript of college grades; are required to submit the original and three additional copies of the application packet. **Deadline:** March 1. **Contact:** GFWC of MA Headquarters, Attention: Women's Italian Club of Boston Scholarship, PO Box 679, Sudbury, MA, 01776-0679; Email: gfwcma@aol.com.

4899 ■ Communication Disorder/Speech Therapy Scholarship *(Graduate/Scholarship)*

Purpose: To support students in their pursuit of communication disorder/speech therapy education. **Focus:** Speech and language pathology/Audiology. **Qualif.:** Applicants must be maintaining legal residences in Massachusetts.

Funds Avail.: Up to $500. **Duration:** Annual. **To Apply:** Applicants must submit a completed application form along with a personal statement (maximum of 500 words) addressing professional goals and financial need; a letter of reference from the department chair (original on school letterhead); and official transcript of college grades; applicants are required to submit the original and additional three copies of the application packet. **Deadline:** March 1. **Contact:** GFWC Massachusetts c/o Music Chairman, 245 Dutton Rd, P.O. Box 679, Sudbury, MA, 01776-0679.

4900 ■ Music Scholarship for Undergraduate in Voice *(Undergraduate/Scholarship)*

Purpose: To support undergraduate voice majors. **Focus:** Music, Vocal. **Qualif.:** Applicants must be Massachusetts residents and undergraduate students currently enrolled in a four-year accredited college, university or school of music, majoring in voice.

Funds Avail.: $500. **Duration:** Annual. **To Apply:** Applicants must submit a completed application form along with a personal statement (maximum of 500 words) addressing professional goals, financial need, experience and repertoire; letter of recommendation from college department head, major professor or voice instructor (original on college letterhead); and official transcript of college grades. **Deadline:** March 1. **Contact:** GFWC Massachusetts c/o Music Chairman, 245 Dutton Rd, P.O. Box 679, Sudbury, MA, 01776-0679.

4901 ■ Nickels for Notes Music Scholarship *(Undergraduate/Scholarship)*

Purpose: To support students majoring in Piano, Instrument, Music Education, Music Therapy or Voice. **Focus:** Education, Music; Music therapy; Music, Piano; Music, Vocal. **Qualif.:** Applicants must be senior students in a Massachusetts high school who will major in Piano, Instrument, Music Education, Music Therapy or Voice.

Funds Avail.: $500. **Duration:** Annual. **To Apply:** Applicants must submit a completed application form along with a personal statement (maximum of 500 words) addressing professional goals, experience and repertoire (if applicable) and financial need; a letter of recommendation from either High School Principal or Music Instructor (original, on school letterhead); and official transcript of

high school grades. **Deadline:** March 1. **Contact:** GFWC Massachusetts c/o Music Chairman, 245 Dutton Rd, P.O. Box 679, Sudbury, MA, 01776-0679.

4902 ■ Pennies for Art Scholarship *(Undergraduate/Scholarship)*

Purpose: To support talented students in their educational pursuits. **Focus:** Art. **Qualif.:** Applicant must be a senior in a Massachusetts high school, or home schooled, and have achieved the standards for graduation set by the town of residence.

Funds Avail.: Up to $500. **Duration:** Annual. **To Apply:** Applicants must submit a completed application form together with a personal statement (maximum of 500 words) addressing professional goals and financial need; a letter of recommendation from high school art instructor (original on school letterhead); official transcript of grades; and a portfolio of three examples of original artwork, matted, not framed, not larger than 12″ X 18″ overall dimension (printed name and address on the back of each example and on the portfolio). **Deadline:** March 1. **Contact:** GFWC Massachusetts c/o Music Chairman, 245 Dutton Rd, P.O. Box 679, Sudbury, MA, 01776-0679.

4903 ■ Women's Italian Club of Boston Scholarships *(Undergraduate/Scholarship)*

Purpose: To support students of Italian heritage in their educational pursuits. **Focus:** Music. **Qualif.:** Applicant must be a senior in a Massachusetts high school, or home schooled, and have achieved the standards for graduation set by the town of residence.

Funds Avail.: $1,000. **Duration:** Annual. **To Apply:** Applicants must submit a completed application form together with a personal statement addressing goals, Italian heritage and work experience; official transcript of high school grades; and two letters of recommendation from counselor or teachers (original on school letterhead); required to submit one original and two additional copies of the application packet. **Deadline:** March 1. **Contact:** GFWC of MA Headquarters, Attention: Women's Italian Club of Boston Scholarship, PO Box 679, Sudbury, MA, 01776-0679; Email: gfwcma@aol.com.

4904 ■ General Motors Foundation

300 Renaissance Ctr.
Detroit, MI 48265-3000
Free: 866-636-2273
E-mail: gmprioritycare@gm.com
URL: www.gm.com
Social Media: www.facebook.com/generalmotors
www.linkedin.com/company/general-motors
twitter.com/GM

4905 ■ Buick Achievers Scholarship Program *(Undergraduate/Scholarship)*

Purpose: To support students who demonstrate excellence in the classroom and communities to attend college. **Focus:** Business; Design; Engineering; Mathematics and mathematical sciences; Science; Technology. **Qualif.:** Applicants must be high school seniors or college undergraduate students who plan to enroll full-time and major in a specified course of study that focuses on engineering, technology, design or business at an accredited four-year college or university in the United States or Puerto Rico; must be US citizens and have a permanent residence in the United

Awards are arranged alphabetically below their administering organizations

States or Puerto Rico. **Criteria:** Scholarships will be awarded based on participation and leadership in community and school activities, interest in the automotive industry, academic achievement and financial need. Special consideration will be given to those who are first-generation college students, females, minorities, military veterans or dependents of military personnel.

Funds Avail.: $25,000. **Duration:** Annual. **To Apply:** Applicants must visit the website for the online application process or may contact Scholarship America for more information.

4906 ■ Genesee Finger Lakes Chapter of the Air and Waste Management Association (GFLAWMA)

PO Box 92006
Rochester, NY 14692
URL: gflawma.wildapricot.org

4907 ■ GFLC AWMA Scholarship Program
(Undergraduate, Graduate/Scholarship)

Purpose: To support and recognize R.I.T. environmental management students. **Focus:** Environmental science.

Funds Avail.: $1,000. **Duration:** Annual.

4908 ■ Geological Society of America (GSA)

3300 Penrose Pl.
Boulder, CO 80301-1806
URL: www.geosociety.org
Social Media: www.facebook.com/GSA.1888
www.instagram.com/geosociety
twitter.com/geosociety
www.youtube.com/geosociety

4909 ■ Farouk El-Baz Student Research Grants
(Graduate, Undergraduate, Doctorate, Master's/Grant)

Purpose: To encourage and support desert studies by students in their senior year of undergraduate studies, or at the Master's or Ph.D. level. **Focus:** Geology. **Qualif.:** Applicants must be GSA members in their senior year of their undergraduate studies, or at the Master's or Ph.D. level. **Criteria:** Applicants must be past graduate student research grant recipients.

Duration: Annual. **To Apply:** Applicants must submit a one-page description of proposed research under title; letter of recommendation by university research advisor. **Contact:** Program Manager, Research Grants, Geological Society of America, PO Box 9140, Boulder, CO, 80301-9140 USA Or Email: researchgrants@geosociety.org.

4910 ■ Geological Society of America Graduate Student Research Grants *(Doctorate, Graduate/Grant)*

Purpose: To Support graduate student research in the geosciences and ultimately enhance the geoscience workforce. **Focus:** Geology. **Qualif.:** Applicants must be GSA members currently enrolled in a North American or Central American university or college in an earth science degree program (with a geologic component). **Criteria:** Recipients will be selected based on the qualifications of the candidate and their academic standing.

Funds Avail.: $2,500. **Duration:** Annual. **Number Awarded:** Varies. **To Apply:** Applicants must fill out the online application form electronically. **Deadline:** February 3. **Contact:** Matt Dawson Geological Society of America

P.O. Box 9140 Boulder, CO 80301-9140 Phone: +1-303-357-1025 researchgrants@geosociety.org.

4911 ■ Georgelis Injury Law Firm, P.C.

2168 Embassy Dr.
Lancaster, PA 17603
Ph: (717)394-3004
Fax: (717)824-4970
E-mail: info@georgelislaw.com
URL: www.georgelislaw.com
Social Media: www.facebook.com/GeorgelisLawFirm
www.linkedin.com/company/georgelis-law-firm-p-c-
twitter.com/georgelislaw
www.youtube.com/channel/UCj_j9T3PGms2Pf8TFamkBbQ

4912 ■ Georgelis Injury Law Firm, P.C. Scholarship Award *(Graduate/Scholarship)*

Purpose: To help students with passion and vision gain a law education and support the need for moral, ethical, principled, and hard working attorneys. **Focus:** Law. **Qualif.:** Applicant must be enrolled in, or preparing to attend imminently, a law school within the United States for the upcoming academic term. **Criteria:** Essays will be evaluated and graded on the following criteria: feasibility; substance; uniqueness; perspective; creativity; insight; presentation; and spelling, grammar, and punctuation.

Funds Avail.: $1,500. **Duration:** Annual. **Number Awarded:** 1. **To Apply:** Applicant must submit essay; applicant should include the following in the body of the email: name, address, phone number, and school of enrollment, along with brief paragraph about self and career-related goals and ambitions; essays must be between 750 and 1000 words--no exceptions. **Deadline:** March 31. **Contact:** Email: info@GeorgelisLaw.com.

4913 ■ Georgetown University

37th & O St. NW
Washington, DC 20057
Ph: (202)687-0100
URL: georgetown.edu
Social Media: www.facebook.com/georgetownuniv
www.instagram.com/georgetownuniversity
www.linkedin.com/school/georgetown-university
twitter.com/georgetown
www.youtube.com/georgetownuniversity

4914 ■ ARIT Summer Fellowships for Intensive Advanced Turkish Language Study *(Graduate, Undergraduate/Fellowship)*

Purpose: To promote American and Turkish research and exchange related to Turkey. **Focus:** Foreign languages; General studies/Field of study not specified. **Qualif.:** Applicant must be a full-time students and scholars affiliated at academic institutions; must be citizen, national, or permanent resident of the United States; must currently enrolled in an undergraduate or graduate level academic program, or be faculty; must have minimum B average in current program of study; must perform at the high-intermediate level on a proficiency-based admissions examination.

Funds Avail.: No specific amount. **Duration:** Annual. **Number Awarded:** Approximately 18. **To Apply:** Applicants must submit complete application information; transcripts

Awards are arranged alphabetically below their administering organizations

and three letters of reference; application fee in the amount of $25. **Deadline:** 'February. **Contact:** Dr. Sylvia Önder, Director; Division of Eastern Mediterranean Languages Department of Arabic and Islamic Studies, Georgetown University; 210 North Poulton Hall, 1437 - 37th Street N.W., Washington, D.C. 20007; Email:aritfellowship@ georgetown.edu or aritoffice@gmail.com. `

4915 ■ Georgetown Working League (GWL)

PO Box 262
Georgetown, ME 04548
URL: georgetownworkingleague.org

4916 ■ Benjamin Riggs Scholarship *(Undergraduate/ Scholarship)*

Purpose: To provide financial assistance to students seeking higher education. **Focus:** General studies/Field of study not specified. **Qualif.:** Applicants must be students seeking higher education who reside in Georgetown, Maine; must have been accepted or wait-listed at an accredited school for further advances in education. **Criteria:** Selection will be based on the committee's criteria.

Funds Avail.: No specific amount. **Duration:** Annual; one year. **To Apply:** Applicants must submit complete application form from high school guidance counselor; copy of most recent transcript; computer generated essay; and copy of school or college acceptance letter or waitlist letter. **Deadline:** April 30. **Contact:** Georgetown Working League, Scholarship Committee, PO Box 262, Georgetown, ME, 04548.

4917 ■ Georgetown Working League Scholarship *(Undergraduate/Scholarship)*

Purpose: To provide financial assistance to students seeking higher education. **Focus:** General studies/Field of study not specified. **Qualif.:** Applicants must be students seeking higher education who reside in Georgetown, Maine; must have been accepted or wait-listed at an accredited school for further advances in education. **Criteria:** Selection will be based on the committee's criteria.

Funds Avail.: No specific amount. **Duration:** Annual; one year. **Number Awarded:** 1. **To Apply:** Applicants must submit complete application form from high school guidance counselor; copy of most recent transcript; computer generated essay; and copy of school or college acceptance letter or waitlist letter. **Deadline:** April 30. **Contact:** Georgetown Working League, Scholarship Committee, PO Box 262, Georgetown, ME, 04548.

4918 ■ Josephine Hooker Shain Scholarship *(Undergraduate/Scholarship)*

Purpose: To provide financial assistance to students seeking higher education. **Focus:** General studies/Field of study not specified. **Qualif.:** Applicants must be students seeking higher education who reside in Georgetown, Maine; must have been accepted or wait-listed at an accredited school for further advances in education. **Criteria:** Selection will be based on the committee's criteria.

Funds Avail.: No specific amount. **Duration:** Annual; one year. **To Apply:** Applicants must submit complete application form from high school guidance counselor; copy of most recent transcript; computer generated essay; and copy of school or college acceptance letter or waitlist letter. **Deadline:** April 30. **Contact:** Georgetown Working League, Scholarship Committee, PO Box 262, Georgetown, ME, 04548.

4919 ■ Riggs Cove Foundation Scholarship *(Undergraduate/Scholarship)*

Purpose: To provide financial assistance to students seeking higher education. **Focus:** General studies/Field of study not specified. **Qualif.:** Applicants must be students seeking higher education who reside in Georgetown, Maine; must have been accepted or wait-listed at an accredited school for further advances in education. **Criteria:** Selection will be based on the committee's criteria.

Funds Avail.: No specific amount. **Duration:** Annual; one year. **Number Awarded:** 1. **To Apply:** Applicants must submit complete application form from high school guidance counselor; copy of most recent transcript; computer generated essay; and copy of school or college acceptance letter or waitlist letter. **Deadline:** April 30. **Contact:** Georgetown Working League, Scholarship Committee, PO Box 262, Georgetown, ME, 04548.

4920 ■ Robinhood Marine Center Scholarship *(Undergraduate/Scholarship)*

Purpose: To provide financial assistance to students seeking higher education. **Focus:** General studies/Field of study not specified. **Qualif.:** Applicants must be students seeking higher education who reside in Georgetown, Maine; must have been accepted or wait-listed at an accredited school for further advances in education. **Criteria:** Selection will be based on the committee's criteria.

Funds Avail.: No specific amount. **Duration:** Annual; one year. **To Apply:** Applicants must submit complete application form from high school guidance counselor; copy of most recent transcript; computer generated essay; and copy of school or college acceptance letter or waitlist letter. **Deadline:** April 30. **Contact:** Georgetown Working League, Scholarship Committee, PO Box 262, Georgetown, ME, 04548.

4921 ■ Woodex Bearing Company Scholarship *(Undergraduate/Scholarship)*

Purpose: To provide financial assistance to students seeking higher education. **Focus:** General studies/Field of study not specified. **Qualif.:** Applicants must be students seeking higher education who reside in Georgetown, Maine; must have been accepted or wait-listed at an accredited school for further advances in education. **Criteria:** Selection will be based on the committee's criteria.

Funds Avail.: No specific amount. **Duration:** Annual; one year. **To Apply:** Applicants must submit complete application form from high school guidance counselor; copy of most recent transcript; computer generated essay; and copy of school or college acceptance letter or waitlist letter. **Deadline:** April 30. **Contact:** Georgetown Working League, Scholarship Committee, PO Box 262, Georgetown, ME, 04548.

4922 ■ Georgia Association of Broadcasters (GAB)

6 W Druid Hills Dr. NE, Ste. 330
Atlanta, GA 30329-2150
Ph: (770)395-7200
URL: gab.org
Social Media: www.facebook.com/GABroadcasters
www.linkedin.com/company/georgia-association-of
 -broadcasters
www.pinterest.com/pin/create/button
twitter.com/gabroadcasters

Awards are arranged alphabetically below their administering organizations

4923 ■ E. Lanier (Lanny) Finch Scholarship
(Undergraduate/Scholarship)

Purpose: To provide financial assistance to deserving students who will carry on the tradition of excellence in Georgia's broadcasting industry. **Focus:** Broadcasting. **Qualif.:** Applicant must be registered as a full-time student at a fully accredited college or university; a rising junior or senior studying for a degree in some aspect of the broadcasting industry and a bona fide resident of the state of Georgia. **Criteria:** Selection participating member stations will select the winning candidates; no one field within the broadcasting industry will receive preferential consideration; allowances will be made for varying levels of experience; judges will consider scholastic records, extracurricular activities, community involvement and leadership potential; there will be no discrimination on the basis of race, color, religion, national origin, sex or age.

Funds Avail.: $1,500. **Duration:** Annual. **To Apply:** Applicants form can be downloaded online; must complete the form, and attach additional sheets as necessary. **Remarks:** Established in 2005. **Contact:** Georgia Association of Broadcasters, Scholarship Committee, 6 W Druid Hills Dr. NE, Ste. 330, Atlanta, GA 30329; E-mail: admin@gab.org.

4924 ■ Georgia Association of Water Professionals (GAWP)
1655 Enterprise Way
Marietta, GA 30067
Ph: (770)618-8690
Fax: (770)618-8695
URL: www.gawp.org
Social Media: www.facebook.com/Gawp.org
twitter.com/tweet_gawp
www.youtube.com/channel/
  UCc8IGWDvgCQfx9KIO86g_dQ

4925 ■ GAWP Graduate Scholarships *(Graduate/Scholarship)*

Purpose: To provide financial assistance to Georgia Association of Water Professionals members and their children who want to pursue their education. **Focus:** General studies/Field of study not specified. **Qualif.:** Applicants must hold an active, individual membership in GAWP; must be graduates of an accredited college or university. **Criteria:** Applicants will be selected by the Scholarship committee based on their academic achievements.

Funds Avail.: $2,000. **To Apply:** Applicants must complete the application available in the website. **Remarks:** Established in 2003.

4926 ■ Philip R. Karr, III Scholarship Fund
(Graduate/Scholarship)

Purpose: To provide financial assistance to GAWP members and their children who want to pursue their education. **Focus:** General studies/Field of study not specified. **Qualif.:** Applicants must be residents of Georgia, who are entering or attending a college or university graduate school located in Georgia; must be graduates of an accredited college or university. **Criteria:** Applicants will be selected by the Scholarship committee based on their academic achievements.

Funds Avail.: $2,000. **Duration:** Annual; one year. **Number Awarded:** 1. **To Apply:** Applicants are required to submit a short essay (not to exceed 1,500 words); must complete the application available on the website. **Deadline:** February 28. **Remarks:** Established in 1996.

4927 ■ Georgia Engineering Foundation (GEF)
Harris Tower, Ste. 700
233 Peachtree St.
Atlanta, GA 30303
Ph: (404)521-2324
Fax: (404)521-0283
E-mail: info@gef.org
URL: www.gefinc.org

4928 ■ Georgia Engineering Foundation Scholarships *(Graduate/Scholarship)*

Purpose: To provide financial assistance to those students who are in need. **Focus:** Engineering. **Qualif.:** Applicants must be Georgia students who are preparing for a career in engineering or engineering technology; must be U.S citizens; must be enrolled in an engineering or engineering technology ABET-accredited program leading to a B.S or graduate degree. **Criteria:** Preference will be given to students who meet the criteria.

Funds Avail.: $1,000-$5,000. **Duration:** Annual. **Number Awarded:** Varies. **To Apply:** Applicants must submit a photo; this can be a casual photo in jpg format and can be electronically uploaded in the application; will be asked to bring a copy of their most recent official transcript with them to the interview. **Remarks:** Established in 1985. **Contact:** Scholarship Chair, Peyton Lingle; Email: scholarship-chair@gefinc.org.

4929 ■ Georgia Gerontology Society
PO Box 7905
Atlanta, GA 30357
Ph: (404)780-3380
E-mail: administrator@georgiagerontologysociety.org
URL: www.georgiagerontologysociety.org
Social Media: www.facebook.com/
  GeorgiaGerontologySociety
www.linkedin.com/company/georgiagerontologysociety
twitter.com/ggs30357
www.youtube.com/user/GaGerontologySociety

4930 ■ Virginia M. Smyth Scholarship *(Graduate/Scholarship)*

Purpose: To offer financial support to a person committed to embarking upon, or seeking to advance, a career in aging. **Focus:** Gerontology.

Funds Avail.: $3,000. **Duration:** Annual. **To Apply:** Applicants must submit 1-2 page essay that describes career goals and commitment to the field of Aging; current resume or curriculum vitae; statement of financial need (narrative, no more than 1 page); two letters of recommendation from professor or professional familiar with student's abilities/accomplishments/goals; official transcript from current college or university. **Remarks:** Established in 1998. **Contact:** PO Box, 7905, Atlanta, GA, 30357; Email: administrator@georgiagerontologysociety.org.

4931 ■ Georgia Library Association
PO Box 30324
Savannah, GA 31410
Social Media: twitter.com/glalibrary

Awards are arranged alphabetically below their administering organizations

4932 ■ GLA Beard Scholarship *(Master's/ Scholarship)*

Purpose: To provide financial assistance towards completing a Master's degree in library science for candidates who show strong potential to inspire and motivate their peers in the profession and in professional associations. **Focus:** Library and archival sciences. **Criteria:** Selection will be based on the application and supporting documents; residents of Georgia will be given preference, but not a requirement.

Funds Avail.: $1,500. **Duration:** Annual. **Number Awarded:** 1. **To Apply:** Applicants must complete the application form; must submit a proof of admission to an American Library Association-accredited Master's program, two letters of reference, official transcripts of all academic coursework and short essay stating the reasons why choosing to become a librarian and ultimate professional goals. **Deadline:** May 15. **Remarks:** The scholarship is made possible by friends and colleagues of the late Charles Edward Beard who served libraries and the library profession for almost 40 years with distinction and dedication. **Contact:** Email: glascholarships2020@gmail.com (for sending all documents, except transcripts), GLA Scholarship Committee Vice-Chair, c/o West Georgia Regional Library, 5329 Fayette Avenue Madison, WI 53713.

4933 ■ GLA Hubbard Scholarships *(Master's/ Scholarship)*

Purpose: To recruit excellent librarians for Georgia and provide financial assistance towards completing a Master's degree in library science. **Focus:** Library and archival sciences. **Criteria:** Selection will be based on the application and supporting documents; residents of Georgia will be given preference, but not a requirement.

Funds Avail.: $3,000. **Duration:** Annual. **Number Awarded:** 1. **To Apply:** Applicants must complete the application form; must submit a proof of admission to an American Library Association-accredited Master's program, two letters of reference, official transcripts of all academic coursework and short essay stating the reasons why choosing to become a librarian and ultimate professional goals. **Deadline:** May 15. **Remarks:** The scholarship is made possible by the family and friends of Mr. C. S. Hubbard, an early supporter of libraries in Georgia. **Contact:** Email: glascholarships2015@gmail.com.

4934 ■ Georgia Press Educational Foundation (GPEF)

3066 Mercer University Dr., Ste. 100
Atlanta, GA 30341-4137
Ph: (770)454-6776
Fax: (770)454-6778
E-mail: mail@gapress.org
URL: gapress.org/georgia-press-educational-foundation
Social Media: www.facebook.com/GAPressAssociation
twitter.com/gapressassoc

4935 ■ Durwood McAlister Scholarship *(Undergraduate/Scholarship)*

Purpose: To provide financial assistance for college students seeking journalism degrees in Georgia. **Focus:** Journalism; Publishing. **Qualif.:** Applicant must be an outstanding student, either a high school senior or a college undergraduate, majoring in print journalism at a Georgia college or university; parents of applicant must be legal residents of Georgia for two years or applicant must be resident of the state for three years; individual need must be established; and applicant should be recommended by a high school counselor, principal, college professor, and/or Georgia Press Association member. **Criteria:** Financial need, career plans, grades, interviews, journalism experience at school publications and recommendations of advisers, principals, teachers, counselors, or Georgia Press Association members are all factors in selection.

Funds Avail.: $1,500. **Duration:** Annual. **To Apply:** Scholarship application can be obtained from the GPEF website; the following documents must be enclosed in the application: most recent grade transcript; anticipated budget; school photograph; copy of SAT scores; parents'/applicant's tax return; and recommendations of high school counselor, principal, college professor, or Georgia Press Association member. **Deadline:** March 1. **Remarks:** The Scholarship is named in honor of Durwood McAlister, former editor of The Atlanta Journal. Established in 1992.

4936 ■ Morris Newspaper Corporation Scholarship *(Undergraduate/Scholarship)*

Purpose: To provide financial assistance for college students seeking journalism degrees in Georgia. **Focus:** Journalism; Publishing. **Qualif.:** Applicant must be an outstanding student, either a high school senior or a college undergraduate, majoring in print journalism at a Georgia college or university; parents of applicant must be legal residents of Georgia for two years or applicant must be resident of the state for three years; individual need must be established; and applicant should be recommended by a high school counselor, principal, college professor, and/or Georgia Press Association member. **Criteria:** Financial need, career plans, grades, interviews, journalism experience at school publications and recommendations of advisers, principals, teachers, counselors or Georgia Press Association members are all factors in selection.

Funds Avail.: $1,500. **Duration:** Annual. **To Apply:** Application details are available online at gapress.org/scholarships-internships/. **Deadline:** March 1. **Remarks:** The scholarship was established to honor Charles Morris. Established in 1987.

4937 ■ William C. Rogers Scholarship *(Undergraduate/Scholarship)*

Purpose: To assist Georgia residents attending Georgia colleges and universities who are pursuing careers in journalism and mass communication. **Focus:** Communications; Journalism; Media arts; Public affairs; Public relations. **Qualif.:** Applicant must be a student of the Grady College of Journalism and Mass Communication at the University of Georgia; parents of applicant must be legal residents of Georgia for two years or applicant must be resident of the state for three years; individual need must be established; and applicant should be recommended by a high school counselor, principal, college professor, and/or Georgia Press Association member. **Criteria:** Financial need, career plans, grades, interviews, journalism experience at school publications and recommendations of advisers, principals, teachers, counselors or Georgia Press Association members are all factors in selection.

Funds Avail.: $1,500. **Duration:** Annual. **To Apply:** Scholarship application can be obtained from the GPEF website; the following documents must be enclosed in the application: most recent grade transcript; anticipated budget;

Awards are arranged alphabetically below their administering organizations

school photograph; copy of SAT scores; parents'/applicant's tax return; and recommendations of high school counselor, principal, college professor, or Georgia Press Association member. **Deadline:** March 1. **Remarks:** The scholarship was established in memory of William Curran Rogers Sr., who was editor and publisher of the Swainsboro Forest-Blade for more than 30 years. Established in 1981.

4938 ■ Gerber Foundation
4747 W 48th St., Ste. 153
Fremont, MI 49412-8119
Ph: (231)924-3175
E-mail: tgf@gerberfoundation.org
URL: www.gerberfoundation.org

4939 ■ Daniel Gerber, Sr. Medallion Scholarship
(Undergraduate/Scholarship)

Purpose: To support graduating seniors from Newaygo County with the expenses of higher education. **Focus:** General studies/Field of study not specified. **Criteria:** Selection is made based on overall academic achievements, recommendations, leadership qualities, and involvement in diverse curricular, extracurricular, and community activities.

Funds Avail.: $10,600 (Over 4 years). **Duration:** Annual. **To Apply:** Applications must be completed through the online system. **Deadline:** February 28. **Remarks:** Established in 2002. **Contact:** The Gerber Foundation, 4747 W 48th S.t, Ste. 153, Fremont, MI, 49412; Phone: 231-924-3175; Email: tgf@gerberfoundation.org.

4940 ■ Gerber Foundation Merit Scholarship
(Graduate/Scholarship)

Purpose: To support graduating seniors from Newaygo and Muskegon Counties with the expenses of higher education. **Focus:** General studies/Field of study not specified. **Criteria:** Selection based on overall academic achievements, recommendations, and involvement in diverse curricular, extracurricular, and community activities.

Funds Avail.: $2,600. **Duration:** Annual. **To Apply:** Applications must be completed through the online system. **Deadline:** February 28. **Remarks:** Established in 1999. **Contact:** The Gerber Foundation, 4747 W 48th S.t, Ste. 153, Fremont, MI, 49412; Phone: 231-924-3175; Email: tgf@gerberfoundation.org.

4941 ■ German Historical Institute (GHI)
1607 New Hampshire Ave. NW
Washington, DC 20009-2562
Ph: (202)387-3355
Fax: (202)387-6437
E-mail: info@ghi-dc.org
URL: www.ghi-dc.org
Social Media: www.facebook.com/GHIWashington
www.instagram.com/ghi_washington
twitter.com/GHIWashington

4942 ■ German Historical Institute Doctoral and Postdoctoral Fellowships *(Doctorate, Postgraduate/ Fellowship)*

Purpose: To European and North American doctoral students as well as postdoctoral scholars to pursue research projects that draw upon primary sources located in the United States. **Focus:** German studies; History, American. **Qualif.:** Applicants must be German and

American doctoral students and post-doctoral scholars in the fields of German history, the history of German-American relations, historical role of Germany and the USA in international relations. **Criteria:** Scholarship recipients will be selected based on the jury's review of the application materials.

Funds Avail.: 2,000 Euros for doctoral students; 3,400 Euros for post-doctoral scholars. **Duration:** Annual. **To Apply:** Applicants send the following materials using the online application form or (as a pdf); must submit two copies of: cover letter; curriculum vitae; A copy of your most recent diploma or transcripts; Project description (no more than 2,000 words); Research schedule for the fellowship; At least one letter of reference. **Deadline:** April 1; October 1. **Contact:** For submission: Email: fellowships@ghi-dc.org; For question: Bryan Hart; Email: hart@ghi-dc.org.

4943 ■ German Historical Institute Fellowships at the Horner Library *(Postdoctorate, Master's/ Fellowship)*

Purpose: To provide travel subsidy and allowance to PhD and MA students for their research. **Focus:** General studies/Field of study not specified. **Qualif.:** Applicants must be PhD or MA students. **Criteria:** Scholarship recipient will be selected based on the selection committee's review of the application materials.

Funds Avail.: $1,000-$3,500. **Duration:** Up to four weeks. **Number Awarded:** 2-4. **To Apply:** Applicants must submit a (two-page) project description; curriculum vitae, copies of transcripts; and the name of the referee; applications (in English or German) should be made electronically to the GHI.; must submit a (two-page) project description; curriculum vitae, copies of transcripts; and the name of the referee; applications (in English or German) should be made electronically to the GHI. **Deadline:** March 1. **Contact:** For submission: Email: fellowships@ghi-dc.org; For question: Bryan Hart; Email: hart@ghi-dc.org.

4944 ■ German Marshall Fund of the United States (GMF)
1744 R St. NW
Washington, DC 20009
Ph: (202)683-2650
Fax: (202)265-1662
E-mail: dba@gmfus.org
URL: www.gmfus.org
Social Media: www.facebook.com/gmfus
www.instagram.com/german_marshall_fund
twitter.com/gmfus
www.youtube.com/user/GermanMarshallFund

4945 ■ APSA Congressional Fellowships *(Other/ Fellowship)*

Purpose: To expand public knowledge and awareness of the U.S. Congress around the world. **Focus:** Political science. **Criteria:** Selection will be based on applicants' commitment to transatlantic relations, quality of their written and oral presentation, preparation for the program, professional excellence and current and future involvement in the public policy in Germany.

Funds Avail.: No specific amount. **To Apply:** Applicants must submit the application form (available at the website); a curriculum vitae with accompanying cover letter; two fellowship-specific letters of reference; and an essay addressing the significance of the Congressional Fellowship

Awards are arranged alphabetically below their administering organizations

program for the applicants' future career and what value they would bring to a congressional office or committee. **Contact:** Ursula Soyez, Senior Program Officer; Email: usoyez@gmfus.org.

4946 ■ Marshall Memorial Fellowship *(Other/ Fellowship)*

Purpose: To provide a unique opportunity for emerging leaders from U.S. and Europe to explore policies, institutions and culture on the other side of the Atlantic. **Focus:** General studies/Field of study not specified. **Qualif.:** Applicants must be leaders from all professional backgrounds, including business, government, and civil society.

Funds Avail.: No specific amount. **Duration:** Annual. **Number Awarded:** 75. **To Apply:** Applicants must complete the online application, which currently includes an application form, essays, a resume/CV and two letters of recommendation; should also submit a letter of recommendation; upon submitting the applications to the selection partner, candidates will be further informed of the interview and selection process. **Deadline:** July 1. **Contact:** Email: leadershipprograms@gmfus.org.

4947 ■ Transatlantic Fellows Program *(Other/ Fellowship)*

Purpose: To develop a range of program and initiatives and build important networks of policymakers and analysts in the Euroatlantic community. **Focus:** General studies/ Field of study not specified. **Qualif.:** Applicants must be policy-practitioners, journalists, business people and academics. **Criteria:** Selection will be based on the committee's criteria.

Funds Avail.: No specific amount. **Duration:** Annual. **To Apply:** Applicants may contact GMF office for more information on the application process.

4948 ■ Urban and Regional Policy Fellowship *(Other/Fellowship)*

Purpose: To provide opportunities for practitioners and policy-makers working on economic and social issues at the urban and regional policy levels to meet with their counterparts across the Atlantic and discuss policies and measures that have been implemented. **Focus:** General studies/Field of study not specified. **Criteria:** Selection will be based on the committee's criteria.

Duration: Annual. **To Apply:** Applicants should see the program summary on the website for further details on the program and application process. **Contact:** Bartek Starodaj, program coordinator; Email: bstarodaj@gmfus.org.

4949 ■ Peter R. Weitz Prize *(Other/Prize)*

Purpose: To acknowledge excellence and originality in reporting European or transatlantic affairs in the American media. **Focus:** General studies/Field of study not specified. **Qualif.:** Must be journalists covering European issues for American newspapers, magazines and online media, whether they are correspondents based in Europe or cover Europe from the United States. **Criteria:** Selection will be made by a jury of senior American and European journalists based on work published either in print or online by American news media during the previous calendar year.

Funds Avail.: $10,000. **Duration:** Annual. **To Apply:** Applicants may contact the German Marshall Fund office for the application process. **Deadline:** March 15. **Remarks:** Established in 1999. **Contact:** For more information on the Peter R. Weitz Prize and other opportunities for journalists,

please contact Kristina Field at kfield@gmfus.org.

4950 ■ German Society of Pennsylvania (GSP)
611 Spring Garden St.
Philadelphia, PA 19123
Ph: (215)627-2332
Fax: (215)627-5297
E-mail: info@germansociety.org
URL: www.germansociety.org

4951 ■ German Society Scholarships *(Undergraduate/Scholarship)*

Purpose: To provide financial assistance for students majoring in German language and literature. **Focus:** Foreign languages; German studies. **Qualif.:** Applicants must be a resident of the greater Delaware valley and a high school senior intending to major in German, or a German major or minor at one of the colleges or universities (double majors are also eligible). **Criteria:** Selection is based on the student's achievement and promise; financial need may also be considered.

Funds Avail.: $2,500. **Duration:** Annual. **To Apply:** Applicants must submit a completed application form; a German writing sample (up to one typewritten page); recent transcript; and two letters of reference. **Deadline:** March 9. **Contact:** Scholarship Awards Committee German Society of Pennsylvania 611 Spring Garden Street Philadelphia, PA 19123 Tel.: 215-627-2332 FAX: 215-627-5297 info@germansociety.org.

4952 ■ Getty Foundation
1200 Getty Ctr. Dr.
Los Angeles, CA 90049
Ph: (310)440-7300
E-mail: communications@getty.edu
URL: www.getty.edu/foundation
Social Media: www.facebook.com/gettyfoundation
twitter.com/gettyfoundation

4953 ■ Getty Conservation Guest Scholars *(Professional development/Grant)*

Purpose: To provide an opportunity for professionals to pursue scholarly research in an interdisciplinary manner across traditional boundaries in areas of interest to the international conservation community. **Focus:** Conservation of natural resources. **Qualif.:** Applicants must be conservators, scientists or professionals who have attained distinction in conservation and allied fields; should have at least five years experience in the field of conservation and should have an established record of publications and other contributions to the field. **Criteria:** Selection is based on a competitive basis; they are reviewed by committee and evaluated by the conservation institute based on: past achievements; their qualifications to undertake the project; how the project would benefit from the resources at the Getty, including its library and collections; how the project would contribute to the advancement of practice in the conservation field.

Funds Avail.: $3,500 per month. **Duration:** Annual; three or six consecutive months. **To Apply:** Applicants are required to complete and submit the online Getty conservation guest scholar grant application form. **Contact:** Phone: 310-440-7374; Email: researchgrants@getty.edu.

4954 ■ Getty Foundation Library Research Grants *(Professional development/Grant)*

Purpose: To provide partial, short-term support for costs relating to travel and living expenses to scholars whose research requires use of specific collections housed in the Getty Research Institute; A Library Research Grant is not a prerequisite for obtaining access to the Research Library. **Focus:** Library and archival sciences. **Qualif.:** Applicants must be scholars of all nationalities and at any level who demonstrate a compelling need to use materials housed in the research library, and whose place of residence is more than eighty miles from the Getty center.

Funds Avail.: $800-$3,000. **Duration:** Annual; up to six weeks to two months . **To Apply:** Applicants will be required to complete and submit the online Getty library research grant application form which includes uploading a project proposal; curriculum vitae; selected bibliography of Getty research library collections you wish to consult; and proposed estimated travel costs; must have two confidential letters of recommendation forwarded by their recommenders via e-mail to the Getty foundation; recommenders should attach a scanned original letter to the e-mail or may provide the recommendation in the body of the email; in all cases, confidential come directly from the recommender's e-mail account and must clearly indicate the applicant's name and "library research grant" in the subject line, and include the recommender's name and title. **Deadline:** October 15. **Contact:** Phone: 310-440-7374; Email: researchgrants@getty.edu.

4955 ■ Getty GRI-NEH Postdoctoral Fellowships
(Postdoctorate/Fellowship)

Purpose: To support emerging scholars who are working on projects related to the Getty Research Institute's annual theme. **Focus:** General studies/Field of study not specified. **Qualif.:** Applications are welcome from scholars of all nationalities. **Criteria:** Selection is based on a competitive basis; they are reviewed by committee and evaluated by the conservation institute based on: the overall quality of the application; the proposed project bears upon the annual research theme; applicant's past achievements; and the project would benefit from the resources at the Getty, including its library and collections.

Duration: Annual. **To Apply:** Applicants are required to complete and submit the online fellowship application form, which includes completing an online information form and uploading a project proposal, doctoral dissertation plan or abstract, curriculum vitae, writing sample, selected bibliography and confirmation letter of academic status; are required to have two confidential recommendation letters forwarded by their recommenders via e-mail to the Getty foundation. **Deadline:** October 1. **Contact:** Phone: 310-440-7374; Email: researchgrants@getty.edu.

4956 ■ Getty Postdoctoral Fellowship in Conservation Science *(Postdoctorate/Fellowship)*

Purpose: To provide a unique two-year research and learning experience in the field of conservation science. **Focus:** Chemistry; Conservation of natural resources; Physical sciences.

Funds Avail.: No specific amount. **Duration:** Two-year.

4957 ■ Getty Postdoctoral Fellowships
(Postdoctorate/Fellowship)

Purpose: To support emerging scholars who are working on projects related to the Getty Research Institute's annual theme. **Focus:** General studies/Field of study not specified. **Qualif.:** Applications are welcome from scholars of all nationalities. **Criteria:** Selection is based on a competitive basis; they are reviewed by committee and evaluated by the conservation institute based on: the overall quality of

the application; the proposed project bears upon the annual research theme; applicant's past achievements; and the project would benefit from the resources at the Getty, including its library and collections.

Funds Avail.: $30,000. **Duration:** Annual; nine months. **To Apply:** Applicants are required to complete and submit the online fellowship application form, which includes completing an online information form and uploading a project proposal, doctoral dissertation plan or abstract, curriculum vitae, writing sample, selected bibliography and confirmation letter of academic status; are required to have two confidential recommendation letters forwarded by their recommenders via e-mail to the Getty foundation. **Deadline:** October 1. **Contact:** Phone: 310-440-7374; Email: researchgrants@getty.edu.

4958 ■ Getty Predoctoral Fellowships *(Doctorate/Fellowship)*

Purpose: To support emerging scholars who are working on projects related to the Getty Research Institute's annual theme. **Focus:** General studies/Field of study not specified. **Qualif.:** Applications are welcome from scholars of all nationalities. **Criteria:** Selection is based on a competitive basis; they are reviewed by committee and evaluated by the conservation institute based on: the overall quality of the application; the proposed project bears upon the annual research theme; applicant's past achievements; and the project would benefit from the resources at the Getty, including its library and collections.

Funds Avail.: $25,000. **Duration:** Annual; nine months. **To Apply:** Applicants are required to complete and submit the online fellowship application form, which includes completing an online information form and uploading a project proposal, doctoral dissertation plan or abstract, curriculum vitae, writing sample, selected bibliography and confirmation letter of academic status; are required to have two confidential recommendation letters forwarded by their recommenders via e-mail to the Getty foundation. **Deadline:** October 1. **Contact:** Pre - and Postdoctoral Fellowships; Phone: 310-440-7374; Email: researchgrants@getty.edu.

4959 ■ Getty Scholar Grants *(Professional development/Grant)*

Purpose: To support and encourage established scholars, or writers who have attained distinction in their fields. **Focus:** Art; Humanities; Social sciences. **Qualif.:** Applicants must be scholars, artists or writers who have attained distinction in their fields; are also accepted from researchers of all nationalities who are working in the arts, humanities or social sciences. **Criteria:** Selection is based on a competitive basis; they are reviewed by committee and evaluated by the conservation institute based on: past achievements; their qualifications to undertake the project; how the project would benefit from the resources at the Getty, including its library and collections; how the project would contribute to the advancement of practice in the conservation field.

Funds Avail.: $65,000. **Duration:** Annual; from 3 to 9 consecutive months. **To Apply:** Applicants are required to complete and submit the online Getty residential scholar application form which includes completing an online information sheet and uploading a project proposal, curriculum vitae and optional writing sample. **Deadline:** October 1. **Contact:** Getty Scholar Grants; Phone: 310-440-7374; Email: researchgrants@getty.edu.

Awards are arranged alphabetically below their administering organizations

4960 ▪ Gettysburg College - Eisenhower Institute

818 Connecticut Ave. NW, Ste. 400
Washington, DC 20006
Ph: (202)628-4444
E-mail: ei@gettysburg.edu
URL: www.eisenhowerinstitute.org
Social Media: www.facebook.com/EisenhowerInstitute
www.facebook.com/Gburg.College
instagram.com/eisenhowerinstitute
www.instagram.com/gettysburgcollege
www.linkedin.com/school/gettysburg-college
twitter.com/gettysburg
www.youtube.com/user/GettysburgCollege/featured

4961 ▪ The Dwight D. Eisenhower/Ann Cook Whitman Washington, D.C. Scholarship Program
(Undergraduate/Scholarship)

Purpose: To assist graduating African-American seniors from the District of Columbia public education system in obtaining an undergraduate degree in furtherance of their education and leadership skills. **Focus:** General studies/Field of study not specified. **Qualif.:** Applicant must be an African-American senior student from any of four eligible high schools (Spingarn, H.D. Woodson, Ballou, and Eastern) pursuing an undergraduate education; and have a 2.8 GPA or above (can be waived for applicants with strong needs or qualifications). **Criteria:** Selection is based on need and merit.

Funds Avail.: $4,000 each year for four years. **Duration:** Annual. **Number Awarded:** 2. **To Apply:** Applicants must submit a completed application form; academic transcript; a statement of career aspirations (maximum of 500 words); identification of colleges or universities applied to; a letter of recommendation from a faculty member or the guidance counselor; and another letter of recommendation from a member of the Washington, DC community, other than a family member. **Deadline:** April 13. **Contact:** Eisenhower Institute; Email: ei@gettysburg.edu.

4962 ▪ Conrad N. Hilton Scholarships
(Undergraduate/Scholarship)

Purpose: To help American students study abroad with strong international orientation to their studies. **Focus:** Business administration; Economics; Government; History; International affairs and relations. **Qualif.:** Applicant must be a Gettysburg College senior or junior undergraduate student planning to study abroad; have at least a 3.0 cumulative GPA (can be waived for applicants with strong needs or qualifications); and must be social science or interdisciplinary majors. **Criteria:** Selection is based on merit.

Funds Avail.: $2,750. **To Apply:** Applicants must submit an academic transcript; a resume; a statement of career aspirations (maximum of 1, 000 words); a letter of recommendation from the candidate's faculty advisor or department chair; and a copy of a (10-15 page) paper (within the last four months) from a course in the applicant's major field of study; submit it at Gettysburg College. **Deadline:** March 15. **Contact:** CGE E-mail: cge@gettysburg.edu, Phone No: 717-337-6866.

4963 ▪ Clifford Roberts Graduate Fellowships
(Doctorate/Fellowship)

Purpose: To support study and education dealing with the role of government in a free society, the relationship between international and domestic issues and improved understanding of world affairs. **Focus:** Public affairs. **Qualif.:** Applicants must be at an advanced stage of their doctoral candidacies, preferably preparing a dissertation. **Criteria:** Selection is based on merit; Institute will consider the applications of less advanced graduate students or persons who recently earned their PhD and pursuing the Institute's field of interest.

Funds Avail.: $10,000. **To Apply:** Applicants must submit a curriculum vitae; a statement describing the nature and scope of the dissertation; a 10- to 15-page writing sample on a topic related to the dissertation; a 1, 000-word statement of career aspirations; two letters of recommendation; and other required materials by the university; submit materials at the participating universities. **Deadline:** March 19. **Remarks:** The program is available only at the participating universities. **Contact:** Erika Butts, Ph No: 717-337-6685, Email: ei@gettysburg.edu.

4964 ▪ Ann Cook Whitman Scholarships for Perry High School *(Undergraduate/Scholarship)*

Purpose: To assist graduating seniors from Perry High School, Perry, Ohio, based on need and merit, in obtaining an undergraduate degree in furtherance of their education and leadership skills. **Focus:** General studies/Field of study not specified. **Qualif.:** Applicant must be a high school senior student at Perry High School planning to receive an undergraduate education; and have an average of B and above (can be waived for applicants with strong needs or qualifications). **Criteria:** Selection is based on need and merit.

Funds Avail.: $4,000 each year for four years. **Duration:** Annual. **Number Awarded:** 2. **To Apply:** Applicants must submit an academic transcript; a resume; a statement of career aspirations (maximum of 1, 000 words); a letter of recommendation from the candidate's faculty advisor or guidance counselor; another letter of recommendation from a member of the Perry, Ohio community other than a family member; and documentation from Perry High School on its needs-based assessment procedures for its nominees; submit materials at the Perry High School. **Deadline:** April 3. **Contact:** Application materials should be forwarded to David Wemer at dwemer@gettysburg.edu.

4965 ▪ Gibbons P.C.

One Gateway Ctr.
Newark, NJ 07102-5310
Ph: (973)596-4500
Fax: (973)596-0545
URL: www.gibbonslaw.com

4966 ▪ John J. Gibbons Fellowship in Public Interest & Constitutional Law *(Professional development/Fellowship)*

Purpose: To provide law students who wants to have a practical experience and training in the public sector. **Focus:** Law. **Qualif.:** Applicant must be a person of high academic achievement and professional accomplishment served as a judicial clerk or have been actively working in the field of public interest law. **Criteria:** Selection is based on the person of high academic achievement and professional accomplishment.

Funds Avail.: No specific amount. **Duration:** Annual. **Number Awarded:** 1. **To Apply:** Applicants must submit a completed application form together with a law school transcript; two letters of recommendation; resume; and a

---

Awards are arranged alphabetically below their administering organizations

writing sample. **Deadline:** March 2. **Contact:** For Submissions: Gibbons Fellowship Program, Gibbons P.C., 1 Gateway Ctr., Newark, New Jersey, 07102-5310.

4967 ■ GibsonSingleton VA Injury Attorneys

4073 George Washington Memorial Hwy.
Hayes, VA 23072
Free: 855-781-6777
URL: www.gibsonsingleton.com
Social Media: www.facebook.com/GibsonSingleton
www.instagram.com/gibsonsingletonlawyers
twitter.com/gsinjurylaw

4968 ■ Text=Wrecks Scholarship *(Graduate, College/Scholarship)*

Purpose: To help a student pay for college while also highlighting the dangers of texting and driving. **Focus:** General studies/Field of study not specified. **Qualif.:** Applicant must be a high school senior on track to graduate or a college student enrolled in an accredited four-year university or college, or currently enrolled in a two year college and planning to transfer to a four-year university or college upon completion; have maintained a 3.0 or higher GPA; and be a U.S. citizen or permanent residents (DACA recipients are welcome to apply).

Funds Avail.: $1,000. **Number Awarded:** 1. **To Apply:** Application and essay should be submitted online. **Deadline:** May 13. **Contact:** Scholarship Manager; Email: beth@gibsonsingleton.com; URL: www.gibsonsingleton.com/scholarship/.

4969 ■ Keith Gilmore Foundation (KGF)

5160 Skyline Way NE
Calgary, AB, Canada T2E 6V1
Free: 888-836-7242
E-mail: kgf@hereford.ca
URL: keithgilmorefoundation.com
Social Media: www.facebook.com/keithgilmorefoundation

4970 ■ Keith Gilmore Foundation - Diploma Scholarships *(Other/Scholarship)*

Purpose: To offer scholarship to those individuals who have their career leading to the field of agriculture. **Focus:** Agriculture, Economic aspects; Communications; Journalism. **Qualif.:** Applicants must be individuals enrolled in a recognized diploma program in agriculture, journalism and/or communications, leading to a career in the field of agriculture. **Criteria:** Selection of recipients is based on academic merit, contribution to school and/or community and indication of academic promise.

Number Awarded: 1,500 Canadian dollars. **To Apply:** Application forms are available online.

4971 ■ Keith Gilmore Foundation - Postgraduate Scholarships *(Postgraduate/Scholarship)*

Purpose: To provide support for the education of the aspiring students. **Focus:** Agriculture, Economic aspects; Communications; Journalism; Veterinary science and medicine. **Qualif.:** Applicants must be entered in senior undergraduate (entering the final year), veterinary, or post-graduate studies. A person may only receive this scholarship once. **Criteria:** Selection of recipients is based on academic merit, contribution to school and/or community and indication of academic promise.

Funds Avail.: $10,000. **Duration:** Annual. **Number Awarded:** Varies.

4972 ■ Keith Gilmore Foundation - Undergraduate Scholarships *(Undergraduate/Scholarship)*

Purpose: To provide educational support to students who are in need. **Focus:** Agriculture, Economic aspects; Communications; Journalism; Veterinary science and medicine. **Qualif.:** Applicant must be an individual enrolled in an undergraduate degree program in agriculture, veterinary medicine, journalism and/or communications at a recognized university, leading to a career in the field of agriculture. **Criteria:** Selection of recipients is based on academic merit, contribution to school and/or community and indication of academic promise.

Funds Avail.: $10,000. **Duration:** Annual. **Number Awarded:** Varies. **To Apply:** Application forms are available online at www.keithgilmorefoundation.com.

4973 ■ Girls Incorporated of the Greater Capital Region

962 Albany St.
Schenectady, NY 12307-1513
Ph: (518)374-9800
E-mail: info@gcr.girls-inc.org
URL: www.girlsinccapitalregion.org
Social Media: www.facebook.com/girlsinccapitalregion
instagram.com/GirlsIncGCR
twitter.com/GirlsIncGCR

4974 ■ Dorothea E. Allen Scholarship *(Undergraduate/Scholarship)*

Purpose: To assist current or former members of Girls Incorporated in enhancing their potentials and talents. **Focus:** General studies/Field of study not specified. **Qualif.:** Applicants must be current or former members of Girls Inc. of the Greater Capital Region; must be high school seniors; must possess an interest and/or talent that will benefit the community and the country. **Criteria:** Preference for applicants who have promise and potential in enhancing their talents.

Duration: Annual. **To Apply:** Applicant must submit the completed application form along with the following: two letters or recommendation; official transcript of high school records or GED scores; a clearly written essay describing the educational or training program in which the applicant wishes to participate. **Deadline:** April 6. **Contact:** URL: girlsinccapitalregion.org/about-us/scholarship-awards/.

4975 ■ William G. Broughton Fellowship for Outstanding Achievement *(Undergraduate, Graduate, Vocational/Occupational, Other/Fellowship)*

Purpose: To assist a present or former member of Girls Incorporated in pursuing study in any field in which she/he has a developing talent or ability. **Focus:** General studies/Field of study not specified. **Qualif.:** Applicants must be a current or former members of Girls Inc. of the Greater Capital Region; must possess an interest and/or talent which has exceptional potential that could be developed through additional training. **Criteria:** Selection based solely on merit and potential, not financial need, age, sex, race or other background factors.

Duration: Annual. **To Apply:** Applicant must submit completed application form along with the following: two

Awards are arranged alphabetically below their administering organizations

letters of recommendation; a transcript of high school records, GED scores, or college/university records; a clearly written description of the educational or training program in which the applicant wishes to participate. **Deadline:** April 6. **Contact:** URL: http://girlsinccapitalregion.org/about-us/scholarship-awards/.

4976 ■ Anna C. Hume Scholarship *(Undergraduate/Scholarship)*

Purpose: To help girls pay for higher education and supplement normal sources of financial aid. **Focus:** General studies/Field of study not specified. **Qualif.:** Applicants must be current or former members of Girls Inc. of the Greater Capital Region; must be high school seniors accepted at an accredited post-secondary institution; must demonstrate an academic record or experience that would indicate success in the chosen course of study (B average or higher). **Criteria:** Selection will be based on the committee's criteria.

Duration: Annual. **To Apply:** Applicant must submit completed application form along with the following: transcript of high school record or GED scores; personal letter clearly stating career goals and financial need; two letters or recommendation. **Deadline:** April 6. **Remarks:** The scholarship was established in memory of Anna C. Hume by members of the Hume family. **Contact:** URL: girlsinccapitalregion.org/about-us/scholarship-awards/.

4977 ■ GJEL Accident Attorneys

2 Theatre Square
Orinda, CA 94563
Ph: (866)218-3776
E-mail: lawfirm@gjel.com
URL: www.gjel.com
Social Media: www.facebook.com/GJELAttorneys
twitter.com/gjelblogger
www.youtube.com/user/GJELattorneys

4978 ■ Safe Teen Driver Scholarship *(Undergraduate, Vocational/Occupational, College/Scholarship)*

Purpose: To help students challenge themselves to become better drivers and/or better passengers. **Focus:** General studies/Field of study not specified. **Qualif.:** Applicants must be graduating high school seniors enrolling in the fall semester or currently enrolled students in a college, trade school, or university. **Criteria:** Selection will be based solely on the quality of writing and the applicant's eligibility.

Funds Avail.: $1,000. **Number Awarded:** 1. **To Apply:** Application and requirements available at www.gjel.com/scholarship. **Deadline:** December 31. **Contact:** Email: casey@gjel.com.

4979 ■ GLAAD

5455 Wilshire Blvd., Ste. 1500
Los Angeles, CA 90036-4204
Ph: (212)629-3322
Fax: (212)629-3225
E-mail: auction@glaad.org
URL: www.glaad.org
Social Media: www.facebook.com/GLAAD
instagram.com/glaad
twitter.com/glaad

4980 ■ Design and Multimedia Internships - New York *(Undergraduate, Graduate/Internship)*

Purpose: To promote understanding, increase acceptance, and advance equality. **Focus:** Media arts. **Qualif.:** Applicants must have the following qualifications: strong proficiency in the Adobe Suite; knowledge of design for web and print media; experience and/or enthusiasm in using visual media for social change; excellent verbal, written and visual communications skills; serious attention to detail; tech and Internet savvy; video editing experience is a plus; experience with HTML, CSS, and/or Drupal are a plus; be genuinely concerned and conversant about LGBTQ issues and have a passion and desire to make a difference. The ideal candidate would be someone who is passionate about LGBTQ, love info graphics, makes gifs for fun and has a strong interest in the intersection of good design and social good. All GLAAD interns are required to be students attending an institution with courses leading to a degree, certificate or diploma, such as college or graduate school. Interns must have graduated from high school. **Criteria:** Selection will be based on the committee's criteria.

Funds Avail.: No specific amount. **To Apply:** The following must be included in application: a brief cover letter outlining their interest and experience specific to the position; a current resume; the title of the position must appear in the first line of the email; an online portfolio of recent work demonstrating proficiency in graphic design across web and print media; one original and effective piece of visual content (optional) for distribution on GLAAD's social media channels that is related to an area of GLAAD's work or mission. **Deadline:** Varies. **Contact:** Human Resources at jobs@glaad.org.

4981 ■ Faith Initiatives Internships - New York *(Undergraduate, Graduate/Internship)*

Purpose: To promote understanding, increase acceptance, and advance equality. **Focus:** Journalism; Media arts. **Qualif.:** Applicants must have the following qualifications: an extremely positive attitude; demonstrated interest in advocacy work around LGBT and progressive issues; skills in communication or journalism; research and writing skills; interest in religion and LGBT issues; computer proficiency in word processing, database work, email and Internet research; ability to manage multiple tasks to meet deadlines and to be a self-starter; creative thinker who is able to work with people of diverse races, ages, ethnicities and sexual identities; willingness to learn, grow and be inspired to greatness. All GLAAD interns are required to be students attending an institution with courses leading to a degree, certificate or diploma, such as college or graduate school. Interns must have graduated from high school. **Criteria:** Selection will be based on the committee's criteria.

Funds Avail.: No specific amount. **To Apply:** The following must be included in application: a brief cover letter outlining their interest and experience specific to the position; a current resume. The title of the position must appear in the first line of the email. **Deadline:** Varies. **Contact:** jobs@glaad.org.

4982 ■ Foundation Relations Internships - Los Angeles *(Undergraduate, Graduate/Internship)*

Purpose: To promote understanding, increase acceptance, and advance equality. **Focus:** Media arts. **Qualif.:** Applicants must have the following qualifications: a self-starter and creative thinker with interest in foundation relations and grant writing; excellent written and verbal communication skills; ability to work in a fast paced environment, with limited supervision; computer proficient in word processing, email and Internet research; genuinely concerned and conversant about LGBT issues and have a passion and desire to make a difference; able to work collaboratively and effectively with people of diverse races, ages, ethnici-

Awards are arranged alphabetically below their administering organizations

ties and sexual identities; interest fundraising, media and LGBT issues; good organizational and time management skills. All GLAAD interns are required to be students attending an institution with courses leading to a degree, certificate or diploma, such as college or graduate school. Interns must have graduated from high school. **Criteria:** Selection will be based on the committee's criteria.

Funds Avail.: No specific amount. **To Apply:** Applicants must submit a brief cover letter outlining their interest and experience specific to the position and their current resume; the title of the position must appear in the first line of the email. **Contact:** jobs@glaad.org.

4983 ■ GLAAD Communications/PR Internships - New York *(Undergraduate, Graduate/Internship)*

Purpose: To promote understanding, increase acceptance, and advance equality. **Focus:** Communications; Public administration. **Qualif.:** The ideal candidate will have had previous internship experience or coursework related to public relations. The successful applicants will be: self-starter and creative thinkers with interest and experience in public relations; knowledgeable about LGBT media outlets and familiar with LGBT newspapers and blogs; successful and experienced in drafting media pitches, press releases, new articles and other communications materials; computer proficient in word processing, database work, email and Internet research; genuinely concerned and conversant about LGBT issues and have a passion and desire to make a difference; able to work collaboratively and effectively with people of diverse races, ages ethnicities and sexual identities. All GLAAD interns are required to be students attending an institution with courses leading to a degree, certificate or diploma, such as college or graduate school. Interns must have graduated from high school. **Criteria:** Selection will be based on the committee's criteria.

Funds Avail.: No specific amount. **Duration:** Annual. **To Apply:** Applicants must submit a brief cover letter outlining their interest and experience specific to the position and their current resume; the title of the position must appear in the first line of the email. **Contact:** E-mail: interns@ glaad.org.

4984 ■ GLAAD Spanish-Language and Latino Media Internships - Los Angeles *(Undergraduate, Graduate/Internship)*

Purpose: To provide equal employment opportunity to all employees and applicants for employment without regard to their race, color, religious creed, sex, gender identity, gender expression, age, national origin, ancestry, citizenship status, physical or mental disability, medical condition, pregnancy, marital or veteran status, sexual orientation, height and weight, or other personal characteristics as may be protected by applicable law. **Focus:** Communications; Journalism; Public relations. **Qualif.:** Candidates must be fluent in both English and Spanish. Fluent oral, verbal, reading and writing Spanish-language skills are a must; have a strong written and oral communication skills; have a professional demeanor and appearance; have a strong organizational skills, ability to manage multiple tasks to meet deadline, and desire to be a self-starter; have an ability to work under pressure; have an interest in Spanish language media and the desire to learn more about media outreach and media work in general. Skills necessary to create a more diverse and inclusive environment are a plus. All GLAAD interns are required to be students attending an institution with courses leading to a degree, certificate or diploma, such as college or graduate school. Interns must have graduated from high school. **Criteria:**

Selection will be based on the committee's criteria.

Funds Avail.: No specific amount. **Duration:** Annual. **To Apply:** Applicants must submit a brief cover letter outlining their interest and experience specific to the position and their current resume; the title of the position must appear in the first line of the email. **Contact:** interns@glaad.org.

4985 ■ GLAAD Youth Issues Internships - New York *(Undergraduate, Graduate/Internship)*

Purpose: To support those from LGBT community in acquiring knowledge related to youth issues. **Focus:** Communications; Journalism. **Qualif.:** Applicants should have a demonstrated interest in progressive communications, local and grassroots activism or advocacy work around issues of LGBT equality; have good written and oral communication skills; have an Internet research skills. Some experience and a working knowledge and understanding of the media and its history of covering trans issues are a plus. All GLAAD interns are required to be students attending an institution with courses leading to a degree, certificate or diploma, such as college or graduate school. Interns must have graduated from high school. **Criteria:** Selection will be based on the committee's criteria.

Funds Avail.: No specific amount. **Duration:** Annual. **To Apply:** Applicants must submit a brief cover letter outlining their interest and experience specific to the position and their current resume. The title of the position must appear in the first line of the email.

4986 ■ News and Rapid Response Internship *(Undergraduate, Graduate/Internship)*

Purpose: To provide equal employment opportunity to all employees and applicants for employment without regard to their race, color, religious creed, sex, gender identity, gender expression, age, national origin, ancestry, citizenship status, physical or mental disability, medical condition, pregnancy, marital or veteran status, sexual orientation, height and weight, or other personal characteristics as may be protected by applicable law. **Focus:** Media arts. **Qualif.:** Applicants must have the following qualifications: an extremely positive attitude; demonstrated interest in advocacy work around LGBT and progressive issues, progressive communications or journalism; exceptional research and writing skills; computer proficiency in word processing, database work, email and Internet research; strong oral communication skills; knowledge of, and commitment to, gay, lesbian, bisexual and transgender issues; the ability to work effectively with people of diverse races, ages, ethnicities and sexual identities; willingness to learn, grow and be inspired to greatness. All GLAAD interns are required to be students attending an institution with courses leading to a degree, certificate or diploma, such as college or graduate school. Interns must have graduated from high school. **Criteria:** Selection will be based on the committee's criteria.

Funds Avail.: No specific amount. **To Apply:** Applicants must submit a brief cover letter outlining their interest and experience specific to the position and their current resume; the title of the position must appear in the first line of the email. **Contact:** E-mail: interns@glaad.org.

4987 ■ Special Events Internship- New York *(Undergraduate, Graduate/Internship)*

Purpose: To provide students the opportunity to gain experience in event management and fundraising in a professional work environment. **Focus:** Media arts. **Qualif.:** Applicants must have the following qualifications interest in

Awards are arranged alphabetically below their administering organizations

fundraising, events, media and LGBT issues; good organizational and time management skills; willingness and ability to work well with others; knowledge of Microsoft Office; polished written and verbal communication skills; knowledge of and commitment to the LGBT community; ability to work in a fast paced environment; must be able and willing to pick up 40 lbs. All GLAAD interns are required to be students attending an institution with courses leading to a degree, certificate or diploma, such as college or graduate school. Interns must have graduated from high school. **Criteria:** Selection will be based on the committee's criteria.

Funds Avail.: No specific amount. **To Apply:** Applicants must submit a brief cover letter outlining their interest and experience specific to the position and their current resume. The title of the position must appear in the first line of the email. **Contact:** E-mail: interns@glaad.org.

4988 ■ Special Events Internships - Los Angeles
(Undergraduate, Graduate/Internship)

Purpose: To provide students the opportunity to gain experience in event management and fundraising in a professional work environment during a 12-week internship. **Focus:** Media arts. **Qualif.:** Applicants must have the following qualifications interest in fundraising, events, media and LGBT issues; good organizational and time management skills; willingness and ability to work well with others; knowledge of Microsoft Office; polished written and verbal communication skills; knowledge of and commitment to the LGBT community; ability to work in a fast paced environment; must be able and willing to pick up 40 lbs; all GLAAD interns are required to be students attending an institution with courses leading to a degree, certificate or diploma, such as college or graduate school; interns must have graduated from high school. **Criteria:** Selection will be based on the committee's criteria.

Funds Avail.: No specific amount. **To Apply:** Applicants must submit a brief cover letter outlining their interest and experience specific to the position and their current resume; the title of the position must appear in the first line of the email.**Contact:** E-mail: interns@glaad.org.

4989 ■ Sports Internships - Los Angeles
(Undergraduate, Graduate/Internship)

Purpose: To provide students the opportunity to engage with journalists and industry professionals in print, broadcast, radio and online outlets. **Focus:** Communications; Journalism. **Qualif.:** Applicants should have a demonstrated interest in both LGBT issues and professional and/or amateur sports, as well as interest in local and grassroots activism or advocacy work around issues of LGBT equality; have good written and oral communication skills; have Internet research skills. Some experience and a working knowledge and understanding of the sports media and its history of covering LGBT issues are a plus. All GLAAD interns are required to be students attending an institution with courses leading to a degree, certificate or diploma, such as college or graduate school. Interns must have graduated from high school. **Criteria:** Selection will be based on the committee's criteria.

Funds Avail.: No specific amount. **To Apply:** Applicants must submit a brief cover letter outlining their interest and experience specific to the position and their current resume. The title of the position must appear in the first line of the email.

4990 ■ Trans Issues Internships - New York
(Undergraduate, Graduate/Internship)

Purpose: To provide students the opportunity to engage with journalists in print, broadcast, radio and online outlets

to ensure fair, accurate and inclusive media coverage of the LGBT community. **Focus:** Communications; Journalism. **Qualif.:** Applicants should have a demonstrated interest in progressive communications, local and grassroots activism or advocacy work around issues of trans equality; have good written and oral communication skills; have an Internet research skills. Some experience and a working knowledge and understanding of the media and its history of covering trans issues are a plus. All GLAAD interns are required to be students attending an institution with courses leading to a degree, certificate or diploma, such as college or graduate school. Interns must have graduated from high school. **Criteria:** Selection will be based on the committee's criteria.

Funds Avail.: No specific amount. **To Apply:** Applicants must submit a brief cover letter outlining their interest and experience specific to the position and their current resume. The title of the position must appear in the first line of the email.

4991 ■ J. Robert Gladden Orthopaedic Society (JRGOS)
9400 W Higgins Rd., Ste. 500
Rosemont, IL 60018
Ph: (847)698-1633
E-mail: jrgos@aaos.org
URL: www.gladdensociety.org
Social Media: facebook.com/gladdensociety
instagram.com/gladdensociety
twitter.com/gladdensociety

4992 ■ J. Robert Gladden Orthopaedic Society PGY5 ABOS Board Preparation Scholarship *(Professional development/Scholarship)*

Purpose: To assist minority orthopedic residents in preparation for their certifying examinations. **Focus:** Medicine, Orthopedic. **Qualif.:** Applicant must be a JRGOS member; must be a PGY 5 resident in an accredited residency program; must be a member of an under represented minority as defined by the AAMC. **Criteria:** Selection is based on submission of documents.

Funds Avail.: No specific amount. **Duration:** Periodic. **Number Awarded:** Up to 10. **To Apply:** Applicants must submit an essay of 500 words of less that includes what this opportunity means to you/your career advancement and how your involvement in JRGOS will further its mission; may not receive any other funding to attend this course; must provide a letter of approval from Chief of Service. **Deadline:** January 15.

4993 ■ J. Robert Gladden Orthopaedic Society Traveling Fellowship Support *(Professional development/Fellowship)*

Purpose: To support the travel of young JRGOS practicing surgeons to visit institutions both within the United States and international in order to broaden their expertise within their fields and disseminate their research ideas through academic exchange. **Focus:** Medicine, Orthopedic. **Qualif.:** Applicants must be members of JRGOS in good standing with 2-3 years in practice. **Criteria:** Preference will be given to those applicants that elect to work with a Senior JRGOS member.

Funds Avail.: $2,000 to $5,000. **To Apply:** Applicants must submit completed application form, which includes: proposed visitation site address; duration of travel; proposal

Awards are arranged alphabetically below their administering organizations

including anticipated experience and enrichment potential; sponsor letter from responsible individual at visitation site and; applicants' CV. **Deadline:** January 20.

4994 ■ Glass Art Association of Canada (GAAC)

c/o Marcia DeVicque
9840 Porlier Pass
Galiano Island, BC, Canada V0N 1P0
E-mail: gaacanada@gmail.com
URL: gaacanada.ca
Social Media: www.facebook.com/GAACanada
instagram.com/GaaCanada

4995 ■ GAAC Project Grants *(Undergraduate, Professional development/Grant)*

Purpose: To support the development of a project that benefits the artist's studio practice and promotes excellence in Canadian Glass. **Focus:** Art. **Qualif.:** Applicants must be students currently enrolled in a glass program in Canada or abroad, or practicing professionals who are not currently attending college or university. **Criteria:** Selection will be based on the submitted project proposal.

Funds Avail.: 1,000 Canadian dollars (student); 1,500 Canadian dollars (professional). **Duration:** Annual. **To Apply:** Applicants must submitted their project proposal to Gabby Wilson via email along with their contact information, indicating whether they are students or professionals. Applicants' curriculum vitae, digital images with corresponding information, and biography should be uploaded at the GAAC Artist Directory. Project proposals should be 1-2 page detailed description of applicants' project and its benefits to their studio practice, including a budget outlining expenses, submitted as a Word document file, labeled lastname_firstname_proposal.doc. **Deadline:** June 11. **Contact:** Project proposal should be submitted to Gabby Wilson at gaac.submissions@gmail.com.

4996 ■ Gleaner Life Insurance Society (GLIS)

5200 W US Highway 223
Adrian, MI 49221
Ph: (517)265-7745
Fax: (517)265-7745
E-mail: gleaner@gleanerlife.org
URL: www.gleanerlife.org
Social Media: www.facebook.com/GleanerLife
www.linkedin.com/company/gleaner-life-insurance-society
twitter.com/GleanerLife

4997 ■ Gleaner Life Insurance Society Scholarship *(Graduate/Scholarship)*

Purpose: To strengthen the brotherhood; to help Gleaner family members pursuing their post-secondary education. **Focus:** General studies/Field of study not specified. **Qualif.:** Applicants must be member who graduating in senior or high school; must enroll as a full-time student taking 12 or more semester credit hours. A minimum grade point average of 2.5 is required for application. **Criteria:** Selection will be based on panel of judges based on score, academic record, leadership, quality of activities and community involvement, letters of recommendation, Explanation about financial need.
Funds Avail.: $2,250. **Number Awarded:** 1.

4998 ■ Glendale Latino Association (GLA)

PO Box 806
Verdugo City, CA 91046

E-mail: info@glendalelatinoassociation.com
URL: www.glendalelatinoassociation.com/about
Social Media: www.facebook.com/
GlendaleLatinoAssociation

4999 ■ Glendale Latino Association Scholarships *(Undergraduate/Scholarship)*

Purpose: To provide encouragement and financial support to Latino students pursuing higher education in colleges and universities. **Focus:** Aeronautics; Engineering; Mathematics and mathematical sciences; Photography; Physics; Science. **Qualif.:** Applicants must have Latino heritage and be graduating from a Glendale Unified School District public/private high school, Allan F. Daily Continuation High School, or Glendale Community College; applicant must be committed to attending a two or four year college/university or a career technical institution; applicants must have demonstrated educational excellence and extraordinary citizenship. **Criteria:** Special consideration will be given to students who have performed community service.

Funds Avail.: $500 - $2,000. **Duration:** Annual. **Number Awarded:** Varies. **To Apply:** Applicants must submit Letters of Recommendation; Personal Essay about Latino heritage, as well as the importance of education; Official Academic Transcripts; FSA Student Aid Reports (SAR); must submit proof of community service or Community Service Confirmation Form. Application form is available online at www.glendalelatinoassociation.com. **Deadline:** March 23. **Contact:** Community Foundation of the Verdugos, 111 East Broadway, Ste., 200, Glendale, CA, 91205.

5000 ■ Glens Falls Foundation

2 Progress Blvd.
Queensbury, NY 12804
Ph: (518)926-8372
E-mail: administrator@glensfallsfoundation.org
URL: www.glensfallsfoundation.org
Social Media: www.facebook.com/glensfallsfoundation
twitter.com/thegffoundation

5001 ■ Gilberto and Lennetta Pesquera Medical School Scholarships *(Graduate/Scholarship)*

Purpose: To assist qualified students who have graduated from local area schools and have successfully completed the first year of medical school. **Focus:** Education, Medical; Medicine. **Qualif.:** Applicant must have graduated from local area schools and have successfully completed the first year of medical school. **Criteria:** Selection will be based on the committee criteria.

Funds Avail.: $4,000. **Duration:** Annual. **Number Awarded:** 4. **To Apply:** Applicants should submit a completed application form; official medical school transcripts; brief personal statement describing applicant's academic and occupational goals, interests and activities; names, phone numbers and e-mail addresses of two personal references. **Deadline:** fourth Friday of June. **Contact:** Pesquera Scholarship Committee Chairman; Email: administrator@glensfallsfoundation.org.

5002 ■ Harry B. Pulver Scholarships *(Undergraduate/Scholarship)*

Purpose: To provide financial assistance to area students attending Dartmouth College or Harvard University. **Focus:** General studies/Field of study not specified. **Qualif.:** Applicants must be in their incoming freshmen college year;

Awards are arranged alphabetically below their administering organizations

must be residents of Warren, Washington, or Saratoga Counties in New York State; must have good moral character; good academic standing and financial need. **Criteria:** Selection will be based on submitted documents and specific criteria.

Funds Avail.: $8,000. **Duration:** Annual; maximum of four years. **To Apply:** Applicants must submit a completed application form; financial aid letter from Dartmouth College or Harvard University; copy of high school transcript including grades through the first semester of the senior year; complete list of extracurricular activities and volunteer work; at least two letters of recommendation; documentation that the applicants will be attending Dartmouth or Harvard; an essay on how the scholarship will assist the applicants in achieving undergraduate goals. **Deadline:** May 15. **Contact:** The Glens Falls Foundation, 2 Progress Blvd., Queensbury, NY, 12804; Phone: 518-926-8372.

5003 ■ Global Business Travel Association (GBTA)

1101 King St., Ste. 500
Alexandria, VA 22314
Ph: (703)684-0836
Fax: (703)783-8686
E-mail: info@gbta.org
URL: www.gbta.org
Social Media: www.facebook.com/GBTAonFB
www.linkedin.com/company/global-business-travel
　-association
twitter.com/GlobalBTA
www.youtube.com/user/GBTATV

5004 ■ Mike Kabo Global Scholarships *(Professional development/Scholarship)*

Purpose: To provide individuals with the opportunity to attend the two day Global Leadership Program (GLP) session and NBTA's International Convention and Exposition. **Focus:** Travel and tourism. **Qualif.:** Applicant must be a corporate travel professional from the buyer community; a resident outside of the United States of America; a member of NBTA or one of its Paragon Partner Members. **Criteria:** Recipients will be selected by the NBTA Foundation and the National Business Travel Association based on standard recipient review and selection procedures including: value of experience to corporate enterprise and travel management; educational background; responsibilities within company; potential growth; and industry involvement.

Funds Avail.: No specific amount. **Number Awarded:** 1. **To Apply:** Applicants must complete the form available at the website and must include an essay (500-1000 words) stating why they are interested in receiving this scholarship and how it would help their professional growth or bring value to the company. **Deadline:** June 15. **Contact:** Magda Halim; Phone: 703.236.1164; E-mail: mhalim@gbtafoundation.org.

5005 ■ Global Scholarship Alliance (GSA)

1700 Madison Road
Cincinnati, OH 45206
URL: globalscholarship.net

5006 ■ GSA Scholarships for International Nurses *(Undergraduate, Master's/Scholarship)*

Purpose: To support both local and international nursing students in further enhancement of their skills in the field of nursing. **Focus:** Nursing. **Criteria:** Selection will be based on the committee's criteria.

Funds Avail.: $500-$1,000. **To Apply:** Applicants must complete and return a Scholarship Agreement in which they agree to: meet GSA standards for selection; be admitted to a GSA approved University Partner; secure US nursing license and US visa; complete their education obligations; enroll, attend classes, maintain an adequate GPA, remain in good standing with the university, and graduate within a prescribed timeframe; maintain compliance with visa work restrictions and complete practical training and on-campus employment obligations; remain in visa status throughout the program period; repay the scholarship amount plus interest if they fail to fulfill their program obligations pursuant to the terms of their Scholarship Agreement; repay the Scholarship Amounts plus interest if they fail to complete their graduate program within the prescribed timeframe; begin fulfilling home service obligation according to visa requirements within thirty days of completing their graduate program and any subsequent practical training.Applicants can make appeal or request GSA offices in their country for seeking information about the program and for the processing of applications.

5007 ■ Global Sustainable Electricity Partnership (GSEP)

393 Saint-Jacques St., Ste 258
Montereal, QC, Canada H2Y 1N9
Ph: (514)392-8876
Fax: (514)392-8900
URL: www.globalelectricity.org
Social Media: www.linkedin.com/company/global
　-sustainable-electricity-partnership
twitter.com/GSEP_Official
www.youtube.com/user/globalelectricity

5008 ■ e8 Sustainable Energy Development Post-Doctoral Scholarship Programme *(Master's/Scholarship)*

Purpose: To support outstanding students pursuing advanced studies in sustainable energy development, and to promote the efficient generation and use of electricity. **Focus:** Energy-related areas. **Qualif.:** Applicants must be citizens of the developing country/territory on the List of official development aid recipients identified by the Development Co-operation Directorate (DAC) of the Organisation for Economic Co-operation and Development (OECD) and committed to returning to their home country/territory after their studies to contribute to its development; have Graduates with excellent grades in the top 20% of their class.

Funds Avail.: Up to $23,000. **Duration:** Biennial. **Number Awarded:** 10. **To Apply:** Applicants must provide an electronic copy of all the documents; Passport (photo page only) or birth certificate; Admission letter from your university program; a copy of your complete university transcript (s); Academic Reference Form must be completed by a faculty member or professor at your current or previous university who knows your academic abilities; need to provide one reference letter from either an academic or personal referee. **Deadline:** March 9.

5009 ■ Goddard Systems Inc.

555 Croton Rd., Ste. 300
King of Prussia, PA 19406
URL: www.goddardschoolfranchise.com

Awards are arranged alphabetically below their administering organizations

Social Media: facebook.com/Goddardsystemsinc
instagram.com/goddardsystemsinc
linkedin.com/company/goddard-systems-inc-
twitter.com/goddardsystems
youtube.com/user/GoddardSchool

5010 ■ The Anthony A. Martino Memorial Scholarship *(Undergraduate/Scholarship)*

Purpose: To provide scholarships for students who demonstrate the work ethic and perseverance that exemplified Martino's commitment to his career, family and community. **Focus:** General studies/Field of study not specified. **Qualif.:** Applicants must be graduates of a Goddard School pre-kindergarten or kindergarten program; must be high school seniors who are U.S. citizens, permanent residents or non-U.S. citizens living legally in the United States.

Funds Avail.: $10,000. **To Apply:** Applicants must provide one 30- to 120-second video addressing the question, "How did your Goddard School experience influence your career path or education?" Video essays should be saved to a USB drive or DVD and mailed with the completed application. The written essay and video submitted with each application must be the original work of the applicants and may not contain the work, including the intellectual property, of others, such as non-original music. Applicants must submit a transcript from all high schools attended and must indicate a cumulative GPA. **Deadline:** March 12. **Contact:** ATTN: Scholarship, Goddard Systems, Inc., 1016 W Ninth Ave., Ste. 140, King of Prussia, PA, 19406.

5011 ■ Godparents for Tanzania
PO Box 20221
Roanoke, VA 24018
Ph: (540)339-7770
E-mail: info@godparents4tz.org
URL: www.godparents4tz.org
Social Media: www.facebook.com/godparents4tz
www.instagram.com/godparents4tz
twitter.com/godparents4tz

5012 ■ Godparents for Tanzania Scholarship *(Undergraduate/Scholarship)*

Purpose: To provide financial assistance for projects that are intended to help educate young people in Tanzania. **Focus:** General studies/Field of study not specified. **Criteria:** Recipients will be selected based on multiple criteria including academic ability, family circumstances and financial need.

Funds Avail.: $1,000 each. **Duration:** Annual. **Number Awarded:** 50.

5013 ■ Goethe Society of North America (GSNA)
Bowdoin College, 7700 College Station
Brunswick, ME 04011-8477
Ph: (207)798-7079
Fax: (207)725-3348
E-mail: btautz@bowdoin.edu
URL: goethesociety.org

5014 ■ Gloria Flaherty Scholarship *(Graduate/Scholarship)*

Purpose: To provide financial aid to worthy graduate students who wish to further their education in areas related to the interests promoted by the society. **Focus:** General studies/Field of study not specified. **Qualif.:** Applicants must be graduate students working on Goethe and/or the Age of Goethe; must able to complete the research project before receiving a doctoral degree.

Funds Avail.: $500 plus a waiver of the conference fee. **Duration:** Annual. **To Apply:** Applicants should send their dissertation prospectus as email attachments and a separate attachment of recommendation letter from their dissertation advisers. **Remarks:** Established in 2008.

5015 ■ Golden Belt Community Foundation (GBCF)
1307 Williams St.
Great Bend, KS 67530
Ph: (620)792-3000
Fax: (620)792-7900
E-mail: gbcf@goldenbeltcf.org
URL: goldenbeltcf.org
Social Media: www.facebook.com/GoldenBeltCF
twitter.com/goldenbeltcf

5016 ■ Mingenback Family Scholarship Fund *(Undergraduate, Graduate/Scholarship)*

Purpose: To provide financial assistance to medical students with personal and professional commitment to the community. **Focus:** Education, Medical.

Funds Avail.: No specific amount. **To Apply:** Application must include college or law school transcript(s) and written personal statement. **Remarks:** The award was established in honor of Dr. John Mingenback, he was known, embodied the characteristics of a servant leader.

5017 ■ Golden Door Scholars
1423 Red Ventures Dr.
Fort Mill, SC 29707
E-mail: info@goldendoorscholars.org
URL: www.goldendoorscholars.org
Social Media: www.facebook.com/GoldenDoorScholars
www.instagram.com/goldendoorscholars
twitter.com/goldendoorschol

5018 ■ Golden Door Scholarship *(Graduate/Scholarship)*

Purpose: To support DACA students in paying for higher education. **Focus:** General studies/Field of study not specified. **Qualif.:** Applicant must be a DACA-eligible student studying for an undergraduate degree at a Golden Door partner school (applicants studying at non-partner schools will be considered on an individual basis). **Criteria:** Recipients will be academically successful students who are involved in extracurricular activities and have shown leadership qualities and determination despite the barriers their status presents.

Funds Avail.: Up to $30,000. **To Apply:** Application must be completed at www.goldendoorscholars.org/apply-now.

5019 ■ Golden Key International Honour Society (GKIHS)
1040 Crown Pointe Pky., Ste. 900
Atlanta, GA 30338
Ph: (678)689-2200

Awards are arranged alphabetically below their administering organizations

Fax: (678)689-2297
Free: 800-377-2401
E-mail: memberservices@goldenkey.org
URL: www.goldenkey.org

5020 ■ Boeing Business Scholarships
(Undergraduate/Scholarship)

Purpose: To financially assist students studying business. **Focus:** Business. **Qualif.:** Applicants must be U.S. undergraduate members currently enrolled in classes in a degree-granting program. **Criteria:** Selection will be based on academic achievement, and demonstrated leadership qualities.

Funds Avail.: $1,000. **Number Awarded:** 1. **To Apply:** Applicants must submit a letter of recommendation from a professor in the discipline; and a current, comprehensive official academic transcript.

5021 ■ GEICO Life Scholarship *(Undergraduate/Scholarship)*

Purpose: To support undergraduate student members for outstanding academic achievement while balancing additional commitments such as family or career. **Focus:** General studies/Field of study not specified.

Funds Avail.: $1,000.

5022 ■ Golden Key Advisor Professional Development Grant *(Professional development/Grant)*

Purpose: To support Golden Key chapter advisors in attending professional development conferences or in pursuing research within their academic disciplines. **Focus:** General studies/Field of study not specified.

Funds Avail.: $1,000. **Duration:** Annual.

5023 ■ Golden Key Graduate Scholar Award
(Graduate/Scholarship)

Purpose: To support a post-baccalaureate member studying at an accredited university anywhere in the world. **Focus:** General studies/Field of study not specified.

Funds Avail.: $10,000. **Duration:** Annual.

5024 ■ Goldia.com
PO Box 5557
New York, NY 10185
Ph: (212)840-6099
E-mail: service@goldia.com
URL: www.goldia.com
Social Media: www.facebook.com/goldiacom
www.pinterest.com/goldiacom
twitter.com/goldiacom

5025 ■ Goldia.com Jewelry Scholarships
(Undergraduate, Graduate/Scholarship)

Purpose: To offer a scholarship to students towards their academic costs for the current academic year. **Focus:** Gemology. **Qualif.:** Applicants must be residents of the United States, Brazil, India, South Korea, Australia, Japan, United Kingdom or Canada; must be currently enrolled full-time in college or an alumni. **Criteria:** Submitted materials will be judged based on punctuation, grammar, clarity and organization, and content.

Duration: Annual. **To Apply:** Applicants must visit the website to fill out a survey related to jewelry; must also answer one of the last three essay questions in the survey with 750 words or less.

5026 ■ Golf Canada
1333 Dorval Dr., Ste. 1
Oakville, ON, Canada L6M 4X7
Ph: (905)849-9700
Fax: (905)845-7040
Free: 800-263-0009
E-mail: info@golfcanada.ca
URL: golfcanada.ca
Social Media: www.facebook.com/TheGolfCanada
www.linkedin.com/company/golf-canada
twitter.com/TheGolfCanada

5027 ■ Suzanne Beauregard Scholarships
(Undergraduate, Graduate/Scholarship)

Purpose: To support young golfers who wish to pursue their studies. **Focus:** General studies/Field of study not specified. **Qualif.:** Applicants (Canadian citizen born or resident in the territory governed by Golf Quebec) must have completed at least one full year in a post-secondary degree program and show a minimum average of 70%; must be full-time students at a university, college or CEGEP; must demonstrate a record of athletic and academic excellence; must be members in good standing of Golf Quebec; must demonstrate regular participation in community and or extracurricular activities. **Criteria:** Candidates will be judged based on the information contained within their applications and support materials.

Funds Avail.: $2,000 each. **Duration:** Annual. **Number Awarded:** 2. **To Apply:** Application forms are available online and must be sent to Golf Canada Foundation. **Deadline:** June 30. **Remarks:** The scholarship was named in the honor of Suzanne Beauregard. **Contact:** E-mail: foundation@golfcanada.ca.

5028 ■ Canadian Seniors' Golf Association Scholarships *(Undergraduate/Scholarship)*

Purpose: To provide financial assistance to young Canadian men and women. **Focus:** Athletics; General studies/Field of study not specified. **Qualif.:** Applicants must be Canadian citizen or landed immigrant; a minimum average of 70% in the last two years of high school/CEGEP and have graduated (minimum Grade 12) or in graduate year of high school/CEGEP (and will graduate by June 2017); completed at least one full year in a post-secondary degree program and show a minimum average of 70% in EACH year of the program; experience in competitive golf at a regional, provincial or national level; accepted at a Golf Canada Foundation recognized college or university and have been named or will be named to the institution's golf team. **Criteria:** Selection will be based on the information contained in their applications and support materials.

Funds Avail.: $3,000. **Duration:** Annual. **Number Awarded:** 2. **To Apply:** Application form are available online and must be sent to Golf Canada Foundation. **Deadline:** June 30. **Contact:** Golf Canada Foundation, Ste. 1, 1333 Dorval Dr., Oakville, Ontario, L6M 4X7; Telephone: 905-849-9700, ext 275; Toll Free: 800-263-0009; Fax: 905-845-7040; E-mail: mbarnard@golfcanada.ca.

5029 ■ Entertainment Media Internships - Los Angeles *(Undergraduate, Graduate/Internship)*

Purpose: To promote understanding, increase acceptance, and advance equality. **Focus:** Media arts. **Qualif.:** Ap-

Awards are arranged alphabetically below their administering organizations

plicants must have the following qualifications: knowledge of entertainment industry and/or lesbian, gay, bisexual and transgender issues; strong written and oral communication skills and strong organizational skills; an ability to manage multiple tasks to meet deadlines and desire to be a self-starter; attention to detail and the ability to think creatively; computer proficiency in word processing, spreadsheets, database work, email and Internet research; ability to work collaboratively and effectively with people of diverse races, ages, ethnicities, orientations and gender identities. All GLAAD interns are required to be students attending an institution with courses leading to a degree, certificate or diploma, such as college or graduate school. Interns must have graduated from high school. **Criteria:** Selection will be based on the committee's criteria.

Funds Avail.: No specifc amount. **Duration:** Annual. **To Apply:** Applicants must submit a brief cover letter outlining their interest and experience specific to the position and their current resume; the title of the position must appear in the first line of the email. **Contact:** jobs@glaad.org.

5030 ■ Geordie Hilton Academic Scholarships
(Undergraduate/Scholarship)

Purpose: To assist a promising university student. **Focus:** Business administration; Sports studies. **Qualif.:** Applicants must be university students studying towards a degree in sport/business administration; must show a minimum average of 80% in the last two years of high school or CEGEP and have attained a graduation diploma (minimum Grade 12); must have completed at least one full year of education in a post-secondary degree program at a recognized institution; must intend to continue in an undergraduate or graduate program in sport/business administration; must have experience in competitive golf at a regional, provincial or national level; must have participated in community and/or extracurricular activities; must be Canadian citizens or landed immigrants. **Criteria:** Selection will be based on the information contained in their applications and support materials.

Funds Avail.: $5,000. **Number Awarded:** 1. **To Apply:** Application form are available online and must be sent to Golf Canada Foundation. **Deadline:** June 30. **Remarks:** Established in memory of Geordie Hilton by friends and family. **Contact:** Golf Canada Foundation, Ste. 1, 1333 Dorval Dr., Oakville, Ontario, L6M 4X7; Telephone: 905-849-9700, ext 275; Toll Free: 800-263-0009; Fax: 905-845-7040; E-mail: mbarnard@golfcanada.ca.

5031 ■ Golf Course Superintendents Association of America (GCSAA)
PO Box 13347
Lawrence, KS 66049-3859
Ph: (785)841-2240
Fax: (785)832-3643
Free: 800-472-7878
E-mail: mbrhelp@gcsaa.org
URL: www.gcsaa.org
Social Media: www.facebook.com/GCSAAFB
twitter.com/GCSAA

5032 ■ GCSAA Scholars Competition
(Undergraduate/Scholarship)

Purpose: To encourage students who wish to pursue a career in golf course management. **Focus:** Turfgrass management. **Qualif.:** Applicants must be undergraduate

students who are currently enrolled in two or more years of an accredited program related to golf course management; must have completed the first year (24 credit hours or equivalent); and must be GCSAA members. **Criteria:** Selection will be evaluated based on academic achievement, potential to become a leading professional, employment history, extracurricular activities, recommendation of a superintendent with whom students have worked with and a current academic advisor.

Funds Avail.: $500-$6,000. **Duration:** Annual. **Deadline:** June 1. **Contact:** Mischia Wright, associate director, development; Phone: 800-472-7878 ext. 4445; Email: mwright@gcsaa.org.

5033 ■ GCSAA Student Essay Contest *(Graduate, Undergraduate/Prize)*

Purpose: To provide assistance to students pursuing degrees in turfgrass science. **Focus:** Agricultural sciences; Turfgrass management. **Qualif.:** Applicants must be undergraduate and graduate students pursuing degrees in turfgrass science, agronomy, or any related fields to golf course management; and must be GCSAA members.

Funds Avail.: First prize is $2,000; second prize, $1,500; third prize, $1,000. **Duration:** Annual. **Number Awarded:** 3. **Deadline:** March 31. **Contact:** Mischia Wright, EIFG; Email: mwright@gcsaa.org.

5034 ■ Dr. James Watson Fellowship Program *(Doctorate, Graduate/Fellowship)*

Purpose: To provide financial assistance for the future educators and researchers of the turfgrass industry. **Focus:** Turfgrass management. **Qualif.:** Applicants must be candidates for masters' or doctoral degrees in fields related to golf course management. **Criteria:** Selection will be evaluated based on academic achievement, potential to become a leading professional, employment history, accomplishments in research and education, communication skills, peer recommendation.

Funds Avail.: $5,000. **Duration:** Annual. **Number Awarded:** 3. **To Apply:** Applicants must submit their transcript of records, advisor's report and superintendent's Report; the essay component must not exceed two double-spaced pages; additional application forms can be obtained from the environmental institute for golf or may visit the GCSAA website. **Deadline:** October 1. **Remarks:** Established in 1998. **Contact:** URL: www.gcsaa.org/education/scholarships; Mischia Wright, Email: mwright@gcsaa.org; Phone: 785-832-4445.

5035 ■ Golf Guides Zone
3003 Hickman St.
Burr Ridge, IL 60527
Ph: (630)419-7385
URL: www.golfguideszone.com
Social Media: www.instagram.com/golfguideszone
www.pinterest.com/golfguideszone
twitter.com/golfguideszone

5036 ■ Annual Golf Scholarship *(Graduate, Postgraduate/Scholarship)*

Purpose: To promote and motivate students to take part in golf. **Focus:** Sports studies. **Qualif.:** Applicants must be students who are studying in such graduate and postgraduate courses as sports science, international sports management, sports tourism, and other related courses. **Criteria:**

Awards are arranged alphabetically below their administering organizations

Persuasiveness, creative writing ability, impactful thoughts or logics, ability to express, and influential writing subject.

Funds Avail.: $1,000. **Duration:** Annual. **Number Awarded:** 1. **To Apply:** Write essay (1,000-1,500 words) on topics provided at www.golfguideszone.com/scholarship. Submit in PDF or DOC format, along with your personal information (including first and last name, phone number and Email address), school/college/university name, current study course, and copy of school ID. **Deadline:** March 20. **Contact:** www.golfguideszone.com/scholarship; E-mail: scholarship@golfguideszone.com.

5037 ■ Gonzaga University School of Law

721 N Cincinnati St.
Spokane, WA 99220-3528
Ph: (509)313-5790
Fax: (509)313-5744
URL: www.law.gonzaga.edu
Social Media: www.facebook.com/GonzagaLawSchool
www.instagram.com/gonzagalaw
twitter.com/GonzagaLaw

5038 ■ Thomas More Scholarship *(Undergraduate/Scholarship)*

Purpose: To help individuals in the pursuit of their educational goals. **Focus:** Law. **Qualif.:** Applicants must be entering a law school as first year students, and have a 3.5 GPA or higher and have taken the LSAT scores in the top quartile. **Criteria:** Recipients will be selected based on academic achievement, life, and work experience.

Funds Avail.: No specific amount. **Duration:** Annual. **Number Awarded:** 5. **To Apply:** Applicants must submit their completed application and two letters of recommendation. **Deadline:** April 15. **Remarks:** Established in 1980. **Contact:** Program Coordinator, Thomas More Scholarship Program, Gonzaga University School of Law, PO Box 3528, Spokane, WA, 99220-3528; Fax: 509-313-5840; Email: tmscholarship@lawschool.gonzaga.edu.

5039 ■ Goodman Acker P.C.

17000 W 10 Mile Rd., 2nd Fl.
Southfield, MI 48075
Ph: (248)793-2010
URL: www.goodmanacker.com
Social Media: www.facebook.com/GoodmanAckerPC
www.instagram.com/goodmanackerlawfirm
twitter.com/goodmanacker
www.youtube.com/user/goodmanacker

5040 ■ Goodman Acker Scholarships *(Graduate/Scholarship)*

Purpose: To assist students who are completing and pursuing their degree in law school. **Focus:** Law. **Qualif.:** Applicants must be students who are currently attending or have been accepted to an accredited law school in the United States; must be enrolled at an accredited 4-year university and have been accepted to a law school; must have academic achievement as reflected by a minimum 3.0 GPA; must be U.S. citizens. **Criteria:** Essays will be judged by a panel from Goodman Acker and associated parties. Submissions will be judged on academic achievement and essay submission.

Funds Avail.: $1,000. **To Apply:** Applicants must submit the following: complete online application form and essay;

certified official copy of law school transcript or undergraduate transcript; and if entering law school, copy of acceptance letter; essay must be no more than three pages long (double spaced, Time New Roman, size 12 font) answering one of the following essay topics: "As a victim, what are the top 10 things you should ask your personal injury lawyer?" and "how would the world be different if there were no personal injury lawyers?".

5041 ■ Goodwin Procter L.L.P.

100 N Ave.
Boston, MA 02210
Ph: (617)570-1000
Fax: (617)523-1231
URL: www.goodwinlaw.com
Social Media: www.facebook.com/JoinGoodwin
instagram.com/join_goodwin
www.linkedin.com/company/goodwin-law
twitter.com/goodwinlaw

5042 ■ 1L and 2L Diversity Fellowship Programs *(Undergraduate/Fellowship)*

Purpose: To help support students who plan to work in public interest law positions. **Focus:** Law. **Qualif.:** Applicants must be full-time, first or second-year law students from underrepresented backgrounds enrolled in ABA-accredited law schools. **Criteria:** Selection will be based on the committee's criteria.

Funds Avail.: $10,000 (1L students); $15,000 (2L students). **Duration:** Annual. **To Apply:** Application and details available online at www.goodwinlaw.com/careers/diversity-fellowships. **Contact:** Email: fellowships@goodwinprocter.com.

5043 ■ Google LLC

1600 Amphitheatre Pky.
Mountain View, CA 94043
Ph: (650)253-0000
Fax: (650)253-0001
URL: www.google.com
Social Media: www.facebook.com/Google
www.instagram.com/google
www.linkedin.com/company/google
twitter.com/google

5044 ■ AISES Oracle Academy Scholarship *(Graduate, Undergraduate/Scholarship)*

Purpose: To encourage and support the students pursuing degrees in Computer Science. **Focus:** Computer and information sciences; Engineering, Computer. **Qualif.:** Applicants must be currently pursuing a degree in Computer Engineering or Computer Science; must be full-time undergraduate student at an accredited college/university or graduate student; must have a 3.5 (on a 4.0 scale) or higher cumulative GPA; must be current AISES members. **Criteria:** Selection will be based upon factors such as academic performance (GPA and academic record), the student's personal essay (demonstrates character, commitment, goals), strength of recommendation letters, and other activities the student has undertaken including jobs, volunteer efforts, internships, extra-curricular activities etc.

Funds Avail.: $2,500 (for undergraduate students); $10,000 (for graduate students). **To Apply:** Applicants must

Awards are arranged alphabetically below their administering organizations

complete the OASIS general application and also include the following: resume; two letters of recommendation; essays. **Deadline:** March 31. **Contact:** Brianna Hall, Email: bhall@aises.org, Phone: 720-552-6123, Ext. 119.

5045 ■ China and East Asia Google PhD Fellowships (Doctorate/Fellowship)

Purpose: To recognize outstanding graduate students doing exceptional work in computer science, related disciplines, or promising research areas. **Focus:** Computer and information sciences. **Qualif.:** Applicants must be full-time graduate students pursuing a PhD; enrolled in a participating university and nominated by that university; completed graduate coursework by the Fall of the award year, when the Fellowship begins. **Criteria:** Selection will be based on the committee's criteria.

Funds Avail.: $10,000 US. **Duration:** 1 Year. **To Apply:** For each student nomination, the university will be asked to submit: name of fellowship for which student is being considered; student CV; transcript of current and previous academic records; research/dissertation proposal (recommended length 4-5 pages, no longer than 8); 2-3 letters of recommendation from those familiar with the nominee's work (at least one coming from the thesis advisor); short (1-page) CV of advisor. **Deadline:** May-June.

5046 ■ Google European Doctoral Fellowships (Doctorate/Fellowship)

Purpose: To provide educational support to students doing exceptional research in Computer Science or closely related areas. **Focus:** Computer and information sciences. **Qualif.:** Applicants must be full-time graduate students pursuing a PhD; enrolled in a participating university and nominated by that university; completed graduate coursework by the Fall of the award year, when the Fellowship begins. **Criteria:** Selection will be based on the committee's criteria.

Funds Avail.: No specific amount. **Duration:** 3 Year. **To Apply:** For each student nomination, the university will be asked to submit: name of fellowship for which student is being considered; student CV; transcript of current and previous academic records; research/dissertation proposal (recommended length 4-5 pages, no longer than 8); 2-3 letters of recommendation from those familiar with the nominee's work (at least one coming from the thesis advisor); short (1-page) CV of advisor. **Deadline:** November.

5047 ■ Google US/Canada PhD Fellowships (Graduate, Doctorate/Fellowship)

Purpose: To recognize outstanding graduate students doing exceptional work in computer science, related disciplines, or promising research areas. **Focus:** Computer and information sciences. **Qualif.:** Applicants must be full-time graduate students pursuing a PhD; enrolled in a participating university and nominated by that university; completed graduate coursework by the Fall of the award year, when the Fellowship begins. **Criteria:** Selection will be based on the committee's criteria.

Duration: 2 Year. **To Apply:** For each student nomination, the university will be asked to submit: name of fellowship for which student is being considered; student CV; transcript of current and previous academic records; research/dissertation proposal (recommended length 4-5 pages, no longer than 8); 2-3 letters of recommendation from those familiar with the nominee's work (at least one coming from the thesis advisor); short (1-page) CV of advisor. **Deadline:** November.

5048 ■ Women Techmakers Udacity Scholarship (Graduate, Undergraduate/Scholarship)

Purpose: To support and encourage women to excel in computing and technology and become active role models and leaders in the field. **Focus:** Computer and information sciences; Engineering, Computer. **Qualif.:** Applicants must identify as a woman; Have fluency or near-fluency in English; be at least 18 years of age at the time the application is submitted; commit to finishing the Nanodegree program within one year. **Criteria:** Selection will be based on the strength of each candidate's academic background and demonstrated leadership; essays will be evaluated by judges.

Funds Avail.: $10,000 (for students in the US); 5,000 Canadian Dollars (for students in Canada). **Duration:** Annual. **To Apply:** Applicants may apply online; must submit their general background information; current resume; academic transcripts from your current and prior institutions (if you have earned a prior degree); responses to four essay questions; two letters of reference from a professor, instructor, adviser or supervisor. **Deadline:** June 9. **Remarks:** The scholarship was established to honor Dr. Anita Borg. Established in 2004. **Contact:** Email: WTMScholars@google.com.

5049 ■ The Gordon Foundation
11 Church St., Ste. 400
Toronto, ON, Canada M5E 1W1
E-mail: info@gordonfn.org
URL: gordonfoundation.ca
Social Media: www.facebook.com/TheGordonFoundation
www.instagram.com/thegordonfoundation
www.linkedin.com/company/walter-and-duncan-gordon
 -foundation
twitter.com/TheGordonFdn
www.youtube.com/channel/
 UCuVsmOFcn9Stevm3bOQN_gQ

5050 ■ Jane Glassco Northern Fellowship (Professional development/Fellowship)

Purpose: To recognize the leadership potential among young northern Canadians eager to address policy challenges facing the North. **Focus:** Canadian studies.

Funds Avail.: $5,000. **Duration:** Annual. **To Apply:** Completed application package should include: completed Application form; copy of resume or curriculum Vitae; two (2) letters of reference (one from a community organization); proof of Canadian citizenship or permanent resident status. **Deadline:** October 1. **Remarks:** The Gordon Foundation honoured Jane by launching the Jane Glassco Northern Fellowship, to help link young northerners with support to build their own futures and amplify their voice on public policy issues. **Contact:** Selection Committee - Jane Glassco Northern Fellowship, The Gordon Foundation, 11 Church St., Ste. 400, Toronto, ON, M5E 1W1; Fax: 416-601-1689; Email: info@gordonfn.org.

5051 ■ Government Finance Officers Association of United States and Canada (GFOA)
203 N LaSalle St., Ste. 2700
Chicago, IL 60601-1210
Ph: (312)977-9700
Fax: (312)977-4806
URL: www.gfoa.org

Awards are arranged alphabetically below their administering organizations

Social Media: www.facebook.com/GFOAofUSandCanada
www.instagram.com/gfoa_
www.linkedin.com/company/gfoa
twitter.com/GFOA
www.youtube.com/channel/
    UC9WdpnRDXE6nzxzRbkkMFOA

5052 ■ Daniel B. Goldberg Scholarship (Graduate/ Scholarship, Recognition)

Purpose: To support outstanding performance in graduate programs by students preparing for a career in state and local government finance. **Focus:** Finance. **Qualif.:** Applicants must be current full-time students in a graduate program that prepares students for careers in state and local government finance and are expecting to be enrolled in the spring semester of the current year in a baccalaureate degree or its equivalent; be citizens or permanent residents of the United States or Canada; and have not been winners of scholarship program administered by the GFOA of the US and Canada. **Criteria:** Selection will be assessed on the basis of their plans to pursue a career in state or local government finance; past academic record and work experience; letters of recommendation from academic advisor; strength of coursework and demonstrated connection between coursework and career goals.

Funds Avail.: $15,000. **Duration:** Annual. **Number Awarded:** 1. **To Apply:** Applicants must submit completed application form; letter of recommendation. **Remarks:** Established in 1985.

5053 ■ Frank L. Greathouse Government Accounting Scholarship (Graduate, Undergraduate/Award, Scholarship)

Purpose: To recognize outstanding performance in accounting studies by students preparing for a career in state and local government finance. **Focus:** Finance. **Qualif.:** Applicants must be current full-time undergraduate or graduate students in an accounting program preparing for a career in state and local government finance (both advanced undergraduate and graduate students); be citizens or permanent residents of the United States or Canada; be recommended by the academic advisor or the accounting program chair; and, have not been past winners of a scholarship program administered by the Government Finance Officers Association of the US and Canada. **Criteria:** Selection will be assessed on the basis of their plans to pursue a career in state or local government finance; past academic record and work experience; letters of recommendation from academic advisor; strength of coursework and demonstrated connection between coursework and career goals.

Funds Avail.: $10,000. **Duration:** Annual. **Number Awarded:** 2. **To Apply:** Applicants must submit completed application form; letter of recommendation. **Remarks:** Established in 1985.

5054 ■ Minorities in Government Finance Scholarship (Graduate, Undergraduate/Scholarship)

Purpose: To recognize outstanding performance by minority students, and support them, in their preparation for careers in state and local government finance. **Focus:** Business administration; Economics; Finance; Political science; Public administration. **Qualif.:** Applicants must be current full- or part-time upper-division undergraduate or graduate students in public administration, accounting, finance, political science, economics or business administration (with a specific focus on government or nonprofit management); belong to one of the following groups (as defined by the U.S. Census Bureau): Black or African American, American Indian or Alaska Native, Asian, Native Hawaiian or other Pacific islander, Hispanic or Latino; be citizens or permanent residents of the United States or Canada; be recommended by academic advisor, the dean of the graduate program (graduate students) or department chair (undergraduate students); and be students who have not received scholarships administered by the Government Finance Officers Association of the United States and Canada. **Criteria:** Recipients will be selected on the basis of their: plan to pursue a career in state and local government finance; past academic record and work experience; strength of past coursework and present plan of study; and undergraduate and graduate grade point averages.

Funds Avail.: $9,000. **Duration:** Annual. **Number Awarded:** 1. **To Apply:** Applicants must submit the following: application form; statement of proposed state and local government finance career plan and if applicable, plan of graduate study; undergraduate and graduate grade transcripts; resume; and academic advisor's, department chair's or dean's letter of recommendation; and other letters of recommendation (optional).

5055 ■ Graduate Fellowships for Science, Technology, Engineering, and Mathematics Diversity (GFSD)

3716 S Hope St., Ste. 348
Los Angeles, CA 90007-4344
Ph: (213)821-2409
Fax: (213)821-6329
Free: 800-854-6772
E-mail: gfsd@stemfellowships.org
URL: stemfellowships.org

5056 ■ NPSC Fellowship (Graduate/Fellowship)

Purpose: To increase the number of American citizens with graduate degrees in the physical sciences and related engineering fields, emphasizing recruitment of a diverse applicant pool. **Focus:** Astronomy and astronomical sciences; Chemistry; Computer and information sciences; Engineering, Chemical; Engineering, Electrical; Engineering, Mechanical; Geology; Materials research/science; Physics. **Qualif.:** Applicants must be American citizens with one or two paid summer internships with a government agency; must establish a lasting relationship with the sponsor. **Criteria:** Selection shall be based on academic standing (GPA), undergraduate and graduate course work and grades, research experience at a university or the industry, letters of recommendation, and GRE general tests.

Funds Avail.: Amount varies. **Duration:** Annual; up to 6 years. **Number Awarded:** Varies. **To Apply:** Applicants must complete the application; letters of recommendation. **Remarks:** Established in 1989. **Contact:** Phone: 800-854-6772; Email: npsc@npsc.org.

5057 ■ Graduate Women in Science (GWIS)

PO Box 7
Mullica Hill, NJ 08062
E-mail: info@gwis.org
URL: www.gwis.org
Social Media: www.facebook.com/pg/GWISci
www.instagram.com/gwisci/

Awards are arranged alphabetically below their administering organizations

twitter.com/GWISci

5058 ■ Eloise Gerry Fellowships *(Graduate/ Fellowship)*

Purpose: To encourage research careers in the sciences for women. **Focus:** Science. **Qualif.:** Applicants must be enrolled as a graduate student, or engaged in post-doctoral or early-stage junior faculty academic research, and demonstrates financial need. **Criteria:** Selection is based on scientific merit, fields of study and requested funding amounts.

Funds Avail.: $10,000. **Duration:** Annual. **Number Awarded:** 2. **To Apply:** Applicants must submit a completed application form together with the abstract of the proposed project (maximum of 200 words, 12 point font, 0.75 in margins); a project proposal description; a proposed budget; two letters of recommendation (sent directly by the authors to fellowships applications@gwis.org, with the name of the applicants as the subject line); copies of animal/human subjects approval or collecting permits; an application process fee of $25. Entire application (except the recommendation letters and fee) must be sent electronically as a single, complete PDF document with "SDE/GWIS Application" an applicant's name in the subject line to fellowships applications@gwis.org. **Deadline:** January 10. **Contact:** GWIS Fellowships Coordinator at fellowships@gwis.org.

5059 ■ Nell I. Mondy Fellowships *(Graduate/ Fellowship)*

Purpose: To help increase knowledge in the fundamental sciences and to encourage research careers in the sciences by women. **Focus:** Science. **Qualif.:** Applicant must be enrolled as a graduate student, or engaged in post-doctoral or early-stage junior faculty academic research, and demonstrates financial need. **Criteria:** Selection is based on scientific merit, fields of study and requested funding amounts.

Duration: Annual. **Number Awarded:** 2. **To Apply:** Applicant must submit a completed application form together with the abstract of the proposed project (maximum of 200 words, 12 point font, 0.75 in margins); a project proposal description; a proposed budget; two letters of recommendation (sent directly by the authors with the name of the applicant as the subject line); copies of animal/human subjects approval or collecting permits; an application process fee of $25. Entire application (except the recommendation letters and fee) must be sent electronically as a single, complete PDF document with "SDE/GWIS Application" an applicant's name in the subject line. **Deadline:** January 10. **Contact:** GWIS Fellowships Coordinator at fellowships@gwis.org.

5060 ■ SDE Fellowship *(Graduate, Postgraduate/ Fellowship)*

Purpose: To increase knowledge in all the natural sciences, and to encourage research by women. **Focus:** Science. **Qualif.:** Awards will be made to women holding a degree from a recognized institution of higher learning, of outstanding ability and promise in research, who are performing hypothesis-driven research at any institution in the U.S. or abroad. Must be Graduate Women in Science members. Financial need of research funding is a requirement for the application. **Criteria:** Selection will be based on career level (e.g. graduate student vs. assistant professor) of the candidate.

Funds Avail.: Maximum of $10,000. **Duration:** Annual. **Number Awarded:** 1. **To Apply:** Application instructions

are available online. **Deadline:** January 10.

5061 ■ Sigma Delta Epsilon Fellowship (SDEF) *(Graduate/Fellowship)*

Purpose: To encourage research careers in the sciences for women. **Focus:** Science. **Qualif.:** Applicants must be enrolled as a graduate student, or engaged in post-doctoral or early-stage junior faculty academic research, and demonstrates financial need. **Criteria:** Selection is based on scientific merit, fields of study and requested funding amounts.

Duration: One year. **Number Awarded:** 2. **To Apply:** Applicants must submit a completed application form together with the abstract of the proposed project (maximum of 100 words, 12 point font, 0.75 in margins); a project proposal description; a proposed budget; two letters of recommendation (sent directly by the authors to fellowships applications@gwis.org, with the name of the applicants as the subject line); copies of animal/human subjects approval or collecting permits; an application process fee of $25. Entire application (except the recommendation letters and fee) must be sent electronically as a single, complete PDF document with "SDE/GWIS Application" an applicant's name in the subject line to fellowships applications@gwis.org. **Deadline:** January 10. **Contact:** GWIS Fellowships Coordinator at fellowships@gwis.org.

5062 ■ Vessa Notchev Fellowship (VNF) *(Graduate/ Fellowship)*

Purpose: To help increase knowledge in the fundamental sciences and to encourage research careers in the sciences by women. **Focus:** Science. **Qualif.:** Applicant must be enrolled as a graduate student, or engaged in post-doctoral or early-stage junior faculty academic research and demonstrates financial need. **Criteria:** Selection is based on scientific merit, fields of study and requested funding amounts.

Duration: Annual. **Number Awarded:** 2. **To Apply:** Applicant must submit a completed application from together with the abstract of the proposed project (maximum of 100 words, 12 point font, 0.75 in margins); a project proposal description; a proposed budget; two letters of recommendation (sent directly by the authors with the name of the applicant as the subject line); copies of animal/human subjects approval or collecting permits; an application process fee of $25. Entire application (except the recommendation letters and fee) must be sent electronically as a single, complete PDF document with "SDE/GWIS Application" and applicant's name in the subject line. **Deadline:** January 10. **Contact:** GWIS Fellowships Coordinator at fellowships@gwis.org.

5063 ■ Grain and Feed Association of Illinois (GFAI)

3521 Hollis Dr.
Springfield, IL 62711-9440
Ph: (217)787-2417
Fax: (217)787-8671
E-mail: info@gfai.org
URL: www.gfai.org
Social Media: www.facebook.com/GrainAndFeed
twitter.com/GrainAndFeed
www.youtube.com/channel/UCYYIxkA6k5KsIvXdwoX2Q4g

5064 ■ GFAI Industry Immersion Scholarship Program *(Undergraduate/Scholarship)*

Purpose: To provide financial assistance to students interested in pursuing a career in the grain and feed

Awards are arranged alphabetically below their administering organizations

industry, while also raising awareness of the many career opportunities that are available. **Focus:** Agricultural sciences. **Qualif.:** Resident of Illinois; a full-time freshman, sophomore or junior at an accredited college or university.

Funds Avail.: $3,500.00. **Number Awarded:** 1. **To Apply:** Visit www.gfai.org/scholarship-program.html for application and details; must be interested in a career in the grain handling or feed industries; submit a transcript and three (3) professional letters of recommendation from school adviser, faculty, employer. **Contact:** E-mail: jbrooks@gfai.org.

5065 ■ Grand Canyon Historical Society (GCHS)

PO Box 1667
Grand Canyon, AZ 86023
URL: www.grandcanyonhistory.org
Social Media: www.facebook.com/grandcanyonhistory

5066 ■ Grand Canyon Historical Society Scholarships *(Graduate/Scholarship)*

Purpose: To develop and promote appreciation, understanding and education of the earlier history of the inhabitants. **Focus:** Environmental conservation; Historic preservation; History. **Qualif.:** Applicant must be include any work that results in original research concerning historical individuals, events, sites, organizations, businesses or environmental issues in the Grand Canyon region.

Funds Avail.: $1,500. **To Apply:** Applicants must submit a research project concerning historical individuals and environmental issues in the Grand Canyon region; one-page application letter with a short biography that includes name, address, phone, number, undergraduate or graduate degrees, current degree program, department and advisor; and must submit a short paragraph describing how this award would be applied on the proposed project. **Contact:** Grand Canyon Historical Society Scholarship and Research Grant; c/o Margaret Hangan PO Box 1667 Grand Canyon, AZ 86023; Email: scholarships@grandcanyonhistory.org.

5067 ■ Grand Haven Area Community Foundation (GHACF)

1 S Harbor Dr.
Grand Haven, MI 49417
Ph: (616)842-6378
Fax: (616)842-9518
E-mail: info@ghacf.org
URL: www.ghacf.org
Social Media: www.facebook.com/
  grandhavenareacommunityfoundation
www.instagram.com/grand_haven_found
www.linkedin.com/company/grand-haven-area-community
  -foundation
www.pinterest.com/ghacf
twitter.com/ghacf

5068 ■ Barbara and Nicole Heacox Foreign Study & Travel Scholarship *(Undergraduate/Scholarship)*

Purpose: To improve and enhance the quality of life in the Tri-Cities area by serving as a leader, catalyst and resource for philanthropy; to strive for community improvement through strategic grantmaking in such fields as arts, education, health, environment, youth, social services and other human needs. **Focus:** General studies/Field of study not

specified. **Qualif.:** Applicant must be a northwest Ottawa County Tri-Cities Area high school student, or college student wanting to pursue educational or travel opportunities in foreign countries; financial need is a primary consideration. **Criteria:** Recipients are selected based on financial need; academic achievement; leadership ability; community and volunteer service; creativity; and special circumstances.

Funds Avail.: No specific amount. **Duration:** Annual. **To Apply:** Applicants must submit completed application form; current high school or college transcript; Student Aid Report (SAR) from the Free Application for Federal Student Aid (FAFSA) with EFC number, unless applying for scholarships that do not consider financial need; and letter of recommendation. Applicants must also provide a course description. **Deadline:** March 1. **Contact:** Grand Haven Area Community Foundation, Lauren Grevel, 1 S Harbor, Grand Haven, MI, 49417; Email: lgrevel@ghacf.org.

5069 ■ Bertha M. Fase Memorial Scholarship *(Undergraduate/Scholarship)*

Purpose: To provide scholarship assistance to a Grand Haven High School student. **Focus:** Education. **Qualif.:** Applicants must be Grand Haven High School graduating seniors with a 3.5 GPA or better; must plan to pursue studies in the field of Education. Applicants must demonstrate interest in youth through volunteer mentoring (for consideration); student who is a member of St. Paul's United Church of Christ will be given special consideration. **Criteria:** Recipients will be selected based on academic achievement; leadership ability; creativity; community and volunteer service; financial need; and special circumstances.

Funds Avail.: No specific amount. **Duration:** Annual. **To Apply:** Applicants must submit completed application form; current high school or college transcript; Student Aid Report (SAR) from the Free Application for Federal Student Aid (FAFSA) with EFC number, unless applying for scholarships that do not consider financial need; and letter of recommendation. **Deadline:** March 1. **Contact:** Grand Haven Area Community Foundation, Lauren Grevel, 1 S Harbor, Grand Haven, MI, 49417; Email: lgrevel@ghacf.org.

5070 ■ Charles (Charlie) A. Bassett Endowed Scholarship *(Undergraduate/Scholarship)*

Purpose: To improve and enhance the quality of life in the Tri-Cities area by serving as a leader, catalyst and resource for philanthropy; to strive for community improvement through strategic grantmaking in such fields as arts, education, health, environment, youth, social services and other human needs. **Focus:** General studies/Field of study not specified. **Qualif.:** Applicants must be graduating seniors from Spring Lake high school who have played on the tennis team. **Criteria:** Recipients will be selected based on positive thought, strong personal conviction and outstanding character; financial need is not a priority.

Funds Avail.: No specific amount. **Duration:** Annual. **To Apply:** Applicants must submit completed application form; current high school or college transcript; Student Aid Report (SAR) from the Free Application for Federal Student Aid (FAFSA) with EFC number, unless applying for scholarships that do not consider financial need; and letter of recommendation. **Deadline:** March 1. **Contact:** Grand Haven Area Community Foundation, Lauren Grevel, 1 S Harbor, Grand Haven, MI, 49417; Email: lgrevel@ghacf.org.

5071 ■ Charles and Eleanor Rycenga Education Scholarship *(Undergraduate/Scholarship)*

Purpose: To improve and enhance the quality of life in the Tri-Cities area by serving as a leader, catalyst and resource

Awards are arranged alphabetically below their administering organizations

for philanthropy; to strive for community improvement through strategic grantmaking in such fields as arts, education, health, environment, youth, social services and other human needs. **Focus:** General studies/Field of study not specified. **Qualif.:** Applicants must be graduating seniors of Grand Haven, Spring Lake or Western Michigan Christian high school; must have the desire to continue their education at an accredited four-year college, junior college, trade school or apprenticeship, preferably in Michigan. **Criteria:** Recipients are selected based on financial need.

Funds Avail.: No specific amount. **Duration:** Annual. **To Apply:** Applicants must submit completed application form; current high school or college transcript; Student Aid Report (SAR) from the Free Application for Federal Student Aid (FAFSA), unless applying for scholarships that do not consider financial need; and letter of recommendation. **Deadline:** March 1. **Contact:** Grand Haven Area Community Foundation, Lauren Grevel, 1 S Harbor, Grand Haven, MI, 49417; Email: lgrevel@ghacf.org.

5072 ■ Dake Community Manufacturing Scholarship
(Undergraduate/Scholarship)

Purpose: To provide encouragement and support to a student with an interest in manufacturing education. **Focus:** Manufacturing. **Qualif.:** Applicants must be current high school graduating seniors from Northwest Ottawa County, Muskegon County or Oceana County; must be high school graduating seniors, current college students or adult students; interested in career manufacturing education including: industrial, vocational, and technical training. **Criteria:** Recipients are selected based on financial need; academic achievement; leadership ability; creativity; community and volunteer service; and special circumstances.

Funds Avail.: No specific amount. **Duration:** Annual. **To Apply:** Applicants must submit: completed application form; current high school or college transcript; Student Aid Report (SAR) from the Free Application for Federal Student Aid (FAFSA), unless applying for scholarships that do not consider financial need; and letter of recommendation. **Deadline:** March 1. **Contact:** Grand Haven Area Community Foundation, Lauren Grevel, 1 S Harbor, Grand Haven, MI, 49417; Email: lgrevel@ghacf.org.

5073 ■ Daniel L. Reiss Memorial Scholarship
(Undergraduate/Scholarship)

Purpose: To improve and enhance the quality of life in the Tri-Cities area by serving as a leader, catalyst and resource for philanthropy; to strive for community improvement through strategic grantmaking in such fields as arts, education, health, environment, youth, social services and other human needs. **Focus:** General studies/Field of study not specified. **Qualif.:** Applicants must be graduating Grand Haven high school students who have at least a 3.8 GPA; must plan to pursue studies at Grand Valley State University or Western Michigan University in an Aeronautical Engineering or Political Science program study. **Criteria:** Recipients are selected based on demonstrated academic excellence and financial need.

Funds Avail.: No specific amount. **Duration:** Annual. **To Apply:** Applicants must submit completed application form; current high school or college transcript; Student Aid Report (SAR) from the Free Application for Federal Student Aid (FAFSA) with EFC number, unless applying for scholarships that do not consider financial need; and letter of recommendation. **Deadline:** March 1. **Contact:** Grand Haven Area Community Foundation, Lauren Grevel, 1 S Harbor, Grand Haven, MI, 49417; Email: lgrevel@ghacf.org.

5074 ■ David and Sharon Seaver Family Scholarship Fund in Memory of Timothy D. Seaver
(Undergraduate/Scholarship)

Purpose: To improve and enhance the quality of life in the Tri-Cities area by serving as a leader, catalyst and resource for philanthropy; to strive for community improvement through strategic grantmaking in such fields as arts, education, health, environment, youth, social services and other human needs. **Focus:** Business. **Qualif.:** Applicants must be graduating seniors of Grand Haven high school who plan to pursue a career in Business. **Criteria:** Recipients are selected based on financial need; creativity; community and volunteer service; leadership ability; and special circumstances.

Funds Avail.: No specific amount. **Duration:** Annual. **To Apply:** Applicants must submit: completed application form; current high school or college transcript; Student Aid Report (SAR) from the Free Application for Federal Student Aid (FAFSA), unless applying for scholarships that do not consider financial need; and letter of recommendation. **Deadline:** March 1. **Remarks:** The Scholarship was established in memory of Timothy D. Seaver. **Contact:** Grand Haven Area Community Foundation, Lauren Grevel, 1 S Harbor, Grand Haven, MI, 49417; Email: lgrevel@ghacf.org.

5075 ■ Erickson Education Scholarship
(Undergraduate/Scholarship)

Purpose: To improve and enhance the quality of life in the Tri-Cities area by serving as a leader, catalyst and resource for philanthropy; to strive for community improvement through strategic grantmaking in such fields as arts, education, health, environment, youth, social services and other human needs. **Focus:** Education. **Qualif.:** Applicants must be graduating seniors of Grand Haven or Spring Lake high schools who have excelled not only academically but who have also demonstrated leadership qualities and an outstanding record of community involvement; financial need is a consideration. **Criteria:** Recipients will be selected based on the following: financial need; academic achievement; leadership ability; creativity; community and volunteer service; and special circumstances.

Funds Avail.: No specific amount. **Duration:** Annual. **To Apply:** Applicants must submit completed application form; current high school or college transcript; Student Aid Report (SAR) from the Free Application for Federal Student Aid (FAFSA) with EFC number, unless applying for scholarships that do not consider financial need; and letter of recommendation. **Deadline:** March 1. **Contact:** Grand Haven Area Community Foundation, Lauren Grevel, 1 S Harbor, Grand Haven, MI, 49417; Email: lgrevel@ghacf.org.

5076 ■ Floto-Peel Family Scholarship Fund
(Undergraduate, Vocational/Occupational/Scholarship)

Purpose: To improve and enhance the quality of life in the Tri-Cities area by serving as a leader, catalyst and resource for philanthropy; to strive for community improvement through strategic grantmaking in such fields as arts, education, health, environment, youth, social services and other human needs. **Focus:** Business; Nursing. **Qualif.:** Applicants must be Tri-Cities area residents planning to attend a two-to-four year college, university or vocational school; must plan to study in the field of nursing or business; must have 2.5 GPA. **Criteria:** Recipients are selected based on financial need; academic achievement; leadership ability; community and volunteer service; creativity; and special circumstances.

Awards are arranged alphabetically below their administering organizations

Funds Avail.: No specific amount. **Duration:** Annual. **To Apply:** Applicants must submit completed application form; current high school or college transcript; Student Aid Report (SAR) from the Free Application for Federal Student Aid (FAFSA) with EFC number, unless applying for scholarships that do not consider financial need; and letter of recommendation. **Deadline:** March 1. **Contact:** Grand Haven Area Community Foundation, Lauren Grevel, 1 S Harbor, Grand Haven, MI, 49417; Email: lgrevel@ghacf.org.

5077 ■ John L. and Victory E. Frantz Scholarship
(Undergraduate/Scholarship)

Purpose: To improve and enhance the quality of life in the Tri-Cities area by serving as a leader, catalyst and resource for philanthropy; to strive for community improvement through strategic grantmaking in such fields as arts, education, health, environment, youth, social services and other human needs; to assist high school graduating seniors of northwest Ottawa County to pursue a college education. **Focus:** General studies/Field of study not specified. **Qualif.:** Applicants must be high school graduating seniors of northwest Ottawa County. **Criteria:** Recipients are selected based on demonstrated academic excellence and financial need.

Funds Avail.: No specific amount. **Duration:** Annual. **To Apply:** Applicants must submit completed application form; current high school or college transcript; Student Aid Report (SAR) from the Free Application for Federal Student Aid (FAFSA), unless applying for scholarships that do not consider financial need; and letter of recommendation. **Deadline:** March 1. **Contact:** Grand Haven Area Community Foundation, Lauren Grevel, 1 S Harbor, Grand Haven, MI, 49417; Email: lgrevel@ghacf.org.

5078 ■ Gauthier Family Scholarship Fund
(Undergraduate/Scholarship)

Purpose: To support students from the Tri-Cities area pursuing studies in Mechanical or Electrical Engineering. **Focus:** Engineering. **Qualif.:** Applicants must be high school students from the Tri-Cities area who wish to pursue studies in mechanical or electrical engineering at Michigan Technical Institute. **Criteria:** Recipients are selected based on demonstrated academic excellence and financial need.

Funds Avail.: No specific amount. **Duration:** Annual. **To Apply:** Applicants must submit completed application form; current high school or college transcript; Student Aid Report (SAR) from the Free Application for Federal Student Aid (FAFSA) with EFC number, unless applying for scholarships that do not consider financial need; and letter of recommendation. **Deadline:** March 1. **Contact:** Grand Haven Area Community Foundation, Lauren Grevel, 1 S Harbor, Grand Haven, MI, 49417; Email: lgrevel@ghacf.org.

5079 ■ Geri Coccodrilli Culinary Scholarship
(Undergraduate/Scholarship)

Purpose: To provide scholarship assistance to a Tri-Cities area students. **Focus:** Culinary arts. **Qualif.:** Applicants must be graduating high school seniors from the Tri-Cities area and Fruitport high school who wish to pursue studies in the Culinary Arts. **Criteria:** Recipients are selected based on leadership ability; community involvement; financial need; creativity; and academic achievement.

Funds Avail.: No specific amount. **Duration:** Annual. **To Apply:** Applicants must submit: completed application form; current high school or college transcript; Student Aid Report (SAR) from the Free Application for Federal Student Aid (FAFSA) with EFC number, unless applying for scholar-

ships that do not consider financial need; and letter of recommendation. **Deadline:** March 1. **Contact:** Grand Haven Area Community Foundation, Lauren Grevel, 1 S Harbor, Grand Haven, MI, 49417; Email: lgrevel@ghacf.org.

5080 ■ Grand Haven Offshore Challenge Scholarship
(Undergraduate/Scholarship)

Purpose: To improve and enhance the quality of life in the Tri-Cities area by serving as a leader, catalyst and resource for philanthropy; to strive for community improvement through strategic grantmaking in such fields as arts, education, health, environment, youth, social services and other human needs. **Focus:** Natural resources. **Qualif.:** Applicants must be graduating high school seniors from the Tri-Cities area who plan to pursue a career in natural resources such as fisheries, wildlife and environmental water quality at any public or private college or university. **Criteria:** Recipients are selected based on demonstrated academic excellence and financial need.

Funds Avail.: No specific amount. **Duration:** Annual. **To Apply:** Applicants must submit completed application form; current high school or college transcript; Student Aid Report (SAR) from the Free Application for Federal Student Aid (FAFSA) with EFC number, unless applying for scholarships that do not consider financial need; and letter of recommendation. **Deadline:** March 1. **Contact:** Grand Haven Area Community Foundation, Lauren Grevel, 1 S Harbor, Grand Haven, MI, 49417; Email: lgrevel@ghacf.org.

5081 ■ H. Wayne VanAgtmael Cosmetology Scholarship *(Undergraduate/Scholarship)*

Purpose: To improve and enhance the quality of life in the Tri-Cities area by serving as a leader, catalyst and resource for philanthropy; to strive for community improvement through strategic grantmaking in such fields as arts, education, health, environment, youth, social services and other human needs. **Focus:** Cosmetology. **Qualif.:** Applicants must be residing in Tri-Cities area; high school graduates; and planning to attend a certified cosmetology program at a Cosmetology School such as Aveda Institute, CHIC University of Cosmetology, French Academy of Cosmetology, or Booker Institute of Cosmetology. **Criteria:** Recipients are selected based on academic excellence and financial need.

Funds Avail.: No specific amount. **Duration:** Annual. **To Apply:** Applicants must submit: completed application form; current high school or college transcript; Student Aid Report (SAR) from the Free Application for Federal Student Aid (FAFSA), unless applying for scholarships that do not consider financial need; and letter of recommendation. **Deadline:** March 1. **Contact:** Grand Haven Area Community Foundation, Lauren Grevel, 1 S Harbor, Grand Haven, MI, 49417; Email: lgrevel@ghacf.org.

5082 ■ Harold and Eleanor Ringelberg Scholarship
(Undergraduate/Scholarship)

Purpose: To improve and enhance the quality of life in the Tri-Cities area by serving as a leader, catalyst and resource for philanthropy; to strive for community improvement through strategic grantmaking in such fields as arts, education, health, environment, youth, social services and other human needs. **Focus:** General studies/Field of study not specified. **Qualif.:** Applicants must be Grand Haven High School graduating seniors with a minimum 3.8 GPA; must plan to pursue a college degree at Michigan State University; must have attended Grand Haven Christian School prior to high school. **Criteria:** Recipients are selected based on academic achievement.

Awards are arranged alphabetically below their administering organizations

Funds Avail.: No specific amount. **Duration:** Annual. **To Apply:** Applicants must submit: completed application form; current high school or college transcript; Student Aid Report (SAR) from the Free Application for Federal Student Aid (FAFSA) with EFC number, unless applying for scholarships that do not consider financial need; and letter of recommendation. **Deadline:** March 1. **Contact:** Grand Haven Area Community Foundation, Lauren Grevel, 1 S Harbor, Grand Haven, MI, 49417; Email: lgrevel@ghacf.org.

5083 ■ Eileen Harrison Education Scholarships
(Graduate, Undergraduate/Scholarship)

Purpose: To provide financial assistance to students pursuing an undergraduate or graduate degree in education. **Focus:** Education. **Qualif.:** Applicants must be residents of Fort Atkinson area, graduates of Fort Atkinson high school or employees of Fort Atkinson School District; must be currently pursuing an undergraduate or graduate degree in Education (graduate students may be full or part-time students); must attend a four-year degree granting college or university; must obtain a GPA of 3.0 on a 4.0 scale; must be in good standing in undergraduate/graduate program. **Criteria:** Selection will be based on evaluation of submitted documents and specific criteria.

Funds Avail.: No specific amount. **Duration:** One year. **To Apply:** Applicants must submit a completed application form; an essay describing commitment to education; high school or college transcripts including undergraduate study and any graduate work completed to date; test scores; two recommendation letters. **Deadline:** February 15. **Contact:** Fort Atkinson Community Foundation, at the above address.

5084 ■ Hierholzer-Fojtik Scholarship *(Undergraduate/Scholarship)*

Purpose: To provide scholarship assistance to a Tri-Cities area students. **Focus:** Law. **Qualif.:** Applicants must be Grand Haven high school graduates planning to pursue law as a career. **Criteria:** Recipients are selected based on financial need; academic achievement; leadership ability; creativity; community and volunteer service; and special circumstances.

Funds Avail.: No specific amount. **Duration:** Annual. **To Apply:** Applicants must submit completed application form; current high school or college transcript; Student Aid Report (SAR) from the Free Application for Federal Student Aid (FAFSA) with EFC number, unless applying for scholarships that do not consider financial need; and letter of recommendation. **Deadline:** March 1. **Contact:** Grand Haven Area Community Foundation, Lauren Grevel, 1 S Harbor, Grand Haven, MI, 49417; Email: lgrevel@ghacf.org.

5085 ■ Hoffman Family Scholarship *(Undergraduate/Scholarship)*

Purpose: To improve and enhance the quality of life in the Tri-Cities area by serving as a leader, catalyst and resource for philanthropy; to strive for community improvement through strategic grantmaking in such fields as arts, education, health, environment, youth, social services and other human needs. **Focus:** General studies/Field of study not specified. **Qualif.:** Applicants must be graduating seniors of Grand Haven or Spring Lake high school who plan to pursue an education in the areas of environment or social services; academic grade point excellence is not required. **Criteria:** Recipients are selected based on demonstrated academic excellence and financial need.

Funds Avail.: No specific amount. **Duration:** Annual. **To Apply:** Applicants must submit completed application form;

current high school or college transcript; Student Aid Report (SAR) from the Free Application for Federal Student Aid (FAFSA), unless applying for scholarships that do not consider financial need; and letter of recommendation. **Deadline:** March 1. **Contact:** Grand Haven Area Community Foundation, Lauren Grevel, 1 S Harbor, Grand Haven, MI, 49417; Email: lgrevel@ghacf.org.

5086 ■ James W. Junior and Jane T. Brown Scholarship *(Undergraduate, Vocational/Occupational/Scholarship)*

Purpose: To assist men and women in the Tri-Cities in returning to school to further their education after a period of working. **Focus:** General studies/Field of study not specified. **Qualif.:** Applicants must be residents of Tri-Cities seeking to return to school to pursue their education after a period of working; must be over the age of 21 and have financial need. **Criteria:** Recipients are selected based on financial need; academic achievement; leadership ability; community and volunteer service; creativity; and special circumstances.

Funds Avail.: No specific amount. **Duration:** Annual. **To Apply:** Applicants must submit: completed application form; current high school or college transcript; Student Aid Report (SAR) from the Free Application for Federal Student Aid (FAFSA) with EFC number, unless applying for scholarships that do not consider financial need; and letter of recommendation. **Deadline:** March 1. **Contact:** Grand Haven Area Community Foundation, Lauren Grevel, 1 S Harbor, Grand Haven, MI, 49417; Email: lgrevel@ghacf.org.

5087 ■ Kevin Ernst Memorial Scholarship
(Undergraduate/Scholarship)

Purpose: To support students from the Tri-Cities area pursuing studies in the field of mathematics or accounting. **Focus:** Mathematics and mathematical sciences. **Qualif.:** Applicants must be students in the foundation's service area who wish to continue their education in the field of mathematics. **Criteria:** Recipients are selected based on financial need; academic achievement; leadership ability; creativity; community and volunteer service; and special circumstances.

Funds Avail.: No specific amount. **Duration:** Annual. **To Apply:** Applicants must submit completed application form; current high school or college transcript; Student Aid Report (SAR) from the Free Application for Federal Student Aid (FAFSA) with EFC number, unless applying for scholarships that do not consider financial need; and letter of recommendation. **Deadline:** March 1. **Contact:** Grand Haven Area Community Foundation, Lauren Grevel, 1 S Harbor, Grand Haven, MI, 49417; Email: lgrevel@ghacf.org.

5088 ■ Kyle R. Moreland Memorial Scholarship
(Undergraduate/Scholarship)

Purpose: To provide assistance to a Grand Haven High School graduating senior student. **Focus:** General studies/Field of study not specified. **Qualif.:** Applicants must be Grand Haven high school graduating seniors planning to attend a two or four-year college degree program; must be active in their Christian faith community; must have participated on high school golf or tennis team; must have a 3.0 GPA or above; scholarship is also open to current graduates of Spring Lake high school and/or Western Christian Michigan high school. **Criteria:** Recipients are selected based on academic performance.

Funds Avail.: No specific amount. **Duration:** Annual. **To Apply:** Applicants must submit completed application form;

Awards are arranged alphabetically below their administering organizations

current high school or college transcript; Student Aid Report (SAR) from the Free Application for Federal Student Aid (FAFSA) with EFC number, unless applying for scholarships that do not consider financial need; and letter of recommendation. **Deadline:** March 1. **Contact:** Grand Haven Area Community Foundation, Lauren Grevel, 1 S Harbor, Grand Haven, MI, 49417; Email: lgrevel@ghacf.org.

5089 ■ Paul J. Laninga Memorial Scholarship
(Undergraduate/Scholarship)

Purpose: To improve and enhance the quality of life in the Tri-Cities area by serving as a leader, catalyst and resource for philanthropy; to strive for community improvement through strategic grantmaking in such fields as arts, education, health, environment, youth, social services and other human needs. **Focus:** Accounting; Business. **Qualif.:** Applicants must be graduating high school seniors of Northwest Ottawa county who plan to attend a public university; must be pursuing education and long-term careers in the areas of business and/or accounting. **Criteria:** Recipients will be selected based on academic achievement; financial need; leadership ability; community and volunteer service; creativity; and special circumstances.

Funds Avail.: No specific amount. **Duration:** Annual. **To Apply:** Applicants must submit completed application form; current high school or college transcript; Student Aid Report (SAR) with EFC number from the Free Application for Federal Student Aid (FAFSA), unless applying for scholarships that do not consider financial need; and letter of recommendation. **Deadline:** March 1. **Contact:** Grand Haven Area Community Foundation, Lauren Grevel, 1 S Harbor, Grand Haven, MI, 49417; Email: lgrevel@ghacf.org.

5090 ■ Jack W. Leatherman Family Scholarship
(Undergraduate, Vocational/Occupational/Scholarship)

Purpose: To improve and enhance the quality of life in the Tri-Cities area by serving as a leader, catalyst and resource for philanthropy; to strive for community improvement through strategic grantmaking in such fields as arts, education, health, environment, youth, social services and other human needs. **Focus:** General studies/Field of study not specified. **Qualif.:** Applicants must be current Grand Haven high school seniors who are pursuing vocational or technology training and/or certification or plan to attend any 2- or 4-year accredited public college/university. **Criteria:** Recipients are selected based on financial need; preference shall be given to students who faced or overcame adversity in life. Strong motivation and desire to achieve will be considered in lieu of past academic performance.

Funds Avail.: No specific amount. **Duration:** Annual. **To Apply:** Applicants must submit: completed application form; current high school or college transcript; Student Aid Report (SAR) from the Free Application for Federal Student Aid (FAFSA), unless applying for scholarships that do not consider financial need; and letter of recommendation. **Deadline:** March 1. **Contact:** Grand Haven Area Community Foundation, Lauren Grevel, 1 S Harbor, Grand Haven, MI, 49417; Email: lgrevel@ghacf.org.

5091 ■ Leo Zupin Memorial Scholarship
(Undergraduate, Vocational/Occupational/Scholarship)

Purpose: To support students from Michigan accredited public college/university. **Focus:** Mathematics and mathematical sciences. **Qualif.:** Applicants must plan to attend any Michigan two-to-four year accredited public college, university, vocational or technology training and/or certification institution; must be students wishing to pursue a degree in mathematics. **Criteria:** Recipients are selected based on financial need, motivation, desire to achieve and academic performance; preference will be given to Applicants who have faced and overcome adversity in their lives.

Funds Avail.: No specific amount. **Duration:** Annual. **To Apply:** Applicants must submit completed application form; current high school or college transcript; Student Aid Report (SAR) from the Free Application for Federal Student Aid (FAFSA) with EFC number, unless applying for scholarships that do not consider financial need; and letter of recommendation. **Deadline:** March 1. **Contact:** Grand Haven Area Community Foundation, Lauren Grevel, 1 S Harbor, Grand Haven, MI, 49417; Email: lgrevel@ghacf.org.

5092 ■ Louise Wachter Wickham Scholarship
(Undergraduate/Scholarship)

Purpose: To assist local graduating high school seniors interested in obtaining a college degree in elementary education. **Focus:** Education. **Qualif.:** Applicants must be graduating high school seniors interested in obtaining a college degree in elementary education; must have a good (but not necessarily perfect) academic record. **Criteria:** Recipients are selected based on academic performance; financial need; leadership ability; creativity; community and volunteer service; and special circumstances.

Funds Avail.: No specific amount. **Duration:** Annual. **To Apply:** Applicants must submit completed application form; current high school or college transcript; Student Aid Report (SAR) from the Free Application for Federal Student Aid (FAFSA) with EFC number, unless applying for scholarships that do not consider financial need; and letter of recommendation. **Deadline:** March 1. **Contact:** Grand Haven Area Community Foundation, Lauren Grevel, 1 S Harbor, Grand Haven, MI, 49417; Email: lgrevel@ghacf.org.

5093 ■ Marion A. and Ruth K. Sherwood Business Scholarship *(Undergraduate/Scholarship)*

Purpose: To provide scholarship assistance to a Tri-Cities area High School student. **Focus:** Education. **Qualif.:** Applicants must be planning to pursue a career in the field of Education. **Criteria:** Recipients are selected based on academic excellence and financial need.

Funds Avail.: No specific amount. **Duration:** Annual. **To Apply:** Applicants must submit completed application form; current high school or college transcript; Student Aid Report (SAR) from the Free Application for Federal Student Aid (FAFSA) with EFC number, unless applying for scholarships that do not consider financial need; and letter of recommendation. **Deadline:** March 1. **Contact:** Grand Haven Area Community Foundation, Lauren Grevel, 1 S Harbor, Grand Haven, MI, 49417; Email: lgrevel@ghacf.org.

5094 ■ Marjorie M. Hendricks Environmental Education Scholarship *(Undergraduate/Scholarship)*

Purpose: To assist an upperclassman or graduate student majoring in environmental science field. **Focus:** Environmental science. **Qualif.:** Applicants must be Tri-Cities area residents or graduates of a Tri-Cities high school, attending a university and majoring in an environmental science course of study. **Criteria:** Recipients are selected based on financial need; first priority will be given to students attending GVSU or Aquinas College.

Funds Avail.: No specific amount. **Duration:** Annual. **To Apply:** Applicants must submit completed application form; current high school or college transcript; Student Aid Report (SAR) from the Free Application for Federal Student Aid

Awards are arranged alphabetically below their administering organizations

(FAFSA) with EFC number, unless applying for scholarships that do not consider financial need; and letter of recommendation. **Deadline:** March 1. **Contact:** Grand Haven Area Community Foundation, Lauren Grevel, 1 S Harbor, Grand Haven, MI, 49417; Email: lgrevel@ghacf.org.

5095 ■ Marvin R. and Pearl E. Patterson Family Scholarship *(Undergraduate/Scholarship)*

Purpose: To improve and enhance the quality of life in the Tri-Cities area by serving as a leader, catalyst and resource for philanthropy; to strive for community improvement through strategic grantmaking in such fields as arts, education, health, environment, youth, social services and other human needs. **Focus:** Art. **Qualif.:** Applicant must be a high school graduate of any Tri-Cities area public school or a non-traditional older student with established residency in the Tri-Cities area; first consideration will be to students studying graphic or fine arts; however consideration may be given to studies in environment, forestry or related fields. **Criteria:** Recipients will be selected based on academic achievement; leadership ability; community and volunteer service; creativity; and special circumstances.

Funds Avail.: No specific amount. **Duration:** Annual. **Deadline:** March 1. **Contact:** Grand Haven Area Community Foundation, Lauren Grevel, 1 S Harbor, Grand Haven, MI, 49417; Email: lgrevel@ghacf.org.

5096 ■ Michael Herman Scholarship *(Undergraduate, Vocational/Occupational/Scholarship)*

Purpose: To improve and enhance the quality of life in the Tri-Cities area by serving as a leader, catalyst and resource for philanthropy; to strive for community improvement through strategic grantmaking in such fields as arts, education, health, environment, youth, social services and other human needs. **Focus:** General studies/Field of study not specified. **Qualif.:** Applicants must be a current high school graduate of any Tri-Cities area; intending to pursue a degree or certification at any two- or four-year accredited college, university or vocational/technical school; middle-income families are encouraged to apply. **Criteria:** Recipients will be selected based on financial need; community and volunteer service; creativity; leadership ability; and special circumstances.

Funds Avail.: No specific amount. **Duration:** Annual. **To Apply:** Applicants must submit the following: a completed application form; current high school or college transcript; Student Aid Report (SAR) from the Free Application for Federal Student Aid (FAFSA), unless applying for scholarships that do not consider financial need; and letter of recommendation. **Deadline:** March 1. **Contact:** Grand Haven Area Community Foundation, Lauren Grevel, 1 S Harbor, Grand Haven, MI, 49417; Email: lgrevel@ghacf.org.

5097 ■ Miller G. Sherwood Family Scholarship *(Undergraduate/Scholarship)*

Purpose: To improve and enhance the quality of life in the Tri-Cities area by serving as a leader, catalyst and resource for philanthropy; to strive for community improvement through strategic grantmaking in such fields as arts, education, health, environment, youth, social services and other human needs. **Focus:** Environmental science. **Qualif.:** Applicants must be graduating seniors of Grand Haven or Spring Lake high school who plan to pursue an education in the areas of environment or social services; academic grade point excellence is not required. **Criteria:** Recipients are selected based on financial need; academic achievement; leadership ability; community and volunteer service;

creativity; and special circumstances.

Funds Avail.: No specific amount. **Duration:** Annual. **To Apply:** Applicants must submit completed application form; current high school or college transcript; Student Aid Report (SAR) from the Free Application for Federal Student Aid (FAFSA) with EFC number, unless applying for scholarships that do not consider financial need; and letter of recommendation. **Deadline:** March 1. **Contact:** Grand Haven Area Community Foundation, Lauren Grevel, 1 S Harbor, Grand Haven, MI, 49417; Email: lgrevel@ghacf.org.

5098 ■ Millicent Mary Schaffner Endowed Memorial Scholarship *(Undergraduate/Scholarship)*

Purpose: To improve and enhance the quality of life in the Tri-Cities area by serving as a leader, catalyst and resource for philanthropy; to strive for community improvement through strategic grantmaking in such fields as the arts, education, health, environment, youth, social services and other human needs. **Focus:** General studies/Field of study not specified. **Qualif.:** Applicants must be female students who have a strong motivation to continue their education at an accredited four-year college. **Criteria:** Recipients are selected based on financial need.

Funds Avail.: No specific amount. **Duration:** Annual. **To Apply:** Applicants must submit completed application form; current high school or college transcript; Student Aid Report (SAR) from the Free Application for Federal Student Aid (FAFSA), unless applying for scholarships that do not consider financial need; and letter of recommendation. **Deadline:** March 1. **Contact:** Grand Haven Area Community Foundation, Lauren Grevel, 1 S Harbor, Grand Haven, MI, 49417; Email: lgrevel@ghacf.org.

5099 ■ North Ottawa Hospital Auxiliary Scholarship *(Undergraduate/Scholarship)*

Purpose: To provide scholarship assistance to a Tri-Cities area students. **Focus:** Nursing. **Qualif.:** Applicants must be from the Tri-Cities area; currently enrolled as college students who have taken their core requirements and been accepted into their health-care related program of study. **Criteria:** Recipients are selected based on financial need, academic achievement, extracurricular activities, work history, educational goals and personal aspirations.

Funds Avail.: No specific amount. **Duration:** Annual. **To Apply:** Applicants must submit completed application form; current high school or college transcript; Student Aid Report (SAR) from the Free Application for Federal Student Aid (FAFSA) with EFC number, unless applying for scholarships that do not consider financial need; and letter of recommendation. **Deadline:** March 1. **Contact:** Grand Haven Area Community Foundation, Lauren Grevel, 1 S Harbor, Grand Haven, MI, 49417; Email: lgrevel@ghacf.org.

5100 ■ Pat and John MacTavish Scholarship *(Undergraduate/Scholarship)*

Purpose: To improve and enhance the quality of life in the Tri-Cities area by serving as a leader, catalyst and resource for philanthropy; to strive for community improvement through strategic grantmaking in such fields as arts, education, health, environment, youth, social services and other human needs. **Focus:** Science. **Qualif.:** Applicants must be high school or college students seeking to pursue any of the following areas of study: math, chemistry, geology, technical writing, physics or computer science. **Criteria:** Recipients are selected based on demonstrated academic excellence and financial need; preference to female students.

Awards are arranged alphabetically below their administering organizations

Funds Avail.: No specific amount. **Duration:** Annual. **To Apply:** Applicants must submit: completed application form; current high school or college transcript; Student Aid Report (SAR) from the Free Application for Federal Student Aid (FAFSA) with EFC number, unless applying for scholarships that do not consider financial need; and letter of recommendation. **Deadline:** March 1. **Contact:** Grand Haven Area Community Foundation, Lauren Grevel, 1 S Harbor, Grand Haven, MI, 49417; Email: lgrevel@ghacf.org.

5101 ■ P.E.O. Chapter DS Scholarship *(Undergraduate, Vocational/Occupational/Scholarship)*

Purpose: To improve and enhance the quality of life in the Tri-Cities area by serving as a leader, catalyst and resource for philanthropy; to strive for community improvement through strategic grantmaking in such fields as arts, education, health, environment, youth, social services and other human needs. **Focus:** General studies/Field of study not specified. **Qualif.:** Applicants must be graduating female students or non-traditional students who graduated from any Tri-Cities area public or private high school; must plan to pursue a degree or certification at any two or four-year accredited college, university, vocational or technical school; planning to attend Cottey College, the college owned and supported by P.E.O.; international will be given priority. **Criteria:** Recipients are selected based on academic performance.

Funds Avail.: No specific amount. **Duration:** Annual. **To Apply:** Applicants must submit: completed application form; current high school or college transcript; Student Aid Report (SAR) from the Free Application for Federal Student Aid (FAFSA) with EFC number, unless applying for scholarships that do not consider financial need; and letter of recommendation. **Deadline:** March 1. **Contact:** Grand Haven Area Community Foundation, Lauren Grevel, 1 S Harbor, Grand Haven, MI, 49417; Email: lgrevel@ghacf.org.

5102 ■ Jacob L. Reinecke Memorial Scholarship *(Undergraduate/Scholarship)*

Purpose: To provide scholarship assistance to a Grand Haven High School student. **Focus:** General studies/Field of study not specified. **Qualif.:** Applicants must be Grand Haven high school graduating seniors planning to attend a two-to-four year college, university or trade school; consideration will be given to male students who participated in high school athletics, specifically basketball or baseball; must have a 3.0 GPA or above. **Criteria:** Recipients are selected based on hard-working attitude and strong motivation to succeed.

Funds Avail.: No specific amount. **Duration:** Annual. **To Apply:** Applicants must submit completed application form; current high school or college transcript; Student Aid Report (SAR) with EFC number from the Free Application for Federal Student Aid (FAFSA), unless applying for scholarships that do not consider financial need; and letter of recommendation. **Deadline:** March 1. **Contact:** Grand Haven Area Community Foundation, Lauren Grevel, 1 S Harbor, Grand Haven, MI, 49417; Email: lgrevel@ghacf.org.

5103 ■ Rick and Beverly Lattin Education Scholarship *(Undergraduate/Scholarship)*

Purpose: To provide financial assistance to graduates of Spring Lake or Grand Haven High school who demonstrate financial need. **Focus:** Business. **Qualif.:** Applicants must be current graduates of Spring Lake or Grand Haven high school who demonstrate financial need; must be pursuing skills in the area of business or technical training and plans

to attend either Grand Valley State University or Western Michigan University. **Criteria:** Recipients are selected based on financial need; academic achievement; leadership ability; community and volunteer service; and special circumstances. Strong consideration will be given to students who are pursuing skills in the area of business or technical training.

Funds Avail.: No specific amount. **Duration:** Annual. **To Apply:** Applicants must submit completed application form; current high school or college transcript; Student Aid Report (SAR) from the Free Application for Federal Student Aid (FAFSA), unless applying for scholarships that do not consider financial need; and letter of recommendation. **Deadline:** March 1. **Contact:** Grand Haven Area Community Foundation, Lauren Grevel, 1 S Harbor, Grand Haven, MI, 49417; Email: lgrevel@ghacf.org.

5104 ■ David and Jinny Schultz Family Scholarship *(Undergraduate/Scholarship)*

Purpose: To improve and enhance the quality of life in the Tri-Cities area by serving as a leader, catalyst and resource for philanthropy; to strive for community improvement through strategic grantmaking in such fields as arts, education, health, environment, youth, social services and other human needs. **Focus:** General studies/Field of study not specified. **Qualif.:** Applicants must be a local resident wishing to continue their education in a college, university, vocational or technical setting; Financial need is a consideration but academic excellence is not. **Criteria:** Recipients are selected based on financial need.

Funds Avail.: No specific amount. **Duration:** Annual. **To Apply:** Applicants must submit completed application form; current high school or college transcript; Student Aid Report (SAR) from the Free Application for Federal Student Aid (FAFSA), unless applying for scholarships that do not consider financial need; and letter of recommendation. **Deadline:** March 1. **Contact:** Grand Haven Area Community Foundation, Lauren Grevel, 1 S Harbor, Grand Haven, MI, 49417; Email: lgrevel@ghacf.org.

5105 ■ Scott A. Flahive Memorial Scholarship *(Undergraduate/Scholarship)*

Purpose: To provide scholarship assistance to a Tri-Cities area students. **Focus:** Law. **Qualif.:** Applicants must be students pursuing career in the field of law enforcement and/or criminal justice. **Criteria:** Recipients are selected based on demonstrated academic excellence; financial need; leadership ability; community and volunteer service; creativity; and special circumstances.

Funds Avail.: No specific amount. **Duration:** Annual. **To Apply:** Applicants must submit: completed application form; current high school or college transcript; Student Aid Report (SAR) from the Free Application for Federal Student Aid (FAFSA) with EFC number, unless applying for scholarships that do not consider financial need; and letter of recommendation. **Deadline:** March 1. **Contact:** Grand Haven Area Community Foundation, Lauren Grevel, 1 S Harbor, Grand Haven, MI, 49417; Email: lgrevel@ghacf.org.

5106 ■ Seth Koehler Central High School *(Undergraduate, Vocational/Occupational/Scholarship)*

Purpose: To provide educational financial assistance to a graduating senior from Central High School. **Focus:** General studies/Field of study not specified. **Qualif.:** Applicants must be graduating seniors from Central high school; must have plan to attend any two-to-four year college, university, vocational or technical school. **Criteria:** Recipients are

Awards are arranged alphabetically below their administering organizations

selected based on financial need; academic achievement; leadership ability; community and volunteer service; creativity; and special circumstances.

Funds Avail.: No specific amount. **Duration:** Annual. **To Apply:** Applicants must submit completed application form; current high school or college transcript; Student Aid Report (SAR) from the Free Application for Federal Student Aid (FAFSA) with EFC number, unless applying for scholarships that do not consider financial need; and letter of recommendation. **Deadline:** March 1. **Contact:** Grand Haven Area Community Foundation, Lauren Grevel, 1 S Harbor, Grand Haven, MI, 49417; Email: lgrevel@ghacf.org.

5107 ■ Ken and Sandy Sharkey Family Scholarship
(Undergraduate/Scholarship)

Purpose: To improve and enhance the quality of life in the Tri-Cities area by serving as a leader, catalyst and resource for philanthropy; to strive for community improvement through strategic grantmaking in such fields as arts, education, health, environment, youth, social services and other human needs. **Focus:** General studies/Field of study not specified. **Qualif.:** Applicants must be graduating seniors from Grand Haven high school who demonstrate civic responsibility and plan to be involved in improving their community in the future; must have a 3.0 minimum GPA. **Criteria:** Recipients are selected based on academic performance; leadership ability; community and volunteer service; financial need; and special circumstances.

Funds Avail.: No specific amount. **Duration:** Annual. **To Apply:** Applicants must submit completed application form; current high school or college transcript; Student Aid Report (SAR) from the Free Application for Federal Student Aid (FAFSA), unless applying for scholarships that do not consider financial need; and letter of recommendation. **Deadline:** March 1. **Contact:** Grand Haven Area Community Foundation, Lauren Grevel, 1 S Harbor, Grand Haven, MI, 49417; Email: lgrevel@ghacf.org.

5108 ■ Marion A. and Ruth K. Sherwood Engineering Scholarship *(Undergraduate/Scholarship)*

Purpose: To provide scholarship assistance to a Tri-Cities area High School student. **Focus:** Engineering. **Qualif.:** Applicants must be a graduating senior of a Tri-Cities high school pursuing a degree in Engineering. Applicants must have a 3.0 minimum GPA and financial need is considered. **Criteria:** Recipients are selected based on academic excellence; financial need; leadership ability; creativity; community and volunteer service; and special circumstances.

Funds Avail.: No specific amount. **Duration:** Annual. **To Apply:** Applicants must submit: completed application form; current high school or college transcript; Student Aid Report (SAR) from the Free Application for Federal Student Aid (FAFSA) with EFC number, unless applying for scholarships that do not consider financial need; and letter of recommendation. **Deadline:** March 1. **Contact:** Grand Haven Area Community Foundation, Lauren Grevel, 1 S Harbor, Grand Haven, MI, 49417; Email: lgrevel@ghacf.org.

5109 ■ Edward P. Suchecki Family Scholarship
(Undergraduate/Scholarship)

Purpose: To improve and enhance the quality of life in the Tri-Cities area by serving as a leader, catalyst and resource for philanthropy; to strive for community improvement through strategic grantmaking in such fields as arts, education, health, environment, youth, social services and other human needs. **Focus:** Business. **Qualif.:** Applicants must be graduating high school senior athletes from Grand

Haven high school, preferably planning to pursue a career in business. **Criteria:** Recipients are selected based on financial need.

Funds Avail.: No specific amount. **Duration:** Annual. **To Apply:** Applicants must submit completed application form; current high school or college transcript; Student Aid Report (SAR) from the Free Application for Federal Student Aid (FAFSA), unless applying for scholarships that do not consider financial need; and letter of recommendation. **Deadline:** March 1. **Contact:** Grand Haven Area Community Foundation, Lauren Grevel, 1 S Harbor, Grand Haven, MI, 49417; Email: lgrevel@ghacf.org.

5110 ■ Henry D. and Ruth G. Swartz Family Scholarship *(Undergraduate/Scholarship)*

Purpose: To improve and enhance the quality of life in the Tri-Cities area by serving as a leader, catalyst and resource for philanthropy; to strive for community improvement through strategic grantmaking in such fields as arts, education, health, environment, youth, social services and other human needs. **Focus:** Computer and information sciences. **Qualif.:** Applicants must be graduating high school seniors from Grand Haven high school, Spring Lake high school, Holland Christian high school or Western Michigan Christian high school in North Ottawa County; must be pursuing a career in engineering, computer science, pre-law or medicine. **Criteria:** Recipients are selected based on leadership ability, community involvement and academic achievement; creativity; financial need; and special circumstances; preference will be given to those students pursuing a career in engineering, computer science, pre-law and medicine.

Funds Avail.: No specific amount. **Duration:** Annual. **To Apply:** Applicants must submit completed application form; current high school or college transcript; Student Aid Report (SAR) from the Free Application for Federal Student Aid (FAFSA); and letter of recommendation. **Deadline:** March 1. **Contact:** Grand Haven Area Community Foundation, Lauren Grevel, 1 S Harbor, Grand Haven, MI, 49417; Email: lgrevel@ghacf.org.

5111 ■ Terry Linda Potter Scholarship
(Undergraduate/Scholarship)

Purpose: To improve and enhance the quality of life in the Tri-Cities area by serving as a leader, catalyst and resource for philanthropy; to strive for community improvement through strategic grantmaking in such fields as arts, education, health, environment, youth, social services and other human needs. **Focus:** Health education. **Qualif.:** Applicants must reside in the Northwest Ottawa County area; must demonstrate scholastic ability and academic performance, interest in pursuing further education, preferably in a health-related field, financial need, and acceptance at an accredited two- or four-year college. **Criteria:** Recipients are selected based on financial need; academic achievement; leadership ability; creativity; community and volunteer service; and special circumstances.

Funds Avail.: No specific amount. **Duration:** Annual. **To Apply:** Applicants must submit completed application form; current high school or college transcript; Student Aid Report (SAR) from the Free Application for Federal Student Aid (FAFSA) with EFC number, unless applying for scholarships that do not consider financial need; and letter of recommendation. **Deadline:** March 1. **Contact:** Grand Haven Area Community Foundation, Lauren Grevel, 1 S Harbor, Grand Haven, MI, 49417; Email: lgrevel@ghacf.org.

Awards are arranged alphabetically below their administering organizations

5112 ■ Tom Gifford Scholarship *(Undergraduate/Scholarship)*

Purpose: To improve and enhance the quality of life in the Tri-Cities area by serving as a leader, catalyst and resource for philanthropy; to strive for community improvement through strategic grantmaking in such fields as arts, education, health, environment, youth, social services and other human needs. **Focus:** General studies/Field of study not specified. **Qualif.:** Applicants must be planning to attend Amherst College within 30 months of high school graduation; those who will be attending one of the top ten colleges or universities (based in the current year US News and World Report) will be considered if no Amherst applicant is available; also available to graduates of Spring Lake high school who have been a student for three semesters immediately prior to graduation and who attended SLHS for atleast three years. **Criteria:** Recipients are selected based on demonstrated academic excellence and financial need.

Funds Avail.: No specific amount. **Duration:** Annual. **To Apply:** Applicants must submit: completed application form; current high school or college transcript; Student Aid Report (SAR) from the Free Application for Federal Student Aid (FAFSA) with EFC number, unless applying for scholarships that do not consider financial need; and letter of recommendation. **Deadline:** March 1. **Contact:** Grand Haven Area Community Foundation, Lauren Grevel, 1 S Harbor, Grand Haven, MI, 49417; Email: lgrevel@ghacf.org.

5113 ■ West Michigan Nursery and Landscape Association Scholarship *(Undergraduate/Scholarship)*

Purpose: To assist graduating high school seniors and currently enrolled college students to pursue a horticulture or green industry career. **Focus:** Horticulture. **Qualif.:** Applicants must be graduating high school seniors or currently enrolled college students planning to pursue a horticulture or green industry career at a two-or-four-year college or university; must be residents of Ottawa, Oceana, Newaygo, Muskegon or Allegan Counties. **Criteria:** Recipients are selected based on demonstrated academic excellence and financial need.

Funds Avail.: No specific amount. **Duration:** Annual. **To Apply:** Applicants must submit completed application form; current high school or college transcript; Student Aid Report (SAR) from the Free Application for Federal Student Aid (FAFSA), unless applying for scholarships that do not consider financial need; and letter of recommendation. **Deadline:** March 1. **Contact:** Grand Haven Area Community Foundation, Lauren Grevel, 1 S Harbor, Grand Haven, MI, 49417; Email: lgrevel@ghacf.org.

5114 ■ Women's Club of Grand Haven Scholarship *(Undergraduate/Scholarship)*

Purpose: To improve and enhance the quality of life in the Tri-Cities area by serving as a leader, catalyst and resource for philanthropy; to strive for community improvement through strategic grantmaking in such fields as the arts, education, health, environment, youth, social services and other human needs. **Focus:** General studies/Field of study not specified. **Qualif.:** Applicants may be non-traditional students; Tri-Cities adult resident seeking to gain additional education of career training at a college, university, technical or vocational school; must be a student whose secondary education has been delayed or interrupted. **Criteria:** Recipients are selected based on financial need, academic achievement, community service and college plans; preference will be given to a female, age 21 or older, with demonstrated financial need.

Funds Avail.: No specific amount. **Duration:** Annual. **To Apply:** Applicants must submit completed application form; current high school or college transcript; Student Aid Report (SAR) from the Free Application for Federal Student Aid (FAFSA) with EFC number, unless applying for scholarships that do not consider financial need; and letter of recommendation. **Deadline:** March 2. **Contact:** Grand Haven Area Community Foundation, Lauren Grevel, 1 S Harbor, Grand Haven, MI, 49417; Email: lgrevel@ghacf.org.

5115 ■ Zenko Family Scholarship *(Undergraduate/Scholarship)*

Purpose: To provide assistance to students to further their education. **Focus:** General studies/Field of study not specified. **Qualif.:** Applicants must be Tri-Cities graduates of Spring Lake, Grand Haven or Fruitport high school; and have made their own financial contribution through employment to further their education at an accredited four-year college, junior college, trade school or apprenticeship. **Criteria:** Recipients are selected based on financial need.

Funds Avail.: No specific amount. **Duration:** Annual. **To Apply:** Applicants must submit completed application form; current high school or college transcript; Student Aid Report (SAR) from the Free Application for Federal Student Aid (FAFSA), unless applying for scholarships that do not consider financial need; and letter of recommendation. **Deadline:** March 1. **Contact:** Grand Haven Area Community Foundation, Lauren Grevel, 1 S Harbor, Grand Haven, MI, 49417; Email: lgrevel@ghacf.org.

5116 ■ Grand Island Community Foundation
1811 W 2nd St., Ste. 365
Grand Island, NE 68803
Ph: (308)381-7767
Fax: (308)384-4069
E-mail: info@gicf.org
URL: www.gicf.org
Social Media: www.facebook.com/GICommunityFoundation
www.instagram.com/gicommunityfoundation/

5117 ■ Henry and Maria Ahrens Charitable Trust Scholarship *(Undergraduate, Graduate/Scholarship)*

Purpose: To provide financial support to students pursuing an education in the medical field. **Focus:** Dentistry; Medical technology; Medicine; Nursing. **Qualif.:** Applicants must have graduated from a Hall County Nebraska high school; much be current college or non-traditional students who are enrolled in medical career schooling, including physicians, dentists, nursing, technicians, and LPNs.

Funds Avail.: No specific amount. **Duration:** Annual. **To Apply:** Application form and details available online at www.gicf.org/communities/scholarships/scholarship-directory/greater-grand-island-community-foundation-scholarships. **Deadline:** February 15. **Remarks:** The scholarship was established to honor the memory of Henry and Maria Ahrens. Established in 1995. **Contact:** Email: scholarships@gicf.org.

5118 ■ Edgar Barge Memorial Scholarship *(Undergraduate/Scholarship)*

Purpose: To provide financial support to students in pursuit of furthering their education and pursuing their dreams. **Focus:** General studies/Field of study not specified. **Qualif.:** Applicants must be a graduating high school seniors

Awards are arranged alphabetically below their administering organizations

who are registered parishioners at Blessed Sacrament Church in Grand Island, NE, who have been confirmed and attend Mass regularly. **Criteria:** Selection is based on the online application.

Funds Avail.: No specific amount. **Duration:** Annual. **To Apply:** Application form and details available online at www.gicf.org/communities/scholarships/scholarship-directory/greater-grand-island-community-foundation-scholarships. **Deadline:** February 15. **Remarks:** The scholarship was established to honor the memory of Edgar Barge. Established in 2005. **Contact:** Email: scholarships@ gicf.org.

5119 ■ Karen A. Connick Memorial Scholarship
(Undergraduate/Scholarship)

Purpose: To provide financial support to students in pursuit of furthering their education and pursuing their dreams. **Focus:** General studies/Field of study not specified. **Qualif.:** Applicants must be graduating seniors from Doniphan-Trumbull High School or Giltner High School. **Criteria:** Selection is based on the online application.

Funds Avail.: No specific amount. **Duration:** Annual. **To Apply:** Application form and details available online at www.gicf.org/communities/scholarships/scholarship-directory/greater-grand-island-community-foundation-scholarships. **Deadline:** February 15. **Remarks:** The scholarship was established to honor the memory of Karen A. Connick. Established in 2005. **Contact:** Email: scholarships@gicf.org.

5120 ■ Doniphan Community Foundation Scholar-ships
(Undergraduate, Community College, Vocational/Occupational/Scholarship)

Purpose: To provide financial support to students in pursuit of furthering their education and pursuing their dreams. **Focus:** General studies/Field of study not specified. **Qualif.:** Applicants must be Doniphan-Trumbull High School graduating seniors. **Criteria:** Selection is based on the online application.

Funds Avail.: No specific amount. **Duration:** Annual. **To Apply:** Application form and details for specific scholarships available online at www.gicf.org/communities/scholarships/scholarship-directory/doniphan-community-foundation-scholarships. **Deadline:** February 15. **Remarks:** Administered on behalf of the Doniphan Community Foundation. **Contact:** Email: scholarships@gicf.org.

5121 ■ Howard and Gladys Eakes Memorial Scholarship
(Undergraduate/Scholarship)

Purpose: To provide financial support to students in pursuit of furthering their education and pursuing their dreams. **Focus:** General studies/Field of study not specified. **Qualif.:** Applicants must be children or stepchildren of a current Eakes Office Solutions employee who has been employed a minimum of one year; must be graduating high school seniors with a minimum 3.0 GPA. **Criteria:** Selection is based on the online application.

Funds Avail.: No specific amount. **Duration:** Annual. **To Apply:** Application form and details available online at www.gicf.org/communities/scholarships/scholarship-directory/greater-grand-island-community-foundation-scholarships. **Deadline:** February 15. **Remarks:** The scholarship was established to honor the memories of Howard and Gladys Eakes. Established in 2001.

5122 ■ Hall County Medical Society Scholarship
(Undergraduate, Graduate/Scholarship)

Purpose: To provide financial support to students in pursuit of furthering their education in medical fields. **Focus:** Den-

tistry; Medical technology; Medicine; Nursing. **Qualif.:** Applicants must be graduates of a Hall County Nebraska high school; must be a current college or non-traditional student who are enrolled in medical schooling, including physicians, dentists, nurses, technicians, and LPNs. **Criteria:** Selection is based on the online application.

Funds Avail.: No specific amount. **Duration:** Annual. **To Apply:** Application form and details available online at www.gicf.org/communities/scholarships/scholarship-directory/greater-grand-island-community-foundation-scholarships **Deadline:** February 15. **Remarks:** Established in 2003.

5123 ■ Jim and Dee Price Family Scholarship
(Undergraduate, Community College, College, University/Scholarship)

Purpose: To provide financial support to students in pursuit of furthering their education and pursuing their dreams. **Focus:** General studies/Field of study not specified. **Qualif.:** Applicant must be graduating seniors from Grand Island High School with a minimum 3.0 GPA; must be attending university, college, or community college in Nebraska in the upcoming school year; open to both traditional and non-traditional students. **Criteria:** Preferences are given to students with disabilities.

Funds Avail.: No specific amount. **Duration:** Annual. **To Apply:** Application form and details available online at www.gicf.org/communities/scholarships/scholarship-directory/greater-grand-island-community-foundation-scholarships. **Deadline:** February 15. **Remarks:** The scholarship was established by Jim and Dee Price. Established in 2005.

5124 ■ Carl C. and Abbie Rebman Trust Scholar-ship
(Undergraduate/Scholarship)

Purpose: To provide financial support to students in pursuit of furthering their education and pursuing their dreams. **Focus:** Automotive technology; Nursing. **Qualif.:** Applicant must be a Hall County resident or their parent/guardian must be a Hall County resident; must attend Central Community College in Grand Island, Hastings, or Columbus; must be studying in the fields of nursing, or automotive, mechanics, or diesel technology; open to traditional and non-traditional students. **Criteria:** Selection is based on the online application.

Funds Avail.: No specific amount. **Duration:** Annual. **To Apply:** Application form and details available online at www.gicf.org/communities/scholarships/scholarship-directory/greater-grand-island-community-foundation-scholarships. **Deadline:** February 15. **Remarks:** The scholarship was established by Carl C. Rebman. Established in 1989. **Contact:** Email: scholarships@gicf.org.

5125 ■ TeamMates Mentoring Program Scholarship
(Undergraduate/Scholarship)

Purpose: To provide financial support to students in pursuit of furthering their education and pursuing their dreams. **Focus:** General studies/Field of study not specified. **Qualif.:** Applicants must be a Grand Island High School graduates and TeamMate mentees with a match date no later than their 9th grade year and be matched with a mentor at time of graduation; available up to 25th birthday to students who graduated with the class of 2019 and beyond. **Criteria:** Selection is based on the online application.

Funds Avail.: No specific amount. **Duration:** Annual. **To Apply:** Application form and details available online at

Awards are arranged alphabetically below their administering organizations

www.gicf.org/communities/scholarships/scholarship-directory/greater-grand-island-community-foundation-scholarships. **Deadline:** February 15. **Remarks:** Established in 1999. **Contact:** Email: scholarships@gicf.org.

5126 ■ Wyman and Cleo Woodyard Family Scholarship (Undergraduate, University, College/Scholarship)

Purpose: To provide financial support to students in pursuit of furthering their education and pursuing their dreams. **Focus:** General studies/Field of study not specified. **Qualif.:** Applicants must be Hall County high school graduating seniors seeking Bachelor's degrees at a Nebraska college or university; must have at least 3.0 GPA and a class rank in the top 25%.

Funds Avail.: No specific amount. **Duration:** Annual. **To Apply:** Application form and details available online at www.gicf.org/communities/scholarships/scholarship-directory/greater-grand-island-community-foundation-scholarships. **Deadline:** February 15. **Remarks:** The scholarship was established by Wyman and Cleo Woodyard Family. Established in 2007. **Contact:** Email: scholarships@gicf.org.

5127 ■ James P. and Joy Y. Zana Scholarship (Undergraduate/Scholarship)

Purpose: To provide financial support to students in pursuit of furthering their education and pursuing their dreams. **Focus:** Arts. **Qualif.:** Applicants must be graduating seniors from Grand Island High School who are pursuing a major or minor in Fine Arts. **Criteria:** Selection is based on the online application.

Funds Avail.: No specific amount. **Duration:** Annual. **To Apply:** Application form and details available online at www.gicf.org/communities/scholarships/scholarship-directory/greater-grand-island-community-foundation-scholarships. **Deadline:** February 15. **Remarks:** The scholarship was established in memory of James P. Zana. Established in 2007. **Contact:** Email: scholarships@gicf.org.

5128 ■ Grand Lodge of Saskatchewan

1930 Lorne St.
Regina, SK, Canada S4P 2M1
Ph: (306)522-5686
Free: 877-661-2231
E-mail: glsask@accesscomm.ca
URL: www.saskmasons.ca
Social Media: www.facebook.com/saskmasons/
twitter.com/saskmasons

5129 ■ Murray Montague Memorial Scholarship (Undergraduate/Scholarship)

Purpose: To provide financial support to students in the higher learning institutions. **Focus:** General studies/Field of study not specified. **Qualif.:** Applicants must be Saskatchewan High School graduates who proceed to an institution of higher learning anywhere in Canada; must be registered for a full academic load for a full academic year as required by the institution chosen. **Criteria:** Selection will be based on academic achievement, leadership skills, community and school activities and special awards.

Funds Avail.: 1,000 Canadian Dollars. **Duration:** Annual. **Number Awarded:** 1. **To Apply:** Applicants must submit the following requirements: completed application form; official final transcript of grade 12 marks issued by the

saskatchewan ministry of education; character reference from a community leader; letter of reference from the high school principal or guidance counselor; letter from the applicants outlining extracurricular activities and educational goals. **Deadline:** August 6. **Contact:** Scholarship selection committee, The grand lodge of saskatchewan ancient free & accepted mansons, 1930 lorne st, Regina, saskatchewan, S4P 2M1; Phone: 306-522-5686; Toll free: 877-661-2231; Email: glask@accesscomm.ca.

5130 ■ Grand Rapids Community Foundation (GRCF)

185 Oakes St. SW
Grand Rapids, MI 49503
Ph: (616)454-1751
Fax: (616)454-6455
E-mail: grfound@grfoundation.org
URL: www.grfoundation.org
Social Media: www.facebook.com/GRCommFound
twitter.com/GRCommFound

5131 ■ Achille & Irene Despres, William & Andre Scholarship (Undergraduate/Scholarship)

Purpose: To provide financial assistance to those students who are in need. **Focus:** General studies/Field of study not specified. **Qualif.:** Applicants must be of Mexican heritage; must be Kent or Ottawa residents; must be enrolled in an accredited college or university; must have demonstrated financial need; must have a cumulative GPA of at least 2.75. **Criteria:** Priority will be given to those students with financial need.

Funds Avail.: No specific amount. **Duration:** Annual. **To Apply:** Applicants must complete the following: general online application; list of awards, volunteer activities, employment/school extra-curricular activities; academic transcript from most recent semester (High School Students must include first semester senior year). Applicants must also submit a personal essay that includes: reasons for choice of college, chosen course of study, career goals, plans for financing education, and information on past activities benefitting community. **Deadline:** April 1. **Contact:** Ruth Bishop, Education Program Officer; Phone: 616-454-1751 Ext. 103; Email: rbishop@grfoundation.org.

5132 ■ Aim High Jerry Clay Scholarship (Undergraduate/Scholarship)

Purpose: To support students in their pursuit of higher education and future career choices. **Focus:** Welding. **Qualif.:** Applicants must be students from Kent, Barry, Ionia, Montcalm, Muskegon, Newaygo, or Ottawa County pursuing a full-time undergraduate degree or certification in the welding technology field of study at an accredited program located at or affiliated with Grand Rapids Community College or Ferris State University; must also have demonstrated financial need. **Criteria:** Selection will be based on the Foundation's criteria.

Funds Avail.: No specific amount. **Duration:** Annual. **To Apply:** Applicants must contact the Foundation for further information. **Deadline:** April 1. **Contact:** Ruth Bishop, Education Program Officer; Phone: 616-454-1751 Ext. 103; Email: rbishop@grfoundation.org.

5133 ■ Altrusa International of Grand Rapids Scholarship (Undergraduate/Scholarship)

Purpose: To provide financial support to those students who are in need. **Focus:** General studies/Field of study not

Awards are arranged alphabetically below their administering organizations

specified. **Qualif.:** Applicants must be students from Kent, Allegan, Iona, Ottawa, Montcalm or Muskegon counties (6 months residency minimum); must be entering or returning to college after sitting out of school for two years; must demonstrate financial need. **Criteria:** Priority will be given to those students with financial need.

Funds Avail.: No specific amount. **Duration:** Annual. **To Apply:** Applicants must complete the following: general online application; list of awards, volunteer activities, employment/school extra-curricular activities; academic transcript from most recent semester (High School Students must include first semester senior year). Applicants must also submit a personal essay that includes: reasons for choice of college, chosen course of study, career goals, plans for financing education, and information on past activities benefitting community. **Deadline:** April 1. **Contact:** Ruth Bishop, Education Program Officer; Phone: 616-454-1751 Ext. 103; Email: rbishop@grfoundation.org.

5134 ■ Arts Council of Greater Grand Rapids Minority Scholarship *(Undergraduate/Scholarship)*

Purpose: To support students of color in their pursuit of higher education and future career choices. **Focus:** Performing arts; Visual arts. **Qualif.:** Applicants must be students of color (African American, Hispanic, Native American, Pacific Islander) attending a non-profit public or private college/university; must be majoring in Fine Arts including all visual and performing art forms; must be Kent County residents; must have a minimum 2.5 GPA; and must have a financial need. **Criteria:** Selection will be based on the Foundation's criteria.

Funds Avail.: No specific amount. **Duration:** Annual. **To Apply:** Applicants must complete the following: general online application; list of awards, volunteer activities, employment/school extracurricular activities; academic transcript from most recent semester (high school students: must include first semester senior year). Must provide a personal essay that includes: reasons for choice of college, chosen course of study, career goals, plans for financing education, and information on past activities benefitting the community. **Deadline:** April 1. **Contact:** Ruth Bishop, Education Program Officer; Phone: 616-454-1751 Ext. 103; Email: rbishop@grfoundation.org.

5135 ■ Audrey L. Wright Scholarship
(Undergraduate/Scholarship)

Purpose: To provide financial support to deserving students. **Focus:** Education--Curricula; Foreign languages. **Qualif.:** Applicants must be residents of Kent County (3 years minimum); must be pursuing an undergraduate degree in Foreign Language or Education; must have financial need; must have a minimum of 3.0 GPA. **Criteria:** Preference will be given to those students who meet the criteria.

Funds Avail.: No specific amount. **Duration:** Annual. **To Apply:** Applicants must complete the following: general online application; list of awards, volunteer activities, employment/school extra-curricular activities; academic transcript from most recent semester (High School Students must include first semester senior year). Applicants must also submit a personal essay that includes: reasons for choice of college, chosen course of study, career goals, plans for financing education, and information on past activities benefitting community. **Deadline:** April 1. **Contact:** Ruth Bishop, Education Program Officer; Phone: 616-454-1751 Ext. 103; Email: rbishop@grfoundation.org.

5136 ■ Dr. Noyes L. Avery, Jr. & Ann E. Avery Scholarship *(Undergraduate, Graduate/Scholarship)*

Purpose: To provide financial assistance to those students who are in need. **Focus:** Medicine. **Qualif.:** Applicants must be full-time students from Kent County (3 years minimum) who are attending the University of Michigan for a medical doctor degree; must have a minimum of 3.0 GPA; must have financial need. **Criteria:** Preference will be given to those students who meet the criteria.

Funds Avail.: No specific amount. **Duration:** Annual. **To Apply:** Applicants must complete the following: general online application; list of awards, volunteer activities, employment/school extra-curricular activities; academic transcript from most recent semester (High School Students must include first semester senior year). Applicants must also submit a personal essay that includes: reasons for choice of college, chosen course of study, career goals, plans for financing education, and information on past activities benefitting the community. **Deadline:** April 1. **Contact:** Ruth Bishop, Education Program Officer; Phone: 616-454-1751 Ext. 103; Email: rbishop@grfoundation.org.

5137 ■ Black Men Building Resources Scholarship
(Undergraduate/Scholarship)

Purpose: To support African American students from Kent County in their pursuit of higher education and future career choices. **Focus:** General studies/Field of study not specified. **Qualif.:** Applicants must be African American male or female students; must be residing in Kent County and graduated or received a GED from a Grand Rapids area high school; must also have demonstrated financial need. **Criteria:** Selection will be based on the Foundation's criteria.

Funds Avail.: No specific amount. **Duration:** Annual. **To Apply:** Applicant must complete the following: general online application; list of awards, volunteer activities, employment/school extracurricular activities; academic transcript from most recent semester (high school students: must include first semester senior year). Must also submit a personal essay that includes: reasons for choice of college, chosen course of study, career goals, plans for financing education, and information on past activities benefitting community. **Deadline:** April 1. **Contact:** Ruth Bishop, Education Program Officer; Phone: 616-454-1751 Ext. 103; Email: rbishop@grfoundation.org.

5138 ■ Harry and Lucille Brown Scholarship
(Undergraduate/Scholarship)

Purpose: To provide financial support to those students who are in need. **Focus:** General studies/Field of study not specified. **Qualif.:** Applicants must be residents of Kent County (3 year minimum); must have financial need; must be pursuing an undergraduate degree at any accredited college in the U.S; must have a minimum of 3.3 GPA. **Criteria:** Selection will be based on the Foundation's criteria.

Funds Avail.: No specific amount. **Duration:** Annual. **To Apply:** Applicants must complete the following: general online application; list of awards, volunteer activities, employment/school extra-curricular activities; academic transcript from most recent semester (High School Students must include first semester senior year). Applicants must also submit a personal essay that includes: reasons for choice of college, chosen course of study, career goals, plans for financing education, and information on past activities benefitting community. **Deadline:** April 1. **Contact:** Ruth Bishop, Education Program Officer; Phone: 616-454-

Awards are arranged alphabetically below their administering organizations

1751 Ext. 103; Email: rbishop@grfoundation.org.

5139 ■ Camilla C. Johnson Scholarship
(Undergraduate/Scholarship)

Purpose: To provide financial support to those deserving students. **Focus:** General studies/Field of study not specified. **Qualif.:** Applicants must be senior students at Union High School entering college full-time in the fall; must have financial need; must have a cumulative of 2.6 GPA. **Criteria:** Selection will be based on the Foundation's criteria.

Funds Avail.: No specific amount. **Duration:** Annual. **To Apply:** Applicant must complete the following: general online application; list of awards, volunteer activities, employment/school extra-curricular activities; academic transcript from most recent semester (high school students: must include first semester senior year). Applicant must also submit a personal essay that includes: reasons for choice of college, chosen course of study, career goals, plans for financing education, and information on past activities benefitting community. **Deadline:** April 1. **Contact:** Ruth Bishop, Education Program Officer; Phone: 616-454-1751 Ext. 103; Email: rbishop@grfoundation.org.

5140 ■ Carolyn Gallmeyer Scholarship
(Undergraduate/Scholarship)

Purpose: To provide financial support to those students who are in need. **Focus:** General studies/Field of study not specified. **Qualif.:** Applicants must be Kent County residents who are pursuing an undergraduate degree at any U.S college; must have financial need and a minimum 2.75 GPA. **Criteria:** Recipients will be selected based on financial need.

Funds Avail.: No specific amount. **Duration:** Annual. **To Apply:** Applicant must complete the following: general online application; list of awards, volunteer activities, employment/school extra-curricular activities; academic transcript from most recent semester (high school students: must include first semester senior year). Applicant must also submit a personal essay that includes: reasons for choice of college, chosen course of study, career goals, plans for financing education, and information on past activities benefitting community. **Deadline:** April 1. **Contact:** Ruth Bishop, Education Program Officer; Phone: 616-454-1751 Ext. 103; Email: rbishop@grfoundation.org.

5141 ■ Llewellyn L. Cayvan String Instrument
Scholarship *(Undergraduate, Graduate/Scholarship)*

Purpose: To assist those students with talent in musical instruments by supporting them financially. **Focus:** Music. **Qualif.:** Applicants must be undergraduate or graduate level students studying the violin, viola, violoncello, or the bass violin. **Criteria:** Priority will be given to those students with financial need.

Funds Avail.: No specific amount. **Duration:** Annual. **To Apply:** Applicants must complete the following: general online application; list of awards, volunteer activities, employment/school extra-curricular activities; academic transcript from most recent semester (High School Students must include first semester senior year). Applicants must also submit a personal essay that includes: reasons for choice of college, chosen course of study, career goals, plans for financing education, and information on past activities benefitting community. **Deadline:** April 1. **Contact:** Ruth Bishop, Education Program Officer; Phone: 616-454-1751 Ext. 103; Email: rbishop@grfoundation.org.

5142 ■ Christine Soper Scholarship *(Undergraduate/Scholarship)*

Purpose: To provide financial support to those students who are in need. **Focus:** General studies/Field of study not specified. **Qualif.:** Applicants must be Kent County residents (3 years minimum) who will be attending Aquinas, Calvin, Cornerstone, Davenport, GRCC, GVSU or Kendall; must have financial need; must have a minimum cumulative GPA of 3.0. **Criteria:** Priority will be given to those students with high financial need.

Funds Avail.: No specific amount. **Duration:** Annual. **To Apply:** Applicant must complete the following: general online application; list of awards, volunteer activities, employment/school extra-curricular activities; academic transcript from most recent semester (high school students: must include first semester senior year). Applicant must also submit a personal essay that includes: reasons for choice of college, chosen course of study, career goals, plans for financing education, and information on past activities benefitting community. **Deadline:** April 1. **Contact:** Ruth Bishop, Education Program Officer; Phone: 616-454-1751 Ext. 103; Email: rbishop@grfoundation.org.

5143 ■ Paul Collins Scholarship *(Undergraduate/Scholarship)*

Purpose: To provide financial assistance to deserving students. **Focus:** Art; Art industries and trade. **Qualif.:** Applicants must be undergraduate level students studying Fine or Applied Arts at Aquinas, Calvin, GVSU, GRCC or Kendall; must be residents of Kent County; must have a minimum of 2.5 GPA, financial need and demonstrate artistic talent. **Criteria:** Priority will be given to those students with financial need.

Funds Avail.: No specific amount. **Duration:** Annual. **To Apply:** Applicant must complete the following: general online application; list of awards, volunteer activities, employment/school extra-curricular activities; academic transcript from most recent semester (high school students: must include first semester senior year). Applicant must also submit a personal essay that includes: reasons for choice of college, chosen course of study, career goals, plans for financing education, and information on past activities benefitting community. **Deadline:** April 1. **Contact:** Ruth Bishop, Education Program Officer; Phone: 616-454-1751 Ext. 103; Email: rbishop@grfoundation.org.

5144 ■ Gerald M. Crane Music Award Scholarship
(Undergraduate/Scholarship)

Purpose: To provide funding to students for their music lessons, seminars, workshops, summer enrichment programs, music concerts, instruments, books, vocal music lessons or any other kinds of musical materials. **Focus:** Music. **Qualif.:** Applicants must be high school music students in Kent or Ottawa County who are requesting money for music lessons, seminars, workshops, summer enrichment programs, music concerts, instruments, books, vocal music lessons or any other kinds of musical materials. **Criteria:** Selection will be based on the Foundation's criteria.

Funds Avail.: $250 to $1,000. **Duration:** Annual. **To Apply:** Applicants must complete the following: general online application; list of awards, volunteer activities, employment/school extra-curricular activities; academic transcript from most recent semester (high school students: must include first semester senior year); a personal essay that includes: reasons for choice of college, chosen course of study, career goals, plans for financing education, and information

Awards are arranged alphabetically below their administering organizations

on past activities benefitting community. **Deadline:** April 1. **Remarks:** The Scholarship Fund was established by caring people who wished to honor Mr. Crane's devotion to the musical arts. Established in 1997. **Contact:** Grand Rapids Community Foundation, 185 Oakes SW Grand Rapids, MI, 49503; For Question: 616-454-1751.

5145 ■ Darooge Family Scholarship *(Undergraduate/Scholarship)*

Purpose: To support students in their pursuit of higher education and future career choices. **Focus:** Construction. **Qualif.:** Applicants must be high school seniors residing in Kent County and entering college to pursue an undergraduate degree in a construction-related field of study at an accredited two or four year college/university/trade school in Michigan; must also have financial need. **Criteria:** Selection will be based on the Foundation's criteria.

Funds Avail.: No specific amount. **Duration:** Annual. **To Apply:** Applicant must complete the following: general online application; list of awards, volunteer activities, employment/school extracurricular activities; academic transcript from most recent semester (high school students: must include first semester senior year). Must also submit a personal essay that includes: reasons for choice of college, chosen course of study, career goals, plans for financing education, and information on past activities benefitting community. **Deadline:** April 1. **Contact:** Ruth Bishop, Education Program Officer; Phone: 616-454-1751 Ext. 103; Email: rbishop@grfoundation.org.

5146 ■ Donald and Florence Hunting Scholarship *(Undergraduate/Scholarship)*

Purpose: To provide financial assistance to those students who are in need. **Focus:** General studies/Field of study not specified. **Qualif.:** Applicants must be senior students at Rockford High School who will be entering college in the fall; must have demonstrated financial need. **Criteria:** Priority will be given to those students with financial need.

Funds Avail.: No specific amount. **Duration:** Annual. **To Apply:** Applicant must complete the following: general online application; list of awards, volunteer activities, employment/school extra-curricular activities; two letters of recommendation; academic transcript from most recent semester (high school students: must include first semester senior year). Applicant must also submit a personal essay that includes: reasons for choice of college, chosen course of study, career goals, plans for financing education, and information on past activities benefitting community. **Deadline:** April 1. **Contact:** Ruth Bishop, Education Program Officer; Phone: 616-454-1751 Ext. 103; Email: rbishop@grfoundation.org.

5147 ■ Donald J. DeYoung Scholarship *(Undergraduate/Scholarship)*

Purpose: To support current or former wards of the court in their pursuit of higher education and future career choices. **Focus:** General studies/Field of study not specified. **Qualif.:** Applicants must be young people currently residing in the West Michigan area who are wards of the court or previously have been a ward of the court and have been discharged successfully; should be referred by a caseworker or probation officer; non-traditional students are also encouraged to apply; scholarship may be used at any educational institution within the United States; must be accepted at a college/university or training school to apply. **Criteria:** Selection will be based on the Foundation's criteria.

Funds Avail.: $1,000 to $2,000. **Duration:** Annual. **To Apply:** Applicants must submit an application form (available at the website) and a recommendation letter from a caseworker. **Deadline:** April 1. **Remarks:** Established in 1997. **Contact:** Ruth Bishop, Education Program Officer; 185 Oakes SW Grand Rapids, MI, 49503; Phone: 616-454-1751; Email: rbishop@grfoundation.org.

5148 ■ Dorothy B. & Charles E. Thomas Scholarship *(Undergraduate/Scholarship)*

Purpose: To provide financial assistance to those students who are in need. **Focus:** General studies/Field of study not specified. **Qualif.:** Applicants must be Kent County residents (3 years minimum) who will be attending Aquinas, Calvin, Cornerstone, Davenport, GRCC, GVSU or Kendall; must have a minimum of 3.0 GPA; must have financial need. **Criteria:** Priority will be given to those students with financial need.

Funds Avail.: No specific amount. **Duration:** Annual. **To Apply:** Applicant must complete the following: general online application; list of awards, volunteer activities, employment/school extra-curricular activities; academic transcript from most recent semester (high school students: must include first semester senior year). Applicant must also submit a personal essay that includes: reasons for choice of college, chosen course of study, career goals, plans for financing education, and information on past activities benefitting community. **Deadline:** April 1. **Contact:** Ruth Bishop, Education Program Officer; Phone: 616-454-1751 Ext. 103; Email: rbishop@grfoundation.org.

5149 ■ Economic Club Business Study Abroad Scholarships *(Undergraduate/Scholarship)*

Purpose: To support students in their pursuit of higher education and future career choices. **Focus:** General studies/Field of study not specified. **Qualif.:** Applicants must be residents of Kent, Allegan, Ottawa or Muskegon County for at least three years, or resident students at a public college or university in the West Michigan area for at least two years; must be full-time undergraduate students (second year or above) pursuing a degree in business and will be studying abroad through a public college or university; must have a minimum GPA of 3.0; and must also exhibit financial need. **Criteria:** Selection will be based on the Foundation's criteria.

Funds Avail.: $2,000. **Duration:** Annual. **To Apply:** Applicants must complete the following: general online application; list of awards, volunteer activities, employment/school extra-curricular activities; academic transcript from most recent semester (high school students: must include first semester senior year); a personal essay that includes: reasons for choice of college, chosen course of study, career goals, plans for financing education, and information on past activities benefitting community. **Deadline:** April 1. **Remarks:** Established in 2000. **Contact:** Grand Rapids Community Foundation, 185 Oakes SW Grand Rapids, MI, 49503.

5150 ■ Economic Club of Grand Rapids Scholarship *(Undergraduate/Scholarship)*

Purpose: To support students in their pursuit of higher education and future career choices. **Focus:** Business. **Qualif.:** Applicants must be undergraduate students pursuing a degree in business; must be residents of Kent or Ottawa County for a minimum of three years with demonstrated financial need; and must have a minimum GPA of 3.0. **Criteria:** Selection will be based on the Foundation's criteria.

Awards are arranged alphabetically below their administering organizations

Funds Avail.: No specific amount. **Duration:** Annual. **To Apply:** Applicant must complete the following: general online application; list of awards, volunteer activities, employment/school extracurricular activities; academic transcript from most recent semester (high school students: must include first semester senior year). Must also submit a personal essay that includes: reasons for choice of college, chosen course of study, career goals, plans for financing education, and information on past activities benefitting community. **Deadline:** April 1. **Contact:** Ruth Bishop, Education Program Officer; Phone: 616-454-1751 Ext. 103; Email: rbishop@grfoundation.org.

5151 ■ Geraldine Geistert Boss Scholarship
(Undergraduate/Scholarship)

Purpose: To provide financial support to those students who are in need. **Focus:** General studies/Field of study not specified. **Qualif.:** Applicants must be full-time students with financial need residing in Kent County (5 years minimum) and pursuing an undergraduate degree at an accredited college in Michigan; must have a minimum of 3.0 GPA. **Criteria:** Selection will be based on financial need.

Funds Avail.: No specific amount. **Duration:** Annual. **To Apply:** Applicants must complete the following: general online application; list of awards, volunteer activities, employment/school extra-curricular activities; academic transcript from most recent semester (High School Students: must include first semester senior year); an essay about yourself that includes: reasons for choice of college, chosen course of study, career goals, plans for financing education, and information on past activities benefitting community. **Deadline:** April 1. **Contact:** Ruth Bishop, Education Program Officer; Phone: 616-454-1751 Ext. 103; Email: rbishop@grfoundation.org.

5152 ■ Grand Rapids Scholarship Association
(Undergraduate/Scholarship)

Purpose: To provide financial assistance to those students who are in need. **Focus:** General studies/Field of study not specified. **Qualif.:** Applicants must be Kent County residents (3 years minimum) who will be attending Aquinas, Calvin, Cornerstone, Davenport, GRCC, GVSU or Kendall; must have financial need and must have a 3.0 minimum GPA. **Criteria:** Priority will be given to those students with financial need.

Funds Avail.: No specific amount. **Duration:** Annual. **To Apply:** Applicants must complete the following: general online application; list of awards, volunteer activities, employment/school extra-curricular activities; academic transcript from most recent semester (High School Students must include first semester senior year). Applicants must also submit a personal essay that includes: reasons for choice of college, chosen course of study, career goals, plans for financing education, and information on past activities benefitting community. **Deadline:** April 1. **Contact:** Ruth Bishop, Education Program Officer; Phone: 616-454-1751 Ext. 103; Email: rbishop@grfoundation.org.

5153 ■ Grand Rapids University Prep Founders' Scholarship *(Undergraduate/Scholarship)*

Purpose: To support students in their pursuit of higher education and future career choices. **Focus:** General studies/Field of study not specified. **Qualif.:** Applicants must be senior students at Grand Rapids University Prep Academy; must be pursuing an undergraduate degree or certification at an accredited two- or four-year college/ university or trade school program located within the United

States; must have a financial need; and must have a minimum cumulative GPA of 2.5. **Criteria:** Selection will be based on the Foundation's criteria.

Funds Avail.: No specific amount. **Duration:** Annual. **To Apply:** Applicants must contact the Foundation for further information. **Deadline:** April 1. **Contact:** Ruth Bishop, Education Program Officer; Phone: 616-454-1751 Ext. 103; Email: rbishop@grfoundation.org.

5154 ■ Guy D. & Mary Edith Halladay Music Scholarship *(Graduate, Undergraduate/Scholarship)*

Purpose: To provide financial assistance to deserving students. **Focus:** Music. **Qualif.:** Applicants must be residents of Kent County (2 years minimum) who are majoring in Music at any college or university in the U.S; must have financial need; must have a cumulative GPA of 3.0. **Criteria:** Priority will be given to those students with high financial need.

Funds Avail.: No specific amount. **Duration:** Annual. **To Apply:** Applicants must complete the following: general online application; list of awards, volunteer activities, employment/school extra-curricular activities; academic transcript from most recent semester (High School Students must include first semester senior year). Applicants must also submit a personal essay that includes: reasons for choice of college, chosen course of study, career goals, plans for financing education, and information on past activities benefitting community. **Deadline:** April 1. **Contact:** Ruth Bishop, Education Program Officer; Phone: 616-454-1751 Ext. 103; Email: rbishop@grfoundation.org.

5155 ■ Hackett Family Scholarship *(Undergraduate/ Scholarship)*

Purpose: To support students in their pursuit of higher education and future career choices. **Focus:** General studies/Field of study not specified. **Qualif.:** Applicants must be senior students or have graduated from any GR public high school in Grand Rapids, Michigan, and attending an accredited college/university or skilled trade school of their choice. **Criteria:** Preference will be given to women of color.

Funds Avail.: No specific amount. **Duration:** Annual. **To Apply:** Applicant must complete the following: general online application; list of awards, volunteer activities, employment/school extracurricular activities; academic transcript from most recent semester (high school students: must include first semester senior year). Must also submit a personal essay that includes: reasons for choice of college, chosen course of study, career goals, plans for financing education, and information on past activities benefitting community. **Deadline:** April 1. **Contact:** Ruth Bishop, Education Program Officer; Phone: 616-454-1751 Ext. 103; Email: rbishop@grfoundation.org.

5156 ■ Guy D. & Mary Edith Halladay Graduate Scholarship *(Undergraduate/Scholarship)*

Purpose: To provide financial support to those students who are in need. **Focus:** General studies/Field of study not specified. **Qualif.:** Applicants must be residents of Kent County (2 years minimum); and must be graduate level students at a Michigan college; must have demonstrated financial need and must have a minimum of 3.0 GPA. **Criteria:** Preference will be given to those who meet the criteria.

Funds Avail.: No specific amount. **Duration:** Annual. **To Apply:** Applicants must complete the following: general

Awards are arranged alphabetically below their administering organizations

online application; list of awards, volunteer activities, employment/school extra-curricular activities; academic transcript from most recent semester (High School Students must include first semester senior year). Applicants must also submit a personal essay that includes: reasons for choice of college, chosen course of study, career goals, plans for financing education, and information on past activities benefitting community. **Deadline:** April 1. **Contact:** Ruth Bishop, Education Program Officer; Phone: 616-454-1751 Ext. 103; Email: rbishop@grfoundation.org.

5157 ■ Harry J. Morris, Jr. Emergency Services
(Undergraduate/Scholarship)

Purpose: To support students in their pursuit of higher education and future career choices in the field of emergency services. **Focus:** Emergency and disaster services; Fires and fire prevention; Paramedics. **Qualif.:** Applicants must be residents of Kent, Allegan, Barry, Ionia, Ottawa, Montcalm, Muskegon or Newaygo County; must be pursuing an undergraduate degree or certificate at an accredited education program in Michigan in the field of emergency medical technician, paramedic, or firefighting training; must have a minimum GPA of 2.5 or verified GED certificate; and have demonstrate a financial need. **Criteria:** Selection will be based on the Foundation's criteria.

Funds Avail.: No specific amount. **Duration:** Annual. **To Apply:** Applicant must complete the following: general online application; list of awards, volunteer activities, employment/school extracurricular activities; academic transcript from most recent semester (high school students: must include first semester senior year). Must also submit a personal essay that includes: reasons for choice of college, chosen course of study, career goals, plans for financing education, and information on past activities benefitting community. **Deadline:** April 1. **Contact:** Ruth Bishop, Education Program Officer; Phone: 616-454-1751 Ext. 103; Email: rbishop@grfoundation.org.

5158 ■ Jack Family Scholarship *(Undergraduate/ Scholarship)*

Purpose: To provide financial assistance to those students who are in need. **Focus:** General studies/Field of study not specified. **Qualif.:** Applicants must be undergraduate students residing in Kent County (3 years minimum) who demonstrate financial need; must have a minimum of 3.3 GPA. **Criteria:** Priority will be given to those students with high financial need.

Funds Avail.: No specific amount. **Duration:** Annual. **To Apply:** Applicants must complete the following: general online application; list of awards, volunteer activities, employment/school extra-curricular activities; academic transcript from most recent semester (High School Students must include first semester senior year). Applicants must also submit a personal essay that includes: reasons for choice of college, chosen course of study, career goals, plans for financing education, and information on past activities benefitting community. **Deadline:** April 1. **Contact:** Ruth Bishop, Education Program Officer; Phone: 616-454-1751 Ext. 103; Email: rbishop@grfoundation.org.

5159 ■ Jacob R. & Mary M. VanLoo & Lenore K. VanLoo Scholarship *(Undergraduate/Scholarship)*

Purpose: To provide financial assistance to those students who are in need. **Focus:** General studies/Field of study not specified. **Qualif.:** Applicants must be Kent County residents (3 years minimum) who will be attending Grand Rapids Community College or Grand Valley State Univer-

sity; must have financial need; must have a minimum of 3.0 GPA. **Criteria:** Selection will be based on financial need.

Funds Avail.: No specific amount. **Duration:** Annual. **To Apply:** Applicants must complete the following: general online application; list of awards, volunteer activities, employment/school extra-curricular activities; academic transcript from most recent semester (High School Students must include first semester senior year). Applicants must also submit a personal essay that includes: reasons for choice of college, chosen course of study, career goals, plans for financing education, and information on past activities benefitting community. **Deadline:** April 1. **Contact:** Ruth Bishop, Education Program Officer; Phone: 616-454-1751 Ext. 103; Email: rbishop@grfoundation.org.

5160 ■ Joshua Esch Mitchell Aviation Scholarship
(Undergraduate/Scholarship)

Purpose: To provide financial support to those students who study flight science. **Focus:** Aviation. **Qualif.:** Applicants must be U.S citizens; must be enrolled full or part-time at a college or university in the United States providing an accredited flight science curriculum; must be 2nd year students or above with a minimum of 2.75 GPA; must be pursuing studies in the field of professional piloting with an emphasis in General Aviation, Aviation Management, or Aviation Safety. **Criteria:** Selection will be based on the committee's criteria.

Funds Avail.: No specific amount. **Duration:** Annual. **To Apply:** Applicants must complete the following: general online application; list of awards, volunteer activities, employment/school extra-curricular activities; academic transcript from most recent semester (High School Students: must include first semester senior year); An essay about yourself that includes: reasons for choice of college, chosen course of study, career goals, plans for financing education, and information on past activities benefitting community. **Deadline:** April 1. **Contact:** Ruth Bishop, Education Program Officer; Phone: 616-454-1751 Ext. 103; Email: rbishop@grfoundation.org.

5161 ■ Ladies Literary Club Scholarship
(Undergraduate/Scholarship)

Purpose: To support students in their pursuit of higher education and future career choices. **Focus:** Arts. **Qualif.:** Applicants must be students who are also residents of Kent, Ottawa, Muskegon, Allegan, Montcalm, or Barry County; must be majoring in literary arts at any accredited Michigan college or university; must have a financial need; and must have a minimum GPA of 3.0. **Criteria:** Selection will be based on the Foundation's criteria.

Funds Avail.: No specific amount. **Duration:** Annual. **To Apply:** Applicant must complete the following: general online application; list of awards, volunteer activities, employment/school extracurricular activities; academic transcript from most recent semester (high school students: must include first semester senior year). Must also submit a personal essay that includes: reasons for choice of college, chosen course of study, career goals, plans for financing education, and information on past activities benefitting community. **Deadline:** April 1. **Contact:** Ruth Bishop, Education Program Officer; Phone: 616-454-1751 Ext. 103; Email: rbishop@grfoundation.org.

5162 ■ Lavina Laible Scholarship *(Undergraduate/ Scholarship)*

Purpose: To provide financial assistance to those students who are in need. **Focus:** General studies/Field of study not

Awards are arranged alphabetically below their administering organizations

specified. **Qualif.:** Applicants must be female students in their third year or above of undergraduate studies at the University of Michigan; must be Kent County residents; must have financial need; must have a minimum of 3.0 GPA. **Criteria:** Selection will be based on the Foundation's criteria.

Funds Avail.: No specific amount. **Duration:** Annual. **To Apply:** Applicants must complete the following: general online application; list of awards, volunteer activities, employment/school extra-curricular activities; academic transcript from most recent semester (High School Students must include first semester senior year). Applicants must also submit a personal essay that includes: reasons for choice of college, chosen course of study, career goals, plans for financing education, and information on past activities benefitting community. **Deadline:** April 1. **Contact:** Ruth Bishop, Education Program Officer; Phone: 616-454-1751 Ext. 103; Email: rbishop@grfoundation.org.

5163 ■ John T. & Frances J. Maghielse Scholarship
(Undergraduate/Scholarship)

Purpose: To provide financial assistance to students who are in need. **Focus:** General studies/Field of study not specified. **Qualif.:** Applicants must be graduates of Grand Rapids Public High School; must be Kent County residents; must be currently pursuing a full-time undergraduate degree in the field of Education at any Michigan public or private college/ university; must have financial need and must have a minimum of 3.0 GPA. **Criteria:** Priority will be given to those students with financial need.

Funds Avail.: No specific amount. **Duration:** Annual. **To Apply:** Applicants must complete the following: general online application; list of awards, volunteer activities, employment/school extra-curricular activities; academic transcript from most recent semester (High School Students must include first semester senior year). Applicants must also submit a personal essay that includes: reasons for choice of college, chosen course of study, career goals, plans for financing education, and information on past activities benefitting community. **Deadline:** April 1. **Contact:** Ruth Bishop, Education Program Officer; Phone: 616-454-1751 Ext. 103; Email: rbishop@grfoundation.org.

5164 ■ Margery J. Seeger Scholarship
(Undergraduate/Scholarship)

Purpose: To provide financial assistance to those students who are in need. **Focus:** General studies/Field of study not specified. **Qualif.:** Applicants must be Kent County residents (3 years minimum) who are pursuing an undergraduate degree at any accredited college in the U.S.; must have financial need; must have a minimum of 3.3 GPA. **Criteria:** Preference will be given to those students who meet the criteria.

Funds Avail.: No specific amount. **Duration:** Annual. **To Apply:** Applicants must complete the following: general online application; list of awards, volunteer activities, employment/school extra-curricular activities; academic transcript from most recent semester (High School Students must include first semester senior year). Applicants must also submit a personal essay that includes: reasons for choice of college, chosen course of study, career goals, plans for financing education, and information on past activities benefitting community. **Deadline:** April 1. **Contact:** Ruth Bishop, Education Program Officer; Phone: 616-454-1751 Ext. 103; Email: rbishop@grfoundation.org.

5165 ■ Mathilda & Carolyn Gallmeyer Scholarship
(Undergraduate/Scholarship)

Purpose: To provide financial assistance to those students who are in need. **Focus:** Art. **Qualif.:** Applicants must be Kent County residents (5 years minimum); must be pursuing Painting or Fine arts; must demonstrate artistic talent, financial need and a minimum of 2.75 GPA. **Criteria:** Selection will be based on financial need.

Funds Avail.: No specific amount. **Duration:** Annual. **To Apply:** Applicants must complete the following: general online application; list of awards, volunteer activities, employment/school extra-curricular activities; academic transcript from most recent semester (High School Students must include first semester senior year). Applicants must also submit a personal essay that includes: reasons for choice of college, chosen course of study, career goals, plans for financing education, and information on past activities benefitting community. **Deadline:** April 1. **Contact:** Ruth Bishop, Education Program Officer; Phone: 616-454-1751 Ext. 103; Email: rbishop@grfoundation.org.

5166 ■ Fred & Lena Meijer Scholarships
(Undergraduate/Scholarship)

Purpose: To support Meijer team members or their dependents in their pursuit of higher education and future career choices. **Focus:** General studies/Field of study not specified. **Qualif.:** Applicants must be students who are Meijer team member or children (natural, legally adopted, or stepchildren) of Meijer team member who have been employed for at least one year by the time of the application deadline. **Criteria:** Selection will be based on the Foundation's criteria.

Funds Avail.: $3,000-$10,000. **Duration:** Annual. **To Apply:** Application is submitted via online. **Deadline:** April 1.

5167 ■ Melbourne & Alice E. Frontjes Scholarship
(Undergraduate/Scholarship)

Purpose: To provide financial assistance to those students who are in need. **Focus:** General studies/Field of study not specified. **Qualif.:** Applicants must be Kent County residents (3 years minimum) who are pursuing an undergraduate degree at Central Michigan University, Western Michigan University, GRCC, University of Michigan or Michigan State University; must have demonstrated financial need and have a minimum of 2.75 GPA. **Criteria:** Priority will be given to those students with financial need.

Funds Avail.: No specific amount. **Duration:** Annual. **To Apply:** Applicants must complete the following: general online application; list of awards, volunteer activities, employment/school extra-curricular activities; academic transcript from most recent semester (High School Students must include first semester senior year). Applicants must also submit a personal essay that includes: reasons for choice of college, chosen course of study, career goals, plans for financing education, and information on past activities benefitting community. **Deadline:** April 1. **Contact:** Ruth Bishop, Education Program Officer; Phone: 616-454-1751 Ext. 103; Email: rbishop@grfoundation.org.

5168 ■ Michael J. Wolf Scholarship *(Undergraduate/Scholarship)*

Purpose: To support students in their pursuit of higher education and future career choices. **Focus:** General studies/Field of study not specified. **Qualif.:** Applicants must be senior graduating students from a Grand Rapids Public High School; must be residing in the City of Grand

Awards are arranged alphabetically below their administering organizations

Rapids; must be pursuing an undergraduate degree at the University of Michigan; must demonstrate a financial need; and must have a minimum GPA of 3.0. **Criteria:** Selection will be based on the Foundation's criteria.

Funds Avail.: No specific amount. **Duration:** Annual. **To Apply:** Applicant must complete the following: general online application; list of awards, volunteer activities, employment/school extracurricular activities; academic transcript from most recent semester (high school students: must include first semester senior year). Must also submit a personal essay that includes: reasons for choice of college, chosen course of study, career goals, plans for financing education, and information on past activities benefitting community. **Deadline:** April 1. **Contact:** Ruth Bishop, Education Program Officer; Phone: 616-454-1751 Ext. 103; Email: rbishop@grfoundation.org.

5169 ■ Mildred E. Troske Music Scholarship
(Undergraduate/Scholarship)

Purpose: To provide financial support to those students who are in need. **Focus:** General studies/Field of study not specified. **Qualif.:** Applicants must be residents of Kent County (2 years minimum) who are studying music at a camp or are undergraduate music majors; must have demonstrated financial need; must have a minimum of 3.0 GPA. **Criteria:** Priority will be given to those students with financial need.

Funds Avail.: No specific amount. **Duration:** Annual. **To Apply:** Applicants must complete the following: general online application; list of awards, volunteer activities, employment/school extra-curricular activities; academic transcript from most recent semester (High School Students must include first semester senior year). Applicants must also submit a personal essay that includes: reasons for choice of college, chosen course of study, career goals, plans for financing education, and information on past activities benefitting community. **Deadline:** April 1. **Contact:** Ruth Bishop, Education Program Officer; Phone: 616-454-1751 Ext. 103; Email: rbishop@grfoundation.org.

5170 ■ NAIFA West Michigan Scholarship
(Undergraduate/Scholarship)

Purpose: To support students in their pursuit of higher education and future career choices. **Focus:** Business; Finance. **Qualif.:** Applicants must be residents of Kent or contiguous counties; must be students pursuing a full-time undergraduate (third year or above) or graduate degree as business/financial majors at Michigan public or private colleges/universities; must have financial need; and must have minimum 3.0 GPA. **Criteria:** Selection will be based on the Foundation's criteria.

Funds Avail.: No specific amount. **Duration:** Annual. **To Apply:** Applicant must complete general online application; list of awards, volunteer activities, employment/school extra-curricular activities; academic transcript from most recent semester (high school students: must include first semester senior year); a personal essay that includes: reasons for choice of college, chosen course of study, career goals, plans for financing education, and information on past activities benefitting community; must provide two letters of recommendation. **Deadline:** April 1. **Contact:** Ruth Bishop, Education Program Officer; Phone: 616-454-1751 Ext. 103; Email: rbishop@grfoundation.org.

5171 ■ Orrie & Dorothy Cassada Scholarship
(Undergraduate/Scholarship)

Purpose: To provide financial assistance to those students who are in need. **Focus:** General studies/Field of study not

specified. **Qualif.:** Applicants must be residents of Kent County (3 years minimum) who will be attending Aquinas, Calvin, Cornerstone, Davenport, GRCC, GVSU or Kendall; must have financial need and a 3.0 minimum GPA. **Criteria:** Priority will be given to those students with financial need.

Funds Avail.: No specific amount. **Duration:** Annual. **To Apply:** Applicants must complete the following: general online application; list of awards, volunteer activities, employment/school extra-curricular activities; academic transcript from most recent semester (High School Students must include first semester senior year). Applicants must also submit a personal essay that includes: reasons for choice of college, chosen course of study, career goals, plans for financing education, and information on past activities benefitting community. **Deadline:** April 1. **Contact:** Ruth Bishop, Education Program Officer; Phone: 616-454-1751 Ext. 103; Email: rbishop@grfoundation.org.

5172 ■ Patricia & Armen Oumedian Scholarship
(Undergraduate/Scholarship)

Purpose: To provide financial support to those students who are in need. **Focus:** Engineering. **Qualif.:** Applicant must be a second year or above full-time student at Kettering or transferring from GRCC to Kettering; must be a resident of West Michigan or currently be employed by a West Michigan Kettering co-op employer; must demonstrate financial need and have a minimum 3.0 GPA. **Criteria:** Selection will be based on the Foundation's criteria.

Funds Avail.: No specific amount. **Duration:** Annual. **To Apply:** Applicant must complete the following: general online application; list of awards, volunteer activities, employment/school extra-curricular activities; academic transcript from most recent semester (high school students: must include first semester senior year). Applicant must also submit a personal essay that includes: reasons for choice of college, chosen course of study, career goals, plans for financing education, and information on past activities benefitting community. **Deadline:** April 1. **Contact:** Ruth Bishop, Education Program Officer; Phone: 616-454-1751 Ext. 103; Email: rbishop@grfoundation.org.

5173 ■ Peggy (Kommer) Novosad Scholarship
(Graduate, Postgraduate/Scholarship)

Purpose: To provide financial support to those students who are in need. **Focus:** Business; Law. **Qualif.:** Applicants must be residents of Kent County who are currently completing or have already earned an undergraduate degree from GVSU or MSU and will be pursuing a full-time graduate or post-graduate degree in business or law at any accredited university in Michigan; must have financial need and a minimum of 3.5 GPA. **Criteria:** Priority will be given to those students with financial need.

Funds Avail.: No specific amount. **Duration:** Annual. **To Apply:** Applicant must complete the following: general online application; list of awards, volunteer activities, employment/school extra-curricular activities; academic transcript from most recent semester (high school students: must include first semester senior year). Applicant must also submit a personal essay that includes: reasons for choice of college, chosen course of study, career goals, plans for financing education, and information on past activities benefitting community. **Deadline:** April 1. **Contact:** Ruth Bishop, Education Program Officer; Phone: 616-454-1751 Ext. 103; Email: rbishop@grfoundation.org.

5174 ■ Reach for Your Goal Scholarship
(Undergraduate/Scholarship)

Purpose: To support students in their pursuit of higher education and future career choices. **Focus:** General

Awards are arranged alphabetically below their administering organizations

studies/Field of study not specified. **Qualif.:** Applicants must be residents of Kent County; must be high school seniors who have been accepted into an accredited Michigan trade school, college or university; must have a financial need; and must have a minimum 3.0 GPA. **Criteria:** Selection will be based on the Foundation's criteria.

Funds Avail.: No specific amount. **Duration:** Annual. **To Apply:** Applicant must complete the following: general online application; list of awards, volunteer activities, employment/school extracurricular activities; academic transcript from most recent semester (high school students: must include first semester senior year). Must also submit a personal essay that includes: reasons for choice of college, chosen course of study, career goals, plans for financing education, and information on past activities benefitting community. **Deadline:** April 1. **Contact:** Ruth Bishop, Education Program Officer; Phone: 616-454-1751 Ext. 103; Email: rbishop@grfoundation.org.

5175 ■ Josephine Ringold Scholarship
(Undergraduate/Scholarship)

Purpose: To provide financial support to those students who are in need. **Focus:** General studies/Field of study not specified. **Qualif.:** Applicants must be Kent County residents (3 years minimum) who will be attending Aquinas, Calvin, Cornerstone, Davenport, GRCC, GVSU or Kendall; must have financial need and a 3.0 minimum GPA is required. **Criteria:** Preference will be given to those students who meet the criteria.

Funds Avail.: No specific amount. **Duration:** Annual. **To Apply:** Applicants must complete the following: general online application; list of awards, volunteer activities, employment/school extra-curricular activities; academic transcript from most recent semester (High School Students must include first semester senior year). Applicants must also submit a personal essay that includes: reasons for choice of college, chosen course of study, career goals, plans for financing education, and information on past activities benefitting community. **Deadline:** April 1. **Contact:** Ruth Bishop, Education Program Officer; Phone: 616-454-1751 Ext. 103; Email: rbishop@grfoundation.org.

5176 ■ Robert L. & Hilda Treasure Mitchell Scholarship *(Undergraduate/Scholarship)*

Purpose: To provide financial assistance to deserving students. **Focus:** General studies/Field of study not specified. **Qualif.:** Applicants must be pursuing an undergraduate degree at any accredited college or university in the United States; must be Kent County residents (3 years minimum); must demonstrate financial need; must have a minimum of 3.3 GPA. **Criteria:** Priority will be given to those students with financial need.

Funds Avail.: No specific amount. **Duration:** Annual. **To Apply:** Applicant must complete the following: general online application; list of awards, volunteer activities, employment/school extra-curricular activities; academic transcript from most recent semester (high school students: must include first semester senior year). Applicant must also submit a personal essay that includes: reasons for choice of college, chosen course of study, career goals, plans for financing education, and information on past activities benefitting community. **Deadline:** April 1. **Contact:** Ruth Bishop, Education Program Officer; Phone: 616-454-1751 Ext. 103; Email: rbishop@grfoundation.org.

5177 ■ Roger and Jacquelyn Vander Laan Family Scholarship *(Undergraduate/Scholarship)*

Purpose: To support students in their pursuit of higher education and future career choices. **Focus:** General

studies/Field of study not specified. **Qualif.:** Applicants must be seniors at South Christian high school; must be entering a full time program in the fall at any accredited college, university, vocational or technical school; must be majoring in healthcare, education, or business; must have a financial need; and must have a minimum 3.0 GPA. **Criteria:** Selection will be based on the Foundation's criteria.

Funds Avail.: No specific amount. **Duration:** Annual. **To Apply:** Applicants must contact the Foundation for further information. **Deadline:** April 1. **Contact:** Ruth Bishop, Education Program Officer; Phone: 616-454-1751 Ext. 103; Email: rbishop@grfoundation.org.

5178 ■ Ronald T. Smith Family Scholarship
(Undergraduate, Graduate/Scholarship)

Purpose: To support individuals in their pursuit of higher education and future career choices. **Focus:** General studies/Field of study not specified. **Qualif.:** Applicants must be students who are employees of or spouses/domestic partners or children (natural, legally adopted, or stepchildren) of employees of Bodycote Grand Rapids or Holland Plants; must be pursuing an undergraduate or graduate degree at any accredited college/university or trade school in the United States; must have a financial need; and must have a minimum GPA of 2.5. **Criteria:** Selection will be based on the Foundation's criteria.

Funds Avail.: No specific amount. **Duration:** Annual. **To Apply:** Applicants must complete the following: general online application; list of awards, volunteer activities, employment/school extra-curricular activities; academic transcript from most recent semester (high school students: must include first semester senior year); a personal essay that includes: reasons for choice of college, chosen course of study, career goals, plans for financing education, and information on past activities benefitting community. **Deadline:** April 1. **Contact:** Ruth Bishop, Education Program Officer; Phone: 616-454-1751 Ext. 103; Email: rbishop@grfoundation.org.

5179 ■ Rosemary Cook Education Scholarship
(Undergraduate/Scholarship)

Purpose: To support students from Kent County who are majoring in education. **Focus:** Education. **Qualif.:** Applicants must be students who are Kent County residents; must be graduates of a Grand Rapids Public High School; must be pursuing an undergraduate degree in Education full-time at any accredited Michigan public or private college/university; must have a financial need; and must have a minimum GPA of 2.75. **Criteria:** Selection will be based on the Foundation's criteria.

Funds Avail.: No specific amount. **Duration:** Annual. **To Apply:** Applicants must contact the Foundation for further information. **Deadline:** April 1. **Contact:** Ruth Bishop, Education Program Officer; Phone: 616-454-1751 Ext. 103; Email: rbishop@grfoundation.org.

5180 ■ Dave & Laurie Russell Family Scholarships for Habitat for Humanity of Kent County Families
(Undergraduate/Scholarship)

Purpose: To support students in their pursuit of higher education and future career choices. **Focus:** General studies/Field of study not specified. **Qualif.:** Applicants must be students who are Habitat for Humanity of Kent County home owners or immediate family member (spouses/partners, children, stepchildren) residing in the home, and pursuing an undergraduate degree or certifica-

Awards are arranged alphabetically below their administering organizations

tion at an accredited vocational trade program, two- or four-year college or accredited graduate level program located in the United States; must also have demonstrated financial need. **Criteria:** Selection will be based on the Foundation's criteria.

Funds Avail.: No specific amount. **Duration:** Annual. **To Apply:** Applicant must complete the following: general online application; list of awards, volunteer activities, employment/school extracurricular activities; academic transcript from most recent semester (high school students: must include first semester senior year). Must also submit a personal essay that includes: reasons for choice of college, chosen course of study, career goals, plans for financing education, and information on past activities benefitting community. **Deadline:** April 1. **Contact:** Ruth Bishop, Education Program Officer; Phone: 616-454-1751 Ext. 103; Email: rbishop@grfoundation.org.

5181 ■ Sherman L. & Mabel C. Lepard Scholarship
(Undergraduate/Scholarship)

Purpose: To provide financial assistance to deserving students. **Focus:** General studies/Field of study not specified. **Qualif.:** Applicants must be pursuing an undergraduate degree at any accredited college or university in the U.S; must be Kent County residents (3 years minimum); must have demonstrated financial need; must have a minimum of 3.3 GPA. **Criteria:** Priority will be given to those students with high financial need.

Funds Avail.: No specific amount. **Duration:** Annual. **To Apply:** Applicant must complete the following: general online application; list of awards, volunteer activities, employment/school extra-curricular activities; academic transcript from most recent semester (high school students: must include first semester senior year). Applicant must also submit a personal essay that includes: reasons for choice of college, chosen course of study, career goals, plans for financing education, and information on past activities benefitting community. **Deadline:** April 1. **Contact:** Ruth Bishop, Education Program Officer; Phone: 616-454-1751 Ext. 103; Email: rbishop@grfoundation.org.

5182 ■ Gladys Snauble Scholarship *(Undergraduate/Scholarship)*

Purpose: To provide financial support to those students who are in need. **Focus:** General studies/Field of study not specified. **Qualif.:** Applicants must be senior students at Cedar Springs High School who will be entering college in the fall; must have financial need. **Criteria:** Priority will be given to those students with financial need.

Funds Avail.: No specific amount. **Duration:** Annual. **To Apply:** Applicants must complete the following: general online application; list of awards, volunteer activities, employment/school extra-curricular activities; academic transcript from most recent semester (High School Students must include first semester senior year). Applicants must also submit a personal essay that includes: reasons for choice of college, chosen course of study, career goals, plans for financing education, and information on past activities benefitting the community. **Deadline:** April 1. **Contact:** Ruth Bishop, Education Program Officer; Phone: 616-454-1751 Ext. 103; Email: rbishop@grfoundation.org.

5183 ■ Dr. William E. & Norma Sprague Scholarship
(Undergraduate, Graduate/Scholarship)

Purpose: To provide financial assistance to those students who are in need. **Focus:** Medicine. **Qualif.:** Applicants must be full-time students and permanent residents in the Michigan counties of Kent, Allegan, Barry, Ionia, Montcalm, Muskegon, Newaygo or Athens County, Ohio, who are pursuing a full-time undergraduate or graduate degree in medicine at Ohio University; must have financial need; must have a minimum of 3.0 GPA. **Criteria:** Priority will be given to those students with high financial need.

Funds Avail.: No specific amount. **Duration:** Annual. **To Apply:** Applicants must complete the following: general online application; list of awards, volunteer activities, employment/school extra-curricular activities; academic transcript from most recent semester (High School Students must include first semester senior year). Applicants must also submit a personal essay that includes: reasons for choice of college, chosen course of study, career goals, plans for financing education, and information on past activities benefitting community. **Deadline:** April 1. **Contact:** Ruth Bishop, Education Program Officer; Phone: 616-454-1751 Ext. 103; Email: rbishop@grfoundation.org.

5184 ■ Stephen Lankester Scholarship
(Undergraduate/Scholarship)

Purpose: To provide financial assistance to those students who are in need. **Focus:** General studies/Field of study not specified. **Qualif.:** Applicants must be Kent County residents (3 years minimum); must be attending an undergraduate program at a Michigan college; must have financial need; must have a minimum of 3.0 GPA. **Criteria:** Priority will be given to those students with high financial need.

Funds Avail.: No specific amount. **Duration:** Annual. **To Apply:** Applicant must complete the following: general online application; list of awards, volunteer activities, employment/school extra-curricular activities; academic transcript from most recent semester (high school students: must include first semester senior year). Applicant must also submit a personal essay that includes: reasons for choice of college, chosen course of study, career goals, plans for financing education, and information on past activities benefitting community. **Deadline:** April 1. **Contact:** Ruth Bishop, Education Program Officer; Phone: 616-454-1751 Ext. 103; Email: rbishop@grfoundation.org.

5185 ■ Thomas D. Coffield Scholarship
(Undergraduate/Scholarship)

Purpose: To provide financial assistance to those students who are in need. **Focus:** General studies/Field of study not specified. **Qualif.:** Applicants must be senior students at Central High School who will be entering a two or four-year accredited college or university; must have a 2.5 minimum GPA; must have demonstrated financial need. **Criteria:** Selection will be based on the Foundation's criteria.

Funds Avail.: No specific amount. **Duration:** Annual. **To Apply:** Applicant must complete the following: general online application; list of awards, volunteer activities, employment/school extra-curricular activities; two letters of recommendation; academic transcript from most recent semester (high school students: must include first semester senior year). Applicant must also submit a personal essay that includes: reasons for choice of college, chosen course of study, career goals, plans for financing education, and information on past activities benefitting community. **Deadline:** April 1. **Contact:** Ruth Bishop, Education Program Officer; Phone: 616-454-1751 Ext. 103; Email: rbishop@grfoundation.org.

5186 ■ Dorothy J. Thurston Graduate Scholarship
(Undergraduate/Scholarship)

Purpose: To provide financial assistance to those students who are in need. **Focus:** General studies/Field of study not

---

Awards are arranged alphabetically below their administering organizations

specified. **Qualif.:** Applicants must be Kent County residents who are pursuing full or part-time study at any accredited school in Michigan; must have financial need; must have a minimum of 3.0 GPA. **Criteria:** Priority will be given to those students with financial need.

Funds Avail.: No specific amount. **Duration:** Annual. **To Apply:** Applicants must complete the following: general online application; list of awards, volunteer activities, employment/school extra-curricular activities; academic transcript from most recent semester (High School Students must include first semester senior year). Applicants must also submit a personal essay that includes: reasons for choice of college, chosen course of study, career goals, plans for financing education, and information on past activities benefitting community. **Deadline:** April 1. **Contact:** Ruth Bishop, Education Program Officer; Phone: 616-454-1751 Ext. 103; Email: rbishop@grfoundation.org.

5187 ■ U-M Alumnae Club (University of Michigan) Scholarships *(Undergraduate/Scholarship)*

Purpose: To support female students in their pursuit of higher education and future career choices. **Focus:** General studies/Field of study not specified. **Qualif.:** Applicants must be female students entering the second year or above at the University of Michigan; must have a permanent residency (three years minimum) in Kent or adjoining counties of Allegan, Barry, Ionia, Montcalm, Muskegon, Newaygo, or Ottawa; must have a financial need; and must have a minimum GPA of 3.0. **Criteria:** Selection will be based on the Foundation's criteria.

Funds Avail.: No specific amount. **Duration:** Annual. **To Apply:** Applicants must complete the following: general online application; list of awards, volunteer activities, employment/school extra-curricular activities; academic transcript from most recent semester (high school students: must include first semester senior year); a personal essay that includes: reasons for choice of college, chosen course of study, career goals, plans for financing education, and information on past activities benefitting community. **Deadline:** April 1. **Contact:** Ruth Bishop, Education Program Officer; Phone: 616-454-1751 Ext. 103; Email: rbishop@grfoundation.org.

5188 ■ Keith C. Vanderhyde Scholarship *(Undergraduate/Scholarship)*

Purpose: To provide financial assistance to those students who are in need. **Focus:** General studies/Field of study not specified. **Qualif.:** Applicants must be senior students or graduates of Ottawa Hills High School who are pursuing a full-time undergraduate degree; must demonstrate financial need; must have a minimum of 3.0 GPA. **Criteria:** Priority will be given to those students with financial need.

Funds Avail.: No specific amount. **Duration:** Annual. **To Apply:** Applicants must complete the following: general online application; list of awards, volunteer activities, employment/school extra-curricular activities; academic transcript from most recent semester (High School Students must include first semester senior year). Applicants must also submit a personal essay that includes: reasons for choice of college, chosen course of study, career goals, plans for financing education, and information on past activities benefitting community. **Deadline:** April 1. **Contact:** Ruth Bishop, Education Program Officer; Phone: 616-454-1751 Ext. 103; Email: rbishop@grfoundation.org.

5189 ■ Virginia Valk Fehsenfeld Scholarship *(Undergraduate/Scholarship)*

Purpose: To provide financial support to those students who are in need. **Focus:** General studies/Field of study not

specified. **Qualif.:** Applicants must be full-time undergraduate students pursuing a degree in Dietetics, Nutrition, Education or General Human Services; must be residents of Kent County, must have financial need and minimum of 3.4 GPA. **Criteria:** Selection will be based on the Foundation's criteria.

Funds Avail.: No specific amount. **Duration:** Annual. **To Apply:** Applicant must complete the following: general online application; list of awards, volunteer activities, employment/school extra-curricular activities; two letters of recommendation; academic transcript from most recent semester (high school students: must include first semester senior year). Applicant must also submit a personal essay that includes: reasons for choice of college, chosen course of study, career goals, plans for financing education, and information on past activities benefitting community. **Deadline:** April 1. **Contact:** Ruth Bishop, Education Program Officer; Phone: 616-454-1751 Ext. 103; Email: rbishop@grfoundation.org.

5190 ■ Vivian M. Kommer Scholarship *(Undergraduate/Scholarship)*

Purpose: To support students in their pursuit of higher education and future career choices. **Focus:** Business. **Qualif.:** Applicants must be senior students at West Catholic High School entering undergraduate studies in business or pre-law; must demonstrate financial need; and have a minimum GPA of 3.0. **Criteria:** Selection will be based on financial need.

Funds Avail.: No specific amount. **Duration:** Annual. **To Apply:** Applicants must complete the following: general online application; list of awards, volunteer activities, employment/school extra-curricular activities; academic transcript from most recent semester (high school students: must include first semester senior year); a personal essay that includes: reasons for choice of college, chosen course of study, career goals, plans for financing education, and information on past activities benefitting community. **Deadline:** April 1. **Contact:** Ruth Bishop, Education Program Officer; Phone: 616-454-1751 Ext. 103; Email: rbishop@grfoundation.org.

5191 ■ Chad Vollmer Scholarships *(Undergraduate/Scholarship)*

Purpose: To support students who will attend Grand Rapids Community College for their pursuit of higher education and to encourage them in their future career choices. **Focus:** General studies/Field of study not specified. **Qualif.:** Applicants must be senior high school students at Central High School and will attend Grand Rapids Community College; must have a financial need; must have a 2.3 minimum GPA to renew; and must have an acceptable work history. **Criteria:** Selection will be based on the Foundation's criteria.

Funds Avail.: No specific amount. **Duration:** Annual. **To Apply:** Applicant must complete the following: general online application; list of awards, volunteer activities, employment/school extracurricular activities; academic transcript from most recent semester (high school students: must include first semester senior year). Must also submit a personal essay that includes: reasons for choice of college, chosen course of study, career goals, plans for financing education, and information on past activities benefitting community. **Deadline:** April 1. **Contact:** Ruth Bishop, Education Program Officer; Phone: 616-454-1751 Ext. 103; Email: rbishop@grfoundation.org.

Awards are arranged alphabetically below their administering organizations

5192 ■ Walter C. Winchester Scholarship
(Undergraduate/Scholarship)

Purpose: To support students in their pursuit of higher education and future career choices. **Focus:** General studies/Field of study not specified. **Qualif.:** Applicants must be senior students graduating from a Grand Rapids Public High School; have demonstrate financial need; and have a minimum 3.3 GPA. **Criteria:** Selection will be based on the Foundation's criteria.

Funds Avail.: No specific amount. **Duration:** Annual. **To Apply:** Applicants must complete the following: general online application; list of awards, volunteer activities, employment/school extra-curricular activities; academic transcript from most recent semester (high school students: must include first semester senior year); a personal essay that includes: reasons for choice of college, chosen course of study, career goals, plans for financing education, and information on past activities benefitting community. **Deadline:** April 1. **Contact:** Ruth Bishop, Education Program Officer; Phone: 616-454-1751 Ext. 103; Email: rbishop@grfoundation.org.

5193 ■ Donald M. Wells Scholarships
(Undergraduate/Scholarship)

Purpose: To provide financial assistance to those students who are in need. **Focus:** General studies/Field of study not specified. **Qualif.:** Applicants must be senior students or graduates of Central high school who are pursuing undergraduate studies at GRCC, University of Chicago or University of Michigan; must have financial need and must have a minimum of 2.5 GPA. **Criteria:** Preference will be given to those students who meet the criteria.

Funds Avail.: No specific amount. **Duration:** Annual. **To Apply:** Applicant must complete the following: general online application; list of awards, volunteer activities, employment/school extra-curricular activities; academic transcript from most recent semester (high school students: must include first semester senior year). Applicant must also submit a personal essay that includes: reasons for choice of college, chosen course of study, career goals, plans for financing education, and information on past activities benefitting community. **Deadline:** April 1. **Contact:** Ruth Bishop, Education Program Officer; Phone: 616-454-1751 Ext. 103; Email: rbishop@grfoundation.org.

5194 ■ Elmo Wierenga Alumni Scholarship
(Undergraduate/Scholarship)

Purpose: To provide financial support to those students who are in need. **Focus:** General studies/Field of study not specified. **Qualif.:** Applicants must be senior students at Ottawa Hills high school pursuing full-time undergraduate studies at any 2 or 4-year accredited school in the U.S; must have financial need and a minimum of 2.5 GPA. **Criteria:** Priority will be given to those students with financial need.

Funds Avail.: No specific amount. **Duration:** Annual. **To Apply:** Applicants must complete the following: general online application; list of awards, volunteer activities, employment/school extra-curricular activities; academic transcript from most recent semester (High School Students must include first semester senior year). Applicants must also submit a personal essay that includes: reasons for choice of college, chosen course of study, career goals, plans for financing education, and information on past activities benefitting community. **Deadline:** April 1. **Contact:** Ruth Bishop, Education Program Officer; Phone: 616-454-1751 Ext. 103; Email: rbishop@grfoundation.org.

5195 ■ Violet Wondergem Health Science Scholarships
(Undergraduate/Scholarship)

Purpose: To support students majoring in a health service related field. **Focus:** Health care services. **Qualif.:** Applicants must be residents of Kent or Ottawa County; must be majoring in a health service related field at any accredited Michigan college or university; must have a financial need; and must have a minimum 3.0 cumulative GPA. **Criteria:** Selection will be based on the Foundation's criteria.

Funds Avail.: No specific amount. **Duration:** Annual. **To Apply:** Applicants must contact the Foundation for further information. **Deadline:** April 1. **Contact:** Ruth Bishop, Education Program Officer; Phone: 616-454-1751 Ext. 103; Email: rbishop@grfoundation.org.

5196 ■ Grand Rapids Trans Foundation
PO Box 2674
Grand Rapids, MI 49501
URL: grtransfoundation.org
Social Media: facebook.com/grtransfoundation
instagram.com/grtransfoundation

5197 ■ Grand Rapids Trans Foundation Academic Scholarship *(Undergraduate, Two Year College, Vocational/Occupational/Scholarship)*

Purpose: To help transgender students with education-related expenses while pursuing a degree or certificate in Kent County, MI. **Focus:** General studies/Field of study not specified. **Criteria:** Selection will be based upon essay and financial need.

Funds Avail.: $2,500. **Duration:** One year. **Number Awarded:** Varies. **To Apply:** Application materials available at grtransfoundation.org/scholarship. **Contact:** Email: applications@grtransfoundation.org.

5198 ■ Granger Business Association (GBA)
PO Box 427
Granger, IN 46530
Ph: (574)271-4235
E-mail: info@grangertoday.com
URL: www.grangerbusinessassociation.org
Social Media: www.facebook.com/
GrangerBusinessAssociation

5199 ■ Granger Business Association College Scholarship *(Graduate/Scholarship)*

Purpose: To help defray college expenses of students from Granger area. **Focus:** General studies/Field of study not specified. **Qualif.:** Applicants must reside in the 46530 zip code and demonstrate financial need. **Criteria:** Selection criteria for selection include (but not limited to) academics; extra curricular activities; volunteer work and personal narratives.

Funds Avail.: $1,000 each. **Duration:** Annual. **Number Awarded:** Typically 10. **To Apply:** Applicants must complete the application form; attach most recent official high school transcripts; one (1) letter of recommendation from a teacher, counselor, or coach; one (1) letter of recommendation from a member of the Granger community or an employer; must provide a short essay of the questions listed in the application form. **Contact:** Kathy Smith, Scholarship Chairman; Phone: 574-243-7746; PO Box 427, Granger, IN, 46530.

Awards are arranged alphabetically below their administering organizations

5200 ■ Granite Bay Cosmetic Surgery
5220 Douglas Blvd.
Granite Bay, CA 95746
Ph: (916)242-2662
URL: www.granitebaycosmetic.com
Social Media: www.facebook.com/
   granitebaycosmeticsurgery
twitter.com/granitebaycs

5201 ■ SPROWT Scholarship for Women
(Undergraduate/Scholarship)

Purpose: To support and empower California women who are following a non-traditional educational path as they pursue higher education. **Focus:** General studies/Field of study not specified. **Qualif.:** Applicant must be female and a resident of California pursuing education at a California higher education institute. Applicant must also be a nontraditional student as defined by the National Center for Education Statistics by meeting one or more of the following criteria: delayed enrollment into higher education; part-time college student; works full-time; has dependent other than a spouse; is a single parent; or done not have a high school diploma. **Criteria:** Selection based on female California residents pursuing education at a California higher education

Funds Avail.: $2,500. **Number Awarded:** 1. **To Apply:** Applicant must complete the application form and provide original essay answers. **Contact:** www.granitebaycosmetic.com/sprowt-scholarship/.

5202 ■ Grant Law Office
1 Concourse Parkway,Ste 800
Atlanta, GA 30328
Ph: (404)846-4676
Fax: (404)995-3950
Free: 866-775-9231
E-mail: submit@waynegrant.com
URL: www.grantlawoffice.com
Social Media: www.facebook.com/GrantLawOffice
www.instagram.com/grantlawoffice
twitter.com/grantlawoffice
www.youtube.com/user/theGrantFirm

5203 ■ Best Foot Forward Scholarship *(Undergraduate, College, University/Scholarship)*

Purpose: To help a student in Georgia pay for college. **Focus:** General studies/Field of study not specified. **Qualif.:** Applicant must be a high school senior in Georgia on track to graduate, or currently attending a college or university in Georgia, or currently enrolled in a two-year college and planning to transfer to a four-year university or college; current high school students in Georgia planning to attend a college outside of Georgia may also apply. Applicant must have a 3.0 or higher cumulative GPA and be a citizen or permanent resident of the U.S. (DACA recipients are welcome to apply).

Funds Avail.: $1,000. **Number Awarded:** 1. **To Apply:** Application and essay must be submitted online. **Deadline:** April 22. **Contact:** Scholarship Manager; Email: submit@ waynegrant.com; URL: www.grantlawoffice.com/ scholarship/.

5204 ■ Grass Foundation
PO Box 11342
Takoma Park, MD 20913

E-mail: info@grassfoundation.org
URL: www.grassfoundation.org
Social Media: www.facebook.com/groups/grassfoundation
twitter.com/grassfoundation

5205 ■ Grass Fellowships at the Marine Biological Laboratory *(Doctorate, Postdoctorate/Fellowship)*

Purpose: To support investigator-designed, independent research projects by scientists early in their career. **Focus:** Biophysics; Neurology; Neurophysiology; Neuroscience. **Qualif.:** Applicants must be early investigators (late stage predoctoral trainees and beyond) including those with prior experience at MBL or with the Grass Foundation; international Fellows (i.e., not US citizens or resident aliens). **Criteria:** Selection is based on demonstrated commitment to a research career and no prior research experience at the MBL.

Funds Avail.: No specific amount. **Duration:** Annual. **Number Awarded:** Varies. **To Apply:** Applicants must complete the application; letters of recommendation. **Deadline:** December 5. **Contact:** Dana Mock-Munoz de Luna, Grass Fellowship Program Coordinator at MBL; Phone: 508.289.7521; Email: gfp@grassfoundation.org.

5206 ■ Gravure Education Foundation (GEF)
PO Box 25617
Rochester, NY 14625
Ph: (201)523-6042
Fax: (201)523-6048
E-mail: gaa@gaa.org
URL: www.gaa.org/about/gravure-education-endowment

5207 ■ Alcoa Scholarship *(Undergraduate, Graduate/ Scholarship)*

Purpose: To identify and cultivate the next generation of talented gravure operators. **Focus:** Printing trades and industries; Publishing. **Qualif.:** Applicants must be undergraduate or graduate students enrolled in a full-time basis in one of the GEF designated learning resource centers; must have GPA of 3.0 or greater on a 4.0 scale. **Criteria:** Selection will be based on demonstrated leadership and academic accomplishments.

Funds Avail.: $1,500. **Duration:** Annual. **Number Awarded:** 1. **To Apply:** Applicants must submit an essay of 300-500 words describing "my Interest in gravuretechnology and the print communications industry"; and a student copy of college/university transcripts. **Deadline:** March 1. **Remarks:** In collaboration with ALCOA Foundation. **Contact:** URL: gaa.org/awards/gravure-education-endowment-scholarships/.

5208 ■ The Cerutti Group Scholarship
(Undergraduate/Scholarship)

Purpose: To identify and cultivate the next generation of talented gravure operators. **Focus:** Printing trades and industries; Publishing. **Qualif.:** Applicants must be enrolled full-time at a college, university or technical school designated by GEF as a Gravure Resource Center or an Educational Partner Program; must be sophomore, junior, senior, or graduate students at the time the scholarships are awarded; declared major in printing, graphic arts, or graphic communications must be demonstrated; must demonstrate leadership development efforts through clubs or associations, sports, community participation, or volunteer activity; must exhibit scholarly performance and

Awards are arranged alphabetically below their administering organizations

demonstrate academic success; with a GPA of 3.0 or greater (on a 4.0 scale) is required. **Criteria:** Recipients will be chosen based on submitted materials.

Funds Avail.: $1,500. **Duration:** Annual. **Number Awarded:** 1. **To Apply:** Application is available online at: gaa.org/awards/gravure-education-endowment-scholarships/. **Deadline:** March 1. **Remarks:** The scholarship is made possible with Cerutti Group. **Contact:** John Berthelsen, VP-Development, PGSF, Phone: 608-575-3904; Email: jberthelsen@printing.org.

5209 ■ Harry V. Quadracci Memorial Scholarship (Undergraduate, Graduate/Scholarship)

Purpose: To provide financial assistance to students and encourage them to be involved in Gravure industry. **Focus:** Graphic art and design; Printmaking; Publishing. **Qualif.:** Applicants must be undergraduate or graduate students; must be enrolled full-time at any of the printing management/graphic arts programs at one of the GEF designed learning resource centers; must maintain a GPA of 3.0 or greater (on a 4.0 scale) is required. **Criteria:** Selection will be based on demonstrated leadership and academic accomplishments.

Funds Avail.: $1,000. **Duration:** Annual. **Number Awarded:** 1. **To Apply:** Applicants must submit an essay of 300-500 words describing "My interest in gravure technology and the print communications industry"; must submit a "student copy" of their college/university transcripts; and mail or e-mail completed application and must have completed the attached GEF scholarship application form. **Deadline:** March 1. **Contact:** URL: gaa.org/awards/gravure-education-endowment-scholarships/.

5210 ■ Robert "Bob" Strahan Memorial Scholarship (Undergraduate, Graduate/Scholarship)

Purpose: To identify and cultivate the next generation of talented gravure operators. **Focus:** Printing trades and industries; Publishing. **Qualif.:** Applicants must be undergraduate or graduate students enrolled full-time at any of the GEF-funded colleges or universities; must be majoring printing, graphic arts or any fields of study related in graphic communications. **Criteria:** Applicants will be selected based on merit.

Funds Avail.: $1,500. **Duration:** Annual. **To Apply:** Application is available online at: gaa.org/awards/gravure-education-endowment-scholarships/. **Deadline:** March 1.

5211 ■ Werner B. Thiele Memorial Scholarship (Graduate, Undergraduate/Scholarship)

Purpose: To promote gravure as a print process for high quality packaging; and to encourage and assist young people as they enter the industry. **Focus:** Printing trades and industries; Publishing. **Qualif.:** Applicant must be at least a sophomore in college at the time of the award with a minimum GPA of 3.0.

Funds Avail.: $1,000. **Duration:** Annual. **Number Awarded:** 1. **To Apply:** Application is available online at: gaa.org/awards/gravure-education-endowment-scholarships/. **Remarks:** The award was established in memory of Werner "Dutch" B. Thiele, founder of Thiele-Engdahl, Inc.

5212 ■ Grays Harbor Community Foundation (GHCF)

705 J St.
Hoquiam, WA 98550

Ph: (360)532-1600
Fax: (360)532-8111
E-mail: info@gh-cf.org
URL: gh-cf.org

5213 ■ Grays Harbor Community Foundation Scholarships (Undergraduate, Graduate/Scholarship)

Purpose: To support outstanding undergraduate and vocational students from Grays Harbor County. **Focus:** General studies/Field of study not specified. **Qualif.:** Applicants must be residents of grays harbor; have graduated from a grays harbor county high school; undergraduate students enrolled as full-time (12 credits minimum) at an accredited college or university or trade or vocational school and have earned a cumulative GPA of 3.0 (or equivalent b average) both in high school and college. **Criteria:** Selection shall be based on applicant outstanding character, a proven work ethic, and the promise of useful citizenship.

Funds Avail.: No specific amount. **Duration:** Annual. **To Apply:** Applicants must submit an application form along with a personal essay; resume and transcripts. **Deadline:** March 1. **Contact:** Community Foundation Office; Phone: 360-532-1600; E-mail: jessica@gh-cf.org.

5214 ■ Great Lakes Athletic Trainers Association (GLATA)

PO Box 436
Crystal Lake, IL 60039
URL: www.glata.org
Social Media: www.facebook.com/Great-Lakes-Athletic-Trainers-Association-139592369427501/

5215 ■ GLATA Living Memorial Doctorate Scholarship (Doctorate/Scholarship)

Purpose: To honor the memory and accomplishments of the deceased members of the GLATA by providing scholarships to students who want to pursue their graduate studies. **Focus:** General studies/Field of study not specified. **Qualif.:** Applicant must be a Certified Athletic Trainer member of District IV who has completed all requirements for a terminal degree, excluding their dissertation.

5216 ■ GLATA Living Memorial Graduate Scholarship (Graduate/Fellowship, Scholarship)

Purpose: To honor the memory and accomplishments of the deceased members of the GLATA by providing scholarships to students who want to pursue their graduate studies. **Focus:** General studies/Field of study not specified.

Funds Avail.: $10,000. **Number Awarded:** 1.

5217 ■ Great Lakes Commission (GLC)

1300 Victors Way, Ste. 1350
Ann Arbor, MI 48108
Ph: (734)971-9135
URL: www.glc.org
Social Media: www.facebook.com/greatlakescommission
www.instagram.com/greatlakescommission
www.linkedin.com/company/greatlakescommission
twitter.com/GLCommission

5218 ■ Great Lakes Commission Sea Grant Fellowship (Graduate/Grant, Fellowship)

Purpose: To provide the funds to work and advance the environmental quality and sustainable economic develop-

Awards are arranged alphabetically below their administering organizations

ment goals. **Focus:** Natural resources; Public health. **Qualif.:** Applicants must be graduate or professional students in the field of public policy, public health, natural resources, aquatic sciences or other related field at an accredited institution of higher education in the United States; must have completed their graduate or professional degree within the six months immediately prior to the time of application. **Criteria:** Evaluations will be based on academic status; communication skills; diversity and appropriateness of background; and interests to fellowship experience.

Funds Avail.: $42,000. **Duration:** One year. **To Apply:** Applicants must complete the required documents; personal and academic resume (maximum of two pages); education and career goal statement (1, 000 words or less); two letters of recommendation with at least one from the student's major professor; a letter of endorsement from the sponsoring Sea Grant Director; a copy of undergraduates and graduates transcript of records. Must be sent to the Great Lakes Commission. **Deadline:** February 16. **Contact:** Great Lakes Commission, 2805 S. Industrial Hwy., Ste.100 Ann Arbor, MI 48104, Phone: 734-971-9135, Email:tcrane@ glc.org.

5219 ■ Great Lakes Section Institute of Food Technologists

MI
URL: www.greatlakesift.org
Social Media: www.facebook.com/groups/
127237630781544

5220 ■ Clifford L. Bedford Scholarship Award
(Undergraduate/Scholarship)

Purpose: To support an undergraduate student pursuing a career in food industry. **Focus:** Food science and technology. **Qualif.:** Applicants must be undergraduate students who intend to pursue a career in the food industry; program leading to associate or bachelor's degrees and intends to pursue a career in the food industry and is a member of the Great Lakes IFT Section; must have at least 3.0 GPA; must be active members of IFT and GLS-IFT; must be enrolled in an accredited Michigan college or university. **Criteria:** Selection shall be made on the basis of both academic and non-academic performance.

Funds Avail.: $1,000. **Duration:** Annual. **To Apply:** Applicants may visit the website for the online application; must submit two signed letters of recommendation (in pdf form) emailed or uploaded directly by persons who are recommending the students; letters must be from faculty members or employers familiar with the scholarship applicant's training and other abilities. **Deadline:** February 24. **Contact:** GLS-IFT Scholarship Award Committee: greatlakesift@gmail.com.

5221 ■ Great Lakes Section Diversity Scholarship
(Graduate, Undergraduate/Scholarship)

Purpose: To support students pursuing careers in the food industry. **Focus:** Food science and technology. **Qualif.:** Applicant must be a full-time minority student with a declared curriculum of food industry; must have at least 3.0 GPA; must be active members of IFT and GLS-IFT; must be enrolled in an accredited Michigan college or university. **Criteria:** Selection of all award recipients will be made by the Scholarship Awards Committee as outlined by the GLS-IFT by-laws; Shall be made on the basis of academic performance, research accomplishments and professional potential in the food industry.

Funds Avail.: $1,000. **Duration:** Annual. **To Apply:** Applicants may visit the website for the online application; must submit two signed letters of recommendation (in pdf form) emailed or uploaded directly by the person who is recommending the student; letters must be from faculty members or employers familiar with the scholarship applicant's training and other abilities. **Deadline:** February 24.

5222 ■ Greater Seattle Business Association (GSBA)
400 E Pine St., Ste. 322
Seattle, WA 98122-2300

5223 ■ Greater Seattle Business Association Scholarships (GSBA Scholarships) *(Undergraduate, Graduate/Scholarship)*

Purpose: To LGBTQ and allied students who exhibit leadership potential, demonstrate strong academic abilities, and are actively involved in school and community organizations. **Focus:** General studies/Field of study not specified. **Criteria:** Preference is given to students who identify as LGBTQ, members of LGBTQ families, or straight allies who've been supportive of the LGBTQ community.

Funds Avail.: up to $13,000. **Duration:** Annual. **Number Awarded:** Varies. **To Apply:** Application includes an essay in which applicants are asked to describe their involvement and leadership within the LGBTQ community. **Deadline:** October 11. **Remarks:** Established in 1990.

5224 ■ Greater Valley Chamber of Commerce
10 Progress Dr., 2nd Fl.
Shelton, CT 06484
Ph: (203)925-4981
E-mail: info@greatervalleychamber.com
URL: www.greatervalleychamber.com
Social Media: www.facebook.com/thegreatervalleychamber
www.instagram.com/greatervalleychamber
www.linkedin.com/company/greater-valley-chamber-of
-commerce
twitter.com/Valley_Chamber
www.youtube.com/user/GreaterValleyChamber

5225 ■ Gerald J. and Helen Bogen Fund
(Undergraduate/Scholarship)

Purpose: To support those most in need of financial aid to assist their pursuing studies beyond the secondary school level to an accredited junior or senior college. **Focus:** General studies/Field of study not specified. **Qualif.:** Applicants must be graduating students from any of the following schools: Ansonia, Derby, Oxford, Seymour, Shelton High Schools, or Emmett O'Brien Vocational Technical School. **Criteria:** Selection will be given to applicants whose applications imply their academic ability, need of financial aid, and those who have showed good citizenship and concern in the community during their high school years.

Funds Avail.: No specific amount. **Duration:** Annual. **Number Awarded:** 2 (1 male and 1 female). **To Apply:** Applicants must complete an attached application form, available online, with complete signatures; high school transcript; financial aid acknowledgement form which indicates the family's contribution (provide single side pages only without staples). **Deadline:** March 31. **Remarks:** Established in 1984.

Awards are arranged alphabetically below their administering organizations

5226 ■ Julia B. DeCapua Fund (Undergraduate/Scholarship)

Purpose: To support students achieve their academic goals. **Focus:** General studies/Field of study not specified. **Qualif.:** applicants must be defined as tax-exempt organizations under Section 501(c)(3) or any applicable statute of the Internal Revenue code. **Criteria:** Selection preference will be given to applicants who are pursuing teaching as a vocation; need financial aid; and have good academic ability.

Funds Avail.: No specific amount. **Duration:** Annual. **To Apply:** Applicants must complete an attached application form, available online, with complete signatures; high school transcript; financial aid acknowledgement form which indicates the family's contribution (provide single side pages only without staples). **Remarks:** Established in 1996.

5227 ■ Herman and Bess Glazer Scholarship Fund (Undergraduate/Scholarship)

Purpose: To support those most in need of financial aid to assist their pursuing studies beyond the secondary school level to an accredited junior or senior college. **Focus:** General studies/Field of study not specified. **Qualif.:** Applicants must be graduating students from any of the following schools: Ansonia, Derby, Oxford, Seymour, Shelton High Schools, or Emmett O'Brien Vocational Technical School. **Criteria:** Selection preference will be given to applicants whose applications imply their need of financial aid in pursuing studies beyond secondary level to an accredited junior or senior college.

Funds Avail.: No specific amount. **Duration:** Annual. **Number Awarded:** 2. **To Apply:** Applicants must complete an attached application form, available online, with complete signatures; high school transcript; financial aid acknowledgement form which indicates the family's contribution (provide single side pages only without staples). **Deadline:** March 31. **Remarks:** Established in 1979.

5228 ■ Greater Washington Society of Certified Public Accountants (GWSCPA)

1015 15th St., NW Ste 600,
Washington, DC 20005
Ph: (202)347-3050
E-mail: info@gwscpa.org
URL: www.gwscpa.org
Social Media: www.facebook.com/Greater-Washington
-Society-of-CPAs-126722140706344
twitter.com/TheGWSCPA

5229 ■ GWSCPA Scholarship Fund (Undergraduate/Scholarship)

Purpose: To support students aspiring to become a Certified Public Accountant. **Focus:** Accounting. **Qualif.:** Applicants must be attending a university with an accredited accounting program located within a 25 mile radius of the White House; must be US citizen and resident permanent legal US; must have overall GPA of 3.2 or above. **Criteria:** Selection is based on the application materials submitted.

Funds Avail.: $3,000-$5,000 each. **Duration:** Annual. **Number Awarded:** Varies. **To Apply:** Applicants must submit their completed application form; official transcript with current semester course list; updated resume; at least one letter of recommendation from an accounting professor at the school in which the student is enrolled; essay limited

to 500 words - "The Importance of the CPA Credential to Me"; financial need statement. **Deadline:** March 31. **Remarks:** Established in 1963. **Contact:** GWSCPA Scholarship Fund, 1140 Connecticut Ave, NW, Ste 606, Washington, DC, 20036; Phone:202-347-3050; Email: kbedell@gwscpa.org.

5230 ■ Greek Orthodox Archdiocese of America

8 E 79th St.
New York, NY 10075
Ph: (212)570-3500
Fax: (212)570-3569
E-mail: administration@goarch.org
URL: www.goarch.org
Social Media: www.facebook.com/goarch
www.instagram.com/goarch
www.pinterest.com/goarch
twitter.com/goarch

5231 ■ Greek Orthodox Archdiocese of America Paleologos Graduate Scholarships (Graduate/Scholarship)

Purpose: To provide financial assistance towards the education of young people from the Orthodox Christian community. **Focus:** General studies/Field of study not specified.

Funds Avail.: $5,000. **Duration:** Annual. **To Apply:** Applicants must submit a completed application form; academic records including undergraduate and graduate transcripts (past and present); statement of financial need; a copy or transcript of baptismal or chrismation certificate; resume or curriculum vitae; scholarship proposal; a personal statement (optional); five recommendation letters. **Deadline:** May 1. **Contact:** Paleologos Graduate Scholarship Committee, Greek Orthodox Archdiocese of America, 8 E 79th St., New York, NY, 10075; Email: scholarships@goarch.org.

5232 ■ Andy Green, Attorney at Law., P.C.

111 SW Columbia, Ste. 1390
Portland, OR 97201
Ph: (503)471-1385
Fax: (503)327-8014
E-mail: info@andygreenlaw.com
URL: www.andygreenlaw.com

5233 ■ The Persons in or Affected by Recovery Scholarship (Undergraduate, Graduate/Scholarship)

Purpose: To support the education of full-time undergraduate or graduate students. **Focus:** General studies/Field of study not specified. **Qualif.:** Applicants must be enrolled in a 2-year, 4-year, graduate level or certification program.

Funds Avail.: $1,000. **Number Awarded:** 1. **To Apply:** Submit essay (500-1,000 words); may be accompanied by supporting diagrams, schematics, illustrations, and photographs. Include name, contact information, institution, major, and expected date of graduation.**Deadline:** July 1.

5234 ■ Green Knight Economic Development Corporation (GKEDC)

PO Box 4
Pen Argyl, PA 18072-0004

Awards are arranged alphabetically below their administering organizations

E-mail: questions@gkedc.com
URL: gkedc.org

5235 ■ Green Knight Economic Development Corporation Scholarships *(Undergraduate/Scholarship)*

Purpose: To support students who wish to continue higher education. **Focus:** General studies/Field of study not specified. **Qualif.:** Applicants must be graduating high school seniors who live in the Pen Argyl School District and who will be continuing their education in a college program. **Criteria:** Selection will be based on the aforesaid qualifications and compliance with the application process.

Funds Avail.: $4,000. **Duration:** Annual. **To Apply:** Applicants must submit a completed scholarship application form together with a one-page essay. Guidance counselor must sign and the date the last page of the application verifying the SAT scores, class rank and GPA. **Deadline:** May 8.

5236 ■ The Greenlining Institute

360 14th St., 2nd Fl.
Oakland, CA 94612
Ph: (510)926-4001
Fax: (510)926-4010
E-mail: info@greenlining.org
URL: greenlining.org
Social Media: www.facebook.com/Greenlining
www.instagram.com/greenlining
www.linkedin.com/company/thegreenlininginstitute-
twitter.com/greenlining
www.youtube.com/channel/UCKxMsA3yBiLiz_3g-dTiFlg

5237 ■ Greenlining Institute Policy Fellowship *(Undergraduate/Fellowship)*

Purpose: To encourage emerging leaders interested in learning to take the lead on race and advocate for change on an institutional and structural level. **Focus:** Leadership, Institutional and community.

Funds Avail.: $55,000 per year/Health Benefits. **Duration:** Annual. **To Apply:** Applications may only be submitted online via Formstack. Do not email, fax, or drop off a paper application. Your application will not be reviewed if submitted in any other format.

5238 ■ GreenMatch

80-83 Long Ln.
London EC1A 9ET, United Kingdom
Ph: 44 020 3608 0130
URL: www.greenmatch.co.uk

5239 ■ Community Service Scholarship - GreenMatch *(Undergraduate, Graduate/Scholarship)*

Purpose: To encourage and empower young individuals to play their part in helping the community the green initiatives and activities. **Focus:** General studies/Field of study not specified. **Qualif.:** Applicants are required to submit the following documents along with their application: participants must provide proof that they are either currently enrolled or have been accepted at an accredited university in 2018;applicants must submit pictures or documents of a community service act that they have been a part of, along with their application; an essay describing a community

service activity that you have participated in; applicants are required to indicate their acceptance through the consent form and send it along with their application. **Criteria:** To participate write an essay with the content language must be in English.

Funds Avail.: $1,000. **Number Awarded:** 1. **To Apply:** Applicant must submit a 1,000-word essay on the following topic: Describe a community service activity or initiative you have participated in. The essay should consider these points: 1. What does green living mean to you?; 2. Why do you think this specific community service activity is important, and what should people know about it? Essay and other documents should be sent to scholarship@greenmatch.co.uk. **Deadline:** October 31. **Contact:** Email: scholarship@greenmatch.co.uk Phone: +44 020 3608 0130.

5240 ■ Greenwich Scholarship Association (GSA)

PO Box 4627
Greenwich, CT 06831
E-mail: gsaapplications@gmail.com
URL: greenwichscholarship.org

5241 ■ Greenwich Scholarship Association Scholarships (GSA) *(Undergraduate/Scholarship)*

Purpose: To assist students to attend a public, private or parochial school to pursue their studies. **Focus:** General studies/Field of study not specified.

5242 ■ Griffin Foundation

303 W Prospect Rd.
Fort Collins, CO 80526
Ph: (970)482-3030
Fax: (970)484-6648
URL: www.thegriffinfoundation.org

5243 ■ Griffin Foundation Scholarships *(Undergraduate/Scholarship)*

Purpose: To support qualified applicants who have an associate degree from a junior or community college. **Focus:** General studies/Field of study not specified. **Qualif.:** Applicants must have an associate degree or at least 60 hours from a junior or community college and seeking to complete a baccalaureate degree; have a cumulative GPA of at least a 3.5 on a 4.0 scale in all college level work; and, be admitted as full-time, on-campus students in a baccalaureate degree program at the participating university they have selected; must have reasonable expectations of completing within two years (four semesters) a baccalaureate degree at the Participating University they enter under this scholarship; maintain at least a 3.0 GPA at the Participating University to remain eligible to continue to receive the scholarship. **Criteria:** Selection will be on a competitive basis by ranking applicants in the following areas for their activities since graduation from high school: scholarship; leadership and service; personal traits; and financial need.

Funds Avail.: $5,000. **Duration:** Annual. **To Apply:** Application form can be downloaded from the Griffin Foundation website; must type or print their application legibly; must attach three letters of recommendation, at least one of which is from a college faculty member, counselor or administrator who can comment on applicants qualifications (be sure recommendations are signed); must attach

Awards are arranged alphabetically below their administering organizations

an official copy of grade transcript(s) from each college attended; scholarship can only be used at Colorado State University (Fort Collins Campus), the University of Northern Colorado, or the University of Wyoming (Larimie Campus). **Deadline:** March 1.

5244 ■ Guajardo & Marks LLP
12221 Merit Dr., Ste 945
Dallas, TX 75251
Ph: (972)774-9800
URL: www.guajardomarks.com
Social Media: www.facebook.com/GuajardoMarks
www.linkedin.com/company/guajardo-&-marks-llp

5245 ■ Guajardo & Marks Law School Scholarship
(Graduate/Scholarship)

Purpose: To encourage and award creative authorship. **Focus:** Law. **Qualif.:** Applicants must be U.S. citizens or authorized to work in the United States; must be commencing law school (1L) in August of the current year; must have a published article in print or digital media. **Criteria:** Selection will be based on the creativity, originality and ability to clearly convey a complex message of the submitted sample writings.

Funds Avail.: $1,000. **Duration:** Annual. **To Apply:** Applicants must prepare a completed scholarship application form, copy of law school acceptance letter, and copy of previously published article or link to its online location.

5246 ■ Harry Frank Guggenheim Foundation (HFG)
42 W 54th St.
New York, NY 10019
Ph: (646)428-0971
Fax: (646)428-0981
E-mail: info@hfg.org
URL: www.hfg.org
Social Media: www.facebook.com/Harry-Frank
  -Guggenheim-Foundation-1289303851153689
www.linkedin.com/company/harry-frank-guggenheim
  -foundation
www.in.pinterest.com/pin/247486942002750182
twitter.com/HFGuggenheim

5247 ■ Harry Frank Guggenheim Dissertation Fellowships *(Doctorate/Fellowship)*

Purpose: To support the doctoral candidates to enable them to complete the thesis in a timely manner and are only appropriate for students approaching the final year of their Ph.D. work. **Focus:** Humanities; Social sciences. **Criteria:** Recipients will be selected based on the comparison of the candidates' theses.

Funds Avail.: $20,000 each. **Duration:** Annual. **Number Awarded:** 10. **To Apply:** Applications are submitted online; applicants must submit the following: project title; abstract and survey; advisor's letter and advisor's abbreviated curriculum vitae; applicant's curriculum vitae and graduate school transcript; project description; protection of subjects; other support. **Deadline:** February 1. **Contact:** The Harry Frank Guggenheim Foundation, 42 W 54th St., New York, NY 10019; Phone: 646-428-0971; Fax: 646-428-0981; Email: info@hfg.org.

5248 ■ Harry Frank Guggenheim Foundation Research Grants *(Professional development/Grant)*

Purpose: To support research that can increase understanding and amelioration of urgent problems of violence and aggression in the modern world. **Focus:** Humanities; Social sciences. **Criteria:** Recipients are selected based on the project proposal; priority is given to research that can increase understanding and amelioration of urgent problems of violence and aggression in the modern world.

Funds Avail.: $15,000 to $40,000. **Duration:** Annual. **Number Awarded:** 10. **To Apply:** Applications are submitted online; applicants must submit the following: project title; abstract and survey; Co-Principal Investigators; Budge; Budget Justification; Research Plan; referee Comments; curricula vitae and lists of relevant publications for the principal investigator(s) and all professional personnel; applicant's curriculum vitae; project description; electronic signature; protection of subjects; other support. **Deadline:** August 1. **Contact:** The Harry Frank Guggenheim Foundation, 42 W 54th St., New York, NY 10019; Phone: 646-428-0971; Fax: 646-428-0981; Email: info@hfg.org.

5249 ■ John Simon Guggenheim Memorial Foundation
90 Park Ave.
New York, NY 10016
Ph: (212)687-4470
Fax: (212)697-3248
URL: www.gf.org
Social Media: www.facebook.com/GuggFellows
twitter.com/GuggFellows

5250 ■ John Simon Guggenheim Memorial Fellowships - United States & Canadian Competition
(Graduate, Postgraduate, Undergraduate/Fellowship)

Purpose: To support individuals in their respective research and artistic creations. **Focus:** Arts; Humanities; Natural sciences; Social sciences. **Qualif.:** Applicants must be U.S. or Canadian citizens. **Criteria:** Selection will be based on committee's criteria.

Funds Avail.: No specific amount. **Duration:** Annual. **Number Awarded:** Varies. **To Apply:** Applicants must submit a completed application form online. **Deadline:** September 17. **Remarks:** Established in 1926. **Contact:** John Simon Guggenheim Memorial Foundation, 90 Park Ave., New York, NY, 10016, USA.

5251 ■ Gulf and Caribbean Fisheries Institute (GCFI)
Florida Fish and Wildlife Conservation Commission
2796 Overseas Hwy., Ste. 119
Marathon, FL 33050
Ph: (305)289-2330
Fax: (305)289-2334
URL: www.gcfi.org
Social Media: twitter.com/gcfi_fisheries

5252 ■ GCFI Student Travel Awards *(Undergraduate/Award)*

Purpose: To recognize and support students who are about to present research related to the Gulf of Mexico and Caribbean Regions. **Focus:** Water resources. **Qualif.:** Applicant must be Caribbean/ Mexican students and another one will be for the U.S./Canadian/European students; must be member of GCFI members.

Funds Avail.: $750 each. **Duration:** Annual. **Number Awarded:** 2. **To Apply:** Applicant must include letter from

Awards are arranged alphabetically below their administering organizations

the advisor, must be in English; must submit a statement of financial need and an estimated cost of the entire travel; a short letter to the Student Awards Committee detailing the importance of the GCFI to their future career goals; must submit a letter of "certification", stating the current academic standing of the student, verifying full time status, and progress toward degree completion. **Deadline:** August 31. **Contact:** Email: studentawards@gcfi.org.

5253 ■ Ronald L. Schmied Scholarship (Other, Undergraduate/Scholarship)

Purpose: To encourage students with interest in marine recreational fisheries. **Focus:** Fisheries sciences/management.

Duration: Annual. **Remarks:** Established in 1998. **Contact:** Dr. Stephen Holland, Chair, at sholland@ufl.edu.

5254 ■ Gwynedd Mercy University
1325 Sumneytown Pke.
Gwynedd Valley, PA 19437
URL: www.gmercyu.edu
Social Media: www.facebook.com/GMercyU
www.linkedin.com/company/gwynedd-mercy-college
www.linkedin.com/school/gwynedd-mercy-university
twitter.com/GMercyU

5255 ■ Gwynedd Mercy University Presidential Scholarship (Undergraduate/Scholarship)

Purpose: To provide full tuition scholarships to a limited number of first-time students (renewable for up to three years). **Focus:** General studies/Field of study not specified. **Qualif.:** Applicant must be attending Gwynedd Mercy University; have a cumulative high school GPA of at least 3.5; have a minimum SAT score of 1360; and attend an interview with an admissions counselor. **Criteria:** Selection based on a full-tuition scholarship awarded to a limited number of selected first-time students.

Funds Avail.: Full tuition. **To Apply:** Applications must be submitted online. **Contact:** Email: admissions@gmercyu.edu; URL: www.gmercyu.edu/admissions-aid/financial-aid-tuition/types-aid/scholarships.

5256 ■ Hagley Museum and Library
298 Buck Rd. E
Wilmington, DE 19807-0630
Ph: (302)658-2400
E-mail: askhagley@hagley.org
URL: hagley.org
Social Media: www.facebook.com/
   HagleyMuseumandLibrary
instagram.com/hagleymuseum/
www.instagram.com/hagleymuseum
twitter.com/hagleymuseum
www.youtube.com/user/HagleyMuseum

5257 ■ Henry Belin du Pont Dissertation Fellowships (Doctorate, Graduate/Fellowship)

Purpose: To support graduate students conducting research for their dissertation. **Focus:** General studies/Field of study not specified. **Qualif.:** Applicants must be graduate students who have completed all coursework for the doctoral degree and conducting research for their dissertation. **Criteria:** Selection is based on demonstrated

superior intellectual quality and presentation of a persuasive methodology for the project. Applicants must show that there are significant research materials at Hagley pertinent to the dissertation.

Funds Avail.: $6,500. **Duration:** Up to 4 months. **To Apply:** Applicants must be projecting abstract (maximum length: 150 words); curriculum vitae; dissertation proposal of any length or a project description of approximately 1,500 words indicating the scope of your research and the existing scholarship with which you engage; summary of the Hagley research materials that you will use in your dissertation and how they are pertinent to your project (maximum length: 500 words); contact information for two recognized scholars who have agreed to write letters in support of your application. **Deadline:** November 15. **Contact:** Dr. Roger Horowitz, Email: rhorowitz@hagley.org.

5258 ■ Henry Belin du Pont Research Grants (Graduate/Grant)

Purpose: To support research and study in the library, archival and artifact collections of the Hagley Museum and Library. **Focus:** Library and archival sciences. **Qualif.:** Applicants must be pursuing an advanced research and study in the library, archival and artifact collections of the Hagley Museum and Library, and must be from out of state.

Funds Avail.: $200-$400. **Duration:** Up to 8 weeks. **Number Awarded:** Varies. **To Apply:** Applicant must project abstract (maximum length: 150 words); curriculum vitae; project description indicating the scope of applicant's research and the existing scholarship with which you engage (maximum length: 1000 words); summary of the Hagley research materials that you plan to consult during your residency and how they are pertinent to your project (maximum length: 500 words); please include the number of weeks requested for research at Hagley. **Deadline:** March 31, June 30 and October 31. **Contact:** Dr. Roger Horowitz; Email: rhorowitz@hagley.org.

5259 ■ Hai Guin Scholarship Association of Boston
23 Bradley Rd.
Arlington, MA 02474
Social Media: www.facebook.com/
   HaiGuinScholarshipAssociationOfMa/

5260 ■ Hai Guin Scholarships (Undergraduate, Graduate/Scholarship)

Purpose: To provide financial assistance to Massachusetts students of Armenian descent. **Focus:** General studies/Field of study not specified. **Qualif.:** Applicants must be undergraduate or graduate students of Armenian descent who are permanent residents of Massachusetts and have completed one full year at the college/university to which scholarship will be applied.

Funds Avail.: $2,000. **To Apply:** Applicants should see the sponsor's Facebook page for application details. **Contact:** Attn: Scholarship Chairman.

5261 ■ Half Chrome
360 Comstock Dr.
Elgin, IL 60124
E-mail: info@halfchrome.com
URL: www.halfchrome.com
Social Media: www.facebook.com/HalfChromeDrones
www.youtube.com/c/HalfChrome

Awards are arranged alphabetically below their administering organizations

5262 ■ Half Chrome Drones Scholarship *(Other/ Scholarship)*

Purpose: To provide help to students with an interest in technology and/or UAVs. **Focus:** Technology. **Qualif.:** Applicant must be a graduating high school senior (home schooling acceptable), already graduated, or possessing a GED; must be planning to pursue a degree at an accredited post-secondary institution in the U.S. in the upcoming school year; must have a minimum 3.0 GPA. **Criteria:** Selection will be based on the creativity of the submitted video.

Funds Avail.: $1,000. **Number Awarded:** 1. **To Apply:** Application and video details available online at www.halfchrome.com. **Deadline:** May 1. **Contact:** Email: drones@ halfchrome.com.

5263 ■ George and Mary Josephine Hamman Foundation
3336 Richmond, Ste. 310
Houston, TX 77098
Ph: (713)522-9891
Fax: (713)522-9693
E-mail: hammanfdn@aol.com
URL: www.hammanfoundation.org

5264 ■ George and Mary Josephine Hamman Foundation Scholarships *(Undergraduate/ Scholarship)*

Purpose: To provide undergraduate scholarships for Houston area high school seniors. **Focus:** General studies/ Field of study not specified. **Criteria:** Selection based on academics and financial need.

Funds Avail.: $20,000. **Duration:** Annual. **Number Awarded:** 70. **To Apply:** Applicants must write for the one-page scholarship application and the three-page financial qualification statement or it may be downloaded from the website; completed scholarship applications must be submitted with these documents (in the following order) financial qualification Statement; complete, legible, signed copy of parents'/guardians' and student's most recent federal income tax return (including all schedules) plus, if applicable, corporate or partnership returns; proof of ACT and/or SAT results and high school transcript. **Deadline:** February 16th.

5265 ■ Harry Hampton Memorial Wildlife, Inc.
PO Box 2641
Columbia, SC 29202
Ph: (803)600-1570
E-mail: jim.goller@hamptonwildlifefund.org
URL: www.hamptonwildlifefund.org

5266 ■ Harry Hampton Fund Scholarship
(Undergraduate/Scholarship)

Purpose: To promote higher education in the natural resources area **Focus:** Biology; Environmental science; Fisheries sciences/management; Forestry; Wildlife conservation, management, and science; Zoology. **Qualif.:** Applicants must be full-time residents of South Carolina; must be seniors in public or private high school in South Carolina; must attend an institution of higher learning in South Carolina; must have a major in natural resources discipline such as wildlife biology, fisheries biology, forestry, marine

science or environmental science; general biology, premedical biology and veterinary science are not eligible; must maintain a GPR of 2.5 or above. **Criteria:** Selection criteria will be determined by the board of directors of the Harry Hampton Wildlife Fund.

Funds Avail.: $5,000. **Duration:** Annual. **To Apply:** Applications are available on the website and must be submitted on or before the due date along with applicants' essay and autobiography, transcript of high school grades, college board scores, rank in high school class and a recent photograph. **Deadline:** January 31. **Remarks:** Established in 1992. **Contact:** Hampton Fund Scholarships, PO Box 2641, Columbia, SC, 29202; Phone: 803-600-1570; Email: jim.goller@hamptonwildlifefund.org.

5267 ■ Hampton Roads Community Foundation
101 W. Main Street, Suite 4500
Norfolk, VA 23510
Ph: (757)622-7951
Fax: (757)622-1751
E-mail: info@hamptonroadscf.org
URL: www.hamptonroadscf.org
Social Media: www.facebook.com/hamptonroadscf
www.linkedin.com/company/hampton-roads-community
-foundation
twitter.com/HamptonRoadsCF
www.youtube.com/user/HamptonRoadsCF

5268 ■ Ellis W. Rowe Memorial Scholarship
(Graduate/Scholarship)

Purpose: To provide financial support to qualified individuals who want to pursue their educational goals. **Focus:** Agriculture, Economic aspects; Biology, Marine; Humanities; Nursing. **Qualif.:** Applicants must be students from Gloucester County; must be studying marine science, nursing, ministry, medicine, humanities, agriculture, biology or any other basic science. **Criteria:** Selection of recipients will be based on financial need and the scholarship criteria; preference will be given to students from the York District attending Virginia Wesleyan College or another Methodist college.

Funds Avail.: No specific amount. **Duration:** Annual. **To Apply:** Applicants must complete the application form available from the website; provide a copy of their transcripts, recommendation letter and statement of family income. **Deadline:** March 1. **Contact:** Robin Foreman-Wheeler, Vice President for Administration; Phone: 757-622-7951; Email: scholarships@hamptonroadscf.org.

5269 ■ Enid W. and Bernard B. Spigel Architectural Scholarship *(Graduate/Scholarship)*

Purpose: To provide financial support to qualified individuals who want to pursue their educational goals. **Focus:** Landscape architecture and design. **Qualif.:** Applicants must be Virginia residents who are junior, senior or graduate students in architecture, architectural history or architectural preservation. **Criteria:** Selection of recipients will be based on financial need and the scholarship criteria; preference will be given to students from the York District attending Virginia Wesleyan College or another Methodist college.

Funds Avail.: No specific amount. **Duration:** Annual; For 2 years. **To Apply:** Applicants must complete the application form available from the website; provide a copy of their

Awards are arranged alphabetically below their administering organizations

transcripts, recommendation letter and statement of family income. **Deadline:** March 1. **Contact:** Robin Foreman-Wheeler, Vice President for Administration; Phone: 757-622-7951; Email: scholarships@hamptonroadscf.org.

5270 ■ Florence L. Smith Medical Scholarship
(Graduate/Scholarship)

Purpose: To provide financial support to qualified individuals who want to pursue their educational goals. **Focus:** Education, Medical. **Qualif.:** Applicants must be Virginia residents attending Eastern Virginia Medical School, University of Virginia School of Medicine or Virginia Commonwealth University School of Medicine; must be from Virginia. **Criteria:** Selection of recipients will be based on financial need and the scholarship criteria.

Funds Avail.: No specific amount. **Duration:** Annual. **To Apply:** Applicants must complete the application form available from the website; provide a copy of transcripts from their postsecondary education; and attach a statement of financial need. **Deadline:** March 1. **Contact:** Robin Foreman-Wheeler, Vice President for Administration; Phone: 757-622-7951; Email: scholarships@ hamptonroadscf.org.

5271 ■ Hampton Roads Association of Social Workers Scholarship *(Graduate/Scholarship)*

Purpose: To provide financial support to qualified individuals who want to pursue their educational goals. **Focus:** Social work. **Qualif.:** Applicants must be graduate students in social work; must be from Virginia; students are eligible for one year of scholarship support. **Criteria:** Selection of recipients will be based on financial need and the scholarship criteria.

Funds Avail.: No specific amount. **Duration:** Annual. **To Apply:** Applicants must complete the application form available from the website; provide a copy of their transcripts, recommendation letter and statement of family income. **Deadline:** March 1. **Contact:** Robin Foreman-Wheeler, Vice President for Administration; Phone: 757-622-7951; Email: scholarships@hamptonroadscf.org.

5272 ■ Tara Welch Gallagher Environmental Scholarship *(Graduate/Scholarship)*

Purpose: To provide financial support to qualified individuals who want to pursue their educational goals. **Focus:** Environmental technology. **Qualif.:** Applicants must be full-time graduate students from the Hampton Roads Sanitation District service area studying environmental health, environmental chemistry, biology or civil or environmental engineering at a public Virginia university. **Criteria:** Selection of recipients will be based on financial need and the scholarship criteria.

Funds Avail.: No specific amount. **Duration:** Annual. **To Apply:** Applicants must complete the application form available from the website; provide a copy of transcripts, recommendation letter and statement of family income. **Deadline:** March 1. **Contact:** Robin Foreman-Wheeler, Vice President for Administration; Phone: 757-622-7951; Email: scholarships@hamptonroadscf.org.

5273 ■ Louis I. Jaffe Memorial Scholarship-NSU Alumni *(Graduate/Scholarship)*

Purpose: To provide financial support to qualified individuals who want to pursue their educational goals. **Focus:** General studies/Field of study not specified. **Qualif.:** Applicants must be graduates of Norfolk State University who

are enrolled in a graduate program at any institution; must be from anywhere in Virginia. **Criteria:** Selection of recipients will be based on financial need and the scholarship criteria; priority will be given to applicants from Hampton Roads.

Funds Avail.: No specific amount. **Duration:** Annual; For 2 years. **To Apply:** Applicants must complete the application form available from the website; must provide a copy of transcripts, recommendation letter and statement of family income. **Deadline:** March 1. **Contact:** Robin Foreman-Wheeler, Vice President for Administration; Phone: 757-622-7951; Email: scholarships@hamptonroadscf.org.

5274 ■ Louis I. Jaffe Memorial Scholarship-ODU
(Graduate/Scholarship)

Purpose: To provide financial support to qualified individuals who want to pursue their educational goals. **Focus:** Art history; Humanities. **Qualif.:** Applicants must be students at Old Dominion University studying humanities or must be students at any other University studying art history. **Criteria:** Selection of recipients will be based on financial need and the scholarship criteria.

Funds Avail.: No specific amount. **Duration:** Annual. **To Apply:** Applicants must complete the application form available from the website; provide a copy of their transcripts, recommendation letter and statement of family income. **Deadline:** March 1. **Contact:** Robin Foreman-Wheeler, Vice President for Administration; Phone: 757-622-7951; Email: scholarships@hamptonroadscf.org.

5275 ■ Lewis K. Martin II, M.D. and Cheryl Rose Martin Scholarship Fund *(Graduate/Scholarship)*

Purpose: To provide financial assistance to qualified individuals who want to pursue their educational goals. **Focus:** Education, Medical. **Qualif.:** Applicants must be Virginia residents pursuing medical school at the University of Virginia School of Medicine. **Criteria:** Selection of recipients will be based on financial need and the scholarship criteria.

Funds Avail.: No specific amount. **Duration:** Annual. **To Apply:** Applicants must complete the application form available from the website; provide a copy of transcripts from their postsecondary education; and attach a statement of financial need. **Deadline:** March 1. **Contact:** Robin Foreman-Wheeler, Vice President for Administration; Phone: 757-622-7951; Email: scholarships@ hamptonroadscf.org.

5276 ■ William F. Miles Scholarships *(Graduate/Scholarship)*

Purpose: To provide financial support to qualified individuals who want to pursue their educational goals. **Focus:** Religion. **Qualif.:** Applicants must be students preparing for leadership in the field of religious service. **Criteria:** Selection of recipients will be based on financial need and the scholarship criteria; recipients are recommended by Westminster Chapter No. 99, Order of the Eastern Star.

Funds Avail.: No specific amount. **Duration:** Annual. **To Apply:** Applicants must complete the application form available from the website; provide a copy of their transcripts, recommendation letter and statement of family income. **Deadline:** April 1. **Contact:** Robin Foreman-Wheeler, Vice President for Administration; Phone: 757-622-7951; Email: scholarships@hamptonroadscf.org.

5277 ■ Palmer Farley Memorial Scholarship
(Graduate/Scholarship)

Purpose: To provide financial support to qualified individuals who want to pursue their educational goals. **Focus:**

Awards are arranged alphabetically below their administering organizations

Communications. **Qualif.:** Applicants must be students pursuing the creative brand management track at the Virginia Commonwealth University Brand center. **Criteria:** Selection of recipients will be based on financial need and the scholarship criteria.

Funds Avail.: No specific amount. **Duration:** Annual; Renewable up to 2 years. **To Apply:** Applicants must complete the application form available from the website; provide a copy of their transcripts, recommendation letter and statement of family income. **Deadline:** May 1. **Contact:** Robin Foreman-Wheeler, Vice President for Administration; Phone: 757-622-7951; Email: scholarships@hamptonroadscf.org.

5278 ■ Richard D. and Sheppard R. Cooke Memorial Scholarship *(Graduate/Scholarship)*

Purpose: To provide financial support to qualified individuals who want to pursue their educational goals. **Focus:** Religion. **Qualif.:** Applicants must be students at Union Theological Seminary in Richmond who are candidates for the ministry; must be enrolled in a degree program. **Criteria:** Selection of recipients will be based on financial need and the scholarship criteria; preference will be given to students from the Norfolk churches within the Presbytery of Eastern Virginia.

Funds Avail.: No specific amount. **Duration:** Annual. **To Apply:** Applicants must complete the application form available from the website; provide a copy of transcripts, recommendation letter and statement of family income. **Deadline:** April 1. **Contact:** Robin Foreman-Wheeler, Vice President for Administration; Phone: 757-622-7951; Email: scholarships@hamptonroadscf.org.

5279 ■ Drs. Kirkland Ruffin & Willcox Ruffin Scholarships *(Graduate/Scholarship)*

Purpose: To provide financial assistance to qualified individuals who want to pursue their educational goals. **Focus:** Education, Medical. **Qualif.:** Applicants must be students from Norfolk attending Eastern Virginia Medical School. **Criteria:** Selection of recipients will be based on financial need and the scholarship criteria.

Funds Avail.: No specific amount. **Duration:** Annual. **To Apply:** Applicants must complete the application form available from the website; provide a copy of transcripts from their postsecondary education; and attach a statement of financial need. **Deadline:** March 1. **Contact:** Robin Foreman-Wheeler, Vice President for Administration; Phone: 757-622-7951; Email: scholarships@hamptonroadscf.org.

5280 ■ Hy Smith Endowment Fund *(Undergraduate/Scholarship)*

Purpose: To provide financial support to qualified individuals who want to pursue their educational goals. **Focus:** Religion. **Qualif.:** Applicants must be students at Virginia Theological Seminary in Alexandria who are candidates for the ministry; must be residents of the geographic region served by the Diocese of Southern Virginia. **Criteria:** Selection on applicants will be based on financial need and the scholarship criteria. Recipients are recommended by the Eastern Star Training Awards Committee for Religious Leadership of Westminster Chapter No. 99.

Funds Avail.: No specific amount. **Duration:** Annual. **To Apply:** Applicants must complete the application form available from the website; provide a copy of the transcripts, recommendation letter and statement of family income.

Deadline: April 1. **Contact:** Robin Foreman-Wheeler, Vice President for Administration; Phone: 757-622-7951; Email: scholarships@hamptonroadscf.org.

5281 ■ Victor and Ruth N. Goodman Memorial Scholarship *(Graduate/Scholarship)*

Purpose: To provide financial assistance to qualified individuals who want to pursue their educational goals. **Focus:** Education, Medical. **Qualif.:** Applicants must be students studying medicine or other health professions; students should be pursuing degrees leading to careers as medical practitioners. **Criteria:** Selection of recipients will be based on financial need and the scholarship criteria.

Funds Avail.: No specific amount. **Duration:** Annual. **To Apply:** Applicants must complete the application form available from the website; provide a copy of their transcripts, recommendation letter and statement of family income. **Deadline:** March 1. **Contact:** Robin Foreman-Wheeler, Vice President for Administration; Phone: 757-622-7951; Email: scholarships@hamptonroadscf.org.

5282 ■ Handweavers Guild of America, Inc. (HGA)

1255 Buford Hwy., Ste. 211
Suwanee, GA 30024
Ph: (678)730-0010
Fax: (678)730-0836
E-mail: hga@weavespindye.org
URL: www.weavespindye.org
Social Media: www.instagram.com/instahga/
www.pinterest.com/weavespindye/
twitter.com/weavespindye

5283 ■ Convergence Assistantship Grants *(Undergraduate/Grant)*

Purpose: To provide opportunity to students to assist internationally known instructors and to participate in the Convergence experience. **Focus:** Art. **Qualif.:** Applicant must be currently enrolled in an accredited academic program and available to attend a Training Class Saturday at the Convention Center. **Criteria:** Selection will be based on the submitted application materials.

Funds Avail.: Varies. **To Apply:** Awardee must submit a Letter of Nomination from the Professor; must provide the Convergence complete registration form and personal statement.

5284 ■ The Dendel Scholarship *(Graduate, Undergraduate/Scholarship)*

Purpose: To further the education in the field of fiber arts, including training for research, textile history and conservation. **Focus:** Art. **Criteria:** Selection will be based on artistic and technical merit rather than financial needs.

Funds Avail.: $2,000. **Duration:** One year. **To Apply:** Applicants should submit two letters of recommendation from people who are knowledgeable about their work and work habits; must be sure to include their daytime phone number and email; official transcript; images of work; image record. **Deadline:** February 1. **Contact:** Contact: Handweavers Guild of America, Inc.; 1255 Buford Highway, Suite 209 Suwanee, GA 30024; Telephone: (678) 730-0010; Email: hga@weavespindye.org.

5285 ■ Mearl K. Gable II Memorial Grant *(Other/Grant)*

Purpose: To provide educational opportunities to members for study in non-accredited programs for any skill level (not

---

Awards are arranged alphabetically below their administering organizations

including the Certificate of Excellence program or any certified program) and may be used for research and studies connected with the fiber arts. **Focus:** Art. **Qualif.:** Recipients must be HGA members. **Criteria:** Selection will be based on the submitted application.

Funds Avail.: $100. **To Apply:** Application form must be printed and must have the following: Name of school or provider of instruction, title and short description of course (attach brochure); must provide a resume of the background, current activities, and future goals in the fiber field. **Deadline:** March 1. **Remarks:** Established in 2000. **Contact:** Contact: Handweavers Guild of America, Inc.; 1255 Buford Highway, Suite 209 Suwanee, GA 30024; Telephone: (678) 730-0010; Email: hga@weavespindye.org.

5286 ■ Silvio and Eugenia Petrini Grants (Other/Grant)

Purpose: To provide educational opportunities to members for study in non-accredited programs for any skill level. **Focus:** Art. **Qualif.:** Recipients must be HGA members. **Criteria:** Selection of applicants will be based on application materials.

Funds Avail.: $300. **To Apply:** Application forms are available on the website. **Deadline:** March 1. **Remarks:** Established in 1994. **Contact:** Contact: Handweavers Guild of America, Inc.; 1255 Buford Highway, Suite 209 Suwanee, GA 30024; Telephone: (678) 730-0010; Email: hga@weavespindye.org.

5287 ■ The Haraldson Foundation
25025 Interstate 45,Ste. 320
The Woodlands, TX 77380-3058
URL: www.haraldsonfoundation.org

5288 ■ Haraldson Foundation Scholarships
(Undergraduate, Graduate/Scholarship)

Purpose: To assist University of Texas-bound high school seniors who have high SAT or ACT scores. **Focus:** General studies/Field of study not specified. **Qualif.:** Applicants must be high school seniors planning to attend the University of Texas, or currently enrolled in a University of Texas undergraduate or graduate program; have volunteered in community service activities; demonstrated academic excellence, leadership and character; and have financial need; must maintain a 3.0 GPA each semester and must complete at least 12 hours of course work each semester. **Criteria:** Selection will be based on committee's criteria.

Funds Avail.: No specific amount. **Duration:** Annual. **Number Awarded:** Varies. **To Apply:** Applicants complete ??financial information; high?? school ??transcript; 2 essays (400 words max). **Deadline:** December 1. **Remarks:** Established in 1992. **Contact:** The Haraldson Foundation, 4747 Research Forest Dr., Ste. 180, Box # 257, The Woodlands, TX, 77381; Email: ebmills@haraldsonfoundation.org.

5289 ■ Harbor Breeze Corp.
100 Aquarium Way, Dock No. 2
Long Beach, CA 90802
Ph: (562)432-4900
E-mail: harborbreezecruises@gmail.com
URL: 2seewhales.com
Social Media: www.facebook.com/harborbreezecorp
instagram.com/harborbreezecruises

youtube.com/user/HarborBreezeCruise

5290 ■ Captain James H. Peterson Memorial Scholarships *(Undergraduate/Scholarship)*

Purpose: To assist deserving students in their future endeavors. **Focus:** General studies/Field of study not specified. **Qualif.:** Applicants must be American citizens, permanent residents, or hold a valid student visa; must have plans to be enrolled as college/university students within the United States; must have a cumulative GPA of at least 3.0; submit the essay and that must be the applicant's original work. **Criteria:** Selection will be based on the submitted essay.

Funds Avail.: $2,500. **To Apply:** Applicants must submit an original essay that answers the following questions: How do you foresee social media and advertising evolving in the future? What will the next generations of customers expect? How can Harbor Breeze Cruises, as a whale watch operations, engage these customers going into the future? How can Harbor Breeze Cruises stand out from the competition going forward in the future?; must also submit a letter of recommendation and their photo online. **Deadline:** April 30.

5291 ■ Hardanger Fiddle Association of America (HFAA)
PO Box 23046
Minneapolis, MN 55423-0046
Ph: (612)568-7448
URL: www.hfaa.org
Social Media: www.facebook.com/groups/21061116655/about

5292 ■ Bernt Balchen, Jr. and Olav Jorgen Hegge Hardingfele Scholarships *(Other/Scholarship)*

Purpose: To provide support for the hardingfele students who are intending to attend the HFAA Annual Workshops. **Focus:** Music. **Qualif.:** Applicants must have an experience in playing a string instrument in either classical or folk tradition; need not play or own a hardingfele; should also be able to learn by ear in a group environment; HFAA membership is not required for application; must be over age 18 as of January 1 and under age 35 as of December 31 of the award year. **Criteria:** Scholarship will be given to the applicants who best meet the requirements.

Funds Avail.: No specific amount. **Duration:** Annual. **To Apply:** Applicants must submit a completed online application form; a personal statement; musical resume; a letter of reference from a person not related to the applicant, preferably an instructor or a fellow musician; three copies of a 3-5 minute recording that demonstrates your bowed stringed instrument playing ability in classical or folk tradition. If submitting as hard copy, mail three copies of a CD, or if submitting electronically, email a sound file in MP3 format. **Deadline:** April 15. **Contact:** HFAA Balchen-Hegge Scholarship Committee, c/o Georgia Beatty, 20-21 Woodbine St., Apt. 3R, Flushing, NY 11385; Email:scholarships@hfaa.org.

5293 ■ Hardwick & Pendergast PS
555 S Renton Village Pl., Ste. 640
Renton, WA 98057
Ph: (425)228-3860
Fax: (425)226-4988
Free: 888-991-9088

Awards are arranged alphabetically below their administering organizations

URL: www.hardwickpendergast.com
Social Media: www.facebook.com/HardwickPendergast
www.instagram.com/hardwickpendergast
twitter.com/wainjurylawyers

5294 ■ Make Your Mark Scholarship *(Graduate, College/Scholarship)*

Purpose: To pay it forward and help deserving students make their own impact. **Focus:** General studies/Field of study not specified. **Qualif.:** Applicant must be a high school senior on track to graduate, a college student enrolled in an accredited four-year college or university, or a student currently enrolled in a two-year college and planning to transfer to a four-year college or university; have maintained a minimum 3.0 GPA; and be a U.S. citizen or permanent resident (DACA recipients are welcome to apply).

Funds Avail.: $500. **Number Awarded:** 2. **To Apply:** Applicant must submit essay and complete application online. **Deadline:** April 29.

5295 ■ Hardy Wolf & Downing Injury Lawyers
477 Congress St.
Portland, ME 04101
Ph: (207)523-3499
Free: 800-992-7333
URL: hardywolf.com
Social Media: www.facebook.com/MaineLawyer
twitter.com/hardywolflaw

5296 ■ Hardy, Wolf & Downing Scholarships *(Undergraduate, Graduate/Scholarship)*

Purpose: To provide financial assistance to students who want to pursue their dreams in legal profession. **Focus:** Law enforcement. **Qualif.:** Applicants must be high school students who plan to attend an accredited U.S. college; college students attending an accredited U.S. College; or law students currently accepted or enrolled in an ABA-accredited law school; applicants must either be active, retired or immediate family relatives of such members of any branch of U.S. military or any branch of law enforcement. **Criteria:** Selection will be based on the strength of the applicants' essays.

Funds Avail.: $5,000. **To Apply:** Applicants must write an essay on the following topics for members and family members of U.S. military - "what is/are the greatest challenge(s) facing veterans when they return home from serving their country?"; for members of law enforcement and family members of law enforcement workers - "what is/are the greatest challenge(s) facing law enforcement personnel today?"; essays must be 1500-2000 words in length; applications must be submitted via email; all materials must be submitted in Word of PDF format; must provide their full name and all current contact information including mailing address, email address and phone number and must complete and sign the attached PDF application form and submit with other required materials (proof of attendance or acceptance at school, proof of minimum 3.0 GPA from the school of the applicants currently attend or most recently attended, and proof of personal affiliation or family affiliation with any branch of the U.S. military or law enforcement agency).

5297 ■ Bryce Harlow Foundation
P.O. BOX 15879
Washington, DC 20003

Ph: (703)402-9094
E-mail: info@bryceharlow.org
URL: bryceharlow.org
Social Media: www.facebook.com/bryceharlowfoundation
twitter.com/BryceHarlow

5298 ■ Bryce Harlow Fellowship *(Graduate/Fellowship)*

Purpose: To provide financial assistance to students who are pursuing a career in professional advocacy through public affairs, government relations or lobbying. **Focus:** Government; Public affairs. **Qualif.:** Applicant must be undertake graduate level studies on a part-time basis and work full-time. **Criteria:** Selection will be as follows: Bryce Harlow Foundation Fellowship Committee will review and select finalists from all of the application and evaluate them based on demonstrated strong interest in public affairs, government relations or lobbying; professional achievement and leadership potential; academic achievement and potential; and financial need.

Funds Avail.: $8,000. **Remarks:** Established in 1985.

5299 ■ Harness Horse Youth Foundation (HHYF)
16575 Carey Rd.
Westfield, IN 46074-8925
Ph: (317)867-5877
Fax: (317)867-1886
URL: www.hhyf.org
Social Media: www.facebook.com/Harness-Horse-Youth-Foundation
www.instagram.com/harnesshorseyouthfoundation
twitter.com/HHYFexperience
www.youtube.com/channel/UCA2JGeiQxLG5PxGjC0_u_Jw/videos

5300 ■ Charles Bradley Memorial Scholarships *(Undergraduate/Scholarship)*

Purpose: To provide financial assistance to the children or relatives of racing officials who were members of the North American Judges and Stewards and licensed pari-mutuel officials. **Focus:** General studies/Field of study not specified. **Qualif.:** Applicants must be at least seniors in high school but no older than 25 years of age. **Criteria:** Candidates will be assessed based on scholastic achievement, grade point average, financial need, completeness of application and quality of essay.

To Apply: Applicants must complete and submit application form; must attach (1, 000 words) typewritten statement including background, career goals and experiences; a copy of the latest transcript; two letters of recommendation. **Contact:** ellen@hhyf.org.

5301 ■ Gallo Blue Chip Scholarships *(Undergraduate/Scholarship)*

Purpose: To support the continuing education of the children of harness racing families in New York, New Jersey and Pennsylvania. **Focus:** General studies/Field of study not specified. **Qualif.:** Applicants must be child of harness horse trainer or caretaker licensed in New York, New Jersey; must have been raised and/or reside in the three-state region; must be at least high school seniors; must be (plan to) enrolled as full-time students (minimum 12 credit hours). **Criteria:** Applicants will be evaluated based on demonstrated scholastic achievement, including but not

Awards are arranged alphabetically below their administering organizations

limited to their GPA, financial need and quality of essay.

Funds Avail.: $15,000. **Duration:** Annual. **To Apply:** Applicants must submit a completed application form and must attach a copy of transcripts; parent's current racing commission license; resume; and 1, 000-word essay explaining the accomplishments, plans or career goals and relationship to New York and New Jersey region. **Deadline:** April 30.

5302 ■ Curt Greene Memorial Scholarships
(Undergraduate/Scholarship)

Purpose: To provide financial support for senior high school students who may or may not be pursuing harness racing but demonstrates passion for the sport. **Focus:** General studies/Field of study not specified. **Criteria:** Candidates will be assessed based on scholastic achievement, grade point average, financial need, completeness of application and quality of essay.

Funds Avail.: $2,500. **Duration:** Annual. **To Apply:** Applicants must complete and submit application form. **Deadline:** April 30. **Contact:** Contact: Harness Horse Youth Foundation; 2711 Friar Tuck Road, Anderson IN 46013; Phone: 317-908-0029; Email: Ellen@hhyf.org.

5303 ■ Harness Tracks of America (HTA)
c/o Tom Aldrich
Northfield Park
10705 Northfield Rd.
Northfield, OH 44067
Ph: (330)467-4101
E-mail: info@harnesstracks.com
URL: www.harnesstracks.com

5304 ■ Harness Tracks of America Scholarship Fund *(Undergraduate/Scholarship)*

Purpose: To provide financial assistance to students for post-secondary education. **Focus:** General studies/Field of study not specified. **Qualif.:** Students attending college or graduate school; children of licensed owners, trainers, drivers, caretakers, or racetrack personnel. **Criteria:** Selection is based on academic merit, financial need and active harness racing involvement.

Funds Avail.: $5,000. **Duration:** Annual. **Number Awarded:** 3. **To Apply:** Applicants must submit completed application form together with essays; official academic transcripts; federal tax forms; student aid report; fee rates schedule; and any other supporting documents. Letters of recommendation are not required but may be included. **Deadline:** June 24. **Remarks:** Established in 1973. **Contact:** Harness Tracks of America Scholarship Committee, Coordinator Heather McColloch, Northfield Pk., 10705 Northfield Rd., Northfield, OH, 44067; Email: hmccolloch@mgmnorthfieldpark.com.

5305 ■ Harris Corporation
1025 W NASA Blvd.
Melbourne, FL 32919
Ph: (321)727-9100
Fax: (321)727-9344
Free: 800-442-7747
URL: www.harris.com
Social Media: www.facebook.com/harriscorp
www.linkedin.com/company/harris-corporation
twitter.com/harriscorp

www.youtube.com/user/HarrisCorporation

5306 ■ National Merit Harris Corporation Scholarship Program *(Undergraduate/Scholarship)*

Purpose: To financially assist high school students. **Focus:** General studies/Field of study not specified. **Qualif.:** Applicants must be high school students who are children of Harris Corporation current employees; must be U.S. citizens or have applied for permanent residence; those who do not take the PSAT/NMSQT because of illness, emergency or other circumstance but meet all the requirements will be accepted. **Criteria:** Selection is based on PSAT/NMSQT scores; academic records; activities and contributions to school and community; recommendation letter; and essay about characteristics, plans, and goals.

Funds Avail.: $2,000 per year. **Duration:** Annual; 4 years. **Number Awarded:** 2. **To Apply:** Applicants must obtain a copy of PSAT/NMSQT Official Student Guide and take the qualifying exam.

5307 ■ Harris Personal Injury Lawyers Inc.
301 Mission Ave., Ste. 203
Oceanside, CA 92054
Ph: (760)231-9970
Fax: (760)231-9919
URL: harrispersonalinjury.com
Social Media: www.facebook.com/HarrisPersonalInjury
www.instagram.com/harrispersonalinjury
www.linkedin.com/company/harris-personal-injury-lawyers
twitter.com/HarrisPI

5308 ■ Injury Scholarship *(Undergraduate/Scholarship)*

Purpose: To provide financial assistance to college students who have suffered a serious injury, and are committed to demonstrating determination to rebuild their lives by attending college **Focus:** General studies/Field of study not specified. **Qualif.:** Applicants must be college students who have suffered a serious injury and have committed to demonstrating a determination to rebuild their life by attending college. **Criteria:** Selection will be based on the committee's criteria.

Funds Avail.: $1,000. **Duration:** Semiannual. **Number Awarded:** 1. **To Apply:** Application must be submitted online. Applicants must write a essay of 500 words which explains their injury experience. Including What college they are attending or planning on attending. **Deadline:** August 14, fall semester; February 12, spring semester.

5309 ■ John A. Hartford Foundation (JAHF)
55 E 59th St., 16th Fl.
New York, NY 10022-1713
Ph: (212)832-7788
Fax: (212)593-4913
URL: www.jhartfound.org
Social Media: www.facebook.com/johnahartford
www.linkedin.com/company/1687203
www.linkedin.com/company/johnahartfordfoundation
twitter.com/johnahartford
www.youtube.com/user/JHARTFOUND

5310 ■ The Paul B. Beeson Emerging Leaders Career Development Award in Aging(K76) *(Professional development/Grant)*

Purpose: To sustain and promote the careers of clinically-trained faculty who are pursuing research in aging. **Focus:**

Awards are arranged alphabetically below their administering organizations

Gerontology. **Qualif.:** Applicant must be clinically trained (primarily physician) early-stage investigators.

Funds Avail.: $600,000 to $800,000. **Duration:** Annual. **Remarks:** The award was established to honor Dr. Paul B. Beeson. Established in 1994.

5311 ■ Hartford Foundation for Public Giving (HFPG)

10 Columbus Blvd., 8th Fl.
Hartford, CT 06106
Ph: (860)548-1888
Fax: (860)249-3561
E-mail: hfpg@hfpg.org
URL: www.hfpg.org
Social Media: www.facebook.com/HartfordFoundation
twitter.com/HartfordFdn
www.youtube.com/user/HartfordFoundation

5312 ■ Frederick G. Adams Scholarship Fund
(Undergraduate/Scholarship)

Purpose: To supports students from the Greater Hartford region who are pursuing a four-year college degree. **Focus:** General studies/Field of study not specified. **Qualif.:** Applicants must be graduating seniors who live in or are attending school in Greater Hartford; must be entering a four-year college or university. **Criteria:** Selection will be based on the committee's criteria.

Funds Avail.: $3,000. **Duration:** Annual. **Number Awarded:** 1. **To Apply:** Applicant must download and fill out the online application and attach the following requirements: letter of recommendation from their guidance counselor or a teacher; official high school transcript, including SAT or ACT scores; copy of the essay they submitted with their college application (if applicant did not have to submit one, they must write a brief essay, no more than 2 pages, regarding their future goals); copy of pages 1 and 2 of applicant's parents' or guardians' most recent completed federal tax form 1040; and mail everything to Hartford Foundation College Scholarship Program. **Deadline:** January 15. **Remarks:** The scholarship chose to honor Dr. Adams with a scholarship fund because of his lifelong dedication to education as the highest pursuit.

5313 ■ Alliance Francaise of Hartford Harpin/ Rohinsky Scholarships *(Undergraduate/Scholarship)*

Purpose: To provide educational assistance for graduating high school seniors who live in or are attending school in Greater Hartford. **Focus:** French studies. **Qualif.:** Applicants must be entering a four-year college or university (full-time enrollment); must pursue French studies in college; must have a financial need; must rank top third of their class; and must be active volunteers in school, community, or other extracurricular activities. **Criteria:** Selection will be based on the committee's criteria.

Funds Avail.: $3,000. **Duration:** Annual. **Number Awarded:** 1. **To Apply:** Applicant must download and fill out the online application and attach the following requirements: letter of recommendation from their guidance counselor or a teacher; official high school transcript, including SAT or ACT scores; copy of the essay they submitted with their college application (if applicant did not have to submit one, they must write a brief essay, no more than 2 pages, regarding their future goals); copy of pages 1 and 2 of applicant's parents' or guardians' most recent completed federal tax form 1040; and mail everything to Hartford

Foundation College Scholarship Program. **Deadline:** January 15.

5314 ■ American Marketing Association-Connecticut Chapter, Anna C. Klune Memorial Scholarship *(Graduate/Scholarship)*

Purpose: To assist in the personal and professional career development of marketing professionals in addition to advancing the science and ethical practice of the marketing discipline. **Focus:** Marketing and distribution. **Qualif.:** Applicants must: be a Connecticut resident, may or may not be studying in Connecticut; be a second-year MBA students; be a Marketing or related major; demonstrated leadership record; have entrepreneurial/innovative spirit. **Criteria:** Selection will be based on the committee's criteria.

Funds Avail.: $1,000 - $1,500. **Duration:** Annual. **Number Awarded:** 1. **To Apply:** Applicants may obtain application materials from the AMA-CT website. **Deadline:** February 16.

5315 ■ John Bell and Lawrence Thornton Scholarship Fund *(Undergraduate/Scholarship)*

Purpose: To supports Hartford-area students who attend Hampton University. **Focus:** General studies/Field of study not specified. **Qualif.:** Applicant must be a Greater Hartford resident; must demonstrate academic excellence, financial need, extracurricular activities and community service; must have a GPA of 3.0 and above; and must be rising sophomore and rising junior status. **Criteria:** Selection will be based on the committee's criteria.

Duration: Annual. **Number Awarded:** Varies. **To Apply:** Applicants may obtain application materials from Connecticut River Valley Chapter National Hampton University Alumni Association, Inc. Scholarship Committee. **Deadline:** January 15.

5316 ■ Brian A. Aselton Memorial Scholarship *(Undergraduate/Scholarship)*

Purpose: To provide educational assistance for students entering or enrolled as undergraduate students at Manchester Community College. **Focus:** Criminal justice. **Qualif.:** Applicant must be a student; their parent is active duty with East Hartford, South Windsor, or Hartford Police Department as of January 1, 2020 (must not have retired or resigned prior to this date); first-time applicants: minimum C average, or 2.0 gpa, in the last marking period; renewal applicants: minimum 2.5 cumulative gpa. **Criteria:** Selection will be based on the financial need.

Duration: Annual. **Number Awarded:** 1-10. **To Apply:** Applicants may obtain the application materials from the Manchester Community College. **Deadline:** February 1.

5317 ■ Brian Cummins Memorial Scholarship *(Undergraduate/Scholarship)*

Purpose: To provide scholarship for college junior or senior or graduate students enrolled in a full-time program to teach blind and visually impaired students in Connecticut. **Focus:** General studies/Field of study not specified. **Qualif.:** Applicant must be CT resident or attending school in CT; full-time student; enrolled in a program to teach blind & visually impaired students in CT. **Criteria:** Selection will be based on the committee's criteria.

Funds Avail.: $2,500. **Duration:** Annual. **Number Awarded:** Varies. **To Apply:** Applicants can obtain the application at the National Federation of the Blind CT's website. **Deadline:** September 1. **Contact:** National

Awards are arranged alphabetically below their administering organizations

Federation of the Blind of Connecticut, 111 Sheldon Rd, Unit 420; Manchester, CT 06045; info@nfbct.org; Phone:(860) 289-1971.

5318 ■ C. Rodney Demarest Memorial Scholarship
(Undergraduate/Scholarship)

Purpose: To provide scholarship for students who are legally blind. **Focus:** General studies/Field of study not specified. **Qualif.:** Applicants must be graduating high school seniors or college students residing or attending school full-time in Connecticut; must be legally blind; must demonstrate financial need, community service and academic excellence. **Criteria:** Selection will be based on the committee's criteria.

Funds Avail.: $3,000. **Duration:** Annual. **Number Awarded:** 1. **To Apply:** Applicants may obtain application materials from National Federation of the Blind of CT. **Deadline:** September 1. **Contact:** National Federation of the Blind of Connecticut, 111 Sheldon Rd, Unit 420; Manchester, CT 06045; info@nfbct.org; Phone:(860) 289-1971.

5319 ■ The College Club of Hartford Scholarships
(Undergraduate/Scholarship)

Purpose: To provide scholarship for graduating high school students. **Focus:** General studies/Field of study not specified. **Qualif.:** Applicants must be graduating public high school seniors residing in Avon, Bloomfield, Canton, East Hartford, Farmington, Glastonbury, Hartford, Manchester, Newington, Rocky Hill, Simsbury, West Hartford, Wethersfield or Windsor; must be attending in an accredited two or four-year school; must demonstrate financial need and community service; must be on a class rank upper 10% (Applicant's grades through 2nd quarter of senior year are required); and must be students who attend Trinity College or St. Joseph College in Connecticut. **Criteria:** Selection will be based on the financial need.

Funds Avail.: $1,500. **Duration:** Annual. **Number Awarded:** Varies. **To Apply:** Applicants may visit the website at http://www.collegeclubofhartford.org/scholarships to obtain an application. **Deadline:** March 23. **Contact:** Patricia Kane, Chairperson, The College Club of Hartford, 222 North Hollow Road, East hartland, CT 06027.

5320 ■ Connecticut Association of Latinos in Higher Education Scholarships *(Undergraduate/Scholarship)*

Purpose: To award a scholarship to the students entering or enrolled as undergraduates in an accredited college or university. **Focus:** General studies/Field of study not specified. **Qualif.:** Applicants must be a high school senior/ged equivalent or undergraduate college student; must be latinx student from Connecticut; must demonstrated financial need; must accepted to or attending an accredited institution of higher education; must cumulative gpa of 2.75 or greater for all completed course work at the time of application; must attend full time and be seeking their first undergraduate degree; must demonstrated community service within the latinx community. **Criteria:** Selection are based on scholarship chair.

Funds Avail.: $1,000. **Duration:** Annual. **Number Awarded:** Varies. **To Apply:** Applicants must submit completed application; letter of acceptance from college or university (for high school seniors or GED Students); two letters of recommendation - one must be from a teacher; official high school or college transcript; Copy of either: Federal Student Aid Report or undocumented/DACA students must submit the State of Connecticut Student Aid

Report; essay. **Deadline:** June 30. **Contact:** Dr. Wilson Luna, Scholarship Chair, Gateway Community College, 20 Church St., New Haven, CT, 06510; Email:70harvest@gmail.com.

5321 ■ Connecticut Mortgage Bankers Social Affairs Fund *(Undergraduate/Scholarship)*

Purpose: To provide scholarship assistance to Connecticut. **Focus:** Business; Real estate. **Qualif.:** Applicants must be entering a four-year college or university (full-time enrollment) pursuing a career in business, mortgage or real estate; must have a financial need; must be on a class rank - top third with good academic record; and must be active volunteers in school, community, or other extracurricular activities. **Criteria:** Selection will be based on the financial need.

Funds Avail.: $3,000. **Duration:** Annual. **Number Awarded:** 1. **To Apply:** Applicant must download and fill out the online application and attach the following requirements: letter of recommendation from their guidance counselor or a teacher; official high school transcript, including SAT or ACT scores; copy of the essay they submitted with their college application (if applicant did not have to submit one, they must write a brief essay, no more than 2 pages, regarding their future goals); copy of pages 1 and 2 of applicant's parents' or guardians' most recent completed federal tax form 1040; and mail everything to Hartford Foundation College Scholarship Program.

5322 ■ Dr. Frank and Florence Marino Scholarship
(Undergraduate/Scholarship)

Purpose: To provide educational support to those students who are attending medical school in Connecticut. **Focus:** Medicine. **Qualif.:** Entering 2nd, 3rd, or 4th year medical student in the Fall 2020 Attended Connecticut public or parochial school for at least 8 years (K-12) and graduated from a Connecticut public or parochial high school. **Criteria:** Selection will be based on the committee's criteria.

Funds Avail.: $1,000-$2,000. **Duration:** Annual. **Number Awarded:** 1-5. **To Apply:** Applicants may obtain an application from the financial aid office of their medical school or may contact Sarah Carlson. **Deadline:** February 1. **Contact:** Sarah Carlson, Hartford Foundation for Public Giving, 10 Columbus Blvd., 8th Fl., Hartford, CT, 06106; Phone: 860-548-1888; Fax: 860-249-3561; Email: scarlson@hfpg.org.

5323 ■ Dr. Nicholas J. Piergrossi Memorial Scholarship *(Undergraduate/Scholarship)*

Purpose: To provide support to first-year students who are attending at University of Connecticut School of Dental Medicine. **Focus:** Dentistry. **Qualif.:** Applicants must be residents of Connecticut who demonstrates financial need and academic excellence. **Criteria:** Selection will be based on the financial need.

Funds Avail.: $1,000. **Duration:** Annual. **Number Awarded:** 1. **To Apply:** Applicants may obtain application materials from University of Connecticut School of Dental Medicine. **Deadline:** February 1.

5324 ■ Dr. Sidney Rafal Memorial Scholarship
(Undergraduate/Scholarship)

Purpose: To provide assistance to students who are attending the University of Connecticut School of Dental Medicine. **Focus:** Dental hygiene; Dentistry. **Qualif.:** Applicant must be a pioneer in the field of geriatric dentistry

Awards are arranged alphabetically below their administering organizations

as a clinician, author, teacher, and editor. **Criteria:** Selection will be based on the committee's criteria.

Funds Avail.: $500 - $1,000. **Duration:** Annual. **Number Awarded:** 1. **To Apply:** Applicants may obtain application materials from University of Connecticut School of Dental Medicine. **Deadline:** February 16.

5325 ■ Dorothy E. Hofmann Pembroke Scholarship
(Undergraduate/Scholarship)

Purpose: To support students in Greater Hartford region. **Focus:** General studies/Field of study not specified. **Qualif.:** Applicants must be female residents of Harford, currently enrolled in a public, private, charter or magnet high school in the 29 town Greater Hartford region; must be planning to attend in one of the following colleges/universities: Trinity College, University of Hartford, University of Connecticut, University of Saint Joseph, Central CT State University, Brown University. **Criteria:** Selection will be based on the financial need.

Funds Avail.: No specific amount. **Duration:** Annual. **Number Awarded:** 2. **To Apply:** Applicants may contact the Foundation for the application process and other information. **Deadline:** February 1. **Contact:** Sarah Carlson, Hartford Foundation for Public Giving, 10 Columbus Blvd., 8th Fl., Hartford, CT, 06106; Phone: 860-548-1888; Fax: 860-249-3561; Email: scarlson@hfpg.org.

5326 ■ Charles Dubose Scholarships
(Undergraduate/Scholarship)

Purpose: To provide scholarship to the students attending five-year accredited colleges or universities offering Architecture. **Focus:** Architecture. **Qualif.:** Applicants must completed a two years of Bachelor in Architecture Program; be a Connecticut connection; demonstrated financial need and academic excellence. **Criteria:** Selection will be based on the committee's criteria.

Funds Avail.: $1,200-$5,000. **Duration:** Annual. **Number Awarded:** 1-2. **To Apply:** Applicants may obtain application materials from the Connecticut Architecture Foundation's website at www.aiact.org. **Deadline:** April 21. **Contact:** Diana Harp Jones, Connecticut Architecture Foundation, 370 James St. Ste. 402, New Haven, CT 06513. Phone: 203-865-2195; Fax: 203-562-5378.

5327 ■ Elmer Cooke Young-Ethel Taylor Young Scholarship Fund *(Undergraduate/Scholarship)*

Purpose: To provide financial assistance for high school graduates who are pursuing their academic dreams. **Focus:** General studies/Field of study not specified. **Qualif.:** Applicants students must be graduating seniors from Glastonbury or Windsor High School; must demonstrate financial need; must be on a class rank - top third with good academic record; and must be active volunteers in school, community, or other extracurricular activities. **Criteria:** Selection will be based on the committee's criteria.

Duration: Annual. **To Apply:** Applicant must download and fill out the online application and attach the following requirements: letter of recommendation from their guidance counselor or a teacher; official high school transcript, including SAT or ACT scores; copy of the essay they submitted with their college application (if applicant did not have to submit one, they must write a brief essay, no more than 2 pages, regarding their future goals); copy of pages 1 and 2 of applicant's parents' or guardians' most recent completed federal tax form 1040; and mail everything to Hartford Foundation College Scholarship Program.

5328 ■ Farmington UNICO Scholarship Fund
(Undergraduate/Scholarship)

Purpose: To provide financial assistance to Farmington students or adjacent communities who are members of UNICO. **Focus:** General studies/Field of study not specified. **Qualif.:** Applicant must be a Farmington or West Hartford resident; be a graduating high school senior; demonstrate financial need and academic excellence. **Criteria:** Selection will be based on the committee's criteria.

Duration: Annual. **To Apply:** Applicant must download and fill out the online application and attach the following requirements: letter of recommendation from their guidance counselor or a teacher; official high school transcript, including SAT or ACT scores; copy of the essay they submitted with their college application (if applicant did not have to submit one, they must write a brief essay, no more than 2 pages, regarding their future goals); copy of pages 1 and 2 of applicant's parents' or guardians' most recent completed federal tax form 1040; and mail everything to Hartford Foundation College Scholarship Program.

5329 ■ Harry A. Donn Scholarship *(Undergraduate/Scholarship)*

Purpose: To support students from the Greater Hartford region who are pursuing four-year college degrees. **Focus:** General studies/Field of study not specified. **Qualif.:** Applicants must be entering a four-year college or university (full-time enrollment); demonstrate financial need; be on a class rank - top third with good academic record; be active volunteer in school, community, or other extracurricular activities. **Criteria:** Selection will be based on the committee's criteria.

Funds Avail.: $3,000. **Duration:** Annual. **Number Awarded:** 1. **To Apply:** Applicant must download and fill out the online application and attach the following requirements: letter of recommendation from their guidance counselor or a teacher; official high school transcript, including SAT or ACT scores; copy of the essay they submitted with their college application (if applicant did not have to submit one, they must write a brief essay, no more than 2 pages, regarding their future goals); copy of pages 1 and 2 of applicant's parents' or guardians' most recent completed federal tax form 1040; and mail everything to Hartford Foundation College Scholarship Program. **Deadline:** January 15.

5330 ■ Ida L. Hartenberg Charitable Scholarships
(Undergraduate/Scholarship)

Purpose: To provide scholarship to the graduating high school senior who lives in or attends school in Greater Hartford. **Focus:** Teaching.

Funds Avail.: $3,000. **Duration:** Annual. **Number Awarded:** 1.

5331 ■ Hartford Grammar School Scholarship Fund
(Undergraduate/Scholarship)

Purpose: To award scholarship to a graduating high school senior from a public high school in the City of Hartford. **Focus:** General studies/Field of study not specified. **Qualif.:** Applicants must be entering a four-year college or university (full-time enrollment); demonstrate financial need; be on class rank with good academic record; be an active volunteer in school, community, or other extracurricular activities. **Criteria:** Selection will be based on the committee's criteria.

Funds Avail.: $3,000. **Duration:** Annual. **Number Awarded:** 1. **To Apply:** Applicant must download and fill

Awards are arranged alphabetically below their administering organizations

out the online application and attach the following requirements: letter of recommendation from their guidance counselor or a teacher; official high school transcript, including SAT or ACT scores; copy of the essay they submitted with their college application (if applicant did not have to submit one, they must write a brief essay, no more than 2 pages, regarding their future goals); copy of pages 1 and 2 of applicant's parents' or guardians' most recent completed federal tax form 1040; and mail everything to Hartford Foundation College Scholarship Program. **Deadline:** January 15. **Remarks:** Established in 1657.

5332 ■ Herman P. Kopplemann Fund
(Undergraduate/Scholarship)

Purpose: To award a scholarship to a graduating high school senior who lives in or attends school in Greater Hartford. **Focus:** General studies/Field of study not specified. **Qualif.:** Applicants must be entering a four-year college or university; demonstrate financial need; be on a top third with good academic record; be an active volunteer in school, community, or other extracurricular activities; has been a newspaper carrier in Hartford County. **Criteria:** Selection will be based on the committee's criteria.

Funds Avail.: $3,000. **Duration:** Annual. **Number Awarded:** 1. **To Apply:** Application form can be downloaded on-line. Applicants must complete the scholarship application. Applicants must also attach the following requirements: letter of recommendation from their guidance counselor or a teacher; official high school transcript. Including SAT or ACT scores; copy of the essay they submitted with their college application. If applicants did not have to submit one, they should write a brief (no more than two pages) essay regarding their future goals; copy of pages 1 and 2 of parents' or guardians' most recent completed federal tax form 1040. **Deadline:** January 15. **Remarks:** Established in 1990.

5333 ■ The Interracial Scholarship Fund of Greater Hartford *(Undergraduate/Scholarship)*

Purpose: To provide scholarship awards to students from the Greater Hartford region who are pursuing a four-year college degree. **Focus:** General studies/Field of study not specified. **Qualif.:** Applicant must be a graduating high school senior who lives in or attends school in Greater Hartford; be in top third of class with good academic record; be active volunteer in school, community, or other extracurricular activities; be involved in community service. **Criteria:** Selection will be based on the committee's criteria.

Funds Avail.: $3,000. **Duration:** Annual. **Number Awarded:** 1. **To Apply:** Applicant must download and fill out the online application and attach the following requirements: letter of recommendation from their guidance counselor or a teacher; official high school transcript, including SAT or ACT scores; copy of the essay they submitted with their college application (if applicant did not have to submit one, they must write a brief essay, no more than 2 pages, regarding their future goals); copy of pages 1 and 2 of applicant's parents' or guardians' most recent completed federal tax form 1040; and mail everything to Hartford Foundation College Scholarship Program. **Deadline:** January 15.

5334 ■ James L. and Genevieve H. Goodwin Scholarship *(Undergraduate/Scholarship)*

Purpose: To provide financial assistance to those students who are in need. **Focus:** Forestry. **Qualif.:** Applicants must be enrolled in an undergraduate or graduate curriculum in

silviculture or forest resource management; and must be a Connecticut resident. **Criteria:** Selection will be based on the committee's criteria.

Funds Avail.: $1,000-$5,000. **Duration:** Annual. **Number Awarded:** 1 - 10. **To Apply:** Applicants may complete the General Scholarship Application and include a personal statement indicating why they are interested in Forest Management and submit to Connecticut forest and Park Association, Inc. **Deadline:** March 20. **Contact:** Eric Hammerling, Executive Director; Connecticut Forest and Park Association, Inc; 16 Meriden Rd., Rockfall, CT, 06481; Phone: 860-346-2372; Fax: 860-347-7463; Email: info@ctwoodlands.org.

5335 ■ The Walter S. Kapala Scholarship Trust
(Undergraduate/Scholarship)

Purpose: To support students who are in need of help with their college finances. **Focus:** General studies/Field of study not specified. **Qualif.:** Applicant must be entering a four-year college or university in the fall after high school graduation; demonstrate financial need and have an academic excellence. **Criteria:** Selection will be based on the committee's criteria.

Funds Avail.: $3,000. **Duration:** Annual. **To Apply:** Applicants must complete and submit the general scholarship application available at the website. **Deadline:** January 15.

5336 ■ Lebbeus F. Bissell Scholarship Fund
(Undergraduate/Scholarship)

Purpose: To provide educational assistance to graduating high school seniors of Rockville, or Ellington High Schools. **Focus:** General studies/Field of study not specified. **Qualif.:** Applicants must demonstrate academic excellence, financial need, extracurricular activities and community service. **Criteria:** Selection will be based on the committee's criteria.

Funds Avail.: $3,000. **Duration:** Annual. **Number Awarded:** 3. **To Apply:** Applicants may obtain application materials from Guidance Departments of Rockville, Tolland or Ellington High Schools or from Lebbeus F. Bissel Scholarship Advisory Committee. **Deadline:** February 1. **Remarks:** Established in 1971.

5337 ■ Manchester Scholarship Foundation - Adult Learners Scholarship *(Undergraduate/Scholarship)*

Purpose: To support adults who were returning to or beginning a college education after a lapse since high school graduation. **Focus:** General studies/Field of study not specified. **Qualif.:** Applicant must be adults of age 21 or older who resided in Manchester for at least six months prior to the application deadline who have been accepted to a college or other post secondary school; plans to attend school part time. **Criteria:** Selection will be based on thw demonstrated financial need.

Funds Avail.: $600 for one course; $1,000 for two courses. **Duration:** Annual. **Number Awarded:** Varies. **To Apply:** Applicants may obtain application materials from their Guidance Office or from Manchester Scholarship Foundation, Inc. **Deadline:** April 15. **Contact:** Ms. Carol Powell, Adult Learner Scholarship Chairperson; Phone: 860-649-2153; Email: johngp@cox.net.

5338 ■ Maria Gonzalez Borrero Scholarship Fund
(Undergraduate/Scholarship)

Purpose: To provide funds for the education of Hispanic descent graduating students from City high schools who

Awards are arranged alphabetically below their administering organizations

are preparing for a career in a health-related field. **Focus:** Health care services. **Qualif.:** Applicants must be entering a four-year college or university (full-time enrollment) pursuing a health-related field; must demonstrate financial need; must be top third with good academic record; and must be active volunteers in school, community, or other extracurricular activities. **Criteria:** Selection will be based on the committee's criteria.

Funds Avail.: $3,000. **Duration:** Annual. **Number Awarded:** 1. **To Apply:** Applicant must download and fill out the online application and attach the following requirements: letter of recommendation from their guidance counselor or a teacher; official high school transcript, including SAT or ACT scores; copy of the essay they submitted with their college application (if applicant did not have to submit one, they must write a brief essay, no more than 2 pages, regarding their future goals); copy of pages 1 and 2 of applicant's parents' or guardians' most recent completed federal tax form 1040; and mail everything to Hartford Foundation College Scholarship Program. **Deadline:** January 15. **Remarks:** The Scholarship Fund was established to recognize the tremendous contribution Ms. Borrero made to the Latino community in Hartford through her work in founding and directing the Hispanic Health Council. Established in 1990.

5339 ■ Mary Main Memorial Scholarship
(Undergraduate/Scholarship)

Purpose: To provide a scholarship to the graduating senior or college student residing or attending school full-time in Connecticut. **Focus:** General studies/Field of study not specified. **Qualif.:** Applicants must be legally blind and demonstrate financial need, community service, and academic excellence. **Criteria:** Selection will be based on the committee's criteria.

Funds Avail.: $3,000. **Duration:** Annual. **Number Awarded:** 1. **To Apply:** Applicants may obtain application materials from the National Federation of the Blind of Connecticut's website. **Deadline:** September 15. **Contact:** National Federation of the Blind of Connecticut 477 Connecticut Blvd. Ste. 217, East Hartford, CT 06108; Phone: 860-289-1971; Fax: 860-291-2795; Email: info@nfbct.org.

5340 ■ ARTC Glenn Moon Scholarships
(Undergraduate/Scholarship)

Purpose: To provide scholarship for graduating seniors from any public or private high school in Connecticut. **Focus:** Education. **Qualif.:** Applicants must be graduating seniors from any public or private high school in Connecticut who are about to enter a four-year college or university and major in teaching career education. **Criteria:** Selection shall be based on Academic record; Character and Personality including community service Interests and Educational Activities; Financial Need will be determined by the Student Aid Report (SAR).

Funds Avail.: One $2,000 renewable, two 1-year nonrenewable. **Duration:** Annual. **Number Awarded:** 2. **To Apply:** Application is available online. **Deadline:** March 31. **Contact:** Judy Morganroth, Chairperson, Association of Retired Teachers of Connecticut - Glenn Moon Scholarship Fund, Inc. 26 Route 87, Columbia, CT 06237; Phone: 860-228-1245; Email: freuenwald@yahoo.com.

5341 ■ Peter T. Steinwedell Scholarship *(Graduate/Scholarship)*

Purpose: To provide a scholarship to graduate students in the field of education. Strong preference for students pursu-

ing a teaching career. **Focus:** Education. **Criteria:** Selection will be based on the financial need and academic excellence; preference for students pursuing a teaching career.

Funds Avail.: $1,000-$1,500. **Duration:** Annual. **Number Awarded:** 1-2. **To Apply:** Applicant must download and fill out the online application and attach the following requirements: letter of recommendation from their guidance counselor or a teacher; official high school transcript, including SAT or ACT scores; copy of the essay they submitted with their college application (if applicant did not have to submit one, they must write a brief essay, no more than 2 pages, regarding their future goals); copy of pages 1 and 2 of applicant's parents' or guardians' most recent completed federal tax form 1040; and mail everything to Hartford Foundation College Scholarship Program. **Deadline:** February 1. **Contact:** Sarah Carlson, Hartford Foundation for Public Giving, 10 Columbus Blvd., 8th Fl., Hartford, CT, 06106; Phone: 860-548-1888; Fax: 860-249-3561; Email: scarlson@hfpg.org.

5342 ■ Mary C. Rawlins Scholarships *(Graduate/Scholarship)*

Purpose: To award financial support to the graduating high school senior. **Focus:** General studies/Field of study not specified. **Qualif.:** Applicants must be a resident of Connecticut; graduating high school senior; be entering a two- or four-year college or university; have a GPA of 2.5 or higher at end of Fall semester. **Criteria:** Selection will be based on the committee's criteria.

Funds Avail.: $500-$1,000. **Duration:** Annual. **Number Awarded:** 1-2. **To Apply:** Applicants may obtain application materials from Division of Criminal Justice, The CTAAAP Scholarship Committee. **Deadline:** March 14. **Contact:** Division of Criminal Justice, The CTAAAP Scholarship Committee, 300 Corporate Place Rocky Hill, CT 06067; Marcia Bonitto at mbpanama4@aol.com.

5343 ■ Rhea Sourifman Caplin Memorial Scholarship *(Undergraduate/Scholarship)*

Purpose: To provide a scholarship to the Jewish high school senior or college students. **Focus:** Health care services; Nursing. **Qualif.:** Applicants must be Greater Hartford residents; be pursuing nursing or health care profession; have a minimum B average in sciences; have a good citizenship and active involvement in the community. **Criteria:** Selection will be based on the committee's criteria.

Funds Avail.: $1,000-$2,000. **Duration:** Annual. **Number Awarded:** 1-2. **To Apply:** Applicants may obtain application materials from Jewish Community Foundation of Greater Hartford's website at http: //www.jchartford.org/scholarships. **Deadline:** April 15. **Contact:** Jewish Community Foundation of Greater Hartford, 333 Bloomfield Ave. Ste. D West Hartford, CT 06117; Phone: 860-523-7460; Fax: 860-231-0576; Email: grants@jchartford.org.

5344 ■ Sylvia Parkinson Fund *(Undergraduate/Scholarship)*

Purpose: To support medical students the University of Connecticut School of Medicine who intended to practice in the Hartford area. **Focus:** Medicine. **Qualif.:** Applicants must be a deserving medical students and prospective medical students attending fully accredited medical schools. **Criteria:** Selection will be based on the committee's criteria.

Duration: Annual. **Number Awarded:** 3-6. **To Apply:** Applicants may obtain application materials from University of

Awards are arranged alphabetically below their administering organizations

Connecticut School of Medicine. **Deadline:** February 1. **Remarks:** Established in 1975.

5345 ■ Symee Ruth Feinberg Memorial Scholarship Fund *(Undergraduate/Scholarship)*

Purpose: To provide a scholarship to needy Hartford residents under age 22 who are seeking careers in human services and have experience helping others. **Focus:** General studies/Field of study not specified. **Qualif.:** Applicants must be entering a four-year college or university; must be pursuing a career in human services; must be a class rank of top third with good academic record; must be an active volunteer in school, community or other extracurricular activities. **Criteria:** Selection will be based on the financial need.

Funds Avail.: $3,000. **Duration:** Annual. **Number Awarded:** 1. **To Apply:** Applicant must download and fill out the online application and attach the following requirements: letter of recommendation from their guidance counselor or a teacher; official high school transcript, including SAT or ACT scores; copy of the essay they submitted with their college application (if applicant did not have to submit one, they must write a brief essay, no more than 2 pages, regarding their future goals); copy of pages 1 and 2 of applicant's parents' or guardians' most recent completed federal tax form 1040; and mail everything to Hartford Foundation College Scholarship Program. **Deadline:** January 15.

5346 ■ The Town and County Club Scholarship *(Undergraduate/Scholarship)*

Purpose: To support adult women who are pursuing their educational goal. **Focus:** General studies/Field of study not specified. **Qualif.:** Applicants must be a female adult learner; must be a resident of Greater Hartford region; must be enrolled full or part-time in an accredited community undergraduate college or university in the Greater Hartford region; must have a completion of 15 semester hours or the equivalent of academic work with a 2.5 GPA; and must demonstrate financial need. **Criteria:** Selection will be based on the committee's criteria.

Funds Avail.: $4,000. **Duration:** Annual. **Number Awarded:** maximum of $5, 000. **To Apply:** Applicants may contact the Town and County Club or access the website www.towncounty.com for application form. **Deadline:** February 16.

5347 ■ W. Philip Braender and Nancy Coleman Braender Scholarship Fund *(Undergraduate/ Scholarship)*

Purpose: To support scholarships for students with financial need in the Greater Hartford region. **Focus:** General studies/Field of study not specified. **Criteria:** Selection will be based on the financial need.

Duration: Annual. **To Apply:** Applicant must download and fill out the online application and attach the following requirements: letter of recommendation from their guidance counselor or a teacher; official high school transcript, including SAT or ACT scores; copy of the essay they submitted with their college application (if applicant did not have to submit one, they must write a brief essay, no more than 2 pages, regarding their future goals); copy of pages 1 and 2 of applicant's parents' or guardians' most recent completed federal tax form 1040; and mail everything to Hartford Foundation College Scholarship Program.

5348 ■ Walter "Doc" Hurley Scholarship Fund of Greater Hartfort *(Undergraduate/Scholarship)*

Purpose: To Provide Graduating high school senior who lives in or attends school in Greater Hartford. **Focus:** General studies/Field of study not specified. **Qualif.:** Applicant must be entering a four-year college or university (full-time enrollment); must have class rank upto top third with a good academic record; must be an active volunteer in school, community, or other extracurricular activities; must participate in a wide variety of scholastic and other extracurricular activities. **Criteria:** Selection will be based on the financial need.

Funds Avail.: $3,000. **Duration:** Annual. **Number Awarded:** 1. **To Apply:** Applicants may obtain application materials from eligible high school guidance office. Applications will not be mailed to students. Valid applications must include: Student Air Report (SAR) from FAFSA showing Estimated Family Contribution (EFC); three letter of recommendation (teacher, guidance counselor, and non-educational person); typed essay (no more than 1 1/2 pages); High School Transcript; SAT or ACT scores. All materials must be submitted to Doc Hurley Scholarship Foundation, Inc. Recommendation of high school vice principal, counselor or community leaders. **Deadline:** January 15. **Contact:** Hartford Foundation for Public Giving College Scholarship Program; One Scholarship Way Saint Paul, MN, 56082; Phone: 800-537-4180; Email: hartfordfoundation@scholarshipamerica.org.

5349 ■ William G. and Mayme J. Green Fund *(Undergraduate/Scholarship)*

Purpose: To support scholarships for graduates of Hartford High School and Newington High School who are pursuing a degree in nursing. **Focus:** Nursing. **Qualif.:** Applicants must: be entering a four-year college or university (full-time enrollment) pursuing a degree in Nursing; must demonstrate financial need; be on the class rank - top third with a good academic record; be an active volunteer in school, community, or other extracurricular activities. **Criteria:** Selection will be based on the committee's criteria.

Funds Avail.: $3,000. **Duration:** Annual. **Number Awarded:** 1. **To Apply:** Application form can be downloaded online. Applicants must complete the scholarship application. Applicants must also attach the following requirements: letter of recommendation from your guidance counselor or a teacher; official high school transcript. Including SAT or ACT scores; copy of the essay you submitted with your college application. If you did not have to submit one, write a brief (no more than two pages) essay regarding your future goals; copy of pages 1 and 2 of your parents' most recent completed federal tax form 1040. Mail everything to Hartford Foundation College Scholarship Program. **Deadline:** January 15.

5350 ■ Hartford Public Library (HPL)

500 Main St.
Hartford, CT 06103-3075
Ph: (860)695-6300
Fax: (860)722-6900
E-mail: reference@hplct.org
URL: www.hplct.org
Social Media: www.facebook.com/HartfordPublicLibrary
www.instagram.com/hplct
twitter.com/HPLCT
www.youtube.com/user/hplct

Awards are arranged alphabetically below their administering organizations

5351 ■ Caroline M. Hewins Scholarship *(Graduate, Undergraduate/Scholarship)*

Purpose: To support students planning to specialize in library work with children. **Focus:** Library and archival sciences. **Qualif.:** Applicants must have received, or about to receive, a four year undergraduate degree and have applied for admission to a library school accredited by the American Library Association. **Criteria:** Preference will be given to applicants who plan to pursue a career in public library service.

Funds Avail.: $4,000. **Duration:** Annual. **To Apply:** Applicants must submit a completed application form along with transcript of credits through the first semester of the senior year and an evidence of application to an accredited school of library service. **Remarks:** The Scholarship was established as a tribute to one of the great pioneers in American Librarianship, Caroline M. Hewins in special recognition of her creative work for children throughout the country. Established in 1926. **Contact:** Marie Jarry, Director of Central Public Services, Hartford Public Library, 500 Main St., Hartford, CT, 06103; Phone: 860-695-6300; Email: mjarry@hplct.org.

5352 ■ Hartford Whalers Booster Club (HWBC)

PO Box 273
Hartford, CT 06141
URL: whalersbc.org
Social Media: www.facebook.com/whalersbc
www.instagram.com/whalersbc
www.linkedin.com/whalersbc
twitter.com/WhalerWatch
www.youtube.com/hwbc

5353 ■ Hartford Whalers Booster Club Scholarship *(Undergraduate/Scholarship)*

Purpose: To provide scholarship to those students who are outstanding in academic and as hockey players. **Focus:** General studies/Field of study not specified. **Qualif.:** Applicants must intend to play collegiate hockey; have an outstanding hockey ability; be a Connecticut resident; have an academic excellence. **Criteria:** Selection will be based on the committee's criteria.

Funds Avail.: $1,000. **Duration:** Annual. **To Apply:** Applicant must complete the General Scholarship Application and include a letter of recommendation from their hockey coach outlining applicant's hockey performance and submit both to Hartford Whalers Booster Club. **Deadline:** March 8.

5354 ■ Harvard Business Services Inc.

16192 Coastal Hwy.
Lewes, DE 19958
Ph: (302)645-7400
Free: 800-345-2677
E-mail: info@delawareinc.com
URL: www.delawareinc.com
Social Media: www.facebook.com/Delawareinc
www.linkedin.com/company/harvard-business-services-inc-
twitter.com/#!/delawareinc
www.youtube.com/user/delawareinc1?ob=0&feature
=results_main

5355 ■ Student Entrepreneur Scholarship *(Undergraduate, Graduate/Scholarship)*

Purpose: To help entrepreneurial students pay for their education. **Focus:** Business. **Qualif.:** Applicant must be at least 18 years old and enrolled in a full-time undergraduate or graduate business or entrepreneurship program at an accredited U.S. college or university. **Criteria:** Selection will be made for Harvard Business Services staff and based on fulfillment of the eligibility criteria and the essay.

Funds Avail.: $1,000. **Number Awarded:** 1. **To Apply:** Applicant must also write and submit a 500 to 1,000 word essay describing their planned or existing business, including a description of the business and the inspiration behind it, why they believe it will succeed and/or continue to grow, and how their college education is directly contributing to their ability to succeed. **Deadline:** February 28.

5356 ■ Harvard-Smithsonian Center for Astrophysics (CFA)

60 Garden St.
Cambridge, MA 02138
Ph: (617)495-7100
E-mail: advancement@cfa.harvard.edu
URL: www.cfa.harvard.edu

5357 ■ CfA Postdoctoral Fellowship *(Postdoctorate/ Fellowship)*

Purpose: To advance knowledge of the Universe through research in astronomy and astrophysics and in related areas of fundamental physics and geophysics. **Focus:** Geophysics; Physics. **Qualif.:** Applicants must be outstanding researchers displaying significant promise in theory, observation, instrumentation and/or laboratory experiments; must be first-author refereed journal paper and who already received their Ph.D. at the time of application.

Funds Avail.: Approximately $68,000 with a research budget of $16,000. **Duration:** Annual. **Number Awarded:** 1. **To Apply:** Applicants submit the information via online.

5358 ■ Clay Postdoctoral Fellowship *(Postdoctorate/ Fellowship)*

Purpose: To support an outstanding researcher(s) displaying significant promise in theory, observation, instrumentation, and/or laboratory experiments. **Focus:** Geophysics; Physics. **Qualif.:** Applicants must be outstanding researchers displaying significant promise in theory, observation, instrumentation and/or laboratory experiments.

Funds Avail.: Approximately $69,000, plus a research budget of $16,000. **Duration:** Annual. **Number Awarded:** Varies. **To Apply:** Applicants submit the information via online. **Deadline:** October 30.

5359 ■ SAO Predoctoral Fellowship *(Graduate/ Fellowship)*

Purpose: To advance the knowledge of the Universe through research in astronomy and astrophysics and in related areas of fundamental physics and geophysics. **Focus:** Geophysics; Physics. **Qualif.:** Applicants must be graduate students wishing to carry out all or part of their thesis research at the Smithsonian Astrophysical Observatory.

Funds Avail.: $31,284. **Duration:** Annual; up to 6 months. **To Apply:** Applicants submit the information via the online; Curriculum Vitae; reference electronically.

5360 ■ Harvard University - Arnold Arboretum

125 Arborway
Boston, MA 02130-3500

Awards are arranged alphabetically below their administering organizations

Ph: (617)524-1718
Fax: (617)524-1418
E-mail: arbweb@arnarb.harvard.edu
URL: www.arboretum.harvard.edu
Social Media: www.facebook.com/ArnoldArboretum
.Harvard
www.instagram.com/arnold_arboretum/
twitter.com/ArnoldArboretum
www.youtube.com/user/ArnoldArboretum

5361 ■ Arnold Arboretum Deland Award for Student Research *(Graduate, Undergraduate/Grant)*

Purpose: To support research expenses and, in some cases, living expenses incurred during the research period. **Focus:** Biology; Botany. **Qualif.:** Applicant must be an advanced undergraduate or graduate student. **Criteria:** Selection of recipients will be based on the educational background of the student and their readiness to conduct the proposed research; the quality of the proposed research; and the relevance of the proposed research to the living collections of the Arnold Arboretum; preference is given to students whose research utilizes the living collections of the Arnold Arboretum.

Funds Avail.: Up to $10,000. **Duration:** Annual. **To Apply:** Applicants submit the online applications should include the following: cover letter; research statement; research budget; project timeline; curriculum vitae; two letters of recommendation. **Deadline:** February 1. **Contact:** Email: arbscholars@fas.harvard.edu.

5362 ■ Harvard University Faculty of Arts & Sciences - Institute for Quantitative Social Science - Henry A. Murray Research Archive

CGIS Knafel Bldg.
1737 Cambridge St.
Cambridge, MA 02138
E-mail: support@dataverse.org
URL: murray.harvard.edu

5363 ■ Jeanne Humphrey Block Dissertation Award *(Postdoctorate/Award)*

Purpose: To encourage and recognize an outstanding individual for the excellent dissertation regarding social sciences. **Focus:** Social sciences. **Qualif.:** Applicants must be Harvard Ph.D. students (3rd year or above) in the social sciences. **Criteria:** Award decision will be based on: significance to science research; innovation and; investigator evaluation.

Funds Avail.: $2,500. **Duration:** Annual; each Spring. **To Apply:** Completed applications along with the required documents must submit through email in the subject line as Jeanne Block Memorial Fund Application; required documents: dissertation paper maximum of two pages; letter of recommendation from dissertation adviser; completed application form; CV/Resume and; project budget. Dissertation must utilize data archived in the Harvard Data verse. **Deadline:** March 13. **Contact:** Email: funding@iq.harvard.edu.

5364 ■ Harvard University Law School (HLS)

1563 Massachusetts Ave.
Cambridge, MA 02138
URL: www.law.harvard.edu
Social Media: www.facebook.com/harvardlaw

www.instagram.com/harvardlaw
twitter.com/harvard_law
www.youtube.com/user/HarvardLawSchool

5365 ■ Henigson Human Rights Fellowship *(Graduate, Master's, Juris Doctorate/Fellowship)*

Purpose: To encourage the HLS students to build human rights work and to expand their interest in working in the field. **Focus:** Human rights; Law. **Criteria:** Selection preference will be given to HLS JD and LLM students from the current graduating class.

Funds Avail.: Up to $27,000 plus $1,500 toward international health insurance. **Duration:** Annual. **To Apply:** Applicants must submit their curriculum vitae, including information about classes, work and extracurricular activities in public interest and human rights inside and outside of Harvard Law School; a personal statement (500 words maximum) about the applicant's relevant experience, interest, and future aspirations with respect to public interest and human rights work; a project description; a letter and supporting materials from sponsoring organization detailing their purpose, function, and particular interest in the work of the applicant; two or three letters of recommendation including at least one from an HLS professor; and an HLS transcript. **Deadline:** March 15. **Remarks:** The fellowship was established by Robert '55 and Phyllis Henigson. **Contact:** Human Rights Program, Harvard Law School, WCC Clinical Wing, 3rd Fl., Cambridge, MA, 02138; Phone: 617-495-9362; Email: hrp@law.harvard.edu.

5366 ■ Satter Human Rights Fellowship *(Graduate, Master's, Juris Doctorate/Fellowship)*

Purpose: To support and promote human rights defense in response to mass atrocity or widespread and severe patterns of rights abuse. **Focus:** Human rights; Law. **Qualif.:** Applicants must be Harvard Law School J.D. students (3Ls expecting to receive the J.D. degree, as well as recent J.D. graduates); and/or, Harvard Law School LL.M. students who expect to receive the LL.M. degree.

Funds Avail.: Up to $45,000 stipend. **Duration:** Annual. **To Apply:** Applicants must submit their curriculum vitae, including information about classes, work and extracurricular activities in public interest and human rights inside and outside of Harvard Law School; a personal statement (500 words maximum) about the applicants' relevant experience, interest, and future aspirations with respect to public interest and human rights work; a project description; a letter and supporting materials from sponsoring organization detailing their purpose, function, and particular interest in the work of the applicant; two or three letters of recommendation including at least one from an HLS professor; and an HLS transcript. **Deadline:** March 15. **Remarks:** The fellowship was established by Muneer A. Satter, '87. **Contact:** Human Rights Program, Harvard Law School, WCC Clinical Wing, 3rd Fl., Cambridge, MA, 02138; Phone: 617-495-9362; Email: hrp@law.harvard.edu.

5367 ■ Harvard University Law School - Program on Negotiation (PON)

501 Pound Hall
1563 Massachusetts Ave.
Cambridge, MA 02138
Ph: (617)495-1684
Fax: (617)495-7818
E-mail: pon@law.harvard.edu
URL: www.pon.harvard.edu

Awards are arranged alphabetically below their administering organizations

Social Media: www.facebook.com/Program-on-Negotiation
-at-Harvard-Law-School-13682273086
www.linkedin.com/company/the-program-on-negotiation
twitter.com/HarvardNegoti8
www.youtube.com/user/ponhls

5368 ■ PON Graduate Student Grants *(Graduate/Grant)*

Purpose: To support cutting-edge research at the graduate level. **Focus:** Consulting; Law. **Qualif.:** Applicants must be graduate students conducting or planning to conduct research; students from any Boston-area school may apply. **Criteria:** Grant applications will be evaluated on the basis of: academic merit; originality and; potential for producing material for an academic paper or thesis.

Funds Avail.: $1,000. **Duration:** One year. **To Apply:** Applicants must submit a cover letter indicating that if the fellowship is accepted, the applicant plans to reside in the Cambridge area; a detailed description of proposed research (no longer than 15 pages); a research budget indicating all expenses and other possible sources of financial support; a resume; a departmentally approved dissertation proposal, and two letters of recommendation, one of which must be from the faculty member who will be supervising research at the student's home university. **Deadline:** November 19, May 1. **Contact:** Polly Hamlen, Program on Negotiation at Harvard Law School, 1563 Massachusetts Ave., Pound Hall 501, Cambridge, MA, 02138; Phone: 617-496-9383; Email: mhamlen@law.harvard.edu.

5369 ■ PON Next Generation Grants *(Doctorate, Postdoctorate/Grant)*

Purpose: To support research in negotiation and conflict resolution by non-tenured faculty and doctoral students. **Focus:** Consulting; Law. **Qualif.:** Applicants must be non-tenured faculty or doctoral students from any school or department within PON's inter-university consortium (Harvard, MIT, and Tufts Fletcher School); post-doctoral students with a formal affiliation to Harvard or one of the consortium schools of PON are also eligible to apply. **Criteria:** Selection will be based on academic merit; originality and potential for yielding publishable material in leading academic journals.

Funds Avail.: $5,000-$10,000. **To Apply:** Applicants must submit a three to five page proposal electronically together with the following: description of the proposed research, justifying the request for funds; qualification of Applicants to carry out the research, referencing appropriate courses or training that provide the basis for competency in the proposed method; budget including all other sources of support for the project; curriculum vitae and; for students: name and contact information for a faculty member familiar with the students' work. **Deadline:** May 31, November 19, and May 30.

5370 ■ PON Summer Fellowships *(Graduate/Fellowship)*

Purpose: To forge new links between our academic community and worldwide organizations involved in the practice of negotiation and dispute resolution, and to encourage students to reach for opportunities that would otherwise not be available to them due to financial constraints. **Focus:** Consulting; Law. **Qualif.:** Applicants must be returning graduate students at schools in the Boston-area; eligible internships and research projects must be unpaid, undertaken in partnership with a public, non-profit or academic

organization, and a minimum of eight weeks in duration; fellowship must have already secured or applied for the position/project for which they are seeking PON summer fellowship support; grants will be dispersed once documentation confirming the internship or project is provided by the host organization or, in the case or research projects, by a supervising faculty member. **Criteria:** Selection will be based on the Committees' criteria.

To Apply: Applicants must complete and submit the following requirements: cover page; letter from host organization (internship) or academic supervisor (research); resume or curriculum vitae; project proposal; budget detailing estimated expenses; letter of recommendation and; Signed Acknowledgement of Risk and General Release Form (to be provided by PON if/when a fellowship is awarded). **Deadline:** March 20. **Contact:** Polly Hamlen, Email: mhamlen@law.harvard.edu.

5371 ■ Hasbrook & Hasbrook
400 N Walker Ave., No. 130
Oklahoma City, OK 73102
Ph: (405)698-3040
Fax: (405)607-9765
URL: www.oklahomalawyer.com

5372 ■ Make Us Proud Scholarships *(Undergraduate/Scholarship)*

Purpose: To support students to achieve their educational goals. **Focus:** General studies/Field of study not specified. **Qualif.:** Applicants must be U.S. citizens living and attending school in the United States; must be graduating high school seniors or college freshmen or sophomores who have completed no more than 60 credit hours. **Criteria:** Selection will be based on the relevance to one of the practice areas, composition and creativity of the submitted essay.

Funds Avail.: $1,000. **Duration:** Annual. **To Apply:** Applicants must write a 140-word essay and 140-character tweet-worthy summary of the essay on a topic related to one of Hasbrook & Hasbrook's nine practice areas. The essay may inform or advocate or both. Applicants must submit a cover page that contains the following information: name; address; date of birth; phone number; email; current school; school planning to attend next semester. A cover page, essay and tweet must be submitted as a single PDF document and a photo of yourself via email attachments. **Deadline:** August 31. **Contact:** Email: scholarship@hasbrooklaw.com.

5373 ■ Hawaii Community Foundation
827 Fort Street Mall
Honolulu, HI 96813
Ph: (808)537-6333
Fax: (808)521-6286
Free: 888-731-3863
E-mail: info@hcf-hawaii.org
URL: www.hawaiicommunityfoundation.org
Social Media: www.facebook.com/
  HawaiiCommunityFoundation
www.instagram.com/hawaiicommunityfoundation
twitter.com/HCFHawaii
www.youtube.com/channel/UCMG3KmXI-eQkAexvf
_L12kw

Awards are arranged alphabetically below their administering organizations

5374 ■ 100th Infantry Battalion Veterans Memorial Scholarship Fund *(Undergraduate, University, College, Vocational/Occupational/Scholarship)*

Purpose: To help descendants of the 100th Battalion Veterans of WWII pursue post-secondary studies. **Focus:** General studies/Field of study not specified. **Qualif.:** Applicants must be undergraduate or graduate students enrolled full-time in an accredited two- or four-year, not-for-profit institution with the United States (including U.S. territories); must be a direct descendant of a 100th Infantry Battalion World War II veteran; must demonstrate a willingness to promote the legacy of the Battalion; must have a minimum 3.0 GPA and be active in extracurricular activities and community service. **Criteria:** Special attention will be noted for volunteer work connected with the activities of the Battalion Veterans organization including, but not limited to, educational programs, annual memorial services, and the anniversary banquet.

Duration: Annual. **To Apply:** Applicant must submit a personal statement and a separate essay on the historical significance of the Battalion and what life stories these soldiers have to teach all American citizens. Application is available online on sponsor's website. **Contact:** Email: scholarships@hcf-hawaii.org.

5375 ■ A&B Ohana Scholarship Fund *(Undergraduate, College, Two Year College, Vocational/Occupational/Scholarship)*

Purpose: To help students in Hawaii pursue post-secondary studies. **Focus:** General studies/Field of study not specified. **Qualif.:** Applicants must be enrolled full-time in an accredited two- or four-year, not-for-profit institution within the United States (including U.S. territories); must be residents of Hawaii and demonstrate financial need. **Criteria:** Financial need; preference will be given to a dependent child of a full-time employee of Alexander & Baldwin Inc.

Duration: Annual. **To Apply:** Applications are available on the sponsor's website. Scholarships are renewable for up to four consecutive years as long as the parent/guardian remains employed by A&B and the student's GPA remains above 2.7; must reapply each year. **Contact:** Email: scholarships@hcf-hawaii.org.

5376 ■ AAUW Honolulu Branch Education Funds *(Undergraduate, Graduate, Master's/Scholarship)*

Purpose: To help female students in Hawaii pursue post-secondary education, especially in STEM fields. **Focus:** General studies/Field of study not specified. **Qualif.:** Applicants must be female students enrolled in accredited, four-year, not-for-profit institutions in Hawaii; must be residents of Hawaii; must have a minimum 3.0 GPA. **Criteria:** Financial need; preference will be given to students majoring in STEM (science, technology, engineering, math) fields.

Funds Avail.: $10,000. **Duration:** Annual. **Number Awarded:** 2. **To Apply:** Must submit two letters of recommendation with application. **Remarks:** Sponsored by the Honolulu branch of the American Association of University Women. **Contact:** Email: scholarships@hcf-hawaii.org; URL: honolulu-hi.aauw.net/scholarships/.

5377 ■ ABC Stores Jumpstart Scholarship Fund *(Undergraduate, University, College, Vocational/Occupational, Graduate/Scholarship)*

Purpose: To assist students in pursuing post-secondary studies. **Focus:** General studies/Field of study not speci-

fied. **Qualif.:** Applicants must be undergraduate or graduate students enrolled full or part-time at an accredited two or four-year institution; must be employees or dependents of employees of ABC Stores or Company Island Gourmet Markets; must be residents of Hawaii, Nevada, Guam, or Saipan; must have a minimum 2.7 GPA. **Criteria:** Financial need.

Duration: Annual. **To Apply:** Application is available online on Foundation's website. **Contact:** Email: scholarships@hcf-hawaii.org.

5378 ■ Aiea General Hospital Association Scholarship *(Undergraduate, College, Two Year College, University/Scholarship)*

Purpose: To help students in Hawaii pay for post-secondary studies in health care fields. **Focus:** Health sciences. **Qualif.:** Applicants must be undergraduate students enrolled full-time in an accredited, two or four-year, not-for-profit institution within the United States (including U.S. territories); must be majoring in a health-related field; must be a resident of one of the following Leeward O'ahu zip codes: 96701, 96706, 69707, 96782, 96792, or 96797; must have a minimum 2.5 GPA. **Criteria:** Financial need.

Duration: Annual. **To Apply:** Must submit two letters of recommendation with application. **Remarks:** Established by the Aeia General Hospital Board of Directors when the hospital closed to give back to the area residents. Established in 1985. **Contact:** Email: scholarships@hcf-hawaii.org.

5379 ■ Daniel K. and Millie Akaka Ohana Scholarship Fund *(Undergraduate/Scholarship)*

Purpose: To assist Hawaiian students in pursuing undergraduate degrees. **Focus:** General studies/Field of study not specified. **Qualif.:** Applicants must be residents of Hawaii with a substantial connection to Hawaii; must be full time students at an accredited, two- or four-year institution; must have good academic standing and a minimum 2.0 GPA; must demonstrate good character, including community service, leadership, and civic involvement. **Criteria:** Preference will be given to previous recipients who were awarded the immediate prior year if they continue to meet eligibility requirements. Preference will also be given to applicants majoring in education, environmental studies, healthcare related fields, or music; candidates with higher academic standing, including a 3.0 or higher GPA; and those with a class standing of undergraduate college sophomore or above.

Duration: Annual. **To Apply:** Application form and details are available on Foundation's website. **Remarks:** Established by Ohana 100 (the Daniel Kahikina Akaka Family Foundation) in memory of U.S. Senator Daniel K. Akaka, and his wife, Millie.

5380 ■ Anthony Alexander, Andrew Delos Reyes & Jeremy Tolentino Memorial Fund *(Undergraduate, University, College, Two Year College/Scholarship)*

Purpose: To help graduating students from Mililani High School pursue post-secondary education. **Focus:** General studies/Field of study not specified. **Qualif.:** Applicant must be residents of Hawaii and current graduating seniors at Mililani High School; must be enrolling full-time in an accredited, two- or four-year, not-for-profit institution in the United States (including U.S. territories); must have a minimum 2.7 GPA. **Criteria:** Financial need.

Duration: Annual. **To Apply:** Applicants must submit a personal statement and an essay on the subject of drinking

Awards are arranged alphabetically below their administering organizations

and driving under the influence, highway safety, or another related subject. **Remarks:** Established to memorialize Anthony Alexander, Andrew Delos Reyes, and Jeremy Toletino who were all students at Mililani High School. Established in 2003. **Contact:** Email: scholarships@hcf-hawaii.org.

5381 ■ Aloha Prince Hall Hawaii Foundation Fund Scholarship *(Undergraduate, College, University/ Scholarship)*

Purpose: To support graduating seniors who are pursuing post-secondary degrees. **Focus:** General studies/Field of study not specified. **Qualif.:** Applicants must be graduating high school seniors pursuing undergraduate degrees at accredited, four-year colleges or institutions; must be residents of Hawaii; must have a minimum 2.7 GPA. **Criteria:** Preference for those with high academic achievement, high financial need, community service, and/or extracurricular activities.

Duration: Annual. **To Apply:** Application details are available on the Foundation's website. **Contact:** Email: scholarships@hcf-hawaii.org.

5382 ■ Bank of Hawaii Foundation Scholarship Fund *(Undergraduate, University, College, Two Year College/Scholarship)*

Purpose: To help young people have an opportunity to succeed. **Focus:** General studies/Field of study not specified. **Qualif.:** Applicants must be full-time undergraduate students enrolled in an accredited, two or four-year institution within the United States (including U.S. territories); must be children or grandchildren of an active-status employee of Bank of Hawaii Corporation or any of its subsidiaries with at least one year of active employment; must be high school graduates with a minimum 2.0 GPA.

Duration: Annual. **To Apply:** Application details available on Foundation's website. **Contact:** Email: scholarships@hcf-hawaii.org.

5383 ■ Bick Bickson Scholarship Fund *(Undergraduate, Graduate/Award)*

Purpose: To help deserving students in Hawaii pursue careers in marketing, law, or travel industry management. **Focus:** Law; Marketing and distribution; Travel and tourism. **Qualif.:** Applicants must be undergraduate or graduate students enrolled full-time in an accredited institution in the United States (including U.S. territories) and majoring in marketing, law, or travel industry management; must be residents of Hawaii; must have good academic standing or maintain a minimum 2.0 GPA. **Criteria:** Financial need.

Duration: Annual. **To Apply:** Application and details available on Foundation's website. **Remarks:** Established to honor Irwin "Bick" Bickson, a lawyer and entrepreneur, who was a leader in the tourism industry in Hawaii. **Contact:** Email: scholarships@hcf-hawaii.org.

5384 ■ Booz Allen Hawaii Scholarship Fund *(Undergraduate, Four Year College, University/ Scholarship)*

Purpose: To provide scholarship grants to Hawaiian residents planning to attend accredited four-year universities or colleges. **Focus:** General studies/Field of study not specified. **Qualif.:** Applicants must be full-time, undergraduate students attending an accredited, four-year, not-for-profit institution within the United States (including U.S. territories); must be a resident of Hawaii; must have a

minimum 3.0 GPA and leadership in community service. **Criteria:** Financial need; preference is for STEM majors.

Duration: Annual. **To Apply:** Application and details available on Foundation's website. **Remarks:** Established in 2007. **Contact:** Email: scholarships@hcf-hawaii.org.

5385 ■ Candon, Todd, & Seabolt Scholarship Fund *(Undergraduate, Four Year College, University/ Scholarship)*

Purpose: To help Hawaiian students pursue degrees in accounting and finance. **Focus:** Accounting; Finance. **Qualif.:** Applicants must be full-time, junior or senior undergraduate students majoring in accounting and/or finance at an accredited, four-year, not-for-profit institution in the United States (including U.S. territories); must be residents of Hawaii; must have a minimum 3.2 GPA. **Criteria:** Financial need; preference may be given to previous recipients.

Duration: Annual. **To Apply:** Application and details available on the Foundation's website. **Contact:** Email: scholarships@hcf-hawaii.org.

5386 ■ Castle & Cooke George W.Y. Yim Scholarship Fund *(Undergraduate, Graduate, Two Year College, Four Year College, University/Scholarship)*

Purpose: To help Hawaiian students pursue post-secondary education. **Focus:** General studies/Field of study not specified. **Qualif.:** Applicants must be full-time, undergraduate or graduate students attending an accredited, two or four-year, not-for-profit institution in the United States (including U.S. territories); must be a dependent of a current employee with at least one year of service with a Castle & Cooke Hawaii-affiliated company; must be residents of Hawaii. **Criteria:** Financial need.

Duration: Annual. **To Apply:** Application and details available on Foundation's website. **Remarks:** Established in 1995. **Contact:** Email: scholarships@hcf-hawaii.org.

5387 ■ Castle & Cooke Mililani Technology Park Scholarship Fund *(Undergraduate, University, Four Year College/Scholarship)*

Purpose: To recognize outstanding students from Central O'ahu and to encourage studies in high technology fields. **Focus:** Engineering; General studies/Field of study not specified; Science. **Qualif.:** Applicants must be full-time students attending an accredited, four-year, not-for-profit institution within the United States (including U.S. territories); must be residents of Hawaii and graduating seniors from Leilehua, Mililani, or Waialua High Schools; must have a minimum 2.7 GPA. **Criteria:** Financial need; preference is given to students majoring in high technology fields, such as science and engineering.

Duration: Annual. **To Apply:** Application and details are available on Foundation's website. **Contact:** Email: scholarships@hcf-hawaii.org.

5388 ■ Catrala - Hawaii Scholarship Fund *(Undergraduate, University, Two Year College, Four Year College/Scholarship)*

Purpose: To provide financial support for high school seniors, with a preference for students pursuing degrees in travel industry management, business, or marketing. **Focus:** Business; General studies/Field of study not specified; Marketing and distribution; Travel and tourism. **Qualif.:** Applicants must be graduating high school seniors enrolling full-time in an accredited, two or four-year, not-for-profit institution with the United States (including U.S. ter-

---

Awards are arranged alphabetically below their administering organizations

ritories); must be residents of Hawaii; must maintain a 2.5-3.5 GPA and have demonstrated community service leadership. **Criteria:** Financial need; preference for applicants intending to pursue degrees in travel industry management, business, or marketing.

Duration: Annual. **To Apply:** Application and details available on Foundation's website. **Contact:** Email: scholarships@hcf-hawaii.org.

5389 ■ Ben and Vicky Cayetano Scholarship Fund
(Undergraduate, College, University, Two Year College/Scholarship)

Purpose: To provide opportunities in higher education to exceptional Hawaiian students - especially those who have demonstrated perseverance and determination in the face of difficult financial and social obstacles. **Focus:** Education; Engineering; General studies/Field of study not specified; Law; Medicine; Political science; Radio and television. **Qualif.:** Applicants must be enrolled full-time in an accredited, two- or four-year, not-for-profit institution within the United States (including U.S. territories); must be residents of Hawaii and graduating seniors from Hawaii public high schools; must have a minimum 3.5 GPA (2.7 GPA for renewals) and demonstrated financial need. **Criteria:** Preference will be given to students with the greatest financial need and those majoring in engineering, medicine, political science, radio technology, law, and education.

Duration: Annual. **To Apply:** Applicants must submit two letters of recommendation (not needed for those reapplying), a personal statement, and an essay on the following topic: Fast forward 40 years, now you are in your late 50s. Reflect on your adult life and list the major accomplishments. Explain why you consider them significant. Application and further details available on Foundation's website. **Remarks:** Established in memory of Brandon F. Cayetano. **Contact:** Email: scholarships@hcf-hawaii.org.

5390 ■ Central Pacific Bank Scholarship Fund
(Undergraduate/Scholarship)

Purpose: To assist CPB employees and their dependents in affording undergraduate education. **Focus:** General studies/Field of study not specified. **Qualif.:** Applicants must be full- or part-time, undergraduate, degree-seeking students attending an accredited, two- or four-year, not-for-profit institution within the United States (including U.S. territories); must be an active employee of CPB and/or subsidiary or affiliated company with a minimum of one year of service, or be the dependent child or grandchild of the same; must have demonstrated financial need. **Criteria:** Preference are as follows, in order of priority: recipients who were awarded in the immediate prior year, if recipients continue to meet the eligibility requirements and are in good academic standing; for new awardees, high school seniors, undergraduate freshmen, sophomores, juniors, and seniors (in that order); demonstrated financial need; cumulative 2.7 GPA or higher.

Duration: Annual. **To Apply:** Application form and details are available on the Foundation's website. **Remarks:** Established in 2010.

5391 ■ Camille C. Chidiac Fund Scholarship
(Undergraduate, Four Year College, Two Year College, Vocational/Occupational/Scholarship)

Purpose: To help students in Hawaii attend post-secondary education. **Focus:** General studies/Field of study not specified. **Qualif.:** Applicants must be full-time students attend-

ing an accredited, two or four-year, not-for-profit institution in the United States (including U.S. territories); must be residents of Hawaii and graduating seniors from Ka'u High School; applicants must have a minimum 2.7 GPA. **Criteria:** Financial need.

Duration: Annual. **To Apply:** Required to include a statement on why it is important for Hawaii students to be internationally aware with application. **Remarks:** Established in 1991. **Contact:** Email: scholarships@hcf-hawaii.org.

5392 ■ Donald W. F. Ching Memorial Scholarship Fund *(Undergraduate, Two Year College, Four Year College/Scholarship)*

Purpose: To help students in Hawaii pursue post-secondary education. **Focus:** Aviation; International affairs and relations; Travel and tourism. **Qualif.:** Applicants must be full-time, undergraduate students attending an accredited, two- or four-year, not-for-profit institution; must be an employee or dependent of an employee of Hawaiian airlines; must be majoring in aviation, international relations, or travel industry management; must be residents of Hawaii, have a minimum 3.0 GPA, and demonstrate financial need. **Criteria:** Preference will be given to applicants who are the first generation in their family to attend college.

Duration: Annual. **To Apply:** Application form and details are available on Foundation's website.

5393 ■ Dolly Ching Scholarship *(Undergraduate, Two Year College, Four Year College/Scholarship)*

Purpose: To help students in Hawaii pursue post-secondary education. **Focus:** General studies/Field of study not specified. **Qualif.:** Applicants must be residents of Hawaii who are attending an accredited, two- or four-year, not-for-profit institution in the United States (including U.S. territories); must have a minimum 2.7 GPA and demonstrate financial need. **Criteria:** Preference will be given to applicants attending a University of Hawaii system school.

Duration: Annual. **To Apply:** Application form and details are available on Foundation's website. **Remarks:** Established in 1994.

5394 ■ Bal Dasa Scholarship Fund *(Undergraduate, University, College, Two Year College, Vocational/Occupational/Scholarship)*

Purpose: To help Waipahu High School graduates pursue post-secondary education. **Focus:** General studies/Field of study not specified. **Qualif.:** Applicants must be residents of Hawaii and graduates of Waipahu High School; must be enrolled full-time in an accredited, two- or four-year, not-for-profit institution within the United States (including U.S. territories); must have a minimum 2.7 GPA. **Criteria:** Financial need; preference may be given to previous recipients.

Duration: Annual. **To Apply:** Application details are available on Foundation's website. **Contact:** Email: scholarships@hcf-hawaii.org.

5395 ■ Deja Vu Surf Hawaii Scholarship Fund
(Undergraduate, Two Year College, Four Year College/Scholarship)

Purpose: To support the success of Kauai students. **Focus:** General studies/Field of study not specified. **Qualif.:** Applicants must be residents of Kaua'i, Hawaii, and the first generation in their family to attend college; must be attend-

Awards are arranged alphabetically below their administering organizations

ing an accredited, two- or four-year, not-for-profit institution within the United States (including U.S. territories); must have a minimum 2.0 GPA and demonstrate financial need. **Criteria:** Preference will be given to students who have been in foster care.

Duration: Annual. **To Apply:** Application form and details are available on Foundation's website.

5396 ■ Diamond Resort Scholarship Fund
(Undergraduate, Two Year College, Four Year College/ Scholarship)

Purpose: To provide financial support to graduating seniors from public schools in Maui County who display excellence in academic achievement, leadership, and community service. **Focus:** General studies/Field of study not specified. **Qualif.:** Applicants must be residents of Hawaii and graduating seniors from public high schools in the County of Maui; must be attending an accredited, two- or four-year, not-for-profit institution in the United States (including U.S. territories); must have a minimum 3.0 GPA and demonstrate financial need.

Duration: Annual. **To Apply:** Application form and details are available on Foundation's website. **Remarks:** Established in 2013.

5397 ■ Allan Eldin & Agnes Sutorik Geiger Scholarship Fund *(Undergraduate, Graduate/Scholarship)*

Purpose: To help students in Hawaii pursue degrees in veterinary science. **Focus:** Veterinary science and medicine. **Qualif.:** Applicants must be sophomore, junior, or senior undergraduate students or graduate students enrolled full-time in an accredited, four-year, not-for-profit institution within the United States (including U.S. territories); must be majoring in veterinary science; must be residents of Hawaii; must have a minimum 3.0 GPA. **Criteria:** Financial need; preference given to previous recipients.

Duration: Annual. **To Apply:** Application details available on Foundation's website. **Remarks:** Established in 2005. **Contact:** Email: scholarships@hcf-hawaii.org.

5398 ■ Blossom Kalama Evans Memorial Scholarship Fund *(Undergraduate, University, Four Year College, Two Year College/Scholarship)*

Purpose: To help students in Hawaii pursue post-secondary education, especially in Native Hawaiian or Hawaiian Studies. **Focus:** General studies/Field of study not specified. **Qualif.:** Applicants must be full-time students attending an accredited, two or four-year, not-for-profit institution in Hawaii; must be residents of Hawaii. **Criteria:** Financial need; preference given to those who major in Native Hawaiian or Hawaiian Studies.

Duration: Annual. **To Apply:** Must include a statement on how their knowledge will be used to serve the needs of the Native Hawaiian community. Application and further details available on Foundation's website. **Remarks:** Created by the family of Blossom Kalama Evans with donations from the Big Island Girls Golf Club. **Contact:** Email: scholarships@hcf-hawaii.org.

5399 ■ Ambassador Minerva Jean Falcon Hawaii Scholarship *(Undergraduate, Graduate, Two Year College, College, University/Scholarship)*

Purpose: To help students in Hawaii pursue post-secondary education. **Focus:** General studies/Field of study not specified. **Qualif.:** Applicants must be full-time undergraduate or graduate students at accredited, two or four-year institutions in Hawaii; must be residents of Hawaii who graduated from high schools in Hawaii; must have a minimum 2.7 GPA. **Criteria:** Financial need; preference will be given to applicants of Filipino ancestry.

Duration: Annual. **To Apply:** Application details are available on the Foundation's website. **Remarks:** Established to honor Minerva Jean Falcon, the Honolulu Consul General of the Republic of the Philippines from 1996-2000. **Contact:** Email: scholarships@hcf-hawaii.org.

5400 ■ Victoria S. and Bradley L. Geist Scholarships *(Undergraduate, University, College, Vocational/ Occupational/Scholarship)*

Purpose: To assist students who have been in the foster system to pursue post-secondary education. **Focus:** General studies/Field of study not specified. **Qualif.:** Applicants must have their primary residences in Hawaii; must plan to attend a two- or four-year college, university, or vocational school and enroll at least half-time; must have past or present placement in foster care within the State of Hawaii and not have been reunited with birth parents before 14th birthday; must be a U.S. citizen.

Duration: Annual. **To Apply:** Applications are available on the sponsor's website. **Remarks:** Established in 1981. **Contact:** Email: scholarships@hcf-hawaii.org.

5401 ■ Doris and Clarence Glick Classical Music Scholarship Fund *(Undergraduate, Graduate, Two Year College, Four Year College, University/ Scholarship)*

Purpose: To help students in Hawaii pursue post-secondary education in music fields, especially classical music. **Focus:** Music; Music, Classical. **Qualif.:** Applicants must be residents of Hawaii who are majoring in music, with an emphasis on classical music, and who demonstrate financial need. **Criteria:** Preference will be given for the following: attending an accredited, two-or-four year, not-for-profit institution in the United States (including U.S. territories); enrolled as a full-time student with a minimum 2.7 GPA; be an undergraduate or graduate student.

Duration: Annual. **To Apply:** Application form and details are available on Foundation's website. **Remarks:** Established by the will of Clarence Glick, a long time teacher at the university of Hawaii, to perpetuate the Glick's love of classical music. Established in 1996.

5402 ■ Anna K. Gower and Annabelle K. Gower Scholarship Fund *(Undergraduate, University, College, Two Year College, Vocational/Occupational/ Scholarship)*

Purpose: To assist Native Hawaiian students who display academic merit and good character in paying for post-secondary education. **Focus:** General studies/Field of study not specified. **Qualif.:** Applicants must be residents of Hawaii and of Native Hawaiian ancestry; must be enrolled full-time in an accredited, two or four-year, not-for-profit institution in the United States (including U.S. territories). **Criteria:** Financial need.

Duration: Annual. **To Apply:** Application details available on the Foundation's website. **Remarks:** Established in 2015. **Contact:** Email: scholarships@hcf-hawaii.org.

5403 ■ Celeste Hayo Memorial Scholarship Fund
(Undergraduate, College, University/Scholarship)

Purpose: To help students from Kekaulike High School pursue post-secondary education. **Focus:** General studies/

Awards are arranged alphabetically below their administering organizations

Field of study not specified. **Qualif.:** Applicants must be undergraduate students attending an accredited, two- or four-year, not-for-profit institution with the United States (including U.S. territories); must be residents of Hawaii and graduates of King Kekaulike High School; must have a minimum 2.5 GPA and demonstrated financial need. **Criteria:** Preference will be given to the following: high school and former high school athletes; students pursuing careers in the medical field, especially nursing; students who have performed community service.

To Apply: Application form and details are available on the Foundation's website. **Remarks:** Established to honor Celeste Hayo, a graduate of King Kekaulike High School who lost her life in a moped accident in Bali.

5404 ■ HCF Community Scholarships Fund
(Undergraduate, Graduate/Scholarship)

Purpose: To assist students in Hawaii aiming to further their education. **Focus:** General studies/Field of study not specified. **Qualif.:** Applicants must be residents of Hawaii; must be full-time undergraduate or graduate students who have plan to attend an accredited two- or four-year college or university; must be the first in their families to attend college or have other unique circumstances; must demonstrate financial need. **Criteria:** Preference is based on the following: first in family to attend college; maintain a 3.3-3.8 GPA; demonstrate a commitment to the community in Hawai'i; be a college sophomore.

Funds Avail.: No specific amount. **Duration:** Annual. **To Apply:** Applications are available on the sponsor's website. **Contact:** Email: scholarships@hcf-hawaii.org.

5405 ■ David L. Irons Memorial Scholarship Fund
(Undergraduate, Two Year College, Four Year College/ Scholarship)

Purpose: To benefit and support deserving Punahou students pursuing post-secondary education. **Focus:** General studies/Field of study not specified. **Qualif.:** Applicants must be residents of Hawaii and graduating seniors from Punahou School; must be attending an accredited, two- or four-year, not-for-profit institution in the United States (including U.S. territories); must be full-time students and demonstrate financial need. **Criteria:** Preference will be given to students attending an educational institution in the state of Indiana.

Duration: Annual. **To Apply:** Application form and details are available on Foundation's website. **Remarks:** Established by the family of David L. Irons, who was known for his fairness, sense of justice, commitment to the community, sense of humor, and concern and interest in the legal system.

5406 ■ Arthur Jackman Scholarship *(Community College, Vocational/Occupational/Scholarship)*

Purpose: To help students on the island of Hawaii attend training programs that will help them gain employment. **Focus:** Technology. **Qualif.:** Applicants must be residents of the island of Hawaii enrolled full-time in an AS or AAS career and technical degree program at a University of Hawaii Community College; must have a minimum 2.7 GPA. **Criteria:** Financial need; preference give to those enrolled at Hawai'a Community College; preference may be given to past recipients.

Duration: Annual. **To Apply:** Application details available on the Foundation's website. **Remarks:** Established by the granddaughter of Arthur Jackman, a man who came to

America in the early 1900s and built his business working from the bottom up of the steel industry. **Contact:** Email: scholarships@hcf-hawaii.org.

5407 ■ Dan & Pauline Lutkenhouse & Hawaii Tropical Botanical Garden Scholarship and Educational Fund *(Undergraduate, Graduate/Scholarship)*

Purpose: To help local youth pursue undergraduate or graduate degrees. **Focus:** Agricultural sciences; Medicine; Nursing; Science. **Qualif.:** Applicants must be undergraduate or graduate students attending an accredited, two- or four-year, not-for-profit institution in the United States (including U.S. territories); must be full-time students and have a minimum 2.7 GPA; must be residents of the Hilo Coast and the Hamakua Coast, north of the Wailuku River; must be majoring in agriculture, science, medicine, or nursing; must demonstrate financial need.

Duration: Annual. **To Apply:** Application form and details are available on the Foundation's website. **Remarks:** Established by Mr. & Mrs. Lutkenhouse, founders of the Hawaii Tropical Botanical Garden, to benefit the youth in the community in which they live.

5408 ■ Cora Aguda Manayan Fund Scholarship
(Undergraduate/Scholarship)

Purpose: To open the doors of education to students. **Focus:** General studies/Field of study not specified. **Qualif.:** Applicants must be residents of Hawaii who have Filipino ancestry and are attending an accredited, not-for-profit institution in the continental United States; must demonstrate financial need.

Duration: Annual. **To Apply:** Application form and details are available on the Foundation's website. **Remarks:** Established by Dr. Cora Manayan, a prominent doctor and community activist in Hawaii.

5409 ■ Craig D. Newman Memorial Scholarship
(Undergraduate/Scholarship)

Purpose: To help students in Hawaii pursue undergraduate education. **Focus:** Education; General studies/Field of study not specified; Maritime studies; Travel and tourism. **Qualif.:** Applicants must be full-time, undergraduate students attending an accredited, two- or four-year, not-for-profit institution with the United States (including U.S. territories); must be residents of Hawaii and graduates of Lana'i High School; must have a minimum 2.7 GPA and demonstrate financial need. **Criteria:** Preference will be given to students in the field of education, travel industry management, or maritime industry studies.

Duration: Annual. **To Apply:** Application form and details are available on the Foundation's website. **Remarks:** Established by C. Jean Shewey in honor of her late son Craig D. Newnan, who founded Expeditions, the only passenger ferry running between Lahaina, Maui, and Manele Harbor, Lana'i.

5410 ■ Charles & Mitch Ota Foundation Scholarship
(Undergraduate, Two Year College, Four Year College/ Scholarship)

Purpose: To benefit students from Maui that participated in the AVID program to attend a college or university, with the intention to support scholarship recipients through their undergraduate degrees. **Focus:** General studies/Field of study not specified. **Qualif.:** Applicants must be high school seniors or previous graduates of Maui High School or King Kekaulike High School; must have participated in the

Awards are arranged alphabetically below their administering organizations

Advancement Via Individual Determination (AVID) program while in high school (preferably for at least 3 years); must be enrolled full-time in an accredited, two- or four-year, public or private not-for-profit post-secondary institution in Hawaii (outside Maui County) or on the continental United States; must have a minimum 2.7 GPA. **Criteria:** Preference is given to current high school seniors.

Duration: Annual. **To Apply:** Application form and details are available on the Foundation's website. **Remarks:** Established in the memory of lifelong Maui residents Charles and Mitch Ota who shared a deep love for their island home and left a lasting legacy. Established in 2020.

5411 ■ Doris Hardinger Roome Scholarship Fund (Undergraduate, Graduate, Two Year College, Four Year College/Scholarship)

Purpose: To assist undergraduate and graduate students who participate in community service and show leadership abilities. **Focus:** General studies/Field of study not specified. **Qualif.:** Applicants must be full-time undergraduate or graduate students at a two- or four-year college or university; must be residents of Hawaii; must have a minimum 2.7 GPA and demonstrate financial need. **Criteria:** Preference for students with strong community service experience and for renewal candidates.

Duration: Annual. **To Apply:** Application form and details are available on Foundation's website. **Remarks:** Established in memory of Doris Hardinger Roome, a longtime resident of Kailua.

5412 ■ Albert and Dorothy Shigekuni Scholarship Fund (Undergraduate/Scholarship)

Purpose: To help students in Hawaii pay for college in the University of Hawaii system. **Focus:** General studies/Field of study not specified. **Qualif.:** Applicants must be undergraduate students enrolled full-time in a University of Hawaii System school; must be residents of Hawaii; must have a minimum 3.1 GPA. **Criteria:** Financial need; preference given to those pursuing one semester or one year abroad through the University of Hawaii system, but who have not previously traveled outside of Hawaii.

Duration: Annual. **To Apply:** Application details available on sponsor's website. **Remarks:** Established in 2013. **Contact:** Email: scholarships@hcf-hawaii.org.

5413 ■ The Jane Suganuma Memorial Scholarship Fund (Undergraduate, Graduate, University, College, Two Year College/Scholarship)

Purpose: To help students in Hawaii pursue degrees in graphic arts. **Focus:** Graphic art and design. **Qualif.:** Applicants must be undergraduate or graduate students enrolled full-time in an accredited, two or four-year, not-for-profit institution within the United States (including U.S. territories); must be majoring in graphic arts; must be residents of Hawaii and graduates of a Hawaiian high school; must have a minimum 2.7 GPA. **Criteria:** Financial need.

Duration: Annual. **To Apply:** Application details are available on the Foundation's website. **Remarks:** Established in 1987. **Contact:** Email: scholarships@hcf-hawaii.org.

5414 ■ Alan and Grace Tenn Scholarship Fund (Undergraduate, Graduate/Scholarship)

Purpose: To help students in Hawaii pursue college degrees in education. **Focus:** Education; Teaching. **Qualif.:** Must be senior undergraduate or graduate students majoring in education at an accredited institution in Hawaii; must be residents of Hawaii, with a preference for residents from Hawaii Island; must have a minimum 2.7 GPA. **Criteria:** Financial need; preference will be given to students planning to teach or provide counseling within the education system.

Duration: Annual. **To Apply:** Submit two letters of recommendation and application. **Contact:** Email: scholarships@hcf-hawaii.org.

5415 ■ Alma White - Delta Chapter, Delta Kappa Gamma Scholarship (Undergraduate, University, College, Two Year College/Scholarship)

Purpose: To help students in Hawaii pursue college degrees in education. **Focus:** Education. **Qualif.:** Applicants must be enrolled in an accredited, four-year, not-for-profit institution within the United States (including U.S. territories); must be majoring in education; must be residents of Hawaii. **Criteria:** Financial need.

Duration: Annual. **To Apply:** Application details are available on Foundation's website. **Remarks:** Established in honor of Alma White, a long-term teacher and principal in Hawaii. **Contact:** Email: scholarships@hcf-hawaii.org.

5416 ■ Clarence and Virginia Young Trust Scholarship (Undergraduate/Scholarship)

Purpose: To support Hawaii public high school graduates pursuing education degrees at University of Hawaii campuses. **Focus:** Education. **Qualif.:** Applicants must be residents of Hawaii and graduates of a public high school in Hawaii; must be enrolled as full-time students at University of Hawaii-Manoa, University of Hawaii-Hilo, University of Hawaii-Maui, or University of Hawaii-West O'ahu; must be majoring in education, have a minimum 3.0 GPA, and have demonstrated financial need. **Criteria:** Preference is for renewal applicants.

Duration: Annual. **To Apply:** Application form and details are available online on the Foundation's website. **Remarks:** Established in 2015.

5417 ■ Hawaii Lodging & Tourism Association (HLTA)
2270 Kalakaua Ave., Ste. 1702
Honolulu, HI 96815-2519
Ph: (808)923-0407
Fax: (808)924-3843
E-mail: info@hawaiilodging.org
URL: www.hawaiilodging.org
Social Media: www.facebook.com/HawaiiLodging/?fref=ts
twitter.com/hawaiilodging

5418 ■ Clem Judd Jr. Memorial Scholarship (Undergraduate/Scholarship)

Purpose: To support students who have the potential to work toward the standard of excellence. **Focus:** Hotel, institutional, and restaurant management. **Qualif.:** Applicants must be students who are Hawaii residents of Hawaiian ancestry enrolled full-time at an accredited university/college in the United States; majoring in hotel/lodging management and have a minimum 3.0 GPA (on a 4.0 scale). **Criteria:** Selection will be based on the citizenship and leadership as demonstrated through activities and college performance.

Funds Avail.: $1,000. **Duration:** Annual. **Number Awarded:** Up to 2. **To Apply:** Applicants must submit the

Awards are arranged alphabetically below their administering organizations

following application checklist (enclosures required with application): proof of residency (either Hawaii state identification card or Hawaii state driver's license); most recent official transcript from current college; autobiography; career goals essay; recommendation from university professor, counselor, or dean; and photograph (optional); current official transcript (or most current transcript if not in school now); letter of recommendation from a college professor, counselor or dean; Personal statement, 500 words or less, addressing the following question: What is your best example of community service in which you have made a difference? and Where in your background would we find evidence of your leadership potential? and how would you apply that in the hospitality industry?. **Deadline:** June 30. **Contact:** Clem Judd Jr. Memorial Scholarship Committee, Hawaii Hotel Industry Foundation, 2270 Kalakaua Ave., Ste. 1702, Honolulu, HI, 96815; Phone: 808-923-0407; Email: jcaires@hawaiilodging.org.

5419 ■ R.W. "Bob" Holden Memorial Scholarships
(Undergraduate/Scholarship)

Purpose: To support students who have the potential to work toward the standard of excellence. **Focus:** Hotel, institutional, and restaurant management. **Qualif.:** Applicants must be students who are Hawaii residents enrolled full-time at an accredited university/college in the United States; majoring in hotel/lodging management and have a minimum 3.0 GPA (on a 4.0 scale). **Criteria:** Selection will be based on the citizenship and leadership as demonstrated through activities and college performance.

Funds Avail.: $1,000 each. **Duration:** Annual. **Number Awarded:** 3. **To Apply:** Applicants must submit the following application checklist (enclosures required with application): proof of residency (either Hawaii state identification card or Hawaii state driver's license); most recent official transcript from current college; autobiography; career goals essay; recommendation from university professor, counselor, or dean; and photograph (optional); current official transcript (or most current transcript if not in school now); letter of recommendation from a college professor, counselor or dean; Personal statement, 500 words or less, addressing the following question: What is your best example of community service in which you have made a difference? and Where in your background would we find evidence of your leadership potential? and how would you apply that in the hospitality industry?. **Deadline:** June 30. **Contact:** R.W. Bob Holden Scholarship Committee, Hawaii Hotel Industry Foundation, 2270 Kalakaua Ave., Ste. 1702, Honolulu, HI, 96815; Phone: 808-923-0407; Email: jcaires@hawaiilodging.org.

5420 ■ Hawaii Pacific Gerontological Society (HPGS)
PO Box 3714
Honolulu, HI 96812
Ph: (808)722-8487
Fax: (808)235-3650
URL: hpgs.org

5421 ■ Hpgs Graduate Scholarships *(Graduate/Scholarship)*

Purpose: To support graduate, law and medical students registered in a program of study focused on gerontology or geriatrics. **Focus:** Gerontology; Medicine; Geriatric. **Qualif.:** Applicants must be enrolled in a degree program at any UH campus, HPU, BYU- Hawaii, or Chaminade; two or

more semesters to complete before graduation; must have GPA of 3.0 or higher. **Criteria:** Selection is based on the submitted application materials.

Funds Avail.: $2,000. **Duration:** Annual. **Number Awarded:** 3. **To Apply:** Application forms are available online; applicants must submit one copy of latest transcript; one letter of recommendation. **Deadline:** July 8. **Contact:** Christy Nishita; E-mail: cnishita@hawaii.edu.

5422 ■ HPGS Undergraduate Scholarships
(Undergraduate/Scholarship)

Purpose: To support professionals pursuing their career related to gerontology or geriatrics. **Focus:** Gerontology; Medicine, Geriatric. **Qualif.:** Applicants must be undergraduate student majoring in Nursing or Social Work; must have a serious interest in professional work related to aging, long-term care, and/or death and dying. **Criteria:** Selection is based on the submitted application materials.

Funds Avail.: $1,000. **Duration:** Annual. **Number Awarded:** 3. **To Apply:** Application forms are available online; applicants must provide a proof of residency in the State of Hawaii; One letter of recommendation from academic adviser, professor or former professors, or supervisor; copy of latest college or university transcript; essay. **Deadline:** July 8. **Contact:** Christy Nishita; E-mail: cnishita@hawaii.edu.

5423 ■ Healing Springs Ranch
100 S Texas St.
Tioga, TX 76271
Free: 866-656-8384
URL: www.healingspringsranch.com
Social Media: www.facebook.com/healingspringsranch
www.linkedin.com/in/healing-springs-ranch-1a7039122

5424 ■ Addiction Treatment Scholarship
(Undergraduate/Scholarship)

Purpose: To provide financial assistance to a college student who has experienced recovery from drug or alcohol addiction, either directly, or witnessed recovery through a loved one or friend. **Focus:** Substance abuse. **Qualif.:** Application should be a U.S. citizen or authorized to work/attend university/college in the U.S. **Criteria:** Essay should clearly convey a complex message as to how personal and social hurdles were conquered during addiction.

Funds Avail.: $1,000. **To Apply:** Applicant should complete the online application and include a copy of university/college acceptance letter. **Deadline:** June 15.

5425 ■ Health Effects Institute (HEI)
75 Federal St., Ste. 1400
Boston, MA 02110-1817
Ph: (617)488-2300
Fax: (617)488-2335
URL: www.healtheffects.org
Social Media: www.instagram.com/unitycollege/
www.linkedin.com/school/unity-college/
www.pinterest.com/unitycollege/
twitter.com/unitycollege
twitter.com/HEIresearch

5426 ■ Walter A. Rosenblith New Investigator Award
(Postdoctorate/Award)

Purpose: To provide funding for outstanding investigators who are beginning independent research on the health ef-

Awards are arranged alphabetically below their administering organizations

fects of air pollution. **Focus:** Air pollution. **Qualif.:** Must be scientists of any nationality holding a PhD, ScD, MD, DVM, or DrPH degree or equivalent; can reside in the US or elsewhere; at the time of application the candidate should have two to seven years of research experience after obtaining the highest degree and must be in an assistant professor or equivalent position at an academic or research institution. **Criteria:** Selection will be based on the research proposal, letters of support, institutional support, and the applicant's career development and mentoring plan.

Funds Avail.: $500,000. **Duration:** Annual. **Number Awarded:** 1 to 2. **To Apply:** Applicants must submit full application form; applications should be in PDF format with a maximum file size of 20 MB; required font size is 11 point with 1-inch margins, single spaced; full application consists of two equally important parts: (1) a formal proposal for a research project of up to three years and associated materials; and (2) evidence of the candidate's qualifications and outstanding research potential as well as a mentoring plan; Specific budget requirements; cover letter from the applicant describing their interest in the award and how this project fits with their career goals; Two letters of reference from well-established scientists familiar with the candidate's professional capabilities but who are not directly involved in the proposed project; One letter from the department chair, dean or other administrative official from the candidate's present institution; A description of the mentoring plan and letters from the candidate's mentor(s) indicating the commitment of the mentor(s) to providing consultation to the candidate on a regular basis; Three recent publications and a list of all publications by the candidate. **Deadline:** September 2. **Remarks:** This award is named for Professor Walter A. Rosenblith who served as the first Chair of HEI's Research Committee and as a member of the HEI Board of Directors; professor Rosenblith's vision of science and standard of excellence enabled HEI to quickly develop a strong scientific program. **Contact:** Health Effects Institute, 75 Federal Street, Suite 1400 Boston, MA 02110, USA Phone: 617-488 2322; Email: funding@healtheffects.org; all prospective applicants are required to send their CV to Dr. Eleanne van Vliet, Email: evanvliet@healtheffects.org.

5427 ■ Health Physics Society (HPS)

950 Herndon Pky, ste 450
Herndon, VA 20170
Ph: (703)790-1745
Fax: (703)790-2672
E-mail: hps@burkinc.com
URL: www.hps.org
Social Media: facebook.com/pages/Health-Physics-Society
 -News-Cafe/157387224301493
www.facebook.com/HealthPhysicsSociety
www.instagram.com/healthphysicssociety
twitter.com/hps_org
www.youtube.com/channel/
 UCOWmRRcBHOAfxud3jmGAAUg

5428 ■ Burton J. Moyer Memorial Fellowship
(Graduate, Undergraduate/Fellowship)

Purpose: To support students enrolled in bonafide U.S. graduate programs in health physics or a closely related field. **Focus:** Health sciences; Radiology. **Qualif.:** Applicants must be full-time entering or continuing students enrolled in U.S. graduate programs in health physics or related field, previous HPS Fellowship holders are ineligible. **Criteria:** Selection is based on the application.

Funds Avail.: $10,000 cash; $800 travel grant to be used to attend the HPS annual meeting. **Duration:** Annual. **Number Awarded:** 1. **To Apply:** Applicants must complete the online application; applicants must submit the copies of all undergraduate and graduate transcripts, and a summary of your health physics. **Deadline:** February 27. **Remarks:** Established with a bequest from the late Burton J. Moyer by Northern California Chapter of the HPS. **Contact:** Place the supporting materials to: Jill Drupa, Health Physics Society; 1313 Dolley Madison Blvd., Ste. 402, McLean, VA 22101; Phone: 703-790-1745; Fax: 703-790-2672; Email: jdrupa@burkinc.com.

5429 ■ J. Newell Stannard Fellowship *(Graduate, Undergraduate/Fellowship)*

Purpose: To support students enrolled in bonafide U.S. graduate programs in health physics or a closely related field. **Focus:** Health sciences; Radiology. **Qualif.:** Applicants must be full-time entering or continuing students enrolled in U.S. graduate programs in health physics or related field; previous HPS Fellowship holders are ineligible. **Criteria:** Selection is based on the application.

Funds Avail.: $5,000 cash; $800 travel grant. **Duration:** Annual. **To Apply:** Applicants must complete the online application; applicants must submit the copies of all undergraduate and graduate transcripts, and a summary of your health physics. **Contact:** Supporting material should be emailed:Jill Drupa Health Physics Society 950 Herndon Parkway, Suite 450 Herndon, VA 20170 phone: 703-790-1745 fax: 703-790-2672 jdrupa@burkinc.com.

5430 ■ Robert S. Landauer, Sr. Memorial Fellowship *(Graduate, Undergraduate/Fellowship)*

Purpose: To provide financial support to students enrolled in bonafide U.S. graduate programs in health physics or a closely related field. **Focus:** Health sciences; Radiology. **Qualif.:** Applicants must be full-time entering or continuing students enrolled in U.S. graduate programs in health physics or related field, previous HPS Fellowship holders are ineligible. **Criteria:** Selection is based on the application.

Funds Avail.: $5,000 cash; $800 travel grant. **Duration:** Annual. **To Apply:** Applicants must complete the online application; applicants must submit the copies of all undergraduate and graduate transcripts, and a summary of your health physics. **Remarks:** The award was established in honor of Robert S. Landauer. **Contact:** Place the supporting materials to: Jill Drupa, Health Physics Society; 1313 Dolley Madison Blvd., Ste. 402, McLean, VA 22101; Phone: 703-790-1745; Fax: 703-790-2672; Email: jdrupa@burkinc.com.

5431 ■ Richard J. Burk, Jr., Fellowship *(Graduate, Undergraduate/Fellowship)*

Purpose: To support students enrolled in bonafide U.S. graduate programs in health physics or a closely related field. **Focus:** Health sciences; Radiology. **Qualif.:** Applicants must be full-time entering or continuing students enrolled in U.S. graduate programs in health physics or related field, previous HPS Fellowship holders are ineligible. **Criteria:** Selection is based on the application.

Funds Avail.: $5,000 cash; $800 travel grant. **Duration:** Annual. **To Apply:** Applicants must complete the online application; applicants must submit the copies of all undergraduate and graduate transcripts, and a summary of your health physics. **Deadline:** February 27. **Contact:** Place the supporting materials to: Jill Drupa, Health Physics Society; 950 Herndon Parkway, Suite 450 Herndon, VA 20170;

Awards are arranged alphabetically below their administering organizations

phone: 703-790-1745; fax: 703-790-2672; Email: jdrupa@ burkinc.com.

5432 ■ Robert Gardner Memorial Fellowship *(Graduate, Undergraduate/Fellowship)*

Purpose: To support students enrolled in bonafide U.S. graduate programs in health physics or a closely related field. **Focus:** Health sciences; Radiology. **Qualif.:** Applicants must be full-time entering or continuing students enrolled in U.S. graduate programs in health physics or related field, previous HPS Fellowship holders are ineligible. **Criteria:** Selection is based on the application.

Funds Avail.: $5,000 cash; $800 travel grant. **Duration:** Annual. **Number Awarded:** 1. **To Apply:** Applicants must complete the online application; applicants must submit the copies of all undergraduate and graduate transcripts, and a summary of your health physics. **Deadline:** December 1. **Contact:** Place the supporting materials to: Jill Drupa, Health Physics Society; 1313 Dolley Madison Blvd., Ste. 402, McLean, VA 22101; Phone: 703-790-1745; Fax: 703-790-2672; Email: jdrupa@burkinc.com.

5433 ■ Health Resources in Action
2 Boylston St. 4th Fl.
Boston, MA 02116
Ph: (617)451-0049
URL: www.hria.org
Social Media: www.linkedin.com/company/health -resources-in-action
twitter.com/hriaction

5434 ■ Charles A. King Trust Postdoctoral Research Fellowship *(Postdoctorate/Fellowship)*

Purpose: To support postdoctoral scientists in non-profit academic, medical or research institutions in Massachusetts. **Focus:** Biological and clinical sciences; Health sciences. **Qualif.:** Applicants must be working in an academic or medical research institution in the state of Massachusetts and have required minimum or maximum years of experience; must hold a fellowship position under the supervision of a faculty member; each applicant must be working under the supervision of an established scientist who is the designated Mentor.

Funds Avail.: $95,350 to $110, 650 per year, inclusive of a $2,000 expense allowance. **Duration:** Annual; two years. **Remarks:** Established in 1936. **Contact:** Lindsey Phelan, MA, Grants Officer, The Medical Foundation; Email: lphelan@hria.org.

5435 ■ Davis Foundation Postdoctoral Fellowships *(Doctorate, Master's/Fellowship)*

Purpose: To support postdoctoral fellows working in non-profit academic, medical and research institutions in the United States. **Focus:** Health sciences. **Qualif.:** Applicant must have MD, PhD or equivalent awarded from an accredited domestic or foreign institution; have completed no more than three years of full-time postdoctoral research experience by the time funding begins; conduct the proposed research project at a hospital, university or other non-profit research institution where applicant holds their postdoctoral fellowship appointment. **Criteria:** Selection will be based on the committee's criteria.

Funds Avail.: $141,000-$177,000. **Duration:** Annual; three years. **To Apply:** Applicants must submit a research project which focuses the relevant aspects of the biological causes

of anorexia nervosa and bulimia nervosa as defined by clinical criteria; must upload a signed letter of support from their research project mentor; and supply two confidential letters of recommendation, one of which must be from thesis advisor for Applicants holding a PhD. If the thesis advisor is unavailable to write a letter of recommendation, a brief explanation of unavailability must be included in the uploaded document. Complete application process required an online submission as well as a mailed copy of the application materials that are submitted online. **Contact:** Jeanne Brown, Program Officer; Phone: 617-279-2240, ext. 709; Email: jbrown@hria.org.

5436 ■ Deborah Munroe Noonan Memorial Research Fund *(Professional development/Grant)*

Purpose: To support innovative clinical and service system research and demonstration projects from both nonprofit organizations and academic institutions that serve children with physical or developmental disabilities and associated health-related complications. **Focus:** Disabilities; Medical research. **Qualif.:** Applicants must hold a position within a nonprofit institution or organization; project must address the target age range of birth through 23 years old; statewide health services research projects that include the majority of disabled children within the Fund's geographic area will also be considered eligible. **Criteria:** Selection will be based on the committee's criteria.

Funds Avail.: $80,000. **Duration:** Annual; 1 Year. **To Apply:** Application must be completed online and the proposal uploaded as a PDF by the deadline; in addition, three hard copies of the uploaded PDF must be mailed. The complete application includes an application face sheet, project summary, proposal (eight pages excluding bibliography), curriculum vitae, proposed budget and letter(s) of support and letter(s) of collaboration. Research projects must be conducted within the Fund's geographic area of interest. **Deadline:** March 15. **Remarks:** Established in 1947. **Contact:** Jeanne Brown, Program Officer; The Medical Foundation; Email: jbrown@hria.org.

5437 ■ Victoria S. and Bradley L. Geist Scholarships *(Undergraduate, University, College, Vocational/ Occupational/Scholarship)*

Purpose: To assist students who have been in the foster system to pursue post-secondary education. **Focus:** General studies/Field of study not specified. **Qualif.:** Applicants must have their primary residences in Hawaii; must plan to attend a two- or four-year college, university, or vocational school and enroll at least half-time; must have past or present placement in foster care within the State of Hawaii and not have been reunited with birth parents before 14th birthday; must be a U.S. citizen.

Duration: Annual. **To Apply:** Applications are available on the sponsor's website. **Remarks:** Established in 1981. **Contact:** Email: scholarships@hcf-hawaii.org.

5438 ■ Charles H. Hood Foundation Child Health Research Awards Program *(Doctorate/Award)*

Purpose: To support newly independent faculty, provide the opportunity to demonstrate creativity, and assist in the transition to other sources of research funding. **Focus:** Medical research. **Qualif.:** Applicants must be researchers who are within five years (PhD scientists) or seven (physician-scientists); must be working in nonprofit academic, medical or research institutions within the six New England states. **Criteria:** Selection will be based on the Applicants' showing of potential for a future career as an

Awards are arranged alphabetically below their administering organizations

independent investigator in research relevant to child health.

Funds Avail.: $165,000 ($82,500 per year inclusive of 10% indirect costs). **Duration:** Annual; up to two years. **Deadline:** January 1; July 1. **Remarks:** Established in 1942. **Contact:** Charlene Mancusi, Program Officer, The Medical Foundation; Email: cmancusi@hria.org.

5439 ■ Klarman Family Foundation Grants Program in Eating Disorders Research (Professional development/Grant)

Purpose: To provide strategic investment in translational research that will accelerate progress in developing effective treatments for anorexia nervosa, bulimia nervosa and binger eating disorder. **Focus:** Medical research. **Qualif.:** Applicants must be investigators who hold a faculty appointment at nonprofit academic, medical or research institutions in the United States, Canada and Israel. **Criteria:** Selection will be based on the submitted application and research project.

Funds Avail.: $400,000 ($200,000 per year, up to two years); $150,000 (one-year pilot studies). **Duration:** Annual; two years. **To Apply:** Application form can be obtained at the website. The complete application process requires an online submission as well as four printed copies of the uploaded PDF; the following sections must be completed for the online submission: institution's tax ID number; eligibility quiz; application data; research project information; research classification; research area; certification; attachment (document upload). The following attached documents and forms must be combined and converted into one PDF file in the order for upload: application face sheet; table of contents; research project summary and performance sites; nontechnical summary; biosketch(es) of Applicants and co-investigator(s); department or division chair's letter; letter of collaboration; budget forms; research proposal. **Remarks:** Established in 2002. **Contact:** Gay Lockwood, Senior Program Officer at glockwood@hria.org or 617-279-2240, x702.

5440 ■ Lymphatic Research Foundation Additional Support for NIH-funded F32 Postdoctoral Fellows Awards (Postdoctorate/Award)

Purpose: To help foster career interest in the field of lymphatic research by offering additional funds for F32 postdoctoral research projects. **Focus:** Medical research. **Qualif.:** Applicants must be postdoctoral fellows who are currently working in a field relevant to the lymphatic system. **Criteria:** Selection will be based on the committee's criteria.

Funds Avail.: No specific amount. **To Apply:** Applicants must visit the website to obtain an application form.

5441 ■ Lymphatic Research Foundation Postdoctoral Fellowship Awards Program (Postdoctorate/Fellowship)

Purpose: To expand and strengthen the pool of outstanding junior investigators in the field of lymphatic research. **Focus:** Medical research. **Qualif.:** Applicants must be postdoctoral scientists in academic, medical or research institutions throughout the world. **Criteria:** Selection will be based on the committee's criteria.

Funds Avail.: $87,396-$98,304. **Duration:** Two years. **To Apply:** Applicants must visit the website to obtain an application form. **Deadline:** January 15.

5442 ■ Robert E. Leet and Clara Guthrie Patterson Trust Mentored Research Award: Clinical, Health Services (Doctorate, Postdoctorate/Grant)

Purpose: To accelerate clinical research by offering K23 and K08 Award Recipients the resources to explore research activities not supported by NIH K Awards. **Focus:** Medical research. **Qualif.:** Applicants must be mentored investigators conducting clinical research across a range of research disciplines, broadly defined to include patient-oriented research and translational laboratory research; must have a doctoral degree (MD, DMD, Ph.D. or other); Degrees obtained outside the United States must be equivalent to these doctoral degrees; there are no institutional limitations on the number of applicants who may submit to this program. **Criteria:** Selection will be based on the committee's criteria.

Funds Avail.: $90,000 ($45,000 per year). **Duration:** Annual; two year. **Number Awarded:** 2. **To Apply:** Application include data institution where proposed research will be conducted, Applicant's contact information and educational background; project Title, Keywords, Project Summary, Non-technical Summary and Mentor; information; research Classification; research area; letters of support; one PDF document is required for upload. **Deadline:** July 3. **Remarks:** Established in 1980. **Contact:** Jeanne Brown, Program Officer; The Medical Foundation; Email: jbrown@hria.org.

5443 ■ Smith Family Awards Program for Excellence in Biomedical Research (Advanced Professional, Professional development/Award)

Purpose: To launch the careers of newly independent biomedical researchers with the ultimate goal of achieving medical breakthroughs. **Focus:** Medical research. **Qualif.:** Applicants must be full-time faculty member at a nonprofit academic, medical, or research institution in Massachusetts, at Brown or Yale University; must have completed their postdoctoral training.

Funds Avail.: $300,000 ($100,000 per year inclusive of 5% overhead). **Duration:** Annual; up to 3 years. **To Apply:** Applicants must be internally selected by their institutions; any school or college within an academic institution in Massachusetts may each submit up to two applications; each hospital or free standing biomedical research facility in Massachusetts may also submit two applications; two applications will also be accepted from Brown University and two applications from Yale University; these applications may be submitted from any academic department or school within Brown or Yale or one of their affiliated entities after going through these institutions' internal review process; the department or division Chair must explain how the award will enhance the Applicants' research career. **Deadline:** July 27. **Remarks:** Established in 1992. **Contact:** Lindsey Phelan, MA, Grants Officer, The Medical Foundation; Email: lphelan@hria.org.

5444 ■ Thome Foundation Awards Program in Age-Related Macular Degeneration Research (Professional development/Grant)

Purpose: To support translational research that will lead to improved therapies for individuals suffering from age-related macular degeneration. **Focus:** Visual impairment. **Qualif.:** Applicants must hold a faculty appointment at a nonprofit academic, medical or research institution in the United States; scientists who have conducted research exploring the biological causes of related disorders and/or similar translational research programs are encouraged to

Awards are arranged alphabetically below their administering organizations

apply; preference will be given to originality of ideas, regardless of faculty seniority.

Funds Avail.: $500,000 ($250,000 per year). **Duration:** Annual; two years. **To Apply:** Applicants must complete and submit online application; initial proposal application must be submitted to the online application system; Applicants who are invited to submit Full Proposals will be notified by email; the full proposal application includes the Application face Sheet, Department or Division Head Letter, Budget Forms, Budget Justification, Applicants' Biosketch and a 10-page Research Proposal. **Deadline:** August 30. **Contact:** Lindsey Phelan, Grants Officer, The Medical Foundation at HriA, Thome Foundation AMD Program, 4th Fl., 2 Boylston St., Boston, MA, 02116; Email: Lphelan@hria.org.

5445 ■ Thome Foundation Awards Program in Alzheimer's Disease Drug Discovery Research
(Professional development/Grant)

Purpose: To support pilot studies towards innovative drug discovery research that will lead to improved therapies for individuals suffering from Alzheimer's disease. **Focus:** Alzheimer's disease. **Qualif.:** Applicants must hold a faculty appointment at a nonprofit academic, medical, nongovernmental or research institution in the United States; the sponsoring institution accepts responsibility for the scientific, administrative and financial management of overall projects including any subcontracts used for the project. **Criteria:** Selection will be based on the committee's criteria.

Funds Avail.: $500,000 two-year grants ($250,000 per year). **Duration:** Two years. **To Apply:** The initial proposal must be submitted via the online application system; applicants who are invited to submit full research proposals will be notified by email; the full proposal includes the application face sheet, department or division head letter, budget forms, budget justification, applicant's biosketch and a 10-page research proposal. **Deadline:** September 9. **Contact:** Lindsey Phelan, MA, Grants Officer, The Medical Foundation; Email: lphelan@hria.org.

5446 ■ Healthcare Information and Management Systems Society (HIMSS)
33 W Monroe St., Ste. 1700
Chicago, IL 60603-5616
Ph: (312)664-4467
Fax: (312)664-6143
E-mail: himss@himss.org
URL: www.himss.org
Social Media: www.facebook.com/HIMSSpage
www.instagram.com/himssglobal
www.linkedin.com/company/himss
twitter.com/himss
www.youtube.com/himss

5447 ■ Dvora Brodie Scholarships *(Graduate, Postgraduate, Undergraduate/Scholarship)*

Purpose: To provide financial support to a HIMSS student member who exhibits excellence and future leadership potential in the healthcare information and management system industry. **Focus:** Health care services. **Qualif.:** Applicant must be a member in good standing of HIMSS attending a school in New England, or originally be from the New England area; and the primary occupation of the applicant at the time the scholarship is awarded must be that of a student in an accredited undergraduate, Masters, or

PhD program related to the healthcare information management systems field. **Criteria:** Recipient will be selected according to merit, financial need, and other factors.

Funds Avail.: No specific amount. **Duration:** Annual. **To Apply:** Applicants must submit a completed application form. **Contact:** scholarships@himss.org.

5448 ■ Healthcare Information Management Systems Scholarships *(Graduate, Postgraduate, Undergraduate/Scholarship)*

Purpose: To provide financial assistance to students in healthcare and IT-related fields. **Focus:** Health care services. **Qualif.:** Applicants must be a member in good standing of HIMSS and a student in an accredited undergraduate, Master's or PhD program related to the healthcare information or management systems field; The specific degree program is not a critical factor, although it is expected that programs similar to those in industrial engineering, operations research, bioinformatics, health informatics, computer science and information systems, mathematics, and quantitative programs in business administration, clinical disciplines, and health administration will predominate; Undergraduate applicants must be at least a first-term junior when the Scholarship is awarded; Is not currently serving on one of HIMSS boards; Cannot be currently employed by HIMSS, nor engaged in a consulting contract with any component of HIMSS; Award judges are ineligible; Previous Foundation Scholarship recipients are ineligible.

Funds Avail.: $5,000. **Duration:** Annual. **Number Awarded:** 2. **To Apply:** Applicants must submit a completed application form; Two letters of recommendation provided by any of the following: peers, colleagues, managers, or professors; We discourage nominees from submitting letters of recommendation written by Selection Committee judges; Resume/curriculum vitae. **Contact:** E-mail: scholarships@himss.org.

5449 ■ Northern California Chapter of HIMSS Scholarships *(Graduate, Postgraduate, Undergraduate/Scholarship)*

Purpose: To provide financial assistance for a student in healthcare informatics who exhibits academic excellence and future leadership potential in the healthcare information and management systems industry. **Focus:** Health care services. **Qualif.:** Applicants must be a member in good standing of HIMSS or member of National HIMSS and who have achieved academic success and attend a college in Northern California are eligible to apply.

Funds Avail.: $5,000. **Duration:** Annual. **Number Awarded:** 12. **Contact:** Email: norcal.info@himsschapter.org.

5450 ■ Richard P. Covert, Ph.D., LFHIMSS Scholarships for Management Systems *(Graduate, Postgraduate, Undergraduate/Scholarship)*

Purpose: To provide financial assistance to students pursuing a degree in Management Engineering. **Focus:** Engineering. **Qualif.:** Applicants must be a member in good standing of HIMSS and the primary occupation of the applicant at the time the scholarship is awarded must be that of student in an accredited undergraduate, Masters or PhD program related to the healthcare information management systems field; Undergraduate applicants must be at least a first-term junior when the scholarship is awarded; Current member in good standing of HIMSS; Is not currently serv-

Awards are arranged alphabetically below their administering organizations

ing on one of HIMSS boards (HIMSS NA, HIMSS Analytics, PCHAlliance, etc.); Cannot be currently employed by HIMSS, nor engaged in a consulting contract with any component of HIMSS; Award judges are ineligible; previous Foundation Scholarship recipients are ineligible.

Funds Avail.: $5,000. **Duration:** Annual. **To Apply:** Applicants must submit a completed application form; two letters of recommendation provided by any of the following: peers, colleagues, managers, or professors; Resume/ curriculum vitae; We discourage nominees from submitting letters of recommendation written by Selection Committee judges. **Contact:** E-mail: scholarships@himss.org.

5451 ■ Healthline Media

660 Third St.
San Francisco, CA 94107
Ph: (415)281-3100
E-mail: info@healthline.com
URL: www.healthline.com
Social Media: www.facebook.com/healthline
www.instagram.com/healthline
www.pinterest.com/healthline
twitter.com/healthline

5452 ■ The Healthline & NORD Stronger Scholarship *(Undergraduate/Scholarship)*

Purpose: To assist and empower college students making a positive impact on rare and/or chronic disease(s). **Focus:** General studies/Field of study not specified. **Qualif.:** Applicant must be a junior or senior undergraduate student and a current U.S. resident; must have a minimum 3.0 GPA; must have demonstrated involvement in the advancement of treatment or assistance for rare and/or chronic disease(s), either through research, patient advocacy, raising awareness, or community building.

Funds Avail.: $5,000. **Duration:** Annual. **Number Awarded:** 4. **To Apply:** Application is available online at aim.applyists.net/Healthline. **Deadline:** April 30.

5453 ■ Hearing Foundation of Canada

32 Britain Street, Suite 100
Toronto, ON, Canada M5A 1R6
URL: www.hearingfoundation.ca

5454 ■ THFC Medical Research Grants *(Professional development/Grant)*

Purpose: To support medical research into different areas of hearing loss. **Focus:** Hearing and deafness; Medical research. **Qualif.:** Applicants must be young investigators. Research must be in the categories of basic or clinical research, and focus on biological and clinical projects rather than the psycho-social aspects of hearing loss. **Criteria:** Selection will be based on the scientific merit of the research proposals of the applicants.

Funds Avail.: Up to 25,000 Canadian Dollars. **To Apply:** Applicants must submit a proposal that should be relevant to the cause, prevention, intervention, morbidity, economic or personal impact, and cure of hearing loss; applications from individuals with or without institutional affiliations will be considered; applications should be in narrative form and no longer than five single-spaced typewritten pages in length; two additional pages of supportive attachments from figures or other related data are acceptable, but they must be relevant; all applications must include the following cover

sheet to be completed by the Principal Investigator; include PI name bottom of every page; co-investigator(s) cover page for each co-investigator; proposed research form, signed by PI; curriculum vitae form for all research personnel; proposed research description, signed by PI; the format for all submission text must be 12 point font, one inch margins and single spaced. **Contact:** Questions can be directed to Jamie Wood, Manager of Programs, at jwood@ hearingfoundation.ca.

5455 ■ Helicopter Foundation International (HFI)

1920 Ballenger Ave., 4th Fl.
Alexandria, VA 22314-2898
Ph: (703)683-4646
E-mail: haifoundation@rotor.org
URL: www.helicopterfoundation.org
Social Media: www.facebook.com/helicopterfoundation
twitter.com/heliexpo

5456 ■ Commercial Helicopter Pilot Rating Scholarships *(Other/Scholarship)*

Purpose: To assist private helicopter pilot candidates who wish to obtain their commercial helicopter ratings. **Focus:** Aviation. **Qualif.:** Applicants must already have their private pilot's license and be enrolled in a commercial helicopter rating program at an FAA-approved Part 141 school or international equivalent. **Criteria:** Recipients will be selected based on skills and abilities to be commercial helicopter pilots and interest in pursuing a career as pilot in the helicopter industry.

Duration: Annual. **Number Awarded:** 1. **To Apply:** Applicants must submit resume; airman certificates; pilot information; maintenance or Flight School Certification; two Signed Letters of recommendation.

5457 ■ Helicopter Foundation International Maintenance Technician Certificate Scholarships *(Other/Scholarship)*

Purpose: To assist candidates who wish to obtain Maintenance Technician certificate. **Focus:** Aviation. **Qualif.:** Applicants must already be enrolled in a Maintenance Technician Certificate program at an FAA-approved Part 147 school or international equivalent. **Criteria:** Recipients are selected based on financial need.

Duration: Annual.

5458 ■ Michelle North Scholarships for Safety *(Other/Scholarship)*

Purpose: To assist private helicopter pilot candidates who wish to obtain their commercial helicopter ratings. **Focus:** Aviation. **Qualif.:** Applicants must be pilots who have already attained a commercial rating and demonstrate an outstanding aptitude for safe flying and aviation best practices. **Criteria:** Recipients are selected based on the aforesaid qualifications.

Funds Avail.: No specific amount. **Duration:** Annual. **Number Awarded:** 1. **To Apply:** Applicants must submit resume; airman certificates; pilot information; maintenance or Flight School Certification; two Signed Letters of recommendation. **Deadline:** November 30. **Contact:** Email: scholarships@rotor.org.

5459 ■ Bill Sanderson Aviation Maintenance Technician Scholarships *(Postgraduate/Scholarship)*

Purpose: To assist private helicopter pilot candidates who wish to obtain their commercial helicopter ratings. **Focus:**

Awards are arranged alphabetically below their administering organizations

Aviation. **Qualif.:** Applicants must be about to graduate from an FAA approved Part 147 AMT school or be recent recipients within the last three years of an Airframe and Powerplant Certificate. **Criteria:** Recipients are selected based on demonstrated interest in the field of aviation.

Funds Avail.: Maximum of $1,600. **Duration:** Annual. **To Apply:** Applicants must have two references; references should be from employers, professionals, representatives of community organizations, etc. **Deadline:** November 30. **Contact:** Email: safety.assistant@rotor.org.

5460 ■ Hellenic Times Scholarship Fund (HTSF)

823 11th Ave., 5th Fl.
New York, NY 10019
Ph: (212)986-6881
Fax: (212)977-3662
E-mail: htsfund@aol.com
URL: www.htsf.org

5461 ■ Hellenic Times Scholarships (Undergraduate, Graduate/Scholarship)

Purpose: To provide financial support to Greek descent students. **Focus:** General studies/Field of study not specified. **Qualif.:** Applicants must be a members of the community and corporations who purchase tables and make donations. **Criteria:** Selection will be based on necessity and merit.

Funds Avail.: No specific amount. **Duration:** Annual. **To Apply:** Applicants must submit a completed application form, applicants' photo, official school transcripts and a copy of tax returns. Winners are required to submit a copy of their Bursar tuition bill.

5462 ■ Hellenic University Club of Philadelphia (HUC)

PO Box 42199
Philadelphia, PA 19101-2199
Ph: (215)483-7440
URL: hucphiladelphia.org
Social Media: www.facebook.com/hucphiladelphia
instagram.com/huc_philly
twitter.com/HUCPhila

5463 ■ Christopher Demetris Memorial Scholarships (Undergraduate/Scholarship)

Purpose: To support students who are of Eastern Orthodox faith, and in need. **Focus:** Greek studies. **Qualif.:** Applicants must be of Greek descent, U.S. citizens or lawful permanent residents of Berks, Bucks, Chester, Delaware, Lancaster, Lehigh, Montgomery or Philadelphia Counties in Pennsylvania or Atlantic, Burlington, Camden, Cape May, Cumberland, Gloucester or Salem Counties in New Jersey. Students who are declared majors in Greek Studies may also apply, regardless of their heritage. They must be also enrolled full-time in a degree program at an accredited four-year college or university; high school seniors accepted for enrollment in such a degree program may also apply. **Criteria:** Selection will be based on merit and financial need.

Funds Avail.: $2,000. **Duration:** Annual. **To Apply:** Application form can be obtained from the HUCPhila website; Applicants must complete the application form and mail to Scholarship Chairman. Applicants must also provide one

letter of recommendation and scholastic transcripts. **Deadline:** April 1.

5464 ■ Dr. Michael Dorizas Memorial Scholarships (Undergraduate/Scholarship)

Purpose: To provide scholarship for students with outstanding academic qualifications and financial need. **Focus:** Greek studies. **Qualif.:** Applicants must be of Greek descent, U.S. citizens or lawful permanent residents of Berks, Bucks, Chester, Delaware, Lancaster, Lehigh, Montgomery or Philadelphia Counties in Pennsylvania or Atlantic, Burlington, Camden, Cape May, Cumberland, Gloucester or Salem Counties in New Jersey. Students who are declared majors in Greek Studies may also apply, regardless of their heritage; they must be also enrolled full-time in a degree program at an accredited four-year college or university; high school seniors accepted for enrollment in such a degree program may also apply. **Criteria:** Selection will be based on academic merit and financial need.

Funds Avail.: $5,000. **Duration:** Annual. **To Apply:** Application form can be obtained from the sponsor's website. Applicants must complete the application form and mail to Scholarship Chairman. Applicants must also provide one letter of recommendation and scholastic transcripts. **Deadline:** April 1. **Remarks:** The scholarship was established in honor of the late Dr. Michael Dorizas, a widely respected Philadelphia educator, lecturer and athlete. **Contact:** URL: hucphiladelphia.org/huc-scholarship-program.

5465 ■ Hellenic University Club of Philadelphia Founders Scholarship (Undergraduate/Scholarship)

Purpose: To provide scholarships for students with outstanding academic qualifications and financial need. **Focus:** General studies/Field of study not specified; Greek studies. **Qualif.:** Applicants must be of Greek descent, U.S. citizens or lawful permanent residents of Berks, Bucks, Chester, Delaware, Lancaster, Lehigh, Montgomery or Philadelphia Counties in Pennsylvania or Atlantic, Burlington, Camden, Cape May, Cumberland, Gloucester or Salem Counties in New Jersey. Students who are declared majors in Greek Studies may also apply, regardless of their heritage; they must be also enrolled full-time in a degree program at an accredited four-year college or university; high school seniors accepted for enrollment in such a degree program may also apply. **Criteria:** Selection will be based on academic merit and financial need.

Funds Avail.: $5,000. **Duration:** Annual. **To Apply:** Application form is available at sponsor's website. **Deadline:** April 1. **Remarks:** The scholarship was established to honor the deceased founders of the Hellenic University Club of Philadelphia. **Contact:** URL: hucphiladelphia.org/huc-scholarship-program.

5466 ■ Nicholas S. Hetos, DDS, Memorial Graduate Scholarship (Graduate, Doctorate/Scholarship)

Purpose: To provide scholarships for students with outstanding academic qualifications and financial need. **Focus:** Dentistry. **Qualif.:** Applicants must be of Greek descent, U.S. citizens or lawful permanent residents of Berks, Bucks, Chester, Delaware, Lancaster, Lehigh, Montgomery or Philadelphia Counties in Pennsylvania or Atlantic, Burlington, Camden, Cape May, Cumberland, Gloucester or Salem Counties in New Jersey. Applicants must be also enrolled full-time in a degree program at an accredited four-year college or university, and be senior undergraduate or graduate students with financial need

Awards are arranged alphabetically below their administering organizations

pursuing studies leading to a Doctoral of Dental Medicine (D.M.D.) or Doctoral of Dental Surgery (D.D.S.) Degree. **Criteria:** Selection will be based on merit and financial need.

Funds Avail.: $2,000. **Duration:** Annual. **To Apply:** Application form can be obtained from the sponsor's website. Applicants must send their name and address to Scholarship Chairman along with one letter of recommendation and scholastic transcripts. **Deadline:** April 1. **Remarks:** The scholarship was established to honor Dr. Nicholas S. Hetos, Philadelphia dentist, past president and founding member of the Hellenic University Club of Philadelphia. This scholarship is funded by Dr. Maria G. Hetos. Established in 2001. **Contact:** URL: hucphiladelphia.org/huc-scholarship-program.

5467 ■ Dr. Nicholas Padis Memorial Graduate Scholarship *(Graduate/Scholarship)*

Purpose: To provide educational support to students of Greek descent who are pursuing graduate degrees. **Focus:** General studies/Field of study not specified. **Qualif.:** Applicants must be of Greek descents, U.S. citizens or lawful permanent residents of Berks, Bucks, Chester, Delaware, Lancaster, Lehigh, Montgomery or Philadelphia Counties in Pennsylvania, Atlantic, Burlington, Camden, Cape May, Cumberland, Gloucester or Salem Counties in New Jersey; and must be a graduating senior undergraduate or graduate student pursuing a graduate degree full-time at an accredited university or professional school. **Criteria:** Selection will be based on students who have the highest academic achievement.

Funds Avail.: $5,000. **Duration:** Annual. **To Apply:** Application form can be obtained from the sponsor's website. Applicants must send their name and address to Scholarship Chairman, along with a transcript, resume, two letters of recommendation, essay and page 1 of FAFSA Student Aid Report. **Deadline:** April 1. **Remarks:** The scholarship was established to honor Philadelphia physician, first president and founding member of the Hellenic University Club of Philadelphia, Dr. Nicholas Padis. Established in 1986. **Contact:** URL: hucphiladelphia.org/huc-scholarship-program.

5468 ■ Dr. Peter A. Theodos Memorial Graduate Scholarship *(Graduate/Scholarship)*

Purpose: To provide scholarship for students with outstanding academic qualifications and financial need. **Focus:** Medicine. **Qualif.:** Applicants must be of Greek descent, U.S. citizens or lawful permanent residents of Berks, Bucks, Chester, Delaware, Lancaster, Lehigh, Montgomery or Philadelphia Counties in Pennsylvania or Atlantic, Burlington, Camden, Cape May, Cumberland, Gloucester or Salem Counties in New Jersey. They must be also enrolled full-time in a degree program at an accredited four-year college or university leading to a Doctor of Medicine (MD) degree and have a financial need. **Criteria:** Selection will be based on academic merit and financial need.

Funds Avail.: $1,500. **Duration:** Annual. **To Apply:** Application form can be obtained from the sponsor's website. Applicants must send their name and address to the Scholarship Chairman and provide one letter of recommendation and scholastic transcripts. **Deadline:** April 1. **Remarks:** The scholarship was established to honor Philadelphia physician, past president and founding member of the Hellenic University Club of Philadelphia, Dr. Peter A. Theodos. The scholarship is funded by Mrs. Peter A. Theodos. Established in 1988. **Contact:** URL:

hucphiladelphia.org/huc-scholarship-program.

5469 ■ Dimitri J. Ververelli Memorial Scholarship for Architecture and/or Engineering *(Undergraduate/ Scholarship)*

Purpose: To provide educational support to students who are in need. **Focus:** Architecture; Engineering. **Qualif.:** Applicants must be of Greek descent, U.S. citizens or lawful permanent residents of Berks, Bucks, Chester, Delaware, Lancaster, Lehigh, Montgomery or Philadelphia Counties in Pennsylvania or Atlantic, Burlington, Camden, Cape May, Cumberland, Gloucester or Salem Counties in New Jersey. Applicants must be also enrolled full-time in an architecture or engineering degree program at an accredited four-year college or university; high school seniors accepted for enrollment in such a degree program may also apply. **Criteria:** Selection will be based on merit and financial need.

Funds Avail.: $2,000. **Duration:** Annual. **To Apply:** Application form can be obtained from the sponsor's website. Applicants must complete the application form and mail to Scholarship Chairman. Applicants must also provide one letter of recommendation and scholastic transcripts. **Deadline:** April 1. **Remarks:** The scholarship was established by Mrs. Anastasia Ververelli to honor her husband, Dimitri J. Ververelli, a past president of the Hellenic University Club of Philadelphia. **Contact:** URL: hucphiladelphia.org/huc-scholarship-program.

5470 ■ Helmer, Conley & Kasselman PA
111 White Horse Pike
Haddon Heights, NJ 08035
Ph: (856)547-7888
Fax: (856)547-7797
URL: www.helmerlegal.com
Social Media: www.facebook.com/helmerlegal
www.linkedin.com/company/helmer-legal
twitter.com/helmerlegal
www.youtube.com/user/helmerlegal

5471 ■ Helmer, Conley & Kasselman Annual College Scholarship *(Undergraduate/Scholarship)*

Purpose: To help students with the financial burdens that come along with a college degree (tuition, housing, textbooks, etc.) **Focus:** Law. **Qualif.:** Applicant must be a high school senior enrolling in an undergraduate program for the next semester, or currently enrolled in college; be pursuing or intending to pursue a degree in law leading to bar eligibility and a license to practice law; and reside and be studying in the United States. **Criteria:** Selection will be based on a combination of writing skills, academic qualifications, and extracurricular activities.

Funds Avail.: $500. **Duration:** Annual. **Number Awarded:** Varies. **To Apply:** Applicant must write an essay (1,000 to 1,700 words) that explains what inspired them to become a lawyer, including what interests them most in the if field, how they plan to apply what they learn to their future career, and what impact they will have on the greater community. Essay must be submitted via email along with the following information: full name, phone number, address, current school and GPA, intended college and major, any extracurricular or volunteer activities, and social media links (if applicable). **Deadline:** November 15. **Contact:** Email: lynnhelmer@helmerlegal.com; URL: www.helmerlegal.com/college-scholarship/.

Awards are arranged alphabetically below their administering organizations

5472 ■ Helsell Fetterman

1001 4th Ave., Ste. 4200
Seattle, WA 98154
Ph: (206)292-1144
Fax: (206)340-0902
E-mail: dakhbari@helsell.com
URL: www.helsell.com
Social Media: www.facebook.com/pages/Helsell-Fetterman
www.linkedin.com/company/helsell-fetterman-llp
twitter.com/helsell

5473 ■ Richard S. White Fellowship *(Undergraduate/Fellowship)*

Purpose: To assist law students in their educational pursuit. **Focus:** Law. **Qualif.:** Applicants must be second year law students in good standing pursuing a law degree at an ABA-accredited law school. **Criteria:** Applicants must possess an academic record, leadership abilities and a commitment to personal and professional initiatives that indicate promise for a successful legal career; demonstrate an interest and commitment to both the practice areas represented at Helsell Fetterman and to building a practice in the Seattle area.

Funds Avail.: $7,500. **Duration:** 12 weeks. **To Apply:** Applicants must prepare a 1- to 2-page personal statement on a topic of their choice that allows the firm to fully evaluate their candidacy and ability to enrich the diversity of the legal community; completed application form must be submitted together with the following: current resume; copy of final undergraduate transcript and current law school transcript, unofficial is acceptable; legal writing sample up to 10 pages; three professional and/or academic references with contact information. **Deadline:** July 11. **Contact:** Email: rswfa@helsell.com.

5474 ■ Hemingway Foundation and Society

c/o Gail Sinclair, Vice Pres. and Treas.
Rollins College
1000 Holt Ave. 2770
Winter Park, FL 32789
Ph: (215)753-3626
URL: www.hemingwaysociety.org
Social Media: www.facebook.com/HemingwaySociety
twitter.com/theEHSociety

5475 ■ Ernest Hemingway Research Grants *(Other/Grant)*

Purpose: To provide funds for scholars and students who are doing research in the Ernest Hemingway Collection. **Focus:** General studies/Field of study not specified. **Qualif.:** Applicant must be a scholar and student interested or doing research in Ernest Hemingway Collection. **Criteria:** Selection will be based on expected utilization of the Hemingway Collection. preference is given to dissertation research by Ph.D. candidates working in newly opened or relatively unused portions of the collection, but all proposals are welcome and will receive careful consideration.

Funds Avail.: Up to $5,000. **Duration:** Annual. **To Apply:** Applicants must submit the online application form and must be accompanied by a brief proposal (three to four pages) in the form of a letter describing the planned research and its significance; must submit two letters of recommendation from academic or other appropriate references; must provide a sample of applicant's writing, a

project budget, and a curriculum vitae. **Deadline:** November 1. **Contact:** Ernest Hemingway Collection John F. Kennedy Presidential Library and Museum, Columbia Point, Boston, MA 02125; Fax: 617-514-1625; E-mail: stephen.plotkin@nara.gov.

5476 ■ Jim & Nancy Hinkle Travel Grants *(Graduate/Grant)*

Purpose: To assist graduate students to attend the biennial international conferences. **Focus:** General studies/Field of study not specified. **Qualif.:** Applicants must be member in good standing of the Hemingway Society; must currently be enrolled in a graduate degree program, and must be planning to present a paper at the conference. **Criteria:** Selection will be based on the following criteria: clarity, originality, and value in furthering Hemingway scholarship, criticism, or instruction. Application from previous Hinkle winners are welcome, applications from students who have not won before will be given priority.

Funds Avail.: No specific amount. **Duration:** Annual. **To Apply:** Application must include the following information: (1) Full name of Applicants, (2) address, phone, email, (3) Social Security Number, (4) Paper title & abstract, (5) Degree program and school, (6) Letter of recommendation. **Remarks:** Established in 1992.

5477 ■ Lewis-Reynolds-Smith Founders Fellowship *(Graduate/Fellowship)*

Purpose: To support the development of a Hemingway-related project. **Focus:** General studies/Field of study not specified. **Qualif.:** Applicants must be a graduate student, independent scholar, or post-doctoral up through the rank of assistant professor. **Criteria:** Selection will be based on the following criteria: clarity, originality, and feasibility, criticism, or instruction; and the likelihood of its publication.

Funds Avail.: $1,000 each. **Duration:** Annual. **Number Awarded:** 2. **To Apply:** Applicants must submit as a Microsoft word attachment or send by mail the following information and agreements: (1) Full name and Social Security Number, (2) Addresses, phone numbers and email address (including summer and between session), (3) Degree program and school, (4) Verification of graduate enrollment status or awarded degree (if appropriate); must have the description of Hemingway Project (200-word limit). **Deadline:** February 15. **Remarks:** The Fellowship was established in honor of Michael Reynolds. Established in 1998.

5478 ■ Hemophilia Federation of America (HFA)

999 N Capitol St. NE, Ste. 201
Washington, DC 20002
Ph: (202)675-6984
Fax: (202)675-6983
Free: 800-230-9797
E-mail: info@hemophiliafed.org
URL: www.hemophiliafed.org
Social Media: www.facebook.com/hemophiliafed
www.instagram.com/hemophiliafed
twitter.com/hemophiliafed
www.youtube.com/user/VoicesHFA/videos

5479 ■ HFA Educational Scholarship *(Undergraduate/Scholarship)*

Purpose: To assist students with a bleeding disorder in attaining their post-secondary education from a college,

Awards are arranged alphabetically below their administering organizations

university or trade school. **Focus:** General studies/Field of study not specified. **Qualif.:** Applicant must be a person with a bleeding disorder. **Criteria:** Applicants are judged upon the committee's criteria.

Funds Avail.: $2,000 to $4,000. **Duration:** Annual. **Number Awarded:** 4. **To Apply:** Applicants must submit an essay (see application for essay prompt); transcript (official or unofficial); acceptance letter/enrollment verification letter; two letters of reference (one professional reference, the other from a medical professional/HTC). **Deadline:** May 15.

5480 ■ Mike Hylton Memorial Scholarship
(Undergraduate/Scholarship)

Purpose: To encourage educational pursuits among men with bleeding disorders through providing financial assistance. **Focus:** General studies/Field of study not specified. **Qualif.:** Applicants must be a United States resident; men diagnosed with hemophilia or von Willebrand Disease or their immediate family member; minimum grade point average of 2.5 on a 4.0; employees and family members affiliated with BioMatrix and it's family of companies are not eligible to apply. **Criteria:** Recipients are chosen based on combined merit and need.

Funds Avail.: $1,000. **To Apply:** Applicants are encouraged to submit their applications electronically along with letter of medical Verification; copy of most recent Transcripts; copy of ACT or SAT scores; outline of work Experience or resume; proof of admission to the college/university/technical school (required for incoming freshman); 300 to 400 word Essay. **Deadline:** August 1. **Remarks:** The scholarship was established in memory of Mike Hylton, man of great character and steadiness. He was a thoughtful, analytical and spiritual individual, patient and tolerant of others, but certainly willing and capable to express his opinions and beliefs. **Contact:** HFA Scholarship Admin, 999 N Capitol St. NE, Ste. 201, Washington, DC, 20002; Phone: 202-675-6984; E-mail: scholarship@hemophiliafed.org.

5481 ■ Millie Gonzalez Memorial Scholarship
(Undergraduate/Scholarship)

Purpose: To encourage educational pursuits among women with bleeding disorders through providing financial assistance. **Focus:** General studies/Field of study not specified. **Qualif.:** Applicants must be a United States resident; men diagnosed with hemophilia or von Willebrand Disease or their immediate family member; minimum grade point average of 2.5 on a 4.0; employees and family members affiliated with BioMatrix and it's family of companies are not eligible to apply. **Criteria:** Recipients are chosen based on combined merit and need.

Funds Avail.: $1,000. **To Apply:** Applicants are encouraged to submit their applications electronically along with letter of medical Verification; copy of most recent Transcripts; copy of ACT or SAT scores; outline of work Experience or resume; proof of admission to the college/university/technical school (required for incoming freshman); 300 to 400 word Essay. **Deadline:** August 1. **Remarks:** The scholarship was established in memory of Millie Gonzalez, devoted wife and mother as well as a pioneer dedicated to advocacy, Millie promoted awareness of the unique struggles faced by women with a bleeding disorder and those caring for an individual affected by a bleeding disorder. **Contact:** HFA Scholarship Admin, 999 N Capitol St. NE, Ste. 201, Washington, DC, 20002; Phone: 202-675-6984; E-mail: scholarship@hemophiliafed.org.

5482 ■ Thomas J. Henry Law
4715 Fredericksburg, Ste. 507
San Antonio, TX 78229
Ph: (210)874-2615
Fax: (888)956-8001
E-mail: info@thomasjhenrylaw.com
URL: thomasjhenrylaw.com
Social Media: www.facebook.com/tjhlaw
linkedin.com/in/thomasjhenrylaw
twitter.com/thomasjhenrylaw
youtube.com/user/thomasjhenrylaw

5483 ■ Thomas J. Henry Leadership Scholarship Program *(Undergraduate, Graduate/Scholarship)*

Purpose: To provide financial support to college and university students. **Focus:** General studies/Field of study not specified. **Qualif.:** Applicants must be enrolled in, or planning to enroll in, an accredited college or university; applicants currently enrolled in a college or university must have a minimum GPA of 2.8; must be aged 18 and older. **Criteria:** Finalist essays may be posted on social media to be voted on via likes, shares, tweets, and Google +1s; social voting is not the sole basis of the final decision, but may influence the eventual outcome, which is determined by Thomas J. Henry staff.

Funds Avail.: $1,000. **Duration:** Semiannual. **To Apply:** Submit essay between 750 and 1,000 words (Microsoft Word document preferred) and should be submitted via email. **Deadline:** July 1; November 1. **Contact:** Email: submissions@thomasjhenrylaw.com; URL: thomasjhenrylaw.com/giving/scholarships/.

5484 ■ Herb Society of America (HSA)
9019 Kirtland Chardon Rd.
Kirtland, OH 44094
Ph: (440)256-0514
Fax: (440)256-0541
E-mail: herbs@herbsociety.org
URL: www.herbsociety.org
Social Media: www.facebook.com/The-Herb-Society-of
 -America-10720845126
www.pinterest.com/HerbSocietyAmer
twitter.com/HerbSociety1933

5485 ■ Herb Society of America Research Grant
(Professional development/Grant)

Purpose: To provide support to students, professionals and individuals engaged in research on the horticultural, scientific, and/or social applications or use of herbs throughout history. **Focus:** Horticulture. **Qualif.:** Applicant must be U.S. residents; may be students, professionals, or individuals.

Funds Avail.: $5,000. **Duration:** Annual. **Deadline:** December 1.

5486 ■ Horticulture Scholarship from Frances Sylvia Zverina *(Undergraduate/Scholarship)*

Purpose: To provide financial assistance to students who are in need. **Focus:** Horticulture. **Qualif.:** Applicants must be citizens of the United States who have completed the 2nd/Sophomore year of undergraduate study; must be attending an accredited college or university in the State of Ohio and have achieved a grade point average of 3.2 or

Awards are arranged alphabetically below their administering organizations

above. **Criteria:** Recipients are selected based on demonstrates financial need and plans a career in horticulture and allied fields; who demonstrate exceptional dedication to horticulture and whose career goals involve teaching, work in the public or nonprofit sector, and sustainable agriculture. **Funds Avail.:** $9,000. **Number Awarded:** 1. **To Apply:** Applicants must submit a completed application form; essays; transcripts and Recommendation Letters; should have the applicant's name in the subject line. **Deadline:** February 28.

5487 ■ Horticulture Scholarship of the Western Reserve Herb Society *(Undergraduate/Scholarship)*

Purpose: To support students with their studies in horticulture or any related fields. **Focus:** Horticulture. **Qualif.:** Applicants must be citizens of the United States who have completed the 2nd/Sophomore year of undergraduate study; must be attending an accredited college or university and have achieved a grade point average of 3.2 or above. **Criteria:** Recipients are selected based on demonstrates financial need and plans a career in horticulture and allied fields; who demonstrate exceptional dedication to horticulture and whose career goals involve teaching, work in the public or nonprofit sector, and sustainable agriculture. **Funds Avail.:** $7,500. **Duration:** Annual. **Number Awarded:** 1. **To Apply:** Applicants must submit a completed application form; essays; transcripts and Recommendation Letters; should have the applicant's name in the subject line. **Deadline:** February 28.

5488 ■ Nashville Unit Scholarships *(Undergraduate/ Scholarship, Grant)*

Purpose: To provide financial assistance to those students who are in need. **Focus:** Horticulture. **Qualif.:** Applicants must be permanent residents of Tennessee; must be current college freshman, sophomore or junior students who are American citizens. **Criteria:** Recipients are selected based on financial need and academic performance. **Funds Avail.:** $1,500. **To Apply:** Applicants must submit a completed application form and two letters of reference. **Deadline:** February 1.

5489 ■ Pennsylvania Heartland Unit Scholarship *(Undergraduate/Scholarship)*

Purpose: To provide support to students who are active within the field of horticulture. **Focus:** Horticulture. **Qualif.:** Applicants must be third or fourth year students of an associate degree program within the study of horticulture; must be residents of Berks, Montgomery, York, Lancaster or Schuylkill county. **Funds Avail.:** $2,000 and $1,000. **Duration:** Annual. **Number Awarded:** 2. **To Apply:** Applicants must submit: a completed application form; two letters of reference from which one must come from an advisor or professor and one from a reference of the student's choice; must submit an official school transcript; and an essay stating their reasons for choosing the field of horticulture and future plans. **Deadline:** April 1. **Contact:** Jeannette Lanshe, jetlan1@aol.com.

5490 ■ South Texas Unit Scholarship *(Undergraduate/Scholarship)*

Purpose: To provide support to students who are in need. **Focus:** Horticulture. **Qualif.:** Applicants must be students who are studying agronomy, horticulture, botany or a closely-related discipline at an accredited four-year college or university; must be either permanent residents of Texas or attending an accredited college or university in Texas; must have completed two full years of college and be entering their junior or senior year of studies.

Funds Avail.: $1,000. **Duration:** Annual. **To Apply:** Applicants must submit a completed application form and recommendation letter from professor or guidance counselor. **Deadline:** May 1. **Contact:** Education Committee Chairman, South Texas Unit of The HSA, PO Box 6515 Houston, TX 77265-6515.

5491 ■ Herbert Law Office
1154 Boylston St.
Boston, MA 02215-3695
URL: www.masshist.org
Social Media: www.facebook.com/lancasterlawyer1995
twitter.com/herbertlawoffi1

5492 ■ Herbert Law Office Scholarship Contest *(Undergraduate/Scholarship)*

Purpose: To provide financial aid to students, encourage students to understand their personal motivation for a career in the legal field, and inspire students to pursue a career in law. **Focus:** Law. **Qualif.:** Applicant must be a high school senior or college freshman in the U.S. who is studying, or plans to study, in the field of law. **Criteria:** Selection is based on the best video essay submitted.

Funds Avail.: $1,000. **Number Awarded:** 1. **To Apply:** Applicant must record a video (one to two minutes long, in plain English) explaining why the want to be a lawyer. Video must be published on the applicant's YouTube channel with the title "Herbert Law Office Scholarship Contest" and this link in the description: www.herbertlawoffice.com/scholarship-for-college-students. Applicant must also share the video on their Facebook page and the sponsor's Facebook page. Instead of a video, applicant may submit a 1,000 to 1,500 word essay on the same subject via email. **Deadline:** August 15. **Contact:** Marc Herbert; Email marcherbertscholarship@gmail.com.

5493 ■ Hereditary Disease Foundation (HDF)
601 W 168th St., Ste. 54
New York, NY 10032
Ph: (212)928-2121
Fax: (212)928-2172
E-mail: cures@hdfoundation.org
URL: www.hdfoundation.org
Social Media: www.facebook.com/
  HereditaryDiseaseFoundation
twitter.com/hdfcures

5494 ■ Hereditary Disease Foundation Basic Research Grants Program *(Advanced Professional/ Grant)*

Purpose: To support projects that contribute in identifying and understanding the fundamental defects in Huntington's disease and related disorders. **Focus:** Huntington's disease. **Qualif.:** Applicants are those who are conducting research on Huntington's disease. **Criteria:** Selection is reviewed by the Scientific Advisory Board. Consideration is given to treatments and cures for Huntington's disease. Selected applicants will receive a written notification of the funding decision. **Funds Avail.:** Up to $75,000. **To Apply:** Applicant must complete the online application form along with letter of intent. **Deadline:** April 17.

Awards are arranged alphabetically below their administering organizations

5495 ■ Hermann Law Group PLLC

1 University Plaza Dr., No. 108
Hackensack, NJ 07601
Ph: (201)862-9700
Fax: (617)859-0074
E-mail: info@nymetrodisability.com
URL: www.nymetrodisability.com
Social Media: www.facebook.com/hermannlawgroup
www.linkedin.com/company/insler-&-hermann-llp
twitter.com/hermannlaw

5496 ■ Hermann Law Group, PLLC Safety Scholarship Contest *(Undergraduate/Scholarship)*

Purpose: To provide financial aid to students, encourage students to understand their personal motivation for a career in the legal field, and inspire students to pursue a career in law. **Focus:** Law. **Qualif.:** Applicant must be a high school senior or college freshman in the U.S. who is studying, or plans to study, in the field of law. **Criteria:** Selection is based on the best video essay submitted.

Funds Avail.: $1,000. **To Apply:** Applicant must record a video (one to two minutes long, in plain English) explaining why the want to be a lawyer. Video must be published on the applicant's YouTube channel with the title "Hermann Law Group, PLLC Scholarship Contest" and this link in the description: www.nymetrodisability.com/safety-scholarship-for-law-students. Applicant must also share the video on their Facebook page and the sponsor's Facebook page. Instead of a video, applicant may submit a 1,000 to 1,500 word essay on the same subject via email. **Deadline:** August 15. **Contact:** Gabe Hermann; Email: HermannScholarship@gmail.com.

5497 ■ Herpetologists League (HL)

PO Box 4022
Topeka, KS 66604
Ph: (785)550-6904
E-mail: herpleaguemember@gmail.com
URL: www.herpetologistsleague.org
Social Media: www.facebook.com/HerpetologistsLeague
www.instagram.com/herpetologistsleague
twitter.com/herpleague

5498 ■ E.E. Williams Research Grant *(Master's, Doctorate/Grant)*

Purpose: To support the research of graduate students. **Focus:** Biology; Herpetology. **Qualif.:** Applicants must be members in good standing of The Herpetologists' League; must be MS or PhD candidates, registered and in good standing in a degree-granting program; project must be original work, authored and conducted by the applicants. Projects that are already fully supported by other sources are not eligible. **Criteria:** Selection will be based on the committee's criteria.

Funds Avail.: $1,000. **Duration:** Annual. **Number Awarded:** 1. **To Apply:** Application forms can be obtained at the website. Proposals must be maximum 1, 200 words, double spaced, with 12 pt. font and one inch margins. Name the file with applicants' name and category. Applicants must include the cover page, available at the website, a detailed budget, as well as sources, and amounts of current and pending support. Applicants must clearly designate the proposal category on the cover page. Arrange in advance for one letter of support to be sent

separately by the supporter. Include a two-page CV that includes telephone, email and mailing addresses. Send complete application as a single PDF electronically to Ann Paterson. **Deadline:** December 15. **Contact:** complete application as a single PDF to Ann Paterson at apaterson@wbcoll.edu with.

5499 ■ The Herpetologists' League Graduate Research Award *(Graduate/Award)*

Purpose: To support graduate students devoted to studying herpetology. **Focus:** Herpetology. **Criteria:** Selection will be based on the committee's criteria.

Funds Avail.: $200-$500. **Duration:** Annual. **Number Awarded:** Up to 5. **To Apply:** Applicants must submit an abstract, of which they must be the senior author and have done the majority of the work, by the deadline for submission of abstracts to the Joint Meetings, indicating their desire to complete for the HL Graduate Research Award; must give the oral presentation at the meeting. **Deadline:** April 9.

5500 ■ Jones-Lovich Grants in Southwestern Herpetology *(Master's, Doctorate/Grant)*

Purpose: To support herpetological field research in the American Southwest. **Focus:** Herpetology. **Qualif.:** Applicants must be members in good standing of The Herpetologists' League; must be MS or PhD graduate students; must be registered and in good standing in a degree-granting program; the project must be original work that is authored and conducted by the applicants; the research must involve amphibians or reptiles from the southwestern United States and northwestern Mexico. **Criteria:** Selection will be based on the committee's criteria.

Funds Avail.: $1,000. **Duration:** Annual. **Number Awarded:** 1. **To Apply:** Applicants must submit a 1, 200 words proposal, excluding citations, budget, cover page or CV, double-spaced, with one inch margins and 12-pt. Font; must also include the following a cover page provided at the HL website; a detailed budget, as well as sources and amounts of current and pending support; a two-page CV that includes applicants' telephone number, email and mailing address; arrange in advance for one letter of support to be sent separately by the supporter to Carol Spencer. **Deadline:** January 4. **Contact:** Carol Spencer at atrox@berkeley.edu.

5501 ■ The Hertz Foundation

2300 First St., Ste 250
Livermore, CA 94550
Ph: (925)373-1642
E-mail: amanda@hertzfoundation.org
URL: www.hertzfoundation.org
Social Media: www.facebook.com/pages/The-Fannie-John-Hertz-Foundation/345993548787387
twitter.com/hertzfoundation
youtube.com/user/hertzfoundation

5502 ■ Hertz Foundation Graduate Fellowship Award *(Graduate/Fellowship)*

Purpose: To support the students of the applied physical, biological and engineering science who are willing to morally commit to make their skills available in time of national emergency. **Focus:** Engineering; Science. **Qualif.:** Applicants must be students of the applied physical, biological and engineering sciences who are citizens or permanent residents of the United States of America, and who are willing to morally commit to make their skills available to the United States in time of national emergency; must be college seniors wishing to pursue the PhD degree in any of the fields of particular interest to the Foundation, as well as graduate students already in the process of doing so. **Criteria:** Selection is based on merit.

Funds Avail.: $32,000; $38,000; $6,000. **Duration:** Annual. **To Apply:** Applicants must visit the website to create a log in and password to view and access the application; must submit the necessary application requirements and other documents asked by the Foundation. **Deadline:** October 23.

5503 ■ Hertz Doctoral Thesis Prize (Graduate/Prize)

Purpose: To support graduate students in the applied physical, biological, and engineering sciences for the purpose of solving difficult, real-world problems. **Focus:** Engineering; Science. **Qualif.:** Applicant must be the fellows who publish exemplary graduate theses with applications to real-world problems. **Criteria:** Selection will be based on the overall excellence and pertinence to high-impact applications of the physical sciences.

Funds Avail.: $5,000. **Duration:** Annual. **Number Awarded:** Varies. **To Apply:** Applicants are required to furnish the Foundation with copies of doctoral dissertation upon receiving the Ph.D.; may contact the Foundation for the application process and other details.

5504 ■ Higher Education Consortium for Urban Affairs (HECUA)
2233 University Ave. W, Ste. 210
Saint Paul, MN 55114
Ph: (651)287-3300
Fax: (651)659-9421
E-mail: hecua@hecua.org
URL: hecua.org
Social Media: www.facebook.com/HECUAoffcampus
instagram.com/hecua_offcampus
www.linkedin.com/company/higher-education-consortium
  -for-urban-affairs-hecua-
twitter.com/HECUA_offcampus

5505 ■ HECUA Scholarship for Community Engagement (Undergraduate/Scholarship)

Purpose: To support students who have worked for social change and whose future goals will be strengthened by a HECUA semester program. **Focus:** Urban affairs/design/planning. **Qualif.:** Applicants must be currently enrolled in one of HECUA's member colleges/universities; must be enrolled in HECUA program (semester-long or short-term programs, abroad or in the U.S. are all eligible); must have a demonstrated commitment to working for social change.

Funds Avail.: Up to $750 for semester-long programs; $350 for short-term programs. **To Apply:** Applicants must submit the following requirements: Scholarship for Community Engagement Application Form; reflective essay answering to questions of "How have past experiences led you to consider yourself a person who values community engagement?" and "How do you expect the HECUA program will enable you to further your goals and projects for social change?" A complete program application to one of HECUA's semester-long or short-term programs must be on file at HECUA. **Deadline:** December 1 (for Spring); April 15 (for Fall).

5506 ■ HECUA Scholarship for Social Justice (Undergraduate, Graduate/Scholarship)

Purpose: To fund the first generation college students with low-income to support their studies. **Focus:** Education. **Qualif.:** Applicants must be first generation college students, or students from a low-income family, or students of color who are currently enrolled in one of HECUA's member colleges/universities in a semester-long domestic or international HECUA program (HECUA's short-term programs are not eligible); students to be considered enrolled, their application must have been accepted by the HECUA Student Services Department and the student must have subsequently submitted a completed and signed participation agreement letter and a non-refundable program deposit. **Criteria:** Selection will be based on the committees' criteria.

Funds Avail.: Up to $1,500. **To Apply:** Applicants must submit scholarship application form, copy of students' FAFSA form and reflective essay composed of: drawing of the Applicants' life experience and personal and academic goals; explanation of the Applicants on how they believe they can contribute to and receive from a program with the mission to equip students with the knowledge, experiences, tools and passion to address nowadays pressing social justice issues and; reflect on how the HECUA program will benefit the Applicants, people, issues and communities they care about. **Deadline:** April 15; December 1.

5507 ■ Highlands Ranch Dental Group
9385 S Colorado Blvd., Ste. 102
Highlands Ranch, CO 80126
Ph: (720)439-2984
E-mail: highlandsranch@highlandsranchdentalgroup.com
URL: highlandsranchdentalgroup.com
Social Media: www.facebook.com/
  HighlandsRanchDentalGroup

5508 ■ Highlands Ranch Dental Group Scholarship (Undergraduate, High School/Scholarship)

Purpose: To help a student attend college. **Focus:** General studies/Field of study not specified. **Qualif.:** Applicants must be high school students that reside or attend school in Highlands Ranch, Colorado. **Criteria:** Essays will be judged on the following criteria: effort, creativity, accuracy, popularity, and quality.

Funds Avail.: $2,000. **Number Awarded:** 1. **To Apply:** Applicant must submit a one to three page essay (which may include photos, graphics, and other visual elements) on one of the following topics: Why do you think Highlands Ranch is a great place to live; Why you don't think Highlands Ranch is a great place to live; How you would improve Highlands Ranch. Application details are available online at highlandsranchdentalgroup.com/scholarship-official-rules/. **Deadline:** April 1.

5509 ■ Hill Country Master Gardeners
3775 Hwy 27
Kerrville, TX 78028
Ph: (830)257-6568
E-mail: kerr@ag.tamu.edu
URL: www.hillcountrymastergardeners.org

5510 ■ Hill Country Master Gardeners Horticulture Scholarship (Undergraduate, Graduate/Scholarship)

Purpose: To provide financial support to two undergraduate or graduate students at Texas A&M, Texas Tech, Tarle-

Awards are arranged alphabetically below their administering organizations

ton State or Stephen F. Austin State University. **Focus:** Horticulture. **Criteria:** Selection will be based on the committee's criteria.

Funds Avail.: $2,000. **Duration:** Annual. **Number Awarded:** 2. **To Apply:** Application forms are available online; two typed or printed letters of recommendation; one letter must be from an instructor; other may be from a recent employer, club advisor, church leader or other qualified person, excluding family members; transcript must include yourmost recent semester. **Deadline:** May 31. **Contact:** Chairman, HCMG Scholarship Committee, Hill Country Master Gardeners Association, PO Box 290464, Kerrville, TX, 78029.

5511 ■ The Hirair and Anna Hovnanian Foundation

37 Hanrapetutyan St.
0010 Yerevan, Armenia
E-mail: info@hovnanianfoundation.am
URL: www.hovnanianfoundation.am

5512 ■ The Hirair and Anna Hovnanian Foundation Presidential Scholarship *(Undergraduate/Scholarship)*

Purpose: To provide financial assistance to those students who are in need. **Focus:** General studies/Field of study not specified. **Qualif.:** Applicants must be students of Armenian ethnic origin who demonstrate financial need and outstanding academic achievements; must maintain a minimum 2.75 GPA. **Criteria:** Consideration will be given to all students of Armenian descent who apply and meet Villanova University's general admissions requirements.

Funds Avail.: No specific amount. **To Apply:** Applicants may contact the Association for the application process and other required materials. **Deadline:** March 15 for incoming freshman; April 15 all other students. **Contact:** Villanova University, Office of Student Financial Assistance, 800 Lancaster Ave., Villanova, PA, 19085.

5513 ■ Hirair and Anna Hovnanian Foundation Scholarship *(Undergraduate/Scholarship)*

Purpose: To provide financial assistance to students of Armenian origin. **Focus:** General studies/Field of study not specified. **Qualif.:** Applicants must be of Armenian origin (could be Armenian or other country citizens) who are pursuing Bachelor's or Master's degree at any local state universities, including American University of Armenia and French University. **Criteria:** Students seeking degrees in the fields of Agriculture, Hospitality, Mining, IT, Nursing/Medicine, Languages/Foreign Languages, Teaching, Business/Management, Law, Journalism, Physics/Science, and Arts will be given priority

To Apply: Application form and details available at www.hovnanianfoundation.am/scholarships/.

5514 ■ Hispanic Association of Colleges and Universities (HACU)

8415 Datapoint Dr., Ste. 400
San Antonio, TX 78229
Ph: (210)692-3805
Fax: (210)692-0823
E-mail: hacu@hacu.net
URL: www.hacu.net
Social Media: www.facebook.com/HACUnews
twitter.com/hacunews

5515 ■ HACU/Denny's Hungry for Education Scholarships *(Undergraduate, Graduate/Scholarship)*

Purpose: To students that share the company's goal of ending childhood hunger in local communities. **Focus:** General studies/Field of study not specified. **Qualif.:** Applicants must be full or part-time undergraduate or graduate students attending a two-year or four-year HACU-member institutions; must possess a minimum cumulative GPA of 2.5; must be citizens or permanent residents of the United States. **Criteria:** Selection will be based on the committee's criteria.

Funds Avail.: $1,000. **Number Awarded:** 5. **To Apply:** Applicants must submit a 500-word essay on how Denny's can help in the fight against childhood hunger in the United States together with enrollment verification form and transcript. **Deadline:** November 22.

5516 ■ HACU/KIA Motors America, Inc. STEAM Scholarships *(Undergraduate, Graduate/Scholarship)*

Purpose: To assist STEAM students in defraying some of the educational expenditures. **Focus:** Arts; Engineering; Mathematics and mathematical sciences; Science. **Qualif.:** Applicants must be full-time sophomore or junior undergraduate students or graduate students attending a four-year HACU-member institution within the United States or Puerto Rico; must possess a minimum cumulative GPA of 3.0; must be in a STEAM field. **Criteria:** Selection will be based on the committee's criteria.

Funds Avail.: $3,400. **Number Awarded:** 10. **To Apply:** Application is available online. Applicants must fill out the application form and provide the following: documents showing that they are currently enrolled or accepted by a college, university, or institution; resume; scholarship essay; official transcript; enrollment verification form; and letter of recommendation. **Deadline:** May 24. **Contact:** Email: scholarship@hacu.net.

5517 ■ Hispanic Dental Association (HDA)

2 Talon Ct.
Sewell, NJ 08080
Ph: (855)337-9992
E-mail: support@hdassoc.org
URL: www.hdassoc.org
Social Media: www.facebook.com/HDAssoc
www.linkedin.com/company/hispanic-dental-association
twitter.com/hdassoc

5518 ■ Colgate-Palmolive/HDA Foundation Scholarships *(Master's, Postgraduate/Scholarship)*

Purpose: To support students for meritorious work who seek scientific and applied clinical knowledge during their academic journey of their dental professional program. **Focus:** Dental hygiene; Dentistry. **Qualif.:** Applicant must be a member of the Hispanic Dental Association who has been accepted into or is currently enrolled in an accredited Masters or above program in a Dentistry Related Field; must have an undergraduate or graduate degree in an oral health related field (dental hygienist, dentistry etc.) from the U.S. or abroad; and must have permanent resident status in the U.S. **Criteria:** Selection is based on students' commitment and dedication to improving the oral health of the Hispanic community; community service (volunteer efforts in school, medical facilities, church, etc.); leadership skills; and scholastic achievement.

Funds Avail.: Up to $4,000. **To Apply:** Applicants must submit a complete application. **Deadline:** July 15.

Awards are arranged alphabetically below their administering organizations

5519 ■ Procter & Gamble Professional Oral Health/ HDA Foundation Scholarships (Undergraduate/ Scholarship)

Purpose: To support promising students as they enter into their academic training. **Focus:** Dental hygiene; Dental laboratory technology; Dentistry. **Qualif.:** Applicant must be a student member of the Hispanic Dental Association who has been accepted into an accredited dental, dental hygiene, dental assisting or dental technician program; and must have permanent resident status in the U.S.; must have a minimum GPA of 3.0 on a 4.0 scale; must show interest in improving the oral health of the Hispanic community; must show evidence of commitment and dedication to serve the Hispanic community. **Criteria:** Selection is based on students' commitment and dedication to improving the oral health of the Hispanic community; community service (volunteer efforts in school, medical facilities, church, etc.); leadership skills; and scholastic achievement.

Funds Avail.: $2,000 for Dental Students; $1,000 for Dental Auxiliaries. **To Apply:** Applicants must submit a complete application and must be typed in English. **Deadline:** July 15. **Contact:** Hispanic Dental Association Foundation, 4557 Dogwood Ln., Brownsburg, IN 46112; Phone: 317-714-0037; Email: hdafoundationscholarships@gmail.com.

5520 ■ Dr. Juan D. Villarreal/HDA Foundation Scholarships (Undergraduate/Scholarship)

Purpose: To support promising students as they enter into their academic training. **Focus:** Dental hygiene; Dentistry. **Qualif.:** Applicant must be a student member of the Hispanic Dental Association who has been accepted into or is currently enrolled in an accredited dental school or dental hygiene program in the state of Texas (student may be at any stage of the undergraduate program, first through the fourth year); and must have permanent resident status in the U.S. **Criteria:** Selection is based on students' commitment and dedication to improving the oral health of the Hispanic community; community service (volunteer efforts in school, medical facilities, church, etc.); leadership skills; and scholastic achievement.

Funds Avail.: $1,000; $500. **To Apply:** Applicants must submit a complete application. **Deadline:** July 15. **Contact:** Hispanic Dental Association Foundation, 4557 Dogwood Ln., Brownsburg, IN 46112; Phone: 317-714-0037; Email: hdafoundationscholarships@gmail.com.

5521 ■ Hispanic Faculty Staff Association (HFSA)
PO Box 8184
Austin, TX 78713
E-mail: hfsa@utexas.edu
URL: sites.utexas.edu/hfsa
Social Media: www.facebook.com/UTHFSA
www.instagram.com/uthfsa
twitter.com/UTHFSA

5522 ■ Jamail/Long Challenge Grant Scholarships (Undergraduate, Graduate/Scholarship)

Purpose: To support deserving Hispanic students at The University of Texas at Austin. **Focus:** General studies/Field of study not specified. **Qualif.:** Must be a current, full-time undergraduate, graduate or transfer students at The University of Texas at Austin. **Criteria:** Recipients are selected based on academic performance.

Funds Avail.: $1,000. **Duration:** Annual. **To Apply:** Applicants must complete the online continuing & transfer scholarship provided by the office of student financial services; must select.

5523 ■ Hispanic Lawyers Association of Illinois (HLAI)
27 N. Wacker Dr., Ste., No. 462
Chicago, IL 60606
Ph: (312)620-5303
E-mail: communications@hlai.org
URL: www.hlai.org
Social Media: www.facebook.com/hispaniclawyersIllinois
www.instagram.com/hispaniclawyersillinois
www.linkedin.com/company/hispanic-lawyers-association -of-illinois
twitter.com/hlaitweets

5524 ■ Kaplan Scholarships (Undergraduate/ Scholarship)

Purpose: To support college and law students through HLAI's JD mentor program. **Focus:** Law. **Qualif.:** Applicants must be law students who demonstrate a genuine interest in pursuing a legal career. **Criteria:** Scholarship will be given based on merit.

Funds Avail.: No specific amount. **To Apply:** Applicants must submit completed application along with two short essays about your commitment to public interest law and to serving the legal and social needs of the Hispanic community. They must also provide a copy of law school transcript. **Contact:** Kaplan Scholarships, 321 S Plymouth Court, Ste. 600, Chicago, IL, 60604; Phone: 312-345-9200; E-mail: hlai-cs@att.net.

5525 ■ Hispanic Metropolitan Chamber (HMC)
333 SW 5th Ave., Ste. 100
Portland, OR 97204
Ph: (503)222-0280
E-mail: info@hmccoregon.com
URL: www.hmccoregon.com

5526 ■ Oregon Latino Scholarship Fund (Graduate, Undergraduate/Scholarship)

Purpose: To provide a long-term source of college scholarship for Latino students. **Focus:** General studies/Field of study not specified. **Criteria:** Selection is based on academic achievements, extracurricular activities in the community and a written essay.

Funds Avail.: No specific amount. **Duration:** Annual. **To Apply:** Applicants must submit a completed application form together with the required materials.

5527 ■ Hispanic Scholarship Fund (HSF)
1411 W 190th St., Ste. 700
Gardena, CA 90248
Ph: (310)975-3700
Fax: (310)349-3328
URL: www.hsf.net
Social Media: www.facebook.com/ HispanicScholarshipFund
www.instagram.com/hsfphotos/
www.linkedin.com/company/hispanic-scholarship-fund
twitter.com/HSFNews
www.youtube.com/user/HSFvideos

Awards are arranged alphabetically below their administering organizations

5528 ■ Becas Univision Scholarship Program
(Undergraduate, Graduate/Scholarship)

Purpose: To assist students of Hispanic heritage obtain a college degree. **Focus:** General studies/Field of study not specified. **Criteria:** Selection will be based on the committee's criteria.

To Apply: Applicants must complete and submit the FAFSA or state based financial aid application. **Deadline:** February 15.

5529 ■ The Gates Millennium Scholars
(Undergraduate/Scholarship)

Purpose: To provide greater access and opportunity to higher education for outstanding students from underrepresented backgrounds. **Focus:** Education; Engineering; Library and archival sciences; Mathematics and mathematical sciences; Public health; Science. **Qualif.:** Applicant must be high school seniors; must be undergraduate students (all years); must be community college students transferring to four year universities; graduate students; must be of Hispanic heritage; must minimum of 3.0 GPA on a 4.0 scale (or equivalent) for high school students; must be a minimum of 2.5 GPA on a 4.0 scale (or equivalent) for undergraduate and graduate students; enroll full-time in an accredited, not-for-profit, four-year university, or graduate school, in the US, for the 2020-2021 academic year; must be US Citizen, Permanent Legal Resident, DACA or eligible non-citizen; must emphasis on STEM majors. **Criteria:** Recipients will be selected based on the merits of the application.

Funds Avail.: No specific amount. **To Apply:** Applications must be submitted using the HSF online application system. **Deadline:** February 15.

5530 ■ Hispanic Scholarship Fund General College Scholarship Program (HSF) *(Undergraduate/Scholarship)*

Purpose: To assist students of Hispanic heritage in obtaining a college degree. **Focus:** General studies/Field of study not specified. **Qualif.:** Applicant must be of Hispanic heritage; U.S. citizen or legal permanent resident with a valid permanent resident card or passport stamped I-551; have a minimum 3.0 GPA on a 4.0 scale or the equivalent; must apply for federal financing aid using the Free Application for Federal Student Aid (FAFSA) at www.fafsa.ed.gov; must be pursuing first undergraduate or graduate degree; must have plans to enroll full-time in a degree seeking program at a two-year or four-year U.S. accredited institution in the U.S., Puerto Rico, U.S. Virgin Islands or Guam. **Criteria:** Recipients will be selected based on the merits of the application.

Funds Avail.: $1,000 to $15,000. **To Apply:** Applications must be submitted using the HSF online application system; Student Aid Report (SAR); and school or HSF enrollment verification form. Submit all required documents in one envelope. **Deadline:** January 1.

5531 ■ HSF/Marathon Oil College Scholarship Program *(Undergraduate/Scholarship)*

Purpose: To provide students the opportunity to participate in a possible paid 8-10 week summer internship at various Marathon Oil Corporation locations. **Focus:** Accounting; Engineering, Chemical; Engineering, Civil; Engineering, Electrical; Engineering, Mechanical; Engineering, Petroleum; Geology; Geophysics; Land management; Logistics; Marketing and distribution; Transportation. **Qualif.:** Applicant must be high school seniors; must be undergraduate students (all years); must be community college students transferring to four year universities; graduate students; must be of Hispanic heritage; must minimum of 3.0 GPA on a 4.0 scale (or equivalent) for high school students; must be a minimum of 2.5 GPA on a 4.0 scale (or equivalent) for undergraduate and graduate students; enroll full-time in an accredited, not-for-profit, four-year university, or graduate school, in the US, for the 2020-2021 academic year; must be US Citizen, Permanent Legal Resident, DACA or eligible non-citizen; must emphasis on STEM majors. **Criteria:** Preference will be given to the applicants who best meet the requirements.

Funds Avail.: Amount varies. **To Apply:** Applications must be submitted using the HSF online application system. **Deadline:** February 15.

5532 ■ HSF/Wells Fargo Scholarship Program
(Undergraduate, Graduate, High School/Scholarship)

Purpose: To assist students of Hispanic heritage obtain a university degree. **Focus:** General studies/Field of study not specified. **Qualif.:** Applicant must be high school seniors; must be undergraduate students (all years); must be community college students transferring to four year universities; graduate students; must be of Hispanic heritage; must minimum of 3.0 GPA on a 4.0 scale (or equivalent) for high school students; must be a minimum of 2.5 GPA on a 4.0 scale (or equivalent) for undergraduate and graduate students; enroll full-time in an accredited, not-for-profit, four-year university, or graduate school, in the US, for the 2020-2021 academic year; must be US Citizen, Permanent Legal Resident, DACA or eligible non-citizen; must emphasis on STEM majors. **Criteria:** Awards are based on merit; amount based on relative need among the scholars selected.

Funds Avail.: $500 to $5,000. **To Apply:** Applications must be submitted using the HSF online application system. **Deadline:** February 15.

5533 ■ Historians of Islamic Art Association (HIAA)
c/o Simon Rettig, Treasurer
1127 C St. SE, Unit 4
Washington, DC 20003
E-mail: historiansofislamicart@gmail.com
URL: www.historiansofislamicart.org
Social Media: www.facebook.com/groups/
  historiansofislamicart
www.instagram.com/historiansofislamicart
twitter.com/hiaa_art

5534 ■ HIAA Graduate Student Travel Grants
(Graduate/Grant)

Purpose: To defray the travel costs of students who are presenting papers at the Annual Meeting. **Focus:** Area and ethnic studies. **Qualif.:** Applicants must be graduate students who have been invited or accepted to present papers at an annual meeting of a professional society. **Criteria:** Preference will be given to Applicants whose papers will be presented at HIAA-sponsored panels.

Funds Avail.: $500. **Duration:** Annual. **Number Awarded:** Varies. **To Apply:** Applicants must submit a cover letter summarizing the application; a separate sheet listing the Applicants' name, institutional affiliation and status (e.g. Ph.D. candidate; 3rd year), email address, name of the

Awards are arranged alphabetically below their administering organizations

primary institutional advisor, conference title, dates and venue, paper title, and itemized travel budget; a letter of support from the advisor; abstract of the paper to be presented; and the notification of acceptance from the conference/session organizer(s). **Deadline:** November 15. **Contact:** Dr. Nancy Micklewright, Head of Scholarly Programs and Publications, FreerlSackler, Smithsonian's Museums of Asian Art; Email: searssj@si.edu.

5535 ■ Margaret B. Ševçenko Prize in Islamic Art and Culture (Doctorate, Graduate/Prize)

Purpose: To support young scholars who have unpublished articles on any aspect of Islamic visual culture. **Focus:** Art history; Culture. **Qualif.:** Applicants must be junior scholars (pre-dissertation to three years after the PhD degree) on any aspect of Islamic visual culture; must be a member of HIAA. **Criteria:** Selection will be based on submitted articles.

Funds Avail.: $500. **Duration:** Annual. **Number Awarded:** 1. **To Apply:** Applicants must submit their attachments (must be in DOC, DOCX or PDF format) with the authors' contact information. A letter of recommendation should be sent separately by an advisor or referee through e-mail. **Deadline:** November 15. **Remarks:** The Prize is named in memory of Margaret Bentley Shevchenko, the first and long-serving Managing Editor of Muqarnas, a journal devoted to the visual culture of the Islamic world and sponsored by the Aga Khan Program for Islamic Architecture at Harvard and at MIT. **Contact:** Šev?enko committee chair, Hala Auji, sevcenko.hiaa@gmail.com.

5536 ■ Ho-Chunk Nation
W9814 Airport Road
Black River Falls, WI 54615
Ph: (715)284-0764
URL: ho-chunknation.com
Social Media: www.facebook.com/HoChunkNation
www.instagram.com/hochunknation/
www.linkedin.com/company/ho-chunk-nation/about/
twitter.com/HoChunkNationPR

5537 ■ Josephine P. White Eagle Scholar (Undergraduate, Graduate/Scholarship)

Purpose: To provides financial resources to help enrolled Ho-Chunk members complete a progressive postsecondary degree. **Focus:** Business; Education; Health sciences; Law. **Qualif.:** Applicants must be enrolled members of the Ho-Chunk Nation; must be accepted into a non-profit Title IV institution offering graduate level degrees within the borders or jurisdiction of the United States. They must be interested in the fields of Education, Business, Health Sciences and Law; must be enrolled in a full-time basis; must have GPA of 3.0 on a 4.0 scale. Those who are accepted in an approved Title IV law school must be accredited by the American Bar Association.

Funds Avail.: '$24,000 for full time and $18,000 for part time. **To Apply:** Applicants must submit submit a copy of the admissions letter from the Graduate School.

5538 ■ Hogg Foundation for Mental Health
Lake Austin Centre, 4th Fl.
3001 Lake Austin Blvd.
Austin, TX 78703
Ph: (512)471-5041
E-mail: Hogg-Grants@austin.utexas.edu

URL: www.hogg.utexas.edu/funding.html

5539 ■ HFMH Bilingual Scholarships for Mental Health Workforce Diversity (Graduate/Scholarship)

Purpose: To raise awareness of, and begin to meet the need for, more cultural and linguistic diversity in the state's mental health workforce. **Focus:** Social work. **Qualif.:** Applicants must be accepted as new students by a Texas graduate social work program that is accredited or in candidacy for accreditation by the National Council on Social Work Education; must be fluent in English and a second language chosen by the school, typically Spanish; must commit to work in Texas after graduation providing mental health services for a period equal to the timeframe of the scholarship; must meet any additional selection criteria required by the program of their choice. **Criteria:** Selection will be based on the committee's criteria.

Funds Avail.: Amount varies. **To Apply:** Students must apply for the scholarship through their school and should contact their graduate program's office for more information. **Remarks:** Established in 2008.

5540 ■ Hollis NorEasters Snowmobile Club
234 Silver Lake Rd.
Hollis, NH 03049
URL: www.noreasters.org
Social Media: www.facebook.com/groups/hollisnoreasters

5541 ■ Nor' Easters Scholarship (Undergraduate/Scholarship)

Purpose: To support the education of a student member. **Focus:** General studies/Field of study not specified.
Duration: Annual.

5542 ■ Nor' Easters Scholarships - Two-year Program (Undergraduate/Scholarship)

Purpose: To support the education of a student member. **Focus:** General studies/Field of study not specified. **Criteria:** Selection is based on the application.

Funds Avail.: $1,000. **Duration:** Annual. **Number Awarded:** 1. **To Apply:** Applicant must submit a completed application form along with the required documents. **Deadline:** April 4.

5543 ■ Joseph A. Holmes Safety Association (JAHSA)
PO Box 9375
Arlington, VA 22219
Ph: (304)256-3223
Fax: (304)256-3319
E-mail: mail@holmessafety.org
URL: www.holmessafety.org
Social Media: www.facebook.com/holmessafety
www.linkedin.com/company/joseph-a-holmes-safety
 -association
twitter.com/JosephAHolmes

5544 ■ Joseph A. Holmes Safety Association Scholarship (High School/Scholarship)

Purpose: To provide financial assistance to students to help their educational costs in a field related to mining health and safety. **Focus:** Mining. **Qualif.:** Applicants must be enrolled in an accredited college or university in the

Awards are arranged alphabetically below their administering organizations

United States. Other qualifications are that you must be: pursuing a degree in a mining-related major, pursuing a degree in health or safety in the mining industry. **Criteria:** Selection will be based on demonstrated outstanding academic achievement, financial need, GPA, leadership and future career interest in a mine related field.

Funds Avail.: Amount varies. **To Apply:** Applicants must submit a completed application form together with transcript of grades for the last three years of completed education; completed financial disclosure information; short essay (200-300 words); typed essay must be double spaced and in a size 12-inch font; and list of extracurricular activities and/or a list of other academic achievements. **Deadline:** May 1. **Contact:** Joseph A. Holmes Safety Association, PO Box 9375, Arlington, VA, 22219; Email: scholarship@ holmessafety.org.

5545 ■ Holocaust and Human Rights Center of Maine (HHRC)

University of Maine at Augusta
46 University Dr.
Augusta, ME 04330-1644
Ph: (207)621-3530
Fax: (207)621-3534
E-mail: infohhrc@maine.edu
URL: www.hhrcmaine.org
Social Media: www.facebook.com/HHRCMaine
www.instagram.com/hhrcmaine
twitter.com/hhrcme

5546 ■ The Lawrence Alan Spiegel Remembrance Scholarship *(Undergraduate/Scholarship)*

Purpose: To support students who submitted a winning essay. **Focus:** General studies/Field of study not specified. **Qualif.:** Applicants must be high school seniors or homeschoolers who are residents of Maine and who have been accepted at any accredited and Title IV eligible college, university or technical school. **Criteria:** Applicants are evaluated by a panel of judges based on submitted essay.

Funds Avail.: $1,000. **Duration:** Annual. **To Apply:** Applicants must write an essay on. **Deadline:** May 1. **Contact:** Holocaust and Human Rights Center of Maine, Michael Klahr Center, UMA, 46 University Dr., Augusta, Maine, 04330; Phone: 207-621-3530; Email: infohhrc@maine.edu.

5547 ■ Home Builders Association of Kentucky (HBAK)

1040 Burlington Ln.
Frankfort, KY 40601
Fax: (502)875-5480
Free: 800-489-4225
URL: www.hbak.com
Social Media: www.facebook.com/HBAofKy
twitter.com/hbaofky

5548 ■ The Betty Bell Scholarship Fund *(Undergraduate/Scholarship)*

Purpose: To assist students in obtaining higher education in a building industry related field. **Focus:** General studies/ Field of study not specified. **Qualif.:** Applicant must be a student presently enrolled in an institution of higher education; a member, spouse, child, or employee of a member of the association; live in the jurisdiction of the Home Builders

Association of Kentucky; and, exhibit good character. **Criteria:** Selection will be based on the submitted applications, personal references, recommendations and scholastic records.

Funds Avail.: $500. **Duration:** Annual. **To Apply:** Applicants must complete the application for the award; must secure a written recommendation from two people other than family members, who can offer personal references for the Applicants. Applications must be mailed or delivered to the Home Builders Association of Kentucky. **Deadline:** April 15.

5549 ■ The Tommy Bright Scholarship Fund *(Undergraduate/Scholarship)*

Purpose: To assist students in achieving a more comprehensive understanding of how the United States government operates. **Focus:** General studies/Field of study not specified. **Qualif.:** Applicants must be students presently enrolled in high school or college; live in the jurisdiction of the Home Builders Association of Kentucky; be the children or grandchildren of a member or member' employee of the HBAK and exhibit good character. **Criteria:** Selection will be based on the submitted applications, personal references, recommendations and scholastic records.

Funds Avail.: $1,000. **Duration:** Annual. **To Apply:** Applicants must complete the application for the award; must secure a written recommendation from two people other than family members, who can offer personal references for the Applicants. Applications must be mailed or delivered to the Home Builders Association of Kentucky. **Deadline:** April 15. **Remarks:** The award was established in honor of Tommy Bright who was a very active member of the Home Builders Association of the Bluegrass. **Contact:** Mail to: HBAK, Tommy Bright Scholarship, 1040 Burlington Ln., Frankfort, KY, 40601.

5550 ■ Homeless Children's Education Fund

1 Hope Sq., 1901 Centre Ave., Ste. 301
Pittsburgh, PA 15219
Ph: (412)562-0154
Fax: (412)562-1109
E-mail: info@homelessfund.org
URL: www.homelessfund.org
Social Media: www.facebook.com/homelesseducation
instagram.com/homelessfund412
twitter.com/homelessfund

5551 ■ Hope Through Learning Award *(Undergraduate/Award)*

Purpose: To assist currently or formerly homeless youth in attending post-secondary education or training. **Focus:** General studies/Field of study not specified. **Qualif.:** Applicants must be currently residing in Allegheny County; must be 24 years of age or younger; must be high school graduates or GED recipients, or due to complete secondary education at the end of the school year; must be accepted into a postsecondary education or career program (e.g. college, university, community college, business school, technical school, vocational school, career training, internship, apprenticeship) for the first time, and are scheduled to begin classes/training before the end of the current year; and must be experiencing or have experienced homelessness during school attendance years. **Criteria:** Selection will be based on commitment to education despite homelessness; compelling challenges due to homelessness; financial need for college; academic achievement

Awards are arranged alphabetically below their administering organizations

and accomplishments; writing style and ability; statement of goals and career interests; and community involvement.

Funds Avail.: $2,500 each. **Duration:** Annual. **Number Awarded:** Varies. **To Apply:** Applicants must fill all sections in the application form and should be submitted along with the resume; high school transcript (in sealed envelope with counselors signature or school stamp over seal); copy of post-secondary program acceptance letter; two recommendation letters (letters should be on letterhead and include the authors title, address, phone number, email address, and signature; each letter should be in a sealed envelope and signed over the seal; examples include teachers, mentors, clergy, community leaders, case managers, or homeless housing staff, excluding any family members); and two to three pages of essay responding to each item (describing their experience with homelessness and how such condition affected their education; how they overcome the challenges of housing instability to succeed in school; and what do they think should be done, or would they do, to increase awareness or address the issue of student homelessness). Application must be completed through the online form at homelessfund.org/hope/. **Deadline:** May 31.

5552 ■ Homus
4318 Oakwood Ave.
New York, NY 10021
URL: homus.org
Social Media: www.facebook.com/homus.org
twitter.com/homus_org

5553 ■ Homus E-Commerce Research Scholarship
(College, University, Undergraduate, Graduate, Community College, Vocational/Occupational, Professional development/Scholarship)

Purpose: To help students achieve their educational goals. **Focus:** General studies/Field of study not specified. **Qualif.:** Applicant must be a student pursuing a degree and above 18 years old.

Funds Avail.: $3,000. **Number Awarded:** 1. **To Apply:** Application form and essay details available online at homus.org. **Deadline:** February 28.

5554 ■ Honor Society of Phi Kappa Phi - North Dakota State University Chapter 10
1210 Albrecht Blvd.
Fargo, ND 58102
Fax: (701)231-8959
Free: 800-608-6378
URL: www.ndsu.edu/pkp
Social Media: www.facebook.com/ndsu.fargo
www.instagram.com/ndsu_official
twitter.com/ndsu
www.youtube.com/user/NDSUofficial

5555 ■ Matilda B. Thompson Scholarship
(Undergraduate/Scholarship)

Purpose: To provide scholarship to members of Phi Kappa Phi. **Focus:** General studies/Field of study not specified. **Qualif.:** Applicants must be members of Phi Kappa Phi and enrolled at NDSU for the fall semester.

Funds Avail.: $100 - $300. **Duration:** Annual. **Number Awarded:** Varies. **To Apply:** Applicants may visit the website to obtain an application: www.ndsu.edu/pkp/

about.html#scholarships. **Deadline:** January 10. **Remarks:** The scholarship is named in honor of a former NDSU dean of women and professor of mathematics who chaired many drives to obtain contributions for Phi Kappa Phi local scholarships. **Contact:** Suzanne Kelley, Editor in Chief, NDSU Press, Minard 204F, Dept. 2360, P.O. Box 6050, Fargo, ND 58108-6050.

5556 ■ Hoover Presidential Foundation
302 Parkside Dr.
West Branch, IA 52358
Ph: (319)643-5327
Fax: (319)643-2391
E-mail: info@hooverpf.org
URL: www.hooverpresidentialfoundation.org
Social Media: www.facebook.com/HooverPresFoundation
www.linkedin.com/company/hooverpresidentialfoundation
twitter.com/HooverPresFndn
www.youtube.com/channel/UCjt8AUAk99PqSqd1amC_mSw

5557 ■ Herbert Hoover Uncommon Student Award
(Undergraduate/Scholarship)

Purpose: To encourage academic excellence and innovativeness among young students of Iowa by providing educational assistance. **Focus:** General studies/Field of study not specified. **Qualif.:** Applicants must be students in their junior level in an Iowa high school or a home schooled program in the spring of the current year, with a high school graduation date of spring of the following year. **Criteria:** Selection shall be based on the project proposal and letters of recommendation of selected students from Iowa High School. (Grades, test score, essays and financial need are not evaluated).

Funds Avail.: $1,500 each (for finalists); additional $5,000 each (for any three finalists). **Duration:** Annual. **Number Awarded:** Up to 15. **To Apply:** Applicants must submit a completed application form, project proposal (at least 2-3 pages) and two letters of recommendation. **Deadline:** March 15. **Contact:** Email: DmcConnaha@HooverPF.org.

5558 ■ Hope for the Warriors
8003 Forbes Pl.,Ste. 201
Springfield, VA 22151
Free: 877-246-7349
E-mail: info@hopeforthewarriors.org
URL: www.hopeforthewarriors.org
Social Media: www.facebook.com/HopeForTheWarriors
www.instagram.com/hope4warriors
twitter.com/Hope4Warriors
youtube.com/HopeForTheWarriors
www.youtube.com/c/HopeforthewarriorsOrgH4W

5559 ■ Restoring Self Scholarship *(Undergraduate/Scholarship)*

Purpose: To identify, recognize and reward exceptional spouses/caregivers to aid in their continued education at a reputable, accredited college or trade school as they assume critical roles in the financial well being of their families. **Focus:** General studies/Field of study not specified. **Qualif.:** Applicants must be students seeking any undergraduate degree. **Criteria:** Selection will be based on eligibility, commitment to succeed as indicated by academic

Awards are arranged alphabetically below their administering organizations

achievement, personal goals, letters of recommendation, resume and an original essay response.

Funds Avail.: No specific amount. **Duration:** Annual. **To Apply:** Applicants must submit a completed application form along with the proof of service, proof of injury/death, original essay, two-page questionnaire and one letter of recommendation. **Deadline:** September 30. **Contact:** E-mail: scholarships@hopeforthewarriors.org.

5560 ■ Horatio Alger Association of Distinguished Americans (HAADA)

99 Canal Center Plz., Ste. 320
Alexandria, VA 22314-1588
Ph: (703)684-9444
Free: 844-422-4200
URL: horatioalger.org
Social Media: www.facebook.com/HoratioAlgerUS
www.instagram.com/horatioalgerassociation
www.linkedin.com/company/horatio-alger-association
twitter.com/horatioalgerus
www.youtube.com/user/HAATEAMATQ

5561 ■ Horatio Alger Ak-Sar-Ben Scholarships
(Undergraduate/Scholarship)

Purpose: To provide financial assistance to students in the state of Nebraska and western Iowa. **Focus:** General studies/Field of study not specified. **Qualif.:** Applicants must be enrolled full time as high school seniors, progressing normally toward graduation and planning to enter college not later than the fall following graduation; must have a strong commitment to pursue a bachelor's degree at an accredited institution (students may start their studies at a two-year institution and then transfer to a four-year institution); must have critical financial need ($50, 000 or less adjusted gross income per family is preferred; if higher, an explanation must be provided); must be involved in co-curricular and community activities; must have a minimum grade point average of 2.0; must be residents of Nebraska or western Iowa; be citizens or permanent residents of the United States. **Criteria:** Recipients will be selected based on financial need.

Funds Avail.: $6,000. **Duration:** Annual. **Number Awarded:** 50. **To Apply:** Applicants must submit an official transcript; a copy of parents/guardians federal tax return; have one letter of support and must be logged in to the application process at the HAA website. Faxes/e-mails will not be accepted. Students must download the certification page from the HAA web site, complete it and obtain the proper signatures prior to mailing. **Deadline:** October 25.

5562 ■ Horatio Alger Delaware Scholarships
(Undergraduate/Scholarship)

Purpose: To provide financial assistance to students in the state of Delaware. **Focus:** General studies/Field of study not specified. **Qualif.:** Applicants must be U.S. citizens who are residents of Delaware, enrolled full time as high school seniors in the United States, and progressing normally toward graduation in spring/summer of the current year with the plan to enter a college in the United States no later than the fall following graduation; must also: be involved in co-curricular and community service activities; display integrity and perseverance in overcoming adversity; demonstrate critical financial need ($55, 000 or lower adjusted gross family income is required); and, exhibit a strong commitment to pursue and complete a bachelor's

degree at an accredited non-profit public or private institution in the United States (students may start their studies at a two-year institution and then transfer to a four-year institution). **Criteria:** Selection will be based on the aforesaid qualifications and compliance with the application process.

Funds Avail.: $10,000. **Duration:** Annual. **Number Awarded:** 8. **To Apply:** Applicants must have one letter of support and must be logged in to the application process at the HAA website. Faxes/e-mails will not be accepted. Students must download the certification page from the HAA web site, complete it and obtain the proper signatures prior to mailing. **Deadline:** October 25. **Remarks:** The scholarships are made in honor of John W. Rollins, Sr.

5563 ■ Horatio Alger District of Columbia, Maryland and Virginia Scholarships *(Undergraduate/ Scholarship)*

Purpose: To support deserving students from the Washington D.C., Metro area in the following counties: District of Columbia, Maryland, Virginia. **Focus:** General studies/Field of study not specified. **Qualif.:** Applicants must be U.S. citizens (residents of District of Columbia, Maryland, and/or Virginia) enrolled full time as high school seniors in the United States, and progressing normally toward graduation in spring/summer of the current year with the plan to enter a college in the United States no later than the fall following graduation; must also: be involved in co-curricular and community service activities; display integrity and perseverance in overcoming adversity; demonstrate critical financial need ($55, 000 or lower adjusted gross family income is required); and, exhibit a strong commitment to pursue and complete a bachelor's degree at an accredited non-profit public or private institution in the United States (students may start their studies at a two-year institution and then transfer to a four-year institution). **Criteria:** Selection will be based on the aforesaid qualifications and compliance with the application process.

Funds Avail.: $10,000. **Duration:** Annual. **Number Awarded:** 10. **To Apply:** Applicants must have one letter of support and must be logged in to the application process at the HAA website. Faxes/e-mails will not be accepted. Students must download the certification page from the HAA web site, complete it and obtain the proper signatures prior to mailing. **Deadline:** October 25. **Remarks:** The scholarships are made possible through its funder, Anthony Welters.

5564 ■ Horatio Alger Florida Scholarships
(Undergraduate/Scholarship)

Purpose: To provide financial assistance to students in the counties of Broward, Martin and St. Lucie in the state of Florida. **Focus:** General studies/Field of study not specified. **Qualif.:** Applicants must be U.S. citizens who are Florida residents, enrolled full time as high school seniors in the United States, and progressing normally toward graduation in spring/summer of the current year with the plan to enter a college in the United States no later than the fall following graduation; they must also: be involved in co-curricular and community service activities; display integrity and perseverance in overcoming adversity; demonstrate critical financial need ($55, 000 or lower adjusted gross family income is required); and, exhibit a strong commitment to pursue and complete a bachelor's degree at an accredited non-profit public or private institution in the United States (students may start their studies at a two-year institution and then transfer to a four-year institution). **Criteria:** Selection will be based on the aforesaid qualifications and compliance with the application process.

Awards are arranged alphabetically below their administering organizations

Funds Avail.: $10,000. **Duration:** Annual. **Number Awarded:** 45. **To Apply:** Applicants must have one letter of support and must be logged in to the application process at the HAA website. Faxes/e-mails will not be accepted. Students must download the certification page from the HAA web site, complete it and obtain the proper signatures prior to mailing. **Deadline:** October 25. **Remarks:** The scholarships are made in honor of John A. Moran.

5565 ■ Horatio Alger Georgia Scholarships
(Undergraduate/Scholarship)

Purpose: To provide financial assistance to students in the state of Georgia. **Focus:** General studies/Field of study not specified. **Qualif.:** Applicants must be U.S. citizens who are Georgia residents, enrolled full time as high school seniors in the United States, and progressing normally toward graduation in spring/summer of the current year with the plan to enter a college in the United States no later than the fall following graduation; must also: be involved in co-curricular and community service activities; display integrity and perseverance in overcoming adversity; demonstrate critical financial need ($55, 000 or lower adjusted gross family income is required); and, exhibit a strong commitment to pursue and complete a bachelor's degree at an accredited non-profit public or private institution in the United States (students may start their studies at a two-year institution and then transfer to a four-year institution). **Criteria:** Selection will be based on the aforesaid qualifications and compliance with the application process.

Funds Avail.: $10,000. **Duration:** Annual. **Number Awarded:** 25. **To Apply:** Applicants must have one letter of support and must be logged in to the application process at the HAA website. Faxes/e-mails will not be accepted. Students must download the certification page from the HAA web site, complete it and obtain the proper signatures prior to mailing. **Deadline:** October 25. **Remarks:** The scholarships are funded by O. Wayne Rollins Foundation.

5566 ■ Horatio Alger Idaho University Scholarships
(Undergraduate/Scholarship)

Purpose: To provide educational support to students who are in need. **Focus:** General studies/Field of study not specified. **Qualif.:** Applicants must attend Idaho State University and be enrolled in the College of Business; must have critical financial need based on the Student Aid Report; must be residents of the State of Idaho; must have a minimum cumulative grade point average of 2.0 or better. **Criteria:** Recipients will be selected based on the committee's review of all applications.

Funds Avail.: $55,000. **Duration:** Annual. **Number Awarded:** 2. **To Apply:** Applicants must submit an official high school and college transcript of records; a copy of parents/guardians federal income tax return; must provide a copy of Student Aid Report (SAR); and have one letter of support and must be logged in to the application process at the HAA website. Faxes/e-mails will not be accepted. Students must download the certification page from the HAA web site, complete it and obtain the proper signatures prior to mailing. **Deadline:** March 15.

5567 ■ Horatio Alger Illinois Scholarships
(Undergraduate/Scholarship)

Purpose: To provide financial assistance to students in the state of Illinois. **Focus:** General studies/Field of study not specified. **Qualif.:** Applicants must be U.S. citizens who are residing in Illinois, and enrolled full time as high school seniors in the United States, and progressing normally

toward graduation in spring/summer of the current year with the plan to enter a college in the United States no later than the fall following graduation; must also: be involved in co-curricular and community service activities; display integrity and perseverance in overcoming adversity; demonstrate critical financial need ($55, 000 or lower adjusted gross family income is required); and, exhibit a strong commitment to pursue and complete a bachelor's degree at an accredited non-profit public or private institution in the United States (students may start their studies at a two-year institution and then transfer to a four-year institution). **Criteria:** Selection will be based on the aforesaid qualifications and compliance with the application process.

Funds Avail.: $10,000. **Duration:** Annual. **Number Awarded:** 17. **To Apply:** Applicants must submit an official high school transcript; a copy of parents/guardians federal income tax return; and have one letter of support and must be logged in to the application process at the HAA website. Faxes/e-mails will not be accepted. Students must download the certification page from the HAA web site, complete it and obtain the proper signatures prior to mailing. **Deadline:** October 25. **Remarks:** The scholarships are funded by Brinson Foundation & Doris K. Christopher.

5568 ■ Horatio Alger Indiana Scholarships
(Undergraduate/Scholarship)

Purpose: To provide financial assistance to students in the state of Indiana. **Focus:** General studies/Field of study not specified. **Qualif.:** Applicants must be U.S. citizens who are residing in Indiana, and enrolled full time as high school seniors in the United States, and progressing normally toward graduation in spring/summer of the current year with the plan to enter a college in the United States no later than the fall following graduation; must also: be involved in co-curricular and community service activities; display integrity and perseverance in overcoming adversity; demonstrate critical financial need ($55, 000 or lower adjusted gross family income is required); and, exhibit a strong commitment to pursue and complete a bachelor's degree at an accredited non-profit public or private institution in the United States (students may start their studies at a two-year institution and then transfer to a four-year institution). **Criteria:** Selection will be based on the aforesaid qualifications and compliance with the application process.

Funds Avail.: $10,000. **Duration:** Annual. **Number Awarded:** 10. **To Apply:** Applicants must submit an official high school transcript; one copy of parents/guardians federal income tax return; and have one letter of support and must be logged in to the application process at the HAA website. Faxes/e-mails will not be accepted. Students must download the certification page from the HAA web site, complete it and obtain the proper signatures prior to mailing. **Deadline:** October 25. **Remarks:** The scholarships are funded by Suzanne and Walter Scott Foundation.

5569 ■ Horatio Alger Kentucky Scholarships
(Undergraduate/Scholarship)

Purpose: To provide financial assistance to students in the state of Kentucky. **Focus:** General studies/Field of study not specified. **Qualif.:** Applicants must be U.S. citizens who are Kentucky residents, and enrolled full time as high school seniors in the United States, and progressing normally toward graduation in spring/summer of the current year with the plan to enter a college in the United States no later than the fall following graduation; must also: be involved in co-curricular and community service activities; display integrity and perseverance in overcoming adversity; demonstrate critical financial need ($55, 000 or lower

Awards are arranged alphabetically below their administering organizations

adjusted gross family income is required); and, exhibit a strong commitment to pursue and complete a bachelor's degree at an accredited non-profit public or private institution in the United States (students may start their studies at a two-year institution and then transfer to a four-year institution). **Criteria:** Recipients will be selected based on financial need.

Funds Avail.: $10,000. **Duration:** Annual. **Number Awarded:** 10. **To Apply:** Applicants must submit an official high school transcript; a copy of parents/guardians federal income tax return; have one letter of support and must be logged in to the application process at the HAA website. Faxes/e-mails will not be accepted. Students must download the certification page from the HAA web site, complete it and obtain the proper signatures prior to mailing. **Deadline:** October 25. **Remarks:** The scholarships are funded by Horatio Alger Endowment Fund.

5570 ■ Horatio Alger Lola and Duane Hagadone Idaho Scholarships *(Undergraduate/Scholarship)*

Purpose: To provide scholarships to students in the State of Idaho. **Focus:** General studies/Field of study not specified. **Criteria:** Selection will be based on the aforesaid qualifications and compliance with the application process.

Funds Avail.: $10,000. **Duration:** Annual. **To Apply:** Applicants must submit an official high school transcript; a copy of parents/guardians federal income tax return; and have one letter of support and must be logged in to the application process at the HAA website. Faxes/e-mails will not be accepted. Students must download the certification page from the HAA web site, complete it and obtain the proper signatures prior to mailing.

5571 ■ Horatio Alger Louisiana Scholarships *(Undergraduate/Scholarship)*

Purpose: To provide financial assistance to students in the state of Louisiana. **Focus:** General studies/Field of study not specified. **Qualif.:** Applicants must be U.S. citizens enrolled full time as high school seniors in the United States, and progressing normally toward graduation in spring/summer of the current year with the plan to enter a college in the United States no later than the fall following graduation; must also: be involved in co-curricular and community service activities; display integrity and perseverance in overcoming adversity; demonstrate critical financial need ($55, 000 or lower adjusted gross family income is required); and, exhibit a strong commitment to pursue and complete a bachelor's degree at an accredited non-profit public or private institution in the United States (students may start their studies at a two-year institution and then transfer to a four-year institution). Furthermore, Applicants must pursue a bachelor's degree at a college in Louisiana. **Criteria:** Selection will be based on the aforesaid qualifications and compliance with the application process.

Funds Avail.: $10,500. **Duration:** Annual. **Number Awarded:** 25. **To Apply:** Applicants must submit an official high school transcript; a copy of parents/guardians federal income tax return; have one letter of support and must be logged in to the application process at the HAA website. Faxes/e-mails will not be accepted. Students must download the certification page from the HAA web site, complete it and obtain the proper signatures prior to mailing. **Deadline:** October 25. **Remarks:** The scholarships are made possible through its funder, William J. Doré.

5572 ■ Horatio Alger Minnesota Scholarships *(Undergraduate/Scholarship)*

Purpose: To provide financial assistance to students in the state of Minnesota. **Focus:** General studies/Field of study not specified. **Qualif.:** Applicants must be U.S. citizens who are Minnesota residents, enrolled full time as high school seniors in the United States, and progressing normally toward graduation in spring/summer of the current year with the plan to enter a college in the United States no later than the fall following graduation; must also: be involved in co-curricular and community service activities; display integrity and perseverance in overcoming adversity; demonstrate critical financial need ($55, 000 or lower adjusted gross family income is required); and, exhibit a strong commitment to pursue and complete a bachelor's degree at an accredited non-profit public or private institution in the United States (students may start their studies at a two-year institution and then transfer to a four-year institution). **Criteria:** Selection will be based on the aforesaid qualifications and compliance with the application process.

Funds Avail.: $10,000. **Duration:** Annual. **Number Awarded:** 10. **To Apply:** Applicants must submit an official high school transcript; a copy of parents/guardians federal tax return; have one letter of support and must be logged in to the application process at the HAA website. Faxes/e-mails will not be accepted. Students must download the certification page from the HAA web site, complete it and obtain the proper signatures prior to mailing. **Deadline:** October 25. **Remarks:** The scholarships are funded by Al and Cathy Annexstad and Horatio Alger Scholarship Fund.

5573 ■ Horatio Alger Missouri Scholarships *(Undergraduate/Scholarship)*

Purpose: To provide financial assistance to students in the state of Missouri. **Focus:** General studies/Field of study not specified. **Qualif.:** Applicants must be U.S. citizens who are Missouri residents and enrolled full time as high school seniors in the United States, and progressing normally toward graduation in spring/summer of the current year with the plan to enter a college in the United States no later than the fall following graduation; must also: be involved in co-curricular and community service activities; display integrity and perseverance in overcoming adversity; demonstrate critical financial need ($55, 000 or lower adjusted gross family income is required); and, exhibit a strong commitment to pursue and complete a bachelor's degree at an accredited non-profit public or private institution in the United States (students may start their studies at a two-year institution and then transfer to a four-year institution). **Criteria:** Selection will be based on the aforesaid qualifications and compliance with the application process.

Funds Avail.: $10,000. **Duration:** Annual. **Number Awarded:** 10. **To Apply:** Applicants must submit an official high school transcript; a copy of parents/guardians federal income tax return; have one letter of support and must be logged in to the application process at the HAA website. Faxes/e-mails will not be accepted. Students must download the certification page from the HAA web site, complete it and obtain the proper signatures prior to mailing. **Deadline:** October 25. **Remarks:** The scholarships are made possible through its funder, Paul Anthony Novelly.

5574 ■ Horatio Alger Montana Scholarships *(Undergraduate/Scholarship)*

Purpose: To provide financial assistance to students in the state of Montana. **Focus:** General studies/Field of study not specified. **Qualif.:** Applicants must be U.S. citizens enrolled full time as high school seniors in the United States, and progressing normally toward graduation in spring/summer of the current year with the plan to enter a college in the United States no later than the fall following graduation; must also: be involved in co-curricular and community service activities; display integrity and perseverance in overcoming adversity; demonstrate critical financial need ($55, 000 or lower adjusted gross family income is required); and, exhibit a strong commitment to pursue and complete a bachelor's degree at an accredited non-profit public or private institution in the United States (students may start their studies at a two-year institution and then transfer to a four-year institution). Furthermore, they must pursue a bachelor's degree at the University of Montana, The University of Montana-Western, The University of Montana-Missoula College of Technology, Helena College of Technology of The University of Montana, or Montana Tech of The University of The University of Montana. **Criteria:** Selection will be based on the aforesaid qualifications and compliance with the application process.

Funds Avail.: $10,000. **Duration:** Annual. **Number Awarded:** 50. **To Apply:** Applicants must submit an official high school transcript; a copy of parents/guardians federal tax return; have one letter of support and must be logged in to the application process at the HAA website. Faxes/e-mails will not be accepted. Students must download the certification page from the HAA web site, complete it and obtain the proper signatures prior to mailing. **Deadline:** October 25. **Remarks:** The scholarships are made possible through the funding from Phyllis and Dennis Washington.

5575 ■ Horatio Alger National Scholarships
(Undergraduate/Scholarship)

Purpose: To assist high school students who have faced and overcome great obstacles in their young lives. **Focus:** General studies/Field of study not specified. **Qualif.:** Applicants must be U.S. citizens enrolled full time as high school seniors in the United States, and progressing normally toward graduation in spring/summer of the current year with the plan to enter a college in the United States no later than the fall following graduation; they must also: be involved in co-curricular and community service activities; display integrity and perseverance in overcoming adversity; demonstrate critical financial need ($55, 000 or lower adjusted gross family income is required); and, exhibit a strong commitment to pursue and complete a bachelor's degree at an accredited non-profit public or private institution in the United States (students may start their studies at a two-year institution and then transfer to a four-year institution). **Criteria:** Selection will be based on the aforesaid qualifications and compliance with the application details.

Funds Avail.: $25,000. **Duration:** Annual. **Number Awarded:** 106. **To Apply:** Applicants must submit an official high school transcript; a copy of parents/guardian federal income tax return; and have one letter of support and must be logged in to the application process at the HAA website. Faxes/e-mails will not be accepted. Students must download the certification page from the HAA web site, complete it and obtain the proper signatures prior to mailing. **Deadline:** October 25.

5576 ■ Horatio Alger North Dakota Scholarships
(Undergraduate/Scholarship)

Purpose: To provide financial assistance to students in the state of North Dakota. **Focus:** General studies/Field of study not specified. **Qualif.:** Applicants must be U.S. citizens who are North Dakota residents, enrolled full time as high school seniors in the United States, and progressing normally toward graduation in spring/summer of the current year with the plan to enter a college in the United States no later than the fall following graduation; must also: be involved in co-curricular and community service activi-

ties; display integrity and perseverance in overcoming adversity; demonstrate critical financial need ($55, 000 or lower adjusted gross family income is required); and, exhibit a strong commitment to pursue and complete a bachelor's degree at an accredited non-profit public or private institution in the United States (students may start their studies at a two-year institution and then transfer to a four-year institution). **Criteria:** Recipients will be selected based on financial need.

Funds Avail.: $10,000. **Duration:** Annual. **Number Awarded:** 12. **To Apply:** Applicants must submit an official high school transcript; a copy of parent's/guardian's federal tax return; have one letter of support and must be logged in to the application process at the HAA website. Faxes/e-mails will not be accepted. Students must download the certification page from the HAA web site, complete it and obtain the proper signatures prior to mailing. **Deadline:** October 25. **Remarks:** The scholarships are funded by BNSF Railway Foundation.

5577 ■ Horatio Alger Pennsylvania Scholarships
(Undergraduate/Scholarship)

Purpose: To provide financial assistance to students in the State of Pennsylvania. **Focus:** General studies/Field of study not specified. **Qualif.:** Applicants must be U.S. citizens who are Pennsylvania residents, enrolled full time as high school seniors in the United States, and progressing normally toward graduation in spring/summer of the current year with the plan to enter a college in the United States no later than the fall following graduation; they must also: be involved in co-curricular and community service activities; display integrity and perseverance in overcoming adversity; demonstrate critical financial need ($55, 000 or lower adjusted gross family income is required); and, exhibit a strong commitment to pursue and complete a bachelor's degree at an accredited non-profit public or private institution in the United States (students may start their studies at a two-year institution and then transfer to a four-year institution). **Criteria:** Selection will be based on the aforesaid qualifications and compliance with the application process.

Funds Avail.: $10,000. **Duration:** Annual. **Number Awarded:** 29. **To Apply:** Applicants must submit an official high school transcript; have one letter of support and must be logged in to the application process at the HAA website. Faxes/e-mails will not be accepted. Students must download the certification page from the HAA web site, complete it and obtain the proper signatures prior to mailing. **Deadline:** October 25. **Remarks:** The scholarships are funded by Neubauer Family Foundation and Alan B. Miller.

5578 ■ Horatio Alger South Dakota Scholarships
(Undergraduate/Scholarship)

Purpose: To provide financial assistance to students in the state of South Dakota. **Focus:** General studies/Field of study not specified. **Qualif.:** Applicants must be U.S. citizens who are South Dakota residents, enrolled full time as high school seniors in the United States, and progressing normally toward graduation in spring/summer of the current year with the plan to enter a college in the United States no later than the fall following graduation; they must also: be involved in co-curricular and community service activities; display integrity and perseverance in overcoming adversity; demonstrate critical financial need ($55, 000 or lower adjusted gross family income is required); and, exhibit a strong commitment to pursue and complete a bachelor's degree at an accredited non-profit public or private institution in the United States (students may start their studies at a two-year institution and then transfer to a four-year institu-

Awards are arranged alphabetically below their administering organizations

tion). **Criteria:** Selection will be based on the aforesaid qualifications and compliance with the application process.

Funds Avail.: $10,000. **Duration:** Annual. **Number Awarded:** 31. **To Apply:** Applicants must submit an official high school transcript; a copy of parents/guardians federal tax return; have one letter of support and must be logged in to the application process at the HAA website. Faxes/emails will not be accepted. Students must download the certification page from the HAA web site, complete it and obtain the proper signatures prior to mailing. **Deadline:** October 25. **Remarks:** The scholarships are funded by MidAmerican Energy Foundation and Dean Buntrock.

5579 ■ Horatio Alger Texas Scholarships
(Undergraduate/Scholarship)

Purpose: To provide financial assistance to students in the state of Texas. **Focus:** General studies/Field of study not specified. **Qualif.:** Applicants must be U.S. citizens who are Texas residents, enrolled full time as high school seniors in the United States, and progressing normally toward graduation in spring/summer of the current year with the plan to enter a college in the United States no later than the fall following graduation; must also: be involved in co-curricular and community service activities; display integrity and perseverance in overcoming adversity; demonstrate critical financial need ($55, 000 or lower adjusted gross family income is required); and, exhibit a strong commitment to pursue and complete a bachelor's degree at an accredited non-profit public or private institution in the United States (students may start their studies at a two-year institution and then transfer to a four-year institution). **Criteria:** Selection will be based on the aforesaid qualifications and compliance with the application process.

Funds Avail.: $10,000. **Duration:** Annual. **Number Awarded:** 21. **To Apply:** Applicants must have one letter of support and must be logged in to the application process at the HAA website. Faxes/e-mails will not be accepted. Students must download the certification page from the HAA web site, complete it and obtain the proper signatures prior to mailing. **Deadline:** October 25. **Remarks:** The scholarships are funded by Ebby Halliday Scholarship.

5580 ■ Horatio Alger Utah Scholarships
(Undergraduate/Scholarship)

Purpose: To provide financial assistance to students in the state of Utah. **Focus:** General studies/Field of study not specified. **Qualif.:** Applicants must be U.S. citizens who are Utah residents, enrolled full time as high school seniors in the United States, and progressing normally toward graduation in spring/summer of the current year with the plan to enter a college in the United States no later than the fall following graduation; must also: be involved in co-curricular and community service activities; display integrity and perseverance in overcoming adversity; demonstrate critical financial need ($55, 000 or lower adjusted gross family income is required); and, exhibit a strong commitment to pursue and complete a bachelor's degree at an accredited non-profit public or private institution in the United States (students may start their studies at a two-year institution and then transfer to a four-year institution). **Criteria:** Selection will be based on the aforesaid qualifications and compliance with the application process.

Funds Avail.: $10,000. **Duration:** Annual. **Number Awarded:** 7. **To Apply:** Applicants must have one letter of support and must be logged in to the application process at the HAA website. Faxes/e-mails will not be accepted. Students must download the certification page from the

HAA web site, complete it and obtain the proper signatures prior to mailing. **Deadline:** October 25. **Remarks:** The scholarships are made possible by its funder, John A. Moran.

5581 ■ Horatio Alger Washington Scholarships
(Undergraduate/Scholarship)

Purpose: To provide financial assistance to students in the state of Washington. **Focus:** General studies/Field of study not specified. **Qualif.:** Applicants must be U.S. citizens who are Washington residents, enrolled full time as high school seniors in the United States, and progressing normally toward graduation in spring/summer of the current year with the plan to enter a college in the United States no later than the fall following graduation; they must also: be involved in co-curricular and community service activities; display integrity and perseverance in overcoming adversity; demonstrate critical financial need ($55, 000 or lower adjusted gross family income is required); and, exhibit a strong commitment to pursue and complete a bachelor's degree at an accredited non-profit public or private institution in the United States (students may start their studies at a two-year institution and then transfer to a four-year institution). **Criteria:** Selection will be based on the aforesaid qualifications and compliance with the application process.

Funds Avail.: $10,000. **Duration:** Annual. **Number Awarded:** 10. **To Apply:** Applicants must have one letter of support and must be logged in to the application process at the HAA website. Faxes/emails will not be accepted. Students must download the certification page from the HAA web site, complete it and obtain the proper signatures prior to mailing. **Deadline:** October 25. **Remarks:** The scholarships are made possible by its funder, Joseph Clark.

5582 ■ Horatio Alger Wyoming Scholarships
(Undergraduate/Scholarship)

Purpose: To provide financial assistance to students in the state of Wyoming. **Focus:** General studies/Field of study not specified. **Qualif.:** Applicants must be U.S. citizens who are Wyoming residents, enrolled full time as high school seniors in the United States, and progressing normally toward graduation in spring/summer of the current year with the plan to enter a college in the United States no later than the fall following graduation; must also: be involved in co-curricular and community service activities; display integrity and perseverance in overcoming adversity; demonstrate critical financial need ($55, 000 or lower adjusted gross family income is required); and, exhibit a strong commitment to pursue and complete a bachelor's degree at an accredited non-profit public or private institution in the United States (students may start their studies at a two-year institution and then transfer to a four-year institution). **Criteria:** Selection will be based on the aforesaid qualifications and compliance with the application process.

Funds Avail.: $10,000. **Duration:** Annual. **Number Awarded:** 5. **To Apply:** Applicants must have one letter of support and must be logged in to the application process at the HAA website. Faxes/e-mails will not be accepted. Students must download the certification page from the HAA web site, complete it and obtain the proper signatures prior to mailing. **Deadline:** October 25. **Remarks:** The scholarships are funded by the Suzanne and Walter Scott Foundation.

5583 ■ Horch Roofing
2414 Camden Rd.
Warren, ME 04864

Awards are arranged alphabetically below their administering organizations

Ph: (207)273-1111
Fax: (207)273-1322
E-mail: office@horchroofing.com
URL: horchroofing.com
Social Media: www.facebook.com/HorchRoofing
www.instagram.com/horchroofing

5584 ■ Horch Roofing Trade School Scholarship
(Vocational/Occupational/Scholarship)

Purpose: To encourage students to study and find gainful employment within the trades. **Focus:** Construction; Education, Vocational-technical; Heating, air conditioning, and refrigeration; Welding. **Qualif.:** Applicant must be a high school senior who will attend a college/trade school or to a current college/trade school student who resides in the state of Maine. **Criteria:** Selection committee will look for a candidates with a proven passion for the trades and enthusiasm to pursue a career in skilled work.

Funds Avail.: $1,000. **Duration:** Annual. **Number Awarded:** 2. **To Apply:** Applicant must submit the following: completed application; brief letter addressed to the scholarship committee and containing background information and a brief explanation of career goals; a letter of recommendation from the applicant's high school teacher/ college professor, administrator, coach, mentor, or employer; a complete high school/college transcript with cumulative GPA and class standing. Application materials are available at horchroofing.com/horch-roofing-trade-school-scholarship/. **Deadline:** May 1.

5585 ■ Horticultural Research Institute (HRI)
525 9th St. NW, Ste. 800
Washington, DC 20004
Ph: (202)789-2900
E-mail: jenniferg@americanhort.org
URL: www.hriresearch.org
Social Media: www.facebook.com/hriresearch
twitter.com/HORTRESEARCH

5586 ■ Bryan A. Champion Memorial Scholarship
(Undergraduate/Scholarship)

Purpose: To provide financial support to students who aim to achieve higher education in horticulture and related fields. **Focus:** Horticulture. **Qualif.:** Applicants must be horticulture students enrolled full- or part-time in programs at the following schools only: The Ohio State University, The Ohio State University Agricultural Technical Institute, Kent State University-Salem, Clark State Community College, Owens Community College, Columbus State Community College, Cuyahoga Community College, Cincinnati State Technical & Community College, and the University of Cincinnati. **Criteria:** Selection will be based on the committee's criteria.

Funds Avail.: $1,000. **To Apply:** Applicants must submit a completed application form along with their statement of purpose, college transcripts, recommendation letter on school letterhead, and a resume. To be submitted by the student directly to the ONLA office.

5587 ■ HostGator.com L.L.C.
5005 Mitchelldale, Ste. 100
Houston, TX 77092
Ph: (713)574-5287
Free: 866-964-2867

URL: www.hostgator.com
Social Media: www.facebook.com/HostGator
instagram.com/hostgator
linkedin.com/company/hostgator-com
twitter.com/hostgator
youtube.com/user/hostgator

5588 ■ HostGator Technology Scholarship *(Community College, Undergraduate, Graduate/Scholarship)*

Purpose: To help students pay for post-secondary education. **Focus:** General studies/Field of study not specified. **Qualif.:** Applicants must be enrolled in an Associate's degree, Bachelor's degree, or graduate-level program at an accredited two- or four-year college or university. **Criteria:** Selection is based on the originality, quality, and innovation of the essay response.

Funds Avail.: $1,500. **Duration:** Annual. **Number Awarded:** 3. **Deadline:** August 30. **Contact:** E-mail: scholarship@hostgator.com.

5589 ■ HostingAdvice.com
15 SE 1st Ave., Ste. B
Gainesville, FL 32601
URL: www.hostingadvice.com
Social Media: www.facebook.com/HostingAdviceCom
twitter.com/Hosting_Advice

5590 ■ HostingAdvice.com Future Web Developers Annual Scholarship *(Undergraduate/Scholarship)*

Purpose: To support development in the IT sector. **Focus:** Computer and information sciences; Information science and technology. **Qualif.:** Applicants must be U.S. residents, graduating high school seniors or college students with a minimum 3.5 GPA, majoring in a computer-science related field.

Funds Avail.: $1,000. **Duration:** Annual. **To Apply:** Complete application; submit official transcripts; write an original essay of 500 to 1,000 words, topic available on website. **Deadline:** September 30. **Contact:** Email: Danielle@ hostingadvice.com; URL: www.hostingadvice.com/ scholarship/.

5591 ■ Houghton Mifflin Harcourt Co.
125 High St.
Boston, MA 02110
Free: 800-323-9239
E-mail: rpc_customer_service@hmhco.com
URL: www.hmhco.com
Social Media: www.facebook.com/houghtonmifflinharcourt
instagram.com/hmhbooks
www.linkedin.com/company/houghton-mifflin-harcourt
pinterest.com/hmhbooks
twitter.com/HMHCo
youtube.com/user/HMHCoTV

5592 ■ Gerda and Kurt Klein Scholarships
(Undergraduate/Scholarship)

Purpose: To recognize and support high school students who foster ethnic and religious tolerance and actively minimize bigotry within their community. **Focus:** General studies/Field of study not specified. **Qualif.:** Applicant must be a high school student who works to affect change in the

Awards are arranged alphabetically below their administering organizations

community by fostering ethnic and religious tolerance and acting against bigotry and hatred. **Criteria:** Award is given based on the submitted application materials.

Funds Avail.: No specific amount. **Duration:** Annual. **To Apply:** Applicants may visit the website to verify the application process and other pieces of information. **Remarks:** Established in 2007.

5593 ■ House of Puerto Rico San Diego (HPRSD)
PO Box 81982
San Diego, CA 92138
Ph: (619)234-3445
E-mail: hprsd@houseofpuertorico.com
URL: www.houseofpuertorico.com
Social Media: www.facebook.com/HouseofPuertoRico

5594 ■ Casilda Pagan Educational/Vocational Scholarships *(Graduate, Undergraduate, Postgraduate/Scholarship)*

Purpose: To assist individuals attain their educational and professional goals. **Focus:** General studies/Field of study not specified. **Criteria:** Selection will be based on need, goal, motivation, application and contribution.

Funds Avail.: No specific amount. **Duration:** Annual. **To Apply:** Applicants must submit a personal essay (minimum of 250 words) including educational goals, financial needs, contribution to community service through the house of Puerto Rico, prior history of community service; proof of current enrollment in an educational or vocational institution; transcripts reflecting most recent academic achievement; three recommendation letters from teachers, counselors, employers or community leaders; completed application form; any additional materials that could enhance application. **Deadline:** July 31. **Contact:** Joe Carballo at jcarballo@san.rr.com.

5595 ■ Houston Geological Society (HGS)
14811 St. Marys Ln., Ste. 250
Houston, TX 77079
Ph: (713)463-9476
Fax: (281)679-5504
E-mail: office@hgs.org
URL: www.hgs.org
Social Media: www.facebook.com/hgs.org
www.instagram.com/hgsorg
www.linkedin.com/groups/2455924/profile
twitter.com/HouGeoSoc
www.youtube.com/user/HGSGeoEducation

5596 ■ W.L. Calvert Memorial Scholarships *(Graduate/Scholarship)*

Purpose: To assist graduate students to pursue a career in some area of economic geology. **Focus:** Earth sciences. **Qualif.:** Applicants must be graduate students who are admitted to a graduate degree program leading to an M.S. or Ph.D. at any accredited U.S. college or university; must be U.S. citizens who are interested in earth sciences or any related field of study. **Criteria:** Applicants will be chosen based on academic record, demonstrated the potential to complete graduate degree requirements as attested by professional earth scientists in academia, government and industry; financial need will be a secondary consideration.

Duration: Annual. **To Apply:** Applicants must complete the application form and must provide an evidence of their acceptance for a graduate study. Application form can be downloaded on sponsor's website. **Deadline:** June 15. **Remarks:** Established in 1974. **Contact:** URL: www.hgs.org/wl-calvert-memorial-scholarship.

5597 ■ HGS Foundation Undergraduate Scholarships *(Undergraduate/Scholarship)*

Purpose: To provide scholarships to deserving undergraduate students majoring in geosciences. **Focus:** Geosciences. **Qualif.:** Applicants must be juniors and seniors in the current academic year; must be enrolled full-time carrying a normal academic load in geosciences; and must be U.S. citizens. **Criteria:** Recipients will be selected based on academic achievement.

Funds Avail.: $1,500. **Duration:** Annual. **To Apply:** Applicants must contact the head of geosciences department for further information. **Remarks:** Established in 1984. **Contact:** URL: www.hgs.org/hgs-undergraduate-foundation-fund.

5598 ■ Houston Intellectual Property Law Association (HIPLA)
Houston, TX 77010
E-mail: lpeschel@jw.com
URL: www.hipla.org
Social Media: www.facebook.com/Houston-Intellectual
-Property-Law-Association-HIPLA-399454887195461

5599 ■ HIPLA Fellowship *(Undergraduate/Fellowship)*

Purpose: To promote development and understanding of the Intellectual Property Law to law students. **Focus:** Law. **Criteria:** Selection is based on student's qualifications and on submitted application materials.

Funds Avail.: Up to $3,000. **Duration:** Annual; At least six weeks. **Number Awarded:** Varies. **To Apply:** Applicants must submit a resume, a letter describing interest in intellectual property law, a letter from the court or USPTO stating that student has been accepted for an internship and a description of any circumstances to be considered. **Deadline:** November 12. **Contact:** Ron Haggerty, Email:ron@ronhaggertylaw.com and Ira Jamshidi, Email:ira.jamshidi@hoganlovells.com.

5600 ■ HIPLA Scholarships for University of Houston Law Center Students *(Graduate, Undergraduate/Scholarship)*

Purpose: To provide financial support to students pursuing a degree in law. **Focus:** Law. **Qualif.:** Applicants must be University of Houston Law Center student who have demonstrated interest in intellectual property law, have completed at least 30 hours of law study and have not previously received a HIPLA scholarship or fellowship. **Criteria:** Selection will be based on students who have interned for a Houston Federal Judge, the U.S. Court of Appeals for the Federal Circuit, or the USPTO.

Funds Avail.: $3,000. **Duration:** Annual. **Number Awarded:** Up to 3. **To Apply:** Applicants must submit an application form; resume; a letter describing your interest in intellectual property law, a letter from the court or the USPTO. **Deadline:** November 12. **Contact:** Houston Intellectual Property Law Association, Palak Shah, Shook, Hardy & Bacon LLP, 600 Travis, Ste. 3400, Houston, TX, 77002-2926; Email: pshah@shb.com.

Awards are arranged alphabetically below their administering organizations

5601 ■ HoustonMovers.com
609 Main St.
Houston, TX 77002
URL: www.houstonmovers.com
Social Media: www.facebook.com/TopHoustonMovers

5602 ■ The HoustonMovers.com Scholarship
(Undergraduate/Scholarship)

Purpose: To help talented students pay for college. **Focus:** General studies/Field of study not specified. **Qualif.:** Applicants must be graduating high school seniors or undergraduate students in the United States who have maintained a minimum 3.0 GPA over the previous school year.

Funds Avail.: $500. **Duration:** Annual. **Number Awarded:** 1. **To Apply:** Complete application and submit a 500 to 750 word essay on the topic, tell us about your hometown. What makes it unique, why do you love living there? **Deadline:** September 1. **Contact:** Email: scholarship@ HoustonMovers.com; URL: www.houstonmovers.com/scholarship.

5603 ■ Houtan Scholarship Foundation
300 Central Ave.
Egg Harbor Township, NJ 08234
E-mail: info@houtan.org
URL: www.houtan.org

5604 ■ Houtan Scholarship *(Graduate/Scholarship)*

Purpose: To support students who have high academic performance and proven interest in promoting Iran's great culture. **Focus:** Area and ethnic studies.

Funds Avail.: $3,500. **Duration:** Annual. **Deadline:** June 1. **Contact:** Houtan Scholarship Foundation 300 Central Ave., Egg Harbor Twp., NJ, 08234, USA; Email: info@houtan.org.

5605 ■ Howard Hughes Medical Institute (HHMI) - Janelia Farm Research Campus
19700 Helix Drive
Ashburn, VA 20147
Ph: (571)209-4000
E-mail: rubing@janelia.hhmi.org
URL: www.janelia.org
Social Media: www.facebook.com/HHMIJRC
www.instagram.com/hhmijanelia
twitter.com/HHMIJanelia

5606 ■ Undergraduate Scholars Program *(Graduate/Scholarship)*

Purpose: To provide an outstanding research experience, an opportunity to network with colleagues at all career levels, and a chance to form lifelong scientific collaborations and friendships. **Focus:** Neuroscience; Technology. **Criteria:** Applicants are evaluated on the basis of their recommendation letters and descriptions of previous research, as well as their statement of how they will contribute to a Janelia lab.

Funds Avail.: $5,000. **Duration:** Annual. **Number Awarded:** 16. **To Apply:** Applicants must submit statement of rationale; statement of career goals; description of prior independent research (not research as part of a course or a lab); identification of Janelia scientists they would like to

work and why list of completed science and math courses or an unofficial college transcript; names of two references for submit a letter of recommendation; both letters of reference must be received before the full application can be submitted. **Remarks:** Established in 2007.

5607 ■ HSMAI Global
7918 Jones Branch Dr., Ste. 300
McLean, VA 22102
Ph: (703)506-3280
Fax: (703)506-3266
E-mail: info@hsmai.org
URL: www.hsmai.org
Social Media: www.facebook.com/HSMAI
www.linkedin.com/company/hsmai
twitter.com/hsmai
www.youtube.com/user/HSMAI1

5608 ■ HSMAI Foundation Scholarship *(Graduate/Scholarship)*

Purpose: To provide financial assistance to students pursuing associate, baccalaureate and graduate degrees in Hospitality Management or related fields. **Focus:** Hotel, institutional, and restaurant management. **Qualif.:** Applicant must be enrolled as a student in a hospitality management or related curriculum; pursuing a degree; must have hospitality work experience; must demonstrate an interest in a career in hospitality sales and marketing; must be in good academic standing. **Criteria:** Recipients are evaluated based on Grade Point Average, Industry-related work experience, Presentation of application, Involvement in HSMAI, Responses to essay questions, Recommendations, and Extracurricular involvement.

Funds Avail.: No specific amount. **Duration:** Annual. **To Apply:** Applicants must submit completed typed application form; transcript from current college or university; two recommendation forms; current resume; and three personal essays. Applicants must send their completed applications to Foundation Scholarship Committee. **Remarks:** Established in 1983. **Contact:** Email: ktindell@hsmai.org.

5609 ■ Hubbell Canada L.P.
870 Brock Rd. S
Pickering, ON, Canada L1W 1Z8
Ph: (905)839-1138
Fax: (905)839-9108
Free: 800-465-7051
E-mail: infohclp@hubbell-canada.com
URL: hubbell-canada.com
Social Media: www.linkedin.com/company/hubbell -canada-lp

5610 ■ Hubbell Canada LP "Electrical Industry Leadership" Scholarship Awards *(Undergraduate/Scholarship)*

Purpose: To support students who have demonstrated interests in a career path that will drive innovation and leadership in the electrical industry in Canada. **Focus:** Electronics; Engineering, Electrical. **Qualif.:** Applicants must be students enrolled in a Canadian university who have completed at least their first year of study in Business, Engineering or Science with a minimum cumulative

Awards are arranged alphabetically below their administering organizations

average of 80%. **Criteria:** Selection will be based on the applicants' eligibility and other criteria of the committee.

Funds Avail.: 3,500 Canadian Dollars. **Duration:** Annual. **To Apply:** Applicants may visit the website for them to create an account to apply for the scholarship, as well as for the other application materials required. **Deadline:** May 31. **Remarks:** The scholarship is co-sponsored by the Hubbell, Inc.

5611 ■ Hudson River Foundation (HRF)

17 Battery Pl., Ste. 915
New York, NY 10004
Ph: (212)483-7667
Fax: (212)924-8325
E-mail: info@hudsonriver.org
URL: www.hudsonriver.org
Social Media: www.facebook.com/HudsonRiverFoundation
twitter.com/harborestuary

5612 ■ Mark B. Bain Graduate Fellowship *(Doctorate, Master's, Graduate/Fellowship)*

Purpose: To support advanced graduate students conducting research on the Hudson River system. **Focus:** General studies/Field of study not specified. **Qualif.:** Applicants must be enrolled in an accredited doctoral or master's program, must have thesis advisor and advisory committee (if appropriate to the institution), and must have thesis research plan approved by the student's institution or department. **Criteria:** Selection is based on the submitted application and materials.

Funds Avail.: $15,000 for doctoral students; $11,000 for Master's level students. **Duration:** Annual. **Number Awarded:** up to 6. **To Apply:** Applicants must submit a proposal cover page; a description of the thesis project (maximum of 10 pages); a timetable for the completion of the research; an estimated cost of supplies, travel, etc.; applicant's curriculum vitae; a letter from the University stating that the Applicants will receive a tuition waiver or reimbursement for the period of the fellowship; and two letters of recommendation (one from an advisor, mailed directly to the Foundation). **Deadline:** March 9. **Remarks:** Established with a bequest from the late Dr. Mark B. Bain for his outstanding contributions to Hudson River science. **Contact:** Applications should be mailed to: Graduate Fellowship Committee, Hudson River Foundation, 17 Battery Pl., Ste. 915, New York, NY 10004; Electronic submission: Email: info@hudsonriver.org; Helena Andreyko; Phone: 212-483-7667.

5613 ■ Tibor T. Polgar Fellowship *(Graduate, Undergraduate/Fellowship)*

Purpose: To provide summertime grant and research funds for college students to conduct research on the Hudson River. **Focus:** General studies/Field of study not specified. **Qualif.:** Applicants must be undergraduate or graduate students who will conduct research on the Hudson River. **Criteria:** Selection is based on submitted application materials.

Funds Avail.: $3,800. **Duration:** Annual. **Number Awarded:** 8. **To Apply:** Applications should include a letter of interest in the program, a short description (4-6 pages) of the research project, a timetable of the research, an estimated cost of supplies and travel expenses, a letter of support from student's advisor and curriculum vitae. **Deadline:** August 21. **Remarks:** Established with a bequest from

the late Tibor T. Polgar, a major contributor to the early development of the Foundation. **Contact:** Polgar Fellowship Committee, Hudson River, Foundation, 17 Battery Pl., Ste. 915, New York, NY, 10004; For questions: Helena Andreyko, Phone: 212-483-7667.

5614 ■ Howard Hughes Medical Institute (HHMI)

4000 Jones Bridge Rd.
Chevy Chase, MD 20815-6789
Ph: (301)215-8500
URL: www.hhmi.org
Social Media: www.facebook.com/HowardHughesMed
twitter.com/hhminews
www.youtube.com/c/hhmi

5615 ■ Gilliam Fellowships for Advanced Study *(Postdoctorate, Master's, Graduate/Fellowship)*

Purpose: To offer an extraordinary opportunity to pursue graduate studies in the life sciences. **Focus:** Biomedical research. **Qualif.:** Applicant must adviser-student pairs from eligible disciplines must be nominated by the HHMI-designated institutional representative. Prospective fellows must be I) U.S. citizens, U.S. permanent residents, undocumented childhood arrivals, or undocumented.**Criteria:** Fellowships are awarded on the basis of the candidate's promise as a scientific investigator and potential for leadership in the scientific community, as reflected by academic records, relevant educational and personal experiences, previous accomplishment and goals, research experience, proposed research plan, references and scores attained on the Graduate Record Examination general test or the Medical College Admission Test.

Funds Avail.: $50,000. **Duration:** Annual; up to 3 years. **To Apply:** Applicants are expected to complete an application, which will be made available electronically to all eligible Exceptional Research Opportunities Program (EXROP) students. The application will be submitted via HHMI's web-based competition system at www.hhmi.org/competitions. A complete application consists of the following items: applicant information including name, current and permanent addresses, email address and other pertinent information; educational history including names of all colleges and universities attended, dates of attendance and degrees obtained; all undergraduate transcripts (to be sent to HHMI directly by institutions attended); list of relevant honors, awards and professional activities; educational and personal experiences relevant to applicant's career goals and objectives; research experiences, including dates, project summary and the applicant's role in the project; list of publications, presentations and posters, if applicable; proposed research plan with literature cited; leadership statement demonstrating leadership potential and/or how receipt of the Gilliam Fellowship will help advance scientific careers of underrepresented students; three letters of reference sent directly to HHMI. Letters should be from those who can speak best to potential as a scientist, and one from HHMI program director; recent score on the Graduate Record Examination General Test or Medical College Admission Test. **Deadline:** December 10.

5616 ■ HHMI International Student Research Fellowships *(Doctorate/Fellowship)*

Purpose: To support outstanding international pre-doctoral students studying in the United States who are ineligible for fellowships or training grants through U.S. federal agencies. **Focus:** Biomedical research. **Qualif.:** Applicants must

Awards are arranged alphabetically below their administering organizations

be in their 3rd or 4th year of a PhD program in the biomedical or related sciences at a designated nominating institution; have demonstrated exceptional talent for research; have entered laboratory in which they will conduct their dissertation research; must not be U.S. citizens, non-citizens or permanent residents of the United States. **Criteria:** Selection will be based on their promise as scientific investigators.

Funds Avail.: $43,000. **Duration:** Up to 3 years. **To Apply:** Application will be submitted online using HHMI's web-based competition system at www.hhmi.org/competitions. A complete application will consist of the following: applicant information, including name, contact information and email address; graduate degree information, including name of department/program, date of entry into the graduate program and name and email address of the dissertation advisor(s); description of intended dissertation research with a limited bibliography of key references; brief discussion of the significance and innovation of the intended research project; research experiences, including dates, project summary and the applicant's role in the project; list of publications, presentations and posters, if applicable; list of relevant honors, awards and professional activities; letters of reference. One letter must be from the applicant's dissertation advisor. Other letters should be from those who can speak best to the applicant's potential as a researcher. These letters must be uploaded in the competition system by the reference writer; educational history, including names of all colleges and universities attended, dates of attendance and degrees obtained; graduate transcripts (to be uploaded by the applicant); scores on the GRE or MCAT and TOEFL.

5617 ■ HHMI Medical Research Fellowship
(Undergraduate/Fellowship)

Purpose: To support students to pursue biomedical research training. **Focus:** Biomedical research. **Qualif.:** Applicants must be enrolled in a medical, dental or veterinary school located in the United States; fellowship research may be conducted at any academic or nonprofit institution in the United States, except the National Institutes of Health. **Criteria:** Selection will be based on applicant's ability and promise for a research career as a physician-scientist or medically trained researcher and the quality of the training that will be provided.

Funds Avail.: Totally $43,000. **To Apply:** Applicants must submit their components (including research proposal), along with mentor's components (and co-mentor, if applicable), Dean's confirmation, and two reference letters.

5618 ■ Hughes Memorial Foundation
223 Riverview Dr., Ste. I
Danville, VA 24541
Ph: (434)799-2412
Fax: (434)799-3089
URL: www.hughesmemorialfoundation.org
Social Media: www.facebook.com/
HughesMemorialFoundation

5619 ■ Hughes Memorial Foundatio n *(Other/Scholarship)*

Purpose: To provide financial assistance to needy students and be able to further their career. **Focus:** General studies/Field of study not specified. **Qualif.:** Applicants must be needy at-risk children living in the Virginia counties of Pittsylvania, Halifax, Mecklenburg, Charlotte, Campbell, Bed-

ford, Franklin, Henry, and Patrick; the North Carolina counties of Stokes, Rockingham, Caswell, and Person; and the cities of Virginia and North Carolina that are located geographically within those counties; must have a minimum of 2.5 GPA. **Criteria:** Selection will be based on financial need;accuracy and completeness of application;full-time status (minimum of 12 credit hours).

Funds Avail.: No specific amount. **Duration:** Annual. **Number Awarded:** Varies. **To Apply:** Applicants must submit a completed application form for Federal Student Aid; Student aid report; parents' Federal Income Tax Return; parents or guardians' federal income tax return used in the completion of the FAFSA or for most current filing period; official transcripts from all high schools or colleges attended. **Deadline:** April 1. **Contact:** For submissions, Hughes Memorial Foundation, Scholarship Applications, 223 Riverview Dr., Ste. I, Danville, VA, 24541.

5620 ■ Huguenot Society of South Carolina
138 Logan St.
Charleston, SC 29401-1941
Ph: (843)723-3235
Fax: (843)853-8476
URL: www.huguenotsociety.org
Social Media: www.facebook.com/
HuguenotSocietyOfSouthCarolina

5621 ■ Huguenot Society of South Carolina Graduate Scholarship *(Graduate/Scholarship)*

Purpose: To support students working toward a graduate degree in history. **Focus:** History. **Qualif.:** Applicants must be students working toward a graduate degree in history.

Funds Avail.: $1,000. **Duration:** Annual. **Number Awarded:** 1. **To Apply:** Applicants must submit two hard copies of the essay, as well as a cover letter giving full name, address, telephone number, details of the undergraduate degree and also the graduate degree currently in progress, and the thesis and significance of the paper. The text should not exceed 25 typed and double-spaced pages, excluding footnotes, illustrations and bibliography (one-inch margins for the top, bottom, left, and right). All submissions must include footnotes and any other necessary documentation. Titles of the works cited in the essay and notes should be typed in italics and indexed if possible, using the standards set forth in the Chicago Manual of Style, 15th Edition. The essay must be a work of scholarship on a Huguenot topic; may examine any aspect of the religious, political, economic, social, or intellectual history of the French or Walloon Protestants from the sixteenth century to the present; may deal with any appropriate geographical area. Submissions must be original, not previously published and not under consideration by another publication. The author of the winning essay will be asked to submit a copy of their paper on a MS Word-Compatible CD. **Deadline:** December 31. **Contact:** Huguenot Society of South Carolina, 138 Logan St., Charleston, South Carolina 29401-1941; Phone: 843-723-3235.

5622 ■ Mary Mouzon Darby Undergraduate Scholarship *(Undergraduate/Scholarship)*

Purpose: To financially support undergraduate students. **Focus:** General studies/Field of study not specified. **Qualif.:** Applicant must be of Huguenot descent and either a member of the Huguenot Society of South Carolina or the child or grandchild of a current member of the Society; must be an undergraduate student.

Awards are arranged alphabetically below their administering organizations

Funds Avail.: $1,000. **Duration:** Annual. **Deadline:** December 31. **Remarks:** Established in 2007. **Contact:** Huguenot Society of South Carolina, 138 Logan St., Charleston, SC 29401-1941; Phone; 843-723-3235.

5623 ■ Human Race Theatre Company
126 N Main St., Ste. 300
Dayton, OH 45402-1766
Ph: (937)461-3823
Fax: (937)461-7223
E-mail: contact@humanracetheatre.org
URL: www.humanracetheatre.org
Social Media: www.facebook.com/humanracetheatre
instagram.com/humanracetheatre
twitter.com/HRTC_Dayton
youtube.com/user/HumanRaceTheatre

5624 ■ Stephen Schwartz Musical Theatre Scholarship *(Undergraduate/Scholarship)*

Purpose: To support student singers or actors in the greater Dayton area. **Focus:** Theater arts. **Qualif.:** Applicants must have a permanent address in Montgomery County or one of seven contiguous counties (Preble, Darke, Miami, Clark, Greene, Warren or Butler) or be currently enrolled at a college in one of the eight counties previously listed. **Criteria:** Selection will be based upon their application, letter of recommendation and their video submission.

Duration: Annual. **Number Awarded:** 2. **To Apply:** Applicants must submit a completed application along with a letter of recommendation and video. **Remarks:** Established in 2007. **Contact:** President and Artistic Director, Kevin Moore; Phone: 937-461-3823 X 3115; Email: kevin@humanracetheatre.org.

5625 ■ Human Resources Research Organization (HUMRRO)
66 Canal Center Plz., Ste. 700
Alexandria, VA 22314-1578
Ph: (703)549-3611
Fax: (703)548-2860
E-mail: socialmedia@humrro.org
URL: www.humrro.org
Social Media: www.facebook.com/Human-Resources
  -Research-Organization-HumRRO-161583990533313
www.linkedin.com/company/humrro
twitter.com/HumRROorg
www.youtube.com/user/humrro

5626 ■ Meredith P. Crawford Fellowship in I-O Psychology *(Doctorate/Fellowship)*

Purpose: To provide financial support while the student completes dissertation in the field of Industrial-Organizational (I-O) Psychology, or in a field congruent with the objectives of the Society for Industrial Psychology. **Focus:** Psychology. **Qualif.:** Applicants must be a doctoral candidate in I-O Psychology or a closely related discipline whose dissertation topic has been proposed and approved by graduate faculty. **Criteria:** Applicants will be evaluated on the basis of merit, research promise, academic achievement and professional productivity.

Funds Avail.: $12,000 stipend. **Duration:** Annual. **Number Awarded:** 1. **To Apply:** Applicants must provide a completed application form, a personal statement, three completed recommendation forms and an official transcript from each institution attended for graduate academic work. **Deadline:** July 1. **Contact:** Human Resources Research Organization; Email: fellowship@humrro.org.

5627 ■ Human Rights Campaign (HRC)
1640 Rhode Island Ave. NW
Washington, DC 20036-3278
Ph: (202)628-4160
Fax: (202)347-5323
URL: www.hrc.org
Social Media: www.facebook.com/humanrightscampaign
www.instagram.com/humanrightscampaign
twitter.com/HRC

5628 ■ McCleary Law Fellows Program *(Graduate, Undergraduate/Fellowship)*

Purpose: To provide training opportunities for law students. **Focus:** Law. **Criteria:** Selection is based on the submitted application materials.

Funds Avail.: No specific amount. **To Apply:** Applicants must submit, via e-mail, a cover letter; resume; brief legal writing sample.

5629 ■ Human Rights in China (HRIC)
110 Wall St.
New York, NY 10123
Ph: (212)239-4495
E-mail: hrichina@hrichina.org
URL: www.hrichina.org
Social Media: twitter.com/hrichina

5630 ■ Robert L. Bernstein Fellowships in International Human Rights *(Graduate/Fellowship)*

Purpose: To enable an NYU Law School graduate to devote a year to full-time human rights work at HRIC. **Focus:** Human rights; Law. **Criteria:** Selection will be based on the committee's criteria.

Funds Avail.: $50,000 plus benefits. **To Apply:** Application must include the following: cover letter, resume, two letters of recommendation, at least one individually written and edited writing sample; an official transcript, an essay of no more than 250 words, describing one key human rights challenge facing China. **Deadline:** October 22. **Remarks:** The award was established in honor of Mr. Bernstein, Director and Chair Emeritus of HRIC and founding chair and director emeritus of human rights. **Contact:** HRIC, Fellowship Committee, 110 Wall St., New York, NY, 10005; Email: fellowships@hrichina.org.

5631 ■ Human Rights Resource Center (HRRC)
University of Minnesota Law School
229 19th Ave. S, Ste. N-120
Minneapolis, MN 55455
Ph: (612)626-0041
Fax: (612)625-2011
Free: 888-473-3828
E-mail: humanrts@umn.edu
URL: www.hrusa.org

5632 ■ Upper Midwest Human Rights Fellowship Program *(Graduate/Scholarship, Fellowship)*

Purpose: To promote social justice by providing practical experience related to international human rights. **Focus:**

Awards are arranged alphabetically below their administering organizations

Human rights. **Qualif.:** Applicants must be law students and graduate students at the University of Minnesota.

Funds Avail.: $1,000 - $5,000 for transportation, lodging, and food expenses incurred during the fellowship period. **Duration:** Annual. **To Apply:** Applicants must submit a complete application form available online; must provide the confirmation letter from host; transcript (from last ten years only); a cover letter/resume; one letter of reference; and a 2-3-page essay detailing the following: (1) Significance of the experience for their academic or professional training, (2) Relationship of the fellowship to future goals, (3) How the host organization will benefit from a fellowship, (4) Description of the key aspects of a current human rights issue in the country/location of the proposed fellowship and how the sponsoring organization addresses it; (5) Description of how they will use their new human rights experiences in their community upon their return home. **Deadline:** February 6. **Contact:** Willa Gelvick, Fellowship Coordinator at 612-626-2226 or hrfellow@umn.edu.

5633 ■ Human Rights Watch (HRW)
350 5th Ave., 34th Fl.
New York, NY 10118-3299
Ph: (212)290-4700
URL: www.hrw.org
Social Media: www.facebook.com/HumanRightsWatch
www.instagram.com/humanrightswatch
twitter.com/hrw
www.youtube.com/user/HumanRightsWatch

5634 ■ Alan R. and Barbara D. Finberg Fellowships
(Graduate/Fellowship)

Purpose: To support and mentor graduates of law schools or graduates of journalism, international relations, area studies, or other relevant disciplines. **Focus:** Area and ethnic studies; International affairs and relations; Journalism; Law. **Criteria:** Selection is based on Applicant's qualifications and submitted application materials.

Funds Avail.: $55,000. **Duration:** one year. **To Apply:** Applicants must submit a complete application packet which includes a cover letter; resume (curriculum vitae); two letters of recommendation; at least one unedited, unpublished writing sample; and an official law or graduate school transcript. Applications should be sent by e-mail, under a single cover and as PDF files with the name of the fellowship being applied in the subject line. **Deadline:** October 8. **Contact:** E-mail: fellowship@hrw.org.

5635 ■ Aryeh Neier Fellowships *(Graduate/Fellowship)*

Purpose: To support and mentor recent law school graduates. **Focus:** Law. **Criteria:** Selection is based on Applicant's qualifications and submitted application materials.

Funds Avail.: $55,000. **Duration:** Annual; two years. **To Apply:** Applicants must submit a complete application packet which must include a cover letter; resume (curriculum vitae); two letters of recommendation; at least one unedited, unpublished writing sample; and an official law or graduate school transcript. Applications should be sent by e-mail, under single cover and as PDF files with the name of the fellowship being applied in the subject line. **Deadline:** October 15. **Contact:** E-mail: fellowship@hrw.org.

5636 ■ Leonard H. Sandler Fellowships *(Graduate/Fellowship)*

Purpose: To support and mentor graduates of Columbia Law School. **Focus:** Law. **Criteria:** Selection is based on

Applicant's qualification and submitted application materials.

Funds Avail.: $55,000. **Duration:** one year. **To Apply:** Applicants must submit a complete application packet which must include a cover letter; resume (curriculum vitae); two letters of recommendation; at least one unedited, unpublished writing sample; and an official law or graduate school transcript. Applications should be sent by e-mail, under a single cover and as PDF files with the name of the fellowship being applied in the subject line. **Deadline:** October 15. **Contact:** E-mail: fellowship@hrw.org.

5637 ■ The Humane Society of the United States (HSUS)
1255 23rd St., NW, Ste. 450
Washington, DC 20037
Ph: (202)452-1100
Free: 866-720-2676
E-mail: donorcare@humanesociety.org
URL: www.humanesociety.org
Social Media: www.facebook.com/humanesociety
www.instagram.com/humanesociety
twitter.com/HumaneSociety
www.youtube.com/user/hsus

5638 ■ Shaw-Worth Memorial Scholarship
(Undergraduate/Scholarship)

Purpose: To help students achieve their dreams of working in the service of animals, the environment and humankind. **Focus:** Animal rights. **Qualif.:** Applicants must be high school seniors who have made contributions to animal protection; must be from New England public, private and vocational schools. **Criteria:** Recipients will be selected based on submitted application materials; scholastic standing and financial need are not the basis for the award.

Funds Avail.: Up to $3,500. **To Apply:** Applicants must submit letter of narrative statement of achievements and attitude towards animal protection. Applicants must submit a documentation of activities such as recommendations from at least three persons and description of future plans for humane work. Supporting letters from teachers, mentors, supervisors, peers and other observers are not required but may help. Applications should include the student's home address and phone numbers. **Deadline:** March 25. **Remarks:** Established in 1965. **Contact:** Shaw-Worth Memorial Scholarship, 1255 23rd St. NW, Ste. 450, Washington, DC, 20037.

5639 ■ Humboldt State University - Schatz Energy Research Center (SERC)
1 Harpst St.
Arcata, CA 95521
Ph: (707)826-4345
E-mail: serc@humboldt.edu
URL: schatzcenter.org

5640 ■ Schatz Energy Fellowships for Graduate Studies *(Graduate/Fellowship, Recognition)*

Purpose: To provide training and experience to graduate students who intend to focus on renewable energy or energy efficiency related work. **Focus:** Energy-related areas. **Qualif.:** Applicants must be admitted to the Environmental Resources Engineering (ERE) and Energy, Technol-

Awards are arranged alphabetically below their administering organizations

ogy, and Policy (ETaP) graduate program at Humboldt State University and intend to focus on renewable energy or energy efficiency related work. **Criteria:** Selection is based on the application.

Funds Avail.: $15,000. **Duration:** Annual. **To Apply:** All applicants who indicate an interest in energy systems are automatically considered for the three clean energy fellowships. In your graduate application essay, please discuss the line of research or project work that you propose to pursue at HSU, and how your prior studies and experience have prepared you for this pursuit. **Deadline:** February 1. **Contact:** Email: serc@humboldt.edu.

5641 ■ Hungarian American Coalition (HAC)
2121 Decatur Pl. NW
Washington, DC 20038
Ph: (202)296-9505
Fax: (202)775-5175
E-mail: hac@hacusa.org
URL: www.hacusa.org
Social Media: www.facebook.com/
HungarianAmericanCoalition

5642 ■ Dr. Elemer and Eva Kiss Scholarship Fund
(Undergraduate/Scholarship)

Purpose: To provide partial annual scholarships to Hungarian students to pursue studies at U.S. colleges and universities. **Focus:** General studies/Field of study not specified.

Funds Avail.: $500-1,000. **Duration:** Annual. **To Apply:** Applicants must provide proof of scholarship and other sources of financial support; record of excellent academic standing; and two letters of recommendation regarding the applicant's personal and academic achievements. **Deadline:** September 1. **Remarks:** The scholarship was renamed as a special memorial by the family and friends of Dr. Elemer and Eva Kiss, of Chevy Chase, Maryland. Dr. and Mrs. Kiss, members of the Coalition since its founding in 1991, left Hungary after the 1956 Hungarian revolution, and settled with their family in Maryland; they demonstrated a life-long commitment to education both in Hungary and in the United States. Established in 1997. **Contact:** Email: scholarship@hacusa.org.

5643 ■ Hungarian-American Enterprise Scholarship Fund (HAESF)
300 Fore St.
Portland, ME 04101
Ph: (207)553-4130
E-mail: llyons@ciee.org
URL: www.haesf.org
Social Media: www.facebook.com/HAESF

5644 ■ HAESF Graduate Scholarships *(Graduate/Scholarship)*

Purpose: To provide opportunities for Hungarian Society leaders to receive an international education that leads to professional occupations. **Focus:** General studies/Field of study not specified. **Qualif.:** Applicants must be recent graduate students who have obtained their five-year program in any Hungarian university. Applicants who have obtained their three years of education under the old curriculum and continued their remaining two years under the new higher education system are eligible to apply; must maintain a minimum of 3.0 GPA; must hold a Hungarian

passport; and must be accepted to an American university/college, or certificate-granting institution. **Criteria:** Applicants will be judged based on potential future contributions to Hungarian Society; professional objectives to the values and mission of HAESF; articulated professional goals; professionalism; strength of recommendations; ability to serve as ambassadors of Hungary; communication skills; diversity of majors and professional interests; project proposal.

Funds Avail.: $18,000. **To Apply:** Applicants must fill out the HAESF Professional Internship Program Application form; must submit a personal statement, current curriculum vitae, a copy of transcript of records (translated in English), a letter signed in English which includes the average of all subjects taken and any related to the major field of study, a copy of diploma, copies of relevant certificates of completion and three letters of reference discussing the Relationship with applicants; Internship's relevance for applicant's future and career goals; Assessment of applicant's character, abilities, strength and weaknesses; English language communication skill. **Contact:** HAESF's Program Officer, at the above address or Email: info@haesf.org.

5645 ■ HAESF Professional Internship Program
(Doctorate/Internship)

Purpose: To provide opportunities for Hungarian society leaders to have an international training experience. **Focus:** Agriculture, Economic aspects; Art; Business; Communications; Media arts; Medicine; Public administration; Public health; Social sciences.

Duration: 6 months.

5646 ■ Senior Leaders & Scholars Fellowship
(Other, Professional development/Fellowship)

Purpose: To help mid-level and senior-level Hungarian professionals who are pursuing their projects in the United States. **Focus:** Business; Public administration. **Qualif.:** Applicants must be individual professional development.

Deadline: September 30.

5647 ■ Beatrice Hunter Cancer Research Institute (BHCRI)
5850 College St., Ste. 2L-A2
Halifax, NS, Canada B3H 4R2
Ph: (902)494-8970
Fax: (902)494-8472
E-mail: admin@bhcri.ca
URL: bhcri.ca
Social Media: facebook.com/bhcri
twitter.com/BHCRI

5648 ■ BHCRI Bridge Funds *(Advanced Professional, Professional development/Grant)*

Purpose: To support professionals in their cancer-related research. **Focus:** Oncology.

Funds Avail.: 25,000 Canadian Dollars per annum. **Duration:** Up to 2 years. **To Apply:** Applicant should check sponsor website for current availability of this award: bhcri.ca/investigator-awards.

5649 ■ BHCRI Cancer Research Training Program (CRTP) Awards *(Graduate, Postdoctorate, Advanced Professional, Professional development/Grant)*

Purpose: To provide training and funding to graduate students, medical residents, postdoctoral fellows, and clini-

Awards are arranged alphabetically below their administering organizations

cal research fellows involved in cancer research at recognized institutions in Atlantic Canada. **Focus:** Oncology. **Qualif.:** Applicants must be graduate students, medical residents, postdoctoral fellows, or clinical research fellows involved in cancer research at recognized institutions in Atlantic Canada. Meanwhile, supervisors must be senior scientists, associate members or honorary members (qualifying a senior scientists or associate members) of the Institute.

Funds Avail.: No specific amount. **Duration:** Annual. **To Apply:** Applicants must submit a signed cover letter which includes confirmation of cancer-related research; completed application form (provided at the BHCRI website), signed and dated; completed funding overlap declaration, signed and dated; and full common curriculum vitae of applicants with appropriate Tri-Council formatting. Send complete application package via e-mail or mail the original application to the BHCRI. **Deadline:** October 1.

5650 ■ BHCRI Matching Funds (Advanced Professional, Professional development/Grant)

Purpose: To support professionals in their cancer-related research. **Focus:** Oncology. **Qualif.:** Applicants must be BHCRI senior scientists, associate members or honorary members (qualifying as senior scientists or associate members) in good standing and whose project is clearly focused on cancer.

Funds Avail.: 25,000 Canadian Dollars per annum. **Duration:** Up to 3 years. **To Apply:** Applicant should check sponsor's website for current availability of this award: bhcri.ca/investigator-awards.

5651 ■ BHCRI Miscellaneous Funds (Advanced Professional, Professional development/Grant)

Purpose: To support professionals in their cancer-related research. **Focus:** Oncology. **Qualif.:** Applicants must be BHCRI Senior Scientists, Associate Members, or Honorary Members (qualifying as Senior Scientists or Associate Members) in good standing and whose project is clearly focused on cancer.

Funds Avail.: 10,000 Canadian Dollars. **To Apply:** Application form and details available online at bhcri.ca/investigator-awards.

5652 ■ BHCRI Seed Funds (Advanced Professional, Professional development/Grant)

Purpose: To support professionals in their cancer-related research. **Focus:** Oncology. **Qualif.:** Applicants must be Principal Investigators including BHCRI Senior Scientists, Associate Members or Honorary Members (qualifying as Senior Scientists or Associate Members in Atlantic Canada) in good standing and whose project is clearly focused on cancer.

Funds Avail.: 10,000 Canadian Dollars. **To Apply:** Application form and details available online at bhcri.ca/investigator-awards.

5653 ■ BHCRI Studentship Awards (Undergraduate, Graduate, Advanced Professional/Grant)

Purpose: To support cancer research by students. **Focus:** Oncology. **Qualif.:** Applicants must be at recognized institutions across Atlantic Canada. Supervisors must be a Scientist, Senior Scientist, Associate Member or Honorary Member (qualifying as a Scientist, Senior Scientist or Associate Member) of the Institute.

Funds Avail.: 5,000 Canadian dollars each. **Duration:** Annual. **Number Awarded:** Up to 6. **To Apply:** Application

details available at bhcri.ca/studentship-awards.

5654 ■ Huntington Ingalls Industries, Inc. (HII)
4101 Washington Ave.
Newport News, VA 23607
Ph: (757)380-2000
URL: www.huntingtoningalls.com
Social Media: www.facebook.com/
  HuntingtonIngallsIndustries
www.instagram.com/huntingtoningalls
www.linkedin.com/company/huntingtoningalls
twitter.com/hiindustries
www.youtube.com/c/huntingtoningalls

5655 ■ HII Scholarship Fund (Community College, Two Year College, Four Year College, Undergraduate, University/Scholarship)

Purpose: To help dependents of company's employees afford a college education. **Focus:** General studies/Field of study not specified. **Qualif.:** Applicants must be dependent children of Huntington Ingalls Industries (HII) employees and enrolled in post-secondary (two- or four-year) programs. **Criteria:** Scholarship and financial need are both considerations in selection.

Funds Avail.: $1,500 to $3,000. **Duration:** Annual. **Number Awarded:** Up to 50. **To Apply:** Register for an account at sponsor website; provide current transcripts and completed application. **Deadline:** April 16. **Contact:** Email: hii-scholarship@scholarshipamerica.org; URL: apply.scholarsapply.org/hii-scholarship/register.php.

5656 ■ Huntington's Disease Society of America (HDSA)
505 8th Ave., Ste. 902
New York, NY 10018
Ph: (212)242-1968
Free: 800-345-4372
E-mail: hdsainfo@hdsa.org
URL: hdsa.org
Social Media: www.facebook.com/HDSofA
instagram.com/hdsanational
www.linkedin.com/company/huntington's-disease-society
  -of-america
twitter.com/HDSA

5657 ■ HDSA Research Grants (Graduate/Grant)

Purpose: To provide seed funding for new or innovative research projects. **Focus:** Huntington's disease. **Criteria:** Recipients are selected based on the potential of their research.

Funds Avail.: No specific amount. **To Apply:** Applicants may visit the website or contact Huntington's Disease Society of America for more details.

5658 ■ The Donald A. King Summer Research Fellowship (Undergraduate/Fellowship)

Purpose: To provide support to young scientist for their research. **Focus:** Huntington's disease. **Qualif.:** Applicants must be undergraduate life sciences students, pre-medical students, and first-year medical students who are currently attending accredited institutions in the United States; the students will conduct full-time research, under the direction

Awards are arranged alphabetically below their administering organizations

of a mentor, investigating a subject relevant to Huntington's disease. **Criteria:** Recipients are selected according to the potential of their research.

Funds Avail.: $4,000. **Duration:** Annual. **To Apply:** Applicant must complete the online application form outlining their project, and can only submit the form with an endorsement from a faculty mentor who will supervise the student. **Remarks:** The Fellowship was established in honor of Donald King, served as HDSA's Chairman of the Board from 1999 to 2003. **Contact:** Leora Fox; E-mail: lfox@hdsa.org.

5659 ■ Don King Student Fellowships
(Undergraduate/Fellowship)

Purpose: To sponsor HD investigations that can be conducted over a 10-week period. **Focus:** Huntington's disease. **Qualif.:** Applicants must be matriculated undergraduate life sciences students, pre-medical students, and first-year medical students who are currently attending accredited institutions in the United States where HDSA sponsors ongoing HD research. **Criteria:** Selection is based on the academic credentials, scientific merit of the proposed project and the relevance of the proposal to HD.

Funds Avail.: $4,000. **Duration:** Annual. **Deadline:** March 3.

5660 ■ Hydro Research Foundation (HRF)
8200 Shaffer Pkwy Ste. 270585
Littleton, CO 80127
Ph: (720)722-0473
E-mail: info@hydrofoundation.org
URL: www.hydrofoundation.org
Social Media: www.instagram.com/hydrofoundation
www.linkedin.com/company/hydro-research-foundation
  -students

5661 ■ Hydro Research Foundation Fellowships
(Advanced Professional/Fellowship)

Purpose: To stimulate new student research and academic interest in research and careers in conventional or pumped storage hydropower. **Focus:** Hydrology. **Qualif.:** Applicants must be Master's or Post-Master's graduate students enrolled full-time at a U.S. university. **Criteria:** Fellows will be selected based on research vision, innovation, academic performance, potential for leadership and overall strength of the research proposal.

Funds Avail.: Approximately $55,000-$141,000 over the one to three year period of study. **Duration:** Annual. **Number Awarded:** Varies. **To Apply:** Applicants must complete an application form; must submit a research proposal, release form, copy of transcript(s), copy of GRE scores, resume, two references, letter of support from university department, supporting documents (optional).

5662 ■ Hydrocephalus Association (HA)
4340 East-West Hwy., Ste. 905
Bethesda, MD 20814-4447
Ph: (301)202-3811
Fax: (301)202-3813
Free: 888-598-3789
E-mail: info@hydroassoc.org
URL: www.hydroassoc.org
Social Media: www.facebook.com/HydroAssoc
www.instagram.com/hydroassoc

www.linkedin.com/company/hydrocephalus-association
www.pinterest.com/hydroassoc/
twitter.com/hydroassoc
www.youtube.com/user/hydroassoc/featured

5663 ■ Anthony Abbene Scholarship Fund
(Undergraduate/Scholarship)

Purpose: To provide financial assistance to capable and promising young adults who live with the ongoing challenges and complexities of hydrocephalus. **Focus:** General studies/Field of study not specified.

Funds Avail.: $1,000 each. **Duration:** Annual. **Number Awarded:** 2. **To Apply:** Applicant must submit one letter of reference is required from someone who care share important insight about your character; Scholarship applicants with an incomplete Application and/or Recommendation Letter will not be eligible for the scholarship. **Remarks:** The Scholarship was established in honor of Anthony Abbene. Established in 2002. **Contact:** E-mail: scholarship@hydroassoc.org.

5664 ■ Gerard Swartz Fudge Memorial Scholarship
(Postgraduate/Scholarship)

Purpose: To offer scholarships to young adults with hydrocephalus. **Focus:** General studies/Field of study not specified. **Qualif.:** Applicants must be between 17 and 30 years old and have hydrocephalus; scholarship funds must be used for educational purposes such as a two or four-year college, a high school post-graduate year to prepare for college, technical or trade school, an accredited employment-training program or a post-graduate program; scholarship funds may be used for tuition, books, housing or an expense directly related to the education experience; Scholarship applicants must have hydrocephalus; no financial qualifications will be used in determining scholarship recipients.

Funds Avail.: $1,000 each. **Duration:** Annual. **Number Awarded:** 2. **To Apply:** Applicant must submit one letter of reference is required from someone who care share important insight about your character; Scholarship applicants with an incomplete application and/or recommendation letter will not be eligible for the scholarship. **Deadline:** April 15. **Remarks:** This fund was established by the Fudge family. Their son, Gerard, had hydrocephalus and died in 1992 at the age of 22 in the midst of his college experience. Established in 1994. **Contact:** E-mail: scholarship@hydroassoc.org.

5665 ■ Justin Scot Alston Memorial Scholarship
(Undergraduate/Scholarship)

Purpose: To provide financial assistance to capable and promising young adults who live with the ongoing challenges and complexities of hydrocephalus. **Focus:** General studies/Field of study not specified.

Funds Avail.: $1,000. **Duration:** Annual. **Number Awarded:** 1. **Remarks:** The Scholarship was established in loving memory of her son, Justin Scot Alston, who died in 2004. **Contact:** E-mail: scholarship@hydroassoc.org.

5666 ■ Morris L. and Rebecca Ziskind Memorial Scholarship *(Undergraduate/Scholarship)*

Purpose: To offer scholarships to young adults with hydrocephalus. **Focus:** General studies/Field of study not specified.

Funds Avail.: $1,000 each. **Duration:** Annual. **Number Awarded:** 2. **To Apply:** Applicant must submit one letter of

Awards are arranged alphabetically below their administering organizations

reference is required from someone who care share important insight about your character; Scholarship applicants with an incomplete application and/or recommendation letter will not be eligible for the scholarship. **Remarks:** The fund was established in 2001 by Rebecca Ziskind and her family in memory of Rebecca's husband, Dr. Morris Ziskind. Dr. Ziskind had normal pressure hydrocephalus. After Rebecca Ziskind's death in 2005, the couple's three surviving children and their spouses Carrie and Dee Norton, Jerome and Rosemary Ziskind, and Janet and Charles Tarino graciously endowed this fund in loving memory of both parents. Established in 2001. **Contact:** E-mail: scholarship@hydroassoc.org.

5667 ■ Mario J. Tocco Hydrocephalus Foundation Scholarships *(Undergraduate/Scholarship)*

Purpose: To provide financial assistance to capable and promising young adults who live with the ongoing challenges and complexities of hydrocephalus. **Focus:** General studies/Field of study not specified.

Funds Avail.: $1,000. **Duration:** Annual. **Number Awarded:** 1. **To Apply:** Applicant must submit one letter of reference is required from someone who care share important insight about your character; Scholarship applicants with an incomplete application and/or recommendation letter will not be eligible for the scholarship. **Deadline:** April 30. **Remarks:** The Scholarship was established in loving memory of Greg's grandfather, Mario, and in honor of the Hydrocephalus Foundation, Inc. of Saugus, MA. Established in 2007. **Contact:** E-mail: scholarship@hydroassoc.org.

5668 ■ Hydrocephalus Canada (HC)
16 Four Seasons Pl., Ste. 111
Toronto, ON, Canada M9B 6E5
Ph: (416)214-1056
Fax: (416)214-1446
Free: 800-387-1575
E-mail: info@hydrocephalus.ca
URL: www.hydrocephalus.ca
Social Media: www.facebook.com/
 SpinaBifidaHydrocephalusOntario
www.instagram.com/hydrocephaluscanada
www.linkedin.com/company/hydrocephalus-canada/
twitter.com/SBH_Ontario

5669 ■ Dr. E. Bruce Hendrick Scholarship Program *(All/Scholarship)*

Purpose: To encourage and support students with spina bifida and/or hydrocephalus to develop independence and responsibility for their own future educational directions, and to assist students to pursue higher education with the ultimate goal of obtaining a degree or graduate certificate or diploma. **Focus:** General studies/Field of study not specified. **Qualif.:** Applicants must be Canadian citizen with spina bifida and/or hydrocephalus residing in the province of Ontario. **Criteria:** Selection is based on applicant's motivation, self-awareness and goal setting, as well as potential for success.

Funds Avail.: No specific amount. **Duration:** Annual. **To Apply:** Applicants must submit a completed application form along with academic transcripts; completed medical assessment form; one letter of reference from an adult other than a family; one letter of reference from a teacher, principal or guidance counselor; and a personal letter. **Deadline:** April 30. **Remarks:** Named in honor of Dr. E. Bruce Hendrick as a tribute to his dedication, on-going support and outstanding service to our members. **Contact:** Hydrocephalus Canada, Dr. E. Bruce Hendrick Scholarship Program, 16 Four Seasons Pl., Ste. 111. Toronto, Ontario, M9B 6E5; Phone: 800-387-1575; Fax: 416-214-1446; Email: info@hydrocephalus.ca.

5670 ■ Hylan Dental Care
3447 W 117th St.
Cleveland, OH 44111
Ph: (216)251-8812
URL: www.drbradhylan.com
Social Media: www.facebook.com/HylanDentalCare
www.instagram.com/hylandentalcare_
www.linkedin.com/in/bradley-hylan-47545121
twitter.com/HylanDentalCare

5671 ■ Hylan Family Scholarship *(Two Year College, Four Year College/Scholarship)*

Purpose: To assist students pursuing further education who are passionate about the way they communicate with other people in the world and wish to make it a better place. **Focus:** General studies/Field of study not specified. **Qualif.:** Applicants must be high school seniors or college students intending to attend college in the upcoming fall semester at an accredited community college, online college, or university. **Criteria:** Quality of essay, which reveals the student with the most promise.

Funds Avail.: $2,500. **To Apply:** Submit essay (500-750 words) that answers the prompt, "Pick an experience from your life and explain how it has influenced your educational and personal development." Submission must include proof of upcoming college attendance. **Deadline:** June 30.

CPSIA information can be obtained
at www.ICGtesting.com
Printed in the USA
BVHW050131200121
598186BV00007B/117

9 780028 670348

7